Death Metal

Garry Sharpe–Young

Zonda Books Limited, New Plymouth

Death Metal
By Garry Sharpe-Young

ISBN 978-0-9582684-4-8

Copyright © Garry Sharpe-Young, 2008.

First published in 2008 by Zonda Books Limited, New Plymouth, New Zealand.

Find us on the World Wide Web at www.zondabooks.com

First Edition, March 2008.

All rights reserved. No part of this publication may be reproduced, stored in a retrieval system, or transmitted in any form or by any means, electronic, mechanical, photocopying, recording or otherwise, without the prior permission of the copyright owner.

While every precaution has been taken in the preparation of this book, the publisher and author assumes no responsibility for errors or omissions, or for damages resulting from the use of the information contained herein.

National Library of New Zealand Cataloguing-in-Publication Data

Sharpe-Young, Garry.
Death metal / Garry Sharpe-Young. 1st ed.
ISBN 978-0-9582684-4-8
1. Death metal (Music) 2. Rock groups. I. Title.
781.66—dc 22

Contents

1917 1	AGE OF AGONY 19
21 LUCIFERS 1	AGE OF RUIN 20
5 BILLION DEAD 1	AGGRESSOR 20
8 FOOT SATIVA 1	AGONIZED 20
9TH PLAGUE 2	AGONY 20
A CANOROUS QUINTET 2	AGONY 21
A COLD REALITY 3	AGORAPHOBIC NOSEBLEED 21
A GRUESOME FIND 3	AGREGATOR 22
A MIND CONFUSED 3	AGRESSOR 22
A PERPETUAL DYING MIRROR 4	AGRETATOR 23
A.W.A.S. 4	AKMA 23
ABADDON 4	ALCHEMIST 23
ABADDON 4	ALFA ERIDANO AKHERNAR 24
ABED 4	ALICE IN DARKLAND 24
ABHORRENCE 5	ALIENGATES 24
ABHORRENCE 5	ALISTER 24
ABHOTH 5	ALL SHALL PERISH 24
ABIGAIL 6	ALLFATHER 25
ABIGAIL WILLIAMS 6	ALMA MATER 25
ABLAZE IN HATRED 6	ALTAR 26
ABLAZE MY SORROW 6	AMAGORTIS 26
ABNORMYNDEFFECT 7	AMARAN 26
ABOMINANT 7	AMOK 27
ABORDA 7	AMON 27
ABORTED 7	AMON AMARTH 27
ABORTION 8	AMORAL 29
ABORTUS 9	AMORPHIS 29
ABOSRANIE BOGOM 9	AMPHITRYON 32
ABRAMELIN 10	AMPUTATION 32
ABRANIA 10	ANAEMICA 32
ABRASIVE 10	ANAL BLAST 32
ABSCESS 10	ANAL CUNT 33
ABSCESS 10	ANAL PUTREFACTION 34
ABSIDIA 11	ANAL VOMIT 34
ABSOLUTE DEFIANCE 11	ANARCHUS 34
ABSORBED 11	ANASARCA 35
ABSTAIN 12	ANATA 35
ABSYNTHIUM 12	ANATOMI-71 36
ABYSMAL DAWN 12	ANATOMY 36
ABYSSAL SUFFERING 13	ANCESTRAL STIGMATA 36
ABYSSOS 13	ANCIENT NECROPSY 37
ACCELERATOR 13	ANCIENT RITES 37
ACCURSED 13	ANESTHESY 38
ACCURSED DAWN 13	ANGELKILL 38
ACHERON 14	ANGELUS INFERNUS 39
ACRID 15	ANGOR 39
ACRIMONY INC. 15	ANGUISH SUBLIME 39
ACROHOLIA 15	ANHKREHG 39
ACROSTICHON 15	ANIMA DAMNATA 39
ADAGIO 16	ANIMAL FORESKIN 40
ADENINE 16	ANIMOSITY 40
ADRAMELECH 16	ANNIHILATION 40
ADRIFT 17	ANNULATION 41
AECRON 17	ANPHISBENAH 41
AEON 17	ANTAGONIST 41
AETURNUS DOMINION 17	ANTARCTICA 41
AFFLICTED 17	ANTARKTIS UTOPIA 41
AFTER THE LAST SKY 18	ANTIGAMA 42
AFTERDEATH 18	ANVIL OF DOOM 42
AGATHOCLES 18	APHASIA 42

APHELON	43
APHOTIC	43
APIARY	43
APOKALYPTIC RAIDS	43
APOKRIFOS	44
APOSTASY	44
APPROACHED BY A GOD	44
ARCANUM	45
ARCANUM	45
ARCH ENEMY	45
ARCHITECTURE OF AGGRESSION	48
ARISE	48
ARKHAM	48
ARMINIUS	49
ARS MORIENDI	49
ARSON	49
ARTERY ERUPTION	49
AS DUSK UNFOLDS	49
AS IT BURNS	50
ASCENSION	50
ASERAPHYMN	50
ASESINO	50
ASHMOLEAN	51
ASMODINA	51
ASPHYX	51
ASPHYXIATOR	52
ASSEMBLENT	52
ASSUCK	52
ASUNDER	52
AT THE GATES	53
AT WINTER'S END	54
ATEM	54
ATHEIST	54
ATHELA	55
ATHERETIC	56
ATHROX	56
ATOMSMASHER	56
ATOMVINTER	56
ATROCITY	56
ATROCITY	58
ATSPHEAR	58
AUBERON	58
AUGURY	59
AURA	59
AURORA	59
AURORA BOREALIS	59
AUTERE	60
AUTOPSY	60
AUTOPSY TORMENT	61
AUTUMN DWELLER	61
AUTUMN LEAVES	61
AUTUMN NOSTRUM	62
AUTUMNAL REAPER	62
AVATAR	62
AVULSED	63
AVULSION	64
AXEGRINDER	64
AZARATH	64
B-LOW	64
BAAL	65
BAALPHEGOR	65
BACKYARD BURIAL	65
BALATONIZER	65
BALVAZ	66
BANE OF EXISTENCE	66
BANISHED	66
BAPHOMET	66
BASTARD SAINTS	66
BEDIMMED	67
BEHEADED	67
BELCHING BEET	67
BELIAL	67
BENEATH THE MASSACRE	68
BENEDICTION	68
BENIGHTED	69
BENUMB	70
BESTIAL DEFORM	70
BESTIAL DEVASTATION	70
BETRAYER	71
BETWEEN THE BURIED AND ME	71
BEYOND BELIEF	72
BEYOND INSANITY	72
BEYOND SERENITY	73
BEYOND THE EMBRACE	73
BEYOND THE SIXTH SEAL	73
BEYOND WITHIN	74
BIRDFLESH	74
BLACK CRUCIFIXION	75
BLACKSHINE	75
BLACKSMITH	76
BLAKK MARKET	76
BLASPHEMER	76
BLASPHEREION	76
BLASTMASTERS	76
BLEAK CROWD	77
BLEAK DESTINY	77
BLEED OF HATE	77
BLINDEAD	77
BLINDED BY FAITH	77
BLINDED COLONY	78
BLO.TORCH	78
BLOCKHEADS	78
BLOOD DUSTER	78
BLOOD FREAK	79
BLOOD RED THRONE	79
BLOOD RETCH	80
BLOOD STORM	80
BLOODBATH	81
BLOODREAPING	81
BLOODRIDE	81
BLOODSHED	82
BLOODSTREAM	82
BLOODWRITTEN	82
BLOODWRITTEN	83
BLOODY GORE	83
BLOODY SIGN	83
BLOODY WINGS	83
BLUDGEON	84
BLUDGEON	84
BLUDGEON	84
BODY CORE	84
BOLT THROWER	85
BONESCREW	86
BORN HEADLESS	87
BORN OF FIRE	87
BOWEL STEW	87
BOWTOME	87
BRAINCHOKE	87
BREEDING CHAMBER	88
BRODEQUIN	88
BROKEN HOPE	88
BRUJERIA	89
BRUTAL	89
BRUTAL TRUTH	90
BRUTALITY	91
BRUTE CHANT	91
BURDEN OF GRIEF	92
BURGUL TORKHAÏN	92

BURIAL GROUND	92
BURIED DREAMS	93
BURN IN SILENCE	93
BURNING SKIES	93
BUTCHERS	94
BUTCHERY	94
BUTTOCKS	94
BY NIGHT	94
C.A.I.N.	94
C.C.C.	95
CADACROSS	95
CADAVER	95
CADAVER INC.	96
CADAVERIC INCUBATOR	96
CADAVEROUS CONDITION	97
CADUCITY	97
CALEDONIAN	98
CALLENISH CIRCLE	98
CANINUS	99
CANNIBAL CORPSE	99
CANOPY	101
CANTAR	101
CANTARA	102
CAPHARNAUM	102
CAPTOR	102
CARBONIZED	103
CARCASE INC.	103
CARCASS	103
CARDINAL SIN	105
CARNAGE	105
CARNAL FORGE	106
CARNAL GRIEF	106
CARNIFIED	107
CARRION CARNAGE	107
CARTILAGE	107
CARVE	107
CASKETGARDEN	108
CASTRUM	108
CATAFALC	108
CATAMENIA	108
CATARACT	109
CATASEXUAL URGE MOTIVATION	110
CATASTROPHIC	110
CATATONIC SCHIZOPHRENIA	111
CATTLE DECAPITATION	111
CAUSEMOS	112
CAUTERIZED	112
CELEBORN	113
CELEBRANT	113
CELESTIAL CROWN	113
CELTIC FROST	114
CENOTAPH	116
CENTINEX	117
CENTURIAN	118
CEPHALECTOMY	119
CEPHALIC CARNAGE	119
CEREMONIAL EXECUTION	120
CEREMONIAL OATH	120
CEREMONY	120
CHAIN COLLECTOR	120
CHAINGUNN	120
CHANGER	121
CHAOSBREED	121
CHAOSYS	121
CHASTISEMENT	122
CHEMICAL DISASTER	122
CHILDREN OF BODOM	122
CHOPCORE	125
CHRYSALIS	125
CHTHONIC	125
CHTON	126
CHURCH BIZARRE	126
CIANIDE	127
CIBORIUM	127
CINERARY	127
CIPHER SYSTEM	128
CIRCLE OF DEAD CHILDREN	128
CIRRHOSIS	128
CLIMATE	128
CLONE	129
CLOTTED SYMMETRIC SEXUAL ORGAN	129
CO-EXIST	129
COALESCE	130
COCK AND BALL TORTURE	130
CODEON	131
COERCION	131
COFFIN TEXTS	131
COLDWAY	131
COLDWORKER	132
COLLAPSE 7	132
COMECON	132
COMMIT SUICIDE	132
COMPOS MENTIS	133
CONGESTION	133
CONSOLATION	133
CONSTRUCDEAD	133
CONTEMPT	134
CORAM LETHE	134
CORIOR	135
CORPORATION 187	135
CORPSE CARVING	135
CORPSE VOMIT	135
CORPSE VOMIT	135
CORPSEFUCKING ART	136
CORPUS MORTALE	136
CORPUS OMNI DOMINI	136
CORRUPTION	137
COUNCIL OF THE FALLEN	137
CRACK UP	137
CRADLE TO GRAVE	138
CREMAINS	138
CREMATORIUM	138
CRIMINAL	139
CRIMSON THORN	140
CRIPPLE BASTARDS	140
CROMLECH	141
CROWHEAD	142
CROWN OF THORNS	142
CRUCIFER	142
CRUCIFIER	143
CRUCIFIX	143
CRUELTY	144
CRYHAVOC	144
CRYOGENIC	144
CRYPT OF KERBEROS	144
CRYPTOPSY	145
CRYSTAL AGE	146
CURRICULUM MORTIS	146
CUTTHROAT	146
CYBORG	147
D-COMPOSE	147
D.S.K.	147
DAATH	147
DAEMON	148
DAEMON	148
DAEMUSINEM	148
DAGOBA	148
DAHMER	149

DAMNABLE	149
DAMNATION	149
DAMNATION	150
DAN SWANÖ	150
DARK	150
DARK DISCIPLE	151
DARK EMBRACE	151
DARK FAITH	151
DARK FLOOD	151
DARK REALITY	152
DARK REMAINS	152
DARK SECRET	152
DARK SUNS	152
DARK TRANQUILLITY	153
DARKANE	155
DARKEN	156
DARKIFIED	156
DARKNESS REMAINS	157
DARKSIDE	157
DARTH	157
DAUNTLESS	158
DAWN CREATION	158
DAWN OF AZAZEL	158
DAWN OF DISEASE	159
DAWN OF RELIC	159
DAYLIGHT DIES	159
DE LIRIUM'S ORDER	160
DEAD BY DAWN	160
DEAD END WORLD	160
DEAD INFECTION	160
DEAD SAMARITAN	161
DEAD TO FALL	161
DEAD TROOPER	162
DEADPOOL	162
DEADSPAWN	162
DEATH	162
DEATH BREATH	165
DEATH BY DESIGN	166
DEATH DU JOUR	166
DEATH OF MILLIONS	166
DEATH REALITY	166
DEATHBOUND	167
DEATHCON	167
DEATHGUY	167
DEATHLESS	168
DEATHSTRIKE	168
DEATHWITCH	168
DEBAUCHERY	169
DECADENCE	169
DECAMERON	169
DECAPITATED	170
DECAY	171
DECEPTION	171
DECOLLATION	171
DECOMPOSED	171
DECORYAH	171
DECREPIT	172
DECREPIT BIRTH	172
DECRYPT	172
DEEDS OF FLESH	172
DEEPRED	173
DEFACED CREATION	173
DEFEATED SANITY	174
DEFENDER KFS	174
DEFILED	174
DEFILEMENT	175
DEFLESHED	175
DEFLORACE	176
DEFORMITY	176
DEHUMANIZED	176
DEHYDRATED	177
DEICIDE	177
DEIFECATION	179
DEIVOS	180
DELIGHT	180
DELIRIUM X TREMENS	180
DELLAMORTE	180
DEMENTIA	181
DEMENZIA	181
DEMILICH	181
DEMISOR	182
DEMONICAL	182
DEMONICON	183
DEMONIUM	183
DENIAL FIEND	183
DEPRAVITY	183
DEPRECATED	183
DEPRESSION	184
DEPRESY	185
DERANGED	185
DERKETA	186
DESCENDING	187
DESCENDING	187
DESECRATED DREAMS	187
DESECRATION	187
DESENSITISED	187
DESOLATE	188
DESPISE	188
DESPISED ICON	188
DESPOILMENT	188
DESTINITY	189
DESULTORY	189
DETERIORATION	189
DEUTERONOMIUM	189
DEVASTACION	190
DEVIANCE	190
DEVILDRIVER	190
DEVILISH	191
DEVILISH IMPRESSIONS	191
DEVILYN	191
DEVISER	192
DEVOURED	192
DEVOURMENT	192
DEW-SCENTED	193
DIABOLIC	194
DIABOLIC INTENT	195
DIABOLICAL	195
DIABOLIQUE	195
DIES IRAE	196
DIES IRAE	196
DIM MAK	196
DIMENSION ZERO	197
DIN-ADDICT	197
DISAFFECTED	198
DISARMONIA MUNDI	198
DISARRAY	198
DISASTROUS MURMUR	199
DISAVOWED	199
DISBELIEF	199
DISCIPLES OF MOCKERY	200
DISCIPLES OF POWER	200
DISCORDANCE AXIS	201
DISCRUCIOR	201
DISFEAR	201
DISFIGURED	202
DISFIGURED CORPSE	202
DISGORGE	202
DISGORGE	203

DISGRACE	203
DISGUST	204
DISGUST	204
DISHARMONIC ORCHESTRA	204
DISILLUSION	204
DISINCARNATE	205
DISINFECT	205
DISINTER	205
DISINTER	205
DISLIMB	206
DISLOYAL	206
DISMAL EUPHONY	207
DISMEMBER	207
DISORDER	209
DISORDER	209
DISPATCHED	209
DISPIRITED	210
DISRUPT	210
DISSECTION	210
DISSENTER	213
DISTRAUGHT	213
DIVINE EMPIRE	214
DIVINE NOISE ATTACK	214
DIVINE RAPTURE	215
DIVINE:DECAY	215
DOG FACED GODS	215
DOLORIAN	215
DOMAIN	216
DOME SERVICE	216
DOMINION	216
DOMINUS	216
DOWNTHROAT	217
DOXOMEDON	217
DRAMATVM	217
DRAWN AND QUARTERED	217
DREAM OF NEBIROS	218
DRIPPING	218
DROWNED	218
DROWNED IN LIFE	219
DSK	219
DWELLING MADNESS	219
DYING EMBRACE	219
DYING FETUS	219
DYSANCHELY	221
DYSENTRY	221
DÄRATH	221
EBONY TEARS	221
ECHOES OF SILENCE	222
ECITON	222
EDENBEAST	222
EDENSHADE	222
EDGECRUSHER	222
EDICIUS	223
ELENIUM	223
EMBALMING THEATRE	223
EMBEDDED	223
EMBERS LEFT	224
EMBODIMENT	224
EMBRACING	224
EMBRAZE	225
EMBRYONIC	225
EMETH	225
ENACTMENT	226
END OF GREEN	226
END ZONE	226
ENDLESS	227
ENDLESS TORMENT	227
ENDYMAERIA	227
ENFORCE	227
ENFORSAKEN	227
ENGORGE	228
ENGORGED	229
ENGRAVE	229
ENMORTEM	229
ENRAGED	229
ENSIFERUM	230
ENTER CHAOS	230
ENTER MY SILENCE	231
ENTHRALLED	231
ENTHRALLMENT	231
ENTOMBED	232
ENTRE LA BASURA	235
ENTWINED	235
EPICEDIUM	235
EQUINOX	235
ERRATA	236
ESQARIAL	236
ESSENCE OF EXISTENCE	236
ESTERTOR	236
ESTUARY	237
ESTUARY OF CALAMITY	237
ETERNAL	237
ETERNAL AUTUMN	237
ETERNAL DARKNESS	238
ETERNAL DEFORMITY	238
ETERNAL DEMENTIA	238
ETERNAL DIRGE	238
ETERNAL GRAY	238
ETERNAL LIES	239
ETERNAL OATH	239
ETERNAL RUIN	240
ETERNAL SOLSTICE	240
ETERNAL SUFFERING	240
ETERNAL TEARS OF SORROW	240
ETERNAL TRAGEDY	241
ETHEREAL COLLAPSE	241
EUCHARIST	241
EULOGY	242
EUTHANAUSEA	242
EVEMASTER	242
EVENTIDE	243
EVERGREY	243
EVIL DEAD	244
EVIL INCARNATE	244
EVIL POETRY	245
EVILHEART	245
EVOKE	245
EVOKED CURSE	246
EX INFERIS	246
EXCARNATED	246
EXCESS OF CRUELTY	246
EXCESSUM	247
EXCRUCIATE	247
EXCRUCIATION	247
EXHUMATOR	248
EXHUMED	248
EXIT 13	249
EXMORTEM	250
EXMORTIS	251
EXOMORTIS	251
EXOTO	251
EXOUSIA	251
EXPOSED GUTS	252
EXPULSION	252
EXSECRATUS	252
EXTERMINATOR	252
EXTOL	253
EXTREEM ECZEEM	253

EXTREME NOISE TERROR	254
EXULCERATE	254
EYE SEA	255
FACE DOWN	255
FALCHION	255
FALCIFORM	255
FALL OF SERENITY	256
FALLEN YGGDRASIL	256
FALSE REALITY	256
FATAL DEMEANOR	257
FEARER	257
FEAROFHATRED	257
FEEBLE MINDED	257
FETUS EATERS	257
FINAL BREATH	258
FINAL DAWN	258
FLAGELLATION	258
FLASHOVER	258
FLESH	258
FLESH GRINDER	259
FLESH PARADE	259
FLESHCRAWL	259
FLESHGRIND	260
FLESHLESS	260
FLESHMOULD	261
FLESHTIZED	261
FOREIGN OBJECTS	261
FORENSICK	261
FOREST STREAM	262
FORGARÐUR HELVÍTIS	262
FORGOTTEN SUNRISE	262
FORNICATION	262
FRACTAL POINT	263
FRAGILE HOLLOW	263
FRAGMENTATION	263
FRAGMENTS OF UNBECOMING	263
FROM BEYOND	264
FROM THE DEPTHS	264
FUCK THE FACTS	264
FUELBLOODED	264
FUNEBRARUM	265
FUNERAL AGE	265
FUNERAL INCEPTION	265
FUNERAL MASK	265
FUNERAL ORATION	265
FUNERATUS	265
FUNERUS	266
FURBOWL	266
FURIA	266
FURIOUS TRAUMA	266
FURY161	267
GADGET	267
GALLERY OF DARKNESS	267
GALLHAMMER	267
GARDEN OF DECAY	268
GARDEN OF SHADOWS	268
GARDENIAN	268
GARDENS OF GEHENNA	269
GATHERING DARKNESS	269
GENERAL SURGERY	269
GENOCIDE SUPERSTARS	270
GHOST	270
GHOSTORM	271
GHOULS	271
GHOULUNATICS	271
GLASS CASKET	271
GOD AMONG INSECTS	272
GOD FORBID	272
GOD FORSAKEN	273
GOD MACABRE	274
GODDAMNED X	274
GODGORY	274
GODKILLER	274
GODLESS	275
GODLESS TRUTH	275
GOETIA	275
GOJIRA	275
GOLEM	276
GOLGOTHA	276
GOMORRHA	277
GOOSEFLESH	277
GORATORY	277
GORE	277
GORE BEYOND NECROPSY	278
GOREFEST	278
GORELORD	279
GOREMENT	279
GOREROTTED	279
GORESOAKED	280
GORETRADE	280
GOREZONE	281
GORGASM	281
GORGUTS	281
GORTICIAN	282
GORY BLISTER	282
GOTHIC	282
GOTHIC	283
GRAVE	283
GRAYMALKIN	284
GRENOUER	284
GRIMORIA	285
GRIND BUTO	285
GRIND INC.	285
GRIND MINDED	285
GROG	285
GROINCHURN	286
GROTESQUE	286
GROTESQUE IMPALEMENT	287
GROTESQUEUPHORIA	287
GUIDANCE OF SIN	287
GUTROT	287
HACAVITZ	288
HACRIDE	288
HADEZ	288
HAEMORRHAGE	288
HAGGARD	289
HANGING GARDEN	289
HARMONY DIES	290
HATE	290
HATE ETERNAL	291
HATE FACTOR	292
HATEPLOW	292
HATESPHERE	292
HEADHUNTER D.C.	293
HEARSE	294
HEAVEN SHALL BURN	294
HEAVENWOOD	295
HEDFIRST	295
HELLHAMMER	295
HELLICON	296
HERMAN RAREBELL	296
HERR SUFFOKATOR	296
HEXENHAMMER	296
HIBERNUS MORTIS	297
HILASTHERION	297
HIMSA	297
HOLOCAUSTO CANIBAL	298
HOMOIRATUS	298

HORFIXION	299
HORRESCO REFERENS	299
HORRICANE	299
HORRIFIED	299
HOUR OF PENANCE	299
HOUWITSER	300
HUMAN	300
HUMAN BLOODFEAST	301
HYMIR	301
HYPERBOREA	301
HYPNOS	301
HYPNOSIA	302
HYPOCRISY	302
HYPOCRITE	304
ILL FARES THE LAND	304
ILLDISPOSED	304
ILLOGICIST	305
IMAGES OF VIOLENCE	305
IMMEMORIAL	306
IMMERSED IN BLOOD	306
IMMOLATION	306
IMMORTAL RITES	307
IMMORTAL SOULS	307
IMPACT WINTER	308
IMPALED	308
IMPALED NAZARENE	309
IMPEDIGON	311
IMPENDING DOOM	312
IMPERIAL	312
IMPERIAL DOMAIN	312
IMPERIAL SODOMY	313
IMPERIOUS	313
IMPERIOUS MALEVOLENCE	313
IMPETIGO	313
IMPIOUS	314
IMPULSE MANSLAUGHTER	314
IMPURITY	315
IN BATTLE	315
IN FLAMES	315
IN GREY	318
IN SOMNIS	318
IN THA UMBRA	319
IN THY DREAMS	319
IN VAIN	319
IN-QUEST	319
INACTIVE MESSIAH	320
INCANTATION	320
INCAPACITY	323
INCARNATE	323
INCENDIUM	323
INCESTUOUS	324
INCREDIBLE PAIN	324
INCUBATOR	324
INCUBUS	324
INEARTHED	324
INEVITABLE END	325
INFAMY	325
INFECTED PUSSY	325
INFERIA	326
INFERNAL	326
INFERNAL DREAMS	327
INFERNÄL MÄJESTY	327
INFERNAL METHOD	328
INFERNAL TORMENT	328
INFESTATION	328
INFINITED HATE	329
INFINITUM OBSCURE	329
INFLICTION	329
INGRAVED	329
INGROWING	329
INGURGITATING OBLIVION	330
INHUMAN VISIONS	330
INHUMATE	330
INHUME	331
INIQUITY	331
INNOCENCE PURE MUTILATED	331
INSANE ASSHOLES	332
INSANITY	332
INSANITY	332
INSATANITY	332
INSISION	332
INSOMNIUM	333
INSURRECTION	334
INTENSE HAMMER RAGE	334
INTENSE MOSH	334
INTERNAL BLEEDING	335
INTERNAL SUFFERING	335
INTESTINAL DISGORGE	336
INTO ETERNITY	336
INTO THE MOAT	337
INVERTED	337
INVOCATOR	337
IRON LUNG	338
IRONY OF CHRIST	338
IRREVERENCE	338
IRRITATE	338
ISACAARUM	339
ISLAND	339
ISOLATED FIELDS	339
ISOLE	339
JACK SLATER	340
JIGSORE TERROR	340
JOHNNY TRUANT	340
JOÃO	340
JUDECCA	341
JUDGEMENT DAY	341
JUGGERMATH	341
JUNGLE ROT	341
KAAMOS	342
KABAK	342
KACHANA	343
KADATH	343
KALIBAN	344
KALIBAS	344
KALISIA	344
KALOPSIA	344
KAOTHIC	344
KARKADAN	345
KARMASSACRE	345
KARNAK	345
KAT	346
KATAFALK	346
KATAKLYSM	346
KATAPLEXIA	348
KATATONIA	348
KATATONIA: TRIBUTE	350
KAZJUROL	351
KEEN OF THE CROW	351
KEKAL	351
KEYDRAGON	352
KHAOSPHERE	352
KHERT-NETER	352
KILL FOR SATAN	352
KILL THE ROMANCE	352
KILLHARMONIC	353
KILLING CULTURE	353
KINETIC	353
KINGDOM OF THE LIE	353

KISS OF DEATH	353
KIUAS	354
KOLDBORN	354
KONKHRA	354
KOROVA	355
KORRODEAD	355
KORRUPTION	355
KRABATHOR	356
KRISIUN	356
KRONOS	357
KRUEGER	357
KRYZALID	358
KUTABARE	358
L.O.S.T.	358
LACRIMA CHRISTI	358
LAKUPAAVI	359
LAMENT	359
LECHEROUS NOCTURNE	359
LEGACY	359
LEGION	360
LEGION	360
LEGION OF THE DAMNED	360
LEHAVOTH	361
LENG TCH'E	361
LET ME DREAM	361
LETHAL CURSE	362
LETHERIA	362
LETHIAN DREAMS	362
LEUKORRHEA	362
LIERS IN WAIT	363
LIGATURE	363
LIGHT THIS CITY	363
LIMB FROM LIMB	364
LITHURIA	364
LIVIDITY	364
LIVING SACRIFICE	365
LOCKUP	365
LONG VOYAGE BACK	366
LORD BLASPHEMER	366
LORD GORE	366
LORDS OF DARKNESS	367
LOS SIN NOMBRE	367
LOST SOUL	367
LOUDBLAST	368
LOUDPIPES	368
LOVE FORSAKEN	368
LOWBROW	369
LUCIFERASE	369
LUCIFERION	369
LUNA FIELD	369
LUNATIC GODS	370
LUST OF DECAY	370
LYCANTROPHY	370
M-26	370
M-90'S	371
M.A.S.A.C.R.E.	371
M.S.I.	371
MACABRE	371
MACABRE END	372
MACHETAZO	372
MACHINERY	373
MAHAVATAR	373
MALAMOR	373
MALEDICTION	374
MALEFACTOR	374
MALEVOLENCE	374
MALEVOLENCE	375
MALEVOLENT CREATION	375
MALICE GARDEN	377
MALIGNANCY	377
MALIGNANT INCEPTION	378
MALIGNANT TUMOUR	378
MANGLED	378
MANGLED TORSOS	379
MANIAS	379
MARAMON	379
MARE DIBERE	379
MARTTYYRIOPERAATIO	380
MARTYR	380
MASACRE	380
MASOCHRIST	381
MASQUE OF INNOCENCE	381
MASSACRE	381
MASTER	382
MASTIC SCUM	383
MAUSOLEUM	384
MAZE OF TORMENT	384
MEATHOLE INFECTION	384
MEGASLAUGHTER	385
MELANCHOLIC SEASONS	385
MENTAL DEMISE	385
MENTAL HOME	385
MENTAL HORROR	386
MERCENARY	386
MERLIN	387
MESS AGE	387
METALLISK ESEL HIVES	387
METANOIA	388
MICTLAN	388
MIDIAN	388
MIDVINTER	388
MINAS TIRITH	389
MINDFLAIR	389
MINDGRINDER	389
MINDROT	389
MINDSNARE	390
MISCREANT	390
MISERY	390
MISERY INDEX	391
MISTRESS	392
MITHRAS	392
MOLESTED	392
MOMENT MANIACS	393
MONASTERY	393
MONSTERWORKS	393
MONSTROSITY	394
MOONSHINE	395
MORBID ANGEL	395
MORBOSIDAD	398
MORBUS	398
MORDANT	398
MORDICUS	398
MORGOTH	399
MORGUL	399
MORNALAND	399
MORPHEUS	400
MORPHEUS DESCENDS	400
MORS PRINCIPIUM EST	400
MORS SUBITA	401
MORTA SKULD	401
MORTAL DECAY	401
MORTAL FORM	402
MORTALITY	402
MORTEM	402
MORTICIAN	402
MORTIFER	403
MORTIFICATION	403
MORTIFIED	404

MORTUARY	404
MORTUM	405
MORTUS POETRY	405
MORTYFEAR	405
MOURNING	405
MUCOPUS	405
MURDER CORPORATION	406
MURDER IN ART	406
MURDER SQUAD	406
MUTILATED	406
MUTILATION	406
MY DYING BRIDE	407
MY SILENT WAKE	408
MYGRAIN	408
MYRKSKOG	409
MYSTICA	409
MYTHIC	409
MYTHOPOEIA	410
NAIL WITHIN	410
NAILDOWN	410
NAPALM DEATH	410
NASUM	415
NATAN	416
NATASTOR	416
NATRON	417
NAUMACHIA	417
NECARE	417
NECROCIDE	418
NECRODEATH	418
NECRODEMON	418
NECROFOBIA	419
NECROMANCER	419
NECRONOMICON	419
NECROPHAGIA	419
NECROPHAGIST	421
NECROPHILISMA	421
NECROPHOBIC	421
NECROPOLIS	422
NECROPRIEST	422
NECROSADISTIC GOAT TORTURE	422
NECROSIS	422
NECROTIC CHAOS	423
NECROVORE	423
NEAPS	423
NEGLIGENT COLLATERAL COLLAPSE	423
NEMBRIONIC	424
NEMBRIONIC HAMMERDEATH	424
NEMESIS	424
NEMESIS IRAE	424
NEOLITH	425
NEOLITHIC	425
NEOPLASMAH	425
NEPAL	425
NEPENTHE	426
NEPENTHE	426
NEPHASTH	426
NERLICH	426
NERVECELL	427
NERVOCHAOS	427
NETHERBIRD	427
NETTLETHRONE	428
NEURAXIS	428
NEUROSIS	428
NEUROSIS INC.	429
NEVOLUTION	429
NEWBREED	430
NIGHT IN GALES	430
NIGHTRAGE	430
NIHILIST	431
NILE	431
NINNGHIZHIDA	433
NO DAWN	433
NO MERCY	433
NOBILITAS NIGRA	433
NOCTAMBULANT GRIMNESS	434
NOCTURNAL BREED	434
NOCTURNUS	435
NOIZ	435
NOMAD	435
NOMENMORTIS	436
NOMICON	436
NOMINON	436
NORDOR	437
NORSETH	438
NORTHER	438
NOSFERATOS	438
NOSTROMO	439
NOUMENA	439
NOVEMBRE	439
NOWEN	440
NUCLEAR DEATH	440
NUNSLAUGHTER	440
NYCTOPHOBIC	443
NYIA	443
OBITUARY	444
OBLITERATION	445
OBSCENE	445
OBSCENE CRISIS	445
OBSCENE EULOGY	446
OBSCENITY	446
OBSCURANT	446
OBSECRATION	447
OBTRUNCATION	447
OCEANS OF SADNESS	447
OCTOBER TIDE	448
OF TREES AND ORCHIDS	448
OFFENSE	448
OMINOUS	448
OMINOUS	448
OMNIUM GATHERUM	449
OMNIUM GATHERUM	449
OPETH	449
OPPRESSOR	452
OPPROBIUM	452
ORIGIN	452
ORIGIN BLOOD	453
ORPHANAGE	453
ORPHANED LAND	453
ORTANK	454
OSSUARY	454
P.C.P.	455
PAGAN	455
PAGANIZER	455
PAINSTRUCK	455
PANDEMIA	456
PANTOKRATOR	456
PANZERCHRIST	457
PANZERSCHRECK	457
PARABELLUM	457
PARACOCCIDIOIDOMICOSISPROCTITISSARCOMUCOSIS	457
PARENTAL ADVISORY	458
PARRICIDE	458
PARRICIDE	458
PASSENGER	459
PATHOGEN	459
PATHOLOGIST	459
PATHS OF POSSESSION	460

PENTACLE	460	REPULSION	482
PERNICIOUS	460	REQUIEM	482
PERSECUTION	461	REQUIEM	482
PERSECUTION	461	REQUIEM	483
PESSIMIST	461	RESPONSE NEGATIVE	483
PESTILENCE	462	RESURRECTED	483
PHANTASM	462	RESURRECTION	483
PHANTASMA	463	RESURRECTURIS	484
PHAZM	463	RESUSCITATOR	484
PHLEGETHON	463	RETALIATION	484
PHOBIA	463	RHESTUS	485
PIG DESTROYER	464	RIBSPREADER	485
PLEURISY	464	RISE	485
POLLUTED INHERITANCE	464	RITUAL CARNAGE	486
POSTMORTEM	465	ROOT	486
POVERTY	465	ROSE FUNERAL	487
PRECIPICE	465	ROSICRUCIAN	487
PREJUDICE	465	ROTTEN SOUND	488
PRIMEVAL	466	ROYAL ANGUISH	488
PROCREATION	466	RUDRA	489
PROFANE OMEN	466	RUNIC	489
PROFANITY	467	S.N.I.F.F.	489
PROJECT: FAILING FLESH	467	S.O.B.	489
PROMETHEAN	467	S.U.P.	490
PROMISQES	467	SACRAMENTUM	490
PROPHECY	468	SACRAPHYX	490
PROPHECY OF DEATH	468	SACRASPHEMY	491
PROSTITUTE DISFIGUREMENT	468	SACRED CRUCIFIX	491
PSICORRAGIA	468	SACRED SIN	491
PSYCHOFAGIST	469	SACRED TEARS	492
PSYCHOTOGEN	469	SACRIFICE	492
PSYCROPTIC	469	SACRIFICIAL SLAUGHTER	493
PSYOPUS	470	SACRIFICIUM	493
PSYPHERIA	470	SACROSANCT	493
PULMONARY ABSCESS	470	SADIST	494
PUNGENT STENCH	470	SADISTIC INTENT	494
PUNISHED EARTH	471	SADUS	494
PUNISHMENT	472	SAMAEL	495
PURGATORY	472	SAMMATH NAUR	497
PUTREFY	472	SANATORIUM	497
PUTRIFACT	473	SANCTIFICATION	498
PUTRILAGE	473	SANCTIMONY	498
PYAEMIA	473	SANGUINARY	498
PYORRHOEA	473	SARCASM	498
PYPHOMGERTUM	474	SARCOFAGO	499
PYREXIA	474	SARCOPHAGUS	499
PYURIA	474	SARGATANAS REIGN	499
QUEST OF AIDANCE	474	SARPANITUM	500
QUO VADIS	475	SATANIC SLAUGHTER	500
R.U. DEAD?	475	SATANIZED	501
RAISE HELL	475	SATARIEL	501
RAMPAGE	476	SATURNUS	502
RAVAGE	476	SAXORIOR	502
RAVAGER	476	SAYYADINA	503
RE-PULSE	477	SCABBARD	503
REALITY GREY	477	SCAFFOLD	503
REBAELLIUN	477	SCAR SYMMETRY	504
RECLUSION	477	SCARIOT	504
RED HARVEST	477	SCARVE	505
REDRUM	479	SCATTERED REMNANTS	506
REGURGITATE	479	SCAVENGER	506
REGURGITATION	480	SCENT OF FLESH	506
REGURGITATION	480	SCEPTIC	506
REIGN OF DECAY	480	SCEPTIC	506
REIGN OF TERROR	480	SCEPTICAL SCHIZO	507
RELEVANT FEW	481	SCHEITAN	507
RENAISSANCE	481	SCREAMING AFTERBIRTH	507
RENASCENT	481	SCULPTURED	508
REPUDIATE	482	SCURVY	508

SEAR	508
SEARING MEADOW	508
SECT OF EXECRATION	509
SEEDS OF SORROW	509
SEMPER TYRANNIS	509
SENTENCED	509
SEPSISM	511
SEPTIC BREED	511
SEPTIC FLESH	511
SERBERUS	512
SERENADE	512
SERMON	513
SERPENS AEON	513
SERPENT	513
SERPENT OBSCENE	513
SERPENTOR	513
SEVERE TORTURE	514
SEVERED SAVIOR	514
SEXTRASH	514
SHADOW'S VEIL	515
SHADOWBREED	515
SHADOWS LAND	515
SHADOWS OF SUNSET	515
SHEOLGEENNA	516
SHOT INJECTION	516
SHROUD	516
SICKENING HORROR	516
SIEGE OF HATE	516
SIKSAKUBUR	517
SILENT AGONY	517
SILENT SCYTHE	517
SILENT SOULS	517
SINISTER	518
SINNERS BLEED	519
SINS OF OMISSION	519
SIX FEET UNDER	520
SKELETAL EMBRACE	521
SKINLESS	521
SKLEROTIKZ	522
SLAUGHTER	522
SLOW AGONY	523
SLUDGE	523
SLUGATHOR	523
SOILENT GREEN	524
SOILS OF FATE	525
SOILWORK	525
SOLAR DAWN	527
SOLARISIS	528
SOLITARY	528
SOMBER	528
SOMBERLAIN	529
SONIC SYNDICATE	529
SORCERY	529
SORROW	530
SOTAJUMALA	530
SOUL DEMISE	530
SOUL EMBRACED	531
SOUL REAPER	531
SOULBURN	531
SOULDRAINER	531
SOULFALLEN	532
SOULFORGE	532
SOULGRIND	532
SOULHAVOC	533
SOULLESS	533
SOULLESS HEART	533
SOULS ON FIRE	533
SOULSCAR	533
SPAWN OF POSSESSION	534
SPAZZ	534
SPHERE	534
SPINAL CORD	535
SPIRAL MADNESS	535
SQUASH BOWELS	535
STABWOUND	536
STARGAZER	536
STATE OF INTEGRITY	536
STEEP	536
STILLBIRTH	537
STILLBORN	537
STRONG INTENTION	537
SUBLUSTRIS	537
SUBTENEBRAS	538
SUFFER	538
SUFFERAGE	538
SUFFOCATE BASTARD	538
SUFFOCATION	539
SUFFOKATOR	540
SUHRIM	540
SUICIDE	540
SUICIDE CULTURE	541
SUICIDE SILENCE	541
SUICIDE SOLUTION	541
SUMMONER	541
SUPURATION	542
SURROGOAT	542
SUTURE	542
SWALLOW THE SUN	542
SWARRRM	543
SWEDISH MASSACRE	543
SWEET SORROW	543
SWOLLEN	544
SWORDMASTER	544
SYMPATHY	544
SYRACH	544
SYSTEM SHOCK	545
SYSTEM:OBSCURE	545
SÉANCE	545
TAKETH	545
TENEBRARUM	546
TERROR	546
TERRORIZER	546
TEXTURES	547
THALES	547
THANATOS	547
THAT OLD BLACK MAGIC	548
THE ABSENCE	549
THE ABYSS	549
THE ACCURSED	549
THE AGONY SCENE	550
THE APPARATUS	550
THE BEAUTY OF DYING	551
THE BEREAVED	551
THE BERZERKER	551
THE BLACK DAHLIA MURDER	551
THE CHASM	552
THE CIRCLE OF ZAPHYAN	553
THE COUNTY MEDICAL EXAMINERS	553
THE CROWN	553
THE DECAY THEORY	554
THE DEVIANT	554
THE DILLINGER ESCAPE PLAN	555
THE DUSKFALL	556
THE ELYSIAN FIELDS	556
THE EMBODIMENT	557
THE EMBRACED	557
THE ENCHANTED	557
THE EVERSCATHED	558

THE EXORIAL	558
THE FALLEN	558
THE FLESH	558
THE FORSAKEN	559
THE FUNERAL PYRE	559
THE LOCUST	559
THE LUST I SEEK	560
THE MEADS OF ASPHODEL	560
THE MEATSHITS	561
THE MONOLITH DEATHCULT	562
THE NUMBER TWELVE LOOKS LIKE YOU	562
THE PLAGUE	562
THE PROJECT HATE	563
THE RED CHORD	564
THE REVENGE PROJECT	564
THE SCOURGER	564
THE SEVENTH DELIRIUM	565
THE TOMBERS	565
THEORY IN PRACTICE	565
THIS ENDING	565
THORAZINE	566
THORIUM	566
THORNAFIRE	566
THOU SHALT SUFFER	567
THRALLDOM	567
THROCULT	567
THROMDARR	568
THRONE OF CHAOS	568
THRONEAEON	568
THRONEUM	569
THROUGH THE EYES OF THE DEAD	569
THURISAZ	570
THY DISEASE	570
THY FLESH CONSUMED	570
THY LEGACY	571
THY SERPENT	571
THYABHORRENT	571
TIAMAT	571
TIBURON	573
TO SEPARATE THE FLESH FROM THE BONES	573
TOMBTHROAT	574
TORCHBEARER	574
TORN	575
TORTHARRY	575
TORTURE ETERNAL	575
TORTURE KILLER	575
TORTURE SQUAD	576
TOTAL DEVASTATION	576
TOTAL FUCKING DESTRUCTION	576
TOTTEN KORPS	577
TOXICDEATH	577
TOXOCARA	577
TRASOS	577
TRAUMA	577
TREBLINKA	578
TRIBULATION	578
TRIVIUM	578
TROLLHEIM'S GROTT	580
TUBE	580
TUSKA	580
TWILIGHT	580
TYPHOID	581
ULCERATE	581
ULTIMATUM	581
UMBRAE	582
UNANIMATED	582
UNBOUND	582
UNCANNY	582
UNCURBED	583
UNDER MOONLIGHT SADNESS	584
UNDER THREAT	584
UNDERCROFT	584
UNGODLY	585
UNHOLY GHOST	585
UNHOLY GRAVE	585
UNHOLY TRINITY	586
UNKNOWN	586
UNLEASHED	586
UNREAL OVERFLOWS	587
UNSANCTUM	587
UNSEEN TERROR	587
URKRAFT	588
V:28	588
VADER	588
VAKARM	591
VAULTAGE	591
VEHEMENCE	591
VENGEANCE RISING	592
VERMIN	592
VERMINOUS	592
VEULIAH	593
VIBRION	593
VICIOUS	593
VICIOUS ART	593
VICTIM	594
VICTIMIZER	594
VICTIMS OF INTERNAL DECAY	594
VIGILIA MORTUM	595
VIHALIHA	595
VII ARCANO	595
VILE	596
VIOLATION	596
VIOLENT ASYLUM	596
VIOLENT HEADACHE	596
VIRULENCE	597
VIRULENT BLESSING	597
VISCERAL BLEEDING	597
VITAL REMAINS	598
VITALITY	599
VITUPERATION	599
VOLATILE	599
VOMIT	599
VOMIT REMNANTS	599
VOMITORY	600
VOMITURITION	600
VORE	601
VULGAR PIGEONS	601
VULTURE	601
WACO JESUS	601
WARGASM	602
WARHAMMER	602
WARHEAD	602
WATCH ME FALL	602
WATCH MY DYING	602
WEB	603
WEHRWOLFE	603
WELKIN	603
WINDHAM HELL	603
WINGS	604
WINTER	604
WITCHERY	604
WITCHES SABBATH	605
WITHERED	605
WITHERED BEAUTY	605
WITHERED EARTH	606
WITHERED GARDEN	606
WITHIN Y	606
WITHOUT GRIEF	606

WOMB	607
WOMB OF MAGGOTS	607
WORLD OF LIES	607
WORMFOOD	607
WORSHIP FACTORY	608
WOUNDS	608
WRATHAGE	608
XANTOSSA	608
XENOFANES	609
XENOMORPH	609
XERPENTOR	609
XYSMA	609
YATTERING	610
YOUR SHAPELESS BEAUTY	610
ZARATHUSTRA	611
ZEENON	611
ZENITE	611
ZIRCONIUM	611
ZOLTAR	612
ZOMBIE VOMIT	612
ZONARIA	612
ZUBROWSKA	612
ZYKLON	612

1917

BUENOS AIRES, ARGENTINA — *Alejandro Sabransky (vocals / guitar), Pansa (bass).*

1917 debuted in Lima, Buenos Aires during 1996 with the demo tape 'Bienvenido A La Nada'. The group had been founded as a quartet of vocalist Marcos, Alejandro Sabransky, bass player Pansa and drummer Fernando some two years earlier. In 1997 the band featured on a three way split demo entitled 'Memorias De Muerte' but then Pansa exited. With this core member out of the picture the band went into hiatus. However, the recruitment of Damien on bass the following year re-activated the band resulting in the EP 'Inti Huacay'. Marcos would then quit, necessitating Sabransky's assumption of the lead vocal role.

1917's next career move was to record fresh tracks for a series of compilation albums for release in Argentina, Portugal and Italy. Upon completion of sessions for use on a Hurling Metal collection Pansa made a return as both Fernando and Damien opted out. The band laid down a full length album 'Genesis & Horror' for Hurling Metal then cut further songs for a three way split CD, alongside SLOW DEATH and SLOW AGONY, billed as 'Sudamerica Brutal Volume II' for issue in December 2002.

Southern Hellish issued the April 2005 album 'Neo-Ritual'. 1917 included their rendition of 'Blood Red' on the June 2006 Hurling Metal Records SLAYER tribute album "Al Sur Del Abismo (Tributo Argentino A Slayer)'.

Inti Huacay EP, Independent (1998). Inti Huacay (Part I) / Redención / Ruinas Sobre Ruinas / Encadenados Al Sufrimiento / Repression And Guilt / Voces Infames / Inti Huacay (Part II).
GENESIS & HORROR, Hurling Metal (2002). Kondores / Hijos De La Contradicción / El Arte De Ser Decadencia / Fatalidad / Agonico Orden / Brotherhood Of Barbarism / El Beso Del Verdugo / Shadows Of Sorrow.
SUDAMERICA BRUTAL VOL. II, Hurling Metal (2002) (Split album with SLOW DEATH and SLOW AGONY). Intro / Cuervo Sin Alas / Tierra De Suenos Muertos / Luz Y Abismo / El Arte De Ser Decadencia.
VISION, Hurling Metal HMR028 (2004). In Tenebra / La Vieja Sangre / Piel De Martir, Carne De Asesino / Mercader De Voluntades / Simbolod Muertos / Visiones / Realidad Desmembrada / Anidadndo Entre Serpientes.
NEO-RITUAL, Southern Hellish (2005). Intro / Negras Alas Del Bien / Principe De Los Dolidos / Sin Voluntad / Neo-Ritual / Necedad Inquebrantable / Perpetuas / Condenados A Existir / La Verdad Del Miserable / Outro.

21 LUCIFERS

FALUN, SWEDEN — *Erik Skoglund (vocals), Tobias Ols (guitar), Nicklas Lindh (guitar), Pär Eriksson (bass), Olle Ferner (drums).*

A Falun based Death / Thrash unit 21 LUCIFERS was formulated in 2002 by former FIVE MORE VICTIMS vocalist / guitarist Erik Skoglund, ex-WITHOUT GRIEF bassist Ola Berg and BLUDGE drummer Björn Åström. Two Grindcore orientated tracks would be recorded after which the trio settled on a band name of GRIDLOCK. Subsequently another WITHOUT GRIEF member, guitarist Nicklas Lindh, enrolled and steered the band into Thrashier territory. With Skoglund opting to concentrate purely on vocals a third WITHOUT GRIEF man was enlisted as second guitarist in the form of Tobias Ols.

21 LUCIFERS issued the 2002 demo 'Retaliation', recorded at Black Lounge Studios and produced by Jonas Kjellgren. Changes in the 21 LUCIFERS line-up during 2003 saw the incorporation of bassist Pär "Sodomizer" Eriksson and drummer Olle Ferner, both having credits with AVSMAK. The demo 'Hope Fades' emerged in 2004, prompting a label deal with the Dutch record company Karmageddon Media. Recording at Black Lounge Studios the band wrapped up their debut album 'In The Name Of . . .' in October.

21 LUCIFERS signed to JMT Music in December 2005.

Retaliation, 21 Lucifers (2002) (Demo). Hate Will Prevail / Kill Or Blood / Self Pollution / Five Infernal Years / Retaliation.
Hope Fades, 21 Lucifers (2004) (Demo). Hope Fades / Man Made Misery / Killing At Will / Addicted To Chaos.
IN THE NAME OF . . ., Karmageddon Media (2005). In The Name Of . . . / . . . Violence / Art Of Chaos / Greed Spreader / Die Dead Gone / Hate Will Prevail / Hope Fades / Perfect Hell / Broken / Kill Or Blood / Manmade Misery / Surprise! You're Dead! / Killing At Will / Where Apathy Dwells / Self Pollution / Quid Pro Quo / 5 Infernal Years / Retaliation.
IN THE NAME OF . . ., JMT Music JMT30303 (2006). In The Name Of . . . / . . . Violence / Art Of Chaos / Greed Spreader / Die Dead Gone / Hate Will Prevail / Hope Fades / Perfect Hell / Broken / Kill Or Blood / Manmade Misery / Surprise! You're Dead! / Killing At Will / Where Apathy Dwells / Self Pollution / Quid Pro Quo / 5 Infernal Years / Retaliation.

5 BILLION DEAD

ORLANDO, FL, USA — *Strain (vocals), Alex Vieira (guitar), Matt Wagner (bass), Chris (drums).*

Orlando, Florida Metalcore band featuring New York native 'Strain' (a.k.a. Gary Dufner) on vocals, CAPHARNAUM guitarist Alex Vieira and EQUINOX and MORTEM A.D.'s Matt Wagner W (a.k.a. 'Darkness') on bass. Dufner had previously fronted New York outfits ETERNAL CHAOS, ACID and PLATO'S CAVE before relocating to Florida and singing for DNS then DEFORM NATION in 2000, the latter act featuring ex-UNDERCORE and future 5 BILLION DEAD drummer Chris.

5 BILLION DEAD's eponymous 2004 EP would be Recorded at Audiohammer Studios by Jason Suecof and mastered by the esteemed Jim Morris at the famed Morrisound Recording studio. Not only would the EP host bonus video tracks but also a free Roadrunner Records sampler album 'Summer Of Metal'. Vieira would second himself out to CANNAE for US touring in mid 2005.

In 2006 word arrived of a new band unit entitled DEAD MENS DREAMS, featuring singer Strain, bassist Matt Wagner plus STILLKEPT, SLANG, MINDSCAPE 9 and RESPONSE NEGATIVE guitarist Claudzilla and RESPONSE NEGATIVE drummer Jim.

5 Billion Dead, Hate The World (2004). Parts / Buried In Sand / Hate The World / Reality Filter.

8 FOOT SATIVA

AUCKLAND, NEW ZEALAND — *Ben Read (vocals), Gary Smith (guitar), Christian Humphreys (guitar), Romilly Smith (bass), Jamie Saint Merat (drums).*

West Auckland modern Metal band 8 FOOT SATIVA, comprising lead vocalist Justin Niessen, UK born guitarist Gary Smith, bass player Brent Fox and Sam Sheppard on the drums, established themselves during 1998. Rapidly building a large local following the band broke through into national radio and TV rotation, so much so that the band was scoring more viewer support than many international Pop artists. Prior to the issue of debut album 'Hate Made Me', arriving via Intergalactic Records in March 2002, the group played a number of gigs around the country, including opening for PANTERA and CORROSION OF CONFORMITY at the Auckland Town Hall early 2001. A line-up change shortly after release of 'Hate Made Me', which reached no. 43 on the national New Zealand charts, saw Sam Sheppard of SINATE and O.C.D. ('Obsessive Compulsive Disorder') taking over from original drummer Speed.

The December 2002 headline trek across New Zealand, dubbed 'The Hate Made Us All' tour, was capitalised on by gaining valuable supports to visiting artists such as DISTURBED in February 2003. The group would also attract attention in the USA with an appearance at the Austin, Texas SXSW event. Spreading their international reach even further 8 FOOT SATIVA would be one of the very few Kiwi acts to accomplish

8 FOOT SATIVA (pic: Jonathan Pilkington)

a full world tour, taking in shows in London, Toronto, Hong Kong, Sydney and New York. Roadrunner Records licensed the debut for Australian release that same year.

8 FOOT SATIVA's second album 'Season For Assault' arrived in October of 2003. The group performed at the Auckland METALLICA headlined 'Big Day Out' festival in January of 2004. August and September shows throughout New Zealand saw the band allied with FRANKENBOK with SUBTRACT handling opening honours in the North Island and SYNDIKAT in the South Island. 'Season For Assaults impact spread further when renowned Swedish label Black Mark records picked the album up for European license. The band worked their way across Australia in May and June forming up the 'Army Of Darkness' trek in union with FRANKENBOK, FULL SCALE and SUNK LOTO. A third effort for Intergalactic, 'Breed The Pain', was delivered in December 2004.

With 8 FOOT SATIVA making waves internationally, it came as a shock for fans to see both Matt and Sam Sheppard breaking away to re-forge SINATE mid 2005. From this point on the band's experienced numerous changes starting with the recruitment of new drummer Corey Friedlander, a veteran of FINAL EVE and RELENTLESS ATTRITION, and a short-lived return of vocalist Justin Niessen. Vocalist Ben Read, of ULCERATE and IN DREAD RESPONSE, replaced Niessen in late 2005 with additional guitarist William Cleverdon joining around the same time. However, Cleverdon would be superseded by Christian Humpreys.

In May 2007 the band released the self-financed 'Poison Of Ages' album, this witnessing a drift into contemporary Metalcore, subsequently scoring major label distribution through Universal. 8 FOOT SATIVA supported MOTÖRHEAD and ROSE TATTOO in New Plymouth that October.

HATE MADE ME, Intergalactic IR007 (2002) (New Zealand release). Before Your Suffering / Hate Made Me / Fuel Set / Cocktease / Believer / It's All So Real / Grown Aggression / Stolen Life / Kick It All Away / 8 Foot Sativa / Engine / Invention. Chart position: 43 NEW ZEALAND.
HATE MADE ME, Roadrunner (2003) (Australian release). Before Your Suffering / Hate Made Me / Fuel Set / Cocktease / Believer / It's All So Real / Grown Aggression / Stolen Life / Kick It All Away / 8 Foot Sativa / Engine / Invention.
SEASON FOR ASSAULT, Intergalactic IR666 (2003) (New Zealand release). What's Lost Tomorrow / For Religions To Suffer / Hatred Forever / Chelsea Smile / Disorder / Escape From Reality / Destined To Be Dead / Season For Assault / The Abused / Gutless. Chart position: 6 NEW ZEALAND.
SEASON FOR ASSAULT, Roadrunner (2004) (Australian release). What's Lost Is Tomorrow / Escape From Reality / For Religions To Suffer / Destined To Be Dead / Hatred Forever / Season For Assault / Chelsea Smile / The Abused / Disorder / Gutless.
SEASON FOR ASSAULT, Black Mark BMCD177 (2004) (European release). What's Lost Is Tomorrow / Escape From Reality / For Religions To Suffer / Destined To Be Dead / Hatred Forever / Season For Assault / Chelsea Smile / The Abused / Disorder / Gutless.
BREED THE PAIN, Intergalactic IR011 (2005) (New Zealand release). Perpetual Torment / Breed The Pain / I Live My Death / Mentally Castrated / Altar Of Obscenity / Human Abattoir / Brutal Revenge / The Punishment Within / Genetic Treason.
BREED THE PAIN, Roadrunner (2005) (Australian release). Perpetual Torment / Breed The Pain / I Live My Death / Mentally Castrated / Altar Of Obscenity / Human Abattoir / Brutal Revenge / The Punishment Within / Genetic Treason.
BREED THE PAIN, Black Mark BMCD182 (2005) (European release). Perpetual Torment / Breed The Pain / I Live My Death / Mentally Castrated / Altar Of Obscenity / Human Abattoir / Brutal Revenge / Punishment Within / Genetic Treason.
POISON OF AGES, Black Mark (2007). For The Birds / Crosses For Eyes / Napalm Existence / Exeunt / The Great Western Cliff-Hanger / Emancipate / Ashes Of The Arsonist / We, The Termites / Pirates And Capitalists / Thumbs, Eye-Sockets, Love.

9TH PLAGUE

HELSINGBORG, SWEDEN — *Tony Richter (vocals), Johan Lindberg (guitar), Kristofer Örstadins (guitar / bass), Rafael Andersson (drums).*

9TH PLAGUE is a Helsingborg Death/Black Metal band created in June of 2000 by vocalist Tony Richter, guitarist Johan Lindberg and drummer Rafael Andersson, later enrolling THE DARKSEND guitarist Stefan Stigert. Richter, besides being owner of 'Nekrologium' fanzine, has a track record with a whole slew of extreme Metal bands such as SLIMESUCKERS, CORRUPTION, DEMISE, SLAVESTATE, ASMODEUS, GARDENS OF OBSCURITY, THE DARKSEND, SPIRITUAL TORTURE, SMÄRTA, LEGION OF DEATH and, in 1998, NOCTURNITY. Both Lindberg and Andersson's prior history saw terms with DET GLÖMDA, ABUSUS AD MORTEM and MANDATORY CARNAGE. The guitarist had also served with EPITAPH OF ETERNITY whilst Andersson had membership of SABBATIC GOAT.

By December of 2000 this opening formation had cut the demo track 'Demonic Conjuration'. The following year saw an abortive attempt to commit the song 'Sacrilegious Predestination' to tape. Meantime, the first 9TH PLAGUE track 'Demonic Conjuration was chosen for inclusion on the compilation album 'Voices Of Death part IV: The Metal Crusade'.

The self financed 'Spreading The Satanic Gospel' EP emerged in December 2002, these sessions marking the introduction of ex-NECROPIA and SACRIFICIAL THORNS bassist Kristofer Örstadius. With Stigert's departure, Örstadius made the switch over to guitar as the group garnered further exposure courtesy of track inclusions on Ignite Production's 'Migraine In The Membrane' compilation and on samplers from 'Vampira' and 'Random' fanzines. Subsequently a cassette version of 'Spreading The Satanic Gospel' emerged as a split offering entitled 'United In Real Brutality' shared with Serbian act MUTILATION. A demo, 'Age Of Satanic Enlightenment', was issued in April 2004 and that August Tobbe Hellman of NOMINON, DION FORTUNE and OBSCENE repute took over bass duties. However, this latest candidate exited in June 2005.

9TH PLAGUE issued the demo 'Triumph Of Diabolism' in August 2006.

Spreading The Satanic Gospel, 9th Plague (2002) (Demo). Visions Of An Unknown God / Revelation Of My Name / Restore The Demonic Earth / Temple Of Belial.
United In Real Brutality, (2003) (Split demo with MUTILATION). Visions Of An Unknown God / Revelation Is My Name / Restore The Demonic Earth / Temple Of Belial.
Age Of Satanic Enlightenment, 9th Plague (2004) (Demo). Betwixt And Between / Beyond The Flesh / The Voice Of Ancient Blasphemy.
Triumph Of Diabolism, 9th Plague (2006) (Demo). Renewed Vow Of Blasphemy / The God Of Ekron Resurrected / The Shrine Of Satan.

A CANOROUS QUINTET

KUNGSÄNGEN, SWEDEN — *Mårten Hansen (vocals), Linus Nirbrant (guitar), Lei Pignon (guitar), Jesper Löfgren (bass), Fredrik Andersson (drums).*

Formed in 1991, the Kungsängen / Stockholm based A CANOROUS QUINTET, a brutal Death / Black Metal act, released their 17 minute 1993 'The Time Of Autumn' demo having undergone a multitude of line-up changes up to that point. An October 1994 EP, 'As Tears' released through Chaos Productions, saw a band roster comprising singer Mårten Hansen, guitarists Leo Pignon and Linus Nirbrant, bass player Jesper Löfgren and Fredrik Andersson on drums. The group released two albums for No Fashion Records, 1996's 'Silence Of The World Beyond', recorded at Abyss Studios with HYPOCRISY's Peter Tägtgren acting as producer, and 'The Only Pure Hate' in 1998 crafted at Sunlight Studios with Tomas Skogsberg behind the desk. However, A CANOROUS QUINTET would fold that same year. Guitarist Leo Pignon later forged a similar Black Metal outfit NIDEN DIV. 187 with members of DAWN and THY PRIMORDIAL releasing two albums 'Towards Judgement' and 'Impergium' on Necropolis Records. Drummer Fredrik Andersson is better known for his role in premier Swedish Black Metal band MARDUK. Andersson also boasts credits with AMON AMARTH, TRIUMPHATOR and ALLEGIANCE.

Vocalist Mårten Hansen guested on OCTOBER TIDE's 1999 album 'Grey Dawn'. By 2000 both guitarist Linus Nirbrant and Andersson were involved with GUIDANCE OF SIN. The following year Andersson's services were requested by AMON AMARTH. The drummer also found space, alongside Pignon, to launch side venture CURRICULUM MORTIS in union with Mattias Leinikka from GUIDANCE OF SIN as lead vocalist. The debut demo 'Into Death' surfaced in 2003.

Andersson started up a fresh project band in 2003, LAID TO REST being a Death / Thrash Metal project featuring KAPUT! and ORCHARDS OF ODENWRATH guitarist Zack Z. Former members of A CANOROUS QUINTET, Mårten Hansen, Leo Pignon, Linus Nirbrant, Jesper Löfgren and Fredrik Andersson, embarked upon a new band project, THE PLAGUE, in early 2005. This act evolved further into THIS ENDING during 2006.

Promo '94, A Canorous Quintet (0) (Demo).
The Time Of Autumn, A Canorous Quintet (1993) (Demo). Revert To Life / Untitled / The Time Of Autumn / Searching.
As Tears EP, Chaos CHAOSCD 02 (1994). Through Endless Illusions / The Joy Of Sorrow / When Happiness Dies / Strangeland.
SILENCE OF THE WORLD BEYOND, A Canorous Quintet NFR 019 (1996). Silence Of The World Beyond / Naked With Open Eyes / Spellbound / The Orchid's Sleep / The Black Spiral / The Last Journey / In The Twilight Of Fear / Burning, Emotionless / Dream Reality.
THE ONLY PURE HATE, No Fashion NFR028 (1998). Selfdeceiver (The Purest Of Hate) / Embryo Of Lies / Red / The Void / Everbleed / The Complete Emptiness / Retaliation / Realm Of Rain / The Storm / Land Of The Lost.

A COLD REALITY

WALTHAM, MA, USA — *Jimmy Campbell (vocals), Justin Joseph (guitar), Brian Higgins (guitar), Neil Souza (bass), Josh Hamwey (drums).*

Waltham, Massachusetts Death / Thrash Metal band COLD REALITY, featuring ex-SLAUGHTERED AT DAWN guitarist Justin Joseph, debuted with a June 2001 demo 'The Silence Remains No Longer', actually taken from a live radio broadcast on WBRS 100.1 FM, with second promotion session 'Remnants Of A Shattered Dream' following in August 2002. COLD REALITY's first, self-financed album, 'As Fading Moments Elapse Into Memories', was delivered in January 2003. However, throughout much of the following year the group remained in stasis, eventually splitting with singer John Reid in October. Guitarist Justin Joseph, previously active with THE INTRICATE SLAUGHTER PROCESS, initiated side projects ABREACTION and AS A DEAD ROSE WITHERS. Returning to the studio, A COLD REALITY cut an October 2003 pre-production demo with Joseph taking lead vocals.

The band re-introduced former singer Jimmy Campbell in August 2004 and added new guitarist Brian Higgins in October.

The Silence Remains No Longer, A Cold Reality (2001). Frozen In Time (Intro) / Staring At The Sky / Strong / Passion Within / Forsaken Soul.
Remnants Of A Shattered Dream, (2002). My Flesh, My Blood / Staring At The Sky / Passion Within.
AS FADING MOMENTS ELAPSE INTO MEMORIES, (2003). The Fallen Angel / My Flesh, My Blood / Your Voice Remains / Remnants Of A Shattered Dream / Staring At The Sky / Prayer For The Living / Passion Within / Forsaken Soul / Deliverance.
My Flesh, My Blood, (2003). Your Voice Remains / My Flesh, My Blood / Prayer For The Living / Remnants Of A Shattered Dream.
A Cold Reality, (2003). Children Of Babylon / Seventh Seal / Empty / Cleanse / Ignorance, I Slay / Of The Everlasting.

A GRUESOME FIND

TOLEDO, OH, USA — *Naberius (vocals), Lord Ryan Mininger (guitar), Jim Albrecht (bass), Lord Cessna (drums).*

Toledo's A GRUESOME FIND assimilate Black and Death styles to forge "True Ohioan Bleath Metal". The group was brought to life in April of 1998 by former CARRION guitarists Lord Ryan Miniger and Jason Reynolds with drummer Jason Trumble. Subsequent line-up changes were settled with the induction of singer Mark of the Damned and bassist Boe Skadeland. Following initial gigging the vocalist was let go and another CARRION veteran, Greg Smith, took command of the drums. The latter's stay would be brief though and before long Jim Little was manning the drum kit as Duke of CARRION assumed vocal responsibilities. This version of A GRUESOME FIND would ultimately grind to a halt though with Reynolds and Skadeland finding a new calling with KRYPTIK EMBRACE.

Re-formulating, Lord Miniger and Mark of the Damned allied themselves with bass player Isaac Cain and drummer DeathCrush for recording of the 2002 EP 'Ravens Of The Full Moon Eclipse'. However, upon completion of these sessions Naberius of REFLECTIONS OF DEATH repute took over the role of frontman. Isaac Cain exited in January 2005 but, following extensive auditions to fill the vacancy, Cain rejoined the ranks in May 2005.

The album 'Minions Engage' was issued in August 2005 through Crash Music. The group's roster in May 2007 comprised Lord Mininger "Razorwire & synth", Naberius "Lyrical tyranny", Lord Albrecht "Lower detonation", Jim Albrecht from Michigan Death Metal band GENOCYA, and Lord Cessna "Battery" from FOREVER LOST. In June the band commenced recording the album 'Of Blood And Nobility' at Dimmworks studios in Akron with producer Mike Carlton.

Ravens Of The Full Moon Eclipse EP, Vile Art (2002). Ravens Of The Full Moon Eclipse / Upon The Throne Of Chaos / Slaughter Of The Lamb / Embodying The Spirit Of Evil.
THE FIRE THAT BURNS IN HELL, Vile Art (2003). The Fire That Burns In Hell / Summoning The Nocturnal Spirit / When Darkness Falls / Blasphemous Bloodstorm / Bring Forth / Devoid Of Humanity / ... As The Wind Blows In Darkness.
MINIONS ENGAGE, Crash Music (2006). Minions Engage / Curse Of Shedim / Nightmare Within / Tree Of Despair / Shroud Of Darkness / Conquerors Of The Darkland / Blood Red Moon / Pawns Of The Deceiver / Wrath / Triumph.

A MIND CONFUSED

STOCKHOLM, SWEDEN — *Johan Thörngren (vocals), Konstantin Papavassilion (guitar), Richard Wyoni (guitar), Nicklas Eriksson (bass), Thomas Aberg (drums).*

Stockholm Death Metal band comprising singer Johan Thörngren, guitarists Konstantin Papavassilou and Richard Wyoni, bassist Nicklas Eriksson and drummer Thomas Aberg. A MIND CONFUSED released a 1995 demo, 'Poems Of A Darker Soul', followed by the 7" single 'Out Of Chaos Spawn' in 1996, a limited edition of 1000 copies pressed by Near Dark Productions.

The June 1997 A MIND CONFUSED 'Anarchos' album, again issued via Near Dark Productions, saw a production credit going to DISMEMBER's Fred Estby. The album would resurface some five years later in Russia courtesy of the Irond label.

Upon the demise of A MIND CONFUSED guitarists Konstantin Papavassilou and Nicklas Eriksson forged KAAMOS. The latter would also be operational with Thrashers SERPENT OBSCENE.

Poems Of A Darker Soul, Near Dark Productions NDP001 (1995). Eternal Sleep / Dreams Of An Erotic Salvation / A Mind Confused / Poems Of A Darker Soul / Morningstar In Zenith / Forever Autumn.

A Mind Confused, A Mind Confused (1995) (Demo). Vengeance / The Shine Of Silver / Fears Of The Serpent / The Kingdom That One Was / Father Of Betrayal.

Out Of Chaos Spawn, Near Dark Productions NDP004 (1996) (Limited edition 1000 hand numbered copies). Out Of Chaos Spawn / Enchantress Of The Dark.

ANARCHOS, Near Dark Productions NDP009 (1997). Bloodpoem / Consecration Of Death / Seducer Of Pain Divine / Obliteration / Ophidia Astrum / Suffer My Deeds / Sanctum Black / Anarchos / Eternal Sleep / Out Of Chaos Spawn.

A PERPETUAL DYING MIRROR

IRAPUATO, MEXICO — *Isaías Huerta (vocals / keyboards), Marce Méndez (guitar), Saúl Flores (guitar), Héctor García (bass), Jesús Bravo (drums).*

In late 1994 erstwhile personnel from SUPPLICIUM, vocalist / keyboard player Isaías Huerta and guitarist Marce Méndez brokered the formation of a new Irapuato based Doom Death Metal force entitled A PERPETUAL DYING MIRROR. By 1996 the band had attained a stable line-up incorporating Huerta, Mendez, rhythm guitarist Carlos Piceno, bass player Héctor García with Jesús Bravo of AGONY LORDS and SOULS ON FIRE repute on the drums. A demo, 'Towards A Constellation View' was recorded and given valuable distribution courtesy of Nighthaunt Records.

In May of 2001 Piceno was usurped by Saúl Flores. This revised version of A PERPETUAL DYING MIRROR laid down a three track demo 'Hermeticum Elohim Chiim'. Isaías Huerta would found old school Death Metal band NECROCCULTUS in 2003.

TOWARDS A CONSTELLATON VIEW, Sempiternal Productions SP 018 (2002). Thy Tragedian Shine (Astral Sublimity Of Night) / Within The Mirror Phosphorescence / An Autumndawn For Eternity / The Forgotten I / All Perpetual Veils / Towards A Constellation View / Hermeticum Elohim Chiim / Pilgrimage Of Dying Ones / Fullmoon In Scorpivs.

A.W.A.S.

BONN, GERMANY — *Viktor Kröker (vocals), Konni Epp (guitar), Eddy Littau (bass), Martin Epp (drums).*

Bonn based Christian Death Metal. Originally billed as TORMENT upon their 1999 foundation the group subsequently took on the title A.W.A.S. ("Acoustic War Against Satan"). The opening formation counted the Epp siblings, guitarist Konni and bassist Martin, alongside dual vocalists Martin E. and Viktor Kröker with Ruben W. on the drums. In 2000 Martin E. switched over to drums as Ruben departed. Stephan Dyck entered the fold in April 2004, initially on bass, but then switching to guitar.

The demo 'Time To Choose' emerged in 2003. Bassist Martin Kuhn would be superseded by Eddy Littau. A.W.A.S. recorded a self-financed album, entitled 'Hope', during 2006. A.W.A.S. parted ways with guitarist Stephan Dyck. Open Grave Records re-released the 'Hope' album in February 2007.

Time To Choose, A.W.A.S. (2003). Time To Choose / Darkness / A.W.A.S. / Love.

HOPE, Open Grave (2007).

ABADDON

OBERHAUSEN, GERMANY — *Markus Esch (vocals), Diana Link (vocals), Daniel Esch (guitar), David Diedrichs (guitar), Steffen Schmitz (bass), Darius Widera (keyboards).*

ABADDON, founded in Oberhausen during 1995, debuted three years later with the demo 'The Infernal Revelation'. In 1998 frontman Markus Esch acted as guest vocalist on NEBULAR MOON's 'Mourning' release. ABADDON's 2001 self-financed album 'De Occulta Philosophia' was recorded at Prolog-Studios in Dortmund by a line-up comprising vocalists Markus Esch and Leif Pannewig, bassist Steffen Schmitz, guitarists Daniel Esch and Sebastian Bossmann, keyboard player Dorothea Pomsel and drummer Lars Tschentschel. Shortly after recording Bossmann was involved in an auto accident, and would be duly replaced by SOULSLIDE and EXECRATE's David Diederichs.

In September of 2002 both Tschentschel and keyboard player Simone Dyllong exited. Darius Widera of NEBULAR MOON, SYNESTHESY and SACRASPHEMY repute enrolled on keyboards. In May of 2003 SACRASPHEMY's Lukas Raupp took over the drum position. ABADDON commenced work on a proposed second album, 'Exprimere Confessionem', that same year.

In March of 2004 Raupp was forced out of the band due to "sudden deafness". Former sticksman Lars Tschentschel made a return for live work.

DE OCCULTA PHILOSOPHIA, Abaddon Independent (2001). De Occulta Philosophia / Nunquam Mores / Ambrosi De Mysteriis / Origines Conta Celsum / Dein Sancta Sanctorum / Illuminationem / Omnia, Lucili / Cathechesi Prima / Requiem.

ABADDON

LAARBEEK, HOLLAND — *Sander Bevers (vocals / guitar), Frank de Groot (guitar), Bas de Kruyff (bass), Dirk Verspaget (keyboards), Ralf Bloemers (drums).*

Laarbeek based Black-Death Metal band. Formulated in 1994, openly and directly inspired by OBITUARY, the trio of guitarist Sander 'Zandor' Bevers, bass player Bas de Kruyff and drummer Gijs van de Kerkhof created the group's first incarnation known as SIMPLY DEATH. Before long Bevers decamped but would make a return as the group morphed into CONTRA MALICE and opted to pursue a Black Metal direction. This new unit subsequently inducted Frank de Groot as second guitarist.

1997 saw the exit of van de Kerkhof. Regrouping with the incorporation of female singer Danielle Claassen and drummer Dirk 'Draego' Verspaget the band yet again switched titles, this time to ABADDON. The tribulations would be far from over though and in 1999 both new recruits broke ranks. Maurits 'Maus' van Sambeek took the drumming vacancy and oddly Verspaget also rejoined but this time as a keyboard player. In this incarnation ABADDON laid down the 'Death In Magenta' EP.

ABADDON pulled in DR. ROCK drummer Ralf Bloemers in October of 2002, using this manoeuvre to switch to a self styled Heavy Death Metal style. Verspaget is also active as drummer for DEPREDATION and TOMBE.

Into the Twilight Kingdom, Independent (1998). Where Will You Be / Darkening Of Eden / Inside … / Nocturnal Seduction / Gods Of All Gods.

Death in Magenta, Independent (2000). Death In Magenta / Victims Of Nature / Conjuring Heaven / Ending World.

ABED

TEL AVIV, ISRAEL — *Ran Yerushalmi (vocals), Matan Berkowitz (guitar), Guy Bloom (guitar), Gal Yaron Meirson (bass), Dror Goldstein (drums).*

Tel Aviv technical Death Metal act ABED, dating to 2001 and founded by guitarists Matan Berkowitz and Guy Bloom, was originally fronted by the FRANTIC and MATRICIDE credited Yotam 'Defiler' Avni and also features ETERNAL GRAY's Dror Glodstein on the drums. Releases included the single 'Mechanical Scythe' issued in July of 2002, this track also appearing on the 'Holy Shit' compilation album, a demo entitled 'Operation: Silence' in 2003, produced by Ami Haronyan at Spawn Studios, and a further EP in March of 2004 '281-219', recorded at Mighty Wobble Studios by Yoni Bar Illan.

Avni sessioned onstage with ORPHANED LAND in 2004. That same year the group drafted new vocalist Ran Yerushalmi. ABED issued an EP, entitled 'The Coming Of Soon', in June 2006.

Mechanical Scythe, Abed (2002). Mechanical Scythe.
Operation : Silence, Abed (2003) (Promo). Operation : Silence / Elegy Of Joy / Mechanical Scythe / Operation : Silence / Fields / Xipix.
281-219, Abed (2004). 281-219.
The Coming Of Soon, Abed (2006). Cement / The Coming Of Soon / Cold Smoke / Redeemabilty.

ABHORRENCE

SÃO JOSÉ DO RIO PRETO, SP, BRAZIL — *Rangel Arroyo (vocals / bass), Marcello Marzari (bass), Fernando (drums).*

Brazilian ultra speed Death Metal founded in 1997. ABHORRENCE arrived with the three track 1997 demo 'Ascension' which would later be pressed onto CD in America by the Wild Rags label. The band cut a further demo tape 'Triumph In Blasphemy' prior to signing to Florida's Evil Vengeance label for the album 'Evoking The Abomination'. Not only did the album benefit from sleeve artwork courtesy of MOTÖRHEAD artist Joe Petagno but the finished tapes were mastered by MORBID ANGEL man Erik Rutan. French imprint Listenable Records licensed the album for Europe.

ABHORRENCE also featured on the Relapse 1999 4 way split CD 'Brazilian Assault' in alliance with MENTAL HORROR, NEPHASTH and OPHIOLATRY Original bass player Kleber Varnier would later make way for Marcello Marzari.

Ascension EP, Seraphic Decay (1998). Reborn To Vengeance / Communication With The Dead / Horde Of The Demons.
BRAZILIAN ASSAULT, Relapse (1999) (Split album with MENTAL HORROR, NEPHASTH and OPHIOLATRY). Triumph In Blasphemy / Hellish Annihilation / Abhorer Existence.
EVOKING THE ABOMINATION, Evil Vengeance (1999). Abattoir / Evoking The Abomination / Sacrificial Offerings / Hellish Annihilation / Storming Warfare / Abhorrer Existence / Reborn To Vengeance / Triumph In Blasphemy.
IMPALING THE CHRISTIAN RACE, Malignant Art Distribution (2005) (Split album with OPHIOLATRY). Evoking The Abomination / Shatterer Merciless / Blackest Execration / Sacrificial Offerings (Live).

ABHORRENCE

HELSINKI, FINLAND — *Jukka Kolehmainen (vocals), Kalle Mattsson (guitar), Tomi Koivusaari (guitar), Juice Ahlroth (bass), Kimmo Heikkinen (drums).*

One of Finland's earliest Death Metal combos, now noted for having included a pre-AMORPHIS guitarist Tomi Koivusaari in the ranks. The Helsinki group, operating in a proto Death-Grind style, was founded by the erstwhile DISASTER trio of vocalist Jukka 'Shrike' Kolehmainen, guitarist Kalle Mattsson, and bassist Jussi 'Juice' Ahlroth. These three would be joined by drummer Kimmo Heikkinen and the VIOLENT DISASTER credited Tomi Koivusaari.

As DISASTER morphed into ABHORRENCE during 1989, the demo 'Vulgar Necrolatry' would be recorded in early February 1990. The band would sign to the US Seraphic Decay label for a blue vinyl single, 'Pestilential Mists' issued in July, these sessions being produced by STRATOVARIUS guitarist Timo T. Tollki. Another pressing was released on grey vinyl with black and green artwork. However, ABHORRENCE would be vocal in their condemnation of this imprint in later years. In August 1990 the rehearsal demo 'Macabre Masquerade' saw release.

Toward the close of ABHORRENCE's career drums were in the hands of Mikael 'Arkki' Arnkil of ANTIDOTE repute. However, just one year after their formation the band splintered. Koivusaari had already by this stage activated AMORPHIS, offering Kolehmainen a chance at the vocal position, an offer he declined. Relapse Records in the USA, unaware of the demise of ABHORRENCE, offered an album contract some six months later to which Koivusaari, and AMORPHIS, replied.

Post ABHORRENCE Jukka Kolehmainen became a DJ, operating his own 'Stoner Hands Of Doom' club night, and a journalist for 'Suomi Finland Perkele Metal' magazine. He would also contribute lyrics to the track 'Adoration Of Abscessed Cadavers' on the debut FUNEBRARUM album. Ahlroth joined SPIHA for a brief term whilst Arnkil continued on with ANTIDOTE before joining IMPALED NAZARENE as a bass player.

The ABHORRENCE 7" single of 1990 'Pestilential Mists' combined with the demo of the same year 'Vulgar Necrolatry' would witness a CD re-release as a split single shared with the early AMORPHIS demo 'Disment Of Souls'.

Vulgar Necrolatry, Abhorrence (1990) (Demo). Intro: The Cult / Vulgar Necrolatry / Pleasures Of Putrid Flesh / Devourer Of Souls.
Pestilential Mists EP, Seraphic Decay SCAM-010 (1990) (Purple vinyl). Pestilential Mists / Holy Laws Of Pain / Caught In A Vortex / Disintegration Of Flesh.
Macabre Masquerade, Abhorrence (1990) (Demo). Pestilential Mists / The Macabre Masquerade / Adoration Of Abscessed Cadavers / Vulgar Necrolatry / Caught In A Vortex.
Abhorrence EP, (2000) (Split single with AMORPHIS). Pestilential Mists / Holy Laws Of Pain / Caught In A Vortex / Disintegration Of Flesh / Intro / The Cult / Vulgar Necrolatry / Pleasure Of Putrid Flesh / Devourer Of Souls.

ABHOTH

VÄSTERÅS, SWEDEN — *Anders Eckmann (vocals), Anfinn Skulevold (guitar), Jörgen Kristensen (guitar), Dag Nesbö (bass), Mats Blückert (drums).*

ABHOTH, hailing from Västerås, date back to 1988 when they went under the guise of MORBID SALVATION ARMY. The original line-up included vocalist Jörgen Bröms, guitarists Staffan Johansson and Jörgen Kristensen, bass player Kristian Fabretto and drummer Carl-Åke Johansson. That same year a new rhythm section was drafted in the form of Fredrik Gustavsson on bass and Jonas Ståhlhammer on the drums. ABHOTH would also lose the services of Johansson, the guitarist later turning up in UTUMNO. Following issue of an opening demo 'The Matter Of Splatter' bass player Dag Nesbö would be pulled in during 1990. A second demo, 'Forever To Be Vanished', was delivered in 1991.

Ståhlhammer, going on to join GOD MACABRE, JEHOVAH SUNRISE and in 1993 UTUMNO, would be superseded by Mats Blückert the following year. Bröms departed in 1990 to join AFFLICTED. Nesbö too would depart to journey on to COERCION.

ABHOTH issued the single 'The Tide' during 1992 for the French label Corpse Grinder Records. It is worth noting that ABHOTH guitarist Jörgen Kristensen and drummer Mats Blyckert have also sessioned for SUFFER in their time. Kristensen also cites credits with BMC SPLEEN and, in 2002, DEAD AWAKEN.

Following the single release, Mats Blückert departed, making room for Claes Ramberg on bass and drummer Jens Klovegård. ABHOTH demoed again, 'Dormant Reality', arriving in 1994. Further changes saw the introduction of Magnus Wall on bass in 1996. Under the revised title of CHIMERA a demo 'Recovery From Life' surfaced in 1999. Klovegård teamed with THRONEAEON / GODHATE that same year with Wall joining his former comrade in 2002. Wall also held membership of SEPTIC BREED. The family ties continued into 2003 as Ramberg supplanted Wall in GODHATE. Wall joined MAUSOLEUM to record their demo September 2003 'Fluctuating Senses' and also enrolled into Power Metal band HATERUSH, figuring on the 2004 opus 'Mark Of The Warrior'.

Claes Ramberg joined the ranks of IN AETERNUM in February 2006. Ex-drummer Mats Blückert enrolled himself into GODHATE that April.

A Matter Of Splatter, Abhoth (1989) (Demo). Intro / Reduced To A Pulp / Liquefied Skeleton / Fatal Inversion / Protained Existence / Evisceration.

Rehearsal 1990, Abhoth (1990) (Instrumental rehearsal demo).

Forever To Be Vanished There In, Abhoth (1991) (Demo). Recantation Of The Forsaken / Forever To Be Vanished There In / Darkness Greets.

The Tide, Corpse Grinder CGR007 (1992). The Tide / Configuration.

Dormant Reality, Abhoth (1994) (Demo). Condemned To Misery / Infinite Blessing / The Realm Of Immortality / Dormant Reality.

ABIGAIL

BUCHAREST, RUMANIA — *BB Hanneman (vocals / guitar), Vlad Buşcă (bass / vocals), Dragoş Hălmagi (keyboards), George Angel Tudor (drums).*

Bucharest Doom Death Metal band ABIGAIL was instigated during 1994, issuing the demo 'These Are The Ruins Of Mine' that same year. Second session 'Together And More' arrived in 1996. Early ABIGAIL band member guitarist Dragoş Grigorescu would exit to forge HOVERCRAFT then SERENITY.

ABIGAIL's membership of vocalist / bassist Vlad Buşcă, guitarist BB Hanneman, keyboard player Dragoş Hălmagi and drummer George Angel Tudor founded melodic Death Metal band L.O.S.T. in March of 2004. Tudor also held DUST credits whilst Buşcă held a tradition with TORNADO and CRONOS. Hanneman also cites prior affiliations with ADRENALINE, CRONOS, ICON OF SIN and MAGMA. An ex-ABIGAIL drummer, Gabi Dama, would feature as a member of GRAVEN.

These Are The Ruins Of Mine, Abigail (1994) (Demo). Intro / Die Before The Rise / Outcast / Find The Light Into Me / Dawn / Dies Irae / Missa Pro Defunctis / Outro / The Threat.

Together And More, (1996) (Demo). The Forever Sin / Together And More / Outcast / Serenity / The Sigh / Kogaion / Empirium / Anno Domini.

Bitter Tears, (1997). Bitterness... Tears / Sonet / Desire / CXLII.

Sonnets EP, Bestial (1998). Bitterness... Tears / Sonet / Insight / Desire / CXLII.

ABIGAIL WILLIAMS

PHOENIX, AZ, USA — *Connor Woods (vocals), Kenneth Rothschild (guitar), Tom Brougher (bass), Ashley Jurgemeyer (orchestration), Killer Kowalski (drums).*

Phoenix, Arizona Metalcore outfit ABIGAIL WILLIAMS, founded in 2004 by guitarist Kenneth Rothschild and comprising personnel from KYDS VS. COLUMBUS, JOB FOR A COWBOY and N17 also includes VEHEMENCE members guitarist Bjorn Dannov and bass player Mark Kozuback, the latter having replaced former four-stringer Tom Brougher. The three track demo 'Gallow Hill' arrived in 2005.

A mass exodus in January 2006 saw singer Connor Woods, Bjorn Dannov, Andy Schroeder and Mark Kozuback all exiting. This foursome stuck together, cutting demos before the close of the month billed as THE SYMMETRY IN CHAOS. ABIGAIL WILLIAMS, now down to a trio, signed to Candlelight Records in March. An album would be recorded with the TESTAMENT, DEATH, AGENT STEEL, CANCER, DISINCARNATE and OBITUARY guitarist credited JAMES MURPHY acting as producer.

A UK tour in October, alongside BRING ME THE HORIZON, was cut short when drummer Zach Gibson injured his wrist during a show in Edinburgh. Candlelight Records issued the 'Legend' EP in January 2007. The following month ABIGAIL WILLIAMS set to work on a full-length album.

In March 2007 it was learned that Mark Kozuback and Ken "Sorceron" had united with singer Marshall Beck, of REBIRTH, DESCEND and VEXATION, in a new conceptual Death Metal project called REIGN OF VENGEANCE. Soon afterwards an official band statement read "ABIGAIL WILLIAMS has decided to disband. It's no secret that the band has had more than its fair share of lineup problems and the time has now come to close the doors."

Gallow Hill, Abigail Williams (2005). Forced Ingestion Of Binding Chemicals / Melquiades (The Great Work) / A Perfect Knot.

Legend, Candlelight (2007). From A Buried Heart / Like Carrion Birds / The Conqueror Wyrm / Watchtower / Procession Of The Aeons.

ABLAZE IN HATRED

TURKU, FINLAND — *Mika Ikonen (vocals / guitar / keyboards), Juhani Sanna (guitar), Miska Lehtivuori (bass), Eve Kojo (keyboards), Antti Hakkala (drums).*

Turku based ABLAZE IN HATRED, created in the Autumn of 2004 and issuing the September 2005 opening demo 'Closure Of Life', features prominent members of the Finnish Metal underground in frontman Mika Ikonen of SEARING MEADOW, guitarist Juhani Sanna from KOLONNA, bassist Miska Lehtivuori of FALL OF THE LEAFE, THUS GROWING MISERY, ETERNAL GRIP, DARK AGES, BILE, BLACK FALL and SEARING MEADOW with Antti Hakkala from SEARING MEADOW on drums. Keyboard player Eve Kojo operates with both EMBERS LEFT and MYGRAIN. The 'Closure Of Life' session was recorded at Noisecamp Studios in Turku with producer Kari Nieminen.

ABLAZE IN HATRED signed to Firebox Records in October 2005. The album 'Deceptive Awareness' arrived in September 2006 through sub-division Firedoom Music.

Closure Of Life, Ablaze In Hatred (2005) (Demo). When The Blackened Candles Shine / To Breathe And To Suffocate / Constant Stillness.

DECEPTIVE AWARENESS, Firedoom Music FDOOM 011 (2006). Lost (The Overture) / When The Blackened Candles Shine / To Breathe And To Suffocate / Ongoing Fall / Constant Stillness / Howls Unknown / Closure Of Life.

ABLAZE MY SORROW

FALKENBURG, SWEDEN — *Martin Qvist (vocals), Magnus Carlsson (guitar), Roger Johansson (guitar), Anders Brorssomn (bass) / Alex Bengtsson (drums).*

Falkenberg's ABLAZE MY SORROW debuted in 1993 with a line-up of vocalist Martin Qvist, a man who boasts terms with APOCRYPHA, ANCIENTS REBIRTH and FALL FROM GRACE, guitarist Magnus Carlsson, ANCIENTS REBIRTH bassist Anders Brorsson and drummer Fredrik Wenzel and soon issued a demo in early 1994 entitled 'For Bereavement We Cried'. However, Fredrik Wenzel departed in mid 1994 in favour of Alex Bengtsson and a second demo, issued in 1995.

Following recording of the 1996 debut album, 'If Emotions Still Burn', guitarist Roger Johansson was substituted by Dennis Linden. Singer Fredrik Arnesson, previously a member of CROMLECH, was drafted to record March 1998's 'The Plague'. Anders Lundin, bassist for CROMLECH, teamed up with the band to act as live guitarist in mid 1998. Both Arnesson and Lundin decamped in 1999. Martin Qvist was re-instated as frontman. However, Qvist departed once again during September 2001. ABLAZE MY SORROW promptly enlisted Kristian Lönnsjö from Death Metal act DEIFICATION as substitute. Lönnsjö is also known for his work with acts such as MORIA, TRYMHEIM and ZAHRIM.

Qvist would front Black Metal act IMMEMOREAL for their 2001 debut 'Temples Of Retribution'. He would also be found as a member of DEIFICATION the same year.

For Bereavement We Cried, Ablaze My Sorrow (1993) (Cassette demo). Incipit Tragoedia / For Bereavement We Cried / Laugh, Enchanters Dream / Nightfall / Into Insignificance / Trespassers.
Ablaze My Sorrow, Ablaze My Sorrow (1995) (Cassette demo). The Rain That Falls … / Denial (The Way Of The Strong) / My Last Journey.
IF EMOTIONS STILL BURN, No Fashion NFR015CD (1996). If Emotions Still Burn / The Rain That Falls … / Rise Above The Storming Sea / Denial (The Way Of The Strong) / The Battle / My Last Journey / As I Face The Eternity / My Revenge To Come (+ Hidden track).
THE PLAGUE, No Fashion NFR026 (1998). Dusk … / The Truth Is Sold / Into The Land Of Dreams / Mournful Serenade / The Return Of The Mighty Raven / I Will Be Your God / Plague Of Mine / As The Dove Falls Torn Apart / Suicide / … Dawn.
THE PLAGUE, Avalon Marquee MICP-10128 (2000) (Japanese release). Dusk … / The Truth Is Sold / Into The Land Of Dreams / Mournful Serenade / The Return Of The Mighty Raven / I Will Be Your God / Plague Of Mine / As The Dove Falls Torn Apart / Suicide / … Dawn / Rapist Of Life / Garden Of Sin.
ANGER, HATE AND FURY, No Fashion NFR059 (2002). Erased/Relived / Suicidal / Where The Strong Live Forever / Machine Supreme / Paradies / Retention Of Illusion / Thou Shalt Forever Suffer / Shrouded Are The Pleasures Of Flesh / Heartless / Slit Wide Open / Ad Libitum / Internet Access To Special Ablaze My Sorrow Website (Data track).

ABNORMYNDEFFECT

CHISINĂU, MOLDAVIA — *Mircea (vocals), Radu (guitar), Oleg (bass), Shtefan (drums).*

Chisinău brutal Death Metal band ABNORMYDEFFECT, self styled as "New age ultra-violent Grindcore", started life during January 2003 under an original title of BUTCHERS, then featuring ex-FOETER MORTIS vocalist / guitarist Mircea, guitarist Radu, bass guitarist Dima and drummer Shtefan. BUTCHERS performed just one gig before folding, duly re-forming and introducing new members singer Stas and bassist Oleg. However, Stas then exited upfront of the group's first, six-track demo, 'Don't Worry, Be Happy'. Second session 'Ineffable Trance' followed in July 2004, the title track of which was also used as a three way split demo shared with DRUGSTORE and DISENTOMB. That September the group evolved into ABNORMYDEFFECT. Their first gig under this new banner came in November 2004 at the St. Petersburg 'Petrogrind' festival alongside SCRAMBLED DEFUNCTS, INFERIA, DISENTOMB, SLUGATHOR and FLESHGORE.

The band released the 2005 demo 'Inside Nowhere—Outside Nothing'.

Inside Nowhere—Outside Nothing, Abnormyndeffect (2005). Cure For Obscure / 723 / Inside Nowhere / Mortul / Outside Nothing.

ABOMINANT

BARDSTOWN, KY, USA — *Michael Ray Barnes (vocals), Timmie Ball (guitar), Buck Wiedeman (guitar), Mike May (bass), Craig Netto (drums).*

Founded in 1993 with the union of former EFFIGY members guitarist Buck Weidman and drummer Craig Netto together with erstwhile SARCOMA personnel guitarist Timmie Ball and bass player Mike May. Songs for a proposed split CD with fellow Kentucky act CATACLYSM were laid down but were duly shelved when their supposed partners split. ABOMINANT issued their tracks as a demo tape regardless.

Weidman would break ranks to join the Air Force leaving ABOMINANT to soldier on as a trio. Before long CATACLYSM singer Mike Barnes was added to the ranks debuting on the late 1994 demo 'Never Truly Dead'. However, the band's second attempt at a commercially released outing was scuppered when label Arctic Circle Records collapsed after ABOMINANT had recorded tracks for a scheduled mini album. Wild Rags Records signed the band to release this material with fresh songs for the 'Unspeakable Horrors' album.

Founder member Weidman would return to bolster the guitar sound but ABOMINANT once more suffered at the hands of their label when Wild Rags imploded. For the bands fourth album 'Ungodly' ABOMINANT cut a deal with Deathgasm Records.

'Ungodly', which included a version of SACRAFICE's 'Reanimation', featured guest vocals from ESTUARY OF CALAMITY vocalist Ash Thomas.

ABOMINANT included their version of METALLICA's 'Battery' to the tribute album 'Overload 2'.

UNSPEAKABLE HORRORS, Wild Rags (1996). Intentionally Accused / Corruption Morality / Calls From Beyond / Lost / The Ecstasy Of Sufferance / Abominant / Child Of The Sky / Age Of Chaos / Unspeakable Horrors.
IN DARKNESS EMBRACE, Wild Rags (1998). Shadows Land / Desecration Of Life / A Time Of Remembrance / Dark Endless Time / Eternal Emptiness / In Mourning / Fatalities Of War / The Nexus / Untitled.
THE WAY AFTER, Wild Rags WRR117 (1999). The Way After / Taogehtssik / Tomorrows End / Goddess Of The Night / The Beauty Of Our Savage Ways / Desire / Echoes of Sorrow / Visual Conquest / Severed Dreams.
UNGODLY, Deathgasm (2000). Dawn Of Despair / Treasures Of Darkness / On Death's Wings / Pinnacle Of Hate / The Fallen / The Dark Mystery / Beyond Spectral Plains / Re-Animation.
UPON BLACK HORIZONS, Deathgasm DG 09 (2002).

ABORDA

BURSA, TURKEY — *H. Fatih Akin (vocals), Kenan Selen (guitar), Alper Aktas (bass), Okaner Ertugrul (drums).*

ABORDA is fronted by the ASSASSINATION, ANTEDILUVIAN and PESTEATEN credited H. Fatih Akin. Founded in 2003 in Burra under a formative title of RAMPAGE, the band underwent line-up changes, exchanging a rhythm section of bassist Eren Olgon and drummer Serhat Karakas for the EVISCERATION pairing of Mehmet Tuz and Enis Tiryaki respectively. The latter also has ties to MELANCHOLIA. Extreminal Productions issued the live EP 'Pirate War' in August 2004. The demo 'Merciless Killing Methods' arrived in 2005. ABORDA, losing the services of lead guitarist Emre Soyler, subsequently pulled in bass player Alper Aktas and drummer Okaner Ertugrul.

Pirate War, Extreminal Productions (2004). Merciless Killing Methods / Pirate War (Aborda) / Flying Human Fleshes / Old Fashioned Aggressions.

ABORTED

BEVEREN, BELGIUM — *Gurgloroth Sven (vocals), Niek (guitar), Christophe (guitar), Koen (bass), Frank (drums).*

Leading brutal Death Metal band ABORTED was forged in Beveren during 1995, led by Gurgloroth Sven (a.k.a. vocalist Sven De Caluwé), also including drummer Steven, bassist Koen ("Bassturbations") and guitarist Niek ("Bulging sick string mayhem"). A second guitarist Christophe augmented the band in 1997 and later Steven would relinquish the drum stool to Frank. ABORTED debuted with the 1998 demo 'The Necrotorous Chronicles'. For these sessions, distributed by Esophagus Records and limited to just 200 hand numbered copies, Sven De Caluwé was to go under the pseudonym 'Inguio Urvan'. Another demo, 'The Splat Pack', arrived that same year. Uxicon Records took the group on to release the May 1999 full-length debut The Purity Of Perversion, this vinyl outing restricted to 500 units. The band then issued a split album with CHRIST DENIED in March 2000 and, due to their rapidly rising profile, Soulreaper Records duly re-issued The Purity Of Perversion.

The 'Engineering The Dead' album emerged in July 2001 through French imprint Listenable Records. In 2002 the Bones Brigade label allied ABORTED with DROWNING, BRODEQUIN and MISERY INDEX for the split outing 'Created To Kill'. The Belgians included a cover version of NAPALM DEATH's 'Suffer

The Children'. ABORTED, incorporating session drummer Dirk Verbeuren of French act SCARVE, set about recording a Jacob Hansen produced album 'Goremageddon: The Saw And The Carnage Done' during November 2002. This record included a cover version of CARCASS' 'Carnal Forge'. Promotion saw the band on tour in Europe with IMMOLATION.

Frontman Gurgloroth 'Svencho' Sven De Caluwé would donate guest vocals to the 2002 'Angel Inside' album from fellow Belgian Death Metal act WELKIN. De Caluwé was also active with Grindcore act LENG TCH'E. An ABORTED 2003 10" vinyl EP, 'Extirpated Live Emanations', hosted tracks recorded at the band's 2002 concert in Lille, France paired with US act EXHUMED. 500 hand numbered copies saw release.

To coincide with European tour dates in April 2004 partnering CANNIBAL CORPSE the band issued a special EP release 'The Haematobic'. This outing comprised three new songs, a cover of ENTOMBED's 'Drowned' plus studio and live video clips. Long term drummer Frank bowed out at this juncture, live dates seeing Dirk Verbeuren stepping back in as substitute. Gilles Delecroix, BELENOS, GRONIBARD and BURGUL TORKHAIN, having taken the drum position in March.

In December of 2004 ABORTED entered Antfarm Studios in Denmark with producer Tue Madsen to commence work on the album 'The Archaic Abattoir', due in early 2005 through Listenable Records. Guest vocal appearances on the album included Bo Summer of ILLDISPOSED, Michael Bogballe from MNEMIC and Jacob Bredahl of HATESPHERE. Quite surreally the band requested fans participate in the manufacture of a limited edition version of the record, complete with 'evidence bag', by asking them to send in hair cuttings and nail clippings. The fans that contributed would be entitled to the special edition, complete with their name as 'victim' on the evidence report. North American versions of 'The Archaic Abattoir', issued in May through Olympic Recordings, would come in different sleeve art.

Guitarist Bart Vergaert quit in May, a band statement revealing the ex-member was "tired of playing this kind of music". Nevertheless, ABORTED, drafting Stephane Souteyrand of French act YYRKOON as replacement, played East Coast dates with LENG TCH'E, IMPALED and MALIGNANCY and appeared at the 'Maryland Death Fest' prior to filming a promotional video for the track 'Dead Wreckoning' with director Darren Doane. North American road work continued throughout 2005, witnessing October and November shows packaged with CRYPTOPSY, CEPHALIC CARNAGE, SUFFOCATION and WITH PASSION. However, the band parted ways with guitarist Thijs de Cloedt and bassist Frederic Vanmassenhove in December, quoting "personal issues."

The band announced European tour dates for January 2006, traversing Poland, Germany, Holland, France, Belgium, Ireland, Switzerland, Austria, Italy and the UK, alongside a heavyweight cast of GRAVE, HURTLOCKER, DEW-SCENTED, VESANIA and CRYPTOPSY. With guitarist Stephane Soutereyand's wife in the latter stages of pregnancy the six-stringer stood down for these dates. The ABORTED band line-up therefore added new faces Seb of GENITAL GRINDER and BALROG on plus Matty of EMETH on guitar with Olivia Scemama of NO RETURN, GARWALL, PHAZM and BALROG repute on bass.

Scandinavian gigs would be announced for August in collaboration with CRYPTOPSY and VESANIA. The band parted ways with both drummer Gilles Delecroix and bass player Olivia Scemama in October. The latter was superseded by EMETH's Peter Goemaere, who debuted with the band in Tel Aviv, Israel. Later that same month the group commenced tracking a fresh album 'Slaughter & Apparatus: A Methodical Overture' with producer Tue Madsen at the Antfarm in Denmark. Drums on the record were taken care of by Dave Haley from Australian band PSYCROPTIC whilst standing in as session drummer for live work would be Etienne Galo from NEGATIVA. Two cover versions

ABORTED (pic: Dimitri Borellini)

were laid down during the sessions, namely 'Slaughtered' from PANTERA and 'Surprise! You're Dead' from FAITH NO MORE. Studio guests on the album included Jeff Walker of CARCASS plus Jacob Bredahl and Henrik Jacobsen of HATESPHERE.

ABORTED announced Dan Wilding as their next drummer in February 2007.

THE PURITY OF PERVERSION, Uxicon (1999). Intro / Act Of Supremacy / The Lament Configuration / The Sanctification Of Fornication / Organic Puzzle / Necro-Eroticism / Highway 1-35 / Gurgling Rotten Feces / Wrenched Carnal Ornaments.
ABORTED, Soulreaper (2000) (Split CD with CHRIST DENIED). Eructations Of Carnal Artistry / Sea Of Cartilage / Symposium Of Semiology / Better Impaled Than Crucified / Castration In The Name Of God / The Uncreation.
THE PURITY OF PERVERSION, Soulreaper (2000). Intro / Act Of Supremacy / The Lament Configuration / The Sanctification Of Fornication / Organic Puzzle / Necro-Eroticism / Highway 1-35 / Gurgling Rotten Feces / Wrenched Carnal Ornaments.
ENGINEERING THE DEAD, Listenable POSH030 (2001). The Holocaust Incarnate / Nailed Through Her Cunt / To Roast & Grind / Engineering The Dead / Eructations Of Carnal Artistry / Sphinctral Enthrallment / Skullfuck Crescendo / Exhuming The Infested.
CREATED TO KILL, Bones Brigade (2002) (Split album with BRODEQUIN, DROWNING and MISERY INDEX). Generic Murder Concept / Suffer The Children.
GOREMAGEDDON—THE SAW AND THE CARNAGE DONE, Olympic Recordings OLY0232-2 (2003). Meticulous Invagination / Parasitic Flesh Resection / The Saw And The Carnage Done / Ornaments Of Derision / Sanguine Verses (... Of Extirpation) / Charted Carnal Effigy / Clinical Colostomy / Medical Deviance / Sea Of Cartilage / Nemesis / Meticulous Invagination (Video).
Extirpated Live Emanations, Listenable (2003) (Split 10 vinyl EP with EXHUMED). Eructations Of Carnal Artistry (Live) / Necro Eroticism (Live) / To Roast & Grind (Live).
The Haematobic, (2004). Gestated Rabidity / Drowned / Voracious Haemaglobinic Syndrome / The Sanctification Of Refornication / Parasitic Flesh Resection (Live) / The Holocaust Incarnate (Live) / Meticulous Invagination (Video) / The Saw & The Carnage Done (Video) / Parasitic Flesh Resection (Live video) / The Holocaust Incarnate (Live video) / Eructations Of Carnal Artistry (Live video).
THE ARCHAIC ABATTOIR, Listenable POSH068 (2005). Dead Wreckoning / Blood Fixing The Bled / Gestated Rabidity / Hecatomb / The Gangrenous Epitaph / The Inertia / A Cold Logistic Slaughter / Threading On Vermillion Deception / Voracious Haemoglobinic Syndrome / Descend To Extirpation.
SLAUGHTER & APPARATUS: A METHODICAL OVERTURE, Century Media (2007). The Chondrin Enigma / A Methodical Overture / Avenious / The Spaying Séance / An Carnage Basked In Its Ebullience / The Foul Nucleus Of Resurrection / Archetype / Ingenuity In Genocide / Odous Emanation / Prolific Murder Contrivance / Underneath Rorulent Soil / Surprise! You're Dead!

ABORTION

NITRA, SLOVAKIA — *Anton Varga (vocals / bass), Mario Matulay (guitar), Richard Oros (drums).*

Nitra Grindcore pioneers ABORTION have been on the underground scene since 1988, at first a trio comprising vocalist / bassist Anton 'Lepra' Varga, guitarist Robert and drummer Charlie, ex-members of ATOM DEATH, F.O.D. and SACRAMENT. The band issued no less than five demos prior to debut album 'Murdered Culture'. Antecedent releases included the 1990 rehearsal recordings 'Dead World' and the following year's 'Disgusting Nation', 1992's 'ImpurityPerversityLove??', September 1993's 'Godmaggots' and the December 1996 set 'Sense Of Humor', subsequently issued as a 7" single. Guitarist Mario Matulay would be superseded by Libor Hanulay. A further demo, 'Charity', was released in July 1997. Copremesis allied ABORTION with AGATHOCLES for a 1999 7" split single 'We Never Forget!!!'

In 2001 Copremesis Records put two ABORTION tracks onto a cassette shared with AGATHOCLES, MALIGNANT TUMOUR and DIN-ADDICT. The November 2002 outing 'Have A Nice Day', issued via Obscene Productions, included a cover version of GODFLESH's 'Suction'. The 'Gonna Be Worse' album was delivered in July 2004. Obscene Productions released 'The Gonzo Music' in 2006, this set featuring cover versions of D.R.I.'s 'Mad Man' and the FILTHY CHRISTIANS 'Who Cares'.

MURDERED CULTURE, Rock Extremum RER 001 (1998). Intro—System State / Never / Nothin' But Trouble / Plastic Man / Sport Ideals Of Death / Murdered Culture / Beautiful Machines / The Sacred Truth Of Stupidity / The Big Red Bear Is Dying / Little Fascist Miracle / Trust Me / Unforsaken / Intro Pussy—Social Certainty / Temple Of Rats / Idol / Perfect Product / Intro Dracula—Life From Memories / He Loved Badness / Animal Dreams / I'm Witness—Jehowas / Myself Knows It Too.

ABORTION, Copremesis (2001). (Split cassette album with AGATHOCLES, MALIGNANT TUMOUR and DIN-ADDICT). Intro / False Friends / Why?? / McDeath / Punk Is Dead / Lies Id Life / Trust Me.

HAVE A NICE DAY, Obscene Productions OBP 048 (2002). Intro—Forever Money / God Loves Ignorant / I Disgrace For Its Nation / Religion Slaughter / Safeguard Tradition / Comrade Punk / Have A Good Time Friends / I Am Not Bad / You Are Suspect / Give Me Leader / Earth On Today / Black Fashion / Life Is War / That Which Not Belong To You / Kill Your Politics / Speech Me Lie / Always Forward / Railway Song / Suction / For God . . . For Nation—Animal Dream / Nacht und Nebel / Justice For The Rich / Too Weak / Fucking System / J.F.T.R.

GONNA BE WORSE, Obscene Productions (2004). Dead Laughter / Rebels Getting Older / Cancer Wins / Im For Sale / The End Is Near / Serial Killer Star / No Talk To Communists / False Babble / A Slave Or A Man / Money Is Your God / Keep It Silent / I'm Not Permanently Sick / Slut City / Pig Power / Icky Ficky / We All Are Snakes / Fucking Ignorant / Instant Life / Power Of Humour / Last Drink / Heavy Mental / N.W.O. / Filth.

ABORTUS

SYDNEY, NSW, AUSTRALIA — *Mark White (vocals), Gooch Trajkovski (guitar), George Kozoroski (bass), Dave Upston (drums).*

Sydney Death Metal combo ABORTUS debuted with the 1999 album 'Judge Me Not'. During December of 2001 ABORTUS toured Europe alongside ANCIENT RITES and MYSTIC CIRCLE. Headline Australian shows, dubbed the 'Violent Elimination' tour, took the band through April, after which Dave Upston of INFERIS would replace former drummer Michael Stojcevski. ABORTUS once again lent support to leading German Black Metal band MYSTIC CIRCLE's October 2002 Australian tour.

In August of 2004 the band evolved into HERRATIK, taking this course in order to distance themselves from the Splatter / Gore branch of Death Metal. The revised formula saw the addition of rhythm guitarist Wader and strengthening of the MYSTIC CIRCLE ties by announcing that Necrodemon was to record session drums. Pre-production recording for a re-debut album had taken place at Amethyst Studios in Sydney during April, these sessions presided over by Astennu (a.k.a. Jamie Stinson) of LORD KAOS, CARPE TENEBRUM, COVENANT and STRONGER THAN HATE repute.

Abortus II, (1998). I Wanna Play (But Not Your Way) / (Untitled).

Abortus, (1998). Redemption / Solstice / Minutes / (Untitled).
JUDGE ME NOT, Battlegod Productions (1999). Seperatism / Tortured / The Shit That Grits Your Teeth / Soul-Less / Judge Me Not / 2U 4U Fuck You / All That Was / Re-Pray.
PROCESS OF ELIMINATION, Code 666 (2001). Abort Us / Revenge Now Sworn / Redemption / The Calm Before The . . . / Process Of Elimination / Worm / Dollar Sign Smile / God Vision / Devil I'll Be / Sadist—Fy.

ABOSRANIE BOGOM

RUSSIA — *Shit Eater (vocals / guitar / bass), Anal Impregnator (vocals / drums).*

Scatology themed "AnalGoregrind" outfit. Initially ABOSRANIE BOGOM was quoted as a trio involving Shit Eater (a.k.a. Jash) on vocals and bass, A Pile Of Boars Masturbation on guitar and drummer Bloody Diarrhoea. First product would be the 35 track August 1999 demo 'Isus Pokritiy Ponosom'. Most of these tracks would be under 30 seconds in length.

The split demo '4 Way Regurgitation' emerged in 2000 pitching the band alongside SLOUGH, INTESTINAL DISGORGE and DEMONIC ORGY. Shit Eater was then joined by Corpsebutcher (Ryan) from INTESTINAL DISGORGE to record the 2001 CD-R 'Coprotherapy'. This set closed with a cover version of GUT's 'Lips—The Passage To Pleasure'.

A split album in alliance with Finland's DECAY emerged in January 2002 dubbed 'Anal Eruption'. That July the band featured alongside Brazilian bands DEFECACAO ORAL, PHAGOCYTOSIS, CHIFRAS DE SATA and VAGINAL AUTOPSY, on a split album dubbed 'Putridphilia' issued by Brazil's Coco Records. Mexican imprint American Line Productions issued the 'Coprotherapy' album, adding the 'Faecalized' EP tracks, in August 2003. That same year Fecal Matter Discorporated included ABOSRANIE BOGOM on the '6 Way Scatological Splat' split album in union with SMOTHERED BROTHERS, DSO, AMOEBIC DYSENTRY plus UTERUS AND FECULENCE.

The band featured tracks on the five way split album 'Uncontrolled Laxative Abuse' released in 2004 by Last House On The Right Records in collaboration with ANAL PENETRATION from Holland, CUMGUN from Canada, SARCOPHAGIA CARNARIA from France and Malta's STENCH OF NECROPSY.

Isus Pokritiy Ponosom, (1999) (Demo). Pauk's Ugly Legs / Shit On Ugly Legs / Pauk is a Faggot / Defecated By God / Jesus Covered With Diarrhoea / Shit In A Sack / Gum Stuck Up The Ass / Anal Lips / Bump In Cunt / Malikov Is A Rachitis / Retarded Mongrel / Anal Smell / Goats Green Peas / Shit Of Polar Bear / Anus In Fog / Thick Fresh Diarrhoea / Unwiped Ass-Hole / Got Dirty With Shit / Saulty Cunt / Faggot In A Cage / Clit Squeezed By A Door / Bloody Turd / Face Covered With Hippopotamuses Sperm / Spermed Eyes / Blister On The Ass Of An Old Lady / Shit On Rails / Dirty Cunt Of Cow / Santa Claus Crapped In The Chimney / Coprophiliac (Shit Fucker) / Someone Crapped / Cunt In A Bear's Lair / Tampax Commercials / Wounded Turd / March Of The Dead Clowns / Bielorussian Partizan Hacked To Small Pieces In The Sewers, Under A Pile Of Nazi Shit.

4 Way Regurgitation, (2000) (Split demo with SLOUGH, INTESTINAL DISGORGE and DEMONIC ORGY).

PUTRIDPHILIA, Coco (2002) (Split album with DEFECACAO ORAL, PHAGOCYTOSIS, CHIFRAS DE SATA and VAGINAL AUTOPSY).

Faecalized, (2002).

COPROTHERAPY, American Line Productions LA 061 (2003). Forced To Swallow Feces / The Art Of Cum-Farting / Turd Radar / Bitch With A Bleeding Rectum / Taking A Turd From A Baby (Give Me Back My Turd) / Head Trapped In A Pigs Rectum / Defecate Your Own Vomit / Scatological Sex School Education / Satisfaction From Sipping A Glass Of Steaming Stool / No, That's Not Chocolate, My Dear / The Fear of Flushing / Shit Xmas Mince Pies Metal Poser Obliteration / Shit-Cauterized Infected Wounds / Excrementhrone / Anal Miscarriage / Pregnant With Turds / Shit-Feast Surprise Party / Turd Rugby Insanity / Clinical Death Of An Excrement / Archaeological Excavations Of Prehistoric Faeces / Copro-Therapy Treatment / $10,000,000 Granny Shit Eating Competition / Castration Of An Uncircumsized Excrement / Anal Dentist / Turd Impregnation / Genetic Engeneering Of Faecal DNA / The Anal Bible / Eternal Constipation / Lips—The Passage To Pleasure.

ABRAMELIN

MELBOURNE, VIC, AUSTRALIA — *Simon Dower (vocals), Mark Schilby (guitar), Tim Aldridge (guitar), Justin Wornes (bass), Ewan Harriott (drums).*

Melbourne Death Metal unit initially formed under the title of ACHERON in 1988 by guitarist David Abbot. ACHERON issued the 1990 demo 'Eternal Suffering' and 1991 single 'Deprived Of Afterlife' on French label Corpsegrinder although shortly after Abbott, together with drummer Jason Dutton departed. The latter would be later found in CHRISTBAIT and, as 'Snorkelbender', in Thrash Black Metal act SITHLORD. The band pulled in replacements Mark Schilby on guitar and BLOOD DUSTER drummer Ewan Harriott as the band changed titles to ABRAMELIN in order to avoid confusion with the American ACHERON.

A 1994 mini album 'Transgression From Acheron' was followed by a full length album 'Abramelin', the latter including a cover version of DEAD CAN DANCE's 'Cantara'. The band travelled to Europe gaining exposure as support to NAPALM DEATH. In 1996 they backed CATHEDRAL and PARADISE LOST on their Australian dates.

During recording of ABRAMELIN's 'Deadspeak' album during 1998 the band split acrimoniously. Vocalist Simon Dower and guitarist Tim Aldridge regrouped pulling in DAMAGED drummer Matt Skitz for session work and re-recorded the album from scratch for a 2000 release. The 2003 incarnation of ABRAMELIN would comprise Dower, Aldridge, second guitarist Matt Wilcock of STEEL AFFLICTION (also anonymously a member of THE BERZERKER) and bass player Grant Karajic.

Drummer Euan Harriott temporarily joined the ranks of BLACK MAJESTY for live work in July of 2004.

TRANGRESSION FROM ACHERON, Thrust (1994). Human Abattoir / Humble Abode / Dearly Beloved / Relish The Blood.
ABRAMELIN, Thrust (1995). Misfortune / Grave Ideals (Nekromaniak) / Spiritual Justice / Humble Abode / Stargazer: The Summoning / Stargazer: Stargazer II / Deprived Of Afterlife / Invocation / Cantar.
DEADSPEAK, Shock (2000). Pleasures / Your Casualty / Waste / Bleeding Hearts / The Germ Factory / Fresh Furnace / Plaque.

ABRANIA

VÄSTERÅS, SWEDEN — *Annika Wilbe (vocals), Jonas Lind (vocals), Peter Strömberg (guitar), Daniel Rejment (bass), Stefan Larsson (drums).*

ABRANIA is a Västerås based melodic Death Metal band founded in 1999. Demo releases included 'Calling My Name' in April 2001 and the 'Dyin' Screams' set of 2005. The band involved vocalist Jho Abrai, guitarists Peter Strömberg and Jerry Engström, bassist Andreas Silfver plus Martin Lindqvist on drums. Ex-ABRANIA band members include guitarist Daniel Andersson, bassist Daniel Rejment and drummer Daniel Forssten. Third session, the self-financed EP 'Only A Dream' arrived in March 2006. By this juncture ABRANIA comprised singers Annika Wilbe, of INSIDE MARILYN, and Jonas Lindh, guitarist Peter Strömberg, bass player Daniel Rejment with Stefan Larsson on the drums.

Calling My Name, Tårtan (2001) (Demo). Calling My Name / Abrania Moon / Chased In Desperation / Better Off Dead / Let 'em Roll / Whisless Nights / Kiss Of Death.
Dyin' Screams, Abrania (2005) (Demo). The Kick In Our Faces / Shout Out / Equal To You / Dyin' Screams / From The Endline.
Only A Dream, Abrania (2006). Only A Dream / Killed By Life / Clarity / Holdin' Rain.

ABRASIVE

STUTTGART, GERMANY — *Ralf Köhler (vocals / guitar), Alex Ringwald (bass), Alexander Mäckle (drums).*

Stuttgart, Baden Württemberg Death Metal formation ABRASIVE was founded by vocalist / guitarist Ralf Köhler, bassist Alex Ringwald drummer and Alexander Mäckle in April 1999. Both Köhler and Mäckle have association with TARGOST with the latter also having HILARION ties. A debut EP, entitled 'Victim', followed in 2000. A second recording session, resulting in the 'Desire' EP for Semen Demon Records, saw the inclusion of second guitarist Björn Dähn. Live performances included the 'Skull Fucked Fest' in Strasbourg in 2002 and the Ludwigshafen Death Fest in 2003.

ABRASIVE signed to Nice To Eat You Records to issue the 'Devotion (Hymns To Subcutaneous Human Pleasure)' album in December 2004. Björn Dähn left the band and was replaced by Tobias Berger in 2005, who was in turn superseded by Tino Lamprecht in 2006 before ABRASIVE returned to the original trio format in February 2007.

Abrasive, Semen Demon Productions (1999). Master Of My Own / Leave / Pussyfied / Life Goes On / Last Step / Pierced From Within.
VICTIM, Semen Demon Productions (2000). Welcome / Master Of My Own / Leave / Pussyfied / Victim / Life Goes On / Last Step / Pierced From Within.
Desire, Semen Demon Productions SDP 002 (2002). Get Fucked / Late Night Demon Bondage Queen / Desire / Unknown / Taste Me / Everlasting Pain.
DEVOTION (HYMNS TO SUBCUTANEOUS HUMAN PLEASURE), Nice To Eat You (2004). Drowning In Sin / Between You / Melting / In My Dreams / Devotion / Just Flesh / Internal Devourment / Addicted To Your Flesh / Desire / Like A Virgin / Under My Skin.

ABSCESS

CAMPINAS, SP, BRAZIL — *Erik Müller (vocals), Alexandre Junior (guitar), Glauco Oliveira (guitar), Wagner F. (bass), Caio Cezar (drums).*

Gore soaked Campinas Death Metal act ABSCESS debuted with the 'Pestilent Emanation' demo in 1993. The band had been started as a Grindcore act in 1991, founded by the brothers guitarist Glauco Oliveira and drummer Caio Cezar. After a succession of line up changes, seeing vocalist Pedro Amatuzzi, lead guitarist Ricardo Oleski and bass players Renato Santos and Daniel Sousa all exiting, ABSCESS settled with the introduction in 1994 of singer Erik Müller, second guitarist Alexandre Junior and bassist Wagner F. They would also share a three way split album 'Death Or Glory Vol.1' with EXTORSION and PSYCHONEUROSIS on the Heavy Metal Rock label. Glauco Oliveira and Caio Cezar founded KEMÖTH during December of 2002.

DEATH OR GLORY VOL. 1, Heavy Metal Rock (1995) (Split album with PSYCHONEUROSIS and EXTORSION). Violation / Irreversible Process / Cut Off Members / Crematory Oven / Pits Of Depression.

ABSCESS

USA — *Chris Reifert (vocals / drums), Clint Bower (guitar), Danny Coralles (guitar), Freeway Migliore (bass).*

ABSCESS included AUTOPSY and DEATH member Chris Reifert in the ranks. Before debuting commercially ABSCESS released a string of underground cassettes in the form of 1994's eponymous demo, the follow up 'Raw Sick & Brutal Noise', 1995's 'Filthy Fucking Freaks' and 'Crawled Up From The Sewer'. The original incarnation of the band saw Chris Reifert on vocals and drums, guitarists Clint Bower of HEXX repute and AUTOPSY man Danny Coralles with Freeway Migliore on bass as well as additional drums. The formative demos would be collected together for CD release as the 1995 'Urine Junkies' album. A limited edition pink vinyl EP 'Throbbing Black Werebeast' and the 'Seminal Vampires And Maggotmen' album arrived in 1996. The line-up maintained its solidity until 1998 when Joe Allen was brought in on bass for the 'Open Wound' 7" single.

In 2000 two split singles found their way onto the market. The 'Open Wound' material was recycled for an alliance with

MACHATAZO whilst a 10" limited edition surfaced shared with DERANGED. During the same year Reifert had created THE RAVENOUS band project with Killjoy of NECROPHAGIA and S.O.D. bassist Dan Lilker.

In 2002 ABSCESS, comprising of Chris Reifert, Clint Bower, Danny Coralles and erstwhile VON bass player Joe Allen set to work on a new record provisionally titled 'Through the Cracks Of Death' for August issue on Peaceville Records. Reifert, Coralles and Allen also announced the formation of the less than quaintly billed Punk side endeavour EATMYFUK. The Dutch Displeased Records label issued a December 2004 album entitled 'Damned And Mummified'. Vinyl and CD versions would sport completely different artwork.

ABSCESS partnered with EXHUMED, SKARP and INSANITY for a short burst of US dates in August 2005. ABSCESS' seventh album, entitled 'Horrorhammer', was issued in March 2007 via Tyrant Syndicate Productions, the label headed up by DARKTHRONE guitarist/vocalist Nocturno Culto.

URINE JUNKIES, Relapse (1995). Aching Meat / Urine Junkies / Crawled Up From The Sewer / 29th Lobotomy / Horny Hag / Depopulation / Zombification / Blacktooth Beast / The Scent Of Shit / Altar Toy / Suicide Fuck / Raw Sewage / Die Pig Die / Inbred Abomination / Unquenchable Thirst / Abscess / Bloodsucker / Abscess.

SEMINAL VAMPIRES AND MAGGOTMEN, Relapse RR 6945 (1996). Naked Freak Show / Freak Fuck Fest (Naked Freak Show II: Orgy Of The Gaffed) / Patient Zero / Zombie Ward / Mud / Stiff And Ditched / Fatfire / I Don't Give A Fuck / Burn, Die And Fucking Fry / Global Doom / Removing The Leech / Pinworms / Gonna Mow You Down / Disgruntled / Tunnel Of Horrors / Worm Sty Infection / Dirty Little Brats / The Scent Of Shit.

Throbbing Black Werebeast EP, (1996) (Pink vinyl). Speed Freak / For Those I Hate / Fuckface / Throbbing Black Werebeast / Leave The Skin / Wriggling Torsos / Fucking Hell.

Open Wound EP, (1998). Leech Boy / Open Wound / Flesh Candy / To Die Again.

TORMENTED, Listenable POSH023 (2000). Rusted Blood / Filth Chamber / Tormented / Madness And Parasites / Deathscape In Flames / Street Trash / Halo Of Disease / Scratching At The Coffin / Ratbag / Death Runs Red / Wormwind / From Bleeding Skies / Madhouse At The End Of The World.

Abscess EP, (2000) (Split EP with DERANGED. Limited edition of 300 copies). Swimming In Blood / Brain Destroyer / Lunatic Whore.

Open Wound EP, (2000) (Split single with MACHETAZO). Leech Boy / Open Wound / Flesh Candy / To Die For.

THROUGH THE CRACKS OF DEATH, Peaceville CDVILE 116 (2002). Raping The Multiverse / Mourners Will Burn / Through The Cracks Of Death / Escalation Of Violence / Serpent Of Dementia / An Asylum Below / Tomb Of The Unknown Junkie / Monolithic Damnation / Die For Today / 16 Horrors / Vulnavia.

DAMNED AND MUMMIFIED, Displeased D-00143 (2004). Through The Trash Darkly / Empty Horizon / Swallow The Venom / Caverns Of Hades / The Dead Are Smiling At Me / Twilight Bleeds / Lust For The Grave / The Dream Is Dead / Damned And Mummified / Inferno Of Perverse Creation / Tattoo Collector / Tirade Of Hallucinations.

ABSIDIA

SCHANBACH, GERMANY — *Daniel Dietelbach (vocals), Arne Link (guitar), Peter Bastian (bass), Marc A. Hartmann (drums).*

Schanbach, Hardcore edged Death Metal band. Under a formative billing of COUNTLESS a 1999 demo tape was released entitled 'Dawn of All Evil'. Initially the band had formed as a quartet comprising lead vocalist Daniel Dietelbach, guitarist Markus, bassist Phillip and drummer Felix. A few gigs later Roland was enrolled on the drums. They would switch to ABSIDIA, adding second guitarist Arne Link, shortly after, recording the album 'Written In Minor Key' in June 2000, this featuring the hidden track 'Museum'. Phillip then departed, leaving the unit without a bassist for several months until Peter Bastian was installed for recording of a split 7" single shared with XMAROONX on Captain Crap On Crap Chords Records.

In late 2001 the group was offered to cut tracks for a proposed split album in union with SIX REASONS TO KILL. However, the departure of Roland stalled progress. Marc A. Hartmann of MAN VS. HUMANITY took command of the drums for recording of the split album 'Morphology Of Fear'.

ABSIDIA folded in late 2003, the guitar pairing of Roland Boeffgen and Arne Link along with drummer Marc A. Hartmann uniting with MORTIFER singer Dennis Mueller to forge THE CRIMSON DIVINE.

WRITTEN IN MINOR KEY, Per Koro PK 034 (2001). Press The Button / A Faint Smell Of . . . / To Overcome The Barrier / Blood Has Been Shed / Never Again Denying Their Lives / Let The Shades Fall Down / Museum.

MORPHOLOGY OF FEAR, (2002) (Split album with SIX REASONS TO KILL). Conspiracy Theory / No Longer Willing To Wither / Written In Minor Key / Reversal Of A Broken Hearted.

ABSOLUTE DEFIANCE

JAKARTA, INDONESIA — *Nino Aspiranta (vocals), Bimo Morbid (guitar), Edwin Haikal (bass), Andyan Gorust (drums).*

Jakarta brutal Death Metal first convened during February 1998 as VILE. The initial line-up comprised vocalist Dedi, bassist Ade, guitar player Bimo Morbid and drummer Anto. Dedi lasted the duration of their inaugural gig and was swiftly replaced by ex-SADISTIS man Sapto. Early gigs would see VILE wearing their American Nu-Death Metal influences proud performing cover songs by the likes of CRYPTOPSY, DEEDS OF FLESH and DYING FETUS.

The line-up changed for second time with the introduction of bassist Edwin and drummer Ghebes, recording a cassette release for the Jakarta based Dementia Records. However, after these recordings VILE replaced Sapto with Fahmi Haraif, previously known for his bass work with IMPIOUS in January of 2000. A heavy gigging schedule ensued after which Ghebes relinquished his position in early 2001 to Andyan Gorust of SIKSAKUBUR. Yet another switch in frontman shortly after put TRAUMA's Nino Aspiranta at the microphone stand.

With this new formation VILE cut a cassette album 'Systematic Terror Decimation' for the local Edelweiss Productions label. These tapes were subsequently licensed to the Dutch Displeased label, adding three extra tracks featuring Haraif on lead vocals. Due to the presence of the American VILE the Indonesians opted for a name change to ABSOLUTE DEFIANCE.

SYSTEMATIC TERROR DECIMATION, Displeased FBP-003 (2002). Butchered Human Corpse / Maggot Infestator / Carnal Dissection / Anonymity Of The Mass Death / Obscure Of Disfigured / Deranged Epidemic / Dehumanized / Feeding The Famished Zombie / Kaleidoskope Pembantaian / Neraka Di Bumi (Final Holocaust) / Exhuming The Truth / Self Fulfilled Prophecy / Heinous Oppressor.

ABSORBED

HOOGEVEEN, HOLLAND — *Jim Klaarmond (vocals), Ferdy Dolserum (guitar), Jeroen Vrielink (guitar), Jeroen Pomper (bass), Michel Jonker (drums).*

A Hoogeveen group heavily inspired by the Swedish Death Metal sound. ABSORBED was founded by former INSOMNIA personnel guitarist Ferdy Dolsersum and drummer Michel Jonker during 1997. A series of line-up changes finally resolved themselves towards the close of the year as Dolsersum and Jonker were joined by Jeroen Pomper on bass and guitarist Dennis de Lange. This unit proceeded perform live and to cut a three track demo session issued during 1998.

ABSORBED debuted with the 1999 mini album 'Sunset Bleeding' for the Resuscitate label after which they parted ways with guitarist Dennis De Lange. His replacement Jeroen Vrielink (a.k.a. 'Tumor') was pulled from the ranks of Grindcore band CEREBRAL TUMOR. With this revised line-up ABSORBED cut the 2002 full length record 'Visions In Bloodred'. A split 7" single with Hardcore merchants S.A.G. was also scheduled for which ABSORBED recorded a cover version of ENTOMBED's 'Left Hand Path'.

ABSORBED would tour Europe in October of 2002 on a package billing with LAST DAYS OF HUMANITY and PUNGENT STENCH. However, guitarist Ferdy Dolserum exited to forge MASSIVE ASSAULT. In 2003 the band announced that, due to musicians commitments to other bands, ABSORBED was to cease activity. Michel Jonker pursued his role as guitarist with MAKILADORAS whilst Jeroen Vrielink teamed back up with ex-guitarist Ferdy Dolserum in MASSIVE ASSAULT.

ABSORBED, comprising Fredda, Michel, Jeroen, Tumor and Jim, made a one off return to appear at the Groningen 'GMC Fest' in 2005.

Absorbed, (1998). From Dark Shadows / World Of Dismemberment / Rotting Below.
SUNSET BLEEDING, Resuscitate RESUS 005 (2000). Sunset Bleeding / Maximum Deformity / The Christgrinder / Nihilistic Butchering / Absorbed.
VISIONS IN BLOODRED, (2002). Exile The Breeding Spawn / Lost In Human Carnage / World Of Dismemberment / Twisted Backwards / Ripping Revelations / Enter The Blood Dominion / Back To Infinity / Angelic Visions In Bloodred / Foul Worlds Decay / Fleshpile / Regulate The Killings.

ABSTAIN

USA — An amalgam of Grind and Hardcore bolstered by politically charged commentary. ABSTAIN's 1997 outing 'Defy', which included a brace of DISRUPT cover versions 'Tortured In Entirety' and 'Religion Is A Fraud', came formatted as a 3" CD album. The band would share a 1998 album 'Live Aboard The M.S. Stubnitz', released by the Australian In League Wit' Satan concern, with Sweden's ARSEDESTROYER.

The band would feature on a string of split 7" singles in collusion with NASUM, UNHOLY GRAVE, DENAK and naturally industrious Belgians AGATHOCLES. The 1998 'Dead Generation' split single in union with Spain's DENAK on the Polish Dwie Strony Medalu label included a cover of the AGATHOCLES track 'Senseless Trip'.

DEFY, Relapse (1997). My Generation / Superiority Complex / Discriminating Nation / Why / The Feeding / No Values / Pseudoscience / Choke / Circle Of Fools / Poetic Justice / Tortured In Entirety- Religion Is A Fraud / House Of Straw.
Religion Is War, Yellow Dog (1998) (Split single with NASUM). Religion Is War.
Hate In The Head, (1998) (Split single with UNHOLY GRAVE). Hate In The Head.
LIVE ABOARD THE M.S. STUBNITZ, In League Wit' Satan (1998) (Split album with ARSEDESTROYER). Superiority Complex / Mass Action / Discriminating Nation / Choke / My Generation / Our True Nature / No Values / Pseudoscience / Self Infliction / Why / Mediawhore / Burn Down The Mall / Terrorizer.
Dead Generation EP, Dwie Strony Medalu (1999) (Split single with DENAK). Self Infliction / The Feeding / Senseless Trip.
Fuck Your Values, (1999) (Split single with AGATHOCLES). Fuck Your Values.

ABSYNTHIUM

BELGIUM — *Bert (vocals), Peter Bloemen (guitar), Jochen Schrijvers (guitar), Joris Meeuwissen (bass), Ruud Gysen (drums).*

The first formation of Death / Black act ABSYNTHIUM was assembled in November 1996 by ex-SIGNS OF DARKNESS, GOTMOOR and FRAME OF MIND guitarist Peter Bloemen and bassist Kevin Schutters, this pair enrolling guitarist Bob Ceyssens and Evy Hoydonkx on flute in February of the following year. Singer Jurgen Erken was incorporated that November but then Ceyssens, Hoydonkx and subsequently Erken all decamped. Restructuring, ABSYNTHIUM enlisted SIGNS OF DARKNESS guitarist Wouter Winters and William Bloemen of DOWNFALL on drums for the band's debut gig, Bloemen taking on lead vocal responsibilities for the occasion. September of 1998's marked the introduction of CULPABLE HOMICIDE guitarist Niki Driessen but just two months later longstanding band member Kevin Schutters exited.

ABSYNTHIUM shifted shape once more, Winters moving over to bass and drummer J.P. Theevissen coming in during May of 1999. Unhappy with being delegated bass, Winters left and the band pulled in Kurt Koppens as replacement. This latest candidate did not last the course and, with the departure of Theevissen, the band was whittled back down to a duo and, with Driessen's defection, a solo concern of Bloemen's.

ABSYNTHIUM was rebuilt during early 2001, Bloemen drawing back in Kurt Koppens on bass guitar. Guitar at first was the responsibility of Jochen Schrijvers but he would soon be usurped by returning member Wouter Winters and by May Bart Hubrechts had been added as frontman. Koppens was unceremoniously ejected once again, due to official sources stating "because his playing improved much slower than the growth of his ego". Hubrechts added bass to his duties whilst Kristof became the new drummer. Predictably this line up did not last as Hubrechts and Kristof bowed out. September of 2001 saw Ruud Gysen of SIGNS OF DARKNESS next in line for drums as Kevin Vangelooven of LAST FUNERAL, THE QUIESCENT and CELEBRANT became the new singer.

Joris Meeuwissen became the new bass man in March of 2002, after which Winters bade his farewell yet again, being replaced by the musician he had originally substituted for— Jochen Schrijvers. In September of 2002 Vangelooven was forced to relinquish the vocal role due to throat problems. Bloemen once again became lead singer until April of 2003 when he too would be afflicted with throat difficulties. Former member Bart Hubrechts was asked to rejoin as ABSYNTHIUM also added new bass guitarist Wesley Van Gaver. This latest addition's tenure would prove brief though and Joris Meeuwissen was duly reinstated. The turbulence continued throughout the year as Hubrechts left, was replaced by Raymond who then quit in November. Bert then took up the challenge.

ABSYNTHIUM crafted a new demo at Grindhouse Studios, entitled 'Vortex Within', during November of 2004. A further session, 'Hatestorm', emerged in mid 2005.

Hatestorm, Absynthium (2005). The Void / Ominous Future Present / Everdark Anthem / I, Hate / Nonexistence.

ABYSMAL DAWN

LOS ANGELES, CA, USA — *Charles Elliott (vocals / guitar), Jamie Boulanger (guitar), Carlos Arriola (bass), Terry Barajas (drums).*

Los Angeles Death Metal trio ABYSMAL DAWN, founded in December 2003, features RISE and INHUMAN VISIONS credited vocalist / guitarist Charles Elliot, INHUMAN VISIONS guitarist Jamie Boulanger and drummer Terry Barajas. A self titled, three song demo, engineered by Sacha Dunable of ANUBIS RISING, was published in 2004. During the latter half of 2005 the group pulled in the OBSCURE, PROTOTYPE and ARTISAN credited Mike Bear as stand in bassist.

ABYSMAL DAWN signed to Crash Music Inc. in January 2006 for the album 'From Ashes'. That same month the band appointed ex-SAVAGERY man Carlos Arriola into the bass position. US dates for September and October 2006 saw the band hooking up with KRISIUN, CATTLE DECAPITATION, DECAPITATED and SIX FEET UNDER. In December the band was added to the DISMEMBER / GRAVE West Coast tour.

Bass player Carlos Arriola departed in January 2007. Regrouping, ABYSMAL DAWN pulled in Mike Cosio of GRAVE DESECRATION and EXCRETION as new four-stringer in March.

Abysmal Dawn, Abysmal Dawn (2004). Blacken The Sky / Solitude's Demise / State Of Mind.

ABYSSAL SUFFERING

PARIS, FRANCE — *Ivan (vocals), David (guitar), John (guitar), Mental (bass), Guillaume (keyboards), Alex (drums).*

Paris based Death Metal band ABYSSAL was created as TRAUMASPHERE in November 2000, releasing a demo under this title billed 'Voidcall' in 2001. At this stage the band comprised a duo of Ivan handling vocals, guitars and bass with Guillaume drums and keyboards. The ABYSSAL SUFFERING tag was adopted for a set of live tapes in 2003, 'Live At 'La Basse Cour', Nanterre', featuring a cover versions of NAPALM DEATH's 'Suffer The Children' and MORBID ANGEL's 'Day Of Suffering', purely for local distribution. The band suffered membership problems, resulting in Ivan declaring the band as of January 2005 to be a solo project. The demo 'Soul Pioneer' followed in July 2005.

Live At 'La Basse Cour', Nanterre, (2003). Civilization? / Eradicated / Cortically Disabled / Suffer The Children / Anthem To The Piteous / Organic Brain Lost In Vacuum / Day Of Suffering.

Soul Pioneer, Abyssal Suffering (2005). Dawn Of The Miserable / Die Dreaming / Soul Pioneer.

ABYSSOS

SUNDSVALL, SWEDEN — *Christian Rehn (vocals / guitar), Daniel Meidal (bass), Andreas Söderlund (drums).*

ABYSSOS is a Sundsvall based vampiric Black Death Metal band, created in January 1996 by vocalist / guitarist Christian Rehn, bass player Daniel Meidal and HOLOCAUST drummer Andreas Söderlund. A demo in February 1996, 'Wherever Witches Might Fly', recorded at Hedberska Studios with INSALUBRIOUS members guitarist Niklas Johansson and singer Vincent Dahlqvist acting as guests, marked their arrival via Spiritual Winter Productions. This same set was re-issued in September, adding two tracks. Positive press coverage duly secured a deal with the British Cacophonous label. They issued their debut album 'Together We Summon The Dark' during 1997, this having been recorded that May at Academy Studios in Yorkshire.

Rehn and Söderlund returned to Yorkshire to craft the second opus 'Fhinsthanian Nightbreed' in November of 1998. Session vocals would be handled by John Östlund (a.k.a. Odhinn Sandin) of IN BATTLE, ODHINN, DIABOLICUM, VALKYRIA and NORRSKEN. Further backing vocals came courtesy of Stefan Carlsson, Af Fhinsta and A.K. Anger.

Frontman Christian Rehn would also be an active member of Black Metal band SARGOTH during this period. Another Black Metal act operating in parallel would be INSALUBRIOUS, its line-up including ABYSSOS credited players such as Rehn, guitarist Niklas Johansson, singer Vincent Dahlqvist, guitarist Daniel Meidal and drummer Andreas Söderlund.

In 2003 word arrived of a fresh ABYSSOS recording, to be entitled 'Delomelanicon', but this did not transpire. Rehn marked a significant return in 2004 as part of ANGTORIA, alongside his MOAHNI MOAHNA credited brother Tommy and fronted by the high profile singer Sarah Jezebel Deva, a lady who has made her mark on the extreme Metal scene as complimentary vocalist for CRADLE OF FILTH, COVENANT, THERION and MORTIIS.

Wherever The Witches Might Fly, Spiritual Winter Productions (1996) (Cassette demo). As The Sky Turns Black Again / Return Of The Nightgale / Through The Gloom Into The Fire.

Wherever The Witches Might Fly, Spiritual Winter Productions (1996) (Reissue of cassette demo). As The Sky Turns Black Again / Return Of The Nightgale / Through The Gloom Into The Fire / Hills Of A Thousand Sins / Wherever The Sleeping Beauty Lies.

TOGETHER WE SUMMON THE DARK, Cacophonous NIHIL 26CD (1997). We Hail Thy Entrance / Misty Autumn Dance / Banquet In The Dark—Black Friday / Lord Of The Sombre Reborn / In Fear They Left The World Unseen / As The Sky Turns Black Again / Love Eternal / Together We Summon The Dark / I've Watched The Moon Grow Old / Through The Gloom And Into The Fire.

FHINSTHANIAN NIGHTBREED, Cacophonous NIHIL33 CD (1999). Masquerade In The Flames / Finally I Kissed The Pale Horse / Where Angels Fear To Tread / She Only Flies At Night / Worthless For Sale? / Fhinsthanian Nightbreed / Queen Covered In Black / Wherever The Witches Might Fly / Firebreathing Whore.

ACCELERATOR

SWITZERLAND — *Fredi Zaugg (vocals / guitar), Sascha Von Arx (guitar / keyboards), Roger Friedrich (bass), Adi Krebs (drums).*

ACCELERATOR's 1997 debut album 'The Prophecy' saw guest vocals from Patrick Schaad with female vocals from Esther Hofer. The band, created in late 1993 as a trio of vocalist / guitarist Fredi Zaugg, ex-GOMORRHA bassist Roger Friedrich and drummer Adi Krebs, had previously gone under the titles of DEAD END and APOPLEXY. As ACCELERATOR they had made their mark with the 1995 demo session 'The Dark Side'.

Following the release of 'The Prophecy' Von Arx departed and Esther Hofer took over the role of guitarist / keyboard player. ACCELERATOR's 2003 line up comprised vocalist Stefan Gehri , vocalist / guitarist Fredi Zaugg, guitarist / keyboard player Esthi Hofer, bass player Sascha von Arx and drummer Adi Krebs.

ACCURSED

WAUWATOSA, WI, USA — *Gabe Catanzaro (vocals / keyboards), Jeremy Nesthus (guitar / bass), Joe Hartmann (drums).*

Wisconsin's ACCURSED was assembled in April of 1993, initially comprising Ryan Olson at vocals, Jeremy Nesthus on guitar, Gabe Catanzaro on bass and drummer Joe Hartmann. ACCURSED published the opening tape 'Horror Within', in June of 1993, followed by a December demo 'A Curse Called Life', recorded at Firebird Studios and the final session to feature singer Ryan Olson. 1994's 'Lament' single track demo would see Catanzaro having switched to the lead vocal role. This song also saw inclusion on a compilation album issued by the Visceral Productions label. An eponymous 1995 cassette preceded the album 'Meditations Among The Tombs', recorded at Allegra Studios for Visceral Productions. ACCURSED ceased activity during 1996.

Horror Within, (1992). Horror Within / Psalm Of A Dead Dreamer / Blood Is Life / Accursed.

A Curse Called Life, (1994). Morbid Departure / Psalm Of A Dead Dreamer / Premeditated Sacrifice / Blood Is Life.

Accursed, (1994). Door To December / Cimmerian Darkness.

Rehearsal 1995, (1995). The Last Sunrise / Oceans Of Time / Where Icicles Form.

MEDITATIONS AMONG THE TOMBS, Visceral Displeased (1995) (Limited edition 1000 copies). The Last Sunrise / Malum In Se / Oceans Of Time / Psalm Of A Dead Dreamer / Meditations Among The Tombs / Land Of Whispers / Embers For The Sacred Fire / Bridal Lust / Where Icicles Form / Funerals For Kings Unknown.

Lament, (1995). Lament.

ACCURSED DAWN

BLACKSBURG, VA, USA — *Brett Coverdale (vocals), Chuck Henry (guitar), Brian Blickle (guitar), Will Barry (bass), Brian Switzer (drums).*

Blacksburg, Virginia based ACCURSED DAWN, originally entitled LYING IN ASHES, was founded in the Autumn of 2002 upon the demise of Black Metal act SHADAR HARAN. Guitarists Chuck Henry and Brian Blickle recruited drummer Brian Switzer from Metalcore act SHRED OF HOPE. Vocals would be handled by former AVULSION and SHADOWS man Brett Coverdale whilst ex-BLACK REIGN man Philip D'Arcangelis took on bass duties. ACCURSED DAWN debuted with the 2003 EP 'Eternal Twilight', followed by promotional session 'With A Mortal Grace' in 2004.

Will Barry of HIT BY A HEARSE joined as bassist in May of 2004. The band would then enter the studio to record the album 'Manifest Damnation (The Creation Affect)'. Gigs in March 2005 saw ACCURSED DAWN using the services of fill-in band members, after which they set out to audition fresh personnel. The band called it quits in May 2006. Brian Switzer joined up with THE KNIFE TRADE, Brian Blickle hooked up with BARONESS whilst Will Barry united with VALKYRIE.

Eternal Twilight, Mercury (2003). Beneath A Sun So Cold / The Becoming / Eternal Twilight / Dead Of Winter.

With A Mortal Grace, (2004). With A Mortal Grace / Beneath A Sun So Cold / The Becoming / Eternal Twilight / Dead Of Winter.

MANIFEST DAMNATION, Pop Faction (2005). Conquest Of A Dying Culture / Last Requiem For The Storm / Euphony To The Night-Treader / The Thunder Swarm / The Breath That Enkindles Insurrection / Dead Of Winter / Flight From Serpent Wings / Triumphs Of A Dying Breed.

ACHERON

COLUMBUS, OH, USA — *Vincent Crowley (vocals / guitar), Michael Estes (guitar), Reverend Peter Gilmore (keyboards), Tony Laureano (drums).*

Death metal musically but with clear Satanic overtones in the lyrics, ACHERON is perhaps one of the more genuine of the American exponents of Black Metal. Mentor and frontman Vincent Crowley is the founder of the irreligious underground movement 'Order of the evil eye' whilst renowned Church of Satan priest Reverend Peter Gilmore adds keyboards and contributes lyrically. ACHERON marked their arrival with the live 1989 demo tape 'Messe Noir'. At this juncture ACHERON comprised singer Michael Smith, guitarist Vincent Crowley, bassist David Smith and drummer Ron Hogue. These recordings would later see a 1995 release on 7" single format by Reaper Records limited suitably to 666 copies. Ex-MORBID ANGEL, INCUBUS and NOCTURNUS drummer Mike Browning has also appeared with ACHERON on their 1993 'Hail Victory' album alongside Crowley and guitarists Tony Blakk and Vincent Breeding. The B side to the 1998 single 'Necromanteion Communion' featured a cover version of BATHORY's 'Raise The Dead'. In 1999 the band executed their interpretation of MERCYFUL FATE's 'Room Of The Golden Air', featured on 'The Unholy Sounds Of The Demon Bells—A Tribute To Mercyful Fate' collection issued via Poland's Still Dead Productions.

Former ACHERON guitarist Pete Slate would found the Black Death act EQUINOX, later drafting another ACHERON veteran Tony Blakk. Guitarist Michael Estes busied himself with a side project act BURNING INSIDE assembled by renowned ICED EARTH, DEMONS & WIZARDS, DEATH and CONTROL DENIED drummer Richard Christy and BLACK WITCHERY guitarist Steve Childers.

Drummer Tony Laureano sessioned for AURORA BOREALIS and MALEVOLENT CREATION. By 2000 he was a member of Dutch act GOD DETHRONED. Another former member, keyboard player Adina Blaze, would join LILITU. Crowley created WOLFEN SOCIETY with DARK FUNERAL guitarist Lord Ahriman and Jeff Gruslin of VITAL REMAINS in 2000.

Full Moon Productions issued a CD of rare early ACHERON material during 2001 entitled 'Compendium Diablerie—The Demo Days'. That same year Vincent Crowley would notably resign from the Church of Satan organisation. During July of 2002 major news was delivered as it was confirmed Crowley had joined the prestigious Black Death Metal veterans INCANTATION for their North American 'Summer Of Blasphemy' tour.

A 2003 album, 'Tribute To The Devil's Music', comprised entirely of cover versions. ACHERON paid homage to tracks such as BLACK SABBATH's 'Black Sabbath', DEATH's 'Evil Dead', CELTIC FROST's 'Dawn Of Megiddo', IRON MAIDEN's 'Wrathchild', KREATOR's 'Flag Of Hate', MOTÖRHEAD's °(Don't Need Religion', MERCYFUL FATE's 'Room Of Golden Air', KISS'

ACHERON

'War Machine', BATHORY's 'Raise The Dead', JUDAS PRIEST's 'Devil's Child' and VENOM's 'Countess Bathory'.

In February of 2004 Michael Estes parted ways with the band with the practicalities of distance from the guitarist's Orlando, Florida base and the rest of the band living in Columbus, Ohio cited as reasoning. ACHERON enlisted a temporary replacement in the form of Stacey Connolly from LIFE IS LOST. Christopher Wiford of THE CONQUERING would be installed on guitar in June.

Polish gigs for November saw ACHERON included on the billing of the 'Conquer Records Winter 2004' festivals. With Kyle Severn unable to attend due to personal issues, ACHERON re-drafted James Strauss for these shows.

In early 2005 ACHERON issued a statement demonstrating a shift in their ideology proclaiming "Let it been know that ACHERON is not a Church of Satan-linked band anymore. Vincent Crowley, who formerly was a Magister/Priest for their organization, resigned back in 2000. ACHERON in no way indorses any type of organized religious groups." New product would be signalled in the form of an album billed 'Sanctum Regnum: The Predator Manifesto' and a DVD release '17 Years Of Pure Hell'.

South American label Dying Music announced a 2006 re-issue of 'Rites Of The Black Mass' for 2006, this version hosting extra demo tracks.

Messe Noir, (1989). Intro / Prayer Of Hell / As Thou Wilt / Midnight Offering / Alla Xul / So It Is Done.

Eternal Suffering, (1990). Eternal Suffering / Morbid Love / Cold Blood / Penetrate My Hunger.

Rites Of The Black Mass, (1991). To Thee We Confess / Thou Art Lord / Ave Sathanas / Summoning The Master / One With Darkness / Prayer To Hell / Unholy Praises / Cursed Nazarene / The Enochian Key / Let Us Depart.

Alla Xul, Gutted (1992). Alla Xul / One With Darkness.

RITES OF THE BLACK MASS, Turbo 007 (1992). Intro / Prayer Of Hell / Intro / Unholy Praises / Intro / Cursed Nazarene / Intro / The Enochian Key / Intro / Let Us Depart / Intro / To Thee We Confess / Intro / Thou Art Lord / Intro / Ave Satanas / Intro / Summoning The Master / Intro / One With Darkness.

HAIL VICTORY, Metal Merchant (1993). Unholy Praises / Seven Deadly Sins / Satanic Erotica / Prayer Of Hell / 666 / God Is Dead / Alla Xul / One With Darkness.

SATANIC VICTORY, Turbo (1994). Unholy Praises / Seven Deadly Sins / Satanic Erotica / Prayer Of Hell / 666 / God Is Dead.

LEX TALIONIS, Turbo (1994). Legions Of Hatred / Enter Thy Coven / Slaughterisation For Satan / Voices Within / Purification Day / Inner Beasts / The Entity / I.N.R.I. (False Prophet) / Lex Talionis March (outro).

Messe Noir, Reaper (1995). Intro / Prayer Of Hell / As Thou Wilt / Midnight Offering / Alla Xul / So It Is Done.

LEX TALIONIS- SATANIC VICTORY, Blackened BLACK006CD (1997). Legions Of Hatred / Enter Thy Coven / Slaughterisation For Satan / Voices Within / Purification Day / Inner Beasts / The Entity / I.N.R.I. (False Prophet) / Lex Talionis March (outro) / Unholy Praises / Seven Deadly Sins / Satanic Erotica / Prayer Of Hell / 666 / God Is Dead.

ANTI GOD- ANTI CHRIST, Moribund (1997). Fuck The Ways Of Christ / Shemhamforash (The Ultimate Blasphemy) / Blessed By Damnation / Baptism For Devlyn Alexandra / Total War.

THOSE WHO HAVE RISEN, Full Moon (1998). Nosferatu Prelude / Lifeforce (The Blood) / Hekal Tiamat / Necromanteion Communion / Out Of Body / Undead Celebration / Final Harvest / Shurpu Kishpu / The Calling / Immortal Sigil.

Necromanteion Communion, (1998) (Picture disc). Necromanteion Communion / Raise The Dead.

COMPENDIUM DIABLERIE—THE DEMO DAYS, Full Moon Productions FMP029CD (2001). Prayer Of Hell / As Thou Wilt / Midnight Offering—Alla Xul / So It Is Done / To Thee We Confess / Ave Satanas / Thou Art Lord / Ave Satanas / Summoning The Master / One With Darkness / Prayer Of Hell / Unholy Praises / Cursed Nazarene / The Enochian Key / Let Us Depart / Alla Xul / Blessed By Damnation / Hekal Tiamat / Necromanteion Communion.

Xomaly EP, Warlord WR05CD (2002). Predator Revealed / Xomaly / Resurgence Of The Unholy / The Kindred.

TRIBUTE TO THE DEVIL'S MUSIC, Black Lotus BLR CD048 (2003). Black Sabbath / Evil Dead / Dawn Of Meddigo / Wrathchild / Flag Of Hate / (Don't Need) Religion / Room Of Golden Air / War Machine / Raise The Dead / Devil's Child / Countess Bathory / Ave Satanas.

REBIRTH: METAMORPHOSING INTO GODHOOD, Black Lotus BLRCD055 (2003). Chaos Invocation / Church Of One / Xomaly / Bow Before Me / The Kindred / A Long Time Ago / Golgotha's Truth / Betrayed (A Broken Pact) / The 9th Gate.

ACRID

HAGUE, HOLLAND — *Mark Pilk (vocals / guitar), Claus Toet (guitar), Arjan Heijden (bass), Frank Debij (drums).*

Hague based Death Metal unit came together during 1994. Just prior to recording their first demo original guitarist Itay was forced out, returning to fulfill his military obligations in his homeland of Israel. ACRID duly drafted Claus Toet for recording of the 'Bitter ...' sessions. A second demo, 'Withered', arrived in 1996 upfront of the debut album 'Amalgamate', recorded at Excess Studios in Rotterdam and released by Polar-Bear Records.

Further demoing saw the band entering Excess Studios in September 1999 to craft the Tryad' session. Plans were made for an album, given a working title 'Unveiling', but in March of 2000 vocalist / bassist Marcel Zonneveld opted out. Deciding to recruit from within, guitarist Mark Pilik assumed lead vocal duties whilst Arjan Heijden was recruited on bass for recording of more demos in 2001, 2002 and the 'Draw The Line' session in 2003. ACRID spent the early half of 2005 crafting a new album entitled 'Prism'.

AMALGAMATE, Polar Bear (1999). Valentine / For The Sake Of ... / Amalgamate / The Darkness Of A Question / The Complete / Withered / The Speaking Eyes / Your Burning Silhouette / Gray Harmony.

Tryad, (1999). Blood Velvet / Clear / Trust.

Demo 2001, (2001). F.C.K.D. / Divine Cruelty / Empty.

Demo 2002, (2002). Art Of War / Sin / Souvereign.

Demo 2003—Draw The Line, (2003). It Begins / A Matter Of Light And Death / Parasite / Draw The Line.

ACRIMONY INC.

IZMIR, TURKEY — *Altug Kaptan (vocals), Emre Meydan (lead guitar), Hakan Yavuz (rhythm guitar), Aykut Cerezcioglu (bass), Cagil Undar (drums).*

ACRIMONY INC. date to 1999, although previously known simply as ACRIMONY. Line-up changes would see the rhythm section of bassist Sevket Cin and drummer Enis Fakioglu replaced by Aykut Cerezcioglu and Cagil Undar respectively. Debut product would be a January 2001 demo entitled 'Burning Lives'. The band evolved into ACRIMONY INC. for a 2002 demo. At this juncture the band comprised vocalist Altug Kaptan, lead guitarist Emre Meydan, rhythm guitarist Hakan Yavuz, bassist Aykut Cerezcioglu and drummer Cagil Undar. A further demo arrived in 2004 but by the time of a 2004 promotional session the group had switched title yet again to UNDONE.

Acrimony Inc., Acrimony Inc. (2002). Transient Lifetime / Silent Farewell / Existence Confined / Prime Of Life.

Promo CD II, (2003). Idee Fixe / Gallows Bird / Sun/Dawn/Obsession / Expiry.

ACROHOLIA

BELGRADE, SERBIA — *Ilija (vocals), Bane (guitar), Slobodan Bosnic (bass), Uros Smiljanic (drums).*

Belgrade Grindcore band ACROHOLIA was forged as a trio of guitarist Bane, bassist Oliver and Uros Smiljanic on the drums in 1991. Adding singer Ilija the group cut two demos during 1992 with a third set crafted in 1995. Songs from these sessions found their way onto various compilation albums released in Yugoslavia, Europe, North America and the Middle East. The Austrian label Capeet Tapes would re-issue the third ACROHOLIA demo as a split release shared with ENTRAILS MASSACRE and YACOPSAE. Subsequently the same songs were released as split 7" single with INTESTINAL DISEASE by Abnormal Beer Terrorism.

In 2002 a fourth demo comprised, entitled 'Ubistvo Sveta', comprised 27 original tracks alongside two NAPALM DEATH cover versions. This release would be promoted by a promotional video, lasting just 54 seconds. Oliver gave way to Suvi before Slobodan Bosnic enrolled on bass. Rock Express Records released the 'Ecocide' album in 2003.

ECOCIDE, Rock Express (2003). Stone Face / Face Skin Harm / Genderless / Butterfly In Flesh / Trial And Error / Pogrom / Bringer Of Fire—Astigmata / Intoxinitiation / Free Like Maggots / Angel Tongue / Abortion Engine / Anniversary Of Defeat / Unholy / Protein Donor / A Monument To Fertility / Ecstasis/Metastasis / Necessity / Sense / The Fallen / Syndicate Of Pigs / Tomorrow And Tomorrow And Tomorrow / Fracture / The Kill / Deceiver / More Than Once / Motions I Dream / Ecocide / Upwards And Sidewise / The Cradle.

ACROSTICHON

TILBURG, HOLLAND — *Corinne van der Brand (vocals / bass), Michel Meeuwissen (guitar), Jos van der Brand (guitar), Serge Smolders (drums).*

Formed in Tilburg during 1989 by the vocalist / bassist Corinne van der Brand with guitarists Richard Schouten and Jos van der Brand and drummer Vincent, this Dutch Black Metal outfit soon added drummer Roeland to the cause. The 'Prologue' demo was cut in 1990. The drum position would switch once again with the recruitment of Serge Smolders, Roeland eventually going on to GREEN LIZARD, and by the end of 1990 could be found opening for CARCASS, followed by gigs with MORBID ANGEL, DEATH and SODOM. In January 1991 the demo 'Dehumanized' was delivered, alongside an officially sanctioned live cassette.

The American independent label Seraphic Decay issued ACROSTICHON tracks as part of a multi-band split album in 1991, the group donating four tracks and sharing vinyl with

MINCH, DISGRACE, GOREAPHOBIA, TOXAEMIA and ABHORRENCE.

Seraphic Decay duly signed the quartet, although the group's debut album, 'Engraved In Black' issued in 1993, was produced by Colin Richardson against their will. ACROSTICHON, now with Michel Meeuwissen having usurped Schouten, signed to the Double Noise label for the 1995 album 'Sentenced. In 1998 Jos van der Brand, Michel Meeuwissen and drummer Serge Smolders founded Thrash act OUTBURST issuing the demo 'Victory For A Soul'. In 2003 Jos van den Brand temporarily joined the ranks of THE MONOLITH DEATHCULT for live work. The guitarist would also score credits with MASTER.

Prologue, (1990). Immolation Of The Agnostic / Havoc / Mentally Deficient / Elaborate Ritual.
Acrostichon Live, (1990). Havoc / Mentally Deficient / Elaborate Ritual / Xenomorphic Mania.
CD SAMPLER, Seraphic Decay (1991) (Split album with MINCH, DISGRACE, GOREAPHOBIA, TOXAEMIA and ABHORRENCE). Dehumanized / Thriving On Chaos / Exasperation / Lost Remembrance.
Lost Remembrance, Seraphic Decay (1991). Lost Remembrance / Dehumanized / Mentally Deficient.
Dehumanized, (1991). Dehumanized / Thriving On Chaos / Exasperation / Lost Remembrance.
ENGRAVED IN BLACK, Modern Primitive PRIM2CD (1993). Immolation Of The Agnostic / Walker Of Worlds / Dehumanized / Mentally Deficient / Lost Remembrance / Zombies / Havoc / Relics / Engraved In Black.
SENTENCED, Double Noise (1995). Sentenced / Snapshot / Forgotten / Guilt / Sleepless / Victims / Scarred / Shelter / Pain.

ADAGIO

BRAZIL — *Fabiano (vocals), Daniel Factor (guitar), M. Fernando (bass), Alessandro (keyboards), Rogério (drums).*

ADAGIO was created in 1995, an opening demo tape entitled 'Sustenuto' seeing a recording line up of vocalist Jeferson, guitarists Mario Crest and Martin with Rogério on the drums. Subsequently Ricardo 'Ratão' enrolled on bass. Crest opted out in 1997, being superseded by Douglas as ADAGIO also welcomed in new bass man M. Fernando for a second demo set 'Feeling's Of Harmony'. Themistocles was inducted on keyboards during 1998 as the band put in high profile support slots to MOONSPELL in São Paulo and ROTTING CHRIST in Santos.

In November of 1998 the band completed a third demo 'Winter', these sessions seeing Priscila as guest vocalist. In 2000 Priscila formally joined the band alongside Jeferson. A new keyboard player was found in Alessandro and then Fabiano took over the lead vocal role. Guitarist Daniel Factor would be the latest recruit.

ROMANTIC SERENADES, Megahard (1999). A World Dreams / Ocean Of Tears / Beautiful Like Sadness / Red Flowers As The Passion / Darkness Forever / Romantic Serenades In The Dawn / Your Soft Touch / My Last Good-bye / ... To The Death.
THE BIRTH OF MISERY, Demise (2001). Lamiai / Tears Of Blood / Succubus / Mater Mors / The Search / The Bone Dance / Loneliness / Stylus Carnibus / Nightmare.
THE BIRD OF MYSER, Megahard (2001).

ADENINE

MONTRÉAL, QC, CANADA — *Martin Quintal (vocals), Pascal Charron (guitar), Michael Kosow (guitar), Christian Choquette (bass), Mathieu Groulx (drums).*

Scandinavian styled Death from Montréal. ADENINE was forged during December of 1999 by erstwhile TRANSCENDENCE guitarist Philippe Coupal. Initially a stand in bassist from NEURAXIS was employed, being replaced by the WINTER BESTOWED and TRAILS OF ANGUISH credited bass player Sebastian Painchaud. The bass position would change once more over to Christian Choquette. ADENINE's debut album 'Govern The Unaligned' would see Pierre Remillard of OBLIVEON acting as producer. The track 'Hindrance' gained further exposure with its inclusion on the Neoblast 'Quebec Invasion' compilation. Upon completion of these sessions the band introduced guitarist Jonathan Phillips as replacement for Philippe Coupal.

ADENINE folded during 2002 with drummer Mathieu Groulx going on to AUGURY whilst ex-member Philippe Coupal involved with RED SUN and TRANCE OF MINE.

GOVERN THE UNALIGNED, NBR-01-04 (2001). Hidebound / Quantum / Disdain / Hindrance / Quarantine / Deceived / Hybrid / Asunder / Soulsight.

ADRAMELECH

LOIMAA, FINLAND — *Marko Silvennoinen (vocals), Jari Laine (guitar), Tommi Rantanen (bass), Jarkko Rantanen (drums).*

A Loimaa Death Metal band formed by bass player Jani Aho, Jusi Tainio on drums and former DISINTERED vocalist / guitarist Jarkko Rantanen in Loimaa during 1991, ADRAMELECH sought out a vocalist and second guitarist to join the founding trio and came up with Tuomas Ala-Nissila and Erik Parviainen respectively, Rantanen switching to drums after Tainio departed.

The band recorded the 1992 'Grip Of Darkness' demo, featuring new bassist Mikko Aarnio, that led to a deal with the French Adipocere label.

Following the release of the 7" vinyl 'Spring Of Recovery' single in December 1992 and a show with DEMILICH, BEHERIT and CRYPT OF KERBEROS in 1993, Seppo Taatila, previously with DEMIGOD, joined and contributed to the recording of 'The Fall' sessions, released in June 1995. The band then featured on a compilation released by the Spanish label Repulse with the track 'Heroes In Godly Blaze'.

The liaison with the Spaniards led to a two album deal with Repulse, the first fruits of which was the commercial release on CD of 'The Fall' tape.

The 'Psychotasia' album arrived in June 1996. ADRAMELECH were to lose bassist Aarnio after the 'Psychotasia' album and also added the ex-vocalist of DEMIGOD towards the end of 1996. For the May 1998 mini-album 'Seven', a five track affair featuring two new studio tracks, a brace of live cuts and a re-recording of 'Ancestral Souls' re-titled 'Captured In Eternal Lost', the band comprised Rantanen, bassist Phillipe La Grassa and drummer Seppo Taatila. 'Pure Black Doom' ensued during April 1999.

ADRAMELECH were still undergoing line-up ructions in 2001 when in September guitar player Ali Leiniö departed. An album, entitled 'Terror Of Thousand Faces', was recorded but process proved arduous as their singer quit before completion of the tracks. The album finally emerged in June 2005 through Xtreem Music. EMISSARY's Marko Silvennoinen took over on lead vocals. Mikko Aarnio was to be replaced on bass by Tommi Rantanen, a scene veteran of UNCREATION'S DAWN, FOREVER WINTER, IMPIOUS HAVOC, NIGHTSIDE and VORDVEN.

Human Extermination, Adramelech (1991) (Demo). Intro / Carnivore Corpse Feast / Human Extermination / Sarcophagus / Pestilential Mists.
Grip Of Darkness, Adramelech (1992) (Demo). Mortal God / Grip Of Darkness / Ancestral Souls / Dreamdeath.
Spring Of Recovery, Adipocere AR 006 (1992). Dethroned / Mortal God / Revived.
The Fall, Repulse RPS 006 MCD (1995). As The Gods Succumbed / Heroes In Godly Blaze / Séance Of Shamans / The Fall Of Tiamat.
PSYCHOTASIA, Adramelech RPS 015 CD (1996). Heroes In Godly Blaze / Psychostasia / Séance Of Shamans / The Book Of The Worm / Thoth (Lord Of Holy Words) / Mythic Descendant / As The Gods Succumbed / Across The Gray Waters.
Seven, Repulse RPS 030 MCD (1998). Seven / The Sleep Of Ishtar / Captured In Eternal Lost / As The Gods Succumbed (Live) / Across The Grey Waters (Live).

PURE BLACK DOOM, Severe SVR-001 (1999). Centuries Of Murder / Thule / Abominations 459 / Season Of The Predator / Thingstead / Lord Of The Red Land / Evercursed / The Book Of The Black Earth / Spawn Of The Suffering.

PSYCHOTASIA / SEVEN / THE FALL, Blackend BLACK051CD (2003). Heroes In Godly Blaze / Psychostasia / Séance Of Shamans / The Book Of The Worm / Thoth (Lord Of Holy Words) / Mythic Descendant / As The Gods Succumbed / Across The Gray Waters / Seven / The Sleep Of Ishtar / Captured In Eternal Lost / As The Gods Succumbed (Live) / Across The Grey Waters (Live) / As The Gods Succumbed / Heroes In Godly Blaze / Séance Of Shamans / The Fall Of Tiamat.

TERROR OF THOUSAND FACES, Xtreem Music XM 030 CD (2005). Intro / Halls Of Human Tragedy / Bleeding For Supremacy / Suicide, Terrorize / I Don't Care About Your Murder / Slain In The Grace Of Thy Name / Book Of Flesh / Terror Of Thousand Faces / Orphica Holodemiurgia.

ADRIFT

TAMPA, FL, USA — *Mark Elm (vocals), Analia Pizzaro (guitar), Jack Owen (guitar), Michael Capuano (bass), Kevin Astl (drums).*

Guitarist Jack Owen of veteran Gore mongers CANNIBAL CORPSE united with the EPITAPH and RESURRECTION credited drummer Kevin Astl and female second, classically trained, guitarist Analia Pizzaro in a brand new "Aggro Hard Rock" Tampa, Florida based band project called ADRIFT in the Summer of 2001. ADRIFT would be completed with the addition of PATH OF MAN vocalist Mark Elm with bassist Michael Capuano coming onboard in mid 2003.

The band completed work on their debut EP at Audiohammer Studios in Sanford, Florida in February of 2004. CAPHARNAUM leader Jason Suecof scored production and engineering credits. The EP was mastered at Morrisound Studios by Jim Morris. ADRIFT set to work on a full length album in August, working at ARS Studios in Winter Park with producer, John Hughes II.

Adrift, Adrift (2006). The Calling / Vague Unconsciousness / Memory / What You've Become.

AECRON

ASIKKALA, FINLAND — *E. Hereticius (vocals / guitar / drums), Krim Reaper (guitar), J. Karjalainen (bass).*

Asikkala Thrash Metal band AECRON comprises vocalist / guitarist / drummer E. Hereticius (a.k.a. E. Paavola), of ARGANATH, AZAROK, FUNERIUM and TYR repute, alongside guitarist Krim Reaper (K. Höök) and bassist J. Karjalainen. The outfit, initiated in 2005, at first traded under the THÖ ROJEKTI banner, this antecedent unit featuring formative personnel guitarist J. Niemeläinen and drummer V. Härkönen. THÖ ROJEKTI issued a 2004 EP 'Kalman Kaunis Tyttö', the demo 'Thö Rojekti', another 2004 EP 'White Man', the video 'Songs That We Destroyed' and an EP 'Aecron' in 2005.

As AECRON, Stay Brutal distributed the May 2005 demo 'Old Scars'. The 'Rehearsal Scheisse' set followed in July.

Old Scars, Aecron (2005) (Demo). War / Fallen / No Sign Of (Fucking) Life / White Man / Kalmankaunis / Veljeni / New God / Aecron / The Unknown Harmony.

Rehearsal Scheisse, Aecron (2005) (Demo). Fallen / War / Veljeni / No Sign Of (Fucking) Life / (Untitled).

AEON

ÖSTERSUND, SWEDEN — *Tommy Dahlström (vocals), Daniel Dlimi (guitar), Zeb Nilsson (guitar), Johan Hjelm (bass), Nils Fjällström (drums).*

Death Metal act AEON was forged in Östersund during mid 1999 by a quartet of erstwhile DEFACED CREATION players, namely singer Tommy 'Blackblood' Dahlström, guitarist Zeb 'Nathzion' Nilsson, bassist Johan Hjelm and Arttu Malkki on the drums. Dahlström and Nilsson also hold credits with DIABOLICUM. Subsequently Morgan Nordbakk was added as second guitarist. Demos produced by Johan Hjelm and recorded at the Courthouse Studios in Östersund in late 1999 apparently prompted offers of contracts from Near Dark Productions, Wicked World and Black Mark but AEON held out for a better offer. The group duly signed with Deathvomit, a subsidiary of US label Necropolis Records, to issue all six demo tracks as the 'Dark Order' EP.

Nordbakk was superseded by Daniel Dlimi, this latest recruit citing credits with DIVINE DESECRATION, SANCTIFICATION, SOULDRAINER and THE EQUINOX OV THE GODS. AEON replaced Malkki with Nils Fjellström of CHASTISEMENT, SOULDRAINER and SANCTIFICATION during June of 2002. Fjellström joined IN BATTLE in 2003 with Dlimi following in 2004.

AEON signed to Unique Leader Records for a 2004 album 'Bleeding The False'. In September 2006 the group, bringing in new bassist Max Carlberg, switched labels to Metal Blade Records. Live work in October 2006 was suspended when Tommy Dahlström had an appendix operation.

Aeon, Aeon (0).

Aeon, Aeon (1999) (Demo). The Return Of Apolluon / Eternal Hate / With Blood They Pay / The Awakening / Bloodlust / Hell Unleashed.

Dark Order, Deathvomit DVR009 (2001). The Return Of Apolluon / Eternal Hate / With Blood They Pay / The Awakening / Bloodlust / Hell Unleashed.

BLEEDING THE FALSE, Unique Leader ULR 60026-2 (2005). Cenobites / Soulburner / Morbid Desire To Burn / Biblewhore / Forever Nailed / Satanic Victory / Enchanter / Bleeding The False / Doorknocker / Bow Your Heads / I Hate Your Existence / God Gives Head In Heaven / Hell Unleashed / Outro / God Gives Head In Heaven (Country version).

AETURNUS DOMINION

CENTRAL COAST, NSW, AUSTRALIA — *Jester (vocals), Demented (vocals /. guitar), Thrax (guitar / vocals), Spud (bass), Ozi (drums).*

New South Wales Death Metal band forged in 2003, issuing the 'Terrorize' demo that same year. Upfront of September 2004 recordings AETURNUS DOMINION parted ways with singer Jester. Guitarist Demented duly took over the role of vocalist as the band persevered as a quartet. The 'Semper Tyrannis' album was originally released in June of 2004 as a self financed effort, being subsequently re-issued by Statue Records. AETURNUS DOMINION line-up changes in 2005 saw the exit of guitarist Spud and bassist Rat, replaced by the TRITURA duo of Thrax and Lex. However, Spud returned, ousting Lex.

AETURNUS DOMINION paid tribute to late PANTERA and DAMAGEPLAN guitarist "Dimebag" Darrell Abbott with their rendition of 'Mouth For war' being donated to 'The Art Of Shredding—A Tribute To Dime' assembled by DarkStar Records.

The band teamed up with fellow Australian act THE FUROR and Dubai, United Arab Emirates band NERVECELL for the "Metalstock Road Rage" Tour, commencing at Australia's Arthouse in Melbourne on Friday, March 30th 2007, followed by five more shows including Adelaide, Wagga Wagga, Wollongong, Canberra and Sydney.

Terrorize, (2003). Aeternus Dominion / Unsanitized / Traumatic Amputation / Solitude Of My Soul / Global Cremation Suicide / Meathook / Terrorize.

SEMPER TYRANIS, Statue (2004). Holocaust / God Has Failed / Aeternus Dominion / They Wait / Unsanitized / Global Cremation Suicide / Meathook / Unholy / Cyanide.

AFFLICTED

SWEDEN — *Joakim Broms (vocals), Jesper Thorsson (guitar), Joacim Carlsson (guitar), Fredrik Ling (bass), Yasin Hillborg (drums).*

Previously known as AFFLICTED CONVULSION and launched in 1988 by ex-DEFIANCE guitarist Jesper Thorsson, his guitar partner Joacim Carlsson previously having been with DISMEMBER. AFFLICTED released the first demo in 1990, titled 'Beyond Redemption'. The decision to drop the word 'Convulsion' from the band name was taken once vocalist Joakim Broms had joined. Further demos followed in 1991 entitled 'The Odious Reflection' and 'Wanderland', prior to the band's first single ('Viewing The Obscene') on Thrash Records.

The band suffered a change in membership when bassist Fredrik Ling was ousted in favour of Phillip Von Segebaden following the 'Astray' single in 1992. During 1993 AFFLICTED recorded the track 'Seven Gates Of Hell' for the VENOM tribute album 'Promoters Of The Third World War' and bass for these sessions was handled by Mikael Lindevall of PROBOSCIS.

The 1995 album 'Dawn Of Glory' witnessed a radical shift in style as Broms quit to join Deathsters ABHOTH and in came vocalist Michael Van De Graaf. Joacim Carlsson left after the second album's release to join PROBOSCIS then the Roadrunner signed FACE DOWN. Despite the changes in roster, AFFLICTED have still been able to tour Scandinavia consistently, including shows with ENTOMBED, THERION and DISMEMBER.

Von Segebaden issued the first album from his side project band DEFENDER in 1999 titled 'They Came Over The High Pass'. His AFFLICTED colleagues vocalist Michael van der Graaf and drummer Peter Nagy also contributed. In 2004 guitarist Joacim Carlsson, then enrolled in the ranks of GENERAL SURGERY, formed up part of the resurrected FACE DOWN.

Promo & Rehearsal Tracks, Afflicted (1990) (Demo). Consumed In Flames / In Years To Come / Untitled / The Root.

The Odious Reflection, Afflicted (1990) (Cassette demo). Intro / The Root ... / Utilization / The Doomwatchers Prediction / In Years To Come.

Ingrained, Thrash THR009 (1991). Viewing The Obscene / The Empty Word.

Wanderland, Afflicted (1991) (Demo). Astray / Tidings From The Blue Sphere / Spirit Spectrum / Ivory Tower.

Rising To The Sun, Nuclear Blast ST 45 NB063 (1992). Rising To The Sun / Ivory Tower.

Nuclear Blast EP, Nuclear Blast (1992) (Split blue 7" vinyl EP with SINISTER, HYPOCRISY and RESURRECTION). In Years To Come.

Wanderland EP, Relapse 019 (1992). Astray / Spirit Spectrum.

PRODIGAL SUN, Nuclear Blast NB 0063-2 (1992). Prodigal Sun / Harbouring The Soul / In Years To Come / Tidings From The Blue Sphere / The Empty Word / Astray / Rising Into The Sun / Spirit Spectrum / The Doomwatcher's Prediction / Consumed In Flames / Ivory Tower.

Promo 1993, Afflicted (1993) (Cassette demo). Raging Into Battle / Dragon Breath.

DAWN OF GLORY, Massacre MASS CD055 (1995). Son Of Earth / Dawn Of Glory / The Oracle / Last Incarnation / Raging Into Battle / Scattered / I Am Vengeance / Cross My Heart / Niflheim.

Relapse Single Series Vol. 5, Relapse RPE 6650-2 (2005) (Split CD single with CANDIRU, MORTICIAN and MYTHIC). Astray / Spirit Spectrum.

AFTER THE LAST SKY

STOKE ON TRENT, STAFFORDSHIRE, UK — *Benjamin Hoare (vocals), Matt Doughty (guitar), James Goad (guitar), Shane Turner (bass), Simon Heywood (drums).*

Stoke on Trent, Staffordshire "Blackcore" Death Metal band AFTER THE LAST SKY operated previously as ANIMOSITY, being founded in late 1997, debuting with a March 1999 demo, entitled 'We Fear ...', recorded at Framework Studios in Birmingham with producer Paul Siddens. Working with Paul Hodson of HARD RAIN, A.N.D. and the BOB CATLEY band acting as engineer a second, self-titled session arrived in 2001. 'Awakening To A Black-Core Dawn' followed in 2002, this set of tracks laid down in Telford and produced by CANCER drummer Karl Stokes. Line-up changes saw the exit of guitarist Duncan Rathband in November 2002 and James Harper duly switched from bass to guitar in March 2003.

ANIMOSITY evolved into AFTER THE LAST SKY in 2004, drafting new bassist Shane Turner of STILLBORN DECAY that March. A posthumous collection of tracks, suitably titled 'Animosity Are Fucking Dead ... Get Over It', was delivered that same year. First product under this new branding would be a split EP 'The Essence Of Our Art Is Hatred' shared with Nottingham based Grind outfit INERT, actually a side act of Benjamin Hoare's. Second guitarist James Goad, of STONE GOLEM, was added to the ranks in December.

AFTER THE LAST SKY guitarist Matthew Doughty also operates with Noisecore merchants FUCKHATEPROPAGANDA. Drummer Simon Heywood holds ties to FIRETHORN and THE POWER OF ISILDOR.

The Essence Of Our Art Is Hatred, Circus of the Macabre (2004) (Split EP with INERT. Art School Lebensborn / Dragons Teeth Harvest / Regretting Those Drunken Words.

AFTERDEATH

LISBON, PORTUGAL — *Sergio Paulo (vocals), Nuno Maciel (guitar), José Ramos (bass), Mário Rui (drums).*

Lisbon Death Metal act AFTERDEATH, founded in 1990 mix a blend of Thrash Metal and Hardcore on their 1995 album 'Backwords'. The band comprised singer Sergio Paulo, guitarist Nuno Maciel, bassist José Ramos and drummer Mário Rui. AFTERDEATH tested the water with a brace of demos 'Unreal Sight' and 'Behind Life', the first of these seeing a recording line-up including erstwhile THORNADO personnel guitarist Virgílio Neto, bass player Roberto Monteiro and drummer Filipe Martins.

This new formation recorded the track 'Dark Atmosphere' for inclusion on the compilation 'Sometimes Death Is Better' released by the Belgian Shiver Records label. In February of 1994, AFTERDEATH recorded a further demo 'Unreal Sight' but then once again went through line-up changes, at first re-installing Nuno Maciel but soon substituting him for Vítor Silva. In addition, José Ramos assumed bass duties. In July of 1995 AFTERDEATH recorded the album 'Backwords' at Rec n' Roll Studios with producer Luís Barros of TARANTULA fame. However, the band had once again undergone a membership overhaul. AFTERDEATH's final performance would be the song "World Deformed By Man' included on the 'Guardians of Metal Vol. IV' compilation released through Guardians of Metal.

Behind Life, (1992). Intro / Digital Horizons / Afterdeath / Heart Of Fire / Fortune.

Unreal Sight, (1994). Justice Manipulation / Live For Today / Speaks On Your Thoughts / Hunger Calling / Deep In Natural Art.

BACKWORDS, Guardians Of Metal (1995). Caught In The Web / Swallowed / Drowning / Within My Self / Eye For War / Undertow / Digital Horizons / Without Words / Confidence Betrayed / View (From Behind) / Dye In Agony.

AGATHOCLES

BELGIUM — *Matty A.G. Dupont (vocals / guitar), Steve (vocals / guitar), Jan A.G. Frederickx (vocals / bass), Burt A.G. Beyens (drums).*

Belgian Grindcore act AGATHOCLES evolved out of the Punk scene in the early 80's. At first a loose collective AGATHOCLES as a fully fledged band was created in around 1985. They have built a reputation as undisputed leaders of the split 7 single phenomenon. The self-titled 'Mince-Core' outfit have issued an exhaustive roster of singles, many split efforts with other bands and albums including a split album with Colombians AVERNO in 1995. This is part of a continuing trend as AGATHOCLES have shared vinyl and CD space with the likes of

NYCTOPHOBIC, CARCASS GRINDER, SMEGMA, BLOOD and PUTRID OFFAL among many others.

The band has featured on a number of compilation albums in addition to the singles and album listed. AGATHOCLES energy seems to know no bounds, by 1996 the band had also performed over 400 gigs. As well as 7 singles AGATHOCLES are not averse to alliances on cassette and tapes over the years have witnessed unions with DRUDGE, LUNATIC INVASION, BULLSHIT PROPAGANDA, INCONTINENTIA, EXTREME STROKE, IMPEDIGION, MUGGLES, VOLTIFIBIA, SHIT, DEFECATION PURULENTIA and Italians CRIPPLE BASTARDS.

During 1999 AGATHOCLES shared a joint album venture 'Hunt Hunters' on Czech label Obscene Productions, with SUPPOSITORY, the band of erstwhile AGATHOCLES guitarist Matti.

The band shared an EP 'Show Your Colors Vol. 3' with Japanese Grind band WORLD DOWNFALL in 2004. AGATHOCLES signed to Dutch label Displeased Records in early 2005 for a new album, commencing recording in November.

Agathocles, Innerforce Wreckords (1989) (Split 7" single with DISGORGE). Threshold To Senility / Consuming Endoderme Pus / Splattered Brains / Forced Pollutions / The Accident.
THEATRE SYMOLISATION OF LIFE, Cyber Music (1992). Burning Water / Lack Of Personality / Four Walls / Theatric Symbolisation Of Life / Like An Ivy / Suffocation / Kill Your Idols / The Truth Begins Where Man Stops To Think / Train / The Tree / What A Nerve / Alternative- Another Trend / Mutilated Regurgitator / The Accident / Threshold To Senility / Forced Pollutions / Consuming Endoderme Pus / Playing With Lifes / Splattered Brains / Well Of Happiness / Judged By Appearance / Solitary Minded / Trust? Not Me / Lay Off Me / Threshold To Senility / Mutilated Regurgitator / Gorgonised Dorks / Lay Off Me / Consuming Endoderme Pus / Let It Be For What It Is.
USE YOUR ANGER- LIVE, 199 (1993).
Distrust And Abuse EP, Boundless Records (1993). Sieg Shit / Hatronomous / Hideous Headchopping / Bigheaded Bastards / Get Off Your Ass / Distrust And Abuse.
Screenfreak, Regurgitated Semen (1993) (Split single With CARCASS GRINDER). Screenfreak.
Pigs In Blue, Bizarre Leprous (1993) (Split single With PLASTIC GRAVE). Pigs In Blue.
No Use . . . (Hatred) EP, Boundless (1993). Go Fucking Nihilist / Hatred Is The Cure / No Use . . . (Hatred) / An Abstract.
CLICHE- LIVE, 199 (1993).
Wiped From Surface, Elephant (1994) (Split single with ROT). Wiped From Surface / Debalace Their Policy / Go Fucking Nihilist (Live).
BLACK CLOUDS DETERMINATE, Cyber CYBER10 (1994). Bastard Breed (Intro) / Scorn Of Humanity / Sentimental Hypocrisy / Megalomaniac Stupidity / Hangman's Dance / Black Clouds Determinate / Ubermensch Hilarity / Triple Murder Flesh / Europe's Fairy Tale / Musicianship- Musicianshit / Confront Your Images / Mister Hardcore Syndrome / For White Lies / Technological Boom-Technological Doom / Destroy To Create / Bigheaded Bastard / Hate Birth / Sieg Shit / Well Of Happiness / Birds (Poem) Agarthy / Theatric Symbolization Of Life / Bigheaded Bastard / Lack Of Personality / Squeeze Anton / What Mankind Creates / Distrust And Abuse / Teachers / Hideous Headchopping / Mutilated Regurgitator / Get Off Your Ass / Hate Birth.
Who Shares The Guilt EP, Poserslaughter (1995) (Split single with NASUM). Who Shares The Guilt.
RAZOR SHARP DAGGERS, Bones Brigade (1995). A Start At Least / Clean The Scene / A For Arrogance / Thy Kingdom Won't Come / Media Creations / All Gone / Swallow Or Choke / Razor Sharp Daggers / Enough / Throwing Away Crap / Cracking Up Solidarity / Lunatic / Didn't Ask / Twisting History / Deserves To Die / Age Of The Mutants / Zero—Ego / Gear Wheels / Dear Friends / Hormone Mob / Hash-Head, Farmer's Death / Dare To Be Aware / Kiss My Ass / All Love Dead / Fear Not / Sieg Shit / Hatronomous / Hideous Headchopping / Bigheaded Bastards / Get Of Your Ass / Distrust And Abuse / Hippie Cult / Provoked Behaviour / Black Ones—Systemphobic / Anthropodislogical / Labelisation / What Mankind Creates / No! / Rejected Adaption / An Abstract / Faded Novelty / Senseless Trip / Here And Now / Is It Really Mine?
Back To 1987 EP, Morbid 660773 (1996). Big One / The Fog / Teachers / Accident / Mutilated Regurgitator / Consuming Endoderme Pus / Splattered Brains / Christianity Means Tyranny / Squeeze Anton / Introyy / Threshold To Senility.
No Gain- Just Pain, MCR Company MCR099 (1996) (Split single with UNHOLY GRAVE). No Gain- Just Pain / The Sin I Regret / Insufferable Beings? / Do All The Sick Experience Healing? / L'Ardoise Vierge.
HUMARROGANCE, Morbid MR 037CD (1997). Humarrogance / Because / Model Citizen / Let's Feel Alright / As Years Pass By / It Bothers Me / One Day Fly / White Horse / Ain't I / Beam Me Up, Scotty / Ice Brick / Culture Of Degradation / Closed Down / Alright, Let's Feel / Kneel And Pay / Failure / I Can't Stand / Smelling The Odours Of Death / The Bastards Have Landed / Mince-Core.
Live And Noisy EP, Bad People BPR009 (1997). Live And Noisy.
THANKS FOR YOUR HOSTILITY, Morbid MR 03 (1997). Criminalization Of Strange Behaviour / Life Control / Until It Bleeds / End Of The Line / Doctors Wished Me / Knock Back / Thanks For Your Hostility / Hatred Is The Cure / Be Your God / Distraction / Remember / Cheers Mankind Cheers / Strangulation / Foul / Un Use . . . Hatred / My Reason / No One's Right / Sheer Neglect / Is There A Place? / Go Fucking Nihilist / Progress Or Stupidity? / Try! / He Cared / Mankind's Not Kind / Reduced To An Object / Ego-Generosity / . . . .
Spud EP, P.O.E. (1998) (Split EP with NUCLEAR DEVASTATION). Intro—Christianity Means Tyranny / Is There A Place? / Distraction / A For Arrogance / Lay Off Me / Msheep—Systemphobic.
MINCE CORE, Controverse (1999). Threshold To Senility / Consuming Endoderme Pus / Splattered Brains / Forced Pollution / The Accident / Mutilated Regurgitator / Playin' With Lives / Trust Not Me / About A Fascist.
HUNT HUNTERS, Obscene Productions (1999) (Split album with SUPPOSITORY). Without A Clue / Careless Wish / Rip The Book / Irreversible Decision / Decimation Of Rights / Slaves To The Beat / Back In Town / Sick Shows Sell / Hunt Foxhunters.
ROBOTIZED, 19 (1999) (Split album with DEPRESSION). Drug Induced Fantasies / Kids For Cash / Get A Life / No Remorse / Robotized / Thanks For Your Hostility / Criminalization Of Strange Behaviour / Is It Really Mine? / Wir Fahren Gegen Nazis.
Kicked And Whipped EP, Impaler Of Trendies Productions (2001) (Split EP with WORSHIP). Making Punk A Farce Again / Kicked And Whipped / Hip Off.
Show Your Colors Vol. 3, (2004) (Split EP with WORLD DOWNFALL). What For? / Dope, Dole, Dumb / Your Standards / Fist The Rapists / Sack The GATT / Fucking Right (Were Left) / Last In, First Out / Lowlife Scumbags / A For Arrogance / Zero Tolerance.
AGATHOCLES, N:C:U (2004) (Split album with KADAVERFICKER. Limited edition 1000 copies). Fucking Right, We Are Left / What For? / Last In, First Out / Sack The Gatt.
Your Standards EP, Agromosh (2004) (Split EP with KUOLEMA). Your Standards / Dope, Dole, Dumb / Fist The Rapists / Lowlife Scumbags.
MINCER, Displeased D-00141 (2006). Dethrone The Tyrant / Matadores Del Libertad / Maze Of Papers / Empty Frame / War Fetisjists Kill / Carved Face Fashion / Forced To Masturbate / Ergos—Thanatos / Archives And Files / Yuppie Career Freak / Diary Of White Trash / Bass The Gabbers / Kurose / Expendable Goods / Class War Necessity / Logical Exodus / Misery = Destiny / Pricks At Gigs / Goredom—Boredom / Where It Belongs / Mincer.

AGE OF AGONY

ZALAEGERSZEG, HUNGARY — *Kálmán Pápai (vocals), Lajos Nagy (guitar), Krisztián Tóth (guitar), Balázs Kovács (drums).*

AGE OF AGONY, fronted by Kálmán Pápai, is a blasphemous Zalalövö, Zalaegerszeg based Death Metal act formulated during 2002. Previous to this date the group had operated under the brand SILENT AGONY. Created in 1995, SILENT AGONY comprised Kálmán Pápai on vocals, guitarists Péter Méhes and Lajos Nagy, bass player Krisztián Tóth with Balázs Kovács. In this guise they issued demos 'Agony' in 1999 and 'Poisoned Tears' in 2001.

The group would go through a succession of early guitarists including Krisztián Varga, from ART OF BUTCHERY, MONASTERY and SEAR BLISS, Péter Méhes and Viktor Apagyi before stabilising with Lajos Nagy solely handling six-string duties as they evolved into AGE OF AGONY. A three track, self-titled demo emerged that same year, with a second set billed 'The Dark Conquers All' following in 2003. AGE OF AGONY struck a deal with Kárpátia Productions for the 2005 debut album 'War, Hate, Blasphemy'.

In 2006 the band shared a split 7" single on Terranis Productions with SLUGATHOR. This set, limited to 300 hand numbered copies, included a cover version of NUNSLAUGHTER's 'She Lives By Night'.

Age Of Agony, Age Of Agony (2002) (Demo). Age Of Innocence / XIII Century / Via Dei.

The Dark Conquers All, Age Of Agony (2003) (Demo). Intro / The Dark Conquers All / Answer / Evolution / The Last Moment (1966).

WAR, HATE, BLASPHEMY, Kárpátia Productions (2005). Grey / Age Of Innocence / External / XIII. Century / On Bloody Pathways / Via Dei / Answer / The Prime / Winter (I Die With You).

Slugathor / Age Of Agony, Terranis Productions (2007) (Split 7" vinyl single with SLUGATHOR. Limited edition 300 copies). Reign Of The Supreme (SLUGATHOR) / Tormentor (SLUGATHOR) / Question (AGE OF AGONY) / She Lives By Night (AGE OF AGONY).

AGE OF RUIN

WASHINGTON, DC, USA — *Derrick Kozerka (vocals), Daniel Fleming (guitar), Joe (bass), Colin Kerez (drums).*

AGE OF RUIN is a Washington D.C. act that aims to mould Scandinavian style Death Metal with American Hardcore. The group's inaugural 1998 formation counted vocalist Derrick Kozerka, guitarist Daniel Fleming, bass player Chris Fleming and drummer Pat Owens. In this incarnation AGE OF RUIN recorded the self financed 2000 album 'Black Sands Of The Hourglass', followed by the EP 'Autumn Lanterns' EP for the Tribunal label. For this second release the band augmented their sound with the addition of second guitarist Brian Kershey. Teaming up with label mates FACEDOWN and HYDE the band traversed the USA and Canada promoting the EP throughout 2002. AGE OF RUIN also put in valuable appearances at the Washington D.C. and Virginia Beach 'Vans Warped' festivals.

Before the close of the year AGE OF RUIN cut the Ken Olden produced EP 'The Longest Winter Woes' for Baltimore based DFF Records. Upon completion Owen exited. Colin Kerez of Maryland's HADDONFIELD took over the drum stool. Meantime Brian Kershey bowed out to prioritise his other act CARVED IN STONE.

In January of 2004 AGE OF RUIN let vocalist Derrick Kozerka go in favour of SAMADHI veteran Ben Swan.

BLACK SANDS OF THE HOURGLASS, (2000). Footsteps In The Catacombs Of Yesterday / The Crimson Fails Forever / Shadows Cast In Candlelight / Terror / Cracks In The Mirror / Black Sunrise / Angel Dusted Dreamlock / Withered Rose / Echoes In Stained Glass.

Autumn Lanterns EP, Tribunal (2002). Tainted Ghost Catharsis / No Kiss Cuts As Deep / Hung Upon The Weakest Branch / Glowing Embers / Water To Wine, Blood To Ink.

The Longest Winter's Woes EP, DFF (2003). The Harlequin's Kiss / Two Sliver Tongues / Dimmer / Passage Of The Winters Woes / The Crimson Fails Forever / Bleed For Better Days.

AGGRESSOR

TALLINN, ESTONIA — *Villem Tarvas (vocals / guitar), Kristo Kotkas (guitar), Marek Piliste (bass), Marko Atso (drums).*

Tallinn Thrash / Death outfit AGGRESSOR date to 1989, first making their mark on the Estonian Metal scene with the 1990 demo session 'Indestructible' and debuting live on 17th April that year. Band line-up comprised vocalist / guitarist Villem Tarvas, guitarist Kristo Kotkas, bassist Marek 'Cram' Piliste with Marko Atso on the drums. A 1991 demo preceded the cassette album 'Procreate The Petrifications', this recorded at the Townhall Studios in May of 1992, released on the Theka label and promoted with gigs in Moscow. 'Of Long Duration Anguish' followed in 1994 for Fugata Records. During 1999 a change in style prompted a name change to NO BIG SILENCE.

'Procreate The Petrifications' was re-issued in 2004 with bonus demo tracks. Drummer Marko Atso subsequently figured as a member of LOITS, HUMAN GROUND and SOLWAIG.

Aggressor, (1991). Meaningless Life / Don't Be So Stupid / Lifestyle / Legal Requirement.

AGGRESSOR

PROCREATE THE PETRIFACTIONS, Theka EHL 001 (1993). Legal Requirement / Wrong Faith / Meaningless Life / Fire Below The Ash / Procreate The Petrifications / Fear The Future / Never End The Odds / Lifestyle / Widow's Mourning / Don't Be So Stupid.

OF LONG DURATION ANGUISH, Fugata FUGCD 1001 (1994). Path Of The Lost God / Unholy Trinity / The Dark Tower / Sanctimonious / Fled Into Immunity / Enchantress Of Desires / Immaculate Conception / Those Who Leave In The End / Of Long Duration Anguish / Russian Vodka.

AGONIZED

COVILHÃ, PORTUGAL — *Nuno Pereira (vocals), Marco Silva (guitar), Gonçalo Paiva (bass), Paulo Grandão (drums).*

Covilhã Death Metal band. AGONIZED published the 2003 demo 'Victim Of His Own Fear'. The band comprises the DISFIGURED HUMAN MIND credited Nuno Pereira on vocals, ex-BRAIN WASH, MAJESTIK and OVERDRIVE guitarist Marco Silva, ex-DAMNATORY and MIND KILLER bassist Gonçalo Paiva and former HEL and DARK AGRESSION drummer Paulo Grandão.

The band also put in an appearance at the 2003 'Steel Warriors Rebellion VI' festival alongside ENTHRONED, INTERNAL SUFFERING, KATATONIA, FINNTROLL, HOLOCAUSTO CANIBAL, NEOPLASMAH, PITCH BLACK, CORPUS CHRISTII, IN THY FLESH, AXE MURDERERS, ATTICK DEMONS, THANATOSCHIZO, FLAGELLUM DEI and ETERNAL MOURNING,

Victim Of His Own Fear, Agonized (2003). Smashing The Pride / Terminal Stage / Agonized Feelings / Victim Of His Own Fear.

AGONY

CANADA — *Michel Brisebois (vocals), Stephane Gauvreau (guitar), Filip Ivanovic (guitar), Jimmy Dunphy (bass), Martin Auger (drums).*

A French language brutal Death Metal band that has borne many tragedies during its lifespan. The band first came together billed as OPROBRIUM during 1992. At this juncture the group incorporated vocalist Sebastien Boucher, guitarists Stephane Gauvreau and Remy Labelle, bassist Augustin Savard with BRAIN DAMAGE's Francois Sercia on the drums. Both Savard and Labelle had previously held down membership in THE MINDS MISUNDERSTOOD.

However, in that first year of operation Labelle was murdered by his younger brother. One of Labelle's friends, Richard Hudson, succeeded him on guitar. The band underwent further turmoil as Boucher was forced out due to health concerns necessitating Gauvreau adding lead vocals to his responsibilities.

In 1993 AGONY recorded the demo 'Eve Of Destruction', produced by OBLIVEON's Pierre Remillard. This tape included the track 'Homicide', relating to the death of Labelle. As Hudson decamped, in order to found ELEMENTS, Martin Heroux of HECATOMB took the lead guitar position. The band's next demo, produced by another Canadian Death Metal name Jean-Francois Dagenais of KATAKLYSM, would be entitled 'Death

By Suffocation In A Vagina'. A further session, 'Apocalyptic Dawning', was also handled by Dagenais.

Drummer Erick Beaudeath sadly committed suicide on July 7th 1997. AGONY's 1998 album, entitled 'L.I.F.E.' and once again seeing Dagenais behind the desk, witnessed the recording debut of former NEURAXIS lead vocalist Michel Brisebois and guitarist Fred. It would also mark the last appearance of bassist Elvis Fretas who left following recording.

During 1999 AGONY pulled in guitarist Filip Ivanovic of HIDDEN PRIDE and ULTIMATUM repute along with drummer Martin Auger from NEURAXIS and OBSCENE CRISIS for a further promo offering 'Awakening Of The Avenger'. Martin Maurais assumed drum responsibilities shortly after.

L.I.F.E., Warfare (1998). Self-Butchery / Perpetual Breeders / Blood Addiction . . . Feasting on Human Components / Obsédé / Kick The Bucket / L.I.F.E.

AGONY

CZECH REPUBLIC — *Mrcy (vocals), Milan (guitar), Stanley (bass), Petra (keyboards), Tom (drums).*

AGONY, forged by ex-MUTE CRY members vocalist / guitarist Mrcy and bass player Viky in 1993, debuted with the 1995 cassette 'Face Of Death'. Band line up at this juncture comprised vocalist / guitarist Mrcy, second guitarist P.A.T., bassist Viky and drummer Rob. The second session 'The Abandonment' arrived in December of 1996, the group now having evolved to see MALFORMED THOUGHT keyboard player Martin and drummer Michal alongside Mrcy and Viky. Signing to Obscene Productions AGONY cut the 1997 'Black Velvet' single and mini album '". . . From Red Heaven' in December of that same year. The membership had undergone further changes, introducing MANSLAUGHTER UNION's Richard on lead vocals and Tom on the drums.

The full length album 'Ashes To Ashes, Dust To Dust', produced by Vaclav Vlachy, saw issue in February of 1999 through Sheer Records. AGONY then underwent a further radical overhaul of personnel. Joining Mrcy and Tom would be female singer Kristin of RETURN TO INNOCENCE repute, the ASHELA duo of guitarist Milan and bassist Standa with keyboard man Elvis. This version of the band figured on the promotion recording 'In Nomine'. The 2003 album 'Call The Rain' found Petra, previously with EXTREME, on keyboards. AGONY entered Hacienda Studios in October of 2004 to record the album 'My Turn To Die' for IFA Records.

Face Of Death, (1995). Inner Insanity / Out Of Life / Dying Heart / Bad Religion / Euthanasia / Interment Alive / Léthe.

The Abandonment, (1996). Rest In(tro) Peace / F.T.F.T.D. / Believer / Purification Of Soul / Immortal / Skyline From Silence / The Abandonment / Quo Vadis (. . . In Sleep).

Black Velvet, Obscene Productions (1997). Black Velvet (Part I) / Black Velvet (Part II).

FROM RED HEAVEN, Obscene Productions (1997). The Scream Of Angels / When Moon's Dying..Your Beauty Fades / Losing Eternity / Under A Killing Dark Sun / Dirge Of Fallen Gods.

ASHES TO ASHES, DUST TO DUST, Sheer (1999). Introduction / Trilogy Of Doom: I. Chapter Of Blood / Trilogy Of Doom: II. Chapter Of Destiny / Trilogy Of Doom: III. Chapter Of Salvation / Skyline From Silence / Autos Da Fé / Black Velvet / Darkness / Sadness & Pain (The Fadeless) / In The Army Now.

In Nomine . . . , (2002) (Promotion release). In Nomine . . . .

CALL THE RAIN, I.F.A. (2003). From Dusk Till Dawn / Doom Theatre / 4U / Winter Flower / Dream Way / In Nomine . . . / Last Wish / Call The Rain / Skyline From Silence.

MY TURN TO DIE, IFA (2004). Introduction / Sometimes / Stronger Than You / Black Rose / Welcome To My Empire / Endless Remorses / Whatever Shall I Do / The Mirror Of The Night / . . . Alone / My Turn To Die.

AGORAPHOBIC NOSEBLEED

VA, USA — *Jay Randall (vocals), Scott Hull (guitar).*

Grindcore act led by ANAL CUNT guitarist Scott Hull. Both Hull and vocalist Jay Randall also busy themselves with other acts as diverse as PIG DESTROYER and JAPANESE COMEDY TORTURE HOUR. Randall also operates THREE RING INFERNO in alliance with Jacob Bannon of CONVERGE and contributed electronics to Boston Doom mongers ISIS's 1999 'Red Sea' EP. Randall was also entrenched in the HOUSE OF LOW CULTURE project in 2000. Resulting in an album 'Submarine Immersion Techniques' for the Crowd Control Activities label, HOUSE OF LOW CULTURE also involved James Plotkin and Stephen O'Malley of ATOMSMASHER and Aaron Turner of ISIS.

AGORAPHOBIC NOSEBLEED employed Richard of ENEMY SOIL and Aaron of Ulcer on vocals prior to the recruitment of Randall. Although the band employs a drum machine Jason of SUPPURATION handles bass guitar.

The band would partner in the studio with ISIS to contribute their rendition of 'Boris' to a 2005 MELVINS tribute album, 'We Reach: The Music Of The Melvins', through Fractured Transmitter Records. AGORAPHOBIC NOSEBLEED compiled the retrospective collection 'Bestial Machinery: The Collected ANB Discography Volume 1', a two disc collection of early material including demo tracks and material originally only found on 7" vinyl splits with acts such as CATTLEPRESS, LACERATION and ENEMY SOIL.

HONKY REDUCTION, Relapse (1998). Black Ink On Black Paper / Polished Turd / Filthy Murder Shack / The Withering Of Skin / Empowerment / The House Of Feasting / Die And Get The Fuck Out Of The Way / Insipid Conversations / Vexed / Circus Mutt (Three Ring Inferno) / Lives Ruined Through Sex (For Anita) / Clawhammer And An Ether Rag / NYC Always Reminds Me / Her Despair Reeks Of Alcohol / Chump Slap / Burned Away In Sleep / Grief Is Not Quantifiable / Cloved In Twain / Torn Apart By Dingos / Pagan Territories / Hat Full Of Shit (For Cletus) / McWorld / How Sean Threw His Back Out Sneezing / Bones In One Bag (Organs In Another) / Acute Awareness (For Wood) / Two Shits To The Moon.

THE POACHER'S DIARIES, Relapse RR6409 (1999).

FROZEN CORPSE STUFFED WITH DOPE, Relapse RLP6530 (2002). (Intro) Engineering Of A Pill Frenzy / Bitch's Handbag Full Of Money / Unwashed Cock / Kill Theme For American Apeshit / Built To Grind / Crap Cannon / Razor Blades Under The Dashboard / Repercussions In The Life Of An Opportunistic, Psuedo Intellectual Jackass / Doctored Results / Ceremonial Gasmask / Hang The Pope / Bovine Caligula / Machine Gun / Protection From Enemies / Dead Battery / Manual Trauma / Time Vs. Necessity / Blind Hatred Finds A Tit / Grandmother With Aids / 5 Band Genetic Equalizer 2 / Hungry Homeless Handjob / Chalking The Temporal God Module / Narcissistic Stimulant / North American Corpse Desecration / Cryogenic Husk / Shit Slit / Sword Swallower / Ceramic God Product / Ambulance Burning / 5 Band Equalizer / Drinking Games / Bullshit Gets Up And Walks Around / The Fatter You Fall Behind / Double Negative / Organ Donor / Someone's Daughter / Contaminated Drug Supply / Fuckmaker.

ALTERED STATES OF AMERICA, Relapse RR 6533 (2003) (Box set). Wonder Drug Wonderland / Spreading The Dis-ease / Ark Of Ecoterrorism / Living Lolita Blow Job / Thawing Out / The Need For Better Body Armor / Freeze-Dried Cemetery / Children Blown To Bits By The Busload / Scoring In Heaven / Fuck Your Soccer Jesus / Guided Tour / Honky Dong / Famous Last Words / Osaka Milk Bar / Drive By Blowjob On A Bicycle / Ten Pounds Of Remains / Utter Mental Retardation And Reversal Of Man / Neotropolis Euphoria / Snitch Olympics / Crawling Out Of The Cradle Into The Casket / Removing Locator Tooth / Aum Shinrikyo / The Protocols Of The Elders Of Zion / The Tokyo Subway Gassing / The Star Of David / Shintaro Ishihara And The Rape Of Nanking In World War 2 / Mahikari / Micro-Tidal Wave / Crop Dusting / LSD As Chemical Weapon / Illegal Manufacture / Drugging The Control Group / Alice In La La Land / Apocalypse As Mescaline Experience / The Artificial Religious Experience / Pussy Hair Prayer Rug / Distortion In Eden / Serpent Of The Gay Pride Rainbow / Snaking Adam's Black Apple / Like A Cretin On Christmas Eve / Boston Hardcore Caligula / Fantasizing Hydrahead / Lamb Of The Rotisserie Go / Holiday Bowl Full Of Asshole / Enter The House Of Feasting / Passing Blunts And Cunts At Relapse / When Taking A Shit Feels Sexy / Poland Springfield Acidbag / Rectal Thermometer / Lemonade And A Snickers Bar / Necro-Cannabalistic Tendencies In Young Children / Bombs With Butterfly Wings / Watching A Clown Point A Gun At A Small Dog /

Mosquito Holding Human Cattleprod / For Just Ten Cents A Day / Mental Changes: Altered Consciousness / Radical Modernism / Human Enhancement / Juxtaposed Impacts / Unprecedented Experiment / Transparent Enclosure / Bong Hit Wonder / Opening To Personals Ad By Richard Johnson / Relapse Refusing U.N. Weapons Inspectors / Neural Linguistic Programming / The Fag vs. The Indian / Black Metal Transvestite / Debbie Does Dishes / Marine Pornography / Keeping A Clean Kennel / Baby Mill Part 1 / Firearms For All Faiths / Domestic Solution / Definition Of Death / Discolored / Scott Hulk On Intramuscular Steroids / 4 Leaches / Group Taking Acid As Considered Conspiracy Against The Government / Small Room And A Six-Pack / Deviant Arousal / Unbound By Civilized Properties / They All Burned! / Shotgun Funeral / Homophobic Assbleed / Exacting Revenge On Pets / Baby Mill Part 2 / Narcoterrorist Megalomaniac / Releasing A Dove From A Ghetto Rooftop / Bipartisan Buttfuck / Bent Over The Cross / A Chance At Reprisal / Altered Ego / Pin The Tail On The Donkey / Latter Day Mormon Ritual / 5 Band Genetic Equalizer Part 3 / Absurd Boast / Burning Social Interest / Whore Torn Vet / Obi Wan Kaczynski / Placing A Personal Memo On The Boss's Desk.
BESTIAL MACHINERY, Relapse (2005). 5% Control / Scrutinized / Hollowpoint / Conform To Death / Life Is Pain / Profit Is The Motive / Snake Charmer / Chasing A Dream / Allegiance / Information / Loss For Words / Your Insecurity / Rich Get Richer / Ode To A Junkie / Crawl Of The Mind / What I Did On My Summer Vacation / One More Drink / Forgotten In Space / Letter Bomb / El Topo / Vapor Lock / Victims As Dogs / Dead Above The Neck / The Executioner VS. The Sodomite / From Above / Green Inferno / 100 Dead Rabbits / Circle Of Shit / Amputee / Eight Girls Instead Of Nine / Sex On The Flag / The Newlyweds Are Raped / Mule / 10.000 Bullets / Centipede / Lithium Daydream / Doubled Over / Suicide Note #1 / From Filth To Defilement / Who Can Wreck The Infinite / Morphine Constipation / Unholy BMX Fights The Nod (Morphine Constipation Remix) / Exceptional Waste / Fat Fucking Chance / Holy Mountain / Sweetback / Arrival Of Bees / Where You Like / Powertrip / Worthless / Pain In Living / Lose Your Will / Unbelievable Stress / Another Useless Asshole / My Life Is A Money Pit / Debilitating Headache / Powerfail / Paradigm / The Power Of Dolemite / Cut To Happy Hour / Military Scientist / Kool-Aid Feedbag / The Big Fuck You / Computer Lethargy / Non-Action / Anti-Septic / Hessian Bodyfarm / Solvent / Glade, A Straw, And A SandwichBag / Headglass / DC5 / Hungry Child / I'd Rather Be Sleeping / I Don't Need Society / Black Ass, White Dick / Black Market Blastbeats / Death Takes A Shit 2 / Ketamine And Kryptonite / Pud Rock / Hammer Fight / Gravework / Can You Dig? / Retardo Montalbon / Death Takes A Shit / Panic Gasp / Hooker Bomb / Pigs Smell Fear / Fuck Your Soccer Mom / Baby Cannon / You Have No Rights / Just A Band / Obscene / Gorrendously Mutilated / Habitrail For Humanity / Inappropriate Response / Nickel Plated Knuckle Fuck / Recovering Contraband From A Constricted Airway / Nice Ass / Pinkworld / Hysterical Misery / My Own Rules / Intro / Mobilize / Measure The Bite Marks / 7.5% / The Alcoholic Pain / Eyes Like Two Pissholes In The Snow / Pediatric Burn Unit / I Smell Really Bad / Ten Fucking Steps / The Grief That Summer Brings / Driven To Succeed / So Many Car Phones, So Few Bullets / McCarthy Witch Hunt / The River / Harvey / Hate Disguised As Legislation / Fucking Move Prick / The Pros And Cons Of The CIA / Scare Tactics / If You Thought Elvis / Disease Bomb / Gratuitous Wound Photos / Broken Political Wing / Full Metal Swimsuit / Swimming In The LaBrea Tar Pits / Tough Guy Bullshit / I Feel Dumb / Ritalin Attack / Absolutely No Samples / Silence / Driven To Succeed 2 / Bloated And Complacent / Privy To War / Typical Tough Guy Bullshit / Man's Hate / I Gave You My Life / Control / Ladies And Gentlemen.
PCP TORPEDO, (2006).

AGREGATOR

TATABÁNYA, HUNGARY — *Tamás Mikus (vocals / guitar), Tibor Preil (guitar), Dávid Szabó (guitar), Roland Liviczki (bass), Peter Boros (drums).*

Tatabánya Death Metal combo AGREGATOR, created in 1997, debuted with a 2000 Doom Death styled demo billed 'Puszta Lét'. AGREGATOR issued the 2001 cassette 'Túlontúl', this second effort displaying self-professed Scandinavian leanings. Guitars for these sessions were handled by Lajos Bencze, subsequently replaced by László Seller of SUNDONE, whilst vocals were delegated to guitarist Tamás Mikus. Tibor Preil then usurped Seller.

Touring for AGREGATOR included appearances at festival events in Hungary such as 'Gothica', 'Káosz', 'Zed!' and the 'Sziget' event, sharing stages with international bands HOLY MOSES, MYSTIC CIRCLE, DEICIDE and DESASTER. Dávid Szabó was added on guitar as Miklós Tóth departed. In July 2004 the band played the 'Rockmaraton' festival in Rumania. After recording sessions for the debut album 'A Semmi Ágán' for the Peron Music Foundation label, that autumn the group toured Hungary packaged with TESSTIMONY and CASKETGARDEN.

AGREGATOR released the 'Szürkület' album in 2006.

Pusztalét, Agregator (2000) (Demo). Sötét éden / Puszta lét / Hattyútánc / Bármi, ami árt / Vándor a porban / Demise / Painting The Chaos / Without Colours / The Apostate.

Túlontúl, Agregator (2001). Halotti beszéd / Túlontúl / Por és Hamu / Remény / Az életút / EdenEast / OnePowered / Stampede / High Water Mark.

SZÜRKÜLET, Agregator (2006). Horizont / Soha már / Zuhanás / Les Gueules Cassées / Ha lesz hajnal / . . . de a bűn még ég / Szürkület / A rengeteg / Krómszín ég alatt.

AGRESSOR

ANTIBES, FRANCE — *Alex Colin-Tocquaine (vocals / guitar), Adramelech (guitar), Joel Guigou (bass), Gorgor (drums).*

Antibes Black-Thrash Metal trio that recorded their first demo in November 1986, AGRESSOR released a couple more demos and played dates with APOCALYPSE and LIVING DEATH. The band signed to Swedish label Black Mark Production for the 1987 album, subtly titled 'Satan's Sodomy', graced with an album cover showing the immediate after effects of buggery with the devil!

The line-up at this juncture was as a trio of vocalist / guitarist Alex Colin-Tocquaine, bassist J.M. Libeer and drummer Jean Luc Falsini. This incarnation recorded the first two demos 'Merciless Onslaught' and 1987's 'Satan's Sodomy'. Things swiftly changed for the group when AGRESSOR added new drummer Thierry and ex-HELLRAISER bassist Laurent in 1988. The group then signed to Noise, recording 'Neverending Destiny', after which both new men split leaving Alex Colin-Tocquaine to soldier on alone. Thierry joined LOUDBLAST.

Undaunted, Alex put together a brand new line-up of his band, thus the 1992 version of AGRESSOR, which recorded the 'Towards Beyond' album, consisted of Colin-Tocquaine, ex-OUTBURST guitarist Patrick Gibelin, ex-OUTBURST bassist Joel Guigon and ex-DEATH POWER drummer Stéphane Guegan.

Gibelin had quit by the time AGRESSOR returned to the studio to cut the ensuing 'Symposium Of Rebirth' album, his place being taken by new guitarist Manu Ragot. The TERRORISER cover track 'After World Obliteration', incidentally, features a guest vocal performance from NAPALM DEATH's Barney Greenaway. AGRESSOR toured as guests to CRADLE OF FILTH on their British tour of June 1996.

The band returned to the studio for the 'Medieval Rites' album. Employing a vast array of traditional instrumentation the multi-faceted release would see both Krell and Christina from Norwegians BLOODTHORN guesting. Also donating their services would be former MERCYFUL FATE drummer Morten Neilsen, ROTTEN SOUND and ENOCHIAN CRESCENT drummer Kai Hahto and the journeyman Death Metal guitarist JAMES MURPHY.

November of 1999 found AGRESSOR on the road in Europe on a package billing in collusion with BLOODTHORN and Finns AND OCEANS. The line up for these shows would see Colin-Tocquaine and Guigo joined by WITCHES guitarist Bernard Queral and Kai Hahto on drums.

Colin-Tocquaine would also session for touring purposes with American occult ancestral Metal act ABSU and renew the relationship with BLOODTHORN by sessioning on their 2000 album 'Under The Reign Of Terror'. As if this activity was not enough, the guitarist would also announce that he had joined another veteran French Metal combo LOUDBLAST. Meantime, Guigou had re-activated his former outfit OUTBURST.

The January 2001 incarnation of AGRESSOR cited a roster of Colin-Tocquaine, guitarist Adramelech, bassist Joel Guigou and drummer Gorgor. Both Adramelech and Gorgor were previously with Black Metal band BELEF. Gorgor also drummed for Grindcore band IMPERIAL SODOMY. Season Of Mist issued an album 'The Spirit Of Evil' during March 2002 comprising rarities plus three live tracks.

Season Of Mist issued the 'Deaththreat' album in November 2006.

SATAN'S SODOMY, Black Mark Production BMCD 36 (1987). Satan's Sodomy / Brainstorm / Blood Feast / Uncontrolled Desire / Black Church / It's Pandemonium.
LICENSED TO THRASH, New Wave 024 (1987). Satan's Sodomy / Brainstorm / Bloodfeast / Uncontrolled Desire / Black Church / It's Pandemonium.
NEVERENDING DESTINY, Black Mark N 0154-2 (1990). Paralytic Disease / The Unknown Spell / Element Decay / Voices From Below / Blood Feast / Neverending Destiny / Prince Of Fire / Dark Power / The Arrival / Brainstorm / Bloody Corps.
TOWARDS BEYOND, Black Mark BMCD 23 (1992). Intro / Primeval Transubtantion / The Fortress / Positionic Showering / Antediluvian / Epileptic Alra / Hyaldid / The Crypt / Future Past- Eldest Things / Turkish March.
SYMPOSIUM OF REBIRTH, Black Mark Production BMCD 55 (1994). Barabas / Rebirth / Negative Zone / Apocalyptic Prophecies / Erga Meam Salutem / Overloaded / Theology / Civilisation / Wheel Of Pain / Abhuman Dreadnought / Torture / Dor Fin-I-Guinar / After World Obliteration.
MEDIEVAL RITES, Season Of Mist (1999). Medieval Rites / Bloodshed / The Woodguy vs. The Black Beast / The Sorcerer / Spirit Of Evil / Wandering Soul / Tye-Melane Melda / God From The Sky / Welcome Home / Ondolinde / Burial Desecration / Tribal Dance / At Night.
THE SPIRIT OF EVIL, Season Of Mist (2002) (Limited edition. 1000 copies). The Spirit Of Evil (Extended version) / God From The Sky / The Sorceror / Wandering Soul / Brainstorm (Live) / Bloodshed (Live) / God From The Sky (Live).
DEATHTHREAT, Season Of Mist (2006).

AGRETATOR

HELSINGBORG, SWEDEN — *Pierre Richter (vocals / guitar), Christofer Malmström (guitar), Jörgen Löfberg (bass), Peter Wildoer (drums).*

Helsingborg's AGRETATOR was assembled under the title DEMISE in 1990, initiated by the erstwhile GOD B.C. pairing of guitarist Pierre Richter and bass player Jesper Granath. Pulling in drummer Peter Wildoer, the group cut a demo 'Prophecy' in 1991. Both later addition to the ranks, guitarist Christofer Malmström, and Wildoer had also been involved with eighties Power Metal band ZANINEZ. A second session, entitled 'Visions' in 1992, then secured a deal with Crypta Records for the 'Delusions' album. However, at this juncture the group discovered the existence of the US based DEMISE and duly switched title to AGRETATOR, being a compromise on two favoured name suggestions 'Aggressor' and 'Agitator'.

AGRETATOR subsequently issued a self-financed EP 'Distorted Logic', recorded at Studiofabriken in Malmö, in 1996 before folding in 1998. The core of AGRETATOR, guitarist Christofer Malmström, bassist Jörgen Löfberg and Peter Wildoer all went on to DARKANE. Wildoer also figured in TIME REQUIEM, ARCH ENEMY, on their 1998 'Stigmata' album, and ARMAGEDDON.

An early singer, Tony Richter, joined GARDENS OF OBSCURITY and THE DARKSEND. A proliferation of other ventures included, besides being owner of 'Nekrologium' fanzine, a track record with a whole slew of extreme Metal bands such as SLIMESUCKERS, CORRUPTION, DEMISE, SLAVESTATE, ASMODEUS, SPIRITUAL TORTURE, SMÄRTA, LEGION OF DEATH and, in 1998, NOCTURNITY.

DELUSIONS, Crypta 8211-2 (1994). Prophecy / Critical Dimensions / Bustering Madness / An Infirm Soul / Pointless Objection / Merciless Living / Human Decay / Internal Severity / Pictures.
Distorted Logic, Agretator (1996). Chains Of Retribution / Distorted Logic / Water / Virtual Tragedy / Non-Human Level.
Infected, Agretator (1997) (Unreleased demo). Impure Inside / Inner Acts / Soul Divine.

AKMA

HAUKIPUDAS, FINLAND — *Lasse (vocals), Ville (lead guitar), Antti (rhythm guitar), Juha-Antti Karppinen (bass), Joni (keyboards), Henri (drums).*

Haukipudas based Death Metal act AKMNA was founded "during school lunch breaks" in 2001 by lead guitarist Ville and Henkka, soon drawing in rhythm guitarist Antti and singer Lassi. Completing the formation would be bassist Jaakko, replaced in 2002 by Otto. AKMA's inaugural offering would be the demo 'Kill Tempo Noise Machine', recorded at Paja Studios and delivered in December 2003.

Following an initial round of gigs, including the 'Metalliaurinko' festival, Juha-Antti Karppinen stepped into the bass position. A 2004 session, 'Artificial Artistic Shit', was recorded at Q Studios in Oulu but never released publicly. 'Prologue To Assassination' arrived in February 2005.

Kill Tempo Noise Machine, Akma (2003) (Demo). Voice / K-Illuminate / Anywhere.
Artificial Artistic Shit, Akma (2004) (Unreleased demo). Suffocated / For The Better World / Innocent / Running With Scissors / K-Illuminate (Unleash Hell version).
Prologue To Assassination, Akma (2005) (Demo). Intro / Dead Flowers / Hollow Me / Shrapnels Of Glass / Mortified / For The Better World / Nin9.

ALCHEMIST

CANBERRA, ACT, AUSTRALIA — *Adam Agius (vocals / guitar), Roy Torkington (guitar), John Lindsey Bray (bass), Rodney Holder (drums).*

Although self styled Progressive Death Metal band ALCHEMIST, hailing from the capital city of Canberra, had been created in 1987, putting out the demo cassette 'Eternal Wedlock' that year, they debuted commercially with the track 'Escapism' included on the 1993 Roadrunner 'Redrum' compilation album. European label Lethal Records issued their 'Jar Of Kingdom' album later the same year.

Guitarist Andrew lost his place to Roy Torkington for the second album 'Lunasphere' issued in 1995. ALCHEMIST have opened for numerous European Metal bands in Australia including KREATOR, NAPALM DEATH, CATHEDRAL and PARADISE LOST.

ALCHEMIST recorded a version of 'Eve Of The War' from Jeff Wayne's 'War Of The World's in 1998. The band signed to the American Relapse label for October 2001's 'Organism' opus. A domestic release surfaced on Chatterbox Records whilst the Dutch Displeased imprint took the record on for European markets. Live work throughout Australia in March and April of 2000 saw the band uniting with CRYOGENIC and PSI CORE for the 'World War III' tour.

Promoting their fifth album, 2003's 'Austral Alien', ALCHEMIST united with SUPERHEIST for a string of July Australian gigs. 'Austral Alien' fared well for the band internationally, critics and fans alike impressed with ALCHEMIST's grasp of almost Psychedelic brand of Metal. International touring in 2004 found ALCHEMIST packaged with CULT OF LUNA and TEXTURES for October gigs in the UK. The band also put in a showing at the Dutch 'Progpower' festival in Baarlo.

Eternal Wedlock, (1987). I Am Free / Kill For It / Just Let Me Die / Eternal Wedlock.
Demo '91, (1991). Enhancing Enigma / Escapism / Imagination Flower / Womb Syndrome.
JAR OF KINGDOM, Lethal (1993). Abstraction / Shell / Purple / Jar Of Kingdom / Wandering And Wondering / Found / Enhancing Enigma / Whale / Brumal: A View From Pluto / Worlds Within Worlds.

LUNASPHERE, Thrust-Shock (1995). Soul Return / Lunation / Unfocused / Luminous / Clot / Yoni Kunda / My Animate Truth / Garden Of Eroticism / Closed Chapter.
SPIRITECH, Trust-Shock THRUST 022 (1997). Chinese Whispers / Road To Ubar / Staying Conscious / Beyond Genesis / Spiritechnology / Inertia / Hermaphroditis / Dancing To Life / Figments.
Eve Of The War, Shock (1998). Eve Of The War / Yoni Kunda (Live) / Chinese Whispers (Live) / Yoni Kunda (Remix) / Brumal: A View From Pluto / Worlds Within Worlds.
ORGANISM, Relapse RLP6499 (2001). Austral Spectrum / The Bio Approach / Rampant Micro Life / Warring Tribes, Eventual Demise / Single Sided 6. Surreality / New Beginning / Tide In, Mind Out / Eclectic / Escape: From The Black Hole.
AUSTRAL ALIEN, Chatterbox CB030 (2003). First Contact / Great Southern Wasteland / Solarburn / Alpha Cappella Nova Vega / Older Than The Ancients / Back Ward Journey / Nature On A Leash / Grief Barrier / Epsilon / Speed Of Life / Letter To The Future.
EMBRYONICS, (2006). Chinese Whispers / Abstraction / Unfocused / Enhancing Enigma / Dancing To Life / Brumal / Lunation / Staying Conscious / Shell / Garden Of Eroticism / Jar Of Kingdom / Paisley Bieurr / Yoni Kunda (Live to air) / Closed Chapter (Live to air) / Eve Of The War / Beyond Genesis / Yoni Kunda / Purple / Imagination Flower / Spirittechnology / Soul Return / Road To Ubar / Found / Clot / Worlds Within Worlds / My Animated Truth / Closed Chapter / Chinese Whispers.

ALFA ERIDANO AKHERNAR

CATEMACO, MEXICO — *Horda (vocals), Adhara (guitar / bass), Xolotl (guitar), Zorvan (keyboards), Encke (drums).*

The brutal Death / Black Metal band ALFA ERIDANO AKHERNAR was founded in Catemaco during 1999 following the disintegration of SACRONOCTURNE. The group's opening line up combined vocalists Insano and Horda, guitarists Adhara and Gerardo with keyboard player Zorvan and Encke on the drums. With debut demo sessions concluded Gerardo broke ranks. Undaunted, ALFA ERIDANO AKHERNAR set about touring Mexico as a quintet, finally bringing in a substitute guitarist Xolotl, previously with MORTUM, in September of 2001.

Insano was next to leave, opting out after recording of a 2002 demo.

The album 'The Magnificent Rebirth Of A Mighty Old Empire' was issued through Aztec War Metal Productions in August 2004. The ALFA ERIDANO AKHERNAR line-up at this juncture comprised vocalist Golgota, guitarist / bassist Adhara, keyboard player Zorvan and drummer Encke.

Alfa Eridano Akhernar, (2000). Castigo Divino / Perfume De Los Muertos / Predicadores Del Mal / Orgullo Y Honor Ancestral / Sueños Eróticos / Venganza A Los Antiguos Dioses / Masacrando A Jesucristo.
Demo 2002, Alfa Eridano Akhernar (2002). Putrefacción Total / Sacrificios Maya / Batallas Mexicas / Maldad Eterna.
THE MAGNIFICENT REBIRTH OF A MIGHTY OLD EMPIRE, Aztec War Metal Productions (2004). Argumentum Ad Baculum / Mexica's Battles / Inhuman Ritual Of Submission And Blood / ... To Aztec Glory / Alienate Armies To Serve Our Greed / Hail King Victorious / The Magnificent Rebirth Of A Mighty Old Empire.

ALICE IN DARKLAND

ITALY — *Alberto (vocals), Alice Chiarelli (vocals / keyboards), Andy (guitar), Andrew Frederich (guitar), Dhilorz (bass), Rullo (drums).*

ALICE IN DARKLAND is a Doom Metal band conceived by the LACUNA COIL keyboard player Alice Chiarelli and debuting in 1999 with the 'Bewitching The Mind' promotion recording. The 2000 demo 'Through Violet Perversion' would see VISION DIVINE and LABYRINTH man Mat Stancioiu on the drums. Lino Sistu, of ABNEGATE, NODE and SUNGIFT, then took the drum stool but would later leave for Power Metal act POWER SYMPHONY. Guitarist Andy would opt out to found STYGIAN in February of 2000, another ALICE IN DARKLAND guitarist Andrea Frederich would also join STYGIAN in October of the following year.

ALICE IN DARKLAND bowed in officially in March of 2002, issuing 'The Evil's Entrails' album Nocturnal Music. The band would employ a succession of drummers during this period including ex-OPHIDIAN man Gianluca, erstwhile NODE member Loris Pacaccio and ANCIENT's Grom (a.k.a. Diego Meraviglia). The band settled on a stable line up comprising new members second guitarist Andrew Frederich, ANCIENT and INFLICTION bass player Dhilorz from Ancient and drummer Alessandro 'Rullo' Durini of STYGIAN and EMPTYMIST. Durini joined SILENCE in 2004.

THE EVIL'S ENTRAILS, Nocturnal Music (2002).

ALIENGATES

SWITZERLAND — *David Oberthaler (vocals), Manfred Aigner (guitar), Loki (guitar), Reto Hardmeier (bass), Mischa Demarmels (drums).*

ALIENGATES is a Ziglschlacht based melodic Death Metal band. The 2001 'Dark Days Quantum' EP, recorded at Die Klangfabrik, would be followed by a demo session 'Funeral Feast' during 2003. Between these recordings the band had inducted bassist Roman Friedrich in the Spring of 2002 but guitarist Pascal Beer left that September, being superseded by Philipp Schalcher.

April of 2004 witnessed a major overhaul for the band with a split that left only vocalist David Oberthaler and drummer Mischa Demarmels remaining. New faces would be guitarist Manfred Aigner and bassist Reto Hardmeier. FLESHCRAWL's Oliver Grbavac would be also enlisted on guitar but he decamped in October, being substituted by Loki.

Dark Days Quantum, (2001). Manual For A Dark Age / Fever The Mind / Saintfilth / Dark Days Quantum / Heartless / Blind Leads Blind.

ALISTER

JAGODINA, SERBIA — *Igor Miladinovic Raven (vocals), Marko Ognjanovic Boldie (guitar), Marko Vuckovic Wolfy (guitar), Ivan Petrovic (bass), Milos Simic (keyboards), Marko Stosic Goofie (drums).*

Jagodina Death-Thrashers forged in 1998 under the previous title of POLTERGEIST. Their first demo, 'The Snakepit', was recorded in Cesnjak Studios, Kragujevac during September of 1999. Cutting four more tracks that Winter at ZIP Studios in Jagodina, including the song 'Alone' featuring Huanita Matic Hana as guest female vocalist, the group collated these recordings as the 'Powerbeat' demo release.

ALISTER's debut album 'Obscurity', laid down at Paradox Studios in Smederevo, would include guest appearances from the PSYCHOPARADOX and ALOGIA triumvirate of Miroslav Brankovic, Branislav Dabic and Ana Useinovic. Live work across Serbia was prolific, including a support slot to PAUL DIANNO, before the band entered the same studios as previous to cut second record 'Memories And Dreams' for One Records during August of 2002. ALOGIA's Srdjan Brankovic would guest.

MEMORIES AND DREAMS, One Records (2002). Flames / See You On The Other Side / Awake / Fiction / Living Hell / The Abyss / In My Memories / Dreams / Raven's Chant / Dark Depth / Life Is Just A Dream ... / If / Light The Darkness / Cicatrice.

ALL SHALL PERISH

OAKLAND, CA, USA — *Craig Betit (vocals), Beniko Orum (guitar), Mike Tiner (bass), Matt Kuykendall (drums).*

Oakland, California Metal band manifested during 2002 and featuring the ANTAGONY credited guitar duo of Caysen Russo and Beniko Orum. The former also holds associations with HACKSAW TO THE THROAT. Although ALL SHALL PERISH have been manoeuvred into the Metalcore genre their music displays strong Gothenburg style Death Metal tendencies.

ALL SHALL PERISH

An opening demo scored the interest of Japanese label Amputated Vein Records, who financed the sessions for debut album 'Hate.Malice.Revenge' for August 2003 issue. The band set about tackling an exhaustive touring schedule, opening for such acts as BLEEDING THROUGH, DYING FETUS, BRUJERIA, AS I LAY DYING, SIX FEET UNDER, HATE ETERNAL, DIECAST, BETWEEN THE BURIED AND ME, MORTICIAN and UNDYING. 2004 was closed out with a nationwide tour partnered with VEHEMENCE and CREMATORIUM. That December the group signed to Nuclear Blast America for a re-release of 'Hate.Malice.Revenge' in early 2005.

ALL SHALL PERISH forged a touring alliance with CREMATORIUM, THE RED DEATH and VEHEMENCE for US dates in May 2005. Back on the road in April, the band, having parted ways with guitarist Caysen Russo "due to differences", formed up a billing combining AGNOSTIC FRONT, LOVE IS RED and MARTYR A.D. The band formed up with a Summer package touring bill comprising HATE ETERNAL, INCANTATION, INTO ETERNITY and KRISIUN for US gigs in June. However, in early July the band was forced to drop off these dates, citing a $3,000 repair bill for their van as making the tour financially unviable. That November ALL SHALL PERISH announced the induction of new frontman, ex-GUNMETAL GREY singer Eddie Hermida. First product released by the revised formation would be the demo track 'Eradication'.

The band cut a new album, 'The Price Of Existence', in early 2006 for an August release. Tour dates across North America to coincide would be backed by SUICIDE SILENCE, LIGHT THIS CITY, TOO PURE TO DIE and NIGHTS LIKE THESE. October and November US concerts were backed by ARSIS and THE FACELESS. A short mid-December stint put the band alongside THROWDOWN, THE WARRIORS and XDEATHSTARX.

2007 was opened by a round of touring pitched alongside TERROR, THE WARRIORS, WAR OF AGES and STICK TO YOUR GUNS. The group then announced "The Trendkiller" US tour commencing February 1st 2007 as an alliance with SWORN ENEMY, KATAKLYSM, TOO PURE TO DIE and BLOOD RUNS BLACK. They would then unite with CALIBAN, BLEEDING THROUGH and I KILLED THE PROM QUEEN for the European 'Darkness Over Europe' tour commencing mid-February and running through until March 25th.

All Shall Perish, (2003). Herding The Brainwashed / The Spreading Disease / For Far Too Long.

HATE.MALICE.REVENGE, Nuclear Blast NB 1401-2 (2005). Deconstruction / Laid To Rest / Our Own Grave / The Spreading Disease / Sever The Memory / For Far Too Long … / Never Ending War / Herding The Brainwashed.

THE PRICE OF EXISTENCE, Nuclear Blast NB 1670-2 (2006). Eradication / Wage Slaves / Day Of Justice / There Is No Business To Be Done On A Dead Planet / Better Living Through Catastrophe / Prisoner Of War / Interlude / We Hold These Truths / The True Beast / Promises / The Last Relapse.

ALLFATHER

BC, CANADA — *Justin Hagberg (guitar), Jasper van der Veen (guitar), Adam Angus (bass), Paul Jacobsen (drums).*

ALLFATHER was initially assembled as a trio of vocalist Paul Jacobsen, guitarist Justin Hagberg and drummer Craig Stewart during 1996. As such the band created the opening demo 'Render To The Unlight' that same year'. Subsequently the band would morph with Jacobsen taking over the drumming role and Cam Pipes being inducted to handle bass. In this formation ALLFATHER recorded the 1998 six track mini album 'Wrath Of The Bloodthirsty'. For live work the band introduced lead vocalist Chad Klassen.

A further recording, a five track promotion issue, was distributed in 1999 after which Adam Angus took command of the bass role. ALLFATHER's next move was to participate in a four way split album release. Released by Realms of Darkness Productions this unique outing billed as 'Lead Us To War And Final Glory' allied ALLFATHER with Hungarian act NEBRON and American bands GNOSTIC and HORDES OF THE LUNAR ECLIPSE.

In September of 2004 Justin Hagberg joined 3 INCHES OF BLOOD. A full length album, 'Weapon Of Ascension', would be readied for January 2005 issue as the band acquired Jasper van der Veen on guitar, a former member of Dutch act FLUISTERWOUD. Chad Klassen resigned from the band following this release.

Wrath Of The Bloodthirsty, (1998). Thy Quest Of Abyssal Plight / Flesh Of The Ancient Bode / Prince Of Many Faces / Wrath Of The Bloodthirsty / Ageless Eternity / Choose Who My Destiny.

Promo 2000, (2000). Bringer Of The Tides Of Disorder / Unbonding Of Thine Forgotten Hymn / And With God Bereft / Dog Lords Resurgence / Hoch Und Steil Leben.

LEAD US TO INTO FINAL GLORY AND WAR, Realms Of Darkness Productions DHR012 (2002) (Split album with GNOSTIC, HORDES OF THE LUNAR ECLIPSE and NEBRON). Warlust / With Glory Unbound / Artifice / Tyranny, Revenge! / Ancestral Resurrection.

Allfather, Invictus Productions (2003). Bringer Of The Tides Of Disorder / Unbonding Of Thine Forgotten Hymn / And With God Bereft / Dog Lords Resurgence / Hoch Und Steil Leben / Sealed In Blood (Live).

WEAPON OF ASCENSION, Invictus Productions IP005 (2005). Evolution To Supremacy / Forever Unconquerable / Flight Into Exile / Hail! Tyrants Of War / Storm Assault / Through Ages Wrought / Invictus / Of Man And Valour / Blood And Soil / In The Face Of Nobility / Progeny Of Vengeance / Path Of Glory.

ALMA MATER

LUARCA, SPAIN — *Cesar Alvarez (vocals), Dan García (guitar), Ricardo Alvar Rozas (guitar), Manuel García (bass), Sonia Alvarez (keyboards), Mario García (drums).*

Luarca Gothic tinged Death Metal band ALMA MATER's origins lay in the 1999 musical partnership of guitarist Miguel Pérez and bassist Manuel García. Subsequent recruits were to be singer Cesar Alvarez, second guitarist Dan García and Mario García on the drums. In this formation, once they had acquired a drum kit (!), the band began rehearsals in August of that year. Early attempts to introduce another guitarist and keyboard player failed to gel but the group did take onboard the title ALMA MATER, in homage to the MOONSPELL song of the same name.

Incorporating Sonia Alvarez on keyboards ALMA MATER, sharing the stage with local acts REPLICA, SHOCK!! and ROADHAUSE, undertook their inaugural gig on 19th August 2000. Throughout June and October 2002 the band laid down tracks for the 'Rising Tide' EP. Following its release in July of 2003 ALMA MATER welcomed guitarist Ricardo Alvar Rozas into the fold.

Rising Tide EP, Independent (2003). Wicked Illness / Funeral Pyre / The Eyes Of Remorse / Born Again / My Buried Love / Searching The Bright.

ALTAR

HARDENBERG, HOLLAND — *Edwin Kelder (vocals), Bert Huisjes (guitar), Marcel Van Haaff (guitar), Nils Vos (bass), Marco Arends (drums).*

Blasphemous Death Metal band ALTAR, based out of Hardenberg, released a 1992 demo titled 'And God Created Satan To Blame For His Mistakes'. Signing to Displeased Records the band opened with 1994's 'Youth Against Christ', recorded at Franky's Recording Kitchen with producers Ronny van der Wey and Berthus Westerhuis. At this juncture ALTAR comprised vocalist Edwin Kelder, guitarists Bert Huisjes and Marcel Van Haaff, bass guitarist Nils Vos and Marco Arends on the drums.

The second album, 1996's 'Ego Art' once again laid down at Franky's Recording Kitchen, features ex-MANDATOR guitarist Marcel Verdermen, replacing Marcel van Haaf, and new drummer Marco De Groot, previously of BLIND JUSTICE. ALTAR, evolving once again with the incorporation of guitarist Richard Ludwig and drummer Sjoerd Visch, would cover the ACCEPT classic 'Fast As A Shark' for their 1998, Attie Bauw produced 'Provoke' outing. Meantime, the ousted ALTAR drummers found employ, Marco Arends subsequently worked with GOD DETHRONED whilst Marco De Groot featured in Gouda Deathsters ROUWEN.

ALTAR switched labels to US concern Pavement Music for the 1999 set 'In The Name Of The Father'. Limited editions of this outing included a rendition of IRON MAIDEN's 'The Trooper' and bonus original 'I Am Your Provider'.

The 2000 release 'Until Heaven Forbids' was a stop gap release intended to plug the gap until the arrival of the 'Red Harvest' album for Crash Music. 'Until Heaven Forbids' would not only witness a cover version of IRON MAIDEN's 'The Trooper' but spoof its famous cover art too. One new track, 'I Am The Provider', bolstered by a collection of demos, live cuts and a video clip for 'God Damn You'. A further album, 'Red Harvest', saw issue in April 2001 on Spitzenburg Records but ALTAR folded that same Autumn.

Drummer Sjoerd Visch left the group in September 2001 to be replaced by INRI's William Vliereman. Visch founded a high profile Death Metal formation billed as MONOLITH which erstwhile ETERNAL CONSPIRACY members guitarist Michiel Dekker (also citing credits with DEAD HEAD) and vocalist / bassist Martijn Moes, former EXPOSING INNARDS guitarist Corvin Keurhorst and singer Robin Kok of EXPOSING INNARDS and SLAYNE. Visch is also involved with Gothic Metal band TO ELYSIUM.

A reformed ALTAR would be assembled by guitarists Marcel Verdurmen and Richard Ludwig, enrolling bassist Reinier de Vries and former DEVIOUS singer Arnold Oudemiddendorp. Ex-drummer Sjoerd Visch joined BEYOND BELIEF in 2005.

And God Created Satan To Blame For His Mistakes, (1992). Throne Of Fire / Forced Imprudence / Psycho Damn / Cross The Bridge Of False Prophecies / Dismantling The God.
YOUTH AGAINST CHRIST, Massacre MASS CD 056 (1994). Throne Of Fire / Jesus Is Dead! / Divorced From God / Hypochristianity / Forced Imprudence / Psycho Damn / Cross The Bridge Of False Prophecies / Cauterise The Church Council.
EGO ART, Displeased D00046 (1996). Eidelon / I Take / Ego Art / C.C.C. / Truly Untrue / Pathetic Priest / Destructive Selection / Egoverment / Follow Me / Tonight This Country Will Die.
PROVOKE, Displeased (1998). Cleaning Day / Route 666 / W.E.B. / Ode / Silent Force / Wrong Night / Judgementality / Wasted World / 2000 Years / Fast As A Shark / R.I.P.
UNTIL HEAVEN FORBIDS, Displeased (2000). I Am Your Provider / The Trooper / Throne Of Fire (Live) / Psycho Damn (Live) / Throne Of Fire (Demo) / Forced Imprudence (Demo) / Psycho Damn (Demo) / 'Cross The Bridge Of False Prophecies (Demo) / God Damn You (Video).
IN THE NAME OF THE FATHER, Displeased (2000). Holy Mask / Spunk / God Damn You / In The Name Of The Father / I Spit Black Bile On You / Hate Scenario / Pro Jagd / Walhalla Express / In Our Dominion.
RED HARVEST, Displeased (2001). Sick / The Stress Factor / Spikes And Pain / On The Throne / The Unbeliever / Red Harvest / Generation X / To My Friends (R.I.P.) / Punishment For Decency.

AMAGORTIS

SWITZERLAND — *Stefan Grimm (vocals), Daniel Baeriswyl (vocals / guitar), Nathalie Lambert (bass), Stefan Jeckelmann (drums).*

Düdingen based Death Metal act AMAGORTIS was founded as a trio of erstwhile MY OWN ENEMY personnel, guitarists Daniel 'Dänu' Baeriswyl and David Luterbacher with Stefan 'Stöf' Jeckelmann on the drums during June of 2001. Enrolling vocalist Andreas Hirschi a debut demo was set to tape, after which bassist Nathalie 'Nätta' Lambert was inducted in time for a second demo session that December. The band evolved further as Silvio Zbinden was inducted as singer in December of 2002. However, his stay would be brief and, in a temporary measure Baeriswyl took the frontman role. In March of 2003 Luterbacher exited and Stefan Grimm took the vocal position in the Summer.

AMAGORTIS self financed their debut album 'Abominable', recorded live at the Amagortis Kitchen Studios over a four-day period, in 2004.

ABOMINABLE, Amagortis (2004). Intro / Cannibal Obsession / Sadistic Enemy / Abominable / Terrorizing Voice / History Bodies / Slaughtered Corpse / Evil Shit / Savage Traces / Madness.

AMARAN

STOCKHOLM, SWEDEN — *Johanna De Pierre (vocals), Kari Kainulainen (guitar), Ronnie Backlund (guitar), Mikael Andersson (bass), Robin Bergh (drums).*

Female fronted Stockholm based Metal act, incorporating erstwhile personnel from MOURNING SIGN, that employ both trad Heavy Metal styles combined with the aggression of Death Metal. The band was formulated by guitarists Kari Kainulainen and Ronnie Backlund, shortly after adding bass player Mikael Andersson and singer Johanna De Pierre. The title of AMARAN was decided upon in January of 2001, a debut demo session arriving in April. AMARAN would complete their line-up with the inclusion of Robin Bergh on drums.

The French Listenable label picked up the band for an inaugural album, 'A World Depraved', released in 2002. In early 2003 the band announced a title of 'Pristine In Bondage' for a second outing, recorded at Studio Underground in Västerås, Sweden. Bassist Mikael Andersson exited in May, being swiftly replaced by Ronnie Bergerståhl, known previously for his role as drummer with JULIE LAUGHS NO MORE. In October that same year Bergerståhl also teamed up with MYNJUN and arch Black-Death Metal act CENTINEX as their new drummer.

European package tour dates for January of 2004 found the group in league with AFTER FOREVER, DARK MOOR and French veterans NIGHTMARE. However, guitarist Ronnie Backlund fractured his right arm just upfront of these gigs and was forced to sit out the dates. Esa Orjatsalo of Finnish band DREAMTALE stepped in as substitute. Next in line for enrollment would be drummer Pär Hjulström, taking over percussion duties for the band's '2000 Decibel' festival appearance in May. Ex-drummer Robin Bergh joined melodic Metal band CELLOUT. In March of 2004 Pär Hjulström, retaining his position with AMARAN, also enrolled himself into Progressive Death Metal band ATHELA and would also join MARAMON. Leading up to the band's appearance the October 'Barlo' festival in Holland AMARAN united with KATATONIA for a run of Scandinavian and European gigs.

In November guitarist Kari Kainulainen quit, announcing his frustration at the band's lack of progress. He would concentrate his efforts on a new outfit billed SIBLIANCE. Meantime, Ronnie Bergerståhl joined WORLD BELOW in December. AMARAN lost the services of Johanna De Pierre in July 2005. As the year closed, so did the lifespan of AMARAN, the band announcing during late December "This year comes to an end and we are sad to say that AMARAN does the same."

Promo 2001, Amaran (2001) (Demo). Received A Kiss / Rusty Warhorse / Imperfect / Lullaby.

A WORLD DEPRAVED, Listenable POSH038CD (2002). Faith Healer / Rusty Warhorse / Void / Daffodil / Lullaby / Imperfect / Little Victory / Karma In Flesh / Received A Kiss / Ode.

PRISTINE IN BONDAGE, Avalon Marquee MICP-10414 (2003) (Japanese release). Atropine / Revolution Without Arms / Coming Home / Inflict / Without Stains / Katharsis / 24 Pills / Wraith / Crow Me / Primal Nature / As We Fly / Seven Long Years / Nocturnal.

PRISTINE IN BONDAGE, Listenable POSH056 (2004) (First pressing, CD slipcase version). Atropine / Revolution Without Arms / Coming Home / Inflict / Without Stains / Katharsis / 24 Pills / Wraith / Crow Me / Primal Nature / As We Fly.

AMOK

BERGEN, NORWAY — *Necrocum (vocals), Lava (guitar / drum programming), Iscariah (bass).*

AMOK, conceived in Bergen during 2001, is a Grind imbued retro-Thrash venture of Norwegian underground elite. Featured musicians would be AETERNUS and TAAKE vocalist / guitarist Radomir Michael Nemec (a.k.a. 'Larva'), bass player Stanley and CULT OF CATHARSIS drummer Tormod Haraldson (a.k.a. 'Mord'). Subsequently Lava re-invented the group to incorporate MYSTICUM's Necrocum on lead vocals and the NECROPHAGIA, WURDULAK and IMMORTAL credited Iscariah on bass guitar.

AMOK delivered the demos 'Sadistic Attack', seeing AUDIOPAIN's Sverre Dæhli adding a guest guitar solo to the track 'Toxic Slayer', in 2001 and 'Lava Dictatorship' the following year. This latter session featured a cover of the SEX PISTOLS 'Bodies' with a guesting Tore Bratseth of OLD FUNERAL, DESEKRATOR and BÖMBERS as guest vocalist. A further demo, 'Effective Mass-Torture', arrived in 2003. That same year Witchhammer Productions re-issued the 'Lava Dictatorship' sessions as a split cassette, limited to 500 copies, shared with AUDIOPAIN's 'Revel In Desecration' demo. The following year Perverted Taste re-published 'Sadistic Attack' with a bonus track on a 10" grey vinyl split in alliance with TAAKE.

Iscariah would found GRIMFIST and also be an active member of the British based Pagan collective THE CLAN DESTINED, led by ex-SKYCLAD frontman Martin Walkyier. Both Mord and Stanley would feature on DEATHCON's 2004 'Zerohuman' EP. Stanley joined AETERNUS in the Autumn of 2004.

AMOK crafted a new album during November 2004, at first branded 'Urinal Graveyard' then switched to 'Necrospiritual Deathcore', being signed to the newly established label Planet Satan Revolution. Iscariah and Mord's next band project would be DEAD TO THIS WORLD. In mid 2006 Mord joined the live line-up of BLACK HOLE GENERATOR.

'Necrospiritual Deathcore' arrived in September 2006, these sessions seeing guests including Kybermensch, Taipan of ORCUSTUS, U. Höst of TAAKE and Fabban Malfeitor from ABORYM.

Sadistic Attack, Amok (2001) (Demo). Ebola To The People / Flamethrower / Chemical Dissection / Nuclear Warbeast / Toxic Slayer.

Lava Dictatorship, Amok (2002) (Demo). Ebola To The People / Nuclear Warbeast / Necro-Guerrilla / Atomic Warfare Fetish / Flamethrower / Project A.I.D.S. / Organized Hate / Chemical Dissection / Skullfucked / Toxic Slayer / Bodies.

Effective Mass-Torture, Amok (2003) (Demo CD single). Effective Mass-Torture / Project A.I.D.S. / Nuclear Warbeast / Skullfucked.

Lava Dictatorship, Witchhammer Productions WHP-025D (2003) (Split demo with AUDIOPAIN. Limited edition 500 copies). Ebola To The People / Nuclear Warbeast / Necro-Guerrilla / Atomic Warfare Fetish / Flamethrower / Project A.I.D.S. / Organized Hate / Chemical Dissection / Skullfucked / Toxic Slayer / Bodies.

SADISTIC ATTACK, Perverted Taste PT 666674 (2004) (Split album with TAAKE. Limited edition 1000 copies. 10" grey vinyl). Ebola To The People / Flamethrower / Chemical Dissection / Nuclear Warbeast / Toxic Slayer / Ranch Apocalypse.

A Norwegian Tribute To VON, Holycaust S810-11 (2006) (Split gatefolded double red vinyl 7" with TAAKE, URGEHAL and NORWEGIAN EVIL). Von.

NECROSPIRITUAL DEATHCORE, Planet Satan Revolution PSR 002 (2006). Necropsy Cunt / Geitehelvete / Channelling Black Horns / Effective Mass-Torture / Organ Ejaculator / Providentialism / Postapokalyptisk Korstog / Goatflesh Removal (Corpus Christi) / Goatflesh Removal (Memento Mori) / Goatflesh Removal (Gloria In Excelsis Deo).

AMON

TAMPA, FL, USA — *Glen Benton (vocals / bass), Brian Hoffman (guitar), Eric Hoffman (guitar), Steve Asheim (drums).*

DEICIDE, emerging from the cult troupe AMON founded in 1987, was the first American Black styled Death Metal band to push the novelty factor into the realms of the dangerous. Early shows had arch protagonist vocalist / bassist Glen Benton drenched in the blood of a pig bedecked in studded body armour sporting an upside down cross the frontman had burned into his own forehead. Quite remarkably for a Death-Black Metal band DEICIDE maintained a rock solid line-up since its inception for fifteen years, comprising Benton, brothers Eric Hoffman and Brian Hoffman on guitars, and Steve Asheim on drums, and continues to maintain a strong unyielding fan base.

AMON released two demos, August 1987's 8 track garage recording 'Feasting The Beast' and 'Sacrificial' in December 1989. This second session scored a deal with Roadrunner Records. The name DEICIDE arrived in June 1990 with an eponymous album recorded in February of that year by Scott Burns at Morrisound Recording, re-crafting all six 'Sacrificial' tracks for this opus. That same year Glen Benton featured as a backing vocalist on another ground breaking recording, CANNIBAL CORPSE's 'Eaten Back To Life'. Further controversy was whipped up after the second album, 1992's 'Legion', when two New Jersey teenagers tortured and killed a dog leaving its carcass hanging in a tree. When questioned by authorities the youngsters claimed inspiration from DEICIDE. With all this notoriety the band built up a loyal fan base with surprising speed and Roadrunner Records were quick off the mark in re-issuing the AMON demos re-credited to DEICIDE and marketed as 'Amon: Feasting The Beast'.

Feasting The Beast, Amon demo (1987). Feasting The Beast / Sacrificial Suicide / Day Of Darkness / Oblivious To Nothing.

Sacrificial, (1989). Lunatic Of God's Creation / Sacrificial Suicide / Crucifixation / Carnage In The Temple Of The Damned / Dead By Dawn / Blaspherereion.

AMON AMARTH

STOCKHOLM, SWEDEN — *Johan Hegg (vocals), Johan Söderberg (guitar), Olavi Mikkonen (guitar), Ted Lundström (bass), Fredrik Andersson (drums).*

Hailing from Tumba, a suburb of Stockholm, AMON AMARTH, titled after the Mount Doom of J.R.R. Tolkien's 'Lord of the Rings' trilogy, trace their roots back to 1992, formatively taking the title SCUM for a 1991 demo. Purveyors of quality, crushing Death Metal, AMON AMARTH's particular brand of aggression is brazenly stained with Norse mythology and the Viking sagas.

Once SCUM folded, the musicians regrouped, originally adopting the name NIFELHEIM before discovering another Swedish act holding prior claim. AMON AMARTH at this stage involved growler Johan Hegg, guitarists Olavi Mikkonen and Anders Hansson, with Nico Kaukinen on drums. The band would also feature erstwhile ETERNAL OATH bassist Ted

Lundström. It would be the latter who suggested the AMON AMARTH moniker.

The unit's first available recording was to have been 1993's 'Thor Arise' demo, constructed at Lagret Studio and which featured a rendition of the BLACK SABBATH anthem 'Sabbath Bloody Sabbath', though this was withheld. It was to be a full year before second demo, 1994's 'The Arrival Of The Fimbul Winter', made it onto the tape trading scene leading to a deal with Singapore based label Pulverised Records.

Following the release of supremely melodic, yet blistering debut 'Sorrow Throughout The Nine Worlds' mini-album, produced by HYPOCRISY's Peter Tägtgren, in April 1996 drummer Nico Kaukinen opted out to be replaced by Martin López. This first release caused some degree of controversy when journalists pointed out that the flaming "sun-cross" on the cover art was unfortunately close to a recognised racist symbol. AMON AMARTH had merely chosen the device because of its Viking origins but would have to deflect questioning on this symbology. Fortunately, positive press resulting from the music contained on 'Sorrow Throughout The Nine Worlds' scored the band a deal closer to home as the German branch of Metal Blade snapped the band up. AMON AMARTH's sophomore release, February 1998's thundering 'Once Sent From The Golden Hall', was again produced by Peter Tägtgren, who also commandeered September 1999's 'The Avenger'. However, a change in line-up would see Anders Hansson, opting out immediately before a June 1998 European tour aligned with DEICIDE, SIX FEET UNDER and BRUTAL TRUTH, superseded by Johan Söderberg prior to these sessions. New drummer Fredrik Andersson, also engaged with A CANOROUS QUINTET and ALLEGIANCE, was inducted once these dates had concluded/

AMON AMARTH, supported by PURGATORY, undertook a tour of Germany in December 2000. A new album, 'The Crusher', featuring a re-recorded 'Risen From The Sea' originally found on the band's debut demo, would arrive in May 2001. Limited edition digipacks hosted a cover rendition of POSSESSED's 'Eyes Of Horror'. That year Fredrik Andersson launched a side venture bearing the title CURRICULUM MORTIS, this project also featuring Leo Pignon of A CANOROUS QUINTET on guitar and Mattias Leinikka from GUIDANCE OF SIN on vocals.

After MARDUK and VADER co-headlined gigs in Europe, a projected US tour was cancelled in the wake of the New York World Trade Center disasters. North American shows were scheduled in again for January 2002 but headline act MARDUK withdrew, leaving AMON AMARTH to persevere on their own then returning to hit Europe flanking VOMITORY in April. Following AMON AMARTH's appearance at the August 2002 'Wacken Open Air' festival in Germany the band went straight into the recording studio to cut a brand new album 'Versus The World'. Limited "Viking" editions of this album came with a bonus CD comprising the band's initial demo recordings, the 'Sorrow Throughout The Nine Worlds' tracks plus a German language version of 'Victorious March' entitled 'Siegreicher Marsch'.

The band was due to form up part of the much vaunted HALFORD spearheaded 'Metal Gods' 2003 North American tour but this ambitious run of dates collapsed after just a handful of gigs. Nevertheless, the band's live schedule intensified with September North American dates dubbed 'The Art Of Noise 2'. This run of shows saw the band allied with KREATOR, VADER, NILE and GOATWHORE. The band would be confirmed as headliners for the 'X-Mass Festivals' European tour commencing in London on December 7th, heading up a strong billing incorporating DESTRUCTION, DEICIDE, NILE, GRAVEWORM, DEW-SCENTED, MISERY INDEX and DISBELIEF.

Andersson started up a fresh project band in 2003, LAID TO REST being a Death / Thrash Metal project featuring KAPUT! and ORCHARDS OF ODENWRATH guitarist Zack Z. In 2004 AMON AMARTH would donate their rendition of 'The Eyes Of Horror' to the 'Seven Gates Of Horror' tribute album assembled by the Dutch Karmageddon Media label in homage to pioneering Bay Area Thrash act POSSESSED.

AMON AMARTH announced the concept behind their 2004 studio album 'Fate Of Norns' as referring to "the three Norns— or "goddesses of fate"—Urd, Skuld and Verdandi who in Scandinavian mythology sits at the root of Yggdrasil—the world tree—weaving the fate of every man."

An incentive for fans to attend German pre-release shows in Bochum and Ludwigsburg in September came in the form of a taster album shared with FRAGMENTS OF UNBECOMING, DISILLUSION and IMPIOUS. Initial, limited edition copies of the regular album came with a bonus DVD, 'Live at Grand Rokk', a forty five minute disc comprising three camera video footage of AMON AMARTH performing live in Reykjavik, Iceland on 5th March, 2004.

The band united with IMPIOUS and German Death Metal crew DISILLUSION for October European tour dates. Dates were announced alongside CANNIBAL CORPSE too, but the band withdrew, claiming it was "economically impossible". Meantime, 'Fate Of Norns' scored well on the European charts, hitting number 31 in Germany and number 56 in Austria. AMON AMARTH toured Mexico in February 2005 with support from EVILHEART and MEN AT ARMS. European Summer festivals would be punctuated by a short Euro tour partnered with CATARACT and IMPIOUS.

In May 2006 AMON AMARTH entered Fascination Street studios in Örebro to commence work on a sixth album, 'With Oden On Our Side', with producer Jens Bogren. The album entered the German national chart at number 21, the highest chart entry in Germany of any band on the Metal Blade roster.

The group teamed up with WINTERSUN and TYR for a European tour, covering Germany, Italy, the Czech Republic, Hungary, Poland, France, the UK, Holland, Belgium, Sweden and Norway, beginning in early November. The band teamed up with GOJIRA, SANCTITY and headliners CHILDREN OF BODOM for a North American tour in December.

AMON AMARTH set up UK dates aligned with FINNTROLL and OCTAVIA SPERATI for April 2007. Summer US dates throughout July and August had the band involved in the gargantuan 'Sounds Of The Underground' touring festival accompanied by JOB FOR A COWBOY, NECRO, GWAR, CHIMAIRA, DARKEST HOUR, THE ACACIA STRAIN, HEAVY HEAVY LOW LOW, GOATWHORE, THE NUMBER TWELVE LOOKS LIKE YOU, THE DEVIL WEARS PRADA, THIS IS HELL and EVERY TIME I DIE amongst others. The group acted as direct support to DIMMU BORGIR's 'The Invaluable Darkness Tour 2007' in October and November.

Thor Arise, Amon Amarth (1993) (Demo). Risen From The Sea / Atrocious Humanity / Army Of Darkness / Thor Arise / Sabbath Bloody Sabbath.
The Arrival Of The Fimbul Winter, Amon Amarth (1994) (Demo). Burning Creation / The Arrival Of The Fimbul Winter / Without Fear.
Sorrow Throughout The Nine Worlds, Pulverised ASH001 MCD (1996). Sorrow Throughout The Nine Worlds / The Arrival Of The Fimbul Winter / Burning Creation / The Mighty Doors Of The Speargod's Hall / Under The Graveclouded Winter Sky.
ONCE SENT FROM THE GOLDEN HALL, Metal Blade 3984-14133-2 (1998). Ride For Vengeance / The Dragon's Flight Across The Waves / Without Fear / Victorious March / Friends Of The Suncross / Abandoned / Amon Amarth / Once Sent From The Golden Hall.
THE AVENGER, Metal Blade 3984-14262-2 (1999). Bleed For Ancient Gods / The Last With Pagan Blood / North Sea Storm / Avenger / God, His Son And Holy Whore / Metal Wrath / Legend Of A Banished Man.
THE AVENGER, Metal Blade 3984-14262-2 (1999) (Digipack). Bleed For Ancient Gods / The Last With Pagan Blood / North Sea Storm / Avenger / God, His Son And Holy Whore / Metal Wrath / Legend Of A Banished Man / Thor Arise.
THE CRUSHER, Metal Blade 3984-14360-1 (2001) (Vinyl release). Bastards Of A Lying Breed / Masters Of War / The Sound Of Eight Hooves / Risen From The Sea 2000 / As Long As The Raven Flies / A

Fury Divine / Annihilation Of Hammerfest / The Fall Through Ginnungagap / Releasing Surtur's Fire.
THE CRUSHER, Metal Blade 3984-14360-2 (2001) (CD release). Bastards Of A Lying Breed / Masters Of War / The Sound Of Eight Hooves / Risen From The Sea 2000 / As Long As The Raven Flies / A Fury Divine / Annihilation Of Hammerfest / The Fall Through Ginnungagap / Releasing Surtur's Fire / Eyes Of Horror.
VERSUS THE WORLD, Metal Blade 3984-14410-2 (2002). Death In Fire / For The Stab Wounds In Our Backs / Where Silent Gods Stand Guard / Vs The World / Across The Rainbow Bridge / Down The Slopes Of Death / Thousand Years Of Oppression / Bloodshed / ... And Soon The World Will Cease To Be.
VERSUS THE WORLD (VIKING EDITION), Metal Blade 3984-14410-0 (2002). Death In Fire / For The Stab Wounds In Our Backs / Where Silent Gods Stand Guard / Vs The World / Across The Rainbow Bridge / Down The Slopes Of Death / Thousand Years Of Oppression / Bloodshed / ... And Soon The World Will Cease To Be / Siegreicher Marsch / Sorrow Throughout The Nine Worlds / The Arrival Of The Fimbul Winter / Burning Creation / The Mighty Doors Of The Speargods Hall / Under The Greyclouded Winter Sky / Burning Creation / Arrival Of The Fimbul Winter / Without Fear / Risen From The Sea / Atrocious Humanity / Army Of Darkness / Thor Arise / Sabbath Bloody Sabbath.
AMON AMARTH, Metal Blade (2004) (German promotion release. Split album with FRAGMENTS OF UNBECOMING, DISILLUSION & IMPIOUS). The Fate Of Norns (Album version) / Pursuit Of Vikings (Album version) / Pursuit Of Vikings (Demo version) / Once Sealed In Blood (Demo version) / Ride For Vengeance / The Last With Pagan Blood / Masters Of War / For The Stabwounds In Our Back.
FATE OF NORNS (LIMITED EDITION), Amon Amarth 3984-14498-0 (2004) (CD + DVD). An Ancient Sign Of Coming Storm / Where Death Seems To Dwell / The Fate Of Norns / Pursuit Of Vikings / The Valkyries Ride / Beheading Of A King / Arson / Once Sealed In Blood / Death In Fire (Live video) / The Last With Pagan Blood (Live video) / For the Stabwounds In Our Back (Live video) / Masters Of War (Live video) / The Sound Of Eight Hooves (Live video) / Bloodshed (Live video) / Versus The World (Live video) / Victorious March (Live video). Chart positions: 31 GERMANY, 56 AUSTRIA.
FATE OF NORNS, Metal Blade 3984-14498-2 (2004). An Ancient Sign Of Coming Storm / Where Death Seems To Dwell / The Fate Of Norns / Pursuit Of Vikings / The Valkyries Ride / Beheading Of A King / Arson / Once Sealed In Blood.
WITH ODEN ON OUR SIDE (LIMITED EDITION), Metal Blade 3984-14584-0 (2006) (2 CD). Valhall Awaits Me / Runes To My Memory / Asator / Hermod's Ride To Hel—Lokes Treachery Part 1 / Gods Of War Arise / With Oden On Our Side / Cry Of The Black Birds / Under The Northern Star / Prediction Of Warfare / Where Silent Gods Stand Guard (Live at Wacken 2004) / Death In Fire (Live at Wacken 2004) / With Oden On Our Side (Demo version) / Hermod's Ride To Hel—Lokes Treachery Part 1 (Demo version) / Once Sent From The Golden Hall (Sunlight Studio Recording 1997) / Return Of The Gods (Sunlight Studio Recording 1997).
WITH ODEN ON OUR SIDE, Metal Blade 3984-14584-2 (2006). Valhall Awaits Me / Runes To My Memory / Asator / Hermod's Ride To Hel–Lokes Treachery Part 1 / Gods Of War Arise / With Oden On Our Side / Cry Of The Black Birds / Under The Northern Star / Prediction Of Warfare. Chart positions: 21 GERMANY, 21 SWEDEN, 27 AUSTRIA, 29 GREECE.

AMORAL

HELSINKI, FINLAND — *Niko Kalliojärvi (vocals), Silver Ots (guitar), Ben Varon (guitar), Ville Sorvali (bass), Juhana Karlsson (drums).*

Helsinki technical Death Metal band AMORAL features bassist Ville Seponpoika Sorvali, also active with AHTI, MAY WITHERS and MOONSORROW. The group was assembled during 1996 by guitarist Ben Varon and drummer Juhana Karlsson, subsequently adding second guitarist Silver Ots and vocalist Matti Pitkänen. AMORAL debuted with the demo 'Desolation' in 2001, after which Niko Kalliojärvi the vocal role and Sorvali was added on bass for a second demo entitled 'Other Flesh' the following year. With Sorvali injured, Tomy Laisto of MORBID FLESH stood in on bass temporarily for AMORAL's showing at the June 2003 'Rocklinna Metalfest' event.

The band signed to the UK based Rage Of Achilles label for a debut album 'Wound Creations', recorded at Sonic Pump Studios and issued in May of 2004. The band parted ways

AMORAL (pic: Uzi Varon)

with bassist Ville Sorvali just prior to this, his MOONSORROW commitments having taken precedence. However, the band and its new label would quickly sever ties "due to financial problems", as AMORAL signed a new deal with Spikefarm Records to issue 'Wound Creations'.

AMORAL, OMNIUM GATHERUM, ELENIUM, MANITOU and KIUAS united for the November 2004 'Dead Achilles' tour of Finland.

On 5th January 2005 Ben, Juffi, Erkki, Niko and Silver gathered with Finland's Metal community at Helsinki's Rock 'n' Roll Station to pay homage to the recently murdered PANTERA / DAMAGEPLAN guitarist Darrell 'Dimebag' Abbott by forming up a one off PANTERA tribute band DIMEN NIMEEN ("In Dime's Name!"). Musicians featured in this collective included Alexi Laiho and Roope Latvala of CHILDREN OF BODOM, Atte Sarkima from AJATARRA, Tony Jelencovich of TRANSPORT LEAGUE, Petteri Hirvanen and Nicke of MONSTERBALL, Toni, Pete, Kride and Jukkis of NORTHER, Nico, Euge and OJ from GODSPLAGUE amongst many others.

Throughout March and April 2005 the group undertook European touring packaged with FINNTROLL and Italians GRAVEWORM. The group would act as openers for DARK FUNERAL's February 2006 tour.

AMORAL booked Hämeenlinna Sound Supreme Studios in February 2007 to cut a new album. The following month the group put in Italian dates partnered with GORY BLISTER.

Desolation, Amoral (2001) (Demo). Metamorphosis / Not to Be.
Other Flesh, Amoral (2002) (Demo). Other Flesh / Metamorphosis / Nothing Daunted.
WOUND CREATIONS, Rage Of Achilles ILIAD053 (2004). The Verge / Atrocity Evolution / Silent Renewal / Solvent / The Last Round / Other Flesh / Distract / Nothing Daunted (Gallows Pole Rock n' Roll) / Languor Passage.
WOUND CREATIONS, Spikefarm NAULA055 (2004). The Verge / Atrocity Evolution / Silent Renewal / Solvent / The Last Round / Other Flesh / Distract / Nothing Daunted / Languor Passage / Metamorphosis.
WOUND CREATIONS, Avalon Marquee MICP-10501 (2005) (Japanese release). The Verge / Atrocity Evolution / Silent Renewal / Solvent / The Last Round / Other Flesh / Distract / Nothing Daunted (Gallows Pole Rock n' Roll) / Languor Passage / Metamorphosis / Other Flesh (Video).
DECROWNING, Spikefarm NAULA067 (2005). Showdown / Lacrimal Gland / Decrowning / Tiebreaker / Drug Of Choice / Denial 101 / Control Cancer / Raptus / Warp / Bleeder.

AMORPHIS

HELSINKI, FINLAND — *Tomi Joutsen (vocals), Esa Holopainen (guitar), Niclas Etelävuori (bass), Santeri Kallio (keyboards), Jan Rechberger (drums).*

One of Finland's premier acts. AMORPHIS, whose title derives from the word 'Amorphous' meaning without shape or form, have ploughed their own distinct furrow by combining Death Metal with elements of 70's inspired Progressive Rock and even Psychedelia. Based in Helsinki, AMORPHIS formed in 1990 by erstwhile VIOLENT SOLUTION and ABHORRENCE guitarist Tomi Koivusaari. ABHORRENCE had been initiated during 1989 by Koivusaari, the DISASTER credited singer Jukka 'Shrike' Kolehmainen, second guitarist Kalle Mattsson bassist Jussi Ahlroth along with drummer Kimmo Heikkinen. This unit bulldozed its way onto the local club scene, even putting in a solitary Norwegian gig, with ANTIDOTE's Mika Arnkil on drums, prior to issuing the 'Vulgar Necrolatry' single on the Seraphic Decay label. Although the group received no revenue from this 7" its presence did stir interest from other record companies. However, this was unknown to ABHORRENCE at the time, who went their separate ways in 1990.

Recording their first demo, 'Disment Of Soul', the same year for a January 1991 release, alongside Koivusaari the founding AMORPHIS line-up also comprised guitarist Esa Holopainen, bass player Olli Pekka-Laine with drummer and keyboard player Jan Rechberger. ABHORRENCE singer Jukka Kolehmainen was offered a chance at the lead vocal position but declined the offer. The band was picked up by American label Relapse almost by accident, the record company having made an offer to ABHORRENCE, not realising the group had folded. The newly established AMORPHIS recorded six tracks in May 1991 at TTT Studios in the capital with Timo Tolkki of STRATOVARIUS behind the mixing desk for an intended split album with INCANTATION, but this never appeared. However, two songs, 'Vulgar Necrolatry' / 'Misery Path', made it onto a limited edition 7" single issued in June 1992.

The first album, 'The Karellian Isthmus' taking its title from a historic Finnish battleground, co-produced by the band and Tomas Skogsberg at Stockholm's Sunlight Studios in May 1992, received creditable media response and strong sales upon its release that November, prompting Relapse to release the previously recorded tracks as the 'Privilege Of Evil' mini-album. Deceptively commencing with an acoustic, Celtic imbued lull, at this juncture Amorphis was entrenched in classic Death Metal territory, content to let guitars buzz with expressive, often arabesque imbued riffage over some impressive, near epic tunes. Lending some colour to the vocal department, narrative and clean vocal accompaniment would be provided by SUBURBAN TRIBE and KYYRIA's Ville Tuomi. Importantly, the European license for 'The Karellian Isthmus' would be taken up by Germany's Nuclear Blast label, who marketed the opus aggressively.

The next AMORPHIS album, 'Tales From A Thousand Lakes' once again cut with Tomas Skogsberg and delivered in September 1994, is loosely based on the Finnish national myth of Kalevala. The album featured a cover version of THE DOORS' 'Light My Fire' and includes the first appearance of new keyboard player Kasper Martenson. 'Tales From A Thousand Lakes' received an ecstatic reception from fans, its content quickly being exalted across the Metal underground as perhaps the very pinnacle of atmospheric Death Metal achievement. The group toured North America in 1994 alongside ENTOMBED then Europe with TIAMAT. With interest in the band gathering pace, standout track 'Black Winter Day' headed up an EP release bolstered by album outtakes in January 1995.

Drummer Jan Rechberger was replaced by Pekka Kasari in 1995. Further line-up ructions occurred for the 'Elegy' album with AMORPHIS adding ex-STONE man Kim Rantala on keyboards and vocalist Pasi Koskinen. Retaining the successful formula, the band employed both Sunlight Studios and Tomas Skogsberg but opted to engage engineer Pete Coleman for a final mix down at Parr Street Studios in Liverpool. 'Elegy', lyrically plundering native folklore with inspiration this time coming from the Elias Lönnrot 1840 compiled 'Kanteletar' body of 7,000 verses, gave AMORPHIS their first chart impression in May 1996 when it entered the German national listings at number 67. Reviews would be universally positive, fans accepting the smoother, refined vocal tones of Koskinen and the group's determination to push boundaries, including the alarming interpolation of a traditional Polka refrain in 'Cares'. The song 'My Kantele' would be lifted for a spin off EP release in May 1997 to maintain momentum, this hosting renditions of HAWKWIND's 'Levitation', the British Psych Godfathers being an increasing influence, and KINGSTON WALL's 'And I Hear You Call'.

Side activity found Holopainen putting in an appearance on the LOVE LIKE BLOOD Gothic Rocker's 'Jubileum' mini-album in early 1998. AMORPHIS returned in February the following year, the 'Divinity' single heralding a fresh album, 'Tuonela' produced by Simon Effemy, hitting the German charts at number 46. A transitional staging post, 'Tuonela' took an enormous leap from Metal into retro-Progressive Rock, this 70s vibe solidified by Hammond organ, sitar, flute overlays on 'Rusty Moon' and Sakari Kukko's saxophone. Indeed, Tomi Koivussaari's Death growl on the song 'Greed' marked the last usage of these harsher tones.

Laine left the band in 2000 to be replaced by KYYRIA's Niclas Etelävuori. Rantala also made his exit and was substituted by former KYYRIA member Santeri Kallio. A retrospective compilation, 'Story: 10th Anniversary', was put out in May 2000 to introduce those who had newly discovered the band to their rich back catalogue. Meantime, enterprising souls would pair up tracks from the 1991 AMORPHIS demo 'Disment Of Souls' with early ABHORRENCE tracks for a well timed split release.

The April 2001 album 'Am Universum', which debuted at number 3 on the Finnish national album charts, also achieved the honour of producing a homeland number one single with 'Alone'. AMORPHIS retained the studio partnership with Simon Effemy, committing 'Am Universum to tape at Finnvox studios in Helsinki. Sakari Kukko saxophone this time stretched across the entire body of work, guitars would be downplayed whilst emphasis on keyboards was heightened. Japanese editions closed with an exclusive track, 'Too Much To See'. Touring in America, with complimentary support act OPETH, would commence with an appearance at the New Jersey Metalfest before Canadian gigs and a short run of headliners in the USA.

Various members of AMORPHIS also bided their time with side projects JAMBOR and ALL HUMANS SUBSTITUTES. Koskinen would engage in a side project AJATTARA releasing the 'Itse' album under the pseudonym of Ruoja. During April of 2002 drummer Pekka Kasari announced his retirement from the band, wishing to spend more time with his family. His replacement would swiftly be announced as none other than ex-AMORPHIS man Jan Rechberger.

The band contributed a new recording 'Kuusamo', actually a Finnish language version of the TOTO hit 'Africa', for the soundtrack to a Finnish movie 'Menolippu Mombasaan' in late 2002 as Koskinen's AJATTARA venture got to work on a second album 'Kuolema'. Meantime Tomi Koivusaari, Santeri Kallio and Niclas Etelävuori readied a second album, 'Happosadetta', from their side concern VERENPISARA. Etelävuori would be doubly industrious during this period, also sessioning for Portuguese Gothic Metal pioneers MOONSPELL. Yet another adjunct outfit with strong AMORPHIS connections came with the unveiling of CHAOSBREED in early 2003. Something of a Finnish Metal 'Supergroup' the band comprised lead vocalist Taneli Jarva of SENTENCED and THE BLACK LEAGUE, guitarists Esa Holopainen of AMORPHIS and Marko Tarvonen of MOONSORROW, bass player Oppu Laine of AMORPHIS and MANNHAI repute with former GANDALF drummer Nalle Österman.

In recognition of the band's rising status AMORPHIS revealed in March 2003 that they had signed a new record deal with major label EMI. The first fruits of this union would be the album 'Far From The Sun' preceded by the single 'Day Of Your Beliefs' in April. Naturally the band's experimental bent was unbowed, this time even drafting the Sveaborg Boys' Choir. It would be learned that former HAVANA BLACK singer Hannu Leiden had acted as vocal producer for Pasi Koskinen during recording. Despite all this activity, both Koskinen and bassist Niclas Etelävuori found space to forge a side project band in league with H.I.M. drummer Mika "Kaasu" Karppinen. Coincidently, it would be leant H.I.M. and AMORPHIS members had forged an anonymous Grindcore venture entitled TO SEPARATE THE FLESH FROM THE BONES.

AMORPHIS united with British Goth-Rock veterans PARADISE LOST for Scandinavian dates in October. However, regular drummer Jan Rechberger was forced out due to personal circumstances, his place being taken by Atte Sarkima from VERENPISARA, also a member of Black Metal combo AJATARRA (as 'Malakias III') and a veteran of 80's hair band CHRISTINE, HAVANA BLACK and Prog merchants FIVE FIFTEEN. In the Spring of 2004, as the band entered CCPC Studios in Helsinki to demo new material, 'Far From The Sun' finally secured a North and South American release a full year after its European issue. The US Nuclear Blast version added three bonus tracks, including an acoustic version of the title track, whilst Japanese variants added 'Darkrooms'.

During September 2004 Esa Holopainen and Santeri Kallio took to the road in Finland with LORDS OF THUNDER, a covers band comprising top flight Metal musicians such as Janne Joutsenniemi of SUBURBAN TRIBE, Atte Sarkama from VERENPISARA plus Mikko Herranen of VELCRA and RUST.

AMORPHIS revealed tour plans for an October run of North American shows partnered with TYPE O NEGATIVE. However, in a move that shocked many fans, longtime AMORPHIS singer Pasi Koskinen quit, performing his last gig with the band on August 21st at the Kontu Rock festival. Vocal duties for the North American trek would be delegated to CHARON and ex-POISONBLACK frontman Juha-Pekka Leppäluoto. In the event, the US October dates too would be pulled when a TYPE O NEGATIVE management statement in mid September revealed a medical exam on frontman Pete Steele resulted in "undisclosed anomalies" being discovered.

Esa Holopainen and Santeri Kallio engaged themselves in extracurricular activities with Heavy Metal / Hard Rock covers band LORDS OF THUNDER alongside Janne Joutsenniemi from SUBURBAN TRIBE, Atte Sarkima of VERENPISARA and the VELCRA and RUST credited Mikko Herranen. Performing songs by the likes of WHITESNAKE, IRON MAIDEN and W.A.S.P. the band embarked upon a Finnish tour in late September 2004.

In November it would be revealed that the AMORPHIS collective of guitarists Esa Holopainen and Tomi Koivusaari, bassist Niclas Etelävuori and keyboard player Santeri Kallio had all donated their services to a Country / Blues covers album assembled by CARCASS frontman Jeff Walker.

In January of 2005 the band inducted new singer Tomi Joutsen, a veteran of NEVERGREEN. US AMORPHIS dates scheduled for March had the band partnered with INTO ETERNITY, SINGLE BULLET THEORY and BEYOND THE EMBRACE. The group re-signed with Nuclear Blast records shortly afterward, entering Sonic Pump studios in Helsinki on 1st July to craft a new album 'Eclipse'. First single 'House Of Sleep' topped the Finnish charts in January 2006.

Later that year Tomi Joutsen aided SWALLOW THE SUN as guest vocalist on their cover version of the TIMO RAUTIAINEN & TRIO NISKALAUKAUS song 'Alavilla Mailla'. AMORPHIS utilised Sonic Pump Studios once again in January 2007 to lay down new album tracks.

Disment Of Soul, Amorphis (1991) (Demo). Disment Of Soul / Excursing From Existence / Privilege Of Evil.

Vulgar Necrolatry, Relapse RR-016 (1992). Vulgar Necrolatry / Misery Path.

THE KARELIAN ISTHMUS, Relapse 6045-2 (1992). Karelia / The Gathering / Grails Mysteries / Warriors Trial / Black Embrace / Exile Of The Sons Of Uisilu / The Lost Name Of God / The Pilgrimage / Misery Path / Sign From The North Side / Vulgar Necrolatry.

THE KARELIAN ISTHMUS, Nuclear Blast NB 072-1 PD (1993) (Vinyl picture disc). Karelia / The Gathering / Grails Mysteries / Warriors Trial / Black Embrace / Exile Of The Sons Of Uisilu / The Lost Name Of God / The Pilgrimage / Misery Path / Sign From The North Side.

Privilege Of Evil EP, Relapse RR6024-2 (1993). From Darkness / Black Embrace / Privilege Of Evil / Misery Path / Vulgar Necrolatry / Excursing From Existence.

TALES FROM THE THOUSAND LAKES, Nuclear Blast NB 097-2 (1994) (Digipack). Thousand Lakes / Into Hiding / The Castaway / First Doom / Black Winter Day / Drowned Maid / In The Beginning / Forgotten Sunrise / To Father's Cabin / Magic And Mayhem / Light My Fire.

TALES FROM THE THOUSAND LAKES, Nuclear Blast NB 097-1 (1994) (Vinyl picture disc). Thousand Lakes / Into Hiding / The Castaway / First Doom / Black Winter Day / Drowned Maid / In The Beginning / Forgotten Sunrise / To Father's Cabin / Magic And Mayhem.

Black Winter Day, Relapse 6918-1 (1994) (12" vinyl single). Black Winter Day / Folk Of The North / Moon And Sun / Moon And The Sun Part II—North's Son / Light My Fire.

Black Winter Day, Nuclear Blast NB 117-2 (1995). Black Winter Day / Folk Of The North / Moon And The Sun / Moon And The Sun Part II—North's Son.

TALES FROM THE THOUSAND LAKES, JVC Victor VICP-5566 (1995) (Japanese release). Thousand Lakes / Into Hiding / The Castaway / First Doom / Black Winter Day / Drowned Maid / In The Beginning / Forgotten Sunrise / To Father's Cabin / Magic And Mayhem / Folk Of The North / Moon And Sun / Moon And Sun Part II: North's Son.

ELEGY, Nuclear Blast NB 6141-2 (1996). Better Unborn / Against Windows / The Orphan / On Rich And Poor / My Kantele / Cares / Song Of The Troubled One / Weeper On The Shore / Elegy / Relief / My Kantele (Acoustic Reprise). Chart position: 67 GERMANY.

My Kantele, Relapse 6956-2 (1997) (USA release). My Kantele / The Brother Slayer / The Lost Son (The Brother Slayer Part II) / Levitation / And I Hear You Call.

My Kantele, Nuclear Blast NB 270-2 (1997). My Kantele / The Brother Slayer / The Lost Son (The Brother Slayer Part II) / Levitation / And I Hear You Call.

Clubhits, Nuclear Blast NB 0404-2 (1997) (Split promotion CDEP with DISMAL EUPHONY and STAHLHAMMER). Divinity / Tuonela.

My Kantele, JVC Victor VICP-60038 (1997) (Japanese release). My Kantele / The Brother Slayer / The Lost Son (The Brother Slayer Part II) / Levitation / And I Hear You Call.

Divinity, Spinefarm SPI 76 CD (1999). Divinity / Northern Lights.

TUONELA, Spinefarm SPI 75CD (1999). The Way / Morning Star / Nightfall / Tuonela / Greed / Divinity / Shining / Withered / Rusty Moon / Summer's End. Chart position: 46 GERMANY.

TUONELA, JVC Victor VICP-60673 (1999) (Japanese release). The Way / Morning Star / Nightfall / Tuonela / Greed / Divinity / Shining / Withered / Rusty Moon / Summer's End / Northern Lights.

Amorphis EP, (2000) (Split EP with ABHORRENCE). Disment Of Soul / Excursing From Existence / Privilege Of Evil.

Alone, Spinefarm SPI 117CD (2000). Alone (Radio edit) / Too Much To See / Alone (Album version).

AM UNIVERSUM, Spinefarm SPI 116CD (2001). Alone / Goddess (Of The Sad Man) / The Night Is Over / Shatters Within / Crimson Wave / Drifting Memories / Forever More / Veil Of Sin / Captured State / Grieve Stricken Heart. Chart positions: 3 FINLAND, 75 GERMANY.

AM UNIVERSUM, JVC Victor VICP-61329 (2001) (Japanese release). Alone / Goddess (Of The Sad Man) / The Night Is Over / Shatters Within / Crimson Wave / Drifting Memories / Forever More / Veil Of Sin / Captured State / Grieve Stricken Heart / Too Much To See.

FAR FROM THE SUN, EMI 07243 583923 2 6 (2003). Day Of Your Beliefs / Planetary Misfortune / Evil Inside / Mourning Soil / Far From The Sun / Ethereal Solitude / Killing Goodness / God Of Deception / Higher Ground / Smithereens. Chart positions: 7 FINLAND, 21 GREECE.

Day Of Your Beliefs, Virgin 7243 5522132 2 (2003). Day Of Your Beliefs (Radio edit) / Day Of Your Beliefs (Album version) / Darkrooms. Chart position: 3 FINLAND.

Evil Inside, Virgin 7243 5 52358 2 4 (2003). Evil Inside / Shining Turns To Grey / Follow Me Into The Fire.

FAR FROM THE SUN, Nuclear Blast NB 1330-2 (2004) (USA release). Day Of Your Beliefs / Planetary Misfortune / Evil Inside / Mourning Soil / Far From The Sun / Ethereal Solitude / Killing Goodness / God Of Deception / Higher Ground / Smithereens / Shining Turns To Grey / Follow Me Into The Fire / Darkrooms / Dreams Of The Damned / Far From The Sun (Acoustic version) / Evil Inside (Video).

Relapse Singles Series Vol. 4, Relapse 6659 (2004) (Split release with EXIT-13, PHOBIA and GOREAPHOBIA). Vulgar Necrolatry / Misery Path.
House Of Sleep, Nuclear Blast NB 1601-2 (2006) (Promotion release). House Of Sleep / Stone Woman.
House Of Sleep, Nuclear Blast NB 1601-2 (2006) (Mail order only European single). House Of Sleep / Stonewoman. Chart position: 1 FINLAND.
ECLIPSE (LIMITED EDITION), Amorphis NB 1596-0 (2006). Two Moons / House Of Sleep / Leaves Scar / Born From Fire / Under A Soil And Black Stone / Perkele (The God Of Fire) / The Smoke / Same Flesh / Brother Moon / Empty Opening / Stonewoman. Chart positions: 1 FINLAND, 29 HUNGARY, 56 GERMANY, 69 AUSTRIA.
ECLIPSE, Nuclear Blast NB 1596-2 (2006). Two Moons / House Of Sleep / Leaves Scar / Born From Fire / Under A Soil And Black Stone / Perkele (The God Of Fire) / The Smoke / Same Flesh / Brother Moon / Empty Opening.
The Smoke, Nuclear Blast NB 1716-2 (2006). The Smoke / House Of Sleep (Video). Chart position: 20 FINLAND.
ECLIPSE, Black Lodge BLOD 041LP (2006) (Swedish vinyl release). Two Moons / House Of Sleep / Leaves Scar / Born From Fire / Under A Soil And Black Stone / Perkele (The God Of Fire) / The Smoke / Same Flesh / Brother Moon / Empty Opening / Stonewoman.

AMPHITRYON

SWITZERLAND — *Leberbor (vocals), Tenka (guitar), Maldah (guitar), Algor (keyboards), Pax (drums).*

AMPHITRYON, previously known as SHADOWS OF THE WOOD, released an eponymous 1999 EP. To avoid confusion with the French act bearing the same title the group duly evolved into AMPHITRIUM. A Black / Death Metal act, they trace their history back to an assembly by guitarists Tenka and Maldah with Algor on keyboards. They would remain singerless until 1997 when Leberbor was inducted and the revised name of HAZE was taken on. Bringing in session drummer Pax, a set of demo recordings were made during 1998 with Dhilorz of ANCIENT guesting on bass guitar. Unfortunately, upon completion of these tapes both Leberbor and Pax departed.

Once again adopting a new title the tracks were finally issued in 2002 as an EP credited to AMPHITRYON. That November Giankrush was installed on the drums. Leberbor made a return and in June of 2003 the band cut a two song demo, 'Chrysalis' and 'Silence Is Mine'. That September though the line fluxed once again as Evil S.A.M. took the vocal mantle and, shortly afterward, Algor was to exit as the group, inducting ex-MELANCHOLIA member Jahz on bass, became AMPHITRIUM.

Amphitryon, Amphitryon (2002). Exegi Monumentum / Amphitryon / The Point Of No Return / Odium Generis Humani.

AMPUTATION

NORWAY — *Demonaz Doom Occulta (vocals / guitar), Jørn Inge Tunsberg (guitar), Armagedda (drums).*

A late eighties primitive Death Metal act known for its fostering of key players in the IMMORTAL saga, vocalist / bassist Abbath Doom Occulta (Olve Eikemo), guitarist Demonaz Doom Occulta (a.k.a. Harald Nævdal) and drummer Armagedda. Guitarist Jørn Inge Tunsberg, of OLD FUNERAL and HADES ALMIGHTY repute, would also figure in the IMMORTAL family tree and would gain notoriety for his conviction on church arson charges.

Abbath and Armagedda were both previously in SATAENEL, an outfit that also featured BURZUM's notorious Count Grisnackh. This triumvirate also operated the Death Metal unit OLD FUNERAL alongside Tyr and Alligator. SATAENAL and OLD FUNERAL ran parallel courses until Demonaz broke away to forge AMPUTATION during 1988 with drummer Armagedda and Tunsberg. The latter exited in the Autumn of 1990 to create HADES (NORWAY) and AMPUTATION duly evolved into IMMORTAL. Besides his main employ fronting IMMORTAL Abbath has also gained credits as session drummer for both GORGOROTH and DET HEDENSKE FOLK. Demonaz has been involved with solo ventures DEMONAZ and PERFECT VISIONS.

AMPUTATION issued two demos, 'Achieve The Amputation' in 1989, also featuring guitarist Truls and bassist Jan-Atle, and July 1990's 'Slaughtered In The Arms Of God'. Both would be heavily bootlegged in later years.

Achieve The Mutilation, Amputation (1989) (Cassette demo). Plague Of Death / Merciless Slaughter / Death Is Not The End / Intense Torture.
Slaughtered In The Arms Of God, Amputation (1990) (Cassette demo). Heavenly Grace / Slaughtered In The Arms Of God.

ANAEMICA

ANTWERP, BELGIUM — *Dirk Broeren (vocals), Paul Broeren (guitar), Donald Van Haesbroeck (bass), Jeroen Buysse (drums).*

Antwerp Death Metal act ANAEMICA would evolve into AEONS OF OLD. The band boasted the dubious distinction of being fronted by a serving policeman- Tom Cornelius! 1997 would see the formation of the quartet billed as CATACOMB, this drummer-less unit comprising guitarists Paul Broeren and Dirk Van Haesbroeck, bassist Donald Van Haesbroeck and keyboard player Kevin Van Staey. By that September the title ANAEMICA had been adopted and Jeroen Buysse of SFAGNUM and DROWNING installed on the drums. Subsequently Tom Cornelis completed the band as lead vocalist for their debut gig held at the local school. In September of 1998 Van Staey opted out and the group decided to do without this instrument for a four song February 1999 demo.

Under the ANAEMICA title they would release the 2001 demo 'Great Vengeance ... And Furious Anger'. With Police interruptions of their gigs becoming quite frequent Cornelis was forced to exit and in November 2002 Dirk Broeren took over the vocal reins. Taking on the revised title of AEONS OF OLD lost the services of both rhythm guitarist Dirk Van Haesbroeck and drummer Jeroen Buysse in 2003. However, Van Haesbroeck retained ties to band, acting in the managerial capacity whilst Ian Van Gemeren of AXAMENTA, GURTHANG and ECLIPTICA stepped in to act as substitute for live dates. AEONS OF OLD debuted with the track 'Howl Of Despair' included on the compilation album 'Face Your Underground Vol. 1'.

Anaemica, Anaemica (1999). Supreme Lords Of Mankind / The Abyss Of The Chosen Ones / Walpurgisnacht / The Enochian Keys.
Great Vengeance ... And Furious Anger, (2001). Banished Mercy / Supreme Lords Of Mankind / Human Disintegration / Rapefruit / Ancient Battles / Halewyn.

ANAL BLAST

USA — *Don Decker (vocals), Luke (guitar), Nick Kulczycki (guitar), Bill Lawrence (bass), Tony Garfield (drums).*

ANAL BLAST's 'Vaginal Vempire' album was clad in a witty parody of premier Black Metal act CRADLE OF FILTH's high art album sleeves. The band even willing to morph their logo into 'Anal Of Blast' to complete the effect. Members of ANAL BLAST also indulge themselves with REVEREND POKY BUNGE issuing the 2000 toilet humour infused album 'Butt Outta Hell' through Root Of All Evil Records.

The band are noted for having included pre SLIPKNOT members drummer Joey Jordison, bassist Paul Gray and guitarist Donnie Steele. Also citing membership of ANAL BLAST would be guitarist Tyrannus Vermis, of AZRAEL, and bassist Lord Samaiza, both accredited TERATISM and PENTAGORIA musicians.

VAGINAL VEMPIRE, Nightfall (1998). Smell Your Cunt / Bloody Mary / Nipples, Knees, Ass, Cheeks, Ankles / Pull A Train / Staple Your Pussy Lips Together / Slop Hole / Crimson Smell / Wings Flew Away / Menstral Pancake / Pussy Blood Popsicle / Diaretic Orgasm / Honey / Bloody Hole / Suck Your Shit Off My Dick / Puss Sores / Bloody Brown Mouse / Puss Blood Pentagram (Bloody Cunt Suck Part II) / Spraying Blood- Blood Sprayer / Big Sags / Farm Animal Hammer / Ass Over Snatch / Lubed With Blood / Tampon Tea Bad / Twisted Bonus.

ANAL CUNT

BOSTON, MA, USA — *Seth Putnam (vocals / guitar), Scott Hull (guitar), Tim Morse (drums).*

Dubbed by many as the vilest band on the planet. A.C. (ANAL CUNT) was created by former EXECUTIONER man Seth Putnam in 1988 initially intended as a joke act designed to offend as many people as they could while playing their instruments as badly as possible for an intended life span of a month at the most. Such was the cult the act engendered A.C. are still at it over a decade later delivering a seemingly endless stream of strictly non P.C abuse. Perversely the band, which has never employed a bass guitarist, has become a major attraction in Japan.

A.C.'s debut line-up comprised Putnam, BRATFACE guitarist Mike Mahan and drummer Tim Morse and as such delivered a hint of what was to come with the '47 Song Demo' tape. The '5643 Song EP' on Stridecore Records was limited to a mere 307 copies of various vinyl colours. Acknowledging the band's already established underground status a bootleg 7" split single with PATARENI was leaked onto the market. A.C. members would also surface on other groups recordings with the singer appearing on the SHIT SCUM 'Manson Is Jesus' 7" single as well as sessioning with POST MORTEM.

With this line-up the band toured Europe but split upon their return. A.C.'s debut full length CD 'Fast Boston H.C' was issued by Ecocentric Records in a plain card cover but confusingly would be reissued the same year retitled 'Greatest Hits Vol. 1' with the same catalogue number.

By 1991 Fred Ordonez was on guitar for an infamous split EP with THE MEATSHITS and a further shared effort with PSYCHO. Putnam would also add guest vocals to the track 'Group Pressure' on PSYCHO's 'Riches And Fame' 10" EP. By the following year John Kozik of TOETAG had taken the position for the 'Morbid Florist' EP.

Between 1993 and '94 A.C. operated with two guitarists, with Kozik alongside a returning Ordonez. In this incarnation the band cut an irreverent live cover version of JUDAS PRIEST's 'Breaking The Law' for a 7" single and the album 'Everyone Should Be Killed', released in Europe with new sleeve artwork by British Extreme Metal aficionados Earache Records. However Ordonez made a rapid exit midway through these recordings.

A.C. garnered further media exposure in 1995 by offering an Oi! Version of the BEE GEES Disco hit 'Stayin' Alive'. This outing saw Kozik's guitar partner as Paul Kraynak.

Mainstream act PANTERA were by now open fans of A.C.'s and it came as no surprise that Putnam was credited with backing vocals on their 'Great Southern Trendkill' opus. A.C. undertook their only proper national tour to date in 1996 with Deathsters INCANTATION. Putnam honoured the event with a track 'Kyle From Incantation Has A Moustache' to which Kyle Severn himself graciously contributed drums. The band by now was down to a trio of Putnam, Morse and guitarist Scott Hull. The latter also operating AGORAPHOBIC NOSEBLEED, PIG DESTROYER and JAPANESE COMEDY TORTURE HOUR.

The 1998 acoustic 'Picnic Of Love' album was reportedly recorded for a miserly $100.

In true spoofing style Putnam and Martin released two supposedly 'Black Metal' demos credited to IMPALED NORTHERN MOON FOREST. These recordings would later see an official release as a 7" single on M.T.S. Records.

The band comprised Putnam, guitarist Josh Martin and drummer Nate Lineham for 1999's 'It Just Gets Worse'. PANTERA's Phil Anselmo and Choke of SLAPSHOT also guested on the record. In typical fashion the album ran into trouble before its release with a planned song 'Conor Clapton Committed Suicide Because His Father Sucks' provoking the expected outrage. The song had its title changed for the record. German distributors also rejected the album due to the song 'Hitler Was A Sensitive Man'. Overall A.C. confronted the expected maturity process by delivering a set of songs more extreme than anything they had previously delivered.

By 1999 John Gillis had taken the drum stool as A.C. issued a shared split live album with INSULT. Former drummer Tim Morse later created THE PRETTY FLOWERS and MORSE CODE.

The band announced a cessation of activities in December of 2001. A fifteenth anniversary spate of shows broke out in March 2003 although Putnam and Linehan also busied themselves with a secondary act ADOLF SATAN. ANAL CUNT, crediting Seth Putnam, guitarist Josh Martin and drummer Nate Linehan, officially reformed for a November 10th gig at Bill's Bar in Boston, Massachusetts. The band revealed 2004 was to commence in a suitably heavy fashion, participating in the January 'Extreme The Dojo VII' tour of Japan alongside NASUM, NAPALM DEATH and PIG DESTROYER.

Defenders Of The Hate, (0).
We'll Just Have To, Total Noise TNT 45-05 (1989) (Split single with SEVEN MINUTES OF NAUSEA).
GREATEST HITS VOLUME ONE, Ecocentric ER 104CD (1991).
Live EP, Psychomania 003 (1991).
Unplugged EP, Psychomania 002 (1991).
EVERYONE SHOULD BE KILLED, Earache MOSH 101CD (1993). Some Songs / Some More Songs / Blur Including New HC Song / Even More Songs / Tim / Judge / Spin Cycle / Song / Pavarotti / Unbelievable / Music Sucks / Newest HC Song / Chiff On And Chips / Guy Smiley / Seth / I'm Not Allowed To Like AC Anymore / EX A Blur / GMOTR / I'm Wicked Underground / Blur Including G / Shut Up Mike / Abomination Of Unnecessarily Augmented ... / Radio Hit / Loser / When I Think Of The True Punk Rock Bands / Eddy Grant / MTV Is My Source For New Music / Song Titles Are Fucking Stupid / Having To Make Up Song Titles Sucks / Well You Know, Mean Gene.
Morbid Florist EP, Relapse RR023 (1993). Some Songs / Song No. 5 / Chump Change / Slow Song From Split 7" / Unbelievable / Siege / Grateful Dead / Don't Wanna Dance / Even More Songs / Radio Hit / Some More Songs / Morrisey / Song No. 6 / Guy Lombardo.
OLD STUFF PART TWO, Devour DEVOUR4 (1994).
TOP 40 HITS, Earache MOSH 129CD (1995). Some Hits / Some More Hits / Pepe, The Gay Waiter / Even More Hits / MJC / Flower Shop Guy / Living Colour Is My Favourite Black Metal Band / Lenny's In My Neighborhood / Stayin' Alive (Oil version) / Benchpressing The Effects Of Kevin Sharp's Vocals / Josue / Delicious Face Style / No 19 To Go / Stealing Seth's Idea- The New Book By Jon Chang / Morbid Dead Guy / Believe In The King / Don't Call Japanese Hardcore Japcore / Shut Up Mike Part 2 / Hey, Aren't You Gary Spivey? / Breastfeeding J.M.J. / Bullock's Toenail Collection / Foreplay With A Tree Shredder / 2 Down 5 To Go / I Liked Earache Better When Dig Answered The Phone / Brain Dead / Newest AC Song No 3 / The Sultry Ways Of Steve Berger / Escape (The Pina Colada Song) / Lives Ruined By Music / Still A Freshman After All These Years.
Stayin' Alive (Oi version), Earache (1995). Stayin' Alive (Oi version).
40 MORE REASONS TO HATE US, Earache MOSH 149 CD (1996). Face It, You're A Metal Band / Punching Joe Bonni's Face In / Kill Women / Steroids Guy / Everyone In Allston Should Be Killed / I Noticed That You're Gay / Dead, Gay And Dropped / You Look Divorced / I Hope You Get Deported / Mike Mahan Has Gingivitis / Trapped / You're A Fucking Cunt / Phyllis Is An Old Annoying Cunt / Al Stanku Is Always On The Phone With His Bookie / Bill Scott's Dumb / Harvey Korman Is Gay / You Fucking Freak / Theme From Three's Company / Jeanine Jism Is A Freak / Everyone In Anal Cunt Is Dumb / I Just Saw The Gayest Guy On Earth / Johnny Violent Getting His Ass Kicked By Morrisey / Metamorphosis / I'm Sick Of You / Howard Wulkan's Bald / You're A Trendy Fucking Pussy / Tom Arnold / I Got Athlete's Foot Showering At Mike's / Big Pants, Big Loser / Marc Payson Is A Drunk.
I LIKE IT WHEN YOU DIE, Earache MOSH 169 (1997). Jack Kevorkian Is Cool / Valujet / You've Got No Friends / You Keep A Diary / You Own A Store / You Got Date Raped / Recycling Is Gay / You're A Cop / You Can't Shut Up / You've Got Cancer / We Just Disagree / Hungry Hungry Hippos / You Are An Interior Decorator / Pottery's Gay / Rich Goyette Is Gay / Branscombe Richmond / You Live In Allston / You Are A Food Critic / Just The Two Of Us / Your Band's In The Cut Out Bin / You're Gay / You Look Adopted / Your Cousin Is George Lynch / You Have Goals / You Drive An IROC / You Play On A Softball Team / Because You're Old / You Sell Cologne / Being A Cobbler Is Dumb / You Live In A Houseboat / Richard Butler / 311 Sucks / Your Kid Is Deformed / You Are An Orphan / You're Old (Fuck

You) / You Go To Art School / Your Best Friend Is You / You're In A Coma / Windchimes Are Gay / No We Don't Want To Do A Split 7 With Your Stupid Fucking Band / Rene Auberjonois / The Internet Is Gay / Ha Ha Your Wife Left You / Hootie And The Blowfish / You Went To See Dishwalla And Everclear (You're Gay) / Dropping Drop Dead In McDonalds / Technology's Gay / Your Favourite Band Is Supertramp / I'm In Anal Cunt / You (Fill In The Blank) / Kyle From Incantation Has A Moustache / Bonus Track No. 3.

In These Black Days EP, Hydrahead HH666-12 (1997) (Split EP with EYEHATEGOD). Black Sabbath Tribute.

PICNIC OF LOVE, Off The Records 002 (1998). Picnic Of Love / Greed Is Something We Don't Need / I Wanna Grow Old With You / I'd Love To Have Your Daughter's Hand In Marriage / I Couldn't Afford A Present So I Wrote You This Song Instead / Waterfall Wishes / I'm Not That Kind Of Boy / Saving Ourselves For Marriage / I Respect Your Feelings As A Woman And A Human Being / In My Heart There's A Star Named After You / My Woman, My Lover, My Friend.

LIVE N.Y.C., Wicked Sick 5 (1999) (Split album with INSULT). Some Songs / Slow Song From Split 7 / Newest HC Song No. 4 / Newset HC Song No. 3 / Some More Songs / Foreplay With A Tree Shredder / Pepe The Guy Waiter / Even More Songs / Don't Call Japanese Hardcore Japcore / G.M.O.T.R. / Flower Shop Guy / Theme From The A Team / Radio Hit / Delicious Face Style / Chump Change / Stayin' Alive / Kill Women / Tom Arnold / Escape (The Pina Colada Song) / Lenny's In The Neighborhood / M.J.C. / I'm Still Standing / Art Fag / Guy Lombardo.

IT JUST GETS WORSE, Earache MOSH 195 (1999). I Became A Rape Counsellor So I Could Tell Victims They Asked For It / Easy E Got A.I.D.S. From F. Mercury / I Like Drugs And Child Abuse / Laughing While Lennard Peltier Gets Raped In Prison / I Convinced You To Beat Your Wife On A Daily Basis / I Sent Concentration Camp Footage To America's Funniest Home Videos / Rancid Sucks (And The Clash Sucked Too) / I Paid J. Howell To Rape You / I Pushed Your Wife In Front Of The Subway / Extreme Noise Terror Are Afraid Of Us / You Rollerblading Faggot / I Sent A Thank You Card To The Guy Who Raped You / I Lit Your Baby On Fire / Body By Auschwitz / I Intentionally Ran Over Your Dog / Sweatshops Are Cool / Women: Nature's Punching Bag / I Snuck A Retard Into A Sperm Bank / Your Kid Committed Suicide Because You Suck / I Ate Your Horse / Hitler Was A Sensitive Man / You Robbed A Sperm Bank Because You're A Cum Guzzling Fag / I Made Your Kid Get A.I.D.S. So You Could Watch It Die / I Fucked Your Wife / Into The Oven / I Gave NAMBLA Pictures Of Your Kid / The Only Reason Men Talk To You Is Because They Want To Get Laid, You Stupid / I Made Fun Of You Because Your Kid Just Died / Domestic Violence Is Really, Really, Really Funny / Dictators Are Cool / Dead Beat Dads Are Cool / I'm Really Excited About The Upcoming David Buskin Concert / Being Ignorant Is Awesome / You're Pregnant, So I Kicked You In The Stomach / Chris Barnes Is A Pussy / Tim Is Gay / BT-AC / I Sold Your Dog To A Chinese Restaurant / I Got An Office Job For The Sole Purpose Of Sexually Harassing Women.

THE EARLY YEARS 1988-1991, NG Records 751047-2 (2000).

ANAL PUTREFACTION

ARACAJU, SE, BRAZIL — *Manoel Mendes (vocals), Fábio Andrade (guitar), Leonardo Teixeira (guitar), Guttemberg Ettinger (bass), Ivo Barreto (drums).*

Aracaju Death Grind outfit ANAL PUTREFACTION debuted with the 1993 demo cassette 'What Now?' The group had been assembled during 1991 by vocalist Manoel Mendes, guitarist Ton Mendes and drummer Alexandre. These latter two musicians soon decamped and the band swelled to a quartet with the introduction of guitarist Cláudio, bassist Sérgio Ricardo and ex-NECROFILIA drummer Ivo Barreto. This line up did not hold either though and by the time of recording the 'What Now?' sessions ANAL PUTREFACTION comprised Manoel Mendes and Ivo Barreto alongside guitarists Antônio Gonzaga and Sérgio Ricardo with Kenton Tibbets on bass. A split then resulted in Gonzaga, Tibbets and Barreto exiting.

Manoel Mendes re-built the band by drafting guitarist César and drummer Mingal, with Sérgio Ricardo switching back to bass. However, the band that played live in 1994 had Mendes and Ricardo, back to guitar, onstage with bassist Júnior and ex-member Ton Mendes, by then a member of BLASTER, working the drums.

The 2001 ANAL PUTREFACTION contingent included erstwhile DISAGREEMENT members Leonardo Teixeira on guitar and Guttemberg Ettinger on bass. Second guitar duties were delegated to ex-ATROPOS man Fábio Andrade whilst Ivo Barreto re-assumed the drum role.

Death Is The Faith, Independent (2002). Living In Peace / Corvu's Fate / Strangers Kill For Money / Faith / What Now / Drugstore Cowboys.

ANAL VOMIT

LIMA, PERU — *Milo Possessor (vocals / bass), Sadonizer (guitar), Toñyn Destructor (drums).*

Lima based extreme Metal act forged during 1992. The band offered up a series of uncompromising demos in the form of 1993's 'Pregnancy Rotten', 'Welcome To The Slow Putrefaction' in 1995 and 'Into The Eternal Agony' in 1997. The band comprised vocalist Manfred Beingolea, guitarist Roy Noizer, bassist Milo Possessor and drummer Toñyn Destructor. ANAL VOMIT represented Peru on the 'Sudamérica Brutal' split album partnered with Argentina's CARNARIUM and Paraguay's FUNERAL.

Former ANAL VOMIT personnel Juan 'Abominator' Flores also performs as 'The Corpse' in Grindcore act GORE as does his erstwhile colleague Jesús Gore. The band has also included EPILEPSIA vocalist / bassist Manfred Beingolea and the CADAVER INCUBADOR credited guitarist Walter Profanador. Meantime, Toñyn Destructor divides his duties with fellow Death Metal band SARCOMA.

The From Beyond Productions label issued the 'Demoniac Flagellations' album in November of 2004. Vinyl versions, limited to 666 copies, included the SEPULTURA cover 'Troops Of Doom' whilst the CD variants hosted a different SEPULTURA track, 'Antichrist'. A split release, entitled 'Devotos del Diablo' issued through Warhymns Records and comprising material from the 1997 'Into The Eternal Agony' demo, would be shared with GOAT SEMEN.

The 'Demoniac Flagellations' album would be re-issued in 2006, a limited edition of 666 copies, as a picture disc by From Beyond Productions. This version added a cover version of SEPULTURA's 'Antichrist'.

From Peruvian Hell EP, Legion Of Death (2002). Penetration / The Ancient Legacy / Gods Of Perdition / Desecration Of Priest / Tormented By The Ghouls.

DEMONIC FLAGELLATIONS, From Beyond Productions FBP-042 (2004). Intro / Sendero Siniestro / Temptation And Pleasure / Total Sacrilegious / Seed Of Evil / Signo De La Bestia / Kingdom Of The Cruelty II / Bestial Massacre / Camara De Torturas / Tales Of Sorcery / Antichrist.

DEPRAVATION, From Beyond Productions FBP-060 (2006).

ANARCHUS

MEXICO — *Pancho (vocals), Miguel (guitar), Julio (bass), Adolfo (drums).*

ANARCHUS, formed in 1987, issued a 1998 demo billed as 'Total Hate'. The band's first commercial product would be the 1990 single 'Final Fall Of The Gods' for Rigid Records, followed by a further 7" '500 Years Of Infamy' in 1991 for the Gothic label. A split album shared with MONASTERY, entitled 'In Partibus Infidelium' on the Slap A Ham imprint, would be limited to 1000 copies. A 1995 demo session 'Never Ending War' preceded a further split 7" single, this time in union with AK47 on the Anomie label. To mark the tenth anniversary of ANARCHUS in 1997 the compilation of archive tracks 'Increasing The Hate' was issued.

The band has over the years acted as openers for many high profile visiting international acts, as well as partnering with SADISTIC INTENT for the 1991 Mexican 'Grind' tour. In 2002 Distorted Harmony re-issued the 1988 'Total Hate' demos, adding live tracks from 1991, in CD format. Such was the band's standing that Alarma Records assembled an ANARCHUS tribute album 'Beyond Good And Evil'. Bands paying homage included DISGORGE, MORBOSIDAD, OXIDISED RAZOR, BOWEL STEW, HORRIFIED, PULVERIZED, PURGATORIA and RAVAGER amongst many others. In 2004 ANARCHUS shared a split album with Japanese band UNHOLY GRAVE. Goatsucker Records weighed in with a fifteenth anniversary album 'Vals Of Hate'.

Pancho would feature as guest vocalist on the conceptual Metal project INTO MY WORLD for the 'Project Of Pain' album assembled by ANDARTA members guitarist Lalo Gómez and drummer Manuel Rodríguez, in collaboration with NOBLE KNIGHT bassist Jorge Escobar.

Final Fall Of The Gods EP, (1990).
500 Years Of Infamy, Gothic (1991).
IN PARTIBUS INFIDELUM, Slap A Ham (1993) (Split album with MONASTERY). Money For God / Fatality Of Human Fate / No Fear To Sin / Supreme Creation / 500 Years Of Infamy / Canonized.
Anarchus, Anomie (1996) (Split single with AK47).
PAST, PRESENT … FUTURE?, Obliteration (2001) (Split album with C.S.S.O.). The Entity In The Room / Cirrhosis / Only Death Is Real / Dead Messiah / Brutal Rage / Massive Strike / Vomit In The Church / Flowers To The Pigs / Creation Of A Religion / Jesus Christ / Final Fall Of The Gods / Ishavet Kaller / Antichrist / Labyrinth / First Casualties / Global Slavery / Conditioned.
TOTAL HATE, Distorted Harmony (2002).

ANASARCA

BREMEN, GERMANY — *Michael Dormann (vocals / guitar), Frank (guitar), Chris (bass), Herb (drums).*

Bremen based Death Metal group ANASARCA was forged in 1995 with a union of former VOMITING CORPSES personnel vocalist / bassist Michael and drummer Heiner in union with VAE SOLIS men guitarist Frank and bassist Chris. Initial fruits of this liaison being the demo tape 'Condemned Truth'.

The 'Godmachine' promotional cassette followed in 1996 which launched the track 'The Weird Ways' appearance on the German compilation album 'Deathphobia 3' and on the Spanish released 'Repulsive Assault 2'. The latter would signal a deal with the Iberian Repulse concern but not before Heiner was replaced by Herbert Grimm of EYE SEA.

Promoting the debut album 'Godmachine' ANASARCA toured Europe in conjunction with CENTINEX. Second album 'Moribund' was recorded for the Danish Mighty Music label. Guitarist Frank had departed by this juncture. New recruit in 2000 would be Benjamin Hakbilir of ACT OF FATE, this new formation featuring at the 'Fuck The Commerce III' festival in Neiden. Signing to the Danish label Mighty Music the 'Moribund' album saw release in February 2001 and that July ANASARCA toured Europe with label mates BEHEADED.

Unfortunately, founder Michael Dormann opted to fold the band in November of 2001. The ANASARCA brand would be re-activated in 2003, Dormann working with drummer Herbert Grimm once again for third album 'Dying', issued in March of 2004. Guitarist Joschi was later enlisted.

GODMACHINE, Repulse RPS033 (1998). The Way Into The Light / Godmachine / The Beast (Perverse Penetration) / The Weird Ways / Drowned And Rotten / Like Thorns In My Head / Loss Of Time / Scorn / Corrosive Eclipse / Condemned Truth / Whisper And Cries.
MORIBUND, Mighty Music PMZ 016 (2001). Done In Our Name / No More / If Only / Concrete Tomb / Those Who Have Eyes / 60 Steps / I Will Not Be Broken / A Cloud Of Smoke / I Am / Signs Of Life / Of Life And Death.
DYING, Mighty Music (2004). Hasten Death / Inside My Head / Final Goodbye / Anopheles / Blame Myself / Terminal / Aggressive Killer / Complete Surrender / Inflammation / Dying.

ANATA

VARBERG, SWEDEN — *Fredrik Schälin (vocals / guitar), Andreas Allenmark (guitar), Henrik Drake (bass), Conny Petersson (drums).*

ANATA

Varberg act ANATA began life as a Thrash / Crossover quartet boon soon evolved into a fully fledged lethal Death Metal machine. The band started life in 1993 comprising of vocalist / guitarist Fredrik Schälin, guitarist Matthias Svensson, bass player Martin Sjöstrand and drummer Robert Petersson. ANATA released the June 1995 demo session 'Bury Forever The Garden Of Lie'.

During 1996 both Svensson and Sjöstrand bade their farewell and new recruits guitarist Andreas Allenmark and bass player Henrik Drake were welcomed into the fold for the 1997 demo 'Vast Lands Of My Infernal Dominion'. ANATA signed with French label Season Of Mist for the debut album 'The Infernal Depths Of Hatred'.

ANATA's second effort formed part of the Seasons Of Mist 'War' series pitching the band up against BETHZAIDA. The band covered BETHZAIDA's 'The Tranquility Of Your Last Breath' and MORBID ANGEL's 'Day Of Suffering' whilst BETHZAIDA reciprocated with their take on ANATA's 'Under Azure Skies.

During 2000, ANATA members vocalist and guitarist Fredrik Schälin, guitarist Andreas Alllenmark and bassist Henrik Drake in league with ETERNAL LIES members guitarist Björn Johansson and drummer Conny Pettersson forged the side project ROT INJECTED.

ANATA pulled in ETERNAL LIES drummer Conny Pettersson during early 2001. ANATA signed to Earache/Wicked World in August 2002. Promoting the album 'Under A Stone With No Inscription' a short spurt of UK dates in February of 2004 saw the band ranked alongside DECAPITATED, ROTTING CHRIST and THUS DEFILED. Further shows had the band allied with DISMEMBER, PSYCROPTIC and SANATORIUM for a full European tour commencing 3rd November in Nürnberg, Germany.

ANATA entered StudioMega in Varberg during July 2005 to craft a new album with a title of 'The Conductor's Departure'.

Bury Forever The Garden Of Lie, Anata (1995) (Demo). River / Infectious Souls Of Mine / Lashes Upon His Face / Livid / In My Eyes.
Vast Lands Of My Infernal Dominion, Anata (1997) (Demo). Let The Heavens Hate / Vast Lands / Infernal Gates / Those Who Lick The Wounds Of Christ (One Is The Remedy) / Under Azure Skies.
THE INFERNAL DEPTHS OF HATRED, Season Of Mist SOM 012 (1998). Released When You Are Dead / Let The Heavens Hate / Under Azure Skies / Vast Lands Infernal Gates / Slain Upon His Altar / Those Who Lick The Wounds Of Christ / Dethroned The Hypocrites / Aim Not At The Kingdom High.
WAR VOLUME II: VS. BETHZAIDA, Season Of Mist SOM 022 (1999) (Split album with BETHZAIDA). Let Me Become Your Fallen Messiah / With Me You Shall Fall / Day Of Suffering / The Tranquility Of Your Last Breath.

DREAMS OF DEATH AND DISMAY, Season Of Mist SOM 035 (2001). Die Laughing / Faith, Hope, Self Deception / God Of Death / Metamorphosis By The Well Of Truth / Dreamon / Can't Kill What's Already Dead / Insurrection / The Enigma Of Number Three / Drain Of Blood / The Temple—Erratic.

UNDER A STONE WITH NO INSCRIPTION, Wicked World WICK15CD (2004). Shackled To Guilt / A Problem Yet To Be Solved / Entropy Within / Dance To The Song Of Apathy / Sewerages Of The Mind / Built On Sand / Under The Debris / The Drowning / Leaving The Spirit Behind / Any Kind Of Magic Or Miracle.

THE CONDUCTOR'S DEPARTURE, Wicked World WICK22CD (2006). Downward Spiral Into Madness / Complete Demise / Better Grieved Than Fooled / The Great Juggler / Cold Heart Forged In Hell / I Would Dream Of Blood / Disobedience Pays / Children's Laughter / Renunciation / The Conductor's Departure.

ANATOMI-71

GOTHENBURG, SWEDEN — *Pärra (vocals / guitar), Limpan (vocals / guitar), Ulf (bass), Putto (drums)*.

Gothenburg's ANATOMI-71, a "D-Beat Hardcore" band, debuted with the demos 'Anatomi-71', 'Strykrisk' and 'Lobotomerad vid Födseln' in 2000. Signing to the British label Rage Of Achilles the band, based in Lund, collaborated with American act NEMO for a split album in 2002. The full-length, self-released 'Ännu ett liv åt Helvete' followed, featuring a cover version of AVSKUM's 'There's No Need For Crying'. ANATOMI-71 featured the unreleased song 'Samhällsbärarna' on a Halvfabrikat Records 2003 compilation.

A 2004 split album, shared with RADIOSKUGGA on Halvfabrikat, would see the drum machine previously in employ replaced by human sticksman Putta (a.k.a. Patrik Hultin) of THE KOLONY and BURST. An exclusive track entitled 'Arbetsförnedringen' would be donated to a Halvfabrikat four way split 7" single 'We Come In Peace' in union with APOLGIA, PROTESTERA and KUOLEMA.

Anatomi-71, Anatomi-71 (2000) (CD-R demo). Svarta Bågar Med Tjocka Glas / Hugga Schly / Diskonsum / 28 År / Utbildningsreserv / Hele Ananasringer / Med Tungan Utanför.

Lobotomerad Vid Födseln, Anatomi-71 (2000) (CD-R demo). LA-Personalen Är Gammal / Om Jag Såg Ut Som Dig Skulle Jag Nita Mig Själv / Religion, Nått För Träskiga Individer Som Inte Fattar Bättre / Ni Ska Inte In I Örebro / Telioffer / Dra Härifrån / Ner I Gruset / Ner På Knä (Du Måste) / Diskonsum / Ag Lyssnade Bara På Metal Innan Jag Blev Pop / Lukta På Det Här Och Tänk På En Gubbröv / Utbildningsreserv / Pappa Var Från Nykroppa / Hele Ananasringer / Outro.

Strykrisk, Anatomi-71 (2001) (CD-R demo). Ner På Knä (Du Måste) / Lukta På Det Här & Tänk På En Gubbröv / Pappa Var Från Nykroppa / Jag Lyssnade Bara På Metal Innan Jag Blev Pop / Bärsärkarmarsch I E-moll / 50 Spänn, Det Är Väl Ingen Ersättning? / Jag Läste En Del Kerrang! När Jag Började Lyssna På Rock / Skär Av Dig Hela Jävla Armen Då För Fan Om Du Törs.

ANATOMI-71, Rage Of Achilles ILIAD 027 (2002) (Split album with NEMO). Du Är Inte Ni Med Mig, Gubbjävel / Sänk Eller Åk Hem / Lobotomerad Vid Födseln / Asocialt Kompetent / Dödad (Av Snuten) / Men Ös Då För Fan / Potential Psykopat / Dra Härifrån / Om Jag Såg Ut Som Dig Skulle Jag Nita Mig Själv / Lukta På Det Här Och Tänk På En Gubbröv / Ni Ska Inte In I Örebro / Ner På Knä (Du Måste) / Jag Lyssnade Bara På Metal Innan Jag Blev Pop / LA-Personalen Är Gammal / Telioffer / Pappa Var Från Nykroppa / Diskonsum / Utbildningsreserv / Religion, Nåt För Träskiga Individer Som Inte Fattar Bättre / Hele Ananasringar / Ner I Gruset.

Ännu Ett Liv Åt Helvete, Anatomi-71 (2003) (CD-R demo). Ditt Skitband Har Gjort Mer Pins Än Bra Låtar / Skitjobb, Skitstad, Skitliv / Studiokött / Anatomi-71 Hatar Dig / Den Dagen Jag Står I Kön Till Spybar Är Det Dags För Ett Skott I Pannan / Öppna Landskap / Sluten Anstalt / Bättre Värdelös Än Meningslös / Teaching Graham Finney How To Use A Hammer On His Flatmates Kid / There's No Need For Crying.

ANATOMI-71, Halvfabrikat HALVEP012 (2004) (Split album with RADIOSKUGGA). Hålögd Och Viljelös (Intro) / Punken Räddade Mig Från Livet / Bättre Värdelös Än Meningslös / Sen När Blev Vi Ett Grindband?

We Come In Peace, Halvfabrikat HALVEP015 (2004) (Split single with APOLGIA, PROTESTERA, PERSONKRETS 3:1, ENSAM, 365 DAGAR AV SYND and KUOLEMA). Arbetsförnedringen.

Hej Kom Och Hjälp Mig, Putrid Filth Conspiracy PFC 044 (2005) (7" vinyl EP). I Allmänhetens Intresse? / Käften Full / Ta Din Jävla Glimt I Ögat Och Lämna Mig Ifred / Hej Kom Och Hjälp Mig / Kollektiv Idiot / Hitleraspiranter / Pissattityder.

Hej Kom Och Hjälp Mig, Halvfabrikat HALVCD017 (2005) (CD single). I Allmänhetens Intresse? / Käften Full / Ta Din Jävla Glimt I Ögat Och Lämna Mig Ifred / Hej Kom Och Hjälp Mig / Kollektiv Idiot / Hitleraspiranter / Pissattityder / Med Sjuklig Aptit.

MYT NYA HÖJDER, Halvfabrikat HALVCD024 (2006). Det Sociala Fiaskot / Hytta Med Näven, Digga Med Foten / Far Åt Helvete / En Fix Idé / Discharge Me / Dagisdespoterna / Slentrianparanoian / Du, Du Är Skit / Caramelo / Mot Nya Höjder Av Uselhet / Asocialt Kompetent / Återvändsgränder / Larmet Går / Profitörerna.

ANATOMY

GLADSTONE PARK, VIC, AUSTRALIA — *Marty (vocals), Hippyslayer (guitar), Machen (guitar), J.A. (bass), Wazarah (drums)*.

Black Death Metal band ANATOMY, hailing from Gladstone Park, Victoria, bowed in with the 1991 'Dark Religion' demo following it up with 1992's session 'Those Whose Eyes Are Black'. ANATOMY's 2000 album 'The Witches Of Duthomir' included their take on POSSESSED's 'The Exorcist'. ANATOMY bassist Jay Saunders also busies himself as a member of Melbourne Thrash Black Metal act SITHLORD.

The band would later enroll the BESTIAL WARLUST and GOSPEL OF THE HORNS credited drummer Markus Hellcunt. A split 7" single shared with fellow Aussies LONG VOYAGE BACK, 'Soulcrusher', arrived through the Bleed Records label in November of 2001.

Dark Religion, (1991). Intro—Divine Comedy / Mortal Graved / Yesteryear Restoration / Dark Religion / Reincarnate.

Those Whose Eyes Are Black, (1992). Carrion Of Jesus / Burial Of Armenia / Nucleus / Arrogance Within Humanity / Fallen Inverted Destiny / Forbidden Realms.

Twisting Depths Of Horror EP, Dark Oceans (1994). For A Darkened Soul / Twisting Depths Of Horror / A Scream Of Seven / Burial Of Armenia / Nucleus Eclipse Torn Abyss / Arrogance Within Humanity.

WHERE ANGELS DIE, Destruktive Kommandoh DSTK7662-2CD (1997). Last Pleasures For Those Of The Apocalypse Of Hate / Under The Wings / Armageddon / Forbidden Realms / The Call For Doom / Where Angels Die / The Frozen Darkness.

THE WITCHES OF DUTHOMIR, Bleed (2000). Ambrosia Death / Suncrusher / The Witches Of Dathomir / Just One More Nail / Blood Will Follow Thee ... / Far From The World Of Blue / Cauldron Nebula / The Exorcist.

Soulcrusher, Bleed BLEED 005 (2001) (Split single with LONG VOYAGE BACK). The Witches Of Dathomir / Soulcrusher.

ANCESTRAL STIGMATA

ITALY — *Giuseppe Di Napoli (vocals / guitar), Mario Giannelli (guitar), Roberto Anfuso (bass), Antonio Marcon (drums)*.

An innovative Death Metal outfit, ANCESTRAL STIGMATA issued the highly praised 'Sprit' album in 2001. The group dated back to 1993, founded by Giuseppe Di Napoli with an initial membership roster also counting guitarist A.Pollizzi, bassist Sascha Radtz and drummer D.Cervone. However, that same year Antonio Marcon took over the drum role. In October of 1994 the 'Adumbrate' demo tape was delivered, followed by a second session 'Dark Side Of The Mind' in December 1995.

During 1997 ANCESTRAL STIGMATA presented an all new line up with Di Napoli and Pollizzi joined by bassist Daniele Lucchina and drummer Omar Cappetti. This version of the band recorded a third demo in September, 'De Tranquillitate Animae'. In 2000 Marco Masci superseded Pollizzi.

ANCESTRAL STIGMATA introduced two new players in 2003, guitarist Mario Giannelli and bass player Roberto Anfuso.

SPIRIT, Northern Darkness NDR024 (2001). Intro / Father / Why Hell (Arabesk) / Evidence / Hate Of The Man / Immortal / Enchantica / Albatross / Outro / First Army / My Spirit Is Thine.

ANCIENT NECROPSY

MEDELLIN, COLOMBIA — *Ivan Jaramillo (vocals / guitar), Beto Martinez (drums).*

A Medellín based Death Metal act forged in 1998 under the formative title of ASGARD by vocalist / guitarist Ivan Jaramillo and drummer Yomar Sanches, adding second guitarist Fredy Arias and bassist Mauricio in 2000. However, as the band gradually splintered down to just Jaramillo the project took on a new title of ANCIENT NECROPSY in January 2001. Solo demos entitled 'Demonstration Of Madness And Hate' led to the signing of an album deal with the Czech Nice To Eat You imprint, an eponymous debut being delivered in July of 2003.

The SUPPURATION, AMPUTATED GENITALS and PURULENT credited Betus Brutus (a.k.a. Beto Martinez) enrolled in 2004.

Demonstration Of Madness And Hate, Ancient Necropsy (2001). Ancient Necropsy / Spirits Of Hate / Fucking With An Unholy Witch From Hell / Australopithecus Corpse / Brutal Grind-Core / Abducted By A Killer Martian / Mutilated By An Innocent Child.

ANCIENT NECROPSY, Nice To Eat You (2003). Intro / Ancient Necropsy / Mutilated By An Innocent Child / Fucking With An Unholy Witch From Hell / Spirits Of Hate / Abducted By A Killer Martian / Australopithecus Corpse / Mummified And Rushed To The Space / Brutal Grind-Core / Breeding On A Putrid Womb.

DEFORMED KINGS MUMMIFICATION, Goregiastic (2004). Intro (To Kneel Front Of Your Majesty) / Deformed King's Mummification (The War Has Begun) / Putrid Aromatherapy (Traumatic Feelings Of The Widow Queen) / The Sand Storm Attack / Profaning The Temple Of Bones / Immolation In The Name Of The Kings / Trapped At The Castle Of Torture / Infernal Bloody Chapter / Invoking The Brutal Death Grind Throne / Bend The Head … Because You Will Be Beheaded / My Apocalyptic Domains.

ANCIENT RITES

BELGIUM — *Gunther Theys (vocals / bass), Jan Yrlund (guitar), Erik Sprooten (guitar), Davy Wouters (keyboards), Walter van Cortenberg (drums).*

Formed in 1989, ANCIENT RITES has fast become one of the leading Belgian Black Metal acts. The group's initial line-up comprised vocalist/bassist Gunther Theys, guitarists Johan and Phillip and drummer Stefan. This concoction released the 'Dark Ritual' demo. A year on, however, and ANCIENT RITES was forced to make changes. Firstly, band roadie Walter Van Cortenberg replaced drummer Stefan and then tragedy struck later in the same year when, in August, guitarist Phillip was killed in a car crash. The band enlisted guitarist Bart Vandereycken but soon after Johan departed leaving ANCIENT RITES as a single guitar band. Further personal tragedy would hit the band when erstwhile drummer Stefan committed suicide.

In 1992 the outfit recorded the self financed 'Evil Prevails' EP with second guitarist Pascal. However, Pascal 's tenure was brief and soon ANCIENT RITES were a trio once more. Recording became quite prolific as the band added a track for Tessa Records' 'Detonation' compilation album as well as recording tracks for a Colombian split album on Warmaster Records in union with Swedish band UNCANNY. ANCIENT RITES also joined forces with Greek act THOU ART LORD for a split 7" single.

This activity was followed by intensive gigging across Europe, including dates in Greece with ROTTING CHRIST. A further track was included on a split EP on Molten Lava Records and the band finally released their first full length album, 'The Diabolic Serenades', on After Dark Records in early 1994. During 1995 ANCIENT RITES toured Europe in with CRADLE OF FILTH and subsequently cut a split EP with fellow Belgians ENTHRONED.

1998's 'Fatherland' had Theys and Van Cortenberg joined by guitarists Erik Sprooten, previously with INQUISITOR, and Jan 'Orkki' Örlund of TWO WITCHES and PRESTIGE. A further addition would be keyboard player Domingo Smets, a veteran of AGATHOCLES and RENAISSANCE.

The band dispensed with keyboard player Smets during October of 2001. A quick fire replacement would turn out to be Davy Wouters of DANSE MACABRE and Gothic Doom band OBLIVION. During 2002 Theys would be found involved in various side acts including DANSE MACABRE, LION'S PRIDE and Heavy Metal band IRON CLAD. He also turned up adding guest vocals to two tracks on the Portuguese Black Metal band BLACK WIDOWS 2002 album 'Sweet The Hell'. Erik Sprooten would also guest session on the April 2002 debut IRON CLAD album 'Lost In A Dream'.

Embarking upon a mammoth string of European shows throughout October and November of 2002 the band created part of a deadly union for the 'Generation Armageddon' festival tour. Joining the band would be Greece's SEPTIC FLESH, Ireland's PRIMORDIAL, Norway's BLOOD RED THRONE, and Swedish heavyweights DISMEMBER and IMPIOUS. A live album and accompanying DVD, 'And The Hordes Stood As One' recorded at the Biebob club in Vosselaar, Belgium during June, was slated for early 2003 release. The 'Generation Armageddon' title would be used once more for a second leg of European shows in May of 2003, the band forming a live alliance with BLOOD RED THRONE, THYRFING, SEPTIC FLESH, PRIMORDIAL and SKYFIRE. The group announced that Jan Yrlund was to leave upon fulfillment of these shows, his replacement being none other than former band guitarist Bart Vandereycken. Yrlund joined the Helena Iren Michaelsen fronted IMPERIA in June 2004.

ANCIENT RITES underwent a major change in its formation in January of 2005. Former members keyboard player Domingo Smets and session guitar player Raf Jansen returned although Smets would take the role of bassist, allowing the band to operate with three lead guitarists. The group, entering Spacelab Studio in Germany, signed to French label Season of Mist in November.

Jansen cut tracks for a demo by his solo AHRÁYEPH project in March 2006. The guitarist also mixed and mastered tracks for fellow countrymen THEUDHO's sophomore album, 'The Völsunga Saga'. Raf Jansen quit ANCIENT RITES in January 2007 in order to prioritise his own ventures.

Evil Prevails EP, Fallen Angel (1992). Götterdammerung / Longing For The Ancient Kingdom / Obscurity Reigns (Fields Of Flanders) / Evil Prevails / Black Plague.

Longing For The Ancient Kingdom II, (1992) (Split single with RENAISSANCE). Longing For The Ancient Kingdom II.

From Beyond The Grave II, Molon Lave MLR-SP-025 (1993) (Split single with THOU ART LORD). From Beyond The Grave II.

ANCIENT RITES, Warmaster (1993) (Split album with UNCANNY). Intro / Götterdämmerung / Longing For The Ancient Kingdoms / Obscurity Reigns—Fields Of Flanders / Evil Prevails / Black Plague.

THE DIABOLIC SERENADES, Mascot M 7018-2 (1994). Infant Sacrifices To Baalberith / Crucifixion Justified (Roman Supremach) / Satanic Rejoice / Obscurity Reigns (Fields Of Flanders) / Death Messiah / Land Of Frost And Despair / Ussyrian Empire / Longing For The Ancient Kingdom / Morbid Glory (Gilles De Rais 1404-1440) / Ritual Slayings (Goat Worship Pure) / Evil Prevails / Last Rites / Echoes Of Melancholy (Outro) / From Beyond The Grave II.

BLASFEMIA ETERNAL, Mascot M7017-2 (1996). Blasfemia Eternal / Total Misanthropia / Garden Of Delights (Eva) / Quest For Blood (Le Vampire) / Blood Of Christ (Mohammed Wept) / Epebos Ai Nia / (Het Verdronken Land Van) Sacftinge / Shades Of Eternal Battlefields (Our Empire Fell) / Vae Victis / Fallen Angel.

FATHERLAND, Mascot M 7035 2 (1998). Avondland / Mother Europe / Aris / Fatherland / Season's Change (Solstice) / 13th Of December 1307 / Dying In A Moment Of Splendor / Rise And Fall (Anno Satana) / The Seducer / Cain.

THE FIRST DECADE 1989-1999, Mascot (2000). From Beyond The Grave (1990 demo) / Infant Sacrifices To Baalberith / Death Messiah / Longing For The Ancient Kingdom / Land Of Frost And Despair / Evil Prevails / Last Rites- Echoes Of Melancholy / Total Misantropia / Blood Of Christ (Mohammed Wept) / Fallen Angel (Outro) / (Het Verdronken Land Van) Saftinge / Quest For Blood (Le Vampire) / Avondland / Mother Europe / Aris / Seasons Change / Fatherland / Cain.

DIM CARCOSA, Hammerheart (2001). The Return / Exile (Les Litanies De Satan) / Victory Or Valhalla (Last Man Standing) / ... And The Horns Called For War / North Sea / Götterdämmerung (Twilight Of The Gods) / (Ode To Ancient) Europa / Remembrance / Lindisfarne (Anno 793) / On Golden Fields (De Leeuwen Dansen) / Dim Carcosa.

AND THE HORDES STOOD AS ONE, Hammerheart (2003). The Return / Exile (Les Litanies De Satan) / Victory Or Valhalla (Last Man Standing) / Total Misanthropia / Aris / And The Horns Called For War / North Sea / Infant Sacrifices To Baalberith / Blood Of Christ / Longing For The Ancient Kingdom / Götterdämmerung (Twilight Of The Gods) / Ode To Ancient Europa / (Het Verdronken Land Van) Saeftinge / Overture To The Sun / On Golden Fields (De Leeuwen Dansen) / Mother Europe / Evil Prevails / Fatherland / Dim Carcosa.

RUBICON, Season Of Mist (2006). Crusade / Templar / Mithras / Thermopylae / Rubicon / Invictus / Ypres / Galilean / Cheruscan / Brabantia.

ANESTHESY

BELGIUM — *Frank Libeert (vocals / guitar), Werner Vanlaere (guitar), Chris Decaesteker (bass), Diego Denorme (drums).*

A Thrash Metal act with distinct Death overtones dating to 1986 and formed by ex-VENDETTA guitarist Frank "Liberty" Libeert, ANESTHESY debuted with their 'Seasons Of The Witch' demo. A further demo tape 'Overdose', released in 1989, led to a deal with English label C.M.F.T. Unfortunately, after recording their debut album the record label went bust and the tracks seemed destined to remain unreleased.

Undeterred, ANESTHESY re-recorded some of these songs, releasing them as the self financed 'Just Married' EP in 1991. The band would lose their original drummer Ringo around this juncture pulling in Diego Denorme as replacement. Soon after the release of 'Just Married' ANESTHESY would also induct bassist Chris Decaessteker then second guitarist Werner Vanlaere into the fold.

Further recordings were submitted to the Tessa Records compilation 'Demolition' which led in turn to an album deal with the Black Mark label. Recording of the 1994 'Exaltation Of The Eclipse' record would take its toll on the band though witnessing the departure of Decaesteker. A substitute was duly located in Stefaan Vanijzere.

Tragedy would strike the band on the 15th July 1994. A horrific car crash would injure Vanijzere and kill Libeert. The remaining members vowed to continue and built the band back up to strength with the addition of singer Sven Houfflijn and guitarist David Vandewalle.

This unit prepared the way for their next release 'The Fifth Season' but would be disappointed to find Black Mark failing to renew their option. Vanlaere broke ranks to be replaced by Guy Commeene. Shortly after Vandewalle bade farewell too. His position would be taken by Jason Masschelein and this variant of ANESTHESY eventually committed 'The Fifth Season' to tape for new label Midas Productions.

The group would capitalise on this release by self financing a third effort 1999's 'Let The Mayhem Begin'. Wouter Nottebaert would now assume bass duties and with the recordings completed Reiner Schenk usurped Masschelein.

ANESTHESY supported the likes of NAPALM DEATH, KREATOR, GOREFEST and MORGOTH but would enter a period of inactivity in 2000. Putting closure to this hiatus, the band was resurrected for a July 2004 live show at the Wevelgem 'Metal Assault fest'. Sven Houfflijn joined FLESHMOULD in August of 2004.

JUST MARRIED, Anesthesy (1991). Ace Of Death / Inflammation Of The Bowels / The Ballad Of Jimmy F. / Rerisin' Humanist / Disbelieve / Just Married.

EXALTATION OF THE ECLIPSE, Black Mark BMCD 54 (1994). Primal Exaltation / Beyond Sadness / The Defector / Guardian / Survival Of The Fittest / Intestinal Haemorrhage / The Change / The Ultimate Reincarnation / Enstrangled Minds / The Sun, The Red, The Blood / Eclipticus Finale Exclinatum.

THE FIFTH SEASON, Midas Productions (1998). Black Soul / Tears Of A Mortal / Cruelty / Brutal Expressions / Forgotten Epitaph / Across The Burning Fields / Retribution / Those Left Behind / Perishable Considerations.

LET THE MAYHEM BEGIN, Anesthesy (1999). Introduction / The Pain I Hide / Darknight Slaughter / The Chaos Path / The Final Sleep / Forever Silent / A Walk Through Infinity / The Last Straw.

ANGELKILL

IA, USA — *Blakk (vocals), Jeff Olsen (guitar), Karl Luethman (guitar), Bruce Duncan (bass), John Lord (drums).*

ANGELKILL, founded in 1988 in Iowa by vocalist/guitarist, Blakk, also active with MORTUARY OATH and Black Metal band MASKIM, and offering dark, Heavy Metal with hints of Death Metal and a strong emphasis on the occult and horror themes, debuted with the 'Beyond The Black' demo in 1990, crafted by 'Mistress Blakk' on vocals / guitar, Chad Snow on bass and Rick Hayslett on drums. ANGELKILL followed with 'Artist Of The Flesh'. Throughout the early stages of ANGELKILL Blakk crafted demos with the aid of local session musicians.

It wasn't until 1993 a band lineup was solidified and the band released their indie debut 'Garden of Crosses'. The line-up at the time consisted of Blakk, Steve Swyers on guitar, Mike Kore on guitar, Norm Sales on bass and Brent Fugate on the drums. A period of instability followed with Blakk replacing almost the entire band with the Olson brothers, Jeff Olson on guitar and Johnathan Olson on bass, also adding Darin Sutton on second guitar.

In 1995 ANGELKILL established a relationship with the underground US label, Wild Rags and in early 1996 the label released, 'Artist Of The Flesh' on CD, a re-recording of their 1990 'Beyond The Black' demo with the new line-up and a re-issue of the 'Artist Of The Flesh' demo. Later that same year the band also released 'Beyond The Black', which also was re-recorded version of old demos. Shortly after the band issued a two-song 7 inch vinyl single 'Lady Cadaver' on the South American label, Enigmatic Records.

Through 1996 and 1997 the band continued writing and recording and experiencing still more membership changes. Blakk and Jeff Olson stayed and welcomed newcomers guitarist Karl Luethman, Bruce Duncan on bass and drummer John Lord. Ex-drummer Brent Furgate enrolled into the ranks of Doom outfit CHURCH OF MISERY. Finally in 1998 the band, new line-up intact and still on the Wild Rags label, issued two full-length albums almost simultaneously, namely 'Casket Lullabies' and 'Bloodstained Memories'. Both albums came with the warning, 'Closed Casket For The Hearing Impaired'. 'Casket Lullabies' saw a European issue, albeit unofficial, via the Portuguese label Lustful Records. A lengthy period of inactivity followed, although the band, back to a duo of Blakk and Olson, were said to be recording an album tentatively called, 'Raped, Burned & Enslaved'. Blakk donated backing vocals to GRAVEWURM's 'Warbeast' album and on LISTEN's 'Close Your Eyes And You're There' record.

Beyond The Black, (1990). Castle Blakk / Crystal Madness / Little Girl Down The Lane / Morbid Confessions / Die By The Cross.

Artist Of The Flesh, (1991). Intro / Artist Of The Flesh / Alice Sweet Alice / Born In Blood / Child's Dream / Chained To The Attic / The Worms Of Time (Outro).

GARDEN OF CROSSES, (1993). Garden Of Crosses / Watching Myself Bleed / Abominated Son / I Rule The Ruins / Dancing With The Dead / Little Dolls / Imagined Ugliness / Elizabeth / And Freaks Were Their Names.

Lady Cadaver EP, Enigmatic (1995). Lady Cadaver / Kill The Witch.

BEYOND THE BLACK, Wild Rags WRR082 (1996). The Awakening / Thirteen Candles / Tales From The Crypt / Trial By Fire / Lady Cadaver / Dark Lake / The Chapel / Evil Walks Among Us / Bodies On Ice / Kill The Witch / Beyond The Grave.

ARTIST OF THE FLESH, Wild Rags WRR055 (1996). Intro / Artist Of The Flesh / Alice Sweet Alice / Born In Blood / Child's Dream / Chained To The Attic / The Worms Of Time (Outro) / Castle Blakk /

Crystal Madness / Little Girl Down The Lane / Morbid Confessions / Die By The Cross.
BLOODSTAINED MEMORIES, Wild Rags WRR109 (1998). The Infernal Names / Carnival Of Lost Souls / Unliving Sleep / Spiritual Amputation / Flesh Defiled / Sinners Dance / The Secret Room / Orgy Of Self Mutilation / Dearly Beheaded.
CASKET LULLABIES, Wild Rags WRR108 (1998). Wolfen / Sewnshut Eyes / Impaled Visions / The Curse / Through Oblivion / Moon On The 7th / Master Of Nightmare / Man Eating Man / Crown Of Flies.

ANGELUS INFERNUS

HAMDEN, CT, USA — *Dave Emerson (vocals), Paul Alves (vocals), Matt Levesque (guitar), Jon Donovan (bass), Bill Stefanski (drums).*

Connecticut Death Metal band ANGELUS INFERNUS was manifested during Summer 2004 by two erstwhile LAID TO REST members vocalist Dave Emerson ("Bloodsoaked Deathvomits") and drummer Bill Stefanski ("Hellish Artillery Blasts") alongside three Black Metal scene veterans, vocalist Paul Alves ("Void Shattering Black Screams"), guitarist Matt Levesque ("Christian Slaughtering Battleaxe") and bassist Jon Donovan. The latter soon departed and Ezra Langston was pulled in to record the band's first demo session 'The Awakening Of A Blackheart'.

Following a support gig to ENTOMBED in early 2005 both guitarist Reid Jeanson and Langston exited. New recruits would be Paul Szabados on guitar and bassist Jeff Golden. A live tape, 'Crushing The Christian Scum' limited to 100 copies, was recorded at the Webster Theater, Hartford in February.

The Awakening Of A Blackheart, Angelus Infernus (2004). Awakening Of A Blackheart / Pandemonium / A Future Encased In Nothingness.
Crushing The Christian Scum, (2005). The Awakening Of A Blackheart / A Future Encased In Nothingness / The Reign Of Angels Ablaze / Pandaemonium.

ANGOR

CHILE — *Felipe Roa (vocals / guitar), Jose Ign.Solari (guitar), Felipe Cordova (bass), Luis Castillo (drums).*

ANGOR was founded in 1995 by vocalist / guitarist Felipe Roa and drummer Cristian Espinoza, subsequently introducing bass player Pedro Barrera. Later recruits would be singer Cristian Espinoza and new drummer Cristian Herrera with second guitarist José Solari enrolled in 1997. Line up changes then saw the bass position being handed over to Carlos Briones. However, both Briones and Herrera exited in 1999. Espinoza took over the lead vocal role whilst Felipe Córdova was installed on bass as the group opened with a 1999 EP 'Sin Fin De Tormento'.

Luis Castillo came onboard as new drummer in 2000. Frontman Cristian Espinoza took his leave in 2001 as the band trimmed to a quartet. ANGOR band supported CANNIBAL CORPSE in Santiago during September of 2002.

Sin Fin De Tormento EP, Independent (1999). Muerto Humano / Once / Fracaso / Rapto.

ANGUISH SUBLIME

TEMERIN, SERBIA — *Arpad Takacs (vocals), Aleksandar Crnobrnja (guitar), Draško Pejovic (guitar), Novelja Korać (bass), Vukasin Mandic (drums).*

Melodic Death Metal band ANGUISH SUBLIME, founded in October 1998 by guitarist Aleksandar 'Crni' Crnobrnja and vocalist Aprad Takacs, hail from the small town of Temerin in Vojvodina, Serbia. The duo committed a number of tracks to demo tape but until 2001 would be unable to locate a set of permanent band members with which to work. During this period Takacs would also be active with guitarist Tino Mihajlovic and drummer Nenad Stupar in the Death-Grind combo ANUS DEI and also participating in the short lived Black-Doom project SYNTHESIS DIABOLIQUE. In early 2002 he would join Doom-Death band TALES OF DARK.

ANGUISH SUBLIME received some forward motion in the Summer of 2002 with the introduction of second guitarist Draško Pejovic and in 2003 would be joined by TALES OF DARK drummer Vukašin Mandic. However, this new recruit soon decamped in order to prioritise TALES OF DARK and ex-TORTURA man Darko Stanojevic was drafted in his stead. For a brief period TALES OF DARK guitarist Nikola Cavar stood in as temporary bassist. Further flux saw a return of Mandic to the drum stool as Takacs relinquished his role in ANUS DEI.

In May of 2004 ANGUISH SUBLIME published the seven song demo 'Among The Raven Skies'. To mark the occasion the band put in its inaugural live performance at the NS Riders underground club in Novi Sad. Novelja Korać took on bass duties in 2005.

Among The Raven Skies, Anguish Sublime (2004). Opening The Iron Gates (Intro) / Among The Raven Skies / Where Leprous Angels Breed / Mesmerized In Asphyxiated Delight / Anguish Sublime / Somberdawn Helix / The Forlorn (Outro).

ANHKREHG

CANADA — *Khayr (vocals / bass), Shrapnel (guitar), Infurya (drums).*

Plessisville, Quebec Black Metal act ANHKREHG, founded during 1992, weighed in with a 1994 demo tape 'The Oath Of The Sorcerer King'. The 'Sacrificial Goat' sessions ensued the following year then 'Howls From The North' and the conceptual 'Brutal Witching Metal', both in 1996. The band had been founded by guitarist Blacknight together with vocalist / bassist Khayr. Soon the band would be rounded off with the addition of lead guitarist Killer and drummer Tormentor. It would be this quartet that recorded the opening 'The Oath Of Sorcerer King' tape.

After ANHKREHG's second promotional session both Killer and Blacknight lost their places as the band inducted guitarist Shrapnel. This new version of the band performed at the 'Trifête' festival alongside CRYPTOPSY. The ambitious, historically themed demo 'Brutal Witching Metal', would prompt prolonged touring inside Canada.

ANHKREHG issued the 'Le Mensonge De Massada' album, through the Hyper Active label, in 1997. Promotion dates included supports to DIMMU BORGIR. A further album, 'Lands Of War' cut for Montreal's Frowz Productions and produced by Jean-Francois Dagenais of KATAKLYSM, found Infurya of MALVERY as session drummer. Jean-Francois Dagenais would also handle production duties for the 2004 album 'Against You All ... Motherfuckers', released by Galy Records.

LE MENSONGE DE MASSADA, Hyper Active (1997). Massada / Slave's Rebellion / L'assault Final / Les Enfants De Massada (Mensonge) Message Au Peuple d'Israel / Anhkrehg / The Oath / To The Devil . . . A Daughter / Act III: Terre Promise.
LANDS OF WAR, Frowz Productions FP007 (2000). Intro—The Omen / Revenge Of The Black Godz / Wonderful Lands Of War / Le Champs Des Morts / Dieu Va Punir Israel / En Paix Avec Soi-Meme, En Geurre Avec Les Autres / Revelation X / Nous Sommes Une Partie De La Legion De Baal.
AGAINST YOU ALL ... MOTHERFUCKERS, (2004). War (Intro) / Against You All ... Motherfuckers / Set Me Free / Darksoul / My Rage (Berzerker) / La Mort Reine Du Monde—Howl From The North / Hair / Poetic Wind / Shiva God Of Destruction / La Malediction Finale.

ANIMA DAMNATA

POLAND — *Necrosodomic Corpse Molestator (vocals / guitar), Bestial Crusher Of Holy Prophets (guitar), Nocturnal Harvester Of Christian Lambs (bass), The Great Lord Hziulquoigmzhah Cxaxukluth Vel Necrolucas (drums).*

The anonymous ANIMA DAMNATA credit themselves under their full titles of vocalist / guitarist Necrosodomic Corpse Molestator, guitarist Bestial Crusher Of Holy Prophets, bass player Nocturnal Harvester Of Christian Lambs And A Great Messenger Of Subliminal Satanic Messages and last, but far from least, drummer Master Of Depraved Dreaming And Emperor Of The Black Abyss The Great Lord Hziulquoigmzhah Cxaxukluth Vel Necrolucas.

The anonymous band apparently started out in 1996, shedding various band members along the way but enrolling NECROPHIL singer Glaca in 2000. Although operating without a bass player ANIMA DAMNATA put in gigs with the likes of HYPNOS, DISGORGE, DAMNABLE and DEVILYN. Glaca quit but finally bassist Nocturnal Harvester Of Christian Lambs came onboard in May of 2001.

ANIMA DAMNATA issued the independent album 'Suicidal Allegiance Upon The Sacrificial Altar Of Sublime Evil And Eternal Sin', featuring a cover version of BEHERIT's 'The Gates Of Nanna'. These tapes would be later compiled on a shared a split album 'Gods Of Abhorrence' with THRONEUM in November of 2002. Released by Pagan Records the album was restricted naturally enough to just 666 copies. In mid 2002 'Christfucker', citing ANIMA DAMNATA membership, enrolled himself into WITCHMASTER as bassist. By late 2004 ANIMA DAMNATA was down to just Necrosodomic Corpse Molestator and Necrolucas.

In 2007 the band notably had their music included on the soundtrack to Black Metal porn movie 'Phallusifer–The Immoral Code'.

SUICIDAL ALLEGIANCE UPON THE SACRIFICIAL ALTAR OF SUBLIME EVIL AND ETERNAL SIN, Independent (2001). Black Communion Of Abhorrent Gods Of Universe / Victimize Yourself / Defile The Cross / To Jesus Christ And All His Servants / Sadistic Rape / Feast In The Blood / Shadow Of Despair / Anima Damnata / The Grand Coronation Of Apocalyptic Pain / The Gate Of Nanna.
GODS OF ABHORRENCE, Pagan MOONCD 033 (2002) (Split album with THRONEUM. Limited edition 666 copies). Black Communion Of Abhorrent Gods Of Universe / Victimize Yourself / Defile The Cross / To Jesus Christ And All His Servants / Sadistic Rape / Feast In The Blood / Shadow Of Despair / Anima Damnata / The Grand Coronation Of Apocalyptic Pain / The Gate Of Nanna.

ANIMAL FORESKIN

YLÖJÄRVI, FINLAND — *Roablock Tintin Sakkept (vocals), Peehole-Preparator (guitar), Joakim Soldehed (bass), Arto Ovaskainen (drums).*

The less than tactful Ylöjärvi based Death / Grindcore band ANIMAL FORESKIN debuted with the 2000 demo 'Anal System'. The band's 2001 demo '... Rolling On Shit ...' featured a cover version of AUTOPSY's 'Fuckdog'. ANIMAL FORESKIN released the EP 'Sledgehammer Sodomizer' in 2003. The group involved vocalist Roablock Tintin Sakkept, guitarist Peehole-Preparator, bass player Joakim "Sperm-Splatterer" Soldehed, of WOUNDS and STORMHEIT, and Arto "Anal-Wall Enlarger" Ovaskainen, also of WOUNDS, UNCREATION'S DAWN and STORMHEIT, on the drums.

Ovaskainen, billed as "Däni Manninen" and working with Chico Santiago (a.k.a. Jouni Hertell), handling vocals, guitar and bass, of WOUNDS and KIDUTTAVA HENGENVETO issued tracks credited to INFILTRATOR on a split EP with ANIMAL FORESKIN in March 2006. Only 51 copies were released.

During 2006 The Warlock (a.k.a. Joakim Soldehed), and The Snake (Arto Ovaskainen), issued the January 2007 demo 'The Night Of Sorcery' under the EVIL WITCH banner. The pair also prepared a full-length album, billed 'Temple Of The Iron Witch', for 2007 release.

Anal System, Animal Foreskin (2000) (Demo).
... Rolling On Shit ..., Animal Foreskin (2001) (Demo). Pregnant Boy / Handicapped Pygmy As A Pet / Soak The Fart Back Inside Your Ass / Grandfather Ate His Organs In War / Shave The Animals / Grilled Before Killed / Anal Manual / True African Black Metal / Enlarging Already 58 cm Dick / Bomb In A Womb / Shitting From The Helicopter / Orgiastic Pleasures With A Michael Jackson-Poster / Fuckdog / Massive Mass-Masturbation.
Tracks For Fags, Animal Foreskin (2002) (Demo).
Sledgehammer Sodomizer, Animal Foreskin (2003). Assborn / Lust For Bottled Camel-Cum / Sledgehammer Sodomizer / Brutal Shit Orgy / Voi Jeesus / Fuckdog.
Animal Foreskin / Infiltrator, (2006) (Split EP with INFILTRATOR. Limited edition 51 copies). I Prefer Panda-Porn / Things That Have Been in My Ass / Running Like Retard, Throwing Ball Like a Little Girl / List Of Neighbourhood Pets I've Recently Raped.

ANIMOSITY

STAFFORDSHIRE, UK — *Benjamin Hoare (vocals), Matt Doughty (guitar), Shane Turner (bass), Simon Heywood (drums).*

Stoke on Trent, Staffordshire Death Metal band ANIMOSITY, founded in late 1997, debuted with a March 1999 demo, entitled 'We Fear ...', recorded at Framework Studios in Birmingham with producer Paul Siddens. Working with Paul Hodson of HARD RAIN, A.N.D. and the BOB CATLEY band acting as engineer a second, self-titled session arrived in 2001. 'Awakening To A Black-Core Dawn' followed in 2002, this set of tracks laid down in Telford and produced by CANCER drummer Karl Stokes. Line-up changes saw the exit of guitarist Duncan Rathband in November 2002 and James Harper duly switched from bass to guitar in March 2003.

ANIMOSITY evolved into AFTER THE LAST SKY in 2004. A posthumous collection of tracks, suitably titled 'Animosity Are Fucking Dead ... Get Over It', was delivered that same year.

Guitarist Matthew Doughty also operates with Noisecore merchants FUCKHATEPROPAGANDA. Drummer Simon Heywood holds ties to FIRETHORN and THE POWER OF ISILDOR. Benjamin Hoare fronts Nottingham Grind outfit INERT.

We Fear, Animosity (1999). Full Body Eclipse / Carninogenic Sympathy / The Epic.
Animosity, (2001). Await The Red River / Wound Too Tight And Aiming For Ulcers In Just 5 Years / Crosses Against The Sky.
Awakening To A Black-Core Dawn, (2002). Tsunami / ... But One Lost Soul In The Valley Of Kings ... / Curse The Temple Of Doom.
ANIMOSITY ARE FUCKING DEAD ... GET OVER IT, (2004). Full Body Eclipse / Carninogenic Sympathy / The Epic / Await The Red River / Wound Too Tight And Aiming For Ulcers In Just 5 Years / Crosses Against The Sky / Tsunami / ... But One Lost Soul In The Valley Of Kings ... / Curse The Temple Of Doom.

ANNIHILATION

KIRUNA, SWEDEN — *Phan Cullhaven (vocals / bass), Muerte (guitar), Mr. Rocker (guitar), Deathking (drums).*

Kiruna Death Metal band rooted in the band REDRUM, an act that had previously issued the December 2000 'Murder Industry' demo. REDRUM had been created by former APOCALYPTIC VISIONS and NAGRIM drummer Deathking alongside guitarist Muerte (a.k.a. Mårten Eliasson), former ELEM and AMSVARTNER vocalist / guitarist Phan 'Phanskap' Cullhaven and bassist Tsenjo. With Tjenso's departure in February 2002 Cullhaven took over the bass role as the band name switched to ANNIHILATION. Following an inaugural live performance the group added guitarist Mr. Rocker. The 'Analsex66' demo arrived in January 2003.

Cullhaven is also an active member of VREDE and, alongside Das Übergay (Jonas Auoja), Thrashers DEADLOCK.

Analsex66, Annihilation (2003) (Demo). Jehova / Suicide / Under The Flesh / Soul / Thrash The Cross / The Annihilation Song / The Lies Left Behind.

ANNULATION

SWITZERLAND — *Dominique Weber (vocals / guitar), Martin Rötlisberger (guitar), Patric Bauer (bass), Simon Rüegger (drums).*

Death Metal act ANNULATION, created by vocalist / guitarist Dominique Weber and drummer Simon Rüegger augmented by guitarist Tin and bassist Paddy, debuted with a four song demo in July of 2001. They followed with the first album 'Burning Times', recorded at Studio Schweinesound in Sedel during 2002. In February of the following year Paddy exited and the band utilised Tom of MAROONED as fill in before they acquired a new bassist in Reto D'Amelio.

ANNULATION's 2004 album 'Human Creatures' closed with a live cover version of SEPULTURA's 'Roots Bloody Roots'. The band gained the valuable support to NUCLEAR ASSAULT's 2005 European tour dates throughout June and August.

BURNING TIME, Independent (2002). Burning Time / No Masterhood / Murderer / Fuck All / Away / Die Fucking Beast / Power Of The Night / Call From A Lord.

HUMAN CREATURES, Record & Play (2004). Siege Of Fear / Fuck All / Human Creatures / Soul Get Out / Confused / Crow Song / Murderer / Radical Shift / Roots Bloody Roots (Live).

ANPHISBENAH

PORTO ALEGRE, RS, BRAZIL — *Cesar Decesaro (vocals / bass), Anderson Alves Oliveira (guitar), Ricardo Cury Lopes (guitar), Trouver Silveira Felix (drums).*

ANPHISBENAH date to 1993, finding a stable line up during 1996. Demand for a 1998 demo 'Initiates The Horrendous' would be so high the band duly manufactured the recordings onto a CD EP. The band's line up at this juncture stood at vocalist / bassist Cesar Decesaro, guitarists Anderson Alves Oliveira and Ricardo Cury Lopes with Trouver Silveira Felix on the drums. By 2003 the band had undergone a complete overhaul, ANPHISBENAH now counting Decesaro and Lopes fronting a whole new unit comprising bassist Andre Marques and drummer Jeronimo Trouver. ANPHISBENAH cut the 2004 EP 'Infinite Mutable Fundamental Form' at Studio 1000 in Porto Alegre working with producer Fabio Lentino.

Initiates The Horrendous EP, M.M. Hardgore Music (1999). Rise Supreme / Prophecy Of Chaos / Portal Of Insanity / Blind Guidance.

Infinite Mutable Fundamental Form, (2004). Perpetuation / I Am The Resistance / Marcha Funebre / Testimony / Into The Sickroom / My Church / Rise Supreme.

ANTAGONIST

WHITTIER, CA, USA — *Carlos Garcia (vocals / guitar), Matt Lopez (guitar), Paul Salem (bass), Lord Garcia (drums).*

Whittier, Los Angeles Metalcore band ANTAGONIST date to 1998, initially forged as a quartet of vocalist / guitarist Carlos Garcia, guitar player David Zamora, bassist Marcus Hill and drummer Lond Garcia. First recorded outing would be a 1999 boombox demo. In 2000 ANTAGONIST put out an eponymous album, capitalised on by a 2000 EP 'Winnetka' and then 2001's 'Simple' and 'Time For Pain' singles. The 'Writings On The Wall' EP arrived in 2002. The bass position would be stabilised by Paul Salem, a scene veteran of AS HOPE DIES, BLACKHEART EULOGY and WINDS OF PLAGUE in 2003. A demo, entitled 'Intended To Hurt Or Wound', was distributed at shows during 2003. In May 2004 ANTAGONIST utilised Lovejuice Labs Studios to cut the self-financed EP 'Eschatology'. 1000 copies were manufactured. Another EP, 'Samsara' restricted to just 250 copies, followed in 2005.

Working with producer Scott Siletta the group recorded the full-length album 'The Architecture Of Discord' at Orange Crush Studios in Orange County for 2005 release.

Dwell Records contracted the group for another album, 'An Envy Of Innocence', issued in November 2006. ANTAGONIST joined forces for on a two week tour with fellow California bands LIGHT THIS CITY and THE FACELESS throughout February and March 2007.

Intended To Hurt Or Wound, Antagonist (2003) (Demo). Your Face Deserves A Crowbar / A Lesson In Confusion / Welcome To Your Letdown / Zero The Magic Number / Deloros Has Pretty Eyes.

Samsara, Antagonist (2005). Valor And Villainy / The Renouncement / Immaculate Misconception / Samsara.

THE ARCHITECTURE OF DISCORD, Antagonist (2005). The Nameless Shall Inherit The Earth / Pureza De Sangre / A Dying Sun / The 7th Vile / Your Face Deserves A Crowbar / The Nothing / Self-Strangulation / Redemption / Escape The Aftermath.

Eschatology, Antagonist (2006) (Limited edition 1000 copies). Kyrie Eleison / Redemption / In The Name Of Fear / The 7th Vile / And There Was Silence.

AN ENVY OF INNOCENCE, Dwell (2006). The Chaos We Breathe / Unless … / Liberation / Eyes Wide Shut / Despiertate / The Renouncement / Samsara / Valor And Villainy / Night Light / Heal, My Wound.

ANTARCTICA

RØYKEN, NORWAY — *Rune Andreassen (vocals), Frode Ramsland (guitar), Geir Solli (bass), Morten Skogen (keyboards / drums).*

Black / Death exponents ANTARCTICA debuted in Røyken during 1999, as a trio comprising Rune Andreassen on vocals and bass, guitarist Frode Ramsland with Morten Skogen handling both keyboards and drums, with the 'Bulder Fra Nord' demo session. Following a period of stasis enforced by members obligations to Norway's national military service, bass player Geir Solli was inducted for a second demo 'Erasing Mankind' in 2001. ANTARCTICA issued the third demo 'Unleash The Dogs Of War' on CD in October 2002.

Both vocalist Rune Andreassen and guitarist Frode Ramsland joined DISIPLIN during early 2005. The pair would also activate Death Metal combo SHAARIMOTH in union with Haakon Nikolas Forwald of DISIPLIN and MYRKSKOG.

Bulder Fra Nord, Antarctica (1999) (Demo). Intro / Vise Ord / Vinden / Nattetid / Bulder Fra Nord / Norren Makt / Nattens Barn.

Erasing Mankind, Antarctica (2001) (Demo). Erasing Mankind / Non Existence / Failed Humanity / The Grandure Hate / Deathfields / Eternal Infernal.

Unleash The Dogs Of War, Antarctica (2002) (Demo). When Weapons Decide / So Many Assholes—So Few Bullets / Forever Reign In Terror / Peace Means Nothing But Reloading Your Weapons / Hate Domain.

ANTARKTIS UTOPIA

SAVONLINNA, FINLAND — *Anssi (vocals / guitar), Henkka (vocals / guitar), Jyrki (bass), Miikka (drums).*

ANTARKTIS UTOPIA is a technical Death Metal act hailing from Savonlinna. The group would be founded during 1997, citing an opening line-up of lead vocalist Tero, guitarists Ansgaros (Anssi) and Aapo with A'raz on drums. Early changes saw the disappearance of Tero, superseded by Miika, and the exit of Aapo. Further changes found Klonkku (Henkka) introduced on second guitar and Sampsa taking on the vocal role. A demo emerged in August 2000 but by 2002 ANTARKTIS UTOPIA was down to the trio of Ansgaros, A'raz and Klonkku. Bassist Valtteri was incorporated but did not last the course. Jesse took his position but he too left. To make matter worse A'raz took time out from the band to undertake the very un-metallic pursuit of garden study.

Ansgaros and Klonkku regrouped in 2003, enrolling new drummer Miikka for the three song demo 'Views From Above' in November. ANTARKTIS UTOPIA issued the 'Self-Destruction' demo in November 2005. ANTARKTIS UTOPIA projected album recordings, dubbed '030550', for 2006.

Antarktis Utopia, Antarktis Utopia (2000). Shadow In Beauty / Midnight's Eternity / And The Blind Ones Shall See / Ode To The Meteoric Banishment.

Promo 2002, Antarktis Utopia (2002) (Demo). Shadow In Beauty / Midnight's Eternity / And The Blind Ones Shall See / Ode To The Meteoric Banishment / In Vanishing Point / The World According To A Madman / World Expired / From The Heart Of Hell / Utopian.

Views From Above, Antarktis Utopia (2003) (Demo). Machinery Of Death / The Room / Universal Truths.

Self-Destruction, Antarktis Utopia (2005) (Demo). I Of The Enemy / Possessed By Hyurii / Reactivation.

030550, Antarktis Utopia (2007). Intro / The Shape Of Things To Come / Cold Front / Aeternum Vale / Prelude To … / Cleansing / Harvesters Of Human Flesh / Celestial Deception / Blood Of A Thousand / Shadow In Beauty 2006 / Territory.

ANTIGAMA

POLAND — *Lucasz Myszkowski (vocals), Sebastian Rokicki (guitar), Michal Pietrasik (bass), Krzysztof Bentkowski (drums).*

ANTIGAMA is an avant-garde Grind act forged in Warsaw during 2002. The opening line-up comprised guitarist Sebastian Rokicki of GARDEN OF WORM and DIFFERENT STATE alongside the MONEV, DAMNABLE and SPARAGMOS credited Krzysztof Bentkowski on drums. Building up the band to full strength would be Lukasz Myszkowski, another SPARAGMOS veteran, and Macio Moretti on bass. This unit signed to the Italian label The Flood Records for a debut album 'Intellect Made Us Blind'.

September of 2001 witnessed the 'Grind Manifesto 2001' Polish tour in alliance with DAMNABLE and BRAINWASH. A line-up change in 2002 saw REINFECTION's Michal Pietrasik enrolling on bass guitar to record tracks used for a split CD in union with Jan Fredericx's of AGATHOCLES project entitled JAN AG. A second 'Grind Manifesto 2002' tour then ensued packaged with Italian acts NEFAS and BASTARD SAINTS together with fellow Poles PIGNATION and TOXIC BONKERS.

ANTIGAMA's 2003 campaign opened with the inclusion of their rendition of 'Anything Is Mine' to a GODFLESH tribute album published by French label Nihilistic Holocaust. In July the highly experimental 'Clint Eastwood' would form up their half of a split EP with Japanese band DERANGED INSANE on Mortville Records from the USA.

The group entered Selani Studios in Olsztyn with producer Szymon Czech to craft the 'Discomfort' album for Ohio based Extremist Records in August of 2003, hooking up with THIRD DEGREE and PIGNATION for another round of the 'Grind Manifesto 2003' trek. A shared cassette with ELYSIUM also saw delivery.

The year 2004 was introduced with a ten date national tour partnered with DEFORMED. A further split effort, issued through Antiself Productions, emerged with Australian band OPEN WOUND. In June ANTIGAMA recorded six brand new songs on three way split CD 'The World Will Fall Soon And We All Will Die' allied with THIRD DEGREE and HERMAN RAREBELL on Selfmadegod Records. HERMAN RAREBELL is, confusingly, not the well known ex-SCORPIONS drummer but an ANTIGAMA side project of 'Szklany' (a.k.a. Sebastian Rokicki) and 'Siwy' (Krzysztof Bentkowski) in partnership with THIRD DEGREE vocalist Czarny and bassist Fazi.

Shortly after recording ANTIGAMA put in an appearance at the major 'Obscene Extreme' festival in the Czech Republic prior to tackling recording for a new album. ANTIGAMA released their third full-length album, entitled 'Zeroland', through Selfmadegod Records on November 1st 2005. The album was recorded during March in Olsztyn with producer Szymon Czech.

ANTIGAMA signed to Relapse Records in May 2006. The 'Resonance' album was recorded in December at Studio X in Olsztyn, Poland by engineer Szymon Czech. In March 2007 the group partnered with DRUGS OF FAITH from Virginia, USA for a split 3" CD release via Selfmadegod Records, the band donating two original tracks plus a GOBLIN cover version.

INTELLECT MADE US BLIND, (2003). Pandemorphia / Spare Some Change / Come + Go / A Tendency To Sleep / Synthesis / Everything Is Normal / Savoir-Vivre Mastas / Filth And Pain / Fala / Improv.

THE WORLD WILL SOON FALL AND WE WILL ALL DIE, SelfmadeGod SMG 011 (2004) (Split album with HERMAN RAREBELL and THIRD DEGREE). Imperfection / Search / Questions / In A Room With Blue Walls / Repeatedness / Snuffbabe.

ZEROLAND, SelfmadeGod SMG 021 (2005). Seed / Izaak / Jazzy / Starshit / How / The View / Wounded Butterfly / Sorry / Zeroland.

ANVIL OF DOOM

CÁDIZ, SPAIN — *Beltrán (vocals), Hugo (guitar), Alois (guitar), Paco (keyboards), Ale (bass), Matoto (drums).*

ANVIL OF DOOM are rooted in the 1996 formation AKELARRE, this unit comprising vocalists Darío and Héctor with guitar players Javier Pinto and Álvaro. By 1998 the moniker ANVIL OF DOOM had been adopted with an all new line-up seeing Álvaro and Pinto joined by ex-SOMBRA vocalist Beltrán and former ALABANZA drummer Alonso for a Thrash orientated demo 'My Conscience'.

Subsequent recruits into the ANVIL OF DOOM fold would include bassist David Escudero and drummer Paco Herrera but by 2000 the group had been whittled back down to the duo of Pinto and Beltrán. Bringing in guitarist Hugo the band adopted a more melodic, Scandinavian style stance. The EP 'Died Before Dawn' arrived in September of 2002 through the Xtreem Music label.

Died Before Dawn EP, Xtreem Music (2002). Millennium / … Waiting / H3 / Anvil Of Doom.

DEATHILLUSION, Xtreem Music (2004).

APHASIA

CANADA — *Stéphane Houle (guitar / vocals), Phillipe Moreau (bass / vocals), Simon Chenier (drums).*

Montreal based APHASIA blend Black and Death Metal styles. The group came together as a quartet in 1995 citing a roster of vocalist / guitarist Stéphane Houle, guitarist Jean-Francois Girard, bassist Guillame Couture and drummer Ugo Bosse. In this incarnation APHASIA performed their first gig in March of 1996. A track 'Stormbound' was recorded for an intended compilation album but this release never transpired. Shortly after Couture broke ranks and Girard switched from the guitar role to that of bassist / vocalist.

In March of 1998 the band entered the studio to cut the self financed four track EP 'Beyond The Infinite Horizon', benefiting from the engineering skills of KATAKLYSM's Francois Dagenais. APHASIA would then experience a series of line up ructions, which stalled live progress in promoting the release.

First Bosse made his exit in August of 1998. It would only be in December that APHASIA pulled in substitute Julien Mercer but he too departed shortly after. Simon Chenier eventually took the position. However, the line up was still not settled as Girard too decamped. The vacancy was duly filled by Phillipe Moreau in time for recording of the full length album 'Arcane In Thalassa', released by the newly formed Grind It! Label.

Beyond The Infinite Horizon EP, (1998). Seasonal Stowaway / The Endless Swamp / Quest For Eternal Life / The Bright Sphere Of Forest.

ARCANE IN THALASSA, Grind It! (2001). Devastating Wind / Merging Process / Passion Of Time / Beyond The Infinite Horizon / Learning From The Unknown Image / Cries Form Despair / L'Absolu Ment / Stormbound.

APHELON

CHRISTCHURCH, NEW ZEALAND — *Okoi Jones (vocals / guitar), Brad Kneale (bass), Cam Sinclair (programming / drums).*

APHELON was formed in the Summer of 2000 by Schemata (Okoi Jones) on lead vocals and guitar with Nemesyss (Cam Sinclair) on programming and drums, both previously active with ELDAR V.T.B., issuing a 2000 demo entitled 'Wastelands'. Inspired by the Scandinavian Black/Extreme Metal scene APHELON began writing original material. A period of failed relationships with bass and guitar members saw the bands' line-up go through several changes. However in 2001 a stable line-up was achieved upon entrance of bass player Brad Kneale. APHELON performed at the annual Christchurch 'Satanfest' in 2001 alongside Australians MISERY and domestic acts DAWN OF AZAZEL, MEATYARD and SKULDOM. Released just prior to this event would be the 'Deathdrone' demo, privately issued and restricted to just twenty copies.

Adding second guitarist Kultur (a.k.a. Nik Coulter) the band again played 'Satanfest' in alliance with DAWN OF AZAZEL, SKULDOM, MEATYARD and SINISTROUS DIABOLIS. The band also opened for veteran Austrian Death Metal pioneers PUNGENT STENCH and US outfit INCANTATION. Next demo 'The Ethos Elite', recorded at Ear Candy studios in Christchurch, was released in April 2003 and included a cover version of 'Wipe Out Christianity', originally by SINISTROUS DIABOLIS. During August of 2003 Lycanthropic Fervour Records re-issued 'The Ethos Elite' in CD format, adding an extra track 'Liars Bound', in time for the band's third 'Satanfest' performance, sharing the stage this time with MISERY, MALEVOLENCE, BACKYARD BURIAL, MEATYARD and ODIUSEMBOWL.

In 2004 APHELON contributed the tracks 'The Curse Of Soil And Blood' and 'Opposing The Pityfilth' to the 'Morbid Music Vol. 1' compilation album. The group also saw a further re-issue of 'The Ethos Elite', adding a multimedia section revealing band details, photos and internet links. This version, limited to 50 hand numbered copies, was disseminated to European audiences on tour dates by DAWN OF AZAZEL. That year the band was down to a trio, minus Kultur. APHELON folded in 2006, closing out with an EP entitled 'Blood Blasted Bronze'.

The Ethos Elite, Lycanthropic Fervour LFR001 (2003). The Curse Of Soil And Blood / Opposing The Pityfilth / Liars Bound / A Silent Drowning / Apostles Of My Vices.

The Ethos Elite, Lycanthropic Fervour (2004) (European promotion release). PC CDROM Data Track / The Curse Of Soil & Blood / Opposing The Pityfilth / Liars Bound / A Silent Drowning / Apostles Of My Vices.

SCORN SHALL PREVAIL, Lycanthropic Fervour LFR002 (2005). Paean Empyrosis / Miasma (Scorn Shall Prevail) / The Trial / A Silent Drowning / Bloodborne / Liars Bound / A Will To Terror (We Will Forever) / The Curse Of Soil And Blood / Wipe Out Christianity / Ashen Echoes.

APHOTIC

GREEN BAY, WI, USA — *Chad (vocals / bass), Keith Powers (guitar / keyboards), Steve (guitar), Jason (drums).*

Green Bay, Bleak, ambient Doom-Death. APHOTIC was forged in April of 2000 by former CRAWL and DUSK members, vocalist Chad, bass guitarist / programmer Keith Powers and guitarist Steve. Upon completion of recording the debut 'Aphotic' EP, cut in just seven hours, the band underwent a change switching Powers to guitar and adding bass to Chad's duties. In August of 2001 this format crafted the follow up 'Under Veil Of Dark'. Expanding further with the addition of drummer Jason APHOTIC then recorded third set 'Stillness Grows'. However, this material would not be released.

The 2004 APHOTIC release through Flood The Earth Records compiled all of the band's previous recordings, an eponymous EP, the 'Stillness Grows' material and the 'Under Veil Of Dark' sessions.

Aphotic EP, Independent (2000). Liquid Dread / Glide / Psychoma / A Chance To Live / Panoramic.

Under Veil Of Dark EP, Independent (2001). Precipice / Under Veil Of The Endless Grey Sky / Atmosphere / Free Me.

STILLNESS GROWS, Flood The Earth FTE01 (2004).

APIARY

SAN JOSE, CA, USA — *Jason Ingram (vocals), Mike McClatchey (guitar), Pete Layman (guitar), Dave Small (bass), Adam Elliott (drums).*

San Jose, California's APIARY, manifested by former members of SOMETHING MUST DIE and CLEARING AUTUMN SKIES, signed to Ironclad Recordings, the label formed by UNEARTH frontman Trevor Phipps, in September 2005. APIARY's debut album, 'Lost in Focus', was released in May 2006, recorded at Castle Ultimate Studios in Emeryville, California with Zack Orhen.

In August 2006 the group underwent a major reshuffle, losing vocalist Jason Ingram whilst Peter Layman moved over from his guitar duties into the singer spot and Chris Brock came into the band as new guitarist. APIARY toured the US alongside THE ABOMINABLE IRON SLOTH in September. Further dates, commencing November 17th at Jerry's Pizza in Bakersfield, California, hooked the band up with THE FUNERAL PYRE and DRYLINE into late December. APIARY introduced new singer Makh Daniels, previously with CLEARING AUTUMN SKIES and BETRAY THE SPECIES, in December 2006.

APIARY set out on the 'Two Dollar Brawler' US tour allied with THE HANDSHAKE MURDERS, LIGEIA and BURN IN SILENCE during February and into March 2007. The band hit the US touring circuit again in June as part of the "First Post Tour", featuring THE DESTRO, UNHOLY, YEAR OF DESOLATION and ISCARIOT in rotating stage slots.

LOST IN FOCUS, Metal Blade 7058337 (2006). Pain Is The Reason / Descent / Extract / Omnipresence / Intervention / Bliss In Vain / Forced To Breathe / Lustrum / Peril's Divinity / Solidified Foundation / Fading Imprint / These Walls Are Permanent / Finding A Way Back.

APOKALYPTIC RAIDS

RIO DE JANEIRO, RJ, BRAZIL — *Nekromaniac (vocals / guitar), Sub Umbra (bass), Skullcrusher (drums).*

Rio De Janeiro trio founded in 1997 and massively influenced by the genre defining HELLHAMMER right down to the band name and album cover artwork. The group would operate as 'APOCALYPTIC RAIDS' until 2001, when the subtle incorporation of a 'K' was made. Following the self issued 1999 EP APOKALYPTIC RAIDS signed to the Demise label for 2000's full length 'Only Death Is Real …'

The band- Gustavo Belo—'Adrameleck' (Witch Hunts & Machine Guns), Leon Manssur—'Nekromaniac' (6-String Damnation & Vokills) and A. Aguinaga—'Sub Umbra' (Low Frequency Armageddon). Manssur also has affiliations with NIGHTBREED and EXPLICIT HATE whilst Aguinaga is operational with POETICUS SEVERUS. Belo had usurped 'Hofgodhar' on bass, this former candidate in actuality being Eduardo of NOCTURNAL WORSHIPPER and SONGE D'ENFER.

During 2001 APOKALYPTIC RAIDS shared a split 7" single, 'Maximum Metal Mayhem' released by the underground German label Iron Bonehead Productions, with the American act GRAVEWURM. The 2003 album 'The Return Of The Satanic Rites' saw Skullcrusher (a.k.a. Pedro Rocha of FARSCAPE) installed on the drums. The band returned in 2005 with third outing 'The Third Storm—World War III', this seeing a version of HELLHAMMER's 'Revelations Of Doom'.

Apocalyptic Raids EP, (1999). Evil / The Impaler / Tyrant, Emperor / Apocalyptic Raids.

APOKALYPTIC RAIDS (pic: Victor "Whipstriker")

ONLY DEATH IS REAL . . ., Demise DMS CD019 (2000). The Enemy (Intro) / Evil / Forgotten Tales / Into The Twilight Zone / Eternal Gloom / Angels Of Hell / Humankind Dies / Tyrant, Emperor / Apocalyptic Raids / Tales Of Horror (Outro).

Maximum Metal Mayhem, Iron Bonehead Productions (2001) (Split single with GRAVEWURM). Maximum Metal Mayhem.

THE RETURN OF THE SATANIC RITES, Dark Sun SUN 006 (2003). Apokalyptic Raids / Ready To Go (To Hell) / The Atheist / The Way Of The Warrior / Satanic Slaughter / Impaler / Emperor's Return / Skullkrusher / Voyeur.

THE THIRD STORM—WORLD WAR III, Dark Sun (2005). I'm A Metal Head / Fallen Beyond Hope / Vision Shadows / Manifesto Politicamente Incorreto / Never Forget What You Are / Humankind Dies / Mankind Defeated (Humankind Dies pt. II) / The Power in My Mind / When The World Ends In Fire (Metal Returns) / I'm A Metal Head (Reprise).

APOKRIFOS

MEXICO — *Blasphem (vocals), Demon Mutilator (guitar), Leobardo (guitar), Kan (bass), Ravenous Cujo (drums).*

Tula based Blasphemic Death Metal band APOKRIFOS debuted in 1997 with the demo 'Fatal Demencia'. The group had been forged during 1995 by vocalist Blasphem and guitarist Smith, later pulling in guitarist Dark, bassist George Satanas and drummer Anticristo. The band would evolve further to incorporate guitarist Blacksoul, bassist Kan and drummer Alberto Gargola. Following recording of the demo Carlos 'Wolfman' Barkley took control of the drums.

The self financed March 2003 album 'R. A. M.' ("Ruido Apokaliptiko Milenario") closed out with an ANARCHUS cover version 'Jesus Christ', also featured on the tribute album 'Beyond Good And Evil'.

R.A.M., Apokrifos (2003). Judas / Moscas (El Ejercito De Los Gusanos) / Sex, Oral, Bitch / Promiscuidad / Snta Decepción / R. A. M. / El Ultimo Grito / Jesus Christ.

APOSTASY

NORTH HAVEN, CT, USA — *Ryan Early (vocals), Danielle Gambardella (guitar), Joe Tursi (guitar / vocals), Zach Green (bass / vocals), Gus Griffen (drums).*

APOSTASY was formulated under the formative banner of HOLLOW POINT in the Summer of 2002 by vocalist / guitarist Ryan Early and drummer Nicole Sestito. Subsequently, guitarist John DeAngelo was enrolled as initial writing sessions led to a name switch to DRESSED IN BLACK. Early the next year second guitarist Danielle Gambardella was inducted, freeing Ryan Early up to prioritise lead vocals. Further material was penned, prompting another title switch to CORPORAL DOWNFALL, under which brand the demo 'Black Winter' was crafted.

Yet another name change, to NECROSIS, saw the introduction of keyboard player Jaime Pompilli and bassist Madison Roseberry. The band inaugurated itself on the live front on 16th August 2003 performing a rain shortened set alongside ALL UNDONE. The group then went into a lengthy period of stasis, broken with the acquisition of Dave Guckian on bass. The revised formation first performed live on 1st November, at the Polish National Alliance in Wallingford.

NECROSIS then unraveled as both Sestito and Guckian exited. Shortly after this defection Pompilli too opted out. The beginning of 2004 marked a new beginning as the remaining band members took on another title change to become APOSTASY. Bassist Zach Green was adopted in February and APOSTASY's stage debut, complete with drum machine, came on 13th March at a gig dubbed 'Rebfest', held in John DeAngelo's basement. The band put in two more gigs with the drum machine before being offered an album deal through Statue Records of California. Brett Pieper was installed on the drum stool and Rob Spalding for 'Shadows Of The Apocalypse' album recordings commencing in August. However, progress in the studio was minimal and Spalding was let go. The existing tapes would be scrapped and work began afresh, this time billing the album 'Invocation'.

Following a support gig to STRAPPING YOUNG LAD in Hartford in April of 2005 APOSTASY dispensed with Pieper's services. Drummer Mike Formanski would then be replaced by Gus Griffen. January of 2006 ushered in further changes with the recruitment of guitarist Joe Tursi.

Live At Rebfest, EarlCore Productions (2004). The New Millennium Holocaust / Damian / Anything To Belong / Dressed In Black / Society Is The Enemy / Pledge Your Allegiance / Sin America / Cataclysm Theory / Happy Song / Bloodlust.

Thornton Wilder Hall (Live), EarlCore Productions (2004). Bloodlust / Cataclysm Theory / Pledge Your Allegiance / Society Is The Enemy / Interstate Hate Song / The New Millennium Holocaust.

Black Summer Tour Demo, EarlCore Records (2004). Twilight Sonata / Bloodlust / Cataclysm Theory / Interstate Hate Song (Demo) / Malefaction (Demo) / The New Millennium Holocaust (Live) / Interstate Hate Song (Remix) / The New Millennium Holocaust (Live Video).

Shadows Of Autumn Tour Sampler, EarlCore Productions (2004). Exordium / No Tomorrow / 44 Minutes / Interstate Hate Song / Cataclysm Theory (Demo) / Nuclear Sunrise (Live) / Sin America (Live) / Bloodlust (Live) / Prelude To The Endtimes.

Spring Sampler, EarlCore Productions (2005). Intro / In God We Trust / Interstate Hate Song / No Tomorrow / 44 Minutes / Bloodlust 2003 / Society Is The Enemy (Live) / Pledge Your Allegiance (Live) / Nuclear Sunrise (Techno version) / Abortion 0235.

Shadows Over Stony Creek (Live), EarlCore Productions (2005). Intro / In God We Trust / No Tomorrow / The New Millennium Holocaust / Bloodlust / Nuclear Sunrise / Pledge Your Allegiance / Interstate Hate Song / Abortion 0235.

DISSECTION OF THEOCRACY, EarlCore Productions (2005). Invocation / Nuclear Sunrise / Vatican In Flames / In God We Trust / The New Millennium Holocaust / Eye Of The Storm / No Tomorrow / Pledge Your Allegiance / Interstate Hate Song / U.S.S.R. / Aftermath.

Summer Campaign Sampler, EarlCore Productions (2005). In God We Trust (Demo) / Interstate Hate Song (Video Edit) / No Tomorrow (2005 Demo) / Cataclysm Theory (2004 Demo) / 44 Minutes.

THE END OF PARADISE, (2006). Revelation 12 / Humanitarian Genocide / Building Bridges To Burn / Oracle Of Desolation / Tunguska / A Thousand Ways To Destroy A Man / My Declaration / Tsavo / Disaster Holiday / The End Of Paradise / Where The River Flows.

TRANSCENSION, Sonic Overload (2006). Invocation / Tunguska 1908 / Building Bridges To Burn / A Thousand Ways To Destroy A Man / Nuclear Sunrise / Transcension / Aftermath.

APPROACHED BY A GOD

QUÉBEC, QC, CANADA — *Kevin Pettinella (vocals), Jérome Boucher (guitar), Maxime Huard (guitar), Mathieu Robichaud (bass), Louis Thivierge (drums).*

Québec Death Metal band APPROACHED BY A GOD was created by vocalist Kevin Pettinella and guitarist Jérôme Boucher in September 2004. Inducting guitarist Maxime Huard, bass player Nicolas Chabot and drummer Mario Forgue the group's live inauguration came in Québec City in April 2005. Forgue was replaced by Simon Frosst, who was in turn to exit a year later, after which Nicolas Chabot decamped.

APPROACHED BY A GOD issued a self-titled 2006 EP, these sessions featuring UTLAGR drummer François Fortin. Upon completion of these tracks the band enlisted a new rhythm section comprising bassist Mathieu Robichaud and drummer Louis Thivierge.

Approached By A God, Approached By A God (2006) (Demo). Urban Apocalypse / Find Your Daughter Before She Gets Killed / Deleted Scene / Cut Yourself.

ARCANUM

VIENNA, AUSTRIA — *Peter Kernstock (vocals), Gabriel Lafranco (guitar), Julian Dölcher (guitar), Rudolf Galler (bass), Peter Langenecker (drums).*

ARCANUM is a Vienna Death Metal act forged in 2004. The group features ex-DIABOLICA singer Peter Kernstock plus two erstwhile INJECTION members, guitarist Gabriel Lafranco and drummer Peter Langenecker. Manuel Höller took on secondary guitar duties whilst Rudolf Galler initially handled bass. ARCANUM bassist Bernadette S., another DIABOLICA veteran, was inducted and in this formation the group won the Black Lagoon 'Battle of the Bands' contest. Bernadette was then replaced by Rudi.

The demo 'Chaos Arise' was issued in April 2006. ARCANUM brought in second guitarist Julian Dölcher and re-instated Rudolf Galler. Noisehead Records released the album 'What If You Die Tomorrow . . .' in February 2007.

Chaos Arise, Arcanum (2006) (Demo). Intro / Legio Astartes / Ygramul / Chaos Arise / Fimbul Winter.

WHAT IF YOU DIE TOMORROW . . . , Noisehead (2007). Prologue / Chaos Arise / One Bullet Left / Behind The Paradise / Urkraft / Legio Astartes / Cerberus / Dunelord / Damien's Torture / Fimbul Winter / Ragnaröck.

ARCANUM

FINLAND — *Taavi Forssell (vocals / guitar), Heikki Aronen (guitar), Juha Kettunen (bass), Tuukka Jääskeläinen (keyboards), Marco Lauriola (drums).*

ARCANUM was a precursor to DAWN OF CREATION. The incepting ALFTHAR unit had formulated as a school band during May of 1999 and quoted a membership roster of vocalist Taavi Forssell, guitarists Esa Rauhala and Heikki Aronen, bassist Antti Vaha, keyboard player Mika Kurvinen with Marco Lauriola on the drums. This formation cut one demo, 'Dark Northern Land', and played one gig before both Vaha and Kurvinen both departed.

Regrouping, the band drafted Tuukka Jääskeläinen on keyboards then Juha Kettunen on bass guitar but then suffered the loss of Rauhala. With Forssell taking on guitar duties, a decision was taken to re-name the band DUSK in late 1999. Demos were recorded in 2001 but an unsatisfied band chose not to release these tracks. In 2003 DUSK morphed into ARCANUM, laying down the demo 'Children Of The Night' at Hyvinkää's Rockstar Studios.

Line-up changes saw the exit of both guitarist Heikki Aronen and keyboard player Tuukka Jääskeläinen. Re-billed as DAWN CREATION the band, having acquired guitarist Jan Jokinen and keyboard player Heidi Hakoinen, issued the demo 'System Overload' in 2004.

Children Of The Night, Arcanum (2003) (Demo). Children Of The Night / Crimson Sky / Deathrow / Fallen Angel.

ARCH ENEMY

HALMSTAD, SWEDEN — *Angela Gossow (vocals), Mike Amott (guitar), Christopher Amott (guitar), Sharlee D'Angelo (bass), Daniel Erlandsson (drums).*

Old style extreme Metal band ARCH ENEMY, based in Halmstad, feature ex-members of CARNAGE, CARCASS and EUCHARIST. Despite ploughing a niche market ARCH ENEMY have managed to attain a degree of commercial success, particularly in Japan. A switch in singers and a quite awesome live campaign would transfer their European and Asian support to the USA, ARCH ENEMY breaking onto the Billboard charts in 2003 with 'Anthems Of Rebellion'.

Frontman Johan Liiva previously played with CARNAGE and FURBOWL whilst guitarist Mike Amott, best known for his role in CARCASS, was also once a CARNAGE member early on and, in addition to ARCH ENEMY, performed in parallel in SPIRITUAL BEGGARS. Christopher Amott, Mike's younger brother, would appear to be following in his brother's footsteps by not laying all his eggs in one basket by also contributing to his side band ARMAGEDDON, whilst drummer Daniel Erlandsson occasionally sat in with IN FLAMES and was previously with EUCHARIST.

The opening ARCH ENEMY album, 1996's 'Black Earth' produced by Fredrik Nordström at Studio Fredman and originally released through Wrong Again Records, a mix of Thrash and Death elements but delivered in a quite unique style, would prove to be a genuine groundbreaking release, the resulting word of mouth amongst the Metal cognoscenti prompting huge world wide sales and respect. 'Black Earth' found ARCH ENEMY more of a solo effort conducted by Mike Amott rather than a full band release, the guitarist composing all of the material and, in spite of sleeve credits to the contrary giving Johan Liiva bass credits, both guitar and bass. The record scored considerable success in Japan and a video clip for the song 'Bury Me An Angel' provided valuable global awareness. The band contributed a cover of 'Aces High' to the Toy's Factory Records tribute to IRON MAIDEN, namely the cheesily titled compilation album 'Made In Tribute'.

Christopher Amott, working in collaboration with along with IN THY DREAMS vocalist Jonas Nyrén and drummer Daniel Erlandsson, launched his side band entitled ARMAGEDDON shortly afterward, the album 'Crossing The Rubicon' arriving in 1997.

For their next record, ARCH ENEMY pulled in ARMAGEDDON bass player Martin Bengtsson to allow Liiva to prioritise his vocals whilst Peter Wildoer, of ARMAGEDDON, Helsingborg's AGRETATOR and earlier ZANINEZ, was recruited onto the drum stool for the next recording sessions. Fredrik Nordström once again manned the desk as ARCH ENEMY's second outing, April 1998's 'Stigmata', benefited from an upward label shift over to Germany's Century Media Records. Japanese editions boasted three extra tracks, 'Damnation's Way', 'Vox Stellarum' and 'Bridge Of Destiny'.

The band shifted shape again in 1999, Sharlee D'Angelo, also an active member of WITCHERY and MERCYFUL FATE as well as citing credits with SINERGY and DISMEMBER, assumed the role of permanent bassist, whilst Daniel Erlandsson was again invited to handle drum duties once again. That March the group undertook their first dates in South America co-headlining with fellow Swedes HAMMERFALL and also performed at the famed 'Dynamo' festival in the Netherlands. In the Autumn the band hit Europe for a full-scale tour, sharing stages on a package bill with DARK TRANQUILLITY, IN FLAMES and CHILDREN OF BODOM. However, US touring would see Dick Lövgren, a seasoned campaigner quoting credentials with ARMAGEDDON, CROMLECH, IN FLAMES and EUCHARIST amongst many others, installed in the four-string position.

ARCH ENEMY built up quite a global reputation with tours

of Japan and Europe. The band also opened for CRADLE OF FILTH in 1999, a support slot gained by admitted nepotism as Daniel Erlandsson's older brother Adrian had favourably gained the CRADLE OF FILTH drummer's job. Japanese versions of the Fredrik Nordström produced 'Burning Bridges' album, issued in July 1999, hosted extra tracks including a cover version of EUROPE's 'Scream Of Anger' plus a newly re-recorded version of 'Fields Of Desolation'. A live album, 'Burning Bridges In Japan', saw issue in Japan but fan pressure prompted a wider international release. Again the band recruited a temporary bassist for live action in 2000, Roger Nilson of SPIRITUAL BEGGARS, THE QUILL and FIREBIRD taking on the obligation this time around.

ARCH ENEMY would transform into a completely new beast for the next studio outing. The Amott siblings would be joined by German singer and journalist Angela Nathalie Gossow, previously with Cologne based acts ASMODINA and MISTRESS. Gossow had been prolific on the local scene, heading up ASMODINA for a November 1991 six song demo 'Your Hidden Fear' followed in February 1994 by 'The Story Of The True Human Personality' session. A further three track promotion outing was delivered in 1996 and the 'Inferno' album arrived in January of 1997 before a move was made to Death Rockers MISTRESS, featuring on two demos, May 1999's 'Worship The Temptress' and 2000's 'Party In Hell'. This band briefly operated as DEVIL IN THE DETAILS during which time Gossow opted out.

Ensconcing themselves in the familiar surrounds of Studio Fredman, the new unit worked with co-producer Fredrik Nordström, mixing the final tracks in league with erstwhile SABBAT guitarist Andy Sneap, to craft their comeback opus 'Wages Of Sin'. Any concerns over the incorporation of a female into the formula were blown away within seconds of Gossow's aural introduction, her bile, spit and venom easily outstripping her predecessor whilst the schizophrenic, twisted tongues approach, ranging from seductive whispers to trollish rumbles, gave ARCH ENEMY an entirely new character. 'Wages Of Sin' also marked a further turning point, often overlooked in the magnitude of Gossow's arrival, in that the Amotts shifted gear down to precision intimidation rather than the chaotic crunch that had previously driven all before them.

The ARCH ENEMY 'Wages Of Sin' album, arriving in April 2001, would see a belated North American release but did come complete with not only a bonus track 'Lament Of A Mortal Soul' and a video clip for 'Ravenous' but a whole separate CD of rarities. Included on the latter would be an unreleased version of JUDAS PRIEST's 'Starbreaker' plus covers of IRON MAIDEN's 'Aces High', EUROPE's 'Scream Of Anger' and a glut of bonus tracks originally only to be found on Japanese albums. The band would perform at the prestigious 2001 Japanese 'Beast Feast' Festival during August at the 30'000 capacity Yokohama Arena alongside SLAYER, V.O.D., STATIC X and SEPULTURA among others.

The ousted Johan Liiva announced the formation of a new endeavour in late 2001 billed as NONEXIST in union with Matte Modin of DEFLESHED and ANDROMEDA's Johan Reinholdz issuing the 'Deus Deceptor' album. However, by early 2002 the man had made a reappearance in HEARSE alongside former FURBOWL members drummer Max Thornell and guitarist Mattias Ljung for a debut 'Dominion Reptilian' album.

ARCH ENEMY toured Japan once again during March 2002 and put in debut British shows, as support to OPETH, in May. The band would be confirmed as one of the headline attractions at the mammoth 'Beast Fest' event in Japan during December of 2002, preceded by UK headliners with support coming from CORPORATION 187 and Hungarians WITHOUT FACE.

ARCH ENEMY guitarist Michael Amott laid down a guest solo on recording sessions by THE HAUNTED in November. As 2003 broke ARCH ENEMY put in January headline dates in Sweden, once again supported by CORPORATION 187. In April the band recorded new versions of 'Beneath The Skin', 'Young Man, Old Soul', 'Mantra' as well as a cover version of BACHMAN TURNER OVERDRIVE's 'Not Fragile' for a BBC radio session.

Sharlee D'Angelo was embroiled in a brand new side venture in early 2003 dubbed FIREGOD. This union saw the bassist uniting with an esteemed cast of MERCYFUL FATE and KING DIAMOND guitarist Mike Wead, the KING DIAMOND, DREAM EVIL and NOTRE DAME credited guitarist Snowy Shaw and drummer Simon Johansson of MEMORY GARDEN and ABSTRAKT ALGEBRA.

ARCH ENEMY, promoting new studio album 'Anthems Of Rebellion', would land a first by headlining the Busan International Rock Festival at Daedepo Beach in Korea on 8th August. The group then allied with HATE ETERNAL, EVERGREY and THE BLACK DAHLIA MURDER for a short but intensive run of US dates coming in mid August before pairing up with NEVERMORE for co-headline European gigs throughout September and October. The closing shows of this trek would be pulled though as ARCH ENEMY were dealt the quite unique blow of suffering from a bug infestation on their tour bus. Maintaining their road presence a lengthy string of US Jägermeister sponsored dates commencing 9th October and running through until mid December saw the band hooked up with SLAYER and HATEBREED. 'Anthems Of Rebellion', breaking the charts across Europe would prove to be Century Media's fastest ever selling record to date. In the USA the record took just three months to sell over 25,000 copies. UK dates in December allied the band with AKERCOCKE.

The band's profile rose higher into 2004 as ARCH ENEMY lent support to IRON MAIDEN's Canadian January dates and the British veterans four show run at New York City's Hammerstein Ballroom then Japanese gigs. European headline dates in February and March saw ZYKLON and STAMPIN' GROUND as support. However, gigs in Osnabruck, Essen and Antwerp would be pulled when Angela Gossow lost her voice. US gigs in April had the band scheduled as heavyweight support to MACHINE HEAD, although the band missed the first show, in Philadelphia on the 25th, due to an apparent delay in processing Angela Gossow's work visa. As it transpired the group then pulled out of the entire tour, headliners MACHINE HEAD issuing a sarcastic press statement claiming the band had withdrawn "because singer Angela 'Gossard' broke a fingernail which had recently been through a vigorous French manicure".

Returning to Japan as headliners, ARCH ENEMY put in a short burst of June dates. Meantime Daniel Erlandsson debuted his new act in mid 2004, REVENGIA issuing the opus 'A Decade In The Dark'. Michael Amott took time out to record a guest guitar solo for the song 'Murder Fantasies' on the latest KREATOR album. Amott's parallel act SPIRITUAL BEGGARS entered Studio Fredman in Gothenburg, Sweden in July with producer Fredrik Nordström to cut a new album. ARCH ENEMY's Sharlee D'Angelo would cut the bass guitar for these tracks.

November 'Headbanger's Ball III' US touring partners would be CRADLE OF FILTH, BLEEDING THROUGH and HIMSA. That same month a US issue of 'Dead Eyes See No Future' saw release whilst December saw the band on the road in Europe, forming up the 'Hammered at Xmas' tour in alliance with THE HAUNTED and DARK TRANQUILLITY. A London show would be filmed for DVD use. A 2005 compilation inclusion of note would be the track 'We Will Rise' featured on the 'Code Red' album, an exclusive collection given to US Marine Corps soldiers active duty in the Middle East.

In mid 2005 Greek guitarist Gus G. (a.k.a. Kostas Karamitroudis) of NIGHTRAGE, MYSTIC PROPHECY, DREAM EVIL and FIREWIND joined ARCH ENEMY as the group's touring guitarist for the US 'Ozzfest' festival dates after Christopher Amott bowed out of that band in order to "fully concentrate on his studies". The 'Doomsday Machine' arrived in stores worldwide during July. Japanese variants on the Toys Factory label added the traditional bonus tracks, live versions of 'Heart Of Darkness' and 'Bridge Of Destiny'. In the USA, the album sold just under 12,000 copies in its first week of release to debut at no. 87 on the Billboard charts.

Building the band back up to strength, new guitarist Fredrik Åkesson was inducted, a scene veteran of such acts as ONE CENT, TAURUS, TALISMAN, the JOHN NORUM band, KRUX, TIAMAT and SOUTHPAW. ARCH ENEMY's September and October European headline dates, taking in the UK, France, Belgium, Holland, Germany, Norway, Sweden and Denmark, saw strong support from TRIVIUM. The two bands stuck together for Japanese gigs in October. However, the UK dates were re-scheduled for December when co-headliner DARK TRANQUILLITY withdrew. STRAPPING YOUNG LAD duly joined forces for the tour. Meantime, the band engaged in touring throughout November in the USA sharing stages with ALL THAT REMAINS, MNEMIC and A PERFECT MURDER.

ARCH ENEMY, CHIMAIRA, NEVERMORE and HATE ETERNAL announced US shows for April 2006. That same month it was learned Gossow was set to feature as guest singer on the all female Greek Black Metal band ASTARTE's 'Demonized' album. ARCH ENEMY's Mexican debut came in May with shows in Monterrey and Mexico City. The band put in a significant appearance at the METALLICA and KORN headlined 'Download' festival in Castle Donington, UK on June 10th. ARCH ENEMY joined up with the MEGADETH headlined 'Gigantour' North American festivals in early September, sharing billing with OPETH, LAMB OF GOD, OVERKILL, INTO ETERNITY, SANCTITY and THE SMASHUP. The group returned to Scandinavia in November, heading up the 'Close Up made me do it' tour alongside COLDWORKER and PATH OF NO RETURN. December continental concerts were supported by Dutch act TEXTURES.

In January 2007 it was learned that Angela Gossow had contributed guest vocals to the AMASEFFER "Holy" project fronted by VANDEN PLAS vocalist Andy Kuntz in union with Israeli musicians guitarists Yuval Kramer, Hanan Abramovitch and drummer Erez Yohanan. South American concerts in February witnessed large crowds in Chile, Argentina and Brazil.

Guitarist Christopher Amott rejoined the ranks of ARCH ENEMY in March.

ARCH ENEMY (pic: Katja Kuhl)

Arch Enemy, Arch Enemy (1996) (Demo). Bury Me An Angel / Dark Insanity / Eureka / Idolatress.

BLACK EARTH, Wrong Again WAR011CD (1996). Bury Me An Angel / Dark Insanity / Eureka / Idolatress / Cosmic Retribution / Demoniality / Transmigration Macabre / Time Capsule / Fields Of Desolation.

BLACK EARTH, Toy's Factory TFCK-88792 (1996) (Japanese release). Bury Me An Angel / Dark Insanity / Eureka / Idolatress / Cosmic Retribution / Demoniality / Transmigration Macabre / Time Capsule / Fields Of Desolation / Losing Faith / The Ides Of March.

STIGMATA, Toy's Factory TFCK-87149 (1998) (Japanese release). Beast Of Man / Stigmata / Sinister Mephisto / Dark Of The Sun / Let The Killing Begin / Black Earth / Hydra / Tears Of The Dead / Diva Satanica / Damnations Way / Vox Stellarum / Bridge Of Destiny.

STIGMATA, Century Media 77212-2 (1998). Beast Of Man / Stigmata / Sinister Mephisto / Dark Of The Sun / Let The Killing Begin / Black Earth / Tears Of The Dead / Vox Stellarum / Bridge Of Destiny.

BURNING BRIDGES, Toy's Factory TFCK-87184 (1999) (Japanese release). The Immortal / Dead Inside / Pilgrim / Silverwing / Demonic Science / Seed Of Hate / Angelclaw / Burning Bridges / Scream Of Anger / Fields Of Desolation.

BURNING BRIDGES (LIMITED EDITION), Century Media 77276 (1999). The Immortal / Dead Inside / Pilgrim / Silverwing / Demonic Science / Seed Of Hate / Angelclaw / Burning Bridges / Diva Satanica / Hydra.

BURNING BRIDGES, Century Media 77276-2 (1999). The Immortal / Dead Inside / Pilgrim / Silverwing / Demonic Science / Seed Of Hate / Angelclaw / Burning Bridges.

BURNING JAPAN LIVE 1999, Toy's Factory TFCK-87217 (2000). The Immortal / Dark Insanity / Dead Inside / Diva Satanica / Pilgrim / Silverwing / Beast Of Man / Bass Intro / Tears Of The Dead / Bridge Of Destiny / Transmigration Macabre / Angelclaw.

WAGES OF SIN, Toy's Factory TFCK-87245 (2001) (Japanese release). Enemy Within / Burning Angel / Heart Of Darkness / Ravenous / Savage Messiah / Dead Bury Their Dead / Web Of Lies / The First Deadly Sin / Behind The Smile / Snow Bound / Shadows And Dust.

Burning Angel, Toy's Factory TFCK-87281 (2002) (Japanese release). Burning Angel / Lament Of A Mortal Soul / Starbreaker.

WAGES OF SIN, Century Media 77383-2 (2002) (2 CD). Enemy Within / Burning Angel / Heart Of Darkness / Ravenous / Savage Messiah / Dead Bury Their Dead / Web Of Lies / The First Deadly Sin / Behind The Smile / Snow Bound / Shadows And Dust / Lament Of A Mortal Soul / Ravenous (Video) / Starbreaker / Aces High / Scream Of Anger / Diva Satanica / Fields Of Desolation '99 / Damnation's Way / Hydra (Instrumental) / The Immortal (Video).

BLACK EARTH, Regain 002AS (2002). Bury Me An Angel / Dark Insanity / Eureka / Idolatress / Cosmic Retribution / Demoniality / Transmigration Macabre / Time Capsule / Fields Of Desolation / Losing Faith / The Ides Of March / Aces High.

STIGMATA, Dream On PARK-9023 (2003) (South Korean release). Beast Of Man / Stigmata / Sinister Mephisto / Dark Of The Sun / Let The Killing Begin / Black Earth / Hydra / Tears Of The Dead / Diva Satanica / Damnation's Way / Vox Stellarum / Bridge Of Destiny.

BURNING BRIDGES, Dream On PARK9024 (2003) (South Korean release). The Immortal / Dead Inside / Pilgrim / Silverwing / Demonic Science / Seed Of Hate / Angelclaw / Burning Bridges / Scream Of Anger / Fields Of Desolation.

ANTHEMS OF REBELLION, Toy's Factory TFCK-87322 (2003) (Japanese release). Tear Down The Walls / Silent Wars / We Will Rise / Dead Eyes See No Future / Instinct / Leader Of The Rats / Exist To Exit / Marching On A Dead End Road / Despicable Heroes / End Of The Line / Dehumanization / Anthem / Saints And Sinners.

ANTHEMS OF REBELLION (LIMITED EDITION), Century Media 77483-2 (2003) (European release). Tear Down The Walls (Intro) / Silent Wars / We Will Rise / Dead Eyes See No Future / Instinct /

Leader Of The Rats / Exist To Exit / Marching On A Dead End Road / Despicable Heroes / End Of The Line / Dehumanization / Anthem / Saints And Sinners / Lament Of A Mortal Soul (Live) / Behind The Smile (Live) / Diva Satanica (Live) / Leader Of The Rats (Remix) / Dead Eyes See No Future (Remix).

ANTHEMS OF REBELLION, Century Media 77483-2 (2003). Tear Down The Walls / Silent Wars / We Will Rise / Dead Eyes See No Future / Leader Of The Rats / Exist To Exit / Marching On A Dead End Road / Despicable Heroes / End Of The Line / Dehumanization / Anthem / Saints And Sinners. Chart positions: 42 FINLAND, 60 SWEDEN, 69 USA, 69 GERMANY, 97 HOLLAND.

ANTHEMS OF REBELLION (LIMITED EDITION), Century Media 77483-2 (2003) (USA release). Tear Down The Walls (Intro) / Silent Wars / We Will Rise / Dead Eyes See No Future / Instinct / Leader Of The Rats / Exist To Exit / Marching On A Dead End Road / Despicable Heroes / End Of The Line / Dehumanization / Anthem / Saints And Sinners / Lament Of A Mortal Soul (Live) / Behind The Smile (Live) / Diva Satanica (Live) / Exist To Exit (Remix) / Leader Of The Rats (Remix) / Dead Eyes See No Future (Remix).

Dead Eyes See No Future, Toy's Factory TFCK-87358 (2004) (Japanese release). Dead Eyes See No Future / Burning Angel (Live) / We Will Rise (Live) / Symphony Of Destruction / Kill With Power / Incarnated Solvent Abuse.

Dead Eyes See No Future, Century Media 82762-9 (2004) (European release). Dead Eyes See No Future / Burning Angel (Live in Paris 2004) / We Will Rise (Live in Paris 2004) / Heart Of Darkness (Live in Paris 2004) / Symphony Of Destruction / Kill With Power / Incarnated Solvent Abuse / We Will Rise (Enhanced video clip).

Arch Enemy, Century Media 8234-2 (2005) (Split promotion release with NEVERMORE). Nemesis / I Am Legend—Out For Blood.

Doomsday Machine Two-Song Sampler, Century Media 41270-6 (2005) (Promotion release). Nemesis / I Am Legend—Out For Blood.

DOOMSDAY MACHINE, Toy's Factory TFCK-87388 (2005) (Japanese release). Enter The Machine / Taking Back My Soul / Nemesis / My Apocalypse / Carry The Cross / I Am Legend / Out For Blood / Skeleton Dance / Hybrids Of Steel / Mechanic God Creation / Machtkampf / Slaves Of Yesterday / Heart Of Darkness (Live) / Bridge Of Destiny (Live).

DOOMSDAY MACHINE (LIMITED EDITION), Century Media 77583 (2005) (CD + DVD). Enter The Machine / Taking Back My Soul / Nemesis / My Apocalypse / Carry The Cross / I Am Legend / Out For Blood / Skeleton Dance / Hybrids Of Steel / Mechanic God Creation / Machtkampf / Slaves Of Yesterday / Intro / Dead Eyes See No Future / Ravenous / Nemesis (Video).

DOOMSDAY MACHINE, Century Media 77583-2 (2005). Enter The Machine / Taking Back My Soul / Nemesis / My Apocalypse / Carry The Cross / I Am Legend/Out For Blood / Skeleton Dance / Hybrids Of Steel / Mechanic God Creation / Machtkampf / Slaves Of Yesterday. Chart positions: 23 SWEDEN, 34 GERMANY, 74 AUSTRIA, 81 UK, 87 USA.

ARCHITECTURE OF AGGRESSION

PRETORIA, SOUTH AFRICA — *Vanzyl Alberts (vocals / guitar), William Bishop (bass), Anton Alberts (drums).*

Pretoria Death Metal combo ARCHITECTURE OF AGGRESSION, founded in 1995, comprised the Alberts brothers, vocalist / guitarist Vanzyl and drummer Anton, together with bassist Brian Liebenberg. The band relocated to London in early 1998, returning to South Africa in October 2000. Toward the close of 2001 Nardus, of SHADOWLORD, assumed the bass position. Subsequently William Bishop, of FUZIGISH, took over on bass. A self-financed album, entitled 'Manifest Destiny', was released in September 2004. This set included a promotional video for the song 'Subtle Forms Of Self Destruction'.

Signing to Witchdoctor Records, ARCHITECTURE OF AGGRESSION worked with engineer J.P. de Stefani to record second album 'Democracy : Consent To Domination' for issue in September 2006.

MANIFEST DESTINY, Architecture Of Aggression (2004). God Kill / Hated Truth / Preaching Death / Subtle Forms Of Self Destruction / Anonymity / Manifest Destiny / Subtle Forms Of Self Destruction (Video).

DEMOCRACY: CONSENT TO DOMINATION, Witchdoctor (2006). Pillars Of Democracy / Establish Dominance / Democracy—Consent To Domination / God Of The New Millennium / The Evil Of Two Lessers / Enslaved (Part 1) / Race Of Sheep (Enslaved Part 2) / Truth Behind The Truth / Lonely Are The Wise / Unsound Method / Systems Of Control / In God We Trust—Through God You're Crushed.

ARISE

ALINGSAS, SWEDEN — *Erik Ljungvist (vocals / guitar), L.G. Jonasson (guitar), Patrick Skoglow (bass), Daniel Bugno (drums).*

ARISE, founded in Alingsas during 1994 and titled in honour of the SEPULTURA album of the same name, blend traditional Swedish style Death Metal with retro Thrash influences. The group was assembled by a triumvirate of erstwhile HOLOCAUST members guitarist Erik Ljungqvist, bassist Patrick Skoglow and drummer Daniel Bugno. Second guitars were on hand from L.G. Jonasson, an ex-member of FUTURE DEVELOPMENT.

Initially the band was fronted by vocalist Jorgen Sjolander who was in turn replaced by Bjorn Andvik. When Andvik decamped Ljungvist took over the lead vocal role as ARISE switched from playing covers to writing original material. They then proceeded to issue a rush of demos including 'Hell's Retribution', 'Resurrection' and 1999's 'Statues'.

ARISE cut an April 2000 session 'Abducted Intelligence' with KING DIAMOND man Andy LaRocque at the production helm. This last tape duly securing a deal with the Finnish Spinefarm label.

ARISE would also contribute a version of 'Communication Breakdown' to the Dwell Records LED ZEPPELIN Death Metal tribute album 'Dead Zeppelin'. Japanese issues of the debut album 'A Godly Work Of Art' include an extra track, namely of cover of METALLICA's 'Motorbreath'. ARISE cut a new album, 'The Beautiful New World', at StudioMega in Bollebygd during 2004.

ARISE lent support to MORBID ANGEL's March 2005 Swedish dates. That December the band parted ways with guitarist/vocalist Erik Ljungqvist and bassist Patrik Skoglow due to "differences in opinion."

Arise, Arise (1998) (Cassette demo). The Last Of Centuries / Forsaken / Crucified Within.

Statues, Arise (1999) (Demo). Purgatory Unleashed / Statues / New Omen.

Resurrection, Arise (1999) (Demo). Intro / Abducted Intelligence / Black Souls / Cellbound / Infinite Sorrow (Outro).

Hell's Retributiton, Arise (2000) (Demo). Black Souls / Delusion Of Life.

Abducted Intelligence, Arise (2000) (Demo). Abducted Intelligence / Cellbound / Black Souls / Delusion Of Life.

THE GODLY WORK OF ART, Spinefarm SPI 121CD (2001). A Godly Work Of Art / Generations For Sale / Within / Delusion Of Life / Haterush / Cellbound / Wounds / Abducted Intelligence / ... And The Truth Is Lies / Motorbreath.

KINGS OF THE CLONED GENERATION, Spinefarm SPI 179CD (2003). Strangled Love / Stains Of Blood / Another World To Consume / Kings Of A Cloned Generation / Corroded / Way Above Life / Nuclear Ray Infected / Stick To The Line / Master Of Gravity / Wasted Life.

THE BEAUTIFUL NEW WORLD, Spinefarm SPI 235CD (2005). How Long Can You Pretend? / A New World / Profit From The Weak / Dreams Worthy Gods / King Of Yesterday, Slave Of Today / Of Life And Death / Expendable Heroes / Inject The Machine / Misery / Broken Trust / Tribute To The Flesh.

THE BEAUTIFUL NEW WORLD, Woodbell WBEX-25008 (2005) (Japanese release). How Long Can You Pretend? / A New World / Profit From The Weak / Dreams Worthy Gods / King Of Yesterday, Slave Of Today / Of Life And Death / Expendable Heroes / Inject The Machine / Misery / Broken Trust / Tribute To The Flesh / A Godly Work Of Art / Generations for Sale / Within / Haterush / Wounds / Abducted Intelligence / Motorbreath.

ARKHAM

LINDENHURST, NY, USA — *Derek Schilling (vocals / guitar), Ryan Lipynsky (guitar), Ted Bouklos (bass), Anthony Dalessio (drums).*

Lindenhurst, New York's ARKHAM was a Long Island band that took on the new title of DECIMATION upon the departure of a prior vocalist. DECIMATION included PSYCHOMANTHIUM personnel guitarist Derek Schilling and drummer Anthony Dalessio with Jennifer 'Satanzangel' Schilling on keyboards. DECIMATION announced a 2000 recording entitled 'Purification Through Suffering'.

During 2002 the band returned under a revised billing of ARKHAM A.D. with a new recording dubbed 'Bloodfiend'. The band was now crediting itself as former ASSASSIN NATION singer Doug, vocalist / guitarist Derek Schilling (a.k.a. 'Derekonomicon') of KRYPTIK, NEGLECT and DEATH HAMMER, Rion (Ryan Lipynsky) of UNEARTHLY TRANCE, THRALLDOM, MOTIVE and DEATH HAMMER, Ted Bouklos ('Theo Darkly') of CROWN and CLEANSER on bass and Anthony "The Lunatic" Dalessio on drums.

THE WRATH, Clean (1998).

ARMINIUS

DORDRECHT, HOLLAND — *Ben de Graaff (vocals), Walter De Groot (guitar), Willem Van Balen (guitar), Henk Van De Berg (bass), Lex Van De Heuvel (drums).*

Dordrecht "Destructive terror blasting deathmetal". ARMINIUS, taking their title from the Germanic general Arminius who destroyed three Roman legions in the hart of the Teutenborger Wald in A.D. 7, came together during 1998, built upon a founding line up of guitarist Willem van Balen, bassist Jasper Pol and drummer Fabian Haringa. In 2000 both Pol and Haringa opted out, being replaced by guitarist Walter de Groot and drummer Lex van de Heuvel. These changes signalled a change of tack to a more technically orientated brand of Metal. Subsequently Henk van de Berg was inducted on bass and Michael Philippo of HEADHAUNTER as lead vocalist. The 'Storms Below' EP arrived in 2003. Further changes saw Ben de Graaff taking over as frontman. Walter de Groot exited in October 2004.

Storms Below, Arminius (2003). Arminivs / Fortress Of Hexa / Burning The Legions / Four Wings / Torched Horizon / Storms Below.
Storms Below, Independent (2003). Arminivs / Fortress Of Hexa / Burning The Legions / Four Wings / Torched Horizon / Storms Below.

ARS MORIENDI

AUSTRIA — *Michael Wegleitner (vocals / guitar), Heiko Ernstreiter (guitar), Thomas Iberer (bass), Christian Keimel (drums).*

ARS MORIENDI, a self-styled "Fucking Thrash Metal" band, was manifested in August 1998 by guitarist Heiko Ernstreiter and drummer Christian Keimel. That September Michael Wegleitner took up the role of vocalist / guitarist and in January 2000 the group debuted with the demo 'World Of Hate'. Bassist Michael Kriegl was installed in February 2001, being replaced in April 2003 by Thomas Iberer.

The band issued the self financed 'Dissimulated' EP in 2004. ARS MORIENDI acquired second guitarist Joachim Liebminger, a veteran of RISING PASSION and DOOMED ERA, in October.

Austrian shows in December 2006 were conducted with PERISHING MANKIND and EVENTIDE.

Ars Moriendi, (2000). Ars Moriendi / Kaltes Fleisch / The Past Catches Me / World Of Hate.
Dissimulated, Ars Moriendi (2004). Endless Silent Sleep / Crossing The Line / Dark Crusade / Fainted I Am blind / God's Oppressive Arms.

ARSON

SOUTH AMBOY, NJ, USA — *Anthony Ezzi (vocals), Keith Dilliplane (guitar), Ken Pescatore (guitar), Kyle Hasselbrink (bass), Keith Hasselbrink (drums).*

South Amboy, New Jersey's ARSON, a volatile mix of Death, Grind and even Prog tendencies. The band, which featured former E-TOWN CONCRETE guitarist Ken Pescatore, vocalist Arthur Willhelm, second guitarist Dan Gonzalez and the sibling rhythm section of bassist Kyle and drummer Keith Hasselbrink, was formed in late 1998.

ARSON released the debut 'Words Written In Blood' EP during 1999 and a 2000 7" single 'Less Perfect Than Death' the following year. Promoting these releases, ARSON became familiar fixture on the East Coast touring scene. Further momentum was gained by the band's third outing, the full length 'Lacerate The Sky', recorded at Trax East Recording Studios and issued by Resurrection A.D. Records.

During 2002 vocalist Anthony Ezzi would temporarily front THE BLACK DAHLIA MURDER for live work after they lost the services of their singer. Guitarist Ken Pescatore exited in 2003, being replaced by Garrett. Ezzi would guest on SET ABLAZE's debut 'The Other Side Of Serenity' the same year. ARSON appeared at the New Jersey 'March Meltdown VI' in 2004.

Words Written In Blood, Resurrection A.D. RR 13 (1999). Words Written In Blood / Myth / I Lost All / Severed / Avoid The Sun.
Less Perfect Than Death, Resurrection RR15 (2000). Less Perfect Than Death / Engraved.
LACERATE THE SKY, Resurrection A.D. RR 21 (2002). Indefiance / Cast In Shadows / Perfect Truth / My Empty Grave / Remnants / Closed Wounds / Motives For Nightmares / Changeling / Limb From Limb / Proceed To Protend.

ARTERY ERUPTION

CLOVIS, CA, USA — *Brian (vocals / bass), Grant (guitar), Brandon Pratt (guitar), Darren Williams (drums).*

ARTERY ERUPTION was conceived as a trio comprising Brian on vocals and drums, guitarist Grant and bassist Miguel Macias during the mid nineties. Second guitar player Brandon Pratt was incorporated during 1999 but would depart after demo recordings in August of 2002. Signing to Sevared Records ARTERY ERUPTION cut the uncompromising 'Reduced To A Limbless Sexslave' album in 2003. For these sessions the group focussed Brian on the lead vocal role and introduced Darren Williams to handle drums. Brandon Pratt was then welcomed back into the fold as Brian then added bass guitar to his responsibilities when Macias opted later that year.

ARTERY ERUPTION projected a split album release in collaboration with MANGLED ATROCITY for 2004.

REDUCED TO A LIMBLESS SEXSLAVE, Sevared (2003). Reduced To A Limbless Sexslave / Rage—Induced Infant Assfuck / Drinking The Menses Of A Dead Slut / Shot Gun Blasts In The Ass / Jacking Off On An Inside-out Butthole / Petrified Fecal Sodomization / Getting A Woodie In Your Sweats, And Setting It On Fire / Full—Nelson Cunt—Bust.

AS DUSK UNFOLDS

FAIRFAX, VA, USA — *Paul Karaffa (vocals), Ryan Tolson (guitar), Dan Boyd (bass), Jack Mclarty (drums).*

Fairfax, Virginia Metalcore band had an unusual start in that founders guitarist Ryan Tolson, and then bass player Andy Nees, originally assembled the band with a view towards a Jazz Blues direction. With the recruitment of drummer Jack Mclarty they instead opted for Metal. Initially a twin guitar band, the formative AS DUSK UNFOLDS endured an ever revolving door of guitarists. The group settled on a single guitar format but Andy Nees would be replaced by Dan Boyd. In 2005 the group supported the likes of STRAPPING YOUNG LAD, KRISIUN, THE AGONY SCENE, INCANTATION and HATE ETERNAL.

In June of 2005 the band folded with the departure of both singer Paul Karaffa and drummer Jack Mclarty. Meantime, Ryan Tolson busied himself with side project FOUR BARRELL. In August FOUR BARRELL drummer Matt took over drums for a resurrected AS DUSK UNFOLDS.

A TWILIGHT TO REMEMBER, As Dusk Unfolds (2004). Darkness Unfolds / Winter Last Breath / Nightsky Falling / When Vengeance Calls My Name / Behold, The Reaper / Dirge For The Past / Hope Turns To Disaster / A Time To Bleed / Tomorrow I'll Come / Sunset.

AS IT BURNS

GRONINGEN, HOLLAND — *Arend Doornheim (vocals), Rocco Rundervoort (guitar), Joost Brouwer (guitar), Floris Maathuis (bass), Gert Plas (keyboards), Jacco Veenstra (drums).*

Groningen band AS IT BURNS, styling itself as "Atmospheric Blackened Death Thrash Metal", was formulated during 1997 by Jeroen Smit on the drums and guitarist Joost Brouwer. Internal manouevres found new man Rocco Rundervoort taking on bass, later switching to guitar as Smit swapped his role of drummer to handle bass duties. Gert Plas, also active with Black Metal band WINTER OF SIN, would take up the keyboard role. An opening session 'Soured', recorded on 4 track, led in turn to the 1999 self financed album 'Obsolete Prophecies'. AS IT BURNS then added Jacco Veenstra of avant-garde Doom act VOLEG on the drums.

The 'Mortal Dusk' effort, the band's first for Cold Blood Industries, would be recorded at Franky's Recording Kitchen with producers Berthus Westerhuys and Jens van der Valk during August of 2002. The band once again utilised Franky's Recording Kitchen studio and producer Jens van der Valk for January 2005 recordings. However, with Cold Blood Industries having collapsed, the band pursued this next album as a self financed effort.

OBSOLETE PROPHECIES, Independent (1999). Eternal Bloodhunt / Soured / Voices Of Darkness / Repay With Death / Slave Of Conspiracy / The Obsolete Prophecy / Amid The Abundance / Domains Of Satan / Wasted / Bachannal Of Lust.

As It Burns, (2000). Host Of Fear / Beyond Humanity / Iconoclasm Hysteria / Bachannal Of Lust / Eternal Bloodhunt / Amid The Abundance.

INFERNO, Independent (2001). Inferno (Intro) / Hosts Of Fear / The Inexorable Mirage Of Nemesis / Iconoclasm Hysteria / Ignorant Accosters Of Christ / Beyond Humanity / Stormknights / Reflections (Outro).

MORTAL DUSK, Cold Blood Industries (2003). Mortal Dusk / Selective Amnesia / God Is A Souvenir / Holy Waste / Silent Might / Eternal / Suicide Prophet / The Pulse Of Anger / A Tortured Face / The Skintrade.

ASCENSION

EGLING, GERMANY — *Juergen Zeisberger (vocals / guitar), Christoph Nadler (guitar), Oliver Winterholler (bass), Martin Szillat (drums).*

ASCENSION is an Egling Death Metal band assembled in 1993 as BLACK FUTURE citing a line-up comprising vocalist / guitarist Stefan Angerer, guitarist Christoph Nadler, Fabian Quoll, bassist Oliver Winterholler and Tobias Quoll on drums. The group switched title to DECAY and the first product would be a 1995 demo 'Downwards', after which Peter Giel took the drum position. In 1996, now titled ASCENSION, the band drafted Jürgen Zeisberger on guitar and the following year Holger Schmalisch enrolled on drums and then Davud Böhm as lead vocalist. The demo 'Walking On The Psychopath' followed. 2001 witnessed further changes, introducing RED TO GREY's Robin Fischer and ex-LAST SALVATION drummer Martin Szillat.

During 2003 Matthias Urban of Augsburg Thrashers STORM sessioned on bass.

Walking On The Psychopath, (2001). Into Coppice / Black In Men / Two / Me, The Lunatic / Vertigo / Bloodred Letter Day / Paying The Debt Of Nature.

ASCENSION, Ascension Ind. (2003). Rising / Writhing / Black In Men / The Grimace Of Angst / Bloodred Letter Day / Road Leads To …? / … Nowhere / Swallowing Emptiness / Mors Interruptum / Second Ascension.

ASERAPHYMN

KNOXVILLE, TN, USA — *Jason Fields (vocals), Jay R. Presley (guitar), Kevin Pippen (guitar), Scott Dunlap (bass / vocals), Jeremy Gregg (drums).*

ASERAPHYMN was founded in Knoxville, Tennessee during March of 2004 by DEMONICIDE and TERMINAL PLAN drummer Jeremy Gregg, fresh from touring with ORIGIN, contacted his TERMINAL PLAN band mate, guitarist Jay R. Presley, with a view to forging a new band unit. Gregg had also previously been involved with ENTER SELF and MURDER CONSTRUCT. Next to enroll would be ex-ENTER SELF guitarist Wes LcQuire, singer Derek Holman and erstwhile BESIEGED bassist Scot Dunlap. June saw the departure of LcQuire to join WERMOD and another TERMINAL PLAN veteran, Kevin Pippen, duly filled the vacancy. Recording at Underground Recording Studio in Knoxville, ASERAPHYMN crafted four tracks, two of which were released as a demo.

The band's debut live show came on 7th July 2004 at the Electric Ballroom International venue in Knoxville. However, before the month closed, Holman exited to join ELDERS OF THE APOCALYPSE. He would be superseded by ex-TERMINAL PLAN guitarist Jason Fields.

The debut album 'Blood, Bone & Hate' was recorded during Spring 2005. A limited edition concert recording followed, 'Live at the M.U.S.E.', restricted to just 100 copies.

BLOOD, BONE & HATE, Aseraphymn (2005). Lion Storm / Abhorent / Usurper's Circle / Ishaigarab / Discipline Of Calus.

LIVE AT THE M.U.S.E., (2005) (limited edition 100 copies). Astoreth (Live) / Usurper's Circle (Live) / Ishaigarab (Live) / Pyre Of The Enconsecrate (Live) / Abhornet (Live) / Discipline Of Calous (Live).

ASESINO

USA — *Tony Campos (vocals / bass), Dino Cazares (guitar), Raymond Herrera (drums).*

ASESINO is a BRUJERIA / FEAR FACTORY, Spanish language, old school Death Metal / Grind spin off established by guitarist Dino Cazares and drummer Raymond Herrera billed as "Asesino" and "Grenudo" respectively. Vocals and bass would be taken care of by STATIC-X man Tony Compos (a.k.a. "Maldito X"). Following recording of the 2002 Kool Arrow album 'Corridos De Muerte', Herrera stepped down, being superseded by Emilio Márquez of SADISTIC INTENT.

The band played a run of dates with STATIC-X, AMERICAN HEAD CHARGE and BLOODSIMPLE in June 2005. That same year Campos guested on the DIA DE LOS MUERTOS project album 'Day Of The Dead' assembled by BODY COUNT bassist Vincent Price, and guitarist Andres Jaramillo and drummer Alfonso Pinzon from the Colombian metal act AGONY.

ASESINO joined the tail end of the October 'Blackest Of The Black' tour in California, sharing stages in Dallas, San Antonio and Los Angeles with DANZIG, CHIMAIRA, BEHEMOTH, HIMSA and MORTIIS.

In January 2006 ASESINO entered Undercity Studios in Los Angeles to record new album 'Solo Putos Muertos Quedan', this effort being produced by Dino Cazares with Logan Mader, ex-MACHINE HEAD, SOULFLY and MEDICATION, acting as engineer. On September 2nd, Cazares debuted his new project band before a headline ASESINO set at the Whisky A Go Go in Hollywood, California. This band involved Tommy Vext of VEXT on lead vocals, Risha Eryavec from DECREPIT BIRTH on bass plus the VITAL REMAINS, DECREPIT BIRTH and NILE credited Tim Yeung on drums.

CORRIDOS DE MUERTE, Kool Arrow (2002). Asesino / Rey De La Selva / Despedazando Muertos / Sequestro Nuestro / Amor Marrano / Luchador Violador / El Patron Mando / Cyko Maton / Carnicero / Chota Sucia / Donde Esta Mi Corte / La Ejecucion / Corrido Del Asesino.

CRISTO SATANICO, Hawino (2006).

ASHMOLEAN

BELGIUM — *Nik Mertens (vocals), Wim Melis (guitar), Wim Meeuws (bass), Bart Boeckx (keyboards), Guy Vernelen (drums).*

Created in 1996 this Death Metal act cited a founding line up of twin lead vocalists Nik Mertens and Rob Slegers, guitarist Wim Melis, bassist Jeff Boeckx and drummer Jan Boeckx. Adding Bart Boeckx on keyboards ASHMOLEAN released the six song 'Close … As Red In Blood' demo tape in April 1997. A self financed promotion EP entitled 'Elegy's For Your Embrace' was delivered in 1998 after which both Jeff Boeckx and Jan Boeckx departed. ASHMOLEAN regrouped by enlisting Wim Meeuws on bass and Guy Vernelen on the drums. This line up debuted with the 2001 EP 'Daylightstruggle'.

Raf Aarts, previously with Thrashers SCARRED MIND, joined as second guitarist in August of 2002.

Elegy's For Your Embrace EP, Independent (1998). One Final Kiss / Whispers Of The Dawn / She, Evil / Denial Of Dreams / A Carnal Desire / Elegy's For Your Embrace.

Daylight Struggle EP, Independent (2001). Deus Ex Machina / Daylight Struggle / Cloud Nine / Pulverized / Soulstrangler / Scarlatine.

ASMODINA

COLOGNE, GERMANY — *Angela Gossow (vocals), Mike (guitar), Pete (guitar), Dave (bass), Aki (drums).*

Not to be confused with the other German Metal act bearing the same title. This ASMODINA, based in Cologne, was an early port of call for Angela Gossow, later to front MISTRESS and the high profile act ARCH ENEMY. The band issued the November 1991 six song demo 'Your Hidden Fear' followed in February 1994 by 'The Story Of The True Human Personality' session. A further three track promotion outing was delivered in 1996 and the 'Inferno' album arrived in January of 1997.

Gossow joined MISTRESS to feature on the demos 'Worship The Temptress' in December 1999 and 'Party In Hell' during 2000. The group subsequently took on a new title of DEVIL IN THE DETAILS when Gossow quit to join ARCH ENEMY for their 2001 album 'Wages Of Sin'. DEVIL IN THE DETAILS issued the 'Groove Styler' album in August 2002.

INFERNO, PRP (1997). Forgotten Tears / Blood / Impregnate The Beast Inside / Another Golgotha / Abuse / Nocturnal Obsession / Pleasure Abuse.

ASPHYX

OLDENZAAL, HOLLAND — *Martin Van Drunen (vocals / bass), Eric Daniels (guitar), Bob Bagchus (drums).*

The highly influential ASPHYX was a leading force on the European Death Metal scene, forging a path for a swathe of bands to follow in their wake. ASPHYX date back to 1987 when the band was formed in Oldenzal by drummer Bob Bagchus with former members Tonny Brookhuis on guitar and Chuck (a.k.a. Christian Colli) handling vocals and bass. The fledgling band took its cue from international pioneers, at first performing cover versions such as DEATH´s 'Infernal Death', CELTIC FROST´s 'Nocturnal Fear' and MAYHEM´s 'Necrolust'. Soon getting to grips with composing original material, the band swiftly cut the rehearsal demo 'Carnage Remains' then issued the first demo entitled 'Enter The Domain', recorded that December.

Replacing Colli briefly with Benno Kremers then with Theo Loomans, the following year the band expanded from a trio to a quartet in April 1989 with the introduction of second guitarist Eric Daniels. ASPHYX's second tape, 'Crush The Cenotaph', saw issue in July, this release garnering the band favour across the international underground and selling over 5,000 copies in the process. Meantime, maintaining their roots, both Bagchus and Loomans operated the HELLHAMMER tribute concern EVOKER. A third effort, 1989's two track 7" 'Mutilating Process', gained distribution via Nuclear Blast Records subdivision Gore Records. Brookhuis left Asphyx after these sessions. In 1990 ASPHYX's fame was such that a gig in Hardenberg saw PARADISE LOST as support act.

Frontman Martin Van Drunen split from Dutch techno-thrashers PESTILENCE in late 1990 due to personality clashes within the band and, shortly after his departure, he hooked up with ASPHYX replacing Theo Loomans. ASPHYX went into the studio to record a projected debut album for the UK based CMFT Productions to be entitled 'Embrace The Death'. However, due to record company financial problems these tapes never saw a commercial release. Nevertheless, unofficial tapes soon circulated amongst the Metal underground, bolstering the band's standing.

The band's second album attempt, and what was to be their debut album, 'The Rack', released in April 1991, was recorded on a minimalist budget in a deliberate attempt to achieve a deliberately primitive sound. Worldwide sales approaching 30'000 copies were boosted by a European tour alongside ENTOMBED, proving ASPHYX had chosen the right path.

'Crush The Cenotaph', issued in 1992, was a mini-album produced by Waldemar Sorychta and containing reworks of pre-Van Drunen era material and live tracks. Full-length album 'Last One On Earth', laid down at Harrows Studios, arrived that October. Live work comprised an extensive European tour with BENEDICTION and BOLT THROWER.

Clearly the tour was more enjoyable for Van Drunen than most as, clearly impressed by each other, the bassist / vocalist duly joined BOLT THROWER in 1994. Van Drunen had also made time outside the ASPYHX camp to guest as lead vocalist for Swedish Death Metal band COMECON, appearing on their 1993 album 'Converging Conspiracies'.

The revised line-up of ASPHYX thus emerged, comprised new vocalist / bassist Ron Van Pol, guitarist Eric Daniels and drummer Sander Van Hoof for an eponymous album of July 1994, having been crafted at Stage One Studio in Bühne, Germany with Andy Classen of HOLY MOSES behind the desk. Further ructions hit the ASPHYX line-up in 1995 as Daniels briefly joined ETERNAL SOLSTICE and original vocalist Theo Loomans returned. Loomans contributed bass and vocals to the 'God Cries' album of May 1996.

The 'Embrace The Death' sessions finally found a release in 1996 through Century Media with extra tracks from the 'Mutilating Process' 7' single.

Despite the constant line-up changes ASPHYX continued to build on their popularity in the Death Metal market with consistent album sales. However, the band, made up of Daniels, Bagchus and erstwhile PENTACLE vocalist / bassist Wannes Gubbels, changed titles to SOULBURN for 1998's 'Feeding On Angels' album. Tragically Loomans was killed the same year. An open verdict was recorded, but the musician had been killed in his car, hit by a train whilst stationary across rail tracks.

SOULBURN invariably included such ASPHYX classics as Abomination Echoes', 'Vermin' and 'The Sickening Dwell' in their live set and once rehearsals got underway for a further album the band members realised the new material was sounding much more in an ASPHYX vein, so duly reverted back to their former title.

A 2000 album, 'On The Wings Of Inferno' recorded at Harrow Production Studios in Losser, found ASPHYX, back to their more familiar band as a mark of respect to Loomans, as a duo of Wannes Gubbles, Eric Daniel and Bog Bagchus. However, after its release ASPHYX announced their retirement.

Martin Van Drunen resurfaced in mid 2002 debuting his new act DEATH BY DAWN on the European live circuit. Early 2005 found Martin Van Drunen and erstwhile PESTILENCE bassist Jeroen Paul Thesseling collaborating with KING LOCUST guitarist Niels Drieënhuizen in a new band entitled PROJEKT TABUN. The trio entered Studio Het Lab in Schaarsbergen to put down initial recordings.

From Beyond Productions released a limited edition vinyl variant of debut 'Embrace The Death' in June 2005. The reissue added liner notes from drummer Bob Bagchus and new artwork.

In January 2007 it would be learned that Martin Van Drunen had joined forces with THANATOS guitarists Stephan Gebédi and Paul Baayens, GOREFEST drummer Ed Warby and former HOUWITSER bass player Theo van Eekelen in a new band unit.

Enter The Domain, (1988). Intro / Vault Of The Vailing Souls / Cadaver Camp / Thoughts Of An Atheist.

Crush The Cenotaph, (1989). Crush The Cenotaph / Rite Of Shades / Abomination Echoes / Thoughts Of An Atheist.

Mutilating Process, Nuclear Blast (1990) (Limited edition 1000 copies). Mutilating Process / Streams Of Ancient Wisdom.

Promo '91, (1991). The Sickened Dwell / Conjuration Of Choronzon / Diabolical Existence.

THE RACK, Century Media 84 9716 (1991). The Quest Of Absurdity / Vermin / Diabolical Existence / Evocation / Wasteland Of Terror / The Sickening Dwell / Ode To A Nameless Grave / Pages In Blood / The Rack.

Crush The Cenotaph EP, Century Media 799723-2 (1992). Crush The Cenotaph / Rite Of Shades / The Krusher / Evocation (Live) / Wasteland Of Terror (Live).

LAST ONE ON EARTH, Century Media 84 9734-2 (1992). Bismarck / The Krusher / Serenade In Lead / Last One On Earth / The Incarnation Of Lust / Streams Of Ancient Wisdom / Food For The Ignorant / Asphyx (Forgotten War).

ASPHYX, Century Media 77063-2 (1994). Prelude Of The Unhonoured Funeral / Depths Of Eternity / Emperors Of Salvation / 'Til Death Do Us Part / Initiation Into The Ossuary / Incarcerated Chimaeras / Abomination Echoes / Back Into Eternity / Valleys In Oblivion / Thoughts Of An Atheist.

EMBRACE THE DEATH, Century Media CD 77141-2 (1996). Intro / Embrace The Death / The Sickened Dwell / Streams Of Ancient Wisdom / Thoughts Of An Atheist / Crush The Cenotaph / Denying The Goat / Vault Of The Vailing Souls / Circle Of The Secluded / To Succubus A Whore / Eternity's Depths / Outro / Mutilating Process / Streams Of An Ancient Wisdom.

GOD CRIES, Century Media 77117-2 (1996). God Cries / It Awaits / My Beloved Enemy / Died Yesterday / Cut-Throat Urges / Slaughtered In Sodom / Frozen Soul / Fear My Greed / The Blood I Spilled.

ON THE WINGS OF INFERNO, Century Media 77263-2 (2000). Summoning The Storm / The Scent Of Obscurity / For They Ascend ... / On The Wings Of Inferno / 06/06/2006 / Waves Of Fire / Indulge In Frenzy / Chaos In The Flesh / Marching Towards The Styx.

ASPHYXIATOR

CHICAGO, IL, USA — *Demogorgon (vocals / guitar), Moloch (guitar), Sehkmet (guitar), Mortus (bass), Leviathan (drums).*

Chicago Gore-Grind outfit ASPHYXIATOR is fronted by Mike "Demogorgon", a scene veteran of FOREST OF IMPALED, GODS OF GORE and SOUL SKINNER. Drummer Adam "Leviathan" holds credits with SOUL SKINNER, DISINTER and BORDERLINE. The band went through various line-up changes with formative members including guitarist James Russel "Xaphan", bassists Mike Fic "Abaddon" and Steve "Angel Ripper".

ASPHYXIATOR's 2005 album 'Ex-Mortem Asphyxiation' included a cover version of BEHEMOTH's 'As Above, So Below'. In April the band added the MIDGET PARADE credited guitar team of Raziel and Mictian. A second album, entitled 'No Breath, After Death', was projected.

EX-MORTEM ASPHYXIATION, Asphyxiator (2005). Suffocating The Unborn / Xaphan's Crucifixtion / Resurrection Of Ex- Mortem / Drinking The Blood Of The Dead / Watching You Burn / Sadistic Vengeance / Change Of Faith / Sacrificial Lamb / Gassed, Skinned And Impaled / Feasting On Post Mortal Skin / Apocalyptic Armageddon / Killing You Within / As Above, So Below.

ASSEMBLENT

SARDOAL, PORTUGAL — *Sérgio Marques (vocals), Filomena Francisco (vocals), Daniel Campos (guitar), Carlos Santos (bass), Pedro Lopes (keyboards), César Bento (drums).*

Melodic Death Metal band ASSEMBLENT published the demo 'Assemblent' in May 2003. The band had been created in 1998 by former members of DAWN and ABYSMO, singer Sérgio Marques, guitarist Daniel Campos, bassist Carlos Santos, keyboard player Tânia Gaspar with César Bento on the drums. Pedro Lopes took over on keyboards in 2002. The following year ASSEMBLENT entered Estúdio Zero in Tomar to record their first demo. Filomena Francisco was introduced to add female vocals in 2004.

ASSEMBLENT's debut Miguel Fonseca produced March 2006 album 'Equilibrium' featured a guest appearance on the track 'Silent Cries' by MOONSPELL frontman Fernando Ribeiro.

Assemblent, Assemblent (2003). Equilibrium / Heartwork / Silent Cries.

EQUILIBRIUM, Nemesis (2006). Equilibrium / Heartwork / From Red Core To Black Sky / A Dying Moment / Silent Cries / Into My Sleep / Grammaton Cleric / Subtellurian Darkness / Fears / Terria.

ASSUCK

ST. PETERSBURG, FL, USA — *Steve Heritage (vocals), Pete Jay (bass), Rob Proctor (drums).*

St. Petersburg, Florida Grind act ASSUCK made quite an impression despite their brief lifespan. Founded in 1992 by vocalist / guitarist Steve Heritage the band went through a succession of line-ups. The 1995 line-up included vocalist Paul Pavlovich, bassist Pete Jay and the NASTY SAVAGE credited drummer Rob Proctor. Bass guitar during 1996 was delegated to INHUMANITY and SCROTUM GRINDER's Steve Kosiba.

Daryl Kahan, erstwhile drummer for New York Hardcore act CITIZEN'S ARREST as well as figuring on the debut BORN AGAINST single, would front the band for a European tour. He would subsequently join arch Black Metal act ABAZAGORATH under the stage pseudonym of 'Morgul'. He would also lead FUNEBRARUM. During 2001 Daryl Kahan would also be located fronting Spanish band VOICE OF HATE.

Blindspot EP, (1992). Blood And Cloth / Automate / Within Without / Blindspot / By Design / Spine / Infanticide.

MISERY INDEX, Sound Pollution (1996). QED / Salt Mine / Corners / Dataclast / Blight Of Element / Talon Of Dominion / Unrequited Blood / Wartorn / Sum And Substance / Riven / Reversing Denial / Lithographs / Intravenous / A Monument To Failure / In Absence.

ASUNDER

OAKLAND, CA, USA — *Dino Sommese (vocals / drums), Geoff Evans (guitar), John Gossard (guitar), Salvador Raya (bass), Alex Bale-Glickman (cello).*

ASUNDER is an Oakland, Californian Doom / Death outfit forged in 1998 by DYSTOPIA vocalist / drummer Dino Sommese and SKAVEN guitarist Geoff Evans uniting with second guitarist Seth Baker and vocalist / bassist Brit Hallett. A two song demo, restricted to just 50 copies, was cut in December 1999. Subsequently these tracks would be used for a split EP release shared with Texas Crustcore band LIKE FLIES ON FLESH.

The band went into stasis for roughly a year until they would reconvene for live shows alongside HIGH ON FIRE and GRIEF. In August of 2000 a further demo emerged, entitled 'Of Wind And Wings'. Shortly after, ASUNDER expanded their range of sounds by incorporating cellist Alex Bale-Glickman and substituting Baker for John Gossard, a veteran of San Francisco bands THE GAULT, WEAKLING and IRON MAIDEN covers act IRON VEGAN. Bass would be handled by Salvador Raya of INSIDEOUS.

ASUNDER then set to work with recording engineer Billy Anderson on an album project 'Under The Vast Indifference Of The Same Sky'. Nuclear War Now Productions would sign the band for a lavish, gatefold vinyl variant of this opus in 2004.

In 2007 the band donated their interpretation of 'Who Rides The Astral Wings' to a THERGOTHON tribute album assembled by Russia's Solitude Productions.

Asunder, Asunder (1999) (Split EP with LIKE FLIES ON FLESH). Eulogy Pt. I / The Fall Of Elders / Tides Of Ruin.

A CLARION CALL, Nuclear War Now! (2004). Twilight Amaranthine / Crown Of Eyes / A Clarion Call.

AT THE GATES

GOTHENBURG, SWEDEN — *Tomas Lindberg (vocals), Anders Björler (guitar), Martin Larsson (guitar), Jonas Björler (bass), Adrian Erlandsson (drums).*

AT THE GATES are recognised as pioneers of the Gothenburg NWoSDM (New Wave of Swedish Death Metal) sound. A very aggressive technical Thrash act in the vein of America's finest, but with added twists and a touch of the avant-garde, this quintet, was initially known as GROTESQUE. This antecedent outfit had been forged by ex-ORAL guitarist Alf Svensson, billed under a stage name of 'The Haunting'. Vocals would be handled by 'Goatspell' (a.k.a. Tomas Lindberg) with 'Necrolord' (a.k.a. 'Bullen' Kristian Wahlin) on secondary guitars. The group's original rhythm section comprised bassist Nuctemeron with the SORHIN and ARCKANUM credited Shamaatae (Johan S. Lager) on drums. Subsequently 'Offensor' (a.k.a. Tomas Eriksson) manned the drums. Recordings issued under the GROTESQUE banner included the demos 'Ripped From The Cross', a three song rehearsal session in 1988, and 'The Black Gate Is Closed' laid down on April 5th 1989. The Dolores label issued the 'Incantations' mini-album in 1990, pressed in both lilac and black vinyl editions. However, that same year the band folded.

In February 1990 Lindberg, joining forces with guitarist Bjorn Mankner and identical twins Anders Björler and Jonas Björler, on guitar and bass respectively, forged INFESTATION. A two song rehearsal demo, 'When Sanity Ends', was recorded at Fågeln studio and issued in August but INFESTATION collapsed shortly thereafter. Lindberg and the two brothers then hooked up with Alf Svensson plus drummer Adrian Erlandsson, and duly created AT THE GATES.

As AT THE GATES the first product to emerge was the mini-album 'Gardens Of Grief' on Dolores Records in May 1991. The 'At The Gates' anthem was poignantly dedicated to late MAYHEM singer Dead (Per Yngve Ohlin), who had committed suicide that April. Svensson's involvement with AT THE GATES would be brief, as the man soon departed later, going on to form the extraordinary OXIPLEGATZ and releasing the 'Fairy Tales (Selatyriaf)' album in 1994 and 'Worlds And Worlds' in 1996.

'The Red In The Sky Is Ours', delivered in July 1992 and despite being an ultra-heavyweight affair, featured guest violinist Jesper Jarold. Presenting their work in the live scenario, AT THE GATES toured Europe in 1992 opening for MY DYING BRIDE. Their third album, 1993's 'With Fear I Kiss The Burning Darkness', was produced by noted Death Metal desk man Tomas Skogsberg and again received solid reviews. DISMEMBER's Matti Kärki notably provided some additional growls for good measure. AT THE GATES appeared at the MTV/Peaceville show at Nottingham's Rock City alongside ANATHEMA and MY DYING BRIDE before once more touring Europe with ANATHEMA and opening act CRADLE OF FILTH in January 1994.

'Terminal Spirit Disease' was produced by Fredrik Nordström and includes a selection of live tracks culled from the previous three releases alongside new studio material, the first to feature the new guitarist Martin Larsson, embellished by cellist Peter Andersson and violinist Ylva Wåhlstedt. To back up its release

AT THE GATES

the band once more hit the road with ANATHEMA and MY DYING BRIDE. The band toured Europe in early 1995 with SEANCE. That same year a short lived but significant AT THE GATES connected project emerged entitled TERROR, this being a union of the AT THE GATES triumvirate of guitarist Anders Björler, bass player Jonas Björler and drummer Adrian Erlandsson with the notorious DISSECTION frontman Jon Nödtveidt. TERROR issued a solitary demo prior to collapse.

AT THE GATES switched labels moving to Earache Records, First product of this liaison was the November 1995 'Slaughter Of The Soul' album, which featured a version of Australian act SLAUGHTERLORD's track 'Legion' as a Japanese bonus track. KING DIAMOND guitarist Andy La Rocque guested on the track 'Cold'. Clocking in at an all too brief 34 minutes, the Fredrik Nordström produced 'Slaughter Of The Soul' was nonetheless startlingly close to Death Metal perfection. AT THE GATES also contributed their rendition of 'Captor Of Sin' to the SLAYER tribute album 'Slatanic Slaughter'.

Despite 'Slaughter Of The Soul' proving to be their highest selling effort, AT THE GATES met on July 27th 1996 and decided to split. Adrian Elandsson immediately fired up THE HAUNTED, rehearsing the very next day with former ORCHRISTE, SÉANCE and SATANIC SLAUGHTER guitarist Patrik Jensen. Both Anders Björler and Jonas Björler soon joined this formation. Adrian Erlandsson founded H.E.A.L. and later joined premier British Black Metal act CRADLE OF FILTH in 1999.

Lindberg became vocalist for GREAT DECEIVER releasing the 2000 album 'Jet Black Art'. Lindberg joined DISINCARNATE in 1999, the band assembled by former DEATH, TESTAMENT and CANCER guitarist JAMES MURPHY. By mid 2000 Lindberg was fronting LOCKUP, the side project of NAPALM DEATH men Shane Embury and Jesse Pintado with DIMMU BORGIR drummer Nick Barker.

'Slaughter Of The Soul' would be re-issued in 2002 adding a glut of extra tracks including the SLAUGHTERLORD 'Legion' Japanese bonus cut, two working demos, an outtake from the album sessions 'The Dying', the cover of SLAYER's 'Captor Of Sin' as well as a rendition of NO SECURITY's 'Bister Verklighet'.

A 2004 tribute album, 'Slaughterous Souls—A Tribute to At The Gates' released in September through Drowned Scream Records, comprised such artists paying homage as TAETRE, GODHATE, MÖRK GRYNING, MOONSKIN, DARKNESS BY OATH, SOUL DEMISE, ETERNAL OATH, ETERNAL GRAY, ILLDISPOSED, ENTER CHAOS, DETONATION, MISANTHROPE, PAGANIZER and VILE. In addition IN AETERNUM weighed in with a cover of 'Blood Run From The Altar', originally by GROTESQUE.

Earache Records issued a picture disc vinyl edition of 'Slaughter Of The Soul' in October 2006, this re-issue was restricted to 1,500 copies.

Gardens Of Grief, At The Gates (1991) (Demo). Souls Of The Evil Departed / At The Gates / All Life Ends / City Of The Screaming Statues.

Gardens Of Grief EP, Dolores DOL 005 (1991) (12" vinyl single). Souls Of The Evil Departed / At The Gates / All Life Ends / City Of The Screaming Statues.

THE RED IN THE SKY IS OURS, Deaf DEAF 10 (1992) (Vinyl release). The Red In The Sky Is Ours / The Season To Come / Kingdom Gone / Through Gardens Of Grief / Within / Windows / Claws Of Laughter Dead / Neverwhere / The Scar / Night Comes, Blood Black.

THE RED IN THE SKY IS OURS, Deaf DEAF 10 (1992) (CD release). The Red In The Sky Is Ours / The Season To Come / Kingdom Gone / Through Gardens Of Grief / Within / Windows / Claws Of Laughter Dead / Neverwhere / The Scar / Night Comes, Blood Black / City Of Screaming Statues.

WITH FEAR I KISS THE BURNING DARKNESS, Deaf DEAF 14 (1993). Beyond Good And Evil / Raped By The Light Of Christ / The Break Of Autumn / Non-Divine / Primal Breath / The Architects / Stardrowned / Blood Of The Sunsets / The Burning Darkness / Ever-Opening Flower / Through The Red.

WITH FEAR I KISS THE BURNING DARKNESS, Deaf DEAF 14 (1993) (Vinyl release). Beyond Good And Evil / Raped By The Light Of Christ / The Break Of Autumn / Non-Divine / Primal Breath / Stardrowned / Blood Of The Sunsets / The Burning Darkness / Ever-Opening Flower / Through The Red.

Gardens Of Grief, Peaceville Collectors CC7 (1994) (7" yellow vinyl single). Souls Of The Evil Departed / All Life Ends.

TERMINAL SPIRIT DISEASE, Peaceville VILE 47 (1994). The Swarm / Terminal Spirit Disease / And The World Returned / Forever Blind / The Fevered Circle / The Beautiful Wound / All Life Ends (Live) / The Burning Darkness (Live) / Kingdom Gone (Live).

Demo 1995, At The Gates (1995) (Demo). Suicide Nation / Unto Others / Captor Of Sin.

SLAUGHTER OF THE SOUL, Earache MOSH 143 (1995). Blinded By Fear / Slaughter Of The Soul / Cold / Under A Serpent Sun / Into The Dead Sky / Suicide Nation / World Of Lies / Unto Others / Nausea / Need / The Flames Of The End.

SLAUGHTER OF THE SOUL, Toy's Factory TFCK-88754 (1995) (Japanese release). Blinded By Fear / Slaughter Of The Soul / Cold / Under A Serpent Sun / Into The Dead Sky / Suicide Nation / World Of Lies / Unto Others / Nausea / Need / The Flames Of The End / Legion.

Cursed To Tour, Earache (1996) (Promotion release. Split with NAPALM DEATH). Slaughter Of The Soul / World Of Lies / Legion / The Dying.

GARDENS OF GRIEF / IN THE EMBRACE OF EVIL, Century Media 8040-2 (2001) (Split album with GROTESQUE). Souls Of The Evil Departed / At The Gates / All Life Ends / City Of The Screaming Statues.

SUICIDAL FINAL ART, Peaceville CDVILED 86 (2001). The Red In The Sky Is Ours / Kingdom Gone / Windows / Ever Opening Flower (Demo) / The Architects / Raped By The Light Of Christ / Primal Breath / Blood Of The Sunsets / The Burning Darkness / The Swarm / Terminal Spirit Disease / Forever Blind / The Beautiful Wound / Blinded By Fear / Slaughter Of The Soul / Terminal Spirit Disease (Video) / The Burning Darkness (Video).

AT WINTER'S END

HELSINKI, FINLAND — *Harri Vähänissi (vocals), Aleksi Juutinen (guitar), Jaakko Nieminen (guitar), Jani Immonen (bass), Jukka Outinen (drums).*

Gothic laden Death Metal band AT WINTER'S END was forged in Helsinki during late 1996 by guitarists Aleksi Juutinen and Jaakko Nieminen. The first incarnation of the band, which included bassist Topi Ruotsalainen, issued the demo session 'Nectar for the Withering' in Spring of 1997. A further tape, 'Hallowed Membrance', ensued in January 1998 prompting the inclusion of the track 'Twilight Entrance' as part of the 'Suomi Finland Perkele' compilation album.

However, in April of 1998 Ruotsalainen opted out of the picture, duly being replaced by Jani Immonen. With this line-up, AT WINTER'S END managed to perform a set of shows in Greece returning home for support gigs to LULLACRY, GANDALF and SOULGRIND.

The 'Divine Empire' EP surfaced in 1999. AT WINTER'S END drummer Jukka Outinen also cites membership of LULLACRY.

Divine Empire EP, At Winter's End (1999). Divine Empire / Solitude Embracing / The Last Despair.

When The Day Is Gone, At Winter's End (2000). When The Day Is Gone / Another Sweet Failure.

ATEM

KEMI, FINLAND — *Antti Kalasniemi (vocals), Mikko Laukkanen (guitar), Olli Heikkinen (guitar), Ilkka Kuusisto (bass), Pentti Penttilä (drums).*

Originally entitled MORGUE the band, founded in 1995 in the Northern Finnish town of Kemi, issued the 'Something Beautiful' demo in 2000, signalling their name switch to ATEM. Two earlier tapes, an eponymous session and 1996's 'Once Dead' had been delivered under the band's previous title. MORGUE's original formation incorporated lead vocalist Antti Kalasniemi, guitarists Olli Heikkinen and Petri Lackman, bass player Ilkka Kuusisto and Pentti Penttilä on drums.

The band boosted their sound in 2002 with the addition of second guitarist Mikko Laukkanen, a member of THE MIDWINTER and THE LEECHWALKER. ATEM cut the 'Yöhön' promo that year, including the title track to the compilation album 'Metal Ostentation 3'. Besides holding down their ATEM duties Kalasniemi, Kuusisto and Penttilä all operate with AIVOPESUKONE. Heikkinen is active with KYY.

Something Beautiful, Atem (2000) (Demo). Sunt Lacrimae Rerum / Tale Of Stoned Garden / Jester / Fourth Toast For The Past.

Yöhön, Atem (2002) (Demo). Yöhön / Do Shadows Sleep.

Vihaolemus, Atem (2003) (Demo). Hämäräntakainen / Alku Uuden Kurjuuden / Hallan Hakkaama / Kun Mennyt Murtuu.

Uhri, Atem (2006) (Demo). Kuolleena Voit Vain Kuunnella / Jonka Hautaa Korpit Karttaa / Muistona Kiven Alla.

ATHEIST

SARASOTA, FL, USA — *Kelly Shaefer (vocals / guitar), Rand Burkey (guitar), Roger Patterson (bass), Steve Flynn (drums).*

Sarasota, Florida's "Jazz-Death" outfit ATHEIST started out life originally titled R.A.V.A.G.E. The band, regrettably lasting just three albums, excelled in highly complex innovation taking Thrash into uncharted realms. Although held in awe by their peers ATHEIST found it tough going on the commercial circuit. Guitarist Rand Burkey's distinction came from not only playing his guitar left handed but performing this feat on a regular but upside down guitar with the strings aligned for a right handed player.

Under the R.A.V.A.G.E title the band contributed tracks 'Brain Damage' and 'On They Slay' to the 1987 'Raging Death' compilation album. Going even further back, to 1984, Kelly Shaefer had forged OBLIVION, this unit inducting Steve Flynn on drums. The following year OBLIVION, then fronted by singer Scrappy and pulling in Roger Patterson on bass, evolved into R.A.V.A.G.E. The group, minus Scrappy, recorded the five-track demo 'Rotting In Hell' in August 1985, later commonly known as 'Kill Or Be Killed'. The band expanded, augmented by second guitarist Mark Schwartzberg, for second demo 'On We Slay'. The band then contributed the tracks 'Brain Damage' and 'On They Slay' to the 1987 'Raging Death' compilation album released on the Godly Records label.

As ATHEIST their first undertaking was the 1987 demo 'Hell Hath No Mercy'. The group issued a 1988 demo, entitled 'Beyond', featuring the tracks 'No Truth', 'Choose Your Death', 'Beyond', 'On They Slay' and Brain Damage'. Promoting this, they would support the likes of TESTAMENT, SNFU, DEATH ANGEL and OBITUARY prior to signing to European label Active Records. The band had originally signed a deal with the US label Mean Machine Records, a subsidiary of Three Cherries Records, but the label was on the verge of bankruptcy so an arrangement was made with Active to take the band. The Scott

Burns produced debut album 'Piece Of Time', worked up at Morrisound Recording in Tampa, was issued in February 1990.

On February 12th 1991 ATHEIST suffered a huge blow. A major auto accident involving the entire band tragically resulted in Roger Patterson being killed. Persevering, the band added ex-CYNIC bassist Tony Choy to record 'Unquestionable Presence', released in October 1991. Flynn would opt out after completion of dates with CANNIBAL CORPSE. Choy exited too accompanying Dutch Death Metal crew PESTILENCE for their 1991 world tour. He would later find an alternate, and more sedate, career as a Jazz musician on a cruise boat.

The May 1993 'Elements' album was, at the band's admission, thrown together in haste in order to fulfill their label contract but would still prove a worthy effort. Josh Greenbaum would handle drums in the studio. A European set of dates ensued alongside BENEDICTION which saw Shaefer joined by guitarist Frank Emmi and drummer Marcel DeSantos. ATHEIST then bowed out of public view. With the albums deleted, no official product would be forthcoming for over a decade.

Shaefer's NEUROTICA side project would blossom into a full time venture. The ex-ATHEIST man was still at it in 2001 launching the 'Living In Dry Years' album produced by none other than Brian Johnson of AC/DC fame. Shaefer acquired the rights to all ATHEIST material for a round of long overdue CD re-releases. Emmi would later figure in GENTLEMEN DEATH. Burkey would hook up with erstwhile CRIMSON GLORY vocalist MIDNIGHT for a project band.

In 2001 Shaefer, Burkey, Emmi and Flynn announced the reformation of ATHEIST. Meantime, Darren McFarland joined UNKNOWN CURE. In October 2002 Kelly Shaefer would be revealed to be involved in a project of the highest magnitude, fronting the new band of the erstwhile GUNS N' ROSES triumvirate of guitarist Slash, bassist Duff McKagan and drummer Matt Sorum. However, his tenure would be short-lived as this band unit pulled in ex-STONE TEMPLE PILOTS frontman Scott Wieland and duly evolved into VELVET REVOLVER. Shaefer launched a fresh band project, STARRFACTORY. Included on this new project would be the guitar pairing of ex-E3 and SERRAPHINE man Donny Jaurols and Noah Thompson of MEGABLATTA repute with erstwhile SANCTUARY drummer Dave Budbill. The singer also featured as a guest artist on the 2003 'Moments Of Clarity' Progressive Rock album by CRYPTIC VISION. Meantime, Word arrived in late 2003 that Rand Burkey was preparing a new band project entitled RANDOM XAOS.

In September 2004 Kelly Shaefer, switching to the guitar role, teamed up with ex-BURIAL frontman Mike Callahan in a Southern Florida based project called UNHEARD. However, in early 2005 it was learned that Shaefer, alongside UNHEARD band mate guitarist Donny Jaurols, would also be plugging a brand new band venture BIG MACHINE sponsored by no less than AC/DC's Brian Johnson.

ATHEIST drummer Steve Flynn resurfaced in 2005, forging a brand new band project, entitled GNOSTIC, with ENDERS GAME, AOS and CAUSTIC THOUGHT vocalist Kevin Freeman, CORPSEWORM and SEVERED guitarist Sonny Carson and CORPSEWORM, AOS and CAUSTIC THOUGHT bassist Stephen Morley.

The entire ATHEIST catalogue would be the subject of a reissue campaign by Relapse Records in 2005. The collection commenced in July with a foil stamped box set, limited to 1000 copies, comprising vinyl versions of each ATHEIST plus the R.A.V.A.G.E. 'On They Slay' 7" EP. ATHEIST announced a reformation in January 2006 to perform at the Italian 'Evolution' festival and Germany's 'Wacken Open Air' event. Line-up was announced as comprising the classic formation of Kelly Shaefer, guitarist Rand Burkey, bassist Tony Choy and drummer Steve Flynn. However, Burkey was forced out due to "legal problems". GNOSTIC's Chris Baker substituted. The band also pulled in second guitarist Sonny Carson of GNOSTIC to cover for Shae-

ATHEIST (pic: Dimitri Borellini)

fer, the frontman's abilities being hampered by tendonitis and carpal tunnel syndrome.

During ATHEIST's European run of dates Tony Choy suffered a sizable accident when he fell through an unsecured part of the large outdoor stage at Italy's Evolution Festival on July 16th. Fortunately the musician was uninjured but, having broken all his bass strings, had to be loaned another instrument to finish the set.

ATHEIST live dates continued into 2007 with European shows including appearances in June at the Hellfest in France as well as Graspop Metal Meeting in Belgium.

PIECE OF TIME, Active ATV8 (1990). Piece Of Time / Unholy War / Room With A View / On They Slay / Beyond / I Deny / Why Bother? / Life / No Truth.

UNQUESTIONABLE PRESENCE, Active ATV20 (1991). Mother Man / Unquestionable Presence / Your Life's Retribution / Enthralled In Essence / An Incarnation's Dream / The Formative Years / Brains / And The Psychic Saw.

ELEMENTS, Music For Nations MFN 150 (1993). Green / Water / Samba Briza / Air / Displacement / Animal / Mineral / Fire / Fractal Point / Earth / See You Again / Elements.

ATHELA

SWEDEN — *Jacob Alm (vocals / guitar), Johan Andren (guitar), Alexander Nordquist (guitar), Elin Lavonen (bass), Pär Hjulström (drums).*

ATHELA, founded during 1999 by bass player Jacob Alm of SLUMBER and Progressive Black Metal band MORNALAND, issued an opening demo entitled 'Unspoken Wish'. Session guitar for this recording came courtesy of PLATINA and ETERNALLY DEVOURED man Patrik Karlsson. The band's early line-up included SARTINAS bassist Patrick Andersson, guitarists Patrick Pira and Alexander Nordquist with Alm's sister on keyboards. Upon completion of these recordings female bass player Elin Lavonen of ETERNALLY DEVOURED, BEATSQUAD, SNEEZING HABIT and MINK and guitarist Johan Andren were enrolled. Drummer Adam Hobr then made up the numbers.

In 2001 ATHELA lost the services of Andersson then Hobr. Rehearsals continued using the esteemed figure of Dennis Ekdahl of RAISE HELL, SINS OF OMISSION, MÖRK GRYNING, BLOODSHED and MYSTIC PROPHECY. repute as stand in. These sessions would be so productive they would be issued as the 'Spectral' demo.

ATHELA released a one track, fourteen minute self-financed single 'Reliance' during 2003. ATHELA added AMARAN drummer Pär Hjulström to the ranks in March of 2004.

Unspoken Wish, Athela (2000) (Demo). Unspoken Wish.

Spectral, Athela (2002) (Demo). Untitled / Untitled / Untitled / Untitled.
Reliance, Athela (2003). Reliance.

ATHERETIC

LAC ST-JEAN, QC, CANADA — *Alexandre Leblanc (vocals), Dany Leblanc (guitar), Dominic Lapointe (bass), Jean-Sébastien Gagnon (drums).*

ATHERETIC, initially based in Lac St-Jean / Baie-Comeau, Quebec, began their activities on the Death Metal front as a Speed Metal covers band named BRAIN DEAD in 1991. Switching title to SATANIZED the band issued the demo 'In Search Of Beyond' during 1997 but by 1999, with a relocation to Montreal and recruitment of former ETERNAL and DORIS singer Wayne McGrath and former B.A.R.F. and GORE bassist Dominic 'Forest' Lapointe, had adopted the new guise of ATHERETIC. A two track demo was distributed during 1999. Signing to Neoblast Records, the debut album 'Adhesion, Aversion...', produced by Sebastien Gilbert at Peter Pan Studios, was delivered in May 2001.

Singer Wayne McGrath was replaced by Alexandre Leblanc, of POINT BLANK RAGE, in 2003. Bassist Dominique Lapointe, also active with AUGURY, enrolled into the ranks of QUO VADIS for Summer 2004 shows. The album 'Apocalyptic Nature Fury', released in May 2006, was recorded by Jean-François Dagenais of KATAKLYSM.

Atheretic, Atheretic (1999) (Demo). Disciple Enslaved By Faith / Bacteria (Compound Parasitism).
ADHESION, AVERSION, Neoblast NBR 01-05 (2001). Intro / Hermetic Seclusion / Compelled To Destitution / Hunter Of Seasons (Orimig Tro) / Disciples Enslaved By Faith / Adhesion, Aversion Of The Matter / Element / Bacteria Compound Parasitism.
APOCALYPTIC NATURE FURY, Galy (2006). Nature Laughs Last / Evolution / The Invisible Force / Solaris / Aquatic Redemption / Equinox / Of Dust & Soil / Sphere / Hunter Of Seasons.

ATHROX

ALKMAAR, HOLLAND — *Dennis M. Alma (vocals), Edsart Udo de Haas (guitar), Merijn Pronk (bass), Menno Duursma (drums).*

Alkmaar Death Metal band ATHROX was created as ATROX in 1998 but upon having an early concert review mis-spelling the band name, duly adopted the mistaken brand as their own. The band comprised ex-CRIST RAPING vocalist Dennis M. Alma, guitarist Edsart Udo de Haas, former DEIFICATION guitarist Lennart Engel, erstwhile CRIST RAPING and YAOTZIN bassist Merijn Pronk with another ex-DEIFICATION man, Menno Duursma, on drums. The band recorded a 1999 demo at Waterman Studio in Bergen.

Alma and Pronk also hold credits with Black Metal act THE DROWNED whilst Edsart Udo de Haas, Lennart Engel and Menno Duursma are involved with THE LIQUID UNDERGROUND. Engel also has an affiliation with THE RAVEN whilst Duursma has ties to MISSING LINK, ZI XUL, NOMANSLAND and THE LOST BOYS.

Athrox, Athrox (1999). Ben Hur / Rock / Angel Skull / Sound Of Silence / Slow / The Long Song.

ATOMSMASHER

USA — *Speedranch (vocals), James Plotkin (guitar), David Witte (drums).*

"Glitchgrind" act ATOMSMASHER, founded in 2000, feature drummer Dave Witte, a scene veteran of acts such as HUMAN REMAINS, DISCORDANCE AXIS, MELT-BANANA and BURNT BY THE SUN, in union with O.L.D. and KHANATE guitarist James Plotkin and JANSKY NOISE's Speedranch. Plotkin's diverse array of extreme music projects included work under the 'Jupiter Crew' pseudonym for a 1996 two track EP credited to JUNGLE CONCRETE on Possible Records plus solo albums billed as FLUX, 'Protoplasmic' in 1997, and ROMANCE, 'Bleak Memories' on Noise Museum in 1999. Collaborations featured Plotkin with Bill Yurkiewicz in NAMANAX, KRANK's 'A Peripheral Blur' outing in 1998 and with Mark Spybey for DEAD VOICES ON AIR. Other leftfield projects saw SOLARUS and TRIFFID PROJECT. Plotkin would issue two worthy 1996 releases, the solo album 'The Joy Of Disease' and a collaboration with SCORN's Mick Harris simply billed as PLOTKIN / HARRIS for the 'Collapse' album.

A self titled ATOMSMASHER album emerged in 2001 through Double H Noise Industries. ATOMSMASHER, maintaining the same line-up, evolved into PHANTOMSMASHER for a 2002 album in Ipecac Records.

October 2004 found Dave Witte enrolling into the ranks of Richmond, Virginia outfit MUNICIPAL WASTE. Witte forged a creative union with Chris Dodge of SPAZZ entitled EAST WEST BLAST TEST, issuing the 2005 album 'Unpopular Music For Popular People'. In 2006 Plotkin forged KHLYST with Runhild Gammelsäeter of THORR'S HAMMER.

ATOMSMASHER, Double H Noise Industries (2001). Caught In Your Orbit / Zanzibar / Thunderspit / Phantom Smasher / Gilgamesh / Skitchy / Very Much Want Head Return / Placebo / Skull Shot / Someone Is Trying To Kill Me / Pokemon Gangbang.

ATOMVINTER

GOTHENBURG, SWEDEN — *Andréaz (vocals), Micke (guitar), Peter (bass), Christer (drums).*

Gothenburg Punk / Death Metal band ATOMVINTER, founded in 1991, issued a self-titled 1995 album through Distortion Records. The group was created by vocalist / guitarist Andréaz, bassist Peter and GBG PUNX, E471 and HERSTORY drummer Christer. Subsequent additions saw the inclusion of guitarist Christian and drummer Joel. However, both these new musicians soon departed. In 1992 ATOMVINTER regrouped, shifting Andréaz to bass, drafting Micke on guitar and seeing Christer return on drums.

Following recording of the album the band pulled in new bassist Brink to record tracks for a 10" vinyl split effort shared with SVART SNÖ for Fäk Åff Räckårds. Tracks were also included on the Fettvadd Records compilation 'Things That Make No Sense'. Another line-up change saw DISORGANISED's Peter employed on bass. In 2000 ATOMVINTER cut nine new tracks intended for a split release with US act RIOTOUS.

ATOMVINTER, Black Sun DISTCD 12 (1995). Sinnes / Kurd / Hej Säpol / Nyliberal / Danska Poliser Är Harda / Sexualakt / Djävla Tvättsvamp / Sla Tillbaka / Du / 790 Dagar / Kärra / Västra Frölunda, / Angered / Nazifasoner / Videodrome.

ATROCITY

LUDWIGSBURG, GERMANY — *Alex Krull (vocals), Matthias Röderer (guitar), Richard Scharf (guitar), Oliver Klasen (bass), Michael Schwarz (drums).*

Founded in Ludwigsburg during 1985, initially billed as INSTIGATOR citing a line-up of erstwhile RIPPER vocalist Alex Krull, guitarists Mathias Röderer and Frank Knodel, bassist René Tometschek and Gernot Winkler on the drums. Re-billed as ATROCITY, they issued the October 1988 five track demo 'Instigators'. The band duly signed to Nuclear Blast Records and, enlisting BELCHING BEET drummer Michael Schwarz, released the 'Blue Blood' EP in 1989. The single was intended to come in two limited edition formats—as a gatefold cover, green vinyl version of 200 copies and a gatefold-cover, blue vinyl variant limited to a slightly more generous 500 copies. However, a mistake during manufacturing would produce a third, highly sought after run of just 50 copies in black vinyl, mispressed with RIGHTEOUS PIGS tracks on one side. The sleeve artwork presented problems as ATROCITY's original intention to depict Lady Diana and Prince Charles splattered in blood was vetoed by the printing company. Undaunted, the band photocopied the sleeves by hand.

The follow up came with the Scott Burns produced 'Hallucinations' album, recorded in Florida the following year and clad in distinctive H.R. Giger artwork. For these sessions ATROCITY re-aligned its line up, inducting guitarist Richard Scharf and bassist Oliver Klasen. The departing Tometschek subsequently formed MIGHTY DECIBEL, releasing an EP 'Relieve The Distress'.

ATROCITY toured Europe as support to CARCASS in 1990, SODOM in 1991 and DEICIDE in 1992. That year the 'Todessehnsucht' album was delivered for Roadrunner Records, this effort seeing the band branching out into grand orchestral arrangements. Without consent from the band Roadrunner issued the record in North America under the anglicised title 'Longing For Death'. The 1993 European "Todessehnsucht über Deutschland' headline tour saw DARK MILLENIUM as support. Proposed US dates allied with DEATH would unfortunately be curtailed.

In 1994 ATROCITY, drafting Markus Knapp to substitute for Klasen, signed to the Massacre label for the 'Blut' album. In keeping with the vampiresque theme of the project Krull and band mates travelled to Transylvania in order to imbibe some creative energies. Although the production of 'Blut' would be slated by the group the promotion, including video clips shot for 'Calling The Rain' and 'Miss Directed', was high. In support of the record the band supported OBITUARY on their British tour, following cancellation by EYEHATEGOD, and also put in shows alongside PITCH SHIFTER, CREMATORY and HATE SQUAD. In early 1995 the band underwent a line-up change, substituting Scharf and Markus Knapp for guitarist Torsten Bauer, citing credits with ENSLAVED, BATTLE ANGEL, STRADIVERI and THRASH MASSACRE, and bassist Chris Lukhamp of SCARAB, WHITE KRAUTS and CORPUS CHRISTI, respectively.

Not content to rest on their laurels, ATROCITY undertook some brave experimentation of sounds for their two 1995 releases. 'Calling The Rain' was graced with an ethnic lead vocal from Alex's sister Yasmin Krull whilst 'Die Liebe' was a joint project with electronic band DAS ICH,

To promote the 'Willenskraft' album ATROCITY toured Germany on a package tour with strong support from IN FLAMES, HEAVENWOOD and TOTENMOND. Strangely the band began to attract media attention for supposed far right political imagery but ATROCITY made their feelings clear on this issue at the 'Wacken Open Air' festival in 1996 as they symbolically destroyed a giant swastika during 'Willenskraft', encouraged by applause from thousands of fans. Drummer Michael Schwarz busied himself in a variety of extracurricular band projects including Mincecore act BELCHING BEET, Crustcore merchants ACCION MUTANTE and Gothic veterans UMBRA ET IMAGO.

Experimenting further still, the 1997 single 'Shout' is ATROCITY's interpretation of TEARS FOR FEARS hit song and also includes a version of D.A.F.'s 'Verschwende Deine Jugend'. Following the tradition of diversity set previously, the 'Shout' single proved to be a taster for the 'Werk 80' album, a collection of cover versions by pop artists such as O.M.D., DAVID BOWIE, DURAN DURAN, FRANKIE GOES TO HOLLYWOOD, HUMAN LEAGUE and even SOFT CELL. The album's impact was sustained with a later 'Festivals edition' adding three extra tracks, a cover of D.A.F.'s 'Das letzte mal', 'Die Deutschmaschine' and 'Verschwende deine Jugend'. The band's prolonged tenacity finally paid rewards when they achieved their first chart album, 'Werk 80' entering the German placings at number 33, the sales figures for which must in some respect be married to a tasteful advertising campaign featuring the two models chosen for the single and album artwork. The momentum would be maintained by the 33 track retrospective 'Non Plus Ultra' compiled of ATROCITY's latest hits plus videos and archive and rare material.

ATROCITY would delve into cover versions once more during 2000, releasing a version of SIMON & GARFUNKEL's 'The Sound Of Silence' as a single. The accompanying album, 'Gemini', would be issued in two different versions. Variants with a red sleeve would include the old wartime marching song track 'Lili Marleen' in English whilst blue covers offered the track in German.

In September 2002 ATROCITY would hook up with IN EXTREMO for a short run of dates in Mexico. During recording of tracks for a new studio album slated for 2003 issue the group, bringing in former FROM THY ASHES and TEABAG guitarist Sebastian Schult, contributed a cover version of THE SISTERS OF MERCY's 'More' for a tribute album.

Guitarist Thorsten Bauer rejoined the band in April 2003 as that same year he also sessioned on the ERBEN DER SCHÖPFUNG 'Twilight' album, produced by Alex Krull with Martin Schmidt on session drums. July bore witness to some high profile Rock n' Roll wedding bells as Krull married long term girlfriend THEATRE OF TRAGEDY singer Liv Kristine Espenæs. This marital union spilled over into a creative force with the announcement of a brand new band LEAVES EYES, seeing Liv Kristine Espenæs Krull and Alexander Krull founding a fresh venture with members of ATROCITY.

The 2004 ATROCITY album 'Atlantis', recorded at Mastersound Studio in Fellbach, Germany under the production guidance of Alex Krull, emerged in April. A single, 'Cold Black Days', preceded it. The group would be engaged in a search for a new drummer in early October when Martin Schmidt announced his intention to leave. Extensive tour dates saw ATROCITY hooking up with LEAVES' EYES, BATTLELORE and ELIS for October gigs throughout Europe and Scandinavia, upfront of a further mainland trek in November allied once again with LEAVES' EYES, BATTLELORE and Norwegians SIRENIA.

As 2005 opened ATROCITY announced they had acquired the services of drummer Moritz Neuner. Heavily in demand on the underground Metal scene, Neuner prior credits included acts such as ST. LUCIFER, SHADOWCAST, DARKWELL, GRAVEWORM, ABIGOR, EVENFALL, DORNENREICH, SIEGFRIED, ANGRY ANGELS, NECROLOGY and KOROVA. During October ATROCITY joined the US road partnership dubbed the 'International Extreme Music Festival' in collaboration with BYZANTINE, NIGHTRAGE, EPOCH OF UNLIGHT, HELL WITHIN, LEAVES' EYES and LILITU.

Aiming to repeat their previous successful 1997 experiment, throughout 2006 the band worked on new recordings for 'Werk 80 II'. Moritz Neuner sessioned on Spanish act DARK EMBRACE's 'The Rebirth Of Darkness' album in November.

Blue Blood, Nuclear Blast NB 23 (1989) (Limited edition on green vinyl of 200 copies, blue vinyl 500 copies). Blue Blood / When The Fire Burns Over The Sea / Humans Lost Humanity.

HALLUCINATIONS, Nuclear Blast NB 038 (1990). Deep In Your Subconsciousness / Life Is A Long And Silent River / Fatal Step / Hallucinations / Defeated Intellect / Abyss Of Addiction / Hold Out (To The End) / Last Temptation / Blue Blood / When The Fire Burns Over The Sea / Humans Lost Humanity.

TODESSEHNSUCHT, Roadrunner RR 9128-2 (1992). Todessehnsucht / Godless Years / Unspoken Names / Defiance / Triumph At Dawn / Introduction / Sky Turned Red / Necropolis / A Prison Called Earth / Todessehnsucht Reprise / Arcangel.

BLUT, Massacre MAS CD033 (1994). Trial / Miss Directed / In My Veins / Blood Lust Undead Trance / I'm In Darkness / Calling The Rain / Moon-Struck / Ever And Anon / Begotten Son (Of Wrath) / Into The Maze / Leicenfeier / Goddess In Black / Threnody (The Spirit Never Dies) / Soul Embrace / Land Beyond The Forest.

DIE LIEBE, Swan Lake MAS CD069 (1995). Die Liebe / Moonstrucker / Bloodlust (Undead Trance) / Misdirected / Parentalia / Trial By Ordeal / Unschuld / Von Leid Und Elend Und Seelenqualen / Die Todgeweihten.

CALLING THE RAIN, Swan Lake MAS CD071 (1995). Calling The Rain (video edit) / Back From Eternity / Departure / Land Beyond The

Forest / Migrant's Shade / Dir Geburt Eines Baumes / Calling The Rain (remix) / Ancient Sadness.

WILLENSKRAFT, Massacre MAS CD099 (1996). Scorching Breath / Deliverence / Blood Stained prophecy / Love Is Dead / We Are Degeneration / Willenskraft / For Ever And A Day / Seal Of Secrecy / Down Below / The Hunt.

The Definition Of Kraft & Wille EP, Massacre MAS CD 114 (1996). Deliverance (Come To My World-Mix) / Willenskraft (Remix) / Scorching Breath (Remix) / Gottes Tod.

Tainted Love, Massacre MASCD143 (1997). Tainted Love / Tainted Love (Albrin mix) / Die Deutschmaschine / Deliverance (Wow! Mix).

Das Letzte Mal, Massacre MAS CD0146 (1997) (German promotion release). Das Letzte Mal.

Shout (Edit), Massacre MAS CD141 (1997). Shout (Edit) / Shout / Verschwende Deine Jugen.

WERK 80, Massacre MAS CD138 (1997). Shout / Rage Hard / Wild Boys / The Great Commandment / Send Me An Angel / Tainted Love / Der Mussolini / Being Boiled / Don't Go / Let's Dance / Maid Of Orleans. Chart position: 33 GERMANY.

WERK 80: FESTIVAL EDITION, Massacre MASCD168 (1998). Shout / Rage Hard / Wild Boys / The Great Commandment / Send Me An Angel / Tainted Love / Der Mussolini / Being Boiled / Don't Go / Let's Dance / Maid Of Orleans / Das Letzte Mal / Die Deutschmaschine / Verschwende Deine Jugend.

Taste Of Sin, Massacre (2000). Taste Of Sin / Taste Of Sin (Ich sterbe schon remix) / Taste Of Sin (Slam-bam Greg Bimson remix) / Pictures Of Matchstick Men.

The Sound Of Silence, (2000). Sound Of Silence (Single mix) / Sound Of Silence (Mezzo mix) / Sound Of Silence (Edit Version).

GEMINI, Motor Music 549 315-2 (2000). Taste Of Sin / Zauberstab / Tanz mit dem Teufel / Liebesspiel / Wilder Schmetterling / Sound Of Silence / Das / Gebot / Sometimes … A Nightsong / Seasons In Black / Lili Marleen.

GEMINI, Motor Music (2000). Taste Of Sin / Zauberstab / Tanz mit dem Teufel / Liebesspiel / Wilder Schmetterling / Sound Of Silence / Das 11. Gebot / Sometimes … A Nightsong / Seasons In Black / Lili Marleen. Chart position: 95 GERMANY.

Cold Black Days, Napalm (2004). Cold Black Days / Cold Black Days (Radio mix) / Antediluvian World / Cold Black Days (Das Ich remix).

ATLANTIS, Napalm NPR143 (2004). Reich Of Phenomena / Superior Race / Gods Of Nations / Ichor / Enigma / Morbid Mind / Omen / Cold Black Days / Atlantean Empire / Clash Of The Titans / Apocalypse / Lost Eden / The Sunken Paradise / Aeon / Ein Volk.

ATROCITY

TORRINGTON, CT, USA — *Rob Wedda (vocals), Jesse Piechowski (guitar), Rich Flint (bass), Jeff White (drums).*

The Torrington, Connecticut Grindcore act ATROCITY, formed in early 1985 and having officially debuted with a scarce 1989 7" single 'Hatred Birth', often had their 'Infected' album, released by British label Metalcore Records, mistakenly attributed to the German ATROCITY. The group, involving vocalist Rob Wedda, guitarist Scott Reynolds, bassist Rich Flint and Jeff White on drums, had issued a string of demos, 'Toxic Death', 'Ravaged By Disease', 'Mangled', upfront of the single. The band's final album, 1992's 'Art Of Death' featuring new guitarist Jesse Piechowski, saw CD versions carrying three extra tracks in 'Winds Of Famine', 'In Protest Of What' and 'False Front'. ATROCITY folded in 1993.

ATROCITY reunited during 2006, signing with Open Grave Records to release an EP comprising alternate versions of previously released songs recorded during the 1990 'Infected' sessions. ATROCITY further initiated recordings for a full-length album and donated a cover version of 'I See A Darkness' for a JOHNNY CASH tribute album entitled 'A Metal Tribute To The Man In Black'.

THE ART OF DEATH, (1992). Pol Pot / Unpure To Christ / Confined / Delirium Tremens / Let The Killing Begin / Waste The Good Suffering / Warped Progress / Maggot Feed / Blood Harvest / I Am God—I Am Death / Depression / Progress Of Suicide / Scarred / Collapsing In Seizure / A Tranquil Place / The Art Of Death / Parade Of The Morbid / Homicidal Cunt / Charred Remains / Suicidal.

CONTAMINATED, Open Grave OGR010CD (2007). Contamination / Awaiting Demise / Nuclear Manslaughter / Personal Decimation / Enslaved In Turmoil / Unseen Death / Slave To Conformity / Redeemed By Confession / Cycle Of Despair / Infected.

ATSPHEAR

MÓSTOLES, SPAIN — *Rafael Fernández Melero (vocals), Sergio Lara Gonzalez (guitar), Manuel Probanza (guitar), Carlos Delgado Peinado (bass), Víctor Hernández (drums).*

Móstoles, Madrid based Death Metal band ATSPHEAR was created during 2001 but stabilised its line-up in May 2003 counting singer Rafael Fernández Melero, guitarists Sergio Lara Gonzalez and Manuel Probanza, bassist Carlos Delgado Peinado with Víctor Hernández on drums. The original band unit had been created under the title DARK CRYSTAL by Sergio Lara Gonzalez, ex-NIGHTFALL members Manuel Probanza, Víctor Hernández and Alberto. Carlos Delgado Peinado, of AKALLABETH, joined in February 2002 whilst Rafael Fernández Melero enrolled in May 2003. ATSPHEAR released the demo 'Atmosphere X', produced by Javier Rubio and recorded at Rock Soul studios in Madrid, in January 2004.

Zero Records released the album 'New Line System' in May 2005. These sessions, again produced by Javier Rubio, were laid down at Korsakov Studies. A promotional video for the song 'Atmosphere X' was directed by Carlos Delgado.

Atmosphere X, Atsphear (2004) (Demo). Introspective / Atmosphere X / Between Love & Hate / Savior / beLIEve / Portrait Of A Suicide.

NEW LINE SYSTEM, Zero (2005). Atmosphere X / Psycho Circle / Supernova / Your Strain / beLIEve / F@mily / Hall Of Mirrors / Sensory / Electrostatic Nation / Between Love & Hate / State Of Coma.

AUBERON

SWEDEN — *Fredrik Degerström (vocals), Johan Asplund (guitar), Magnus Lindblom (guitar), Johan Westerlund (guitar), Pekka Kiviaho (bass), Morgan Lie (drums).*

Swedish Death Metal band with Progressive leanings founded as school band OBERON in 1988. Originally a trio of vocalist and guitarist Fredrik Degerström, 12 year old drummer Morgan Lie and guitarist Andreas. OBERON cut their first demo 'Follow The Blind' with Degerström handling bass duties.

The band's first guitarist Andreas quit to follow the Punk path and in came Jon Andersson on guitar and former MISHRAK man Johan Westerlund on bass for recording of the 'Insane' demo. The band also pulled in guitarist Nils Norberg but he departed for NOCTURNAL RITES in mid 1996. That same year Degerström united under the pseudonym of 'Spider' with the NOCTURNAL RITES duo of guitarist Frederik 'Psycho' Mannberg and bassist Nils 'Snake' Eriksson to record the 'Under The Guillotine' album as retro-Thrashers GUILLOTINE.

Upon signing to the Black Mark label a nameshift to AUBERON occurred as the band discovered other acts with their previous moniker. Guitarist Magnus Lindblom was added after the release of the February 1998 album 'The Tale Of Black'. The record featured Andreas Stoltz of HOLLOW as session guest.

AUBERON guitarist Pekka 'Power' Kiviaho created PERSUADER for 'The Hunter' album. During 2000 AUBERON underwent a line-up shift pulling in two new guitarists in Jonathan Holmgren and Anders Johansson. AUBERON would issue 'Crossworld' during April 2001, once again seeing HOLLOW's Andreas Stolz as guest musician.

In early 2005 it would be revealed ex-member Pekka Kiviaho had joined ONE MAN ARMY AND THE UNDEAD QUARTET, the new project of ex-THE CROWN singer Johan Lindstrand.

Follow The Blind, Auberon (1993) (Demo).

Insane, Auberon (1995) (Demo).

Infinite Beauty, Black Mark (1998) (Promotion release). Infinite Beauty / A Whispering Wind / The Dance.

THE TALE OF BLACK, Black Mark BMCD 103 (1998). Intro / Infinite Beauty / Secrets / A Whispering Wind / The End Of All / The Dance / A Farewell Of Creation / The White Ship / Fearless / For All Time.

CROSSWORLD, Black Mark BMCD 145 (2001). Intro—Crossworld / Vanitys Fall / The Beast Within / Hellborn / Ex Oblivione / Gaia / I See Her / A Bleeding Work Of Art / Forbidden.

Scum Of The Earth, Auberon (2004) (Demo). Mirror Image / Scum Of The Earth / Fear / Hypnos.

AUGURY

MONTREAL, QC, CANADA — *Arianne Fleury (vocals), Patrick Loisel (guitar), Mathieu Marcotte (guitar), Dominic Lapointe (bass), Etienne Gallo (drums).*

Montreal Death Metal combo AUGURY was initiated in late 2001 when guitarist Mathieu Marcotte exited his prior act SPASME. Building up a band unit, he was joined by SEPTEMBER 12 and ROSTRUM, Paraguayan born soprano vocalist Arianne Fleury and the ATHERETIC, QUO VADIS, B.A.R.F. and SATANIZED credit Dominic 'Forest' Lapointe. This trio would subsequently be bolstered with the recruitment of KRAZILEC and FORESHADOW guitarist Patrick Loisel in February 2002. That June, drummer Mathieu Groulx completed the line-up. However, Groulx soon exited, being superseded by Étienne Gallo of DISEMBARKATION and NEURAXIS repute.

The band entered Wild Studio in late November 2003 with producers by Yannick St-Amand and KATAKLYSM's Jean-Fancois Dagenais to craft the debut album 'Concealed' for Galy Records. Adipocere Records licensed 'Concealed' for European distribution in 2005. AUGURY partnered with UNEXPECT for Canadian touring in April 2006.

CONCEALED, Galy GALY-026 (2004). Beatus / … Ever Know Peace Again / Cosmic Migration / Nocebo / Alien Shores / In Russian Dolls Universes / Becoming God / The Liar Of Purity / From Eden Estranged / … As Sea Devours Land.

AURA

EINDHOVEN, HOLLAND — *Peter Brinkman (vocals / guitar), Mark van Dooren (guitar), Martijn Luppens (bass), Michel Jolie (keyboards), Bas van den Boom (drums).*

Eindhoven melodic Death Metal band AURA began life in 1991, formed by vocalist / guitarist Peter Brinkman, bass player Martyn Luppens and Ruby Soffner on second guitar. The group went through a succession of drummers including Peter van de Linden in 1993, Sander van Balen and Molly "The Beast". Signing to Hammerheart Records AURA released the 1996 EP 'Shattered Dawnbreak'.

AURA drafted another new drummer in 1998, Bas van den Boom, at the same juncture expanding their sound with the incorporation of keyboard player Michel Jolie. The demo 'Sect' arrived in 2000. The album 'Hidden' saw release in 2004, after which AURA evolved into SCENARIO II.

Shattered Dawnbreak, Hammerheart (1996). Your Ignorant Ways / This Shattered Dawnbreak / Moonsymmetry XXI: Empires Ablaze / (An Ode To) The Autumnlands.
Promo 2000 Sect, Independent (2000). Sect / In Sylvan Enchantment / 750ms / Absynth.

AURORA

AABENRAA, DENMARK — *Claus Frøland (vocals), Thomas Broberg (guitar), Jens Ecklon Asmussen (guitar), Niels Kvist (bass), Morten Sørensen (drums).*

Aabenraa based, Gothic styled Progressive Death Metal band forged during 1994 and featuring former personnel from ASMODEUS. The opening line up comprised singer Claus Frølund, guitarists Thomas Broberg and Allan Iversen, bass player Carsten Terp and drummer Morten Gade Sørensen. Broberg held a track record with PARRICIDE whilst Terp was ex-DRAIN and HORIZONTAL SPEED. Sørensen was also to be found manning the drum kit for SCORNFUL during 1995.

A demo 'Childhood Memories' and a single entitled 'I'll Cry Alone' was released under the AURORA BOREALIS banner, the group truncating their title in 1997. Signing to the Serious Entertainment label the group debuted with the Jacob Hansen produced 'Eos' album. 'Sadiam', another Hansen produced offering, capitalised on this achievement but Iversen opted out that same year, being superseded by HORIZONTAL SPEED man Anders Vestergaard. As a diversion, both Frøland and Sørensen would also be active with NEPENTHE.

Further side activities found Terp operational with DAMION and Sørensen with SCAVENGER. Retaining his position in AURORA Sørensen joined WUTHERING HEIGHTS in 2001. AURORA would switch Terp for new bass man Niels Kvist in 2002. Upon completion of the 'Dead Electric Nightmares' album Jens Ecklon Asmussen supplanted Vestergaard the following year.

Both Morten Gade Sørensen and Niels Kvist would also be active with melodic Power Metal band PYRAMAZE, cutting the 'Melancholy Beast' album in 2003.

I'll Cry Alone, Prutten PRUT001 (1997). I'll Cry Alone / Black Tears.
EOS, Serious Entertainment SE009CD (1998). Aurora Borealis / I'll Cry Alone / Ethereal Goddess / Elyzium / Blue / Danzing Summer / Psychedelia / Black Tears / Numbed Eyes / Childhood Memories.
Sadiam, Serious Entertainment SE017CD (1999). Beloved / To Hell / Sadiam / Home.
DEVOTION, Serious Entertainment SE019CD (2000). Mrs. Pink / It's Just / Devotion / All The Things / Slow Down / In This Room / Catharthis / You.
DEAD ELECTRIC NIGHTMARES, Lucretia LU20012-2 (2002). Black Heavy Cat / Metaphysical Electric / New God Rising / Martyr Of Life / A Perfect Light / Watching, Falling, Breathing / Two Dice And A Silent Disguise / Causa Sui / Jack / Chains Of God.

AURORA BOREALIS

ATLANTA, GA, USA — *Ron Vento (vocals / guitar), Jason Ian-Vaughn Eckart (bass), Derek Roddy (drums).*

Essentially a one man project of former LESTREGUS NOSFERATUS man Ron Vento. AURORA BORALIS, based out of Atlanta, Georgia, first employed ACHERON, MALEVOLENT CREATION, NILE and ANGEL CORPSE drummer Tony Laureano for the 'Mansions Of Eternity' album. By the time of 'Praise The Archaic- Lights Embrace' bassist Jason Ian-Vaughn Eckart and MALEVOLENT CREATION drummer Derek Roddy were employed.

The band is prolific on the tribute scene having cut 'After Forever' for the BLACK SABBATH tribute 'Hell Rules', Altar Of Sacrifice' for the SLAYER homage 'Gateway To Hell', JUDAS PRIEST's 'Metal Meltdown' for the 'Hell Bent For Metal' opus and 'We Rock' for the DIO collection 'Awaken The Demon'.

The band signed to the Die Hard Music label, promptly resulting in a re-issue of the 'Northern Lights' album complete with a glut of extra material. AURORA BOREALIS returned in January 2003 with a new album 'Time, Unveiled'. Drums for these sessions were handled by erstwhile HATE ETERNAL man Tim Yeung.

Ex-AURORA BOREALIS drummer Tony Laureano subsequently joined high status Norwegian Black Metal band DIMMU BORGIR. AURORA BOREALIS returned in April 2006 with the 'Relinquish' album released through Nightsky Productions.

MANSIONS OF ETERNITY, (1998). Crowned With Embalmment / Weighing Of The Heart / Valley Of The Kings / Slave To The Grave / Sixteenth Charm.
PRAISE THE ARCHAIC- LIGHTS EMBRACE, Nightsky Productions NSP001 (1999). Offerings Of Jade And Blood / A Gaze Into Everdark / In The Depths Of A Labyrinth / Aggressive Dynasty / War Of The Rings / For Your Comprehension / Constellation Embellished With Chaos / Calm Before The Storm.
NORTHERN LIGHTS, Nightsky Productions NSP003 (2000). Thrice Told / Enter The Halls / Images In The Nightsky / Draco / Sky Dweller / Hydrah / Dream God / Distant.
TIME, UNVEILED, Die Hard Music (2003). Triumph Again / Sky Burial / Searching / Transversing The Tide / Berserker / The Last Day / Reign / Sixteenth Chamber / Slave To The Grave.
RELINQUISH, Nightsky Productions (2006). Myths Of The Light / Let The Games Begin / Ravaged By Fire / God Wills It / The Red Flag / River Through The Skies / Tonight We Feast / Black Snow.

AUTERE

TURKU, FINLAND — *Jemmy W. (vocals), Jussi Kaumi (guitar), Petri Huhtala (guitar), Markus Virtanen (bass), Tatu Turunen (drums).*

Melodic Death Metal band AUTERE was conceived in Turku during September 2002, initiated by two bored security guards, guitarist Juha-Matti Helmi and drummer Jaakko Pellotsalo. The group would be constructed with the addition of Markus Virtanen on bass, second guitar player Jussi Kaumi and singer Jemmy W. Just as the band readied itself to craft a debut demo in July 2003, Pellotsalo exited. Tatu Turunen was duly enrolled but in October of 2004 the unit suffered a further blow when founder Juha-Matti Helmi took his leave. Nevertheless, an EP, entitled 'Lines & Fragments', was rendered at Popstudios in Loimaa during May 2005.

AUTERE drafted replacement six-stringer Petri Huhtala in mid 2005.

Autere, Autere (2004) (Demo). Autere / Waste For Nothing.
Lines & Fragments, Autere (2005). Begone XVIII / Tactical Warfare Wonder / Surveillance System / Explicit / Slow Motion Death / Making Of (Video).

AUTOPSY

SAN FRANCISCO, CA, USA — *Eric Cutler (vocals / guitar), Chris Reifert (drums / vocals), Danny Corrales (guitar), Ken Sovari (bass).*

The truly horrific AUTOPSY, originally known as THE ABORTED, was formed in San Francisco during 1987 when drummer Chris Reifert left DEATH following their 'Scream Bloody Gore' album. The band debuted in December that year with a four-track demo executed at ATR studios in Lafayette comprising 'Human Genocide', 'Embalmed', 'Stillborn' and 'Mauled To Death', these sessions featuring Eric Eigard on bass. Guitarist Eric Cutler sang lead vocals on 'Mauled To Death' whilst Reifert handled lead vocals on the other three tracks. A second demo, 'Critical Madness' issued in July 1988, found the inclusion of guitarist Danny Corrales and Ken Sorvari on bass.

The highly influential British underground label Peaceville Records duly picked the group up. The debut 1989 album 'Severed Survival' came adorned in a sickening sleeve, involving an unfortunate individual being ripped to pieces with the band logo rendered in lumps of flesh. This first edition rapidly became a collectors item when replied by the more generally known doctors cover. Demand was heightened by blood red vinyl editions and, naturally, a picture disc. Where AUTOPSY made their mark on the scene was by their incorporation of proto-sludge sluggishness as a counter foil to the death metal abrasion. They would carry this defining trait throughout their catalogue.

The group utilized SADUS bassist Steve DiGeorgio for the 'Severed Survival' recording sessions, conducted under the production guidance of METAL CHURCH guitarist John Marshall at Starlight Studios, but the band soon re-enlisted Ken Sorvari in time for European live work with BOLT THROWER and PESTILENCE. A stopgap EP, 'Retribution For The Dead', emerged in 1991. In 1990 prior to a further European tour bassist Ken Sovari left to be replaced by Eric's bother Steve Cutler. The band then executed dates in Holland throughout February aligned with PESTILENCE and BOLT THROWER on the 'Bloodbrothers' tour. SUFFOCATION bassist Josh Barohn also featured as a member the same year. Barohn was later to found WELT and IRON LUNG.

Steve Cutler departed following the 1991 'Mental Funeral' album, these self-produced tracks being laid down in just six days at Different Fur Studios in San Francisco. AUTOPSY played a 1992 festival in Detroit on a bill with MORTICIAN, VITAL REMAINS and REPULSION in which the band played as a trio due to Eric Butler breaking his hand. AUTOPSY re-enlisted the services of DiGiorgio for the March 1992 'Fiend For Blood' EP before adding ex-SUFFOCATION bassist Josh Barohn on a permanent basis. The spasmic Thrash / Doom collision 'Acts Of The Unspeakable', released that October, was hyped as AUTOPSY's most "sickest fuckin' album ever"- until July 1995's scatological comeback 'Shitfun'. This outing, clad in one of the grossest sleeves yet to adorn a Metal album to date, saw a guesting Clint Bower of HEXX repute on bass guitar. 'Shitfun' deliberately dove to uncharted depths of decadence with such fecally inclined material as 'I Shit On Your Grave', 'I Sodomise Your Corpse' and 'Shiteater'. The album's presentation, and change in direction to incorporate primitive Grind-Punk alienated a large sector of their existing audience.

Although 'Shitfun' had made an undeniable mark, AUTOPSY was to split. Chris Reifert created ABSCESS and by 2000 THE RAVENOUS with ANTHRAX, NUCLEAR ASSAULT and S.O.D. bassist Dan Lilker and NECROPHAGIA's Killjoy. In early 2002 Reifert guested on the 'Murderous, Ravenous' by MURDER SQUAD, the Swedish 'All star' Death Metal project of DISMEMBER and ENTOMBED members.

The specialist Death Metal label Necroharmonic Productions would issue a 9 track double 7" coloured vinyl live single 'Tortured Moans Of Agony' in 1998. The same label would combine AUTOPSY's early demos plus two 1990 era live tracks for the 2000 CD release 'Ridden With Disease'. Reifert continued on the path of the absolute in extreme the following year, announcing the formation of a fresh project subtly entitled EATMYFUKK.

A career retrospective DVD, entitled 'Dark Crusades'. Clocking in at 3 hours this set included numerous concert films including the band's last ever live show on July 29th 1994 at Ruthies Inn, San Francisco. Necroharmonic Productions added to the archives with vintage live tapes issued as the 2004 'Dead As Fuck' album.

Demo '87, Autopsy (1987) (Demo). Human Genocide / Embalmed / Stillborn / Mauled To Death.
Critical Madness, Autopsy (1988) (Demo). Charred Remains / Ridden With Disease / Critical Madness.
SEVERED SURVIVAL, Peaceville VILE 12 (1989) (Vinyl banned cover). Charred Remains / Service For A Vacant Coffin / Disembowel / Gasping For Air / Ridden With Disease / Pagan Saviour / Impending Dread / Severed Survival / Critical Madness / Embalmed / Stillborn.
SEVERED SURVIVAL, Peaceville VILE 12 CD (1990) (CD release). Charred Remains / Service For A Vacant Coffin / Disembowel / Gasping For Air / Ridden With Disease / Pagan Saviour / Impending Dread / Severed Survival / Critical Madness / Embalmed / Stillborn.
Retribution For The Dead, Peaceville VILE 24 (1991). Retribution For The Dead / Destined To Fester / In The Grip Of Winter.
MENTAL FUNERAL, Peaceville VILE 25 (1991). Mass Of Burnt Decay / In The Grip Of Winter / Fleshcrawl / Torn From The Womb / Slaughterday / Dead / Robbing The Grave / Hole In The Head / Destined To Fester / Bonesaw / Dark Crusade / Mental Funeral.
LIVE FROM THE GRAVE, Autopsy (1992) (12" vinyl). Severed Survival / Hole In The Head / Flesherawl / Torn From The Womb / Bonus Track / Service For A Vacant Coffin / Embalmed / Destined To Fester / Robbing The Grave / Charred Remains.
Fiend For Blood, Peaceville VILE 29 (1992). Fiend For Blood / Keeper Of Decay / Squeal Like A Pig / Ravenous Freaks / A Different Kind Of Mindfuck / Dead Hole.
ACTS OF THE UNSPEAKABLE, Peaceville VILE 33 (1992). Meat / Necrocannibalistic Vomitorium / Your Rotting Face / Blackness Within / An Act Of The Unspeakable / Frozen With Fear / Spinal Extractions / Death Twitch / Skullptures / Pus-Rot / Battery Acid Enema / Lobotomized / Funerality / Tortured Moans Of Agony / Ugliness And Secretions / Orgy In Excrements / Voices / Walls Of The Coffin.
SHITFUN, Peaceville VILE 49 (1995). Deathmask / Humiliate Your Corpse / Fuckdog / Praise The Children / The Birthing / Shit Eater / Formaldehigh / I Sodomise Your Corpse / Geek / Brain Damage / Blood Orgy / No More Hate / Grave Violators / Maim Rape, Kill Rape / I Shit On Your Grave / An End To The Misery / The 24 Public Mutilations / Bathe In Fire / Bowel Ripper / Burnt To A Fuck / Excremental Ecstasy.
RIDDEN WITH DISEASE, Necroharmonic Productions SLEAZY 001 (2000). Human Genocide / Embalmed / Stillborn / Mauled To Death / Charred Remains / Ridden With Disease / Critical Madness / Severed Survival / Service For A Vacant Coffin.

Tortured Moans Of Agony, Necroharmonic Productions (2001). Fiend For Blood (Live) / Charred Remains (Live) / Dead (Live) / Fleshcrawl (Live) / Slaughterday (Live) / Death Twitch (Live) / Twisted Mass Of Human Decay (Live) / Torn From The Womb (Live) / Shiteater (Live).

TORN FROM THE GRAVE, Peaceville CDVILE 84 (2001). Charred Remains / Disembowel / Gasping For Air / Severed Survival / Ridden With Disease / Service For A Vacant Coffin / Retribution For The Dead / Robbing The Grave / Twisted Mass Of Burnt Decay / Fleshcrawl / Torn From The Grave / Slaughterday / Dark Crusade / Mental Funeral / Fiend For Blood / Squeal Like A Pig / Funereality / An Act Of The Unspeakable / Frozen With Fear / Spinal Extraction / Death Twitch / Walls Of The Coffin / Shiteater / Humiliate Your Corpse / Brain Damage / Blood Orgy / Bowel Ripper.

DEAD AS FUCK, Necroharmonic Productions SLEAZY 006 (2005). Dead / Fiend For Blood / Twisted Mass Of Burnt Decay / Deathtwitch / Slaughterday / Fleshcrawl—Torn From The Womb / Charred Remains / Shiteater / Pus / Rot / Gasping For Air / Severed Survival / Hole In The Head / Torn From The Womb / Fiend For Blood / Service For A Vacant Coffin / Embalmed / Destined To Fester / Robbing The Grave / Charred Remains.

AUTOPSY TORMENT

SWEDEN — *Devil Lee Rot (vocals), Harri (guitar), Daniel Scyphe (bass), Sexual Goatlicker (drums).*

A notorious name among Death Metal circles. AUTOPSY TORMENT would spawn the equally renowned PAGAN RITES. The band first emerged with the Grindcore 1989 demo session 'Splattered' but had adopted a more Death Metal style for the 1991 effort 'Darkest Rituals'. The 'Nocturnal Blasphemy' and 'The Seventh Soul Of Hell' demos were delivered the following year. The band folded in 1994 as vocalist David Lee Rot (a.k.a. Thomas Karlsson) and drummer Sexual Goatlicker (a.k.a. Karl Vincent) forged PAGAN RITES. Rot also became the singer for TRISTITIA.

However, by the following year original bass player Daniel Scyphe recreated the band with Rot, Goatlicker and Jimi on bass. A reunion show in Gothenburg witnessed a non appearance from Rot necessitating Ustumallagen from DENIAL OF GOD deputizing.

AUTOPSY TORMENT laid down recordings for a 2001 release. 'Orgy Of The Dead' would be released in two variants, both hosting completely different sleeve designs, a 7 track CD version and a vinyl issue with an extra track 'Gory To The Brave'. In 2003 the Time Before Time label issued a shared CD-R in collaboration with DEVIL LEE ROT, 'Premature Torture', limited to 333 copies.

Die Todesrune issued the 'Graveyard Creatures' album in April 2005.

Jason Lives, Autopsy Torment (1989) (Rehearsal demo). Jason Lives / Eating Human Flesh By Humans / Human Holocaust / Putrefaction / Splattered.
Darkest Rituals, Autopsy Torment (1991) (Demo). Intro—Darkest Rituals / Rotting Flesh / Blasphemy Priest / Consumed Christ.
Splattered, Autopsy Torment (1991) (Cassette demo). Behemoth (Intro) / Injury Corpse / Splattered / From The Past Comes The Zombies / Virus Of Carcass / Outro.
Moon Fog, Slaughter (1992) (Cassette EP limited to 100 copies). Darkway Of Live / Moon Fog / Darkest Rituals / The Nice Suffering.
Darkest Rituals, Sombre (1992) (7" single. Limited edition 500 copies). Intro—Darkest Rituals / Rotting Flesh / Blasphemy Priest / Consumed Christ.
Nocturnal Blasphemy, Autopsy Torment (1992) (Cassette demo). Nocturnal Blasphemy / Moon Fog / Invocation To Satan / Beyond The Fearless Cries.
Autopsy Torment, Autopsy Torment (1992) (Demo). Satanic Sadist / Beyond The Fearless Cries / Moon Fog / Invocation To Satan / The Nice Suffering / Darkway Of Live.
The 7th Soul Of Hell, Autopsy Torment (1992) (Cassette demo). The 7th Soul Of Hell / Into The Lake Of Fire / Moonfog / Crucified In Flames / Darkest Rituals.
ORGY WITH THE DEAD, City Of The Dead (2001) (CD release). Orgy With The Dead / Humanipulation / I, The Morbid And Grotesque / Only Pleasure In Life … Death / Human Puzzle / Mark Of The Devil / Stiff Cold Lover (Orgy Part II).
ORGY WITH THE DEAD, Miriquidi Productions MPLP02 (2001) (Vinyl release). Orgy With The Dead / Humanipulation / I, The Morbid And Grotesque / Only Pleasure In Life … Death / Human Puzzle / Mark Of The Devil / Stiff Cold Lover (Orgy Part II) / Gory To The Brave.
PREMATURE TORMENT, Time Before Time DEATH004 (2003) (Split CD-R with DEVIL LEE ROT limited to 333 copies). Eating Human Flesh By Humans / Premature Torture / Parasite / Die In Pain / Masturbate The Dead / Bloody Fury / Orgy With The Dead / Humanipulation / The Morbid And Grotesque / Only Pleasure In Life … Death / Human Puzzle / Still Cold Lover.
TORMENTORIUM, Painkiller PKR029 (2003) (Vinyl album limited to 500 copies). Preludium (Welcome To Tormentorium) / Tormentorium / Human Puzzle / I, The Morbid And Grotesque / Kill Till I Die! / Death By Metal / Humanipulation / Death Comes Slow / Gory To The Brave / Eating Human Flesh By Humans / Bred For Murder / Orgy With The Dead.
TORMENTORIUM, Painkiller PKR029 (2003). Preludium (Welcome To Tormentorium) / Tormentorium / Human Puzzle / I, The Morbid And Grotesque / Kill Till I Die! / Death By Metal / Humanipulation / Death Comes Slow / Gory To The Brave / Eating Human Flesh By Humans / Bred For Murder.
GRAVEYARD CREATURES, Die Todesrune DTM012 (2005) (Vinyl release). Entering The Graveyard / Psychopath Onslaught / Necromance / Bloody Fury / Parasite / Into The Crypt Of Darkness / Die In Pain / Masturbate The Dead / Slaughterhouse / Blood To Survive / Tormented Pain / Bringer Of Torment / Feeble Creep / Graveyard Creatures / Splattered.
GRAVEYARD CREATURES, Die Todesrune DTM012 (2005) (CD release). Entering The Graveyard / Psychopath Onslaught / Necromance / Bloody Fury / Parasite / Into The Crypt Of Darkness / Die In Pain / Masturbate The Dead / Slaughterhouse / Blood To Survive / Tormented Pain / Bringer Of Torment / Feeble Creep / Graveyard Creatures.

AUTUMN DWELLER

VÄSTERÅS, SWEDEN — AUTUMN DWELLER is a solo Death / Thrash Metal concern of the Västerås based Joakim Jonsson, a man citing affiliations with a multitude of acts such as SKYRUNNER, VORTEX, GANGJÄRN, KOBOLDERS, DREADSTATE, SKYFIRE, SKINFECTED, Black Metal combo DUST, MORNALAND and THE MIST OF AVALON. Lyrical contributions are courtesy of erstwhile MORNALAND man Tommy Öberg and Andreas Johansson of SKINFECTED.

The project's first recordings, 'A Level Beyond' featuring John Grahn of GANGJÄRN as guest vocalist on the track 'Beams Of The Divine', emerged in 1998. A 2003 single, 'Eve Of Salvation', included a rendition of the A-HA hit 'Take On Me'. Vocals for these sessions were donated by Henrik Wenngren of SKYFIRE, VICIOUS, DUST, ZAVORASH and MORNALAND repute.

In January of 2004 Jonsson teamed up with AXENSTAR to act as touring bassist for European dates. The following month he would record drums for a new SKYFIRE album.

A LEVEL BEYOND, Autumn Dweller (1998) (Unreleased album).
A Level Beyond, The Riddle (1998). Daydreamer / Beams Of The Divine / Cold Birds.
Eve Of Salvation, Autumn Dweller (2003). Eve Of Salvation / Take On Me.

AUTUMN LEAVES

RIBE, DENMARK — *Torsten Madsen (vocals), Thomas Andersen (guitar), Flemming C. Lund (guitar), Boris Tandrup (bass), Egil H. Madsen (drums).*

Formed in Ribe during 1993 as Death Metal exponents under the name of DECRIAL, the Danish group adopted the name AUTUMN LEAVES upon recording their first demo tape. At this juncture the group included guitarist Tommy Christensen. A second demo session, titled 'Hope Springs Eternal' in June 1995, succeeded in selling over 1'000 copies. By 2002 guitarist Flemming C. Lund had formed up part of the newly reconstituted veteran Thrash Metal act INVOCATOR.

Flemming C. Lund and bassist Boris Tandrup would work up a Thrash side project in early 2004. Dubbed SCAVENGER the band also included Morten Sørensen from AURORA, WUTHERING HEIGHTS and PYRAMAZE on drums. This new formation, bringing onboard RAUNCHY singer Kasper Thomsen, evolved into THE ARCANE ORDER in 2005.

Hope Springs Eternal, Autumn Leaves (1995) (Demo). On The Verge Of Tears / Forever The Destiny / Hope Springs Eternal / Weakening Trip.

EMBRACED BY THE ABSOLUTE, Serious Entertainment SE 005CD (1997). Blood / Forever The Destiny / Universal Hood / On The Verge Of Tears / Rise From Your Nest / Serpent / Hope Springs Eternal / The Surface Anger / Weakening Trip / Embraced By The Absolute.

AS NIGHT CONQUERS DAY, Serious Entertainment SE 014CD (1999). The Reign Supreme / Revolution 21 / Another Day, Another Demon / Empty Black Stare / Resigning From Life / As Night Conquers Day / Autumn Fever / The Present Past / Shadowland / The Discovery.

AUTUMN NOSTRUM

MONHEIM, GERMANY — *Tommy (vocals), Sönke (guitar), Marcus Riewaldt (guitar), Christoph (bass), Lars Wehner (drums).*

Monheim Death Metal band debuted with the 'Autumn Nostrum' album in 1996. The group had been forged in the Autumn of 1994 by teenagers guitarist Sönke, bassist Christoph and drummer Lars Wehner, going under such formative titles as KORYPHEUS and ANACOSTIA. The group would be rounded out by guitarist Marcus Riewaldt and vocalist / keyboard player Tobias. A later addition would be keyboard man Philip for recording of the opening demo in the Autumn of 1996 at Skyline Studios.

An eponymous demo followed in 1998 but then Tobias exited in favour of new frontman Tommy. A further change saw Philip dispensing with the keyboards and adopting the role of second lead vocalist. The limited edition 7" single 'Fuck You Ass' of 1999 would signal the band's final release, AUTUMN NOSTRUM folding in 2000. The group actually split twice, first when Philip left, then reforming before Wehner quit. Unable to replace their drummer the group threw in the towel. However, they would be briefly re-activated for a one off gig supporting Brazilians KRISIUN at the Wermelskirchen AJZ.

AUTUMN NOSTRUM members Christoph, Marcus Riewaldt and drummer Lars Wehner subsequently joined SUIDAKRA.

AUTUMN NOSTRUM, Autumn Nostrum (1996). Lust Infernal / Autumnal Storms / Beyond My Gate / Lord Of Deceit / Melodie Der Trauer / Dream The Autumnal Storm.

Autumn Nostrum, Autumn Nostrum (1998). My Scorn / Angel's Jab / Masquerade / Benevolence Denied / Till Our Worlds Collide / Last Eventide.

Fuck You Ass, (1999). Fuck You Ass / Dead Eyes Shining.

AUTUMNAL REAPER

ARNHEM, HOLLAND — *Royy Vermeulen (vocals / bass), Dave van Beers (guitar), Vincent Wassink (guitar), Joost Westdijk (drums).*

AUTUMNAL REAPER is a blasphemous Death Metal band hailing from Arnhem. The group started out as a trio of vocalist / bassist Royy Vermeulen, guitarist Roeland de Haas and drummer Dennis Wolsink in 1991 billed as RAGING DEATH, carrying this title until 1993. A brace of demos preceded the self-financed 1999 album 'Of Pure Damnation', which was in turn followed up by a further demo in 2000, 'Studio Demolition'. Whilst recording a second album, 'March Of The Reaper', it would be learnt that Roeland de Haas was suffering from cancer. The album saw release in May of 2003, unfortunately de Haas had died on 28th February that year. Other musicians employed by AUTUMNAL REAPER for these sessions would included guitarists Woodrow Wegkamp and Fulco Helmig plus drummer BLOODPHEMY Quint Meerbeek.

AUTUMNAL REAPER was reconstructed by Vermeulen, drafting the HER ENCHANTMENT credited Dave van Beers on guitar, second guitarist Vincent Wassink from MORTAL FORM and the veteran figure of BOLTHORN, THRONAR and HEIDEVOLK drummer Joost Westdijk (a.k.a. 'Masterblaster').

OF PURE DAMNATION, Autumnal Reaper (1999). Of Pure Damnation / Under The Sign Of The Black Mark / Cursed / From Oblivion To Conquer / Magisterial Of Malevolence / Ex Infernis / Morbid Massacre / Glacier Wastelands / Both Ends Of The Funeral Path (Outro).

MARCH OF THE REAPER, Autumnal Reaper (2003). 2000 Thirteen / March Of The Reaper / Storming Towards Victory / Ancient Enigma / Four Horsemen Of The Apocalypse / On Killing Grounds / My Beloved Enemy / I Eat Christians / Inverted Crusade / The Skullcrusher / Total Desolation.

Live Demolition, Ex Infernis Productions (2004). Intro / March Of The Reaper / The Skull Crusher / Ancient Enigma / Four Horsemen Of The Apocalypse / On Killing Ground / Inverted Crusade / Morbid Massacre / I Eat Christians / Reaper Hordes Roar (Outro).

AVATAR

GOTHENBURG, SWEDEN — *Johannes Michael Gustaf Eckerström (vocals), Jonas Jarlsby (guitar), Simon Andersson (guitar), Henrik Sandelin (bass), John Alfredsson (drums).*

AVATAR is a Gothenburg melodic Death Metal band established during 2001 as LOST SOUL by vocalist Christian Rimmi and drummer John Alfredsson. Guitarists Viktor Ekström and Daniel Johansson, together with bass player John Isacsson, formed up the first band unit. Unfortunately, with members expressing an interest in pursuing a funk direction, the line-up soon fragmented and Alfredsson remained staunch in his Metal objectives. Jonas Jarlsby was inducted on guitar followed a name switch to AVATAR fuelled by a fully revised cast of second guitar player Kim Egerbo, CLASSIC MOLLY singer Johannes Eckerström and bassist Niklas Green. The latter was soon ousted and replaced by KREMATORIUM and SEMINARIUM's Björn Risberg. However, the group folded once again when both Eckerström and Risberg departed.

AVATAR was re-founded in 2003 as Eckerström and Risberg returned to the ranks, the former bassist now occupying the guitar role. Henrik Sandelin came in on bass and Risberg's place was taken by Simon Andersson.

A first set of demo tracks, entitled 'Personal Observations', would be recorded at Studio Gain in December 2003 and released the following January. The follow up, '4 Reasons To Die' issued in November, saw the guest inclusion of NIGHTRAGE and FIREWIND guitarist Marios Iliopoulos on the track 'Apocalypse Showtime'. The Blood Stained Art label put out a single, 'My Shining star' in 2005 as a limited run of 300 copies. This release was given out only at the semifinal of Musik Direkt in Vänersborg on April 2nd. A second single, 'And I Bid You Farewell', arrived in October.

AVATAR signed to GAIN Music Entertainment for a full-length album 'Thoughts Of No Tomorrow'. The band joined forces with fellow Swedish metal artists SONIC SYNDICATE and INEVITABLE END for the 'Sweden United–Metal' tour commencing in late January 2006. AVATAR then supported EVERGREY on their European and Scandinavian shows throughout October and November.

AVATAR recorded fresh album tracks in February 2007.

Personal Observations, Avatar (2004) (Demo). Saviour / Soul Prison / War Song / The Meeting.

4 Reasons To Die, Blood Stained Art BSA001 (2004). Tied, Torn And Twisted / My Shining Star / Apocalypse Showtime / Stranger.

My Shining Star, Blood Stained Art BSA002 (2005) (Limited edition 300 copies). My Shining Star / Break (Live) / My Shining Star (Live) / War Song (Live) / My Shining Star (Video).

And I Bid You Farewell, Blood Stained Art BSA003 (2005). And I Bid You Farewell / War Song.

THOUGHTS OF NO TOMORROW, Gain Productions GPCD28 (2006). Bound To The Wall / And I Bid You Farewell / Last One Standing / War Song / The Willy / My Shining Star / My Lie / Stranger / The Skinner / Sane? / Slave Him Meltdown.

AVULSED

SPAIN — *Dave Rotten (vocals), José Cabra (guitar), Juancar (guitar), Lucky (bass), Furni (drums).*

AVULSED was created in 1992 by vocalist Dave Rotten, bassist Lucky, drummer Toni and HAEMORRAGE man Luisma. With this line-up a demo tape, 'Embalmed In Blood', emerged and by November of that year guitarist Jose Cabra was enrolled. Five months later a second effort, 'Deformed Beyond Belief' was issued as AVULSED began playing live scoring gigs with CANCER, CEREBRAL FIX, GOMORRHA and INTOXICATION pushing sales of the demo beyond the 1,200 mark. A live tape, 'Live In Perfect Deformity' was also issued.

The hard work paid off in September 1993 when Greek label Molon Lave Records offered a contract. AVULSED's 'Deformed Beyond Belief' sessions becoming one half of a split CD shared with Greek act ACID DEATH. During December of that year Toni quit and AVULSED made up the ranks with former INTOXUCATION man Furni.

1994 found AVULSED gigging alongside Lusimas's side project HAEMMORAGE. Releases that year saw the 'Carnivoricity' 7" EP emerging through the German Malodorous Mangled Innards label featuring two originals and a cover of 'Demoniac Possession' by Chilean act PENTAGRAM. A mini album of the same name was issued in June adding extra tracks including more covers in 'As I Behold I Despise', originally by Finnish act DEMIGOD, and a take on BRUJERIA's 'Matando Guerros'.

Discontent within the AVULSED ranks as to their guitarists commitment to their act forced Lusimas dismissal as AVULSED drafted erstwhile SACROPHOBIA guitarist Juancar for gigs with HELLBOUND and VADER followed by European dates in February 1996 together with SINISTER, CREEPMIME and DARKSEED.

Lucky departed just prior to the release of 'Eminence In Putrescence' in November 1996. In now a now established tradition the record would contain a cover version, this time a rendition of BARON's 'Resisire'. Colombian label Quirofamo Productions would issue a collection of early demos and live cuts, including a cover of the ASPHYX track 'Mutilating Process', billed as 'Seven Years Of Decay' in September of 1999.

The 'Stabwound Orgasm' album would amply illustrate the band's ascendancy selling more than double it's predecessor in Europe alone. In Russia the album, complete with bonus tracks, was licensed to Irond Records. World War III Records would also take the album for North America.

As 2001 AVULSED announced the signing of a new record deal with the Avantgarde label. The band would headline the Murcia 'Clash Of The Helmets' festival the following month, topping a bill over SOLARIS, THE AWAKENING and ETERNAL CRY. During March AVULSED issued a limited edition mini album 'Bloodcovered' comprising entirely of cover songs. Bands honoured included MORBID ANGEL's 'Immortal Rites', CARCASS' 'Embryonic Necropsy And Devourment', CANNIBAL CORPSE's 'Edible Autopsy' and SODOM's 'Magic Dragon' and a live version of SEPULTURA's 'Inner Self'.

Touring would find AVULSED appearing in America at the April 'Metal Meltdown' festival in New Jersey and closer to home at the Portuguese 'Steel Warriors Rebellion' festival.

A new studio album, 'Yearning for The Grotesque', initially set for a November 2002 release through the Italian Avant-Garde Music label was pushed back to an early 2003 release. However, the record hit a further obstacle when the pressing plant refused to reproduce the band's original suggestions for cover art. AVULSED signed with Slovakian label Metal Age Productions in January of 2004 for the release of the band's fourth album. The group entered VRS Studios in Madrid to record 'Gorespattered Suicide' in July. The album, which included a cover of MOTÖRHEAD's 'Ace Of Spades', would be mixed by HATE ETERNAL's Erik Rutan at Mana Recording Studios in Florida.

AVULSED

AVULSED's 2005 'Gorespattered' world tour took the band to Japan, Australia and New Zealand in April followed by festival appearances at the German 'Fuck The Commerce' event, the London 'Deathfest' and Czech 'Obscene Extreme' show.

The group opened 2006 with the EP 'Reanimations' through Electric Chair Music, this set including a brace of new tracks in 'River Runs Red' and 'Foetal Consolation', a remake of a song from their 1992 debut demo 'Unconscious Pleasure' plus three cover songs, W.A.S.P.'s 'I Wanna Be Somebody', GOREFEST's 'Mental Misery and EXODUS' 'Piranha'. Bonus tracks comprised no less than eight AVULSED cover versions performed by five Spanish acts, TERRORISTARS, KAOTHIC, WITCHES' SABBATH, BYLETH and ABYFSS, plus three international bands in Argentina's IN ELEMENT, Algeria's CARNAVAGE and TWISTED FATE from Australia.

DEFORMED BEYOND BELIEF, Molon Lave (1994) (Split album with ACID DEATH). Achieving The Perfect Deformity (Intro) / Addicted To Carrion / Bodily Ransack / Gangrened Divine Stigma / Infanticide.

Carnivoricity EP, Malodorous Mangled Innards (1994). Carnivoricity / Cradle Of Bones / Demoniac Possession.

CARNIVORISITY, Repulse RPS 007 (1995). Carnivoricity / Cradle Of Bones / Demoniac Possession / Morgue Defilement / Bodily Ransack / As I Behold I Despise / Gangrended Divine Stigma / Cradle Of Bones / Deformed Beyond Belief / Matando Gueros.

EMINENCE IN PUTRESCENCE, Repulse RPS 017 CD (1996). Hidden Perversion / Sweet Lobotomy / Powdered Flesh / Goreality / Gangrened Divine Stigma / Frozen Meat / Ecstasy For Decayed Chunks / Killin Astral Projections / Bodily Ransack / Resistiré.

CYBERGORE, Repulse RPS 029 CD (1998). Frozen Beat / Addicted To Red Bull / Sweet Bakalaotomy / Hash Perversions / Powered Fish / Petisuis Lobotomy / Gorroneality / Pastivoracity / Beyond Monotony / Emixnence In Popurrence.

SEVEN YEARS OF DECAY, Quirofamo Productions (1999). Skinless ('98 version) / Addicted To Carrion ('96 version) / Powdered Flesh / Ecstasy For Decayed Chunks / Morgue Defilement / Deformed Beyond Belief / Achieving The Perfect Deformity (Intro) / Addicted To Carrion / Bodily Ransack / Gangrened Divine Stigma / Malodorous Mangled Innards / Infanticide / Denial (Intro) / Unconscious Pleasure / Clandestinely Autopsied / Mutilating Process (Live).

STABWOUND ORGASM, Repulse RPS 043 CD (1999). Amidst The Macabre / Stabwound Orgasm / Compulsive Hater / Eminence In Putrescence / Exorcismo Vaginal / Anthro-Pet-Phagus / Homeless Necrophile / Nice Rotting Eyes / Skinless / Coprotherapy / Virtual Massacre.

BLOODCOVERED, Avulsed AD001 (2001) (Limited edition. 500 copies). Immortal Rites / Embryonic Necropsy And Devourment / Edible Autopsy / Magic Dragon / Inner Self (Live).

YEARNING FOR THE GROTESQUE, Avantgarde AV 069 (2003).

AVULSION

BUFFALO, NY, USA — *Tony S. (vocals), Ryan P. (vocals), Matt Kennedy (guitar), Eric Wilhelm (guitar), Roger DiPirro (bass), Kenny Brand (drums).*

AVULSION, hailing from Buffalo, New York, began life in 1992 and rank as one of the areas first ever Grindcore practitioners. The 'Dying Nation' demo arrived in 1993 and in 1996 AVULSION issued two 7" singles, 'Green Scare' being a split release with LACERATION on Clean Plate Records and 'Living Life Through The Five Senses' through Recalcitrant Noise Records, a further shared effort this time with FORCED EXPRESSION. The debut album, 'The Crimson Foliage Hits', followed for 625 Records.

Line up changes put the band into hiatus for a while but they returned with two tracks included on the compilation album 'World Demise' on Fifteen Inch Records. 2001 saw a split release 'Prince Of A Thousand Enemies' shared with San Francisco's IMPATIENCE OR INDIFFERENCE, Rochester, New York's HIDE THE BODIES and Los Angeles band AGITATE 96.

Green Scare, (1995).
Avulsion, Clean Plate (1996) (Split single with LACERATION).
Living Life Through The Five Senses, Recalcitrant Noise (1996).
THE CRIMSON FOLIAGE HIT, 625 (1998).
Prince Of A Thousand Enemies, (2001) (Split single with HIDE THE BODIES, IMPATIENCE OR INDIFFERENCE & AGITATE 96).
CRIMES AGAINST REALITY, (2003).

AXEGRINDER

LONDON, UK — *Trev (vocals), Matt (bass), Steve (guitar), Daryn (drums).*

An underground British Metal band that was created in 1986 from various anarchist London Punk bands, including STONE THE CROWZ, the band were originally titled TYRANTS OF HATE with drummer Jel, of THE PROUDHORNS, at the drum stool. As the band began to lean towards more slower, Metal material, a change of name to AXEGRINDER came about. In 1986 they recorded their 'Grind The Enemy' demo at Reel to Reel studios in Brixton. Jel was superseded by Darryn from GUTROT and concert demo cassette, 'Live 11-7-87', hosted tracks recorded at the William Morris club, Wimbledon supporting CIVILISED SOCIETY. Further studio tracks were cut for an intended 7" single, but this never transpired and the material was distributed as 'The Squat Tape' demo in 1988. This led to interest from Peaceville Records guru Hammy, actually lead singer of CIVILISED SOCIETY. AXEGRINDER subsequently appeared on the 'A Vile Peace' compilation album which, in turn, led to an offer of a full album. The 'Rise Of The Serpent Men' sessions, co-produced by the band and Hammy, were recorded at Lion studios in Leeds between May and August 1988. The album track 'Life Chain' was remixed for inclusion on the compilation album 'Hiatus'. AXEGRINDER later recruited guitarist Cliff Evans, who featured on two tracks, 'Evilution' and new song ' Requi-Anthem', included on the Peaceville video compilation 'Vile Visions' alongside PARADISE LOST and DEVIATED INSTINCT filmed at the Queens Hall, Bradford in 1990. After the band's demise, Cliff formed Death Metal band FLESH.

Peaceville found an opportunity to give 'Rise Of The Serpent Men' a CD release by including the tracks on a split album shared with PROPHECY OF DOOM in 1990. Trev, Steve and Daryn created WARTECH enlisting bassist Chris.

Grind The Enemy, Axegrinder (1986) (Demo). Intro / Aftermath / Master Race / One Law / Grind The Enemy / Armistice / Thealphobia / Damnation Of The Living / Special Brew.
Live 11-7-87, Axegrinder (1987) (Live demo). Intro / Black Days Ahead / Damnation Of The Living / Butcher Of Jerusalem / In Death She Waits / Where Evil Dwells.
The Squat Tape, Axegrinder (1988) (Demo). Never Ending Winter / Black Days Ahead / Hellstorm / The Final War / Life Chain.
RISE OF THE SERPENT MEN, Peaceville VILE7 (1989). Never Ending Winter / Hellstorm / Life Chain / War Machine / Evilution / Rise Of The Serpent Men / The Final War.

AZARATH

TCZEW, POLAND — *Bruno (vocals / bass), Thrufel (guitar), Bart (guitar), Inferno (drums).*

Ultra extreme, blasphemic Death Metal. AZARATH, based in Tczew, featured Inferno of BEHEMOTH and WITCHMASTER on drums and Bart of DAMNATION on guitar. Vocalist / bassist Bruno has credits with DAMNATION and CENOTAPH whilst second guitarist D. was also a DAMNATION and BEHEMOTH veteran. The group debuted in 1998 with the demo 'Traitors'. To promote the 'Demon Seed' album AZARATH teamed up with VADER, HATE and ELYSIUM for Polish dates in June 2002.

The follow up 'Infernal Blasting' arrived in 2003. AZARATH's 2000 demo tracks would be issued a split album 'Death Monsters' in 2004, shared with STILLBORN on the Time Before Time label. Guitarist D would be superseded by Thrufel of YATTERING and SHADOWS LAND. The album 'Diabolic Impious Evil' arrived in September 2006 through Pagan Records.

AZARATH guitarist Thrufel announced the side project MASACHIST, a union with drummer Daray, of VADER, VESANIA and NEOLITHIC, in December 2006.

DEMON SEED, Pagan MOONCD 029 (2001). Earthly Morgue / Doombringer / Awaiting Eternity Of Fire / Heaven's Light Demise / Taedium Vitae / Destroy Yourself / Deathlike Silence / Traitors / Mindloss / Nightskies Burial Ground.
INFERNAL BLASTING, Pagan MOONCD 036 (2003). Legacy Of Tyrant God / Nuclear Revelation / False God / Burn In Hell / Demonspeed / Christscum / Damned To Hell / Infested With Sin / Joy Of Mutilation / Born to Rot.
DEATH MONSTERS, Time Before Time DEATH 21 (2004) (Split album with STILLBORN). Thousand Faced-Bitch (STILLBORN) / Anti-God, Anti-Human (STILLBORN) / Wrath, Death & Destruction (STILLBORN) / Earthly Morgue (AZARATH) / Doombringer (AZARATH) / Heavens Light Demise (AZARATH) / Nightskies Burial Ground (AZARATH).
DIABOLIC IMPIOUS EVIL, Pagan MOON CD 046 (2006). Whip The Whore / Baptized In Sperm Of The Antichrist / Devil's Stigmata / Anti-Human, Anti-God / For Satan My Blood / Screamin' Legions Death Metal / Intoxicated By Goat Vomit / Angels' Assassins / Beast Inside / Goathorned's Revenge.

B-LOW

HOLLAND — *Marinus Moerland (vocals), Patrick Mangnus (bass / tape loops), Bastiaan van Zwieten (bass / samples / programming), Jos Wübbels (vocals / drums).*

Doom styled Industrial-Death Metal founded in November of 1995. B-LOW bowed in with a 2001 demo 'Demotivation Remake 2B'. Somewhat controversially B-LOW's 2003 album 'Ground Zero Souvenirs' not only came clad in a photographic depiction of the September 11th World Trade Centre disaster but opened up musically with a distorted US anthem, the sound of jets, explosions and a "Going down" elevator message. The entire record proved to be 9-11 based. B-LOW's track 'Two Towers Down' featured on the 2003 compilation album 'Blown To Pieces II' released by Fearsome Records.

Novelly, B-LOW employed two bassists with Patrick 'B2' Mangnus supplying both distorted bass and "wrecking" vocals whilst Bastiaan 'Bastard' van Zwietan delivered "blurry" bass and "sissy" vocals. The main "freak vox" singing came from drummer Jos 'Midget' Wübbels. The band drafted new singer Marinus "Lichtbringer" Moerland in the Spring of 2004.

Demotivation Remake 2B, (2001). Serenade To Sickness / Death To The Dance / Natural Suffering / Sonically Transmitted Disease.
GROUND ZERO SOUVENIRS, Almost God (2003). Int(R)o The Basement / Two Towers Down / I'm Proud ... God Bless ... (God Fakes America) / Genocide Generation / Always And Never / Suicide Shop / Ground Zero Souvenirs.

BAAL

MEXICO — *Jesus Mendoza (vocals), Alexandro Mendoza (guitar), Alberto Delgado (bass), Antonio Ortiz (drums).*

BAAL is a Vera Cruz Death Metal band harking back to a formation during 1995. The founding quartet comprised singer Jesus Mendoza, guitarist Christian Rodriguez, bass player Alberto Delgado and drummer Fernando Perez. During 1997 Mendoza bailed out, being replaced by Leo Ganem. However, within a year BAAL then lost the services of both their new frontman and their drummer. Mendoza was duly re-instated at the microphone and Antonio Ortiz took on drums as Filipo Figueroa boosted the band's compliment on second guitar. In this incarnation BAAL cut the 'Passages To Eternity' album for Toaj Records.

Figueroa would then be usurped by Alexandro Mendoza as BAAL cut their second offering 'State Of Aggression' for American Line Productions.

STATE OF AGGRESSION, American Line Productions LA 057 (2002).

BAALPHEGOR

GIRONA, SPAIN — *Miguel Herrera (vocals), David Fernandez (guitar), Marc Plana (guitar), Jose Hernandez (bass), Alfred Berengena (drums).*

Girona based Death Metal band BAALPHEGOR began life in 1996 as a quartet comprising lead vocalist Jesús Díaz, guitarists David Fernández and Jordi Massanes with Alfred Berengena on drums. Shortly after formation Raimon Jaramillo was introduced on bass and David Sallarés supplanted Massanes. Upon completion of the band's first batch of gigs Miguel Herrera was incorporated as BAALPHEGOR's new singer.

For the band's first demo in 1998 José Hernández took the bass position. However, shortly after Sallarés quit and BAALPHEGOR opted to persevere as a quartet. Recordings were undertaken for a proposed album but the band deemed the resulting tapes as unsatisfactory and shelved the project. For some time in 2000 the group performed live with Regius as their new frontman but Herrera subsequently made a return in May of 2001.

Marc Plana, previously with REALITAT CAÒTICA and PHOBIA, was added to the band as they set about recording their first album once more 'The End Of Descent'.

The band contributed their rendition of DEATH's 'Lack Of Comprehension' to the 'Together As One' 2003 tribute album assembled by the Spanish Mondongo Canibale label.

THE END OF DESCENT, (2003). Always Here / Your Father Is Dead / Seven / The End Of Descent / Surrounded By Dead / The Pact / Mental Slide / Voodoo / Noted My Putrefaction / Their Warlock King / Eaten Alive.

BACKYARD BURIAL

LOWER HUTT, NEW ZEALAND — *Blaps Warmonger (vocals), Bobby Hellford (guitar), Psychdroid Shitfux (guitar), Cyborg Slut (bass), Human Hating War Machine (drums).*

Lower Hutt Grindcore claiming on their 2001 EP to involve vocalists Blaps, guitarist Bobby Hellford and Shitfux, bass player Dan Druff and drummer 'The artist formally known as the South Island splayer'. BACKYARD BURIAL began as Death / Doom act MEAT SURGEON during 1998 comprising Mike on drums, Dave on guitar and later adding bassist Ryan and vocalist Matt. However, before the close of the year Dave had relocated to Australia. Switching the band title to BACKYARD BURIAL the group, with Ryan now on guitar, persevered as a trio. Under this new guise the band bowed in with the six track demo 'Deviance In Society' displaying a musical shift towards more Grind orientated territory. BACKYARD BURIAL, inducting Nathan on bass, put in their inaugural gig in mid 1999 at the Wellington 'Punkfest'. For their second gig Nathan maneuvered to guitar and Aiden came in to take on bass responsibilities.

The 2001 '$2 Pe.ep', produced by Nich Cunningham, was recorded in Auckland. Subsequent gigs saw a support to visiting Australians MISERY and headline gigs across the North Island of New Zealand. Aiden would then leave and Gregg of DISCENTER was enrolled in time for further recordings. With the 'Repeat Offender' album wrapped up the band introduced guitarist Mark of ABRACADAVER and FALCIFORM bassist Jason Hislop into the fold.

By the 2002 album 'Repeat Offender' BACKYARD BURIAL purported to comprise vocalist Blaps Warmonger ("Vocals & sickness"), guitarists Bobby Hellford ("String splatter") and Psychdroid Shitfux ("Chugs & chunks"), bassist Cyborg slut ("Low end terrorist") and drummer Human Hating War Machine ("Drums & guns"). That same year guitarist Mark and drummer Mike struck up the avant-garde Metal endeavour SIDEPROJECT.

BACKYARD BURIAL acted as support to notorious Austrian Death Metal combo PUNGENT STENCH on their March 2005 New Zealand dates at the Wellington date.

Deviance In Society, Backyard Burial (1999) (Demo). Cutting Up The Cadaver / Disciple Of Goatlord / Deviance In Society / Necrolisurgic / 666 Atrocities / From Life To Death.

The $2 PE-EP, Backyard Burial (2001). Digging Up The Dead / If It Came Down To It I'd Eat You / You've Got Tourettes Syndrome / Psychotic Amok In The Morgue / Backyard Bugs.

REPEAT OFFENDER, Backyard Burial (2002). First She Raped Him Then She Killed Him / Spunking Batter Chunks / The Bone Collector / Masturbation Over Catholic Bitch / The Host / Persecuted By Fundamentalists / Religion & Politics / Home Invasion / Amok In The Church on PCP.

HEDONISTIC CRAVINGS, Backyard Burial (2005). Ice In Your Veins / You Show Me Yours . . . / You Sleep, We Creep / I Always Inhale / Hedonistic Cravings / Burnt Morals / Deviance In Society / Cactus Coffin.

A Promising Young Law Student, Backyard Burial (2007) (CD single). A Promising Young Law Student.

BALATONIZER

PALERMO, ITALY — *Mario Musemeci (vocals), Marco Failla (guitar / drums / programming / samples), Rodan Di Maris (bass).*

BALATONIZER is a Palermo, Sicily based Grind-Crust Death Metal band. The band was formed in 1998 by erstwhile UNTORY guitarist Marco Failla, singer Mario Musumeci and Rodan Di Maria on bass, together with long-term friends Massimo and Giovanni on drums and secondary vocals. A demo, entitled 'Balatonizer' featuring a cover version of EXTREME NOISE TERROR's 'In It For Life', followed in 1999, after which both Giovanni and Massimo exited. Fresh demos were recorded, the thirteen track 2002 'Occlused In Ottusity' set, employing Claudio Di Prima of THY MAJESTIE as session drummer.

The album 'Occlused In Ottusity' was released by US label Devil Doll Records in July 2004.

Balatonizer, Balatonizer (1998) (Demo). Raschios / C.E.P. / Anal By Anal / Putrification Of The Mind / Brutal Devastation / Infernus / Tipardo / In It For Life / Petra Lavica Etnea / Satanas / Diabolos / Barbapapà.

Occlused In Ottusity, Balatonizer (2002) (Demo). Brutal Devastation / Caimmè / Eaten / Scacciatiasta / Reborn In Ignorance / Ottenebrated Perseverance Through Mental Disorder / C.E.P. / Anfame / Ciccio Tagliavia / Pulverization After Intimidation / Sucaman / Putrification Of The Mind / From The Obsolation To The Obeteration.

OCCLUSED IN OTTUSITY, Devil Doll (2005). Intro / Muscular Prevarication / Corporal Usurpation / Ciccio Tagliavia / Brutal Devastation / Caimme / Anfame / C.E.P. / Petra Lavica Etnea / Abominations Of Triviality / Diabolos / Occlubinated Eyes Convergence / Scacciatiesta / Pulverization After Intimidation / Inebetit / Eaten / Cerebral Regression / Guttural Satisfaction / Macabrotic Poetry / Microscopic Brain / From The Obsolation To The Obeteration / Putrification Of The Mind / A'cinta No! / Sbigottit /

Primitivity 46 / Reborn In Ignorance / Se So Sa / Sucaman / Ottenebrated Perseveration Through Mental Disorder / Occlused In Ottusity / Anal By Anal / Tristeza.

BALVAZ

FREDRIKSTAD, NORWAY — *Lasse (vocals / guitar), Lars Lie (guitar), Jon Bakker (bass), Øyvind Olsen (drums).*

Fredrikstad Death Metal band. BALVAZ feature former members of BRAINDEAD. Demos included a self titled 1987 effort, the 1989 session 'Kællus Tapus', which featured Anders Odden of CADAVER on bass guitar, and 'Phlegm' in 1990. BALVAZ also issued an eponymous 1990 7" single through Virulence Records but folded during 1992.

Members vocalist / guitarist Lasse and guitarist Lars Lie went on to DISGUSTING. Lie also featured in the ranks of PENDULUM. Bassist Jon Fredrik Bakker holds credits with KAMPFAR, CARPATHIAN FULL MOON, CREMATOR, GRUESOME, NECROSENTIENT MORTIS FEED and PENDULUM. Drummer Øyvind Olsen went on to DECAY LUST.

Balvaz, Balvaz (1987) (Demo). Mens Insano.
Kællus Tapus, Balvaz (1989) (Demo). Illusions / Hate / Inside You.
Phlegm, Balvaz (1990) (Demo). Phlegmous / Fusion / Blemish / Freak / Contrafibularities.
Balvaz, Virulence (1990) (7" vinyl single). Phlegmous / Fusion / Blemish / Contrafibularities.

BANE OF EXISTENCE

ROCKLAND, MA, USA — *Doug Rinaldi (vocals), Jim Ash (guitar), Brandon Adelizzi (bass), Mike Butkewicz (drums).*

Massachusetts Death Metal. Originally going by the name of DISMALBIO this Death Metal act evolved during late 1999, built up by guitarist Jim Ash and drummer Mike Butkewicz. This pairing was soon joined by Randy Odierno on bass, known for his terms of office with the infamous Doom act GRIEF as well as his role as drummer with DISRUPT. Doug Rinaldi was soon after inducted on lead vocals. However, once initial demos had been completed Odierno left the frame. Lucas took on the bass position but would leave in August of 2001 to join LEUKORRHEA. BANE OF EXISTENCE duly took on former DREAD and WARHEAD man Brandon Adelizzi to fill the vacancy. The band pressed up a limited edition CD sampler entitled 'Denounced' for give aways at gigs that year. As well as the title track the EP included two live cuts, 'The Art Of Fisting' and 'The Approaching', recorded at the Lowell 'Gorewhore Fest' in November of 2000.

A full length album 'Humanity's Splintered Salvation' was recorded during 2002. Mike Butkiewicz made a return in late 2003 with an extreme Metal band entitled NOOSEBOMB, this unit including GRIEF and DISRUPT pairing of Jeff Hayward and Randy Odierno. The new group debuted with the 'Brain Food For The Braindead' album. Ultrasound Productions finally issued 'Humanity's Splintered Salvation' in 2004.

BANE OF EXISTENCE announced they were to part ways with vocalist Doug Rinaldi in April 2005, performing their last gig with the departing singer on 3rd June at O'Brien's in Allston. The band also severed ties with second guitarist Greg Armstrong. August saw the addition of ex-ACEPHALUS and DESPOILMENT members vocalist Dusty Lyon and guitarist Chris Farmerie.

Bane Of Existence, Independent (2001). Denounced / The Art Of Fisting / Evisceration / Iconoclast / Cankerous.
Bane Of Existence, (2001). Denounced / Art Of Fisting / Evisceration / Iconoclast / Cankerous.
Promo 2003, (2003). From Soiled Heart To Infected Tongue / Iconoclast.
HUMANITY'S SPLINTERED SALVATION, Ultrasound (2004). From Soiled Heart To Infected Tongue / Subjugate / The Approaching / Denounced / Art Of Fisting / Iconoclast / Apocalyptic Disenchantment / Solace In The Arms of The Dead / Cankerous.

BANISHED

VISLANDA, SWEDEN — *Tony Svensson (vocals), Daniel Gustavsson (guitar), Kristoffer Ståhlgren (guitar), Christian Linell (bass), Jonas Mårtensson (drums).*

BANISHED is an old school Death Metal combo trading under the banner of PUTREFACTION between 1996 and 1999. The band's first formation, manifested at school in Vislanda, counted lead vocalist Tony Svensson (a.k.a. 'Sigismund Ninja'), guitarists Daniel Gustavsson and Loffe Knutsson with Kristoffer Hytinkoski on bass and Jonas Mårtensson ('Jutta Ninja') on the drums. Although PUTREFACTION considered themselves a Black Metal band their set would be peppered with covers by acts such as PARADISE LOST, PROPAIN and KISS. The band's first sign of line-up troubles came with a rehearsal fist fight between Svensson and Hytinkoski, resulting in the latter's departure. The ex-bassist went on to front TOETAG. Minus a bass player, PUTREFACTION undertook their debut gig switching bass between Knutsson and Gustavsson.

Finally Robin was installed on bass guitar, but then Knutsson departed. Robin then switched to guitar as Christian Linell ('Firtal') assumed the bass role as, in late 1999, PUTREFACTION evolved into BANISHED. An initial set of demos entitled 'Land Of The Immortal' was committed to tape and, shortly after, Gustavsson, Mårtensson and Robin fired up Black Metal side project HYPERBOREAN in league with Örebro musicians.

Gustavsson exited to prioritise HYPERBOREAN, with BANISHED recruiting Kristoffer Ståhlgren ('Krizzt o Fear') of SUPERION in his stead. Further demos ensued dubbed 'Feeding The Monster', witnessing a change in musical direction from Death Metal to Death Rock n' Roll. Gustavsson made a return in May of 2004.

Land Of The Immortal, Banished (2000) (Demo). Dark Clouds / The Clue / Land Of The Immortal.
Feeding The Monster, Banished (2003) (Demo). Soul Possessed / Feeding The Monster / In Cold Blood.
Hail Sejtan, Banished (2005) (Demo). Legalize Murder / Cunthunter / Just Do It.

BAPHOMET

BIETGHEIM, GERMANY — *Thomas Hertler (vocals), Gernot Kerrer (guitar), Hansi Bieber (bass), Manuel Reichart (drums).*

Founded during 1986 in Bietgheim, BAPHOMET released a brace of demos prior to signing with Massacre Records in 1990, releasing the debut album 'No Answers' the following year. Bass on the debut was contributed by POLTERGEIST's Marek Felis.

BAPHOMET went on the road in Europe to promote the album's release, opening for the likes of BATTLEFIELD, ATROCITY and MYSTIK. They toured again throughout Germany in October 1992 as support to CANNIBAL CORPSE.

For the second album, 'Latest Jesus', which included a cover version of HALLOWS EVE's 'Lethal Tendencies', BAPHOMET supported GRAVEDIGGER in Germany.

Thomas Hertler was to quit the group after touring in support of the 'Trust' album thanks to the age old 'musical differences' excuse.

NO ANSWERS, Massacre MASS CD001 (1991). No Answers / Past And Present / The Fence / Act Of Jealousy / Elm Street / Time Has Come / Identified / Rise Of Baphomet / Terror Of Thoughts.
LATEST JESUS, Massacre MASS CD007 (1992). A Second To None / Lethal Tendencies / State Of Censorship / Latest Jesus / Coalition Of The Lost / Born Of No Name / Near Dawn / Full Moon Eyes.
TRUST, Massacre CD027 (1993). Betrayed / Mind The Doubt / What Went Wrong / Everlast / Intense / Low Life / Attitude / Prove / Trust.

BASTARD SAINTS

ITALY — *Marino Andrea (vocals), Quintiero Fiorenzo (guitar), Coviello Fabio (bass), Benvenuto Alessandro (drums).*

Blasphemous Death Metal. Bassist Coviello Fabio of NEFAS would session on the 2000 split album shared with Spaniards CHRIST DENIED. This relationship between NEFAS and BASTARD SAINTS was strengthened with the issue of a shared EP in August of 2001 'Ropes Above An Abyss Of Fury'. In 2002 the band conducted the Polish 'Grind Manifesto 2002' tour packaged with fellow Italians NEFAS and Polish outfits PIGNATION, ANTIGAMA and TOXIC BONKERS.

Former BASTARD SAINTS drummer Gianpaolo Ferrotti joined MINDSNARE in March of 2003. Another BASTARD SAINTS sticksman Simone teamed up with Death Metal act PSYCHOFAGIST in April that same year.

BASTARD SAINTS, Macabre Mementos (2000) (Split album with CHRIST DENIED). Disinfect With Terrorism / Jesus Chew Angel's Tongue / Inhale The Futuristic Filthiness / No Morality / Sick Mans Sperm's Crawls On Holy Virgin Tear-Stained Face / Tear Up My Brain And Stab It.
Ropes Above An Abyss Of Fury EP, The Flood (2001) (Split EP with NEFAS).

BEDIMMED

JÄRVENPÄÄ, FINLAND — *Tami Hintikka (vocals), Juha Lappalainen (guitar), Timo Ahlström (guitar), Timo Riuttamäki (bass), Jussi-Pekka Manner (drums).*

Järvenpää Death / Thrashers BEDIMMED issued the demo 'Scars Healing In Reverse' in July 2005 as their opening gambit. Frontman Tami Hintikka holds a tradition with DISINTER, PILGRIM and TRAILS OF BEREAVED. Second guitarist Timo Ahlström enrolled in June. The group's inaugural live performance took place that September, at the 'Heviosasto' festival with Juha Pöysä acting as stand in bassist, acting as replacement for original four-stringer Erkka Korpi. Subsequently Timo Riuttamäki took on bass duties.

BEDIMMED guitarist Juha Lappalainen and drummer Jussi-Pekka Manner maintain side ventures SONS OF ARAGORN, SKULLFUCKER and THE LAKEND CONNECTION. Manner also operates with SHREWDRIVER.

BEDIMMED commenced recording of a second demo session, entitled 'Sounds Of Terminal Torment', in 2006.

Scars Healing In Reverse, Bedimmed (2005) (Demo). Heal Me / Reverse Evolution / Scar Over A Scar.

BEHEADED

MALTA — *Lawrence Joyce (vocals), David Bugeja (guitar), David Cachia (bass), Chris Brincat (drums).*

A rare Maltese Death Metal formation. BEHEADED was founded in 1991 by the trio of vocalist Marcel Scalpello, guitarist David Bugeja and drummer Chris Brincat. Later additions were guitarist Tyson Fenech and bassist David Cachia. Under this incarnation BEHEADED released a 1995 promotional cassette 'Souldead'.

Fenech would depart in favour of Omar Grech for recording of the debut album 'Perpetual Mockery' issued by the Swedish X-Treme label. Scalpelle would then leave as BEHEADED pulled in Lawrence Joyce for a second outing 'Resurgence Of Oblivion'. November of 2004 saw BEHEADED on the road in Europe allied with PREJUDICE.

European dates throughout September of 2005 had the band hooked up with Dutch act BRUTUS and US headliners MORTAL DECAY.

PERPETUAL MOCKERY, X-Treme (1998). Transcendental Iniquity / Perpetual Mockery / Inborn Lust / Subconscious Deliverance / Void Of Empathy / Ethereal Passages / Vae Victus (Prayer For The Vanquished) / Omnipotent Carnage / Souldead / Suffer In Silence.
RESURGENCE OF OBLIVION, Mighty Music (2001). Transmutation Of Veracity / Exhortation Of Benevolence / Resurgence Of Oblivion / Paramnesis Dream / Suffer Some More.

RECOUNTS OF DISEMBODIMENT, (2002). Broken Thoughts Of Righteousness / Horde Of The Stolen Sun / Recounts Of Disembodiment / Consecrated Absurdities / Compelling Derangement / Inherited Plague / Fed Upon Odium / Disdain / Spreading Contagion / Unbound.

BELCHING BEET

GERMANY — *Sven Vöhringer (vocals), Winnie Hoffman (guitar), Bernd Biedenbach (bass), Michael Schwarz (drums).*

Grindcore mongers BELCHING BEET date back to 1987. The group's inaugural line up comprised vocalist Dirk Neuhäuser, guitarist Winnie Hofmann, bassist Peter Scholz and drummer Michael Schwarz. However, just after recording their first demo Neuhäuser decamped. BELCHING BEET pulled in new singer Michael Wattolla for a second tape. With the rise of the global Grindcore movement the band was ideally placed to support many visiting influential acts. An EP 'You Know The Holes Are Empty' was delivered in 1989 followed up by a split album 'Kill For Fun' with Australians RUPTURE in 1991. Despite this progress the band ceased operations in 1993.

BELCHING BEET was revitalised in 1997, Hoffman, Schwarz and Wattolla drawing in bass player Bernd Biedenbach for the demo 'Nothing'. Their 1999 split album with fellow Germans MINDFLAIR included a cover version of EXTREME NOISE TERROR's 'Another Nail In My Coffin', TERRORIZER's 'Storms Of Stress' as well as a tongue in cheek take on the PATRICK HERNANDEZ Disco hit re-dubbed 'Porn To Be Alive'. Schwarz, also active with Gothic act UMBRA ET IMAGO as well as ATROCITY, would team up with Crustcore outfit ACCION MUTANTE in 1998. Wattolla opted out in mid 2000, being replaced by Sven Vöhringer.

The Hernandez spoof, alongside a rendition of the SEPTIC DEATH track 'Terrorain', also featured on a split picture disc single shared with MALICIOUS in 2001. A split album in collaboration with MUCUPURULENT was planned for 2002. Winnie Hoffman joined Schwarz as a member of ACCION MUTANTE that same year. Bernd Biedenbach, also having SPLASHDOWN credits, would join DUST & BONES in the guitar role.

You Know That The Holes Are Empty EP, Masters Of Mayhem And Noise (1989). Holes Are Empty / Silent Death / Programmed War / Endless Cage / Tornado / Bloodbath / Animals (Can't Build A World) / Belching Blues.
KILL FOR FUN, Ecocentric (1991) (Split album with RUPTURE). Kill For Fun / Why Don't You Care? / Fresh Fruit And Vegetables / Asphalt Victims / Tears In My Eyes / Dying For Beauty / Astrolink / Profit's Eye / Outro.
BELCHING BEET, Deliria Noise Outfitters (1999) (Split album with MINDFLAIR). Nuclear Romance / Lose Control / Nothing / World Without Warning / Sometimes I Imagine / Shame Of Mankind / Seize The Day / No Time / Another Nail In The Coffin / Storm Of Stress / Porn To Be Alive / Trapped In Silence.
Terrorain, Unterfett Rex (2001) (Split picture disc single with MALICIOUS). Terrorain / Porn To Be Alive.

BELIAL

OULU, FINLAND — *Jarno Antilla (vocals / guitar), Jani Lehtosaari (bass), Reima Kellokoski (drums).*

Oulu's BELIAL date to April 1991, with the demo 'The God Of The Pits' bringing them to the attention of the Death Metal Underground. At this stage the group comprised vocalist Jarno Koskinen, guitarists Jarno Antilla and MUTILATION's Jukka Valppu, former OBFUSCATION bassist Jani Lehtosaari and drummer Reima Kellokoski. However, Jukka Valppu quit to form MYTHOS in 1992. The band's earliest recordings proved to be so popular on the tape trading circuit that BELIAL's initial demos were later pressed and issued by Moribund Records.

Having participated in the recording of the 'Wisdom Of Darkness' and 'Never Again' albums, frontman Koskinen left to form ETERNITIES. Having replaced him with new singer Jarno Antilla for the much more adventurous and melancholic '3' album,

BELIAL was rocked by a further departure in early 1996 when bassist Jani Lehotosaari joined IMPALED NAZARENE.

BELIAL personnel were later involved in the PLAN E endeavour, a union that culminated with the 'E Is For Your Ears' release performing with the BELIAL / IMPALED NAZARENE rhythm section of bassist Jani Lehtosaari and drummer Reima Kellokoski, LEGENDA bassist Niko Karpinnen as well as ex-BELIAL keyboard player Reetta Saisa. In 2002 Lehtosaari joined SINVISION.

Jukka Vappu returned in 2006 with a new band unit entitled VIOLENT HAMMER, a Kuusamo based Death Metal band involving frontman Matti Viitala, DEATHMANTRA guitarist Lasse Limma, bass player Kalle Salmivaara and drummer Ari Mikkola.

The Gods Of The Pit, Moribund (1991) (Demo). The Invocation / Voices Beyond / Dead Zone / For The Beasts.

WISDOM OF DARKNESS, Lethal LRC002 (1992). Intro / The Invocation / Of Servant Of Belial / Lost Souls / Rise Of Hecate / Hypocrisy Of The God's Sons / Voices Beyond.

NEVER AGAIN, Lethal LRC 666 (1993). Firestorm / The Red One / Dragons Kiss / Swan Song / As Above So Below / The Sun / About Love / Pain-Flood / Clouds / Desires / On You.

THE GODS OF THE PIT PT. II, Moribund DEAD-05 (1993). The Invocation / Voices Beyond / Deceased / For Them / Piece By Piece (Remix).

After Taste 1 1/2, E-Records SHIT-2 (1994) (One sided 7" vinyl single limited to 50 copies). After Taste 1 1/2.

After Taste, BringMeTheHeadOfMichaelPiesch SHIT-1 (1994) (7" vinyl single limited to 500 copies). Clouds / The Invocation (Live) / Punkshit (Live) / Piece By Piece (Live).

3, Witchhunt WIHU 9418 (1995). Other Channel / Mr. Blue Sky High / I Want You To Die / The End / Exit / You / Holes And Boots / One Way In And Out On Valium / Nautilus / Saturnus / One Day / Sinä Inhotat Minua Rakkaani / Hate Song.

BENEATH THE MASSACRE

MONTRÉAL, QC, CANADA — *Elliot Desgagnés (vocals), Christopher Bradley (guitar), Dennis Bradley (bass), Justin Rousselle (drums).*

Montréal, Québec Death Metal band founded in 2004. Early BENEATH THE MASSACRE members included guitarist Jonathan Dubeau, of BURN MY EYES, FECALPHELIAC and BUILT ON LIES, plus Chris Pépin of SOMBRE NOSTALGIE. The group stabilised with a roster comprising singer Elliot Desgagnés, guitarist Christopher Bradley, bass player Dennis Bradley with Justin Rousselle on drums.

BENEATH THE MASSACRE, issuing the 'Evidence Of Inequity' mini-album through Galy Records, put in Canadian shows in September 2005 supporting NEURAXIS. However, these gigs would be cut short when the group's van sustained major damage in an accident outside Thunder Bay in Ontario. The band returned to Canada in October in union with FROM A SECOND STORY WINDOW and ION DISSONANCE.

The band, signing a new label deal with Prosthetic Records, partnered with Belgian Deathsters LENG TCH'E plus FUCK THE FACTS for a Canadian tour commencing in May 2006. The group worked with producer Yannick St-Amand at Yan's Room Studio on a new album, mixed by ex-OBLIVEON guitarist Pierre Rémillard. Further dates included shows at the Toronto 'Terror Fest', the 'Robot Mosh Fest' in Milwaukee then July US 'Trails Unto The Sick' concerts allied with VICTIMAS and NEURAXIS in July, which included the San Antonio 'Better Off Dead Fest' and Albuquerque 'Gathering of the Sick Fest'. In August the 'Fusion of Brutality' dates hooked the band up with SLEEP TERROR.

BENEATH THE MASSACRE had their track 'Profitable Killcount' included on a 2006 Cyclone Records compilation album, issued only in Japan "as a free gift from the Canadian Metal scene". The band's full-length album 'Mechanics Of Dysfunction' again produced by Yannick St-Ammand and mixed by

BENEATH THE MASSACRE

Pierre Rémillard, saw issue in February 2007 via Prosthetic Records.

BENEATH THE MASSACRE confirmed for the band's first headline appearances in the United States throughout March and April supported by ARSIS and ION DISSONANCE. The band's next tour outing was to be the 'Summer Slaughter' trek across the USA throughout June and July, seeing NECROPHAGIST headlining on a mammoth package billing with DECAPITATED, CEPHALIC CARNAGE, CATTLE DECAPITATION, THE FACELESS, AS BLOOD RUNS BLACK, ARSIS and ION DISSONANCE.

EVIDENCE OF INEQUITY, Galy (2005). Comforting Prejudice / Profitable Killcount / Totalitarian Hypnosis / Regurgitated Lullaby For The Borndead / Never More.

MECHANICS OF DYSFUNCTION, Prosthetic (2007). The Surface / Society's Disposable Son / The System's Failure / The Stench Of Misery / Untitled / Modern Age Slavery / The Invisible Hand / Better Off Dead / Long Forgotten / Sleepless.

BENEDICTION

BIRMINGHAM, WEST MIDLANDS, UK — *Dave Ingram (vocals), Darren Brookes (guitar), Peter Rew (guitar), Frank Healy (bass), Ian Treacy (drums).*

A Birmingham act formed in February 1989, BENEDICTION is sadly more noted in their home country for having supplied vocalist Mark 'Barney' Greenway to NAPALM DEATH than their musical achievements. However, outside of Britain, BENEDICTION, affectionately known in their home city as "The Bennies", have garnered a sizeable following through ever improving albums and constant touring.

The group, borne out of an earlier band entitled STILLBORN, debuted with 'The Dreams You Dread' demo in June 1989 which secured the band a deal with German label Nuclear Blast, a stable base of operations for the band to the present day. The opening formation found Greenway backed by guitarists Peter Rewinski and Darren Brookes, bassist Paul Adams with Ian Treacy on the drums. The inaugural audio generated by this union came with a split 7" single, 'Confess All Goodness', shared with Austrian gore-mongers PUNGENT STENCH. From the outset it was clear that the group was intent on breaking down genre stereotypes, effortlessly amalgamating Thrash and Death stylings, capping mid-paced, low end rumblings with Greenways effective, if thoroughly indecipherable, roar.

Following the release of the September 1990 first album, entitled 'Subconscious Terror' and co-produced by the band together with NAPALM DEATH's Mick Harris, Dave Ingram stepped in for Greenaway on vocals and contributed to promotion activity during the year which included British supports to PARADISE LOST and AUTOPSY.

The band undertook a further British tour opening for BOLT THROWER prior to recording their follow up at Silverbirch Studios in Birmingham, the Paul Johnston produced effort 'The

Grand Leveller', this outing seeing BOLT THROWER's Karl Willetts guesting on the track 'Jumping At Shadows' and closing out with a rendition of CELTIC FROST's 'Return To The Eve'. Before the record came out the band undertook further headlining dates throughout 12 countries, capitalised on by selected British and German dates upon its release. 1991 shows included gigs with label mates DISMEMBER and MASSACARA.

At the dawn of 1992 BENEDICTION hit the road once more with BOLT-THROWER on a bill including ASPHYX that enabled the band to embark on the 'World Violation' world tour across the European continent, the USA, Canada and also played a date in Tel Aviv, Israel. In October BENEDICTION released the 'Dark Is The Season' EP, which featured a reworking of the old ANVIL chestnut 'Forged In Fire' with former singer Barney Greenway guesting. The group endured another line-up change when bassist Paul Adams departed, BENEDICTION favouring ex-CEREBRAL FIX man Frank Healy to take his place.

The April 1993 album 'Transcend The Rubicon' opened up more new ground as the band tackled a one take studio jam of THE ACCUSED's 'At the Wrong Side of the Grave' and reworked the songs 'Artefacted Irreligion' and 'Spit Forth The Dead' from the 'Subconscious Terror' sessions. BENEDICTION topped the bill of a European tour with ATHEIST and CEMETERY as support. Dates included visits to Ireland, Portugal and Mexico. BENEDICTION, backed by an interim EP 'The Grotesque / Ashen Epitaph', supported BOLT THROWER on their American club tour, but found themselves as headliners on latter dates as problems hit BOLT THROWER forcing their withdrawal. BENEDICTION also appeared at the legendary Milwaukee Metalfest during the same year, on a bill alongside fellow heavyweights BIOHAZARD and SLAYER. The travelling cost the group the services of drummer Ian Treacy though, the skinsman quitting and being superseded by the 18 year old Neil Hutton in time for the Nuclear Blast New Year festivals in January 1995. 'The Dreams You Dread' arrived in June, being promoted with a European trek aligned with DEATH.

That Year Neil Hutton and Dave Ingram formed the side project WARLORD UK, releasing the 'Maximum Carnage' album on Nuclear Blast in 1996. The album included covers of AMEBIX and SLAYER songs.

Frontman Dave Ingram lent a helping hand to BOLT THROWER for a batch of live dates during 1997, when their vocalist Martin Van Drunen bailed out without warning. However, the 'helping hand' turned out to be more permanent and BENEDICTION promptly pulled in Dave Hunt to fill the vacated vocal position. BENEDICTION's March 1998 album 'Grind Bastard', the first to have erstwhile SABBAT guitarist Andy Sneap in control of the faders, ambitiously included covers of both JUDAS PRIEST's 'Electric Eye' and TWISTED SISTER's 'Destroyer'. Digipack variants hosted another cover, in 'We Are the League' originally by the ANTI-NOWHERE LEAGUE. Once again the group forged a touring partnership with DEATH, Chuck Schuldiner's last live expedition, prior to uniting with Norwegian Black Metal combo IMMORTAL.

BENEDICTION would make a return with the September 2001 record 'Organised Chaos' once again produced by Andy Sneap. Road work had the band in familiar company, co-headlining a January 2002 European expedition with BOLT THROWER backed up by FLESHCRAWL. Once these commitments had been fulfilled drummer Neil Hutton opted out to join STAMPIN' GROUND. In September 2004 the band headed up the 'Thunderstorm Over Europe' tour allied with GODHATE and NOMINON. The group also rendered their interpretation of SLAYER's 'Necrophiliac' for the 2004 Blackened tribute album 'Slatanic Slaughter'.

In early 2005 the band announced the high profile addition of CRADLE OF FILTH, LOCK UP and DIMMU BORGIR drummer Nick Barker to the ranks. Barker made his live debut with the band at Austria's 'Devil Days' festival on 10th June. Initial recordings laid down by the new formation included a cover version of SACRILEGE's 'Lifeline' including the guesting BOLT THROWER duo of vocalist Karl Willetts and guitarist Barry Thompson.

Nuclear Blast once again handled the 2006 BENEDICTION album, 'Killing Music'. In April the band revealed they had laid down studio cover versions of 'Seeing Through My Eyes' by BROKEN BONES, 'Into the Void' by BLACK SABBATH, and 'Banned from the Pubs' by PETER & THE TEST TUBE BABIES. In early May the band announced a temporary suspension of activities due to Nick Barker breaking his foot in what was described as "an incident in Estonia".

Despite working up new album tracks in early 2007 BENEDICTION band members would be involved in a variety of outside activities. Nicholas Barker would be helping out TESTAMENT on their live dates, Dave Hunt contributing vocals to both MISTRESS and ANAAL NATHRAKH whilst Frank Healy was playing bass in the reformed CEREBRAL FIX, sessioning for ANAAL NATHRAKH and instigating side project THE BURNING DEITIES.

The Dreams You Dread, (1990) (Demo). Experimental Stage / Subconscious Terror / Artifacted Irreligion / Bonesaw.
Confess All Goodness, Nuclear Blast NB 031 (1990) (Split 7" single with PUNGENT STENCH). Confess All Goodness.
SUBCONSCIOUS TERROR, Nuclear Blast NB033 (1990). Intro-Portal To Your Phobias / Subconscious Terror / Artefacted Irreligion / Grizzled Finale / Eternal Eclipse / Experimental Stage / Suspended Animation / Divine Ultimatum / Spit Forth The Dead / Confess All Goodness.
THE GRAND LEVELLER, Nuclear Blast NB048 (1991). Vision In The Shroud / Graveworm / Jumping At Shadows / Opulence Of The Absolute / Child Of Sin / Undirected Aggression / Born In A Fever / The Grand Leveller / Senile Dementia / Return To Eve.
Experimental Stage, Nuclear Blast NB 057 (1992). Experimental Stage / The Grand Leveller / Senile Dementia.
Return To The Eve, Nuclear Blast NB 058PDS (1992). Return To The Eve / The Grand Leveller / Senile Dementia.
Dark Is The Season EP, Nuclear Blast NB 059 (1992). Foetus Noose / Forged In Fire / Dark Is The Season / Jumping At Shadows / Experimental Stage.
Wrong Side Of The Grave, Nuclear Blast (1993) (7" picture disc). Wrong Side Of The Grave / Artefacted Religion / Spit Forth The dead.
TRANSCEND THE RUBICON, Nuclear Blast NB073 (1993). Unfound Mortality / Nightfear / Paradox Alley / Bow To None / Painted Skulls / Violation Domain / Face Without Soul / Bleakhouse / Blood From Stone / Wrong Side Of The Grave / Artefacted-spit Forth.
The Grotesque / Ashen Epitaph, Nuclear Blast NB 088-2 (1994). The Grotesque / Ashen Epitaph / Violation Domain (Live) / Subconscious Terror (Live) / Visions In The Shroud (Live).
THE DREAMS YOU DREAD, Nuclear Blast NB120 (1995). Down on Whores (Leave Them All For Dead) / Certified . . . ? / Soulstream / Where Flies Are Born / Answer To Me / Griefgiver / Denial / Negative Growth / Path Of The Serpent / Saneless Theory / The Dreams You Dread.
GRIND BASTARD, Nuclear Blast (1998). Deadfall / Agonised / West Of Hell / Magnificat (Irenicon) / Nervebomb / Electric Eye / Grind Bastard / Shadow World / Bodiless / Carcinova Angel / We The Freed / Destroyer / I.
ORGANISED CHAOS, Nuclear Blast NB0522 (2001). Suicide Rebellion / Stigmata / Suffering Feeds Me / Diary Of A Killer / The Temple Of Set / Nothing On The Inside / Easy Way To Die / Don't Look In The Mirror / This Graveyard Earth / Charon / I Am The Disease / Organised Chaos.

BENIGHTED

SAINT ETIENNE, FRANCE — *Julien Truchan (vocals), Olivier Gabriel (guitar), Liem N'Guyem (guitar / bass), Fred Fayolle (drums).*

Founded in May 1998, the brutal Black-Death Metal act BENIGHTED, based in the Saint Etienne region, comprises erstwhile members of DISHUMANISED in vocalist Julien Truchan, guitarist Olivier Gabriel and Chart, guitarist Liem N'Guyem of OSGILIATH and drummer Fred Fayolle of Black Metal combo

DARKNESS FIRE. A self-financed debut in 2000 led in turn to a contract with Adipocere Records for the 2002 follow up 'Psychose', after which Remi was inducted on bass guitar for April dates partnered with FURIA, CARCARIASS and RAIN.

The 'Insane Cephalic Production' album, produced by Christian Kholemannsleiner in August 2003, surfaced through Adipocere Records in February of 2004. DESTINITY vocalist Mick guested on the track 'Perpueral Cannibalism'. BENIGHTED had recruited WINDS OF TORMENT bassist Bertrand in November of 2003 but a new bassist Eric was drafted in May 2004.

2005 album 'Identisick', recorded at Kohlekeller Studios and featuring both Kris of KRONOS and Leif Jensen from DEW-SCENTED as guests, included a cover version of NAPALM DEATH's 'Suffer The Children'. Signing to Osmose Productions, the band cut new album tracks in the summer of 2007 at Kohlekeller Studio.

BENIGHTED, Independent (2000). The Diabolical Reign Of The Four Fallen Angels / Werewolf´s Nightmare / Last Part Of Humanity / Nocturne / Benighted Transcendence / Abysses Of Sadness / Infernal Killings.
PSYCHOSE, Adipocere (2002). Prémices Psychotigués / Paranoia / Dégénérescence / Banished / Arcanes Démoniaques / Aversion Fanatique / Lost In Catalepsy / From Desire To Disgust / Internal Sufferings / Claustrophobia / Feasting On The Disinterred Corpse / Unleash Hell / Slay The Benighted.
I.C.P., Adipocere CDAR83 (2004). Bestial Bleeding / Stay Brutal / Foetus / Deviant / Perpueral Cannibalism / Self-Proclaimed God / Dementia (The Precocious Symptoms Of Mental Perversion) / Phlebotomized / Insane Cephalic / Insomnies.
IDENTISICK, Adipocere CDAR106 (2006). Nemesis / Collapse / Identisick / Sex-Addicted / Mourning Affliction / The Twins / Ransack The Soul / Blind To The World / Spiritual Manslaughter / Iscarioth.

BENUMB

CA, USA — *Pete Ponitkoff (vocals), Dave Hogarth (guitar), Rob Koperski (guitar), Tim Regan (bass), John Goteli (drums).*

Californians BENUMB, led by the Russian émigré Paul Pontikoff, trod a fine line between Hardcore and Death Metal. BENUMB issued a string of shared 7 singles with the likes of SHORT HATE TEMPER, THE DUKES OF HAZZARD, SUPPRESSION and APARTMENT 213 oddly all featuring untitled tracks.

Kopeski would later be credited as penning lyrics for NU-Metal platinum act KORN on the track 'Helmet In The Bush'. Both Pontikoff and Gotelli would found VULGAR PIGEON issuing the 'Genetic Predisposition' single and 'Summary Execution' album. The duo also Both operate Christian Death Metal band TORTURED CONSCIENCE.

A 2002 BENUMB album issued by Robotic Empire would be shared as a split release with PIG DESTROYER.

Split, Same Day (1995) (Split single with SHORT HATE TEMPER).
Gear In The Machine EP, Relapse (1997). Consumed / No Hope / A.A.D. / Deprivation / Beyond Fucked.
Split, Rape An Ape (1997) (Split single with THE DUKES OF HAZZARD).
Split, Stenchasaurus (1997) (Split single with APARTMENT 213).
SOUL OF THE MARTYR, Relapse (1998). Driven Out / No Regret / L.N.F. / Nothing Personal / Sick / Monetary Gain / Oblivious / Stood Up And Sold Out / C.T.O.A. / I.H.M.U.S.T. / Blind / Struggle On / Purpose / Crawl, Stagger, Fall / Self Righteous / Stuck Pig / Self Inflicted / T.P.U. / T.Y.G. / Agony I / Agony II / Consumed / No Hope / A.A.D. / Of My Own / Deprivation / Beyond Fucked / Reoccurrence / Lost Perception / Perseverance / Overwhelmed, Overcome / Nothing For Nothing / A.D.S. / Choke.
Split, Monkeybite (1999) (Split flexi single with SUPPRESSION).
WITHERING STRANDS OF HOPE, Relapse (2000). Synopsis Of Ignorance Within The Society At Large / Once And Never Again / Underbelly / Minimum Wage Intellectual / Pass The Buck / Suffer / Epileptic / Integration / Realization Of Fact / Oxygen Thief / Just Short Of The Line / Serenity Within Chaos / WTO: Disintegration Of The Working Class / Three Down, One To Go / Laceration Of Belief / Survival Between Maggots / Amongst The Fallen / Articulation Of Hypocrisy / Abundant Knowledge, Infinite Stupidity / Father To The Fatherless / Imminent Departure / Flesh For Flesh / Dissection Of Grace / Embodiment Of Despair / Ascend From Persecution / Years Of Unjust / Cause And Reject / Genocide / Statistics / Division Within Division / Successful Failure / Closing Argument.
BENUMB, Robotic Empire (2002) (Split album with PIG DESTROYER). Path Of The Righteous / Whats Done Is Done / Stealing From The Blind.
BY MEANS OF UPHEAVAL, Repulse RR 6559 (2003). Cesspool Of Human Sewage / Rise From Squander / That Which Is Set In Stone / Programming The Caranial Void / Decimation To All That Which Resembles Compromise / Mesmerized By The Insignificant / Regurgitation Of The Bacteria Which Threatens The Present State Of Self / Judicial Failure / Clouding The Source Of Salvation / Devour, Discard, Advance / Swallow Conviction—Defeat Guilt / Breathing Life Into Predestined Failure / S.A.N.D.E.R.S. / Seeping Into The Blood System / Oppressing Binds Of Silence / Medicated Into Submission / Hierarchal Gluttony / Guilty Of Which You Accuse / Free Trade, Global Slavery / Engraved Into The Psyche / Gutted Out—Spit On / Fixation Of Complacent Self-Loathing.
BENUMB, Thorp THP57 (2005). Ageless Pain / 0% Down Enslavement For Life / Abatement Of The Weak Incarnation / Free Trade Abolishment / Chemically Involved Circumstances / Internalized Subjective Opposition / Pay Now Suffer Later / Christmas Morning In The House of Poverty Two Week After Bi-Partison Procrastination on a State and Local Level Failed to Provide Extensions on Existing Unemployment Claims, Before Leaving On Paid Holiday Vacation / Manufacturing Opportunity To Prolong The Abusive Cycle.

BESTIAL DEFORM

RUSSIA — *Kirill Ulanenkov (vocals / guitar), Timur Madayev (guitar), Aleksandr Petrov (bass).*

St. Petersburg blasphemic Death Metal combo BESTIAL DEFORM debuted during 1992 with the EP 'Worship To Madness'. The band underwent a major overhaul that same year, dispensing with guitarist Andrey Shnurov, bass player Sergey Utkin and drummer Viktor Kuzmichev. Replacements would be located in the form of Dmitriy Ivanov on guitar, former MECCA bassist Sergey Zelenyuk and drummer Mikhail Lind of GREAT SORROW repute. This version of BESTIAL DEFORM cut the EPs 'Malebranche' in 1993 and 'The Mystic' in 1994 as well as albums 'Together We'll Destroy The World' in 1994 and, signing to RAE Music, the 'Bellum Contra Omnes' set of 1996.

BESTIAL DEFORM shifted shape once more in 1997, with Ivanov, Zelenyuk and Lind all exiting.

Worship To Madness, Bestial Deform (1992). Re-Animator / Senseless Massacre / Treponem Pele / Asmodeus.
Malebranche, Bestial Deform (1993). For The Great Evil / Piece Of Flesh.
TOGETHER WE'LL DESTROY THE WORLD, Bestial Deform (1994). Intro / I Am Evil, I Am Death / Conjuration / Re-Animator / Name Of The Light / Piece Of Flesh / For The Great Evil / Outro.
The Mystic, Bestial Deform (1994). In The Sound Of Torment / Together We'll Destroy The World / Bestial Deform.
BELLUM CONTRA OMNES, RAE Music (1996). Intro (Heaven Of Demons) / Before The World Was Made! / My War / Conjuration / Name Of The Light / Flame Of Eternal And Gentle Pain / From Hell / I'm Evil, I'm Death / In The Sound Of Torment / For The Great Evil / Outro.

BESTIAL DEVASTATION

ATESSA, ITALY — *Torturer (vocals / guitar), Animal (bass / vocals), Lord Destroyer (guitar), Brutal (drums).*

Atessa Grindcore band BESTIAL DEVASTATION was founded under an original title of VIOLENCE during April 2002, debuting a year later with the demo 'Sores, Blood & Pus'. The band further enhanced their profile with inclusions on the compilation albums 'Atlantida Vol.22' and 'Register Of Zombies'. June of 2004 witnessed the recording of tracks for a split release to be shared with OBSCENE on Redrum Records. Three tracks also found their way onto the September released compilation album 'Metalson 1'. BESTIAL DEVASTATION then signed to Deadsun Records for their full length debut. 'Splatter Mania' arrived in July.

and the 'Death Metal' festival alongside MESSIAH, GRAVE and MORGOTH in Zabrze.

BETRAYER pulled in new guitarist Ripper, another ex-SLAUGHTER player. For a period in late 1991 Berial joined VADER as bassist. A further membership change in the BETRAYER ranks saw guitarist Northon replaced by Ryju. At this same juncture Northon, together with Molly, joined another Death Metal act CONDEMNATION.

BETRAYER activity on the domestic live front included shows such as a 1992 support to CANNIBAL CORPSE and SINISTER in Bydgoszcz, the 1992 'Shark Attack' festival, the 1993 'Metalmania' festival in Zabrze with THERION, MESSIAH, CANNIBAL CORPSE, CARCASS and DEATH and the 1994 'Metalmania' event sharing the stage with SAMAEL, UNLEASHED, CANNIBAL CORPSE and MORBID ANGEL.

In January 1994 BETRAYER recorded the 'Calamity' debut album at Modern Sound Studio in Gdynia for Morbid Noizz Productions. With the band's demise both Molly and Ryju joined MORTIFY.

CALAMITY, Morbid Noizz MN 002 (1995). After Death / Down With The Gods / In Sacrifice / From Beyond The Graves / Maze Of Suffering / Before Long You Will Die / Wrathday / Sickness Of The Human Race.

BETWEEN THE BURIED AND ME

NC, USA — *Tommy Rogers (vocals / keyboards), Paul Waggoner (guitar), Nick Fletcher (guitar), Jason King (bass), Mark Costello (drums).*

BETWEEN THE BURIED AND ME is an eclectic, Crossover Progressive Death Metal unit hailing from North Carolina. A diverse array of influences would be brought to bear by founding members vocalist Tommy Rogers and guitarist Paul Waggoner both of UNDYING and PRAYER FOR CLEANSING alongside Will Goodyear from THE VOIDS and PRAYER FOR CLEANSING. Rogers had also fronted New York Hardcore band FROM HERE ON, recording an album, 'Hope For A Bleeding Sky' released as a limited run of 700 copies in 2001. The band would be rounded out by ex-AZAZEL musicians guitarist Nick Fletcher and bassist Jason King. BETWEEN THE BURIED AND ME parted ways with Nick Fletcher in November of 2003.

The band allied themselves with CAVE IN and CONVERGE for a mammoth series of US dates in the Fall of 2004. However, guitarist Shane Blay exited in September, the band drafting Dustie Waring from GLASS CASKET as stand in. Further membership casualties were sustained in January of 2005 with the exit of both Kevin Falk and Jason Roe. Recruited as replacement drummer would be GLASS CASKET's Blake Richardson. Meantime, Falk promptly joined EVERY TIME I DIE.

BETWEEN THE BURIED AND ME announced a new album for Victory Records in 2005 would be titled 'Alaska'. Promoting this release, the band put in Autumn US dates in partnership with THE RED CHORD, THE ACACIA STRAIN and FROM A SECOND STORY WINDOW. Going into September, the band formed up package shows backed by CEPHALIC CARNAGE, THE BLACK DAHLIA MURDER, and INTO THE MOAT. Back on the road in November, Canadian and US gigs would be union with THE DILLINGER ESCAPE PLAN and HELLA. The band opened 2006 with US dates throughout February and March backed by EVERY TIME I DIE, BLEEDING THROUGH and HASTE THE DAY.

'Ozzfest' loomed for the 2006 summer touring season, the group sharing the festival stages with OZZY OSBOURNE, SYSTEM OF A DOWN, HATEBREED, LACUNA COIL, DISTURBED, BLACK LABEL SOCIETY, UNEARTH, BLEEDING THROUGH, NORMA JEAN, A LIFE ONCE LOST, STRAPPING YOUNG LAD, THE RED CHORD, FULL BLOWN CHAOS, WALLS OF JERICHO, ALL THAT REMAINS and ATREYU.

BETWEEN THE BURIED AND ME June 2006 album, 'The Anatomy Of', comprised entirely of cover versions. Renditions

BESTIAL DEVASTATION

BESTIAL DEVASTATION issued a split album, 'Total Fucking Gore!' shared with Singapore's DEMISOR, through Scrotum Jus Records in January 2006.

Sores, Blood & Pus, Bestial Devastation (2003). Intro / Cutting & Grinding Human Flesh / Perversion / Necronomicon: The Book Of The Dead Men / Smashing You Ass {Necrosodomy} / Vomit On ***** / The Thor's Hammer.
WISH YOU DIED HERE, Redrum REDRUM004 (2005) (Split album with OBSCENE). Io Necrofilo / Brutalized Pussy / Armin Meiweis / E.E. / Wish You Died Here / Last Cannibal Supper / Party With The Dead / Fuck. Remove. Collect ... Vaginal Apparatus.
SPLATTER MANIA, Deadsun DSR041 (2005). Bestialized / Perverse Female Disfiguration / Self-Defecation / Splatter Mania / Charlie Don't Shit / Blek Tamarr' Pt. I / Postmortem Fellatio / The Sublime Art Of Devastation / The Thor's Hammer / Cockless Man / Keep On Playin' / My Name Is Brokenass (Anal Fistula) / Vai Mezza / No ... I Want A Whole Pizza / Blek Tamarr' Pt. II / In Memory Of Dr. Satan / Bestial Devastation.
TOTAL FUCKING GORE!, Scrotum Jus SJR001 (2006) (Split album with DEMISOR). Smashed & Squashed / Genital Necrosis (Cockless Man II) / Crème de Chatte / Freakiller / Psycho Proctologist / Voodoo Curse / Emergenza Vruscl' / You're Gay / 115, Hotel de Paris.

BETRAYER

SŁUPSK, POLAND — *Berial (vocals / bass), Ripper (guitar), Riju (guitar), Molly (drums).*

BETRAYER was formed in Słupsk during 1990 as an aggressive Thrash Metal band. That same year the group recorded an improvised studio demo tape 'Forbidden Personality' with Molly on both drums and vocal. Subsequently joined by ex-SLAUGHTER vocalist / bassist Berial the band adopted a fresh Death Metal stance. In 1991 BETRAYER recorded at CCS Studio in Warsaw a six track demo billed 'Necronomical Exmortis'. These sessions featured the late guitarist Morris and subsequently distributed through Carnage Records. That year BETRAYER performed at the 'S'thrash'ydlo' festival in Ciechanow

BETWEEN THE BURIED AND ME (pic: Paul Brown)

recorded included THE DOORS 'People Are Strange', DEPECHE MODE's 'Little 15', SMASHING PUMPKINS 'Geek U.S.A.', BLIND MELON's 'Change', PANTERA's 'Cemetery Gates', SEPULTURA's 'Territory', SOUNDGARDEN's 'The Day I Tried To Live', MÖTLEY CRÜE's 'Kickstart My Heart', PINK FLOYD's 'Us And Them', QUEEN's 'Bicycle Race', METALLICA's 'Orion' and 'Blackened', and FAITH NO MORE's 'Malpractice'.

The group maintained their road ethic, hooking up with NORMA JEAN, FEAR BEFORE THE MARCH OF FLAMES, MISERY SIGNALS, THE FULLY DOWN and THE CONFESSION for the 'Radio Rebellion' tour set to kick off October 6th in Nashville. The band teamed up with DARKEST HOUR and MISERY SIGNALS for a UK tour in December.

Between The Buried And Me, (2002). More Of Myself To Kill / What Have We Become / The Use Of A Weapon.
BETWEEN THE BURIED AND ME, Lifeforce LIFE027 (2002). More Of Myself To Kill / Arsonist / Aspirations / What We Have Become / Fire For A Dry Mouth / Naked By The Computer / Use Of A Weapon / Shevanel Cut A Flip.
THE SILENT CIRCUS, Victory VR210 (2003). Lost Perfection: a) Coulrophobia / Lost Perfection: b) Anablephobia / Camilla Rhodes / Mordecai / Reaction / Shevanel Take 2 / Ad A Dglgmut / Destructo Spin / Aesthetic / The Need For Repetition.
ALASKA, Victory VR262 (2005). All Bodies / Alaska / Croakies And Boatshoes / Selkies: The Endless Obsession / Breathe In, Breathe Out / Roboturner / Backwards Marathon / Medicine Wheel / Primer / Autodidact / Laser Speed.
THE ANATOMY OF, Victory (2006). Blackened / Kickstart My Heart / Day I Tried To Live / Bicycle Race / Three Of A Perfect Pair / Us And Them / Geek U.S.A. / Forced March / Territory / Change / Malpractice / Little 15 / Cemetery Gates / Colorblind. Chart position: 151 USA.

BEYOND BELIEF

KAMPEN, HOLLAND — *A.J. Van Drenth (vocals / guitar), Robbie Woning (guitar), Michiel Dekker (bass), Sjoerd Visch (drums).*

Formed in 1986, BEYOND BELIEF featured two ex-DEADHEAD members guitarist Robbie Woning and bassist Ronnie Van Der Way alongside frontman A.J. Van Drenth and drummer Jacko Westendorp. Another early bassist would be Artino Selles. Having released the 'Remind The Skull' demo in 1990, recorded at Heaven's Shores Studios in Kampen, the contributed two exclusive tracks to a 1992 DSFA Records compilation then a further demo, 'Stranded', cut at Franky's Recording Studios, followed in 1992. BEYOND BELIEF toured their native Holland with CREEPMINE, ANCIENT RITES and DEADHEAD.

BEYOND BELIEF signed with Shark Records from Germany, recording the album 'Towards The Diabolical Experiment', at T&T Studios in Gelsenkirchen with producer Tim Buktu, for release in 1993. That June Artino Selles made his exit. Re-entering Franky's Recording Studios with producer Berthus Westerhuis in 1994 BEYOND BELIEF laid down the second album 'Rave The Abyss'. Live work marked the introduction of new bassist Wicliff Wolda. In side activity, Van Drenth initiated Black Metal project THRONE in union with ASPHYX drummer Bob Bagchus, releasing the demo 'The Ultimate Blasphemy'.

1996 proved to be the year BEYOND BELIEF came to a close. Robbie Woning departed and although EP recordings billed 'The Terror' were recorded with new guitarist Ronald, the group folded. The following year Van Drenth and Wicliff joined forces with PLEURISY drummer Edwin to create Death Metal band C-TANK, this alliance producing 'The Hellfeast' EP. Van Drenth then manifested LEGION, crafting the EP 'Unhallowed Ground' with collaborations from THE MONOLITH DEATHCULT vocalist Robin Kok.

In 2003 Painiac Records issued the limited edition retrospective 'Dawn' vinyl compilation, collecting together the 'Remind The Skull' and 'Stranded' demos. Van Drenth joined up with THE MONOLITH DEATHCULT for live shows. Meantime, Robbie Woning scored credits with GOD DETHRONED and worked as producer on two albums for SEVERE TORTURE.

BEYOND BELIEF was reformed during 2004, quoting a membership of Drenth, the MONOLITH, LEGION, TOXOCARA and ETERNAL CONSPIRACY credited Martijn Moes on guitar, bassist Wicliff Wolda and drummer Arjen Hurkmans. The band re-inaugurated itself on the live scene on 19th September 2004 at the 'Doom Day III' festival at Rotterdam's Baroeg. BEYOND BELIEF evolved further in 2005, now seeing Woning re-installed alongside MONOLITH and ETERNAL CONSPIRACY bassist Michiel Dekker and the ALTAR and MONOLITH veteran drummer Sjoerd Visch.

Remind The Skull, (1991). Intro / Shades Of Sorrow / Fade Away / Menticide / Done With Fate / Remind The Skull / Another / Soul Within / Timeless Dark.
Stranded, (1992). Intro / Forsaken / Stranded / Silent Are The Holy / Prophetic Countdown.
TOWARDS THE DIABOLICAL EXPERIMENT, Shark 029 RTD (1993). Intro: Ave / Shapes Of Sorrow / Stranded / The Experiment / The Nameless / Silent Are The Holy / Fade Away / Untouched / Prophetic Countdown / Kissing In XTC / The Finishing Touch / Outro: Never.
RAVE THE ABYSS, Shark 102 (1995). Rave The Abyss / Cursed / Blood Beach / High On The Moon / The Burning Of Redlands / Crushed Divine / The Grand Enigma / Tyrants Of The Sun / Lost.

BEYOND INSANITY

HAMAR, NORWAY — *Ander Langberg (vocals), Victor Bauman (guitar), Alexander Dalbakk (guitar), Svein-Ivar Sarassen (bass), Frank Nikolaisen (drums).*

Hamar based BEYOND INSANITY comprises the EVOLUTION DENIED, TROLL-MYR and MÖRKEGJEMSEL pairing of Anders Langberg and guitarist Victor Bauman. Langberg also cites credits with PHANTASMAGORIA, EMBER and EXPLICIT KARMA. Guitarist Alexander Dalbakk is active with EMBER, EVOLUTION DENIED and TROLL-MYR whilst drummer Frank Nikolaisen and bassist Svein-Ivar Sarassen are both also involved with PESTIFEROUS. Nikolaisen also holds MONOKHROM credits whilst Sarassen has ties to SUBVERSOR, CARPTICON and VIDSYN.

BEYOND INSANITY supported PANTHEON I on Summer 2004 Norwegian dates. That July Bauman added ABOMINAT to his list of band credentials, installing himself as their new drummer. Sarassen, billed 'Decepticon', joined QUADRIVIUM.

Superior, Beyond Insanity (2004) (Demo). Superior / Survival Of The Fittest / Game Of Death.

BEYOND SERENITY

SAARBRÜCKEN, GERMANY — *Torsten Kroke (vocals), Karsten Gries (guitar), Marc Barbian (guitar), Jochen Lehmann (bass), Charly Grammes (drums).*

Saarland Death Metal act not to be confused with the Danish outfit of the same title. The group was formulated in Saarbrücken during August of 1995 as a trio of guitarist Karsten Gries, bass player Torsten Kroke and Matthias Kleinbauer on drums. BEYOND SERENITY's first offering was the demo 'Dark One', these sessions seeing the introduction of Jochen Lehmann on bass and Marc Barbian on second guitar. By the Spring of 1998 Kleinbauer had been substituted by Charly Grammes.

May of 2000 found BEYOND SERENITY as a trio of Kroke, now handling both lead vocals and bass, Gries and Grammes, recording the EP 'Product Of Civilisation'. Shortly afterward Marc Bollow took command of the drum stool. In this incarnation BEYOND SERENITY cut the 'Total Control' album.

A body blow was dealt to the band in March of 2002 when founder member Torsten Kroke exited. Nelly Thomas took the role of frontman, Florian Klein bass whilst Patrick Mayer came in on second guitar.

Product Of Civilisation EP, Independent (2000). Unborn Dead / Dead Kiss / Product Of Civilization / Memory Of Death / Unreal / God's Pray.
TOTAL CONTROL, Independent (2001). Die In Your Mind / Sinner's Pain / Total Control / Bloodnight Terror / Product Of Civilization / Day Of Suffering / Dismembered Souls / Unreal / Blood For God / Revenge / Dead Cold Night.

BEYOND THE EMBRACE

NEW BEDFORD, MA, USA — *Shawn Gallagher (vocals), Alex Botelho (guitar), Oscar Gouveia (guitar), Jeff Saude (guitar), Adam Gonsalves (bass), Mike Bresciani (drums).*

An extreme yet melodic Metal six piece unit out of New Bedford, Massachusetts. BEYOND THE EMBRACE, founded by lead vocalist Shawn Gallagher and lead guitarist Oscar Gouveia in January of 2000, fuse retro Bay Area Thrash style persuasions with cutting edge Death Metal bolstered by the enhanced delivery of three guitars. Originally the pack of Gouveia, guitarists Jeff Saude and Alex Botelho, drummer Mike Bresciani and Fil Aroujo had been together as the act PARANORMAL. Regrouping, with Adam Gonsalves coming onboard as bassist, the new band debuted with a 1999 three song demo, which included a rendition of IRON MAIDEN's 'The Trooper', soon catching the ear of Metal Blade Records.

BEYOND THE EMBRACE would part ways with drummer Mike Bresciani shortly after recording their debut album for Metal Blade Records. He would be replaced by former VOICES FORMING WEAPONS and ROSWELL man Kevin Camille. The band would form up part of the fifth annual summer 2002 'Death Across America' dates headlined by KATAKLYSM and backed up by DIVINE EMPIRE and MISERY INDEX. In May of 2003 the band tagged onto the closing half of the US OPETH and LACUNA COIL nationwide tour.

BEYOND THE EMBRACE introduced former MARAZINE man Chris Parlon on bass in April of 2004. The band, promoting the 'Insect Song' album through Metal Blade, set out on tour with this new formation in May as openers to PRONG, however, gigs in Baltimore and Binghampton, New York were cancelled as Shawn Gallagher was afflicted with a throat infection. High profile Summer gigs had the band opening for ICED EARTH and TRIVIUM. Unfortunately the band was put out of commission yet again when guitarist Jeff Saude broke his leg onstage at a festival in July. Suffering still further, the guitarist then was hospitalized for two weeks due to a blood clot and a case of pneumonia.

BEYOND THE EMBRACE teamed up with BYZANTINE and CHILDREN OF TRAGEDY for the 'Sofa King Metal' tour commencing 24th September at the Sound Factory in Charleston, West Virginia. Unfortunately the group had to withdraw from the latter portion of this trek due to a combination of factors including getting rid of their van, having the replacement van in for repairs whilst their drummer was rushed to hospital to treat a serious infection in his foot.

2005 found Oscar Gouveia gaining production credits on the debut TRANSFIX demo. US dates scheduled for March of 2005 had the band partnered with INTO ETERNITY, SINGLE BULLET THEORY and headlining Finns AMORPHIS. A further announced short run of dates in June had the group in union with CRISIS and M.O.D. but the band pulled out of these shows before the tour kicked off. In September BEYOND THE EMBRACE acted as support to the Swedish Operatic Metal band THERION. November witnessed a line-up change as BEYOND THE EMBRACE parted ways with longtime drummer Kevin Camille. The following month KAGE's Steve Bolognese was announced as replacement.

The group backed noted Norwegian Progressive Metal band GREEN CARNATION for a run of US gigs throughout March 2006. Drummer Steve Bolognese joined Canadian band INTO ETERNITY in December.

AGAINST THE ELEMENTS, Metal Blade (2002). Bastard Screams / Mourning In Magenta / Compass / Rapture / Drowning Sun / Against The Elements / Release / The Bending Sea / Embers Astray / The Riddle Of Steel.
INSECT SONG, Metal Blade (2004). Fleshengine Breakdown / Plague / My Fall / ... Of Every Strain / Redeemer / Insect Song / Ashes / Weak And The Wounded / Absent / Within.

BEYOND THE SIXTH SEAL

WEYMOUTH, MA, USA — *Mike McKenzie (vocals), Adam Wentworth (guitar), Justin Chappell (guitar), Matt Woods (bass), Brendan Roche (drums).*

Weymouth, Massachusetts Metalcore band BEYOND THE SIXTH SEAL was founded during 1998 by Brendan Roche and Justin Chappell. Debut product would be a 1999 demo entitled 'Genocide Empire', recorded as a trio with Justin Chappell on lead vocals and bass, Rob Devlin on guitar and Brendan Roche on drums. By the time of the follow up 2000 'The White Demo' Chappell had switched to guitar, THE RED CHORD's Adam Wentworth was installed on bass and Lawrence Kwong was onboard as frontman. Voice of Life delivered a 2001 EP entitled ' A Homicide Divine'. Band line-up at this juncture comprised singer Lawrence Kwong, guitarists Justin Chappell and Adam Wentworth, bassist Rob Devlin with Brendan Roche on drums. European and US touring then ensued. In 2002 the band laid down a demo, 'Knives & Guns'.

Lifeforce Records then issued full-length album 'Earth And Sphere' in 2002. For these sessions BEYOND THE SIXTH SEAL pulled in Matt Woods on bass, from AMERICAN NIGHTMARE, and Mike McKenzie, of THE RED CHORD, on vocals. In September 2003 the group partnered with THE RED CHORD for a series of UK dates. However, the band then folded.

BEYOND THE SIXTH SEAL was to surface once again as a studio project of Mike McKenzie, Brendan Roche and bassist Greg Weeks of THE RED CHORD, signing to Metal Blade Records for the April 2007 album 'Resurrection Of Everything Tough'.

Genocide Empire, Beyond The Sixth Seal (1999) (Demo). Forest Of The Impaled / Saint Slaughter / Nordic Invasion / Order Of The Death's Head.

The White Demo, Beyond The Sixth Seal (2000) (Demo). In The Long Drawn Days / Drawn From Autumn / Enslaved / A Revelation For The Forsaken.

A Homicide Divine, Voice Of Life (2001). A Homicide Divine / Beneath The Barren Fields / The Gates Of Redemption / A Revelation For The Forsaken / Drawn From Autumn.

EARTH AND SPHERE, Lifeforce 60032-2 (2002). Medusan / Idols In Human Form / A Potent Wind / Faceless / Awaken / A Homicide Divine / Lift High The Banner Of Falseness / The Birthing Apparatus / A Subtle Texture.

Knives & Guns, Beyond The Sixth Seal (2002) (Demo). In The Long Drawn Days / Drawn From Autumn / Enslaved / A Revelation For The Forsaken.

RESURRECTION OF EVERYTHING TOUGH, Metal Blade (2007). Nothing To Prove / My Terrifying Ally / I Die At 35 / Revelry / Stricken / The Twisted Ladder / Feral Dreamer / The Law You Have Sworn / Forward Thinking / Yawning Of The Gale / Everything Tough / Blood Of A Ghost / Monument.

BEYOND WITHIN

SUDBURY, ON, CANADA — *Todd Pidgeon (vocals), Chris Finlay (guitar), Chad Condratto (guitar), John MacRae (bass), Paul Larochelle (drums).*

Sudbury, Ontario melodic Death Metal band BEYOND WITHIN self financed the 2003 'Belligerence' album. The band was initiated during March of 2002 by guitarist Chris Finlay and drummer Paul Larochelle, inducting Jesse on bass and a short-lived vocalist Dan Brousseau, being swiftly replaced by Todd Pidgeon. Subsequent recruits would be second guitarist Chad Condratto and bassist Scott Souci. Initially the group took on the title of HOLLOW POINT but after a few weeks discovered this name was taken. Their second choice, SWORN ENEMY, suffered the same fate and they finally settled on BEYOND WITHIN. After just three gigs Souci was usurped by John MacRae.

The 'Belligerence' outing featured four live video tracks filmed at Club Rockit in Toronto. The band added keyboard player Darren in April of 2004.

BELLIGERENCE, Beyond Within (2003). Satisfaction Of Freedom / No Glory / In Sleep / Words / Devilution / Why! / The Rider / What's This World / Insanity's Call / Serve No One / Trapped Deep / I Am Diseased / Existence Of Nothing.

BIRDFLESH

SWEDEN — *Achmed Abdulex (vocals / guitar), Magnus Moshbastard (vocals / bass), Smattro Ansjovis (vocals / drums).*

One of Scandinavia's leading Grind Metal acts. BIRDFLESH, founded in October of 1992, issued the promotional tapes 'The Butcherbitchtape' in 1994, and 'Demo Of Hell' in 1995. Two songs from this session were also issued on the 'Sometimes Death is Better 2, 3 & 4' Compilation CD Box set released by the Belgian Shiver label.

Further demos 'Fishfucked' arrived in 1997. However, in August of 1997 Alex went on an eight month sabbatical throughout South East Asia during which period BIRDFLESH was put on ice. Meantime both Andreas and Magnus worked with their other acts as well as forging a fresh Japanese inspired Grindcore band together NAPALM GORE.

With Alex back from his travels the newly reconvened BIRDFLESH released their fourth demo, 'We Were 7 Who 8 Our Neighbours On A Plate' in August 1998. Successive releases included the 'Trip To The Grave' 7" single, the 'Morbid Jesus' split EP shared with Poland's SQUASH BOWELS and another split, 'Misery Of The Defenceless' in union with CARCASS GRINDER.

The band would tour Japan in 1999 as running mates with D-RIVER. For the 2002 Razorback album 'Night Of The Ultimate Mosh' BIRDFLESH enlisted the father of drummer Adde Mitrouliu (a.k.a. Smattro Ansjovis) and Apostolos Ansjovis to perform guest clarinet. Also guesting on these sessions would be Jörgen of DETHRONEMENT, Cab of HYPNOSIA and Tobbe Eng and Tobbe Ander from JIGSORE TERROR all on backing vocals.

Adde exited in early 2002, joining SAYYADINA for a European tour and also finding his way into the ranks of GENERAL SURGERY. 2002 also saw BIRDFLESH cramming no less than 19 tracks onto a 7" format album 'Carnage On The Fields Of Rice'. The band cut a whole swathe of new tracks in June of 2003, these being earmarked for use on split singles shared with THE KILL, FRIGHTMARE and EMBALMING THEATER. BIRDFLESH, bringing in Cab Castervall of HYPNOSIA repute as live guitarist, united with NEURAXIS and HELLBLAZER for European shows in September.

The Butcherbitchtape, Birdflesh (1994) (Cassette demo). Morbid Hatt / Butcherbitch / Twisted Eyes In Beauty.

Demo Of Hell, Birdflesh (1995) (Demo). 782 / Splatterart / Pukebox / Gimme 5!? / Violent Silence.

Fishfucked, Birdflesh (1997) (Demo). Fried Eyes / Fishfucked / Brown Banana / I Don't Give A Fuck.

Trip To The Grave EP, Burning Death BDR001 (1998). The Hungry Vagina / Trip To The Grave / Burgers Of The Fucking Dead / Land Of The Sick / Walk Of Insanity / Mutilation Boogie & Masturbation Blues / Sweat Of The Old Man / Teenage Mutilator / The Brutal Corpse / More Garlic / Bodily Dismemberment.

We Were 7 Who 8 Our Neighbours On A Plate, Birdflesh (1998) (Demo). 782 / Destruction And Eternal Carnage / Warstorm / Page Rage / Flower Power Violence / The Bugman / Party On! / Sox, T-shirts And Ties / Criminal Cat / Tipp Tapp / Dental Torture.

Trip To The Grave, Birdflesh (1998). Burgers Of The Fucking Dead / More Garlic / Mutilation Boogie & Masturbation Blues / Sweat Of The Old Man / Teenage Mutilator / The Hungry Vagina.

Wo-Man?!, Fudgeworthy FUDGE 025 (1999) (Split EP with SQUASH BOWELS). Destination Shanghai / Blood On The Rice / Dead In The Paper / Forbidden Fetus / Morbid Jesus / Prostitution Of Mankind / Hai Banzai / Ninjas From The Grave Of Satan.

Misery Of The Defenceless, Underground Warder Productions UWP003 (1999) (Split 7" vinyl EP with CARCASS GRINDER). Northern Garden / Misery Of The Defenceless / The Hedgehog Sickness / Death To Flies.

Birdflesh / The Dead, Nocturnal Music NMCD 028 (2001) (Split EP with THE DEAD). Sillman / Summergrind / Handicapitation / I Must Not Live / Dead Delicious / Astray And Fooled.

ALIVE AUTOPSY, Leather Rebel LRR 2001 (2001). Barbarian Bar / Electrodeath / Skyrat / Kick On The Cross / Victim Of The Anal Abscess / Alive Autopsy / Bullchrist / Repulsive Regurgitation / The Gay And The Demon / Crazy Island / Loser Of The Universe / The Return Of The Blasphemous Birdgorrilla / Mongolized / Ken Is Dead / Motorbed / I Will Always Hate You / Murderfire / Teenage Mutilator (Live) / Arabian Dreams (Live) / Vicious World (Live) / Destination Shanghai (Live) / Walk Of Insanity (Live).

NIGHT OF THE ULTIMATE MOSH, Putrid Filth Conspiracy PFC 026 (2002) (Vinyl release). Coffinfucker / Master Of Violence / Gore In Gore Out / Arabian Psycho / Night Of The Ultimate Mosh / The Rolling Massgrave / Above, Where Are You? / Catmouth / Gut To Kill / Bloodshed Attack / Eternal Emotions / Slaughter Of Flies / Bowelthrasher / Kid Of The Brown Vomit / The Evil Pig / Everything Is Shit / Dance On The Frozen Desert / Crowes In The Nose / Death And Insanity / Carmolesting Dead / Suicide Maniac / Victim Of The Grind / Fried Eyes.

Carnage On The Fields Of Rice, Nuclear Barbecue Party NBP005 (2002). Napalm Gore / Suicide Kamikaze / The Land Of The Rising Sun / Anal Misery / Assbuttmen / Oral Hell / Gorilla Death / Goatboy / The Sound Of The Hound / Harvester Of Sorrow / Carnage On The Fields Of Rice / Brutal Pregnancy / Paralysed Head / Race Behind The Rice / Samurai Overdrive / Murderblood / 1000 Gorillas Unleashed / Rise From The Rice / Yota Komuza.

NIGHT OF THE ULTIMATE MOSH, Razorback RR 013 (2002). Coffinfucker / Master Of Violence / Gore In Gore Out / Arabian Psycho / Night Of The Ultimate Mosh / The Rolling Massgrave / Above, Where Are You? / Catmouth / Gut To Kill / Bloodshed Attack / Eternal Emotions / Slaughter Of Flies / Bowelthrasher / Kid Of The Brown Vomit / The Evil Pig / Everything Is Shit / Dance On The Frozen Desert / Crowes In The Nose / Death And Insanity / Carmolesting Dead / Suicide Maniac / Victim Of The Grind.

SWEDISH ASSAULT, Relapse 6556 (2003) (Split CD with SAYYADINA, ASSEL, GENOCIDE SUPERSTAR, GADGET and DISFEAR). Trip To The Grave / Walk Of Insanity / Mutilation Boogie And Masturbation Blues / Teenage Mutilator / Barbarian Bar / Alive Autopsy / Kick On The Cross / Mongolized.

Catbomb, Regurgitated Semen RSR 46 (2003) (Split vinyl EP with THE KILL). Catbomb / The Cannibal And The Corpse / No Fucking Heaven / Lipbalm Death.

KILLING ROSENKELLER, Haunted Hotel HHR02 (2004) (Live cassette release limited to 200 copies). Night Of The Ultimate Mosh / Morbid Jesus / Anal Misery / The Cannibal And The Corpse / Teenage Mutilator / Out To Kill / Victim Of The Grind / Fried Eyes / Coffinfucker / Misery Of The Defenceless / Alive Autopsy / Walk Of Insanity / The Rolling Massgrave / Vicious World.

Death Metal Karaoke, Rescued From Life (2004) (Split EP with EMBALMING THEATRE). Death Metal Karaoke / Carnival Of Slime / Blind Butcher / Blast From The Ass / Vikings From The North.

TIME TO FACE EXTINCTION, Civilisation CR 024 (2004) (Split album with CATHETER). Nightmare On Bahamas / I Love Myself And I Want To Die / Maggot Hotel / The Insane Winds / Wildpig Massacre / Deathgore Of The Fleshmaster / Trapped In The Ass Of The Dead / Mongo Business / Speeder Man / Sons Of Samurai.

LIVE @ GIANTS OF GROUND, Power It Up # 29 (2005). Gut To Kill / Night Of The Ultimate Mosh / The Cannibal And The Corpse / Carnival Of Slime / Catmouth / Master Of Violence / Anal Misery / Gore In Gore Out / Misery Of The Defenceless / No Fucking Heaven / Teenage Mutilator / Deathgore Of The Fleshmaster / Walk Of Insanity / Bowelthrasher / Ken Is Dead / Victim Of The Grind / The Rolling Massgrave / Coffinfucker / The Evil Pig / Alive Autopsy / Fried Eyes / Destination Salzgitter / Morbid Jesus.

MONDO MUSICALE, Dental DR 190210 (2006). Mongo Musicale / Wigdestroyer / Then You Know / Mongoloid Wannabe / Arabian Jesus / Wedlock / Crocophile / Born Tired / After-Ski Obliteration / Bass Of Thunder / Mr. Big Head / Dear Driver / The Friendly Call / Handicapitation / Drums Of Death / Whirlpool Whiplash / Dancefloor Dismemberment / Nightgrinder / Colombian Tie / Guitars Of Steel / The Day Hell Came To Town / Dying Cable / Moonwalk Massacre / Victims Of The Cat / Ladies Night / Birdo Might.

BLACK CRUCIFIXION

ROVANIEMI, FINLAND — *Timo Livari (vocals), Juha Kullpi (guitar), Henrik Esa Juujärvi (bass), Jari Pirinen (drums).*

BLACK CRUCIFIXION was established as a Rovaniemi based side concern of members guitarist Holocausto Vengeance (a.k.a. Juha Kullpi) and drummer Sodomatic Slaughter (a.k.a. Jari Pirinen) of arch Black Metal band BEHERIT in union with guitarist / vocalist Fornicator and bassist Blacksoul (a.k.a. Arjo Wennström or 'Black Jesus'). Pirinen was also previously a member of KADATHERON and GOAT VULVA. Wennström held ties to PARADE OF SOULS.

BLACK CRUCIFIXION arrived in 1992 touting the two track demo 'Flowing Downwards'. The band, installing Henrik Esa Juujärvi, also from PARADE OF SOULS, on bass and having issued 'The Promethean Gift' EP for the Austrian Lethal label in 1993, this seeing V. Jauhiainen contributing backing vocals. They then commenced work on a planned album with a provisional title 'Faustian Dream'. However, this endeavour was never realised and the group eventually evolved into PROMETHEAN, releasing the 1997 album 'Gazing The Invisible'. In 1999 the Soul Seller label re-issued 'The Fallen One Of Flames' demo as a 10" single.

BLACK CRUCIFIXION returned during 2006, returning to the 'Faustian Dream' concept, having adopted a much smoother approach with clean vocals in a Death / Doom format. Meantime, Juujärvi, together with PARADE OF SOULS man Veijo Pulkkinen and ex-BLIND PILOTS and RAUTAKANKI guitarist Kimmo Nissinen had forged the experimental Metal outfit ONSÉGEN ENSEMBLE.

FAUSTIAN DREAM, Paragon PRG26021 (0). Faustian Dream / As Black As The Roses (As Weak As My Smile) / Bible Black Tyrant / Wrath Without Hate / Where Will You Hide / Winterkill / Scandinavian Melancholy / Frailest / Faustian Scream.

Flowing Downwards, Fallen Pages Productions (1992) (Cassette demo limited to 250 copies). Intro / Flowing Downwards / Master Spirit / Outro.

Promethean Gift EP, Lethal LMCD 222 (1993). Promethean Gift / Serpent Of Your Holy Garden / Journey Into Myself (Through A Ritual) / Flowing Downwards.

The Fallen One Of Flames, SoulSeller SSR 002 (1999) (10" vinyl single). Intro / Flowing Downwards / Master Spirit / Goddess Of Doom / Outro.

The Fallen One Of Flames, SoulSeller SSR 002 (2001) (MCD). Intro / Flowing Downwards / Master Spirit / Goddess Of Doom / Outro.

The Fallen One Of Flames, Paragon PRG26017 (2005) (MCD). Intro / Flowing Downwards / Master Spirit / Goddess Of Doom / Outro.

FAUSTIAN DREAM, SoulSeller SSR 008 (2006). Faustian Dream / As Black As The Roses (As Weak As My Smile) / Bible Black Tyrant / Wrath Without Hate / Where Will You Hide / Winterkill / Scandinavian Melancholy / Frailest / Faustian Scream.

BLACKSHINE

STOCKHOLM, SWEDEN — *Anders Strokirk (vocals / guitar), Joakim Stabel (guitar), Fredrik Holmberg (bass), Anders Freimanis (drums).*

Stockholm based riff hungry yet adventurous Metal band, the young Swedish act, billed as 'Goth n' Roll', started life as HETSHEADS issuing the 1995 Repulse album 'We Hail The Possessed'. The band would opt to veer away from Death Metal and rebilled themselves as BLACKSHINE, scoring a deal with the German G.U.N. label and toured in Germany prior to their debut album, 'Our Pain Is Your Pleasure' appearing in the stores. BLACKSHINE would open for U.D.O. in Europe and BRUCE DICKINSON in Scandinavia.

Switching to the SPV label BLACKSHINE parted ways with drummer Anders Freimanis, enrolling erstwhile FACE DOWN and GODBLENDER man Hakan Eriksson in his stead for the January 2001 'Soulless And Proud' album. The band put in a short run of dates supporting ENTOMBED in Sweden during November. Meantime BLACKSHINE singer Anders Strokirk would lend his vocal abilities as session guest on NECROPHOBIC's 'Bloodhymns' record.

BLACKSHINE would be allocated the support slot for the IN FLAMES tour of Germany in October 2002 but later lost this spot to SOILWORK. More than adequate compensation was delivered when BLACKSHINE were confirmed as opening act to the European jaunt of LACUNA COIL and SENTENCED. In September 2004 the band, having completed work on a new album 'Lifeblood' with new man Stipen of MERCILESS, DIA PSALMA/STREBERS and TRANSPORT LEAGUE repute on drums, confirmed they had parted ways with SPV/Steamhammer Records and had inked a new deal with Escapi New Media Entertainment. Stipen joined HARMS WAY in mid 2005. Line-up changes in November saw drummer Stefan Carlsson replaced by KAAMOS and REPUGNANT man Chris Barkensjö (a.k.a. 'Chris Piss').

The following February Barkensjö enrolled himself into the ranks of FACE DOWN. BLACKSHINE signed to German label Dockyard 1 in July. That same year BLACKSHINE personnel were also involved with the Team Hamarby IF supporting "Klack Metal" band BAJEN DEATH CULT.

II, Blackshine (1996) (Cassette demo). My Pain Is Your Pleasure / For A Better Day / The Shadow / Lost To Eternity.

OUR PAIN IS YOUR PLEASURE, Great Unlimited Noises GUN 145 (1997). My Pain Is Your Pleasure / Blow My Mind / The Dead Is The Winner / The Beast Within / Cul-De-Sac / Shade / Forever Goodbye / Lost To Eternity / My Own God / Razor Blades / Liquid Serenity.

SOULLESS & PROUD, Steamhammer SPV 085-72532 (2002). Love Our Hell / Soulless And Proud / Sacrifice / Chocked With Feathers / Another Twist / Light The Fuse / Servants Of The Harvest / Shadowman / Blackheart Brain / Outcast / Full Moon Rising.

LIFEBLOOD, Dockyard 1 DY100372 (2006). Cure In The Shape Of Noise / Born A Denier / Lifeblood / Stonefog / Powerghoul / Unbroken / Burn The World / Face The Bastard God / Dwell In Black / Second Rate Blasphemer / Denial Of Pain.

BLACKSMITH

JYVÄSKYLÄ, FINLAND — *Kai Leikola (vocals / bass), Christian Jörgensen (guitar), Mikko Luontama (guitar), Turo Marttila (keyboards), Juha Pesonen (drums).*

BLACKSMITH was a Jyväskylä Melodic Death Metal band, founded in 1996. The group recorded the January 1999 session 'Beneath A Thick Satin Moon' at Watercastle Studio in Jyväskylä with a recording line up comprising vocalist / bassist Kai Leikola, guitarist Christian Jörgensen, keyboard player Turo Marttila and drummer Juha Pesonen. 'Outcast / Forlorn' followed in 2000, this outing seeing the band joined by second guitarist Mikko Luontama. However, obligatory military service put the band on hold for much of the year.

Only Leikola would remain as the transition to SOULFALLEN took place in 2002. New personnel would be Tuomas Ekholm as keyboard player and drummer Jimmy Salmi for a 2004 EP 'Dark Remains'.

Beneath A Thick Satin Moon, Blacksmith (1999). Beneath A Thick Satin Moon / The Mask Of Inhuman Misery / Of Mourning And Grief / The Eclipse.

Outcast / Forlorn, Blacksmith (2000). Midnight's Caress / The Darkened Veils Of Remembrance And Past Times / Beyond The Grim Horizon / The Remains Of An Utter Desire / A Shred Of Hope / ... Only To Be Cast Away.

BLAKK MARKET

FLORIANOPOLIS, SC, BRAZIL — *Fernando Melleu (vocals), Thiago Rocha (guitar), Alexandre Schneider (guitar), Felippe Chiella (bass).*

BLAKK MARKET is a Thrash / Death act hailing from Florianopolis, first assembled during 2002 with a line up comprising vocalist / bassist Fernando Melleu, guitarists Thiago Rocha and Alexandre Schneider, both previously with DESPOTIC, and drummer Marlon Sens. Schneider would soon opt out and Felippe Chiella, another DESPOTIC veteran, enrolled on bass, freeing Melleu up to concentrate on lead vocals. Marlon Sens vacated the drum stool in May of 2004, this gap soon filled by yet another DESPOTIC man—Alexandre Sell. Expanding their sound the group briefly inducted ANATRIZ keyboard player Julio Stotz. This formation lasted some two months before Alexandre Schneider rejoined.

BLAKK MARKET's November 2004 demo 'Hateful Affection', limited to 350 copies, would include a video for the track 'Twisted Broadcast'. In 2005 BLAKK MARKET contributed their version of 'Indians' to the Collision Records ANTHRAX tribute album 'Indians ... NOT! Brazilian Tribute to Anthrax'.

Drummer Alexandre Sell exited in 2006. BLAKK MARKET commenced recording the album 'Self-improvement: Suicide' at AML Studios with producer Alexei Leão in early November.

Hateful Affection, Blakk Market (2004) (Limited edition 350 copies). Twisted Broadcast / The Wheel Keeps Turning / Putrefaction Guaranteed / The Dawn Of The Dead / Twisted Broadcast (Video).

BLASPHEMER

DEWSBURY, WEST YORKSHIRE, UK — *Cristiniano Cagna (vocals / guitar), Matthew Firth (guitar), Jason Wright (bass), Andrew Miller (drums).*

Dewsbury Death Metal band BLASPHEMER came together during 1990. Recording at Academy Studios, the band debuted with a 1992 four song demo. A second set, 'Dominion', arrived in 1994 with a third 1995 session scoring the band a deal with Peaceville Records. It would be at this juncture the group opted to switch title to DOMINION although just prior to the name switch, BLASPHEMER donated the track 'The Joyful Tears Of Sorrow' to the compilation 'Under The Sign Of The Sacred Star'. As DOMINION, the band promoted session singer and erstwhile ballet student Michelle Richfield to the lead vocalist role. However, her angelic strains still compete in the mix with the Death growls of guitarists Mass Firth and Cristiano 'Arno' Cagna.

DOMINION released two critically acclaimed albums, 'Interface' and 'Blackout', before folding. Guitarist Mass Firth joined EBONY LAKE following the album 'On The Eve Of The Grimly Inventive'. However, this band folded shortly after, with Firth joining Wakefield brutal Death Metal band NAILED.

Demo '92, Blasphemer (1992). Take Me Now ... I'm Dying / Immortality / Sutcliffe / Blasphemer.

Dominion, (1994). Dominion / Squandered Opportunity / Liquidate The Nazarene / Consciousness Surrounds.

Demo '95, (1995). The Sea Of Selfishness / The Joyful Tears Of Sorrow / Parasite.

BLASPHEMER DEMOS '92-'95, (2001). Take Me Now ... I'm Dying / Immortality / Sutcliffe / Blasphemer / Dominion / Squandered Opportunity / Liquidate The Nazarene / The Sea Of Selfishness / The Joyful Tears Of Sorrow / Parasite.

BLASPHEREION

CHARELOI, BELGIUM — *Dan Vandenplas (vocals / guitar), Patrick Rosa (guitar), Eddy Satin (guitar), Fabrice Depireux (drums).*

Chareloi based BLASPHEREION evolved from MORBID DEATH, a late eighties Death Metal trio, publishing the demos 'Demoniac' in 1988, 'Sin Of Pride' in 1989 and 1990's 'Diabolic Force'. The following year the band evolved into BLASPHEREION. The band comprised vocalist / guitarist Dan Vandenplas, DYING CORPSE bassist Franck Lorent and drummer Fabrice Depireux with guitarists Patrick Rosa and 'Eddy Satin' also being credited. BLASPHERION debuted for the French label Osmose Productions with the album 'Rest In Peace'.

During 1993 Vandenplas and Lorent, taking on the guises of 'Cernunnos' and 'Lord Sabathon' respectively, founded a further Death Metal unit entitled SLANESH and the Black Metal act ENTHRONED. The latter would rapidly rise to international recognition but on 19th April 1997 Cernunnos committed suicide. His replacement in ENTHRONED would be Fabrice Depireux (a.k.a. 'Namroth Blackthorn').

REST IN PEACE, Osmose Productions OPCD 003 (1991). Church Of Lies / Bells Of Pain / Demon's Blood / Decadence Life / Apocalyptic Visions / It's Still There / R.I.P. / Inside My Eyes / At The Bound Of Madness / Future Earth.

BLASTMASTERS

FL, USA — BLASTMASTERS is a June 2004 founded, Florida based Death Metal band led by former DIABOLIC and UNHOLY GHOST drummer Lee 'Aantar' Coates. Coates' comrades included the EVIXION and AS UNDER credited bass player Jesse Jolly and guitarist R.J.

The group cut a self-titled demo in August at Diet Of Worms Studios with producer Juan "Punchy" Gonzalez of MORBID ANGEL and UNHOLY GHOST repute. The following month the project was reported to have added second guitarist Jerry Mortellaro, also of DIABOLIC and UNHOLY GHOST, but within days this statement was denied. Oddly, a further report in December stated Mortellaro had in fact been involved, aiding on the composition of three songs, but had opted out due to his commitment to UNHOLY GHOST.

February 2006 saw an announcement detailing BLASTMASTERS credited players guitarist Jeff Parrish and bassist Jesse Jolly's induction into an all new band billed PROMETHEAN HORDE alongside PATHS OF POSSESSION and DARK FAITH singer Nick Goodyear, ex-HELL ON EARTH guitar player Mike W, LULL ME TO LARVAE keyboard player Mike Goodyear and ROYAL ANGUISH drummer JR Daniels.

In June 2006 BLASTMASTERS members Aantor Coates, guitarist R.J. and bassist Jesse Jolly reforged DIABOLIC.

Blastmasters, Blastmasters (2004). Implemented Digital Control / The Beheadings / La Fin Du Monde.

BLEAK CROWD

OULU, FINLAND — *Tommi Suomala (vocals), Janne Kauppi (guitar), Ville Hakala (guitar), Kimmo Kuoppamaa (bass), Timo Anttonen (drums).*

Dark, melancholic Metal band BLEAK HOUSE was manifested in Oulu during 1999 by the will of the erstwhile UNBLESSED guitar pairing of Janne Kauppi and Ville Hakala. In October 2000 the band, enrolling RED and JOINT DEPRESSION bassist Kimmo Kuoppamaa, cut an opening demo 'Memory Of A Life'. A second demo session entitled 'Mourn' arrived in mid 2001 and before the year was out the band had been joined by a new singer, Tommi Suomala.

BLEAK CROWD's next demo, 'Of Existence', saw delivery in 2002. The group's next move was to self-finance the 2003 album 'In Solitude'. Jouni Juurikka supplied backing vocals. A single, 'God-Given Goddamn Misery', followed up in 2004.

The Memory Of A Life, Bleak Crowd (2000) (Demo). Breaking Point / It's All Over / Only One Morning / Still Can't Let You Go / Memory Of A Life.
Mourn, Bleak Crowd (2001) (Demo). Emily / Heartbreaker / These Days / Still Can't Let You Go / Forget The Pain.
Of Existence, Bleak Crowd (2002) (Demo). No Ending / Of Existence / Until You're Cold Inside.
IN SOLITUDE, Bleak Crowd (2003). A Long Crawl From Cradle To Grave / Until You're Cold Inside / Shroud / In Solitude / Autumn Dyer / Never Die In Me / Kill Me / A Seal Upon Your Eyes / No Ending / Mirror Of Your Grace / Of Existence / Back Inside (Dialogue With The Mirror).
God-Given Goddamn Misery, Bleak Crowd (2004). God-Given Goddamn Misery / Lie / Blind On A Leash / Torch Of Souls.
Into The Stars, Bleak Crowd (2005). Fight Against The Wall / The Mountain / Into The Stars / Somewhere Somehow.

BLEAK DESTINY

MISSISSAUGA, ON, CANADA — *Boyan Guerdjikov (vocals), Alex Koumpan (guitar), Chris Lantz (guitar), Marko Vukovic (bass), Clare Buchanan (keyboards).*

Mississauga's BLEAK DESTINY was assembled by Ukrainian guitarist Alex Koumpan and CORPORATE RIOT bassist and Serbian native Marko Vukovic, enlisting Chris Lantz, a veteran of ENFORCED POWER, P.U.S., SOLEMN RIFF and ACACIA, as second guitarist. The group would be rounded out with the addition of singer Alon Tamir, keyboard player Clare Buchanan and Polish drummer Michael 'Chopper' Walczak. With Tamir opting out to pursue a career in the military, the Bulgarian born Boyan "Warlock" Guerdjikov of BURIED DREAMS and BY FEAR IF FALL took the vocal position in May of 2004.

That September the band organized and promoted two successful festivals, 'Ashes of Autumn 2004' and a Chuck Schuldiner tribute show. In October Michael Walczak decided to leave the band due to personal reasons. Thereafter, BLEAK DESTINY played three shows with ex-CORPORATE RIOT/current MORTIFY drummer Lenny Isac filling in. BLEAK DESTINY also published the demo '… At The Gates Of Zhongdu' in October.

BLEAK DESTINY folded, with ex-members guitarist Alex Koumpan, bassist Marko Vukovic and keyboard player Clare Buchanan forging SYMETARY. Boyan Guerdjikov was to front NEPHELIUM.

… At The Gates Of Zhongdu, Bleak Destiny (2004). Zhongdu / Currents Of Sorrow.

BLEED OF HATE

PERU — *Gustavo (vocals), Jorge P. (guitar), Coco (guitar), Giovanni (bass), Omar (drums).*

Peruvian Death Metal band BLEED OF HATE holds its roots in prior act VORAZ, constructed in late 1999 by bassist Giovanni and guitarist Coco, second guitarist Vitaly, singer Ronnie and drummer Hans. Line-up troubles spelled the end for VORAZ but Giovanni and Coco stuck together to forge BLEED OF HATE, drafting vocalist Ana, guitarist Luis and drummer Omar. This version of the band cut a three song demo in December 2003, 'Bleed Of Hate Demo 1 2k3', before both and Luis exited, the latter to join DISINTER. BLEED OF HATE regrouped, drawing in Gustavo of NARKAN on vocals and Guillermo of MERTHUR on guitar to record a six song CD for release in August 2005. Subsequently Jorge Rengifo usurped Guillermo before he too was replaced, by Coco.

Bleed Of Hate Demo 1 2k3, (2003). Pagan Krieg / To Human / Evil Speech.
NEW BLOOD… MORE VICTIMS, Sangre Fria-Gate of Horrors (2005). Psycho Denied (Intro) / These Walls / Hate To Love / I Deny / Wrong / Victims Of Society / Southern Storm (Intro) / Anarkoblacks.

BLINDEAD

GDYNIA, POLAND — *Nick Wolverine (vocals), Havoc (guitar), Dead Man (guitar), Mike (bass), Konrad (drums).*

Gdynia Doom Death outfit BLINDEAD feature vocalist Nick Wolverine of NEOLITHIC and TIMES NEW ROMAN with BEHEMOTH man Havoc on guitar. The group started out billed as INCORRECT PERSONALITY in 1999 with a line-up comprising guitarist Havoc and bassist Mike, subsequently adding second guitarist Dead Man then singer Patryk and drummer Konrad. Demos followed in the Winter of 2000 and 2002, after which Patryk departed. Nick Wolverine stepped in as replacement.

The promo recording 'Dig For Me…' was recorded in 2003. Bassist Zima opted out in April 2004. BLINDEAD issued the 'Devouring Weakness' album through Empire Records in July 2006. Further Polish dates, dubbed the 'Torment Tour', witnessed a strong union with HELL-BORN, MASSEMORD and HERMH throughout November and December.

Dig For Me…, Blindead (2003) (Demo). Dig For Me… / Taste My Pain.
DEVOURING WEAKNESS, Empire (2006). Suicidal / Memory Of Loss / Mindscape / Drug Disorder / The Time / Devouring Weakness.

BLINDED BY FAITH

LÉVIS, QC, CANADA — *Tommy Demers (vocals), Daniel Gingras (guitar), Pascal Côté (guitar), Vincent Roy (bass), Danny Émond (keyboard), Luc Gaulin (drums).*

Yet another heavy act from the prolific province of Quebec, BLINDED BY FAITH was formed in Lévis during 1996. The band play a Gothic Doom-Death style with lyrics with a medieval flair. After a few line-up changes and a number of local gigs the band managed to produce a seven-track debut release, entitled 'Veiled Hideousness', in late 1999. Guitarist Sebastian Lessard was replaced by Pascal Cote in 2000 and the band continued to be active and play local gigs including the prestigious Polliwog Festival. BLINDED BY FAITH issued their second album, 'Under An Occult Sun' on Galy Records, in 2003.

BLINDED BY FAITH were joined by ex-MOONLYGHT, ASGARD, NO TURN AROUND, SORCIER DES GLACES and PASSAGE drummer Luc Gaulin in January 2006. The group utilised New Rock studios in Québec commencing November 3rd, working with producer Yannick St-Amand on new album tracks dubbed 'Weapons Of Mass Distraction'.

VEILED HIDEOUSNESS, Tuxedo Productions TUX001 (1999). Somber Harbinger / Behind The Placid Mask Of The Starlit Cosmos / Veiled Hideousness / My Burnt Wings / Reptilian Shudder / A Slumber In Cobwebs / Melania.
UNDER AN OCCULT SUN, Galy GALY-008 (2003). Tear The Purple Curtain / A Perfect Imperfection / Burning Rebellion / The World Has Something To Offer / Under An Occult Sun / Submit To The Summit / The Last Missive / Reptilian Shudders / The Triumph Of Treachery.

WEAPONS OF MASS DISTRACTION, Galy (2007).

BLINDED COLONY

KARLSHAMN, SWEDEN — *Johan Schuster (vocals), Tobias Olsson (guitar), Johan Blomstrom (guitar), Roy Erlandsson (bass), Staffan Franzen (drums).*

Karlshamn melodic Death Metal band previously known as STIGMATA, formed in January 2000 by guitarist Johan Blomström, second guitarist Tobias Olsson and singer Niklas Svensson. BLINDED COLONY released their debut album, 'Divine', during 2003 via Italy's Scarlet Records. BLINDED COLONY parted ways with Svensson in January of 2005, bringing in substitute Johan Schuster of TDPP and solo project PLOUGHBILL. The revised version of the band cut a self-titled demo that March, recording at Soundpalace Studios 2005 with producer Johan Blomstrom.

BLINDED COLONY contracted with Pivotal Rockordings in March 2006 to record a new album, 'Bedtime Prayers', once again utilising Sound Palace Studios. Originally intended for a 2006 issue, the album was pushed back into January 2007. A promotional video for the song 'Once Bitten, Twice Shy' was directed by Thomas Tjäder.

BLINDED COLONY partnered with EKTOMORF and KAYSER for European tour dates throughout February and into March 2007.

Tribute To Chaos, Blinded Colony (2002) (Demo limited to 100 copies). Contagious Sin / Discrown The Holy / Selfobtained Paranoia / Demoniser DCLXVI / Anno Domini 1224.
DIVINE, Scarlet SC 067-2 (2003). Contagious Sin / Thorned & Weak / Legacy (Slave In The Name Of Christ) / Selfobtained Paranoia / Lifeless Dominion / Discrown The Holy / Kingdom Of Pain / Demonizer DCLXVI / Anno Domini 1224.
Blinded Colony, Blinded Colony (2005) (Demo). Aaron's Sons / Swallow And Sleep / In Here / Need.
BEDTIME PRAYERS, Pivotal Rockordings (2007). My Halo / Bedtime Prayers / Once Bitten, Twice Shy / Need / Revelation, Now! / 21st Century Holocaust / Aarons Sons / In Here / Heart.

BLO.TORCH

DEN HAAG, HOLLAND — *Chris van der Valk (vocals), Marvin Vriesde (guitar), Hassan Moechtar (guitar), Sander Koole (bass), Pascal Rapailles (drums).*

Den Haag Thrash Metal act. BLO.TORCH lost the services of singer Michel De Wilde in early 2002. Guitarist Marvin Vriesede would join German Thrashers DEW SCENTED on a temporary basis that year for tour work. The band added new singer Chris van der Valk during November for a new demo recording billed as 'Plan B'.

During June of 2003 Vriesde united with fellow Dutchmen SEVERE TORTURE. BLO.TORCH cut a new Hans Pietersen produced studio album 'Volatile' at Excess Studio in Rotterdam for 2004 release. In March the band won a cash prize, festival appearances and 500 singles as the winners of the 'Grote Prijs van Zuid-Holland' competition. BLO. TORCH returned with the 'Volatile' album in 2004.

With guitarist Martin Vriesde otherwise occupied out on the road with SEVERE TORTURE and DEW-SCENTED the band pulled in Rory Hansen as substitute for Summer 2005 shows.

The Plot Sickens ..., (1997). The Plot Sickens / King Of Karnage / Abandoned / March Of The Worm.
BLO-TORCH, Wicked World WICK008 (1999). Spanish Sun / Mount Ygman / King Of Karnage / Inkblack Sky / Panzerstorm / Quatrain / Seem To Be The Enemy / March Of The Worm / Bloodstains.
Promo 2001, (2001). Razorjob / Lightblockers.
Plan B, (2002). Razorjob / The Ties That Blind / Vermin Circle / Scattered Ashes Lay.
VOLATILE, (2004). Consumed By Indifference / Split Soul Massacre / Razorjob / Perish With The Pitiful / Justifiable Homicide / Votives In Suspension / Aberrant Dream / The Ties That Blind / Vermin Circle / Endtime.

BLOCKHEADS

NANCY, FRANCE — *Xav (vocals), Antoine (guitar), Payot (bass), Nico (drums).*

Marbaches, Nancy Grindcore outfit forged in 1989 with an opening formation of vocalist Xav (a.k.a. Xavier Chevalier), guitarist Ben, bass player Xaxa and drummer Oli, subsequently adding second guitarist Pierre. This latest recruit would bow out in 1991, to join YELLOW FLOWERS, and would be replaced by Fred. Next to defect would be Xaxa, substituted by Bruno from AMIBE and ANAGNORISIS.

BLOCKHEADS marked their entry into the world of Grind with a 1993 demo 'Haashaastaak'. Following recording the band shifted shape once more, drafting ANAGNORISIS drummer Benoît, this line up recording the debut 1995 album 'Last Tribes'. Despite this obvious progress the group splintered, with Benoît, Ben and Fred all leaving. A new look band duly arose, drafting the DEATH TO PIGS, CATARIS and HALBA'S DOGS credited Ludo on guitar, ex-CATARIS man Payot on bass and drummer Nico of NAUSEA GODS and in January of 1998 BLOCKHEADS issued the 'Watch Out' album. Ludo would then be usurped by DHIBAC veteran Antoine.

Signing to the Bones Brigade label the first two albums would be compiled into one release and put out as 'From Womb To Genocide' in 2000, this preceding a brand new studio album 'Human Parade'. Raph would then be the latest inductee, taking his role as new bass man. Shared releases in 2002 found BLOCKHEADS sharing a split single with Swiss act NOSTROMO, covering NOSTROMO's 'Selfish Blues' whilst their partners took on the BLOCKHEADS 'Unwillingly And Slow', and a cassette release with CEMENTERIO SHOW.

LAST TRIBES, (1995). Moloch / Masked Masses / Unwillingly And Slow / D.Y.B.M. / Womb / Flies Reward / Paroxysm Of Speeches / Butterfly / Millennium Utopia / Regression.
WATCH OUT, (1998). First Genocide / Generally Accepted Ideas / Polymorphic Perdition / Horned Totem / Artificial Day / McDollars / Avagdu / G.O.D.S. / Opportunist / Circle Of Consumption / Dog Bomb / Between Human And Animal / Crom Cruach / Ekun / Will Nature Soon Forget.
FROM WOMB TO GENOCIDE, Bones Brigade (2000). First Genocide / Generally Accepted Ideas / Polymorphic Perdition / Horned Totem / Artificial Day / McDollars / Avagdu / G.O.D.S. / Opportunist / Circle Of Consumption / Dog Bomb / Between Human And Animal / Crom Cruach / Ekun / Will Nature Soon Forget / Seismosore / Moloch / Masked Masses / Unwillingly And Slow / D.Y.B.M. / Womb / Flies Reward / Paroxysm Of Speeches / Butterfly / Millennium Utopia / Regression / Haashaastaak.
Blockheads, Waiting For An Angel WFAA 015 (2002) (Split release with NOSTROMO). Selfish Blues / War To War.
HUMAN PARADE, Bones Brigade BB 013 (2002). Face Yourself, Make Up Your Mind! / Sometimes / Reek Of Deceit / Enmeshed / Primate Way / Ephemeral / Rupture / Lamenting Spirit / Positive Incentive / (...) / G.M.O. / It Will Eat You / Dreamland / A.C.T. / Dead Men Working / Shaman Pulse / Micropig / Hide Your Face / War To War / Logic Of Chaos.

BLOOD DUSTER

MELBOURNE, VIC, AUSTRALIA — *Tony Forde (vocals), Matt Collins (guitar), J.J. LaWhore (guitar), Jason P.C. (bass), Matt Rizzo (drums).*

Quite uniquely Melbourne's BLOOD DUSTER have somehow managed to mould lethal Grindcore with traditional 70's style Southern Rock and Rockabilly rhythms spiced up with a large dose of grossed out humour. The band, often performing naked onstage, opened up with an inaugural 1990 line up of bassist Jason 'P.C.' Fuller, drummer Brick and a guitarist (possibly) called Fred, opened up proceedings with the 1992 demo 'Menstrual Soup'. Guest vocals on the closing track 'Swine In Shit' came courtesy of Leigh Cornish. Brick would be forced into retiring from music suffering with a badly injured knee whist Fred (?) reportedly also retired but in his case to a mental home!

BLOOD DUSTER signed to Wild Rags Records in America for a proposed first album. However, the record 'Fisting The Dead', would eventually emerge on the domestic Dr. Jim label. Line up at this stage comprised of Jason P.C., drummer Shane Rout, vocalist Tony Forde and guitarist Brad. However, Rout would break ranks to join Black Metal band LORD LUCIFER at the same time as Brad made his exit.

Second outing 'Yeest', replete with a deliberately shocking medical photograph for a cover and apparently so named as to copy exactly another local act's album title, would be re-issued by Relapse in America combined with the previous mini album. Fin Allman was now on guitar with ORDER OF CHAOS man Matt Rizzo on drums.

For 1998's 'Str8 Outta Northcote' Rout made a return on drums as Allman departed. BLOOD DUSTER then drafted NO GRACE six stringer Matt 'Lowpartz' Collins, second guitarist Josh ('J.J. La Whore') of POD PEOPLE and reinstituted Rizzo. The quaintly titled 'Cunt' album sees a cover of IMPETIGO's 'Dis-Organ-Ized'. The band signed to the French label Season Of Mist for an eponymous January 2004 album. Topping the year would be an appearance at METALLICA headlined 'The Big Day Out' festival plus support dates to THE HAUNTED. A single, 'Six Six Sixteen', employed a sleeve photograph mimicking the debut W.A.S.P. album. Australian gigs in June would be curtailed when Tony Forde shattered his collarbone and received a head would requiring stitches at a gig in Geelong.

In side activity, both Fuller and La Whore were members of MEGAWATT WINGED AVENGER whilst Bassist Jason P.C. also operated Stoner band DERN RUTLIDGE. BLOOD DUSTER personnel would also be engaged with THE DAY EVERYTHING BECAME NOTHING.

BLOOD DUSTER supported SLAYER and MASTODON on April 15th 2007 at the Vodafone Arena in Melbourne.

Menstrual Soup, (1992). Knee Deep In Menstrual Blood / Ted / Dr. Artery / Dirty Platter / Swine In Shit.

Yeest EP, Dr. Jim 014 (1993). Albert / Northcote / Motherfuckin' / Chuck / Showered With Affection Part 2 / Strop / Nasty Chicks.

FISTING THE DEAD, Dr. Jim 8 (1995). Intro / Vulgar Taste / Kill, Kill, Kill / Bitch / Intro / Mortician / Sadomasifuck / Rectal Spawn / Intro / Grossman The Meatman / Blood Fart / Knee Deep In Menstrual Blood (The Bleeding Bitch Returns) / Intro / Chunky Bit / Intro / Simultaneous Pleasure Pinch / Intro / Theatre Of The Macabre / Gimmie Some Lovin' / Raping The Elderly / Intro / Anal Feast / Fisting The Dead / Intro / Derek.

YEEST, Relapse (1995). Albert / Northcote / Motherfuckin' / Chuck / Showered With Affection Part II / Strop / Nasty Chicks / Vulgar Taste / Kill, Kill, Kill / Bitch / Mortician / Sadomasifuck / Rectal Spawn / Grossman The Meatman / Bloodfart / Knee Deep In Menstrual Blood Part II / Chunky Bit / Simultaneous Pleasure Pinch / Theatre Of The Macabre / Gimme Some Lovin' / Raping The Elderly / Anal Feast / Fisting The Dead / Derek.

YEEST, Dr. Jim (1995). Vulgar Taste / Kill, Kill, Kill / Bitch / Mortician / Sadomasifuck / Rectal Spawn / Grossman The Meatman / Bloodfart / Knee Deep In Menstrual Blood Part II / Chunky Bit / Simultaneous Pleasure Pinch / Theatre Of The Macabre / Gimme Some Lovin' / Raping The Elderly / Anal Feast / Fisting The Dead / Derek.

STR8 OUTTA NORTHCOTE, Relapse (1998). Givin' Stiff To The Stiff / Hippie Kill Team / Metal As Fuck / I Hate Girls And Crusty Punx / Chop Chop / Tittie / Motherload / The Meat Song (Stiffy In McDonalds) / Death Squad / Instrumental I / The Simple Life / Where Does All The Money Go When Releasing A Full Length Album? / It's Just Not Metal / Celebrating 35% Pig Fat / F.S.S. / Ooh Aah / Derek II / Roll Call / Shoved Up Your Pisshole / Ballad Of Hoyt / Pure Digital Silence.

CUNT, Relapse (2000). We Are The Word Police / Big Fat Arse / Another Slack Arsed Aussie Band / Pronstoresiffi / Pissing Contest / I Just Finished Sucking Off Metalheads In The Mens Urinals / Hoochie Mumma / I Love It When Joe Pesci Swears / Stock Takin' / Lets All Fuck / A Track Suit Is Not Appropriate Metal Apparel / The Corpse Song / Fuck You Scene Boy / Is Killing Clones Illegal / Don't Call Me Home Boy Ya Cunt / Spefeven / The Object Is To Shift Some Units / Sweet Meat / Dis-Organ-Ized.

I Wanna Do It With A Donna, (2003) (White vinyl. Limited edition 1000 copies). I Wanna Do It With A Donna / Midnight Nambla.

D.F.F. EP, High Voltage HVR005 (2003). Thespiritodsorethroathaslongsincedied / Painfullnoiseentitled"htabbaskcalb" / Orneryhornery / D.F.F. / 66.6onyourFMdial / Tickettoride / htabbaskcalb Part 2 / Let's Fuck.

Six Six Sixteen, High Voltage HVRS001 (2004). Intro-Pledge Of Allegiance / Six Six Sixteen / Love Piss / It's A M.A.N.S. World / I Wanna Be Your Pimp.

BLOOD DUSTER, Season Of Mist SOM 086 (2004). ForThoseAboutToFuck / Idi:54 / SixSixSixteen / CockJunkie / Sellout / IWannaDoItWithADonna / FruityRelationships / HerionPunk / Sk8ergrrl / BadHabits / OnTheStage / VeganFeast / DrinkFightFuck / TonyGoesToCourt (Skit) / OnTheHunt / CurrentTrends / Underground / DrugFiend / Achin'ForAn'A'Cup / DahmerTheEmbalmer / She'sAJunkie / NuCorporate / OrneryHornery / 66.6OnYourFMDial / TicketToRide + PainfulNoise entitled 'HTABBASKCALB' / Let's Fuck.

BLOOD FREAK

ANAHEIM, CA, USA — *Jason Grinter (vocals / bass), Jon Sellier (guitar), Andy Reed (drums).*

Anaheim Gore-Grinders BLOOD FREAK, created in August 1988 by PUTRIFIED MASS and POGO THE CLOWN members vocalist / bassist Jason Grinter and drummer Andy Reed, cut tracks at Sonic Tracks Studios for an album in July 1990, intended to be titled 'Blood, Blood, And More Blood!'. However, the band fell apart in the studio. It was not until November 2003 that Razorback Records released the sessions, together with 1988 demos, as 'Sleaze Merchants'. BLOOD FREAK subsequently re-united, signing an album deal with Razorback Records for a new album to be entitled 'Live Fast, Die Young, & Leave a Flesh-Eating Corpse'. However, tragedy of the worst kind hit the band in mid August 2005 when, travelling from Anaheim to commence recordings in Seattle, their van suffered an accident near Portland, killing all three band members.

SLEAZE MERCHANTS, Razorback (2003). Warning / Feast Of The Undead / Blood, Blood, And More Blood! / Grinding Up The Dead / Bloodthirsty Butchers From Beyond / Flesheaters From Outerspace / The Gruesome Gorehounds / Infested With Worms / The Cult Of The Cannibal Freaks / I Rip Your Flesh / Gobble Up Your Guts / The Slaughterhouse / You Are What We Eat! / Werewolf A-Gore-Gore / Kill! Kill! Kill! / A Brutal Orgy of Ghastly Terror! / Awakening The Beast / Insane For Gore / (Untitled) / I Said ... Murder! / Dr. Cannibal / A Happy Ending.

MULTIPLEX MASSACRE, Razorback (2006).

BLOOD RED THRONE

KRISTIANSAND, NORWAY — *Mr. Hustler (vocals), Død (guitar), Tchort (guitar), Erlend Caspersen (bass), Freddy B (drums).*

BLOOD RED THRONE is the retro Death Metal project of erstwhile EMPEROR man Tchort (a.k.a. Terje Vik Schei). The band was convened in Kristiansand after both Tchort and guitarist 'Død' (Daniel Olaisen) both quit SATYRICON during 1999 and operate as a side project in parallel to Tchort's activities with GREEN CARNATION. Bass duties would fall to Erlend Caspersen of APOSTASY, UNSPOKEN NAMES, MR. CUCUMBER and DISMAL EUPHONY. Olaisen also performed with SCARIOT whilst Tchort also finds the time to rank as bassist with CARPATHIAN FOREST. For recording of the 'Deathmix 2000' demo session BLOOD RED THRONE utilised the services of vocalists Ronnie Thorsen of SCARIOT and Vidoor Helseth. A cut from these tapes would find its way onto the Necropolis 'Nordic Metal II' compilation.

The anonymous 'Mr. Hustler' (Flemming Gulch) would take over duties at the microphone for the debut album 'Monument Of Death'. Issued by the Dutch Hammerheart label 'Monument Of Death' would see a later license to North America courtesy of the Martyr Music group. The first 1000 copies, dubbed "The Suicide Kit", are apparently signed with the real blood of the band members.

BLOOD RED THRONE announced touring activity for June 2002, forming part of the 'Generation Armageddon' festival

BLOOD RED THRONE

package in league with Swedish acts DISMEMBER, SATARIEL and NECROPHOBIC, Dutchmen SINISTER and Danes MERCENARY. That same year Flemming Gulch and Daniel Olaissen initiated side venture COBOLT 60, cutting the album 'Meat Hook Ballet'.

As a stop gap mini-album, 'A Taste For Blood', comprising of unreleased promo tracks, a MASSACRE cover version and a cut from the 'Nordic Metal II' compilation, was readied for 2002 release BLOOD RED THRONE announced the induction of new drummer Espen Antonsen. A second, full length album, the Endre Kirkesola produced 'Affiliated With The Suffering', was projected for October release. Embarking upon a mammoth string of European shows throughout October and November of 2002 BLOOD RED THRONE created part of a deadly union for the 'Generation Armageddon' festival tour. Joining the band would be Greece's SEPTIC FLESH, Ireland's PRIMORDIAL, Belgium's ANCIENT RITES, and Swedish heavyweights DISMEMBER and IMPIOUS. This title would be used once more for a second leg of European shows in May of 2003, the band forming a live alliance with ANCIENT RITES, THYRFING, SEPTIC FLESH, PRIMORDIAL and SKYFIRE.

The band spent the early part of 2004 crafting a new studio album 'Altered Genesis'. The recording line-up for this opus comprised vocalist Mr. Hustler, guitarist Tchort and Død, bassist Erlend Caspersen with session drums from Bernt A. Moen. European dates for June saw an alliance with VADER and MALEVOLENT CREATION.

The band altered its line-up, introducing singer Vald and drummer Anders Faret Haave, the latter of APOSTASY and GROUND ZERO SYSTEM, for November European shows ranked alongside MORTICIAN and AKERCOCKE. Although the tour saw MORTICIAN pulling out in dramatic circumstances, as frontman Will Rahmer was arrested in Poland on 13th November under the charge robbery with a dangerous weapon, the tour continued. Members of AKERCOCKE and BLOOD RED THRONE pooled talents to cover vocals and bass duties in order for MORTICIAN to continue the dates.

In early 2006 Erlend Caspersen joined the ranks of US Death Metal band VILE to conduct their 'Gutting Europe' tour during March and April. In October he teamed up with Santa Cruz, California Death Metal band DECREPIT BIRTH.

BLOOD RED THRONE entered Jailhouse Studios in Horsens, Denmark in early February 2007 to record a fourth studio album.

Deathmix 2000, Blood Red Throne (2000) (Demo). Ravenous War Machine / The Children Shall Endure ... / Dream Controlled Murder / Mary Whispers Of Death.
MONUMENT OF DEATH, Hammerheart HHR100 (2001). Portrait Of A Killer (Testimony Of The Dying) / Souls Of Damnation / The Children Shall Endure ... / Dream Controlled Murder / Mary Whispers Of Death / Ravenous War Machine / Malignant Nothingness / Monument Of Death / Path Of Flesh.
A Taste For Blood, Hammerheart HHR125 (2002). Ravenous War Machine / The Children Shall Endure ... / Mary Whispers Of Death / Monument Of Death / Cryptic Realms / Malignant Nothingness.
AFFILIATED WITH THE SUFFERING, Hammerheart HHR126 (2003) (Digipack). Unleashing Hell / A Dream Of Death / Bleeders Lament / Mandatory Homicide / Death Inc. / Razor Jack / Chaos Rising! / Gather The Dead / Affiliated With The Suffering / Malediction / Mercy Killings / Deadly Intentions.
AFFILIATED WITH THE SUFFERING, Hammerheart HHR126 (2003). Unleashing Hell / A Dream Of Death / Bleeders Lament / Mandatory Homicide / Death Inc. / Razor Jack / Affiliated With The Suffering / Gather The Dead / Chaos Rising! / Malediction.
A TASTE FOR BUTCHERY, Hammerheart America 3 (2003) (Split album with SEVERE TORTURE). Ravenous War Machine / The Children Shall Endure / Mary Whispers Of Death / Monument Of Death / Cryptic Realms / Malignant Nothingness.
ALTERED GENESIS, Earache MOSH285 (2005). Death To Birth / Incarnadine Mangler / Tortured Soul Appearance / Eye-Licker / Mephitication / Arterial Lust / Flesh To Destroy / Ripsaw Resentment / Altered Genesis—Creation And Sudden Demise / Smite / State Of Darkness / Deliberate Carnage.

BLOOD RETCH

PONTYPRIDD, WALES, UK — *Eddie Richards (vocals), Lee Jones (guitar), Terence Monk (guitar), Matt Wilson (bass), Jamie Jones (drums).*

Pontypridd Death Metal act BLOOD RETCH was fronted by 'Eddie Richards' (a.k.a. Gareth Bonetto). The vocalist, who had previously been a member of PRECISION AND KAOS, forged the band with guitarist Lee Jones in August 2003. That October, the band line-up was bolstered with the addition of bassist Frosty alongside Steve Smith and Gareth Williams. However, these three all soon departed. In November Matt Wilson was installed ion bass and in December Jamie Jones secured the drum position. Terence Mark was acquired as second guitarist in February 2004 to record the split EP 'Demons' and album 'Pain Is My Weakness'.

Tragedy struck the band on 14th March 2005 when Gareth Bonetto was found hanged at his Yr Hendre home in Nantgarw, near Pontypridd, apparently the result of suicide. The singer had only just been discharged from Royal Glamorgan Hospital.

PAIN IS MY WEAKNESS, Blood Retch (2005).

BLOOD STORM

USA — *Mezzadurus (vocals / guitar), Axarcuth (guitar), Deyaxulgaat (bass), MacCriunna (drums).*

BLOOD STORM, a highly rated Black / Death Metal fusion, is the act of ABSU touring member Mezzadurus (real name Chris Gamble). The vocalist / bassist had previously fronted the renowned Death Metal combo GOREAPHOBIA, an act that released a solitary EP on Relapse Records. Drummer Telco Coraxo has a background with NAMTARU and PERVERSERAPH. BLOOD STORM emerged with a brace of demos with 1995's 'Iron Flames Of Battle' and the following year's 'Death By The Storm Wizard'. Following the release of the debut album 'Atlantean Wardragon' on French label Osmose Productions both these earlier recordings would be reissued on CD in 1998.

BLOOD STORM put on an impressive old school black metal performance at the 1997 Milwaukee Metalfest. A restricted release vinyl EP 'An Attack Of Sonic Torment', shared with MORIA, would include a cover version of EXCITER's 'War Is Hell'. The 2001 BLOOD STORM album 'Ancient Wraith Of Ku' included a cover version of SLAUGHTER's 'The Curse'. By the summer of 2001 both Mezzadurus and Teloc Coraxo had forged an alliance with Dana Duffey for a resurrection of the notorious DEMONIC CHRIST.

Drummer Telco Coraxo would session on the 1998 KRIEG album 'Rise Of The Imperial Hordes'. He would also provide the same duties for the PERVERSERAPH mini album 'Savage Messiah'. BLOOD STORM put in appearances at the 2002

'Destruction' festivals in New York and New Jersey utilizing the services of drummer Vaz from Florida's BLACK WITCHERY.

An extreme Metal package tour of the USA, dubbed the 'Hellstorm Of Unholy Legions', saw August 2005 dates in union with KULT OV AZAZEL, TERATISM and HORN OF VALERE.

DEATH BY THE STORMWIZARD, Nightfall (1996). Vision Of The Soothsayer / Yuggothian Slayers / Expulsion Of Wrath / Volkruun Ihuul Zhahruus / Serpent Of The Icecross / Crypts Of Sorcery / Clavicula Salomonis (Of The Lightless Fire) / Spell Of The Burning Wind / Savior Under The Sword / Destroyer / Calling Lands Of Blood Storm.

THE ATLANTEAN WARDRAGON, Cacophonous (1997). Spell Of The Burning Wind / All Of One Doom / Iron Flames Of Battles / The Atlantean Wardragon / Destroyer / Yuggothian Slayers / Steel Burning Thunder.

An Attack Of Sonic Torment (Live), Hellframe (1999) (Split EP with MORIA). Destroyer / Clavicula Solomnis / War Is Hell.

PESTILENCE FROM THE DRAGON STAR, Soul Sold (1999). Wrath And Vengeance / Death Thunder / The Chaos Magician / The Angel Web / Sirius Rebellion / Successor To The Plague Gods / Oruthaaht Xun Xihron (The Intellect Devourer) / Nibiru Assassins / Invader Of Darkness.

ANCIENT WRAITH OF KU, Metal War Productions (2001). Intro / Quantum Nihilism / Cold Flesh Of Space / Intro / Spectral Holocaust / Shrieks Of Torture / Intro / Ancient Wraith / Kmo A'Ajei Virus / Intro / Haunters Of The Dead / V.V.V.V.V. (Vi Veri Vniversum Virus Vici) / Intro / Possession By The KU / Outro / The Curse.

BLOODBATH

STOCKHOLM, SWEDEN — *Dan Swanö (vocals), Peter Tägtgren (vocals), Blackheim (guitar), Martin Axenrot (bass).*

A genuine Death-Black Metal supergroup endeavour. The unholy Stockholm based union includes DAN SWANÖ, an industrious figure claiming involvement with a slew of acts including NIGHTINGALE, UNICORN, EDGE OF SANITY, INFESTDEAD, ODYSSEY and PAN-THY-MONIUM amongst others, OPETH's Mikael Akerfeldt, KATATONIA and DIABOLICAL MASQUERADE's guitarist Blackheim and KATATONIA and OCTOBER TIDE bassist Jonas Renske. The 'Breeding Death' EP, recorded in January 1999, was released in February 2000, preceding their album debut. The debut full-length 'Resurrection Through Carnage' album arrived in November 2002 courtesy of Century Media Records. With OPETH's rise to global popularity Akerfeldt would be forced to relinquish his position.

In March of 2004 the band would be joined by singer Peter Tägtgren, frontman for HYPOCRISY and PAIN, and drummer Martin 'Axe' Axenrot of BLASPHEMOUS, MORGUE, COVEN, TRIUMPHATOR, WITCHERY, SATANIC SLAUGHTER and N.C.O. repute. A sophomore album 'Nightmares Made Flesh' would at first be scheduled for Autumn release, once again through Century Media. US versions hosted not only an extra two tracks, in the form of previously unreleased demos from the 'Breeding Death' sessions, but all new artwork from Wes Benscoter too. However, the North American launch would then be pushed back even further to March 2005.

BLOODBATH revealed their live debut, conducted by a revised cast of musicians, would be held at the August 'Wacken Open Air' festival in Germany. However, Peter Tägtgren was to back out, due to "conflicting schedules", and the band announced Mike Åkerfeldt would make a return for the gig. That same month Martin Axenrot temporarily joined the ranks of OPETH for European touring, covering for regular drummer Martin López who was forced out due to medical concerns.

Dan Swanö opted out in July 2006. In November the group re-issued its 1999 EP 'Breeding Death', adding demo recordings of the tracks 'Breeding Death' and 'Ominous Bloodvomit'.

Breeding Death EP, Century Media 77255-2 (2000). Breeding Death / Ominous Bloodvomit / Furnace Funeral.

RESURRECTION THROUGH CARNAGE, Century Media 8155-2 (2002). Buried By The Dead / Like Fire / Trail Of Insects / The Soulcollector / Bathe In Blood / Death Delirium / Cry My Name / Ways To The Grave / So You Die / Mass Strangulation.

NIGHTMARES MADE FLESH, Century Media 77555-2 (2004). Outnumbering The Day / Year Of The Cadaver Race / Draped In Disease / Cancer Of The Soul / The Ascension / Eaten / Brave New Hell / Stillborn Saviour / Feeding The Undead / Bastard Son Of God / Soul Evisceration / Blood Vortex.

NIGHTMARES MADE FLESH, Century Media 8255-2 (2005) (USA release). Outnumbering The Day / Year Of The Cadaver Race / Draped In Disease / Cancer Of The Soul / The Ascension / Eaten / Brave New Hell / Stillborn Saviour / Feeding The Undead / Bastard Son Of God / Soul Evisceration / Blood Vortex / Breeding Death (Demo version) / Ominous Bloodvomit (Demo version).

Breeding Death EP, Century Media CMD001 (2005) (Vinyl picture disc. Limited edition 500 copies). Breeding Death / Ominous Bloodvomit / Furnace Funeral.

Breeding Death, Century Media (2006). Breeding Death / Ominous Bloodvomit / Furnace Funeral / Breeding Death / Ominous Bloodvomit.

BLOODREAPING

MEXICO — *Antimo Buonanno (vocals), Eduardo Guevara (guitar), Roberto Roman (bass), Saul Martinez (drums).*

Queretaro based BLOODREAPING was forged initially as a late 1999 side project of PYPHOMGERTUM members guitarist Eduardo Guevara and drummer Jorge Rubio utilising Antimo Buonanno of DISGORGE, IMPIETY, RAVAGER, HACAVITZ and DEMONIZED as session vocalist. Victor Reza would act as both studio drummer and producer for the debut 'Feasting The Weak' album, released by the Emerald City label in 2000. The band would then go into stasis as Guevara busied himself as a member of DISGORGE and Buonanno prioritised work with CENOTAPH.

Reconstituting BLOODREAPING in 2001 the group drafted ex-PYPHOMGERTUM bass player Roberto Roman and former PROHIBITORY drummer Miguel Ventura for a rhythm section. However, Ventura was soon to abandon the project and Saul Martinez of GENOCIDE repute took over. Further tribulation hit the band the following year when Roman defected, BLOODREAPING enlisting Fernando Salgado as replacement. BLOODREAPING welcomed back original bassist Roberto Roman in April of 2003 for recording of the 'Ignis Penumbra' album.

Guevara and Martinez are also active with a further side venture billed as RAPED GOD.

FEASTING THE WEAK, Independent (2001). Boiling Through Mastication / Freezing Slaughter / As My Knife Cuts / Diabolic Profanation / Seeds Of Destruction / Feasting The Weak / Excrement Ward / Sacrilegious Dismemberment.

IGNIS PENUMBRA, Sempiternal Productions SP 021 (2003).

BLOODRIDE

VISBY, SWEDEN — *Andreas Bergstedt (vocals), Magnus Martinsson (guitar), Andreas Hemmander (guitar), Eric Ljungberg (bass), Jocke Ytterberg (drums).*

Visby Death Metal act BLOODRIDE, at first known as ASRAEL, was assembled during 2002 by vocalist Johan Aldén, guitarists Andreas Hemmander of LIKFÄRD and Magnus Martinsson of THE DRAPES, bassist Danne Petterson with Jocke Ytterberg of THE DRAPES on drums. Subsequently, Andreas Bergstedt of GEBURAH and ADESPICA took over bass duties. In this formation the group first performed live in the hometown of Visby during June 2003.

With Aldén relocating, Bergstedt assumed vocal responsibilities as the group evolved into BLOODRIDE during 2004. Eric Ljungberg was then acquired to cover on bass. The demo 'First Murder' was recorded in September. Bergstedt would also be active with other projects, FAIDUM, alongside Ytterberg, and POST TRAUMATIC STRESS RELEASE.

First Murder, Bloodride (2004) (Demo).

Carnage Awaiting, Bloodride (2005) (Demo). Carnage Awaiting / Obedience To None.

BLOODSHED

STOCKHOLM, SWEDEN — *Erik Wall (vocals), Tommy Åberg (guitar), Mats Nehl (guitar), Robin Verho (bass), Martin Karlsson (drums).*

Raw Death / Black Metal act conceived in Stockholm by guitarist Joel and drummer Mikael as SCYTHE during 1996. The following year guitarist Tommy Åberg, singer Glenn and bassist Stange would join the band for the demo cassette 'When The Night Betrays The Light'. In 1998 Stange was replaced by Robin and SCYTHE evolved into BLOODSHED for the next promotional tape, 1999's 'Laughter Of Destruction'.

BLOODSHED signed to the Code 666 label and released the 'Skullcrusher' EP in May 2001. Another track, the exclusive 'Kiss Of Cruelty', would find its way onto the compilation album 'Better Undead Than Alive'. BLOODSHED would land support gigs to FINNTROLL in Finland during December 2001 although drummer Mikael was unable to make the excursion. The group duly enrolled the temporary services of the much travelled Dennis Ekdahl of RAISE HELL, also known for his work with MÖRK GRYNING, MYSTIC PROPHECY and SINS OF OMISSION.

February 2002 was an eventful time for BLOODSHED. Besides starting the recording of their upcoming debut album 'Inhabitants Of Dis', Tommy had jumped in on tour with FINNTROLL on four dates in Holland and Belgium to replace vocalist Katla who was suffering from vocal problems. Around this same time the label Ledo Takas released a limited edition white 7" vinyl version of the 'Skullcrusher' EP.

The following year remained rather calm while the band promoted their debut album and began rehearsing new material. February 2004 saw the band begin recording their upcoming EP 'Blade Eleventh' at Necromorbus Studio. Around this time the band's line-up went through some major changes. Prior to the recordings guitarist Joel decided to leave the band, and shortly after Mikael and Glenn threw in the towel. Replacements were found in singer Erik Wall, guitarist Johannes Pedro and INSISION, PANDEMONIC, FLAGELLATION credited Marcus Jonsson on drums. BLOODSHED made their live debut with this new line-up at the Bands Battle Festival 2004 in Germany on May 14th.

Due to touring commitments with INSISION, Marcus Jonsson continued only as session drummer playing a few live shows under 2005. By July the band had attained the services of drummer Martin Karlsson from MYKORRHIZA, SIN, STAIRLAND. Further changes took place in September as Johannes Pedro was replaced by Mats Nehl on guitars. The band's 'Blade Eleventh' demos would subsequently be released as a 7" vinyl single through Horrorfiend Records. Cursed Division finally issued the much delayed CD EP of 'Blade Eleventh' in October 2005, adding the rare compilation track 'Kiss of Cruelty' plus 'Scythe—Blade Of Destruction' and 'Act Of Retaliation' from the 'Laughter Of Destruction' demo.

With a stable line-up once again, in January 2006 BLOODSHED would rehearse and prepare to record their new full-length album 'Stale Cold Cell Recital'. In late March the band entered Necromorbus Studios with producer Vidar Widgren. BLOODSHED parted ways with drummer Martin Karlsson in June, drafting ex-DECADENCE man Patrik Frögéli in September.

Laughter Of Destruction, Cursed Division CURSEXX1 (1999) (Cassette demo). Once A Future Might / Abyss Ascendant / Scythe—Blade Of Destruction / Without A Reason / Act Of Retaliation / Segerstrid.
Skullkrusher EP, Code 666 CODE006 (2001). Preparation—Aggression / Skullcrusher / Let The Bloodshed Begin / Laughter Of Destruction / The Ultimate Overthrow.
Skullcrusher EP, Ledo Takas LETA 005 EP (2002) (7" bone-white vinyl single). Preparation—Aggression / Skullcrusher / Let The Bloodshed Begin / Laughter Of Destruction / The Ultimate Overthrow.
INHABITANTS OF DIS, Code 666 CODE011 (2002). Death By Hanging / Mark Of The Cursed / Paradoxal Experience / Release / Dark Trace / Kiss Of Cruelty / Blood Music / Deceit / City Of Dis / Doomsday Device / Psychosomatic Revelation.
Blade Eleventh, Bloodshed (2004) (Demo). Dead Men Walking / Shapeshifter Enemy / Intro / Living Palindrome.
Blade Eleventh EP, Cursed Division CURSE001 (2005). Dead Men Walking / Shapeshifter Enemy / Intro / Living Palindrome / Kiss Of Cruelty / Scythe—Blade Of Destruction / Act Of Retaliation.
STALE COLD CELL RECITAL, Cursed Division (2006). General Exodus / Call / Haereticus / Into . . . / Pieces / Headless Idol / Death Indulgence / Cravings / High End Return / Prophecies Of Man.

BLOODSTREAM

UK — *Robb Philpotts (vocals), Richard Peart (guitar), John Hanslip (guitar), Ian Bell (bass), Adam Goldsmith (drums).*

BLOODSTREAM made their mark as a heavyweight Female fronted Metal band, formulated by guitarists Richard Pearl, previously with THE INQUISITION, and John Hanslip in 1995. BLOODSTREAM performed their debut gig in Bradford during July of 1997, headlining over NEOPHYTE, BULLWEEK and KRAWL. The band, citing a line up comprising Rick Peart on vocals and guitar, John Hanslip on guitar, Phil Shillham on bass and drummer Ste Ward debuted with the demo 'If It Moves . . . Kill It' that same year. By October of 1999 the EP 'Scarlet' emerged. This release was restricted to 500 copies.

For a period during 2000 BLOODSTREAM was fronted by singer Vinny. The group also put in an appearance at the Bradford 'Metal Inquisition' festival in 2000, sharing the stage with THE LORD WEIRD SLOUGH FEG, TWISTED TOWER DIRE, WYTCHFYNDE, SOLSTICE and THUS DEFILED. Subsequently female singer Brick, having previous affiliations with HYBERNOID, was added to the line up in mid 2001 and Ian Bell, a veteran of NECROMANCER, PURITY CRIES, DAWN RAISER and INSANE VIOLENCE, took command of the bass position. A full length album, 'Black Storm Harvest, surfaced in December of 2002. Guest vocals on the track 'Blood And Sand' came courtesy of erstwhile SABBAT and SKYCLAD vocalist Martin Walkyier. BLOODSTREAM grabbed a valuable support slot to ANTHRAX in March of 2003.

In mid 2004 Brick, having exited in February, was replaced by new singer Robb Philpotts of THE ENCHANTED. Further changes in the line up saw longstanding drummer Steve Ward opting out in favour of Adam Goldsmith, previously with THE SEVEN MACHINE. A November EP, recorded at Dreamcatcher Studios in Bingley and entitled 'Death—Speed—Hate', would include cover versions of ANTHRAX's 'Only' and DEAD KENNEDY's 'California Uber Alles'.

In mid 2005 Robb Philpotts would be found dividing his time between BLOODSTREAM and acting as temporary guitarist for Birmingham Death Metal band ENDLESS TORMENT.

If It Moves . . . Kill It, (1997). Body Hammered / Reclaiming Serenity / No Way Out / Day 13 / Life Is Prison.
Scarlet, (2000). Slow Decline / Poverty Trap / Revenge Not Hate / Alone Once More.
BLACK STORM HARVEST, (2002). Captives / Life Expectancy Unknown / Ghost Room / The Weak / Last Victim / D.N.Y.P. / Blood And Sand / Obey / Impurity.
Death-Hate-Speed, (2005). Epiphany / Day 13 / From Hatred To Ashes / California über alles / Only.

BLOODWRITTEN

WARSAW, POLAND — *Bastard (vocals), Thanathos (guitar), Hypnos (guitar), Chaos (bass), Matt (drums).*

Warsaw's BLOODWRITTEN released an eponymous 1998 demo, the line-up for which comprised Bastard on vocals and guitar, Thanathos on guitar, bassist Ostry and drummer Arek. By the time of recording the 2000 album 'Pages In Blood' the band was seemingly back up to strength with Bastard and Thanathos being joined by bassist Wampir and drummer Taylor Hod. However, Thanathos committed all the bass guitar to tape for the sessions and Wampir was duly ejected. Regrouping, BLOODWRITTEN incorporated second guitarist Hypnos and bassist Chaos, the latter from Prog-Rock outfit WINSOME JESTER. Live work then ensued but progress was stalled by the departure of Taylor Hod as a result of time honoured "musical differences".

In July 2002 the band drafted CASSIOPEIA's DeAmon as new drummer. Unfortunately this latest candidate exited within a matter of months to join NAMTAR. Next in line for the drum stool would be DarKiron, his tenure lasting little over a year. BLOODWRITTEN was forced into a lengthy hiatus, this finally broken with the arrival of CONDEMNATED drummer Matt for recording of the three song 'Reborn' demo.

BLOODWRITTEN returned in December 2006 with the demo 'Iniquity Intensity Insanity'. These sessions were recorded at Hertz Studio by Bracia Wiesławscy.

PAGES IN BLOOD, Bloodwritten (2000). Preludium—Evocation Of Yog-Sothoth / Chapter One—Ancient Gods Born Again /Dog-Star / Chapter Two—Witches' Forest /Blood Magick / Chapter Three—Świt /Nigdy Więcej / Chapter Four—Moon Maniac /Atonement Through Pain / Chapter Five—Thanathos /Let Us Dream / Chapter Six—Temptations In E-minor /Father In Darkness / Postludium—Closing Ceremony.

Reborn, (2004). Intro / Moon Speaks My Name / The Throne / Praise the Black Sorcery.

Iniquity Intensity Insanity, Bloodwritten (2006) (Demo). Taste Insanity / The Forgotten Empire / Sworn To Darkness / Reborn Through Fire / Seed Of Destruction / Incantations Carved in Flesh / In Blood It Shall Be Written.

BLOODWRITTEN

RALEIGH, NC, USA — *Dave Sanchez (vocals / guitar), Roland Arthur (guitar), Steve Busi (bass), Rob Miller (drums).*

Raleigh, North Carolina Death Metal act conceived in May of 2000 by frontman Dave Sanchez, a veteran of ISCARIOT and Punk act NEGATIVE STATE, in union with Power Metal formation WIDOW, SORROW BEQUEST and VISCERAL REMAINS guitarist Johnny Wooten. BLOODWRITTEN's inaugural album 'We Live In Darkness', which ambitiously included a trilogy based on the poems of Lord George Byron, found this pair joined by SORROW BEQUEST, ULLER and WIDOW lead guitarist Chris Bennett, WEIRDING WAY bassist Steve Busi and drummer Tim Haisman from FALSE PROPHET, WIDOW, LEADFOOT and NEGATIVE STATE.

Two demo tracks 'Echoes Of Sadism' and 'Dormant Crown' would be combined as a split release shared with ISCARIOT in 2002. BLOODWRITTEN's next offering would be the November 2003 outing 'Everything Beautiful Dies'. At this juncture the band added GROSS REALITY and FACEPLANT lead guitarist Roland Arthur and drummer Trey Spikes. The latter would be replaced by Rob Miller.

WE LIVE IN DARKNESS, Independent (2000). Cycle Of Ages / Darkness Part I / Absent Twilight / Darkness Part II / Bleeding Of The Heart / Darkness Part III / Revealer of the Shadows / Waters Of Despair / Outro.

Bloodwritten, (2002) (Split EP with ISCARIOT). Echoes Of Sadism (Demo) / Dormant Crown (Demo).

EVERYTHING BEAUTIFUL DIES, (2003). Intro / Echoes Of Sadism / Dormant Crown / Apocryphal Phase / Crimson Collapse / Soul Betrayer.

BLOODY GORE

INDONESIA — *Ipank (vocals), Rio (guitar), Mithos (bass), Sonny (drums).*

BLOODY GORE came together during August of 1996, according to official statements with the sole aim of "creating the most sick, extreme and repulsive form of music". Initially the band was a joint initiative of vocalist Ipank, guitarists Mithos and Rio, bassist Feby and drummer Sonny. Subsequently Ewien took over bass duties but this latest recruit then opted out, necessitating Mithos switching instruments to cover the vacancy. In this guise BLOODY GORE cut a two song demo tape in November of 1998, a track from which was featured on the 'Brutally Sickness' compilation tape released by Indonesian label ESP Productions. June of 1999 saw the release of their self-financed and produced debut 'Stench Of Your Perversion'.

Ipank exited in order to prioritise his day job and BLOODY GORE enrolled erstwhile DELIRIUM TREMENS man Donny Iblis as their new frontman. The band signed a label deal with Uxicon Records, based in Belgium, for the album 'Blood Driven Vehemence'. With the departure of drummer Sonny BLOODY GORE announced they were to fold in early 2002. The BLOODY GORE duo of guitarist Rio and bassist Mithos stuck together to rapidly found a further Death Metal venture FUNERAL INCEPTION in alliance with vocalist Donny Iblis and drummer Pandi SDS, recording a debut album 'Anthems Of Disenchantment' for the French Warpath label.

STENCH OF YOUR PERVERSIONS, (1999). Intro—Provoking Horror / Leaping Organism / Bodily Levitation / A Distorted Lifeform / Fetuses Decorated With Blood / Fields Of The Dead Bodies.

BLOOD DRIVEN VEHEMENCE, Uxicon (2001). Slices Of Flesh Are Being Devoured / Eaten By Worms / Bathing Your Soul With Gore Tears / Shrivel And Rot / Blood Driven Vehemence / Unrecognizable Mutilations / Drowned In Impurity.

BLOODY SIGN

GUEBERSCHWIHR, FRANCE — *Hagent (vocals), Kalevi (guitar), Deimos (bass), Ilmar Uibo (drums).*

Gueberschwihr based Black / Death Metal band featuring ARCHAEUS bassist Deimos. The inaugural band unit of 1995 comprised singer Wilhelm Aldagurth, guitarists Kalevi and Frédéric with Ilmar on drums. Their debut undertaking would be a July 1997 demo tape entitled 'The Nocturnal Moans Of The Fallen Angel' with 'Dionysos Contre Le Crucifie' following a year later. Aldagurth exited in 2001 and BLOODY SIGN duly reorganised their line up, switching Kalevi to vocals and pulling in Nathaniel on bass.

A third demo, 'Primitive Horde', was crafted in December of 2001. However, a further switch found Nathaniel on vocals and Kalevi back to guitar. BLOODY SIGN toured Estonia in 2002, taking this opportunity to cut three new songs at the Guano Records studios in Tallinn. Nathaniel exited in September, Hagent assuming the role of frontman. More tribulation came as Frédéric opted out, being superseded by Deimos (Thomas).

The self financed album 'Vana Vigala Loïts' was released in 2003, this including a live version of 'Master Of Nothing' recorded at La Laiterie that April and a cover PESTILENCE's 'Parricide'.

Ilmar Uibo found himself in the news in November of 2004 when he was selected to act as stand in drummer for INCANTATION's 'Clash Of The Demigods' European tour. Deimos exited in January of 2005, leaving Hagend to fulfill bass duties to record tracks for a split release shared with Germany's RADEMASSAKER.

BLOODY SIGN crafted their second album, 'Explosion Of Elements' featuring a cover version of 'Apocalyptic Warriors' originally by MASSACRA, at Dissonant Studio in Italy during early 2006. The band unveiled European tour plans, taking in France, Spain and Portugal alongside road mates Cincinnati Deathsters ESTUARY, for April and May 2006.

VANA VIGALA LOITS, Bloody Sign (2003). Possessed By Ancient Earth / Unleashing The Power Of The Bloody Sign / Conquering Pain / Vana Vigala Loïts (Part I) (Intro) / Vana Vigala Loïts (Part II) / Parricide / Banished / Master Of Nothing (Live).

BLOODY WINGS

BERGAMO, ITALY — *Giulio Pizzuto (vocals / guitar), Matteo Barbetta (guitar), Pierpaolo Boninelli (keyboards), Aurelio*

Pizzuto (drums).

Doom Death act BLOODY WINGS was formulated in Bergamo, Lombardia during the Autumn of 2002 by vocalist / guitarist Giulio Pizzuto, at that active alongside his keyboard playing sibling Aurelio, a student at the Bergamo Conservatory, as a member of Progressive Metal band NEVER NAMED. Aurelio assumed the role of drummer in this new act as Pierpaolo Boninelli was inducted in the keyboard role, then Fabio Facoetti on bass guitar. BLOODY WINGS first impressions would be made with a four song demo in March of 2003, after which Facoetti exited. In July Luca Cortinovis became the band's new bassist and Guido Pagano was added as second guitarist.

BLOODY WINGS would lose both its latest candidates in the Spring of 2004, swiftly drafting ex-BRUTAL MURDER man Matteo Barbetta on lead guitar as replacement and during the Summer Stefano Ruocco was installed on bass. Within a matter of weeks the bass role had switched again though, Antonio Cassella of 17 DAYS being the latest recruit and on 14th November 2004 the group entered Zero Crossing Studios to lay down more material, completing these tracks in February 2005.

Cassella left, being substituted by Omar from CHEMICAL DAMAGE.

Bloody Wings, Bloody Wings (2003). My Beautiful Friend Suicide / Intimation Of Sadness / Sweet Oblivion / Monologue Of A Vampire.

BLUDGEON

LONDON, UK — *Zach White (vocals), Tim Sheehan (guitar / bass / drum programming).*

BLUDGEON is a London, brutal Death Metal band manifested by frontman Zach White ("vokillz") and guitarist Tim Sheehan ("guttars") during 1996. The following year the demo 'Mainstay Of Hatred' was recorded on a 4-track machine. The formative version of the band suffered from a succession of line up changes and it was not until 2000 that a second demo session, entitled 'A Cannibals Fixation', emerged. 100 copies were circulated throughout the extreme Metal underground, gaining airplay as far away as the USA.

BLUDGEON entered the recording studio once again in March of 2001 to craft the 'Realm Of Decay' promo, this garnering the band a deal with Fleshfeast Productions, the demo tracks being slated for a three way split release, "And Then There Were Three' released by Life Fluid Productions to be shared with Australia's CORPSE CARVING and TWITCH OF THE DEATH NERVE. On the live front, BLUDGEON formed up a brief spate of touring ranked alongside Japan's VOMIT REMNANTS and Czech act GODLESS TRUTH, as well as opening for US acts GORATORY and SKINNED plus Sweden's VISCERAL BLEEDING.

Bassist Victor Prokofjevs would be incorporated for recording of a full length album 'Devoted To Lunacy', but then exited making BLUDGEON a duo once again.

AND THEN THERE WERE THREE, Life Fluid Productions (2005) (Split album with CORPSE CARVING and TWITCH OF THE DEAD NERVE). Intro / Rigor-mortal Intercourse / Omophagic Cravings For The Pyrolosis Infested / Exuviation Of The Stigmatiferous / Martyr Of A Condemned Existence.

BLUDGEON

CHICAGO, IL, USA — *Mark Duca (vocals / guitar), Carlos Alvarez (guitar), Chris Studtmann (bass), Ryan Blazek (drums).*

Brutal Thrash Metal act BLUDGEON, dating to 1997, initially featured the scene veteran Cazz Grant of GRAND BELIAL'S KEY, CRUCIFIER, INFERNAL HATRED and DECEIVERON on drums for the 1998 'Inner Hell' demo. A formative bassist would be Vince Papi, a veteran of HEARSE and CRUCIFIER. The group, mentored by frontman Mark Duca, enlisted MIXED BREED guitarist Carlos Alvarez in 2000 and enrolled a fresh rhythm section of bassist Eric Karol and drummer Matt 'Chewy' Dezynski the following year. BLUDGEON would be the first band to sign to MANOWAR's Magic Circle Music imprint distributed through Metal Blade Records. Naturally, BLUDGEON would support MANOWAR in America during 2002 and also travel to Europe with the musclebound Metal veterans during November. A live CD / DVD package 'Crucified Live' was scheduled for September 2003. That same year Carlos Alvarez joined GODHELPUS.

BLUDGEON, now with Chris Studtmann on bass and Ryan Blazek on the drums, returned with the 'World Controlled' album in June 2006. On November 18th the band appeared at the Monterrey Metal Fest event at the at the Coca Cola Auditorium in Mexico alongside BLIND GUARDIAN, CATHEDRAL, U.D.O., EDGUY, OBITUARY, DEICIDE, LEAVES' EYES, SADUS, VAINGLORY, HYDROGYN and JOE STUMP'S REIGN OF TERROR.

CRUCIFY THE PRIEST, Magic Circle Music (2002). Smoke Screen / Idle Distinction / Tortured Through Lies / Zero Tolerance / Last Rites / Voluntary Manslaughter / Crucify The Priest / Abandoned / Bound / Inner Hell / Turmoil / Stained In Blood.

WORLD CONTROLLED, Magic Circle Music MCA 02150-2 (2006). Unholy Murder / Carnage Begins / Bitter Emptiness / Consumed By Anger / Infidel / World Controlled / Save Your Servant / Refuse The Truth / Hunt Or Be Hunted / Awakening / Out Of Reach.

BLUDGEON

PA, USA — *Chris Yuastella (vocals), Jeff Anderson (guitar), Vince Papi (guitar), Kevin Coates (drums).*

Pennsylvania Death Metal band BLUDGEON released a 1997 demo entitled 'Maniac Nun With A Bat', distributed through The Crucifier Brotherhood. 'Abandon All Hope' followed in 2001, after which, due to the presence of several US acts bearing the same title, the band switched names to MEGATON.

The group comprised vocalist / guitarist Cazz Grant ('The Black Lourde of Crucifixion') of AMISEGARDAUQ, BRETHREN, GRAND BELIAL'S KEY, CRUCIFIER, DECEIVERION, INFANTRY and INFERNAL HATRED repute, guitarist "Drottin Bane" (a.k.a. Jeff Anderson) having credits with BRETHREN, AMISEGARDAUQ, CRUCIFIER and HEARSE, second guitarist "Ordog" (Vince Papi) of CRUCIFIER and HEARSE plus CORPUS ROTTEN man Kevin Coates on drums. Following the debut demo BLUDGEON added ABOMINOG vocalist Chris Yuastella. Granr exited in 2000.

Maniac Nun With A Bat, The Crucifier Brotherhood (1997) (Demo). Smother Your Children / Barbaric Through The Ages / Cleansed In Fire / Cleaved By Axeblast.

BODY CORE

HÄSSLEHOLM, SWEDEN — *Dan Hejman (vocals / samples / congas / maracas), Markus Wallén (guitar), Micke Jonsson (guitar), Nicklas Wallén (bass / flute / accordion), Håkan Johansson (drums).*

Hässleholm, Skåne based Death Metal band dating to 1997. The band debuted in December 2000 with the demo 'I Kill You In My Dreams'. Follow ups included 2002's 'Welcome To Our Dying World' and 'Idle Mind Amputation' in June 2003. BODY CORE guitarist William Ekeberg, having replaced Daniel Larsson, would also be active with BROKEN DAGGER and TRYMHEIM. The album 'Blunt Force Trauma' arrived in January 2004.

BODY CORE, minus William Ekeberg and finding Micke Jonsson on second guitar, returned in January 2005 with the demo 'Rancid Cerebral Lobotomy'. Adding a touch of the avant-garde to proceedings singer Dan Hejman now employed samples, congas and maracas whilst bass player Nicklas Wallén also handled both flute and accordion.

I Kill You In My Dreams, Dustbin (2000) (Demo). Intro: Block 8 / Head Games / Close Encounter / I'm Not You.

Parasite, Body Core (2001) (Demo). No 360 / Parasite / Bone White Lover / Body And Soul.

Welcome To Our Dying World, Dustbin (2002) (Demo). Body And Soul / Life Leech / Parasite / No 360 / Bone White Lover / Necroleptic / Ghost Of Silence.

Idle Mind Amputation, Body Core (2003) (Demo). Shovel In The Ground / Further Torture / Grotesque I-II.

BLUNT FORCE TRAUMA, Dustbin (2004). Random Acts Of Violence / Blunt Force Trauma / Shovel In The Ground / Further Torture / Epiphany / Body And Soul Part II / Close Encounter / Prophecy / IX / Idle Mind Amputation / Grotesque Part I & II / Life Leech / Necroleptic.

Rancid Cerebral Lobotomy, Dustbin (2005) (Demo). Enshrouded With Hate / Rancid Cerebral Lobotomy / Absence Of Organd (Scarlet Infinity) Pt. 1-2.

BOLT THROWER

BIRMINGHAM, WEST MIDLANDS, UK — *Karl Willetts (vocals), Barry Thomson (guitar), Gavin Ward (guitar), Jo-Anne Bench (bass), Andy Whale (drums).*

Founded in Birmingham during September 1986, BOLT THROWER gained notoriety on the local Metal scene with a unique, war obsessed heaviness. At this early point the band featured vocalist Alan West, guitarist Barry Thomson, bassist Gavin Ward and drummer Andy Whale. The name BOLT THROWER is taken from a siege device in a Games Workshop 'Warhammer' fantasy role playing game. Famously, the initial idea for the band had been formulated in a pub toilet in Coventry by Ward and Thompson. First product would come in the form of an April 1987 demo session 'In Battle There Is No Law'. With Ward switching to the guitar role BOLT THROWER drafted Alex Tweedy to cover on bass.

Following a September 1987 demo, 'Concessions In Pain', the fledgling band, still utilising Ward as temporary bassist as new man Tweedy had failed to commit, added bassist Jo-Anne Bench. The second demo resulted in a four song Radio One session on the John Peel show, recorded in January 1988. This airing led to an album deal with Vinyl Solution Records, but not before West's departure.

The band brought in vocalist Karl Willetts, actually the official BOLT THROWER van driver up to that juncture, to record the debut 1988 album at Loco Studios in Wales, the Andrew Fryer produced 'In Battle There Is No Law'. BOLT THROWER also submitted a separately recorded version of the album track 'Drowned In Torment' to a free fanzine split EP alongside INSTIGATORS, H.D.Q. and CULTURE SHOCK. Although support for the band was rising on the Metal underground, the group felt Vinyl Solution's Hardcore ethic was restrictive and duly switched label's to Nottingham's burgeoning underground imprint Earache Records. A notable gig that July saw the band supporting DEATH ANGEL and WARFARE at London's Astoria. BOLT THROWER also scored a further John peel session, cutting more tracks for Radio One play in November.

The group's first album for Earache, October 1989's 'Realm Of Chaos: Slaves To Darkness' recorded at Slaughterhouse Studios, was to sell in excess of 50'000 copies worldwide and utilised expansive gatefold artwork from Games Workshop that carried on the theme of futuristic fantasy wargaming. The world of gaming also infused the lyrical content of 'Realm Of Chaos' too, both 'Plague Bearer' and 'World Eater' borrowing heavily from gaming titles. Musically, 'Realm Of Chaos' was the first record to introduce Bolt Thrower to an international audience, critics polarizing between jaw dropping appreciation for the super low bottom end, with guitars dragged right down to A, and guttural grind or horrified by the unashamed unsophistication. Meantime, Vinyl Solution would re-issue the debut on CD, this variant coming complete with totally different artwork to the original.

Having performed well on the Earache organised "Grindcrusher" tour of 1989 shoulder to shoulder with CARCASS, MORBID ANGEL and NAPALM DEATH, and after contributing a track to the compilation album of the same name, the band then executed dates in Holland throughout February 1990 with AUTOPSY and PESTILENCE on the 'Bloodbrothers' tour. A third John Peel session was undertaken in July 1990.

The release of the next studio affair in September 1990 proved fortuitous, 'Warmaster' again crafted at Slaughterhouse but with noted desk man Colin Richardson now in control, being cut coincidentally just prior to the complex burning down. For this offering BOLT THROWER curtailed the speed somewhat and defined some degree of clarity by pitching guitars at C#. Even with this fine tuning, 'Warmaster' would still make for a monstrously ugly Death Metal album.

The 'Cenotaph' EP arrived in January 1991. BOLT THROWER once more toured Europe, this time as part of the 'War Mass' package with support from US outfit NOCTURNUS and Sweden's UNLEASHED. That October the group conducted a package tour of the USA together with BELIEVER and Toronto Thrashers SACRIFICE before engaging in further European shows, where they were supported by BENEDICTION and ASPHYX. In 1991 the three John Peel sessions saw commercial release on CD format.

The band drew back from their Grind influences and changed tack towards a Doom edged feel for October 1992's 'The IVth Crusade' album, reprising their studio creativity with Colin Richardson. Whilst retaining the militaristic stance, the band went for a more classical feel, adapting a medieval Eugène Delacroix painting for the album cover. European dates to open up 1993 witnessed a strong union with Poles VADER and Swedes GRAVE. This activity was backed by an EP release comprising a remixed 'Spearhead' alongside new material. Unfortunately BOLT THROWER's first Australian tour in September 1993, supported by ARMOURED ANGEL, ended in debacle when the band were stuck without a flight home.

Eventually managing to make it back to Britain the Birmingham bunch undertook another American club tour in July 1994 with fellow Brummies BENEDICTION as support, but failed to complete the schedule. The album of that year, 'For Victory', witnessed strong sales. Colin Richardson again took production honours and once more Bolt Thrower's imagery took a further leap in history, the record sleeve depicting marines yomping across the tundra of the Falkland Islands. Initial copies came with a free bonus live disc recorded in Manchester during 1992. Ex-PESTILENCE, ASPHYX and SUBMISSION vocalist Martin Van Drunen joined the band in 1994 replacing the departed Willets and drummer Martin Kearn was added in the line-up shuffle. Taking their Metal to the European masses, the band undertook the 1995 'No Guts, No Glory' tour in union with BRUTALITY and CEMETARY. They hit the continent again the following year, making a statement on the 'Fuck Price Politics' expedition with SENTENCED, EXPRESSION OF POWER and THE VARUKERS.

Severing connections with Earache Records in early 1997 and signing to American label Metal Blade, before recording on a brand new album could commence, Van Drunen, suffering from a disease which made his hair fall out, quit unexpectedly on the eve of some European festivals. BOLT THROWER killed time by throwing in a few live gigs with BENEDICTION's Dave Ingram guesting.

As BOLT THROWER went into the studio in late 1997 it was announced that 19 year old Alex Thomas had succeeded skinsman Kearns and that Willets had rejoined. With this line up the band cut the 1998 album 'Mercenary' for new label Metal Blade Records. This offering, despite the lengthy hiatus between recordings, re-established BOLT THROWER's fan base and gave the group a showing in the national German album charts too. Although Willetts had performed on the album it would be a re-instated Dave Ingram, having recently quit BENEDICTION, who took up the vocal mantle for live work packaged with CROWBAR and TOTENMOND. Confusingly Thomas would then leave and the drummer he had usurped in the first instance duly took over once again in time for BOLT THROWER's second showing at the major German 'Full Force' festival.

In December 1999 Dave Ingram made time to session on a demo for Danish act ATOBIC, an alliance between INIQUITY and CORPUS MORTALE guitarist Brian Eriksen and drummer Peter Olsen.

BOLT THROWER toured Europe in January 2001 supported by FLESHCRAWL and HEAVEN SHALL BURN to push a new album 'Honour, Valour, Pride'. Further road work had the band in familiar company, co-headlining a January 2002 European expedition with BENEDICTION backed up by FLESHCRAWL. Martin Van Drunen resurfaced in mid 2002 debuting his new act DEATH BY DAWN on the European live circuit. BOLT THROWER would be confirmed as one of the headline acts at the October 'Westfalen' festival in Dortmund, Germany. BOLT THROWER would be finalised for the running order of the 'Rock Hard' magazine festival at the Gelsenkirchen Amphitheatre for June 2003 but withdrew at short notice to allow singer Dave Ingram to be present at the birth of his first child. BOLT THROWER announced the departure of Ingram, apparently due to the singer "suffering with health and personal problems", in August of 2004. The singer later revealed he had been suffering with mental difficulties, but once recovered, duly founded FULL SCALE HATRED, this new band subsequently evolving into DOWNLORD.

In November BOLT THROWER welcomed the return of original vocalist Karl Willetts, soon re-entering the recording studio to craft a new album. Willetts also re-recorded the vocal lines on the 'Honour, Valour, Pride' album, , this effort seeing production credits going out to former MARSHALL LAW bassist Andy Faulkner. Digipack variants hosted an exclusive track, 'Covert Ascension'.

Early 2005 found former singer Martin Van Drunen and erstwhile PESTILENCE bassist Jeroen Paul Thesseling collaborating with KING LOCUST guitarist Niels Drieënhuizen in a new band entitled PROJEKT TABUN. The trio entered Studio Het Lab in Schaarsbergen to put down initial recordings. Back on the BOLT THROWER front, vocalist Karl Willetts and guitarist Barry Thompson would guest on a cover version of SACRILEGE's 'Lifeline' recorded by fellow Brummies BENEDICTION.

In May the band entered Sable Rose Studios, again collaborating with Andy Faulkner as producer, to craft a new album for Metal Blade Records. 'Those Once Loyal' emerged in November and gave the band its highest charting record in Germany, debuting at number 76. To coincide, former label Earache re-issued the 'Realm Of Chaos' opus, re-mastered and clad in all new artwork.

European headline shows in January and February 2006 witnessed strong backing from MALEVOLENT CREATION, NIGHTRAGE and NECROPHAGIST. Gigs for April across Europe were scheduled originally to see GOREFEST as support but these plans were changed and KATAKLYSM, GOD DETHRONED and DOWNLORD took over the opening roles. The group projected dates in North America but then cancelled these plans. A statement claimed Metal Blade Records had "refused to financially back the band ... Despite trying to work out other ways to make this happen, the band found they were unable to finance a tour of this scale on their own and therefore had to stop any further planning of the tour. Regrettably, it looks like while BOLT THROWER are signed to Metal Blade Records they will be unable to tour the States."

The band's appearance at the Gelsenkirchen 'Rock Hard' festival in Germany during June was taped and subsequently the track 'Killchain' was included on the 'Rock Hard' magazine

BOLT THROWER

compilation album 'Rock Hard: Das Festival 2006'.

The Peel Sessions EP, Strange Fruit (1988). Forgotten Existence / Attack In The Aftermath / Psychological Warfare / In Battle There Is No Law.

IN BATTLE THERE IS NO LAW, Vinyl Solution SOL 11 (1988). In Battle There Is No Law / Challenge For Power / Forgotten Existence / Denial Of Destiny / Concession Of Pain / Attack In The Aftermath / Psychological Warfare / Nuclear Annihilation / Blind To Defeat.

REALM OF CHAOS, Earache MOSH 13 (1989). Eternal War / Through The Eye Of Terror / Dark Millennium / All That Remains / Lost Souls Domain / Plague Bearer / World Eater / Drowned In Torment / Realm Of Chaos / Outro.

WARMASTER, Earache MOSH 29 (1990). Intro: Unleashed (Upon Mankind) / What Dwells Within / The Shreds Of Sanity / Profane Creation / Destructive Infinity / Final Revelation / Cenotaph / War Master / Rebirth Of Humanity / Afterlife.

THE PEEL SESSIONS 1988-90, Strange Fruit DEI 8118-2 (1991). Forgotten Existence / Attack In The Aftermath / Psychological Warfare / In Battle There Is No Law / Drowned In Torment / Eternal War / Realm Of Chaos / Domination / Destructive Infinity / Warmaster / After Life / Lost Souls Domain.

Cenotaph EP, Earache MOSH CD 33 (1991). Cenotaph / Destructive Infinity / Prophet Of Hatred / Realm Of Chaos (Live).

THE IVTH CRUSADE, Earache MOSH 70 (1992). The Fourth Crusade / Icon / Embers / Where Next To Conquer / As The World Burns / This Time It's War / Ritual / Spearhead / Celestial Sanctuary / Dying Creed / Through The Ages (Outro).

Spearhead EP, Earache MOSH 73 (1993). Spearhead (Extended remix) / Crown Of Life / Dying Creed / Lament.

FOR VICTORY, Earache MOSH 120 (1994). War / Remembrance / When Glory Beckons / For Victory / Graven Image / Lest We Forget / Silent Demise / Forever Fallen / Tank (MK 1) / Armageddon Bound.

WHO DARES WINS, Earache MOSH 208 (1998). Cenotaph / Destructive Infinity / Prophet Of Hatred / Realm Of Chaos (Live) / Spearhead (Extended remix) / Crown Of Life- Dying / Creed / Lament / World Eater '94 / Overlord.

MERCENARY, Metal Blade 14147-2 (1998). Zeroed / Laid To Waste / Return From Chaos / Mercenary / To The Last.... / Powder Burns / Behind Enemy Lines / No Guts, No Glory / Sixth Chapter. Chart position: 87 GERMANY.

HONOUR, VALOUR, PRIDE, Metal Blade 14386-2 (2001). Contact Wait Out / Inside The Wire / Honour / Suspect Hostile / 7th Offensive / Valour / K-Machine / A Hollow Truce / Pride.

THOSE ONCE LOYAL, Metal Blade 14506-2 (2005). At First Light / Entrenched / The Killchain / Granite Wall / Those Once Loyal / Anti-Tank (Dead Armour) / Last Stand Of Humanity / Salvo / When Cannons Fade. Chart position: 76 GERMANY.

BONESCREW

BOSTON, MA, USA — *Steven Flynn (vocals / guitar), Dan Kelly (bass), Keith Starkweather (keyboards), Chris Haskell (drums).*

BONESCREW, forged by former SUBJUGATOR personnel vocalist / guitarist Steven Flynn and drummer Steven Blair in 1999, debuted with the 2000 demo 'Bound Beaten Screwed'. Musically the band offer up a compelling hybrid of Doom laced Industrial Metal. Following this release erstwhile JOE STUMP drummer Max took Blair's position. Keyboard player Joe Baptiste bowed out in March of 2001, being replaced by Keith Starkweather that same month. Drummer Max was next to exit in September and as a temporary measure former member Steven Blair stepped in to plug the gap. The band utilised the temporary services of NIKULYDIN's Steve Asaro for live work to close out 2002.

ASK FOR NOTHING, Savagelane (2003). Purge / Dust / Ask For Nothing / Open Wound / Perpetual Decline / It's Raining / I'll Get Mine / New World Orbit / Collapsed / Innocence.

BORN HEADLESS

HOBART, TAS, AUSTRALIA — *Ewen G (vocals), Rowan Thompson (guitar), Rowan M (bass), Pat Moane (drums).*

Hobart, Tasmania Death Metal band BORN HEADLESS debuted with a self-titled 2001 demo. The group had been founded in late 1999 by guitarist Jason Peppiatt, previously of YORTA and Black Metal band BOLVERK, and YORTA credited drummer Pat Moane, being completed by bass player Mark Sawford.

Life Fluid Productions issued the 'Headless Henchmen' album in 2004, this release recorded with new lead vocalist Corwyn Kenny and with Peppiatt originally playing both guitar and bass. Final sessions to complete the record saw engineer Dave Luck contributing bass parts. BORN HEADLESS then underwent a radical makeover as Peppiatt, joining PSYCROPTIC as singer, was replaced by Rowan Thompson and Rowan M assumed bass duties. The group added new singer Ewen G in May.

Born Headless, Born Headless (2001). Immortal Remains / Stained Wars Of Coloured Earth / Headless Henchmen / Deceiving The Gods / Blackend Skies.
HEADLESS HENCHMEN, Life Fluid Productions (2004). Butchered Hope / Headless Henchmen / Vision Of The Beast Within / Dungeons Of Abraxus / Empowered Existence / Rise Of The Overlord / Roman / No More Shall Remain / Scalps Of Scythia / Skull Crusher / Stained Wars Of Coloured Earth.

BORN OF FIRE

STOCKHOLM, SWEDEN — *Mr. Dim (vocals), Fredrik Lindgren (guitar), Richard Cabeza (bass), Peter Stjärnvind (drums).*

BORN OF FIRE is a 2001 Stockholm assemblage led by guitarist Mr. Dim, ENTOMBED, REGURGITATE, KRUX, MERCILESS, MURDER SQUAD and LOUDPIPES drummer Peter Stjärnvind, guitarist Freddie Lindgren of UNLEASHED, TERRA FIRMA, CELESTIAL PAIN and LOUDPIPES and bassist Rickard Cabeza, citing credits with DISMEMBER, GENERAL SURGERY, UNANIMATED, SATYRICON, DAMNATION and MURDER SQUAD. The EP 'Chosen By The Gods' was issued through Primitive Records in 2001.

Cabeza added to his long list of extreme Metal citations in the Spring of 2002, acting as tour bassist for premier Black Metal act DARK FUNERAL's North American dates. Mr. Dim and Lindgren then put their energies into a new project, HARMS WAY being assembled in the winter of 2003

Chosen By The Gods, Primitive Art PAR025 (2001). Chosen By The Gods / The Art Of Dying.

BOWEL STEW

ITALY — *Omar (vocals / guitar), Ombre (bass), Riccardo (drums).*

Founded as a Death Metal act entitled MONOLITH during January of 1996, the early incarnation of the band comprised vocalist / guitarist Omar, guitarist Ambrogio, bass player Darko and Riccardo on drums. As MONOLITH the band cut a July 1998 demo which included a rendition of CANNIBAL CORPSE's infamous 'Hammer Smashed Face'. With the departure of both Ambrogio and Darko in 1999 the band took on a more sinister musical direction. The band pulled in Ombre on bass and adopted the new title of BOWEL STEW, marking this transition by covering 'The Pulsating Feast' for a REGURGITATE tribute album issued by Bizarre Leprous Productions.

BOWEL STEW's 2002 album 'Necrocannibal Rites', released by the Belgian Disgorgement Of Squash Bodies label, included a cover version of GUT's 'Perpetual Sperm Injections'. The album tracks are interjected by narratives from notorious gore flicks such as 'Zombie New Millennium', 'Roadkill', 'Deadly Spawn', 'Anthropophagous', 'Damonenbraut', 'Das Komabrutale Duell' and 'White Cannibal Queen'.

BOWEL STEW figure on numerous tribute collections having donated tracks such as 'Another Lie' to the Shit Worm Productions UNHOLY GRAVE homage and 'Theme from the A-Team' for an ANAL CUNT collection on My Lai Records.

NECROCANNIBAL RITES, Disgorgement Of Squash Bodies (2002). Invocation Of Necrocannibal Rites / Bizarre Ovine Gang Bang / Anal Abortion Of Mongoloid Foetus / Intracranial Malignant Tumour / Mondo Cane / Splatter House / Fulci Metal Jacket / Disgorgement Of Squash Clitoris / Coprophiliac Atrocities / Lymphatic Varicosities In The Scrotum / Abnormal Rectal Constipation / Bowel Stew / Stench Of Rotten Gore / Syphilitic Warfare / Purulent Disfigurement / Massacesi Commando / Perpetual Sperm Injections / Demented Acts Of Anatomical Quartering.

BOWTOME

BALINGEN, GERMANY — *Marc Etter (vocals / bass), Thomas Keringer (guitar), Dennis Reith (guitar), Andreas Mayer (drums).*

Balingen Death Metal unit assembled by former FUNERAL MARCH personnel guitarist Thorsten Witteck and drummer Vorken Mahlenbrey alongside erstwhile OSCULUM bassist Marc Etter during 1998. Guitarists Robert Kerner and Max Endele were introduced in 2000. As a trio, BOWTOME issued a live demo 'Cum On Me', recorded in 1999 at the Eberthalle in Balingen. Subsequently new members singer Maik Schlereth and ex-DEFINITION UNKNOWN guitarist Dennis Reith were added.

Following release of the 2001 'Crush The Planet' EP Thorsten Wittek was replaced by ex-OSCULUM man Bernd 'Usiel' Sturm. Fractures then saw Schlereth and Mahlenbrey, this duo forging DARK ASSAULT. Johannes 'Deathgrinder' Wehrmann, a veteran of STORMHUNTER and IRONY, took command of the drums. His tenure would be brief though as Andreas Mayer was then acquired as new sticksman. Thomas Keringer joined as second guitarist in 2003. BOWTOME's next release would be the demo 'First Time Murder'.

Cum On Me, (2000). Blasphemy / I Die / Brainshot / Killfuck / The Oath / Withburn / Bow To Me.
Crush The Planet EP, Independent (2001). Addicted To Kill / No Brain, No Pain / Cum On My Face / Cannibalistic Torture / Crush The Planet.
Sick, Gun ... Dead, (2002). Sick, Gun ... Dead / Soldiers Revenge.
First Time Murder, (2004). First Time Murder.

BRAINCHOKE

BRAINTREE, ESSEX, UK — *Mark (vocals), Paul Martin (guitar), Kieran (guitar), Dave (bass), Simon (drums).*

Essex Grindcore outfit dating to January 2000. BRAINCHOKE members Paul Martin and Dave also operate with SUFFERING whilst other personnel cite credits with INIMENTER. In support of the 'Migraine Music' album, released in November 2000, the band toured nationwide sharing stages with artists such as THE HAUNTED, AKERCOCKE, HECATE ENTHRONED and DESECRATION.

The 2002 'Mental Clarity' EP, sporting re-recorded speedier versions of 'D.T.D.' and 'Chair Or Chamber' from the debut, would be followed by the band's inclusion in 'Terrorizer' magazine's top ten unsigned bands poll. A subsequent cover mount

CD had BRAINCHOKE donating a unique four minute medley. In 2003 BRAINCHOKE issued the 'Microchipped And Mindcontrolled' album for Grindethic Records, a split affair shared with FETUS EATERS.

MIGRAINE MUSIC, MBTC Productions (2000). In The Arms Of Morpheus / Mental S.O.S. / Brainchoked / D.T.D. / Incarcerated In Spite / For All To Remember / Chair Or Chamber / Mind Cannon / Soaked In Nihilism / Cretinous Disorder / Crimson Tide / Awaken (Your Soul) / Single Figure I.Q. / Entrance Barred / Corridors Of The Maze.

Mental Clarity EP, MBTC Productions (2001). Alone By The Lake / Short n' Sour / Memory Mislaid / Unbelievable Opulence / D.T.D. / Chair Or Chamber.

MICROCHIPPED AND MINDCONTROLLED, Grindethic Records (2003) (Split album with FETUS EATERS). The Quickening / Memory Mislaid / Jester Of Belial / Anonymous Anxiety / Disassemble (Your Soul) / Chair Or Chamber / Soaked In Nihilism / Microchipped And Mindcontrolled / Alone By The Lake / Mental S.O.S. / Single Figure I.Q. / D.T.D. / Mind Cannon.

BREEDING CHAMBER

KOTKA, FINLAND — *Aapo Koivisto (vocals), Olli Liukkonen (guitar), Janne Vihavainen (guitar), Tommi Vehmas (bass), Petri Sallansalo (drums).*

A brutal, old school Death Metal act. BREEDING CHAMBER, hailing from Kotka, was manifested under the original title of POLARKRAKEN during 2002 by the NEXT IN LINE pairing of guitarist Olli Liukkonen and drummer Petri Sallansalo. Joining this pair would be Tommi Vehmas of ID:EXORCIST on bass, being completed with Janne Pöllänen on lead guitars and Lauri Yläjussila on vocals. However, following issue of the 'Kill Your Pain' demo, the latter two recruits were to exit in 2003, replaced in 2003 by Janne Vihavainen and OMNIUM GATHERUM's Aapo Koivisto respectably. BREEDING CHAMBER followed up with the 'Final Breath' demo session in 2004. Third session 'Inside, Looking Out' followed that same year.

Kill Your Pain, Breeding Chamber (2003) (Demo). Into A Chaos / Values / My Own Devil / Bonus (Joke).

Final Breath, Breeding Chamber (2004) (Demo). Final Breath / Deathblow / Worms.

Inside, Looking Out, Breeding Chamber (2004) (Demo). Voices / Testimony / My Own Devil.

BRODEQUIN

KNOXVILLE, TX, USA — *Jamie Bailey (vocals / bass), Mike Bailey (guitar), Chad Walls (drums).*

Death Metal band BRODEQUIN, named after a French medieval leg crushing torture device, include former BESIEGED and ENTER SELF drummer Chad Walls in the ranks. The debut album 'Instruments Of Torture' was self financed but later re-issued by Extremis Records.

BRODEQUIN's Jamie Bailey would deputise as a drummer for DISGORGE on their 2002 American tour dates. A permanent replacement would be found in the form of FOETOPSY's Jon Engman.

Drummer Chad Walls would later figure in DISLIMB and INEXTYA. He also featured in PUSTULATED. Jamie Bailey united with ex-DISGORGE vocalist Matti Way to found LITURGY in 2003. BRODEQUIN marked a return in December of 2004 with the album 'Methods Of Execution', released by Unmatched Brutality Records.

INSTRUMENTS OF TORTURE, Extremist (1999). Spinning In Agony / Soothsayer / Ambrosia / The Virgin Of Nuremburg / Duke Of Exeter / Infested With Worms / Burnt In Effigy / Strappado / Hollow / Feast Of Flesh.

FESTIVALS OF DEATH, Unmatched Brutality (2002). Mazzetello / Judas Cradle / Trial By Ordeal / Torches Of Nero / Vivum Excoriari / Lake Of The Dead / Blood Of The Martyr / Gilles De Rais / Flow Of Maggots / Bronze Bowl / Auto De Fa.

BROKEN HOPE

CHICAGO, IL, USA — *Jeremy Wagner (vocals), Brian Griffin (guitar), Shaun Glass (bass), Ryan Stanek (drums).*

Very much in the Gore-Metal mould. Chicago's BROKEN HOPE have nevertheless put a healthy work ethic to their advantage touring America constantly to back up a string of blood curdling releases. The band formulated in 1989 when vocalist Jeremy Wagner and bassist Joe Ptacek joined CRYPT, an act featuring drummer Ryan Stanek. CRYPT folded and the trio duly founded BROKEN HOPE. The band's first demo secured a deal with Grindcore Records for their debut 'Swamped In Gore'.

BROKEN HOPE stepped up a gear by signing to Metal Blade Records for their sophomore effort 'Bowels Of Repugnance', this album seeing erstwhile SINDROME bassist Shaun Glass joining the fold. The band toured persistently and hard alongside acts such as DEICIDE and SIX FEET UNDER. A further album 'Loathing' cemented BROKEN HOPE's grip on the scene.

1995's 'Repulsive Conception' featured BROKEN HOPE's version of the TWISTED SISTER track 'Captain Howdy'. The album also saw AGENT STEEL / CANCER / DEATH guitarist JAMES MURPHY as guest on the track 'Engorged With Impiety'.

The band parted ways with Metal Blade masking any doubts over their career by touring America with support from Poland's VADER and MONSTROSITY before dates in Chile with German's SODOM.

Stanek, DeMumbrum and Griffin forged the side act EM SINFONIA in the ensuing downtime during which Glass departed. The bass player would dispense with Death Metal, switching tack completely and opting to found Nu-Metal band SOIL in alliance with a triumvirate of former OPPRESSOR personnel guitarist Adam Zadel, bassist Tim King and drummer Tom Schoefield. With SOIL seemingly on the ascendancy during 2002 BROKEN HOPE's Brian Griffin would be found to be on the road with the band as well, acting as live sound engineer.

In April of 2002 it would be announced that BROKEN HOPE was no more. Guitarist Jeremy Wagner and vocalist Scott Creekmore revealed they would be using material projected for the next album 'Flesh Mechanic' for a fresh band project. This new unit transpired to be EARTHBURNER, the two ex-BROKEN HOPE men pulling in the talents of FLESHGRIND guitarist Steve Murray, PUTRID PILE bass player Shaun LaCanne and drummer Jeff Bumgardner. Wagner would also devote time to his other band concern LURCH. Wagner also revealed plans for a further project with Electronic / Hardcore remix DJ DELTA 9 entitled BECOMING.

In July guitarist Brian Griffin and bassist Sean Baxter unveiled a new project called INCIVISM, setting to work on an album with a projected title of 'Voluntary Exile'. Former BROKEN HOPE guitarist Jeremy Wagner launched a new project entitled LUPARA in November. In July of 2005 Sean Baxter would be announced as frontman for THY DIVINE EMPIRE, the act assembled by ex-DIVINE EMPIRE members J.P. Soars and Duane Timlin.

BOWELS OF REPUGNANCE, Metal Blade CDZORRO 64 (0). Repugnance / The Dead Half / Coprophagia / She Came Out In Chunks / Peeled / Hobo Stew / Decimated Genitalia / Preacher Of Sodomy / Remember My Members / Waterlogged / Embryonic Tri-Clops / Drinking The Ichor / Felching Vampires.

SWAMPED IN GORE, Grind Core International (1991). Borivoj's Demise / Incinerated / Swamped In Gore / Bag Of Parts / Dismembered Carcass / Devourer Of Souls / Awakened By Stench / Gorehog / Gobblin' The Guts / Cannibal Crave / Claustrophobic Agnostic Dead.

REPULSIVE CONCEPTION, Metal Blade (1995). Dilation And Extraction / Grind Box / Chewed To Stubs / Engorged With Impiety / Swallowed Whole / Erotic Zoophilism / Pitbull Grin / Into The Necrosphere / Essence Of Human Pain / The Internal Twin / Penis Envy / For Only The Sick / Freezer Burnt / Imprim's Obscurity / Captain Howdy.

LOATHING, Metal Blade (1997). Siamese Screams / Translucence / The Cloning / Reunited / High On Formaldehyde / A Window To Hell /

Skin Is In / Auction Of The Dead / He Was Raped / I Am God / Deadly Embrace.
GROTESQUE BLESSINGS, Martyr Music (1999). Wolf Among Sheep / Chemically Castrated / Necro-Fellatio / Christ Consumed / War Maggot / Earth Burner / Internal Inferno / Razor Cunt / Hate Machine.

BRUJERIA

USA — *El Brujo (vocals), El Asesino (guitar), El Cynico (bass), El Angelito (drums).*

Although a supposedly anonymous Mexican Death Metal band BRUJERIA ("Witchcraft") was in fact initially led by FEAR FACTORY guitarist Dino Cazares and drummer Raymond Herrera in collusion with NAPALM DEATH members and FAITH NO MORE's Billy Gould. BRUJERIA's unique marketing ploy was to adopt the personas of anonymous Mexican drug barons and, for a while, they fooled the Metal world until their identities were leaked. The initial 1989 formation comprised guitarist El Asesino (Dino Cazares) and bassist Güero Sin Fe (Billy Gould), this pair cutting the singles 'Demoniaco' for Nemesis in 1990 and 'Machetazos' through Alternative Tentacles the following year.

The band shifted shape in 1993 as singer El Brujo (Juan Brujo), drummer Greñudo (FEAR FACTORY's Raymond Herrera) and bass player Fantasma (Pat Hoed of DOWN BY LAW) were inducted. With this entry into the wider public arena, artwork featuring a photograph of a charred severed head and brutally unrefined grindcore, BRUJERIA naturally caused controversy from the outset. A sickened sense of humour prevailed over the entire affair as evidenced by songs such as 'Matando Güeros' ("Killing White Boys"), 'Molestando Ninos Muertos' ("Molesting Dead Children") and 'Chinga Tu Madre' ("Fuck Your Mother").

The band's second slice of depravity, 'Raza Odiada', arrived in August 1995. The sleeve's shock value was to be more refined this time around, a heroic portrait of the Zapatista Army of National Liberation guerila leader Insurgente Marcos. The audio content opened with a satirical speech by DEAD KENNEDYS leader Jello Biafra pouring diatribe against "brown skinned" immigrants choking California. Brujeria's response, a hail of gunfire, acted as an inceptor into a deluge of grind.

Ex-CRADLE OF FILTH, DIMMU BORGIR and LOCK UP drummer Nick Barker contributed to the 2000 album 'Brujerizmo'. That same year BRUJERIA's 'Marijuana' EP through Billy Gould's own Kool Arrow label commendably spoofed the Pop hit the 'Macarena' in Death Metal style.

A BRUJERIA offshoot sprang up in late 2001, the 'Corridos de Muerte album' was released via Kool Arrow/Demoniaco billed as ASESINO ('Assassin'), which featured Cazares and Herrera alongside STATIC X frontman Tony Campos.

The break up of FEAR FACTORY in 2002 would also seemingly bear repercussions on BRUJERIA as SADISTIC INTENT drummer Emilio Márquez was reported to have supplanted Herrera in both BRUJERIA and ASESSINO. These rumours would soon be quickly denied but in fact Márquez (El Sadístico) did join ASESINO. The official formation of BRUJERIA in July of 2003 stood at vocalist El Brujo, guitarist El Asesino (Cazares) and drummer Hongo Jr. (Nick Barker). BRUJERIA united with SOULFLY for the September 'Aztlan Fest '03' US tour, these dates, also including DELINQUENT HABITS and Mexico's Ska-Punks CABRITO VUDU, designed to showcase international Latin artists.

A July 2004 BRUJERIA gig in McAllen, Texas was cancelled after Cazares was reportedly bitten on the leg by a brown recluse spider, causing a massive infection. Suffering from fevers and hallucinations the guitarist was hospitalized for two days. Nevertheless, BRUJERIA still performed two sold out, back to back shows in Los Angeles at the Key Club that same month, the group's debut shows in the city breaking a 14 year ban. Every other attempt by the band to play Los Angeles had been previously blocked by protest. In January of 2005 BRUJERIA founder Dino Cazares announced his decision to quit.

ASESINO released 'Cristo Satanico' in 2006. Back on the road in 2006, BRUJERIA, having added a new rhythm section of Angelito ((Tony Laureano of NILE and MALEVOLENT CREATION) on drums and El Cynico (CARCASS man Jeff Walker) on bass, announced Chile, Argentina and Mexico shows for January then partnered with CEPHALIC CARNAGE for US shows in February. The group notably saw the inclusion of former CARCASS bassist/vocalist Jeff Walker. Spanish shows in September, retaining Walker in the line-up, saw Spanish metal band HORA ZULÚ as support.

Back on the campaign trail, BRUJERIA undertook US concerts in March 2007 supported by CEPHALIC CARNAGE.

¡Demoniaco!, Nemesis NEM 26 (1990). Seis Seis Seis / Sacrificio / Santa Lucía / Papa Capado.
¡Machetazos!, Alternative Tentacles VIRUS 113 (1992). Padre Nuestro / Molestando Niños Muertos / Grito De Los Soldados Poseidos / Machetazos (Sacrificio II) / Castigo del Brujo / Cristo de la Roca.
MATANDO GÜEROS, Roadrunner RR 9061-2 (1993). Para De Venta / Leyes Narcos / Sacrificio / Santa Lucía / Matando Güeros / Seis Seis Seis / Cruza La Frontera / Grenudos Locos / Chingo De Mecos / Narcos Satanicos / Desperado / Culeros / Misas Negras (Sacrificio III) / Chinga Tu Madre / Verga Del Brujo / Están Chingados / Molestando Niños Muertos / Machetazos (Sacrificio II) / Castigo Del Brujo / Cristo De La Roca.
Tribute To Pablo Escobar EP, Alternative Tentacles VIRUS 142 (1994). El Patron / Hermanos Menendez.
RAZA ODIADA, Roadrunner RR 8923-2 (1995). Raza Odiada / Colas De Rata / Hechando Chingazos / La Migra / Revolucion / Consejos Narcos / Almas De Venta / La Ley De Plomo / Los Tengo Colgando / Sesos Humanos / Primer Meco / El Patrón / Hermanos Menendez / Padre Nuestro / Ritmos Satánicos.
Marijuana, Tee Pee TP-011CD (2000). Marijuana / Matando Güeros '97 / Pito Wilson (Live) / Henchando Chingazos (Live) / Matando Güeros (Live) / Radio Advertisement (Hidden track).
BRUJERIZMO, Roadrunner RR 8504-2 (2000). Brujerizmo / Vayan Sin Miedo / La Tracion / Pititis, Te Invoco / Laboratorio Cristalitos / Division Del Norte / Marcha De Odio / Anti-Castro / Cuiden A Los Ninos / El Bajon / Mecosario / El Desmadre / Sida De La Merte.
MEXTREMIST! GREATEST HITS, Kool Arrow KACD010 (2001). Seis Seis Seis / Santa Lucia / Sacrificio / Machetazos / Padre Nuestro / Molestando Ninos Muertos / Castigo Del Brujo / Matando Gueros '97 / Nacro-Peda / Bruja Cirujano / Asesino / Hechando Chingasos (Live '97) / Poseido / Cristo De La Roca / Papa Capado / Seran Mios Para Siempre (Fantasma remix) / Mecosario (Pinche Peach Torsido remix) / Marijuana (Escobar remix—DJ Juju).

BRUTAL

HOBART, TAS, AUSTRALIA — *Father Time (vocals / guitar / drum programming), Brutal Dave (guitar), Thor (bass).*

Hobart, Tasmania Death Metal band BRUTAL, self styled "most brutal band in Austfuckingralia", issued the demo 'Fukin Brutal', including a cover version of METALLICA's 'Fade To Black', in April 2004. These sessions would be conducted by Father Time as a solo venture, after which Brutal Dave enrolled to handle guitar and drums. Subsequent membership evolution saw the introduction of bassist Thor Hammer and drum machine Hal 9000.

The follow up 'Bombs Over Hollywood' followed just days later. In May BRUTAL spewed out no less than four demos in quick succession, 'What's That Fucking Noise?', 'Live Brutalation!', 'Guts n' Roses' and 'Shageggdog'. In June 'The Shocking Truth Behind Tom Piper's Braised Steak And Onion' arrived. At one juncture, for the January 2005 demo 'Sellouts', BRUTAL would don ludicrous animal costumes and credit themselves as vocalist Pumpkin Head Christmas Pig, lead guitarist Gorerilla String Chumpchase, rhythm guitarist / bassist Shit Features with Giant Lobster on drums. Whittled back down to a trio,

BRUTAL then saw Jake Cunt installed on drums before Brutal Dave left, replaced by Eddie Van Wimplen.

In mid 2005 BRUTAL announced a reformation of their "classic" line-up with plans to record a full-length album.

Fukin Brutal, Brutal Demo (2004). Fukin' Brutal / I Love People Pie / Grind With Me Baby! / Legacy / Legacy (Extended version) / Fade To Black.

Bombs Over Hollywood, (2004). Brutal Grind / Legacy (Extended vocal version) / American Mutant / Bringer Of Change.

What's That Fucking Noise?, (2004). Dirty Harry Rules / Brutal Gets All The Chicks / Steer Clear Of AIDS / Volcano Head.

Live Brutalation!, (2004). Anti-Goth / I Love People Pie.

Guts n' Roses, (2004). Lovely Little Bunnys / Cheese Hole / I Dropped My Can Of Coke.

Shageggdog, (2004). Bogan, Jock Holocaust / You're My Russian Mailorder Girl.

The Shocking Truth Behind Tom Piper's Braised Steak And Onion, (2004). Bursting Out Of The Baby / The Shocking Truth Behind Tom Piper's Braised Steak And Onion / Slip The Bitch A Mickey.

Sellouts, (2005). BJH / I Just Stole Your Kids / Tribute To China / I Wish I Had A Flamethrower.

BRUTAL TRUTH

NEW YORK, NY, USA — *Kevin Sharp (vocals), Brent McCarty (guitar), Dan Lilker (bass), Rich Hoak (drums).*

BRUTAL TRUTH, New York Grindcore exponents with a definite thirst for speed, would be created during a lull in NUCLEAR ASSAULT activities during 1990 when the distinctive figure of lanky, mop topped bassist Dan Lilker, previously with high profile Thrash outfit ANTHRAX and spoof offshoot act S.O.D., assembled a band to indulge his love of Hardcore. Recruiting guitarist Brent McCarty and drummer Scott Lewis the line-up was finalized with the addition of vocalist Kevin Sharp.

Early demo recordings made by the band whilst still a trio were issued on the bootleg EP 'The Birth Of Ignorance' on Liberated Records. In time, Lilker split from a flagging NUCLEAR ASSAULT to concentrate fully on BRUTAL TRUTH. With Lilker's pedigree a deal was quickly on the table and the band signed to grindcore exponents Earache Records for their debut October 1992 Colin Richardson produced effort 'Extreme Conditions Demand Extreme Responses'. Opening with the 33 second burst of 'P.S.P.I.', BRUTAL TRUTH careered through the most ferocious Grindcore yet to be committed to tape, all punctuated by anti-capitalistic vitriol, disturbing narrative and industrial sound samples looted from an array of construction tools. A 1992 7 " single 'Ill Neglect' also saw the light of day featuring a raucous cover of THE BUTTHOLE SURFERS 'The Shah Sleeps In Lee Harvey's Grave'.

BRUTAL TRUTH paid their live dues in America opening for CATHEDRAL, CARCASS and NAPALM DEATH prior to guesting for FEAR FACTORY in Europe. During the tour Lewis departed and was supplanted by former NINEFINGER man Rich Hoak.

Pushing the boundaries of extremity even further BRUTAL TRUTH forged a liaison with Coventry techno act LARCENY to record the February 1993 'Perpetual Conversion' 7", the B side of which featured a version of BLACK SABBATH's 'Lord Of This World'.

The October 1994 album 'Need To Control', again overseen by Colin Richardson and hosting a take on THE GERMS 'Media Blitz', was formatted uniquely enough to make an impact with it being a boxed set of 5, 6, 7, 8 and 9 inch vinyl. Bonus cuts included CELTIC FROST's 'Dethroned Emperor' and PINK FLOYD's seminal 'Wish You Were Here'. Just as this album was being released Lilker was dabbling in another project titled EXIT 13, together with Lewis, and guesting on the 'No Matter What The Cause' album by Germans HOLY MOSES up front of a BRUTAL TRUTH tour encompassing Australia, Japan and America. European dates in April through to June 1994 saw the band packaged with MACABRE and Austria's PUNGENT STENCH.

The band, feeling that Earache Records did not have the necessary commitment, broke away from the label in search of another deal. It was to be a full two years before BRUTAL TRUTH signed up with American label Relapse Records. During this interim the quartet was far from inactive however contributing tracks to the 'Nothings Quiet On The Western Front' compilation and issuing split EPs with SPAZZ, complete with 'Rumours', originally by DIE KREUZEN, and MELVINS, the latter boasting the MELVINS cover version 'Zodiac'. Another 1996 Relapse EP, 'Machine Parts', involved five different live recordings of 'Collateral Damage' fronted up by EXIT 13's Bill Yurkiewicz and NAPALM DEATH's Barney Greenaway.

BRUTAL TRUTH's third full-length, 'Kill Trend Suicide' issued in October 1996, was laid down at the Cutting Room in New York and produced by Billy Anderson. Successive releases included a brace of split EPs, shared with CONVERGE, another Hydra Head 7" outing featuring BLACK SABBATH's 'Cornucopia', and RUPTURE.

In 1997 Hoak teamed up with CORROSION OF CONFORMITY's Mike Dean to record a project album under the band name of NINE FINGER.

BRUTAL TRUTH made an appearance in a porn movie 'Studio X' in 1997. The band played two songs live and even took a part in acting although not in some of the more 'animated' scenes. Lilker took time out to resurrect S.O.D. as the original line-up toured America one last time.

The September 1997 album 'Sounds Of The Animal Kingdom', recorded that June at Baby Monster Studios in New York, broke BRUTAL TRUTH into fresh audiences and includes a somewhat unlikely cover of jazz maestro SUN RA's 'It's After The End Of The World'. Featured as guest vocalist on the track 'Postulate Then Liberate' would be EXIT 13's Bill Yurkiewicz who also acted as producer. The Japanese release added bonus cover versions in AGATHOCLES's 'Hippie Cult', NAUSEA's 'Cybergod' and BLACK SABBATH's 'Cornucopia'.

BRUTAL TRUTH undertook a demanding 90 date tour of North America to wind up 1997 on a touring package combining CANNIBAL CORPSE, IMMOLATION and OPRESSOR.

Despite steady progress and increased sales BRUTAL TRUTH split following completion of an Australian tour in September 1998. Lilker resumed activity with S.O.D. for their 'Bigger Than The Devil' album, the bassist also operating Black Metal band HEMLOCK as a side endeavour. Yet another venture found Lilker assembling THE RAVENOUS in 2000 for the 'Assembled In Blasphemy' album. Included were NECROPHAGIA's Killjoy and Chris Reifert of AUTOPSY.

Hoak re-emerged in 2000 with his subtly titled new band TOTAL FUCKING DESTRUCTION. Meantime, BRUTAL TRUTH received a posthumous honour from The Guinness world book of records organisation, being awarded the world recognised title for "Shortest Music Video Ever" for their 1994 'Collateral Damage' promotional clip, involving 48 still images blurred in rapid succession for a duration of 2.18 seconds. Lilker surprisingly announced the reformation of the classic NUCLEAR ASSAULT line-up for an appearance at the 2002 'Wacken Open Air' Metal festival in Germany. Kevin Sharp made waves in late 2003 with his induction into the Grind 'supergroup' VENOMOUS CONCEPT, this outfit seeing the guitarist partnered with the illustrious underground Metal veterans guitarist Buzz Osbourne of MELVINS and FANTOMAS repute and the NAPALM DEATH rhythm section of bassist Shane Embury and drummer Danny Herrera.

Lilker would be in the driving seat for OVERLORD EXTERMINATOR in early 2004, a Black Metal combo featuring Adam Bonacci from WITHERED EARTH on vocals and COMMIT SUICIDE's Lee on bass guitar. This band's presence would be first marked by internet demos posted in February. That same Autumn the bassist forged CRUCIFIST, a Death / Black Metal band featuring singer Ron Blackwell, ORODRUIN and NIGHT

CONQUERS DAY guitarist John Gallo with Mike Waske of ORODRUIN on drums.

BRUTAL TRUTH reunited in May 2006 in order to record a version of 'Sister Fucker' for an EYEHATEGOD benefit album, 'For The Sick—A Tribute To Eyehategod', released on Emetic Records. In September and October Lilker temped for SOULFLY's North American dates after regular bassist Bobby Burns suffered a mild stroke.

2007 BRUTAL TRUTH concerts were announced for the UK in February and Japan during March as part of the 'Extreme The Dojo V. 17' festivals.

Birth Of The Ignorance, Brutal Truth (1990). Birth Of Ignorance / Stench Of Prophet / Antihomophobe / Consumer Mentality.

Ill Neglect, Earache 7 MOSH 80 (1992). Ill Neglect / The Shah Sleeps In Lee Harvey's Grave / Hear Nothing From You / Pre Natal Homeland.

EXTREME CONDITIONS DEMAND EXTREME RESPONSES, Brutal Truth MOSH 069 (1992). P.S.P.I. / Birth Of Ignorance / Stench Of Profit / Ill-Neglect / Denial Of Existence / Regression-Progression / Collateral Damage / Time / Walking Corpse / Monetary Gain / Wilt / H.O.P.E. / Blockhead / Anti-Homophobe / Unjust Compromise.

Perpetual Conversion, Earache MOSH 84CD (1993) (Split CD with LARCENY). Perpetual Conversion / Perpetual Larceny / Walking Corpse / Lord Of This World / Bedsheet.

Godplayer, Earache (1994) (USA promotion release). Godplayer / Wish You Were Here... Wish You'd Go Away.

B.I.T.B., Earache MOSH 110B (1994) (Free EP with 'No Need To Control' album). B.I.T.B. / Dethroned Emperor / Painted Clowns / Wish You Were Here.

NEED TO CONTROL, Earache MOSH 110 (1994). Collapse / Black Door Mine / Turn Face / Godplayer / I see Red / Iron Lung / Bite The Hand / Ordinary Madness / Media Blitz / Judgement / Brain Trust / Choice Of A New Generation / Mainliner / Displacement / Crawlspace.

Brutal Truth, (1996) (Split EP with SPAZZ). Pork Farm / Rumours / Foolish Bastard.

KILL TREND SUICIDE, Relapse RR 6948-2 (1996). Blind Leading The Blind / Pass Some Down / Let's Go To War / Hypocrite Invasion / Everflow / Zombie / Homesick / Humanity's Folly / I Killed My Family / Kill Trend Suicide.

Cornucopia, Hydrahead (1997) (Split EP). Cornucopia.

Brutal Truth / Rupture, Rhetoric (1997) (Split 7" vinyl picture disc with RUPTURE). Vision / I See Red (Live) / Stench Of Profit (Live).

SOUNDS OF THE ANIMAL KINGDOM, Relapse RR 6968-2 (1997). Dimentia / K.A.P. / Vision / Fuck Toy / Jiminez Cricket / Soft Mind / Average People / Blue World / Callous / Fisting / Die Laughing / Dead Smart / Sympathy Kiss / Pork Farm / Promise / Foolish Bastard / Postulate Then Liberate / Machine Parts / In The Words Of Sun Ra / Unbaptise / Cybergod.

Machine Parts + 4, Deaf American Recordings DA-02000 (1998) (Limited edition 1000 copies red vinyl). Spare Change / Machine Parts / Collateral Damage (Live At Faces, Rhode Island) / Collateral Damage (Live At G Willikers, New Jersey) / Collateral Damage (Live At Milwaukee Metalfest) / Collateral Damage (Live At G Willikers) / Collateral Damage (Live In Baltimore) / Fucktoy / Kill Trend Suicide.

GOODBYE CRUEL WORLD! LIVE FROM PLANET EARTH+13, Relapse RR 6425-2 (1999). Intro / Dementia / K.A.P. / Choice Of A New Generation / Birth Of Ignorance / Stench Of Profit / Walking Corpse / Sympathy Kiss / Pork Farm / Jemenez Cricket / Repeat At Length / Media Blitz / Fucktoy / Ill-Neglect / Kill Trend Suicide / Cornucopia / Godplayer / I Killed My Family / Time / Denial Of Existence / Hippie Cult / Callous / Zodiac / No Sleep / Cybergod / Cornucopia / Born To Die / Spare Change / Machine Parts / Collateral Damage x 5 / Fucktory / Kill Trend Suicide / Bubblebop Shop / Boredoms Cover 2 / Telly (With Bucky) / Blind Leading The Blind / Pass Some Down / Vision / Fisting / Die Laughing / Let's Go To War / Zombie / Homesick / Everflow / Dead Smart / Soft Mind / Dethroned Emperor / It's After The End Of The World / Callous / Average People / Black Door Mine / Promise / Foolish Bastard / Bite The Hand / Collateral Damage.

FOR DRUG CRAZED GRINDFREAKS ONLY, Solardisk SOLD-005 (2000). K.A.P. / Dead Smart / Blind Leading The Blind / Let's Go To War / Choice Of A New Generation / Walking Corpse / Fisting / Homesick / Stench Of Profit / Jemenez Cricket / (untitled).

BRUTALITY

FL, USA — *Scott Reigal (vocals), Mausolus Arguelles Von Kiszka (vocals / guitar), Demian Heftel (guitar), Jeff Acres (bass), Jim Coker (drums).*

BRUTALITY's debut album, recorded naturally at Morrisound studios, featured a line up of vocalist Scott Reigal, guitarists Don Gates and erstwhile EULOGY man Jay Fernandez, bassist Jeff Acres and drummer Jim Coker. Fernandez would make his exit to be replaced by Brian Hipp for 1995's 'When The Sky Turns Black'.

By the time of BRUTALITY's last outing 'In Mourning' Both Hipp and Gates had been superseded by erstwhile NASTY SAVAGE man Danny Gray and ex-DEGRADATION member Dana Walsh. However, pre- recording Gray made way for former EXECRATION guitarist Pete Sykes.

Ex member Brian Hipp would enjoy a fleeting appearance with premier British Black Metal band CRADLE OF FILTH during 1995 and later resurfaced as a member of DIABOLIC.

Coker and Sykes were operational with CONTORTED in 1997, a union with former EULOGY guitarist Dave Sawyer and bassist Ed Webb of EULOGY and DIABOLIC. In late 2002 BRUTALITY reformed and set to work on a comeback album billed as 'From The Ashes'. The revised band unit numbered original members vocalist Scott Reigel, guitarist, founding member Larry Sapp and bass player Jeff Acres as well as members of one-time BRUTALITY side endeavour ASTAROTH. However, despite signing to the Polish label Still Dead Productions by October of 2003 the new album had still not surfaced. BRUTALITY at this juncture comprised Reigal, Acres, guitarists Mausolus Arguelles Von Kiszka and Demian Heftel with drummer Jim Coker.

In early 2005 BRUTALITY announced they were to disband, blaming Still Dead Productions and claiming they had "completely backed out of their end of the deal". In May reports emerged that guitarist Mausolus Arguelles Von Kiszka has died. That same month ex-BRUTALITY guitarist Brian Hipp joined UNHOLY GHOST.

Hell On Earth, Gore GORE 007 (1991). Hell On Earth.

SCREAMS OF ANGUISH, Nuclear Blast NB 075 (1993). These Walls Will Be Your Grave / Ceremonial Unearthing / Sympathy / Septicemic Plague / Crushed / Spirit World / Exposed To The Elements / Cries Of The Forsaken / Cryptorium / Spawned Illusion.

WHEN THE SKY TURNS BLACK, Nuclear Blast NB115-2 (1995). When The Sky Turns Black / Race Defects / Awakening / Electric Funeral / Foul Lair / Screams Of Anguish / Esoteric / Artistic Butchery / Violent Generation / Shrine Of The Master.

IN MOURNING, Nuclear Blast (1996). Obsessed / The Past / Destroyed By Society / Waiting To Be Devoured / Died With Open Eyes / In Mourning / Subjected To Torture / Calculated Bloodshed / Extinction.

BRUTE CHANT

RIGA, LATVIA — *Sandis Korps (vocals), Jānis Aizkalns (guitar), Dainis Daikis (bass), Dzintars Vīksna (drums).*

Technical Death Metal act BRUTE CHANT, featuring SANCTIMONY guitarist Jānis Aizkalns, was founded in Riga during 1998. The group was rounded out by vocalist Sandis Korps, bass player Dainis Daikis with Dzintars Vīksna on drums. An opening demo session in 1999, entitled 'Defect God', was issued as a split cassette shared with GOLDPRICK by Moral Insanity Productions. These same tracks were re-issued by Klasma in 2000 as 'A Return Of The Beginning... Of The End', this time in collaboration with LUNATIC TERROR's 'The Reason Of All' demo.

Father Records released the album 'Killer Each Of You' in 2002. BRUTE CHANT folded after this release.

Defect God, Moral Insanity Productions (1999) (Split demo with GOLDPRICK). Backwards / Amok / Red-Baiting / Zengra.

BURDEN OF GRIEF

A RETURN OF THE BEGINNING ... OF THE END, Klasma (2000) (Split album with LUNATIC TERROR). Is There A God (LUNATIC TERROR) / Avoid The Drugs (LUNATIC TERROR) / Corruption (LUNATIC TERROR) / Sickness (LUNATIC TERROR) / Learn To Survive (LUNATIC TERROR) / Backwards (BRUTE CHANT) / Amok (BRUTE CHANT) / Red-Baiting (BRUTE CHANT) / Zengra (BRUTE CHANT).
KILLER EACH OF YOU, Father Productions FAP 003 (2002). Brother (Mechanical) / Another Level / Olympiad / D.C.M. (Dead Cows Milk) / Hair Scoff / Seminal Salute / Pink Noise / Unface / Carnal / Betons.

BURDEN OF GRIEF

GERMANY — *Mike Huhmann (vocals), Phillip Hanfland (guitar), Johannes Rudolph (guitar), Florian Bauer (bass), Carsten Schmerer (drums).*

Working with former HOLY MOSES guitarist Andy Classen BURDEN OF GRIEF laid down their debut album 'Haunting Requiems' in protracted sessions throughout 1997 and 1999 for the Grind Syndicate Media label. Recording line-up for this first effort comprised singer Mike Huhmann, guitarists Philipp Hanfland and Oliver Eikenberg, bassist Ulrich Busch with Christoph Schellöh on the drums. The band, bringing in Christian Nürnberg on drums, then signed to the Massacre label, once again crafting their next record 'On Darker Trails' with Andy Classen.

BURDEN OF GRIEF cut their third album 'Fields Of Salvation' in 2003 with producer Tommy Hansen. During the same sessions the band laid down a cover version of RUNNING WILD's 'Raise Your Fist' for a Remedy Records tribute 'The Revivalry—A Tribute To Running Wild'. By this juncture the band had evolved further with Busch switching from bass to guitar to cover for a departed Eikenberg. An all new rhythm section would be installed in bassist Dirk Bulmahn and drummer Carsten Schmerer.

BURDEN OF GRIEF celebrated their tenth anniversary with a special performance at their annual 'Art Of Darkness' festival on 13th November at Stadthalle in Scherfede, Germany. Drummer Carsten Schmerer announced his intention to leave in November. New man Sebastian Robrecht was installed on the drum stool in February 2005. Meantime, Magick Records, a division of the Cleopatra Label Group, licensed 'Fields Of Salvation' for US release, adding a live version of 'Reborn'.

Membership changes witnessed the departure of both guitarist Ulrich Busch and bassist Dirk Bulmahn. They would be superseded by guitarist Johannes Rudolph from GUTLOCK and bassist Florian Bauer of TWILIGHT PROPHECIES. BURDEN OF GRIEF's fourth album, 'Death End Road' released in March 2007, was recorded at Krachgarten Tonstudio in Kassel, Germany and was mixed at Jailhouse Studios in Denmark with producer Tommy Hansen.

ETERNAL SOLAR ECLIPSE, Burden Of Grief (1999). Smashed To Pieces / Paradox Reality / Deliverance / Eternal Solar Eclipse / A Duet Of Thoughts / Prowler.
HAUNTING REQUIEMS, GSM (2000). Smashed To Pieces / Paradox Reality / Deliverance / Eternal Solar Eclipse / A Duet Of Thoughts / Prowler / My Beauty's Embrace / In The Name Of My Blood / Days Of Anguish / Immense Infinity / Gedankenwelt.
ON DARKER TRAILS, Massacre (2001). On Darker Trails (Intro) / Cold Fire / Demonized / Reborn / Another Sphere Of Life / Stigmata / Frozen Pain / Under Burning Skies / Master Of Puppets.
FIELDS OF SALVATION, Remedy (2004). Desaster And Decay / Dead Soul Decline / The Nightmare Within / Engaged With Destiny / Fields Of Salvation / Slowly Pass Out / Yearning For Salvation / The Silent Killing / Don't Fear The Creeper.
DEATH END ROAD, Remedy (2007). Death End Road / Vita Reducta / Swallow The Sun / The Game / Running Scared / The Killer In Me / Drown In Sorrow / Schizophrenic / Passion Of The Night / Road Of Visions / Smashed To Pieces '07 / Immense Infinity '07.

BURGUL TORKHAÏN

FRANCE — *Arno Strobl (vocals), Ben Moritz (guitar), Fabian Desgardins (guitar), Kristofer Lorent (bass), Olivier Canton (drums).*

Grind merchants BURGUL TORKHAÏN are fronted by Arno Strobl of CARNIVAL IN COAL. Guitars come courtesy of UNTOLD, CAARCRINOLAS, VAKARM, DESCAMISADOS and D.S.K.'s Benoît Moritz and DECLINE IN HUMANITY's Fabien 'Fack' Desgardins with the rhythm section of bass player Kristofer Lorent and drummer Olivier 'Oliviersticks' Canton pulled from TRIDUS ELASTICUS. The group was actually conceived by bassist Kristofer Lorent during 1998 when he was a member of YYRKOON.

The 2001 album 'The Adventures Of Burgul Torkhaïn' was recorded with GRONIBARD and BELENOS drummer Gilles Delecroix sessioning and LUCRETIA's Pat Frescura on guitar. Two tracks originally intended for YYRKOON, 'Under The Green Moon' and 'Amothep', would make the final running order. Meantime, as a backdrop to BURGUL TORKHAÏN's progress Lorent had exited YYRKOON to join DEMENTIA. However, shortly after the self financed release of 'The Adventures Of Burgul Torkhaïn' in October of 2001 Lorent skipped camps again, hopping from DEMENTIA to TRIDUS ELASTICUS. Signing to Thundering Records, 'The Adventures Of Burgul Torkhaïn' was granted a re-release the following year.

Assembling a band unit to perform the album live, Lorent drafted Arno Strobl, guitarist Ben Moritz, Fabian Desgardins and Olivier Canton. The band debuted live at the 7th 'Rotonde' Fest in Hirson, France on 31st May 2003, appearing on a billing alongside SAXON, PARADISE LOST, SONATA ARCTICA and SHAMAN. Their second gig would prove even more prestigious, the group being the first ever French act to perform at the STRATOVARIUS headlined 'Tuska' festival in Helsinki, Finland. That same year Canton would divide his duties by enrolling into the ranks of Death-Thrashers KRYZALID.

Kristofer Lorent took time out to feature on the MONOLITHE 'II' album in 2004. As Moritz exited in March of 2004 the band would be reduced to a trio of Kristofer, Fack and Oliversticks for recording of the album originally entitled 'Bestiary—3 Years Of Encounters' but then switched to 'Ke-Ptalas: The Talisman Of Chaos'. These sessions saw MALEDICTION's Sylvian Mollard acting as guest back up singer.

THE ADVENTURES OF BURGUL TORKHAÏN, Independent (2002). An Old Man In An Old Smoky Pub / Under The Green Moon / Burgul Torkhaïn / The Mechanical Perverts / The Monastery / Ke-Ptalas Ben Amothep / People Of The Sea / The Prophecy / Amothep / The Choice / The Mountain Of Tal-Dagor.

BURIAL GROUND

VALLADOLID, SPAIN — *David (vocals / guitar), Dani (guitar), Tachu (guitar / bass), Miguel (drums).*

Valladolid Death Metal band BURIAL GROUND was founded during 1991. A first set of recordings, co-produced by Angel Corbacho, emerged in April 1992 as a demo billed 'The Lurking Fear'. Band members at this time included Sergio Canuto and Dave Devour. Their next offering was the self-funded concert recording 'Live In Ourense With Absorbed', taped on March 12th at Casa Da Xuventude in Ourense, issued in April 1993, featuring cover versions of CARCASS' 'Incarnated Solvent Abuse' and OBITUARY's 'Slowly We Rot'. BURIAL GROUND folded in 1994.

In 2006 ex-BURIAL GROUND frontman Dave Devour founded old school Death Metal band UNCONSECRATED including vocalist Shadowolf, of OAK, WINTERFROST and WOLFTHRONE.

The Lurking Fear, Burial Ground (1992) (Demo). Punished To Challenge The God (Intro) / The Yellow Sign / Over Dismal Beach / Big Breed / Vestige Of A Forgotten World / At The Wall Of Punishment/The Final Pain (Outro).

LIVE IN OURENSE WITH ABSORBED, Burial Ground (1993). The Yellow Sign / Over Dismal Beach / Beyond The Foolishness / The Show Of Violence / Slowly We Rot / Sadness / Big Breed / Sweet And Silent / Henry / Ways Of Pleasure / Incarnated Solvent Abuse / Anguish / Vestige Of A Forgotten World.

Demo 93, Burial Ground (1993) (Demo). Intro -The Spiritual Shelter / Ways Of Pleasure / Sad Awake / Your Heart (My Torment).

BURIED DREAMS

MEXICO — *Erich Olguín (vocals), Antonio De Yta (guitar), Ndua Valdespino (guitar), Ezequiel Mendoza (bass), Ivan Sartos (keyboards), Daniel Romero (drums).*

Deathsters BURIED DREAMS, named after the CARCASS song, began life in January 1995 as a quartet. Their early gigs would be plagued by line up problems but finally the band got down to recording a debut demo entitled 'The World Beyond'. This tape secured an entry into a national 'Underground Heavy Metal' contest. BURIED DREAMS duly won the first prize of an album recording and support to two international acts. By February of 1997 the band had signed to the Oz Productions label. The group's first commercial recordings were planned as a split album to be shared with DIES IRAE but the label soon opted to record full length albums from each band.

Promoting the 'Beyond Your Mind' debut BURIED DREAMS toured extensively as headliners and support to CANNIBAL CORPSE, HELLOWEEN, IMPALED NAZARENE and HYPOCRISY. Further shows had the band heading up their own Mexican 'Tourmentor' package alongside UNDER MOONLIGHT SADNESS, SHAMASH, DISGORGE and THE ZEPHYR. For these dates BURIED DREAMS line up, having undergone recent changes, stood at vocalist Erick Olguin, guitarists Ndua Valdespino and Antonio De Yta, bass player Ezequiel Mendoza, keyboard player Ivan Santos and Oscar Doniz on drums.

In October of 1999 the band travelled to Gothenberg, Sweden to record with the esteemed Death Metal producer Fredrik Nordstrom. These sessions, including a cover version of their CARCASS theme tune, resulted in the 'Perceptions' album. Whilst in Europe the band also put in a live show in Berlin, Germany in November. With 'Perceptions' released in April of 2000 BURIED DREAMS once more set off on tour, also appearing at the 'Milwaukee Metal Fest XIV'. Daniel Romero, of CANSERBERIA and AWAKENING, would later join the band as their new drummer.

BEYOND YOUR MIND, Oz Productions (1997). The Sword And The Cross / Black Dragon / Reflexions Of The Light / The Battle / Beyond Your Mind / Limits Of Fantasy / Looking Through The Fire / Irony / Moxtla / Her Beauty.

PERCEPTIONS, Oz Productions (2001). Illhamiqui / The Riddle / The Mind's Subconscious / At The End / Cosmic Prophecies / 360 / Perceptions / God's Of Fire / Buried Dreams.

NECROSPHERE, Oz Productions (2002). Io / Remorse / Andromeda Strain / The Shadow Murderer / Redemption / Immortal Echoes / Inside Reality / Death Beneath / Mictlanmatini / Preemptive Solution / Death Beneath (Demo).

BURN IN SILENCE (pic: Bruce Bettis)

BURN IN SILENCE

BRIGHTON, MA, USA — *Chris Harrell (vocals), Mike Casavant (guitar), Alan Glassman (guitar), Max Lavelle (bass), Ben Schulkin (keyboards), Darren Cesca (drums).*

Brighton, Massachusetts based Metalcore band BURN IN SILENCE had already supported the likes of SHADOWS FALL, MORBID ANGEL and DAMAGEPLAN before recording the debut Ken Susi produced EP 'Pure As Your First Day'. Drummer Darren Cesca has scene associations with VIRULENCE, GORATORY and PILLORY.

BURN IN SILENCE entered the studio with producer Ken Susi of UNEARTH in late December 2005 to record the band's Prosthetic Records debut entitled 'Angel Maker'. Final product was mixed by Tue Madsen. US gigs in March 2006 saw an alliance with BLACK MY HEART, CASSIUS and TOO PURE TO DIE. For an April leg of these dates the latter act was replaced by MISERY SIGNALS. July shows were backed by JACKNIFE, CLIFTON and THE AUTUMN OFFERING. BURN IN SILENCE hooked up with Indiana Thrashers YEAR OF DESOLATION for dates across August into October. November concerts in North America would be aligned with MISERY INDEX, INTRONAUT and YAKUZA.

Darren Cesca joined ARSIS during January 2007. BURN IN SILENCE set out on the 'Two Dollar Brawler' US tour allied with THE HANDSHAKE MURDERS, LIGEIA and APIARY during February and into March 2007. That same month Alan Glassman joined DESPISED ICON.

ANGEL MAKER, Prosthetic (2006). Lines From An Epitaph / Rebirth / Age in Which Tomorrow Brings / Embrace The Plague / Primal Human Pain / Angel Maker / Judging Hope / Well Adjusted / Watching Dead Leaves Fall / World Of Regret.

BURNING SKIES

BRISTOL, UK — *Merv (vocals), Liam (guitar), Ben (guitar), Andie (bass), Phil (drums).*

BURNING SKIES is a Bristol / Southwest Deathcore act forged in September 2002 by former FOOTHOLD members guitarist Liam, bass player Andie and Stu on drums. The demo 'A Premonition Of Things To Come', cut in 2003, secured a deal with Lifeforce Records for the February 2004 debut 'Murder By Means Of Existence'. A Summer European tour to promote this release saw the band partnered with A TRAITOR LIKE JUDAS. Drummer Stu was replaced by Phil in 2005.

BURNING SKIES issued the 'Desolation' album in October 2006. The band then announced they were to team up with MISERY INDEX, COLDWORKER and NECROPHAGIST for a European tour beginning in February 2007. However, guitarist Ben opted out beforehand.

MURDER BY MEANS OF EXISTENCE, Lifeforce (2004). Intro / Murder By Means Of Existence / Individual Hate Complex / Nacroleptic Suicide Attempt / Forever Endeavour / Emo Assassination / Thrash Gordon / Erase This Decay (And Disappear) / (Untitled) / Hatred Remains / Symptoms Of Perversion / Preaching To The Silent.

DESOLATION, Lifeforce (2006). Intro / R.K.D. / Sweet Sound Of Violence / Bauer Power / Desolation ... (For The Denial Of Ignorance) / Damaged / Fairytale Supremacy / Caught In The Circle / Lurid Demolition / Could You Sink Any Lower?

BUTCHERS

CHISINÃU, MOLDAVIA — *Mircea (vocals / guitar), Radu (guitar), Oleg (bass), Shtefan (drums).*

Chisinãu brutal Death Metal band BUTCHERS, self styled as "New age ultra-violent Grindcore", started life during January 2003, then featuring ex-FOETER MORTIS vocalist / guitarist Mircea, guitarist Radu, bass guitarist Dima and drummer Shtefan. BUTCHERS performed just one gig before folding, duly re-forming and introducing new members singer Stas and bassist Oleg. However, Stas then exited upfront of the group's first, six-track demo, 'Don't Worry, Be Happy' in 2003. Second session 'Ineffable Trance' followed in July 2004, the title track of which was also used as a three way split demo shared with DRUGSTORE and DISENTOMB. That September the group evolved into ABNORMYDEFFECT. Their first gig under this new banner came in November 2004 at the St. Petersburg 'Petrogrind' festival alongside SCRAMBLED DEFUNCTS, INFERIA, DISENTOMB, SLUGATHOR and FLESHGORE.

The band released the 2005 demo 'Inside Nowhere—Outside Nothing'.

Don't Worry, Be Happy, Butchers (2003).
Ineffable Trance, (2004). Mortul / Birds / 436 / Follow The Yellow Brick Road / 723 / 832 / River Of Blood.
Butchers vs Disentomb vs Drug-Store, (2004) (Split demo with DISENTOMB and DRUGSTORE). Ineffable Trance.

BUTCHERY

KARLSKOGA, SWEDEN — *Christer Elgh (vocals), Martin Jansson (guitar), Robert Lundgren (bass), Tobias Israelsson (drums).*

Karlskoga's BUTCHERY, featuring Robert Lundgren of AHRIMAN credit, was forged during 1999 by the guitar pairing of Jonathan O. Gonzales and Juha Helttunen along with drummer Tobbe Israelsson. Subsequently Christer Elgh took on lead vocal responsibilities and bass was delegated to Lundgren. A set of demos was recorded at Kumlabunkern Studios but the end result was unsatisfactory and therefore not made public. Persevering, the band entered Black Lounge Studios in September 2000 for a demo entitled 'The Coming'. This tape secured a deal with Voice Of Destruction Records but progress was then curtailed when both Gonzales and Helttunen decamped. As a side concern, both guitarist Juha Helttunen and drummer Tobias Israelsson founded STRANGULATION.

BUTCHERY, adding new guitarist Martin Jansson in March 2002, released the demo 'Repulsive Christ Curse'.

The Coming..., Butchery (2000) (Demo). Repeating Madness / Ancient Wrath / The Coming....
Repulsive Christ Curse, Butchery (2002) (Demo). The Gift / Filthfuck / Repulsive Christ Curse.

BUTTOCKS

VARTEIG, NORWAY — *Thomas Andresen (vocals / guitar), Frank Wilhelmsen (guitar), Glenn Spitz (bass), Pål Solli (drums).*

Death Metal combo BUTTOCKS, hailing from Varteig, released a 1990 demo 'Urcemurcel Turkus' prior to evolving into ALGOL, re-emerged with the 1992 demo cassette 'The Priests Are Laughing'. The group had actually been initiated as a Punk act in February 1989 under the brand SÉANCE, using this title for a few months before changing singers and switching to BUTTOCKS, featuring vocalist / guitarist Thomas Andresen, bass player Glenn Spitz and drummer Pat Solli (a.k.a. Pål Solli). The band also featured the WITCHHAMMER and DECAY LUST credited guitarist Frank Wilhelmsen to record the 'Urcemurcel Turkus' songs in December 1989. A second demo followed in March 1991. Wilhelmsen was replaced in September by Kjell-Ivar Andersen as the transition was made to ALGOL.

Capitalising on 'The Priests Are Laughing', the five track 'Witchsleep' promotional tape, recorded on an 8 track at McQuake's Studio, arrived in 1993. Signing to Effigy Records the band put out the 1996 album 'Entering the Woods Of Enchantment'. However, following release Thomas Andresen relocated, taking the ALGOL brand name with him. Ultimately, ALGOL dissolved. Frontman Thomas Andresen resurfaced in 2004 in SINCERA, a Metal band forged by Bjørn Andre Mathisen of FESTER.

Urcemurcel Turkus, Buttocks (1990) (Demo). Intro / Dark Sides / No Fun / Evil Dead / Hymns Of The Satanic Empire / Bowels / Nightmare / Outro.

BY NIGHT

FALKENBURG, SWEDEN — *Adrian Westin (vocals), Andre Gonazales (guitar), Simon Wien (guitar), Henrik Persson (bass), Per Qvarnstrom (drums).*

Falkenburg's BY NIGHT heralded their arrival upon the Death Metal scene with an eponymous, two-song 2000 demo. Further sessions, the five-track 'Derelict' in 2001 and 'Lamentations' the following year, were subsequently delivered. Lead vocalist Adrian Westin is also active with AGGRESSIVE SERPENT and, alongside guitarist Andre Gonazales, TRENDKILL. In 2004 the group shared a split album with CIPHER SYSTEM on the Lifeforce label. The full-length 'Burn The Flags' followed in February 2005. Throughout October and November of 2005 the band engaged in the "The Monster Mosh Down" dates across Germany, Switzerland, Austria, Holland and the UK partnered with Germans DISBELIEF, Hungarian act EKTOMORF and Israel's BETZEFER.

BY NIGHT scheduled time at StudioMega in Varberg in May 2006 to cut a new album 'A New Shape Of Desperation'.

By Night, By Night (2000) (Demo). Frozen Future Haze / Fight With The Darkness.
Derelict, By Night (2001) (Demo). Awakening / Lost To The Tormentor / Greed And Misery / Derelict / Of Infatuation.
Lamentations, By Night (2002) (Demo). Lamentation / Unseen Oppression / Obsessed To Hate.
BY NIGHT, Lifeforce LFR 043-2 (2004) (Split album with CIPHER SYSTEM). Lamentation / Unseen Oppression / Obsessed To Hate.
BURN THE FLAGS, Lifeforce LFR 050-2 (2005). Between The Lines / Part Of Perfection / One And The Same / Raise Your Voice / Completed / Behind In Silence / Unseen Oppression / At The End Of The Day / Dead Or Confused.
A NEW SHAPE OF DESPARATION, Lifeforce LFR 063-2 (2006). It Starts Within (Intro) / The Truth Is Sold / People Like You / Through Ashes We Crawl / Same Old Story / Dead Eyes See No Future / Walls Of Insecurity / Idiot / Forsaken Love / Cursed By The Thought / Time Is Running Out (Outro).

C.A.I.N.

PLOUGHKEEPSIE, NY, USA — *Quinton Gardner (vocals), Nate Satkewich (guitar), Adam Fletcher (guitar), Jon Dilks (bass), Tommy Soden (keyboards), Christoph Rühlmann (drums).*

Ploughkeepsie's C.A.I.N. ("Christ Aborted In Nativity") was formed in September 2000 by erstwhile THE MISERY CHORDS vocalist Quinton Gardner and guitarist Nate Satkewich, subsequently enlisting KINMA, KANNEPHORA and GRAPES OF WRATH bass player Jon Dilks and ex-TURNSTYLE and MALICE IN WONDERLAND drummer Dan Brunnemer. Satkewich cited prior credits with a string of outfits such as DESPITE THE SUN, HAMMURABI'S CODE, COUP DE GRAS, DISSIGHT and STRONGHOLD.

Following a debut live performance keyboard player Tommy Soden of FILTHY ROBOT was brought onboard. C.A.I.N. issued the 2001 four song EP 'If You Set Yourself On Fire The World Will Pay To Watch You Burn'. The group brought in second guitarist Adam Fletcher of URBAN LEGEND repute although Brunnemer exited in January of 2002. C.A.I.N. enlisted local Jazz musician Tucker Dalton as a temporary substitute before adding Christoph Rühlmann to fill the vacancy in February. By the following year had lost Rühlmann's services, the sticksman relocating back to his native Germany.

Quinton Gardner is also active with CEMETERY WOMB.

If You Set Yourself On Fire The World Will Pay To Watch You Burn, Independent (2001). Luna's Requiem / Imprisoned In Flesh / . . . Of Razor Blades And Membranes / Terminat Hora Diem.

C.C.C.

TÜRI, ESTONIA — *Ank (vocals), Ben (guitar), Jaanus (guitar), Kaido Kaidis (bass), Lauri (drums).*

C.C.C. was a Türi based, blasphemous Death Metal band. The group, established in 1992, comprised vocalist Ank (Ants Lill), of FORFEIT, DISCRUCIOR, SORTS, SUPPURATION, DAWN OF GEHENNA, MUST MISSA, THARAPHITA and MEINARDUS repute, guitarists Ben and Jaanus, the latter of FORFEIT, bassist Mantas of SORTS, MANATARK, PIRIT and LOITS plus drummer Lauri of PIRIT and FORFEIT. A rehearsal demo, 'Seven Rites', was recorded in Särevere during December 1993. Also credited on bass guitar after 1994 would be Kaido Kaidis of FORFEIT and DISCRUCIOR. A further demo, 'Per Mortem Ad Astra', arrived in 1994 but by the following year C.C.C. had disbanded.

Seven Rites, C.C.C. demo (1993). Martyrium / Hoc Diaboli Opus Est / Sacrificium / Blasphemia / Sacrilegium / Omnia Pymetha / Crematio.
Per Mortem Ad Astra, (1994). Civitas Diaboli / E.A. / Per Mortem Ad Astra.

CADACROSS

FINLAND — *Sami Aarnio (vocals), Jukka Salo (vocals), Nina Laakso (vocals), Georg Laakso (guitar), Tino Ahola (guitar), Jukka-Pekka Miettinen (bass), Antti Ventola (keyboards), Kimmo Miettinen (drums).*

CADACROSS started life as a straightforward Death Metal band upon their inception in 1997. The founding line-up comprised guitarist Georg Laakso, drummer Janne Salo, bassist Jarkko Lemmetty and guitarist Tommi Saari. A demo 'Bloody War' put together the following year would apparently prove so disillusioning the band halted activities and opted for a complete re-think. In 1999, maintaining his footing with CADACROSS, Georg Laasko joined TURISAS. When they reconvened a more melodic Metal approach was decided upon, adding keyboard player Mathias Nygård, frontman of TURISAS, as evidence of this. In this guise CADACROSS recorded a full album's worth of material dubbed 'So Pale Is The Light'.

SVARTMOOR frontman Sami Aarnio would be installed as lead vocalist in 2000. Guitarist Tommi Saari would bail out signalling what would be for CADACROSS just the start of many line-up fluxs. Tino Aloha of Folk Metal band TURISAS took Saari's place but then Nygard decamped. The keyboard role would be handed over to Olli Laitola. Fortunately the group was picked up by Low Frequency Records in January of 2001 to issue 'So Pale Is The Light' on CD.

The same June drummer Janne Salo bade his farewell, being replaced by Kimmo Miettinen (a.k.a. Mor Vethor) of ARTHEMESIA, ENSIFERUM and DARK REFLECTIONS repute. Laitala was the next casualty, keyboards next delegated to TURISAS man Antti Ventola. CADACROSS cut a new album, 'The Northern Crown', for 2002 release through Low Frequency Records. New recruits that year would be second vocalist Jukka Salo and ARTHEMESIA and ENSIFERUM bassist Jukka-Pekka Miettinen (a.k.a. Mor Voryon).

CADACROSS entered Steeltrack Studios in Hämeenlinna in May of 2004 in order to cut their third opus. During 2005 Tino Ahola forged a new Power Metal styled band billed TIMEKEEPER.

Power Of The Night, Cadacross (1997) (Demo). Dawn Breaks Behind My Eyes / Falling Down / Martyrdom / Power Of The Night Part I / Power Of The Night Part II.
Bloody Way, Cadacross (1998) (Demo). Bloody Way / Burning Down / Mind Is Burning / Make Your Mind.
SO PALE IS THE LIGHT, Low Frequency LFR 3140-05 (2001). Intro / Twilight / So Pale Is The Light / Battle Of North / Might Of Sword / Dawn Breaks Behind My Eyes / Turmion Taival.
CORONA BOREALIS, Low Frequency LFR 3140-30 (2002). Northern Crown / Among The Stars / Kings Of Grim / Morning Star / Learn The Dark / Flaming Ember / Bring Out Your Dead / Forest Remains Victor / Wreath Of Seven Stars / Turmion Taival.
CORONA BOREALIS, Teichiku TKCS-85053 (2002) (Japanese release). Northern Crown / Among The Stars / Kings Of Grim / Morning Star / Learn The Dark / Flaming Ember / Bring Out Your Dead / Forest Remains Victor / Wreath Of Seven Stars / Turmion Taival / Wreath Of Seven Stars (Version).

CADAVER

RÅDE, NORWAY — *Ole Bjerkebakke (vocals / drums), Anders Odden (guitar), Espen Sollum (guitar), Rene Jansen (bass).*

Renowned Råde Death Metal unit CADAVER, brought into being by Ole Bjerkebakke and Anders Odden during 1988, put out the November rehearsal tape 'Into The Outside' then opened proceedings officially with the July 1989 demo 'Abnormal Deformity', recorded at Kællen studios in Torp and distributed by Rapax Productions. These sessions were conducted by Ole Bjerkebakke on vocals and drums, Anders Odden on guitar with Renè Jansen handling bass. That same year Odden sessioned as bassist the BALVAZ demo 'Kællus Tapus'. A live CADAVER demo, 'Sunset At Dawn' featuring new second guitarist Espen Sollum, followed in September. Five further studio tracks were recorded in January 1990, but not made available to the public.

CADAVER's November 1990 'Hallucinating Anxiety' album was also issued, minus one track 'Hypertrophyan', as a split CD with CARNAGE. For the second release, October 1992's '... In Pains' issued through Earache Records, bassist Rene Jansen made way for Eilert Solstad. Anders Odden now handled all guitar duties. The CADAVER debut plied pure Death Metal whilst the sophomore attempt '... In Pains', produced by Kjetil Kællen Johansen at Rhythm Studios in Bidford, saw more technical Thrash elements creeping in.

In spite of being recognised genre leaders CADAVER folded with guitarist Anders Odden founding APOPTYGMA BERZERK and performing sessions on both SATYRICON's 'Rebel Extravaganza' and MAYHEM's 'Grand Declaration Of War'. Odden would breathe life back into CADAVER, now billed as CADAVER INC., during 1999. In this guise, the band's reliance on uncompromising Death Metal subject matter and images, and in particular their spoof 'Murder clean up service' website has even prompted investigation by the Norwegian government.

The new look band would be fronted by LAMENTED SOULS and AURA NOIR vocalist Apollyon, also known as a one time member of DHG and DØDHEIMSGARD. On bass would be L.G. Balvaz of DISGUSTING, HYDR HYDR and BALVAZ whilst drums would be allocated to Czral, a true veteran of the scene citing credits with SATYRICON, ULVER, VED BUENS ENDE, INFERNO, AURA NOIR, VIRUS, DIMMU BORGIR and DØDHEIMSGARD. CADAVER INC.'s 5 track EP 'Primal' would land a deal with the Earache concern for the 2001 'Discipline' opus. Both Fenriz of DARKTHRONE and erstwhile EMPEROR member Faust would

CADAVER

be on hand to add to these recording sessions. Touring the same year would see the band on the road for an extensive European tour in league with EXTREME NOISE TERROR.

In 2004 the group, once more billed simply as CADAVER, signed to the UK based Candlelight label for the 'Necrosis' album, produced by Bjørn Boge at Sound Residence Studio in Oslo. Meantime, Odden also busied himself with another act MAGENTA. News emerged in September that "after 15 years of underground service", CADAVER had decided to call it a day.

Anders Odden joined the touring line-up of CELTIC FROST in 2006.

Into The Outside, Cadaver (1988) (Rehearsal cassette demo). Intro / Maelström / Hypertrophyan / Fisken Skrek I Vannet / Into The Outside / Morgue Riffling / Den Tørre Sangen.

Abnormal Deformity, Rapax Productions (1989) (Cassette demo). Twisted Collapse / Corrosive Delirium / Abnormal Deformity / Erosive Fester / Cannibalistic Dissection / Hypertrophyan.

Sunset At Dawn, Cadaver (1989) (Live cassette demo). Corrosive Delirium / Erosive Fester / Abnormal Deformity / Twisted Collapse / Cannibalistic Dissection / Hypertrophyan.

Cadaver, Cadaver (1990) (Unreleased demo). Ignominous Eczema / Hallucinating Anxiety / Innominate / Maelström / Bodily Trauma.

HALLUCINATING ANXIETY, Necro NECRO 004 (1990) (Vinyl release). Tuba / Ignominious Eczema / Corrosive Delirium / Hallucinating Anxiety / Cannibalistic Dissection / Hypertrophyan / Petrified Eyes / Inniminate / Twisted Collapse / Abnormal Deformity / Maelstrom / Mental Abhorrence / Bodily Trauma.

HALLUCINATING ANXIETY, Necro NECRO 003/004 (1990) (Split CD album with CARNAGE). Tuba / Ignominious Eczema / Corrosive Delirium / Hallucinating Anxiety / Cannibalistic Dissection / Petrified Eyes / Inniminate / Twisted Collapse / Abnormal Deformity / Maelstrom / Mental Abhorrence / Bodily Trauma.

... IN PAINS, Earache MOSH 71CD (1992). Bypassed / Mr. Tumour's Misery / Into The Outside / Blurred Visions / Runaway Brain / Inner Persecution / In Distortion / Thy Misanthrope / Ins-Through-Mental / During The End.

NECROSIS, Candlelight CANDLE095CD (2004). Necro As Fuck / Decomposed Metal Skin / Evil Is Done / Odium / Awakening / Goat Father / Unholy Death / The Etching Cleanser / Heartworm.

Cadaver / Voice Of Hate, Temple Of Darkness TOD004 (2006) (Split EP with VOICE OF HATE limited to 666 hand numbered copies. First 200 in white vinyl, 466 in grey vinyl). Decomposed Metal Skin.

CADAVER INC.

RÅDE, NORWAY — *Apollyon (vocals), Neddo (guitar), L.J. Balvaz (bass), Czral (drums).*

CADAVER INC. is essentially a regeneration of the infamous early 1990s Råde based Death Metal combo CADAVER. The band's reliance on uncompromising Death Metal subject matter and images, and in particular their spoof 'Murder clean up service' website has even prompted investigation by the Norwegian government.

Guitarist and founder member Anders Odden ('Neddo') would be involved with APOPTYGMA BERZERK following the dissolution of CADAVER and would also feature on such SATYRICON's 'Rebel Extravaganza' and MAYHEM's 'Grand Declaration Of War'. Odden would breathe life back into CADAVER, now billed as CADAVER INC., during 1999.

The new look band would be fronted by LAMENTED SOULS and AURA NOIR vocalist Apollyon, also a one time member of DHG and DØDHEIMSGARD. On bass would be L.G. Balvaz of DISGUSTING, HYDR HYDR and BALVAZ whilst drums would be allocated to Czral (a.k.a. Carl Michael Eide or 'Aggressor') a true veteran of the scene citing credits with SATYRICON, ULVER, VED BUENS ENDE, INFERNO, AURA NOIR, VIRUS, DIMMU BORGIR and DØDHEIMSGARD. CADAVER INC.'s 5 track EP 'Primal', issued on Rapax Productions in 2000, would land a deal with the Earache concern for the April 2001 'Discipline' opus. Both Fenriz of DARKTHRONE and erstwhile EMPEROR member Faust would be on hand to add to these recording sessions.

Touring the same year would see the band on the road for an extensive European tour in league with EXTREME NOISE TERROR. In 2004 the group, once more billed simply as CADAVER, signed to the UK based Candlelight label for the 'Necrosis' album. Neddo also operated side project MAGENTA.

Czral got himself into the news in somewhat bizarre circumstances when he plummeted from a five-story building in Oslo on 26th March 2005. Severely injured, the musician underwent two major operations immediately after the event.

Anders Odden joined the touring line-up of CELTIC FROST in 2006.

Primal EP, Rapax Productions (2000). Primal / Killtech / Die Like This / Murderhead / Manic.

DISCIPLINE, Earache MOSH 242 (2001). Primal / Deliverance / Murderhead / Rupture / Die Like This / Point Zero / Killtech / Reptile Robots / Manic / Snapper Organs / Discipline.

LIVE INFERNO, Rapax Productions (2002). Tuba (Intro) / Die Like This / Murderhead / Rupture / Innominate / Primal / Deliverance / Snapper Organs / Mr. Tumours Misery / Point Zero / Killtech / Discipline / Manic / Reptile Robots.

CADAVERIC INCUBATOR

HELSINKI, FINLAND — *Necroterror (vocals / bass), Corpse Humiliator (guitar), Kim Humiliator (drums).*

Helsinki Grind act CADAVERIC INCUBATOR, founded by Necroterror, ("4-string deathbuzz / sepulchral vomit"), and Corpse Humiliator, ("6-string hacksaw / pitch black breath"), in late 2004, released a 2005 demo entitled 'Resurgence Of Morbidity'. Necroterror is in fact Antti Oinonen, of APOPLEXY, DEEP RED, EXCREMENT and SLUGATHOR repute, whilst Corpse Humiliator is Ilkka Paasonen of DEEP RED. Initially drums were in control of Mental (Teemu Mutka) of ACABÓ EL SILENCIO, AZAGHAL, CARCASE INC., DEEP RED, JUMALATION and NERLICH. Kim Humilator was next in line to provide "penetrator hammer".

In November 2006 CADAVERIC INCUBATOR shared a three way split album on the SoulFlesh Collector label with FETAL DECAY and Russian act MORTALIZED.

Resurgence Of Morbidity, Cadaveric Incubator (2005) (Demo). The Cadaveric Incubator Theme / Rejoice In Rot / Cold In Casket / Necrophagous Urge / The Undead Fiend / Resurgence Of Morbidity.

CADAVERIC INCUBATOR / FETAL DECAY / MORTALIZED, SoulFlesh Collector SFC05-001 (2005) (Split album with FETAL DECAY and MORTALIZED). The Cadaveric Incubator Theme (CADAVERIC INCUBATOR) / Rejoice In Rot (CADAVERIC INCUBATOR) / Cold In Casket (CADAVERIC INCUBATOR) / Necrophagous Urge (CADAVERIC INCUBATOR) / The Undead Fiend (CADAVERIC INCUBATOR) / Resurgence Of Morbidity (CADAVERIC INCUBATOR) / Aggressive and Fucked (FETAL DECAY) / One Or Billion (FETAL DECAY) / Try To Kill (FETAL DECAY) / Lethal Creatures (MORTALIZED) / Cremation

(MORTALIZED) / Bloody Junket (MORTALIZED) / People Hunting (MORTALIZED) / Sasha The Cannibal (MORTALIZED) / Consternation Day (MORTALIZED) / Mortifer (MORTALIZED) / Horror Delivery (MORTALIZED) / Searching For Blood (MORTALIZED) / Killed By Axe (MORTALIZED) / Sacrifice (MORTALIZED).

CADAVEROUS CONDITION

AUSTRIA — *Wolfgang Weiss (vocals), René Kramer (guitar), Peter Droneberger (bass), Paul Droneberger (drums).*

CADAVEROUS CONDITION, a Death Metal band with strong, traditional Folk influences, revamped the Deutsche Welle hit 'Eisbär' in true Death Metal style for their 1993 debut, 'In Melancholy', recorded that April at the Vienna Power Station by Michael Zastoupil and released by domestic label Lethal Records. The group recording line-up involved singer Wolfgang Weiss, guitarist René Kramer, bass player Peter Droneberger with Paul Droneberger on drums. An EP, 'Eisbär 90210', arrived in 1994 as the debut product for Starry Records, as a limited edition of 500 units.

The second album, 1995's '"For Love" I Said', featured a guest appearance by WEREWOLF vocalist Hagen on the track 'In June, As I Killed Time'. The album, recorded at Cosmix Studios with producer Cornelius Dix, closed out with a rendition of THE UNDERTONES 'Teenage Kicks'. The 'Tryst' album, a shared set in alliance with TODD DILLINGHAM, followed in 1996. CADAVEROUS CONDITION included two TODD DILLINGHAM covers in their contributions to the disc, 'Lakeside Down' and 'Up The Ass Of A Swan'. These sessions now saw Jürgen Weinhofer on bass guitar.

Switching to the Perverted Taste imprint, CADAVEROUS CONDITION broke a lengthy silence in 2001 with 'The Lesser Travelled Seas' set. This album was laid down at two locations, Noirmont Point with Andreas Dockl and Future Studios working with Michael Strasser and Axel Rab. Maintaining their tradition of cover versions, the record saw inclusion for a take on DEATH IN JUNE's 'Heaven Street'. Studio guests included Richard Leviathan, supplying narration, and violinist Matt Howden.

CADAVEROUS CONDITION would act as support to veteran gore mongers PUNGENT STENCH's Austrian leg of their 'Holy Inquisition' 2002 tour. A collection of concert recordings, some dating back to 1993, was released as a hand numbered limited edition 'Live' album in 2002. Only 33 copies were manufactured. A further rarity that year surfaced as part of an Italian compilation album 'Audacia Imperat!' on Oktagon Records and an exclusive live recording of 'Nostalgia'.

The album 'What The Waves Were Always Saying', produced by former band member Peter Droneberger at Lifebook Studio, was a free give away for the band's May 2003 concerts in Reykjavik, Iceland. Besides CADAVEROUS CONDITION tracks the album boasted a cover version of the REPTILICUS 'Snaketime' and the inclusion of 'Playe IV' by another Icelandic band, PRODUCT 8. In early 2004 bassist Peter Droneberger rejoined the band, supplanting Manfred Bayer. That year the group issued a split 10" release 'Time' through Eis & Licht Records, shared with Folk Noir band CHANGES. The title track featured vocalists from both bands alongside the violin of SIEBEN and SOL INVICTUS credited Matt Howden. Richard Leviathan of OSTARA also acted as sessioneer. A compilation collection, 'The Past Is Another Country', strangely only saw release in Turkey and Iran.

'To The Night Sky' saw issue in August 2006 via Oak Knoll Productions. Guest vocals on the song 'Sleep On The Wind' were handled by Patrick Leagas of SIXTH COMM and DEATH IN JUNE. The album also featured a cover version of BONNIE PRINCE BILLY's 'Black'.

IN MELANCHOLY, Lethal LRC 008 (1993). Katzentanz / To Be / Beautiful / Marian / The Flower / Shine / The Sadness Out Of Me / You Remain / Depart (With Me) And I Wait / May Fragments Not Dissolve / Eisbär.

Eisbär 90210, Starry STARRY 1 (1994) (Limited edition 500 copies). Underneath Stars Without A Sky / Eisbär 90210 / Fall Apart / Nadja / Eisbaer.

"FOR LOVE" I SAID, Lethal LRC 23 (1995). M / Tayst / A Song For / All The Vastness / What The Moon Brings / In June, As I Killed Time / Your And My Dead Stars / I Love You / The Ever Bleating Fools / Cold / . . . And The Forgotten / Teenage Kicks.

TRYST, Starry SQD 02 (1996). Motherdust / Shine / Lakeside Down / Wings But No Body / Nostalgia / Undertaker / Up The Ass Off A Swan / Who Will Buy My Records When I'm Dead / It Really Matters / I'll Protect Myself / Meg The Gypsy / Luminous Glow / Never Want To See You (Again) / I'll Be There / Nice Device / Never Want To Sleep With You Again / Wings.

THE LESSER TRAVELLED SEAS, Perverted Taste PT 041 (2001). The Moon And The Scars / Young Blood / Time / The Lonely Have No Right To Share The Summer Sun / Lesser Travelled Seas / Tesco Girl / I Came To Leave / Lead Me / First Song / Arrival / Heaven Street / The Nothing Out Of Me / A Dream Within A Dream / Outro.

LIVE, Starry STARRY 3 (2002) (Limited hand numbered edition of 33 copies). The Moon And The Scars / The Lesser Travelled Seas / Summer / I Came To Leave / Eisbaer / Lead Me / Marian / Tryst / Katzentanz / To Be / Shine.

WHAT THE WAVES WERE ALWAYS SAYING, Starry STARRY 4 (2003) (Free gig album). Now We Make The Past Undone / To The Distant Grey / Snaketime / Shores Of Yesterday / The Once And Future King / Tesco Girl / Plate IV / And Never Return.

TIME, Eis & Licht EIS039 (2004) (Split album with CHANGES). Time / And Never Return / Shores Of Yesterday / A Dream Within A Dream.

THE PAST IS ANOTHER COUNTRY, Starry STARRY 5 (2004) (Turkish release). The Once And Future King / Now We Make The Past Undone / The Moon And The Scars / Young Blood / And I Wait / You And My Dead Stars / Underneath Stars Without A Sky / The Lonely Have No Right To Share The Summer Sun / The Lesser Travelled Seas / Time / What The Moon Brings / Wings But No Body / Nostalgia / To The Distant Grey / To Be / Tryst / Tesco Girl / Shine / Lead Me / A Dream Within A Dream.

TO THE NIGHT SKY, Oak Knoll Productions OKP 015 (2006). Fireship / The Loneliest Grave / Destroy Your Life / There Is No Death And There Are No Dead / At The Crossroads / North Isles Motel / Repent / Black / Sleep On The Wind / The Once And Future King / To The Distant Grey / Now We Make The Past Undone / My Ocean Is Shipless / I Woke From A Sleep That Lasted All My Life.

CADUCITY

AALST, BELGIUM — *Tony (vocals), Jens (guitar), Vinnie Borduwe (guitar), Steven Suys (bass), Marino Kerkhove (drums).*

Aalst Death Metal combo forged in 1989. The band's original formation included a rhythm section of bassist Dirk Piers and drummer Bert Van Thuyne. Adding singer Guy Nirion the band cut the 1993 demo 'Incarnated: The Abhorer's Tale'. CADUCITY issued the follow up demo 'The Imperishable Mystery' in 1993. A debut album, 'The Weiliaon Wielder Quest', emerged through Shiver Records in 1995.

The band hit the recording studio in Belgium during the fall of 1996 and soon after the same label released sophomore outing 'Whirler Of Fate' in 1997 which musically contained many Thrash and Power Metal elements as well. The pair of releases comprised a long, elaborate and somewhat confusing concept story about a quest with knights, gypsies, a crow, a Council of Twelve and a number of other mystic characters.

In 2000 CADUCITY underwent line-up changes, inducting vocalist Medhi and ECTOPIA guitarist Wesley Carrez. Another latter recruit would be ANESTHESY guitarist Jason Masschelein, bowing out to join IMPEDIGON. The retrospective collection 'Gentle Annihilation Of The Enthroned' emerged in 2004.

THE WEILIAON WIELDER QUEST, Shiver SHRO12 (1995). Entry: Thus Begins Our Fair Journey / Vision For The Morrigon / Praseodymium / The Whimsical Crafts Of Enchantment / Strength Of Cruid Fire / Gymbrea's Enriching Wisdom Part One, Two And Three.

WHIRLER OF FATE, Shiver SHR 020 (1997). Crow and Hooves, Lightningdome Part I / Crow and Hooves, Lightningdome Part II / Arcane Churning Yearning / Niobilatika / The Sprinkling Snarl of My Ravishing Blade / Beneath In his Benighted Dwelling, The Paramount Shrieks With Laughter / Be' eth The Clairvoyant The Whirler Of Fate / When Your Dear God Falls to Perishment.

CALEDONIAN

FINLAND — *Ari Nieminen (vocals), Riina Rinkinen (vocals), Petri Immonen (guitar), Mikko Paavilainen (keyboards), Narttu (drums).*

CALEDONIAN started life as a quartet in 1998 fronted by singer Ari Nieminen. Formative associates included guitarists Salla Lindsröm and Jarmo Puikkonen, bassist Tuomas Kataja and drummer Juha Heimonen. Debut demo, 'Our Heavenly Womb?', arrived in 2000. 'Re-Create Me' followed in March of 2001. The group subsequently incorporated Riina Rinkinen of SILENTIUM on female vocals as the departing Nieminen relocated to Helsinki to join DAUNTLESS. Firebox Records issued the 'Acolyte' album in 2002 but shortly after release the band was vocal-less, quoting a line-up of guitarists Ville Leppänen and Petri Immonen, bassist Hermanni, former MORNINGSTAR keyboard player Mikko 'Mice' Paavilainen and drummer Narttu.

CALEDONIAN ultimately ground to a halt in the Summer of 2003, leaving a parting message to fans "It is time to quit when a band is more of a burden and full of misfortune than it's about the joy of playing and moving forward".

Our Heavenly Womb?, Caledonian (1999) (Demo). Prelude / Coherent Black Light Part I: Towards Hall Of Night / Coherent Black Light Part II: The Reveal / Justice / Coherent Black Light Part III: Epilogue / Nuijasota—Battle Of Finlandia / Outro.

Re-Create Me, Caledonian (2001) (Demo). Depth Of Her Love / Lust For Celtic Dark / Ragdoll.

ACOLYTE, Caledonian DR003 (2002). Intro / Depth Of Her Love / Lust For Celtic Dark / Ragdoll / Silkrose / Sparrow Inside Black Ruins / Opera Of Forgotten Words.

CALLENISH CIRCLE

AC HOLTUM-BORN, HOLLAND — *Patrick Savelkoul (vocals), Jos Evers (guitar), Ronny Tyssen (guitar), Roland Schuschke (bass), Gavin Harte (drums).*

AC Holtum-Born based CALLENISH CIRCLE was, in its original incarnation as GENOCIDE in 1992 by vocalist Patrick Savelkoul and guitarist Jos Evers, a straight Death Metal act. Numerous line-up changes afflicted the ranks until 1994 when, opting to switch titles to CALLENISH CIRCLE, the band issued the 1995 'Lovelorn' demo tape.

The tape made an enormous impression gaining the band the honour of "Demo of the month" in the well respected Dutch Rock magazine Aardschock and eventually winding up voted third best demo of the year. A string of contributions to various compilation releases ensued before CALLENISH CIRCLE landed a deal with Hammerheart Records.

The band opened proceedings with the 1996 Hans Swagerman produced 'Drift Of Empathy' album featuring a line up of Savelkoul, Evers, guitarist Ronny Tyssen, bassist John Gurissen and drummer Gavin Harte. This line up remained stable for the 'Escape' EP issued by Polar Bear Records and until recording of the 'Graceful . . . Yet Forbidding' opus which found bass player Roland Schuschke usurping Gurissen. Released by the DSFA label 'Graceful . . . Yet Forbidding' would become the victim of turbulent times for the label and in the end only saw limited release in the Benelux countries. The band attained the rights to the record licensing it to the Norwegian EdgeRunner imprint as well as various cassette releases in Eastern Europe and Asia.

CALLENISH CIRCLE signed to Metal Blade Records in the Fall of 2001 for their 'Flesh-Power-Dominion' opus produced by former HOLY MOSES guitarist Andy Classen. The record would contain two cover versions, namely DEATH's 'Pull The Plug' and more unexpectedly GOLDEN EARRING's 'When The Lady Smiles'. Upon the album release CALLENISH CIRCLE would form part of a European package tour in alliance with VOMITORY and AMON AMARTH.

By mid 2002 guitarist Ronny Tyssen was also ensconced in the Dutch / Belgian Doom 'Supergroup' LES FAIDITS assembled by ex SENGIR members singer Jurgen Cobbaut and guitarist Kris Scheerlinck. Bassist Roland Schuschke would break away from CALLENISH CIRCLE in late June. A replacement would soon be named in CHEMICAL BREATH, STORMRIDER and FORM man Rene Rokx as the band confirmed a run of low countries headline gigs for September supported by Ireland's PRIMORDIAL and Denmark's MERCENARY. The band's continuing ascendancy would be further progressed as CALLENISH CIRCLE was confirmed as participants in the April 2003 European 'No Mercy' festivals. The group formed up part of a heavyweight billing comprising TESTAMENT, DARKANE, DIE APOKALYPTISCHEN REITER, NUCLEAR ASSAULT, PRO-PAIN, MALEVOLENT CREATION, DEATH ANGEL, and MARDUK. Dutch dates in May had the band packaged with DISMEMBER and FLESH MADE SIN. UK and European dates projected into October of 2003, dubbed the 'Bonded By Metal' trek, found the band forming up a billing comprising EXODUS, AGENT STEEL, NUCLEAR ASSAULT, MORTICIAN, OCCULT and GOD DETHRONED. Filling in on bass would be former GENETIC WISDOM guitarist Ralph Roelvink.

In March of 2004 the band drafted the STORMRIDER and SPEEDICA credited Spike on drums. A short burst of Benelux dates in September saw CALLENISH CIRCLE united with DISMEMBER, OCCULT and HEARSE. That same month the Karmageddon Media label assembled together all of the band's early works in a retrospective compilation entitled 'Forbidden Empathy'. This set comprised the albums 'Drift Of Empathy' and 'Graceful . . . Yet Forbidding', the 'Escape' EP, the entire 'Lovelorn' demo and the track 'The Dreamers Path' from the 1996 sampler 'And the Ravens Left The Tower'.

September 2004 gigs alongside DISMEMBER, OCCULT and HEARSE would see a return for Gavin Harte behind the drum kit. In January of 2005 Patrick Savelkoul recorded a guest appearance on the track 'War Of Wars' for Spanish Thrash Metal band LEGEN BELTZA. Working with producer Gail Liebling, CALLENISH CIRCLE spent the Summer of 2005 recording a new album '[Pitch.Black.Effects]' at aRe U Recordings in Holland. The final mix was undertaken at Antfarm Studio in Denmark with Tue Madsen whilst mastering duties were handled once again by Peter Neuber at Mega Wimp Sound in Germany.

[Pitch.Black.Effects]", was released in the in January 2006 via Metal Blade Records. CALLENISH CIRCLE performed their first Baltic States show as headline act at the 'Green Christmas' festival held in Rakvere, Estonia during December 2006. That same month it was learned that Patrick Savelkoul was involved with AFTER FOREVER guitarist/songwriter Sander Gommans new project HDK.

CALLENISH CIRCLE announced they were disbanding in February 2007.

DRIFT OF EMPATHY, Hammerheart (1996). Inner Sense / Mental Affection / Slough Of Despond / Solitude / Last Words / The Dreamers Path / Disguised Ignorance / Where The Moon Meets The Sea / Scars.

Escape EP, Polar Bear (1998). Silent Tears / Escape / Broken / Mirror Of Serenity.

GRACEFUL . . . YET FORBIDDING, EdgeRunner EDGE002CD (2000). No Reason / Forgotten / Inner Battle / Beyond . . . / Broken / Oppressed Natives / Silent Tears / Passionate Dance / Caught By Deceit / Shadows Of The Past / Alone.

FLESH-POWER-DOMINION, Metal Blade (2002). Obey Me / For What It's Good For . . . / Witness Your Own Oblivion / Take Me Along / Bleeding / Your Final Swansong / Suffer My Disbelief / They've Chosen / Pull The Plug / When The Lady Smiles.

MY PASSION / YOUR PAIN, Metal Blade (2003). Soul Messiah / Dwelling In Disdain / Forsaken / What Could Have Been . . . / This Truculent Path / My Hate Unfolds / Misled / My Passion / Conflicts / Your Pain / Out Of The Body.

FORBIDDEN EMPATHY, Karmageddon Media (2004). No Reason / Forgotten / Inner Battle (Intro) / Beyond / Broken / Oppressed Natives / Silent Tears / Passionate Dance (Intro) / Caught By Deceit / Shadows Of The Past / Alone (Outro) / Silent Tears / Epacse / Broken / Mirror Of Serenity / Inner Sense / Mental Affection / Slough Of Despond / Solitude / Last Words / The Dreamers Path / Disguised

Ignorance / Where The Moon Meets The Path / Scars / Slough Of Despond / Disguised Ignorance / Lovelorn / Shadows / The Dreamers Path.

PITCH.BLACK.EFFECTS, Metal Blade (2005). The Day You Regret / Ignorant / Behind Lines / Schwarzes Licht / Sweet Cyanide / Blind / Guess Again / Self-Inflicted / As You Speak / Pitch Black.

CANINUS

BROOKLYN, NY, USA — *Budgie (vocals), Basil (vocals), Belle Molotov (guitar), Sudz Exodus (guitar), Buddy Bronson (bass), Curry Lightning (drums).*

Taking Death and Grindcore Metal vocals to their most extreme and logical conclusion is Brooklyn's CANINUS (pronounced "K—9—us"), a band employing two dogs, pit bull terriers Budgie and Basil rescued from animal refuge, as lead vocalists. The group, a strictly vegan affair, was formed during 1992, with early line-up changes seeing drummers L. Ron Howard, Rocky Raccoon and Thunder Hammer Attack giving way to Curry Lightning.

CANINUS issued the self-financed album 'Now The Animals Have A Voice' in 2004. The following year a split album, shared with HATEBEAK, emerged on the Reptilian label. A split 7" single in alliance with CATTLE DECAPITATION arrived in December 2005.

NOW THE ANIMALS HAVE A VOICE, Caninus (2004). Intro / Basil #1 / Brindle Brickheads (Unprecedent Ferocity) / Bite The Hand That Breeds You / Studio Guy Gets Pissed / Fear Of Dog (Religious Myths) / Budgie #1 / New Yorkie Crew (Loyal Like A Stone) / No Dogs, No Masters / Human Rawhide / Misunderstood Machines / Locking Jaws / Canine Core (Demo) / Fuck The A.K.C.

CANINUS / HATEBEAK, Reptilian (2005) (Split album with HATEBEAK). Bird Seeds Of Vengeance (HATEBEAK) / Bird Bites, Dog Cries (HATEBEAK) / Feral Parrot (HATEBEAK) / Abbra Cadaver (Intro) (CANINUS) / Ecuadorians In Disassociate T-shirts (CANINUS) / Canine Incisors (CANINUS) / God Eat God World (CANINUS) / Sensationalize : Demonize (CANINUS).

CANNIBAL CORPSE

BUFFALO, NY, USA — *George Fisher (vocals), Pat O'Brien (guitar), Jeremy Turner (guitar), Alex Webster (bass), Paul Mazurkiewicz (drums).*

Premier Gore merchants CANNIBAL CORPSE, since their debut 1990 album 'Eaten Back To Life', have stayed the course over an impressive stream of uncompromising albums. The band's album artwork has remained deliberately provocative with many releases being issued in tamer variants of the original shockers. Indeed, certain releases are completely banned in certain territories. By 2000 the band, based in Tampa, Florida, had shifted half a million records.

The band was conceived in Buffalo, New York during 1988 in the wake of the break down of two antecedent acts TIRANT SIN and BEYOND DEATH. Recording in Niagara Falls the band's eponymous five song demo, opening with 'A Skull Full Of Maggots', soon secured a recording contract with Metal Blade Records. The CANNIBAL CORPSE line-up that debuted on the hard hitting Scott Burns produced 'Eaten Back To Life', this first dose of detestation delivered in August 1990, comprised vocalist Chris Barnes, dual guitarists Bob Rusay and Jack Owen, bassist Alex Webster and drummer Paul Mazurkiewicz. Unfortunately for protectors of morality, material such as 'Rotting Head', 'Shredded Humans' and 'Edible Autopsy' merely provided a hint of what was to come. Two notable studio guests included DEICIDE's Glen Benton and OPPROBRIUM's Francis Howard on backing vocals for the songs 'Mangled' and 'A Skull Full Of Maggots'.

Scott Burns also manned the desk for July 1991's 'Butchered At Birth'. Once again Glen Benton figured as backing singer, making his presence felt on 'Vomit The Soul'. By this juncture the band's gore soaked imagery and uncompromising song titles was beginning to make sharp inroads into the mainstream media. The record sleeve, a dismembered female corpse presided over by a pair of zombies with baby corpses hanging in the background, saw 'Butchered At Birth' being totally banned from retail sale in Germany. In America many stores carried the album in a plain white sleeve.

'Tomb Of The Mutilated', yielded for public consumption in September 1992 and once more crafted by Scott Burns at Morrisound Studios, maintained the momentum. CANNIBAL CORPSE put in extensive road work in North America, Europe and even Russia. 'Tomb Of The Mutilated' provided no respite in either the ferocity of the band's music or the hideous nature of their album sleeves, this offering clad in artwork depicting two decomposing corpses engaged in oral sex. A March 1993 EP 'Hammer Smashed Face' would include a cover of POSSESSED's 'The Exorcist' and a surprise rendition of BLACK SABBATH's 'Zero The Hero', these both originally included as exclusive Japanese bonus tracks on 'Tomb Of The Mutilated'. European variants were boosted up to five songs with the inclusion of 'Meat Hook Sodomy' and 'Shredded Humans'. The track 'Hammer Smashed Face' had been thrust into the public limelight when comic actor Jim Carrey had insisted it be included in the soundtrack to his hit movie 'Ace Ventura—Pet Detective'.

'The Bleeding', laid down at Morrisound during late 1993, provided increased sales upon its issue in April 1994, tipping over 100,000 units in the USA alone. This outing found Rusay ejected in favour of Rob Barrett, a veteran of DARK DECEPTION, SOLSTICE and MALEVOLENT CREATION. Lyrically the band plumbed new depths of depravity illustrated with beyond the pale song titles 'Stripped, Raped And Strangled', 'She Was Asking For It' and 'Fucked With A Knife'. Naturally the original album decoration, a tapestry of corpses, was censored. Global touring found the band adding both Australia, and South America to their familiar path of Europe and the USA. A three month stint in the USA that Summer had CYNIC acting as show openers. However, it was the last CANNIBAL CORPSE album to feature Chris Barnes, the vocalist opting out to concentrate on his side project act SIX FEET UNDER. Barnes would fuel this band into a highly successful venture in its own right. Barnes had defected during recording of the next studio record, at that stage going under a working title of 'Created To Kill'.

CANNIBAL CORPSE's 1996 line-up for the re-titled 'Vile' album comprised of mainstay guitarists Jack Owen and Rob Barrett, bassist Alex Webster, drummer Paul Mazurkiewicz and ex-MONSTROSITY vocalist George 'Corpsegrinder' Fisher. Japanese copies would add 'The Undead Will Feast' and a video of 'Devoured By Vermin' to the running order. 'Vile' would give the band their only Billboard chart position to date, peaking at no. 151 in May. More importantly 'Vile' would be credited as the first ever Death Metal record to break into Billboard. CANNIBAL CORPSE also made it into the households of North America in an unexpected fashion when Republican vice-presidential candidate Bob Dole branded the group as practitioners of a "numbing exposure to graphic violence and loveless sex". Democrat senator Joseph Lieberman also weighed in on this moral crusade.

Touring for 'Vile' would be exhaustive and would see CANNIBAL CORPSE performing gigs for nearly a full year, including guest spots in the USA to both ANTHRAX and the MISFITS. European gigs in the Spring would be bolstered by support from IMMOLATION and VADER whilst a round headlining round of US dates saw support from BRUTAL TRUTH, IMMOLATION and OPPRESSOR. Japanese touring that year saw DEFILED as opening act. The intensity of the band's live set during this period would be captured on the concert video 'Monolith Of Death'. Once again CANNIBAL CORPSE broke records as 'Monolith Of Death's sales made it the highest selling Death Metal video ever.

The band added former NEVERMORE guitarist Pat O'Brien for the 'Gallery Of Suicide' opus, these sessions in April 1998 utilising a new producer in Jim Morris. Once more the Japanese edition boasted extra exclusive material in a cover of SACRIFICE's anthem 'Sacrifice'. Another change of producer to Colin Richardson did not sway the band away from their course for the follow up 'Bloodthirst', recorded at Village Studios in El Paso, Texas. This time the lucky Japanese were treated to a take on POSSESSED's 'Confessions' as their bonus incentive. The world campaign that followed comprised two North American treks and no less than three separate European tours. September 1998 gigs in Europe had INFERNAL MAJESTY and DARK FUNERAL as running mates. Promoting the 'Bloodthirst' opus, the band was back on the road in Europe during October of 1999, heading a billing comprising MARDUK, ANGEL CORPSE, AETERNUS and DEFLESHED.

From February 2000 shows at the Rave in Milwaukee and the Emerson Theatre in Indianapolis CANNIBAL CORPSE's inaugural live album, 'Live Cannibalism', was culled, arriving in September. A full six tracks would be excised from the German edition as material from the band's first three albums was illegal in that territory.

Ex-member Barrett founded HATEPLOW with a moonlighting Phil Fasciana of MALEVOLENT CREATION to issue the 2000 album 'The Only Law Is Survival'. Guitarist Pat O'Brien announced his Death Metal 'Super' combo CEREMONY centred upon MORBID ANGEL vocalist / bassist Steve Tucker and DISASTRONAUT guitarist Greg Reed. Erstwhile EMPEROR drummer Trym was recruited into CEREMONY during 2002. Renowned Spanish Death Metal act AVULSED would honour CANNIBAL CORPSE committing a cover version of 'Edible Autopsy' to their March 2001 'Bloodcovered' mini album.

The group, enjoying somewhat of a renaissance with their recent 'Gore Obsessed' album, would embark on a further round of American dates billed alongside INCANTATION, DARK FUNERAL and PISSING RAZORS, commencing on the 24th April in Los Angeles. 'Gore Obsessed', the eighth studio album, marked a slight shift in emphasis with the employment of Neil Kernon as producer. Initial variants of the record hosted a "secret" bonus track with a cover of METALLICA's 'No Remorse'. Japanese editions also hosted a live cut of 'Compelled To Lacerate'. European headliners would be scheduled commencing September 19th 2002 in Eindhoven, Holland with a month's worth of dates supported by DEW SCENTED and SEVERE TORTURE.

The band announced the release of a DVD version of 'Monolith Of Death' and a six track limited numbered release EP 'Worm Infested' for mid 2002 release, comprising three 'Gore Obsessed' outtakes, a cover of ACCEPT's 'Demon's Night', 'Confessions' originally by POSSESSED and No Remorse originally by METALLICA. CANNIBAL CORPSE would be back on European soil in September for an extensive run of dates heading up a package bill comprising DEW SCENTED, SEVERE TORTURE and VIU DRAKH. The band returned to the road in the USA in November, allied with touring compatriots HATE ETERNAL, MACABRE and CATTLE DECAPITATION. Southern state gigs in December found MALEVOLENT CREATION as support. The band scheduled a headline run of dates throughout Europe in April of 2003. Guitarist Jack Owen united with the EPITAPH and RESURRECTION credited drummer Kevin Astl and female second guitarist Analia Pizzaro in a brand new "Aggro Hard Rock" band project called ADRIFT in November.

The band, promoting a mammoth four disc career retrospective box set '15-Year Killing Spree' comprising three audio CDs and a DVD, put in a run of headline gigs commencing 12th February in Houston, Texas that had the band traversing North America in league with EXHUMED, HYPOCRISY and VILE. They then formed up part of the 2004 European heavyweight 'No Mercy' festivals commencing 29th March, sharing billing with SPAWN OF POSSESSION, HYPOCRISY, KATAKLYSM, CARPATHIAN FOREST, VOMITORY, PREJUDICE and EXHUMED. US shows in July and August found THE BLACK DAHLIA MURDER and Polish act DECAPITATED as openers.

Also in 2004 CANNIBAL CORPSE would donate their rendition of 'Confessions' to the 'Seven Gates Of Horror' tribute album assembled by the Dutch Karmageddon Media label in homage to pioneering Bay Area Thrash act POSSESSED. Just upfront of a US tour in July partnered with THE BLACK DAHLIA MURDER and SEVERED SAVIOR Jack Owen quit the band in order to prioritise his ADRIFT venture. He closed his fifteen tenure with the explanation that his "heart just wasn't in it anymore". Rumours soon put ORIGIN's Jeremy Turner in the frame to fill the vacancy, who duly completed the remaining scheduled dates. In October Owen temporarily joined the ranks of DEICIDE for European touring.

CANNIBAL CORPSE's North American road campaign continued into the Winter packaged with NAPALM DEATH, MACABRE, KATAKLYSM and GOATWHORE. George Ficher missed the bands 16th November show at The World in Pittsburgh, hospitalised due to a sudden illness caused by a viral lung infection. The band proceeded to run through an instrumental set, capped with a guest vocal appearance from KATAKLYSM frontman Maurizo Iacono.

In side activity, Alex Webster founded MACHINATIONS OF DEMENTIA, a technical extreme Metal project co-masterminded by guitarist Ron Jarzombek of WATCHTOWER and SPASTIC INK repute. Initially this band included LAMB OF GOD drummer Chris Adler but he would bow out in December 2005 due to other commitments.

CANNIBAL CORPSE drafted former guitarist Rob Barrett, whose previous tenure lasted between 1993 and 1997, into the ranks for the band's show at the 'Northwest Death Fest' in Seattle on 3rd April. Following a one off 13th August performance at the 'Party.San Open Air' festival in Germany the band then scheduled recordings for a new album, 'Kill', at Mana Studios in Tampa, Florida in October with producer Erik Rutan. In December it would be officially confirmed that Rob Barrett had rejoined CANNIBAL CORPSE.

'Kill' arrived in March 2006, bowing in on the US national album charts at number 170 having sold over 7,000 copies in its first week of sale. The band formed up a European 'No Mercy' festival package for dates across Germany, Austria, France, Switzerland, Belgium and Holland in April, ranked alongside KATAKLYSM, GRIMFIST and LEGION OF THE DAMNED. The group subsequently engaged in a gigantic roving festival billing with the US 'Sounds Of The Underground' tour throughout the summer, commencing in Cleveland, Ohio on July 8th, partnered with IN FLAMES, TRIVIUM, AS I LAY DYING, GWAR, TERROR, THE BLACK DAHLIA MURDER, BEHEMOTH, THE CHARIOT and THROUGH THE EYES OF THE DEAD. That August, on the band's Vancouver stop in Canada, Fisher and Barrett took time out to guest on INFERNAL MAJESTY's five track EP, 'Demo'n God', featuring on a re-recorded version of the song 'S.O.S.', from the band's 'None Shall Defy' album.

Australian gigs in October saw PLAGUE and PSYCROPTIC as support with New Zealand gigs being backed by ULCERATE. November saw US dates backed by NECROPHAGIST, UNMERCIFUL and DYING FETUS. The group joined forces with Danish act URKRAFT and Holland's DISAVOWED for extensive European dates in February and March 2007. To coincide, Metal Blade's 25th anniversary was celebrated with the reissuing of the band's 1996 fifth studio album 'Vile', complete with an additional four-track DVD filmed at San Francisco's Berkeley Square on February 3rd 1997.

Alex Webster took time out to deputise on HATE ETERNAL recordings in April. US concerts that same month had the band aligned with PSYOPUS and JOB FOR A COWBOY. CANNIBAL CORPSE lined up two shows in Reykjavik, Iceland in June and July.

Cannibal Corpse, Cannibal Corpse (1989) (Demo). A Skull Full Of

CANNIBAL CORPSE (pic: Jesse Angelo)

Maggots / The Undead Will Feast / Scattered Remains, Splattered Brains / Put Them To Death / Bloody Chunks.

EATEN BACK TO LIFE, Metal Blade ZORRO 12 (1990). Shredder Humans / Edible Autopsy / Put Them To Death / Mangled / Scattered Remains, Splattered Brains / Born In A Casket / Rotting Head / The Undead Will Feast / Bloody Chunks / A Skull Full Of Maggots / Buried In The Backyard.

BUTCHERED AT BIRTH, Metal Blade ZORRO 26 (1991). Meat Hook Sodomy / Gutted / Living Dissection / Under This Rotted Flesh / Covered With Sores / Vomit The Soul / Butchered At Birth / Rancid Amputation / Innards Decay.

TOMB OF THE MUTILATED, Metal Blade 3984-14003-2 (1992) (USA release). Hammer Smashed Face / I Cum Blood / Addicted To Vaginal Skin / Split Wide Open / Necropedophile / The Cryptic Stench / Entrails Ripped From A Virgin's Cunt / Post Mortal Ejaculation / Beyond The Cemetary.

Hammer Smashed Face EP, Metal Blade M ZORRO 57 (1993). Hammer Smashed Face / The Exorcist / Zero The Hero / Meat Hook Sodomy / Shredded Humans.

THE BLEEDING, Metal Blade ZORRO 67 (1994). Staring Through The Eyes Of The Dead / Fucked With A Knife / Stripped, Raped And Strangled / Pulverised / Return To The Flesh / The Pick Axe Murders / She Was Asking For It / The Bleeding / Force Fed Broken Glass / An Experiment In Homicide.

VILE, Metal Blade 3984-14220-2 (1996) (Digipack). Devoured By Vermin (Video) / Devoured By Vermin / Mummified In Barbed Wire / Perverse Suffering / Disfigured / Bloodlands / Puncture Wound Massacre / Relentless Beating / Absolute Hatred / Eaten From Inside / Orgasm Through Torture / Monolith / Staring Through The Eyes Of The Dead (Live) / Hammer Smashed Face (Live).

VILE, Metal Blade 3984-14104-2 (1996). Devoured By Vermin / Mummified In Barbed Wire / Perverse Suffering / Disfigured / Bloodlands / Puncture Wound Massacre / Relentless Beating / Absolute Hatred / Eaten From Inside / Orgasm Through Torture / Monolith. Chart position: 151 USA.

GALLERY OF SUICIDE, Metal Blade (1998) (European release). I Will Kill You / Disposal Of The Body / Sentenced To Burn / Blood Drenched Execution / Gallery Of Suicide / Dismembered And Molested / From Skin To Liquid / Unite The Dead / Stabbed In The Throat / Chambers Of Blood / Headless / Every Bone Broken / Centuries Of Torment / Crushing The Despised.

GALLERY OF SUICIDE, Metal Blade 14151 (1998) (USA release). I Will Kill You / Disposal Of The Body / Sentenced To Burn / Blood Drenched Execution / Gallery Of Suicide / Dismembered And Molested / From Skin To Liquid / Unite The Dead / Stabbed In The Throat / Chambers Of Blood / Headless / Every Bone Broken / Centuries Of Torment / Crushing The Despised.

BLOODTHIRST, Metal Blade 14274 (1999). Pounded Into Dust / Dead Human Collection / Unleashing The Bloodthirsty / The Spine Splitter / Ecstasy In Decay / Raped By Beast / Coffinfeeder / Hacksaw Decapitation / Blowtorch Slaughter / Sickening Metamorphosis / Condemned To Agony.

LIVE CANNIBALISM, Metal Blade 14302 (2000). Starring Through The Eyes Of The Dead / Fucked With A Knife / Stripped, Raped And Strangled / Fucked With A Knife / Unleashing The Bloodthirsty / Dead Human Collection / Gallery Of Suicide / Perverse Suffering / The Spine Splitter / I Will Kill You / Devoured By Vermin / Disposal Of The Body / Sacrifice / Confessions.

GORE OBSESSED, Metal Blade 3984-14390-2 (2002). Savage Butchery / Hatchet To The Head / Pit Of Zombies / Dormant Bodies Bursting / Compelled To Lacerate / Drowning In Viscera / Hung And Bled / Sanded Faceless / Mutation Of The Cadaver / When Death Replaces Life / Grotesque. Chart position: 71 GERMANY.

Worm Infested EP, Metal Blade METAL 14432 CD (2002). Systematic Elimination / Worm Infested / Demon's Night / The Undead Will Feast / Confessions / No Remorse.

THE WRETCHED SPAWN, Metal Blade METAL 14475 CD (2004) (USA release). Severed Head Stoning / Psychotic Precision / Decency Defied / Frantic Disembowelment / The Wretched Spawn / Cyanide Assassin / Festering In The Crypt / Nothing Left To Mutilate / Blunt Force Castration / Rotted Body Landslide / Slain / Bent Backwards And Broken / They Deserve To Die.

THE WRETCHED SPAWN, Metal Blade 3984-14469-2 (2004) (German release). Severed Head Stoning / Psychotic Precision / Decency Defied / Frantic Disembowelment / Rotten Body Landslide / Cyanide Assassin / Festering In The Crypt / Nothing Left To Mutilate / Blunt Force Castration / Slain / The Wretched Spawn / Bent Backwards And Broken / They Deserve To Die. Chart position: 74 GERMANY.

KILL, Cannibal Corpse 3984-14560-2 (2006). The Time To Kill Is Now / Make Them Suffer / Murder Worship / Necrosadistic Warnings / Five Nails Through The Neck / Purification By Fire / Death Walking Terror / Barbaric Bludgeonings / The Discipline Of Revenge / Brain Removal Device / Maniacal / Submerged In Boiling Flesh / Infinite Misery. Chart positions: 59 GERMANY, 170 USA, 187 FRANCE.

KILL, Metal Blade 3984-14560-0 (2006) (CD + DVD). The Time To Kill Is Now / Make Them Suffer / Murder Worship / Necrosadistic Warnings / Five Nails Through The Neck / Purification By Fire / Death Walking Terror / Barbaric Bludgeonings / The Discipline Of Revenge / Brain Removal Device / Maniacal / Submerged In Boiling Flesh / Infinite Misery / Shredded Humans (DVD) / Puncture Wound Massacre (DVD) / Fucked With A Knife (DVD) / Stripped, Raped And Strangled (DVD) / Decency Defied (DVD) / Vomit The Soul (DVD) / Unleashing The Bloodthirsty (DVD) / Pounded Into Dust (DVD) / The Cryptic Stench (DVD) / They Deserve To Die (DVD) / Dormant Bodies Bursting (DVD) / Gallery Of Suicide (DVD) / Pit Of Zombies (DVD) / The Wretched Spawn / Devoured By Vermin / A Skull Full Of Maggots / Hammer Smashed Face.

CANOPY

STOCKHOLM, SWEDEN — *Fredrik Huldtgren (vocals), Erik Björkman (guitar), Jonatan Hedlin (guitar), Daniel Ahlm (bass), Peter Lindqvist (drums).*

Stockholm Death Metal band founded in 2002. Guitarist Jonatan Hedlin is also operational with THE REVEREND JOHN LOATHE, OCEAN ROOM and CORPULENT MOTH. CANOPY was founded by Hedlin and second guitarist Erik Björkman, drawing in the rhythm section of bassist Daniel Ahlm and drummer Peter Lindqvist during 2003. In February 2004 the band inducted FACING DEATH singer Fredrik Huldtgren.

Corpulent MothCANOPY signed with Disconcert Music in November 2006 for debut album 'Serene Catharsis'. This album, recorded at Sawmill studios in Stureby, featured guests Antonio Ravina da Silva on vocals, guitarist Fredrik Segell and fretless bassist Johannes Zetterberg.

During Day One, Canopy (2004) (Demo). Common Walls / During Day One / Symbiotic / Shades Of Truth.

Will And Perception, Canopy (2005) (Demo EP). Decipher / Perception / For The Sickened Voice To Hear / Void / Will.

SERENE CATHARSIS, Canopy (2005). And Oceans / The Lie That You Once Told / Firmament (Part I) / Firmament (Part II) / Concentric / Last Point Of Reference / The Bleeding Earth / We Are Not To Be Of This World / Subtle / Serene Catharsis.

SERENE CATHARSIS, Disconcert Music DM0989-2 (2006) (US release). And Oceans / The Lie That You Once Told / Firmament (Part I) / Firmament (Part II) / Concentric / Last Point Of Reference / The Bleeding Earth / We Are Not To Be Of This World / Subtle / Serene Catharsis.

CANTAR

BELGIUM — *Ruben Drijkoningen (vocals / guitar), Filip Goris (guitar), Filip Vandeputte (bass), Tom Slegers (keyboards), Caroline Boven (violin), Kristof Naulaerts (drums).*

CANTAR's inaugural steps into the Doom-Death scene would be with the 1995 'Victim Of Your Imagination' demo. The group had been conceived a year earlier by vocalist / guitarist Ruben Drijkoningen and drummer Kristof Naulaerts, making up numbers with the introduction of Filip Goris on bass and, in April of 1995, Hanne on violin. Initially a stand in keyboard player was utilised until the addition of Elke that June. With this formation CANTAR recorded the opening demo. Subsequently Filip Goris switched roles to guitar and THE DARKENING's Tom B. was enrolled to cover bass duties. A second demo was projected but internal strife put a halt to proceedings as Elke exited.

Getting back into motion the 1997 "Beyond The Last Breath' promo session found Tom Slegers contributing keyboards. The group then embarked upon recording of an ambitious trilogy billed as 'Lament'. However, this endeavour stalled in the studio and in 2001 both Hanne and Tom B. bowed out. The sessions were completed with the use of a guesting professional violinist. 2003 saw CANTAR adding bassist Filip Vandeputte and violin player Caroline Boven. CANTAR entered Redtape Studios in early 2005 to craft more demos.

CANTAR, Independent (2003). Impressions Of The Forlorn / A Paroxysm Called Desire / Lake Of Redemption / Phantasmagoria / Carpe Mortem / Crimson Shades Called To The Crypt / Insanity Kingdom.

CANTARA

DROUWENERVEEN, HOLLAND — *Dick Barelds (vocals / bass), Jens Van Der Valk (guitar), Pascal Grevinga (guitar), Freddy Leenders (drums).*

Drouwenerveen's CANTARA, established during 1992 comprised an elite cast of Dutch Metal players in KATAFALK and WINTER OF SIN frontman Dick Barelds, the GOD DETHRONED, AUTUMN and SALACIOUS GODS credited guitarist Jens van der Valk, SINISTER, INCURSION, GOD DETHRONED and SARDONIC guitarist Pascal Grevinga and drummer Freddy Leenders.

The line-up changed to incorporate former AWAKENING man Peter Kamminga as lead singer plus a new rhythm section of bassist Mats van der Valk (ak.a. 'Grä Gmorg') of SALACIOUS GODS, SEIZURE, FRAME, MEADOWS, AEOLIAN and FEAR ME, and drummer Chris Oldenburger of INCURSION and SALACIOUS GODS. The 1993 demo 'All Beauty' preceded an EP 'Dark'. The Teutonic Existence label published a 1998 EP 'Fields Of Everlasting Serenity'. Kamminga later joined SEIZURE as Mats van der Valk assumed the lead vocal role.

Dark, Smalltime SPCD001 (1993). Dark / The Shades Of Love / Shredding Memories (A Trilogy Part III) / Exposure Of Involuntary Frustrations (Of Misery) / Odi Et Amo (Outro).
All Beauty, (1993). Grief / Intro / Treading On Thorns / Cherish / The Shades Of Love / Godforsaken.
Fields Of Everlasting Serenity, Teutonic Existence TER-012 (1998). Daytime Starlight / Fields Of Everlasting Serenity / Longgone Memory / In Time / The Mourning Sky.

CAPHARNAUM

FL, USA — *Matt Heafy (guitar), Jason Suecof (vocals / guitar), Alex Vieira (guitar), Mike Poggione (bass), Jordan Suecof (drums).*

Florida Death Metal band CAPHARNAUM comprised vocalist / guitarist Jason Suecof and drummer Jordan Suecof both of MONSTROSITY repute. The group, originally based in Connecticut, dates back to 1993 and a formative line-up of then 13 year old Jason Suecof, singer Frank Vega, bass player Andy Dickens and 9 year old drummer Jordan Suecof. The membership would be fluid until settling upon a roster of Suecof, vocalist Tony Espinoza, guitarist Kevin Schremmer and bass player Shawn Greenlaw. Demos included the 1997 session 'Reality Only Fantasized', issued on album by Pathos Productions, and follow up 'Plague Of Spirits'. Erstwhile CAPHARNAUM members vocalist Tony Espinoza and guitarists Kevin Schremmer and Ryan Adams, in union with Adam Schmidt on bass and drummer Steve LaMonica, subsequently forge CATALYST.

CAPHARNAUM, now featuring the Suecof siblings alongside MARTYR, QUO VADIS and GORGUTS guitarist Daniel Mongrain, vocalist Matt Heafy from TRIVIUM and bassist Mike Poggione, signed to the Willowtip label in November 2003 for a debut album 'Fractured', recorded at Jason Suecof's own AudioHammer Studios.

CAPHARNAUM personnel are also behind the tongue in cheek Black Metal act GARGAMEL. Jason Suecof, under his alter ego of Fornicus "Fuckmouth" McFlappy, also operates the satiristic extreme Metal act CROTCHDUSTER. Quite surreally, although this band utilises a drum machine, percussion credit is given to a non human member—Cain the dog. Cain actually features on the recordings in the form of panting. CROTCHDUSTER issued the 'Big Fat Box Of Shit' album in 2004.

In October of 2004 Dan Mongrain acted as stand in guitarist for CRYPTOPSY. CAPHARNAUM issued the 'Fractured' album through Earache Records in February 2005. On the production front, Jason Suecof scored credits on CANNAE's 'Gold Becomes Sacrifice' album. Guitarist Alex Vieira also operates with Metalcore band 5 BILLION DEAD. Vieira would second himself out to CANNAE for US touring in mid 2005.

In early 2006 bassist Mike Poggione joined LECHEROUS NOCTURNE.

REALITY ONLY FANTASIZED, Pathos Productions (1997). Eternal Descent / Night Terror / Sinister Perceptions / Sightless / Drawn-In Misery / Journey Beyond / Delusional Imprisonment / Soul Dissolved.
FRACTURED, Earache MOSH 311CD (2005). Ingrained / Fractured / Perpetuate Catatonia / Machines / Icon Of Malice / Reins Of Humanity / The Scourge Trial / Refusal.

CAPTOR

VINGÅKER, SWEDEN — *Magnus Fasth (vocals), Niklas Kullström-Lindblom (guitar), Fredrik Olofsson (guitar), Jacob Nordangård (bass), Angelo Mikaj (drums).*

Vingåker / Katrineholm Death-Thrash Metal combo CAPTOR can trace the band history back through many line-up changes as far back as 1986. The opening unit, formed by guitar player Jacob Nordangård, Christer "Putte" Johansson and Juha "Gonzo" Mäyre, took on a variety of short-lived titles including GONZOLA, MIDAS TOUCH and PESTILENCE. The CAPTOR brand was adopted after the SLAYER song 'Captor Of Sin'. During 1988 drummer Christer Johansson switched over to guitar and Lars-Ingvar Eriksson enrolled as the new drummer. However, obligatory military service forced a temporary disbandment the following year.

CAPTOR was re-formulated in the autumn of 1989 by Jacob Nordangård, moving from guitar to bass, and Lars-Ingvar Eriksson in alliance with new guitarist Niklas Kullström-Lindblom. In 1991 CAPTOR was featured on the Extreme Close-Up sampler, sponsored by Swedish Rock magazine Close Up Magazine. The first demo recorded in 1991 was titled 'Memento Mori'. A further tape, 'Domination', followed in 1992. Newly incorporated on drums would be Angelo Mikaj.

Bassist / vocalist Jacob Nordangård was to lose his place following the debut album, December 1993's Andreas Ahlenius produced 'Lay It To Rest' issued on the Euro label and recorded at Gävle Ljudstusio. CAPTOR opted to recruit two new members in his place, the jobs going to bassist Christoffer Andersson and vocalist Magnus Fasth. A 1995 EP, entitled 'Refuse To Die', was recorded at IndoCaptor Studio with producer Fredrik Olofsson.

The Drowned' opus, cut at Roasting House Studio, followed in July 1996 for the Danish imprint Diehard Music. A Japanese release was put out by Avalon Marquee hosting an extra track 'Down'. Third opus 'Dogface' emerged in March 1998. That year Fredrik Olofsson was superseded by Jonnie Carlsson. 2000 found both Fasth and Mikai forging KODEEN.

CAPTOR, switching towards a distinctly Nu-Metal styled direction, released the 'Alien Six' album on Turkish label Hammer Müzik in October 2001. Ex-member Jacob Nordangård joined THE DOOMSDAY CULT.

Memento Mori, Captor (1992) (Demo). Possessed / Vision Of Fear / Metamorphosis / Fundamental Influence / Memento Mori.

Domination, Captor (1992) (Demo). T. D. L. (Traumatic Depressive Lunacy) / Trail Of Death / Domination.

LAY IT TO REST, Euro EURO 933-CD (1993). Intro / Traumatic Depressive Lunacy / Utilized / Aspects Of Positive Thinking / Jaws Of Lust / Domination / Let Revolution Speak / Possessed / Depression / Trail Of Death / Lay It To Rest / Fundamental Influence.

Refuse To Die, Dolphin Productions DMPCDS 07 (1995). Refuse To Die / My Head / Insane / More Life / Circle Of Hate.

DROWNED, Diehard PCD-34 (1996). So Bold As Cold / Disbelieve / Mother / Zombiehead / Hostile Reality / Refuse To Die / Insane / Lost / Confession / More Life / Pray / Sick.

DROWNED, Avalon Marquee MICY-1011 (1997) (Japanese release). So Bold As Cold / Disbelieve / Mother / Zombiehead / Hostile Reality / Refuse To Die / Insane / Lost / Confession / More Life / Pray / Sick / Down.

Diehard Checkpoint # 1, Diehard (1998) (Split promotion CD single with KONKHRA, TAETRE and NAOP). Disconnect.

DOGFACE, Diehard PCD-42 (1998). Disconnect / Bleed With Me / All My Pain / Filthy / Lofi / I Told You / Hate Is Hate / Lakafak / So / Unfair / L.F.S.

ALIEN SIX, Hammer 20010 115016 01 (2001). Shout Up / Cold Inside / Burn / Do You Want To Be Me / Break It / Me, Myself And Them / Scum / Porch / Hold Me, Save Me / Not So Far / Head / Fake Is The World Around Me / Why.

CARBONIZED

STOCKHOLM, SWEDEN — *Christofer Johnsson (vocals / guitar), Lars Rosenberg (bass), Piotr Wawrzeniuk (drums).*

Formed by former CONSPIRACY bass player Lars Rosenberg as a studio quintet in Stockholm during 1988, CARBONIZED released the 'Auto-Da-Fe' demo in September the following year. The band's first line-up had comprised of Rosenberg, vocalist Matti Karki, guitarist Jonas Derouche and ex-CONSPIRACY drummer Per Ax. Guitarist Henrik "Hempa" Brynolfsson, another CONSPIRACY veteran, also joined the band but would swiftly exit, taking Ax with as the duo forged EXCRUCIATE. The band regrouped, drawing in guitarist Zoran Jovanovic and drummer Markus Rüden. Further changes in 1989 introduced guitarist Stefan Ekström. However, Ekström and Röden left to join MORPHEUS. Nicklas Larsson then manned the drums.

Following the release of the 'No Canonisation' 7" single on the Thrash label during 1990 vocalist Matti Karki opted to join DISMEMBER, although the group did add ex-ROBOTS drummer Piotr Wawrzeniuk. The new line-up recorded the demo 'Recarbonised' in 1990, but soon after Rosenberg left to join ENTOMBED, effectively putting CARBONIZED on ice for live work. Nevertheless, CARBONIZED added THERION member guitarist Christofer Johnsson in favour of Jonas Derouche to record the 'For The Security' debut album.

CARBONIZED were to suffer further membership problems in April 1992 when Wawrzeniuk joined THERION. Nevertheless, the band cut a new album 'Disharmonization' with producer Thomas Skogsberg at the famous Sunlight Studios in a rapid three days during that Autumn. 'Disharmonization' emerged in December 1992.

The 'Screaming Machines' album was issued by the Foundation 2000 label in April 1996. Both of these latter outings witnessed a drastic alteration in the band's playing style, being described by one reviewer as "Freaked out psychedelic Jazz Metal".

Au-To-Dafe, Carbonized (1989) (Demo). Final Chapter / Paradise Lost / Au-To-Dafe.

No Canonisation, Thrash THR 003 (1990). No Canonisation / Statues / Au-To-Dafe.

Recarbonized, Carbonized (1990) (Demo). Intro / Recarbonized / For The Security / Two Faces / The Monument / Outro.

Cronology Of Death, Thrash Your Brain 001 (1991) (7" vinyl single free with Slovenian 'Blackout' magazine, limited to 500 hand numbered copies, split with SENTENCED, BLUUURGH... and XENOPHOBIA). The Monument.

FOR THE SECURITY, Thrash THR 011 (1991). Recarbonized / Hypnotic Aim / Euthanasia / Blinded Of The Veil / Syndrome / Reflections Of The Dark / Third Eye / Purified (From The Sulfer) / For The Security / Monument.

DISHARMONIZATION, Foundations 2000 FDN 2006-2 (1992). Frozen Landscapes / Vladtepes / Lord Of Damnation / Silent Journey / Spanish Fly / Succubus / Night Shadows / The Voice Of Slained Pig / Confessions / Spacecraft / Whip Me Darling.

SCREAMING MACHINES, Foundation 2000 FDN 2013-2 (1996). My Hate / Circles / For Those Who Play / High Octane / Psychodelica / Golden Rain / Fever / I Wanna Die / Fist / Common Enemy / Screaming Machines.

CARCASE INC.

RIIHIMÄKI, FINLAND — *Juhani Anton Jokisalo (vocals), Markus Rantala (guitar), Jani Vesanen (guitar), Mikael Seppanen (bass), T. Kristian (drums).*

Death Metal combo CARCASE INC. was manifested in Riihimäki during Spring of 2002 by guitarists Jani Vesanen and Markus Rantala alongside drummer DEEPRED Teemu Mutka. Bassist Jouni Valkki joined shortly after then completed the line up with LET ME DREAM singer Tuukka Koskinen. CARCASE INC.'s first trip to the recording studio in the Autumn of 2002 resulted in the demo 'Mental Suicide'. However, before the close of the year Valkki exited, replaced in early 2003 by Mikael Seppanen for the second demo 'Disposal Human Waste'.

CARCASE INC. enrolled new drummer T. Kristian in 2004, (a.k.a. Toni Kostiainen) of FLEGETON, YEARNING, SAATTUE and TWILIGHT OPHERA. The band introduced a new singer in the form of Juhani Anton Jokisalo, also operational with APOCRYPHAL VOICE, ABSENT VOICE and going under the pseudonym of Kasdaye for fellow Black Metal outfit EX CALIGA.

CARCASE INC. folded in 2005.

Mental Suicide, Carcase Inc. (2002) (Demo). Diagnosis / Mental Suicide / Screaming Chaos / Malfunction Of Brains.

Disposal Human Waste, Carcase Inc. (2003) (Demo). Intro / Beyond Control / The Seeds Of Madness And Hatred / Daylight Demons.

CARCASS

LIVERPOOL, UK — *Jeff Walker (vocals / bass), Bill Steer (guitar), Ken Owen (drums).*

Certainly to be counted as originators of the gore-Death genre, CARCASS was a Liverpool based extreme Metal band formed in 1985 and masterminded by ex-NAPALM DEATH man Bill Steer and ex-ELECTRO HIPPIES vocalist / bassist JEFF WALKER, CARCASS' 1988 debut album, 'Reek Of Putrefaction', sparked immediate controversy with its cover depicting a collage of human flesh.

Bill Steer had first made his presence felt with DISATTACK, releasing a Hardcore / Punk "Dis-core" styled six song demo under that title, 'A Bomb Drops...', in March 1986. DISATTACK comprised Steer, vocalist Pek, bassist Paul and drummer Middie. The guitarist was an active promoter of extreme music, being co-publisher, alongside Middie and Pek, of the fanzine 'Phoenix From The Crypt'. Jeff Walker was to enroll, initially as bassist, and Ken Owen took over on drums as the transition to CARCASS was implemented. Steer and Walker's first musical experiences together were learning to play JUDAS PRIEST cover versions as a bedroom band, but this brand of traditional Metal soon gave way to something far more sinister.

The group's first set of CARCASS recordings came in 1987 with a thirteen track demo cassette entitled 'Flesh Ripping Sonic Torment'. Lead vocals on this session were provided by Sanjiv, this singer (the band never learned his surname), exited soon afterward. With Walker adopting the vocal role, a further five tracks were released in cassette form in 1988 dubbed 'Symphonies Of Sickness'. This set secured a recording contract with Nottingham's Earache Records.

Although CARCASS played intense Death Metal more than extreme enough to match the visuals, the group has since claimed that the whole point of 'Reek Of Putrefaction's sleeve art was in order to get it banned. Instead, it just sold more copies. Where CARCASS had scored a first was in their enthusiastic looting of medical text books in order to find inspiration. Previously the genre had stuck to hackneyed themes of Satanic practices, occult lore and historical brutality but CARCASS found richer, and far more realistic, realms to plunder. Due to 'Reek Of Putrefaction', fans discovered that words such as Uterogestation, Mucopurulence, Pyosisified and Detruncation, not previously deemed suitable for public consumption, were all too horrifyingly real. CARCASS went beyond mere shock value though, it soon being learned that behind the slabs of raw meat were a set of earnest vegetarians.

Radio One DJ John Peel, known for his adventurous tastes in music, pulled CARCASS into the BBC studios on December 13th, 1988 to record a session for his show. Produced by Dale Griffin these four tracks aired to the nation in January 1989 and would be followed up by a commercial release, 'The Peel Sessions EP', that same year. Band members notably credited themselves as W.G. Thorax Embalmer (Bill Steer), J. Offalmangler (Jeff Walker) and K. Grumegargler (Ken Owen).

Steer departed from NAPALM DEATH to concentrate fully on CARCASS just before recording of 1989's the 'Symphonies Of Sickness'. That same year the Mexican label Distorted Harmony issued a three track live EP, 'Live St. George's Hall, Bradford 15.11.89', comprising concert recordings from both the title's venue and London University. Although having the appearance of a budget bootleg, this 7" vinyl was originally authorised by the band, but would be heavily bootlegged in later years. On the live front, the group participated in the Earache organised "Grindcrusher" tour of Europe shoulder to shoulder with BOLT THROWER, MORBID ANGEL and NAPALM DEATH.

CARCASS added Swedish guitarist Mike Amott, previously with CARNAGE, in March 1990 to thicken their live sound. That year, German shows saw ATROCITY as support act whilst Dutch gigs had ACROSTICHON opening. As the Grind wave peaked, February 1992's 'Necrotism—Descanting The Insalubrious' album, recorded at Amazon Studios in Simonswood with producer Colin Richardson, rapidly sold in excess of 100'000 copies. The combination of Colin Richardson behind the desk, Mike Amott on second guitar and a greater proficiency from the founding members took CARCASS to new heights of creativity and technical proficiency.

CARCASS played a brace of back to back Mexican gigs in March 1992 supported by CENOTAPH, DEADLY DARK and HARDWARE. Road work to promote the ensuing 'Necrotism' and the June 1992 'Tools Of The Trade' EP included last minute support dates alongside French Thrashers LOUDBLAST on DEATH's British tour when PESTILENCE pulled out. This was followed up by the epic Earache records 'Gods Of Grind' tour, featuring CARCASS, CATHEDRAL, ENTOMBED and CONFESSOR.

Amott departed after October 1993 album's 'Heartwork's completion in order to return to Sweden to form the highly rated SPIRITUAL BEGGERS and ARCH ENEMY. CARCASS, meantime, had endeavoured to mature in order to rid themselves of the Death Metal tag and progress musically. 'Heartwork', laid down that summer at Parr Street Studios with Colin Richardson, displayed a far greater degree of musicianship than its predecessors with classic Heavy Metal influences very much on display, especially on the guitar solos. The album also benefited from an HR Giger photographed sculpture, entitled 'Preserve Life', as its cover, as opposed to the expected dead meat.

In order to replace Amott CARCASS recruited ex VENOM guitarist, American born Mike Hickey for live work. The band toured Britain in December 1993 as guests alongside HEADSWIM to Rap Metallers BODY COUNT before a mammoth European and American tour. Sales of 'Heartwork' were strong, over 50'000 in America alone, and towards the end of the American dates the band were signed to Columbia Records. In June Hickey was replaced (later turning up in CATHEDRAL and CRONOS), by ex DEVOID guitarist Carlo Regadas.

In late 1995 Walker opted to tour with YEAR ZERO on a temporary basis whilst CARCASS waited for Columbia Records to release the new album. However, Columbia in America dropped the band during November resulting in the departure of Steer.

Although CARCASS regrouped and resigned the already recorded album to previous label Earache, Steer's departure left his former colleagues to carry on under the new banner of BLACKSTAR adding ex-CATHEDRAL and YEAR ZERO guitarist Mark Griffiths to the cause.

Ken Owen suffered a brain haemorrhage in his sleep in February 1999. This illness was to put the drummer into a coma for ten months and following surgery, in March 2000, Owen only left hospital in February 2001.

Steer had re-emerged in 1999 fronting BLACKSMITH. By the following year he had created FIREBIRD with CATHEDRAL's Leo Smee and SPIRITUAL BEGGERS Ludwig Witt. The CARCASS brand was kept in the public eye in 2001 with the issue of 'Requiems Of Revulsion' by Deathvomit Records, this being a tribute collection witnessing homage by such acts as REGURGITATE, PIG DESTROYER, DISGORGE, GENERAL SURGERY, DEAD INFECTION, AVULSED, IMPALED, VULGAR PIGEONS, NASUM, CATTLE DECAPITATION, ROTTEN SOUND, HAEMORRHAGE and ENGORGED.

Earache Records re-issued the first two CARCASS albums 'Reek Of Putrefaction' and 'Symphonies Of Sickness' in late 2002, restored with the banned sleeve art. Both albums had previously been unavailable with the original covers since 1992. Jeff Walker made a return to action in 2004, producing an album for Liverpool's DIAMANTHIAN. In October, Walker would act as guest vocalist on the NAPALM DEATH album 'The Code Is Red... Long Live The Code', featuring on the track 'Pledge Yourself To You'.

CARCASS frontman JEFF WALKER surprised many in October when he revealed he recorded a solo album comprising exclusively of Country and Blues covers ranging across such artists as SKEETER DAVIS, HANK WILLIAMS, JOHNNY CASH, CONNIE SMITH, and JOHN DENVER. Conducted naturally with an extreme Metal angle, the record, 'Welcome To Carcass Cuntry', besides including CARCASS colleagues Bill Steer and Ken Owen, featured a whole host of guest contributors including former CARCASS colleague Bill Steer, the H.I.M. duo of frontman Ville Valo, ex-FAITH NO MORE bassist Bill Gould and drummer Gas Lipstick and the AMORPHIS collective of guitarists Esa Holopainen and Tomi Koivusaari, bassist Niclas Etelävuori and keyboard player Santeri Kallio. Repaying the favour, Walker acted as studio guest for the AMORPHIS / H.I.M. side project TO SEPARATE THE FLESH FROM THE BONES debut album 'Utopia Sadistica'. Walker also contributed to the 'No End In Sight' album from THIS IS MENACE, a collaborative project of PITCHSHIFTER members bassist Mark Clayden and drummer Jason Bowld.

January 2006 found Walker joining infamous "Mexican" Death Metal band BRUJERIA for South American dates.

Flesh Ripping Sonic Torment, (1987). Genital Grinder / Regurgitation Of Giblets / Festerday / Limb From Limb / Rotten To The Gore / Excreted Alive / Malignant Defecation / Fermenting Innards / Necro-Cannibal Bloodfeast / Psychopathologist / Die In Pain / Pungent Excrutiation / Face Meltaaargh.

CARCASS (pic: Linda Aversa)

Symphonies Of Sickness, (1988). Reek Of Putrefacation / Slash Dementia / Embryonic Necropsy And Devourment / Cadaveric Incubator Of Endoparasites / Ruptured In Purulence.

REEK OF PUTREFACTION, Earache MOSH 6 (1988). Genital Grinder / Regurgitation Of Giblets / Maggot Colony / Pyosisified (Rotten To The Gore) / Carbonized Eye Sockets / Frenzied Detruncation / Vomited Anal Tract / Festerday / Fermenting Innards / Excreted Alive / Suppuration / Foeticide / Microwaved Uterogestation / Feast On Dismembered Carnage / Splattered Cavities / Psychopathologist / Burnt To A Crisp / Pungent Excruciation / Manifestation Of Verrucose Urethra / Oxidised Razor Masticator / Mucopurulence Excretor / Malignant Defecation.

The Peel Sessions EP, Strange Fruit SFPS 073 (1989). Crepitating Bowel Erosion / Slash Dementia / Cadaveric Incubator Of Endo Parasites / Reek Of Putrefaction.

Live St. George's Hall, Bradford 15.11.89, Distorted Harmony (1989) (Mexican release). Embryonic Necropsy And Devourment / Swarming Vulgar Mass Of Infected Virulency / Pungent Excruciation.

SYMPHONIES OF SICKNESS, Earache MOSH 18 (1989). Reek Of Putrefaction / Exhume To Consume / Excoriating Abdominal Emanation / Ruptured In Purulence / Empathalogical Necroticism / Embryonic Necropsy And Devourment / Swarming Vulgar Mass Of Infected Virulency / Cadaveric Incubator Of Endoparasites / Slash Dementia / Crepitating Bowel Erosion.

NECROTISM—DESCANTING THE INSALUBRIOUS, Earache MOSH 42 (1992). Inpropagation / Corporeal Jigsaw Quandary / Symposium Of Sickness / Pedigree Butchery / Incarnated Solvent Abuse / Carneous Cacophony / Lavaging Expectorate Of Lysergide Composition / Forensic Clinicism / The Sanguine Article.

Tools Of The Trade, Earache MOSH 49 (1992). Tools Of The Trade / Incarnated Solvent Abuse / Pysofied (Still Rotten To The Gore) / Hepatic Tissue Fermentation II.

Embodiment, Columbia CSK6274 (1993) (USA promotion release). Embodiment.

Buried Dreams, Earache (1993) (UK promotion release). Buried Dreams.

No Love Lost, Columbia CSK6004 (1993) (USA promotion release). No Love Lost.

Heartwork, Earache MOSH 108 (1994). Heartwork / This Is Your Life / Rot n' Roll.

Heartwork, Earache (1994). Heartwork.

HEARTWORK, Earache MOSH 97 (1994). Buried Dreams / Carnal Forge / No Love Lost / Heartwork / Embodiment / This Mortal Coil / Arbeit Macht Fleish / Blind Bleeding The Blind / Doctrinal Expletives / Death Certificate. Chart position: 54 UK.

SWANSONG, Earache MOSH 160 (1996). Keep On Rotting In The Free World / Tomorrow Belongs To Nobody / Black Star / Cross My Heart / Child's Play / Room 101 / Polarized / Generation Hexed / Firmhand / R**k The Vote / Don't Believe A Word / Go To Hell. Chart position: 58 UK.

CARDINAL SIN

GOTHENBURG, SWEDEN — *Dan Ola Persson (vocals), Magnus Andersson (guitar), John Zwetsloot (guitar), Alex Losbäck (bass), Jocke Göthberg (drums).*

Gothenburg's CARDINAL SIN, whose musicians openly state to be rooted in 80's Metal, boast ex-MARDUK members guitarist Magnus 'Devo' Andersson and drummer Jocke 'Grave' Göthberg. Guitarist John Zwetsloot forged the band upon his exit from DISSECTION. Following this line-up's recording of the 'Spiteful Intent' EP the rhythm section was completed in 1995 with the addition of bassist Alex Losbäck and a new vocalist was added in the form of Dan Ola Persson, the latter a veteran of ENTITY and THE ANCIENTS REBIRTH. CARDINAL SIN performed just one concert before folding.

Göthberg, also citing credits with GRIMORIUM and DIMENSION ZERO, created DARKIFIED. John Zwetsloot made his mark with DECAMERON, the original THE HAUNTED line-up and NIFELHEIM while Andersson went on to front OVERFLASH.

CARDINAL SIN was resurrected during 2003 comprising a member roster of Persson, Zwetsloot, the SARGATANAS REIGN duo of guitarist Kristoffer 'Ushatar' Andersson and bassist Niklas Samuelsson along with drummer Janne Pakkanen. Andersson also has affiliations with NEFANDUS, LAUG TIMOR, KRET and MINION whilst Samuelsson has SHADOWS OF GRIEF and ANTIPATHY credits. During May of 2004 Magnus 'Devo' Andersson had rejoined MARDUK as bass player. Kristoffer Andersson joined THE LEGION in June.

Spiteful Intent EP, Wrong Again WAR 010 CD (1996). Spiteful Intent / Probe With A Quest / The Cardinal Sin / Language Of Sorrow.

CARNAGE

STOCKHOLM, SWEDEN — *Matti Kärki (vocals), David Blomkvist (guitar), Mike Amott (guitar), Johnny Dordevic (bass), Fred Estby (drums).*

Despite only having performed three gigs, Stockholm's CARNAGE, who featured ex-DISMEMBER drummer Fred Estby and former CARBONISED and DISMEMBER singer Matti Kärki in their line-up, play a pivotal part in the historical lineage of Swedish Death Metal.

The band debuted with a live single in 1989, which was recorded by Estby, guitarist Mike Amott, bassist Johnny Dordevic and vocalist / guitarist Johan Axelsson. Although recorded in Stockholm it only saw a release in Mexico. A debut album 'Dark Recollections' emerged during 1990 as a split affair with CADAVER. Much of this material was re-recorded material from two earlier DISMEMBER demos, 1988's 'Dismembered' and 1989's 'Last Blasphemies'. Axelsson soon left to join JESUS EXERCIZE then FURBOWL and was replaced by another ex-DISMEMBER man, namely David Blomqvist.

In the wake of the band's split, Mike Amott later joined UK outfit CARCASS before forming SPIRITUAL BEGGARS and higher profile ARCH ENEMY. Dordevic joined ENTOMBED as lead vocalist. Estby, Blomqvist and Kärki reformed DISMEMBER. The drummer also carved himself out a considerable reputation on the production front.

The 'Dark Recollections' album would see a re-issue through Earache Records in 2000 with bonus demo tracks and different artwork.

The Day Man Lost..., Carnage (1989) (Cassette demo). Crime Against Humanity / Aftermath / The Day Man Lost....

Infestation Of Evil, Carnage (1989) (Cassette demo). Torn Apart / Infestation Of Evil.

Torn Apart (Live), Distorted Harmony DH003 (1989) (Mexican 7" vinyl single). Torn Apart (Live) / Crime Against Humanity (Live) / The Day Man Lost (Live) / Infestation Of Evil (Live).

DARK RECOLLECTIONS, Necrosis NECRO3 (1990). Dark Recollections / Torn Apart / Blasphemies Of The Flesh / Infestation Of Evil / Gentle Exhuming / Deranged From Blood / Malignant Epitaph / Self Dissection / Death Evocation / Outro.

CARNAL FORGE

SALA, SWEDEN — *Jens C. Mortensen (vocals), Johan Magnusson (guitar), Jari Kuusisto (guitar), Petri Kuusisto (bass), Stefan Westerberg (drums).*

The founding line-up of Sala Thrashers CARNAL FORGE comprised DELLAMORTE man Jonas Kjellgren, drummer Stefan Westerberg of IN THY DREAMS and STEEL ATTACK personnel guitarist Jari Kuusisto and bassist Dennis Vestman. Following the debut album 'Who's Gonna Burn' Vestman departed to be replaced by another IN THY DREAMS man Petri Kuusisto. Vocalist Jonas Kjellgren was temporary guitarist with CENTINEX between 1999 and September 2000.

In 2001 guitarist Johan Magnusson made his exit prompting bassist Petri Kuusisto to switch over to guitars whilst former SLAPDASH and ROSICRUCIAN man Lars Lindén assumed bass duty. Lindén already had a CARNAL FORGE connection being responsible for the band's website as well as providing artwork for second album 'Firedemon'

A fresh CARNAL FORGE album 'Please Die!' would be cut during the summer of 2001.The band would land a valuable European tour on a strong package billing with NILE, THE HAUNTED and THE FORSAKEN. Drummer Stefan Westerberg stepped in as a temporary replacement in the ranks of CENTINEX for their winter European dates in 2002.

In October Guitarist Jonas Kjellgren and drummer Stefan Westerberg along with ex-S.I.B. and TURABUS frontman Mikael Danielsson allied themselves in a new Progressive Doom Metal venture WORLD BELOW, bowing in with a demo 'Sacrifices To The Moon'. The following year yet another CARNAL FORGE side project emerged as Westerberg and guitarist Petri Kuusisto founded ASPERITY working alongside vocalist/bassist Peter Kronberg and guitarist Johan Jahlonen for the album 'The Final Demand'. Kuusisto would also act as session guest on the 2004 debut album from VICIOUS 'Vile, Vicious & Victorious'.

CARNAL FORGE made a return in April of 2004 with the 'Aren't You Dead Yet' opus, released by Century Media in Europe and Soundholic in Japan. They also entered the DVD age with 'Destroy Live', featuring concert footage from a January 2004 Krakow, Poland show and 2003 New York and Tokyo dates. European dates for the Spring in alliance with MISERY INDEX were cancelled due to "economic difficulty as well as an unsolvable schedule". The band drafted LEECH, ex-REVOLVER and SLAPDASH man Jens C. Mortensen as their new singer in August. This new line-up would be inaugurated with September European dates partnering with PRO-PAIN and France's DISTURB.

Meantime, Jonas Kjellgren proved industrious throughout 2004, acting as producer for TORCHBEARER's album 'Yersinia Pestis' and forging a brand new melodic Death Metal combo, fronted by the INCAPACITY, UNMOORED, SOLAR DAWN and TORCHBEARER credited Christian Älvestam, entitled SCAR SYMMETRY for an album 'Symmetric In Design'. That same year Petri Kuusisto would be found as guitarist in another side act, SOULSKINNER.

In January 2007 CARNAL FORGE signed a worldwide deal with Candlelight Records.

WHO'S GONNA BURN, Wrong Again WAR 0006 (1998). Who's Gonna Burn / Sweet Bride / Twisted / Godzilla Is Coming Thru' / Other Side / Part Animal—Part Machine / Born Too Late / Evilizer / Maggotman / Confuzzed.

CARNAL FORGE

FIREDEMON, Century Media 77312-2 (2000). Too Much Hell Ain't Enough For Me / Covered With Fire (I'm Hell) / I Smell Like Death (Son Of A Bastard) / Chained / Defacer / Pull The Trigger / Uncontrollable / Firedemon / Cure Of Blasphemy / Headfucker / The Torture Will Never Stop / A Revel In Violence.

FIREDEMON, Century Media 8012-2 (2000) (USA release). Too Much Hell Ain't Enough For Me / Covered With Fire (I'm Hell) / I Smell Like Death (Son Of A Bastard) / Chained / Defacer / Pull The Trigger / Uncontrollable / Firedemon / Cure Of Blasphemy / Headfucker / The Torture Will Never Stop / A Revel In Violence.

PLEASE … DIE!, Century Media 77398-2 (2001). Butchered, Slaughtered, Strangled, Hanged / Hand Of Doom / Fuel For Fire / Totalitarian Torture / Everything Dies / Slaves / Welcome To Your Funeral / Please … Die! (Aren't You Dead Yet?) / Becoming Dust / No Resurrection / A World All Soaked In Blood / A Higher Level of Pain.

THE MORE YOU SUFFER …, Soundholic TKCS-85056 (2003) (Japanese release). H.B.F. Suicide / Deathblow / Ripped & Torn / Destroy Life / Cursed / Divine Killing Breed Machine / Deep Rivers Of Blood / Breaking Boundaries / Into Oblivion / My Bloody Rampage / Baptized In Fire / Let Me Bleed / Hits You Like A Hammer / Bullet Proof Godmaterial.

THE MORE YOU SUFFER …, Century Media 74982-2 (2003) (European release). H.B.F. Suicide / Deathblow / Ripped & Torn / Destroy Life / Cursed / Divine Killing Breed Machine / Deep Rivers Of Blood / Breaking Boundaries / Into Oblivion / My Bloody Rampage / Baptized In Fire / Let Me Bleed.

Deathblow, Century Media (2003) (Promotion CD single). Deathblow.

THE MORE YOU SUFFER …, Century Media 8198-2 (2003) (USA release). H.B.F. Suicide / Deathblow / Ripped & Torn / Destroy Life / Cursed / Divine Killing Breed Machine / Deep Rivers Of Blood / Breaking Boundaries / Into Oblivion / My Bloody Rampage / Baptized In Fire / Let Me Bleed.

AREN'T YOU DEAD YET?, Century Media 75982-2 (2004) (European release). Decades Of Despair / My Suicide / Burn Them Alive / Waiting For Sundown / Exploding Veins / Sacred Flames / Inhuman / The Final Hour / Totally Worthless / The Strength Of Misery.

AREN'T YOU DEAD YET?, Soundholic TKCS-85097 (2004) (Japanese release). Decades Of Despair / My Suicide / Burn Them Alive / Waiting For Sundown / Exploding Veins / Sacred Flames / Inhuman / The Final Hour / Totally Worthless / The Strength Of Misery / Ruler Of Your Blood.

AREN'T YOU DEAD YET?, Century Media 8298-2 (2004) (USA release). Decades Of Despair / My Suicide / Burn Them Alive / Waiting For Sundown / Exploding Veins / Sacred Flames / Inhuman / The Final Hour / Totally Worthless / The Strength Of Misery.

TESTIFY FOR MY VICTIMS, Candlelight (2007). Testify For My Victims / Burning Eden / Numb (The Dead) / Godsend Gods End / End Game / Questions Pertaining The Ownership Of My Mind / Freedom By Mutilation / Subhuman / No Longer Bleeding / Biological Waste Matter / Lost Legion / Ante Mori.

CARNAL GRIEF

ARBOGA, SWEDEN — *Per Jonas Carlsson (vocals), André Alvinzi (guitar), Johan Lindgren (guitar), Johan Olsen (bass), Aaron Henrik Brander (drums).*

CARNAL GRIEF was formulated in Arboga during 1997 by erstwhile POWER PIG members guitarist Johan Lindgren and bass player Johan Olsen. The band's debut product would be the 1997 demo tape 'Embraced By The Light, a track from which appeared on the 'From The Underground' from X-treme Records, followed by a further session 'Cradlesongs' a year later. During mid 1999 the band lost the services of guitarist Johan Larsson and Per Magnus Andersson filled the vacancy.

CARNAL GRIEF's 'Wastelands' 1999 demo included a cover version of W.A.S.P.'s 'I Wanna Be Somebody'. CARNAL GRIEF drummer Henrik Brander would also be an active member of Thrash Metal act MAUSOLEUM. CARNAL GRIEF returned in February 2004 with the 'Out Of Crippled Seeds' album through Trinity Records.

During 2005 CARNAL GRIEF announced a revised band formation counting singer Per Jonas Carlsson, guitarists André Alvinzi and Johan Lindgren, bass player Johan Olsen with Aaron Henrik Brander on drums. This unit cut sophomore album 'Nine Shades Of Pain'. CARNAL GRIEF contracted with GMR Music in June 2006 for the release of their second album.

That same year André Alvinzi co-forged COLDWORKER in 2006, an alliance with NECRONY and NASUM drummer Anders Jakobson, RUIN and CHAIN OF HATE guitarist Anders Bertilsson, PHOBOS singer Joel Fornbrandt plus Oskar Pålsson of RELENTLESS as bassist.

Embraced By The Light, Carnal Grief (1997) (Demo). Reflections Of The Past / The Hate That Dwells Within / Mythomania / Embraced By The Light.

Cradlesongs, Carnal Grief (1998) (Demo). Rapid Eye Fiction / Entangeled In Chaos / Twin Sister / Theatre Of The Flesh.

Wastelands, Carnal Grief (1999) (Unreleased demo). Selfclaimed King / Insanitary / Just Another R.P.G. / Lovesong / I Wanna Be Somebody.

OUT OF CRIPPLED SEEDS, Trinity TRHK-003 (2004). The New Era / Selfclaimed King / Insanitary / Entrapment Concealed / Just Another RPG / Entangeled In Chaos / Poem Of The Impossible / Theatre Of The Flesh / Rapid Eye Fiction / Twin Sister / Deadlands.

NINE SHADES OF PAIN, GMR Music GMRCD 90-02 (2006). Information Feed / Epitaph / Catatonic / Elsewhere / The Perpetual Grey / Chronolies / Tin Winged Angel / A Passion For Hate / Crown Of Might / Charts Of Temporal Diversity.

CARNIFIED

BRAZIL — *Serafim Vila (vocals), Ricardo Sanct (guitar), Rafael Pires (guitar), Ricardo Sobrinho (bass), Saulo Andrade (keyboards), Vicente Azevêdo (drums).*

Salvador based Death Metal unit constructed in 1997 with an opening membership of vocalist Serafim ("Mifares") Villa, guitarists Rafael ("Liaphar") Pires "Liaphar" and Ricardo ("Khir") Carvalho, bass player Ricardo ("Odrack") Sobrinho, keyboard player Saulo ("Oluas") Andrade with Vicente ("Etneciv") Azevêdo on the drums. The band donated a track to the compilation album 'The Winds Of A New Millennium II' prior to cutting successive demo tapes 'Carnified' and 'O Primeiro Elo'.

CARNIFIED guitarist Thony D'Assys would join MYSTIFIER during 1998. Two further CARNIFIED guitarists, the MALEFACTOR and HELL'S MESSENGERS credited José Felipe and Marcos Franco founded FROZEN in 1998. Ricardo Sanct teamed up with MALEFACTOR in 2001.

WHERE THE GODS BLEED, Maniac (2001). On The Komenom's Way / Black Legacy / By The Eyes Of The Guardian / Sini's Revenge / Symphony For Sohram / The Black Moon Of Ol-Huas / The Cry Of A Witch / Impaled Knights From The Third Moon.

CARRION CARNAGE

LINKÖPING, SWEDEN — *Daniel Linder (vocals / guitar), Stefan Jörbo (guitar), Cyrus Djahedi (bass), Jakob Selbing (drums).*

Linköping Death Metal band CARRION CARNAGE was manifested during 2001 by guitarist Daniel Linder in union initially with Ulf Ståhl and Johan Dyyk. Linder also has association with SVARTUS KRÅKUS SATANICUS. This trio soon fractured without recording, the latter going on to WELTSCHMERZ and EYES OF ICE. In 2002 Stefan Jörbo of CHROME enrolled on guitar and this duo entered La Bomba Studios to craft the demo 'Evil'. Upon completion of these sessions Linder switched instruments to take command of the drums.

In 2003 Janne Hyyttiä was taken on to cover guitar and bass but would exit before the year was out. Back to a duo once again, the March 2003 album 'Mass Murder Rampage' featured a rendition of SIX FEET UNDER's 'No Warning Shot'. As the year closed ex-PURGAMENTUM man Jakob Selbing was inducted on drums for CARRION CARNAGE's inaugural live performance.

In side activity, CARRION CARNAGE members, guitarist Johan Hertil, bass player Pelle Djahedi and drummer Daniel Linder, forged the extracurricular project SNIPPA (Swedish for 'Cunt') in 2003 working with vocalist Magnus "Strigge" Strigner. This venture evolved into the less brazen ZNIPPA before taking on the TOTAL INCINERATION tag for a 2003 demo entitled 'Perverse Suffering'.

CARRION CARNAGE's March 2004 album 'Awaiting Salvation Of Death' included a cover versions of CANNIBAL CORPSE's 'Hammer Smashed Face' and NILE's 'Ruins'

MASS MURDER RAMPAGE, Carrion Carnage (2003). I Crave / Die By The Knife / No Warning Shot / Fear Of Dying / Revenge Of The Zombie / Evil (Re-recorded) / Murder Mankind.

Evil, Carrion Carnage (2003) (Demo). Evil / Evil (Video).

AWAITING SALVATION OF DEATH, Carrion Carnage (2004). Blood Anthem (Intro) / Closer To Extinction / Hideous Disfigurement / Destined To Suffer / The Eye Of Horus / Tortured Souls / Awaiting Salvation Of Death / Hammer Smashed Face / Ruins.

Oppressed By Fear, Carrion Carnage (2004) (Demo). Intro / Oppressed By Fear.

CARTILAGE

VAASA, FINLAND — *Mikki Salo (vocals), Karri Suoraniemi (vocals / guitar), Mikko Hannuksela (guitar), Harri Huhtala (bass), Kai Hahto (drums).*

Vaasa Death Metal combo CARTILAGE debuted in 1991 with the tape 'In Godly Flesh' before releasing a split album 'The Fragile Concept Of Affection' with Sweden's ALTAR through Drowned Productions in 1992. The erstwhile CARTILAGE collective of guitarist Mikko Hannuksela, bassist Harri Huhtalla and drummer Kai Hahto would found VOMITUTITION. Hahto later added ROTTEN SOUND and ENOCHIAN CRESCENT to his list of credits, going by the pseudonym of Caer Hallam Generis in the latter act. Meantime guitarist Karri Suoraniemi (re-billed as W.G. Victor) and singer Mikki Salo founded WINGS, issuing the EP 'Thorns On Thy Oaken Throne'. Suoraniemi too would later re-emerge in ENOCHIAN CRESCENT whilst Salo busied himself with his own label Woodcut Records.

In Godly Flesh, Cartilage (1991) (Demo). Intro / Carnival Of Souls / The Altar / To Your Scattered Bodies Go / Infernal Paradise ... The Journey.

THE FRAGILE CONCEPT OF AFFECTION, Drowned Productions DC013 (1992) (Split CD release with ALTAR). The Underworld / Afterlife Sorrow (Infernal Paradise II) / Why Do I Watch The Dawn? / Consanguine To Understanding / Blessing In Depths / Intro—The Altar / Ether Depression.

THE FRAGILE CONCEPT OF AFFECTION, Hard Vinyl (1992) (Split vinyl album with ALTAR). The Underworld / Afterlife Sorrow (Infernal Paradise II) / Why Do I Watch The Dawn? / Consanguine To Understanding / Blessing In Depths.

CARVE

SWEDEN — *Rogga Johansson (vocals / guitar), Emil Koveroth (guitar), Oskar Nilsson (bass), Matthias Fiebig.*

Founded in 2000, CARVE comprises members of Sweden's extreme Death Metal elite with a line-up of former PAGANIZER members vocalist / guitarist Rogga Johansson and drummer Matthias Fiebig alongside PORTAL guitarist Emil Koveroth and OBSCURITY bass player Oskar Nilsson. Johansson also has a tradition with DEAD SUN, DERANGED and, as a drummer, with Black Metal band BLODSRIT. CARVE signed to the Brazilian Black Hole Productions label for their 2002 opus 'Stillborn Revelations'.

Johansson would be a prominent guest artist on the EDGE OF SANITY 'Crimson II' album. In 2004 he founded RIBSPREADER with erstwhile PAGANIZER man Andreas Carlsson on guitar and the esteemed DAN SWANÖ on drums and lead guitars.

Hunters Rise From Turmoil, Carve (2001) (Demo). Imothep / Burn The Dead / Creatures With Wings / Circle Of Damnation / Operation Re-Crucifixion / Hunters Rise From Turmoil.

STILLBORN REVELATIONS, Black Hole Productions BHP002 (2002). Darker Skies / Millennium / As Wolves Are Fed / Flatline / Imhotep / Burn The Dead / Creatures With Wings / Circle Of Damnation / Operation Re-Crucifixion / Hunters Rise From Turmoil / Stillborn Revelations.

Carve, Carve (2002) (Demo). Promoting Total Death / Brutal Way To Die / Only Ashes Remain.

REVEL IN HUMAN FILTH, Black Hole Productions BHP010 (2004). Storms Across A Dead Planet / Hatred Unbound / Soulrape Unleashed / Dim View To Afterlife / Amongst The Ruins / Humanity Delete / Fall From Disgrace / Evangelicum (Revel In Human Filth).

CASKETGARDEN

MOSONMAGYARÓVÁR, HUNGARY — *István Cseh (vocals), Balázs Tóth (guitar), Péter Musitz (guitar), Gábor Őri (bass), Attila Cseh (drums).*

Mosonmagyaróvár Melodic Death Metal group CASKETGARDEN was assembled as a trio of guitarists Péter Musitz and Balázs Tóth with drummer Attila Cseh during 1998. Vocalist István Cseh enrolled the following year for recording of two demos, 1999's 'An Ever Rounding Circle' and '... Of Grief' in 2000. This latter session was widely distributed across Europe, scoring the band much favourable press. Rock Express Records combined the two sessions for a single cassette release, issuing this version in Serbia, Slovenia, Croatia, Bosnia, Bulgaria and Romania.

CASKETGARDEN shed their old bassist in favour of Gábor Őri in 2001. In this incarnation the band cut 'The Non Existant' promo, duly securing a label deal with Czech concern Metal Age Productions. The group stepped up its live campaign, traversing Serbia, Austria, Switzerland and Italy supporting the likes of NIGHTWISH, ANTHRAX, PUNGENT STENCH, DEW SCENTED and CHILDREN OF BODOM. The album 'This Corroded Soul Of Mine', recorded at Studio Denevér, arrived in September of 2003. CASKETGARDEN united with AGREGATOR, TESTIMONY and BLOOD RAINBOW for an Autumn tour to coincide with this release.

The Non-Existent, Casketgarden (2002) (Demo). Non-Existent / The Day When Silence Died / 7th Scar.

THIS CORRODED SOUL OF MINE, Metal Age Productions (2003). Human Corrosive Disease / I Witness / Grief 100% / Song Of Tears / The Day When Silence Die / Immortality Inc. / Non-Existent / 7th Scar / Widow Mother Earth / Across The Vast Oceans Of Time.

OPEN THE CASKET, ENTER THE GARDEN, Metal Age Productions MAP 059 (2006). The First Handful Of Soil (Intro) / Open The Casket / Spirit Unseen, Body Unknown / Why The Vultures Cry / One More Lie / A Grief History / Poisonvein 1010011010 / To Relive My Carnage / Alone As God / Enter The Garden.

CASTRUM

UKRAINE — *Georgius (vocals), Cornelius (guitar / bass / keyboards), Werkoff (drums).*

CASTRUM, based in Uzhgorod in the Ukraine, are fronted by Hungarian vocalist Georgius (real name George Kudla). The band was founded in 1994 by guitarist / bassist Cornelius (real name Kornel Kontros), Georgius and drummer Lancelot. CASTRUM issued no less than three demo tapes in 1996 namely 'Burial Of Affection', 'Flames By Impiety' and 'Pleasure In The Deeds Of Horror'. After these recordings Lancelot was superseded by Werkoff. All three members also operated in CHAMOS.

Werkoff was to depart having his position filled by Doni of SOULREST. Another change would see Sharapoff coming in on bass guitar. The Ukrainian Metal Force label would issue a compilation of early CASTRUM material as 'The Leading Spirit Of Medieval Tortures' cassette album. Yet another line up ruction witnessed Sharapoff being supplanted by new four stringer Roma.

CASTRUM would then sign to Canadian label Bloodbucket Productions for their debut CD release 'Hatenourisher'. Metal Force would release the album in tape format.

THE LEADING SPIRIT OF MEDIEVAL TORTURES, Metal Force MF002 (1999). Burial Of The Affection (Intro) / Book Of Malediction / Brand / Undying Hatred (Outro) / Tears Of Eternal Expiation (Intro) / Gilles De Rais (Le Bon Sire) / Calvary Of Grandier / Unprecedented Torture / Book Of Malediction / Brand / Painful Sighs In Castrum / Night Of Saint Bartholomew / Source Of Hate / Rapid Death.

HATENOURISHER, Bloodbucket Productions BPCD1304 (2001). Hatenourisher / Painful Sighs In Castrum / Book Of Malediction / Brand / Night Of Saint Bartholomew / Unprecedented Torture / Source Of Hate / Rapid Death.

MYSTERIOUS YET UNWEARIED, Bloodbucket Productions BP 1307 (2003). The Gate Of The Universal Mystery / The Undiscovered Dimension / Sinister Omens / Suffocating Thugs / Unrestrained Power / Desert Of Darkness / The Art Of Homicide / Invisible Force Of Fear / The Essence Of The Past Still Haunts Us / Dark Paths To The Ancient Thrones.

CATAFALC

SELJA, ESTONIA — *Eero Soomere (vocals), Mihkel Muru (guitar), Ando Enns (guitar), Raino Suurna (bass), Eero Mitt (drums).*

CATAFALC is a brutal Death Metal band hailing from the remote Selja settlement in Pärnu County, launched by vocalist Eero Soomere, guitarist Ando Enns and drummer Eero Mitt during 1999. In May of 2001 the trio entered W-House Studios to record the single demo track 'Impotent Scene'. Jan Talts enrolled as bassist for the band's inaugural gig, held on 26th October at the Bremen Bar in Tallinn. CATAFALC's third gig, at the Nõmme Kultuurimaja venue in January 2002, would be captured on the recording 'Hard Rock Club Live 19.01.2002'.

The band switched bassist over to Jogane Munno (a.k.a. 'Uziel' of IGNORABIMUS). Toward the close of 2003 the group utilised MusicWorks Studios, working with Arne Holm to craft the album 'Pain Performance'. Second guitarist Mihkel Muru was inducted upon completion of these sessions.

Hard Rock Club Live 19. 01. 02, (2002). Nr. One / Small World / Masturbate With Gun / Impotent Scene / Even Evil Can Cry / Blessed With Pain / Impotent Scene.

PAIN PERFORMANCE, Catafalc (2004). Masturbate With Gun / Small World / Progressive Surgery / Blessed With Pain / Death In Deathrow / I Come, Blood On My Hands / Even Evil Can Cry / Broken Bone / Impotent Scene.

CATAMENIA

OULU, FINLAND — *Olli-Jukka Mustonen (vocals), Riku Hopeakoski (guitar), Ari Nissilä (guitar), Toni Kansanoja (bass), Veikko Jumisko (drums).*

A Black/Death Metal sextet from Oulu, founded during 1995 by guitarist Riku Hopeakoski and singer Mika Tönning, the former also active with UNWRAP. The group took on the title CATAMENIA ("Menstration flow") simply for the sound of the word, unaware of its meaning. Opening demos included a three song 1995 session and follow up 'Winds' in 1996. The group signed with Germany's Massacre Records and set about recording their debut in September 1997. CATAMENIA opened their commercial account in January 1998 with the release of the debut album, 'Halls Of Frozen North', produced by Gerhard Magin at Commusication Studios in Beindersheim, Germany. The band at this juncture comprised singer Mika Tönning, guitarists Riku Hopeakoski and Sampo Ukkola, bass player Timo Lehtinen, the DOLORIAN credited keyboard player Heidi Riihinen with Toni Tervo on the drums.

Following the issue of the Tomas Skogsberg produced January 1999 album 'Morning Crimson', cut at Sunlight studios in Stockholm and which would see ATROCITY vocalist Alex Krull lending his talents in the studio on backing vocals, CATAMENIA underwent some upheaval with the departure of both guitarist Sampo Ukkola and drummer Toni Tervo. Replacements would be found in the form of Ari 'WarTechs' Nissilä on guitar, a member of UNWRAP, and occupying the drum stool, none other than Sir Luttinen of IMPALED NAZARENE and LEGENDA.

The band got back to business with a third album for Massacre, issued in August 2000 and entitled 'Eternal Winter's Prophecy', recorded at Tico-Tico Studios with producer Ahti Kortelainen. In September 2001 yet more ructions assailed the line-up as Sir Luttinen and keyboard player Heidi Riihinen decamped. New man on the drums would turn out to be Janne Kusmin, also a member of WRATHAGE, KALMAH and SOULHAMMER. Newly installed on keyboards would be Tero Nevala, a scene veteran of BLODSOFFER, DEAD MAN'S GRIP, DOROTHA, as 'Syvämetsän Saatana', NATIONAL NAPALM SYNDICATE and WRATHAGE.

CATAMENIA crafted the 'Eskhata' album at SoundMix Studios with producer Mika Pohjola. Upon completion of this record, which arrived in stores during April 2002, the band renewed its contract to Massacre Records for a further three albums, commencing with February 2003's 'ChaosBorn', laid down at Neo Studio in Oulu with Kari Vähäkuopus and Immu Ilmarinen manning the production desk. Installed on drums for these sessions was Veikko 'Moottorisaha' Jumisko with guest vocals courtesy of Kakke Vähäkuopus.

The band underwent a line-up change in December 2004, bassist Timo Lehtinen exiting in favour of Mikko Hepo-oja, another UNWRAP member. Shortly afterward Mika Tönning also decamped. CATAMENIA's 2005 album 'Winternight Tragedies', seeing vocals from Ole-Jukka Mustonen and WarTechs, included a cover version of SATYRICON's 'Fuel For Hatred'. Mustonen's prior credentials included membership of DOROTHA, as 'Verisperma the Necrophile', and WRATHAGE. Female session vocals came courtesy of Nevala's girlfriend Heidi Sainio. Yet another change then marked the introduction of the BURNING POINT and BLACK SWAN credited Toni Kansanoja on bass.

CATAMENIA returned in August 2006 with 'Location: COLD'. This album, closing with a cover version of W.A.S.P.'s ' I Wanna Be Somebody', was recorded at Mastervox Studios and produced by Vähäkuopus and Immu Ilmarinen once again. The group roster changed in the studio as Olli-Jukka Mustonen was forced to stand down due to throat problems. In his stead the group utilised Antti Haapsamo from MORS SUBITA, CATALEPTIC and SEMENTII for much of the vocal work. Tero Nevala decamped, informing his colleagues of his decision at the train station in St. Petersburg in the midst of Russian dates.

That November Polish label Metal Mind Productions issued a live DVD, 'Bringing The Cold To Poland'. February 2007 witnessed European dates aligned with ADORNED BROOD and BLACK UNICORN, backed by a promotional video for the track 'Location: COLD'.

Demo '95, Catamenia (1995) (Demo). Legacy / Child Of Sunsets / Pimeä Yö.
Winds, Catamenia (1996) (Demo). Land Of The Autumn Winds / Awake In Darkness / Into Infernal / The River Winds.
Winds, Catamenia (1996) (Demo). Land Of The Autumn Winds / Awake In Darkness / Into Infernal / The River Winds.
HALLS OF FROZEN NORTH, Massacre MAS CD0153 (1998). Dreams Of Winterland / Into Infernal / Freezing Winds Of North / Enchanting Woods / Halls Of Frozen North / Forest Enthroned / Awake In Dark / Song Of The Nightbird / Icy Tears Of Eternity / Burning Aura / Child Of Sunset / Land Of The Autumn Winds / Pimeä Yö / Outro.
Catamenia, Massacre (1999) (Shaped CD single). Winternacht / Talviyön Varjot / Dreams Of Winterland / Aurora Borealis / Into Infernal / Freezing Winds Of North.
Massacre Classix Shape Edition, Massacre MAS SH0202 (1999) (Shaped picture disc). Winternacht / Talviyön Varjot / Dreams Of Winterland / Aurora Borealis / Into Infernal / Freezing Winds Of North.
MORNING CRIMSON, Massacre MAS CD0190 (1999). Aurora Borealis / Talviyön Varjot / . . . And Winter Descends / In Blood They Lay / Beauty Embraced By The Night / Passing Moment Of Twilight Time / Cast The Stars Beyond / Morning Crimson / The Forests Of Tomorrow / Towards The Winds Of Winter (Shores Of Sendar) / When The Frost Took The Lakes / Shadeweaver's Season / Winternacht.
ETERNAL WINTER'S PROPHECY, Massacre MAS CD0258 (2000). Gates Of Anubis / Soror Mystica / Blackmansions / Kingdom Of Legions / Half Moons, Half Centuries / Forever Night / Dawn Of The Chosen World / Eternal Winter's Prophecy / In The Void / The Darkening Sun / In The Capricorn's Cradle.
ESKHATA, Massacre MAS CD0317 (2002). Storm / Rain Of Blood / Flames / Vortex / Coexistence Circle / Landscape / Karma / Astral Tears / Time In My Hands / Beyond The Starlight / Eskhata.
CHAOS BORN, Massacre MAS CD0376 (2003). Kuolon Tanssi / Calm Before The Storm / The Fallen Angel Pt. I / The Fear's Shadow / Mirrorized Thoughts / Lost In Bitterness / The Era / The Fallen Angel Pt. II / One With Sorrow / Hollow Out—Chaos Born.
WINTERNIGHT TRAGEDIES, Massacre MAS CD0450 (2005). The Heart Of Darkness / Verikansa / Strength And Honor / The Crystal Stream / Kaamos Warrior / My Blood Stained Path / Perintö Pohjolan / Iced Over / The Ancient / Fuel For Hatred.
LOCATION: COLD, Massacre MAS CD0524 (2006). Tribe Of Eternity / Gallery Of Fear / Coldbound / Tuhat Vuotta / Closed Gates Of Hope / Zero Gravity / Location:COLD / The Day When The Sun Faded Away / Expect No Mercy / I Wanna Be Somebody.

CATARACT

SWITZERLAND — *Fedi (vocals), Simon (guitar), Greg (guitar), Kay Brem (bass), Ricki (drums).*

A brutal Hardcore edged, 'War Metal' act out of Switzerland, founded during 1998 by ex-MINE guitarist Simon and drummer Ricki. Adding second guitarist Greg of BLUE WATER BOY and CEASE, along with bassist Michi and ELISON vocalist Mosh CATARACT's line-up was completed that October. A whole string of releases including a demo, a 7" single, an EP on CD, compilation album appearances and a European support tour to GRADE led to recording of the debut full length album 'Golem'. The band had actually recorded 'Golem' under their own steam but the American Ferret Music label soon picked it up for CD release. The Lifeforce label issued a vinyl version for European consumption. Promotion in Europe included opening gigs for BROTHERS KEEPER.

In March 2001 CATARACT announced a new vocalist in erstwhile DARK DAY DUNGEON man Ferdi. North American dates had CATARACT touring the East Coast with the likes of POISON THE WELL, BANE, NORA and MOST PRECIOUS BLOOD among others and putting in a showing at the 'Hellfest' event. A limited edition green vinyl single 'Martyr's Melodies' was released by Life Recordings to coincide with these gigs. Several short bursts of touring in Europe included shows in the Czech Republic, France, Spain, Austria, Germany, Belgium, Holland and Switzerland. The band forged a road alliance with SIX FEET UNDER, DARK FUNERAL, DISBELIEF, DYING FETUS, WYKKED WYTCH and NILE for the 'No Mercy Festivals 2005' European tour beginning in early March. A short Euro tour in August saw the group partnered with AMON AMARTH and IMPIOUS.

As 2006 opened the band commenced recording a new album at Antfarm Studios in Denmark with producer Tue Madsen. CATARACT parted ways with bassist Michael Henggeler in June, pulling in TRIBES OF CAIN man Kay Brem as substitute. The band formed up the UK and European "Hell On Earth" tour in September and October. Joining them would be GOD FORBID, Germany's MAROON, HEAVEN SHALL BURN, FULL BLOWN CHAOS, PURIFIED IN BLOOD from Norway and A PERFECT MURDER. Live work in December across Europe was to see the band hooking up with SIX FEET UNDER, GOREFEST, DARZAMAT and KRISIUN for the 'X-Mass' festivals. However, the group then dropped off this tour.

CATARACT parted ways with guitarist Simon Fullemann in January 2007. DISPARAGED and NÄCHTLICH THRÄNET man Tom Kuzmic took over the vacancy the following month.

Cataract EP, Infinite (1998) (Limited edition. 400 copies).

War Anthems, Join The Teamplayer (1999) (Limited edition 2500 copies).

GOLEM, Ferret Music (2000). Loss Of A Smile / Where I Belong / I Regret / Two Seconds / Ruin And Rule / Blinded By Darkness / Within Four Walls / Coward / Source Of The Collapse (Part 1).

Martyr´s Melodies, Life Recordings LIFE025 (2001) (Green vinyl).

Martyr´s Melodies EP, Lifeforce LIFE 025 (2002). Martyr's Melodies / Red Clouds / Forsaken Cries / Someone Does / Final Expression.

GREAT DAYS OF VENGEANCE, Lifeforce 035/036 (2003). Devon / The Weapon / Rest / The Volcano Effect / Lost Compassion / Sinner From Birth / Great Days Of Vengeance / Save Their Aim / Forsaken Cries / Scars / The Dying.

WITH TRIUMPH COMES LOSS, Metal Blade (2004). Killing Tool / Nothing's Left / Vanished In The Dark / Skies Grew Black / As We Speak / Godevil / Fuel / Reborn From Fire / Saving Shelter / Hallow Horns / With Triumph Comes Loss.

KINGDOM, Metal Blade (2006). Kingdom's Rise / War Of Cultures / On This Graveyard / Denial Of Life / Tongues Spitting Hate / March With Your Battleforce / Sacrificed For The Wealth / Definition Of The Scared / Legions At The Gates / Unforgotten / For Their Sins.

CATASEXUAL URGE MOTIVATION

TOKYO, JAPAN — *Sadochist Ejaculata (vocals / guitar), Cyber EMF (drum programming).*

Extreme grinding act with an obvious murder fixation. Tokyo based CATASEXUAL URGE MOTIVATION was created in 1992 and involves vocalist / guitarist Sadochist Ejaculata (a.k.a. Tomoaki Kanai) and drum programmer Cyber MF. A principle figure is lyricist Sadochist Spermata (Yuzin Kanai), who also handles all the band's artwork. CATASEXUAL URGE MOTIVATION emerged with the September 1994 'Catharsis' demo tape following this effort with further cassettes 'Rape Trauma Syndrome' in 1995 and 'Bizarre Abnormality'. A 7" split single shared with SLOUGH on Extermination Records in 1995 featured a SLOUGH cover version, 'Fucked By A Priest'.

The group would be included on a 4 way split single 'Hungry Urinary Urn' alongside C.S.S.O., MALIGNANT TUMOUR and N.C.C. A shared tape 'What Do You Kill For' in 1996 witnessed an alliance with NEGLIGENT COLLATERAL COLLAPSE. The same year the band shared another tape with GOROPSY and issued a live session entitled 'Satsujin'. A further shared 7" release would witness an alliances with Poland's SQUASH BOWELS. This latter split EP, 'Necrophallus', included a cover version of IMPETIGO's 'Boneyard'.

The 1997 album included a cover version of IMPETIGO's 'Defiling The Grave'. CATASEXUAL URGE MOTIVATION would change their name to VAMPYRIC MOTIVES shortly after the release of the 2000 re-release of the 'Encyclopedia Of Serial Murders' album. The band reformed during 2002 in order to contribute new material to a Razorback Records compilation album 'Nekronicle'.

Catharsis, Catasexual Urge Motivation (1994) (Demo). Sonic Hate Spleen Rupture / Never Spend My Time In Wholesome / Vivid Stains Of Hematomania's Delirium / Hate From The Womb.

Rape Trauma Syndrome, Catasexual Urge Motivation (1995) (Demo). Sonic Hate Spleen Rupture / Hate From The Womb / Vivid Stains of Hematomania's Delirium / Never Spend My Time In Wholesome / To Kill, And Kill Again.

C.U.M. / Slough, Extermination (1995) (Split 7" single with SLOUGH). Intro (CATASEXUAL URGE MOTIVATION) / Bleeding For Spermqueen (CATASEXUAL URGE MOTIVATION) / Sexual Terrorist (CATASEXUAL URGE MOTIVATION) / Fucked By A Priest (CATASEXUAL URGE MOTIVATION) / Fucked By A Priest (SLOUGH) / Carving In Jimmy (SLOUGH) / Fist Fuck (SLOUGH).

Necrophallus EP, Extermination (1996) (Split EP with SQUASH BOWELS). I Am As Beautiful As I Have Killed / Mass Murder, The Only Way To Become God / Boneyard.

FANTASY WANTS VICTIM, (1996).

ENCYCLOPEDIA OF SERIAL MURDERS, Deliria (1997). Mutilation, Rape And Serial Murder As A Modern Metaphor / Supraliminal Psychosadistic Motivation / Bleeding For Spermqueen / Hate From The Womb / I Have A Good Knife For Penetration / Philosophical Diary Of A Habitual Murderer / Joy To The Kill ... Be My Victim / King Of The Degenerates In The End Of The Century / Multiple Parasexuality Disorder / Mass Murder, The Only Way To Become God / Homicidal Patterns: Disorganized- Organized / Murder Is Art Accepted By Many Artists / The Man Who Aimed At Maximum Murder To The Greatest Pleasure / Murder Is Better Than Birth / He Shot Her Down And Ate Her Flesh, And Then Said Excuse Me For Living But I Preferred To Be Eaten Rather Than To Eat / What Was The Spark That Touched Off A Murder / I Am As Beautiful As I Have Killed / I'll Confess Everything That I Ever Killed 5 People And The One Was A Little Girl / Defiling The Grave / Declaration Of A Serial Killer ... Mental Terrorism / Campaign For Legalized Murder / Vivid Stains In Hematomania's Delirium.

NEKRONIKLE, Razorback (2003). Vivid Stains Of Hematomania's Delirium '94 (Remastered) / Sonic Hate Spleen Rupture / Hate From The Womb / Vivid Stains Of Hematomania's Delirium / Never Spend My Time In Wholesome / To Kill, And Kill Again / I Am As Beautiful As I Have Killed / Mass Murder, The Only Way To Become God / Bleeding For Spermqueen / Sexual Terrorist / Fucked By A Priest Part 2 / Supraliminal Psychosadistic Motivation / Homicidal Patterns: Organized / Disorganized / Their Eyes Were Watching The Knife In My Hand / Philosophical Diary Of A Habitual Murderer / World Record 222 Mass Murder A Day / Boneyard / Addicted To Mutilating And Murdering Itself / Where There's Killing, There's My Way / Murder: It's A Proof Of One's Conscience And A Necessary Evil Most Necessarily / It's A Pure Fuckin' Hatred! Showcase Of Cruelty And Bloodshed / Rape And Slaughter Like An American Murderer / Campaign For Legalize Murder (New version) / The Legacy Of A Serial Killer Lives On Forever Due To Their Uncanny Ability To Capture The Interest Of The Worlds Spectators Through The Extreme Quality, Quantity, Method And Results Of Their Actions / After Beating Unconscious In A Deserted Street, I Bind Her Hands And Feet With Wire, Duct Tapes On Her Mouth And Places A Burlap Sack Over Her Head / Whore Is Beautiful Like A God, And God Is Voluptuous Like A Whore / Murderhatekillkillkill.

CATASTROPHIC

USA — CATASTROPHIC was the new Death Metal vehicle for former OBITUARY guitarist Trevor Peres. CATASTROPHIC debuted in 2001 with the unashamed retro-Death sounds of 'The Cleansing' album.

The band would figure as part of the gargantuan European 'No Mercy' touring festival package in March and April of 2002. Also on the billing would be VADER, IMMORTAL, DESTROYER 666, HYPOCRISY, DISBELIEF, MALEVOLENT CREATION and OBSCENITY. American support dates to the mighty MANOWAR were also projected.

Bassist Brian Hobbie helped launch PSYCHOMANTHIUM in early 2004, an "old-school Speed/Thrash metal" band featuring vocalist Martin Missy from the eighties cult German band PROTECTOR and latterly Swedish act RUINS OF TIME. Also featured would be the ARKHAM 13 pairing of guitarist Derek 'Derekonomicon' Schilling and drummer Ant Ichrist. The band signed to Poland's Still Dead Productions for a debut album 'Death Attack'.

The band's next road alliance, suitably dubbed 'European Decimation', took in April 2005 gigs throughout Italy, Portugal, the UK, Holland and Germany in partnership with INCANTATION, FUNERUS, JUNGLE ROT and HEXENHAMMER.

THE CLEANSING, Metal Blade CD 085-103202 (2001). Hate Trade / Balancing The Furies / Enemy / Lab Rats / Messiah Pacified / The Cleansing / Pain Factor / Jesters Of The Millennium / The Veil / Blood Maidens / You Must Bleed / Terraform.

CATATONIC SCHIZOPHRENIA

SOFIA, BULGARIA — *Catatonic (vocals / guitar), TheDarkLich (vocals), Z.Zdravsteen (guitar), Dex (keyboards).*

CATATONIC SCHIZOPHRENIA is a Sofia based Death Metal band dating to 1985. Initially the project operated as a solo venture for two 2004 demos, 'Kampong' (Malaysian for village) and the Tolkien inspired 'Hobbit's Needs', this session featuring such bizarre song titles as 'In The Forest Bush I Have a Bowel Movement' and 'Unstoppable Pickling Onions'. The album 'Tension' followed. The endeavour then expanded to incorporate guitarist Z. Zdravsteen for a single entitled 'Nine Heroes'. CATATONIC SCHIZOPHRENIA, back to a solo concern, then readied a further album, 'We Kill'.

The project then grew to a full band status for next session 'Crusader Kings', a line-up being credited as Catatonic on vocals and guitar, TheDarkLich on "Papal vocals / Communist vocals", Z.Zdravsteen on guitar, Dex on keyboards and Spacerunner "Narrator / Promoter". The 2005 album 'We Kill' included a cover version of RHAPSODY's 'Emerald Sword'. CATATONIC SCHIZOPHRENIA sense of humour was amply displayed on the September 2005 'Crusader Kings' album with closing track 'Dead Meat' being listed as a "Somalian bonus track".

TENSION, (2004). Thunder / Magic Of The Shaman / ShiTude / Siren's Call / Worst Song Part I / The Final Countdown / Death Of The Dragon (Burpumental) / Worst Song Part II / Speedorama / Memmingen / Tension.

Kampong, Catatonic Schizophrenia (2004). Imodiumadness / Splendidoramisimo / Howler / Balladesque Massacre / Buttend.

Hobbits' Needs, (2004). Hobbit / In The Forest Bush I Have a Bowel Movement / Arwen's Cry (Interlude) / The Oak Wood / Unstoppable Pickling Onions / Sauron's Last Laughter (Interlude) / Epic Endo.

Nine Heroes, (2005). Nine Heroes (ft.Drogo) / Kohyan / Extremely Silent / Z for Zpeed! (ft.Z. Zdravsteen) / ProgreZZing (ft.Z.Zdravsteen).

WE KILL, (2005). Call Of The North / Emerald Sword / The Green Warrior / The Kombat / Midtro / Imperial Rage / The Sword Bearer / Notpalc Alyal / Inoperable / The End ....

CRUSADER KINGS, (2005). Ab Aeterno / King Of Kings / Prelude To Madness / The Moonstruck Minstrel / Decision (Narration) / The Brethren Slaughter / Holy Crusade / Malicious Joy Of The Insane / The Dawn Of Defeat / Final Encounter / Dead Meat.

CATTLE DECAPITATION

SAN DIEGO, CA, USA — *Travis Ryan (vocals / guitar), Josh Elmore (guitar), Troy Oftedal (bass), Dave Astor (drums).*

San Diego Death Metal band, founded in 1996. Pushing a militant vegetarian message, backed up by suitably horrific graphics, CATTLE DECAPITATION quickly found prominence. Eschewing the standard fare of demons and monsters, the group has successfully employed the cow motif throughout much of its product, using this docile bovine supplier of meat quite uniquely as a figure of horror.

Drummer Dave Astor would be known for his work with Sci-Fi 'Horrorcore' act THE LOCUST, an act which featured former CATTLE DECAPITATION guitarist Gabe Serbian as drummer. As CATTLE DECAPITATION they bowed in with a 7" single 'Ten Torments Of The Damned' that same year. Only 4,000 singles were produced, the single's artwork, a cow awaiting execution from the decapitating blow of an axe, an understated portent of what was to come. However, shortly after their frontman suddenly decamped without warning. The group was brought back up to strength with the enrolment of erstwhile STRANGULATION drummer Travis Ryan, the CATTLE DECAPITATION duo having been impressed by Ryan's vocal performance on a session by his other act ANAL FLATULENCE. With Ryan's induction Astor and Serbian would switch roles, Serbian becoming the band's guitarist.

Under this incarnation the group released their debut 1999 album, 'Human Jerky', through the Reno, Nevada based Satan's Pimp label. Issued in 'urinary tract infection' coloured vinyl the first pressing of 1'000 sold out in it's first week. Establishing a precedent for album covers designed to shock, 'Human Jerky' was emblazoned with a decapitated cow against a background of pulped meat.

A follow up followed remarkably quickly as CATTLE DECAPITATION were keen to prove they were far from a one off and 'Hovomore', issued in 'cow' coloured vinyl, emerged on the Three One G imprint in April 2000. Three tracks from this outing would be re-cut with Spanish vocals for the 'iDecapitacion!' 7" green vinyl single released by Accident Prone Records. These same three songs would form part of the three way split EP, alongside TICWAR and Nebraska's ARMITRON, 'The Science Of Crisis' released by the Toyo label.

The band, adding Troy Oftedal on bass, would include a demo version of 'The Regurgitation Of Corpses' to a Metal Blade Records compilation 'Uncorrupted Steel', prompting a deal with Metal Blade for a 2002 album 'To Serve Man'. Again the band caused consternation with their choice of artwork, a human being, divided in the manner of butchers meat cuts, spilling his intestines onto a plate. After this session CATTLE DECAPITATION recruited guitar player Josh Elmore. CATTLE DECAPITATION would also include their rendition of the CARCASS track 'Burnt To A Crisp' to the Necropolis Records tribute compilation 'Requiems Of Revulsion'.

The Metal Blade debut would run into immediate controversy in Germany where distribution company SPV reportedly refused to handle the album due to the unnerving and disturbing artwork of Wes Benscoter. November 2002 shows found the band on the road in North America on a package billing with CANNIBAL CORPSE, HATE ETERNAL and MACABRE.

The group severed ties with Dave Astor in May of 2003, pulling in former CREATION IS CRUCIFIXION man Michael Laughlin as substitute. Laughlin's first task with the band was to lay down the track 'Cloacula: The Anthropophagic Copromantik' for the 'Uncorrupted Steel II' compilation. Meantime Scott Miller took time out from the CATTLE DECAPITATION schedule to work with Los Angeles based "Power-Noise-Industrial" Metal band PRO DEATH.

The band announced touring plans for the US in November of 2003, forming up a billing comprising HATE ETERNAL, DEICIDE and KRISIUN. Recording sessions for a new album billed as 'Humanure' were curtailed in January of 2004 after bassist Troy Oftedal broke his wrist. The Bill Metoyer produced 'Humanure' album immediately stoked controversy, being banned in Germany, with its gut wrenching sleeve artwork depicting a cow excreting human remains. However, before the close of August the band admitted defeat, claiming they had "received too many complaints that people are unable to find the album". The album was re-pressed with an inoffensive barren wasteland cover.

US shows in September saw the band forming up a four way package billing alongside DEICIDE, GOATWHORE and JUNGLE ROT. The band announced plans for a split release in collaboration with CANINUS for 2005 through Wartorn Records.

CATTLE DECAPITATION returned in the summer of 2006 with new studio album 'Karma.Bloody.Karma', again continuing the anti-meat trade theme with an album cover depicting a cow as the war goddess Kali. Produced by Billy Anderson, the album included guest appearances from Joey Karam of THE LOCUST and John Wiese of SUNN 0))) and BASTARD NOISE. Shortly after recording the band parted ways with Michael Laughlin, citing "personal reasons" and drafted ex-UNHOLY GHOST and ROYAL ANGUISH man J.R. Daniels. However, they were rejoined by Michael Laughlin for August shows in Los Angeles and San Diego. Subsequent live dates saw alliances with NECROPHAGIST and FROM A SECOND STORY WINDOW. US dates projected for September and October 2006, to see the band hooking up with KRISIUN, SIX FEET UNDER, DE-

CATTLE DECAPITATION

CAPITATED and ABYSMAL DAWN, were cancelled, the band claiming their fill-in drummer was not cut out for touring. Further shows saw touring unions with DAATH, GOATWHORE and LAIR OF THE MINOTAUR. New man behind the drum kit would be ex-DYING FETUS, MISERY INDEX, HATE ETERNAL and CHIMAIRA veteran Kevin Talley, who also performed double drum duties each night with DAATH. Meantime, former drummer J.R. Daniels joined the ranks of ANGEL CORPSE.

The group was rejoined by drummer Michael Laughlin in January 2007 then teamed up with MARDUK, SETHERIAL and MONSTROSITY for the "Chaos Metal Attack Mexico 2007" tour. European concerts, along with DYING FETUS, SKINLESS and WAR FROM A HARLOT'S MOUTH, witnessed shows across Germany, France, Italy, Austria, Belgium, Holland, Norway, Denmark Ireland and the UK in May. The band's next tour outing was to be the 'Summer Slaughter' trek across the USA throughout June and July, seeing NECROPHAGIST headlining on a mammoth package billing with DECAPITATED, CEPHALIC CARNAGE, BENEATH THE MASSACRE, THE FACELESS, AS BLOOD RUNS BLACK, ARSIS and ION DISSONANCE.

10 Torments Of The Damned, Humanure Atrocities (1996). Priest Of Ass / The Axe Will Fall / Mad Cow Conspiracy / Parasitic Infestation / Projectile Vomit / Flesheating Disease / Species Of Feces / Bodysnatcher / Christ On Crack / Nightcrawler.
HUMAN JERKY, Satan's Pimp PMP031 (1999). Cloned For Carrion / Parasitic Infestation (Extracted Pus, Mistaken For Yogurt, And Gargled) / Unclogged And Ready For Spewage / Gestation Of Smegma / Mute Rain / Flesh-Eating Disease (Flu-Like Symptoms Of E-Coli With Complete Digestive Shutdown) / The Decapitation Of Cattle / Constipation Camp / Intro To Carnage / Cream Of The Crop / Mad Cow Conspiracy (Bloated Bovine-Home To Flies And Anthrax Spores) / Veal And The Cult Of Torture / Stench From The Dumpster / Body Snatcher (Viscrea Intact-Ripe For Devourment) / Roadkill Removal Technician / Bovine, Swine, And Human-Rinds / Bludgeoned, Beaten, And Barbequed / Colon-Blo.
¡Decapitacion! EP, Accident Prone AP009 (2000) (Green marble vinyl). Tripas De Pepe / Vino De Lo Sanguifero / Queso De Cabeza.
HOVOMORE, Three One G 31G14 (2000). Mauled / Joined At The Ass / Open Human Head Experiments With Bleach Lacquer And Epoxy / Diarrhea Of The Mouth / Headcheese / Colostomy Jigsaw Puzzle / Pepe's Trepes / Release The Gimp / The Roadside Dead (Detrunked Stumpification Through Roadcrash) / Carnal Fecophelia Due To Prolonged Exposure To Methane / Icepick Gag Reflex / Bathing In A Grease Disposal Unit / Molested/Digested / Win Of The Sanguine / Ride 'Em Cowboy / Human Jerky And The Active Cultures.
The Science Of Crisis EP, Toyo 4 (2000) (Split EP with TICWAR and ARMITRON). Tripas De Pepe / Vino De Lo Sanguifero / Queso De Cabeza.
TO SERVE MAN, Metal Blade 14405-2 (2002). Testicular Manslaughter / I Eat Your Skin / Writhe In Putrescence / Land Of The Severed Meatus / The Regurgitation Of Corpses / Everyone Deserves To Die / To Serve Man / Colonic Villus Biopsy Performed On The Gastro-intestinally Incapable / Pedeadstrians / Long-pig Chef And The Hairless Goat / Hypogastric Combustion By C-4 Plastique / Deadmeal / Chunk Blower.
HUMANURE, Metal Blade 14450-2 (2004). Scatology Domine (Intro) / Humanure / Reduced To Paste / Bukkake Tsunami / Cloacula: The Anthropophagic Copromantik / Chummified / Applied Human Defragmentation / The Earthling / Polyps / Lips & Assholes / Men Before Swine (Outro).
HUMANURE, Metal Blade MBCY-1003 (2005) (Japanese release). Scatology Domine (Intro) / Humanure / Reduced To Paste / Bukkake Tsunami / Cloacula: The Anthropophagic Copromantik / Chummified / Applied Human Defragmentation / The Earthling / Polyps / Lips & Assholes / Men Before Swine (Outro) / I Eat Your Skin (Live) / Reduced To Paste (Live).
War Torn Presents Cattle Decapitation & Caninus, War Torn WTR004 (2005) (Split 7" EP with CANINUS). Birth. Cancer. Death / No Future / Chili Dispenser / The Recapitation Of Cattle / Thrombosis All-In / Turn On The Masters.
KARMA.BLOODY.KARMA, Metal Blade 14575-2 (2006). Intro / Unintelligent Design / Success Is ... (Hanging By The Neck) / One Thousand Times Decapitation / The Carcass Derrick / Total Gore / Bereavement / Suspended In Coprolite / Alone At The Landfill / Karma.Bloody.Karma / The New Dawn / Of Human Pride & Flatulence.

CAUSEMOS

ESPOO, FINLAND — *Simo Autio (guitar), Antti Lauri (guitar), Pekka Johansson (bass), Rainer Tuomikanto (drums).*

CAUSEMOS is an Espoo based melodic Death Metal unit dating as far back as 1989, with members trading under the stage names Spoonboy, Mike Hell and S. Autio. The first incarnation of the band had been initiated by school friend guitarists Simo Autio and Mikael Vedenpää, working with bassist Jürgen Schreiber and drummer Jukka Vesamaa. In 1993 Schreiber was ousted as the band took on the title of BIOPSY. Introducing vocalist / bassist Petri Ervonmaa in 1994 the band adopted a revised title of CARNAGE. The following year Rainer Tuomikanto took command of the drums. Shortly afterward, CARNAGE became INTHRAL.

A demo, 'Reborn', was issued and concert work undertaken in Espoo. Between 1997 and 1999 INTHRAL recorded a brace of demos at Brutal Art Sound Lab studios with Jani Holopainen on vocals. Neither of these were released due to the band's dissatisfaction with the quality. Holopainen took his leave in 1999. It would not be until the autumn of 2000 that the group shifted shape to move Simo Autio over to lead vocals. Re-branded CAUSEMOS, they also expanded further with the induction of keyboard player Risto Kokkonen.

A demo surfaced in March 2001 but Spoonboy (Ervonmaa) decamped in mid 2003. Kokkonen decamped in 2004. Rebuilding the band, Pekka Johansson took on bass guitar duties in 2005 and, in 2006, Vedenpää was replaced by Antti Lauri. CAUSEMOS released the September 2006 demo 'Severed Senses Combined'. A release party concert was held at Kantis restaurant in Helsinki.

Demo '01, Causemos (2001) (Demo). Regressive Initiation (Prologue) / Drowning In Tears / Darklit Skies / Delusion / Less Than Nothingness / Celestial Conclusion (Epilogue).
Severed Senses Combined, Causemos (2006) (Demo). With The Pain / Silent / Arboretum.

CAUTERIZED

DENMARK / SOUTH AFRICA — *Kim M. Jensen (vocals), Shukri Adams (guitar / bass), Antti Kivilahti (drum programming).*

A truly international politically minded Grindcore act founded in Cape Town, South Africa during 1998 by guitarist Shukri Adams, a veteran of acts such as DEADLOCK and DRAKENKULUS. Initially CAUTERIZED was established as an adjunct to Adams endeavours with Black Metal band SOLOMON'S KEY. Andrew Glover of SOLOMON'S KEY occupied the lead vocal position for the 1998 demo recording 'Serratura'. Shortly after recording Adams relocated to England, joining OVERLORD as guitarist but maintaining his interest in CAUTERIZED. The band's debut, 'Tolerance Through Abhorrence' found Glover replaced at the microphone by OVERLORD man Richard Austin. Adams then moved to Denmark, drafting Finnish drum programmer Antti Kivilahti in 1999.

During 2000 CAUTERIZED added Kim M. Jensen, previously a member of NOAIDA and SATURATE, as their new singer. The March 2001 album 'Retribute' comprised entirely of cover versions. Featured were AUTOPSY's 'Stillborn' and 'Fuckdog', PUNGENT STENCH's 'Embalmed In Sulphuric Acid' BRUTAL TRUTH's 'Wilt', DEATH's 'Zombie Ritual', DESTRUCTION's 'Curse The Gods', GRAVE's 'Into The Grave' and MASSACRE's 'Corpsegrinder'. The album was recorded in both South Africa and Denmark. A further 2001 album, confusingly entitled 'Retribution', featured all original tracks with the exception of a homage to GROINCHURN with a rendition of 'What Goes Around'.

Both Adams and Jensen also operate as members of Hardcore act LITANY. Adams pursues a variety of other projects too including Black Metal bands THY SOUL DEVOURED and SOLOMON'S KEY. Kivilahti busies himself with SCUMFUSION and QUETZALCOATL. CAUTERIZED cut a split offering shared with DECAY in 2003.

TOLERANCE THROUGH ABHORRENCE, Cauterized (1998). Suicide Gene / Crowbar Abortion / The Immaculate Deception / Bleed The Leech / Not Even Human / Silence Is Consent / Dawn Of The Age Of Ignorance / Cauterization / Everywhere To Hide / Delirium / Giving In To Hate / Sledgehammer Dissection / Fucked By The System / The Prelude To Extinction / Truth Be Damned.
Serratura, Cauterized (1998) (Demo). Bleed The Leech / Dawn Of The Age Of Ignorance / Sledgehammer Dissection / Crowbar Abortion / Not Even Human / Cauterization By Magma / Human Battering Ram / The Prelude To Extinction.
RETRIBUTION, Cauterized (2001). One Settler, One Bullet / Controlled Drowning / Decompiled / Sadomasochrist / Perpetual Hate / What Goes Around / Shoot Them in The Face / Reichburner / Vote With Your Fists / In Search of The Perfect Abhorrence / Retribution / You Are Nothing.
RETRIBUTE, Cauterized (2001). Stillborn / Embalmed In Sulphuric Acid / Wilt / Zombie Ritual / Fuckdog / Curse The Gods / Into The Grave / Corpsegrinder.
Dead Infection Tribute, Cauterized (2003) (Split single with DECAY). From The Anatomical Deeps / Maggots In Your Flesh.

CELEBORN

SWEDEN — *Jörgen Bylander (vocals / bass), Magnus Sahlgren (guitar), Jon J Klingberg (guitar), Kjell-Erik Eriksson (electric violin), Robert Eriksson (drums).*

Death Metal band CELEBORN recorded the 'Etherial' demo in 1992. The group also cut tracks, 'Exalted' and 'Astral Tide', at Rockhuset Studios in Östersund for inclusion on a 1993 split album 'Metal North' in collaboration with QUICKSAND DREAM, LEFT HAND SOLUTION, TOXIC WASTE and UNHOLY.

CELEBORN members raised their individual profiles in subsequent years with bassist Jörgen Bylander working with DEFACED CREATION, CONDAMNED, DEFACED CREATION, SANCTIFICATION and DERANGED, guitarist Magnus Sahlgren would journey on to TIAMAT, sessioning on the 1994 'Wildhoney' album and tour, DISMEMBER in 1998 and LAKE OF TEARS, second guitarist Jon J Klingberg finding prominence with WHALE whilst drummer Robert Eriksson enrolled into THE HELLACOPTERS and SEWER GROOVES.

Etherial, Celeborn (1992) (Demo). Etherial Skies / The Quest / Cosmic Sphere.
METAL NORTH, Massproduktion MASS CD-57 (1993) (Split album with LEFT HAND SOLUTION, TOXIC WASTE, UNHOLY and QUICKSAND DREAM). Exalted / Astral Tide.

CELEBRANT

BREE, BELGIUM — *Kurt Straetemans (vocals), Bart Straetemans (guitar), Geert Thaens (guitar), Jan Jacobs (bass), Mark Van Develde (drums).*

Bree, Limburg technical Death Metal outfit CELEBRANT are fronted by THE QUIESCENT and ABSYNTHIUM credited vocalist Kevin Vangeloven. The group's formation dates to January of 1994, being conceptualised by guitarist Geert Thaens and drummer Pascal Mooren. First in line for the lead vocal position was to be Pier Fieddelaers, followed shortly after by second guitarist Bart Straetemans. This band unit cut the opening December 1994 demo 'Nocturnal Goddess' at Music-house Studios. CELEBRANT would adopt a new musical stance for the second demo, 'Blessing The Blackness' released in April 1996, shifting from a Dark metal style to more of a Black / Death approach. Subsequent to these recordings the band was strengthened with the arrival of bassist Geert Vercouteren.

CELEBRANT took on a new singer during 1997, inducting former LAST FUNERAL man Kevin Vangelooven. That same year Vercouteren made his exit and Jan Jacobs was installed on bass in July. Augmenting their sound, the group incorporated keyboard player Jurgen Vanderhaegen in April of 1998 and in this formation CELEBRANT entered the Dyprins Digital Studios in January of 1999 to lay down tracks for 'Slaughter Of Eden'. This demo surfaced in June, shortly after which Vanderhaegen opted to take the role of guitarist with RAPTURE. The group opted to persevere minus keyboards. Next to decamp, in July of 2000, would be Jan Jacobs.

Tragedy struck CELEBRANT in October of 2000 when drummer Pascal Mooren died suddenly of a cardiac vein failure. It would take the band many months to get over this loss but by mid 2001 they would be back in action again with SKULL COLLECTOR's Mark Van Develde on the drum stool. Ex-RESUSCITATION bassist Eddy Duwyn joined the fold in July. Vangelooven, maintaining his position with CELEBRANT, joined ABSYNTHIUM in late 2001.

The 2004 album 'Dark Memories From Beyond' included a cover version of SLAYER's 'Black Magic'. CELEBRANT re-enlisted former bassist Jan Jacobs in September. They would also switch vocalists, seeing Kevin Vangeloven exiting and a replacement being swiftly located in Kurt Straetemans, brother of Bart. However, in February of 2005 original singer Pier Fieddelaers returned to the fold as Kurt Straetemans duly joined SKULL COLLECTOR.

DARK MEMORIES FROM BEYOND, (2004). Intro / Garden Of Eternal Lust / The Only Truth Is Myself / Pandemonium / Nocturnal Goddess / Reborn In Blood / Intro / The Satanic Mass / The Mirror Of The Soul / Age Of Sadness / In Nomine / Blessing The Blackness / Beyond The Darkside / Outro / Garden Of Evil / The Satanic Mass (Re-recorded) / My Church / Black Magic.

CELESTIAL CROWN

TARTU, ESTONIA — *DeVol (vocals), Alone Diana (vocals), The Serpent (guitar), Shel (guitar).*

Originating from Tartu, Estonia CELESTIAL CROWN was by vocalist Denis and Aleksander ('Shel') during 1999. In October of that year the duo recorded the opening session 'Invasion Of Suicidal Angels' in a home studio. In the Spring of 2000 lead guitarist Sergei boosted the numbers as subsequently CELESTIAL CROWN expanded to a quartet with the augmentation of female vocalist Diana. With this unit the band debuted live in October 2000, testing their songs and performance in front of friends in the humble surroundings of a garage.

CELESTIAL SEASON's 'The Embraced' album would see release through the Mexican Doom label. The band returned in 2005 with the album 'A Veiled Empire' released by Divenia Records. 'Suicidal Angels', featuring a cover version of NIGHTWISH's 'Two For Tragedy', followed in March 2006.

Invasion Of Suicidal Angels EP, Independent (2000). Under The Black Sun / Trapped In The Dark / Your Touch / Nocturnal Insanity / Holy Waters / Embittered With Grief / A Wish.
THE EMBRACED, Doom DOOM-01-016 (2002). With The Autumn Winds / Dreams Of Elizabeth / The Embraced / Your Touch /

Nocturnal Insanity / Dark Dance / From Dance To Fall / Return To The Haunted Shores / Epitaph In Two Parts.
A VEILED EMPIRE, Divenia Music DNA004 (2005). Veil Of Eternity / Sacrifice In Red / Eclipsed My Hope / Deep Within / Night By The Silent Waters / Stone Heart / For The End Of The Days / For One Love / So Let Thy Will Shalt Be / New Aeon / Into Eternity / Consecration / A Sea.
SUICIDAL ANGELS, Divenia DNA013 (2006). Under The Black Sun / Trapped In The Dark / Holy Waters / Embittered With Grief / A Wish / Supreme Domination / Two For Tragedy / Return To The Haunted Shores (Suicidal Edit).

CELTIC FROST

ZÜRICH, SWITZERLAND — *Tom G. Warrior (vocals / guitar), Martin Eric Ain (bass), Reed St. Mark (drums).*

A highly influential Zürich Thrash Metal act who pushed the musical boundaries of the genre to the limit, CELTIC FROST blended a fusion of extreme aggression with classical and jazz leanings to create a unique 'avant-garde' eclectic style. This reputation was forged by the group's obsessive attention to detail and meticulous planning, their intended career path having been strategized fully even before their first record hit the shelves. At their peak the band looked set to rival the big name American speed Metal outfits for world domination but would spectacularly crash to earth due to one of the most disastrous style changes ever witnessed.

CELTIC FROST had a strange genesis as mentor and renowned 'death grunter' Tom G. Warrior (a.k.a. Thomas Gabriel Fischer) and bassist Martin Eric Ain were members of what was generally acknowledged to have been one of the worst bands ever- HELLHAMMER. Tom himself started out musically in GRAVE HILL who were heavily influenced by the NWoBHM bands such as DIAMOND HEAD and VENOM.

HELLHAMMER actually started out under the HAMMERHEAD banner. Initially bass guitar was handled by the 14 year old Michael Baum, who in turn transferred these duties to Fischer, then wishing to be known as 'Satanic Slaughter'. Of note is that Baum then journeyed on to Los Angeles to found AOR act SIERRA before enrolling into TRIBE OF GYPSIES.

During the August of 1982 Fischer, transferring from bass to guitar, was now fronting a trio of Priestly and drummer Jörg Neubart (a.k.a. 'Bloodhunter'). Inspired apparently by Newcastle upon Tyne NWoBHM band RAVEN and their Gallagher brothers team Fischer and Priestly adopted the joint stage surnames of 'Warrior'. Neubart became 'Bruce Day'.

Their debut demo, 'Triumph Of Death', was widely regarded as one of the worst examples of a Heavy Metal band ever. 'Metal Forces' magazine editor Bernard Doe in particular cited it as the most appalling thing he had ever heard. History however would dictate that HELLHAMMER would later be recognized as one of the root catalysts of the Black Metal genre. Although in later years band members have admitted their knowledge of music was basic to say the least when the HELLHAMMER recordings were made nevertheless the band were in possession of an artistic vision which would undoubtedly shape the Metal scene over many years.

In 1983 HELLHAMMER enrolled bass player Martin Eric Ain and drummer Stephen Priestly from SCHIZO. However, invited to submit a fresh demo to Berlin's Noise Records HELLHAMMER very nearly split as Ain felt he did not have the necessary talent to go through with the session!

Still, positive or negative press encouraged Noise to sign the band and the Berlin based label released the 'Apocalyptic Raids' EP which had no details as to what RPM the record should be played at; sounding just as strange at 33RPM as it did at 45.

Metal Blade Records released the EP in America with an extra two tracks. Demand for HELLHAMMER also warranted a bootleg 7" single issued by Necromantic union, a pairing of a live cut of 'Buried And Forgotten' and a rehearsal recording 'Messiah'.

The original CELTIC FROST line-up in May 1984, so named after a combination of song titles and lyrics on a CIRITH UNGOL album sleeve, comprised Warrior, Ain and drummer Isaac Darso. The latter lasted precisely one rehearsal before being usurped by SCHIZO's Stephen Priestly on a temporary basis as a session drummer for recording. At this stage CELTIC FROST were still working on NWoBHM favourites such as songs by ANGEL WITCH and ARAGORN.

With HELLHAMMER's reputation preceding them, magazines reviews polarized at either the genius or dreadful end of the spectrum, CELTIC FROST retained their previous deal with Noise Records by submitting a master plan detailing the names of all future releases. The strategy called for an initial demo to be entitled 'A Thousand Deaths' but the label soon persuaded the band that this should form the basis of an opening commercially available product.

CELTIC FROST's first product, the mini-album, 'Morbid Tales' was recorded with Martin Eric Ain's former colleague in SCHIZO drummer Stephen Priestly. Guesting in the studio on additional vocals would be Horst Müller and Hertha Ohling plus violinist Oswald Spengler. As soon as the sessions were completed though Priestly decamped. CELTIC FROST set about negotiations with American drummer Jeff Cardelli of Seattle act LIPSTICK. However, the band hired another American, ex-CROWN drummer Reed St. Mark (real name Reid Cruickshank).

As with HELLHAMMER media views on 'Morbid Tales', issued in June 1984, ranged in their extremity from excellent to dire. European editions of 'Morbid Tales' comprised six tracks whilst a US license, through Metal Blade Records, added two extra tracks in 'Morbid Tales' and 'Return To The Eve'. The controversy stoked up by these opposing views would serve the band well. CELTIC FROST were still at this juncture wearing the stage make up later to be given the name 'corpse paint' by later generations of Black Metal bands. A further EP, 1985's 'The Emperors Return' issued in both regular format and as a limited run, highly sought after picture disc, followed to equally polarised reviews and even condemnation from the band themselves. By now CELTIC FROST were being acknowledged as leaders in their field.

CELTIC FROST's inaugural live performances came with a run of shows opening for German bands BEAST and MASS in Germany and Austria. Planned shows in Italy with ASTAROTH were shelved.

Ain had been asked to leave during recording of the next album 'To Mega Therion', surfacing in October 1985, and CELTIC FROST pulled in Dominic Steiner of the Glam Rock act JUNK FOOD. The album, which saw the band utilizing timpanis, French horns, courtesy of Wolf Bender, and operatic vocals courtesy of Claudia-Maria Mokri, plus credited sound effects from Horst Müller and Urs Sprenger, would be the first to be graced with lavish album sleeve artwork from the renowned artist H.R. Giger.

Friction between the band members resulted in Steiner's dismissal as soon as 'To Mega Therion' had been completed. For CELTIC FROST's debut show outside of Europe, at the 30th November 1985 'World War III' festival in Montreal alongside VOIVOD, POSSESSED, DESTRUCTION and NASTY SAVAGE, Martin Eric Ain was drawn back in the bass position.

Warrior also worked as producer for fellow Swiss Metal band CORONOR, a gesture they in turn repaid by becoming CELTIC FROST's road crew.

February 1986 had CELTIC FROST back on the live circuit, touring Europe sharing billing with HELLOWEEN and GRAVE DIGGER. Later shows saw a headline at the Belgian 'Metalysee' festival, the band's debut in England in London with GRAVE DIGGER and HELLOWEEN supporting at London's Hammersmith Palais and also touring in North America alongside RUNNING WILD and VOIVOD throughout June.

With CELTIC FROST's status rising sharply, the 1986 'Tragic

Serenades' EP was issued to keep fans happy between albums. The EP consisted of remixed tracks from 'Into Mega Therion', both 'The Usurper' and 'Jewel Throne' with bass substituted by Martin Eric Ain, alongside newly recorded 'Return To The Eve'.

The group's third full-length opus, 'Into The Pandemonium' released in November 1987, provided fans with another bizarre offering comprising tracks such as a cover of WALL OF VOODOO's 'Mexican Radio' and the Rap cut 'One In Their Pride'. Before the album had been recorded New York based guitarist Ritchi Desmond was briefly linked with a position in the band, but, having travelled to Switzerland to work with the group Desmond returned home citing "too many conflicting attitudes" as the reason why he failed to join CELTIC FROST. Warrior countered that Desmond brought uninvited family members along to the audition and looked nothing like his submitted photograph. Desmond was to front SABBAT for their 'Mourning Has Broken' album and subsequent disastrous tour.

During a break in recording the band played a series of European gigs with ANTHRAX, CRIMSON GLORY and even METALLICA. The finalised sessions witnessed a further expansion in CELTIC FROST's aural dynamics with the employment of a swathe of session contributors. Claudia-Maria Mokri once again featured as a spotlighted additional vocalist and additional singers included Thomas Berter, Marchain Regee Rotschy and Manü Moan. Classical instruments were cut by violinists Malgorzata Blaiejewska Woller and Eva Cieslinski, cellist Wulf Ebert, French Horn player Anton Schreiber with Jürgen Paul Mann on viola. Additional guitar work was provided by Andreas Dobler.

For live work to promote 'Into The Pandemonium', CELTIC FROST added second guitarist Ron Marks and toured Britain in winter of 1987 with support from KREATOR then North America on a bill with EXODUS and ANTHRAX. The tour succeeded in dumbfounding many of the band's established fans with such radical tracks as the aforementioned 'Mexican Radio' cover and the band was dogged throughout it's duration by legal wrangles with Noise Records. Disillusioned, Marks quit to be replaced by former JUNK FOOD guitarist Oliver Amberg. Upon their return to Europe CELTIC FROST hit further problems when Martin Ain decided to abandon the music business entirely, so Warrior quickly drafted in Curt Victor Bryant.

CELTIC FROST was in a state of flux besieged by business and financial problems. Even an offer from director Ken Russell to lay down the soundtrack to the movie 'The Lair Of The White Worm' had to be declined because the group was in such disarray. However, the final blow to the classic line-up came when Reed St. Mark upped and left to join MINDFUNK and his position was filled by a returning Stephen Priestly. This was the line-up that was to record the disastrous 'Cold Lake' album produced by Tony Platt at Hansa Studios and Sky Trak Studios in Berlin, a record that severely damaged the band's career in Europe.

With this effort, CELTIC FROST appeared to ditch all of their former pretensions artistically and even adopted a new 'Glam' image, much to the horror of their most hardcore following. Tom dropped the 'Warrior' from his stage name and became plain Thomas Gabriel Fischer, even sporting an L.A. GUNS T-shirt on official press photos. Fans would be quick to spot that CELTIC FROST were now crediting one Michelle Villaneva as "Wardrobe and styling artist". 'Cold Lake' was to emerge in September 1988.

It was heavily rumoured in the European media that the band had, in a SPINAL TAP style move, adopted Tom's girlfriend as manager and that the new look was her masterplan for CELTIC FROST's step into the big league. CELTIC FROST themselves maintained that tracks like 'Teaze Me' were a parody of Glam Rock, but fans were outraged and the Rock press universally attacked the album. A single, 'Cherry Orchards', was announced then shelved. The European tour, commencing in late February with UK shows supported by DESTRUCTION, fared badly with audiences deserting in droves. However, in America 'Cold Lake' was in actual fact making serious sales headway and a U.S. tour beginning in March 1989 was judged a success.

In late 1989 the badly bruised CELTIC FROST announced a return to their former style and regrouped with Ron Marks. Martin Eric Ain was also persuaded to put down some guest bass tracks and contribute lyrics. The Roli Mossiman produced 'Vanity / Nemesis' album was cited by many as the band's best record to date, but the legacy of 'Cold Lake' still haunted the quartet to such a degree that sales suffered.

CELTIC FROST only managed minimal touring to back up the release of April 1990's 'Vanity / Nemesis', including a British tour backed by Thrashers SLAMMER. Earlier German dates had been cancelled, due to the band's perilous business state, but CELTIC FROST endured through two Dutch shows and the entire UK leg. By now Warrior was to be seen spotted playing a guitar emblazoned with his wife's name 'Michelle', the lady in question also having become a backing singer for the band. CELTIC FROST performed their last ever concert on 29th May 1990 at the Derby Assembly Rooms. New management hooked up a deal with major label BMG in North America. However, the deal was shelved at the last minute leaving CELTIC FROST high and dry.

Warrior took the band into an even more radical direction when he mooted the idea of working with ex-THE TIME guitarist Jesse Johnson on a projected Funk-Metal project. Stephen Priestly meantime would perform drums for French act TREPONEM PAL's 1991 'Aggravation' album.

Following a 1992 four track demo, featuring the tracks 'Honour Thy Father', 'Seeds Of Rapture', 'Icons Alive' and Oh Father', the band searched in vain for a new deal. Initial tapes were laid down with Priestly on drums but sessions in Texas saw Reed St. Mark back behind the kit and Renée Hernz on bass. Nothing came of this latest venture and CELTIC FROST effectively split; Marks relocating to America to form STEPCHILD then SUBSONIC.

1992 Noise released a CELTIC FROST epitaph in the form of 'Parched With Thirst Am I And Dying'; a collection of rare and unreleased studio out-takes as the band bowed out. In more recent years Martin Ain produced the debut album from doom band SADNESS in 1995, whilst Tom Warrior was found fronting new venture APOLLYON SUN in 1996.

Late 2001 would herald renewed rumours, at first vehemently denied and then later confirmed, of a full-blown CELTIC FROST reunion with Tom G. Warrior, Martin Eric Ain and Reed St. Mark, along with Fischer's long-time songwriting partner and co-founder of APOLLYON SUN, guitarist/producer Erol Unala, all participating. By November a projected album title of 'Probe' had emerged but it would not be until April 2003 that a demo track entitled 'Ground' was posted online. The CELTIC FROST camp also disseminated a revised and apparently spurious album working title of 'Dark Matter Manifest'. Meantime, Martin Eric Ain contributed vocals to Los Angeles based HATESEX's Industrial take on the SLAYER track 'Black Magic'.

In June of 2004 Tom G. Fischer announced he had plans for a solo album for 2005 release although CELTIC FROST persevered with composing new material with drummer Franco Sesa. The band would also have their classic cut 'Dawn Of Megiddo' chosen as a pioneering piece of music for a compilation assembled by DARKTHRONE drummer Fenriz, released through Peaceville Records and entitled 'Fenriz Presents The Best Of Old School Black Metal'.

Employing drummer Franco Sesa, CELTIC FROST revealed a new set of demos had been completed in May 2005 and entered Horus Sound Studios in Hannover in August to track the album, given a working title 'Dark Matter Manifest'. HYPOCRISY and PAIN mentor Peter Tägtgren would be selected as producer.

For tour work CELTIC FROST drafted the APOPTYGMA BERZERK, SATYRICON, CADAVER, and MAYHEM credited Anders Odden on guitar. Live campaigning for 2006 included scheduled appearances at Sölvesborg's 'Sweden Rock' festival in June, Helsinki's 'Tuska' festival in July, Germany's 'Wacken Open Air' and Norway's Bergen 'Hole In The Sky' events in August. However, the band's June 3rd 'Rock Hard' festival in Gelsenkirchen was cancelled that same day. Martin Eric Ain announced from the stage that Thomas Gabriel Fischer had been rushed to hospital with acute kidney problems, subsequently diagnosed as a kidney stone.

According to Nielsen SoundScan the 'Monotheist' album sold just under 2,500 copies in its first week of sale in North America. In the band's homeland of Switzerland the record entered the charts at number 41. US dates would be projected for September. The band filmed a promotional video for the track 'A Dying God Coming Into Human Flesh', directed by Jessie Fischer in Zurich prior to launching into a 47 date US tour, commencing September 12th at West Springfield, Virginia's Jaxx venue, backed by SAHG and 1349. The tour generated favourable reviews but closed on a sour note, as Tom G. warrior revealed on his official blog, stating "Out of petty, pathetic vengefulness for being confronted, in a highly professional manner one might add, for utterly failing to do his job, one of those who travelled with us in North America in September, October, and November 2006, and was paid by us no less, destroyed one of the band's sacred back-up Iceman guitars as soon as unwatched for a moment after the end of the tour".

Japanese dates were scheduled for January 2007 dubbed the "Extreme The Dojo" alongside SATYRICON and NAGLFAR. The band then shifted shape, drafting V. Santura of the German Black Metal group DARK FORTRESS as new touring guitarist.

Preceded by a one off solo gig on March 6th, held at the Mascotte club in Zurich, CELTIC FROST headed up a package billing with KREATOR, LEGION OF THE DAMNED and WATAIN for a lengthy run of European dates. Scandinavian concerts saw Sweden's WOLF acting as openers. Back on North American soil, the band forged a union with TYPE O NEGATIVE and BRAND NEW SIN for dates in April.

MORBID TALES, Noise N0017 (1984). Into The Crypt Of Rays / Visions Of Mortality / Procreation (Of The Wicked) / Return To Eve / Danse Macabre / Nocturnal Fear.
Emperors Return EP, Noise N0024 (1985). Dethroned Emperor / Circle Of The Tyrants / Morbid Tales / Suicidal Winds / Visual Aggression.
TO MEGA THERION, Noise N0031 (1985). Innocence And Wrath / The Usurper / Jewel Throne / Dawn Of Megiddo / Eternal Summer / Circle Of Tyrants / (Beyond The) North Winds / Fainted Eyes / Tears In A Prophet's Dream / Necromantical Screams.
Tragic Serenades EP, Noise N0041 (1986). The Usurper / Jewel Throne / Return To Eve.
I Won't Dance, Noise N0094 (1986). I Won't Dance / One In Their Pride / Tristesses De La Lune.
INTO THE PANDEMONIUM, Noise N0065 (1987). Mexican Radio / Mesmerised / Inner Sanctum / Sorrows Of The Moon / Babylon Fell / Caress Into Oblivion / One In Their Pride / I Won't Dance / Rex Irae (Requiem / Opening) / Oriental Masquerade.
COLD LAKE, Noise NUK 125 (1988). Intro-Human / Seduce Me Tonight / Petty Obsession / (Once) They Were Eagles / Cherry Orchards / Juices Like Wine / Little Velvet / Blood On Kisses / Downtown Hanoi / Dance Sleazy / Roses Without Thorns / Tease Me / Mexican Radio (New Version).
Wine In My Hand (Third From The Sun), Noise (1990) (Promotion release). Wine In My Hand (Third From The Sun) / Heroes / Descent From Babylon.
VANITY/NEMESIS, Noise/EMI EMC 3576 (1990). The Heart Beneath / Wine In My Hand (Third From The Sun) / Wings Of Solitude / The Name Of My Bride / This Island Earth / The Restless Seas / Phallic Tantrum / A Kiss Or A Whisper / Vanity / Nemesis / Heroes.
PARCHED WITH THIRST AM I AND DYING, Noise N0191-2 (1992). Idols Of Chagrin / A Descent To Babylon / Return To The Eve / Juices Like Wine / The Inevitable Factor / The Heart Beneath / Cherry Orchards / Tristesses De La Lune / Wings Of Solitude / The Usurper / Journey Into Fear / Downtown Hanoi / Circle Of The Tyrants / In The Chapel In The Moonlight / I Won't Dance / The Name Of My Bride / Mexican Radio / Under Apollyon's Sun.
Montheist Sampler, (2006) (Promotional release). Progeny / Ground.
MONOTHEIST, EMI 5051099750012 (2006) (Vinyl release). Progeny / Ground / A Dying God Coming Into Human Flesh / Drown In Ashes / Os Abysmi Vel Daath / Temple Of Depression / Obscured / Domain Of Decay / Ain Elohim / Totengott / Synagoga Satanae / Winter (Requiem, Chapter Three: Finale).
MONOTHEIST, Century Media CD 77500-2 (2006). Progeny / Ground / A Dying God Coming Into Human Flesh / Drown In Ashes / Os Abysmi Vel Daath / Temple Of Depression / Obscured / Domain Of Decay / Ain Elohim / Totengott / Synagoga Satanae / Winter (Requiem, Chapter Three: Finale). Chart positions: 12 GREECE, 41 SWITZERLAND, 57 FINLAND, 67 GERMANY, 194 FRANCE.

CENOTAPH

MEXICO — *Edgardo Gonzalez (vocals), Samuel Ocadiz (guitar), Eduardo Guevara (guitar), Fernando Garcilazo (bass), Oscar Clorio (drums).*

An illustrious Mexican Death Metal act founded in 1989, issuing the demo 'Rise Of Excruciation', featuring an AUTOPSY cover version 'Ridden With Disease', that same year. Although traditionally Death Metal musically CENOTAPH employ strong Satanic themes. A 7" single, 'Tenebrous Apparitions', saw issue through Distorted Harmony Records in 1990 followed up by 'The Eternal Disgrace' double 7" EP released by Baphomet Records. Recording line up for these sessions comprised vocalist / bassist Daniel Corchado, guitarists César Sánchez and Guillermo Hérnadez with Oscar Clorio on drums. CENOTAPH's first full length opus, 'The Gloomy Reflection Of Our Hidden Sorrows', arrived on Horus Records in 1992.

Ex-member Daniel Corchado would go on to forge the highly rated and industrious act THE CHASM. He would be later joined by Julio Viterbo for THE CHASM 2000 album 'Procession To The Infraworld'. For a period THE CHASM would also number another erstwhile CENOTAPH man in their ranks, bassist Robert Valle.

Following a Milwaukee Metalfest performance CENOTAPH folded but recently have regrouped. The 1992 album 'The Gloomy Reflection Of Our Hidden Sorrows' would be re-issued in 1998, adding tracks from the rare 'Tenebrous Apparitions' 7" single. Ex-CENOTAPH bassist Rodolfo Riveron relocated to Seattle, Washington to forge SINDIOS.

Rise Of Excruciation, (1989). Reek From The Grave / Colony Undead / The Last Infection / Rise Of Excruciation / Ridden With Disease.
Tenebrous Apparitions, Distorted Harmony (1990). Larvs Of Subconscious / Repulsive Odor Of Decomposition.
The Eternal Disgrace, Baphomet (1991). Dissection / Tenebrous Apparitions.
Cenotaph, (1991). Repulsive Odor Of Decomposition / Larvs Of Subconscious / Dissection / Tenebrous Apparitions.
THE GLOOMY REFLECTION OF OUR HIDDEN SCROLLS, Horus Corporation (1992). Requiem For A Soul Required / Ashes In The Rain / ... A Red Sky / Evoked Doom / Tenebras Apparitions / The Spiritless One / Infinite Meditation Of An Uncertain Existence In The Cosmic Solitude / Repulsive Odor Of Decomposition.
EPIC RITES (9 EPIC TALES OF DEATH RITES), Oz Productions CDOZ001 (1996). Intro / Crying Frost / Lorn Ends / Navegate / Towards The Umbra / As The Darkness Borns / Angered Tongues / Epic Rites / Dethroned Empire / Thornes Of Fog.
RIDING ON BLACK OCEANS, (1998). The Solitudes / Severance / Grief To Obscuro / Macabre Locus Celesta / Among The Abrupt / Infinitum Valet / The Silence Of Our Black Oceans / Soul Profundis / Ectasia Tenebrae.
SAGA BELICA, Oz Productions (2002). Iron Peaks And Fists / Holocausto Riot / Everlasting Command / Hurricane Cenotaph / Owners Torment / Lambs For Wolfs / Necrocommandments / Saga Belica.

CENTINEX

HEDEMORA, SWEDEN — *Johan Jansson (vocals), Johan Ahlberg (guitar), Jonas Kjellgren (guitar), Martin Schulman (bass), Ronnie Bergerståhl (drums).*

Renowned Hedemora Death Metal act that have increasingly bolstered their sound and imagery with Satanic lyrical references. CENTINEX opened their career in September 1990 issuing the debut demo cassette 'End Of Life', recorded at the famous Sunlight Studios, the following year. The band signed to Swedish label Underground for release of the album 'Subconscious Lobotomy', again recorded at Sunlight, which saw a limited release of 1000 copies. The CENTINEX line-up at this juncture comprised twin vocalists Erik and Mattias Lamppu, guitarist Andreas Evaldsson, bass player Martin Schulman and drummer Joakim Gustafsson.

A further three track demo session, entitled 'Under The Blackened Sky, followed. Gigging took CENTINEX throughout Sweden, Finland and Poland during 1993. CENTINEX's next cassette release 'Transcend The Dark Chaos', released on the band's own novelly titled Evil Shit Productions in 1994, was repressed by Sphinx Records. The second CENTINEX full-length album 'Malleus Malefaction' was recorded for the Wild Rags label and produced by Peter Tägtgren of HYPOCRISY.

1996 saw the release of a shared 7" single in collusion with INVERTED and a fresh band roster retaining Lamppu, Schulman and Evaldsson but with new faces in UNCURBED guitarist Kenneth Wiklund and drummer Kalimaa. The band also featured on a split EP with Sweden's VOICES OF DEATH and German act BAPHOMET.

The 'Reflections' CD was released in March 1997, later in the year being licensed to Slovakian Rock Extremum Records for a tape version. Early 1997 found CENTINEX on tour in Scandinavia as guests to CRADLE OF FILTH. However, a split in the ranks came the following year when both Lamppu and Evaldsson made their exit. The 'Reborn Through Flames' album was delivered during June of 1998, being made available on tape format through Polish Novum Vox Mortis Records. The Norwegian Oskorei Productions would issue the 'Shadowland' 7EP, a limited two track vinyl, the same year. Gigging took CENTINEX into Germany, Spain, Portugal and Holland.

The 'Bloodhunt' album, issued in June 1999 by Repulse, would also be delivered by Oskorei Productions in a limited edition 10" vinyl format restricted to just 300 copies. It was to be July 1999 before CENTINEX enrolled UNCANNY, MOONDARK, INTERMENT, PYOSISFIED and DELLAMORTE drummer Kennet Englund. For touring later in the year CENTINEX pulled in PEXILATED, SICKENSIDE, DELLAMORTE and CARNAL FORGE man Jonas Kjellgren on guitar and the PYOSISFIED, HATRED, SIDEBURNERS, ASOCIAL, FLESHREVELS, UNCURBED, INTERMENT, FULMINATION, FROSTHEIM and DELLAMORTE credited vocalist Johan Jansson. CENTINEX undertook two European tours during the year with shows across Germany, Holland, Belgium, France, the Czech Republic and Slovakia. The same year had CENTINEX contributing their version of 'Ripping Corpse' to a Full Moon Productions KREATOR tribute album. Both the 'Subconscious Lobotomy' and 'Malleus Maleficarum' albums were re-mixed and edited for a re-release but legal problems forced Repulse to cancel the schedule.

2000 witnessed yet more ructions when Kjellgren and Englund decamped. Replacements were AZURE vocalist Robban Kanto and drummer Johan. The 'Apocalyptic Armageddon' 7" EP saw release in February through the German Deadly Art concern. In September of 2000 Repulse issued the 'Hellbrigade' album with the Japanese Soundholic label following suit in December. The following year it would be picked up by World War III Records in America, Picoroco Records in South America and Irond Records in Russia. Nocturnal Music would also weigh in with a limited edition vinyl version. The band appeared at several Swedish summer-festivals and journeyed across Scandinavia and Europe once more performing in Finland, Germany, Belgium, Holland, France, Switzerland, Spain, Austria and the Czech Republic.

In April of 2001 the group signed a new worldwide deal with the English Candlelight label, cutting the first album for their new partners, entitled 'Diabolical Desolation', at Black Lounge studios during July and August. CENTINEX would also share vinyl with the infamous American act NUNSLAUGHTER with their take on SODOM's 'Enchanted Land' for the 'Hail Germania' EP on the Belgian Painkiller label.

In October 2001 guitarist Kenneth Wiklund would break ranks and Johan Ahlberg of SUBDIVE would subsequently secure the position. With this revised line-up CENTINEX would put in their inaugural gig on American soil followed up be festivals across Sweden and Germany.

'Diabolical Desolation' was released in Europe on March 11th 2002, the release date for North America being April 30th. A subsequent limited edition vinyl version would be issued through Finland's Northern Sound Records. Restricted to 1000 copies this variant came in a gatefold sleeve clad in all new layout and artwork. European dates slated for November saw the band making up a bill including headliners DEICIDE alongside MYSTIC CIRCLE. For these shows the band roped in CARNAL FORGE skinsman Stefan Westerberg as regular drummer Kennet Englund was unable to commit.

The British Candlelight label announced it was to re-release the CENTINEX back catalogue for 2003 adding a significant number of bonus tracks to each release. A new album, 'Decadence—Prophecies Of Cosmic Chaos', including an instrumental track 'A Dynasty Of Obedience' composed by ARCANA's Peter Pettersson, was projected for 2003 release but then pushed back into 2004. The group severed ties with drummer Kennet Englund in August, inducting Ronnie Bergerståhl of JULIE LAUGHS NO MORE, AMARAN and MYNJUN repute in October. CENTINEX toured Finland in April of 2004 allied with DEATH DU JOUR and Swedish act REPUGNANT.

Swedmetal Records issued a limited edition 'Live Devastation' 7" single in September, this comprising 'Towards Devastation', recorded live in Borlänge, Sweden and 'Bloodhunt', recorded live in Lappeenranta, Finland. In November the band signed a new album deal with Cold Records, a subsidiary of Metal Blade, for the 'World Declension' opus. Ronnie Bergerståhl joined WORLD BELOW in December. In addition, A WORLD BELOW / CENTINEX split 7" EP, entitled 'Doomed Death Blow', would be released by UK imprint Conquer Records, limited to 500 copies. Promoting 'World Declension', released in North America through Candlelight Records, CENTINEX announced European touring in union with IMPIETY for October 2005. However, these gigs would be cancelled.

In March 2006 the band issued a press release closing their career, stating ""We hereby announce that after 16 years in the business the Swedish Death Metal act CENTINEX call it quits." A farewell live performance was scheduled for May 13th in Eskilstuna, Sweden. Beforehand, Martin Schulman, Johan Jansson and Ronnie Bergerståhl announced the formation of a new combo dubbed DEMONICAL. Johan Jansson joined REGURGITATE in September.

Centinex, Centinex (1991) (Rehearsal cassette demo).
End Of Life, Centinex (1991) (Cassette demo). The Aspiration / Fear / Bells Of Misery / Dreams Of Death.
SUBCONSCIOUS LOBOTOMY, Underground UGR05 (1992) (Limited edition 1000 copies). Blood On My Skin / Shadows Are Astray / Dreams Of Death / Orgy In Flesh / End Of Life / Bells Of Misery / Inhuman Dissections Of Souls / The Aspiration / Until Death Tear Us Apart.
Under The Blackened Sky, Wild Rags WRR-CEN (1993) (Cassette EP). Cranial Dismemberment / Only Slices Remains / Thorn Within.
TRANSCEND THE DARK CHAOS, Sphinx SIXR 003 (1994) (Cassette EP). Transcend The Dark Chaos / Thorns Of Desolation / Eternal Lies / At The Everlasting End.

CENTINEX

MALLEUS MALEFICARUM, Wild Rags WRR 043 (1996). Upon The Ancient Ground / Dark Visions / Sorrow Of The Burning Wasteland / Transcend The Dark Chaos / Thorns Of Desolation / Eternal Lies / At The Everlasting Evil.
Sorrow Of Burning Wasteland, Voices Of Death VOD 003 (1996) (Split single with INVERTED. Limited edition 600 copies). Sorrow Of Burning Wasteland.
REFLECTIONS, Diehard RRS 954 (1997). Carnal Lust / Seven Prophecies / Before The Dawn / The Dimension Beyond / My Demon Within / In Pain / Undivined / Darkside / Into The Funeral Domain.
Shadowland, Oskorei Productions OP 004 (1998) (Lilac vinyl. Limited edition 500 copies). Shadowland / Eternal Lies.
REBORN THROUGH FLAMES, Repulse RPS 032CD (1998). Embraced By Moonlight / Resurrected / Summon The Golden Twilight / The Beauty Of Malice / Under The Guillotine / Through Celestial Gates / Molested / In The Arch Of Serenity.
BLOODHUNT, Repulse RPS 042CD (1999) (CD release). Under The Pagan Glory / For Centuries Untold / Luciferian Moon / Bloodhunt / The Conquest Infernal / Like Darkened Storms.
BLOODHUNT, Oskorei Productions OP 008 (1999) (10" vinyl single). Under The Pagan Glory / For Centuries Untold / Luciferian Moon / Bloodhunt / The Conquest Infernal / Like Darkened Storms / Mutilation.
Apocalyptic Armageddon, Deadly Art DAP 095 (2000) (7" grey vinyl single limited to 500 copies). Apocalyptic Armageddon / Seeds Of Evil / Everlasting Bloodshed.
HELLBRIGADE, Repulse RPS 046CD (2000) (European CD release). Towards Devastation / On With Eternity / The Eyes Of The Dead / Emperor Of Death / Last Redemption / Blood Conqueror / Neverending Hell / Nightbreeder / Hellbrigade.
HELLBRIGADE, Soundholic TKCS-85003 (2000) (Japanese release). Towards Devastation / On With Eternity / The Eyes Of The Dead / Emperor Of Death / Last Redemption / Blood Conqueror / Neverending Hell / Nightbreeder / Hellbrigade / Apocalyptic Armageddon / Seeds Of Evil / Everlasting Bloodshed.
HELLBRIGADE, Soundholic TKCS-85003 (2000) (Japanese release). Towards Devastation / On With Eternity / The Eyes Of The Dead / Emperor Of Death / Last Redemption / Blood Conqueror / Neverending Hell / Nightbreeder / Hellbrigade / Apocalyptic Armageddon / Seeds Of Evil / Everlasting Bloodshed.
DIABOLICAL DESECRATION, Candlelight CANDLE 065CD (2002). Demonic Warlust / Forthcoming Terror / Spawned To Destroy / Soulcrusher / Diabolical Desecration / On Violent Soil / Total Misanthropia / The Bloodline / A War Symphony / Hellfire Twilight.
Hail Germania, Hell's Headbangers HELLS EP001 (2003) (Split single with NUNSLAUGHTER. Limited edition 1000 copies). Enchanted Land.
Deathlike Recollections, Sword & Sorcery STEEL 003 (2003). Blood On My Skin / Shadows Are Astray.
DECADENCE—PROPHECIES OF COSMIC CHAOS, Candlelight CANDLE 089 (2004) (CD version). Arrival Of The Spectrum Obscure / Misanthropic Darkzone / Hollowsphere / Target: Dimension XII / Deathstar Unmasked / A Dynasty Of Obedience / Mechanical Future / Cold Deep Supremacy / New World Odyssey.
DECADENCE—PROPHECIES OF COSMIC CHAOS, Hells Headbangers HELLS LP 003 (2004) (Vinyl version. Limited edition 566 copies). Arrival Of The Spectrum Obscure / Misanthropic Darkzone / Hollowsphere / Target: Dimension XII / Deathstar Unmasked / A Dynasty Of Obedience / Mechanical Future / Cold Deep Supremacy / New World Odyssey.
DECADENCE—PROPHECIES OF COSMIC CHAOS, Soundholic TKCS-85100 (2004) (Japanese release). Arrival Of The Spectrum Obscure / Misanthropic Darkzone / Hollowsphere / Target: Dimension XII / Deathstar Unmasked / A Dynasty Of Obedience / Mechanical Future / Cold Deep Supremacy / New World Odyssey / Towards Devastation (Live) / Bloodhunt (Live) / Arrival Of The Spectrum Obscure (Video).
Live Devastation, Swedmetal SM-01-7 (2004) (7" vinyl single limited to 500 copies). Towards Devastation / Bloodhunt.
WORLD DECLENSION, Regain RR 081 (2005). Victorious Dawn Rising / Purgatorial Overdrive / The Destroyer / As Legions Come / Sworn / Synthetic Sin Zero / Flesh Is Fragile / Wretched Cut / Deconstruction Macabre.
WORLD DECLENSION, Candlelight CANDLE 227 (2005) (USA release). Victorious Dawn Rising / Purgatorial Overdrive / The Destroyer / As Legions Come / Sworn / Synthetic Sin Zero / Flesh Is Fragile / Wretched Cut / Deconstruction Macabre.
METAL PACK VOL. 9, Candlelight TANGLA0009 (2005) (4 CD box set). Towards Devastation / On With Eternity / The Eyes Of The Dead / Emperor Of Death / Last Redemption / Blood Conqueror / Neverending Hell / Nightbreeder / Hellbrigade / Apocalyptic Armageddon / Seeds Of Evil / Everlasting Bloodshed / Upon The Ancient Ground / Dark Visions / Sorrow Of The Burning Wasteland / Transcend The Dark Chaos / Thorns Of Desolation / Eternal Lies / At The Everlasting End / Cranial Dismemberment / Only Slices Remain / Torn Within / Mutilation / Ripping Corpse / Under The Pagan Glory / For Centuries Untold / Luciferian Moon / Bloodhunt / The Conquest Infernal / Like Darkened Storms / Embraced By Moonlight / Resurrected / Summon The Golden Twilight / The Beauty Of Malice / Under The Guillotine / Through Celestial Gates / Molested / In The Arch Of Serenity / Shadowland / Eternal Lies / Arrival Of The Spectrum Obscure / Misanthropic Darkzone / Hollowsphere / Target: Dimension XII / Deathstar Unmasked / A Dynasty Of Obedience / Mechanical Future / Cold Deep Supremacy / New World Odyssey.

CENTURIAN

PUTTEN, HOLLAND — *Jerry Brouwer (vocals / bass), Rob Oorthuis (guitar), Oskar van Paradijs (guitar), Wim van der Valk (drums).*

A Putten based, vicious Black Metal act rooted in a prior Thrash / Death formation known as INQUISITOR. Two members of INQUISITOR, Rob Oorthuis and drummer Wim van der Valk founded CENTURION in January of 1997, soon enlisting vocalist Seth van der Loo and undertaking live gigs. This trio completed recordings for a promotional CD entitled 'Of Purest Fire', after which bass player Patrick Boley was inducted into the fold. The American Full Moon Productions label would pick up 'Of Purest Fire' for commercial release in April of 1998, the title track also featuring on the compilation album 'Tribute To Hell'. Dark Angel Records would also release 'Of Purest Fire' in cassette form.

The full length 'Choronzonic Chaos Gods', packaged complete with sleeve artwork executed by Oorthuis in his own blood, arrived the following year. However, both van der Loo and Boley opted out in December of 2000 in order to concentrate on their priority act SEVERE TORTURE. The band would then draft vocalist / bass player Jerry Brouwer and additional guitar player Oskar van Paradijs, both members of Death Metal band ZI XUL, in January of 2001. This revised version of CENTURION cut a cover of MORBID ANGEL's 'Blasphemy' for a tribute album 'Scream Forth Blasphemy'.

The 'Liber Zar Zax' album, for new label Listenable Records, surfaced in October of 2001 and was picked up by Olympic Records for North American distribution in February the following year. The Perverted Taste imprint would subsequently release a limited vinyl version. CENTURION undertook dates across the UK in March of 2002 billed with Polish Death Metal veterans VADER and Thrashers DEW SCENTED.

Of Purest Fire EP, Full Moon Productions (1998). Intro: Evoking Demonstorms / Hell At Last / Soultheft / Blasphemy / Better Of Burning / God Got Killed / Of Purest Fire / Damnation For The Holy.
CHOROZONIC CHAOS GODS, Full Moon Productions (1999). Damned And Dead / The Law Of Burning / Hail Caligula!!! / Misanthropic Luciferian Onslaught / Let Jesus Bleed / Blood For Satan / Soul Theft / Cross Of Fury / In The Name Of Chaos.

LIBER ZAR ZAX, Listenable (2001). The Reading (ZarZax Unto Zax) / Heading For Holocaust / Colosseum Of Blood / Hell At Last / Ritually Slaughtered For Satan / Feeding Flesh To The Vortex / Conjuration For Choronzon / Speech Of The Serpent / Committed To Hell / Fornicating The Nazarene / Dead Black Nucleus.

CEPHALECTOMY

TRURO, NS, CANADA — *Jason Nichols (vocals), Rob DeCoste (guitar), Corey Andrews (guitar / drums).*

Novia Scotia's "Mystigrind" Death Metal combo CEPHALECTOMY released the demo 'Gateway To The Gods' in 1997, this session being crafted by a line up of vocalist/guitarist Corey Andrews, bassist Jason Nichols, and drummer Clayton Horne. However, Horne was to exit the ranks, according to the band due to his "lack of interest and evil spirit". SPUR drummer Chad Mitchell briefly held membership before CEPHALECTOMY opted to persevere as a duo. The 'Dark Waters Rise' session arrived the following year. DICHOTIC's Raland Kinley would aid on guest vocals.

The band signed to Discorporate Music in 1999 for the album 'Sign Of Gods', with 'Eclipsing The Dawn' following in March of 2004.

SIGN OF CHAOS, Discorporate Music (2000). Upon Winged Elemental Crests / Dimensional Manifestation Of Ashen Forms / Through The Ethereal Vortex Of Archaic Life / The Ravaged Crimson Fields Of Evanescence / Phantoms Of The Fallen Ruins Of Kia / Spaces Between The Realms Of Existence / Gates To The Spheres Of Astral Frost / Unto The Darkly Shining Abyss.

ECLIPSING THE DAWN, Discorporate Music DCM006 (2004). Of Grievance And Exhumation . . . (The Fallen) / Espousing The Lore Of Ancient Mythos / Discerning Thee Apocryphal Divinity / Invocate The Tempests To Castigation / The Squalid Eyes Of Impending Treachery / The Ghosts Of Reprisal And Strife / Dragons Upon The Mountains Of Mashu / The Sundering Of Eternal Sentience.

CEPHALIC CARNAGE

DENVER, CO, USA — *Lenzig (vocals), Zac (guitar), Steve (guitar), Jawsh Mullen (bass), John (drums).*

CEPHALIC CARNAGE, a self-styled "Rocky Mountain hydrogrind" band, marked their entrance onto the Doom-Death scene with a triumvirate of demos in 1994's 'Scrape My Lungs', 1996's 'Fortuitous Oddity' and a further self titled release in 1997. Upfront of the opening 'Conforming To Abnormality' album for Headfucker Records the band released a split tape in union with ADNAUSEUM. CEPHALIC CARNAGE covered a version of SLAYER's 'Jesus Saves' for the tribute album Gateway To Hell II' on Dwell Records. The band also recorded a split album with ANAL BLAST on Nightfall Records. Ex-bassist Doug Williams would join ORIGIN during 1999.

CEPHALIC CARNAGE toured North America in 2000 on a package bill with INTERNAL BLEEDING and DEEDS OF FLESH. By September of 2002 the band would be acting as opening act for the veteran German Thrash duo KREATOR and DESTRUCTION.

The band undertook the 'North American Contamination' tour alongside MASTODON, Santa Barbara's UPHILL BATTLE and Philadelphia's DYSRHYTHMIA in May of 2003. CEPHALIC CARNAGE enrolled Patrick Russel of SERBERUS and EMBER repute as stand in guitarist. The band united with MADBALL, HATE ETERNAL, TERROR and headliners HATEBREED for the North American 'Rise Of Brutality' tour commencing 10th September.

The band entered the DVD generation by filming their January 2004 show at the Denver, Ogden Theatre gig for release as a concert package. Supported by NOISEAR and CONTROL ELEMENT, the gig was a free event. CEPHALIC CARNAGE would enter the studio to cut a new album, 'Anomalies', in September with producer Dave Otero. The record would be promoted by a Darren Doane directed promotional video for the track 'Dying Will Be The Death Of Me'.

CEPHALIC CARNAGE (pic: Jesse Angelo)

May of 2005 saw the band announcing North American shows partnered with SHADOWS FALL, TERROR and ZAO. Road work was set to continue throughout 2005, witnessing announced October and November shows packaged with CRYPTOPSY, SUFFOCATION, ABORTED and WITH PASSION. However, in June the band dropped off this tour. Going into September, the band formed up package shows backed by BETWEEN THE BURIED AND ME, THE BLACK DAHLIA MURDER, and INTO THE MOAT.

Bassist Jawsh Mullen exited in January 2006 to prioritise his education and other acts MUNIMULA, STUNTCOCK and CARNICERIA. In April the group hit the US campaign trail once again, this time with A LIFE ONCE LOST, SCARLET and THROUGH THE EYES OF THE DEAD in tow. CEPHALIC CARNAGE teamed up with DARKEST HOUR and DEAD TO FALL for an extensive European tour in June.

The group, working with longtime collaborator Dave Otero, commenced fresh album recordings in late January 2007 resulting in the 'Xenosapien' set. Back on the campaign trail, CEPHALIC CARNAGE lent support to BRUJERIA on US dates in March. The group teamed up with TED MAUL and AKERCOCKE for a tour of the UK and Ireland in May. The band's next tour outing was to be the 'Summer Slaughter' trek across the USA throughout June and July, seeing NECROPHAGIST headlining on a mammoth package billing with DECAPITATED, BENEATH THE MASSACRE, CATTLE DECAPITATION, THE FACELESS, AS BLOOD RUNS BLACK, ARSIS and ION DISSONANCE.

CONFORMING TO ABNORMALITY, Headfucker (1999). Anechoic Chamber / Jihad / Analytical / Wither / Regalos De Mora / Extreme Of Paranoia / AZT / Waiting For The Millenium.

EXPLOITING DYSFUNCTION, Relapse (2000). Hybrid / Driven To Insanity / Rehab / Observer To The Obliteration Of Planet Earth / On Six / Gracias / Crypto Sporidium / The Ballad Of Moon / Of Smoke / Warm Hand On A Cold Night (A Tale Of Onesomes) / Invertus Induca (The Marijuana Convictions) / Molestandos Plantas Muertos! / Eradicate Authority / Paralyzed By Fear / Exploiting Dysfunction.

LUCID INTERVAL, Relapse (2002). Scolopendra Cingulata / Fortuitous Oddity / Anthro Emesis / The Isle Of California / Pseudo / Friend Of Mine / Rebellion / Zuno Gyakusatsu / Black Metal Sabbath / Cannabism / Lucid Interval / Misguided / Redundant / Arsonist Savior.

Halls Of Amenti, Willowtip WT-017 (2002). Halls Of Amenti.

PERVERSION . . . AND THE GUILT AFTER, Willowtip (2003) (Split album with ANAL BLAST). I Live At Your Mom's House / Strung Out / Exhumed Remains / Britches / The Struggle / Trailer Park Meth Queen / Phantom Pharter / Trailer Park Meth Queen / Perversions And The Guilt After / Stepped In Cowshit Blues / Father Pederast / Once More Without Feeling / Shut Up / Novicane / Shrup Po' boy / Celebrate / Occular Penile Recepticle / 17 Minutes Of Your Time.

ANOMOLIES, Relapse (2005). Scientific Remote Viewing / Wraith / Counting The Days / The Will Or The Way / Piecemaker / Envivore / Dying Will Be The Death Of Me / Inside Is Out / Sleeprace / Kill For Weed / Litany Of Failure / Ontogeny Of Behavior.

CEREMONIAL EXECUTION

MJÖLBY, SWEDEN — *Robert Kardell (vocals), Matte Frisk (guitar), Jimmy Johansson (guitar), Björn Ahlqvist (bass), David Andersson (drums).*

Mjölby Death Metal act forged in early 2003 by former members of BLUMP, guitarists Matte 'Flesh' Frisk and Jimmy 'Dolla' Johansson along with ex-GUTS, SINNERS FATE and MEADOWS IN SILENCE drummer David 'Deathroll' Andersson. CORNERPIT's Robert 'Gorebert' Kardell assumed the vocal role and initially THY PRIMORDIAL, INDUNGEON, NIDEN DIV. 187 and CARCAROTH man Jonas Albrektsson took on bass duties but he soon bowed out. Björn Ahlqvist of GUTS and DEMONS TO PREFER took over the bass role.

CEREMONIAL EXECUTION issued the October 2003 demo 'Ceremonial Execution'. A split 7" vinyl single with BORIGOR arrived in 2004 through Erode Records. The album 'Death Shall Set Us free' was released in September 2005. CEREMONIAL EXECUTION closed 2006 with their December 'Black God Rising' single on Blood Harvest Records.

Ceremonial Execution, Ceremonial Execution (2003) (Demo). Parasite / Abdominal Goring With Broken Bottle / Vermin / Everything Dies.
Ceremonial Execution / Borigor, Erode 002 (2004) (Split 7" vinyl single with BORIGOR). Parasite / Abnormal Goring With A Broken Bottle.
DEATH SHALL SET US FREE, Ceremonial Execution (2005). Rotten Remains / Parasite / Drowned In Blood / Abdominal Goring With Broken Bottle / Death Is Certain / Ceremonial Execution / Everything Dies / Mass Consumption / Intestinal Collapse.
Black God Rising, Blood Harvest (2006) (7" vinyl single). Life Denied / Black God Rising / Autopsy Of My Dying Bride.

CEREMONIAL OATH

GOTHENBURG, SWEDEN — *Anders Friden (vocals), Anders Iwers (guitar), Mikael Andersson (guitar), Thomas Johansson (bass), Markus Nordberg (drums).*

A melodic Death Metal band founded in Gothenburg during 1989 by erstwhile guitarist Anders Iwers, ex-FORSAKEN guitarist Mikael Andersson, bassist Jesper Strömblad and former CRYSTAL AGE vocalist Oscar Dronjak. Both Iwers and Dronjac also featured as part of Black / Thrash act DESECRATOR, this antecedent act having released the 1989 demo cassette 'Wake The Dead' and in 1990, a three song demo 'Black Sermons'.

CEREMONIAL OATH debuted in 1992 with a single, 'The Lost Name Of God', on Corpsegrinder Records. Unfortunately, the band was hit by the departure of Strombold, who left to join IN FLAMES, and Dronjac, having decided to reunite with CRYSTAL AGE, following the release of the debut album 'The Book Of Truth'. Anders Iwers would join high profile acts CEMETARY then TIAMAT.

Interestingly, both Strömbold and Dronjac were to come to the fore in 1997 with their Trad Metal side project band HAMMERFALL which, with their debut album 'Glory To The Brave', quite unexpectedly broke the national German charts wide open.

CEREMONIAL OATHS's eventual second album, 'Carpet', included a guest performance by AT THE GATES vocalist Tomas Lindberg. It also featured a version of IRON MAIDEN's 'Hallowed Be Thy Name'. The group has also submitted a version of 'Disposable Heroes' for the METALLICA tribute album 'Metal Militia'.

Ceremonial Oath, Ceremonial Oath (1991) (Demo). The Lost Name Of God / For I Have Sinned / The Praise.
Lost Name Of God, Corpse Grinder CGR 005 (1992). Lost Name Of God / For I Have Sinned / The Praise.
THE BOOK OF TRUTH, Modern Primitive 38102242 (1993). Prologue (Sworn To Avenge) / The Invocation / For I Have Sinned (The Praise) / Enthroned / Only Evil Prevails / Thunderworld (Welcome To Forever) / Lords Of Twilight / Ceremonial Oath / The Lost Name Of God / Book Of Truth B / Hellbound.
CARPET, Black Sun BS02 (1995). The Day I Buried / Dreamsong / Carpet / The Shadowed End / One Of Us / Nightshade / Immortalised / Hallowed Be Thy Name.

CEREMONY

TAMPA, FL, USA — *Steve Tucker (vocals / bass), Pat O'Brien (guitar), Greg Reed (guitar), Shannon Purdon (drums).*

A Death Metal 'Super' combo centred upon MORBID ANGEL vocalist / bassist Steve Tucker, CANNIBAL CORPSE, ex-NEVERMORE, MONSTROSITY and CANNIBAL CORPSE guitarist Pat O'Brien and DISASTRONAUT guitarist Greg Reed. The EMPEROR, ENSLAVED and ZYKLON credited drummer Trym Torson (a.k.a. Kai Johnny Mosaker) was recruited in 2002.

Tucker duly rejoined MORBID ANGEL for the 2003 album 'Heretic', but would leave the band again, exiting just prior to proposed Mexican dates in August 2004. Apparently Tucker had suffered "massive anxiety attack and had to be hospitalized". The frontman soon responded, stating that he had contracted a lung infection "due to my excessive travel and the variety of weather and environments that I endure in these travels."

Greg Reed would be involved with the 2004 Alt-Rock act UNDERCURRENT, a project comprising former MORBID ANGEL frontman Steven Tucker, SUBVINYL man Anthony Gentry on bass and DISINTER drummer Tomaz. March of 2005 found Tucker acting as stand-in bassist for NILE's European festival dates.

The Days Before The Death EP, Hammerheart (2000). Parade The Insane / Instrumental / Crucifixion / Sculpted Humanity.

CHAIN COLLECTOR

KRISTIANSAND, NORWAY — *Kjetil Nordhus (vocals), Gøran Bomann (guitar), Kjell Jacobsen (guitar), Anders Kobro (drums).*

Kristiansand act incorporating the IN THE WOODS and GREEN CARNATION duo of vocalist Kjetil Nordhus and drummer Anders Kobro. The latter also has credits with SCARIOT and CARPATHIAN FOREST whilst Nordhus also has ties to TRAIL OF TEARS. Guitarist Gøran Bomann holds CARPATHIAN FOREST, PANTACULUM, NEON GOD and APOSTASY connections whilst second guitarist Kjell Jacobsen is a founding member of NEON GOD.

CHAIN COLLECTOR's demo 'Forthcoming Addiction', recorded by Endre Kirkesola at DUB Studios during February and March 2004, landed a two album deal with the Portuguese label Sound Riot. The band set to work on an album with producer Endre Kirkesola in October. In September 2005 CHAIN COLLECTOR revealed they had licensed to Germany's Massacre Records for 'The Masquerade' album for distribution across Europe, Canada, South America and Australia.

In early 2007 Kjetil Nordhus ended his collaboration with both TRAIL OF TEARS and CHAIN COLLECTOR in order to prioritise GREEN CARNATION. The group signed with Sublife Productions in April.

Fourthcoming Addiction, Chain Collector (2004). Wicked Mask / Winter Princess / Crucifixion / Fallen Angel.
THE MASQUERADE, Sound Riot SRP.035 (2005). Hierarchy Of Murder (Code Of Silence) / Harvester / Neverwhere / And Then There Was None / Crucifixion / Project Savior / Tapping The Vein / Fallen Angel / Wicked Mask / Winter Princess.

CHAINGUNN

WILKESBORO, NC, USA — *Russell Shumate (vocals), Jason Tedder (guitar), Brian Williams (guitar), Steven Adams (bass), Erik McCray (drums).*

Wilkesboro-Charlotte, North Carolina Death Metal band. CHAINGUNN guitarist Brian Williams has a tradition with OVERLORDE, K OCTAVE and OCTOBER 31. His fellow six stringer Jason Tedder is also a K OCTAVE member. The band's original rhythm section of May 2002 comprised bassist Joel McGee and drummer Dennis Warren of CRYPTAMERIA repute.

When Warren relinquished his position to DARKMOON's Scott Pletcher. When Pletcher exited for WEHRWOLFE he was duly superseded by DESECRATOR man Erik McCray. However, with McCray's departure the band went into hiatus.

In 2006 CHAINGUNN reformed around guitarist Jason Tedder and singer Russell Shumate. The band issued 'Show Me Your War Face'. In August drummer Mark Bare was replaced by Tom Berry of OBEY BIZARRE and K OCTAVE.

SHOW ME YOUR WAR FACE, Chaingunn (2006). Time To Pray / Your Pain Is Forever / No Glory No Guts / You Die Here / Show Me Your War Face / It Has A Name / Judge Jury Executioner / The Kill Machine / Mommie Dearest.

CHANGER

REYKJAVIK, ICELAND — *Egill (vocals), Johann (guitar), Fannar (guitar), Gisli (bass / vocals), Kristjan B. Heidarsson (drums).*

Death Metal with Metalcore traits. Reykjavik's CHANGER features the POTENTIAM rhythm section of bass player Berti and drummer Kristjan B. Heidarsson. The latter, also citing credits with OBSCURED SIGNAL, DARK HARVEST, PORNEA as well as SHIVA and working from his hometown of Akureyri, would initiate the project as a solo venture during November of 1999. In his guise CHANGER released the album 'January 109' in January of 2000. This album, issued by Hardkjarni Records, was limited to just 50 copies. Relocating to the capitol Reykjavík, Kristjan B. Heidarsson drafted guitarist Jói, second guitarist Hudson of SKURK and bassist Snorri. Subsequent changes saw Berti taking the position and Magnus enrolling as frontman.

The band first performed live in March of 2001, after which CHANGER issued the Kristján Edelstein produced 'Inconsistency' EP. Live work in Iceland saw an appearance at the 'Icelandic Airwaves' festival as well as supports to INSTIL, AMON AMARTH and MASTODON. During February of 2004 the band cut the album 'Scenes', recorded at I.V. Studios in Reykjavik with producer Óskar Ingi Gíslason.

In early 2006 CHANGER recorded a new EP, entitled 'Breed The Lies', mixed and mastered at Antfarm Studios in Denmark by producer Tue Madsen. January 2007 witnessed a line-up change as CHANGER parted ways with guitarist Fannar. After two gigs as a four-piece, CHANGER announced a replacement guitarist Unnar.

JANUARY 109, Hardkjarni (2000) (Limited edition 50 copies). Gates Of Instability / Armageddon / Decisions / Slow / In Dreams / Fields Of Fear / Religion In Flames / Quicksilver.
Inconsistency, Changer (2001). Feelings: Deleted / Lost Chances / Religion In Flames / Fields Of Fear.
Sept 2001 Demo, Changer (2001) (Demo). Fudge / New Eden Attitude / Spunk.
Fudge, Changer (2002) (Rehearsal demo). Vicious / Go On / Stand Up And Lie / Fudge / Untitled.
SCENES, Inconsistency (2004). Vicious / Go On / The New Eden Attitude / Craving Romancer / Rough Mix / Fudge / Scenes / The Lord Is A Monkey / Spönk / Kill The Human.
Breed The Lies, Inconsistency (2006). Breed The Lies / Recaptured Sanity / Path Of Anguish / Odium.

CHAOSBREED

HELSINKI, FINLAND — *Taneli Jarva (vocals), Esa Holopainen (guitar), Marko Tarvonen (guitar), Oppu Laine (bass), Nalle Österman (drums).*

CHAOSBREED, unveiled in early 2003, is a something of a Helsinki Metal 'Supergroup'. The band comprised lead vocalist Taneli Jarva of SENTENCED and THE BLACK LEAGUE, guitarists Esa Holopainen of AMORPHIS and Marko Tarvonen of MOONSORROW, bass player Oppu Laine of AMORPHIS and MANNHAI repute with former GANDALF drummer Nalle Österman. The band would debut with the demo 'Unleashed Carnage' with a commercial inauguration courtesy of a split 7" single shared with RYTMIHÄIRIÖ issued through Rising Realm Records. This single contained rough mixes of 'Sink In Hell', 'Slutrush' and the CARNAGE cover version 'The Day Man Lost'. The group's demo would subsequently see CD format release in North America and Europe through Crash Music Inc. in January 2004. A full blown album, entitled 'Brutal', would be cut at CCPC Studios with producers Santeri Kallio and Niclas Etelävuori.

A further split single in union with RYTMIHÄIRIÖ would be cut in March of 2004, this outing comprising two new tracks and a cover of MASTER's 'Funeral Bitch'. Plans would also be underway for another split 7" in alliance with TO SEPARATE THE FLESH FROM THE BONES. With Oppu Laine committed to a MANNHAI gig the same day as CHAOSBREED's performance at the Helsinki 'Tuska' festival the band pulled in Janne Perttilä of RYTMIHÄIRIÖ as substitute. A Jyväskylä gig in August was cancelled when Taneli Jarva injured his back during a show in Oulu with THE BLACK LEAGUE.

CHAOSBREED lent support to GRAVE's March 2004 Finnish dates and their return run in May upfront of a European leg. However, the band revealed it had parted ways with both vocalist Taneli Jarva and guitarist Esa Holopainen. CHAOSBREED then retracted earlier statements, revealing that Jarva and Holopainen would be participating in gigs throughout May with GRAVE. Within days the confusion grew as CHAOSBREED then put out a press release pulling out of the GRAVE shows.

An interesting diversion came in on 4th August when CHAOSBREED members Oppu Laine and Nalle Österman put in a one off tribute show to THE DOORS with a band entitled THE BLUE HORSE. With Österman switching his traditional role as drummer over to lead singer for the evening, THE BLUE HORSE also comprised lead guitarist Markku "Crazy" Heiskanen of HAVANA BLACK, ex-AMORPHIS and MANNHAI keyboard player Kasper Martenson and MANNHAI drummer Mikko "Junior" Pietinen.

Unleashed Carnage, Chaosbreed (2003) (Demo). Wretched Life / Rotting Alive / F/C/D/C (Freedom Corps Death Crush).
Unleashed Carnage, Rising Realm REALM 004 (2003). Intro—Prelude To Death / Wretched Life / Rotting Alive / F/C/D/C (Freedom Corps Death Crush) / Friendly Fire.
BRUTAL, Century Media 77475-2 (2004). Wretched Life / Casket Ride / Faces Of Death / Moralized / Rotting Alive / Demon Skunk / Shitgrinder / Symptoms Of The Flesh / F/C/D/C (Freedom Corps Death Crush) / An Evil Eye / Rotting Alive (Live video) / F/C/D/C (Live video).
Chaosbreed Mixtape, Century Media (2004) (Promotion release. Cassette marketing article for album release party limited to 50 copies). Moralized (Album version) / Casket Ride (Live at Stella Star Club July 2003) / Ridden With Disease (Live at Stella Star Club July 2003) / Supposed To Rot (Live at Stella Star Club July 2003) / Moralized (Live at Nosturi September 2003) / The Day Man Lost (Live at Nosturi September 2003) / F/C/D/C (Instrumental rehearsal April 2004) / Gypsy Doom (Instrumental rehearsal March 2004).
Chaosbreed / Rytmihäiriö, Homorock PARITUS-69 (2004) (Split 7" vinyl single with RYTMIHÄIRIÖ). Rabid Outburst / Crippled Beyond Belief / Funeral Bitch.

CHAOSYS

SÖDERTÄLJE, SWEDEN — *Stefan Lindstedt (vocals), Tomas Åkvik (guitar), Holger Thorsin (guitar), Johan Risberg (bass), Tommy Enström (drums).*

CHAOSYS is a Södertälje based Death / Thrash outfit formulated during 2003 from pedigree extreme Metal talent. Lead vocalist Stefan Lindstedt cites a tradition with WEB OF SOLITUDE and THE KRISTER OUTLOOK EXPRESS, guitarist Tomas Åkvik held membership of THE KRISTER OUTLOOK EXPRESS and BRUTALITY OF ANGER whilst second guitarist Holger Thorsin has NOCTES, FIST FIRST, 138, CONSTELLATION and CONCEALED credits. The band's rhythm section comprising bassist Johan Risberg and drummer Tommy Enström boast a heritage with FAREWELL ETERNITY. Risberg also has TIDERLAG connections.

CHAOSYS delivered the EP 'The Inperfection Is Yours' in 2004. CHAOSYS credited guitarist Oak joined NALE in December 2006.

Demo 2003.02.23, Chaosys (2003) (Demo). P.M. Faith Proclaimed / Deus Ex / Mass Submission.

The Inperfection Is Yours, Chaosys (2004). SPS / Signed Yours Faithfully / Humanity 6.8.

Development Of The Human Mind, Chaosys (2005) (Demo). Retardeadnation / Alteration.

CHASTISEMENT

ÖSTERSUND, SWEDEN — *Johan Klitkou (vocals), Marcus Edvardsson (guitar), Tommy Larsson (guitar), Nicklas Linnes (bass), Nils Fjellström (drums).*

CHASTISEMENT, created during 1995 by the guitar duo of Fredrik Magnusson and Marcus Edvardsson, is a melodic Death Metal unit from the northern town of Östersund. In 1997 drummer Nils Fjellström, also active with AEON, SANCTIFICATION and IN BATTLE, joined the fold. CHASTISEMENT recorded the demos '... But Lost We Are' in 1999 and 'Alleviation Of Pain' during 2002. The band underwent a major overhaul in 2002 as bassist Per Gabrielsson lost out to Nicklas Linnes, Magnusson was replaced by Tommy Larson and Johan Klitkou was introduced on lead vocals.

Besides their endeavours with CHASTISEMENT Klitkou, Edvardsson, Larsson and Fjellström are also involved with SOULDRAINER. Tommy Larsen joined JAGGERNAUT then in August of 2005 enrolled into the ranks of DREAM EVIL. However, in February 2006 the bassist joined HEED, the group assembled by erstwhile LOST HORIZON members singer Daniel Heiman and guitarist Fredrik Olsson.

2006 witnessed the formation of neo-Thrash Metal act ENDLESS TORTURE, a union between Marcus Edvardsson, A*TEEM vocalist Peter Mellgren plus Tom Åsvold, from PAINCRAZE and DIMENSION34, on drums.

Chastisement, Chastisement (1997) (Demo).

... BUT LOST WE ARE, Chastisement (1999). Rapid Fluid / Exposed Hatred / At the Garden of Eden / Conclusion; Pain! / My Father / But Lost We Are / Life Denied.

ALLEVIATION OF PAIN, Chastisement (2002). Another Pace / Destructutorial / Soul Evasion / The Journey / Tsavo—The Land Of Slaughter / Time Zone Zero / Disowned / World Beyond / Joie De Vivre / Redeemer / I Am You / Disgust / A New Dawn.

LIVE AT GAMLA TINGSHUSET ÖSTERSUND, Chastisement (2003). The Journey (Intro) / Tsavo—The Land Of Slaughter / Time Zone Zero / Disowned / Another Pace / Destructutorial / Disgust / Teaser / Redeemer / Life Denied / Rapid Fluid / A New Dawn / Soul Evasion.

ALLEVIATION OF PAIN, Rage Of Achilles ILIAD050 (2004) (UK release). Another Pace / Destructutorial / Soul Evasion / The Journey / Tsavo—The Land Of Slaughter / Time Zone Zero / Disowned / World Beyond / Joie De Vivre / Redeemer / I Am You / Disgust / A New Dawn.

CHEMICAL DISASTER

BRAZIL — *Leao Gazzano (vocals), Fernando Nonath (guitar), Fabio Brunelli (bass), Arthur Justo (drums).*

An early Brazilian Death Metal band. CHEMICAL DISASTER released the 'Ressurrection' album through the Cogumelo label in 1993 but suffered line up fractures afterward. Guitarist Diego Gonzales relocated to Argentina, singer Luis Carlos exited and other members defected to join the band BLACK METAL. Another formative member, guitarist Marcelo Miranda would gain credits with CANIS LUPUS (as 'Lord Vargathron'), NERVOCHAOS and OLAM EIN SOF.

The band began to rebuild itself slowly, bringing in guitarist Fernando Nonath in 1993, singer Leao Gazzano in 1996 and

CHILDREN OF BODOM

finally bass player Fabio Brunelli two years later. CHEMICAL DISASTER re-recorded two tracks, 'Sexual Maniac' and 'The Sinner', from their debut for the comeback album 'Scraps Of A Being'.

RESSURRECTION, Cogumelo (1993). Ressurrection / Ghastly Altar / Disagreement / Pleasures Of Pain / Realm Of Darkness / Suffer 'Till Die / Sexual Maniac / Along With Death / On Your Left / Stormy Life / Town Of The Damned / The Sinner / Clash Of Souls.

CHILDREN OF BODOM

ESPOO, FINLAND — *Alex Laiho (vocals / guitar), Ale Kuoppala (guitar), Henkka Seppäiä (bass), Janne Wirman Pimeys (keyboards), Jaska Raatikainen (drums).*

A powerful, modern Metal act from the town of Espoo, named after Finland's infamous Lake Bodom, the scene of a horrific, unsolved attack on June 5th 1960 that left three teenagers dead. The children had died from multiple stab wounds but a sole survivor, Nils Gustafsson, was famously declared insane and institutionalized after he had blamed the attack on the Grim Reaper. This medieval harbinger of death character would feature prominently on all of the group's output to date.

Founder member and vocalist Alex "Wildchild" Laiho made his name as part of THY SERPENT, maintaining CHILDREN OF BODOM, created in 1993 with drummer Jaska Raatikainen, as a going concern. Initially the group had gone under the title of INEARTHED, issuing a batch of melodic Death Metal demos commencing with 'Implosion Of Heaven', recorded at Munkkiniemen Studios in August 1994 and released that December. These tracks would be laid down as a duo of Laiho and Raatikainen.

INEARTHED followed this opening tape with second set 'Ubiquitous Absence Of Remission' in July 1995, recording this time at Astia Studios. Interestingly, melodies from the track 'Translucent Image', which featured female guest vocals from Nina Keitel, would re-surface in SINERGY's 'Beware The Heavens' at a later date. Once again composed and performed by Laiho and Raatikainen, the tape does make mention of bassist Samuli Miettinen and new member rhythm guitarist Alexander Kuoppala. A third demo, entitled 'Shining', was committed to tape at Astia Studios in February 1996 utilising keyboard player Jan Peri Pirisjoki. A line-up change found bassist Samuli Miettinen superseded by Henkka Seppala.

As INEARTHED the group scored a label deal in Belgium but a better offer from the highly respected Finnish Spinefarm concern convinced the band their way. At this stage the band, now with Janne Wirman Pimeys on keyboards, switched title to CHILDREN OF BODOM recording the Anssi Kippo, Alex Laiho and Jaska Raatikainen produced 'Something Wild' debut.

The album was issued in Finland in February 1997 and picked up for European license by the German Nuclear Blast corporation shortly after, emerging on the continent in April 1998, and successively via Toy's Factory in Japan. Adding a degree of colour to the mix, the group employed movie narrative from 'Ben Hur' as an intro to 'The Nail', the opening section of 'Deadnight Warrior' being taken from the film 'It' and even Mozart's Symphony no. 25 was re-worked for 'Red Light in My Eyes, Pt 2'. The group recorded an additional track, 'Children Of Bodom', which, when released as a single alongside tracks from CRYHAVOC and WIZZARD, scored the unprecedented achievement of hitting the number 1 spot on the charts. The band supported DIMMU BORGIR on their 1997 Finnish dates and in February of the following year hooked up with HYPOCRISY, COVENANT and BENEDICTION for mainland European gigs. For these shows, a friend of the band, Erna, substituted for Wirman Pimeys who could not get time out of schooling. With album sales on a sharp rise, CHILDREN OF BODOM were back out on the road in Europe during September, performing as part of another package bill with DISMEMBER, AGATHODAIMON, RAISE HELL and NIGHT IN GALES. Once again Wirman Pimeys had to sit it out and Kimberley Goss of AVERNUS, DIMMU BORGIR and THERION repute filled in. A one off concert in St. Petersburg, Russia, pairing with IMPALED NAZARENE, resulted in Alex Laiho opting to join the fellow Finns when CHILDREN OF BODOM's schedule allowed. As such, Laiho perform with IMPALED NAZARENE in February 1999 on their tour of North America and Mexico.

CHILDREN OF BODOM scored a further national number 1 single with 'Downfall' in early 1999. The single also contained a cover version of STONE's 'No Commands'. The 'Hatebreeder' album would also witness the band's presence in the national German album charts for the first time peaking at number 75. Humour was again in evidence, the intro narrative for opening song 'Warheart' being lifted from Milos Forman's 'Amadeus' movie and the keyboard introduction to 'Black Widow' brazenly borrowing from 80s TV series 'Miami Vice'.

Touring began with inaugural dates in Japan during the summer, concert recordings from Club Citta, Tokyo then surfacing as 'Tokyo Warhearts–Live In Japan', followed by a familiar all-Scandinavian Nuclear Blast package European venture allied with IN FLAMES, DARK TRANQUILITY and ARCH ENEMY. This time Janne Wirman Pimeys was finally in his rightful place behind the keyboards. In band down time Wirman, under the title of WARMEN, cut a solo album titled 'Unknown Soldier'.

In May 2000 another partnership with IMPALED NAZARENE conducted Greek gigs in Thessaloniki and Athens with Alex Laiho performing double guitar duty each night. The ensuing October album 'Follow The Reaper' record, cut at Abyss Studios in Sweden with the HYPOCRISY pairing of Peter Tägtgren and Lars Szöke acting as producer and engineer respectively, found the Japanese version with an extra bonus track, a version of OZZY OSBOURNE's 'Shot In The Dark'. Fans were quick to spot the band's now traditional oddball habit of planting the unexpected with the bridge section of 'Bodom After Midnight' in homage to 'The Rock' movie whilst speeches in 'Taste Of My Scythe' came transplanted from 'Exorcist 3'.

As a precursor of what was to come the band's 'Hate Me' single of October 2000, featuring a cover version of W.A.S.P.'s 'Hellion', swiftly reaped Platinum sales status in Finland by selling over 10'000 copies. Raatikainen deputised for SINERGY toward the close of the year before CHILDREN OF BODOM supported PRIMAL FEAR for a European tour across Germany, Austria, Italy, Spain and France in February 2001. Their 'Follow The Reaper' album quickly shifted over 50'000 copies in Europe, attaining a number 46 placing in the German national charts and reaching the top five in Finland. In October the band featured on the Spinefarm compilation 'Metal Rocks' with an exclusive cover version of IRON MAIDEN's 'Aces High'.

Jaska Raatikainen, along with TAROT and SINERGY bassist Marco Hietala and TAROT keyboard player Janne Tolsa would also convene a 2001 endeavour dubbed VIRTUOCITY. Raatikainen would also find time to session on the EVEMASTER EP 'Wither'.

CHILDREN OF BODOM broke their silence in mid 2002 unveiling plans for an August single comprising a new track 'You're Better Off Dead' coupled with a cover version of the RAMONES 'Somebody Put Something In My Drink'. Upon release this single was swiftly certified with Gold sales status. By October the band had flagged up 'Hate Crew Deathroll' as a projected title for their next Anssi Kippo produced studio album. Upon release the record crashed into the national Finnish album charts at number one, soon racking up in excess of 15,000 domestic sales and duly attaining gold status.

Jaska Raatikainen forged a project band in 2004 entitled GASHOUSE GARDEN, comprising such scene notables as NORTHER lead guitarist Kristian Ranta, CRAYDAWN guitarist Jaakko Teittinen and the SINERGY, KOTIPELTO, WARMEN credited Lauri Porra on bass. Heading up the band would be female singer Mertsa, located whilst singing AC/DC covers with her band CHINA CAT. An opening set of demos was recorded at Janne Wirman's studio in Helsinki.

CHILDREN OF BODOM live dates in Japan, allied with none other than Metal God HALFORD, were announced for February 2003. Rhythm guitarist Alexander Kuoppala left the CHILDREN OF BODOM ranks following the band's appearance at the July Helsinki 'Tuska' festival.

The band, announcing that the noted figure of SINERGY, LATVALA BROS, WALTARI and ex-STONE man Roope Latvala had joined up as session guitarist for the remainder of their world tour, debuted this new look line up in Moscow on 16th August. They would be back in the Far East for a further run of Japanese shows that September, partnering up with SOILWORK. That same month 'Hate Crew Deathroll' saw release in the USA on the Century Media label. In the interim Alexi Laiho gained co-production credits on GRIFFIN's album 'No Holds Barred'. In Japan, the Toy's Factory Records label revealed an exclusive compilation album entitled 'Bestbreeder (1997-2000)'.

CHILDREN OF BODOM united with DIMMU BORGIR, NEVERMORE and HYPOCRISY for US dates in November. During a gap in the band's schedule Laiho reunited with his ex-SINERGY comrade Tommi Lillman, founding KYLÄHULLUT, or "village idiot", alongside lead singer on Finnish punk band KLAMYDIA Vesa Jokinen. The band issued the 'Keisarinleikkaus' EP in May of 2004.

An extensive North American trek throughout April and May of 2004 had the band partnered with ICED EARTH and Swedish Progressive Metal band EVERGREY. An EP, 'Trashed, Lost & Strungout', novelly included covers of ALICE COOPER's 'Bed Of Nails' and ANDREW W.K.'s 'She Is Beautiful'. The single, backed by a promotional video for the title track directed by Patric Ullaeus, would impressively debut on the Finnish charts at no. 1. Despite all this activity Alexi Laiho found time to act as producer for the GRIFFIN album 'No Holds Barred'. Meantime Roope Latvala guested on SOULGRIND's 'The Origins Of The Paganblood' album.

The band would tour Brazil in August. October shows across the US had the band partnering with LAMB OF GOD, FEAR FACTORY and THROWDOWN.

On 5th January 2005 Alexi Laiho and Roope Latvala gathered together with Finland's Metal community at Helsinki's Rock 'n' Roll Station to pay homage to the recently murdered PANTERA / DAMAGEPLAN guitarist Darrell 'Dimebag' Abbott by forming up a one off PANTERA tribute band DIMEN NIMEEN ("In Dime's Name!"). Other musicians featured in this collective included Atte Sarkima of AJATTARA and VERENPISARA, Tony Jelencovich from TRANSPORT LEAGUE, Petteri Hirvanen and Nicke of MONSTERBALL, Toni, Pete, Kride and Jukkis of NORTHER and Nico, Euge and OJ from GODSPLAGUE amongst many others.

In early 2005 the Back On Black label re-issued 'Something Wild', 'Hatebreeder' and 'Follow The Reaper' on limited edition vinyl picture discs. CHILDREN OF BODOM's new studio album title would be revealed as 'Are You Dead Yet?'. Unfortunately, the similarity to CARNAL FORGE's recent 'Aren't You Dead Yet?' drew immediate comparisons.

CHILDREN OF BODOM's single 'In Your Face', issued in August, surprisingly included a cover version of BRITNEY SPEARS' 'Oops I Did It Again'. The album 'Are You Dead Yet?' saw release on 14th September in Finland and 19th September for the rest of the world. A limited edition vinyl picture disc, restricted to just 2000 copies, would be pressed up by Universal in Germany. In keeping with the band's left-field choice of cover songs, Japanese variants of the record added a rendition of the Glam Rock classic 'Talk To Dirty To Me' originally by POISON. 'Are You Dead Yet?' debuted at number 1 in Finland and in Japan at number 17, where it sold 21,000 copies in its first week of release. Meantime, the 'Humppasirkus' album from fabled Finnish Humppa Metal band ELÄKELÄISET sported a rendition of CHILDREN OF BODOM's 'Hate Me' re-branded 'Vihann Humppaa' ("I Hate Humppa").

US tour dates commenced in November, partnered with TRIVIUM and AMON AMARTH. The group then hooked up with EKTOMORF and ONE MAN ARMY AND THE UNDEAD QUARTET for European and Scandinavian gigs commencing in Germany during late December and finalizing in Finland in February 2006. North American gigging witnessed a union with BULLET FOR MY VALENTINE and CHIMAIRA in March. Summer 2006 US dates commencing in June, dubbed the "Unholy Alliance—Preaching To The Perverted" tour, saw the group packaged with headliners SLAYER plus MASTODON, LAMB OF GOD and THINE EYES BLEED as support. The group also joined the European leg of the 'Unholy Alliance', comprising SLAYER, IN FLAMES, LAMB OF GOD and THINE EYES BLEED, in October. CHILDREN OF BODOM teamed up with AMON AMARTH, SANCTITY and GOJIRA for a North American tour in December.

The band was announced as performing at the Dubai, United Arab Emirates 'Desert Rock' festival in March 2007 but withdrew when Alexi Laiho injured his shoulder, tripping over at a bowling alley. CHILDREN OF BODOM's performance of the song 'Everytime I Die', filmed at the BÖHSE ONKELZ farewell show in Lausitzring, Germany in 2005, was featured on a four-DVD BÖHSE ONKELZ box set.

On February 16th CHILDREN OF BODOM was honoured with the "Band of the Year" award at the Finnish Metal Awards, which were held during the Finnish Metal Expo at the Cable Factory in Helsinki, Finland.

SOMETHING WILD, Spinefarm SPI 49CD (1997). Deadnight Warrior / In The Shadows / Red Light In My Eyes (Part I) / Red Light In My Eyes (Part II) / Lake Bodom / The Nail / Touch Like Angel Of Death.

CHILDREN OF BODOM

The Carpenter, Spinefarm SPI 46CD (1997) (Split single with NIGHTWISH and THY SERPENT). Red Light In My Eyes, Part II.
Children Of Bodom, Spinefarm SPI 59CD (1998) (Split single with WIZZARD and CRYHAVOC). Children Of Bodom.
SOMETHING WILD, Toy's Factory TFCK-87155 (1998) (Japanese release). Deadnight Warrior / In The Shadows / Red Light In My Eyes (Part I) / Red Light In My Eyes (Part II) / Lake Bodom / The Nail / Touch Like Angel Of Death / Children Of Bodom / Mass Hypnosis.
Downfall, Spinefarm SPI 73CD (1998). Downfall / No Commands. Chart position: 1 FINLAND.
HATEBREEDER, Spinefarm SPI 69CD (1999). Warheart / Silent Night, Bodom Night / Hatebreeder / Bed Of Razors / Towards Dead End / Black Widow / Wrath Within / Children Of Bodom / Down Fall. Chart position: 75 GERMANY.
HATEBREEDER, Toy's Factory TFCK-87180 (1999) (Japanese release). Warheart / Silent Night, Bodom Night / Hatebreeder / Bed Of Razors / Towards Dead End / Black Widow / Wrath Within / Children Of Bodom / Down Fall / No Commands.
TOKYO WARHEARTS—LIVE IN JAPAN 1999, Nuclear Blast NB 0440-2 (1999). Intro / Silent Night, Bodom Night / Lake Bodom / Warheart / Bed Of Razors / War Of Razors / Deadnight Warrior / Hatebreeder / Touch The Angel Of Death / Downfall / Towards Dead End.
TOKYO WARHEARTS—LIVE IN JAPAN 1999, Vinyl Collector's VC 012 (1999) (Vinyl release). Intro / Silent Night, Bodom Night / Lake Bodom / Warheart / Bed Of Razors / War Of Razors / Deadnight Warrior / Hatebreeder / Touch The Angel Of Death / Downfall / Towards Dead End / No Commands.
Hate Me!, Spinefarm SPI 98CD (2000). Hate Me! / Hellion.
FOLLOW THE REAPER, Spinefarm SPI 99DP (2000) (Finnish digipack). Follow The Reaper / Bodom After Midnight / Children Of Decadence / Every Time I Die / Mask Of Sanity / Taste Of My Scythe / Hate Me! / Northern Comfort / Kissing The Shadows / Don't Stop At The Top.
FOLLOW THE REAPER, Spinefarm SPI 99CD (2000). Follow The Reaper / Bodom After Midnight / Children Of Decadence / Every Time I Die / Mask Of Sanity / Taste Of My Scythe / Hate Me! / Northern Comfort / Kissing The Shadows.

FOLLOW THE REAPER, Toy's Factory TFCK-87236 (2000) (Japanese release). Follow The Reaper / Bodom After Midnight / Children Of Decadence / Every Time I Die / Mask Of Sanity / Taste Of My Scythe / Hate Me / Northern Comfort / Kissing The Shadows / Shot In The Dark / Hellion.
FOLLOW THE REAPER, Spinefarm SPI 99CD (2001). Follow The Reaper / Bodom After Midnight / Children Of Decadence / Every Time I Die / Mask Of Sanity / Taste Of My Scythe / Hate Me / Northern Comfort / Kissing The Shadows / Hellion. Chart positions: 46 GERMANY, 85 ITALY.
SOMETHING WILD (DELUXE EDITION), Nuclear Blast NB 1017-2 (2002). Deadnight Warrior / In The Shadows / Red Light In My Eyes (Part I) / Red Light In My Eyes (Part II) / Lake Bodom / The Nail / Touch Like Angel Of Death / Children Of Bodom / Mass Hypnosis / Silent Scream / Don't Stop At The Top.
You're Better Off Dead, Spinefarm SPI 159 (2002). You're Better Off Dead / Somebody Put Something In My Drink.
HATE CREW DEATHROLL (SPECIAL EDITION), Spinefarm SPI 165SP (2003). Needled 24/7 / Sixpounder / Chokehold (Cocked 'n Loaded) / Bodom Beach Terror / Angels Don't Kill / Triple Corpse Hammerblow / You're Better Off Dead / Lil' Bloodred Ridin' Hood / Hate Crew Deathroll / Silent Scream / Hidden Internet Link To Needled 24/7 Video.
Needled 24/7, Spinefarm SPI 163PD (2003) (Picture disc). Needled 24/7 / Silent Scream.
HATE CREW DEATHROLL, Universal Japan UICO-1048 (2003) (Japanese release). Needled 24/7 / Sixpounder / Chokehold (Cocked 'n Loaded) / Bodom Beach Terror / Angels Don't Kill / Triple Corpse Hammerblow / You're Better Off Dead / Lil' Bloodred Ridin' Hood / Hate Crew Deathroll / Silent Scream / Somebody Put Something In My Drink.
HATE CREW DEATHROLL, Spinefarm SPI 165CD (2003). Needled 24/7 / Sixpounder / Chokehold (Cocked 'n Loaded) / Bodom Beach Terror / Angels Don't Kill / Triple Corpse Hammerblow / You're Better Off Dead / Lil' Bloodred Ridin' Hood / Hate Crew Deathroll. Chart positions: 1 FINLAND, 36 SWEDEN, 45 GERMANY, 74 FRANCE.
Trashed, Lost & Strungout, Spinefarm SPI 207CD (2004). Trashed, Lost & Strungout / She Is Beautiful.
Trashed, Lost & Strungout, Spinefarm SPI 207EP (2004). Trashed, Lost & Strungout / Knuckleduster / Bed Of Nails / She Is Beautiful / Trashed, Lost & Strungout (Video) / Trashed, Lost & Strungout (Video: Live in Helsinki) / Children Of Bodom's Night Out (Video). Chart positions: 1 FINLAND, 27 CANADA.
In Your Face, Spinefarm SPI 244CD (2005). In Your Face / Oops I Did It Again / In Your Face (Censored radio edit). Chart position: 1 FINLAND.
ARE YOU DEAD YET?, Spinefarm SPI 230CD (2005). Living Dead Beat / Are You Dead Yet? / If You Want Peace ... Prepare For War / Punch Me I Bleed / In Your Face / Next In Line / Bastards Of Bodom / Trashed, Lost And Strungout / We're Not Gonna Fall. Chart positions: 1 FINLAND, 16 GERMANY, 16 SWEDEN, 17 JAPAN, 42 AUSTRIA, 67 FRANCE, 79 SWITZERLAND, 80 ITALY, 82 CANADA.
In Your Face, Spinefarm SPI 244DVD (2005) (DVD single). In Your Face (Video 2.0) / In Your Face (Video 5.1) / All Night Long (Sh*t-Faced Bastards Of Bodom) / Sixpounder (Live at Wacken Open Air).
In Your Face, Island (2006) (UK promotion CD single). In Your Face.
In Your Face, Island MCST 40439 (2006) (12" vinyl picture disc). In Your Face / She Is Beautiful.
In Your Face, Island MCSTD 40439 (2006) (CD single). In Your Face / Knuckleduster / Bed Of Nails / In Your Face (Video).
ARE YOU DEAD YET? (DELUXE EDITION), Universal Japan UICO-9015 (2006) (CD + DVD, Japanese release). Living Dead Beat / Are You Dead Yet? / If You Want Peace ... Prepare For War / Punch Me I Bleed / In Your Face / Next In Line / Bastards Of Bodom / Trashed, Lost And Strungout / We're Not Gonna Fall / Oops! I Did It Again / Talk Dirty To Me / Living Dead Beat (Live) / Follow The Reaper (Live) / Hate Crew Deathrole (Live) / Trashed, Lost & Strungout / Sixpounder / Everytime I Die (Live At Tuska Open Air) / All Night Long (COB Remarkable Record Session Recovery Story) / Trashed—Lost In Helsinki / Downfall (Live At Tuska Open Air).
ARE YOU DEAD YET?, Universal Japan UICO-1086 (2006). Living Dead Beat / Are You Dead Yet? / If You Want Peace ... Prepare For War / Punch Me I Bleed / In Your Face / Next In Line / Bastards Of Bodom / Trashed, Lost And Strungout / We're Not Gonna Fall / Oops! I Did It Again / Talk Dirty To Me.
CHAOS RIDDEN YEARS—STOCKHOLM KNOCKOUT LIVE, Spinefarm SPI 299CD (2006). Living Dead Beat / Sixpounder / Silent Night, Bodom Night / Hate Me! / We're Not Gonna Fall / Angels Don't Kill / Deadbeats I / Bodom After Midnight / Bodom Beach Terror—medley / Follow The Reaper / Needled 24/7 / Clash Of The Booze Brothers / In Your Face / Hate Crew Deathroll / Are You Dead Yet? / Latvala / Lake Bodom / Everytime I Die / Downfall. Chart positions: 28 FINLAND, 75 GERMANY.

CHOPCORE

NJ, USA — *John Paoline (vocals), Brian Keeley (guitar), John Hartman (guitar), Rich Cusato (bass), Dan Jefferson (drums).*

Formed in 1998 CHOPCORE deliver Hardcore with a distinct Death edge. The formative band line-up underwent many changes until it arrived at what the band calls its "family unit" comprising lead vocalist John Paoline, formerly of South Jersey's Gore Grind act MORTAL DECAY, guitarists Brian Keeley of CIRCLE OF FEAR, bassist Rich Cusato and Jim Cawood. This combo cut the 1999 demo 'Fuck That Noise'. Subsequently, with Cawood's departure in June of 2002, Dan Jefferson of FORCE OF NATURE took over drum duties. Also inducted at the same juncture would be second guitarist John Hartman, also from MORTAL DECAY.

CHOPCORE's activities on the live circuit saw them acting as openers for such acts as PRO-PAIN, MASTERMIND, DRI and INTERNAL BLEEDING before signing to Metal Age Productions for the album 'Bloody Little Mess'.

BLOODY LITTLE MESS, Metal Age Productions (2002). Bloody Little Mess / Thread Of The Universe / Mama Cass / Twentyninethirty / Reborn Deprived / Dance Phobia / Your Dream My Loss / Chain Of Violent Acts / Hollow.

CHRYSALIS

MONTPELLIER, FRANCE — *Sébastien (vocals), Aurélie Potin Suau (vocals / guitar), Loic Tezenas (guitar), François Subtil (bass), Fabien Sabatier (drums).*

CHRYSALIS is a Montpellier based melodic Death Metal band created during 1995. The band, fronted by female vocalist Aurélie Potin Suau, came together as a union of KALISIA and of HEGEMON members going under the banner of SUSPERIA for the first eighteen months of their existence. Re-billed as CHRYSALIS the group, comprising vocalist / guitarist Aurélie, second vocalist Cedric Guillermin, guitarist Jean-Philippe Bleys, bassist Jerome Pinelli, keyboard player Dominique Dijoux and drummer Ben, cut the 1999 'Between Strength And Frailty' EP for the Adipocere label. However, the group would fracture after this release.

CHRYSALIS regrouped for a 2002 promotion recording, this effort seeing Aurélie, Guillermin and Dijoux joined by guitarist Loic Tezenas, bassist François Subtil, and drummer Fabien Sabatier. CHRYSALIS ceased activity in August of 2003 with Aurélie and Tezenas embarking upon a fresh project entitled EILERA, issuing the 'Facettes' album in April 2003.

Between Strength And Frailty, Adipocere (2001). Eruption Within / "Plague, Sweet Plague" / Innocence Denied / Inadequacy.

CHTHONIC

TAIPEI, TAIWAN — *Freddy (vocals / violin), Jesse (guitar), Doris (vocals / bass), Luis (vocals / keyboards), A-Jay (drums).*

Taiwan's leading Metal band, CHTHONIC, founded in Taipei during 1995, are a radical extreme Metal band employing theatric use of face paint onstage and flavouring their music with a generous infusion of Black and Folk Metal alongside oriental sounds including Oceanic drums and frontman Freddy's employment of an ancient two stringed violin, the Er-hu.

The group's opening line-up would comprise frontman Freddy, with guitarist Ellis, bassist Yu, keyboard player Ambrosia and drummer Terry. Wang would then take over the drum position and Zac would be added as second guitarist. CHTHONIC's opening album would be 1999's 'Where the Ancestors' Souls Gathered', subsequently embarking upon a tour of fifteen colleges and universities throughout Taiwan. For those shows the CHTHONIC roster saw Freddy and Ambrosia joined by an all new cast of guitarist Null, bassist Doris and drummer A-Jay. The follow up, '9th Empyrean' now with Jesse installed on lead guitar, saw both Far Eastern and Western releases, the latter through the US based Nightfall label. Although dealing in mythology the band proved unafraid to take on the authorities with this outing, the album describing an epic battle between Chinese Han spirits and the spirit gods of Taiwan's aboriginal people.

The band, having replaced Ambrosia with Vivien, debuted in North America in 2002 with an appearance at the 'Metal Meltdown' festival before travelling onto Japan in August where, united with DARK FUNERAL, the group performing in Nagoya, Osaka, Nagano and Tokyo. The year closed with a special one off performance seeing CHTHONIC onstage with the world renowned lion drum performers and a classical Chinese orchestra group at the National Taiwan University. The group would return to the USA in 2003 for a gig at the 'Milwaukee Metalfest' event. The band's third album, 'Relentless Recurrence'—a concept piece themed on an old Taiwanese ghost story 'Natao-ji', was recorded at Borsing Studios in Århus, Denmark. Luis would then take the keyboard role.

During August 2003 the band scooped the 'Best band' accolade at the 14th 'Golden Melody' awards, generally acknowledged to be the biggest music award of mandarin countries. CHTHONIC scored another major coup when their track 'Satan's Horns' was chosen as the theme tune for the Taiwanese version of the major horror flick 'Jason Vs. Freddy'.

CHTHONIC released its fourth album, 'Seediqbale', on October 3rd 2006 through Down Port Music. Throughout the summer months of 2007 the band toured the USA as part of the OZZY OSBOURNE headlined 'Ozzfest' dates. The group also partnered with NILE for a series of 'Off-Fest' dates.

Deep Rising, (1998). Deep Rising / Fuck Or Die / Fuck Or Die (Special version).

WHERE THE ANCESTOR'S SOULS GATHERED, (1999). Drift Out To Mystery / Across The Sea / Breath Of Ocean / Mother Isle Disingrated, Aboriginal Gods Enthroned (MI) / Deep Rising / Yen Geh Shin / Bloody Cloud / Holy War / Nightmare.

Nightmare, (1999). Nightmare.

9TH EMPYREAN (INTERNATIONAL VERSION), Nightfall (2000). Breath Of Ocean / Mother Isle Disingrated, Aboriginal Gods Enthroned (MI): 2-1 / MI: 2-2 / MI: 2-3 / MI: 2-4 / MI: 2-5 / MI: 2-6 / MI: 2-7.

RELENTLESS RECURRENCE, (2002). (Chinese title) / (Chinese title) / (Chinese title) / (Chinese title) / (Chinese title) / (Chinese title) / (Chinese title) / (Chinese title) / (Chinese title) / (Chinese title).

SEEDIQBALE, Down Port Music (2006).

CHTON

TRONDHEIM, NORWAY — *Terje (vocals), Torstein (guitar), Øyvind (guitar), Christer Lunde (bass), Vyl (drums).*

Trondheim Death Metal quintet. An eponymous two song demo CD arrived in 2001. The group in its formative stages, and including the erstwhile FROST members guitarist Torstein Parelius and drummer Vidar Berg alongside LUMSK guitarist Øyvind, was originally entitled NIL ADMIRARI. GRIFFIN man Marius Karlsen also became embroiled at one stage. The Spring of 2002 saw ETERNAL SILENCE and ex-AWAKE man Terje (a.k.a. 'Drakon') take up the microphone. Torstein also became an active participant as bassist with MANES as well as holding down membership of GASKAMMER.

CHTON later recruited Kenneth, also of EXALTED, on bass guitar. Signing to Retribute Records the band cut the 'Chtonian Lifecode' album at Godt Selskap Studios in mid 2004. Studio guests included Attila Csihar of ABORYM, MAYHEM and TORMENTOR repute and Frediablo of NECROPHAGIA and GRIMFIST. Gigs in Bergen, Oslo, Kristiansand and Trondheim during the Autumn of 2004 saw Vyl (a.k.a. Vegar Larsen) of

CHTON (pic: Lars Wara)

APTORIAN DEMON and KEEP OF KALESSIN manning the drum kit. Drummer Vidar Berg officially exited in May, being superseded by Vyl. CHTON subsequently recruited former PROFANIA bassist Christer Lunde.

First Blood, Chton (2001) (Unreleased demo). Flies To Faces / Come Full Circle / Hammered (Down) / Depopulator Grotesk.

Chton, Chton (2002) (Demo). Book Of Black Earth / Crawling Chaos.

Two Tales Of Terror, Time Before Time DEATH011 (2003) (Split cassette EP with SUPREME LORD limited to 333 copies). Book Of Black Earth / Crawling Chaos.

CHTONIAN LIFECODE, Retribute RET018 (2004). Invitation To Hell / Enemie / Book Of Black Earth / Flies To Faeces / Chtonian Lifecode / Unholy Communion / The Horror, The Horror / Crawling Chaos / Hammered (Down).

Death Awaits, Chton (2005) (Demo). Scavenger Of A Dead World / Contagion (The Disease) / Dobermanifesto / Unholy Communion (Video) / Book Of Black Earth (Video) / Xhaos Xultus Xhton (Video).

CHURCH BIZARRE

AALBORG, DENMARK — *Jens Pedersen (vocals), A. Larsen (guitar), Henrik Engkjær (guitar), C. Norgaard (bass), Lars Groth (drums).*

Aalborg / Ringe Thrash Metal act CHURCH BIZARRE, first publishing an eponymous 2004 demo, is a project of VICTIMIZER members. Band members cite a wealth of other project credentials, vocalist Jens Pedersen (a.k.a. 'Killhailer') with AD NOCTUM, CRUCIFIX, FORLIS, KILL, SANCTUS DAEMONEON and UNDERGANG, guitarist A. Larsen with ALTAR OF OBLIVION, second guitarist Henrik Engkjær with DEUS OTIOSUS, EXECRATOR and FULL MOON LYCANTHROPY, bassist C. Norgaard (a.k.a. 'Vuml') with FORLIS and SICK ROOM 7 and drummer Lars Groth with CRUCIFIX, DEMON REALM and LUNAR CAUSTIC. The group employed Jim Voltage on session drums, another seasoned veteran of such acts as KILL, KARNARIUM, EVOKED CURSE, CROSS BOW, DEVIL LEE ROT and PAGAN RITES. Also going through the ranks would be bassist Lenny Blade, of BEYOND DEATH, BULLET, DEVIL LEE ROT, FUNERAL, HYPNOSIA, INCINERATOR, NOMINON and PAGAN RITES plus drummer Galheim (a.k.a. Michael Pedersen), of AD NOCTUM, DENIAL OF GOD, EXMORTEM, HELLSERMON, LIVJATAN, MARERIDT and PANZERCHRIST.

The project was at first assembled as a covers band, performing Death classics by the likes of NUNSLAUGHTER and DEATH. The first sessions included three originals and the NUNSLAUGHTER cover version 'Devil Metal'. Kuravilu Productions re-issued this cassette with a revised track order and new cover art that December. A further promotional session, 'Advance Hell 2005' including the DISSECTION cover 'Son Of The Mourning', arrived in 2005. That November Hells Headbangers put out the 7" vinyl EP 'Evoked Or Not - Evil Will Come'. Horror Records issued the EP 'Enigma Of Hate' in January 2006. CHURCH BIZARRE's debut full-length album, 'Sinister Glorification' was delivered by Hells Headbangers in 2007. A cassette version was distributed by Satanic Propaganda Records.

Evoked Or Not - Evil Will Come, Hells Headbangers (2005) (7" vinyl gatefold sleeve). Judging Eyes (Intro) / Evoked Or Not - Evil Will

Come / Chapel Of Suffering / Son Of The Mourning / Return Of The Gemini / Burning Sentence (Outro).

Enigma Of Hate, Horror (2005) (7" vinyl single). Intro / The Horned Majesty / Consumed By The Southern Cross / Enigma Of Hades / Devil Metal.

SINISTER GLORIFICATION, Hells Headbangers (2007). Voltaris Of Blood (Intro) / Sinister Glorification / Into The Dark (Where Witches Burned) / Redeemer And The Scythe / The Mighty Sword Of Cain / Inscribed In The Black Book Of Death / Enter The Temple Of Shadows / Prophet Of Disease / Ubrarum Regni Novem Portis / Foaming Mouth Of Mankinds Tomb.

CIANIDE

CHICAGO, IL, USA — *Mike Perun (vocals / bass), Steve Coroll (guitar), Jim Bresnahen (guitar), Andy Kuizin (drums).*

Chicago Death Metal act CIANIDE was created as a trio of singer / bassist Mike Perun, guitarist Steve Caroll during 1988. An early vocalist would be SEVERED's Bill Thurman but he would depart prior to any recording. Caroll also operates as the lead vocalist for Black Death Thrashers LORDES WERRE appearing on their 1999 'Demon Crusades' album.

After an opening 1990 demo, entitled 'Funeral', featuring Carlos Mendoza on drums, CIANIDE, having newly inducted drummer Jeff Kabella, struck a deal with the Grindcore International label for their 1992 debut 'The Dying Truth'. Second effort 'A Descent Into Hell' during 1994 included a version of SLAUGHTER's 'Death Dealer'.

Kabella left in 1995 and was replaced by Andy Kuizin for 1996's limited edition demo release 'Rage War'. The group would also make their presence felt on the Dwell Records CELTIC FROST tribute album 'In Memory Of Celtic Frost' with their interpretation of 'Dawn Of Meggido'. Second guitarist Jim Bresnahen was drafted for 1998's 'Death, Doom And Destruction'. That same year CIANIDE paid tribute to MASTER by covering 'The Truth' for a 7" single released through Lost Horizon. The Cryonics label would re-issue the 'Rage War' sessions as a regular CD release in 1999.

Paying homage to TWISTED SISTER, the band donated their take on 'Tear It Loose' to the 2001 tribute album 'Destroyer' on Dwell Records. A further split single, released in 2002, would be shared with NUNSLAUGHTER. The group trimmed down to a trio in 2003 with the departure of guitarist Jim Bresnahen.

CIANIDE's 2004 rehearsal recordings album 'Dead And Rotting', released on CD through the Polish Time Before Time imprint and on vinyl by From Beyond Productions limited to 666 hand numbered copies and seeing a further SLAUGHTER rendition in 'Metal Never Bends'. From Beyond Productions also compiled a demo retrospective entitled 'Ashes To Ashes'. That year the group also cut tracks for a split 7" in union with SCEPTER through Hells Headbanger Records. A brand new studio album, billed as 'Hell's Rebirth', would at first be projected for issue via Merciless Records but the band parted ways with the label, instead signing these recordings over to From Beyond Productions. The same label also scheduled a 2005 compilation of archive demos and unreleased tracks.

Funeral, Cianide (1990). Funeral / Choose your Death.
Second Life, Cianide (1991) (Demo). The Dying Truth / Mindscape / Human Cesspool / The Suffering / Second Life.
THE DYING TRUTH, Grindcore International (1992). Mindscape / Human Cesspool / The Suffering / Scourges At The Pillar / Crawling Chaos / The Dying Truth / Funeral / Second Life.
Cianide Kills, Cianide (1993) (Demo). Gates Of Slumber / Eulogy / The Undead March / In Darkness.
A DESCENT INTO HELL, Red Light (1994). Gates Of Slumber / Eulogy / The Undead March / The Luciferian Twilight / Beyond The Fallen Horizon / Darkness / Death Dealer / Mountains In Thunder.
DEATH, DOOM AND DESTRUCTION, Lost Horizon (1998). Rage War / This World Will Burn / Metal Never Bends / Envy And Hatred / Salvation / The Power To Destroy / Deadly Spawn / (We Are All) Doomed.
The Truth, Lost Horizon (1998). The Dying Truth '96 / The Truth.
RAGE WAR, Cryonics (1999). Rage War / Metal Never Bends / Envy And Hatred / Deadly Spawn / (We Are) The Doomed / Scourging At The Pillar / Envy and Hatred / Gates Of Slumber / Second Life.
Live In Studio, (1999). Scourging At The Pillar / Envy & Hatred / Gates Of Slumber / Second Life.
DIVIDE AND CONQUER, Merciless MRCD0013 (2000). Divide And Conquer / Throne Of Blood / Death Machine / Armed To The Teeth / Apocalyptic Fear / Filled With Hate / One Thousand Ways To Die / Battle Scarred / Bastardized / Remain In Hell.
Cianide, Merciless (2002) (Split single with NUNSLAUGHTER). Trust No One / Choose Your Death.
DEAD AND ROTTING, Cianide (2004) (Limited edition 666 hand numbered copies). Divide And Conquer / Scourging At The Pillar / The Undead March / Mindscape / Ragewar / Gates Of Slumber / Death Machine / Envy And Hatred / Death Dealer / Second Life / The Dying Truth / Metal Never Bends.
HELL'S REBIRTH, From Beyond Productions FBP-040 (2005). Age Of Hell's Rebirth / Death Metal Maniac / Trust No One / Curse Of The Dead / Fires That Consume / World Abyss / Powerhead / Sickened To Behold / Wormfeast.
Cianide / Machetazo, Hell's Headbangers (2005) (Split 7" picture disc with MACHETAZO). Black Earth.

CIBORIUM

PORTUGAL — *José Carlos Marques (vocals / guitar), João Lopes (guitar), João Pereira (bass), Antónia Beirade (keyboards), Bruno Guilherme (drums).*

Portuguese Gothic flavoured Death Metal founded by former MAFETASY members vocalist / guitarist José Marques and guitarist João Lopes. After inducting keyboard player Antónia Beirante and bassist Armando Barradas the band debuted with a two song 1996 demo 'On The Strayed Pyx', recorded at Pé de Vento Studios. CIBORIUM's inaugural album, 'Colossal Crags', was recorded in November 1997 at Rec n' Roll Studios, with production courtesy of TARANTULA drummer Luís Barros. The record was issued on the Grade label in September 1998.

On the eve of live promotion, Marecos left, being replaced by Bruno Guilherme. Further changes found Ricardo Simões taking over on keyboards, but his term was short lived. On January 2001, João Sequeira joined CIBORIUM handling the lead vocal duties for the 2002 album 'Overgrowing Human Void'.

COLOSSAL CRAGS, Grade (1998). The Wraith / Thy Soot / Catalepsy / Scion / Avigarzitor / Lugubrious Voyager.

CINERARY

CHICAGO, IL, USA — *Matti Way (vocals), Danny Louise (guitar), Mike Dooley (bass), Rick Myers (drums).*

Chicago Death Metal act CINERARY evolved from INCESTUOUS, an act founded in 1999 by ex GORGASM drummer Derek Hoffman. A series of line-up changes led to the solo INCESTUOUS release 'Brass Knuckle Abortion' after which the band opted for a name change to CINERARY.

Personnel at this point were ex DISGORGE vocalist Matti Way, former SMEGMA and CUMCHRIST guitarist Danny Louise ('Wrench'), Mike Dooley from CORPSE VOMIT on bass and DISGORGE drummer Rick Myers. Founder member Hoffman had rejoined GORGASM in January 2001 and would also be found deputizing for LIVIDITY.

Wrench also operated BRETHREN with ex-INCESTUOUS and DYSPHORIA vocalist 'Sick' Nick Hernandez, Jeff and Jim from CIANIDE and Nefarious of MACABRE. The September 2001 mini-album, 'Rituals Of Desecration'- the first release for the Deepsend label, found BRODEQUIN man Jamie Bailey on bass guitar.

In 2006 Rick Myers forged SARCOLYTIC alongside Steven Watkins, Mark Denton and Jon Zig from IMAGES OF VIOLENCE.

RITUALS OF DESECRATION, Deepsend DSR001 (2001). Undying / Inheriting The Deified / Recapitated / Rituals Of Desecration / Hung By Intestines / God Of Cremation.

CIPHER SYSTEM

GOTHENBURG, SWEDEN — *Daniel Schöldström (vocals), Johan Eskilsson (guitar), Magnus Öhlander (guitar), Henke Carlsson (bass), Peter Engström (keyboards / samples), Pontus Andersson (drums).*

Gothenburg's CIPHER SYSTEM was previously known from a 1995 formation as ETERNAL GRIEF, issuing the demos 'Path Of Delight' in 1998 under this formative name. Toward the close of 1999 the group cut the follow up demo 'Raped By Chaos', these sessions being mixed by Anders Fridén of IN FLAMES, after which singer Daniel Schöldström decamped. 'Awakening Of Shadows' followed in 2000 before ETERNAL GRIEF evolved into CIPHER SYSTEM. The band maintained a low profile throughout 2002 but by the end of the year persuaded Schöldström to return for the 'Demo 2003', recorded at Studio Fullmoon.

Signing to the Lifeforce label CIPHER SYSTEM cut a split album with BY NIGHT. Their debut full-length 'Central Tunnel 8' album, released in October 2004, was crafted with producer Patrik J Sten at Studio Fredman.

In March 2007 it was revealed that Henric Carlsson had teamed up with tattooed Swedish platinum selling solo artist Sara Löfgren, SUNDOWN, BESEECH, CEMETARY 1213 and FATAL EMBRACE credited guitarist Manne Engström, BESEECH guitarist Robert Vintervind with Christian Silver of SUNDOWN and CEMETARY on drums. This union titled itself TWDSO ("THOSE WE DON'T SPEAK OF").

Eyecon, Cipher System (2002) (Demo). In Perfection / Life Surrounds / 24 Hrs Left.
Promo 2003, Cipher System (2003) (Demo). What If / Receive, Retrieve And Escalate / Sufferstream.
CIPHER SYSTEM BY NIGHT, Lifeforce LFR 043-2 (2004) (Split album with BY NIGHT). What If / Receive, Retrieve And Escalate / Sufferstream.
CENTRAL TUNNEL 8, Lifeforce LFR 048-2 (2004). In Perfection / 24 Hours Left / What If / State Unknown / Central Tunnel Eight / Life Surrounds / C.S.I. / Sufferstream / Receive, Retrieve & Escalate / Complete / Slow Chemical—Controle H (Outro).

CIRCLE OF DEAD CHILDREN

PITTSBURGH, PA, USA — *Joe Horvath (vocals), Jason Andrews (guitar), Alf Kooser (bass), Mike Bartek (drums).*

Pittsburgh Grindcore act. During September of 2003 vocalist Joe Horvath and guitarist Jason Andrews fired up a side venture entitled SLEEPWALKER in union with erstwhile CIRCLE OF DEAD CHILDREN bassist Alf Kooser and members of Pittsburgh act SADIS EUPHORIA. CIRCLE OF DEAD CHILDREN, unable to locate a full time drummer, proceeded on with the services of SADIS EUPHORIA man drummer Mike Bartek. Problems in the percussion department dogged the band into 2004 as well, their drummer breaking his wrist in a snowboarding accident.

CIRCLE OF DEAD CHILDREN re-signed to Willowtip Records for the July 2005 album 'Zero Comfort Margin', produced by TODAY IS THE DAY's Steve Austin. Drummer Mike Bartek was ejected in June 2006 in obviously acrimonious circumstances, the band issuing a statement claiming their erstwhile colleague had "defecated on any concepts of friendship and respect possible and stooped lower than we thought even he would ever go".

CIRCLE OF DEAD CHILDREN added drummer Matt Francis to its line-up in February 2007.

STARVING THE VULTURES, Willowtip WT 003 (1999). Ursa Major / Eldorado / Where The Hive Hangs / Sunday's Agenda? / Tranquilizer / Four Walls And A Feeling / When Silence Glorifies Pestilence (Faint) / Sons Of Nameless / Doom Farmer / Calm / Freethinkers Fight Song / Return To Water / Heidi's Arrow / Imprint This Stake With Your Name.
Exotic Sense Decay, Willowtip (2000). Pigeon vs. Crow / A Wooden Heart Never Bleeds / Wotton / Grabbing N / Skull Of A Hermit / Brain Of A Faery / 10 Fingers (My Last Ten Minutes) / Scarecrow Trailer Park.
THE GENOCIDE MACHINE, Deathvomit (2001). Migration / The Genocide Machine / Cremationism (Become The Flame) / From Eros To Thanatos / Corpses Of Refinement a.k.a. The Men Behind The Sun / Only One Per Coffin / Barbarians And Henchmen / Isabella's Nightmare / Two-Week Notice / Extreme Cannibal Smoke! / Digestive Ceremony / When We Make The Clouds Scream / Beethoven's Children / It's A Bloody Day When You Get Your Head Nailed To A Kross / Wormpaste (Bled Through The Earth) / Ch / oR / Ctrl * Alt * Delete.
HUMAN HARVEST, Displeased D-00117 (2003). A Family Tree To Hang From / We Wear The Gimp Mask / Salt Rock Eyes / Bring Her A Mushroom Cloud Pt. 1 / No Tolerance For Silence / Destiny Of The Slug / Sleepwalker / Harvest At Dawn (Enter Fertility) / Corsage Of Fresh Meat And Rotten Pride / Oak And Iron / Mother Pig / Rocket / King Cobra Vs Queen Bee / Buzzard Blizzard / White Trash Headache / Shadows Of The Narcissist / My Supernatural (Bell Ring Slowly) / Alkaline.
ZERO COMFORT MARGIN, Earache (2005). Forward Through The Copper Sun / Zero Comfort Margin / No Tears Fall Through Hollow Eye-sockets / Chemical Goat / Whimper / Android: 120 Ampere Opiate / Host(age) / Bohemian Grave / The System As The Master Deceiver / Born On A Bomb Shell / Strip Naked For The Killer / A Homage To Tombstone Granite / Footprints In Fire / Playdumb / For Black Eyes Only a.k.a. Depopulate: Tears Of Illuminati.

CIRRHOSIS

UBERLÂNDIA, MG, BRAZIL — *Luiz Fernando (vocals), Marlon (guitar), Rodrigo (guitar), Jaurez (bass), Fernando (drums).*

CIRRHOSIS was originally conceived by SARCOFAGO's Wagner Antichrist in late 1988. The founder would return to his home base of SARCOFAGO leaving the remaining band members to stabilise a line up comprising lead vocalist Luiz Fernando, guitarists Rodrigo and Marlon, bassist Jaurez and Fernando on the drums. In this incarnation CIRRHOSIS signed to the Cogumelo label, releasing a split album with LUCIFER 'Alcohol Rules'. The group put in extensive touring but folded sometime during 1993.

CIRRHOSIS resumed action in 2002 citing a fresh roll call incorporating Jaurez on vocals and bass, guitarists Henrique and Marcos with Fernando appointed on drums. The resulting 'Alcoholic Death Noise' album was produced by Geraldo Minelli of SARCOFAGO and includes a cover version of SARCOFAGO's own 'Midnight Queen'.

ALCOHOLIC DEATH NOISE, Cogumelo CG 0060 (2002). The Sin / Sexual Delight / Alcoholic Death Noise / An Eye For An Eye / No Future / Welcome To Miseries / Humanity / Beyond The Slavery Of Sin / Repulsive Impulses / Midnight Queen.

CLIMATE

POLAND — *Sebastian Bardzal (vocals / guitar), Daniel Wojtowicz (guitar), Lukasz Popielnicki (bass), Dr. Boss (drums).*

CLIMATE is a Chelmie based Death Metal band dating back to 1994, issuing their opening Heavy Metal styled demo 'Escape From Reality' that same year. The group comprises ex-PROJECT X, MURDERGRAM, TORMENT vocalist / guitarist Sebastian Bardzal, erstwhile PIGALL guitar player Arkadiusz Stalega, former TORMENT man Piotr Tymoszuk on bass and the PARRICIDE, TORMENT and MELANCHOLY CRY credited drummer Tomasz Luc. A new album, 'The Final Prophecy' including a rendition of PINK FLOYD's 'Another Brick In The Wall', was recorded in September 2003.

The 2004 line up comprised vocalist / guitarist Sebastian Bardzal, guitarist Daniel Wojtowicz, bass player Lukasz Popielnicki and drummer Dr. Boss.

HIGHER, (2001). To Be Higher / Mercyful Pain / When You Will Want To Forget Me / Name Of Hate / Horn Of Plenty / Whenever / Escape From Reality / The Light In The Tunnel / News At Night / Screaming Race.
The Wheel Of Time EP, (2002). Early Death / The Choice / Mercyful Pain / Infinity / Tragical Consequences.
Evil Comes From ... EP, (2003). From The Abyss / The Great Attack Of Chaos / Infernal Dream / War Against War.

THE FINAL PROPHECY, (2004). My Mistake Our Pain / The Choice / The Great Attack Of Chaos / Death Is Around Us / War Against War / Scream Of The Dead / Tragical Consequence / Infernal Dream / Another Brick In The Wall.

CLONE

ÅSBRO, SWEDEN — *Jonny Westerback (vocals / guitar), Henrik Tranemyr (guitar), Mikael Nilsson (bass), Tobhias Ljung (drums).*

CLONE came together in Åsbro during 1998, the product of bassist Mikael Nilsson and JONNY WONG guitarist Henrik Tranemyr's desire to create a new Metal band. Before long the founding duo was joined by singer Jonny Westerback and second guitarist Tonka. JONNY WONG Tobhias Ljung stood in for the initial sessions. By November of 1999 Jimmy Johansson had assumed the lead vocal mantle. CLONE did not enjoy much luck during 2000, recording a demo, which the band judged unfit to release, and recording a version of 'Welcome To Dying' for a BLIND GUARDIAN tribute album. This latter session was also deemed not up to par and the group unsurprisingly parted ways with Johansson as Westerback and Ljung took over the vocal duties.

The band pulled in singer Mikael Reini and a second stab at cutting a demo gave more favourable results. During June of that year the band learned of the death of their original singer Jimmy Johansson, the former frontman dying peacefully in his sleep in Spain. CLONE, despite dispensing with Reini, issued the November 2002 demo 'Inverted Icons', produced by DIONYSUS drummer Ronny Milianowicz.

The band subsequently switched title to THE BEREAVED, issuing the album 'Darkened Silhouette' in 2004 through Greek label Black Lotus Records.

Clone, Clone (2000) (Unreleased demo).

Clone, Clone (2001) (Demo).

Inverted Icons, Clone (2002) (Demo). Hollow Child / Silverspoon / Angels Ablaze / Lines In Shape.

CLOTTED SYMMETRIC SEXUAL ORGAN

JAPAN — *Narutoshi (vocals), Sumito (guitar), Takeshi (drums).*

Notorious Japanese premier Grindcore act C.S.S.O. (CLOTTED SYMMETRIC SEXUAL ORGAN) began life entitled GUSTRIC JUICE with a line up of vocalist Narutoshi, guitarist Sumito, drummer Takashi and Gan-Tyan. The band's singer would depart for MAGGOTY CORPSE whilst Sumito teamed up with GRUDGE. However, the pair would return to action with GUSTRIC JUICE soon evolving the band into ALTERNATIVE DEADBODY.

Under this new guise the band cut a demo with MAGGOTY CORPSE drummer Junji sessioning. Shortly after recording the band morphed again into C.S.S.O. pulling in EUTHANASIA drummer Makato then Susumu.

During 1996 C.S.S.O. toured Europe sharing billing with Poland's DEAD INFECTION and Spain's HAEMORRHAGE. This union resulted in the release of a split EP in collusion with DEAD INFECTION.

The band's shared EP in alliance with Austria's MASTIC SCUM and RAPE, included versions of NAPALM DEATH's 'Control' and CARCASS' 'Genital Grinder'. In 1998 Susumu made way for Takeshi.

2000 found the group appearing on the 'Transoriental X-Press' shared album combined with French artists DESECRATION and INFECTED PUSSY. The year would also see the group's debut European album release 'Nagrö Läuxes VIII' on Germany's Morbid Records.

C.S.S.O. would also contribute their version of 'Cannibal Ballet' to the IMPETIGO tribute album 'Wizards Of Gore'. Further split EP's ensued with Australians THE BLOODY VICE, Sweden's BIRDFLESH and a 2002 three way split 'Three Way Of Armageddon' with NUCLEAR DEVESTATION and TOTAL FUCKING DESTRUCTION in 2002 for Japan's Obliteration Records..

Tijikuwa Hejimagari, Morbid (1993) (Split single with THE MEATSHITS). Tijikuwa Hejimagari / Bra Bara Man / I'm Sorry I Was Born / Boric Acid Dumpling.

Alkanoid, Gulli (1994) (Split single with BLAST OF SILENCE). Alkanoid / Itch / Putrid Cadaver Part II / Zombie Fuck.

Putrid Cadaver Part II, M.M.I. (1994) (Split single with VIVISECTION). Putrid Cadaver Part II / Zombie Fuck / Nuclear Karate Man.

Split, Underground Warder (1997) (Split single with DEMISOR).

Genital Grinder, Ohne Maulkorb Productions (1997) (Split single with MASTIC SCUM and RAPE). Genital Grinder / Slithering Maceration Of Ulcerous Facial Tissue (Sampling version) / General Surgery / Fear?! (70's mix) / Regurgitate / Control.

C.S.S.O., Relapse (1997). Shake It Up Bokan / Diversion Of Former Customary Trite Composition / Don't Play Guitar Sitting On Chair / Long Hair Mathematics Teacher / Hey Tonny! (a.k.a. Anal Bloody Anal) / Eclectic Birth.

Worst EP, Morbid (1998) (Split single with DEAD INFECTION). Baka Sen / Worst.

GRINDWORK, Grindwork Productions (1999) (Split album with NASUM, VIVESECTION and RETALIATION).

Hungry Urinary Urn, Bizarre Leprous Productions (1999) (Split single with MALIGNANT TUMOUR, NEGLIGENT URGE COLLAPSE and CATASEXUAL URGE MOTIVATION). Hungry Urinary Urn.

TRANSORIENTAL X-PRESS, Necrophile Productions (2000) (Split album with DESECRATION and INFECTED PUSSY).

NAGRÖ LÄUXES VIII, Morbid (2000). Daddy's Home / Explanatory Notes Of Pilferige / 256 / Very, Very Blue Belly / Perversion / Kyushikanga / Spartan / Intro / Bara Bara Man / Richly Coloured Moist Elegy / I'd Chokyo / Alkanoid / Rolling The Zen / Psycho 65 / Boric Acid Dumpling / Penisnatcher / The Song Without Rice / A Trigonometrical Of Mokuba / Intro / Zombie Fuck.

LIVE, Riot City Japan (2000). Into The Dogma / Into The Dead / (Japanese title) / (Japanese title) / Terrorize / 305 / Hail Impetigo / The Kill / I Hope You Die In A Hotel Fire / Impro Session / 893K / Alkanoid.

ARE YOU EXCREMENTS, Morbid (2001).

Split, Ubble Gubble (2001) (Split single with BIRDFLESH).

Living Dead A Go Go, The Spew Records (2001) (Split single with THE BLOODY VICE). Living Dead A Go Go.

Three Way Of Armageddon, Obliteration (2002) (Split EP with NUCLEAR DEVESTATION and TOTAL FUCKING DESTRUCTION). Kenji Shige Is Guilty / Kenji Shige Is Guilty / Kenji Shige Is Guilty / Kenji Shige Is Guilty / Kenji Shige Is Guilty / Kenji Shige Was Guilty / Diversion (Live) / Stage Dive (Live) / 893 K.

CO-EXIST

GLASGOW, SCOTLAND, UK — *Dawson (vocals), Charlie (guitar), JJ (guitar), Danny (bass), Quzzy (vocals / drums).*

Glasgow Death / Grindcore act CO-EXIST, founded during 1998, feature MURDER ONE, MEDULLA NOCTE and LAZARUS BLACKSTAR vocalist Paul Catten. The band had initially been formed as an adjunct to CONFUSION CORPORATION by bassist Danny, drummer Quzzy and guitarist Charlie, subsequently enlisting second guitarist JJ. The Undergroove label issued the album 'Surgical Removal Of The Teeth, Toenails And Drilling Of The Kneecaps', recorded at Redeye Studio in Clydebank, in September 2005. Although Catten features on the album he would be replaced by Dawson, another erstwhile CONFUSION CORPORATION member. CO-EXIST partnered with REFLUX and EDEN MAINE for UK touring in March 2005.

SURGICAL REMOVAL OF THE TEETH TOENAILS AND DRILLING OF THE KNEECAPS, Undergroove (2005). Urge To Mutilate / Surgeon Without License / Choke Chain / Fear Of Sharks / Teeth Meet Fist / Septic / I Am The Leper / Pulling Teeth / A Secret Plan / Blackmail / Let's Grind / Spite Engine / Grinddogs / Black Fuel / Stitch / Man Beats Man / Lifelong / Stress Related Killing.

COALESCE

KANSAS CITY, MO, USA — *Sean Ingram (vocals), Jes Steineger (guitar), Nathan Ellis (bass), James DeWees (drums).*

Kansas City Hardcore Metal act COALESCE debuted with a five track mini album issued in August of 1996. Early global exposure had been reaped by sharing a high profile split EP with premier genre outfit NAPALM DEATH. The band was rooted in the early 90s band BREACH founded by guitarist Jes Steineger, bassist Stacy Hilt and drummer Jim Redd. As BREACH parted ways with their lead vocalist Sean Ingram, of RESTRAIN, would be invited to take the position and upon his acceptance the band name duly switched to COALESCE.

During 1995 the group made its first inroads into the American Rock psyche by touring as guests to 108 and BLOODLET, many marvelling at the group's insistence on breaking Hardcore norms by employing discordant guitar riffs, jarring time signatures and copious amounts of feedback. This exposure would come to the attention of NAPALM DEATH resulting in the split EP and subsequent European media exposure.

COALESCE would undertake lengthy bouts of touring but would fold in 1995. Regrouping the following year with Nathan Ellis having taken Hilt's post they would sign to Philadelphia's Edison label for the 'Functioning On Impatience' album.

The 1999 album 'Nothing New Under The Sun' was comprised entirely of LED ZEPPELIN cover versions, most in typical highly charged COALESCE style, with a guesting Matt Pryor of THE GET UP KIDS, but 'That's The Way' and 'Thank You' performed acoustically. Another label leap had COALESCE signing to the Relapse concern for the '0:12—Revolution In Just Listening' album. Despite progress COALESCE would announce their dissolution even before the album arrived in the stores.

Posthumously the group donated three tracks to a split EP with BOY SETS FIRE on The Hydra Head label released in January 2000, although one of these tracks 'Bob Junior' being a new recording by Ingram and Ellis together with drummer Ed Rose billed as MIASIS.

News emerged in the spring of 2001 that Ingram and Dewees were involved in a twin drummer collaboration billed as AMERICAN SPECTATOR in union with ZAO drummer Jesse Smith together with TFU personnel bassist Don Clark and guitarist Ryan Clark. Ingram would later be spotted performing live vocal duties for the DILLINGER ESCAPE PLAN. COALESCE would reform for the third time later the same year. Ingram and DeWees persuading original bassist Stacy Hilt to rejoin. New face on the guitar was Corey Whitehead, also billed as a member of THETA and ESOTERIC. However, the band ceased activity in 2002. COALESCE drummer James DeWees also operated as a member of THE GET UP KIDS and REGGIE AND THE FULL EFFECT.

COALESCE, comprising Jes Steineger, Nathan Ellis, Sean Ingram, and Nathan Richardson, re-united for a gig at the 20th August 2005 'Hellfest'.

Split EP, Earache MOSH 168 CD (1996). A Safe Place / Harvest Of Maturity.
002 EP, Earache MOSH 140 (1996). 73-C / Grain Of Salt / Simulcast.
COALESCE, Second Nature 1 (1996). On Their Behalf / The Harvest Of Maturity / Simulcast / A Safe Place / One At A Time.
FUNCTIONING ON IMPATIENCE, Edison (1998). You Can't Kill Us All / Reoccurring Ache Of / A New Language / My Love For Extremes / On Being A Bastard / Measured In Gray / A Disgust For Details.
012: REVOLUTION IN JUST LISTENING, Relapse (1999). What Happens On The Road Always Comes Home / Cowards.Com / Burn Everything That Bears Our Name / White The Jackass Operation Spins Its Wheels / Sometimes Selling Out Is Waking Up / Where The Hell Is Ricky Thorne These Days? / Jesus In The Year 2000 / Next On The Shit List / Counting Murders And Drinking Beer (The $46'000 Escape) / They Always Come In Fall.
THERE IS NOTHING NEW UNDER THE SUN, Hydra Head 35 (1999). Immigrant Song / Heartbreaker / Black Dog / Out On the Tiles / Whole Lotta Love / That's The Way / Thank You.
Coalesce EP, Hydra Head 30 (2000) (Split EP with BOY SETS FIRE). Vehicle / In The Wilderness / Bob Junior.
A SAFE PLACE, Second Nature 11 (2000). 73-C / Grain Of Salt / Simulcast / A Safe Place / Blend As Well.
GIVE THEM ROPE, Edison 6 (2000). Have Patience / One On The Ground / Cut To Length / For All You Are / Still It Sells / Chain Smoking / Did It Pay The Rent / Every Reason To / I Am Not The First / This Is The Last / I Took A Year.

COCK AND BALL TORTURE

GERMANY — *Tobi (guitar), Timo (bass), Sascha (drums).*

The delightfully named Grindcore act COCK AND BALL TORTURE was created in 1997 by erstwhile CARNAL TOMB members. Their first product, the demo tape 'Cocktales', would be later re-issued on CD in 1998 in a limited run of 550 copies but would run foul of the censors due to its pornographic cover art. Shredded Records would give the EP a further re-release of 1000 copies with different artwork.

COCK AND BALL TORTURE have shared a string of split singles and EPs with the likes of LIBIDO AIRBAG, Poland's SQUASH BOWELS, GROSSMEMBER and Mexico's DISGORGE.

The split 'Big Tits, Big Dick' EP in collaboration with LAST DAYS OF HUMANITY included a cover version of MUCUPURULENT's 'Suborbital Ejaculation'. The band shared a four way split EP with FILTH, NEGLIGENT COLLATERAL COLLAPSE and DOWNTHROAT for Bizarre Leprous Productions in 2001. COCK AND BALL TORTURE's contributions included a swathe of cover songs including NASUM's 'See The Shit (With Your Own Eyes)', GUT's 'Dead Girls Don't Say No', SQUASH BOWELS 'Hasta la Vista Baby', LAST DAYS OF HUMANITY's 'Consuming Purulent Sputum' and SUPPOSITORY's 'Doorway To Destruction'.

Another MUCUPURULENT rendition surfaced on the 2002 EP 'Where Girls Learn To Piss On Command', COCK AND BALL TORTURE tackling 'Zombie Squad 69' as well as AHUMADO GRANUJO's 'Cold Turkey'. In 2004 the 'Sadochismo' album was released in the ex-USSR territories via Moral Insanity Productions, this license hosting two bonus tracks.

Band members also operate BRADYPHAGIA.

Cocktales EP, Shredded (1998). The Taste Of Animal Sperm (The Orgasm Of A Hyena) / After Master / Fresh Ejaculata / Scrotum Blast / Horney Hosier / The Cock And Ball Torture / Cuntkiller / Sperm-Orgy / She Sucks As Hard As She Can / Hymen / Phrenetic Pussy Slasher / Frenzy Lesbians / Pussy Commando / Drowned In Sperm / Randy Rectum Fistfuck / Colonel Cunt.
Veni, Vidi, Spunky EP, Bizarre Leprous Productions (1999) (Split single with SQUASH BOWELS). F.B.I.—Funny Butt Injector / Exhymed (Hymen Part II) / Anal Intruder 2000 / Dildo Debacle / Shaven Smooth Snatch / Diarrhea Derby / Clit-Doris.
OPUS (SY) VI, Shredded (2000). Anal Sex Terror / Candy Teen Pussy Pleasers / Feakal Fatal / Anna'n'ass / Fat Sex Mama / Spunky Monkey / King Anus III / Big Tit Slappers / Lesbian Duo Dildo Fuck / Spank Me / Fuck Me / Fill Me / Rosetta Twist / Panda Penis / Koala Cunt / Bi-Bee / Anal Lilly Pissing Chick / Fist Fuck Family / Torture'lini Ball'o'nese / Important Impotence / Juicy Lucy / Vulvurine Cooze Blues / Whorrorbitch.
Anal Cadaver EP, Noweakshit (2000) (Split single with GROSSMEMBER).
Zoophilia EP, Stuhlgang (2000) (Split CD single with LIBIDO AIRBAG). Tapir Tits / Scato Scampi / Pinguine / Dingo Dong.
Barefoot And Hungry EP, Lofty Storm LSR011 (2001) (Split single with DISGORGE). Titty Torture Bondage Boys / Poontang Clan / Tampon Terrorizer / Lesbian Latex Legion.
Cock And Ball Torture EP, Bizarre Leprous Productions (2001) (Split EP with FILTH, NEGLIGENT COLLATERAL COLLAPSE & DOWNTHROAT). See The Shit (With Your Own Eyes) / Dead Girls Don't Say No / Hasta La Vista Baby / Consuming Purulent Sputum / Doorway To Destruction.
Big Tits, Big Dicks EP, Flesh Feast Productions (2001) (Split single with LAST DAYS OF HUMANITY). Cunt Caviar / Sexcretion / Buttman Goes To Rio / Suborbital Ejaculation.
Where Girls Learn To Piss On Command EP, Stuhlgang (2002). Where Girls Learn To Piss On Command / Tampon Removal / Barefoot & Hungry / Barbaric Teenage Orgasm Simulator / Cold Turkey / Zombie Squad 69.

SADOMACHISMO, Ablated (2002). Where Girls Learn To Piss On Command / Heterosexual Testosterone Compressor / Enema Bulldozer / Instant Onanizer / Whoredom Sonata / Aphrodisianus / Colon Latino / Kamikaze Incest / Caudal Armada / Multiple Slave Sex / Klistier Power / Faggot Filter / Cellulite Convoy / G Spot Gigolo / Supreme Genital Goddess.

EGOLEECH, Morbid MR 108 (2004). Another Arch Abraded / Close Your Eyes And Bear It / Blindfold|Bare|Submissive / Complex 27 / Be Raped|Bereaved / She No Longer Cared / Sharp And Slender / Sono Sterile Theory / Thickening / Six Holes Cut / Thirty Degrees Backwards / Contagious / One Inch Left.

CODEON

HELSINKI, FINLAND — *Vesa Mattila (vocals), Sami Raatikainen (guitar), Asko Sartanen (guitar), Lauri Mailasalo (bass), Joni Varon (drums).*

Helsinki technical Death Metal band forged by guitarist Sami Raatikainen in October 2002, hooking up with bass player Lauri Mailasalo, then drummer Mats Lindewvist that December. Singer Vesa Mattila held ties to BODIES and FINAL DAWN. An initial line-up fractured, leaving Raatikainen to handle all guitar work on a 2003 demo. The band then drafted the IMPERANON and NAILDOWN credited Asko Sartanen on second guitar.

A self-funded EP in June 2005, 'On My Side', secured a recording contract with Dies Irae Records for a re-release in December. Another membership change saw Lindewvist replaced by Joni Varon. CODEON guitarist Sami Raatikainen joined German Death Metal band NECROPHAGIST in February 2006.

Vesa Mattila fronts SAATANAN MARIONETIT under the alter ego 'Aargh Satan' and performs bass with BLACK TEMPLE.

Demo 2003, Codeon (2003) (Demo). Fatal Soul Collision / Backstabbers' Parade / Tidal Complete.

On My Side EP, Codeon (2005). Fatal Soul Collision 2004 / Decay Life / On My Side / Cold Trigger / The Dying Race.

On My Side EP, Dies Irae IRAE 003 (2005). Fatal Soul Collision 2004 / Decay Life / On My Side / Cold Trigger / The Dying Race.

COERCION

STOCKHOLM, SWEDEN — *Kenneth Nyman (vocals / bass), Rickard Thulin (guitar), Pelle Ekegren (drums).*

Stockholm Death Metal act COERCION came together in 1992 as a quintet of frontman Kenneth Nyman, guitarists Rickard Thulin and L. Ortega, bassist Pelle Liljenberg and drummer G. Johnston. By the following year the first demo 'Headway' had emerged and COERCION would follow this with a further tape 'Human Failure'. COERCION's line-up had evolved by this point as Stefan Persson had taken Ortega's position. The band scored a deal with domestic label Chaos Records but much to their frustration no product was instigated. However, German label Perverted Taste would pick up the band for the debut album 'Forever Dead'. New members at this juncture, with the departure of Persson, were guitarist Steffe Söderberg and drummer Tor Frykholm. Subsequently Persson went on to DREAD and Heavy Metal act STONFROG in September 1997.

Shortly after the 'Forever Dead' sessions Frykholm broke ranks and Pelle Ekegren took over drum duties. COERCION's turmoil did not end there though as Liljenberg would make his exit immediately prior to gigs in Germany and Poland on a package bill with IMPENDING DOOM, CRYPTIC TALES and PURGATORY.

With Söderberg also leaving COERCION trimmed down to a trio to record the sophomore March 1999 album 'Delete'. Thulin entered the ranks of MYNJUN and would also be inducted into IMPERIOUS during 2004. Drummer Pelle Liljenberg joined veteran act GRAVE in early 2004.

Headway, Coercion (1993) (Demo). Urge To Kill / Coughing Blood / Take The Pain / Blind Witness.

Headway (Remix), Coercion (1994) (Demo re-issue). Blind Witness / Coughing Blood / Urge To Kill.

Human Failure, Coercion (1994) (Demo). Human Failure / Dead Meat / Crawling In Filth / March.

FOREVER DEAD, Perverted Taste PT021 (1997). Coughing Blood / Blind Witness / Cursed With Existence / Dead Meat / Crawling In Filth / Breeding The Enemy / Down We Go / Human Failure / March / Forever Dead / Scattered / Grief (Beyond Relief).

DELETE, Perverted Taste PT025 (1999). Come The Storm / Once I Cared / Eclipsed / Mental Turmoil / The Pointless Routine / Delete / Burst / Anticlimax / Without Aim / Discontinued / Life Denied / Evolution Reversal.

Lifework, Animate 100913 (2003). Man Vs Logic / Push And Hold / Consumed / Four Walls / Passive Tool.

COFFIN TEXTS

LOS ANGELES, CA, USA — *Robert Cardenas (vocals / bass), Richard Gonzalez (guitar), Marce Castro (drums).*

Los Angeles Death Metal act forged by former ENTETY and ENGRAVE vocalist / bassist Robert Cardenas, ex-ENTETY guitarist Richard Gonzalez and drummer Marce Castro from DEMOLITION. The band undertook a US Midwest tour during 1996 aligned with WICKED INNOCENCE, INFAMY and CREMATORIUM.

Dwell Records would issue the Egyptian themed debut album 'Gods of Creation, Death & Afterlife' in April of 2000, this including a cover rendition of BLACK SABBATH's 'Disturbing The Priest'. Other recordings surfacing that year included takes on VENOM's 'One Thousand Days In Sodom' for the tribute album 'In the Sign of the Horns', MORBID ANGEL's 'Thy Kingdom Come' for the 'Scream Forth Blasphemy' collection and an interpretation of 'Crypts Of Eternity' donated to the SLAYER homage 'Gateway To Hell'.

Cardenas would join DIABOLIC for European touring in late 2002. Upon completion of these dates the singer joined up with INFAMY. COFFIN TEXTS, now featuring new drummer Ariel Alvarado, issued a three song promotional CD 'Tomb Of Infinite Ritual' in 2003.

Marce Castro rejoined in June 2004 as COFFIN TEXTS signed to the German Morbid Records label. A second album, 'Tomb Of Infinite Ritual', was set to be recorded at Injected Senses Studio in Temecula with producer Gary Miranda for September release. In late 2004 Mars Castro joined up with ABATTOIR lead vocalist Steve Gaines, also holding scene credentials with the likes of BLOODLUST, PAGAN WAR MACHINE, DREAMS OF DAMNATION and TACTICS, in a brand new band unit ANGER AS ART alongside HANGAR 18 and RAVEN MAD guitarist William Rustrum and NEW EDEN bassist Javier Marrufo.

Robert Cardenas joined Florida's DIABOLIC as their new frontman in December 2006.

GODS OF CREATION, DEATH & AFTERLIFE, Dwell (2000). Ethereal Conjuration / Their Bodies, Our Souls / Revengeful Entity / The Grand Gallery (Final Judgement) / Coffin Texts / Earthbound / Crypts of Eternity / Disturbing The Priest.

COLDWAY

TORNIO, FINLAND — *Jonas Sjödin (vocals), Markus Pitkänen (guitar), Risto Ruotsalainen (guitar), Juhani Impiö (bass), Tero Konola (drums).*

Death Metal band COLDWAY was created in Tornio during the Winter of 2001 by ex-BLODSOFFER guitarist Markus Pitkänen, bass player Juhani Impiö and Joni Salo on drums. Singer Jonas Sjödin was enrolled in August of 2003 and in February 2004 Jouni Gauriloff (a.k.a. Gxanthe) of ORIGINY and RUTTOLAPSET joined as second guitarist. This latest candidate would soon be replaced by Risto Ruotsalainen. Drummer Tero Konola, ENTERAINNUTIN, KOLLAPSE, KELLARICORE and RELATIVITY, was added in 2004. Gauriloff soon departed. BLODSOFFER's Mikko Nikula then took over on lead vocals.

COLDWAY recorded the demo 'Deathwish Overload' in June 2006.

Coldway, Coldway (2004) (Demo). Pitiful Faceless / With Light Along / Forever Bleeding.

Coldway, Coldway (2005) (Demo). Bleeding Flesh / Pain Is A Lie / At The Heart Of Death.

Deathwish Overload, Coldway (2006) (Demo). Deathwish Overload / Stains On The Wall.

COLDWORKER

ÖREBRO, SWEDEN — *Joel Fornbrant (vocals), Anders Bertilsson (guitar), André Alvinzi (guitar), Oskar Pålsson (bass), Anders Jakobson (drums).*

Örebro's Grindcore combo COLDWORKER comprise members of such bands as NASUM, RELENTLESS, CARNAL GRIEF, RUIN and PHOBOS. NECRONY and NASUM drummer Anders Jakobson formulated the project in January 2006, first recruiting INSIDIOUS, RUIN and CHAIN OF HATE guitar player Anders Bertilsson and RELENTLESS bass player Oskar Pålsson. André Alvinzi of CARNAL GRIEF enrolled as second guitarist in March with ex-PHOBOS man Joel Fornbrant installed as frontman the following month. A debut album, 'The Contaminated Void', was self-produced during 2006 and mixed by EDGE OF SANITY's Dan Swanö. Japanese editions added a cover version of PANTERA's 'Far Beyond Driven'. In July COLDWORKER announced signature to Relapse Records. A manufacturing fault would result in an inadvertent collectable, as the artwork for the CD variant, different to the vinyl version, was printed with inked silhouettes on frosted vellum instead of the intended clear. 2000 copies were released in this form.

The group toured Scandinavia in November, forming up the 'Close Up made me do it' tour alongside ARCH ENEMY and PATH OF NO RETURN.

The band replaced André Alvinzi with INSIDIOUS and RUIN's Daniel Schröder in January 2007. COLDWORKER then announced they were to team up with MISERY INDEX, NECROPHAGIST and BURNING SKIES for a European tour beginning in February.

THE CONTAMINATED VOID, Relapse 6716-2 (2006). The Interloper / D.E.A.D. / An Unforgiving Season / The Contaminated Void / Death Smiles At Me / A Custom-Made Hell / Return To Ashes / Strain At The Leash / Flammable / Antidote / They Crawl Inside Me Uninvited / Waiting For Buildings To Collapse / Heart Shaped Violence / Generations Decay.

COLLAPSE 7

AUSTRIA — *Mario Klausner (vocals / bass), Werner Freinbichler (guitar), Gerald Huber (guitar), Michael Gregor (drums).*

Apocalyptic Death Metal band COLLAPSE 7 is founded upon the former SCENT OF PARADISE and PATHETIC axis of vocalist / bassist Mario Klausner and guitar player Werner Freinbichler. On drums is the esteemed figure of Michael Gregor, a.k.a. 'Silenius' of HOLLENTHON, KREUZWEG OST, PAZUZU, SUMMONING, ABIGOR, AMESTIGON and RAVENTHRONE. Secondary guitars come courtesy of Gerald Huber, another ex-PATHETIC man.

Outside activities found Klausner enrolling into the ranks of BELPHEGOR in 1998 and then joining PUNGENT STENCH in 2001. That same year, alongside Freinbichler, he would also join HOLLENTHON's live line-up.

COLLAPSE 7 signed to Napalm Records for the 2004 album 'In Deep Silence', produced by Martin Schirenc.

IN DEEP SILENCE, Napalm NPR 144 (2004). Intro / Infernal Apocalypse / In Deep Silence / Empty As We Are / A Prophet's Speech / Blessed With Pain / Into Obscurity / Legions Of Blackness / Tombs Of Depravity / A Suicidal Sickness / Within The Light / Faith In Flames.

COMECON

SWEDEN — *Martin Van Drunen (vocals), Pelle Strom (guitar), Rasmus Ekman (guitar), Anders Green (drums).*

Previously known in a more Hardcore vein as KRIXJHÄLTERS under which title they released three records, an eponymous debut EP, the 1987 mini-album 'Hjälter Skelter' and 1989's full blown album 'Evilution'. A name change and musical shift was adopted to OMNITRON ensued in an effort for more global recognition.

Going back to their Hardcore Metal roots the band renamed themselves again this time to COMECON and engaged the MORBID and ENTOMBED credited vocalist Lars-Göran Petrov as a guest on the debut Tomas Skogsberg engineered 'Megatrends In Brutality' album. Also featured in this line-up would be erstwhile AGONY guitarist Pelle Ström, guitarist Rasmus Ekman and drummer Anders Green. Oddly the album was issued with a conflicting song order to that stated on the sleeve. Upon completion of this album Petrov rejoined ENTOMBED.

Dutchman Martin Van Drunen, formerly with PESTILENCE and ASPHYX, contributed vocals to 1993's 'Converging Conspiracies' drums being handled by Fredrik Palsson. Van Drunen subsequently joined BOLT THROWER.

Obviously intent on sticking to tradition, the band's third album, 'Fable Frolic', found MORGOTH frontman Marc Grewe singing lead vocals. Jonas Fredriksson would be found manning the drums. In keeping with the quirky nature of the band the album cover sported the less than metal artwork of three sheep.

Branded By Sunlight, CBR S 134 (0). Branded By Sunlight.

Branded By Sunlight, CBR S 134 (1991) (Split 7" vinyl promotion single with MERCILESS). Branded By Sunlight.

MEGATRENDS IN BRUTALITY, Century Media 9735-2 (1991). The Dog Days / Wash Away The Filth / Slope / Teuton Tantrums / The Mule / Armed Solution / The Future Belongs To Us / Conductor Of Ashes / Good Boy Benito / Omnivorous Excess / Ulcer.

CONVERGING CONSPIRACIES, Century Media 77057-2 (1993). Democrator / The Ethno-Surge / Community / Aerie / Bleed/Burn / Morticide / Worms / Pinhole View / The Whole World / God Told Me To / Dipstick / The House That Man Built.

FABLE FROLIC, Century Media 77094-2 (1995). Soft, Creamy Lather / How I Won The War / Bovine Inspiration / Frogs / Ways Of Wisdom (Serves Two) / Propelling Scythes / The Family Album / Imploder / It Wears Me Down / Anaconda Charms Grass Snake / Icons Of Urine / Sunday Stroll / Canvas Of History / Turnover!

COMMIT SUICIDE

PITTSBURGH, PA, USA — *Scott (vocals), Neal (guitar), Damien (guitar), Dan (bass), Lee (drums).*

Innovative Pittsburgh Grindcore act. The debut album, originally slated to be titled 'Fornicating In The Aftermath', would be picked up by the new Willowtip extreme Metal label for January 2002 release rebilled as 'Human Larvae (Earthly Cleansing)'. COMMIT SUICIDE would also lay down tracks, including a take on DEATH's 'Open Casket', for a split EP shared with MISERY INDEX.

Lee would be in the bass seat for OVERLORD EXTERMINATOR in early 2004, a Black Metal combo assembled by Danny Lilker of NUCLEAR ASSAULT, THE RAVENOUS, BRUTAL TRUTH and ANTHRAX reputation and also featuring Adam Bonacci from WITHERED EARTH on vocals. This band's presence would be first marked by internet demos posted in February.

COMMIT SUICIDE folded in September of 2004.

HUMAN LARVAE (EARTHLY CLEANSING), Willowtip WT012 (2002). Ablation / Silence Beyond The Delicate / Cyclic Vomiting / Black Falls / Through The Light / Automated Sheep Crutch / When Nothing Exists / Your Mind Dies / Hollow / American Werewolf / Epiphany / Just Wanted To Look / Human Larvae.

COMPOS MENTIS

DENMARK — *Jesper Heinsvig (vocals / guitar), Ryan Kristensen (guitar), Dan Damgaard (bass), Bo Damgaard Christensen (keyboards), Andreas Posselt (drums).*

Death Metal band COMPOS MENTIS came together in January 1996, initially as, under their own admission, a METALLICA jam band. By 1998 a Black and Death Metal slant was evident, confirmed on the debut April 1999 demo 'Vulturous'. The band then added the keyboards of Bo Damgaard Christensen to the line-up, this version of the band bowing in with the track 'Brave And Lonely' included on the Serious Entertainment label 'Extremity Rising Vol. 4'. A further self-financed effort 'Quadrology Of Sorrow', issued in October 2000, would score a deal with the Lost Disciple label. COMPOS MENTIS would prepare a debut album 'Fragments Of A Withered Dream' during 2002 for release in January the following year.

Completing a new album entitled 'Gehennesis', the band inducted Ken Holst from ADVERSARY as new guitarist during July 2006. Keyboard player Bo Damgaard closed a seven year tenure in September, bowing out "due to lack of time".

COMPOS MENTIS projected the 'Gehennesis' album for 2007 release through Mighty Music. Shortly afterwards the group announced the addition of keyboard player Rune Klausen to the ranks.

Vulturous, Compos Mentis (1999) (Demo). Abuse / Unreal Penetration / Sacrifice.

Quadrology Of Sorrow, Compos Mentis (2000) (Demo). Divine Wrath / Beyond Salvation / Visions Of Tragedy / Till The End Of Eternity.

FRAGMENTS OF A WITHERED DREAM, Lost Disciple LDR 0016 (2003). Drained / Temptation / My Inner Beast / Within Me / Dead Among The Dead / The Prophecy / Black Clouds Gather / The Innate God.

GEHENNESIS, Mighty Music (2007). The Drunken Diamond / The Mind's Eye / In The Womb Of Winter / Portrait Of An Attempted Escape / Downfall / My Suicidal Valentine / Faustian / Circle Of One / Tale Of The Shadow / In The Heart Of The Diamond's Secret.

CONGESTION

RIIHIMÄKI, FINLAND — *Tuuka Koskinen (vocals), Jani Koskela (vocals / guitar), Juhana Stolt (guitar), Marko Tuominen (bass), Jari Koskela (keyboards), Marko Jokinen (drums).*

A Riihimäki Doom / Death Metal act that also incorporate elements of Black Metal into their sound. The band date back to 1989 when vocalist / guitarist Jani Koskela and drummer Janne Peltoranta forged CONGESTION. Teemu Peltoranta would join the duo on keyboards in 1991 and guitarist Marko Pitkanen would be installed but quickly departed. Around this timeframe an opening, untitled three song demo was recorded, this session featuring a cover version of CELTIC FROST's 'Dethroned Emperor'. The demo 'Third Dimension' was then laid down after which Marko Tuominen was enrolled for bass duties and a further tape arrived 'Bed Of The Ancient River'. CONGESTION would also tackle their first live gigs during 1993 but Teemu Peltoranta was to depart, replaced by Jari Koskela for a Finnish tour guesting for Argentinean act VIBRION.

The band's demo, 'Bed Of The Ancient River', had by this stage come to the attention of the French Adipocere label and, switching title to LET ME DREAM, the group issued their debut album 'My Dear Succubus' in 1995.

Third Dimension, Congestion (1992) (Demo). Intro—Unblessed / When I Ride To Beyond / A Gift From Heaven.

Congestion, Congestion (1992) (Demo). Object Of Palaeontology / Unblessed / Dethroned Emperor.

Bed Of The Ancient River, Congestion (1993) (Cassette demo). Burnt Into My Mind / Wind Convoys / Bed Of The Ancient River.

Promo '94, Congestion (1994) (Demo). Throne Of Dominating Force / When The Sun Rises In The South / Burnt Into My Mind / A Clear Line Of Sanity.

CONSOLATION

HOLLAND — *Manloxx (vocals), Yehudi (guitar), Dennis (guitar), Rein (bass), Toep (drums).*

Originally known as GORE-FLIX and formed in 1989, the Dutch quintet changed titles to CONSOLATION due to increasing line-up changes.

the new handle the group submitted the track 'Eye Of The Storm' to the 1992 compilation album 'And Justice For None' before new vocalist Manoloxx, of BUBONIC PLAGUE and CARDINAL, was added later in the year.

Having signed to Displeased Records, CONSOLATION released their debut CD, a split effort with NEMBRIONIC HAMMERDEATH, in 1993, following it up in 1996 with the 'Brave Melvin From The Southern Point' record. CONSOLATION members united with personnel from NEMBRIONIC in early 2002 announcing a new, less than subtly titled, act FUCKFACE. In March of 2005 Manoloxx joined Black Metal band APOCRYPHA.

BEAUTY FILTH, Displeased (1993) (Split album with NEMBRIONIC HAMMERDEATH). We Mourn / Christianity Exposed / Crusaders / Beautyfilth / No Hope, No Fear / Locked / Part-Time God / Snowfall.

BRAVE MELVIN FROM THE SOUTHERN POINT, Displeased D-00031 (1996). Murder / Ephemera / Godmode / A Clean Whistle And American Meat / Moribund / Truckload Of Hatred / Red Rum / Stahlhelm / The Truth / Dominion Fails / Brave Melvin From The Southern Point / Sin / The Darkest Black.

STAHLPLAAT, Displeased (1998). Fireblade / Motocation / Cold Blooded Cold / Camel Song / Dead Thrill / Holocauster / Route 666 / Killjoy / Funeral Pyre / Murder Death Kill / Hellwalker I: Beyond The Darkest Black / Hellwalker II: Wheels Of Steel / Hellwalker III: Black Tar / Speedstar.

CONSTRUCDEAD

STOCKHOLM, SWEDEN — *Jonas Sandberg (vocals), Rickard Dahlberg (guitar), Christian Ericson (guitar), Joakim Harju (bass), Erik Thyselius (drums).*

A traditionally motivated old school Death Metal band out of Stockholm, CONSTRUCDEAD arose in May 1999, centred upon the triumvirate of drummer Erik Thyselius and guitarists Rickard Dahlberg and Christian Ericson, all previously involved with ARIZE, this act having put out a brace of 1998 demos. Bass player Joakim 'Harju' Hedestedt would be pulled in from the collapsing FACE DOWN. During these formative months THYRFING vocalist Henrik Svegsjö operated as frontman briefly before ex-EMBODIMENT man Jonas Sandberg secured the lead vocal role. Drummer Erik Thyselius also operates as a member of TERROR 2000.

CONSTRUCDEAD debuted with a self-financed December 1999 demo EP 'The New Constitution' and followed this with another EP 'Turn' in March 2000. This latter release would see SOILWORK's Peter Wichers guesting. The band put in a valuable overseas performance with a showing at the Dutch 'Stonehenge' festival billed alongside a heavyweight billing of ENTHRONED, HOUWITZER, ABSORBED, DEADHEAD, GOSPEL OF THE HORNS and HAMMERHAWK. Erik Thyselius would also find time to session for the notorious GENERAL SURGERY.

Another EP 'As Time Bleeds' was duly issued upfront of another European festival gig at the Czech 'Nuclear Storm' festival in July 2001. CONSTRUCDEAD signed to the Japanese Soundholic label for their first full length album 'Repent'. The album included a guest guitar session from Magnus Soderman. Japanese versions issued on the Teichiku label added a bonus track 'Metamorphosia'.

The band parted ways with singer Jonas Sandberg in September of 2002, shortly after announcing the replacement as Daniel Regefelt. However, within weeks Regefelt was out of the picture and GODSIC frontman Peter Tuthill was duly enrolled. The group would also sever ties with Cold Records.

Second album 'Viladead', recorded and mixed at Helsingborg's Queenstreet Recording with producer Richard Larsson, emerged in January of 2004. The record featured guest appearances by SOILWORK vocalist Björn "Speed" Strid and ex-SOILWORK drummer Henry Ranta on the track 'Bitter End'. Subsequently bass guitarist Joakim Hedestedt and drummer Erik Thyselius formed up part of the resurrected FACE DOWN. That August CONSTRUCDEAD drafted ex-CARNAL FORGE guitarist Johan Magnusson as their new bass man, entering Fear And Loathing Studios in late October to craft the EP 'Wounded'.

Working with director Charlie Granberg, CONSTRUCDEAD filmed their 1st April 2005 appearance at Kolingsborg venue in Stockholm for a live DVD release. However, the band was dealt a blow in May when Peter Tuthill quit in order to resurrect his previous group DOG FACED GODS. In early 2006 Tuthill announced new formation NAILSTATE to the world, being a union of Paul Mäkitalo (a.k.a. 'Themgoroth') of DARK FUNERAL and INFERNAL, Gustaf Jorde, ex-DEFLESHED and Stefan Norgren from ETERNAL OATH.

Jens Broman from THE DEFACED and HATELIGHT filled the spot as vocalist during the recording of 'The Grand Machinery'. This revised version of CONSTRUCDEAD made its live debut on 7th July at the 'Sundsvall Gatufestival' in Sundsvall. Touring throughout Scandinavia, the UK and Europe in October saw the band supporting SOILWORK. Broman also rejoined THE DEFACED that same month.

'The Grand Machinery' saw a belated Japanese release through Teichiku Records in February 2006, this version adding another three tracks. CONSTRUCDEAD entered Studio Cosmos on December 2nd with producer Jocke Skog to cut new tracks.

The New Constitution, Soundsation Production (1999) (Demo). Second Coming / The New Constitution / A.D.O.T.S.U.
Turn, Soundsation Production (2000) (Demo). Turn / Evil As I / Omission / Inhuman Condition.
As Time Bleeds, Soundsation Production (2000) (Demo). Moral In Corrosion / As Time Bleeds / Through Parasite Eyes / Repent.
God After Me, Soundsation Production (2001) (Demo). God After Me / My Undying Hate / Turn / Repent.
REPENT, Teichiku TKCS-85038 (2002) (Japanese release). God After Me / Repent / As Time Bleeds / My Undying Hate / Moral In Corrosion / Through Parasite Eyes / I've Come To Rule / The Rain / To War / At Any Cost / Metamorphosia / Turn (Demo version).
REPENT, Cold COLD001CD (2002). God After Me / Repent / As Time Bleeds / My Undying Hate / Moral In Corrosion / Through Parasite Eyes / I've Come To Rule / The Rain / To War / At Any Cost / Metamorphosia.
VIOLADEAD (LIMITED EDITION), Black Lodge BLOD 006DG (2003). Pinhook / Rise / Bricks / Hate / Wounded / Cancer / The Saviour / Disbelief / New Skin / Re-Arrange / Turn / Bitter End / Evil As I (Demo version) / Inhuman Condition (Demo version).
VIOLADEAD, Teichiku TKCS-85080 (2003) (Japanese release). Pinhead / Rise / Bricks / Hate / Wounded / Cancer / The Saviour / Disbelief / New Skin / Re-Arrange / Turn / Bitter End / Evil As I (Demo version).
VIOLADEAD, Black Lodge BLOD 006CD (2004). Pinhook / Rise / Bricks / Hate / Wounded / Cancer / The Saviour / Disbelief / New Skin / Re-Arrange / Turn / Bitter End.
Wounded, Black Lodge BLOD 021CD (2005). Wounded / Human Harvest / Misery / Save Me / Wounded (Video).
THE GRAND MACHINERY, Black Lodge BLOD 026CD (2005). Grand Machinery / A Cog In The Machinery / The Lustfull / In A Moment Of Sobriety / 8 Inches Of Flesh / The Cynical Revolution / Treachery / The Eye Of Revelation / Pater Noster / Rusty Armour / Forever Cin / Hatelist.
THE GRAND MACHINERY, Teichiku TKCS-85138 (2006) (Japanese release). Grand Machinery / A Cog In The Machinery / The Lustfull / In A Moment Of Sobriety / 8 Inches Of Flesh / The Cynical Revolution / Treachery / The Eye Of Revelation / Pater Noster / Rusty Armour / Forever Cin / Hatelist / Human Harvest / Misery / Save Me.

CONTEMPT

KOŠICE, SLOVAKIA — *Lubo Loksa (vocals / guitar), Peter Madaros (guitar), Dodo Kesely Toth (drums).*

Kosice based CONTEMPT deliver uncompromisingly brutal Death Metal. Previously known as DESECRATOR, vocalist / guitarist Lubo Loksa, bassist Bajuz, drummer Robo and later with the addition of second guitarist Ivo, under which title the band issued the 1990 demo 'Corner'. However, the group judged the final results so disparagingly the tape was never released to the public.

The band was put on hold during 1991 as Lubo undertook his military draft. During this period Bajuz would be replaced by Mato. Newly billed as CONTEMPT the band embarked upon a string of demo sessions commencing with 1992's 'Cruel Mercy'. Once again the recordings were deemed unfit for the masses and withheld. Following 1993's eight song 'Fanaticism' tape both Ivo and Matto left the ranks. The 'Paradise Garden' tape emerged in 1995 and shortly after INFINITY FURY bassist Erik was welcomed into the CONTEMPT family. A March 1997 demo, 'Eyes', included a cover version of MEKONG DELTA's 'Sabre End'.

In March 2001 CONTEMPT recorded 11 tracks for their debut album. At the same sessions three cover versions of VADER, NILE and DARK FUNERAL were also executed for use as extra tracks on foreign license versions. The album, 'The Secret Around Us' released by Empire Records, arrived in 2002. CONTEMPT's drummer Robo also played with NOMENMORTIS.

The band embarked upon a ten date tour of Poland during October 2002 co-headlined by MONSTROSITY and Swedes VOMITORY backed by TRAUMA, SCEPTIC, LOST SOUL and DISSENTER. Follow up album 'When Angels Begin To Cry' arrived in 2003.

Paradise Garden?, Contempt (1995) (Demo). Intro / Your Drug / Lost People / Paradise Garden / Der Rausch / Nostalgic Cry.
Eyes, Contempt (1997) (Demo). Never / We Are Techno / Why? / Fourth / More Scorn / Eyes Are Closed / Sabre End.
THE SECRET AROUND US, Empire EMP009 (2002). Intro / Blind Eyes Can't Speak / Who Am I? / My End / Not Any Question / A Dead Stone / The Nightwind / The Secret Around Us / Go My Boy Go And Die / Choke On Your Shame / The Dark Rain / You Must Die!!!
Fanaticism, Contempt (2003) (Demo). Intro / Identism / Under Threat Of Death / Holy Lies / F.I.T.H (Flames Into The Heaven) / Lost Future / Therapy.
WHEN ANGELS BEGIN TO CRY, Empire EMP 021 CD (2003). Intro—I Shall Rule / 33 / Death Is Eternal / Hate / Holy Lies / Once You All Will Die When Our Overcast Day Shall Come / Mercy / Suicide / When Angels Begin To Cry / Who Is The Untrue? / Fortune Will Be Gone / I Am The Truth Of Life.

CORAM LETHE

ITALY — *Mirco Borghini (vocals), Leonardo Fusi (guitar), Francesco Bargagni (guitar), Giacomo Occhipinti (bass), Francesco Miatto (drums).*

CORAM LETHE, forged in August of 1999, feature vocalist Mirco Borghini and drummer Francesco Miatto, both previously with Black Metal band LACHYRMA CHRISTI. Guitarist Leonardo Fusi is ex-STORMLORD and Tuscan Thrash act SPLEEN whilst the band was rounded out by erstwhile UTOPIA bassist Giacomo Occhipinti.

CORAM LETHE's debut demo, 'Reminiscence', was recorded at GRM Studios in Certaldo during March and April of 2000. Subsequently live promotion found the band acting as openers for TANKARD and, on the recording front, donating a rendition of 'Symbolic' to an Italian DEATH tribute album.

The band cut further demos at Fear Studio in Alfonsine and Studio 73 in Ravenna, between July and September 2003. Second guitarist Francesco Bargagni, of IMPHERYA and HELLWRATH, was incorporated during 2004. CORAM LETHE signed to the British based Rage Of Achilles label for a debut album. However, by October the band revealed they had then switched to Finland's Rising Realm Records. The group's debut album, 'The Gates Of Oblivion' recorded at Fear Studio in Alfonsine and Studio 73 in Ravenna, was scheduled for release in January 2005.

THE GATES OF OBLIVION, Crash Music (2005). The Angels Fell / Shouts Of Cowards / Dying Water Walk With Us / Episode / Instinct / I, Oblivion / Hands Of Lies / Pain Therapy For A Praying Mantis / Ruling Emptiness / Sleet.

CORIOR

FRANCE — *Alex Mahéo (vocals / guitar), Manu Marteau (guitar), Jibus Ménard (bass), Marc Herbert (drums).*

CORIOR, founded during 1998 as INNER SELF, at first involved vocalist / guitarist Alexandre Mahéo, second guitarist Mickaël Salaün, bassist Olivier Busson and drummer Marc Herbert. In 1999 the COORIOR title, adding lead singer Olivier Valen but losing Salaün. The following year a slight name change saw a switch to CORIOR.

The group debuted with a split live album in 2001 shared with LEGACY OF PAIN. The band line up for these recordings comprised Mahéo, second guitarist Luc Hoyet, Busson and Herbert. Subsequent releases included the 2002 EPs 'The Death-Metal Chatel Crew', recorded in January minus Hoyet, and 'The New Metal Chatel Crew'. This second session found Jibus Ménard on bass guitar and Manu Marteau entrenched on second guitar.

The album 'Like A Stray Animal' emerged in 2003.

LIKE A STRAY ANIMAL, Corior (2003). Out Of Order / Armed And Soul / Again And Against / Torment / Dead Bodies / Saturate / Blizzard.

CORPORATION 187

LINKÖPING, SWEDEN — *Filip Carlsson (vocals), Olof Knutsson (guitar), Magnus Pettersson (guitar), Viktor Klint (bass), Robert Eng (drums).*

Linköping Thrash Metal band. CORPORATION 1987 was established during 1995 the opening line-up comprised ex-DAISY CHAIN singer Pelle Severin, guitarist Olof Knutsson, former RABID CREW guitarist Magnus Pettersson with Robert Eng on the drums. Pettersson, Knuttsson and Eng had all previously worked together as part of a SLAYER tribute band. CORPORATION 187's 1998 self-titled demo saw Pettersson handling bass duties.

In 1999 the band employed SÉANCE credited Johan Ekström on bass guitar. Signing to Earache Records subsidiary Wicked World CORPORATION 187 released debut album 'Subliminal Fear', recorded at Studio Underground and Studio Helltower, in February 2000. Gigs across Europe had the band packaged with DECAPITATED and LOCKUP. However, Severin then took his leave and Filip Carlsson, having already been involved in the band's formative SLAYER homage days, took on the bass role. Carlsson's many scene credentials included terms with DAISY CHAIN, ANCIENT DIGGER OF GRAVES, DEMONS TO PREFER, HÖST, SATANIC SLAUGHTER, SPITEFUL and THORNCLAD. Changes during 2002 witnessed Ekström's departure but the inclusion of DEMONS TO PREFER, THORNCLAD and RABID CREW bassist Viktor Klint.

CORPORATION 187 European gigs in April 2002, promoting second offering 'Perfection In Pain', mixed by HYPOCRISY's Peter Tägtgren, saw a union with road partners LORD BELIAL and SATANIC SLAUGHTER. The band then acted as support act to ARCH ENEMY's December 2002 UK gigs following up on this by remaining as guests for their January 2003 Swedish dates.

SUBLIMINAL FEAR, Wicked World WICK9 (2000). Hope Is Lost / Caught Inside Your Mind / Straw Coloured Corpse / Paralyzed / Subliminal Fear / Souls / With Your Sins / Hypnotic Illusion / Frustration / Low Pitched.

PERFECTION IN PAIN, Wicked World WICK14CD (2002). Religious Connection / Ghosts Of Confusion / Liquid Truth / My Life To Kill / Thursday Night Aggression / Perfection In Pain / 2nd Pain / Strange Is Strong / Violated Relation / The Joy Of Being Addicted.

CORPSE CARVING

LAUNCESTON, TAS, AUSTRALIA — *Chris Quince (vocals), Tom Pryer (guitar / programming), Chris Pope (bass).*

Although new onto the Death Metal scene in 2004 Launceston, Tasmania's CORPSE CARVING would announce their arrival by projecting split albums allied with Italians MINCER on the Maltese Pestilent label entitled 'Hacked, Split Then Quartered', as well as Slovakian outfits THORWALD and DECOMPOSITION on Eclipse Records from Japan. Also in the works would be an EP entitled 'Saws, Scalpels And Surgery—Anatomy And The Art Of Dissection', featuring a cover of MORTICIAN's 'Zombie Apocalypse' and a full length album 'Goratorium' For Life Fluid Records. Band members guitarists Jarrod Carter and Tom Pryor also operate with CRANIAL DEVOURMENT.

In July 2005 Life Fluid Productions issued a three way split album, 'And Then There Were Three', shared with British bands BLUDGEON and TWITCH OF THE DEAD NERVE.

AND THEN THERE WERE THREE, Life Fluid Productions (2005). Forceps Gash / Discharging Gorekorrhea / Gutted In A Cesspool / Congenital Corpse / Egregious Visceral Dismemberment / Cadaverous Hacking / Vile Womb Pustule / Gnawing The Amputee / Razorblade Decapitation / Reaping The Remains / Hooker On A Butchers Hook / Incest-A-Cide / Fermenting The Skinned / Whore Of Flatulence.

CORPSE VOMIT

DENMARK — *Molesting Mike (vocals), Anal Al (guitar), Caco Cezo (guitar), Cape Cum (bass), Murder (drums).*

Not to be confused with the American CORPSE VOMIT. Confusingly both acts claim true rights to the name. CORPSE VOMIT's album release, 'Drowning In Puke' issued in December 1999, was delayed by many months due to the controversial nature of the sleeve artwork. The band was formulated during the early nineties as a trio of vocalist / drummer Molesting Mike, guitarist Anal Al and Cape Cum on bass. Their first product was a self-titled 1993 demo. Subsequently the band expanded, incorporating second guitarist Caco Cezo and drummer Murder.

The recording sessions for CORPSE VOMIT's debut album 'Drowning In Puke', which included a cover version of AUTOPSY's 'Gasping For Air', took place over just four days between Christmas and New Year's Eve in 1998 at Soundzone Studios in Copenhagen, being produced, engineered and mixed by Captain Schmidt (a.k.a. Lars Schmidt) of MUTILATOR and CUTTHROAT. Participating guests in the studio included ARTILLERY's Morten and Michael Stützer plus Joey Fernandez of DAEMON, FURIOUS TRAUMA and KONKHRA.

When Mighty Music attempted to release the album the pornographic nature of the sleeve art resulted in two pressing plants in succession, Sonopress and Tocano, turning the album down. Magazines also refused to carry the album artwork in advertisements. CORPSE VOMIT's media response was scathing, Germany's biggest magazine 'Rock Hard' giving it their "Arschbombe des Monats" award.

There are rumours that CORPSE VOMIT frontman 'Molesting Mike' is in reality the vocalist with WITHERING SURFACE.

DROWNING IN PUKE, Mighty Music PMZ007 (1999). Reeking Cunt / In The Grip Of Autumn / Maggots Eating My Dick / The Pus / Drowning In Puke / Hurdibrehan / Disembowelment / Gaydog / Rotten Fetus / Gasping For (Fresh) Air.

CORPSE VOMIT

CHICAGO, IL, USA — *Matt McClelland (vocals / guitar), Pat Clancy (guitar), Mike Dooley (bass), Garrett Scanlon (drums).*

Not to be confused with the Danish CORPSE VOMIT which issued a 2000 album through Mighty Music, the US band was founded in Chicago during 1993 by vocalist / guitarist Matt McClelland, guitar player Pat Clancy and drummer Garrett Scanlon. Two years later CORPSE VOMIT added bass player

Brice Dalzell as the act issued the demos 'Gathering Chemical Children' and 'Bastards Of Forever Filth'. Dalzell left in 1998, forging THE EVERSCATHED alongside vocalist / bassist Bill Frickenstein and drummer Tim Frickenstein of ENMORTEM, as CORPSE VOMIT enlisted Mike Dooling of CINERARY.

McClelland, Scanlan and Clancy also operated CUMCHRIST. Scanlan and Clancy also have another side project entitled L.S.B. During 2005 Matt McClelland, Pat Clancy, Mike Dooley and Garrett Scanlon, working with YAKUZA singer Bruce Lamont, returned en masse with IBEX.

Bastards Of Foreverfilth, Wild Rags (1996). Skull Thorn / Maggot Lamb / Scores Of The Ripe Blade / Seas Of Excrement / This Is My Tainted Blood.

RAPING THE EARS OF THOSE ABOVE, Blackened Moon Productions (1999). Sons Of Famine / Maggot Lamb / Waste / Seas Of Excrement / Mind Scabs / Gathering Chemical Children / Sleeping Dismay / Death Meddle / Crawling Visions / Nothing.

CORPSEFUCKING ART

ITALY — *Jack Limone (vocals), Marco Riccardi (guitar), Andrea Cipolla (guitar), Marco De Ritis (bass), Stuart (drums).*

Originally entitled ENTHRALMENT, releasing the 1994 EP 'Accursed In Divinity' through Cryptic Soul Productions. Founded in Rome during 1994 ENTHRALMENT quoted a line up comprising Max—"gurgling", Andrea Cipolla on guitars, Fabio on bass and drummer Marco for their opening 'Eulogy Of Burning Christ'. The group would switch title to CORPSEGOD for a 1996 EP 'Opinion About Sorrow'. The band evolved further into a more brutal Death Metal vein with a suitable new handle of CORPSEFUCKING ART for a series of Gore-Metal albums.

A line up shuffle at this juncture found Max and Cipolla joined by fresh blood guitarist Massimo, bass player Edo and drummer Marcello. Under this guise CORPSEFUCKING ART contributed the track 'Molesting The Corpse' to the horror movie soundtrack 'Sick-o-pathic' and put in guest slots to both CANNIBAL CORPSE and IMMOLATION in Rome. Re-debuting, the band signed to Sterminio Productions for the 'Puzzle Of Flesh' album in 1999.

The band, drafting a new rhythm section of bassist Marco De Ritis and drummer Stuart, shared their 2001 outing 'Zombieccromicon' as a split release with GORETRADE. Amongst CORPSEFUCKING ART's contributions would be included a rendition of MORTICIAN's ' Bloodcraving'. The 2002 'Splatter Deluxe' album saw a cover of DEICIDE's 'Oblivious To Evil'. Having utilised Tony Ananas on a session basis for the vocals on the album Jack "Sasà" Limone became the band's new singer in September.

A PUZZLE OF FLESH, Sterminio Productions (1999). You Will See The Flesh / Addicted To Murder / They Won't Stay Dead / Hooked And Smashed / A Corpse In The Backyard / Body Beneath / Hammer Torture / Zombified / You Saw The Flash.

ZOMBIECRONOMICON, Coagulated (2001) (Split album with GORETRADE). Corpsex / Four On A Meathook / Homicidal Chainsaw Butchery / Addicted To Murder / Bloodcraving.

SPLATTER DELUXE, Forever Underground (2002). The Freezers Monster / Necromantic / Splatter Deluxe / Pet (ting) Cemetery / Robocorpse / Gore Mon Amour / Suck My Corpse / Dawson's Crypt / Corpsex II (The New Menu) / All You Need Is Gore / Four On A Meathook / Oblivious To Evil / Demented / Pig Pong.

CORPUS MORTALE

DENMARK — *Martin Rosendahl (vocals / bass), Roar Christoffersen (guitar), Brian Eriksen (guitar), Nicholas Maschøln (drums).*

CORPUS MORTALE is an old school styled Death Metal combo forged during 1993 by guitarist Søren Jensen and drummer Nicholas Maschøln. Formative line-up changes ensued, stabilising with the recruitment of vocalist / bassist Martin Rosendahl. The 'Corpus Mortale' demo was recorded the following year and the band was boosted to a quartet with the induction of second guitarist Morten Jensen in 1996 for a second demo session 'Integration'. As a side venture that same year Rosendahl activated Black Metal project ZAHRIM, recording a demo entitled 'Mashshagarannu'.

CORPUS MORTALE encountered problems in 1999 with internal friction centred on the unsatisfactory result of the 'Spiritism' recordings. Both Jensens exited but the group was re-assembled by enlisting INIQUITY vocalist / guitarist Brian Eriksen and the INIQUITY and SATURNUS credited Jens Lee also on guitar. Live work ensued before CORPUS MORTALE entered Soundzone Studios to craft the EP 'Succumb To The Superior'. 2001 would witness CORPUS MORTALE personnel Rosendahl, Lee and Maschøln publishing the 'Denied' demo through an Industrial side concern billed HUMAN MACHINE.

In mid 2001 Lee opted out of CORPUS MORTALE, being superseded by Roar Christoffersen. The album, 'With Lewd Demeanor' produced by Anders Lundemark, was recorded for Neurotic Records in 2003. That same year Rosendahl involved himself with the extreme Metal 'supergroup' STRANGLER. Early 2005 found both Rosendahl and Christoffersen recording a demo 'Music For Tough Guys' with new band SLOW DEATH FACTORY, a high profile union of Danish extreme Metal elite comprising ILLDISPOSED's Morten Gilsted and Per Møller Jensen of INVOCATOR, KONKHRA and THE HAUNTED repute on drums.

Martin Rosendahl provided guest session vocals on USIPIAN's debut July 2005 album, 'Dead Corner Of The Eye', featuring on the tracks 'Selfless' and 'Shadows Of The Once Unseen'.

Corpus Mortale, Corpus Mortale (1995) (Cassette demo). Pythogenic Ecstacy / Malice Shrivelling / Possessed / Faith Designation / Slaves Of Darkness / Too Dark To See.

Integration EP, Corpus Mortale CMCD0196 (1996) (CDEP). Our Lives! / Integrated By Beliefs / Fanatic Adherent / Your Lack Of Faith / Thoughts / Persistence Instead Of Weakness / Abhor The Lies / Die Suffocate.

SPIRITISM, Corpus Mortale (1998) (Unreleased album). The Book Of Blood / Malicious / A Notorious Feeling / Immaterialism / False Prophecies / One Black Destiny / Time Elapses / Another Dead Soul.

Succumb To The Superior EP, Corpus Mortale CMCD0201 (2001). Succumb To The Superior / The Purity Of Dying / Undesirable / Spiritism / Driven Into Possession.

Sombre And Vile, Corpus Mortale (2002) (Demo). Sombre And Vile / Exaltation Of The Macabre / The Illaffected.

WITH LEWD DEMEANOR, Neurotic NRT030001 (2003). Mass Funeral Pyre / Exaltation Of The Macabre / Force Fed Obedience / The Dismal Recurrence / Sombre And Vile / Lucid Dreaming / Succumb To The Superior / Tragical Art / Undesirable / The Illaffected / Too Dark To See.

WITH LEWD DEMEANOR, Neurotic NRT030001 (2003). Mass Funeral Pyre / Exaltation Of The Macabre / Force Fed Obedience / The Dismal Recurrence (Instrumental) / Sombre And Vile / Lucid Dreaming / Succumb To The Superior / Tragical Art (Instrumental) / Undesirable / The Illaffected / Too Dark To See.

Seize The Moment Of Murder, Nuclear Winter NWR 017 (2006) (7" vinyl single). Seize The Moment Of Murder / The Book Of Blood / Slowly We Rot.

A NEW SPECIES OF DEVIANT, Neurotic (2007).

CORPUS OMNI DOMINI

HELSINKI, FINLAND — *Antti Lindell (vocals / guitar), Kaide Hinkkala (vocals / guitar), Jebe Vuolle-Apiala (bass).*

Helsinki Doom / Death band CORPUS OMNI DOMINI, featuring BABYLON WHORES vocalist / guitarist Antti Lindell, first made their presence felt with the June 1993 demo 'Burn The Victims'. Rounding out the line-up would be vocalist / guitarist Kaide Hinkkala, bass player Jebe Vuolle-Apiala, keyboard player Meeba Uotinen with Samuli Katainen on the drums. An EP, 'Monolith Empire', followed for the Wild Rags label in 1996, followed that July by a two-track second demo session. However, CORPUS OMNI DOMINI then folded. Both Antti Lindell and Kaide Hinkkala scored credits in the studio with SHAPE OF DESPAIR.

The band returned in 2005, signing an album deal with Firebox Records.

Burn The Victims, Corpus Omni Domini (1993) (Cassette demo). Through The Gates / Kingdom Of Death / Disaster Area / The Executioner / Inner Self (Live) / End Has Begun (Live).

Monolith Empire EP, Corpus Omni Domini CODCD 001 (1996). Into The Dreams / Monolith Empire / Another Day In Paradise / Imago Mortis.

Label Promo I/96, Corpus Omni Domini (1996) (Demo). They Fade Away ... / Eternally.

Monolith Empire, Wild Rags WRR 101 (1997). Into The Dreams / Monolith Empire / Another Day In Paradise / Acoustic Interlude / Imago Mortis.

CORRUPTION

SANDOMIERZ, POLAND — *P. Horne (vocals), Janusz Kubicki (guitar), Piotr Wacisz (bass), Miroslaw Mroz (keyboards), Grezegorz Wilkowski (drums).*

Doom Death / Stoner influenced Metal outfit established in Sandomierz during 1991. CORRUPTION's early releases included the cassettes 'Absorbed In Misery', issued in November 1991 and sporting a cover version of PUNGENT STENCH's 'Blood, Pus And Gastric Juice', 'The Ultra-Florescence' in 1992 and 'Dawn Of Sullen Oratory'. The band's debut recording line-up comprised lead vocalist P.Horne, guitarist Chicken, bass player Anioł, keyboard man Mirek and drummer Melon. Following the 1996 'Ecstacy' album, this effort seeing the introduction of guitarist Thrashu, a further tape, 'Bacchus Songs', was followed by the 'Junky' promo. The band had morphed further by this stage, pulling in D.J. Abel on vocals and second guitarist Gootek.

CORRUPTION's 2002 album 'Pussyworld' includes covers of BLACK SABBATH's 'Paranoid' and DEEP PURPLE's 'Perfect Strangers'. The band roster had switched once again for this record, now fronted by Rufus and with Gootek having been substituted by Elektryczny. 2003's 'Orgasmusica', featuring a reworked 'Lubricant Rains' from the 'Junky' promo, saw the band back down to a quartet. Nergal of BEHEMOTH added guest vocals to the track 'Revenge'. The band incorporated ex-TWISTED COW guitarist Fala as second guitarist upon completion of these sessions.

Polish headline dates in September 2004 saw ROOTWATER and SO I SCREAM as support. Newly installed on bass would be the LEASH-EYE, ASCALON and GORTAL credited O-Path.

Absorbed In Misery, Corruption (1991) (Rehearsal demo). Unchristian Reality / Abyss Of Disgust / Logical Substitution / Absorbed In Misery / Decadence Within / Blood, Pus And Gastric Juice / Nazi Scum.

The Ultra-Florescence, Carnage (1992) (Demo). Unchristian Reality (Intro) / Enraptured With Illusion / Profane Inherence / Into The Darkness / Sanity Ignored / Effigy The Infirmity / The Ultra-Florescence / Absorbed In Misery / Vicious Constellation (Outro).

Dawn Of Sullen Oratory, Corruption (1993) (Demo). The Sadness / Mystic Whores Fly / Scarlet-Souled / Receive My Sacrifice / Eve In The Shroud / A Heart Of Ashes.

ECSTASY, Sick (1996). Ecstasy / Animals He Served / Winter Winds / Mystic Whores Fly / Wooden Jesus / Receive My Sacrifice / Scarlet—Souled / Eye In The Shroud / Breezy Winds / Sorrows / A Heart Of Ashes / When Love Was Mine.

BACCHUS SONGS, Negative (1996). As Horses Override / Lubricant Rain / Sweet Misery / Bacchus Song / I Distend / Freaky Friday / Ernestine / Ride The Dragon / Meryphillia / Der Ubermensch.

Junky, Corruption (1998) (Demo). Junkie / Die Young / Never Get Old / Pole Nation.

PUSSYWORLD, Metal Mind Productions MMP 0173 (2002). (How Like) Wardog / (Stoned Like) Junkie / (Happily) Wasted / (Almighty Like) Manitou / (Far From) Die Young / (Hear Licentious) Whispering / (Hot-Headed Like) Witcher / (Ready For Next) Pussy Quest (With Shit-Load Of Chainsaw Hash!) / Never Get Old / (Optimistically Look For) The Day After / Paranoid / Perfect Strangers.

ORGASMUSICA, Metal Mind Productions (2003). Blasting Foreskins / Sleeper / The Angel And The Beast / Flying Carpet / In League With The Devil / Revenge / Groovy Liberator / Baby Satan / I Used To Know The Little Red Riding Hood / Demon By My Side / Hate The Haters / Candlelight / Lubricant Rains 2003.

VIRGIN'S MILK, Metal Mind Prductions (2005). 99% Of Evil / Hey You / Murdered Magicians / Lucy Fair / Freaky Friday / Fake Demon / Invisible Cry / Prophet / Disbelief / E.C.E.G.

COUNCIL OF THE FALLEN

PITTSBURGH, PA, USA — *Kevin Quirion (vocals / guitar), Sean Baxter (vocals / bass), Sean Ohtani (guitar), Tim Yeung (drums).*

COUNCIL OF THE FALLEN formed in mid 1997 when drummer Derek Roddy of HATE ETERNAL was introduced to guitarist/vocalist Kevin Quirion. January 2000 sees COUNCIL OF THE FALLEN record a demo CD, aptly titled 'Council Of The Fallen', which was sent off to friends, magazines and record labels. Soon thereafter, Martyr Music Group expressed interest and quickly signed the band. Plans for a full-length album were put in motion and during this time they met Sean Baxter who was playing in BROKEN HOPE and EM SINFONIA, both of which also signed to Martyr Music Group. As plans moved forward, Baxter assumed bass and the main vocal duties on COUNCIL OF THE DAMNED's debut album, 'Revealing Damnation'. Baxter initiated a side venture dubbed INCIVISM in mid 2002, an alliance with BROKEN HOPE colleague Brian Griffin.

The 2003 album 'Deciphering The Soul' was scheduled to include Derek Roddy but his HATE ETERNAL schedules conflicted with studio time. COUNCIL OF THE FALLEN drafted Tim Yeung, another HATE ETERNAL veteran, in his stead. In late 2004 the band partnered with UNHOLY GHOST and THE CLASSIC STRUGGLE for the 'Reigning Florida' tour commencing 31st December at New Smyrna Beach.

In July 2005 Sean Baxter would be announced as frontman for THY DIVINE EMPIRE, the act assembled by ex-DIVINE EMPIRE members J.P. Soars and Duane Timlin.

COUNCIL OF THE FALLEN returned with the 2006 EP 'An Examination Of Being'. These tracks comprised two recording sessions, the first conducted in September 2006 at Mana Studios in Tampa with producer Brian Elliott featuring vocalist / guitarist Kevin Quirion, guitarist Marius Kozlowski, bass player Scott Patrick and drummer Dave Kinkade, the second set of songs cut at Roddy Studios in Deerfield Beach, Florida with just Quirion and drummer Derek Roddy.

Drummer Dave Kinkade quit in March 2007 to prioritise MONARCH and Pennsylvania Death Metal band INSATANITY.

REVEALING DAMNATION, Martyr Music Group MARTYR 0034 (0). Search For Purpose / Eternal Sufferings / Shadowed Horizon / Secrets No Longer / Unveiling The Path / Lying In Wait / Cloaked In Isolation / Demon Winds / Remnants Of Existence / Confronting The Absence / Cast From The Heavens / Realms Of Conquest.

DECIPHERING THE SOUL, Season Of Mist SOM 083 (2003). Longing For Clarity / Acceptance In Silence / No Vision Of Prophecy / Scourge Of Thy Enemy / Distant Memories / Tempting Angelic Pride / Resurgence / Falling Through Decades / Repetition Breeds Insanity.

CRACK UP

GERMANY — *Tim Schnetgöke (vocals / bass), Dirk Oschaltz (guitar), Helvin Pour (guitar), Frank Schlinkert (drums).*

CRACK UP are an industrious German 'Death n' Roll' band. The group arrived in 1994 delivering the demo 'Forsaken Dreams' leading to a deal with We Bite Records for the debut 'Blood Is Life' album. The band would also have a track included on the 'Assassins' compilation album assembled by New York's Thunder Lizard Records. CRACK UP would then sign to the Nuclear Blast concern for the 1997 'From The Ground' record, produced by HOLY MOSES guitarist Andy Classen and including a cover version of FANG's 'Money'. The same year

CRACK UP would guest for UNLEASHED and DRILLER KILLER on tour in Europe and into 1998 would ally themselves with DEW SCENTED and DISBELIEF. These latter dates found DEW SCENTED guitarist Florian taking over regular guitarist Helvin Pour's position on a temporary basis.

1998 would see the band stepping up a gear with the October released 'Heads Will Roll' record, once again produced by Classen. With this album CRACK UP offered up two cover versions, takes on TURBONEGRO's 'Bad Mongo' and the DICTATORS 'Next Big Thing'. At this juncture CRACK UP were employing two guitarists- Helvin Pour and Torben Voight, the latter also a member of CRESTFALLEN.

CRACK UP undertook touring as part of a BENEDICTION and DEATH package billing and also put in shows with HYPOCRISY, IN FLAMES and COVENANT. In September the group put in valuable shows guesting for DISMEMBER, hastily pulled in as substitute for a late cancelling GORGOROTH.

During March of 1999, in the midst of touring, Pour made a hasty exit necessitating the band pulling in Flo of DEW SCENTED once again as a short term replacement. CRACK UP drafted Dirk Oschaltz as a permanent member to plug the gap, the six stringer actually having been an original member of the band previously. However, despite stabilising their line up CRACK UP would part ways with Nuclear Blast and manoeuvred over to the newly established Moonstorm label for the March 2000 'Dead End Run' opus, retaining their relationship with Andy Classen as producer. Following the album release long term drummer Frank Schlinkert decamped in favour of DIECAST's Andy Nohlen.

With this revised line up CRACK UP toured Europe as openers to PRO-PAIN in 2001. Plans were also afoot during 2001 to issue a shared 7" single in union with THE NOW NOISE on Wanker Records.

BLOOD IS LIFE, Corrosion CR 6-501-2 (1996). Blood Is Life / Unburden / Wounded / Voices / Failing / Forever In Me? / Hatred Unfolds / Cycle Of Need / Painted Black / Fading Away.
FROM THE GROUND, Nuclear Blast NB CD 257-2 (1997). From The Ground / Razzberry / Cracked Pack / Money Will Roll Right In / Broomer / Rats / Swab / Glorious / Blood On The Floor / For Fake / Sappy Restrain / Dysorientated / Burrrn! / Worthless / To The Sky.
HEADS WILL ROLL, Nuclear Blast (1998). Well Come / So Far No Good / Only w/ The Devil / The Assassin / Harder They Fall / Off-Kilter / Next Big Thing / Hell's Day / For 2nds I Thought I'd Rather Be Dead / In A Hole / Modern Art / Into The Dirt / Demon / Bad Mongo.
DEAD END RUN, Moonstorm (2000). It's Shit / Dead End Run / Maximum Speed / Stallknecht / Dead Good Motherfucker / Higher / Whores Suck It / Well In The Night / I'm The Only Way / Cut / Microcosm / Heavy Hearted King / Better Dance / Evenflow / Rock The Coffin'.
BUTTOXIN BLOOM, (2005). Leaving Mexico / Hyperventilating / Manic / Depeche Express / Oversized / Johnny Good / Cheesed / Push Me Down / Go To Hell / Fuckrock / Sonic / Tits & Champagne.

CRADLE TO GRAVE

VANCOUVER, BC, CANADA — *Greg Cavanagh (vocals), Denis Barthe (guitar), Glenn Chisholm (bass), Simon Adam (drums).*

Vancouver based CRADLE TO GRAVE feature AGGRESSION credited guitarist Denis "Sasquatch" Barthe. The guitar player founded the band in February of 2002 as an alliance with BOTTOM FEEDER members vocalist Greg Cavanagh and bassist Eric Green, with drummer Matt Fowler enrolling in May of 2003 for the demo 'Lifespan Sessions'.

CRADLE TO GRAVE recorded the 'Hibernation' demo in April of 2004. Signing to Year Of The Sun Records the band entered Turtle Studios in White Rock, British Columbia to record a debut album simply entitled 'CTG'. On a temporary basis, CRADLE TO GRAVE's singer Greg Cavanagh filled in for INFERNAL MAJESTY on a batch of live shows.

CRADLE TO GRAVE

Re-structuring the band line-up, CRADLE TO GRAVE acquired ex-STILL AT A LOSS guitarist Scott Dennis and ex-OMEGACROM drummer Zeus in February 2005. In May 2006 the group parted ways with longtime bassist Eric Green due to "musical differences and irreparable conflicts", with drummer Ryan Mackie following soon afterwards. The group's new rhythm section, announced in July, comprised drummer Simon Adam, ex-EMPYRIA, and bassist Glenn Chisholm, ex-A MURDER OF CROWS.

Lifespan Sessions 2003, Cradle To Grave (2003). Nuclear Flowers / Shut My Eyes / Southern Oak / Just Cause / Crown Of Snakes.
CRADLE TO GRAVE, Year Of The Sun YOTS-22642 (2004). As We Lay Dying / Projectile / Nuclear Flowers / Just Cause / Sunrise Sunset / What I Say / Southern Oak / Shut My Eyes / The Manipulated Dead / Wounded / Across The Sky / Bleeding Heaven / Crown Of Snakes.

CREMAINS

MONTREAL, QC, CANADA — *Chris Eldridge (vocals), Dany Côté (guitar) Yvon Hébert (guitar) Yves Hébert (bass), Pierre Côté (drums).*

Formed in June 1986, one of the very early Death Metal bands in a very insular, yet incredibly prolific Quebec Death Metal scene, CREMAINS managed to release only one mini album in July of 1987. The band's roots trace back to 1985's OBNOXIOUS SLAUGHTER, an act founded by the Hébert twins, bassist Yves and guitarist Yvon, together with frontman Chris Eldridge. In early 1986 drummer Pierre Côté was installed upon the recommendation of VOIVOD's Michel "Away" Langevin and at this juncture the revised title of CREMAINS was taken onboard.

Guitarist Dany Côté then completed the line up for recording of the self financed 'Back From The Graves', issued in July of 1987. A further four songs were tracked in the studio later that same year with the intention of partnering with OBLIVEON's 'Whimsical Uproar' session for a split release. However, the tracks never saw the light of day as CREMAINS fragmented.

Chris Eldridge subsequently joined the eclectic Jazz Hardcore act HAZY AZURE. Guitarist Yvon Hébert died in 1993. Interestingly enough the EP was re-released by a small label called New World Symphony Records in 1994. NWSR started to re-release a number of obscure 80's releases by Quebec Death Metal bands as apart of the Nostalgie Series.

BACK FROM THE GRAVES, (1987). Back From The Graves / Demonology / Valley Of The Dead / Glance Of Death / Nuclear Carnage.

CREMATORIUM

WHITTIER, CA, USA — *Dan Tracy (vocals), Mark Uehlein (guitar), Aaron Ramson (bass), Dan Taylor (drums).*

CREMATORIUM

Californian Deathsters, self-styled as "Murdercore" and founded as PURGATORIA by the Escalon brothers Frank and Marvin, plus guitarist Moshe Alvarez, in 1990. Formative line-up shuffles would see the addition of singer Adam Perez but the exit of bassist Marvin Escalon, quickly substituted by Alex Villalobos, in 1992. The group debuted with the 1993 demo 'Dark Manifestation'. The follow up cassette 'Unholy Massacre' arrived in 1996, promoted through a Midwest tour aligned with WICKED INNOCENCE, INFAMY and COFFIN TEXTS. CREMATORIUM underwent further ruction when both Perez and Alvarez exited. This in turn led to the recruitment of new frontman Dan 'Dismal' Tracy and guitarist Mark Uehlien for the self-financed, 1997 'Epicidiums Of The Damned' album. Founder Frank Escalon quit the band in 1998, effectively putting CREMATORIUM on ice.

On 11th November 2000 the band reformed with Dismal, Mark Uehlien, Alex Villalobos and Frank Escalon, re-debuting at the 'November To Dismember' festival. Moshe Alvarez also rejoined the ranks. An exhaustive schedule of live work ensued, seeing CREMATORIUM opening for the likes of MAYHEM, CRADLE OF FILTH, NILE, GOD FORBID, DRAGONLORD and SHADOWS FALL. CREMATORIUM offered their homage to JUDAS PRIEST by including their version of 'Breaking The Law' to the 'Hell Bent For Metal' tribute album. The band's 2002 EP 'A World Where Only Nightmares Prevail', on the Dismal imprint, included a cover of METALLICA's 'Whiplash'.

Signing with the then fledgling Prosthetic Records label in 2002, CREMATORIUM released 'For All Our Sins' that same year. Alvarez opted out once again during 2003. The band, pulling in a new rhythm section of bassist Aaron Ramson and drummer Trynt Kelley, previously of DOTAGE and DIE SECTION ATE, announced shows across the USA allied with VEHEMENCE, ALL SHALL PERISH and ANIMOSITY for September 2004. November found the band recording a new album in Los Angeles with producer DD Erlich, entitled 'The Process Of Endtime'. Kelley opted out prior to these sessions, to join INITIUM, and was replaced by Taylor Young. Also on the way out would be guitarist Frank Perez and Alex Villalobos, superseded by Aaron Ramson.

CREMATORIUM forged a touring alliance with VEHEMENCE, THE RED DEATH and ALL SHALL PERISH for US dates in May 2005. The band opened for MAYHEM's July 2007 Californian dates.

EPICEDIUMS OF THE DAMNED, Crematorium (1997). Lands Plagued / Disbelief / Coma Of The Soul / Unholy Massacre / Corporate Malignance / Painless, Lifeless / Sufferance Of Life / Unfound Face / Dismal.

FOR ALL OUR SINS, Prosthetic 65619100062 (2002). Seasons Of Nothingness / The Murder Process / Through Adversity / Nightmares Fused Within Reality / Unlearn / A Disconsolate Winter Landscape / The Dying Place / Cast The Stone / Life : Sick / Bright Lights, Grey Skies / Carved From Deceit / Hidden / From Order And Chaos.

A World Where Only Nightmares Prevail EP, Dismal (2002). Cast The Stone / Carved From Deceit / Unlearn / Whiplash.

THE PROCESS OF ENDTIME, Prosthetic 6561910022-2 (2005). Bloodwake / Reconstructed / Drowning As One / Infinitesimal Acculturation / Perils Of The Disillusioned / Dying Under A Binary Star / Turn A Blind Eye / Born Of The Deadtide / Testicular / End Of Days.

CRIMINAL

CHILE — *Anton Reisenegger (vocals / guitar), Rodrigo Contreras (guitar), Juan Fransisco (bass), Jimmy Ponce (drums).*

A notorious Death Metal act from Chile led by Anton Reisenegger, renowned for his exploits with PENTAGRAM. The band was formulated during 1991 in Santiago and, following a brace of 1992 demo tapes 'Criminal' and 'Forked', made an immediate impact with their 1994 inauguration 'Victimized', released by major label BMG in both South America and Japan. The band's second outing 'Dead Souls', produced by Vincent Wojno, has shifted over 10'000 copies in Chile alone.

During January of 2002 both vocalist / guitarist Anton Reisenegger and lead guitarist Rodrigo Contreras relocated to England in an effort to reach a larger international audience. A new look CRIMINAL was formulated bringing in erstwhile CRADLE OF FILTH man Robin 'Graves' Eaglestone on bass, EXTREME NOIZE TERROR and FAILED HUMANITY drummer Zac O'Neil and keyboard player Mark Royce, a veteran of both ENTWINED and PRIMARY SLAVE. Meantime, ex-CRIMINAL bassist Juan Francisco Cueto joined veteran Chilean act DORSO.

The band would act as special guests to renowned and recently reformed Swedish Doomsters CANDLEMASS and Martin Walkyier's RETURN TO THE SABBAT for their performance at the London Mean Fiddler venue in mid July. Further live action ensued at the German 'Wacken Open Air' and 'Summer Breeze' festivals as CRIMINAL touted a three track demo to labels. The band put in a short burst of UK shows during November packaged with DARKANE and DESCENT.

Robin Eaglestone left the band in March of 2003. Undaunted, CRIMINAL cut a new album 'No Gods No Masters' at Springvale Studios in Suffolk during October. Pulling in bass player Staff Glover, the group teamed up with label mates SIX FEET UNDER and FLESHCRAWL for a two-week European tour throughout February and March of 2004. Chilean dates in May would be marred by the disappearance of keyboard player Mark Royce just two days before the concerts. Naturally, Royce was duly ejected from the band.

Confusion arose that Summer when fabled 'Mexican' Death Metal band BRUJERIA announced Brazilian gigs with CRIMINAL as support. However, it would soon be learned that this an act having no ties to the Chilean combo. In August CRIMINAL announced the recruitment of bassist Aldo Celle, hailing from Viña del Mar in Chile. The new line-up debuted on 20th August at the 'Summer Breeze' festival in Abtsgmünd, Germany. However, original bassist Juan "Kato" Cueto returned to the fold in early 2005.

In early 2006 Mark Royce launched a new band venture dubbed COLD LAZARUS. Another erstwhile band member, bassist Robin Eaglestone, teamed up with Norwegian band GRIMFIST for European touring. Meantime, CRIMINAL re-inducted bassist Staff Glover.

LIVE DISORDER, RCA 74321 44951 2 (1996). Psychopath / Self Destruction / White Hell / Under My Skin / Slave Master / New Disorder.

DEAD SOUL, Metal Blade 14238 (1999). Denial / Scapegoat / Collide / Terror / Life Is Agony / No Salvation / Victimized / S.S.S. / Hijos De La Miseria / Slave Master / Nation of Hate / Guilt.

CANCER, Metal Blade (2001). Cancer / Force Fed / Alma Muerta / Savagery / Control / Green / Play God / Above And Beyond / El Azote / Greed Killing.

CRIMINAL

NO GODS, NO MASTERS, Metal Blade (2004). Aberration / Deconstruction / Consumed / No Return / Tidal Wave / Downfall / Idol / Dark Half / Faceless / Violent Change / Bow To None.

SICARO, Metal Blade (2005). Rise And Fall / Time Bomb / Walking Dead / The Root Of All Evil / Shot In The Face / Sicaro / The Land God Forgot / Preacher Of Hate / Touch Of Filth / From The Ashes / Por La Fuerza De La Razon / Self Destruction.

CRIMSON THORN

MINNEAPOLIS, MN, USA — *Luke Renno (vocals / bass), Miles Sunde (guitar), Andy Kopesky (guitar), Kevin Sundberg (drums).*

Christian Death Metal act CRIMSON THORN heralded their coming with the demo session 'The Plagued'. At this stage the band comprised of vocalist / bassist Luke Renno, guitarists Miles Sunde and Paul Jongeward and drummer Dave Quast. By the time of recording the debut album 'Unearthed' Quast had made way for Kevin Sundberg. This album, originally released on the Atomic label would be re-released by the R.E.X. concern with different artwork and once more by Morphine Records coupled with tracks from 'The Plagued' demo.

The 'Dissection' album, originally issued on Morphine but later remarketed by Little Rose Productions, includes a cover version of STRYPER's 'Loud n' Clear'.

CRIMSON THORN would contribute a track to the 2001 LIVING SACRIFICE tribute album. Andy Kopesky made a return to the ranks in May 2005. That same month Miles Sunde and Luke Renno activated side project AXEHEAD INC..

UNEARTHED, Atomic (1995). Unearthed / Decrepit / Cultivate Decay / Ignorant Self / Your Carcass / Asphyxiated / Malignant Masters / Defaced / Comatose / Imminent Wrath / No Exceptions.

DISSECTION, Morphine (1999). Beaten Beyond / Eternal Life / Deepest Affliction / Dissection / Putrid Condemnation / All Authority / Blood Letting / My Salvation / I Ask / 2nd Timothy / Grave Of Rebirth / Psallo / Loud n' Clear.

CRIPPLE BASTARDS

ITALY — *Giulio The Bastard (vocals), Alberto The Crippler (guitar), Fulvio Hatebox (guitar), Andrea (bass), Al Mazzotti (drums).*

Asti based Grindcore act CRIPPLE BASTARDS have over the years forged alliances with many of their international colleagues on a series of split singles. The group came into being when teenagers vocalist / guitarist Alberto (16) and drummer Giulio (13) teamed up with the Punk-Metal band GRIMCORPSES. By 1988 an extreme Metal direction had been decided upon and a name switch to CRIPPLE BASTARDS highlighted this shift. The group also put in their debut 'gig' at a friends birthday party.

The band did get to record a demo in 1989 (a blistering 25 songs in six minutes!) but somehow neglected to distribute it. The two protagonists started a side Hardcore band DISSONANCE in 1990 together with friend Luigi on drums. This unit would see the first occasion Giulio took up lead vocals. Both DISSONANCE and CRIPPLE BASTARDS would share cassette space with K.S.G. (yet another extra curricular project of Giulio and Alberto- this time a sombre ambient affair) for a three way demo tape with CRIPPLE BASTARD laying down no less than 64 tracks. This tape would be given away free by the group members at other bands gigs.

In 1991 DISSONANCE folded but K.S.G. scored five tracks included on the 'Killed By The Machinary Of Sorrow' compilation. CRIPPLE BASTARDS meantime cut their second demo. The band put in their first proper gig proudly announcing that, bar a handful of determined fans, they cleared the venue!

1992 saw CRIPPLE BASTARDS inaugural vinyl appearance with the band donating two tracks from their 1991 demo to the 'Son Of Bblleeauurrggh!' compilation on Slap A Ham Records. In August the band, still a duo of Giulio on vocals along with drums and Alberto on guitar, put in their first foreign show at the Croatian 'Melody' festival. Shortly after the act drafted drummer Michele Delemont but would remain without a bass player for some time to come. Not content with resting on their laurels Giulio and Alberto struck up another side outing HARSH FEELINGS.

Two shared tape releases emerged on the bands own E.U. label in 1993. Live recordings from their Croatian festival performance were allied with tracks from Belgians AGATHOCLES and another 40 demo tracks featured alongside DARK SEASON songs. The band somehow managed to squeeze no less than 44 tracks onto their shared 1993 7" single with Spain's VIOLENT HEADACHE. These tracks were recorded in 1991 as a duo of Giulio and Alberto on a small cassette recorder in the band's rehearsal room. Although he appears on the sleeve artwork drummer Michele did not perform although he did feature on the rare 1993 split single with W.B.I. Early material from the bands GRIMCORPSES era was released on a cassette with more recent CRIPPLE BASTARDS, HARSH FEELINGS and FILTHY CHARITY material.

The band, back to a deadly duo minus Michele, would also manage to put in live dates in Germany. Other recordings that year included 6 new originals for a split single with SOCIAL GENOCIDE, 5 PATARENI cover versions for a tribute album 'Obrade', an AGATHOCLES cover for the 'Kill Your Idols' compilation and even a BEATLES cover.

1994 would prove a taxing year for the band as Alberto struggled with a drug problem. Nevertheless split releases with PSYCHOTIC NOISE and SENSELESS APOCALYPSE. The EP 'Frammenti Di Vita' comprised solely of cover versions with CRIPPLE BASTARDS paying homage to extreme Italian acts such as INDEGESTI, WRETCHED, NEGAZIONE, NABAT, UNDERAGE, IMPACT and BLUE VOMIT. A further split 7" on the German Regurgitated Semen label, in collaboration with PATARENI, included a cover of the KING CRIMSON classic '21st Century Schizoid Man'. However, after these songs were laid to rest Michele quit the band but was persuaded to stay on in order to conclude recording commitments. CRIPPLE BASTARDS did put in a batch of Italian and German gigs with a stand in drummer. Before the end of the year CRIPPLE BASTARD's tenure without a bassist was ended when Brazilian Eduardo joined the band.

In 1995 a whole slew of split singles arrived with PSYCHOTIC NOISE on the Belgian Grinding Madness label, with CAPITALIST CASUALTIES on the American Wiggy Bits double 10" release and PRÉPARATION H for another American label Vicious Interference. With Michele still hanging on the band recorded a mass of material throughout the year that would see the light of day on the full length 'Your Lies In Check' album, a split album with SUPPRESSION and yet more split singles. Some material was also bootlegged in South America on a single split with WRETCHED.

CRIPPLE BASTARDS finally replaced Michele with ex ARTURO man Paulo. An impromptu live jam with Giulio gusting for IMPACT would surface on a split 10" single with PATARENI.

Eduardo returned to Brazil in May of 1996 and a temporary replacement was found in the form of ARTURO's Stefano. This liaison soon broke down as both ARTURO men departed. CRIPPLE BASTARDS remained as a duo until STUNTPLASTICPARK man Gaba made an entrance. The state would intervene though and after just two shows Gaba was forced out in order to fulfill his military service duties. Paulo would deputise in the studio to cut some tracks for a HUSKER DÜ tribute album on Beserk Records before quitting again. The group laid down some more material with Giulio on drums once more until former WELCH and ACREDINE man Walter Dr. Tomas took the post. A new bassist was found in Gigi Pacino.

The new look quartet would perform at some chaotic Italian Hardcore festivals before a date in Slovenia before recording tracks for a split single with I.R.F. Further gigs at Italian Punk festivals followed before Pacino broke ranks. More live shows, this time in Austria, were completed without a bassist but upon their return Panz took the four string position.

As 1997 turned into 1998 there were rumblings of disquiet from founder member Alberto. Although persuaded to stay the course for the next round of recordings by the time of CRIPPLE BASTARDS support tour of Italy to Brazilians RATOS DE PORAO it was with ex HATEBOX man Fulvio on guitar alongside Alberto. Yet again line up problems would blight the band with Panz being fired and Alberto finally packing his bags. ENTROPIA drummer Andrea duly filled the bass slot for a tour of Slovenia, Croatia, Czech Republic and Germany. A series of Belgian shows would see Alberto returning for these and the next round of studio recordings.

1999 predictably saw CRIPPLE BASTARDS in turmoil once again as Dr. Tomas made his exit. Al Mazzotti of Punk band STINKING POLECATS and Thrash Metal band AUTOPSIA was pulled in for live work although Dr. Tomas remained in place for recordings. Tragedy would strike in the midst of European dates though as the band was involved in a serious crash which injured Mazzotti's hand.

1999 would see the issue of the 'Falafel Grind' tribute through the Czech Obscene Productions label. This collection comprised 25 bands paying homage by covering CRIPPLE BASTARDS songs including DEMISOR, BIRDFLESH, HATEBOX, BLOODSUCKERS, ENTROPIA, STRONG INTENTION, MINDLOCK, CARCASS GRINDER, THE BUTTPLUGZ, ACROHOLIA, GROINCHURN and many more.

Cripple Bastards EP, Psychomania (1991) (Split single with VIOLENT HEADACHE). Useful- Useless / Conceptual Indistinction / Zakljucenje / Look In Your Dish / Toxic Sex / Without A Shadow Of Justice / Shame Of You / Ecological Carnage / Flagged Pain / Fucked ... Original Expressions / Standing Violent / Civilized Torment / Resumption! / Thick Glasses Division / HC Funeral / Incurableness Of A Stigmatization / Sick Of Pleasure / I.H.P. / Far Away From My Best Friends / Self Instruction / Against The Stream / Stealthy Loneliness / Rending Aphthous Fevers / What Can Be ... / Animal-Respect / Outside World / Stylized Fear / A Sort Of Repulsion Called 'Intelligence' / My Last Hours / Windows / Mortuary Slab / Irenic / Rigid Freedom / Sincere Smiles / Act Like A Rose / Psychosexuality / Breathing For Fun / Something Wrong / Equality / Alternative- Dressed Puppets / Turn The Corner / Sarcastic Gloom / Allegorical Masturbations / I Dare You.

Frammenti Di Vita EP, Ecocentric (1993). Spero Venga La Guerra / Incubo Di Morte / Troia / Sporca Naia / Mass Media / Vaffanculo / La Nostra Violenza.

War Spoils EP, Useless USE 001 (1993) (Split single with W.B.I. Limited edition of 500 copies). Paranoic / Without A Shadow Of Justice / Round Table / T.L.O.H. / War Spoils / Bane / Frightened-Neglected / What I Thought.

Life's Built On Thoughts EP, A-Wat (1993). S.L.U.T.S. / Living Monuments / Radije Volim ... / Offensive Death / 0:01 / Bonds Of Enmity / Miniaturized Eden / Prisons / The Opinion Of The Poor / Stimmung / Imposed Mortification / Vital Dreams / More Frustrations / Falling Wish / My Serenity / Dealing With A Pressing Problem.

21st Century Schizoid Man EP, Regurgitated Semen (1993) (Split single with PATERNI). Life In General / Disagreeable Selections / 21st Century Schizoid Man / Hydrophobic Web / Mass Media / Grimcorpses.

Images Of War- Images Of Pain, View Beyond (1996) (Split single with SENSELESS APOCALYPSE). Images Of War- Images Of Pain / My Mind Invades / Blue Penguins / Italia Di Merda / Peasants / Self Justice Punks / 1974 / Something Wrong / Walk Away / Ragman.

Massacrecore, Denied A Custom (1997).

YOUR LIES IN CHECK, Ecocentric (1997). Being Ripped Off / Without A Shadow Of Justice / Prejudices And Walls / Images Of War- Images Of Pain / Imposed Mortification / Prospettive Limitate / Intelligence Means ... / Disagreeable Selections / Caught In Your Silence / Prisons / Irenic / September 18th 1993 / A Dispetto Della Discrezione / Watching Through My Chaos / Newscast Slave / Round Table / Italia Di Merda / The Outside World / My Mind Invades / Danas Je Dan Za Lijencine / More Frustrations / Stimmung / Ghiacciaio / What I Thought / Negative Fractures / Ratings / Paranoic / Frightened- Neglected / 1974 / Milicija Die! / Walk Away / Nichilismo Ampliato / Vital Dreams / Blue Penguins / Bonds Of Enmity / Ragman / Windows / Rending Aphthous Fevers / Bane / Living Monuments / War Spoils / We Can Work It Out / Self Justice Punks / Incorporated Grave / D.S.S. (Double Scented Shit) / Sexist Society ... Must Destroy It! / The Last Shipwrecked / Intransigent Simpathy / Polizia, Una Razza De Estinguere / Cormorant / Life In General / Hydrophobic Web / Padroni / Useful- Useless / More Restrictions. Why? / Miniaturized Eden / Something Wrong / 21st Century Schizoid Man / Devozioni? / Nothing On Earth / Invito Alla Riservatezza / Come E Falso Dio / Radije Volim ... / S.L.U.T.S. / Grimcorpses / Offensive Death / My Serenity / Dealing With A Pressing Problem / Necrospore.

Good Taste In Assholism, MCR Company (1998) (Split single with I.R.F.).

Dawn Of Ecology, Havin' A Spazz (1999) (Split single with POPULAR EASY LISTENING MUSIC ENSEMBLE).

Extreme Glorification Of Violence, Nat (1999).

ALMOST HUMAN, Obscene Productions OBP 039 (2001). Pete The Ripper / Negativity / I Wonder Who The Real Cannibals Are / I Dare You / Ring The Curtain Down / Guerra E Pecador / Cleaning My Ass With Zips & Chains / Il Sentimento Non E Amore / Insuppressible Revenge / Sbocco Nihilista / I Hate Her / Get Out And Bite Them / Mondo Plastico / Fuck Politics, Let's Riot / Always Unsatisfied / Jesus And His Crabs / Odium Prevails / Sexual Hysteria / Jurisdictions / Incurableness Of A Junkiefied Nation / Dawn Of Ecology / Punch Drunk / The Girl Who Lives On Heaven Hill / Strejt Edz / No Way—Il Tuo Amico Morto / Haunting My Worst Sleeps / Morte De Tossico / Il Grande Silenzio / Quasi Donna ... Feminista / Misantropo A Senso Unico / Conclusione / Misantropo A Senso Unico / I Hate Her / Me + Her In A Microcosm Of Torture / Italia Di Merda / Il Sentimento Non E Amore / Idiots Think Slower / September, 18th 1993 / Prospettive Limitate / The Mushroom Diarrhoea / Hazardous Waste / Polizia, Una Razza Da Estinguere / Bomb "La Scintilla" / S.L.U.T.S. / Fuck Politics, Let's Riot / Lotta Per Il Potere (Kollettivo) / Jurisdictions / Inside Out / A Dispetto Della Discrezione / Stimmung.

CROMLECH

SWEDEN — *Fredrik Arnesson (vocals), Jonas Eckerström (guitar), Henrik Meijner (guitar), Dick Löfgren (bass), Mattias Bäck (drums).*

Death Metal act CROMLECH was formed in late 1994 under the name DELIRIUM by guitarists Henrik Meijner and Jonas Eckerström, the latter also handling drum duties initially. Mattias Bäck joined as a drummer, after which bass player Anders Lundin and singer Fredrik Arnesson were enrolled as the CROMLECH title was adopted. A 1996 demo succeeded in gaining track inclusions on compilation albums issued through Black Mark Productions and Near Dark Productions.

During 1997 Meijner joined EUCHARIST whilst Arnesson joined the ranks of ABLAZE MY SORROW. Lundin followed suit in 1998. Early the next year CROMLECH rose up once again, recording a second set of demos. They would be then joined by EUCHARIST bassist Dick Löfgren, also holding ARCH ENEMY, LAST TRIBE, MESHUGGAH, TIME REQUIEM and IN

FLAMES credentials. CROMLECH signed to Italian label Beyond Productions to release an EP entitled 'The Vulture Tones'.

The Vulture Tones, Beyond Productions (2000). A Clarity Denied / The Bleeding / The Vulture Tones / Garden Of Sin.

CROWHEAD

SARPSBORG, NORWAY — *Jo-Inge Slangvold (vocals), Øyvind Trindborg (guitar).*

Sarpsborg Electronic Gothic Metal band CROWHEAD is centred on erstwhile SHADOW DANCERS man Jo-Inge Slangvold and Rym Vicious (a.k.a. Øyvind Trindborg), another SHADOW DANCERS former member as well as citing credits with RAGNAROK. CROWHEAD released the 'Love Letter' demo during 2000. The debut 'Frozen' album included two remixes courtesy of Rico Darum and Ted Skogmann of APOPTYGMA BERZERK, the pair also donating their skills on guitar, keyboards and drums, as well as ICON OF COIL's Sebastian.

Studio recordings in late 2003 saw Lex Icon of THE KOVENANT (a.k.a. ex-DIMMU BORGIR man Nagash) acting as session vocalist / bassist.

FROZEN, The Art ARTCD03012 (0) (Mexican release). My Angel / Mad Man / Eternity (Drums Of Death) / Intro / Fire Eye (Kill You) / Love Letter / Frozen (2002) / My Angel (Signal Krem remix) / The Soul Is In The Dark Side (Part 1) / The Soul Is In The Dark Side (Part 2) / Outro.

Love Letter, Neodawn Production NDP 002 (2000) (Demo). Eternity / Through The Eyes Of A Mad Man / Lost Angel.

FROZEN, My Kingdom Music ECHO 001 (2002). My Angel / Mad Man / Eternity (Drums Of Death) / Intro / Fire Eye (Kill You) / Love Letter / Frozen (2002) / My Angel (Signal Krem Remix) / The Soul Is In The Dark Side (part.1) / The Soul Is In The Dark Side (part.2) / Outro.

CROWN OF THORNS

TROLLHÄTTAN, SWEDEN — *Johan Lindstrandt (vocals), Marcus Sunesson (guitar), Marko Trevonen (guitar), Magnus Osfelt (bass), Janne Saarenpaa (drums).*

Not to be confused with Jean Beouvoir's American Melodic Rock act, Trollhättan's CROWN OF THORNS, founded in 1990 by vocalist Johan Lindstrandt and very much in the Grindcore mould, are a much heavier proposition altogether. CROWN OF THORNS first hit the tape trading scene with an impressive demo, 1993's 'Forever Heaven Gone'. Shortly after its release the band got to play the Swedish Hultsfred festival alongside ENTOMBED and IGGY POP but lost guitarist Robert Österberg to Punk act ÖLHÄVERS. His replacement was Marcus Sunesson who cut his teeth with the 1994 demo 'Forget The Light'. This tape scored them a deal with Black Sun Records for the debut album 'The Burning'. CROWN OF THORNS also made their mark on the SLAYER tribute album 'Slaytanic Slaughter' contributing their take on 'Mandatory Suicide'. During this period Lindstrandt would also be deputising for Thrash act IMPIOUS as a drummer, performing on their 'Infernal Predomination' demo.

CROWN OF THORN's sophomore outing 'Eternal Death' continued the trend and yet again the Swedes were adding to another tribute album, this time nailing a cover of 'Arise' for the SEPULTURA homage 'Sepultural Feast'. The band would be put on ice for a period when Lindstrandt was drafted for military service in early 1996. At this juncture IMPIOUS pulled in CROWN OF THORNS guitarist Marko Trevonen as their replacement drummer!

Continued threat of litigation from the American CROWN OF THORNS resulted in the band adopting the title THE CROWN in 1997. Undaunted the band toured Europe in early 1998 on a billing with SACRILEGE resulting directly in a deal with American label Metal Blade for third album 'Hell Is Here'. As THE CROWN the band issued a follow up 'Deathrace King' in 2000.

CROWN OF THORNS was resurrected in 2007, signing to Italian label Frontiers for a new album.

Forever Heaven Gone, Crown Of Thorns (1993) (Demo). Seventh Gate / Deadspawn / Diachronic Damnation / The Lord Of The Rings / Beyond Where Darkness Dwells / Forever Heaven Gone.

Forget The Light, Crown Of Thorns (1994) (Demo). Soullicide Demon-Might / Godless / Neverending Dream / Candles.

THE BURNING, Black Sun BS05 (1995). Of Good And Evil / Soulicide Demon-Might / Godless / The Lord Of The Rings / I Crawl / Forever Heaven Gone / Earthborn / Neverending Dreams / Night Of The Swords / Candles / Forget The Light.

ETERNAL DEATH, Black Sun BS10 (1997). Angels Die / Beautiful Evil Soul / In Bitterness And Sorrow / The Black Heart / World Within / The Serpent Garden / Kill (The Priest) / Misery Speaks / Hunger / Death Of God.

CRUCIFER

FREDERICKSBURG, VA, USA — *Jeff Riddle (vocals / drums), Brian Ronquest (guitar / keyboards), Steve Snyder (bass).*

CRUCIFER was a Fredericksburg, Virginia three-piece Death/Thrash band that had a fairly successful run in the 1990's, at least by underground standards. Originally entitled KILLER INSTINCT, they were notable for the fact that ex-PLATINUM AXE drummer Jeff Riddle also served as lead vocalist. Bassist Steve Snyder was also a member of PLATINUM AXE. The trio, incorporating Brian Ronquest on guitar was formed in late 1990 and quickly established a long and productive relationship with the Wild Rags record label. Their debut four-song demo 'Beyond The Realms' was released in 1991 and CRUCIFER first performed live as support to BELIEVER on 9th February 1991.

In 1992 another release followed in the form of 'Festival Of Death', recorded at SST Studios the previous October. The band followed a common routine of gigging, writing, recording and releasing albums. Later in 1992 they released a two-song seven-inch vinyl promo called 'Pray for The Dead', the first 250 copies of which would be pressed in "Eerie" blue vinyl. They released the 'Pictures of Heaven' album, crafted at Salamone's Recording Studios in October of 1992, and in 1994 the 'Separation' EP. 1996 was a bigger year for the band as Wild Rags also re-issued almost all their material on CD, each album remastered with various bonus tracks. CRUCIFER projected a concept album to be entitled 'The Pharos Curse', although this project was never completed. Another attempt to record an album, provisionally entitled 'Sickly Divine', would also be, apparently, aborted. Material from this session would surface on the Wild Rags compilation entitled, 'World Dies-1989-1998'.

In January 2007 the group announced they were to participate on a four-way split CD in collaboration with Sweden's BESTIAL MOCKERY, fellow US outfit SATHANAS, and Poland's THRONEUM through Time Before Time Records.

Beyond The Realms, Wild Rags (1991).

FESTIVAL OF DEATH, Wild Rags WRR-CRU (1992). Festival Of Death / Pieces / Crucifer / Atheist / Mindrape / Flowers / Eternal Truth.

Pray For The Dead, (1992) (7" single. First 250 copies blue vinyl). Pray For The Dead / Post Nuclear Dream.

PICTURES OF HEAVEN, Wild Rags WRR031 (1993). Pictures Of Heaven / Dawn Of Time / Sister Crematorium / Death Becomes Us / Parallels To Eternity / False Sense Of Hope / Impaled / And Once Again.

Separation, Wild Rags WRR-051 (1994). Separation / The World Dies / Dissatisfied.

SICKLY DIVINE, Wild Rags (1996). Soul Within / No Colour / Deity In Black / Sickly Divine / Green With Envy / Left Hand Path / Destruction / Mirrors / Heart In Hand / Grace / Laughing As I Suffer / Winter.

CRUCIFIER

EDDYSTONE, PA, USA — *The Black Lourde Of Crucifixion (vocals / drums), Madman (guitar), Infernal (guitar), Necrodemius Hammerhorde (bass).*

Dating to September 1990, Pennsylvania Black Metal band CRUCIFIER, centred on Cazz Grant of GRAND BELIAL'S KEY, has issued a whole array of demos starting with 'Humans Are Such Easy Prey' in 1991. Further sessions included 'Crown Of Thorns', 1993's 'By Disgrace Of God' and 1994's 'Powerless Against'. The opening CRUCIFIER formation saw Grant on vocals and drums with Ira Redden and Jeff Anderson handling guitar. A projected demo, to be entitled 'The Unholy Trinity', was "planned, attempted and unfortunately aborted". The line-up shifted shape in January 1991 with the departure of Anderson and the induction of guitarist Dan Kamp and bassist Chris Miller. Redden then exited, paving the way for replacement Mike Machette and in this formation CRUCIFIER recorded the 'Humans Are Such Easy Prey' session. However, in November of 1991 both Machette and Miller opted out.

CRUCIFIER cut their second demo 'Crown Of Thorns', then enrolled new bassist Dan Keaton. The band laid down material for the 'Unparalleled Majesty' EP, through Polish label Pagan Productions, but dismissed Keaton in September 1992. Gary Gandy stepped in as substitute. Following completion of the 'By Disgrace Of God' sessions Kamp made his exit to join INCANTATION. This defection put CRUCIFIER into a state of flux, resulting in a fluid line-up which would include at various stages the likes of Joe Ceresini, Mike Pandorf of SNAG, Joel Prange of WITCHERY, Craig Ross from RAPID VIOLENCE and ex-FACE FIRST man Chris DePetro.

In the Spring of 1994 CRUCIFIER drafted Mark Neto from British band CRUENTUS on bass guitar. Although now just a duo of Grant and Neto, the band, bringing back Dan Kamp and Chris DePetro, put in live work. In May the three song 'Powerless Against' promotional session was recorded with the aid of Nick "The Marauder" Mertaugh on guitar. Additional vocals would be supplied by the GRAND BELIAL'S KEY, THOKK and ANCIENT credited Vlad Luciferian and Jose Infernal of 'Sargatanas' zine. Virginia's Sinistrari Records issued 'Powerless Against', after which Neto departed.

CRUCIFIER members Grant ('The Black Lourde Of Crucifixion'), Der Sturmer and Lilith would all session on the debut GRAND BELIAL'S KEY album 'Mocking The Philanthropist'. Grant founded a new Thrash act BLUDGEON in 1997. CRUCIFIER returned in 1999, sharing the 'Trafficking With The Devil' single with NUNSLAUGHTER. CRUCIFIER duly hired ex-GOREPHOBIA, FACE FIRST and POLTERCHRIST guitarist Spencer "Madman" Murphy and Vince Papi of HEARSE and BLUDGEON on bass guitar. Live performances ensued but both Papi and Murphy left. Nick "The Marauder" Mertaugh was re-recruited on guitar and Jon "Demonic" Chamot took on the bass guitar role. In 2002 Madman returned to the fold.

In September of 2003 the Spanish label Death To Mankind Records issued the album 'Stronger Than Passing Time'. The band line-up fluxed once again, seeing new personnel guitarists Madman and Infernal with Necrodemius Hammerhorde on bass. Hammerhorde also operates with INFERNAL HATRED and his own DECIEVERION project, the latter also seeing contributions from Cazz Grant.

Unparalleled Majesty, Pagan (1993). Sodomy Of Angels / Spirits / Demons Of Filth / Something Wicked This Way Comes.

By Disgrace Of God EP, Pagan (1993). A Mourning In Nazareth / Portraits Of Blasphemy.

Powerless Against, Sinistrari (1994). Chime Of The Goat's Head Bell / Fire & Brimstone / My Lord Of Swine.

Trafficking With The Devil, The Crucifier Brotherhood International (1998) (Split single with NUNSLAUGHTER). Foul Deeds Will Rise.

THE NINTH YEAR, Elegy ER012CD (2002). The Cinerarium / Demons Of Filth / The Funeral / Exhumed Remains Of A Decayed Corpse / Portraits Of Blasphemy / Massacremation Of The Flock / Disembowelment Lunacy / Apocryphal Nativity / Soul Burial / Chime Of The Goat's Head Bell / Portraits Of Blasphemy / A Mourning In Nazareth / Chime Of The Goat's Head Bell / Fire And Brimstone / My Lord Of Swine / Foul Deeds Will Rise.

STRONGER THAN PASSING TIME, Death To Mankind (2003). Sodomy Of Angels / Thine Enemies Destroyed / Kneel To Lilith / Something Wicked This Way Comes / A Mourning In Nazareth / Demons Of Filth / The Rotten Whore Of God / Fire & Brimstone / Spirits / Plunging Pitchforks Through Paradise.

CRUCIFIX

SKJERN, DENMARK — *Simon Skyrme (vocals), Måns (guitar), Morten Hellhound (guitar), Martin Jacobsen (bass), Lars Groth (drums).*

Skjern Death Metal act CRUCIFIX was manifested during 1993 as a covers act by guitar player Morten Agerbo and drummer Lars Groth, subsequently enlisting second guitarist Tommy Johnson, bassist Bo Simonsen then vocalist Hans Henrik. The group gained a track inclusion on the 1995 'Danish Upcommers' compilation album but then would be struck by tragedy when Henrik was killed in a motorbike accident. Simonsen quit shortly afterward but CRICIFIX persevered to record an eponymous demo, Agerbo handling lead vocals. In late 1996 Jesper Hansen took on bass duties.

In November 1997 Morten Flindt joined on guitar and Rene Engholm became the new singer but Agerbo departed at the same juncture. CRUCIFIX gigged extensively throughout Denmark but eventually parted ways with Engholm, the ex-singer joining EVIL PIGS. The group would re-enlist Morten Agerbo.

The band released a live demo, 'Caught Live In Varde', in February 1998. The second CRUCIFIX studio demo, 'Extermination' also issued in 1998, was produced by INVOCATOR's Jacob Hansen. The track 'Into the Unknown' was later released on a compilation album 'Extremity Rising Vol. 4.' Despite this progress, CRUCIFIX ceased activities.

In 2001 the band rose up once again prompted by interest from Diehard Records. However, this version of the band soon splintered. CRUCIFIX returned for a third attempt, with Flindt and Groth drawing in new members guitarist Jeppe Larsen and EVIL PIGS bassist Kristian Ohmer. This latter candidate soon exited and CRUCIFIX found a new frontman in Jens "Killhailer" Pedersen of VICTIMIZER, AD NOCTUM, UNDERGANG and CHURCH BIZARRE repute. Larsen then took his leave, being superseded by Måns.

CRUCIFIX went into a further hiatus during the Autumn of 2003 as Groth and Flindt pursued another band project called LUNAR CAUSTIC. Yet again CRUCIFIX was resurrected, briefly seeing Soeren Kusk handling the microphone in December 2004 before Killhailer returned. JUGGERNAUGHT's Martin Jacobsen was delegated bass.

Working with producer Alberto Gallista, the group cut a new demo, 'Where Angels Rot', in 2005. This release would benefit from a commercial re-issue through Polish label Gruft Prodüktions. That same year Pedersen would sub himself out to KILL for live work. Pedersen opted out during November 2005, prioritising VICTIMIZER and CHURCH BIZARRE, and CRUCIFIX duly drafted new singer Simon Skyrme in January 2006.

Crucifix, Crucifix (1996). Unknown Human / The Blazing Valley / The End Of Life / Funeral Of Silence / Shadows.

Extermination, (1998). Enslaved By The Mind / The Deathwish / Into The Unknown / Gates To The Allmighty.

Caught Live In Varde, (1998). Intro / Into The Unknown / Broken / 7 Gates To The Allmighty / The Blazing Valley / The Deathwish.

Where Angels Rot, Gruft Prodüktions (2005). Violence Of The Flesh / Where Angels Rot / Bloodrush / Perception Of The World / The Cleansing Storm.

CRUELTY

RIO DE JANEIRO, RJ, BRAZIL — *Rubens Sickness (vocals), Júnior (guitar), Renato Medeiros (guitar), André (bass), Valério Shadows (drums).*

CRUELTY was a Rio de Janeiro Death-Thrash Metal act, forged during 1995 as a trio of vocalist / drummer Valério Shadows, guitarist Bruno and bass player Adilon. This version of the band crafted the demo 'Symphony Terrible' in 1998. Both Adilon and Bruno decamped and CRUELTY drafted guitarist Renato Medeiros, ex-former HALLUCINATION, BLOOD AREA, ALIENATION OF WAR, VULGAR singer Rubens Sickness and bassist André for a second set 'Brutal Symphony'. Júnior enrolled as second guitarist, but the band then folded.

Valério forged Black Metal band DURST, both Rubens and Júnior subsequently joining this group. Rubens, going by the stage name of 'Vírus' initiated ESCÓRIA. Valério also made his mark with Portuguese outfit OPUS DRACONIS whilst Renato also operated as a member of DIABLERIE.

Symphony Terrible, Cruelty (1995). Intro / I'm Insane / Cruelty / Don't Need / Symphony Terrible.

Brutal Symphony, Cruelty (1998). Death / Cruelty / Prince Of All Lives / Brutal Symphony / Crudely.

CRYHAVOC

HELSINKI, FINLAND — *Kaapro Ikonen (vocals), Jouni Lilja (guitar), Risto Lipponen (guitar), Kari Myöhänan (bass), Pauli Tolvahen (drums).*

Helsinki's CRYHAVOC began their musical journey entitled PREPROPHECY issuing the acclaimed Death Metal demos 'A Tomb Of Sanity' in 1993 and its follow up 'Season Of Sorrows'. A name switch to RAVENSFALL saw the addition of ABSURDUS rhythm section bassist Taneli Nyholm and drummer Matti Roiha in 1996. However, when ABSURDUS were signed by the British Candlelight label Nyholm and Roiha disembarked back to their priority act. (Nyholm, billed as 'Daniel Stuka', would later join BABYLON WHORES).

A deal was struck with a Singapore based label and RAVENSFALL began preparation for recording of a debut album. Fate intervened when the label in question folded leaving the band high and dry. Noted label Spinefarm came to their rescue and the band, now billed as CRYHAVOC, cut their debut entitled 'Sweetbriers', issued in May 1998.

Sales of the album were high, no doubt aided by the artistic sleeve photo cover imagery, and 'Pitch Black Blues' emerged in August 1999. Touring, despite support dates to THE GATHERING in Europe, would be minimal although a short batch of Finnish dates was conducted with DARK TRANQUILITY and IN FLAMES during October.

'Pitch Black Blues' would be licensed to Brazil through Rock Brigade Records, Japan via Avalon / Marquee and in Poland on cassette format by Mystic Productions.

Children Of Bodom, Spinefarm SPI 59CD (1998) (Split single with WIZZARD and CHILDREN OF BODOM). Repent (Whore).

SWEETBRIERS, Spinefarm SPI 58CD (1998). Bloodtie / Repent (Whore) / Come With Me / Wolfdance / Pagan Uprise / I Fade Away / Armageddon Y'Know / Misanthropy.

PITCH BLACK BLUES, Spinefarm SPI 78CD (1999). Cryscythe / Metamorphosis / The Wind / Snowsong / Spree / The Serpent And Eve / Wild At Heart / Pitch Black Ink.

PITCH BLACK BLUES, Rock Brigade RBR/LCR 1950 (2000) (Brazilian release). Cryscythe / Metamorphosis / The Wind / Snowsong / Spree / The Serpent And Eve / Wild At Heart / Pitch Black Ink / The Key / Wolfdance / Blackheart.

PITCH BLACK BLUES, Avalon Marquee MICP-10179 (2000) (Japanese release). Cryscythe / Metamorphosis / The Wind / Snowsong / Spree / The Serpent And Eve / Wild At Heart / Pitch Black Ink / Bloodtie / Repent (Whore) / Come With Me / Wolfdance / Pagan Uprise / I Fade Away / Armageddon Y'Know / Misanthropy.

CRYOGENIC

SYDNEY, NSW, AUSTRALIA — *Ryan David (vocals), Steve Essa (guitar), Anthony Henning (bass), Darren Jenkin (drums).*

CRYOGENIC, hailing from Sydney, made their first impressions in the early nineties as a Thrash Metal act, the formative membership comprising vocalist / guitarist Russell Player, lead guitarist Steve Essa, bass guitarist Anthony Henning and drummer Chad Bartosik. Although this version of the band demoed they would not progress beyond local compilation albums such as the inclusion of 'Take The Pain' on the 1995 collection 'Warhead Volume 1' and 'Intoxicated' on 1996's 'On Earth Undead'. New impetus was given with the introduction of drummer Darren Jenkin in 1996, the man known for his prior work for MORTALITY.

Following Australian support gigs to FEAR FACTORY in 1997 Player defected. Although their erstwhile singer had already laid down vocal sessions for a debut album 'Suspended Animation', these were wiped and Darren Maloney, another recruit from MORTALITY, re-recorded the album for release. Maloney's Death Metal leanings gave the band a new edge and 'Suspended Animation', released by the domestic Warhead label, would be promoted throughout 1998 with a series of valuable nationwide tours including guest slots to ENTOMBED, STRAPPING YOUNG LAD and CRADLE OF FILTH. The band stepped up a league later that same year by undertaking European dates and, returning home to Australia, opening shows for SLAYER.

An appearance at the 1999 Sydney Big Day Out was to precede issue of a second Tony Jarrett produced album 'Ego-Noria', released by Extreme Music Australia Records. Media and fans began to detect distinct traces of Nu-Metal leanings in the band's sound but progress was unchecked as CRYOGENIC headlined the 'Metal For The Brain' festival and delivered a second 'Big Day Out' set in January 2000. Packaged with PSI-CORE and ALCHEMIST the group then embarked upon the 'World War Three' tour throughout March and into May. Later that same year Essa would act as stand in musician for PSI-KORE.

2001 proved relatively quiet bar a third showing at the Sydney 'Big Day Out'. It would be then learned that the band had parted ways with Maloney. He would be superseded by ex-HENRY'S ANGER man Steve Simmons, this enlistment signalling a shift toward more down tuned, Hardcore musical realms. Unfortunately this phase of the band's career was cut short when, in September of 2002, Simmons was seriously injured in an auto accident, forcing him out of the group. CRYOGENIC re-enlisted singer Ryan David in April of 2003. Before the close of the year the band had not only relocated to Los Angeles but adopted the new title IN THE NAME OF … Their inaugural gig as newly billed US residents would be in Hollywood during December supporting the BEAUTIFUL CREATURES.

SUSPENDED ANIMATION, Warhead WH 23 (1997). One Minute Hit / Mind Over Soul / Severed / Junc / Death Becomes You / Mary Belle / Destructive Minds / Numerical Superiority / Bring It On.

EGO-NORIA, E.M.A. Music EMA101 (1999). Analysis / Directionally One / Death By Misadventure / Conspiracy Theory / Hate My Head / Fall On / T.Y.T.D. (Cliffo) / Full Grown State / Stalemate / Redneck / Shock Value.

CRYPT OF KERBEROS

ESKILSTUNA, SWEDEN — *Christian Eriksson (vocals), Jonas Strandell (guitar), Peter Petersson (guitar), Stefan Källarsson (bass), Jessica Strandell (keyboards), Mattias Borgh (drums).*

Eskilstuna Death Metal band founded in 1990 under the original moniker of MACRODEX, releasing demos under that title, 'Disgorged To Carrion' in February 1989, 'Infernal Excess' in June 1989 and 'Remains Of A Lost Life' the following year. The group, counting a membership of vocalist Christian

Eriksson, guitarists Roger Petterson, ex-TEARS OF GRIEF and INFESTER, plus Peter Petersson, bassist Stefan Karlsson with Mikael Sjöberg on drums, transformed itself into CRYPT OF KERBEROS. After the release of 1991 the 'Visions Beyond Darkness' single guitarist Johan Löhnroth and drummer Mikael Sjöberg split and Jonas Strandell and Mattias Borgh were drafted in to fill the respective vacancies.

CRYPT OF KERBEROS issued a follow up single in 1992 and the 'World Of Myths' album, recorded at Studio Skyline in January 1993. Album track 'The Canticle' would be included on the Displeased Records compilation 'Against All Gods'. In 1995, the group lost the services of both guitarist Jonas Strandell and keyboard player Jessica Strandell. Substituting on guitar would be Johan Hallgren and Marcus Pederson was introduced on bass. With these new members the band wrote and recorded new songs in Studio Underground in Eskilstuna. However, vocals never got to be recorded and these sessions only proceeded to rough mix status. Nevertheless, due to the positive response to the debut album labels such as Earache Records, Inline Records and Roasting House all expressed interest.

CRYPT OF KERBEROS underwent a further line-up change with Pederson relinquishing his bass position. The HOUSE OF USHER credited Stefan Källarsson enrolled but then singer Christian Eriksson exited. The band regrouped, drafting singer Daniel Gildenlöw and keyboard man Peter Jansson and commenced rehearsals for a proposed second album given a working title of 'Nadia'. This material saw the band embarking upon a grandiose concept album with much more melodic overtones than its predecessor. Pre-production tapes were crafted at Studio Skyline but then the band began to fragment, officially splitting in 1995.

With the demise of CRYPT OF KERBEROS, Peter Petersson became a member of ARCANA. Guitarist Johan Hallgren and frontman Daniel Gildenlöw subsequently joined PAIN OF SALVATION. Peter Jansson was inducted into MAZE OF TORMENT.

The Australian label Anatomy Bleed Records planned an archival release to comprise early demos, the two 7" EP's and some rehearsals previous to 'World Of Myths' to be collected together as 'Crypt of Kerberos: The Macrodex of War'.

CRYPT OF KERBEROS announced a band reformation in January 2006.

Visions Beyond Darkness, Sunabel SUNABEL 001 (1991). Visions Beyond Darkness / Darkest Rites.
Crypt Of Kerberos, Crypt Of Kerberos (1991) (Demo). Intro / Sacrifice / Armageddon / Devastator / The End Of Time.
Demo '91, Crypt Of Kerberos (1991) (Demo). Intro: Eternal Suffering / Nocturnal Grasp / Stormbringer / Bleed World / Yule Horror / Shadow Fire.
Cyclone Of Insanity, Adipocere AR004 (1992). Cyclone Of Insanity / The Ancient War.
WORLD OF MYTHS, Crypt Of Kerberos CDAR 013 (1993). The Canticle / Cyclone Of Insanity / Dream … / Stormbringer / The Ancient War / Nocturnal Grasp / The Sleeping God / World Of Myths.
THE MACRODEX OF WAR, Bleed BLEED 009 (2005). Sacrifice / Armageddon / Devastator / The End Of Times / Intro: Eternal Suffering / Nocturnal Grasp / Storm Bringer / Bleeding World / Yule Horror / Shadow Fire / Cyclone Of Insanity / The Ancient War / Dream … / World Of Myths / Guidance / The Beholder / Temptation Denial / Visions Beyond Darkness / Darkest Rites.

CRYPTOSY

MONTRÉAL, QC, CANADA — *Mike DiSavo (vocals), Jon Levasseur (guitar), Alex Auburn (guitar), Eric Langlois (bass), Flo Mounier (drums).*

Montréal's CRYPTOPSY was created during 1992 by erstwhile NECROSIS personnel vocalist Lord Worm (a.k.a. Dan Greening), guitarist Steve Thibault and renowned speed drummer Flo Mounier together with former REACTOR guitarist Dave Galea. The antecedent NECROSIS, formed in 1988, issued two demos, 'Realms Of Pathogenia' in 1991 and 'Necrosis' in 1992, prior to the name change. CRYPTOPSY was rounded off by bassist Kevin Weagle for the opening four song demo session 'Ungentle Exhumation' in July 1993. The early incarnation of CRYPTOPSY was quite theatrical with many shows beginning with Lord Worm rising from a dirt-filled coffin and actually eating large, white worms!

Formative line-up changes would see Galea breaking ranks, to be superseded by Jon Levasseur, whilst Weagle also left the fold as CRYPTOPSY pulled in replacement Martin Fergusson. CRYPTOPSY's debut album, 'Blasphemy Made Flesh' produced by Rod Shearer. Recorded in April 1994 for the independent label Gore Productions and released later in the same year, the album was licensed in Europe to Invasion Records who released it with a different cover.

Further line-up shuffles saw the exit of both Fergusson and Thibault. The band signed to the Swedish Wrong Again concern for the follow up 'Non So Vile', co-produced by OBLIVEON guitarist Pierre Rémillard. 'None So Vile' would be re-issued in 1999 on the Dutch Displeased label in Europe.

Eric Langlois was enrolled as bassist as CRYPTOPSY cut their third album, September 1998's 'Whisper Supremacy', this time for Germany's Century Media label, as a quartet. Guitarist Miguel Roy was added after recording. As the band signed to Century Media the lyrical content and image were toned down considerably causing some critics to call for a return to the gore Metal stylings of the first two releases instead of the hyper-kinetic Death Thrash of the later releases.

CRYPTOPSY suffered another major blow when Lord Worm decided to retire from the band, finding a somewhat more sedate career path as an English teacher. However, this move was on good terms as the previous incumbent introduced the band to his replacement, ex-INFESTATION vocalist Mike DiSavo. Promoting 'Whisper Supremacy', which featured Lord Worm on backing vocals, CRYPTOPSY undertook their inaugural American tour sharing billing with NILE, OPPRESSOR and GORGUTS. Further shows in 1999 saw Roy out of the picture replaced by former SEISME six-stringer Alex Auburn as the band hit the road in the States for another round, this time with Poles VADER. The group would also put in a European showing at the prestigious Dutch Dynamo festival as well as dates in Japan. Promoting fourth album 'And Then You'll Beg' witnessed the 'Pain Cometh' tour with support from CANDIRA.

Mike DiSalvo decided to leave the band his last live performance being the 4th August 2001 'Wacken Open Air' festival date in Germany. Despite this blow CRYPTOPSY's future seemed assured. Century Media USA would show faith by licensing the band's first two albums 'Blasphemy Made Flesh', released on February 20th, and 'None So Vile' for re-release. The label used the original artwork for 'Blasphemy Made Flesh' with a few very minor changes. In August the band announced Martin Lacroix, previously with SPASME, as their new vocalist.

CRYPTOPSY recorded their June 1st appearance in front of 1,800 fans at the Medley in Montreal for a live album, 'None So Live', released in 2003. The band headlined the Detroit, Michigan 'Xtreme Benefest' in November, a two day Death Metal extravaganza aimed at raising funds for scene veteran JAMES MURPHY.

In August 2002 Flo Mounier forged part of a Thrash covers act BLACK CLOUD for a one-off appearance at the Thrashback festival in Montréal on November 9th 2002. This band boasted the prodigious talents of B.A.R.F. frontman Marc Vaillancourt, bassist Jean-Yves 'Blacky' Thériault of VOIVOD infamy alongside GHOULUNATICS frontman Patrick Mireault, Pierre Rémillard of OBLIVEON on guitar and Daniel Mongrain of MARTYR on second guitar. CRYPTOPSY's Alex Auburn substituted temporarily for QUO VADIS in March of 2003. The band parted ways with vocalist Martin Lacroix in October that year. Original vocalist Lord Worm rejoined CRYPTOPSY in December 2003.

Flo Mounier acted as stand in drummer for GHOULUNATICS

during May of 2004, their regular sticksman Brian Craig being put out of action with a sprained ankle. Meantime, Emetic Records re-issued CRYPTOPSY's first two albums, 1994's 'Blasphemy Made Flesh' and 1995's 'None So Vile', as a double vinyl, gatefold package, limited to 1,000 copies worldwide.

CRYPTOPSY put in an impressive swathe of dates right across Canada during September and October 2004, culminating with an appearance at the Trois-Rivieres Metalfest. For the first set of shows former guitarist Miguel Roy acted as stand in for Jon Levasseur. For the second portion, beginning in Québec City, Dan Mongrain of MARTYR and GORGUTS took over. These gigs produced the live DVD release, 'Trois-Rivières MetalFest IV'.

Stand in guitarist Daniel Mongrain exited in May 2005 in order to prioritise MARTYR. That same month the band entered Studio Vortex in Saint-Constant, Québec with producer Sébastien Marsan to work on a new album, 'Once Was Not'. The album arrived that October, with a special 'deluxe' edition, limited to 10,000 copies, clad in an embossed, foil-stamped digipak. Road work continued in late 2005, witnessing October and November shows packaged with SUFFOCATION, CEPHALIC CARNAGE, ABORTED and WITH PASSION. For these gigs CRYPTOPSY recruited Christian Donaldson from MYTHOSIS to fill in on second guitar.

The band returned to Europe in January 2006, backed by a supporting cast of GRAVE, ABORTED, DEW-SCENTED, VESANIA and HURTLOCKER. That same month ex-singer Martin Lacroix joined COVENANCE, a band assembled by MISERY INDEX members Matt Byers on drums and guitarist Bruce Greig.

US East Coast touring was set to resume with EXODUS and IMMOLATION in April but these shows were cancelled due to immigration problems, a slated appearance at the New England Metal and Hardcore Festival on April 29th in Worcester, Massachusetts also affected. Scandinavian gigs would be announced for August and September in collaboration with ABORTED, VISCERAL BLEEDING and VESANIA with the band also hooking up with SHE SAID DESTROY, GOREROTTED and SYLOSIS for a UK run of dates that same month. This trek included a one off support to CELTIC FROST in London.

Ungentle Exhumation, Cryptopsy (1993) (Demo). Gravaged (A Cryptopsy) / Abigor / Back To The Worms / Mutant Christ.
BLASPHEMY MADE FLESH, Black Light Creations I.R. 011 (1994). Defenestration / Abigor / Open Face Surgery / Serial Messiah / Born Headless / Swine Of The Cross / Gravaged (A Cryptopsy) / Memories Of Blood / Mutant Christ / Pathological Frolic.
NONE SO VILE, Wrong Again WAR009CD (1996). Crown Of Horns / Slit Your Guts / Graves Of Your Fathers / Dead And Dripping / Benedictive Convulsions / Phobophile / Lichmistress / Orgiastic Disembowelment.
WHISPER SUPREMACY, Century Media 7921-2 (1998). Emaciate / Cold Hate, Warm Blood / Loathe / White Worms / Flame To The Surface / Depths You've Fallen / Faceless Unknown / Serpent's Coil.
AND THEN YOU'LL BEG, Century Media 8009-2 (2000). And Then It Passes / We Bleed / Voice Of Unreason / My Prodigal Sun / Shroud / Soar And Envision Sore Vision / Equivalent Equilibrium / Back To The Worms / Screams Go Unheard.
AND THEN YOU'LL BEG, JVC Victor VICP-61184 (2000) (Japanese release). And Then It Passes / We Bleed / Voice Of Unreason / My Prodigal Sun / Shroud / Soar And Envision Sore Vision / Equivalent Equilibrium / Back To The Worms / Screams Go Unheard / Slit Your Guts (Live) / Born Headless (Live).
Ungentle Exhumation, Galy / Defen Society CR 012 (2002). Gravaged (A Cryptopsy) / Abigor / Back To The Worms / Mutant Christ.
NONE SO LIVE, Century Media CD 8142-2 (2003). Intro / Crown Of Horns / White Worms / We Bleed / Open Face Surgery / Cold Hate, Warm Blood / Phobophile / Shroud / Graves Of The Fathers / Drum solo / Defenestration / Slit Your Guts.
ONCE WAS NOT, Century Media 8242-2 (2005). Luminum / In The Kingdom Where Everything Dies, The Sky Is Mortal / Carrionshine / Adeste Infidelis / The Curse Of The Great / The Frantic Pace Of Dying / Keeping The Cadaver Dogs Busy / Angelskingarden / The Pestilence That Walketh In Darkness (Psalm 91: 5-8) / The End / Endless Cemetery.
ONCE WAS NOT, JVC Victor VICP-63207 (2005) (Japanese release). Luminum / In The Kingdom Where Everything Dies, The Sky Is Mortal / Carrionshine / Adeste Infidelis / The Curse Of The Great / The Frantic Pace Of Dying / Keeping The Cadaver Dogs Busy / Angelskingarden / The Pestilence That Walketh In Darkness (Psalm 91: 5-8) / The End / Endless Cemetery / Cold Hate, Warm Blood (Live) / We Bleed (Live).

CRYSTAL AGE

GOTHENBURG, SWEDEN — *Oscar Dronjac (vocals / guitar), Moses Jonathon Elfström (guitar), Fredrick Larsson (bass), Hans Nilsson (drums).*

CRYSTAL AGE, a Death Metal band, was forged in Gothenburg by ex-CEREMONIAL OATH vocalist / guitarist Oscar Dronjac and ex-LIERS IN WAIT men guitarist Moses Jonathon Elfström and drummer Hans Nilsson. A debut demo was recorded in January 1994. The group covered METALLICA's 'Damage Inc.' for the 1994 Black Sun Records tribute album 'Metal Militia', before unleashing their debut album the following year. Dronjac had also been a member of Black / Thrash act DESECRATOR, having released the 1989 demo cassette 'Wake The Dead' and a 1990, three song demo 'Black Sermons'.

Interestingly, a band created by Dronjac and bassist Frederick Larsson purely for fun in 1993 was later to overtake CRYSTAL AGE. The trad Metal renaissance band HAMMERFALL, which included Dronjac's erstwhile CEREMONIAL OATH colleague drummer Jesper Strömbold, also of IN FLAMES, as well as members of DARK TRANQUILLITY, exploded into the national German charts during 1997 with their debut album 'Glory To The Brave'.

Larsson relinquished his HAMMERFALL ties just prior to the band gaining prominence, joining Thrashers NONE. He later formulated DEATH DESTRUCTION with his erstwhile NONE colleague, and EVERGREY member, Henrik Danhage and would work with HAMMERFALL vocalist Joacim Cans on his CANS side project. In July 2006 Fredrik Larsson joined the ranks of EVERGREY. Larsson rejoined HAMMERFALL in April 2007.

Promo 1994, Crystal Age (1994) (Demo). Far Beyond Divine Horizons / Star Destroyer / Retaliation.
FAR BEYOND DIVINE HORIZONS, Vic VIC2 (1995). Far Beyond Divine Horizons / Fortune And Glory / The Beauty Of Evil / Son Of Time / Wind Walker / Crystals Of The Wise / On Blooded Wings / Tempt Not Thy Maker / Star Destroyer / Retaliation.

CURRICULUM MORTIS

SWEDEN — *Mattias Leinikka (vocals), Leo Pignon (guitar), Fredrik Andersson (guitar / bass / drums).*

CURRICULUM MORTIS is a 2001 formation spearheaded by the AMON AMARTH, ALLEGIANCE and A CANOROUS QUINTET drummer Fredrik Andersson. He would be joined by Leo Pignon of A CANOROUS QUINTET and NIDEN DIV. 187 on guitar and Mattias Leinikka from SANGUINARY and GUIDANCE OF SIN as lead vocalist. The debut demo 'Into Death' surfaced in 2003.

Andersson started up a fresh project band in 2003, LAID TO REST being a Death / Thrash Metal project featuring KAPUT! and ORCHARDS OF ODENWRATH guitarist Zack Z.

Pignon and Andersson, alongside erstwhile colleagues from A CANOROUS QUINTET, embarked upon a new band project, THE PLAGUE, in early 2005.

Into Death, Curriculum Mortis (2003) (Demo). Kill All Life / Into Death / Walls Of Ice / Frail / Preserve You Forever.

CUTTHROAT

LARVIK, NORWAY — *Pål Borgersen (vocals), Thor Øyvind Mathisen (guitar), Ole Holm Klepaker (guitar), Endre Moe (bass), Per Ivar Ederklep (drums).*

Larvik Death Metal act CUTTHROAT issued the 2003 demo 'Encyclopedia In Brutalism'. Both guitarist Ole Holm Klepaker and lead vocalist Pål Borgersen have a prior tradition with GRAYBONE, the singer also citing credits with SOUL SCARRED and SATAN'S SHADOW. Second guitar player Thor Øyvind Mathisen is an ex-MORBID member whilst bassist Endre Moe has ties to DIMENSION F3H. The CUTTHROAT pairing of Borgersen and drummer Per Ivar Ederklep were previously members of ABSOLUTE STEEL. Ederklep is an ex-member of mid nineties act LEGIONS. The self-financed EP 'Morbid Mental Disorder' saw release in 2005.

In January 2006 guitarist Kenneth Hansen ('Mottvind') of ARCH NEMESIS, DIMENSION F3H and EXTRUDE joined CUTTHROAT.

Encyclopedia In Brutalism, Cutthroat (2003) (Demo). Face Of Death / Buried Dead And Mutilated / Coffin Sweet Coffin / Axe.
Morbid Mental Disorder, Cutthroat Ind. (2005). Face Of Death / Hatch Me If You Can / My Anger, Your Suffering / Coffin Sweet Coffin / Consumed By Maggots / Butchering.

CYBORG

BRØNDBY, DENMARK — *J. Mann (vocals), Bo Lund (guitar), John R. Petersen (guitar), K. Johansen (bass), Jesper Bonnesen (drums).*

Death Metal band CYBORG was created in Brøndby during 1993 with an unlikely line-up of the bizarrely titled Crusher Of Non-Intelligent Livechips on vocals, guitarists Mad Dog Process Exterminator and Infernalizer Of Undeveloped Human Brains and drummer Infector of the New World. This group released the 1993 demo 'Cybernetic Orgasm'.

By 1996 only Crusher Of Non-Intelligent Livechips, more commonly known as J. Mann, was left, adding KONKHRA guitarist Bo Lund and members of DETEST to regenerate CYBORG. Guitarist John R. Petersen would also be active with S.D.I.D. The group subsequently inducted ex-FACELIFT singer Ivan Grossmeyer.

Cybornetic Orgasm, Cyborg (1993) (Demo).
CHRONICLES, Die Hard RRS951 (1996). Cyberchrist / Falling / Chronicles / Father Of Lies / Sow The Child / Day Of The Dog / Powermind / Wrapped In / Human Tissue (Hidden Track).

D-COMPOSE

AMSTERDAM, HOLLAND — *Arthur (vocals), Martin (vocals), Pablo Minoli (guitar), Rafael Gimón (bass), Rafael Gimón (drums).*

Tribal Grindcore act D-COMPOSE, created in 2003 and based in Amsterdam, Holland but featuring a diverse range of musicians including Polish vocalist Arthur, Montevideo, Uruguay born guitarist Pablo Minoli, Venezuelan bassist Rafael Gimón and Cuban drummer Liber Torriente. The band includes MATKA TERESA members vocalists Arthur and Martin, LABERINTO guitarist Pablo Minoli and bass Rafael Gimón of AGRESION. Arthur is also a drummer for ULTRA EXTREME MASTICATION. Rafael Gimón's credits extend to KRUEGER, MYSTICAL DARKNESS and NOXIOUS.

A 2004 session, entitled 'D-Demo', included a cover version of the RAMONES 'I'm Not Jesus'.

D-Demo, D-Compose (2004). La Uno / La Dos / La Tres / La Cuatro / I'm Not Jesus.

D.S.K.

AMIENS, FRANCE — *Nicolas Boury (vocals), Benoît Moritz (guitar), Pierre Antonik (guitar), Kevin Lebas (bass), Marc Le Gigan (drums).*

Amiens Death-Grind act D.S.K. ("Disruption Of Soul And Kind") is rooted in the antecedent Thrash Metal band DESCAMISADOS, the 1997 version counting singer Nicolas Boury, guitarist Olivier Delplace, drummer Sébastien Bizet and bassist David Galimidi. Former vocalist Marc Le Gigan, of BLOWDEAD and fellow Grind outfit BLINDING FEAR, had opted out to undertake compulsory military service. This unit recorded the album 'In Cold Blood'. Immediately following these sessions Bizet exited and Marc Le Gigan was taken back onboard as new drummer and, at the same juncture, Benoît Moritz of EXTRAVAGANZA, UNTOLD, CAARCRINOLAS and VAKARM repute bolstered the line up as second guitarist.

A second set of demos signalled the name change over to D.S.K. and the departure of Delplace to VAKARM. In his stead, Pierre Antonik from TRIDUS ELASTICUS joined the band in October of 2001. Moritz added to his tally of bands by joining BURGUL TORKHAÏN in 2002.

With David Galimidi's defection in November of 2002 the group pulled in DECLINE OF HUMANITY frontman Frédéric Bredin as stand in member. With recordings completed at Walnut Groove Studios for a new album '... From Birth', this closing out with a cover of NAPALM DEATH's 'Walls Of Confinement', for Thundering Records Bredin took his leave the following October and was duly superseded by ex-BRUTAL COCO man Kevin Lebas.

Disruption Of Soul And Kind, Independent (2000). Te Asesinan / In Cold Blood / Drug Me / Forever Lost.
ULTRA DEATH METAL, LIVE3X Productions (2003). Introduction To Not / My Eyes Are Corrupted / En La Ciudad / My Fist / Te Asesinan / With My Organs / The Shell / Politics Of The Worst.
... FROM BIRTH, Thundering (2004). Alive But Broken / My Fist / My Eyes Are Corrupted / En La Ciudad / Repudiate / Introduction To Not / Suffer Is Mine / With My Organs / Death K / The Shell / Policy Of Worst / Walls Of Confinement.

DAATH

ATLANTA, GA, USA — *Sean Farber (vocals), Michael Kameron (vocals / keyboards), Eyal Levi (guitar), Emil Werstler (guitar), Jeremy Creamer (bass), Matt Ellis (drums).*

Atlanta techno-Death Metal act, operational until 2003 under the billing of DIRT NAP. The debut album 'Futility' would see drums sessioned by Kevin Talley of DYING FETUS, SUFFOCATION and MISERY INDEX. DAATH added Sam Cuadra on guitar and Cory Brewer on drums in April of 2004.

A new album, given a tentative title of 'The Hinderers', would be set to be mixed by the esteemed figure of DEATH, TESTAMENT, OBITUARY and CANCER credited guitarist JAMES MURPHY. Kevin Talley contributed drums once again with other studio guests including ARSIS guitarist Jim Malone. Further line-up changes saw the introduction of guitarist Emil Werstler, bassist Jeremy Brewer and drummer Matt Ellis.

DAATH signed to Roadrunner Records in April 2006.

US shows throughout October and into December saw touring unions with CATTLE DECAPITATION, GOATWHORE and LAIR OF THE MINOTAUR. Behind the drum kit would be ex-DYING FETUS, MISERY INDEX and CHIMAIRA veteran Kevin Talley, who also performed double drum duties each night with CATTLE DECAPITATION. To coincide with the issue of 'The Hinderers', the group scheduled a round of British dates in March 2007, packaged with UNEARTH, JOB FOR A COWBOY and DESPISED ICON. The group joined the OZZY OSBOURNE headlined 'Ozzfest' extravaganza for arena dates throughout June and July across the USA. October and November North American shows were packaged with NAGLFAR and DARK FUNERAL.

FUTILITY, Daath (2004). The One / Placenta / Filter / Child Says / Infestation / Concentrate Living / Blender For The Baby / Slow / Just For A Second / Crystasis.
THE HINDERERS, Roadrunner (2007). Subterfuge / From The Blind / Cosmic Forge / Sightless / Under A Somber Sign / Ovum / Festival Mass Soulform / Above Lucium / Who Will Take The Blame? / War Born (Tri-adverserenade) / Dead On The Dance Floor / Blessed Through Misery / The Hinderers.

DAEMON

NELSON, NEW ZEALAND — *Xanataph (guitar), DeadBC (bass), Amoniath (drums).*

DAEMON, hailing from Nelson on New Zealand's south island, have endured turbulent times with persisting line-up fractures leading up to the release of the 1997 'Neodeath' album. The band's roots lay in the 1992 act BLOODWYCH which included vocalist Beezle and guitarist Xanataph. Later additions Jude Haenga on guitar, Jim Whyte on bass and drummer Peter Hockey saw the band evolve into the CARCASS inspired SLASH DEMENTIA.

Kori Barrett took the drum stool as the group morphed yet again into DAEMON. However, Beezle would decamp in late 1993 to be replaced by Steve Doubrey of CATALYST. This line up predictably floundered and after a short spell with a female lead singer Xanataph added the vocal role to his duties. In a period of confusion Barrett made his exit. His replacement Amoniath was in turn ousted by the returning Barrett.

At this juncture DAEMON leader Xanataph forged a side outfit ANALYST with ex member Amoniath and bassist Nostohein from THE ADVERSARY. By 1997 ANALYST had retitled themselves DAEMON to record the 'Neodeath' album.

Later line-ups of DAEMON would see Dead BC on drums and Lord Goatfuck on bass. The latter would bail out, his temporary replacement in 2000 being Thyiendalen on loan from BELTANE.

Demo '93, (1993). Entity Mine / Perdition / Estranged / Resurrection / Die In Fear.
DAEMON, (1996). She Had To Die / Better You Than Me / Blindsight / Shattered / Needless / As I Weep / Left Hand Path / Words / War / Rape The Earth / Herr Director.
NEODEATH, (1997). Neodeath Syndrome / Sulphurous Tablous Infernus / Only Death Is Real / Dog Dam / Tick Tock / An Apparition Is Revealed / Entity Mine.
DEMISE BY WILL, (1998). Lord Of Chaos / Geschidt Christlich Erschlagen / Quest For Eternal Night / An Apparition Is Revealed (Live) / War (Live) / Sulphurous Tablous Infernus (Live) / Entity Mine (Live) / Lord Of Chaos (Live).

DAEMON

SWEDEN / DENMARK — *Anders Lundemark (vocals / guitar), Morgan Pitt (bass), Nicke Andersson (drums).*

DAEMON is the Copenhagen based Death Metal project venture of high profile extreme Metal veterans KONKHRA's Anders Lundemark and drummer Nicke Andersson of ENTOMBED and THE HELLACOPTERS. The debut 1996 'Seven Deadly Sins' album, issued on the Diehard Music label, was produced by DISMEMBER's Fred Estby and saw guest guitar from ENTOMBED's Ulf Cederlund. In 1998 the project introduced drummer Frank Hellmet (a.k.a. Per Möller Jensen) of ARTILLERY, THE HAUNTED, INVOCATOR and KONKHRA repute, guitarist Joey Fernandez (Lars Mayland) of FACELIFT, FURIOUS TRAUMA and KONKHRA plus KONKHRA bass player Thomas "Gnist" Christensen. A 1999 follow up, suitably entitled 'The Second Coming', sported a cover version of BLACK SABBATH's 'Symptom Of The Universe'.

DAEMON's third album, 2002's 'Eye For An Eye', would see Thomas Fagerlind of SWOLLEN, THORIUM and INIQUITY handling bass and the famed Gene Hoglan of DARK ANGEL and STRAPPING YOUNG LAD on drums. Late 2004 saw Fagerlind operating with DOWNLORD, the band led by BOLT THROWER and BENEDICTION singer Dave Ingram.

SEVEN DEADLY SINS, Diehard Music RRS947 (1996). Sloth / Wrath / Greed / Lust / Gluttony / Pride / Envy / The Eight Sin.
THE SECOND COMING, Diehard Music RRS964 (1999). What If... / Come Die With Me / The Truth / My Kingdom Is A Sacred Place / The Prince Of Lies / Make Me Bleed / Way Out Of Hand / Spirit In Flames / Symptom Of The Universe.
Checkpoint #3, Diehard Music (2001) (Split promotion release with AURORA BOREALIS, 2 TON PREDATOR, ILLDISPOSED & NECROSPHERE). Gone Forever.
EYE FOR AN EYE, Diehard Music RRS970 (2002). Intro / Gone Forever / Crucification / Disconnect / Eternal Bliss / Truth Be Known / Kingdom Of Fools / The Beating / Cursed / The Trial / Tailgunner.

DAEMUSINEM

ITALY — *Gianni (vocals), Patrick (guitar), Massimo Altomare (drums).*

Previously known as UNCREATED this mythically inspired Death Metal formation evolved into DAEMUSINEM during 1999, the band taking their name from a local Torino mountain known as being a place of strange occurrences. By 2000 the inaugural demo tape 'Darkside Dimension' fired the interest of the Cold Blood Industries label. A switch in drummers would witness the introduction of drummer Massimo Altomare, known for his work with DYING AWKWARD ANGEL, DARK REALITY, ALLOST, BLACK FLAME and MORTUARY DRAPE, for the debut 2001 album 'Daemusinem Domine Empire'.

DAEMUSINEM guitarist Agony holds membership of both PHENRIS and VINTERFROST. In January 2006 Altomare joined Norwegian Black Metal band DISIPLIN.

DAEMUSINEM DOMINE EMPIRE, Cold Blood Industries CBI 0201 (2001). Daemusinem / Domine Empire / Throne Of Illusions / Witch's Dream / Killers Of The Wood / Burning Souls / The Key Of The Realm Of Deads / Silence In The Water Mother Of Life.

DAGOBA

MARSEILLE, FRANCE — *Shawter (vocals), Izakar (guitar), Werther (bass), Frank Costanza (drums).*

Marseille based DAGOBA debuted with a 1998 demo entitled 'Time To Go'. Although the group secured a valuable support to RAMMSTEIN the line-up fractured. The band's official biography would therefore claim a September 2000 initiation date when surviving member Shawter regrouped with fresh personnel guitarist Izakar, bassist Werther and drummer Frank Costanza. An EP, entitled 'Release The Fury', followed in November 2001.

Album tracks were laid down during early 2003 at Praxis Studio in South of France, then mixed at Philia Studio in Oxford by Dave Chang. DAGOBA, promoting their June released self-titled album for Enternote Records, would lend support to the joint KILL II THIS and SLITHERYN European tour of November 2003. The band then jumped straight into the guest position for SAMAEL dates across Scandinavia, Holland, England and Switzerland. Other notable supports saw gigs with FEAR FACTORY in Amsterdam and MACHINE HEAD in Brussels.

DAGOBA signed to Season Of Mist Records in July 2005. Following a support date to KORN in Toulon, the group utilised Antfarm studios in Denmark in September working with producer Tue Madsen for a new album. A notable guest inclusion on two tracks, 'It's All About Time' and 'The White Guy (Suicide)', would be DIMMU BORGIR and ARCTURUS man Simen 'ICS Vortex' Hestnæs.

In March and April 2006 DAGOBA acted as openers to European shows headed up by IN FLAMES and SEPULTURA. Amongst a series of headline gigs, the group also supported STONE SOUR in Paris during November.

Release The Fury, Dagoba (2001). Rush / Agression Comes Back To You / Something Stronger / Time 2 Go / My Army / Gods Forgot Me.
DAGOBA, Enternote (2003). From Torture To Enslavement / Maniak / The White Guy (And The Black Ceremony) / Something Stronger / Another Day / Fate Contained In A Cristal Ball / Year Of The Scape Goat / Dopesick / Act 1, Part 2 / Rush / The Chaos We're Involved In / Here We Are / 4.2 Destroy / Pornocars / Gods Forgot Me.
WHAT HELL IS ABOUT, Season Of Mist (2006). What Hell Is About ... / Die Tomorrow (... What If You Should ?) / The Fall Of Men / The Man You're Not / Cancer / It's All About Time / The Things Apart / The Things Within / Livin' Dead / 042104 / Morphine—The Apostle Of Your Last War / The White Guy (Suicide).

DAHMER

CANADA — *Sebastian Dionne (vocals / bass), Ti-Fred (guitar), Yvan (drums).*

Canadian Death- Grindcore act with an uncompromising intent to shock. Named after one of the twentieth centurys most infamous mass murderers DAHMER use the serial killer theme throughout all of their controversial releases. DAHMER began with a union in 1995 of guitarists Sebastian Dionne and John with drummer Yvan. Seb would switch instruments to bass. However, due to the guitarist's work commitments the band's debut split single was recorded minus John and indeed without any bass guitar. He would return after recording as DAHMER added second guitarist Ti-Fred. DAHMER issued a self titled demo and a three way split cassette shared with CARCASS GRINDER and DIARRHÉE MENTALE, the latter being Dionne's side project band.

DAHMER's line up, minus John once more, settled down to the trio of Seb, Fred and Yvan with Seb handling bass and vocals.

A stream of split 7" singles would follow including alliances with SATURATION, I.R.F., APARTMENT 213, Spain's DENAK and fellow Canucks WADGE. The bands shared single with SUPPRESSION 'Let's Dance' on Germany's Yellow Dog label displayed DAHMER's wry sense of sick humour as the sleeve depicted a pair of severed feet. The '9 Trak' single, issued on the Canadian Spineless label, would be released with no less than three different covers.

The cover artwork to the 'Dahmerized' album was particularly horrific featuring a photograph of severed head, hands and genitalia. The album itself is made up of songs many of which are titled after notorious murderers. Latterly DAHMER have mixed in political and social commentary in their lyrics alongside the tried and tested murder fixation.

Ex DAHMER members created MESRINE, named after the serial killer Jacques Mesrine their debut 2002 album would unsurprisingly document the tales of infamous Canadian mass murderers.

THE STUDIO SESSIONS: DISCOGRAPHY, Grind It! GIT 006 (2003).

DAMNABLE

POLAND — *Bayn (vocals / guitar), Andy (guitar), Rolly (bass).*

A Polish Death Metal band with a turbulent history. DAMNABLE was created in May of 1992 citing a line up of vocalist Yehovy, guitarist Andy, bass player Clans and drummer Melon. The following year Clans switched to guitar as DAMNABLE pulled in Rolly on bass. In April 1994 Yehovy left the band and to be replaced by Bayn. With this revised line-up DAMNABLE issued a rehearsal tape to act as an opening demo. This offering would land the group a spot on one of the biggest festivals in Eastern Europe, 'FMR Jarocin', and prompt a further recording, the studio session 'Obsession Pain'.

Toward the end of 1996 Clans left the band and Bayn added the role of second guitarist to his duties. In this incarnation DAMNABLE toured Poland in January of 1997 as support act to DERANGED. A third recording, 'In Perdition'. Would be publicly released on cassette through the Polish Immortal Records with Italian concern Cryptic Soul Productions opting to issue the same as a CD variant. However, the Cryptic Soul Production release never transpired. As some consolation the German T&M label coupled two DAMNABLE tracks on a split 7" shared with Spain's arch Grindsters HAEMORRHAGE.

DAMNABLE toured Germany throughout March of 1998 upfront of a run of gigs in the Czech Republic in May. Another split release then ensued, the 'The Futuristic Trial of Mankind' sessions on Novum Vox Mortis Records shared with INCARNATED. For these recordings DAMNABLE cut a cover version of TERRORIZER's 'After World Obliteration'. Subsequent to recording Melon decamped and Sivy was drafted as replacement.

DAMNABLE's next move was to sign to the established American Relapse label to re-issue 'In Perdition' as part of a four way split album in alliance with YATTERING, LOST SOUL and DECAPITATED dubbed 'Polish Assault'. Another set of demos were laid down in 2000 after which Sivy exited, DAMNABLE opting to continue minus a drummer, secured a fresh contract with the German Cudgel Agency label. The band kept their live profile high by touring alongside VULGAR DEGENERATE and BRAINWASH. Festival showings included positions on the 'Fuck The Commerce IV', 'Obscene Extreme III', 'Morbid Festspiele' and 'Brutal Assault' events.

September of 2001 witnessed the 'Grind Manifesto 2001' Polish tour in alliance with ANTIGAMA and BRAINWASH. During 2002 the DAMNABLE credited drummer Krzysztof Bentkowski forged the avant-garde Grind band ANTIGAMA.

DAMNABLE formed up a package billing of LIVIDITY, MASTIC SCUM and the infamous LIVIDITY for European touring in March of 2003.

INPERDITION, Immortal (1997). Intro / Underworld / Paranormal Verdict / Circle Of Time / The Myth / Reincarnation / Re-Reincarnation / To A God Unknown / Self Analysis / Outro.
THE FUTURISTIC TRIAL OF MANKIND, Novum Vox Mortis (1998) (Split album with INCARNATED). Imperceptible / The Futuristic Trial Of Mankind / What For It Everything / Craze Of Entity / After World Obliteration / Inaccessible / Paranormal Verdict / Self Analysis ... / Imperishable.
COMPLETELEY DEVOTED, Cudgel Agency (2001). Farewell To Reality / Vertigo / Completely Devoted / Street News / Beyond Reincarnation / They Will Never Destroy Mountains / Nothing Excuses / I Wish You A Nice Evening? / Futuristic Trial Of Mankind / Damnable I / Unreal Telepathy / Light Song.

DAMNATION

POLAND — *Les (vocals / guitar), Bart (guitar), Nergal (bass), Inferno (drums).*

Black Death Metal act DAMNATION feature two members of BEHEMOTH vocalist / guitarist Les and bassist Nergal. The band formed in 1991 releasing their first demo 'Everlasting Sickness' in 1993. A further tape, 'Forbidden Spaces', followed the next year which led to a deal with Polish label Pagan Records.

Following the debut album's release bassist Dagon was replaced by Nergal. 1997 saw DAMNATION cutting the track 'Porwany Obledem' in homage to Polish extreme Metal pioneers KAT. With DAMNATION's profile rising sharply Pagan Records would issue the band's 'Forbidden Spaces' demo as part of a split album shared with BEHEMOTH. An EP, 'Coronation', followed comprising of three new tracks and a re-recording of 'Land Of Degradation'. The same year also saw the induction of former CONDEMNATION bass player Arthur. Touring Poland in April of 1998 DAMNATION formed part of a package bill with LUX OCCULTA and SACRIVERSUM. Further afield the band played at the German 'Fuck The Commerce II' festival and the Belgian 'With A Dragons Blaze' event.

Vocalist Les was to create a side project titled HELL-BORN together with BEHEMOTH's Lord Ravenlock releasing an eponymous album.

In 2000 DAMNATION's latest release 'Resist' scored international distribution being released by Metal Mind in Poland, Cudgel Agency in Germany and Dark Realm in America. DAMNATION had now shaped up as a quartet of vocalist Raven, guitarists Les and Bart, bassist Holoc and drummer Varien. Bart also busies himself as a member of BEHEMOTH drummer Inferno's side project band AZARATH.

More recently DAMNATION have spread their talents across the burgeoning tribute market featuring on no less than two MORBID ANGEL tributes donating 'Bleed For The Devil' to a Dwell Records album and 'Blasphemy Of The Holy Ghost' to a Hellfire effort. The band also appears on the Necropolis

Records KING DIAMOND tribute with their take on 'A Mansion In Darkness' and offer 'Tribulation' to a No Mercy Records POSSESSED tribute compilation.

The 2003 'Resurrection Of Azzareth' compilation through Conquer Records collected together early material from the mid 90s, including unreleased tracks, as well as the band's KING DIAMOND and MORBID ANGEL covers.

In April 2005 it was reported that Varyon had united with musicians guitarist Wojtek Lisicki of Swedish bands LOST HORIZON and LUCIFERION had united with musicians guitarist Adrian Adamus from North American act FOREST OF IMPALED, Logan Perez on lead vocals and Martin Widel on keyboards in a new extreme Metal project dubbed AGAINST THE PLAGUES.

REBORN, Pagan Moon CD 002 (1995). Pagan Prayer- The Antichrist / The Land Of Degradation / Leaving Into New Reality / From Broken Cross (Bleeding Jesus) / Time Of Prophets / Infestation- Maldoror Is Dead / Forbidden Spaces / The Ruling Truth / Behind The Walls Of Tears / Reborn (Outro).

REBEL SOULS, Last Epitaph Productions LEP010 (1996). Prelude To Rebellion / Who Your God Is / Son Of Fire / Rebel Souls / Azarath-Watching In Darkness / From The Abyssland / Deliverance / Might Returns.

Coronation EP, Last Episode 007300-2 LEP (1997). Coronation / Spell Master / Sworn To The Darkside / The Land Of Degradation.

FORBIDDEN SPACES, Last Epitaph (1997) (Split album with BEHEMOTH).

RESIST, Cudgel Agency CUD 007 (2000). Your Pain Is Not For Me / In Resistance / Confession / Voices Of An Unknown Dimension / Absence In Humanity / Forsaken By Destiny / Against My Enemies / Invisible Force / Down Of My Feet.

DAMNATION

STOCKHOLM, SWEDEN — *Richard Cabeza (vocals / guitar), Björn Gramell (bass), Peter Stjärnvind (drums).*

Stockholm's DAMNATION published the 1994 demo recording 'Divine Darkness'. Its membership included some elite players from the Scandinavian extreme Metal scene including frontman Richard Cabeza of UNLEASHED, DISMEMBER, UNANIMATED, CARBONIZED, GENERAL SURGERY and MURDER SQUAD fame. Cabeza had forged DAMNATION during DISMEMBER down time, returning to his priority act for their 'Massive Killing Capacity' album.

Drummer Peter Stjärnvind is known for his work with ENTOMBED, LOUDPIPES, REGURGITATE, UNANIMATED, MERCILESS, MURDER SQUAD, KRUX and FACE DOWN. Bass player Björn Gramell has CHARRED REMAINS credentials.

Cabeza and Stjärnvind reunited in BORN OF FIRE, working alongside guitarist 'Mr. Dim', and LOUDPIPES man Fredrik Lindgren. This act would bow in with the 7" single 'Chosen By The Gods' on Primitive Art. Richard Cabeza would team up with premier Black Metal act DARK FUNERAL for North American touring in the Spring of 2002.

In August 2004 Threeman Recordings issued the album 'Destructo Evangelia'. Somewhat unusually this outing featured only Peter Stjärnvind. Contributing would be E Watain on vocals with narration on 'When Creations Die' courtesy of Mörk Malign. The record featured cover versions of VULCANO's 'Bloody Vengeance' and BATHORY's 'Armageddon'. That same year Iron Fist Productions re-issued the 'Divine Darkness' demos in 7" single format.

Divine Darkness, Damnation (1994) (Cassette demo). Eternal Black / The Dark Divine / The Mistress—Queen Of Sin / The Return Of Darkness And Evil.

Divine Darkness, Iron Fist Productions IFPEP006 (2004) (7" vinyl EP). Eternal Black / The Dark Divine / The Mistress / Queen Of Sin / The Return Of Darkness And Evil.

Insulter Of Jesus Christ, Iron Fist Productions IFPEP005 (2004) (7" vinyl EP). Insulter Of Jesus Christ / Bloody Vengeance / Night Eternal.

DESTRUCTO EVANGELIA, Threeman Recordings TRECD012 (2004). Invocation Of The Storms / Insulter Of Jesus Christ / Night Eternal / Destructo Evangelia / Bloody Vengeance / When Creation Dies / Eternal Black / Armageddon.

DAN SWANÖ

ÖREBRO, SWEDEN — 'Moontower', released through Black Mark Production, is the 1998 solo outing from the ever industrious EDGE OF SANITY leading force DAN SWANÖ. Hailing from Örebro, Swanö's influence on the Swedish music scene, besides his production work, includes involvement in other acts as diverse as UNICORN, PAN-THY-MONIUM, GODSEND, WOUNDED KNEE and NIGHTINGALE among many others. He first came to attention as part of the late eighties, notorious Crossover act BREJN DEDD. In 1999 he executed his interpretation of MERCYFUL FATE's 'Melissa', featured on 'The Unholy Sounds Of The Demon Bells—A Tribute To Mercyful Fate' collection issued via Poland's Still Dead Productions.

In 2003 a new side project was on the agenda dubbed RIBSPREADER. This unite comprised Swanö, PAGANIZER frontman Rogga Johansson and erstwhile PAGANIZER man Andreas on guitar. The album 'Bolted To The Cross' emerged in April 2004.

Swanö activated "Post-Prog" project SECOND SKY in 2004 for the album 'Skydiving'. He would also provide guest vocals for the 2005 ENFORSAKEN album 'Sinner's Intuition'. Throughout the year his home studio work gained Swanö mixing credentials on albums for EDEN'S FALL, THE PROJECT HATE, ANOTHER LIFE, RIBSPREADER, PAGANIZER, HEARSE, MISERY SPEAKS, SHADOWSPHERE and MILLENCOLIN.

Dan Swanö contributed guest lead vocal tracks to a cover version of MOXY's 'Out Of The Darkness' for inclusion on OVERDRIVE and LOCOMOTIVE BREATH guitarist Janne Stark's November 2006 MOUNTAIN OF POWER tribute collection. Swanö also laid down backing vocals for English Progressive Metal band THRESHOLD's album 'Dead Reckoning'. Swanö's next move was to join DEMIURG, fronted by PAGANIZER and RIBSPREADER mainman Rogga Johansson for the album 'Breath Of The Demiurg', released in February 2007 through Dutch imprint Mascot Records. That summer Swanö produced debut sessions for HAIL OF BULLETS.

MOONTOWER, Black Mark Production BMCD 129 (1998). Sun Of The Night / Patchworks / Uncreation / Add Reality / Creating Illusions / The Big Sleep / Encounterparts / In Empty Phrases.

DARK

GERMANY — *Michael Löchter (vocals), Thorsten Schmitt (guitar). Mathias Fickert (guitar), Christian Betz (bass), Jochen Donauer (drums).*

DARK were created during 1991 as a covers act playing the Death Metal favourites by such artists as SEPULTURA, DEATH and MORBID ANGEL. DARK's first compositions of their own surfaced on the 1994 demo 'Visions', a cassette which was limited to 300 soon sold out copies.

The band debuted commercially for G.U.N. Records in 1997 with the 'Endless Dreams Of Sadness' album. Touring in Europe during March of 1997 saw the band forming up a package billing alongside THERION, SENTENCED, ORPHANAGE and MY DYING BRIDE for the 'Out Of The Dark III' festivals. The group then followed up with 'Seduction' in 1998.

Vocalist Michael Löchter would lose his place for the third album 'Revolution'. Guitarist Mathias Fickert took the lead vocal role on the record which included an ambitious stab at U2's Pride (In The Name Of Love). DARK drummer Jochen Donauer would session on the debut album from Progressive Metal band SUNBLAZE.

ENDLESS DREAMS OF SADNESS, Great Unlimited Noises GUN 117 BMG 74321 44768-2 (1997). Endless Dreams . . . / Nemesis Of Neglect / Dawn Of The Gods / When Love Is Gone / Gaias Masterpiece / Fool / A Taste Of Fear / In Darkness / Brainsickness / Dagobar / Embedded In Illusions / Visions / . . . Of Sadness.

SEDUCTION, Great Unlimited Noises GUN 74321 50237-2 (1997). Another Journey / Dark Clouds Rising / Bloodred Sunrise / Broken

Down / My Desire / Love And Seduction / Sands Of Time / This Falling Veil / Shadowdancer / Angeltear / The Flood.
REVOLUTION, Great Unlimited Noises 74321 66382 2 (1999). Deadzone / Eyes Wide Open / Pride (In The Name Of Love) / Cradle Of Darkness / Unreal / Marble Halls / Edge Of Infinity / Spacedrift / May B!

DARK DISCIPLE

CHESTERTON, MD, USA — *Mat Sergeant (vocals), Rez (vocals / lead guitar), Maddog (drums).*

Baltimore, Maryland Death Metal act forged in March of 1999. The band marked their arrival the following year with the four song 'When The Wicked Inherit The Earth' demo, recorded with a line-up of frontman Bones, guitarists Rez and Craig, bassist Ben and drummer Maddog. DARK DISCIPLE, substituting new guitarist Josh in Craig's place, adopted a deliberately blasphemous stance for the follow up session, 2002's 'Beneath The Inverted Cross', these three songs making a significant impact upon the MP3 charts. However, line up changes had taken their toll and by 2003 the band only counted two surviving founding members. Prior to recording debut album 'Unholy Hate Gore', laid down in just two days during June of 2003 at Hit and Run recording studios in Rockville, Maryland, for the German Morbid Records label, DARK DISCIPLE switched singers, with Bones being substituted by Mat 'Sicko' Sergeant. 'Unholy Hate Gore' emerged in April of 2004.

DARK DISCIPLE geared up for a run of 2004 European dates, beginning on 1st May in Zwickau, Germany, partnered with headliners MONSTROSITY. Unfortunately the tour was cancelled on 4th May with only a handful of dates being conducted. In a rare admission a statement confirmed "Turnouts have been too bad, losing money day by day is no fun for the bands". DARK DISCIPLE was down to a trio by 2005, losing the services of bassist 'G'.

When The Wicked Inherit The Earth, (2001). Dead Cell Manifestation / Wicked Inherit The Earth / I Am Suicide / Curse Of The Zombies.
Beneath The Inverted Cross, (2002). Beneath The Inverted Cross / Revelations In Black / Headless By Dawn.
UNHOLY HATE GORE, Morbid MR 106 (2004). Jesus Loves You / Serving The Priest / Annihilation Of The Living / A Thousand Corpses / Vile Infection / Reign Of Terror / 666 Stab Wounds / Human Killing Machine / Welcome To Purgatory / Unholy Gate Gore.

DARK EMBRACE

LA CORUÑA, SPAIN — *Oscar Asunder (vocals / cello), Cæsar Dark Emperor (guitar), Damien Stillborn (keyboards), Anaea (bass), Alvaro (drums).*

La Coruña, Galicia based Gothic Doom act founded in June of 2000. Initially taking a Black Metal direction the band delivered their opening demo 'Raven's Blood' in May of the following year. This cassette featured cover versions of TIAMAT's 'Dust Is Our Fare', ANATHEMA's 'Sleepless' and CRADLE OF FILTH's 'Summer Dying Fast'. Their September 2003 offering, 'Bitter End', witnessed a change of tack to a more Doom Metal slant. The title track gained extra exposure for DARK EMBRACE by its inclusion on the 'Chariots Arrive Again vol.2' compilation issued by Foreshadow Productions.

Guitarist Jaime Allegue opted out in October of 2003, at first being superseded by Alejandro Varela of RELATIVE SILENCE. Finding a permanent guitarist, Cæsar Dark Emperor, from the band CHAOS SYMMETRY, was added to the ranks in March 2004. The group partnered with Spanish band AGATHODAIMON for Iberian concerts in November 2006. That same month they signed to German label Armageddon Music.

The album 'The Rebirth Of Darkness' was recorded at Stage One studios in Borgentreich, Germany with producer Andy Classen. Sessioning on drums would be Moritz Neuner, an in demand veteran of acts such as ST. LUCIFER, SHADOWCAST, DARKWELL, GRAVEWORM, ABIGOR, EVENFALL, DORNENREICH, SIEGFRIED, ANGRY ANGELS, NECROLOGY, KOROVA, ATROCITY and LEAVES' EYES.

Bitter End, Independent (2003). Dying Breath (Intro) / Bitter End / The Threat Of Flesh And Its Libidinous Storms Of Silence / Fragility Of life.
THE REBIRTH OF DARKNESS, Armageddon Music (2007). Prelude To Darkness / The Threat Of Flesh And Its Libidinous Storms Of Silence / Doomed By Life / Bitter End / Solitude / Dusk Of My Heart (Raven's Blood) / Learning To Live / Children Whispered Screams From Beyond / Fragility Of Life.

DARK FAITH

ORLANDO, FL, USA — *Peter Olen (vocals), Kellan Anderson (guitar), Kevin Shaw (guitar), Paul Thompson (bass), Christian Smith (keyboards), Karsten Anderson (drums).*

Orlando, Florida Death Metal combo created during 1997 by vocalist Peter Olen, guitarist Kellan Anderson and rhythm guitarist Kevin Shaw. This trio would subsequently be joined by bassist Paul Thompson, keyboard player Christian Smith and drummer Karsten Andersen. Olen would also be active CREATION CONSUMED. An opening demo arrived in 1998, featuring a BLACK SABBATH cover version of 'Sweet Leaf', with follow up 'Legacy Of Pain' delivered a year later. DARK FAITH's commercial debut would be the 2002 'Domain' EP. Signing to Splattergod Records the band then issued the split 'Crypt Of Madness' album in 2003, shared with PATHS OF POSSESSION. This set included the DEATH cover 'Zombie Ritual'.

Throughout June 2003 DARK FAITH engaged in the 'Death Worship' US tour alongside running mates SCARABAEUS. The band signed to Poland's Still Dead Productions in 2004, entering the Dimensional Sound Studios Erik Rutan of MORBID ANGEL and HATE ETERNAL repute acting as producer. DARK FAITH united with CRIMSON MASSACRE for US touring throughout June and July. The band added ex-PATHS OF POSSESSION drummer Nick Goodyear shortly afterward.

February 2006 saw an announcement detailing Nick Goodyear's induction into an all new band billed PROMETHEAN HORDE alongside BLASTMASTERS members guitarist Jeff Parrish, also ex-EXECRATION, and bassist Jesse Jolly, additionally citing CRIMSON MASSACRE credentials. They would be joined by ex-HELL ON EARTH guitar player Mike W, LULL ME TO LARVAE keyboard player Mike Goodyear and ROYAL ANGUISH drummer JR Daniels.

DARK FAITH undertook extensive US touring throughout July 2006.

Dark Faith, Dark Faith (1998) (Demo). Dark Faith / Dark Domain / Grinder / Sweet Leaf.
Drunken, Dark Faith (2001) (Demo). Dark Domain / Hellfire Consumed / Hymnal Of Hatred / Blasphemer.
THE CRYPT OF MADNESS, Splattergod (2003) (Split album with PATHS OF POSSESSION. Limited edition 1000 copies). Rending The Shroud / Voice Of Blood / Calling Death Worship / Zombie Ritual / Constrictions Of The Flesh / Storms of Vengeance.

DARK FLOOD

OULU, FINLAND — *Pauli Heikkinen (vocals), Kalle Ruumensaari (guitar), Tuomas Perkkiö (guitar), Ville Ruumensaari (bass), Sampo Heikkinen (keyboards), Henri Meripaasi (drums).*

Oulu based DARK FLOOD features singer Pauli Heikkinen, who also has association with ZEROCROWD and HYBRID DAEMON. The group was assembled as FLOOD by bass player Ville Ruumensaari, guitarists Kalle Ruumensaari and Tuomas Perkkiö plus Henri Meripaasi on drums, during 1996. Re-branded DARK FLOOD and having drafted Pauli Heikkinen as frontman, they released the demos 'Ad Infinitum ...', recorded at Neo Studio, Oulu in October 1998, 'Deep-Sleep-Utopia Demo', laid down at Soundmix Studio in June 2000 with new keyboard player

Sampo Heikkinen and 'In Vain Demo' during 2001. Minortone Entertainment released the album 'Still Liberty' in 2005.

Kalle Ruumensaari acted as stand in live guitarist for REFLEXION in July 2006. In August, upon conclusion of recordings for a new album with producer Kalle Ruumensaari, keyboard player Sampo Heikkinen exited to prioritise his other band LOOPWORK.

Ad Infinitum ..., Dark Flood (1998) (Demo). ... Of Agony / Whisper Of Winds / Whisper of Winds.

The Deep-Sleep-Utopia, Dark Flood (2000) (Demo). Captured By My Ignorance / Thorn Throne / Disguise Of Dawn / Circus Emperium.

In Vain, Dark Flood (2001) (Demo). Vanity's Ground / Nevermelting.

STILL LIBERTY, Minortone Entertainment MT 001 (2005). No Name Carries / State / Nevermelting / Vanity's Ground / Let Me Disappear / For My Sun / A Mere Bleak Story / The Grief Waters / The Waters Turn Silent.

Dark Flood / ZeroCrowd, Minortone Entertainment MT 002 (2006) (Finnish split promotion CD single with ZEROCROWD).

THE DEAD LINES, Minortone Entertainment MT 003 (2006). Intro / Sanctuary Cell / Playground Of Ice / To Reach For The Ground / Never Free, Never Yours / The Monument Of Sin / Discouraged Skies / Deadline / Deaths A Remedy / The Song Of A Somber Light.

DARK REALITY

GERMANY — *Oliver Ramacher (vocals), Martin Heinzelmann (guitar), Phillip Kailer (guitar), Patrick Schmid (bass), Andreas Waldura (wind instruments), Gert Kopf (drums).*

DARK REALITY had been in existence for over two years prior to deciding on their own self financed album. A brace of demos in 1991 and 1992 preceded the 'Umbra Cineris' album launched in 1993. Following the debut drummer Gert Kopf drifted away as did bassist Patrick Schmid. Alex Schiem plugged the gap left by Schmid for the 'Blossom Of Mourning' album.

DARK REALITY are nothing if not ambitious in the lyrical department as 'Gruselet' is based on the works of Christian Morgenstern and 'In The Cathedral' relates a Franz Kafka tale.

DARK REALITY suffered a blow when vocalist Oliver Ramacher upped and left in November 1996. Rather than bring in a new face vocals on the 1997 album 'Oh Precious Haze Pervade The Pain' were dealt with by guitarist Phillip Kailer and Andres Waldura.

UMBRA CINERIS, Dark Reality (1993). Pgn Gloriosa / Draged Miford / Salvation / Das Grauen / Umbra Cineris / Smouldering Remains.

BLOSSOM OF MOURNING, General Inquisitor Torquemado's Witchhunt GIT 004 SPV 084-96902 CD (1997). Am Endes des Weges / Ants Under Glass / In The Cathedral / Sint Lumbi Vestri / Ashen / Gruselett / Gewitterfront / Moping Carol / Will To Deny / Little Chaffinch.

OH PRECIOUS HAZE PERVADE THE PAIN, General Inquisitor Torquemado Releases GIT 006 SPV 084-96932 CD (1997). Rain Oroson / Skytied / Spingono I Vecchi Giorni / Frühling, Elegisch / Futility / Erkenntis / A Glimpse / Lokrischer Traum / Facetting / Sternennacht.

DARK REMAINS

GOUDA, HOLLAND — *RSD Droog (vocals), Frank Kooiman (guitar), Bob Kooger (guitar), Rik van Gageldonk (bass), André van der Ree (drums).*

Gouda based DARK REMAINS was forged in December 1998 by former ETERNAL SOLSTICE members drummer André van der Ree, also holding MOURNING and ARCANE credits, and bassist Ramon Soetebroek in union with guitarist Frank Kooiman. As the formative band evolved the bass position went to Saidi Sapuletej in 1999 whilst Rogier Droog (a.k.a. RSD Droog) of FUNERAL WINDS took the frontman role. In this formation the band signed to Cleansweep Productions for the 'Manifestations' album, after which Rik van Gageldonk became next in line to occupy the bass position and Bob Kooger, of ORDO DRACONIS, inducted on second guitar.

Rik van Gageldonk founded VUIST in May of 2000. During 2005 André van der Ree and Rik van Gageldonk forged WARMASTER, an old-school Death Metal band. Bob Kooger joined the WARMASTER live line-up in 2006. Sophomore album, 'Planet Earth Scourged' recorded at A.M. Studios, was released in September through Burning Misery Records. That same month new singer Erwin was confirmed.

DARK REMAINS donated the track 'Misanthropic Rage' to the 2006 compilation album 'Blown To Pieces 4' issued by FearSomeRecords.

DEATH MANIFESTATION, Cleansweep Productions (2002). Bloodsoaked / Left In Misery / Burned To The Stake / Death Manifestation / Searching For A Manmade Armageddon / Impaled Silhouettes / Into Infinite Decay / Genocide / Abandoned / Heading Towards The Meltdown.

PLANET EARTH SCOURGED, Burning Misery BM-001 (2006). Planet Earth Scorched / Raining Fire / The Vortex Of Existence / No Fallout / Sulphur Winds / Receiving The Terror / Misanthropic Rage / Ageless / Vernichtingskrieg / Planet Earth Scorched (Live Video) / Bloodsoaked (Live Video).

DARK SECRET

ITALY — *Calogero Piscopo (vocals / guitar), Andrea Scimone (bass), Salvatore Morreale (drums).*

DARK SECRET came into being during 1999, issuing their Scandinavian influenced Death Metal demo 'The Hand Of Destiny' as an opening shot. The band line up for these recordings comprised lead vocalist Michele Matrosimone, the guitar team of Calogero Piscopo and Antonio Busciglio, bass player Alessandro Sanfilippo and Franceco Vella on the drums. Successively, a fresh vocalist was found in Cristian Lo Maglio whilst Carlo Gibiino superseded Sanfilippo on the bass. Having issued the album 'The Frozen Memories' in July of 2000 the band would re-formulate itself once more with central figures Piscopo and Vella recruiting Davide Mastrosimone as singer and on bass Marcello Cicismondo. Subsequently Pietro Di Bilio became next in line for the four string position.

The band opened up 2002 with a run of Italian shows co-billed with ADIMIRON dubbed as the "Screamers of death" tour. However, in the summer DARK SECRET hit a major stumbling block when both original member Francesco Vella and their vocalist bowed out. Allessandro Sanfilippo duly took command of the drums. By August the roster was seemingly completed with the incorporation of Stefano Carrara behind the microphone. However, within weeks Aldo Giammusso usurped his predecessor.

DARK SECRET would project a new album 'Evil And Passion' for 2003 issue. The band line-up changed in early 2005, Piscopo now handling lead vocals and inducting a new cast of Andrea Scimone on bass and Salvatore Morreale on the drums.

THE FROZEN MEMORIES, (2000). The Hands Of Destiny / The Swan's Song / What I Gain / In My Veins / Frozen Memories / The Other Voice / Rainsound / Fear Inside.

DARK SUNS

KEMBERG, GERMANY — *Niko Knappe (vocals / drums), Maik Knappe (guitar), Torsten Wenzel (guitar), Christoph Bormann (bass), Thomas Bremer (keyboards).*

DARK SUNS is a Kemberg based Progressive Death Metal act founded upon the demise of local metal bands CARNIVAL OF SOULS and REQUIEM during 1997. The initial formation counted vocalist / drummer Niko Knappe of CARNIVAL OF SOULS, TOTHAMON and BLACK MARIA alongside REQUIEM, BOOR and FAUSTRECHT man Tobias Gommlich on guitar. The following year the band was brought up to a full compliment with the addition of guitarist Maik Knappe, a veteran of BLACK MARIA, CARNIVAL OF SOULS and SEVENTH LANE with bassist Oliver Fricke and keyboard player Thomas Bremer, both from WYCART.

A 1998 demo 'Below Dark Illusion' preceded a series of line up changes. In 2000 SHADES OF SORROW man Michael Beck took over on bass guitar but the following year his position was usurped by another WYCART member Christoph Bormann. signature to Voice Of Life Records for the distribution of a 2002 debut album 'Swanlike'. Gommlich bowed out in 2003, his role being delegated to IMMACONCEPT's Torsten Wenzel.

DARK SUNS signed to Prophecy Productions for the early 2005 album 'Existence'. The band acted as support to Sweden's PAIN OF SALVATION European tour dates.

EXISTENCE, Prophecy Productions (2005). Zero / A Slumbering Portrait / The Euphoric Sense / Her And The Element / Daydream / Anemone / You, A Phantom Still / Gently Bleeding / Abiding Space / Patterns Of Oblivion / One Endless Childish Day.
SWANLIKE, (2005).

DARK TRANQUILLITY

GOTHENBURG, SWEDEN — *Mikael Stanne (vocals), Niklas Sundin (guitar), Martin Henriksson (guitar), Michael Nicklasson (bass), Martin Brändström (keyboards), Anders Jivarp (drums).*

DARK TRANQUILLITY is a Swedish act that has managed to carve out a buoyant international fanbase with their quite unique strain of dark Metal music. The band began life in the characteristic 'Gothenburg' Death Metal style but have diversified with frightening speed with each successive release to carve out their own niche in the Metal world. Later releases employ Electronica, stark piano led pieces, orchestration, female vocal and a heady, often wholly unexpected, juxtaposition of sounds. DARK TRANQUILLITY date back to December 1989, but started life under the rather bizarre moniker of SEPTIC BROILER. In this guise the band, lead vocalist Anders Fridén, the guitar pairing of Niklas Sundin and Mikael Stanne with Martin Henriksson on bass and drummer Anders Jivarp, released a 1990 demo entitled 'Enfeeble Earth'. Only 100 copies of this cassette, co-produced by the band in union with Dragan Tanascovic and Stefan Lindgren, saw distribution.

Switching names to DARK TRANQUILLITY, the band booked three days at Studio Soundscape studios in Gothenburg during March 1991 to lay down tracks for the demo 'Trail Of Life Decayed'. 800 copies would be sent out. Next to see issue would be two now rare 7" singles. The first of these 1992 efforts, the Guttural Records of Mexico manufactured 'Trail Of Life Decayed' EP, was limited to a thousand copies. Dedicated fans soon spotted that the sleeve credited B side track 'A Void Of Tranquillity' was in fact not included, instead 'Vernal Awakening' mistakenly took its place. Only a mere five hundred pressings were made of the 'A Moonclad Reflection' EP, initially bearing the Slaughter Records logo before a second run provided the debut release for the Exhumed Productions label. Both these recordings were re-released in Poland the following year on Carnage Records.

DARK TRANQUILLITY's opening full-length album, August 1993's 'Skydancer' again finding the Dragan Tanascovic and Stefan Lindgren team behind the desk, issued through the Finnish Spinefarm imprint, saw their raging brand of Metal tempered by a guest inclusion for singer Anna-Kajsa Avehall. 'Skydancer' garnered global releases through Toy's Factory in Japan and in Russia where Fono Records handled CDs and Counter Attack produced cassettes. In the wake of this release vocalist Anders Fridén left for IN FLAMES and was replaced internally by Mikael Stanne, by coincidence also having performed with IN FLAMES as singer on their 'Lunar Strain' debut, for the follow up 1995 EP 'Of Chaos And Eternal Night'. The band also employed second guitarist Fredrik Johansson. In between these sessions DARK TRANQUILLITY contributed a version of 'My Friend Misery' to the METALLICA tribute album 'Metal Militia', which was released on Black Sun Records in 1994.

A second album, the landmark 'The Gallery', was produced by Fredrik Nordström at Studio Fredman and issued through French label Osmose Productions in November 1995. Now regarded as a pillar of the Gothenburg sound, 'The Gallery' blended massive riffage strewn with classically wrought lead soloing and philosophical subject matter. Mikael Stanne's performance in particular, plumbing the depths of subterranean belly roars to pure toned chorusing, came in for lashings of praise whilst female accompaniment came courtesy of Eva-Marie Larsson. International versions of 'The Gallery' were beefed up with extra tracks, Japan adding 'My Friend Of Misery' whilst Korean variants saw a rendition of SACRED REICH's 'Sacred Reich' anthem. In addition, a limited edition 10" vinyl box also boasted the SACRED REICH track and a take on KREATOR's 'Bringer Of Torture'. A further stop gap EP then arrived, 'Enter Suicidal Angels' released in November 1996. Involving three tracks cut whilst crafting the next album, 'The Mind's I', the EP also added a somewhat unsuccessful techno amalgam of previous DARK TRANQUILLITY tracks bundled into one entity given a title 'Archetype'.

Stanne contributed guest vocal on DENIAL's debut EP 'Rape Of The Century'. Perhaps a more significant moment in the band's history was the decision taken by Stanne and Sundin to create a trad-Metal side project with former CEREMONIAL OATH drummer Jesper Strömbold and CRYSTAL AGE guitarist Oscar Dronjac titled HAMMERFALL. With the original intention of creating a non serious, kickabout band, HAMMERFALL signed to Nuclear Blast and quite amazingly shifted over 100'000 copies of their debut album 'Glory To The Brave' in Germany alone. Unfortunately for Stanne this was after he had dropped out of the band to concentrate on DARK TRANQUILLITY.

'The Mind's I' came out in April 1997, punctuated by both acoustic guitar passages and the female voices of Sara Svensson, once more demonstrated the band's ability to balance technical finesse with unrelenting, oppressive Metal. Former singer Anders Fridén guested on the song 'Hedon'. In November DARK TRANQUILLITY headlined the Osmose touring extravaganza known as the 'World Domination' tour in headlining over ENSLAVED, BEWITCHED, SWORDMASTER, DEMONIAC and DELLAMORTE.

During early 1999 second guitarist Fredrik Johansson bowed out. DARK TRANQUILLITY duly shifted bassist Martin Henrikson over to the guitar role and inducted Martin Brändström on keyboards. The band, switching to the German Century Media label, re-emerged touting the album 'Projector' in June, the final set to feature Fredrik Johansson. Here the group took a quantum leap forward, with the Death growls stripped away and replaced by cleaner tones, an increased female vocal content from Johanna Andersson, keyboard washes, dominant piano and a switching down in gear towards the neo-Gothique.

DARK TRANQUILLITY toured Japan in September 1999. The band also performed to their biggest audience the same year as part of the Italian 'Gods Of Metal' festival headlined by IRON MAIDEN. The same year Dutch band ETHEREAL SPAWN would cover 'Punish My Heaven' on their debut album.

The vacant bass role was filled by LUCIFERION's Michael Nicklasson in time for recording of July 2000's 'The Haven'. A transitional work, 'The Haven' would see a band reacting to criticism levelled at 'Projector' by re-introducing the Death growls but also increasing the keyboard content. During September DARK TRANQUILLITY formed part of a strong Metal package bill for a lengthy European tour ranked alongside their friends IN FLAMES and Finnish outfits SENTENCED and TO/DIE/FOR. This would be followed up by a short burst of Mexican dates.

The band toured Japan for the second time in April of 2001 co-headlining with Finnish act CHILDREN OF BODOM. Returning to Europe an appearance was put in at the 'Wacken Open Air' festival in Germany. Brändström would then be lent out to TIAMAT frontman Johan Edlund's LUCYFIRE endeavour for live work upfront of DARK TRANQUILLITY's first show in

Istanbul, Turkey in October supported by DISHEARTEN and AFFLICTION. However, drummer Anders Jivarp injured his wrist on the eve of this jaunt and LEFAY's Robin Engström stepped into the breach at short notice.

In early 2002 Brändström would once again loan out his services, this time for TIAMAT. DARK TRANQUILLITY's momentum quickened with the 'Damage Done' album that August reaping worthy media praise and sales. The record would also break into the national German and Swedish album charts. Buoyed by this success an extensive run of European headline dates was organised with co-headliners SINERGY throughout November and December.

The band teamed up with an impressive extreme Metal touring package of NILE, NAPALM DEATH, STRAPPING YOUNG LAD and THE BERZERKER for North American dates in January and February 2003. DARK TRANQUILLITY entered the DVD era in style, their 'Live Damage' collection comprising live footage from the Kraków Krzemionki Studio TVP performance recorded in October of 2002 alongside fan video recordings taken in Athens, Essen and Paris the same year and promo clips for 'Monochromatic Stains' and 'ThereIn'.

DARK TRANQUILLITY celebrated their fifteenth anniversary with the issue of a two CD retrospective compilation 'Exposures—In Retrospect And Denial'. Collected together would be archive material from the demos 'Trail Of Life Decayed' and the 'A Moonclad Reflection' EP along with live and bonus songs and unreleased songs 'Static', 'No One' and 'In Sight'.

During 2004 Niklas Sundin donated guitar parts to Japanese avant-garde Metal act SIGH's controversial 'Gallows Gallery' album. DARK TRANQUILLITY, having wrapped up production of a new album, performed at the fourth annual Busan Rock Festival in South Korea during August of 2004, putting in a small club gig at Seoul's Live Hall venue just beforehand under the pseudonym of 'DAMAGE DONE'. Shortly after the band filmed a promotional video for the track 'Lost to Apathy' with director Roger Johansson. An EP of 'Lost To Apathy' emerged in November, charting on the Swedish singles rankings at number 47.

Live promotion found the band on the road in Europe during December, forming up the 'Hammered at Xmas' tour in alliance with THE HAUNTED and ARCH ENEMY, with US dates in January 2005 packaged with SOILWORK and HYPOCRISY before teaming up with German Thrash veteran's KREATOR for the 'Enemy of God' tour commencing in February. Martin Brändström would then join the ranks of TIAMAT for European dates. Quite spectacularly, new album 'Character' entered the national Swedish charts at no. 3.

DARK TRANQUILLITY's early albums, 1995's 'The Gallery' and 1997's 'The Mind's I', would be set for re-release, both adding a wealth of rare bonus material. Added to 'The Gallery' would be the band's cover versions of KREATOR's 'Bringer Of Torture', SACRED REICH's 'Sacred Reich', IRON MAIDEN's '22 Acacia Avenue', MERCYFUL FATE's 'Lady In Black' and METALLICA's 'My Friend Of Misery'. A 2005 compilation inclusion of note would be the track 'Lost To Apathy' featured on the 'Code Red' album, an exclusive collection given to US Marine Corps soldiers active duty in the Middle East.

DARK TRANQUILLITY announced South American gigs for June, taking in Chile, Guatemala, Mexico, Colombia, Argentina and Brazil. The band revealed plans for September and October European dates, taking in the UK, France, Belgium, Holland, Germany, Norway, Sweden and Denmark, with strong support from ARCH ENEMY and TRIVIUM but then pulled out of these gigs.

In side activity, DARK TRANQUILLITY guitarist Niklas Sundin unveiled a project union with vocalist / bassist Jonatan Nordenstam, and THE PROVENANCE pairing of guitarist Joakim Rosén and drummer Joel Lindell billed LAETHORA. The new

DARK TRANQUILLITY (pic: Dimitri Borellini)

band's debut album, 'March Of The Parasite', was finalised in August. A brief burst of German dates had the band supported by HATESPHERE and CHIMAIRA.

DARK TRANQUILLITY's 2006 season of live campaigning opened up in the USA during February alongside OPETH and DEVIN TOWNSEND.

The group returned to US campaigning in March and April 2007 flanking THE HAUNTED and INTO ETERNITY. To coincide, DARK TRANQUILLITY issued the 'Fiction' album. Japanese editions hosted an extra song 'A Closer End' whilst Australian variants included the instrumental 'Winter Triangle'. Director Roger Johansson shot a promotional video for the song 'Focus Shift' in mid February.

Trail Of Life Decayed, Dark Tranquillity (1991) (Demo). Midwinter (Intro) / Beyond Enlightenment / Vernal Awakening / Void Of Tranquillity.

A Moonclad Reflection EP, Exhumed Productions CORPSE001 (1992) (Limited edition of 500). Unfurled By Dawn / Yesterworld.

Trial Of Life Decayed EP, Guttural (1992) (7" vinyl single limited to 1000 copies). Midwinter (Intro) / Beyond Enlightenment / Vernal Awakening.

Tranquillity, Carnage CARR 057-93 (1993) (Polish cassette release limited to 2000 copies). Midwinter / Yesterworld / Unfurled By Dawn / Beyond Enlightenment / Vernal Awakening / Void Of Tranquillity.

SKYDANCER, Spinefarm SPI 16CD (1993). Nightfall By The Shore Of Time / Crimson Winds / A Bolt Of Blazing Gold / In Tears Bereaved / Skywards / Through Ebony Archways / Shadow Duet / My Faeryland Forgotten / Alone.

Osmose Promo Sampler, Osmose Productions OPCD 1D (1995) (Split promotion CD single with NECROMANTIA, DIABOLOS RISING and ENTHRONED). Punish My Heaven.

Of Chaos And Eternal Night EP, Spinefarm SPI 23CD (1995) (CD single). Of Chaos And Eternal Night / With The Flaming Shades Of Fall / Away.

THE GALLERY, Osmose Productions OP 033 (1995) (10" vinyl box set). Punish My Heaven / Silence, And The Firmament Withdrew / Edenspring / The Dying Line / The Gallery / The One Brooding Warning / Midway Through Infinity / Lethe / The Emptiness From Which I Fed / Mine Is The Grandeur ... / ... Of Melancholy Burning / Bringer Of Torture / Sacred Reich.

THE GALLERY, Osmose Productions OPCD 033 (1995). Punish My Heaven / Silence, And The Firmament Withdrew / Edenspring / The Dying Line / The Gallery / The One Brooding Warning / Midway Through Infinity / Lethe / The Emptiness From Which I Fed / Mine Is The Grandeur … / … Of Melancholy Burning.

THE GALLERY, Toy's Factory TFCK-88769 (1995) (Japanese release). Punish My Heaven / Silence, And The Firmament Withdrew / Edenspring / The Dying Line / The Gallery / The One Brooding Warning / Midway Through Infinity / Lethe / The Emptiness From Which I Fed / Mine Is The Grandeur … / … Of Melancholy Burning / My Friend Of Misery.

Enter Suicidal Angels EP, Osmose Productions OPMCD 049 (1996). Zodijackyl Light / Razorfever / Shadowlit Facade / Archetype.

THE MIND'S I, Osmose Productions OPCD 052 (1997). Dreamlore Degenerate / Zodijackyl Light / Hedon / Scythe, Rage And Roses / Constant / Dissolution Factor Red / Insanity's Crescendo / Still Moving Sinews / Atom Heart 243.5 / Tidal Tantrum / Tongues / The Mind's Eye.

THE WORLD DOMINATION LIVE, Osmose Productions OPCD 068 (1998) (Split CD with ENSLAVED, BEWITCHED, SWORDMASTER, DELLAMORTE and DEMONIAC). Dreamlore Degenerate / Punish My Heaven / Insanity's Crescendo / Zodijackyl Light / Lethe / Constant / Of Chaos And Eternal Night.

THE OFFICIAL DEMO SERIES, Metal Invader (1999) (Split CD with HUNGER and INFERNÄL MÄJESTY free with 'Metal Invader' magazine). Midwinter / Beyond Enlightenment / Vernal Awakening / Void Of Tranquillity.

PROJECTOR, Century Media 77285-8 (1999) (Digipack). FreeCard / ThereIn / UnDo Control / Auctioned / To A Bitter Halt / The Sun Fired Blanks / Nether Novas / Day To End / Dobermann / On Your Time / Exposure.

PROJECTOR, Century Media 77285-2 (1999). FreeCard / ThereIn / UnDo Control / Auctioned / To A Bitter Halt / The Sun Fired Blanks / Nether Novas / Day To End / Dobermann / On Your Time.

PROJECTOR, Toy's Factory TFCK-87186 (1999) (Japanese release). FreeCard / ThereIn / UnDo Control / Auctioned / To A Bitter Halt / The Sun Fired Blanks / Nether Novas / Day To End / Dobermann / On Your Time.

HAVEN, Century Media 77297-2 (2000). The Wonders At Your Feet / Not Built To Last / Indifferent Suns / Feast Of Burden / Haven / The Same / Fabric / Ego Drama / Rundown / Emptier Still / At Loss For Words.

HAVEN, Century Media 77297-8 (2000) (Digipack). The Wonders At Your Feet / Not Built To Last / Indifferent Suns / Feast Of Burden / Haven / The Same / Fabric / Ego Drama / Rundown / Emptier Still / At Loss For Words / ThereIn (Video).

HAVEN, Toy's Factory TFCK-87235 (2000) (Japanese release). The Wonders At Your Feet / Not Built To Last / Indifferent Suns / Feast Of Burden / Haven / The Same / Fabric / Ego Drama / Rundown / Emptier Still / At Loss For Words / Cornered / ThereIn (Video).

DAMAGE DONE, Century Media 77403-8 (2002) (Digipack). Final Resistance / Hours Passed In Exile / Monochromatic Stains / Single Part Of Two / The Treason Wall / Forfat C: For Cortex / Damage Done / Cathode Ray Sunshine / The Enemy / I, Deception / White Noise / Black Silence / Ex Nihilo / Monochromatic Stains (Video).

DAMAGE DONE, Century Media 77403-2 (2002) (CD release). Final Resistance / Hours Passed In Exile / Monochromatic Stains / Single Part Of Two / The Treason Wall / Forfat C: For Cortex / Damage Done / Cathode Ray Sunshine / The Enemy / White Noise / Black Silence / Ex Nihilo. Chart positions: 29 SWEDEN, 83 GERMANY, 146 FRANCE.

DAMAGE DONE, Century Media 77403-1 (2002) (Vinyl release). Final Resistance / Hours Passed In Exile / Monochromatic Stains / Single Part Of Two / The Treason Wall / Forfat C: For Cortex / Damage Done / Cathode Ray Sunshine / The Enemy / I, Deception / White Noise / Black Silence / Ex Nihilo.

DAMAGE DONE, Toy's Factory TFCK-87288 (2002) (Japanese release). Final Resistance / Hours Passed In Exile / Monochromatic Stains / Single Part Of Two / The Treason Wall / Forfat C: For Cortex / Damage Done / Cathode Ray Sunshine / The Enemy / The Poison Well / White Noise / Black Silence / Ex Nihilo / Monochromatic Stains (Video).

Lost To Apathy, Century Media 77585-2 (2004). Lost To Apathy / Derivation TNB / The Endless Feed (Chaos Seed remix) / Undo Control (Live) / Lost To Apathy (Video) / D.T. Screensaver. Chart position: 47 SWEDEN.

CHARACTER, Toy's Factory TFCK-87380 (2005) (Japanese release). The New Build / Through Smudged Lenses / Out Of Nothing / The Endless Feed / Lost To Apathy / Mind Matters / One Thought / Dry Run / Am I 1? / Senses Tied / My Negation / Derivation TNB / Endless Feed (Chaos Seed Remix).

CHARACTER (LIMITED EDITION), Century Media 77603-8 (2005). The New Build / Through Smudged Lenses / Out Of Nothing / The Endless Feed / Lost To Apathy / Mind Matters / One Thought / Dry Run / Am I 1? / Senses Tied / My Negation / Lost To Apathy (Video) / Damage Done (Live in Korea 2004) / The Wonders At Your Feet (Live in Korea 2004) / Final Resistance (Live in Korea 2004) / The Treason Wall (Live in Korea 2004).

CHARACTER, Century Media 77603-2 (2005). The New Build / Through Smudged Lenses / Out Of Nothing / The Endless Feed / Lost To Apathy / Mind Matters / One Thought / Dry Run / Am I 1? / Senses Tied / My Negation. Chart positions: 3 SWEDEN, 30 FINLAND, 57 ITALY, 83 GERMANY.

FICTION, (2007). Nothing To No One / The Lesser Faith / Terminus (Where Death Is Most Alive) / Blind At Heart / Incipher / Inside The Particle Storm / Empty Me / Misery's Crown / Focus Shift / The Mundane And The Magic.

DARKANE

HELSINGBORG, SWEDEN — *Andreas Sydow (vocals), Christofer Malmström (guitar), Klas Ideberg (guitar), Jörgen Löfberg (bass), Peter Wildoer (drums).*

DARKANE founders guitarist Christofer Malmström, bass player Jörgen Löfberg and drummer Peter Wildoer were previously members of noted technical Metal band AGRETATOR. Both Malmström and Wildoer had also been involved with eighties Power Metal band ZANINEZ. The duo forged DARKANE with the enlistment of second guitarist Klas Ideberg of Helsingborg Thrashers HYSTE´RIAH G.B.C., bassist Jörgen Löfberg and singer Lawrence Mackrory, of irreverent Thrashers F.K.Ü. (Freddy Krueger's Ünderwear), and bowed in with the impressive 'Rusted Angel' record. Released originally by Wrong Again Records in Scandinavia, US license was granted to Regain Records who re-issued the album adding extra live tracks.

Ex-vocalist Lawrence Mackrory would guest session on the 1998 THE MIST OF AVALON record as backing singer and also the 1999 ANDROMEDA debut album 'Extension Of The Wish'. He would later found FORCEFEED releasing an EP 'Soil', later changing this band name to SEETHINGS.

DARKANE reconvened for a sophomore Daniel Bergstrand produced opus entitled 'Insanity'. This outing also marked the debut of new vocalist Andreas Sydow. Promoting 'Insanity' the band would put in their inaugural United States show at the 'Milwaukee Metalfest' in 2001. Japanese versions of the album, released on the Toys Factory label, would see a bonus track with a live rendition of 'Convicted'.

Jörgen Löfberg and guitarist Klas Ideberg, along with SOILWORK's drummer Henry Ranta and vocalist Henrik Sjöwall and guitarist Mattias Svensson would forge a project band entitled THE DEFACED. Ideberg is also involved with TERROR 2000.

DARKANE would be set to release a new album, 'Expanding Senses', co-produced by Daniel Bergstrand and former MISERY LOVES COMPANY member Örjan Örnkloo, in August of 2002 through Nuclear Blast. Coincidently the same production team would work on ex-DARKANE member Lawrence Mackrory's SEETHINGS debut album. Mackrory also figured on THE DUSKFALL debut 'Frailty' as a session guest. Peter Wildoer found time in his schedule to act as session drummer for Gothic Metal band DAWN OF OBLIVION.

The band put in a short burst of UK shows during November packaged with CRIMINAL and DESCENT and Dutch gigs supported by FUELBLOODED before travelling to Japan for gigs with MASTODON and HIGH ON FIRE. DARKANE would lend support to BEHEMOTH for gigs in Poland during December.

The band's continuing ascendancy would be further progressed as DARKANE was confirmed as participants in the April 2003 European 'No Mercy' festivals. The group formed up part of a heavyweight billing comprising TESTAMENT, MARDUK, DIE APOKALYPTISCHEN REITER, NUCLEAR ASSAULT, PROPAIN, MALEVOLENT CREATION, DEATH ANGEL, and CALLENISH CIRCLE. An extensive run of European shows in November caught the band packaged with DISBELIEF, MNEMIC, MYSTIC

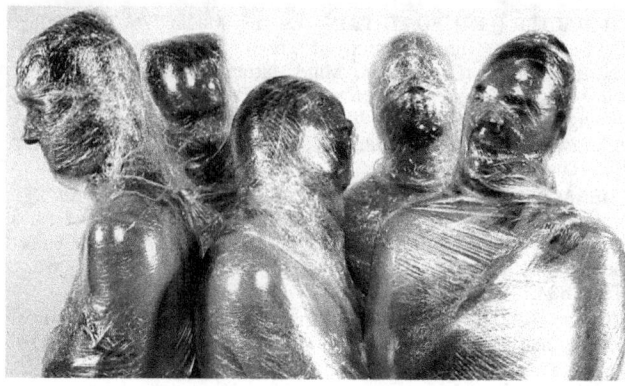
DARKANE (pic: Stefan Ideberg)

PROPHECY and headliners DEATH ANGEL. However, upon completion of these gigs Wildoer, having suffered from a wrist injury dating back to February, was forced out of band activities in order to recuperate.

DARKANE guitarist Christofer Malmström readied a solo project for 2004 release billed as NON-HUMAN LEVEL, this venture including studio contributions from MESHUGGAH bassist Gustaf Hielm, DEVIN TOWNSEND band and GOD AWAKENS PETRIFIED drummer Ryan Van Poederooyen and his DARKANE colleague drummer Peter Wildoer, the latter taking on a lead vocal role. Wildoer eased himself back into the drumming role by working up tracks with Rock n' Roll outfit BEN. Meantime ex-DARKANE frontman Lawrence Mackrory re-emerged in 2004 as bassist for Death Thrashers ENEMY IS US and also sessioned demos for SCAVENGER.

In January 2005 Andreas Sydow contributed guitar work for Spanish Thrash Metal band LEGEN BELTZA's conceptual track dubbed 'War of Wars' included on their album 'Dimension Of Pain'. That same month DARKANE set a working title of 'Layers Of Lies' for their new album, established for June 2005 release. Japanese versions added a traditional bonus track in 'Subliminal Seduction'. Meantime, guitarist Christofer Malmström signed a deal with France's Listenable Records for his solo project, NON-HUMAN LEVEL featuring DEVIN TOWNSEND drummer Ryan van Poederooyen.

October 28th in Lawrence, Kansas, marked the start of a US tour, the band forming up a bill comprising FEAR FACTORY, STRAPPING YOUNG LAD and IT DIES TODAY. Fellow Swedish act SOILWORK was added to the bill from November 8th. Drummer Peter Wildoer joined up with SOILWORK on a temporary basis, covering on summer 2006 shows at the 'Festimad' event in Madrid, Spain plus shows in Piteå and Malmö. Guitarist Klas Ideberg also got in on the temping act, subbing for HYPOCRISY's October North American tour. That same month former singer Lawrence Mackrory sessioned on album recordings for French band SCARVE.

RUSTED ANGEL, War Music WAR0009 (1998). ::Iii:O:Iii:: / Convicted / Bound / Rape Of Mankind / Rusted Angel / A Wisdoms Breed / Chase For Existence / The Arcane Darkness / July 1999 / Frenetic Visions.
RUSTED ANGEL, Toy's Factory TFCK-87168 (1999) (Japanese release). ::Iii:O:Iii:: / Convicted / Bound / Rape Of Mankind / Rusted Angel / A Wisdoms Breed / Chase For Existence / The Arcane Darkness / July 1999 / Frenetic Visions / Relief In Disguise.
INSANITY, Toy's Factory TFCK-87237 (2001) (Japanese release). Calamitas / Third / Emanation Of Fear / Impure Perfection / Hostile Phantasm / Psychic Pain / 000111 / The Perverted Beast / Distress / Inaupicious Coming / Pile Of Hate / Inverted Spheres / Convicted (Live).
INSANITY, Nuclear Blast NB 602-2 (2001). Calamitas / Third / Emanation Of Fear / Impure Perfection / Hostile Phantasm / Psychic Pain / 000111 / The Perverted Beast / Distress / Inaupicious Coming / Pile Of Hate / Inverted Spheres.
EXPANDING SENSES, Nuclear Blast NB 1021-2 (2002). Innocence Gone / Solitary Confinement / Fatal Impact / Imaginary Entity / Violence From Within / The Fear Of One's Self / Chaos Vs Order / Parasites Of The Unexplained / Submission.
EXPANDING SENSES, Toy's Factory TFCK-87290 (2002) (Japanese release). Innocence Gone / Solitary Confinement / Fatal Impact / Imaginary Entity / Violence From Within / The Fear Of One's Self / Chaos Vs Order / Parasites Of The Unexplained / Submission / Growing Hate.
LAYERS OF LIES, Nuclear Blast NB 1459-2 (2005). Amnesia Of The Wildoerian Apocalypse / Secondary Effects / Organic Canvas / Fading Dimensions / Layers Of Lies / Godforsaken Universe / Klastrophobic Hibernation / Vision Of Degradation / Contaminated / Maelstrom Crisis / Decadent Messiah / The Creation Insane.
LAYERS OF LIES, Toy's Factory TFCK-87393 (2005) (Japanese release). Amnesia Of The Wildoerian Apocalypse / Secondary Effects / Organic Canvas / Fading Dimensions / Layers Of Lies / Godforsaken Universe / Klastrophobic Hibernation / Vision Of Degradation / Contaminated / Maelstrom Crisis / Decadent Messiah / The Creation Insane / Subliminal Seduction.

DARKEN

FRANCE — *Silem (vocals), Dave Blanchard (guitar), Alexandre Saba (guitar), Camille Preuvot (bass), José Alfonso (drums).*

This Doom styled Gothic Metal formation was initiated during 1994 by guitarists Alexandre Saba and Dave Blanchard with José Afonso on the drums. The following year Silem joined as lead singer and, in 1996, Camille Preuvot on bass. The band debuted with the demo 'The Silent Bleeding Of Eternity' that October. Signing to Kaly Productions the album 'Arcane XIII' emerged during 1998. However, both Silem and Blanchard exited in 1999. DARKEN drafted Fred as their new frontman and utilised session guitarists, such as Bruno and Wilfrid, for live work. DARKEN folded that same year though, putting in their swan song gig in Marseille in May 1999.

In May of 2000 Saba, Blanchard and Preuvot re-constituted the band under the revised billing of DARK-N, acquiring a new vocalist in David Hanin and with Jerome Constant on the drums. A demo, 'Loading Please wait', arrived in 2001. Line-up changes saw Fred Faucheur replacing Blanchard and Dom taking command of the drums. Both these new candidates exited in November 2004, with Ben being installed on drums. Signing to Thundering Records DARK-N published the album 'Loading Complete' in January 2005.

The Silent Bleeding Of Eternity, (1996). Unlogical Sphere / Sculpture Of Nothingness / Scarlet Trance / The Whispering Mist / The Dream Of Akenaton.
ARCANE XIII, Kaly Productions (1997). A. XIII / Falling / Neo-Mystic: The Whispering Mist / Neo-Mystic: Scarlet Trance / Neo-Mystic: Promethee / Ghostly Runes / Lynk Spacies: Mobbius Ribbon / Lynk Spacies: The Angels Left / The Sculpture Of Nothing.

DARKIFIED

SÖDERKÖPING, SWEDEN — *Martin Gustavsson (vocals), Martin Ahx (guitar), Robert Karlsson (bass), Jocke Göthberg (drums).*

Söderköping based, blackened Death Metal. Guitarist Martin Ahx held TRIMMADELG affiliations, singer Martin "Draupin" Gustavsson has scene ties to AMENOPHIS, ALLEGIANCE and THE CHAINSAWS. DARKIFIED released the demos 'Dark' in May 1991. The group debuted with the January 1992 single 'Sleep Forever'. Both these sessions were recorded at Gorysound Studios and produced by Swanö. Jonas Amundin sessioned on guitar.

Ex-GRIMORIUM, MARDUK and CARDINAL SIN drummer Jocke 'Grave' Göthberg was a key figure in DARKIFIED, EDGE OF SANITY's mentor DAN SWANÖ also making his presence felt contributing keyboards on the March 1995 'A Dance On The Grave' album for Repulse Records. Bassist Robert Karlsson also sings lead vocal for Swanö's act PAN-THY-MONIUM and holds further credits with INCAPACITY, FACEBREAKER, EDGE OF SANITY and SOLAR DAWN.

Dark, Darkified (1991) (Demo). Intro / Howlings From The Darkness / A Summond For The Nameless Horrors / The Forgotten City / Outro—Out From The Darkness.

Sleep Forever, Drowned Products DS003 (1992). Sleep Forever / The Forgotten City / The Whispers In The Darkness.

A DANCE ON THE GRAVE, Repulse RPS005 (1995). Intro / Howling From The Darkness / A Summon For The Nameless / The Forgotten City / Outro—Out From The Darkness / Sleep Forever / The Forgotten City (1992 version) / The Whisperer In The Darkness.

DARKNESS REMAINS

PRINCETON, WV, USA — *Jon Fralick (vocals / guitar), Bob Chapman (guitar), Erik Harvey (bass), Matt Tote (drums).*

Princeton, West Virginia Death Metal band. Established during 2001, DARKNESS REMAINS, forged whilst members were still attending Princeton Junior High School, first numbered guitarist Mark Masri, second guitarist John Fralick and drummer Josh White. This unit, entitled INHUMANE, fractured and ENSCRIPTION then rose up, pulling in RAYA drummer Matt Tote. As the band evolved into DARKNESS REMAINS vocalist Jeff Griffith and bassist Curtis Henson made up the numbers.

Tribunal Records issued the February 2002 debut album 'To Touch The Depths Of Sorrow', after which Griffith took his leave. Follow up 'Mamia' arrived in February 2003, prompting another line-up change as Henson exited. In late summer 2004, guitarist Mark Masri also decided to quit.

Reformulating, the group drew in ABYSMAL DEPTHS man Bob Chapman on guitar. Travis Cook, previously of FALSE HOPE, offered his services on bass guitar. These new members had switched instruments in order to join, both having been formerly employed as drummers. However, Cook soon opted out and in February 2004 Erik Harvey took on bass duties.

DARKNESS REMAINS undertook US "Appalachian Death" touring throughout August 2006 backed by PREMATURE BURIAL.

TO TOUCH THE DEPTHS OF SORROW, Tribunal (2002). Death On Wings / These Ghosts Forever / Under Eternity / The Pawn That Could Not / Warsaw / The Quest / Darkness Remains / A Grave Too Shallow.

LAMIA, Tribunal (2003). The Betrayal / Lamia In Corinth / Serenity's Desire / Heart Of Nails / Untitled / Aura Of Despair / Plagues Not Overcome.

DARKSIDE

WIENER NEUSTADT, AUSTRIA — *Wolfgang Süssenbeck (vocals), Peter Durst (guitar), Pit (guitar), Peter Böhm (bass), Daniel Hanak (keyboards / acoustic guitar), Lukas Siska (drums).*

Wiener Neustadt based atmospheric flavoured Death Metal band DARKSIDE trace their formation back to 1991 founded upon the rhythm section of bassist Peter Böhm and drummer Robert Grögler, later joined by vocalist / guitarist Peter Durst. This triumvirate cut the opening demo 'Depression'. After this first attempt keyboard player Wolfgang Süssenbeck was added to add a degree of depth to the proceedings. For their second demo 'Herbst', Böhm was to concentrate on the lead vocal role whilst new recruit Herbert Knöchel took on the guitar duties. DARKSIDE then embarked on touring as opening act for the likes of KRABATHOR and SCABBARD. These dates established DARKSIDE a sizable fan base in the Czech Republic.

The band self financed their opening 1994 album 'Melancholia Of A Dying World'. The follow up, 1997's 'Shadowfields' saw the band now signed to the Impact Records label. During this timeframe DARKSIDE gained further exposure supporting well-known acts such as THERION, SIX FEET UNDER and BAL-SAGOTH.

In April of 1998 DARKSIDE recorded 'Evolution' in the Hazienda Studio for NSM Records. DARKSIDE would then promptly resume touring putting in dates with MOONSPELL and THERION, playing 46 shows in 16 countries.

In preparation for the group's fourth album both Robert Grögler and Peter Durst left the band, the latter working with DESPERADO INC. To add to their woes the chosen producer apparently was none too keen on the direction of the new material or the performance of the new drummer Bernd Pichlbauer. DARKSIDE subsequently wrote new material and found a new guitarist in Vlastimil Koritar.

Although 'Cognitive Dissonance' initially had Böhm handling both bass and vocal duties it would be Süssenbeck who took the mantle of lead vocalist for live shows and the keyboard player re-recorded the vocals for the album too. DARKSIDE would also enlist the services of a second guitarist, Radek Hajda of Czech outfit SILENT STREAM OF GODLESS ELEGY. Böhm would find time to assist Black Metal band SANGUIS in the studio for their debut album 'Chaosgate Guardians'.

DARKSIDE enlisted Markus Glandecker on guitar during February of 2002. However, following the conclusion of European touring ranked alongside CARNAL FORGE and MORTICIAN, Peter Böhm, bass player and founding member of the band announced his departure. Original singer and guitar player Peter Durst returned to the fold in mid December. DARKSIDE entered X-Line Studios in Bratislava, Slovakia in October 2004 to record the album 'Amber—Skeletal Journeys Through The Void'.

Members would still find time to maintain side project CITIZEN X, recording the 'Satanation' album, whilst bassist Peter Böhm cut an album 'Dressed With Scars' for his side endeavour H8. Also in the works would be an album from CRANIOTOMY, 'Cut A Piece For Your Hunger' released Czech Republic's Grodhaisn Productions, a side venture of drummer Lukas and keyboardist Daniel. Pit and Wolf also engaged in touring with their other act, DEMOLITION.

DARKSIDE supported MOONSPELL dates across Europe in March 2007.

MELANCHOLIA OF A DYING WORLD, Darkside DARKCD001 (1995). Deadly / To The Deceased / Prelude / Melancholia / Emesis Of The Soul / Dying World / Shades Of Grief / Fragmental Aggression / Gedanken / Copcrusher / Pictures In Grey / A Winters Night / The Truth.

SHADOWFIELDS, System Shock IR-C-093 (1997). Intro / Of Vision And Mental Derangement / In Nomine / Shades Of pictures In Grey / In Your Eyes / Noohoorsh / Shadowfields / The Blood On My Hands / Requiem.

EVOLUTION, NSM (1998). In The Beginning / The Gloaming / Souls Of Led Blackness / Evolution? / Traces Of Red / Spiritual Galleries / Pink Frog-Cold Smoke / Whores' Bleeding Magick / Till' (Y)our Bitter End / In Silence.

COGNITIVE DISSONENCE, Season Of Mist SOM 055 (2001). Intro / Legend of the Gods / Hear Evil, Do Evil, Speak Evil / Cognitive Dissonance / The Fallen / Fifth / Hymn To The Chosen Ones / Mechanical Landscape / Caress Of The Sleeping Giant / Bloodbound / S.W.I.H. / Pontifex 666.

DARTH

GERMANY — *Adam Zietek (vocals), Matthias Klinkmann (guitar), Dirk Alberti (guitar), Ralle (drums).*

Death Metal combo forged in 1995, debuting with the track 'Love Is Pain' included on the 1996 compilation album 'Let's Camp Together'. That same year the song 'Permanent Invigilated' featured on a further various artists sampler 'HA-RD '96', the band following up on this with the consecutive 'HA-RD '97' release sporting the track 'Control Part 2'.

DARTH's 1999 line-up comprised lead vocalist Adam Zietek, guitarist Matthias Klinkmann, bassist Florian von Bargen and Daniel Rabe on the drums. The group put in their inaugural live performance in March of 2001, switching drummers to the GOAT OF MENDES, ex- SPLUTTER and MAILVALTAR credited Ralle that December. The 'Amok' demo arrived in 2002, after which DARTH inducted another erstwhile MAILVALTAR man, bassist Dirk Alberti.

DARTH's December 2003 album 'Buttfucked By Destiny', produced by Klinkmann, was recorded at K-Sound Studios in Hagen-Hohenlimburg.

BUTTFUCKED BY DESTINY, Crude Entertainment (2003). Wall Of Ignorance / Empire Of The Lie / I Should Be Dead / Forbidden Happiness / Age Of Depression / Self-Exorcism / Buttfucked By Destiny / Amok / Koma.

DAUNTLESS

HELSINKI, FINLAND — *Ari Nieminen (vocals), Riku Katainen (guitar), Sami Helle (guitar), Tuomo Tukkimaki (bass), Santeri Salmi (drums).*

Helsinki's DAUNTLESS, fronted by erstwhile CALEDONIAN singer Ari Nieminen, began life as MANIAX in 1991. In this guise the group, operating in a Hardcore mould, released the demos 'Face The Fact' in 1995 and 'Prophecy...' in September the following year. The band switched title to DAUNTLESS during 1998, re-debuting with the demo tape 'Cold I Am' after which Riku Katainen was introduced on guitar. The 'Inhuman Kind' session arrived in 1999.

DAUNTLESS issued the demo 'Modern Ways Of Discipline' in January of 2003. Both guitarist Sami Helle and drummer Santeri Salmi, previous to DAUNTLESS being a brief member of DEEPRED, are also active with LOCKFIST. A further demo, 'Obey—Erase—Obey', arrived in October 2005. The band signed to Firebox Records in June 2006. The album 'Execute The Fact' entered the Finnish charts at number 40 in March 2007.

Cold I Am, Dauntless (1998) (Demo). Abuse / Undaunted / Out Of Mind.

Inhumankind, Dauntless (1999) (Demo). Dehumanized / Body Open Wide / Cycle Of Evolution / Traces Of Genocide / All-Enslaving Global Plan / Riot!

Modern Ways Of Discipline, Dauntless (2000) (Demo). The Distorted Facts / Unobtrusive Monitoring / War Without Blood / Overcrowded / All World's Hate.

Ruins MMIV, Dauntless (2004) (Demo). Ruins / Sickest Victory / Blindfolded Solutions.

Obey—Erase—Obey, Dauntless (2005) (Demo). Flow Of Fortune / Shelter = Grave / Four Walls United.

DAWN CREATION

FINLAND — *Taavi Forssell (vocals / guitar), Jan Jokinen (guitar), Juha Kettunen (bass), Heidi Hakoinen (keyboards), Marco Lauriola (drums).*

Originally entitled ALFTHAR, DUSK then ARCANUM, Death Metal band DAWN CREATION debuted with a 2003 demo 'Children Of The Night'. The incepting ALFTHAR unit had formulated as a school band during May of 1999 and quoted a membership roster of vocalist Taavi Forssell, guitarists Esa Rauhala and Heikki Aronen, bassist Antti Vaha, keyboard player Mika Kurvinen with Marco Lauriola on the drums. This formation cut one demo, 'Dark Northern Land', and played one gig before both Vaha and Kurvinen both departed.

Regrouping, the band drafted Tuukka Jääskeläinen on keyboards then Juha Kettunen on bass guitar but then suffered the loss of Rauhala. With Forssell taking on guitar duties, a decision was taken to re-name the band DUSK in late 1999. Demos were recorded in 2001 but an unsatisfied band chose not to release these tracks. In 2003 DUSK morphed into ARCANUM, laying down the demo at Hyvinkää's Rockstar Studios.

Line-up changes saw the exit of both guitarist Heikki Aronen and keyboard player Tuukka Jääskeläinen. Re-billed as DAWN CREATION the band, having acquired guitarist Jan Jokinen and keyboard player Heidi Hakoinen, issued the demo 'System Overload' in 2004.

System Overload, Dawn Creation (2004) (Demo). Modest / Overdozer / As I Say / Death Portrait.

Dawn Creation, Dawn Creation (2005) (Demo). Don't Push It! / Inner Me / Pounding.

DAWN OF AZAZEL

AUCKLAND, NEW ZEALAND — *Rigel Walshe (vocals / bass), Joe Bonnett (guitar), Tony Angelov (guitar), Phill Osborne (drums).*

Exceptionally raw Auckland Black / Death "Militant audio apocalypse" Metal band founded in 1997 by vocalist / bassist Rigel Walshe. DAWN OF AZAZEL's uncomprising musical stance, at first Grind based but edging toward a more technically inclined direction upon later releases, has garnered a burgeoning cult fan base. Formative line-ups proved fluid but the band gained stability with a platform of Walshe, ex-RETICENCE guitarist Joe Bonnett, second guitarist Tom James and drummer Tony Corry, this line-up putting in DAWN OF AZAZEL's inaugural gig on the 5th June 1999 alongside COVEN, VEXT, GUTTERED and NOTHWINGHUNGER. However, James exited soon after.

DAWN OF AZAZEL's first commercial offering was the September 1999 demo 'Of Bloodshed And Eternal Victory'. In keeping with the militaristic themes, the demo cover notably sported the "wolfsangel" Dopplehaken symbol of the 34th Waffen SS panzer grenadier Division Landstorm Nederland. However, the band members would subsequently voice their opposition to any links with neo-fascism. Subsequently, Tony Angelov filled the guitar vacancy but then Corry opted out. The new man behind the drums would be Phil Osbourne. The follow up 'Vita Est Militia Super Terram' session arrived in 2000 and was promoted with support dates to Australia's ATOMIZER. 2001 witnessed an increase in live activity, including an appearance at the Christchurch 'Satanfest' and being topped by Australian gigs in December.

The single of 2002, 'Bloodforged Abdication' released through Hellflames Productions, featured a cover version of 'Plateau Of Invincibility' originally by ORDER FROM CHAOS. DAWN OF AZAZEL undertook their 'Bloodforged Abdication' national tour March through May of 2003 to promote a 7" single bearing the same title. All 500 copies of this single were sold out on pre-order alone. The band signed to the Polish Agonia label later that year, projecting a debut full-length album, 'The Law Of The Strong', for January 2004 and touring Europe in July. Vinyl versions added an extra track in 'In Flagellation Of Eden'.

Guitarists Joe Bonnett and Tony Angelov would also be active on the scene with Death Metal band FORCED TO SUBMIT. Drummer Phil Osborne is a member of Death-Grind outfit GRAYMALKIN with both Walshe and Bonnet having figured in this band's history too. However, DAWN OF AZAZEL's Australian tour of November would be their last gigs with drummer Phil Osborne,"removed from the line-up", and guitarist Antony Angelov. New man on drums would be Martin Cavanagh of FORCED TO SUBMIT, GRAYMALKIN and SKULDOM repute.

In May of 2005 the group revealed it had completed recordings for a new album but had split away from Agonia Records. The 'Sedition' album surfaced through Ibex Moon Records, owned by John McEntee of INCANTATION, in October.

During November Walshe's daytime occupation, as a court escort in the Counties Manukau police district, was the subject of New Zealand media attention when Police Minister Annette King requested a report into a possible conflict of interests. The resulting exposure briefly made DAWN OF AZAZEL's a household name. 2006 live campaigning would be announced with a collaboration with San Diego's DISGORGE and INTENSE HAMMER RAGE for the 'Torturing New Zealand & Australia 2006' tour commencing in late February. The band opened for KORN on May 1st at the SuperTop in Auckland then embarked on US shows commencing in late May hooked up with INCANTATION, SIN OF ANGELS and VITAL REMAINS. Further high profile supports included New Zealand concerts with SKINLESS in November and a guest slot to DEICIDE's Australian and New

Zealand tour in December.

Of Bloodshed And Eternal Victory, (1999). Intro/Conqueror Throned / Triumph Upon Equinox / Conflagration Of The Mortal Soul / March On The Blind.

Vita est Militia Super Terram, (2000). Monarch Of Bloodshed And Eternal Victory (Solar Invictus) / Conqueror Throned / Triumph Upon Equinox / Bloodforged Abdication.

Bloodforged Abdication, Hellflame Productions (2002). Bloodforged Abdication / Plateau Of Invincibility.

THE LAW OF THE STRONG, Agonia (2004). Conqueror Throned / Triumph Upon Equinox / Victory (Iniquity Guides My Blade) / I Stand Unconquered / Conflagration Of The Mortal Soul / Justice Is A Fist / Immortal Dominance / Monarch Of Bloodshed And Eternal Victory (Solar Invictus).

SEDITION, Ibex Moon (2005). Spare None / Swathed In Impurity / The Road To Babalon / Descent Into Eminence / Villany Endures / Sedition / Violence And Uncleanliness / Sin (Amongst The Kings) / Master Of The Strumpets.

DAWN OF DISEASE

OSNABRÜCK, GERMANY — *Thomas Wisniewski (vocals), Alex Miletic (guitar), Sebastian Preuin (guitar), Sven Surendorf (bass), Sebastian Timper (drums).*

Osnabrück, Niedersachsen Death Metal act founded in 2001 by guitar player Alex Miletic and the STYGIAN and URINSTEIN credited drummer Sebastian Timper. DAWN OF DISEASE released a debut mini-album, 'Through Bloodstained Eyes' produced by Sven Sievering at Trollheim Studio, in October 2004 through Unstoppable Media. Recording roster comprised vocalist Thomas Wisniewski, guitarist Alex Miletic, bassist Sven Surendorf and drummer Sebastian Timper.

That following April co-founder Sebastian Timper decamped. A new track, 'Fried Genitals' featuring Carsten Schumacher of CHRONICLE OF TYRANTS as session drummer, was included on various compilation albums such as 'Xtreemities 5', 'Gentle Carnage' and 'Ancient Dreams'.

In mid 2006 DAWN OF DISEASE introduced second guitarist Sebastian Preuin, a man holding tradition with DISEMBODIED and THE VAST. The band parted ways with guitarist Sebastian Preuin in December 2006.

DAWN OF DISEASE inducted new members guitarist Stedi and drummer Mathias in March 2007.

THROUGH BLOODSTAINED EYES, Unstoppable Media (2004). Reincarnation / Through Bloodstained Eyes / Rape The Unborn / Cut Per Cut / Realies (Realize The Lies) / Sadistic Ejaculation / Lust Auf Morden.

DAWN OF RELIC

OULU, FINLAND — *Mika Tonning (vocals), Rauli Roininen (guitar), Teemu Luukinen (guitar), Pekka Mustonen (bass), Pekka Malo (keyboards), Jukka Juntunen (drums).*

Adventurous Death Metal act brought to life in Oulu initially as a keyboard based project by Jukka 'Zann Path' Juntunen during 1993, the debut eponymous demo arriving later that same year. The band's unique brand of Death / Black Metal is heavily infused with H.P. Lovecraft references. Throughout 1994 and into 1996 Path was joined by vocalist Jarno Juntunen and guitar players Rauli Roininen and Pekka Mustonen. DAWN OF RELIC's second demo recording, 1997's 'Of The Ambience', secured a deal with the Wicked World offshoot of Earache Records resulting in the album 'One Night In Carcosa'. Session vocalists for the 'One Night In Carcosa' album were CATAMENIA's Mika Tönning and HORNA's Nazgul Von Armageddon.

The band, severing ties with Wicked World, would then introduce Teemu Luukinen on guitar for a further brace of demo sessions in 2001, 'Wrathcast' and 'Rose Haven'. These tapes secured DAWN OF RELIC the title of best unsigned band from the influential French 'Metallion' magazine and a new contract with the Season Of Mist label for January 2003's 'Lovecraftian Dark'.

The album saw guest sessions courtesy of Alexi Ranta from THE BLACK LEAGUE, Kaisa Jouhki of BATTLELORE, Mikko Hyttinen of R.M.S. and Jarno Juntunen from IGNIS FATUUS.

DAWN OF RELIC, parting ways with bass player Pekka Mustonen, entered Tico Tico Studios in November of 2004 to craft a new album 'Night On Earth'.

Of The Ambience..., Dawn Of Relic (1997) (Demo). Fimbulvetr / Nether Seas Boiling / Welkins Gat / Just A River / Oceans.

ONE NIGHT IN CARCOSA, Wicked World WICK005 (1999). Fimbul Vetr / When Aldebaran Is Visible / The Last Dance Of Sarnath / Kadath Opened / Nether Seas Boiling / Welkins Gat / Just A River / Oceans.

Wrathcast—Traintape 1666/2000, Dawn Of Relic (2001) (Demo). Masquerade Of Sickness / Wrathcast / N.W.S. 1666 / Scions Of The Blackened Earth / The Awakening / The Wail Of Tartarean Well's / Starlit Plateau Of The Leng / Ghoulish Soil Burst / Watchtower Son / Oceanic Children Arise.

Lovecraftian Dark—The Story Of Rose Haven, Dawn Of Relic (2001) (Unreleased demo). Snowfall / Dormant From Kiasmagoria / Phantasm And Evenfall.

LOVECRAFTIAN DARK, Season Of Mist SOM 056 (2003). Throes Matrix: Dawn Over Carcosa / Throes Matrix: Masquerade Of Sickness (The Eve Of Reckoning) / Throes Matrix: Throes Matrix / Throes Matrix: Phosphor / Throes Matrix: Scions Of The Blackened Soil / Throes Matrix: Wrathcast / Throes Matrix: Watchtower Son (Lemurian Guard) / Themes Of Stifled Screams: The Awakening / Themes Of Stifled Screams: Bowels Of Murder / Themes Of Stifled Screams: The Wail Of The Tartarean Wells / Themes Of Stifled Screams: It Dragged Her To Dark... / The Story Of Rose Haven: Snowfall / The Story Of Rose Haven: Dormant From Kiasmagoria / The Story Of Rose Haven: Phantasm And Evenfall.

NIGHT ON EARTH, Season Of Mist SOM 112 (2005). Evenfall (Intro) / Serpent Tongues / September And The One / Birth / Sinbread City / Night On Earth / Nemesis / Room Of Paintings.

DAYLIGHT DIES

NC, USA — *Guthrie Iddings (vocals), Barre Gamblings (guitar / bass), Jesse Haff (drums).*

North Carolina's Death Doomsters DAYLIGHT DIES issued the 2003 'No Reply' album through Relapse Records. The band is rooted in a 1996 musical union between guitarist Barre Gamblings and drummer Jesse Haff, their first recordings being dubbed 'The Long Forgotten' demo. Inducting singer Guthrie Iddings the following year the trio cut a second demo entitled 'Idle'. DAYLIGHT DIES would be boosted to quartet status with the introduction of bassist Egan O'Rourke. In 1998 Jesse Haff would also deputise for SORROW BEQUEST.

Following worldwide touring, which saw the band supporting KATATONIA across Europe and LACUNA COIL in Canada and the USA, vocalist Guthrie Iddings opted out. The band pulled in former WEHRWOLFE frontman Nathan Ellis in January of 2004.

DAYLIGHT DIES, announcing the addition of guitarist Charlie Shackelford to the group's ranks, cut a 2005 album entitled 'Dismantling Devotion' at Volume 11 Studios. The record was mixed by Jens Borden of Fascination Street Studios in Örebro, Sweden. Former bassist Matthew Golombisky lent his talents on the cello. During October the band contracted the album to Candlelight Records.

DAYLIGHT DIES supported MOONSPELL and KATATONIA for a North American tour commencing in October.

Idle EP, Tribunal (2000). Unending Waves / Piano Interlude One / Forfeiture Of Life / Piano Interlude Two / Stronger Days.

NO REPLY, Relapse RR 6536 (2002). The Line That Divides / I Wait / Hollow Hands / Four Corners / Unending Waves / In The Silence / Minutes Pass / Back In The World / Everything That Belongs.

DISMANTLING DEVOTION, (2006). A Life Less Lived / Dead Air / A Dream Resigned / All We Had / Solitary Refinement / Strive To See / Lies That Bind / Dismantling Devotion.

DE LIRIUM'S ORDER

KUOPIO, FINLAND — *Corpse (vocals), S.M. NekroC (guitar), Dr. Lirium (guitar), E.R. Insane (drums).*

DE LIRIUM'S ORDER, manifested in Kuopio during 1998 by guitarist S.M. NekroC ('a.k.a. Nekrocancer') and drummer E.R. Insane, offer a brutal, technical yet melodic brand of Metal. Initially the band started out as a quintet billed as ADRAMAN. Joined by guitarist V. Parviainen, and adopting the revised title of DE LIRIUM'S ORDER, their first experimental recordings, 'Termination In Surreal', would be caught on tape at the Perkele Studios in Kuopio.

The second set, February 2003's 'Morbid Brains', with Corpse, of WINTERWOLF, DEATHCHAIN, TWISTED SILENCE and TROLLHEIM'S GROTT, now having assumed lead vocal duties, was recorded by S.M. NekroC in his own Midgard Studio, these tracks leading to a contract with Woodcut Records in the Summer 2003. DE LIRIUM'S ORDER cut their opening commercial shot, a projected title of 'Extermination Network' being switched to 'Victim no. 52', at Tico Tico Studios in Kemi. Besides Corpse, session vocals came from Rutto von Kuolio.

On 15th April 2005 DE LIRIUM'S ORDER frontman Tuomas "Tuoppi" Lintulaakso was stabbed to death in Helsinki. The following month drummer EpiDemic joined up with SHADE EMPIRE. During 2005 Corpse was also operational with DEMILICH.

TERMINATION IN SURREAL, De Lirium's Order (2002). Introduction / Termination In Surreal / Metempsykhosis / Terve Ruumis, Sairas Sielu / Suolla / Koskenkorva, -30C / Of Hollow And Midwinter Night / Kalpea Muisto / Too Drunk / Convent Orgia / De Lirium's Ultimate Quietus.
Morbid Brains, De Lirium's Order (2003). Abomination / Through The Eyes Of A Murderer / The Sounds Of Mutilation / Masterpiece Of A Morbid Mind.
VICTIM NO. 52, Woodcut CUT 031 (2004). Sanctuary Of Incineration / Abomination / The Art Of Butchering / Masterpiece Of A Morbid Mind / Victim no. 52 / Through The Eyes Of A Murderer / Nightmare In Apartment 213 / Dr. Lirium Orders: Suffering / Pathologist's Perverse Fantasies / The Sunrise.

DEAD BY DAWN

POLAND — *Remik Rybalow (vocals), Mateusz Machnikowski (guitar), Artur Olkowicz (bass), Michal Zielinski (drums).*

DEAD BY DAWN emerged in February 2002, founded by erstwhile NOCTURN members Mateusz 'Mefius' Machnikowski and drummer Tomasz 'Starkey' Starczewski. That June former MESS AGE bassist Andrzej 'Grooby' Osmalek enrolled and in March of the following year the band was completed with the addition of singer Tomek Pawlak. In this formation, DEAD BY DAWN first performed live on 5th July 2003 at the 'Malbork' festival.

Both Osmalek and Pawlak exited in April 2004, being superseded by vocalist Remik 'Remov' Rubalow and the ADS NOCTEM, OBLIVION and MESS AGE credited bassist Artur Olkowicz for recording of demos. These sessions duly scored a label deal with Conquer Records. In March 2005 the band gained a valuable placing on the CRADLE OF FILTH headlined 'Metalmania' festival in Katowice. DEAD BY DAWN replaced drummer Tomasz Starczewski, who had apparently "lowered us with reason of disease", with Michal 'Troll' Zieliński of OBLIVION and DEFUCTO repute for recording of the album 'And Blind Is Leading And Blind'.

Dead By Dawn, Dead By Dawn (2004). The Betrayal / I Know Nothing.

DEAD END WORLD

VÄSTERVIK, SWEDEN — *Jonas Granvik (vocals), Kristian Andrén (vocals), Simon Johansson (guitar), Rogga Johansson (bass), Patrik Johansson (drums).*

Västervik Progressive Death Metal band DEAD END WORLD, announced in mid 2005 and bowing in with a demo billed 'The Isolation', combined an awesome array of Swedish Metal talent. Recorded at both The Barn Studios in Florida, USA and Solna Soundlab Studios in Stockholm the demo was mixed by Mike Wead of MERCYFUL FATE and KING DIAMOND..

Fronting the band would be dual singers Jonas Granvik of WITHOUT GRIEF on "Death vocals" and the STREET TALK, MEMENTO MORI, WUTHERING HEIGHTS and TAD MOROSE veteran Kristian 'Krille' Andrén on "Melodic" vocals. Musicians included guitarist Simon Johansson of FIFTH REASON, ABSTRAKT ALGEBRA and MEMORY GARDEN, bassist Roger Johansson of DEAD SUN, BLODSRIT, CARVE, DERANGED, RIBSPREADER and PAGANIZER with Patrik Johansson holding YNGWIE MALMSTEEN, STORMWIND and WITHOUT GRIEF credits on drums.

Simon Johansson also announced the formation of Progressive Doom outfit FIREGOD, a Swedish / Danish collaboration of high profile Metal veterans involving guitarist Mike Wead (a.k.a. Mikael Vikström), of WITCH, HEXENHAUS, MEMENTO MORI, ABSTRAKT ALGEBRA, KING DIAMOND and MERCYFUL FATE, bass player Hal Patino, of KING DIAMOND, and drummer Snowy Shaw (Tommy Helgesson), ex-KING DIAMOND and DREAM EVIL. Kristian Andrén joined BLOODBOUND in September.

The Isolation, Dead End World (2005) (Demo). The Isolation / A Place Where Everything Is Dead.

DEAD INFECTION

POLAND — *Jaro (vocals), Maly (guitar), Tocha (guitar / bass), Cyjan (drums).*

DEAD INFECTION commenced their Grindcore career with the 1992 cassette 'Start Human Slaughter'. The 1993 'World Full Of Remains' sessioned preceded the gut wrenching debut album, 'Surgical Disembowlment', released later that same year on the Morbid label. The band issued a live recording on cassette format during 1995 with tracks including cover versions of AGATHOCLES' 'Sentimental Hypocrisy' and NAPALM DEATH's 'Prison Without Walls'. During 1996 the band toured Europe in alliance with HAEMORRAGE and Japan's C.S.S.O. These shows would be captured for posterity at a Rotterdam gig for the EP 'Grind Over Europe'. A three way split EP in union with DEAD INFECTION's touring partners the record included a cover version of ULCEROUS PHLEGM's 'Consequence'.

Their 1998 album, 'The Greatest Shits', comprised almost in its entirety of cover versions. DEAD INFECTION tackled tracks such as REGURGITATE's 'Total Dismemberment Of A Female Corpse', EXTREME NOISE TERROR's 'Raping The Earth', GENERAL SURGERY's 'Slithering Maceration Of Ulcerous Facial Tissue', ULCEROUS PHLEGM's 'Consequence', the CARCASS classic 'Pungent Excruciation' and, er... the BEE GEES 'Stayin' Alive'.

The 2001 'Dead Singles Collection' included material originally found on the 'Grind Over Europe '96' compilation. 2003's collection comprised material culled from the 'Poppy-Seed Cake' EP, 'No Pate, No Mind' EP, 'The Greatest Shits' EP and the 'Grind Over Europe' 1996 cassette.

SURGICAL DISEMBOWELMENT, Morbid MR 010 CD (1993). Maggots In Your Flesh / Pathological View On The Alimentary Canal / Torsions / Undergo An Operation / After Accident / Xenomorph / Let Me Vomit / Spattered Birth / Start Human Slaughter / Deformed Creature.
Party's Over EP, Morbid Single Productions (1994) (Split single with BLOOD). From Anatomical Deeps / Life Of A Surgeon / Her Heart In Your Hands / The Firing Ground.
A CHAPTER OF ACCIDENTS, Morbid MR020 (1995). From The Anatomical Deeps / Autophagia / The End Of Love / Hospital / Incident Of Corsica / Airplane's Catastrophe / Little John's Story / Her Heart In Your Hand / Ambulance / Colitis Ulcerosa / Life Of A Surgeon / Fire In The Forest / Damaged Elevator / The Firing

Ground / Tragedy At The Railway Station / Don't Turn His Crushed Face On Me / Torn By The Lion Apart / The Merry-Go-Round.

Grind Over Europe '96, Obliteration (1996) (Split EP with HAEMORRAGE and C.S.S.O.). Airplane Catstrophe / Mru! / Consequence / Her Heart In Your Hands / After Accident / Sinful Life Of Franciszek Bula / The Merry Go-Round / Fire In The Forest / Tragedy At The Railroad Station.

No Pate, No Mind, Obscene Productions (1998). You Can't Help Falling In Love / No Pate, No Mind / He Makes Shit Who Makes Shit Last / Death By The Master Key / We Are All Polish / Where Is The General? / Uncontrollable Flatulence.

Dead Infection EP, Morbid (1998) (Split EP with C.S.S.O.). Mrs. Irene's Story / Poppy Seed Cake / Mysterious Wine / Flying Shit In Outer Space / Gas From Ass / After Accident / How to Stop Drinking.

THE GREATEST SHITS, Obscene Productions (1998). Psalms About Computers / Total Dismemberment Of A Female Corpse / Raping The Earth / D.I. / Clean The Scene / Slithering Maceration Of Ulcerous Facial Tissue / Stayin' Alive / Consequence / Owce / Prison Without Walls / Pungent Excruciation / Psalms About Storage Battery.

DEAD SINGLES COLLECTION, Timmy (2001). Poppy-Seed Cake / Mysterious Wine / Flying Shit In The Outer Space / Gas From Ass / After Accident Part III / No Pate, No Mind / He Makes Shit Who Makes Shit Last / Death By The Master-Key / We Are All Polish / Where Is The General? / Uncontrollable Flatulence / From The Anatomical Deeps / Life Of A Surgeon / Her Heart In Your Hands / The Firing Ground / Consequence / Uncontrollable Flatulence / Merry-Go-Round / Fire In The Forest / Tragedy At The Railway-Station.

THE LETHAL COLLECTION, Obscene Productions (2003). Poppy-Seed Cake / Mysterious Wine / Flying Shit In The Outer Space / Gas From Ass / After Accident (Part II) / No Pate, No Mind / He Makes Shit Who Makes Shit Last / Death By The Master-Key / We Are All Polish / Where Is General? / Uncontrollable Flatulence / From The Anatomical Deeps / Life Of A Surgeon / Her Heart In Your Hands / The Firing Ground / Total Dismemberment Of A Female Corpse / Raping The Earth / D.I. / Clean The Scene / Slithering Maceration Of Ulcerous Facial Tissue / Stayin' Alive / Consequence / Owce / Prison Without Walls / Pungent Excruciation / Consequence (Live) / Uncontrollable Flatulence (Live) / Merry-Go-Round (Live) / Fire In The Forest (Live) / Tragedy At The Railway Station (Live).

DEAD SAMARITAN

HÄMEENLINNA, FINLAND — *Pasi Lehtinen (vocals), Marko Saarinen (guitar), Marcus Moberg (bass), Janne Honkanen (drums).*

Hämeenlinna Death / Thrash act DEAD SAMARITAN, mentored by 20/20 VISION, SHARPEVILLE and AGUSTA BELLS guitarist Marko Saarinen, started out under a formative title of THE BEAUTY OF DYING. During 2000 the band was built up with the incorporation of singer Pasi Lehtinen, BLASHEMIA, JALOSTAMO and ARCADIAN drummer Janne "Homicide" Honkanen with the SHARPEVILLE credited Marcus Moberg on bass. Some six months later Teemu Raunio, of WITHERED GARDEN, was added on second guitar.

In September of 2001 THE BEAUTY OF DYING cut their debut, three song demo 'First Kill'. Their inaugural concert would be held at the Lahti 'Hellbound 3' event on 8th March 2002 sharing the stage with MUSTAN KUUN LAPSET, BEFORE THE DAWN, GLORIA MORTI, NOWEN and FUNERIS NOCTURNUM. Following this gig the band, drafting Jussi Leppänen to replace Raunio, adopted the DEAD SAMARITAN title. A promotional session entitled 'Dark Matter' was laid down in January of 2003. The demo 'Bone Hill Revelation', limited to 200 copies, was issued in July 2004.

Guitarist Jussi Leppänen exited in 2005.

Dark Matter, (2003) (Demo limited to 300 copies). Intro / The Gateway / Dark Matter / Skeleton On Your Shoulder.

Bone Hill Revelation, Dead Samaritan (2004) (Demo limited to 200 copies). Bone Hill Revelation (Intro) / Bleeding Ground / Battered Beyond Recognition / Nemesis Thy Name Is Sacred / Through The Cleansing Fire.

DEAD TO FALL

CHICAGO, IL, USA — *Jonathan Hunt (vocals), Bryan Lear (guitar), Seth Nichols (guitar), Justin Jakimiak (bass), Dan Craig (drums).*

Northern Chicago Metalcore outfit. DEAD TO FALL signed to Victory Records in January 2002 but lost the services of guitarist Matt Hartman that April. Their debut, 'Everything I Touch Falls to Pieces', would see production credits going to Barry Poynter. Live promotion commenced with US East Coast touring sharing stages with CALIBAN prior to inclusion on the nationwide 'Summer Blasphemy' dates packaged with INCANTATION, IMPALED, VEHEMENCE and DECAPITATED. August shows had the band paired with ONE NATION UNDER preceding headliners leading into November opening slots to MASTODON and ATREYU. Drummer Dan Craig then opted out in December.

Back on the road with new drummer Brad King, the group united with REMEMBERING NEVER and UNDYING for gigs throughout April and May 2003. DEAD TO FALL underwent a major split in the ranks during August, both Brad King and guitarist Bryan Lear exiting, leaving only vocalist Jonathan Hunt and bassist Justin Jakimiak remaining. Closing this chapter in their career, DEAD TO FALL put in a final gig with ex-drummer Dan Craig filling in for the evening. New draftees would be former 7 ANGELS 7 PLAGUES guitarist Matt Matera and drummer Evan Kaplan. Gigs scheduled for that December saw a return for founder member Antone Jones on second guitar.

DEAD TO FALL entered Trax East Studios in April 2004 to record a new album with producer Eric Rachel. Nationwide gigs throughout May and June saw the band partnered with SHATTERED REALM and A LIFE ONCE LOST. In November former drummer Dan Craig announced he was working on a new band venture entitled VALE with ex-RIPPING CORPSE bassist Dave Bizzigotti along with guitarists Dan Pocengal and ex-DISCIPLE 13 man Shawn Brandon. The following month Craig was ousted from this new act.

DEAD TO FALL would support MARTYR A.D. and THE HAUNTED for UK shows in February 2004. US gigs throughout May and June of 2005 had DEAD TO FALL packaged with TWELVE TRIBES, LOSA and FIGHT PARIS. The band engaged in US dates throughout February 2006 backing HIMSA, A LIFE ONCE LOST, THE ACACIA STRAIN and DARKEST HOUR. A new Eric Rachel produced album, entitled 'The Phoenix Throne', emerged in April through Victory Records. That same month the group returned to the road backed by FROM A SECOND STORY WINDOW, LIGEIA and ED GEIN. The band teamed up with DARKEST HOUR and CEPHALIC CARNAGE for an extensive European tour in June.

The group hit the road with A LIFE ONCE LOST, NAPALM DEATH, IMPALED, ARSIS and ANIMOSITY throughout November and December as part of the 'Death By Decibels' US tour. To open 2007 in January the band aligned with TOO PURE TO DIE, BLOOD RUNS BLACK and NIGHTS LIKE THESE. The band teamed up with WALLS OF JERICHO, KITTIE, 36 CRAZYFISTS and IN THIS MOMENT for "The Funeral For Yesterday Tour" beginning in early February. With little respite, hey were rapidly back into touring mode once again, forming up a set of European shows throughout May alongside THROUGH THE EYES OF THE DEAD, ION DISSONANCE and DYING FETUS hitting Germany, the UK, Poland, Denmark, Croatia and Belgium.

EVERYTHING I TOUCH FALLS TO PIECES, Victory VR179 (2002). Prologue / Memory / Eternal Gates Of Hell / Like A Bullet / Graven Image / Words Ignored / Cost Of A Good Impression / Tu Se Morta / Doraematu / Preying on the Helpless / Balance Theory.

VILLAINY AND VIRTUE, Victory VR221 (2004). Torn Self / Bastard Set Of Dreams / Stand Your Ground / You've Already Died / Villainy And Virtue / Little Birds / Blood Of The Moon / Cross Section / Master Exploder / Epilogue.

THE PHOENIX THRONE, Victory VR264 (2006). All My Heroes Have Failed Me / Womb Portals / Smoke & Mirrors / Servant Of Sorrow /

Chum Fiesta / Guillotine Dream (Slow Drugs) / Doomed To Failure / Clock Tower Corpse Collector / The Reptile Lord / Death & Rebirth.

DEAD TROOPER

NORWAY — *Andreas Paulsen (vocals / bass), Morten Müller (guitar), Birger Larsen (guitar), Are Sorknes (drums).*

DEAD TROOPER was founded during 1998 by the former SFW and DAMAGE duo of guitarists Morten Müller and Birger Larsen. Müller also had a brief association with CADAVARIZED. Frontman Andreas Paulsen is active with LEFT AMONG THE LIVING. Drummer Are Sorknes has a tradition with GUTHRUM, GRIEF EMPORIUM, OPPOSITE OF SERENITY and MØRKEMANNMENNENE.

DEAD TROOPER released the 2002 'Axewielders' demo. The '100 % Norwegian Thrash Metal' tape, combined with a DVD, arrived in 2004. Parting ways with Paulsen, an EP, 'Spiritual Funeral', was delivered in July 2005. Nico Benz filled in as session bassist Meantime, DEAD TROOPER members Are Sorknes and Birger Larsen worked up the JUJ project alongside SUSPERIA vocalist Athera. DEAD TROOPER would be rejoined by Andreas Paulsen in May.

The band aligned themselves with the 'Venting the Anger' Scandinavian tour of December 2005 featuring SUSPERIA, DEMOLITION and MIKSHA. DEAD TROOPER parted ways with drummer Are Sorknes in January 2006. Paulsen joined Torbjørn Sandvik's GLITTERTIND project in February. BLACK COMEDY drummer Marius Strand was enrolled in July.

Axewielders, Dead Trooper (2002) (Demo). Hail To The King / Violence Spiral / Burning Watchtowers / Dead And Dreaming / Beauty Extoled.
100 % Norwegian Thrash Metal, Dead Trooper (2004) (Demo, CD + DVD). Creed Of God / Dead And Dreaming / Hail To The King / Bloodred And Strong / Mold Of The Unspeakable / Creed Of God (Live) / Mold Of The Unspeakable (Live) / Hail To The King (Live) / Violence Spiral (Live video) / Resurrection (Live video).
Spiritual Funeral, Dead Trooper (2005). Spiritual Funeral / Dead Trooper / Thirst And Envy / Unite To Destroy / The Deathmatch.

DEADPOOL

ADELAIDE, SA, AUSTRALIA — *Adam Ritchie (vocals / guitar), Shane Dedrick (guitar), Ashley Banner (bass).*

Extreme Adelaide Metal band founded during 1994. DEADPOOL comprises talent from such former acts as MARTIRE, ORGY OF PIGS, SUCK KIDNEYS, CHIMERA 9 and HOBSON'S CHOICE. The initial duo of vocalist Andrew McIntyre and guitarist / drum programmer Shane Dedrick were subsequently joined by a second vocalist in Tony Waters and bass player Ashley Banner. In early 1996 second guitarist Adam Ritchie was enrolled and sometime later Waters lost his position. Following tour work McIntyre bowed out and Ritchie assumed lead vocal responsibilities. DEADPOOL have supported the likes of DEICIDE, NAPALM DEATH and STRAPPING YOUNG LAD. Both Waters and Dedrick are active with SLAUGHTER THOU.

DEADPOOL, Dominator (1997). Manipulate / Sturgis / Sica / B.C.B. / S.F.H. / Dreadlord / Lost / Taste / Disturbed / Endemic / Deja-vu / Xeper / Oblique / Haunted / Bloodscream / W.M.F. / H.I.V. / Blak / Digital Blak.

DEADSPAWN

SYDNEY, NSW, AUSTRALIA — *Dave Micallef (vocals / guitar), Aaron Bilbija (guitar), Bob Latsombath (bass), Wayne Morris (drums).*

Premier Sydney Death Metal band. The debut line-up of DEADSPAWN included the former DEPRESSION guitarist Aaron Bilbija alongside six string colleague Darren Jenkins of MORTALITY repute. The latter was soon enticed away into the ranks of CRYOGENIC and Dave Micallef took over the role. By mid 1996 DEADSPAWN, now with NEOPHOBIA man Graham Goode on the drums, performed their inaugural live gig. However, with Goode's priorities to NEOPHOBIA calling on him the drums were handed over to another ex-DEPRESSION member Wayne Morris.

The band cut the 'Emissions Of Power' album for the Warhead label in 1999. Live activity was infrequent save for a showing at the 2001 'Metal For The Brain' festival incorporating SYPHILIS man Peter Peric on bass. Matters would become confusing when Bilbija joined up with SYPHILIS. DEADSPAWN folded as both Micallef and Morris bowed out. Bilbija and Peric swiftly founded INFERNAL METHOD. Bilbija later figured in PSI.KORE's final line-up and by 2002 was operating with the high profile DAYSEND. Wayne Morris subsequently joined him in this outfit.

EMISSIONS OF REALITY, Warhead WHCD25 (1999). Scum / Victim Of The System / Scarblind / Force Fed / Merciless / I / Godshed / Way Of Life / Hunger Breeds.

DEATH

TAMPA, FL, USA — *Chuck Schuldiner (vocals / guitar / bass), Rick Rozz (guitar), Kam Lee (drums). Chuck Schuldiner (vocals / guitar / bass), Rick Rozz (guitar), Chris Reifert (drums). Chuck Schuldiner (vocals / guitar / bass), John Hand (guitar), Chris Reifert (drums). Chuck Schuldiner (vocals / guitar), Terry Butler (bass), Bill Andrews (drums). Chuck Schuldiner (vocals / guitar), Albert Gonzales (guitar), Terry Butler (bass), Bill Andrews (drums). Chuck Schuldiner (vocals / guitar), Mark Carter (guitar), Terry Butler (bass), Bill Andrews (drums). Chuck Schuldiner (vocals / guitar), James Murphy (guitar), Terry Butler (bass), Bill Andrews (drums). Chuck Schuldiner (vocals / guitar), Terry Butler (bass), Bill Andrews (drums). Chuck Schuldiner (vocals / guitar), Paul Masvidal (guitar), Terry Butler (bass), Bill Andrews (drums). Louis Carrisalez (vocals), Walter Thrashler (guitar), Terry Butler (bass), Bill Andrews (drums). Chuck Schuldiner (vocals / guitar), Walter Trachler (guitar), Terry Butler (bass), Bill Andrews (drums). Chuck Schuldiner (vocals / guitar), Paul Masvidal (guitar), Steve DiGeorgio (bass), Sean Reinert (drums). Chuck Schuldiner (vocals / guitar), Paul Masvidal (guitar), Scott Carino (bass), Sean Reinert (drums). Chuck Schuldiner (vocals / guitar), Andy LaRocque (guitar), Steve DiGeorgio (bass), Gene Hoglan (drums). Chuck Schuldiner (vocals / guitar), Craig Locicero (guitar), Steve DiGeorgio (bass), Gene Hoglan (drums). Chuck Schuldiner (vocals / guitar), Ralph Santolla (guitar), Steve DiGeorgio (bass), Richard Christy (drums). Chuck Schuldiner (vocals / guitar), Shannon Hamm (guitar), Scott Clendenin (bass), Richard Christy (drums). Chuck Schuldiner (vocals / guitar), Bobby Koelble (guitar), Kelly Conlan (bass), Richard Christy (drums).*

A genre breaking band, Florida's DEATH, centred upon frontman Chuck Schuldiner, would become one of the prime instigators of the Death Metal movement. Despite an ironclad hegemony enforced by Schuldiner, DEATH endured a bewildering succession of musicians that ultimately led to the group's downfall. Nevertheless, over six studio albums issued in the band's heyday, three are acknowledged as undisputed classics. The band leader's sense of purpose and probity forced DEATH along at a pace his players could often not keep up with as he strived towards Death Metal excellence.

Originally formed in 1984, the band's early demos were recorded with the founding teenage trio of guitarist Chuck Schuldiner, former THATCHER guitarist Rick Rozz (real name Frederick DiLillo) and drummer / vocalist Barney 'Kam Lee' under the name of MANTAS. The first fruits of their labours would be dubbed the 'Emotional' demo, issued in the Spring of 1984. By the summer a second session, recorded within the confines of the Schuldiner's garage, resulted in the 'Death By Metal' demo. MANTAS would then be dismantled but the exact same triumvirate regrouped as DEATH, re-releasing the

'Death By Metal' cassette in September complete with all new DEATH branding, artwork depicting a crude inverted crucifix and two grinning skulls plus an additional song 'Zombie'. That same month the group distributed a MANTAS show recording, thirteen tracks incorporating a rendition of VENOM's 'Poison', as 'Death Live 11/9/84'.

A third studio attempt, the five track 'Reign Of Terror' tape, would be laid down in October 1984, various versions of which sported a fluid track listing including a subsequently discarded instrumental 'Zombie Attack', upfront of an inaugural New Years Eve gig in Tampa as openers to NASTY SAVAGE. This gig would be committed to tape, dubbed 'Infernal Live', and sold to fans through Guillotine magazine.

In March 1985 Rozz made his exit. As a duo, Schuldiner and Lee came up with a further demo, the single track 'Rigor Mortis'. Later, guitarist Matt Olivio and bassist Scott Carlson from the Michigan based GENOCIDE brought DEATH, briefly, up to strength but Lee would then depart. Schuldiner would journey to San Francisco to generate a new band project with drummer Eric Brecht but this venture soon faltered, dispensing just one studio demo session 'Back From The Dead' in October and the concert set 'Live At Ruthies Inn' during December. As Schuldiner returned to Florida his former band mates Rozz and Lee were gearing up for the arrival on the scene of their new act, the influential MASSACRE.

Once again Schuldiner would relocate in an attempt to kick start his career, travelling to Toronto in January 1986 joining Canadians SLAUGHTER for a brief tenure. The SLAUGHTER collusion was fleeting, resulting in just one track 'Fuck Of Death'. Back in Florida, after resurrecting DEATH with drummer Chris Reifert, rehearsals were distributed, including a March 1986 three song tape featuring SLAUGHTER's 'Fuck Of Death'. More recording resulted in the April 'Mutilation' demo, landing the band a deal with Combat Records.

Initially DEATH convened to the Hollywood Music Grinder studios with producer Randy Burns. Also participating would be newly enrolled second guitarist John Hand. However, Hand was reportedly unable to keep pace with DEATH's material and had his services excused without recording a note. The first album 'Scream Bloody Gore', released in March of 1987 in North America by Combat and licensed to Music For Nations subsidiary Under One Flag imprint for a European issue in June, proved a somewhat pedestrian and all too predictable Death Metal outing, proving an unreliable marker for what was to come. DEATH, firmly centred on the erratic talent of Schuldiner, were to develop into a finely honed and technically proficient leader of the genre over successive releases.

Reifert departed in 1987 to form AUTOPSY releasing a four track demo in 1988 and a string of notoriously sickening albums thereafter. Schuldiner reconstituted DEATH by enlisting the bulk of MASSACRE- Rick Rozz on guitar, Terry Butler on bass and Bill Andrews on drums. This line up would undertake DEATH's first North American tour, including a performance at the infamous 'Milwaukee Metalfest'.

The November 1988 'Leprosy' album, produced by Dan Johnson at Morrisound Studios in April of 1988, solidified the band's burgeoning reputation. Although Terry Butler would be accredited bass on the album jacket, it was in reality Chuck Schuldiner that performed these duties. 'Leprosy' provided a staging post, marking the first transitional steps away from the familiar gore soaked subject matter with tentative steps into more philosophical realms laid out over songs of longer duration, a pattern which would increase with each successive release. DEATH, alongside FORBIDDEN, RAVEN and FAITH OR FEAR, would also feature on the live video 'The Ultimate Revenge' recorded in October at the Trocadero Theatre in Philadelphia.

DEATH toured Europe in 1989 alongside GANG GREEN and with support act DESPAIR prior to American dates with DARK ANGEL. However, before recording the third album Rozz returned to his act MASSACRE.

For the 'Spiritual Healing' album, committed to tape at Morrisound with Scott Burns and issued in March 1990, DEATH comprised Schuldiner, bassist Terry Butler and drummer Bill Andrews. Rehearsals were held with guitarist Mark Carter before erstwhile AGENT STEEL and HALLOWS EVE man JAMES MURPHY was drafted in. This latter figure greatly enhanced the cutting edge guitar quality of the band. 'Spiritual Healing' gave a platform for Schuldiner to expand upon his political and social observations such as human cloning, vigilantism and capitol punishment, and, although he was not yet in possession of the musicians to fully implement his ambitions at this stage, experiment with progressive leanings.

Following the album's release Murphy was unceremoniously fired, later joining OBITUARY, British thrash act CANCER, TESTAMENT and Danes KONKHRA as well as issuing solo albums. DEATH set about touring initially as a trio before adding CYNIC's Paul Masvidal on a temporary basis. This inclusion was significant as it provided the first clue towards the next stage of evolution for the band.

1990 American dates with CARCASS and PESTILENCE were completed using the services of ex-EVILDEAD guitarist Albert Gonzalez. DEATH then enlisted former ROTTING CORPSE guitarist Walter Trachsler for the remaining dates of their American tour with KREATOR.

Somewhat bizarrely DEATH toured Britain with KREATOR minus Schuldiner who reportedly was advised to stay in America for health reasons. Ex-DEVASTATION and ROTTING CORPSE drummer Louie Carrisalez filled in on vocals whilst Trachsler substituted on guitar. The fans refused to accept a touring line up minus Schuldiner- in spite of a series of bizarre allegations that he had renounced extreme music and was pursuing a Glam path (!), and the dates were far from a success. Upon their return to America both Butler and Andrews joined MASSACRE.

Schuldiner was quick to resurrect the band finally managing to attain the services of CYNIC's Paul Masvidal full time. Masvidal had in between stints with DEATH guested on the MASTER album of 1991 'On The Seventh Day God Created Master'. Alongside them were former SADUS bassist Steve DiGeorgio and CYNIC drummer Sean Reinert, this line-up recording the 'Human' album, released that October. Japanese editions hosted an uncharacteristic cover version of 'God Of Thunder', originally by KISS. 'Human', despite a less than focussed production, would go down in musical history as one of the quintessential Death Metal releases. Now having the requisite skills at his disposal, a gifted set of musicians and his own talents on the lyrical and songwriting front now realised, Schuldiner's aspirations towards technical yet intense metal had been fulfilled.

For DEATH's 1991 touring line-up Schuldiner was joined by Masvidal, Reinert and bassist Scott Carino. DEATH played a brace of concerts in Mexico during August 1991 supported by SADUS, CENOTAPH, LEPROSSY and BLACK THORN. After US and Canadian dates the band toured Europe as part of a Christmas package in alliance with NAPALM DEATH, DISMEMBER and CANNIBAL CORPSE and then Britain in February 1992 with support from VIOGRESSION. A useful promotional aid came with a video clip for the track 'Lack Of Comprehension'. Later that year Relativity Records would issue the compilation album 'Fate'.

Paul Masvidal and Sean Reinert got back to their project CYNIC in 1993, releasing their debut album 'Focus'. Carino went to FESTER and in 2000 was a member of LOWBROW. The revised version of DEATH now saw the inclusion of KING DIAMOND guitarist Andy LaRocque and DARK ANGEL's Gene Hoglan on drums. For recording of the June 1993 'Individual Thought Patterns' album Steve DiGiorgio stepped in once more. The album was duly backed up by the filming of a second video, for the song 'The Philosopher'. The record was widely predicted at being unable to scale the same glorious heights of 'Human' but reviewers and fans alike agreed that if fell only slightly short. Praise in particular was bestowed upon the veritable shredfest delivered by Schuldiner, LaRocque, DiGeorgio and Hoglan.

Commitments with KING DIAMOND prevented LaRocque from involving himself in live work. DEATH soldiered on enlisting Craig Locicero of FORBIDDEN for European shows and Ralph Santolla of EYEWITNESS for American dates, supported by Dutch act GOREFEST, and subsequent European festivals. Santolla would later come to the fore in the Melodic Rock community with acts such as MILLENIUM and MONARCH.

The 'Symbolic' album, the first for new label Roadrunner emerging in March 1995, was to have been recorded with LaRocque and former WATCHTOWER and RETARDED ELF bassist Doug Keyser but the guitarist was obliged to recording of the KING DIAMOND album 'The Spider's Lullaby' and no fee could be agreed for the bassist. DiGeorgio and LaRocque departed in early 1995 to be replaced by ex-PAIN PRINCIPLE bassist Kelly Conlon and guitarist Bobby Koelble. DEATH toured America with NEVERMORE the same year. Kelly Conlon would team up with MONSTROSITY and later VITAL REMAINS.

Surrounded by this confusion, Schuldiner still somehow managed to pull off another near perfect example of the genre, 'Symbolic' universally recognised as the closing chapter of DEATH's triptych of genius. The fractious nature of the band's existence though had taken its toll.

Schuldiner changed tack completely later the same year putting DEATH on ice and generating a new project CONTROL DENIED very much in the power metal mould. Originally Schuldiner was to work with the original WINTER'S BANE vocalist but he was to be lured away for a more permanent liaison with WICKED WAYS. CONTROL DENIED was now down to Schuldiner, bassist Brian Benson and drummer Chris Williams.

Another version of the band saw Schuldiner and Williams joined by guitarist Shannon Hamm and Scott Clendenin on bass, both of TALONZFURY. Although CONTROL DENIED had recorded an album's worth of material and received offers from various labels Williams would soon depart, replaced by ex-BURNING INSIDE and ACHERON drummer Richard Christy.

The outcome was somewhat inevitable and DEATH announced their reformation in October with a line-up of Schuldiner, guitarist Shannon Hamm, drummer Richard Christy and a returning Steve DiGeorgio on bass, the latter still retaining his fulltime participation in SADUS. DiGeorgio also reunited with another ex-DEATH man guitarist JAMES MURPHY for one of his side projects DISINCARNATE.

DEATH duly returned to the scene in April 1997, back on European soil and heading up the 'Full Of Hate' Easter festivals alongside OBITUARY, ENTOMBED, SAMAEL, NEUROSIS, CROWBAR, KILLING CULTURE and STRAPPING YOUNG LAD. The group signed to the aggressive Nuclear Blast label for 1998's 'Sound Of Perseverance', an album which saw a further progression towards straight heavy metal. Schuldiner was aided in this effort by Hamm, Christy and bassist Scott Clendenin. The album included a stab at JUDAS PRIEST's 'Painkiller'.

Ex-DEATH drummer Gene Hoglan would turn up on the drums for cult Norwegian outfit OLD MAN'S CHILD's 1998 album 'Ill Natured Spiritual Invasion'. Meantime touring found DEATH on the road in Europe with BENEDICTION and America sharing the bill with high profile Swedes HAMMERFALL.

Although 1999 heralded the welcome release of Schuldiner's CONTROL DENIED album, 'The Fragile Art Of Existence', fate dealt a cruel blow when it was announced that the frontman was diagnosed with a brain tumour. The frontman, who had learnt of the disease on his 31st birthday, had an operation in January and spent the bulk of the year in recuperation. The same year the Century Media label would unveil an impressive 5 album vinyl box set.

2000 found Christy back on the drum stool aiding fellow Deathsters INCANTATION for their live commitments before touring with ICED EARTH. DiGeorgio meantime was found to be part of the Metal 'All star' DRAGONLORD project of TESTAMENT guitarist Eric Peterson. Meantime ex drummer Chris Reifert created ABCESS and by 2000 THE RAVENOUS with STORMTROOPERS OF DEATH bassist Dan Lilker and NECROPHAGIA's Killjoy.

Veteran British Hardcore merchants NAPALM DEATH paid homage in their own oblique way by including a DEATH cover on their 'Leaders Not Followers' album, although the song in question was from an early demo and does not appear on any official DEATH release.

Schuldiner, now receiving the experimental drug Vincristine, was still very ill by mid 2001 and the Hammerheart America label organised an online auction to raise funds for a second operation. Among the items auctioned off was one of Chucks own guitar and a Steve DiGiorgio custom bass. The Nuclear Blast label would pitch in by releasing the 'Live In L.A. (Death & Raw)' album. Issued on both CD and double vinyl album formats the recordings were taken direct from the soundboard at the band's Whiskey A Go Go show on the 'Sound Of Perseverance' dates. Across America and Europe the extreme Metal community rallied to the cause putting on numerous benefit shows.

Chuck Schuldiner passed away on the 13th December 2001.

During 2002 DEATH veterans would be active upon the scene. Bassist Kelly Conlon joined the Boston based Progressive Metal act INFINITY MINUS ONE and Gene Hoglan, besides his work with STRAPPING YOUNG LAD, would form part of the reconstituted DARK ANGEL line up. As 2003 drew in plans were announced for a DEATH tribute album involving erstwhile DEATH guitarist JAMES MURPHY, ex-MALEVOLENT CREATION vocalist Brett Hoffmann, ex-MALEVOLENT CREATION and SUFFOCATION drummer Dave Culross and CKY guitarist Deron Miller. This album, by early 2004 being dubbed 'Within The Mind— In Homage To The Musical Legacy Of Chuck Schuldiner' later added the SLIPKNOT pairing of Mick Thomson and Paul Gray, MUDVAYNE's Ryan Martinie and Chad Gray, ICED EARTH drummer Richard Christy, TESTAMENT's Chuck Billy and Eric Peterson, the PAINMUSEUM and HALFORD credited Mike Chlasciak, Jean-François Dagenais of KATAKLYSM, Patrick Mameli from PESTILENCE, Luc Lemay of GORGUTS and Peter Tägtgren of HYPOCRISY. In June both guitarist Matt Bachand and drummer Jason Bittner of SHADOWS FALL also sessioned. DARKEST HOUR guitarist Kris Norris' contributions would be recorded backstage at the 'Ozzfest' Tampa Amphitheater concert.

It would be learned that erstwhile DEATH guitarist Bobby Koelble, having performed on the bands 1995 release 'Symbolic', was now the driving force behind the Latin and World Music inspired, Orlando based JUNKIE RUSH.

Karmageddon Media 2004 releases included the 'Zero Tolerance' archive sets of demo and live material. The first album comprised DEATH's 1985 'Infernal Death' and 1986 'Mutilation' demos alongside previously unreleased demo recordings from CONTROL DENIED. 'Zero Tolerance II' would be made up of the first MANTAS demo 'Death By Metal' from 1984, the 'Reign Of Terror' session from the same year and a DEATH live show recorded at the After Dark club in Texas during the 'Spiritual Healing' tour in 1990. Although as recordings these sets were welcome additions to the Schuldiner legacy, the manner of their release was unfortunately overcast with controversy, with very public legal spats between Chuck's mother and the Dutch label. This bitterness resulted in the final product being sadly sub-par in presentation and backed by almost non existent promotion.

Former band members continued to be active throughout the scene. Paul Masvidal and Sean Reinert re-emerged that year in Prog Rock outfit AEON SPOKE, touting the album 'Above The Buried Cry'. March 2006 found Steve DiGeorgio involving

DEATH

himself in a studio collaboration with singer Björn Strid, of SOILWORK, TERROR 2000 and COLDSEED, Glen Alvelais from FORBIDDEN, TESTAMENT and LD/50 and Jeremy Colson of the STEVE VAI band, MARTY FRIEDMAN, MICHAEL SCHENKER, APARTMENT 26, DALI'S DILEMMA and LD/50 repute.

Announced in April 2006, both DEATH players vocalist Kam Lee and bassist Terry Butler were revealed to have formed retro Thrash / Death Metal combo DENIAL FIEND, co-assembled by an elite cast comprising guitarist Sam Williams, previously with DOWN BY LAW, and erstwhile NASTY SAVAGE drummer Curt Beeson.

Death By Metal, Death (1984) (Demo cassette). Legion Of Doom / Zombie / Power Of Darkness / Death By Metal / Evil Dead (Live).
Live 11/9/84, Death (1984) (Live demo cassette). Mantas / Summoned To Die / Evil Dead / Beyond The Unholy Grave / Reign Of Terror / Power Of Darkness / Poison / Corpse Grinder / Legion Of Doom / Zombie / Witch Of Hell / Slaughterhouse / Death By Metal.
Reign Of Terror, Death (1984) (Demo cassette). Corpse Grinder / Summoned To Die / Witch Of Hell / Reign Of Terror / Slaughterhouse.
Infernal Live, Death (1985) (Live demo cassette). Intro / Infernal Death / Summoned To Die / Evil Dead / Beyond The Unholy Grave / Reign Of Terror / Power Of Darkness / Slaughterhouse / Legion Of Doom / Curse Of The Priest / Archangel / Death By Metal / Corpse Grinder.
Rigor Mortis, Death (1985) (Demo). Rigor Mortis.
Back From The Dead, Death (1985) (Demo). Intro / Back From The Dead / Mutilation / Reign Of Terror / Beyond The Unholy Grave / Baptized In Blood / Legion Of Doom / Skill To Kill.
Live At Ruthies Inn, Death (1985) (Live demo cassette). Back From The Dead / Reign Of Death / Legion Of Doom / Infernal Death / Archangel / Corpsegrinder / Skill To Kill / Baptized In Blood.
Rehearsal #12, Death (1986) (Rehearsal demo). Land Of No Return / Zombie Ritual.
Rehearsal '86, Death (1986) (Rehearsal demo). Fuck Of Death / Land Of No Return / Zombie Ritual.
Mutilation, Death (1986) (Demo). Land Of No Return / Zombie Ritual / Mutilation.
SCREAM BLOODY GORE, Under One Flag FLAG 12 (1987). Infernal Death / Zombie Ritual / Denial Of Life / Sacrificial / Mutilation / Regurgitated Guts / Baptized In Blood / Torn To Pieces / Evil Dead / Scream Bloody Gore / Beyond The Unholy Grave / Land Of No Return.
LEPROSY, Under One Flag FLAG 24 (1988). Leprosy / Born Dead / Forgotten Past / Left To Die / Pull The Plug / Open Casket / Primitive Ways / Choke On It.
SPIRITUAL HEALING, Under One Flag FLAG 38 (1990). Living Monstrosity / Altering The Future / Defensive Personalities / Within The Mind / Spiritual Healing / Low Life / Genetic Reconstruction / Killing Spree.
HUMAN, Roadrunner RC 9238 (1991). Flattening Of Emotions / Suicide Machine / Together As One / Secret Face / Lack Of Comprehension / See Through Dreams / Cosmic Sea / Vacant Planets.
INDIVIDUAL THOUGHT PATTERNS, Roadrunner RR 9079CD (1993). Overactive Imagination / Jealousy / Trapped In A Corner / Nothing Is Everything / Mentally Blind / Individual Thought Patterns / Destiny / Out Of Touch / Philosopher / In Human Form.
SYMBOLIC, Roadrunner RR 8957-2 (1995). Symbolic / Zero Tolerance / Empty Words / Sacred Serenity / 1,000 Eyes / Without Judgement / Crystal Mountain / Misanthrope / Perennial Quest.
THE SOUND OF PERSEVERANCE, Nuclear Blast 27361 63372 (1998). Scavenger Of Human Sorrow / Bite The Pain / Spirit Crusher / Story To Tell / Flesh And The Power It Holds / Voice Of The Soul / To Forgive Is To Suffer / A Moment Of Clarity / Painkiller. Chart position: 60 GERMANY.
LIVE IN L.A. (DEATH & RAW), Nuclear Blast NB 0554-2 (2001). The Philosopher / Spirit Crusher / Trapped In A Corner / Scavenger Of Human Sorrow / Crystal Mountain / Flesh And The Power ... / Zero Tolerance / Zombie Ritual / Suicide Machine / Together As One / Empty Words / Symbolic / Pull The Plug.
LIVE IN EINDHOVEN, Nuclear Blast (2001). The Philosopher / Trapped In A Corner / Crystal Mountain / Suicide Machine / Together As One / Zero Tolerance / Lack Of Comprehension / Flesh And The Power It Holds / Flattening Of Emotions / Spirit Crusher / Pull The Plug.
CHUCK SCHULDINER: ZERO TOLERANCE I, Karmageddon Media (2004). (Untitled) (CONTROL DENIED) / (Untitled) (CONTROL DENIED) / (Untitled) (CONTROL DENIED) / (Untitled) (CONTROL DENIED) / Infernal Death (1985 demo) / Baptized In Blood (1985 demo) / Archangel (1985 demo) / Land Of No Return (1986 demo) / Zombie Ritual (1986 demo) / Mutilation (1986 demo).
CHUCK SCHULDINER: ZERO TOLERANCE II, Karmageddon Media KARMA 056 (2004). Legion Of Doom (1984 demo) / Evil Dead (1984 demo) / Beyond The Unholy Grave (1984 demo) / Power Of Darkness (1984 demo) / Death By Metal (1984 demo) / Corpse Grinder (1985 demo) / Summon To Die (1985 demo) / Zombie (1985 demo) / Witch Of Hell (1985 demo) / Reign Of Terror (1985 demo) / Slaughterhouse (1985 demo) / Living Monstrosity (Live: After Dark Club, Texas, 1990) / Pull The Plug (Live: After Dark Club, Texas, 1990) / Zombie Ritual (Live: After Dark Club, Texas, 1990) / Altering The Future (Live: After Dark Club, Texas, 1990) / Left To Die (Live: After Dark Club, Texas, 1990) / Spiritual Healing (Live: After Dark Club, Texas, 1990) / Defensive Personalities (Live: After Dark Club, Texas, 1990) / Mutilation (Live: After Dark Club, Texas, 1990).

DEATH BREATH

STOCKHOLM, SWEDEN — *Jörgen Sandström (vocals), Robert Persson (guitar), Mange Hedquist (bass), Nicke Andersson (drums).*

Concocted in Stockholm during late 2005, the deliberately retro-styled Death Metal combo DEATH BREATH was initiated by former ENTOMBED drummer and THE HELLACOPTERS frontman Nicke Andersson. He would be joined by frontman Jörgen Sandström, who had previously fronted the Swedish Death Metal act GRAVE, played with Andersson in ENTOMBED as the group's bassist and holds both VICIOUS ART and THE PROJECT HATE credentials, plus guitarist Robert Persson of THUNDER EXPRESS. Bass would be handled by Mange Hedquist. REPULSION vocalist / bassist Scott Carlson also guested on album recordings.

DEATH BREATH signed to Black Lodge Records in May 2006. Upfront of the album release a limited edition single, of the 'Death Breath' anthem, hosted two exclusive tracks in 'Corpses of Death', featuring Markus Karlsson of I QUIT on vocals, and 'Matricide'. Relapse Records issued the 'Stinking Up The Night' album in the USA.

The band parted ways with bassist Magnus Hedquist in early October, simply stating "The reasons for his departure are, shall we say, none of your business". DEATH BREATH made its live debut on October 26th at Debaser Medis in Stockholm. For this show the band unit was expanded with the introduction of guests Scott Carlson, from REPULSION, and Jörgen Sandström, of GRAVE, ENTOMBED and VICIOUS ART.

Black Lodge issued an EP, 'Let It Stink', in February 2007.

Death Breath, Black Lodge BLOD 7002 (2006). Death Breath / Corpses Of Death / Matricide.
STINKING UP THE NIGHT, Black Lodge BLOD 044CDL (2006) (Gatefold digipack CD). Death Breath / Chopping Spree / Heading For Decapitation / Dragged Through The Mud / Coffins Of The Unembalmed Dead / A Morbid Mind / Reduced To Ashes / Christ All Fucking Mighty / Flabby Little Things From Beyond / Cthulhu Fhtagn!
STINKING UP THE NIGHT, Black Lodge BLOD 044CD (2006) (CD release). Death Breath / Chopping Spree / Heading For Decapitation / Dragged Through The Mud / Coffins Of The Unembalmed Dead / A

Morbid Mind / Reduced To Ashes / Christ All Fucking Mighty / Flabby Little Things From Beyond / Cthulhu Fhtagn!

STINKING UP THE NIGHT, Black Lodge BLOD 044PD (2006) (Vinyl picture disc). Death Breath / Chopping Spree / Heading For Decapitation / Dragged Through The Mud / Coffins Of The Unembalmed Dead / A Morbid Mind / Reduced To Ashes / Christ All Fucking Mighty / Flabby Little Things From Beyond / Cthulhu Fhtagn!

STINKING UP THE NIGHT, Black Lodge BLOD 044LP (2006) (Vinyl version). Death Breath / Chopping Spree / Heading For Decapitation / Dragged Through The Mud / Coffins Of The Unembalmed Dead / A Morbid Mind / Reduced To Ashes / Christ All Fucking Mighty / Flabby Little Things From Beyond / Cthulhu Fhtagn!

STINKING UP THE NIGHT, Relapse 766745 (2006) (USA release). Death Breath / Chopping Spree / Heading For Decapitation / Dragged Through The Mud / Coffins Of The Unembalmed Dead / A Morbid Mind / Reduced To Ashes / Christ All Fucking Mighty / Flabby Little Things From Beyond / Cthulhu Fhtagn!

Let It Stink, Black Lodge (2007). Giving Head To The Dead / His Protoplasmic Worship / Maimed And Slaughtered / Dead But Walking / Lycanthropy / Sacrifice / Twisted In Distaste.

DEATH BY DESIGN

FRANCE — *Marc (vocals), Beuz (vocals / guitar), Erick (guitar), Jorys (bass), Nicko (drums).*

Based in the Parisian suburb of Rambouillet DEATH BY DESIGN started life during the mid nineties under the original title of NO SOBRIETY, a Thrash / Death combination, which first demoed during 1998 with 'Sourisathanelas'. NO SOBRIETY featured on a S.U.P. tribute album with their rendition of 'The Accomplishment' on Inner Side Records in 2001, following this with the EP 'Here Comes The Breath', recorded at Sextan Studios in Malakoff. Their efforts were rewarded with a 'Demo of the month' accolade in the French 'Rock Hard' magazine.

Switching the band name to DEATH BY DESIGN, the line up underwent an overhaul, inducting former members of CIRRHOSIS, QUADRYSS and FREEWAY. In this incarnation the band adopted a more brutal approach, utilising both clean and Death vocals as evidenced on the 'Discreation' album, released by Thundering Records in April of 2004.

DISCRETION, Thundering (2004). Infared Eyes / Awake / Evolution Denied / E-Side / Jeffrey / Lost / Inside The Maze / J-Side / Freakshow / Death By Design.

DEATH DU JOUR

TURKU, FINLAND — *T.K. (vocals / guitar), O.M. (guitar), Pasi Bunda (bass), T.F. (drums).*

The origins of Turku's DEATH DU JOUR, a technically Progressive Death Metal unit, can be traced back to the 2000 annual West Coast Holocaust event when vocalist / guitarist T.K. and bassist P.B. (the FALL OF THE LEAFE credited Pasi Bunda) decided to forge a fresh band project. The following year witnessed an evolutionary process of fluid membership but during 2001 guitarist O.M. was located and in the Summer of the following year drummer T.F. With this settled line-up DEATH DU JOUR cut the opening EP 'Gamashinoch'. For release in April 2003.

The band toured Finland in April of 2004 allied with CENTINEX and REPUGNANT. An album, 'Fragments Of Perdition', recorded at Pop-Studio with producer Mika Haapasalo for Golden Lake Productions, was completed in August. The 'Destruction of Finland' tour followed in October allied with GODHATE, INSISION and HATEFORM. 'Fragments Of Perdition' arrived in stores early November.

Gamashinoch EP, Death Du Jour (2003). All Flowers Rot (Transact Exitus) / Artificial Excessive Excessivities / Icing World Hunger / Gamashinoch.

FRAGMENTS OF PERDITION, Golden Lake Productions GOLDCD18 (2004). Grace By Chalice Of Anger / Fragments Of Perdition / Embittering Cicatricies / Harlot Deliverance / Weakmeat Vortex / Satire Of Caustic Lunacy / Triangle Gallows / Dogma—The Suffering.

Gamashinoch EP, Hammermill HMILL 001 (2005). All Flowers Rot (Transact Exitus) / Artificial Excessive Excessivities / Icing World Hunger / Gamashinoch.

DEATH OF MILLIONS

AUSTIN, TX, USA — *Chuck Salvo (vocals), Brian Morrison (guitar), Lee Ribera (guitar), Brendan Bigelow (bass), Mark Perry (drums).*

An extreme Texan Death Metal outfit assembled during 1994 by vocalist Chuck Salvo, guitarist Lee Ribera and Mark Perry on the drums. Second guitarist Brian Morrison was enrolled in 1995 and bass player Brendon Bigelow in 1997. DEATH OF MILLIONS guitarist Lee Ribera has connections with NOKTURNEL whilst drummer Mark Perry has ties to INCANTATION. The band debuted with the 1995 demo 'Ritual Killing' before a 1996 effort 'Frozen'. The group successively displayed their mettle with appearances at the Milwaukee Metal Fest in 1996, 1997, 1998, and 1999. The band also put in showings at the San Antonio 'November To Dismember' event and 2000's 'November To Dismember' gig in Los Angeles.

The 1999 album 'Frozen', released via Singapore's Dies Irae Productions, closed with a cover version of TWISTED SISTER's 'Burn In Hell'. Two further demos, 'Lay in Wait' and 'The Shadow of the Temples', came upfront of a deal with the Blackened label.

Brendan Bigelow co-founded IGNITOR in mid 2004, a "True" Metal band comprising Erika Swinnich, former vocalist of AUTUMN TEARS, alongside former AGONY COLUMN guitarist Stuart Laurence, Pat Doyle of THE OFFENDERS and Beverly Barrington of T.A.N.G.

FROZEN, Dies Irae (1999). Abortion Retrieval / Empty Shell Relief / Dead Corpse / No Excuse / Death Is The Love Drug / Diane / Frozen / Salvational Rot / The Feasting / Majestic Black / Ceremonial Rites / Kidnap Victim #12: Razorblade Artwork / Burn In Hell.

STATISTICS AND TRAGEDY, Blackened BLACK 050 (2003).

DEATH REALITY

MÜGELN, GERMANY — *Jürgen Naumann (vocals), Michael Müller (guitar), Michael Casch (guitar), Tobias Rüster (bass), Martin Ryzerski (drums).*

Mügeln / Sachsen based DEATH REALITY, founded in February 1996 by teenagers drummer Martin Ryzerski, guitarist Michael Gasch and vocalist Jürgen Naumann with later addition Tobias Rüster on bass, released the October 1998 demo 'Ancient Rebirth', selling 300 copies, followed by a 1999 demo 'Butchered Souls'. A second guitarist would be added in the form of MORTAL SCUM's Michael Müller.

The Remission label issued the debut album 'Blasphemous Bleeding' in 2001. DEATH REALITY swiftly maintained the momentum by entering Soundlodge Studio in Oldenburg, under the direction of producer Jörg Uken, to record 'Flesh Still Feeds'. Although unlisted on the album credits the track listing included a cover of OBITUARY's 'Threatening Skies'.

Embalmed With Cunt Liquid EP, Perverted Taste (2001) (Split EP with SCURVY). Eternal Suffocation / Embalmed With Cunt Liquid.

BLASPHEMOUS BLEEDING, Remission (2001). Rise of The Dead / Condemned For Intestine Penetration / Splattered Bones / Chained By Maggots / Butchered Souls / Embalmed With Cunt Liquid / Killing With Pleasure / Blasphemous Bleeding / Mutual Mortifying / Eternal Suffocation / Under My Boots / Violent Domination.

FLESH STILL FEEDS, Remission RMR 003 (2003). Among Cerebral Depths / Flesh Still Feeds / Witness Your Death / Defiled Virginity / A Colder Ejaculation / Spawned Decay / Procreation Of Sickness / We Hate And So We Gather / Massacre Masters / Departed In Tragedy.

BLOODPRINTS, Morbid (2004). Bloodprints / Your Epitaph Is Written / Awaren The Revenge / Trailblazer / Ingenuous Thoughts / Wages Of Eternal Death / Divine Sickening Tragedy / Chamber Of Desolation / Carnal Desires.

DEATHBOUND

VAASA, FINLAND — *Kai Jaakkola (vocals), Petri Seikkula (guitar), Tommi Konu (bass), Mika Q (drums).*

Vaasa Death Metal band. The 2002 DEATHBOUND membership roster boasts a worthy Death Metal pedigree with frontman Kai Jaakkola holding down a reputation with DUSKFALL, NECROMICON and MONSTER SPANK, guitarist Petri Seikkula citing credits with BLACK DAWN as well as AND OCEANS, bassist Tommi Kontz activity with HELLMASKER and drummer Mika Q claiming AND OCEANS, BLACK DAWN and ROTTEN SOUND credentials.

The group has its roots in the early 90's act UNBOUND. By 1995 the title of TWILIGHT had been put into effect, this band starting life with a roster of vocalist Kai Jaakkola, guitarist Petri Seikkula, bassist Tommi Konu and Toni Erkkilä on the drums. In this incarnation TWILIGHT issued a brace of demos 'Twilight', in December 1995, and 'The Melancholy Of The Northern Landscapes' before the band was put on hold due to the intrusion of Finland's national service policy. Activity was sporadic until 1998 when the band regrouped with the addition of BEYOND DREAMS guitarist Fred Andersson and drummer Robert Sundelin of SATARIEL and an ex-member of NECROMICON. Konu, as 'Hellkuntz', participated in recording of the Swedish band HELLMASKER's 'Probably The Best Band In The World' demo. The band recorded the 'Flames Of Madness' demo in September 1999 upon completion of which Andersson's place was taken by NECROMICON's Nick Sundqvist.

During 2000 the decision was taken to revert back to the formative title of UNBOUND due to the increasing media presence of the Italian Power Metal band TWILIGHT. Bringing in Mikael Sandorf on the drums the band laid down a fresh demo 'Elaborate The Torture' in November 2000 before switching the group name again—this time to DEATHBOUND as Blastmor of THYRANE became next in line to occupy the drum stool but by 2002 Mika Q had taken the role.

DEATHBOUND signed to the Woodcut label for a debut May 2003 album release 'To Cure The Insane—With Insanity'. Former drummer Mika Q rejoined DEATHBOUND as the group's bass player in 2004. That November the group entered Soundlab Studios in Örebro, Sweden to commence recording their second album, 'Syringe—Death And Addictions', due in early 2005 via Dynamic Arts Records. Promotion included Finnish shows in December alongside label mates SCORNGRAIN and Sweden's CULT OF LUNA although the band parted ways with Mika Aalto that same month, drafting Sami Latva as substitute. A split seven-inch single with fellow Finns DEATHCHAIN would also be due in January 2006 through Dynamic Arts Records. The following month drummer Sami Latva joined ROTTEN SOUND.

Dynamic Arts re-issued the album 'To Cure the Sane—With Insanity' in May, adding five live tracks recorded at the Tuska Open Air 2005 event, a video for the song 'Doomsday Comfort' plus new artwork. Quoting a title of 'We Deserve Much Worse', DEATHBOUND entered the recording studio on September 11th to craft a new album.

In January 2007 DEATHBOUND supported NAPALM DEATH for touring in Scandinavia and the Baltic States.

Elaborate The Torture, Deathbound (2000) (Demo). Elaborate The Torture / I Am Thy Father's Misery / Initiating The Fires Above.
TO CURE THE SANE WITH INSANITY, Woodcut CUT026 (2003). One Mans Hell Is Another Mans Heaven / Without Pain / Whitecoatparanoia / As Reluctance Grows / Treacherous Breed / Silent City Deathcount / Consumed / The House Of The Silent And Friendly / The Flesh Is The Cage.
DOOMSDAY COMFORT, Dynamic Arts DYN009 (2005). Ghost Among The Dead / Doomsday Comfort / Extinct / Inside The Nothingness / Chokehold / Take Left / For The Rats / I God / Spill The Blood / In The Mud / Hell Today—No Tomorrow / Remake The Improved / Gasmask.
Deathchain / Deathbound, Dynamic Arts DYN007 (2006) (Split single with DEATHCHAIN). Soulburn / Dead And Gone.
WE DESERVE MUCH WORSE, Dynamic Arts DYN019 (2007). Deceiving Shortcuts / End The Guessing / Gain Control / Revolutions Against Nothing / Connected To Confusion / Torn / Debate Or Terminate / Preaching Back To Preachers / Betrayal Wears Your Face / No Disease Like Us / Final Element / A Fraction Of Truth / Never Been Worse / Rockthrowers Among Us / Landmine / Put The Blame On The Devil / Vansinne / Ward 77.

DEATHCON

BERGEN, NORWAY — *V'gandr (vocals / bass), Stanley (lead guitar), Dreggen (rhythm guitar), Mord (drums).*

Bergen Death Metal band DEATHCON, releasing the 2004 'Zerohuman' EP through Perverted Taste Records, feature HELHEIM's V'gandr on lead vocals and bass. V'gandr also fronts Viking Metal band CULT OF CATHARSIS, has sessioned for EINHERJER and performs bass guitar for AETERNUS. DEATHCON also includes the TAAKE and AMOK credited drummer Tormod Haraldson (a.k.a. 'Mord'), CULT OF CATHARSIS guitarist Dreggen and Stanley (Stian) from AMOK on lead guitar. Stanley joined AETERNUS in the Autumn of 2004.

In mid 2006 Mord and Dreggen joined the live line-up of BLACK HOLE GENERATOR. Dreggen also hooked up with GRIMFIST in August.

Zerohuman, Deathcon (2004) (Demo). Waste Of Life / City Without Soul / Delusions Of Grandeur / The Meaning Of Nothing / An Eye For The I.
Zerohuman EP, Perverted Taste PT 095 (2005). Waste Of Life / City Without Soul / Delusions Of Grandeur / The Meaning Of Nothing / An Eye For The I.
MONOTREMATA, Karisma KAR020 (2006). Existence Futile / Waste Of Life / Monotremata / Zerohuman / Delusions Of Grandeur / The Meaning Of Nothing / An Eye For The I / City Without Soul / Delusions Of Grandeur (Megalomania Mix).

DEATHGUY

THAILAND — *Thanit Thepsitrakorn (vocals / bass), Verapol Emaree (guitar), Nuttaphum Prapaiboon (guitar), Suppakit Chuersuwan (drums).*

Bangkok based Blackened Thrash—Death Metal act formed in August 1998. Following DEATHGUY's 1998 'Introduction' EP the founding duo of vocalist / bassist Thanit Thepsitrakorn (Joe) and guitarist Verapol Emaree (Ong) added second guitarist Nuttaphum Prapaiboon (Imm) and ex-ANNULAR ECLIPSE drummer Suppakit Chuersuwan (Link) to the line up. Nuttaphum is also active with Death Metal combo BLACK FIRE whilst Thanit has numerous side projects including Porn Metal band SHE'S GORE.

DEATHGUY's second release, the cassette 'The Secondary Quest', arrived in 2000. Trinity Records compiled earlier demo sessions to assemble the 2002 album release 'The Legend Of Romancer'. Toward the close of that year the single track promotion single 'The Beast' was recorded. Guitarist Nuttaphum Prapaiboon bowed out in 2003 as DEATHGUY switched away from their Black-Death direction into pure, brutal Death Metal.

Signing to Singapore's Vrykoblast Productions, DEATHGUY released 'Concentrate The Annihilation' in 2004 recorded at Ghost Studio in Bangkok, the band credited themselves as Zuppakit "Cerebral Assaulter", Verapol "Krush Kill and Destroy" and Thanit "Vacuum Butchering & Cardiac Excavator". Zilent Zlaughter Productions also issued a three way split EP 'Siamese Brutalism Attack' in union with SHE'S GORE and LACERATE.

THE SECONDARY QUEST—THE LEGEND OF ROMANCER, Trinity THK001 (2000). Ballad Of Sunset / Zero Frontier / Lust Murder / Lake Of Tears / Savage Seraphim / Black Swan / The Promised Land / Beheader / The Beast (Demo) / Marn / Den Sungkom.
Siamese Brutalism Attack, Zilent Zlaughter Productions (2003) (Split EP with SHE'S GORE and LACERATE). Beheader / The Beast.
CONCENTRATE THE ANNIHILATION, Vrykoblast Productions (2004). Hell Dominion (Reign Beyond Suffering / Degust The Blood (Sadistic Cannibal Meal) / Anathematic Damnation (The Fertilization

Of Damn) / Beheader (Human Head Collection) / Necronivora (Silent Murderous Supremacy) / Awake From Within (Cardiac Excavation) / Tyrant (Decaying Of All Civilization) / The Beast (Characteristic Of Devourer) / Cannibal Lust.

DEATHLESS

BARCELONA, SPAIN — *Emilio Canas (vocals), Michel Fidalgo (guitar), Jose Contreras (guitar), Antonio J. Canto (bass), Miquel J. Llodra (keyboards), Carlos Climent (drums).*

A melodic Death Metal band, based in the L´Hospitalet de Llobregat of Barcelona, initially titled LINE OF FIRE upon their formation in 1995. As DEATHLESS the band signed to the Pulverized label and recorded their debut album 'The Time To Be Immortal' during 1997 at Sweden's famous Sunlight Studios with Tomas Skogsberg handling production duties. However, Pulverized and DEATHLESS parted ways and the band would have to wait until 2000 until the record would finally be issued by the domestic Goldtrack label. A cassette variant would see issue in Thailand through the Dark Angel label. Released in Russia by the CD Maximum label in June of 2003, this new version of 'The Time To Be Immortal' added four bonus tracks taken from 2002 demo sessions. Dark Angel also issued the demo 'The Sound Of The New World' as an official cassette release during 2003, adding further demo tracks from 1996 sessions. In Indonesia the Disastrous Sounds imprint also published 'The Sound Of The New World' in early 2004.

DEATHLESS would undergo line up changes with drummer Jose Luis Gonzalez exiting in July of 2002, being superseded in August by Carlos Climent. That December the band added keyboard player Miquel J. Llodra. In September of 2004 the Voliac Rock Productions label re-issued the band's 2002 demo sessions as a 10" vinyl EP 'The Sounds Of The New World', this release restricted to 300 copies.

Promo '96, (1996). Razing Life / Two Ways.
THE TIME TO BE IMMORTAL, Goldtrack GT 011 CD (2000). Razing Life / Torture's Deep Inside My Mind / Two Ways / Under Fear / World's Heartbeat / The Price Of Our Wasting Lives / Where No Sun Shines / Law Of Fire / Holy Sepulchre / Years Later.
THE TIME TO BE IMMORTAL, Dark Angel ANGEL 017 (2000) (Thai cassette release). Razing Life / Torture´s Deep Inside My Mind / Two Ways / Under Fear / World´s Heartbeat / The Price Of Our Wasting Lives / Where No Sun Shines / Law Of Fire / Holy Sepulchre / Years Later.
Promo 2002, Deathless (2002). Worshippers Of Darkness / Distortionated Word / Wrong Again / The Sound Of The New World.
THE TIME TO BE IMMORTAL, CD Maximum CDM 0703-1435 (2003) (Russian release). Razing Life / Torture's Deep Inside My Mind / Two Ways / Under Fear / World's Heartbeat / The Price Of Our Wasting Lives / Where No Sun Shines / Law Of Fire / Holy Sepulchre / Years Later / Worshippers Of Darkness / Distortionated Word / Wrong Again / The Sound Of The New World.
THE SOUNDS OF THE NEW WORLD, Dark Angel DARK 007 MC (2003) (Thai cassette release). Worshippers Of Darkness / Distortionated Word / Wrong Again / The Sound Of The New World / Razing Life (Demo) / Two Ways (Demo) / Holy Sepulchre (Demo) / Under Fear (Demo) / Law Of Fire (Demo) / Where No Sun Shines (Demo) / World´s Heartbeat (Demo) / Years Later (Demo).
THE SOUNDS OF THE NEW WORLD, Disastrous Sounds DS 003 (2004) (Indonesian cassette release). Worshipers Of Darkness / Distortionated Word / Wrong Again / The Sound Of The New World / Razing Life (Demo) / Two Ways (Demo) / Holy Sepulchre (Demo) / Under Fear (Demo) / Law Of Fire (Demo) / Where No Sun Shines (Demo) / World´s Heartbeat (Demo) / Years Later (Demo).
The Sounds Of The New World, Voliac Rock Productions V001MLP (2004) (Limited edition 300 copies). Worshippers Of Darkness / Distortionated Word / Wrong Again / The Sounds Of The New World.

DEATHSTRIKE

CHICAGO, IL, USA — *Paul Speckmann (vocals / bass), Kirk Miller (guitar), Chris Mittelbrun (guitar), Bill Schmidt (drums).*

Project act of MASTER and ABOMINATION's Paul Speckman. DEATHSTRIKE was conceived by drummer Bill Schmidt and Speckmann during 1983, the pair both recent refugees from WARCRY. This unit issued the 'Trilogy Of Terror' demo and also scored a track on Metal Blade's 'Metal Massacre IV' compilation.

Although Schmidt took time out in 1984 to join MAYHEM the DEATHSTRIKE line up was finalised during January of 1985 with the introduction of former TRANSGRESSOR guitarist Chris Mittelbrun, second guitarist Kirk Miller and drummer John Leprich. Recordings would find Leprich struggling with the songs and so Schmidt duly made a return. The 'Fuckin' Death' demo was delivered in that same year.

In the Summer of 1985 Speckmann, Mittelbrun and Schmidt founded MASTER, thus signalling a closure for DEATHSTRIKE. Parallel with DEATHSTRIKE Speckmann would also be active with another project entitled FUNERAL BITCH. Subsequently Mittelbrun re-emerged as a member of SINDROME.

Speckmann teamed up with Czech veterans KRABATHOR in 2002. Schmidt turned up as a member of Glamsters DIAMOND REXX. In 2004 it was learned that guitarist Chris Mittelbrun has resurfaced as "Mick Mars" in the Chicago based MÖTLEY CRÜE tribute band dubbed THE CRÜE.

FUCKING DEATH, Nuclear Blast (1991).

DEATHWITCH

SWEDEN — *Reaper (vocals), Af Necrohell (guitar), Lady Death (bass), Terror (drums).*

DEATHWITCH is a side project act of SACRAMENTUM drummer Niklas 'Terror' Rudolfsson. A demo saw Rudolfsson joined by bassist Lady Death (Karin Blomqvist, also drummer of DRACENA), the mysterious Reaper on vocals and guitarist Af Necrohell (a.k.a. Mia of DRACENA). Following the first album 'Triumphant Devastation' both Lady Death and Alf Necrohell decamped. With the issue of second album 'Dawn Of Armageddon' Rudolfsson's priorities with SACRAMENTUM and SWORDMASTER put DEATHWITCH on ice for a period.

1998's 'The Ultimate Death' was produced by former KING DIAMOND guitarist Andy LaRocque. DEATHWITCH's line-up for this opus being Terror switching from drums to vocals, Doomentor on guitar, DISSECTION bassist Peter Palmdahl ('Carnivore') and new drummer Horror.

Rudolfsson issued a side project album 'Enter The Realm Of Death' under the band name RUNEMAGICK in 1999.

DEATHWITCH scored a deal with Earache Records subsidiary Wicked World for a 2003 album 'Violence Blasphemy Sodomy'. The band's line up at this juncture comprised vocalist / guitarist / bassist Terror, guitarist Slade Doom with drummer Morbid Juttu. In September Slade Doom would be jailed for "undisclosed offences".

TRIUMPHANT DEVASTATION, Desecration DR001 (1996). Intro—Black Dawn / Triumphant Devestation / Flag Of Black Death / Unholy Destruction / Soul Crusher / Bestial Mutilation / Storm Of Damnation / Infernal Gates Of Hell / Under The Black Wings / Deathwitch / Nocturnal Sacrifice / Sadistic Sodomizer.
DAWN OF ARMAGGEDON, Necropolis DR02 (1997). Intro (Dawn Of War) / Jehova Shall Bleed / Angel Execution / Wrath Of Sathanas / Hellfuck Sodomy / Dawn Of Armageddon / Eternal Fornication / Blasphemous Desecration / Beast Of Holocaust / Diabolical Tormentor / Desecration Of The White Christ / Outro (Armageddon) / Intro (Infernal Gate) / Triumphant Devastation / Beast Of Holocaust / Evil Blood / Wrath Of Sathanas / Nocturnal Sacrifice.
THE ULTIMATE DEATH, Necropolis NR028 (1998). Prelude To Grand Darkness / The Ultimate Death / Necromancer's Rites / Violent Carnage / Dark Gift / Grave Symphony / Condemned To The Grave / Witches Morbid Lust / Prelude Top Grand Conquest / Monumental Massacre / Revel In Sin / Monster Perversion / Death Machine / Pestilent Pandemonium / Demon Sabbath / Dawn Of Ymodos Millenium.
MONUMENTAL MUTILATIONS, Necropolis NR035 (1999). Intro -The Return Of Evil / Demonic Witch / Possessed Sadist / Fire Fuck / Jehova Shall Bleed / Total Cremation / Black Feast / Sacrifice In Fire / The Rite Of Darkness / Tettor Doom / Flag Of Black Death / Executioner 1999 / Necromancer.

DEATHWITCH

DEATHFUCK RITUALS, Hellspawn HELL009 (2002). Satanic Orgasm Abyss (Intro) / Order Of Perversion / Deathfuck Rituals / Only Death / Mayhem Masturbator / Ymodos 666 / Fuckonecroholic / On Paths To Sodom / Revelation Of The Goat / Evil Fertilizer / Vampire Slut / Erection Of Lucifer / Repulsions In Heaven (Outro).
VIOLENCE, BLASPHEMY, SODOMY, Wicked World WICK 016 (2004). Inrot / Flamethrower Carnival / Total Morbid / Blood Sucking Fuck / Abhorrent Sadistic Tormentor / Lord Of Ymodos / Witch Of Death / Necrosodomizer / Bitch Finder / Violence Blasphemy / Coffin Fornicator / Worthless Scum / Fuck Off And Die / Death Maniac.

DEBAUCHERY

CREEDMOOR, NC, USA — Andy Pitre (guitar), Brent Smith (guitar), Henrik Dahlstrand (bass), John Snead (drums).

DEBAUCHERY is a Creedmoor-Wendell, North Carolina Death Metal band, initially founded as BEYOND INFINITY during 1989. The opening roster comprised vocalist Mark Moore, guitarists Andy Pitre and Brent Smith, bass player Ritchie Owens with John Snead on drums. Owens was replaced by Jeff Stegal as the group moved away from cover versions into composing originals. In 1990 Brent Smith exited, but soon made a return. Stegal then exited prior to BEYOND INFINITY recording three demo tracks, 'Bedbugs', 'Infernal' and 'Judgenot', although these would not be distributed to the public. That summer, Mark Moore left the band, forging Doom outfit SURREAL in league with Ritchie Owens.

In 1991 Mike Patrum was inducted on bass as the group adopted the new title of DEBAUCHERY. Another unreleased demo, involving two songs 'Quarantine' and 'Non-Terminus', followed upfront of the band's live debut in December 1991 at the Fallout Shelter in Raleigh. Patrum took his leave, being replaced by Jeff Fischer before this latest candidate also left, to join ELDRITCH HORROR. Persevering, DEBAUCHERY cut the four song demo 'Cranial Indulgence' after which Hendrik Dahlstrand took over on bass. The band also included a track on King Fowley's 'Midnight Offerings' compilation album.

DEBAUCHERY during folded after Dahlstrand relocated back to his homeland Sweden and Snead suffered Carpal Tunnel Syndrome. Andy Pitre would join his former band mates in SURREAL. Sadly, Ritchie Owen was killed in an auto accident during 1997. Snead eventually got back into playing, performing with DREAMSCAPES OF THE PERVERSE.

Cranial Indulgence, Debauchery (1993) (Demo). Distrayed Discordial Harmonies / Quarantine / Dunes Of A Fallow Field / Labyrinth Of The Arachne.

DECADENCE

STOCKHOLM, SWEDEN — Kitty Saric (vocals), Kenneth Lantz (guitar), Daniel Green (guitar), Joakim Antman (bass), Erik Röjås (drums).

Female fronted, Stockholm melodic Death Metal band DECADENCE, featuring the ex-DEVASTATOR guitar pairing of Christian Lindholm and Niclas Radberg alongside DEMENTED bassist Kenneth Lantz, issued the 2004 demo 'Land Of Despair'. The band had started life billed as RAVENOUS, but would only undertake two gigs under this title before switching to DECADENCE. Singer Kitty Saric holds credits with DIVINE DOMINION and DEKAPITERA. Lantz shifted to the guitar role as Roberto Vacchi Segerlund was inducted on bass.

Ex-DEAFENING SILENCE drummer Patrik Frögéli would accede to the position as his predecessor Peter Lindqvist bowed out to prioritise his other acts CANOPY and A-BROS. Radberg would be substituted by rhythm guitarist Michael Sjölund of TRAMUMATAGE. The band, issuing the album 'Decadence', shifted shape once again and in 2005 was quoting a line-up comprising Saric, Lantz, second guitarist Daniel Green, bass player Joakim Antman with Erik Röjås on drums.

Ex-drummer Patrik Frögéli joined BLOODSHED in September 2006.

Land Of Despair, Decadence (2004). Despair / Heavy Dose / Among The Fallen / The Bell Tolls For Thee.
DECADENCE, Decadence (2005). Wrathful And Sullen / Heavy Dose / Black Eternity / Decadence / Foyer Of Hell / Among The Fallen / Dagger Of The Mind / War Within.
THE CREATURE, Decadence (2005). Red / Labyrinth / The Creature / Wasteland / Possession / Killing Perseverance / Desperate Secrecy / Inside.
3RD STAGE OF DECAY, HTI 001 (2006). Corrosion / Claustrophobia / 3rd Stage Of Decay / Theater Of The Absurd / Settle The Score / Sculpture / Invert / Endgame.

DECAMERON

SWEDEN — Alex Losbäck (vocals / bass), Johannes Losbäck (guitar), Johan Norrman (guitar), Tobias Kellgren (drums).

Previously known as NECROFOBIC, the Swedes changed titles to DECAMERON in 1991 and released their first demo in 1992 titled 'My Grave Is Calling'. Frontman Alex Losbäck also moonlighted with RUNEMAGICK in the early 90's whilst drummer Tobias Kjellgren is ex-SWORDMASTER. One of the band's original guitarists Johan Norrman quit to join DISSECTION in mid 1994 and also joined SACRAMENTUM. DECAMERON soldiered on utilising the temporary services of LORD BELIAL guitarist Dark. A permanent member was later found in Johnny Lehto. Drummer Tobias Kellgren departed following completion of the debut album, which was issued in 1996.

Kjellgren would later joined DISSECTION in December 1995. By 2002 both Kjellgren and guitarist Johannes Losbäck were resident in Power Metal band SEVENTH ONE, signing to the Massacre label for a debut album 'Sacrifice'. Kellgren joined up as touring member of IN FLAMES during October 2005, as regular drummer Daniel Svensson, awaiting the birth of his second child, sat out these shows.

My Grave Is Calling, Decameron (1992) (Cassette demo). Intro—Mary-Ann Ward / Demogorgon / My Grave Is Calling / Satanized / Whispers Of Sorrow / Carved Upon My Stone.

MY SHADOW..., No Fashion NFR013CD (1996). Mörker / Carpe Nocem / Our Time Has Come / Satanized / Le Roi Triste / The Scar Of Damnation / Sexual Immortality / Skábma / My Shadow... / Prophecy Of Life To Come / Mistress Of Sacrifice.

DECAPITATED

POLAND — *Sauron (vocals), Vogg (guitar), Martin (bass), Vitek (drums).*

As a Teenage Death Metal act DECAPITATED averaged an age of just 17 by the time of their debut album but incredibly drummer Vitek was a mere twelve years old upon their formation in 1996. Both guitarist Vogg and bassist Martin also hold down membership of Black Metal act LUX OCCULTA. In 1997 the trio of vocalist Sauron, guitarist Vogg and Vitek added the 13 year old bassist Martin. DECAPITATED debuted with the demos 'Cemeteral Gardens' in 1997 and 1998's 'The Eye Of Horus'. Further exposure was garnered by the inclusion of tracks on the 2000 Relapse Records 'Polish Assault' compilation alongside YATTERING, LOST SOUL and DAMNABLE.

The first album, recorded for Earache subsidiary Wicked World, was produced by VADER's Piotr Wiwczarek and sees a cover of SLAYER's 'Mandatory Suicide'. DECAPITATED's early demos were pressed up onto CD by Poland's Metal Mind Productions entitled 'The First Damned', adding two live tracks from the 'Thrash 'em All' festival. The band toured as support to VADER in early 2001.

DECAPITATED's February 2002 album 'Nihility' would include a cover version of NAPALM DEATH's 'Suffer The Children'. The band scored a valuable coup later that same year, being chosen to perform at the Polish 'Ozzfest' event in late May. By August DECAPITATED was on the road in North America with tour partners INCANTATION, VEHEMENCE and DEAD TO FALL. The band, shooting a promotional video for the track 'Spheres of Madness' to further promote the album, would form up part of a strong package bill topped by VADER for a run of dates across mainland Europe from late August alongside KRISIUN and PREJUDICE. Vitek took time out to lay down drums on VADER frontman Piotr Wiwczarek's PANZER X project EP 'Steel Fist'.

The February 2004 DECAPITATED album 'The Negatron' would see a bonus track offering of a take on DEICIDE's 'Lunatic Of God's Creation'. A short spurt of UK dates saw the band ranked alongside ROTTING CHRIST, ANATA and THUS DEFILED. The band then united with Norwegian Black Metal elite outfit MAYHEM and Japanese act DEFILED for a European tour commencing early April. US dates scheduled for July and August had DECAPITATED opening for CANNIBAL CORPSE. However, all North American touring plans were cancelled due to the sensitivity in regard to the band's name and the executions of hostage victims in Iraq.

DECAPITATED parted ways with guitarist Jacek Hiro in October, opting to remain a quartet for February 2005 European gigs allied with HATE, CRIONICS and DIES IRAE. The band re-shaped in June when frontman Sauron closed a nine year tenure by announcing his withdrawal. DECAPITATED quickly drew in Covan (a.k.a. Adrian Kowanek), formerly of ATROPHIA RED SUN, as replacement. The band entered Hertz Studios in Bialystok in August to record a new album entitled 'Organic Hallucinosis'. September European dates had DECAPITATED partnered with British act GOREROTTED and Dutch Deathsters DETONATION. Following US gigs in December, DECAPITATED parted ways with bassist Martin, the four-stringer having to deal with military conscription issues, pulling in Richard Gulczynski as replacement.

Live work breaking into 2006, promoting the 'Organic Hallucinosis' album recorded at Hertz Studio in Bialystok, saw the band teaming up with HYPOCRISY, SOILENT GREEN, RAGING SPEEDHORN, NILE and WITH PASSION for a North American tour commencing in early January. In mid February it was learned that bassist Martin had returned to the fold. US dates for September and October 2006 saw the band hooking up with KRISIUN, CATTLE DECAPITATION, SIX FEET UNDER and ABYSMAL DAWN. The band united with headliners FEAR FACTORY and SUFFOCATION for further North American shows in November.

DECAPITATED

The band united with Nancy's PHAZM for extensive European touring throughout February 2007. In May the group toured throughout Australia supporting NILE.

The band's next tour outing was to be the 'Summer Slaughter' trek across the USA throughout June and July, seeing NECROPHAGIST headlining on a mammoth package billing with BENEATH THE MASSACRE, CEPHALIC CARNAGE, CATTLE DECAPITATION, THE FACELESS, AS BLOOD RUNS BLACK, ARSIS and ION DISSONANCE.

DECAPITATED issued a limited edition version of their debut 'Winds Of Creation' on October 8th, this set featuring a bonus DVD containing a full live show filmed in Nottingham on December 20th 2004 with original vocalist Sauron.

Whilst on tour in Russia alongside CRIONICS during late October 2007 Witold Kieltykaand and Adrian Kowanek were both seriously injured in a road accident involving DECAPITATED's tour bus and a truck carrying wood in Gomel, on the Russian/Belarus border. The pair were hospitalised in Novozybkov. Witold Kieltyka died on November 2nd. He was 23 years old.

In mid November DECAPITATED have contracted a deal with Nuclear Blast Records, who commented "This exceptional band has so far recorded four albums, and we're looking forward to the upcoming mix of technical superiority, brutal riffs and blastbeats on album number five. The joy over these awesome news are of course overshadowed by the tragic death of DECAPITATED drummer Witold 'Vitek' Kieltyka."

Cemeteral Gardens, (1997). Intro / Destiny / Way To Salvation / Ereshkigal / Cemeteral Gardens.

The Eye Of Horus, (1998). Intro / The Eye Of Horus / Blessed / The First Damned / Nine Steps / Danse Macabre (Outro) / Mandatory Suicide.

WINDS OF CREATION, Wicked World WICK011 (2000). Winds Of Creation / Blessed / The First Damned / Way To Salvation / The Eye Of Horus / Human's Dust / Nine Steps / Dance Macabre / Mandatory Suicide.

THE FIRST DAMNED, Metal Mind Productions (2001). Intro / The Eye Of Horus / Blessed / The First Damned / Nine Steps / Dance Macabre / Mandatory Suicide / Destiny / Way To Salvation / Ereshkigal / Cemeteral Gardens / Way To Salvation (Live) / Nine Steps (Live).

NIHILITY, Wicked World MOSH255 (2002). Perfect Dehumanisation (The Answer?) / Eternity Too Short / Mother War / Nihility (Anti-Human Manifesto) / Names / Spheres Of Madness / Babylon's Pride / Symmetry Of Zero / Suffer The Children.

THE NEGATION, Wicked World (2004). The Fury / Three-Dimensional Defect / Sensual Sickness / Calling / The Negatron / Long-Desired Dementia / The Empty Throne / Lying And Weak / Lunatic Of God's Creation.

ORGANIC HALLUCINOSIS, Teichiku TKCS-85137 (2006). A Poem About An Old Prison Man / Day 69 / Revelation Of Existence / Post Organic / Visual Delusion / Flash B(l)ack / Invisible Control / Nihility (Anti-Human Manifesto) (Live) / Spheres Of Madness (Live).

DECAY

EGLING, GERMANY — *Stefan Angerer (vocals / guitar), Christoph Nadler (guitar), Fabian Quoll (guitar), Oliver Winterholler (bass), Tobias Quoll (drums).*

Egling Death Metal band assembled in 1993 as BLACK FUTURE citing a line-up comprising vocalist / guitarist Stefan Angerer, guitarists Christoph Nadler and Fabian Quoll, bassist Oliver Winterholler and Tobias Quoll on drums. The group switched title to DECAY and the first product would be a 1995 demo 'Downwards', after which Peter Giel took the drum position. In 1996, now titled ASCENSION, the band drafted Jürgen Zeisberger on guitar and the following year Holger Schmalisch enrolled on drums and then Davud Böhm as lead vocalist. The ASCENSION demo 'Walking On The Psychopath' followed. 2001 witnessed further changes, introducing RED TO GREY's Robin Fischer and ex-LAST SALVATION drummer Martin Szillat.

During 2003 Matthias Urban of Augsburg Thrashers STORM sessioned on bass.

Downwards, (1995). Falling Into Mourning / Doom / Ride The Devil / Besessen / Blumen Im All.

DECEPTION

MIELEC, POLAND — *Deather (vocals / bass), Paweł Dusza (guitar), Dominik Augustyn (drums).*

Mielec Death Metal band DECEPTION was forged during 1998 by guitarist Paweł "Aggareth" Dusza and drummer Dominik "August" Augustyn, subsequently inducting guitarist Marcin Deszcz. DECEPTION's first product would be a Summer 2001 demo, recorded at Hertz Studios and entitled 'Age Of Suffering'. Upon completion of these sessions vocalist / bassist Marcin Malczyński was acquired and in this formation the band put in an inaugural concert at the Tarnow Przepraszam Club sharing the stage with CHRIST AGONY.

Returning to Hertz Studios in September of 2002 the band crafted a second demo, 'Holy Deception'. In 2003 the Czech Record Company Nice To Eat You re-released these recordings under the title 'Permanent Torment'. In the meantime, tracks from 'Holy Deception' saw issue as part of a split EP shared with PUTIDITY through Old Temple.

Signing to the domestic Redrum 666 label the group entered Screw Factory Studios in Dębica to cut the 'Nuclear Wind' album. Both Malczyński and Deszcz then opted out and new vocalist / bassist 'Mumin' (Lukasz Tumidajski) was drafted. DECEPTION headlined the November 2004 'Extreme Blast Attack' tour of Poland alongside SAMMATH NAUR, EFFECT MURDER and PENTHAUSE. DECEPTION issued the 'Praying To Liar' demo in 2005. Tumidajski would be replaced by Deather.

Age Of Suffering, (2001). My Inside / Age Of Suffering / Damnation / Bringing Death / Sorrow.
HOLY DECEPTION, Deception (2002). Bloody Rape / Unholy Darkness / Warriors Of Blasphemy / Lucifer's Legion / Bloody Dusk Of Chaotic Utopia / Broken Faith / In Shadow Of Apocalypse / My Inside / Age Of Suffering / Damnation / Bringing Death / Sorrow.
PERMANENT TORTURE, Nice To Eat You (2003). Bloody Rape / Unholy Darkness / Warriors Of Blasphemy / Lucifer's Legion / Bloody Dusk Of Chaotic Utopia / Broken Faith / In Shadow Of Apocalypse / My Inside / Age Of Suffering / Damnation / Bringing Death / Sorrow.
DECEPTION, Old Temple (2003) (Split album with PUTRIDITY). Warriors Of Blasphemy / Lucifer's Legion / Unholy Darkness / Bloody Dusk Of Chaotic Utopia / In Shadow Of Apocalypse / Broken Faith.
NUCLEAR WIND, RedRum666 (2004). Nuclear Wind / Dead Again / God Perverse / His Slumbery Lies / Modern Apostles / Revenge / Deceitful Sacrifice / Marasm.
Praying To Liar, (2005). Deviant Prophet / Praying To Liar / Apocaliptic Protection.

DECOLLATION

GOTHENBURG, SWEDEN — *John Lesley (vocals / guitar), John Jeremiah (guitar), Charles Von Weissenberg (bass), Nick Sheilds (keyboards), Chris Steele (drums).*

Despite their anglicised pseudonyms DECOLLATION are all Swedish natives rooted in Gothenburg. Bassist Charles Von Weissenberg (real name Tomas Johansson) is ex-CEREMONIAL OATH whilst drummer Chris Steele (real name Kristian Wåhlin) was previously with GROTESQUE and LIERS IN WAIT. Both Wåhlin and vocalist John Lesley (real name Johan Österberg) subsequently went on to Gothic-Electro outfit DIABOLIQUE. Wåhlin also goes under the pseudonym of Necrolord as cover artist for many Black Metal bands. DECOLLATION released the EP 'Cursed Lands', recorded at Sunlight Studios by producer Tomas Skogsberg in February 1992, during 1993 for the French label Listenable Records.

Cursed Lands EP, Listenable POSH004 (1993). Dawn Of Resurrection / Point Of No Return / The Godborn / Cursed Lands.

DECOMPOSED

UK — *Harry Armstrong (vocals / bass), Pete Snasdell (guitar), James Ogawa (guitar), Tim Spear (drums).*

DECOMPOSED issued a 1991 demo recording 'Ego Sum Lex Mundi'. The band, alongside GOMORRAH, formed part of the billing for the 1992 UK package tour 'Underground Titans'. Their solitary album 'Hope Finally Died', produced by Paul Johnson for Candlelight Records, would be recorded at Rhythm Studios in Bidford-On-Avon during April of 1993. Both frontman Harry Armstrong and guitarist James Ogawa later turned up as members of HANGNAIL and Progressive Death Metal band COLLAPSE.

DECOMPOSED member Reverend Al (a.k.a. Ali Reza Hikimi Ghazvini) journeyed through MOURN and MINDFIELD, the latter act with Seamus, a veteran of Punk act TBAC ("Throw Bricks at Coppers"). MINDFIELD evolved into CARNIVAL OF SOULS, and then EVIL KNIEVEL. In 2002 Al founded BLOOD ISLAND RAIDERS.

HOPE FINALLY DIED, Candlelight CANDLE003CD (1994). Inscriptions / Taste The Dying / Falling Apart / At Rest / Instrumental / Procession / (Forever) Lying In State.

DECORYAH

FINLAND — *Jukka Vuorinen (vocals / guitar), Jani Kakko (guitar/bass), Jonne Valtonen (keyboards), Mikko Laine (drums).*

Wistful Finnish Rock charged with a grandiose Darkwave feel, strings and female backing vocals. DECORYAH, although dating back to 1989, only released their debut demo 'Whispers From The Depth' in 1992. A second demo, entitled 'Cosmos Silence', was recorded over three days in December 1992 at ECI-Sound Studio in Turku and released in January the following year. This tape provoked attention from Switzerland's Witchhunt Records prompting a 7" single release. The album 'Wisdom Floats', issued in June 1994, would be recorded at ECI-Sound Studios with engineer Erkki Kujala.

By the recording of their 1996 Metal Blade Records debut, 'Fall Dark Waters', DECORYAH was down to a trio of Jukka Vuorinen on vocals and guitars, Jani Kakko on guitar and drummer Mikko Laine. An array of session musicians embellished the grand scale of the album with strings and female backing vocals. Contributing would be former member Jonne Valtonen sessioning on keyboards, Piritta Vainio on vocals, Maria Aspelund on viola, Sini Koivuniemi with female vocals and flute, Karolina Olin with female vocals and violin and cellist Anna Pursiheimo.

Whispers From The Depths, Decoryah (1992) (Demo). Dark Embrace / Where The Black Dove Lives / Chared / Falling Into Dim.

Ebonies, Witchhunt 9312 (1993). Cosmos Silence / Astral Mirage Of Paradise.

Cosmos Silence, Decoryah (1993) (Demo). Cosmos Silence / Abstract Rays / Solid Blackness / Tranquil Ecstasy / Astral Mirage Of Paradise.

WISDOM FLOATS, Decoryah WIHU 9416 (1994). Astral Mirage Of Paradise / Wisdom Floates / Monoliths / Beryllos / Reaching Melancholia / Circle Immortality / When The Echoes Start To Fade / Cosmos Silence / Intra-Mental Ecstasy / Ebonies / Infinity Awaits.

FALL-DARK WATERS, Metal Blade 3984-14111-2 (1996). Fall-Dark Waters / Submerged Seconds / Envisioned (Waters)? / Some Drops Behind The Essence / Endless Is The Stream / Gloria Absurdiah / Wintry Fluids (Portal) / She Came To Me In The Form Of Water / She Wept In The Woods.

Breathing The Blue EP, Metal Blade 3984-14130-2 (1997). Once / Beneath The Clouded Mind / Breathing The Blue / Let The One Drown / Swinging Shapes At A Lake.

DECREPIT

CLEVELAND, OH, USA — *Rob Molzan (vocals), Tom Rojack (guitar), Duane Morris (guitar), Matt Sorg (bass), Chris Dora (drums).*

Cleveland's DECREPIT, featuring erstwhile MUTILATION and EMBALMER guitarist Duane Morris and ex-BLOOD OF CHRIST bassist Matt Sorg, debuted in 1993 with the demo 'Hymns Of Grief And Pain'. During 1994 DECREPIT was put into hiatus as Morris would figure in the INCANTATION family tree. Morris, second guitarist Gene Lambert and BLOOD OF CHRIST guitarist Tom Rojack, as drummer, founded the Black Metal side venture FUNERAL PYRE. During this period Lambert opted out of DECREPIT, re-founding an all new version of FUNERAL PYRE, but Morris made a return in 1995 to re-activate the band with FUNERAL PYRE colleague Tom Rojack taking Lambert's position.

Upon the band's demise band personnel vocalist Rob Molzan, guitarist Duane Morris and bassist Matt Sorg all resurfaced in FROM THE DEPTHS. Morris also served with SANCTORUM and the infamous NUNSLAUGHTER. Tragically Rojack, shortly after the group had folded, died after falling down some stairs whilst intoxicated. Chris Dora would prove a much in demand drummer for bands such as SOULLESS, INCANTATION, ALL THAT IS EVIL, SPAWN OF SATAN and BLOODSICK.

The 1997 'Acrimonium' album, which included a cover version of BLOODFEAST's 'Face Fate', was released more than a year after the group had folded. Following the issue of two albums FROM THE DEPTHS dissolved with the core membership forging DEAD OF NIGHT, this band consisting of Duane Morris, Matt Sorg Chris Dora alongside NUNSLAUGHTER, SOULLESS and ALL THAT IS EVIL guitarist Wayne Richards alongside the TERROR, BLOOD OF CHRIST and MUTILATION credited Randy Scott on bass.

The Wake, (1994). The Wake / Rise Again.
CREATION OF SIN, Dismal (1995). To Rise Again / The Wake / Pathogenesis / The Gate To Misery / Spirits Of Infirmity / Withered / Mausoleum / The Creation Of Sin / Rotted Congregation.
ACRIMONIUM, Dismal (1997). In Thy Name / Lusting For The Day's End / Angel Of Dark Shadows / Face Fate / Perish / Acrimonium.

DECREPIT BIRTH

SANTA CRUZ, CA, USA — *Bill Robinson (vocals), Matt Sotelo (guitar) Derek Boyer (bass), Tim Yeung (drums).*

Santa Cruz, California Death Metal band. DECREPIT BIRTH's full length debut, '... And Time Begins', was released in 2003 through Unique Leader Records. Bassist Derek Boyer vacated, joining the reformed SUFFOCATION in April 2004. DECREPIT BIRTH drafted new drummer KC Howard of ODIUS MORTEM repute in September. The band announced a road union with PSYCROPTIC and VILE for the 'Bloodletting North America' Summer 2005 tour.

The band partnered with DEEDS OF FLESH, VILE and ODIOUS MORTEM on the 'Bloodletting North America V' tour of the USA in July 2006.

DECREPIT BIRTH members bassist Risha Eryavec and drummer Tim Yeung forged a new band project in mid 2006 allied with Tommy Vext of VEXT on lead vocals and former FEAR FACTORY man Dino Cazares on guitar.

DECREPIT BIRTH got back to live work, pulling in the VILE, BLOOD RED THRONE, APOSTASY, UNSPOKEN NAMES, MR. CUCUMBER, DISMAL EUPHONY and THE ALL SEEING I credited Erlend Caspersen as stand in bassist. In October the band announced a fresh album billed 'Diminishing Between Worlds' for Unique Leader Records. The following month Risha Eryavec returned in the bass position. Tim Yeung deputised as stand in drummer for Western Massachusetts Metal outfit ALL THAT REMAINS North American dates throughout November and December 2006.

DECREPIT BIRTH entered Castle Ultimate studios on May 8th 2007, working with producer Zack Ohren, to begin recording their second album, 'Diminishing Between Worlds'.

... AND THE TIME BEGINS, Unique Leader (2002). Prelude To The Apocalypse / Condemned To Nothingness / Thought Beyond Infinity / The Infestation / Rebirth Of Consciousness / Shroud Of Impurity / Concepting The Era / Of Genocide / ... And Time Begins.

DECRYPT

IN, USA — *Zach Gheaja (vocals), Chris Montez (guitar), Jim Kelly (bass), Brad Vanderzee (drums).*

Founded in 2000, Indiana Death Metal band DECRYPT's debut line-up comprised vocalist / guitarist Chris Montez, bassist Billy O'Neill and drummer Brad Vanderzee. Jim Kelly, previously with RITUAL HOMICIDE, took O'Neill's position in October of 2001. Another RITUAL HOMICIDE member, Zach Gheaja, took on the task of lead vocalist. DECRYPT's self-financed 2002 album 'Transmissions From The Fuckhole' closed out with cover versions of BLONDIE's 'Call Me' and DANZIG's 'Mother'.

DECRYPT guitarist Chris Montez acted as stand in musician for INTERNAL BLEEDING's 2005 US tour work. That October both Montez and Jimbo Kelly joined HUMAN ARTIFACTS, a new band constructed by LIVIDITY's Matt Bishop and Robert Brody of ALCHYMIST repute.

TRANSMISSIONS FROM THE FUCKHOLE, Independent (2002). Greed Disease / Fecal Matter Platter / Looking Through Dark Eyes / Poop Shoot Massacre / Abstract Obscenity / Inanimate Earth / Call Me / Mother.
HOLY EROTIC RAPTURE, Forever Underground FU019 (2003). Holy Erotic Rapture / Armageddon=Satisfaction / Grind A.D. / Escucha Mysica / Immaculate Deception / Intentional Tourettes / Braindead Masses / Greed Disease / Fecal Matter Platter / Lost Cause / Human Supposition / Progressive Holocaust / Mental Restraints.

DEEDS OF FLESH

USA — *Jacoby Kingston (vocals / bass), Erik Lindmark (guitar), Jared Deaver (guitar), Mike Hamilton (drums).*

DEEDS OF FLESH was forged by ex-T.H.C. and CHARLIE CHRIST members Jacoby Kingston, Eric Lindmark and drummer Joey Heaslet in 1993. Following the self financed 'Gradually Melting' EP DEEDS OF FLESH signed to Relapse Records for their sophomore effort 'Trading Pieces'.

With the issuing of third album 'Inbreeding The Anthropophagi' Heaslet made his exit and was supplanted by Brad Palmer. The band also pulled in erstwhile VILE guitarist Jim Tkacz.

Heaslet made his return for the 'Path Of The Weakening' album. This release would sell in excess of 15'000 copies and prompt lengthy bouts of touring in both North and South America after which Tkacz decamped. His position was filled by former PSYPHERIA and IMPALED guitarist Jared Deaver. Later in the year the drum stool was taken over by Mike Hamilton of VILE.

Kingston was unable to fulfill a November 1998 tour of Brazil necessitating the recruitment of DEPRECATED man Derek Boyer to fill in. With the recording of the 2001 album 'Mark Of The Legion', the band hit the road in July and August of on the MONSTROSITY led 'Bloodletting North America Pt. II' tour alongside Dutchmen PYAEMIA, ODIOUS SANCTION and SABBATIC FEAST. Jared Deaver though, then opted to make his exit, joining SEVERED SAVIOR. A swift replacement was named as Aaron Gustafson for DEEDS OF FLESH's billing on the April 2002 'Bloodletting North America III' tour alongside running mates DISGORGE, SEVERE TORTURE and DISAVOWED.

Taking the band into 2004 would be January European dates, the band packaged alongside HATE ETERNAL, DYING FETUS and PREJUDICE. Australian gigs that Summer, the band's first, saw Tasmanians PSYCROPTIC as support.

DEEDS OF FLESH cancelled a batch of gigs in February 2005 when both Jacoby Kingston and Mike Hamilton were injured in a fall from a 20 foot high balcony. The singer sustained a sprained ankle, fractured vertebrae and a compressed disk whilst the drummer suffered a broken arm.

The band lined up with MONSTROSITY, VILE and IMPALED for the 'Gutting Europe 4' European tour beginning in Poland during late March 2006. The group then partnered with DECREPIT BIRTH, VILE and ODIOUS MORTEM on the 'bloodletting North America V' tour of the USA in July 2006.

TRADING PIECES, Repulse (1996). Carnivorous Ways / Born Then Torn Apart / Trading Pieces / Hunting Humans / Impious Offerings / Acid Troops / Deeds Of Flesh / Erected On Stakes / Chunks In The Shower / Blasted / Outro.
INBREEDING THE ANTHROPOPHAGI, Repulse (1998). End Of All / Deeding Time / Breeding The Anthropophagi / Infecting them With Falsehood / Canvas Of Flesh / Ritual Of Battle / Fly Shrine / Gradually Melted.
PATH OF THE WEAKENING, Erebos ERE 017 (1999). Indigenous To The Appalling (Mutinous Humans) / Lustmord / Path Of The Weakening / Summarily Killed / Sounds Of Loud Reigns / Execute The Anthropophagi / I Die On My Own Terms / Sense Of The Diabolic / A Violent God.
MARK OF THE LEGION, Unique Leader Entertainment (2001). Cleansed By Fire / An Eternity Of Feasting And Brawling / Mark Of The Legion / Spewing Profilgacy / Fulfilled In Warfare / Contest Of Wills / Master Of Murder / Ideal Genocide / Drink The Blood.
REDUCED TO ASHES, Unique Leader (2003). Reduced To Ashes / Infested Beneath The Earth / Avowed Depraved / Empyrean / Human Trophies / Banished / Disinterred Archaic Heap / The Endurance.

DEEPRED

FINLAND — *Rodrigo Artiga (vocals), Ile Paasonen (guitar), Antti Oinonen (guitar), Tuomo Latvala (drums).*

Brutal Death Metal act DEEPRED came into being during 1999, founded by guitarists Antti Oinonen and Ile Paasonen with Teemu Mutka on drums, issuing the three track opening demo 'Yours In Murder'. A further effort 'All Will See Rebirth' saw the inclusion of new members vocalist Dani Andersson and bassist Henrik Laine. The band would sign to the American Blunt Force label, owned by Death Metal veterans DYING FETUS, for their debut 'Prophetic Luster' opus, recorded during the Summer of 2000 at Cursed Studios. 'Prophetic Luster' subsequently saw a 2001 European release via Forensick Music.

Changes saw Tommi Havo of MORBID SAVOURING and KHERT-NETER taking over from Andersson upfront of tour dates, which took the band throughout the Czech Republic, Slovakia and Germany in August and September of 2001, also appearing at the Ludwigshafen 'Deathfest' event. Following completion of material for a split release 'The Beating Goes On' with DYING FETUS for Relapse Records, more ructions in the line up signalled the departure of the rhythm section. Santeri Salmi of DAUNTLESS stepped in to fill the drum vacancy briefly, later going on to LOCKFIST, then Tommi Havo bailed out. Mutka made a return to the drum stool.

DEEPRED contributed their version of 'Trap Them And Kill Them' to a 2001 IMPETIGO tribute album. This recording was also to surface on a 2002 split 7" single shared with SLUGATHOR released by Snuff Records of the Czech Republic. The band planned a split-CD with France's LOATHING through Several Bleeds Records in March of 2003.

DEEPRED located a new frontman in Rodrigo 'Fatality' Artiga of El Salvador's KABAK. Drums would then be handed over to Tuomo Latvala, a veteran of DEMIGOD, TORN and TORTURE KILLER.

Yours In Murder, Deepred (1999) (Demo). In Cold Blood / Beyond Deception / Creation .44
Creation .44.
All Will See Rebirth, Deepred (1999) (Demo). All Will See Rebirth / Dismissed From Life / A Relentless Path.
Creation .44, Deepred (2001) (Split CD-R promotion single with SLUGATHOR). Creation .44 / Trap Them And Kill Them.
PROPHETIC LUSTER, Blunt Force BFR 005 (2001). Hi-Speed Confusion / Multiple Errors / Dismissed From Life / Luster / In Cold Blood / A Song For The Lovers / A Relentless Path / Homogenous World / All Will See Rebirth.
Deep Red, (2002). Creation .44 / Trap Them And Kill Them.
Creation .44, Snuff Productions (2002) (Split 7" vinyl single with SLUGATHOR). Creation .44 / Trap Them And Kill Them.
The Beating Goes On, Relapse (2002) (Split 7" vinyl single with DYING FETUS). The Beating Goes On.
Promo 2002, Deepred (2002) (CD-R demo). The Crime / Slow Decay / Trapped Under Grave.
THIS IS A FACE OF HUMANITY..., Several Bleeds SBR 001 (2003) (Split CD album with LOATHING). The Crime / Slow Decay / Trapped Under Grave / Multiple Errors (Live) / The Beating Goes On (Live).
The Crime, American Line Productions LA 059 (2003) (Latin American cassette EP). The Crime / Slow Decay / Trapped Under Grave / Multiple Errors (Live) / Trapped Under Grave (Live) / The Beating Goes On (Live).

DEFACED CREATION

SWEDEN — *Tommy Dahlström (vocals), Jörgen Bylander (guitar), Zeb Nilsson (guitar), Johan Hjelm (bass), Arrtu Malkki (drums).*

Death Metal band dating back to 1993. The group was founded by ex-CELEBORN man Jörgen Bylander on guitar, bassist Zeb Nilsson and vocalist Tommy Dahlström. The opening 1994 demo 'Santeria' still found DEFACED CREATION as a trio utilizing a drum machine. Shortly after guitarist Stefan Dahlberg enrolled but would soon part ways with the band.

A further demo session arrived in 1995 and secured a single deal with the Paranoya Syndrome label for the resulting 7" vinyl EP 'Resurrection'. The band then underwent a period of flux as Nilsson switched to second guitar as the rhythm section was secured by bassist Jocke Wassberg and drummer Arrtu Malkki. This line-up laid down two new songs for release on a split 7" single 'Fall' with ACTERNUM before Wassberg made way for new four stringer Johan Hjelm. The band toured Europe as part of the 'Brutal Summer' package including DYING FETUS and DERANGED.

DEFACED CREATION signed up to the Voice Of Death label for their debut album 'Serenity In Chaos'. A further split single, in alliance with STANDING OUT, also emerged on Rockaway Records.

During mid 2001 Jörgen Bylander, who also divides his time with side project CONDAMNED, joined DERANGED as bass player.

Defaced Creation, Defaced Creation (1995) (Demo). Oceans Of Blood / Emptiness / Mental Genocide / Lady Babylon / Necropedofiliac / My Dark Side / Moon Maiden / Innocent / No Seconds Left / Defaced Creation.
Resurrection, Paranoya Syndrome PS 004 (1996) (7" vinyl EP limited to 300 copies). Devastation / Stillborn / Entering The Gates / Resurrection / Ghouls Attack.

Defaced Creation / Aeternum, Paranoya Syndrome PS 011 (1997) (Split EP with AETERNUM)). Fall / Bloodwar.
Defaced Creation / Standing Out, Rockaway 001 (1998) (Split EP with STANDING OUT). Infernal / Victorious Underworld.
SERENITY IN CHAOS, Voices Of Death VODCD005 (1999). Baptized In Fire / Macabre Exposure Of Fleshly Devotion / Fire Temple / Kill The Light / Devastation / Return In Black / Cannibalistic Feast / Stillborn / The Victorious Underworld / Infernal / Enslave The Christians / Fall.

DEFEATED SANITY

DACHSBACH, GERMANY — *Markus Keller (vocals), Wolfgang Teske (guitar), Christian Kühn (guitar), Jacob Schmidt (bass), Lille Gruber (drums).*

Purist, brutal Death Metal band DEFEATED SANITY emerged in Dachsbach during 1994, their first 1996 demo seeing a line-up of vocalist Robert Colnik, guitarist Wolfgang Teske, bass player Jonas Gruber with Lille Gruber on the drums. A second promotion recording, 'Withdrawn From Beauty', arrived in 1998. As DEFEATED SANITY veered away from previous experimental sounds into a harsh, American brutal style of Death Metal new musicians were recruited in the form of guitarist Christian Münster and bass player Tino Köhler. After cutting a 2000 demo Colnik exited and was duly superseded by Markus Keller. A re-recorded track from the demo, with the addition of Keller's vocals, found its way onto a split single shared with POPPY SEED GRINDER through the Czech Grodhaisn label.

Münster bailed out to join NECROPHAGIST in 2001. DEFEATED SANITY issued a split EP 'Collapsing Human Failures' with Brazilians IMPERIOUS MALEVOLENCE on the Merciless label in 2003. Grindethic Records picked the band up for the debut full-length album 'Prelude To The Tragedy', recorded at Soundforge Studios and released in November 2004. In 2006 the band engaged in UK dates with British band NECROCEST and Czech headliners FLESHLESS in February.

Ex-DEFEATED SANITY guitarist Christian Münzner teamed up with MAJESTY in May 2006. Another line-up change saw the introduction of CEREBRIC TURMOIL bass player Jacob Schmidt. The band wrapped up recordings for the 'Psalms Of The Moribund' album, engineered by Jörg Uken at Soundlodge Studios in Rhauderfehn, Germany for Grindethic Records, in August.

Lille Gruber filled in on drums for Austrian Death Metal outfit BELPHEGOR on their 2007 North American tour dates alongside UNLEASHED and KRISIUN.

The Parasite, Grodhaisn Productions (2000) (Split single with POPPY SEED GRINDER). The Parasite / Forensic Entomology / Horrid Decomposition / Expectoration Of Fear / Retreat Of The Conquered / Transplanting The Incurable.
Collapsing Human Failures EP, Merciless (2003) (Split EP with IMPERIOUS MALEVOLENCE). Collapsing Human Failures.
Prelude To The Tragedy, Defeated Sanity (2004). Liquefying Cerebral Hemispheres / Remnants Of The Dead / Prelude To The Tragedy.
PRELUDE TO THE TRAGEDY, Grindethic (2004). Liquefying Cerebral Hemispheres / Drifting Further / The Parasite / Horrid Decomposition / Tortured Existence / Apocalypse Of Filth / Collapsing Human Failure / Remnants Of The Dead / Prelude To The Tragedy.
PSALMS OF THE MORIBUND, Grindethic (2007). Stoned Then Defiled / Fatal Self Inflicted Disfigurement / Prelude To The Tragedy / Hideously Disembodied / Butchered Identity / Psalms Of The Moribund / Engorged With Humiliation / Arousal Through Punishment / Artifacts Of Desolation.

DEFENDER KFS

VIENNA, AUSTRIA — *Harald Mezensky (vocals), Gregor Marboe (guitar), Martin Arzberger (guitar), Alexander Mayer (bass), Peter Kelman (drums).*

Viennese War Metal outfit forged in July 1998 by former PENDRAGON man Gregor 'Gore' Marboe and guitarist Andy Hammer. Gore's tradition included credits with bands such as JORMUNGARD, ENDKRIEG, PROJECT X, ESCHATA, CRYOSPHERE and even as drummer for KULDEBLOD. In March 1999 DEFENDER KFS rehearsals featured Oliver Schlögl, ex-PENDRAGON and CRYOSPHERE, on bass and Rene Binder, of PARENTAL ADVISORY, on drums. In April Patrick Tamerus took on the lead vocal position.

Following initial demos bassist HateMachine enrolled. Dispensing with some early members, Metzler of JORMUNDGAND took over the lead vocal position and, in October 1999, Beisser (a.k.a. Niko Scharf) of DEVESTATION took control of the drums. In April 2000 Hammer departed and HateMachine filled in on guitar as Axe.L.X. (Alex Burger) of PENDRAGON and CRYOSPHERE became the band's new bass player. Live gigs would be undertaken utilising the services of Bernhard 'Burny' Brem from JORMUNDGAND as session guitarist. After a DEFENDER KFS appearance at the 'Earshot' festival both Beisser and Axe.L.X exited, the latter to concentrate his efforts on his solo venture ESCHATA. Beisser also served a term with PARENTAL ADVISORY.

The band issued the 'Feed The Worms' promotional session in 2004. Bass player Rainer Schmidt exited the following year. In 2006 DEFENDER KFS was put on hold as Marboe was hired by PUNGENT STENCH as replacement for bassist Reverend Mausna. DEFENDER KFS completed work on second album 'Self Impact' in October 2006. That same month saw the introduction of new members bassist Alexander Mayer of MOLOKH, ESOPHAGUS and SEEDS OF SORROW plus guitarist Martin Arzberger, also of MOLOKH.

THE COMMAND, (2000). Northman Salvation / Halls Of Fire / Cold (Mind War) / The Sign Of Hell / Hellfire Seed / Literary Pandemonium / The Command / Labyrinth Of You / Post Mortal Gate.

DEFILED

TOKYO, JAPAN — *Kenji Sato (vocals), Yusuke Sumita (guitar), Haruhisa Takahata (bass), Tadashi Kurihara (drums).*

Discordant, technical Death Metal. Tokyo's DEFILED, manifested during 1992, issuing a brace of demos then debuted commercially in 1994 with the 'Defeat Of Sanity' EP for Bizarre Records. DEFILED secured the support slot for the 1996 CANNIBAL CORPSE Japanese tour and followed this achievement with gigs opening for visiting Western artists such as ARCH ENEMY, TESTAMENT, VADER and MORBID ANGEL. US touring had the band locked in with INCANTATION.

1999's 'Erupted Wrath' album, recorded for Terrorizer Records, saw production duties delegated to Brian Griffin of BROKEN HOPE and EM SINPHONIA. For these sessions the band travelled to Quali-Tone Studios in Chicago whilst the final product was mixed by Jim Morris at the Death Metal Mecca of Morris Sound Studios in Florida. That same year marked DEFILED as Japan's first band ever to play North America's 'Milwaukee Metalfest' and 'New Jersey Metal Meltdown' events. Road work in 2000 had DEFILED partnered with DEMENTOR for a three week European run as well as gigs across Canada, Korea and Malaysia.

The 2001 album 'Ugliness Revealed', released via Baphomet Records, saw Naoki Akamatsu on the drums, subsequently replaced by Yuichi Ishiguro for 2003's 'Divination' released by the French Season Of Mist label.

DEFILED united with Norwegian Black Metal elite outfit MAYHEM and Polish act DECAPITATED for a European tour commencing early April 2004. In late 2005 DEFILED underwent a drastic line-up change, with only guitarist Yusuke Sumita remaining musician from the group's previous formation. The three new charges would comprise singer Kenji Sato, bass player Haruhisa Takahata and Tadashi Kurihara on drums.

Defeat Of Sanity, Bizarre (1994). Rush Of Hostility / Addicted To Occult Oath / Boiled In Limbo / Defiled / Defeat Of Sanity.
ERUPTED WRATH, Nightfall (1999). Fall Into Dilemma / Nihilism / Rush Of Hostility / Erupted Wrath / Defiled / Boiled In Limbo /

Addicted To Occult Oath / Crush The Enemy Rising / Depths Of Psycho / Defeat Of Sanity.
UGLINESS REVEALED, Baphomet (2001). Lies For A Lie / Decimate With Hysteria / Uncovered Plots / To Zero / Disguised / Fatal Intrigue / Embodiment Of Jealousy / Crush The Enemy Rising / Nihilism / Defeat Of Sanity / Ugliness Revealed (Outro).
DIVINATION, Season Of Mist SOM 074 (2003). Downfall / The Dormant Within / Divination / Stench Of Grudge / Fast Decline / Dissolve In Dust / Enraptured / Swollen Insanity / Through The Killing / Fear And Epicureanism / Odour Of Malignancy / Floating Sediment / Eciov Erazzic / Decadence.

DEFILEMENT

CACAK, SERBIA — *Tara Kerac (vocals), Budimir Zivkovic (guitar), Nenad Topalovic (guitar), Ivan Francuski (bass), Marko Gospavic (drums).*

DEFILEMENT is a brutal Death Metal band forged in March of 2003 by guitarist Nenad Topalovic, bass player Ivan Francuski and drummer Marko Gospavic. Initially Vule occupied the vocal position but his brief tenure was ended by the introduction of Tara Kerac. Second guitarist Budimir Zivkovic was enrolled during September of 2003 and in this formation DEFILEMENT undertook their debut gig at the NS Riders Club in October, delivering four original songs and a cover of CANNIBAL CORPSE's 'Hammer Smashed Face'. Subsequent concerts saw supports to VOKODLOK, VADER, CANNIBAL CORPSE and ANCIENT CEREMONY. In December of 2004 DEFILEMENT entered the recording studio to cut the album 'The Sickness Of Brutality'. A demo, entitled 'Sickness', arrived in May 2005.

Necrocathedral, Defilement (2003). Hatred Of The Tormented / Necrocathedral / Morbid / Flesh Eaten & Bones Broken / Defilement / Pagan's War / Preserved Zombie Head / Sekira.
Sickness, (2005). Intro / Mark Of The Undead / Defilement / Hatred Of The Tormented / Morbid / Bones Broken & Flesh Eaten / Rotting Crypt.

DEFLESHED

UMEÅ, SWEDEN — *Lars Löfven (vocals / guitar), Kristoffer Griedl (guitar), Gustaf Jorde (bass), Oscar Karlsson (drums).*

Umeå's DEFLESHED are purveyors of Thrash infused Death Metal, heavy on gross lyrics and impenetrable vocals. DEFLESHED was forged during 1991 with an inaugural line-up of ex-CONVULSION guitarist Lars Löfven, Kristoffer Griedl and drummer Oskar Karlsson. This version of the band managed an eponymous demo before fracturing. Second session 'Abrah Kadavrah' saw the inclusion of erstwhile CREMATORIUM bassist Gustaf Jorde and lead vocals from Johan Hedman. Progress was such that DEFLESHED were included on the Nuclear Blast 'Grindcore' compilation and had three tracks from the demo issued as a 7" courtesy of the Italian Miscarriage label as 'Obsculum Obscenum' in December 1993.

Bassist Gustaf Jorde was added prior to recording of debut November 1994 EP 'Ma Belle Scalpelle' for the German Invasion Records concern. Karlsson left for GATES OF ISHTAR, and subsequently SCHEITAN and RAISED FIST, and in his stead came Matte Modin in time for the February 1996 released 'Abrah Kadavhrah' album. 1997's 'Under The Blade' closed out with a cover version of DESTRUCTION's 'Curse The Gods'.

In 1998 DEFLESHED contributed their version of SEPULTURA's 'Beneath The Remains' for a tribute album. Japanese fans would be in for a treat with the 1999 'Fast Forward' album, their domestic variant including an extra seven live tracks. On the road in Europe during October of 1999, the group joined a heavyweight billing comprising MARDUK, ANGEL CORPSE, AETERNUS and CANNIBAL CORPSE.

The Hammerheart 2000 re-issue of 'Under The Blade' added new artwork and a whole swathe of bonus tracks including a cover of SEPULTURA's 'Beneath The Remains'. That same year 2000 Modin had bailed out to join DARK FUNERAL.

DEFLESHED

The band toured Japan during March 2001. During 2002 ex-drummer Oskar Karlsson was found to be active with THE DUSKFALL and Death n' Roll outfit HELLTRAIN.

A projected extensive run of European tour dates throughout March and April of 2003 found DEFLESHED acting as support act to GRAVE. However, these shows would then be cancelled and the band put together headline dates, dubbed the 'Battle Royal' tour with support from TAETRE. The Regain Records November 2003 re-issue of 'Fast Forward' hosted significant extra tracks in a 2002 version of the title track plus cover versions of NUCLEAR ASSAULT's 'Radiation Sickness', SEPULTURA's 'Beneath The Remains' and DESTRUCTION's 'Curse The Gods'. The band hooked up with DARK FUNERAL for a short burst of Italian dates in March 2004. Guitarist Lars Lofven would also aid THE DUSKFALL for live work.

The band entered Dug Out Studios in Uppsala to record their fifth studio album 'May The Flesh Be With You', sporting a cover rendition of MÖTLEY CRÜE's 'Red Hot'. Gustaf Jorde featured as backing vocalist on THE PROJECT HATE's 2005 album "Armageddon March Eternal (Symphonies Of Slit Wrists)". Festival dates for DEFLESHED in the Summer of 2005 saw the re-inclusion of DARK FUNERAL drummer Matte Modin. However, in November the group announced it was to disband. A farewell show would be scheduled for Christmas day at the Fellini venue in Uppsala.

Ex-DEFLESHED bassist Gustaf Jorde announced new formation NAILSTATE to the world in early 2006, being a union with Paul Mäkitalo (a.k.a. 'Themgoroth') of DARK FUNERAL and INFERNAL, Peter Tuthill, ex-CONSTRUCDEAD and DOG FACED GODS and Stefan Norgren from ETERNAL OATH.

Defleshed (Rotting Inflictioner), Defleshed (1992) (Cassette demo). Satanic Séance / Rotting Inflictioner / Totalitarian Corporal Torment / Vacuited Soul / Phlegm / Defleshed / Rot In Agony.
Abrah Kadavrah..., Defleshed (1992) (Cassette demo). Pulverlized, Pasteurized Eyes / Vastus Ecclesia / Vintras Daughter / Obsculum Obscenum / Open Gates.
Body Art, Defleshed (1993) (Cassette demo). Necromantic Barbeque / Anatomically Incorrect / Mary Bloody Mary / Orbital Cavity Discovery / Forruttenels.
Obsculum Obscenum, Miscarriage MS002 (1993) (7" vinyl single). Obsculum Obscenum / Satanic Source / Phlegm.

Ma Belle Scalpelle, Invasion IR 009 (1994). Gathering Flies / Moribiance Blue Cafe / Simply Fall Towards / Many Mangled Maggots / Ma Belle Scalpelle.
ABRAH KADAVRAH, Invasion IR 019 (1996). Beaten, Loved And Eaten / Mary Bloody Mary / With A Gambrel / In Chains And Leather / Abrah Kadavrah / Gone With The Feaces / Anatomically Incorrect / On Gorgeous Grounds / Body Art ... / ... Pierced Through The Heart.
UNDER THE BLADE, Invasion IR 032 (1997). Farewell To The Flesh / Entering My Yesterdays / Eat The Meat Raw / Sons Of Spellcraft And Starfalls / Metalbounded / Under The Blade / Thorns Of A Black Rose / Cinderella's Return And Departure / Walking The Moons Of Mars / Metallic Warlust / Curse The Gods.
FAST FORWARD, Soundholic SHCD1-0032 (1999) (Japanese release). The Return Of The Flesh / The Heat From Another Sun / Fast Forward / The Iron And The Maiden / Proud To Be Dead / Snowballing Blood / Wilder Than Fire / Feeding Fatal Fairies / Lightning Strikes Thrice / Domination Of The Sub Queen / Speeding The Ways / Entering My Yesterdays / Mary Bloody Mary / Metallic Warlust / Under The Blade / Walking The Moons Of Mars / In Chains And Leather / Thorns Of A Black Rose.
FAST FORWARD, War Music WAR 011 (1999). The Return Of The Flesh / The Heat From Another Sun / Fast Forward / The Iron And The Maiden / Proud To Be Dead / Snowballing Blood / Wilder Than Fire / Feeding Fatal Fairies / Lightning Strikes Thrice / Domination Of The Sub Queen / Speeding The Ways.
Death—The High Cost Of Living, War Music RAW 003 (1999). Entering My Yesterdays / Mary Bloody Mary / Metallic Warlust / Under The Blade / Walking The Moons Of Mars / In Chains & Leather / Thorns Of A Black Rose.
FAST FORWARD, Pavement Music 32340 (2000) (USA release). The Return Of The Flesh / The Heat From Another Sun / Fast Forward / The Iron And The Maiden / Proud To Be Dead / Snowballing Blood / Wilder Than Fire / Feeding Fatal Fairies / Lightning Strikes Thrice / Domination Of The Sub Queen / Speeding The Ways / Under The Blade (Live) / Thorns Of A Black Rose (Live).
ROYAL STRAIGHT FLESH, Teichiku TKCS-85050 (2002) (Japanese release). Hand Over Fist / Fire In The Soul / Friction / Warborn / Feed On The Fallen / Royal Straight Flesh / Back For The Attack / Blood Brigade / Pick Your Poison / Dangerous When Dead / Brakefailure / Fast Forward / Radiation Sickness.
ROYAL STRAIGHT FLESH, Regain RR 0211-109 (2002) (European release). Hand Over Fist / Fire In The Soul / Friction / Warborn / Feed On The Fallen / Royal Straight Flesh / Back For The Attack / Blood Brigade / Pick Your Poison / Dangerous When Dead / Brakefailure.
RECLAIM THE BEAT, Teichiku TKCS-85116 (2005) (Japanese release). Stripped To The Bone / Abstinence For Turbulence / Chain Reaction / Bulldozed (Back To Basic) / Under Destruction / Grind And Rewind / Reclaim The Beat / Red Hot / May The Flesh Be With You / Ignorance Is Bliss / Aggroculture / Over And Out / Needless To Pray.
RECLAIM THE BEAT, Regain RR 051 (2005) (European release). Stripped To The Bone / Abstinence For Turbulence / Chain Reaction / Bulldozed (Back To Basic) / Under Destruction / Grind And Rewind / Reclaim The Beat / Red Hot / May The Flesh Be With You / Ignorance Is Bliss / Aggroculture / Over And Out.
RECLAIM THE BEAT, Regain North America 217 (2005) (USA release). Stripped To The Bone / Abstinence For Turbulence / Chain Reaction / Reclaim The Beat / Grind And Rewind / Under Destruction / Red Hot / Bulldozed (Back To Basic) / Ignorance Is Bliss / May The Flesh Be With You / Needless To Pray / Aggroculture / Over And Out.

DEFLORACE

CZECH REPUBLIC — *Petr Vrbica (vocals), Milan Urbánek (guitar), Mira Mièka (guitar), Pavel Jurek (bass), Martin Krče (drums).*

Moravian Death-Grinders from Nový Jičín created in 1992. DEFLORACE, having first performed live in July of 1993 and including guitarist Jari Vrbica and bassist Jiøí Sosík in the ranks, emerged with the 1994 demo 'Morbid Oratorium'. Follow up promotion efforts included 'Postmortal Abomination', two tracks from which also appeared on the compilation album 'Echoes From The Underworld', and 'Dreams Of A Serial Killer'. This last demo was later pressed up as part of a Leviathan Records split album CD in alliance with INGROWING's 'Perverted Look At The World'.

Ex-DEFLORACE bassist Pavel Jurek and drummer Martin Krče joined MARTYRIUM CHRISTI in 1998.

11 MURDERS, (1998). At The Gein's Is Glee / Dungeon Full Of Suffer / A Happy Man / It Was Václav Mrázek / Eternal Love / Radio Gay Gay / ... And All Of Them Are Dead / Those Were Our Children, My Darling / The Best Of ... / Perverted Soldier (A Green Cannibal) / A Killogramme Of Meat From Fritz.

DEFORMITY

BELGIUM — *Christopher D. Wolff (vocals / bass), Micha (guitar), G (guitar), B. Demonic (drums).*

Extreme Metal band DEFORMITY date back to 1995, founded by drummer Bolle, bassist Wulf and guitarists Gaze and Lookmulle. Shortly after CONGRESS guitarist Michael was also drafted. A live demo, 'Deformity Live Beyond', was cut during 1996 prompting a deal with Goodlife Recordings which subsequently bore fruition with the 1997 'Misanthrope' MCD. The following year DEFORMITY toured Europe and put in appearances on several compilation albums.

1999's 'Murder Within Sin', released by Blasphemour Records in the USA and Next Sentence Records in Europe, found the band growing ever more aggressive. A non album track would also feature on a Blasphemour compilation album. During early 2001 Lookmulle was forced out of the band suffering throat problems and Wulf duly took over the lead vocal role. DEFORMITY signed to the Displeased label for June 2002's 'Superior' outing. In November 2004 ex-DEFORMITY guitarist Dave Vanlokeren joined FLESHMOULD.

Misanthrope EP, Goodlife Recordings (1997). My Creation / Splitting / They Watch / God Defined / A.I.D.G.
177252: God Defined, Goodlife Recordings (1997) (Split single with CONGRESS). 177252: God Defined.
MURDER WITHIN SIN, Blasphemour (1999). Eyes / Bloodfields / Stained Red / Enter Within The Lust Divine / 33 / Angelheart / The Dark Sun / Speak Out My Name / Misanthrope / Burn Down The Heavens / Night Scars.
SUPERIOR, Displeased D-00105 (2002). Dawn Of Omega / Samslaysman / 7 Fathers I / Raven / Time (The Avenger) / The Prophet Game / Daylight Bleeding / Vassago / Eden Is Burning / Shadowcross / L'Ame Des Immortels / Godwind.

DEHUMANIZED

NEW YORK, NY, USA — *Johny Collet (vocals), Rich Nagasawa (guitar), Paul Tovora (guitar), Mike Hussey (bass), George Torres (drums).*

DEHUMANIZED was forged during 1995 by guitarists Rich Nagasawa, of CHARNEL HOUSE repute, and Mike Palacios with George Torres on the drums. This trio cut the opening demo 'Terminal Punishment', after which they added vocalist Mike Zuzio. Honing their live craft the band undertook intensive local gigging opening for the likes of SIX FEET UNDER, IMMOLATION, CANNIBAL CORPSE and BRUTAL TRUTH, all within months of formation.

However, DEHUMANIZED was blighted by an ever fluctuating line up, first signalled by the departure of both Palacios and Zuzio. Enrolling Dave Zatuchney from IMMORTAL SUFFERING to fill the guitar vacancy the band then pulled in bassist Mike Chan and vocalist Jerry Barco. The following year both Zatuchney and Chan exited. Finding Tom Toscano of UMBILICAL STRANGULATION to fill in six string duties DEHUMANIZED continued gigging minus a bassist. In this formation the group entered the recording studio in late December of 1997 to craft the debut album 'Prophecies Foretold', released by Pathos Productions in early 1998.

Drafting former FALLEN CHRIST bassist Sean Morelli DEHUMANIZED embarked upon an exhaustive nationwide campaign to promote the album, appearing at the 'Milwaukee Metalfest', 'Texas Grindfest', 'Ohio Deathfest' and 'New Jersey Metalfest' events as well guesting for bands such as SUFFOCATION, MORBID ANGEL, DEICIDE, OBITUARY, VADER, CRYPTOPSY, BROKEN HOPE, MONSTROSITY and NILE. In spite of this progress the group folded in 2000. Torres would join fellow New York Death Metal crew SKINLESS during October 2001. The drummer would also add session vocals for IRATE.

Nagasawa and Torres resurrected DEHUMANIZED in 2004, assembling an all new look band including singer John Collett, second guitarist Paul Tovora and erstwhile KALOPSIA bassist Mike Hussey. Notable gigs included the 'Maryland Death Fest' in May and the 'Sick Shit Fest 2' in June.

PROPHECIES FORETOLD, Pathos (1988). Prophecies Foretold / Kingdom Of Cruelty / Fade Into Obscurity / Solitary Demise / Infinite Despair / Doomed To Die / Terminal Punishment / Condemned / Drawn By Blood.

PROBLEMS FIRST, New Red Archives (1999). Classified / Educators / Fee To Live / Mommy's Killin' / Fuck You Where's My Brew / Confessions / Coo-Coos / Better Later Days / Convenience / Everyday / Childish & Cowardly / Tragic / Gimme The Scoop.

DEHYDRATED

PIEŠŤANY, SLOVAKIA — *Vlado Pagáè (vocals), Brano Jurak (guitar), Jano Bezovy (guitar), Maros Juliny (drums).*

Brutal grinding Death Metal band DEHYDRATED, based out of Piestany, delivered their opening shot with the 1992 demo cassette 'Festered Mind'. The group had been formed a year earlier by guitarist Vlado Pagáè and two erstwhile BRUTALIZER members bassist Palo and drummer Peter 'Pegas' Hlaváè. The 'Suffering Of Living Mass' session followed swiftly on its heels the same year, both of these tapes being strictly in the traditional Grindcore mould. The band's first commercial release came with four tracks for the 'Burnt' split album shared with BESTIALIT for Metal Age Productions. The 'Ideas' recordings first surfaced in Slovakia in cassette format through Metal Age in 1996 but would be picked up by Copremesis Records for a CD version in 1999 which featured different cover art.

Drummer Hlaváè would depart to join KRABATHOR and later figure in HYPNOS and APOPLEXY. DEHYDRATED regrouped pulling in guitarist Jano Bezovy, vocalist Vlado Pagáè and drummer Maros Juliny.

DEHYDRATED also garnered extra exposure with the inclusion of two tracks on the 'Sometimes Death Is Better' released by the Belgian Shiver label and the homegrown 'Death Metal Made In Slovaki' collection released by Exponent Studio Records.

BURNT, Metal Age Productions (1994) (Split album with BESTIALIT).
IDEAS, Metal Ages MA-0009-4-331 (1996). Hate To God / Common Perfection / Stallion / The Weak King / Stolid / Ode To Solitude / Touch The Sun / The Old House / Poet And Pain / The End / Way Kyky Raga.

DEICIDE

FL, USA — *Glenn Benton (vocals / bass), Eric Hoffman (guitar), Brian Hoffman (guitar), Steve Asheim (drums).*

DEICIDE, emerging from the cult troupe AMON founded in 1987, was the first American Black styled Death Metal band to push the novelty factor into the realms of the dangerous. Early shows had arch protagonist vocalist / bassist Glen Benton drenched in the blood of a pig bedecked in studded body armour sporting an upside down cross the frontman had burned into his own forehead. Benton, whose first son he tactfully named Daemon, rather intriguingly voiced premonitions that he will die aged 33. Needless to say his 33rd Birthday passed without event.

The singer's more than vocal appreciation of a Satanic belief system, his willingness to engage in media sponsored set discussions on good and evil with church members (including the late former TWELFTH NIGHT vocalist and vicar GEOFF MANN) and his apparent witnessed shooting of squirrels in his house (!) put DEICIDE firmly in the Black Metal camp. Quite remarkably for a Death-Black Metal band DEICIDE maintained a rock solid line-up since its inception for fifteen years, comprising Benton, brothers Eric Hoffman and Brian Hoffman on guitars, and Steve Asheim on drums, and continues to maintain a strong unyielding fan base.

AMON released two demos, August 1987's 8 track garage recording 'Feasting The Beast' and 'Sacrificial' in December 1989. This second session scored a deal with Roadrunner Records. The name DEICIDE arrived in June 1990 with an eponymous album recorded in February of that year by Scott Burns at the spiritual home of US Death Metal, Tampa's Morrisound Recording, re-crafting all six 'Sacrificial' tracks for this opus. This winning formula of studio and producer would be cemented for the next three albums.

The 'Deicide' album, issued in June 1990, broke little new ground, if any, musically but Benton's skill in manipulating the media was matched by a half hour savage burst of pure blasphemy driven by Steve Asheim's impressive percussive abilities. Lyrical content was entirely devoted to the practices of Lucifer and his minions with the exception of opener 'Lunatic Of God's Creation' and 'Carnage In The Temple Of The Damned', in deference respectively to Charles Manson and Guyana occultist Jim Jones.

That same year Glen Benton featured as a backing vocalist on another ground breaking recording, CANNIBAL CORPSE's 'Eaten Back To Life'. Further controversy was whipped up after the second album, June 1992's 'Legion', when two New Jersey teenagers tortured and killed a dog leaving its carcass hanging in a tree. When questioned by authorities the youngsters claimed inspiration from DEICIDE. 'Legion', intended as a quick fire response to the furor engendered by the debut, was so rushed that the original sessions clocked in at just over 20 minutes, necessitating the band returned to the studio to bring the second effort up to a satisfactory duration.

So vociferous was the media against DEICIDE that their notoriety spread into areas not normally troubled by Black Metal. Benton's comments regarding his supposed treatment of animals led to bomb threats which blighted a winter 1992 European tour. A more pointed message left with the media, allegedly from the Animal Militia organisation's Manchester cell, informed Benton he would be killed if he stepped on English soil. DEICIDE's British and European shows went according to plan until the Scandinavian leg when a bomb planted at the Fryshuset club in Stockholm, Sweden exploded. The device actually detonated during touring partner's THERION's set, but had been timed to go off in the middle of DEICIDE's originally scheduled stage time. Nobody was seriously hurt, although the bomb caused several minor injuries and blew apart part of a wall and roofing. However, it was unclear as to the object of the assault as support band GOREFEST had also received death threats from another source. Performing in the UK, a fake bomb, constructed out of a clock and wires, was thrown onstage in Manchester, temporarily halting the show. The band finished the remainder of the European tour without major incident.

With all this notoriety the band built up a loyal fan base with surprising speed and Roadrunner Records were quick off the mark in re-issuing the AMON demos re-credited to DEICIDE and marketed as 'Amon: Feasting The Beast'. In a rare guest slot outside of DEICIDE activities Benton aided leading Mexican Thrash act TRANSMETAL with backing vocals on their 1993 'Dante's Inferno' opus.

DEICIDE's third album arrived in April 1995, 'Once Upon The Cross' immediately provoking outrage with its cover art depicting a slaughtered messiah figure. In the USA large stickers were placed over the offending image. However, upon opening the CD case purchasers were confronted by even more graphic artwork portraying an eviscerated Jesus. Once the shock value had been overcome, the record was given enough impetus to land at a suitable number 66 in the national British charts, unfortunately 'Once Upon The Cross' showed minimal progression.

'Serpents Of The Light' slithered out in October 1997, replete once again with provocative artwork showing Jesus with a forked serpent tongue. The album hosted a fourth round of zero tolerance toward Christianity, included concert favourite 'Blame It On God'. Live album 'When Satan Lives' emerged a year later.

The band's July 2000 release, the wryly titled 'Insinerate Hymn', proved to be as uncompromising as ever, the unrelenting river of blasphemy triggered by another stage staple 'Bible Basher'. Rumblings of discontent were boiling to the surface though as the band began voicing dissatisfaction with their label, complaining of an unfavourable degree of promotion and budgeting.

DEICIDE toured as headliners in America during May of 2001 topping a bill comprising MARDUK, GORGUTS and ALL OUT WAR. 'In Torment In Hell' was delivered that September but obviously all was not well in the DEICIDE camp. When reviews pointed towards a roughshod finish, the group claimed Roadrunner Records had released an uncompleted product.

During early 2002 Glen Benton cut session lead vocals for VITAL REMAINS 'Dechristianize' album leading to speculation as to the future of DEICIDE. However, it would soon after be revealed that DEICIDE themselves were in the recording studio cutting a 2002 album. European tour dates slated for November saw the band heading up a bill including BEHEMOTH, DESTROYER 666, DIABOLIC, ANTAEUS and CENTINEX. However, this roster would be subsequently slashed to just DEICIDE, MYSTIC CIRCLE and CENTINEX.

DEICIDE, ending their long relationship with Roadrunner Records, signed to the British Earache label during November. The band would be confirmed as headliners for the 'X-Mass Festivals' European tour commencing in London on December 7th, heading up a strong billing incorporating DESTRUCTION, AMON AMARTH, NILE, GRAVEWORM, DEW-SCENTED, MISERY INDEX and DISBELIEF.

The band announced touring plans for the US in November of 2003, heading up a billing comprising HATE ETERNAL, KRISIUN and CATTLE DECAPITATION.

DEICIDE's February 2004 offering 'Scars Of The Crucifix' came marketed in an array of formats designed to test the budget of the most ardent fan. The U.S. only slipcase version, packaged with die cut inverted cross naturally, contained an extra 'Behind The Scars' DVD and would be restricted to 3,000 copies. Meantime the European digipack variant also added the 'Behind the Scars: Under the Skin of Deicide' DVD plus the incentive of a signature DEICIDE guitar pick. Restricted to 10,000 copies, 9,999 included either a Glen Benton, Eric Hoffman or Brian Hoffman signature pick but hidden inside one copy was a specially minted DEICIDE guitar pick made of metal, the lucky fan who bought this copy winning a BC Rich NJ Beast guitar. In addition, a vinyl version, limited to 2,000 copies and manufactured in heavyweight 180 gramm 12" black vinyl, would be clad in exclusive Paul Booth cover art, different from the artwork on the CD version.

'Scars Of The Crucifix' would generate strong sales, eventually proving to be Earache's highest selling album of the year, debuting at No. 18 on Billboard's Independent Albums Chart and No. 24 on Billboard's Heatseekers Chart in the U.S., hitting both charts higher than any other metal band.

Touring in North America during the Spring was to see DEICIDE on a package billing with SUPERJOINT RITUAL and CLUTCH. However, shortly into these dates it seemed the band had either left or been unceremoniously ejected. Nevertheless, DEICIDE was quick to announce their own September headlining shows, partnered with road mates GOATWHORE, CATTLE DECAPITATION and JUNGLE ROT.

The band's touring history was blighted yet again though in June when, on the eve of scheduled European shows allied with MYSTIC CIRCLE, AKERCOCKE and IN AETERNUM, DEICIDE abruptly pulled out. Recriminations from the tour organisers the Metallysee Booking Agency were both swift and damning. The group had performed just one show at the Dutch 'Dynamo' festival then cancelling a London gig and flying home to Florida. Whilst an official label statement cited DEICIDE's "anger and frustration at the transportation and financial arrangements" in return Metallysee alleged the band had doubled their fee and given faulty air conditioning on a tour bus as an excuse to withdraw. The group also withdrew from the major 'Wacken Open Air' festival in Germany scheduled for August, citing "family reasons". Positive news came with the band's re-signing with Earache Records a re-routed European tour booked for October / November with French Black Metal crew ARKHON INFAUSTUS as guests. However, the group re-shaped itself for these shows, drafting former CANNIBAL CORPSE guitarist Jack Owen as Brian Hoffman would be forced out due to personal reasons. As such, the group was forced to rearrange the first three dates, at Hassalt, Haarlem and Paris, in order to give Owen time to learn the catalogue. Featured on second guitar would be VITAL REMAINS man Dave Suzuki as, according to band reports, Eric Hoffman had not arrived at the airport in time to leave for the tour as scheduled. Suzuki was drafted that same day, flying from Rhode Island to JFK airport in order to meet up with the band and fly on to Madrid, Spain. However, DEICIDE pulled part of the tour due to an apparent "family crisis" (the death of drummer Steve Asheim's father). Following a truncated 45 min concert at the Hard Club in Porto, Portugal on 5th November the band returned to the USA, before regrouping to complete the trek.

Ex-guitarist Eric Hoffman joined UNHOLY GHOST in February 2005, although this would subsequently be refuted. The following month the Hoffman brothers instigated legal proceedings over the rights to the DEICIDE band and announced they were to assemble a brand new DEICIDE. Meantime, Benton's version of DEICIDE collaborated with IMMOLATION, SKINLESS, MISERY INDEX and WITH PASSION for US dates in May. Joining the band for these dates would be guitarist RALPH SANTOLLA, a man known for his melodic work with EYEWITNESS, MILLENNIUM and MONARCH, solo works plus later stints with ICED EARTH and SEBASTIAN BACH.

Glen Benton made time to see inclusion on the ROADRUNNER UNITED 25th anniversary album 'The All-Stars Sessions', featuring on the track 'Annihilation By The Hand Of God' penned by SLIPKNOT's Joey Jordison.

A concert in Chile, at the Gimnasio Nataniel in Santiago on 15th July and actually DEICIDE's third attempt to play in the country, would run into bitter controversy as local church officials attempted to ban the concert. So far reaching was the debate that finally Osvaldo Puccio, General Secretary of the Chilean government, issued a statement affirming the government's position that "in this country, no cultural expression will be censored". Over 3,000 fans attended the gig, with 15 being arrested for public drunkenness and disorderly conduct.

DEICIDE allied with VISCERAL BLEEDING, WYKKED WYTCH and PROSTITUTE DISFIGUREMENT for European shows throughout October and November, taking in the UK, Ireland, France, Belgium, Holland, Germany, Switzerland, Austria, Hungary, Croatia, Czech Republic, Spain and Italy. On December 15th Glen Benton notably joined the ROADRUNNER UNITED conglomerate at the New York Nokia Theater for an all star Metal evening. The singer fronted a cover of OBITUARY's 'The End Complete' featuring SEPULTURA's Andreas Kisser, ex-FEAR FACTORY man Dino Cazares plus the SLIPKNOT rhythm section of bassist Paul Gray and drummer Joey Jordison plus DEICIDE's own 'Dead By Dawn'.

The group ran into further controversy on their February 2006 tour of South America when a concert in Valparaiso, Chile was cancelled. The gig was replaced by a show in Quilpue, but that too was aborted. Local promoters had stirred the wrath of local church and civic organisations by postering the dates with images of Jesus Christ with a bullet hole in the forehead. In somewhat of an ironic twist, bearing in mind DEICIDE's vocal history, guitarist Ralph Santolla stated that he was a Catholic and "against Satanism".

Further trouble followed the band into Europe. A scheduled performance at the 'Hellfest' event in France was cancelled over authorities concerns in relation to grave desecration in Brittany, where tombstones had been vandalised with the DEICIDE song title 'When Satan Rules His World'. Back on US soil, the group entered Morrisound Studios once again to cut a new record 'The Stench Of Redemption', produced by Jim Morris. DEICIDE conducted West Coast "God Killers" shows alongside VITAL REMAINS, seeing Glen Benton doing double frontman duty each night, CREMATORIUM and Oregon's DESOLATION.

The band wound up in chaos again though when on July 14th at Hustlers in Laredo, Texas, guitarist Ralph Santolla was arrested. Reports stated that Glen Benton had voiced his displeasure at being "ripped off" by promoters and had the power cut after just four songs. In the following chaos the police arrived, arresting Santolla after the guitarist had allegedly thrown a can at one of the officers.

In further adverse publicity, DEICIDE had 'The Stench Of Redemption' banned from large Swedish online store Ginza.se, the company citing the blasphemous album sleeve art and controversial lyrical subject matter as their reasoning. In addition, the store apparently also removed all DEICIDE back catalogue. Unfortunately, a day after this press announcement a spokesman for Ginza.se stated the only reason DEICIDE was not represented in their store was because their albums "didn't sell very well".

The band was set to partner with HURTLOCKER, DESOLATION and JUNGLE ROT for US touring throughout September and October but then cancelled these dates after severing ties with their booking agent. Canadian concerts too were suspended, the band citing "due to paperwork issues with the Canadian venues". A fresh round of shows was announced, these including appearances in Guatemala, Costa Rica and Mexico in November. On November 18th the band appeared at the Monterrey Metal Fest event at the at the Coca Cola Auditorium in Mexico alongside BLIND GUARDIAN, CATHEDRAL, U.D.O., EDGUY, OBITUARY, BLUDGEON, LEAVES' EYES, SADUS, VAINGLORY, HYDROGYN and JOE STUMP'S REIGN OF TERROR.

Australian and New Zealand shows, supported by DAWN OF AZAZEL, took place in December. DEICIDE announced they would be hooking up with VISCERAL BLEEDING and PSYCROPTIC for a European tour in January 2007. However, DEICIDE kicked off their European tour on January 5th in Eindhoven, Holland without frontman Glen Benton, who reportedly was forced to stay home to take care of "pressing legal matters". Replacing Benton for the first four dates would be the SEVERE TORTURE, CENTURIAN and NOX credited Seth van Loo. On January 9th, debuting for a concert in Manchester, England, Garbaty Yaha from the Polish Death Metal band DISSENTER joined DEICIDE on bass and vocals. In addition to Yaha, the January 12th London show saw vocal duties divided between Jason Peppiatt of PSYCROPTIC, Martin Pedersen from VISCERAL BLEEDING and Solomon J Lucifer Christ from TED MAUL.

Spanish promoter Matarile withdrew its show offers due to Benton's non-appearance, but these shows were subsequently rescheduled as Benton announced he was to rejoin the band for January 13th in Paris.

A concert DVD, 'Doomsday L.A.' recorded at the Los Angeles Knitting Factory, emerged on Earache in early February. A preceding digital download EP, the 'Doomsday L.A. Live EP", arrived in January.

DEICIDE

DEICIDE, Roadrunner RO 9381 (1990). Lunatic Of God's Creation / Sacrificial Suicide / Oblivious To Evil / Dead By Dawn / Blasphericion / Deicide / Carnage In The Temple Of The Damned / Mephistopheles / Day Of Darkness / Crucifixion.
LEGION, Roadrunner RC 91922 (1992). Satan Spawns The Caco-Daemon / Dead But Dreaming / Repent To Die / Trifixion / Behead The Prophet (No Lord Shall Live) / Holy Deception / In Hell I Burn / Revocate The Agitator.
AMON: FEASTING THE BEAST, Roadrunner RR 9111-2 (1993). Lunatic Of God's Creation / Sacrificial Suicide / Crucifixation / Carnage In The Temple Of The Damned / Dead By Dawn / Blasphereion / Feasting The Beast / Day Of Darkness / Oblivious To Nothing.
ONCE UPON THE CROSS, Roadrunner RR 8949-2 (1995). Once Upon The Cross / Christ Denied / When Satan Rules His World / Kill The Christian / Trick Or Betrayed / They Are All Children Of The Underworld / Behind The Light They Shall Rise / To Be Dead / Confessional Rape. Chart position: 66 UK.
SERPENTS OF THE LIGHT, Roadrunner RR 8811-2 (1997). Serpents Of The Light / Bastard Of Christ / Blame It On God / This Hell We're In / I Am No One / Slaves To The Cross / Creatures Of Habit / Believe The Lie / The Truth Above.
WHEN SATAN LIVES, Roadrunner RR 8704-2 (1998). When Satan Rules His World / Blame It On God / Bastard Of Christ / They Are The Children Of The Underworld / Serpents Of The Light / Dead But Dreaming / Slave To The Cross / Believe The Lie / Trick Or Betrayed / Behind The Light Thou Shall Rise / Deicide / Father Baker's / Dead By Dawn / Sacrificial Suicide.
INSINERATE HYMN, Roadrunner RR 8570-2 (2000). Bible Basher / Forever Hate You / Standing In The Flames / Remnant Of A Hopeless Path / The Gift That Keeps On Giving / Halls Of Warship / Suffer Again / Worst Enemy / Apocalyptic Fear / Refusal Of Penance.
IN TORMENT IN HELL, Roadrunner RR 8482-2 (2001). In Torment In Hell / Christ Don't Care / Vengeance Will Be Mine / Imminent Doom / Child Of God / Let It Be Done / Worry In The House Of Thieves / Lurking Among Us.
SCARS OF THE CRUCIFIX, Earache MOSH 273 (2004). Scars Of The Crucifix / Mad At God / Conquered By Sodom / When Heaven Burns / Fuck Your God / Darkness Come / Enchanted Nightmare / Go Now Your Lord Is Dead / The Pentecostal. Chart position: 140 FRANCE.
THE STENCH OF REDEMPTION, Earache (2006). The Stench Of Redemption / Death To Jesus / Desecration / Homage For Satan / Never To Be Seen Again / The Lord's Sedition / Walk With The Devil In Dreams You Behold / Crucified For The Innocence / Not Of This Earth. Chart positions: 84 GERMANY, 99 FRANCE.
Doomsday L.A. Live EP, Earache (2007) (Digital EP). The Scars Of The Crucifix / The Stench Of Redemption / Desecration.

DEIFECATION

ENSCHEDE, HOLLAND — *Brus (vocals), Iwan (guitar), Jan Ziljstra (guitar), Marijn de Zeeuw (bass), Splatterick Stuivenberg (drums).*

DEIFICATION is an Enschede based brutal Death Metal combo formulated during 1998 by vocalist Willem, guitarist Iwan, bassist Liwu and drummer Gijs. Gigging locally, the quartet achieved its first success by winning the preliminary round of the 'Grote Prijs van Drienerlo' competition. Subsequent appearances included showings at the 'Flatrock' festival in both 1999 and 2000. The band also joined forces with Punk Metal act LIKMNREET for touring.

Bolstering their sound, DEIFICATION acquired Jan Ziljstra as second guitarist. However, both Liwu and Gijs exited in 2000, being substituted by EXTREEM ECZEEM members bassist Marco Olthof and drummer Jan Patrick "Splatterick" Stuivenberg. In March 2001 the band recorded the 'Dystopian Anthropotagonism' demo at Ground Zero Studios in Zutphen, after which Olthof departed. Marijn de Zeeuw duly assumed bass duties. Signing to the German based Unstoppable Media DEIFICATION cut their debut album 'Reciprocreation' for September 2004 release. Drummer Splatterick Stuivenberg was replaced by Floris in January 2004.

RECIPROCREATION, Unstoppable Media (2004). The Abusement Park / Minor Defect / Fetushistic Ectopikleptomaniac / Dystopian Anthropotagonism / Hysterical Hysterectomy / Triggerhappy Childmolester / Fountain Of Youth / Wombraider / Babybrutaliser / Down The Slide, Up The Plate / Found At The Playground.

DEIVOS

POLAND — *Jaroslaw Pienkos (vocals / bass), Tomasz Kolcon (guitar), Krysztof Saran (drums).*

Lublin Death Metal act created during 1997 by the erstwhile RAVENDUSK pairing of vocalist Marcin Górniak and guitarist Maciej Nawrocki. Second guitarist Tomasz Kolcon is also an active member of ENGRAVED whilst frontman Jaroslaw Pienkos and drummer Krysztof Saran operate Black Metal act ABUSIVENESS. Saran is also a member of ECLIPSE. The band's 1999 'Praised By Generations' demo saw Maciej Nawrocki aiding on bass and lead vocals from Marcin Gorniak.

DEIVOS lost the services of both Nawrocki and Górniak in 2001 so Pieñkos added lead vocal responsibilities to his role in order to cover. In this incarnation the group debuted on the live front in April of 2002, supporting PARRICIDE, DAMNABLE and HYPNOS. The 'Hostile Blood' blood EP emerged in early 2003. Subsequently signed by the Bulgarian label Butchery Music 'Hostile Blood' saw a re-issue adding extra demo tracks.

During April of 2004 Krzysztof Saran acted as stand in drummer for PARRICIDE's live dates. DEIVOS inducted ABUSIVENESS guitarist Mścisław in June.

Hostile Blood EP, Independent (2003). Chasm Climber / Hostile Blood / Encircled By Nothingness / Scarcity Of Suffering / Throw Off The Fetters.

DELIGHT

POLAND — *Paulina Maslanka (vocals), Jaroslaw Baran (guitar), Sebastian Wójtowicz (guitar), Piotr Szymanski (bass), Barbara Lasek (keyboards), Tomasz Baran (drums).*

A Gothic Death Metal act forged in 1997 by former SATOR members vocalist Paulina Maslanka, guitarists Jaroslaw Baran and Sebastian Wójtowicz, bassist Piotr Szymanski and drummer Tomasz Polczyk. Quite incredibly DELIGHT's 2002 offering 'The Fading Tale' included a cover version of GEORGE MICHAEL's 'Careless Whisper'. The band participated in the mammoth CLOSTERKELLER headlined tour throughout Poland in November 2003 dubbed the 'Dark Stars' festivals. Joining the band for these dates would be a supporting cast including MOONLIGHT and SACRIVERSUM. The band, promoting the new album 'Anew', would join the 'Dark Stars' festivals yet again in November 2004 with a supporting cast of MOONLIGHT, CLOSTERKELLER, CEMETERY OF SCREAM, DARZAMAT and DESDEMONA.

Signing to Roadrunner Records the band, the very first Polish act on the label, recorded the Rhys Fulber produced album 'Breaking Ground' for issue in January 2007. Live promotion included a tour of Germany, Austria and Switzerland, commencing January 17th at the Zürich Alpenrockhouse, backing EXILIA.

THE LAST TEMPTATION, Metal Mind Productions (2001). Revelation Of A Sinner / Plenitude Is A Perfect Vacancy / The Last Temptation / Daimonion / Time Of Revenge / Farewell / Sator / Eyes That Last I Saw In Tears / The Shapes And The Shadows / The Lamentable Monument Of Stone.

THE FADING TALE, Metal Mind Productions (2002). The Fading Tale / Nymphaea / Carving The Way / The Gates Of The Green / Backwards / Careless Whisper / Orchard / Great Words On The Altars / Sombre Wine.

ETERNITY, Metal Mind Productions (2003). The Hand / Stained Glass / Requiem / Spring Day / Whale's Lungs / I Promise / The Sun / Otherness.

OD NOWA, Metal Mind Porductions (2004). Od Nowa / Za Mało / Między Nami / Wypowiem Twoje Imię / Uwolnij Mnie / Mam Dość / Zmowa Milczenia / To Jest We Mnie / O Tobie / Mój Błękit / Sen.

ANEW, (2004). Anew / More / Emotune / Your Name / Set Me Free / The Pact Of Silence / All That's In Me / About You / Bare Tree / Sleep.

BREAKING GROUND, Roadrunner (2007). Divided / Sleep With The Light On / In Too Deep / Reasons / Fire / Every Time / Emotune / More / Juliet / All Alone / Your Name / Bare Tree.

DELIRIUM X TREMENS

BELLUNO, ITALY — *Alberto Da Rech (vocals), Lorenzo Baldan (guitar), Fabio Della Lucia (guitar), Matteo De Mori (bass), Thomas Lorenzi (drums).*

Death Metal band forged in the Agordo region of Belluno in 1998, then simply billed as DELIRIUM TREMENS. Line-up problems blighted the bands early years leaving core members bassist Matteo 'Pondro' De Mori, citing a tradition with SWEET POISON, THROUGH THE ABYSS and SEVEN DARK EYES, and the GRON, INFERION and THROUGH THE ABYSS credited vocalist Alberto 'Ciardo' Da Rech in search of a whole new band. First in would be guitarists Fabio 'Med' Della Lucia, a veteran of SWEET POISON, BREATHALYSER, DREAMQUEST, BLADES and S-PLATTERS, and Lorenzo Baldan, ex of DESTHEMONA, ELECTRIC EYES and LEGION OF DOOM, followed by drummer Giorgio Murer as the group evolved into DELIRIUM X TREMENS.

This version of the band entered Majestic Studios in Scorzè near Venice in June 2003 to cut the debut EP 'CyberHuman' with producer Marino De Angeli. Upon completion of these sessions Thomas Lorenzi, previously with LAZZARUS, LEGION OF DOOM and CICLOMETRO, took over the drumming role.

DELIRIUM X TREMENS toured Italy with NECRODEATH and METHEDRAS in November 2006.

CyberHuman, Delirium X Tremens (2003). 1000 Wolves / Science / Delirium 9991 / . . . Inside Me / CyberHuman.

DELLAMORTE

AVESTA, SWEDEN — *Jonas Kjellgren (vocals), Johan Jansson (guitar), Matthias Norrman (guitar), Daniel Ekeroth (bass), Sonny Svedlund (drums).*

An infamous Death Metal act with a deeply rooted Thrash bias. DELLAMORTE, created in Avesta, was rooted in the 1990 band INTERMENT, established by erstwhile HATRED and ASOCIAL guitarist Johan Jansson. Vocalist Jonas Kjellgren is ex-PEXILATED and SICKENSIDE. During 1993 INTERMENT evolved briefly into MOONDARK before settling on DELLAMORTE. A 1995 demo, 'Drunk In The Abyss', landed a deal with the Finn label, recording in a mere 4 days the now very scarce but highly sought after album 'Everything You Hate'. The following year a 7 single, 'Dirty', emerged through the Yellow Dog label and prompted the interest of the Kron-H label, a subsidiary of French concern Osmose Productions. DELLAMORTE released the sophomore 'Uglier And More Disgusting' album, produced by Peter Tägtgren of HYPOCRISY, and set about promoting it as part of the 'World Domination' tour billed alongside DARK TRANQUILITY and ENSLAVED. Added exposure was garnered with the subsequent inclusion of DELLAMORTE on the follow up 'World Domination Live' CD and video.

1998 would witness both Jansson and vocalist Jonas Kjellgren, still retaining their allegiance to DELLAMORTE, joining the renowned Deathsters CENTINEX. Paradoxically though, the duo would switch roles in CENTINEX, Jansson becoming a lead vocalist and Kjellgren adopting guitar. DELLAMORTE bassist Daniel Ekeroth would not be left on the sidelines when it came to side ventures, the four-stringer joining INSISION.

Third album, 'Home Sweet Hell' produced once again by Peter Tägtgren, arrived in 1999. DELLAMORTE welcomed in new drummer Kennet Englund, a veteran of MOONDARK, UNCANNY and SUBDIVE. That same June Englund too would team up with CENTINEX.

Besides DELLAMORTE and CENTINEX both Jansson and Kjellgren are members of the SIDEBURNERS. Jansson would also be busying himself with UNCURBED and Kjellgren too had affiliations to another act in the high profile CARNAL FORGE.

Matthias Norrman would tour as bassist for OPETH in 2001, a quiet year for DELLAMORTE with the band only putting in one gig during March. Jonas Kjellgren proved industrious throughout 2004, acting as producer for TORCHBEARER's album 'Yersinia Pestis' and forging a brand new melodic Death Metal combo, fronted by the INCAPACITY, UNMOORED, SOLAR DAWN and TORCHBEARER credited Christian Älvestam, entitled SCAR SYMMETRY for an album 'Symmetric In Design'. Johan Jansson joined REGURGITATE in September 2006.

Shadows Path, Moondrake (1993) (Demo released under the name MOONDRAKE). Shadows Path / Inside The Crypt / The Dawn For Our Race / Dimension Of Darkness / Trespassing Into ... / ... The Abyss / Concealing The Daylight / World Devastator.
EVERYTHING YOU HATE, Finn FINN 016 (1996). Total Agony / Break The Limits / Fuck Off / Pieces / Empty / No Shit / In A Box / In Your Face / Never Bleed / Gotta' Explode / Monster / Syringe Kiss.
Dirty, Yellow Dog YD 006 (1997) (Split 7" vinyl EP with CORNED BEEF). Dirty / Plug Me In / Suchastupiddisgustingfuckedupfuck.
UGLIER AND MORE DISGUSTING, Kron-H 09CD (1997). Uglier And More Disgusting / Sex Machine / Miss Lords / Corpses / The Lies / Fallen Angel Crashes Dead / Dirty / Plug Me In / Wretched / As Much As You Hurt Me / 666 And Pentagrams / So Many Reasons.
Drunk In The Abyss, Dellamorte (1999) (Cassette demo). Never Bleed / Monster / In A Box / Edge Of The World / Syringe Kiss.
HOME SWEET HELL, Kron-H 14CD (1999). Heart Of Darkness / Dellamortesque / Fucked / Home Sweet Hell / Into The Fire / The Tombs Of My Fear / Supercharged / Strategies Of Humanity / Bones / Faustian Soul / The Deathking / Motorkill / The Zoo / Rapes Of Wrath.
Fuck Me Satan EP, PAS 83 (2001) (7" vinyl EP). A Sure Shot / 1000 Dead / Hellhole / I Am King.

DEMENTIA

TÜBINGEN, GERMANY — *Stephan Nowotny (vocals), Jörg Rupp (guitar / vocals), Martin Müller (guitar), Andreas Müller (bass), Stefan Brunn (keyboards), Gerry Mayerhofer (drums).*

Southern German act DEMENTIA was founded as a covers band in 1989, initiated by guitarists Martin Müller, ex-HILARION and MINDTRIP, and Heiko Schach with Andreas Müller on bass. Adopting a Scandinavian style of technical Death Metal, the band debuted with the 1995 demo 'Abiosis', recorded with vocalist Stephan Nowotny and drummer Daniel Duffner. The follow up album, 'Blackstone' recorded by Matthias Ambs at Cat Studios and released in 1996, closed out with a cover version of Canadian cult Metal outfit SACRED BLADE's 'Master Of The Sun'. The 1999 outing 'The Elfstone's Chronicles' would be a conceptual affair based upon Terry Brook's novel 'The Elfstones Of Shannara'. These sessions marked the introduction of keyboard player Jörg Rupp and new drummer Gerry Mayerhofer, previously with MALIGNANT.

DEMENTIA's next offering would be a split single, 'The Whitechapel Horror', shared with FALLEN YGGDRASIL. Stefan Brunn of WISTERON repute would be introduced on keyboards for 2004's 'Nina' album, another concept piece, this time inspired by the 'Sole Survivor' story by Dean Koontz.

Abiosis, Dementia promo (1995). Asleep / Nightfall / Sore / In Blood / Last Embrace / Common Sense.
BLACKSTONE, (1996). Staaplebom / The Secrets Of My Soul / Into Immemorial Silence / Transient Tears / Absence Of Life / Enslaver Of Fate / Of Two Kids / Blackstone / Master Of The Sun.
THE ELFSTONES CHRONICLES, (1999). Ellcrys Downfall / Darklight Awakening / The Druids Return / The Task Of Revelation / Journey To Arborlon / Reapers Prey / Of Witchcraft And Dark Sorcery / Amidst The Bloodfire / The Loss Of Halys Cut / Sarandanon Funeral / On The Edge Of Death / Ellcrys Rebirth.
The White Chapel Horror, (1999) (Split single with FALLEN YGGDRASIL). The White Chapel Horror.
NINA, (2004). Flight No.353 / Bloodsoiled / Decipher Fractions / Mindreaders / Cyberdeath / My Freaks' Syllogism / The Performance Of Fear / The Delusive End.

DEMENZIA

SOFIA, BULGARIA — *Vladimir Ivanovr (vocals / guitar / keyboards), Velizar Gordeev (guitar), Georgi Gigov (bass), Marin Ivanov (keyboards), Zlatomir Ganadiev (drums).*

Sofia Death Metal band DEMENZIA (initially titled DEMENTIA) was created in the Summer of 2003 by members of Black Metal act SHADOWLAND. DEMENZIA comprised frontman Valdemar (a.k.a. Vladimir Ivanovr), guitarist Vile (Velizar Gordeev) and drummer Demented Destructor (Dani). The band's opening demo, 'A.D. 542', made historical reference to the great plague. Bass player Bobi Ivanov enrolled in early 2005.

DEMENZIA underwent a line-up change, bringing in bassist Georgi "Hollow Heart" Gigov, keyboard player Marin "Yourkiller" Ivanov and drummer Zlatomir "Demented Destructor" Ganadiev in 2006. The album 'Different Seasons', recorded at V.I.B Depression Studio, saw release on the Distributor Of Pain label on June 6th 2006.

a.d. 542, Demenzia (2003). Simply Nothing / The Road To The Sin / Sarcastic / The Black Death / Instinct Of The Evil Habit / Heaven Needs Gods / Winter Tale / If Tomorrow Comes.
Demenzia—Mini CD, (2005). Etude "A.D. 542" / Instinct Of The Evil Habit / Ephemeral Failure / Winter Tale.
Demenzia, (2005). Etude A.D.542 / Instinct Of The Evil Habit (Single version) / Ephemeral Failure / Winter Tale.
DIFFERENT SEASONS, Distributor Of Pain (2006). Hollow / Road To The Sin / Death Expectation / My Goddess / Mystical Windmill / Pain / Candles In The Wind / Ephemeral Failure / Monuments Of A Dead Past / For My Empty Soul / Hope ... For Eternal Spring / My Goddess (Dark dub remix).

DEMILICH

KUOPIO, FINLAND — *Antti Boman (vocals / guitar), Aki Hytonen (guitar), Ville Koistinen (bass), Mikko Virnes (drums).*

Without a doubt Kuopio's DEMILICH offer up a unique sick brand of Sludge Death Metal over laden with extreme guttural vocals. Antti Boman's singing style is so outrageous that the band felt the need in the CD booklet to explain that no effects were used during recording.

The band was created during 1990, established by vocalist / guitarist Antti Boman, bass player Jussi Teräsvirta plus drummer Mikko Virnes. The cassette demos 'Regurgitation Of Blood' and 'The Four Instructive Tales ... Of Decomposition' surfaced the following year, after which BARATHRUM guitarist Aki Hytönen was added to the roster. '... Somewhere Inside The Bowels Of Endlessness ...' followed in 1992. At this juncture Ville Koistinen had assumed bass duties. Grinder Productions distributed a further 1992 demo dubbed 'The Echo'.

DEMILICH's commercial debut, 'Nespithe' in February 1993, was released by American label Necropolis and licensed by

Repulse. The European version adds four songs from the demo 'The Four Instructive Tales Of ... Decomposition'.

During 2005 the line-up expanded by introducing guitarist SDS, from BLACK DEATH RITUAL, and bassist Korpse, of DEATHCHAIN, DE LIRIUM'S ORDER, TROLLHEIM'S GROTT, WINTERWOLF and TWISTED SILENCE. DEMILICH announced US tour dates for June 2006 supported by BIOLICH. Releases that year included two compilations of archive demo tracks in 'V34ish6ng 0f Emptiness' through Xtreem Music and the vinyl album 'Em9t2ness Of Van2s1ing' on Morbid Thoughts Records.

DEMILICH bowed out with a swansong show in Kuopio, Finland on July 22nd, 2006.

Regurgitation Of Blood, Demilich (1991) (Cassette demo). Uncontrollable Regret Of The Rotten Flesh.

The Four Instructive Tales ... Of Decomposition, Demilich (1991) (Cassette demo). Introduction—Embalmed Beauty Sleep / Two Independent Organisms -> One Suppurating Deformity / And The Slimy Flying Creatures Reproduce In Your Brains / The Uncontrollable Regret Of The Rotting Flesh.

The Echo—Demo II '92, Grinder Productions (1992) (Cassette demo). egasseM neddiH A—ortnI / The Echo (Replacement) / Erecshyrinol / The Sixteenth Six-Tooth Son Of Fourteen Four-Regional Dimensions (Still Unnamed) / The Cry.

... Somewhere Inside The Bowels Of Endlessness ..., Demilich (1992) (Demo). (Within) The Chamber Of Whispering Eyes / ... And You'll Remain ... (In Pieces Of Nothingness) / The Cry / The Putrefying Road In The Nineteenth Extremity (... Somewhere Inside The Bowels Of Endlessness ...) / Inherited Bowel Levitation—Reduced Without Any Effort.

NESPITHE, Necropolis NCR005 (1993). When The Sun Drank The Weight Of Water / The Sixteenth Six-Tooth Son Of Fourteen Four Regional Dimensions (Still Unnamed) / Inherited Bowel Levitation—Reduced With Any Effort / The Echo (Replacement) / The Putrefying Road In The Nineteenth Extremity (... Somewhere Inside The Bowels Of Endlessness) / (Within) The Chamber Of Whispering Eyes / And You'll Remain ... (In Pieces Of Nothingness) / Erecshyrinol / The Planet That Once Used To Absorb Flesh In Order To Achieve Divinity And Immortality (Suffocated To The Flesh That It Desired ...) / The Cry / Raped Embalmed Beauty Sleep.

NESPITHE, Grinder Productions RPS 014 (1996). When The Sun Drank The Weight Of Water / The Sixteenth Six-Tooth Son Of Fourteen Four Regional Dimensions (Still Unnamed) / Inherited Bowel Levitation—Reduced With Any Effort / The Echo (Replacement) / The Putrefying Road In The Nineteenth Extremity (... Somewhere Inside The Bowels Of Endlessness) / (Within) The Chamber Of Whispering Eyes / And You'll Remain ... (In Pieces Of Nothingness) / Erecshyrinol / The Planet That Once Used To Absorb Flesh In Order To Achieve Divinity And Immortality (Suffocated To The Flesh That It Desired ...) / The Cry / Raped Embalmed Beauty Sleep / Introduction—Embalmed Beauty Sleep / Two Independent Organisms -> One Suppurating Deformity / And The Slimy Flying Creatures Reproduce In Your Brains / The Uncontrollable Regret Of The Rotting Flesh.

NESPITHE, Pavement 76962-32208-2 (2004). When The Sun Drank The Weight Of Water / The Sixteenth Six-Tooth Son Of Fourteen Four Regional Dimensions (Still Unnamed) / Inherited Bowel Levitation—Reduced With Any Effort / The Echo (Replacement) / The Putrefying Road In The Nineteenth Extremity (... Somewhere Inside The Bowels Of Endlessness) / (Within) The Chamber Of Whispering Eyes / And You'll Remain ... (In Pieces Of Nothingness) / Erecshyrinol / The Planet That Once Used To Absorb Flesh In Order To Achieve Divinity And Immortality (Suffocated To The Flesh That It Desired ...) / The Cry / Raped Embalmed Beauty Sleep.

DEMISOR

SINGAPORE — *Fahmy (vocals), Amirul (guitar), Syamsir (bass), Jali (drums).*

Death Metal combo DEMISOR date to 1987, starting out with a line-up comprising guitarists Azizi and Yazid, bassist Dol and Maiden on the drums. Changes saw Dol switching to the drums whilst Botak, editor of 'Living Corpse' fanzine as vocalist. The 1990 demo 'Mastectomy' saw Zul added on bass guitar. However, DEMISOR split shortly after these sessions, leaving Botak and Dol to reforge the band with new bass man Amirul. Subsequently Dol swapped instruments once again, becoming the group's guitarist, whilst Jali took on drums. Once again though internal frictions resulted in a schism as the last remaining founder member Dol exited and lead vocalist Harman and bassist Apang were inducted. Harman's vocals were complimented by second singer John, who in turn was rapidly usurped by Fahmy for recording of the 'Oral Climax' demo of 1992. This version of DEMISOR performed at the 'Perak' festival in Malaysia during 1993 alongside BRAIN DEAD and TORMENTOR. After this show Azizi returned, ousting Apang on bass guitar as the group undertook recordings for a split EP shared with Malaysian Death Metal act NECROTIC CHAOS. Predictably the DEMISOR line up fluxed once again as Botak and Harman decided to quit and Azizi manoeuvred back into his original guitar position.

DEMISOR put in gigs in Indonesia during 1997, after which Azizi was forced out due to immigration problems. Persevering as a trio DEMISOR then performed in Malaysia once again and played live for the first time in Japan. However, the group was put into hiatus shortly after as Fahmy was taken ill and other members dealt with studies.

DEMISOR was reformed by Fahmy, Amirul, Azizi and drummer Zainal to act as support for NAPALM DEATH's Asian dates. Azizi exited once again and as a trio for the second time DEMISOR recorded tracks for a split release shared with Japanese band CARCASS GRINDER. DEMISOR also shared the split 'Reality' EP with Japan's CLOTTED SYMMETRIC SEXUAL ORGAN in 1998. A split cassette, 'Grind Fucker' allied with EXTREME DECAY, was delivered in 2000. Keeping up the tradition of split releases the group united GORE BEYOND NECROPSY for a 7" single on the US label Fudgeworthy Records and also allied with Chinese acts REGICIDE and OPERATING TABLE for a shared CD 'Split Your Face' on Mort Productions.

DEMISOR issued a split album, 'Total Fucking Gore!' shared with Italy's BESTIAL DEVASTATION, through Scrotum Jus Records in January 2006.

Reality EP, Underground Warder Productions (1998) (Split EP with CLOTTED SYMMETRIC SEXUAL ORGAN). Mass Genocide / Espionage Of Conflict / Hypocrite Bastard / Terrified / Code: Abomination.

SPLIT YOUR FACE, Mort Productions (2004) (Split album with REGICIDE and OPERATING TABLE). Why!!?? / Sarcasm Denied / The Inner Anger / Point Of Anger / Raised In Misery / Life Through My Eyes / Capacity Outrage / I See Lies.

DEMONICAL

HOUTLAND, SWEDEN — *Ludde Engellau (vocals), Johan Jansson (guitar), Martin Schulman (bass), Ronnie Bergerståhl (drums).*

With the collapse of longstanding Death Metal combo CENTINEX in March 2006, three band members duly forged old school Death Metal act DEMONICAL. The founding formation, assembled in Houtland, comprised guitarist Johan Jansson, also having association with a swathe of acts such as PYOSISFIED, HATRED, SIDEBURNERS, ASOCIAL, FLESHREVELS, FULMINATION, FROSTHEIM, UNCURBED, INTERMENT and DELLAMORTE, bass player Martin Schulman and drummer Ronnie Bergerståhl, also known for his work with AMARAN and JULIE LAUGHS NO MORE. In April the triumvirate advertised for a frontman. DEMONICAL laid down demo tracks, billed 'Bloodspell Divine', at Necromorbus Studios in July. Johan Jansson joined REGURGITATE in September 2006.

DEMONICAL contracted with Germany's Cyclone Empire Records in November. At the same juncture the group announced the addition of Ludde Engellau from TALION, UNCHASTE and Grind act REMASCULATE as their new vocalist.

On January 18th 2007 DEMONICAL entered Black Lounge Studios, working with producer Jonas Kjellgren, to lay down drum tracks for new album 'Servants Of The Unlight'. On January 28th they switched over to Necromorbus Studios in Stockholm and, with the help of Sverker Widgren, cut the remaining vocal, guitar and bass tracks. A 2007 European tour set to feature DERANGED, MASTER and DEMONICAL was announced but then cancelled by the booking agency "due to economical issues".

Following a brace of late April shows opening for GRAVE, DEMONICAL arranged to support NUNSLAUGHTER with opening act NOMINON on a short European tour in July 2007.

Bloodspell Divine, Demonical (2006) (Demo). Revel In Misanthropia / Unholy Desecration / Feeding The Armageddon / Leipzig 1945.

DEMONICON

MINNEAPOLIS, MN, USA — *Brandon Almendinger (vocals / bass), Anthony Columbus (guitar), Brian Owens (guitar), Patrick Morris (bass), Corey Jones (drums).*

DEMONICON is a Minneapolis extreme Death Metal outfit that originally gelled DOMINION in 1993. The opening line up counted vocalist / bassist Bill Hedal, ex-CRYOGEN, DEBAUCHERY and EVISCERATION guitarist Brian Owens and drummer Mike Curran. The line remained unstable throughout the band's formative years with a succession of second guitar players enrolling and exiting. However, during 1995 Scott Ellingboe made the position permanent. Before the close of the year though Curran had vacated the drum stool in favour of the EVISCERATION and CRYOGEN credited Chad Ludwig. With this line up DOMINION cut the album 'Soul's Redemption'. Promoting the album in 1996 with live work saw the band putting in a showing at the Milwaukee Metalfest, after which Ellingboe was superseded by Corey Jones of THEATRE OF THE MACABRE, NECROMIS and CONTAGION repute.

DOMINION recorded a demo in 1997 and delivered another set at the Milwaukee Metalfest. A deal was secured with Root Of All Evil Records but in 1998 Ludwig exited in order to pursue a career in bodybuilding. Scott Robinson plugged the gap as the band took on the new title of DEMONICON. Unfortunately Robinson upped and left a matter of weeks before the group was scheduled to go into the recording studio. By necessity Corey Jones switched from guitar to drums and ANAL BLAST and SEVERED man Anthony Columbus was drafted in on guitar for the 2000 album 'Condemned Creation'.

High profile gigs in 2002 saw DEMONICON appearing the Milwaukee Metalfest and Chicagoland Deathfest. Frontman and co-founder Bill Hedal dropped out from the band in December of 2002. Replacements would soon be located in the CYPHESCY pairing of vocalist Brandon Almendinger and bass player Pattick Morris.

Drummer Corey Jones is also active with COHERENT LIQUID FORM. Columbus also operates CREEPING CHARLIE. Morris joined up with DEVILINSIDE during January 2005.

SOUL'S REDEMPTION, Independent (1996). Prelude To Chaos / Soul's Redemption / Divine Addiction / Self Inflicted / The Seed / Mind's Eye / Starting Cut.
CONDEMNED CREATION, Root Of All Evil ROE 026 (2001). Resmortevante / The Burning Starts Again / Severed Bloodline / Condemned Creation / Ascension / Blind Darkness / Quietus Infinitum / Exile Ingrown / Enveloping Rage / Infested / Animal Of Instinct / Insidious Seduction.
BLOODLUST, Root Of All Evil ROE 037 (2003). Heretic / Ordained Molestation / Bloodlust / Dismissing Autonomy / Drafting The Phalanx / Convoke The Drones / Schismatic Tirade / Raze Heaven On High / Cathartic Self-destruction.

DEMONIUM

FERNTREE GULLY, VIC, AUSTRALIA — *Andrew George (vocals), Jeremy Landry (guitar), Cam Arief (bass), James Sheean (drums).*

DEMONIUM, hailing from the South Eastern Suburbs of Melbourne, feature THE DESECRATOR drummer James Sheean. The band, created in June of 2002, included a succession of formative guitarists including ex-AGOMMORAH man Jay Sanchez, Luke Zouzoulas, Justin Cook and Tim Anderson. The April 2004 demo 'Death Defying' featured vocals from the late Nick Walker.

DEMONIUM endured another line-up reconstruction in May of 2005. The band shed frontman Anthony Spencer and both guitarists Cameron Arief and Matt Willis and introduced new members vocalist Andrew George, of 'Melbourne Metal Music', David Howells, ex-TRIBURA and SYMBIOSIST, plus Jeremy Landry of MOREDHEL. Further evolution saw the departure of guitarist David Howells and bassist Paul Beaton being replaced by Cam Arief.

Death Defying, Demonium (2004). Schlafen Der Engel / Death Defying / Humanity Defiled / Defleshed.

DENIAL FIEND

TAMPA, FL, USA — *Kam Lee (vocals), Sam Williams (guitar), Terry Butler (bass), Curtis Beeson (drums).*

Announced in April 2006, Tampa, Florida retro Thrash / Death Metal combo DENIAL FIEND was assembled by an elite cast comprising the MASSACRE and DEATH duo vocalist Kam Lee and bassist Terry Butler, also of SIX FEET UNDER, guitarist Sam Williams, previously with DOWN BY LAW, and ex-NASTY SAVAGE drummer Curtis Beeson. Lee also held credits with KAULDRON, CADAVERIZER, URIZEN and SOUL SKINNER. A three track rehearsal demo was recorded on April 23rd.

Further projects were announced for Lee in early 2007 including working with Matt Olivo of REPULSION on a project called MONSTERSHOCK and adding guest studio vocals to recordings from HATEPLOW.

Denial Fiend, Denial Fiend (2006) (Rehearsal demo). Cover Me In Blood / The Thing With 100 Eyes / Frankenstein Conquers The World.

DEPRAVITY

GERMANY — *Birte Krause (vocals), Dennis Geil (guitar), Christian Dasbach (bass), Cornelius Steinke (drums).*

DEPRAVITY was forged in November of 1999 as a Black / Death combo by the former EUPHORIC FAILURE and BLYND pairing of guitarist Dennis Geil and bass player Christian Dasbach alongside vocalist / guitarist Alexander Schwarzin. Formative demos were cut with the aid of a drum machine and in the Summer of 2000 the group enrolled singer Julia Vogelsberg. In this combination DEPRAVITY set about gigging, subsequently inducting a third guitarist in Jens Phillips during 2001.

A line up shift saw the vocal position changing hands over to Birte Krause in December of 2001. This version of DEPRAVITY laid down the opening September 2002 self-financed album 'Bloodbath In Paradise'. The band finally secured a drummer in February of 2003 with Cornelius Steinke duly taking up the position. DEPRAVITY commenced work on a second album, initially under the billing of 'Catering The Dead', in November. Emerging in February of 2004 the sophomore outing had seen a title change to 'Litanies For The World To Suffer'.

BLOODBATH IN PARADISE, (2002). Cradle Of Death / Rotting In Bloom / Towards The Raventhrone / Ages In Nocturnal Solitude / Sanctuary Within The Realm Of Eternal Winter / Highborn Hellspwan / Philtre Of immortal Taste / Phantasmagoria / The I-God / Incarnated Depravity Versus Lethargic Sovereignty.
LITANIES FOR THE WORLD TO SUFFER, Depravity (2004). Moshing Corpses / Mythdirected / On Dark Summits Of Might / Let's Fucking Die / Necroslut / Monster Island Crusade / Wrath Of The Chimera / Grrrrrind! / Into The Whispering Light / Philtre Of Immortal Taste / Sanctuary Within The Realm Of Eternal Winter.

DEPRECATED

USA — *A.J. Magana (vocals), John Remmen (guitar), Matt Sotelo (guitar), Derek Boyer (bass), Torrey Moores (drums).*

Founded in 1996 by former DISGORGE members vocalist A.J. Magana, bassist Derek Boyer and drummer Torrey Moores. DEPRECATED first guitarist was Adam Heast. During November of 1998 Boyer filled in for DEEDS OF FLESH vocalist Jacony Kingston for a series of shows in Brazil.

DEPRECATED pulled in VEHEMENCE and BRIDES OF CHRIST guitarist John Chavez for recording of 'Engulfing Visions'. Meantime DEPRECATED members turned up deputizing for other acts with A.J. Magana fronting DISGORGE as temporary replacement for Matti Way and bass player Derek Bowyer teaming up with DYING FETUS in 2001.

The band added former DECREPIT BIRTH guitarist Matt Sotelo but found that Magana had joined DISGORGE on a full time basis appearing on their 'Dissecting The Apostles' opus.

Deriding His Creation EP, (1997). Deriding His Creation / Mentally Deprived / Realization Of Betrayal / Induced Deception.

DEPRESSION

DEPRESSION (pic: Thor Wanzek)

GERMANY — *Marc Miekeley (vocals), Ron Sanders (vocals), Kai Sattelkau (guitar / bass / drums).*

DEPRESSION is an early German Death-Grind unit, conceived during 1989 by guitarist / bass player and drummer Kai Sattelkau, previously a member of GODS OF GRIND and MORTUUS. As a solo enterprise, Sattelkau recorded the Noisecore styled 'Tal Der Tränen' demo during 1990. The 'Vergessene Welten' session followed in 1992, after which singer Marc Miekeley was inducted into the proceedings, featuring on the third demo, 1993's '... In Verzweiflung'. DEPRESSION would then cease activity as both Sattelkau and Miekely joined DISMAL.

By 1995 DEPRESSION was back, touting a fourth demo 'Erinnerungen'. A debut 7" EP, 'Ein Hauch Von Moder' released on Gulli Records, followed in the Autumn of 1996. Pressed on purple vinyl this single was limited to 800 copies. Their next move was to be the 1997 'Böses Blut' split CD shared with AGATHOCLES and including a cover version of FEAR OF GOD's 'Thy Beauty'. Before the year was out a further split 7" saw release, 'Die Zeiten ändern Sich' being in union with fellow German Grind combo MAGGOT SHOES. This effort, seeing a rendition of IMPETIGO's 'Heart Of Illinois', would be manufactured in orange vinyl and restricted to 500 units.

1998 started out with the issue of archive rehearsal and live recordings as split cassette 'Enjoy Or Die!' with Spanish Noise-Grindcore band HIERBA. Once more DEPRESSION tackled cover tracks in IMPETIGO's 'Boneyard' and BLOOD's 'Dogmatize'. Material left over from 1996 emerged in April of 1998 as the purple vinyl 'Ein Hauch Von Moder Part II' split 7" EP with German Gore act REJECTAMENTA. Finding an alliance with infamous Brazilian band ROT, the 10" album "Und Keiner Weint Uns Nach', recorded in just one day during November of 1998 at Krähativsound Studios and sporting a take on ABSCESS' 'Suicide Fuck', was delivered by Deadly Art Productions in 1999. An initial pressing of 666 hand numbered green coloured vinyl rapidly sold out so a second edition in blue vinyl was released.

DEPRESSION entered the new millennium with the full length album 'Chronische Depression'. Released once more by Deadly Art Productions this record included the by now customary cover, MORTICIAN's 'Bloodcraving'. To celebrate the band's tenth anniversary the album added one track culled from each year of DEPRESSION's existence as bonus material. An extended break from recording would be broken on Christmas of 2001 with the 'Zur Stille Finden' album for Cudgel Agency. Once again a split affair, this time with Spain's HAEMORRHAGE and including their version of AGATHOCLES' 'Enough'. This album also marked the introduction of former DISMAL vocalist Ron sanders to the ranks. Maintaining the relationship with Cudgel Agency 2002's 'Schatten', a split EP with German goremongers GONORRHOEACTION, saw the band taking on ANAL CUNT's 'Radio Hit'.

During 2003 DEPRESSION re-issued all of the 'Ein Hauch Von Moder' session tracks as part of a four way split album on Noise variations in union with INTESTINAL INFECTION, MEATKNIFE and NEW YORK AGAINST THE BELZEBU. The same label also put out the 'Enjoy Or Die!' tape tracks as a split 7" entitled 'Der Wahnsinnliche' with INTESTINAL INFECTION the same year. A KADAVERFICKER split 7" EP was then issued on Gore-A-Go-Go Records. The group honoured DEATH by donating their recording of 'Torn To Pieces' for inclusion on the 'Together As One' collection compiled by Mondongo Canibale Records and also paid homage to GUT by contributing their rendition of 'Vagina Berserker' to a tribute album on Alarma Records.

Quite incredibly, after fifteen years of recorded output DEPRESSION had never played live. They planned to rectify this in September of 2004 with their debut show at the Wermelskirchen 'Deathfest'. That same month a split album shared with Canadian act MESRINE and released by 2+2=5 Records would include cover versions of 'Hate The Kids' from TURBONEGRO and 'Behram' by MESRINE whilst the Canadians repaid the honour by tackling DEPRESSION's 'The Mangler'. Power It Up Records issued a grey coloured vinyl version, limited to 500 copies. Ron Sanders also forged side project APHELION, a Death Metal duo in alliance with Skaldir of HEL and CASCADE.

2005 saw the issue of a split 7" single with FLESHRIPPER, these tracks including a cover version of GUT's 'Vaginaberserker'. Limited to 500 copies, the first 100 would be pressed on orange vinyl.

Ein Hauch Von Moder, Gulli (1996) (Limited edition 800 copies). Flesh Of Mine / Infection / Dogmatize / Amputations For My Rations / Desperation Of My Soul / Greet The Corpses.

Die Zeiten ändern Sich, (1997) (Split EP with MAGGOT SHOES. Limited edition 500 copies). Four-String Violin / Heart Of Illinois / Santanico Pandemonium / Howling At My Backdoor.

BOSES BLUT, Cudgel Agency (1997) (Split album with AGATHOCLES). Bloodheaven / Thy Beauty / You Call Me Beast / Vomit Bowel / Life Is Hard And Then You Die / Burnin' Within / The Mangler / Sathanas (I Am God).

Ein Hauch Von Moder Part II, (1998) (Split EP with REJECTAMENTA. Limited edition 500 copies). Blood On God's Hands / Short Song / The Barbarian / Eroded Epitaph.

Und Keiner Weint Uns Nach, Deadly Art Production (1999) (Split EP with ROT. Limited edition 666 green vinyl, 300 blue vinyl). I Remember My Future / Suicide Fuck / Where Am I? / Sun And Moon / Thy Black Altar / Broken Fragments.

CHRONISCHE DEPRESSION, Deadly Art (2000). Putting The Last Nail / The Ritual / A Murmured Cry / Bloodcraving / Seven Feet Under / The Peeling Session / Gods Of Grind / Never / Cattle Grid / Cruel / Depressionen / I Remember My Future / The Barbarian / Four-String Violin / Bloodheaven / Flesh Of Mine / Defaced / Impious Lands / ... In Desperation / Forgotten Worlds / Vale Of Tears.

Schatten, Cudgel Agency (2002) (Split single with GONORRHOEACTION). I Will Kill Someone During Spring (Spring Time Is Killing Time) / Radio Hit / Suicide Dreams / A Colossal Vision / Men Behind The Sun / Fucked Up By Belief / The Rancid Bowels Of The Vocalists (Part I & II).

ZUR STILLE FINDEN, Cudgel Agency (2002) (Split album with HAEMORRHAGE). (Intro) The Ancient Arrival Of Thy Utter Darkness / No Tumours, Just Rumours / Defaced / (She's) Satan In High Heels / No Need For A God / Under The Pale Moonlight / Enough / The Battle / An Autumn Blaze / I Am The Devil / Jimmy Was In Town.

EIN HAUCH VON MODER: PART I & II, Noise Variations (2003) (Split album with INTESTINAL INFECTION, MEATKNIFE & NEW YORK AGAINST THE BELZEBU). The Visitation Of The Stillborn Souls / Infection / Flesh Of Mine / Dogmatize / Desperation Of My Soul / Amputations For My Rations / Greet The Corpses / Blood On God's Hands / Short Song / The Barbarian / Eroded Epitaph.

Der Wahnsinnliche, Noise Variations (2003) (Split EP with INTESTINAL INFECTION). Defaced / Boneyard / Blood On God's Hands / Short Song (Pt. II) / Greet The Corpses.

DIE TOTEN TAGE KOMMEN . . . , 2+2=5 (2004) (Split album with MESRINE). The Grim Rise Of . . . (Intro) / Human Prey / Maggot Eater / Hate The Kids / Depression Vs. The Devil / Berham / Leichenduft / I Spit In Your Grave (Torture Fuck) / Dare The Pain / Just A Piece Of Flesh / A Farewell / . . . The Reborn Brutality (Outro).

DEPRESY

TRENČIN, SLOVAKIA — *Dragon (vocals), Shimi (guitar), Dirt (guitar), Martych (bass), Elevo (drums).*

An accomplished and highly rated technical Death Metal outfit from the city of Trencin. DEPRESY, forged in August 1991, embarked upon their career path by delivering the 1992 opening demo 'If Dream Will Be Real' followed up by March 1993's 'In Embrace Of The Dying'. DEPRESY's musical and lyrical focus shifted onto the occult after the second demo, evident in the two tracks, 'Without Future' and 'Try Not To Breathe', donated to the Metal Ages Productions compilation album 'Wretched People In The Real World'. The latter song would also turn up on the Station Master collection 'Death Metal Made In Slovakia'.

During August of 1995 DEPRESY convened for a third demo '. . . And Then Came The Tears Of Christ'. Released to the public, this demo soon sold out prompting Shindy Productions to re-issue it in cassette form and later on CD. DEPRESY at this juncture comprised of vocalist Drahos Gabris, guitarists Roman Filo and Roman Spatny and drummer Roman Lasso.

The album 'A Grand Magnificence', comprising of two new tracks, a cover of HYPOCRISY's 'An Elder Spirit's Reincarnation' and a re-recorded take of 'Try Not To Breathe' also came complete with all the tracks from the previous demo. Promoting the release on the live scene DEPRESY appeared at the 'Nuclear Storm', 'Brutal Assault' and 'Festering Blood' festivals.

DEPRESY added bass player Martych in late 1998 upfront of recording the 'Sighting' album. The band featured a brace of tracks, 'The Antichrist's Philosophy' and 'Spiritual Obscure Mysteries' on the 2001 compilation 'MetalWorld Compilation I'.

. . . AND THEN THERE CAME THE TEARS OF CHRIST, Shindy Productions (1995).

A Grand Magnificence EP, Shindy Productions (1997). Unpure Romanticism- Part 1: The Alchemy Of Eternity / Unpure Romanticism- part 2: Drama / Try Not To Breathe / An Elder Spirit's Reincarnation.

A GRAND MAGNIFICENCE, Shindy Productions (1998). Unpure Romanticism—Part I: The Alchemy Of Eternity / Unpure Romanticism—Part II: Drama / Try Not to Breathe / An Elder Spirit's Reincarnation / ..And There Came The Tears With Christ / Heresy, Shadowsnight / Magic Of Eternal Dreaming / Desire / Kisses Of Suffering / Of The Nightfall Heaven's Crash (Opening Of Hells) / Feardimension / Maleficium.

SIGHTING, Shindy Productions (1999). Sighting (Ceremonial Magic) / Lunar Spell / The Antichrist's Philosophy / Monumental Jeremiad Of Dismay / The Forest Below The Midnight Shadow / In Multam Noctem—Nocturnal Blackness / Tale Of Dust / Spirit Obscure Mysteries.

Depresy EP, (2000) (Split EP with NEURAXIS).

PSYCHOMANTIUM PHENOMENON, Shindy Productions (2003). Psychospiritual Mysticism / Blind Equilibrium / NAVb—Carpathian Sonnet Of The Dead / Demonized Muse / Anamnesis / Beyond The Limits Of Language / Metaphysical Implication Of Evil / Crepuscular Conquest / Cosmic Tragedy / Heathen Esoteric Transmissions / Kisses Of Suffering (Reinvoked 1995).

DERANGED

HJÄRUP, SWEDEN — *Per Gyllenbäck (vocals), Johan Axelsson (guitar), Tomas Ahlgren (bass), Rikard Werman (drums).*

Yet another Scandinavian act attempting to out-gross the originators of the genre. Hjärup based DERANGED, debuting with the 1992 demo cassette 'The Confessions Of A Necrophile', contributed a cover of the VENOM track 'In League With Satan' on the 1992 Primitive Art Records tribute album 'Promoters Of The Third World War'. Obliteration Records would then issue the 1993 EP 'The Confessions Continues'. Singer Per Gyllenbäck gained considerable kudos on the Swedish Metal scene with his personal Metal imprint Wrong Again records, giving a valuable kick start to acts such as ARCH ENEMY and IN FLAMES amongst many others.

The band contributed the original cut 'Hammer Cottered Rectum' to the 1993 Repulse Records compilation 'Sometimes Dead Is Better'. The follow ups would come in the form of the 'Upon The Medical Slab' 7" single for MMI Records and an EP 'Architects Of Perversion', recorded at Studio Koket in the Winter of 1993 and featuring a guesting Mike Amott of CARCASS on guest guitar.

In 1995 bassist Jean-Paul Asenov was sacked and superseded by Mikael Bergman. The latter's stay with the band was fairly short-lived and he was fired shortly afterward, which led to guitarist Johan Axelsson performing bass duties on the 'Rated X' sessions, which included a rendition of the ROLLING STONES 'Paint It Black', prior to the band recruiting former INVERTED bassist Dan Bengtsson. Meantime, guitarist Johan Axelsson, bassist Dan Bengtsson and drummer Rikard Wermén were also active with a side act entitled MURDER CORPORATION, fronted by ex-MEGASLAUGHTER vocalist Emil Lilic and issuing the 1996 album 'Blood Revolution 2050'. Around this juncture, Per Gyllenbäck contributed his vocals to an IN FLAMES demo track 'The Inborn Lifeless', later to evolve into 'The Jester Race' album's 'Dead God In Me'.

Sessions were cut for an intended mini-album to be titled 'Sculptures Of The Dead' for the German Invasion label but this material was shelved. These tracks would surface though as part of a limited edition package of the 'Ratex X' album, the first 2000 copies adding the extra disc.

The 'III' album, produced by Berno Paulsson at Berno Studios in May of 1999, emerged in 2000. The French Listenable Records label would take three tracks from these sessions to be paired with ABSCESS for a split album release.

DERANGED put in headline shows in Japan during October and November of 2000. Renewed live work in Europe during May 2001 saw the band on a package billing with IMMOLATION, Australians DESTROYER 666, DECAPITATION and SOUL DEMISE. The Perverted Taste label would the same year re-issue the inaugural 'Rated X' set along with a bonus disc of material from the 'Architects Of Perversion' and unreleased 'Sculptures Of Death' mini-albums.

Following the release of the 2001 eponymous album for Merciless Records frontman Johan Anderberg decamped. DERANGED quickly regrouped announcing a line-up of the DEAD SUN, PAGANIZER and BLODSRIT credited Rogga Johansson on vocals, guitarist Johan Axelsson, Jörgen Bylander of CELEBORN and DEFACED CREATION on bass and drummer Rikard Werman.

By 2002 DERANGED had been whittled down to a trio comprising SKULLFUCK man Calle Fäldt on vocals and bass, guitarist Johan Axelsson and drummer Rikard Wermén. Promoting the 'Plainfield Cemetery' album the group acted as support to KREATOR's October UK shows. Fäldt also acted as live session man for MISTELTEIN that same year. Also in 2002 Johan Axelsson and Rikard Wermén fired up a new outfit billed as KILLAMAN in alliance with being frontman Rune Foss of EXEMPT and RECLUSION, second guitarist Roger Johansson of INSISION and bass player Kaspar Larsen of WITHERING SURFACE.

Fäldt would reunite with his SKULLFUCK colleague John Huldt in the 2004 technical Thrash combo FEARED CREATION, this band also including the MASSGRAV, OMINOUS and THE FORSAKEN credited frontman Anders Sjöholm along with MISTELTEIN bassist Magnus Gillberg.

DERANGED reformed in 2005, signing to French label Listenable Records for a new album, at first billed 'Obscenities In B Flat' but then changed to 'The Red Light Murder Case', recording at Berno Studios in Malmö. The band teamed up with AMPUTATED and SKINNED for the "Bloodjunkies Killing Spree '05" UK tour in November. DERANGED announced European plans for early 2006 in union with Italy's NATRON but subsequently cancelled, apparently due to employment commitments. In April DERANGED severed ties with vocalist/bassist Calle Fäldt citing "personal and musical differences." The band acquired a new singer in the shape of Martin Schönherr, drummer with Malmö Grindsters SPLATTER MERMAIDS.

DERANGED inducted the MONOLITH, END, ARSONIST and PANDEMONIUM credited Tomas Ahlgren as their new bassist in November 2006. The band announced a headlining a European tour commencing in April 2007 with RESURRECTED, EPICEDIUM and DEMONICAL as support.

The Confessions Of A Necrophile, Deranged (1992) (Demo). The Maceration Of A Carbuncular Embryo / Nervus Thoracicus Longus / Orgy Of Infanticide Exposed Corpses / The Confessions Of A Necrophile.

The Confessions Continues ... EP, Obliteration OR001 (1993) (7" vinyl single limited to 1000 copies). Orgy Of Infanticide Exposed Corpses (Part II) / The Confessions Of A Necrophile / Nervus Thoralicius Longus (Part II).

Upon The Medical Slab, MMI MMI 015 (1994) (7" vinyl single limited to 1000 copies). Upon The Medical Slab / Red Disorder.

Architects Of Perversion, Repulse RPS002 (1994). Architects Of Perversion / Coagulated Seminal Fluids / Stairway To Hell / Hammer Cottered Rectum / Rigid Anatomy Art.

RATED X (LIMITED EDITION), Repulse RPS 010 (1996) (2 CD). Black Semen Vengeance / Killing Spree / (Clim) Axe / Narcisstic Sleighride / Unleash My Hunger ... / Razor Tongue / I'm The Love Undertaker / ... As A Wolf / Sixteen And Dead / Paint It Black / Internal Vaginal Bleeding / The Bowels Of My Dismay / Majestic Hole / Sculptures Of The Dead.

RATED-X, Repulse RPS 010 (1996). Black Semen Vengeance / Killing Spree / (Clim) Axe / Narcisstic Sleighride / Unleash My Hunger ... / Razor Tongue / I'm The Love Undertaker / ... As A Wolf / Sixteen And Dead / Paint It Black.

Sculpture Of The Dead EP, Repulse RPS 021MCD (1996). Internal Vaginal Bleeding / The Bowels Of My Dismay / Majestic Hole / Sculptures Of The Dead.

HIGH ON BLOOD, Regain RR9803-001 (1998). Razor Divine / Humanity Feeds On Filth / (Eroti)kill / Raised On Human Sin / High On Blood / Robber Of Life / Nailed Ejaculation / By Knife ... / Haunted By Natural Danger / With The Silence Came Horror / Experience The Flesh.

III, Soundholic SHCD1-0031 (1999) (Japanese release). Ripped, Raped, Randomized / Compulsive Urge To Kill / Consume Excrete / Laugh At Human Tragedies / Through The Realm Of Torture / Festering / III / Thrill Kill / Icon Of Murder / I Thrive On Suffering / Death Tripping / Vermin Of A Sewer World / Relentless / Stagnant Pool / Razor (Rection).

III, Listenable POSH 018 (1999). Ripped, Raped, Randomized / Compulsive Urge To Kill / Consume Excrete / Laugh At Human Tragedies / Through The Realm Of Torture / Festering / III / Thrill Kill / I Thrive On Suffering / Death Tripping / Razor (Rection).

III, Merciless M.R.SRLP018 (1999) (Vinyl album + 7" single). Ripped, Raped, Randomized / Compulsive Urge To Kill / Consume Excrete / Laugh At Human Tragedies / Through The Realm Of Torture / Festering / III / Thrill Kill / I Thrive On Suffering / Death Tripping / Razor (Rection) / Stagnant Pool / Hammer Cottered Rectum / Raised On Human Sin / Razor Divine / Some Kinda Hate.

DERANGED, Listenable POSH 028 (2001). Flesh Rebel / Cum On Command / Dead Hand Strangulation / Endophagy / Injected / La Orgia De Los Muertos / Humanity, God's Failure / Malebolgia / Incurable / Impulse, Prey, Pleasure / Screen Passion.

ABSCESS / DERANGED, Listenable POSH 029 (2001) (Split album with ABSCESS). Vermin Of A Sewer World / Relentless / Stagnant Pool.

DERANGED, Tokuma TKCS-85019 (2001) (Japanese release). Flesh Rebel / Cum On Command / Dead Hand Strangulation / Endophagy / Straight Razor / Injected / La Orgia De Los Muertos / Humanity, God's Failure / Malebolgia / Incurable / Impulse, Prey, Pleasure / Screen Passion.

PLAINFIELD CEMETERY, Listenable POSH 040 (2002). Beaten, Raped, And Left And Left To Fuckin' Die / Stab And Hack / Mutilate And Dumb You / We Lure And Abduct / God Is Dead / Deathgasm / Imbecile Humans—Drag Her Out To Die / Suffering, The Sweet Suffering / Roadside Rendez-Vous / The Deviant Is Dead.

OBSCENITIES IN B-FLAT, Listenable POSH 083 (2006). Long Live The New Flesh / I Torture, Rape, Cum And Kill / Crawl With Me Through The Filth / Coven Of Death / Deflower The Dead / Bodyfluids From Unknown Source / Alive Swarming With Flies / Pray On The Weak / Dead In A Ditch.

DERKETA

PITTSBURGH, PA, USA — *Sharon Bascovsky (vocals / guitar), Heather (bass), Jim Sadist (drums).*

DERKETA, generally acknowledged as the first in their field of all female acts, is a Doom influenced Death Metal formation out of Pittsburgh, Pennsylvania. Taking their title from Stygian Mythology; specifically a goddess of death worshipped by a blood-drinking cult, DERKETA came into being during 1988, founded by vocalist / guitarist Sharon Bascovsky and drummer Terri Heggen. Utilising the services of Kim August from 'Ultimatum' zine on bass DERKETA debuted with a two song demo the following year. In February of 1990 a further session, 'The Unholy Ground', was offered prompting a label deal from Seraphic Decay and a resulting 7" single 'Premature Burial'.

Mary Bielich would stand in on bass during 1991 before opting out, subsequently joining forces with MYTHIC, NOVEMBER'S DOOM and PENANCE. Terri Heggan too exited, founding MYTHIC with Bielich and Dana Duffey.

Recruiting Jim Sadist, previously drummer with NUNSLAUGHTER, Bascovsky re-built the band. This revised unit cut two tracks for inclusion on a split single 'Begotten Son' through Ordealis Records allied with NUNSLAUGHTER and DELIRIA NOISE OUTFITTERS. Rhia of SOMNUS aided on session keyboards for these recordings. The band's next outing would be the track 'Your Rotting Flesh' incorporated on the Master Of Bestial Mockery compilation album 'Mad Max Impaler of Trendies'. Local drummer Jeff "The Troll" took command of drums for this track.

With Jim Sadist back on board and Heather on bass guitar DERKETA's next recording would be the track 'Spirits in The Morgue'. This song was released in December 2002 as part of a 4-way split 7 single 'Behold The Legions Of Hell' with GRAVEWURM, SADO-MANIAC and WITCHBURNER on the Iron Bonehead Productions label.

DERKETA's archive material was due for a compilation issue billed as 'Goddess Of Death' through the Necroharmonic label in 2003. An album of new material, 'In Death We Meet' with Jared Altamare of EVISCUM on drums, was also projected. Bascovsky returned the favour, aiding EVISCUM on bass guitar.

Premature Burial, Seraphic Decay (1990).

Behold The Legions Of Hell, Iron Bonehead Productions (2002) (Split single with GRAVEWURM, SADO-MANIAC & WITCHBURNER). Spirits In The Morgue.

DESCENDING

FJÄLLBACKA, SWEDEN — *Andreas Hedström (vocals / guitar), Daniel Hansson (guitar), Eddie Hellgren (drums).*

Fjällbacka Black / Death Metal endeavour DESCENDING was manifested during 2001, initiated by vocalist / guitarist Andreas Hedström, of EXCESSUM, RETARD and GRIEF OF EMERALD, and drummer Carl Nordblom, a veteran of RETARD, MATRICIDE and HUMAN DEATH. Subsequent inductees would be guitarist Stefan Eliasson and the RETARD, STONEBITCH, MATRICIDE and EXCESSUM credited bassist Kaj Palm (a.k.a. Gimbrynjer). This version of the group recorded the demo 'A World Shaped To Die', released in 2004. The band re-formulated itself in 2005, Hedström dispensing with his entire cast and drawing in fresh members guitarist Daniel Hansson and Eddie Hellgren on drums.

A World Shaped To Die, Descending (2004) (Demo. Limited edition 100 copies). Your World Descend / A World Shaped To Die / The Supremacy Of Darkness.

DESCENDING

GOTHENBURG, SWEDEN — *Kristofer Boström (vocals), Rickard Apelstav (guitar), Anders Lundvall (guitar), Joakim Bryngelsson (bass), Simon Zachrisson (drums).*

Gothenburg's Death Metal band DESCENDING was formulated during mid 2005 by erstwhile members of SCENSKRÄCK, lead guitar player Rickard Apelstav, rhythm guitarist Anders Lundvall and Alexandra Andersson on the drums. That same Summer the bass player Michael Skalenius joined the band. A temporary vocalist was installed but soon departed and in November Kristofer Boström enrolled as new frontman.

DESCENDING lost Andersson's services in 2006, the drummer relocating to the USA. A substitute named Rasti briefly occupied the position prior to Simon Zachrisson filling the vacancy. That Autumn the band recorded tracks for a debut EP entitled 'End Of Eternity'. Upon conclusion of these sessions Skalenius quit to focus on an athletic career. Joakim Bryngelsson took his place.

End Of Eternity, Descending (2005).

DESECRATED DREAMS

SLOVAKIA — *Stano Konechy (vocals), Lubomir Michalovic (guitar), Milan Jozefek (guitar), Marek Navratil (bass), Andrej Simon (drums).*

DESECRATED DREAMS deliver Death Metal with strong Thrash leanings. The band, founded in 1996 by former BARBAROSSA guitarists Lubomir Michalovic and Milan Jozefek, arrived on the scene in 1997 with the demo 'Waiting For The Last Sunset', capitalising on this with a further promotional tape 'Raven Forest' in 1998.

The opening DESECRATED DREAMS album, 2001's 'Feeling Of Guilt' issued by Metal Age Productions, saw the band fronted by Stano Konechy, with Marek Navratil on bass and Mizo Patz on drums. The band featured a brace of tracks, 'The Lost Faith' and 'Animal' on the 2001 compilation 'MetalWorld Compilation I'.

Subsequently erstwhile EMBALMED and BLACK WIDOW drummer Andrej Simon would join the fold. In late 2001 Navratil departed.

FEELINGS OF GUILT, Metal Age Productions (2001). Intro (... In The Darkest Forest) / Mirror Of Damnation / Animal / The Lost Faith / Impure / Mysteries Of The Spiritual World / Pavor Nocturnus / Angel's Whisper / Screaming Eyes / Fallen To The Sin / Breathing Fire.

DESECRATION

NEWPORT, WALES, UK — *Ollie Jones (vocals), Pete Davies (bass), Michael Hourihan (drums).*

Welsh gore mongers of repute. This extreme Newport based act opened proceedings with the gory 'Mangled Remains' demo of 1992. DESECRATION's 1995 debut album 'Gore And Perversion's cover artwork was so extreme the record remained without a label for a lengthy period. Eventually the Arctic Serenades label felt brave enough to sign the act only to have the first pressing seized by the police under the obscene publications act. The album eventually surfaced but mastered from a cassette the police had missed in their raid on frontman Ollie Jones's house.

Without a drummer, vocalist Ollie took up the role for second album 'Murder In Mind', released by Copro Records. The 1998 formation of the band saw Ollie Jones joined by guitarists Glenn Thomas and Paul Arlett with John Wagenaar on bass. DESECRATION toured the UK supporting CANNIBAL CORPSE, IMMORTAL and THUS DEFILED prior to European dates with VADER and MORTICIAN.

The third album, 2000's 'Inhuman', was produced by Dave Chang. A swathe of US dates in December that year found the band supporting veteran Deathsters MONSTROSITY. DESECRATION would re-record their notorious debut 'Gore And Perversion' in November of 2002 with a line-up of Ollie Jones on vocals and guitar, Pete Davies on bass and Michael Hourihan of STORMCROW and PARRICIDE repute on the drums. The Martin Barbour produced re-work surfaced through Copro Records in April of 2003, this revised version re-dubbed 'Gore And PerVersion2'.

DESECRATION united with Birmingham's ENDLESS TORMENT for UK gigs in June of 2004. That same year Michael Hourihan joined up with the reformed Glam band TIGERTAILZ. He would also man the drums with EXTREME NOISE TERROR.

In July 2005 the band put in an appearance at the 'Dungeonfest 555' festival at The Royal Park Cellars in Leeds. Gigs across Europe in November saw the band supporting Sweden's VOMITORY. UK headline dates in March 2007 saw support from SEVERE TORTURE and EVILE. Valuable media exposure came the band's way when Ollie Jones was selected to appear in the BBC 3 reality television show 'Singing With The Enemy'.

GORE AND PEVERSION, Arctic Serenades SERE005 (1995). Raping The Corpse (Desecration) / Human Gore / Penile Dissection / It Cant Be My Grave / Dead Bitch In The Skip / No More Room In The Freezer / Mutilated Genitalia / Immense Suffering / To Kill With A Drill / Pharaonic Circumcision / Copraphiliac Connoisseur / Fontanelle Fornication / L.A.I.

MURDER IN MIND, Copro COP06 (1998). Intro / Murder In Mind / Impaled / Cerebral Annoxia / Stillborn Climax / Beyond Recognition / Bathroom Autopsy / Victimised / I.S. / Obscene Publication / Crave For Rot.

INHUMAN, Copro CD-COPO13 (2000). Insane Savagery / Turning Black / Dig up, Dig in / Asphyxiate On Blood / Life Of Gore / Inhuman / Another Obscene Publication / Death You'll Face / Kill Row / A Message To The Censor.

PATHWAY TO DEVIANCE, Copro COP022 (2002). Cleaver, Saw And Butcher's Knife / Offer The Flesh / King Of The Missing / Bloody Human Carvery / None Of Us Are Saints / Let's Have A Hanging / Swollen / Bathroom Autopsy / They Bled / Frosted Breath.

GORE AND PERVERSION2, Copro (2003). Raping The Corpse (Desecration) / Human Gore / Penile Dissection / It Can't Be My Grave / Dead Bitch In The Skip / No More Room In The Freezer / Mutilated Genitalia / Immense Suffering / To Kill With A Drill / Pharonic Circumcision / Coprophiliac Connoisseur / Fontanelle Fornication / I.A.I.

PROCESS OF DECAY, Copro COP039 (2005). When The Heart Stops Beating / Initial Decay / Bacterial Breakdown / Black Putrefaction / Butyric Fermentation / Maggots In Evidence / Corpse Fauna / Dry Rot / Gravewax.

DESENSITISED

HOLLAND — *Steven (vocals), Susan (guitar), Jeroen Gelissen (bass), Rick (drums).*

DESENSITISED, originally entitled CATAFALQUE, was formed in 1994 by bassist Jozef, guitarist Susan and drummer Rutger in 1994, soon adding lead singer Jo to round off the line up. Still billed as CATAFALQUE the band issued a 1995 demo 'Your Final Ride' before Jo departed. A succession of line up changes forced the band to come to a close. However, the band rose up once more in 1998 with singer Steven, guitarist Susan and drummer Rutger and by September 2001 had adopted the new title of DESENSITISED.

Bass player Jeroen Gelissen of SECTARIAN joined the band prior to release of the album 'Thriving On Carnage', these recordings featuring RIMMSHOT's Mark Raets as session bassist. Rutger announced his intention to leave in mid 2002 but minus a replacement drummer DESENSITISED employed the temporary services of Rutger for gigs until October. The drum position was finally filled in November by Rick of SECTARIAN.

Band members forged side project STATE:CHAOS during 2006 for a demo entitled 'Ashes Of Misery'.

THRIVING ON CARNAGE, Bleedin' Hemorrhoid (2002). Flock / Torchure / Miscloned / Masochistic Masculinity / Cover Up / Hidden In The Ground / Sacred Slaughter.

DESOLATE

BULGARIA — *Ilko Gizdov (vocals / keyboards), Vladislav Stoyanov (guitar), Metodi Pavlov (guitar), Danail Andonov (bass), Ivailo Gamanov (drums).*

DESOLATE came together in November of 1992, incorporated at the hands of lead vocalist Ilko Gizdov, guitarist Mladen Zahariev, bass player Andre Mateev with Nikolay Surbinov on the drums. Demo sessions took the band into the following year when Surbinov was forced out to undertake compulsory military service. Ivailo Gamanov, formerly with DEATH PENALTY, plugged the vacancy for recording of the debut album 'A Shadowed Dying Conscience'. However, DESOLATE would then enter into a protracted hiatus, re-emerging with a revised line up seeing Gizdov adding keyboard duties to his role, Vladislav Stoyanov and Metodi Pavlov taking over the guitar role, Danail Andonov as new bass man and Gamanov retained on the drums. With this version of the group DESOLATE put in their inaugural live gigs in 1996.

'While The Name Is Going Away From The Stone' arrived as a set of demo recordings in February of 1997 and that December DESOLATE cut a second album entitled 'Eventide Of The Orb And Heavens'. Gigs in 1998, allied with German band DARKSEED, spawned the live demo 'Four Elements'.

Former guitarist Vladislav Stoyanov subsequently forged the symphonic Black Metal band DIMENSION OF HARM in 2000.

EVENTIDE OF THE ORB AND HEAVENS, X Rated (2001). At God's Hand / Fireflight / Eventide In Fire / Place For Ourselves / Firmament / Bloodylands / Nightview / While The Name Is Going Away From The Stone.

DESPISE

CZECH REPUBLIC — *Michal Kusák (vocals), David Krédl (guitar), Jaroslav Šantrùèek (guitar), Jaroslav Petøík (bass), Tomáš Prášek (bass), Radim Dvoøák (drums).*

Kolin based, brutal Death Metal act manifested during 1998. The instigating trio comprised guitarist David 'Dejvy' Krédl, bass player Jaroslav 'Beavis' Petřík and LYKATHEA AFLAME and GARBAGE DISPOSAL drummer Tomáš Corn. Changes in 2001 signalled the exit of Corn but the entry into the ranks of vocalist Michal 'Sepp' Kusák and bass player Jaroslav Šantrůček, both of IMPERIAL FOETICIDE. This latter band then subsequently provided two further personnel into the DESPISE fold, Radim Dvořák on drums and second bassist Tomáš Prášek.

The 2001 DESPISE EP 'Confinement In Decrepitude' closed out with a cover version of PYREXIA's 'Confrontation'. A split album of the same session arrived in 2003, shared naturally enough with IMPERIAL FOETICIDE.

DESPISE, together with a guesting Mr. Šimeček of GODLESS TRUTH, planned a split release with US act LUST OF DECAY for 2004.

Confinement In Decrepitude EP, (2001). Room 101 / Mutual Assured Destruction / Separated Entity Alteration / Confrontation.
DESPISE, Grodhaisn GRO 005 (2003) (Split album with IMPERIAL FOETICIDE). Room 101 / Mutual Assured Destruction / Separated Entity Alteration / Confrontation / Millennium Fuck.
Demo 2004, (2004). Philantropic Depravity / Millennium Fuck.

DESPISED ICON

MONTRÉAL, QC, CANADA — *Marie-Hélène Landry (vocals), Steve Marois (vocals), Alan Glassman (guitar), Éric Jarrin (guitar), Sebastien Piché (bass), Alexandre Erian (drums).*

Montréal Deathcore band. DESPISED ICON, created in 2002, includes HEAVEN'S CRY guitarist Éric Jarrin along with DYING DAYS and NEURAXIS drummer Alexandre Erian. The debut album 'Consumed By Your Poison' was released in October 2002 on Galy Records. DESPISED ICON signed to Century Media Records in January 2005. The band's second album, 'The Healing Process', produced by guitarist Yannick St-Amand, was set for April release. That same month a rash of Canadian gigs had the band packaged with ION DISSONANCE and PREMONITIONS OF WAR.

The group announced April 2006 US tour dates combined with MORBID ANGEL, Poles BEHEMOTH and Brazilians KRISIUN. The band would hit the US touring circuit in September forming up a strong billing alongside HATEBREED, EXODUS, THE BLACK DAHLIA MURDER, NAPALM DEATH and FIRST BLOOD. Guitarist Yannick St. Amand opted out in December but stayed associated with the band, producing their next album. The group then pulled in the GORATORY and ex-BURN IN SILENCE credited Alan Glassman as new guitar player.

The group scheduled a round of British dates in March 2007, packaged with UNEARTH, JOB FOR A COWBOY and DAATH.

CONSUMED BY YOUR POISON, (2002). Compel To Copulate / Poissonnariat / Grade A-One / Le Chêne Et Le Roseau / Dead King / Absolu / Fashionable / Interfere In Your Days / Clef De Voûte / Despise The Icons.
THE HEALING PROCESS, Century Media (2005). Bulletproof Scales / Silver Plated Advocate / Immaculate / Warm Blooded / Retina / The Sunset Will Never Charm Us / As Bridges Burn / Harvesting Deceased / End This Day.
THE ILLS OF MODERN MAN, (2007).

DESPOILMENT

MA, USA — *Kev Wood (vocals), Dusty Lyon (guitar), Chris Farmerie (bass), Matt Johnson (drums).*

Massachusetts Death Metal act previously operational as ACEPHALUS. The group was actually conceived as an ACEPHALUS side project in August of 2001 by guitarist Dusty Lyon, bassist Chris Farmerie and Nate Westerlind. A demo, 'Forsaken Penetration', was cut before Westerlind exited from both ACEPHALUS and DESPOILMENT. Further tracks saw ACEPHALUS lead guitarist Jonah Burstein contributing. The demise of ACEPHALUS in March of 2002 signalled a move towards DESPOILMENT, with GUTWRENCH drummer Matt Johnson being drafted. The ACEPHALUS connections were strengthened with the recruitment of erstwhile vocalist Kev Wood. Both vocalist Dusty Lyon and guitarist Chris Farmerie joined fellow Massachusetts Death metallers BANE OF EXISTENCE in August 2005.

Forsaken Penetration, Despoilment (2002). Self-Inflicted War Atrocity / Fucked At Birth / Ravaged By Hate / Hordes Of Pain / Living Dissection / Lust For Blood / Suffer No Longer / Slophole / The Foresight Is Gone.
Despoilment, (2003). A Shallow Grave Awaits / Wartorn.

DESTINITY

LYON, FRANCE — *Mick (vocals), Nico (guitar), Zephiros (guitar), David (bass), Morteüs (drums).*

Lyon based symphonic Black Metal act DESTINITY came into being during July of 1996. At this stage DESTINITY comprised of vocalist Mick, guitarist Zephiros, guitarist / keyboard player Morteüs, guitarist Jim, bass player Benn and drummer Tyraël (Chris). A 1998 demo 'Enigmatic Forest' triggered DESTINITY's signing to AMI Productions for the debut album 'Wepts From The Sky'. The 'Supreme Domination Art' album would follow, initially released by Plaza Records and later picked up by the Malaysia based Psychic Scream Entertainment label. Signing to the Adipocere label DESTINITY issued the January 2003 album 'Under The Smell Of Chaos'. The record, featuring new lead guitarist Lord D.D. and which included a live video track recorded at Salon de Provence in April of 2002, witnessed guest contributors Akaias of AGATHODAIMON, Julien of BENIGHTED and Kohle from CENTURY. Chart was subsequently added to the line up as new bassist as Benn prioritised his other acts RAVENDUSK and the Sumerian Metal band ANKSUNAMON.

Under the banner 'Days Of Suffering' the band allied themselves with ENTHRONED, SETH and AGATHODAIMON for a spate of European dates in April and May of 2003. That November Hrafnagud was inducted as new bassist as the band entered Sonovore Studios with FURIA guitarist Mickael Vallesi acting as producer for 'In Excelsis Dementia'. Lord D.D. exited after these recordings.

DESTINITY underwent a change of direction with the September 2005 album 'Synthetic Existence', adopting a distinct Thrash Metal stance, the group now labelling itself as "Thrashened Extreme Music". The record was crafted between July and August that year with producer Jacob Hansen at Hansen Studios in Denmark and saw Zephiros resuming his lead guitar position. Upon completion of the album both Hrafnagud and Tyraël were excused of their duties. Further evolution saw Morteüs switching from keyboards to drums. David was drafted on bass.

WEPTS FROM THE SKY, AMI Productions (1999). Vanth's Dusk Enigma / Storm's Breath / Desire … / Souls Joined Together Eternally / Supremacy In Madness / The Beautiful Call Of Lord / Ultimate Silence Of The Unspoken / Wepts From The Sky.
SUPREME DOMINATION ART, Psychic Scream Entertainment (2001). The Beginning Of Eternal Sufferings / Wreak Of Sorrow / Beyond The Spiritual Prophecy / Supreme Domination's Art / New Dark Empire / From The Bowels Of The Abyss / The Greatest Dream / The Sermon Of Infinity / Vanth's Dusk Enigma.
UNDER THE SMELL OF CHAOS, Adipocere (2003). Introspection / Under The Smell Of Chaos / Daemonity / Enter My Nightmare / Evil Moon / Psychose / Glutted Wargasm / As The Disease We Shall Spread / Hymns For Minas Morgul / An Astral Travel (Through The Gloomy Ocean Of Sadness) / Dominus Satanas.
IN EXCELSIS DEMENTIA, Adipocere CDAR84 (2004). After The Grace Of Kaos Synopsis / Gloria In Exelcis Ecclesia / Divine Extase / Heffen Kemet / Until Death Desire / Sadistic Massacre / Black Upon The Throne / And Silence / Pleasures Of The Flesh / Forceps Of Hate.
SYNTHETIC EXISTENCE, Adipocere CDAR104 (2005). At The End / In Nuclear Light / Ex Nihilo / Fanatic God Machine / Evolution—Devilution / Deconstruction Of Times / Deshumanised Nature / Neurotic Illness / Synthetic Existence.

DESULTORY

SÖDERTÄLJE, SWEDEN — *Klas Morberg (guitar / vocals), Stefan Pöge (guitar), Jens Almgren (bass), Thomas Johnson (drums).*

Södertälje, Stockholm based Death Metal band formed in 1989, debuting in January 1990 with the four track demo cassette 'From Beyond'. DESULTORY recorded a further 1990 demo at the renowned Sunlight Studios with producer Tomas Skogsberg titled 'Death Unfolds'. This demo, together with a later effort 'Visions', were released together as the 'Forever Gone' limited edition mini-album in 1992 through the House of Kicks label.

DESULTORY signed to Metal Blade Records for the February 1993 album 'Into Eternity', this set featuring DISMEMBER's Matti Kärki aiding on backing vocals for the track 'Depression'. The band toured Britain with CANNIBAL CORPSE in 1994, promoting the Tomas Skogsberg and Fred Estby produced 'Bitterness' opus issued that June, and by the third full-length album, 'Swallow The Snake' in October 1996, DESULTORY had trimmed down to a trio of Johnson, Morberg and his brother Häkan Morberg on guitar. DESULTORY, adding bass player Jojje Bohlin, would evolve into Stoner act ZEBULON issuing the 'Cape Canaria' EP and 'Volume 1' album.

From Beyond, Desultory (1990) (Demo). Eternal Darkness / The Awakening / Cease To Exist / Insanity.
Death Unfolds, Desultory (1990) (Demo). Passed Away / The Chill Within / Death Unfolds.
Visions, Desultory (1991) (Demo). Forever Gone / Depression / Visions.
Forever Gone, House Of Kicks HOK LP002 (1992) (Limited edition 500 copies). Forever Gone / Depression / Visions / Passed Away / The Chill Within / Death Unfolds.
INTO ETERNITY, Metal Blade ZORRO 52 (1993). Into Eternity / Depression / Tears / The Chill Within / Visions / Twisted Emotions / Forever Gone / Passed Away / Asleep.
BITTERNESS, Metal Blade ZORRO 77 (1994). Life Shatters / Left Behind / A Closing Eye / Taste Of Tragedy / Bleeding / Among Mortals / Enslaved / Winter / Cold Bitterness.
SWALLOW THE SNAKE, Metal Blade 3984-14109-2 (1996). Mushroom Smile / The Bitter Man / Before Today, Beyond Tomorrow / Swallow The Snake / In My Veins / Blizzard In My Blood / Zone Traveller / Beneath / King Of The Valley And The Western Sky / Nothing Dies / Silent Suffering.

DETERIORATION

BLOOMINGTON, MN, USA — *James Kahmann (vocals / bass), Ian Wencl (guitar), Joe Kahmann (drums).*

Bloomington, Minnesota Death Metal trio DETERIORATION was manifested in November of 2003, cutting the eight song 'Body Count' demo before the year was out. The group was created by vocalist / bassist Jim Kahmann and guitarist Ian Wencl, both previously members of END OF THE WORLD featuring Jim's younger brother Joe Kahmann. This trio then fired up a Hardcore band in August of 2003, fronted by singer Nic, known as WIDE AWAKE NIGHTMARE. Dispensing with Nic, and adopting a Thrash / Death style DETERIORATION was borne in November.

A self produced album, 'Annihilation', arrived in 2004. The single 'Zombie Ritual' was released that March with an EP 'Slaughtered By Zombies' completed in July.

ANNIHILATION, Deterioration (2004). Prelude To The Massacre / Annihilation / Salem / Rotting Corpses / Fifty Ways To Kill, Fifty Ways To Die / Hacked Apart / He Deserved It / Involuntary Cannibalism / Blinded By The Light / The End Is Here.

DEUTERONOMIUM

JYVÄSKYLÄ, FINLAND — *Miika Partala (vocals / guitar), Kalle Paju (guitar), Manu Lehtinen (bass), J.J. Kontoniemi (drums).*

A Christian Death Metal act, founded in 1993 and based out of Jyväskylä. DEUTERONOMIUM's second album 'Here To Stay' is highly revered among certain circles. The band, featuring ex-CATHACOMB members, began life with a line-up of drummer Jarno Lehtinen, vocalist / guitarist Miika Partala, bass player Manu Lehtinen and Tapio Laakjo debuting with a 1993 demo 'Paths Of Righteousness'. A second session 'Crosshope' in 1996 led to recording of the 'Tribal Eagle' EP. This latter session would be recorded with session drummer Johnny Pesonen. Upon completion of 'Tribal Eagle' DEUTERONOMIUM enlisted drummer J.J. Kontoniemi and second guitarist Kalle Paju.

The first album 'Street Corner Queen', released in May of 1998, proved remarkable for not only pushing a Christian message but also brewing a heady mixture of sounds as diverse as Black Metal and Reggae! Manu Lehtinen would also be making a name for himself as owner of leading Christian Metal label Little Rose Productions. 'Here To stay' arrived in 1999 and interest in the band was strong enough to re-issue 'Street Corner queen', the revised version adding not only the 'Tribal Eagle' tracks but also a cover of ONE BAD PIG's 'Red River'.

Following the 'Here To Stay' DEUTERONOMIUM were down to a duo of guitarist Kalle Paju and bassist Manu Lehtinen. Apparently the band splintered due various band members struggles to maintain a Christian lifestyle. As lead vocalist, Manu Lehtinen subsequently founded the Finnish language Metal band VASKIKÄÄRME in league with guitarists Ville Hämäläinen and Mikko Korpiaho, bassist Jaakko Leinonen and drummer Miika Erkkilä. DEUTERONOMIUM drummer J.J. Kontoniemi would be active with both ICON CLAN and IX SYNDICATE. Miika Partala would front up Punk band NO MAN'S LAND.

Paths Of Righteousness, Deuteronomium (1993) (Demo). Your Destructive Hate / Thoughts Of The Weary / Apostasy (What Happened?) / Stranger In A Strange Land / My Prayer.

Crosshope, Deuteronomium (1996) (Demo). Chains Of Bitterness / Heretical Healers / Fire Of Trials.

Tribal Eagle EP, Deuteronomium DEUCD-001 (1997). Crosshope / Thinking / Tribal Eagle / Blue Moment.

STREET CORNER QUEEN, Little Rose Productions LRP 9801 (1998). Street Corner Queen / Druglord / Spell Of Hell / The Fall / Empty Shell / Human Nature / Bonsai People / Black Raven / C.C.R. / III / Northern Praise / Blue Moment.

HERE TO STAY, Little Rose Productions LRP 9904 (1999). Whirlwind / To Die And Gain / S.S. / My God / Terminator / Statue Of Liberty / Comeback / Fool / Here To Stay / Christ Addict / D.D.D. / Millstone / Dead End.

To Die And Gain, Little Rose Productions LRP 9902 (1999). To Die And Gain / Misleader / To Die And Gain (Demo version).

DEVASTACION

BUENOS AIRES, ARGENTINA — *Walter Ortiz (vocals / guitar), Pablo Maggione (guitar), Gonzalo Giulano (bass), Gustavo Quiroga (drums).*

DEVASTACION is a Buenos Aires Death Metal combo dating to 1987. For recording of the 1993 demo 'Maquinarias De Poder' the band line up stood at vocalist / guitarist Walter Ortiz, lead guitar player Guillermo Lamadrid, bassist Gonzalo Giulano and drummer Gustavo Quiroga. Gigs in early 1995 saw live action throughout Argentina, Bolivia and Peru.

DEVASTACION then entered a period of turmoil after losing the services of their guitarist and drummer. However, in 1997 the band pulled in guitarist Fabian Cejas and re-enlisted Quiroga. The debut album '... Que Lo Pario!!' was released during 2000, after which Cejas was substituted by Pablo Maggione.

... QUE LO PARIO, (1999). Intro / Raza Vengada / Pata, Sudor Y Sangre / Evolucion / Muerte Cumbia / Q'Lo Pario / Resistiendo Al Engano / La Patria Olvidada / Condicion Humana / Tratando De Zafar / El Enganero / La Ruta Interior / El Informador Oficial / Barbara Imposicion.

DEVIANCE

FORSHAGA, SWEDEN — *Mike Wennerstrand (vocals / rhythm guitar), Christer Grenskog (lead guitar), Henrik Bergström (keyboards), Björn Arvidsson (drums).*

Forshaga Death Metal band DEVIANCE was formulated during 2003 by keyboard player Henrik Bergström and Erik as an old school Black Metal project. Building up a band unit, the duo drafted vocalist Mike Wennerstrand, a veteran of acts such as BLACK HEART, MISANTHROPIA, DELIGHTED DARKNESS and AGONIZED, together with guitarist Christer Grenskog, also ex-BLACK HEART, MISANTHROPIA, DELIGHTED DARKNESS and AGONIZED as well as having credits with NIDING and LEGENDARY. Completing the band would be drummer Björn Arvidsson from SAMPHIRE, TOMMYGUN, AGONIZED and INSANITARY.

Founder Erik exited in 2004. DEVIANCE's June 2005 demo comprised an instrumental cover version of DIMMU BORGIR's 'Spellbound (By The Devil)'. The group went into hiatus during 2006 due to national military obligations of two band members. DEVIANCE evolved into VENOMOUS during 2006.

Rehearsal, Deviance (2005) (Demo). Spellbound (By The Devil).

DEVILDRIVER

USA — *Dez Fafara (vocals / guitar), Jeff Kendrick (guitar), Mike Spreitzer (guitar), Jon Miller (bass), John Boecklin (drums).*

DEVILDRIVER, originally going by the title of DEATHRIDE, was conceived during mid 2002 as a side project of COAL CHAMBER frontman Dez Fafara. Far removed from the Nu-Metal clichés of his former outfit, DEVILDRIVER presented a much harder proposition with a keen eye towards Death Metal. The band, also featuring guitarists Dragon (Jeff Kendrick) and Sleeper (Evan Pitts), bassist Shak (Jon Miller) and drummer Junk (John Boecklin), signed to the Roadrunner label for a Ross Hogarth produced debut album. Originally going by the projected title of 'Straight To Hell' the album would subsequently be re-named simply 'Devildriver'.

DEVILDRIVER united with DANZIG and SUPERJOINT RITUAL for the October 2003 'Blackest Of The Black' North American tour. The band got back on schedule in the New Year supporting OPETH on their 'Lamentations Over America Tour 2004' commencing in Redmonton, Canada on 20th January. DEVILDRIVER also landed the support slot to IN FLAMES European dates in April. That Summer the group joined the roving cast of the mammoth BLACK SABBATH, JUDAS PRIEST and SLAYER headed 'Ozzfest' events. DEVILDRIVER missed the July 29th 'Ozzfest' gig at Shoreline Amphitheater in Mountain View, California when their bus broke down.

Touring plans for the Autumn of 2004 saw the band joining up with the DANZIG headed 'Blackest Of The Black' tour, organised by Glenn Danzig and comprising DOYLE, featuring ex-MISFITS guitarist Doyle, Norwegian Black Metal pioneers MAYHEM, Thrash veterans DEATH ANGEL and EYES OF FIRE. However, with just days to go before these dates the entire tour was abruptly cancelled.

DEVILDRIVER had the previously unreleased track 'Digging Up The Corpses' included on the 'Resident Evil: Apocalypse' movie soundtrack. The group maintained momentum by entering Sonic Ranch studio in Tornillo, Texas on 15th November with producer Colin Richardson to cut their second album.

Ex-DEVILDRIVER guitarist Evan Pitts forged BACKMASK in late 2004, an alliance with lead vocalist/guitarist Shane McFee (son of DOOBIE BROTHERS guitarist John McFee) and the HIRAX and TCHILDRES credited drummer Dan Bellinger. Pitts would be substituted in the DEVILDRIVER ranks by Mike Spreitzer. Meantime, US gigs for DEVILDRIVER in May saw a road alliance with THE HAUNTED, MACHINE HEAD and IT DIES TODAY.

Initially announced as an opening act on the SLIPKNOT / SHADOWS FALL US arena tour of Spring 2005 the band was forced to drop off the billing due to "Union enforced time constraints". A new DEVILDRIVER album, 'The Fury Of Our Maker's Hand', shifted over 10,000 copies in its first week of US sales to debut at no.117 on the national Billboard charts. The band had their track 'I Could Care Less' featured on the soundtrack to the 'Rainbow Six Lockdown' game issued by 3volution Productions.

The Summer of 2005 found the group participating in the US 'Sounds of the Underground' touring extravaganza, a col-

DEVILDRIVER (pic: Paul Brown)

laboration between independent labels Ferret Music, Prosthetic Records, Trustkill Records and Metal Blade Records. The mammoth billing for these shows saw the band sharing stages with CLUTCH, OPETH, POISON THE WELL, FROM AUTUMN TO ASHES, CHIMAIRA, NORMA JEAN, EVERY TIME I DIE, STRAPPING YOUNG LAD, THROWDOWN, HIGH ON FIRE, UNEARTH, ALL THAT REMAINS, A LIFE ONCE LOST and GWAR. Regional additions included MADBALL and TERROR, splitting the East and West portions of the tour respectively, THE RED CHORD on the East Coast, FEAR BEFORE THE MARCH OF FLAMES in the Midwest and Southeast and HIMSA for Western gigs. Jon Miller of DEVILDRIVER took over the STRAPPING YOUNG LAD bass position in mid July as their regular bassist, Bryon Stroud, had been previously contracted out to FEAR FACTORY.

Former DEVILDRIVER guitarist Evan Pitts announced another new formation in early 2005 billed VEINGLORY. Meanwhile, Dez Fafara donated his vocals to the ROADRUNNER UNITED 25th anniversary album 'The All-Stars Sessions' released in October, featuring on the track 'Baptized In The Redemption' composed by Dino Cazares, formerly of FEAR FACTORY. The band acted as direct support to GWAR's US dates commencing 7th October in Sayreville, New Jersey, also packaged with A DOZEN FURIES and MENSREA. Maintaining their road ethic, UK gigs in December for DEVILDRIVER saw a strong package billing allied with LAMB OF GOD and THE AGONY SCENE. Subsequently, IN FLAMES, TRIVIUM and DEVILDRIVER pooled their talents for a January 2006 US tour. The group heightened their road profile further by hooking up with BURY YOUR DEAD, REMEMBERING NEVER, IF HOPE DIES and ARTIMUS PYLEDRIVER for the US 'Burning Daylight' tour in May. The band also put in a significant appearance at the METALLICA and KORN headlined 'Download' festival in Castle Donington, UK on June 10th.

The band and producer Jason Suecof utilised Sonic Ranch studios in El Paso Texas for their next album, 'The Last Kind Words', commencing recording on November 13th. Meantime, Jon Miller, Jeff Kendrick and John Boecklin activated instrumental side project BELT-FED in union with PRESSURE 4-5's Joe Schmidt.

DEVILDRIVER supported KATAKLYSM, UNEARTH and headliners Norwegian symphonic black metallers DIMMU BORGIR on their North American tour beginning on April 20th in Cleveland, Ohio.

DEVILDRIVER, Roadrunner (2003). Nothing's Wrong? / I Could Care Less / Die (And Die Now) / I Dreamed I Died / Cry For Me Sky / The Mountain / Knee Deep / What Does It Take (To Be A Man) / Swinging The Dead / Revelation Machine / Meet The Wretched / Devil's Son.
THE FURY OF OUR MAKER'S HAND, Roadrunner (2005). End Of The Line / Driving Down The Darkness / Grinfucked / Hold Back The Day / Sin & Sacrifice / Ripped Apart / Pale Horse Apocalypse / Just Run / Impending Disaster / Bear Witness Unto / Before The Hangman's Noose / The Fury Of Our Maker's Hand. Chart positions: 117 USA, 153 FRANCE.
THE LAST KIND WORDS, Roadrunner (2007).

DEVILISH

FINLAND — *Jaakko Peltonen (vocals / guitar), Juho Peltonen (guitar), Krister Virtanen (bass), Petri Törmä (drums).*

Thrash Metal band DEVILISH is rooted in the predecessor 1998 formation DISCIPLES OF DARKNESS, assembled by drummer Jaakko Peltonen alongside singer Rolle, bassist Andi and guitarist Mika. A 1999 demo, 'This Is A Good Day To Die', was issued, after which Peltonen took over bass duties as Andi departed. Pete was introduced on drums as Peltonen switched instruments again, now taking up rhythm guitar as Krister Virtanen took up bass. Subsequent demos included 'Armageddon Is Here' in 2000 and 'Reign Of Evil' in 2002.

In 2003 Jake's brother Juho entered the band to play lead guitar. With Rolle's exit, Jaako Peltonen took over the vocal responsibilities. DEVILISH recorded the demo 'Possessed By Hellfire' in October 2004.

This Is A Good Day To Die ..., Devilish (1999) (Demo). Disciples Of Darkness / Alone In The Dark / Lost / Human Mind Hell / No Escape From Dying.
Armageddon Is Here, Devilish (2000) (Demo). Armageddon Is Here / Figures In The Dark / Blinded By Faith / Time To Die.
Reign Of Evil, Devilish (2002) (Demo). Reign Of Evil / Armageddon Is Here / Hate Is Me.
Possessed By Hellfire, Devilish (2004) (Demo). Born By Human Fear / Possessed By Hellfire / Revolutionary Suicide / Beast Inside / Armageddon Is Here.

DEVILISH IMPRESSIONS

POLAND — *Quazarre (vocals / guitar), Starash (guitar), Adrian Nefarious (bass), Turqouissa (keyboards), Dragor (drums).*

Avantgarde Death Metal band DEVILISH IMPRESSIONS involved singer Quazarre, guitarist Starash, bassist Adrian Nefarious, keyboard player Turquoissa with Dragor on drums. Both Nefarious and Dragor have LUNA AD NOCTUM connections whilst Quazarre is a member of ASGAARD. The group's formation dated back to a foundation by Turquoissa and Starash during 1998. Enrolling Quazarre, first product was a 2002 demo, 'Eritis sicut Deus; Verbum Diaboli Manet in Aeternum; Vox Verpetilio Act I–Moon Var Dies Iare', recorded at D.J. Wołkos 666 Studio in Opole, for which bass and drum programming were sessioned by Paweł Wołczyk. Nefarious and Dragor were introduced in 2005.

DEVILISH IMPRESSIONS signed to Conquer Music for the 'Plurima Mortis Imago' album release in September 2006. These tracks were laid down at Mamut Studios and Hendrix Studios, Lublin with production credits going to Maciek Mularczyk with a mix by Arek Malczewskito. The track 'Dracula's Mechanized Universe' hosted a re-working of Ludwig Van Beethoven.

Eritis sicut Deus; Verbum Diaboli Manet in Aeternum; Vox Verpetilio Act I–Moon Var Dies Iare, Devilish Impressions (2002) (Demo). Moon / Var / Dies Irae.
PLURIMA MORTIS IMAGO, Conquest (2006). Lunarium–Intro / Rebellion Of Will Manifesto / Visions Of Kingdom To Come ... / Dracula's Mechanized Universe / Funeral Of God / Alpha And Omega Spaces / Crowned To Be Crucified / Smell Of Death / SataniChaoSymphony.

DEVILYN

POLAND — *Novy (vocals / bass), Bony (guitar), Dino (guitar), Basti (drums).*

Death Metal act centred upon frontman Novy and guitarist Bony, being originally formulated as CEREBRAL CONCUSSION during 1992. Live gigs commenced the following year. A demo, 'The Rule', led to a deal with the French Listenable label and a name switch to DEVILYN. The group's line up for the 1996 debut Listenable release 'Anger' was accredited to vocalist / bassist Novy, guitarists Bony and Piotr and drummer Kuba. DEVILYN maintained this line up for 1998's 'Reborn In Pain'. European dates had the group supporting acts such as CANNIBAL CORPSE and KRABATHOR before touring inside Poland saw DEVILYN heading out on their own 1999 'Pain Domination' tour with session guitarist Borowa in tow. However, the band roster shifted to allow Dino (a.k.a. Krystian Wojdas) to take Piotr and Borowa's place on guitar and new drummer Basti (Sebastian Łuszczek), both also members of SPINAL CORD, into the fold. Ex-drummer Kuba would later session for ECLYPSE. Touring in Spain and Portugal during December of 2000 had DEVILYN packaged on a billing with PANDEMIA.

DEVILYN bounced back with the 'Artefact' album, released by the British Blackened label. Upfront of the album release DEVILYN headed a bill of TRAUMA and MYSTERIA for Polish 'Expression Of Horror' dates during January 2002.

Novy joined leading Polish Death Metal act VADER in June of 2003 and would also join the ranks of SPINAL CORD. The DEVILYN album release that year, 'The Past Against The Future', actually comprised 'The Rule' demo from CEREBRAL CONCUSSION along with 2000 promotional recordings. This latter session incorporated a cover of CARCASS' 'Hatework'.

The group entered Hertz Studios in Bialystok during October of 2004 to craft their fourth album for Conquer Records. The band, having replaced bassist Cyprian with Cyclone, toured alongside HATE in early 2005.

ANGER, Listenable POSH009 (1996). Intro / Decline Of Worlds / The Rule / Millenium / Necrosis Of The Ego / Uncrown / Black Mask Of Death / The Burial Ground Of God / Wings Of Night / The Shadows Of Acheron / Anger.
REBORN IN PAIN, Listenable POSH016 (1998). Reborn In Pain / Scoff / Messiah For The Blind Fools / Dead's Prayer / Banished Of Alive / Song Of Suffer / Final Truth / Darkness Feller / Your Fear, My Power / Without Mercy, Without Glory / To Be Awaken In The Nightmares.
ARTEFACT, Blackend BLACK038CD (2001). Soul Snatcher / Aryman's Grace / Psalm / Contempt / Kingdom Of The Blind / Deceived Conscience / Expression Of Horror / Prophet's Crux / Fire Step Follow Me / Sense Scarity / Hatched Out Of ....
THE PAST AGAINST THE FUTURE, Metal Mind Productions (2003). Intro / The Rule / A Shadows Of Acheron / Into Centuries / My Own Creation / Illusions / An Astral Dream / Deceived Conscience / Testimony / The Past Against The Future / Hatework.

DEVISER

GREECE — *Matt Hnaras (vocals / guitar), George Triantafilakis (guitar), Nick Cristogianis (bass / keyboards), Mike Tsembertzis (drums).*

Black Metal outfit DEVISER was founded in 1989. The band's first demo 'Forbidden Knowledge' ensued the following year as did second effort 'Psychic Completion'. In 1993 a further tape surfaced entitled 'Into His Unknown'. DEVISER's debut commercial recording came with the release of 'The Revelation Of Higher Mysteries' 7" EP through the Dutch Teutonic Existence label. Touring to promote the release witnessed gigs in both Greece and Holland before the band returned to the studio to cut another demo session 'Thy Blackest Love', which emerged in 1995. These recordings prompted a deal from another Dutch based label, Mascot, for the 'Unspeakable Cults' inaugural album. A second effort, 'Transmission Chaos', was delivered in 1998.

Toward the close of 2001 bass player Nick Cristogiannis opted out and was duly replaced by Spyros. During October of 2001 DEVISER lost the services of keyboardist Manos Hiotis due to ill health. The band signed to the LSP label for their third album 'Running Sore'. Album cover artwork was from Kris Verwimp, noted for his work with many major league Black Metal bands. Keyboard contributions came courtesy of former bassist Nick Cristogiannis for this release. DEVISER appeared on the billing for the July 2002 'Rockwave' festival in Athens headlined by SLAYER and HALFORD.

The Revelation Of Higher Mysteries, Teutonic Existence (1995). The Revelation Of Higher Mysteries.
UNSPEAKABLE CULTS, Mascot M 7024-2 (1997). Stand & Deliver / Darkness Incarnate / Threnody / When Nightmares Begin / The Rape Of Holiness / Ritual Orgy (Instrumental) / Dangers Of A Real And Concrete Nature / The Fire Burning Bright / In The Horror Field / Afterkill (Outro).
TRANSMISSION TO CHAOS, II Moons TM 1206 2 (1998). Transmission To Chaos / Sailed By Night / Satyr, Hail! / Transcendent Beauty / A Story Of The Wind / Daemonlaetria / The Dark Mood Gathered / Open Shaft To Lunacy / Oneiric Aphasia.
RUNNING SORE, LSP Records LSP008 (2002). Signals From Another World / I Am In Awe / Liber Animus / Bemused Minds / Mourn The Dead / From The Starry Voids / Under the Lunar Skies / She Who Is To Come / Descend Among The Damned.

DEVOURED

EKSJÖ, SWEDEN — *David Hällgren (vocals), Goatfuck Demon (guitar), Pat Penetrator (bass), Eric Svensson (drums).*

DEVOURED an Eksjö based Black / Thrash outfit. The group was created under a former Death Metal guise, featuring singer David Hällgren. With Hällgren replaced by Johan Engdahl the band released an early 2004 demo entitled '... By Maggots', the band also comprising guitarist Oskar Mattelin, bassist Martin Olsson and drummer Eric Svensson as the band evolved into DEMONIUM.

The DEVOURED debut demo was re-released, with an additional cover version of IRON MAIDEN's 'The Trooper', in 2004 by No God Records re-branded 'Dependence On Malevolence'. In June of the following year DEMONIUM released the Black / Thrash orientated demo 'The Witchmaster' saw issue.

... By Maggots, Devoured (2004) (Demo). Devourer / Desecrating St. Peter's Cathedral / Bleed / Devourer (Version).

DEVOURMENT

TX, USA — *Ruben Rosas (vocals), Brian Wynn (guitar), Kevin Clark (guitar), Mike Majewski (bass), Brad Fincher (drums).*

Deathgrind outfit DEVOURMENT was formulated with an original line-up of ex-MEATUS vocalist Wayne Knupp, guitarist Brian Wynn and drummer Brad Fincher. A demo, engineered by future guitarist Braxton Henry, led to the debut album 'Molesting The Decapitated' for the United Guttural label However, by this stage DEVOURMENT had undergone radical line up changes with only Wynn and Fincher surviving. New members comprised of former DETRIMENTAL guitarist Ruben Rosas on vocals, second guitarist Kevin Clark and bassist Mike Majewski.

Following the release of the album DEVOURMENT was apparently put on ice when Rosas was reportedly imprisoned. The band would reconvene drafting original singer Wayne Knupp back into the fold and with Braxton Henry supplanting Wynn.

The 2000 album 'Devourment', issued by the Corpsegristle label, comprised of a new studio recording 'Babykiller', three remastered songs from the 'Impaled' demo and eight tracks culled from the debut 'Molesting The Decapitated' album. PROPHECY bassist Joseph Fontenot was added to the line-up in May 2003. '1.3.8.', with additional studio and demo tracks, saw a European release in September 2004 through the Dutch Displeased label. DEVOURMENT reformed during late 2004 to record a new album 'Butcher The Weak'. Eric Park, of Louisiana's SUTURE and Texan outfits SCARLINE and RHOME, replaced Brad Fincher on the drums in March 2005.

In August 2006 former singer Wayne Knupp announced a fresh band union with Brian Mohler of ARTERY ERUPTION and drummer Alexander Gosselin. Night Of The Vinyl dead issued a vinyl version of the '1.3.8' album, adding three demo tracks and a previously unreleased song 'Babykiller', limited to 500 hand numbered copies.

MOLESTING THE DECAPITATED, United Guttural (1999). Festering Vomitous Mass / Postmortal Coprohagia / Choking On Bile / Molesting The Decapitated / Self Disembowelment / Fucked To Death / Devour The Damned / Shroud Of Encryption.

1.3.8, Corpsegristle CGR004 (2000). Babykiller / Shroud Of Encryption (Demo) / Festering Vomitous Mass (Demo) / Choking On Bile (Demo) / Festering Vomitous Mass / Postmortal Coprophagia / Choking On Bile / Molesting The Decapitated / Self Disembowelment / Fucked To Death / Devour The Damned / Shroud Of Encryption.

1.3.8., Night Of The Vinyl Dead NIGHT005 (2006) (Vinyl version. Limited edition 500 hand numbered copies). Baby Killer / Shroud Of Encryption (Demo) / Festering Vomitous Mass (Demo) / Chocking On Bile (Demo) / Festering Vomitous Mass / Postmortal Coprophagia / Chocking On Bile / Molesting The Decapitated / Self Disembowelement / Fucked To Death / Devour The Damned / Shroud Of Encryption.

DEW-SCENTED

GERMANY — *Leif Jensen (vocals), Hendrik Bache (guitar), Florian Müller (guitar), Alexander Pahl (bass), Uwe Werning (drums).*

Germany's DEW-SCENTED, despite their innocuous title, trade in a vicious amalgam of Thrash Hardcore Doom Heavy Metal. DEW-SCENTED, founded in 1992 and taking their name from the works of Edgar Allan Poe, made their intentions clear with the 1994 opening demo 'Symbolization'. At this juncture DEW-SCENTED comprised vocalist Leif Jensen, guitarists Jörg Szittnick and Ralf "Shotte" Klein, bass player Patrick Heims and drummer Tarek Stinshoff. Further exposure would be gained with the inclusion of the 'Poems Of Dirt' track on a 1995 Major Records compilation. These sessions would lead to a recording contract with the Steamhammer label for the February 1996 'Immortelle' record. An intensive round of live promotion witnessed supports to EDGE OF SANITY, LAKE OF TEARS, SADIST, MORBID ANGEL and ARCH ENEMY as well as a ten date tour through Italy. With these shows over the group then re-assembled itself, bringing in new members guitarist Florian Müller replacing Szittnick and on the drums Uwe Werning.

The 1998 'Innoscent' album, produced by Dan Swanö and issued by Grind Syndicate Medial, would include a cover version of OVERKILL's 'Fatal If Swallowed'. The band's road schedule saw supports to DEATH, DISMEMBER and NIGHT IN GALES, participation in the 'Summer Clash' festival tour alongside DEICIDE, SIX FEET UNDER and BRUTAL TRUTH and an appearance at the 'Wacken Open Air' event.

The 1999 album 'Ill-Natured' would prove a pivotal point in the band's career as their trademark blend of Death and intricate Thrash styles came to the fore. Klein had made his exit beforehand, substituted in the studio by Christian Göllner. Festivals showings found the band making their presence felt throughout the Summer in Europe at the 'Wave Gotik Treffen', 'Fuck The Commerce' and ' Summer Breeze' events. Guest spots included gigs with IMMORTAL, PRIMORDIAL, WARHAMMER, VADER, CRYPTOPSY and TANKARD plus a full blown European tour ranked alongside OVERKILL and ANNIHILATOR. During late 1999 DEW-SCENTED drummer Uwe Werning would loan himself to NIGHT IN GALES for tour work.

DEW-SCENTED returned in January 2001 with the 'Inwards' album, recorded as a four piece of Jensen, Müller, Heims and Werning and produced by ex-HOLY MOSES guitarist Andy Classen. The band would tour Japan during March of 2001 billed alongside NIGHT IN GALES and DEFLESHED. 'Inwards' would see a January 2002 issue in Japan courtesy of Soundholic Records. Japanese versions included an exclusive track, a cover of SLAYER's 'War Ensemble'.

The band tagged onto the Thrash renaissance DESTRUCTION, KREATOR and SODOM 'Hell Comes To Your Town' for dates in Holland and Belgium during early 2002. Second guitarist Hendrik Bache was added to the ranks in March as gigs into France found the band billed with a mini tour package of NO RETURN, SCARVE and RAIN in May. A further run of European shows would be scheduled commencing September 19th in Eindhoven, Holland, a month's worth of dates supporting CANNIBAL CORPSE. For these gigs the band pulled in the BLO.TORCH credited Marvin Vriesde on additional guitar.

Digipack versions of DEW-SCENTED's August 2003 Andy Classen produced album 'Impact', which had Bache contributing studio bass, added a cover version of TURBONEGRO's 'Hobbit Motherfuckers' plus an extra original composition 'Force-Fed [The Bleeding Scheme]'. A double vinyl set of the new album paired 'Impact' with prior album 'Inwards'.

The band inducted OBSCENITY bassist Alexander Pahl and his band mate Marc Andree "Mücke" Dieken, also active with BK 49 and PAIN FOR PLEASURE, on the drums, the latter acting as a temporary stand in for Uwe Wening whilst the regular sticksman attended university. They then geared up for an exhaustive 2004 touring schedule to promote 'Impact' teaming up with KATAFALK and OUTBURST for a German run of dates in September, British club shows with NILE and MISERY INDEX in December which led up to the 'Xmas' European festivals in a heavyweight package comprising DEICIDE, DESTRUCTION, AMON AMARTH, NILE, GRAVEWORM and MISERY INDEX.

DEW-SCENTED entered Stage One Studios in Borgentreich with producer Andy Classen to record a new album 'Issue VI', featuring a cover version of ZEKE's 'Evil Dead', in January 2005. April gigs witnessed a union with Swedish veterans GRAVE although Florian Müller had exited in favour of Marvin Vriesde of BLO.TORCH and SEVERE TORTURE. Returning to Japan, the band performed as part of the 'Extreme The Dojo Vol. 14' tour in union with HIGH ON FIRE and MISERY SIGNALS in June. To coincide with these dates, Soundholic Records issued the 'Issue VI' album complete with exclusive bonus track 'Full-Blown Revenge'. In outside activity, Leif Jensen guested on Saint Etienne Death Metal band BENIGHTED's 'Identisick' album.

During September 2005 the group partnered with Denmark's MERCENARY and US headline act NEVERMORE for European touring. The band announced European tour dates for January 2006, traversing Poland, Germany, Holland, France, Belgium, Ireland, Switzerland, Austria, Italy and the UK, alongside a heavyweight cast of GRAVE, ABORTED, HURTLOCKER, VESANIA and CRYPTOPSY.

2006 shows witnessed the return of guitarist Florian Müller. German concerts in November were conducted with NOISE FOREST and FALLEN YGGDRASIL prior to December gigs aligned with TRIVIUM and Sweden's WOLF. In outside activity, Hendrik Bache donated guest guitar to RECKLESS TIDE's 'Helleraser' album. Alexander Pahl also featured on a new OBSCENITY album.

DEW-SCENTED announced early 2007 recording plans with producer Jörg Uken at Soundlodge Studio. 'Incinerate', mixed by Andy Sneap and arriving in April, featured Jeff Waters of ANNIHILATOR and Gus G. of FIREWIND guesting with guitar solos on the song 'Perdition for All'. Mille Petrozza from KREATOR provided guest vocals on the track 'Retain The Scars'. Shows across Europe for March and April 2007 aligned the band with NAPALM DEATH, BEHEMOTH, ROOT and MOONSPELL.

IMMORTELLE, Steamhammer SPV 085-18262 (1996). In Flames / Silenced / Black Is The Day / Thirst For The Sun / Unending / Afterlife / Afterlove / . . . Yonder . . . / Beloved Elysium / For You And Forever / Poets Of Dirt / Native Soil Venus / Theory Of Harm.

INNOSCENT, GSM (1998). Shatteredinsanity / Bereaved / Burn With Me / Starspangled / The Sicker Things / Everred / The Grapes Of Wrath / Aentity / Underneath / Fatal If Swallowed.

ILL-NATURED, GSM (1999). Embraced By Sin / This Grace / Simplicity In Chaos / Apocalypse Inside / Defiance / Wounds Of Eternity / Idolized / Skybound / The Endless / Hear See Say No . . . .

DEW-SCENTED (pic: Axel Jusseit)

INWARDS, Nuclear Blast NB 704-2 (2002). Bitter Conflict / Unconditional / Life Ending Path / Inwards / Blueprints Of Hate / Locked In Motion / Degeneration / Terminal Mindstrip / Feeling Not / Reprisal.

IMPACT, Nuclear Blast NB 1169-2 (2003). Acts Of Rage / New Found Pain / Destination Hell / Soul Poison / Cities Of The Dead / Down My Neck / One By One / Agony Designed / Slaughtervain / Flesh Reborn / 18 Hours.

ISSUE VI, Nuclear Blast NB 1452-2 (2005). Processing Life / Rituals Of Time / Turn To Ash / Ruins Of Hope / Out Of The Self / The Prison Of Reason / Bled Dry / In Defeat / Never To Return / Vortex / Conceptual End / Evil Dead.

INCINERATE, Nuclear Blast NB 1817-2 (2007). Exordium (Intro) / Vanish Away / Final Warning / That's Why I Despise You / The Fraud / Into The Arms Of Misery / Perdition For All / Now Or Never / Aftermath / Everything Undone / Contradictions / Retain The Scars / Exitus (Outro).

DIABOLIC

TAMPA, FL, USA — *Paul Ouellette (vocals), Brian Malone (guitar), Brian Hipp (guitar), Ed Webb (bass), Aantor Coates (drums).*

Tampa, Florida blasphemous Black Death Metal band DIABOLIC feature former HORROR OF HORRORS, NECROSIS, IMPIETY, EULOGY and EXMORTIS drummer Lee 'Aantor' Coates. Bassist Ed Webb is also a former EULOGY member. DIABOLIC's June 1997 demo 'City Of The Dead' would be reissued as a mini-album by Fadeless Records. The act's debut gig came with a high profile appearance sharing the stage with heavyweights VADER, MONSTROSITY and BROKEN HOPE. Signing to Conquest Music for the 1999 'Supreme Evil' album the band took to the road with gusto in 1998 appearing at the Milwaukee Metalfest and New York Demonfest, the New England Death And Hardcore festival and the Texan November To Dismember gig in 1999.

Touring in North America saw DIABOLIC as part of the 'Death Metal Massacre' package alongside CANNIBAL CORPSE, GOD DETHRONED and HATE ETERNAL. The tour, although a great success, was marred by the band having all their equipment stolen after the first gig. Undaunted, DIABOLIC put in further touring supporting MORBID ANGEL the same year.

Vocalist Paul Ouellette would later be sacked for alleged weakness as bass player Ed Webb took over lead vocal duties. The band would also draft former BRUTALITY and CRADLE OF FILTH guitarist Brian Hipp. With this line-up, DIABOLIC cut a version of SLAYER's 'Killing Fields' for a tribute album. Later shows would see erstwhile ANGEL CORPSE guitarist Gene Palubicki filling in. Bassist Ed Webb would also be operating CONTORTED alongside his erstwhile EULOGY colleague guitarist Dave Sawyer and the BRUTALITY duo of Jim Coker and Pete Sykes.

The band amicably parted ways with vocalist Paul Ouellette, replacing him with ex-COFFIN TEXTS frontman Robert Cardenas. A further shift in personnel occurred as the band parted ways with guitarist Jerry Mortellaro, bringing in Eric Hersemann of Chicago's LORD BLASPHEMER as replacement. European dates slated for November 2002 saw the band making up a bill including headliners DEICIDE alongside BEHEMOTH, DESTROYER 666, CENTINEX and ANTAEUS. However, DIABOLIC along with half of the other bands originally name, would be subsequently dropped from these shows.

Drummer Aantar Coates was apparently asked to leave upon completion of the tour although within days of this announcement the situation was officially reversed, Coates being credited once more as a full member of the group. Confusingly the original press release was believed to have been issued by guitarist Jerry Malone and subsequent statements from the band affirmed that it was in fact Malone out of the picture and not Coates. The band was reported to be reuniting with original guitarist and PESSIMIST founder Kelly McLauchlin, although in actuality this did not transpire. The story did not end there as yet more press statements confirmed that Malone, Eric Hersemann and Robert Cardenas, were to carry on with the band name DIABOLIC and that Coates, together with Kelly McLauchlin and erstwhile members Jerry Ouellette and Paul Mortellaro branched off into a completely new band set up called UNHOLY GHOST. Coates subsequently exited this formation, forged BLASTMASTERS and cutting a Juan Gonzalez produced demo in August.

In 2004 DIABOLIC would donate their rendition of 'No Will To Live' to the 'Seven Gates Of Horror' tribute album assembled by the Dutch Karmageddon Media label in homage to pioneering Bay Area Thrash act POSSESSED. US shows scheduled for September saw the band announced as forming up a four way package billing alongside DEICIDE, CATTLE DECAPITATION and GOATWHORE. However, the group subsequently dropped off this tour. As it transpired, DIABOLIC performed their final show at the Masquerade in Tampa on 20th August. In mid September founder Brian Malone announced the group had folded. Jerry Mortellaro was reported to have joined Aantor Coates in BLASTMASTERS, but within days this statement was denied. DIABOLIC guitarist Eric Hersemann joined HATE ETERNAL in May 2005. That same month guitarist Brian Hipp joined UNHOLY GHOST. Aantar Lee Coates joined the resurrected EXMORTIS in mid 2005.

DIABOLIC marked a return to action in June 2006, assembled by founder member Aantar Lee Coates and his UNHOLY GHOST colleague guitarist Kelly McLauchlin alongside BLASTMASTERS members Jesse Jolly, handling both vocals and bass, with R.J. on second guitar. A new album, 'Shellfire And Tombstones', was produced by Juan "Punchy" Gonzales, of MORBID ANGEL and UNHOLY GHOST, at Diet of Worms studios. Meantime, Eric Hersemann forged the GIGAN project in union with HATE ETERNAL vocalist / guitarist Randy Piro and drummer Grover Norton.

Guitarist Bryan Hipp died on October 21st 2006.

DIABOLIC underwent line-up changes in December, losing both Kelly McLauchlin and Jesse Jolly, the former to regular employment whilst Jolly opted to prioritise his other acts CRIMSON MASSACRE, LULL ME TO LARVAE, AFTER DEATH and PROMETHEAN HORDE. Taking over the role of vocalist / bassist would be ENGRAVE and COFFIN TEXT's Robert Cardenas whilst Josh Cannon took on guitar duties.

DIABOLIC announced a return to action in April 2007, the line-up comprising vocalist / bassist Paul Ouellette, guitarists Jerry Mortellaro and Raymond James with Aantar Coates on drums.

SUPREME EVIL, Conquest Music (1998). Insacred / Sacrament Of Fiends / Ancient Hatred / Treacherous Scriptures / Grave Warnings / Rack Of Torment / View With Abhorrence / Dwelling Spirits / Wicked Inclination / Supreme Evil.

CITY OF THE DEAD, Fadeless (1999). Denounce God / City Of The Dead / Vortex / Encarta / Inborn.
SUBTERRANIAL MAGNETUDE, Conquest Music (2001). Vassago / Forewarning / Extinction Level Event / Fatal Extraction / Deadly Deception / Fleshcraft / Infernalism / Diabolic Perception / Soul Projection / Necromancer Of The Ancient Arts / Subterraneal Magnitude.
VENGEANCE ASCENDING, Olympic OLY0223-2 (2002). Darken The Imagination / All Evils Inside / Vengeance Ascending / The Shallowed / Marked For Banishment / The Inevitable / Possess The Strength / Celestial Pleasures / Cease To Be / Majestic Satanic.
INFINITY THROUGH PURIFICATION, Olympic (2003). From The Astral Plane ... Entwined With Infinity / Spiritual Transition / Satanic Barbarism / Internal Mental Cannibalism / Procession Of The Soul Grinders / Exsanguinated Life / Descending Through Portals Of Misery / Enter The Maelstrom.

DIABOLIC INTENT

ORLANDO, FL, USA — *Anthony Farr (vocals), Chris Migdalski (guitar), Mike Raines (bass), Mop (drums).*

Orlando Death Metal band DIABOLIC INTENT was formulated during 1998 as a quartet comprising singer Anthony Farr, guitarist Chris Migdalski, bassist Mike Raines and drummer Ed Lopes. The band gained valuable experience the following year by supporting CANNIBAL CORPSE in Tallahassee. Subsequently their gig schedule took in opening spots for DYING FETUS, CANDIRIA, MONSTROSITY and KILLSWITCH ENGAGE amongst others.

In 2000 DIABOLIC INTENT entered ARS Studios in Longwood to craft the debut album 'Reborn'. Live promotion for the record would prove exhaustive, lasting nearly two years and including an appearance at the Snakenet metal 'Radio MetalNation' festival in 2002. In 2003 Ed Lopes opted out, to be replaced by Mop for recording of a new album 'The Cold Path Of Man'. Other releases include a DVD 'Failure's Not An Option'.

In early 2006 DIABOLIC INTENT cut their third album 'The Cold Path Of Man' for the Auditory Suicide label at Dark Angel Studios in Joannesburg, South Africa.

REBORN, Diabolic Intent (2000). Machines Of Genocide / Dark Existence / Pain Divine / Scorn / Chalice / Dead Reckoning / Godsick / Reborn / Krew Krie.
THE COLD PATH OF MAN, Diabolic Intent (2004). The Cold Path Of Man (Sufferance Is Imminent) / The Phenomilogical Concept Of Nothingness / Progressive Regression / Purveyors Of Hate And Division / FCC (Forcing Censored Content) / Lessons In Abhorrence.

DIABOLICAL

SUNDSVALL, SWEDEN — *Magnus Ödling (vocals), Hans Carlsson (guitar), Vidar Widgren (guitar), Rickard Persson (bass), Carl Stjärnlöf (drums).*

Founded by rhythm guitarist Vidar Widgren DIABOLICAL, for a formative period known as MISANTHROPIC ORCHESTRA, was founded in Sundsvall during 1996. Going under their early title the band, comprising of Vidar Widgren, vocalist Agilma (a.k.a. Jens Blomdal) and the GARBO rhythm section of bass player Phamarus (Fredrik Hast) and drummer Keuron (Kim Thalén), contributed to the 1997 compilation album 'Voices Of Death' with tracks laid down at Studio Mysak.

During April of 1998 the band underwent the transition to DIABOLICAL, drafting Lars Söderberg the same month. Various bass players were tried out but the final decision was made that Söderberg should handle both bass and drums. In October DIABOLICAL entered the studio, cutting tracks for a split EP with BLAZING SKIES billed as 'Northern Triumphators'. The DIABOLICAL trio for these sessions was credited as Agilma on vocals, Vidar Widgren on guitar and Lars Söderberg on bass and drums. Shortly after the band re-entered the studio to lay down their version of 'No Remorse' to the Black Sun Records METALLICA tribute collection 'Metal Militia Volume 3'. However, pushed for studio time, the band would make it clear they were far from happy with the end result.

DIABOLICAL then entered a period of flux with various members drifting in and out. One who stayed the course was lead guitarist Hans Carlsson, a seasoned campaigner of IN BATTLE, VALKYRIA and ODHINN. A further demo, 'The Dreaming Dead', arrived in August of 1999. This tape saw the introduction of new frontman Magnus Ödling of CAVEVOMIT and SORGHEGARD, Agilma having made the break to concentrate on his priority act HAIMAD.

Another three track demo was issued in the form of 'Deserts Of Desolation', released in May of 2000 as an EP by Cadla Communications in Western Europe, Guano Records in Eastern Europe and the Canadian Death Network for North America. Selling over 3'000 copies of the disc brought DIABOLICAL to the attention of the Italian Scarlet label who signed the band up for the debut P.O. Saether produced album 'Synergy'.

In May of 2001 the group inducted MÖRK GRYNING man Jonas Berndt as stand in live bassist for a short rash of dates in Sweden. Berndt's priorities with his main act meant this union was only temporary though. A fresh rhythm section involved bassist Rickard Persson and drummer Henrik Ohlsson, the latter boasting a wealth of associations to acts such as ADVERSARY, ALTERED AEON, LEGIA, MUTANT, SCAR SYMMETRY and THEORY IN PRACTICE.

To promote the second album, March 2002's 'A Thousand Deaths', DIABOLICAL lined up an extensive European tour, adding the services of HECTORITE and PSYCHO POETRY guitarist Roger Bergsten, as part of a package deal in alliance with AMON AMARTH, VOMITORY, CALLENISH CIRCLE and SINS OF OMISSION. The band would also would tour Poland in November of 2002, co-headlining a package billing also comprising fellow Swedes NECROPHOBIC, British band THUS DEFILED along with Polish outfits CORRUPTION, HELL BORN, MESSAGE and UNNAMED.

The band introduced new drummer ABSENTIA Carl Stjärnlöf in February of 2003, previous sticksman Henric Ohlsson opting to fully concentrate on his other act THEORY IN PRACTICE. Meantime, Ödling forged side venture FENRIA in alliance with bassist Viklund and guitarist Sasrof of BLOODLINE, SETHERIAL and DIABOLICUM. The two track demo 'Helvetesvisioner' was issued in 2005.

Northern Triumphators, Diabolical (1998) (Demo).
SYNERGY, Scarlet (2000). Suicidal Glory / Ashes II / Caged Wrath / Drowned In Blood / Guidance Of Sin / Human Control / The Passenger / Haven.
Deserts Of Desolation EP, Cadla Communications CDN 002 (2000). Ashes (Intro) / Guidance Of Sin / Deserts / The Dreaming Dead.
A THOUSAND DEATHS, Scarlet SC44-2 (2002). A Thousand Deaths / Children Of The Mushroom Cloud / God Of The Underworld / Dead Angel's Choir / Until The Day Arrives / Under My Skin / An Opposite Law / Demonic / Profane Murder.
SYNERGY / A THOUSAND DEATHS, Zenor Recordz 78983 241691 68 (2003) (Brazilian release). Suicidal Glory / Ashes II / Caged Wrath / Drowned In Blood / Guidance Of Sin / Human Control / The Passenger / Haven / A Thousand Deaths / Children Of The Mushroom Cloud / God Of The Underworld / Dead Angel's Choir / Until The Day Arrives / Under My Skin / An Opposite Law / Demonic / Profane Murder.
THE GALLERY OF BLEEDING ART, Zenor Recordz (2007).

DIABOLIQUE

GOTHENBURG, SWEDEN — *Kristian Wåhlin (vocals / guitar), Johan Österberg (guitar), Bino Carlsson (bass), Hans Nilsson (drums).*

Gothenburg's DIABOLIQUE is the brainchild of DECOLLATION, GROTESQUE and LIERS IN WAIT founder Kristian Wåhlin. As a drummer for DECOLLATION Wåhlin went under the pseudonym of 'Chris Steele'. Guitarist Johan Österberg is also ex-DECOLLATION, where he went by the title 'John Lesley'.

Drummer Hans Nilsson is another LIERS IN WAIT member and also has credits with LUCIFERION, CRYSTAL AGE, THE GREAT DECEIVER and DIMENSION ZERO. Bassist Bino Carlsson is a SÉANCE veteran.

The band started operations in the traditional Death Metal mould but would pursue more atmospheric, Gothique soundscapes with each successive recording. French label Listenable issued the 1996 EP 'The Diabolique' as their opening gambit. The debut album, 1997's 'The Wedding Grotesque' released on Black Sun Records, was produced by KING DIAMOND's Andy La Rocque. DIABOLIQUE's album run continued with 'The Black Flower' in 1999, 'Butterflies' in 2000 through Necropolis Records and the almost fully Electro 'The Green Goddess' in 2001.

Wåhlin also goes under the pseudonym of Necrolord as cover artist for many Black Metal bands, executing such memorable sleeve designs as AT THE GATES 'Slaughter Of The Soul', EMPEROR's 'In The Nightside Eclipse', BATHORY's 'Blood On Ice', DARK TRANQUILLITY's 'The Gallery', DISMEMBER's 'Massive Killing Capacity' amongst many others.

The Diabolique, Listenable POSH 011 (1996). Stealing The Fire From Heaven / Blood Of Summer / Beggar Whipped In Wine / Sorrows Piercing Art / Deep Shame Of God.
WEDDING THE GROTESQUE, Black Sun BS 011 (1997). Dark Man / Shaven Angel Forms / Blood Of Summer / Sacrificial Highway / The Unchaste Bittersweet / Sorrow Piercing Art / The Smiling Black / Beggar Whipped In Wine / The Diabolique.
THE BLACK FLOWER, Black Sun BS 018 (1999). Catholic / Dark Rivers Of The Heart / Absinthe / And Deepest Sadness / Yesmine / Eternal Summer / Cannula / Morphine / A Golden Girl From Somewhere / Silver / Play In The Dark.
Butterflies, Necropolis NR044CD (2000). Rain / Losing You / Butterflies / Summer Of Her Heart / Stolen Moments / Beneath The Shade.
THE GREEN GODDESS, Necropolis NR060CD (2001). On Through The Night / Remedy / Innuendo / White Nights / Models / Winter Blue / All For You / Elysee / Snowblind / Substancer.
THE BLACK SUN COLLECTION, Blackend BLACK093DCD (2005) (2CD). Dark Man / Shaven Angel Forms / Blood Of Summer / Sacrificial Highway / The Unchaste Bittersweet / Sorrow Piercing Art / The Smiling Black / Beggar Whipped In Wine / The Diabolique / Catholic / Dark Rivers Of The Heart / Absinthe / And Deepest Sadness / Yesmine / Eternal Summer / Cannula / Morphine / A Golden Girl From Somewhere / Silver / Play In The Dark.

DIES IRAE

POLAND — *Novy (vocals / bass), Mauser (guitar), Hiro (guitar), Docent (drums).*

Death Metal unit created by a pre-VADER Mauser in 1992. The original line up of DIES IRAE comprising of Mauser on guitar and vocals, second guitarist Jaroslaw 'China' Labieniec previously with IMPURITY, bassist Czarny and drummer Gilan. This incarnation of the band would cut the inaugural demo 'Fear Of God'. This outing would be re-issued commercially by Serenades Records in 1994.

China would stand in as temporary live guitarist for VADER in 1996. However, in 1997 Mauser teamed up with VADER full time and DIES IRAE promptly folded. Labieniec would subsequently found NYIA in league with PROPHECY guitarist Szymon Czech.

Mauser would find the opportunity to re-activate the DIES IRAE name in 2000 drafting his VADER colleague Docent (a.k.a. Krzysztof Raczkowski) on drums, SCEPTIC guitarist Jack Hiro and frontman Novy of DEVILYN. This new version of DIES IRAE entered the recording studio in June of 2000 with producer Szymon Czech for the debut 'Immolated' album. The band would sign to the Metal Blade label who issued 'Immolated' during November.

DIES IRAE formed part of a package Death Metal tour of Europe with NILE in January 2001. Novy would join SPINAL CORD as bassist in November of 2003.

The 'Sculpture Of Stone' album emerged in May of 2004, live dates seeing Vitek from DECAPITATED substituting on drums for the injured Docent. February of 2005 saw European gigs allied with HATE, CRIONICS and DECAPITATED. Tragedy hit in August 2005 with the announcement that former drummer Krzysztof Raczkowski had died. The musician, ejected from VADER the previous March, was just 35 years old and had a history of alcohol related problems.

The band undertook the 'Empire Invasion' March 2006 tour of Poland allied with HERMH, VESANIA and THE CHAINSAW.

NAÏVE, Oz Records (2001). Sculpted In Stone / Ice In Dawn / Blurred / Parallel Universe Part I / Shattered Mockery / Slow / In Porous Verves / Shades / Parallel Universe Part II.
IMMOLATED, Metal Blade 3984143562 (2001). Zohak / Message Of Aiwaz / Sirius B / Immolated / The Nameless City / Bestride Shantak / Turning Point / Hidden Lore / Lion of Knowledge.
THE SIN WAR, Metal Mind Productions MMP 0158 (2002). Comrade Of Death / Incarnation Of Evil / Internal War / Horde Of Angry Demons / Infinity / Genocide Generation / The Truth / Beyond Sensual / Another Being Wasted / Nine Angels.
SCULPTURE OF STONE, Metal Mind Productions (2004). Beyond All Dimensions / The Beginning Of Sin / The Art Of An Endless Creation / The Hunger / Trapped In The Emptiness / The Plague / The Oceans Of Filth / Unrevealed By Words / Sculpture Of Stone.

DIES IRAE

BUCHAREST, RUMANIA — *Radu Iordake (vocals), Marian Stoenică (guitar), Sorin Stoian (guitar), Ioachim Stroe (bass), Victor Stoica (drums).*

DIES IRAE is a Bucharest Death-Black orientated Doom Metal outfit dating to 1995 by guitarist Sorin Stoian and bass player Ioachim Stroe. Adding vocalist Radu Iordache and Victor Stoica on drums a self titled February 1996 demo, cut at Kerestely Studios in Bucharest and put in their inaugural live performance at the Hard n' Heavy Cafe in Bucharest in March. In May a further demo recording was laid down at Migas Real Compact Studios working with engineer Adi Ordean. DIES IRAE's next move would be to issue a live demo, captured once more at the Hard n' Heavy Café, in October.

Guitarist Marian Stoenică came onboard in January 1997, leading in turn to a split cassette entitled 'A Perennial Spleen' shared with GOD. Their first full length release, the 1998 'Gargoyles' album, recorded at the Show Factory Studios in Timisoara was issued as a cassette release through Bestial Records.

GARGOYLES, Bestial (1998). Never More Occult / I Built The Symmetry Of Chaos / The Vineyard / My Soul To Ashes / Dervent / Enrapture The Heathen / In A Frown I Found My Hate / The Funeral I've Never Seen / The Wish / Gargoilism.

DIM MAK

RED BANK, NJ, USA — *Scott Ruth (vocals), Shaune Kelley (guitar), Dennis Carroll (bass), Brandon Thomas (drums).*

DIM MAK consist of former RIPPING CORPSE members guitarist Shaune Kelley, vocalist Scott Ruth and drummer Brandon Thomas together with ex-TORTURE KRYPT bassist Dennis Carroll. Eschewing the gore and occult leanings of their former acts DIM MAK, named after an ancient Chinese martial art technique the 'death touch', made their presence felt with numerous compilation appearances prior to signing to the Singapore based Dies Irae label for their 1999 'Enter The Dragon' album. DIM MAK's next move was to join forces with New Jersey's Olympic label, recording the 'Intercepting Fist' album with MORBID ANGEL guitarist Erik Rutan, also an erstwhile RIPPING CORPSE colleague, acting as producer. Denmark's Mighty Music would take the album on for European distribution.

DIM MAK reformed in 2005, now counting in the ranks ORIGIN, THE RED CHORD, ANGEL CORPSE, DYING FETUS, EXHUMED and SKINLESS credited John Longstreth on drums.

The band quickly signed to Willowtip Records to cut an album, 'Knives Of Ice', at Sound Spa Studios in September for an April 2006 release.

ENTER THE DRAGON, Dies Irae (1999). Spirit Of The Dragon / Defy The Clouds / Feel The Pain / Cobra's Eyes / Between Two Fires / Royal Ass Whipping / Insect To Insect / No Rope A Dope / Warchild / Sorry / Tribulations / Gas Poured On Flame / Dark With Demons.
INTERCEPTING FIST, Mighty Music (2002). Phoenix Eye Fist / Tai Pan Snake Venom / Komodo Whip / Shambling / Mindgate / Den Of The Avalanche Dragon / Interceptor / Climbing Knife Mountain / Nine Head Serpentine Sire / Essence Of The Northern Fist / To The Negative Power.
KNIVES OF ICE, Willowtip 44 (2006). Knives Of Ice / Seeing Crows In Silver / Great Worm Of Hell / Devil Finding Mirror / Incident At The Temple At Leng / Notorious Vectors Of Disease / Weakener / Windowpane / Perpetuating Corpses / Monolith.

DIMENSION ZERO

GOTHENBURG, SWEDEN — *Jocke Göthberg (vocals), Jesper Strömblad (bass), Glenn Ljungström (guitar), Hasse Nilsson (drums).*

Gothenburg's DIMENSION ZERO boast a bona fide heavyweight line-up with the inclusion of IN FLAMES guitarist Jesper Strömblad, on bass, ex-IN FLAMES six-stringer Glenn Ljungström, CHAMELEON guitarist Fredrik Johansson, erstwhile GRIMORIUM, MARDUK and DARKIFIED vocalist Jocke Göthberg (billed as "Grave") and also operating as drummer with CARDINAL SIN, plus LUCIFERION and DIABOLIQUE drummer Hasse Nilsson.

DIMENSION ZERO debuted with an April 1994 demo session 'Screams From The Forest'. During 1996 the band drafted guitarists Fredrik Johansson and Glenn Ljungström. They would follow with the 1997 mini-album 'Penetrations Of The Lost World' issued through War Music. In 1998 the band, minus Johansson, donated a Death Metal revision of SEPULTURA's 'Troops Of Doom' to the Black Sun tribute album "Sepulchral Feast" although this saw IN FLAMES drummer and SACRILIGE vocalist Daniel Svensson at the helm. Another track, 'My Demon', would be supplied to a MERCYFUL FATE tribute.

Göthberg returned later the same year as DIMENSION ZERO drew out of the shadows once more depositing 'They Are Waiting For Us' to the 'War Dance' compilation. This act though would be announced as the band's swansong and DIMENSION ZERO duly folded.

By 2000 the band resumed activity. DIMENSION ZERO now listed as Jocke Göthberg, Jesper Strömblad, Glenn Ljungström and new member Daniel Antonsson from PATHOS on Guitar. DIMENSION ZERO reconvened in Gothenburg's Studio Fredman in 2001 to record a full length album 'Silent Night Fever'. DIMENSION ZERO added PATHOS guitarist Daniel Antonsson to the ranks in 2002.

The band's opening EP 'Penetrations From The Lost World' would see a re-issue in 2003, adding two previously unreleased tracks plus a cover of THE BEATLES 'Helter Skelter' and material recorded live in Japan. A brand new studio album 'This Is Hell' followed but minus Glenn Ljungström, who exited in August. The ex-guitarist would subsequently forge PITCHLINE in union with former GARDENIAN vocalist Jim Kjell. Scheduling tour dates for November, DIMENSION ZERO opted to persevere as a quartet.

The band united with IMMEMORIAL and HANDFUL OF RAIN for European dates in February 2004. Guitarist Daniel Antonsson joined SOILWORK as a temporary member in April 2006. DIMENSION ZERO returned to the recording studio to cut tracks for a third album in November 2006. Recordings were wrapped up in mid December.

DIMENSION ZERO rejigged their line-up for an appearance at the Close-Up Båten festival boat cruise leaving Stockholm on February 5th 2007, seeing Jocke Göthberg on vocals, Hasse Nilsson on drums, Jesper Strömblad on guitar alongside PATHOS' Daniel Antonsson with bass supplied by LORD BELIAL guitarist Niclas Andersson. Antonsson was announced officially as new guitarist for SOILWORK in early March.

Screams From The Forest, Dimension Zero (1994) (Demo). Through The Virgin Sky / Dead Silent Shriek / Forgotten ... But Not Forgiven / Everlasting Neverness.
Penetrations Of The Lost World EP, War Music (1997). Through The Virgin Sky / Dead Silent Shriek / Forgotten ... But Not Forgiven / Everlasting Neverness.
Penetrations Of The Lost World EP, Toy's Factory TFCK-87151 (1998) (Japanese release). Through The Virgin Sky / Dead Silent Shriek / Forgotten ... But Not Forgiven / Everlasting Neverness / Troops Of Doom.
SILENT NIGHT FEVER, Toy's Factory TFCK-87274 (2001) (Japanese release). Silent Night Fever / The Murder-Inn / Through The Virgin Sky / Your Darkest Hour / Not Even Dead Yet / They Are Waiting To Take Us / Until You Die / End / Slow Silence / Helter Skelter.
SILENT NIGHT FEVER, Regain RR 0111-010 (2002) (European release). Silent Night Fever / The Murder-Inn / Through The Virgin Sky / Your Darkest Hour / Not Even Dead Yet / They Are Waiting To Take Us / Until You Die / End / Slow Silence.
SILENT NIGHT FEVER, Dimension Zero 7876-2 (2002) (USA release). Silent Night Fever / The Murder-Inn / Through The Virgin Sky / Your Darkest Hour / Not Even Dead Yet / They Are Waiting To Take Us / Until You Die / End / Slow Silence.
PENETRATIONS FROM THE LOST WORLD, Regain RR 0305-028 (2003). Through The Virgin Sky / Dead Silent Shriek / Forgotten ... But Not Forgiven / Everlasting Neverness / Condemned / Helter Skelter / Silent Night Fever (Live) / Not Even Dead (Live) / The Murder Inn (Live) / They Are Waiting To Take Us (Live) / Through The Virgin Sky (Live).
THIS IS HELL, Regain RR 0308-033 (2003). The Introduction To What This Is / Dimension Zero / Immaculate / Blood On The Streets / Into & Out Of Subsistence / The Final Destination / Amygdala / Killing My Sleep / This Light / Di'I Minores.
PENETRATIONS FROM THE LOST WORLD, Toy's Factory TFCK-87309 (2003) (Japanese release). Through The Virgin Sky / Dead Silent Shriek / Forgotten ... But Not Forgiven / Everlasting Neverness / Condemned / Helter Skelter / Silent Night Fever (Live) / Not Even Dead (Live) / The Murder Inn (Live) / They Are Waiting To Take Us (Live) / Through The Virgin Sky (Live).
THIS IS HELL, Toy's Factory TFCK-87335 (2003) (Japanese release). The Introduction To What This Is / Dimension Zero / Immaculate / Blood On The Streets / Into & Out Of Subsistence / The Final Destination / Amygdala / Killing My Sleep / This Light / Di'I Minores / Hellmet.
HE WHO SHALL NOT BLEED, (2007). He Who Shall Not Bleed / Unto Others / A Paler Shade Of White (A Darker Side Of Black) / Hell Is Within / Red Dead Heat / I Can Hear The Dark / Going Deep / Is / Deny / The Was / Way To Shine.

DIN-ADDICT

HUNGARY — *Kisz (vocals), David (guitar / bass), Bakelit (drums).*

Grindcore act DIN-ADDICT is rooted in the 1996 formation NEEDLESS RELIGIONS. This unit soon evolved into NEUROCIDE but then broke up with half of the musicians founding DISSECTIVE FINGERS with the remaining half forging INSISTENCE. These two outfits would morph to create DIN-ADDICT with an inaugural membership of vocalist Zama, guitarist H.L., bassist Jirzsi and drummer Bakelit.

A demo 'Horrible Musical Ejaculation' was recorded in January of 1999, after which Jirzsi exited and Kisz enrolled as secondary singer. Before the close of the year H.L. decamped, his replacement being David. In this guise DIN-ADDICT undertook extensive touring, opening for acts such as INGROWING, CENTINEX, SUFFOCATE, ABORTION and MONOLITH amongst others. A rehearsal tape 'Vivisection Of Reality' led in turn to a further studio demo 'Caution! Fucking Zone!', distributed as a split release shared with SANGRE CON FILTRO. A major gig at the 'Obscene Extreme Fest' in the Czech Republic, and inclusion on the event's compilation sampler, raised the band's profile higher.

DIN-ADDICT underwent a line up change, adding the SANGRE CON FILTRO and NEURAL BOOSTER credited Sangre on bass guitar. In December of 2000 this line up recorded a total on nineteen new tracks at Denevér Studios, including an AGATHOCLES cover, for release as a split release with AGATHOCLES entitled 'We Hate Hungarian Scene'. Live work then saw the band hooking up with HUMAN ERROR and VICTIMS for Austrian dates before traversing Slovakia with MALIGNANT TUMOUR, ABORTION, SUPPOSITORY and SUFFOCATE. A return to the Czech Republic had the band partnered with MALIGNANT TUMOUR once again. Recorded output included tracks on a Czech compilation tape put out by Copremesis Records and three studio and thirteen live songs contributed to an Ironworks split effort.

Ensconcing themselves once more in Denevér Studios in February of 2002 DIN-ADDICT tracked 26 songs for use on split releases shared with OBLITERATE and ENDLESS STRUGGLE. The French Skud Records label issued the OBLITERATE split whilst the union with ENDLESS STRUGGLE surfaced through the Singapore based In Mince We Grind Wreckchords concern. Meantime the AGATHOCLES split emerged in the USA on 7" vinyl format through Nuclear BBQ.

Getting back to road action DIN-ADDICT allied themselves with SUFFOCATE and ABORTION for more Slovakian gigs, following up with Hungarian shows then gigs in Croatia, Slovenia, and Austria with HUMAN ERROR. Signing to Bizarre Leprous Productions a new album, 'Music For Opened Minds', was recorded in the Autumn of 2003. Further output came in early 2004 with a split cassette shared with ABYSMAL TERROR.

We Hate Hungarian Scene, Nuclear Barbecue Party (1997) (Split EP with AGATHOCLES). Intro/Cannabis Jointplex / Off-Shore / Go And Fuck Your Marketing Strategy / Sub-Ways / You're In Broadcasting, Please Lie In The Camera / Musc-Lee: Hero Of Today / Who Am I? / Necro-Punk / Prick Cops/Outro.
PLANET U.S.A., Skud (2002) (Split album with OBLITERATE). Intro / Confess Killers / Ego-Tours / A Haladó Gondolkodás Hatásmechanizmusa / Another Stupid Whore / Saturday Night Fever (Speed Trip) / Child Adopting / Planet U.S.A. / I Hope You Die / Peaceful Anarchy / The Fashion Impose The Life Upon You / Neglect Of Consequence / Extent Of Change / In Wolf Skin / Song About The Millions / Enjoy Din-Addict!
DIN-ADDICT, In Mince We Grind Wreckchords (2002) (Split album with ENDLESS STRUGGLE). Check Your CD Player! / Cunt Cunt Cunt / Dickhunters / There Are Still Too Many Gay / Why? Why? Why? / Silicon Bastard / See Your Enemy / Vérszaros Fasz / Flying Penis / Hey Fucking God! / Jamming In Tirpákland.
MUSIC FOR OPENED MINDS, Bizarre Leprous Productions (2004). You Explored Your Female Sexuality In The Jail / You're Retired / Your Boyfriend's Boyfriend / Another Reason To Stay Home, And Watch TV / Porn, Confirmed By The European Union / You Want To Play In The Underground Scene, Because You're Gay / Scorched Crossroad / Your Life Is Fine / Insidescream / Scream From Your Ass / Killing Carrot / Reduce Your Weight Easily, Die! / Japanese People's Song / Your Girlfriend's Favourite Newspaper Is Cosmopolitan / Will You Suck My Dick, If I Apologize To You? / Nice To Meet You? / Lack Of Intellectual Independence / Thought-Provoking / Being Trendy In 2003 Too / Born Alive, Live Dead / Economy Is Gay / Pop Music Will Never Die / Hate Me! / The Inhuman Selection Game / Re-Routing / Predestinated Slavery / Chains.

DISAFFECTED

PORTUGAL — *José Costa (vocals), Zakk (guitar), António Gião (bass), Fátima Gerónimo (keyboards), Quim Aries (drums).*

DISAFFECTED was created in January 1991 by singer Sérgio Paulo and drummer Quim Aries. Adding Zakk on guitar and Sérgio Monteiro to cover bass they issued two demos prior to gigging. Line up changes ensued as DISAFFECTED recruited bassist António Gião, keyboard player Fátima Gerónimo and a guesting José Costa, vocalist of DARK TALES and SACRED SIN. A tape of a rehearsal landed the band a deal with Skyfall Records in 1995 although shortly after the release of 'Vast' DISAFFECTED lost both their vocalist and drummer Quim Aries, the latter going on to join SACRED SIN.

The debut album, which includes a cover of ACHERON's 'Thou Art Lord', was produced by Marsten Bailey, the Englishman responsible for the HEAVENWOOD album 'Diva'. DISAFFECTED also made a contribution to the SLAYER tribute album 'Slatanic Slaughter' with a cover of 'Seasons In Abyss'. The band ceased activities in 1997.

VAST, Skyfall l (1995). Cold Tranquility / No Feelings Left / Unlimited Vision / The Praxis Of The Non Being / Dreaming I / Dream II (Another Form) / Allusion / Dead Like My Dreams / Vast- The Long Tomorrow / ... And Flesh Will Be My Bride / Thou Art Lord.

DISARMONIA MUNDI

TURIN, ITALY — *Benny Bianco Chinto (vocals), Federico Cagliero (guitar), Simone Palermiti (guitar), Mirco Andreis (bass), Ettore Rigotti (drums).*

Avigliana, Turin Death Metal act created in 2000. Debut album 'Nebularium', fronted by Benny Bianco Chinto of DYING AWKWARD ANGEL, arrived that same year, after which the band splintered, losing Chinto plus guitarists Simone Palermiti and Federico Cagliero. Only drummer Ettore Rigotti and bass player Mirco Andreis going forward, being joined by singer GROUND ZERO Claudio Ravinale. Having signed to Scarlet Records, DISARMONIA MUNDI's May 2004 album 'Fragments Of D-Generation' featured SOILWORK, COLDSEED, DARKANE and TERROR 2000 singer Bjorn Strid on guest vocals.

A third album, 'Mind Tricks' released in June 2006 and closing with a cover version of PANTERA's 'Mouth For War', also featured Bjorn Strid. Japanese variants added a bonus track, a demo version of 'Moon Of Glass'.

NEBULARIUM, Independent (2000). Into D.M. / Blue Lake / Mechanichell / Guilty Claims / Burning Cells / Demiurgo / Nebularium / Awakening.
FRAGMENTS OF D-GENERATION, Scarlet SC 085-2 (2004). Common State Of Inner Violence / Morgue Of Centuries / Red Clouds / Quicksand Symmetry / Swallow The Flames / OceanGrave / A Mirror Behind / Come Forth My Dreadful One / Shattered Lives And Broken Dreams / Colors Of A New Era.
MIND TRICKS, Scarlet SC 121-2 (2006). Resurrection Code / Mindtricks / Celestial Furnace / Nihilistic Overdrive / Parting Ways / Venom Leech And The Hands Of Rain / Liquid Wings / Process Of Annihilation / Last Breed / A Taste Of Collapse / Mouth For War.

DISARRAY

NASHVILLE, TN, USA — *Chuck Bonnett (vocals / guitar), Vance Wright (bass), David Peridore (drums).*

Southern edged Thrashers DISARRAY debuted with a 1993 demo entitled 'Tragic Cause' upfront of a brace of EP releases, 'Widespread Human Disaster' in 1994 and the 1996 set 'Bleed' on the Inner V.O.I.D. label. Fans would also be treated to a live cassette release, 'Spreading The Death Plague', recorded at The Cannery in Nashville in December 1997. The group had been initiated during 1993 by high school friends vocalist / guitarist Chuck Bonnett and drummer Shane Harmon, subsequently bringing onboard rhythm guitarist Jim Johnson and bassist Jerry Lomax. For 'Bleed' Joe 'Hooch' Dotson would contribute additional bass guitar. Dotson switched to guitar and Chris Looney took over bass duties.

The full length album 'A Lesson In Respect' arrived in 1999 on the New Jersey based indie label Eclipse Records. The DISARRAY line up for this outing would see the group format back down to a trio with Dotson re-installed on bass and Tony Moseley taking command of the drums. That same year DISARRAY donated their rendition of 'Tom Sawyer' to the Dwell Records RUSH tribute album 'Red Star'. The following year would witness a whole crop of cover versions for the Dwell concern including 'Just One Fix' for the MINISTRY tribute 'Devilswork', 'Cowboys From Hell' on the PANTERA 'Panther' tribute, 'Delivering The Goods' for the JUDAS PRIEST 'Hell Bent For Metal 2' collection, 'Rise' to a second PANTERA effort 'Southern Death',

'Subliminal' to the SUICIDAL TENDENCIES homage 'Suicide In Venice' and 'Blur The Technicolor' for a WHITE ZOMBIE tribute.

The 2002 DISARRAY album 'In The Face Of The Enemy' was produced by Dave Brockie ('Oderus Ungerus') of GWAR infamy. Both Ungerus and GWAR colleague Balsac would guest on the album. By this juncture Bonnett had been joined by an all new cast of bass player Vance Wright and David Peridore on the drums. DISARRAY toured heavily to promote this outing, sharing stages with CROWBAR, BIOHAZARD, CLUTCH and naturally GWAR. The band wrapped up recording of a new album entitled 'Edge Of My Demise' in early 2005.

Widespread Human Disaster, Independent (1994). Holocaust / Death Plague Jesus / Scarred For Life / Powered By Hate / Agony.

Bleed, Inner V.O.I.D. (1996). Nailed Shut / Future Lost / Bleed / Caught In The Chains / Rust.

A LESSON IN RESPECT, Eclipse (2000). Piss (Back-Stabbing Coward) / Forever Scorned / Mindless / Loss Of Tolerance / Exist To Suffer / Black Truth / Lesson In Respect (Face Down) / Your Fuct World / Failure / Eye Of Disgust / Uncontrollable Killing Addiction / Enslaved Race / Freebird.

Depths Of The Wreckage, Eclipse (2002) (US promotion release). Depths Of The Wreckage / Voice Of Reason / To This Day.

IN THE FACE OF THE ENEMY, Eclipse (2002). Depths Of The Wreckage / To This Day / Voice Of Reason / Open Wounds-Self Inflict / Neverending Quest For Revenge / Path Of No Regrets / This World / Powers That Be / I'll Be Standing / Burned Soul / Life Is Gone.

EDGE OF MY DEMISE, Inner V.O.I.D. (2007). Destroy Me / Punishment For Being Born / Edge Of My Demise / Breaking Point / It's About Time / Severed Ties / Observance Of Human Error / Conform / Threshold Of Pain / Better Days (That Have Never Come) / Foul Stench Of The Damned.

DISASTROUS MURMUR

AUSTRIA — *Harald Bezdek (vocals / guitar), Walter Schweiger (bass), Manfred Perack (drums).*

DISASTROUS MURMUR was formed in 1988 after vocalist / guitarist's Harald Bezdek defection from DISHARMONIC ORCHESTRA, soon debuting with the demo 'Embryonic Utergestation' and 7" single 'Extra Uterine Pregnancy'. For these sessions DISASTROUS MURMUR comprised Bezdek allied with guitarist Manfred Fülöp, bassist Walter Schweiger and drummer Manfred Perack. A 1990 demo recording billed 'Flesh Is What I Need' would score a deal with the French Osmose Productions for the album 'Rhapsodies In Red'. Although Martin Messner took over on drums during 1990 Perack would make a return, sticking with the band until its demise in 1994. The group's swansong 'Folter' album managed to compose an entire album based on various means of horrific torture.

DISASTROUS MURMUR would see a reformation during 1998 at the instigation of drummer Manfred Perack working with Fülöp, Schweiger and LAST DAWN vocalist / guitarist Elmar Warmuth. The revised line-up cut a 2001 album for the Perverted Taste label '… And Hungry Are The Lost'. Both Fülöp and Schweiger opted out but DISASTROUS MURMUR persevered, enlisting LAST DAWN bassist Oliver Neussl. The bass role would change hands once more the following year as another LAST DAWN veteran, Florian Kranz, took over.

Premier American Death Metal act MORTICIAN would cover 'Extra Uterine Pregnancy' on their 2001 album 'Domain Of Death'. DISASTROUS MURMUR undertook a brief spate of dates in November of 2004 co-headlining with BELPHEGOR.

RHAPSODIES IN RED, Osmose Productions OPLP 004 (1992). Disgorged Bowel Movement / Extra Uterine Pregnancy Part 2 / Dinner Is served / Trash, Chunk And Garbage / Masked Killer / Flesh … Is What I Need / satisfaction In The morgue / Into The Dungeon / Desecrating The Grave / Drowned In Blood.

FOLTER, Lethal LRC 848 (1994). The Oral Rectal And Vaginal Pear / Breaking By Means Of The Wheel (Germany 1550-1750) / The Punishment Collar / The Judas Cradle / The Headcrusher / Unfleshed To The Bone / The Saw (Spain 18th Century) / Heretic's Pincers / The Grate.

… AND HUNGRY ARE THE LOST, Perverted Taste (2001). Necrotic Ulcerous Genoplast / Are You Dead / Pigamism Of Remains / Ultimate Masturbation / Land Shark / Little Purple M..?—Penis / Pedigree Insanity / Headless Autophelatio / The Game We Play / Fleshmaster's Birthday / Fotus Controlled Dismemberment.

DISAVOWED

HOLLAND — *Robbert Kok (vocals), Joel Sta (guitar), Nils (bass), Robbe Vrijenhoek (drums).*

Death Metal band founded in September of 1994 under a former title of NOCTURNAL SILENCE and in this guise debuted with a 1995 demo 'Into The Abscess'. Upon completion of these recordings drummer Maarten Winnips opted out and ex-PYAEMIA man Robbert Vrijenhoek was inducted in his stead. Having recovered from this change the band was struck a further blow with the defection of guitarist Dorus Neijboer. Another PYAEMIA member, Joel Sta, took his place. Still billed as NOCTURNAL SILENCE the band issued the 'Plateau' EP in 1998 but subsequently adopted a far more brutal Death Metal stance. In December of 1999 the band illustrated this shift of tack with a three song promo 'Point Of Few'. However, Joel Sta was to exit. The band took this opportunity to take on the new title of DISAVOWED to reflect this change.

In 2005 Joey Sta and Robbet Kok, in alliance with ex-LENG TCH'E bassist Rizzo, and MANGLED, drummer Floris plus lead guitarist Pranger, fired up the Death Metal project ARSEBREED, recording the album 'Munching The Rotten'.

The band signed with Neurotic Records in August 2006, subsequently recording the 'Stagnated Existence' album at Studio Excess in Rotterdam. DISAVOWED joined forces with CANNIBAL CORPSE and Danish act URKRAFT for extensive European dates in February and March 2007.

Point Of View EP, Independent (2000). Rhizome / Reason Rejected / Generative Patterns.

PERCEPTIVE DECEPTION, Unique Leader Entertainment (2001). Rhizome / Abolition Of Impediment / Reason Rejected / Condensed Conditions / Masses Conformed / Unfolding Disposition / Generative Patterns / Critical Emulation / Opposite Extremities.

DISBELIEF

GUNDERNHAUSEN, GERMANY — *Karsten Jäger (vocals), Jan-Dirk Löffler (guitar), Olly Lenz (guitar), Jochen Trunk (bass), Kai Bergerin (drums).*

DISBELIEF's entrance came with a two song demo tape delivered in February 1992, the Gundernhausen based band at this juncture comprising lead vocalist Karsten Jäger, guitarists Denis Musiol and Oliver Lenz with former DEZTROYER man Markus Gnap on the drums. Retaining the same membership roster DISBELIEF capitalised on this opening effort with a five song cassette entitled 'Unbound' the following Summer. The band would then install a fresh rhythm section of bassist Tommy Fritsch and drummer Kai Bergerin for a set of 1995 Rudi Scheitler produced promotion recordings. A further shift in personnel that same year had Jochen Trunk taking over the bass role whilst Fritsch switched to second guitar for yet more demos billed as 'Choice'. This would be the DISBELIEF incarnation that struck a deal with the Grind Syndicate Media label for release of the debut album in May 1997. Production for these sessions would be credited to the veteran figure of erstwhile HOLY MOSES guitarist Andy Classen.

The 'Infected' album arrived in June 1998 after which Jan-Dirk Löffler usurped Fritch for 2001's 'Worst Enemy' and the Heinz Hess produced 'Shine' in March 2002. The band would be confirmed as forming up part of the 2002 'X-Mass Festivals' European tour commencing in London on December 7th, making up a strong billing incorporating DESTRUCTION, AMON AMARTH, NILE, DEICIDE, DEW-SCENTED, MISERY INDEX and DEICIDE.

DISBELIEF returned in October 2003 with the album 'Spreading The Rage', recorded at Stage One Studios in Bühne and produced once more by Andy Classen. Issued by Massacre Records in Europe 'Spreading The Rage' found a US release through Nuclear Blast in March the following year. An extensive run of European shows in November of caught the band packaged with MNEMIC, DARKANE, MYSTIC PROPHECY and headliners DEATH ANGEL. The live schedule would continue well into 2004, with DISBELIEF guesting for PRO-PAIN in Europe in March. The band, alongside SUIDAKRA, would also be confirmed as co-headline act for the May 'Demons From Hell' festival in Coburg, Germany.

Signing to Nuclear Blast Records globally for a projected 2005 album '66 Sick' the band selected Tue Madsen as their producer, recording at Antfarm Studios in Århus, Denmark. However, guitarist Jan-Dirk Löffler would be replaced by Tommy Fritsch. The band forged a road alliance with SIX FEET UNDER, DARK FUNERAL, NILE, DYING FETUS, WYKKED WYTCH and CATARACT for the 'No Mercy Festivals 2005' European tour beginning in early March. Throughout October and November of 2005 the group engaged in the "The Monster Mosh Down" dates across Germany, Switzerland, Austria, Holland and the UK partnered with EKTOMORF, BY NIGHT and BETZEFER.

The group re-contracted with Massacre Records in April 2006, announcing plans to record a seventh album, 'Navigator', at MX studio in Buchen, Germany with producer Michael Mainx in October. The following month DISBELIEF amicably parted ways with guitarist Oliver Lenz. DISBELIEF completed work on 'Navigator' in late December.

DISBELIEF utilized the services of SACRED STEEL guitarist Jonas Khalil for live shows commencing on April 7th 2007 in Eisleben. However, due to scheduling conflicts, guitarist Oliver Lenz rejoined his former bandmates for two shows, on April 13th at Roxy in Flensburg and April 14th at Gleis 1 in Eisenach.

DISBELIEF, Nuclear Blast (1997). Follow / Away / My Life / Scattered Product / God? Master! / In A Cage / Soul Massacre / Why Emotional? / Against The Shadow / The Harmony Within / Behind Those Eyes.
INFECTED, Grind Syndicate SYN003 (1998). Infected / Mindstrip / First / Fetish 97 / Again / Down / Pounding / Without A Kiss / Now.
WORST ENEMY, Massacre MAS CD0278 (2001). Misery / Believe / Survive / All Or Nothing / Denial / Assassinate The Scars / Recession / Living Wreck / Humiliation / Outro.
SHINE, Massacre (2002). No Control / Walk / The Decline / Shine / Me And My World / Alive / Honour Killings / Falling Without Reason / Mad Sick Mankind / Free.
SPREADING THE RAGE, Massacre (2003). The Beginning Of Doubt (Intro) / Ethic Instinct / To The Sky / No More Lies / Spreading The Rage / Inside My Head / Death Will Score / For Those Who Dare / Addiction / It's God Given / Drown / Democracy / Back To Life.
66 SICK, Nuclear Blast NB 1379 (2005). 66 (Intro) / Sick / Floating On High / For God / Continue From This Point / Crawl / Rewind It All (Death Or Glory) / Lost In Time / Try / Edges / Mental Signpost / To Atone For All.
NAVIGATOR, Massacre (2007).

DISCIPLES OF MOCKERY

NJ, USA — *Craig Pillard (vocals / guitar), Mike Boyce (guitar), Ronnie Deo (bass), Jim Roe (drums).*

DISCIPLES OF MOCKERY was founded by the exodus of INCANTATION members guitarist Craig Pillard, bassist Ronnie Deo and drummer Jim Roe in alliance with former ROTTING CORPSE man Mike Boyce on second guitar. Pillard has made a significant impact upon the US extreme Metal scene, being a pivotal member of acts such as AGGRESSIVE INTENT, CARNAGE, PUTRIFACT and DESECRATOR. Pillard had also issued a series of solo demos accredited to NOCTURNAL CRYPT including a self titled 1987 effort, 'Recrudescence Of ...' in 1988 and a rehearsal tape the following year.

The band cut a notorious 3 track live in the studio promotional CD soon dubbed the 'Red' single before cutting the debut album 'Prelude To Apocalypse'. Manufactured in a limited run of a mere 1'000 copies the album was produced by Paul Crook of ANTHRAX.

Pillard departed in 1994, relocating to New York. In the midst of a well documented heroin addiction Pillard teamed up with both CATTLE PRESS and Doom act CEREMONIUM. Freeing himself from his drug habit the man journeyed back home where he reunited with Deo and Roe in WOMB.

The 'Red' single was combined with WOMB tracks for a split CD release by Necroharmonic Productions. The same label would also reissue the one and only album. Pillard forged bass driven Doom-Sludge duo METHADRONE in 2003.

PRELUDE TO APOCALYPSE, Necroharmonic Productions (1998). Literal Upheaval Of The Earth / Our Father Who Art As Nothing / Prelude To Absolution / God Of Love / Behold The Holy Virgin Whore / An Endless Pursuit For A Satisfying Pain / Sustained In Desolation / Dogma / Rotting Immaculate Like You.
Disciples Of Mockery, Necroharmonic Productions (2001) (Split EP with WOMB). Rotting Immaculate Like You / Sustained In Desolation / God Of Love.

DISCIPLES OF POWER

CANADA — *Hart Bachmier (vocals / guitar), Wes Sontag (guitar), Andy Smith (bass), Dean Relf (drums).*

Founded in Medicine Hat, Alberta in 1985, from the ashes of WARTHORN, DISCIPLES OF POWER are one of Canada's longest running Metal acts. The driving force behind the band has always been founder, Hart Bachmier who relocated the band to Edmonton in 1987. After a quick demo called 'Kutulu' in 1987 and another called 'Power Of Death', they appeared on a local, vinyl compilation called 'Writing In Stone' in 1988. DISCIPLES OF POWER were early enough on the Metal scene to score a reasonably secure deal with Fringe Records and they relocated to Ottawa.

In 1989 they released their debut album 'Power Trap' and toured Canada. The band relocated again to briefly to Vancouver where they produced a video for the track 'Crisis'. Yet another relocation and line-up change found the band back in Edmonton where they and recorded their second Fringe album, 'Ominous Prophecy'. More touring followed and the over the next few years the band received critical acclaim for their Death-Thrash style. The band filmed a video for the track 'Nature's Fury' and hosted the 'Power Hour', Much Music's metal video specialty show.

After two releases on Fringe, the band decided to go the independent route releasing another album entitled 'Invincible Enemy' on their own Mind Gash label. Another video followed for the track 'Before The End' and more touring followed. 1993 was a busy year for the band as DISCIPLES OF POWER released total re-working of the debut 'Power Trap' also on Mind Gash. Another video was shot in Edmonton this time for the title track of the re-issue subtitled, The Brutal Re-mix.

In 1995 the band release their 4th full-length 'Mechanikill'. This album was not as well received and the band toured Western Canada very sporadically for the next several years while the band members pursue other projects. Despite many line-up changes the band has a solid reputation, not only for their intense, technical Death Metal but also for their professional image and attitude enhanced by steady touring, videos and the excellent artwork. Steve Chandler provided the art for the first two releases and the following three were done by Shane Hawco of THORAZINE.

In 2000 the band decided to regroup and begins writing and touring a little more extensively including headlining the inaugural show of the Okanagan Metal Fest in Oliver, BC. in the summer of 2001. A further album, 'In Dust We Trust', is projected for release also on the Mind Gash label.

POWER TRAP, Fringe (1989). Shades Of Grey / Powertrap / Ice Demons / Slave To No One / Protector / Night Of The Priest / Crisis / Hidden Worlds / Bitch Of Doom / Disciples Of Power.

OMINOUS PROPHECY, Fringe (1992). Chains Of Reason / Vindicator / Nature's Fury (Betrayed Earth) / Witch Of Lies / Sleeping Dead / The Rising / Skull March / Eternal Purgatory.
INVINCIBLE ENEMY, Mind Gash PPC003 (1993). Afterbirth / Invincible Enemy / Infected Science / Born Unto Death / Injecticide / Lords Of Creation / Return From The Gates / Before The End.
MECHANIKILL, Mind Gash (1996). Introvenus / Wings Of Suicide / Cast The First Stone / Inside (Circles Of Sickness) / Crypts Of The Frozen Soul / Swarming The Throne / Mechanikill / Symphonic Animosity / Waraphoric Structures (Part 1 & 2).
IN DUST WE TRUST, Mind Gash (2002). The Cursing Of Winter / Tripwire / Armoured Ring Of Skull / Widows Web / Pharmacudical Suicide / In Dust We Trust / Dimensions Of The Dragon Sky / Wartorn.

DISCORDANCE AXIS

NEW YORK, NY, USA — *Eva 05 (vocals), Qon (guitar), Dave Witte (drums).*

New York Grindcore unit founded by former HUMAN REMAINS and EXIT 13 drummer Dave Witte. Other members go under pseudonyms although Eva 05 is in actuality Jon Chang and Qon is guitarist Rob Marton. DISCORDANCE AXIS were founded in 1992 emanating from the dissolving of SEDITION. The band bowed in with a split 7" single in alliance with COSMIC HURSE. At this stage the band was actually intended to be a purely one off recording project. Nevertheless DISCORDANCE AXIS returned shortly after to cut tracks for another split affair, this time shared with HELLCHILD. The recordings came dangerously close to being consigned to the vaults as the studio time was originally slated for the recording of a debut album. Apparently the band members got into an argument and disbanded. Three months later the differences were resolved and the tracks that had been cut were issued on the single.

Yet again DISCORDANCE AXIS pursued the split 7" idea in collusion with CAPITALIST CASUALTIES. The band contributed live tracks to a single intended for a miserly production run of just 200 copies. A mistake in the pressing plant left 25 over runs though and these were released with different cover artwork to the main issue.

DISCORDANCE AXIS had their fourth split 7" in 1994 with DEF MASTER. These songs are notable for having no bass guitar at all. Released on the Japanese HG Fact label the single saw a run of 2000 copies. Finally the band got around to their debut album 'Ulterior' released in 1995 by Devour Records. When work in the studio was completed Witte broke ranks to concentrate on HUMAN REMAINS full time. Undaunted the band drafted Rob Proctor of ASSUCK for a tour of Japan the same year. After these dates Witte returned.

Yet another split 7" ensued, this time with PLUTOCRACY on the Slap A Ham label. The record came about by accident though as PLUTOCRACY's tracks were supposed to be back to back with songs donated by ASSUCK. When ASSUCK's tapes failed to arrive DISCORDANCE AXIS plugged the gap.

In 1998 the band put together another split effort, this time with Japanese band MELT BANANA. A cover version of MELT BANANA's 'So Unfilial Rule' was countered by their Japanese colleagues responding in kind by covering 'One Dimensional'.

After DISCORDANCE AXIS had released their second full length album 'Jouhou' Marten, suffering from tendonitis, quit. Steve Procopio of HUMAN REMAINS soon made up the numbers as the band delved into electro sounds for the 1997 single 'Necropolitan'.

1998 saw 'Jouhou' reissued with a compliment of bonus tracks and a brace of live tracks appearing on the 'Snarl Out' compilation album on Slightly Fast Records. Devour Records also collated early, live and rare tracks for the 'Original Sound Version' album.

The 2000 album 'The Inalienable Dreamless' benefited from an international release in both vinyl and CD formats. There was even an ultra limited edition boxed version restricted to just six copies.

Witte created side project ATOMSMASHER in 2000 in union with OLD guitarist James Plotkin and JANSKY NOISE's Speedranch. The drummer would also act as a member of BURNT BY THE SUN with his former HUMAN REMAINS colleague Teddy Patterson.

In March of 2001 DISCORDANCE AXIS was reportedly laid to rest. Marten had been forced out again due to an illness which provoked pain when subjected to loud noises. Not the best complaint to have when a member of a Grindcore band! Former member Procopio was pulled in to fulfill Japanese tour commitments. October of 2004 found Dave Witte enrolling into the ranks of Richmond, Virginia outfit MUNICIPAL WASTE. The drummer also forged a creative union with Chris Dodge of SPAZZ entitled EAST WEST BLAST TEST, issuing the 2005 album 'Unpopular Music For Popular People'.

Information Sniper, HG Fact (1995). Information Sniper / Amphetamine Hollow Tip / Tokyo / So Unfilial Rule / Junk Utopia / Continuity.
ULTERIOR, Devour (1995).
JOUHOU, Devour (1997). Vertigo Index / Panoptic / Aperture Of Pinholes / Information Sniper / Carcass Lottery / Come Apart Together, Come Together Alone / Rain Perimeter / A Broken Tomorrow / Attrition / Nikola Tesla / Flow My Tears The Policeman Said / Jouhou / Damage Style / Arther Scalpul / A Crack In The Cataracts / Numb(ers) / Ashtray Ballpoint / Typeface / Reciprocity / Reincarnation / Alzheimer.
ORIGINAL SOUND VERSION, Devour (1998).
THE INALIENABLE DREAMLESS, Hydrahead (2000). Castration Rite / The Inalienable Dreamless / Sound Out The Braille / Oratorio In Grey Vacuum Sleeve / Angel Present / The Necropolitan / Pattern Blue / The End Of Rebirth / Loveless / Radiant Arkham / Use Of Weapons / Compiling Autumn / Jigsaw / The Third Children / A Leaden Stride To Nowhere / Drowned.
Discordance Axis, HG Fact (2001) (Split EP with 324 and CORRUPTED). Ikaruga / Berserk.

DISCRUCIOR

RAKVERE, ESTONIA — *Ank (vocals), Alo Karus (guitar), Kert Kirsimäe (bass), Massacra (drums).*

Established in 1993, Doom edged Death Metal band DISCRUCIOR was fronted by vocalist Ank (Ants Lill), of FORFEIT, C.C.C., SORTS, SUPPURATION, DAWN OF GEHENNA, MUST MISSA, THARAPHITA and MEINARDUS repute. Bassist Kert Kirsimäe holds ties to ECHOSILENCE and SUPPURATION. The demo 'Mundus Subterraneus', featuring a cover version of BATHORY's '13 Candles', emerged in 1994.

During 1994 line-up changes saw the introduction of bassist Stig Lindeberg from SYMBOLIC STATE, FORFEIT and SCAVENGER, being duly replaced by Ahto, of LOITS, DECEASE and THARAPHITA. Kaido Kaidis of FORFEIT would also be employed on guitar that year. The band had the track 'Pilgrimage' included on the 1996 compilation album 'Sometimes Death Is Better. Part 2-4' on the Belgian Shiver label. In 1997 original drummer Ax was replaced by Massacra, having credits with SUPPURATION, LOITS and THARAPHITA.

Mundus Subterraneus, Discrucior (1994). When The Day'll Come / Mundus Subterraneus / Doom / Isn't For Me / 13 Candles.

DISFEAR

NYKÖPING, SWEDEN — *Jeppe (vocals), Björn (guitar), Frykaman (bass), Jallo (drums).*

Nyköping Crustcore unit. Lost And Found Records issued the album 'A Brutal Sight Of Fear' in August 1993. DISFEAR released a split EP with UNCURBED in 1995. That same May the 'Soul Scars' album emerged via Distortion Records. Original drummer Jallo Lehto would be superseded by Robin Wiberg. The band signed to Kron-H, a subsidiary of French imprint Osmose Productions, for October 1997's 'Everyday Slaughter'.

The band made a return in 2003, newly fronted by the AT THE GATES, GREAT DECEIVER and LOCK UP credited Tomas Lindberg. New recordings would be cut for the Spanish Throne Records concern, surfacing as the 7" EP 'Powerload' in November, restricted to 2000 copies of which 300 were pressed on clear red vinyl.

European gigs in September and October of 2003 saw DISFEAR in alliance with Linköping's NINE and headliners ENTOMBED. For the December 2003 Scandinavian 'Close-Up Made Us Do It' tour alongside ENTOMBED and RAISED FIST, the band pulled in Uffe Cederlund of ENTOMBED as secondary live guitarist. The band switched guitarists again in mid 2004, performing at the 'Pointless Fest' in Philadelphia that August with NASUM guitarist Jon Lindqvist substituting for Cederlund.

DISFEAR teamed up with ROTTEN SOUND for Scandinavian dates in March 2005. Product that year included a split 7" single shared with ZEKE. Gigs on the US West Coast in May 2006 saw a union with PHOBIA, STRONG INTENTION and 9 SHOCKS TERROR.

The group recorded fresh album tracks in August 2007 with CONVERGE guitarist Kurt Ballou acting as producer at his Godcity studio in Salem, Massachusetts.

Disfear, (1992) (7 vinyl single). Disfear.

A BRUTAL SIGHT OF FEAR, Lost And Found LF060CD (1993). A Brutal Side Of War / Judgement Day / Forced To Conform / No Hope Of Survival / Religion / Min Elegi / Undergang / Vietnam Idaq / Det Sista Kriget.

SOUL SCARS, Distortion DISTCD 13 (1995). Soul Scars / Left To Die / The Ultimate Disaster / To Hell And Back / Weak / Sobriety / The Price Of Ignorance / All This Fear / Do As You're Told / The True Face Of War / Grim Reality / After The Revival / Anxious / Disavowed.

EVERYDAY SLAUGHTER, Kron-H 08 (1997). With Each Dawn I Die / Anthem Of Agony / Crimescene: Worldwide / A Race For Power / Spectre Of Genocide / Everyday Slaughter / Subsistence / Totalitarian Control / Frustration / Aftermath / Overkill / Captured By Life / ... In Fear.

MYSANTHROPIC GENERATION, Relapse RR 6554 (2003). Powerload / An Arrogant Breed / Misanthropic Generation / Rat Race / The Final Of Chapters / Never Gonna Last / Demons—Demons—Demons / 26 Years Of Nothing / A Thousand Reasons / The Horns / Dead End Lives / Desperation.

MYSANTHROPIC GENERATION, Howling Bull HWCY-1152 (2003) (Japanese release). Powerload / An Arrogant Breed / Misanthropic Generation / Rat Race / The Final Of Chapters / Never Gonna Last / Demons—Demons—Demons / 26 Years Of Nothing / A Thousand Reasons / The Horns / Dead End Lives / Desperation.

Powerload EP, Throne CHAPTER 05 (2003) (Limited edition 2000 copies). Powerload / The Age Of Conflict / Med En Hälsning Frän Helvetet.

Zeke / Disfear, Relapse RR 6503EP (2005) (Split 7" vinyl EP with ZEKE). Rat Race / No Survivors.

Phantom, (2006) (Limited edition USA tour 7" single). Phantom / Left To Die (Live) / Everyday Slaughter (Live).

DISFIGURED

HICKSVILLE, NY, USA — *Joe Reilly (vocals), John Luyster (guitar), Ryan Schimmenti (bass), Jean Paul Matiuk (drums).*

New York's DISFIGURED, renowned for bassist Ryan Schimmenti's predilection for wearing Graham Bonnet style Hawaiian shirts, was created in 1996 as a trio of former CREHATE members guitarist John Luyster and drummer Jean Paul Matiuk along with SCHIMMENTI. Later former REPUDIATION man Joe Reilly took over lead vocals.

DISFIGURED's debut album 'Prelude To Dementia', recorded in Illinois and produced by BROKEN HOPE's Brian Griffin, includes an unaccredited take on AC/DC's 'Dirty Deeds Done Dirt Cheap' with guest vocals from Frank Rini of INTERNAL BLEEDING and a guitar solo from Chris Matiuk. FLESHGRIND's Rick Lipscomb also adds guest vocals to 'Ridden With Disgust' and 'Witness Your Creation'.

Schimmenti would perform session bass duties on BROKEN HOPE's 'Grotesque Bleedings' album and would later join INTERNAL BLEEDING as temporary frontman supplanting Frank Rini.

PRELUDE TO DEMENTIA, Severed (1999). Prelude To Dementia / Ridden With Disgust / Witness Your Creation / Diffuse / De-Evolve / Dirty Deeds Done Dirt Cheap.

DISFIGURED CORPSE

CZECH REPUBLIC — *Vladis 999 (vocals), Tomba S53 (guitar), Hadgi 666 (bass), Ferenc 777 (drums).*

Ostrava Death—Grind outfit. Forged during 1991 the group debuted that same year by releasing the rehearsal cassette 'The Born In Distress And The Funeral In Borde Of Society' with the studio session 'Fall Down In reality' emerging in 1992. These recordings would subsequently be re-issued by the Bona label as a split EP shared with TOTAL DEATH. The band's line up at this juncture comprised vocalist Vladimír Třískala, guitarists Igor and ex-MORSUS man Pancho de la Mancha, bass guitarist Martin Hadgi Stoklosinski and drummer Frank.

Signing to Sheer Records DISFIGURED CORPSE then put out the full length album 'Flash Of Pain' in 1995. Another cassette then ensued, with 'Evolution' distributed by Obscene Productions that same year.

DISFIGURED CORPSE toured the Czech Republic on the 'Metal Breath' package tour in 2001 partnered with PROMISES, MYTHOPOEIA, ENDLESS, VUVR and ALIENATION MENTAL. Jose Nogando of G.O.R.E. aided with guest backing vocals on the 2003 DISFIGURED CORPSE album 'United He666and'.

FLASH OF PAIN, (1998). Introduction To Your Inward Natures / Suicidal Picture / I Have Recognised / Mental Gripe / F.A.I. / Flash Of Pain / Glass Madness / Your Mind / Right For Life / The Hidden.

MEGA ULTRA INTERGALACTIC CORE, (2000). Keep Away / Free Minds / Broken Desire / Instinct Of Survival / Fly Paper / Rise Up / Pigs / Man Who Steal The Sun / Western Madness / Somewhere / Lost Demons / Hatework / Height / Way Begins / Refuse To Believe / Kinder Surprise / Megaton—Vestige Of Earthly Remains / Attitude / Chaos D.C. / Dead End / Vlakin Is Dead / Middlesome Heart / Springs / Summer (Drinking Monkey Party) / Autumn / Winter Mummary, Its Over / Fuck Of Die !!! / M.F.A.S. (Mutherfuckers Nazi Skins).

UNITED HE666AND, Crystal Production 666 (2002). Holy Propaganda / Me, Mine (Selfish Signs) / Toy Games / Not Understanding / Chill Out / Mind Obsession / Four Seasons: Part I—Der Wolfen In Zoo / Four Seasons: Part II—16 Seconds With Porno Stars / Four Seasons: Part III—Baboons's Pavilion / Four Seasons: Part IV—Freedom Of Hungary (Zappata Said) / Blood / Deliver / Destroy / Lights Out / Life / Instant Purity / Ave Maria / Upper Society / Six. Six. Six / Parasites / Obrij Me Majko ... / Repeater / Four Suicides Enough, Honey (Comrades Are Already Dead) / Viva La Nu Metal (666) / Dehydrant (Boys On The Cocks).

DISGORGE

MEXICO — *Antimo (vocals / bass), Edgar (guitar), Guillermo (drums).*

Grinding Deathsters DISGORGE are one of the most uncompromising extreme Metal bands in the world. Antimo of DISGORGE also operates as frontman for Black Metal band RAVAGER and also DEMONIZED, the latter act in union with the DOMAIN pairing of guitarist Samuel and drummer Oscar. Guitarist Eduardo Guevara is active with PYPHOMGERTUM, RAPED GOD and BLOODREAPING.

The band arrived with the 1995 demo cassette 'Through The Innards'. Previously the band had made their reputation on the live circuit in Mexico and an appearance on the live compilation video 'Audio Visual Aberration II' issued by Bellphegot Records. A second three track cassette emerged in 1996 prompting tour dates which spread into such far flung places as El Salvador and Guatemala. In Mexico itself DISGORGE supported visiting artists such as CANNIBAL CORPSE, MACABRE, INCANTATION and KATAKLYSM.

A further tape entitled 'Chronic Corpora Infest' arrived in 1997 and was later re-issued in CD format, complete with a stomach churning photograph depicting a real autopsy, by American Line Productions. The following year a split 7 single in alliance with Polish Grind merchants SQUASH BOWELS was issued in the Czech Republic. DISGORGE's 1999 'Infestour' took them outside of Mexico into Nicaragua, Costa Rica and back to Guatemala, El Salvador. Domestic dates billed the 'Tormentour' included gigs with SHAMASH and BURIED DREAMS.

DISGORGE's second album 'Forensick' was released by the Spanish Death Metal specialists Repulse Records. For the cover artwork DISGORGE outdid themselves, managing to find one of the most appalling photographs ever to adorn a record. The band released a split EP with COCK AND BALL TORTURE during 2002, this outing including a cover version of GRAVE's 'Inhuman'. 2003 bore the realisation of a further project of Antimo Buonnano and Eduardo Guevara, founding Black-Death Metal trio HACAVITZ in league with drummer Oscar Garcìa, a veteran of RAVAGER, IMPIETY, DOMAIN and DEMONIZED.

Back out on tour in April of 2004 the band partnered with SANATORIUM, AMPUTATED and headliners GOREROTTED for a short burst of UK dates.

CHRONIC CORPORA INFEST, Perpetual (1997). The Vile Sores In Urticariothrocisism Goulashed Decrepitance / Stygmatodermuropyanephrosism On Impetiginose Urogenism / Faecalized / Rancid Bowel Sarcoma / In The Acro Cianotyc Post Clonning Ectopysm / Lymphatic Orgy In A Ulcerated Incubation / Viscose Oseal Fibroma / Gribbled Maggotized Pregnant Inside Into A Fetid Renal Sarna / Pedophilamorphia Of Excreachllemical Endolapse.
Disgorge, (1998) (Split single with SQUASH BOWELS). Spasmobliterance Filtrates Scabs / Urethrive Decortico Xanthomatose Muco Gestated Scallfolds.
FORENSICK, Repulse (1999). Jism Adipose Carbonization / Spasmobliterance Filtrates Scabs / Scid / Urethrive Decortico-xanthomatose Muco Gestated Scaffolds. / Jaundice Of Hookworm / Haemorph Endartemectomized / Purpuric Cytoskeletal Glucid Oxidase / Crevice Flux Warts / Depths Carmesí / Silks Sphinter Anal Lumen.
Goremassacre Perversity EP, Lofty Storm LSR011 (2001) (Split single with COCK AND BALL TORTURE). Goremassacre Perversity / Grotesque Devourment / Inhuman.
NECRHOLOCAUST, Xtreem Music (2003). Raise The Pestilence / Sodomic Baptism / Macabre Realms Of Inhuman Bestiality / Ravenous Funeral Carnage / Necrholocaust / Goremassacre Perversity / Excremental Lust / Boiling Vomit Through My Veins.

DISGORGE

SAN DIEGO, CA, USA — *Matti Way (vocals), Tony Freithoffer (guitar), Eric Flesy (bass), Rick Myers (drums).*

San Diego's DISGORGE mutated from formative act STRANGULATION, the drummer of which- Ryan Travis, would later go on to front Vegan Death Metal act CATTLE DECAPITATION. DISGORGE was created during 1992 by frontman Bryan Ugartechea, guitarist Tony Freithoffer and drummer Ricky Myers. This line-up cut the opening demo 'Cognitive Lust Of Mutilation' the same year but a relocation to San Diego saw the departure of Ugartechea. By the time of DISGORGE's second demo session in 1995 Matti Way had taken over on lead vocals and Eric Flesy had took the bass position.

Further ructions occurred after the debut 1998 album 'Cranial Impalement with both Freithoffer and Flesy decamping. New faces were guitarist Diego Sanchez and former STRANGULATION bassist Ben Marlin. The line-up predictably would not last. DISGORGE members vocalist A.J. Magana, bassist Derek Boyer and drummer Torrey Moores all founded DEPRECATED during 1996.

Following the departure of Matti Way to former GORGASM drummer Derek Hoffman's act INCESTUOUS (later CINERARY) the band utilized the temporary services of DEPRECATED's A.J. Magana. This position became a permanent fixture as Magana rejoined the act full time for recording of the 'Dissecting The Apostles' album. Ricky Myers also joined CINERARY in early 2001.

DISGORGE toured Europe in March of 2001 headlining over GOREOPSY and SANATORIUM. Following recording of the 'Consume The Forsaken' album, for new label Unique Leader Entertainment, Magana exited from the band. A lengthy bout of touring in America throughout the early part of 2002, billed as the 'Bloodletting North America III' dates alongside DEEDS OF FLESH, SEVERE TORTURE and DISAVOWED, would see BRODEQUIN's Jamie Bailey stepping into the breech at short notice.

In December vocalist Levi Fuselier of SABBATIC FEAST enrolled as the band's new frontman. DISGORGE embarked upon the Summer 2003 'Rotting With Your Christ' US dates allied with FUNERUS and headliners INCANTATION. That same year Matti Way united with BRODEQUIN vocalist Jamie Bailey to found LITURGY. DISGORGE signed to Crash Music during 2004, preparing a new studio album entitled 'Parallels Of Infinite Torture'. The band would headline the first Tokyo 'Deathfest' in April 2005 at the Shibuya Cyclone, topping a billing comprising ETERNAL RUIN, Czech act GODLESS TRUTH and Japanese bands VOMIT REMNANTS, DISCONFORMITY and WOUNDEEP. The band toured the South West USA with IMPALED and BLESSING THE HOGS in September.

2006 live campaigning would be announced with a collaboration with DAWN OF AZAZEL and INTENSE HAMMER RAGE for the 'Torturing New Zealand & Australia 2006' tour commencing in late February. DISGORGE also put in a one-off show in Bangkok, Thailand.

CRANIAL IMPALEMENT, Extremities Productions (1998). Deranged Epidemic / Atonement / Cognitive Lust Of Mutilation / Period Of Agony / Cranial Impalement / Penetrate The Unfledged / Malodorous Oblation / Carnally Decimated.
SHE LAY GUTTED, Erebos ERE 018 (2000). Revelations XVIII / She Lay Gutted / Exhuming The Disemboweled / Compost Devourment / Sodomise The Bleeding / False Conception / Womb Full Of Scabs / Disfigured Catacombs / Purifying The Cavity.
CONSUME THE FORSAKEN, Unique Leader Entertainment ULR60008-2 (2002). Demise Of The Trinity / Perverse Manifestation / Manipulation Of Faith / Consecrating The Reviled / Indulging Dismemberment Of A Mutilating Breed / Consume The Forsaken / Dissecting Thee Apostles / Denied Existence / Divine Suffering.
PARALLELS OF INFINITE TORTURE, Crash Music (2005). Revealed In Obscurity / Enthroned Abominations / Atonement / Abhorrent Desecration Of Thee Iniquity / Forgotten Scriptures / Descending Upon Convulsive Devourments / Condemned To Sufferance / Parallels Of Infinite Torture / Asphyxiation Of Thee Oppressed / Ominous Sigils Of Ungodly Ruins.

DISGRACE

FINLAND — *Jukka Taskinen (vocals / guitar), Riku Sanaksenaho (guitar), Anton Kupias (guitar), Jussi Selonen (bass), Miska Koski (drums).*

Although starting life as a straightforward extreme Metal outfit, DISGRACE would evolve into a groovy mixture of Death Metal and 50's Rock n' Roll. The group even recorded an, unreleased, Doom album. DISGRACE debuted, like so many young Scandinavian acts, for the American Seraphic Decay label, releasing a 7" EP 'Depths Of Gods' in 1990. They would also feature tracks on the 'Annihilation Of Antichrist' compilation record issued by the Swiss Witchhunt label the following year.

DISGRACE's Death Metal album 'Grey Misery' on the Modern Primitive label featured guitarist Toni Stranius. The band cut another album for Modern Primitive but the label collapsed before it could be released. DISGRACE then cut the laboured Doom offering 'Vol II: Black Lizards Cry' in 1993, although this record would never see the light of day. Stranius was replaced by Anton Kupias for the 1995 effort 'Superhumandome', this record including reworked tracks from the 'Vol II: Black Lizards Cry' sessions. A seasonal split single, 'Snowy Xmas', arrived in 1997 as a shared effort with TROUBLE BOUND GOSPEL.

By 2000 the band were billing themselves as vocalist Oral Chimpanzee, guitarists Anal Chimpanzee and Jimbo Mini Golf, bass player C.C. Less and drummer King Nobody. The DISGRACE 'Take Me To Your Leader' European tour of March 2004 saw the band partnered with BOOMHAUER and KOMETA.

Depths Of Gods EP, Seraphic Decay SCAM 007 (1990). Depths Of Gods / Deprive My Innermost Soul / Incinerate / Offering.
GREY MISERY, Modern Primitive PRIM-1 (1992). My Dark Paradise / Unity's Interlude Dyes Blind Tomorrow / Abtruse Myth / Obscurity In The Azure / The Chasm / And Below Lies Infinity / Waves Of Hypocrisy Seas / Debris / Immortalitys Open Lake / Transcendental Dimension.
Vacuum Horror, Horror Vacuums EP, Crawfish Recordings FISH001 (1994). Sunwheel / Malachia's Grin / Fields / Love Mountain / Icon / Radioblast.
SUPERHUMANDOME, Morbid SPV 084-12652 CD (1995). Mean Relief / Distress / Dome / One Spiral / Bait / Forever / Ride / The Earth Silence / Christaddictsense / Spleen.
Gula, Greatest Vinyl Collections GVC 101 (1998). Gula / Cut It Off / Down On Elvis / She Loves.
IF YOU'RE LOOKING FOR TROUBLE, Metamorphos (1998). Psyche Rodeo / The Supremes / Cut It Off / Deadbeat / Tequila Desert / Speed Up / Greyhound / She Loves / Rock n' Roll / Explode—Explode / Roadkill Theme.

DISGUST

LILLE, FRANCE — *Benoit (vocals), Frank (guitar), Christoph (bass), Laurent (drums).*

DISGUST is a Lille based Death Metal band established in 1990, debuting with the promotional tape 'Disgusting Anatomy' that same year. The 'Anorexia' demo emerged in October 1993 recorded with a line-up of vocalist / guitarist Frank, bassist Christophe and drummer Christophe. 'Inquisition', produced by Stéphane Buriez of LOUDBLAST, followed in 1997. A former DISGUST guitarist, Geoffres, operating with the band between 1995 and 1996, subsequently founded DOGMATIC STATE.

During 1997 DISGUST incorporated former NECROSIS, NECROS and DAMN NATION man DeVermisMysteriis. Exiting to join Gothic band KRAAL, DeVermisMysteriis established solo concern BLIND LEADING THE BLIND, joined Parisian Gothic band NOVA ET VETERA as keyboard player and found prominence with KARMASSACRE.

Warpath Records issued the Stéphane Buriez produced album 'In Aeternum' in 2000. In 2002 the band drafted bassist Christophe, replacing Stephane, also a member of GERBE OF LIFE. DISGUST projected a split EP in collusion with KABBAL in 2003, although this did transpire.

DISGUST's vocalist Benoit and drummer Laurent both hold DISTASTE ties, the drummer also being ex-INFEST.

Anorexia, Disgust demo (1993). Anorexia / Surgical Inepsy / Cannibal Predominance / Demon / Unlikely Cure.
Inquisition, (1997). Epileptic Ascendancy / Inquisition / A Nursery Tale / Soiled Child Hood / Ill Fitting Society.
IN AETERNUM, Warpath (2000). In Aeternum … / Sample Of Life / Epileptic Ascendancy / Neverending Torment / Gruesome Rejoicing / Intro / A Nursery Tale / My Hate / Soiled Childhood / A Strange Confession / Ill-Fitting Society / Bastards Of God.

DISGUST

JAPAN — *Atsu (vocals), Masumi (guitar), Satoshi (bass), Kiyo (drums).*

DISGUST arrived upon the Japanese Death Metal scene with their 1994 'Deforming Child' demo. After this tape vocalist Atsu and bassist Satoshi joined the line up. Commercially their first outing would be the 1996 split EP shared with DESPERATE CORRUPTION. A further collaborative 7" single in league with Americans HEMDALE was delivered for Visceral Productions during 1997 following which DISGUST cut a cover version of 'A For Arrogance' donated to the AGATHOCLES tribute album 'Kill Your Idols', released by the South African Happy Hamster label. Guitarist Katsuyuki Nakabayashi left the fold in July of 1999 to found Thrashers GRIM FORCE. He would subsequently join RITUAL CARNAGE for their 'Every Nerve Alive' album.

During 2002 drummer Kiyo replaced Sanjun.

Disgust, (1996) (Split EP with DESPERATE CORRUPTION).
Disgust, Visceral Productions (1997) (Split EP with HEMDALE). War Criminal / Suicide Attempt / Change Yourself.
UNDERMANKIND, Mask (2001). Ochlocracy / Susceptive Child / Molested Dignity / Sequence Of Tenses / Blood For God / Political Murder / Ego Pride / Side Effects / Massive Expense On Massive Waist.

DISHARMONIC ORCHESTRA

AUSTRIA — *Patrick Klopf (vocals / guitar), Harald Bezdek (bass), Martin Messner (drums).*

DISHARMONIC ORCHESTRA, among the first European bands to tour Israel, as their name implies are an experimental trio unafraid to mix Metal with Rap and Grindcore. The band was founded in 1987 by vocalist/ guitarist Patrick Klopf and drummer Martin Messner. Two demos resulted in 1987 'The Unequalled Visual Response Mechanism' and 'Requiem For The Forrest' before bassist Harald Bezek departed.

The band drafted Herwig Zamernik in for live dates and soon scored a deal with German extreme label Nuclear Blast. The firsts fruits of this union was a split album with fellow Austrians PUNGENT STENCH and an EP 'Successive Substition'.

order to promote their first full length album 'Expositions Prophylaxe' the trio set out on a series of German festival dates with ATROCITY, CARCASS, ENTOMBED and PUNGENT STENCH. A club tour of America ensued on a billing including AUTOPSY, CANNIBAL CORPSE, IMMOLATION and REPULSION. 1992 was sealed with European dates with ENTOMBED and SINISTER.

Signing to the SPV Steamhammer label DISHARMONIC ORCHESTRA issued the 'Pleasuredome' album before calling it a day. Some 8 year later the band reformed announcing the recording of a fresh studio album billed as 'Ahead' for 2002 release.

SPLIT LP, Nuclear Blast NB019 (1989). Dehumanoid / Distorted Mind / Putrid Stench / Shredded Illusion / Compulsorily Screaming / Interposition / Animal Suffocation.
Successive Substitution, Nuclear Blast NB (1990). Successive Substitution.
EXPOSITIONS PROPHYLAXE, Nuclear Blast NB 037 (1990). Introphlaxe / Inexorable Logic / Life Disintegrating / Sick Dishonourableness / Successive Substitution / Accelerated Evolution / Psycoanalysis / Quintessentially / Unnecessary Institution / Hypophysis / Disappeared With Hermaphrodite Choids / Disharmonisation / The Unequalled Visual Response Mechanism.
NOT TO BE UNIDIMENSIONAL CONSCIOUS, Nuclear Blast NB062 (1992). Perishing Passion / A Mental Sequence / Addicted / Seas With Missing Pleasure / The Return Of The Living Beat / Idiosyncrasy / Like Madness From Above / Time Frame / Mind Seduction.
PLEASURE DOME, Steamhammer SPV 084-76772 (1994). Hyperact / Recommended Suicide / The Silence I Observe / Feel Like Fever Now / The Sick Deepunder / Getting Me Nowhere / Pleasuredome / Stuck In Something / Fall Colours Fall / Overwhelming Tranquility / Where Can I Park My Horse / Off The Road / Sunday mood.
AHEAD, Nuclear Blast NB 1029-2 (2002). Plus One / R.U.S.M.T.S.I.M. / Supervision / Nine9nine / Grit Your Teeth / Keep Falling Down / Dual Peepholes / If This Is It, It Isn't It, Is It? / Idiosyncrated / The Love I Hate / Pain Of Existence / Mindshaver / I.M.S.M.T.S.U.R.

DISILLUSION

LEIPZIG, GERMANY — *Vurtox (vocals / guitar), Rajk Barthel (guitar), Jens Maluschka (drums).*

Leipzig melodic Death Metal act forged during 1994 with an original line up comprising vocalist / guitarist Tobias Spier, second guitarist Vurtox (a.k.a. Andy Schmidt), bassist Markus Espenhain and drummer Alex Motz. A July 1995 demo session, not offered to the public, found the band in neo-Thrash territory. Espenhain quit the following year for MORHYTHM, just upfront of recordings for a second demo 'Subspace Inanity'. The 'Red' demo followed in 1997. These tapes showed DISILLUSION to be veering into more technically challenging spheres of Death Metal. However, with the defection of Spier and Motz the group disbanded in March 1998.

By the following year Vurtox and Motz had began working together once again, sowing the seeds for a DISILLUSION reformation. Motz would eventually bow out and Vurtox took the reins, soon uniting with guitarist Rajk Barthel of DYING IN SILENCE and LOOM. Session men were recruited for offers of live work but the group then re-shaped itself by inducted the PIGS MUST PURGE duo of guitarist Jörg Heinze and drummer Jens Maluschka. At this juncture Vurtox also enrolled into MOSHQUITO as a side venture.

DISILLUSION re-enrolled Rajk Barthel for recording of 2001's 'Three Neuron Kings' demo. A single, 'The Porter' issued through Voice Of Life Records in 2002, preceded a signature to Metal Blade Records and 2003's 'Back To Times Of Splendor' album.

German shows in the Summer of 2004 found the band performing with an expanded line up of an acoustic guitarist, keyboard player, bassist, and two back-up singers, featuring members of fellow Liepzig band DARK SUNS. DISILLUSION lent support to IMPIOUS and AMON AMARTH on European October gigs. The group acquired new bassist Ralf Willis in March 2005. However, this latest candidate exited in early September.

Three Neuron Kings EP, Independent (2001). In Vengeful Embrace / Expired / The Long Way Down To Eden / Three Neuron Kings.
BACK TO TIMES OF SPLENDOR, Metal Blade 3984-14456-2 (2003). And The Mirror Cracked / Fall / Alone I Stand In Fire / Back To Times Of Splendor / A Day By The Lake / The Sleep Of Restless Hours.
GLORIA, Metal Blade (2006). The Black Sea / Dread It / Don't Go Any Further / Avalanche / Gloria / Aerophobic / The Hole We Are In / Save The Past / Lava / To Many Broken Cease Fires / Untiefen.

DISINCARNATE

USA — *Tomas Lindberg (vocals), James Murphy (guitar), Steve DiGeorgio (bass), Nick Barker (drums).*

Although a veteran journeyman guitarist for hire on the Death scene guitarist JAMES MURPHY, whose impressive credits include AGENT STEEL, DEATH, TESTAMENT, CANCER, OBITUARY and KONKHRA, also made time for his own act DISINCARNATE.

The 1993 Colin Richardson produced album 'Dreams Of The Carrion Kind' had Murphy working with fellow guitarist Jason Carman, vocalist Bryan Cegon and drummer Tommy Viator. Guesting vocalists were CANCER's John Walker and MY DYING BRIDE man Aaron Stainthorpe.

The band was reassembled in 1999 with a line-up of Murphy, ex-AT THE GATES singer Tomas Lindberg, SADUS / DEATH bassist Steve DiGeorgio and CRADLE OF FILTH drummer Nick Barker. Before any product could be issued Barker joined DIMMU BORGIR.

Murphy has issued two solo albums to date 'Convergence' in 1996 and 1999's 'Feeding The Machine'. DiGeorgio joined ICED EARTH. Unfortunately the guitarist was diagnosed with a massive brain tumour in 2001.

In February 2004 Roadrunner Records re-issued a remastered version of the 'Dreams Of The Carrion Kind' album, adding three extra demo tracks. During November 2006 Polish label Metal Mind Productions re-issued 'Dreams Of The Carrion Kind' as a digipack, limited to 2000 hand numbered copies.

DREAMS OF THE CARRION KIND, Roadrunner (1993). De Profundis / Stench Of Paradise Burning / Beyond The Flesh / In Sufferance / Monarch Of The Sleeping Marches / Soul Erosion / Entranced / Confine Of Shadows / Deadspawn / Sea Of Tears / Immemorial Dream.
DREAMS OF THE CARRION KIND, Metal Mind Prductions MASS CD DG 0987 (2006) (Polish release digipack. Limited edition 2000 hand numbered copies). De Profundis (Intro) / Stench Of Paradise Burning / Beyond The Flesh / In Sufferance / Monarch Of The Sleeping / Soul Erosion / Entranced / Confine Of Shadows / Deadspawn / Sea Of Tears / Immemorial Dream (Outro) / Stench Of Paradise Burning (Demo) / Soul Erosion (Demo) / Confine Of Shadows (Demo).

DISINFECT

LUDWIGSBURG, GERMANY — *Jochen S. (vocals), Markus Sailor (guitar), Christian Kilian (guitar), Jochen (bass), Tomazsz Janiszewski (drums).*

Ludwigsburg Death Metal act forged during 1999 by erstwhile PROPHECY and OBSCURE guitarist Christian Kilian and ex-SACRIFICIUM guitarist Claudio. Other early recruits would be vocalist Jan, CARRION bassist Schenk and drummer Heiko. Subsequently the band incorporated ex-PALE singer Chris Simper and the REVENGE OF INSANITY credited Olli on drums. Another change in frontman came when Jochen S. was inducted. After gaining national exposure as tour support to SINISTER, the album 'Beinspender' was recorded at Exponent Studios in Slovakia during the Summer of 2001 for Rest In Hell Records. After this release the drew in new members singer Alex and drummer Tomasz Janiszewski.

Ex-DISINECT drummer Tomasz Janiszewski, also active with THE EXORIAL, joined theatric Death Metal band LUNAFIELD during 2003. Another former DISINFECT man, guitarist Markus Sailer, also teamed up with THE EXORIAL whilst formative singer Chris Simper holds MY DARKEST HATE credits.

In late 2004 DISINFECT underwent further member changes, enrolling bassist Klaus and drummer Hannes.

BEINSPENDER, Rest In Hell (2002). Beinspender / One Night Steak / Darmmanifest / After Killing / LII A5 / Inner Fear / Grave New World / Menschenfeind / Foxy Disintegration.

DISINTER

PERU — *Isarel Betran (vocals / guitar), Nimer Gomez (guitar), Kike Ilave (bass), Roberto Leonardi (drums).*

Peruvian Death Metal act founded as DEMIGOD in 1993 by GORE drummer Roberto Leonardi and vocalist / guitarist Iomar. Discovering a band of the same title based in Europe DEMIGOD evolved into DISINTER. New recruits were gathered in with guitarist Pepo, vocalist Leo and bass player Isarel Betran. However, Iomar was to leave and DISINTER pulled in former SUPPLICUM guitarist Cezar. By September of 1995 this latest addition was to leave too and Nimer Gomez came in for the debut demo session 'Laments For The Castle Of Sorrow'.

A further demo, April 1997's 'Unborn', followed after which Leo made his exit necessitating Betran taking over the lead vocal role. New members Enrique 'Kike' Ilave of STEEL MASTER and ICARUS, on bass, and guitarist Pepe Navarette also joined up. During 2002 the Yawar label coupled the two demo recordings for a CD release 'Laments Of The Unborn'. DISINTER subsequently drafted ex-BLEED OF HATE guitarist Luis.

LAMENTS OF THE UNBORN, Yawar (2002). Sowing / Necrophiliac Pleasure / Trapped In The Eternal Dark / Soulgrinder / In Cathalepsya I Dwell / Skinning Me / I Have Come / Rotten Human Scraps / Renacer / Dead Man Way / Into My Brain.

DISINTER

CHICAGO, IL, USA — *Zion (vocals), Preston Schrewsbury (guitar), Mike LeGros (guitar), Bats (bass), Tom (drums).*

Old school Death Metal band founded in 1990 as a side project from EYEGOUGER (as "Pussy Pounder") and PAIN guitarist Preston Schrewsbury with GORGASM's Tom Tangalo, vocalist Evil Eddie, bassist Jay and drummer Judd. After Fred replaced Tangalo DISINTER cut a 1991 demo tape 'Disinterra Et Corpus'. Following a brief burst of local shows DISINTER was put on one side whilst Schrewsbury concentrated on EYE-GOUGER. Schrewsbury would hold further credits with LEDFOOT, KILL, SPIRITUAL DECAY and EXTREMACY.

In February of 1995 Schrewsbury and EYEGOUGER colleague Mike LeGros ("Rectum Wrecker") pulled together a new DISINTER line up, drawing in ex-FUNERAL BITCH and FUNERAL NATION man Dave Chiarella on drums, shortly after finalising the line up the return of Eddie and ex-GORGASM man Bats on bass. This line up recorded the demo 'Storm Of The Witch' in 1996. Pulverizer Records would then sign the band for the 'Desecrated' release. A nine track promotional outing, 'Torn From The Grave', featuring three new songs with new frontman Zion, previously with Dixon's TIBERON.

After the 1997 'With The Blood' demo, Chiarella left to join USURPER re-titling himself Dave Hellstorm. Acquiring a new drummer in Tom from AD INFINITUM, DISINTER issued the EP 'The Beauty Of Suffering' in July of 2000 as a limited edition shaped disc and the album 'Welcome To Oblivion'. Signing to the German label Morbid Records DISINTER then crafted 'Demonic Portraiture', which included a cover version of 'Blinded By Fear' originally by AT THE GATES, for 2001 release. LeGros, maintaining his commitment to DISINTER, would also figure as part of Black Metal act NACHTMYSTIUM and join NOVEMBER'S DOOM in the bass role.

The 'Vedma' demos arrived in 2002 with full length 'As We Burn' following as the second DISINTER release for Morbid Records. The band was set to enter the recording studio in October with producer Chris Djurcic for a new studio album tentatively entitled 'Designed By The Devil, Powered By The Dead'.

DISINTER drummer Tomaz would be involved with the 2004 Alt-Rock act UNDERCURRENT, a project comprising former MORBID ANGEL frontman Steven Tucker, SUBVINYL man Anthony Gentry on bass and CEREMONY and DISASTERNAUT guitarist Greg Reed.

DESECRATED, Pulverizer (1997). Born To Die / Desecrated Corpse / Only To Suffer / Tortures Of The Damned / Death And Resurrection / With The Blood / Escape Thru Pain / The Place Of Bones / Steel Death Bed / Storm Of The Witch.
TORN FROM THE GRAVE, Disinterred Music (1998). Followed From Death / Torn From The Grave / Descendants Of Darkness / Only To Suffer / The Place Of Bones / Storm Of The Witch / Necropolis / Destroyer / Rage.
The Beauty Of Suffering EP, Desecrated Productions (1999). The Beauty Of Suffering / Welcome To Oblivion / Field Of Screams / With The Blood / Not Be Saved.
WELCOME TO OBLIVION, Morbid MR 079 (2000). The Sleeper Awakens / Welcome To Oblivion / Followed From Death / That Which Is Owned / Descendants Of Darkness / Holy Parasites / The Battle Rages On / Twisted Soul / Field Of Screams / Earthern Interment: Torn From The Grave.
DEMONIC PORTRAITURE, Morbid (2001). First And Last In Battle-Strength And Honour / An Eternity Of Pain / The Hunter's Moon / Where We Are Mortal / Woven With Pestilence And War / What Once Was, Again Shall Be / Cyclopean Ruins / Upon The Winds Of Vengeance / Whirling Spectral Voices / Demonic Portraiture.
AS WE BURN, Morbid MR 107 (2004). Go Away And Rot / As We Burn / Black Seas Of Infinity / Born To Darkness / Murals Or Horror / Dig Me No Grave / A Curs Of Pain And Hate (Burn With Me) / Inferno—As We Burn Acoustic Reprise.

DISLIMB

CLEVELAND, OH, USA — *Ryan A. Inman (vocals), Mike Connors (guitar), Rob Lesniak (bass), Chad Wallis (drums).*

Cleveland ultra-brutal Death Metal act convened in the Spring of 2002 by erstwhile NUNSLAUGHTER bassist Rob Lesniak and vocalist Ryan Inman of EMACIATED ENTRAILS. Making up the line-up would be REGURGITATION's Jason Trecazzi on drums and former REGURGITATION and EMACIATED ENTRAILS guitarist Steve Pedley. A demo, billed as 'Abhorrent Defilement', was recorded but never released and this formative version of DISLIMB duly folded.

Inman and Lesniak reconstituted the band by bringing in drummer Chad Walls, a seasoned veteran of BESIEGED, ENTER SELF, PUSTULATED and BRODEQUIN along with guitarist Mike Connors, also citing a string of laudable credits with artists such as DRIPPING, NECROSADIST, FECAL CORPSE and MARKASU. This version of the band cut the self financed promotion EP 'Bleeding Anxiety'. These tapes would be subsequently combined with material from Wisconsin's DYSCRASIA for a split album issued by Comatose Music. Don Wolff of DEFENESTRATION would be a later addition on second guitar for live work.

Decamping from DISLIMB the triumvirate of vocalist Ryan A. Inman, guitarist Mike Connors and Chad Walls formed a new band entitled INEXTYA. Bassist Rob Lesniak persevered with DISLIMB recruiting an entirely fresh roster of members incorporating erstwhile HAPPY RAINBOW DEATH and VIRTUO BRUTALIA vocalist Silent Nick, guitarists Paul Klukan and Don Wolff with Lee Andrews of SNATCH on drums. A new album, 'The Unspeakable Perversity', was readied during 2002.

Late 2003 found Rob Lesniak involved in an all new act entitled NECROTIC DISGORGEMENT, formation centred upon the erstwhile REGURGITATION trio of guitarists Ben Deskins and Tony Tipton with drummer Jason Trecazzi. Joining the fold would be the EROTIC INCISIONS and CLEAN FLESH credited frontman Joe Wolffe. DISLIMB severed ties with vocalist Ryan A. Inman in early 2004. Within weeks the band had folded, with Rob Lesniak and Mike Connors forging a fresh act entitled ALL HOPE IS LOST. Connors subsequently enrolled into the ranks of New Jersey's MOURNING.

Bleeding Anxiety EP, Independent (2002). Bleeding Anxiety / Infatuated With Sickening Thoughts / Deprived Of Humanity / Last Rites Of The III Content / Behind The Green Door.
BLEEDING ANXIETY, Comatose Music (2002) (Split album with DYSCRASIA). Bleeding Anxiety / Infatuated With Sickening Thoughts / Deprived Of Humanity / Last Rites Of The III Content / Behind The Green Door.

DISLOYAL

KĘTRZYN, POLAND — *Lukas (vocals / guitar), Tomash (guitar), Macabre (bass), Yaro (drums).*

DISLOYAL's Macabre (a.k.a. Tomek Korzeniewski) is also known as Lord Thorn in Black Metal act PAGAN TEMPLE. Both Macabre and drummer Yaro (Jarek Pparota) are also active with SOULLESS. Founded in 1997 as a unit of Yaro, vocalist / guitarist Szycha (Slawek Szuszczewicz, guitarist Zaki (Tomek Kaczmarczyk) and bass player Jurek Dacko, the Kętrzyn based Death Metal act debuted with the 'Desire' demo, recorded that December at Selani Studios in Olsztyn. After these recordings Macabre took over from Zaki.

Demonic Records issued the 'Pessimistic' album in 1999, once again utilising Selani Studios. Promotion for record saw nationwide Polish 'Pain Domination' dates in July of 1999 in union with DEVILYN. That September both previous recordings were combined for issue under a new title of 'Avenger' as a limited edition of 500 copies. However, line up changes ensued with both Szycha and Zaki being replaced by PANZERFAUST personnel vocalist / guitarist Lukas and guitarist Tomash.

The EP 'I Am The Plague' followed in 2002.

Desire, Disloyal (1997). Desire / Declaration / Make My Dreams Come True / I Am The God.
PESSIMISTIC, Demonic (1999). Discover The Power / The Dolls Factory / The Quest / Creating An Art / Source Of My Faith / The Pain Of Existence / Sinner's Cry / A Day Of Sorrow.
AVENGER, Demonic (2000). Discover The Power / The Dolls Factory / The Quest / Creating An Art / Source Of My Faith / The Pain Of Existence / Sinner's Cry / A Day Of Sorrow / Desire / Make My Dreams Come True / I Am the God.
I Am The Plague, (2002). Beyond / The Fall / I Am The Plague.

DISMAL EUPHONY (pic: A. Dittman)

DISMAL EUPHONY

HAFRSFJORD, NORWAY — *Anja Natasha (vocals), Frode Clausen (guitar), Ole K. Helgesen (bass), Sven Axel Henriksen (keyboards), Kristoffer Austrheim (drums).*

An act that has engendered a sizeable global fan base for its quite unique approach to the Metal genre. Hafrsfjord's DISMAL EUPHONY is rooted in the 1992 teen Death Metal outfit THE HEADLESS CHILDREN manifested by thirteen year olds Ole K. Helgesen and Kristoffer Austrheim. The following year a name shift to CARNAL TOMB occurred as the duo welcomed onboard lead vocalist Erik Borgen and guitarist Kenneth Bergsagel, proceeding to veer off in a more Black Metal orientated direction. As CARNAL TOMB the quartet managed to commit a solitary song, 'Black Funeral', to tape prior to Borgen's exit. Regrouping, Helgesen took on the lead vocal role but Linn Achre Tveit ('Keltziva') was drafted as secondary singer and Elin Overskott was inducted as keyboard player as the DISMAL EUPHONY title first came into use.

The group released the demo 'Spellbound' on CD prior to a name change to SORIA MORIA SLOTT. However, upon signing to Napalm Records the band reverted back to their previous title for the album fittingly entitled 'Soria Moria Slott'. The line-up, with the exception of seeing Frode Clausen on studio bass, remained solid for the 1997 follow up 'Autumn Leaves— The Rebellion Of Tides' before the group switched labels over to Nuclear Blast, also signaling the departure of both Keltziva and Overskott and the installation of new lead vocalist Anja Natasha.

The 'All Little Devils' album, produced by Waldemar Sorychta of GRIP INC., brought DISMAL EUPHONY to a wider international audience. For the 1999 EP 'Lady Ablaze' Jo-Arild Tonnesen of TWIN OBSCENITY stood in on session bass for the title track whilst Tor Harald Byrkjedal was delegated the four string duties for the song 'Abandon'. Former session man Frode Clausen formed up part of the official band roster for this recording, although this time as a guitarist.

New recruits to DISMAL EUPHONY for the 'Python Zero' album in 2000 were bassist Erlend Caspersen of APOSTASY and reputedly of MR. CUCUMBER(!) with APOSTASY keyboard player Svenn Axel Henriksen. Caspersen also operated with retro Death Metal band BLOOD RED THRONE. Linn Achre Tveit fired up Hard Rock act CAT CALL.

The band suffered a tragedy in September 2004 when the body of former keyboard player Elin Overskott was found in Stavanger. The musician, just 24 years old, had died from a heroin overdose.

In early 2006 Erlend Caspersen joined the ranks of US Death Metal band VILE to conduct their 'Gutting Europe' tour during March and April. In October he teamed up with Santa Cruz, California Death Metal band DECREPIT BIRTH.

Spellbound, Dismal Euphony (1995) (Cassette demo). A Winter's Tale / Spellbound / The Mournful Silence.
Dismal Euphony, Napalm NPR 018 (1996). A Winter's Tale / Spellbound / The Mournful Silence.
SORIA MORIA SLOTT, Napalm NPR 021 (1996). Prolog / Et Vintereventyr / Nattan Løftet Sitt Tunge Ansikt / Alvedans / Trolloundet / Ekko / Isgrav, Det Siste Hvilested / Epilog.
SORIA MORIA SLOTT (LIMITED EDITION), Napalm NPR 021 (1997). Prolog / Et Vintereventyr / Nattan Løftet Sitt Tunge Ansikt / Alvedans / Fortidssjeledrepte? / Trolloundet / Ekko / Isgrav, Det Siste Hvilested / Epilog.
AUTUMN LEAVES (THE REBELLION OF TIDES), Napalm NPR 033 (1997). An Autumn Leaf In The Circles Of Time / Simply Dead / A Thousand Rivers / Mistress Tears / Carven / Spire / In Remembrance Of A Shroud / Splendid Horror.
Clubhits, Nuclear Blast NB 0404-2 (1999) (Split promotion CDEP with AMORPHIS and STAHLHAMMER). Days Of Sodom / Psycho Path.
ALL LITTLE DEVILS, Nuclear Blast NB 0340-2 (1999). Days Of Sodom / Rage Of Fire / Victory / All Little Devils / Lunatic / Psycho Path / Shine For Me Misery / Scenario / Dead Words.
Lady Ablaze EP, Napalm NPR 072 (1999). Lady Ablaze / Abandon / Cabinet Bizarre / 150 MPH / Bortgang.
PYTHON ZERO, Nuclear Blast NB 0501-2 (2001). Critical Mass / Python Zero / Zentinel / Needle / Magma / Birth Reverse / Plasma Pool / Flyineye.

DISMEMBER

STOCKHOLM, SWEDEN — *Matti Kärki (vocals), David Blomqvist (guitar), Martin Persson (guitar), Tobias Christiansson (bass), Fred Estby (drums).*

Stockholm extreme Death Metal act, DISMEMBER have stuck true to a pedantic path, uncontaminated by any notions of mellowing or experimentation in any capacity. DISMEMBER was formed in 1988 as a trio of vocalist / bassist Robert Sennebäck, guitarist David Blomqvist and drummer Fred Estby. This initial line-up only maintained itself for just over a year but did release two demos in the shape of 'Dismembered' and 1989's 'Last Blasphemies'. The first of these tapes included the song 'Substantially Dead', exclusive to these sessions whilst the remaining material was set to resurface, re-worked by CARNAGE. The original DISMEMBER folded in late 1989 with Estby joining forces with CARNAGE, Sennebäck enrolling into UNLEASHED and Blomqvist opting for ENTOMBED. However, shortly before recording of the debut CARNAGE album, 'Dark Recollections', which actually found the earlier DISMEMBER demo tracks included in re-recorded form, Blomqvist jumped ship from his new act to join the band.

CARNAGE dissolved when guitarist Mike Amott quit to British extreme Metal act CARCASS leaving Estby, Blomqvist and GENERAL SURGERY man Matti Kärki, switching from bass to vocals, to resurrect DISMEMBER. Still a trio, this new line-up released the Tomas Skogsberg produced 'Reborn In Blasphemy' demo, this replete with Nicke Andersson of ENTOMBED handling guitar solos.

The band then invited Sennebäck, then still a member of UNLEASHED, to resume his position in the band as rhythm guitarist. DISMEMBER also augmented their sound with the addition of the CARBONISED and GENERAL SURGERY credited Richard Cabeza on bass. Having signed to Germany's Nuclear Blast label, the first hard product to arrive was the inclusion of two of the latest demo tracks on the 'Death Is Just The Beginning' compilation album.

DISMEMBER garnered huge media attention in 1991 with their 'Like An Ever Flowing Stream' debut album. Recorded by Tomas Skogsberg at Sunlight Studios in March 1991, the album again featured a guesting Nicke Andersson, who also designed the band's well recognised logo. Musically the band borrowed heavily from the harsher spectrum of the antecedent US Thrash Metal scene, crunching through a collection of pummeling, sharply defined riff laden numbers.

'Like An Ever Flowing Stream' scored solid media reaction but it was when the album was confiscated by British and Australian customs, for being 'indecent and obscene' (hence the title of their 1993 album), that the wider global Metal population began to pay attention. Her Majesty's customs had objected to song titles and lyrics such as 'Skin Her Alive' and 'Brutal Orgy Of Flesh' and legal proceedings held in Great Yarmouth would give government officials opportunity to brand DISMEMBER's lyrical content as "hideous, frightful and repulsive to the senses ... liable to inspire a sense of violence in the listener". Naturally the court case shot DISMEMBER's name to the forefront of the current wave of Death Metal acts.

The band toured Europe opening for MORBID ANGEL in June 1991 but these dates were curtailed due to disagreements between the two acts. Further live shows included DISMEMBER's appearance at the Rock Hard festivals alongside DEATH, PESTILENCE and NAPALM DEATH.

The band's notoriety was capitalised on by the October 1992 mini-album 'Pieces', the cover of which depicted the band members severed heads, and had Richard Cabeza going by the title Richard Daemon. 'Pieces' generated more live shows in Europe, touring in conjunction with OBITUARY and NAPALM DEATH. DISMEMBER preceded their record's release with a bout of touring in America in 1993 with SUFFOCATION and DEICIDE before hooking up with MORBID ANGEL once more for a European tour. A second full album, 'Indecent And Obscene' released in December 1993, gave their fans more of the same formula which had so outraged H.M. customs. Wrapped in a cover portraying the band's bloodied logo nestling in a cavity left by evisceration, 'Indecent And Obscene' matched the brutality of its visuals with a collection of starkly lethal death metal diamonds.

Following a lay off period, in which Cabeza worked up the DAMNATION project for the 'Divine Darkness' demo, DISMEMBER returned to the fray in early 1995 as part of the Nuclear Blast organised festivals alongside label mates MESHUGGAH, HYPOCRISY and BENEDICTION. A single, 'Casket Garden', was released as a taster for the new album. The follow up 'Massive Killing Capacity', arriving in August 1995, gave DISMEMBER their first German chart album. This album focussed more intently on groove, reining back the speed somewhat and provoking a degree of criticism from the die hards.

The June 1997 EP 'Misanthropic' included DISMEMBER's rendition of AUTOPSY's 'Pagan Saviour'. The full album 'Death Metal', produced by Fred Estby at Sunlight Studios, arrived in August. By now the group had made their intentions clear that, in a climate coloured by many previously extreme bands exploring far more subdued musical options, Dismember were to remain steadfast. In 1998 DISMEMBER enrolled the CELEBORN and TIAMAT credited Magnus Sahlgren on guitar. This unit cut the January 2000 'Hate Campaign' album at Das Boot Studios. By this juncture Cabeza had been replaced by Sharlee D'Angelo (aka Charles Petter Andreason).

Whilst gaining notoriety within the DISMEMBER ranks, bassist Richard Cabeza had also moonlighted for UNANIMATED and was briefly linked with Norway's SATYRICON. Matti Kärki and Cabeza would also collude with ENTOMBED's Uffe Cederlund and Peter Stjärnvind for their MURDER SQUAD project, Pavement Records issuing the 2001 debut Unsane, 'Insane And Mentally Deranged'. DISMEMBER would be announced as headliners of the June 2002 'Generation Armageddon' festivals in Europe fronting a roster of SINISTER, BLOOD RED THRONE, NECROPHOBIC and MERCENARY.

Yet another DISMEMBER offshoot arrived in 2001, BORN OF FIRE, founded by Cabeza alongside guitarist 'Mr. Dim', and the LOUDPIPES duo of Peter Stjärnvind and Fredrik Lindgren. This act would bow in with the 7" single 'Chosen By The Gods' on Primitive Art. Richard Cabeza would team up with premier Black Metal act DARK FUNERAL for North American touring in the Spring of 2002. European dates for November would be announced with DISMEMBER heading up a package bill comprising SPETIC FLESH, SINISTER and THYRFING.

Embarking upon a mammoth string of European shows throughout October and November 2002 DISMEMBER created part of a deadly union for the 'Generation Armageddon' festival tour. Joining the band would be Norway's BLOOD RED THRONE, Greece's SEPTIC FLESH, Ireland's PRIMORDIAL, Belgium's ANCIENT RITES, and fellow Swedish heavyweights IMPIOUS.

By January 2003 DISMEMBER, having signed to Hammerheart Records, where scheduling a new album with the proposed title of 'Where Ironcrosses Grow' for a September release, later pushed back to early 2004. Meantime, Magnus Sahlgren had been replaced by Martin Persson in 2003. The album would be recorded at Sami Studios in Stockholm during December and saw both David Blomqvist and Richard Cabeza handling bass. Also emerging would be a concert DVD entitled 'Live Blasphemies', a two disc set comprising the band's performance from May 27th 2003 at Klubben in Stockholm with a second disc of documentary and home video footage. Dutch dates in May saw CALLENISH CIRCLE and FLESH MADE SIN as support.

With Rickard Cabeza residing in Dallas, Texas, DISMEMBER announced the addition of bassist Johan Bergebäck of NECROPHOBIC and MORPHEUS to the group's ranks in September 2004. A short burst of Benelux dates in that same month saw the band united with CALLENISH CIRCLE, OCCULT and HEARSE. Further shows had DISMEMBER allied with Australians PSYCROPTIC, fellow Swedes ANATA and Slovakian act SANATORIUM for a full European tour commencing 3rd November in Nürnberg, Germany. The band opened 2005 with a January tour of Finland backed by BONEGRINDER and OMNIUM GATHERUM.

Regain Records picked up the DISMEMBER back catalogue for 2005 re-issue, each release being expanded with extra tracks. The first of these, the digipack 'Pieces' EP in June, boasted an additional ten live tracks recorded in Stockholm during 1993. The 'Complete Demos' release collected together promotional sessions 'Dismembered' from 1988, 'Last Blasphemies' from 1989 and 1990's 'Reborn In Blasphemy'. That same year Robert Sennebäck broke an eight year hiatus during 2005, forging SOULDEVOURER in union with GRAVE guitar player Ola Lindgren and NECROPHOBIC drummer Joakim Sterner.

DISMEMBER parted ways with bassist Johan Bergebäck in August. The band's seventh album, 2006's 'The God That Never Was', would once again be produced by drummer Fred Estby at Sami Studios in Stockholm. DISMEMBER teamed up with VITAL REMAINS, GRAVE, DEMIRICOUS and WITHERED for a North American tour beginning in early October. Night Of The Vinyl Dead Records re-issued 'Hate Campaign' as a limited edition of 500 hand numbered splatter vinyl, adding two tracks.

European show announced for November, dubbed the "Masters Of Death", had the band lined up with a supremely heavyweight Scandinavian cast of GRAVE, ENTOMBED and UNLEASHED. The group then set out to unite once more with GRAVE for a US West Coast tour in December. However, these concerts were cancelled.

Co-founder Fred Estby exited in April 2007, stating "My decision to put my family in first hand makes it impossible to keep on touring and commit to the band full-time."

Dismembered, Dismember (1988) (Demo). Deathevokation / Substantially Dead / Defective Decay.

Rehearsal Demo '89, Dismember (1989) (Demo). Deranged From Blood / Blasphemies Of The Flesh / Self Dissection / Death Evocation.

Last Blasphemies, Dismember (1989) (Demo). Deranged From Blood / Blasphemies of The Flesh / Self Dissection.

Reborn In Blasphemy, Dismember (1990) (Demo). Intro / Dismembered / Sickening Art / Defective Decay.

Skin Her Alive, Nuclear Blast NB 047 PDS (1991) (7" vinyl picture disc). Skin Her Alive / Defective Decay.

LIKE AN EVER FLOWING STREAM, Nuclear Blast NB 047-2 (1991) (CD release). Override Of The Overture / Soon To Be Dead / Bleed For Me / And So Is Life / Dismembered / Skin Her Alive / Sickening Art / In Death's Sleep / Deathevocation / Defective Decay.

DISMEMBER

LIKE AN EVER FLOWING STREAM, Nuclear Blast NB 047-1 (1991) (Vinyl release). Override Of The Overture / Soon To Be Dead / Bleed For Me / And So Is Life / Dismembered / Skin Her Alive / Sickening Art / In Death's Sleep.
Pieces, Nuclear Blast NB 060-1 (1992) (12" vinyl single). Intro / Pieces / I Wish You Hell / Carnal Tomb / Soon To Be Dead / Deathvocation.
Pieces, Nuclear Blast NB 060-2 (1992) (European CD single). Intro / Pieces / I Wish You Hell / Carnal Tomb / Soon To Be Dead.
Pieces, Nuclear Blast America NBA RED 6021-2 (1992) (USA CD single). Intro / Pieces / I Wish You Hell / Carnal Tomb / Soon To Be Dead / Torn Apart.
INDECENT AND OBSCENE, Nuclear Blast NB 077-2 (1993). Fleshless / Skinfather / Sorrowfilled / Case Obscene / Souldevourer / Reborn In Blasphemy / Eviscerated (Bitch) / 9th Circle / Dreaming In Red.
Casket Garden, Nuclear Blast NB 130-2 (1995) (CD single). Casket Garden / Wardead / Justifiable Homicide.
MASSIVE KILLING CAPACITY, Dismember NB 123-2 (1995). I Saw Them Die / Massive Killing Capacity / On Frozen Fields / Crime Divine / To The Bone / Wardead / Hallucigenia / Collection By Blood / Casket Garden / Nenia / Life—Another Shape Of Sorrow. Chart position: 85 GERMANY.
MASSIVE KILLING CAPACITY, JVC Victor VICP-5689 (1996) (Japanese release). I Saw Them Die / Massive Killing Capacity / On Frozen Fields / Crime Divine / To The Bone / Wardead / Hallucigenia / Collection By Blood / Casket Garden / Nenia / Life—Another Shape Of Sorrow / Justifiable Homicide.
Misanthropic, Nuclear Blast NB 254-2 (1997). Misanthropic / Pagan Saviour / Shadowlands / Afterimage / Shapeshifter.
DEATH METAL, Nuclear Blast NB 250-2 (1997). Of Fire / Trendkiller / Misanthropic / Let The Napalm Rain / Live For The Fear Of Pain / Stillborn Ways / Killing Compassion / Bred For War / When Hatred Killed The Light / Ceremonial Comedy / Silent Are The Watchers / Mistweaver.
DEATH METAL, Avalon Marquee MICY-1051 (1998) (Japanese release). Of Fire / Trendkiller / Misanthropic / Let The Napalm Rain / Live For The Fear (Of Pain) / Stillborn Ways / Killing Compassion / Bred For War / When Hatred Killed The Light / Ceremonial Comedy / Silent Are The Watchers / Mistweaver / Pagan Saviour / Shadowlands / Afterimage / Shapeshifter.
HATE CAMPAIGN, Nuclear Blast NB 419-2 (2000). Suicidal Revelations / Questionable Ethics / Beyond Good And Evil / Retaliate / Enslaved To Bitterness / Mutual Animosity / Patrol 17 / Thanatology / Bleeding Over / In Death's Cold Embrace / Hate Campaign.
HATE CAMPAIGN, Avalon Marquee MICP-10170 (2000) (Japanese release). Suicidal Revelations / Questionable Ethics / Beyond Good & Evil / Retaliate / Enslaved To Bitterness / Mutual Animosity / Patrol 17 / Thanatology / Bleeding Over / In Death's Cold Embrace / Hate Campaign / Live To Hate / Unhealing Scars.
WHERE IRONCROSSES GROW, Karmageddon Media KARMA 025 (2004). Where Ironcrosses Grow / Forged With Hate / Me-God / Tragedy Of The Faithful / Chasing The Serpent / Where Angels Fear To Tread / Sword Of Light / As The Coins Upon Your Eyes / Children Of The Cross / As I Pull The Trigger.
THE GOD THAT NEVER WAS, Regain RR CD083 (2006). The God That Never Was / Shadows Of The Mutilated / Time Heals Nothing / Autopsy / Never Forget, Never Forgive / Trail Of The Dead / Phantoms (Of The Oath) / Into The Temple Of Humiliation / Blood For Paradise / Feel The Darkness / Where No Ghost Is Holy.

DISORDER

KORTRIJK, BELGIUM — *Dieter Claerboudt (vocals), Frederick Clement (guitar), Alex Engels (guitar), Jonas Calu (drums).*

DISORDER is a Kortrijk, Coutrai based melodic Death Metal band forged as young teens in February of 1998 under the original title of BRAINDEAD. The band's first formation counted drummer Hannes Pype, guitarists Alex Engels and Frederik Clement with Bart Favere on bass. By March the DISORDER title had been settled on and in July the first line up change transpired as Sven Valcke was installed on bass guitar. In this formation the group's inaugural live performance took place in Heule during November.

Valcke exited in the Summer of 1999, being replaced by Clem Vanhee in October. More changes found Hannes Pype opting out in order to prioritise his role as guitarist in MITHRIL. As such, Jonas Calu became the new DISORDER drummer. In 2000 Vanhee decamped and Dieter Claerboudt was enrolled as frontman.

Cold Blood, Disorder (2000). Cry Of The Angels / Gathering Of Death / End The Pain / Twilight Of Darkness.

DISORDER

EL SALVADOR — *Manuel Vega (vocals), Jose Manuel Revelo (guitar), Jorge Montesino (guitar), Julio Rodas (bass), Boris Rodas (drums).*

San Salvador's DISORDER issued the politically charged 'Voces De La Tumba' demo during 2001. The group was conceived as NOSERFER by guitarist Jorge Montesino during 1996, introducing class mate Boris Rodas on the drums the following year. Guillermo Rodriguez was recruited on bass as the formative band crafted their first song 'Diabolical Mutilations'. Next in line for recruitment would be vocalist Manuel Vega and second guitarist José Manuel Revelo. In this incarnation the group debuted live supporting SARNICUM at a show in San Marcos.

Taking on the revised band title of DISORDER the group opted to pursue Spanish language Death Metal. Unfortunately problems arose when Vega suffered throat problems and Rodriguez stepped down. The band drafted Boris' younger brother Julio Rodas, also guitarist for Power Metal band SINDERSIS to cover on bass whilst they sought a replacement. However, at a subsequent gig supporting Guatemalan act NOCTIC IN-OCAT the group, impressed by Rodas skills, offered him full time membership. A remastered version of 'Voces De La Tumba' would be issued in 2002. Latterly Manuel Vega left the band.

Guitarist Manuel Revelo, bassist Julio Rodas and his brother Boris on drums founded DREAMLORE in 2002, issuing the 'Negative Specter' album in December of 2003. Julio Rodas is also a member of Power Metal band SYMBOLIC.

VOCES DE LA TUMBA, (2002). En La Puertas Del Desorden / Campos De Exterminio / Pertrechos De Guerra / Almas En Pena / Espíritus Violentos / Más Allá Del Fuego Tóxico / Ultrotoxofogos / Escuadrones De La Muerte / Voces De La Tumba / Post Scriptum.

DISPATCHED

GNESTA, SWEDEN — *Krister Andersson (vocals), Daniel Lundberg (guitar), Jonas Kimberg (bass), Emanuel Åström (drums).*

Gnesta based Death Metallers DISPATCHED, centred on founder member guitarist Daniel Lundberg and fronted by Krister Andersson, were created in 1991. Jonas Kimbrell was inducted on bass and Emanuel Åström as drummer the following year with Ulrika Forsberg being drafted in 1993. During 1994 the band adopted a fresh rhythm section following the Dan Swanö produced 'Awaiting The End' EP, released in February 1995 by Exhumed Productions. New members were ex-MARBLE ICON bassist Fredrik Larsson and drummer Emanuel Lundberg. The group had recorded an album's worth of material for Exhumed Productions for an intended product labelled 'Blackshadows'. However, the album never saw the light of day and only a smattering of promotional cassettes resulted. Further Dan Swanö sessions resulted in the 1996 release 'Blackshadows' through Toppling Collossus Records.

DISPATCHED folded but mentor guitarist Daniel Lundberg reformed the act in 1996. Dennis Hultin would briefly occupy the guitar position in 1997. Toppling Collossus put out the 'Returned To Your Mind' EP in 1997. Recording at Abyss Studios Tommy Tägtgren took the production reins for both the December 1998 EP 'Promised Land', issued by the German Kshatryas Production label, and the June 2000 Music For Nations album 'Motherwar', the latter witnessing a raunchy cover version of EUROPE's 'The Final Countdown'.

The band, working with Anders Fridén of IN FLAMES as producer, recorded a further album at Studio Fredman during 2001 with a provisional title of 'Terrorizer' but this record remained unreleased for a lengthy period. The DISPATCHED line-up at this numbered Fredrik 'Mussla' Karlsson on lead vocals and keyboards, guitarists Daniel Lundberg and Emil Larsson, bass player Mathias Hellman and Dennis Nilsson on the drums. 'Terrorizer-The Final Chapter...' finally emerged in August 2003 via Medusa Productions. The album hosted a hidden track entitled 'Cyber'.

DISPATCHED, resurrected in April 2004, signed to Rising Realm Records in Finland for a three album deal, commencing with a remastered version of 'Terrorizer'. The Soundholic label issued the record in Japan that July. Crash Music gave 'Terrorizer' a belated USA release in July 2005.

Dispatched Into External, Dispatched (1992) (Demo). Intro / Ruined Minds / Demoniac Of Cannibalism / Hang You In The Tongue / Dispatched Into External / Outro.
Promo-Tape '93, Dispatched (1993) (Demo). The Crusade Of The Northern Gods / Act Of Resurrection.
Promo 2, Dispatched (1993) (Demo). Blackshadows / Darkness / Act Of Resurrection / The End (Outro).
Blackshadows, Exhumed Productions (1994) (Cassette promotion release). Seattle / Tranquility / Horizon Of Dawn I / Darkness / Blue Fire / Harmageddon / Ghastly Gates / Act Of Resurrection / ... Is Born / Blackshadows / Red Zone / Awaiting The End / Horizon Of Dawn II / You Only Know Life / Horizon Of Dawn III.
Awaiting The End EP, Exhumed Productions CORPSE 06 (1995) (7" vinyl single). Blue Fire / Is Born / Awaiting The End / Red Zone.
Blackshadows, Toppling Collossus TCR002 (1996). You Only Know Life / Ghastly Gates / Blackshadows / Act Of Resurrection / Outro.
Returned To Your Mind, Toppling Collossus TCR003 (1997). Restless Mind / Like A River Of Sand / Hate My Life / Canis Lupis.
Promised Land, Kshatryas Production KSP007 (1998). A Griffin Banner / Ravenous Men / Promised Land / Grant Me Rest / The Revealing / Fallen Wind.
MOTHERWAR, Music For Nations CDMFN259 (2000). Intro / Motherwar / To Sleep You Go / She's Lost / Down / Templar / The Final Countdown / Silver Waves / Dispatched.
Motherwar, Music For Nations (2000). Motherwar / Down.
TERRORIZER—THE LAST CHAPTER..., Medusa Productions MP 006 (2003). Terrorizer / Rebellion / Wicked Dreams / Waste Some Steel / Override / Mechanical / I Am Thy Lord / Beneath The World Of Chaos / Under The Ice (Short version) / Cyber (Hidden track).
TERRORIZER, Soundholic TKCS-85099 (2004) (Japanese release). Terrorizer / Rebellion / Wicked Dreams / Beneath The World Of Chaos / Waste Some Steel / Override / Mechanical / I Am Thy Lord / Cyber / Under The Ice / A Trail Of Fear.
TERRORIZER, Crash Music Inc. CMU 61137 (2005) (USA release). Terrorizer / Rebellion / Wicked Dreams / Beneath The World Of Chaos / Waste Some Steel / Override / Mechanical / I Am Thy Lord / Cyber / Under The Ice.

DISPIRITED

FORSHAGA, SWEDEN — *Henrik Ivarsson (vocals), Peter Östlund (guitar), Erik Gustafsson (guitar), Fredrik Thörnesson (bass), Lowe Wikman-Åbom (drums).*

Forshaga's DISPIRITED, fronted by DOMINATION's Henrik Ivarsson and founded in 1999, issued the demo 'Suicide Angel' in 2000, after which the band played three gigs in Iceland as part of a European Union funded project in union with Austrian act MILLSBOMB. A second demo, 'Violent Forms Of Hatred' produced by Ola Sonmark, arrived in 2002. Originally Pontus Nordqvist manned the drums but Roger Larsson would succeed him in 1999. Bassist Mikael Sundin, opting out to take up a career in glassblowing, was replaced by Fredrik Thörnesson in 2002. Yet more changes found Lowe Wikman-Åbom acceding to the drum stool.

DISPIRITED lost singer Henric Ivarsson in January of 2004. The group would be quick to audition Pär Carlsson. Guitarist Peter Östlund would found retro Thrashers THE LAW and, in December 2005, join VOMITORY.

Suicide Angel, Dispirited (2000) (Demo). Suicide Angel / Afflicted / Eyes Of The Agonized / South Passage / Moment Of Truth.
Violent Forms Of Hatred, Dispirited (2002) (Demo). Buried In Betrayal / Infected Souls / Sterilized, Paralyzed, Terrorized, Hated / I Despise Your Life.
Sun City Compilation 4, Hellbilly 009 (2002) (Split CD with HORNED, NECROKÜLT and HAVOC). Sterilized, Paralyzed, Terrorized, Hated.

DISRUPT

MA, USA — *Jay Stiles (vocals), Jeff Hayward (guitar), Terry Savanstano (guitar), Bob Palombo (bass), Randy Odierno (drums).*

The core of DISRUPT would later found the ultra sludge Doom band GRIEF. Drummer Randy Odierno would at first switch to bass, then back to drums before finally leaving GRIEF for BANE OF EXISTENCE. The band has issued a slew of split 7" releases in collaboration with artists such as TUOMIOPAIVAN LAPSET, WARCOLLAPSE, SAUNA, RESIST, DESTROY and DISDAIN.

Singer Jay Stiles would also make his presence felt with STATE OF FEAR. In alliance with DISRUPT guitarist Jeff Hayward he also features in CHICKEN CHEST AND THE BIRD BOYS. Jeff Hayward and Randy Odierno made a return in late 2003 with an extreme Metal band entitled NOOSEBOMB, this unit including BANE OF EXISTENCE drummer Mike Butkiewicz. The new group debuted with the 'Brain Food For The Braindead' album.

REFUSE PLANET, (1991) (Split album with DESTROY). Dog Eat Dog / Suffocation / Subject To Suffering / No Values / Inebriated / Refuse Planet / G.A.M.E. / Consumed By The System.
UNREST, Relapse (1994). Domestic Prison / Mass Graves / Complaint / A Life's A Life / Pay For... / Unrest / Reality Distortion / Down My Throat / Tortured In Entirety / Religion Is A Fraud / We Stand Corrected / Faction Disaster / Human Garbage / Without Sincerity / Neglected / Same Old Shit / For What? / Squandered / Mindlock / Green To Grey / Critics / Dog Eat Dog / Deprived / Give It Back / Victims Of Tradition / Exorbitant Prices Must Diminish / Smash Divisions / Lack Of Intelligence / No Values / Solidarity.

DISSECTION

STRÖMSTAD, SWEDEN — *Jon Nödveidt (vocals / guitar), Johan Norman (guitar), Peter Palmdahl (bass), Ole Öhman (drums).*

If ever a band deserved the description blackened death, it would be Strömstad's Satanic masters DISSECTION. This truly blasphemous band, self-described as the sonic propaganda unit of the Misanthropic Luciferian Order, date back to a formation in 1989, instigated by vocalist / guitarist Jon Nödveidt and bassist Peter Palmdahl. Previous to DISSECTION, Nödtveidt, Palmdahl and drummer Ole Öhman had operated with Thrash Metal band SIREN'S YELL, releasing a 1988 demo comprising the songs 'Dawn Of The Dead', 'The Final War' and 'Show No Mercy'.

DISSECTION's first offering was the rehearsal demo 'Severing Into Shreds', these tracks cut in April 1990. Their live entrance was made that October, acting as support to ENTOMBED. For their next try out, 'The Grief Prophecy', three tracks recorded on December 14th 1990, the band having been temporarily boosted to a quartet with the introduction of rhythm guitarist 'Mäbe' (a.k.a. Mattias Johansson), another erstwhile SIREN'S YELL member at the time employed with NOSFERATU. The cassette was to sport artwork from respected scene figure 'Necrolord' (Kristian Wåhlin), the first design which in turn led to the artist's work appearing on all DISSECTION product bar one. Notably the artwork for a second, April 1991, edition of this tape was rendered by 'Dead' (a.k.a. Per Yngve Ohlin), the late MORBID and MAYHEM frontman.

The group structure had altered in January 1991, having drawn in second guitarist John Zwetsloot. They followed in September with a limited edition single, 'Into Infinite Obscurity', on the French label Corpsegrinder Records. To promote this effort and accompanying shows, the group printed up their first merchandise, these T-shirts the first to bear the infamous flaming trident cross logo. The live set for these early shows had the originals bulked out by covers such as POSSESSED's 'Séance', DEATH's 'Evil Dead' and MAYHEM's 'Freezing Moon'. This latter act had begun to figure ever stronger in DISSECTION's career path. Both Nödtveidt and Öhman guested with MAYHEM at a concert that December held in Askim, Norway and it was known that the DISSECTION frontman had been initiated into what was known as the Norwegian 'Black Circle'.

Nödtveidt would also be demoing with another act billed as SATANIZED, performing a solitary November 1991 gig with this band comprising vocalist Per Alexandersson of NIFELHEIM, second guitarist Johan Norman and DECAMERON drummer Tobias Kjellgren.

A further crop of DISSECTION demos, 'The Somberlain' laid down in March 1992 and a two song 1993 set, featuring a cover of 'Elisabeth Bathory' originally by Hungarian band TORMENTOR, led to an album deal with No Fashion Records. Nödtveidt, going under the pseudonym of Rietas, was also operating his side project THE BLACK at this stage. The debut DISSECTION album, 'The Somberlain', would be constructed at Hellspawn / Unisound studios in March 1993, the sessions overseen by producer DAN SWANÖ, frontman for EDGE OF SANITY amongst many others. For such an extreme concept, DISSECTION's inaugural album surprised many with its sophistication. Although undoubtedly heavy, 'The Somberlain' was also balanced by dexterous musicianship, noticeably John Zwetsloot's classical persuasions, acoustic passages and a keen priority on melody. DISSECTION pointedly dedicated their first offering to the murdered MAYHEM singer Euronymous.

Whilst assembling 'The Somberlain' album throughout 1993 the group members relocated to Gothenburg, sharing rehearsal facilities with AT THE GATES. Meantime, Nödtveidt's extra curricular act THE BLACK released their debut record 'The Priest Of Satan' as 'The Somberlain' arrived in stores in December 1993.

Yet another outside indulgence for Nödtveidt would be the highly experimental OPHTHALAMIA, a fantasy fuelled Metal exercise arranged by It (a.k.a. Tony Särkää) of ABRUPTUM. Nödtveidt's presence, disguised as 'Shadow', was to be felt on the 1994 album 'A Journey In Darkness'.

Internal friction resulted in the exit of John Zwetsloot, the final concert of this incarnation conducted on April 14th 1994 in Oslo. Johan Norman, previously with DECAMERON, SATANIZED and SACRAMENTUM, was drawn into the fold as a quick-fire replacement. John Zwetsloot forged CARDINAL SIN, issuing the 'Spiteful Intents' EP, and later figured briefly in the original line-up of THE HAUNTED.

DISSECTION signed to Germany's major independent Nuclear Blast label that November, but not before releasing two tracks on a compilation album for Wrong Again Records, namely the 1993 demo tracks, 'Elizabeth Bathory' and 'Where Dead Angels Lie'. The Swedes had also contributed SLAYER's 'Anti-Christ' to the Black Sun Records compilation 'Slatanic Slaughter'. That same year a short-lived but significant DISSECTION connected project emerged entitled TERROR, this being a union Jon Nödtveidt with the AT THE GATES triumvirate of guitarist Anders Björler, bass player Jonas Björler and drummer Adrian Erlandsson. TERROR issued a solitary demo prior to collapse.

The DISSECTION quartet ensconced themselves in the familiar surroundings of the Hellspawn / Unisound environs in March 1995 in order to manifest their next opus, 'Storm Of The Light's Bane'. Once completed, the band hit the UK for the first time, putting in three concerts flanking CRADLE OF FILTH. Music was not the only creative force on the agenda though, as that summer Nödtveidt and Norman established an occult denomination known as the Misanthropic Luciferian Order.

On October 10th supporting MORBID ANGEL at Gothenburg's Kåren venue, DISSECTION debuted a new drummer, Tobias Kjellgren, previously with SATANIZED, SWORDMASTER and DECAMERON. The departing Öhman temporarily teamed up with SWORDMASTER then joined OPHTHALAMIA.

'Storm Of The Light's Bane' arrived in November. Framed by two instrumentals, the opening 'At The Fathomless Depths' and a piano finale 'No Dreams Breed in Breathless Sleep' performed by Alexandra Balogh, then girlfriend of ABRUPTUM's Tony Särkkä, the record pursued a more direct Black Thrash approach than its predecessor. The record's clear Satanic aesthetic was tempered by swathes of reverb and supremely melodic, often palm muted riffs and more immediate songwriting, enabling DISSECTION to widen their support.

DISSECTION toured Europe with label mates DISMEMBER in December, this trek encompassing Germany, Austria, Czech Republic, Switzerland and Sweden. Having started 1996 touring in the UK in February as an alliance with AT THE GATES, the band hit the West Coast of North America, on a bill alongside AT THE GATES and MORBID ANGEL, DISSECTION's return shows in Europe throughout April were on a billing with SATYRICON and GORGOROTH. With continental road work extending further, the 1997 'Gods of Darkness' dates placed DISSECTION into an unholy mix alongside CRADLE OF FILTH, DIMMU BORGIR and IN FLAMES. Operations were concluded with an appearance at the 'Wacken Open Air' event, captured on tape, and headlining the Nuclear Blast festivals. This exhaustive regime had affected the group stability though, Palmdahl opting out and the outdoor appearances witnessing a fresh roster now featuring Jon's brother Emil Nödtveidt assuming bass duties. Another defection had Johan Norman withdrawing into anonymity, allegedly under fear of the Misanthropic Luciferian Order.

During a down period in the band's activity frontman Jon Nödtveidt, albeit anonymously, created an Electro Dark Ambient collaborative side project with MIDVINTER's Damien titled DE INFERNALI during 1997 for the album 'Symphonia De Infernali'. Ole Öhman also engaged in side work, enrolling into OPHTHALAMIA in 1997 under the nom de guerre of 'Bone'.

As December dawned DISSECTION's future was thrown into doubt when Nödtveidt, in keeping with recent Black Metal musicians behaviour patterns, was arrested on suspicion of the murder of a 38 year old Algerian homosexual, Josef Ben

Meddaour, some months earlier. The victim had been slain in Keillers Park in Gothenburg. Found guilty of being an accessory to a murder and in possession of an illegal firearm, Nödtveidt would ultimately be incarcerated for eight years, commencing his punishment at the maximum security prison in Kumla before being sent to Tidaholm jail.

Whilst Nödtveidt bided his time composing new material and deepening his esoteric studies, DISSECTION fans were kept interested with the Necropolis Records release 'The Past Is Alive' which collected together the early demos and singles as well as two tracks from SATANIZED, yet another side project outfit that included Nödtveidt, guitarist Johan Norman and drummer Kjellgren.

Despite DISSECTION being inoperative, Nödtveidt's influence upon the scene could still be felt from jail however, Nödtveidt contributing lyrics to DIABOLICUM's 2001 'The Dark Blood Rising (The Hatecrowned Retaliation)' album. The ousted Palmdahl had joined up with RUNEMAGICK for 'The Supreme Force Of Eternity' album. The bassist also appeared on the 1998 album from DEATHWITCH, 'Ultimate Death'.

During July of 2002 reports indicated that the former EMPEROR and THORNS drummer Bård 'Faust' Eithun would be sitting behind the kit for the planned 2003 DISSECTION's comeback release. Purely as a PR exercise let alone a creative union this proposed arrangement stoked controversy as it paired off two convicted murderers, Eithun also having been jailed for a similar crime. Preceding the release of both Nödtveidt, then languishing in Södertälje prison, and Faust the band re-established their credentials with the issue of a live album 'Live Legacy', recorded during 1996 at the German 'Wacken Open Air' festival.

Before the close of 2003 Eithun backed out of DISSECTION, apparently due to a conflict over "the demands of DISSECTION's Satanic concept". The band, recording new material in July, upfront of Nödtveidt release on September 6th, announced UK tour dates for December 2004 with WATAIN as support. Alongside Nödtveidt in this new line-up would be ABORYM and BLOODLINE guitarist Set Teitan, bassist Brice Leclercq of NIGHTRAGE and the INFERNAL, DAWN and DARK FUNERAL credited Thomas 'Alzazmon' Asklund on drums.

Response for the comeback was enthusiastic, with the band's Stockholm gig being moved from the Klubben venue to the Lilla Arenan due to high ticket demand. A new single, entitled 'Maha Kali', described by the band as "a hymn to the wrathful black Hindu goddess of Mahapralaya, the great dissolution of cosmos, Jai Maha Kali," would be made available solely at concert dates and through the band's website. The single entered the national Swedish charts at no. 50.

On 17th November DISSECTION were joined by TORMENTOR, ABORYM and newly re-appointed MAYHEM singer Attila Csihar for renditions of two old school black classics 'Elizabeth Bathory' by TORMENTOR and 'Freezing Moon' from MAYHEM during the band's appearance at Kultiplex in Budapest, Hungary.

DISSECTION's confirmed appearance at the 2005 'Metalist' festival in Israel was cancelled due to objections from event headliner MEGADETH's mainman Dave Mustaine's refusal to play with Satanic bands. Jon Nödtveidt reacted by branding Mustaine "a coward", further lambasting the singer with a tirade stating "you do not dare to face true opponents in faith?! You think this will stop us?! We are Satanists, yes, truly enemies of yours! For we are the antithesis to cowards like you!"

Brice Leclercq exited abruptly in early June just upfront of DISSECTION's appearance at the 'Undead Festival' in Hungary. Undaunted, the band duly performed as a trio with the bass guitar performed by a backing track. Subsequently, Haakon Nikolas Forwald (a.k.a. 'Kshatriya' or 'Savant M') of MYRKSKOG, SLAVIA, KOLDBRANN and DISIPLIN as well as member of the 'Misanthropic Luciferian Order' was installed on bass.

Gigs across South America were scheduled for September but shows in Chile and Venezuela would be cancelled, the band blaming the promoter for not honouring contractual commitment. Returning to Sweden, the band utilised Black Syndicate Studios in Stockholm to record a new album with Nödtveidt's brother Emil Nödtveidt (a.k.a. THE DEATHSTARS' Nightmare Industries) and Skinny Kangur acting as producers.

DISSECTION suffered the loss of Forwald in November, a press statement revealing the bassist had vacated his position "in order to focus on his esoteric and exoteric work in Norway". Rejecting rumours of a band split, as Erik Danielsson was introduced on bass, Jon Nödtveidt stated "We are now heading into a new phase, a darker phase". The following month the album title of 'Reinkaos' was announced, the comeback album bowing in suitably on Walpurgis night, April 30th 2006.

Just upfront of the album release a movie was released in Scandinavian theatres documenting the tragedy of the murder for which Jon Nödtveidt had been convicted. 'Keillers Park', titled after the location where Josef Ben Meddaour had been slain, was directed by Susanna Edwards.

The End Records unveiled an expanded re-issue campaign of re-masters for June. 'The Somberlain' added the 1990 'The Grief Prophecy' and 1991 'Into Infinite Obscurity' demos plus live tracks and rehearsal sessions, whilst 'Storm Of The Light's Bane' was enhanced with a second disc comprising the 1996 'Where Dead Angels Lie' EP, previously unheard 1994 demos and a completely different album mix.

On May 22nd Jon Nödtveidt put out a statement signalling the end of DISSECTION, explaining "I have reached the limitations of music as a tool for expressing what I want to express, for myself and the handful of others that I care about, and I will now move along to other realms of practice. Dissection's work is done and this is our legacy. Salve Satan! Salve Azerate 218!" The band's final performances were set to be a Swedish concert, their first and final Israeli gig and a brace of dates in the USA, on September 1st at the House of Blues in West Hollywood, California and September 6th at B.B. King Blues Club in New York City. DISSECTION's June 24th show in Stockholm, dubbed 'Midsummer Massacre '06', would be filmed and recorded for a DVD and live album. A scheduled show in Tel Aviv, Israel would be curtailed. The band's announced US concerts were then cancelled, Jon Nödtveidt having been denied legal entry into the United States as a result of his 1998 conviction.

Jon Nödtveidt closed DISSECTION's career in a manner befitting his philosophies, committing suicide in August. Band members released a statement claiming "he was more focussed, happier and stronger than ever" and "he chose to end his life by his own hands. As a true Satanist he led his life in the way he wanted and ended it when he felt that he had fulfilled his self-created destiny".

Nödtveidt, 31 years old, was found dead at his apartment in Hässelby, a suburb of Stockholm, on August 16th. Newspapers reported he had surrounded himself by candles and had a copy of Anton LaVey's 'The Satanic Bible'. Nödtveidt had ended his life with a shot to the head. Shortly beforehand he had told friends he was "going to Transylvania". Subsequently, DISSECTION guitarist Set Teitan reportedly commented on an online forum that the book Nödtveidt had open in front of him was "a Satanic grimoire" and not LaVeys work, because "He despised LaVey and 'Church of Satan'."

The Grief Prophecy, Dissection (1990) (Demo). Intro—Severed Into Shreds / The Call Of The Mist / Consumed.

Into Infinite Obscurity, Corpse Grinder CGR 003 (1991). Into Infinite Obscurity / Shadows Over A Lost Kingdom / Son Of The Mourning.

The Somberlain, Dissection (1992) (Demo). Frozen / Feathers Fell / Mistress Of The Bleeding Sorrow / In The Cold Winds Of Nowhere.

Promo '93, Dissection (1993) (Demo). Where Dead Angels Lie / Elisabeth Bathory.

THE SOMBERLAIN, No Fashion NFR 006 (1993). Black Horizons / The Somberlain / Crimson Towers / A Land Forlorn / Heaven's Damnation / Frozen / Into Infinite Obscurity / In The Cold Winds Of

DISSECTION (pic: Dimitri Borellini)

Nowhere / The Grief Prophecy / Shadows Over A Lost Kingdom / Mistress Of The Bleeding Sorrow / Feathers Fell.
THE SOMBERLAIN, JVC Victor VICP-5491 (1994) (Japanese release). Black Horizons / The Somberlain / Crimson Towers / A Land Forlorn / Heaven's Damnation / Frozen / Into Infinite Obscurity / In The Cold Winds Of Nowhere / The Grief Prophecy / Shadows Over A Lost Kingdom / Mistress Of The Bleeding Sorrow / Feathers Fell / Son Of The Mourning.
STORM OF THE LIGHT'S BANE, Nuclear Blast NB 129-2 (1995). At The Fathomless Depths / Night's Blood / Unhallowed / Where Dead Angels Lie / Retribution: Storm Of The Light's Bane / Thorns Of Crimson Death / Soulreaper / No Dreams Breed In Breathless Sleep.
STORM OF THE LIGHT'S BANE, JVC Victor VICP-5636 (1995) (Japanese release). At The Fathomless Depths / Night's Blood / Unhallowed / Where Dead Angels Lie / Feather's Fell / Retribution: Storm Of The Light's Bane / Thorns Of Crimson Death / Feather's Fell / No Dreams Breed In Breathless Sleep.
Where Dead Angels Lie EP, Nuclear Blast NB 167-2 (1996). Where Dead Angels Lie (Demo Version) / Elisabeth Bathori / The Anti-Christ / Feathers Fell / Son Of the Mourning / Where Dead Angels Lie (Album Version).
Where Dead Angels Lie / Bastard Saints, Morbid Noizz Productions 144 (1996) (Polish split cassette release with SINISTER). Where Dead Angels Lie (Demo Version) / Elisabeth Bathori / The Anti-Christ / Feathers Fell / Son Of The Mourning / Where Dead Angels Lie (Album Version).
THE PAST IS ALIVE (THE EARLY MISCHIEF), Necropolis NR017 (1996). Shadows Over A Lost Kingdom / Frozen / Feathers Fell / Son Of The Mourning / Mistress Of The Bleeding Sorrow / In The Cold Winds Of Nowhere / Into Infinite Obscurity / The Call Of The Mist / Severed Into Shreds / Satanized / Born In Fire.
STORM OF THE LIGHT'S BANE / WHERE DEAD ANGELS LIE, Nuclear Blast NB 0646-2 (2002). At The Fathomless Depths / Unhallowed / Night's Blood / Where Dead Angels Lie / Retribution: Storm Of The Light's Bane / Thorns Of Crimson Death / Soulreaper / No Dreams Breed In Breathless Sleep / Where Dead Angels Lie (Demo Version) / Elisabeth Bathory / Anti Christ / Feathers Fell / Son Of Mourning.
LIVE LEGACY, Nuclear Blast NB 650-2 (2003). Intro—At The Fathomless Depths / Retribution—Storm Of The Light's Bane / Unhallowed / Where Dead Angels Lie / Frozen / Thorns Of Crimson Death / The Somberlain.
LIVE LEGACY (LIMITED EDITION), Nuclear Blast NB 650-5 (2003). Intro—At The Fathomless Depths / Retribution—Storm Of The Light's Bane / Unhallowed / Where Dead Angels Lie / Frozen / Thorns Of Crimson Death / The Somberlain / At The Fathomless Depths / Night's Blood / Unhallowed / Son Of The Mourning / Where Dead Angels Lie / Black Horizons / Elisabeth Bathory / Retribution—Storm Of The Light's Bane / The Somberlain.
Maha Kali, Escapi AUD008 (2004). Maha Kali / Unhallowed (Rebirthed version). Chart position: 50 SWEDEN.
THE PAST IS ALIVE (THE EARLY MISCHIEF), Karmageddon Media KARMA082 (2005). Shadows Over A Lost Kingdom / Frozen / Feathers Fell / Son Of The Mourning / Mistress Of The Bleeding Sorrow / In The Cold Winds Of Nowhere / Into Infinite Obscurity / The Call Of The Mist / Severed Into Shreds / Satanized / Born In Fire / Where Dead Angels Lie / Elizabeth Bathory.
REINKAOS, Black Horizon BHM001 (2006). Nexion 218 / Beyond The Horizon / Starless Aeon / Black Dragon / Dark Mother Divine / Xeper-I-Set / Chaosophia / God Of Forbidden Light / Reinkaos / Internal Fire / Maha Kali / Starless Aeon (Video).
Starless Aeon, The End TE071 (2006). Starless Aeon (Album version) / Xeper-I-Set (Album version) / Starless Aeon (Instrumental version) / Starless Aeon (Video).

DISSENTER

POLAND — *Garbaty Yaha (vocals / bass), Rob (guitar), Stoker (guitar), Mlody (drums).*

Veteran Death Metal act DISSENTER previously operated as BLOODLUST, founded in January of 1989 and releasing the demos 'Holocaust' and 'Hideous'. BLOODLUST, inducting guitarist Sivy and drummer Mlody, would raise a high profile on the Polish Metal scene, which included numerous domestic tours as well as dates in Moscow, before folding in 1995. The band had actually entered Spaart Studios in Rzeszow to cut a debut album 'You'll Die' but this would remain unreleased.

Refounded as DISSENTER the group published the demo 'Moral Insanity' in 1997. The band at this juncture comprised singer Maniac, guitarists Heter and Sivy, bass player Garbaty and drummer Mlody. A further demo preceded the 1999 four way split album 'Disco's Out, Slaughter's In' shared with REINLESS, LOST SOUL and NIGHT GALLERY.

DISSENTER underwent a major restructuring for recording of the 2002 album 'Apocalypse Of The Damned', trimming down to a trio featuring Garbaty on lead vocals and bass, guitarist Heter and drummer Mlody. The band embarked upon a ten date tour of Poland during October of 2002 co-headlined by MONSTROSITY and Swedes VOMITORY backed by TRAUMA, SCEPTIC, LOST SOUL and CONTEMPT. Guitarist Heter was forced out during these dates as DISSENTER pulled in the guitar pairing of Rob and Stoker for the 2003 'Contamination' album.

In early 2007 DISSENTER frontman Garbaty Yaha got himself in the news when he was chosen as temporary replacement to front DEICIDE's European dates when mainman Glen Benton was forced to address pressing legal issues in the USA.

DISCO'S OUT, SLAUGHTER'S IN, (1999) (Split album with NIGHT GALLERY, REINLESS and LOST SOUL). Moral Insanity / The End.
BLOODLUST & BLASPHEMY, Beta Studio DISS 03 (2000). With A Crown Of Thorns On Temple / Moral Insanity / Desire … (In My Veins) / In The Empire Of Damnation / … For Kill My Pain / Strange To Heaven / Ruling Of Conscience / The End / … For Kill My Pain (Video).
APOCALYPSE OF THE DAMNED, Cold Blood Industries (2002). Runic Hymn / By The Eyes Of The Dead / Apocalypse Of The Damned / Dead Author / Rotten Soul / The Beginning / Buried / Altar Of Fire / Masters Of Holy Justice / Death's Arena.
CONTAMINATION, Empire (2003). Intro / Contamination / Unholy Sight / In Flames Of Hate / Dawn Of Dignity / Ugly Corpse Of The Angel / Born From The Dead / Dirge Of The Deceased / Death Bringer / Misty Mankind.

DISTRAUGHT

BRAZIL — *André Meyer (vocals), Ricardo Silveira (guitar), Marcos Pinto (guitar), Gustavo Stuepp (bass), Éverson Krentz (drums).*

Porto Alegre Death Metal band DISTRAUGHT emerged touting the demo 'To Live Better'. In 1994 the band shared a three way split CD for Encore Records with SCARS and ZERO VISION. The four tracks submitted for this release were recorded by a DISTRAUGHT line up of lead vocalist André Meyer, guitarist Fernando Soares, bass player Alexandre Figueiro with Hugo Guarana Lobo on the drums.

For their 1998 debut full length album 'Nervous System' Meyer and Guarana Lobo were joined by new recruits Leandro Mohr on guitar and bassist Sandro Magoo. By second opus 'Infinite Abyssal' DISTRAUGHT's line up had been completely overhauled with only Meyer remaining. His new quartet of players numbered guitarists Ricardo Silveira and Marcos Pinto, bassist Gustavo Stuepp and drummer Éverson Krentz.

Their 2002 live album witnessed covers of SLAYER's 'Angel Of Death' and 'Raining Blood' alongside a take on SEPULTURA's 'Escape To The Void'.

ULTIMATE ENCORE, Encore (1994) (Split album with ZERO VISION & SCARS). Time And Fail / Continuation / Inspiring Heroine / Situation Of Pain.

NERVOUS SYSTEM, Encore (1998). New Crime / Cemetery Of The World / The Dreamer / N.T.S. / As Good As The Rain / Sarin / Foot X Violence X Ball / Death Road / Inertia / A Peaceful Place / To Conquest Space Air.

INFINITE ABYSSAL, Encore (2001). Infinite Abyssal / Removing The Rubbish / Umbral / Antibiotic Tendence / Spiritual Reward / The Cut / Science, Philosophy And Religion / Tufão / Dusty Land / Slaves Of Creed.

LIVE BLACK JACK, Encore (2002). Spiritual Reward / Antibiotic Tendence / Angel Of Death—Raining Blood / Removing The Rubbish / Dusty Land / Death Road / Escape To The Void.

DIVINE EMPIRE

BOCA RATON, FL, USA — *Jason Blachowicz (vocals / bass), J.P. Soars (guitar), Derrick Roddy (drums).*

Vicious Death Metal band from Boca Raton, Florida, founded in late 1997 by a trio of MALEVOLENT CREATION defectors vocalist / bassist Jason Blachowicz, guitarist J.P. Soars and drummer Derrick Roddy. After a 1998 six track demo the band debuted commercially for Olympic Recordings with the 'Redemption' album, promoting its release with a lengthy American tour schedule billed alongside GORGUTS, CRYPTOPSY and VADER. A further round of dates in 1999 found DIVINE EMPIRE on the road in the USA and Canada in alliance with EMPEROR, BORKNAGER, WITCHERY and PECCATUM.

Roddy would make his exit upon completion of these shows and Alex Marquez took over drumming duties for second album 'Doomed To Inherit' in 2000. DIVINE EMPIRE's progress would be stalled when Blachowicz was jailed. The singer had been attacked by a drunk wielding a broken bottle and, in resorting to defense, had seriously injured his assailant. The frontman was freed in October 2001. Soars also operates as guitarist with avant-garde Stoners BURNER and WYNJARA.

In May of 2002 drummer Duane Timlin, an esteemed veteran of BROKEN HOPE, FOREST OF IMPALED, SARCOPHAGUS and, under the pseudonym of 'Cryptic Winter' WELTMACHT, was announced as a new band member as DIVINE EMPIRE undertook studio recordings for the 'Nostradamus' through Olympic Recordings. The band would form up part of the fifth annual summer 2002 'Death Across America' dates headlined by KATAKLYSM and backed up by BEYOND THE EMBRACE and MISERY INDEX. The group would act as co-headliners for a North American package tour in May of 2003, completing a bill of SKINLESS, MISERY INDEX and DYING FETUS.

DIVINE EMPIRE entered the recording studio in August of 2004 with producer Jeremy Staska to craft a new album entitled 'Method Of Execution'. In early 2005 Blachowicz assembled a new Death Metal band venture in early 2005 dubbed MURDER 101, including the CHRONZON pairing of singer Rob Rosenzweig and guitarist Samuel Dean with Cesar Placeres of HIBERNUS MORTIS on drums.

The band abruptly severed ties with bassist/vocalist Jason Blachowicz in mid June, an official statement citing "serious personal and legal issues". However, within hours of this statement Blachowicz responded, proclaiming that he was "the owner, heart and soul of DIVINE EMPIRE" and that it was not he, but Soars and Timlin that had been ejected. Jason Blachowicz further revealed he was in the process of recruiting new band members.

Projected promotion for the newly released album included Summer 2005 dates, commencing in Florida during early July, had the band scheduled to be packaged with ORIGIN, ANIMOSITY and headliners MALEVOLENT CREATION. In September the band was set to form up the 'Blitzkrieg 3' tour package, traversing Poland, Germany, Austria, Switzerland, Spain, Portugal, France, Denmark, Belgium, The Netherlands, Italy, Czech Republic, Sweden and Norway in alliance with VADER, ROTTING CHRIST and ANOREXIA NERVOSA but due to the internal ructions would, according to Blachowicz, be forced to withdraw. As the story unfolded though, Soars and Timlin hit back, laying legal claim to the DIVINE EMPIRE brand, that they had the backing of their label Century Media and stating that the tour was on with NILE veteran Chief Spires making up the band numbers. Blachowicz quickly retaliated, himself taking the DIVINE EMPIRE name and forming up a brand new band unit with new players guitarists Marco Martell and the DWELLING MADNESS and VILE EXISTENCE veteran Frank Cusimano with David Kinkade on the drums. However, Frank Cusimano soon backed out.

J.P. Soars and Duane Timlin, slamming the new formation set up by Blachowicz as "a covers band", relinquished the title and announced they were to be titled as THY DIVINE EMPIRE. Joining them would be vocalist / bassist Sean Baxter of BROKEN HOPE, COUNCIL OF THE FALLEN and EM SIMFONIA repute. Timlin's side activities continued unabated, joining Texan Death Metal band INGURGITATE, recording a fourth album for FOREST OF IMPALED and working with Minneapolis Stoner/Grindcore act NEVER AGAIN. In a further twist, Jason Blachowicz rejoined MALEVOLENT CREATION in October. As the year closed, DIVINE EMPIRE drafted second guitarist Chris Defaut.

Divine Empire, (1998). Hidden Hatred / Draped In Black / Criminal Instinct / Redemption / Silent Carnage / Out For Blood.
REDEMPTION, Serious Entertainment (1999). The Awakening / Hidden Hatred / Out For Blood / Witness To Terror / Redemption / Silent Carnage / Induced Expulsion / Born Of Sin / Criminal Instinct / Draped In Black / Pray For Deliverance.
DOOMED TO INHERIT, Olympic (2000). War Torn / Repulsive / Dead And Martyred / Birth Of Legends / Murder Suicide / Truth Be Denied / Self Inflicted / Blood Of Nations / Mandatory Punishment / The Culprit.
NOSTRADAMUS, Century Media (2004). Sacrifice In Vain / Ravaged / Tribulation / They Rise / Manifestation / Season Of Extinction / The Pain Remains / Basher / Aggravated Battery / Cuidate Del Traidor.
METHOD OF EXECUTION, Century Media CD 77521-2 (2005). Vowed Revenge / The Mauler / Surgical Strike / Dungeon Mask / Shadow Of Violence / Prelude To The Storm / Storm Of Hatred / Random Beheadings / Incarcerated / Judge, Jury & Executioner / Terror Zone / Sanctioned Homicide / Impervious Deception / Kill The King / Murderous / Reduced To Ashes.

DIVINE NOISE ATTACK

GERMANY — *Christian Schulze (vocals), Feldbock Feldhofen (guitar), Thomas Stage (guitar), Christian Bartels (bass), Claas Fallet (drums).*

Braunschweig based Death Metal band DIVINE NOISE ATTACK released the 2002 demo 'Soulless Something'. The group, whose core members were previously operational with CORNUCOPIA, is fronted by erstwhile OUR SOULS frontman Christian Schulze. The singer also cites a tradition with ANGEL DUST, CRUCIFIXION and Wolfsburg Death Metal act PROTECTOR. Guitarist Thomas Stage has prior links to Doom band TACTICAL FORTRESS whilst his six string partner Feldbock Feldhofen was active with JIMMI PELZ FISTFUCK. Pre CORNUCOPIA drummer Class Fallet provided percussion for Neumünster Crustcore outfit CONTRAGRESSIVE.

The band credit themselves as vocalist Schulle "Brutal Vocal Artizt", guitarist Thomas Stage "Rythm & Lead Distortion Sounds / Martyr Screams", second guitarist Feldbock Feldhofen "Rythm & Lead Distortion Sounds", bass player Christian "Distortion Basspain" and drummer Claas Fallet "Atomic Blastbeat Clockwork".

TORN APART, Black Attack (2006). Torn Apart / Bombthreat / Warhead / Fields Of Starvation / Bitter End / Isolation / Scum / Soulless Something / Collapse / Diabolical Masterpiece / Disgust / Inferno.

DIVINE RAPTURE

CHESTER HEIGHTS, PA, USA — *Mike Hrubovcak (vocals), J.J. Hrubovcak (guitar), Babak Davodian (guitar), Ryan Moll (bass).*

Chester Heights, Pennsylvania Death Metal band. DIVINE RAPTURE's eponymous debut would oddly include two separate sessions of recordings of the same songs. A 2001 follow up demo would see engineering credits going to MORBID ANGEL guitarist Erik Rutan. Founded by the Hrubovcak brothers, guitarist J.J. and singer Mike, along with guitarist Babak Davodian later conscripts included former EVIL DIVINE bassist Ryan Moll and drummer Justin DiPinto. Subsequently the latter would enroll with MALEVOLENT CREATION.

The band issued a split CD with HATRED through the Under The Baphomet label during 2002 and announced plans for a further split affair in league with CRANIOTOMY for Immortal Souls Productions. The band would also contribute their version of 'World Of Shit (The Promised Land)' for a MORBID ANGEL tribute album on the Hellspawn imprint and DEATH's 'Pull The Plug' for a Mondongo Canibale Distribution release 'Together As One'. A full length DIVINE RAPTURE album, 'The Burning Passion', was also in production. Drummer Justin DiPinto joined up with Black Metal band INSATANITY during December of 2002. J.J. Hrubovcak subsequently enrolled into the ranks of New Jersey's MOURNING. 2005 saw Babak Davodian joining Jersey City Metalcore band RANDALL FLAGG.

In early 2006 the Hrubovcak siblings joined the ranks of VILE to conduct their 'Gutting Europe' tour during March and April.

DIVINE RAPTURE, Hrborrah (1999). Desirous Nonsubsistence / Purging Thy Torrents / Black Moon Harvest / Unyielding Presence / The Well Of Enlightenment / A Glimmer From Beneath / Black Moon Harvest (Raw Primal version) / Desirous Nonsubsistence (Raw Primal version) / Purging Thy Torrents (Raw Primal version) / Unyielding Presence (Raw Primal version) / A Glimmer From Beneath (Raw Primal version).

THE BURNING PASSION, Listenable POSH051 (2003). The Kindling / Your Time Has Come / Severed / My Demon, Your Dove / The Deifying, The Sorrow, The Awakening / Funeral Mist / Affliction Of Faith / Black Moon Harvest / Spirit Storm Serenade / No Future, No Past / The Smothering.

DIVINE:DECAY

HELSINKI, FINLAND — *Alec Hirst-Gee (vocals / guitar), Paul (guitar), Stig Evil (guitar), Timo Nyberg (guitar), Toni Grönros (bass), Pätkä (drums).*

Helsinki Death Metal formation created during 1999 by SUBURBAN TRIBE drummer Alec Hirst-Gee, acting as frontman, HYBRID CHILDREN guitarist Paul, AM I BLOOD bass player Toni Grönros and H.I.M. credited drummer Pätkä (a.k.a. Juhana Rantala). The group debuted with the 1999 'Batcave Sessions' demo, leading up to the Spring 2001 album 'Songs Of The Damned', released by French extreme Metal label Osmose Productions. DIVINE DECAY augmented their sound in 2002 with the incorporation of second guitarist Stig Evil (a.k.a. Timo Nyberg) of GANDALF repute. Janne Joutsenniemi of STONE and SUBURBAN TRIBE repute acted as producer for the 2002 DIVINE:DECAY album 'Songs Of The Damned'. During 2003 the band pulled in a third guitar player, Timo "Stig666Evil" Nyberg previously with GANDALF, for live work. The September 'Maximise The Misery' album found Joutsenniemi resuming his role in the production chair.

Batcave Sessions, Divine:Decay (1999) (Unreleased demo). Alone / Divine:Decay / Hollow / Genocide / Dead Calm / Through My Eyes.

SONGS OF THE DAMNED, Divine:Decay OPCD 111 (2001). Alone / Divine Decay / Song Of The Damned / Hollow / Dead Calm / Bloodline / F# (Wake Up) / Kill The Dead / Through My Eyes / Genocide.

MAXIMIZE THE MISERY, Osmose Productions OPCD 128 (2003). Icons Fall / Weave A Web Of Vanity / Without A Soul / Scars / Killing Innocence / Maximise The Misery / Dead In Me / The Discomfort Of Artificial Euphoria / Filth / Black Hearted Angel (Remorse) / (Hidden Track).

DOG FACED GODS

STOCKHOLM, SWEDEN — *Johnny Wranning (vocals), Conny Jonsson (guitar), Peter Tuthill (bass), Richard Evensand (drums).*

Stockholm's DOG FACED GODS was named after the TESTAMENT song. Vocalist Johnny Wranning and guitarist Conny Jonsson also have credits with EBONY TEARS. Wranning is also an ex-MISCREANT member. Before too long all the membership of EBONY TEARS were involved with DOG FACED GODS operating both bands in tandem. Pelle Saether of ZELLO produced and added guest vocals to the 1998 album. Keyboards came courtesy of ZELLO's Mats Olsson.

Following three EBONY TEARS albums, 1998's 'Tortura Insomnia', 1999's 'A Handful Of Nothing' and 'Evil As Hell' in 2001, Wranning exited that band, forging EYETRAP in November 2000 in collaboration with erstwhile SHATTRD personnel guitarist Fredrik Rhodin, bassist Joakim "Chucken" Rhodin and drummer, Jan Karlsson.

In 2004 the singer announced his new band MURGHATROID, a union with ex-THERION drummer Sam Carpenter (a.k.a. Sami Karppinen). Over his career, drummer Rickard Evensand would wind his way through a succession of acts of rising stature including EBONY TEARS, SORCEROR, Funksters IT'S ALIVE, MANIC DEPRESSION, SOUTHPAW, EYEBALL, SOILWORK, American act CHIMAIRA and the 2004 retro Black-Thrash union DEMONOID.

Peter Tuthill quit his position in CONSTRUCDEAD in May of 2005 in order to resurrect DOG FACED GODS. In early 2006 Tuthill announced new formation NAILSTATE to the world, being a union of Paul Mäkitalo (a.k.a. 'Themgoroth') of DARK FUNERAL and INFERNAL, Gustaf Jorde, ex-DEFLESHED and Stefan Norgren from ETERNAL OATH.

In early 2007 it was revealed Evansand was also involved with a high profile side act, DEAD BY APRIL, featuring M.A.N guitar player Martin Meyerman, DRAGONLAND guitarist Olof Mörck, bassist Staffan Persson of WHEN WE FALL plus the PAINFIELD, DEATHDESTRUCTION and NIGHTRAGE credited singer Jimmie Strimell.

Demo 1997, Dog Faced Gods (1997) (Demo). Structural Damage / Room 18.

RANDOM CHAOS THEORY IN ACTION, Gothenburg Noiseworks GNW 04 (1998). Blindfolded / The Man Inside / God Over All / Face My Rage / Fractured Image / Dirge / Prozac 3105 / Purge / As Worlds Collide… / Swallowtail / The Chaos Factor.

Demo 1999, Dog Faced Gods (1999) (Demo). I.D. / Soul Bleed / Wreak Havoc.

Demo 2000, Dog Faced Gods (2000) (Demo). Metamorphosis / The New Man Of Me / Centrifugal.

DOLORIAN

OULU, FINLAND — *Antti Ittna Haapapuro (vocals / guitar), Ari Kukkohovi (bass / drums), Jussi Ontero (keyboards).*

A multi-faceted act DOLORIAN, based in Oulu and previously entitled TEMPLES BEYOND, employ elements of Black and Death Metal slowed down to labouring Doom crawl. The band themselves describe their music as leaving the listener "spiritually cramped". Both drummer Ari Kukkohovi and vocalist Antti Ittna Haapapuro have credits with Black Metal act BLACK SWAN. Haapapuro also has affiliations with Dark Ambient project HALO MANASH, AEOGA and I. CORAX. DOLORIAN's first recordings came in the form of a 1997 demo, these tracks embellished by keyboards from CATAMENIA's Heidi Riihinen. Subsequently keyboards were handled by Jussi Ontero of WILDCARD and GHOST MACHINERY.

Wounded Love Records, a subsidiary of Avantgarde Music, issued the album 'When All Laughter Has Gone', recorded at Tico-Tico Studios, in 1999. The band stayed with Wounded Love a self-titled follow up, again cut at Tico-Tico, released during 2000. In February 2004 DOLORIAN shared a split 7" single with Swedish act SHINING through Selbstmord Services. That same year Jussi Ontero worked with BURNING POINT.

DOLORIAN returned in April 2006 with the album 'Voidwards'.

WHEN ALL LAUGHTER HAS GONE, Wounded Love WLR017 (1999). Desolated Colours / My Weary Eyes / A Part Of Darkness / When All Laughter Has Gone / Collapsed / Fields / With Scorn I Perish.
DOLORIAN, Wounded Love WLR023 (2000). Grey Rain / Blune Unknown / Hidden—Rising / Cold—Colourless / Nails / Numb Lava / Ambiguous Ambivalence / Eclusion / Faces.
Dolorian, Unpleasant Wax UW 001 (2004) (Split 7" vinyl single with SHINING). Ekstasis (DOLORIAN) / Through Corridors Of Oppression (SHINING).
VOIDWARDS, Wounded Love WLR035 (2006). Dual–Void–Trident / In The Locus Of Bone / Co-il-lusion / Ivory Artery / The Flow Of Seething Visions / The One Whose Name Has No End / The Absolute Halo Is Awakening / Epoch Of Cyclosure / The Fire Which Burns Not / Raja Naga—Rising.

DOMAIN

ŁÓDŹ, POLAND — *Paul (vocals / guitar), V-ac (guitar), Mike (bass), Mitloff (drums).*

Łódź based Black-Thrash Metal band DOMAIN started life as a proto-Black Metal duo in 1989 under the billing of PANDEMONIUM. Although only sporting two members, vocalist / guitarist Paul and colleague Peter 'Zuber', PANDEMONIUM built up a cult following on the live circuit and generated by the demos 'Reh' and February 1992's 'Devilri'. Pulling in bassist Simon a third demo set, 'The Ancient Catatonia', was issued before PANDEMONIUM went into hiatus. Simon would join TENEBRIS whilst Paul founded DOMAIN due to the fact ousted member Zuber put in a legal claim to the PANDEMONIUM band title.

Signing to Morbid Noizz Productions they would debut with the 'Pandemonium' album in 1995. A switch to Apocalypse Productions saw the release of 1999's '… From Oblivion', with former drummer Karol 'Carol' Skwarczewski, a veteran of DEVASTATOR and IMPERATOR, would be superseded by Piotr 'Mittloff' Kozieradzki of HATE, GOETIA and RIVERSIDE repute, and 'Gat Etemmi' in 2002. Studio guests on this latter outing including keyboard player Rober Srzednicki and female vocalist Ewa Frakstein. However, Mittloff departed to prioritise RIVERSIDE. In October of 2003 the SIRIUS, DARK GALLERY, UMBRA SPHERE and STROMMOUSSHELD credited Maelstrom joined the ranks as keyboard player / programmer.

DOMAIN planned a fourth album, entitled 'Namtar The Wizard', for 2004 issue but would in fact revert back to the PANDEMONIUM banner for a comeback album 'Zonei', released by Mystic Productions.

PANDEMONIUM, Morbid Noizz Productions (1995). The Beginning / Blood Of God / Immemorial Legend / Sword Into Heart Of Lies / The Calling / Hagia Sophia / Lost Preexistence / Mirror Of Hate / Somewhere Above / Lost Preexistence (Remix).
… FROM OBLIVION, Apocalypse Productions (1999). Whispered In The Dark / Supernatural / The Maklu Spell / Sunless Domain / Ritual Combat / Asymetrical Megalith / Deathmaker / Fall Into Decay / Devilri / The Enter / Nar Mattaru / Whispered In The Dark (Remix) / Unholy Existence (Live) / Ritual Combat (Live).
GAT ETEMMI, Apocalypse Productions (2002). Asaku Marsuti / The Seven Sibbiti / Ningiszida / The Ancient Ones Monstrous / Gat Etemmi / Anzu Storm / Azag Rite / Dingur Xul / The Gate Of Pazuzu / Summa Amelu Kasip / Shub Nigurath Space Outside / Yog Sothoth Dominion.

DOME SERVICE

DENMARK — *Morten Larsen (vocals), Thor Hansen (guitar), Niels Dranov (guitar), Jonas Heidemann (bass), Anders P. Larsen (drums).*

DOME SERVICE began life as ICON BLEEDING, switching to their present title in the Autumn of 2001. Originally the band had come together in 1995 under the formative handle of DISTEMPERED CAUSE, citing a line-up of vocalist Morten Larsen, guitarist Thor Hansen, bassist Jonas Heidemann with Anders Larsen on the drums. A second guitarist, Niels Dranov, was added upfront of a debut gig at Vordingborg in March of 1996. That year the group, opting for the revised title ICON BLEEDING, laid down the demo 'Lucid'. Benefits from this session included the inclusion of the track 'The Lost Lenore' on the Serious Entertainment compilation album 'Extremity Rising III'. Despite this progress the band remained inactive throughout the following year and only performed twice in 1998.

Rebilled as DOME SERVICE the group began demoing once more in 2002.

Dome Service, Dome Service (2002) (Demo). E Pluribus Unum / Clarity / Day Of Silence.

DOMINION

MINNEAPOLIS, MN, USA — *Bill Hedal (vocals / bass), Brian Owens (guitar), Scott Ellingboe (guitar), Chad Ludwig (drums).*

DOMINION was a Minneapolis extreme Death Metal outfit founded in 1993. The group would subsequently adopt the revised title of DEMONICON for a series of album releases. The opening line up counted vocalist / bassist Bill Hedal, ex-CRYOGEN, DEBAUCHERY and EVISCERATION guitarist Brian Owens and drummer Mike Curran. The line remained unstable throughout the band's formative years with a succession of second guitar players enrolling and exiting. However, during 1995 Scott Ellingboe made the position permanent. Before the close of the year though Curran had vacated the drum stool in favour of the EVISCERATION and CRYOGEN credited Chad Ludwig. With this line up DOMINION cut the album 'Soul's Redemption'. Promoting the album in 1996 with live work saw the band putting in a showing at the Milwaukee Metalfest, after which Ellingboe was superseded by Corey Jones of THEATRE OF THE MACABRE, NECROMIS and CONTAGION repute.

DOMINION recorded a demo in 1997 and delivered another set at the Milwaukee Metalfest. A deal was secured with Root Of All Evil Records but in 1998 Ludwig exited in order to pursue a career in bodybuilding. Scott Robinson plugged the gap as the band took on the new title of DEMONICON. Unfortunately Robinson upped and left a matter of weeks before the group was scheduled to go into the recording studio. By necessity Corey Jones switched from guitar to drums and ANAL BLAST and SEVERED man Anthony Columbus was drafted in on guitar for the 2000 album 'Condemned Creation'.

SOUL'S REDEMPTION, Independent (1996). Prelude To Chaos / Soul's Redemption / Divine Addiction / Self Inflicted / The Seed / Mind's Eye / Starting Cut.

DOMINUS

RINGSTED, DENMARK — *Michael Poulsen (vocals / guitar), Mads Hansen (guitar), Jesper Olsen (bass), Jess Larsen (drums).*

Ringsted Death Metal act founded by Michael Poulsen in 1991, DOMINUS released a self-titled demo followed up by the 'Ambrosius Locus' session of 1992 and a further tape 'Astaroth' in early 1993. The band's first commercially available product came in the form of a track donated to the second in the series of 'Fuck You, We're From Denmark' compilation albums on Progress Records. Poulsen, a lecturer in "Positive Nordic

Satanism", engaged himself in TV discussions concerning his Black Metal stance with a priest on Scandinavian TV.

DOMINUS signed to Greek label Molon Lave releasing a 7" single, 'Sidereal Path Of Colours'. The band's first album, March 1995's 'View To The Dim', saw the band returning to Progress Records. At live shows Poulsen addresses his audience in native Norwegian tongue. Following the debut album DOMINUS underwent a line-up shift, adding ex ILLDISPOSED drummer Lars Hald and bassist Anders Nielsen. 'The First 9' followed in September 1996.

The group then took on an adventurous change in direction, as November 1997's 'Vol. Beat' found DOMINUS adopting a radical musical shift towards 50's Rock n' Roll inspired beat Metal. Quite aptly, the album was recorded at Jailhouse studios by Tommy Hansen.

DOMINUS, complete with a fresh rhythm section of bassist Frans Hellbus and erstwhile FURIOUS TRAUMA drummer Brian Andersen, returned to an earthier sound for the fourth record 'Godfallos' issued in October 2000. However, despite praiseworthy reviews the band announced it was to fold shortly after. Michael Poulsen duly forged a fresh act entitled VOLBEAT. Joining him would be a cast comprising ex-POST and COMMON DELUTION guitarist Teddy Vang, erstwhile PINK APPLE, DOMINUS and NO SOLUTION bassist Anders Kjølholm with Jon Larsen, credited with membership of MORATORIUM and THE SCENT, on the drums. VOLBEAT's inaugural product would be a six song demo 'Beat The Meat'. The band signed to New Aeon Media, a subsidiary of Holland's Karmageddon Media, for a debut 2004 album.

Ambrosius Locus, Dominus (1992) (Cassette demo). Intro: Ambrosius Locus / Blood Falls / Obscurantist / Suffocation To The Holy / The Forth Dimension.
Sidereal Path Of Colours, Molon Lave MLR SP 031 (1993) (7" vinyl single). Sidereal Path Of Colours / De-Ice Dreams.
Astaroth, Dominus (1993) (Demo). Intro / The Darkest Deity / Into The Gods / Spiritual Mountain / Infected Cadaver Flows.
VIEW TO THE DIM, Progress RRS 942 (1995). Symphony Of The Goddess / Tears In Black / Bring Down The Roars / Spiritual Mountain / Awakening Of The Overthrown / View To The Dim / Lost Behind Scars / A Sign From The Cryptic Winter / The Blaze Of Valhalla / Sideral Path Of Colours / The Raven's Eye / Weiv Ot Eht Mid.
THE FIRST 9, Progress PCD-30 (1996). Dancing With Magic / Soul Damnation / Final Journey / The Burning Maid / Ancient Emperor / Next Living Obliging / Confront The 9 / Second Palace / The Crystal Demon / Final Journey (Part II).
VOL. BEAT, Progress PCD-40 (1997). No Matter What ... / Swine For A While, Pigs For A Week / The Path / Give Me The Reason / Beat, Booze, The Hooker's Lose / Billy Gun / Me And I / Action Please / How Sweet They Kill / From The Cradle Goes The Bell / The Call.
GODFALLOS, Progress PCD-57 (2000). Thine / The Act Of Organic Plastic / Seed From The Beast / Manipulated Destiny / Call #3 / Hypercane / The Face That Wouldn't Show / Antichrist / Cabbage / To Seek Her Scent / Angelsitter.

DOWNTHROAT

ANADIA, PORTUGAL — *Ricardo Arsenio (vocals), Hugo Silva (guitar), Marco Paredes (guitar), Ricardo Santos (bass), Paulo Serra (drums).*

Horror Grind merchants DOWNTHROAT, based in Anadia, credited themselves for the 1999 demo tape 'I've Got My Mothers Eyes' as Hugo—"Neoplasmatic strings & high-throat vomits", P.N.—"Uncontrollable & putrescent beat", Kurika—"Subthroat regurgitation", Ricardo—"Four strings' brutalization" and Mosh—"Spill decomposed strings". The band had been manifested by former PUTRESCENCE members Hugo Silva and Ricardo Santos. In December of 1997 the drummer P.N. (a.k.a. Paulo Serra) and guitarist Mosh joined the band, shortly afterward followed by singer Kurika (Ricardo Arsenio).

In 1999 DOWNTHROAT recorded material for the Czech label Bizarre Leprous Productions for split release with NEGLIGENT COLLATERAL COLLAPSE, COCK AND BALL TORTURE and FILTH 'We Both Have The Same Father'. Debut album 'Verminate' arrived in 2002.

I've Got My Mother's Eyes, (1999). Decomposed, Tortured And Devoured / Insane Cannibal Desire / Bloody Dream / The Hunter / Blow Up To Pieces / Ulceral Abdominal Decomposure.
DOWNTHROAT, Bizarre Leprous Productions (2001) (Split album with NEGLIGENT COLLATERAL COLLAPSE, COCK AND BALL TORTURE and FILTH). Monachus Monachus / Kurt The God / Miss Auschwitz '43 / Máj / Bloody Dream / Blow Up To Pieces / Ulceral Abdominal Decomposure.
VERMINATE, Independent (2002). Verminate / I See Blood / Frigid Grandma / Dying In Love / Open Chest With Fruit Salad / Windfall / Convulse Gastric Haemorrhage With Eggs / To Eve The Art Of Gore / Blood, Guts And Ice Cream / Life Is Beautiful / Mom And Dad ... / Face No More / Uncontrollable Discharge Of Blood And Pus.

DOXOMEDON

SINGAPORE — *Paat (vocals), Pearce Arai (guitar), Sham (guitar), Joehanis (bass), Azli (drums).*

DOXOMEDON is a Black Grindcore act founded as LIBATION during 1992 by NECRONANISM vocalist / bassist Paat, guitarist Ash and drummer Zul. This group would switch names to ITNOS for the less than tactfully titled EP 'Christ Mary Bitch' released on the Dutch Superior Creation label in 1994.

ITNOS folded with Zul (as Dajjal) joined ABBATOIR and IMPIETY. Paat reassembled a new band with erstwhile MIXES guitarist Jumaat and former MARTYRDOM drummer Azli for the promotional cassette 'Hymnenic Promonancy'. By 1997 the band had filled out with second guitarist Sham, previously an OSSUARY member.

December 1998 witnessed further changes with the enlistment of ex-HARVESTER guitarist Pearce Arai and former OSSUARY and MARTYRDOM bassist Joehanis. With this line up the group adopted the new title of DOXOMEDON. The band featured on the Dwell Records LED ZEPPELIN tribute 'Dead Zeppelin' with their take on 'Living Loving Maid'.

EVANESCE, Darkartz (1999). Prismythic Refractious / In Portal Somnolent / Embrace In Solace / Evanesce.

DRAMATVM

GUADALAJARA, MEXICO — *Cecilia Ledesma (soprano vocals), Roberto Perez (death vocals/guitar), Alfonso Tobias (guitar), Daniel Estrada (bass), Angela Ramirez (keyboards), Luis Santana (drums).*

The Guadalajara band DRAMATVM was conceived in the Summer of 2003 under a formative title of VESANIA by MELANCHOLY members soprano vocalist Cecilia Ledesma, drummer Abraham Banda and guitarist Roberto Perez in union with guitarist / keyboard player Alfonso Tobias. That October, MELANCHOLY performed its last concert and VESANIA became an active unit. Banda would exit and the following month another MELANCHOLY veteran, German, took over bass whilst Enrique Real was also added to the line up. The bass role was soon taken by Daniel Estrada and In February of 2004 the revised project title of DRAMATVM was adopted. The demo 'Index Dramatvm' followed. Further changes saw the introduction of keyboard player Angela Ramirez in September and drummer Enrique Real being replaced by Luis Santana.

Index Dramatvm, Pancho Villa (2004). Profetia / Violent Storm / Vesania / My Domains / Violent Storm (Instrumental).

DRAWN AND QUARTERED

SEATTLE, WA, USA — *Herb Burke (vocals), Kelly Kuciemba (guitar), Greg Reeves (bass), Matt Cason (drums).*

Uncompromising Death Metal band initially founded in Seattle, Washington as PLAGUE BEARER. Evolved into DRAWN AND QUARTERED in 1996 drafting bassist Greg Reeves the following year. DRAWN AND QUARTERED issued demos and

DRAMATVM (pic: Angela Ramirez)

had their track 'Open Mind' included on the compilation album 'Eat The Evidence' issued on Morta Coil Records. Drummer Matt Cason also operates in side act SERPENT'S AEON. Other band members have also resurrected PLAGUE BEARER.

DRAWN AND QUARTERED completed their fifth album, entitled 'Merciless Hammer Of Lucifer' for Moribund Records, in February 2007. The album was recorded at the Autopsy Room with Jesse O' Donnell and mastered by Kevin Nettlingham. The first 3,000 copies included a bonus CD of rare and unreleased tracks, including the 2002 EP 'Crusaders Of Blasphemy'. Also issued in 2007 would be a limited edition gatefold vinyl pressing of 2005's 'Hail Infernal Darkness'.

TO KILL IS HUMAN, Moribund (1999). Ministry Of Torture / Machete Bloodbath / The Hills Run Red / Open Mind / Carnal Copulation / To Kill Is Human / Implements Of Hell / Christian Extinction / Broken On The Wheel / Punishment By Burning Torment / Mangled Beyond Recognition.
EXTERMINATION REVELRY, Moribund DEAD 45 (2003). Embrace Of Darkness / Incinerated Faithful / The Omens Await / Kill For My Master / Necrophile Decapitator / Worshippers Of Total Death / Sodomized And Butchered / Under The Chainsaw / Abyss Behind My Gaze / Show No Mercy.
RETURN OF THE BLACK DEATH, Moribund (2004).
HAIL INFERNAL DARKNESS, Moribund (2006). Procession Of Pain / Genocide Advocacy / Hail Infernal Darkness / Blood Of A Million Martyrs / Throne Of Desolation (Befowling The Scriptures) / Suffer A Traitor's Fate / Escape To Cremation / Bind, Torture, Kill / Nightghoul Of The Graveyards.

DREAM OF NEBIROS

MONTERREY, MEXICO — *Andres Lobo (vocals), Fernando Zuñiga (guitar), Joel (guitar), Beto (bass), Francisco Melendez (drums).*

Monterrey, Nuevoleon Doom-Death act DREAM OF NEBIROS, oddly describing themselves as "Romantik Anal Metal", was created in 1994. The group operated as Spanish language, Thrash Metal combo BLACK HATE until 1996. In this guise the band cut the 1996 demo 'And The Soul Cannot Trespass The Dream'. The group then evolved into NEBIROS briefly, then DREAM OF NEBIROS. Demos ensued in the form of 'From Passion To Bestiality' in 1998 and 'Ancient Poetry' in 1999.

The band's debut album 'Into The Critical Evolution' emerged in 2001, promoted with an expansive live schedule including supports to MARDUK, INCANTATION, SKINLESS and IMPALED NAZARENE. A change in musical direction to incorporate more sinister, Gothic sounds would be evident on the January 2003 follow up 'Naked In A Morbid Dream'. Tour dates included shows across Germany and a support to HYPOCRISY in March of 2004.

INTO THE CRITICAL EVOLUTION, Dream Of Nebiros (2001). Feel My Shadows Cut / Opening The Gates Of Anal Romance / Eternal Hypocrisy / Rabia Hypocrisy / Bestiality And Incitations In The Heart / I Engrossed / Lost Tears / Adagio / Death's Doom / Ignominy Shows And Soft Confusion / Journey In Autumn.
NAKED IN A MORBID DREAM, (2003). Intro / Pathetic Memories / Only Bizarre Dreams / A Pale Horse / To Prick My Eyes / My Goddess / Diary Of A Sex Addict / My Heart On Black Dimension / To Lure Temptation / Adagio / A Priest And A Dying Man.

DRIPPING

NJ, USA — *Frank Bleakley (vocals), Sebastian Russo (guitar), Tom Keiffer (bass), Bruce Moallem (drums).*

New Jersey Death Metal convened in late 2000 by former CADAVERMENT personnel guitarist Sebastian Russo and drummer Bruce Moallem. An initial line-up included DECEMBER vocalist / guitarist Jerry Sammarco and bassist Tom Keiffer.

Sammarco would quit before the end of the year. The band would soon be boosted back to quartet status with the inclusion of erstwhile UNHALLOWED, CARRION and COMATOSE RUST man Frank Bleakley. In late 2002 Sebastian Russo teamed up with New Jersey's MUTANIS CASTRATION appearing on their EP 'Traces Of A Mutilated Blasphemous Reality'. DRIPPING would also feature DISLIMB and FECAL CORPSE guitarist Mike Connors, later to found ALL HOPE IS LOST and subsequently enrolled into the ranks of New Jersey's MOURNING.

DISINTEGRATION OF THOUGHT PATTERNS DURING A SYNTHETIC MIND TRAVELLING BLISS, Macabre Memento MM 005 (2002). Escape Into Orbital Infinity (Introduction—First Chapter) / Through The Storm (Second Chapter) / Decomposed Fixation (Third Chapter) / Prelude To The Fallen (Interlude) / Passing Through The Spheres Of Abstract Thought (Fifth Chapter) / Within Myself (Sixth Chapter) / Reflecting Identities (Seventh Chapter) / Poisoning Reality (The End).

DROWNED

BELO HORIZONTE, MG, BRAZIL — *Fernando Lima (vocals), Marcos Amorim (guitar), Rafael Porto (guitar), Rodrigo Nunes (bass), Beto Loureiro (drums).*

Belo Horizonte Death Metal combo DROWNED was first assembled in 1994, undergoing various line up changes until settling in 1998 upon the formation comprising lead vocalist Fernando Lima, guitarists Thiago Rodrigues and Marcos Amorim, bass player Rodrigo Nunes and Beto Loureiro on the drums. That year DROWNED laid down the three song demo recording 'Where Dark And Light Divide ...'. Rafael Porto took the place of Rodrigues in March of 2000.

DROWNED signed to Cogumelo Records in March 2001 for the 'Bonegrinder' album, recorded during April and May and released that August. A Brazilian tour to launch the album would be suspended mid way through when guitarist Marcos Amorim was badly injured in a car accident. It would be early 2002 when the band, with Amorim fully recovered and issuing the 'Back To Hell' EP to coincide, reconvened the tour. 'Back To Hell' incorporated demo recordings, covers, new versions of old material, unpublished material and brand new songs. A further run of national dates, commencing in their hometown of Belo Horizonte, kicked off in August 2002.

In February 2003 DROWNED retired to their own studios to cut the 'Butchery Age' album. Released in June, 'Butchery Age' was backed up by a massive nine month long tour, lending support to German Thrash veterans DESTRUCTION along the way. DROWNED added new guitarist Kerley Ribeiro in August 2004 for recording of the album 'By The Grace Of Evil'. An internet only EP, 'By The Evil Alive', was recorded in concert in Belo Horizonte during November 2005.

Rodrigo Nunes exited and Wesley Ribeiro took over bass duties in May 2006. The group returned in September, unveiling a new album title of 'Bio-Violence' for Cogumelo Records.

Where Dark And Light Divide ..., Drowned (1998) (demo). Learn To Obey / Words From The Pit / Where Dark And Light Divide ....
BONEGRINDER, Cogumelo (2001). Who Is The King? / The Most Destructive Art / Men Who Break Bones / Third Master / Spiritual Force To Kill / Words From The Pit / Learn To Obey / Where Dark And

Light Divide . . . / Wisdom Without Direction / Praying For The One Who's Left / Blood Sand / Come And Taste The Victory.

BACK FROM HELL, Cogumelo (2003). Back From Hell / Rhymes Of Death / Demonic Cross / Evil Darkness Inside / The Curse / Bestial Devastation / Bloody Sand / Destroyer / The Laws Of Scourge / The Fucking Twins / Bone Grinder / Wisdom Without Direction.

BUTCHERY AGE, Cogumelo CG-0066 (2003). Butchery Age Has Come / When To Kill Is A Worthy Job / Hate If The Greater Thing To Feel / The Beginning End / Heros Die First / Massacre Is Justice / Cry Your Dead Away / Natural Born Killers / The Peace Comes To Destroy / Armies Of Dead Men / Reign Of Slaughters / Hell Made With A Certain Measure.

BY THE GRACE OF EVIL, Cogumelo CG 0073 (2005). XIII Chapter (Nothing Stops The Killing) / Hell March / No God For Apes / Only A Business / AK-47 / The Son Will Not Return / Godless Field / Kill The Lambs / Poke Your Wounds / All Will Be Fine (If We All Are Dead!!!).

By The Evil Alive, Cogumelo (2005). Hell March / Back From Hell / Who Is The King / . . . Only A Business / Butchery Age Has Come.

BIO-VIOLENCE, Cogumelo (2006). New Rome Arises / Bio-Violence / The Fossil Target / Genesis Of Chaos / Dead Sunshine For A Better World / People Born To Hate People / Eyes Bent For Own Navel / Drown The Revolution / The Friendly Oppressor / Hypnosis Against The Tribes.

DROWNED IN LIFE

LAHTI, FINLAND — *Janne Savolainen (vocals), Tomi Luoma (guitar), Antti Kokkonen (guitar), Raimo Posti (bass), Mika Tanttu (drums).*

Lahti melodic Death Metal act. DROWNED IN LIFE issued the demos 'For Me To Live For' in 2001, laid down at GrassRoots Studios, and 'Nothing Less Than A Rockstar', recorded and mixed at Sonic Pump Studios by Nino Laurenne, during 2002. Vocalist Jouni Sahiluoto exited in November of 2002. A self-financed EP, 'So Goddamn Beautiful', arrived in 2004.

DROWNED IN LIFE members guitarist Antti Kokkonen and drummer Mika Tanttu are also members of PROFANE OMEN. The latter is an ex-BEFORE THE DAWN member. Kokkonen, Tanttu, guitarist Tomi Luoma and bass player Raimo Posti also hold ties to KILL THE ROMANCE. Tomi Luoma has SOLACIDE credentials.

For Me To Live For, Drowned In Life (2001) (Demo). Vanishing Tomorrow / Dark Blue / Bridges / Not The One.

Nothing Less Than A Rockstar, Drowned In Life (2002) (Demo). Dead Child Within / You're Nothing / My Way Down.

So Goddamn Beautiful, Drowned In Life (2004). A Few Chosen Words / Fear New Day / Playground.

DSK

FRANCE — *Nicolas Boury (vocals), Pierre Antonik (guitar), Benoît Moritz (guitar), Kevin Lebas (bass), Marc Le Gigan (drums).*

Ultra Death Metal band DSK started life billed as DESCAMISADOS, including guitarist Olivier Delplace, drummer Sébastien Bizet, bassist David Galimidi and frontman Nicolas Boury and issuing a three track 1998 demo 'In Cold Blood' under that title. Bizet then exited, being replaced by Marc Le Gigan as the group also added second guitarist Benoît Moritz. As DSK ("Disruption of Soul and Kind") a further three song, eponymous demo arrived in 2000, after which Delplace exited to join Death Metal band VAKARM and Pierre from TRIDUS ELASTICUS joined the band in October 2001. Recording for the 'Ultra Death Metal' EP was completed then Galimidi decamped. Fred, singer of DECLINE OF HUMANITY, enrolled to handle both vocals and bass.

The 2004 album 'From Birth', recorded at Walnut Groove Studios, would come with a free album entitled 'Anything To Add?', this comprising demos, unreleased tracks and demos. Fred took his leave to prioritise DECLINE OF HUMANITY and erstwhile BRUTAL COCO man Kevin Lebas filled the gap.

ULTRA DEATH METAL, (2003). Introduction To Not / My Eyes Are Corrupted / En La Ciudad / My Fist / Te Asesinan / With My Organs / The Shell / Politics Of The Worst.

FROM BIRTH, Thundering (2004). Alive But Broken / My Fist / My Eyes Are Corrupted / En La Ciudad / Repudiate / Introduction To Not / Suffer Is Mine / With My Organs / Death K / The Shell / Policy Of Worst / Walls Of Confinement.

ANYTHING TO ADD?, Aberrent Productions (2004). Death K (video) / Policy Of Worst (video) / In Cold Blood / Repudiate / Chrysalis / My Eyes Are Corrupted / Forever Lost / Death K / Policy Of Worst / My Fist / En La Ciudad / With My Organs.

DWELLING MADNESS

BALTIMORE, MD, USA — *Eric Little (vocals / bass), Gary Daniels (guitar), Eddie Braun (guitar), Joe Roffeld (drums).*

Baltimore's DWELLING MADNESS was created during the late 80's as a quintet of vocalist Brian Chandler, guitarists Gary Daniels and Anthony Frederick, bass player Brian Suchy and drummer Benny DiDonato. Extensive line-up changes found a latter day version of the band hinged solely on surviving member Gary Daniels, now handling lead vocals, with new faces guitarist Eddie Braun, bassist Mike Stoecker and Joe Roffeld. DWELLING MADNESS demoed but eventually split.

Daniels teamed up with PESSIMIST during 1998, as did Roffeld following a stint with FORGOTTEN SOULS. During the summer of 2000 DWELLING MADNESS was resurrected by Daniels and Roffeld, bringing in former member Eddie Braun and another former PESSIMIST man Eric Little on vocals and bass. Frank Cusimano, of VILEXISTENCE, enrolled on guitar briefly then went on to the ranks of Jason Blachowicz's restructured DIVINE EMPIRE in July 2005.

The band lost the services of Eddie Braun, drafting Bill Hayden, formerly of F.O.G. and PESSIMIST as substitute. However, shortly afterward Eric Little also departed. Signing with Death Rape Records, DWELLING MADNESS entered the recording studio in March 2005 with producer Drew Mazurek to cut a full-length album 'Spawn Of Malevolence'.

Dwelling Madness, Dwelling Madness (2002). Viral Holocaust / Finger Of God / Blunt Expression Of Disgust / Prelude To Extinction.

DYING EMBRACE

INDIA — *Vikram Bhat (vocals), Jimmy Palkhivala (guitar), Jai Sarge Kumar (bass), Daniel Marc David (drums).*

Bangalore Doom-Death combo formed as MISANTHROPE toward the close of 1991. The formation, counting vocalist Deepak Prasad, guitarist Jimmy Palkhivala and Daniel Marc David on drums, cut an opening demo in 1993. Subsequently Prasad relinquished his role due to health reasons and Palkhivala assumed lead vocal duties until Vikram Bhat, an ex-member of Black Metal band OMINUS LEGIO, took control. Newly billed as DYING EMBRACE, in late 1997 the band, having inducted Jai Sarge Kumar on bass guitar, entered the studio to record a six song mini album entitled 'Serenades Of Depravity' for February 1998 issue. DYING EMBRACE followed up with the 'Grotesque' EP in 2000.

The band secured international interest and signed to the French concern Legion Of Death Records. First product would be a gatefold sleeve double 7" single hosting two new tracks alongside a brace of songs from the 'Grotesque' EP. The US label Bestial Onslaught also weighed in, re-issuing 'Serenades Of Depravity' for the North American market in 2003.

Misanthrope EP, Legion Of Death (2002). Blood Rites / Tromlech Of Hate / The Passing Away / Degeneration.

DYING FETUS

BALTIMORE, MD, USA — *John Gallagher (vocals / guitar), Mike Kimball (guitar), Sean Beasley (bass), Erik Sayenga (drums).*

Baltimore's DYING FETUS, originally titled for maximum shock value DEAD FETUS, was forged in 1991. The 1993 demo 'Bathe In Entrails' witnessed a membership comprising vocalist / bassist Jason Netherton, vocalist / drummer John Gallagher and guitarist Nick Spelelos. The band drafted guitarist Brian Latta in 1994 and drummer Rob Belton to issue demos commercially as the 'Infatuation With Malevolence', using this same title for a compilation of demos the following year. This self financed release led in turn to a deal with Pulverizer Records for the 1996 follow up 'Purification Through Violence'. Promoting this outing DYING FETUS toured North America on a package bill with MONSTROSITY and Canadians KATAKLYSM.

The group, having enlisted former DEITY drummer Kevin Talley, signed to German label Morbid Records for 1998's 'Killing On Adrenaline', with the album being released on their own label, Blunt Force, in the USA. The record betrayed some of DYING FETUS's Hardcore leanings as the band included an INTEGRITY cover song. A subsequent nine week touring spree included a headline performance at the 'Morbid Metalfest' in Germany. However, Latta would leave in December 1998 as DYING FETUS promoted one of their road crew Sparky Voyles, also an erstwhile guitarist with the infamous M.O.D., to plug the gap.

The group re-issued the 'Infatuation With Malevolence' debut through Blunt Force in 1999 complete with extra live tracks recorded in Germany. 2000 bowed in with the six track mini-album 'Grotesque Impalement' and a showing at another German festival, this time headlining the 'Fuck The Commerce III' festival. Before the year was out DYING FETUS had released the full length 'Destroy The Opposition' album through Death Metal specialists Relapse.

Netherton, Voyles and Talley departed in January 2001 to found MISERY INDEX. Netherton's initial replacement being DEPRECATED bass player Derek Boyer, before he was superseded by Sean Beasley from GARDEN OF SHADOWS. DYING FETUS toured America as part of the 'Death Across America' tour billed alongside Poland's VADER and CEPHALIC CARNAGE and DEEDS OF FLESH. The band drafted vocalist Vince Matthews, a veteran of SADISTIC TORMENT, MUCOUS MEMBRANE and AUTUMN DAWN, guitarist Bruce Greig and Erik Sayenga on drums.

DYING FETUS set out on a headline club tour of America in August 2001 with running mates PAINMASK, MASTODON and THE HOODS.

Gallagher, Voyles and Talley would also be operational with a Hardcore side outfit named KNUCKLE DEEP.

By September Netherton's MISERY INDEX band, issuing the 'Overthrow' EP, was to boast further ex-DYING FETUS personnel in guitarist Sparky Voyles and drummer Kevin Talley. The interplay between the two bands was highlighted in December when Voyles and Matthews united to found the Grindcore project CRIMINAL ELEMENT.

Guitarist Bruce Greig left DYING FETUS in March 2002. The band continued to play as a four-piece and joined forces with MONSTROSITY and HOUWITZER for the 'Intervalle Bizarre' European tour during September and October. Adding Mike Kimball to fill the second guitar position the band would form up part of an impressive cast for European 'Xmas Festivals' in December in alliance with SIX FEET UNDER, IMMOLATION, KATAKLYSM, MARDUK and HATE. However, DYING FETUS would pull out of the shows in October blaming a conflict of schedules for recording of a new studio album. The band united with HATE ETERNAL, KATAKLYSM, and INTO ETERNITY for North American dates in February and March 2003. They would act as headliners for a further package tour that May, coinciding with the release of the 'Stop At Nothing' album, topping a bill of SKINLESS, DIVINE EMPIRE and MISERY INDEX. Taking the band into 2004 would be January European dates, the band packaged alongside HATE ETERNAL, DEEDS OF FLESH and PREJUDICE. US shows in May had MALAMOR as support for a first leg prior to hooking up with road partners SUFFOCATION. Scandinavian shows in June saw the band partnering with MALEVOLENT CREATION upfront of planned further European gigs. However, these shows would be cancelled within days of the start date, the band blaming disorganisation by the promoter. Following September gigs in Mexico a further national US tour, dubbed 'Mock The Vote' commencing on 26th October in Norfolk, Virginia, would be as support to GWAR. However, just beforehand DYING FETUS parted ways with vocalist Vince Matthews, stating "This action was taken due to a number of musical, professional, and personal reasons that we feel do not need elaboration at this time." Yet more changes for these gigs saw the addition of session drummer John Longstreth, of ORIGIN, SKINLESS, THE RED CHORD and EXHUMED, in replacement for a temporarily unavailable Erik Sayenga. Meantime, Sayenga fired up side project WARTHRONE, a union with ex-WITCH-HUNT, NECROPSY and SANGUINARY singer Richard Johnson and ex-WITCH-HUNT, WARFAIR and DARK PURITY keyboard player / bassist Kristel.

In February of 2005 former DYING FETUS members Vince Matthews and Bruce Greig allied with the MISERY INDEX credited drummer Matt Byers to forge a new project billed as COVENANCE. Meantime, DYING FETUS forged a road alliance with SIX FEET UNDER, DARK FUNERAL, DISBELIEF, NILE, WYKKED WYTCH and CATARACT for the 'No Mercy Festivals 2005' European tour beginning in early March. Drummer Erik Sayenga left DYING FETUS "due to circumstances beyond his control" in early May. Sayenga was replaced by Duane Timlin.

Ex-drummer Kevin Talley acted as fill in for THE BLACK DAHLIA MURDER in February 2006 and joined the ranks of HATE ETERNAL in March. Another DYING FETUS credited sticksman, Erik Sayenga, recorded for Swedish band MORDICHRIST's debut album.

The band entered Hit & Run Studios in Rockville, Maryland during late September to cut fresh album tracks. November saw US dates for DYING FETUS backing CANNIBAL CORPSE, UNMERCIFUL and Germany's NECROPHAGIST.

DYING FETUS set 'War Of Attrition' as the title of their March 2007 album, recorded at Hit & Run Studios in Rockville, Maryland, issued through Relapse Records. Meantime, Night of the Vinyl Dead announced the vinyl release of 'Killing On Adrenaline', limited to 500 hand numbered copies and pressed in splatter vinyl with color insert. Frankie Nasso acted as director for a promotional video of the track 'Homicidal Retribution'.

European concerts, along with CATTLE DECAPITATION, SKINLESS and WAR FROM A HARLOT'S MOUTH, witnessed shows across Germany, France, Italy, Austria, Belgium, Holland, Norway, Denmark Ireland and the UK in May.

Bathe In Entrails, (1993) (Demo). Bathe In Entrails / Nocturnal Crucifixion / Wretched Flesh Consumption / Grotesque Impalement / Vomiting The Fetal Embryo / Tearing Inside The Womb.

Infatuation With Malevolence, (1994) (Demo). Eviscerated Offspring / Your Blood is My Wine / And The Weak Shall Be Crushed / Visualize Permanent Damnation (In E Minor 440) / Purged Of My Worldly Being.

INFATUATION WITH MALEVOLENCE, Wild Rags WRR-058 (1995). Eviscerated Offspring / Your Blood Is My Wine / ... And The Weak Shall Be Crushed / Purged Of My Worldly Being / Bathe In Entrails / Nocturnal Crucifixion / Wretched Flesh Consumption / Grotesque Impalement / Vomiting The Fetal Embryo / Tearing Inside The Womb.

PURIFICATION THROUGH VIOLENCE, Pulverizer PRCD004 (1996). Blunt Force Trauma / Beaten Into Submission / Skull Fucked / Permanently Disfigured / Raped On The Altar / Nothing Left To Pray For / Nocturnal Crucifixion / Skum (Fuck The Weak).

KILLING ON ADRENALINE, Morbid MR042 (1998). Killing On Adrenaline / Procreate The Malformed / Fornication Terrorists / We Are The Enemy / Kill Your Mother, Rape Your Dog / Absolute Defiance / Judgement Day / Intentional Manslaughter.

Grotesque Impalement EP, Blunt Force BFR004 (2000). Grotesque Impalement / Streaks Of Blood / Bringing Back The Glory / Tearing

Inside The Womb / Final Scream (Prelude To Evil: Davey's Nightmare) / Hail Mighty North—Forest Trolls Of Satan.
DESTROY THE OPPOSITION, Relapse RR 6463-2 (2000). Praise The Lord (Opium Of The Masses) / Destroy The Opposition / Born In Sodom / Epidemic Of Hate / Pissing In The Mainstream / In Times Of War / For Us Or Against Us / Justifiable Homicide.
Vengeance Unleashed, Relapse (2002) (Split single with DEEPRED). Vengeance Unleashed.
STOP AT NOTHING, Relapse RR 6549-2 (2003). Schematics / One Shot, One Kill / Institutions Of Deceit / Abandon All Hope / Forced Elimination / Stop At Nothing / Onslaught Of Malice / Vengeance Unleashed.
WAR OF ATTRITION, Relapse 766704 (2007).

DYSANCHELY

MARTIN, SLOVAKIA — *Lojzo Horak (vocals), Alena Pichlerova (vocals), Nela Horvatova (vocals), Milos Kosak (guitar), Dodo Zachar (guitar), Brando Glida (bass), Milan Lux (drums).*

The melancholic Doom styled Death Metal act DYSANCHELY came into being during 1995 in Martin, fronted by the male vocals of Lojzo Horak and female counterpart Zuza Grujbakova. The 1996 'Messengers Of Destruction' demo announced their arrival, followed up by 'Eternal Sleep' the same year. This latter tape would see DYSANCHELY enhancing their vocal sound with the addition of Alena Pichlerova.

A deal was secured with the Czech label Leviathan but upfront of recording the debut album 'Tears' Grujbakova decided to leave. Her replacement would be Nela Horvatova, later also a member of fellow Slovakian Doom merchants THALARION.

DYSANCHELY would adopt a more Black Metal stance for a cassette album 'Songs Of Sorrow' issued by Russian label Oupiric Productions. This release featured a cover version of KISS' 'God Of Thunder', new tracks and re-worked older material. A three song demo 'Secrets Of The Sun' surfaced in 2003. By this juncture the band unit was down to a quartet of vocalist / bassist Brano Glinda, guitarists Dodo Zachar and Milos Kosák with CRANIOTOMY man Lukash Shushka on drums. Shushka sessioned on GALADRIEL's 2003 album 'World Under Worlds'.

TEARS, Leviathan (1998). Century Of Inquisition / Return To The Hall Of Ages / Shadows Of The World / Eternal Sleep / Cruel Beauty / In The Dust Of Eternity / Tears / Instrument Of Extermination.
SONGS OF SORROW, Oupiric Productions (2000).
SECRETS OF THE SUN, Metal Age Productions MAP 045 (2003). Lullaby / About Man And Evil / Bloody Tears Of Contradictions / Song Of Sorrow / Lost In Beauty / Get What You Deserve / Secrets Of The Sun / Kill Your Love.

DYSENTRY

GERMANY — *Dirk (vocals / guitar), Robby (vocals / guitar), Mark (vocals / bass), Marcel (drums).*

A Grind act forged in 1990 as a trio of vocalist / guitarist Robby, bassist Mark and drummer Rico. By July of 1991 DYSTENTRY had recorded the demo 'Abnormal Faeces'. These sessions attracted the attention of the Poserslaughter label who in turn financed a 7" EP 'Pathological Waste . . . Disemboweled End. An album, '. . . Brings Me No Tears . . .', was released by the Dutch Lowland label in 1993. DYSTENTRY put out the 'Pro Patria' demo in April of 1995 after which second guitarist Dirk was brought into the fold. A further demo 'The Distance' surfaced in 1997.

Following the 'Spheres Of Insanity' album drummer Rico, after a twelve year stint, was replaced by Marcel during 2002. DYSENTRY would busy themselves on a new studio album 'Sickening Thoughts' in the latter half of the year.

Pathological Waste . . . Disemboweled End, Poserslaughter (1991). Pathologists Fun In The Morgue / Dysentery / Cremated Remains / Cadaverizer.
. . . BRINGS ME NO TEARS . . . , Lowland (1993). Sonic Pleasures Of Genital Pathology / With Pins And Chisels / Dermapathological Dreams / Siagolic Cruor / Bacterial Decomposition / A Purulent Torso / Abnormal Faecal / Siagolic Cruor (Mix) / With Pins And Chisels (Mix) / Dermapathological Dreams (Mix) / Cadaverizer II (Mix).
SPHERES OF INSANITY, (2002). Intro / Remains / Repulsive Passion / Mental Disagree / Repugnant Art Displays / To Satisfy The Eagerness / Paradizer / Go To Hell.

DÄRATH

BOGOTÁ, COLOMBIA — *Juan Carlos Ángel (vocals), Jorge A. Holguin (guitar), Juan Felipe Gutierrez (guitar), Daniel Cadena (bass), Jorge E. Rojas (keyboards), Gustavo Forero (drums).*

Bogata Death Metal act DÄRATH, founded in 1992, first emerged two years later with demo recordings featuring a line up of vocalist Juan Carlos Ángel, guitarists Jorge A. "Pyngwi" Holguin and Andrés Felipe 'Dooke' Duque, bass player Juan Diego Atehortua and Luis Enrique Arias on the drums. By 1995 the band had trimmed down to a quartet, losing the services of Dooke. That same year keyboard player Carlos A. Bedoya would be added for a cassette entitled 'Tiempo Perdido'. DÄRATH's debut album, 'El Nacimiento De La Diosa' produced by David Corkidi of KRONOS, was delivered in 1996.

Adding guitarist Juan Felipe Gutierrez and substituting Atehortua for Daniel Cadena and with Gustavo Forero now manning drums DÄRATH, having shed their keyboard player at this point, issued the independent single 'Que El Rock No Muera' in 1998. In 2002 the band, losing Gutierrez, introduced keyboards back into the band courtesy of Jorge Enrique Pardo.

EL NACIMIENTO DE LA DIOSA, Discos Fuentes (1996). Preludio / Cautivo / Yo No Te Debo Amar / Tiempo Perdido / Ciclos Ocultos / Fuego Del Olvido / Eres Sombra / Basta / Noche De Rock / No Puedo Dejarte / Ruinas En Soledad /. Epílogo.
Que El Rock No Muera, Independent (1998). Que El Rock No Muera / Me Faltas Tú.
UFOs, Schizophrenic (1998). UFOs / Cautivo (En Vivo).
TIME STONE, (2003).

EBONY TEARS

STOCKHOLM, SWEDEN — *Johnny Wranning (vocals), Conny Jonson (guitar), Thomas Thun (bass), Iman Zolgharnian (drums).*

Stockholm Death Metal combo dating to 1996. EBONY TEARS vocalist Johnny Wranning also operated with MISCREANT and DOG FACED GODS. Guitarist Conny Jonson is also a DOG FACED GODS man. Eventually the membership of DOG FACED GODS mirrored EBONY TEARS with the recruitment of ex-BULLDOZER bassist Peter Tuthill and drummer Richard Evensand with the two bands functioning in tandem. Evansand has a diverse range of credits spanning Funksters SORCEROR, IT'S ALIVE, SOUTHPAW, MANIC DEPRESSION and EYEBALL. Following three albums, 1998's 'Tortura Insomnia', 1999's 'A Handful Of Nothing' and 'Evil As Hell' in 2001, Wranning exited, forging EYETRAP in November 2000 in collaboration with erstwhile SHATTRD personnel guitarist Fredrik Rhodin, bassist Joakim "Chucken" Rhodin and drummer, Jan Karlsson.

In June of 2003 Evansand was announced as new drummer for the swiftly rising SOILWORK. Before the year was out he had joined US outfit CHIMAIRA. Evansand also racked up credits with DEMONOID, THERION and LIONS SHARE. Johnny Wranning announced his new band MURGHATROID in 2004, a union with ex-THERION drummer Sam Carpenter (a.k.a. Sami Karppinen).

In early 2007 it was revealed Evansand was also involved with a high profile side act, DEAD BY APRIL, featuring M.A.N guitar player Martin Meyerman, DRAGONLAND guitarist Olof Mörck, bassist Staffan Persson of WHEN WE FALL plus the PAINFIELD, DEATHDESTRUCTION and NIGHTRAGE credited singer Jimmie Strimell.

Ebony Tears, (1996) (Demo). Spoon Bender / Nectars Of Eden / Forbidden Thoughts.
TORTURA INSOMNIA, Black Sun (1998). Moonlight / Freak Jesus / Nectars Of Eden / With Tears In My Eyes / Involuntary Existence / Opacity / Spoonbender / Evergrey / Skunk Hour.
A HANDFUL OF NOTHING, Black Sun (1999). Inferno / Harvester Of Pain / A Handful Of Nothing / Scenario / When Depression Speaks / Erised / Cosmical Transformation / The End.
EVIL AS HELL, Black Sun (2001). Deviation / Soulcrusher / Outraged / Negative Creep / Lowdown / Hands Of Doom / Lucified ... Evil As Hell / Demon Ride.

ECHOES OF SILENCE

MONROVIA, CA, USA — *Leviticai.*

Monrovia, California symphonic Black Metal project ECHOES OF SILENCE is mentored by Leviticai as a solo concern. The endeavour began life during 2000, then billed as MIDNIGHT MASQUERADE. Rebranded as ECHOES OF SILENCE the demo 'Echoes In The Night' was released in January 2001, this closing out with the CRADLE OF FILTH cover version 'Saffron's Curse'. Anno Satannas Records released the June 2004 album 'Where No Sun Shines'. The December 2005 album, 'Raven Dusk', featured former GORTHYRMUS man Lord Onigumo on keyboards and guitars. Somewhat strangely, the June 2006 EP 'Tears Of Our Past Lives', restricted to only 20 copies, featured a cover version of 'Machinehead', originally by BUSH.

Echoes In The Night, Echoes Of Silence (2001) (Demo). Lust For The Grave / An Unmarked Grave / Under An Ancient Moon / Lament / Congregation Of Souls / Graveyard Of The Ancients / Into The Mist Of The Night / Vampiric Erotica / Drowning In Despair / Sands Of Time / Saffron's Curse.
WHERE NO SUN SHINES, Anno Satannas (2004). Screams In The Dark / Rituals In Blood / Babylonian Whore / Spiritus Mortis / Where No Sun Shines / The Withering Rose.
Thy Darkest Desires EP, (2005). The Darkside Of The Moon / Thy Darkest Desires / A Doomed Lover / Spiritus Mortis.
WITHIN DARK WATERS, Anno Satannas (2005). The Forest Whispers My Name / Underneath The Past / Lost Chapter / Apparitions Of Hatred / Visions Of Despair / Upon Lost Shores (Within Dark Waters).
RAVEN DUSK, Anno Satannas (2005). The Shadow Garden (Intro) / Midwinter's Night (The Caressing Darkness) / Beyond The Veil Of Sorrow / Ravendusk / In Silent Mourn / A Midnight Masquerade (Outro).
The Fall Of Angels, (2006) (Demo). Chapter One: The Fall Of Mortals / Chapter Two: Hidden In The Dark Shadows / Chapter Three: Streams Of Angel's Blood.
Tears Of Our Past Lives EP, (2006) (Limited edition 20 copies). Till Death Do Us Part / On A Moonless Night / My Remaining Hours (Left To Live) / Machinehead.
YOUR UNDYING BEAUTY, (2006). Candlelight Serenade / Till Death Do Us Part / The Verses Of Autumn / The Asylum Of Souls / On A Moonless Night / Prison Of Tears / My Remaining Hours (Left To Live) / Sewing The Threads Of Damnation / Embrace Of The Night's Wind / Buried In The Crimson Sea / In The Graven Image / The Eternal Sleep / Your Undying Beauty.
DEAD WINTER NIGHTS, (2006). Necromantic Lust / Raped Of Faith And Innocence / The Source Of Dark Light / The Pungent Stench Of A Soul's Decay / Buried Deep In Solitude / Sculptured In Unholiness.

ECITON

COPENHAGEN, DENMARK — *Jesper Bøeck (vocals / bass), T.C. Vibe (guitar), Thomas Berg (guitar), Jesper Frost (drums).*

Copenhagen melodic Death Metal band ECITON began life in 2000 billed as INDESPAIR, releasing the 2004 Lars Schmidt produced album 'Oppressed By Contempt', issued through French label Adipocere Records, under this prior title. Recording line-up would stand at ex-ANXIETY NEUROSIS singer Jesper Bøeck, guitarist T.C. Vibe, bassist Søren Maiboe with Lars Poulsen of AFFLICTION on drums. However, following this release Søren Maiboe died and Paulsen would subsequently depart. Regrouping under the ECITON brand, the group introduced Jesper Frost of INIQUITY and THORIUM on drums together with guitarist Thomas Berg of JEEL, ANXIETY NEUROSIS, JANTEFAX and SATAN ASSAULT.

OPPRESSED, Adipocere CDAR99 (2005). Butchering The Helpless / Cynical Exploitation Of Mankind / Waiting With Regret / The Excitement / Fuck Your World / Slaughter Of The Innocent / Someone Suffers / In Good Faith / Sanguinity Dreams.

EDENBEAST

SONDERBORG, DENMARK — *Steen G. Knudsen (vocals), Kristian Bjorn Olesen (guitar), Christian Przemyslaw Zalewski (guitar), Erik Nielsen (bass), Christian Mindedahl (drums).*

Sonderborg Death Thrashers EDENBEAST date back to an earlier formation entitled NECROPOLIS, which issued two demos, 'Twilight Destinies' in 1998 and 'Ungracious Cruel Art' during 1999. As EDENBEAST they bowed in with a 2003 promotional set entitled 'Prozac Party Songs', recorded at Sonderborghus with producer Asmus Thomsen. In 2004 the band donated their version of 'Blind In Texas' to the W.A.S.P. tribute album 'Shock Rock Hellions—A Tribute To W.A.S.P.' issued through Denmark's Valhalla Records. EDENBEAST guitarist Chris Przemyslaw Zalewski has ties to AURORA.

Both singer Steen Knudsen and bass guitarist Erik M. Nielsen opted out in 2005. Kristian Bjorn Olesen duly switched over to bass.

Prozac Party Songs, Edenbeast Demo (2003). Frameworld / Embrace The Neon Sun / The Heart Cages.
Promo 2004, (2004). Bring Out Your Dead / Mute / Embrace the Neon Sun—Redistorted / The Heart Cages -Redistorted.

EDENSHADE

MACARETA, ITALY — *Lorenzo Morresi (vocals), Stefano Wosz (guitar), Daniele Tiberi (bass), Massimiliano Wosz (keyboards), Roberto Cardinali (drums).*

EDENSHADE is a Macareta based melodic styled Death Metal act dating to 1998 and fronted by ex-SYNAPTIC singer Lorenzo Morresi. The band issued the 'Shades Of Duality' session in 1999 and the 'Love Injuring Criteria' demo, recorded at the Outer Sound Studios in Rome with Giuseppe Orlando and Massimiliano Pagliuso of NOVEMBRE, in December 2000. The band signed to Negatron Records for a debut album but this deal collapsed. A new deal was soon inked with the Atrheia concern and EDENSHADE, working in the studio with former producers Orlando and Pagliuso once again, cut the 'Ceramic Placebo For A Faint Heart' in Rome for a Spring 2003 release.

Keyboard player Matteo Belli exited in late 2003, being replaced by SYNAPTIC's Massimiliano Wosz in January 2004. EDENSHADE recorded a new album in 2005, 'The Lesson Betrayed'. During these sessions the band also cut a cover version of DEPECHE MODE's 'In Your Room'.

Shades Of Duality, (1999). Lost The Spark / Bohemian's Agony / Innocence / My Morbid Grey.
Love Injuring Criteria, (2000). A Fact Of Egoism / The Inconstancy Of April / Love Injuring Criteria / A Particular Shade Of Bliss.
CERAMIC PLACEBO FOR A FAINT HEART, Atrheia (2003). The Pathology Of Incest / A Fact Of Egoism / (Untitled) / Unreasonable Heartbeating Diminuendo / The Inconstancy Of April / The Elegant Curse Of Understanding / Some Pain We Shared / Part 2 / Stigma.9 / Scent Of A MidSummer Dawn.

EDGECRUSHER

IEPER, BELGIUM — *Davy Bauwen (vocals), Jo Decaesteker (guitar), Isaac Delahaye (guitar), Stijn Vanpeteghem (bass), Karel Willemyns (drums).*

Melodic Death Metal band forged as a trio of guitarist Jo Decaesteker, bassist Freddy and drummer Sientje in 1999. Upfront of sessions for the opening demo 'Damnatio Memoriae' the band inducted singer Davy Bauwen and second guitarist

Isaac Delahaye. Upon completion of these tracks Thijs Lanoye took over the bass role.

Sientje exited in the Winter of 2001 and the band utilised GOD DETHRONED drummer Ariën Van Weesenbeek for recording the 2002 demo 'Impressions Of Mankind', subsequently enrolling Michael Maes onto the drum stool. Further line up changes saw the introduction of a fresh rhythm section of bassist Stijn Vanpeteghem and drummer Karel Willemyns.

EDGECRUSHER guitarist Isaac Delahaye joined GOD DETHRONED in August of 2004.

Damnatio Memoriae, Edgecrusher (2000). Ungodly / Drained From Life / Demise Of Words / Instrumental #4 / Eyes Wide Shut / Evilution.

Impressions Of Mankind, Edgecrusher (2002). The Power Of Mankind / The Netherworld / Enslaved By Earth / Evilution / Veiled In Silence / Grief Of A Shattered Soul.

EDICIUS

FRANCE — *Insane (vocals / guitar), Alpha. Eion (bass / keyboards), Icon (drums).*

A Black Metal Grindcore band out of Nancy. EDICIUS was originally borne as a solo project of vocalist / guitarist Insane but subsequently evolved to a trio. After EDICIUS had released the 2000 album 'Adimirantum Noctes' on TFU Productions Alpha. Eion, owner of the label, was added to the band.

Alarmingly the first 100 copies of the April 2002 EDICIUS album 'Ce Que Tu Dois Honorer' came with a free suicide kit! Contained within was a razor, syringe and rubber strap.

EDICIUS members all pursue outside Grindcore projects. Insane operates with DETRITUS DE FOETUS AMORTS, drummer Icon is a member of BLOCK whilst Alpha.Eion has duties with LES CHIOTTES.

ADIMIRANTUM NOCTES, TFU Productions (2000). Effroi Du Néant / L'odeur Du Sang / O.B.S.C.U.R. / Prière / Nécrologie / (Untitled) / Messe Suicide / Peine Eternelle / D.O.D.E.M.N. / Mon Subconscient / C.H.V.I.S. / Pleures . . . Que Je Ris.

AEON, Deadsun (2001). Ogden Blut / Gothic Breed / Tremendous Unknown / Misericordious Insane / Bledemon / At Mo s Phe Res / Ravaged / By Cold Anger / And The Pleasure / Of Death . . . .

CE QUE TU DOIS HONORER, Deadsun (2002). Soul Obedience / Endemic Prosternation / Obitus Lugere / Succulent Crisis / Ex Nihilo / Doléance / Izenblood / Anti-Human Chronicles / Mitleid / Bloodifier.

ELENIUM

VANTAA, FINLAND — *Jukka Pelkonen (vocals), Tommi Leinonen (guitar), Kasperi Heikkinen (guitar), Tuomo Räisänen (bass), Johannes Salo (keyboards), Mikko Niemelä (drums).*

Vantaa raised Death Metal act ELENIUM forged by the trio of vocalist Jukka Pelkonen, guitarist Okko and keyboard player Johannes Salo. Subsequent additions included second guitarist Daavid, bassist Tuomo Räisänen and drummer Mikko. As such ELENIUM was formed officially in August of 1995.

In April of 1998 ELENIUM added former BOREALMS man Tommi Leinonen as second guitarist. ELENIUM released the demo 'This Side Of Paradise' in 1998, re-released that same year as a CD single by Hella Records. Okko decamped in 1999 and unfortunately much of 2000 would see the band on hiatus as various members undertook their national military service. Salo took time out to perform with SOULSTREAM. Kasperi Heikkinen was inducted as second guitarist in the Autumn of 2001.

The three track 'Them Used Gods' demo surfaced in 2002, this session scoring the band an album deal with the British Rage Of Achilles label provisionally billed as 'For Giving—For Getting'. ELENIUM, OMNIUM GATHERUM, AMORAL, MANITOU and KIUAS united for the November 2004 'Dead Achilles' tour of Finland.

In May 2006 Jukka Pelkonen was confirmed as new vocalist for OMNIUM GATHERUM.

This Side Of Paradise, Hella (1998). This Side Of Paradise / Shades Of Grey / Your Immortal Kiss.

FOR GIVING—FOR GETTING, Rage Of Achilles ILIAD046 (2003). Up The Long Ladder / Eye For A Lie / Impostor / Nameless–Faceless / Moments / Subcreator / Under The Mug / Few Gone Wrong / 6-Missing.

EMBALMING THEATRE

SWITZERLAND — A 2000 single, a split effort with Belgian veterans AGATHOCLES entitled 'Even Shakespeare Fed The Worms', for the Czech Paranoia Syndrome label saw EMBALMING THEATRE taking on a cover of EXTREME NOISE TERROR's 'Murder'. Two further split releases arrived in 2001 were shared with UNHOLY GRAVE and FINAL EXIT.

The 'I Can Smell That They Are Dead' album of 2002, which included rendition's of REPULSION's 'Bodily Dismemberment' and AGX's 'Big One', was restricted to a miniscule production of just 50 copies. EMBALMING THEATRE's January 2003 split 7" single 'Web-cam In My Coffin' shared with TERRORISM included a cover version of S.O.B.'s 'Not Me'. The 2003 album 'Sweet Chainsaw Melodies' saw a cover of EXUCLERATION's 'Gastric Purulence'.

Quite incredibly the band shared a track on the July 2005 'Unlawful Grindcore Assembly' 7" split single issued by Nuclear Barbecue Party Records as a collaborative effort with SAYYADINA, PESTILENT DECAY, GATE, WATCH ME BURN, BLOODRED BACTERIA, MIERDA PARA TODOS, CARA DE MIL PUTASOS, FETUS EATERS, DEADFOOD, THE KILL, TU CARNE, WASTEOID, PINATA LAZER, UNHOLY GRAVE, GORED FACE, GODSTOMPER, KERUM, NUKEM, UNHOLY SEMEN, 2 MINUTADREKA and COPROPHAGIGS.

Even Shakespeare Fed The Worms EP, Paranoia Syndrome (2000) (Split single with AGATHOCLES). Intro / Beyond Recall / Even Shakespeare Fed The Worms / Murder.

Catapult For Steaming Cadavers EP, Paranoia Syndrome (2001) (Split single with UNHOLY GRAVE). Intro / Catapult For Steaming Cadavers / Monotonous Copulation Machine / Bite Of The Dead / Anthropophagus / Outro.

I CAN SMELL THAT THEY ARE DEAD, Independent (2002) (Limited edition 50 copies). Intro / Dead, Stolen, Hacked Up And Raped / Undead In The Morgue / Someone Else In My Coffin / The Asian Penis Elevator / Rape The Cadaver / Shoes Made Of Human Skin / Bodily Dismemberment / Catapult For Steaming Cadavers / Bite Of The Dead / Dead, Stolen, Hacked Up And Raped (Live) / Shoes Made Of Human Skin (Live) / Big One (Live).

Cardinal Pad. O Phile EP, Nuclear BBQ Party (2002) (Split EP with FINAL EXIT. Limited edition of 503 copies). Cardinal Pad. O Phile / United Pest Control / Topless But Mummified / Mine In The Voting Booth / Burn Body Burn.

SWEET CHAINSAW MELODIES, Razorback (2003). Intro / Execution By Hanging Is Not A Game / Export Of Corpses / Dive For The Dead / 4 Brains, One Hand And One Foot In My Luggage / Wretched Rat Barbeque / We Ate Daddy / She Ate Her Flesh / A Leg Is In The Mail / Shoes Made Of Human Skin / Intermezzo / Someone Else In My Coffin / Chatroom For Impalers / Dead Stolen, Hacked Up And Raped / Buried Alive II: Breath Of Cancer / Gastric Purulence / Crash The Hearse / Topless But Mummified / Chemical Solution For A Rotten Problem / Corpse On Board / Bags With Heads.

Web-cam In My Coffin EP, Morbid Reality (2003) (Split EP with TERRORISM. Limited edition 1000 copies). Web-cam In My Coffin / Rotten Corpses Wherever I Look / Not Me / Outro.

EMBEDDED

OSNABRÜCK, GERMANY — *Rainer Düsing (vocals), André Danowsky (guitar), Christian Wösten (guitar), Matthias Puhr (bass), Thrawn (drums).*

Osnabrück based old school Death Metal act EMBEDDED was manifested in the Summer 1994 by vocalist / bassist André Müller, guitarist André Danowsky with Jens Wöstmann on drums. A 1996 demo tape would be capitalised on by gigs supporting MANOS, DEW SCENTED and KRABATHOR. Despite this progress EMBEDDED folded during 1998.

Danowsky revived the group in 1999, pulling in vocalist Markus Brunsmann, bass guitarist Ingo Neugebauer and ex-MORBUS drummer Jörg Heemann. That December this version of the band cut the EP 'Fragments Of Horror' over a three day session, releasing this outing in May of 2000. Toward the close of the year EMBEDDED expanded with the addition of second guitarist Kai Schweers. Perverted Taste heightened their profile further with a split cassette release shared with Austrians DISASTROUS MURMUR.

Rainer 'Nefarius' Düsing, of THE VAST, replaced Brunsmann for the group's appearance at the 2001 'Fuck The Commerce IV' festival and the following 'Ludwigshafen Deathfest' in September. 'Banished From The Light', EMBEDDED's debut full length album, emerged through Revenge Productions in November. Dates in Finland, including a gig at the 'Westcoast Holocaust' festival in Turku, found EMBEDDED sharing stages with road partners DEEPRED and Swedish act IMMERSED IN BLOOD. Returning to mainland Europe the group also put in a showing at the Czech 'Obscene Extreme' event in Trutnov.

The band hit line-up troubles in September of 2002 with the departure of both Schweers and Neugebauer. BOUND FOR TOMB and THE VAST man Christian 'Mystif' Wösten took on bass duties. A few gigs later Philipp Jonas enrolled on guitar. EMBEDDED subsequently inducted Thrawn of SECRETS OF THE MOON on the drums and Matthias Puhr on bass, under his pseudonym of 'Ferneus' having prior affiliations with MARTYRIUM, BOUND FOR TOMB and MOSU KUMA.

Rainer Düsing donated guest vocals to KATAPLEXIA's 2005 album 'Catastrophic Scenes'.

FRAGMENTS OF HORROR, Independent (2000). Intro / Death Unfolds / Deliverance / Demonflesh / Fragments Of Horror / A Trace Of Death / The Forsaken Soul.

BANISHED FROM THE LIGHT, Revenge Productions (2001). Triple Corpse Horror / Hackknife Compensation / Creation Of Sin / Banished From The Light / The Scourge Of Oblivion / Stench Of Burning Flesh / The Obscene / World Within / Incarnate Impurity / Sadistic Demise / Loathing.

EMBERS LEFT

KERAVA, FINLAND — *Janne Kauppi (vocals), Ville Matti Vienonen (guitar), Olli Ojala (guitar), Janne Boman (bass), Eve Kojo (keyboards), Kalle Hytonen (drums).*

EMBERS LEFT is a Gothic Metal band, based out of Kerava and established during 1999. First product would be a demo entitled 'Cold Reflection', recorded in 2000 and featuring session keyboards from Risto Kokkonen of CAUSEMOS. Following release of the 2001 EP 'Chords Of Desolation' EMBERS LEFT, comprising now vocalist Janne Kauppi, guitarist Olli Ojala and bassist Janne Boman, added new guitarist Ville Matti Vienonen, keyboard player Eve Kojo and drummer Kalle Hytonen. Ex drummer Tapio Kanko promptly joined up with Deathsters STILLBURNED. A further demo effort, 'Failure', arrived in 2003. The group underwent severe fractures, disbanding in January 2004, re-formulating that June then dissolving again in January 2005.

Eve Kojo has association with both ABLAZE IN HATRED and Helsinki's MYGRAIN.

Cold Reflection, Embers Left (2000) (Demo). I Yearn / Dreaming A Lie / Like A Thorn.

Chords Of Desolation EP, Embers Left (2001). Taken Away / The Lost Name Of Love / Serene Illusion / Message On The Wind / Faithless.

Failure, Embers Left (2003). Stained (Failure pt. 1) / Forever Buried (Failure pt. 2) / Dishearten One.

EMBODIMENT

HARDERWIJK, HOLLAND — *Peter Hagen (vocals / guitar), Erik-Jan Brinker (guitar), Sebastian den Oudsten (bass), Martijn van Gene (drums).*

Harderwijk Death-Thrashers. The band was originally gathered as EMBODIMENT in 1994 by vocalist / guitarists Peter Hagen and Erik-Jan Brinker along with drummer Martijn van Gene and bassist Sebastian den Oudsten. Den Oudsten exited in 1996 to join up with CANISTER, subsequently going on to ART OF PREMONITION. The band put in its first concert on 13th December 1996, after which den Oudsten returned to the ranks as EMBODIMENT entered QSA Studios in Utrecht with producer Vincent Dijkers to craft the demo 'All Because Of Lust' in January 1998.

Bassist Danny van Helden was inducted during 2000 and shortly afterward the group subtly revised its title to THE EMBODIMENT. An EP, 'Razor Cut Reality', emerged in 2002. Peter Hagen went on to join Groningen's ENRAGED in 2004.

All Because Of Lust, Independent (1998). Insanity / 45 Years / Suicidal Thoughts / The Holy Way / Shattered Soul / My Own Misery.

EMBRACING

UMEÅ, SWEDEN — *Matthias Holmgren (vocals / keyboards / drums), Ronnie Björnström (guitar), Peter Uvén (bass), Nicklas Holmgren (drums).*

High standard Death Metal from Umeå. Founded in 1992, the cassette demo 'Beauty Found In Deep Caverns' was issued under a formative band title of MISHRAK. Previous to this a collective of five musicians had assembled under the banner of BEYOND, this unit comprising singer Henrik Nygren, guitarists André Nylund and Johan Westerlund, bassist Peter Lundberg and drummer Matthias Holmgren. Although the MISHRAK demo was committed to tape the group, unsatisfied with the final result, never distributed it to the public. Holmgren enrolled into NAGLFAR in 1995, cutting tracks for the 'Vittra' album, but then returned to MISHRAK.

Line-up changes saw Johan Westerlund quitting the band to play with OBERON (subsequently AUBERON), as well as the departure of Lundberg. Pulling in substitute guitarist Rickard Magnusson, and re-billed as EMBRACING, the second demo, 'Winterburn', arrived in 1995. Signing to the German based Invasion Records label the group debuted commercially with the 1996 album 'I Bear The Burden Of Time', these sessions seeing Jens Kidman from MESHUGGAH behind the desk. Magnusson then opted out and Mikael Widlöf was incorporated on bass. Second album 'Dreams Left Behind' followed a year later. With the demise of Invasion Records EMBRACING struck out on their own, putting out the EP 'Inside You' in 1998 and the 'Rift' session in 1999.

EMBRACING drummer and band founder Matthias Holmgren would lend lead vocals to SKYFIRE's December 1997 demo 'Within Reach'. Holmgren has also performed on the 1999 DEAD SILENT SLUMBER album 'Entombed In The Midnight Hour'. As a session drummer Holmgren features on the 1999 AZURE album 'Moonlight Legend'. EMBRACING drummer Nicklas Holmgren is an ex-NASHEIM member.

Guitarist Ronnie Björnström, of KNIFE IN CHRIST and PROGRESSIVE ACTS, would join the fold in 2002. EMBRACING issued the demo 'The Dragon Reborn' in 2003, ditching bass player Mikael Widlöf in September, after which rhythm guitarist Tomas Elofsson would be auditioned. Khaosmaster Productions re-issued 'I Bear The Burden Of Time' in 2004, adding no less than seven bonus tracks. Meantime, Thrashcorner Records re-issued 'Dreams Left Behind' hosting brand new tracks recorded with new bassist STAR QUEEN and XENOPAGE man Peter Uvén.

Holmgren would also be active with the TIRED TREE project. Ronnie Björnström contributed guest solo work to Black Metal band AZURE's 'King Of Stars—Bearer Of Dark' opus.

I BEAR THE BURDEN OF TIME, Invasion IR 022 (1996). Winterburn / Shades Embrace / On Wings Of Sadness / My Dragon Banner / I Bear The Burden Of Time / They Seldom Return / Thirst For Blood / Eternal Sear / Shapeless / A Last Breath Of Night.

Inside You, (1998). Emerald Eyes / Stop Crying / Inside You / Dragon Rage / Heroes Die In Battle.

DREAMS LEFT BEHIND, Invasion IR 031 (1998). Drown Inside The Illusion / Morningdew / Stolen Memories / Only Greedy Gods / Killers Nature / Long Time No seen / For The Angels For Me / The Good Old Days / Name It Tomorrow / Dreams Left Behind / Lay The Rose upon Her Grave.

Rift, (1999). Stranger / Chased By A Shadow / Precious Discovery / Rift.

EMBRAZE

KIIMINKI, FINLAND — *Lauri Tuohimaa (vocals / guitar), Olli-Pekka Karvonen (guitar), Sami Siekkinen (bass), Heidi Maatta (keyboards), Ilkka Leskela (drums).*

EMBRAZE, an atmospheric Gothically charged Death Metal outfit out of Kiiminki, were formed in late 1994 by frontman Lauri Tuohimaa, ex-CREATURE and KALLISTA KAKKAA, and drummer Ilka Leskela. The latter, also a 'veteran' of KALLISTA KAKKAA, was a mere 12 years old upon the bands formation.

Making up the inaugural unit would be female keyboard player Heidi Maatta, bassist Petri Henell and guitarist Juka Rytkonen. A succession of well received demo tapes, commencing with May 1995's 'Allotria', and consistent gigging would lead eventually to a coveted overall winner award at the Finnish Rock Championships. The group would also add two second places in the same competitions to their tally. An original billing of EMBRACE would soon give way to EMBRAZE

April 1998 saw EMBRAZE committed to commercial recording with the issue of debut album 'Laeh' for Mastervox Records with videos being shot for 'Amid Peals' and 'Charm Of The Wilderness'. The album caught the attention not withstanding it's fusing of Dark Wave and Death Metal but for it's inspired cover version of the KISS 70s Disco classic 'I Was Made For Lovin' You'. Before the close of the year work ensued on a second album and a cover of SLAYER's 'Chemical Warfare' was donated to the 'Straight To Hell' tribute record. Headline touring in Finland billed as the 'Dark Side Of Laeh' dates had AFTERWORLD as running mates.

In January 1999 in the midst of recording sessions both guitarists Janne Regelin and Janne Räsänen exited the ranks. The latter, who as well as acting as bassist for EMBRAZE was holding down guitar duties in ROOSTER, would team up with GRINSTER as a drummer.

However, the band persevered and 1999 would see the band sharing the stage at the 'Nummirock' festival sharing the stage with countrymen CHILDREN OF BODOM and STRATOVARIUS and international artists such as DREAM THEATER, SLAYER and PANTERA. 1999 also brought the April release of the single 'Sin, Love And The Devil' and further recording sessions resulting in their second full-length album entitled 'Intense'.

Requested to return to the 'Nummirock' event once more EMBRAZE rubbed shoulders with bands such as MOTÖRHEAD, SCORPIONS, DANZIG and HAMMERFALL. They then headed for the 'Liosaarirock' Festival to share the stage with ANATHEMA, HENRY ROLLINS and PARADISE LOST. Further line-up shuffles would see both bassist Tony Kaiso and guitar player Markus Uusital decamping. Fresh blood came in the form of the NORMAL FIGURES and MAPLE CROSS duo of Sami Siekkinen on four string duties and guitarist Olli-Pekka Karvonen.

In May 2000 'Endless Journey' would garner valuable international media praise. The record would see global releases by MTM Metal in Germany, NEH Records in America and in Brazil on the Moria imprint.

During March of 2002 Lauri Tuohimaa was announced as part of the formation of a Finnish 'Gothic Metal supergroup' dubbed FOR MY PAIN. Joining him in this endeavour would be the ETERNAL TEARS OF SORROW triumvirate of bassist Altti Veteläinen, guitarist Olli-Pekka Törrö and drummer Petri Sankala, keyboard player Tuomas Holopainen of NIGHTWISH and fronted by REFLECTION vocalist Juha Kylmänen.

In parallel with their main band activity, the bulk of EMBRAZE would also co-exist as Thrash side project MAPLE CROSS. EMBRAZE entered Studio 23 in Oulu during August 2005 to craft a new album. A promotional video clip for the track 'The One' was shot with director Marko Siekkinen.

Finnish and Baltic States concerts in September saw EMBRAZE acting as openers to MOONSPELL.

LAEH, Mastervox MXVCD2 (1998). Charm Of The Wilderness / Dead Spring / Fragments Of Life / Autumn Child / Close My Stage / Mystic / I Was Made For Lovin' You / This Moment / Amid Peals / Sweet Hate / Stream Of Emptiness / Little Reaction.

Sin, Love And The Devil, Mastervox (1999) (Finnish release).

INTENSE, Mastervox MVXCD10 (1999). Sin, Love And The Devil (Single edit) / This Cold Day / Rain And Moon / Endless Journey / Passion / One Moon, One Star / Shame / Sin, Love And The Devil (Album version) / Looking Ahead Into The Embrace Of Hell.

ENDLESS JOURNEY, MTM Metal 1704-7 (2001). Whispers / Lost / Endless Journey / Robot Stud / Passion / Tenderness / One Moon One Star / This Cold Day / Lethal Dance / Looking Ahead To The Embrace Of Hell.

KATHARSIS, Low Frequency (2002). My Star / Beautiful Death / Fear / The Sun Loves Moon / Filthy Angels / Subzero / Frozen Sun / Closed / Calm And Distant / Kiiminkijoki / Sinmaker.

THE LAST EMBRACE, (2006). Carvings On The Gallowstree / Branded / Racing Against Time / Dead Roses / Liquid Fire / Memory Trace Of Our Time / The One / Sleeping Ground / Sun Goes Down / No Solace. Chart position: 29 FINLAND.

EMBRYONIC

AKKERHAUGEN, NORWAY — *Vegard Tveitan (vocals / guitar / bass), Tomas Haugen (guitar / bass), Ronny Johnson (drums).*

Akkerhaugen's EMBRYONIC, initially founded as DARK DEVICE then XERASIA, was a forerunner of THOU SHALT SUFFER. The XERASIA trio comprised vocalist / bassist Finn Arne Nielsen, guitarist Tomas Thormodsæther Haugen with Ronny Johnson on drums. A 1990 live rehearsal demo was issued under the XERASIA banner prior to a name change EMBRYONIC, having replaced Nielsen with Vegard Sverre Tveitan (a.k.a. Ihsahn) and releasing the demo 'The Land Of Lost Souls', recorded in November 1990 at Notodden Lydstudio. Subsequently the act morphed again into THOU SHALT SUFFER during 1991.

Tomas Haugen would later come to the fore as Samoth, citing high profile credits with ARCTURUS, BURZUM, EMPEROR, ILDJARN, ZYKLON, ZYKLON B, SATYRICON, SCUM and GORGOROTH.

The Land Of The Lost Souls, Embryonic (1990) (Demo). Intro / The Land Of The Lost Souls / Throne Of Blood / Morbid Silence.

EMETH

ZELEM-HALEN, BELGIUM — *Tom Kimps (vocals), Matty Dupont (guitar), Peter Goemaere (guitar), Gregory Hal (bass), Tom Ales (drums).*

EMETH is a Zelem-Halen, Limburg based act dating to October 1997 as a Metalcore orientated outfit, adding former NECRODOCHION drummer Tom A. during March of 2001 as they switched to a technical Death Metal stance. Signing to the Brutal Bands label the band entered Excess Studios in Rotterdam during September 2003 to lay down their debut album 'Insidious'. The album saw release in June 2004 and was promoted by European festival performances at the Belgian 'Brame fest' and 'Deathmetal.be' event, the 'Obscene Fest' in the Czech Republic and 'The Mezz' in Holland. US dates in August, dubbed the 'Brutal Domination' tour, had EMETH allied with Colombians INTERNAL SUFFERING, Swedish act STABWOUND and US Deathsters INCINERATE.

Guitarist Peter Goemaere joined the ranks of ABORTED in October 2006. The 2007 album 'Reticulated' was recorded at

Excess Studios. Gurgloroth Sven of ABORTED guested. In June EMETH partnered with FUCK THE FACTS and HEAPS OF DEAD for dates across Ontario, Canada.

INSIDIOUS, Brutal Bands (2004). Impermance Of Being / Catatonic Entanglement / Manifestation / Mitigated Enmity / Endemicy Preordained / Stratum / Archaic Halos / Mimetic Conflation / Aeon.

RETICULATED, (2007). Eleven / Fallacy Of Reason / Karmic Impediment / Heteronomy Of The Will / Concentric Diversions / Predestined To Persevere / Order From Chaos / Synoptical Incoherence / Nescientia.

ENACTMENT

ORADEA, RUMANIA — *Yosha (vocals / guitar), Devi-Ques (programming / keyboards).*

Oradea Progressive Metal act ENACTMENT, a duo comprising vocalist / guitarist Yosha and keyboard player Devi-Ques, was founded as FORSAKEN PRINCEDOM in the spring of 2002. switching title to ENACTMENT the album 'Tides Of Darkness', self-described as "Gothenborgian Death Metal", was released in 2004. Guest appearance included female vocalist Beatrix on the track 'When Stars Disappear' and Vásári Loránt from Lory Studios, who also directed the video for 'Tides of Darkness'.

ENACTMENT would then change style to Progressive Metal. A second album, entitled 'Adamant Rage', saw release in January 2006, with a new guest female vocalist, László Viktória, followed by an EP billed 'Stygian War', recorded as a soundtrack to a computer game. Third album 'Forsaken Princedom' was scheduled for November 2006, this including cover versions of songs by IN FLAMES and IRON MAIDEN. Studio guests included Finnish guitarist DarkShadow and Hungarian female vocalist Morvai Szilvia. Work on a fourth release, 'The Swanson Project', was underway.

TIDES OF DARKNESS, Enactment (2004). Black Enactment / Runaway / Virus / Tides Of Darkness / When Stars Disappear / The Dawn / Under Wicked Skies / Haunted / Mindcrime / God Of Tears / Chaos Scanner.

ADAMANT RAGE, Enactment (2006). Intro / A Drifting File / Adamant Rage / Chaos Scanner / The Inner Side Of Loneliness / Drowning In The Fountain Of My Own Will / Instinct Revisited / Rest In Tears / Module 666 / Subject Of The Transmission.

Stygian War OST, Enactment (2006). Call To Power / If I Could Dream / Ode To An Eagle / Bloodmoon.

THE FORSAKEN PRINCEDOM, Enactment (2006). The Final Breath / Clay Man / Ode To An Eagle / She's A Maniac / Kids / No Prayer For The Dying / Instinct I.T. / Runaway (Live) / Rest In Tears (Live) / Haunted (Live).

She's A Maniac, Enactment (2006). She's A Maniac (Album Version) / Wings Of Light (Demo) / She's A Maniac (Russian Version) / Mod 666 (Edit) / She's A Maniac (Hungarian Version) / KidZ (Stomach-Ache Version).

END OF GREEN

GERMANY — *Michael Huber (vocals / guitar), Oliver Merkle (guitar), Michael Setzer (guitar), Rainer Hampel (bass), Matthias Siffermann (drums).*

Formed in 1991 as a six piece band END OF GREEN first played Punk influenced Rock, but the group got heavier after the firing of the original singer and keyboard player. The group recorded two demos as label interest grew and Nuclear Blast wound up signing them. Bassist Jürgen Hees quit before the recording of the debut album, which was recorded as a trio before END OF GREEN added Rainer Hampel. However, at the end of 1996 the group parted company with Nuclear Blast. During 1999 Michael Setzer, formerly of German Death Rockers INNOMINANDUM enrolled.

Bass player Oliver Merkle and drummer Mathias Sifferman would go on to form the initial line up of Doom act VOODOO SHOCK in league with erstwhile NAEVUS man Uwe Groebel. However, the pair had vacated this band in the Spring of 2001. END OF GREEN's 2002 album 'Songs For A Dying World' included a cover version of TYPE O NEGATIVE's 'Black No. 1'.

The band are active outside of the END OF GREEN parameters. Michael Setzer aids Grindcore band ICHEHERNTION as session guitarist whilst Michael Huber has released demos with the acts NOOSE and DIE FUGE. He would also figure as guest vocalist on the track 'Slope' on the UNDERTOW record 'UnitE'. Rainer Hampel also operates project Band DYING JULIA. Promoting the May 2003 album 'Last Day On Earth' END OF GREEN put in festival performances at the 'Summer Breeze' in Germany', 'Metal Fest' in Austria and the Swiss 'Metal Dayz' events. A full scale European tour in September was plotted allied with label mates UNDERTOW.

END OF GREEN's August 2005 album 'Dead End Dreaming', released through Silverdust Records, entered the German charts at no. 99.

INFINITY, Nuclear Blast 27361 61402 (1995). Left My Way / Away / Seasons Of Black / Infinity / Tomorrow Not Today / Sleep / You / Nice Day To Die / No More Pleasure.

Believe EP, Subzero (1998). My Friend / I Don't / Believe.

BELIEVE, MY FRIEND, Sub Zero SZ 004 (1998). Civ / Eternity / Noise Breath / My Friend / Fallen Angel / My Way / I'm Waiting / Downfall / Weak / Believe . . . .

SONGS FOR A DYING WORLD, Silverdust SD006 (2002). Motor / Only One / Death In Veins / I Hate / Astrobastard / Everywhere / Godsick / Mirror / Black No. 1 / Myra.

Motor EP, Silverdust SD002 (2002). Motor / Onlyone / Black No. 1.

LAST NIGHT ON EARTH, Silverdust (2003). Evergreen / Tormented Sundown / Demons / Dying In Moments / Queen Of My Dreams / Tragedy Insane / Highway 69 / Melanchoholic / Emptiness—Lost Control.

DEAD END DREAMING, (2005). Chart position: 99 GERMANY.

END ZONE

RUSSIA — *Igor Lobanov (vocals / guitar), Oleg Mishin (guitar / keyboards), Roman Senkin (bass), Valeri Dedov (drums).*

Moscow based Gothic Metal band END ZONE was created in 1993 by frontman Igor Lobanov, with bass guitarist Roman Senkin and drummer Valery Dedov joining up shortly after. This trio took over a year in locating a suitable lead guitarist, finally settling on Oleg Mishin. END ZONE employ flute, keyboards and female backing vocals on their increasingly adventurous catalogue.

END ZONE's debut album 'First Bequest' arrived in 1995, released on cassette by the Russian Aria label, and found the band in distinct Thrash- Death territory. Extensive gigging across Russia culminated in an appearance at the Polish 'Shark Attack 7' festival.

During February of 1996 the Metal Agen imprint re-issued 'First Bequest' on CD format. That same year END ZONE inducted keyboardist Alexander Dronov and drummer Oleg Milovanov into the ranks. This version of the band commenced recording a Evgeny Trushin produced entirely instrumental album entitled 'Thalatta Et Thanatos' for Metal Agen. Amongst the compositions would be Metal reworks of classic masters such as Handel, Grieg and Tchaikovsky.

A third album, 'Eclectica' issued in 1998 comprised four new tracks, a cover version of SEPULTURA's 'Refuse/Resist' and an ambitious interpretation of Mussorgsky's 'Khovanschina'. Igor Lobanov would aid with session vocals on Progressive Metal band NORDREAM's 2000 album 'Memories Progression'.

THALATTA ET THANATOS, Metal Agen (1996). Overture / Thalatta / End Zone / Baba-Yaga / Roma / Elements / Death Of Tsar (Dedicated To Russian Emperor Pavel I) / Passacaglia / The Edge Of String (Turbo version) / Parkinson's Ballet / Castle Of Woman Of Mine / Cobalt / Night Of The Sun / Dance Of The Lore / Outflow.

ECLECTICA, Metal Agen (1998). Alpha / The Vortex Of Reality / Hovanchina (Final) / Dual Infinity / The Remedy / Refuse / Resist / Afterwards.

ENDLESS

CANADA — *Justin Serr (vocals / guitar), Shawn Davidson (vocals / bass), Kevin Morgan (drums).*

Death Metal band out of Scarborough, Ontario, created as MORBID FEROCITY during the early 90s. Founding members comprised vocalist / bassist Derek Yee, guitarists Justin Serr and Anthony Prugo with Mike Kirejczyk on drums. A name switch to PAGAN SAVIOR ocurred prior to the departure of Prugo in March of 1992 after which a further title change to ENDLESS was put into force upfront of their inaugural live showing in August of that year. Subsequent notable support gigs in the Toronto area included gigs with both ENTOMBED, INFERNAL MAJESTY and OBITUARY.

In the summer of 1994 Derek Yee parted ways with the band, his position on bass being filled by Shawn Davidson. ENDLESS inducted lead vocalist Tom Ellis in early 1995, this line up recording the demo 'Life Drawing'. Subsequently Ellis decamped, the group responding by utilising both Serr and Davidson to share the lead vocal role. Unfortunately, ENDLESS were struck by another set back in October 1996 as Mike Kirejczyk left the band to concentrate on his university studies. Shortly after he was replaced on drums by a close associate Kevin Morgan.

During late May 1997, the band set to work on their debut album 'Beauty, Tears And The Setting Sun' at Toronto's Studio 92. After several set backs the record was released in April 1998.

BEAUTY, TEARS AND THE SETTING SUN, (1998). Children / Defeat / Doomed / Smoke / A Weeping Mist Reveals / In Stone He Creeps / The Unrest / Shame Of Deeds Past / Cry My Ecstasy / Everlasting Dream.

ENDLESS TORMENT

BIRMINGHAM, UK — *Barney (vocals), Jez (guitar), Robb (guitar), Caygill (bass), Steve (drums).*

Birmingham's ENDLESS TORMENT, created in 2002, underwent a succession of line-up changes marking its evolution from a Death-Gore outfit up to their 2004 Progressive Death Metal stance. After cutting the 2004 demo 'Endless', featuring a cover version of DEATH's 'Symbolic', the band enrolled new guitarist Andy in February and drummer Stu, replacing Tim Wilson, in April. Gigging across the UK in June saw the band uniting with DESECRATION. Yet more member changes found Andy replaced by Si, Robb being installed on bass in place of Dee and Steve taking command of the drums. ENDLESS TORMENT again underwent member changes, installing Caygill on bass as Robb switched back to guitar.

Live work during 2005 saw the installation of Robb Philpotts of THE ENCHANTED and BLOODSTREAM on guitar.

Endless, Endless Torment (2004). Endless / The Elusive Truth / The Utopia Machine / Symbolic.

ENDYMAERIA

TWENTE, HOLLAND — *Michiel Lankhorst (vocals), Bram Ueffing (guitar), Ylona Gerritsen (bass), Silvana Jirka (viola), Ronnie ten Vregelaar (drums).*

A Gothic styled extreme Metal band hailing from Twente, ENDYMAERIA notably included CAEDERE members vocalist Michiel Lankhorst and guitarist Niels Ottink. The group evolved from a prior formation, SIGNS OF ZODIAC, founded in 1998 and which had issued the 2001 demo 'Evil Spirits'. Bassist Ylona Gerritsen had pre-SIGNS OF ZODIAC been a member of ORSMEER whilst drummer Ronnie ten Vregelaar, also an active member of SATANAPHOBIA, had been involved with DEEP REST and PUKE.

Viola player Silvana Jirka, a member of the Apeldoorn Symphony Orchestra, debuted with ENDYMAERIA in May of 2002. Niels Ottink left the ranks in March 2003, being replaced by Bram Ueffing from HILLS OF ETERNITY. However, both Ueffing and keyboard player Joost Schuttelaar exited in December 2004.

Invocation, Endymaeria (2003). Realm Of Betrayal / Land Of Shadows / Invocation.

ENFORCE

PERTH, WA, AUSTRALIA — *Guy Bell (vocals / guitar), Rob Hartley (guitar), George Gallafallou (bass), Troy Watson (drums).*

Perth's technical Death Metal outfit ENFORCE debuted in March 1998 with the 'Premonition' demo. The group had been forged two years earlier by vocalist / guitarist Guy Bell, guitarist Rob Hartley and drummer Tim White, the latter soon to depart because of back injuries. For the 'Premonition' sessions the band installed a fresh rhythm section of bassist Dave Dow and drummer Ben Cody. 300 cassettes were manufactured, which quickly sold out. In May of 1998 Cody backed out and that September Rory Ward was enlisted.

Signing to the Singapore based Sonic Wave International album the August 2000 ENFORCE album 'Campfire Night' was recorded by a line up comprising Bell, Hartley, bassist Thomas Foster and drummer Graeme Stone. For subsequent live work another new rhythm team was drafted in bass player Dave Sandstrom and drummer Troy Watson. George Garofallou took over bass duties in February of 2001, featuring on the second album 'Message Of Death', issued by Graveyard Records in Australia in October of 2003 and by Sonic Wave International in 2004.

ENFORCE lost the services of bassist George Garofallou, due to "personal reasons and commitments to his faith", in December of 2003. A January 2004 support gig to DESTROYER 666 saw ENFORCE performing as a trio minus bass.

ENFORCE paid tribute to late PANTERA and DAMAGEPLAN guitarist "Dimebag" Darrell Abbott with their rendition of 'By Demons Be Driven' being donated to 'The Art Of Shredding—A Tribute To Dime' assembled by DarkStar Records.

CAMPFIRE NIGHT, Sonic Wave International (2000). Nuclear War / As Death Sets In / Slayer / Brutal / Campfire Night / Stalker / N.D.E.F.D. / Infections / Darkness.
MESSAGE OF DEATH, Sonic Wave International (2003). Testinal Embowlment / Expression / Sick, Sick, Sick / The Few, The Many & The Far Inbetween / Message Of Death / Afterburner / Constellation Of Planets / All Of You / Born Of Two Worlds / First Assault.

ENFORSAKEN

ARLINGTON HEIGHTS, IL, USA — *Steven Sagala (vocals), Joe DeGroot (guitar), Steve Stell (guitar), Eric Kawa (bass), David Swanson (drums).*

ENFORSAKEN, originally intended only to be a side venture, was founded in Arlington Heights, Illinois during March of 1998 by guitarist Steve Stell and drummer Pat O'Keefe, members of DEADPORNSTAR and THE FALLEN. A December 1998 demo emerged, both tracks also putting in an appearance on the compilation album 'Orchestrated Chaos 3' on Soulside Records. The exposure afforded by these tracks prompted Wisconsin based Immortal Records to offer ENFORSAKEN a deal but due to lack of personnel of which to form a full band this opportunity had to be turned down. The ENFORSAKEN project would then be laid to rest for a good six months.

During early 2000 ENFORSAKEN would be reinvigorated with the inclusion of THROUGH ASHES members vocalist Steven Sagula and guitarist Joe DeGroot. Newspaper adverts eventually located bassist Eric Kawa to finalise the line up.

Live action then ensued, an early gig found ENFORSAKEN sharing the stage with DISMEMBER, SHADOWS FALL, KATAKLYSM and KRISIUN. Matt Bachand of SHADOWS FALL and Lifeless Records extended an offer and the band debuted with the Chris Djuricic produced 'Embraced By Misery'. The cover art would be executed by Carlos Del Olmo Holmberg, keyboard player for Sweden's SOILWORK. The Lifeforce label would license the album for Germany during September, this version adding a cover version of 'Incarnated Solvent Abuse' by CARCASS as a bonus track.

The band added drummer David Swanson (a.k.a. G Reymond). This latest recruit would double up his duties with his other act VENIFICUM. ENFORSAKEN signed to WWIII Records for North America, the 'Embraced By Misery' album being re-issued with extra tracks and retitled 'Into The Everblack'. Guitarist Joe de Groot also operates Doom band AVIDOST.

US dates had the band united with USURPER, EPOCH OF UNLIGHT and headliners ENSLAVED for a tour of the Midwest and East Coast commencing July. The band pulled in new bassist Adam Simon in December of 2003.

A new studio album, entitled 'The Forever Endeavor', would be set for release in February of 2004. Mastered by the DISINCARNATE, DEATH, CANCER, TESTAMENT and OBITUARY guitarist JAMES MURPHY the esteemed axeman also donated a guitar solo to the track 'All For Nothing'. Japanese versions of 'The Forever Endeavor', issued on 29th September through Soundholic Records, added four additional bonus songs including the cover of CARCASS' 'Incarnated Solvent Abuse'. The band set 'Sinners' Institution' as a provisional title for a 2005 album. However, ENFORSAKEN parted ways with Olympic Recordings that April. In side activity, ENFORSAKEN guitarist Steve Stell re-united with erstwhile drummer Patrick O'Keefe to forge side project THE SOULSELLERS.

The 'Embraced By Misery' EP would see a re-issue in August through Cartel Media, the revised version, clad in all new artwork, adding tracks from the band's 1999 demo plus an electro remix of 'Of Open Wounds' by Novalex. During October ENFORSAKEN revealed that the 'Sinner's Intuition' album, recorded in Wisconsin with producer Chris Djuricic, included guest vocal performances from EDGE OF SANITY, BLOODBATH, NIGHTINGALE and PANTHYMONIUM mentor DAN SWÄNO.

The group ceased operations in June 2006, issuing a statement "After eight years of existence, we have decided to lay ENFORSAKEN to rest". A final show at Chicago's Metro venue was scheduled for August 19th. That same month ENFORSAKEN vocalist Steven Sagala guested on Japanese Metal band SIGH's 'Hangman's Hymn' album.

EMBRACED BY MISERY, Lifeless (2001). Of Open Wounds / The Acting Parts / Embraced By Misery / Dead Light, Dead Night / Into The Everblack / Standing In The Shadows.

THE FOREVER ENDEAVOR, Olympic (2004). Tales Of Bitterness / The Forever Endeavor / A Break From Tradition / Vertigo Equilibrium / Dead Light, Dead Night / Cloaked In Need / The Acting Parts / Poison Me / Redemption The Death Of Vanity / All For Nothing.

ENGORGE

LYNDHURST, NJ, USA — *Kyle Powell (vocals), Omar Davila (guitar), Desmond Tolhurst (bass), Gian Davila (drums).*

Lyndhurst, New Jersey's ENGORGE comprise erstwhile DISCIPLES OF MOCKERY and NEBULA 666 members. Not to be confused with the Dutch Death Metal act of the same name that released the 'Awaiting To Subside' album. The origins of the band lay in vocalist Kyle Powell's early 90s act FRAGMENTATION, an extreme Metal act founded whilst Powell was serving in the USAF at March air force base in California. Beginning life in 1991 FRAGMENTATION, a trio of Aluukard on vocals, Urthon on bass and Fej on both guitar and drums, released a 1993 EP 'Prelude To Evil' and a 1994 full length album 'Black Death' through Powell's own Eviscerated label.

The original ENGORGE band unit, created during 1996 comprised of vocalist Kyle Powell, Craig Pillard of INCANTATION, DISCIPLES OF MOCKERY and WOMB on guitar, second guitarist Mike Boyce of DISCIPLES OF MOCKERY and FAUST, bassist Ronnie Deo, again of INCANTATION, DISCIPLES OF MOCKERY and WOMB and ex FAUST drummer Bill Vessey. Powell had previously acted as a stand in drummer for Death Metal act MORTICIAN. The band announced their arrival in low key fashion with the demo session 'The Winter Of Pathological Hate', restricted to a mere 20 copies.

The band underwent a complete overhaul during 1999, Powell being joined in his endeavour by guitarist Matt Troost, bassist John Tobin and drummer Douglas Maxwell. This quartet issued the six track 'Grave Desecration' demo before Maxwell decamped, later to join SUFFER, the following year. Tobin shifted over to occupy the drum stool whilst Bart Traylor of New Jersey's SANGUINARY took over the bass position.

After a further demo 'Enchanted By The Battles Of Azazel' ENGORGE issued an extremely rare album. The 'Within The Realms Of Blasphemous Fornication' CD was pressed in only 100 copies. By this juncture bass was now in the hands of Mitch Coken, a veteran of New York's HEAD TRAUMA.

Yet again, within the space of a year, ENGORGE's line up shifted with both Troost and Tobin losing their positions. The pair would later wind up with DIEGRINDED LEFTOVERS. Standing alongside Powell, Coken and a returning Mike Boyce for the promo cassette 'Blood, Urine, Semen ... The Order Of Defilement' would be drummer Gian Davila and ex APOTHEOSIS and ABYSMAL MALEVOLENCE guitarist Anthony Prieto.

ENGORGE would not enjoy stability for long. Boyce decamped once again and Powell, Coken and Davila welcomed onboard BLOODTHRONE members guitarists Omar Davila and Josef Magnus. This version of ENGORGE released the promotional mini album 'Necroinsemination' in

By 2002 ENGORGE had been whittled down to a trio of Powell and the Davila brothers, cutting the album 'Dead ... Fuck ... Blackness'.

Guitarist Mike Boyce (as 'Demonian') would wind up as lead vocalist for Black Metal band BLOODTHRONE and later LIFE DECEIVER. During March of 2002 ENGORGE drafted MORTICIAN, HEAD TRAUMA and MALIGNANCY veteran Desmond Tolhurst into the ranks as their new bass player and set about recording a fresh album 'Ravenous Horde Of Darkened Gods' for 2002 issue.

Kyle Powell also operates as vocalist and drum programmer for the Black Metal act DARK AUTUMN HYMNS in league with Cythraul of ABAZAGORATH in tandem with ENGORGE. This side venture issued the cassette demo 'I Am The Horned King', limited to just 50 copies, during 1996. This demo would be slated for a CD re-issue in November 2002. Powell also has a further adjunct to his career with EVOKED DAMNATION, a band venture in alliance with Will Rahmer of MORTICIAN.

Omar Davila, who also has his own Black Metal act MORTE GENESIS, amicably parted ways with the band in September. Stepping in as substitutes would be the twin guitar team Arawn and Dalkiel of Black Metal act ALGOL. Dalkiel would join up first, debuting with the band at a record release party on August 3rd. ENGORGE would then engage in laying down material for the album 'Ravenous Horde Of Darkened Gods'. In January of 2003 longtime drummer Gian Davila bowed out, being replaced by GARDEN OF SHADOWS man Bret O'Connor.

ENGORGE parted ways with bassist Mitch Coken in May of 2004, drafting Randell Salmon of DECOMPOSED for West Coast dates. The summer of 2005 witnessed national US touring, the band heading up a billing alongside NECROPHAGIA, TYPHUS and SUMERIA. These shows included appearances at the 'Return Of Darkness And Evil' and 'Milwaukee Metal Fest' events.

WITHIN THE REALMS OF BLASPHEMOUS FORNICATION, Eviscerated (2000). Intro / Pagan Holiday / Rites Of Crucifixion / Deranged Perversion / Enchanted By The Battles Of Azazel / Morbid Demons / Sexorcist ... / Vampyric Blood / Buried Alive / Outro.

NECROINSEMINATION, Eviscerated (2001) (Promotion release). Intro / Morbid Demons … / Travelling By Orcan Fields / Endless Abyss / Rites Of Crucifixion / Outro.

DEAD-FUCK-BLACKNESS, Dark Horizon DHR013 (2001). Channeling The Antichrist To The Bleeding Altar / Gravedom Within The Chasm / Travelling The Orcan Fields … / Vampyric Blood (New version) / Morbid Demons … / Endless Abyss / Morte Genesis / Rites Of Crucifixion / Enchanted By The Battles Of Azazel / Legions Of The Incubus / Dead … Fuck … Blackness / Blissful Impregnation Of The Lusting Angel Of Christ.

BEREFT OF LORDSHIP … 11 YEARS OF MALICE, Dark Horizon (2007). Intro / NecroBlackDeath Machine / Morbid Demons In The Wake … / Gravedom Within The Chasm / Spiked With Lust Of Hell / Traveling The Orcan Fields To The Gates Of Seht / Endless Abyss / Kingdom Of Blackened Sexual Misanthropy / Ravenous Horde Of Darkened Gods / Legions Of The Incubus / Pathway To My Lustful Ruin / Morbid Demons / Rites Of Crucifixion / Enchanted By The Battles Of Azazel / Buried Alive / Pagan Holiday / The Gift Ov Urthon / Satans Millenium.

ENGORGED

NY, USA — *Dave Tentacle (vocals), Ryan Engorged (guitar), Noah (guitar), Kevin (bass), Shad Justice (drums).*

Classic groove orientated 'slice n' dice' splatter Metal out of Portland. ENGORGED include ex-LORD GORE guitarist Ryan in the ranks. The band debuted with an obviously Horror B movie inspired 1997 demo 'Death Metal Attack' before signing to the newly founded Razorback label to issue the inaugural album 'Death Metal Attack II'.

During 2000 ENGORGED contributed tracks 'Chemically Castrated' on the 'Gore Is Your Master II' and 'Dear Uncle Creepy' to the 'Wizards Of Gore' compilations, both on Razorback Records, and 'Swarming Vulgar Mass Of Infected Virulency' to the Necropolis 'Requiems Of Revulsion' collection. A split single with IMPALED also surfaced the same year. The band's second full length release, simply billed 'Engorged', was delivered through Necropolis subsidiary Deathvomit in June of 2002. Also projected for 2002 was a split album release with Australian extremists FUCK … I'M DEAD through No Escape Records.

ENGORGED personnel also operate in acts such as Black Metal act THY INFERNAL, GOUGER and FORNICATOR.

DEATH METAL ATTACK 2, Razorback (1999). Engorged / House Of The Dead / In Support Of Multi National Corp. / F.A.N.G.S. / Cobra H.I.S.S. / XVY Triad / Genital Finder / Chemically Castrated / Carpet Sharkin' / Sealed With A Klip (Kipland P. Kinkle) / Death Metal Attack II / Engorged / Huge Gaping Hole / XVY Triad / Death Metal Attack / Kings Of Beer / Legalize Child Porn / Raping The Full House Twins / Vomiting Butchers / Fangs / Encore.

Surgery, Drugs, And Rock And Roll, Discos Al Pacino (2000) (Split EP with IMPALED). Surgery, Drugs, And Rock And Roll.

ENGORGED, Deathvomit DVR016 (2002). March Of The Engorged / The Dreadnaught / It Came From Beyond / Cobra Rage / Eaten Alive! / Death Metal Attack III / White Line Nightmare / Slithis / Shockwaves / Beerguts / Night Of The Living Dead / Dawn Of The Dead / Day Of The Dead.

ENGRAVE

USA — Formed by the erstwhile BRAINSTORM triumvirate of Emilio Marquez, Mario Gutierrez and Adrian Villanueva alongside ex ENTITY man Robert Cardenas during March of 1997. A demo quickly ensued upfront of an appearance at the Milwaukee Metafest. This showing prompted S.O.D. Records to offer ENGRAVE a deal for 1998 'The Rebirth' album which included a take on SLAYER's 'Evil Has No Boundaries'..

A 1999 demo session 'The Infernal Bleeding' arrived in 1999 sporting another cover version- this time SEPULTURA's 'Beneath The Remains'. Indeed, ENGRAVE would seemingly excel in the field of covers donating a plethora of tracks to various Dwell Records tribute albums including BLACK SABBATH's 'Johnny The Blade', RUSH's 'Anthem's, JUDAS PRIEST 'Sinner', METALLICA's 'Metal Militia' and MOTÖRHEAD's 'We Are The Road Crew' among others.

ENGRAVE's debut would be re-issued in 2001 by World War III Records complete with a extra three tracks. The band would also lose Villanueva the same year, drafting Jimmy Ash as replacement.

THE REBIRTH, S.O.D. (1998). Minister's Nightmare / The Infernal Bleeding / Secrets Of The Unknown / Morbid Dreams / Liar, Deceiver / Full Moon Rising / Raping The Earth / Storm Of Obliteration.

ENMORTEM

CHICAGO, IL, USA — *Bill Frickenstein (vocals / bass), Brian Laurence (guitar / vocals), Tim Frickenstein (drums).*

Chicago Death Metal trio ENMORTEM, established during 1996, comprised brothers vocalist / bassist Bill Frickenstein and drummer Tim Frickenstein alongside guitar player Brian Laurence. ENMORTEM issued the 1997 demo 'Bleeding The Sorrow', after which Laurence bowed out. Tom Flanagan was drafted on guitar for a second demo session, 1999's tuned down, doomier 'Their Blood I Offer The King'. Later that same year the trio utilised Sheffield Studio to record 'Manifestations Of Infernal Disgust'.

At this juncture the Frickenstein siblings forged side project WARSHIP in collaboration with guitarist Brice Dalzell of CORPSE VOMIT repute. Dalzell then quit CORPSE VOMIT, joining up with ENMORTEM. The quartet version of the band did not last long and Flanagan soon exited. A June 2000 demo cassette 'Barbaric Displeasure' was cut at RK Studios. The group subsequently evolved into THE EVERSCATHED as tracks were laid down for a debut album entitled 'Razors Of Unrest' in 2002. The band also issued the January 2003 demo 'Halted Glory'.

However, a major setback hit the band as Dalzell was severely injured at work, severing a nerve in his fretting arm. Just as Dalzell had fully recovered, a further accident ensued. In early 2005, Bill Frickenstein was to undergo surgery as he was injured too, tearing the bicep on his fretting arm.

A further demo, '… Again The Chains', arrived in June 2005. THE EVERSCATHED signed to Open Grave Records in May 2006 for the album 'Razors Of Unrest'.

Barbaric Displeasure, Enmortem (2000) (Limited edition. 325 copies). Malicious Oblation / Our Dead See / The Blood Red Cemetery / Crimson Onslaught / Halted Glory / Evil Bleeds On.

ENRAGED

GRONINGEN, HOLLAND — *Peter Hagen (vocals / bass), Martijn Linker (guitar), Ralph Evers (guitar), Douwe Talma (drums).*

Groningen Grind-Death act ENRAGED was formulated during 1997 by guitarist Martijn Linker and ex-ASFIVE drummer Douwe Talma. Despite enduring the instability of a fluctuating line up the band did commit to the demo 'Enraged I Revolt' in October of 1998. These recordings were completed with the aid of erstwhile DIABOLIQUE and LEGACY OF HATE vocalist Jitse Schregardus and another ASFIVE member Steven Jongma on bass guitar. These same tracks would be-reissued as the 'Tirade' demo in 1999.

The band was put into hiatus for a period during 1999 when Douwe Talma joined up with MORTUARY I.O.D. for tour work. ENRAGED then re-formulated enlisting Schregardus as a permanent member and adding ex-SPIRITUAL DISSOLVENT guitarist Ralph Evers. A 2001 EP 'Counterblast' was released through So It Is Done Productions and promoted with support dates to YATTERING in March of 2001.

Despite losing the services of Jongma ENRAGED worked up new promo recordings billed as 'Resist Or Serve—Promoting Our Contemptuous Resistance Against Human Treason' in 2003. Dates in 2004 saw ENRAGED aligned with GOREROTTED. That same year the band inducted new frontman Peter Hagen, a veteran of THE EMBODIMENT.

Tirade, Enraged (1999). Drown In Your Lies / Dictated By Misanthropy / Lower Species / Counterblast (Land Of Unknown).

Counterblast EP, So It Is Done Productions (2001). In Fury / Drown In Your Lies / Lower Species / Enraged I Revolt.

Resist Or Serve—Promoting Our Contemptuous Resistance Against Human Treason, Enraged (2004). Intolerable Misconduct / Below The Surface / Resist Or Serve / Confabulated To Defile.

ENSIFERUM

HELSINKI, FINLAND — *Jari Mäenpää (vocals / guitar), Markus Toivonen (guitar), Sami Hinkka (bass), Meiju Enho (keyboards), Oliver Fokin (drums).*

Melodically inspired Helsinki Death Metal band ENSIFERUM started life in 1995, founded by the trio of DARK REFLECTIONS man Markus Toivonen on guitar, Sauli Savolainen on bass and DARK REFLECTIONS drummer Kimmo Miettinen. This trio commenced rehearsals during January 1996 at the Pasila Youth centre in Helsinki. At the close of 1996 they were joined by Jari Mäenpää of IMMEMORIAL on guitar and vocals. ENSIFERUM put on an inaugural concert of sorts at their rehearsal rooms in December of that year. The gig comprised of just one song entitled 'Old Man'. However, Mäenpää's national service army duties stalled band progress for a while.

ENSIFERUM cut a debut three song demo, recorded at Kivi-Studios in November 1997. The following year Jukka-Pekka Miettinen stepped in as the new bass player and Oliver Fokin from ARTHEMESIA filled the drummer's role. Ironically Miettinen moved on to join ARTHEMESIA.

1999 witnessed two demo tapes, the latter of which was produced by Janne Joutsenniemi of SUB-URBAN TRIBE. This session secured a deal with the Spinefarm label for the debut 2001 album, recorded by Tuomo Valtonen in November 2000 at Sundi-Coop Studios in Savonlinna. Studio guests included FINNTROLL and BARATHRUM man Trollhorn on keyboards, Johanna Vakkuri with female vocals and Marita Toivonen on kantele. The band incorporated a fifth member, keyboard player Meiju Enho, upon completion of these sessions.

During 2001 Kimmo Miettinen enrolled into CADACROSS. He would soon be joined by Jukka-Pekka Miettinen, both maintaining their membership of ENSIFERUM. Upon completion of the Flemming Rasmussen produced 'Iron' album, recorded at Sweet Silence studios in Copenhagen, Denmark, ENSIFERUM severed ties with frontman Jari Mäenpää in January of 2004, the singer prioritising his side project WINTERSUN. Nevertheless, the band partnered with FINNTROLL for an extensive European tour in April, pulling in NORTHER's Petri Lindroos as session guitarist/vocalist. That same year Spinefarm Records included an exclusive ENSIFERUM track 'Tale Of Revenge' to their compilation album 'Spinetingler III'.

ENSIFERUM issued the single 'Tale Of Revenge', the B side of which included a cover version of METALLICA's 'Battery', as a taster for their new album 'Iron'. The record was recorded during the Summer of 2003 at Sweet Silence studios in Copenhagen, Denmark with producer Flemming Rasmussen. In October 2004 NORTHER's Petri Lindroos was announced as being a permanent member of the band, replacing Jari Mäenpää. More changes came in December when bassist Jukka-Pekka Miettinen, citing "personal reasons", exited. He would be swiftly replaced by Sami Hinkka. European touring in April 2005 had ENSIFERUM packaged with GRAVEWORM and COMMUNIC. Janne Parviainen of SINERGY, BARATHRUM (as 'Abyssir'), WALTARI, JIMSONWEED, ST. MUCUS and ZWANZINGER repute would temporarily be installed on drums but by September it was revealed this position had been made permanent.

The band was announced as engaged in the 'X-Mass Fest Part II' European tour, set to begin in early December and involving ENTHRONED, UNLEASHED, PRIMORDIAL and MORBID ANGEL. However, these dates would be pulled after UNLEASHED

ENSIFERUM (pic: Dimitri Borellini)

withdrew. Closing the year, the group put on a tenth anniversary celebration concert, taking place December 31st 2005 at the Nosturi venue in Helsinki. This show was filmed for the DVD release '10th Anniversary Live', which entered the Music DVD chart in their home country at number 2.

The band announced an EP release, entitled 'Dragonheads' and recorded at Sonic Pump studios in Helsinki, for early 2006 release. ENSIFERUM engaged in European touring in alliance with KNORKATOR, SPELLBOUND, NOISE FOREST and Israel's ORPHANED LAND during April and May. ENSIFERUM entered Sonic Pump Studios in Helsinki during mid November with producer Janne Joutsenniemi to commence recording its third album, 'Victory Songs'.

A Finnish tour in January 2007 saw the temporary recruitment of Emmi Silvennoinen, of support band EXSECRATUS, on keyboards. The following month the 'One More Magic Potion' entered the Finnish charts at number one. 'Victory Songs' hit number six in March.

Tale Of Revenge, Spinefarm (2000). Tale Of Revenge / Battery.

ENSIFERUM, Spinefarm SPI 112CD (2001). Intro / Hero In A Dream / Token Of Time / Guardians Of Fate / Old Man / Little Dreamer / Abandoned / Windrider / Treacherous Gods / Eternal Wait / Battle Song / Goblins Dance.

IRON, Spinefarm SPI177CD (2004). Ferrum Aeternum / Iron / Sword Chant / Mourning Heart / Tale Of Revenge / Lost In Despair / Slayer Of Light / Into Battle / LAI LAI HEI / Tears.

VICTORY SONGS, Spinefarm SPI274 (2007) (Promotion release). Ad Victoriam / Blood Is The Prince Of Glory / Deathbringer From The Sky / Ahti / One More Magic Potion / Wanderer / Raised By The Sword / The New Dawn / Victory Song.

One More Magic Potion, Spinefarm (2007). One More Magic Potion. Chart position: 1 FINLAND.

VICTORY SONGS, Spinefarm SPI274 (2007). Ad Victoriam / Blood Is The Prince Of Glory / Deathbringer From The Sky / Ahti / One More Magic Potion / Wanderer / Raised By The Sword / The New Dawn / Victory Song. Chart position: 6 FINLAND.

ENTER CHAOS

POLAND — *Lady Martex (vocals), Mr Verymetal (guitar), Mr Ozz (guitar / bass), Mr D. (guitar / bass), Mr Blasphemo (guitar / bass), Mr Raiden (keyboards), Mr L. Rambo (drums).*

Lead vocalist Marta Meger, as 'Lady Martex', broke away from IMMEMORIAL after two albums 'Ius Primae Noctis' and 'Monologue' to found the 'all star' extreme Metal venture ENTER CHAOS. This union, transpiring in January of 2002, pulled in such talents as Raiden from Ambient act AURAL PLANET on programming, former AZARATH and CENOTAPH man D., DAR SEMAI's Verymetal, DEVILYN's Bony and BEHEMOTH's Havoc and TRAUMA's Mister on guitar, Novy of BEHEMOTH, DIES

ENTER CHAOS

IRAE and DEVILYN on the bass and L. Rambo, from DEMISE, DAMNATION and MOON, on the drums.

This unit, albeit with a number of changes seeing Ozz of DEMISE and LUNA AD NOCTEM's Blasphemo coming in on guitar, debuted with the 'Dreamworker' album. The record featured a cover version of 'Cold' originally performed by AT THE GATES. During August of 2002 the 'Dreamworker' album picked up Russian distribution through the maximum label. Meger had another for celebration though as she gave birth to a son Filip a few weeks later. ENTER CHAOS later replaced Blasphemo with the PROPHECY, THIRD DEGREE and NYIA credited guitarist Szymon.

The band donated their rendition of 'Cold' to the AT THE GATES tribute album, 'Slaughterous Souls—A Tribute to At The Gates' released in September 2004 through Drowned Scream Records.

DREAMWORKER, Metal Mind MMP 0157 (2002). Blood Desire / Chaos / ... And The Angels Sing / Dreamworker / Lethal Dreams / Electronic Zombies / Industrial Disease / Synthetic Future / Lost In Ecstasy / Cold.

ENTER MY SILENCE

JYVÄSKYLÄ, FINLAND — *Mikko Kotamaki (vocals), Arto Huttunen (guitar), Tuomas Jappinen (guitar), Ville Lapio (bass), Teemu Hokkanen (drums).*

A melodic Death Metal crew previously operating in their hometown of Jyväskylä as CAPTIVITY. The band created in 1995 a series of demos were issued before bassist Ville Lapio made his exit in 1998, necessitating guitarist Arto Huttunen switching instruments to plug the gap. As 1998 drew to a close the band adopted a new title of ENTER MY SILENCE issuing the four track EP 'Sophia's Eye'.

Lapio made his return as ENTER MY SILENCE signed up to the Danish Mighty Music concern for a 2001 debut album 'Remote Controlled Scythe'. The album saw US release through Mercenary Musik. Lead vocals on this release were laid down by a guesting Mikko Kotamaki of FUNERIS NOCTURNUM (as 'Torment'), TROLLHEIM's GROTT, EMPYREAN BANE and SWALLOW THE SUN. In November 2004 the band entered Studio Watercastle in Jyväskylä to cut their second album. However, later that same month ENTER MY SILENCE parted ways with singer Mikko Kotamäki, replacing him swiftly with Mika Lisitzin.

The band signed to the newly established JMT Music label in October 2005 for a second album entitled 'Coordinate: D1SA5T3R' set for February 2006 release. Unfortunately for the band, JMT Music closed down just weeks later.

Sophia's Eye EP, (1998). Neverdawn / Sophia / The Tide Will Turn / Plastic Night.
REMOTE CONTROLLED SCYTHE, Mighty Music PMZ014-2 (2000). Six. Nothing / Irrelevant / Inhale-Exhale / Articulate / Split / Nevernity / Filter X / The Loss Of The Leading One / Mindfall Effect.
CORDINATE: D1sa5t3r, JMT Music (2006). Thin Red Line / Spin / For A Place In The Sun / Silent Treatment / Coordinate: D1SA5T3R / The Paradox Of Two / Insignificant / Unspoken Words / 9mms To Deliverance.

ENTHRALLED

TROLLHÄTTAN, SWEDEN — *Robert Greén (vocals), Hjalmar Nielsen (vocals / guitar), Hannes Berggren (guitar), Erik Peterson (bass), Mikael Norén (drums).*

Trollhättan Death Metal combo ENTHRALLED date to 1996, at first pursuing a Thrash direction and billed as ENTHRAL. The founder members, producing the demos 'First Chapter' in 1996, as ENTHRAL, and the following year's 'Forever Gone', comprised vocalist / guitarist Hjalmar Nielsen, second guitarist Hannes Berggren, IMPIOUS bass player Erik Peterson and drummer Martin Restin. During 1998 the group became ENTHRALLED, marking this transition with the demo 'Accession'. The song 'They Breed' was contributed to the compilation album 'Voices Of Death III' in 1999 but this would be Restin's last recordings with the band.

For the 2000 sessions, entitled 'Death Is Breeding' and being recorded and mixed by THE CROWN duo of Marko Tervonen and Markus Sunesson, ENTHRALLED inducted fifteen year old Mikael Norén of CONFORMATORY and IMPIOUS on drums. Shortly after Robert Greén was drafted as frontman, this variation of the band debuting with the 'Anthropomorphous' demos of 2002.

Hjalmar Nielsen would join arch Black Metal act LORD BELIAL during 2003. In February ENTHRALLED lost the services of Mikael Norén.

Forever Gone, (1997). Murder Without Regrets / Brutal Denial / As Darkness Falls ... / Forever Gone / Valley Of Tombs.
Accession, (1999). Alone To The Black End / Evil / Black Light / Allseeing Eye / Accession.
Death Is Breeding, Enthralled (2000). They Breed / Riders Of The Hellstorm / Divine Hypocrisy / Emotions In Grief.

ENTHRALLMENT

BULGARIA — *Plamen Bakardjiev (vocals), Hristo Hristov (guitar), Lachez (bass), Ivo Ivanov (drums).*

ENTHRALLMENT came together during 1998, a collection of musicians from prior acts such as CONDEMNED, CORPSE, GRAVEWORM and ODIUM. Original bassist Simeon Totev decamped in 1999 and was duly replaced by Dimitar Tomov as the group cut their debut Emo Marinov produced cassette 'The Scarlet Difference'. Issued by Dark Mist Productions this uncompromising brutal Death Metal outing included a cover version of CANNIBAL CORPSE's 'Stripped, Raped and Strangled'. Shortly after release singer Yasen Kianov exited and ENTHRALLMENT drafted Plamen Bakardjiev.

This new incarnation of the band participated in the May 2000 Shumen open air 'Metal Sound Fest' alongside fellow Bulgarian acts HYPERBOREA, KOROZY, BRAINSTORM, CLAYMORE, DARK INVERSION and SAMHAIN. New recordings billed as 'Burning Fields' emerged as an album through Butchery Music in 2001. The following year Lachez took the bass position as ENTHRALLMENT shared a split release with Swedish band RELENTLESS. Live work in 2003 included a showing at the 'Hellhammer' Serbian festival in union with HYPNOS, FLESHLESS, PYAEMIA, NEGURA BUNGET and KOROZY.

ENTHRALLMENT readied a live album 'Return To The Grave' for 2004 issue. Also in the works would be a split album to be shared with Austrian band BONEMACHINE. A new full length opus, 'Smashed Brain Collection', emerged in 2005 on Grindethic Records. In 2006 the band underwent a line-up change, adding ex-NECROPHILIA guitarist Vasil Furnigov and bassist Martin Nay.

Burning Fields EP, (2001). Fast Explosion / Burning Fields / Massacre / Graveyard.

ENTOMBED

STOCKHOLM, SWEDEN — *Lars Göran Petrov (vocals), Alex Hellid (guitar), Nico Elgstrand (bass), Peter Stjärnvind (drums).*

In the plethora of Death Metal bands to have emerged, Stockholm's ENTOMBED have proven themselves as ranking among the elite. Never less than skull crushingly heavy, the band has carved its own niche in the market with deft musicianship and a unique perspective generating a 'Death-Doom' style. The band's 1993 album 'Wolverine Blues' is generally acknowledged to be a masterpiece of the genre.

A precursor to ENTOMBED was NIHILIST, forged by teenagers under the BRAINWARP banner during 1987. Initiated by drummer Nicke Andersson the first unit involved school friends singer Daniel "Dudde" Strachal, guitarist Alex Hellid and Leif Cuzner on bass. Strachal soon opted out, later resurfacing behind the LOBOTOMY drum kit, and the band briefly rehearsed with Mattias "Buffla" Boström on the microphone. However, upon entering the Stockholm's Studio Z in March 1988 to cut their first set of demos it would be Lars-Göran Petrov, drummer of MORBID (the band that featured a pre-MAYHEM Per 'Dead' Ohlin), employed as session singer. Another MORBID man, Ulf 'Uffe' Cederlund, handled secondary guitar duties for what would be the Leif Martinsson engineered demo 'Premature Autopsy'.

For subsequent live shows the band was joined by Petrov and new bass guitarist Johnny Hedlund as Cuzner switched to guitar. Over two days in December 1988 this formation utilised Sunlight Studios in Stockholm, and a then unknown producer Tomas Skogsberg, in December to craft a further three song demo, 'Only Shreds Remain'. Once leaked onto the tape trading market the NIHILIST name rapidly garnered enthusiastic support. Until this juncture the only cutting edge Death Metal circulating was emanating from the UK and USA. With 'Only Shreds Remain', NIHILIST had initiated what was to be a tidal flow from Scandinavia.

Leif Cuzner was reluctantly forced out of operations when his family relocated to Canada. In his stead came their former session ally Ulf 'Uffe' Cederlund, at the time attempting to kick start his own INFURATION project. Another round of Swedish club dates ensued before a return to recording was prompted at the invitation of 'Metalion' (a.k.a. Jon Kristiansen), owner of the fabled 'Slayer' fanzine. The journalist was attempting to assemble a split release set to feature PARADISE LOST, CARCASS and BOLT THROWER to launch his Head Not Found label, requesting NIHILIST also contribute material. although the band laid down the new track 'Morbid Devourment' for this purpose the proposed release never transpired. The song was then mooted for inclusion on a compilation album 'Brutal Jaevla Död', but this too failed to eventuate.

Persevering, NIHILIST set about constructing the 'Drowned' demo in August 1989, including a cover rendition of REPULSION's 'Radiation Sickness'. The debut single, 1989's 'Severe Burns' on Bloody Rude Defect Records, was originally the demo "Drowned', whilst a second single, 'Radiation Sickness' in 1991, turned out to be a semi-official bootleg. Just after these sessions, internal disagreements froze out Johnny Hedlund. The bass player soon set up anew with the powerful UNLEASHED, whilst the remainder forged ENTOMBED. Around this period Nicke Andersson was also dividing his duties singing with TREBLINKA, the pre-TIAMAT extreme Death Metal combo out of Täby.

The newly named outfit, with David Blomquist on bass, used Sunlight Studios once again on September 23rd 1989 to carve out tracks for the 'But Life Goes On' demo. A contract was secured with leading British label Earache Records and ENTOMBED retained Tomas Skogsberg's services to record their first album that December, Uffe Cederlund and Nicke Andersson both handling bass duties for the occasion, which witnessed re-works of many earlier NIHILIST songs. Following the release of the 'Left Hand Path' debut album in June 1990, ENTOMBED recruited a permanent bass player in former CONSPIRACY, CARBONISED and MONASTARY man Lars Rosenberg.

1991 was a quite eventful year for the outfit as vocalist Lars-Göran Petrov was fired following personal clashes within the band. Orvar Säfström of NIRVANA 2002 briefly took up the role, long enough to feature on the April 1991 EP 'Crawl', but was in turn was replaced by ex-CARNAGE vocalist Johnny Dordevic. The second album, 'Clandestine', released in November 1991, also credited Dordevic with lead vocals, although it was later learned that in fact Nicke Andersson had sang in the studio. Another EP, 'Stranger Aeons' issued in August 1992, also credited Johnny Dordevic when in fact Nicke Andersson had vocalised. Dordevic exited in September.

In the Autumn, the band toured America on the 'Gods Of Grind' billing alongside fellow Swedes UNLEASHED and headliners MORBID ANGEL with the vocal position filled by the reinstated Lars-Göran Petrov. In his sabbatical from ENTOMBED, the vocalist had recorded with both COMECON and MORBID.

The landmark 'Wolverine Blues' opus arrived in October 1993, signalling a radical shift away from the tried and trusted Death Metal and into wholly unexplored areas of groove loaded extreme music which would become known as "Death n' Roll". Longstanding fans were sharply divided in their opinion but with 'Wolverine Blues' the group had successfully avoided the artistically bankruptcy choking many other bands of their ilk. The record came issued in two sleeve variations, one clad in artwork depicting Marvel comics 'X Men' Wolverine cartoon character. This design, unsanctioned by the band, resulted in acrimony with Earache Records and their new US corporate partners Columbia Records. As a marketing ploy, the gamble certainly worked, bringing many new fans into the world of ENTOMBED.

In 1994 ENTOMBED toured Europe heavily as guests to NAPALM DEATH. General opinion was that ENTOMBED consistently stole the show from a flagging headliner. Subsequent North American dates were only marred by the band having to play as a trio in Canada minus Lars-Göran Petrov. The singer had lost his passports when ENTOMBED's tour van was stolen in Cleveland. ENTOMBED persevered with a show in Toronto, Ontario utilizing guitarist Ulf Cederlund as lead vocalist. Further chaos was to impinge itself though when, for the second show in Montreal, Cederlund lost his voice completely, prompting the band to invite audience members to participate to plug the gap.

The only ENTOMBED product to see release during 1994 was the 'Out Of Hand' 7" single, which saw the band covering tracks by such diverse influences as KISS and REPULSION.

Mid-way through 1995 bassist Rosenberg opted to join THERION, having filled in on a temporary basis for live work. ENTOMBED would add ex-GRAVE bassist Jörgen Sandström in his place and would part company with Earache Records in 1996 to sign with major label East West. However, despite finalizing recording of a projected album the band found themselves embroiled in record company politics and the album was shelved. Luckily, a deal was hastily negotiated between East West and leading independent Music For Nations in order for 'DCLXVI—To Ride, Shoot Straight And Speak The Truth' to be released in 1997. Digipack versions of the album came with a free 'Family Favourites' EP which saw ENTOMBED ripping through BLACK SABBATH's 'Under The Sun', VENOM's 'Bursting Out', KING CRIMSON's '21st Century Schizoid Man' and MC5's 'Kick Out The Jams'. 'To Ride, Shoot Straight And Speak The Truth' impacted impressively on the Swedish album charts at number 7.

Aside from ENTOMBED, Nicke Andersson, in the guise of Nicke Royale, also began to dabble with a side Punk project known as THE HELLACOPTERS with Dick Hakansson (a.k.a. Dregan) from BACKYARD BABIES. Andersson issued his first full length album for THE HELLACOPTERS in late 1996 to laudatory reviews. The band received such acclaim, even being requested to support KISS on their Scandinavian dates that Andersson felt obliged to quit his parent act to concentrate fully on THE HELLACOPTERS.

In 1996 Cederlund and Andersson released the 'Seven Deadly Sins' album together with KONKHRA's vocalist Anders Lundemark under the band name of DAEMON. April of 1997 found the band back on European soil, heading up the 'Full Of Hate' Easter festivals alongside OBITUARY, DEATH, SAMAEL, NEUROSIS, CROWBAR, KILLING CULTURE and STRAPPING YOUNG LAD. ENTOMBED themselves would tour the UK as headliners in September and October of 1997, supported by NEUROSIS and BREECH. Incidentally, Uffe Cederlund also dabbled with a Punk crew titled HAYSTACK together with BACKYARD BABIES bassist Johan Blomqvist, the band releasing a 1998 album 'Slave Me'.

ENTOMBED, now with MERCILESS, FACE DOWN, REGURGITATE and LOUD PIPES drummer Peter 'Flinta' Stjärnwind, put in an American tour to kick off 1998. A new ENTOMBED album, 'Same Difference', was greeted in November 1998 by indifferent reviews and only scraped onto the Swedish charts at number 52. The somewhat mellow 'Same Difference' had been hewn out at Polar Studios in Stockholm with Daniel Rey acting as producer. The following year both Petrov and Hellid would make their presence felt as session guests to the 'Wasting The Dawn' album from Finnish vampire Rockers THE 69 EYES.

Opting for a complete rethink after the artistic failure of 'Same Difference' ENTOMBED went back to the very basics. Relieving some of the pressure the group put out a mini-album, entitled 'Black Ju Ju' in November 1999 through leading US Stoner imprint Man's Ruin Records comprising entirely of cover versions. Honoured would be CAPTAIN BEYOND's 'Mesmerization Eclipse', ALICE COOPER's 'Black Juju', HEY ON GLUE's 'Sentimental Funeral', TWISTED SISTER's 'Tear It Loose', JERRY'S KIDS 'Lost', BOB DYLAN's 'The Ballad Of Hollis Brown' and 'Satan', originally by THE DWARVES.

The 2000 album 'Uprising', costing a miserly £4'000, being deliberately under produced by engineer Nico Elgstrand at Das Boot Studios, harked back to past glories. Not only was the old logo revived but the album cover was in fact the artwork from their original 'But Life Goes On' demo tape. If that was not enough ENTOMBED reworked the title track from 'Left Hand Path' retitling it 'Say It In Slugs'. DISMEMBER's Fred Estby laid down drums on two tracks, 'Year In Year Out' and 'Returning To Madness'. US editions of 'Uprising', on Sanctuary's Metal-Is imprint, added three extra tracks. With ENTOMBED's star in the ascension once again, former label Earache issued a set of live tapes culled from a 1992 London Astoria show for the 'Monkey Puss—Live In London' album.

2000 also saw Cederlund and Stjärnvind in collusion with DISMEMBER's Matti Karki and Richard Cabeza for their MURDER SQUAD project album 'Unsane, Insane And Mentally Damaged'. Another ENTOMBED offshoot, the Thrash band BORN OF FIRE, would see Stjärnvind and Cabeza in alliance with Dimman and ex-UNLEASHED and present day LOUD PIPES and TERRA FIRMA bassist Fredda Lindgren. Sandström would also engage publicly with his new act the Gothic-Electro Death Metal unit THE PROJECT HATE.

The band performed an about turn with their next album set, September 2001's 'Morning Star' delving back into prime Death Metal territory and considerably boosting ENTOMBED's album sales as evidenced by a respectable number 41 entry on the Swedish charts.

ENTOMBED would stretch their creativity during February and March 2002 with a series of ambitious concert performances at the Royal Opera Hall in Stockholm. Billed as the 'Unreal Estate' these gigs witnessed a 45 minute ENTOMBED set complimented by a ten year old actor and a ballet troupe! Recordings from these shows surfaced during 2004 as the 'Unreal Estate' album.

Bassist Jörgen Sandström, acting as a guitarist, and drummer Peter Stjärnvind would announce the formation of a new side venture entitled KRUX featuring such prominent players as Leif Edling of CANDLEMASS, guitarist Michael Amott of ARCH ENEMY and vocalist Tomas Person. KRUX signed up to Mascot Records for their debut, although a line-up change saw erstwhile YNGWIE MALMSTEEN and ABSTRAKT ALGEBRA frontman Mats Leven assuming the mantle of lead vocalist. Uffe Cederlund would embark on another high profile side concern entitled WASHOE in alliance with the MISERY LOVES CO. trio of Vocalist Patrick Wirén, bass player Patrick Thorngren and drummer Olle Dahlstedt. The title of this band would be subsequently be switched to ALPHA SAFARI.

Music For Nations released a compilation of ENTOMBED archive cover versions and B sides in 2002 billed as 'Sons Of Satan-Praise The Lord'. In December Cederlund revealed plans for renewed live action with his pre-ENTOMBED band HAYSTACK featuring Johan from the BACKYARD BABIES on bass and Jonas of THE MAGGOTS on drums.

The band's May 2003 album 'Inferno' was produced by Pelle Gunnerfeldt and accelerated the renewed appreciation for the band, hitting number 21 on the domestic charts. Vinyl versions surfaced on the group's own imprint Threeman Recordings and boasted the inclusion of an exclusive extra track 'When Humanity Is Gone'.

September and October European shows had NINE and DISFEAR as support before the band forged a union with KING DIAMOND for US touring throughout October and November. Canadian gigs planned for Toronto and Montreal would be cancelled as drummer Peter Stjärnvind was found to be suffering from "2 pus filled boils in his throat area". Returning home for the December Scandinavian 'Close-Up Made Us Do It' tour alongside DISFEAR and RAISED FIST, Uffe Cederlund doubled up duties as live guitarist for DISFEAR.

In January of 2004 ENTOMBED parted ways with Jörgen Sandström and drafted Nico 'Moosebeach' Elgstrand, formerly of ALBATROSS and TERRA FIRMA, in his stead. Sandström maintained his ties with both THE PROJECT HATE and KRUX as well as joining Stockholm based Death Metal band VICIOUS ART. Another record he featured on would be a 2004 album from THE MIGHTY NIMBUS, featuring on a cover of the SAINT VITUS track 'Born Too Late'. Primitive Art Records released a split single of ENTOMBED and THE COFFINSHAKERS, both acts covering LEE HAZLEWOOD songs. ENTOMBED donated their version of 'Some Velvet Morning'. Lars-Göran Petrov recorded a guest appearance for the E-TYPE Electro Pop album 'Loud Pipes Save Lives'.

North American dates would be announced for March, but then retracted as the band was unable to secure a work visa for Nico Elgstrand in time. The revised band undertook a batch of Australian gigs in April, with support coming from DAYSEND. US versions of the 'Inferno' opus released in August through Candlelight added a bonus disc of extra material dubbed 'Averno' comprising two previously unreleased songs from the 'Inferno' sessions and 'When Humanity's Gone' from the 'Inferno' vinyl format. Also featured would be promotional videos for 'Retaliation' and 'Albino Flogged In Black'. Meantime, Alex Hellid acted as producer for all girl Metal band MISDEMEANOR's second album, 'High Crimes & Misdemeanor' for GMR Music.

ENTOMBED headed up a package billing comprising CROWBAR, PRO-PAIN, and THE MIGHTY NIMBUS for US tour dates in February 2005. A notable gig came in July at the 'Peace And Love' festival in Borlänge, Sweden when erstwhile drummer Nicke Andersson joined the band onstage as fill in guitarist for Uffe Cederlund, the latter on the road with DISFEAR. However, in early September the band put out an official statement that Uffe Cederlund was "no longer in the band". ENTOMBED persevered, also drafting ALPHA SAFARI and ex-MISERY LOVES CO. session drummer Olle Dahlstedt. In early November ENTOMBED revealed 'Serpent Saints' was to be the title of a new album, set for a September 2006 release through Threeman Recordings. The group entered Studioland studio in Upplands Väsby in mid-December.

During late 2005 two ex-ENTOMBED members, Nicke Andersson and Jörgen Sandström, concocted the deliberately retrostyled Death Metal combo DEATH BREATH, being joined by guitarist Robert Persson of THUNDER EXPRESS.

First ENTOMBED product for 2006 would be the EP 'When in Sodom', issued in June. Norwegian concerts in September witnessed support from MANIFEST. European show announced November, dubbed the "Masters Of Death", had the band lined up with a supremely heavyweight Scandinavian cast of DISMEMBER, GRAVE and UNLEASHED. The group was then set unite once more with DISMEMBER, GRAVE plus THE ABSENCE for a US West Coast tour in December. However, ENTOMBED pulled out, stating that "conflicts with the promoter, breach of trust and straight-up lies" had forced their hand.

But Life Goes On, (1989) (Demo). But Life Goes On / Shreds Of Flesh / The Truth Beyond.

LEFT HAND PATH, Earache MOSH 21 (1990). Left Hand Path / Drowned / Revel In Flesh / When Life Has Ceased / Supposed To Rot / But Life Goes On / Bitter Loss / Morbid Devourment / Deceased / Truth Beyond / Carnal Leftovers.

Crawl, Earache MOSH 38T (1991). Crawl / Forsaken / Bitter Loss.

CLANDESTINE, Earache MOSH 37 (1991). Crawl / Severe Burns / Living Dead / Through The Colonnades / Stranger Aeons / Blessed Be / Sinners Bleed / Chaos Breed / Evilyn. Chart position: 44 SWEDEN.

Stranger Aeons, Earache MOSH 52 (1992). Stranger Aeons / Dusk / Shreds Of Flesh.

State Of Emergency, King Kong KK004 (1993) (Split EP with TEDDY BEAR & DOLL SQUAD). State Of Emergency.

Hollowman EP, Earache MOSH 94 (1993). Hollowman / Serpent Speech / Wolverine Blues / Bonehouse / Put Off The Scent / Hellraiser. Chart position: 26 SWEDEN.

Contempt, Columbia CSK 6017 (1993) (US promotion release). Contempt / Black Breath.

Full Of Hell, Columbia CSK 6407 (1993) (US promotion release). Full Of Hell / God Of Thunder / State Of Emergency.

Wolverine Blues, Columbia (1993) (US promotion release). Wolverine Blues.

WOLVERINE BLUES, Earache MOSH 82 (1993). Eyemaster / Rotten Soil / Wolverine Blues / Demon / Contempt / Full Of Hell / Blood Song / Hollowman / Heavens Die / Out Of Hand.

Out Of Hand, Earache MOSH 114 (1994). Out Of Hand / God Of Thunder / Blackbreath.

WOLVERINE BLUES, Columbia 57593 (1994) (USA release). Eyemaster / Rotten Soil / Wolverine Blues / Demon / Contempt / Full Of Hell / Blood Song / Hollowman / Heavens Die / Out Of Hand.

Night Of The Vampire, Earache MOSH 132 (1995) (Split single with NEW BOMB TURKS). Night Of The Vampire.

ENTOMBED, Earache MOSH 125 (1997). Out Of Hand / God Of Thunder / Black Breath / Stranger Aeons / Dusk / Shreds Of Flesh / Crawl / Forsaken / Bitter Loss / Night Of The Vampire / State Of Emergency / Vandal X.

ENTOMBED

Wreckage, Music For Nations CDMGNM233 (1997). Wreckage / Tear It Loose / Satan / Lost / Ballad Of Hollis Brown.

Like This With The Devil, Threeman Recordings (1997). Like This With The Devil / Damn Deal Done.

Family Favourites EP, Music For Nations DISC 2 (1997) (Free EP with album). Kick Out The Jams / 21st Century Schizoid Man / Bursting Out / Under The Sun.

WRECKAGE, Pony Canyon PCCY 01207 (1997) (Japanese release). Wreckage / Lights Out (Live) / Just As Sad (Live) / They (Live) / Wreckage (Indie Cart) / Kick Out The Jams / Tear It Loose / 21 Century Schizoid Man / Bursting Out / Under The Sun.

DCLXVI—TO RIDE, SHOOT STRAIGHT AND SPEAK THE TRUTH, Music For Nations MFN 216 (1997). To Ride, Shoot Straight And Speak The Truth / Like This With The Devil / Lights Out / Wound / They / Somewhat Peculiar / DCLXVI / Parasight / Damn Deal Done / Put Me Out / Just As Sad / Boats / Mr Uffe's Horrorshow / Wreckage. Chart positions: 7 SWEDEN, 75 UK.

MONKEY PUSS—LIVE IN LONDON, Earache MOSH 213 (1998). Living Dead / Revel In Flesh / Stranger Aeons / Crawl / But Life Goes On / Sinners Bleed / Evilyn / The Truth Beyond / Drowned / Left Hand Path.

SAME DIFFERENCE, Music For Nations MFN 244 (1998). Addiction King / The Supreme Good / Clauses / Kick In The Head / Same Difference / Close But Nowhere Near / What You Need / High Waters / 20-20 Vision / The Day, The Earth / Smart Aleck / Jack Worm / Wolf Tickets. Chart position: 52 SWEDEN.

Black Juju EP, Man's Ruin MR099 (1999) (Grey swirl vinyl 10" single). A Mesmirization Eclipse / Vice By Proxy / Black Juju / Sentimental Funeral.

BLACK JU JU, Man's Ruin MR119 (1999). Mezmerization Eclipse / Vices By Proxy / Black Ju Ju / Sentimental Funeral / Tear It Loose / Lost / Ballad Of Hollis Brown / Satan.

UPRISING, Metal Is 73002 (2000) (USA release). Seeing Red / Say It In Slugs / Won't Back Down / Insanity's Contagious / Something Out Of Nothing / Scottish Hell / Time Out / The Itch / Year In Year Out / Returning To Madness / Come Clean / In The Flesh / Superior / The Only Ones / Words.

UPRISING, Threeman Recordings TRECD 005 (2000) (European release). Seeing Red / Say It In Slugs / Won't Back Down / Insanity's Contagious / Something Out Of Nothing / Scottish Hell / Time Out /

The Itch / Year In, Year Out / Returning To Madness / Come Clean / In The Flesh. Chart position: 55 SWEDEN.

MORNING STAR, Threeman Recordings TRECD 006 (2001). Chief Rebel Angel / I For An Eye / Bringer Of Light / Ensemble Of The Restless / Out Of Heaven / Young Man Nihilist / Year One Now / Fractures / When It Hits Home / City Of Ghosts / About To Die / Mental Twin. Chart position: 41 SWEDEN.

SONS OF SATAN—PRAISE THE LORD, Music For Nations MFN 293 (2002). Black Breath / Albino Flogged In Black / March Of The S.O.D. / Sergeant D And The S.O.D. / Some Velvet Morning / One Track Mind / Hollywood Babylon / Night Of The Vampire / God Of Thunder / Something I Learnt Today / 21st Century Schizoid Man / Black Juju / Amazing Grace (Punk version) / Satan / Hellraiser / Kick Out The Jams / Yout' Juice / Bursting Out / State Of Emergency / Under The Sun / Vandal X / Tear It Loose / Scottish Hell / The Ballad Of Hollis Brown / Mesmerization Eclipse / Lost / Amazing Grace (Mellow Drunk version).

INFERNO, Music For Nations MFN 295 (2003). Retaliation / The Fix Is In / Incinerator / Children Of The Underworld / That's When I Became A Satanist / Nobodaddy / Intermission / Young & Dead / Descent Into Inferno / Public Burning / Flexing Muscles / Skeleton Of Steel / Night For Day. Chart position: 21 SWEDEN.

INFERNO + AVERNO, Candlelight CANDLE 124 (2003) (USA slipcase release). Retaliation / The Fix Is In / Incinerator / Children Of The Underworld / That's When I Became A Satanist / Nobodaddy / Intermission / Young & Dead / Descent Into Inferno / Public Burning / Flexing Muscles / Skeleton Of Steel / Night For Day / When Humanity's Gone / There Are Horrors Of 1000 Nightmares / Random Guitar / Retaliation (video edit) / Albino Flogged In Black (video edit) / Retaliation (Enhanced video) / Albino Flogged in Black (Enhanced video).

UNREAL ESTATE, Threeman Recordings TRECD 015 (2004). DCLXVI / Intermission / Chief Rebel Angel / Say It in Slugs / It Is Later Than You Think / Returning To Madness / Mental Twin / Night Of The Vampire / Unreal Estate / In The Flesh / Something Out Of Nothing / Left Hand Path (Outro).

When In Sodom EP, Threeman TRECDEP 022 (2006). When In Sodom / Carnage / Thou Shalt Kill / Heresy / Amen.

ENTRE LA BASURA

ROSARIO, ARGENTINA — *Guillermo Negro Lottero (vocals / guitar), Fabian Giacca (bass), Martin Pliego (drums).*

ENTRE LA BASURA is a Rosario based Death / Grindcore act. The band began in late 1989 under the name ENTRE EL CIELO Y LA BASURA as a trio comprising vocalist / guitarist Guillermo Negro Lottero, bassist Fabian Giacca and drummer Andres Cilentti. The group soon truncated the title to simply ENTRE LA BASURA for initial live work in both Rosario and Buenos Aires, leading up the recording of a self-titled demo. In 1993 the band expanded with the addition of second guitarist Gustavo Biancospino. The April 1994 album 'En el Nombre del Fraude, Del Fisco y los Estados Unidos, OK', recorded at El Camote Studios in Rosario, featured a cover version of V8's 'Brigadas Metalicas'.

Subsequently, Andres Cilentti exited, being temporarily replaced Sergio of ENTERRADO VIVO. In late 1993 Martin Pliego of INTENSE MOSH made the position permanent. The 'Combatiendo al Capital' album followed for Saturno Discos in April 1995. The following year Biancospino opted out. Pablo was recruited as substitute but ENTRE LA BASURA folded before any further gigging could take place. Guillermo Negro Lottero joined INTENSE MOSH.

EN EL NOMBRE DEL FRAUDE, DEL FISCO Y LOS ESTADOS UNIDOS, OK, Entre La Basura (1993). Estado de Venganza Continua / Muerto Por Insano / Sin Opresion / Odio los Extremos / Putrefaccion / Brigadas Metalicas / Ruidos de Muerte / Consumidor Final / Liberacion Animal / Vomit / Sacrifice The Fire.

COMBATIENDO AL CAPITAL, Saturno Discos (1995). La Klase Dirigente / Sistematica Agresion / Esclavo / Sistema Inmunologico Mental / Dictaduras / Hombre Libre / Falsa Democracia / Diskeria Alternativa / Palestina / Los 7 Enanitos.

ENTWINED

COLCHESTER, UK — *Stephen John Tovey (vocals), Lee James (guitar), Simon (bass), James Southgate (drums).*

Colchester based ENTWINED feature erstwhile ESTRANGED members vocalist Stephen John Tovey, bassist Simon and drummer James Southgate. Guitarist Lee James has credits with MORTAL TIDE and METAL STORM. Evolving as ENTWINED during 1995 the band bowed in with the demos 'XIII', produced by Neville Dean at Garden Studios in Essex during February 1996, and 'Her Cherished Mask', laid down at Adelaide Studios in September of that year.

ENTWINED supported MORBID ANGEL on their 1998 European tour supporting the 'Dancing Under Glass' album but would fold shortly after.

Former ENTWINED keyboard player Mark Royce joined PRIMARY SLAVE and then the expatriated Chilean Death Metal band CRIMINAL in March of 2002. In early 2006 Mark Royce launched a new band venture dubbed COLD LAZARUS.

XIII, (1996). The Sleep Of Innocence / Chasing Leaves / Bonfire Of The Vanities / Beside And Beyond.

Her Cherished Mask, (1996). Red Winter Love / Elegance In Death / ... To Suffer Silently / Her Cherished Mask / October Betrothed.

DANCING UNDER GLASS, Earache MOSH194 (1998). The Sound Of Her Wings / Shed Nightward Beauty / Under A Killing Moon / The Forgotten / A Moments Sadness / The Sacrifice Of Spring / Red Winter / Heaven Rise / XIII.

EPICEDIUM

CA, USA — *Rainier O'Donnell (vocals / guitar), Robert Tulk (guitar), Aaron Ramson (bass), Aaron Cross (drums).*

EPICEDIUM is a Southern Californian Death Metal combo instigated by vocalist / guitarist Rainier O'Donnell and drummer Aaron Cross in late 1995. The initial version of the band, which included Dan Dismal, later of CREMATORIUM, would fold but then rise again with new personnel. The group went through a succession of guitarists and bass players including Richard Wiggins, Jerry Dewalt, Nick Gentry, Brian Coleman and Pat Blackstorm. The inclusion of Robert Tulk brought some stability to the band in 1996.

EPICEDIUM cut a five song demo at Moon Studios during 1999. The band's live profile rose considerably with a series of supports to acts such as DEICIDE, SIX FEET UNDER, MOONSPELL, MORTICIAN and MALEVOLENT CREATION. In June of 2003 the group signed to Embryo Records and introduced a new bassist in Steve Edwards to replace Aaron Ramson.

EPICIDIUM, Embryo (2004). Homicidal Repercussion / Lifeforms / The Wrath / Sacrosanta / The Time Of Ruin / Legacy Of Darkness / The Corpse Yard / Repugnance / Plague Of The Innocence / Horrific Eradication.

EQUINOX

TAMPA, FL, USA — *Darkness (vocals / bass), Pete Slate (guitar), Tony Blakk (guitar), Steven Spillers (drums).*

A retro Black defiled Death Metal band from Grand Island, central Florida created during the winter of 1992 by erstwhile ACHERON guitarist Pete Slate, former INCUBUS bassist Mark Lavenia, vocalist Darkness (Matt W.) and drummer Stephen Spillers. Both Slate and Lavenia also held a tradition with the Kam Lee fronted ABHORRENT EXISTENCE during 1987.

EQUINOX debuted with the demo cassette 'Anthem To The Moon' during 1993, featuring a cover version of the KISS track 'The Oath'. Second demo, the three track 'Equinox', was recorded at Morrisound Studios on 6th November 1993, following which Lavenia decamped. Darkness took over the bass role as the band also inducted another ACHERON veteran guitarist Tony Blakk. With this line-up the band cut 'Upon The Throne

Of Eternity' single, a red vinyl pressing limited to 666 copies, for the German based Silencelike Death Records.

During the autumn of 1995 the group secured a deal with the Greek Unisound concern for the debut full length album 'Return To Mystery', recorded at Shock Lizard Studios and engineered by Tom Morris.

By 2000 Lavernia had reunited with Slate in an alliance with ex-MASSACRE drummer Kam Lee founding CAULDRON. EQUINOX made a return during 2003, signing to the Polish Still Dead Productions for the album 'Journey Into Oblivion', once again recording at Morrisound Studios. In the USA the album was issued via DaemonStorm Records.

The EQUINIX credited drummer Gabriel Lewandowski, also citing HELLWITCH and ACHERON affiliations, joined UNHOLY GHOST in May 2005. Matt W. operates with Metalcore band 5 BILLION DEAD.

Anthem To The Moon, (1993). Psychic Rebirth / Dreams Of The Winter Solstice / Divine Ascension / Return To Mystery / The Oath.

Equinox, (1994). Come Forth The Haunting / Divine Ascension / Return To Mystery.

Upon The Throne Of Eternity, Silencelike Death Productions (1995) (Limited edition 666 copies red vinyl). De Sacrificio Summo / The Oath.

Equinox, (1995). Come Forth The Haunting / Divine Ascension / Return To Mystery / De Sacrificio Summo / Path To Eternal Ruin.

RETURN TO MYSTERY, Unisound (1996). Rites Of Red Giving / Return To Mystery / Until The Dawns Mist / The Mourning River / Valley Of The Kings / Dreams Of Winter Solstice / Winds Of Autumn / Infernal Atavism (Descend To Tetragrammaton) / Path To Eternal Ruin.

JOURNEY INTO OBLIVION, Still Dead Productions SDP 03106 (2003). Invasions Of The Angry Dead / Enchantress / Sorcerer / Journey Into Oblivion / Roar Through The Aeons / The Sword Of Sirsir / Divine Ascension / Crystallized / In Remembrance / Séance.

ERRATA

EDINBURGH, SCOTLAND, UK— *Mark Pringle (vocals), George Nisbeet (guitar), Matt Orrock (guitar), Chris Trotter (bass), Hammy (drums).*

Edinburgh Death Metal act ERRATA feature former INVERSUS members vocalist Mark Pringle and guitarist George Nisbet. The latter also holds SUBSTATE credits. They would be joined by second guitarist Conor Cromie whilst the ERRATA rhythm section comprised bassist Guss Mortimer and drummer Hammy (a.k.a. Paul Hameed). The latter held credits with LEECHHATE, TASTE MY SILENCE, RIDGEBACK, ABIGAIL'S GLORIOUS VOICE and RAMAGE INC. Raw Nerve Promotions issued the February 2003 EP 'To Become A War'. Cromie exited in mid 2003.

The demo, 'Broken, But Not Dead', followed in January 2004. However, Mortimer opted out in June. That August, LEECHHATE, RAMAGE INC. and TASTE MY SILENCE guitarist Mat Orrock, who had been covering on bass, switched back to guitar as Chris Trotter enrolled as new bassist. ERRATA folded in January 2005.

To Become A War, Raw Nerve Promotions (2003). Self Administered / Idle And Silent / On That Even Keel / Grindcore / In This, The Year Of Our Lord.

Broken, But Not Dead, (2004). Curse The Day / Amongst The Swarm / Broken, But Not Dead / Last Cold Wind.

ESQARIAL

POLAND — *Marek Pajak (vocals / guitar), Dariusz Witkowski (guitar), Przemyslaw Przybylski (bass), Bartosz Wozniak (drums).*

ESQARIAL date to 1991, opening proceedings with the overlooked 'Refuse' demo before a second session, 'A Conspiracy Of Silence', attracted the attention of the Metal media. The band debuted with the 1998 'Amorphous' album prior to switching to Empire Records for follow up 'Discoveries'. The band's 2002 line-up comprised vocalist / guitarist Marek Pajak, second guitarist Bartek Nowak, bassist P. Ludendorf and Bartosz Wozniak on the drums.

The band's April 2004 album 'Klassika', recorded at Fonoplastykon Studios with producer Marcin Bors, would be a collaborative effort with Grzegorz Kupczyk of CETI, NON IRON and TURBO repute. The band would form up the 'Days Of Destruction' tour, alongside HATE, MUTILATION, ABUSED MAJESTY and PYORRHOEA, throughout Poland that December.

ESQARIAL guitarist Marek Pająk featured on the PANZER X 'Steel Fist' project of VADER's Piotr Wiwczarek.

AMORPHOUS, Pagan (1999). On The Edge / Butcher / Galley (Intro) / Obsession / The Earth / Invocation (Intro) / Silent Lamentation / Amorphous / Centurion (Intro) / Reality (Graveyard Caves) / The earth (Instrumental version).

DISCOVERIES, Empire EMP0006 (2001). World In Flames / Kill All Of Them / Travel In Past / Sacred War / Nightmare / Unreal / Atlantis / New Land / True Lies / Guitar Explosions.

INHERITANCE, Empire EMP 019 CD (2003). Inheritance / Everlasting Wanderers / Broken Link / Flying Over The Treetops / A Pure Formality / Catching The Falling Knife / The Source Of Constraint / The Day When The Sun Went Out / Two Minutes Two Fullmoon / Killing For Killing Time / Fire.

KLASSIKA, Empire EMP CD 035 (2004). Prelude D-Moll / Toy Soldier / Requiem / Eye Of The Cyclone / El Fuego / Timequake / True Lies / Sleeping In The Flame / Moonlight Sonata / Pure Formality.

ESSENCE OF EXISTENCE

SLOVAKIA — *Void (vocals), Astral (vocals / guitar), Technology (guitar), Fear (keyboards).*

ESSENCE OF EXISTENCE, forged by vocalist / guitarist Astral and bassist N'ght in the Autumn of 1993, deliver atmospherically charged Black-Death Metal with elements of the Symphonic. 1995 saw the introduction of guitarist Miki, bass player Technology, keyboard player Maaya and drummer Goldo. A handful of gigs were performed in 1996 before Mango superseded Goldo. However, this latest recruit's tenure would be fleeting and a drum machine, "Unbuing", was delegated the role. ESSENCE OF EXISTENCE underwent yet more changes as Cry replaced Miki and Maaya exited in favour of Fear.

The band bowed in with the 1999 demo 'Of Bloody Tears', recorded at ASI Studios in Frydek Mistek. Upon completion of these sessions Cry decamped in order to join KARRION and Technology shifted position to guitar. A full length album, 'Ephemeris Sun' recorded with new lead singer Void, was recorded in 2002 and arrived in early 2004 through the band's own Sonic Temple imprint. A third effort, 'Tome III: Terra Mentis', would be worked on during 2003.

EPHEMERIS SUN, Sonic Temple (2004). Extinction Of The Species / The Chosen One / The Experiment Theory / Death Vault / Eclipse Of A Distant Star / Time Constancy / Universe Of Pain / Death Scholar / Variations Of Agony / Innovation Of The Ruins (Outro).

ESTERTOR

BOLIVIA — *Marcelo Soto de la Fuente (vocals / guitar), Arturo Salguero (guitar), J. Rommel Neynaga (bass), Pablo Mendoza (drums).*

Doom Death act ESTERTOR was created as a 1996 trio of guitarist Marcelo Soto de la Fuente, bass player Gustavo Mendoza and drummer Pablo Mendoza. The band released the 2002 demo 'Episodes Of The Shadows', this tape also featuring live cover versions of IRON MAIDEN's 'Fear Of The Dark' and IN FLAMES 'The Hive'. Upon completion of these sessions J. Rommel Neynaga took over the bass guitar role. ESTERTOR also took this opportunity to induct second guitarist Arturo Salguero. During March of 2001 ESTEROR gained the honours of supporting HAMMERFALL's Bolivian dates, capitalising on this achievement by opening for fabled Argentinean band RATA BLANCA across Latin America. Live activity continued into

2002, including acting as guests to HORCAS in Santa Cruz, prior to recording the album 'Between Silence And Light' for Moonlapse Productions.

BETWEEN SILENCE AND LIGHT, Moonlapse Productions (2003). Intro (In The Forest...) / Ride To The Unknown / Shadows / Dark Silent Room / Green / Eternal Fall / Lifebuilder / The Follower / Drunk Song (Nietzche) / Hunting Lost Dreams / Sacred Sin (Death In Life...) / Slept Shining Dew / To My Conscience (Outro).

ESTUARY

CINCINNATI, OH, USA — *Zdenka Prado (vocals), Ash Thomas (guitar), Brad Howard (guitar), Steve Eberl (bass), Jesse Wilson (drums).*

Essentially a re-branding of Ohio Death Metal act ESTUARY OF CALAMITY, founded in October of 1992, originally billed as NECROLATRY, and describing themselves as Grinding Doom Death. As a trio of vocalist / bassist Ash Thomas, guitarist Adam Ellis and drummer Jesse Wilson a Death Metal influenced demo arrived in 1993. By May of that same year though, wishing to distance themselves from a plethora of acts of similar name, the band became ESTUARY OF CALAMITY, adding second guitarist Brad Howard at the same juncture. As a newly billed quartet recorded the demo 'Losing Myself In The Cryptic Breeze'.

Although suffering from an obvious lack of financial input 'Losing Myself In The Cryptic Breeze' engendered favourable press reports. Wishing to duplicate the more experimental music displayed on the demo the band inducted keyboard player Leslie Anderson. However, by 1995 the group had folded with Thomas and Anderson forging ahead with THORNS OF THE CARRION.

ESTUARY OF CALAMITY lay dormant until October 1997 when Thomas, Ellis and Anderson resurrected the band. For this revised version Thomas switched to guitar whilst Ellis became bass player. The track 'Unheard In The Storm' would be shopped as a promotional tool as well as cutting 'Mansions In Darkness' for the KING DIAMOND tribute album 'Church Of The Devil'.

The full length album 'The Sentencing' was delivered in May 2000. The band underwent a name change in 2002, simply becoming ESTUARY. In this new guise they would re-debut with the September EP 'Under their new, truncated name and now fronted by ex-GARDEN OF SHADOWS and FORTY DAYS LONGING singer Zdenka Prado the band re-debuted with the September 2002 EP 'Riding The Tides Of Malice'. Shortly afterward Steve Eberl of MORTICITE enrolled on bass guitar.

The band signed to John McEntee of INCANTATION's label Ibex Moon for the full length album 'To Exist & Endure', recorded at Audioasis Studios in Cincinnati during late 2003. ESTUARY supported INCANTATION and CIRCLE OF DEAD CHILDREN on a short burst of East Coast dates in May of 2005.

ESTUARY unveiled European tour plans, taking in France, Spain and Portugal alongside road mates French Deathsters BLOODY SIGN, for April and May 2006. In mid-September the band entered Audioasis Studios in Cincinnati to record second album 'The Craft Of Contradiction'. The band wrapped up these sessions in early February 2007.

Riding The Tides Of Malice, (2002). Riding The Tides Of Malice / Tragedy Born / The Evershielding.

TO EXIST AND ENDURE, Ibex Moon IMR002 (2004). To Exist... / Soul Scarred Captives / Draining The Deptor / Of Weakening Stone / Woven Denial / The Evershielding / Flesh And Blood Dilemma / Silence And Mind / Riding The Winds Of Malice / ... To Endure.

ESTUARY OF CALAMITY

CINCINNATI, OH, USA — *Ash Thomas (vocals / bass), Adam Ellis (guitar), Brad Howard (guitar), Leslie Anderson (keyboards), Jesse Wilson (drums).*

Ohio act founded in October of 1992, originally billed as NECROLATRY, describing themselves as Grinding Doom Death. As a trio of vocalist / bassist Ash Thomas, guitarist Adam Ellis and drummer Jesse Wilson a Death Metal influenced demo arrived in 1993. By May of that same year though, wishing to distance themselves from a plethora of acts of similar name, the band became ESTUARY OF CALAMITY, adding second guitarist Brad Howard at the same juncture. As a newly billed quartet recorded the demo 'Losing Myself In The Cryptic Breeze'.

Although suffering from an obvious lack of financial input 'Losing Myself In The Cryptic Breeze' engendered favourable press reports. Wishing to duplicate the more experimental music displayed on the demo the band inducted keyboard player Leslie Anderson. However, by 1995 the group had folded with Thomas and Anderson forging ahead with THORNS OF THE CARRION.

ESTUARY OF CALAMITY lay dormant until October of 1997 when Thomas, Ellis and Anderson resurrected the band. For this revised version Thomas switched to guitar whilst Ellis became bass player. The track 'Unheard In The Storm' would be shopped as a promotional tool as well as cutting 'Mansions In Darkness' for the KING DIAMOND tribute album 'Church Of The Devil'.

The full length album 'The Sentencing' was delivered in May of 2000. The band underwent a name change in 2002, simply becoming ESTUARY. In this new guise they would re-debut with the September EP 'Under their new, truncated name and now fronted by ex-GARDEN OF SHADOWS singer Zdenka Prado the band re-debuted with the September 2002 EP 'Riding The Tides Of Malice'.

THE SENTENCING, (2000). A Grain Of Sand, A Breath Of Life / At The Dreamscape Ruins / The Spiritual Beheading / The Sentencing / Nightsky Awakening / Unheard In The Storm / Summoned At Daybreak.

ETERNAL

MEDELLIN, COLOMBIA — *Jorge Munox (vocals / drums), Susanna Correa (vocals), Ivan Rios (guitar), Gabriel Sanchez (guitar), Camilo Barrera (bass), Miguel Gongora (keyboards).*

Medellin based Gothic Death Metal act created during 1995. ETERNAL, who seemingly have a penchant for wearing sinister monks cassocks, issued the demo tape 'Dreamworld' in 1997, the band's membership at this time consisting of Jorge Munox on lead vocals and drums, guitarists Ivan Rios and Gabriel Sanchez, secondary vocalist Maria Carolina Echeverry, ex-LIPTHOPIA bassist Jairo Hurtado and keyboard player Hammell Atehortua.

By the time of recording the debut album 'Gothic Dreams' ETERNAL had undergone line up changes with new faces being bass player Camilo Barrera, keyboard player Miguel Gongora and the striking Susanna Correra on soprano vocals.

Gongora would bow out in August of 2001, being replaced on the ivories by Juan Carlos Gomez. The band supported THERION on their Colombian dates.

GOTHIC DREAMS, (2000). Gothic Dreams / Slaves Of Concrete / Garden Of Souls / Freezing Winds / Dark Shine / Princess / Misregard For Fear / Last Day / Broken Promises / Cold Woman.

ETERNAL AUTUMN

MARIESTAD, SWEDEN — *John Carlsson (vocals / guitar), Thomas Ahlgren (guitar), Sami Nieminen (bass), Ola Sundström (drums).*

Founded in 1993, Mariestad based melodic Death / Thrash act ETERNAL AUTUMN underwent numerous line-up changes until the introduction of drummer Andreas Tullson provided some much needed stability. However, the band hired a bass player in quick succession then shortly after vocalist and founder member Daniel quit. The band issued an inaugural demo recording in 1994 before Daniel was to re-enter the fold, although this time taking up the duties of bass player. A 1996 demo was issued after which Daniel made his exit again and Tullson decamped too.

A third effort, the six track 'Moonscape' cassette, witnessed a revised membership comprising vocalist / rhythm guitarist John Carlsson, Thomas Ahlgren on lead guitar, Tobias Vipeklev on bass and drummer Ola Sundström. This last session led to a deal with the Black Diamond label for the 1998 album 'The Storm'. In the midst of laying down the debut Vipeklev was asked to leave necessitating the two guitarists sharing the bass duties. Musically the album was firmly entrenched in traditional Heavy Metal territory although, by the band's admission, the whole affair was liberally injected with a degree of Gothicism.

ETERNAL AUTUMN, now with Sami Nieminen on bass, would cut their version of 'Return Of The Vampire' for the MERCYFUL FATE tribute album 'The Unholy Sounds Of The Demon Bells' issued via Poland's Still Dead Productions. Although a new album '... From The Eastern Forest' was announced for release through the Japanese Soundholic label ETERNAL AUTUMN folded in the summer of 2001.

THE STORM, Black Diamond BDP005 (1999). The Storm / Autumn Fire / In My Recent Shape / As The Last Leaf Fell / Moonscape / Autumn Opus, No 1 / Floating ... / In A Land Dawn Never Reached.

... FROM THE EASTERN FORESTS, Soundholic SHCD1-0037 (2000) (Japanese release). November Frost / The Ashes Of The Witch / Seven Years / Grey Filthy Claws / - / An Eternity In Vengeance Part 2 / Statues.

ETERNAL DARKNESS

ESKILSTUNA, SWEDEN — *Janne (vocals), Jompa (guitar), Tony (guitar), Tero Viljanen (bass), Make Pesonen (drums).*

Eskilstuna Doom / Death outfit dating to 1990. An opening demo that year, entitled 'Ceremony Of Doom' was capitalised on by the 'Suffering' session a year later. Entering Balsta Studios in February of 1992 ETERNAL DARKNESS cut the 'Doomed' EP for the Distorted Harmony label. An album, with a projected title of 'Twilight In The Wilderness', was recorded in 1993 but would remain unreleased.

ETERNAL DARKNESS drummer Make Pesonen was later to be found as an integral member of THE BLACK. In January 2007 Morbid Wrath Records issued the ETERNAL DARKNESS compilation 'Total Darkness'. A vinyl version was restricted to 1000 copies, of which 300 were pressed on white vinyl.

Doomed, Distorted Harmony DH006 (1992). Doomed / Psycopath.
TOTAL DARKNESS, Morbid Wrath (2007). Psychopath (7" EP version) / Doomed (7" EP version) / Ceremony Of Doom (Alternate version) / Zombie Feast / Serve & Obey / Psychopath / Despair / Twilight In The Wilderness / That Day Will Come / A Pleasant Surprise / The Island (Of Fear).

ETERNAL DEFORMITY

DĘBICA, POLAND — *Przemek Kajnat (vocals / bass), Przemek Smyczek (guitar), Arek Szymuś (guitar), Piotr Tomala (keyboards), Tymoteusz Ciastko (drums).*

ETERNAL DEFORMITY came together in Dębica during 1993, based upon an idea formulated by guitarist Arkadiusza Szymusia and drummer Rafała Rybińskiego, being initially augmented by singer Artur Olszewski and second guitarist Przemysław Smyczek. The following year this quartet entered Beat Center Studios to record the cassette 'Forgotten Distant Time'. Extensive road work across Poland ensued but in 1996 the band suffered its first line up change when Tymoteusz Ciastko was installed as new drummer and Przemysław Kajnat added on bass. ETERNAL DEFORMITY's profile was then boosted by a live schedule that saw supports to NUCLEAR ASSAULT, DEPRESY, NIGHT IN GALES and KRABATHOR. A further tape, 'Nothing Lasts Forever' was cut in 1997 with 'In The Abyss Of Dreams ... Furious Memories' arriving in 1999.

THE SERPENT DESIGN, Eternal Deformity (2002). Malleus Malleficarum—Intro / Follow Me / Star Sailor / Uncontrolled / UsoA / HS 32 (New Weapon / Field Of Glory / Sea Of Love / Release Me / E.D. Rhapsody.

ETERNAL DEMENTIA

VERDAL, NORWAY — *Stig A. Kristiansen (vocals / keyboards), Larse (guitar), Ludvik Brandsegg (bass), Tor Erik Simensen (drums).*

Self-styled "authentic" Metal band ETERNAL DEMENTIA was created in Verdal / Mikadhdsasa during 2002 by SKAMBITT and MASHADAR singer Stig A. Kristiansen and ex-RAGNAROK drummer Tor Erik Simensen, also active with SKAMBITT and NO DAWN. Subsequent additions on guitar would be the DEPRAVED pairing of Andreas and Robert Florholmen. The demo 'The Virgin, Sedated And Seduced', mixed and mastered by Tony Waade at Mistral Lydstudio, was published in September of 2004. ETERNAL DEMENTIA underwent changes in mid 2004, adopting another NO DAWN member Ludvik Brandsegg on bass guitar along with keyboard player Ida, but losing both guitarists.

Toward the close of 2004 the band acquired WALLACHIA and AMNESIA guitarist Larse (Lars Stavdal) and set to work on recordings provisionally dubbed 'Tales Of The Demented, Vol. 1'. A new recording of the song 'The Virgin, Sedated And Seduced" with Larse on guitar was scheduled for release in March on a local compilation.

The Virgin, Sedated And Seduced, Eternal Dementia (2004) (Limited edition. 200 hand numbered copies). The Virgin, Sedated And Seduced / Prelude: The Birth / Set Out To Die.

ETERNAL DIRGE

GERMANY — *Timo (vocals / guitar), Pethe (guitar), Boelmi (bass), Ralf (drums).*

This self styled "Neo pagan psycho Metal" band, from Marl, Westfalia, was formed in the mid 80s and released several demos before 'We Are The Dead' led to a record deal. Both of ETERNAL DIRGE's albums, 1994's 'Morbus Ascendit' and 1996's 'Khaos Magick', highlight the group's brand of Death / Thrash Metal with keyboard leanings on a grand scale. Indeed, during the recording of the 'Khaos Magick' album permanent keyboardist Sascha R. joined the group. Touring included an appearance on the 1996 'Full Of Hate' Easter festivals sharing the billing with SIX FEET UNDER and THINK ABOUT MUTATION.

An ex-ETERNAL DIRGE bassist, Karsten Boehnke, scored credits MUSTY GUTS and SUFFOCATE BASTARD.

MORBUS ASCENDIT, HASS Production (1994). Out The Eons / The Crawling Chaos / Exploring The Depths / Blind Idiot God / The Decadence Within / We Are The Dead / Sinustis Maxillaris / Evolved Mutations.
KHAOS MAGICK, Moribund MR024 (1996). I, Unameable / The Threshold Of Sensation / Anthem To The Seeds (Of Pure Demise) / Feaster From The Stars / Rending The Veils / Kallisti / Like Roses In A Garden Of Weed / In Praise Of Biocide / Hymn To Pan / My Sweet Satan.

ETERNAL GRAY

ISRAEL — *Eyal Glottman (vocals / guitar), Dory Bar-Or (guitar / keyboards), Gil Ben Ya'akov (bass), Roy Chen (drums).*

ETERNAL GRAY operated in their formative years under the title BETRAYER. This Death Metal outfit last performed live in the summer of 2001 as support to ROTTING CHRIST but soon after the core members regrouped as ETERNAL GRAY. The 'Kindless' album was recorded in Sweden with Tommy Tägtgren acting as producer. The band revealed recording during 2003

ETERNAL GRAY (pic: Itamar)

of a second outing 'Your Gods, My Enemies' would include the talents of SCARVE drummer Dirk Verbeuren and even MORBID ANGEL frontman Steve Tucker.

The band severed ties with singer Eyal Glottman in April of 2004. As a trio of guitarist / keyboard player Dory Bar-Or, bassist Gil Ben-Ya'akov and drummer Roy Hen ETERNAL GRAY cut the EP 'Deeds Of Hate', restricting this to a thousand hand numbered copies.

The band, inaugurating ABED drummer Dror Goldstein and session guitarist Auria Sapir of MATRICIDE, donated their rendition of 'Blinded By Fear' to the AT THE GATES tribute album, 'Slaughterous Souls—A Tribute to At The Gates' released in September 2004 through Drowned Scream Records.

ETERNAL GRAY enrolled a triumvirate of players in January 2005, vocalist Oren Balbus, guitarist Auria Sapir and drummer Dror Goldstein. An EP, to be titled 'Numb', was recorded but never issued due to membership problems. The group announced fresh album recordings had commenced in early March 2007.

KINDLESS, Raven Music (2002). Sins In The Process Of Creation / Flesh Cycles / Absent Mourn / Inflicting Pain / There Lays Nothing / War Of Chaos / The Unbelievers Die / Intro / World Of Ice / Outro.

ETERNAL LIES

VARBERG, SWEDEN — *Tommy Grönberg (vocals), Björn Johansson (guitar), Erik Månsson (guitar), Marcus Wesslén (bass), Conny Pettersson (drums).*

Varberg based melodic Death Metal. ETERNAL LIES was formulated during late 1998 by 1998 by former AGGRESSIVE SERPENT guitarist Björn Johansson and drummer Conny Pettersson, soon adding second guitarist Jocke Ludwigson and former FATAL EMBRACE singer Tommy Grönberg. Bassist Martin Karlsson of PARAZITE and EUCHARIST completed the roster.

An abortive attempt to lay down a demo recording in 2000 subsequently saw the departure of Ludwigson. At this juncture both Björn Johansson and Conny Pettersson also operate ROTINJECTED in union with ANATA members vocalist and guitarist Fredrik Schälin, guitarist Andreas Alllenmark and bassist Henrik Drake. Conny Pettersson, whilst retaining his ties to ETERNAL LIES, would join the ranks of ANATA in 2001. Nevertheless ETERNAL LIES scored a recording deal with the Arctic Music Group resulting in the September 2002 album 'Spiritual Deception'. Following recording Karlsson relinquished his services, subsequently going on to REVENGIA and Progressive Metal band PARALLEL UNIVERSE. Two personnel from AGGRESSIVE SERPENT, guitarist Erik Månsson and bass player Marcus Wesslén, plugged the vacancies. Pettersson would return the favour by enrolling into AGGRESSIVE SERPENT the following year.

In July of 2004 ETERNAL LIES drafted Tobias Gustafsson, former bass player with EUCHARIST, as their new singer.

SPIRITUAL DECEPTION, Arctic Music Group (2002). Leaving Only Me / Consecrate Life / Newborn Sunrise / Poems / Evaporate / Winter Breeze / A Memory Of Lies / By The Hands Of The Architect / Addicted To Fire / Divided.

ETERNAL OATH

SÖDERTÄLJE, SWEDEN — *Joni Maensivu (vocals), Peter Nagy (guitar / drums), Petri Tarvainen (guitar), Peter Wendin (bass), Par Almquist (keyboards), Ted Jonsson (drums).*

Södertälje Gothic Metal outfit. ETERNAL OATH guitarist Peter Nagy also has credits with HYPOCRITE, WYVERN and MÖRK GRYNING. The band came together during 1991 citing an inaugural line-up comprising vocalist Joni Mäensivu, guitarist Petri Tarvainen bass player Ted Lundström and drummer Ted Jonsson. A later addition saw the ranks swelled with the introduction of second guitarist Daniel Dziuba. This formation cut an opening three track demo in the December 1992. However, shortly after Lundström took leave to join up with AMON AMARTH and a replacement on bass was found in Martin Wiklander. Because of this line-up shuffle the demo remained consigned to the vaults.

A full year later the band set about recording a second demo, a five track session entitled 'Art Of Darkness'. This new material demonstrated ETERNAL OATH's drift away from the basic Death Metal approach. Peter Nagy took Dziuba's position that same year. In February of 1994 a further demo was laid down, prompting the interest of Rat Pack Records and resulting in recording of songs for the mini-album 'So Silent'. The album never emerged on Rat Pack though, ETERNAL OATH severing ties with the label and industriously releasing the record under their own steam in June of 1996.

Wiklander lost interest and decamped and ETERNAL OATH pulled in Peter Wendin as substitute for the debut full length album 'Through The Eyes Of Hatred', issued in May 1999 by the Singapore based Pulverized label. The August 2002 ETERNAL OATH outing 'Righteous', released by the Greater Arts label, would include a cover version of PARADISE LOST's 'Eternal'.

The band donated their rendition of 'The Fevered Circle' to the AT THE GATES tribute album, 'Slaughterous Souls—A Tribute to At The Gates' released in September 2004 through Drowned Scream Records.

In June 2006 ETERNAL OATH parted ways with original singer Joni Mäensivu, bringing in Timo Hovinen of SLOW GROWING NUMB and GAME OVER as replacement. However, in January 2007 announced their decision to disband.

Art Of Darkness, Eternal Oath (1993) (Demo). Eternal Rest / Humanitarian / Unreal Visions / Presence Denied / Walls Of Lost Souls.

SO SILENT, N Wrapped Media NWM01 (1996). The Dawn / Harmonic Souls Departed / So Silent / Insanity / Eternal Rest / Dream Of Rising.

THROUGH THE EYES OF HATRED, Pulverised ASH010CD (1999). Beyond Forgiveness / Without Tears / Angel Of Deception / When The Dreams Die / The Funeral Winds / Lost Somewhere Between / Through The Eyes Of Hatred / The Secret Flame / Soulpoem.

RIGHTEOUS, Greater Art GREAT 08001 (2002). Preserve The Emotions / Into The Dreamscape / Dreams Of The Silent / Righteous / The Destiny Forsaken / Crown Of Emptiness / And I Close My Eyes / Eternal / Unbelieved World / The Tears For Time.

WITHER, Black Lodge BLOD 022CD (2005). Behind Tomorrow / Death's Call / In Despair For My Sins / Godsend / Second Life / Within My World / Act Of Fate / On Bitter Wings / Fallen Virtue / At Your Hands / A Face In The Crowd / Wither.

RE-RELEASED HATRED, Black Lodge BLOD 010CD (2006). The Dawn / Harmonic Souls Departed / So Silent / Insanity / Eternal Rest / Dream Of Rising / Beyond Forgiveness / Without Tears / Angel Of Deception / When The Dreams Die / The Funeral Winds / Lost Somewhere Between / Through The Eyes Of Hatred / The Secret Flame / Soulpoem / The Fevered Circle.

ETERNAL RUIN

BALTIMORE, MD, USA — Joe Ridgely (vocals), Dee Jay Mclain (guitar), Nolan Clyde (guitar), Ryan Engle (bass), Eric Lowery (drums).

Although originally founded in Greencastle, PA Death Metal act ETERNAL RUIN would subsequently shift base to Baltimore, Maryland. Coming together in 2000 the inaugural line up comprised lead vocalist Brian Lawyer, guitarist John Pierce, bassist Ryan Engle and drummer Chris Park. After a swathe of gigs across the tri-state area, and as their music progressed into darker, faster realms, ETERNAL RUIN severed ties with Lawyer, replacing him with Joe Ridgely. In 2001 the band entered the recording studio to capture some of this new material on tape. Although the demo, which featured a guesting Vinnie Matthews of DYING FETUS on backing vocals, garnered healthy reviews the band dissolved.

After a hiatus of just two months ETERNAL RUIN rose once more, bringing onboard returned with a new drummer & guitarist in that of Eric Lowry and Jon Malec respectively. At this juncture the band made the move to Maryland although, after finalizing recording of the EP 'Book Of The Dead', Malec exited. Nolan Clyde entered the fold in early 2003.

The band would feature on the first Tokyo 'Deathfest' in April 2005 at the Shibuya Cyclone, joining a billing comprising GODLESS TRUTH, DISGORGE and Japanese bands VOMIT REMNANTS, DISCONFORMITY and WOUNDEEP.

Book Of The Dead EP, Amputated Vein (2003). Violence In Epic Proportions / Children Of A Depleted Humanity / Excreting Hate / Forced To Contend / Enemy Within.

ETERNAL SOLSTICE

HOLLAND — Kees Van Schouten (vocals), Philip Nutgren (guitar), Victor Van Drie (guitar), Ramon Soeterbroek (bass), Mischa Kak (drums).

Founded in 1989 by vocalist Kees Van Scouten, guitarist Philip Nutgren, bassist Ramon Soeterbroek and original drummer Edwin Roor, when the latter departed two ex-SEMPITERNAL DETHREIGN musicians were added in drummer Mischa Hak and guitarist Victor Van Drie. Hak was also playing drums with MOURNING.

ETERNAL SOLSTICE began recording a proposed split album with MOURNING in 1990 but Van Schouten departed leaving Souterbroek to handle lead vocal duties. It took a further two years for this split album to see a release on Midian Creations Records, during which time ETERNAL SOLSTICE split.

The band was reformed the following year by Nutgren and Soeterbroek together with drummer Eric Boekoe. A demo followed, but the band splintered once more leaving Soeterbroek handling lead vocals. Although drummer Mische Hak performed on the debut full length album 'The Wish Is Father To The Thought', which included a cover version of the SODOM track 'Outbreak Of Evil', ETERNAL SOLSTICE finding a permanent drummer in ex-MOURNING and ARCANE man Andre Van Der Ree.

The band augmented their sound in early 1996 by welcoming ex ASPHYX guitarist Eric Daniels into the ranks. In December of 1998 ex-members André van der Ree and Ramon Soeterboek forged DARK REMAINS.

AT THE DAWN OF ..., Midian Creations MID 001 (1992) (split album with MOURNING).

THE WISH IS THE FATHER TO THE THOUGHT, Displeased (1994). God In The Flesh / Torn Apart / Chamber Of Morpheus / Act Of Settlement / Blasphemous Sermons / Dragged Down To Rot / Sleep Of Death / Demonic Fertilizer / Wrapped In Darkness / Outbreak Of Evil.

HORRIBLE WITHIN, Poseidon PP 35020 (1995). Unholy Trinity DV / Culpable Homicide / The Ceremony Has Begun / Mask The Face Of Death / One Last Vision (Prepare) / By Your Command / T.W.I.F.T.T.T. / Eager For Death / A Wish Beyond / Worn With Age.

DEMONIC FERTILIZER, Poseidon (1997). Inserts / Deep Sleep / Melancholic '97 / Rebirth In Ice / Obscuration / In The Year 2525 / Demonic Fertilizer II / Thrall Rode To The Gallows / Turn Of The Century.

ETERNAL SUFFERING

KINGSTON, MA, USA — Wayne Sarantopoulos (vocals), Chris Glover (guitar), Brian Evans (guitar), Jon Landolfi (bass), Chad Connell (drums).

ETERNAL SUFFERING's beginnings trace back to the Spring of 1994 and the formation of PUTRID by guitarist Brian Evans and drummer Chad Connell. With the introduction of bassist Chris Glover and ENSTRANGLEMENT vocalist Wayne Sarantopolous the band evolved into DISGORGE. However, soon after, with the discovery that DISGORGE was already in use by a plethora of acts, a name switch to ETERNAL SUFFERING was actioned. In late 1996 the band cut the demo 'Remain Forever In Misery'.

During August of 1998 ETERNAL SUFFERING laid down tracks in Triticon Studios in Connecticut for the album 'Drowning In Tragedy'. Bassist Jon Landolfi was inducted subsequent to these sessions. Drummer Chad Connell joined MINCERY in December of 2002.

Members of ETERNAL SUFFERING also operate in Grindcore act EJACULATED WHORE. Both Chris Glover and Wayne Sarantopoulos subsequently activated SCUM BITCH

DROWNING IN TRAGEDY, Extremities Productions (1999). Intro / My Once Shadowed Desire / Drown In The Candles Flame / Let The Dark Waters Flow / The Warmth In Her Torment / Trail Of Blood To The Altar / Love Can Never Conquer Hate / Buried Under Blackend Tears / Rise / To Sadness, Betrothed / T.T.P.

ETERNAL TEARS OF SORROW

OULUNSALO, FINLAND — Altti Veteläinen (vocals), Antti Talala (guitar), Jarmo Puolakanaho (guitar), Olli Pekka-Torro (guitar / keyboards), Pasi Hiltula (keyboards), Petri Sankala (drums).

Oulunsalo Death Metal act with Black overtones although the band themselves are reluctant to label their brand of music "black". The group rose from the ashes of an early 90's act ANDROMEDA, which comprised Altti Verläinen on bass, Jarmo Puolakanaho on guitar, vocalist Mikko Komulainen, guitarist Olli Pekka Törrö and drummer Petri Sankula. ANDROMEDA folded after their rehearsal rooms burnt down but did manage a 1993 demo 'Beyond The Fantasy'.

By the following year Verläinen, Törrö and Puolakanaho founded ETERNAL TEARS OF SORROW bowing in with the tape 'The Seven Goddesses Of Frost'. The group was far from happy with the end result citing the facts that it had been recorded at school on a four track machine. Fortunately a follow up session 'Bard's Burial' secured a deal with the Swedish X-treme Records label. However, although the 'Sinner's Serenade' opus was laid down in 1996 it was to be September 1997 before its release.

The band switched to the Finnish Spinefarm concern for sophomore outing 'Vild Mánnu'. In 1999 Törrö decamped and new members Antti Talala on guitar, bassist / keyboard player Pasi Hiltula and erstwhile ANDROMEDA colleague drummer Petri Sankula were welcomed into the fold.

The 'Chaotic Beauty' album, which includes a cover of EDGE OF SANITY's 'Black Tears', was produced by Mikko Karmila featured backing vocals from SINERGY's Kimberley Goss.

Touring to promote the album resulted in the exit of Talala with Antti Kokko of KALMAH taking his position. ETERNAL TEARS OF SORROW members Altti Veteläinen, keyboard player Pasi Hiltula and drummer Petri Sankala also cite membership of KALMAH.

During March of 2002 the ETERNAL TEARS OF SORROW triumvirate of bassist Altti Veteläinen, guitarist Olli-Pekka Törrö and drummer Petri Sankala announced the formation of a Finnish 'Gothic Metal supergroup' dubbed FOR MY PAIN. Joining them in this endeavour would be guitarist Lauri Tuohimaa of EMBRAZE, keyboard player Tuomas Holopainen of NIGHTWISH and fronted by REFLECTION vocalist Juha Kylmänen.

ETERNAL TEARS OF SORROW folded in January of 2003. Members guitarist Antti Talala and drummer Reiska Pohjola re-united in Gothic Rock outfit SOULRELIC, assembled by SNAKEGOD and TECHNICAL JUSTICE keyboard player Jani Hölli and including Pekka Talala on bass guitar plus BLEAK CROWD singer Tommy Suomala.

The band bounced back in January 2005, announcing their reformation with a signature to Spinefarm Records and a new album 'Before The Bleeding Sun', recorded at Tico-Tico Studios in Kemi and at Note-On Studios in Kuopio. Newly included in the line-up would be the TAROT and VIRTUOCITY credited Janne Tolsa on keyboards and guitarist Risto Ruuth from Oulu's SCRYON. Guest studio vocals came courtesy of vocals by Jarmo Kylmänen of SCYRON, Miriam "Sfinx" Renvåg from RAM-ZET, Tony Kakko of SONATA ARCTICA and Marco Hietala of NIGHTWISH and TAROT. Antti Talala took on double duties, joining TO/DIE/FOR in June. ETERNAL TEARS OF SORROW finally mixed 'Before The Bleeding Sun' in February 2006, with Mikko Karmila at Finnvox Studios in Helsinki, setting a May release date. "Before The Bleeding Sun' entered the national Finnish charts at number 26. In Japan the album emerged on the Avalon Marquee label in October.

For the first ETERNAL TEARS OF SORROW live concert in over six years, held December 31st 2006 at Club Teatria in Oulu, the band underwent a membership change. Drummer Petri Sankala suffered an ankle-related accident and was waiting an operation. His duties would be handled by Tuomo Laikari of RAUTAVAARA INC. Keyboard player Janne Tolsa, sidelined by his other act TAROT, was substituted by Veli-Matti Kananen.

SINNERS SERENADE, X-Treme XTR003 (1997). Another One Falls Asleep / The Law Of The Flames / Dirge / Into The Deepest Waters / Sinners Serenade / My God, The Evil Wind / March / Bard's Burial / The Son Of The Forest / Empty Eyes.
VILD MÁNNU, Spinefarm SPI 068CD (1999). Northern Doom / Burning Flames Embrace / Goashem / Scars Of Wisdom / Nightwinds Lullaby / Raven (In Your Eyes) / Vild Mánnu / Coronach / Nodde Rahgan / Seita.
CHAOTIC BEAUTY, Spinefarm SPI 197CD (2000). Shattered Soul / Blood Of Faith Stains My Hands / Autumn's Grief / The Seventh Eclipse / Bride Of The Crimson Sea / Black Tears / Tar Of Chaos / Bhéan Sidhe / Nocturnal Strains / Flight Of Icarus / Coronach / Nightwinds Lullaby / Burning Flames Embrace.
The Last One For Life, Spikefarm SPI 122CD (2001). The Last One For Life / As I Die.
A VIRGIN AND A WHORE, Spinefarm SPI 123CD (2001). Aurora Borealis / Heart Of Wilderness / Prophetian / Fall Of Man / The River Flows Frozen / The Last One For Life / Sick, Dirty And Mean / Blood Of Hatred / Aeon. Chart position: 39 FINLAND.
BEFORE THE BLEEDING SUN, Spinefarm (2006). Sweet Lilith Of My Dreams / Another Me / Red Dawn Rising / Upon The Moors / Sakura No Rei / Sinister Rain / Lost Rune Of Thunder / Tar Still Flows / Angelheart, Ravenheart (Act I: Before The Bleeding Sun). Chart position: 26 FINLAND.

ETERNAL TRAGEDY

MILAN, ITALY — *Stefania Ponzilacqua (vocals / guitar / bass), Iwan Hendrikx (drums).*

Milan's ETERNAL TRAGEDY has its roots in the epic styled Classic Metal project METAL 'TIL DEATH, dating to 1999. Under this banner the act did not record but, having adopted the ETERNAL TRAGEDY title, debuted in 2001 with a two song demo of 'Dreamworld' and 'Murder Of Souls'. The formative band at this juncture comprised vocalist / guitarist Stefania Ponzilacqua, Valentina Ponzilacqua on bass, Alessandro Patelli on drums and Andrea M. on vocals. However, this alliance soon fractured. Undaunted, Ponzilacqua crafted a July 2004 two song demo billed as 'Voice Of Instinct'. Iwan Hendrikx would subsequently be recruited on drums.

Album recordings in 2006 found ETERNAL TRAGEDY employing some well known figures, the sessions being produced by Tim Aymar of CONTROL DENIED and engineered by Curran Murphy, ex-ANNIHILATOR, and also featuring guest appearances by Kelly Conlon, ex-DEATH and MONSTROSITY, on bass with Robert Falzano, ex-ANNIHILATOR, on drums.

Voice Of Instinct, Eternal Tragedy (2004) (Demo). Eternal Tragedy / Outside Of Mercy.
Voice Of Instinct, Eternal Tragedy (2004). Eternal Tragedy / Outside Of Mercy.

ETHEREAL COLLAPSE

WILKES-BARRE, PA, USA — *Ryan Klubeck (vocals / guitar), Dave Kline (guitar), Tom Colón (bass), Matt Rodriguez (drums).*

Melodic Death Metal band ETHEREAL COLLAPSE, hailing from Wilkes-Barre, Pennsylvania, feature the FALLOUT credited Matt Rodriguez on drums and ex-NIHILISTIC and EPHEMERAL bassist Tom Colón. Frontman Ryan Klubeck was previously with BLIND AMBITION. The band had begun life billed DEITY with an original drummer Zach Baldassari. ETHEREAL COLLAPSE cut a three track demo upfront of the 2004 EP 'Fallen Hope'. After this release bassist Kevin Chlipala was replaced by Tom Colón.

ETHEREAL COLLAPSE maintained a strenuous live schedule, racking up support credits to the likes of GOATWHORE, CATTLE DECAPITATION, EXHUMED, MASTODON, PREMONITIONS OF WAR, IN FLAMES, SLAYER, DYING FETUS, MISERY INDEX, CANNIBAL CORPSE, SHADOWS FALL, THE BLACK DAHLIA MURDER and GOD FORBID amongst others. The band signed to New York's Innerstrength Records in 2005. to cut debut album 'Breaching The Citadel'.

Bassist Tom Colón bowed out in January 2006, prioritising his other act PUTREFIED FLESH.

Fallen Hope, Ethereal Collapse (2004). A Tragedy Divine / Walls Of Eternity / Fallen Hope / Grand Deceiver.
BREACHING THE CITADEL, Innerstrength (2006). A Tragedy Divine / Undo Creation / Walls Of Eternity / As The Mighty Fall / Breaching The Citadel / The Eyes Of Solace / The Nightmare Creature / On The Reins Of Desire.

EUCHARIST

VEDDIGE, SWEDEN — *Markus Johnsson (vocals / guitar), Thomas Einarsson (guitar), Tobias Gustafsson (bass), Daniel Erlandsson (drums).*

One of the first bands to combine Death Metal with strong melodies, these so called pioneers of the 'Göthenberg style'. EUCHARIST, founded in 1989 and hailing from Veddige near Gothenburg, released their debut 'A Velvet Creation' in 1993 for Wrong Again Records although a 1992 demo, recorded whilst most of the band were still only sixteen years old, and an EP 'Greeting Immortality', on the Obscure Plasma label, had preceded it. Apparently the single was issued without the consent of the band. EUCHARIST also had their track 'The View' included on a compilation album 'Deaf Metal Sampler' issued by UK label Deaf Records, a subsidiary of Peaceville.

The debut album was actually recorded under strenuous conditions, the band disliking each other so much they had actually officially split up before commencement of recording. 'A Velvet Creation' was recorded by vocalist / guitarist Markus Johnsson, guitarist Thomas Einarsson, bass player Tobias Gustafsson and drummer Daniel Erlandsson. Tensions were still high though and Johnsson was in particular so disgusted he refused to record any guitars for the album. In the summer of 1994, two further tracks, 'Wounded And Alone' and 'The Predictable End' were recorded for inclusion on a compilation album released by Wrong Again Records, 'W.A.R. Compilation vol 1', released in 1995. These songs saw Matti Almsenius having replaced Einarsson.

EUCHARIST folded once again. Drummer Daniel Erlandsson later joined IN FLAMES, featuring on two tracks on their 'Subterranean' EP, LIERS IN WAIT and DIABOLIQUE. By 1996 Erlandsson and Johnsson were working once again on EUCHARIST.

EUCHARIST reconvened once more in the late 90's cutting two tracks 'The Predictable End' and 'Wounded And Alone' for 1995's Wrong Again Records compilation 'War'. 1996 found the EUCHARIST credited trio of vocalist / bassist Tobias Gustafsson, guitarist Matti Almsenius and drummer Daniel Erlandsson issuing an EP credited to THE END. During 1997 the pairing of Gustafsson and Almsenius were touting a Thrash Metal trio CROAM.

EUCHARIST returned in 1998 with the Fredrik Larnemo produced 'Mirrorworlds' set for Regain Records, this having been recorded at Studio Recordia in Varberg by Markus Johnsson, Daniel Erlandsson and bassist Martin Karlsson. Subsequently, the band drafted second guitarist Henrik Meijner of CROMLECH for live work.

EUCHARIST bass player Martin Karlsson, a prior member of PARAZITE, later joined Varberg's ETERNAL LIES. In 2004 the ETERNAL LIES connection was strengthened further when bassist Tobias Gustafsson enrolled as their new singer.

Greeting Immortality, Obscure Plasma (1992) (7" single). Greeting Immortality / Into The Cosmic Sphere.

Eucharist, Eucharist (1992) (Demo). Intro / Greeting Immortality / March Of Insurrection / Into The Cosmic Sphere / Outro.

A VELVET CREATION, Wrong Again WAR001 (1993). Greeting Immortality / The Religion Of The Blood-Red Velvet / March Of The Insurrection / My Bleeding Tears / Floating / A Velvet Creation / Into The Cosmic Sphere / Once My Eye Moved Mountains.

MIRROR WORLDS, Regain RNA1032 (1998). Mirror Worlds / Dissolving / With The Sun / The Eucharist / Demons / Fallen … / In Nakedness / Bloodred Stars.

EULOGY

USA — *Jason Avery (vocals), Jarret Pritchard (guitar), Jay Medina (guitar), Mike Beardon (bass), Clayton Gore (drums).*

EULOGY, despite only managing a solitary mini album release 'The Essence', was a renowned and influential force in the Florida Thrash / Death Metal transitional scene during the early 90s. The band was originally established in Virginia by vocalist Jason Avery, guitarist Jarrett Pritchard and bass player Mike Beardon. A debut demo was cut with the aid of a drum machine before EULOGY relocated to Florida in order to hook up with drummer 'Aantar' Lee Coates, a veteran citing credits such as NECROSIS, EXMORTIS and IMPIETY. However, within weeks Coates was out of the picture, duly replaced by Clayton Gore.

The band debuted on the live front in January of 1992, opening a gig in Tampa for MONSTROSITY and BRUTALITY. For a brief period EULOGY operated with second guitarist Jerry Mortillero, later of DIABOLIC. However, this line up never performed live or recorded. Back as a quartet the band recorded the 1992 Tom Harris produced demo session 'Dismal'. For these recordings EULOGY introduced Jay Medina on guitar in Mortillero's stead.

Later that same year a deal was scored with the Dutch Cenotaph label and recording commenced for the mini album 'The Essence'. However, in spite of fronting the money for these studio sessions themselves the record was massively delayed, surfacing as late as 1994. A tour of Florida ensued in alliance with GOREPHOBIA and IMMOLATION after which Medina exited. BRUTALITY's Jay Fernandez would deputize but then in another body blow Beardon decamped.

Down to the surviving trio of Pritchard, Avery and Gore EULOGY attempted to regroup bringing in Ed Webb on bass and RIPPING CORPSE man Erik Rutan on guitar. Rutan soon bade his farewell to join premier act MORBID ANGEL and Dave Sawyer stepped into the breach for live work. A demo tape, 'Lesson In Fear', surfaced in January of 1995, a track from which, 'Human Harvest', appeared on the Metal Blade 'Metal Massacre MMXII' compilation.

Shortly after EULOGY folded. Avery became frontman for MONSTROSITY. Jarret Pritchard switched from guitar to bass in order to enroll in CANEPHORA. Beardon had founded ANGEL TRUMPETS, a band operating in parallel with EULOGY that also saw contributions from Fernandez, Avery and Gore. ANGEL TRUMPETS had cut a two song demo in December of 1993. The drummer would also enjoy a brief term with Erik Rutan's ALAS project band.

Webb teamed up with BRUTALITY before joining forces with formative EULOGY drummer Lee Coates in DIABOLIC. Later Webb, ex-EULOGY guitarist Dave Sawyer and the erstwhile BRUTALITY pairing of Pete Sykes and Jim Coker founded CONTORTED. Guitarist Jarret Pritchard forged THE STELLAR CORE. In 2003 Clayton Gore re-surfaced as part of St. Louis, Missouri Black Metal band HARKONIN.

ESSENCE, Cenotaph 077-140782 (1994). The Essence / When The Heavens Bleed / Entombed By Belief / Consecration Of Fools.

EUTHANAUSEA

RIIHIMÄKI, FINLAND — *Janne Tamminen (vocals), Mika Nikkanen (guitar), Ville Nummenpää (guitar), Vesa Salminen (bass), Santtu Penttinen (keyboards), Marko Jokinen (drums).*

Riihimäki based Death / Thrash outfit, created in 1990 with a line-up of singer Janne Tamminen, guitarists Mika Nikkanen and Ville Nummenpää, bass guitarist Vesa Salminen and drummer Marko Jokinen. The band's first recordings, the 7" single 'Songs Of Forgotten Souls', would be overseen by STRATOVARIUS guitarist Timmo Tolkki. A further 1993 session, resulting in the 'Melodying' demo, also saw Tolkki handling production. EUTHANAUSEA then expanded their roster of band members by adding keyboard player Santtu Penttinen for a five song demo 'Satan Is Good'.

EUTHANAUSEA would then record the 1995 EP 'Sleep-Dream-Die-Fly', featuring guest vocalist Katja Nieminen on the song 'Mother's Darkest Lullaby'. Upon completion of these tracks vocalist Janne Tamminen was dismissed, later joining Hardcore merchants ENDSTAND. Nikkanen opted to take over the vocal role and in this incarnation the band submitted two tracks to the compilation album 'Shadows Of Michelangelo'. Adopting a completely new course the band drafted singer Saku Hänninen and switched title to SINSATIONAL. In this guise the group recorded one demo but, after the defection of Penttinen in 1999, would once more re-evolve into EUTHANAUSEA by 2002. The 'Fireworks' EP would be next on the agenda.

Songs Of Forgotten Souls, Independent EUTS-0892 (1992). Songs Of Forgotten Souls / Sadistfaction.

Sleep-Dream-Die-Fly, Independent (1995).

Fireworks, (2003). Fireworks / Helldozer / Sixteen Tons / Technicolor.

EVEMASTER

POHJOLA, FINLAND — *Jarno Taskula (vocals), Tomi Mykkänen (guitar / bass / keyboards).*

EVEMASTER blend a heady mixture of Doom Metal with strong traits of Death and even Black Metal to achieve their sound. Essentially the band is a duo, founded in Pohjola during 1996, of vocalist Jarno Taskula and multi instrumentalist Tomi Mykkänen. EVEMASTER's first demo cassette, 'In Thine

Majesty', would prove so successful it would be later re-pressed as a CD EP.

A deal was struck with the Finnish KTOK label for debut album 'Lacrimae Mundi'. Sessioning on this release would be keyboard player Ansi Kippo, MORTAL GOD guitarist Timo Laihanen and vocalist Nazgul von Armageddon of arch Black Metal band HORNA. The album would be subsequently re-released in digipack format by Polish label AMP Records.

The EVEMASTER duo recruited a live band for gigs in 1999 consisting of guitarist / vocalist T. Vaittinen, bass player M. Gran, keyboard player E. Huikuri and drummer M. Neuvonen. With this line-up EVEMASTER performed at the Katowice 'Metal Maniacs' festival in Poland during May.

Toward the end of 2001 EVEMASTER assembled once again to cut an EP 'Wither', recorded at Astia Studios with producer Anssi Kippo, for new label Vortex Motion. The record included a cover version of TAROT's 'Wings Of Darkness', complete with TAROT, SINERGY and VIRTUOCITY man Marco Hietala lending vocal support. Other studio guests included drummer Jasko Raatikainen of CHILDREN OF BODOM, GRAIN vocalist M. Lindberg and MORTAL GOD guitarist Timo Laihanen once again.

The band, signing to Rising Realm Records, would completely re-record their debut album for a February 2005 release, retitling said opus as 'MMIV Lacrimae Mundi'. Featuring an extra track in a cover version of DIO's 'We Rock' the revised version once more saw Jaska Raatikainen from CHILDREN OF BODOM manning the drums.

Tomi Mykkänen temporarily joined Fantasy Metal band BATTLELORE for European tour dates in October.

In Thine Majesty, (1998). Lacrimae Mundi / The Divine Iamblichus / Epistelium (The Storm Rises).
LACRIMAE MUNDI, KTOK Records (1999). Pandemonium / Whispers / Embraced / Archways / Lacrimae Mundi / Epistelium (The Storm Rises) / Equinox Nocturne.
Wither EP, Vortex Motions Records LFR314037 (2002). Midnight In The Garden Of Evil / Stars—Serenity—Burning / Wings Of Darkness / As I Turn Away.
MMIV LACRIMAE MUNDI, Rising Realm (2005). Pandemonium / Whispers / Embraced / Archways / Lacrimae Mundi / Epistelium (The Storm Rises) / Equinox Nocturne / We Rock.

EVENTIDE

SWEDEN — *Jacob Magnusson (vocals / guitar), Jonas Sjölin (guitar), Niclas Linde (bass), Andreas Kronqvist (keyboards), Max Seppälä (drums).*

EVENTIDE released the 1999 demo, 'Caress The Abstract' recorded at Los Angered studios outside Gothenburg with KING DIAMOND guitarist Andy LaRoque acting as producer, then citing a line-up of Jacob Magnusson on vocals and guitars, guitarist Niclas Linde, bass player Åke Wallebom and drummer Max Seppälä. The 'Caress The Abstract' demo cover was notably executed by Niklas Sundin. A self titled demo, once again crafted at Los Angered Recording, was released in 2000.

The band hit membership tribulation during 2004, this eventually leaving EVENTIDE standing merely as a duo of Magnusson and Seppälä. Re-building the band, new draftees would be Thomas Magnusson on bass and Jonas Sjölin on guitar. However, the latter's tenure proved brief. EVENTIDE returned in September 2005 with the 'No Place Darker' promotional session.

A debut album, 'Diaries From The Gallows', again recorded at Los Angered studios in Gothenburg, saw release in October 2006 through Cartel Media. EVENTIDE were joined by former ZOMBIE AUTOPILOT guitarist Sebastian Olsson. EVENTIDE parted ways with Cartel Media in April 2007.

Caress The Abstract, Eventide (1999). Silence Of Her Fall / Draining Reality / House Of Trauma / Blank / Thoughts Astray.
Eventide Promo 2000, (2000). The Collector's Pride / Banned From Life / Conscience Exhaled.
No Place Darker, (2005). No Place Darker / New Reality / My Closest Demon / Arms Of Silence.
DIARIES FROM THE GALLOWS, Cartel Media (2006). Into Illusion / Killing What Can't Be Handled / My Closest Demon / This Curse / No Place Darker / Standards Of Rebellion / Indifferent / The Skeleton Who Sold Its Skin / Vargavidderna / I, Enemy / Confinement.

EVERGREY

HELSINGBORG, SWEDEN — *Tom S. Englund (vocals / guitar), Henrik Danhage (guitar), Michael Håkansson (bass), Rikard Zander (keyboards), Jonas Ekdahl (drums).*

Highly regarded Progressive Metal band out of Helsingborg, EVERGREY, established during 1996, specialise in maudlin yet intricate works of weighty gravitas headed up by the rustic timbre of Thomas Englund. EVERGREY's 1998 album 'The Dark Discovery', released on the GNW (Gothenburg Noise Works) label, witnessed guest performances from KING DIAMOND's Andy LaRocque, also acting as producer, and FREAK KITCHEN's MATTIAS EKLUNDH. The recording band unit comprised singer Tom Englund, guitarist Dan Bronell, bassist Daniel Nöjd, keyboard player Will Chandra and drummer Patrick Carlsson.

EVERGREY switched to the Hall Of Sermon Gothic Rock specialists for May 1999's 'Solitude, Dominance, Tragedy' outing. The album release party was held in Bochum, Germany at a gig sharing billing with RAGE.

However, bass player Daniel Nöjd decamped and EVERGREY enlisted two new recruits, bassist Michael Håkansson and SOILWORK keyboard player Sven Karlsson, both erstwhile members of Black Metal band EMBRACED. Håkansson also divided his duties with THE FORSAKEN.

European dates saw the band opening proceedings at the German 'Bang Your Head' festival and touring alongside CRIMSON GLORY and KAMELOT. The band would also find studio time the same year to donate their rendition of 'Rising Force' to a YNGWIE MALMSTEEN tribute album.

Before the year was out guitarist Dan Bronelli made his exit too. The band endured by drafting Henrik Danhage. EVERGREY signed to the Inside Out Music label for release of a third album, the September 2001 alien abduction themed conceptual piece 'In Search For Truth'.

Keyboard player Sven Karlsson would be let go later in the year, his replacement being Chris Rehn. By 2002 EVERGREY had installed Rikard Zande in the keyboard role for recording of a new album, 'Recreation Day', with producer Andy LaRocque. Shortly after release of the record in March 2003 drummer Patrick Carlsson severed ties with the band, being superseded by Jonas Ekdahl. EVERGREY allied with HATE ETERNAL, ARCH ENEMY and THE BLACK DAHLIA MURDER for a short but intensive run of US dates coming in August.

EVERGREY undertook a short burst of Danish dates in March 2004 allied with MERCENARY. The band resumed road action, acting as opening band for ICED EARTH and CHILDREN OF BODOM North American Tour in April to promote 'The Inner Circle' album released by Inside Out Music.

Michael Håkansson, maintaining his commitment to EVERGREY, resurrected his former act EMBRACED in June of 2004. That Summer Tom S. Englund and Arnold Linberg acted as production team for the DRAGONLAND album 'Starfall'. EVERGREY revealed they would be filming a 9th October show in Gothenburg for a live DVD release.

EVERGREY members Henrik Danhage and Jonas Ekdahl revealed a raw Metal side project dubbed DEATH DESTRUCTION in union with ex-HAMMERFALL bassist Fredrik Larsson. Meantime, Michael Håkansson sessioned bass on new album recordings for THE PROJECT HATE. EVERGREY, promoting the March 2005 released 'A Night To Remember' album, acted as support to DREAM THEATER frontman JAMES LABRIE's European solo dates in April. The DVD of 'A Night To Remember' impressively topped the national Swedish charts. Henrik

Danhage also made time to guest on the NOCTURNAL RITES album 'Grand Illusion'.

Again working with Inside Out Music the band entered the studio in late 2005 to craft an album with the noted production team of Sanken Sandquist and Stefan Glaumann. 'Monday Morning Apocalypse', issued in March 2006, entered the Swedish album charts at number 6. A brief run of homeland shows followed in April. The band's appearance at the Gelsenkirchen 'Rock Hard' festival in Germany during June was taped and subsequently the track 'She Speaks To The Dead' was included on the 'Rock Hard' magazine compilation album 'Rock Hard: Das Festival 2006'.

EVERGREY drafted former CRYSTAL AGE, DEATH DESTRUCTION, NONE, HAMMERFALL and SHOT INJECTION man Fredrik Larsson on bass in July. Ex-bassist Michael Håkansson duly joined ENGEL. Following an appearance at the 'Canarias MetalZone' festival on the Canary Islands on October 10th, the band toured throughout Europe, the UK and Scandinavia in October and November backed by AVATAR. The following month Henrik Danhage acted as stand in guitarist for IN FLAMES North American dates.

The band had the tracks 'Mark Of The Triangle' and 'Obedience' included on the 'ProgPower USA VIII' DVD compilation in 2007. That April bassist Fredrik Larsson opted out, re-joining HAMMERFALL.

THE DARK DISCOVERY, GNW GNW002 (1998). Blackened Dawn / December 26th / Dark Discovery / As Light Is Our Darkness / Beyond Salvation / Closed Eyes / Trust And Betrayal / Shadowed / When The River Calls / For Every Tear That Falls / To Hope Is To Fear.
SOLITUDE, DOMINANCE, TRAGEDY, Hall Of Sermon 7111 (1999). Solitude Within / Nosferatu / The Shocking Truth / A Scattered Me / She Speaks To The Dead / When Darkness Falls / Words Mean Nothing / Damnation / The Corey Curse.
IN SEARCH OF THE TRUTH, Inside Out Music IOMCD 081 (2001). The Masterplan / Rulers Of The Mind / Watching The Skies / State Of Paralysis / The Encounter / Mark Of The Triangle / Dark Waters / Different Worlds / Misled. Chart position: 59 SWEDEN.
RECREATION DAY, Inside Out Music IOMCD 117 (2003). The Great Deceiver / End Of Your Days / As I Lie Here Bleeding / Recreation Day / Visions / I'm Sorry / Blinded / Fragments / Madness Caught Another Victim / Your Darkest Hour / Unforgivable / Trilogy Of The Damned. Chart positions: 18 SWEDEN, 148 FRANCE.
I'm Sorry, Inside Out Music IOMCD 115 (2003). I'm Sorry / Blinded / The Masterplan (Video).
THE INNER CIRCLE, Inside Out Music IOMCD 165 (2004). A Touch Of Blessing / Ambassador / In The Wake Of The Weary / Harmless Wishes / Waking Up Blind / More Than Ever / The Essence Of Conviction / Where All Good Sleep / Faith Restored / When The Walls Go Down. Chart position: 24 SWEDEN.
A NIGHT TO REMEMBER, Inside Out Music IOMCD 203 (2005). Intro / Blinded / End Of Your Days / More Than Ever / She Speaks To The Dead / Rulers Of The Mind / Blackened Dawn / Waking Up Blind / As I Lie Here Bleeding / Mislead / Mark Of The Triangle / When The Walls Go Down / Harmless Wishes / Essence Of Conviction / Solitude Within / Nosferatu / Recreation Day / For Every Tear That Falls / Touch Of Blessing / The Masterplan.
Monday Morning Apocalypse, Inside Out Music (2006). Monday Morning Apocalypse / Rulers Of The Mind (Live from Gates Of Metal 2005) / Monday Morning Apocalypse (Karaoke version). Chart position: 19 SWEDEN.
MONDAY MORNING APOCALYPSE, Inside Out Music IOMCD 240 (2006). Monday Morning Apocalypse / Unspeakable / Lost / Obedience / The Curtain Fall / In Remembrance / At Loss For Words / Till Dagmar / Still In The Water / The Dark I Walk You Through / I Should / Closure. Chart position: 6 SWEDEN.

EVIL DEAD

USA — *Phil Flores (vocals), Juan Garcia (guitar), Albert Gonzales (guitar), Mel Sanchez (bass), Rob Alaniz (drums).*

EVIL DEAD, a band who were unafraid to take Death Metal to new levels of extremity, were created by guitarist Juan Garcia after he abandoned AGENT STEEL in 1988. Garcia's previous credits also included ABATTOIR. The original version of EVIL DEAD included ex-ABATTOIR bassist Mel Sanchez and erstwhile NECROPHILIA drummer Rob Alaniz. ABATTOIR guitarist Mark Caro was invited to join early on but the liaison didn't pan out and he quickly left the scene after recording a three track demo tape.

Guitarist Albert Gonzalez and vocalist Phil Flores were added a year later and EVIL DEAD would go on to score a deal with the German label Steamhammer Records. The group debuted with the 'Rise Above' EP in 1989 and followed it up with the full blown album 'Annihilation Of Civilization' the same year. Japanese versions of 'Annihilation Of Civilization' included bonus tracks from the European only released EP. However, EVIL DEAD fragmented before their second album, Albert Gonzales was fired and would join DEATH for touring duties.

Rob Alaniz walked out (forming RISE in the process) but Flores and Garcia regrouped by adding guitarist Dan Flores and bassist Karlos Medina (after Sanchez split) for 1991's 'The Underworld'. Drums on the album, which included a version of the SCORPIONS 'He's A Woman, She's A Man', were supplied by former DEFCON man Doug Clawson and backing vocals by METAL CHURCH man David Wayne. DEATH drummer Gene Hoglan also guested.

Rise Above, Steamhammer 557590 (1989). Rise Above / Run Again / Sloe Death / S.T. Riff.
ANNIHILATION OF CIVILIZATION, Steamhammer 847603 (1989). F.C.I.: The Awakening / Annihilation Of Civilization / Living God / Future Shock / Holy Trials / Gone Shooting / Parricide / Unauthorised Exploitation / B.O.H.I.C.A.
THE UNDERWORLD,, Steamhammer 084 76362 (1991). Intro (Comshell 5) / Global Warming / Branded / Welcome To Kuwait / Critic- Cynic / The 'Hood / The Underworld / He's A Woman, She's A Man / Process Elimination / Labyrinth Of The Mind / Reap What You Sow.
LIVE ... FROM THE DEPTHS OF THE UNDERWORLD, Steamhammer (1992). The Underworld / Global Warning / Gone Shooting / Parracide / F.C.I.—Welcome To Kuwait / The 'Hood / Annihilation Of Civilization / Darkness.

EVIL INCARNATE

USA — *Mike Eisenhauer (vocals / bass), Rob Rigney (guitar), Dave Gally (guitar), Andy Vehnekamp (drums).*

A blasphemic Death Metal band of some repute. Previously known as APOLLYON and forged by erstwhile NUM SKULL members frontman Mike Eisenhauer and guitarist Tom Brandauer in 1994. A series of demos started with 'Beyond Blasphemy' in 1994 and 'Deliverance From Salvation'. Brandauer departed and was replaced by former MORBID CORPSES and FEAR SPAWNED RELIGION man Dave Gally The third effort 'Christ Destroyed' was issued before Deathgasm Records compiled these early recordings for the 'Blood Of The Saints' album. These recording were also issued on cassette by the Czech label Ramu Records.

EVIL INCARNATE have also offered tribute by appearing on the Dwell Records releases VENOM 'In The Sign Of The Horns', SLAYER 'Gateway To Hell' and BLACK SABBATH 'Hell Rules Volume 2'. For some of these recordings Scott Creekmore took the lead vocal mantle as Eisenhauer was detained serving a jail sentence.

EVIL INCARNATE drummer Andy Vehnekamp is better known as a member of JUNGLE ROT. Brandauer returned following the exit of Gally.

A second album entitled 'Blackest Hymns Of God's Disgrace', for Death Gasm Records, was recorded in 2000. Another round of tribute appearances saw EVIL INCARNATE committing to tape versions of TWISTED SISTER's 'The Nature Of The Beast' and DESTRUCTION's 'Tormentor'. EVIL INCARNATE clocked up a round of European dates in April of 2001 sharing billing with DISMEMBER and MONSTROSITY. In early 2002 the band was back on the tribute trail offering up MÖTLEY CRÜE's 'Shout At The Devil' and SLAYER's 'Piece By Piece' for WW3 Records collections. A short burst of dates in Mexico during March found the band in alliance with KRABATHOR and MASACHISM.

BLACKEST HYMNS OF GOD'S DISGRACE, Death Gasm (2000). Kingdom Under The Shade Of Night (Intro) / Satanic Victory / Strike The Earth With Bloodshed / Legions Of Christian Pigs / Christ Destroyed / Smoke Of The Holy Ones Burning / The Blackest Hymn Of God's Disgrace / Thy King Cometh / At War With God / Sodomizing Ritual (In The Church Of God) / Those Who Fear The Serpent.

BLOOD OF THE SAINTS, Deathgasm (2000). First Born Of The Wicked / Last Suffer Of Nazarene / Blood Of The Saints / Heaven Lay Burned / His Only Bastard Son / Twist Of The Serpents Head / Raised From The Deep / The Sacrificial Lamb / Dead Corpse Of Jesus Christ / Sculpture Of Impurity.

EVIL POETRY

MEXICO CITY, MEXICO — *Zephiroth (vocals / guitar), Rockarla (bass), Shadowbuilder (drums).*

The Black-Doom styled EVIL POETRY released the 2003 demo 'The Return Of The Black Flames'. The band had been initiated in Mexico City during February of 1998 by guitarist Zephiroth, a former member of MEN AT ARMS, WINTER SOLSTICE NIGHT and KARNAK with drummer Carlos López, previously with GENOCIDE and MORE. Joining the formation would be the MEN AT ARMS, SOULLESS DOMAIN, KARNAK and RAPED GOD credited singer Polo Flores, ex-KARNAK bassist Carlos Díaz and keyboard player Alejandro Besné.

The group underwent a series of line-up changes and by 2002 would be down to a quartet of Zephiroth, WINTER SOLSTICE NIGHT and BEHOLDING SIGNS singer Saack, female bassist Teufelsweib and ex-GORETROCITY drummer Alonso Mijares. However, by that September Saack had quit to front SOULBURNER, being swiftly superseded by Dämmerung.

The demo 'The Return Of The Black Flames', featuring Leonardo Diaz on session bass, saw release in June 2003. EVIL POETRY in 2006 comprised a trio of Zephiroth on vocals and guitar, bassist Rockarla with Shadowbuilder on drums. Antichristian Black Metal Records released the album 'Letheus Nocturnus', recorded at M.A.T. Studio by Miguel Angel Tavera, in April 2006.

The Return Of The Black Flames, Evil Poetry (2003) (Demo). Intro (The Storm) / The Return Of The Black Flames / Bestiality Crescendo / In Hoc Signo Vinces (Outro).

LETHEUS NOCTURNUS, Antichristian Black Metal ABM001 (2006). Drama And Evolution / Beyond The Trees Of The Sacred Forest / Lacus Somniorum / Letheus Nocturnus / Omeyocan Conjure / The Silence Is Behind / Hate.

EVILHEART

MEXICO — *César Bañuelos (vocals), Raúl Borrego (guitar), Ricardo Salazar (guitar), Jorge Torres (bass), Rodolfo Rogers (drums).*

EVILHEART began life as a project of guitarist Raúl Borrego and drummer Rodolfo Rogers during late 1998, rounding out the line up with erstwhile FROM THE ASHES guitarist Alex Fernández, keyboard player Luis Valencia and finally former FINAL DUSK singer vocalist César Bañuelos and ex-FUNERAL bassist Jorge Torres. This would be the formation that debuted live in November of the following year.

Following a bout of touring in Mexico billed alongside MORTAL CANNABIS both Fernández and Valencia exited. Tomás Ramírez stepped in on guitar but this latest recruit would be dismissed in April of 2001. Nevertheless, EVILHEART issued the album 'Summoned To War' prior to inducting Ricardo Salazar, a veteran of acts such as DETONATION, RAPED FLESH and ZADKIEL.

EVILHEART gained prestige by opening for DIMMU BORGIR at their 1st May 2004 Monterrey show. The band set 'Dark In Glory' as the title of their debut album, set for April release through Green Maid Productions. A further valuable gig appearance came in November, with EVILHEART's inclusion on the billing for the 'Monterrey Metal Fest' alongside DIO, TWISTED SISTER, DOKKEN, QUIET RIOT, SHAMAN and HATEBREED. The band supported Swedes AMON AMARTH on their February 2005 Mexican gigs.

SUMMONED TO WAR, Green Maid Productions (2001). Buried In Ice, Virgin Blood On Virgin Snow: Part I—Cold Winter Sunset / Buried In Ice, Virgin Blood On Virgin Snow: Part II—She Died / Amongst The Howls / Escape Towards / Eternity / Enthrallment / Denied Fate Reaching Light Through Darkness Noctlux.

DARK IN GLORY, Green Maid Productions (2004). Prelude To Rebirth / In Other Lands / Lycanthropic Possession / Umarth / The Black Chasm / Dark In Glory / Buried In Ice / Ice Sword Revenge / Therionmorphosis.

EVOKE

MANSFIELD, NOTTINGHAMSHIRE, UK — *Jamie Hunter (vocals / guitar), John Parkin (guitar), Dave Marshall (bass), Ian Bacon (drums).*

EVOKE, a Mansfield based Death Metal band, debuted with a 1994 demo tape before eventually issuing two singles during 1997, the second of which is a split 7" green vinyl affair shared with Germany's KADATH. The group had been founded in August of 1993 incorporating three former DEVIANCE members in guitarist John Parkin, bassist Dave Marshall and drummer Ian Bacon. The rhythm section also held prior positions with CONSPIRATOR. Other original members would be vocalist John Redfern and guitarist Martin Tryner. As such EVOKE debuted with the demo session 'I Am ... My Own God'.

The band's next move was to contribute the track 'Equanimity Lost' to the compilation album 'Sometimes Death Is Better'. Upon completion of these recordings Tryner exited, being superseded by erstwhile LAWNMOWER DEATH and CABALA man Gavin O'Malley. With this revised line up EVOKE cut the 'Behold The Twilight' 7" single in 1996 and a split EP with KADATH. The debut album 'Dreaming The Reality', mixed in Sweden by Dan Swanö, preceded the departure of O'Malley in December of 1997. PIT DOG guitarist James Hogg would be duly inducted in May of 1998. That September Impact Records released 'Dreaming The Reality'.

Hogg's recording debut came in June of 1999 as EVOKE laid down two tracks, including a cover version of CARNAGE's 'Gentle Exhuming' for a split single, subsequently issued in January of 2000 through Paranoia Syndrome Records. Limited to just 300 hand numbered copies this single would be pressed on marbled vinyl. During the summer of 1999 EVOKE allied themselves with MALEVOLENT CREATION, MASTER and KRABATHOR for a short run of UK dates. The remainder of the year would be taken up by recording of the second album 'The Fury Written', produced by SAVAGE guitarist Andy Dawson.

Guitarist James Hogg opted out in April of 2001, the vacancy soon being filled by ex-CRAWLSPACE man Jamie Hunter. In June of 2002 vocalist John Redfern was forced out due to ill health. His place was taken by Jamie Hunter.

Evoke, (1993). Faded Memories / Fear Of What Will Become.
I Am ... My Own God, (1994). Impending Demise / Fade From Reality / Harmonized Visions / Obscure Thoughts / My Gods Called.
As I Bleed, Paranoia Syndrome (1997) (Split 7" with KADATH). As I Bleed / Among Mere Mortals.
Behold The Twilight, Megagrind (1997). Behold The Twilight / Await The Inevitable.
DREAMING THE REALITY, Impact (1998). Intro / The Sign Of Solitude / Through Blood Stared Eyes / Body Rites / Among Mere Mortals / No Repeat / Rouge / Die Before My Eyes / When Beauty Dies / Equanimity Lost / Manipulate The Ridicule / As I Bleed / While You Decay I Live.
THE FURY WRITTEN, System Shock (2000). Intro / The Truth Beyond Your Paradise / Twisted In Chaos / The Miracles Of My Flesh / Masters Of Conquest / Just A Descending Veil / Contemplating Suicide / Beneath The Mirage / Only To Destroy / Embracing Pessimistic Abandonment.

Evoke, Paranoia Syndrome (2000) (Split single with AETERNUM. Hand numbered limited edition 300 copies). The Ancient Enemy / Gentle Exhuming.

EVOKED CURSE

LAHTI, FINLAND — *Orgasmatron (vocals), Necrophiliac (guitar), Imperator (drums).*

Lahti Death Metal combo EVOKED CURSE are fronted by vocalist Orgasmatron (a.k.a. Henry Juvonen) of WITCHTIGER and EVIL ANGEL. The band claims a tradition stretching back to a 1989 formation by guitarist Necrophiliac (a.k.a. 'Fiend' or more commonly Harri Juvonen), a musician holding scene credits with acts such as WITCHTIGER, TRISTITIA, PAGAN RITES, GOATSODOMY and DEVIL LEE ROT. Formative band rosters included a session rhythm section of bassist Tooloud, from GOATSODOMY and EVIL ANGEL, plus drummer Deathskull. EVOKED CURSE subsequently enrolled drummer Imperator (a.k.a. Ilmari Jalas) of SLUGATHOR, ANXIOUS DEATH and WITCHTIGER repute.

First product would be February 1999's demo 'Outburst Of Hell', recorded by Orgasmatron and Fiend. 'Altar Of Sodomy', including a cover version of HELLHAMMER's 'Reaper', arrived in 2000, these tracks recorded with drummer Deathskull. 2002's 'Cursed Unholy Mausoleum' found Imperator manning the drums. EVOKED CURSE published a fourth demo, 'Merciless Revenge' restricted to 50 copies, in 2004.

Three band members, singer H. Necrophiliac Ju Von Nen, bassist Tooloud and drummer Imperator, forged the 2006 Black Metal band SATANIC TORMENT in alliance with guitarist Kaosbringer, of NEUTRON HAMMER, SACRIFICIAL DAGGER and SYÖPÄ.

Outburst Of Hell, Evoked Curse (1999). Intro—The Curse / Evil Sacrifice / Corpsepaint, Leather & Spikes / Bonebreaking And Skullcrushing / Impale Heaven's Virgins.

Altar Of Sodomy, (2000). Upon The Altar (Intro) / Altars Of Sodomy / Whiplashing Metal / Outburst Of Hell / Anal Kiss Of Hell / Verilöyly / Reaper / Outro: Haistakaa Paska.

Cursed Unholy Mausoleum, (2002). Sadistic Savage / Morbid Outrage / The Day Of Metal Inquisition.

Merciless Revenge, (2004) (Limited edition 50 copies). Intro / Merciless Revenge / Morbid Outrage / The Day Of Metal Inquisition / Whiplashing Metal / Outburst Of Hell / Bonebreaking And Skullcrushing / Evoked Apocalypse / Outro.

EX INFERIS

ESCH / ALZETTE, LUXEMBOURG — *Fabrice Mennuni (vocals), Angelo Mangini (guitar), Kevin Muhlen (guitar), Marc Nickts (bass), David Renard (drums).*

Esch / Alzette based EX INFERIS was formulated during 1999 by singer Marti, guitarists Angelo Mangini and Kevin Muhlen with David Renard on drums. They performed their first concert that same February, without a bass player, but Marc Nickts assumed the four-string role in May. EX INFERIS debuted in 2000 with the self-financed EP ' Everything Is Burning ... So Doth Your Soul'. However, Marti took his leave during these sessions and was replaced by Stefano. Live work included UK concerts in April.

The following year Skipworth Records assembled an alliance with GANESHA for the split EP 'Ex Inferis Analyzing Ganesha', these two brand new tracks arriving in June. In June 2002 EX INFERIS included three tracks on a split album, entitled '4 Way Deathmarch', shared with SWORN VENGEANCE, HOSTILITY and EXISTENCE through US label Battlescarred Records.

Another change of frontman saw Fabricio Mennuni enrolling in December 2003. The band funded the full-length 'Defunctus In Heresi', produced by Tony DeBlock and recorded at Midas Studios in Lokeren, for issue in January 2005.

Everything Is Burning ... So Doth Your Soul, Ex Inferis (2000). As Evil Rises / Beyond The Grave / Co-ed Killer / Schizo / Incarcerated / Sadness.

Ex Inferis Analyzing Ganesha, Skipworth (2001) (Split EP with GANESHA). Like A Dead Whisper / Sick Devotion.

4 WAY DEATHMARCH, Battlescarred (2002) (Split album with SWORN VENGEANCE, HOSTILITY and EXISTENCE). Nil Admirare / Like A Dead Whisper / Sooth The Killing.

Ex Infernalis, Ex Inferis (2004). Ex Infernalis / Conduct Of War / Death Eruption / Shadows Burn True.

DEFUNCTUS IN HERESI, Dali Talents Events Creation DALI-MET-002 (2005). Dawn Of The Faith Surgeons / Blood Soaked Apostasy / Adonai / Selfmadegod / From Twilight Came Torment / Stabbed By The Cross / Embers Of Eight / Delusions Of A Derelict Mind / Chants From The Beyond 1 / Seek No Salvation / ... Of innocence And vultures / Defunctus In heresei.

EXCARNATED

MELBOURNE, VIC, AUSTRALIA — *Chris (vocals), Rodney (guitar), Nick (bass), Matt (drums).*

Melbourne Death Metal band previously known as HACKTICIAN. In this former guise the band issued a January 1998 demo restricted to just 20 copies. EXCARNATED donated an exclusive cut of 'Molesting The Faith' to the Australian Metal compilation album 'Legions–Opening Of The Southern Gate' issued by Blacktalon Media in July of 2004. A line-up of vocalist Chris, guitarist Craig, bassist Craig and drummer Mick would evolve into an EXCARNATED roster for 2004 quoting Chris, guitarists Rodney and Tony with Nick on bass guitar. The latter then departed, leaving the band a quartet.

EXCARNATED issued the album 'Purging The Earth' through Life Fluid Productions in April 2006.

Let The Hatred Manifest, (1998). Let The Hatred Manifest / Skinstripper / Excarnated / Orgasm Through Suffocation / I Love You (In Pieces).

Genital Gallery, (1999). Crimson Ecstasy / Orgiastic Abominations / Torso Fucker / Where the Dead Dream.

HOMICIDAL DECIMATION, (2002). The Lament Configuration / Crimson Ecstasy / Beyond Mortal Relapse / Torso Fucker / The Trophy Hunter / Autistic Dementia / Bleached Bodies / Homicidal Decimation / Aristocratic Depravity / Total Bloodshed.

Where The Dead Dream, (2004). Let The Hatred Manifest ('98) / Age Of Murder ('03) / Molesting The Faith ('03) / Where The Dead Dream ('98).

PURGING THE EARTH, Life Fluid Productions LFP008 (2006). Autocratic Annihilation / The Cyanide God / Churning Seas Of Lava / Dogmatic Upheaval / The Face Of Fear / Industrial Manslaughter / Molesting The Faith / Like Fools Praying To A Dead God.

EXCESS OF CRUELTY

LINDEN, BELGIUM — *Johan Detraux (vocals / guitar), Jan Verschueren (guitar), Joris Tallon (guitar), Raf Veulemans (bass), Joeri Caluwaerts (drums).*

Created by a union of former KOROS DAGANAT and NEX personnel during 1991 EXCESS OF CRUELTY began life as a Grindcore unit but would soon start to tread down the path of Black inspired Death Metal. The band first gelled when the Metal band NEX's rhythm section of drummer Joeri and bassist Raf Veulemans teamed up with vocalist Johan and guitarist Joris from Hardcore group KOROS DAGANAT. This initial incarnation of EXCESS OF CRUELTY issued a Grind influenced demo but by their second effort 'Infinite Solitariness' the band had become a fully fledged Death Metal operation.

A 7 single 'Thoughts Of A Forlorn Existence' ensued prior to a further demo 'Stream To Aljira' in 1992. Two years later a further cassette 'Catharsis Tranquillitatis' emerged before the enrollment of second guitarist Jan. The 1996 tape 'Fionnuala' precipitated the departure of Raf and the recruitment of CHEMICAL BREATH four stringer Gerry. Bassist Raf Veulemans joined AEGRIMONIA in June of 2000.

EXCESS OF CRUELTY added AEGRIMONIA guitarist Tim Thijs in April of 2002. During August of 2003 members Johan Detraux, Joeri Caluwaerts and Christophe Vanghinstel alongside KELTGAR man Bas Verdin and TONER's Jan Verschueren, both being former EXCESS OF CRUELTY members founded a fresh act RE:CREATION. The new band debuted live that October at the Kampenhout Jeugdhuis Tonzent venue shortly before EXCESS OF CRUELTY ceased operations. Vanghinstel joined GRACEFALLEN in early 2005.

Thoughts Of A Forlorn Existence, Lowland (1992). The Grave Of Transistoriness / Solitude Of Inner Confinement / Fear.

Stream To Aljira, (1992). Malign Neuroleptic Syndrome / 7 Times Of Heathen / Korihor / Mindwarp Of Tears / The Grave Transitoriness.

UNDER THE IVY OF ITHAMOR, Wood Nymph (1997). The Dreamweavers Illusion / Wafts From Birch And Briar Breath / The Reaper Of The Harvest / Fionuala / Nangara / Beholding The Crimson Tide / When At Eventide / Under The Ivy Of Ithamor / Solemn Sounds Of The Soul / Northern Shekinah Light / The Trooper.

EXCESSUM

RAMLE, ISRAEL — *Ilia Badrov (vocals), Arie Aranovich (guitar), Jonathan Bar-Ilan (guitar), Elad Manor (bass), Shaked Furman (drums).*

Ramle Death / Thrashers EXCESSUM, founded in 2000, feature ex-ARAFEL guitarist Leon Notik (a.k.a. 'Oboroten'), the SOLITARY, MATRICIDE and ACROPOLIS credited Elad 'Romano' Manor on bass guitar and ex-SOLITARY and DEHUMANIZED drummer Shaked Furman. The group was forged by singer Ilia Badrov with guitarist Nomaed Dominus (a.k.a. Boris) under an original billing of DARK SUICIDE.

The EXCESSUM title was adopted in 2001 as second guitarist Nesly was to lose his place to Arie before the band unit was solidified with the incorporation of rhythm section bassist Maor 'Keves' Bitton and Itamar on drums. Nomaed Dominus quit in mid 2002 for Folk Metal act HOLTSCYRM, being swiftly replaced by Notik. Next in line to decamp would be Itamar, seeing Nadav Luzia taking his place briefly before Dor stepped in. However, he too left and Luzia made a return.

EXCESSUM performed their first live concert in June 2003 at the Asylum Club in Tel Aviv, sharing the stage with NATURE'S ELEMENT and DAGOR DAGORATH. In August Firman took over the drum position and Manor took over from former bassist Bitton in December.

Instruction For Self-Destruction, Excessum (2006) (Limited to 1000 copies). Deception / Destination, Life / Suffer And Die / Infernal Existence / Kingdom Loneliness.

EXCRUCIATE

STOCKHOLM, SWEDEN — *Lars Levin (vocals), Johan Rudberg (guitar), Henrik Brynolfsson (guitar), Fredrik Isaksson (bass), Per Ax (drums).*

A pioneering Stockholm Death Metal act, EXCRUCIATE helped define the now widely recognised "Swedish" sound. EXCRUCIATE started life as a trio in 1989 with guitarists Henrik Brynolfsson and Johan Melander together with drummer Per Ax. This line-up, all previously having worked together as comrades in CEMENTERY, CONSPIRACY and the short-lived CRUCIFIED, recorded the 'Mutilation Of The Past' demo the following year before adding bassist Fredrik Isaksson and vocalist Christian Carlsson.

Following the band's commercial debut, a split album with EPITAPH through Infest Records, Carlsson made way for ex-MASTICATION singer Lars Levin. In 1992 Melander opted to leave and in his stead came another erstwhile MASTICATION member Johan Rudberg.

Having signed with Thrash Records, strangely EXCRUCIATE folded soon after the 1993 album 'Passage Of Life'. Henrik Brynolfsson reforged the band in 2001, bringing in MORPHEUS singer David Brink. However, after a three track demo this latest version of EXCRUCIATE collapsed again. Brynolfsson, allying himself with SIN, BLOODSHED and STAIRLAND drummer Martin Karlsson, founded the adventurous Industrial Death Metal unit MYKORRHIZA. With demand for works of the forerunners of Swedish Death Metal increasing globally the Konqueror label collected together the 'Passage Of Life' and 'Hymns Of Mortality' album tracks together with the 'Mutilation Of The Past' demos for a 2003 retrospective release 'Beyond The Circle'.

EXCRUCIATE, Infest INF002 (1991) (Split album with EPITAPH). Sickness Hate / Hymn Of Mortality / Sign Of Suffer / I Pray For Infinity.

PASSAGE OF LIFE, Thrash 852 314 (1992). Confused Mind / Endless Suffocation / Inhumation Postnatal / Eternal Incubation / Anatomical Self-fertilization / Passage Of Life / Sabbath In The Mortuary / Beyond The Circle.

BEYOND THE CIRCLE, Konqueror KR 004 (2003). Confused Mind / Endless Suffocation / Inhuman Postnatal / Eternal Incubation / Anatomical Self-Fertilization / Passage Of Life / Sabbath In The Mortuary / Beyond The Circle / Sickness Hate / Hymn Of Mortality / Sign Of Suffer / I Pray For Infinity / Sabbath In The Mortuary / Eternal Incubation / Inhumation Postnatal / Bubonic Plague / Slow Death / Beyond The Circle / The Mortuary / Sabbath.

EXCRUCIATION

ZURICH, SWITZERLAND — *Eugi Meccariello (vocals), Marc Bosshart (guitar), Mick (bass), Andy (drums).*

EXCRUCIATION was an early example of Swiss Death / Thrash. Founded during late 1984 in Zurich the band was initiated by Joe Venegas and guitarist Mat Arani, soon being joined by lead vocalist Eugi Meccariello, Did Lowinger and Marc Bosshart. In April of 1985 this formation recorded the opening 'Fourth Rider Of The Apocalypse' demo, although this session was never made public. In September of that year Arani was replaced by Andrea Renggli.

In February of 1986 the band released their first demo, 'First Assault', and after that same year their label debut came out, an EP called 'Last Judgement' on the Chainsaw Massacre Record label, an affiliate of We Bite Records label. Shortly after Venagas left the band. EXCRUCIATION continued on as a four-piece for a couple of years and released another demo in the summer of 1988, 'Prophecy Of Immortality', recorded in March and April with the band laid down nine new tracks. Another year passed and EXCRUCIATION recorded a fourth demo called 'The Abyss Of Time', in October of 1989. Soon afterward Greg Hauser was added on second guitar.

Yet another demo surfaced in December of 1990 called 'Act Of Despair'. The long years of work finally paid off to a small degree because the band was finally signed to the Turbo/JL America concern. EXCRUCIATION entered DNS Studios and remixed the 1988, 1989, and 1990 demos to release them as a set billed 'Anno Domini—An Anthology Of The Past' The collection also included one live track called 'Wardance'.

Fourth Apocalyptic Rider, (1985).

First Assault, (1986).

Last Judgement EP, Chainsaw Murder CM 002 (1986). At The Edge Of Madness / The Silence / Hateful Pain / Desperate End (Nuclear Nightmare) / Mirror Of Eternity.

Abyss Of Time, (1989).

Act Of Despair, (1990).

ANNO DOMINI- ANTHOLOGY OF THE PAST, Turbo 38154-1002-4 (1991). The Circle / Hasta La Muerte / The Mask / Oppressive Reality / Pleasure 'n' Pain / Genocide In God's Name / Merciless Destiny / Call Of Desperation / Rage / Odoren Di Morte Dentro Di Me / Wardance (Live).

Prophecy Immortality, (1998).

EXHUMATOR

BELARUS — *Alexander Bourei (vocals / guitar), Pavel Bolokhov (bass), Jouri Golovach (drums).*

Extreme Metal act EXHUMATOR was forged in Minsk, capitol of Belarus, in 1989. The band started out as a quartet of vocalist Slava Korsakov, guitarist Vova Lisishin, bassist Igor Silnichenko and drummer Anton Arkhipov. This line up cut the debut album 'Welcome And Die' and the follow up EP 'Arising Of Suspicions'. Vadim Akimov was added on lead vocals in 1992 to appear on the sophomore album 'Resurrected'. The bass position then switched to accommodate erstwhile ASSUARY man Pavel Bolokhov.

The 1994 demo 'Sacrificial Bleeding' would be the last recording made by Akimov who died the following year. Undaunted EXHUMATOR relocated to Western Europe in order to further their career. Settling in Brussels EXHUMATOR were by now a trio of ex-ANNEXATION frontman Alexander Bourei, Bolokhov and former AUTODOPHE drummer Jouri Golovach. This line up cut the 1998 demo 'Condescension From Dark Side'.

WELCOME AND DIE, (1990).
Arising Of Suspicions EP, (1993).
RESURRECTED, (1993).

EXHUMED

SAN JOSE, CA, USA — *Matt Harvey (vocals / guitar), Mike Beams (guitar), Leon del Muerte (bass), John Longstreth (drums).*

Brutal Death Metal in its most undiluted state. San Jose, California's EXHUMED have made unrelenting progress despite being wrought into ever new incarnations by constant line up changes over the years. The band first made their mark in 1991 with an inaugural roster of frontman Jake Giardina, guitarist Derrel Houdashelt and Matt Harvey, bassist Ben Marrs and drummer Col Jones.

EXHUMED debuted with a stark statement of intent with the demo 'Dissecting The Caseated Omentum'. A 7" single 'Excreting Innards' proved there was to be no concessions to compromise. Ramming the point home EXHUMED would garner valuable exposure for their sick art form guesting for visiting dignitaries such as AUTOPSY, ENTOMBED, CANNIBAL CORPSE and MORBID ANGEL. A whole slew of uncompromising demo cassettes would ensue beginning with 'Gorgasm'.

With the dismissal of Marrs in November 1993 Ross Sewage would front the band as Giardina deputised on bass for 1993's 'Grotesque Putrefied Brains'. Further touring had the band out with heavyweights DISMEMBER, SUFFOCATION and VADER.

Another promotional tape was offered titled 'Cadaveric Splatter Platter'. These sessions had Harvey responsible for both guitar and bass as Giardina bade his farewell. Mark Smith would come in on bass but would soon decamp. Matt Widener was later inducted as permanent bassist. The revised band cut a further demo session 'Horrific Expulsion Of Gore' in late 1994. The following year witnessed an exclusive new track 'Necro-Fornicator' being contributed the Morbid Metal compilation album 'Deterioration Of The Senses' and a shared live cassette in alliance with notorious Spanish Death Metal brethren HAEMMORHAGE. However, Widener would vacate his position and Sewage wound up adding bass guitar to his duties. Having his own graphics company Sewage would be responsible for much of EXHUMED's horrifically graphic artwork.

Another rare track 'Intercourse With A Limbless Cadaver' was included on the 'Orchestrated Chaos' compilation put out by Soulside Records in March of 1996. EXHUMED would share space with the equally twisted Ohian act HEMDALE on a split album 'In The Name Of Gore' and issue a split 7" single with PALE EXISTENCE the same year. Further ructions saw the release of Houdashelt and the swift substitution with Leon Del Muerte.

Del Muerte would figure on recordings made for a four way split EP 'Chords Of Chaos' for Lofty Storm Productions which paired EXHUMED off with NECROSE, BLEEDING DISORDER and EXCRETED ALIVE. The new guitarist would also feature on the compilation track 'Bleeding Heap Of Menstrual Carnage' donated to the 'Accidental Double Homicide' collection on Satan's Pimp Records before leaving the ranks to found IMPALED.

Down to a trio EXHUMED set out on a support tour of America guesting for MORTIIS before hooking up with the European extravaganza 'Grind Over Europe II'. This gargantuan Death package nestled EXHUMED in amongst the likes of VOMITORY, AGATHOCLES, DERANGED, KADATH, HEMDALE and NYCTOPHOBIC. With the fulfillment of these dates EXHUMED, limbering up for dates in Mexico, was back up to strength as a quartet with the induction of ex-BURIAL and BEREAVE guitarist Mike Beams.

During 1997 vocalist / guitarist Matt Harvey (as 'Matt Hellfiend') and drummer Andy 'Col' Jones (as 'Atomic Maniac') founded the retro Thrash side project DEKAPITATOR. Debuting with a split 7" single shared with NUNSLAUGHTER and following this up with a 1999 album 'We Will Destroy,... You Will Obey' DEKAPITATOR succeeded in generating generous praise globally for their efforts.

EXHUMED signed to Death Metal aficionados Relapse Records for the 1998 'Gore Metal' full length debut. The album saw production courtesy of former TESTAMENT, DEATH and CANCER guitarist JAMES MURPHY. Not neglecting the singles market 1998 proved fruitful for EXHUMED collectors as the band graced no less than three split affairs in cahoots with RETALIATION on the 'Tales Of The Exhumed' release for the Italian Headfucker concern, NYCTOPHOBIC as part of the 'Totally Fucking Dead' issue on Germany's Revenge Production label and also with PANTALONES ABAJO MARINERO for 'Indignities To The Dead'.

Sewage would bow out from EXHUMED in 1999 shortly after showings at the Massachusetts Metal & Hardcore Festival and the March Metal Meltdown event. Erstwhile PALE EXISTENCE bassist Bud Burke would fill the gap as EXHUMED undertook the Relapse 'Contamination' American tour alongside label mates TODAY IS THE DAY, BENUMB, NASUM, CEPHALIC CARNAGE, SOILENT GREEN and MORGION.

The 2000 album 'Slaughtercult' would see a later re-issue as a saw shaped CD picture disc. Japanese versions came with an extra four bonus tracks. Touring to promote the album had EXHUMED on the road with VULGAR PIGEON, ABCESS and IMPALED. As 2001 broke EXHUMED kept up the tradition of the split 7" releases cutting a further effort with SANITY'S DAWN entitled 'Emeticide'.

Besides work with DEKAPITATOR both Harvey and Jones would also be in operation with the side project CADAVERIZER. Meantime bassist Bud Burke forged DYING IN YOUR BEAUTY SLEEP, a harsh Death Metal act conceived in union with guitarist Bruce Flores, previously a member of Hardcore act KISSING GIRLS WITH BROKEN JAWS, and bass guitarist Jeff Whalen from SoCal Punk act DESPISED.

A two CD EXHUMED anthology set was projected for early 2003 release entitled 'Platters Of Splatter: Cyclopedic Symposium Of Execrable Errata And Abhorrent Apocrypha 1992-2002'.

A new studio effort, 'Anatomy Is Destiny', fell foul of the censors in Germany when it was deemed that faked 'death' shots of the band members by photographer Alex Solca were too realistic for public consumption. The album was withdrawn from sale in that territory and re-issued with the offending artwork removed. EXHUMED united with KATAKLYSM, DIABOLIC and MALIGNANCY for September US dates before hitting Europe packaged with CEPHALIC CARNAGE and INHUME in October.

The band, pulling in the INFANTICIDE, IMPALED and MURDER CONSTRUCT credited Leon del Muerte on bass once again and drummer John Longstreth of ANGEL CORPSE, ORIGIN and SKINLESS repute, united with CANNIBAL CORPSE for a run of US dates commencing 12th February in Houston, Texas. They would then form up part of the 2004 European heavyweight 'No Mercy' festivals commencing 29th March, sharing billing with SPAWN OF POSSESSION, HYPOCRISY, KATAKLYSM, CARPATHIAN FOREST, VOMITORY, PREJUDICE and headliners CANNIBAL CORPSE. However, by that May Longstreth was ensconced in Metalcore outfit THE RED CHORD and by October had temporarily joined the ranks of DYING FETUS for US touring. He subsequently hooked up with a reformed DIM MAK.

In September Matt Harvey temporarily filled in as frontman for Thrash Metal veterans EXODUS on their Central and South American gigs in Mexico, Brazil, Chile and Argentina after vocalist Steve 'Zetro' Souza was taken ill. The following month Harvey, alongside EXHUMED drummer Col Jones, enrolled into the ranks of REPULSION. Despite these extracurricular activities EXHUMED, having severed ties with Relapse Records, maintained momentum, revealing plans for an album of cover versions entitled 'Regurgitated Requiems: Garbage Daze Re-Regurgitated'. Tracks would include HEXX's 'Twice As Bright, Half As Long', EPIDEMIC's 'In Fear We Kill', the AMEBIX 'The Power Remains', UNSEEN TERROR's 'Uninformed', G.B.H.'s 'Necrophilia', PENTAGRAM's 'The Ghoul', SIEGE's Drop Dead', MASTER's Pay To Die' and METALLICA's 'Trapped Under Ice'. The record would be picked up by Listenable Records for European license.

EXHUMED announced the addition of ex-FUCK THE FACTS and EXPERIMENT IN TERROR drummer Matt Connell to the ranks in November and later that same month revealed former member Leon del Muerte had rejoined in the bass position. Early 2005 found the band filming two shows in Los Angeles at the Alterknit Lounge room of the Knitting Factory for a DVD release. European dates scheduled for May witnessed an alliance with VOMITORY, ROTTEN SOUND and PROSTITUTE DISFIGUREMENT. However, the group parted ways with long-time guitarist Mike Beams upfront of these shows. Ex-UPHILL BATTLE Wes Caley substituted.

Leon del Muerte activated a side project billed INTRONAUT, a Progressive Metal styled band featuring Sacha Dunable, ex-ANUBIS RISING, Danny Walker of UPHILL BATTLE and Joe Lester. A four track demo, entitled 'Null–Demonstration Extended Play Compact Disc', arrived in 2005. EXHUMED partnered with ABSCESS, SKARP and INSANITY for a short burst of US dates in August 2005. European dates were scheduled, then pulled shortly afterwards.

A split EP, 'Something Sickened This Way Comes' shared with Czech band INGROWING released by Obscene Productions, included a cover version of NAPALM DEATH's 'Life'. Matt Connell activated Grindcore side project DRUDGERY in 2006, this band featuring Derek P.C. from ARISE AND RUIN on vocals, guitarist Brent Munger of ARISE AND RUIN plus Steve Ferraro of DEAR BLACK DIARY on bass.

GORE METAL, Relapse (1988). Necromaniac / Open The Abscess / Postmortem Procedures / Limb From Limb / Emulceation / Casket Krusher / Death Mask / In My Inhuman Slaughterhouse / Sepulchural Slaughter / Vagiterian II / Blazing Corpse / Deadest Of The Dead / Sodomy And Lust.

Excreting Innards EP, After World (1992). Festering Sphinctral Malignancy / Perverse Innard Infestation / Coital Mutilation / Disfigured Corpse / Grubs / Cadaveric Splatter Platter.

Split EP, 625 Productions (1996) (Split single with PALE EXISTENCE).

Chords Of Chaos EP, Lofty Storm Productions (1996) (Split EP with BLEEDING DISORDER, NECROSE and EXCRETED ALIVE). Excreting Innards / Vagiterian / Grotesque Putrefied Brains / The Exquisite Flavour Of Gastro-Anal Tripe (Cadaveric Splatter Platter Part II) / Sex, Drinks And Metal.

IN THE NAME OF GORE, Visceral Productions VP004 (1996) (Split album with HEMDALE). Horrendous Member Dismemberment / Septicemia (Festering Sphinctral Malignancy Part II) / Masochistic Copramania / Necrovores: Decomposing The Inanimate / Disinterred, Digested And Debauched / Bone Fucker / The Naked And The Dead / Torso / Dissecting The Caseated Omentum / Death Metal.

Instruments Of Hell EP, Open Wound Records (1997) (Split 7" single with NO COMPLY).

Tales Of The Exhumed EP, Headfucker (1998) (Split single with RETALIATION). Gory Melanoma / Necro-Voyeur.

Indignities To The Dead EP, Discos Al Pacino (1998) (Split single with PANTALONES ABAJO MARINERO).

Totally Fucking Dead EP, Revenge Productions (1998) (Split single with NYCTOPHOBIC).

SLAUGHTERCULT, Relapse (2000). Decrepit Crescendo / Forged In Fire (Formed In Flame) / A Lesson In Pathology / This Axe Was Made To Grind / Carnal Epitaph / Dinnertime In The Morgue / Fester Forever / Deep Red / Infester / Slave To The Casket / Slaughtercult / Funeral Fuck / Vacant Grave.

Emeticide, Deadly Art (2000) (Split single with SANITY'S DAWN). Emeticide / Pus Grinder.

ANATOMY IS DESTINY, Relapse RR 6566 (2003). Anatomy Is Destiny / Waxwork / The Matter Of Splatter / Under The Knife / Consuming Impulse / Grotesqueries / In The Name Of Gore / Arclight / Nativity Obscene (A Nursery Chyme) / Death Walks Behind You / A Song For The Dead.

GARBAGE DAZE RE-GURGITATED, Listenable (2005).

Something Sickened This Way Comes, Obscene Productions (2006) (Split EP with INGROWING. Something Sickened This Way Comes / Consumer Or Consumed / Life.

EXIT 13

MILLERSVILLE, PA, USA — *Bill Yurkiewicz (vocals), Steve O'Donnel (guitar), Dan Lilker (bass), Scott Lewis (drums).*

Grind merchants EXIT 13, based out of Millersville, Pennsylvania, are the result of an extracurricular project assembled by Relapse Records boss Bill Yurkiewicz on vocals, guitarist Steve O'Donnel, and the esteemed ANTHRAX, S.O.D., NUCLEAR ASSAULT and BRUTAL TRUTH credited Dan Lilker on bass together with his former band mate drummer Scott Lewis.

Initially EXIT 13's first product, a brace of 1989 demo cassettes entitled 'Disemboweling Party' and November's 'Eat More Crust', featured a recording membership of Yurkiewicz, O'Donnel, bassist Joel Dipietro with drum duties shared between Bill Shaeffer and Pat McCahan. Follow up Eps included 'The Unrequited Love For Chicken Soup' in 1990 and 'Spare The Wrench, Surrender The Earth' in 1991.

EXIT 13 adopted a revised line-up, inducting the rhythm section of bassist Dan Lilker and drummer Scott Lewis, for 1993's 'Green Is Good'. A 1995 EP, '… Just A Few More Hits', sported cover artwork spoofing VENOM's classic 'Black Metal' album cover. The band's 1996 split EP shared with MULTIPLEX included a cover version of TERRORIZER's 'Storm Of Stress'. A former EXIT 13 drummer Dave Witte was to create DISCORDANCE AXIS and ATOMSMASHER.

Disemboweling Party, Exit 13 (1989) (Demo).

Eat More Crust, Exit 13 (1989) (Demo).

The Unrequited Love For Chicken Soup, (1990).

Spare The Wrench, Surrender The Earth, (1991).

DON'T SPARE THE GREEN LOVE, (1993). Spare The Wrench Surrender The Earth / Only Hypocrisy Prohibits Legality / Only Protest Gives A Hope For Life! / Societally Provoked Genocidal Contemplation / My Minds Mine / Anthropocentric Ecocidal Conundrum / Reevaluate Life! / Gaia / Unintended Lyrical Befuddlement / An Outline Of Intellectual Rubbish / Where Is Exit-13? / Ecotopian Visions / Constant Persistence Of Annoyance / Inbreeding Populations / Self-Misunderstood Cerebral Masturbation / The Funk Song / Get High On Life / Disemboweling Party / Shattnerspackle / Terminal Habitation / Fingernails / Conclusions On Various Religious Frauds / Political Dismay / Impaled / Disemboweling Party.

GREEN IS GOOD, (1993). Anthropocentric-Ecocidal Conundrum / Reevaluate Life / Gaia / Inbreeding Population / Unintended Lyrical Befuddlement / An Outline Of Intellectual Rubbish / Where's Exit-13? / Ecotopian Visions / Constant Persistence Of Annoyance / Self-Misunderstood Cerebral Masturbation / The Funk Song / Get High On Life / Disemboweling Party / Shattnerspackle / (Hidden track).

ETHOS MUSICK, Roadrunner RR 6913-2 (1994). Societally Provoked Genocidal Contemplation / Ethos Musick / Facilitate The Emancipation Of Your Mummified Mentality / Diet For A New America / Anthropocentric Ecocidal Conundrum / Reevaluate Life! / Legalize Hemp Now! (including A Warm Wave Of Euphoria) / Open Season (The Story Of Hunter Slaughter) / My Minds Mine! / Earth First! / Only Protest Gives A Hope Of Life! / Disemboweling Party / An Electronic Fugue For The Imminent Demise Of Planet Earth.

... Just A Few More Hits, (1995). Legalize Hemp Now! / A Man And His Lawnmower / Oral Fixation / Constant Persistence Of Annoyance / Wake Up And Change! / Snakes And Alligators.

EXIT 13 / HEMDALE, Visceral Productions (1996). Gout d'Belgium (EXIT 13) / Black Weakeners (EXIT 13) / Hopped Up (EXIT 13) / Storms Of Stress (EXIT 13) / Societtally Provoked Genocidal Contemplation (Live) (EXIT 13) / Terminal Habitation (Live) (EXIT 13) / Advanced Intestinal Love (HEMDALE) / Gastral Colostomy (HEMDALE) / Demented Surgical Incest (HEMDALE) / Rise Above (HEMDALE) / Are You Pornophoric? (Remix) (HEMDALE) / Extremely Rotten Flesh (HEMDALE).

Exit 13 EP, Visceral Productions (1996). Gout d'Belgium / Black Weakeners.

Exit 13, HG Fact (1996) (Split EP with MULTIPLEX). Hopped Up! (By The Demon Humulus Lupulus) / Storm Of Stress.

SMOKING SONGS, Relapse (1996). Light Up! / Jack, I'm Mellow / If You're a Viper (Blissful Mix) / Stoney Monday / When I Get Low I Get High / Lotus Blossom (Sweet Marijuana) / Willie the Record Releaser / 1'1 (Thirteen Inches of Fun) / Weed / If You're a Viper (Viper Mad Lilker Mix) / Knockin' Myself Out / Hempcake / Sweet Marijuana Brown.

EXMORTEM

ÅRHUS, DENMARK — *Simon Petersen (vocals), Henrik Kolle (guitar), Andreas Schubert (guitar), Rune Koldby (bass), Reno Kiilerich (drums).*

Originally known as MORDOR this Århus Death Metal band date back to 1992 with a line-up of guitarist Henrik Kolle, drummer Mike Neilsen and bassist Mads Weng. It wasn't to be until 1993 when the band added a vocalist in Søren Lønne, recording the 'Souls Of Purity' demo. Still, as MORDOR the band contributed the track 'In Command' to the Progress Records compilation 'Fuck You We're From Denmark. Volume II' in 1994. Weng left soon after its release and Lønne took over bass duties.

Signing to new label Euphonious the band, aware of at least three other Metal acts titled MORDOR, adopted the new title of EXMORTEM.

Following the June 1995 album 'Labyrinth Of Horror' release the band augmented its sound with the addition of second guitarist Martin "Sigtyr" Thim. A further demo tape, 'Dejected ...' preceded the second album 'Dejected In Obscurity'. Later that year Dennis took command of the drum stool for more demos, subsequently being released as a split 7" single 'Berzerker Legions' shared with IMPENDING DOOM in 1999. Bass guitar for these sessions would be delegated to Martin Rosendahl of CORPUS MORTALE, ZAHRIM, USIPIAN and INIQUITY.

Once again EXMORTEM shifted shape, introducing new vocalist Simon Petersen (a.k.a. 'Smerte') of LUSTRATION, HORNED ALMIGHTY and MARERIDT, and drummer Reno Kiilerich in 2000. The third album 'Berzerker Legions' was issued in May of 2001 on the Hammerheart label. The group, bringing onboard bassist Andreas Schubert, from AD NOCTUM, and drummer Michael Pedersen, switched labels once more to the French Osmose Productions for 2002's 'Pestilence Empire'. By 2003 Reno Kiilerich was a member of PANZERCHRIST. Later that same year Kiilerich joined fabled North American Death Metal band VILE.

Projected releases into late 2003 included the 'Pest Campaign 2003' EP through Osmose Productions featuring three

EXMORTEM

live tracks recorded in Valencia, Spain that April alongside a re-recorded version of the 1995 track 'Intoxicated By Death'. Also in the works was the 'Killstorms' 7" single for Ancient Darkness Productions, bearing the unreleased title cut from 1998, re-arranged with new lyrics backed with a cover of AUTOPSY's 'Critical Madness'. A limited edition of 500 copies, half of these came pressed in camouflaged vinyl.

Reno Kiilerich stepped up a further league in March of the following year when he was recruited as session man for DIMMU BORGIR's European, South American and US 'Ozzfest' festival dates. EXMORTEM entered Antfarm Studios in Aarhus on 17th May with producer Tue Madsen to record their fifth studio album, 'Nihilistic Contentment', for Earache Records subsidiary Wicked World. They would be rejoined by drummer Reno Kiilerich in October.

EXMORTEM landed the support to Polish Black Metal band BEHEMOTH's January 2005 UK tour. In keeping with the incestuous nature of the tight knit Danish Metal scene April saw former EXMORTEM drummer Michael Pedersen replacing Reno Kiilerich's role in PANZERCHRIST. Meantime, Kiilerich laid down drums on a new album for OLD MAN'S CHILD.

Line-up changes in May saw bassist Andreas Schubert shifting to the second guitar position and the installation of a session bassist, Rune Koldby of SPECTRAL MORTUARY. The EXMORTEM credited Martin Thim joined ILLDISPOSED in August. In September 2006 EXMORTEM announced it had "ended its co-operation with Earache and Wicked World Records".

Drummer Morten Siersbaek joined DOWNLORD in March 2007.

LABYRINTHS OF HORROR, Euphonious PHONI 001CD (1995). By Death / In The Dark Of The Moon / Bloodshed Of The Holy / In Command / Creation Of Evil / Dark Thy Kingdom / Punishment For The Weak / Labyrinths Of Horror / Necromonicon The Gateway To The Seven Mighty Gates Of Reincarnation.

Dejected ... —Promo '97, Exmortem (1997) (Demo). Obsessed ... / Deathcult / Behold The Mighty Ravenholt.

Promo Anno 1998, Exmortem (1998) (Demo). In The Lustful Flesh Of Sin We're Gathered / The Lustful Flesh Of Sin / In The Name Of Massacretion.

DEJECTED IN OBSCURITY, Euphonious PHONI 008 (1998). Creatures Of The Night / Born Into The World Of Darkness / Deathcult / Land Of No Return / No Redemption / Materialization / Behold The Mighty Ravenholt / Obsessed / Dwell In Darkness / Dawn Of Reincarnation.

Berzerker Legions EP, Perverted Taste PT 25 (1999) (Split 7" vinyl single with IMPENDING DOOM). The Lustful Of Sin / In The Name Of Massacretion.

BERZERKER LEGIONS, Hammerheart HHR103 (2001). Icecold Ugliness (Part1) / Berzerker Legions / Sovereignty / Bonfire Of The Insanities / The Grim Recker / The Conqueror / Deeds Of Hatred / Terror Mundi-The Cult Of Fimbulty / Into The Realm Of Legend / Dawn Of Revelation / The Revolutionary Soul.

PESTILENCE EMPIRE, Osmose Productions OPCD 139 (2002). Ghastly Grotesque / Funerary Sculpture / Pestifer / Malus Invictus /

Death Deceiver / Grand Dome Of Destruction / Icecold Ugliness (Part 2) / Gruesome Icons / A Tyrants Hunger.

Killstorms, Ancient Darkness ADP004 (2003) (limited edition 500 copies). Killstorms / Critical Madness.

Pest Campaign 2003 EP, Osmose Productions OPEP 011 (2004) (10" vinyl EP). Berzerker Legions / Into The Realm Of Legend / Icecold Ugliness / Intoxicated By Death.

NIHILISTIC CONTENTMENT, Wicked World WICK 19CD (2005). Flesh Havoc / Bitter Discipline / The Human Rape Symphony / Black Walls Of Misery / Division Of Genocide Pleasure / Swamp Of Decadence / Symbols Of Inhumanity / Fix Of Negativity / Graveside Mourning Ritual / Parasite Paradise.

EXMORTIS

FREDERICK, MD, USA — *Brian Werking (vocals / guitar), Ted Hartz (guitar), Chris Wiser (bass), Aantar Lee Coates (drums).*

Frederick, Maryland Death Metal band EXMORTIS was raised during 1987 by vocalist / guitarist Brian Werking, bassist Chris Wiser and drummer Aantar Lee Coates, subsequently enlisting second guitarist Ted Hartz. First product would be the July 1988 demo tape 'Descent Into Chaos', featuring the brief addition of singer Mike Simons, followed by 1989's 'Immortality's End'. This set, recorded with Werking handling vocal duties, would see a UK 12" Vinyl release, limited to 1000 copies, through the CCG Underground label. International underground recognition was by now coming the band's way and on the live front EXMORTIS expanded out of the Maryland club scene to conduct live shows across Washington D.C., Virginia, Pennsylvania, Delaware, New York and New Jersey. However, in 1990 the band splintered, with Werking journeying to Pittsburgh, Pennsylvania whilst both Coates and Hartz relocated to Tampa, Florida. Chris Wiser attempted to persevere with the EXMORTIS name, pulling in guitarist Chewka (a.k.a. Michael Marchewka), but this version of the group, having issued the 1993 demo 'Butchers Of The Urban Frontier', folded, Chewka founding HORROR OF HORRORS.

Rage Records released the October 1991 EP 'Fade From Reality', these songs actually being solo tracks constructed at Zax Trax Studios solely by Werking. In 1993 Deaf Entertainment commissioned two brand new tracks, 'Necrotic Visions' and 'Silence Of Darkness', for use on their compilation album 'The History Of Things To Come'. However, these songs were put out under the BLOODLESS brand.

Aantar Lee Coates subsequently made his mark on the extreme Metal scene serving terms of duty with EULOGY, DIABOLIC, UNHOLY GHOST, NECROSIS, IMPIETY, BLASTMASTERS and HORROR OF HORRORS. Brian Werking featured in STATIC IMAGES and SHOCKWERKS.

Brian Werking conducted further recordings under the EXMORTIS name in 1997, donating cover versions to Dwell Records tribute albums honouring DEATH, with 'Baptized In Blood', and MORBID ANGEL, with 'God Of Emptiness'. Other tribute albums Werking contributed to included those in honour of MARILYN MANSON, KRAFTWERK, MINISTRY and WHITE ZOMBIE. In 2001 EXMORTIS re-released both the 'Descent Into Chaos' and 'Immortality's End' demos in a limited edition CD-R of just 250 copies of each.

EXMORTIS reformed in mid 2005, projecting an album entitled 'The Resurrection'.

Descent Into Chaos, Exmortis (1988). Lords Of Abomination / Exmortis / Pathogenic Silence.

Immortality's End, (1989). Intro / Immortality's End / The Resurrection / Beyond The Realms Of Madness / Casual Killing / Outro.

Fade From Reality, Rage JE-00101 (1991). Dreams Of The Dead / Fade From Reality.

EXMORTIS

LEIRIA, PORTUGAL — *Lho (vocals), Fernando (guitar), Sergio Phantas (guitar), Bigodes (bass), Miguel Sousa (drums).*

Leiria Death Metal band EXMORTIS debuted during 1991 with the demo 'From Darkness To Darkness', this set including a cover version of DIEGODS 'Psychotic Aberrance'. EXMORTIS appeared on the MTM Records compilation album 'The Birth Of A Tragedy' issued in 1992 with the track 'Reflections Of The Last Memory'. Another song, 'Through The Looking Glass', saw inclusion on a 1994 compilation 'From Here To Nowhere'. The group comprised vocalist Lho, guitarists Fernando, ex-PARANOIA, and Sergio Phantas, bass player Bigodes and drummer Miguel Sousa. At one time the group also included Paulo "Sexy" of DESECRATION.

EXMORTIS supported THORMENTHOR, DINOSAUR, SACRED SIN, DISAFFECTED and BOWELROT amongst others. The band subsequently evolved into CANKER BIT JESUS.

From Darkness To Darkness, Exmortis (1991) (Demo). Intro-Ancient Tomb / Petrified Pleasures / A Tribute To Thrash / The Abscess / Enslavement Of Obscurity / Psychotic Aberrance.

Exmortis, Exmortis (1994) (Demo). As A Stone / Gift Of Life / Dream Of Deception / D.S.M. / Words Of Insane.

EXOTO

BELGIUM — *Chris Meynen (vocals), Wilek (guitar), Flip Boonen (guitar), Vic Van Der Steen (bass), Molly (drums).*

One of the leading Death Metal acts in Belgium and the Netherlands, EXOTO formed in Mol, Limburg during 1989 and released a live cassette entitled 'Waiting For The Maggots' in 1990. A studio recorded tape, 'And Then You Die', followed in 1991 and gained the honour of being voted 'Demo Of The Month' in the influential Dutch Rock mag 'Aardschock', going on to sell 1,600 copies.

A third demo, 'The Fifth Season', spawned two tracks that would appear on the 'Ashes' EP released by the Midian Creations label in 1992 before the group's first album, 'Carnival Of Souls', arrived in 1994. Sadly, original drummer Didier was killed in a traffic accident in April of the same year. This traumatic event would lead to the band recording the 'A Tribute To Didier' tape in 1995. Still, having been signed by Black Mark Productions after the response by fans to 'Carnival Of Souls', EXOTO were to release the 'A Thousand Dreams Ago' album.

And Then You Die, Exoto (1991). After Death / Cannibalistic Killer / Chorus Of The Doomed / Insomnia / Into The Ritual / Reincarnation / The Things That Here (And Shall Be Again) / Waiting For The Maggots.

The Fifth Season, (1992). Art Of Butchery / Necromantic Love Affair / Ashes From The Past / The Fifth Season.

Ashes EP, Midian Creations (1992). Art Of Butchery / Ashes From The Past.

CARNIVAL OF SOULS, Tessa (1994). Loss Of Identity / Disappearing Silence / Escape The Eternal Sleep / Dignity Of Entrails / Exhume The Beloved / After Death / Immortality As Defence / Necromantic Love-Affair / Ashes From The Past / Final Discorporation / The Visiting Room / Art Of Butchery.

A THOUSAND DREAMS AGO, Black Mark BMCD 81 (1995). The World Before You / Behind Your Mind / Scream Inside / Waveyard / She / Spirit Within Me / Anxious For The Light / Deny The Pain / Thoughts / The Fifth Season / Second Murder / No Regret.

EXOUSIA

MEXICO — *Marco Pérez (vocals), Miriam López (vocals), Carlos Osnaya (guitar), Miguel Martinez (guitar), Victor Bautista Xolocotzin (bass), Eduardo Armijo (drums).*

Formed in January 1999, Christian Death Metallers EXOUSIA recorded their first album 'Serpiente de Bronce' five months later. The second full length album 'Welcome To The Kingdom Of The Light' was released in June of 2001. Frontman Marco Pérez was previously with LAMENT whilst guitarist Miguel Martínez had a tradition with SACRAMENTO and his six string partner Carlos Osnaya is ex-AMBERDAWN. Bassist Víctor Bautista Xolocotzin operated prior to EXOUSIA in NEFROPTOSIS.

The band confirmed an appearance at the first international 'Revolution Metal Fest' held at the Palacio de los Deportes in Mexico City, Mexico on November 20th 2004 alongside fellow Christian artists SAVIOUR MACHINE, STRYPER, MORTIFICATION and NARNIA. The band would be announced as performers at the 'Underground' festival in Helsinki, Finland during August 2005. The band teamed up with an all-Christian package comprising NARNIA, MORTIFICATION and ROB ROCK for a South and Central American tour in November 2006 hitting Mexico, Guatemala, Honduras, Brazil, Argentina, Colombia and Costa Rica.

SERPIENTE DE BRONCE, (1999). Sangre / Serpiente De Bronce / Break The Silence / Huesos Secos / Ven Fuera De Egipto / Ciudad Brutal / Quien Es Tu Señor / Extremo Amor.

WELCOME TO THE KINGDOM OF LIGHT, (2001). Eterna Dimensión / Master of Master's / Yo Creo En Dios / Salvation / Covenant / Welcome to the Kingdom of Light / Puedes Confiar / Extreme Love / Bebed Mi Sangre.

CONQUER, (2002). Conquer / Victory / Vengeance / Intro—Generación / Guerrera / Generación Guerrera / Intro—Te Necesito / Te Necesito / Martyrs / La Historia de Alguien.

EXPOSED GUTS

GERMANY — *Markus Lempsch (vocals / guitar), Philip Akoto (vocals / bass), Karsten Kautz (guitar), Andreas Seewald (drums).*

Ruhr based Grindcore act founded in 1997 by Markus Lempsch and Michael Smykalla. Demos included "Taste Of Human Flesh' in 1998, recorded using a drum machine, and 'Ultimate Gore Assault' during 1999, the latter produced by Alex Cwiertnia of DELIRIOUS. Shortly afterwards EXPOSED GUTS gained exposure with the inclusion of the track 'Rip It From The Mother's Cunt' on the Razorback Records compilation 'A Hog Wild Tale Of Terror'. A further three song promotion session in March of 2000 would see Cwiertnia once again behind the production desk.

Second guitarist Karsten Kautz was added to the line up in May of 2001. Further overhauls saw Philip Akoto taking the bass position in 2002 and the drum role delegated to Andreas Seewald the following year.

THE WAY OF ALL FLESH, Independent (2003). Guts Are Gory / Beyond The Spheres / Innocence / Regorge The Spawn / Blueprints For Bloodshed / World At War / Invisible Prison Cell / Rip It From The Mother's Cunt / Levelled To A New Stage / Pee All Over Me.

EXPULSION

STOCKHOLM, SWEDEN — *Anders Holmberg (vocals / bass), Stefan Lagergren (guitar), Calle Fransson (drums).*

Stockholm's EXPULSION date back to a 1988 band titled RIVER'S EDGE. The Initial line-up for EXPULSION featured former TIAMAT members guitarist Stefan Lagergren, bassist Anders Holmberg and drummer Calle Fransson. The band released its first demo tape, 'Cerebral Cessation', in 1989 and also contributed the track 'Certain Corpses Never Decay' to the compilation cassette 'Hymns Of The Dead Volume Two'. Later the same year EXPULSION recorded a second demo entitled 'Veiled In The Mist Of Mystery'. This tape landed the band a deal with Putrefaction Records for whom they were to record the single 'Soul Upheaval' / 'Lain Hidden'. However, this remains unreleased. Another blow was struck when various members found themselves with impending terms of compulsory national military service. Holmberg thus decided to put the band on ice and joined TRANQUILLITY.

Lagergren and Fransson reformed EXPULSION in 1991 adding vocalist Fredrik Thornqvist and female bassist Chelsea Krook. The following year EXPULSION augmented their sound with the enlistment of second guitarist Chris Vowden, an erstwhile member of ABSURD and member of Black Metal combo GEBURIUM. The band's first gig, supporting GRAVE, soon followed.

Chelsea Krook departed and the returning Anders Holmberg signed up once more in time to record the debut single, a self financed effort.

EXPULSION promptly featured three tracks—'The Other Side', 'Soul Upheaval' and 'As The Last One Leaves'—to the Evil Omen Records compilation album 'Vociferous and Machiavellian Hate'. Coincidentally a further EXPULSION track, 'Let The Raven's Fly', was featured on the Growing Deaf label's compilation 'History Of Things To Come'.

EXPULSION's long awaited debut album, 'Overflow', appeared in 1994 and offered a guest appearance from TIAMAT vocalist Johan Edlund on the track 'At The Madness End'. Both Chris Vowden and Calle Fransson teamed up once more as part of Thrash Metal band STRESSFEST.

In 2007 Vic Records announced the commercial release of an EXPULSION album to comprise both the 'Cerebral Cessation' and 'Veiled In The Mists Of Mystery' plus unreleased tracks.

Bitter Twist Of Fate, Dodsmetallfirma Expulsion (1993) (Limited edition of 600 copies). Bitter Twist Of Fate / With Aged Hands / Lain Hidden / In A Whirling Dust.

OVERFLOW, Godhead GOD011 (1994). Don't Leave Me To Bleed / Let The Raven's Fly / Fallen / With Aged Hands / Dreamvoyage / The Other Side / The Anatomical Range / As The Last One Leaves / At The Madness End / Overflow.

EXSECRATUS

FINLAND — *Leeni-Maria Kristina Tuulentytär Hovila (vocals), Olli Mattila (vocals / guitar), Kimi Rautiainen (guitar), Timo Kauhajärvi (bass), Emmi Silvennoinen (keyboards), Jussi Raatikainen (drums).*

Melodic Gothic Death Metal band EXSECRATUS was formed during spring 2004 by vocalist / guitarist Olli Mattila and N. Hartikainen. Formative members included female vocalist Armi Päivinen and guitarist Elias Vihma. M. Niemelä took over on drums in 2005 but decamped after a brief tenure. That spring Hartikainen also exited in order to fulfill his national military obligations. New bass player Timo Kauhajärvi was enrolled in early 2006. Drummer Jussi Raatikainen of DRAUGNIM, ELENIUM and THYESTEAN FEAST repute, and keyboard player Emmi Silvennoinen then firmed up the membership.

EXSECRATUS issued the two song demo 'Execute' in September 2006. THRACIAR's T. Honkanen donated guest backing vocals. Kimi Rautiainen took over guitar duties whilst Päivinen was supplanted by Leeni-Maria Kristina Tuulentytär Hovila.

For Finnish shows supporting ENSIFERUM in January 2007 EXSECRATUS keyboard player Emmi Silvennoinen doubled up on live duties, performing with both bands.

Execute, Exsecratus (2006) (Demo). For You / Suicide.

EXTERMINATOR

PEER, BELGIUM — *Jacky Cuypers (vocals / guitar), Kris Jacquemin (guitar), Ivan De Hondt (bass), Marc Damiaens (drums).*

Melodic Death Metal band EXTERMINATOR was manifested in January of 1991, cutting opening demo 'Circle Of Violence' at Gobi Sound studio in Maastricht. The band had been founded with a line up of singer Bart Maarten, guitarists Jacky Cuypers and Ronny Serdongs, bassist Rudi Houben and drummer Sigi Loots, debuting on the live front in November of 1991 supporting DEADHEAD. The band suffered a major blow in January of 2002 when a car accident left road crew member Frank dead and Rudi Houben seriously injured. Maarten exited that May, leaving EXTERMINATOR to persevere with Cuypers and Serdongs sharing lead vocals.

Rejecting an offer from Inline Music from Germany, EXTERMINATOR set to work with Andre Gielen to record a self financed EP. However, in June Sigi Loots departed, being swiftly replaced by Mario Goossens. The group folded in May of 1994, but would be re-activated by founder and frontman Jacky Cuypers that same November as a trio featuring new members Jeroen Lemmens on bass and drummer Jules Lemmens. The 'Forgotten Souls' EP saw issue through Tessa Records in February of 1995. The group expanded to a quartet, drafting second guitarist Werner Geijsels.

1997 opened with line up changes, Ivan De Hondt replacing Jeroen Lemmens and Werner Geijsels decamping, to be superseded by Kris Jacquemin. More tribulation hit the ranks when in May, following a support to BENEDICTION, Jules Lemmens vacated the drum stool. Molly would be the new man on the drums and in 1998 the band's profile rose sharply with valuable supports to visiting international artists such as CANNIBAL CORPSE, VADER, INFERNAL MAJESTY, DARK FUNERAL and even an opening slot to EDGE OF SANITY in the Czech Republic. Baruch Van Bellegem was incorporated as their new drummer in July of 1999 in time for album recordings taking place at Studio De Hautregard in Verviers.

EXTERMINATOR would enter into negotiations with the Shiver label to release 'Mirror Images' but finally published it themselves on the band's own I.M.F. imprint. Promotion included an appearance at the SAXON headlined 'Biebob Metalfest' and a headline tour of Spain. A second trek around Spain, in September of 2001 in alliance with Spaniards DIRTY LUST, was completed before Marc Damiaens took command of the drums and in September of the following year EXTERMINATOR once again put in Spanish dates.

In 2004, despite the band being out of action on the live front due to Cuypers suffering from an articular disease, the group scored a deal with the French Deadsun label. Bassist Ivan De Hondt exited in February 2005. A replacement was soon located in the DESPERATION and LEECH credited Alan Coenegrachts.

Circle Of Violence, (1992). Fragments Of An Agony Deranged / Circle Of Violence / In My Sleep / The Unknown Warrior / Criminal Act.
Forgotten Souls, Tessa (1995). Epitome—Intro / Opaque Ordeal / Hysteron Proteron / World Within / Erroneous Idiosyncrasy.
Night Music, (1997). Fragments / Blackened Dead / Mirror Images / Bitter End / Night Music (The Dark Caress) / Epitome / Opaque Ordeal / Hysteron Proteron / World Within / Erroneous Idiosyncrasy.
Realm Of Chaos, (1999). Church Of Chaos / Bitter End / Tragedy . . . Rejoice . . . / Mirror Images.
MIRROR IMAGES, Exterminator (2000). Birth / Liberty . . . Death . . . / Circle Of Violence / Mirror Images / Church Of Chaos / Bitter End / Night Music (The Dark Caress) / The Kill / Tragedy . . . Rejoice . . . .

EXTOL

BEKKESTUA, NORWAY — *Peter Espevoll (vocals), Christer Espevoll (guitar), Tor Magne S. Glidje (guitar), Jor Robert (bass), David Husvik (drums).*

Highly rated technical Progressive Christian Death Metal. EXTOL was formulated in Bekkestua during the beginning of 1994 by drummer David Husvik, guitarist Christer Espevoll and vocalist Peter Espevoll. Within a few months bassist Eystein Holm completed the line-up. Starting life as a regular Metal band the decision to branch out into more challenging sounds focussed the need for a second guitarist. Emil Nikolaisen of ROYAL was inducted and later Ole Borud from Norwegian Doom veterans SHALIACH brought the band up to strength.

First product would be a split outing dubbed 'Northern Lights', in collaboration with ANTESTOR, SCHALIACH and GROMS, issued in 1996 through Steve Rowe of MORTIFICATION's label Rowe Productions. A three song demo cassette entitled 'Embraced' was then delivered in 1997. The impressive 1999 'Burial' debut album would be the first product released in 1999 by the Endtimes Productions label. For the Japanese market 'Burial' was issued by the Avalon label with an extra track. Tooth & Nail took the album on for North America. The stopgap 'Mesmerized' mini-album surfaced in 1999 which included new tracks and remixes.

Borud opted out in order to devote time to solo Pop orientated projects. EXTOL pulled in Tor Magne S. Glidje of LENGSEL in as replacement. Holm would also lose his position with the new man on bass being Jor Robert.

Mid 2003 found EXTOL, promoting the 'Synergy' album recorded at Toproom Studios, on the road in North America partnered with DEMON HUNTER, STILL BREATHING and THE AGONY SCENE. Scandinavian shows in October found the band supporting OPETH. The band severed ties with guitarists Christer Espevoll and Ole Borud in May 2004. Nevertheless, EXTOL entered Toproom Studios once again August to commence work on a new album, shortly afterward announcing the recruitment of the LENGSEL and GANGLION credited guitarists Tor Magne S. Glidje and Ole Halvard Sveen to the group's ranks.

In 2004 the EXTOL credited David Husvik and Christer Espevoll allied themselves with Magnus Westgaard of VARDOGER and Ivar Nikolaisen from SILVER to forge the ABSURD2 project, recording an EP for Endtime Productions. February 2005 saw EXTOL on the road in Europe as opening act for MASTODON and DOZER. Unfortunately the band's scheduled performance at the April 2005 'New England Metal And Hardcore' festival was cancelled as the band was prevented in reaching their destination due to a tornado in Kentucky. EXTOL would be announced as support to OPETH's September European dates. In side activity, Husvik forged the TWISTED INTO FORM band project with SPIRAL ARCHITECT guitarist Kaj Gornitzka.

The band performed at the Halmstad, Sweden Christian Metal Endtime Festival in March 2007 alongside CRIMSON MOONLIGHT, ANTESTOR, DROTTNAR, EVERGRACE, HARMONY, INEVITABLE END, VARDOGER, VIRGIN FOREST and VENI DOMINE.

Northern Lights, Rowe Productions (1996) (Split EP with SCHALIACH, GROMS and ANTESTOR). Vicious Intent / Christianity Misunderstood / Seek The Righteous.
Embraced, (1997). Embraced / The Prodigal Son / Burial.
Mesmerised, Tooth & Nail (1999). Enthralled / The Prodigal Son / Storms of Disillusion / Burial (Sanctum Remix) / Renhetens Elv (Sanctum Remix) / Work of Art (Raison d'Etre Remix).
BURIAL, Endtimes Productions ENDCD01 (1999). Into Another Dimension / Celestial Completion / Burial / Renhetens Elv / Superior / Reflections Of A Broken Soul / Justified / Embraced / Innbydelse / Tears Of Bitterness / Work Of Art / Jesus Kom Till Jorden For Å Dø.
MESMERIZED, Solid State SS25 (1999). Enthralled / The Prodigal Son / Storms Of Disillusions / Burial (Sanctum remix) / Renhetens Elv (Sanctum remix) / Work Of Art (Raison D'Etre remix).
And I Watch, (2000) (Limited edition. 400 copies). And I Watch / Human Frailties Grave.
UNDECEIVED, Endtimes Productions ENDCD07 (2000). Undeceived / Inferno / Time Stands Still / Ember / Meadows Of Silence / Shelter / A Structure Of Souls / Of Light And Shade / Where Sleep Is Rest / Renewal / Abandoned / And I Watch.
SYNERGY, Century Media 8207-2 (2003). Grace For Succession / Paradigms / Psychopath / Blood Red Cover / 26 Miles From Marathon / Confession Of Inadequacy / Scrape The Surface / Thrash Synergy / Aperture / Emancipation / Nihilism 2002.
BLUEPRINT, Century Media (2005). Gloriana / Soul Deprived / In Reversal / Pearl / From The Everyday Mountain Top / Another Adam's Escape / The Things I Found / Lost In Dismay / Essence / Void / The Death Sedative / Riding For A Fall.

EXTREEM ECZEEM

ENSCHEDE, HOLLAND — *Manus (vocals / guitar), Marco Olthof (vocals / guitar), Richard (guitar), Mark (drums).*

EXTREEM ECZEEM, meaning "Extreme fungus or rash", was forged during August of 1996 by Jeroen "The Mad Gerrit"

Hulleman, Manuel "Manus Mc Mollest" Horst and drummer Patrick Jan Stuivenberg. Undergoing a succession of line up changes the February 2000 version of the band would see Richard Schonewille on guitar and Marco Olthof on bass. In this formation EXTREEM ECZEEM undertook their inaugural live appearance on the 21st October at the 'Metal Battle' concert in Atak, Enschede. Their success in this competition saw the group invited up to the semi-final stages and an inclusion on the live album 'Ontzettend Besmettend'. Both Olthof and Stuivenberg would also serve a tenure with DEIFICATION during 2000.

Ronnie Meinders of DEATH SQUAD replaced Stuivenberg in February of 2001, this line up recording the album 'Magnus Contaminus' at the Ground Zero Studios in Zutphen in October of the following year. A further change on the drum stool saw the incorporation of PERNICIOUS veteran Mark Knoop.

MAGNUS CONTAMINUS, Extreem Eczeem (2004). Mummified / Corpsefucker / Deboned / A Quivering Exaltation In Self Excoriation / Pusseater / Into The Meatshredder / Necroforous Cuisine / Silence Of The Limbs.

EXTREME NOISE TERROR

IPSWICH, UK — *Dean Jones (vocals), Phil Vane (vocals), Pete Hurley (guitar), Ali Firouzbakht (guitar), Lee Barrett (bass), Pig Killer (drums).*

Formed in Ipswich during 1985, and signed to Manic Ears Records after just one gig, Ipswich Punk Metal merchants EXTREME NOISE TERROR achieved a great deal of Pop notoriety by performing on KLF's hit single '3AM Eternal'. The inaugural product would be a split LP with Punk outfit CHAOS UK titled 'Radioactive'. Initially a raw Hardcore outfit EXTREME NOISE TERROR developed through Grindcore into a latter day Death Metal combo.

In the group's formative period NAPALM DEATH drummer Micky Harris could be found on vocals, but would leave during 1987 to form SCORN. The same year the band recorded numerous sessions for Radio One DJ John Peel but suffered other changes in personnel with bassist Jerry Clay leaving to make way for Mark Gardiner. Harris was superseded by ex-DOOM drummer Stig (a.k.a. Tony Dickens) and the band recorded their first full length album 'A Holocaust In Your Head', although Gardiner also departed in favour of Mark Bailey. 1990 found Jones and Firouzbakht guesting on RAW NOISE's 'Sound Of Destruction' single.

Following a tour of Japan ENT recorded their third John Peel session and it was this recording that brought the band's unique sound to the attention of KLF mainman Bill Drummond and the two united to record the hit single '3 AM Eternal'. An album, entitled 'The Black Room', was also recorded but never released. Nevertheless, EXTREME NOISE TERROR had their moment of glory at the 1992 Brit Awards when band members fired blanks from machine guns at the audience.

During 1994 the band lost drummer Stig (who quit to join D.I.R.T.) although his position was filled by original skinbasher Pig Killer. Mark Bailey was also replaced during this period by Lee Barrett, who was also a member of DISGUST.

In early 1997 Vane, who also plied his trade with OPTIMUM WOUND PROFILE, was announced as the new vocalist for NAPALM DEATH supplanting the departed Barney Greenaway. Vane had previously been asked by NAPALM DEATH to fill in for Greenaway on an American tour during 1996 due to Barney's fear of flying! Amazingly, Greenaway was, within days, fronting EXTREME NOISE TERROR! And whilst Vane recorded a split EP with NAPALM DEATH he was soon to return to the TERROR, with Greenaway rejoining NAPALM DEATH, but not before he had laid down vocals for the 'Damage 381' album.

For their Earache tenure the band employed former DECEMBER MOON / CRADLE OF FILTH drummer Was Sarginson although by 2000 he had been supplanted by the 19 year old Zac O'Neil.

Band members put in an appearance on the 2000 RAW NOISE album 'The Terror Continues'. Members of EXTREME NOISE TERROR would also feature in the radical Death Metal band FAILED HUMANITY.

For EXTREME NOISE TERROR's 2001 album 'Being And Nothing' the band shifted to Candlelight Records. CRADLE OF FILTH guitarist Gian Pyres puts in a guest appearance. O'Neil would join the expatriated Chilean Death Metal band CRIMINAL in March of 2002. Lee Barrett collaborated with Hungarian vocalist Juliette Kiss, previously from WITHOUT FACE, Tom MacLean of FORLORN HOPE and FUBAR on guitar and Akos Pirisi of BLACK MOLLY manning the drums for a 2005 Progressive Metal project TO-MERA.

EXTREME NOISE TERROR announced February 2007 European tour dates partnered with THE ACCUSED, CRUMBSUCKERS and DRILLER KILLER. US shows saw an alliance with PHOBIA in May. Manning the drums would be Michael Hourihan, of PARRICIDE, DESECRATION, STORMCROW, NECKBRACE and TIGERTAILZ repute.

RADIOACTIVE, Manic Ears ACHE 1 (1986) (Split album with CHAOS UK). System Shit / No Threat / Human Error / Murder / False Profit / Show Us You Care / You Really Make Me Sick / Fucked Up System / Real Life / Only In It For The Music.

PEEL SESSION, Strange Fruit SFPS048 (1987). False Profit / Another Nail In The Coffin / Use Your Mind / Carry On Screaming / Human Error / Conned Through Life / Only In It For The Music Part Two.

THE PEEL SESSIONS '87—'80, Strange Fruit SFPMA208 (1987). Work For Never / 3rd World Genocide (By Arms Trade) / Fact Or Fiction / Subliminal Music Mind Control / Carry On Screaming / Conned Through Life / Only In It For The Music / I'm A Bloody Fool / In It For Life / Deceived / Shock Treatment / False Profit / Another Nail In The Coffin / Use Your Mind / Human Error / No Threat / Take The Strain / Bullshit Propaganda / Murder / Show Us You Care / System Shit / Only In It For The Music #3.

A HOLOCAUST IN YOUR HEAD, Hurt HURT 1 (1987). Statement / Take The Strain / Show Us You Care / Use Your Mind / Only In It For The Music / Deceived / Conned Thru Life / Innocence To Ignorance / Another Nail In The Coffin.

ARE YOU THAT DESPERATE?, Crust (1989). Deceived / Another Nail In The Coffin / Subliminal Music / Murder / Raping The Earth / Punk: Fact Or Faction.

EXTREME NOISE TERROR, Sink Below SINK1 (1989) (Split album with FILTHKICK). Intro / In It For Life / Subliminal Music Mind Control / Work For Bever / Punk: Fact Or Faction / Cruelty To Carnivores / Damaging Noise.

PHONOPHOBIA, Vinyl Japan DISC 1 X (1992). Pray To Be Moved / Knee Deep In Shit / Self Decay / Moral Bondage / Just Think About It / Lame Brain / What Do.

RETRO-BUTION (TEN YEARS OF TERROR), Earache MOSH 83 (1995). Raping The Earth / Bullshit Propaganda / Lame Brain / Work For Never / We The Helpless / Invisible War / Subliminal / Human Error / Murder / Think About It / Pray To Be Saved / Conned Through Life / Deceived / Third World Genocide.

DAMAGE 381, Earache MOSH 173 (1997). Utopia Burns / Punishment Solitude / Icon Of Guilt / Jesus On My Side / Cold World / Damage 381 / Shallow Existence / Chaos Perverse / Crawl / Downside.

BEING AND NOTHING, Candlelight CANDLE057CD (2001). Being And Nothing / Through Mayhem / When Gods Burn / Man Made Hell / Damage Limitation / No Longer As Slaves / One Truth One Hate / Awakening / Non Believer Genocide / Detestation.

FROM ONE EXTREME TO ANOTHER—LIVE, Cherry Red (2002). Deceived / False Prophet / Murder / We The Helpless / Use Your Mind / Take The Strain / Bullshit Propaganda / Conned Through Life / Another Nail In The Coffin / Raping The Earth / Show Us You Care / Interview With Band.

EXULCERATE

SAN ANTONIO, TX, USA — *Aaron Mendiola (vocals), Angel Tarin (guitar), Ryan Varville (guitar), Matt Hernandez (bass), Dennis Sanders (drums).*

Texan Death Metal combo EXULCERATE, founded in June 2003, are fronted by ex-PUTRILAGE singer Aaron Mendiola with former MORTILITY and present day DISEMBOWEL man Dennis Sanders, replacing Lee Eubanks, on drums. The band's first concert, featuring a line up of Mendiola, Eubanks, DISEMBOWEL guitarist Angel Tarin, bassist Eddie Blanquiz, came in late 2003 with an appearance at the 'Death Fest' alongside PYAEMIA, SEVERED SAVIOR, SPAWN OF POSSESSION and GORGASM.

The demo 'Samples Of Sickness' arrived in early 2004, after which ex-RUPTURE CHRIST guitarist, Ryan Varville was inducted into the line-up. A further change came with the exit of Eubank in February, EXULCERATE swiftly finding a replacement in Dennis Sanders from MORTALITY.

The band undertook tour dates as supports to FLESHGRIND and DEAD FOR DAYS during March. These dates resulted in a recording deal offer from United Guttural Records. However, further membership problems afflicted the group as bassist Eddie Blanquiz opted out in May. Another MORTALITY man, Matt Hernandez, filled the vacancy in August to record the debut album 'Remnants Of A Cannibalistic Debauchery'.

Samples Of Sickness, Exulcerate (2004). Intense Stench Of Deterioration / Resurrection Of The Insane Killing Kind.

EYE SEA

GERMANY — *Tolga Kolburan (vocals / guitar), Uwe Rohlfs (vocals / bass), Herbert Grimm (drums).*

"Hyperfast" Grindcore band EYE SEA came into being during 1994, albeit then titled DISILLUSION, an alliance of vocalist / guitarist Tolga Kolburan and bass player Sven. Herbert Grimm of MUTTI'S LEIDEN was enrolled on drums during 1995 but Sven then departed. Uwe Rohlfs of DEMENZ DURCH ALLTAG, another band that Kolburan was active in, filled the vacancy. EYE SEA's first product was the 1996 'BeLIEve' demo, recorded in Poland and limited to just 100 copies.

A second promotional set 'Off Lies: Monodology' preceded the 'Bloodgeon' album. Just prior to recording 'Bloodgeon' the band inducted lead vocalist Damir although this latest recruit would not feature on the recording. The album includes a cover version of the RIGHTEOUS PIGS track 'I Hope You Die In A Hotel Fire'.

Herbert Grimm also operates with ANASACRA.

BLOODGEON, Shredded (2000). Intro / Bludgeon / Evolutionary Failure / Lifes Unavoidable Consequences / I Hope You Die In A Hotel Fire / Righteous / One Eternal Day.

FACE DOWN

HAGERSTEN, SWEDEN — *Marco Aro (vocals), Joacim Carlsson (guitar), Jaokim Hedestedt (bass), Erik Thyselius (drums).*

Originally titled MACHINE GOD upon their formation in Hagersten during 1993 by ex-AFFLICTED and PROBOSCIS duo of guitarist Joacim Carlsson and bassist Joakim 'Harju' Hedestedt, the quite brutal FACE DOWN found themselves snapped up by Roadrunner and this resulted in the release of the critically acclaimed 'Mindfield' debut album. However, drummer Richard Bång left after the album was completed and had his vacant space occupied by ex-UNANIMATED and MERCILESS man Peter Sjärnvind. April of 1996 found the band conducting UK dates with NAPALM DEATH and CROWBAR.

A second album, 'The Twisted Rule The Wicked', emerged through new label Nuclear Blast in 1997. Aro joined THE HAUNTED with ex-members of AT THE GATES. Despite his international success with THE HAUNTED Aro re-activated FACE DOWN in 2004, working with a cast comprising original members, AFFLICTED and GENERAL SURGERY guitarist Joacim Carlsson, bassist Joakim Hedestedt of CONSTRUCDEAD and new drummer Erik Thyselius from CONSTRUCDEAD, GENERAL SURGERY and TERROR 2000. The band signed to Black Lodge Records for a new studio album 'The Will To Power', entering Offbeat Studios in Stockholm during late October. FACE DOWN put in their first concert in over six years supporting PAIN on 12th February at Klubb Kaliber in Mariestad.

The band parted ways with drummer Erik Thyselius in February 2006. The KAAMOS, REPUGNANT and BLACKSHINE credited Christofer Barkensjö (a.k.a. 'Chris Piss') stepped in as substitute. This new unit entered Offbeat Studios on November 24th to cut demo tracks.

MINDFIELD, Roadrunner RR 8902 (1995). Wear / Kill The Pain / Human / Holy Race / Demon Seed / Save Me, Kill Me / Colors / Twelve Rounds / Hatred / One Eyed Man.
THE TWISTED RULE THE WICKED, Nuclear Blast NB 194-2 (1997). Breed / Self Appointed God / Waste / Life Relentless / Autumn Scars / Bed Of Roaches / Top Of The World / Slender Messiah / For Your Misery / Embrace The Moment / Cleansweep / With Unseeing Eyes.
THE WILL TO POWER, Black Lodge (2005). Drained / Blood Tiles / Heroin / Will To Power / Grey / Heretic / The Delusion / War Hog / The Unsung.

FALCHION

LAHTI, FINLAND — *Juho Kauppinen (vocals / guitar / accordion), Jani Laine (guitar), Sami Heinonen (guitar), Seppo Tiaskorpi (bass), Teemu Peltonen (drums).*

Folk orientated Death Metal act FALCHION debuted with the November 2003 demo 'Glory Of The Sword'. The group had been assembled in May of 2002 by KORPIKLAANI and DEMONIC CREMATION vocalist / guitarist Juho Kauppinen, keyboard player Joonas Simonen and Ville Vehviläinen on drums. Subsequently, bass player Seppo Tiaskorpi enrolled in December and Sami Heinonen joined up in March 2003 as rhythm guitar player. During recording of 'Glory Of The Sword' Vehviläinen was drafted into the military. Unfortunately both Simonen and Heinonen also exited at this juncture.

FALCHION regrouped by enlisting Teemu Peltonen of CRODONIUM as drummer and Jani Laine, of CRODONIUM and DEMONIC CREMATION, as rhythm guitar player in October 2003 to complete the demo sessions. In mid 2004 FALCHION recorded their debut album 'Legacy Of Heathens', being released via the Japanese label World Chaos Productions label, at Studio Watercastle in Jyväskylä with producer with Arttu Sarvanne. September saw Sami Heinonen re-enrolled.

Glory Of The Sword, Falchion (2003). Folk In The Golden Town / Cursed To Live / The Darkest Valleys Of Mist / Man Of Spells.
LEGACY OF HEATHENS, World Chaos Production KDM-018 (2005). Immortal Heroes / The Ancient Tale / Folk In The Golden Town / Broken Stone / Journey In The Woods / Swordmaster Of The Dragonland / The Darkest Valleys Of Mist / Burning The Gates / Black Crown.

FALCIFORM

WELLINGTON, NEW ZEALAND — *Jason Hislop (vocals / bass), Nathan Forbes (vocals / guitar), Kent Humphrey (guitar), Hayden Browne (drums).*

Extreme yet technically inclined Death Metal out of Wellington. FALCIFORM, originally entitled DENIAL, was first given life during 1993, initially comprising by guitarists Kent Humphrey and Nathan Forbes with Hayden Browne on drums. Clayton McGregor was incorporated as vocalist / bassist during 1994 but by January of 1995 this latest recruit had opted out and Forbes took over the lead vocal role. A few months later Jason Hislop was drafted to perform the vocals and bass roles.

An inaugural demo was recorded during 1996 followed by sessions for the mini-album 'Catalyst' the year after. In August of 1999 the band opened for BRUTAL TRUTH and finally managed to issue the 'Catalyst' recordings. A new track 'Falciform' would also be laid down for the 'Eruption-Vol. 1 Part 1' compilation album. By mid 2000, having discovered numerous acts worldwide brandishing the DENIAL handle, the group adopted the revised title of FALCIFORM. This new incarnation of the group debuted live as opening act for Australia's ATOMIZER.

FALCIFORM bassist Jason Hislop would also make his mark with Lower Hutt Grindcore act BACKYARD BURIAL. Both Nathan Forbes and Jason Hislop were also operation with the highly regarded Black Metal act ZIRCONIUM. Forbes also found the time to work with MONSTERWORKS. In September 2003 FALCIFORM announced the band was splitting up at the end of the year. The band contributed the track 'King Of Kings' to the 'Morbid Music Vol. 1' 2004 compilation album.

CONTAGION, (2001). Prologue / Heathen Inbreed / Escape Your Fate / Degenerate World / Endorsed By The Faceless / Consumed / (Untitled) / This Incohesion Demands / In Extremis / Falciform.
LIMITS OF POWER, Falciform (2003). Cannibal Christ / Mutation Of Lies / One False Move / The Hierarchy Forsworn / King Of Kings / Illusionary Chaos Machine / Knowing No Masters.

FALL OF SERENITY

GERMANY — *René Betzold (vocals), Alex Fischer (guitar), Eddy Langner (guitar), John Gahlert (bass), Nick Putzmann (drums).*

Death Metal act FALL OF SERENITY evolved from a prior act entitled CONTRITION in 1998, the band at this stage numbering singer Lars, guitarists Alex Fischer and Eddy Langner, bassist Andreas Ferge and drummer Ulli Walther. The band's first release would be the 1999 'Smoldering Doom' opus, restricted to just 500 copies with 100 of these being pressed on grey marbled vinyl. That same year further tracks were laid down for a split album shared with HEAVEN SHALL BURN. For these sessions René Betzold was drafted on backing vocals, this providing the catalyst for the band to employ both René and Lars for dual lead vocals.

Eager to capture their new line up on tape FALL OF SERENITY went back into the studio to cut the demo billed as 'Demonstration Tracks 2000'. However, Andreas made an exit upon completion of these tracks. John Gahlert of OBSCURATION, a side project which also included René, Alex and Eddy alongside IMPENDING DOOM's Patrick W.Engel on drums, soon substituted. FALL OF SERENITY signed to the Voice Of Life label for debut album 'Grey Mans Requiem'. The record, produced by Patrick W.Engel, closed out with cover versions of DISMEMBER's 'Casket Garden' and BLACK SABBATH's 'Electric Funeral'. Lars made a break from the band in 2002.

FALL OF SERENITY bassist John also acts as frontman for Deathcore band SOULGATE'S DAWN. The band drafted new drummer Nick Putzmann for recording of 2004's 'Royal Killing' album. Signing to Lifeforce Records the band issued the 'Bloodred Salvation' album, recorded at Rape Of Harmonies Studios by Ralf Müller and Patrick W. Engel, in 2006, this set featuring a guest appearance by Leif Jensen of DEW-SCENTED. The band hooked up with HATE ETERNAL, SPAWN OF POSSESSION and SHADOWSLAND for European touring in May covering the UK, Germany, France, Spain, Italy, Holland, Hungary, Czech Republic and Belgium.

FALL OF SERENITY parted ways with singer René Betzold in late September, switching bassist John Gahlert over to the lead vocal role whilst new member Simon Brach took over on bass.

Smoldering Doom EP, X83X (2000) (Limited edition 500 copies). Intro / Blood Feud / Fire / When The Sun Falls / Irony Of Fate / Power Struggle / CMS.
GREY MAN'S REQUIEM, Voice Of Life VOL013 (2001). ... The Storms Are Gathering / Cold Sweat / Living The Pain / The Price Of Innocence / Masters Of Chaos / Followed By Hell / Holy Divinity / The Gift Of Fury / Broken Doorways.
ROYAL KILLING, Metal Age (2004). Thirst For Knowledge / Royal Killing / Falling Apart / Mask Of Hatred / The Forthcoming / Children Of A Dying Breed / Lost Horizon / Casting Shadows / Behind The Veil / Demon-(mon)archy.
BLOODRED SALVATION, Lifeforce LFR 061 (2006). Blood Starts Running (Intro) / Out Of The Clouds / A Piece Of You / Dead Eyes / Bloodred Salvation / Raise Your Remorse / As I Watch / Overflowing Senses / Swallowed Lies / Twin Curse.

FALL OF SERENITY

FALLEN YGGDRASIL

BADEN-WÜRTTEMBERG, GERMANY — *Simon (vocals), Rafael (guitar), Denno (guitar), Sulli (bass), Molch (drums).*

Baden-Württemberg Death Metal band FALLEN YGGDRASIL debuted with the 1997 promo cassette 'Frost Bite'. At this juncture the band, already having been through early line-up changes, bore a membership of vocalist Simon, guitarists Rafael and Sascha with drummer Matze.

They would follow up in early 1998 sharing a live recorded tape with Austrian act DECEPTION upfront of a further studio effort billed as 'Odyssey In Sorrow'. August of 2000 witnessed a split 7" EP, limited to 500 copies, in league with DEMENTIA. Shortly after this release Matze left the fold, being replaced by Molch. Further ructions witnessed the departure of both Sascha and keyboard player Phillip. In late 2000 Dierk took the bass position. After the mini album 'In No Sense Innocence' FALLEN YGGDRASIL morphed yet again, drafting bassist Sulli and second guitarist Denno.

German concerts in November 2006 were conducted with NOISE FOREST and DEW-SCENTED.

Fallen Yggdrasil, (2000) (Split single with DEMENTIA. Limited edition 500 copies). You Suicide Me / Nightflowers.
IN NO SENSE INNOCENCE, (2002). New Age Mephisto / You Suicide Me / Crown Of All Creatures / In No Sense Innocence / Odyssey In Sorrow / Nightflower.
BUILDING UP A RUIN TO COME, Supreme Chaos SCR-CD013 (2004).

FALSE REALITY

BRASOV, RUMANIA — *Ioan Crisan (vocals), Silviu Stan (guitar), Catalin Bota (bass), Lucian Popa (keyboards), Cristian Tîrsan (drums).*

Brasov, melodic Death-Black Metal band FALSE REALITY formed in December of 1998 around guitarists Silviu 'Jacuzzi' Stan and Marius Moga, bassist Catalin Bota and drummer Crisan 'Cristian Death' Tîrsan. The latter is active on the local scene, industriously citing membership of ELECTTON, Black Metal band VIELTAVA, Progressive Metal band MIRROR, Hard Rock combo ART and Thrash Metal band SARCASTIC. Subsequently the band was rounded out by singer Ioan 'Judas' Crisan and keyboard player Adrian Irimie. The first line up switch occurred when Lucian 'Lucullus' Popa took over keyboards.

FALSE REALITY put in a significant performance at the Satu-Mare 'Samus Rock Alive' festival in the Summer of 1999, after which they recorded the opening demo 'Escape From Doom'. With this session complete, Moga made his exit. For a period the band operated with one guitarist until Alexandru Iuga filled the vacancy in October of 2000. However, the following year Iuga opted out and FALSE REALITY decided upon a one guitar format.

Signing to Sidekick Records the band cut the EP 'Tales Of Eternity' for 2002 release. That March FALSE REALITY gave their first televised performance from the 'Metalheart' festival in Constanta.

Tales Of Eternity, Sidekicks (2002). Confuse Sunset / Escape From Doom / The Sentence / Virgin's Curse / Under Waters.

FATAL DEMEANOR

OSLO, NORWAY — *Abuse (vocals), Tlaloc (guitar), Berserkr (guitar), Skamslått (bass), Myrdr (drums).*

Oslo Black Metal. The 2003 line-up of FATAL DEMEANOR counted singer Wodan (a.k.a. Morten Lockert), lead guitarist Tlaloc (Henrik Vissmark) and bass player Draupne (Hans Petter Roskifte). The 1349 and PANTHEON-I credited Tjalve (Andrè Kvebek) assumed drum duties. At this juncture the band name was ANTROCITY.

In 2004 Charun (Lars Vissmark) took over the second guitar spot whilst Vold (Martin Sørvold) became the new drummer. A switch in the band's rhythm section saw Draupne and Vold usurped by Skamslått and Myrdr respectively. Rhythm guitarist Charun adopted a new stage name of Berserkr whilst Wodan became Abuse. A demo, 'Morbid Facts', was released in August 2004.

FATAL DEMEANOR guitarist Henrik Vissmark joined THORN-BOUND in November 2004.

Morbid Facts, Fatal Demeanor (2004). Rabid God / Inside Holocaust / Morbid Facts / Rotting Saint.

FEARER

EMDEN, GERMANY — *Tom Zorn (vocals / guitar), Matthias Wiltfang (guitar), Karsten Kleen (bass), Alf Kluge (drums).*

East Frisian, Emden based Death Metal band FEARER were borne out of the break up of the infamous VOMITING CORPSES during 1995. As the VOMITING CORPSES rhythm section of bassist Michael and drummer Heiner forged the high profile ANASARCA vocalist Tom Zorn and guitarist Frank Spinka- enlisting bassist Karsten Kleen, another early VOMITING CORPSES member, and drummer Alf Kluge, founded FEARER, debuting with a 1996 demo 'Mindless'. An EP, 'No Tomorrow', arrived in 1998 after which Frank departed.

FEARER's first full length album 'No Compromise' was delivered in 2000. However, it would be completely re-recorded and re-titled as 'The Grinning Face Of Death' for a subsequent 2001 release. Bizarrely the same recordings would be given a third wind, re-dubbed 'Confession Of Hate' in 2002.

FEARER cited a 2002 line up of Tom Zorn on vocals and guitar, Matthias Wiltfang on guitar, Karsten Kleen on bass and Alf Kluge on drums.

No Tomorrow EP, (1998). No Tomorrow / Notify / Fasten Your Seatbelts / Fasten Your Seatbelts Part 2 / Earth Siege.

NO COMPROMISE, (2000). Stored Experiment / No Compromise / Human Camouflage / Countdown For Murder / Retort Creature / Dark Memories / Lost Species / Painflow / Tombstonesuckers.

CONFESSION TO HATE, Remission (2002). Final Breath (Intro) / Confession To Hate / No Compromise / Painflow / Countdown To Murder / Stored Experiment / Earth Siege / Lost Species / Blind The Meanless / Dark Memories / Retort Creature / Human Camouflage.

BACKFIRE, Remedy (2005).

FEAROFHATRED

LINCOLN, LINCOLNSHIRE, UK — *Steve Cowan (vocals / guitar), Craig Furniss (vocals / guitar), Glenn Gibbs (vocals / bass).*

Lincoln Death Metal band FEAROFHATRED was founded during 1996 by Steve Cowan and Steve Robinson. Demos were recorded but the project was then put into hiatus. Cowan reactivated the band during 2005 to record the 'Unrelent' EP. An album, 'The Year Of Hydrogen', was released in early 2006, after which vocalist / guitarist Craig Furniss was recruited.

FEAROFHATED released the 2006 album 'Fear Of The Night Sky' through Swan Recordings. Glenn Gibbs was then enrolled on bass. FEAROFHATRED vocalist / guitarist Steve Cowan also operated "blackened Thrash" project MÃO PRETA, recording an EP entitled 'Canções Para A Estação Do Outono', scheduled for September 2006 release.

THE YEAR OF HYDROGYN, ThornCult (2006). JC1A100505 / Taken / Egoism / Test / Can't Stay / DeadStone / Always Glad When It's June / Elegy For No One / Cloudloop / Wish I Was Anywhere.

THEFT OF THE NIGHT SKY, ThornCult (2006). Lycanthropic Reign / Blackest Light / Adrenalin Rush / Broken Pieces / Beyond This Life / Destruction Of The Nile / Ingested Vanity / In The Name Of God / Una Famiglia Di Una / Winter.

FEEBLE MINDED

CZECH REPUBLIC — *Honza Zoubek (vocals), Banjo (guitar), Pavel Šatra (guitar), Jaromir (bass), David (drums).*

Rokycany Death-Grind band FEEBLE MINDED date to 1996, at first comprising GRIND 6.4 singer Honzik (Honza Zoubek), guitarist Pavel Šatra, bassist Jaromir and a drum machine. Inducting second guitarist Erik the band issued the demo 'CML-5' in 1999. FEEBLE MINDED's 2001 album 'Hate Feeling' album would be a shared affair split with fellow Czech Grindcore act LIMITS OF NESCIENT. The band replaced Erik with Banjo and added HATE SICK drummer David in November of 2002. However, for recording purposes FEEBLE MINDED would rely on the session talents of Lille Grueber from German band DEFEATED SANITY.

Bassist Jaromir is also operational on the live circuit with "Para-Jazz-Core" band SAVAGE SAUSAGE, Black Metal act SALIX and Doomsters BELTAINE.

HATE FEELING, Grohaisen GRO 001 (2001) (Split album with LIMITS OF NESCIENT).

FETUS EATERS

BURBANK, CA, USA — *Kevin (vocals), Ross (guitar), Erich (bass), Ed (drums).*

Self styled Burbank, California "Vomitcore" outfit featuring WATCH ME BURN guitarist Kevin. Apparently the band's debut gig in 1995 attracted no patrons whatsoever but they would proudly boast two punters at their next show had turned up expecting to see another band. The inaugural demo 'Do You Wanna Get Pregnant?' would be promoted with support gigs to such extreme Metal acts as IMMOLATION, DEICIDE, CEPHALIC CARNAGE and BENUMB amongst others. They would sign to the European Hammerwerk imprint for an eponymous 1999 album. A split 7" single would be shared with Finns IRRITATE on Vulgar Records. FETUS EATERS shared the Regurgitated Semen 2002 'Mediocre' album with German Grind veterans SANITY'S DAWN.

FETUS EATERS, Hammerwerk V61 (1999). C'mon Nobody Really Likes Manowar / Some Slayer / TTT Tom / Some Skynyrd / Chew Chu / You Saxy Thang / Eye Scream Truck / Fuck Yer Mom—Oh By The Way I'm Satan / Beelzebub / God Am A Lie / Seth Is Gay / Beatbox You To Def.

MEDIOCRE, Regurgitated Semen (2002) (Split album with SANITY'S DAWN). WWJD / Cleaning / C'mon, Nobody Really Believes In God / Next Time You Take A Shit, Please Retrieve My Cockring / Nikky Sixx Pinky Holster / Eye Still Can't Believe It's Not Butter / Big Piece Of Shit / Sperm Encrusted Sock / It's Funny When Girls Cry / You Call Your Kids Babys Cuz You Can't Have Kids / I Put Jelly On The Window Sill To Keep The Ants Away From My Dishes / George Dubya Has An IQ Of 91 / If My Pet Cow Died, I'd Eat It / Granny Lactates Cottages Cheese / Holiday In Afghanistan / Little More Hand, Little Less Tooth (C'mon, Nobody Really Likes Pornogrind) / Taste Like Burning / Obituary / Thank You Satan / Need Sobriety / Ohhh ….. / So Heavy, God Can't Lift It / Old Man Chocolate Is Knocking On At The Back Door, And He Ain't Waitin / The Big Guy Downstairs / Sucks To Be Jesus / Stop Crying, Stop Being So Emo, And Take Off That Sweater Mr. Spock / Tardcore.

FINAL BREATH

GEMÜNDEN, GERMANY — *Jurgen Aumann (vocals), Jörg Breitenbach (guitar), Werner Müller (guitar), Thomas Wissel (bass), Heiko Krumpholz (drums).*

Founded in Gemünden in 1993, FINAL BREATH first began playing cover versions of various popular Metal acts. This soon changed however as original songs were written and culminated in the 1995 demo tape 'Soulchange'. A move to CD format saw the band release the 'End Of It All' EP in 1997. Unable to find a suitable label FINAL BREATH went down the self-financed road once more and brought in producer Andy Classen, guitarist with HOLY MOSES to control the sound. The resulting album 'Flash-Burnt Crucifixes' convinced Gutter Records, a division of Massacre Records, to set-up a license contract to publish the album.

2002 saw the release of the full length album 'Mind Explosion' under new label Nuclear Blast, again produced by the renowned Andy Classen. Switching to Remedy Records, FINAL BREATH released 'Let Me Be Your Tank' in October 2004. The band put on a special release party gig on 13th November at the Neustadt am Main Turnhalle venue.

The band forged a touring alliance with Norway's ANCIENT and Danish act ILLDISPOSED for European dates throughout March of 2005. In mid 2005 it was learned that Jurgen Aumann was contributing to the DAWNRIDER project assembled by MAJESTY mentor Tarek "Metal Son" Maghary.

SOULCHANGE, (1995). Intro / Dreamland / Valhalla / Mirror Of Beauty / Final Breath / Life / Dreams Of Sorrow / Soulchange.
END OF IT ALL, (1997). Law Of Nature / End Of It All / Suicide Symphony / Selfpossession / Bust-Art.
FLASH BURNT CRUCIFIXES, Gutter (2000). Violent Death / Going Hellbound / Ratrace / Sociopathically Insane / Exposed To Hatred / Bloodred Sky / The Pact / Killing Machines / Soulcontrol / Chaos.
MIND EXPLOSION, Nuclear Blast (2002). Under Pressure / Mind Explosion / Killed By Lust / Break Down / Nonedescript / White Prison / When Lover Turnes To Hate / The Punisher / To Live And To Die / Careless.
LET ME BE YOUR TANK, Remedy (2004). Intro / Strong Pain / Eyes Of Horror / Greed For Revenge / Empty Eyes / Exposed To Hatred / Let Me Be Your Tank / Bemoaned Animosity / Sociopathically Insane / Coma Divine.

FINAL DAWN

OULU, FINLAND — *Vesa Mattila (vocals / guitar), Marko Leiviskä (guitar), Toni Laine (bass), Mikko Törmänen (drums).*

Oulu Death Metal act FINAL DAWN, describing themselves as "Melodic Aggrometal" was founded in mid 2000 by the former BODIES guitarist/vocalist Vesa Mattila, drummer Mikko Törmänen and bassist Hessu Meriläinen. In the spring of 2001 erstwhile RMS, AM I BLOOD and STILLBURNED guitarist Marko Leiviskä joined the fold. An opening demo, 'Suicide Of Your World', was cut in May of 2001 after which Meriläinen was usurped by Tony Laine of FIREWALL. In this new guise FINAL DAWN laid down the two track 'Aggression Overdrive' promo session that September.

FINAL DAWN signed to the British Rage Of Achilles label in 2002. However, no product eventuated from this liaison and the band switched over to Dutch imprint New Aeon Media, a subsidiary of Hammerheart Records. A collection of tracks recorded at Sonic Pump Studios emerged as the album 'Under The Bleeding Sky' in March 2004.

Singer Vesa Mattila relocate to Helsinki, signalling the end of the band. Here he would front CODEON and, as 'Argh Satan', SAATANAN MARIONETIT. FINAL DAWN was re-activated by Mattila in 2007. New bass player Leonard also performs as drummer with BLACK TEMPLE and BLINDED RAIN.

Suicide Of Your World, Final Dawn (2001) (Demo). Aggression Overdrive / 12 Times / My Pain / Suicide Of Your World / Among Two Storms.
Aggression Overdrive, Final Dawn (2002) (Demo). Aggression Overdrive / My Pain.
UNDER THE BLEEDING SKY, New Aeon Media (2004). Solemn Art / Ardent / Aggression Overdrive / Doze / Regression Is Transgression / Bleeding Sky / What Flows Within / My Pain.

FLAGELLATION

STOCKHOLM, SWEDEN — *Per Lindström (vocals / bass), Daniel Cannerfelt (guitar), Fredrik Klingwall (keyboards), Marcus Jonsson (drums).*

Stockholm Death Metal combo FLAGELLATION started life billed as THORNSPAWN. The group features IN GREY members Per Lindström on vocals and bass, guitarist Daniel Cannerfelt and keyboard player Fredrik Klingwall. Drummer Marcus Jonsson held a tradition with INSISION, PANDEMONIC, CROMB and GENOCRUSH FEROX. Session guitars came courtesy of Toob Brynedal, also of INSISION, CROMB and GENOCRUSH FEROX. The demo 'Spineless Regression' was issued during 1998.

FREDRIK KLINGWALL would also feature in RISING SHADOWS and issued Industrial solo album 'Entrance' in 2006. Both Klingwall and Lindström joined the ranks of MACHINERY in 2006.

FLAGELLATION issued a download EP entitled 'Incinerate Disintegrate' in February 2007 via Last Entertainment Productions. These tracks were recorded at Black Lounge Studio with producer Jonas Kjellgren.

Spineless Regression, Last Entertainment LAST 001 (1998). Necrophilian Dreams / Thornspawn Visions / Spineless Regression.
Incinerate Disintegrate, Last Entertainment (2007) (Download EP). Rendering The Apocalypse / Chaos In The Flesh / Threshold To Madness / Purified By Fire / Incinerate Disintegrate / Vast Desolation.

FLASHOVER

BRASÍLIA, DF, BRAZIL — *Itazil Junior (vocals / guitar), Fernando Cézar (guitar), Daniel Lima (bass), Rafael Alves Pereira (drums).*

Taguatinga, Distrito Federal Death-Thrashers FLASHOVER, founded in October of 1997, feature former DEATH SLAM member Itazil Junior. He would head up a founding line up also comprising bassist Daniel Lima and drummer Fernando Cavalcante. Subsequently second guitar was delegated to Fernando Cézar.

FLASHOVER debuted with the 2001 album 'Infamous Country'. Signing to Lethal Records the band issued the 2003 follow up 'Land Of Cannibals' album. The closing track 'Metal Blood' boasted an array of Brazilian extreme Metal talent, studio guests including Júnior of CORPSE GRINDER, Alex Carmago of KRISIUN, Pedro from WINDS OF CREATION, Nathan of RHEVENGE and Fellipe C.D.C. of DEATH SLAM. Also aiding would be journalist Antonio Rolldão from 'Metal Blood' magazine and Lethal Records own Spyker.

INFAMOUS COUNTRY, (2001). Flesh And Blood / This Life / Infamous Country / Incorporating The Pain / My Revenger / Torment / Under World / Mother Fucker / Pain And Hate / Choose Your Guns.
LAND OF CANNIBALS, Lethal (2003). Land Of Cannibals / Threating Eyes / Repressed Desires / Dogs Of War / Days Of Fight / Kill The Priest / Wrong Place ... Wrong Time / Rise Above The Sky / Die, Die, Die!!! / I Hate Your Life / Metal Blood.

FLESH

STRÄNGNÄS, SWEDEN — FLESH is the 2005 old school Death Metal solo project of Strängnäs based guitarist Peter 'Flesh' Karlsson, a veteran of THE MORTICIAN DEAD, MAZE OF TORMENT and DECEIVER. Karlsson held a wealth of scene credentials, commencing with the 1991 EMBRYO demo 'Damnatory

Cacophony'. With next project HARMONY he featured on demos, 1992's 'Blood Angels' and 'Until I Dream' plus 1994's 'The Radiance From A Star'. THE MORTICIAN DEAD released the 2002 demo 'Necrophalia Retribution' prior to Karlsson joining MAZE OF TORMENT.

The FLESH album, 'Dödsångest' emerged through the Gothenburg based label Iron Fist Productions, being recorded over just three days in June at the Abyss studio with producer Tommy Tägtgren. Karlsson handled lead vocals, guitar and bass whilst DECEIVER's Flingan (a.k.a. Magnus Flink) delivered the drums.

Working with DECEIVER bassist Crille Lundin, Flesh formulated THROWN in 2006 for a debut album, entitled 'The Suicidal Kings Occult', recorded at the Abyss studio with producer Tommy Tägtgren over just five days commencing August 30th 2006. A new FLESH album, 'Temple Of Whores', was released in September through Iron Fist Productions.

TEMPLE OF WHORES, Iron Fist Productions (2006). Temple Of Whores / Taste The Devil's Blood / Visions Of Damnation / Rotten Through The Skin / Baptised On The Demon's Throne / Grotesque Infection / Vultures / Spirits Reborn In Chaos / Invisible Darkness.

FLESH GRINDER

BRAZIL — *Chacal (vocals / guitar), Fábio Görresen (vocals / guitar), Rogerio (bass), Daniel Henriques (drums).*

Splatter-Core outfit FLESH GRINDER, founded in 1993, employ some truly horrific photographic artwork on their albums. The band shared their unique art with fellow Grindcore unit LYMPHATIC PHLEGM for their 2000 opus 'From Rotten Process To Splatter'. The artwork for the 2001 album 'Libido Corporis' was so extreme release was delayed until the band could find a printer willing to handle the product. Not for the faint hearted.

Drummer Johnny subsequently joined Grind act HECATOMB. He would also join Black Metal act FORNICATION during 2003. FLESH GRINDER persevered by enlisting Edilson Roberto of IN NOMINE on the drums. However, Johnny then returned, only to exit once again. By August Daniel Henriques was behind the drum kit as the band cut new material for a proposed split EP for 2004 issue through the Czech based Bizarre Embalming Productions.

ANATOMY AND SURGERY, Lofty Storm LSR003 (1997). Intro: Cerebral Draw / Opthamologic Laceration In An Insane Moribund / Tissue Injury Caused By An Apparent Immunologic Reaction Of Host / Embolia / Surgical Considerations About Embryologic Malformations / Anatomy In Surgery / Congenital Abnormalities Of Basic Mechanics Of Excretory Tubules / Boneyard / Hemorrhagical Convultions Of The Gastric Ligaments / Aberrations Of The Immune Response Seen In Viral Immunity.
S.P.L.A.T.T.E.R., Lofty Storm LSR005 (1999). Intro (Stomachal Emanation) / Chronic Mucocutaneous Candiasis / S.P.L.A.T.T.E.R. / Technics To Extract The Female Reproductive System Thru Anal Canal / Cutaneous Anaphilaxis / Cavernous Sinus Thrombosis / Granulomatous Inflammation With Elliptical Macrophages / Acute Syndrome Resembling Infectious Monucleosis / The Amorphous (Nongibrous) / Chronic And Recurrent Regurgitant Lung Disease / Adverse Effects Seen In Immunologically Compromised Hosts / The Adagio Of Pathologist / Developing Malignant Cancerous Tissue In The 8th Inch Of The Large Intestine.
FROM ROTTEN PROCESS ... TO SPLATTER, Millennium (2000) (Split album with LYMPATHIC PHLEGM). Crematorium / Genital Putrefaction / Sexual Mutilation / Necrophagia / Ophtalmologic Laceration In An Insane Moribund / Hemorrhagical Convultions Of The Gastric Ligaments / Chronic Mucocutaneous Candidiasis / Thecnics To Extract The Female Reproductive System Thru Anal Canal.
LIBIDO CORPORIS, Demise (2001).

FLESH PARADE

NEW ORLEANS, LA, USA — *Jason Pilgrim (vocals), Rene Perez (guitar), Shane Lechler (bass), Todd Capiton (drums).*

Louisiana Grindcore crew FLESH PARADE began life in 1990 touting a Death Metal sound. The original group consisted of vocalist Blake Balu, guitarists Duane Marcel and Joe Militello, bassist C.J. Pierce and drummer Todd Capiton. With this roster FLESH PARADE cut the 1991 demo session 'Meathook'. This incarnation of the group only managed a handful of shows before folding with Balu, Marcel and Pierce all making their exit. The latter member would eventually relocate to Dallas, Texas, finding fame as guitarist for Nu-Metal act DROWNING POOL.

FLESH PARADE regrouped pulling in erstwhile SEVERANCE members vocalist Jason Pilgrim and guitarist Rene Perez. The bass position remained fluid, Ben Marrs of EXHUMED taking the role for a brief period, but officially the band was without a bassist for its second demo 'Hate Life'.

Both Militello and Marrs opted out prior to recording a third demo, 1993's 'Worthless'. Shane Lechler would then fill the bass vacancy. In 1997 FLESH PARADE signed to the Relapse label for the release of a 7" single 'Kill Whitey'. A CD retrospective compilation arrived in 1998.

Kill Whitey EP, Relapse (1997). Monsieur Lebeaux / Backstabber / King Cobra / Bite And Get In It / Fat And Gristle.
FLESH PARADE, Relapse (1998). Monsieur Lebeaux / Backstabber / King Cobra / Bite And Get In It / Fat And Gristle / Worthless / Bite And Get In It / Just A Little / Coping With It / Lighten Up / 'Bout Had It / How About Some Good Stuff?

FLESHCRAWL

GERMANY — *Alex Pretzer (vocals), Stefan Hanus (guitar), Mike Hanus (guitar), Markus Amann (bass), Bastian Herzog (drums).*

FLESHCRAWL's first demo tape in 1991 was titled 'Festering Flesh'. This was quickly followed by the self financed mini album 'Lost In A Grave'.

1993's 'Impurity' release was produced by EDGE OF SANITY's Dan Swanö. Prior to recording the third album, 'Bloodsoul', bassist Amann quit leaving Mike Hanus to take up four string duty.

Although the group pursued a Doomier direction in the early part of their career they have since progressed into a pure Death Metal outfit.

2000 found FLESHCRAWL on tour in Europe as part of the 'No Mercy' festival package alongside Poland's VADER, America's VITAL REMAINS and Brazilians REBAELLIUN.

FLESHCRAWL's 'As Blood Rains From The Sky ...' album sees covers of EXCITER's 'Swords Of Darkness' and CARNAGE's 'The Day Man Lost'. More covers were in evidence on the 2001 'Soulskinner' album, this time a take on JUDAS PRIEST's 'Metal Gods'.

In April of 2002, following a decade of service, guitarist Stefan Hanus announced his departure from the band. Oliver Gbravac would duly take the vacancy, performing live with FLESHCRAWL for the first time at the 'Wacken Open Air' festival. Grbavac would also enroll himself into Swiss Death Metal band ALIENGATES during 2003 as a side concern, but left that formation in order to prioritise FLESHCRAWL. The group teamed up with label mates CRIMINAL and SIX FEET UNDER for a two-week European tour throughout February and March of 2004.

FLESHCRAWL inducted new bassist Nico Scheffler in April 2007. The band utilised Toninfusion studios in Ulm during May to track a new album provisionally titled 'Structures Of Death' with taking place in early June at Studio Underground in Sweden.

Lost In A Grave EP, Morbid (1991). Lost In A Grave.
IMPURITY, Black Mark BMCD 48 (1993). From The Dead To The Living / Withering Life / Reincarnation / Subordinated / Disfigured / After Obliteration / Stiffen Souls / Center Of Hate / Inevitable End / Incineration.
BLOODSOUL, Black Mark BMCD 88 (1996). Bloodsoul / In The Dead Of Night / Embalmed Beauty Sleep / Contribution Suicide / The Age Of Chaos / Recycling The Corpses / Nocturnal Funeral / Tomb Of Memories.

FLESHCRAWL

AS BLOOD RAINS FROM THE SKY ... WE WALK THE PATH OF ENDLESS FIRE, Metal Blade 14295 (2000). March Of The Dead (Intro) / Path Of Endless Fire / Under The Banner Of Death / As Blood Rains From The Sky / Embraced By Evil / The Dark Side Of My Soul / Swords Of Darkness / Impure Massacre Of Bloody Souls / Creation Of Wrath / Graves Of The Tortured / Feed The Demon's Heart / The Day Man Lost.

SOULSKINNER, Metal Blade 3984-1 4389-2 (2001). Soulskinner / Dying Blood / Carved In Flesh / Breeding The Dead / The Forthcoming End / Deathvastation / Legions Of Hatred /.Forced To Kill / Rotten / Metal Gods.

MADE OF FLESH, Metal Blade (2004). Beneath A Dying Sun / Made Of Flesh / Scourge Of The Bleeding Haunted / Into The Depths Of No Return / Flesh Bloody Flesh / Forged In Blood / Damned In Fire / Demons Of The Dead / Carnal Devourment / When Life Surrenders.

FLESHGRIND

IL, USA — *Rich Lipscomb (vocals / guitar), Steve Murray (guitar), James Genenz (bass), Alan Collado (drums).*

Incarnated during 1993 FLESHGRIND's initial line-up roster included vocalist / guitarist Rich Lipscomb, Steve Murray on guitar, bassist Casey Ryba and drummer Dave Barbolla. This unit recorded the 'Holy Pedophile' demo produced by BROKEN HOPE's Brian Griffin. The bands next effort, 1995's 'Sorrow Breeds Hatred (Bleed On Me)' again produced by Griffin, led to a deal with the Pulveriser label for the 'Destined For Defilement' album. The album saw the exit of Ryba in favour of Ray Vasquez. However, it transpired that Pulverizer were unable to manufacture the CD and so FLESHGRIND issued the album on their own imprint.

Both Vasquez and Barbolla broke away from the band as FLESHGRIND inducted drummer Alan Collado of EUPHORIC EVISCERATION and James Genenz of Doom band AVERNUS. Touring ensued with Canadian dates in union with SUFFOCATION and an American nationwide tour with MORTICIAN.

Lipscomb would add guest session vocals to DISFIGURED's debut album 'Prelude To Dementia' appearing on the tracks 'Witness Your Creation' and 'Ridden With Disgust'. In the Spring of 2002 guitarist Steve Murray would unite with the erstwhile BROKEN HOPE duo of guitarist Jeremy Wagner and vocalist Scott Creekmore for a new band unit billed as EARTHBURNER. Also involved would be PUTRID PILE bass player Shaun LaCanne and drummer Jeff Bumgardner.

FLESHGRIND would induct Derek 'Dirty Sanchez' Hoffman, formerly of GORGASM, INCESTOUS and LIVIDITY, as their new drummer in August. The band soon set to work on a new studio opus 'Murder Without End'. Meantime James Genenz found spare time to donate his services as bassist to DEAD OF WINTER. August of 2004 saw Hoffman uniting with former GORGASM members guitarist Tom Tangalos and bassist Russ Powell in a new band called DEPTHS OF AGONY. By December the SCREAMING AFTERBIRTH and FOETOPSY credited Jesse Kehoe had taken command of the FLESHGRIND drum stool.

In June 2005 FLESHGRIND bassist James Genenz joined JUNGLE ROT in the guitar role. Frontman Rich Lispcomb opted out in September and that October FLESHGRIND's story closed as the band announced ""We regretfully wish to inform everyone that FLESHGRIND has officially called it quits".

DESTINED FOR DEFILEMENT, Pulverizer (1998). Whacked / Burning Your World / Chamber Of Obscurity / Sordid Degradation / Rape Culture / Lurid Impurity / Organ Harvest / Frozen In A Voiceless Scream / Litany Of Murder.

FLESHGRIND LIVE, (2001) (Split album with RESURRECTED). Sorrow Breeds Hatred ... Bleed On Me / Litany Of Murder / Ejaculate On Entrails / The Supreme Art Of Derangement / Anger.

THE SEEDS OF ABYSMAL TORMENT, Season Of Mist (2001). Destroying Your Will / Desire For Control / Monarch Of Misery / Disdain The Mournful / The Deviating Ceremonies / Hatred Embodied / Seas Of Harrow / A Legion Of Illusions / The Supreme Art Of Derangement / Hogtied And Hatefucked.

MURDER WITHOUT END, Olympic Recordings OLY 0233-2 (2003). Murder Without End / Sycophantic / Duct-Taped And Raped / Enslaved To My Wrath / Displayed Decay / Perversion Of Innocence / In Sickness Intertwined / Libertine Atonement / Pistolwhipped / Holy Pedophile.

FLESHLESS

DĚČÍN, CZECH REPUBLIC — *Vladimír Prokoš (vocals), Michael (guitar), Ludek (guitar), Vitys (drums).*

Notorious Czech Death Metal act. FLESHLESS, hailing from Décín and featuring former ZVRATOR vocalist Vladimir alongside erstwhile personnel from GARBAGE DISPOSAL, cut the October 1993 demo 'Stench Of Rotting Heads' following up a year later with a second demo 'Grinding'. A 1996 split offering 'Free Off Pain' shared with MASTIC SCUM arrived via Ohne Maulkorb Productions with a further split cassette, in union with DISFIGURED, issued through Obscene Productions. Subsequently the band drafted former GARBAGE DISPOSAL Honza Čížek on bass and DIECHRIST's guitarist Jarda. FLESHLESS contributed their rendition of 'Každý Z Nás' to a 1999 MASTER'S HAMMER tribute album compiled by Redblack Productions.

FLESHLESS performed in the USA during 2000, appearing at both the Milwaukee Metal Fest and November To Dismember events. Touring across North America saw the band partnered with LIVIDITY whilst European dates had the band forming up a package billing of VOMIT REMNANTS, PESSIMIST and LIVIDITY. The 2001 'Nice To Eat You' album closed out with a cover version of ROOT's 'Hrbitov'. None too surprisingly two manufacturing plants turned the album away due to its graphic sleeve art.

In 2006 FLESHLESS engaged in the 'To Kill For Skin' tour, putting in UK dates with Germany's DEFEATED SANITY and British band NECROCEST in February.

GRINDGOD, Obscene Productions OBP 030 (1999). Daemonic Exordium ... / Perverted Intention / Exhumed Brutality / Evil Odium / Grindgod / Doomed Glorification Of Blasphemy / A Piece Of Flesh / Beautiful Enough To Kill / Kazdý Z Nás / Art Of Horrification / Death And Dying / ... Final Desolation / I Will Grind Your Fingers / Dismembered / Eternal Suffer / Positive / Noise I. / Intro / Mental Dreams / Faces At Decomposition / Fleshless / Land Of Emptiness / Sexual Carnage (Remix).

ABHORRENCE OF CADAVERIC, Obscene Productions (2000). Intro / Blood Of Whore / Pain Is Domain / Abhorrence Of Cadaveric / A Damp Smell Of Rotting Ovulation / Kdyz Ti Svítí Zelená / With Blood On The Hands / I'm The Part Of You / Free Of Pain / Tears Of Dying Children.

NICE TO EAT YOU, Obscene Productions OBP 043 (2001). Nice To Eat You / The Body Bag Blues / Culture Meat / Noise Part III / Red Stars Hypocrisy / Where's Mine Resurrection / Defy The Fear / Headscratcher / A Roadkill Recipe / Breathe And Bleed / Hrbitov.

SENSUAL DEATH IMITATION, Obscene Productions (2003). Torture Me / Sensual Death Imitation / Scream Of Decapitated / Incinerated / Parasites / Disconnected / Surrounded By Hell / Survival Extortion / Foetal Purulent.

FLESHMOULD

BELGIUM — *Sven Houfflijn (vocals), Reinier Schenk (vocals / guitar), Dave Vanlokeren (guitar), Bjorn Demeyer (bass), Roel Ghesquiere (drums).*

Self styled "Ultimate technical cyber Death Metal" band, founded in 2000, centred on the veteran figure of guitarist Reinier Schenk of ANESTHESY, MALISHA, BATTALION, YOSH and FUTURE TENSE repute. The opening 'Fleshmould 2K' sessions, recorded at DK-Studio in Destelbergen, saw Schenk joined by bassist Bjorn Demeyer and drummer Steev DC. Guesting would be female singer Petra Gryson with Marco Born adding sequencing parts. The album 'Incompatible Fragments', cut in late 2002 at ShumCot SoundLab in Aartrijke, had Schenk and Demeyer now augmented by guitarist Dirk Derdaele, previously vocalist / guitarist for BEYOND THE GATES, vocalist for CATAFALQUE and pivotal member of UNCHAINED, and drummer Roel Ghesquiere, previously with AT THE FRONT.

FLESHMOULD introduced ex-ANESTHESY, CRYPTICAL REALM and IMPEDIGON singer Sven Houfflijn as frontman in August of 2004. in November another new recruit was inaugurated, ex-DEFORMITY guitarist Dave Vanlokeren in substitution of Dirk Derdaele. This new formation debuted on the 2005 EP 'Apocalyptus Rexx', recorded at Shumcot Soundlab in Aartrijke.

FLESHMOULD cut a new album for Shiver Records, 'The Lazarus Breed', in February 2006.

INCOMPATIBLE FRAGMENTS, Fleshmould (2003). Hunger / Mess-iah / Blind / Salted Wounds / D-prived / Watthu / Senile Decay / Rool / NME / Clone 03.
Apocalyptus Rexx, (2005). Bitter Harvest / Apocalyptus Rexx / AOM / Icarian Fall / Messiah 2005.
THE LAZARUS BREED, Shiver (2006). Argus / God Of Nihil / Apocalyptus Rexx / Structures In Decline / Eternal Shifting Portals / Bitter Harvest / Havoc / (I Am Your) Thorn.

FLESHTIZED

HUNTSVILLE, AL, USA — *Rob Kline (vocals), Sonny Lombardozzi (guitar), Jason Flippo (bass), Gary White (drums).*

Huntsville, Alabama Death Metal act FLESHTIZED was founded during the Spring of 1996, soon displaying their wares with demos including 1998's 'Tower Of Pain'. A self financed June 2001 mini album 'Divide And Conquer', limited to 1000 copies, followed after which second guitarist Adam Parker quit the line-up. During this period FLESHTIZED drummer Gary White took time out to deputize for UPHEAVAL whilst bassist Garth Lovvorn would session with SPINECAST on the live front and appear on their demo 'Nightmare Of Depravity'.

With the first effort soon selling out the Danish Mighty Music label picked the band up for the full length Jacob Hansen produced album 'Here, Among Thorns'. Included, much to reviewers surprise, would not only be a not for note perfect cover version of MORBID ANGEL's 'Rapture' but three guitar solo instrumentals and a bass solo. FLESHTIZED also cut a version of the CANNIBAL CORPSE track 'Hammer Smashed Face', a song the band had been performing live for many years, for a Dwell Records tribute album.

FLESHTIZED bassist Garth Lovvorn also operated the side project LISIYA GORI in union with BLOODSTAINED DUSK frontman Daggeth, guitarist Jim Mullis and SPINECAST drummer Lance Wright. The trio of Lovvorn, Mullis and Wright would subsequently forge Christian Thrash Metal band TEMPLE OF BLOOD. Meantime, Gary White would also be active with CONVERGENCE FROM WITHIN.

Casey Robertson would decamp in mid 2002, later joining two high profile acts in the Death Metal band REGURGITATION and Black Metal group EPOCH OF UNLIGHT. Following a hiatus, FLESHTIZED reformed in February of 2004, announcing their line up as the PESSIMIST, HATRED UNLEASHED and PSYCHOTOGEN credited vocalist Rob Kline, INCANTATION and SEVEN GATES guitarist Sonny Lombardozzi, bassist Garth Lovvorn and drummer Gary White. Lombardozzi was noted for his dexterity in playing both left handed and right handed on a unique double headed guitar.

FLESHTIZED morphed once more in mid 2004 as both Lovvorn and Robertson made their exit. Making up the numbers would be bassist Jason Flippo of BLOODSTAINED DUSK and QUINTA ESSENTIA repute. Lombardozzi subsequently joined CASTRATION.

DIVIDE & CONQUER, (2001). Divide & Conquer / Choice Of Consequence / Self / Delivered Into Suffering / Come Cerberus.
HERE, AMONG THORNS, Mighty Music PMZ019-2 (2001). Ill Divine / Deplorable / Everything Dies / Here Among Thorns / Feral Earth / Bound In Unity / Rise Of The Fallen / Clash Dimension / Rapture.

FOREIGN OBJECTS

USA — *Deron Miller (guitar), James Murphy (guitar), Jess Margera (drums).*

FOREIGN OBJECTS is a technical Death Metal band forged by CKY members guitarist Deron Millar and drummer Jess Margera. In August of 2004 they would be joined by guitarist JAMES MURPHY, a man held in high esteem and having racked up playing credits with TESTAMENT, DEATH, OBITUARY and CANCER.

The October 2004 album 'Universal Culture Shock/Undiscovered Numbers And Colors', through Distant Recordings, was a two-disc compilation hosting the 'Universal Culture Shock' album, which was recorded in 1998 but then shelved, and the 'Undiscovered Numbers And Colors' EP, which was originally released in 1995. Also featured would be live video material captured from a gig at the Henderson Auditorium in 1996, one of the only two shows that FOREIGN OBJECTS had ever played to that point.

UNIVERSAL CULTURE SHOCK / UNDISCOVERED NUMBERS AND COLORS, Distant (2004). Test It Out / They Come In Peace / Chemical Control / Puzzles / Genesis 12a / F.O.#10 / Planetary / Disengage The Simulator / Big Boy / F.O.#8 / Victory / The Undiscovered Numbers & Colors / Far Cry Behind / The Other Side Of The End Of The Universe / Delve / Destination Undefined.

FORENSICK

BILBAO, SPAIN — *Rafa (vocals), Juanma Blanco (guitar), Raúl Arauzo (bass), Igor (drums).*

Bilbao brutal Death Metallers FORENSICK began life in 2001 as a two man operation conducted by guitarist / "grunter" Oscar and drummer Igor. An inaugural demo, entitled 'Sick Rehearsal Promo', was issued before Jorge of NECROLUST was introduced on second guitar. Adding Juanma Blanco on bass they band recorded the EP 'Splattered Innards' for Genital Herpess Records, finally released in February 2004. Upon completion of these sessions Oscar departed, being substituted by BIOPSIA frontman Victor. Next to go was Jorge, FORENSICK reacting by switching Juanma Blanco to guitar before the bass position was filled in December 2002 by LUMINA MORTE, VIRTUAL TIME, NO FEELING and ABRA MACABRA veteran Raúl Arauzo. Also new into the fold would be singer Jonathon.

The group underwent line up changes in the first quarter of 2004, bring in new guitarist Maciej of DISBRAINER, GYROBRAIN, ELBERETH and DORMANTH repute in March and then adding new singer Rafa, a veteran of DECLINE and TYPHARETH, in April. Ex-vocalist Jonathon joined THIRD WORLD'S MOURNING. The former FORENSICK team of guitarists Juanma Blanco and Jorge Araiz along with bassist Raúl Arauzo forged Gothic Metal act IN LOVING MEMORY.

Signing to Necromance Records the band, having lost the services of Maciej Z. in August, entered X Recording Studios in

Mieres, Asturias in October to cut their debut album 'Reign Of Survival Horror' for February 2005 issue.

Sick Promo Rehearsal Tape 2001, Forensick (2001) (Rehearsal demo). Haemorrhagic Wounds / Impaled & Decapitated / The Instinct Of Perturbed Mind / Vomit Of Flesh.

Live At Bilborock (31-05-2003), Forensick (2003) (Demo). Haemorrhagic Wounds / Asymmetric Existence / Wrath.

Splattered Innards, Genital Herpes (2004). Vomit Of Flesh / The Instinct Of A Perturbed Mind / Intro / Haemorrhagic Wound / Intense Bleeding / Impaled And Decapitated / Fetus Molester / Wrath (Live).

REIGN OF SURVIVAL HORROR, Forensick (2005). Survival Horror / Black Plague / Agoraphobia / . . . Whispering / Dominion / Wrath / Asymmetric Existence / Ebony Vernix . . . / Haemorrhagic Wounds 2004 / Cryptosynthesis / Diary / Artificial Light.

FOREST STREAM

RUSSIA — *Sonm The Darkest (vocals), Wizard Omin (guitar), Berserk (guitar), Silent Anth (bass), Elhella (keyboards), Kir (drums).*

FOREST STREAM is a bleak, Gothic Metal band forged in Chernogolovka during 1995 by the former ANESTESIA pairing of guitarist Ungel and drummer Sonm the Darkest. Wizard Omin was incorporated on second guitar soon after. Ungel would depart in 1997 as Silent Anth took over on bass for the debut 1999 demo 'Snowfall'. A second promotion recording, 'Last Season Purity', came in 2000.

The band signed to the Elitist arm of Earache Records for their debut, recording 'Tears Of Mortal Solitude' at the S&O Home Studio, Chernogolovka during June of 2002. FOREST STREAM added drummer Kir in early 2004. FOREST STREAM contributed their version of 'Without God' to the Northern Silence Productions KATATONIA tribute double album 'December Songs' released in December 2006.

TEARS OF MORTAL SOLITUDE, Elitist MOSH904CD (2002). Autumn Elegy / Legend / Last Season Purity / Snowfall / Mel Kor / Whole / Black Swans / The Winter Solstice / The Steps of Mankind.

FORGARÐUR HELVÍTIS

SELFOSS, ICELAND — *Siggi Pönk (vocals), Venni (guitar), Gimsi (guitar / drums), Maddi (bass), Maggi (drums).*

FORGARÐUR HELVÍTIS, based in Selfoss, debuted with the 'Brennið Kirkjur' ('Burning Churches') demo. These tracks would re-surface as part of a split 7" single release in league with DEVIATE of South Africa in 1997. The band's tenth anniversary concert would be captured on the 2001 live album 'Afmæli í Helvíti' included on which would be cover versions of NAPALM DEATH's 'Lucid Fairytale', BRUTAL TRUTH's 'Walking Corpse', TERRORIZER's 'Corporation Pull In', NAILBOMB's 'Walking Away' and even DARKTHRONE's 'Under A Funeral Moon'. FORGARÐUR HELVÍTIS also committed three live tracks to the 'Dordingull.com' benefit concert album in 2002. With drummer Maggi departing guitar player Gimsi took on the drum role for the 'Gerningaveður' record in 2002.

FORGARÐUR HELVÍTIS would be active in a variety of other bands. Vocalist Siggi Pönk fronts Punk band DYS, both guitarist Gimsi and Venni are also employed with Death Metal band MÚSPELL and PORGUNNUR NAKIN. Bass player Maddi is also in the ranks of both PORGUNNUR NAKIN and MUSPELL as well as Black Metal act ARMSVARTNIR.

Forgarður Helvítis EP, View Beyond (1997) (Split single with DEVIATE). Guð Er Stærsta Lygi í Heimi / Bónusfólk / Eðlileg Hegðun Er Hundleiðinleg / Hóra / Heilalínuritið Er á Núlli / Samansaumuð Augu / Dautt Fólk Er Ekki Kúl / Örlag / Brennið Kirkjur / Hey Tussa / Takk / Vonbrigði / Upprisa / Viðurkenning / Þú Ert Ekki Til / Kjöt Með Gati.

HELVÍTI SESSIONS 2000, Independent (2000). Freedom Is Shit / Ljóð Til Þín / Leikur Trúðanna / Legsteinn Grafar Minnar / Krossfest Börn / Vítahringur ömurleikans / Eðlislægur Fasismi / Vængbrotnir Englar / Gelding óskhyggjunnar / Þar Sem Hamingjan Ræður Ríkjum / Guð Er Stærsta Lygi I Heimi / Bónusfólk / Eðlileg Hegðun Er Hundleiðinleg / Hóra / Heilalínuritið Er á Núlli / Samansaumuð Augu / Dautt Fólk Er Ekki Kúl / Örlag / Brennið Kirkjur / Hey Tussa / Takk / Vonbrigði / Upprisa / Viðurkenning / Þú Ert Ekki Til / Kjöt Með Gati / Aumt Stolt / Messírass / Mannleg Grimmd.

AFMAELI I HELVITI, (2001). Kjöt Með Gati / Vítahringur ömurleikans / Wasting Away / Lucid Fairytale / Corporation Pull In / Walking Corpse / Under A Funeral Moon.

GERNINGAVEOUR, Independent (2002). Án þess Að Depla Auga / Baráttusöngur / Legsteinn Grafar Minnar / Ferðasýn / Í Forgarðinum / Fjandafæla / Krossfest Börn / Gerningaveður / Gelding óskhyggjunnar / Vítahringur ömurleikans / Ljósbrjótur / Guð Er Stærsta Lygi í Heimi / Vængbrotnir Englar / Tormentor / Þar Sem Hamingjan Ræður Ríkjum / Skuggahiminn / Eðlislægur Fasismi / Heljarslóð.

FORGOTTEN SUNRISE

TALLINN, ESTONIA — *Anders Meltz (vocals), Margus Gustavson (guitar), Jan Talts (bass), Tarvo Valkm (drums).*

A band from Tallinn formed in 1992. After the debut demo, 'Behind The Abysmal Sky', appeared FORGOTTEN SUNRISE signed to the Finnish label Rising Realm. The band's debut CD, the 1994 'Forever Sleeping Greystones' EP, highlighted their melodic Death Metal laced with plentiful Doom influences to good effect; the group utilizing violin, flute, keyboards and female backing vocals in the mix. Line-up changes saw the exit of guitarist Margus "Kusti" Gustavson, keyboard player Margus "George" Aro and drummer Tarvo Valm in 1995. The latter went on to work with HUMAN GROUND. Introduced on guitar in 1997 would be Keijo Koppel.

A self titled EP followed in 1998, then the 'a.Nimal f.Lesh—Looma Liha' EP of 2001 and 'Ple:se Disco-Nnect Me' EP, the latter featuring no less than thirteen variants on the same song.

FORGOTTEN SUNRISE returned with 'Ru:mipu:dus' in 2004 through My Kingdom Music.

Behind The Abysmal Sky, (1993). Intro: Sunrise / Rottening Art / Alive In The Grave / Indifference / Son Of Sun / Knock-Outro: Solstice.

Forever Sleeping Greystones, Rising Realm REALM 003 (1994). Unknown Land Of Silence / Ode To The Depressive Timedance / Enjoyment Of Sunrise / In Your Eyes.

Forgotten Sunrise EP, (1998). Waves & Flames / Hero-In-Gre:npiece / Into Flesh I Was Born / Sombrefog / Midwinter Dreamlights / Sombrefog (El Diablo Plastic Wrapper remix) / Hero-In-Gre:npiece The Alchemist Soft Switch remix) / Into Flesh I Was Born (El Diablo Come Upon remix).

a.Nimal f.Lesh—Looma Liha EP, (2001). K-Os Tik-Tak / Vhatsoewer / Surroundcosmos / My First Day Was My Birthday / Christ Your Name / Surroundcosmos (Clean version) / K-os Tik-Tak (Karmo Koppel End Of The Reverse Side remix) / Christ Your Name (Karmo Koppel Drastic remix).

Ple:se Disco-Nnect Me EP, (2003). Ple:se Disco-Nnect Me (Clean version) / Ple:se Disco-Nnect Me (Device remix) / Ple:se Disco-Nnect Me (Unidentified Off_Line remix) / Ple:se Disco-Nnect Me (Bongirl Death By Pop-Gun remix) / Ple:se Disco-Nnect Me (Jubei Clean Sucks remix) / Ple:se Disco-Nnect Me (Cyclone-B Vocals Up remix) / Ple:se Disco-Nnect Me (Device Easy Feeling remix) / Ple:se Disco-Nnect Me (Mess Twice Second Face remix) / Ple:se Disco-Nnect Me (Galaktlan remix) / Ple:se Disco-Nnect Me (GGFH Diskonekt "Long Time Dead" remix) / Ple:se Disco-Nnect Me (Jubei Dirty Socks remix) / Ple:se Disco-Nnect Me (DJ Brain Disconnected remix) / Ple:se Disco-Nnect Me (Original version).

RU:MIPU:DUS, My Kingdom Music (2004). Outumnyo:nic / Never(k)now / The Doubletalker & The Sle:perspe:ker / Vhatsoewer / (Life) 24H / Surroundcosmos / Into Flesh I Was Born / Thou-Sand-Men / Ple:se Disco-nnect Me / Over The Deathbringer Stars / The Doubletalker & The Sle:perspe:ker (GGFH Rage Filled remix) / Never(k)now (Video).

FORNICATION

BRAZIL — *Elcio (vocals), Gerson (guitar), Adriano (guitar), Hernan (bass), Flavio (drums).*

Black / Death act created in 1993. FORNICATION has released two demos, 'Eternal Sufferance' in 1996 and 'Elegy To

Forgotten Soul' during 1998. FORNICATION, enlisting INFERNAL's Mauricio Amorim on drums, spent 2003 working on a new album titled 'Descendants Of The Degenerated Race'. Subsequently Johnny of HECATOMB and FLESH GRINDER repute took the drum position.

Guitarist Gerson is also a member of Grindcore act HORRIFIC DISTURBANCE. The band contributed their rendition of DEATH's 'Regurgitated Guts' to the 'Together As One' 2003 tribute album assembled by the Spanish Mondongo Canibale label. The band united with Dutch act SUPPOSITORY and Polish acts INFATUATION OF DEATH and SCABIES for the 'Grind Tour de Pologne' November 2004 tour of Poland.

DESCENDENTS OF THE DEGENERATED RACE, Black Hole Productions BHP 007 (2003). Omnipotent Ones / Malignant Devotion / Triumph Of Evil / Dreadful Feelings Of Sufferance / Black Souls Disguised By The Light / Degenerated Race / Malicious Benevolence / Regurgitated Guts / Mistress Of Darkness / Under Spell Of Full Moon.

FRACTAL POINT

SWITZERLAND — *Antoine Nessi (vocals), Guilherme Vorpe (guitar), Carlo Di Biase (drums).*

FRACTAL POINT is a Geneva based Death Metal unit originating in 1999. An opening 2001 demo would be capitalised on by the 2002 'Analysis Of Dimensions' EP with a further demo, 'At The Beginning', arriving in 2003. The opening demo saw a band line up comprising vocalists André Joye of RECTAL HUMILIATION and STUMP FUCKING's Thomas Jeanmonnod, guitarists Guilherme Vorpe and RECTAL HUMILIATION's Olivier Joye, bass player Carlo Di Biase with AD NAUSEUM, STURMGESCHÜTZ and STUMP FUCKING's Julien Riesen on the drums. This line up, bar the omission of Jeanmonnod, featured on 'Analysis Of Dimensions'. Laurent Wenghart took over on second guitar for the 'At The Beginning' sessions.

Drummer Julien Riesen joined COMPLEX VENDETTA in September of 2002.

FRACTAL POINT issued the 2004 album 'The Bizarre Machinery Of Universe' through Deadsun Records.

Fractal Point, (2001). Metric Dimension (Cosmic Stairs) / Retained? / Dimension III (Focused Perceptions) / Dimension II (Arranged Memories) / Spacetime / Disturbed Visons / Material Substance / Saturnian.
Analysis Of Dimensions EP, Independent (2002). Retained? / Dimension II / Dimension III / Disturbed Visions / Metric Dimension.
At The Beginning, (2003). Intro / At The Beginning / Material Substance / Dark Matter / Saturnian.
THE BIZARRE MACHINERY OF UNIVERSE, Deadsun (2004). 10-2[s] / At The Beginning / Saturnian / Chaos Unification / Cosmic Fields / Parallel Worlds / Material Substance / The Dimensional Experiment / Dark Matter / Celestial Corpse.

FRAGILE HOLLOW

HELSINKI, FINLAND — *Aleksi Ahokas (vocals / guitar / bass), Sami Koikkalainen (guitar), Harri Petjakko (guitar), Teo (bass), Tea Dickman (keyboards) Oli Wall (drums).*

Helsinki based atmospheric Doom Death founded in 1997 by vocalist / guitarist Aleksi Ahokas and guitarist Sami Koikkalainen under an early billing of PROPHET. Ahokas also held credits with EXCELSIOR, RAIN PAINT, SNOWGARDEN, ROTTEN TORTURE, COLD SWEAT, DIABLERIE, EXCELSIOR and RAPTURE. The group emerged brandishing a 1997 demo tape 'The Sky Takes You Away' followed by a three track session 'Gone' in 1998. A single 'Miles Away' was delivered in 1999 upfront of a further promotion effort 'Death Becomes You' in 2000. A second single, the four track 'Broken Promise', paved the way for a fourth demo entitled 'Dirty' in 2001.

The February 2002 album 'Fragile Prologue' would, besides PROPHET band members guitarist Sami Koikkalainen and drummer Pete Raatikainen, also include a number of notable guests. Henri Urponpoika Sorvali a.k.a. 'Trollhorn' of FINNTROLL and MOONSORROW would donate keyboards, DENIGRATE guitarist Seppo Nummela added an 'eighties style' guitar solo whilst DIABLERIE and TRIONES frontman Henri Villberg weighed in with 'growl' vocals. The band would later adopt the new title of FRAGILE HOLLOW so as to avoid confusion with the global plethora of acts all laying claim to the title PROPHET.

FRAGILE HOLLOW's 2003 'Effete Mind' album, released on the Italian label Avantgarde Music, surprisingly included a cover version of DURAN DURAN's 'Come Undone'. Both Teo and Markus exited after completion. FRAGILE HOLLOW put in 2004 concerts in St. Petersburg and Moscow to promote 'Effete Mind'.

The band contributed their rendition of 'Saw You Drown' to the KATATONIA tribute album 'December Songs' in 2005.

EFFETE MIND, Avantgarde AV 071 (2003). I Am Not You / FragileHollow / Disgusting / Come Undone / I Don't Believe In Love / Have You Seen A Girl? / Dirty / Confusion / Are We Through? / Leaving You / I Am Sorry.

FRAGMENTATION

CA, USA — *Aluukard (vocals), Urthon (bass), Fej (guitar / drums).*

FRAGMENTATION was the early act from Kyle Powell of ENGORGE repute, being an extreme Metal act founded whilst Powell was serving in the USAF at March air force base in California. FRAGMENTATION, a trio founded during 1991 of Aluukard on vocals, Urthon on bass and Fej on both guitar and drums, released a 1993 EP 'Prelude To Evil' and a 1994 full length album 'Black Death' through Powell's own Eviscerated label.

Powell relocated to New Jersey to forge the original ENGORGE band unit, created during 1996 comprising of Powell, Craig Pillard of INCANTATION, DISCIPLES OF MOCKERY and WOMB on guitar, second guitarist Mike Boyce of DISCIPLES OF MOCKERY and FAUST, bassist Ronnie Deo, again of INCANTATION, DISCIPLES OF MOCKERY and WOMB and ex FAUST drummer Bill Vessey. Previous to this Powell had acted as a stand in drummer for Death Metal act MORTICIAN.

ENGORGE announced their arrival in low key fashion with the demo session 'The Winter Of Pathological Hate', restricted to a mere 20 copies. A string of demo and album releases would follow.

Prelude To Evil EP, Eviscerated (1993). Ascension Of Darkness / Pentagram.
BLACK DEATH, Eviscerated (1994). Ascension Of Darkness / Pentagram / Black Satin Blood / Lilith / Slayer Of The Unborn / Bloody Anal Intrusion / Maggots / Mistress Winter.

FRAGMENTS OF UNBECOMING

GERMANY — *Stefan Weimar (vocals / guitar), Sascha Ehrich (guitar), Wolfram Schellenberg (bass), Ingo Maier (drums).*

FRAGMENTS OF UNBECOMING is a Scandinavian style Death Metal elite grouping from some of Germany's most extreme acts. The band comprised the ex-VENERAL DISEASE pairing of vocalist / guitarist Stefan Weimar and drummer Ingo Maier, former MORTIFIED guitarist Sascha Ehrich and erstwhile DISEMBOWLED bass player Wolfram Schellenberg. The latter, as 'Ewool', contributed bass to TOMBTHROAT's EP 'Evil Fuckin' Zombie Riot' in January 2000.

FRAGMENTS OF UNBECOMING signed to the Metal Blade label for the January 2004 'Skywards—A Sylphe's Ascension' album. The band introduced singer Sam Anetzberger, also active with LEGACY, in November. However, Anetzberger dropped out in January of 2005 to prioritise LEGACY once again. FRAGMENTS OF UNBECOMING projected a new album release, 'Sterling Black Icon', for the Summer.

SKYWARDS—A SYLPH'S ASCENSION, Metal Blade (2004). Up From The Blackest Of Soil / The Seventh Sunray Enlights My Pathway / Shapes Of The Pursuers / Skywards–A Sylphe's Ascension / Mesmerized / Entangled Whispers In The Depth / Evensong / Scattered To The Four Winds / On A Scar's Edge Infinity / Loud Pulse / Fear My Hatred / Life's Last Embers.
STERLING BLACK ICON, Metal Blade (2006). Carmine Preface / Sterling Black Icon / Weave Their Barren Path / Dear Floating Water / Breathe In The Black To See / Ride For A Fall / A Faint Illumination / Live For The Moment, Stay 'Til The End / Scythe Of Scarecrow / Onward To The Finger Of God / Stand The Tempest / Chambre Noire.

FROM BEYOND

PROSTĚJOV, CZECH REPUBLIC — *P.D.Z. (vocals / bass), S.O. (guitar), L.H. (guitar), T.J. (drums).*

FROM BEYOND is a Prostějov Death Metal act, founded in 1992 and fronted by Petr Zapletal. Demos included 1996's 'Born' and an eponymous 1998 cassette. The group also included tracks 'The Tempter' and 'Cydonia' on the compilation album 'U Nás Doma' on Organika S.R.O. The 'Endtime' demo saw release in 2000 and the following year a further brace of tracks, 'Undercover' and 'Entrancing Flame' featured on the compilation 'MetalWorld Compilation I'.

'Where Hell Begins', featuring a version of 'Assassin' originally by Chicago Doomsters TROUBLE, arrived in 2003. Guitarist Z.V. was replaced by L.H. in October 2004. FROM BEYOND issued the 'Endtime' album through Sonic Temple Records in 2005.

From Beyond, (1998). Assassin / Max And Marlin / On Surface / Cropcircles / Devil's Preachers / M. I. B. / The Tempter / Independence Day / Cydonia.
Endtime, From Beyond Demo (2000). Area 51 / Entrancing Flame / Memento Mori (Endtime) / Black Sky / Undercover / Stigmaticon / Revelations (Life Or Death) / Conspiracy Of Shadows.
WHERE HELL BEGINS, (2003). Marche Funebre (Intro) / Where Hell Begins / Earth Fiasco / Nibiru / Inhuman Eyes / Pain Within / Assassin / I. D. Theory / Progeria Of The Mankind.
ENDTIME, Sonic Temple STR 002 (2005). Area 51 / Entrancing Flame / Memento Mori (Endtime) / Black Sky / Undercover / Stigmaticon / Conspiracy Of Shadows / Assassin / Max And Marlin / On Surface / Cropcircles / Devil's Preachers / M. I. B. / Independence Day.

FROM THE DEPTHS

CLEVELAND, OH, USA — *Rob Molzan (vocals), Brian Bertram (guitar), Matt Sorg (guitar), Duane Morris (bass), Rob Newlin (drums).*

Cleveland Euro styled Death Metal band manifested by players from the acclaimed DECREPIT, guitarist Duane Morris and Matt Sorg. Morris also had a tradition with MUTILATION, EMBALMER, Black Metal act FUNERAL PYRE and as touring member for INCANTATION. Drummer Rob Newlin was previously a member of Sarasota, Florida Death Metal band BURIAL. The band would also initially employ keyboard player Brian Boston. Line up changes saw the defection of singer Rob Molzan, necessitating Duane Morris adding lead vocals to his role, and the recruitment of SOULLESS and NUNSLAUGHTER bassist Wayne Richards.

FROM THE DEPTHS issued a demo entitled 'Bereavement', pressed up into an EP release, after the release of their 1996 debut album. The follow up record, 1998's 'Elysium', closed out with cover versions of SLAYER's 'Epidemic' and IRON MAIDEN's 'Iron Maiden' theme.

Duane Morris would also be an active member of SANCTORUM, first as bass player then as vocalist / guitarist, during the lifespan of FROM THE DEPTHS. He would subsequently enroll in the infamous NUNSLAUGHTER.

As FROM THE DEPTHS dissolved the core membership forged DEAD OF NIGHT, this band consisting of Duane Morris, Matt Sorg and Wayne Richards alongside the TERROR, BLOOD OF CHRIST and MUTILATION credited Randy Scott on bass with DECREPIT and INCANTATION drummer Chris Dora.

FROM THE DEPTHS, Dismal (1996). Intro: Into Mystery And Beyond / The Magic Of The October Moons / The War Of The Captive Spirits / Fuck That Witch / Curse Of The Scarecrow / Bring Forth The Detractor / Apparitions Of Myself / Dawn Of The Crimson Harvest / And They Shall Rise Again / It Lurks / Autumn Colored Day / The Wraths Of The Other Realms / From The Depths / Outro: The Echoes Of Distant Dreams.
Bereavement EP, Dismal (1997). Bereavement / Absentina / Anagoge / Last Dawn.
ELYSIUM, Nightfall (1998). Separation / Sunshine / Regret / Elysium / Dark Angel / Thy Bright Night / Forever / Epidemic / Iron Maiden.

FUCK THE FACTS

QC, CANADA — *Mel Mongeon (vocals), Topon Das (guitar), Mathieu Vilandré (guitar), Steve Chartier (bass), Tim Olsen (drums).*

Notorious Quebec Grindcore act. The band contributed their rendition of DEATH's 'Empty Words' to a 2003 tribute album assembled by the Spanish Mondongo Canibale label. That same year saw the inclusion of their rendition of 'Devastator' to a GODFLESH tribute album published by French label Nihilistic Holocaust.

FUCK THE FACTS recorded tracks for a split CD in union with French act SERGENT SLAUGHTER in mid 2004. Ex-FUCK THE FACTS drummer Matt Connell joined the ranks of veteran US Death Metal combo EXHUMED in November.

FUCK THE FACTS parted ways with guitarist Dave Menard and bassist Marc-Andre Mongeon in May of 2005. Drafted as stand ins for live work in July, supported by BRIEF RESPITE and THE MASS, would be the BAD TRIPPE and INSURRECTION credited Mathieu Vilandré on guitar and Steve Chartier of ORGANIZED CHAOS on bass.

FUCK THE FACTS signed to Relapse Records in April 2006 to lay down a new album, 'Stigmata High-Five', at Studio En-Phase in Montreal. The band partnered with Belgian Deathsters LENG TCH'E plus GORGASM and BENEATH THE MASSACRE for a Canadian tour commencing 1st May Ottawa, Ontario.

Bastardising Canada Summer 2002 Tour EP, (2002). N.S.S.T.S. / The Burning Side / Terror Bomb / Smokin' A Fatty (live).
STIGMATA HIGH FIVE, Relapse (2006).

FUELBLOODED

DEN BOSCH, HOLLAND — *Vital Welten (vocals), Danny Tunker (guitar), Michiel Rutten (guitar), Michel Steenbekkers (bass), Norbert Moen (drums).*

A Den Bosch Melodic Death / Thrash Metal act previously known as SACRAMENTAL SACHEM. This former act dated back to 1989 and had issued the albums 'Recrucifixtion' in 1995 and 'Anxiety' in 2001. Formative drummer Luciano Marras also held ties to SCAVENGER.

FUELBLOODED released a four track demo in 2002, promoting this with supports to DARKANE. The band re-debuted with the 2004 Stephen van Haestregt produced album 'Inflict The Inevitable'. FUELBLOODED added ex-FORM guitarist Danny Tunker, replacing Michiel Stekelenburg, in February 2005.

FUELBLOODED signed to British label Copro Records in early 2006 for the album 'Inflict The Inevitable'. Uniting with fellow Dutch Deathsters DETONATION, the band put in UK tour dates in early May. FUELBLOODED parted ways with singer Vital Welten in September.

Promo 2002, Fuelblooded (2002). Poisonous / Dissector Of Souls / Constructive Destruction / The Silence.

FUNEBRARUM

NJ, USA — *Daryl Kahan (vocals), Nick Orlando (guitar), Dan Dornbierer (guitar), Dave Wagner (bass), Brian Jiminez (drums).*

Death Metal act FUNEBRARUM, created during 1999, out of New Jersey boast some pedigree players. Fronted by vocalist Daryl Kahan is an erstwhile member of ASSUCK, Hardcore act CITIZEN'S ARREST, drummer for BORN AGAINST as well as pivotal member (as 'Morgul') of premier Black Metal act ABAZAGORATH. Guitarist Nick Orlando is known for his work with Doomsters EVOKEN and NYARLATHOTEP. This pairing convened FUNEBRARUM during August of 1999 in an attempt to nostalgically resurrect some retro-Scandinavian style Death Metal. The band, debuting with the 'Triumphant Ascent' demo cassette, would be rounded out by second guitarist Dan Dornbierer, ABAZAGORATH bassist Dave Wagner and drummer Brian Jiminez. The 'Tombs Of The Sleeping Darkness' demo session arrived in 2000. In keeping with their Scandinavian influences former ABHORRENCE singer Jukka Kolehmainen contributed lyrics to the track 'Adoration Of Abscessed Cadavers'. During 2001 Daryl Kahan would also be located fronting Spanish band VOICE OF HATE.

FUNEBRARUM recorded a split album in alliance with Swedish Death Metal act INTERMENT for release by Conqueror Of Thorns Records in December 2006. Further new product, in the form of the full-length album 'Perish Beneath', was issued in January 2007 by Necroharmonic Productions.

TOMBS OF SLEEPING DARKNESS, (2001).

FUNERAL AGE

FALL CITY, WA, USA — *Kevin Bedra (vocals / guitar), Chris Mannino (guitar), Rob Steinway (bass), Mike Sillifrant (drums).*

FUNERAL AGE is a direct descendent of SUICIDE CULTURE. The 2003 EP sessions 'Fistful of Christ', issued through Thousand Funerals Music, were originally intended to be a SUICIDE CULTURE release but band members felt the switch in musical direction was great enough to warrant a change of name. Guesting as vocalist would be former SUICIDE CULTURE man Paul English, also of VS. THE WORLD and ALCHEMY.

Line up changes saw SEVERED SAVIOR bassist Tom Stoltz giving way to Greg Hartung. The bass position changed again in 2004 as Rob Steinway of SHADED ENMITY and EVANGELIST was enrolled. Guitarist Chris Mannino also holds SHADED ENMITY and EVANGELIST affiliations.

Fistful Of Christ, Thousand Funerals Music (2003). … Bloodshed Begin / Fistful Of Christ / Promised Land Of Lies / Upon The Grave Of Angel's Wing / Halo Of Suffering / Requiem Of The Condemned / The Funeral Ages.

FUNERAL INCEPTION

INDONESIA — *Doni (vocals), Rio (guitar), Mithos (bass), Pandi SDS (drums).*

Technical, US styled Death Metal. The erstwhile BLOODY GORE duo of guitarist Rio and bassist Mithos stuck together following their former act's demise in early 2002 to rapidly found a further Death Metal venture FUNERAL INCEPTION in alliance with vocalist Doni, a prior member of DELIRIUM TREMENS, ORDOTH and KERANGKENK, and drummer Pandi, an erstwhile recruit of DISGUSTING GOD and VILE. Pandi also is active in both CRYPTICAL DEATH and SADISTIS. FUNERAL INCEPTION recorded a debut album 'Anthems Of Disenchantment' in May 2002 at Palu Studios in Jakarta for the French Warpath label. The Rottrevore label would manufacture cassette variants for Indonesia. Bassist Mithos exited in March of 2003, being superseded by Praza. A new FUNERAL INCEPTION album, 'Countdown To Apocalypse', was prepared for 2003.

ANTHEMS OF DISENCHANTMENT, Warpath (2002). … Of Banished And Depraved Existence / Man Destined To Fail / Bathing Your Soul With Gore Tears / Violence Speaks Louder Than Words / Unrecognizable Mutilations / Sons Of The Unclean / Holy Halls Of Paranoia / I Am My Own Enemy / Planting The Seeds Of Hate / Slices Of Flesh Are Being Devoured.

FUNERAL MASK

FL, USA — *Jason Hildebrand (vocals / guitar), Ron Wojcik (guitar), Brian Divver (bass), Duane Large (drums).*

Florida Death Metal band FUNERAL MASK, formulated in 1999, issued their debut, self titled demo in March 2000 with second session 'Catapulting Corpses' delivered in December of 2001. Guest vocalist for the song 'Pictures Of Dismemberment' would be CORPUS ROTTUS and CEMETERY EARTH singer Brian 'Bundy' Swafford.

Frontman Jason Hildebrand's prior acts include HAZARAX, CEMETERY EARTH, NECROTION and VIATICUM with second guitarist Ron Wojcik and drummer Duane Large are also ex-CEMETERY EARTH members, the latter also holding credits with LIFE and INCITE. Bassist Brian Divver holds a prior tradition with OBLIVIAX, RITUAL LAW and LIFE.

Catapulting Corpses, (2001). Cemetery Life / Pictures Of Dismemberment / Catapulting Corpses.
Funeral Mask, Funeral Mask (2002). Not Dead Enough / Funeral Mask / Deathcry / Giza.

FUNERAL ORATION

TARANTO, ITALY — *The Old Nick (vocals), Luca (guitar / keyboards), Malfeitor Fabban (bass), Rodolfo Russo (drums).*

A Taranto Death Metal band formed in 1989, FUNERAL ORATION, not to be confused with the Dutch Hardcore band of the same title, has only one surviving member from the original line-up, guitarist Luca being that man. Bassist Malfeitor Fabban is well known on the Italian scene as mentor behind the notorious Black Metal band ABOYRM and lead vocalist for Ambient Doom project VOID OF SILENCE.

Having released two demos 'Domine A Morte' and 'XXX A.S. 1995 E.V.' and a 7" EP FUNERAL ORATION toured Italy extensively before line-up changes forced the group to adopt a slightly bizarre Black Metal direction in 1993.

Having issued a new, two track demo and the 'Christic Depravations' live video Avantgarde Records stepped in to offer the Italian outfit a deal, with debut album 'Sursum Luna' arriving in 1996. FUNERAL ORATION drummer Rodolfo Russo joined AVANGUARD in 2003. He also involved himself with SOVRAN and THANATOID.

SURSUM LUNA, Avantgarde AV 017 (1996). Beltane's Night / Pregnant Whore / Intermezzo I / Me A Morte Libera Domine / Intermezzo II / The Age Of Apotheosis / Intermezzo III / Sursum Luna (Lunesta Trilogia) / Intermezzo IV / Stigmata / Intermezzo V / Pagan Joy / Finale.

FUNERATUS

MOCOCA, SP, BRAZIL — *Fernando (vocals / bass), Andres (guitar), Gustavo (drums).*

Death Metal trio FUNERATUS, hailing from Mococa, came together in 1993 citing a line up of vocalist / bassist Fernando, guitarist Andres and drummer Flavio. During August of 1995 Flavio made his exit and FUNERATUS welcomed onboard Rodrigo as their new drummer. This line up cut the 1996 demo session 'The First Baptism'.

In 1999 FUNERATUS featured tracks on a split album 'Upcoming Old Apparition' with DESCEREBRATION issued by the Millenium label. After these recordings Rodrigo left. For live work the band took on the temporary services of Ronaldo from ANCESTRAL MALEDICTION. A new record deal was struck with the Mutilation label for the 2001 album 'Storm Of Vengeance'.

Both Ronaldo and Bruno of HORNED GOD were utilised as session drummers for this work. FUNERATUS inducted Gustavo as a permanent drummer shortly after.

Upcoming Apparition EP, Mutilation (2000) (Split EP with DESCEREBRATION). Crawling In The Darkness (Intro) / Upcoming Apparition / Saint Of Killers / Feast Of The Undead / Universatan.

STORM OF VENGEANCE, Mutilation (2001). Storm Of Vengeance / Soaked Blood Sword / The Death Is Laughing / Behind The Crucifix / The Eyes Of Destruction / Winged Evil / Universatan / Miserable Mortals / The Cortège (Intro).

FUNERUS

JOHNSTOWN, PA, USA — *Brad Heiple (vocals / guitar), John McEntee (guitar), Jill McEntee (bass), Kyle Severn (drums).*

The origins of FUNERUS lay in the 1990 Pennsylvania band CREATIVE SICKNESS, manifested by vocalist / guitarist Brad Heiple and drummer Jason Foust. Originally steeped in American Thrash and Death Metal the unit apparently took on a new lease of life once having heard an album by Sweden's ENTOMBED. So drastic was the subsequent switch in musical style that the revised band title of FUNERUS was taken onboard. Minus a bass player, FUNERUS nonetheless managed to record a brace of demos. Finally Jill Daily was recruited, bringing with her a unique brand of "sewage slinging tractor-bass".

During 1994 the band gigged with ROTTREVORE, DECREPIT and BLOOD COVEN amongst others but would then be struck a blow with the departure of Heiple. An enforced hiatus ensued, during which time Jill Daily married John McEntee of INCANTATION repute. Yearning to get FUNERUS back together Jill, now Jill McEntee, assembled a one off line up for a gig on 21st November 1998 at the Boratkos Tavern in Johnstown, Pennsylvania. Her band mates for this event comprised vocalist Jim D., guitarist Belial Koblak and drummer Chris Allen.

A FUNERUS gig scheduled to open for INCANTATION in 2002 attracted the attention of Heiple, who was enticed back into the fold. Subsequently John McEntee and drummer Kyle Severn made up the numbers.

FUNERUS united with DISGORGE for US touring in October of 2003. The band's next road alliance, suitably dubbed 'European Decimation', took in April 2005 gigs throughout Italy, Portugal, the UK, Holland and Germany in partnership with CATASTROPHIC, INCANTATION, JUNGLE ROT and HEXENHAMMER.

FESTERING EARTH, Ibex Moon (2003). In The Trees / D.N.R. / Stagnant Seas / Suffering Life / Nebulous Existence / Polluted Excess / Shade / Web Of Deceit / Festering Earth.

FURBOWL

VÄXJÖ, SWEDEN — *Johan Axelsson (vocals / guitar), Nicke Stenemo (guitar / keyboards), Max Thornell (drums).*

A Växjö based Death Goth Metal band formed in 1991 as DEVOURMENT by ex-CARNAGE man Johan Axelsson and former JESUS EXERCISE and DEVOURMENT drummer Max Thornell, FURBOWL's first demo, 'The Nightfall Of Your Heart' featured the ever busy ex-CARCASS guitarist Mike Amott making a guest appearance. Bassist Johan 'Liiva' Axelsson would join Mike Amott in his highly successful late 90's act ARCH ENEMY.

After the release of debut album 'Those Shredded Dreams', Axelsson left to be superseded by Per Jungberger. Nicklas Stenemo of MUDDLE was drafted on guitar in 1993. After 'The Autumn Years' album emerged in 1994 the band adopted the new name WONDERFLOW. With Liiva decamping from ARCH ENEMY following three high profile albums as lead vocalist he would pick up the bass guitar once again to found a fresh project with erstwhile FURBOWL colleagues guitarist Mattias Ljung and drummer Max Thornell billed as HEARSE.

THOSE SHREDDED DREAMS, Step One SOR004 (1992). Damage Done / Nothing Forever / Razorblades / Desertion / Sharkheaven / Those Shredded Dreams.

THE AUTUMN YEARS, Black Mark BMCD47 (1994). Bury The Hatchet / Cold World / Dead And Gone / The Needle / Is This Dignity / Weakend / Baby Burn / Stabbed / Road Less Travelled / Still Breathing.

FURIA

FRANCE — *Nicolas Perchaud (vocals), Michaël Vallesi (guitar), Sébastien Lobut (guitar), Guillaume Mauceli (bass), Isabelle Vailler (keyboards), Médéric Moge (drums).*

FURIA, a Death edged Heavy Metal band, came together in June of 1997. The group debuted with a 1998 cassette demo 'Darkside Of Apocalypse'. A further demo followed in 1999, after which drummer Sebastien Gilot departed, with a third set, 'Le Jardin D'Eden' arriving in 2000. Upon completion of the album 'On Search Of The Past', released by Adipocere Records in September of 2001, singer Nicolas Perchaud exited. FURIA lost the services of guitarist Sébastien Lobut in May 2005, shortly before release of the 'Re-birth' EP. In October the band announced signature to Season Of Mist Records for a third album entitled 'Kheros'.

Keyboard player Mehdi Khadouj left in June 2006 to prioritise his other band BEYON-D-LUSION.

A LA QUETE DU PASSE, Adipocere CDAR53 (2001). Chapitre I : Prologue / Chapitre II : A La Quête Du Passé / Chapitre III : Gorthoth, Le Passeur Du Fleuve De L'oubli / Chapitre IV : Le Temple Des Putains Démoniaques / Intermède / Chapitre V : Le Jardin D'Eden / Chapitre VI : Incantation à Cébil / Chapitre VII : Le Sacrifice De La Vierge / Chapitre VIII : Le Baptême Du Diable / Chapitre IX : Et La Lumière Fut ... / Chapitre X : L'antre Des Morts / Chapitre XI : Une Quête Sans Lendemain / Chapitre XII : Les Larmes Du Destin.

UN LAC DE LARMES ET DE SANG, Adipocere CDAR71 (2003). Fereme Les Yeur ... / Un Lac De Larmes Et De Sang / Elmira, L'image D'un Destin / Les Revelations D'un Temps Passe / Auto-Psy D'un Damne / Mecanique De L'infamie / Le Judgement D'une Conscience / Les Deux Mondes ... / Mental En Perdition / Memoires D'outre-Tombe / Gailen ... / L'oratoire De La Folie / La Mort De L'ame.

Re-birth, Adipocere (2005).

KHEROS, Season Of Mist (2006).

FURIOUS TRAUMA

COPENHAGEN, DENMARK — *Lars Schmidt (vocals / guitar), Henrik B. Jacobsen (guitar), Claus Weiergang (bass), Allan Tschicaja (drums).*

A Copenhagen based Thrash-Death Metal band formed during the late eighties with first product being the 1988 demo 'Tempora Mutantur' (notably dedicated to Cliff Burton). FURIOUS TRAUMA's line-up at this juncture comprised singer Klaus Hansen, guitarists Lars Schmidt and Morten Gilsted, bassist W. and drummer Henrik Quaade. This was followed by the 'Profit Counts' session by which stage the band had shifted shape to see Schmidt joined by an all new cast of guitarist Samir Belmaati, bassist Kaare Strøm Hansen and Brian Andersen on the drums.

After the release of their debut album, 'Primal Touch' in 1993, the band hit the road and can count support slots to MOTÖRHEAD and KREATOR amongst their biggest gigs. FURIOUS TRAUMA also appeared at the July 1993 Roskilde Festival, opening for ANTHRAX, SUICIDAL TENDENCIES, MIDNIGHT OIL and PORNO FOR PYROS. However, line-up changes occurred in 1994 with frontman Lars Schmidt joining KONKHRA and also losing their drummer; Morten Nielsen of BLACK ROSE, FORCE MAJEURE, CRIME ACADEMY and MERCYFUL FATE replacing the latter. The 'Eclipse' album emerged in 1995 through Euphonious Records.

1996's 'Strange Ways' EP contained cover versions of ARTILLERY's 'The Challenge' and KISS' 'Strange Ways' plus a CD-ROM portion containing video clips for 'Chaos Within' and 'My

Dying Time' plus a band interview. Signing to French label Season Of Mist FURIOUS TRAUMA issued 'Roll The Dice' in 1999. Ex-FURIOUS TRAUMA drummer Brian Anderson joined DOMINUS in 2000.

FURIOUS TRAUMA's 2004 band line-up comprised Lars Schmidt, the HATESPHERE and KOLDBORN credited Henrik B. Jacobsen on guitar, GUTRIX and ZOSER MEZ bassist Claus Weiergang and drummer Allan Tschicaja.

Tempora Mutantur, Skaldic Art (1988). The Trinitytest / Brainstorm / R.F.F. / Trash Yer Guts Out.
Profit Counts, (1990). Prepare Retaliation / Fast n' Furious / Taking Over / Scumbags / Muslim Aggression / Chaotic Thoughts.
PRIMAL TOUCH, CBOD (1993). Born Of The Flag / Adult Lust / Kick Ass / Slam The Fays / White Slavery / Ridin' With Sioux / Liquid Materia / In Your Dreams.
Strange Ways EP, Euphonious PHONI 006 (1996). Chaos Within / My Dying Time / Born Under The Flag (New Version) / Way To Perfection / The Challenge / Strange Ways / Chaos Within (Video) / My Dying Time (Video).
ECLIPSE, Euphonious PHONI 002 (1996). Hustler / Smalltalker M.F. / Chaos Within / Stop The Bastards / My Dying Time / Sacred Bond / Swallow My Conscience / Silent Forever / Subject To Surgery / Another Face In The Crowd.
ROLL THE DICE, Season Of Mist (1999). Intro / Roll The Dice / On Top Of The World / Alive / The Fifth Season / Opinions / Worth To Live / Hole In My Pocket / Memory And Mind, pt. 1 / Weightless / Focus Intact / In The Tombs / Memory And Mind, pt. 2.

FURY161

GUADALAJARA, SPAIN — *Rubén (vocals), Ramiro (guitar), David Vega (guitar), Ivan (bass), David (drums).*

Guadalajara Death Metal band FURY161 were founded in 1999 by DOLOR members vocalist Rubén and bassist Ivan plus A DESTAJO personnel guitarists Edu and Ramiro with Hector on drums. Reyes from THE ART OF BLASPHEMY replaced Edu in 2001. FURY161 released the demos 'My Inner Secret' in 2002. The group was set to put down more demo tracks, to be titled 'Demon's With Angel Skin', but instead went into hiatus.

They returned with 'Black Bomber' during 2006. FURY161 planned a debut album to be titled Soul's Secret Memories'. In July 2006 the band incorporated new guitarist David Vega of HUMANO, TORSO, CABEZA DE TURCO and CHAMBER 313.

Black Bomber, Fury161 (2006) (Demo).

GADGET

GÄVLE, SWEDEN — *Emil Englund (vocals), Rikard Olsson (guitar), Fredrik Nygren (bass), William Blackmon (drums).*

Gävle Grindcore act GADGET, featuring William Blackmon of WITHERED BEAUTY and Rikard Olsson of DISKONTO, NAGANA, PANZERSCHRECK and SHITSTORM, featured their track 'Boredom Suits Me Fine' on the Relapse Records compilation 'Contaminated 5.0'. Initially GADGET had been initiated as a solo concern of Blackmon during 1997, this formative version recording a solitary demo before going into hiatus. The project was resurrected in 1999. A split 7" single shared with EXHUMED surfaced on Relapse Records in 2001. In 2003 GADGET hired Gothenburg studio Phlat Planet and Fredrik Reinedahl for the production of the debut album 'Remote'.

The band united with fellow Swedes RELEVANT FEW for a run of September 2004 German "Born to Booze, Live to Grind" tour dates. Promoting 'The Funeral March', in Spring 2007 GADGET, following a run of headline shows in March, hooked up with THE ACACIA STRAIN, ALL THAT REMAINS and MISERY SIGNALS for European dates.

Promo 00, (2000). Unrest / Empty / Fields / That's Just It? / Wishing It'd Be Different / Nothing / Boredom Suits Me Fine / I Want Out / It Sucks / Disorder.
Promo December 2000, (2000). New Era / Autumn / XI Days / Filled With Nothing / Keep Out / Unrest.
Gadget, Relapse (2001) (Split EP with EXHUMED). Unrest / Fields / XI Days / Inget Val.
REMOTE, Relapse (2004). Still / For What Cause / Crestfallen / Death And Destruction / Unreachable / The Sentinel / Wake Up The Dead / Fuel / Rid The Darkness / Failure / Connected / Tear You Apart / Dethrone / Förbrukad / Remote / Enigmatic / Tema: Skit.
FUNERAL MARCH, Relapse 766687 (2006).

GALLERY OF DARKNESS

GERMANY — *Konstantin Lühring (vocals), Florian Engelke (guitar), Karsten Schöning (guitar), Thorsten Nieland (bass), Florian Neumeyer (drums).*

Oldenburg based GALLERY OF DARKNESS guitarists Karsten Schöning and Florian Engelke pursued their craft with OF TREES AND ORCHIDS during the mid 90s. In late 1997 the pair decided on a straightforward Death Metal direction and duly created a fresh band involving vocalist Konstantin Lühring and drummer Holger Lüken of Black Metal outfit FUNERAL PROCESSION. This unit, with Engelke handling bass duties as well as guitar, recorded the March 2000 mini album 'Sea Of Silence'

Following recording Holger split away from the band and GALLERY OF DARKNESS drafted Florian Neumeyer from THE AWAKENING as substitute. Shortly after, ACT OF FATE,s Thorsten Nieland enrolled to become the group's first bass player.

Both Florian Engelke and Karsten Schöning operate side project INGURGITATING OBLIVION issuing the 'Thought Cathedral' album. Vocalist Konstantin Lühring fronts DESPONDENCY, an act that also features INGURGITATING OBLIVION drummer Dirk Janßen and debuted with the 'Distinction' album. This record has GALLERY OF DARKNESS's Florian Engelke contributing bass parts. Nieland can also be found as a member of Grind band GOREZONE.

GALLERY OF DARKNESS have now disbanded.

SEA OF SILENCE, (2000). Desperate Soliloqzuy Of A Dying One / Sea Of Silence / Forlorn (Part I) / I Am The Sleeping Forest / Forlorn (Part II) / Gallery Of Darkness.
Instinct EP, Independent (2001). Alienation Feeds Existence / Purity Of Anger / Fire Walk With Me.

GALLHAMMER

TOKYO, JAPAN — *Mika Penetrator (vocals / guitar), Vivian Slaughter (vocals / bass), Risa Reaper (drums).*

GALLHAMMER is an all female, Tokyo based Death / Black Metal trio incorporating members of DEATH COMES ALONG and MEAT SLAVE. First product would be simply titled 'The First Reh-Tape', a cassette issued just upfront of the band's debut gig at the Koiwa Death Fest. An eponymous studio demo followed that July with a third demo, 'Endless Nauseous Days', arriving in March 2004. An August 2004 demo, entitled 'The Worship' and restricted to just 66 copies, comprised cover versions of HELLHAMMER's 'Revelations of Doom', BURZUM's 'Lost Wisdom' and ;Axeman' originally by AMEBIX.

GALLHAMMER contracted to Mexican label Goatsucker Records for their inaugural full-length album 'Gloomy Lights', released in August 2004. That October GALLHAMMER featured tracks on a split release entitled 'Kill You I' issued via SSKJL Records in alliance with DEATHCOUNT, PEST and ROOKIE OUTSIDER. Five tracks would be contributed for a four way split releases in collaboration with Split with 77, DXIXE and FUGUE in January 2005. The group signed to UK label Peaceville Records in December. The double set 'The Dawn Of . . . ' arrived in January the following year.

The First Reh-Tape, Gallhammer IAK-001 (2003) (limited edition 30 copies). / .
Gallhammer, IAK-002 (2003). / / / / (Live).
Endless Nauseous Days, (2004). Endless Nauseous Days / Ishiki Kondaku (Live) / Insane Beautiful Sunnyday Slaughter (Live).

GALLHAMMER

The Worship, (2004) (Limited edition 66 copies). Axeman / Lost Wisdom / Revelations Of Doom.
GLOOMY LIGHTS, Goatsucker (2004). Endless Nauseous Days / Crucifixion / Tomurai : May Our Father Die / Beyond The Hate Red / Lost My Self / State Of Gloom / Aloof And Proud Silence / Color Of Coma.
THE DAWN OF . . . , Peaceville CDVILEF147 (2007). Speed Of Blood / Crucifixion / May Our Father Die / Aloof And Proud Silence / Hallucination / Selfish Selfless / Insane Beautiful Sunnyday Slaughter / Beyond The Red Hate / Friction / At The Onset Of The Age Of Despair / Crucifixion (Rehearsal 2006) / May Our Father Die (Rehearsal 2006) / Endless Nauseous Days / Blind My Eyes / May Our Father Die / Song Of Fall / Hallucination / Crucifixion / Song Of Fall / Hallucination / Blind My Eyes / Crucifixion / At The Onset Of The Age Of Despair / Speed Of Blood / Lust Satan Death / Beyond The Hate Red / Crucifixion / Blossom In The Raven River / Beyond The Hate Red / May Our Father Die / Lust Satan Death / Endless Nauseous Days / Beyond The Hate Red / Crucifixion / Speed Of Blood / Hallucination.

GARDEN OF DECAY

BELGIUM — *Quentin Demelenne (vocals), Claude Remade (vocals), Vince Tamiset (guitar), Stéphane Hubert (guitar), Phillipe Beck (bass), Nicolas Bodard (drums).*

GARDEN OF DECAY is a Belgian melodic Death Metal band fronted by both male and female lead vocals, founded by guitarist Stéphane and drummer Nicolas Bodard. A former guitarist, Ludovic, was replaced by ex-SCATOPHAGUS and ALASTHOR guitarist Vince Tamiset during 2003. An EP, 'We Generate', emerged in May 2004.

GARDEN OF DECAY parted ways with founder member, female singer Claude Remacle, citing "musical differences", in June 2006. In early March 2007 the band folded, stating ""After five years of blood, sweat and beers, and following the departure of our bass player and founding member Philippe Beck, we've decided to put GARDEN OF DECAY to rest."

We Generate, Independent (2004). Intro—Regenerate / Visions / Chaos Song / The Sands Of Time.

GARDEN OF SHADOWS

GAITHERSBURG, MD, USA — *Chad (vocals), Mary (guitar), Brian (guitar / keyboards), Sean (bass), Bret (drums).*

Mystically inspired epic Death Metal from Maryland with evident influences directly culled from the Greek Metal scene. The band previously operated under the guise of FUNERAL OPERA. GARDEN OF SHADOWS, who employ female ex-BIOVORE guitarist Mary, came into being during 1995 but would soon after dispense with their rhythm section of bass player Dave and drummer Kevin. Former SADISTIC TORMENT man Bret took the drumming position.

In 1997 the band cut the demo 'Heart Of The Corona' after which new bass player Sean was inducted. He too soon decamped to be superseded by Owen to record the eight and a half minute track 'Shards Of The Sphere'. This song would be added to the original demo recordings for a CD release on X Rated Records.

Owen would switch to guitar as keyboard player Scott left. Further fluctuations in the line up witnessed the departure of Owen and the reenlistment of Sean on bass. Signing to the British Wicked World label, a subsidiary of the Earache concern, GARDEN OF SHADOWS set to work on the 'Oracle Moon' album taking a break to perform at the Czech 'Brutal Assault' festival.

Sean would join DYING FETUS in February 2001 as GARDEN OF SHADOWS utilized the temporary services of the bassist of FROM WITHIN for live work. Ex-vocalist Zdenka Prado would join ESTUARY in mid 2002.

ORACLE MOON, Wicked World WICK010 (2000). Oracle Moon / Citadel Of Dreams / Into Infinity / Dissolution Of The Forms / Continuum / Desert Shadows / Twilight Odyssey.

GARDENIAN

GOTHENBURG, SWEDEN — *Jim Kjell (vocals), Niclas Engelin (guitar), Hákan Skoger (bass), Thym Blom (drums).*

Melodic Death Metal from a Gothenburg act founded during April 1996 by former HEADPLATE frontman Jim Kjell and drummer Thym Blom. Later recruits were former IDIOTS RULE and SARCAZM guitarist Niclas Engelin and bassist Hákan Skoger. The band was championed in their early years by Jesper Strömblad of IN FLAMES who secured the deal with the French concern Listenable Records to put out the June 1997 album 'Two Feet Stand'. GARDENIAN's Nuclear Blast debut, August 1999's 'Soulburner', included guest lead vocals from ex-ARTCH vocalist Erik Hawk. This outing also found former ICE AGE singer Sabrina Kihlstrand adding her distinctive touch on backing vocals.

Niclas Engelin embroiled himself in yet another in the very long line of Swedish side ventures with PASSENGER, a late 2002 band endeavour also incorporating his erstwhile IN FLAMES colleague frontman Anders Fridén, HEADPLATE bassist Håkan Skoger and ex-TRANSPORT LEAGUE drummer Patrik J. Sten.

The band shifted shape quite dramatically in early 2003, inducting TIME REQUIEM and MAJESTIC singer Apollo Papathanasio and erstwhile GOOSEFLESH bassist Robert Hakemo, the latter also citing membership of Grindcore act RELEVANT FEW. Papathanasio was also to be found fronting SANDALINAS, a joint Spanish / Swedish collaboration centred on guitarist Jordi Sandalinas. Kriss Albertsson, who had previously performed bass in the group, remained a member, but only as a touring/session guitarist.

GARDENIAN folded in early 2004, although a new project soon rose up entitled KEROZENE. This new unit saw Engelin and ex-bassist Robert Hakemo joined by drummer Patrik J. Sten, of PASSENGER and an ex-TRANSPORT LEAGUE member, along with vocalist Mikael Skager. The band cut recordings for their debut album early in the year, mixing it at Studio Fredman in

Gothenburg during April. Meantime, vocalist Jim Kjell joined forces with ex-IN FLAMES guitarist and founder of DIMENSION ZERO, Glenn Ljungström, to create PITCHLINE.

In March 2005 a new Metal formation was announced with ENGEL, a Gothenburg based quintet featuring Niclas Engelin and Robert Hakemo in union with guitarist Marcus Sunesson, ex-THE CROWN, drummer Morbid Mojjo (a.k.a. Daniel Moilanen), a veteran of MINDSNARE, SANDALINAS, RUNEMAGICK, DRACENA, RELEVANT FEW and LORD BELIAL together with vocalist Mangan Klavborn. Meantime, ex-vocalist Apollo Papathanasio guested on VITALIJ KUPRIJ's 2005 opus 'Revenge' and in November joined Greek outfit FIREWIND. In August 2006 Robert Hakemo joined M.A.N.

TWO FEET STAND, Listenable POSH008 (1997). Two Feet Stand / Flipside Of Reality / The Downfall / Awake Of Abuse / Netherworld / Do Me Now / Murder... / Freedom / Mindless Domination / The Silent Fall.
TWO FEET STAND, Avalon Marquee MICP-1034 (1997) (Japanese release). Two Feet Stand / Flipside Of Reality / The Downfall / Awake Of Abuse / Netherworld / Do Me Now / Murder... / Freedom / Mindless Domination / The Silent Fall / Ecstasy Of Life.
SOULBURNER, Nuclear Blast NB 0397-2 (1999). As A True King / Powertool / Deserted / Soulburner / If Tomorrow's Gone / Small Electric Space / Chaos In Flesh / Ecstasy Of Life / Tell The World I'm Sorry / Loss / Black Days.
SINDUSTRIES, Nuclear Blast NB 0533-2 (2000). Self Proclaimed Messiah / Doom And Gloom / Long Snap To Zero / Courageous / Heartless / The Suffering / Scissor Fight / Sonic Death Monkey / Sindustries / Funeral.

GARDENS OF GEHENNA

MÜNCHBERG, GERMANY — *Andreas Opel (vocals / guitar), Alexander Kaul (guitar), Birgit Lages (bass), Hagen Fitz (drums).*

Münchberg Death-Doom outfit GARDENS OF GEHENNA, comprising frontman Andreas Opel (who also operates as guitarist for Power Metal band ANACONDA), bass player Birgit Lages, guitarist Holger Fiedler, drummer Thomas Drechsel and keyboard player Michaela Marek, came into being during 1995. Although a regular on the live circuit throughout Germany since the losing the services of Dreschel GARDENS OF GEHENNA have utilised the use of a drum machine on stage for many years. Two demo sessions were delivered during 1996 and the band garnered extra exposure by a track inclusion on the Belgian Shiver label series of compilation albums 'Sometimes Death Is Better'. The group reaped valuable live exposure performing as opening act on select dates of the 'Heaven Shall Burn' MARDUK, GEHENNA and MYSTICUM tour as well as shows supporting DAS ICH.

The debut album, 'Mortem Saluta' produced by DAS ICH member Bruno Kramm, was recorded in January of 1997 and subsequently issued by the Shiver label in February of 1998. Despite this progress the group underwent serious line up changes which eventually saw only Opel and Lages remaining. Temporarily Martin F. Jungkunz of DESPAIRATION was employed as live guitarist. GARDENS OF GEHENNA was brought back up to strength with the addition of guitarist Christian Wachter and keyboard player Michael Schöner. This new formation signed to the Last Episode label for a second album ,'Dead Body Music' once again produced by Bruno Kramm, released in July of 2000.

Upfront of recording the third album 'The Mechanism Masochism' the band included their version of 'A Prelude To Agony' on a TYPE O NEGATIVE tribute album in 2001.

GARDENS OF GEHENNA added second guitarist Bastian Rosner from Black Metal band ETERNAL SILENCE in 2002. However, this latest inductee left the fold in April of 2003. The band would re-enlist former member Martin Buchmann as stand in. The 2004 version of the band was counted as a quartet comprising vocalist / guitarist Andreas Opel, guitarist Alexander Kaul, bassist Birgit Lages with Hagen Fitz on drums.

MORTEM SALUTA, Shiver (1998). Nebelmond / Beyond The Gates Of Dusk / Blood / Those Who Walk The Shadows / Mortem Saluta / Iconoclasm / Prophecy / Nebelmond (DAS ICH remix).
DEAD BODY MUSIC, Last Episode (2000). Requiem / Iesaiah 14:12 / Tod Und Teufel / Gethsemane / Beautiful Blackness / Lacrimae Rerum / From A Silent Yearning Dark / Dust Of Life.
MECHANISMS OF MASOCHISM, Prophecy (2003). A Dissonant Prelude To Divine Decay / The Downfall Of Jezira / Demon's Diaspora.

GATHERING DARKNESS

SANTANDER, SPAIN — *José Lavín Cabello (vocals), Nicolas Cuesta Fernandez (guitar), Fernando Gómez Aedo (bass), Jesús Quintana Claver (drums).*

Santander, Cantabria Doom-Death outfit GATHERING DARKNESS, fronted by 'Uruksoth' (a.k.a. José Lavín Cabello), was assembled during 1998. Line-up changes saw the departing of guitarists Julo, Mon and Ramón. Drummer Chus would be replaced by Jesús Quintana Claver. First product would be an April 2000 demo 'Surrounded By Thorns'.

During 2002 GATHERING DARKNESS members guitarist 'H-Astur' and drummer 'JhesuQ' founded Death Metal sideband OPROM ("Orbital Processor Request From Outer Materia") in alliance with vocalist Erun-Dagoth (a.k.a. Javier Sixto) of BRIARGH, DAEMONLORD, MOONSHINE, FORESTDOME, BAGRONK, WOLFTHRONE, FLOWING CRIMSON and CRYSTALMOORS and bassist Thorgen of FATAL PORTRAIT.

A second GATHERING DARKNESS session 'Suffering Into My Dreams' arrived in 2003. Grotesque Productions issued the debut album 'Beholders Of The Pain Planet' in January 2005.

Surrounded By Thorns, Gathering Darkness (2000). Martyr / My Ardent Desire / A New Fallen Angel / Stream Tears / Last Crusade / 100 Tears To My Ocean.
Suffering Into My Dreams, (2003). Configuration Of Pain / The Cold Of The Limbs / Decay / Back To The Grief / A New Fallen Angel / 100 Tears To My Ocean / Martyr.
The New Beginning, (2004). Visions Of An Astral Dream / Arquitecture Of Pain.
BEHOLDERS OF THE PAIN PLANET, Grotesque Productions (2005). Intro / Necrocosmos / Arquitecture Of Pain / The Room Of Flesh / Visions Of An Astral Dream / Human Daemon / Civic XXY / Blind Of Anger / Time To Suffer.

GENERAL SURGERY

STOCKHOLM, SWEDEN — *Grant McWilliams (vocals), Joacim Carlsson (guitar), Johan Wallin (guitar), Glen Sykes (bass), Adde Mitrouliu (drums).*

Formed in 1989, Stockholm's GENERAL SURGERY is the side project of various members of Swedish Death Metal acts. The original line-up comprised of then UNLEASHED guitarist Richard Cabeza on vocals, CARBONISED guitarist Jonas De Rouche, Grant McWilliams on bass and then CARBONISED vocalist Matti Kärki on drums. The project's first demo was titled 'Erosive Offals'.

McWilliams departed prior to the second demo 'Pestiferous Anthropophagia'. GENERAL SURGERY's line-up then virtually disintegrated, leaving only Kärki remaining. Cabeza soon returned to the fore with DISMEMBER. New recruits were AFFLICTED guitarist Joacim Carlsson and drummer Matts Nordrup. Grant McWilliams also rejoined. GENERAL SURGERY were then offered a deal by American label Grind 'Til Global Perfection. Tracks were recorded which would eventually become the 'Internecine Prurience' demo. Also recorded would be a three track demo attributed to MEAT MISSILE. Following recording of further GENERAL SURGERY songs with producer Tomas Skogsberg, Kärkki quit to concentrate full time as vocalist for DISMEMBER.

The tracks recorded for the American EP were to surface as the 'Necrology' EP on Relapse Records in 1991. The initial 1000 copies came in blood red vinyl and, as the pressings soon sold out, Relapse reissued the EP on CD, with two extra tracks, in 1994.

With GENERAL SURGERY on hold, Matts Nordrup would surface in CREMATORY. GENERAL SURGERY would reform in 1999 citing a new line-up of Matti Kärkki on vocals, Grant McWilliams on vocals, guitarist Joacim Carlsson, bassist Richard Cabeza and NASUM man Anders Jakobson on drums. The band soon got back into action contributing their version of 'Empathological Necroticism' to a Deathvomit CARCASS tribute album. However, Jakobsen would depart and the group pulled in the temporary services of Erik Thyselius of Stockholm's CONSTRUCDEAD. Chris 'Piss' Barkensjö of REPUGNANT and KAAMOS would take the drum stool in February of 2001. By 2002 it would be the BIRDFLESH, DETHRONEMENT and SAYYADINA credited Adde Mitrouliu (a.k.a. Smattro Ansjovis) enrolled as new drummer. Richard Cabeza would team up with premier Black Metal act DARK FUNERAL for North American touring in the Spring of 2002.

A GENERAL SURGERY split album shared with THE COUNTY MEDICAL EXAMINERS was issued by Razorback Records in 2003. In September of that year GENERAL SURGERY boosted their numbers with the addition of SCURVY, BOMBSTRIKE and REPUGNANT credited second guitarist Johan 'Bosse' Wallin. Further split releases were projected with Spanish Horror-Grind outfit MACHETAZO and the bizarre Japanese band BUTCHER ABC, both via Escorbuto Recordings.

Bassist Andreas Eriksson decamped in January of 2004, the band drafting REGURGITATE's Glen Sykes as temporary fill in. As such, GENERAL SURGERY announced that they were to perform live for the first time in over fourteen years, this momentous event taking place Club Nocturnal in Gothenburg on Valentine's day. By May guitarist Johan Wallin and REGURGITATE bassist Glenn Sykes had enrolled full time. That same year guitarist Joacim Carlsson and former drummer Erik Thyselius formed up part of the resurrected FACE DOWN.

Promoting the album 'Left Hand Pathology', released through Listenable Records, GENERAL SURGERY were set to engage in the 'Pathology Over Europe' tour in March 2006, supported by GRIMNESS 69, but cancelled when singer Grant McWilliams left. However, in mid June the group revealed that McWilliams had returned and newly installed on bass would be Dr. Mikael Van Touminen of FINGERSPITZENGEFÜHL and THE GROKENBERGERS. GENERAL SURGERY teamed up with IMPALED and BUTCHER ABC for the "Gore Over Japan Tour" in September.

In March 2007 a collection of retro-Punk tracks was laid down at Studio Garaget by NICE IDIOT, a project featuring Mikael Van Tuominen, Joacim Carlsson with MASSGRAV's Johan Norsebäck on bass and Ove Wiksten, of SAYYADINA and I QUIT!, on drums. The following month bassist Dr. Mikael Van Tuominen took his leave and was replaced by former band member Andreas Eriksson.

Erosive Offals, (1990) (Demo). Sneezing Pus / Erosive Offals / Mortified Flesh.

Pestisferous Anthropophagia, (1990) (Cassette demo). Slithering Maceration Of Ulcerous Facial Tissue / The Succulent Aftermath Of A Subdural Haemmorhage / Grotesque Laceration Of Mortified Flesh.

Internecine Prurifence, (1990) (Demo). Ominous Lamentation / Slithering Maceration Of Ulcerous Facial Tissue / Severe Catatonia In Pathology / Crimson Concerto / An Orgy Of Flying Limbs And Gore / Grotesque Laceration Of Mortified Flesh.

Necrolgy, Relapse (1991) (7" single). Ominous Lamentation / Slithering Maceration Of Ulcerous Facial Tissue / Grotesque Laceration Of Mortified Flesh / Severe Catatonia In Pathology / Crimson Concerto.

NECROLOGY, Nuclear Blast NB092-2 (1993). Ominous Lamentation / Slithering Maceration Of Ulcerous Facial Tissue / Grotesque Maceration Of Mortified Flesh / Severe Catatonia In Pathology / Crimson Concerto / The Succulent Aftermath Of A Subdoural Haemmorhage / An Orgy Of Flying Limbs And Gore.

GENERAL SURGERY, Razorback RR17 (2003) (Split album with THE COUNTY MEDICAL EXAMINERS). Pre-Bisectal Corrosive Immersion / Lab Rat / Mortuary Wars / Cauterization Frenzy / Reception Of Cadavers / Decomposer / Convivial Corpse Disposal Methodology.

Filth / General Surgery, Bones Brigade (2004) (Split EP with FILTH). Unruly Dissection Marathon / Scalpel Infestation / Fully-Mechanized Corpse Thresher / The League of Extraordinary Grave Robbers.

Demos, Buio Omega (2004) (Double 7" package). Sneezing Pus / Erosive Offals / Mortified Flesh / Slithering Maceration Of Ulcerous Facial Tissue / The Succulent Aftermath Of A Subdural Haemmorhage / Grotesque Laceration Of Mortified Flesh / Ominous Lamentation / Slithering Maceration Of Ulcerous Facial Tissue / Grotesque Laceration Of Mortified Flesh / Severe Catatonia In Pathology / Crimson Concerto / An Orgy Of Flying Limbs And Gore.

General Surgery, Escorbuto Recordings (2004) (Split single with MACHETAZO). Necrodecontamination / Forensic Farce / Viva! Blunt Force Trauma / Cold Storage Fever.

LEFT HAND PATHOLOGY, Listenable (2006). If These Walls Could Talk / Ambulance Chaser / Fulguration / Arterial Spray Obsession / Necrodecontamination / The League Of Extraordinary Grave Robbers / The Admirable Teachings Of Burke & Hare / Capricious Provisional Cadaver Grater / Decomposer / Viva! Blunt Force Trauma / Cold Storage Fever / Mucopurulent Mayhem / Mortuary Wars / Convivial Corpse Disposal Methodology.

GENOCIDE SUPERSTARS

ÖREBRO, SWEDEN — *Danny Violence (vocals / guitar), Mieszko Talarczyk (vocals / guitar), Richard A.D. (vocals / bass), Matt von Superstars (drums).*

Örebro's GENOCIDE SUPERSTARS previously went under the title GENOCIDE SS, releasing two albums under that banner. With the change in name came a change in musical style, the Grindcore of yore giving way to a dirty, Punk Rock n' Roll sound. The band was formed during 1994 by guitarists Danny Violence and Mieszko Talarczyk, the latter of SHAGIDIEL and NASUM repute. The NECRONY and NASUM credited Richard A.D. handled bass. Drummer Matt Von Superstars (a.k.a. Mathias Borg) is active with Thrashers 2 TON PREDATOR. Debut offering, 'Hail The New Storm', arrived in 1996 through Distortion Records.

2004 ended on a tragic note for the band as Mieszko Talarczyk was caught in the tidal waves that engulfed the Indian Ocean just after Christmas. Taking a holiday with his girlfriend on Thailand's Phi Phi Island, Mieszko's girlfriend Emma was injured and hospitalised whilst the singer was reported missing. Tragically, Talarczyk was later learned to have lost his life.

HAIL THE NEW STORM, Distortion (1996). The Final Doom / Mord / A New Wave Of Hatred / The New Storm / Demonomania / As The Machinegun Rivers Flow / Genocide SS / VIII / No Use, Just Die / Face The Stormtroopers / The Massive Genocide Experience / Through The Blood / Bombs Shall Cloud The Sky / Ten Miles Behind Enemy Lines / It's Time To Die (U Scum) / The Ultimate Declaration Of War / War Is Certain / The Bleeding Fields / The Leader Of The Fucking Assholes.

WE ARE BORN OF HATE, Distortion (1999). We Are Born Of Hate / Fuck The Enemy / Under Attack / Going Down To Die / Feed Me Hate / Warchrist Supreme / Be My Bitch / Extinction Extinction / They Walked In Line / In The Mist Of The Aftermath / Blackout / Firestorm / Victory Or Genocide / Dead In The Shadows / Crazy Motorcycle / Devastating Power / Bloodred City Streets.

SUPERSTAR DESTROYER, Relapse (2003). The Hateball Is Rolling / Destroyer Of The Worlds / Moro II / Final Descent / Hatestomp / Stairsweeper / Air-A Prelude To Hell / Superstar Destroyer / Danger Danger / Superstar Confession / In Misery Embraced / Like Roadkill / Warchild / Outlaw Song.

GHOST

POLAND — *Krzysztof Berlik (vocals), Dariusz Engler (guitar), Roman Pegza (guitar), Mieczyslaw Klimek (bass), Krzysztof Jankowsky (drums).*

GHOST is a Gdansk based Death Metal unit founded during 1988 with an opening line up comprising singer Krzysztof Berlik, guitarists Dariusz Engler and Roman Pegza, bass player Ryszard Lakomiec and drummer Marek Szczabel. In 1989 Krzysztof Jankowski took command of the drum stool for recording of the 'Noc Demona' demo tape. The band issued the 1993 'Bad

Obsession' demo, these sessions witnessing a further switch in personnel as Mieczyslaw Klimek came in on bass guitar.

The GHOST line up would remain stable until 2000 when new faces included Piotr Kawalerowski on bass, Lukasz Kumanski on the drums and the employment of YATTERING guitarist Radoslaw Cwalinski for live work.

THE LOST OF MERCY, Loud Out CD 0011 (1994). Anthem Of Vengeance / Morbid Game / Flag Of Shadowmaster / Alien / Bestial Rites / Cross Of Stone / Extreme Reality / The Day After / Kings Of Darkness / Fight For Your World.

GHOSTORM

VILNIUS, LITHUANIA — *Marius Berenis (vocals), Sarunas Tamulaitis (guitar), Rytis Tankevicius (guitar), Andrius Daugirdas (bass), Linus Buda (drums).*

GHOSTORM, a technical Death Metal band out of Vilnius, debuted with a 1994 demo 'The End Of All Songs'. These sessions included June 1993 tracks laid down by guitarist Sarunas "Omenas" Tamulaitis and DISSECTION drummer Meinardas "Brazas" Brazaitis with other DISSECTION members vocalist Lauras and bassist Liudas sessioning alongside October songs crafted by Tamulaitis, Brazaitis, singer Marius Berenis, bass player Andrius Daugirdas and guitarist Rytis Tankevicius.

They would follow up with the Black Mark released 'Frozen In Fire' two years later. The album was recorded at Unisound studios in Sweden and produced by EDGE OF SANITY's Dan Swanö. Bassist Andrius Daugirdas also featured as a member of VOLIS. Guitarist Sarunas Tamulaitis held a prior tradition with CONSCIOUS ROT whilst singer Marius Berenis has ties to REGRIDOR. Second guitar duties went to Rytis "Taraila" Tankevicius of REGRIDOR. Drummer Meinardas Brazaitis, of DISSECTION, would be replaced by Linas "Smarve" Buda.

Prior to disbanding the group put in concerts under a revised billing of GO-STORM.

The End Of All Songs, (1994). The Sea / Frost / Bird / Never ... / Within The Rain.
FROZEN IN FIRE, Black Mark BMCD 65 (1995). Fraud Of Dark / There / Solitude / Frost / Dreamland / Come Back / The Sea / At Boundary / Unnormal.
BLACK BOX, Pagan (1997). Boxes / In Hate We Trust / Legend / Circles In The Sand / Gardens Of The Scorpion / Daughter / Bedstories / Out Of Darkness.

GHOULS

ITALY — *Massimiliano Franceschini (vocals), Antonio Poletti (guitar / bass).*

GHOULS was manifested during 1995 by singer Massimiliano Franceschini in league with bass guitarist Fabrizio Franceschini. Demos were recorded that same year, after which an unnamed guitarist and drummer exited due to "personal issues". In 1998 Franceschini contacted CARNAL RAPTURE vocalist / guitarist Emilio Trillò and erstwhile NOVEMBRE guitarist Antonio Poleti to record a new set of demo recordings billed 'Rebaptized In Blasphemy'. Drums for these sessions would be handled by Giuseppe Orlando of CATACOMB, ROSAE CRUCIS and NOVEMBRE. Upon completion of these tracks both Trillò and Poleti made the decision to enroll as fulltime GHOULS members. Utilising Orlando's percussive services once again a further batch of demo tracks, 'Promo 2000', was recorded.

During 2001 the band incorporated a fresh rhythm section of bassist Michele Viti and drummer Mauro Mercurio, both holding credits with HOUR OF PENANCE. However, before long Viti quit and the bass position was delegated to Silvano Leone from FEARWELL for another promotional session dubbed 'Promo 2003'.

In 2004, GHOULS replaced Mercurio with Alessio Brugiotti of ARS ONIRICA and TERRORSTATE, the latter a side project convened by Antonio Poletti and Silvano Leone. That same year 'Nighthorn' of GHOULS recorded session bass on the LORD VAMPYR album 'De Vampyrica Philosophia'. By early 2007 GHOULS was operating simply as a duo of Max Franceschini on vocals and Antonio Poletti handling guitars and bass.

Ghould 1996, (1996). Absolute Dominion / Antichrist / Fear / Evil & Hate.
Rebaptized In Blasphemy, (1998). Ghouls / Rebaptized In Blasphemy / My Life For Your Death.
Promo 2000, Ghouls (2000). Divine Chosen / I'm The Living Swear / Eternal Damnation.
Promo 2003, (2003). Marquise De Sade / Slut In Black / Phallic Soul.

GHOULUNATICS

CANADA — *Patrick Mireault (vocals), Jarrod Martin (guitar), Patrick Gordon (guitar), Gary Lyons (bass), Brian Craig (drums).*

GHOULUNATICS issued the demo 'Mystralengine' in 1995. The band issued two albums consecutively in May 2004, the 'Sabacthany' studio effort recorded at Wild Studio by Yannick St-Amand and mixed and mastered by Pierre Rémillard, whilst a live album 'It's Alive!' was captured at a Halloween 2003 show in Montreal.

In August of 2002 Patrick Mireault forged part of a brand new Thrash act BLACK CLOUD. This band boasted the prodigious talents of bassist Jean-Yves 'Blacky' Thériault of VOIVOD infamy alongside B.A.R.F. vocalist Marc Vaillancourt, CRYPTOPSY frontman Flo Mounier, Pierre Rémillard of OBLIVEON on guitar and Daniel Mongrain of MARTYR on second guitar. Gigs in May of 2004 saw CRYPTOPSY's Flo Mounier filling in on drums, regular drummer Brian Craig having sprained his ankle.

In 2006 Patrick Gordon forged LES ÉKORCHÉS, a purely acoustic project featuring vocalist Marc Vaillancourt from B.A.R.F. and BLACK CLOUD, cellist Philippe Mius d'Entremont from MARUKA plus drummer Michel Langevin from VOIVOD. Indica Records released the Glen Robinson 'Les Ékorchés' album in February 2007.

CARVING INTO YOU, (1999). Carving Into You / Brother Worm / Timeless Time / Plenitude / L'eveil du Drag On / Trial / Drowning / Nature Morte / Creepy Crawly / Presence Presence.
MYSTRALENGINE, (2000). Interlude / Cold Fish / Blood Curdling Tale / Mystralengine / Devours and Adores / Nature Morte / Howling Season / Mighty Empire / Lifeless Story / Carving Into You (Live) / Plentitude (Live) / Creepy Crawly (Live) / Nature Morte (Live) / Buttman & Rocco (Live).
KING OF THE UNDEAD, (2002). King Of The Undead / Mobster Fiesta Extravaganza / Melodrame / Tower 311 / Oh God! The Stench / Pernicious Sentence / Suspicious Minds / Brother Worm (The Slimy One) / LAIC / Red Shovel / Exuviae / Agony Column.
SABACTHANY, Galy (2004). Beastial Behaviour / Ashes To Ashes, Costs A Lot / Alone With The Seasons / Sabacthany / Wind Up Dead / Axe, My Deadly Friend / Nothing More / Two Legged Disease / Fresh Meat Without Chemicals / Mr.Reggid's Garden / Grave Concern / Roadkill Parade / Right To Pass.
CRYOGENIE, Galy (2006). Exerese / 1412 De Malines / Raz-de-Mariage / Monstrueusement Votre / Engrenage / Cryogenie / Guerrier Pixelise / L'Invite / Eclats de Gerveau / Vox Clamatis In Deserto.

GLASS CASKET

WINSTON-SALEM, NC, USA — *Adam Cody (vocals), Blake Tuten (guitar), Dustie Waring (guitar), Sid Menon (bass), Blake Richardson (drums).*

GLASS CASKET, previously entitled GADREL but taking on the new title inspired by the 'Snow White' fable, was originally assembled in Winston-Salem, North Carolina during the Summer of 2001. As GADREL the band issued a now highly sought after EP. Lyrically, GLASS CASKET employs Christian themes although the band has stated that the membership involves both Christian and non-Christian musicians. The core line-up comprised lead vocalist Adam Cody, guitarists Dustie Waring and Ian Tuten with Blake Richardson on drums. Several months later, Sid Menon, from the Indie group UPHELD, was acquired to fill the bass guitar position. Waring also held prior live experience with ACEDIA and formative high school outfit NARAYAN alongside Adam Cody, Blake Tuten and drummer Sanjay.

As GLASS CASKET, an opening three track demo secured the interest of Century Media affiliate Abacus Recordings and GLASS CASKET entered the studio with producer Jamie King to craft debut album 'We Are Gathered Here Today ...' Bastardised Recordings took the album on for a European license.

GLASS CASKET guitarist Dustie Waring acted as temporary live filling for BETWEEN THE BURIED AND ME in September of 2004. Drummer Blake Richardson followed suit in January 2005. Vocalist Adam Cody joined VEHEMENCE as temporary frontman for touring in the Spring then in September announced he was enrolling into the ranks on a permanent basis.

WE ARE GATHERED HERE TODAY ..., Abacus Recordings CD 0003-2 (2004). Pencil Lead Syringe / And So It Was Said / Fisted And Forgotten / Fearfully And Wonderfully Made / Cellar Door / Chew Your Fingers / Scarlet Paint And Gasoline / In Between The Sheets / A Gray A.M. You Will Never Get To See.

A DESPERATE MAN'S DIARIES, Abacus Recordings (2006). Phenomenon / Too Scared To Live / Genesis / Less Like Humans / A Cork Stops The Whinning / Post Trumatic Death / I Slept / The Redeemer / Name Above All Names.

GOD AMONG INSECTS

SWEDEN — *Emperor Magus Caligula (vocals), Kenth Philipson (guitar), Tomas Elofsson (bass), Tobias Gustafsson (drums).*

Retro Death Metal act forged in October of 2003 by the elite cast of guitarist Lord K (a.k.a. Kenth Philipson) of LEUKEMIA, ROSICRUCIAN, ODYSSEY, LAME, HOUSE OF USHER and THE PROJECT HATE repute, fellow THE PROJECT HATE singer Jörgen Sandström, bassist Tomas Elofsson from SANCTIFICATION, PROSERPHINE and DIVINE DESECRATION along with VOMITORY drummer Tobias Gustafsson. The group, replacing Sandström with lead vocalist Emperor Magus Caligula of DARK FUNERAL, signed to Threeman Recordings for a debut album. The band cut 'World Wide Death' in March of 2004 at Abyss Studios with engineer Tommy Tägtgren, claiming this outing would probably be their one and only musical statement.

In early 2004 Sandström also enrolled himself into VICIOUS ART, a Death / Thrash act forged by former DARK FUNERAL and DOMINION CALIGULA members Mattias 'Dominion' Mäkelä and Robert 'Gaahnfaust' Lundin. Another record he featured on would be a 2004 album from Stoners THE MIGHTY NIMBUS, featuring on a cover of the SAINT VITUS track 'Born Too Late'.

'World Wide Death' ran into problems just before release when its graphic cover, a deliberately naive depiction of a crucifixion victim wrapped in barbed wire, was banned by German authorities, forcing albums to be sold in a slip case. GOD AMONG INSECTS put on a 4th September record release party gig at Kelly's in Örebro, supported by Norwegian band MYRKSKOG. Tomas Elofsson joined the ranks of IN BATTLE as session guitarist in September.

GOD AMONG INSECTS entered Abyss Studios with producer Tommy Tägtgren in August 2005 to craft a new record. In November Kenth Philipson joined the touring ranks of VOMITORY as fill-in guitarist for the recently departed Ulf Dalegren for gigs UK, Ireland, The Netherlands and Sweden.

WORLD WIDE DEATH, Threeman Recordings (2004). Legions Of Darkness / A Gush Of Blood / Headless Nun Whore / Wretched Hatching / Chainsawed Christians / Purified In Carnage / Uprising Of The Rotten / Severe Facial Reconstruction / Uhr-Nazuur.

ZOMBIENOMICON, Threeman (2006). The First House / F(wh)oreplay / Zombie Torture / They Came In Thousands / Toth'

GOD AMONG INSECTS

Tauun / Marching Into War / 12th Dimension / Fucked By The Dead / Weaklings / The Bashing Of Skulls.

GOD FORBID

NEW BRUNSWICK, NJ, USA — *Bryon Davis (vocals), Doc Coyle (guitar), Dallas Coyle (guitar), John Outcalt (bass), Corey Pierce (drums).*

New Brunswick, New Jersey's New Wave of American Heavy Metal band GOD FORBID, founded by drummer Corey Pierce and ex-FEINT 13 guitarist Dallas Coyle issued early product on the independent 9 Volt label. The band had evolved from its earlier inception as MANIFEST DESTINY through to INSALUBRIOUS before settling on GOD FORBID. During May 1997 GOD FORBID were joined by vocalist Bryon Davis and in September of the same year by erstwhile WOMB bassist John 'Beeker' Outcalt. Guitarist Doc Coyle would deputize on a temporary basis for AS DARKNESS FALLS in 1998. 9 Volt issued the 'Out Of Misery' EP in September 1998.

Upon signing to German concern Century Media, just after the New Jersey 'Metalfest' appearance, for the highly praised April 2001 'Determination' album, GOD FORBID upped their American touring plans appearing with AMEN and SHADOWS FALL for a March tour then hooking up with the NEVERMORE, OPETH and CHILDREN OF BODOM dates in April. Touring in Britain would be supported by LABRAT and CO-EXIST.

In September 2001 the band's 'Out Of Misery' EP would benefit from a re-release to capitalise on the band's burgeoning status, adding bonus live tracks, including a take on SEPULTURA's 'Propaganda', recorded at New York's infamous CBGB's club. GOD FORBID toured the States in alliance with HATEBREED, CONVERGE and POISON THE WELL and then promptly announced another bout of North American touring, commencing 16th January 2002, in alliance with headliners GWAR and SOILENT GREEN. Further shows would be scheduled with SHADOWS FALL and KILLSWITCH ENGAGE but the band subsequently withdrew from these gigs in order to place their efforts towards songwriting.

In 2003 the band cut a rendition of the GUNS N' ROSES track 'Out Ta Get Me', with producer Chris Pearce, for use on a Law Of Inertia tribute album. Also emerging would be a re-press of GOD FORBID's long out of print debut album 'Reject The Sickness', released via the band's own PR Records label. The band got back into tour mode in August, headlining US dates over ATREYU, DARKEST HOUR and UNDEROATH. The group would be back on the road in October for the five week 'Headbanger's Ball' dates alongside KILLSWITCH ENGAGE, SHADOWS FALL, UNEARTH and LAMB OF GOD. The band gave themselves no respite, thereafter hopping onto the MUSHROOMHEAD national tour into November. The band resumed live activity in 2004, headlining a February run of US dates with running mates WALLS OF JERICHO, BLOOD HAS BEEN SHED and FULL BLOWN CHAOS.

In an unexpected move, GOD FORBID donated their rendition of 'Out Ta Get Me' to the GUNS N' ROSES tribute album 'Bring You To Your Knees' released by Inertia Records in March. The next road trek was set to be a month's duration co-headline tour in June of 2004 with label mates KILLSWITCH ENGAGE, CHIMAIRA and SHADOWS FALL upfront of an appearance at the mammoth 'Ozzfest' touring festival headlined by BLACK SABBATH, JUDAS PRIEST and SLAYER. A brief burst of September headline gigs, supported by A LIFE ONCE LOST, NORMA JEAN and THE RED CHORD, would be filmed by director Zach Merck for a promotional video.

The band allied with SOULFLY and DEATH BY STEREO for North American shows in March 2005, UK headline shows then extended live work into April and May with headliners supported by CALIBAN, IT DIES TODAY and FULL BLOWN CHAOS. A compilation inclusion of note would be the track 'Soul Engraved' featured on the 'Code Red' album, an exclusive collection given to US Marine Corps soldiers active duty in the Middle East.

Just one day after completion of touring, GOD FORBID commenced work on a new album 'IV: Constitution Of Treason' in May, utilising the services of Jason Suecof at Audiohammer Studios in Florida and Eric Rachel at Trax East in New Jersey. Gigs in July had the band partnered with FULL BLOWN CHAOS and HIMSA. 'IV: Constitution Of Treason' sold over 8'300 copies in its first week of sale to debut at no. 119 on the US Billboard charts.

The band then announced further US dates alongside MESHUGGAH, THE HAUNTED and MNEMIC throughout October. Roadwork continued apace in November as the group toured Europe traversing Holland, the UK, France, Belgium, Spain, Germany, Austria, Switzerland, Denmark and Sweden in union with MANNTIS and THE HAUNTED. 2006 was opened up with US road work throughout January aligned with ANTHRAX, MANNTIS and SWORN ENEMY. March had the band scheduled for 'The Crusade III: Ascend Above The Ashes' concerts in the UK and Ireland alongside TRIVIUM and BLOODSIMPLE. The band put in a significant appearance at the GUNS N' ROSES headlined 'Download' festival in Castle Donington, UK on June 11th.

GOD FORBID headed up the UK and European "Hell On Earth" tour in September and October. Joining them would be Swiss act CATARACT, Germany's MAROON, FULL BLOWN CHAOS, PURIFIED IN BLOOD from Norway and A PERFECT MURDER. December 2006 had the band aligned with PROTEST THE HERO and THE HUMAN ABSTRACT for a run of shows across Canada.

2007 US dates commenced on January 4th at the First Unitarian Church in Philadelphia, Pennsylvania with a first headlining leg backed by GOATWHORE, MNEMIC, THE HUMAN ABSTRACT and ARSIS. On February 2nd BYZANTINE joined this touring entourage in the stead of THE HUMAN ABSTRACT.

GOD FORBID toured Australia, New Zealand, Mexico, Puerto Rico and Alaska, all for the first time, in March. HATEBREED teamed up with GOD FORBID, EVERGREEN TERRACE, THE ACACIA STRAIN and AFTER THE BURIAL for the North American "Monsters Of Mayhem II Tour" commencing mid-May.

Out Of Misery EP, 9 Volt 9V004 (1998). Mind Eraser / Habeeber / Madman / Nosferatu / Inside.

REJECT THE SICKNESS, 9 Volt 9V008 (1999). Amendment / Reject The Sickness / N2 / No Sympathy / Assed Out / Ashes Of Humanity (Regret) / Dark Waters / Heartless / Weather The Storm / The Century Fades.

DETERMINATION, Century Media 8066-2 (2001). Dawn Of The New Millennium / Nothing / Broken Promise / Divide My Destiny / Network / Wicked / Determination Part I / Determination Part II / Go Your Own Way / God's Last Gift / A Reflection Of The Past / Dead Words On Deaf Ears.

OUT OF MISERY, We Put Out 2 (2001). N2 / Mind Eraser / Habeeber / Madman / Nosferatu / Inside / No Sympathy (Live) / N2 (Live) / Reject The Sickness (Live) / Ammendment (Live) / Propaganda (Live).

GONE FOREVER, Century Media 8166-2 (2004). Force-Fed / Anti-Hero / Better Days / Precious Lie / Washed Out World / Living Nightmare / Soul Engraved / Gone Forever / Judge The Blood.

Better Days, Century Media 8150-2 (2004). Better Days / Allegiance / Wicked (Demo) / Reject The Sickness / Mind Eraser.

GONE FOREVER, Toy's Factory TFCK-87350 (2004) (Japanese release). Force-Fed / Anti-Hero / Better Days / Precious Lie / Washed Out World / Living Nightmare / Soul Engraved / Gone Forever / Judge The Blood / Allegiance / Mind Eraser.

GONE FOREVER (LIMITED TOUR EDITION), Century Media 8166-0 (2004). Force-Fed / Anti-Hero / Better Days / Precious Lie / Washed Out World / Living Nightmare / Soul Engraved / Gone Forever / Judge The Blood / Allegiance / Wicked (Demo) / Reject The Sickness / Mind Eraser / Anti-Hero (Video) / Better Days (Video).

IV: Constitution Of Treason (Two-Song Sampler), Century Media (2005) (Promotion release). Chains Of Humanity / The End Of The World (Edit).

IV: CONSTITUTION OF TREASON, Century Media 8266-2 (2005). The End Of The World / Chains Of Humanity / Into The Wasteland / The Lonely Dead / Divinity / Under This Flag / To The Fallen Hero / Welcome To The Apocalypse (Preamble) / Constitution Of Treason / Crucify Your Beliefs.

IV: CONSTITUTION OF TREASON, Toy's Factory TFCK-87397 (2005) (Japanese release). The End Of The World / Chains Of Humanity / Into The Wasteland / The Lonely Dead / Divinity / Under This Flag / To The Fallen Hero / Welcome To The Apocalypse (Preamble) / Constitution Of Treason / Crucify Your Beliefs / We Are No More.

To The Fallen Hero, Century Media (2006) (Limited tour single). To The Fallen Hero / The End Of The World / Antihero / Precious Life / To The Fallen Hero (Video) / The End Of The World (Video).

GOD FORSAKEN

OULU, FINLAND — *Mika Hankaniemi (vocals), Hannu Kujanen (guitar), Sami Ketola (bass), Teemu Hautaniemi (drums).*

Previously known as PUTRID, Finnish quartet GOD FORSAKEN suffered an almost immediate setback just after the debut 1992 release, 'Dismal Gleams Of Desolation', when vocalist Mika Hankaniemi fell victim to hearing problems in late 1993. The band was able to record a further demo with guitarist Hannu Kujanen handling most of the vocal duties prior to Hankaniemi's return. However, shortly after recording the demo drummer Juha Pohto quit to be temporarily replaced by MYTHOS member Teemu Hautaniemi. A European tour with ANATHEMA and PYOGENESIS followed with Hautaniemi until a new drummer, Jani Viskari, could be found. This liaison was short-lived however and in late 1994 original drummer Pohto rejoined.

Severe line-up struggles hit the band in early 1995 after the recording of 'The Tide Has Turned' with both bassist and drummer being sacked. Quick stand-ins were found in former colleague Hautaniemi and bassist Sami Ketola.

Teemu Hautaniemi subsequently worked with BARCODE and Stoners FIREWALL.

DISMAL GLEAMS OF DESOLATION, Adipocere AR 008 CD (1992). Loveless / Dismal Glease Of Desolation / Waiting For The Unknown / The End Of Eternity / Who Lives Will See / In My Darkness / Exhaling Timeless Tedium / There Were Seven Suns Shine.

THE TIDE HAS TURNED, Adipocere AR 025 CD (1995). November / Forsaking The World / Until Death Joins Us Again / Jupiter / Astral Voyager 69 / The Tide Has Turned / Nowhere To Be Found / Giving It All away / It's All The Same in The End / She Dies / Goodbye.

Tomorrow Is Never, Northern Darkness (2001). Silver Skulls / Mustang / Tomorrow Is Never.

Electric Releases, KTOK (2003). Devil May Care / The Pillar / Bloodhound.

GOD MACABRE

KARLSTAD, SWEDEN — *Per Boder (vocals), Ola Sjöberg (guitar), Jonas Ståhlhammar (guitar), Thomas Johansson (bass), Niclas Nilsson (drums).*

Previously operating as MACABRE END, this Karlstad act would rank among the forerunners of the Swedish Death Metal scene. As MACABRE END the group put out the 'Consumed by Darkness' single through Corpse Grinder Records. Adopting the GOD MACABRE title in 1990 the band signed to the German label Mangled Beyond Recognition Records for an album 'The Winterlong'.

Rhythm guitarist Ola Sjöberg would go on to join his fellow ex-MACABRE END colleague Per Boder in Stoners SNAKE MACHINE as bassist, a band which subsequently evolved into SPACE PROBE TAURUS with Sjöberg taking on lead vocal duties. Guitarist Jonas Ståhlhammar journeyed on through ABHOTH, UTUMNO and JEHOVA SUNRISE.

Relapse Records in the USA re-issued 'The Winterlong' in remastered form during 2002.

THE WINTERLONG, MBR MANGLED 6 (1995). Into Nowhere / Lost / Teardrops / Ashes Of Mourning Life / Spawn Of Flesh / Lamentation / In Grief.

GODDAMNED X

VIENNA, AUSTRIA — *Helmut Lechner (vocals / guitar), Manfred Kargl (guitar), Bernhard Schuberth (bass), Georg Hauser (drums).*

Vienna Death Metal combo forged in 2003. Leading up to the release of the 2004 EP 'Marching Through The Inferno' GODDAMNED X had gained a reputation on the Austrian live circuit supporting the likes of BEHEMOTH, IMPALED NAZARENE, BENEDICTION and PUNGENT STENCH. The band was founded in February of 2003 by guitarist Manfred Kargl upon his exit from Black Metal band ATENOUX. Initially the band included second guitarist Arek and bassist Bernhard Schuberth from Viennese Thrash/Death Metal band DAYS OF LOSS. Arek would soon depart but a drummer was found in Georg 'Schurl' Hauser of Linz outfit FESTERING FLESH. The band was rounded in October of 2003 out by singer Helmut 'Hoemal' Lechner, previously with Black Metal band BASTARD.

GODDAMNED X debut live show came in March of 2004 as opening act to FUROR DIABOLIS, IMPURITY and SUIDAKRA. In April the group entered the studio to craft the EP 'Marching Through The Inferno' but during these sessions Lechner quit his then other act AMPLIFIED to prioritise GODDAMNED X. Gigs throughout the Summer witnessed a performance at the 'Kaltenbach Open Air' festival and supports to URGEHAL, MASTER, THUNDERBOLT, ILLDISPOSED, HOLY MOSES and STERNENSTAUB amongst others.

In November of 2004 the group opened for DISMEMBER and DISSECTION.

Marching Through The Inferno, Goddamned X (2004). The Way Of All Flesh / Drugged To Extremes / Marching Through The Inferno / The Last Temptation / Burn The Heretic.

GODGORY

KARLSTAD, SWEDEN — *Matte Andersson (vocals), Stefan Olsson (guitar), Mikael Dahlqvist (guitar), Fredric Danielsson (bass), Thomas Heder (keyboards), Erik Andersson (drums).*

Karlstad melodic Death Metal outfit GODGORY are amongst a number of rising new groups to have been produced by EDGE OF SANITY's DAN SWANÖ, the man having worked on the GODGORY January 1996 debut 'Sea Of Dreams'. The band was created in 1992 bowing in with an April 1994 demo session which scored a contract offer from the German Invasion label. At this juncture the band comprised of vocalist Matte Andersson, guitarists Mikael Dahlqvist and Stefan Olsson, bassist Fredric Danielson and drummer Erik Andersson.

For the follow up album 'Shadow's Dance' the band brought onboard the keyboard talents of Thomas Heder and an additional guitarist Henrik Lindström. However, shortly after the album's release Matte Andersson and Erik Andersson would ask the remaining band members to leave.

GODGORY refugees Dahlqvist, Heder and Danielsson, allying themselves with vocalist Matthias Sandqvist and drummer Bruno Anderson, would forge Progressive Metal act WORD OF SILENCE. Olsson would rename himself Stefan Grundel.

The remaining duo contacted Nuclear Blast Records securing a placing on the 'Beauty In Darkness Volume 3' compilation with a new song 'Conspiracy Of Silence'. Minus the best part of a full band former members were recalled to aid in the studio. This pattern of utilizing Dahlqvist, Lindström, Heder and Danielsson was repeated for the 1999 'Resurrection' album.

Vocalist Matte Andersson also fronted a side project band GRAVE FLOWERS releasing the 2000 album 'Solace Me'. GODGORY contributed a version of THIN LIZZY's 'This Is The One' to a Nuclear Blast tribute album.

SEA OF DREAMS, Invasion IR 021 (1995). Intro / Sick To The Gore / Walking Among The Dead / Inside My Head / Sea Of Dreams / Surrounded By Dreams / Corporal Infection / Key To Eternity / In Silence Forever / Deathwish / Religious Fantasy.

SHADOW'S DANCE, Invasion IR 025 (1996). Abandon / Tear It Down / Rotten In Peace / Leavetaking / God's Punishment / Make You Pay / In The Ocean Sky / Shadow's Dance.

RESURRECTION, Nuclear Blast NB 371-2 (1999). Resurrection / Crimson Snow / Adultery / My Dead Dreams / Death In Black / Collector Of Tears / Waiting For Lunacy To Find Me / Princess Of The Dawn.

WAY BEYOND, Nuclear Blast (2000). Journey / Payback / Another Day / Tear It Down / Caressed By Flames / Farewell / Sea Of Dreams / Holy War.

GODKILLER

MONACO — Extreme Satanic Death Metal act GODKILLER hail, quite bizarrely from the millionaire's playground known as the the principality of Monaco.

Formed in 1994 the band, centred upon one Duke Satanaël (a.k.a. Benjamin Labarrere) previously operating between 1988 and 1994 as an Industrial Metal project THE PUPPET, released their debut demo 'Ad Majorem Satanae Gloriam' the same year. It was a tape GODKILLER swiftly capitalised on in February of the following year by offering a further tape entitled 'The Warlord'. The group since released albums for Avantgarde Records subsidiary Wounded Love.

GODKILLER concentrate on medieval paganistic themes and are so fundamentalist in their beliefs that mainman Duke Satanaël even denounces Anton La Vey's Church of Satan as being 'weak'!!

THE REBIRTH OF THE MIDDLE AGES, Wounded Love WLR010 (1996). Hymn For The Black Knights / From The Castle In The Fog / Path To The Unholy Frozen Empire / Blood On My Swordblade / The Neverending Reign Of The Black Knights.

IN GOD WE TRUST, Wounded Love (1997).

THE END OF THE WORLD, Wounded Love WLR014 (1998). The End Of The World / The Inner Pain / Down Under Ground / Following The Funeral Path / Day Of Suffering / Nothing Left But Silence / Still Alive / Waste Of Time / De Profundis.
DELIVERANCE, Wounded Love WLR021 (2000). Nothing Is Sacred / Wailing / At Dusk / When All Hope Is Gone / Dust To Dust / For My Days Are Vanity / Wisdom / I Am A Stranger In The Earth / Deliverance.

GODLESS

ONESTI, RUMANIA — *Vlad (vocals), Coca (vocals), Razvan (guitar), Adi-arm (guitar), Dan (bass), Stefan (keyboards), Andi (drums).*

Gothic, Death Doom act GODLESS has its roots in the preceding Doom outfit NERGAL. This band, hailing from Onesti, would undergo line up changes in the Summer of 1999 by incorporating female singer Coca and ex-G.D.F. guitarist Adi-arm to the already existing formation of singer Vlad, guitarist Razvan, bassist Dan, keyboard player Stefan and drummer Romeo. A rough demo was cut but not circulated. However, a second demo, entitled 'Vanity', would see exposure, backed by a promotional video for the track 'Desertaciune-Uselessness'.

The Summer of 2000 brought about a switch on the drum stool as Andi, from Blues Rockers SONIC, took over from Romeo. The band took on a new direction at this point, adopting a harder stance by dispensing with both female vocals and keyboards for the 2001 'Firemetal' sessions.

FIREMETAL, Godless (2001).
FORBIDDEN SKY, (2004).

GODLESS TRUTH

OLOMOUC, CZECH REPUBLIC — *Zdenel Simacek (vocals), Petr Svancara (guitar), Michael Rucil (guitar), Bizarro (drums).*

GODLESS TRUTH was founded in Olomouc during 1994 but only guitarist Petr Svancara survives from the original incarnation of the band. The group, which specializes in American style 'groove' Death Metal, debuted with a 1994 demo session 'Another Disease' followed by a 1996 tape 'Desperation'. However, over the next two years the group fractured to such a degree only Petr was left. The band's manager Zdenek Simacek assumed the role of lead vocalist as GODLESS TRUTH secured a deal with the French Deadsun label. Session drummer Olda was enrolled for recording of 1998's 'Desperation', basically the band's former cassette plus two new tracks.

In April of 1999 the band drafted Jirka and set about touring with American act LIVIDITY. Further dates in August of 1999 had GODLESS TRUTH ranked alongside PESSIMIST and FLESHLESS. The touring activity would continue into the year 2000 with shows in March billed with Belgian act PREJUDICE before summer gigs in union with FLESHLESS once again and Japan's VOMIT REMNANTS. To close the year GODLESS TRUTH hooked up with Californians DISGORGE on their subtly titled 'Kill The weak Europeans' tour.

In September of 2001, following a gig in Prague with DYING FETUS and CRYPTOPSY drummer George was asked to leave. His replacement, Bizarro (a.k.a. Paul) of DEMIMONDE was pulled in a few weeks later. The band featured a brace of tracks, 'Next Step' and 'Worthless Human Being' on the 2001 compilation 'MetalWorld Compilation I'.

The band would feature on the first Tokyo 'Deathfest' in April 2005 at the Shibuya Cyclone, joining a billing comprising ETERNAL RUIN, DISGORGE and Japanese bands VOMIT REMNANTS, DISCONFORMITY and WOUNDEEP.

DESPERATION, Deadsun (1998). Hatred / Lost In Yourself / Hope For The Life / Theres No God / Individual / Doors / Deceptive Beauty Part I / Deceptive Beauty Part II / Silentium / Dont Believe.
BURNING EXISTENCE, Deadsun (1999). Burning Existence / Indeed Painful / Disgusted / Camellot / No Reason To Die / Feebleminded / Gruesome Awakening / June 1994 / Fatal Preacher.
SELF REALIZATION, Shindy Productions (2001). Ninetyseven / Worthless Human Being / Disdain / He's Not / Constructing The Future / Next Step / Isolated Victim / Predetermined Disfiguration / I Take Your Life / Crooshpetz (Unwelcomed Bonus).

GOETIA

POLAND — Death- Black Metal band GOETIA, the product of one Nashat-Tchort, was founded in Warsaw during early 1996. From GOETIA's early days vocalist / bassist Nashat-Tchort struggled to maintain a stable line up. The band managed a rehearsal tape but suffered an ongoing series of membership shuffles. As such, Nashat-Tchort resolved to record the 'Enthroned Upon Dark Skies' utilising session musicians guitarist Grg and drummer Darek Z. This tape and CDR would be distributed commercially by Battle Hymn Productions.

GOETIA's next attempt, 'Wolfthorn', was originally intended to be a second cassette release but the improved quality of the recording and the underground status afforded 'Enthroned Upon Dark Skies' generated an offer for a full blown CD release through the British Mordgrimm label. Tape versions were issued through the Greek Demonian Productions concern. Nashat-Tchort employed Darek Z on drums once again with Paul Z aiding on guitar.

'Mare Tenebrarum', recorded during August of 2000, would be issued by Mordgrimm in late 2001. 'Mare Tenebrarum' included four tracks originally slated for an EP recorded by Nashat-Tchort, guitarist Grg and HATE drummer Piotr 'Mittloff' Kozieradzki, announced as 'Thy Infinite Darkness' but shelved. The main album sessions would be laid down by Nashat-Tchort, guitarist Grg, keyboard Cedamus, drummer Mittloff and sampler Robert K.

A third album, 'Hail Satan!' in 2001, saw release through the Greek ISO666 label and Apocalypse Productions in Poland. The Italian Black Blood concern would weigh in with a vinyl pressing. Mittloff, although firing up a further band venture in the Progressive Rock styled RIVERSIDE, would maintain his position on drums whilst J. M. took on the guitar role.

ENTHRONED UPON DARK SKIES, Battle Hymn Productions HYMN 001 (1998). Thy Kingdom Come (Intro) / Evil One / The Law (Intro) / Hawk-Headed God Enthroned / Dawn Of Blackness (Intro) / Sworn To The Abyss / Voice Of Void (Intro) / Black Magic / Thy Kingdom Came (Outro).
Wolfthorn EP, Mordgrimm GRIMM 10 (2000). Intro / Wolfthorn / Adoration / The Flame Of Lucifer / Let Their Dream Be Dead.
HAIL SATAN!, Iso666 IS11 (2001). Hail Satan (Antichristus Summus) / Communion Of Hatred / The Alchemy Of Sacred Evil (Christian Holocaust) / Vineyards: Thy Blood / Into The Cathedral Of Grief / Lust.
MARE TENEBRARUM, Mordgrimm GRIMM 11 (2001). Liturgy (Intro) / Thy Infinite Darkness / Hawk-Headed God Enthroned / Paths Of Seth / Blood Spell Of Goetia / The Blasphemy / Sphinx / Sworn To The Abyss / Ira (Wrath) / Mare Tenebrarum / Baptized In Suffering / Adoration.

GOJIRA

BAYONNE, FRANCE — *Joseph Duplantier (vocals / guitar), Christian Andreu (guitar), Jean-Michel Labadie (bass), Mario Duplantier (drums).*

Initially billed as GODZILLA the Bayonne based band released the 1996 'Victim' demo and second promotional session 'Possessed' during 1997. Under the revised GOJIRA title, actually the original Japanese Toho Studios title for Godzilla, the 'Saturate' demo session arrived in 1999, with 'Wisdom Comes' following in 2000. The group retired to a Belgian recording studio to cut their debut full-length album, the fully self-financed 'Terra Incognita'. Another solo enterprise, the EP 'Maciste All Inferno', arrived in 2003 whilst Boycott Records issued the single 'Indians' and album The Link. A follow up DVD and album, The Link Alive, followed in April 2004.

GOJIRA

GOJIRA featured the track 'Remembrance' on the 2005 Listenable Records French Metal compilation 'Revolution Calling'. The album 'From 'Mars To Sirius' debuted on the French national charts at number 44.

The band's appearance at the Gelsenkirchen 'Rock Hard' festival in Germany during June 2006 was taped and subsequently the track 'Clone' was included on the 'Rock Hard' magazine compilation album 'Rock Hard: Das Festival 2006'.

The band hooked up with OBITUARY and GOREROTTED for a run of UK dates in August 2006. The band united with Denmark's HATESPHERE for further UK October dates. GOJIRA teamed up with AMON AMARTH, SANCTITY and headliners CHILDREN OF BODOM for a North American tour in December. The band packaged up with LAMB OF GOD, TRIVIUM and MACHINE HEAD for a lengthy run of North American dates commencing on February 16th 2007 at the Palladium Ballroom in Dallas, Texas. In July 2007 it was revealed that Joseph Duplantier was forming up a side project band with the high profile SEPULTURA siblings Igor and Max Cavalera plus SOULFLY's Mark Rizzo entitled INFLIKTED. Duplantier guested on Finnish cello band APOCALYPTICA's 'Worlds Collide' album.

Saturate, (1999). On The B.O.T.A. / Clone / Saturate / Deliverance.

Wisdom Comes, (2000). Lizard Skin / Satan Is A Lawyer / Locked In A Syndrom / Fire Is Everything / Love / Wisdom Comes / Terra Incognita.

TERRA INCOGNITA, Independent (2001). Clone / Lizard Skin / Satan Is A Lawyer / 04 / Blow Me Away You (Niverse) / 5988 Trillions De Tonnes / Deliverance / Space Time / On The B.O.T.A. / Rise / Fire Is Everything / Love / 1990 Quatrillions De Tonnes / In The Forest.

Maciste All Inferno, (2003). Maciste 01 / Maciste 02 / Maciste 03.

THE LINK, Boycott (2003). The Link / Death Of Me / Connected / Remembrance / Torii / Indians / Embrace The World / Inward Movement / Over The Flows / Wisdom Comes / Data.

THE LINK ALIVE, Boycott (2004) Limited Edition 500 Copies Live CD. Connected / Remembrance / Death Of Me / Love / Embrace The World / Space Time / Terra Inc. / Indians / Wisdom Comes / Blow Me Away You (Niverse) / Lizard Skin / Inward Movement / The Link / Clone / In The Forest.

FROM MARS TO SIRIUS, Listenable POSH074 (2005). Ocean Planet / Backbone / From The Sky / Unicorn / Where Dragons Dwell / The Heaviest Matter Of The Universe / Flying Whales / In The Wilderness / World To Come / From Mars / To Sirius / Global Warming. Chart position: 44 FRANCE.

GOLEM

BERLIN, GERMANY — *Andreas Hilbert (vocals / guitar), Carsten May (guitar), Rainer Humeniuk (bass), Eric Krebs (drums).*

GOLEM, a Grind style Death Metal band out of Berlin, formed in July of 1989, at first as a trio comprising vocalist / guitarist Andreas Hilbert, bassist Max Grützmacher and drummer Michael Marschalk. The band issued the opening demo 'Visceral Scab' in January of 1991. Two tracks off the demo tape were subsequently released as the 'Visceral Scab' 7" vinyl EP on Cannibalized Serial Killer Records.

Tragically, GOLEM was hit with the death of two band members in separate car accidents during 1992, taking the life of Grützmacher, and 1993 with the demise of second guitarist Jens Malwitz. Having recorded a solitary demo, 'Recall The Day Of Incarnation' featuring Rico Spiller of FERMENTING INNARDS on bass and Ruben Wittchow of T.A.O.R. aiding on the drums, the group was signed by Invasion Records and released the debut album, 'Eternity: The Weeping Horizons' in 1996. These sessions, recorded at the famous Unisound Studios, saw a return to action for former drummer Michael Marschalk.

In 1996 Spiller decamped. For much of the following year GOLEM remained a duo but in 1998 guitarist Carsten May and bassist Rainer Humeniuk, both from Senftenbergs PROGERIA, enrolled. Signing to the Ars Metalli label the second album 'The 2nd Moon' was cut in July of that year, being released in January of 1999. Gigging across Germany would prove prolific but then progress was stalled as Marschalk exited once again. Momentum was resumed when Eric Krebs from Berlin Death-Thrashers SINNERS BLEED occupied the drum position in 2000.

Splitting from Ars Metalli GOLEM switched to the Grind Syndicate label to lay down their third opus during February of 2003. 'Dreamweaver' would see an April 2004 release.

Visceral Scab, (1992). Visceral Scab / Mutilated Organs.

ETERNITY: THE WEEPING HORIZONS, Invasion IR 021 (1996). Throne Of Confinement / Mental Force / In My Favorite Darkness / Dedication / Emotionally Astray / Incarnated Beast / Message From The Past / The Fall / Beyond The Future Skies.

THE 2ND MOON, Ars Metalli ARSCD 008 (1998). The Wanderers / Departure / The Shortening Of The Way / Heretics / Old Father Eternity / God Emperor / Honoured And Hated / Renewal / The 2nd Moon.

DREAMWEAVER, Nuclear Blast NB 1173-2 (2004). Al-Ghanor / Starchild / Remote Control / Breeder / Afterglow / Rose / Tomb / Diaspora / Faces / The Tower / Dreamweaver / Le Sacre Du Printemps.

GOLGOTHA

SPAIN — *Amon Lopez (vocals), Vicente J. Paya (guitar), Ivan Ramos (guitar), Toni Soler (bass), Jose Nunez (keyboards), Ruben Alarcon (drums).*

More of a project than an actual band, Spain's GOLGOTHA was the brainchild of UNBOUNDED TERROR's Vicente J. Paya, who felt he needed a vehicle for songs that he'd written that didn't fit the concept of his main outfit. The debut GOLGOTHA release, the 'Caves Of Mind' mini album, which included a cover version of BLACK SABBATH's 'Snowblind' and was recorded with a line up of Paya, Gustavo Garcialo, David Garcialo and vocalist Amon Lopez.

It received glowing reviews in Europe and this gave Paya the incentive to put something a little bit more permanent together, adding DEHUMANIZED members Ivan Ramos and Ruben Alarcon amongst others. The 1995 outing 'Melancholy' featured the female vocals of Carmen Jaime. Metal Age Productions released the 'New Life' album in 2006. The record included a cover version of EMERSON, LAKE & PALMER's 'Knife Edge'.

G

CAVES OF MIND, Repulse (1994). Lake Of Memories / Calachos Julisbol (Memories) / Embrace Me (Into The Cold Darkness) / Immaterial Deceptions / Snowblind.

MELANCHOLY, Repulse RPS011 (1995). Lonely / Lake Of Memories / Nothing / Raceflections / Lost / Immaterial Deceptions / Stillness / Virtualis Demens / Caves Of Mind.

The Way Of Confusion EP, Repulse (1997). The Way Of Confusion / Embrace Me (New version) / Snowblind.

ELEMENTAL CHAPTERS, Repulse (1998). Emotionless / Dark Tears / The Way Of Confusion / The Wood In Me / Lifetrappers / Answers / Save Me, Kiss Me / The Proverb / Internal Fight / Love Gun / Elemental Changes.

NEW LIFE, Metal Age Productions MAP 058 (2006). Forever Gone / Never, Never Again / Trapped In Two Worlds / Repentance / I Am Lost / Broken Emotions / Need You / New Life / Knife Edge / Lake Of Memories (2005 version).

GOMORRHA

GERMANY — *Timo Just (vocals), Jan Hempel (vocals / guitar), Robert Friedel (guitar), Renè Möller (bass), Florian Schairer (drums).*

Jena Death Metal acted created during 1995, originally billed as PAIN, as a quartet comprising vocalist / guitarist Jan Hempel, guitarist Robert Friedel, bass player Rene´ Möller with Florian Schairer on the drums. Taking on the GOMORRHA title the group debuted in February of 1997 with the demo 'Die Nacht Des Todes', this capitalised on with a second session 'Ready To Kill'. The self financed album 'Time of Apocalypse' followed in 1999. October 2002 'Autumnal Killing' shows found GOMORRHA sharing stages with Czech act FLESHLESS and PANDEMIA. The band toured Germany in April of 2003 partnered with FLESHLESS once more and Colombians PURULENT billed as the 'Killing Easter' tour.

TIME OF APOCALYPSE, Independent (1999). Bloody Destiny / Time Of Apocalypse / Forever Dead / Depression / Fuckin Like An Animal / Pain In Head / Die Nacht Des Todes / Never Again.

SEXUAL PERVERSITY BY AUTOPSY, Nice To Eat You (2003). Sexual Perversity By Autopsy / That's Me Gerontophily / Eating Dead Flesh Of A Grannycunt / Cry Of Defloration / Pedophilistic Execution / Animal Peace / Love, Peace And Excrements / Fuck Bizarre / Perverse Bakerman / Fatal Aggression / Necrophagous Serial Killer / The Price Is Your Skin / The Milwaukee Monster.

GOOSEFLESH

TROLLHÄTTAN, SWEDEN — *Kristian Lampila (vocals / guitar), Tommy Scalisi Svensson (guitar), Robert Hakemo (bass), Lars Berger (drums).*

Trollhättan based Crossover Metal band forged by RAT SALAD bassist Micael Larsson and guitarist Tommy Scalisi Svensson as a side project to their priority act in 1995. Replacing Larsson with Robert Hakemo, GOOSEFLESH released the demos 'The Wraith' and 'Glow' in 1996 and 'Welcome To The Suffer Age' in 1997. These latter recordings would subsequently see commercial release as an EP issued through the Spanish Goldtrack label. The band submitted their rendition of 'Slave New World' to the SEPULTURA tribute album "Sepultural Feast'. The full length 'Chemical Garden' album was recorded originally for the German High Gain label but the closure of this label necessitated the securing of fresh deals. The record finally surfaced in Europe through Digital Dimension and in Japan via Dolphin Entertainment.

GOOSEFLESH folded in 2001 with vocalist Kristian Lampila and bassist Robert Hakemo founding MINDSNARE. Svensson and drummer Lars Berger founded ELECTRIC EARTH. Ex-bassist Micael Larsson would be back on the circuit with BLACK SABBATH tribute band SABBRA CADABRA.

Hakemo joined GARDENIAN in early 2003. In early 2004 the bassist was part of a band collaboration entitled KEROZENE, a union between guitarist Niclas Engelin, of SARCAZM, PASSENGER, GARDENIAN and IN FLAMES repute, drummer Patrik J. Sten, also of PASSENGER and an ex-TRANSPORT LEAGUE member, along with vocalist Mikael Skager. In August 2006 Robert Hakemo joined M.A.N.

Welcome To Suffer Age, Goldtrack (1998). Suffer Age / Blinded / Killing Stone / Seeds Of Terror / Fine Tuned War Machine.

CHEMICAL GARDEN, High Gain 0055332HGR (1999). Burning Soul / Godbreed / Cut That Never Heals / Thin Skinned Jesus / Wraith / The Syndicate / Art Of Treachery / Controller / Sore Throat / Voices / Denial / Absence.

GORATORY

FRAMINGHAM, MA, USA — *Adam Mason (vocals), Alan Grassman (guitar), Zach Pappa (bass), Darren Cesca (drums).*

Framingham, Massachusetts gore Metal. GORATORY's debut album cover infamously portrayed a photograph of a disemboweled rape victim. Created in May of 2000 by erstwhile COMPOST PILE musicians vocalist / bassist Dana Santello and drummer Jay. Later additions included another ex-COMPOST PILE man Max Lavelle on bass, as Dana switched to guitar, and vocalist Nick, the latter holding scene associations with BOTULISM, FUCKFEST, LECHEROUS and VINCULUM TERMINATII. Parallel to GORATORY, guitarist Alan Grassman, Max, and singer Adam Mason were all operational with TWISTED SACRIFICE.

At the time of recording the 2001 'Sexual Intercorpse' album GORATORY comprised a six piece line-up of vocalists Adam Mason and Joe Peck, guitarists Dana Santello and Alan Grassman, bass player Max Lavelle and drummer Jay Blaisdell. GORATORY, trimming down to a quartet of Mason, Grassman, Lavelle and Blaisdell, signed to the Japanese Amputated Vein label during 2002 for recording of the 'Orgasm Induced Diarrhea' album. Amputated Vein would also re-issue the debut complete with extra tracks.

The 2003 7" single 'Your Mutha's A Lazy-Eyed Chow-Bearing Slut But I Fucked Her Anyways' on Undecent Records witnessed an all new GORATORY line-up seeing the introduction of bassist Zach Pappas and the VIRULENCE and PILLORY credited Darren Cesca on drums. This band roster also cut the 2004 album 'Rice On Suede'.

GORATORY signed with UK based Grindethic Records in early 2006. Adam Mason temporarily joined the ranks of New York's MUCOPUS for European touring in September 2006. Darren Cesca joined ARSIS in January 2007. Alan Glassman joined DESPISED ICON in March.

SEXUAL INTERCORPSE, (2001). Pus Filled Maggots / Retrograde Defecation / Mutilate And Modify / Into The Grinding Machine / Wrestling With Feces / Infant Skin Suitcase / Fisting The Elderly.

ORGASM INDUCED DIARRHEA, Amputated Vein AVR002 (2002). George Clinton And The Nine Year Old Gutter Slut / Donkey Punch / Total Eclipse Of The Fart / Severed Fuck Stump / The Wrath Of Piper's Pit / Kiz Nizel Mi Dills Nufus / Preschool Prowler / Pig Fucker / Golden Shower Gladiators / Cream Of Fetus / Cottagecheesecum.

Your Mutha's A Lazy-Eyed Chow-Bearing Slut But I Fucked Her Anyways, Undecent (2003). Your Mutha's A Lazy-Eyed Chow-Bearing Slut But I Fucked Her Anyways / Cottagecheesecunt.

RICE ON SUEDE, Amputated Vein (2004). Anally Injected Death Sperm / Rice On Suede / 8 Seconds Of Fury / Headie Mung Festizzeo / Whose Spine Is It Anyway / Fuckhole / Hang Em' And Bang Em' / Your Mutha's A Lazy-Eyed Chow Bearing Slut But I Fucked Her Anyways / Mutilate Remodified.

GORE

BRAZIL — *Robot (vocals / bass), Lizandro (guitar), Rubem Zachis (drums).*

Rio De Janeiro Grind act GORE are among the very sickest of the sick. The band think nothing of using the most depraved of photographic images for record sleeves. A burst of gut wrenching demo sessions heralded GORE's arrival opening with the 1992 tape 'Psychonecropsypatholic', 1993's 'Open Doors To The Morgue' and 1994's 'To A Life Consumed By Decay'.

The band took a mere 3 days to record their debut 1996 album 'Consumed By Slow Decay'. In 2000 GORE featured tracks on the 'Six Ways To The Holocaust' compilation album and shared a split 7" single with WTN for Mexican label American

Line Productions. A split album with LAST DAYS OF HUMANITY also emerged.

2001 found the release of another shared album, this time with NEURO-VISCERAL EXHUMATION and the full length 'Ungrotesque'. Ex-drummer Rubem 'Corpse Fucker' Zachis forged CATIVEIRO for a 2002 split album 'Assembly Of The Most Ferocious'.

CONSUMED BY SLOW DECAY, Lofty Storm LSR001 (1995). Fetus Jejuni / Incomplete Evacuation / Hysterical Extraction Of Facial Tissue / Intestinal Pestilence / Dissimulated Incabation And Maximum Infection / Phlatulent Manifestation Of Alcaligenes Feacalis / Exposed Guts / Syndrome Of Intensive Regurgitation / Attenuated Mutant Worms / Inquisitive Corporal Recremation / Unfinished Radiation / Frenetic Fetishchism For Human Pieces In Decomposition / Human Limbs Mutilated / Cycle Of Suffocation / Cannibal Zoophilism With Extreme Sexual Aberration / Consummated Cancer.

GORE BEYOND NECROPSY

KANAGAWA, JAPAN — *Mamoru (vocals), Kiyonobu (guitar), Akinobu (bass), Hironori (noise), Hayato (drums).*

Kanagawa Grind act GORE BEYOND NECROPSY set the scene with the disturbing 1992 demo 'I Recommend You Amputation'. First product was the 7" EP 'This Is An EP You Want' in 1993 followed by a 1994 live tape. Their shared album with notorious Electro-Anarchists MERZBOW 'Rectal Anarchy' was far from subtle, the album cover graced by an enlarged anus and the song content comprising of warped cover versions. In 1997 GORE BEYOND NECROPSY toured Australia with Victoria's WARSORE and returned the compliment by arranging Japanese dates for WARSORE and issuing a split 7" single.

The band managed to cram over 50 tracks into just under 25 minutes on their 1999 album 'Noise A Go Go'. A split single with Swedish Grindsters ARSEDESTROYER arrived in 2000 and the pair toured Japan the same year.

This Is An EP You Want, M.M.I. (1993). A Dozen Of ... / Six Dimensional Perversion / Floating Flesh / Bizarre Bazaar / A.N.U.S.
Split, Blurred (1995) (Split single with SENSELESS APOCALYPSE).
Split, Mangrove (1995) (Split single with MERZBOW).
Faecal Noise Holocaust EP, Cyillusions (1995).
Split, (1997) (Split single with DISGORGE).
Split, Mink (1997) (Split single with MINCH).
Split, Sterilized Decay (1998) (Split single with WARSORE).
RECTAL ANARCHY, Relapse (1998) (Split album with MERZBOW). Punks Not Dead / Chaos Disorder / Pretty Vacant Panty / Love Me / The Sunlight Path / Between Nothingness and Eternity / Split Crotch Disorder / Snatch Punk / Pussy Poking Disorder Chaos / In Tight Disorder / Tits 4 Chaos / Finger Friggin in Grind / Melon & Mounds / There Way All the Mosh / Say Ah! / That Takes Balls / Ski Meat Funky / Jeff Stryker Super Star / Mods Action Ultra-Shit / Ten Groovy Wheel Drive / A Horse Named / Heritage Banner Dictate Passion Hate / Force Dead Face Apathy Under the Rectal Anarchy / London Calling Chaos Damnation Action Violent / Parracide Blaze of Socialized / Agent Orange Country War Feast / Release from Agony State of Procession / Morbid Shit Confusion Anarchy Violent / Manta Size Shit Body Pollution Hate / Up Her Shit Emotion Disregarded / He Can Fly Them Against Cruel No Harm Shit.
Sounds Like Shit EP, Blurred (1998).
NOISE A GO GO, Relapse (1999). Intro / Faecal Gor Gore Attack / Chain Of Torture / Horrendous Nazi Infection / Gore Gore Warscars / Mild Shit Taste / Brainwashed Media Slave / Garbage In The Sewage / Sulfuric Acid Dream / Poultry Within / Kill The Cock Rock Greedy Hog / Intro / Dead Dog Idolization / Fartstorm / Deaf, Dumb, Blind / Filth Sounds Of Hatred / Cock Rock Asshole / Gurgling Spiral Repulsion / Global Tumor / Negative Thoughts Whirling Around / Born Deformed / Raping The Arse / Cock Rock Roach / Trash Of The Hemorrhoids / Mind Plague / Puke Yourself / The Worst Shit In The World / Boiling Detestation / Noise A Go Go! / Intro / Arsebleed / Horrendously Analdrilled / From The Cradle To The Grave / Dead Life Goes On / Subliminal State Control / Cock Rock Incineration / Pain To Be Slain / Shittier Than Shit / Instant Necropsy / Power Of Media Arrogant Mass Control / Uncleanly Devoured Visions / It's The Gore Gore Goreality / Intro / Huma BBQ Burning Hell / Stench Of Carnage ... / Corporate Ghouls / Driller Killer From Outer Space / Disease Bondage / The End Of Life / Intro / Bad Taste Grotesqueen / Divine's Dead / Grudge / Harshit Shock / Chaos, Disorder & Confusion / Steaming, Bubbling Cadaverous Odor / Shitgobbling Hate Generation / Outro.
GO FILTH GO, Infernal (1999).
Split, Devour (2000) (Split single with ARSEDESTROYER).

GOREFEST

HOLLAND — *Jan Chris De Koeyer (vocals / bass), Frank Haarthorn (guitar), Alex Van Schiak (guitar), Marc Hoogedoorn (drums).*

Highly influential Death Metal act on the Dutch scene, GOREFEST emerged in late 1989 with the above listed line-up and swiftly debuted with the 'Tangled In Gore' demo recorded in December 1989, which led to a great deal of record company interest. A further demo, titled 'Horrors In A Retarded Mind', secured a support tour in Belgium and Holland to CARCASS and a deal with Foundation 2000 Records. Live tracks from the CARCASS tour were subsequently included on the D.F.S.A. compilation 'Where Is Your God Now?'.

Although GOREFEST parted company with guitarist Alex Van Scaik in 1990 they toured Europe with REVENANT before suffering another departure, this time losing the services of drummer Mark Hoogedorn. However, following the release of the debut album, 'Mindloss', GOREFEST complemented their line-up by adding former AGGRESSOR and ELEGY drummer Ed Warby and guitarist Boudewyn Bonebakker. The group toured as support to DEICIDE in Europe in 1992 before a successful American tour opening for DEATH ensued.

1994's 'Fear' EP was intended to include a cover version of KRAFTWERK's 'Autobahn', but the famed German Electro band refused permission for its use. However, a demo version of the track did appear on a Nuclear Blast compilation. After a break of nearly two years a brand new studio effort 'Soul Survivor' surfaced through the major German independent label Nuclear Blast in 1996. GOREFEST performed at the Dynamo festival the same year.

In early 1998 the group, promoting 'Chapter 13' for fresh label SPV, scored a major coup as the support band for JUDAS PRIEST's comeback 'Jugulator' tour that was set to open in Europe during March. Strangely, GOREFEST folded toward the end of 1998.

News emerged in 2002 of erstwhile GOREFEST members activities. Jan-Chris De Koeijer, in union with Iljan Mol and Erwin Polderman of ORPHANAGE created the Electro-Dance act COLDPOP CULTURE. Frank Harthoorn re-surfaced in Stoner band THE SPEED KINGS. By October of 2004 it transpired that GOREFEST had reformed.

Ed Warby acted as stand in for a hospitalised André Borgman of AFTER FOREVER for their 11th February show at the Heineken Music Hall in Amsterdam. GOREFEST signed to Nuclear Blast Records in March. The label promptly announced a re-issue of the band's back catalogue, putting out 'Mindloss' with extra demo tracks, combining 'False' and 'Erase' along with extra demos and pairing 'Soul Survivor' with 'Chapter 13' and unreleased rarities. GOREFEST entered Excess studio in Rotterdam with engineer Hans Pieters in July to record their fifth studio album. In December leading Spanish Death Metal band AVULSED covered 'Mental Misery' on their EP 'Reanimations'.

GOREFEST announced a reformation for 2005, re-signing with Nuclear Blast Records to issue the 'La Muerte' album in October. To open 2006 the band hooked up with RESURRECTURIS, MASTER and LUNA FIELD for 'The Glorious Dead: European Exorcism' European tour set to commence 16th February in Holland. However, in late January the band pulled the entire tour. GOREFEST was then announced as tour support to BOLT THROWER's April European jaunt, but once again saw dates pulled when the headline act opted for other bands to partner with. Live work planned in December across Europe was to see the band hooking up with DARZAMAT, BELPHEGOR, TRAIL OF TEARS, PROSTITUTE DISFIGUREMENT and

MADDER MORTEM for the 'X-Mas' festivals set to commence December 8th at the Berlin K17 venue. However, this entire trek was cancelled just days beforehand.

In January 2007 it would be learned that Ed Warby had joined forces with THANATOS guitarists Stephan Gebédi and Paul Baayens, former PESTILENCE and ASPHYX singer Martin Van Drunen and former HOUWITSER bass player Theo van Eekelen in a new band unit dubbed HAIL OF BULLETS. That same month GOREFEST themselves demoed up new album material and entered the studio in March to craft a fresh album. Ed Warby also joined Swedish band DEMIURG in March.

MINDLOSS, Foundation 2000 (1990). Intro / Mental Misery / Putrid Stench Of Human Remains / Foetal Carnage / Tangled In Gore / Confessions Of A Serial Killer / Horrors In A Retarded Mind / Loss Of Flesh / Decomposed / Gorefest.

Live Misery, Cenotaph (1991). Live Misery.

THE EINDHOVEN INSANITY- LIVE AT THE DYNAMO, Nuclear Blast NB091-2 (1993). The Glorious Dead / State Of Mind / Get A Life / Mental Misery / From Ignorance To Oblivion / Reality- When You Die / The Mass Insanity / Confessions Of A Serial Killer / Eindhoven Roar.

FALSE, Nuclear Blast NB069 (1993). The Glorious Dead / State Of Mind / Reality- When You Die / Get A Life / False / Second Face / Infamous Existence / From Ignorance To Oblivion / The Mass Insanity.

Fear, Nuclear Blast NB122 (1994). Fear / Raven / Horrors '94 / Fear (Live).

ERASE, Nuclear Blast NB110 (1994). Low / Erase / I Walk My Way / Fear / Seeds Of Hate / Peace Of Paper / Goddess In Black / To Hell And Back.

SOUL SURVIVOR, Nuclear Blast NB 143-2 (1996). Freedom / Forty Shades / River / Electric Poet / Soul Survivor / Blood Is Thick / Dogday / Demon Seed / Chameleon / Dragonman.

Freedom (Single Edit), Nuclear Blast (1996). Freedom (Single Edit) / Tired Moon / Goddess In Black (Orchestral Version) / Freedom (Album Version).

CHAPTER 13, SPV Steamhammer 085-18862 P (1998). Chapter Thirteen / Broken Wing / Nothingness / Smile / The Idiot / Repentance / Bordello / F.S. 2000 / All Is Well / Unsung / Super Reality / Serve The Masses.

LA MUERTE, Nuclear Blast NB 1494-2 (2005). For The Masses / When The Dead Walk The Earth / You Could Make Me Kill / Malicious Intent / Rogue State / The Call / Of Death And Chaos / Exorcism / Man To Fall / The New Gods / 'till Fingers Bleed / La Muerte.

GORELORD

NORWAY — A solo Death Metal venture from guitarist Frediablo, known for his other activities in DERIDE. The debut 'Force Fed On Human Flesh', produced by Killjoy of NECROPHAGIA and RAVENOUS and issued on the man's Baphomet label, found BLOODTHORN drummer Jehmod assisting in the studio.

Frediablo would also feature significantly in Killjoy's WURDULAK Black Metal endeavour 'Ceremony In Flames'. Toward the close of 2001 Frediablo made an opening for a further side venture in union with DERIDE's Ole Walanet and the IMMORTAL pairing of Horgh and Iscariah. This as yet unnamed alliance bowing in with the demo session 'Ghouls Of Grandeur'.

Recording in early 2002 had Frediablo piecing together a second GORELORD opus 'Zombie Suicide Part 666'. A further project of Frediablo also emerged in 2004, initially billed as SEVEN GATES OF HELL, but then switched to CHAMBER OF STRENGTH. Recording at Godfed Studios in Norway this solo venture would be self described as "an intense hybrid of Death, Hardcore and modern Metal". Meantime, Frediablo's Black Metal project HEMNUR published the 'Ravnsvart' demo in October, also crafting a debut album 'Untamed Norwegian Black Metal' for early 2005 issue through Baphomet Records. The guitarist also readied a new GRIMFIST recording and a third GORELORD album, 'Norwegian Chainsaw Massacre', due in May 2005 via Coffin Records. That August, Frediablo relinquished his associations with NECROPHAGIA, GORELORD, WURDULAK and CHAMBER OF STRENGTH to prioritise GRIMFIST. 'Norwegian Chainsaw Massacre' finally arrived, a year late, in April 2006.

FORCE FED ON HUMAN FLESH, Baphomet S8TN 6602 (2001). Dismembered Virgin Limbs / Crushed Skull On Christian Shoulders / Crucified Goat Drenched In Blasphemic Blood / Force Fed On Human Flesh / Necrophilic Orgy In Entrails & Cum / Chainsaw Ripping Skin / Alive When Fucking The Dead / Maggots Impaled / Hell's Kitchen.

ZOMBIE SUICIDE PART 666, Season Of Mist SOM 067 (2002). The Stench Of Flesh Decomposing / Screams Choked To Silence / Dreams Of The Macabre / Horror, Gore & Unreligion / Outback / Shrieks Of The Undead / Cunfucked Face Of Death / Four Ways To Heaven, One Way To Hell / I Am Master Here / Alive When Fucking The Dead (Demo) / Necrophiliac Orgy In entrails & Cum (Demo).

NORWEGIAN CHAINSAW MASSACRE, Coffin (2006). Outback Part II / Dying Or Dreaming / All Hail The Gods Of Horror / Flesh To Feed / Man Of Shit / Deathbreed / Hammered / The Rising Of The Undead / Sprayed With Gasoline / The Glorification Of Violence / The Final Cut.

GOREMENT

NYKÖPING, SWEDEN — *Jimmy Karlsson (vocals), Patrik Fernlund (guitar), Daniel Eriksson (guitar), Nicklas Lilja (bass), Mattias Berglund (drums).*

Nyköping Death Metal combo created in 1990. Original singer Mikael Bergström would be superseded by Jimmy Karlsson. GOREMENT's debut would be with the 1991 demo cassette 'Obsequies', followed up that same April by the 'Human Relic' session. In November the After World label issued the 'Obsequies' material as a 7" single. Switching to the notorious Poserslaughter Records GOREMENT put out the 1992 single 'Into Shadows'.

Crypta Records took the band on for the solitary album 'The Ending Quest'. An August 2004 compilation, entitled 'Darkness Of The Dead' and issued by Necroharmonic, comprised the album alongside the 'Human Relic' demo, the 'Obsequies' and 'Into Shadows' singles plus an unreleased 1995 track.

The erstwhile GOREMENT trio of guitarists Patrik Fernlund and Daniel Eriksson with bassist Nicklas Lilja subsequently founded the Death Doom outfit PIPERS DAWN. This band released the 1994 demo 'Moonclad' prior to folding.

Obsequies, After World AWR005 (1991). Intro / Process Of Cent / Gruesome Modification Of Form / Obsequies Of Mankind.

Into Shadows, Poserslaughter (1992). Into Shadows / The Memorial.

THE ENDING QUEST, Crypta DA 8207-2 (1994). My Ending Quest / Vale Of Tears / Human Relic / The Memorial / The Lost Breed / Silent Hymn (For The Dead) / Sea Of Silence / Obsequies Of Mankind / Darkness Of The Dead / Into Shadows.

DARKNESS OF THE DEAD, Necroharmonic Productions (2004). My Ending Quest / Vale Of Tears / Human Relic / The Memorial / The Lost Breed / Silent Hymn (For The Dead) / Sea Of Silence / Obsequies Of Mankind / Darkness Of The Dead / Into Shadows / Intro—Darkness Of The Dead / Human Relic / Moulder Within / Intro—Process Of Cent / Gruesome Modification Of Form / Obsequies Of Mankind / The Memorial / Into Shadows / Profound Harmony.

GOREROTTED

LONDON, UK — *Mr. Gore (vocals), Baby Slice (vocals), Dick Splash (guitar), Fluffy (guitar), Mr. Smith (bass), Rushy (drums).*

An infamous London Gore Metal act. GOREROTTED lost vocalist Graham 'Nutty Strangeways' Hodis in late 1999. Ex-BEYOND FEAR bassist Steve Smith, also of 7TH CHILD, also operates a side project entitled INFECTED DISARRAY. This new unit would include GOREROTTED drummer John Insane (also of ZARATHUSTRA and BRUTAL INSANITY), guitarist Lal, second guitarist Paul of BRAINCHOKE and SUFFERING and fronted by former ZARATHUSTRA singer Eddie.

Signing to the Metal Blade label GOREROTTED conjured up a sophomore album 'Only Tools And Corpses' for October 2003 release. The band would hit the road in Europe the following month, supporting PUNGENT STENCH. Back out on tour in April of 2004 the band partnered with SANATORIUM, AMPUTATED and Mexican act DISGORGE for a short burst of UK dates. This activity would be backed up by the filming of an

GOREROTTED

GORETRADE

extreme, zombie orientated, promotional video for the 'Only Tools And Corpses' album's title track directed by Adam Powell.

GOREROTTED announced they had lost the services of singer and founder member Mr. Gore in August. The band had just previously performed at the 'Kaltenbach Open Air' festival in Austria minus Mr. Gore, the singer detained in the UK due to personal reasons. Touring across Europe was maintained, the group hooking up with VOMITORY for gigs in August, including the German festivals 'Party.San Open Air' and 'Summer Breeze', and with INHUME during December.

GOREROTTED entered Aexxys-Art Studio in Munich, Germany during February 2005 to begin recording third album 'A New Dawn For The Dead'. September European dates had GOREROTTED partnered with Poland's DECAPITATED and Dutch Deathsters DETONATION. GOREROTTED supported UK tours for OBITUARY in June 2006, alongside GOJIRA, and then hooked up with CRYPTOPSY, SHE SAID DESTROY and SYLOSIS in August. This trek included a one off support to CELTIC FROST in London.

Throughout March 2007 the band toured Europe forming up the "A Splatterday Night Part Two" dates with PUNGENT STENCH and GRIMNESS 69 closing with a run of Spanish shows. The band's US debut came at the Maryland Deathfest in Baltimore during May.

Her Gash I Did Slash EP, (1999). Limb From Limb / Her Gash I Did Slash / Stab Me Til I Cum / Carrion Smelling.
MUTILATED IN MINUTES, Dead Again (2001). Hack Sore / Bed 'Em, Behead 'Em / Stab Me Till I Cum / Cut, Gut, Beaten, Eaten / Corpse Fucking Art / Put Your Bits In A Concrete Mix / Mutilated In Minutes, Severed In Seconds / Gagged, Shagged, Bodybagged / Severed, Sawn And Sold As Porn.
ONLY TOOLS AND CORPSES, Metal Blade (2003). Zombie Graveyard Rape Bonanza / Hacked In The Back And Dumped In A Sack / Fuck Your Ass With Broken Glass / Only Tools And Corpses / Her Gash I Did Slash / Can't Fit Her Limbs In The Fridge / Village People Of The Damned / Masticated By The Spasticated / To Catch A Killer.
A NEW DAWN OF THE DEAD, Metal Blade (2005). .... And Everything Went Black / Pain As A Prelude To Death / Nervous Gibbering Wreck / Adding Insult To Injury / Fable Of Filth / Dead Drunk / A Very Grave Business / Horrorday In Haiti / Selection And Dissection Of Parts For Resurrection / I Am The Black Wizard.

GORESOAKED

HELSINKI, FINLAND — *Patrik Nuorteva (vocals), Konsta Kaikkonen (guitar), Pekka Koivisto (guitar), Yrjö Gävert (bass), Perttu Saarsalmi (drums).*

Death Metal band GORESOAKED, fronted by Patrik "Pate" Nuorteva and initially including female bassist Siiri Korhonen of MENSURA, released the demos 'Genital Butchery', produced by Glen Loit at Heltec Studios in April 2004, and 'Death Metal Ejaculation', laid down at Dauntless Studio by Santeri Salmi in September 2005. New bassist Yrjö Gävert, of NORTHWORLD, was introduced after this second release.

Singer Patrik Nuorteva is also active with LANA and MENSURA, the latter act alongside GORESOAKED band mate drummer Perttu Saarsalmi. Guitarist Konsta Kaikkonen is also a member of NORTHWORLD whilst second guitar player Pekka Koivisto has an affiliation with THY LEGACY.

Genital Butchery, (2004). Genital Dismembering / Fucked With An Axe 'Til Death.
Death Metal Ejaculation, Goresoaked (2005). Postmortal Haemorrhoids / Teaching A Retard To Play / Coprourinal Eucharistia / Rectal Goatfistfucking.

GORETRADE

DOSQUEBRADAS, COLOMBIA — *Cesar Vera (vocals / guitar), Mauricio (guitar), Nestor (bass), Carlos (drums).*

In famous Dosquebradas, Risaralda based gore-mongers GORETRADE were established during early 1999 by vocalist / guitarist Cesar Vera and drummer Anderson Montoya, later adding Hernan "Corpse" and James Correa. Live work ensued but GORETRADE then shifted shape, inducting Andres Garcia, of INTERNAL SUFFERING, on bass and Alex Avalo on guitar. In this formation the group recorded the album 'Ritual Of Flesh' in New York. Split releases also saw issue, GORETRADE sharing vinyl with CARNAL from Colombia, on Supreme Musick, and CORPSEFUCKING ART from Italy, 'Zombiecronomicon'.

Next album 'Perception Of Hate', released through From Beyond Productions in November 2006, witnessed a line-up of Cesar Vera, guitarist Mauricio, WASTELAND bassist David with Carlos "Cacha" on drums. Following recording David was replaced by Nestor.

ZOMBIECRONOMICON, Coagulated (2001) (Split album with CORPSEFUCKING ART). Corpsex (CORPSEFUCKING ART) / Four On A Meathook (CORPSEFUCKING ART) / Homicidal Chainsaw Butchery (CORPSEFUCKING ART) / Addicted To Murder (CORPSEFUCKING ART) / Bloodcraving (CORPSEFUCKING ART) / Postmortem Incision (GORETRADE) / Serial Killer (GORETRADE) / The Horror Of Gore (GORETRADE) / Carnal Access (GORETRADE) / Killing Virgin Women (GORETRADE).
GORETRADE / CARNAL, Supreme Musick (2001) (Split album with CARNAL). Unholy Masturbation (GORETRADE) / Cannibal Instinct (GORETRADE) / Human Butchery (GORETRADE) / Laceration

(GORETRADE) / Blasphemous Feelings (CARNAL) / Vampire's Night (CARNAL) / The Seventh Demon (CARNAL) / Holy Decay (CARNAL).
RITUAL OF FLESH, From Beyond Productions FBP-010 (2003). Piercing Her Throat / Ritual Of flesh / Ambushing The Ignorance / Bloodstained Altars / Bloody Beings / Hell's Dominion Butchery / ... And Your Blood Will Be Lust / Born Of A Murderer / Postmortem Incision / Laceration.
Revenge Shall Be Mine Promo 2006, (2006) (Promotion release). Revenge Shall Be Mine.
PERCEPTION OF HATE, From Beyond Productions FBP-058 (2006). Impregnate With Deceit / Perception Of Hate / Drifting Towards Extinction / Revenge Shall Be Mine / Someone To Kill!!! / Righteous Retribution / Rising From Defeat / Derogate / Ritual Of Flesh (2006 version).

GOREZONE

OLDENBURG, GERMANY — *Torben Waleczek (vocals), Thilo Neidhöfer (guitar), Markus Krügel (guitar), Torsten Nieland (bass), Markus Strehlau (drums).*

GOREZONE was previously active on the Oldenburg Death Metal circuit under an earlier guise of WOLFSHADE. With this name the group issued the 1997 demo 'Carry The Twin' and its 1999 follow up 'Eats The World Alive!'. In the summer of 2000 bassist Torsten Nieland, whilst maintaining his membership of both GOREZONE and his other band ACT OF FATE, joined Speed Metal band GALLERY OF DARKNESS. GOREZONE side projects include EBOLA BEACH PARTY, an alliance of vocalist Torsten Waleczek and guitarist Markus Krügel with Axel Rolfs from DEAMONS EMBRACE and the erstwhile ACT OF FATE and THE SEVENTH SEAL man Alexander Oberdick.

With Sebastian Bösche suffering an accident, ex-MEASLY CORPSE man Markus Strehlau took over on drums.

ERASE THE SCUM, Independent (2001). Open Fire / Erase The Scum / Gorezone / Total Absorbtion / Human Demise / Spasmodical / Anal Service / Murder/Death/Kill / Tool Time.

GORGASM

CHICAGO, IL, USA — *Tom Tangalos (vocals / guitar), Tom Leski (vocals / guitar), Russ Powell (vocals / bass), Derek Hoffman (drums).*

A notorious name in Death Metal circles fronted by former DISINTER man Tom Tangelos. Chicago's GORGASM's repute is well justified, their particular brand of brutally harsh Metal inspiring many. The band was created out of the disintegration of CREMATORIUM during 1994 with an inaugural demo being cut in 1996 before the arrival of powerhouse drummer Derek Hoffman. Tangalos would take time out during 1998 to act as guest lead vocalist foe AD INFINITUM, appearing on their 'Dies Irae' demo.

Hoffman would decamp to found the equally illustrious INCESTUOUS in alliance with ex-DISGORGE vocalist Matti Way, former SMEGMA and CUMCHRIST guitarist Danny Louise ('Wrench') and Mike Dooley from CORPSE VOMIT on bass recording the 'Brass Knuckle Abortion' album. INCESTUOUS would in turn, following Hoffman's departure and his replacement by Ricky Myers of DISGORGE, into CINERARY.

In January of 2001 Hoffman regrouped with GORGASM to cut the much anticipated second album 'Bleeding Profusely' for the Extremities Productions label. The drummer would also be seen on the live circuit deputizing for another arch Death Metal band LIVIDITY and by August of 2002 had teamed up with FLESHGRIND. The band added Brian Baxter of REGURGITATION on bass during November.

August of 2004 saw former GORGASM members guitarist Tom Tangalos, bassist Russ Powell and drummer Derek Hoffman re-uniting in a new band called DEPTHS OF AGONY. By late 2005 Tangalos, Hoffman, TORN BETWEEN bassist Jeremy Barger and ex-RELLIK singer James Eads had fired up another new band unit, WORMS INSIDE.

Newly installed on drums would be Tomasz Pilasiewicz of DISINTER, CORPHAGY and UNDERCURRENT repute to record demos in April 2006 at Studio One in Racine, Wisconsin. The band, announcing a new album title of 'Kuntkiller', partnered with Belgian Deathsters LENG TCH'E plus FUCK THE FACTS for a Canadian tour commencing 1st May 2006 Ottawa, Ontario.

STABWOUNDS INTERCOURSE, Pulverizer (1998). Necrosodomy / Disemboweled / Stabwounds Intercourse / Coprophiliac / Horrendous Rebirth / Clitoral Circumcision.
BLEEDING PROFUSELY, Extremities Productions EXT005 (2001). Bleeding Profusely / Morbid Overgrowth / Stripped To Bone / Fucking The Viscera / Voracious / The Essence Of Putrescence / Post Coital Truncation / Severed Ecstasy / Lesbian Stool Orgy / Fisticunt / Disembodied.

GORGUTS

QUÉBEC, QC, CANADA — *Luc LeMay (vocals), Sylvian Marcoux (guitar), Eric Giguere (bass), Stephane Provender (drums).*

Highly regarded and innovative Jazz flavoured Death Metal act GORGUTS was founded in Québec during 1989. In 1990 the band released a pro-demo called '... And Then Comes Lividity', which caught the attention of some record companies and they were soon signed to Roadrunner Records. The group at this stage comprised vocalist / guitarist Luc Lemay, bassist Eric Giguere, drummer Stephane Provencher with Gary Chouinard on second guitar. Very early on the band established themselves as one of the leading Death Metal acts forging associations with a number of Florida bands. GORGUTS even had Chris Barnes, ex-CANNIBAL CORPSE, SIX FEET UNDER, and journeyman guitarist JAMES MURPHY of OBITUARY, CANCER, appear on the debut, 1991's Scott Burns produced 'Considered Dead', recorded at Morrisound Studios, in Tampa, Florida, as guest stars. Murphy donated a solo to 'Inoculated Life' whilst Barnes' unmistakable tones were lent to 'Bodily Corrupted', 'Rottenatomy' and 'Hematological Allergy'. At this juncture the quartet, spearheaded by the gut wrenching growls of vocalist Luc LeMay, comprised guitarist Sylvian Marcoux, bass player Eric Giguere and drummer Stephane Provender.

However, GORGUTS returned from a 1993 European tour promoting the second album, 1993's 'Erosion Of Sanity', to discover they had been dropped by Roadrunner Records. The band also splintered at this juncture losing both their drummer and a guitarist. New faces were PURULENCE guitarist Steve Hurdle and PSYCHIC THROB bass player Steve Cloutier. This new formation signed to Olympic Recordings.

Following the recording of the Pierre Remillard produced 'Obscura' opus GORGUTS drafted Steve McDonald as drummer in September 1998 to replace the recently departed Patrick Robert. With this line up GORGUTS undertook the 'Death Across America' tour alongside running mates NILE, CRYPTOPSY and OPPRESSOR.

Before the close of 1999 guitarist Daniel Mongrain, whilst retaining his ties to his own act MARTYR, would join GORGUTS replacing Hurdle and appearing on their 'From Wizdom To Hate' album.

Luc LeMay would guest on MARTYR's 2000 album 'Warp Zone'. Steve McDonald would also unite with ASGARD in mid 2002. However, on October 19th the sad news was learned that McDonald had committed suicide by hanging himself. Apparently the drummer had been battling depression for many years.

Luc Lemay made studio time in early 2004 to donate his services to the DEATH tribute album 'Within The Mind' assembled by JAMES MURPHY. In October of that year Dan Mongrain acted as stand in guitarist for CRYPTOPSY. During the Autumn of 2005 former GORGUTS members Steve Hurdle and Luc Lemay returned to the fore with a new project called NEGATIVA, the band being completed by Dominic Lapointe of QUO VADIS, AUGURY and ATHERETIC on bass alongside Etienne

Gallo from AUGURY on drums. Lemay revealed in October that GORGUTS had been laid to rest and that he intended to concentrate on his career as a self-taught furniture maker.

'Considered Dead' and 'Erosion Of Sanity' were re-issued in CD format during November 2006 by Displeased Records in Europe and Caroline in the USA the following January.

... And Then Comes Lividity, Gorguts (1990) (Demo). ... And Then Comes Lividity / Haematological Allergy / Inflicted Maturity / Metempsukhosis / Calamitous Mortification.

CONSIDERED DEAD, Roadrunner RC 92731 (1991). Bodily Corrupted / Considered Dead / Disincarnated / Drifting Remains / Haematological Allergy / Inoculated Life / Stiff and Cold / Waste Of Immortality.

EROSION OF SANITY, Roadrunner RR91142 (1993). With The Flesh He'll Create / Condemned To Obscurity / Erosion Of Sanity / Orphans Of Sickness / Hideous Infirmity / Path Beyond Premonition / Odours Of Existence / Dormant Misery.

OBSCURA, Olympic Recordings 008 633129-2 (1999). Obscura / Earthly Love / The Carnal State / Nostalgia / The Art Of Sombre Ecstasy / Clouded / Subtle Body / Rapturous Grief / La Vie Est Prelude / Illuminatus / Faceless Ones / Sweet Silence.

FROM WISDOM TO HATE, Season Of Mist (2001). Inverted / Behave Through Mythos / From Wisdom To Hate / The Quest For Equilibrium / Unearthing The Past / Elusive Treasures / Das Martyrium Des ... / Testimonial Ruins.

CONSIDERED DEAD, Metal Mind Productions MASS CD DG 0988 (2006) (Polish release. Limited edition 2000 hand numbered copies). ... And Then Comes Lividity / Stiff And Cold / Disincarnated / Considered Dead / Rottenatomy / Bodily Corrupted / Waste Of Mortality / Drifting Remains / Hematological Allergy / Inoculated Life / Considered Dead (Demo) / Rottenatomy (Demo).

EROSION OF SANITY, Metal Mind Productions MASS CD DG 0989 (2006) (Polish release. Limited edition 2000 hand numbered copies). With Their Flesh, He'll Create / Condemned To Obscurity / The Erosion Of Sanity / Orphans Of Sickness / Hideous Infirmity / A Path Beyond Premonition / Odors Of Existence / Dormant Misery / A Path Beyond Premonition (Demo) / Dissecting The Adopted (Demo).

GORTICIAN

WASHINGTON, LA, USA — *Timothy Archer (vocals / bass), Tony Buzby (guitar), Jason Christie (drums).*

Although a renowned name in underground circles GORTICIAN's historical background is shrouded in mystery due to a campaign of misinformation emanating from the band themselves. The group was convened around 1990 by frontman Junior, former GRENDEL and MAD MONK man Timothy Archer, guitarist Tony Buzby and drummer Ronnie Berthelot. This initial line up would splinter within weeks as Matt took over the drum stool and Junior bailed out.

By 1993 GORTICIAN had settled on a power trio line up of Archer on vocals and bass, Buzby on guitar and drummer Jason Christie, the latter previously with Las Vegas act ENTITY. Reportedly the band's three track demo 'Eaten, Beaten & Crucified', with guest guitars from CHAOS HORDE guitarist Mike, was deemed so offensive the band was jailed under obscenity laws. Various stories put the group members sentences as ranging from three months in jail to a few hours incarceration with a $50 fine. There is also an urban legend that PMRC campaigner Tipper Gore incited her followers to burn the entire production run of the cassette with only one copy escaping her wrath.

GORTICIAN finally got around to a commercial release with the 2000 'Transmigration Into Hell' album released on their own Bleeding Erection label. Earlier works, including a less than reverential take on the STRAY CATS 'Stray Cat Strut' anthem, were collected on the compilation 'The Wonder Years'.

Christie, under his pseudonym of High C, also operates in the Rap Metal side project THE GUYS WHO WEAR BLACK TOO MUCH led by Lord Vic Naughty of RAMPAGE.

GORTICIAN, with guest vocalist Jeremy Whitman of DESPONDENCY, would contribute their version of VENOM's '1000 Days In Sodom' to an online tribute album.

THE WONDER YEARS, Unsung Heroes (2000). Kick The Chair / Orgy With The Dead / The Next Religion / Alien Abduction / Caesarian Salad / Vagina Dentata / Orgy With The Dead (1993 version) / Vagina Dentata (1993 version) / Beaten, Mocked And Crucified (1993 version) / Ugly Police Incident / Death Trip / Mind Of A Lunatic / Stray Cat Strut / Alien Abduction (Special Surgery mix).

TRANSMIGRATION INTO HELL, Bleeding Erection (2000). The Next Religion / Alien Abduction / Avatar In The Abattoir / Labyrinths Animator / The Avengers / Olmec Assimilation / Blazing Morgue / Empire Of Perversion / Knight Of The Brazen Serpent / In The Shadow Of The Accursed Mountains / Hypocrisy And Downfall / Twilight Cycle.

GORY BLISTER

MILAN, ITALY — *Adri (vocals), Raff (guitar), Fredrick (bass), Joe La Viola (drums).*

Technically minded, Milan based Death Metal band GORY BLISTER made their opening impressions with a brace of demo tapes in 1991 and 1993. The 1999 album 'Art Bleeds' was re-issued in 2003 by French label Sekhmet Records. Two GORY BLISTER members would also feature in the ranks of Thrash—Death act NODE, frontman Daniel Botti and drummer Joe La Viola. Bassist Michele Brustia of THY NATURE is an ex-GORY BLISTER member.

By 2004 GORY BLISTER's line-up comprised vocalist Adri, guitarist Raff, bassist Fredrick (replacing Bruce Teah) and drummer Joe La Viola. The band would be requested to donate their cover of '1000 Eyes' to a Chinese DEATH tribute album, 'Unforgotten Past—A Tribute to Chuck Schuldiner', published in October of 2004 by AreaDeath Productions.

GORY BLISTER signed to Holland's Mascot Records in January 2005 for the album 'Skymorphosys', recording at Fear Studios with producer Gabriele Ravaglia.

GORY BLISTER parted ways with vocalist Adry Bellant in January 2007 A replacement frontman was swiftly found in the shape of Clode, formerly of SALMORAR and HATEFILES. The group flanked Finnish band AMORAL on Italian shows in February.

Cognitive Sinergy, (1996). Cognitive Sinergy / The Voyage Out / Where Thoughts Flow / Premonition On The Ageless Land / Spoil.

ART BLEEDS, Sekhmet (2003). Primordial Scenery / As Blood Moves / Art Bleeds / Mermaids Beloved / Anticlimax / Cognitive Sinergy / Snowfall / A Gout From The Scar / Comet ... And Her Trail Of Spiritual Dust / Never Let Me Down.

SKYMORPHOSYS, Mascot (2006).

GOTHIC

FRANCE — *Goth (vocals / guitar), The Xela (bass), Wax (drums).*

Parisian Gothic (!) styled Death Rockers GOTHIC first came together in 1992 as a quartet of bassist The Xela (apparently only 11 years old at the time!), guitarist / vocalist Goth, Demetus and drummer Rony. The following year GOTHIC, all still teenagers at this stage, recorded the 1993 'Pain Before Insane' demo cassette with second guitarist Wolf now on board.

Before the band could play live both Wolf and Demetus departed. This did not affect the group's progress however and subsequent gigs generated the second demo, a live recording titled 'Pleasures Of Brutality' in 1994, limited to 100 copies. 1995 saw their efforts coming to fruition with the self financed mini album, 'Brutal Conditions Of Extreme Alchemy', emerging.

Rony was to leave the fold in advance of GOTHIC recording a second album, titled 'Prelude To Killing'. GOTHIC drafted a new sticksman in the form of Wax. The 'Criminal Art Motivations' album emerged through Mafia Underground Productions in 1999.

GOTHIC band members are also active in FAST FORWARD, a project band involving TREPONOM PAL drummer D.

BRUTAL CONDITIONS FOR EXTREME ALCHEMY, Gothic (1995).

PRELUDE TO KILLING, Gothic (1997). A Third Seasons Of Murders / Doctrine For Monkeys / Smile A Day / Die Later / Fun Projects And … Death / Closed.

CRIMINAL ART MOTIVATIONS, Mafia Underground Productions (1999). Lethal Injection: The Substance / Bring The Pain / To Create To Use To Exterminate / Story Of A Dead Man / C.R.I.M.E. / The Macabre Underground (+ Foeturpurical) / Like A Razor / Return To The Cold Chamber / 4 Elements / Doctrine For Monkeys / Death To The Core (Fast Forward Remix).

GOTHIC

GENOA, ITALY — *James Jason (vocals / keyboards /. Synthesizers), Davy Jones (guitar), John Ruin (programming), David Bosch (artwork).*

GOTHIC is a Genoa based, Dark Electro multimedia project led by James Jason. The project evolved in September of 1989, blending Death, Grindcore and gloom and originally billed as CRYPTIC SANCTUM, but adopting the GOTHIC title for demo recordings in December of that year billed 'Into The Gothic Gloom'. Follow ups 'Into The Deep Tartarus' arrived in September 1990, 'Into The Cave' in June 1991, 'Whispers From The Grave' in June 1992 and ' … And From Hell Came The Revenge' in February 1993. The December 1993 session marked a musical transition for the band, 'The Pestilence … Post Contagium' delving into keyboard orientated Doom. November 1994's 'Dreaming The Apocalypse' continued this trend.

GOTHIC's eight demo, 'Dark Dimension', saw release in September 1995 with the experimental 'Cold Winds Of Suicide' delivered in January 1997. That year, the introduction of artist David Bosch signalled GOTHIC's move into multimedia. Ultimately, this would culminate in the October 2000 double CD 'Fleeing The Rainland'.

Former band colleagues include guitarists Frederick Thomas, Mr. R and Mr. D, with bassists Jordan and Andy Under and drummer Chris Joint and Ricky F. The May 2004 'Grim' album included additional DVD content replete with not only the traditional video but also paintings and poetry.

GRIM, Théâtre de la Mort 08 XI (2004). In Wickedness / Forlorn / I Give Up (Defeat's Dance) / Wintered Wings / Splinters Inside / Feed My Frenzy / Lurking Limbo / Between The Endless Tides / Integrationsstatus: Negativ (!?!)—beginne entpersonalisierungsprozess oder einleiten (a) oder [dein] system anhalten (b) ??? [Die Entscheidung liegt bei Uns, danke] / Down In Your Shrine / Noir (Czarny):
Néant—Eloignement—Dévoilement—Torpeur—Effroi—Néant / Barren Moors / "… poiché … la Morte … è sulle colline …" / Victim Of Distress / Am I … ?

GRAVE

VISBY, SWEDEN — *Jörgen Sandström (vocals / guitar), Ola Lindgren (guitar), Jonas Torndal (bass), Jensâ Paulsson (drums).*

Visby's GRAVE are one of the founders of the Swedish Death / Doom Metal scene releasing their first demo, 'Sick Disgust Eternal', in August 1988 following a name change from CORPSE. The trio responsible for these tracks comprised Jörgen Sandström handling lead vocals, guitar and bass guitar, Ola Lindgren on guitar and drummer Jensâ Paulsson. The band unit had been raised at high school on the isle of Gotland, first branded RISING POWER, in honour of the AC/DC song of the same name on the 'Flick Of The Switch' album, then DESTROYER and ANGUISH before adopting CORPSE in 1986 for the demo 'Black Dawn'. A name switch to GRAVE was marked by the 'Sick Disgust Eternal' sessions. Parallel to this, Sandström, Lindgren and Paulsson, together with bass player Jonas Edwardsson, cut the 'Painful Death' demo credited to PUTREFACTION in 1989. However, these tracks would be sucked into the GRAVE catalogue.

Two further demos, February 1989's 'Sexual Mutilation' and August 1989's 'Anatomia Corporis Humanum', recorded at Yellowhouse Studio, gained the band an enviable cult status. The latter demo was also to be issued as a four track EP by German imprint M.B.R Records.

Prophecy Records published four tracks as part of a collaborative album shared with DEVIATED INSTINCT and DEVOLUTION during 1991. GRAVE had been snapped up by another German label, Century Media Records, and put out the full-length 'Into The Grave' album in August 1991. Putting down these tracks at Stockholm's Sunlight Studios with producer Tomas Skogsberg, GRAVE would use these facilities as a base of operations throughout their career. Now placed onto a global stage, GRAVE's music garnered laudatory reviews, fans entranced by the bludgeoning nature of their rustic, simplistic riffing, oppressively mutated bass and subterranean roar of Jörgen Sandström. The band toured Europe as guests to Florida thrashers MALEVOLENT CREATION in September 1991 shortly followed by dates opening for ENTOMBED.

In 1992 bassist Jonas Torndal quit and frontman Jörgen Sandström took over four string duties. Second album 'You'll Never See' was recorded in June. A January 1994 EP, '… And Here I Die … Satisfied', included a re-worked version of the early CORPSE track 'Black Dawn'.

Following the release of June 1994's 'Soulless', GRAVE toured North America in a headlining capacity prior to hooking up with the CANNIBAL CORPSE and SAMAEL tour as support. Further dates had the band putting in an appearance on the 'Full Of Hate' festivals and acting as openers for MORBID ANGEL. Following this bout of activity Sandström wound up joining ENTOMBED in 1995. GRAVE persevered as a duo with Lindgren now responsible for vocals for the 1996 Tomas Skogsberg produced 'Hating Life' record, laid down at Sunlight Studios. A double concert recording, 'Extremely Rotten Live', arrived in April 1997.

GRAVE, centred upon vocalist / guitarist Ola Lindgren, Jensâ Paulsson and bassist turned guitarist Jonas Torndal, who had previously vacated his post in 1992, reconvened in September 2001. New man on bass would transpire to be the THERION credited Fredrik Isaksson. This unit set to work on the Tomas Skogsberg produced 'Back From The Grave' album. First editions of the record came packaged with a bonus disc of archive tracks compiled from the demos 1988's 'Sick Disgust Eternal', 1989's 'Sexual Mutilation' and 'Anatomia Corporis Humani' tapes. Subsequent European live dates would bear witness to the introduction of COERCION drummer Pelle Ekegren into the fold, regular skinsman Jensâ Paulsson being temporarily out of action. By February it was learned Paulsson was out of the picture for good, GRAVE inducting KAAMOS, GENERAL SURGERY and REPUGNANT man Cristofer Barkensjö as permanent replacement.

A projected extensive run of European tour dates throughout March and April 2003 found DEFLESHED as support act. However, these shows would then be cancelled. There would be no let up on the live front for the summer though, GRAVE teaming up with IMMOLATION, CREMATORIUM and GOATWHORE for US shows in June, the band's first North American shows in over seven years. The band would then ally themselves with the gargantuan 'Bonded By Metal Over Europe' roving gigs in October, ranked alongside EXODUS, NUCLEAR ASSAULT, AGENT STEEL, BEHEMOTH, MORTICIAN, CARNAL FORGE, OCCULT and CALLENISH CIRCLE.

GRAVE parted ways with drummer Christofer Barkensjö in early 2004 as he opted out to prioritise his other act KAAMOS. The band duly replaced him with replacing him with the COERCION credited Pelle Liljenberg for recording of a new album in April at Abyss Studios by producers produced by Tommy and Peter Tägtgren, this opus going by a working title of 'Fiendish Regression'. Included in the running order would be a cover version of SAINT VITUS Doom classic 'Burial At Sea' and a re-recording of an archive 1989 song named 'Autopsied'.

December 2004 touring saw GRAVE in union with ROTTING

CHRIST prior to hooking up with GOD DETHRONED for Low Countries shows in January 2005 and a further run across Europe partnered with THIRD MOON and Swiss act DISPARAGED. Gigs in Finland during March saw support from CHAOSBREED and SCENT OF FLESH followed by German concerts allied with DEW SCENTED. A run of dates in Finland during May had CHAOSBREED and DELIRIUM'S ORDER as support.

Jörgen Sandström announced the formation of a deliberately retro-Death Metal band project entitled DEATH BREATH in collaboration with his erstwhile ENTOMBED colleague and THE HELLACOPTERS frontman Nicke Andersson with THUNDER EXPRESS man Robert Persson on guitar. Ola Lindgren too got involved in extracurricular activity, forging SOULDEVOURER in union with the DISMEMBER and UNLEASHED credited Robert Sennebäck and NECROPHOBIC drummer Joakim Sterner.

GRAVE announced European tour dates for January 2006, traversing Poland, Germany, Holland, France, Belgium, Ireland, Switzerland, Austria, Italy and the UK, alongside a heavyweight cast of HURTLOCKER, ABORTED, DEW-SCENTED, VESANIA and CRYPTOPSY. Tracks for a new album, 'As Rapture Comes' including a cover version of ALICE IN CHAINS' 'Them Bones', would be constructed at Studio Soulless in Stockholm, being subsequently mixed by Peter Tägtgren at The Abyss Studio.

The band teamed up with VITAL REMAINS, DISMEMBER, DEMIRICOUS and WITHERED for a North American tour beginning in late September. This signalled a clear rejuvenation for the band as European shows announced for November, dubbed the "Masters Of Death", had the band lined up with a supremely heavyweight Scandinavian cast of DISMEMBER, ENTOMBED and UNLEASHED. The seemingly tireless group then set out to unite once more with DISMEMBER for a US West Coast tour in December. However, these concerts were cancelled.

Sick Disgust Eternal, (1988) (Demo). Into The Grave / Annihilated Gods / Infernal Massacre.
Anatomia Corporis Humani, M.B.R. (1989). Extremely Rotten Flesh / Brutally Deceased / Septic Excrements / Reborned Miscarriage.
Sexual Mutilation, (1989) (Demo). Intro / Slow Death Deformed / Reality Of Life / Morbid Way To Die / Sexual Mutilation / Outro / Death Of The Bumblebee.
Anatomia Corporis Humani, (1989) (Demo). Extremely Rotten Flesh / Brutally Deceased / Septic Excrements / Reborned Miscarriage.
Promo 1989, (1989) (Demo). Autopsied / Eroded / Hating Life.
GRAVE, Prophecy SRT 91L2878 (1991) (Split album with DEVIATED INSTINCT and DEVOLUTION). Into The Grave / Reborned Miscarriage / Eroded / Putrefaction Remains.
Tremendous Pain, Century Media (1991) (Promotion release). Tremendous Pain / Putrefaction Remains / Haunted / Day Of Mourning / Eroded / Inhuman.
INTO THE GRAVE, Century Media 84 9721 (1991). Deformed / In Love / For Your God / Obscure Infinity / Hating Life / Into The Grave / Extremely Rotten Flesh / Haunted / Day Of Mourning / Inhuman / Banished To Live.
YOU'LL NEVER SEE, Century Media CD 9733 (1992). You'll Never See / Now And Forever / Morbid Way To Die / Obsessed / Grief / Severing Flesh / Brutally Deceased / Christ(ns)anity.
... And Here I Die ... Satisfied, Century Media 77066-2 (1994). ... And Here I Die ... Satisfied / I Need You / Black Dawn / Tremendous Pain / Day Of Mourning / Inhuman.
SOULLESS, Century Media CD 77070 (1994). Turning Black / Soulless / .I Need You / Bullets Are Mine / Bloodshed / Judas / Unknown / And Here I Die / Genocide / Rain / Scars.
HATING LIFE, Century Media 77106-2 (1996). Worth The Wait / Restrained / Winternight / Two Of Me / Beauty Within / Lovesong / Sorrowfilled Moon / Harvest Day / Redress / Still Hating Life.
EXTREMELY ROTTEN LIVE, Century Media 77162-2 (1997). Extremely Rotten Flesh / Turning Black / Restrained / Winternight / Haunted / Two Of Me / Hating Life / You'll Never See / Lovesong / Sorrowfilled Moon / Rain / Soulless / And Here I Die ... / Into The Grave / Reborn Miscarriage.
BACK FROM THE GRAVE, Century Media 77411-2 (2002) (Includes bonus disc of demos). Intro / Rise / Behold The Flames / Dead Is Better / Receiver / No Regrets / Resurrection / Below / Bloodfed / Thorn To Pieces / Into The Grave (Demo) / Annihilated Gods (Demo) / Infernal Massacre (Demo) / Deformed (Demo) / Reality Of Life (Demo) / Morbid Way To Die (Demo) / Sexual Mutilation (Demo) / Extremely Rotten Flesh (Demo) / Brutally Deceased (Demo) / Septic Excrements (Demo) / Reborn Miscarriage (Demo).
FIENDISH REGRESSION, Century Media 77511-0 (2004). Last Journey / Reborn / Awakening / Breeder / Trial By Fire / Out Of The Light / Inner Light / Bloodfeast / Heretic / Burial At Sea / Autopsied.
AS RAPTURE COMES, Century Media (2006). Intro—Day Of Reckoning / Burn / Through Eternity / By Demons Bred / Living The Dead Behind / Unholy Terror / Battle Of Eden / Epic Obliteration / Them Bones / As Rapture Comes.
ENRAPTURED, Metal Mind Productions MMP DVD 0095 (2006) (CD + DVD. Limited edition). Intro / Deformed / Burn / You'll Never See ... / Turning Black / Christi(ns)anity / Breeder / Bullets Are Mine / Unholy Terror / Extremely Rotten Flesh / Rise / Soulless / By Demons Bred / And Here I Die / Heretic / Outro / Reborn Miscarriage / Into The Grave / Rise / Into The Grave / Interview / Photo Gallery / Intro / Deformed / Burn / You'll Never See ... / Turning Black / Christi(ns)anity / Breeder / Bullets Are Mine / Unholy Terror / Extremely Rotten Flesh / Rise / Soulless / By Demons Bred / And Here I Die / Heretic / Outro / Reborn Miscarriage / Into The Grave.

GRAYMALKIN

AUCKLAND, NEW ZEALAND — *Gareth Craze (vocals), Michael Rothwell (guitar), Phil Kusabs (bass), Phil Osborne (drums).*

East Auckland Death-Grind act GRAYMALKIN employ DAWN OF AZAZEL drummer Phil Osborne. The band was conceived as a duo of Osborne and INFAUSTUS, PARASPHERE and GRENADE KILLS THREE guitarist Michael Rothwell during 1999 and made initial impressions with the demos 'Pleased To Meat You' in 1999 and 'Deciphering The Deranged' the following year. Expanding to a full band unit GRAYMALKIN incorporated DAWN OF AZAZEL and FORCED TO SUBMIT man Joe Bonnet on bass guitar.

Wellington's 'Bludgeoning and Burning' festival in May of 2002 bore witness to the inaugural GRAYMALKIN live performance, the group utilising the services of DAWN OF AZAZEL's Rigel Walshe and SKULDOM and FORCED TO SUBMIT's Martin Cavanagh as stand in members for this performance. Shortly afterwards Gareth Craze was enrolled into the vocal position. The band's debut recording 'Revenge On Mankind' would be cut during December of 2002 at Rockbottom Studios.

In mid 2003 Bonnet decamped on good terms and the VASSAFOR, SPINE, CANIS, ENTROPY and GUEVARA credited bassist Phil Kusabs plugged the vacancy. The delayed release of 'Revenge On Mankind' fortuitously coincided with GRAYMALKIN's support slots to INCANTATION's New Zealand tour. The band contributed the track 'Malice' to the 'Morbid Music Vol. 1' 2004 compilation album. In 2004 Osborne joined leading Black Metal combo DAWN OF AZAZEL but was "removed from the line-up" before the close of the year. Ironically, another GRAYMALKIN veteran, Martin Cavanagh, took over the DAWN OF AZAZEL drum stool. 2005 demos from Kusabs solo project VASSAFOR also saw Cavanagh on the drums.

REVENGE ON MANKIND, Jailbait (2003). Malice / Parliament Of Whores / Deviant Pregnancy / Marched At Gunpoint / Avowed / Introperversion / Salvation Through Incest.

GRENOUER

PERM, RUSSIA — *Andrew Merzlyakov (vocals), Alexander Shatov (guitar), Viatcheslav Koltchin (bass), Sergei Lyalin (drums).*

Perm based Death Metal band founded in 1992, debuting with 1993's 'Death Of A Bite' demo. The 1997 GRENOUER line-up comprised Andrew "The Indian" Merzlyakov on vocals, guitarist Alexander Shatov, bassist Viatcheslav Koltchin-bass and Sergei Lyalin on drums. The band issued a cassette only album 'Border Of Misty Times' on the Metal Agen imprint. The 'Gravehead' album arrived in 1999 followed by 'The Odour O' Folly' in 2001, the latter boasting a Blac-Death cover version of the A-HA Pop hit 'Take On Me'.

During 2001 GRENOUER was sporting a line up incorporating Merzlyakov, Koltchin, Lyalin and guitarists Denis Davidoff and Alexander Sokolov. The band would also operate a parallel industrial side endeavour billed as COD. GRENOUER signed to the CD Maximum label for the 2003 offering 'Presence Of War'. Recorded at Navahohut Studios in Moscow it was mastered at the world famous Finnvox Studios in Finland. That year also saw the inclusion of their rendition of 'I Me Mine' to a GODFLESH tribute album published by French label Nihilistic Holocaust. GRENOUER suffered a setback in September 2005 when the band lost all their instruments and equipment in a fire at their rehearsal complex, apparently caused by an "unqualified welder". Sessions for recording of a fifth album, to have taken place at Astia Studios in Finland, were postponed.

GRAVEHEAD, (1999). The Time Spool / Down Under Dome Of Heaven / Conversing The Dolt / King's Ebony Blade / Predominant Nature / Riddle Of Steel / Alone In The Dark / Salt Of Mayhem / Mystery.

THE ODOUR O'FOLLY, (2001). Your Beast Tonight / Confident / Stabbed By Touch / Soulhunters (Spiritual Archers) / Skittle Man / Death Ought To Wait For Me / In-Sekt / Take On Me / Mind Ruins.

PRESENCE OF WAR, CD Maximum CDM1776 (2004). Mercenary Fields / Sex Optica / The Choice Of Flesh / The Last Bullet Magic / Crash, Crash, Crash / Clonetwigs / Sheitan / Communist Skinhead / A Farewell To Arms.

GRIMORIA

TOULOUSE, FRANCE — *Sire Cédric (vocals), Nilas (guitar), Emmanuelle Dal-Grande (guitar), Rémy (bass), Tenebras (drums).*

Founded in Toulouse during 1996, the first formation of GRIMOIRE counted Tenebras on vocals and bass, Funerarium on guitar and Lord Von Catharsis on drums. Second guitarist Ostrak joined the fold in September of that year and Zagoth took over keyboards in March of 1997. GRIMORIA released the tapes 'Démonologie' in April 1998 and 'The Black Procession' in May of 1999. Both Catharis and Zagoth bowed out in 2000.

In 2000 GRIMORIA had the track 'The Wind Of Chaos' included on the Autumn Productions compilation album 'The Real Underground Vol. 1'. A split album with IRAVEN arrived in 2001, the band at this juncture featuring Nils on vocals and bass, vocalist Ilahen, guitarist Ostrak and keyboard player Elenya. The band donated their rendition of 'Pain Injection' to the 2002 Holy Record S.U.P. tribute 'A Tribute To S.U.P'. The band featured on the third installment of 'The Real Underground' compilations, 2003's volume III featuring the song 'Le Lac Des Souffrances'.

The 2005 GRIMORIA formation was quoted at vocalist Sire Cédric, guitarists Nilas and Emmanuelle Dal-Grande, bassist Rémy with Tenebras on the drums. The band projected an album entitled 'Le Seuil'.

WINDS OF CHAOS, Mono-Emotional (2001) (Split album with IRAVEN). The Wind Of Chaos / Le Lac Des Souffrances / Reflection Of A Broken Mirror / The Achievement.

GRIND BUTO

INDONESIA — *Frank Yudo (vocals / bass), Henk J. John (guitar),.*

Muslim Grindcore unit out of Indonesia. GRIND BUTO was forged as a quartet in the mid nineties comprising vocalist / bassist Frank Yudo, guitarist Henk J. John, guitarist Jameel and drummer Eddy. Both Jameel and Eddy would depart, the exiting guitarist subsequently joining AAARGH, and GRIND BUTO persevered as a duo. The pairing of Yudo and John delivered the December 1997 cassette 'In Hell Beast From' following it with the 'Extreme Damage' session.

GRIND BUTO issued the 1998 'The Malevolence' tape upfront of a split single shared with Belgian veterans AGATHOCLES. A collaborative album 'Santa Is Satan' was shared with MURDER CORPORATION in 2000.

The Malevolent, Uxicon (1999) (Split EP with AGATHOCLES). Carnal Carnivore / Massacre.

SANTA IS SATAN, Psychic Scream (2000) (Split album with MURDER CORPORATION). Prelude Butcher / Brutal Tragedy / Damage / Carnal Carnivore / In Hell Beast From / Mass Devour.

GRIND INC.

KREFELD, GERMANY — *Tom Strater (vocals), Christoph Mieves (vocals), Jan Pelser (guitar), Jochen Pelser (bass), Adriano Ricci (drums).*

GRIND INC. is a Krefeld Grindcore act sporting an all star cast of extreme Metal elite. Featuring the dual vocals of HATE FACTOR and CRIKEY man Christoph Mieves and erstwhile CORONATION man Tom Strater the band was rounded out by HATE FACTOR and ex-TORTURE CHAMBER guitarist Jan Pelser with HATE FACTOR and ex-PREMATURE man Jochen Pelser on bass and drummer Adrian Ricci, a veteran of BLOOD RED ANGEL, TORTURE CHAMBER, CORONATION and NIGHT IN GALES.

GRIND INC. put out the 'Defined To Kill' demo in 2004, signing to Morbid Records for a debut 2005 album 'Executed'.

In March 2006 GRIND INC. parted ways with bass player Jochen Pelser, citing "personal reasons", replacing him with Thomas Granzow, guitarist for RESURRECTED. Morbid Records released the band's second album, 'Inhale The Violence', in May.

EXECUTED, Morbid (2005). Executed / Non-Existence / Defining The Art Of Pure Brutality / Intense Zombie Butchery / 40 Incisions / Obsession / Murder & Slaughter Repeat / Overkill Infernalized / Splattered In Virginia / Beware Of God / Kill For This Peace / Forever Blood / Forced To Eat Their Guts While Dying / What To Fuck / Forced To Consume / The Sin That Makes Us Forget.

INHALE THE VIOLENCE, Morbid (2006). Intro—Absorbing Brutality / Dead Body Costume / Rebirth Of An Ancient Time / Cold Irregular Truth / Glorification Of Violence / Congregation Of The Extreme / Intro—Harbinger For The Doomed / Inhale The Swarm / Scanning The Molecules / While The Vile Wept / The Grinding Process / Peace By Pieces.

GRIND MINDED

HOLLAND — *David Brans (vocals), Jerry Duinkerken (guitar), Jasper Bolderdijk (bass), Erwin Koerts (drums).*

Grind styled Death Metal band founded in 1997 by from guitarist Jerry Duinkerken and Bakvet of CrustPunk outfit STICK TO THE PAN in alliance with bassist Henk Zinger, also a member of GOD DETHRONED, and vocalist Robert from Metalcore unit BLINDSIDED. At first GRIND MINDED was of side project status but as both STICK TO THE PAN and BLINDSIDED folded, eventually became priority. Line up shuffles saw Robert replaced by Arjen as frontman. David Brans of DUST and TRICK LIGHT subsequently took the role for the 2001 'Your Suffering Will Be Legendary' album.

Henke Zinger exited in January 2006 in order to prioritise GOD DETHRONED. He would be replaced by GRINROTH bassist Jasper "Boldey" Bolderdijk.

YOUR SUFFERING WILL BE LEGENDARY, Filthy (2001). Tomorrows Ashes / Hatecore / Six Feet Under / World Domination / Goddestructeve / Inconsummatus.

GROG

PORTUGAL — *Pedro Pedra (vocals), Hugo (guitar), Ivo Martins (guitar), Alex (bass), Rolando Barros (drums).*

GROG is a brutal Death Metal combo hailing from Oeiras and founded during 1991 by vocalist Pedro Pedra, guitarist Joao, bass player Marco and drummer Johnny. The group, originally operating as DEATHEATH, made their presence felt with the Grind-Gore rehearsal demo 'The Bluuuaaarrrggghhh Rehearsal '92' tape. A studio recording, 'A Nauseating Sweet Taste', followed in 1993, after which Hugo superseded Joao. A two song promo was then cut, then signing to German label Born To Booze Records, the 7" single '95 Stabwounds To Your Throat'. All 500 copies soon sold out. GROG switched to the Skyfall label for the debut album, 'Macabre Requiems' issued in 1996, but then fell apart.

Pedra reconstituted the band in 1998, drafting guitarists Nuno Loureiro, of SQUAD and PAINSTRUCK, and Paulo, bass player Ivo Martins of PAINSTRUCK and drummer Bruno Berto. Unfortunately Paulo soon left, followed by Berto. Pulling in Beto on drums GROG laid down the 1999 demo 'Regurgitape'. Altering the band set up in 2000, Simão Santos was installed on bass guitar as Ivo Martin shifted to guitar. This unit secured a deal with Shockwave Records for the April 2001 album 'Odes To The Carnivorous'. Ronaldo Barros, a scene veteran of NEO-PLASMAH, NEPHYST and SACRED SIN would be next in line to man the drum stool, first featuring on a live cassette distributed by Lucidist & Requiem Productions billed as 'Madness, Horror And Guts Live'.

MACABRE REQUIEMS, Skyfall (1996). Embrace My Cold Body / Tribal Flesh Ceremony / Dawn Of The Living Dead / Monstrous Anatomic Deformation / Splashterized Autopsy / Excreted And Vomited Abortions / Spontaneous Gore / Cannibal Feast / Rotten Grave / Sado-Masoquist Butchery / Cannibalistic Devourement / Blood In My Face / Drowned In The Pleasure Of Tortured Flesh.
ODES TO THE CARNIVOROUS, Shockwave (2001). Ode To The Carnivorous (Prelude To Brutality) / Corpse Reanimation (The Mutants Revenge) / Fornicators Delirium / Dead Art Collector / Cult Of Blood / Terrified / Necrogeek (The Doctor's Diary) / Realm Of The Soulless / Raped By A Virgin / Narcissistic Skinblade Reflection.

GROINCHURN

SOUTH AFRICA — *Christo Bester (vocals / bass), Mark Chapman (vocals / guitar), Sergio Christina (drums).*

South Africa's premier Death Metal outfit. The obviously Grind act GROINCHURN convened in 1994 as a trio of vocalist / bassist Christo Bester, vocalist / guitarist Mark Chapman and drummer Sergio Christina. This line up has remained steadfast until the present day. GROINCHURN debuted with the demos 'Human Filth' and 'Every Dog Has Its Decay'. 1995 witnessed a glut of 7" single releases with GROINCHURN sharing split 7" singles with CAPTAIN 3 LEG for the American Fudgeworthy label and WOYCZECH on the German Painart imprint. A live 7" EP entitled 'Totally Fucking Alive' was also issued by the Czech label Icy Illusion.

Promoting the inaugural album 'Six Times Nine' GROINCHURN toured Europe with KRABATHOR and SANITY'S DAWN securing a deal with the German Morbid label along the way. Fudgeworthy would also issue the record in America on a limited edition 10" vinyl format.

Second album 'Fink' witnessed the band returning the favour to KRABATHOR as both acts put in a string of South African shows. GROINCHURN would also bring CRYOGENIC over for gigs in their homeland too before renewed touring efforts in Europe.

GROINCHURN were back in action with KRABATHOR once more in Europe during 2000 promoting the 'WhoamI' release prior to American shows with TOTAL FUCKING DESTRUCTION.

SIX TIMES NINE, 1999 (0).
Totally Fucking Alive EP, Icy Illusion (1995).
Split, Painart (1995) (Split single with WOYCZECH).
Split, Fudgeworthy (1995) (Split single with CAPTAIN 3 LEG).
Bow To The Gimplord, Morbid (1998) (Split single with HAEMMORHAGE). Bow To The Gimplord / I Don't Think So / Stayin' Alive.
ALREADY DEAD, Morbid (1998). Already Dead / Let's Put The Fun Back Into Fundamentalists / Satan Spawn, The Idiots / Toad-Lee / Genocidal Tendency / Contraceive.
FINK, Morbid (1998). Generic / Repetition Works / Already Dead / Change Is Change / Whole / More / Ugly People / Bridges Burn / Principles Of Mass Suggestion / The Big Picture / Just Passing Through / More Different Than Different / Being Ripped Off / Open / What About Them Injuns / Sein / The Clock Is Ticking / I Want To Be White / Hollow / Ninety Nine / I Will Say It.
WHOAMI, Morbid MR74 (2000). You Know's A Lie / Untitled / Fickle World / Quiet Please / Rotaludom / Blown Off Course / Da Vitameen Green / Coughin' / Eluide / Killkillkill / Re-Evolution / Puppy Love / Buy The Way.

GROTESQUE

GOTHENBURG, SWEDEN — *Tomas Lindberg (vocals), Alf Svensson (guitar), Kristian Wahlin (guitar), Thomas Eriksson (drums).*

A Gothenburg Death Metal band created during August 1988 by ex-ORAL guitarist Alf Svensson, billed under a stage name of 'The Haunting', GROTESQUE later evolved into the highly regarded AT THE GATES. Vocals would be handled by 'Goatspell' (a.k.a. Tomas Lindberg) with 'Necrolord' (a.k.a. 'Bullen' Kristian Wahlin) on secondary guitars. The group's original rhythm section comprised bassist Nuctemeron with the SORHIN and ARCKANUM credited Shamaatae on drums. Subsequently 'Offensor' (a.k.a. Tomas Eriksson) manned the drums. Recordings issued under the GROTESQUE banner included the demos 'Ripped From The Cross', a three song rehearsal session in 1988, and 'The Black Gate Is Closed' laid down on April 5th 1989. The Dolores label issued the 'Incantations' mini-album in 1990, pressed in both lilac and black vinyl editions. However, that same year the band folded.

In February 1990 Lindberg, joining forces with guitarist Bjorn Mankner and identical twins Anders Björler and Jonas Björler, on guitar and bass respectively, forged INFESTATION. A two song rehearsal demo, 'When Sanity Ends', was recorded at Fågeln studio and issued in August but INFESTATION collapsed shortly thereafter. Lindberg and the two brothers then hooked up with Alf Svensson plus drummer Adrian Erlandsson, and duly created AT THE GATES.

In 1996 Black Sun Records put out the compilation 'In The Embrace Of Evil', this comprising the 'Incantation' sessions, re-mastered songs from an unreleased demo set 'In The Embrace Of Evil' alongside two brand new recorded tracks 'Church Of The Pentagram' and 'Ripped From The Cross', laid down by Thomas Lindberg, Alf Svensson and Kristian Wahlin.

Guitarist Kristian Wahlin joined LIERS IN WAIT. Svensson formed OXIPLEGATZ. Tomas Lindberg forged THE CROWN. By 2000 Lindberg was fronting THE HAUNTED and would go on to feature in another high profile project LOCKUP. The pedigree and impression made upon the scene by its members lent the 'In The Embrace Of Evil' GROTESQUE album to an American CD re-release in 2001 courtesy of Century Media Records.

A 2004 AT THE GATES tribute album 'Slaughterous Souls—A Tribute to At The Gates' released by Drowned Scream Records included a take of GROTESQUE's 'Blood Run From The Altar' from IN AETERNUM.

Breaking a sixteen year silence, GROTESQUE, alongside NIR-VANA 2002 and INTERMENT, reunited for a one off, non-public concert held on January 26th 2007 at Kafé 44 in Stockholm. GROTESQUE relented for a regular audience show, backed by WITCHERY and GRAND MAGUS, at the Storan venue in Gothenburg on April 20th.

Ripped From The Cross, (1988). Ripped From The Cross / Shadows Of Lost Life / Moondance Prophecy.
The Black Gate Is Closed, (1989). Bestial Summoning / Blood Runs From The Altar / Angels Blood.
Rehearsal Demo, (1989). Angels Blood / Fall Into Decay / Rise Of Armageddon.
INCANTATIONS, Dolores DOL004 (1991). Incantations / Spawn of Azahoth / Nocturnal Blasphemies / Submit To Death / Blood Runs From The Altar.
IN THE EMBRACE OF EVIL, Black Sun BS007 (1996). Thirteen Bells Of Doom / Blood Runs From The Altar / Submit To Death / Fall Into Decay / Seven Gates / Angels Blood / Nocturnal Blasphemies / Spawn Of Azathoth / Incantation / Church Of The Pentagram / Ripped From The Cross.

GROTESQUE IMPALEMENT

KARLSRUHE, GERMANY — *Sebastian Knab (vocals), Stefan Linder (guitar), Norman Gerstner (guitar), Dersep (bass), Christian Krischke (drums).*

Badenian Death Metal hailing from Karlsruhe. GROTESQUE IMPALEMENT was manifested during February of 2000 at the hands of guitarist Norman Gerstner and drummer Christian Krischke. Subsequent recruits would be frontman Sascha Wagner, second guitarist Stefan Linder and bassist Mathias Mössner. At first this combo went by the title of MUTILATION. In September of 2001 Wagner exited, his place being soon filled by Sebastian Knab and in this guise the group took on the new name of GROTESQUE IMPALEMENT.

A further change came in August of 2002 when Mössner opted out. Sebastian 'Dersep' Kappenberger took his position on bass for recording of the EP 'Exposition Of The Impaled', produced by Patrick Damiani and recorded at Tidal Wave Studios in Karlsruhe.

EXPOSITION OF THE IMPALED, Independent (1987). Exposition Of The Impaled / Necrolust / The Shadow.

GROTESQUEUPHORIA

LONG ISLAND, NY, USA — *Sam Lara (vocals / guitar), Doug Randazzo (guitar), Eric Sandalic (bass), Gabe Madsen (drums).*

Long Island Death Metal quartet previously traded under the titles of EXUVIATE then the female fronted BUTCHERY. The self financed debut, 'Euphoric Discordance', arrived in 2002. The bands roots go back as far as 1995, and the band SANGUINARY CARNAGE comprising of vocalist / guitarist Sam Lara, erstwhile EXUVIATE guitarist Doug Randazzo and drummer Rich Hervey. This act was completed the following year when EXTRA HOT SAUCE guitarist Eric Sandalic switched instruments to fill the bass position.

When the band's original rehearsal complex burnt down the act relocated to Holtsville, soon inducting lead vocalist April Taylor. Lara now concentrated on guitar playing and a name switch to BUTCHERY was adopted. The band made their entrance officially with the 1998 demo session 'Blackest Blood'. Throughout 1998 and 1999 BUTCHERY put in support slots in New York City to numerous visiting artists including DEICIDE, IMMOLATION, KRISIUN, INTERNAL BLEEDING, DEHUMANIZED, NILE, INCANTATION, DISFIGURED, GORGUTS, ANGEL CORPSE and VADER amongst others. The group also delivered strong performance at the 1999 'March Metal Meltdown' festival in Asbury Park, New Jersey.

During the summer of 1999, work on the full length album commenced. However, during the pre-production stages internal disputes culminated in the departure of Hervey. The remaining band members duly re-adopted the new title of Randazzo's erstwhile band EXUVIATE.

In early 2000, after selling some 700 copies of the EXUVIATE CD, the band enrolled ex-ABHORANCE drummer Gabe Madsen through the time tested method of a 'musicians wanted' ad. The group's line up was still unstable though and after Taylor neglected to show up for a gig in Pennsylvania she was fired. The lead vocal role was brought in house as Sam Lara re-assumed the duties of lead vocalist, backed up by both Madsen and Randazzo.

During 2001, after a set at the 'Milwaukee Metal Fest' the band set to work on a further CD. At this juncture yet another new band title came to pass and GROTESQUEUPHORIA was decided upon with Randazzo keeping EXUVIATE for the title of a side project venture. A new album entitled 'Conquered By Corruption' was laid down in 2003 but Randazzo then bailed out to join PERPETUAL SUFFERING and Sandalic switched back to the lead guitar role. In August of 2003 the band enrolled the IMMORTAL SUFFERING and SPAWN credited Leo Bakman on guitar.

EUPHORIC DISCORDANCE, (2002). Cursed To Live / Dead / Sadistic Symphony / Torch Of Revenge / Shadow Of The Dwell / Death Bed Repentance / Ritual Manifestation / Grotesque Mutation / Pavement Of The Concentration Camp / Intro / The Coming Plague / Burial.

GUIDANCE OF SIN

STOCKHOLM, SWEDEN — *Mattias Leinikka (vocals), Jesper Lofgren (guitar), Linus Nirbrandt (guitar), L.E. Simnell (bass), Tobbe Sillman (drums).*

Stockholm "Death Rollers" founded by guitarists Jesper Lofgren and Linus Nirbrant during 1994, both formerly with the highly rated A CANOUROUS QUINTET. The act was originally conceived as a side project act with ex-SANGUINARY vocalist Leini (a.k.a. Mattias Leinikka) and AMON AMARTH, A CANOROUS QUINTET and MARDUK drummer Fredrik Andersson. Interest in the groups endeavours following a 1997 demo 'Soul Disparity' prompted a deal with the Danish label Mighty Music Label for the album 'Soul Seducer'.

Following this album GUIDANCE OF SIN pulled in erstwhile SANGUINARY and SPAZMOSITY bassist L.E. Limnell. Andersson would decamp to concentrate on AMON AMARTH and Tobbe Sillman, of THE DEAD, duly filled the vacancy.

The 2000 released '6106' album, released again through Mighty Music, sees a cover of MOTÖRHEAD's 'Killed By Death'. GUIDANCE OF SIN would fold the following year. In 2001 Andersson and Leinikka spearheaded a fresh outfit dubbed CURRICULUM MORTIS, joined by Leo Pignon of A CANOROUS QUINTET and NIDEN DIV. 187 on guitar. Switching to the guitar role, ex-GUIDANCE OF SIN drummer Tobbe Sillman created VICIOUS ART in 2002 with ex-DARK FUNERAL members guitarist Matti Mäkelä and drummer Robert Lundin.

Linus Nirbrant gained mixing credits on VOTUR's 2003 'Planet Cemetery' EP.

Linus Nirbrant and Jesper Löfgren, alongside erstwhile colleagues from A CANOROUS QUINTET, embarked upon a new band project, THE PLAGUE, in early 2005.

Soul Disparity, (1997). Goddess Of Lies / Soul Disparity / Turning To Reality / The God Who Didnt Forgive.

Acts, Nocturnal Music (1999). Act / In The Hour Of Peril.

SOULSEDUCER, Mighty Music (1999). Guided By Sin / Soulseducer / Desire / Prosecution Of The True Meaning / Dawn Of The New Religion / Fated ... / Goddess Of Lies / Soul Disparity / Turning To Reality / The God Who Didnt Forgive.

6106, Mighty Music (2000). Mans Journey / Dont Let God Come Near / In The Hour Of Peril / Nosferatus Head / Breaking The Circle / Acts / Rock Of The 20s / 6106 / The Primeval Myth Of A Vampyre / Killed By Death.

GUTROT

DETROIT, MI, USA — *Brian Forge (vocals), Chris (guitar), Jon Halcomb (guitar), Kevin Carron (bass), Zach Gibson (drums).*

GUTROT was created during the Summer of 2003, originally conceived as a side project of MULCH conceived by guitarist Jon Halcomb and singer Brian Forge. Subsequent recruits would be CURATE drummer Zach Gibson and MULCH colleague Kevin Carron on bass guitar. However, after demoing two tracks the band was stopped in its tracks due to "financial problems'. Whilst GUTROT was in stasis though, with Gibson having joined MUTILATED, the demo circulated and drew a positive response.

The group was re-founded in 2003, adding ex-SOLSTICE member Chris as second guitarist. Signing to the Amputated Vein label GUTROT delivered six tracks for inclusion on a split album 'Excruciatingly Euphoric Torment' shared with DYSENTERY in 2004. The band would lose the services of both guitarists Chris and Jon Halcomb in May, drafting Kevin as one replacement.

Zach Gibson resigned from his posts in both GUTROT and MUTILATED in June of 2004 in order to join THE BLACK DAHLIA MURDER.

EXCRUCIATINGLY EUPHORIC TORMENT, Amputated Vein (2004) (Split album with DYSENTERY). Legless And Helpless / Gorging On Menstrual Chunks / Incestual Rimjob / Fatal Anal Penetration / Teabagging The Dead / Cock Snot Covered Twat.

HACAVITZ

QUERETARO, MEXICO — *Antimo Buonnano (vocals / guitar), Eduardo Guevara (guitar), Oscar García (drums).*

Queretaro Black / Death Metal band HACAVITZ signed to French label Osmose Productions for their opening 2004 EP. Frontman Antimo Buonnano is noted for his work with such extreme acts as DISGORGE, PYPHOMGERTUM, RAVAGER, IMPIETY, BLOODREAPING and DEMONISED. Drummer Oscar García is a veteran of RAVAGER, IMPIETY, DOMAIN and DEMONIZED whilst guitarist Eduardo Guevara holds credits with BLOODREAPING, RAPED GOD, CENOTAPH and PYPHOMGERTUM.

A May 2005 single, the single track 'Lusting The Dead Of The Night' on FTF Productions, was restricted to 666 copies. HACAVITZ signed a deal with Moribund Records in 2005, issuing the 'Venganza' album in November. The album saw European release in January 2006. Despite the loss of longstanding guitar player Eduardo Guevara, the follow up record, billed 'Katun', was completed in February 2007.

Hacavitz, Osmose Productions (2004). Conquista / Fervour Of Dead / Ravage.
Lusting The Dead Of The Night', FTF Productions (2005) (limited edition 666 copies). Lusting The Dead Of The Night'.
VENGANZA, Moribund (2005). Night Winds / Ultimate Covenant / Tsita Ndte / Fathom Thee Eerie / Old Rancor / Lusting The Dead Of The Nite / Venganza / Mixtla Miquiztli / Lightning Bolts Of Dead / Viaje A Mictlan.

HACRIDE

POITIERS, FRANCE — *Samuel Bourreau (vocals), Adrien Grousset (guitar), Benoist Danneville (bass), Olivier Laffond (drums).*

Technical Death Metal act HACRIDE, taking the title from "Acrid" and created during 2001 in Poitiers, opened with a 2003 demo entitled 'Cyanide Echoes' produced by Matthieu Metzger. Recording line-up involved singer Samuel Bourreau, guitarist Adrien Grousset, former LATRODECTUS bass player Benoist Danneville with Olivier Laffond on drums.

The band featured the track 'The Daily Round' on the 2005 Listenable Records French Metal compilation 'Revolution Calling'. The band issued their debut album 'Deviant Current Signals', recorded by Franck Hueso, in 2005.

HACRIDE issued the follow up 'Amoeba' in February 2007. This set, recorded at L'Autre Studio and co-produced by the band with Frank Hueso, included a cover version of OJOS DE BRUJO's 'Zambra'. The band toured France and Switzerland in May 2007 partnered with KLONE and AYGGHON.

Cyanide Echoes, Klonosphere (2003) (Demo). Cold / This Place / Down.
DEVIANT CURRENT SIGNAL, Listenable POSH069 (2005). Human Monster / TYPO / This Place / Polarity / Flesh Lives On / Protect / Cold (Demo) / Down (Demo).
AMOEBA, Listenable POSH091 (2007). Perturbed / Fate / Vision Of Hate / Zambra / Liquid / Cycle / Deprived Of Soul / Strength / Ultima Necat / On The Threshold Of Death.
AMOEBA, Listenable POSH091 (2007). Perturbed / Fate / Vision Of Hate / Zambra / Liquid / Cycle / Deprived Of Soul / Strength / Ultima Necat / On The Threshold Of Death.

HADEZ

PERU — *John Agressor (vocals / guitar), Christ Death (guitar), Abel Sedition (bass), Daniel Demolition (drums).*

HACRIDE

Death Metal combo HADEZ was forged in 1986 by Rafo Basura, Armando Mutante and Toñin Destructor, subsequently adding guitarist John Agressor and vocalist / bassist Kike Satanás Eyaculation. With Destructor's departure the band opened proceedings with the three track demo 'Guerreros de la muerte'. After these sessions Christ Death took over bass guitar and Ron King was enrolled as lead vocalist, this line up cutting two further demos 'Altar Of Sacrifice' in 1989 and 'Hadez Attack' during 1990.

The HADEZ line up for the 'Extreme Badness On The World' demo of 1992 comprised guitarists John Agressor and Christ Death, bass player Abel Sedition and drummer Daniel Demolition. A debut album, entitled 'Aquelarre', emerged in 1993, followed by 'Even If You Die A Thousand Times' for Guerreros de la Muerte Records.

AQUELAREE, Brutal (1996).
EVEN IF YOU DIE A THOUSAND TIMES, 199 (2000).

HAEMORRHAGE

SPAIN — Spain's HAEMORRHAGE are noted not only for the ferocity of their unique brand of Goregrind but their stomach churning single and album covers. Indeed, the 1999 split single with Czech act INGROWING depicts a truly horrendous photograph of a young child mauled by a dog. Debuted with the 'Grotesque Embryopathology' demo and have also issued a split promo CD on Morbid Records with CHRIST DENIED in addition to 1995's 'Emetic Cult' album.

The 2000 album 'Loathesongs' includes many cover versions, not only of the expected kind with renditions tracks by CARCASS, DEFECATION, ENTOMBED, REGURGITATE, IMPALED NAZARENE, IMPETIGO and SUICIDAL TENDENCIES of but also a take on UFO's 'Doctor Doctor'. The band would also feature three tracks as part of a four way split EP 'Rotten To The Gore' shared with OBLITERATE, EMBOLISM and SUFFOCATE. A split tape would also arrive courtesy of Shindy Productions, 'Dawn In The Rotting Czech', shared with MASTIC SCUM and recorded in the Czech Republic in July of 2000.

HAEMORRHAGE donated a version of 'Staph Terrorist' to the Razorback IMPETIGO tribute album 'Wizards Of Gore'.

The 2001 album 'Scalpel, Scissors And Other Forensic Instruments', on the Czech Copremesis label, collated early HAEMORRHAGE material including cover versions of KORTATU's 'Zu Atrapatu Artek' and GENERAL SURGERY's 'Slithering Of The Ulcerous Facial Tissue'. The same year the band shared a live split album, culled from their tenth anniversary gig at the Silcoma Rock Club, for the German Cudgel Agency label 'Live At The Morgue' with DEPRESSION.

The 2002 album 'Home Sweet Morgue' would be issued in Germany by Morbid Records with differing sleeve artwork. To promote the record HAEMORRHAGE undertook European dates an April billed alongside CRYPTOPSY, SPAWN and PROFANITY.

Guitarist Lucima was previously a member of AVULSED. Dani and Ramon debuted a new side project GREENFLY in 2003, issuing the album 'Globalization'.

Obnoxious EP, Morbid Single Productions MSP 03 (1994) (7" split single with CHRIST DENIED). Grotesque Embryopathology / Fermented Post Mortem Disgorgement / Cadaveric Metamorphose / Anatomized / Via Anal Introspection.

EMETIC CULT, Steamhammer SPV 84-12482 (1995). Necromantic / Uncontrollable Proliferation Of Neoplasm / Decrepit Dejection / Dilacerate The Sweet Diabetic Diabolism / Deranged For Loathsome / Excaving The Iliac Fossaty / Grotesque Embryopathology / Intravenous Molestation Of Obstructionist Arteries (O-Pus) / Via Anal Inspection / Fermented Post Mortem Disgorgent / Cadaveric Metamorphose / Anatomised / Pernicious Dyseptic Inoculation / Foetal Mincer / Expectorating Pulmonary Mucu-purulence.

Decom-Poser, (1997) (7" split single with DAMNABLE). Decom-Poser / Malignant Cancroid Formation / Excavating The Iliac Fossaty.

GRUME, Morbid (1997). Incinerator Of Cadaveric Leftovers / Exquisite Eschatology / Torrentlike Eventeration / Dissect, Exhume, Devour ... / Putrescent Necromorphism / Cartilageous Pulped Offals / Decom-Posers / Fragments (Anatomical Blues) / In Nephritic Blue / Ectopic Eye / Intravenous Molestation Of Obstructionist Arteries (O-Pus II) / Rectovaginal Fistula / Formaldehyde / Far Beyond The Forensic Pathology.

The Cadaverous Carnival EP, Upground (1998) (7" split single with DENAK). The Sickening Aroma Of A Rectal Carcinoma / Cirrhoetic Liver Distillation / Worm Infested Cavities / Zu Atrapatu Artek.

Surgery For The Dead EP, Morbid (1998) (7" split single with GROINCHURN). Enshrouded In Putilage / Surgery For The Dead / Slithering Maceration Of Ulcerous Facial Tissue.

ANATOMICAL INFERNO, Morbid MR049 (1998). Enshrouded In Putrilage / A Cataleptic Rapture / Surgery For The Dead / Treasures Of Anatomy / Necrectic Garbage / Putritorium / Dawn In The Rotting Paradise / Aftertaste Of Putrefaction / Worm Infested Cavities / I'm A Pathologist / Cirrhectic Liver Distillation / Witness Of Forensic Horror / Dying On A Mass Of Chyme And Rancid Excrement / Set The Morgue On Fire.

Putrefaction (I Still Remind), Copremesis (1999) (7" split single with INGROWING). Putrefaction (I Still Remind) / Anatomized / Rectovaginal Tissue.

Rotten To The Gore EP, Erebos Productions ERE 020 (2000). Pyosified (Rotten To The Gore) / Unlock The Morgue / Fester Feast.

LOATHE SONGS, Morbid MR 070 (2000). Intro- Megaton / Vestige Of The Earthly Remains / Pyosfied (Rotten To The Core) / Premature Autopsy / Disgorging Fetus / Oozing Molten Gristle / Dear Uncle Creepy / Fascist Pig / M.A.D. / Satanic Masowhore / Doctor Doctor.

LIVE IN THE MORGUE, Cudgel Agency (2001). Treasures Of Anatomy / Necrotic Garbage / Pyosified / Deranged For Loathsome- Putrescent Necromorphism / Anatomized / Decom-Posers / Disgorging Foetus / Excavating The Iliac Fossa / Oozing Molten Gristle / Staph Terrorist / I'm A Pathologist.

SCALPEL, SCISSORS AND OTHER FORENSIC INSTRUMENTS, Copremesis (2001). Decom-Poser / Fragments (Anatomical Relics) / Dissect, Exhume, Devour,... / Torrent Like Eventeration / Malignant Canceroid Formation / Intravenous Molestation / Excavating The Iliac Fossa / Uncontrollable Proliferation Of Neoplasm / Rectovaginal Fistula / Enshrouded In Putrilage / Surgery For The Dead / Slithering Maceration Of Ulcerous Facial Tissue / The Sickening Aroma Of A Rectal Carcinoma / Cirrhoetic Liver Distillation / Worm Infested Cavities / Zu Atrapatu Artek / Extreme Ulceration.

Do You Still Believe In Hell? EP, Fudgeworthy FUDGE 31 (2001). Exquisite Eschatology / Decom-Posers / Excavating The Iliac Fossa.

MORGUE SWEET HOME, Morbid MR 092 (2002). Mortuary Riot / Oozing Molten Gristle / Midnight Mortician / Virulent Mass Necropsy / Funeral Carnage / Obnoxious (Surgeon Of The Dead) / Exhuming Impulse / Unlock The Morgue / Sublime Surgical Epitaph / Morgue Sweet Home / Mangled Surgical Epitaph / The Forensic Requiems / Dirge For The Sick / Intravenous Molestation Of Obstructionist Arteries (O-Pus IV).

APOLOGY FOR PATHOLGY, Morbid (2006). Posthumous Predation / Feasting On Purulence / Frenzied Genital Carbonization / Antemortem Thanatopraxis / Disgorging Innards / Festerfeast / Excruciating Denervation Of The Limbar Spine / Edible Necrectomy / Intravenous Molestation Of The Obstructionist Arteries (O-Pus V) / Cadaveric Metamorphose / Furtive Dissection / Surgical Extravaganza / Syndicate Of Sickness / Apology For Patholgy.

HAGGARD

GERMANY — *Asis Nasseri (vocals / guitar), Markus Reisinger (vocals / guitar), Taki Saile (vocals / piano), Andreas Nad (bass), Vera Hoffman (violin), Katherina Quast (cello), Luz Marsen (drums).*

HAGGARD, mentored by vocalist / guitarist Asis Nasseri, was founded in late 1991 and released their first demo, 'Introduction', the following year, the band touring heavily supporting the likes of DEICIDE, BIOHAZARD, AGRESSOR, ANATHEMA and PYOGENESIS. During these formative years HAGGARD would evolve from a straightforward melodic Death Metal combo into a full blown 16 piece Metal orchestra.

1993 saw HAGGARD's first self financed mini album 'Progressive' and in 1994 they toured Europe as support to AMORPHIS and DESULTORY. In 1995 the group issued the 'Once ... Upon A December's Dawn' promo tape, promoting this release by touring with Danes ILLDISPOSED and DISGUST. By now the group had inducted a violinist, cellist, soprano vocalist and pianist and for the first time HAGGARD took a line-up roster out on the road comprising of 16 musicians.

The follow up album, 'And Thou Shalt Trust ... The Seer' released by the Serenades label in 1997, proved to be an ambitious affair with German, English and Latin lyrics atop a heady mix of Metal. Classical and mediaeval music. HAGGARD toured alongside RAGE in 1997 and ATROCITY in February of 1998. Later that same year HAGGARD had elevated themselves to headliner status undertaking a September batch of European dates with guests SOLEFALD and Norway's TRISTANIA. The group's debut live album 'Awaking The Gods', culled from headline shows in Mexico, would arrive in August of 2001.

Following issue of the 'Eppur Si Muove' album HAGGARD underwent line-up changes, unceremoniously dumping both bassist Robin Fischer and singer Gaby Koss, the latter rather tactlessly described by Nasseri as "not good enough". Suzanne took over the vocal position. The group also acquired two cellists, Johannes and Claudia.

PROGRESSIVE, Progressive (1993). Charity Absurd / Mind Mutilation / Incapsuled / Progressive / Daddy Was Her First Man.

ONCE ... UPON A DECEMBER'S DAWN, Progressive (1995). Perpetual Motions / The Tragedy / Afterlife / The Lost Forgiveness / Circle Of Dreams.

AND THOU SHALT TRUST ... THE SEER, Serenades SR011 (1997). Chapter 1: The Day As Heaven Wept / Chapter 2: Origin Of A Crystal Soul / Chapter 3: In A Pale Moon's Shadow / Chapter 4: De La Morte Noire / Chapter 5: Lost (Robin's song) / Chapter 6: A Midnight Gathering.

AWAKING THE CENTURIES, Drakkar (2000). Rachmaninov: Choir / Pestilencia / Heavenly Damnation / The Final Victory / Saltorella La Manuelina / Awaking The Centuries / Statement zur Lage der Musica / In A Fullmoon Procession / Menuett (I) Prophecy Fulfilled / Menuett (II) And The Dark Night Entered / Courante / Rachmaninov: Choir. Chart position: 64 GERMANY.

AWAKING THE GODS- LIVE IN MEXICO, Drakkar (2001). Intro- Rachmaninov Choir / Mediaeval Part / Lost / Prophecy Fulfilled- And The Dark Night Entered / Menuett / Origin Of A Chrystal 50 Vl / Awakening The Centuries / Courante / In A Full Moon Procession / Final Victory / In A Pale Moon's Shadow.

EPPUR SI MUOVE, Drakkar (2004). All' Inizio H La Morte / Menuetto In Fa-minore / Per Aspera Ad Astra / Of A Might Divine / Gavotta In Si-minore / Herr Mannelig / The Observer / Eppur Si Muove / Larghetto / Epilogo Adagio / Herr Mannelig (Short version). Chart position: 47 GERMANY.

HANGING GARDEN

FINLAND — *Ari Nieminen (vocals), Mikko Kolari (guitar), Saku Manninen (guitar), Matti Reinola (bass / keyboards), Janne Jukarainen (drums).*

Gothic Doom Metal combo HANGING GARDEN comprises an elite cast of players. Led by CALEDONIAN and DAUNTLESS vocalist Ari Nieminen the band also includes SHAMRAIN guitarist Mikko Kolari, EXIT WOUNDS guitarist Saku Manninen and bassist / keyboard player Matti Reinola of GRAYSCALE and SHAMRAIN. Janne Jukarainen, another scene adept cites credentials with BEEZEBUB, GAURITHOTH, GRAYSCALE, NAILDOWN, SHAMRAIN and SOURCE OF DEMISE.

HANGING GARDEN was formulated during mid 2004 by Ari Nieminen and Matti Reinola. First product would be a two track demo in February 2006, these songs securing a deal in April with Spinefarm Records.

Hanging Garden, Hanging Garden (2006) (Demo). Sleep Of Ages / This Dead Scene / Dark Waters.

HARMONY DIES

BERLIN, GERMANY — *Martin Pomp (vocals / bass), Mike Hoffman (guitar), Kai Mertens (guitar), Robert Kotlarski (drums).*

Berlin Death Metal act HARMONY DIES date to 1992. The band made their presence felt on the Metal underground scene with the demo tapes 'Living Corpses' in 1992 and 'Slope' coming in 1993. A split single with Brazilian Death veterans KRISIUN emerged in 1994 on the Morbid label. More demos then ensued with 'Third Output Of Incompetence' delivered in 1994 and a 1995 promo session preceding the 1996 'Slaughtered' EP.

Signing to the Ars Metalli label, HARMONY DIES industrious release schedule continued on with 1998's 'Don't Trust' album and 2000 follow up 'I'll Be Your Master'. Poserslaughter Records issued a split 7" single, 'Hybrid Manifestation' shared with SPAWN, in 2002. Morbid Records issued the 'Impact' album in 2003.

HARMONY DIES added new guitarist Ulf Binder in October of 2002.

Slaughtered, Folter (1996). Decision For War / Slaughtered / Eternal Cycle / Like Yourself / Where The Dead Are.
Decision For War, Harmony Dies (1996) ('Slaughtered' EP). Decision For War / Slaughtered / Eternal Cycle / Like Yourself / Where The Dead Are.
DON'T TRUST, Ars Metalli (1997). Execution / Pray To God / Something Dies / Dwell In Darkness / Living Corpses / Perhaps / Flying / Schmerz / Pulsating Uterine / Menstrual / Song Of Sirens / From Behinds.
I'LL BE YOUR MASTER, Ars Metalli ARSCD028 (1998). I'll Be Your Master / Final Confrontation / Inner Pleasure / Tuning / Wasted Minds / No Longer / Markmens Destiny / Eating Flesh / The Unbecoming / Another Song Of Sirens.
IMPACT, Morbid MR 104 (2003). Narcotic / Blessing / Toxicated / Illfated / Impact / Farewell / Inside / Suffering / InstruMental / Silence / Subliminal.

HATE

WARSAW, POLAND — *Adam The First Sinner (vocals / guitar), Hellbeast (guitar), Cyprian (bass), Hexen (drums).*

Debuting with the 1992 'Abhorrence' demo tape HATE, having started life in Warsaw during 1990 initially entitled INFECTED, cited a line-up of Adam The First Sinner on vocals and guitar, lead guitarist Quack, bass player Martin and drummer Piotr 'Mittloff' Kozieradzki, the latter also a long term session member of GOETIA. The 1994 follow up 'Evil Art' saw Daniel taking the bass role. A third tape, the eight track 'The Unwritten Law' issued in 1995, found Quack replaced by Ralph. This HATE line up was maintained for the band's first album, the vinyl issue 'Daemon Qui Fecit Terram' released by the Vox Mortiis label in 1996. 'Lord Is Avenger' followed in 1998.

HATE's 1999 mini-album 'Victims' included four new tracks alongside cover versions of NAPALM DEATH's 'Kill' and SLAYER's 'Postmortem'. This latter track would re-surface on the Dwell SLAYER tribute album 'Gateway To Hell Volume II'. Cyprian would now be the band's new bass player. That same year Mittloff would prove influential in resurrecting DOMAIN, subsequently featuring on their 'From Oblivion' record.

With HATE's reputation burgeoning the Polish apocalypse Productions label re-issued a collection of early material as the 2000 box set 'Evil Decade Of Hate'. Mittloff would also deputise in the studio for THUNDERBOLT's 'The Sons Of The Darkness' record. HATE also scored a North American release through the World War III imprint, repackaging the 'Victims' and 'Lord Is Avenger' outings as one retitled 'Holy Dead Trinity' the following year. Mittloff then featured on a second DOMAIN outing, 'Gat Etemmi'.

In September 2000 guitarist Ralph was replaced by Kaos. A brand new HATE studio album, 'Cain's Way', was delivered in June 2001 via Apocalypse Productions for domestic Polish release. That October Mittloff made his exit to found a Progressive Rock outfit RIVERSIDE, HATE pulling in substitute Hellrizer- a man with credits with such artists as PASCAL, GOETIA and GORTAL. With this revised line-up HATE headlined a short run of gigs in Belarus before embarking on the Polish 'Thrash 'Em All' tour in November in alliance with KRISIUN, VADER and BEHEMOTH.

A further series of Polish gigs found HATE hooking back up with VADER with support act AZARATH in June 2002. As HATE busied themselves with a new studio album provisionally titled 'Awakening Of The Liar' the esteemed British Candlelight label took on 'Cain's Way' for a European issue, with all new artwork, in July. Roadwork included the band forming up part of an impressive cast for European 'Xmas Festivals' in December in alliance with SIX FEET UNDER, IMMOLATION, KATAKLYSM, DYING FETUS and MARDUK. Later gigs in Holland added veteran Thrashers EXODUS to the bill.

HATE signed to France's Listenable Records for a February 2004 album 'Awakening Of The Liar'. The band would head up the 'Days Of Destruction' tour, over ESQARIAL, MUTILATION, ABUSED MAJESTY and PYORRHOEA, throughout Poland that December. February 2005 saw European gigs allied with DIES IRAE, CRIONICS and DECAPITATED. The band entered Hertz Studio in Bialystok in the Summer for a new album 'Anaclasis' for an October release through Listenable Records.

In November HATE announced the addition of ex-CHAOSPHERE and DAMNED guitarist Hellbeast. Drummer Hellrizer was let go in December due to a quoted "weakening dedication to HATE's" activities", and would be replaced by Hexen in January 2006.

The band formed up the Polish 'Rebel Angels' tour in April 2007 featuring DARZAMAT, CRIONICS and SAMMATH NAUR.

DAEMON QUI FECIT TERRAM, Vox Mortiis (1996). Animate The Blood / In Satan We Trust / Inflict The Pain / Almost You Are Dead / Merry Christless / Heaven Like A Hole / Lords Of Sin / An Eye For An Eye / Died In Vain / Deamon Qui Fecit Terram / Cadentia.
LORD IS AVENGER, Novum Vox Mortis (1998). Share Your Blood With Daemon / World Has To Die / Dead And Mystified / Intransigence Of Evil / Enter The Hell / Convocation / Lord Is Avenger / Paradise As Lost / Pagan Triumph / Vexation Of My Spirit / Satan's Horde.
VICTIMS, Metal Mind Productions (1999). Holy Dead Trinity / No Life After Death / Victims / God Overslept / The Kill / Postmortem.
EVIL DECADE OF HATE, Apocalypse Productions (2000).
HOLY DEAD TRINITY, World War III BLACK 044 (2001) (USA release). Holy Dead Trinity / No Life After Death / Victims / God Overslept / The Kill / Share Your Blood With Daemon / World Has To Die / Dead And Mistified / Enter The Hell / Convocation / Lord Is Avenger / Paradise As Lost / Pagan Triumph / Satan's Horde.
CAIN'S WAY, Apocalypse Productions BLACK 045 (2001). Apocalypse / The Sin Becomes / Sectarian Murder / The Fifth Eternally Despised / Thorough Hate To Eternity / Shame Of The Creator / Resurrected But Failed / Cain's Way / Holy Dead Trinity / Future Is Mayhem / From Cain To Cadmon.
AWAKENING OF THE LIAR, Listenable POSH057 (2003). Flagellation / Anti-God Extremity / Close To The Nephilim / Immolate The Pope / The Shroud / The Scrolls / Awakening Of The Liar / Serve God Rely On Me / Grail In The Flesh / Spirit Of Gospa.
ANACLASIS—A HAUNTING GOSPEL OF MALICE AND HATRED, Listenable POSH077 (2005). Anaclasis / Necropolis / Hex / Malediction / Euphoria Of The New Breed / Razorblade / Immortality / Fountains Of Blood To Reach Heavens.

HATE ETERNAL

TAMPA BAY, FL, USA — *Erik Rutan (vocals / guitar), Alex Webster (bass), Tim Yeung (drums).*

HATE ETERNAL is one of the two bands led by MORBID ANGEL and ex-RIPPING CORPSE guitarist Erik Rutan and CANNIBAL CORPSE bassist Alex Webster. Erik Rutan also operates a Symphonic female fronted Metal project titled ALAS. These two concerns shared equal space on a 1997 industry promo release entitled 'Engulfed In Grief'.

The Tampa Bay based project signed up with Wicked World, a death metal subsidiary of UK label Earache Records. For recording of the October 1999 'Conquering The Throne' album HATE ETERNAL pulled in ex-INTERCINE bassist Jared Anderson, drummer Tim Yeung and SUFFOCATION and WELT guitarist Doug Cerrito. Rutan would still be assisting MORBID ANGEL as live guitarist and establishing his reputation behind the controls as a noted producer, having handled Brazilian act KRISIUN's 2000 album amongst many others.

HATE ETERNAL toured as support to CANNIBAL CORPSE and DETHRONED with the band's latest line-up including former MALEVOLENT CREATION drummer Derek Roddy.

Anderson would be drafted into the ranks of MORBID ANGEL for their 2001 UK dates when regular frontman Steve Tucker was forced to bow out. However, HATE ETERNAL would go beyond the side project stage when a new album, 'King Of All Kings', was announced for September 2002 release. Gigs to promote the release would include a run of shows in Brazil the same month.

Erstwhile HATE ETERNAL drummer Tim Yeung would be employed as session drummer for the 2002 AURORA BOREALIS album 'Time, Unveiled'. Coincidentally, Derek Roddy had also previously sat in with AURORA BOREALIS on earlier albums. November 2002 shows found the band on the road in North America on a package billing with CANNIBAL CORPSE, CATTLE DECAPITATION and MACABRE. The band then toured the UK in December with support from KATAKLYSM and DERANGED.

HATE ETERNAL, bringing in Randy Piro, at first only intended as temporary replacement for Jared Anderson, united with DYING FETUS, KATAKLYSM, and INTO ETERNITY for North American dates in February and March of 2003. Erik Rutan suffered a cracked vertebrae when the band's van went off the road in Wisconsin on 8th March. The singer was released from hospital and persevered with the tour. Jared Anderson backed out of band activities in order to commit himself to a drug rehabilitation programme. Rutan was recovered enough to mix the album 'Total Death' from leading Colombian Death Metal band MASACRE.

HATE ETERNAL allied with ARCH ENEMY, EVERGREY and THE BLACK DAHLIA MURDER for a short but intensive run of US dates in August before hooking up with HATEBREED, MADBALL, TERROR and CEPHALIC CARNAGE for September shows. The band announced further touring plans for the US in November of 2003, forming up a billing comprising DEICIDE, KRISIUN and CATTLE DECAPITATION. Taking the band into 2004 would be January European dates, the band headlining over DYING FETUS, DEEDS OF FLESH and PREJUDICE.

Erik Rutan gained mixing credits for Swedish act IN BATTLE's 2004 album 'Welcome To The Battlefield', the guitarist also donating a solo to the track 'Serpent'.

HATE ETERNAL announced the addition of second guitarist Eric Hersemann of LORD BLASPHEMER and DIABOLIC to the group's ranks in May of 2005. The group headed up a Summer package touring bill comprising KRISIUN, INCANTATION, INTO ETERNITY and ALL SHALL PERISH for US gigs in June. However, with INCANTATION forced out of the Canadian leg, due to "legal issues", JUNGLE ROT took over the vacant support slot for those gigs. This tour preceded a batch of Australian shows. A new album, 'I, Monarch' preceded by a Shane Drake

HATE ETERNAL (pic: Jesse Angelo)

directed promotional video for the title track, arrived on 28th June through Earache Records. 'I, Monarch', came in three formats, a regular CD, a limited edition slipcase CD with different cover art and a vinyl picture disc restricted to 1000 copies.

Erik Rutan spent December 2005 acting as producer for CELLADOR's 'Enter Deception' album. As 2006 opened, drummer Derek Roddy teamed up with BLOTTED SCIENCE, a technical extreme Metal project masterminded by guitarist RON JARZOMBEK of WATCHTOWER and SPASTIC INK repute alongside CANNIBAL CORPSE bassist Alex Webster. Meantime, erstwhile drummer Tim Yeung forged DIVINE HERESY with ex-FEAR FACTORY guitarist Dino Cazares.

HATE ETERNAL announced European gigs for April 2006 but would cancel these and lose the services of drummer Derek Roddy beforehand. A new set of shows resulted in an April US trek alongside ARCH ENEMY, CHIMAIRA, NEVERMORE and GOD FORBID, these shows later adding TEMPLE OF BRUTALITY. Kevin Talley of CHIMAIRA, DYING FETUS and MISERY INDEX stepped in as substitute drummer. The band then hooked up with SPAWN OF POSSESSION and SHADOWSLAND for European touring in May covering the UK, Germany, France, Spain, Italy, Holland, Hungary, Czech Republic and Belgium. Standing in on drums would be the DIMMU BORGIR, DEW-SCENTED, VILE, OLD MAN'S CHILD and PANZERCHRIST credited Reno Kiilerich.

Former HATE ETERNAL vocalist Jared Anderson died in his sleep on Saturday, October 14th at the age of 30.

Former member Tim Yeung deputised as stand in drummer for Western Massachusetts Metal outfit ALL THAT REMAINS North American dates throughout November and December 2006. Before the close of the year ex-drummer Derek Roddy joined TODAY IS THE DAY. As 2007 broke, HATE ETERNAL members Randy Piro and Eric Hersemann revealed they had teamed up in a new band called GIGAN.

The group signed with Metal Blade Records in January 2007. HATE ETERNAL parted ways with bassist Randy Piro in March. Alex Webster from CANNIBAL CORPSE handled bass duties on new recordings.

Alas / Hate Eternal, (1997) (Split demo with ALAS). Messiah Of Rage / Sacrilege Of Hate / Saturated In Dejection.

CONQUERING THE THRONE, Wicked World WICK006 (1999). Praise Of The Almighty / Dogma Condemned / Catacombs / Nailed To Obscurity / By His Own Decree / The Creed Of The Chaotic Divinity / Dethroned / Sacrilege Of Hate / Spiritual Holocaust / Darkness By Oath / Saturated In Dejection.

KING OF ALL KINGS, Earache MOSH 260 CD (2002). Our Beckoning / King Of All Kings / The Obscure Terror / Servants Of The

Gods / Beyond Redemption / Born By Fire / Chants In Declaration / Rising Legions Of Black / In Spirit (The Power Of Mana) / Powers That Be.

I, MONARCH, Earache MOSH 286 CD (2005). Two Demons / Behold Judas / The Victorious Reign / To Know Our Enemies / I, Monarch / Path To The Eternal Gods / The Plague Of Humanity / It Is Our Will / Sons Of Darkness / Faceless One.

I, MONARCH, Tokuma TKCS-85131 (2005) (Japanese release). Two Demons / Behold Judas / The Victorious Reign / To Know Our Enemies / I, Monarch / Path To The Eternal Gods / The Plague Of Humanity / It Is Our Will / Sons Of Darkness / Faceless One / I, Monarch (Session) / Son Of Darkness.

HATE FACTOR

GERMANY — *Christoph Mieves (vocals), Jan Pelser (guitar), Jochen Pelser (guitar), Manuel Bolze (bass), Christian Lehmkuhl (drums).*

Krefeld-Uerdingen Death Metal HATE FACTOR debuted in April of 2001 with the EP 'The Bad Breed'. The Pelser siblings, TORTURE CHAMBER lead guitarist Jan and rhythm guitarist Jochen of PREMATURE, together with drummer Christian Lehmkuhl, all members of SCYTHE, created the band in February of 2000. Peter Thomassen enrolled on bass that Summer, but decamped within a couple of months.

In an attempt to locate a suitable single the fledgling HATE FACTOR cut the purely instrumental demo '100% Of Pure Fuckin' Hate'. Christoph Mieves of CRIKEY, actually a rejected former applicant for the vocal spot in SCYTHE, convinced the band he had what it took. The bass was taken care of in the Spring of 2001 as former RIMJOB guitar player Manuel Bolze took on the task. This was the line up that crafted the EP 'The Bad Breed' and undertook their inaugural live performance on 18th August in Düsseldorf.

A second EP 'Mind Forged Killings' was published in 2002. The HATE FACTOR triumvirate of singer Christoph Mieves and guitarists lead player Jan Pelser and rhythm man Jochen Pelser also operate Grindcore band GRIND INC.

The Bad Breed, Hate Factor (2001). The Hate Factor / No One / Bad Breed / Kneel To The Bastard / My Blackest Seed / Death Parade / In The Hand Of The Obscene.

Mind Forged Killings, (2002). M.F.K. / Psychopath Massacre / Fight The War / Grown In Anger / Extinct!

HATEPLOW

FL, USA — *Kyle Simon (vocals), Rob Barrett (guitar), Phil Fasciana (guitar), Julian Hollowell (bass), Dave Culross (drums).*

Florida's HATEPLOW, initially convened as an amateur studio project, feature MALEVOLENT CREATION guitarists Rob Barrett and Phil Fasciana. Barrett is also an erstwhile member of CANNIBAL CORPSE. HATEPLOW was first assembled with drummer Larry Hawke in 1994. With the project becoming a more serious venture ex-SICKNESS vocalist Kyle Symon and former REVENANT bassist Tim Scott were inducted to make up the numbers as a deal was scored with Pavement Records.

However, just before recording of the debut album 'Everybody Dies' Hawke was arrested and sentenced to a lengthy jail sentence. Thankfully for the band Hawke was able to lay down his drum tracks before being incarcerated. Tragedy would strike later though as Hawke, trying to save the life of his pet dog, died in a fire at his home in May of 1997.

Former MALEVOLENT CREATION, INCANTATION and SUFFOCATION man Dave Culross would take the drummers position for the second album 'The Only Law Is Survival. The bass position would also undergo a change with the inclusion of HIBERNUS MORTIS and ACRIMONIUM's Doug Humlack.

Just prior to a February 2001 European jaunt alongside IN AETURNUM and MALEVOLENT CREATION Humlack backed out. Julian Hollowell, a.k.a. Xaphan- guitarist with Black Metal merchants KULT OV AZAZEL, would fill in on four string duties.

The band toured Europe in June of 2003 alongside Finland's ROTTEN SOUND and Germany's DEBAUCHERY.

A live album, entitled 'Moshpit Murder' and recorded in Detroit, Michigan during the band's "The Only Law is Survival" 2000 tour in support of S.O.D., would be issued through Arctic Music in September of 2004. Bonus tracks included the band's original 1996 demo.

EVERYBODY DIES, (1998). Everybody Dies / Stalker / Prison Bitch / $20.00 Blow Job / Challenged / The Gift Over / Crack Down / In The Ditch / Ass To Mouth Resuscitation / Compound / Ante Up / Anally Annie / Denial / Born With Both.

THE ONLY LAW IS SURVIVAL, Pavement Music (2000). The Only Law Is Survival / Shattered By Disease / F.T.M. / Emotional Catastrophe / Should I Care? / Outcast / Addicted To Porn / Traitor / Without Weapons / Payback / Incarcerated (Intent To Sell) / Random Acts Of Violence / Resurgence Of Hate.

MOSHPIT MURDER, Arctic Music (2004). Crack Down / Everybody Dies / The Only Law Is Survival / Traitor / FTM / Prison Bitch / Without Weapons / Stalker/Born With Both / In The Ditch / $20 Blow Job / Anally Annie / Ante Up / Born With Both / Everybody Dies / In The Ditch / Addiction / Stalker / The Gift Giver / Payback.

HATESPHERE

DENMARK — *Jacob Bredahl (vocals), Peter Lyse Hansen (guitar), Ziggy (guitar), Mikael Ehlert (bass), Morten Toft Hansen (drums).*

Death-Thrash act which includes featuring RAUNCHY drummer Morten Toft Hansen in the ranks. Early demo works, 'Condemned Future' in April 1995, 'Disconnected' in 1997 and 'Spring'98', were conducted under the formative banner of NECROSIS. Rebranded, the group re-debuted with an eponymous album in April 2001 for the Italian Scarlet label. The 2002 album 'Bloodred Hatred', produced by Tommy Hansen, was recorded in Jailhouse Studios in Horsens, Denmark. The band hooked up with INFLICTION for January 2003 tour dates followed by April European gigs ranked alongside MASTODON and THE HAUNTED.

Drummer Morten Toft Hansen exited in May 2003 in order to focus his energies on RAUNCHY. The band substituted him with Anders Gyldenøhr in July. The band's December 2003 EP, 'Something Old, Something New, Something Borrowed And Something Black', issued through Italy's Scarlet Records saw live tracks alongside cover versions of OZZY OSBOURNE's 'Bark At The Moon' and ANTHRAX's 'Caught In A Mosh'.

The 'Ballet Of The Brute' album, recorded at Jailhouse Studios with producer Tommy Hansen, arrived in 2004. INVOCATOR's Jacob Hansen guested on the track 'Warhead'. A further studio session found HATESPHERE laying down the track 'Hvornår Er Det Søndag Igen?!' for a collection of tribute songs to local football team AGF. The band would be chosen, alongside fellow Scandinavian acts THE HAUNTED, MNEMIC, MERCENARY, RAUNCHY, MELTED, BLINDFAULT and STOMPED, to form up the "Nordic Threat" show for the Popkomm 2004 music convention at the Silver Wings in Berlin on 29th September. Bassist Mikael Ehler and drummer Anders Gyldenøhr teamed up with resurrected veteran Thrash act ARTILLERY for a one off gig in November at The Rock venue in Copenhagen. Jacob Bredahl took time out to aid ABORTED as guest backing vocalist on their album 'The Archaic Abattoir'. The singer also activated side project ALLHELLUJA in alliance with Italian drummer Stefano Longhi.

HATESPHERE's January 2005 'The Killing EP' would include a cover version of SUICIDAL TENDENCIES 'Trip At The Brain'. The band then tagged onto KREATOR and DARK TRANQUILLITY's 'Enemy Of God' European tour prior to March / April shows as guests to MORBID ANGEL. HATESPHERE entered Jailhouse Studios with producer Tommy Hansen in early June to craft a new album 'The Sickness Within' for September issue. A brief burst of German dates had the band supporting CHIMAIRA and DARK TRANQUILLITY.

HATESPHERE

The band united with French tech-Thrashers GOJIRA for UK October 2006 dates. Later that same month Mikael Ehlert acted as stand in bassist for KOLDBORN whilst both Jacob Bredahl and Henrik Jacobsen sessioned on ABORTED's 'Slaughter & Apparatus: A Methodical Overture' album. HATESPHERE, RAUNCHY and VOLBEAT pooled their talents for the 'Danish Dynamite' European tour in November and December.

HATESPHERE's 2007 album, entitled 'Serpent Smiles And Killer Eyes', emerged in April.

That same month Danish label Futhermocker issued an exclusive HATESPHERE 7" single, limited to 220 hand numbered copies, containing the songs 'Drinking With The King Of The Dead' and an exclusive cover version of CORROSION OF CONFORMITY's 'Vote With A Bullet'.

Concerts in Denmark and Norway during May saw support from Norway's STONEGARD.

In May HATESPHERE undertook tour dates in China, commencing at the Beijing Midi Festival in Haidian Park. HATESPHERE played the mainstage of the festival on May 1st, followed by a May 2nd concert at The Star Live, Beijing with Norwegian act EL CACO and three Chinese bands, NARAKAM, SUFFOCATED and YAKSA. Upon their return, the band flanked Norwegian act STONEGARD for a series of Scandinavian shows then engaged in German shows partnered with Belgium's ABORTED leading up to numerous European festival appearances.

HATESPHERE, Soundholic TKCS-85013 (2001) (Japanese release). Hate / Picture This / Addicted Soul / Bloodsoil / Down For Good / No Sense / Preacher / Dead / Ill Will / Restrain.

HATESPHERE, Scarlet SC 027-2 (2001). Hate / Picture This / Addicted Soul / Bloodsoil / Down For Good / No Sense / Preacher / Dead / Ill Will.

BLOODRED HATRED, Soundholic TKCS-85045 (2002). Intro / Believer / Hell Is Here / Insanity Arise / Disbeliever / Plague / Low Life Vendetta / Deeper And Deeper / Kicking Ahead / Addicted Soul / Under Water.

BLOODRED HATRED, Scarlet SC 054-2 (2002). Intro / Believer / Hell Is Here / Insanity Arise / Disbeliever / Plague / Low Life Vendetta / Deeper And Deeper / Kicking Ahead.

Something Old, Something New, Something Borrowed And Something Black EP, Scarlet SC 077-2 (2003). Release The Pain / Bark At The Moon / Caught In A Mosh / Low Life Vendetta (Live) / Bloodsoil (Live) / Plague (Live) / Hate (Live).

BALLET OF THE BRUTE, Scarlet SC 087-2 (2004). The Beginning And The End / Deathtrip / Vermin / Downward To Nothing / Only The Strongest ... / What I See I Despise / Last Cut, Last Head / Warhead / Blankeyed / 500 Dead People.

BALLET OF THE BRUTE, Soundholic TKCS-85098 (2004) (Japanese release). The Beginning And The End / Deathtrip / Vermin / Downward To Nothing / Only The Strongest ... / What I See I Despise / Last Cut, Last Head / Warhead / Blankeyed / 500 Dead People / Release The Pain / Bark At The Moon / Caught In A Mosh.

The Killing EP, Steamhammer SPV 056-99262 (2005). The Will Of God / You're The Enemy / Murderous Intent / Trip At The Brain.

THE SICKNESS WITHIN, Steamhammer SPV 085-99662 (2005). The White Fever / The Fallen Shall Rise In A River Of Blood / Reaper Of Life / Sickness Within / Murderous Intent / The Coming Of Chaos / Bleed To Death / Heaven Is Ready To Fall / Seeds Of Shame / Chamber Master / Marked By Darkness. Chart position: 87 DENMARK.

Sickness Within, Steamhammer (2005) (Promotion release). Sickness Within / Reaper Of Life.

THE SICKNESS WITHIN, Soundholic TKCS-85130 (2005) (Japanese release). The White Fever / The Fallen Shall Rise In A River Of Blood / Reaper Of Life / Sickness Within / Murderous Intent / The Coming Of Chaos / Bleed To Death / Heaven Is Ready To Fall / Seeds Of Shame / Chamber Master / Marked By Darkness / You're The Enemy / The Will Of God / Trip At The Brain.

Drinking With The King Of The Dead, Futhermocker (2007) (7" vinyl single. Limited edition 220 hand numbered copies). Drinking With The King Of The Dead / Vote With A Bullet.

SERPENT SMILES AND KILLER EYES, Steamhammer (2007). Lies And Deceit / The Slain / Damned Below Judas / Drinking With The King Of The Dead / Forever War / Feeding The Demons / Floating / Let Them Hate / Absolution.

HEADHUNTER D.C.

SALVADOR, BA, BRAZIL — *Sérgio Baloff (vocals), Paulo Lisboa (guitar), Fábio Nosferatus (guitar), Paulo Alcântara (bass), Daniel Beans (drums).*

Salvador, Bahia's HEADHUNTER D.C. came together in 1987, founded by guitarist Paulo Lisboa alongside an inaugural band complement comprising vocalist Eduardo Falsão, bassist Luciano and drummer Iaçanã Lima. However, within the first year of operation Ualson Martins took over the bass slot. HEADHUNTER D.C. released tracks on a demo cassette 'Hell Is Here' during 1989. Originally intended as an EP release these tapes found their way into North America courtesy of Wild Rags distribution. Subsequent to these recordings Sérgio Baloff assumed the frontman responsibilities as Cogumelo Records took the band on for the 1991 album 'Born ... Suffer ... Die ...'. This album served to propel HEADHUNTER D.C. to the upper echelons of the South American Death Metal scene.

After laying down a second album, 'Punishment At Dawn', the group drafted Túlio Constantin on the drums and throughout 1993 and 1994 undertook extensive touring across Brazil. Once these shows were finalised a fresh rhythm section of bass player Alberto Alpire and drummer André Moysés was installed.

HEADHUNTER D.C. underwent a major restructure in 1998 with Lisboa and Baloff being joined by second guitarist Fábio Nosferatus, bassist Alex Mendonça and drummer Thiago Nogueira. By 2000 Paulo Alcântara was the new man on bass but then Mendonça subsequently returned. HEADHUNTER D.C. drummer Daniel Beans is also active with INSAINTIFICATION and PANDORA.

BORN ... SUFFER ... DIE, Cogumelo (1991). Am I Crazy? / Decomposed / Death Vomit / Hell Is Here / Headhunter D.C. / Beneath The Hate / Suicidal Soldier / Winds Of Death / Prepare To Die / Disunited / Why Wars?

BORN ... SUFFER ... DIE, Cogumelo (1991). Intro—Am I Crazy? / Decomposed / Death Vomit / Hell Is Here / Headhunter D.C. / Beneath The Hate / Suicidal Soldier / Winds Of Death / Prepare To Die / Disunited / Why Wars?

PUNISHMENT AT DAWN, Cogumelo (1993). Forgotten Existence / Intense Infanticide / Hallucinations / Punishment At Dawn / Bloodbath / Searching For Rottenness / Terrible Illusion / Deadly Sins Of The Soul.

PUNISHMENT AT DAWN, Cogumelo (1993). Forgotten Existence / Intense Infanticide / Hallucinations / Punishment At Dawn / Bloodbath / Searching For Rottenness / Terrible Illusion / Deadly Sins Of The Soul.

... AND THE SKY TURNS BLACK, Mutilated Records (2000).

... AND THE SKY TURNS BLACK, Mutilation (2000). ... And The Sky Turns Black / Falling Into Perdition / Beyond The Deepest Lie / The Glory / From Dream To Nightmare / Eternal Hatred / Conflicts Of The Dark And Light.

BRAZILIAN DEATH CULT LIVE VIOLENCE, Cogumelo (2002). Forgotten Existence / Intense Infanticide / Decomposed / Death Vomit / Disunited / Search For Rottenness / Bloodbath / Terrible Illusion / Winds Of Death / Buried Alive / Deadly Sins Of The Soul.

BORN ... SUFFER ... DIE, Cogumelo CG 0058 (2002). Intro—Am I Crazy? / Decomposed / Death Vomit / Hell Is Here / Headhunter D.C. / Beneath The Hate / Suicidal Soldier / Winds Of Death / Prepare To Die / Disunited / Why War? / Intro—Hell Is Here / Suicidal Soldier / Prepare To Die / Headhunter D.C. / Why Wars? / Death Vomit / Am I Crazy? / Winds Of Death (Live) / Decomposed (Live).

HEARSE

SWEDEN — *Johan Liiva (vocals / bass), Mattias Ljung (guitar), Max Thornell (drums).*

HEARSE was founded by erstwhile ARCH ENEMY man Johan Liiva on vocals and bass. Liiva also fronts NONEXIST. For the HEARSE project, which signed to the Hammerheart label for a debut album 'Dominion Reptilian', Liiva was joined by ex-FURBOWL personnel guitarist Mattias Ljung and drummer Max Thornell. HEARSE opened proceedings with a 7" EP entitled 'Torch' in August 2002, preceding an album 'Dominion Reptilian'.

The band cut a sophomore album, the Jonas Elder produced 'Armageddon Mon Amour' recorded at Basement Audio System in Stockholm, for release in early 2004. Initially it would be announced this release was to be through Holland's Karmageddon Media label but the band then switched to the UK Candlelight concern. A short burst of Benelux dates in September 2004 saw the band united with CALLENISH CIRCLE, OCCULT and DISMEMBER.

In January 2005 HEARSE completed recordings at Stockholm's The White Chapel Studios with Jonas Edler for the album 'The Last Ordeal', set for a Summer release through Karmageddon Media. An EP, fronted by a cover rendition of KIM WILDE's 'Cambodia', was issued in late January to precede the album. HEARSE switched over to the Cold label in July.

DOMINION REPTILIAN, Hammerheart (2002). Dominion Reptilian / Torch / Cosmic Daughter / Contemplation / Rapture In Twilight / Well Of Youth / Abandoned / End Of Days / So Vague / The Unknown / Avalon.

Torch, Hammerheart (2002) (Limited edition). Torch / Avalon.

ARMAGGEDON MON AMOUR, Candlelight (2004). Mountain Of The Solar Eclipse / Turncoat / Crops Of Waste / In Love And War / Ticket To Devastation / Tools / Cambodia / Sodi / Play Without Rules / Determination / Armageddon Mon Amour.

THE LAST ORDEAL, Karmageddon Media KARMA085CD (2005). Pathfinder / Quintessence / Shackles Of Guilt / Ambrosia / Una Lucha A Muerte / Bountyhunter / Demon Curd / Aggravation / The Last Ordeal.

Cambodia, Karmageddon Media (2005). Cambodia / The Accused / Wheels Of Misfortune / Torch / Avalon / Well Of Youth (Demo) / Raptured In Twilight (Demo) / Dominion Reptilian (Demo) / So Vague (Demo).

IN THESE VEINS, Dental (2006). House Of Love / Corroding Armour / Intoxication / Naked Truth / Crusade / Among The Forlorn / Atrocious Recoil / Hearse / In These Veins.

HEAVEN SHALL BURN

GERMANY — *Marcus (vocals), Alexander Dietz (guitar), Maik (guitar), Eric (bass), Matthias (drums).*

A socially conscious Hardcore cum Thrash / Death Metal band. The band's lyrical themes have developed to deal with such subjects as veganism, racism and social rights issues. HEAVEN SHALL BURN was originally conceived billed as CONSENSE during the Autumn of 1996 with a debut demo recording following in early 1997. The band's roster would shift allowing the introduction of lead vocalist Markus and bass player Eric upfront of a second promotion recording. Live work ensued after which the Deeds Of Revolution label offered a contract to release HEAVEN SHALL BURN's mini album 'In Battle There Is No Law, issued in 1998. Shortly after second guitarist Patrick Schleitzer joined the fold.

A split release shared with FALL OF SERENITY followed in 1999 after which HEAVEN SHALL BURN signed up to the Impression label. This union brought forth the April 2000 'Asunder' album. That same year a further split offering found HEAVEN SHALL BURN paired with CALIBAN for a Lifeforce Records release. After extensive touring throughout Spain, Portugal, Swiss, Italy, the Benelux and the Czech Republic the group settled down to craft the 'Whatever It May Take' record. Of interest to collectors was that 'Whatever It May Take' was issued in Brazil with completely different artwork, a revised song running order and a bonus track. Live work in 2002 saw an appearance at the massive 'With Full Force' festival in Germany as well as gigs as far afield as Iceland.

The band signed to Germany's Century Media Records in early 2004 for the April album 'Antigone'. This outing would also see release in vinyl format via Lifeforce Records and licensed in South America through Brazil's Liberation Records. A promotional video for the track 'The Weapon They Fear' was shot at an April gig in Chemnitz by director Marc Drywa. Gigs included a 30th May appearance at the Brazilian 'Liberation Fest V' in Sao Paulo.

To aid victims of the December 2004 Indian Ocean tsunamis HEAVEN SHALL BURN, in collaboration with THE HAUNTED and NAPALM DEATH, participated in the issue of a special single release. The band donated the DIE SKEPTIKER cover version 'Strassenkampf' featuring guitarist Patrick Schleitzer on vocals. These singles, restricted to just 1000 hand numbered copies, would be for sale only at NAPALM DEATH's Bochum and London shows in January 2005. The band hooked up with a further multi-package billing, dubbed 'Hell On Earth', for Autumn European touring alongside running mates AS I LAY DYING, EVERGREEN TERRACE, AGENTS OF MAN, END OF DAYS and NEAERA. Long-time guitarist Patrick Schleitzer then opted out, putting on a final farewell gig with the band on 18th November in Saalfeld, before being swiftly replaced by Alexander Dietz.

In June 2006 the band revealed a new album title, 'Deaf To Our Prayers', was inspired by the poem 'The Silesian Weavers' by German poet Heinrich Heine. 'Deaf To Our Prayers', recorded at Rape Of Harmonies Studios in Thüringen, entered the national German charts at number 65. The band formed up the UK and European "Hell On Earth" tour in September and October. Joining them would be GOD FORBID, MAROON, CATARACT, FULL BLOWN CHAOS, PURIFIED IN BLOOD from Norway and A PERFECT MURDER. Upon completion of these shows guitarist Alexander Dietz temporarily joined the ranks of NEAERA for live work.

IN BATTLE THERE IS NO LAW, Deeds Of Revolution (1998). Partisan / Forthcoming Fire / Thoughts Of Superiority / Mandatory Slaughter / Remember The Fallen.

THE SPLIT PROGRAM, Lifeforce LIFE019 (2000) (Split album with CALIBAN). Suffocated In The Exhaust Of Our Machines / No Single Inch / The Seventh Cross / One More Lie.

ASUNDER, Impression LIFE018 (2000). To Inherit The Guilt / Cold / Betrayed Again / Deification / Pass Away / Open Arms To The Future / The Drowned And The Saved / Where Is The Light / Asunder / The Fourth Crusade.

WHATEVER IT MAY TAKE, Lifeforce LIB011 (2002) (Brazilian release).

WHATEVER IT MAY TAKE, Lifeforce (2002). Behind A Wall Of Silence / The Worlds In Me / The Martyrs' Blood / It Burns Within / Implore The Darker Sky / The Few Upright / Whatever It May Take / Ecowar / Naked Among Wolves / The Fire / Casa De Cabocio / Implore The Darken Sky (Classic version).

ANTIGONE, Century Media (2004). Echoes (Intro) / The Weapon They Fear / The Only Truth / Architects Of The Apocalypse / Voice Of The Voiceless / Numbing The Pain / To Harvest The Storm / Rìsandi Von (Outro) / Bleeding To Death / Tree Of Freedom / The Dream Is Dead / Deyjandi Von (Outro).

DEAF TO OUR PRAYERS, Century Media (2006). Counterweight / Trespassing The Shores Of Your World / Profane Believers / Stay The Course / The Final March / Of No Avail / Armia / mybestfriends.com / Biogenesis (Undo Creation) / Dying In Silence / The Greatest Gift Of God. Chart positions: 50 GREECE, 65 GERMANY.

HEAVENWOOD

PORTUGAL — *Ernesto Guerra (vocals), Ricardo Dias (guitar), Bruno Silva (bass), Luiz Ferreira (drums).*

Initially known as DISGORGED upon their formation in 1992, recording the introductory demo tape 'As Illusive As A Dream' in late 1994, tragedy struck the band the following year when their bass player committed suicide. By 1995 the group comprised guitarist Miguel Cardoso, bassist Rui with Zé on drums, shortly afterward being joined by singer Nelo and guitarist Ricardo Dias. A further demo, entitled 'Emotional Wound', surfaced in June 1995. The band signed to Germany's Massacre Records after a name change to HEAVENWOOD and a musical shift away from the Death Metal of DISGORGED. Changes in the ranks saw Cardoso superseded by Mário Rui Lemos to record 'Diva' album, produced by Gerhard Magin in the Communication Studios, Germany. Japanese versions added an extra exclusive track 'Frozen Image'. The band was soon on the road in Europe promoting the record touring saw shows with ATROCITY and IN FLAMES.

In their homeland, HEAVENWOOD opened for the likes of CRADLE OF FILTH, MOONSPELL and GENOCIDE. The 1998 album 'Swallow' sees THEATRE OF TRAGEDY's Liv Kristine and GAMMA RAY's Kai Hansen guest. Guitarist Ricardo Dias exited in March 2005. He would found an all new act in union with former HEAVENWOOD bass player Fitti and SECRECY drummer Luiz Ferreira. However, in 2007 Luiz Ferreira joined HEAVENWOOD.

DIVA, Massacre MASS CD106 (1996). Frozen Images / Emotional Wound / Flames Of Vanity / Since The First Smile / Tears Of Grief / Moonlight Girl / Judith Heavenward / Weeping Heart / Frithiof's Saga / Lament.

SWALLOW, Massacre MASS CD 0158 (1998). Heartquake / Soulsister / Rain Of July / Suicide Letter / Shadowflowers / Luna / Season '98 / At Once And Forever / Downcast.

HEDFIRST

POLAND — *Przemek Witkowski (vocals), Janek Fronczak (guitar), Kuba Tomaszewski (guitar), Lukasz Wojtasik (bass), Arkadiusz Lukasiak (drums).*

HEDFIRST arrived upon the scene during 2000, subsequently inducting former NOIZGATE singer Przemek "Bayer" Witkowski, ex-VESTIS guitarist Janek Fronczak and bassist Lukasz Wojtasik as they evolved from a covers band into HEADFIRST. The band issued the June 2001 demo 'Checkpoint'. As an opener, this tape seeing covers of SEPULTURA's 'Refuse/Resist' and VERBAL ABUSE's 'I Hate You'. That August Pawel "Vesta" Wesolowski supplanted Lobacz and before the close of the year the revised title of HEDFIRST had been adopted.

The band, reprising the VERBAL ABUSE cover, cut their debut eponymous album for release in May of 2002. However, Wesolowski was then to exit and founder member Lukasz Wojtasik took his place. The Crash Music label picked up the 'Hedfirst' album for re-release in mid 2003, HEDFIRST supporting this with a national Polish tour ranked alongside HUNTER.

October 2005 gigs, billed 'Metal Union Road Tour', had the group sharing stages with FRONTSIDE, SUNRISE and AL SIRET.

HEDFIRST, Crash Music (2003). Fathers Son / Headfirst / Crowd / Beyond Past / Blame / Locked / Message On The First / Last Man Standing.

SCARISMATIC, Metal Mind Productions (2005). Scarismatic / Primal Hate / Truth Against Truth / Time For Fight / Broken Root / Defeat / Dead End / Sleepers / Scars / Wasted / The End Is Always The Beginning.

HELLHAMMER

NÜRENSDORF, SWITZERLAND — *Satanic Slaughter (vocals / guitar), Savage Damage (bass), Bloodhunter (drums).*

Formerly known as HAMMERHEAD, this bizarre and primitive extreme Nürensdorf—Zürich Metal outfit, which would in time evolve into the equally revered CELTIC FROST, was founded in 1982. The influence of the band would reverberate over decades throughout the Thrash and Black Metal genres. Previous to HAMMERHEAD frontman Thomas Gabriel Fischer and bassist Steve had been involved with various fledgling acts emulating their NWoBHM heroes VENOM.

HELLHAMMER's origins lay in the formative unit HAMMERHEAD. Initially bass guitar was handled by the 14 year old Michael Baum, who in turn transferred these duties to Fischer, then wishing to be known as 'Satanic Slaughter'. Of note is that Baum then journeyed on to Los Angeles to found AOR act SIERRA before enrolling into TRIBE OF GYPSIES.

Their debut 1982 rehearsal demo, saw the group apparently inspired by Newcastle upon Tyne NWoBHM band RAVEN and their Gallagher brothers team as Fischer, bassist Steve Patton, previously known as 'Savage Damage' and drummer Peter Stratton all adopting the joint stage surnames of 'Warrior'. During August 1982, HELLHAMMER shifted shape again, drafting drummer Jörg Neubart (a.k.a. 'Bloodhunter') and transferring from bass to guitar. Neubart subsequently became 'Bruce Day'.

In 1983 HELLHAMMER enrolled drummer Stephen Priestly from SCHIZO. Hellhammer followed up with their first studio demo, the July 1983 nine track 'Death Fiend'. Only a very limited distribution of this cassette, via Prowlin' Death Promotions, saw the light of day. This first official set witnessed a band still very much in its embryonic stages, chock full of copycat NWoBHM riffs and pre-pubescent lyrics such as opening line She's got my joystick right in her mouth from the song 'Bloody Pussies'. The band had actually committed a total of 17 tracks to tape, surfacing first on 'Death Fiend', then on the infamous 'Triumph Of Death'.

Clad in exactly the same artwork as its predecessor, once 'Triumph Of Death' made it outside of the tape trading underground and into the mainstream it provoked extreme opinions. Horrifically recorded, 'Triumph Of Death' offered an ugly wall of sound, choking doom styled riffs matched in intensity by stampeding bass and tortured vocals. HELLHAMMER's image, lifted straight from fantasy board games, had the trio complementing the music decked out in bullet belts, leather and spikes. Ambitiously the legend adorning the cassette issued the challenge 'VENOM are killing music ... HELLHAMMER are killing VENOM'.

Whilst leading French magazine 'Enfer' hailed it as a classic, the UK's 'Metal Forces' magazine editor Bernard Doe cited it as the most appalling thing he had ever heard. History however would dictate that HELLHAMMER would later be recognized as one of the root catalysts of the Black Metal genre. Although in later years band members have admitted their knowledge of music was basic to say the least when the HELLHAMMER recordings were made, nevertheless the band were in possession of an artistic vision which would undoubtedly shape the metal scene over many years.

The group pulled in bass player Martin Eric Ain ('Slayed Necros') to lay down more demos, 'Satanic Rites', that December in Sound Concept studios. However, invited to submit a fresh demo to Berlin's Noise Records HELLHAMMER very nearly split as Ain felt he did not have the necessary talent to go through with the session.

Still, positive or negative press encouraged Noise to sign the band and the Berlin based label released the Horst Müller engineered 'Apocalyptic Raids' EP in March 1984, which had no details as to what RPM the record should be played at; sounding just as strange at 33RPM as it did at 45. An unconfident label only ordered up a first pressing of 1200 copies, which soon flew out of stores. This inaugural press was the only official one to include a lyric sheet. Subsequent quick fire re-presses resulted in a variation of colours and tones on the sleeve artwork, making for unintentional greater collectability.

Metal Blade Records released the EP in America with an extra two tracks. Demand for HELLHAMMER also warranted a bootleg 7" single issued by Necromantic union, a pairing of a live cut of 'Buried And Forgotten' and a rehearsal recording 'Messiah'.

HELLHAMMER mainman 'Satanic Slaughter' later swapped identities to become Tom G. Warrior and started the avant-garde Metal legends CELTIC FROST in May of 1984 retaining the deal with Noise. CELTIC FROST issued a stream of critically praised outings before fizzling out.

Still an influence in some circles over ten years later, Sweden's ABYSS covered the HELLHAMMER track 'Massacra' on their 1995 album 'The Other Side'. Leading American Death Metal unit INCANTATION would wear their influences with pride too committing a cover of 'The Third Of Storms' to their inaugural demo session. Arch Black Metal protagonists DARKTHRONE would commit 'The Usurper' to an early demo which would later find the light of day on the 'Live In Frostland' bootleg. Fellow Swiss Metal act SAMAEL too would cover HELLHAMMER on their early demos with 'The Third Of The Storm'.

Warrior forged a new project in the late 90's billed as APOLLYON SUN. By late 2001 a full blown CELTIC FROST reunion had been announced but would prove protracted. In 2004 the band would have their classic cut 'The Third Of Storms' chosen as a pioneering piece of music for a compilation assembled by DARKTHRONE drummer Fenriz, released through Peaceville Records and entitled 'Fenriz Presents The Best Of Old School Black Metal'.

Rehearsal Demo, Hellhammer (1982) (Rehearsal demo). Triumph Of Death.

Triumph Of Death, Hellhammer (1983) (Demo). Intro / Crucifixion / Maniac / When Hell's Near / Decapitator / Blood Insanity / Power Of Satan / Reaper / Death Fiend / Triumph Of Death / Metallic Storm / Ready For Slaughter / Dark Warriors / Hammerhead.

Death Fiend, Hellhammer (1983) (Demo). Maniac / Angel Of Destruction / Hammerhead / Bloody Pussies / Death Fiend / Dark Warriors / Chainsaw / Ready For Slaughter / Sweet Torment.

Satanic Rites, Hellhammer (1983) (Demo). Intro / Messiah / The Third Of The Storms / Buried And Forgotten / Maniac / Eurynomos / Triumph Of Death / Revelations Of Doom / Reaper / Satanic Rites / Crucifixion / Outro.

DEATH METAL, (1984) (Four way split album with HELLOWEEN, RUNNING WILD and DARK AVENGER). Revelations Of Doom / Messiah.

Apocalyptic Raids EP, Noise N008 50-1668 (1984). The Third Of The Storms (Evoked Damnation) / Massacra / Triumph Of Death / Horus / Agressor.

HELLICON

STOCKHOLM, SWEDEN — *Pehr Hägg (vocals), Joakim Antman (guitar), Mattias Frånberg (guitar), Johannes Borg (bass), Robert Wernström (drums).*

Melodic Death Metal band HELLICON, hailing from the Haninge suburb of Stockholm, was established in 2001 as a unit of singer Pehr Hägg (a.k.a. 'Mol Allena'), guitarists Joakim Antman ('Dark Ant') and Mattias Frånberg ('Nox Noctis'), bass player Karl-Oskar Brosell and Robert Wernström ('Ert Crush') on the drums. The band's live debut came as support to STEEL ATTACK in November 2001. The group's recording inauguration came in July of the following year with the 'Helliconia' demo session, cut at Oak Farm Studios in Handen. Line-up changes saw Alexander 'Sir Mërbid' Swahn, located working at McDonalds, then assuming bass duties as Mërb exited to prioritise his other act MUSHROOM FOREST. HELLICON entered Oxroad Studios in Brandbergen with producer Guran Florén in September 2003 to craft the demo 'A New Beginning'. These tracks saw Per Rinaldo of HEAD and PAINTED DEVIL on guest backing vocals. Johannes Borg took the bass position in early 2005.

Helliconia, Hellicon (2002). Arise (Intro) / Helliconia / Tell Me / The Prize (I'll Pay).

A New Beginning, (2004). Falling Through / I Surrender / In Agony / A New Beginning.

HERMAN RAREBELL

POLAND — *Czarny (vocals), Szklany (guitar), Sojovy (bass), Siwy (drums).*

Quite surreally, not HERMAN RAREBELL of SCORPIONS repute, probably the most successful German Rock drummer of the age, but a Polish Grindcore band. The project decided to name themselves HERMAN RAREBELL during 2003, featuring on a three way split CD 'The World Will Fall Soon And We All Will Die' allied with THIRD DEGREE and ANTIGAMA on Selfmadegod Records. The combo was in fact an ANTIGAMA side project of 'Szklany' (a.k.a. Sebastian Rokicki) and 'Siwy' (Krzysztof Bentkowski) in partnership with THIRD DEGREE vocalist Czarny and bassist Fazi. The album included a cover version of DEFECATION's 'Mutual Trust'.

HERMAN RAREBELL's 2006 album, 'Too Late For Peace...', saw cover versions of two NAPALM DEATH tracks, 'Multinational Corporations' and 'Instinct Of Survival', plus a rendering of DOOM's 'Rags To Riches'.

THE WORLD WILL FALL SOON AND WE WILL ALL DIE, SelfmadeGod SMG 011 (2003) (Split album with ANTIGAMA and THIRD DEGREE). Herman Rarebell / The Dreams Of Gunther Von Hagens / Aftermath / Eyehatepope / Fick Dich Selbst / Iron Snake / Mutual Trust.

TOO LATE FOR PEACE..., SelfmadeGod (2006). A Sample to Taste, Pt. I / A Sample to Taste, Pt. II / Observation / Too Late for Peace... / Alcoholocaust / Hermania / Rags To Riches / /.../ / Cage Of Life / Firing Squad / A Toy / Radio M / Red Ideology / Multinational Corporations / Instinct Of Survival.

HERR SUFFOKATOR

OULU, FINLAND — *Herr Kriegmeister (vocals), Dieqo Death (guitar), Ettra718 (bass), Jonas Lindberg (drums).*

HERR SUFFOKATOR, previously known as SUFFOKATOR, is a Grind project mentored by vocalist Herr Kriegmeister. Under various pseudonyms, such as J.S., Caine Infest, J.S. GRVHM and I.C. Cholera, frontman Herr Kriegmeister (real name Joni Soini) also manifested VACUI SEGNO, CHOLERA, TRSX, FROM THE NORTH and ARAS. Billed as SUFFOKATOR, Hellbourg Records debuted the solo endeavour with a July 2005 EP split with SPLITZEN. Skullyard Records followed swiftly that same month with another split EP, 'Fear The Suffocater', this time in collaboration with NÄKKILEPÄ KANADAAN. Quick fire successive releases included the 'Massacrematory' and 'Chambers' EPs in August. That September the compilation 'Complikation' was issued.

Skullyard Records released the 'Suffoaction' EP in 2006. For live work HERR SUFFOKATOR included SPLITZEN guitarist Dieqo Death, the FROM THE NORTH and TYR credited Ettra718 on bass plus drummer Jonas Lindberg, of F and FORNJOTR.

Suffoaction, Skullyard (2006). Suffoaction / Your Corpse / Captivity / Chymos / Kannibaali / Homicide.

HEXENHAMMER

GERMANY — *Frank Hürland (vocals), Christian Gubernat (guitar), Maik Hoffmann (guitar), Ingo Kuhoff (bass), Daniel Steigüber (drums).*

HEXENHAMMER started out as a 1999 three man project of guitarist Andreas Klapper, bass player Ingo Kuhoff and Jürgen Langner on the drums. With Daniel Steigüber of NECROPHOBIA and EPHEL DUATH replacing Langner the group committed to the demo 'Deathfuck Autopsy'. Another EPHEL DUATH member, Frank Hürland, supplied vocals. Subsequently the band enlisted Christian Gubernat on guitar but then later lost the services of Klapper. He would be superseded by ex-NOCTURNAL DESIRE man Maik Hoffmann in May of 2001.

In November of 2002 HEXENHAMMER went into a studio in Kassel with BURDEN OF GRIEF drummer Carsten Schmerer acting as producer for an eponymous EP. Twilight Records issued the debut album 'Divine New Horrors' in February 2005. The band helped forge a heavyweight road alliance, suitably dubbed 'European Decimation', took in April gigs throughout Italy, Portugal, the UK, Holland and Germany in partnership with CATASTROPHIC, FUNERUS, JUNGLE ROT and INCANTATION.

Hexenhammer EP, Independent (2003). Exhumed & Consumed / Toxic Sanity / Raped With A Chainsaw.

DIVINE NEW HORRORS, Twilight (2005). Hell Force One / Blasting Composition / Litany Of Curses / Less Than Nothing / Devouring Embryos / Exhumed & Consumed / Bloodkicked / Rebel Amok Suicide / Enter My Tomb / Self / Tortured Existence / Devil's Breath.

HIBERNUS MORTIS

HIALEAH, FL, USA — *Alex Campbell (vocals / guitar), David Miller (guitar), Cesar Placeres (drums).*

Hialeah's HIBERNUS MORTIS, created in December 1995 by former ACRIMONIUM band personnel vocalist Adam Fleury, guitarist Doug Humlack and drummer Cesar Placeres, initially issued the 'The Existing Realms Of Perpetual Sorrow' album under their own steam. Notably featured on backing vocals would be SICKNESS vocalist Kyle Symon and J.P. Soars of MALEVOLENT CREATION and DIVINE EMPIRE. An early bassist, Ralf Varela, would be switch to guitar and have his former position superseded by Yasser Morales. First product would come in the form of a 1998 demo 'Into The Thresholds Of Dead Winter', with 'Live Manslaughter' following in 2000. On the live front the band acted as support to MORBID ANGEL, DEICIDE, CANNIBAL CORPSE, INCANTATION, MALEVOLENT CREATION, HATE ETERNAL, MAYHEM, IMMOLATION, MONSTROSITY, KRISIUN, ANGEL CORPSE and DISMEMBER.

Signing to the Horns Up label, "The Existing Realms Of Perpetual Sorrow' record would be re-issued adding two brand new studio tracks, two live cuts, and a cover of SLAYER's 'South Of Heaven'. Drummer Cesar Placeres assembled a new Death Metal band venture in early 2005 dubbed MURDER 101, also including the CHRONZON pairing of singer Rob Rosenzweig and guitarist Samuel Dean and the MALEVOLENT CREATION and DIVINE EMPIRE credited Jason Blachowicz on bass. Humlack also holds HATEPLOW credentials whilst Placeres also has a tie in with TOMB.

Placeres rebuilt the band in 2005, inducting CAPRA HIRCUS and TOMB guitarist Alex Campbell and the ENEMY AGAINST ENEMY, SONNY CHIBA DEATH CULT, TOMB and TYRANNY OF SHAW credited second guitarist David Miller.

THE EXISTING REALMS OF PERPETUAL SORROW, (2002).

HILASTHERION

FINLAND — *William Rönn (vocals / guitar), Niclas Buss (vocals / guitar / keyboards), Henrik Fellman (bass), Joel Björkstrand (drums).*

Christian melodic Death Metal band HILASTHERION was established during 2003 by Anders Olin and William Rönn. HILASTHERION released the album 'Taken From Darkness' through Victoryzine Records during June 2006. Recording membership comprised lead vocalist / guitarist William Rönn, Niclas Buss of PARAKLETOS and NORTHERN FLAME, handling guitar and keyboards, bass player Henrik Fellman and the CRIMSON MOONLIGHT, DIVINEFIRE, SABAOTH, ESSENCE OF SORROW, ETERNIUM, RENASCENT, AM I BLOOD and SINS OF OMISSION credited Jani Stefanovic on drums. Emil Stenros and Simon Granlund provided backing vocals. After the album was completed HILASTHERION drafted new drummer Joel Björkstrand.

TAKEN FROM DARKNESS, Victoryzine (2006). Taken From Darkness / See The Pain In His Face / Jesus Rules / Why (Song Of Despair) / A Sinner's Song Of Desperation / Battle Of The Flesh / The End Is Not The End / Save My Soul / Sick And Rotten World / Judgement Day / A Fallen One / Story Of John.

HIMSA

SEATTLE, WA, USA — *John Pettibone (vocals), Kirby Charles Johnson (guitar), Sammi Curr (guitar), Derek Harn (bass), Chad Davis (drums).*

HIMSA, "To wage wrath and destruction" in Sanskrit, was assembled in Seattle by former personnel from acts such as TRIAL, GENUINE, HARKONEN and CHRIST with ANONYMOUS and JESSICA lead vocalist Christian in October 1998, debuting with a 7" eponymous EP and the Paul Speers produced 1999 'Ground Breaking Ceremony' album. For these outings Mike Green manned the drums. Founder members guitarist Brian Johnson, bassist Derek Harn and second guitarist Aaron Edge all held TRIAL credentials. Christian and Edge would soon decamp, the latter going on to THE SIX MINUTE HEARTSTOP. During 2000 the band operated with three guitarists for a period as the membership ebbed and flowed.

The band unit would be rocked by line-up changes but by the recording of November 2001's 'Death Is Infinite' EP, originally projected as a split album to be shared with PRETTY GIRLS MAKE GRAVES, HIMSA comprised erstwhile NINE IRON SPITFIRE and UNDERTOW vocalist John Pettibone, guitarist Brian Johnson and Kirby Johnson, bassist Derek Harn, electronics man Clay Layton and drummer Tim Mullen. In this formation the group strayed away from their Hardcore roots and steered towards a very identifiable Scandinavian style of technical Thrash / Death Metal.

April 2002 West Coast shows saw the band supporting BREAKING THROUGH. Following recording of the 2003 opus 'Courting Tragedy And Disaster', issued by Prosthetic Records, HIMSA replaced guitarist Sammi Curr with Matt Wicklund. Breaking in Wicklund and new drummer Steve Fournier HIMSA set about a rash of East Coast dates in July partnered with AS I LAY DYING and THE AGONY SCENE. Maintaining their live presence the group hooked up with SHADOWS FALL and THIS DAY FORWARD for October dates, running into a further leg into Canada allied with DEATH BY STEREO.

HIMSA shot a promotional video for the track 'A Girl In Glass' in June 2004, this short directed by Kevin Leonard upfront of Summer dates with label mates BYZANTINE in July and leading up to a full US tour with SHADOWS FALL, AS I LAY DYING and REMEMBERING NEVER. November 'Headbanger's Ball III' US touring partners would be CRADLE OF FILTH, BLEEDING THROUGH and ARCH ENEMY. Nationwide touring throughout February of 2005 saw the band packaged with THE ACCUSED, 3 INCHES OF BLOOD and COUNTDOWN TO LIFE. The group entered AntFarm Studios in Denmark with producer Tue Madsen in May to record the 'Hail Horror' opus. Live work extended throughout the mid-year period in an alliance with SCARS OF TOMORROW, THE AGONY SCENE and THE ESOTERIC on the 'Dirty Black Summer' trek, commencing 13th June in Sacramento, California. Just upfront of these gigs the band parted ways with guitarist Matt Wicklund, re-drafting former member Sammi Curr in his stead. Wicklund, announcing his intention to marry fiancé and former adult film star Jasmin St. Claire, explained he had exited due to "professional and personal reasons".

Gigs in July had the band partnered with FULL BLOWN CHAOS and GOD FORBID. The band joined forces with the DANZIG headlined 'Blackest of the Black' US dates commencing in September, these shows accompanied by CHIMAIRA, BEHEMOTH, MORTIIS and THE AGONY SCENE. That same month Wicklund returned to the scene, uniting with erstwhile CRADLE OF FILTH personnel keyboard player Martin Powell and guitarist James McIlroy in a brand new band project called PREY.

HIMSA launched a new album, 'Hail Horror', in February 2006, Japanese versions adding extra track 'I, Possession'. The band engaged in US dates that same month backed by DARKEST HOUR, A LIFE ONCE LOST, THE ACACIA STRAIN and DEAD TO FALL. UK and European gigs in April and May, taking in Germany, Holland, Belgium, Austria, Italy, Switzerland, Denmark and Sweden, had the band hooked up with running mates DEATH BY STEREO and THE BANNER.

HIMSA singer John Pettibone fronted an all new project band dubbed THE VOWS involving bass player Rob Moran of UNBROKEN and SOME GIRLS, drummer Ryan Murphy of ENSIGN and UNDERTOW plus the CHAMPION guitar pairing of Aram Arslanian and Chris Williams. This unit signed with Indecision Records for an EP release. Another HIMSA related project, IAMTHETHORN, comprised Johnny Pettibone and Aaron Edge plus Jerad Shealey of RECEDER on bass plus Joe Axler, from SKARP, BOOK OF BLACK EARTH and SPLATTERHOUSE, on drums.

The group announced touring plans for the summer of 2006, kicking of the 'Sthress' tour in July alongside POISON THE WELL, IT DIES TODAY, SHADOWS FALL, DARKEST HOUR, BURY YOUR DEAD, SUFFOCATION, THROWDOWN and STILL REMAINS. The band contributed their version of 'Maladjusted' to the SICK OF IT ALL tribute album 'Our Impact Will Be Felt' assembled by Abacus Recordings for January 2007 release.

Revealed in early 2007 would be OPHIDIAN, a project between former HIMSA guitarist Matt Wicklund with the NILE, ACHERON, AURORA BOREALIS, GOD DETHRONED, MALEVOLENT CREATION, DIMMU BORGIR, SYSTEM:OBSCURE, NIDINGR and ANGEL CORPSE credited Tony Laureano on drums.

HIMSA commenced fresh album recordings on April 23rd, utilising Steve Carter to engineer guitar, bass and drums before DEVIN TOWNSEND took over for vocal work. Tue Madsen provided the final mix.

GROUND BREAKING CEREMONY, Revelation (1999). Daylight Savings / The Great Depression / Another Version Of The Twist / Ground Breaking Ceremony / Carrier / Mud / Cremation / The Date Is Here / Tapas / White Out.
Death Is Infinite EP, Revelation (2001). Born To Conquer / Twist / Hellbent And Hammered / Exhale.
Himsa, Revelation (2003). Blackout / Flood In The Market / Sink In.
COURTING TRAGEDY AND DISASTER, Prosthetic (2003). Dominion / Rain To The Sound Of Panic / A Girl In Glass / Kiss Or Kill / Jacob Shock / Cherum / It's Night Like This That Keep Us Alive / Loveless And Goodbye / Scars In The Landscape / Sense Of Passings / When Midnight Breaks.
HAIL HORROR, Prosthetic (2006). Anathema / Sleezevil / The Destroyer / Pestilence / Wither / Wolfchild / Seminal / They Speak In Swarms / Calling In Silent / Send Down Your Reign.

HOLOCAUSTO CANIBAL

PORTUGAL — *Carlos (vocals), Nuno (guitar), Zé Pedro (bass), João (drums).*

HOLOCAUSTO CANIBAL was manifested during the Autumn of 1997, assembled by erstwhile members of acts such as NEPHRIT, WEB, DYING SEASON, WINTERSHADES and IMPIOUS in vocalist Ricardo Silva, guitarist Nuno, bassist Zé Pedro and drummer João Lamela. The first line up change occurred in October 1998 when Silva was asked to leave. New man Carlos would be drafted for recording of the rehearsal demo 'oPus I'. The sale of over 1000 cassettes prompted a debut album, 'Gonorreia Visceral' being laid down at Rec n' Roll Studios in September 1999, being released by So Die Music in February 2000. João Lamela quit shortly afterward and HOLOCAUSTO CANIBAL persevered with a drum machine for the national 'Chaos And Disorder' tour packaged with THANATOSHIZO and THE FIRSTBORN.

The group would re-introduce Ricardo Silva as lead vocalist and enrolled Ivan on the drums and in November 2000 undertook a further headline tour, dubbed 'Portuguese Bastards', with support from GOLDENPYRE and CORPUS CHRISTII. Next product would be the video 'Gore, Vulva e Holocaustos' comprising live footage, interviews and suitably gory moments from cult movies. The album 'Sublime Massacre Corporeo' emerged in 2002.

HOLOCAUSTO CANIBAL shared a 2003 split album with Italian Grind act GRIMNESS. The album cover was horrific even by Grindcore standards. The band also put in an appearance at the 2003 'Steel Warriors Rebellion VI' festival alongside ENTHRONED, INTERNAL SUFFERING, KATATONIA, FINNTROLL, ATTICK DEMONS, NEOPLASMAH, PITCH BLACK, CORPUS CHRISTII, IN THY FLESH, AXE MURDERERS, AGONIZED, THANATOSCHIZO, FLAGELLUM DEI and ETERNAL MOURNING,

GONORREIA VISCERAL, So Die Music (2000). Vagina Convulsa / Holocausto Canibal / Empalamento / Antropofagia Auto Infligida / Septicemia Vaginal / Carnificina Psicopata / Gorgasmos … … Orgasmicos Espasmos Gore / Faixa Oito.
HOLOCAUSTO CANIBAL, Grindmind (2003) (Split album with GRIMNESS). Amizade Fàlica / Fornicada Pelo Bisturi / Acupuntura Genital / Perspective Disdiadococinèsicas [Gorgasmos … Orgàsmicos Espasmos Gore v.2k3] / Limbonicas Convulsoes Espirais / Canzana Bienorragica (Live) / Sàdica Flagelacao Hiperbòlica (Live).
SUBLIME MASSACRE CORPOREO, (2003). Psicótico Prelúdio / Cadavérica Ejaculação Espasmódica / Canzana Blenorrágica / Necro-Felação / Sádica Flagelação Hiperbólica / Micose Cotovelar / Embrio Progéria / Violada Pela Moto Serra / Reinfecção Clitórica—Septicemia Vagi-Anal 2001 / Sufocada Pelo Semen / Porno Hardgore / Paradigmas Sub Cutâneos–Verborreicas Incursões Pela Terminologia Forense / Purulento Climax Chill Out / Necro-Felação Invertida / Faixa 15 / Your Mother Ate My Dog! / Zingayah! You Got The Bite! / I Kick Ass For The Lord! / What! No Pudding?

HOMOIRATUS

GREECE — *Thomas Bairachtaris (vocals), Alex (guitar), Aggelos (bass), Argyris (drums).*

Thessaloniki Deathcore act. Forged in early 1998, the opening demo 'Absence Of Progress' featured a line up of vocalist / guitarist Alex, guitarist Kostas and drummer Argyris. After these sessions Jim enrolled as the band's singer and in this formation HOMOIRATUS donated the track 'False Criteria' to the 1999 compilation album 'Vibes From Bellow' issued by Psiclone Sinphonies. Membership fluctuations saw the addition of bassist Aggelos in November and the incorporation of vocalist Mitch, but shortly after the departure of Kostas. This version of the band signed to the Arctic Music Group to record debut album 'Human Consumes Human'.

HOMOIRATUS was fronted by vocalist Thomas Bairachtaris, a veteran of EXHUMATION and EVADE, for the 2002 EP 'The Knowledge … Their Enemy '. However, upon completion of 2003's 'Apocalypse' album Bairachtaris made his exit, leaving the band as a trio. Undaunted the band engaged in October European tour dates packaged with KONKHRA, ILLNATH and CORPUS MORTALE.

HUMAN CONSUMES HUMAN, Arctic Music (2001). Life—Like Violence / Dead Upon Conception / Project : New World / Absence Of Progress / Homo Sapiens ? / Crawling Principles / Hideousness Show / False Criteria / Sonus In Terrorem / Human Parts Inc. / King Of Logic / Slavery / Freedom / Tomahawk Cruise Messiah / S.H.I.T.

The Knowledge … Their Enemy, Arctic Music (2002). Protection Through Surveillance / Roots Bloody Roots / Tomahawk Cruise Messiah / Homo Sapiens? / Project New World (Video) / Tomahawk Cruise Messiah (Video).
APOCALYPSE, (2003). Another Daybreak Gone / The Age Of Numbers / So Many Nulls / Disintegrating Rotor's Authority / Soulconscienceworkshop / One Last Breath / Sci-Vi / Constructing Stature / E-Land Phobia / Binary Clone Epoch / On Fertile Ground / Equipollence.

HORFIXION

CANADA — *Samuel Landry (vocals / guitar), Simon Auger (guitar), Richard Gélinas (bass).*

Death / Thrash act HORFIXION started out as a covers band HORRIFIC ILLUSION during 1993, conceived by vocalist / guitarist Samuel Landry and guitarist Kevin St-Yves. With the recruitment of bass player Richard Gélinas and drummer Alexandre Noel during 1996 the group adopted the HORFIXION title, their debut demo 'Let The Nightmare Begin …' arriving in late 1999. During 2000 Erik Doucet took over bass duties for a follow up demo session entitled 'Rage'. However, Doucet would then be superseded by a returning Gélinas, this version of the group cutting the album 'Disynchronize'. Session drums came courtesy of the MARTYR, BLACK CLOUD and GORGUTS credited Daniel Mongrain.

As 2002 dawned Simon Auger supplanted St-Yves as HORFIXION laid down second album 'Instigators Of Chaos'. Studio guest included Patrice Hamelin of MARTYR on the drums.

DISYNCHRONIZE, Independent (2000). Maze Of Mind / Voiceless Scream / Disynchronize / Rage / Human Machine / Tears Of Sand / Deserted Landscape / Danger Zone / Nightmare / Désynchronisé.
INSTIGATORS OF CHAOS, Independent (2002). Intro / Instigators Of Chaos / Another Man / Minefield / Misfortune / Emotional Storm / Evolutive Revolution / Le Retour De La Grande Faucheuse / V.A.B. / Magma.
SELF INFLICTED HELL, Galy GALY 024 (2004). Immaculate Destruction / Self Inflicted Hell / Insane Poetry / Twisted Inner Mind / Godless Faith / Deconstructing My Life / Digitalizing Existence / Thoughtless / Rendez-vous Avec La Mort.

HORRESCO REFERENS

FRANCE — *Rash (vocals / guitar), Guillaume (guitar), Pascal (bass), David (drums).*

HORRESCO REFERENS is a self styled "Lust Metal" band out of Paris, apparently combining Power Metal, Thrash, Death with a touch of Black Metal for good measure. The band debuted in 1994 with the demo 'In Darkness I Grow', at this juncture comprising a line up of lead vocalist Rash, the MISANTHROPE credited guitarist Xavier, bass guitarist Mario and drummer Phineas. Maintaining this membership roster HORRESCO REFERENS, and working with producer Stéphane Buriez, 'The Cesspit' debut album emerged in 1997. The group drafted a fresh rhythm section of Pascal on bass and Nicolas behind the drum kit in 2001.

Signing to Anvil Corporation the next record, '… Of Our Souls' released in 2003, witnessed a line up switch with Guillaume of Black Metal act LOCI INFERNI taking the guitar spot and David inducted on the drums. Promotional tour work across Europe found the band sharing stages with artists such as ENTHRONED, KATATONIA, KILLING MODE and VANDEN PLAS.

Ex-drummer Foued Moukid joined THE OLD DEAD TREE in September of 2004.

THE CESSPIT, Anvil Corporation (1999). Still Awake … / D.E.E.P. (The Cesspit Part II) / Ahmanem VI / Outlive / In The Mists / Virginborn / Everlasting Climax / Dimension Zero / … The Silent Wisdom.
… OF OUR SOULS, Anvil Corporation (2003). … Of … / Gorgeous / Sarx / Purity Of Sex / Last Letter / … Our … / Where Sentiments Live / Deceptes / The Rain / Suicide Planet / … Souls.

HORRICANE

TALLINN, ESTONIA — *ERX (vocals), PCHN (guitar), ANZ (guitar), VX (bass), DZDZ (keyboards), MDX (drums).*

Tallinn Death Metal band with a rich heritage and known as the "Lynch lawyers death squad". The group was founded in 2002 and comprises vocalist ERX (a.k.a. Erki Hirv) of ASSAMALLA, guitarists PCHN (Andre Pichen) of ASSAMALLA and WHISPERING FOREST and ANZ (Andreas Löhmus) from [03] and MEINARDUS, 5 string bass player VX (Veigo Peetsalu) of KALM and ASSAMALLA, keyboard player DZDZ (Georg Gurjev) of KALM and INSTIGATOR OF GRIEF and the DECEASE, [03], SUPPURATION and ECHOSILENCE credited MDX (Risto Mötus) on drums. An opening demo, 'The Lynch-Lawyers' Death Squad', was cut at Zorg Studios in early 2004. Notable gigs that year saw supports to VADER, FEAR FACTORY, MORTIIS and, in December, PARADISE LOST.

HORRICANE signed to Sweden's Black Mark Records for a debut album 'The Lynch-Lawyers'. In November 2005 the group added new guitarist 'WRZ', actually ex-RECYCLE BIN man Jaan Varts. The group severed ties with Black in February 2007.

The Lynch-Lawyers' Death Squad, Horricane (2004). Coup De Grace / Fraction In Your Eyes / The Lynch-Lawyers' Death Squad / Demon-Strate / Nitro Boost Turmoil.

HORRIFIED

GREECE — *Gore (vocals), Stavros (guitar), Thanos (bass), Stelios (drums).*

Lethargic, laboured medieval flavoured Death Metal. HORRIFIED came into being during 1989 as a quartet of vocalist Gore, guitarist Timos, bassist Kostas and drummer Stelios. The 'Prophecy Of Gore' demo was summoned up in 1990 after which Kostas was supplanted by Bill who, in turn, was shortly after replaced by Thanos.

In this incarnation HORRIFIED signed to the Black Power label. The first fruits of this relationship would be the 1991 12 single 'Eternal God' for which Spiros was inducted as rhythm guitarist. However, Timos would decamp thereafter and in came Stavros for 'The Ancient Whisper Of Wisdom' 7 release. Promoting this release HORRIFIED put in numerous support shows to bands such as ROTTING CHRIST and SEPTIC DEATH.

The full length album 'In The Garden Of Unearthly Delights' would herald the introduction of Mina as female backing vocalist. In spite of the obvious forward momentum HORRIFIED split.

HORRIFIED reunited in 1998, signing to the Black Lotus label for the 'Animal' outing. The band's profile rose sharply in 1999 with live supports to visiting international artists such as IMMORTAL, SODOM, MERCYFUL FATE and MANOWAR. The band's third album, 'Deus Diabolus Inversus', was produced by Fredrik Nordstrom in 2002. Guesting would be OPETH's Michael Akerfeldt.

IN THE GARDEN OF THE UNEARTHLY DELIGHTS, Black Power BPR008 (1991). The Awakening / Elisaph / Early Dawn Enraged / Crawling Silence / Down At The Valley Of The Great Encounter / Dying Forest / Baptized In Venereal Blood / Poetry Of War / Unbridled God / Dancing Next To Dying Souls.
ANIMAL, Black Lotus BLRCD 004 (1996). Hypnos / Forbidden Knowledge / Ghost / Redemption / Davolja Varos / Under The Roots / Evol Morena / Empty Moment / Funny Man.
DEUS DIABOLUS INVERSUS, Black Lotus BLR CD045 (2003). Deus Diabolus Inversus / Battle Of The Serpents Within / Requiem For A Caged Lust / Selenes And Endymions Son / Ascending Path: A Star Child Is Born / Aphorism / Monolith: Test Teach Transform / Once Upon A Time? / The Seven Gifts Of Sin / Doberman / Incects / Avatar Of The Age Of Horus / Argentum Astrum.

HOUR OF PENANCE

ROME, ITALY — *Francesco Paoli (vocals), Giulio Moschini (guitar), Silvano Leone (bass), Mauro Mercurio (drums).*

Rome based brutal Death Metal band founded during 1999, initially as a covers band paying homage to the Florida Death Metal scene. The opening line-up comprised guitarists Enrico Schettino and Francesco De Honestis plus Mauro Mercurio of EYECONOCLAST on drums. Michele Viti handled vocals and bass. The first demo session was recorded in October 2000 at Outer Sound Studios in Rome with engineering credits going to NOVEMBRE's Giuseppe Orlando and Massimiliano Pagliuso. The HOUR OF PENANCE rhythm section of bassist Michele Viti and drummer Mauro Mercurio founded side project GHOULS in 2001. That same year Morabito, De Honestis and Mercurio made space to create another project, BENIGHTED, this subsequently evolving into RUST OF REASON.

In September the HOUR OF PENANCE utilised the same familiar studio setting to record another original song plus a DEICIDE cover version for use on an intended split release to be shared with CADAVERIC CREMATORIUM on Warlord Records. However, this never eventuated. Francesco De Honestis then exited to be substituted by Stefano Morabito, formerly of FAUCES and CHTHONIAN NEMETON.

HOUR OF PENANCE put in a notable live performance on June 1st 2002 at the Gothenburg 'Deathfest'. After this show Morabito then decamped and De Honestis returned.

Spanish label Xtreem Music released the 'Disturbance' album in April 2003, these tracks recorded at 16th Cellar Studio. The group at this stage involved Viti, Schettino, Mercurio and guitarist Francesco De Honestis. Line-up changes then hit the band as guitarist Francesco De Honestis was superseded by a returning Giulio Moschini. In January 2005 HOUR OF PENANCE drafted new vocalist Alex 'Necrotorture' Manco of SPLATTERED CAVITIES and NECROTORTURE. New bassist Silvano Leone, of FEARWELL, was introduced in February. The same label put out follow up 'Pageantry For Martyrs' in June 2005.

In March 2006 the group supported KRISIUN and DEATHBOUND for shows in Spain, France, Switzerland and Italy. However, in September guitarist Enrico Schettino exited, followed shortly afterward by Alex Necrotorture. The group swiftly pulled in new frontman Francesco Paoli, of TYRANNIC ETHICAL RECONSTRUCTION. HOUR OF PENANCE entered 16th Cellar Studios in Rome on December 18th 2006 to record a new three-song demo. The band signed with Unique Leader Records in March 2007.

Hour Of Penance, Hour Of Penance (2000) (Demo). Confined In Flesh / First Killed Then Judged / Introspective Genius And Hatred / Hour Of Penance / Soul Addicted.

DISTURBANCE, Xtreem Music XM 005 (2003). Der Zorn Gottes (intro) / Rise And Oppress / Mystification As Law / From Hate To Suffering / Inhaling Disbelief / N.E.M.A. / Spires / Soul Addicted / Dawn Of Cerberus / Blood Tribute.

PAGEANTRY FOR MARTYRS, Xtreem Music (2005). Towards Our Storm / Shreds Of Martyr / End Of Relief / Celebrating Collective Terror / Far Beyond Humiliation / Life In A Pain Amplifier / Exiled Innocence / Naked Knife Absolution / Deranged Parasite / Egomanisch / (Untitled).

Hour Of Penance, Hour Of Penance (2007) (Demo). Misconception / Slavery In A Deaf Decay / Hierarchy Of The Fools.

HOUWITSER

HOLLAND — *Stan (vocals), Michel Alderliefsten (guitar), Alex (guitar), Theo Van Eekelen (bass), Aad Kloosterwaard (drums).*

HOUWITSER is a Death Grind side project from SINISTER's Mike and drummer Aad Kloosterwaard in conjunction with JUDGEMENT DAY's Theo Van Eekelen. The band debuted in the Spring of 1999 with 'Death ... But Not Buried' after which Mike vacated the frontman role. HOUWITSER pulled in Arjaaan 'Djortzzz' Kampman for second offering 'Embrace Damnation'. Following tour work HOUWITSER added to their guitar arsenal with the incorporation of another SINISTER veteran Alex. Shortly afterward Kampman relinquished his standing to new frontman Stan. Both Kloosterwaard and Van Eekelen also held down membership of the reformed THANATOS although by August 2001 Kloosterwaard would vacate his position with THANATOS to concentrate his efforts on HOUWITSER and SINISTER. The band strengthened the SINISTER connection by inducting guitarist Michel Alderliefsten. The band joined forces with DYING FETUS and MONSTROSITY for the 'Intervalle Bizarre' European tour during September and October of 2002 although they would lose the services of guitarist Michel Alderliefsten beforehand.

Former HOUWITSER singer Mike van Mastrigt resurfaced in late 2002 in a new band union DEATH SQUAD working with ex-RADIATHOR guitarist Walter Tjwa, second guitarist J.G. and drummer Michel.

Aad Kloosterwaard founded the old school US styled Death Metal side project INFINITED HATE in August 2003. Opening with the demo 'Primitive Butchery', recorded at the AM studios in Gouda, these tapes featured SINISTER members Rachel Kloosterwaard and Ron van de Polder. INFINITED HATE signed to Displeased Records for a 2004 debut. Also in 2004 HOUWITSER would donate their rendition of 'March To Die' to the 'Seven Gates Of Horror' tribute album assembled by the Dutch Karmaggedon Media label in homage to pioneering Bay Area Thrash act POSSESSED.

Aad Kloosterwaard exited in the Spring to concentrate on INFINITED HATE. Unable to secure a replacement drummer HOUWITSER duly cancelled all announced shows and in July called it a day. Kloosterwaard and guitarist Alex immediately fired up a new project dubbed NO FACE SLAVE. In October 2006 Aad Kloosterwaard sessioned guest vocals on demos for SUPREME PAIN. Retaining his SINISTER ties, he subsequently joined this old school Death Metal band, which featured Erwin Harreman on bass and guitar and Robert Kovacic of SCAFFOLD on drums. In March 2007 SUPREME PAIN signed a deal with the US based label Comatose Music, owned by Steve Green of LUST OF DECAY, for a debut album 'Cadaver Pleasures'.

In January 2007 it would be learned that former HOUWITSER bass player Theo van Eekelen had joined forces with THANATOS guitarists Stephan Gebédi and Paul Baayens, former PESTILENCE and ASPHYX singer Martin Van Drunen and GOREFEST drummer Ed Warby in a new band unit dubbed HAIL OF BULLETS.

DEATH BUT NOT BURIED, Displeased D00063 (1999). Intro / Dead's A Fact / Shredded To Pieces / Terror Legion / Sixtynineher / Monkey In Control / Ravishing Chaos / D.P.W. / Sliced & Diced / War, Blood & Honey / Fistfull Of Vixen / World's Parasites / Support Satan / Trip Of Fire / I Shape The Suffering.

EMBRACE DAMNATION, Displeased (2000). Onslaught Of Hate / Feeding On Fools / Embrace Damnation / Catenated / Stabbing Overdose / Command Respect / Vile Amputation / Feel The Consequence / Unholy Orgasm / Leeches Come / Consuming Cadavers / Mentally Mutilated.

RAGE INSIDE THE WOMB, Osmose Productions (2002). Slaughter Confession / Nailing The Torso / Score Of Corpses / Gutted In The Gutter / A Bite Of A Diseased Rat / Rage Inside The Womb / Vengeance Needs Blood / Unleash The Fury / 37 Stabwounds / Exposed To Poison.

DAMAGE ASSESSMENT, Osmose Productions OPCD 151 (2003). Clean Till The Bone / Damage Assessment / Hunger For The Feast / Liquidating The Venomous / Mean And Malice / Paradise To Purgatory / Parasomy / Skineater.

HUMAN

CHRISTCHURCH, NEW ZEALAND — *Scott Spatcher-Harrison (vocals / guitar), Vaughn Richardson (vocals / bass), Kezz Brewster (vocals / guitar), Paul Harrison (drums).*

Death Metal / Grindcore act from Christchurch, HUMAN debuted with the 'Organ Splatters' demo in 1992. This was followed by a raft of demos including 'Vomit Discreetly' and 'Things That Make You Go ...' both in 1993, 'Not So Famous

Game Show Themes' during 1995, 'Playtime For The Sex Machine' in 1996 with both '69 Minutes Of Self Abusement' and 'Stampede Of Stupidity' delivered in 2002.

1999 saw the release of HUMAN's first full length CD 'The Sound Of Yellow'. The band produced a video 'Paytoilet Of Despair' in 2003. HUMAN shot a video clip for the song 'Night Of The Living Bread' at The Dux De Lux in Christchurch during September of 2004. Line-up changes saw Mitchell Hopley replacing Tim Facoorey on guitar. The latter founded TAINTED in October 2004.

HUMAN returned in January 2005 with the album 'Blood Bucket', released by Dead Guy in New Zealand with worldwide distribution through German label Pikaz Music. Subsequently, Kezz Brewster superseded Hopley.

In 2006 HUMAN teamed up with Auckland's TRIAL BY FIRE for the "Scourge, Purge, And Burn Tour" co-headlining New Zealand tour, commencing October 12th in Christchurch.

Foreskin Face, Subcide Productions (1993). Foreskin Face / Crunchy Frog.
SIXTY NINE MINUTES OF SELF ABUSEMENT, (1998). Dipped In Shit / Graveyard Gourmet / Internal Pain / Umbilical Strangulation / Open Heart Brain Surgery / Maggots / Cacophonic Organ Splatter / An Insatiable Lust For Excretions / Scrotal Shock Torture / Decomposing Rectum Muscle / Crunchy Frog / Turning Green And Starting To Smell (1 & 2) / Trapped In A Meat Locker / Spermfire / Foreskin Face / Wave Goodbye To Both Your Hands / Easter Basket Full Of Carnage / Dance Of The Amputees / Toilet Flesh / Hoopsciously Drangled / Trails Of A Man Called Barry / Do You Love Me? / I Ate Him In Self Defence / Masturbate To Survive / Back From The Groove / My Grandmother's Not Your Type / Don't Call Me Gerald / Donkies In Bondage / Can I Borrow A Pen?
THE SOUND OF YELLOW, Suffocating Discs (1999). Easter Basket Full Of Carnage / Dipped In Shit / Toilet Flesh / Hoopsciously Drangled / Bright Green Body In A Big Black Coffin / Underwater Undertaker / Maggots / Wave Goodbye To Both Your Hands / Moonshine Highway / D.R.M / Scrotal Shock Torture / Umbilical Strangulation.
BLOOD BUCKET, Dead Guy (2005). Night Of The Living Bread / Better Dead Than Dinner / Dayt Ripper / Home Necronomics / Choked In The Dark / Leathers And Feathers / Run With Scissors / A Bugger Of A Night In Blud / Stampede Of Stupidity / Paytoilet Of Despair / Paytoilet Of Despair (Video) / Night Of The Living Bread (Video).

HUMAN BLOODFEAST

REGENSBURG, GERMANY — *Sebastian Heim (vocals), Marcus Merl (vocals / guitar), Tobias Köppl (guitar), Stephan Fimmers (bass), Joachim Wolf (drums).*

Regensburg Death Metal combo, founded during October 1999 by singer Andreas Mausch, vocalist / guitarist Marcus Merl, second guitarist Andreas Schneid and Joachim Wolf and drums. After initial 2000 demos Schneid was replaced by Martin Buchmann and Stephan Fimmers was enrolled to cover bass duties. In November of 2001 HUMAN BLOODFEAST entered the recording studio to lay down tracks for the debut 'Damned To Rot'. Although the band scored numerous support gigs to the likes of CRYPTIC WINTERMOON, FLESHLESS, DISBELIEF, FLESHCRAWL, PROFANITY and ILLDISPOSED, Buchmann was to exit. Filling the vacancy would be Tobias Köppl.

HUMAN BLOODFEAST lost the services of Andreas Mausch in the Spring of 2003, the frontman opting out due to health reasons. A temporary replacement was located in Sebastian Heim, this posting later becoming permanent. The band's next recording would be the self financed 'Bath Of Bugs' EP, cut at Aexxys Art Studios in September.

The band hooked up with SYCRONOMICA, ILLEGIMITATION and EQUILIBRIUM for the "Blasting Bavaria" tour of Germany in November of 2004.

DAMNED TO ROT, Independent (2002). Intro / I'm Alive / Me In You / The Beast Inside / Follow The Bloodline / Orgasm Through Mutilation / Twisted Desires / Damned To Rot / In My Head / Addicted To Flesh / Flesh Eating Mother.
Bath Of Bugs, Independent (2003). Bath Of Bugs / Schizophrenic Butchering / Perverse Lust / Orgasm Through Mutilation.
SHE COMES GUTTED, Possessed (2006).

HYMIR

UTRECHT, HOLLAND — *Pablo de Groot (vocals), Kay van Kalsbeek (guitar), Daan Douma (guitar), Sander Leune (bass), Tom Gorissen (keyboards), Per Hoogendoorn (drums).*

Utrecht Death-Black Metal outfit HYMIR was created during late 2005 by erstwhile TYRANNY FOREST and MYSTIC REALM members vocalist / guitarist Pablo de Groot and drummer Per Hoogendoorn. Other MYSTIC REALM veterans, second guitarist Kay van Kalsbeek and bass player Bob Kuitenbrouwer, were quick to enroll. HYMIR was rounded out by keyboard player Thomas Dirkse. Subsequently Daan Douma was pulled in for live work as guitarist but soon took on this position on a permanent basis.

Kay van Kalsbeek and Thomas Dirkse both exited, but the guitarist then returned. Tom Gorissen assumed the keyboard role to record the 2007 EP 'Perish', recorded by Quintijn Verhoef at Independent Recordings studio. The band took on new bassist Sander Leune, also associated with DIP-SWITCH.

Perish, Hymirr (2007). Expugno (Intro) / Perish / Mars Almighty / Bleak / Conquer And Smite / For Never To Return Again.

HYPERBOREA

SOFIA, BULGARIA — *Kiril Kirilov (vocals), Yordan Kanchev (guitar), Andrei Andronov (guitar), Vladimir Ivanov (bass), Zhivko Kyosev (drums).*

Sofia Death Metal act HYPERBOREA was initiated during 1997 by guitarists Krum Doinov and Ilia Dimitrov, soon drawing in singer Kiril Kirilov. Differences saw the departure of Dimitrov though, who was initially replaced by Plamen Petkov, who subsequently switched to bass. The band's debut live show took place in early 1998 at the Sevastopol Metal club with Stoyan 'Epizod' on the drums. Changes then saw the introduction of drummer Ivaylo 'Murtvo' Baev and guitarist Yordan 'M.O.P.' Kanchev. This version of HYPERBOREA put up an intensive gigging schedule across the country.

In 1999 Baev exited and HYPERBOREA persevered by recruiting guest musicians including Pencho Penchev of VILE and RAINDOGS, Tzvetan Tzonev and Alex Gueorguiev of PRIMITIVE ANGEL GOSPODEN. Finally, in May of 2002, the band inducted ex-UXORICIDE guitarist Jivko Kyossev to fill the vacancy on a permanent basis. Planen departed that Autumn and WARTIME guitarist Andrei Andronov substituted on bass before the Spring of 2003 found Vlado Ivanov assuming the position.

Between June and November 2003 HYPERBOREA set about recording their debut album 'Architecture Of Mind'. In January 2004 the band marked it's first live appearance abroad, performing in Bucharest in Rumania, this show at the A Club, supported by KRATOS and AVATAR, to 500 Metal fans being broadcast on national television.

'Architecture Of Mind' saw arrival in June of 2004 on Butchery Music. Following release, the band, seeing temporary inclusion of Lyubo "Chewbaca" in lieu of Yordan Kanchev, supported VADER. Andrei Andronov would then be installed to replace Krum.

ARCHITECTURE OF MIND, Butchery Music (2004). Intro / Nosferatu / Call Of The Master / Mortified / Hyperborea / The Lamarchand's Box / Unseen Hand / Hypocrisy / Odium / Disrooted Past (Outro).

HYPNOS

CZECH REPUBLIC — *Bruno (vocals / bass), R.A.D. (guitar), Skull (drums).*

Czech trio HYPNOS are in fact KRABATHOR men vocalist Bruno and drummer Skull, the latter also holding MASTER

HYPNOS

credits. The 2000 album 'In Blood We Trust' sees Mikka 'Sir' Luttinen of IMPALED NAZARENE involved. HYPNOS toured Europe in December 2000 as part of an almighty Death Metal package that included ENSLAVED, MORBID ANGEL, BEHEMOTH, THE CROWN and DYING FETUS. In November of 2001 guitarist Daniel M. bowed out- apparently to pursue a career as an undertaker! His replacement would be Mills.

HYPNOS collected a set of rarities for the 2004 album 'Demo(n)s' issued through Metal Age Productions. That same year Skull forged Metalcore band BAD FACE in union with former DECAY vocalist Pawel, ex-HYPNOS, STAGNANT and SHAARK guitarist R.A.D. and former DEPRESION guitarist Dan.

XXX, Morbid MR 066 (2000). Intro / The End Of God / X / Nath And Her Gun / XX / Phantasma Plasma / Mother / XXX / Neverland / XXXX? / Riddle / Mother (Father Edit) / The End Of God (Resurrection mix).

Hypnos EP, Morbid (2000). Infernational / Breeding The Scum / The Cave / In Blood We Trust.

IN BLOOD WE TRUST, Morbid (2000). Incantation / Burn The Angels Down / Fatal Shrine Of Sky / Infernational / Lovesong / Open The Gates Of Hell / Sacrilegious / Across The Battlefields / Breeding The Scum / In Blood We Trust / After The Carnage (Outro).

THE REVENGE RIDE, Morbid (2001). Ravens Opera DMoll / Crystal Purity Of Treachery / Evil Awaken / Regicide / Journey Into Doom / Endorsed By Satan / Spider-Werk / I Am The Wind / Lost / Heroism Of New Era.

DEMO(N)S (THE COLLECTION 1999-2003), Metal Age Productions (2004). Supernatural Race Disharmony / Krieg—The Alpha Paradox / Journey Into Doom / Regicide / Breeding The Scum / Crystal Purity Of Treachery / In Blood We Trust / Infernational / Breeding The Scum / The Cave / In Blood We Trust.

HYPNOSIA

SWEDEN — *Cab Castervall (vocals / guitar), Hampus Klang (guitar bass), Mike Sjöstrand (drums).*

Vaxjo based Thrash styled Deathsters HYPNOSIA first emerged brandishing the four track April 1996 'Crushed Existence' demo tape. At this juncture the band comprised Cab Castervall on vocals and guitar, Carl-Petter Berg on second guitar, bass player Klas Gunnarsson and drummer Mike Sjöstrand. For the follow up demo, 1997's 'The Storms', HYPNOSIA lost the services of Gunnarsson and Mattias 'Slask' Werdenskog took over on bass. HYPNOSIA also had the track 'The Last Remains' included on the VOD Records compilation 'Voices Of Death'.

The February 1998 mini album 'Violent Intensity' saw a vinyl release in November of 1999 by the Dutch Soulseller Productions imprint which included an exclusive extra track in HYPNOSIA's rendition of SODOM's 'Outbreak Of Evil'. For these recordings the band numbered Cab Castervall on vocals and guitar, Johan Orre on second guitar and drummer Mike Sjöstrand. Session bass guitar came courtesy of Mange Roos. Further line up ructions forced the departure of Johan Orre in January of 1999, being replaced by Daniel Sporrenstrand of XENOFANES repute. In April Hampus Klang enrolled on bass but with the exit of Sporrenstrand this latest recruit switched over to lead guitar.

HYPNOSIA covered POSSESSED's 'My Belief' on vinyl variants of their October 2000 album 'Extreme Hatred'. Digipack versions of the record included the entire 'Violent Intensity' album as a bonus. By November HYPNOSIA had solved their ongoing problems with a permanent bassist with the introduction of Lenny Blade.

In March of 2002 Castervall unveiled a Black-Death side project billed as FUNERAL in union with Chrille from SOIL OF THE UNDEAD. That same year Werdenskog featured as vocalist on SOIL OF THE UNDEAD's demo 'Seduced By Mental Desecrations'. HYPNOSIA performed a brief run of dates in the low countries but despite announcing plans for a new album provisionally entitled 'World Sacrifice' HYPNOSIA folded in June of 2002. Cab Castervall would turn up on tour in Europe in September of 2003 as live guitarist for infamous Grind act BIRDFLESH.

Former HYPNOSIA drummer Mikael Sjöstrand passed away on 8th January 2004 following a battle with skin cancer. He was just 27 years old.

VIOLENT INTENSITY, Iron Fist Productions (1998). Funeral Cross / Haunting Death / Undead / Perpetual Dormancy / Mental Terror / The Storms.

EXTREME HATRED, Hammerheart (2000). Extreme Hatred / Circle Of The Flesh / The Last Remains / Operation Clean Sweep / Comatose / Act Of Lunacy / Gates Of Cirith Ungol / My Belief / Hang 'Em High / Traumatic Suffering.

HYPOCRISY

STOCKHOLM, SWEDEN — *Peter Tägtgren (vocals / guitar), Andreas Holma (guitar), Mikael Hedlund (bass), Horgh (drums).*

HYPOCRISY was formed in Ludvika, Stockholm by guitarist Peter Tägtgren in October 1991. As well as HYPOCRISY, Tägtgren has carved out a considerable and esteemed catalogue of work with other musical concerns such as the industrial solo concept PAIN, LOCKUP, THE ABYSS and BLOODBATH. He also does dual duty as a producer in constant demand, operating from his Abyss Studios base racking up recognition on the other side of the desk with acts such as CHILDREN OF BODOM, DIMMU BORGIR, THERION, CELTIC FROST, DARK FUNERAL, DESTRUCTION and IMMORTAL amongst many others.

HYPOCRISY were initially known as SEDITIOUS. Long before this venture, both Tägtgren and drummer Lars Szöke had previously been members of CONQUEST, an act dating back as far as 1984. HYPOCRISY was established when Tägtgren had returned from North America where he had put in tenures as a member of both MALEVOLENT CREATION and MELTDOWN.

SEDITIOUS was set to debut as a solo concern with the 1991 demo cassette 'Rest In Pain'. This would not see distribution though as Tägtgren was unsatisfied with his vocal performance. A second attempt to re-cut the same tracks, adding 'Nightmare' and 'Left To Rot', emerged as the first public airing of HYPOCRISY.

HYPOCRISY's line-up was augmented by bassist Mikael Hedlund, EPITAPH guitarist Jonas Österberg and erstwhile VOTARY vocalist Masse Broberg. As HYPOCRISY the band soon secured a deal with Germany's Nuclear Blast Records issuing the debut 'Penetralia' album in 1992. Stylistically HYPOCRISY pursued a narrow path of Florida styled Death Metal, laden with ripping guitar chaos and uncompromisingly blasphemous subject matter. That same year Österberg and Szöke released the 'Tranquility' album from their other act EPITAPH. The following year US label Relapse Records put out the EP 'Pleasure Of Molestation', these four tracks then being re-recorded for the next album. By this stage HYPOCRISY were whittled down to a quartet, with Peter Tägtgren handling guitars.

For the second album, 'Osculum Obscenum' released again by Nuclear Blast during October 1993, HYPOCRISY covered VENOM's seminal 'Black Metal'. Tour dates included shows with DEICIDE and CANNIBAL CORPSE. However, on tour vocalist Masse Broberg was reported to have suffered a breakdown, necessitating Tägtgren taking over lead vocals. Subsequently, Broberg hooked up with DARK FUNERAL, taking the alter ego persona of Emperor Magus Caligula.

Following the dates HYPOCRISY decided to carry on as a trio, of Tägtgren, Hedlund and Szöke, releasing the 'Inferior Devoties' mini-album, which included the SLAYER cover 'Black Magic'. This track also appeared on the SLAYER tribute compilation album 'Slatanic Slaughter Volume One'.

In 1995 HYPOCRISY toured such far flung places as Mexico and Portugal promoting their 'The Fourth Dimension' album. This record had been laid down in March 1994 at Park Studios in Stockholm, observing a band exploring new directions, wresting themselves away from the Satanic lyrical content and replacing buzzsaw riffage with more melancholic chord patterns. 'The Fourth Dimension' was also the first Hypocrisy body of work to prominently highlight keyboards. Japanese versions added the 'Inferior Devotees' material.

During 1995 the band released the 'Maximum Abduction' chicken (!) shaped CD mini-album, which included a cover of KISS' 'Strange Ways'. In 1996 Tägtgren fulfilled duties as stand in guitarist for MARDUK on their European tour as well as working on a solo project PAIN. Tägtgren, Hedlund and Szöke, curiously all swapping instruments for the occasion, also pursued a side project act entitled THE ABYSS, releasing two albums; The Other Side' and 'Summon The Beast'.

The alien themed 'Abducted' album, recorded at Tägtgren's own Abyss Studio complex, arrived in February 1996. A notable HYPOCRISY release would be the 'Roswell 47' 7" single shared as a split release with MESHUGGAH. For concerts, the group expanded with the introduction of second guitarist Mathias Kamijo, known for his roles in PAIN, THE ABYSS and ABEMAL. Kamijo would regularly reprise this role on future tours.

The fifth album, October 1997's 'The Final Chapter' included a cover version of 'Evil Invaders' originally by Canadian Thrashers RAZOR. As 'The Final Chapter' saw the light of day, Tägtgren announced that this would signal HYPOCRISY's final fling, citing that he wished to concentrate on PAIN. However, this announcement combined with the resulting good reviews granted to 'The Final Chapter' persuaded Tägtgren to change his mind.

HYPOCRISY issued their first live album 'Hypocrisy Destroys Wacken' in March 1999, recorded as a quartet including second guitarist Matthias Kamijo. As well as the thundering live set captured on tape at the world famous German festival on August 8th 1998, the album closed out with four studio tracks, 'Time Warp', 'Until The End', 'Fuck U' and 'Beginning Of The End'.

They followed up quickly with another critically acclaimed studio album in June, given a provisional name of 'Cloned' but eventually delivered simply titled 'Hypocrisy'. This tour de force, which benefited enormously from an increased songwriting input from both Hedlund and Szöke, transported the trademark Hypocrisy rawness into all new vistas of sound, generating the most richly atmospheric outing to date. After summer festival shows, a European campaign in September took out running mates THE KOVENANT, GARDENIAN, DISMAL EUPHONY and DISBELIEF.

Peter Tägtgren also involved himself in the commercially successful LOCKUP project with NAPALM DEATH bassist Shane Embury and guitarist Jesse Pintado with DIMMU BORGIR drummer Nick Barker. Although the LOCKUP album sold spectacularly well in Germany Tägtgren backed out of the project before live work ensued.

2000 found Tägtgren busier than ever with a further PAIN album 'Rebirth', which garnered a healthy and lengthy placing in the national Swedish album charts, as well as a fresh HYPOCRISY effort, the retro flavoured 'Into The Abyss', released in August.

The band, installing a new second live guitarist in SCATTERED CORPSES member Andreas Holma and promoting the 'Catch 22' album, would figure as part of the gargantuan European 'No Mercy' touring festival package in March and April of 2002. Also on the billing would be VADER, CATASTROPHIC, DESTROYER 666, IMMORTAL, DISBELIEF, MALEVOLENT CREATION and OBSCENITY.

HYPOCRISY cut a new album for 2004 release entitled 'The Arrival'. Recording would not run smoothly though and upon completion the whole album would be remastered and remixed. Fan demand would persuade the band to re-record 'The Abyss' for this record, the song originally only included as a bonus track on 'The Fourth Dimension'. A rare outside influence found Silenoz of DIMMU BORGIR co-credited as composer for the track 'New World' and a switch in drummers found the IMMORTAL, LOST AT LAST, PAIN and GRIMFIST credited Horgh (a.k.a. Reidar Horghagen) taking over from Lars Szöke in January 2004.

Peter Tägtgren donated a guest vocal appearance for the 2004 KATAKLYSM album 'Serenity In Fire', appearing on the track 'For All Our Sins'. He also contributed his services to a tribute album 'Within The Mind', assembled by guitarist JAMES MURPHY in honour of the late DEATH mentor Chuck Schuldiner, and added to his roster of official projects by joining the Blackheim and DAN SWANÖ mentored BLOODBATH.

HYPOCRISY put in a run of co-headline gigs commencing 12th February in Houston, Texas that had the band traversing North America in league with EXHUMED, CANNIBAL CORPSE and VILE upfront of a run of South American gigs. They then formed up part of the 2004 European heavyweight 'No Mercy' festivals commencing 29th March, sharing billing with SPAWN OF POSSESSION, CANNIBAL CORPSE, KATAKLYSM, CARPATHIAN FOREST, VOMITORY, PREJUDICE and EXHUMED.

Horgh relinquished his GRIMFIST position in June in order to prioritise HYPOCRISY. The band performed an unusual concert dubbed the '34'000 Ton Metal Cruise' on 25th September, performing onboard the Münchenbryggeriet car ferry in Stockholm, Sweden alongside TANKARD, AMON AMARTH, SKYCLAD, TAD MOROSE, STORMWARRIOR and WOLF. US dates for January 2005 had the band packaged with DARK TRANQUILLITY and SOILWORK. In February Peter Tägtgren worked in the studio as producer for German Thrash Metal veterans DESTRUCTION. That August he would ensconce himself in Horus Sound Studios in Hannover, producing the 'Monotheist' comeback album for CELTIC FROST then engage in promotion for the HYPOCRISY 'Virus' record launched in September before getting back to work on a new record for PAIN.

'Virus' found HYPOCRISY engaging in a more technical direction and would prominently feature new guitarist Andreas Holma, a man with a Jazz background. Notably, Gary Holt of EXODUS guested on the track 'Scrutinized'. European gigs that November, allied with EXODUS, saw support from KEEP OF KALESSIN. Live work breaking into 2006 saw the band teaming up with NILE, SOILENT GREEN, RAGING SPEEDHORN, DECAPITATED and WITH PASSION for a North American tour commencing in early January. The band joined the 'Metal Hammer' sponsored 'European Neckbreaker's Ball' 2006 tour, also featuring SCAR SYMMETRY, SOILWORK and ONE MAN ARMY AND THE UNDEAD QUARTET, commencing 11th April in Denmark.

Guitarist Andreas Holma quit in September, the band claiming the musician was "not motivated anymore" as the cause. Holma duly announced solo project UNCHARTED WATERS. HYPOCRISY utilized the services of DARKANE's Klas Ideberg as a session guitarist for its North American "Machines At War

Tour" with FEAR FACTORY, SUFFOCATION and DECAPITATED kicking off on October 26th in San Francisco, California.

PENETRALIA, Nuclear Blast NB 067-2 (1992). Impotent God / Suffering Souls / Nightmare / Jesus Fall / God Is A ... / Left To Rot / Burn By The Cross / To Escape Is To Die / Take The Throne / Penetralia.

Pleasure Of Molestation, Relapse 6040 (1993). Pleasure Of Molestation / Exclamation Of A Necrofag / Necronomicon / Attachment To The Ancestor.

OSCULUM OBSCENUM, Nuclear Blast NB 080-2 (1993). Pleasure Of Molestation / Exclamation Of A Necrofag / Osculum Obscenum / Necromonicon / Black Metal / Inferior Devoties / Infant Sacrifices / Attachment To The Ancestor / Althotas.

Inferior Devoties EP, Nuclear Blast NB 098-2 (1994). Inferior Devoties / Symbol Of Baphomet / Mental Emotions / God Is A Lie / Black Magic.

THE FOURTH DIMENSION, Nuclear Blast NB 112-2 (1994). Apocalypse / Mind Corruption / Reincarnation / Reborn / Black Forest / Never To Return / Path To Babylon / Slaughtered / Orgy In Blood / The North Wind / T.E.M.P.T. / The Fourth Dimension / The Arrival Of The Demons / The Abyss.

Roswell 47, Nuclear Blast (1996) (Split single with MESHUGGAH. Limited edition 1000 copies). Roswell 47.

Maximum Abduction EP, Nuclear Blast NB 145-2 (1996). Roswell 47 / Carved Up / Request Denied / Strange Ways.

Carved Up, Relapse RR-030 (1996) (7" purple swirl vinyl). Carved Up / Beginning Of The End.

ABDUCTED, Nuclear Blast NB 133-2 (1996). Gathering / Roswell / Killing Art / The Arrival Of The Demons (Part Two) / Buried / Abducted / Paradox / Point Of No Return / When The Candle Fades / Carved Up / Reflections / Slippin' Away / Drained.

THE FINAL CHAPTER, Nuclear Blast NB 283-2 (1997). Inseminated Adoption / A Coming Race / Dominion / Inquire Within / Last Vanguard / Request Denied / Through The Window Of Time / Shamateur / Adjusting The Sun / Lies / Evil Invaders / The Final Chapter.

HYPOCRISY DESTROYS WACKEN, Nuclear Blast NB 376-2 (1999). Roswell 47 / Inseminated Adoption / A Coming Race / Apocalypse / Osculum Obscenum / Buried / Left to Rot / The Fourth Dimension / Pleasure of Molestation / Killing Art / The Final Chapter / Time Warp / Til´ the End / Fuck U / Beginning of the End.

HYPOCRISY, Nuclear Blast NB 388-2 (1999). Fractured Millennium / Apocalyptic Hybrid / Fusion Programmed Minds / Elastic Inverted Visions / Reversed Reflections / Until The End / Paranormal Mysteria / Time Warp / Disssconnected Magnetic Corridors / Paled Empty Sphere / Selfinflicted Overload. Chart position: 85 GERMANY.

INTO THE ABYSS, Nuclear Blast NB 529-2 (2000). Legions Descend / Blinded / Resurrected / Unleash The Beast / Digital Prophecy / Fire In The Sky / Total Eclipse / Unfold The Sorrow / Sodomized / Deathrow (No Regrets). Chart position: 63 GERMANY.

10 YEARS OF CHAOS AND CONFUSION, Nuclear Blast NB 630-2 (2001). Penetralia (Re-recorded) / The Fourth Dimension (Re-recorded) / Osculum Obscenum (Re-recorded) / Apocalypse (Re-recorded) / Killing Art / Deathrow / Left To Rot (Re-recorded) / Until The End / Pleasures Of Molestation (Re-recorded) / A Coming Race / Fractured Millenium / Roswell 47 / Fire In The Sky / The Final Chapter.

CATCH 22, Nuclear Blast NB 710-2 (2002). Don't Judge Me / Destroyed / On The Edge Of Madness / A Public Puppet / Uncontrolled / Turn The Page / Hatred / Another Dead End (From Another Deadman) / Seeds Of The Chosen One / All Turns Black / Nowhere To Run. Chart position: 78 GERMANY.

THE ARRIVAL, Nuclear Blast NB 1230-2 (2004). Born Dead Buried Alive / Eraser / Stillborn / Slave To The Parasites / New World / The Abyss / Dead Sky Dawning / The Departure / War Within. Chart positions: 43 FINLAND, 71 AUSTRIA.

VIRUS, Nuclear Blast NB 1141-2 (2005). Intro / Warpath / Scrutinized / Fearless / Craving For Another Killing / Let The Knife Do The Talking / A Thousand Lies / Incised Before I've Ceased / Blooddrenched / Compulsive Psychosis / Living To Die. Chart positions: 58 SWEDEN, 75 AUSTRIA, 76 GERMANY.

HYPOCRITE

STOCKHOLM, SWEDEN — *Johan Haller (vocals / bass), Niclas Åberg (guitar), Henrik Hedborg (guitar), Peter Nagy (drums).*

Stockholm Death Metallers HYPOCRITE started out life in 1989, founded by vocalist / bassist Johan Haller and guitarist Niclas Åberg, under the name of DARK TERROR. Formative demos included 'Ruler Of The Dark' in 1991, 'Welcome To Abaddon' in 1992 and 1993's 'Dead Symbols'. HYPOCRITE's 1994 7" single was a split effort with ELECTROCUTION on the Italian Molten Metal label. The band released their debut album 'Edge Of Existence' in June 1996 through the Italian label Flying Records. Notable guest singers included ENTOMBED's Lars-Göran Petrov and Thomas Vikström of CANDLEMASS.

During 1997 guitarist Henrik Hedberg contributed guest lead vocals to the WYVERN demo 'The Ancient Sword'. For the 1998 Fred Estby produced album 'Into The Halls Of The Blind', recorded at Das Boot Studios, HYPOCRITE were down to a trio of vocalist / bassist Johan Haller, guitarist Henrik "Headbang" Hedborg and drummer Peter Nagy. No Fashion Records re-issued a remixed version of 'Edge Of Existence' in 1999.

Nagy has racked up credits playing for MÖRK GRYNING, WYVERN, DEFENDER, INFLICTION and ETERNAL OATH.

Ruler Of The Dark, (0). Buried Alive / Rulers Of The Dark / Genocide.

Welcome To Abaddon, (1992). Antichrist / Welcome To Abaddon / The Scream ....

Dead Symbols, (1994). Heaven's Tears / Sanctuary Of The Sleeping God / Beyond The Edge.

Heaven's Tears, Molten Metal MOLTEN010 (1994) (Split single with ELECTROCUTION). Heaven's Tears.

EDGE OF EXISTENCE, Offworld OW005 (1996). Vita Dolorosa / Deep Within This Flower Of Sin / Edge Of Existence / The Scream ... / Voices From The Dark Side / Heaven's Tears / A Black Wound / When I'm Gone / Sanctuary Of The Sleeping God / Welcome To Abaddon / Forsaken by Christ / Beyond The Edge.

INTO THE HALLS OF THE BLIND, No Fashion NFR032 (1998). Dreadful Shadow / In Blood We End / Mind Reaper / Slavery Society / Blood Blind / Eye Of The Serpent / Dark Blue Velvet / Son Of The Sungod / Into The Halls Of The Blind / Of A Fiend Kind / Awakening Of The God.

ILL FARES THE LAND

BELGIUM — *Roel Ulenaers (vocals), Bart Put (guitar), Jan Bogaerts (guitar), Bart Vanderheyden (drums).*

ILL FARES THE LAND began life in 1997 as a Metalcore outfit dubbed HERETIC. A series of membership realignments, seeing singer Bart Roman exiting for PERSONAL VENDETTA and the departure of bassist Bert Ulenaers, marked a shift towards Death Metal and the adoption of the new title ILL FARES THE LAND for the 1999 demo 'Souls Aground On The Reefs Of Sin'. This tape secured a deal with the Uxicon label for the album release 'Nonentity'.

Bassist Jurgen Hondshoven quit to join CRAWLSPACE in 2001. In November of 2002 Filip Dupont, of GORATH, MAHLSTRØM, P:407 and THE QUIESCENT repute, was enlisted on bass but would not stay the course. Dupont subsequently joined Viking Metal project THEUDHO during 2005 as bassist.

NONENTITY, Uxicon (2003). The Defeated Prophecy (Progression Into Privilege II) / Insufferable Insolence / Worlds Beyond The Grave / Signs Proclaiming Apocalypse / Ages Of Chaos / Devouring Of The Soul (Progression Into Privilege I).

ILLDISPOSED

ÅRHUS, DENMARK — *Bo Summer (vocals), Jakob Batten (guitar), Martin Thim (guitar), Jonas Kloge (bass), Thomas Jensen (drums).*

Århus based ILLDISPOSED date from early 1991 and the group's first demo was titled 'The Winter Of Our Discontempt', which led to a deal with Nuclear Blast Records. In late 1992 the band contributed the track 'Reversed' to the Progress Red label's 'Fuck You, We're From Denmark' compilation album and toured Europe as support to WARGASM and SINISTER in December 1993. During 1994 Envoldsen left to join ANGEL

ACCELERATOR DEATH and guitarist Martin Gilsted stepped in to replace Hans Wagner, who was suffering from alcohol problems.

In early 1995 drummer Lars Hald took over for a few live shows. The 1995 album 'Submit' saw Rolf Rognvard Hansen, previously known as guitarist for CAUSTIC, taking over the drum stool as Hald teamed up with PANZERCHRIST. Live shows in Germany to promote the album, noted for guitarist Lasse Bak performing many gigs stark naked, saw ILLDISPOSED playing alongside HAGGARD and DISGUST.

The 1998 effort 'There's Something Rotten ...' found Gilsted supplanted by ex-roadie Tore Mogensen. Bo Summer joined PANZERCHRIST for their third album 'Soul Collector'. The 2000 album 'Retro' was comprised entirely of cover versions. Bands honoured included CARCASS' 'Reek Of Putrefaction', AUTOPSY, DARKTHRONE 'Cromlech', VENOM, AC/DC's 'Beating Around The Bush' and MOTÖRHEAD's 'Killed By Death'. In February 2002 ILLDISPOSED drafted a new drummer, Thomas Sølvkæde Muskelbuks.

The band was back in the news as 2003 closed when guitarist Lasse Bak was arrested at a football match in Aarhus. The musician was charged for "drunk and offensive behavior", receiving a fine for "throwing a ½-litre tankard containing urine at a superintendent of Aarhus Police". More concrete news had the band entering the recording studio that February to prepare a new album.

The band donated their rendition of 'Slaughter Of The Soul' to the AT THE GATES tribute album, 'Slaughterous Souls—A Tribute to At The Gates' released in September 2004 through Drowned Scream Records. ILLDISPOSED was announced as support to DEATH ANGEL's European 2004 tour but pulled out due to "financial problems with the promoter". Nevertheless, ILLDISPOSED's October 2004 album '1-800 Vindication' would hit no. 85 on the national Danish charts, the highest rating ever for a Death Metal album. Bo Summer took time out to aid ABORTED as guest backing vocalist on their album 'The Archaic Abattoir'.

Ex-ILLDISPOSED guitarist Morten Gilsted bounced back in January 2005 with the SLOW DEATH FACTORY demo 'Music For Tough Guys', a high profile union of Danish extreme Metal elite comprising vocalist Martin Rosendahl of STRANGLER, CORPUS MORTALE and INIQUITY, CORPUS MORTALE's Roar Christofferson on bass guitar and Per Møller Jensen of INVOCATOR, KONKHRA and THE HAUNTED repute on drums.

ILLDISPOSED forged a touring alliance with Norway's ANCIENT and German act FINAL BREATH for European dates throughout March of 2005. Upon completion of these gigs the band parted ways with guitarist Lasse Bak and persevered as a quartet. ILLDISPOSED toured Germany packaged as part of the 'Wacken Open Air Roadshow' with REGICIDE, SUIDAKRA and HOLY MOSES during May 2005. In August the band introduced EXMORTEM guitarist Martin Thim into the ranks.

ILLDISPOSED readied a new album, 'Burn Me Wicked', for April 2006 release through Roadrunner Records. Following European touring with DEADSOIL and 37 STABWOUNDZ, the band flew to New Zealand to headline the 'Metal In The Beast—666—Metal Day Out' festival.

Announcing a working title of 'Det' Noget Lort Jim' ILLDISPOSED set to work on fresh album tracks in January 2007. The band scheduled UK headline dates for February with support from AMENTI.

RETURN FROM TOMORROW—ATTITUDES AND LONG TERM ADJUSTMENT OF PATIENTS SURVIVING CARDIAC ARREST, Nuclear Blast SPV 56- 1416732 (1994). Depersonalisation / Return From Tomorrow / On Death And Dying / Darkness Weaves With Many Shades / Impact / Withering Teardrops / Instrumental Outro.

FOUR DEPRESSIVE SEASONS, Nuclear Blast NB 103 (1994). Forbidden Summer Poetry / Reversed / Weeping Souls Of Autumn Desires / Life Equals Zero (A Love Song) / Deathwork Orange / The Winter Of Discontempt / Wardance Of The Technocracy / Never Ceasing Melancholic Spring / Inherit The Spring / With The Lost Souls On Our Side.

SUBMIT, Progress PCD 21 (1995). Purity Of Sadness / A Frame Of Mind / Vesuvio / The Hidden Acne / Memories Expanded / Slow Death Factory / Submit / Flogging A Dead Horse / Die Kingdom.

THERE'S SOMETHING ROTTEN IN THE STATE OF DENMARK, Serious Entertainment SE013CD (1998). Cyclus I-III / Pimp / Near The Gates / We Lie In The Snow / Not A Vision—1991 / Wake Up Dead / Instrumentally Illdisposed / There's Something Rotten ... / Horsens Highway.

RETRO, Cyclone (2000). Cromlech / None Shall Defy / Reek Of Putrefaction / Rapture / Nightmare / Gasping For Air / Open Casket / Killed By Death / Out Of The Body / Intoxicated / Beating Around The Bush.

1-800 VINDICATION, Roadrunner (2004). Believe In Me / Dark / Now We're History / When You Scream / Jeff / In Search Of Souls / Still Sane / You Against The World / No More Time / The Final Step. Chart position: 85 DENMARK.

BURN ME WICKED, Roadrunner (2006). Shine Crazy / Case Of The Late Pig / Back To The Street / Our Heroin Recess / Throw Your Bolts / Burn Me Wicked / Fear The Gates / Slave / Nothing To Fear ... Do It / The Widow Black / Illdispunk'd. Chart position: 58 DENMARK.

KOKAIINUM, Cyclone (2006). A Warm Welcome / Just Like A Clockwork / Richard Scarry / Illdisposed / Forever Young / Intellargent / Kokaiinum / A Girl And Her Boss / Fear Bill Gates.

ILLOGICIST

AOSTA, ITALY — *Luca Minieri (vocals / guitar), Diego Ambrosi (guitar), Emilio Dattolo (bass), Sergio Ponti (drums).*

Aosta based technical Death Metal band ILLOGICIST was manifested in the Summer of 1997 by guitarist Luca Minieri and drummer Remy Curtaz. Initial recording sessions, the 'Polymorphism Of Death' demos of February 2002 recorded at One Voice Studio with producer Daniele Giordana, were crafted with the core duo expanding to incorporate bassist Roberto Zeppa and former NEFARIUM guitarist Fabio Filippone. However, upon completion of these tracks both Zeppa and Filippone opted out and ILLOGICIST duly drafted Diego Ambrosi on guitar and Emilio Dattolo to handle bass.

The band utilised One Voice Studio once again at the end of October 2002 for the recording of a new EP entitled 'Dissonant Perspectives'. This scored a deal with US label Crash Music Inc. Curtaz exited briefly, but returned to cut the album 'Subjected', laid down at the band's own Dissonant Studios but mixed at the fabled Finnvox Studios in Helsinki by master engineers Mikko Karmila and Mika Jussila. The album surfaced in July 2004. Live work to promote this opus saw the introduction of new drummer Sergio Ponti. Projecting a new album to be recorded in November 2005 ILLOGICIST severed ties with Crash Music Inc.

The group announced signature with Willowtip Records in November 2006. Marco Minnemann laid down session drums for new album recordings.

Polymorphism Of Death, (2002). Warped / Visions Of Decay / Grimaces.

Dissonant Perspectives, (2003). The Soul Feeder / Knowledge Curse / Dissonant Perspectives.

SUBJECTED, Crash Music Inc. (2004). Into Your Mind / The High Price Of Confidence / Knowledge Curse / Every Straight Lie / Dissonant Perspectives / Subjected / Introspection / The Soul Feeder / The Last Show.

IMAGES OF VIOLENCE

AUSTIN, TX, USA — *Jon Zig (vocals), Steven Watkins (guitar), Dobber Beverly (guitar), Mark Denton (bass), Larry Jackson (drums).*

Blasphemous Death Metal from Austin, Texas featuring SECT OF EXECRATION guitar player Steven Watkins and ACERBUS drummer Larry Jackson. Singer John Zig has carved a reputation on the art front, his work gracing sleeve designs by many

US Death Metal releases. The first IMAGES OF VIOLENCE offering, a 2003 demo entitled 'Burnt', closed out with a cover version of NAPALM DEATH's 'Suffer The Children'. Deep Send Records followed with a 2004 EP 'Cadaverous Recomposition'. The band also employs Dobber Beverly, better known as drummer for INGURGITATE, SECT OF EXECRATION and BRACED FOR NAILS, on second guitar.

In 2004 IMAGES OF VIOLENCE members guitarist Steven Watkins, bass player Mark Denton and vocalist Jon Zig united with drummer Rick Myers of DISGORGE and CINERARY to forge the SARCOLYTIC project. Houston based Ossuary Industries released the IMAGES OF VIOLENCE album 'Degrade The Shapeless' on June 6th 2006.

Burnt, Images Of Violence (2003) (Demo). Juxtaposed In Opposition / Consumed By My Merciless Vengeance / As Greedy As A Pig / Suffer The Children.

Cadaverous Recomposition EP, Deep Send (2004). Voracious Devouring / Erotically Discolored / Spontaneous Act Of Selfish Depression / As Greedy As A Pig / Cadaverous Recomposition / Suffer The Children.

DEGRADE THE SHAPELESS, Ossuary Industries (2006). Pernicious Desire / Nocturnal Visits / Cleanse The Impure / Degrade The Shapeless / Spread For Worship / Among The Dead That Seem Living / Mephitic Possessor / Perverse Caress / Tools Of Severance.

IMMEMORIAL

GDAŃSK, POLAND — *Karolina Czertowicz (vocals), Frost (guitar / bass), Tadra (guitar), Fizyk (drums).*

Gdańsk Death Metal act conceived in Elbląg during June of 1997 and lent immediate distinction courtesy of the uncompromising vocals of Marta Meger. The group debuted with the mini album 'Ius Primae Noctis', delivered in 1998. This release was backed up by promotion afforded by the promo video clip 'Betrothal With The Death', this track also being included as part of a sampler compilation entitled 'Blood To Come' given away with the Polish 'Thrash 'Em All' magazine. World-wide reaction to the album on the international Death Metal scene was both swift and unanimously positive.

Meger, re-billing herself as 'Lady Martex', broke away from IMMEMORIAL to found the 'all star' extreme Metal venture ENTER CHAOS. This union, transpiring in January of 2002, pulled in such talents as Raiden from Ambient act AURAL PLANET on programming, former AZARATH and CENOTAPH man D., DAR SEMAI's Verymetal, DEVILYN's Bony and BEHEMOTH's Havoc and TRAUMA's Mister on guitar, Novy of BEHEMOTH, DIES IRAE and DEVILYN on the bass and L. Rambo, from DEMISE, DAMNATION and MOON, on the drums. This unit, albeit with a number of changes, debuted with the 'Dreamworker' album.

Working with producer Szymon Czech IMMEMORIAL, and adding new members vocalist Karolina Czertowicz and erstwhile BEHEMOTH and HEFEYSTOS bassist Rafa 'Frost' Bauer, the band prepared for a new studio album 'After Deny' in 2003. Moldy exited in January of 2004, the group reacting by switching Frost from bass to guitar. IMMEMORIAL united with Sweden's DIMENSION ZERO and DETONATION for European dates in February. The band line up at this juncture would be credited as vocalist Karla, guitarist / bassist Frost, guitarist Tadra and drummer Fizyk. However, Karla departed in March 2005.

IUS PRIMAE NOCTIS, (1998). Only Sadness (Intro) / Betrothal With The Death / Temptress The Remembrance / Another Reality / Ius Primae Noctis / Immemorial Wars / Love And Hate (Outro).

MONOLOGUE, Conquer CR 003 (2001). Forsaken In Nonentity / A Monologue / Wander Through Life / Demons Of Fate / Under Delusion / Born To Redeem / A Nightmare / Seized With Darkness.

AFTER DENY, Conquer (2003). Angel Of Sorrow / Suicide / Wooden Box / Tanatos / Corrupted By Death / Day Of Anger / Homeless Corpse / Evil Fills Me / Carrion / Longing For A Sin / Depression.

IMMERSED IN BLOOD

SWEDEN — *Stefan Lundberg (vocals), Robert Tyborn Axt (guitar), Johan Ohlsson (guitar), Joel Andersson (bass), Joakim Unger (drums).*

Gothenburg Death Metal act IMMERSED IN BLOOD debuted with the 1999 demo tape 'Eine Kleine Deathmusik'. The band was rooted in the demise of the highly rated INVERTED in 1998, a band that had issued two albums for the Belgian Shiver label. Three erstwhile INVERTED members, singer Stefan Lundberg, also a member of SKYMNING and holding prior credits with VEXATOR, FORLORN EMPIRES and CARNAL DEFORMATION, guitarist Johan Ohlsson, also a participant in Industrial Deathsters BLESSED, and bassist Joel Andersson allying themselves with second guitarist Robert Tyborn Axt, another veteran of VEXATOR, FORLORN EMPIRES and CARNAL DEFORMATION, and the SUPREME MAJESTY, SARGENT CARNAGE, VEXATOR and DOMINATION credited drummer Joakim Unger. The group played their debut gig in March 1999, cutting the opening demo just two months later.

Songs from the 'Eine Kleine Deathmusik' sessions along with two newly recorded tracks were donated to a three way split album 'Sweets For My Sweet Chapter 1' shared with CONFESSIONS OF OBSCURITY and OUTCAST issued by Lowlife Records in 2001. In September of that year Downfall Records issued the EP 'Relentless Retaliation'. Switching labels to the Arctic Music Group the full length 'Killing Season' arrived in 2003.

Joakim Unger left the band in mid 2003.

Bassist Joel Andersson joined the ranks of NOMINON in June of 2004. IMMERSED IN BLOOD added new members guitarist Christian Strömblad and Jonny Bogren in January 2005.

Relentless Retaliation EP, Downfall (2001). Relentless Retaliation / Collector Of Souls / Genuine Suicide Attempt / Celestial Carnage / Serpent Of Chaos.

KILLING SEASON, Arctic Music Group (2003). Salvatorial Rape / Recession / Rectal Force Ecstasy / We Have A Bleeder / Killing Season / Supreme Bukkake / Elite/Perfected / Percussive Control / Letum Non Omnia Finit / Azura.

IMMOLATION

NEW YORK, NY, USA — *Ross Dolan (vocals / bass), Bill Taylor (guitar), Robert Vigna (guitar), Steve Shalaty (drums).*

Anti-Christian Metal band IMMOLATION was created in Yonkers, New York during February 1988 by frontman Ross Dolan, drummer Neal Boback and two erstwhile RIGOR MORTIS members, guitarists Robert Vigna and Thomas Wilkinson. Two demos, in July 1988 and June 1989, ensued prior to the July 1991 'Dawn Of Possession' album and the recruitment of drummer Craig Smilowski. These tracks had been constructed under the guidance of Harris Johns at Musiclab Studios in Berlin for Roadrunner Records. 'Dawn Of Possession' quickly found appreciation on a crowded market due in main to its convoluted and writhing unorthodoxy, pinch harmonics, atonal riffing and abundance of minor keys forming up a disturbing avalanche of unpredictability.

In January 1995 Repulse Records collected together the band's earlier demos, RIGOR MORTIS sessions, plus live tapes from New Rochelle, New York in December 1988 and Belle Vernon, Pennsylvania in June 1989, for release as the 'Stepping On Angels ... Before Dawn' compilation. IMMOLATION, switching labels to Metal Blade, issued the February 1996 'Here In After' album. Former FALLEN CHRIST and DISASSOCIATE drummer Alex Hernández joined upon completion of the 'Here In After' sessions. Touring saw shows in Europe with CANNIBAL CORPSE.

In July 1998 the group entered Millbrook Sound Studios to forge 'Failures For Gods' with producer Paul Orofino, Metal

Blade releasing this set a full year later. An exercise is unabashed, near indecipherable technicality, the album's subtleties were regretfully lost in a muddy mix.

IMMOLATION toured America in 2000 sharing billing with SIX FEET UNDER. Fourth album 'Close To A World Below' slunk out in November, rectifying many of the sound quality problems of its predecessor.

John McEntee of INCANTATION deputized for Vigna on later tours. With Vigna returning to action former ANGEL CORPSE man Bill Taylor would take over from Wilkinson in 2001.

Touring in Europe during May found IMMOLATION as headliners over DERANGED, DESTROYER 666, DECAPITATED and SOUL DEMISE. The band signed to Olympic Records for North America and the French Listenable label for Europe to issue the October 2002 'Unholy Cult' effort, again produced by Paul Orofino. The band would also schedule a European headlining tour in December in alliance with DERANGED, backed by Germany's Black Metal act MYSTIC CIRCLE and Sweden's INSISION. Further concerts witnessed the band forming part of an impressive cast for European 'X-mas Festivals' in December alongside SIX FEET UNDER, MARDUK, KATAKLYSM, DYING FETUS and HATE. Later gigs in Holland added veteran Thrashers EXODUS to the bill. There would be no let up on the live front in 2003, IMMOLATION teaming up with CRADLE OF FILTH for European gigs throughout March and April then GRAVE and GOATWHORE for US shows in June. Hernández was forced to drop off the US tour in June when he developed a hernia. He was replaced by Steve Shalaty who since become a permanent member.

During early 2004 Russ Dolan donated his services to a tribute album 'Within The Mind' assembled by guitarist JAMES MURPHY in honour of the late DEATH mentor Chuck Schuldiner. Former IMMOLATION drummer Alex Hernández joined Uruguayan Death Metal band REQUIEM AETURNAM for recording their album 'The Philosopher' in May 2004. Meantime, IMMOLATION themselves entered the studio in July with mainstay producer Paul Orofino for their seventh studio album, 'Harnessing Ruin', set for February 2005 release through Listenable Records and March in the USA via Olympic Recordings. The band collaborated with DEICIDE, WITH PASSION, SKINLESS and MISERY INDEX for US dates in May 2005.

North American touring resumed with EXODUS and CRYPTOPSY in April 2006. IMMOLATION cut new album tracks, dubbed 'Shadows Of The Light', with producer Paul Oforino at Millbrook Sound Studios in New York during November. The band also put down material for an EP billed 'Hope And Horror', released in tandem with a live DVD filmed at B.B. King's Blues Club in New York City. 'Shadows Of The Light' was delivered in May 2007 through Century Media.

SUFFOCATION teamed up with IMMOLATION and SKINLESS for a North American tour beginning late October.

'88 Demo, Immolation (1988) (Demo). Immolation / Dawn Of Possession.

Immolation, Immolation (1989) (Demo). Internal Decadence / Burial Ground / Despondent Souls.

DAWN OF POSSESSION, Roadracer RC 9310-2 (1991). Intro Everlasting Fire / Despondent Souls / Dawn Of Possession / Those Left Behind / Internal Decadence / No Forgiveness (Without Bloodshed) / Burial Ground / After My Prayers / Fall In Disease / Immolation.

1994 Promotional Demo, Metal-Core (1994). Away From God / Towards Earth / Christ's Cage.

STEPPING ON ANGELS ... BEFORE DAWN, Repulse RPS004CD (1995). Relentless Torment / Holocaust / Rigor Mortis / Warriors Of Doom / Immolation / Dawn Of Possession / Internal Decadence / Burial Ground / Despondent Souls / Infectious Blood / Despondent Souls (1990) / Burial Ground (Live) / Infectious Blood (Live) / Immolation (Live) / Despondent Souls (Live) / Dawn Of Possession (Live).

HERE IN AFTER, Metal Blade 14102-2 (1996). Nailed To Gold / Burn With Jesus / Here In After / I Feel Nothing / Away From God / Towards Earth / Under The Supreme / Christ's Cage.

FAILURES FOR GODS, Metal Blade 14197 (1999). Once Ordained / No Jesus, No Beast / Failures For Gods / Unsaved / God Made Filth / Stench Of High Heaven / Your Angel Died / The Devil I Know.

CLOSE TO A WORLD BELOW, Metal Blade 14349 (2000). Higher Coward / Father, You're Not A Father / Furthest From The Truth / Fall From A High Place / Unpardonable Son / Lost Passion / Put My Hand In The Fire / Close To A World Below.

UNHOLY CULT, Olympic OLY 0227-2 (2002). Of Martyrs And Men / Sinful Nature / Unholy Cult / Wolf Among The Flock / Reluctant Messiah / A Kingdom Divided / Rival The Eminent / Bring Them Down.

HARNESSING RUIN, Listenable POSH065 (2005). Swarm Of Terror / Our Savior Sleeps / Challenge The Storm / Harnessing Ruin / Dead To Me / Son Of Iniquity / My Own Enemy / Crown The Liar / At Mourning's Twilight.

HARNESSING RUIN, Listenable POSH065 (2005) (Digipack). Swarm Of Terror / Our Savior Sleeps / Challenge The Storm / Harnessing Ruin / Dead To Me / Son Of Iniquity / My Own Enemy / Crown The Liar / At Mourning's Twilight / Harnessing Ruin (Video).

SHADOWS IN THE LIGHT, Listenable POSH 095 (2007). Hate's Plague / Passion Kill / World Agony / Tarnished / The Weight Of Devotion / Breathing The Dark / Deliverer Of Evil / Shadows In The Light / Lying With Demons / Whispering Death.

IMMORTAL RITES

GERMANY — *Phillip Frick (vocals / guitar), Dominic Haufe (guitar), Ralf Hauber (bass), Sascha Lorenz (drums).*

Schwäbisch Gmünd melodic Death Metal combo dating to 1995. The band comprises singer / guitarist Phillip Frick, guitarist Dominic 'Dolly' Haufe, bassist Ralf Hauber and drummer Sascha Lorenz. IMMORTAL RITES would release the 1999 EP 'Beyond The Gates Of Pain' as a self financed effort. The following year these sessions, adding extra live material, saw increased distribution throughout Eastern Europe in cassette variants issued by Beverina Productions.

IMMORTAL RITES debut 'Art Of Devolution', issued in North America through Khaosmaster Productions, was produced by Alex Krull of ATROCITY. Studio guests included Alex Krull and Martin Schmidt from ATROCITY as well as the THEATRE OF TRAGEDY and LEAVES' EYES credited Liv Kristine. The album would see a European release in March 2004 via Morbid Records. The album release was followed by appearances at the 'Summer Breeze', 'Fuck The Commerce' and 'Morbide Festspiele' events plus shows with UNLEASHED, BEHEMOTH, MYSTIC CIRCLE, DISBELIEF, and GOD DETHRONED, among others.

Parting ways with Morbid Records, during October 2006 IMMORTAL RITES recorded its second full-length album, billed as 'Source Code @ Converter's Day', at Audiospezialist Studios in Germany with ex-ATROCITY/LEAVES' EYES drummer Martin Schmidt acting as producer. The mastering of these sessions took place at Unisound Studios in Sweden by EDGE OF SANITY mastermind DAN SWANÖ.

BEYOND THE GATES OF PAIN, (1999). The Shadowsouls / Tormenting Emotions / Beyond The Gates Of Pain / Weeping Tears / The Script Of Sadness.

ART OF DEVOLUTION, Morbid MR 105 (2004). Eugenic (Intro) / Fatal Exploited / Dressed In Amazing Red / Digital God / United Scars Anthem / Mirror Reflections / Hallucinations Overture / The Utter Dark / Pathetic Patterns / The Cadaverizer.

IMMORTAL SOULS

KOKKOLA, FINLAND — *Aki Särkioja (vocals / bass), Esa Särkioja (guitar), Pete Loisa (guitar), Jupe Hakola (drums).*

A Finnish melodic Death Metal act, IMMORTAL SOULS was convened in late 1991 by the Särkioja brothers vocalist / bassist Aki and guitarist Esa. The latter is also active with INHUMAN and, alongside guitarist Pete Loisa, WHATEVER. Aki Särkioja's history witnessed membership of such acts as HOPE, THE WOLVES, THE RIGGS, CATHACOMB, VIIS VEIS, DBM and D.O.D.

IMMORTAL SOULS, pulling in drummer Jupe Hakola, issued the opening demo 'Vision Of Hell' in 1993. The new face of Atti Nykyri would be manning the drums for the follow up 'Immortal Souls' in 1995 but Hakola returned for the 1997 set 'Reflections Of Doom'.

Signing to the Dutch Fear The Dark label IMMORTAL SOULS issued the 'Ice Upon The Night' album, recorded at Sonic Pump Studios in Helsinki, in March 2003. Dates in Germany and Holland followed and the group also scored a placing at the prestigious 'Tuska' festival. The band licensed then 'Ice Upon The Night' album to Facedown Records for US release. With Jupe Hakola resigning, IMMORTAL SOULS inducted JP Koivisto of SILENT VOICES as their new drummer in March 2004.

Divine Wintertime EP, (1998). Snow Soul / Divine Wintertime / Morning Mist / Christ Mass.

The Cleansing, Little Rose Productions (2000). The Cleansing / Until / The Prophet / Icebound.

UNDER THE NORTHERN SKY, Little Rose Productions (2001). Frostmind / The Cleansing / The Cold Northwind / Blue Flamed Fire / Snowfalls / Dark Night Under The Northern Sky / Love Demise / Metsäkukkia / Winterheart / Painthings.

ICE UPON THE NIGHT, Fear Dark (2003). Everwinter / Welcome To North / Sacrifice / Painbearer / Edge Of The Frost / Coldstreets / You / Suicidalive / Man Of Sorrow.

IMPACT WINTER

PERTH, WA, AUSTRALIA — *SVRT 666 (vocals), Slutbuster (guitar), Kill Machine (guitar), Lord Humongous (bass), Maelstrom (drums).*

Black Metal hailing from Victoria Park in Perth, Western Australia. IMPACT WINTER was founded during 1995 by vocalist SVRT 666, also operating the GOATRAPIST project, and bassist Lord Humongous. A demo cassette, simply entitled 'Die' and restricted to 150 copies, emerged in 1995. Second set 'Destroy The World' was manufactured in 500 copies for release in 1998.

A series of line-up changes would see guitarist Asmodeus dropping by the wayside and drummer Cuntfucker, from STORM OF HATRED, and guitarist Slutbuster being installed in 1999. That year Meat Cleaver distributed IMPACT WINTER's third demo 'Hellvomitindarkinsanity'.

Sabnak (a.k.a. David Lance) of HYPERCENTER, took over bass duties in 2000. Cuntfucker decamped in 2003, being superseded by Maelstrom of AVANTGARD and WARDAEMONIC repute. Secondary guitar duties would be delegated to THE FUROR, GOATRAPIST and HATED BY HUMANITY man Kill Machine.

A full-length album, billed as 'God Is Dead', would be readied for 2007 release.

Die, Impact Winter (1995) (Demo. Limited edition 150 copies). Intro / Total Destruction Of Life / Infernal Ascent / First After Satan / Blood And Iron.

Destroy The World, Impact Winter (1998) (Demo. Limited edition 500 copies). Black Seas Beyond The Stars / Destroyer Of Worlds / God Is Dead / Serpent Crown / Unlife.

Hellvomitindarkinsanity, Meat Cleaver (1999) (Demo). Kicking The Shit Out Of The Servants Of God / Unlife.

IMPALED

CA, USA — *Leon Del Muerte (vocals / guitar), Sean McGrath (guitar), Ross Sewage (bass), Raul Varela (drums).*

Californian Death Metal band IMPALED feature erstwhile members of EXHUMED. Founded in 1995 by erstwhile INFANTICIDE personnel guitarist Jared Deaver, bassist Ron Dorn and vocalist Jeremy Frye alongside INHUMATION guitarist Sean McGrath and drummer Raul Varela. Almost as soon as the band had gelled Frye decamped suddenly necessitating Deaver and McGrath to assume shared lead vocal duties.

With this line up IMPALED issued the 1997 four track demo 'Septic Vomit'. However, quite alarmingly Deaver would contract throat cancer forcing him to forsake vocal duties. Leon Del Muerte of EXHUMED and INFANTICIDE was enlisted as lead singer for support gigs to SUFFOCATION and DEICIDE.

A second demo ensued with Dorn's position on bass being taken by Tom Persons of Black Metal act ENTHRONED. Bad luck forced its hand once more though as Deaver was injured and Persons decamped back to ENTHRONED. Plugging the gap Del Muerte took over Deaver's guitar role and EXHUMED Ross Sewage was implemented on bass.

This incarnation of IMPALED cut the 'From Here To Colostomy' demo with the track 'Immaculate Defecation' being donated to the Razorback compilation 'Gore Is Your Master'. Other songs from this session would figure on a split 7" single release issued by Italian label Headfucker Records in union with CEPHALIC CARNAGE.

IMPALED contributed their rendition of 'I Work For The Streetcleaner' to the 2001 Razorback Records IMPETIGO tribute album 'Wizards Of Gore'. The 'Choice Cuts' album of the same year, issued by Necropolis subsidiary Deathvomit Records, included the IMPETIGO cover as well as a rendition of 'Carneous Cacoffiny' originally by CARCASS and various outtakes and demo recordings.

Leon Del Muerte made his exit during November of 2001 to assemble a new project MURDER CONSTRUCT in league with ORIGIN vocalist / bassist Paul Ryan and TERMINAL PLAN drummer Jeremy Gregg. Meantime, bassist Ross Sewage was operational with the female fronted Black Metal outfit LUDICRA. IMPALED embarked upon a mid 2002 North American trek billed as the 'Summer of Blasphemy' tour packaged with co headliners INCANTATION alongside DECAPITATED and FALL TO DEAD. The band's 2002 album stirred controversy when the original cover art was banned in European territories.

Leon del Muerte, switching to the bass role, joined EXHUMED in early 2004 for an extensive series of global dates. Inducting new guitarist Jason Kocol of MADERA ROAD, PUNY HUMANS, QOQOL and SLAUGHTERHOUSE FLIES repute the band entered Take Root studios in San Francisco during early May with Trey Spruance of MR. BUNGLE acting as producer. The band also donated their version of 'On Your Knees' to the W.A.S.P. tribute album 'Shock Rock Hellions—A Tribute To W.A.S.P.' issued through Denmark's Valhalla Records.

In November of 2004 Sean McGrath announced the formation of a brand new "Full on" Heavy Metal band to feature ex-SACRILEGE B.C. and GRINCH guitarist Sean Smithson and ex-GRINCH, VERBAL ABUSE, MACHINE HEAD, KONKHRA, TESTAMENT, THE SERVANTS and ATTITUDE ADJUSTMENT drummer Chris Kontos.

IMPALED's March 2005 album 'Death After Life', recorded at Take Root Studios in San Francisco with producer Trey Spruance, saw issue through Century Media Records. The band played May East Coast dates packaged with LENG TCH'E, MALIGNANCY and ABORTED. The band seemingly booked to tour further with MORTICIAN and THINE EYES BLEED but withdrew from these dates, slamming the organisers for "unprofessional booking practices". The band toured the South West USA with BLESSING THE HOGS and DISGORGE in September. The band lined up with DEEDS OF FLESH, VILE and MONSTROSITY for the 'Gutting Europe 4' European tour beginning in Poland during late March 2006.

IMPALED teamed up with GENERAL SURGERY and BUTCHER ABC for the "Gore Over Japan Tour" in September hitting Osaka, Nagoya and Tokyo. The group hit the road with A LIFE ONCE LOST, DEAD TO FALL, NAPALM DEATH, ARSIS and ANIMOSITY throughout November and December as part of the 'Death By Decibels' US tour.

THE DEAD SHALL DEAD REMAIN, Death Vomit (2000). Introduction / Faeces Of Death / Flesh And Blood / Trocar / Spirits Of

The Dead / Immaculate Defecation / Faecal Rites / Back To The Grave / All That Rots / Gorenography / Bloodbath / XXX.

CHOICE CUTS, Death Vomit DVR010 (2001). Nightsoil / Until Death / Carneous Cacoffiny / I Work For The Streetcleaner / All That Rots (1998 Unreleased version) / Spirits Of The Dead (1998 Unreleased version) / Immaculate Defecation (Demo) / Flesh & Blood (Demo) / Fecal Rites (Demo) / From Here To Colostomy (Demo) / With Shit I Am Adorned (1998 Unreleased version) / Ingestion Of Colotomic Funk / With Shit I Am Adorned.

MONDO MEDICINALE, Deathvomit DVR013 (2002). The Hippocritic Oath / Dead Inside / Raise The Stakes / Operating Theatre / Choke On It / We Belong Dead / The Worms Crawl In / To Die For / Rest In Fæces / Carpe Mortem.

DEATH AFTER LIFE, Century Media (2005). Goreverture / Mondo Medicale / Gutless / Theatre Of Operations / Preservation Of Death / Wrought In Hell / Resurrectionsists / Critical Condition / The Dead Shall Dead Remain / Medical Waste / Dead Alive / Coda Morte.

IMPALED NAZARENE

OULU, FINLAND — *Sir Mikka Luttinen (guitar), Tuomo Louhio (guitar), Jarno Anttila (guitar), Mikael Arnkil (bass), Reima Kellokoski (drums).*

IMPALED NAZARENE date back to November 1990 and have created a unique niche market for themselves in the Death Metal scene with their own brand of 'Cyber-Punk' Metal. The Oulu based band have leaned more towards Punk with each successive release and have landed themselves in hot water with the Finnish authorities by branding Russians as "Red scum". Bassist 'The fuck you man' is in fact SENTENCED's Taneli Jarva. The band's inaugural line-up comprised siblings Mika Luttinen on vocals and drummer Kimmo Luttinen, guitarists Ari Holappa and Mika Pääkkö plus bass player Anti Pihkala. Both Luttinen brothers were previously members of MUTILATION. The first song composition assembled by IMPALED NAZARENE was entitled 'Condemned To Hell', although early live sets also included MUTILATION numbers 'The Crucified' and 'Morbid Fate'.

IMPALED NAZARENE's presence was first felt in February 1991 when the debut demo emerged titled 'Shemhamforash'. The tape, which sported cover versions of DEICIDE's 'Crucifixation' and EXTREME NOISE TERROR's 'Conned Thru Life', was laid down by Eero Vuolukka on a primitive two track and saw the departure of Pihkala in favour of Harri Halonen. Was the first audio product to witness IMPALED NAZARENE's peculiar bent of blending the occult and sexual perversion, song titles such as 'Disgust Suite and 'Worms In Rectum' being the first in a long line of increasingly eccentric euphonies.

In April 1991 IMPALED NAZARENE put in their first live gig as support to BEHERIT in Kempele. Further shows ensued as openers to SENTENCED. The second demo session, 'Taog Eht Fo Htao Eht' ("The Oath Of The Goat") recorded at Tico Tico Studios in Keme by Ahti Kortelainen quickly followed in August. A noticeable shift in emphasis was focussed by Satanic themed song titles and artwork bearing a crude inverted crucifix. This ten track tape was capitalised on by a festival appearance at the Oulu 'Days Of Darkness' event alongside AMORPHIS. As an interesting diversion, Mikka Luttinen was issuing some less than savoury demos bearing the titles 'Glumph' and 'Never Mind Burzum ... Here's Anus Cunt' from his twisted ANUS CUNT project.

A 7" single 'Goat Perversion' was released by the Italian Nosferatu concern in February 1992, after which both Holappa and Halonen decamped. 'Goat Perversion' had been produced by Ahti Kortelainen once again at Tico Tico the previous September. Although seemingly hosting four tracks the EP in fact bore a fifth, unaccredited, song in IMPALED NAZARENE's rendition of 'The Black Vomit', originally by cult blasphemous Brazilian band SARCOFAGO. Undeterred by the loss of two key players, IMPALED NAZARENE gigged for a while as a power trio. New recruit Taneli Jarva was drafted for in October recording a second single for French label Osmose Productions pairing 'Sadogoat' with a JOHNNY CASH cover 'Ghost Riders'. However, that same month, Pääkkö broke ranks and Jarno Anttila deputised on guitar. This roll would soon turn into a full time tenure.

Retaining Ahti Kortelainen as producer the debut February 1993 full-length album, 'Tol Cormpt Norz Norz Norz' on Osmose Productions, saw initial limited edition copies including an extra thirteen tracks comprising the earlier demos. Credits for the album, apparently "recorded faraway in pain and mistery XXVII Anno Satanas", went out to Mikaakim (Mika Luttinen) and Kimmoomik (Kimmo Luttinen) with Jarno Anttila and Taneli Jarva only given session status. Musically Tol Cormpt Norz Norz Norz' purveyed the very harshest of blackened Grindcore with the barked vocals making lyrics totally unintelligible. Sales were strong enough to break the Finnish national top forty album charts. IMPALED NAZARENE's third single, 'Satanic Masowhore', was backed on the flip side with their cover version of EXTREME NOISE TERROR's 'Conned Thru Life'. In July the band entered Tico Tico studios to record tracks to compile their second album 'Ugra-Karma' and the 'Satanic Masowhore' 7" EP. The 'Ugra Karma' effort, out in December and on which the group proclaimed their support for "nuclear energy and the destruction of the environment", came deceptively clad in a serene Madame Koslovsky depicting an Indian Goddess, which would come back to haunt the band in later years.

The band toured Europe with ANCIENT RITES in January 1994 upfront of recording third album 'Suomi Finland Perkele', switching from a previously announced intended album title of 'Hail To Finland'. Issued in October sporting three different coloured sleeve designs, the record's perceived right wing lyrics draw controversy and instructions were issued by French authorities to withdraw the album from the stores. Fortunately, sales were not unduly harmed as misinformation led to the band's previous album, 'Ugra Karma', being removed from racks. 'Suomi Finland Perkele' doubled the controversy when attention was drawn to the album dedication, the song 'Winter War' being "dedicated to those glorious who died by red scum". Embroiled in the resulting press frenzy, IMPALED NAZARENE set out on tour around Europe during April 1995 with Americans ABSU and Australia's SADISTIK EXEKUTION.

IMPALED NAZARENE were set to utilise Tico Tico once again in August for a planned EP given a working title 'Hamnasnas', but was shelved due to in fighting in the band. Bassist Taneli Jarva and founder member Sir Kimmo Luttinen decamped abruptly to concentrate on his solo projects ISÄNMAA, cutting the demo 'Yli Peltojen, Vetten Ja Tunturien', and LEGENDA. After Kimmo Luttinen's departure he also operated in parallel BEHERIT and would session for CATAMENIA. Reima Kellokoski took the IMPALED NAZARENE drum stool for October tour dates in Europe with MINISTRY OF TERROR and KRABATHOR. The group also put in their first British show headlining a Halloween event at London's Astoria.

In early 1996 the band added ex-BELIAL and OBFUSCATION bassist Jani Lehtosaari for recording of the 'Latex Cult', released in April 1996, and 'Motörpenis' EP outings. Both Jarva and the wayward Luttinen would later found THE BLACK LEAGUE.

The 'Motörpenis' mini-album featured covers of tracks from Finnish Punk acts FAFFBEY and TERVEET KADET as well as GANG GREEN's 'Alkohol'. Pushing 'Latex Cult', April 1996 had the band out on their lengthiest trek around Europe to date as part of the 'No Mercy' touring festival. IMPALED NAZARENE sharing the stage with CANNIBAL CORPSE, IMMOLATION, ROTTING CHRIST, KRABATHOR and GRAVE.

Recovering after these dates the band laid down an exclusive track 'I Am The Killer Of Trolls', in October 1996 at Tico Tico, for the compilation album 'World Domination II'. 1996 was rounded off by a further bout of European touring with ANGEL CORPSE and GEHENNAH in December.

The band found themselves back in trouble in 1997 when

the Hare Krishna movement objected to the use of artwork on the earlier 'Ugra Karma' album. Eventually this concern would be addressed outside of court, resulting in a re-issue of the record with new cover art. A relatively quiet year for the band excepting their legal woes, IMPALED NAZARENE put down instrumental demos in preparation for their next outing.

During the summer of 1998 the group, again on the road marketing the 'Rapture' album issued that April, put in further prominent international shows playing the Milwaukee Metalfest, gigs in Canada and a series of dates in Mexico. Film from the band's 'Tuska' festival appearance was used for a promotional video for the song 'Penis & Circes'. In September 1998 the band drafted THY SERPENT, CHILDREN OF BODOM and SINERGY guitarist Alex Laiho, this alliance having been cemented at a one off concert in St. Petersburg, Russia pairing IMPALED NAZARENE and CHILDREN OF BODOM. However, Laiho's commitments kept him out of the line-up for another round of European shows this time with DRILLER KILLER and RITUAL CARNAGE. Laiho did perform with the band in February 1999 on their second visit to North America and Mexico but cut short his commitment returning to Finland. Nevertheless, IMPALED NAZARENE undertook their first Japanese shows as a quartet. The band would not let up the live work and by April were back in Europe as part of the 'No Mercy III' festivals in alliance with PECCATUM, LIMBONIC ART, THE CROWN, EMPEROR and MORBID ANGEL. Still as a four piece the band also put in shows in far flung Australia and New Zealand, these latter shows in the August being supported by MALEVOLENCE. Surprisingly, here the group suffered its first concert casualty as a result of local community pressure when a concert in Wollongong, Australia was prevented. In New Zealand, both Mika Luttinen and Jarno Anttila were lucky to survive a car crash on the way to an Auckland concert. Upon their return to Finland in August, IMPALED NAZARENE took to Astia Studios in Lappeenranta to forge another album.

Erstwhile band member Sir Luttinen would find the time to become drummer for fellow Finns CATAMENIA. Meantime, IMPALED NAZARENE's 2000 release saw a split effort with DRILLER KILLER on Lehtosaari's Solardisk imprint. New album 'Nihil' surfaced in February 2000. A brace of Finnish gigs to coincide, sharing the stage with FINNTROLL and THRONE OF CHAOS, witnessed a brief re-acquaintance with Alex Laiho, after which the group appeared at the chaotic New Jersey 'March Metal Meltdown'. Tomi Ullgren of SHAPE OF DESPAIR and THY SERPENT was enlisted on guitar for the 'Assault The Weak' tour of France. This trek would be highlighted by a refusal by authorities for the band to sell any Satanic themed merchandise and IMPALED NAZARENE's conviction that they were being tailed by French "secret police". In May another partnership with CHILDREN OF BODOM conducted Greek gigs in Thessaloniki and Athens with Alex Laiho performing double duty each night. The 'Decade Of Decadence' ten year anniversary collection was cut at Astia in August and delivered in November.

The band's status was now such that several bootleg singles and albums, most notably 'Live In The Name Of Satan', seeped onto the market. In the autumn of 2000 it was announced that both Laiho and Lehtosaari, the latter joining SINVISION, had fled the fold with new members plugging the gap being THY SERPENT and BARATHRUM guitarist Teemu Raimovanta (a.k.a. 'Somnium')of FINNTROLL and bass player Mikael Arnkil, known previously as drummer for ANTIDOTE and ABHORRENCE. A concert at the Nosturi venue in Helsinki in December 2000 saw a group roster with Tomi Ullgren on guitar and Raimoranta temporarily on bass as Arnkil had not learned the set.

In March 2001 IMPALED NAZARENE renewed their business relationship with Osmose Productions, re-signing for a further two albums. Czech gigs in April debuted Mikael Arnkil on bass but with Jarno Anttila unable to attend Tomi Ullgren deputised. Major Finnish festival appearances, at Tuska Open Air and at Koria Open Air in July, were preceded by a Down By The Laituri at Turku gig notable for a one off re-adoption of corpsepaint. In September 2001 IMPALED NAZARENE issued the 'Absence Of War Does Not Mean Peace' album, promoted by a video for the track 'Hardboiled And Still Hellbound' enhanced by the presence of porn actress Rakel Liekki. Successive live work involved shows at the London X-Mass festival, in Italy and, as a union with FINNTROLL, in Moscow in March 2002. In July a memorable performance at the With Full Force event in Leipzig, Germany caught IMPALED NAZARENE hitting the stage at 4.35 am. Another gig at Tuska Open Air followed, with a show at Ilosaari Rock held on the very same day. Further festivals included Headbanger's Fest in Lisbon, Portugal and the group's Norwegian debut as headliner at the Bergen A Hole In The Sky show. Another first came with a gig in Tallinn, Estonia in October with the year being capped in December with the X-Mass festival European tour together with MARDUK, IMMOLATION, EXODUS, SIX FEET UNDER, KATAKLYSM, MACABRE, RAGNAROK, HATE ETERNAL and ANTAEUS.

During early 2003 IMPALED NAZARENE drummer Reima Kellokoski (a.k.a. 'Repe F.W. Misanthrope') established the blackened Death Metal side concern SHADOW CUT.

IMPALED NAZARENE man Teemu 'Somnium' Raimoranta died on 16th March 2003 at the exceptionally young age of just 25. Apparently the guitarist suffered fatal injuries from a fall off Helsinki's Pitkäsilta bridge onto ice below. At the time official reports stated Raimoranta had met his death accidentally although subsequently Mikka Luttinen claimed he had jumped voluntarily. The band brought in ANTIDOTE guitarist Tuomo Louhio for recording of the album 'All That You Fear'. Gigs were announced for early 2004 in league with THE LEGION but these dates would then be cancelled.

The band performed an unusual concert dubbed the '34'000 Ton Metal Cruise' on 25th September, performing onboard the Münchenbryggeriet car ferry in Stockholm, Sweden alongside TANKARD, AMON AMARTH, HYPOCRISY, TAD MOROSE, STORMWARRIOR, SKYCLAD and WOLF.

IMPALED NAZARENE, working with their sound engineer Tapio Pennanen, would plan on recording three Italian gigs in September, in the towns of Milan, Catania, Ascoli, for a live album. Unfortunately the band arrived at Milan to find their equipment had not arrived, forcing them to use the support band's gear, and both shows in Catania and Ascoli could not provide adequate digital recording gear. Undaunted, the group resolved to record a subsequent show in Stockholm but only captured three songs on tape due to a mid show electricity cut. IMPALED NAZARENE's bad luck carried on into Russia when, just before a concert in Moscow, Mika Luttinen claimed he was drugged. After passing out and being revived by smelling salts, Luttinen and the band performed the show. The group announced they would attempt to record a December gig at the Tavastia club in Helsinki to finally get the tracks for the live record 'Death Comes In 26 Carefully Selected Pieces'.

European shows for January 2005 found IMPALED NAZARENE in union with YYRKOON and PHAZM. In June IMPALED NAZARENE confirmed they had re-signed with Osmose Productions for two more albums, first entering Sonic Pump studios with producer Tapio Pennanen on November 21st to begin recording the new album 'Pro Patria Finlandia'. IMPALED NAZARENE embarked on a lengthy round of European dates throughout April and May 2006 seeing staged supports first from Switzerland's DARK RISE, then Italians RESURRECTURIS before MASTER and ZUUL FX jumped onboard to close the dates. Swedish Death Metal act ZONARIA were later added to the bill. Italian concerts in November, in Padova, Rome and Bologna, saw HANDFUL OF HATE as support.

In 2007 both the 1996 'Latex Cult' and 1998 'Rapture' albums were re-issued as expanded formats with all new artwork and

IMPALED NAZARENE

remastered by Mika Jussila at Finnvox studio. 'Latex Cult' added bonus material in the form of live tracks recorded at La Laiterie club in Strasbourg in 1996, 'Total War—Winter War', 'Soul Rape', 'Punishment Is Absolute' and 'Mortification/Blood Red Razor Blade'. The 'Rapture' re-issue hosted cover versions of SODOM's 'Burst Command ´til War' and 'Nuclear Metal Retaliation', plus eight live tracks, also taken from the same Strasbourg show, in 'Transvestite', a TERVEET KÄDET cover, 'Motorpenis', 'Bashing In Heads', 'I Eat Pussy For Breakfast', 'Whore', 'Violence I Crave', 'Goat Perversion' and 'Hoath: Darbs Lucifero'.

Shemhamforash, (1991) (Demo cassette). Intro / Condemned To Hell / The Crucified / Disgust Suite O:P I / Morbid Fate / Disgust Suite O:P II / Worms In Rectum / Conned Thru Life / Crucifixation.

Taog Eht Fo Htao Eht, (1991) (Demo cassette). Nuctemeron Of Necromanteion / Condemned To Hell / Impurity Of Dawn / The Crucified / Infernus / Morbid Fate / Ave Satanas / In The Name Of Satan / Fall To Fornication / Damnation (Raping The Angels).

Goat Perversion, Nosferatu SKRELEETS 001 (1992). Noisrevrep Taog / In The Name Of Satan / Noisrevrep Eht Retfa / Damnation (Raping The Angels).

Sadogoat, Osmose Productions OPEP 001 (1993) (7" single). Ghost Riders / Sadogoat.

TOL CORMPT NORZ NORZ NORZ, Osmose Productions OPCD 010 (1993). Apolokia / I Al Purg Vompo / My Blessing (The Beginning Of The End) / Apolokia II: Aikolopa 666 / In The Name Of Satan / Impure Orgies / Goat Perversion / The Forest (The Darkness) / Mortification Blood Red Razor Blade / The God (Symmetry Of Penis) / Condemned To Hell / The Dog (Art Of Vagina) / The Crucified / Apolokia III: Agony / Body-Mind-Soul / Hoath: Darbs Lucifero / Apolokia Finale XXVII AS / Damnation (Raping The Angels). Chart position: 40 FINLAND.

Satanic Masowhore, Osmose Productions OPEP003 (1993) (7" single). Satanic Masowhore / Conned Thru Life (Diabolic penis mix).

UGRA-KARMA, Osmose Productions OPCD 018 (1993). Goatzied / The Horny And The Horned / Sadhu Satana / Chaosgoat Law / Hate / Gott Ist Tot (Antichrist War Mix) / Coraxo / Soul Rape / Kali-Yaga / Cyberchrist / False Jehova / Sadistic 666—Under A Golden Shower.

SUOMI FINLAND PERKELE, Osmose Productions OPCD 026 (1994). Intro / Vituursen Multi Huipennus / Blood Is Thicker Than Water / Steel Vagina / Total War—Winter War / Quasb—The Burning / Kuolema Kaikille (Paitsi Meille) / Let's Fucking Die / Genocide / Ghettoblaster / The Oath Of The Goat.

LATEX CULT, Osmose Productions OPCD 038 (1996). 66 6 S Foreplay / 1999: Karmakeddon Warriors / Violence I Crave / Bashing In Heads / Motorpenis / Zum Kotzen / Alien Militant / Goat War / Punishment Is Absolute / When All Golden Turned To Shit / Masterbator / The Burning Of Provinciestraat / I Eat Pussy For Breakfast / Delirium Tremens.

Motörpenis, Osmose Productions OPMCD 039 (1996). Motörpenis / Whore / S/M Party / Transvestite / Alkohol.

RAPTURE, Osmose Productions OPCD 069 (1998) (CD edition). Penis Et Circes / 6 Degree Mindfuck / Iron Fist With An Iron Will / Angels Rectums Do Bleed / We're Satan's Generation / Goatvomit And Gasmasks / Fallout Theory In Practice / Burst Command 'Til War / The Pillory / The Return Of The Nuclear Gods / Vitutation / J.C.S. / Inbred / Phallus Maleficarum.

RAPTURE, Osmose Productions OPPIC 069 (1998) (Vinyl edition). Penis Et Circes / 6 Degree Mindfuck / Iron Fist With An Iron Will / Angels Rectums Do Bleed / We're Satan's Generation / Goatvomit And Gasmasks / Fallout Theory In Practice / Burst Command 'Til War / Healers Of The Red Plague / The Pillory / The Return Of The Nuclear Gods / Vitutation / J.C.S. / Nuclear Metal Retaliation / Inbred / Phallus Maleficarum.

UGRA-KARMA, Osmose Productions OPCD 018 (1998). Goatzied / Horny And The Horned / Sadhu Satana / Chaosgoat Law / Hate / Gott Ist Tot (Antichrist War mix) / Coraxo / Soul Rape / Kali-Yaga / Cyberchrist / False Jehova / Sadistic 666—Under A Golden Shower / Satanic Masowhore / Conned Thru Life (Diabolical Penis mix).

NIHIL, Spinefarm SPI 101CD (2000). Cogito Ergo Sum / Human Proof / Wrath Of The Goat / Angel Rectums Still Bleed—The Sequel / Porteclipse Era / Nothing's Sacred / Zero Tolerance / Assault The Weak / How The Laughter Died / Nihil.

Impaled Nazarene Vs. Driller Killer, Solardisk SOLDB004 (2000) (Split single with DRILLER KILLER). Impotent Mankind / I Couldn't Care Less.

DECADE OF DECADENCE, Osmose Productions OPCD 108 (2000). Intro / Condemned To Hell / The Crucified / Disgust Suite Op. I / Morbid Fate / Disgust Suite Op. II / Worms In Rectum / Conned Thru Life / Crucifixation / Nuctermeron Of Necromanteion / Condemned To Hell / Impurity Of Doom / The Crucified / Infernus / Morbid Fate / Ave Satanas / In The Name Of Satan / Fall To Fornication / Damnation (Raping The Angels) / Noisrevrep Taag / In The Name Of Satan / Noisrevrep Taag / Damnation (Raping The Angels) / The Black Vomit / Ghost Riders / Sadogoat / I Am The Killer Of Trolls / Kill Yourself / Burst Command Til War / Nuclear Metal Retaliation / Instrumental I / Instrumental II / Instrumental III.

ABSENCE OF WAR DOES NOT MEAN PEACE, Spinefarm SPI 136CD (2001). Strategem / Absence Of War / The Lost Art Of Goat Sacrificing / Prequel To Bleeding / Hardboiled And Still Hellbound / Into The Eye Of The Storm / Before The Fallout / Humble Fuck Of Death / Via Delorosa / Nyrkilla Tapettava Houra / Never Forgive / Satan Wants You Dead / The Madness Behind.

ALL THAT YOU FEAR, Osmose Productions OPCD 152 (2003). Kohta Ei Naura Enää Jeesuskaan / Armageddon Death Squad / The Endless War / The Maggot Crusher / Curse Of The Dead Medusa / Suffer In Silence / Halo Of Flies / Recreate Thru Hate / Goat Seeds Of Doom / Even More Pain / Tribulation Hell / Urgent Need To Kill / All That You Fear.

DEATH COMES IN 26 CAREFULLY SELECTED PIECES, Osmose Productions OPCD 172 (2005). Intro / The Horny And The Horned / Armageddon Death Squad / Goat Perversion / 1999: Karmageddon Warriors / Motorpenis / Kohta Ei Naura Enää Jeesuskaan / The Endless War / Sadhu Satana / Ghettoblaster / Coraxo / Soul Rape / Sadistic 666—Under A Golden Shower / Zero Tolerance / The Maggot Crusher / Let's Fucking Die / Tribulation Hell / We're Satan´s Generation / Cogito Ergo Sum / Goat Seeds Of Doom / Condemned To Hell / Intro S.F.P. / Sadogoat / Vitutuksen Multihuipennus / The Lost Art Of Goat Sacrificing / Total War–Winter War.

PRO PATRIA FINLANDIA, Osmose Productions OPCD 178 (2006). Weapons To Tame A Land / Something Sinister / Contempt / For Those Who Have Fallen / Cancer / Neighbourcide / This Castrated World / Leucorrhea / Kut / I Wage War / Goat Sodomy / One Dead Nation Under Dead God / Psykosis / Hate–Despise–Arrogance. Chart position: 38 FINLAND.

IMPEDIGON

BELGIUM — *Hendrik Vanwynsberghe (vocals), Fire (guitar), Jason Masschelein (guitar), Wouty (bass), Kevin Strubbe (drums).*

IMPEDIGION are rooted in the August 1993 founded act CALAMITAS. Ongoing line up changes eventually forced a new title of IMPEDIGION, marking their entrance onto the scene with the October 1994 demo 'Butchered by Beliefs'. At this juncture the band operated in a straight forward unrefined Scandinavian Death Metal style but would opt to introduce a keyboard player and introduce more melody for their next effort 'Pilgrims From The Age Of Fire ...'. Tragedy would strike the band though over the Christmas of 1995 when founder member Steven succumbed to cancer.

Vowing to persevere IMPEDIGION released their debut album in 2002 through LSP Records. The band line-up would include the ANESTHESY and CADUCITY credited Jason Masschelein on guitar with AFTER ALL's Kevin Strubbe on drums.

IMPEDIGON singer Hendrik Vanwynsberghe has an impressive roll call of credits for GARDENS OF GRIEF, DEATH ANOS, ANAL TORTURE (as 'Toiletseat'), DARK TEARS and Thrashers DEMONIZER.

AS DESIRES FADES..., LSP Records LSP006 (2002).

IMPENDING DOOM

GERMANY — *Andy Kaufmann (vocals), Patrick W. Engel (guitar), Marcus Regel (guitar), Manne (bass), Patrick W. Engel (drums).*

German Black Death Metal unit IMPENDING DOOM evolved from an earlier 1993 act BLACK PROPHECY featuring guitarists Marcus Regel and Uwe Rodel, bass player Thomas Born and drummer Pierre Krüger. With the addition of Andreas Kaufmann as frontman during 1995, and the subsequent replacement of Rodel by Patrick W. Engel and enlistment of Olaf Riegler on keyboards the band retitled itself IMPENDING DOOM.

Under their new guise IMPENDING DOOM opened proceedings with the 'Messias Abaddon' demo session achieving healthy sales around the 600 mark. Gigs as support to OCCULT, MAYHEMIC TRUTH and KRABATHOR led in turn to a mini tour with GORGOROTH and MYSTIC CIRCLE through Germany and the Netherlands and a further bout of live action in the winter of 1997 with PURGATORY and COERCION.

Their promotional tape 'Pagan Fires' and a split 7" single in alliance with ATANATOS spurred a deal with the Perverted Taste label for debut album 'Caedes Sacrilegae'. Following this release the band lost the services of Riegler but opted to persevere minus keyboards.

IMPENDING DOOM's sophomore effort, 'Signum of Hate' issued in 1998, started to pull in positive media reviews. Vinyl versions of this release added two exclusive cuts in the form of covers of MORBID ANGEL's 'Chapel Of Ghouls' and CELTIC FROST's 'Dethroned Emperor'. A split 10" single, a take on DARKTHRONE's 'Cromlech', also arrived the same year shared with EXMORTEM. Live work saw support to SODOM and an appearance at the 'Fuck The Commerce II' festival. The group would then sign to the Cudgel Agency label for a third album 'Apocalypse III- The Manifested Purgatorium'. Christhunt Productions would handle the vinyl versions with obligatory extra tracks.

IMPENDING DOOM would pay homage to the extreme Czech act MANIAC BUTCHER by appearing on a 2002 tribute album. Bassist Manne opted out in September signalling the recruitment of ex-ANAEL man Mellhammer the following month. Drummer Patrick W. Engel is also active with ATANATOS, OBSCURATION (in league with members of FALL OF SERENITY) and Thrashers BURIED GOD.

Thuringian Circle EP, (1996) (Split single with ATANATOS). Pagan Fires.
CAEDES SACRILEGAE, Perverted Taste (1997). Caedes Sacrilegae / Aeon Of Dreams / Be My Blood Of The Night / Dracul's Passion By The Light Of The Bloodmoon / My Goddess / Autumn Silence / Funeral Pile / Revelation Of Baphomet / Downfall Of God / Impending Doom.
Cromlech, (1998) (Split single with EXMORTEM). Cromlech.
SIGNUM OF HATE, (1998). The Age Of Antichrist / Armageddon Tales / Demon- (Mon)Archy / Land Of Burning Coffins / Hellhammer / Sumerian Awakening / The Rebirth / Domination Of Suffering Souls / Forward To Golgotha / Stigma (Signum Of Hate) / Metal To The Metals.
BLASPHEMY INCARNATE, Merciless (2000). Dead But Dreaming / Atone For Your Mistake / Revelation Of Baphomet / Burn The House Of God (Live) / Obscure Funeral (Live) / Dethroned Emperor (Live) / Raining Blood (Live).
Impending Doom EP, (2001) (Split single with GOATFIRE). Luciferian Curse / Headshot Christ.
APOCALYPSE III: THE MANIFESTED PURGATORIUM, Cudgel Agency CUD009 (2001). Hatespawn / Burn The House Of God / Chaos God / Obscure Funeral / Bloodpraised Agony / Revokation Of Creation / Atone For Your Mistake / Frozen Empire / Where Sinners Bleed.
BEYOND THE ALTAR OF OBSCURITY—A DECADE IN BLASPHEMY, Voice Of Life (2003). Dead But Dreaming / The Great Pale Hunter / Bloodpraised Agony / Headshot Christ / Raining Blood / Obscure Funeral / Burn The House Of God / Cromlech / Sumerian Awakening / Chapel Of Ghouls / Armageddon Tales / Draculs Passion By The Light Of The Fullmoon / Hellhammer / Dethroned Emperor / Caedes Sacrilegae / Aeon Of Dreams / Be My Blood Of The Night / Screams Of A Raven / Funeral Pile—My Throne Of Fire / Pagan Fires / Nosferatu / With Hate And Impurity / Soulbrothers / My Goddess / Downfall Of God / Infernal Bleeding / Black Prophecy / The Beginning.

IMPERIAL

FRANCE — Marseille Black-Death Metal act forged in 1992. IMPERIAL are renowned for their uncompromising lyrical and musical stance. Following three demo tapes, including 'War Spirit' in 1994 and 'The Red Moon' in 1995, IMPERIAL cut a debut album, 'Aux Crépuscules', for Osmose Productions during 1997. A mini album 'Thrasheurs 13' arrived the following year upfront of a second full length effort 'Malmort'. IMPERIAL have also recorded cover versions of BULLDOZER's 'Desert' for a 2000 split EP with legendary Japanese Black- Thrashers SABBAT and also paid homage to their allies with a version of SABBAT's own 'Reek Of Cremation' on the 'Sabbatical Worldwide Harmageddon' tribute album.

A ten year anniversary single emerged on the Dream Evil label in 2002, limited to just 333 red vinyl copies 'Ten Years Of Imperial' included four tracks spanning IMPERIAL's first ever 1992 recording 'Dark', the previously unreleased 'Cannibale' up to two brand new tracks 'L'Enfermé' and 'Le Mange-Crottes'.

AUX CREPUSCULES, Osmose Productions (1997). Le Narcissique / Aux Crepuscules / Montre Ton Regard / Orage Find / Un Adieu / La Femme Brulee / Vermin / Les Cavaliers De L'oubli / La Lune Rouge / Imperial / Thrasheurs 13.
THRASHEURS 13, Osmose Productions (1998). Thrasheurs 13 / Censure / Gouvener / Rebellion / Les Tableaux Rouges.
MALMORT, Osmose Productions (2000). Malmort / Gouvener / Paolla / Les Filles Mort Ne Disent Jamias 'Non' / Le Metal / Caranaval / Domination / La Chiennasse / Confesse / L'Historie De Bobby Qui S'Est Abye, Qui Revient, Et Que Sa Copine Trove Qu'll Pue L'Egout / Paraboles.
Ten Years Of Imperial EP, Dream Evil (2002) (Limited edition. 333 copies. Red vinyl). Dark / Cannibale / Blood: L'Enfermé / Le Mange-Crottes.

IMPERIAL DOMAIN

UPPSALA, SWEDEN — *Tobias V. Heideman (vocals), Peter Laitinen (guitar), Philip Borg (guitar), Alvaro Romero (drums).*

Uppsala melodic Death Metal band IMPERIAL DOMAIN feature guitarist Peter Laitinen of Black Metal band GOATWORSHIP and the AZOTIC REIGN and LOCH VOSTOK credited drummer Alvaro Romero Torres. Founded in June 1994 the group originally included guitarist Anders Eklöf, bassist Erik Wargloo and drummer Kalle Wallin. Following two demos, September 1995's 'The Final Chapter' and August 1996's 'In The Ashes Of The Fallen' recorded at Egghell studio in Enköping, the Singapore based Pulverised label released the debut album 'In The Ashes Of The Fallen' during 1998, this being the first product to feature Alvaro Romero Torres. Konqueror Records issued 'The Ordeal' album in 2003.

The Final Chapter, Imperial Domain (1995) (Demo). Where Silence Reign / The Final Chapter / From Time Immemorial / The Enchantress.
In The Ashes Of The Fallen, Imperial Domain (1996) (Demo). Like Fire In The Night / Where Life And Death Collide / But No One Hears / In The Ashes Of The Fallen.
IN THE ASHES OF THE FALLEN, Pulverised (1998). Like Fire In The Night / From Time Immemorial / Crystal Walls / The Enchantress / Where Life And Death Collide / Midnight Madness / But No One Hears / The Final Chapter / In The Ashes Of The Fallen / In The Arms Of Morpheus.

THE ORDEAL, Konqueror (2003). The Final Parade / White Dust Valley / The Wind Cries Her Name / Foolish Nation / The Shield / A Portrait Of Chaos / Dreamdemons / The Ordeal / When The Last Rain Falls.

IMPERIAL SODOMY

MANDELIEU, FRANCE — *Mordred (vocals), Mordrir (guitar), Bleuargh (guitar), Blaspho (bass), Orifist (drums).*

South of France Grindcore act. Mandelieu based IMPERIAL SODOMY comprise BELEF personnel vocalist Mordred (a.k.a. Morrdrëd), guitarist Mordrir and drummer Orifist (Romain Goulon). The latter also operated as drummer for AGRESSOR. Founded during 1997 the initial formation counted vocalist Ikkar, guitarist Reek, bassist Disaster and drummer Gorgor. This line-up produced the 1998 self financed EP 'Piss Of Love'. Bluargh was introduced on second guitar as Disaster took the lead vocal role. Signing to Criminal Records the 'Tormenting The Pacifist' album emerged in 2001, after which Orifist usurped Gorgor. A new demo, entitled 'Suffering', emerged in 2003.

Musically the band credited themselves as Mordred "Hammer drill barbecue", Mordrir "Six strings grind panzer", Bleuargh "Six strings extrem BTP", Blasphomet "Hateful tractor axe" and Orifist "Eternal sub-machine gun".

The band readied a second album, 'Demolished', for issue through Diamond Productions in 2004. Romain Goulon, also having ties to DISHARMONY and KAOTEON, joined Progressive Metal band KRYSALYD in early 2005. Orifist temporarily manned the drums for SCAVENGOURS that same year.

Piss On Love EP, (1998). Human Beast / Symphony Of Criminals / Out Of Here / Quick Hippie Molestation / Delirium Absynthia.
TORMENTING THE PACIFIST, Criminal (2001). Pacifistfucking / 70% Vol. / Symphony Of Criminals / Disorder Bringers / Violence / In Flesh I Trust / Dead Wishes / Basic Instincts / Lobotomized.
DEMOLISHED, Diamond Productions DIAM 005 (2004). Cool Shit / Castrated / Suicidation / I Hate Humans / Disfigured Lacerator / Flesh Corruption / Mortal Unleashed / Chaos & Muscles / Death Forge / Death Is All.

IMPERIOUS

SWEDEN — *Johan Thorén (vocals / guitar), Adam Skogvard (guitar), Rickard Thulin (bass), Chris (drums).*

Stockholm's IMPERIOUS began life in 1997 under the initial billing of OBSCURA. This opening trio, fronted by vocalist / guitarist Johan Thorén, cut an eponymous demo the following year with a second set 'In Agony' maintaining momentum. A 2001 demo, entitled 'From Suffering', would be crafted with the aid of session musicians but nevertheless scored a deal with the UK based Retribute label. Whilst crafting debut album 'In Splendour', recorded at Subsonic studio in December 2002 and engineered by Stefan Olsson, the revised tag of IMPERIOUS would be adopted.

With the departure of longstanding member Emil, IMPERIOUS enrolled the MYNJUN team of guitarist Adam Skogvard and bassist Rickard Thulin in June of 2004. Skogvard also operates PHANINDRA and BOOK OF HOURS whilst Thulin has COERCION connections.

IN SPLENDOUR, Retribute RET015 (2003). In Splendour / Fall Below / From Suffering / Kingdom Of Deceit / God Lied / One With Nothingness / Somer Rapture / Uncreate With Might / Impaled / Descend Into Oblivion / Lament.

IMPERIOUS MALEVOLENCE

CURITIBA, PR, BRAZIL — *Rafahell (vocals / bass), Mano (guitar), Maia (guitar), Antonio Death (drums).*

Curitiba based IMPERIOUS MALEVOLENCE trade in brutal Black inspired Death Metal. The band announced it's arrival with the 1995 demo session 'From Eternal Vacuum Storms' citing a line up of vocalist Guilherme, former INFERNAL guitarist Mano, bass player Rafahell and drummer Jaao.

A major shift in line up occurred with both Guilherme and Jaao leaving the picture upfront of the 1999 eponymous debut album issued by Deafen Music. Rafahell took on lead vocal duties whilst the band was brought back up to strength with the addition of second guitarist Maia and erstwhile CITOMEGALODEATH drummer Antonio Death. The band would tour Europe in 2000 putting in gigs in Germany and Belgium topped off with an appearance at the Czech 'Brutal Assault' festival alongside MACABRE and MORTICIAN performing to a crowd of 3'000.

IMPERIOUS MALEVOLENCE announced a new album slated for 2002 entitled 'Hatecrowned'. The band featured on the 2005 Moondo Records four way split 7" single 'Warriors Of The Morbid Moon' shared with ANTHROPOPHAGICAL WARFARE, DISFORTERROR and METACROSE. This release was limited to 400 copies.

IMPERIOUS MALEVOLENCE, (1999). Seeds Of Pain / Misery Of Existence / Into Dark Ages / When The Ancient Come / Imperious Malevolence / No Return / The End Of Millennium / Bloody Dawn / To Kill Or Be Killed / A Complete Slavery.

IMPETIGO

BLOOMINGTON, IL, USA — *Stevo De Caixo (vocals / bass), Mark (guitar), Scotty (guitar), Dan (drums).*

Pioneering and highly revered Death Metal band from Illinois. IMPETIGO was created in 1987 as a trio of Stevo De Caixeo on vocals and bass, guitarist Mark and drummer Dan. Following the debut demo 'All We Need Is Cheez' second guitarist Scotty was added. A 1989 demo 'Giallo' secured a deal with German label Wild Rags. However, their new record company's printers refuse to press up sleeves for the debut album 'Ultimo Mondo Cannibale' fearing possible legal action. The local Bloomington council also banned the artwork deeming it obscene and pornographic. The album eventually emerged with toned down artwork, although the original design would emerge on a limited edition picture disc.

A now rare 7" single 'Biuo Omega' followed then a split EP shared with German band BLOOD and the 'Faceless' EP before a second full length outing 'Horror Of The Zombies'.

IMPETIGO only managed some 30 gigs during the band's lifetime before folding in 1993. De Caixeo later founded INSOMNIA but after recording an as yet unreleased album this act folded.

IMPETIGO's underground status was such that a 2000 tribute album 'Wizards Of Gore' emerged on Razorback Records featuring such artists as BLOOD DUSTER, MORTICIAN, IMPALED, DECEASED, EXHUMED and VASTION. In 2006 Razorback reissued the first two IMPETIGO albums, adding extra live tracks, the 'Faceless' EP material and restoring 'Ultimo Mondo Cannibale' with its intended, banned, artwork. 'Horror Of The Zombies' too included added live recordings and artwork that was unused at the time.

Stevo De Caixo launched new band project CONVULSIONS in December 2006, an alliance with bassist Greg Mattingly of FORSAKEN, NOTHING and SON OF DOG and drummer Maniac Neil, of FRIGHTMARE, LORD GORE and BLOOD FREAK.

ULTIMO MONDO CANNIBALE, Wild Rags WRR020 (1990). Maggots / Dis-Organ-Ised / Intense Mortification / Revenge Of The Scabby Man / Veneral Warts / Bloody Pit Of Horror / Dear Uncle Creepy / Bitch Death Teenage Mucous Monsters From Hell / Zombie / Jane Fonda Sucks (Part 2) / Red Wigglers / Harbinger Of Death / Unadulterated Brutality / Mortado / Heart Of Illinois / My Lai.
Boneyard, Iron (1991) (Split EP with BLOOD). Boneyard / Cannibal Apocalypse.
Faceless EP, Wild Rags WRR031 (1991). Sinister Urge / Faceless / Dis-Organ-ised / Bloody Pit Of Horror.

Biuo Omega EP, Wild Rags (1992). Harbinger Of Death / Revenge Of The Scabby Man / Dear Uncle Creepy / Bitch Death Teenage Mucous Monsters From Hell.

HORROR OF THE ZOMBIES, Wild Rags WRR035 (1992). Boneyard / Work For The Streetcleaner / Wizard Of Gore / Morturia / Cannibale Ballet / Trap Them And Kill Them / Cannibal Lust / Defiling The Grave / Staph Terrorist / Breakfast In The Manchester Morgue (Let Sleeping Corpses Lie).

H.B.O. Theme- Who's Fucking Who? (Live), Bloodbath BIMI021 (1999) (Split EP with TRANSGRESSOR). H.B.O. Theme- Who's Fucking Who? (Live) / My Lai / Jane Fonda Sucks.

Late Night Necrophiliac Fun, (2000) (Split single with INGROWING). I Work For The Street Cleaner (Live.

BIUO OMEGA, Obscene Productions OBP 035 (2000). Harbinger Of Death / Revenge Of The Scabby Man / Dear Uncle Creepy / Bitch Death Teenage Mucous Monsters From Hell / H.B.O. Theme: Who's Fucking Who? (Live) / My Lai / Jane Fonda Sucks.

IMPIOUS

TROLLHÄTTAN, SWEDEN — *Martin Akesson (vocals), Valle Adzic (guitar), Robin Sörqvist (guitar), Erik Peterson (bass), Ulf Johansson (drums).*

Trollhättan based Thrash orientated Death Metal act. Created in early 1994 by guitarists Vladimir 'Valle' Adzic and Martin Akesson IMPIOUS originally relied on a drum machine for initial demos. In late 1994 CROWN OF THORNS and THE CROWN vocalist Johan Lindstrandt manned the drum stool and a temporary bassist was enlisted. IMPIOUS put in their inaugural gig in May 1995 supporting LORD BELIAL and got to grips with their debut publicly available demo session entitled 'Infernal Predomination'. The track 'Dominated By Tales' would also surface on the compilation album 'Vad Hander'.

In early 1996 Lindstrandt was drafted for his military service. This move put CROWN OF THORNS on ice temporarily but freed up their guitarist, Marko Trevonen, to replace Lindstrandt as the new IMPIOUS drummer. With this makeshift line up a second demo tape 'The Suffering' was produced by KING DIAMOND guitarist Andy La Rocque. Shortly after recording Ulf Johansson, also involved in Power Metal band POWER SUPREME and DRACONIAN, took the drum stool on a more permanent basis. IMPIOUS would donate their version of SEPULTURA's 'Inner Self' to the Black Sun tribute album 'Sepulchural Feast'. A further cover saw the band tackling METALLICA's 'One' but more significantly the group's first album, 1998's 'Evilized', saw release. Promotion witnessed a rash of dates in the Low Countries in cahoots with Dutch veterans SINISTER.

Akesson would then decide to concentrate on the lead vocal role and as such IMPIOUS manoeuvred Robin Sörqvist, also known as singer for POWER SUPREME, over to guitar. The numbers were made up with the induction of ENTHRALLED bass player Erik Peterson. This revised version of the band cut the 'Terror Succeeds' album which saw release in America by way of licensing to the Century Media label.

In March of 2002 drummer Ulf Johansson, opting out to become bass player for the TV series band TRIBAL INK, made way for Mikael Norén, another ENTHRALLED man and also holding CONFORMATORY credits. IMPIOUS announced the imminent arrival of a mini album entitled 'Deathsquad' as a taster for their next full length effort. 'Deathsquad' was slated to feature new material plus cover versions of MÖTLEY CRÜE's 'Live Wire', METALLICA's 'Trapped Under Ice', the ANTHRAX song 'Medusa' and 'Soldiers Of Hell' by RUNNING WILD.

Embarking upon a mammoth string of European shows throughout October and November of 2002 IMPIOUS created part of a deadly union for the 'Generation Armageddon' festival tour. Joining the band would be Norway's BLOOD RED THRONE, Greece's SEPTIC FLESH, Ireland's PRIMORDIAL, Belgium's ANCIENT RITES, and fellow Swedish heavyweights DISMEMBER. Allied with NECROPHOBIC and SATARIEL, the band toured mainland Europe in January of 2003.

During 2004 IMPIOUS would donate their rendition of 'Fallen Angel' to the 'Seven Gates Of Horror' tribute album assembled by the Dutch Karmaggedon Media label in homage to pioneering Bay Area Thrash act POSSESSED. The band, setting 'Hellucinations' (subsequently truncated to 'Hellucinate') as the title of their fourth album, recorded at Studio Mega with producer Valle Adzic and mixed by Chris Silver and Valle Adzic, due for October through Metal Blade Records. However, this title would be subsequently changed to 'The Killer'. IMPIOUS announced shows with fellow Swedes AMON AMARTH and German Death Metal crew DISILLUSION for Winter European tour dates. Meantime, Karmaggedon Media published the 'Born To Suffer' outing in November, this release including a swathe of cover versions including 'Fallen Angel' originally by POSSESSED, 'Trapped Under Ice' by METALLICA, 'Soldiers Of Hell' by RUNNING WILD, 'Live Wire' by MÖTLEY CRÜE, 'Inner Self' by SEPULTURA and 'One' from METALLICA.

Ex-IMPIOUS singer Johan Lindstrand re-emerged in early 2005 with his band ONE MAN ARMY AND THE UNDEAD QUARTET, also featuring the IMPIOUS credited Valle Adzic on bass. A short Euro tour in August saw the group partnered with AMON AMARTH and CATARACT. Johan Lindstrand spread his talents by also signing up as new frontman for INCAPACITY in December.

IMPIOUS wrapped up fresh album recordings, billed as 'Holy Murder Masquerade', in October 2006. Thomas Backelin from LORD BELIAL guested.

EVILIZED, Black Sun (1998). Dying I Live / Don't Kiss My Grave / Born To Suffer / Haven (A Leap In The Dark) / Facing The Nails / Anthem For The Afflicted / The Faded Paradise / Painted Soul / Extreme Pestilence / Inside / Evilization.

TERROR SUCCEEDS, Black Sun BS21 (2000). Soulexcursion / Terror God / Retaliation / Nuclear Storm Demise / The Punishment / Dimension Hell / Black Death / Diseased / The Loss Of Life / Nightmare Resurrection.

THE KILLER, Hammerheart (2002). Intro / Burn The Cross / Dead Eyes Open / Caught In Flesh / The Deathsquad / Sick Sex Six / The Hitman / Kill For Glory / Stabbed 69 Times / Needles Of Sin / Digital Devil.

HELLUCINATIONS, Metal Blade (2004). Inject / Wicked Saints / Infernique / Hellucinations / Show Me Your God! / Death Wish Scar / Toxic Paranoia / Needles Nervosa / Bloodspill Revelation / Suicide Park.

BORN TO SUFFER, Karmageddon Media (2004). Deathsquad / Hitman / Dead Eyes Open / Digital Devil / Born To Suffer / Facing The Nails / Painted Soul / Fallen Angel / Trapped Under Ice / Soldiers Of Hell / Live Wire / Inner Self / One.

HOLY MURDER MASQUERADE, Metal Blade (2007). The Confession / Bound To Bleed (For A Sacred Need) / T.P.S. / Bloodcraft / Holy Murder Masquerade / Death On Floor 44 / Slaughtertown Report / Three Of One / Everlasting Punishment / Purified By Fire / Dark Closure.

IMPULSE MANSLAUGHTER

CHICAGO, IL, USA — *Karl Patton (vocals), Chris Hanley (guitar), Nick Stevens (bass), Glen Herman (drums).*

Punk influenced Death / Thrash outfit. Chicago's IMPULSE MANSLAUGHTER would be one of the very first signings to the Nuclear Blast label, debuting in 1986 with the yellow vinyl 7" single 'Burn One Naked And Nuke It'. The band's original formation saw Chris Hanley on bass guitar before he adopted the lead guitarist role. The album 'He Who Laughs Last … Laughs Alone' followed in 1987. Bassist Nick Stevens would depart in late 1987 and Chris Hanley duly switched from guitar to bass again to cover whilst Mike Schaffer was drafted as guitarist. With Schaffer opting out in early 1988 to join ABOMINATION Hanley moved back to the guitar role and Vince Vogel of SCREECHING WEAZEL came onboard in the bass role.

IMPULSE MANSLAUGHTER's 1988 album 'Logical End' included cover versions of MOTÖRHEAD's 'Stone Deaf Forever' and the ROLLING STONES 'Gimme Shelter'.

John Tolczyk was added on second guitar in 1989. Further tribulation came in 1990 when longstanding drummer Glen Herman quit, being replaced by Dan Duchaine. The following year Chris Hanley left the band for a solo project entitled NO CLASS and was duly superseded by Rob Lanam. John Tolczyk was kicked out at the end of 1991, the ex-member going on to found EYEGOUGER. He would eventually be replaced by Rick McKelvy in late 1992.

In 1993 the band shared a split 7" EP with PROVOCATION but folded that same year. Duchaine would later feature in FECK.

Burn One Naked And Nuke It, Nuclear Blast NB025 (1986). Sack O'Shit / Ratbag / Slithis / Nothing / Sedation / Chaos / Contradiction / Oatmeal.

HE WHO LAUGHS LAST … LAUGHS ALONE, Nuclear Blast NB0003-1 (1987). Batman And The Oracle Of Pevile Savage / Vomit Heads / We're All Bored Here / Suffer In Silence / Walls / They Start The War / Premature Evacuation / Crimes / Too Late / Pills / This World / Sedation / Cheer Up You Fucker / Kein Spiel / Oatmeal II / 1987 Schitzoid Sam / Pattonstein's Disease / Piss Me Off.

LOGICAL END, Walkthrufyre (1988). Drag / Face It / Not Quite Sure / Missing Children / Gimme Shelter / Crimson Dreams / No Deals / Let Them Die / Stone Dead Forever / Borderline Retard.

SOMETIMES, Nuclear Blast (1992).

LIVE AT WFMU, Beer City BEER CITY 129 (2004). Blanket Of Fear / Sedation / Media / They Start The War / Not Quite Sure / Dogshit Extravaganza / Premature Evacuation / Crimes / Pills / Kein Spiel / Gutterhead / Nothing / Mighty Harness / A Hell On Earth / Deceived / Given / Rat Bastard / Blanket Of Fear / Gutterhead / Given / Media / Dogshit Extravaganza / Chaos / Mighty Harness / Sometimes / Face It / Missing Children / Borderline Retard / Pills / Piss Me Off / The Oracle Of Penile Savage / Vomitheads / They Start The War / Crimes / Sedation / Kein Spiel / Pattonsteins Disease / Drink Smoke Vomit.

IMPURITY

KĘTRZYN, POLAND — *Bazyl (vocal / guitar), Lony (bass), Cinek (drums).*

IMPURITY, forged in Kętrzyn during 1987 under the formative title of DAMNATION, would include the noted figure of a pre-VADER, DIES IRAE, NYIA and SWEET NOISE guitarist Jaroslaw 'China' Labieniec. The opening DAMNATION combo comprised vocalist / guitarist Bazyl, bassist Mogil (MYCOSIS NAILZ man Pawel Kaminski) and drummer Pietkin. As the group evolved into IMPURITY, Max of DR. WATT took over on drums for the demo 'In Pain We Trust'. VADER's Peter also sessioned bass for 'In Pain We Trust'.

A further re-shuffle introduced China on guitar and bassist Lony. Another personnel shift saw China replaced by Tomaszek, who was in turn substituted by NECROSOUL, BLASPHEREREION and KINGDOM OF THE LIE's Edek (a.k.a. Daniel Ejmont) as Cinek became the drummer. Bazyl subsequently became a highly respected tattoo master in Olsztyn.

In Pain We Trust, Impurity (1990). Hellbound / Immense Decay / Last Sufferings.

IN BATTLE

SUNDSVALL, SWEDEN — *John Odhinn Sandin (vocals), Otto Wiklund (drums / vocals), John Frölén (guitar / bass).*

Hailing from Sundsvall, IN BATTLE was an amalgamation in 1996 of ODHINN members guitarist John 'Fröléti' Frölén, Ostlund and drummer Otto Wiklund with SETHERIAL's Sjödin. Signing to the Austrian Napalm label the band delivered their eponymous debut in 1997. IN BATTLE's line up for the 1998 album 'The Rage Of The Northmen' was down to a duo of Wiklund and Frölén. The band resurfaced in 2003 sporting a revised line-up. Joining vocalist John Odhinn Sandin and guitarist John Frölén would be ex-DIABOLICAL guitarist Hasse Karlsson, bassist Marcus Edvardsson, of CHASTISEMENT, SANCTIFICATION and SOULDRAINER, and drummer Aeon (a.k.a. Nils Fjällström). Sandin has a string of credits ranging across such extreme Metal bands as VALKYRIA, ABYSSOS, INHUMAN, ODHINN and UNCHAINED 2000. This unit recorded the demo 'Soul Metamorphosis', subsequently scoring a label deal with Metal Blade subsidiary Cold Records.

The band's third album, 2004's 'Welcome To The Battlefield', would see production credits going to the MORBID ANGEL and HATE ETERNAL veteran Erik Rutan, who also contributed a guitar solo to the track 'Serpent'. In January 2004 the group introduced AEON, SOULDRAINER and STUM credited Daniel Dlimi on guitar, switching Frölen to bass duties. In September the band inducted session guitarist Tomas Elofsson, from GOD AMONG INSECTS, PROSERPHINE and SANCTIFICATION. The band teamed up with UNLEASHED and YATTERING for a European tour commencing in late November prior to commencing work on a new album, 'Terrorkings', once again with Erik Rutan acting as producer. The group also announced they were now endorsed by the Swedish clothing company 'For Vikings Only'.

IN BATTLE supported Poland's BEHEMOTH on their 'Hate Means Hate' European tour in March 2005. The group severed ties with Cold Records the following month. Contracting with Nocturnal Art Productions for Europe and Candlelight for US distribution, the band prepared fourth album 'Kingdom Of Fear' for 2006 issue.

Otto Wiklund committed suicide on August 13th 2006.

January 2007 found IN BATTLE back in recording mode, cutting tracks for the album 'Kingdom Of Fear', for Nocturnal Art Productions.

IN BATTLE, Napalm NPR 031 (1997). Ruler Of The Northern Sphere / Enchant Me / Ar Av Kold / Doom Of The Unbeloved / Odhinn / A Sign Of Northern Triumph And Glory / I Ofred Vi Drar Fram / The Nocturnal Moon / De Hangdas Furste / Lokes Att / Helhorde / In Battle.

THE RAGE OF THE NORTHMEN, Napalm NPR 050 (1998). From The Flesh And Bones Of Our Enemies / The Rage Of The Northmen / The Specter Of Hate / The Conqueror / The Destroyer Of Souls / Muspelheim The Dominion Of The Flame / Storms Of War / Armies Of The Northern Realms / Endless War.

WELCOME TO THE BATTLEFIELD, Metal Blade (2004). Shunned By Life / Madness In The Realm Of War / Eldjättar / Scorched World / Soul Metamorphosis / Despoter / Serpents / The Blood Divine / Stonefaced Mountains / King God / Mass Produced Hybrid Humans.

IN FLAMES

GOTHENBURG, SWEDEN — *Anders Fridén (vocals), Jesper Strömblad (guitar), Björn Gelotte (guitar), Peter Iwers (bass), Daniel Svensson (drums).*

IN FLAMES is a high ranking Gothenburg Metal band, founded in late 1990, and widely recognised as one of the catalysts and practitioners of the melodic Death Metal genre. The band's eminence rose sharply in Europe and with tireless touring the band elevated themselves into the US charts. Early line-up fluidity was nailed down by 1999's 'Colony', this stability giving the band a solid platform from which to conquer the globe. As the band has broadened its appeal, stage-posted on 2002's 'Reroute To Remain', a dilution in aggression has alienated a core of older fans but each successive album has overall strengthened IN FLAMES' position with increased global sales.

The quintet only assumed the name IN FLAMES in 1993 after membership changes. One of these formative members, guitarist Ander Iwers later of TIAMAT, backed out in 1992. The founding triumvirate comprised CEREMONIAL OATH guitarist Jesper Strömblad, bassist Johan Larsson and second guitarist Glenn Ljungström. The band's debut, three track August 1993 demo cassette, featuring 'In Flames', 'Upon An Oaken Throne' and 'Clad In Shadows', secured a deal with Wrong Again Records. Guest lead guitar contributions came courtesy of TIAMAT's Anders Iwers. Upon being offered a deal the protoband claimed to have a full album's worth of material ready to go, and so hastily had to compile the entire debut set in just 24 hours.

IN FLAMES line-up for the debut album 'Lunar Strain', recorded by engineer Fredrik Nordström at Studio Fredman and released in August 1994, found the original trio supported by sessioning friends such as Anders Iwers, guitarist Carl Näslund, CEREMONIAL OATH guitarist Oscar Dronjak, female singer Jennica Johansson on 'Everlost (Part II)', violinist Ylva Wåhlstedt on the instrumental 'Hårgalåten' and the DARK TRANQUILLITY pairing of vocalist Mikael Stanne and drummer Anders Jivarp.

By the time of the five track 'Subterranean' mini-album in 1995, IN FLAMES had added EUCHARIST drummer Daniel Erlandsson, although Anders Jivarp did also contribute once again. Session vocals were handled by Henke Forss, holding DAWN, FUNERAL FEAST, NIDEN DIV. 187 and RETALIATION credentials. Upon the album's release the band found a new frontman in ex-CEREMONIAL OATH and original DARK TRANQUILLITY singer Anders Fridén as further flux saw Erlandsson losing his place to Björn Gelotte.

Following two critically acclaimed albums IN FLAMES contributed a cover version of 'Eye Of the Beholder' for the METALLICA tribute album 'Metal Militia Volume 1' compiled by Black Sun Records. Being as the band had no lead vocalist at this juncture, ANCIENT SLUMBER frontman Robert Dahne lent his lungs for this recording.

IN FLAMES tried out various vocalists in an attempt to gain some degree of stability. Demo tracks included at this juncture witnessed the inclusion of MARDUK's Jocke Göthberg on the song 'Dead Eternity' and DERANGED's Per Gyllenbäck, and label boss at Wrong Again Records, on 'The Inborn Lifeless', later to evolve into the following album's 'Dead God In Me'.

IN FLAMES eventually re-enlisted Fridén in time to record 'The Jester Race' released in February 1996, the album that was to really push the band to the forefront. The band had gravitated upwards to the major German independent Nuclear Blast label, this concern able to fully promote and market the band internationally. Studio sessions, conducted ably once again by Fredrik Nordström at Studio Fredman, found Oscar Dronjak adding vocals to 'Dead Eternity', Kaspar Dahlqvist of TREASURELAND donating his keyboard skills to 'Wayfaerer' and DARK TRANQUILLITY's Fredrik Johansson laying down lead guitar on 'December Flower'. Japanese variants of 'The Jester Race', clad in completely different artwork to the European tank design, added two exclusive tracks with demos of 'Dead Eternity' and 'The Inborn Lifeless'.

Backed up by numerous laudatory press reviews IN FLAMES set out on the Spring 'Out Of The Darkness' festival package in Germany together with DIMMU BORGIR, CRADLE OF FILTH and DISSECTION. 1997 witnessed the arrival of the Japanese IRON MAIDEN tribute album, 'Made In Flames' put out through the Toys Factory label. IN FLAMES contributed with their version of 'Murders In The Rue Morgue'. Jesper Strömblad was to enter the national German charts in late 1997, although not with IN FLAMES. The guitarist was the unofficial sixth member of trad Metal outfit HAMMERFALL assembled by his colleague Oscar Dronjak. The fellow Swedes debut peaked at number 34 in the charts with the 'Glory To The Brave' debut bearing many co-write credits to Strömblad.

With IN FLAMES on hold the band took the opportunity to realign their line-up, dispensing with Ljungström and Larsson. Two new players, guitarist Niklas Engelin and bassist Peter Iwers of CHAMELEON, were quickly slotted in following recording of October 1997's 'Whoracle' album. This record would be preceded by a taster picture-disc EP, 'Black-Ash Inheritance'. Obviously, not wishing to enter the realms of predictability, quite surreally the 'Whoracle' album included a version of DEPECHE MODE's 'Everything Counts'. Japanese versions, issued via the Toy's Factory label, added three extra tracks in 'Goliaths Disarm Their Davids', 'Acoustic Medley' and a live version of 'Behind Space'. Importantly, Whoracle was the first In Flames product to register on the charts, reaching number 78 in Germany. Mid 1998 had the band supporting DIMMU BORGIR, hitting the continental festivals in earnest and undertaking their debut appearances in Japan. That same year Daniel Svensson, citing SACRILEGE and DIMENSION ZERO credentials, took command of the drums, giving the group its now solid line-up.

The opening gambit of the new look IN FLAMES, 'Colony', hit stores across Europe, as well as charts in Germany, Sweden and Finland, in May 1999. Produced by Fredrik Nordström, who also gained extra credits for Hammond organ, slide guitar and "some other hippie stuff", 'Colony' also found EUROPE guitarist KEE MARCELLO (Kjell Lövbom) donating his soloing skills to the track 'Coerced Coexistence'. Peter Iwers stood down temporarily to devote time to his new born daughter and Dick Lövgren of ARCH ENEMY and ARMAGEDDON repute filled in as substitute. After a season on the summer European festival circuit and shows in the USA and Japan, the latter gigs seeing a return for Iwers, IN FLAMES closed 1999 with a December 18th concert in London flanking CRADLE OF FILTH and ARCH ENEMY.

'Clayman' took the band into higher reaches of the European charts in July 2000. Although this record maintained the same formula of musicians and producer as its predecessor, the album gave the first hints of a change in direction, the more abrasive edges now beginning to see refinement. 'Clayman' also hosted the song 'Only For The Weak', a track which would go on to establish itself as the band's anthem. A limited edition release, packaged in a 3D cover, was bolstered by the inclusion of an extra song 'World Of Promises', a radical adaptation on melodic Rockers TREAT's original.

IN FLAMES toured America in 2000 on a billing with EARTH CRISIS and SKINLAB. The band was announced as support for CLUTCH's summer 2001 American dates but then pulled out. The Swedes would however get on the road in the UK during November supporting the infamous SLIPKNOT, this combination certainly placing the group in front of fresh audiences. It would then be back to America in April 2002 forming a more traditional package billing with ICED EARTH and JAG PANZER. IN FLAMES would also be announced as part of the billing of the SLAYER topped American 'Extreme Steel' festivals. With live work finally at a close IN FLAMES set to work on a new studio record 'Reroute To Remain', produced by Daniel Bergstrand and set for September release. The band's 1994 rendition of 'Eye Of The Beholder' resurfaced on a Nuclear Blast METALLICA tribute collection.

As 'Reroute To Remain' gave the band an unprecedented number 5 placing in the Swedish charts a month's worth of North American dates commenced in San Francisco on September 16th backed up by SENTENCED, KILLSWITCH ENGAGE and LACUNA COIL. October headliners in Germany would be scheduled with support from PAIN and BLACKSHINE, although the latter act would subsequently be substituted by SOILWORK.

Anders Fridén embroiled himself in yet another in the very long line of Swedish side ventures by fronting up PASSENGER, a late 2002 band endeavour also incorporating his erstwhile IN FLAMES colleague and GARDENIAN guitarist Niclas Engelin, HEADPLATE bassist Håkan Skoger and ex-TRANSPORT LEAGUE drummer Patrik J. Sten.

IN FLAMES would be back on the North American touring circuit in March 2003 on a package billing allied with Industrialists MINISTRY and Nu-Metal act MUDVAYNE. An EP launched in Spring entitled 'Trigger' saw the inclusion of a GENESIS cover 'Land Of Confusion'. Title track of this EP also found its way onto the 'Freddy Vs. Jason' movie soundtrack. As an aside, a novel promotional video for the SOILWORK track 'Rejection Role' saw the band in a turf war with the members of IN FLAMES.

The band resumed touring in North America for a month

long headline trek commencing 26th June in Toronto, Canada. Support acts comprised SOILWORK, CHIMAIRA and UNEARTH. Toward the close of 2003 guitarists Björn Gelotte and Jesper Strömblad found time in their schedule to activate an all new project dubbed ALL ENDS as a collaboration with "musical artist" Tinna Karlsdotter and Björn's sister Emma Gelotte.

The band, re-signing to Nuclear Blast Records, set 'Soundtrack To Your Escape' as the title of a new 2004 album produced by Daniel Bergstrand and ex-MISERY LOVES COMPANY man Örjan Örnkloo. A single, 'The Quiet Place', would be promoted with a video shot by director Patric Ullaeus. Quite spectacularly, the single landed at no. 2 in the national Swedish charts upon release. 'Soundtrack To Your Escape' sold an impressive 10,659 copies during its first week of US release to debut at no. 145 on the Billboard charts. It would also go top five in Sweden.

Meantime, Regain Records re-issued the archive albums 'Lunar Strain' and 'Subterranean', both hosting extra tracks. European dates in April saw DEVILDRIVER as support act.

As Nielsen SoundScan reports showed that 'Soundtrack To Your Escape' was healthily selling around 3,000 units a week in the USA, the UK's 'Metal Hammer' magazine presented IN FLAMES with their 'Best Underground Act' award in June. IN FLAMES put in Australian dates in September, allied with CHIMAIRA. Two special shows later that same month, held at the Los Angeles Roxy and New York's infamous C.B.G.B.'s would be recorded for a live album. The band would perform two sets each night, the first comprising the entire 'Soundtrack To Your Escape' album before closing the night with back catalogue tracks. Returning to Sweden, guitarists Björn Gelotte and Jesper Strömblad would swiftly set to work composing new material. The band closed out the year with a special performance on 27th December at the Carling Apollo Hammersmith in London alongside LACUNA COIL, CALIBAN and CHIMAIRA. As part of the show IN FLAMES performed a cover of PANTERA's 'Fucking Hostile' as a tribute to murdered PANTERA / DAMAGEPLAN guitarist "Dimebag" Darrell Abbott.

IN FLAMES grabbed the high profile support to JUDAS PRIEST's February 2005 European dates. Throughout the Spring the band would be ensconced in Dug-Out Studios in Uppsala crafting the new album, given a working title 'Crawl Through Knives' but subsequently switched to 'Come Clarity'. The group also opened for MÖTLEY CRÜE on their two Finnish dates in early June. The band's lavish DVD set 'Used & Abused— In Live We Trust' topped the Swedish charts in July upon release.

IN FLAMES united with MOTÖRHEAD and GIRLSCHOOL for UK gigs throughout October and December. Daniel Svensson, awaiting the birth of his second child, sat out these shows as Tobbe Kellgren, a seasoned campaigner holding credits with DECAMERON, DISSECTION, SWORDMASTER, SOULREAPER, SEVENTH ONE, WOLF and SATANIZED, stepped in as substitute. The band restructured its label dealings for 'Come Clarity', retaining Nuclear Blast for Europe but switching to Ferret Records for the USA. Quite spectacularly, the album crashed into the number one position on both the Swedish and Finnish album charts. Importantly, 'Come Clarity' would sell 24,000 copies in the United States in its first week of release to debut at number 58 on the Billboard chart.

IN FLAMES, TRIVIUM, DEVILDRIVER and Pennsylvania's ZAO pooled their talents for a January 2006 US tour. European shows throughout April and May witnessed veteran Brazilian Thrashers SEPULTURA and Frenchmen DAGOBA as opening acts. The band put in a significant appearance at the GUNS N' ROSES headlined 'Download' festival in Castle Donington, UK on June 11th. The group subsequently engaged in a gigantic roving festival billing with the US 'Sounds Of The Underground' tour throughout the summer, commencing in Cleveland, Ohio on July 8th, partnered with AS I LAY DYING, TRIVIUM, CANNIBAL CORPSE, GWAR, TERROR, THE BLACK DAHLIA MURDER,

IN FLAMES

BEHEMOTH, THE CHARIOT and THROUGH THE EYES OF THE DEAD. During this trek Nuclear Blast announced that 'Soundtrack To Your Escape' had surpassed 100,000 sales in the USA.

IN FLAMES joined the European leg of the 'Unholy Alliance' tour, comprising SLAYER, CHILDREN OF BODOM, LAMB OF GOD and THINE EYES BLEED, in October. Further North American shows followed with SEEMLESS and LACUNA COIL in December. For these concerts IN FLAMES re-enlisted former guitarist Niklas Engelin to fill in for Jesper Strömblad, who was "sitting out the group's current tour in order to deal with some personal issues'. Björn Gelotte then stood down temporarily, due to impending fatherhood, and Henrik Danhage from EVERGREY stood in.

To close the year, Black Lodge Records released a limited-edition 7" vinyl single from on December 13th comprising 'Come Clarity' / 'Only For The Weak'. 2007 opened for IN FLAMES in fine style as 'Soundtrack To Your Escape' became the band's second album to pass the 100,000 sales marker in the USA.

IN FLAMES were in pre-production mode by mid-February. Meantime, NightOfTheVinylDead reissued the 1997 EP 'Black-Ash Inheritance' as a limited edition shaped picture disc vinyl.

Demo '93, (1993). In Flames / Upon An Oaken Throne / Clad In Shadows.

LUNAR STRAIN, Wrong Again WAR003 (1994). Behind Space / Lunar Strain / Starforsaken / Dreamscape / Everlost (Part I) / Everlost (Part II) / Hårgalåten / In Flames / Upon An Oaken Throne / Clad In Shadows.

SUBTERRANEAN, Wrong Again WAR006 (1995). Stand Ablaze / Ever Dying / Subterranean / Timeless / Biosphere.

THE JESTER RACE, Nuclear Blast NB 168-2 (1996). Moonshield / The Jester's Dance / Artifacts Of The Black Rain / Graveland / Lord Hypnos / Dead Eternity / The Jester Race / December Flower / Wayfearer / Dead God In Me.

WHORACLE, Nuclear Blast NB 284-2 (1997). Food For The Gods / Gyroscope / Dialogue With The Stars / The Hive / Jester Script Transfigured / Morphing Into Primal / Worlds Within The Margin / Episode 666 / Everything Counts / Whoracle. Chart position: 78 GERMANY.

Black Ash Inheritance EP, Nuclear Blast NB 251 (1997) (CD picture disc). Goliaths Disarm Their Davids / Gyroscope / Acoustic Medley / Behind Space (Live).

COLONY, Nuclear Blast NB 399-2 (1999). Embody the Invisible / Ordinary Story / Scorn / Colony / Zombie Inc. / Pallar Anders Visa / Coerced Coexistence / Resin / Behind Space '99 / Insipid 2000 / The New World. Chart positions: 34 SWEDEN, 34 FINLAND, 69 GERMANY.

CLAYMAN, Nuclear Blast NB 499-2 (2000). Bullet Ride / Pinball Map / Only For The Weak / ... As The Future Repeats Today / Square Nothing / Clay Man / Satellites And Astronauts / Brush The Dust Away / Swim / Suburban Me / Another Day In Quicksand. Chart positions: 17 SWEDEN, 21 FINLAND, 43 GERMANY, 61 POLAND.

THE TOKYO SHOWDOWN—LIVE IN JAPAN 2000, Nuclear Blast NB 636-2 (2001). Bullet Ride / Embody The Invisible / Jotun / Food For The Gods / Moonshield / Clayman / Swim / Behind Space / Only For The Weak / Gyroscope / Scorn / Ordinary Story / Pinball Map / Colony / Episode 666. Chart positions: 31 FINLAND, 43 SWEDEN.

REROUTE TO REMAIN, Nuclear Blast NB 624-2 (2002). Reroute To Remain / System / Drifter / Trigger / Cloud Connected / Transparent / Dawn Of A New Day / Egonomic / Minus / Dismiss The Cynics / Free Fall / Dark Signs / Metaphor / Black & White. Chart positions: 5 SWEDEN, 5 FINLAND, 23 GERMANY, 67 AUSTRIA, 70 ITALY, 72 NORWAY, 81 FRANCE.

Cloud Connected, Nuclear Blast NB 1083-2 (2002). Cloud Connected / Colony (Live) / Cloud Connected (Mpeg Video).

Trigger EP, Nuclear Blast NB 1130-2 (2003). Trigger (Single edit) / Watch Them Feed / Land Of Confusion / Cloud Connected (Club Connected remix) / Moonshield (C64 Karaoke version) / Trigger (Video) / Cloud Connected (Video).

The Quiet Place, Nuclear Blast NB 1249 (2004). The Quiet Place / My Sweet Shadow (Remix) / Värmlandsvisan (Live at the Queen Street Bar 2004) / The Quiet Place (Video) / Studio Recording Session (Video) / Screensaver. Chart position: 2 SWEDEN.

SOUNDTRACK TO YOUR ESCAPE, Nuclear Blast NB 1231 (2004). F(r)iend / The Quiet Place / Dead Alone / Touch Of Red / Like You Better Dead / My Sweet Shadow / Evil In A Closet / In Search For I / Borders And Shading / Superhero Of The Computer / Dial 595-Escape / Bottled / Discover Me Like Emptiness. Chart positions: 2 SWEDEN, 13 FINLAND, 28 GERMANY, 32 HUNGARY, 35 AUSTRIA, 36 NORWAY, 82 FRANCE, 132 UK, 145 USA.

SOUNDTRACK TO YOUR ESCAPE, Nuclear Blast NB 1445 (2005) (Double CD). F(r)iend / The Quiet Place / Dead Alone / Touch Of Red / Like You Better Dead / My Sweet Shadow / Evil In A Closet / In Search For I / Borders And Shading / Superhero Of The Computer / Dial 595-Escape / Bottled / The Quiet Place (Video) / Touch Of Red (Video) / Watch Them Feed (Live At Wacken Open Air 2003) / Only For The Weak (Live At Wacken Open Air 2003) / The Making Of "Soundtrack To Your Escape" (Feat. producer Daniel Bergstrand).

COME CLARITY, Nuclear Blast NB 1309-2 (2005). Take This Life / Leeches / Reflect The Storm / Dead End / Scream / Come Clarity / Vacuum / Pacing Death's Trail / Crawling Through Knives / Versus Terminus / Our Infinite Struggle / Vanishing Light / Your Bedtime Story Is Scaring Everyone.

COME CLARITY, Nuclear Blast NB 1309-2 (2006). Take This Life / Leeches / Reflect The Storm / Dead End / Scream / Come Clarity / Vacuum / Pacing Death's Trail / Crawling Through Knives / Versus Terminus / Our Infinite Struggle / Vanishing Light / Your Bedtime Story Is Scaring Everyone. Chart positions: 1 SWEDEN, 1 FINLAND, 6 GERMANY, 16 AUSTRIA, 23 GREECE, 27 NORWAY, 27 CANADA, 30 SWITZERLAND, 52 DENMARK, 58 USA, 67 UK, 88 SPAIN, 89 FRANCE.

COME CLARITY: SPECIAL EDITION, Nuclear Blast NB 1309-0 (2006) (Double CD + DVD). Take This Life / Leeches / Reflect The Storm / Dead End / Scream / Come Clarity / Vacuum / Pacing Death's Trail / Crawling Through Knives / Versus Terminus / Our Infinite Struggle / Vanishing Light / Your Bedtime Story Is Scaring Everyone / Live Performance In Rehersalroom.

Come Clarity, Black Lodge (2006) (7" vinyl single). Come Clarity / Only For The Weak.

Black Ash Inheritance, NightOfTheVinylDead NIGHT009SH (2007) (Shaped vinyl picture disc limited to 555 hand numbered copies). Goliaths Disarm Their Davids / Gyroscope / Acoustic Medley / Behind Space (Live).

IN GREY

STOCKHOLM, SWEDEN — *Joakim Croneström (vocals), Niklas Axelsson (guitar), Dennis Starkenberg (drums).*

Stockholm's IN GREY, founded by guitarist Niclas Axelsson, was originally created as the Death Metal band TEARS OF LUNA in 1992 as a trio of Axelsson, bassist Guillaume Le Hucke and drummer Andre B. However, Le Hucke, re-billed as 'Israphael', soon vacated his post to join KATATONIA. Still under this formative title the group, then comprising singer Dennis Liljedahl, guitarist Joakim Bergenvall and drummer Andre Teilman, released two demos, 1994's 'The Journey' and 'Skydancer' in 1995. That same year guitarist Anders Nyström (a.k.a. Blakkheim) of BLOODBATH, KATATONIA, BEWITCHED, DIABOLICAL MASQUERADE and ANCIENT RITES was inducted. The band adopted the IN GREY title for the 1996 'Time Circles' set. After this session the band went into hiatus as Nyström prioritised KATATONIA.

IN GREY made a return in 1998, Liljedahl, Axelsson, guitarist Joakim Luleå and drummer Dennis Starkeberg issuing a 1999 demo 'Seasons Change' cut at Subsonic Studios. The band, borrowing ex-KATATONIA bassist Mikael, put in their debut gig at the Stålverket festival.

The next set of recordings, 2000's 'Mask', featuring Johan Erikson on bass, saw a radical shift into more subdued, Gothic areas, this trend being continued with the 2001 'Above' demo and, after enrolling FLAGELLATION's Per Lindström on bass guitar, the 2003 album 'Sulphur Tears'. That same year FLAGELLATION's Daniel Cannerfelt would be installed on second guitar. It seems Elvis Aleman was also briefly positioned on guitar.

The 2004 version of IN GREY had Axelsson and Starkeberg being joined by new recruits singer Joakim Cronestrom, guitarist Igor Jevtic and RISING SHADOWS, FLAGELLATION, ANIMA MORTE and GOATSODOMIZER keyboard player Fredrik Klingwall. This line-up cut the four song demo 'MMIV'. The band parted ways with Klingwall in November 2005.

FREDRIK KLINGWALL departed to join Progressive Metal band LOCH VOSTOK in December 2005 and issued Industrial solo album 'Entrance' in 2006. IN GREY lost the services of bassist Per Lindström in April. Both Klingwall and Lindström joined the ranks of MACHINERY in 2006.

The Journey, In Grey (1994) (Demo).

Skydancer, In Grey (1995) (Demo).

Time Circles, In Grey (1996) (Demo). Crystallized / Awakened / Beg For More / Blackness.

Seasons Change, In Grey (1999) (Demo). Seasons Change / In Heaven / Like This / I Think.

Mask, In Grey (2000) (Demo). Once Again / Mask / The Same.

Above, In Grey (2001) (Demo). Above / I Amaze.

SULPHUR TEARS, Last Entertainment LAST 002 (2003). Intro / Sulphur Tears / Life Has Changed / At The Edge / As Passion Turns To Hate / I Amaze / Above / Mask / Instrumental / A Sun That Never Sets.

MMIV, In Grey (2004) (Demo). Heaven Cries / My Nectar / Liyah / Everytime I Burn.

XII, In Grey (2004) (Demo). The End Is The Beginning / Once Again / Bittersweet / Black River.

LIYAH, Last Entertainment LAST 003 (2006). The End Is The Beginning / Once Again / My Nectar / Everytime I Burn / Bittersweet / Into Oblivion / Heaven's Cry / Emptiness / Alone I Weep / Liyah / Black River.

IN SOMNIS

VLAANDEREN, BELGIUM — *Moribundus (vocals), D. Vermeersch (guitar), S. (bass), A. Binamé (flute), K. Villez (drums).*

IN SOMNIS is a West Vlaanderen Doom act featuring PANTHEÏST drummer K. 'Soporifer' Villez and bassist 'S' (a.k.a. Stijn van Cauter). 'S' would be involved in a bewildering array of projects including UNTIL DEATH OVERTAKES ME, FALL OF THE GREY WINGED ONE, BEYOND BLACK VOID, I DREAM NO MORE, THE SAD SUN, DE MONSTRORUM MMXIII, FORBIDDEN FIELDS and THE ETHEREAL.

The genesis of IN SOMNIS dates back to 1992 and ideas formulated by singer Moribundus and guitarist D. Vermeersch. For a lengthy period the project would be purely hypothetical until the arrival of drummer K. 'Soporifer' Villez in June of 1997 saw the project picking up momentum. Formative line up changes saw the removal of an unwanted bassist, the exit of female member A. 'Mab' Binamé and then departure of D. Vermeersch in July of 1999. With the defection of a further guitarist IN SOMNIS by 2000 was down to a duo of Moribundus and Soporifer.

The pair resolved to rebuild the group, re-drafting both D. Vermeersch and Mab, the latter now employed on flute. A second guitarist was located with Login but he would leave in the Spring of 2001. New inductees the following year would be guitarist Johan Bekaert and keyboard player M. 'Argiël' Matthys.

Nulll Records would issue the debut album 'The Memory You've Become' in 2003, of note being the track 'Heer Halewyn' with lyrics from an anonymous 14th century writer. Dates across the Lowlands in April 2004 saw IN SOMNIS on a package billing with US act WHILE HEAVEN WEPT and Ireland's MOURNING BELOVETH. The band parted ways with guitarist Johan Bekaert and keyboard player Argiël shortly after. That July the group pulled in new personnel, guitarist Lethe and keyboard player Kyrinla, both also active members of LETHIAN DREAMS.

THE MEMORY YOU'VE BECOME, Nulll 020 (2003). My Siren / Galatea / The Goblet / A Memory You Become / A Goddess Reborn / Heer Halewyn / Like Death,... Forever / Alone / Lost In Dreams.

IN THA UMBRA

PORTUGAL — *Bruno J.S. Correia (vocals / guitar), Bob H.J. Sneijers (guitar), Scott (bass), João Marques (drums).*

IN THA UMBRA first made their presence felt with the 1996 demo 'Of The Singing Dusk ... Mystic Charms, A Funeral Sky And The Withering Light'. The Algarve band had been forged that January by Brün K. Diaboliih, guitarist Bob H. J. Sneijers, bassist Scott and drummer João Marques. Following release of the debut album 'Descend Supreme Sunset' in 1998 the band signed to the Hibernia label for a follow up single 'The Göatblöd 666'.

Recording began in 2002 of a sophomore album, with the project initially entitled 'O' Night Old Night'. The album title would subsequently be switched to 'Midnight In The Garden Of Hell'. Just prior to release founder guitarist Bob H. J. Sneijers opted out, being superseded by Bruno Miguel Bernardo of TEASANNA SATANNA. This revised version of the band cut the 'Pentagramma' EP, this including two live tracks and renditions of CELTIC FROST's 'Into The Crypts Of Rays' and MOTÖRHEAD's 'Ace Of spades'. During 2002 the bass position was assumed by another TEASANNA SATANNA member, Calhau Jr.

IN THA UMBRA entered Straka Studios in Albufeira during August of 2004 to craft the album 'Nigrium Nigrius Nigro'.

DESCEND SUPREME SUNSET, Art Music Group (1998). As Dusk Weaves The Night / Flowers For A Funeral / The Moon Lay Hidden Beneath A Cloud / Like Ravens 'Neath Nightskies / If Thou Wouldst Shadow Me / Leanan Sidhe / Descend Supreme Sunset / Epilogue-Harvester of Armageddon.
The Göatblöd 666, Hibernia (1999). To Chaos And The Chant O' Nymph / Crescent.
Pentagramma, (2002). Through Lycanthropie's Trod Communion / Once Atrocities Has Hacked Upon Daylight's Throat / To Chaos And The Chant O'Nymphs / Chrysalid / Ace Of Spades / Into The Crypts Of Rays / Blooming Wolf's Bane Scent / Like Raven's Neath Nightskies (Live) / The Spring Breathes Horrors (Live).

IN THY DREAMS

SALA, SWEDEN — *Jonas Nyrén (vocals), Kakan Stuvemark (guitar), Jari Kuusisto (guitar), Fredrik Eriksson (bass), Stefan Westerberg (drums).*

A Sala based melodic Death Metal unit. Guitarist Hakan Stuvemark is an erstwhile member of Deathcore unit WOMBBATH. Vocalist Jonas Nyrén is known also frontman for ARCH ENEMY guitarist Christopher Amott's side endeavour ARMAGEDDON. IN THY DREAMS, after debuting with the mini album 'Stream Of Dispraised Souls' in 1997, would suffer when their label Wrong Again took a lengthy hiatus.

The same year drummer Stefan Westerberg and guitarist Jari Kuusisto, both also operating as members of STEEL ATTACK, founded a further side act entitled CARNAL FORGE in alliance with STEEL ATTACK personnel Johan Magnusson and Dennis Vestman along with Jonas Kjellgren of DELLAMORTE and CENTINEX.

The record company finally re-emerged as War Music issuing the greatly delayed Pelle Saether produced 'The Gate Of Pleasure' in 1999.

IN THY DREAMS replaced vocalist Jonas Nyrén with Thomas Lindfors. 'Highest Beauty', once more with production duties delegated to Saether, was delivered in November 2001. Japanese editions came complete with an exclusive bonus track 'Side Thoughts Swirl Chaotically'.

In February 2007 it was announced that Stefan Westerberg had joined forces with a brand new, melodic Death Metal inclined project called KRYPTILLUSION. Kristofer Nilsson of UNDIVINE handled lead vocals whilst Mike Wead, of KING DIAMOND and MERCYFUL FATE, featured on lead guitar and Fredrik Groth from THE STORYTELLER assumed bass duties.

STREAM OF DISPRAISED SOULS, Wrong Again WAR014 (1997). Fateless / Glistening Truth / Fleeing Illusion / Dreams Within / Stream Of Dispraised Souls.
THE GATE OF PLEASURE, War Music (1999). Into Infinity / A Man Of Dreams / Deadly Desires / Master Of Lies / Blinded / Probing Insanity / Indoctrinated Lies / Feeing Illusion / Forgiven Sins.
HIGHEST BEAUTY, War Music (2001). Highest Beauty / Surrealistic Insanity / Hatred / Spirits Forge / Control / Selfpity Human / Lower Regions / Razor Sharp / Weeping Twilight / Upon Your God.

IN VAIN

KRISTIANSAND, NORWAY — *A. Frigstad (vocals), S. Nedland (vocals / keyboards), J. Haaland (guitar), Even Fuglestad (guitar), Kristian Wikstøl (bass), Stig Reinhardtsen (drums).*

Kristiansand Death Metal band founded in late 2003 by singer A. Frigstad and guitarist J. Haaland. In May 2004 IN VAIN utilised Ansgar Studio in Kristiansand to cut tracks for the EP 'Will The Sun Ever Rise'. The group added bassist J. Sehl in mid 2005 to record a second EP entitled 'Wounds'. IN VAIN subsequently recruited guitarist Magnus Olav Tveiten, in November, then drummer Stig Reinhardtsen, in December.

Ole Vistnes replaced J. Sehl in May 2006. In November IN VAIN announced new members bassist Kristian Wikstøl and guitarist Even Fuglestad. A debut album, 'The Latter Rain', was recorded for 2007 release.

VREID, BATTERED and IN VAIN teamed up for the "Northern Brigade" tour beginning in Belgium during late March 2007.

Will The Sun Ever Rise, In Vain (2004). As I Wither / Caught Within / A Vision By Night.
Wounds, In Vain (2005). October's Monody / Det Rakner / In Remembrance / Epilogue.

IN-QUEST

ARENDONK, BELGIUM — *Mike Löfberg (vocals), Douglas (guitar), Jan (guitar), Manu (bass), Gert (drums).*

Arendonk's militaristic Death Metal band IN-QUEST would be notably fronted by ABORTED and LENG TCH'E frontman vocalist Sven De Caluwé. Under the pseudonym 'Inguio Urvan' he also claims a heritage with infamous scat-Grind act ANAL TORTURE. The group had been active for over ten years on the underground extreme Metal scene, enduring many line up changes prior to enrolling new guitarist Douglas in 1999 and De Caluwé for the 2003 EP 'Destination: Pyroclasm'.

The band had earlier been prolific on the Grindcore scene where, billed as SYSTEM SHIT, they had issued three demos before taking on the IN-QUESt title in 1994. Capitalising on a 7" single 'Rewarded With Ingratitude' and a demo 'Xylad Valox' IN-QUEST had debuted commercially in 1997 with the 'Extrusion: Battlehymns' album released by Teutonic Existence. At this juncture the band comprised a quartet of vocalist NG, guitarist Wim, bassist Manu and drummer Gert. Switching labels to Shiver the 1999 record 'Operation Citadel' saw the addition of rhythm guitarist Jan.

IN-QUEST's third album, 'Epileptic', recorded at CCR Studios by Kris Belaen and released in April of 2004 through Goodlife Records, included a cover of PRO-PAIN's 'In For The Kill'. By this juncture the band was crediting its members as SDC 'Deathscreams and Battle Commands', GM 'Mechanic Artillery', Douglas V 'Aerial Bombardements', JG 'Tankattacks' and MVT 'Anti-Aircraft Battery'. However, just weeks after the release of the record, De Caluwé quit. The band drafted Mike Löfberg as replacement. IN-QUEST supported FEAR FACTORY and MNEMIC on several European dates in December.

IN-QUEST's May 2005 album, 'The Comatose Quandary', closed out with an unaccredited hidden track entitled 'Remote Batch Disposal'.

EXTRUSION: BATTLEHYMNS, Teutonic Existence (1997). Extrusion—Battlehymns / Matrimonium / Encrust Excrement Crevice / Anti-Disestablishmentarianism / Xylad Valox / Opus: Questor Mastodon / Inspiration Of Thou Madness / Coroner's Inquest.

OPERATION: CITADEL, Shiver SHR 035 (1999). Cross Cursed / Festung Stalingrad / Coital Amnesia / Bombattack Trauma / Battle Domination / Operation Citadel / Necklacing.

Destination Pyroclasm, Soulreaper (2003). Stahlmacht: Destruction Unbound / Scorched: A Reign Of Fire / Sequence 2172: Dehumanized / Battle Domination 2003.

EPILEPTIC, Goodlife Recordings GL 093 (2004). Neurofractal Bypass / The Imminence Of Disposition / Reverberating Human Callousness / Deprivation Synapse / Retrospected Void / In For The Kill / Epileptic / Scorched / Placid Vortex.

THE COMATOSE QUANDRIES, Goodlife GLR 101 (2005). Diffuse Pattern Recognition / Audiotoxic Binaries / Socioneural Geneticism / Cryotron FreQuency / The Frozen; Nuclear Aftermath / The Comatose Quandary / Warpath / Systematic Arhythmetic Hate / Operation; Citadel "Pulse Shattering Biowaste" / Sigmoid Signal / Resilient Androtronic Carnage / Remote Batch Disposal (Hidden track).

INACTIVE MESSIAH

GREECE — *John Minardos (vocals), Jim Koutsoukis (guitar), Lefteris Christou (bass), Chris Benetsanopoulos (keyboards), Katerina Stavropoulou (drums).*

INACTIVE MESSIAH was created under the title WOMB OF MAGGOTS, initiated as a trio comprising bass player Lefteris Christou, keyboard player Chris Benetsanopoulos and drummer Katerina Stavropoulou in April of 2001. Following an eponymous demo cut with the aid of session players Jim Koutsoukis enrolled on guitar. Singer John 'Mineiros' Minardos came in just prior to recording the debut album for Sleaszy Rider Records. 'Life Odium' included a cover version of KREATOR's 'Phobia'. Makis of NEGATIVE CREEPS aided in a guest role and former EN-GARDE vocalist Elisabeth Kotronia makes her presence felt on the title track 'Life Odium'.

Live shows throughout 2002 saw supports to SEPTIC FLESH and ROTTING CHRIST in Greece and also the undertaking of gigs in Bulgaria and Rumania. In 2004 the group switched title to INACTIVE MESSIAH, duly signing to Black Lotus Records. The self titled album saw SEPTIC FLESH members guesting, Chris A. appearing on the track 'Marble Smiling Face' and Fotis V. contributing guest vocals to 'Tell Me A Reason'.

INACTIVE MESSIAH, Black Lotus (2004).

INCANTATION

JOHNSTOWN, PA, USA — *Craig Pillard (vocals / guitar), John McEntee (guitar), Ronnie Deo (bass), Jim Roe (drums).*

A highly influential act, Johnstown, Pennsylvania's INCANTATION straddle the borderline between Black and Death Metal. INCANTATION are cited by many of today's acts as being a direct inspiration. INCANTATION came together in August 1989 with a line-up of erstwhile BLOOD THIRSTY DEATH members guitarist Brett Makowski and bassist Aragon Amori, plus ex-REVENANT men John McEntee and Paul Ledney, the latter of whom had also previously performed with G.G. Allin's Connecticut Cocksuckers. As 1990 drew in this line-up cut INCANTATION's inaugural rehearsal demo in January, a tape which included a cover version of HELLHAMMER's 'Third Of The Storm'.

A major fall out occurred with McEntee being left alone as Makowski, Amori and Ledney decamped en masse to found the notorious Black Metal act PROFANATICA releasing a string of highly controversial EPs. That March INCANTATION was citing a line-up of McEntee, bassist Ronnie Deo and the ex-DECAY pairing of guitarist Sal Seijo and drummer Peter Barnevic. The latter two had been located from an ad posted in a local music store whilst Deo had responded to a musicians wanted posting in the 'East Coast Rocker'. In June another set of demos was laid down. At this juncture McEntee was also acting as substitute guitarist for fellow Death Metal unit MORTICIAN. This union prompted MORTICIAN frontman Will Rahmer to act as guest vocalist for the 7" 'Entrantment Of Evil' single. After recording both Seijo and Barnevic would part ways with the band.

By August of the same year INCANTATION was back up to strength having enrolled Bill Venner on guitar and Jim Roe on drums, again located via the 'East Coast Rocker'. Unfortunately Venner's tenure was fleeting although he did provide a worthy service in executing INCANTATION's now familiar logo. As a quartet of Rahmer, McEntee, Deo and Roe Incantation performed at the October 'Day Of Death' festival in Buffalo. Meantime, 'Entrantment Of Evil' had emerged as a violet vinyl 7" in September on the Seraphic Decay label.

November 1990 saw the induction of former PUTREFACT guitarist Craig Pillard. The new guitarist had also issued a series of solo demos accredited to NOCTURNAL CRYPT including a self titled 1987 effort, 'Recrudescence Of ...' in 1988 and a rehearsal tape the following year. The 'Entrantment Of Evil' sessions would be re-issued by Relapse Records in February 1991, limited to 500 red vinyl copies, with a second pressing on regular black vinyl following in May due to demand.

With Rahmer's commitments to MORTICIAN increasing his position was made vacant and Pillard subsequently stepped into the lead vocal role too. This line-up released the single 'Deliverance Of Horrific Prophecies', this November 1991, originally intended as a split EP to be shared with AMORPHIS. This outing was to be their inaugural new product for Relapse Records. The group undertook the its first North American national tour billed alongside ANAL CUNT and PHLEGM. With the dates completed in November 1992 Deo opted out.

INCANTATION brought in ex-CRUCIFER man Dan Kamp on bass for recording of the track 'Emaciated Holy Figure', donated to the track listing of the Nuclear Blast 'Death Is Just The Beginning Volume II' compilation. Further touring would see the band out on the road with AUTOPSY, VITAL REMAINS and MORGUE. However, both Roe and Kamp broke ranks following these shows.

It would be August 1993 when INCANTATION announced the recruitment of a fresh rhythm section in NECROSION bassist Dave Niedrist and DETERIOROT drummer John Brody. With a tour awaiting in the wings and recording of the debut album 'Onward To Golgotha' to be completed the band solved matters by re-employing Roe to handle drums in the studio whilst Brody learnt the material for the live setting.

'Onward To Golgotha', produced by Steve Evetts at Trax East Studios, provided a fresh perspective to the US Death Metal scene, being one of the first high profile albums not to be tarred with the Morrisound / Florida trademarks. Instead, INCANTATION went in for a swarming set of riffs, low register growls corralled by a thick, choking production. Although the record was not by any means a genre cornerstone, it did possess enough individuality to set the band on its way.

'Mortal Throne Of Nazarene' was set as the title of INCANTATION's second album, a self-produced effort engineered by Garris Shipon at Excello Recording Studios in March 1994. However, following INCANTATION's second set and European dates in conjunction with SINISTER and DEADHEAD, frontman Craig Pillard broke away from the group. Before long bassist Ronnie Reo and drummer Jim Roe joined him to found WOMB, an act that evolved into DISCIPLES OF MOCKERY. Competition between DISCIPLES OF MOCKERY and INCANTATION was so fierce by this stage that at the 1994 Deathstock festival in New York Pillard's band played a full set of INCANTATION numbers just before INCANTATION themselves took the stage. Confusion reigned in Death Metal circles when an alternate mix of INCANTATION's 'Mortal Throne Of Nazarene', first issued that November, was re-released under the new title of 'Upon The Throne Of Apocalypse' with a reversed track order and a sticker proclaiming 'Pagan Disciples Of Mockery'!! (Later Pillard's mob became WOMB again but reverted to DISCIPLES OF MOCKERY for the 1999 three track promotion CD).

Amidst all this INCANTATION regrouped enlisting Duane Morris on vocals and guitar for a package tour in alliance with MORGUE, AFTERLIFE, ANAL CUNT and MORPHEUS DESCENDS. MALEVOLENT CREATION were originally slated as headliners but with their cancellation INCANTATION were elevated to headline status. With the tour rolled up the band familiarly fractured yet again, this time Brody and Niedrist bidding their farewell.

INCANTATION relocated entirely to Ohio with only founder member John McEntee creating a completely revised line up. Morris was retained as frontman with ex-BLOOD OF CHRIST bassist Randy Scott and ESCALATION ANGEL man Kyle Severn being recruited on drums.

An American tour with FEAR OF GOD and Swedes GRAVE was nearly curtailed when Scott decided not to go along for the ride. Stoically the band carried on without bass as a trio of McEntee, guitarist Duane Morris and drummer Kyle Severn. In March 1995 Mike Donnelly of DISGORGED teamed up with the band as INCANTATION performed a short tour of Mexico in 1995 sharing a bill with IMMOLATION and ACID BATH. Further confusion followed as Morris then bailed out only to return shortly after. The problem re-occurred halfway through touring as Morris upped and left once again. Daniel Corchado of Mexican acts CENOTAPH and THE CHASM was hastily drafted to complete the dates.

Donnelly was next to leave and INCANTATION took on yet another guise by pulling in bassist Mary Ciullo, MORTICIAN and DEATHRUNE man Mike Saez on guitar and a re-enlisted Will Rahmer on vocals. This unit demoed and put in three shows in New York, Pennsylvania and Cleveland.

In March 1996 McEntee and Severn were joined by MALIGNANCY bassist Kevin Hughes and vocalist / guitarist Nathan Rossi of ROTTREVORE for American dates with MORTICIAN and ANAL CUNT. Rossi would then bow out and former member Craig Pillard took the frontman mantle once again for recording of 'The Forsaken Mourning Of Angelic Anguish'. Mike Saez would also be involved in this line-up on a session basis. Hughes took his leave and once more INCANTATION called on Daniel Corchado, this time acting in the bass role. Tragically that same year former bassist Aragon Amori died.

The October 1997 mini-album, produced by Bill Korecky, features a cover of DEATH's 'Scream Bloody Gore'. Corchado would occupy the frontman spot for a burst of touring and Saez was invited onboard for American touring with VITAL REMAINS and European dates with AVULSED, ADRAMELECH and DEEDS OF FLESH. Saez would be unable to commit to later gigs and so, switching Corchado to guitar INCANTATION performed as a trio minus bass. Despite this ebb and flow of members, the 'Diabolical Conquest' album was released in April 1998 through Roadrunner Records.

In April 1998 Bob Yench, a veteran of MORPHEUS DESCENDS and BRIMSTONE, filled the bass position. INCANTATION set about touring with MORBID ANGEL and VADER but Corchado was obliged to leave mid way through these dates. With an appearance at the 'Milwaukee Metalfest' already booked the band took onboard Tom Stevens as vocalist / guitarist. Stevens had previous credits with SAVAGE DEATH, EXILE, BRIMSTONE, NOKTURNEL and MORPHEUS DESCENDS. This line-up was to undertake further shows in Canada with MORBID ANGEL but Severn was found to be ineligible to cross the Canadian border. Chris Dora of INTEGRITY, SOULLESS and DECREPIT quickly stepped in to save the day.

The band then suffered a major blow was, returning home from a gig in Dallas, Texas, their van overturned. Both McEntee and Severn were badly injured. Following the accident Severn decided to retire from the band. Clay Lytle of FATAL AGGRESSION would occupy the drum stool for INCANTATION's appearance at the 1998 'Chilean Metalfest'. Ranked alongside DEATH and CANNIBAL CORPSE the band performed to over 7'000 South American fans in one night. After the gig Lytle dropped out.

INCANTATION moved bases to Pennsylvania, recruiting a new sticksman Rick Boast of NECROTOMIE. The band hooked up with ANGEL CORPSE and Brazilians KRISIUN for the nationwide American 'Diabolical Extermination' tour before Boast too left. Chris Dora would once again act as stand in for the band's March 1999 'Metal March Meltdown' festival in New Jersey's Asbury Park. In April Mark Perry (a.k.a. 'Tophetareth') of Texan act DEATH OF MILLIONS became the latest in a long line of INCANTATION drummers. A headline tour of Canada ensued after which Perry opted out. In July 1999 Stevens too took his leave in order to resurrect his NOKTURNEL act.

For a batch of dates in Argentina the reliant Chris Dora came in on drums and past member Mike Saez also rejoined as frontman. The 2000 album 'The Infernal Storm' was recorded with session drummer Dave Culross of MALEVOLENT CREATION and the band pulled in DEATH, CONTROL DENIED and ICED EARTH man Richard Christy for tour work.

Ex-drummer Kyle Severn was back in the fold by August 2000 for American gigs with NILE and IMPALED. Severn also involved himself with the high profile WOLFEN SOCIETY project featuring ACHERON's Vincent Crowley, VITAL REMAINS singer Jeff Gruslin and DARK FUNERAL guitarist Lord Ahriman. Severn would also perform gigs with ACHERON and commit to studio sessions for a single.

INCANTATION geared up for a month long tour of the States in early 2001 in alliance with IMMOLATION and GOATWHORE. However, the dates would be abruptly curtailed at a gig in Queens, New York. The band's van was broken into outside the Voodoo Lounge venue before the show then various band members and friends became embroiled in a vicious fight. Saez had stepped in to prevent a fight involving his former DEATHRUNE band mate Chris Shaw. As it turned out Shaw was stabbed in the back and face no less than seven times. The intervening Saez also received major wounds to his arm. Another friend Pete Schulz also received deep lacerations to the arm.

The attacker fled from the venue but was chased and caught by Kyle Severn who apprehended the man and held him until police caught up with him. The injuries to Saez were so severe that the tour was cancelled. Saez would later be rushed into hospital at a later date with stomach pains but would make a full recovery.

INCANTATION switched labels from Relapse to Necropolis and put in a series of hugely successful Brazilian shows with a guesting REBAELLION in May of 2001 after which Yench decided to exit the band. The Sao Paulo gig would be recorded, albeit only from the soundboard, for a live album 'Live—Blasphemy In Brazil 2001'. Released by Mutilation Records it would be limited to 2000 copies all of which quickly sold out. Joe Lombard took over bass for a set of German dates in August.

Planned touring of Europe for February of 2002 backed up by INFERNAL POETRY and INIQUITY was postponed when Severn suffered a back injury. The group would embark on a further round of American dates, headlined by CANNIBAL CORPSE and billed alongside DARK FUNERAL and PISSING RAZORS, commencing on the 24th April in Los Angeles. A new studio album, 'Blasphemy' produced by Bill Korecky, arrived in June upfront of a headline North American trek billed as the 'Summer of Blasphemy' tour packaged with IMPALED, DECAPITATED and FALL TO DEAD. These dates would kick off on July 25th at the Al Rosa Villa venue in Columbus, Ohio with later shows on the schedule adding DRAGONLORD to the bill. Major news arrived shortly after the confirmation of these dates as Vincent Crowley of ACHERON and WOLFEN SOCIETY had joined the band. Further gigs had the band headlining throughout Europe in August with support from PANDEMIA.

In February of 2003 the band inducted new guitarist Lou 'Sonny Lombardozzi' as John McEntee took over the lead vocal role. Lombardozzi was noted for his dexterity in playing both left handed and right handed on a unique double headed guitar.

In this formation the group undertook the 'Rotting With Your Christ' US tour that month partnered with PUNGENT STENCH, BEYOND THE EMBRACE and RUNE. INCANTATION struck New Zealand and Australia in June but would be involved in a high speed car crash on their way to a gig in Bexley, Australia. Severn, McEntee and Lombardozzi were all injured albeit not seriously. However, Kyle Severn's chest injuries forced him out of a scheduled appearance at the 'Bloodlust' festival in Sydney. Local bands rallied to support so INCANTATION could perform a shortened set with PSYCROPTIC's Dave Haley standing in on three songs whilst ASTRIAAL man Gryphon took on 'Ibex Moon', a song his band had been performing live as a cover. INCANTATION recovered to embark upon their Summer 'Rotting With Your Christ' US dates allied with FUNERUS and DISGORGE. Both McEntee and Severn would be doubling live duties with FUNERUS, actually the band mentored by McEntee's wife and bass player Jill. South American gigs in November found INCANTATION shifting shape once more, inducting Thomas Pioli of HEMLOCK, CEREMONIUM and OBLITERATION repute. This would be a re-recruitment for Pioli, who had earlier played bass guitar for INCANTATION's 1992 'Onward To Golgotha' dates.

INCANTATION signed a deal with France's Listenable Records in early 2004 for European licensing and, shortly after, announced signature with Olympic Records for the USA. The band entered the Mars Recording Compound in Cleveland, Ohio with producer Bill Korecky on 5th March to track their eighth full length album 'Decimate Christendom' scheduled for early July release. European shows that November dubbed the 'Clash Of Demigods' saw the band forming up a package billing with KRISIUN, RAGNAROK and BEHEMOTH. However, Kyle Severn was forced to withdraw from these gigs due to the unexpected death of his mother. Filling in on drums for the tour will be Ilmar Uibo from the French Black Metal band BLOODY SIGN.

To open 2005 the band hooked up with THE CHASM, MORTICIAN and ARSIS for the 'Winter Migration Broootality' US tour commencing early January. The band's next road alliance, suitably dubbed 'European Decimation', took in April gigs throughout Italy, Portugal, the UK, Holland and Germany in partnership with CATASTROPHIC, FUNERUS, JUNGLE ROT and HEXENHAMMER. INCANTATION then formed up with a Summer package touring bill comprising HATE ETERNAL, KRISIUN, INTO ETERNITY and ALL SHALL PERISH for US gigs in June. However due to "legal issues" the band was forced to skip the Canadian dates of this trek, instead filling the gap with East Coast shows supported by CIRCLE OF DEAD CHILDREN and ESTUARY. Lombardozzi subsequently worked with FLESHTIZED and CASTRATION.

Gigs in Poland during September saw support from GORTAL and SPHERE.

Gigs in Mexico during February 2006 saw Roberto Lizárraga of INFINITUM OBSCURE installed on bass guitar. Bill Korecky and the band cut tracks for a new album at Mars Recording Compound during April/May. US shows commencing in late May had INCANTATION hooked up with VITAL REMAINS, SIN OF ANGELS and New Zealanders DAWN OF AZAZEL. The group then announced the "Decimate Spain" shows in July flanking IRREDEMPTION, after which further sessions were conducted on seventh album 'Primordial Domination'.

Relapse Records re-issued the classic 'Onward To Golgotha' in October, adding a DVD comprising three full live sets from the 1992 line-up. INCANTATION, backed by INTERNAL SUFFERING and YEAR OF DESOLATION, opened up another lengthy US tour commencing November 1st 2006 at the Modern Exchange in Southgate, Michigan.

The band joined a heavyweight casting of CARPATHIAN FOREST, MALEVOLENT CREATION, HARM, ROTTING CHRIST and NEURAXIS for the 'Domination' European tour, commencing on February 14th 2007 at the Warsaw Progresja venue in Poland before hitting Germany, Austria, the Czech Republic, Italy, Belgium, France and Holland. For these shows, former INCANTATION member Jim Roe filled in for drummer Kyle Severn.

Incantation, Incantation (1990) (Rehearsal demo). Profanation / Unholy Massacre / Third Of The Storms.

Demo #1, Incantation (1990) (Demo). Profanation / Devoured Death / Entrantment Of Evil / Eternal Torture.

Entrantment Of Evil, Seraphic Decay SCAM 003 (1990). Entrantment Of Evil / Eternal Torture / Devoured Death / Unholy Massacre.

Deliverance Of Horrific Prophecies EP, Relapse RR 012 (1991). Deliverance of Horrific Prophecies / Profanation.

ONWARD TO GOLGOTHA, Relapse RR 6037-4 (1992) (Cassette Release). Golgotha / Devoured Death / Blasphemous Creation / Rotting Spiritual Embodiment / Unholy Massacre / Entrantment Of Evil / Christening The Afterbirth / Immortal Cessation / Profanation / Deliverance Of Horrific Prophecies.

ONWARD TO GOLGOTHA, Relapse RR 6037-2 (1992). Golgotha / Devoured Death / Blasphemous Creation / Rotting Spiritual Embodiment / Unholy Massacre / Entrantment Of Evil / Christening The Afterbirth / Immortal Cessation / Profanation / Deliverance Of Horrific Prophecies / Eternal Torture.

MORTAL THRONE OF NAZARENE, Relapse RR 6905-2 (1994). Demonic Incarnate / Emaciated Holy Figure / Iconclasm Of Catholicism / Essence Ablaze / Nocturnal Dominium / The Ibex Moon / Blissful Bloodshower / Abolishment Of Immaculate Serenity.

UPON THE THRONE OF APOCALYPSE, Relapse RR 6922-2 (1996) (Limited edition 1000 copies). Abolishment Of Immaculate Serenity / Blissful Bloodshower / Ibex Moon / Nocturnal Dominium / Essence Ablaze / Iconoclasm Of Catholicism / Emaciated Holy Figure / Demonic Incarnate.

The Forsaken Mourning Of Angelic Anguish, Repulse RPS020CD (1997). Shadows From The Ancient Empire / Lusting Congregation Of Perpetual Damnation (Eternal Eden) / Triumph In Blasphemy (Interlude) / The Forsaken Mourning Of Angelic Anguish / Scream Bloody Gore / Twisted Sacrilegious Journey Into The Darkest Neurotic Delirium / Outro.

TRIBUTE TO THE GOAT, Elegy ER02 (1997). Devoured Death / Profanation / Unholy Massacre / Blissful / United in Repugnance / Nefarious Warriors / Twisted Sacrilegious Journey Into Our Darkest Neurotic Delirium / Abomination / Devoured Death / Entrantment Of Evil / Eternal Torture / Profanation.

THE FORSAKEN MOURNING OF ANGELIC ANGUISH, Relapse RR 6974-2 (1997). Shadows From The Ancient Empire / Lusting Congregation Of Perpetual Damnation (Extreme Eden) / Triumph In Blasphemy (Interlude) / Forsaken Mourning Of Angelic Anguish / Scream Bloody Gore / Twisted Sacrilegious Journey Into The Darkest Neurotic Delirium / Outro / The Ibex Moon / Blasphemous Cremation / Essence Ablaze / Blissful Bloodshower.

DIABOLICAL CONQUEST, Incantation RR 6982-2 (1998). Impending Diabolical Conquest / Desecration (Of The Heavenly Graceful) / Disciples Of Blasphemous Reprisal / Unheavenly Skies / United In Repugnance / Shadows Of The Ancient Empire / Ethereal Misery / Unto Infinite Twilight—Majesty Of Infernal Damnation.

THE INFERNAL STORM, Relapse RR 6442-2 (2000). Anoint The Chosen / Extinguishing Salvation / Impetuous Rage / Sempiternal Pandemonium / Lustful Demise / Heaven Departed / Apocalyptic Destroyer Of Angels / Nocturnal Kingdom Of Demonic Enlightenment.

THE INFERNAL STORM, Moria MO 3 (2000) Brazilian release). Anoint The Chosen / Extinguishing Salvation / Impetuous Rage / Sempiternal Pandemonium / Lustful Demise / Heaven Departed / Apocalyptic Destroyer Of Angels / Nocturnal Kingdom Of Demonic Enlightenment / Hell Awaits.

LIVE—BLASPHEMY IN BRAZIL TOUR 2001, Mutilation MUT 013 (2002) (Limited edition of 2000). Intro / Anoint The Chosen / Unholy Massacre / Shadows From The Ancient Empire / The Ibex Moon / Ethereal Misery / Forsaken Mourning Of Angelic Anguish / Apocalyptic Destroyer Of Angels / Devoured Death / Essence Ablaze / Disciples Of Blasphemous Reprisal / Blissful Blood Shower / Sempiternal Pandemonium / Profanation / Impending Diabolical Conquest / Lustful Demise / Deliverance Of Horrific Prophecies.

BLASPHEMY, Necropolis NR073 (2002). Blasphemy / The Fallen / A Once Holy Throne / Crown Of Decayed Salvation / Rotting With Your Christ / His Weak Hand / The Sacrilegious Apocalypse Of Righteousness And Agonizing Dementia (The Final Defilement Of Your Lord) / Deceiver (Self-Righteous Betrayer) / Descend Seraphic Irreverence / Uprising Heresy / Misanthropic Indulgence / Outro (Part 1) / Outro (Part 2).

Relapse Singles Series Vol. 3, Relapse RR 6588-2 (2004) (Split release with ROTTREVORE, REPULSION & MONSTROSITY). Deliverance Of Horrific Prophecies / Profanation.

DECIMATE CHRISTENDOM, Listenable POSH060 (2004). Decimate Christendom / Dying Divinity / Oath Of Armageddon / Blaspheme The Sacraments / Merciless Tyranny / Horns Of Eradication / Unholy Empowerment Of Righteous Deprivation / Thorns Of Everlasting Persecution / No Paradise Awaits / Eternal Darkness Under Conquered Skies / Feeble Existence / Exiling Righteousness.

PRIMORDIAL DOMINATION, Ibex Moon (2006). Primordial Domination / The Fallen Priest / Dissolute Rule / Begin Apocalypse / Hailed Babylon / Lead To Desolation / Doctrines Of Reproach / The Stench Of Crucifixion / Extirpated Dominus / Conquered God.

INCAPACITY

SKÖVDE, SWEDEN — *Andreas Axelsson (vocals), Christian Älvestam (guitar), Robert Ivarsson (guitar), Anders Edlund (bass), Henrik Schönström (drums).*

INCAPACITY, established during 2002, is a Skövde based heavyweight amalgam of Swedish Death Metal talent. Featured would be EDGE OF SANITY and INFESTDEAD lead vocalist Andreas "Dread" Axelsson, UNMOORED and SOLAR DAWN guitarist Christian Älvestam, PAN-THY-MONIUM and ASHES guitarist Robert Ivarsson, SOLAR DAWN bassist Anders Edlund with the UNMOORED, SOLAR DAWN and TRAUMATIZED credited Henrik Schönström on drums. The industrious Älvestam has an extended roll call of band endeavours such as CARNAL-IZED, ANDUIN '98, EVENDIM, LORD OF THRONES, ORGY OF FLESH, SATTYG, RED SKIES DAWNING, THE STINK BUG COLLECTIVE and DEN TIDLÖSA EVIGHETEN.

The debut 2003 'Chaos Complete' album was produced by CARNAL FORGE frontman Jonas Kjellgren. A June 2004 INCAPACITY album '9th Order Extinct', was recorded at Soundlab Studios in Örebro with producer Mieszko. For a one off gig on 1st October at the Belsepub in Gothenburg supporting IMPIOUS the band would be fronted by THE CROWN frontman Johan Lindstrand. That same year Christian Älvestam would be found fronting Jonas Kjellgren's SCAR SYMMETRY band for their 'Symmetric In Design' debut.

In December 2005 INCAPACITY would be joined on vocals by the high profile figure of Johan Lindstrand of ONE MAN ARMY AND THE UNDEAD QUARTET, also formerly of THE CROWN and IMPIOUS. Lindstrand also guested on Austrian Death Metal band DECOMPOSED CRANIUM's third album, 'Death Roulette'. Christian Älvestam donated guest vocals to ZONARIA's 2006 debut album 'Rendered In Vain', featuring on the track 'Attending Annihilation'.

CHAOS COMPLETE, Cold (2003). Reptillian Breed / Third Degree Suffering / Amputate God / Demon King / Paradise Crushed / Fervent Hate / Cancerchrist / Deathcrush / Injection Divine / Faceshifters.

9TH ORDER EXTINCT, Metal Blade (2004). Wide Of The Mark / Grand Future Disease / Winged With Fire / File Under Torture / Cross-Fixed / Shadows Of The Watcher / Christless Ways / Infinite Time Decay / A Plague Of Their Own / Overdose On Purity.

INCARNATE

KANNUS, FINLAND — *Markus Tavasti (vocals), Juha Kellokoski (guitar), Jukka Kiviniemi (bass), Lasse Löytynoja (drums).*

INCARNATE is a Kannus based Death Metal band dating to 1999. Promotion releases included 'Deathsigns' in 2003 and a 2004 set 'Expectations Of Exhumation'. Originally the band operated as a duo with Lasse Löytynoja, of YDIN, ARSKA and GESCHÜSZTURM, handling vocals and drums with Jussi Yli-Korpela on guitar. Subsequently Markus Tavasti, another ARSKA and GESCHÜSZTURM veteran, was enrolled on lead vocals then second guitarist Juha Kellokoski of ZOMBIE VOMIT. INCARNATE underwent further changes in 2002, adding Jukka Kiviniemi of NONSENSE on bass guitar but losing co-founder Yli-Korpela, the guitar spot being filled by Kalle Niskala to record 'Deathsigns'. Prior to the second session 'Expectations Of Exhumation' INCARNATE dropped Niskala from the ranks, the erstwhile guitarist duly founding DEVIL'S OWN.

Lasse Löytynoja and Markus Tavasti would also be active with ZOMBIE VOMIT. The singer also held membership of GOATDOMAIN and KURALUTKU.

Deathsigns, Incarnate (2003). Keeper Of The Undead / Haunted Be Thy Grave / Stained In Blood / Deathsigns.

Expectations Of Exhumation, Incarnate (2004). A Threat To End Of Life / Demented / Post-Chaos Sundown / Dead Corpse Incarnation.

INCENDIUM

VAASA, FINLAND — *Aki Hahto (vocals), Hannu Perälä (guitar), Antti Haapala (guitar), Mika Hirvikoski (bass), Petri Kahra (keyboards), Henna Sjöberg (violin), Otto Väisänen (drums).*

Vaasa Death Metal act INCENDIUM published the February 1999 'Incendium' demo as their opening gambit. The group had previously operated as BLACK SHRINE, releasing a 1998 demo, recorded at Test Music Studios, under this formative title. The name switch came with the departure of former members singer Juha and guitarist Toni. Regrouping, the unit drew in three new musician singer Aki Hahto, guitarist Unski and keyboard player Jarno. Upon completion of the 'Incendium' sessions, drummer Hannu Perälä opted out, being replaced by Teemu. However, the band stalled in 2000 with the exit of both Unski and Jarno.

Keyboard player Petri Kahra joined the fold in mid 2001, Perälä returned in the guitar role and Otto Väisänen took on drum duties. The 2004 'After Silence' demo, laid down at Black Room studios, followed. Drummer Otto Väisänen would be found as a member of Industrial Metal endeavour RADICAL M PROJECT during 2003, involving ALL IN ME vocalist / guitarist Esa Uusimaa, DIECELL guitarist Sami Puolakka, former THROES OF DAWN bass player Matti Suomela with SHADEMBRACE singer Jenny Malmberg.

INCENDIUM released the 'When Daylight Is Gone' demo in 2005. A further effort, 'Crawling Quietly', followed in June 2006.

Incendium, Incendium (1999). The Meaning / Hate Guides My Way / Far Away / Wind Is My Breath.
After Silence, (2003). Drowning In You / Crush / Life Sarcasm / Wither.
When Daylight Is Gone, (2005). Devastated Life / Stoned / Weak / Letter.
Crawling Quietly, Incendium (2006) (Demo). Infection / Sad One In The Mirror / Sum Of Misery / Entity / Black Hole.

INCESTUOUS

CA, USA — *Matti Way (vocals), Danny Louise (guitar), Mike Dooley (bass), Rick Myers (drums).*

INCESTUOUS was an act founded in 1999 by ex-GORGASM drummer Derek Hoffman. A series of line up changes led to the solo INCESTUOUS release 'Brass Knuckle Abortion' after which the band opted for a name change to CINERARY. Personnel at this point were ex-DYSPHORIA vocalist 'Sick' Nick Hernandez, former SMEGMA and CUMCHRIST guitarist Danny Louise ('Wrench'), Mike Dooley from CORPSE VOMIT on bass. Following recording of the album former DISGORGE vocalist Matti Way took the role of frontman. Founder member Hoffman had rejoined GORGASM in January 2001 and INCESTUOUS plugged the gap with Ricky Myers of DISGORGE.

Wrench also operates BRETHREN with ex-INCESTUOUS and DYSPHORIA vocalist 'Sick' Nick Hernandez, Jeff and Jim from CIANIDE and Nefarious of MACABRE.

BRASS KNUCKLE ABORTION, United Guttural (1999). In Blasphemous Tongue / Flesh Enslaved / Ethnic Cleansing / Desolation / Infanticide / Brass Knuckle Abortion / Nailed Unmercifully.

INCREDIBLE PAIN

OSNABRÜCK, GERMANY — *Patrick Bankmann (vocals), Markus Speckmann (guitar), Kai Pohlmann (bass), Björn Eder (drums).*

Bremen and Osnabrück Death Metal band INCREDIBLE PAIN began life in 2001 as LAWBREAKER. The band's first formation counted two vocalists, Patrick Bankmann and Marco Wietelmann, guitarist Markus Speckmann and drummer Björn Eder. In February of 2002 this roster was expanded with the introduction of Kai Gevers on bass, later replaced by Kai Pohlmann.

INCREDIBLE PAIN debuted with the February 2003 demo 'Enter The Realms Of Pain', produced by Lars Brokob at NFZ Tonstudio Sulingen. The band recorded their debut, self financed album 'Screaming In Agony' produced by Torsten Sauerbrey, at Metalsound Studios in Osterode during April of 2004.

Enter The Realms Of Pain, (2003). No Time To Waste . . . / Future Fear / War / Jack The Ripper / You Will Die Now . . . / No Salvation.
SCREAMING IN AGONY, Incredible Pain (2004). Collateral Damage / Painstorming / Killer / Black Death / Heart Of A Nation / T.O.S. / Witchhunt / This Pain / Sniper Attack / Nights Of Fear.

INCUBATOR

OLDENBURG, GERMANY — *Chris Mummelthey (vocals), Sven Schade (guitar), Michael Hahn (guitar), Steve Becker (bass), Dominique (drums).*

An Oldenburg in Holstein Death Metal band with an offbeat sense of humour, INCUBATOR, founded by ANGER guitarist Michael Hahn and SCHIZOPHRENIA frontman Christian Mummelthey, debuted in 1990 with a self-titled demo. A second demo 'No Aggression', followed. The group, expanding to incorporate second guitarist Sven Schade, bassist Stefan Becker and drummer Dominique Thomsen, signed to West Virginia Records for the 1991 album 'Symphonies Of Spiritual Cannibalism'. The band engaged ex-HOLY MOSES man Andy Classen to produce, who also took the reins for 1992's concept outing 'McGillroy The Housefly'. That same year Michael Hahn and Sven Schade also put out the STONEHANGE side project opus 'Death Is The Crown Of All'. A membership shift saw the departure of Michael Hahn and bassist Steve Becker. INCUBATOR drafted replacements drummer Kim Sievers and bass player Marcel Wroblewski respectively.

The third album, 1993's 'Hirnnektar' recorded at Stage One Studio for Steamhammer Records, is notable for featuring a cover of PINK FLOYD's 'Set The Controls For The Heart Of The Sun'. Tragically drummer Dominique Thomsen committed suicide in 1995.

The 'MCMETALXCVIII' album, recorded at Rosenquartz Studio, followed in 2000, for new label Chameleon Records. INCUBATOR at this juncture saw Mummelthey joined by Wroblewski, having switched to lead guitar, second guitarist Stefan Volkmann, bassist Stefan Hoppe with Michael May on drums. 'Divine Comedy', issued via Godz Greed and featuring keyboards courtesy of Christof F., arrived the following year.

Frontman Christian Mummelthey subsequently founded the Industrial edged Grindcore band THE SIXTH INCUBATOR, releasing 'Live-Reincarnation-Ground-Zero' in 2002, 'The Skullcrusher Sessions' EP' in 2003 and 'Inphonoir' during 2003.

Christian Mummelthey re-activated INCUBATOR in August 2006 drawing in Axel Boldt on drums, DEFORMITY bassist Wolf and SUBCUTANE's Oliver on guitar. Shortly afterwards ex-INCUBATOR man Stefan Hoppe joined SUBCUTANE. The new April 2007 roster involved guitarist Marcel Wroblewski, bass player Wolfgang Snijders and drummer Axel Boldt.

McGILLROY THE HOUSEFLY, West Virginia WVR 84-57242 (1992). Thinkin' Green—Believe In Grey / Prisons Of Gore / (No Name) / Raped By A Stranger / Chaos Ego / Identität / Stories Enter Controlled Dept / Brain Eliminator / Games Of A Moon murder / Forced / Playing A Game . . . .
HIRNNEKTAR, Steamhammer SPV 084-76732 (1993). Taste Yourself / Leben / Spiritätze / Words Can't Hurt / And I Live In Between / S.K.S. Syndrom / So Sad (In The Mind Of Us All / Set The Controls For The Heart Of The Sun / Your Life Is Done.
MCMETALXCVIII, Godz Greed (2000). Resist / Inc. Murdering / Hirnnektar / Bio Shock / Pray / Fear 2 Fear / 666 x 3 / Gillroys House / Hard Heart / Gods Greed.

INCUBUS

TAMPA, FL, USA — *Sterling Von Scarborough (vocals / bass), Gino Marino (guitar), Mike Browning (drums).*

Florida's short-lived INCUBUS featured NOCTURNUS and MORBID ANGEL drummer Mike Browning. The band's April 1987 demo 'God Died On His Knees' would also be pressed up as a 7" single the following year. Frontman Sterling Von Scarborough featured as bassist on MORBID ANGEL's 1991 album 'Abominations Of Desolation' and guitarist Gino Marino, previously with TERROR, also figured in the 1992 version of MORBID ANGEL. Previous to Scarborough's enrollment into MORBID ANGEL a formative version of INCUBUS existed in Georgia with Scarborough in league with Steve 'Skellator' Shoemaker and drummer Rich Fuscia.

By 1993 Scarborough, in union with guitarist Danny Klein and old comrade Rich Fuscia had founded USURPER. Subsequently Scarborough had a further stab at resurrecting INCUBUS. The early INCUBUS recordings found their way onto a bootleg compilation 'Harmony Dies Vol. I' alongside rare NECROVORE and MORBID ANGEL tracks.

In 1995 Sterling Von Scarborough, under the pseudonym 'Nocticula', published a demo, restricted to just 66 copies, under the banner LIBER NOCTICULA.

God Died On His Knees, (1989). God Died On His Knees / Reanimator's Multilation / Engulfed In Unspeakable Horror.

INEARTHED

ESPOO, FINLAND — *Alexi Laiho (vocals / guitar), Alexander*

Kuoppala (guitar), Henkka Seppala (bass), Jani Pera Pirisjoki (keyboards), Jaska W. Raatikainen (drums).

INEARTHED was the proto-version of CHILDREN OF BODOM, a powerful, modern Metal act from the town of Espoo, named after Finland's infamous Lake Bodom, the scene of a horrific, unsolved attack in 1960 that left three teenagers dead. Founder member and vocalist Alex Laiho made his name as part of THY SERPENT, maintaining CHILDREN OF BODOM, created in 1993 with drummer Jaska Raatikainen, as a going concern. Initially the group had gone under the title of INEARTHED, issuing a batch of melodic Death Metal demos commencing with 'Implosion Of Heaven', recorded at Munkkiniemen Studios in August of 1994 and released that December. These tracks would be laid down as a duo of Laiho and Raatikainen.

INEARTHED followed this opening tape with second set 'Ubiquitous Absence Of Remission' in July of 1995, recording this time at Astia Studios. Interestingly, melodies from the track 'Translucent Image', which featured female guest vocals from Nina Keitel, would re-surface in SINERGY's 'Beware The Heavens' at a later date. Once again composed and performed by Laiho and Raatikainen, the tape does make mention of bassist Samuli Miettinen and new member rhythm guitarist Alexander Kuoppala. A third demo, entitled 'Shining', was committed to tape at Astia Studios in February 1996 utilising keyboard player Jan Peri Pirisjoki. A line-up change found bassist Samuli Miettinen superseded by Henkka Seppala.

As INEARTHED the group scored a label deal in Belgium but a better offer from the highly respected Finnish Spinefarm concern convinced the band their way. At this stage the band, now with Janne Wirman Pimeys on keyboards, switched title to CHILDREN OF BODOM recording the 'Something Wild' debut.

Besides their high profile activities with CHILDREN OF BODOM Laiho has also racked up credits with SINERGY and IMPALED NAZARENE whilst Raatikainen has figured as a member of VIRTUOCITY.

Implosion Of Heaven, Inearthed (1994). Chaos / Shards Of Truth / Implosion Of Heaven / Tss, Ahh!!!

Ubiquitous Absence Of Remission, (1995). Intro / Translucent Image / Possessed / Shamed.

Shining, (1996). Talking Of The Trees (Sanctuary) / Vision Of Eternal Sorrow / Homeland / Homeland II: Shining (The 4th Kingdom).

INEVITABLE END

JÖNKÖPING, SWEDEN — *Andreaz Hansen (vocals), Joakim Malmborg (guitar), Emil Westerdahl (bass), Christoffer Johansson (drums).*

Christian Death Metal band INEVITABLE END hail from Jönköping. The group was forged during 2003, first putting down demos onto tape in April the following year. Line-up problems then struck, with singer Magnus Semerson and bassist Joakim Bergqvist both exiting. Ex-guitarist Jonas Arvidsson going on to session for CRIMSON MOONLIGHT. New frontman would be Norwegian Andreaz Hansen of BLEEDIENCE and VIXIVI.

INEVITABLE END, promoting the demo 'Reversal', joined forces with fellow Swedish Metal artists AVATAR and SONIC SYNDICATE for the 'Sweden United–Metal' tour commencing in late January 2006. The band performed at the Halmstad, Sweden Christian Metal Endtime Festival in March 2007 alongside CRIMSON MOONLIGHT, ANTESTOR, DROTTNAR, EVERGRACE, HARMONY, VENI DOMINE, VARDOGER, VIRGIN FOREST and EXTOL.

Inevitable End, Inevitable End (2004) (Demo). Redeemed By Fire / End Of All Battles / Parade Of Chaos.

Reversal, Inevitable End (2005) (Demo). Redintegration / Past Darkness / Indweller.

INFAMY

LOS ANGELES, CA, USA — *Joshua Heatley (vocals / bass), Memo Mora (guitar), Mark Casillas (guitar), James Brijalva (drums).*

Los Angeles Death Metal INFAMY made their first impressions upon the scene with the September 1995 demo 'Count The Dead'. The band undertook a Midwest tour aligned with WICKED INNOCENCE, CREMATORIUM and COFFIN TEXTS during 1996. The debut album 'The Blood Shall Flow' arrived in mid 1997. Mark Casillas of INSIDIOUS joined the band after this release. Frontman Joshua 'Jagger' Heatley died in March of 1998. Tragically, his replacement, Daryl Parvin, died in February 2003.

The band entered Shiva Industries with producer Matt Fisher, ex-MINDROT and EYES OF FIRE, in December 2004 to record the demo 'Gates Of Purgatory'. At this juncture INFAMY comprised vocalist / bassist Robert Cardenas of DIABOLIC, COFFIN TEXTS, ENGRAVE and ENTITY repute, ex-ENTITY guitarist James Grijalva and drummer Mark Casillias. Line-up changes in June of 2005 saw Hans Faber of UNSANCTIFIED taking over the bass position from Cardenas. However, Faber was out of the picture within weeks.

THE BLOOD SHALL FLOW, Qabalah Productions QAB005 (1998). The Maggots Are In Me / Bodily Disembowelment / Onslaught Of Carnage / Cranial Implosion / Putrid Infestation / Salem's Burning / Mass Cremation / Lacerated / The Blood Shall Slow / Cryptobiaosis.

INFECTED PUSSY

FRANCE — A Grindcore act with a sense of humour. INFECTED PUSSY have shared cassette releases with SUBLIME CADAVERIC DECOMPOSITION, Poland's SQUASH BOWELS and DEAD INFECTION as well as a four way demo with ORAL CLIMAX, TERMINAL 8 and DISOBEY.

Despite being limited to a 7 vinyl single format INFECTED PUSSY managed to cram over 50 songs onto their 'Touch Me' release.

INFECTED PUSSY purport to comprise band members entitled "Hot Dog Hamburger Of Anal Shit Decomposition In The Woods Of Fukai", "Ultra Creator Of Space Sounds From The Dark Ages Of Shintoigerbatose Since The Beginning Of Noise In Japan", "Manga Perversion On TV Lover Of Sex Sins In The Era Of Cum199x", "Silence Of The Celtic Wind In Winter And I Can Fly In The Space Like The Spoutnik (Verizmikroparrtou)" and "Lancelot The Pipoting King Of Lucum And Master Of Pizza Hut".

Touch Me EP, Panx Productions (1996). The Spoutnik In Your Cunt (Aygemalle V) / Why Should My Anus Vomit? / Bananapizza / Knorr Periodic Bloody Infusion (Qu'est-ce Que Tu Nous Mijotes Encore?) / Punk As Drunk (Or As Ardilouze) / Ougl !!! (Satan: Keep All In Your Fuckin' Mouth, Please) / Attack Of The Azantac (Phil Is Proud Again To Have A New Treatment) / Ulsirous Teisseire (Si T'es Sport, T'es Sirop Chlore) / Cool Tie-Dye Shirt ! (No, It's Sperm) / Du Bekommst Eine Nulle!! / Couscous Of Sand / Basilic Instinct / Do You Want A Big Stick, Pal? / Impaled On A Cactus / Footfucking: A Nike Air 180 (size 52) In Your Hole / Destroy Carrefour As Pearl Harbour / The S Of Space (Cake) / Batman For Saturday Night Fever (With Robinou) / Fight The Balls Of The Dragon / I Like Uro-Guro / Starsky And Hutch On The Periph (Horrible Accident: Sabotage) / Spermicide Ice Cream, Spermicide Scream / Why Can't The Fetus Shit? / Do You Remember D.N.S.? (Masterdedicace) / M.S. Means: Miss Senegal, Master of Sodomy, Moule de Souris, Michel Sardou, Monica Seles, But Not Meat Shits (If You Have Found Over Anagrams, Don't Hesitate To Send Us Them Quickly) / Repainting The Toilets With Undigerated Choucroute / Agathoricles (Make Me Free) / T.G.V.: The Green Vulva / Staying A Larve / Snesni Nasx / Ya Mo. Fuck Miaou!!! / Gastric Dunk, Plastic Funk / Necrophil's Stomach (Aygemalle VI) / The Tits Can Travel / Bejour, Bejour … / … In The Wind Total / Pyromania Shoesman / I Am Crade / Prout On The Train / Rent A Car (En Sac) / The Fabulous Return Of Leguman (My Hero) / Asterocarotte / Es Kuzededer Ange! / Miaou Miam Crokette Plouf, Chacha Kosto / TVAss / Shit In My Kalbut: The Night Was Hot! / The Siamois Are Making Caca In The Same Time / Ken The Survivor Kills Albator (In

Monopoly) / I Like The Blak Metol As Much As Folklo Country Music / Salut Dibool / Stinky Kindy / Zizi Pipi Fini: Ziiiiiiiippppp.

INFECTED PUSSY, Flesh Feast Productions (1999) (Split album with MUCUPURULENT). Your Cunt Is My Oyster / Overzealous Cops / Lady Di Crashed Down (High Prized Coffin Offered By Mercedes) / Welcome In France: Your Pass Now / You Are A Pitoufos (Cenkorloingrenschtroumpfeuh?) / Tim & Sprittou / Nasal Diarrhoea (With Gluing Things, Ya Know?) / Liquid Shit (With Stinking Things, Ya Know?) / Best TV Sluts Election (Or Who's Miss [Add Here The Name Of Your Country]) / Fresh Krem(lin) / Spermshower / Elastic Cunt / Straddling Legs In The Summer Tube (Wet Underwear) / Abnormal Facial Proeminence / You Thought It Was A Flatulence (But You Shit On You) / Experimentations In Excrementations (Dr. Uro Sez Ya) / Fist Fucked Yourself To The End / Pornart In My Mind / Buy In Intercourse (Come Down Supermarket) / Hardboiled Yeggs (Will Understand Who Want To . . .) / Can You Die 'Coz Of A Nightmare? / Campagne For Champain / Brontosoidal Dick / Debilus Profondis / GfaimGfroidGenvideferpipiGsquad (TAGUEULE!!!) / Kan-s-skonsaret? / Ferrarillusions / AsteroHdentagueul!! / Retrocketpunch / Fatal Dersch / Menthol Lesion / Mr. T For Tantouze / Pegaze Is A Ridiculous Name (Pet & Gaz) / www.losers.com / A Poireau In The Ass (Walking Down The Street) / Mornings Erections / Ambidexstral Masturbation / Anused & Virgined / Spoke To Me! (Yes Captain) / Mental Distortions Shocking Conformists / Black Pus (Under A Tooth) / AAAAALLLAAARRRMMMM!!!! / Totalitariracismu$$ / Dr. Molotov (Absolut Dangerous) / Revitalising Abdoul's Virility / Maked Up Girls On TV, Big Headed Sluts Everyday / Bidibulle's Party (Metamorphosis Partouzation) / Finedenzidizenmanatraktive? / Pumar Extravaganza / 'Till I Get Enough . . . Continue The Torture / Spirit Of A Gouine / Intergalactical Rave / No Doubt: You Stink Cheez' / Let Me Be The Arm Handling The Knife / Next Victim Please / Panic In The Cine (Satyr Acts) / I've Killed My Angel / Caracterial Thrashes / Choregraphies For MTV / Rape The System / A Cross Between The Boops And Lies Between The Lips / Motherfuckers' Legions / City R n' R Orchestra / Awards For Cowards / Double Abdominal Female Muscles / No Pills Guy / Stations' Security / Passionaked / Yang Tse Swimming Bad / One Finger On Keyboard Music (Radio Teen'aged Music) / Let Me Hit Your Corpse / Paranoid Imagination / Madonnass / Guys With Suits / We Are The Slamming Gaulois!! / Doc Marteen's Massage (We're Old On Stage) / Carsher Shower / Jtechidsu!! / Pineball (Hitcouzinhit) / A-larm!!!! / Rotten Bollox And Putrefied Dick / A Verruca On The Top . . . / Malozabdopipiododo / Bourrinman / Infected Pussy / Harshiterrorizenucleatedistortionoize.

INFERIA

LAHTI, FINLAND — *Jani Huttunen (vocals / guitar), Jarmo Hyytiä (guitar), Juha Merilaakso (bass), Taito Soramäki (drums).*

'Porn Grind' act INFERIA emerged in Lahti during 1991 with the 'Funeream' demo. A succession of promotion releases followed including 'Decursus Morbi' in November the following year, seeing the band comprising a trio of Jani Huttunen on vocals, guitar and bass, guitarist Jani Nikkilä and drummer Tero Järvinen, and 'Curible Orpheus' in March 1993. Heikki Isosipilä assisted on session bass for this last session. Further recordings in 1993 found Reijo Kortesniemi joining on vocals and Harri Kujala on bass. By October Petri Malinen had been instated on bass for the EP 'Spawned At The Dawn'.

1995 saw live dates throughout Poland after which INFERIA signed to the German Fireline label for the 'Masterpiece' album. Both Kortesniemi and Malinen opted out in 1998.

In August of 2001 INFERIA drafted Olli Herranen as their new bassist. The group underwent some major ructions in late 2001 with drummer Tero Järvinen making his exit. Soon pulled in as replacement would be Taito Soramäki. In March of 2002 Jarno Dahl became the band's new singer. A concert recording, 'Turpasauna - Live At Jyväskylä', emerged in 2002. The band's 2004 line up saw Jani Huttunen on vocals and guitar, Jarmo Hyytiä on guitar, Juha Merilaakso on bass and drummer Taito Soramäki.

666 Strings Records released the album 'Fucking Is A Great Way To Get To Know New People' in 2007.

Spawned At The Dawn, Invasion IR007 (1995). Under The Skin Of The Split Body / The Art Of Self Mutilation / Lunatics Anal Fanatics / Spawned At The Dawn / They Bleed And Bleed.

MASTERPIECE, Fireline (1995). Assortment Memorial / Covered In Semen / Onslet / Mallet Rape / An Image Of Masturbate So Brutally / Unbridled Perversity / Contusions Around The Vagina / Cystous Gullet / The Boiling Of Excrement Baths / Illicit Intercourse / Mortify One's Flesh / Tears More Than Cuts / Place Was Full Of Bodies.

PARENTAL ADVISORY, (1998). Explicit Lyrics / Cunt / Georgeous Oral Sex / Another Slut / Filthy 2 Minutes Handjob / Glad In Rubber / Massive Mutual Orgasm / Murder / Hot Golden Mouthwash / Harmless Voices / Auburn Spermed Sexuality.

TURPASAUNA 2002 - LIVE IN JYVÄSKYLÄ, Inferia (2002). Roadtrain Amputee / Excuse Me, Are You Cigarez / Cunt / Pussy Farts / Hot Golden Mouthwash / Filthy Two Minutes Handjob / Holecheck(king) / Mortify One's Flesh / Anusferatu / Mike Horner / Harmless Noises / Fast Cock Story / Balls Nailed To The Kitchen Table / Cum Eye.

Explosive Copulation, (2004). Distort To Pieces / Discharging Porn / Orgasm Through The Dead / Naked, Tasted, Crushed / Explosive Copulation.

RELEASE FOR BURIAL ORGIES, Nice To Eat You NTEY 13 (2005). Intro / Fucked From Behind / Red Raw Sore / Born In Penis Erection / Cunt / The Smell Of Anal Intercourse / Hot Golden Mouthwash / Cum Eye / Sadomize / Cock And Roll Show / Anusferatu / Extreme Oral Hacking / From Perversion To Sperm Overdose / Goldenshowers By Blood / Pussy Farts / Preferred Vaginal Looks / Cum Shot Victim.

FUCKING IS A GREAT WAY TO GET TO KNOW NEW PEOPLE, 666 Strings 13 (2007). Intro / Then Finger My Hole / The Flick / Balls Nailed To The Kitchen Table / Porn Addictdick / Assterix / External Vaginal Orifice / How To Eat Pussy / Reputation As An Expert / Attractive Penis / Lets Fist Again / Rhythm Of Ecstasy / Cuntrol / Ready And Willing / Impress / Tongue Intercourse.

INFERNAL

BRAZIL — *Marcelo Koehler (vocals), Luga (guitar), Danilo Zolet(guitar), Covero (bass), Mauricio Amorim (drums).*

Curitiba based INFERNAL, founded in 1986, trade in European influenced Thrash / Speed Metal that would later give way to more Death Metal persuasions The group's initial formation cited a line up of vocalist Paulo, guitarists Danilo Zolet and Marcelo Dos Anjos, bassist Covero (real name Renate Augusto de Alburquerque) and drummer Jonas. INFERNAL's inaugural gig, opening for MX in 1988, would already signal the start of a constant stream of line up ructions- new faces for the show being guitar player Lineau and frontman Marcelo Paulista.

In 1989 INFERNAL got around to cutting their first demo session 'The First Stage' but ran into immediate controversy with the media for the lyric "Speak Portuguese or die" in the track 'Brazoo'.

Another shift in line up found Mano on guitar and CREEPIN' DEATH and STEEL WAR man Mauricio Amorim on drums the following year for a sophomore cassette 'Cathedral Of Despair'. The track 'Fear Of Death' also garnered further exposure included on the compilation album 'Vampiros De Curitiba'.

INFERNAL debuted commercially in 1991 with the 7" single 'Of Weakness And Cowardice' but shortly after Mano decamped. Juliano Oening would fill the vacant guitar spot for a mammoth show in Araucária to over 4'000 people.

Paulista would be the next in line to leave creating Black Metal band AMEN CORNER. Marcelo Koehler would then take the mike stand for the inaugural album 'Drowning In The Chalice Of Sin'. For session work INFERNAL drafted Mano of HECATOMB but at the closure of recording ex guitarist Mano rejoined. The returning six stringer made it back in time to lay down lead guitar solos on the album. (Sadly Oening would later be killed in a car accident).

A heavy gig schedule across Brazil then ensued but Mano would bid farewell yet again, creating Death Metal band IMPERIOUS MALEVOLENCE.

HECATOMB's Mano assisted in the interim until INFERNAL recruited ex HAMMERDOWN member Poyoka. However, following a gig in Asunción, Paraguay in May '97 Poyoka too left. Daniel of SUBVERSIVE was to replace him but an injury to the new guitarist's left hand soon forced his dismissal. Ex CYTOMEGALODEATH man Luis Gabriel Maluf da Silva a.k.a.

'Luga' took over for recording of a second album 'Ritual Humiliation'

Of Weakness And Cowardice EP, (1991). Prelude To The Feast / The Feast Divine / True Reality.

DROWNING IN THE CHALICE OF SIN, (1993). Smash Thy Enemy / Bloody Rain / Il Passagio- The Ends Of Hell / Morbid Dream / Reaping Lives / Drowning In The Chalice Of Sin / Eternal Battle / Insurrection Day / The Endless Well Of Torment / Cathedral Of Despair.

RITUAL HUMILIATION, (2001). Intro: Bestial Overture / Die (Slow, Painful Death) / Absent Light / Secret Code / Ritual Humiliation / A Study In Blood And Darkness / Before My Turn, Agonizing / Plains Of Desolation / Intermezzo: The Nightmare / Sights Of The Unreal / Unholy Life / Invitation To Delirium / Cities Of Horror / Like Men Bleed / Rise, Charge, Obliterate / Finale: P.M.L.T.R.C.

INFERNAL DREAMS

PORTUGAL — *Carlos Mendes (vocals), Vitor Mestre (guitar), Rui Figueirado (bass), Pedro Fernandes (keyboards), Paulo Mateus (drums).*

INFERNAL DREAMS formation can be accredited to the 1994 musical union of rhythm guitarist Kim Mira and drummer Paulo Mateus. Subsequent additions the following year brought singer Carlos Mendes and Rui Figueiredo on bass for a set of 1995 demos. Upon completion keyboard player Lourenço Azevedo was enrolled and in this formation INFERNAL DREAMS debuted commercially with the track 'Blood Tears' included on the Guardians Of Metal compilation album 'Southern Assault Vol.I'.

The band would then re-group, drawing in the guitar pairing of Jorge Santos and erstwhile AFTER DEATH man Vitor Mestre. Further tribulation though resulted in the departure of both Azevedo and Santos. Pulling in Pedro Josué on keyboards recordings were undertaken for the album 'And I Dream . . . ', this being picked up for distribution by the Guardians Of Metal label.

AND I DREAM . . . , Guardians Of Metal (1999). Echoes (Intro) / Contact (Reach Beyond) / And I Dream . . . / In The Night / The Cursed Ones / Last Moment / Infernal Dreams / Cascade Of Thoughts / Obscure / Thanatos (Outro).

INFERNÄL MÄJESTY

TORONTO, ON, CANADA — *Chris Bailey (vocals), Steve Terror (guitar), Kenny Hallman (guitar), Psycopath (bass), Rick Nemes (drums).*

Heavily studded Toronto Thrash Metal combo INFERNÄL MÄJESTY first delivered the four track 'Infernäl Mäjesty' demo cassette in 1986, cut at TRIUMPH's Metal Works studios. Opening band formation comprised singer Chris Bailey, guitarists Kenny Hallman and Steve Terror, bass player Psycopath with Rick Nemes on drums. Both Hallman and Terror had previously operated with LACED, the guitarist also having conducted live operations with THE ASTRID YOUNG BAND. After a brief flirtation with the title OVERLORD, the group switched to INFERNÄL MÄJESTY.

INFERNÄL MÄJESTY's debut 1987 album 'None Shall Defy' was released through Roadrunner Records, the New York office having been forwarded a demo through a European fan, and gained glowing reviews. A near flawless execution of pure Thrash, 'None Shall Defy' blazed brightly but unfortunately lack of marketing meant its merits were largely overlooked. Despite this impact, the alliance with Roadrunner soon came to a halt. The band subsequently released the demos 'Nigresent Dissolution', recorded at Wellesley studios in 1988, and the Brian Taylor produced 'Creation Of Chaos', during 1992. This second session marked a shift in band personnel, new man on vocals being Vince with bassist Steve Terror replaced by Bob Quelch with Kevin Harrison on drums, Rick Nemes having vacated to join INNER THOUGHT. Quite bizarrely INFERNÄL MÄJESTY found themselves the subject of mainstream media attention when Vince was jailed, charged with Vampyric activity. Apparently the vocalist had slashed his girlfriend's wrist and sucked her blood. Vince, who went on to front BLOODWURM, died of a heroin overdose on October 14th 2001.

Dutch label Displeased Records re-issued 'None Shall Defy' in 1997, adding the 'Nigresent Dissolution' demo tracks as bonus material. With interest renewed, INFERNÄL MÄJESTY resurrected itself, with original vocalist Chris Bailey, for live work across Europe. In March 1997 a brace of brand new songs, 'Where Is Your God?' and 'Gone The Way Of All Flesh', were donated to the 'Kanada' compilation album. The group, contracting with domestic label Hypnotic Records and with Chay McMullen now installed on bass, returned to the studio for August 1998's 'Unholier Than Thou'. The band then blasted Europe, touring alongside CANNIBAL CORPSE and DARK FUNERAL that September. An April 2000 live album, 'Chaos In Copenhagen' recorded on October 14th 1998 at the Loppen Club in the Danish capital, added two cover versions of INFERNÄL MÄJESTY tracks by other acts, namely DAWN's 'Night Of The Living Dead' and CHRIST DENIED's take on 'Overlord'.

The 2002 line-up of INFERNÄL MÄJESTY, lead vocalist Chris Bailey, guitarists Steve Terror and Kenny Hallman, bassist Kiel Wilson, and ex-GRUDGE drummer Kris DeBoer, cut a four track demo. Eric Dubreuil was incorporated on bass guitar during October for recording at Profile Sound Studios in Vancouver of a new album 'One Who Points To Death'. The record, produced by Sho Murray and mastered by OBLIVEON's Pierre Rémillard at Wild Studios in St-Zenon, Quebec, was slated for April 2004 issue through the Greek Black Lotus label in Europe whilst North American release was handled by Canada's Galy Records. On a temporary basis, CRADLE TO GRAVE's singer Greg Cavanagh filled in a batch of live shows.

INFERNÄL MÄJESTY, having located new singer Brian Langley previously of MECHA MESSIAH, undertook a six week long Canadian tour with support act DEAD JESUS. The kick off show came as a support to METAL CHURCH at The Cobalt in Vancouver on 20th June. According to the band they lost out on support gigs to W.A.S.P. in August because the headline act deemed INFERNÄL MÄJESTY as "too heavy for the bill". European shows scheduled for September would be cancelled due to work visa problems. The band were soon back on the road, acting as support alongside fellow Canadians 3 INCHES OF BLOOD for Norwegian Black Metal act SATYRICON's US dates commencing December 2nd in San Francisco. However, INFERNÄL MÄJESTY abruptly dropped off these dates just prior to commencement.

The band announced touring plans for European dates in early 2005 in partnership with Thrash veterans HIRAX. A new album, recorded in December and entitled 'Systematical Extermination' and produced by KATAKLYSM's Jean-François Dagenais, would then be readied, this marking the recording debut with the band Brian Langley.

A December 2006 five track EP, 'Demo'n God', featured a re-recorded version of the song 'S.O.S.', from the band's 'None Shall Defy' album, complete with George "Corpsegrinder" Fisher of CANNIBAL CORPSE fame lending his vocal talents along with Rob Barrett, of CANNIBAL CORPSE and MALEVOLENT CREATION, adding guest guitar.

Infernäl Mäjesty, (1986) (Demo). Overlord / Night Of The Living Dead / Skeletons In The Closet / S.O.S.

NONE SHALL DEFY, Roadrunner RR 49609 (1987). Overlord / R.I.P. / Night Of The Living Dead / S.O.S. / None Shall Defy / Skeletons In The Closet / Anthology Of Death / Path Of The Psyco / Into The Unknown / Hell On Earth.

Nigresent Dissolution, (1988) (Demo). Into The Unknown / Hell On Earth.

Creation Of Chaos, (1992) (Demo). Power Intrusion / What's What / Into The Unknown / Those About To Die.

UNHOLIER THAN THOU, Hypnotic HYP 1062 (1998). Roman Song / The Hunted / Where Is Your God? / Death Roll / Gone The Way Of All Flesh / Unholier Than Thou / Black Infernal World / The Art Of War.

INFERNAL MAJESTY

CHAOS IN COPENHAGEN, Hypnotic (2000). Birth Of The Power / Unholier Than Thou / Where Is Your God? / R.I.P. / Night Of The Living Dead / The Hunted / Night Of The Living Dead / Overlord.

ONE WHO POINTS TO DEATH, Black Lotus BLR 066 (2004). Death Of Heaven / Pestilential Eternity / Honey Tongue Of Satan / Cathedral Of Hate / Hysterion Proteron / Angels And Acid / Virgin Blood Tastes Purest At Night / One Who Points To Death.

SYSTEMATICAL EXTERMINATION, Black Lotus (2006). Against All Gods / Return / Heathenism / Burnt Beyond Recognition / Systematical Extermination / From Paradise To Hell / Crusade / Nation Of Assassins.

INFERNAL METHOD

SYDNEY, NSW, AUSTRALIA — *Joss Separovic (vocals / guitar), Peter Michael Peric (guitar), Andrew Lilley (guitar), Lee Glanzmann (bass), Grahame Goode (drums).*

Sydney melodic Death Metal band INFERNAL METHOD is the brainchild of former SYPHILIS, AUTOMATION and DEADSPAWN guitarist Peter Michael Peric. The band was formulated by incorporating ex-DEPRESSION vocalist Shane Thompson, another erstwhile DEPRESSION and DEADSPAWN man guitarist Aaron Bilbija, bass player Michael Kordek and drummer Graham Goode. The latter is an experienced player citing credits with AUTOMATION, CRYOGENIC and NEOPHOBIA.

Guitarist Aaron Bilbija quit to join PSI.KORE, and later the highly successful DAYSEND, whilst bass player Michael Kordek too opted out to enroll into DAYSEND as rhythm guitarist. By coincidence ex-PSI.KORE guitarist Andrew Lilley took Bilbija's place and SYPHILIS bassist Lee Glanzmann brought the band back up to strength. The group acquired the services of American Jonah Weingarten on keyboards in January of 2002 but he lasted just one gig. A three song Demo CD comprising the bands initial works was released in May. Shane Thompson was ousted making way for new frontman SHACKLES and SAMSARAS WOUNDS singer Joss Separovic.

Weingarten would unite with the Danish melodic Power Metal band PYRAMAZE, cutting the 'Melancholy Beast' album in 2003. Grahame Goode acted as temporary drummer for Heavy Metal band DUNGEON's June 2004 support gigs to EDGUY. In July INFERNAL METHOD announced they were calling it a day. Weingarten joined US act LILITU in October whilst Pete Peric joined DUNGEON on bass guitar in November. However, as 2005 opened both Peric and Goode broke away from DUNGEON in order to re-forge INFERNAL METHOD. The band supported Swedes INSISION during July and ARCH ENEMY in November.

The band announced they were to flank KILLRAZOR as support to leading Polish Death Metal act VADER's April 2007 Australian dates. However, just previous to these shows the band folded.

Demo 2002, Infernal Method (2002). Reanimating The Wicked / The Burning Earth / Of Words, Will And Power.

INFERNAL TORMENT

SILKEBORG, DENMARK — *Scott Jensen (vocals), Jacob Hansen (guitar), Poul Winhyer (guitar), Steffan Larsen (bass), Martin Boris (drums).*

Sick, sick, sick Death Metallers, Silkeborg's INFERNAL TORMENT concoct some rather Extreme Metal allied to lyrics that put better known Grind acts to shame. INFERNAL TORMENT sing about bizarre sexual practices, such as eating excreta, in lurid detail. After seeking legal advice the band's record company only agreed to print the lyrics on the sleeve of the debut album if they were in reverse type and the first 3000 copies of their debut album even came complete with a free sick bag.

INFERNAL TORMENT formed in 1993 and released various demos, including the 1993 'Incapability On The Cross' and 1994's 'Instincts' tape, before contributing the track 'No Longer A Virgin' to the 'Fuck You, We're From Denmark' compilation album on Progress Records in 1994 and supported INVOCATOR on tour later the same year.

The band added ex-CONDEMNED guitarist Poul Winther prior to recording the debut album, 'Man's True Nature' recorded at Borsing Studios and released in December 1995, the CD cover for which was immediately banned thus garnering INFERNAL TORMENT further promotion. The offending image, a murderer impaling his naked, decapitated with a garden fork, was replaced by a simple logo design. The July 1998 album 'Birthrate Zero' included a hidden cover version of IRON MAIDEN's 'Seventh Son Of A Seventh Son'.

Singer Scott Jensen and drummer Heinz Kristensen forged DAWN OF DEMISE in 2003.

Incapability On The Cross, Infernal Torment (1993) (Demo). The Undertaker / Passive By Nature / Forest Of Lechery / Lepperfuck / Dead But Masturbating / Incapability On The Cross / Paradise Of Pain.

Instincts, Infernal Torment (1994) (Demo). No Longer A Virgin / Uncontrollable Lechery / Instincts / On The Hunt For Her Flesh.

MAN'S TRUE NATURE, Progress (1995). Taking Advantage Of A Virgin / Motherfuck / Uncontrollable / Perverted / Instincts / The Undertaker / Baby-Battering-Bill / No Longer . . . / On The Hunt For Fresh Flesh / When Daddy Comes Home.

BIRTHRATE ZERO, Diehard (1998). The Razor Twist / Product Of Society / Birthrate Zero / The End Of Civilization / 443556 / Murder The World / Race / Eliminate / Inhaled / Fuck The Whales / Seventh Son Of A Seventh Son.

INFESTATION

HOVÅS, SWEDEN — *Tomas Lindberg (vocals / bass), Anders Björler (guitar), Björn Mankner (guitar), Jonas Björler (drums).*

Hovås, Gothenburg based Death Metal band INFESTATION only saw operations between February and September in 1990. Despite the brief life span, the band featured a clutch of well known performers on the extreme Metal scene with vocalist / bassist Tomas Lindberg, guitarist Anders Björler, second guitarist Björn Mankner and Jonas Björler on drums. Lindberg's credits include AT THE GATES, BEN-HUR, CONQUEST, THE CROWN, DISFEAR, THE GREAT DECEIVER, GROTESQUE, HIDE, LIERS IN WAIT, LOCKUP, NIGHTRAGE, SKITSYSTEM and WORLD WITHOUT END. The Björler twins found prominence with AT THE GATES, THE HAUNTED and TERROR.

A two song INFESTATION rehearsal demo, 'When Sanity Ends', was recorded at Fågeln studio and issued in August. Just weeks later, Lindberg and the two brothers then hooked up with Alf Svensson plus drummer Adrian Erlandsson, and duly created AT THE GATES.

At one stage INFESTATION also included Anders Malmström of IMMEMORIAL and PROPHANITY repute. Anders Malmström joined NOMINON as new bassist in October 2006.

When Sanity Ends, Infestation (1990) (Rehearsal demo). Disfigured / Carved Out.

INFINITED HATE

HOLLAND — *Rachel Kloosterwaard (vocals), Ron van de Polder (guitar), Aad Kloosterwaard (drums).*

INFINITED HATE was founded in August of 2003 by the SINISTER, THANATOS and HOUWITSER credited drummer Aad Kloosterwaard. The project, offering old school US styled Death, opened with the self financed 'Primitive Butchery', recorded at the AM studios in Gouda, these tapes featuring SINISTER members vocalist Rachel Kloosterwaard and guitarist Ron van de Polder. INFINITED HATE signed to Displeased Records for an April 2004 debut 'Revel In Bloodshed'.

Swiftly recording their second album that same year, the 'Heaven Termination' set saw session drums delivered by the much in demand SCARVE member Dirk Verbeuren, a man also holding credits with ABORTED, LYZANXIA, ETERNAL GRAY, MORTUARY and SOILWORK. Meantime, regular drummer Aad Kloosterwaard kick started the Death Metal side venture BLAST KORPS.

In October 2005 line-up changes saw Rachel Heyzer-Kloosterwaard relinquishing her role and drummer Aad Kloosterwaard taking over as the group's lead vocalist. In October 2006 Aad Kloosterwaard sessioned guest vocals on demos for SUPREME PAIN. Retaining his SINISTER ties, he subsequently joined this old school Death Metal band, which featured Erwin Harreman on bass and guitar and Robert Kovacic of SCAFFOLD on drums. In March 2007 SUPREME PAIN signed a deal with the US based label Comatose Music, owned by Steve Green of LUST OF DECAY, for a debut album 'Cadaver Pleasures'.

PRIMITIVE BUTCHERY, Independent (2003). Haunting Noises / Bound By Hate / Arrival Of Doom / Dreadful Gore / Built For The Kill / Primitive Butchery / Tribute To The Dead / Terminal Conclusion.
REVEL IN BLOODSHED, Independent (2004). Ill Formed Beast / Tribute To The Dead / Chaos Called Underworld / Bound By Hate / Dreadful Gore / Haunting Noises / Primitive Butchery.

INFINITUM OBSCURE

MEXICO — *Roberto Lizarraga (vocals / guitar), Carlos Escobar (bass), Joel Marquez (drums).*

Tijuana Death Metal band INFINITUM OBSCURE, created in 2000 by vocalist / guitarist Roberto Lizarraga, feature ex-NINTH LEVEL guitarist, erstwhile DIABLA VESTA MORTAR bassist Carlos Escobar and former SADISTIC INTENT drummer Joel Marquez. The band issued a September 2003 split album 'Ipsus Universum', produced by Ed Talorda of San Diego's MORTUUS TERROR and shared with Chicago's ANCIENT GODS through Utterly Somber Creations.

Noel Bello decamped I December of 2004, his last gig being a support to Polish act BEHEMOTH in Tijuana. Escobar was then forced out due to a hernia injury. However, Bello returned to form up a live line up, alongside fellow sessioneer Lorenzo Kemp of MAN DESTROYS HIMSELF, for Californian shows in June of 2004. During this period Lizarraga was also being utilised as bassist for leading Mexican Death Metal act THE CHASM.

IPSUS UNIVERSUM, Utterly Somber Creations (2003) (Split album with ANCIENT GODS). The Ninth Gate / Shunned By Thy Dark Light / Storm Of Impious Hatred / Beyond A Dying Sun.

INFLICTION

MILAN, ITALY — *Björn Gosses (vocals), Riky (guitar), Gianluca (guitar), Hilo (bass), Jan (keyboards), Cristian Z. (drums).*

Milan based Death Metal unit. Formed in 1995 INFLICTION debuted with the demo 'Heretical' prior to adding Jan on keyboards for the follow up session 'The Bleeding Dreams'. Numerous line up changes finally settled with the recruitment of lead vocalist I.R. of MELANCHOLIA and Dhilorz from ANCIENT on bass guitar. The album 'The Faint Smell Of Suicide' surfaced in May of 2002. Released by the German Voice Of Life label 'The Faint Smell Of Suicide' included guest sessions from Aphazel of ANCIENT, Björn Gosses of NIGHT IN GALES as well as both Goth Gorgon and Draakh Kimera of MÖRK GRYNING. Gosses would also land credits for designing the album cover.

INFLICTION pulled in Björn Goosses of esteemed German Metal band NIGHT IN GALES for vocals on their second album 'Earshot'. INFLICTION established tour dates in Europe throughout January in league with Danes HATESPHERE. Goosses left the band in January 2006.

THE FAINT SMELL OF SUICIDE, Voice Of Life (2002) (Limited edition 1000 copies). Intro / A Credit To Dementia / Soulquake Bizarre / As Coward Meets Coward / Faint Smell Of Suicide / Prelude / The Blood That I Crave / Hypochrist / Unmorning / Pleasure Called Hate / Vanishing Point.
THE SILENCER, Cruz Del Sur CRUZ14 (2005). Eyeseeblack / Redhouse / Poisonradio / Nocturnal / Sleepers / Welcome / Paperlife / Thirtyseven / Breathe / Closer / The Voice / Eyeseeblack (Video).

INGRAVED

ITALY — *Antas (vocals), Argonath (guitar), Interitus (guitar), Enoch (bass), M16 (drums).*

Death Metal act INGRAVED came together in April of 2001, a formation of vocalist Antonio, guitarists Gianluigi 'Interitus' and Damiano 'Hades' De Parigi, bass player Sandro 'Enoch' with Mario 'M16' on the drums. With this line up the band cut the opening EP 'From The Eyes Of Pain' and the October 2002 follow up 'Complete Domination'. However, Gianluigi would then exit, being replaced by Giuseppe 'Argonath'. Tragedy struck INGRAVED on 21st December 2002 when De Parigi was killed in an auto accident.

Opting to persevere despite this loss INGRAVED toured Italy and Slovenia in early 2003 in union with GOD DETHRONED and THE CROWN. Upon completion of these dates Gianluigi rejoined.

From The Eyes Of Pain EP, Independent (2001). Disconnect—Dead / Dark Messiah / ErotiKrist.
Complete Domination EP, Independent (2002). Necro.Sad.Instinct (Intro) / Last Prophecy / Loving Flesh (Complete Domination) / Domina Peccatorum (Amrita Latex Goddess) / Erotokrist (Abyssic version).

INGROWING

CZECH REPUBLIC — *Patrik Vlakin Staněk (vocals / bass), Eddie (guitar), Pouzar (guitar), Zbyna (drums).*

Grindcore act INGROWING, hailing from České Budějovice, debuted in 1996 with the 'Perverted Look At The World' tape. Band members vocalist Vlakin and guitarist Pouzar, along with ex-INGROWING drummer Milan and Chymus from ISACAARUM would also be operational with Noise act LEWD. The trio of trio of Vlakin, Pouzar and Milan are also active with PLASTIC GRAVE.

INGROWING would share their Leviathan Records album 'Perverted Look At The World' with DEFLORACE and issue a split live cassette in alliance with GRIDE. A split cassette 'Deformed' shared with CONTRASTIC surfaced in 1997 as well as a collaborative 7" EP through Epidemie Records in partnership with MALIGNANT TUMOUR. A further live document, entitled

'Succumb To Self-abusement', was put out as a split effort with GRIDE once more.

The band would then participate in one of the most infamous Grindcore releases, the 1999 'Creation Of Another Future' 7" single through Copremesis in league with Spaniards HAEMORRHAGE. The group contributed their rendition of 'Duše Nesmrtelných' to a 1999 MASTER'S HAMMER tribute album compiled by Redblack Productions. INGROWING also included their version of 'Bitch Death Teenage Mucous Monster From Hell' to the 2001 Razorback IMPETIGO tribute album 'Wizards Of Gore'.

Promoting the album 'Cloned & Enforced' INGROWING engaged with ISACAARUM for the 'Bondage Enforcers' tour of Europe in April 2006. A split EP release, 'To Clone And To Enforce', shared with EXHUMED, included a cover version of REGURGITATE's 'Total Dismemberment Of A Female Corpse'.

CYBERSPACE, Tentamen (1998). Underture / Cyberspace Floats Through Me / Touretted / Polyanghuulaar Dereems / Sunken / Surreal Ego Ravening / We Created Another Future / Sexual Inferiority / Mournful Inferiority / Mournful Dejection / Synergy Pertual (The Unplugged Factory... Unperpetualism) / Intro / Virus Bioforge / Just Only Weeping Decadence / Sadomasochistic Grind-Mind Fucker / Agnosis / Pithecanthrope Syndrome / Cortex Combustion.

Creation Of Another Future EP, Copremesis (1999) (Split single with HAEMORRHAGE). Sexual Inferiority / Cyberspace Floats Through Me / Radio Hit.

Peristatica IX, (2000) (Split single with IMPETIGO). Peristatica IX / Bitch Death Teenage Mucous Monster From Hell.

SUICIDE BINARY REFLECTIONS, Obscene Productions OBP 040 (2001). Suicide... (Intro) / Binary Reflections / Dreams Torn Asunder / Chemical Emotions / Ethereality Section / Enigmatism / Cryogenics / Biomechanized Earth Flutes / Deflated / D.C. Sucks!!! (Ultimate Intermezzo) / Hyperspace Souls / Demodeus / The Onerous Physical / ... Successful (Outro).

SUNRAPE, Obscene Productions OBP 051 (2003). Here Comes The Sun / Exposed To The Light / Erradicated / Annelid Cult / Fragmented Oracle / Four Murders Guaranteed (DC Sucks Part II) / The Darkness Inverted / Sunrape / Virtua Bleed / Nebular / Not Enough (Budweis City Babies Revenge) / Spectral Passages / Illumination / Raped.

To Clone And To Enforce, Obscene Productions (2006) (Split EP with EXHUMED). Biomechanized / Dance Of Submission / Total Dismemberment Of A Female Corpse.

INGURGITATING OBLIVION

GERMANY — *Ulrich Kreienbrink (vocals), Karsten Schöning (vocals), Florian Engelke (guitar), Sascha Hermesdorf (guitar), Henning Dinkla (bass), Florian Neumeyer (drums).*

INGURGITATING OBLIVION released two albums, 1998's 'Fragmente aus dem Fliessenden' and 2000's 'Thought Cathedral', under their former title OF TREES AND ORCHIDS. A supremely inventive Oldenburg based Death Metal act convened in 1997 at the hands of former GALLERY OF DARKNESS guitarist Florian Engelke, lead vocalist Marcel Schomakers, bass player Felix Engelke and Heinz Kassens on the drums. Atypically the band trod a somewhat oblique Metal path, blending elements of classical German literature such as the works of Wolfgang Borchert with extreme melodies. This avant-garde approach would be amply illustrated by the debut album 'Fragmente aus dem Fliessenden', recorded by Florian Engelke and Heinz Kassens along with new guitarist Karsten Schöning of GALLERY OF DARKNESS and DEFORMED. A later addition was to be bass player Dennis Eickenhorst.

During early 2001 Kassens opted out to prioritise his Stoner band THE MILLSTONE. Heinz Dirk Janssen of DESPONDENCY swiftly enrolled to fill the drum vacancy but then Eickenhorst exited. Nevertheless, OF TREES AND ORCHIDS regrouped in the recording studio to cut the sophomore album 'Thought-Cathedral'. The membership for this occasion comprised Engelke, Schöning, Janssen and bass player Sascha Hermesdorf.

OF TREES AND ORCHIDS evolved into INGURGITATING OBLIVION in the midst of recording the August 2001 album 'Cadence And Perspective'. Lead vocal responsibilities were handed over to Ulrich Kreienbrink in early 2002. Janssen made the decision to concentrate on his main act DESPONDENCY in August of that year. Florian Neumeyer of THE AWAKENING and GALLERY OF DARKNESS plugged the gap. This signalled a radical overhaul of the band with Schöning laying down his guitar to become a co-lead singer and Henning Dinkla of THE AWAKENING taking the bass role as Hermesdorf switched to guitar.

By 2003 INGURGITATING OBLIVION were going by the stage pseudonyms of Killrich Corpse Rotter, H.D. Hatecraft, S. Corpsegrinder Grinder H., K. The Chasm S., Flobotter, and F. Cthulhu E.

CADENCE AND PERSPECTIVE, Independent (2001). A Poet's Fingernails / La Gitana / Descent To The Temple / Nothingness / Slumbering In Relativity.

INHUMAN VISIONS

LOS ANGELES, CA, USA — *Rick Fowler (vocals / bass), Charles Elliott (guitar), Jaime Boulanger (guitar), Mike Radke (drums).*

Los Angeles melodic Death Metal act INHUMAN VISIONS, fronted by Rick Fowler and created in 1991, debuted in 1993 with a four song demo, followed in 1995 with the self financed album 'Inhuman Throughout Myself'. Early band members would include guitarists Erick Marin and Ron Ascoli, the ARTISAN, OBSCURE and PROTOTYPE credited bassist Mike Bear (a.k.a. Mike Brew) and keyboard player Joe Lester. A later recruit would be RISE guitarist Charles Elliott. An EP, 'Symptoms Of The Manipulated', would be released in February of 2001, launched with a special gig at the Hollywood Whiskey A Go Go.

INHUMAN VISIONS folded in April of 2002. An attempt was made at a resurrection but in December of 2003 guitarists Charles Elliott and Jaime Boulanger opted out in order to prioritise their other act ABYSMAL DAWN.

INHUMAN THROUGHOUT MYSELF, Inhuman Visions (1995). Dismal Hope / Denial / Consumed By Emptiness / Lost / Mindless Task / Betrayal / Crush / Broken Promises / Inhuman / 4/20.

Symptoms Of The Manipulated, (2001). Freedom Lacking / Wasted Breath / Symptoms / Blasphemous Lies / No Progress / Born Again / The End (A Sermon).

INHUMATE

STRASBOURG, FRANCE — *Christophe (vocals), David (guitar), Fred (bass), Yannick (drums).*

Strasbourg Grind band created in 1990 by guitarist David, bassist Fred, vocalist Olivier and drummer Stephane. By the following year Stephane had vacated his position for APOPLEXY and Sebastien had taken over the lead vocal spot. New drummer was Valentin. In 1993 INHUMATE cut their debut demo 'Abstract Suffering'. In late 1994 the band saw Valentin leave for LES MARAUDERS and Sebastien decamp to CEREBRAL COMMOTION. New faces were singer Christophe and drummer Yannick, bother former GOD EATER personnel. INHUMATE's second 7 track demo arrived in May 1995 billed as 'Grind Your Soul'. The debut album, 'Internal Life', was delivered in September of 1996 with 'Ex-Pulsion' arriving in November 1997.

The band would subsequently feature on a whole slew of split cassette releases during the mid 90s included amongst which were alliances with FUNERAL MARCH in 1996, DISEMBOWEL and TRAUMA TEAM in 1998, MAGGOT SHOES, EXHUMATOR and SANGUINARY in 1999 and BLOODSHED, PULMONARY FIBROSIS, TRAUMATISM, DEPRAVED and MUCUPURULENT during 2000. INHUMATE shared a split EP with ALIENATION MENTAL in 2001. The 2000 album 'Growth' would see various re-pressings globally with Witchhammer Records in Thailand, Mad Lion in Poland and Music Box in Malaysia all licensing the album for cassette formats. The band self financed the 2004 offering 'Life'.

INTERNAL LIFE, Grind Your Soul GYS001 (1996). Alone / My Sweet Love / Putrefaction / Blood / Welcome / D.P.B. / Piece Of Meat / Screams / I Want To Kill Some … / Tatanka / The Dream / Why? / Obsession / Earth Fucking Earth / The Bullet / Incest (Just A Kiss).

EX-PULSION, Grind Your Soul GYS002 (1997). The Key / Therapy For Dogs / Sodomy / The Chosen One / Perfection / In Quest / Blind / Efluves / Grind Inc. / Desperate / Trance / History / Mother Fuck Her Grindub.

GROWTH, Grind Your Soul GYS003 (2000). I Want To Kill Some … (Part III) / Underground / Copyright / The Fright / Clock / Grind God / Time / The Golden Cage / Vanite? / N.S.C. / Urges! / Karamazov / Grind To The Core / Satyriasis / Bread And Games / Muensterturm / D.I.Y.F.

LIFE, Independent (2004). No Answer / A Trip / Blasted (History Of A Dive) / Destinity? / Labyrinth / I Wan't To Kill Some … (Part IV) / Sickness Is The Law / Sons Of Earth / The Fight / For Lust / N.D.S. / The Scorpion / Thank You / Rage / One Day / Life?

INHUME

HOLLAND — *Johan (vocals), Joost (vocals), Harold Gielen (guitar), Ben (guitar), Loek Peeters (bass), Michiel (drums).*

Dutch Grindcore act INHUME was convened in late 1994 issuing an inaugural demo tape at the close of 1995. Early live work found the band guesting for AGATHOCLES, DEAD INFECTION, BENEDICTION, ALTAR and NYCTOPHOBIC among others. A live shared cassette with SUPPOSITORY was issued in 1996 followed up by a further split tape in union with Ecuador's MUNDO DE MIERDA. 1997 saw further studio work for a promotional demo produced by Erwin Hermsen of MANGLED. A European tour in collaboration with Swedish acts DERANGED and VOMITORY was arranged but curtailed when guitarist Richard and drummer Roel broke ranks.

Replacements would be found in guitarist Harold Gielen and NEE drummer Michiel. The latter's tenure proved fleeting though as after a matter of days he would quit to concentrate on his main act. Nevertheless, a split single with BLOOD would be embarked upon.

As 1999 opened SINISTER's Erik De Windt took the drum stool but only lasted a few months after which the circle was closed as original drummer Roel was re-enlisted. Coincidently Joost would front SINISTER for a period. De Windt wound up with Australians DESTROYER 666 and by mid 2002 also took on drum duties with PROSTITUTE DISFIGUREMENT.

Vocalist Joost, bassist Loek and guitarist Ben are also members of DROWNING IN TEARS. Loek Peeters and Harold Gielen also operated with MANGLED and the bassist also held down duties in DISRUPT. Harold Gielen forged Mathcore Metal band CHARLIE*ADLER, in 2003, alongside former COLLISION man Wouter Wagemans on lead vocals, guitarist Johan van Gestel of GAAR, KUTABARE and VLEISBOEUM, second guitarist Roel in 't Zandt from GRAMOXONE with Niek van Lin from CONCUBINE, SIN and VLEISBOEUM on the drums.

Inhume EP, (1998) (Split EP with BLOOD). Airplane Crash / Gargling Guts / 4 Months Below.

DECOMPOSING FROM INSIDE, Bones Brigade (2000). Gargling Guts / Squirming Parasites / Human Fucking Guinea Pig / Schizophrenic Pulp / Unforeseen Annihilation / Forbidden Hunger / Airplane Crash / Splenetic Views / Blood, Sperm, Shit / Tiamat / Meatcleaver / Tumorhead / Foul Mouths Below / Inescapable Destiny / Regressive Progressive / The Missing Limb / Dead Man Walking / Destructive Impulse / Invisible Death.

IN FOR THE KILL, Osmose Productions OPCD146 (2003). Incineration Of The Body By Own Will / Process To Decelerate / Inhume / Genetic Intervention / Prelude To Human Confinement / Scourging / In For The Kill / Decimated Content / Ignorance Of The Elevated / Bitch Redecoration / Bowel Movement / Profound Presumption / Fucked With Paranoia / Blood Orgy At 7th Street / Sodomizing Encounter / Retreat From Morality.

CHAOS DISSECTION ORDER, Osmose Productions (2007). Superior Existence / Plague Injected / Oppressing The Weak / Chaos Dissection Order / Retaliate / Severely Deteriorated Flesh / Dismal / Abhorrent / Grind Culture / Hollow / Exhume / Swift Genocide / Illuminati / Human Slave Colony / Bewildered By Rage / Hate/Kill.

INIQUITY

DENMARK — *Brian Petrwosky (vocals / guitar), Lars Friis (guitar), Thomas Christensen (bass), Jesper Frost (drums).*

Death Metal band INIQUITY date to 1989 releasing the debut demo tape 'Words Of Despair' in 1991. Further demos, such as 1992's 'Entering Deception', and various appearances on compilation albums followed before their debut album, 1996's 'Serenadium' released through Emanzipation Records. The founding quartet had comprised CORPUS MORTALE vocalist / bassist Martin Rosendahl, guitarists Brian Eriksen and Jens Lee with drummer Jesper Frost. As a side venture in 1996 Rosendahl activated Black Metal project ZAHRIM, recording a demo entitled 'Mashshagarannu'.

During 1997 INIQUITY fractured with vocalist / guitarist Mads Haarløv and drummer Jacob Olsen forging SWOLLEN to issue the EP 'The Breathless Waiting' in 1996 and a 1998 demo. INIQUITY also suffered the loss of both Rosendahl and Lee that same year. SWOLLEN then folded and both Haarløv and SWOLLEN bassist Thomas Fagerlind subsequently joined INIQUITY. Three tracks from the 1998 SWOLLEN demos emerged on INIQUITY's 1999 'Five Across The Eyes' release. Production for this album was handled by ex-INVOCATOR frontman Jacob Hanson. Meantime, ex-band members Brian Eriksen and Jens Lee joined up with CORPUS MORTALE in 1999. INIQUITY drafted second guitarist Kræn Meier from SACRIFICIAL in 2001 for the 'Grime' opus.

The Mighty Music label would release a compilation album 'Iniquity Bloody Iniquity' in early 2003 comprising archive demo material plus brand new tracks. Both Haarløv and Rosendahl would form up the extreme Metal 'supergroup' STRANGLER. Drummer Jesper Frost joined melodic Death Metal act ECITON in early 2005 before moving on to join DOWNLORD, the band led by ex-BENEDICTION and BOLT THROWER vocalist Dave Ingram and INIQUITY colleague Thomas Fagerlind.

SERANADIUM, Progress RRS953 (1996). Tranquil Seizure / Prophecy Of The Dying Watcher / Serenadium / Spectral Scent / Mockery Retained To Obturate / Encysted And Dormant / Son Of Cosmos / Retorn.

THE HIDDEN LORE, (1998). Desiderated Profligacy / Notable Diversity / Achromatic Chronicles / The Hidden Lore.

FIVE ACROSS THE EYES, Mighty Music (1999). Inhale The Ghost / Surgical Orb / Sidereal Seas / Random Bludgeon Battery / From Tarnished Soil / Reminscene / Pyres Of Atonement / The Rigormortified Grip / Forensic Alliance.

GRIME, (2002). Tides Of Vengeance / The Bullets Breath / Border Into Shadow / Bloodletting / Spawn Of The Abscess / Thawed For Breeding / Stygian / The Last Incantation / Poets Of The Trench / Part II.

INIQUITY BLOODY INIQUITY, Mighty Music PMZ 032 (2003). Revel In Cremation / Madman Of The Trade / Extreme Unction / Bloodletting / The Bullet's Breath / Inhale The Ghost / The Rigormortified Grip / Cocooned / Desiderated Profligacy / The Hidden Lore / Encysted And Dormant / Retorn / Entangled / Torn / Prophecy Of The Dying Watcher / The Bullet's Breath (Video).

INNOCENCE PURE MUTILATED

SETE LAGOAS, MG, BRAZIL — *Jiusepe Gáspari (vocals / guitar), Renato Duarte (bass), Júlio Lanza (drums).*

Heavy Metal act INNOCENCE PURE MUTILATED was founded during 1994 by drummer Júlio Lanza, recruiting Jiusepe Gáspari on vocals then bassist Marcelo Morais. The latter exited in 1995 and the band soldiered on without a permanent bassist, recording the demo 'No More Be Good' in 1998. Renato Padrão was enrolled on bass guitar in 2000, recording the single 'Next Emanation'. However, Padrão then left. In 2002 the band introduced Alípio Teixeira on keyboards and André Leão on bass, shortly afterward adopting the ESPADA

NEGRA title. A two track demo arrived in 2004, followed by the self-financed album 'Kingdom Of Fear' in April the following year.

No More Be Good, Innocence Less Mutilated (1998). No More Be Good / Supreme / Vulvagine / Death Notice / Ethnic Stupidity / The Suicidal Friend / The Bells Shadows / Coffee Break.

INSANE ASSHOLES

VENICE, ITALY — *Maurizio Insane (vocals), Tommy (guitar), Alessandro (bass), Marco the Asshole (drums).*

INSANE ASSHOLES was founded by Maurizio Insane ("puke, insults, gore & chainsaw engineer") and G.F.H. drummer Stefano Buraz during 1999. Initially Fede and Francesco were employed on guitar and Manuel covered bass duties. In 2000 Tommy ("panzer guitars") assumed guitar duties. 2001 saw the drum position handed over to Marco ("human skin drums & beer"), a scene veteran of LUMAKA INFEROCITA, GRUNTER SCREAMS, N.A.B. and WARMONGER. This revised formation laid down the debut 2002 album 'Stralci di Oblio'.

INSANE ASSHOLES 2003 album 'Nella Stanza', released by NoBrain Records, would be a split offering shared with GRUNTER SCREAMS. That December Alessandro ("pigsfukker bass") enrolled as new bassist.

STRALCI DI OBLIO, Insane Assholes (2002). No Prey / Niente / Being Ripped Off / Carbonara Crew / Pensiero Incongruo / Mente Vuota / Ripper / C.P.S. / Michael Myers.

NELLA STANZA, NoBrain (2003) (Split album with GRUNTER SCREAMS). Pigs / To Love, To Protect, To Kill, To Rip / Loser / Who's The Cannibal? / Nella Stanza / Laugh Of The Bastard / Peter Jackson / Leatherface Is A Grinder / The War Of Zombies / The March Of Carbonara's Eaters / Delirium / Ripper (Live) / Niente (Live).

INSANITY

BRAZIL — *George Frizzo (vocals / bass), Alberto Lopes (guitar), Bruno Gabai (drums).*

Fortaleza's INSANITY was founded in 1989, the opening line up comprising George Frizzo on lead vocals and bass guitar, lead guitarist Alberto Lopes and drummer Bruno Gabai. INSANITY, adding second guitarist Fábio Andrey, issued the 'Friday The 13th Massacre' and 'In Search Of Reason' demos in 1990 followed by the 'Cryogenization' 7" single. INSANITY's next move was to cut the opening album 'Phobia' and donate a track to the DORSAL ATLANTICA tribute album 'Omnisciens'. However, Andrey would defect to THE MIST in April of 1996.

Bruno Gabai would front SIEGE OF HATE as a side pursuit.

The band donated their rendition of 'As If By Magic' to a ROTTING CHRIST tribute album, entitled 'An Evil Existence For Rotting Christ', released through Recordshop Productions in June of 2004.

Cryogenization EP, (1991).
PHOBIA, Heavy Metal Rocks (1993). The 7th Day Of Creation / Dismal Lullaby / Pleasure Of Pain / Mistakes Of Oblivion / Pay For Your Faith / Night Of The Living Deads / Innocent Laughter / Sadness / ... And The Bloodshed Goes On.
MIND CRISIS, Muvuca (1998). Subconscious Damage / Massive Thought Control / The Monitor / Confiner / Strain / Sleeper Effect / Infections / Contemplations / Hopeless / Another Cut / Neurosis / Feed Me / Unsafe.

INSANITY

CA, USA — *Dave Gorsuch (vocals / guitar), Scott Dodge (guitar), Lou Gilberto (bass), Bud Mills (drums).*

Northern California Bay Area act INSANITY stood out from the regular Thrash pack by delivering an intense brand of proto-Death Metal. The original line up counted vocalist Joe DeZuniga, guitarist Dave Gorsuch, bassist Keith Ellison and drummer Bud Mills. INSANITY debuted live on the 19th of October 1985 as opening act for SACRILEGE and DEATH. INSANITY circulated the 1986 rehearsal recording 'Fire, Death, Fate' and would soon foster a genuine cult following.

Progress was stalled though as INSANITY hit a series of major obstacles. Firstly Mills was incarcerated in jail for a ten month spell and then DeZuniga became ill suffering from heart problems. The band managed to lay down one further rehearsal recording before DeZuniga died tragically young on 16th May 1987. INSANITY struggled on with an ever fluctuating line up and would issue the 'Death After Death' album in 1993. Bud Mills joined Bay Area Deathsters POVERTY in 1998. Following issue of the 'Poverty Sucks' demo, Mills and band colleagues guitarist Scott Dodge and bassist Lou Gilberto, alongside Dave Gorsuch, re-founded INSANITY. The 'Sacrefixion' demo arrived in 2001, pre-empting an EP comprising all new material. That same year INSANITY folded yet again, Mills, Dodge and Gilberto subsequently re-forging POVERTY.

DEATH AFTER DEATH, Black Lung (1993). Attack Of Archangels / Fire, Death, Fate / In Memory / Rotting Decay / Morbid Lust / Blood For Blood / Possession / Death After Death.
Sacrefixion EP, Black Lung (2002). Sacrefixion / Blind / Mortification.

INSATANITY

PA, USA — *Chris Lytle (vocals), Kevin McClintock (guitar), Ed Drozdowsky (guitar), Lou Suppa (bass), Justin DiPinto (drums).*

Philadelphia extreme Metal band INSATANITY released a plethora of demos prior to signing to Greek label Unisound for their debut 1996 album. The group had been founded in mid 1992. Frontman Chris Lytle had operated as bassist / vocalist with a whole swathe of acts including STAID, OCONUS, INHUMANITY, DARK SUN and DIVINATION. Bass player Lou Suppa had a history with SAPREMIA and SPEEDCHRIST. Drummer Matt Mazzenga is also ex-OCONUS. Guitarist Ed Drozdowsky was also an active participant in MAIL ORDER BRIDE whilst his six string partner Kevin McClintock, an ex-ETHEREAL member, divides his duties with POLTERCHRIST.

INSATANITY bowed in with an eponymous demo in 1993 following it the same year with 'Ad Maiorem Satanae Glorium' and 'Unholiness Rising' in 1995.

The debut album, 'Divine Decomposition', was released by the Greek Unisound Records concern in January of 1996. However, by July of 1997 INSATANITY had signed with the Mortal Coil label and issued their second CD outing, 'Vengeance From Beyond The Grave', a shared CD in league with fellow Death Metal outfit IMMORTAL SUFFERING.

An EP, 'The Plague Of Amon', was prepared for 2002 release. During December 2002 drummer Justin DiPinto of DIVINE RAPTURE and MALEVOLENT CREATION repute replaced Matt Mazzenga.

2007 album recordings saw the inclusion of the MONARCH, DIVINE EMPIRE, MALEVOLENT CREATION and COUNCIL OF THE FALLEN credited Dave Kinkade on drums.

DIVINE DECOMPOSITION, Unisound (1996). Begotten, Not Made / Shemhamforash / Diabolical Indignation / Transfiguration / Divine Decomposition / Under The Baphomet / Rex Judaeorum / Angels Of The Apocalypse / The Blood Is The Life.
VENGEANCE FROM BEYOND THE GRAVE, Mortal Coil (1997) (Split album with IMMORTAL SUFFERING). Holocaust Divinity / At One with Infinity / Vengeance From Beyond The Grave / Mortification / The Great Abstinence / Unjaded.

INSISION

STOCKHOLM, SWEDEN — *Carl Birath (vocals), Roger Johansson (guitar), Daniel Ekeroth (bass), Marcus Jonsson (drums).*

Stockholm's INSISION debuted with the 1998 demo cassette 'Meant To Suffer'. The group had been founded the year previous by a union of erstwhile ILLDOOM and EMBALMER personnel citing an opening line-up of vocalist Johan Thornberg, guitarists Jonas Ahonen and Patrick Muhr and drummer Thomas Daun. Thornberg, Muhr and Daun had all been members of SACRIFICE BITCH. Before long Muhr exited and former DISFIGURED man Roger Johansson took his position.

With this line up INSISION cut the 1999 mini album 'The Dead Live On' for Heathendoom Music. However, further line up changes would witness the departure of both Ahonen and Thornberg. Replacements would soon be located in ex-AZATOTH and SUPERIOR Carl Birath and bassist Daniel Ekeroth, bassist of the renowned DELLAMORTE.

Gigging saw INSISION acting as opening act for HYPOCRISY, DARK FUNERAL, THE HAUNTED and MERCILESS. In March of 2001 the band drafted GENOCRUSH FEROX and CROMB guitarist Torbjörn "Toob" Brynedal, debuting as a quintet as support to Mexicans DISGORGE.

A further tape, 2001's 'Revelation Of The Sadogod', would include a cover version of DEATH's 'Zombie Ritual'. INSISION, utilising the tracks laid down in the 'Revelation Of The Sadogod' sessions, would share a split 10" single on Nuclear Winter Records with Greek act INVERACITY during 2002. A deal would be announced with the Earache Records subsidiary Wicked World for a forthcoming 2002 full length album 'Beneath The Folds Of Flesh'.

Immortal Souls Productions would re-issue 'The Dead Live On' in 2002 adding two bonus tracks including a cover of DEATH's 'Zombie Ritual'. British shows in late 2002 saw a batch of shows in December headlined by THE BERZERKER and including LABRAT and RED HARVEST. In March of 2004 the band entered Soundlab Studios with NASUM mainman Mieszko Talarczyk at the production helm for a new album going under the working title 'Revealed and Worshipped'.

With the album scheduled for July release the band announced plans to tour Europe in June on a heavyweight package billing comprising SUFFOCATION, DEMENTOR and DISGORGE. However, INSISION suffered a double blow in May of 2004 when drummer Thomas Daun departed and guitarist Toob Brynedal was forced to sit out the band's shows "for medical reasons out of our control." The band announced the 'Destruction of Finland' tour in October allied with GODHATE, DEATH DU JOUR and HATEFORM. Scandinavian dates as part of the 'Close Up' magazine sponsored 'Close Up Made Me Do it' tour had the band allied with TOTALT JÄVLA MÖRKER and THE HAUNTED in February of 2005. Australian shows in July saw support from INFERNAL METHOD.

INSISION announced they had parted ways with Wicked World Records in July 2006. The group entered Black Lounge studios in Avesta on October 16th to craft new album 'Ikon'. This album was signed over to Dental records in December.

Meant To Suffer, Insision (1998) (Demo). Paedophilia Cum Sadissimus / Meant To Suffer / Drain Your Soul / I Am The Worm.

THE DEAD LIVE ON, Heathendoom Music HDMCD010 (1999). Corridors Of Blood / Paedophilia Cum Sadissmus / The Dead Live On / She Speaks No More / Exaggerated Torment.

Promo 2000, Insision (2000) (Demo). Ex-Oblivion / Impamiiz Graa / Rewind Into Chaos / Entangled In Thorns.

Revelation Of The Sado God, Insision (2001) (Demo). Intro / Before My Altar / Sadogod / Trapped Within / Zombie Ritual / The Revelation (Outro).

Revelation Of The Sadogod EP, Nuclear Winter NWR 004 (2001) (Split 10" single with INVERACITY). Intro—Before My Altar / Sadogod / Trapped Within / Zombie Ritual / Outro—The Revelation.

THE DEAD LIVE ON, Immortal Souls Productions ISP 054 (2002). Corridors Of Blood / Paedophilia Cum Sadissimus / The Dead Live On / She Speaks No More / Exaggerated Torment / Trapped Within / Zombie Ritual.

BENEATH THE FOLDS OF FLESH, Wicked World WICK013 (2002). World Impaled / Trapped Within / Sado God / Temple Of Flesh / Rewind Into Chaos / Impamiiz Graa / My Fever / Before My Altar / Ex Oblivion.

INSISION

Revelation Of The Sadogod EP, Revenge Productions RVP 11 (2002) (Split CD EP with INVERACITY). Intro—Before My Altar / Sadogod / Trapped Within / Zombie Ritual / Outro—The Revelation.

REVEALED AND WORSHIPPED, Wicked World WICK017 (2004). No Belief / The Foul Smell Of Humans / Imminent Vision / In The Gallows / The Cleansing / Revealed And Worshipped / The Unrest / Grotesque Plague Mass / We Did Not Come To Heal / Havoc / The Ideas Of Revolution.

INSOMNIUM

JOENSUU, FINLAND — *Niilo Sevanen (vocals / bass), Ville Vänni (guitar), Ville Friman (guitar), Markus Hirvonen (drums).*

Joensuu based dark Metal band. Vocalist / bassist Niilo Sevanen and drummer Tapani Pesonen started their musical career with a covers band entitled PAISE ('Abcess' in Finnish). Later acts included Grunge orientated outfits DISHARMONY and STONECROW. During 1996 guitarists Markus Hirvonen and Ville Friman joined Sevanen and Pesonen, opting to pursue a full on Metal direction as INSOMNIUM was borne. In 1998 Pesonen was forced out in order to conduct his national military service. INSOMNIUM regrouped switching the dexterous Hirvonen over to drums and pulling in second guitarist Timo Partanen.

INSOMNIUM marked their entrance upon the Metal scene with a 2000 demo 'Underneath The Moonlit Waves'. The band added WATCH ME FALL guitarist Ville Vänni in March of 2001. Signing to the British Candlelight label INSOMNIUM debuted in 2002 with 'In The Halls Of Awaiting'. The band released their second album, 'Since The Day It All Came Down' recorded at Media Works Studios, during May 2004.

During 2004 Ville Vänni forged Death-Thrashers HATEFORM in union with singer Petri Njysvär" Nyström and the ex-MORBID DREAM triumvirate of guitarist Tomy Speedy Laisto, bassist Joni Jontte Suodenjärvi and drummer Tuomas Reisari Vähämaa.

The album 'Above The Weeping World' was released through Candlelight Records during October 2006, hitting number 9 on the Finnish charts. Preceding this release the group toured the UK backing ENSLAVED, ZYKLON and 1349.

INSOMNIUM

IN THE HALLS OF AWAITING, Candlelight CANDLE 066 (2002). Ill Starred Son / Song Of The Storm / Medeia / Dying Chant / The Elder / Black Waters / Shapes Of Deep Green / The Bitter End / Journey Unknown / In The Halls Of Awaiting.
SINCE THE DAY IT ALL CAME DOWN, Candlelight (2004). Nocturne / The Day It All Came Down / Daughter Of The Moon / The Moment Of Reckoning / Bereavement / Under The Plaintive Sky / Resonance / Death Walked The Earth / Disengagement / Closing Words / Song Of The Forlorn Son.
ABOVE THE WEEPING WORLD, Candlelight (2006). The Gale / Mortal Share / Drawn To Black / Change Of Heart / At The Gates Of Sleep / The Killjoy / Last Statement / Devoid Of Caring / In The Groves Of Death. Chart position: 9 FINLAND.

INSURRECTION

BRAZIL — *Vino Fernandes (vocals), Marcelo Roffer (guitar), Mauro Rodrigues (guitar), Josias Rodrigues (bass), Alisson Lino (drums).*

Founded in Belo Horizonte during 1992 INSURRECTION's debut line up comprised singer Vino Fernandes, guitarists Marcelo Roffer and Cláudio Lettro, bass player Marconi Kristull and drummer Cláudio Márcio. INSURRECTION's February 1993 album 'Dim As Your Mind' was released as a shared effort with DEATH DIVINE. By the time of these recordings Célio Oliveira had taken over bass responsibilities. A further change witnessed the introduction of new drummer Marcelo Zap for 1994 demo sessions.

Entering into a period of instability INSURRECTION laid down tracks for a proposed album to be entitled 'Morbid Dreams Of Incantation'. With recording taking place between 1996 and 1999 the band at this juncture numbered new recruits guitarist Fernando Fernandes, bassist Mallú Hanndres and drummer Guilherme Cosse. The 2002 formation had MISBELIEVER, WALPURGIS NIGHT and SOULLESS drummer Alisson Lino enrolled alongside ex- MORTAL SCENERY guitarist Mauro Rodrigues and bass player Josias Rodrigues. This version of the band cut promotion recordings dubbed 'Secret Garden'.

DIM AS YOUR MIND, Miragem (1993) (Split album with DEATH DIVINE). Possession Of Souls / Master Of Death / Evil / I Know Way / Dim As Your Mind / Lethal Dose / Celebrum Working / Slave Of Death.

INTENSE HAMMER RAGE

BURNIE, TAS, AUSTRALIA — *Chris (vocals / bass), Ricey (vocals / guitar), A.B. (vocals / drums).*

Burnie, Tasmanian trio INTENSE HAMMER RAGE go all out to shock with their brand of gut churning Grindcore. The band themselves subtly describe their own particular brand of Death Metal as "Putridfoulfesteringdeathgrindcuntcore". INTENSE HAMMER RAGE announced their arrival with a 1995 tape 'The 24cm Makita Brand Circular Saw' capitalized on by the following years 'Massive Sphinkta Release'. Although a quartet at this stage the band would dispense with their vocalist, for reasons as the band put it succinctly of being "lazy, whinging, so called vocalist".

1998 witnessed INTENSE HAMMER RAGE's debut CD 'Devogrindporngorecoreaphile'. With the expected obscene cover artwork the album swiftly sold out of its first production run. American label Extremist Records would re-issue the record as half of a shared release with DROGHEDA.

Further recordings resulted in the 'Gory B' eight song session released on cassette in Japan by Obliteration Records. The band, utilizing their subtly titled own label Slut Kunting Whore Productions, would later issue it on CD. A Spanish label, Flesh Feast Productions, would also pick up 'Gory B' pairing it for CD release with the 'Massive Sphinkta Release' demo.

American label Razorback put out the 2001 album 'Avagoyamugs' but the extreme lyrical content of this work resulted in an immediate ban in Australia. So keen were the authorities to censor the product that band members would later be prosecuted and fined for importing the album as a prohibited product. Split singles in collaboration with ENGORGED and N.V.E. were also planned for 2001. A former INTENSE HAMMER RAGE singer, Craig 'Spills' Spilsbury, later turned up as frontman for CRANIAL DEVOURMENT.

2006 live campaigning would be announced with a collaboration with San Diego's DISGORGE and New Zealand's DAWN OF AZAZEL for the 'Torturing New Zealand & Australia 2006' tour commencing in late February.

DEVOGRINDPORNGORECOREAPHILE, Intense Hammer Rage (1998).
GORY B., Obliteration (1999) (Japanese release).
DEVOGRINDPORNGORECOREAPHILE, Extremist (2000) (Split album with DROGHEDA). There's A Baby On My Knob / Reclusive Existence Of A Forgotten Entity / I Blame You / The Mechanism Of Defecation / Siamese Sluts Of Fused Flesh / Fucking Dead Babies Cause I'm A Sick Cunt / Axx Scenting The Gore / I Dreamt I Had A Vagina / With Her Cunt She Fucks / Pussy Lips Kissing To The Wrist / Wet Bones / Look Inside Her Insides Insides / Human Pie / Pervert The Meat / Gore, Gore And More Fucking Gore / Addicted To The Splatter / Leaking Reeking Pregnant Cunt / Sticky Mugoid Discharge.
AVAGOYAMUGS, Razorback (2001). Choking On A Chocolate Log / My Fist, Her Face, Same Time, Same Place / The Third Of Five To Have Her Alive / Homesick Abortion / Premature Ejaculraper / The Promise Of Horror And Worse To Come / I'd Rather Be Retarded / Any Old Snuff Film Starring Your Kid As The Corpse / Laugh At You, You're Dying / Meatarian Cannibal / The Corpse In Question Didn't Say No / Babysitter / Pre-Teen Sex Scene / To Men Who Masturbate Over Dying Children / The Art Of Fucking Kids.

INTENSE MOSH

ROSARIO, ARGENTINA — *Jose M. Galvano (vocals), GR Mateo (guitar), Guillermo Negro Lottero (guitar), Fernando Herrera (bass), Martin Pliego (drums).*

Rosario based Hardcore styled Death Metal band INTENSE MOSH was created during 1988 by guitarist Ignacio, vocalist Jose Miguel Galvano and drummer Esteban Olive under a formative title of HARDCORER. The first track the band composed would be a Rap style homage to local football club Rosario Central. Olive departed, paving the way for the installation of the INSANE rhythm section bassist Fernando Herrera and drummer Martin Pliego, the latter also active with Grind outfit ENTRE LA BASURA. These changes signalled the name switch to INTENSE MOSH.

Subsequently, second guitarist GR Mateo was acquired. INTENSE MOSH debuted in March 1991 with the demo 'Brewed In Rosario', recorded at in El Camote Records studio, Rosario. On the live front, the band debuted that December. Subsequent shows saw the band supporting LOGOS, HERMETICA, SICK OF IT ALL, CABEZONES, DIE TOTEN HOSEN and A.N.I.M.A.L. amongst others. The 'Dulce Y Cariñoso' album followed in 1993. This would also see a Spanish release, as a split outing shared with KOMADREJA.

Second album '17 Susurros en tus Oidos Vol. 2' followed in 1996, although the band lost the services of founder Ignacio during recording, being swiftly replaced by ENTRE LA BASURA man Guillermo Negro Lottero. Next to leave would be Martin Pliego, prompting the split of the band. INTENSE MOSH regrouped in 2002 for a one off show at Piripincho's Theatre.

Brewed In Rosario, (1991). Mision "V" / M.P.M. / El Papa Tiene S.I.D.A. / Injusticia / Enfermo (El Retorno del Budin Contaminado) / Kasimiro.

DULCE Y CARINOSO, Pinhead PH 002 (1993). Unos Gramos Son Pasion / Frutos del Horror / Viejo Bodegon / Deudas Personales / Olmedo / M.F.H. / Santas Toxinas / Actitud / Las Manos de J.D. / M.E.U.P.E.L.M.

17 SUSURROS EN TUS OIDOS VOL. 2, Intense Mosh PH 010 (1997). 11.25 / M.F.H. / Sin Sentimiento / Y Hoy No Estas … / Viejo Bodegón / A Mi No Me Convences / Las Manos De Jean Dominique / Amplitud Mental / Olmedo / T.V. / Santas Toxinas / M.P.M. / El Gran Campeón / Misión V / Actitud / Caer / Desgrazzia.

INTERNAL BLEEDING

NEW YORK, NY, USA — *Ray Lebron (vocals), Chris Pervalis (guitar), Guy Marchais (guitar), Jason Carbone (bass), Brian Tolley (drums).*

Billing themselves as "Total fucking slam" INTERNAL BLEEDING debuted in 1991 with a line up of singer Brian Richards, guitarists Chris Pervalis and Anthony Miola, bassist Tom Slobowski and drummer Brian Tolley. The band would endure repeated line up changes with only Pervalis and Tolley remaining as anchors. 1991 had the band releasing the 'One Dollar' demo followed by a second effort 'Invocation Of Evil' in 1993.

Richards would be replaced by the wonderfully named Eric Wigger but by the time of the debut album 'Voracious Contempt' Frank Rini was fronting the band. Although the album was mixed by Scott Burns the band were far from happy with the end result although in Death Metal circles the album is regarded as a near classic of the genre.

The band toured America during 1996 on a Death Metal package bill alongside SIX FEET UNDER and IMMOLATION. Rini, who when he wasn't growling for a Death Metal band was plugging away at his day job as a policeman, would guest on DISFIGURED's 'Prelude To Dementia' album.

Rini made way for the former DISFIGURED, and apparently Hawaiian shirt obsessed, Ryan Schimmenti. This liaison proved only temporary though as INTERNAL BLEEDING drafted Ray Lebron for the 'Driven To Conquer' album. The record was produced by Brian Griffin of BROKEN HOPE.

Miola would make his exit to have his place taken by ex-PYREXIA man Guy Marchias. Jason Carbone would take Hobbie's position in 2000. INTERNAL BLEEDING made another change in December of 2001 bringing in Jerry Lowe of BODYFARM as the group's new vocalist for the 2002 Olympic album 'Hatefuel'. In mid 2002 long-term guitarist Guy Marchais was replaced with Frank Buffalino.

The band announced a run of live dates alongside PYREXIA and MORTAL DECAY in July of 2003. However, these would seemingly be without founder member Chris Pervalis, who quit in June, and by early July INTERNAL BLEEDING, unable to field a full line up, had withdrawn from the tour. Bassist Jason Carbone also backed out but Pervalis was duly replaced by the REPUDILATION, GFY and 420 credited Matt Ferrara. This newest member also happened to be a participant in PUNCHYOURFACE, the side project of INTERNAL BLEEDING personnel guitarist Frank Buffalino and vocalist Jerry Lowe.

INTERNAL BLEEDING would set 'Hatefuel' as a projected title for a new 2004 opus, recorded at Full Force Studios and engineered by Terrance Hobbs, but by May had switched to a revised branding of 'Onward To Mecca'. North American touring throughout August and September had the band packaged with SIX FEET UNDER. In October INTERNAL BLEEDING were rejoined by founding guitarist Chris Pervelis, following the exit of Frank Buffalino.

The band drafted the temporary services of guitarist Chris Montez from DECRYPT and MUCOPUS drummer Kyle Eddy for a two month US trek partnered with BODIES IN THE GEARS OF THE APPARATUS and STRONG INTENTION in mid 2005. In October 2006 it was announced that four of the original members of INTERNAL BLEEDING, Frank Rini, Chris Pervelis, Brian Hobbie and Bill Tolley, were set to forge a new band.

Invocation Of Evil EP, Gutted (1993). Beyond The Gates Of Tartus (Intro) / Despoilment Of Rotting Flesh / Ruthless Inhumanity / Gutted Human Sacrifice / Epoch Of Barbarity.

Perpetual Degradation EP, Now You're Dead Music (1994). Anointed In Servitude / Conformed To Obscurity / Prophet Of The Blasphemies / Inhuman Suffering.

VORACIOUS CONTEMPT, Pavement (1996). Languish In Despair / Anointed In Servitude / Reflection Of Ignorance / Epoch Of Barbarity / Gutted Human Sacrifice / God Of Subservience / Prophet Of The Blasphemers / Humanicide / Inhuman Suffering / Despoilement Of Rotting Flesh.

THE EXTINCTION OF BENEVOLENCE, Pavement (1997). Prepare For Extinction / Ocular Introspection / Prevaricate / Ruthless Inhumanity / Plagued By Catharsis / Conformed To Obscurity / Genetic Messiah / Cycle Of Vehemence.

DRIVEN TO CONQUER, (1999). Rage / Driven To Conquer / Falling Down / Six Shots In Dallas / Conditioned / Inhuman '99 / Invisible / Slave Soul / Anthem For A Doomed Youth.

INTERNAL SUFFERING

COLOMBIA — *Fabio (vocals), Leandro (guitar), Andres (bass), Fabio Ramirez (drums).*

INTERNAL SUFFERING, previously entitled SUFFER, feature erstwhile RITUAL guitarist Leandro. The band supported visitors to Colombia INCANTATION and SODOM during 1997. Original drummer Jorge would decamp to be replaced with Edwin as the band signed with the Spanish Repulse concern for their debut album 'Supreme Knowledge Domain'. However, after recording Edwin made his exit and Fabio took the drum stool. In a round of musical chairs this new enlistee would soon break ranks and Edwin was inducted back into the fold.

INTERNAL SUFFERING cut the 6 track mini album 'Unmercyful Examination' for the Japanese Macabre Mementos label. A split album, 'Vatican's Bombardment' to be shared with Americans STENCH OF DECREPITY for Fleshfeast Productions, was mooted but never transpired.

Touring in 2001 found INTERNAL SUFFERING on the road in America alongside BRODEQUIN and Japan's VOMIT REMNANTS. In March of 2002 the band opened shows in Colombia for CANNIBAL CORPSE. The band would also announce a fresh record deal with the Dutch Displeased label for the May 'Chaotic Matrix' album. Promotion found the band on the road in America including a date at the 'Ohio Deathfest'. Further gigs had INTERNAL SUFFERING billed with the package 'Chaos Over America' tour alongside GORGASM, CATTLE DECAPITATION and SUTURE. Displeased would also announce the re-issue later that same year of 'Supreme Knowledge Domain', remastered, clad in new artwork and with bonus tracks. The band hit Europe for a three month live trek in mid 2003 packaged alongside SANATORIUM and THRONEAEON. They also put in an appearance at the 2003 Portuguese 'Steel Warriors Rebellion VI' festival alongside ENTHRONED, ATTICK DEMONS, KATATONIA, FINNTROLL, HOLOCAUSTO CANIBAL, NEOPLASMAH, PITCH BLACK, CORPUS CHRISTII, IN THY FLESH, AXE MURDERERS, AGONIZED, THANATOSCHIZO, FLAGELLUM DEI and ETERNAL MOURNING,

Original drummer Fabio Ramirez, having since made his name with INFERNAL HATE and CARNAL, made a return to the INTERNAL SUFFERING drum position in November of 2003. Progress would be marred though as guitarist Leandro broke his arm. Back in action, the band entered Mana Studios in Tampa, Florida in April of 2004 to record a new album 'Choronzonic Force Domination'. Erik Rutan of MORBID ANGEL would be at the production helm. The band headed up the 'Brutal Domination' US tour that August, heading up a pack comprising INCINERATE, STABWOUND and EMETH.

INTERNAL SUFFERING signed with Unique Leader Records in mid 2005, entering Mana Recording Studios with HATE ETERNAL's Erik Rutan acting as producer. The band lined up with INCANTATION and YEAR OF DESOLATION for a further US tour, opened up another lengthy US tour commencing November 1st 2006 at the Modern Exchange in Southgate, Michigan.

SUPREME KNOWLEDGE DOMAIN, Supreme Music SM001 (2000). Mighty Triumphant Return / Valley Of The Impaled / Evil Sorcerers / Daemons Awakening / Outside Dwellers / Threshold Into The Unknown / Enter The Gate Of Death / Beyond The Mystic Portal Of Madness / Supreme Knowledge Domain / Summoning The Ancient Ones.

UNMERCYFUL EXTERMINATION, Macabre Memento (2001). Unmercyful Examination / Dominating Thunderous Force / Breeders Of Chaos / Outside Dwellers (New Hyper Brutality Impaled version) / Catacombs Devourer / Decapitation Of The Weak.

CHAOTIC MATRIX, Displeased D-00098 (2002). Chaotic Matrix: Prelude I- Onward To Termination / Colossal Vortex: Prelude II- Phenomenal Spectrum / Lurking Monstrosity: Prelude III- Ancient Oceans Dweller / Cosmic Ancient Mountain: Upcoming Chaos I- The Tree Of Knowledge / Reborn In Victory: Upcoming Chaos II- The Unholy Manuscript / Cataclysmic Origin: Upcoming Chaos III- Unleashed Astral Chaos / Vatican Bombardment: Uprising Hecatomb I- Dominion Of The Xul / Destroyer Entity: Uprising Hecatomb II- Center Of Destruction / The Antiquary Horror: Interlude- At The Edge Of Madness / Decapitation Of The Weak: Uprising Hecatomb III- Arrival Of The Highest Hierarchy.

CHORONZONIC FORCE DOMINATION, Displeased D-00136 (2004). Choronzonic Force Domination / Summon The Gods Of Chaos / Across The Tenth Aethyr / Baphomet Invocation / Legion / Dagon's Rising / Dispersion And Darkness / Orbiting Chaosphere / Enter The Gate Of Death.

INTESTINAL DISGORGE

TX, USA — *Pissy (vocals), Josh (guitar), Nick (bass), Ryan (drums).*

Grindcore merchants INTESTINAL DISGORGE bowed in with the 1999 demo 'Festering Excrement'. A split cassette with EJACULATED WHORE followed prior to an appearance on a 4 way compilation tape in collaboration with SLOUGH, DEMONIC ORGY and ABOSRAINE BOSOM.

2000's 'Drowned In Rectal Sludge' album credited the INTESTINAL DISGORGE membership as vocalist "The Consumer Of Festering Rectal Slime", guitarists "The Imbiber Of Disgusting Urinary Discharge" and "The Colon Grinding Corpse Butcher" and drummer "The Feces-Caked Barbecuer Of Anal Sausage". The band would split up before the release of their 2001 album 'Whore Splattered Walls'.

DROWNED IN RECTAL SLUDGE, Lofty Storm LSR006 (2000). Rectum Grinder / Plastered In Runny Filth / Toilet Intercourse / Bathing In Fecal Bathwater / Corrosion Of Green Anal Walls / Gastrointestinal Splatter Spray / Gorging On Fizzing Malignant Entrails / Imbibing Rancid Micturation / Intestinal Collapse And Melting / Extensive Obliteration Of The Rectal Orifice / Exploding Juicy Cancerous Guts / Caked In Grimy Rectal Filth / Vomiting Rancid Grime / Sleeping In Grime Soaked Bedsheets / Swimming In Child Innards / Torrents Of Festering Purulency / Trembling In Torrents Of Diarrhea / Life Story Of A Coprophagic / Soaking Wet With Urination / Disemboweled And Deliciously Barbecued / Foaming Genital Corpulence / Colonic Eruption / Butchered Rotting Human Carcasses / Soaked With Intestinal Chyme / Cascade Of Gastrointestinal Crap / Bloody Feces Syndrome / Vomiting Fecal Paste / Face Down In A Toilet Full Of Vomit And Feces / Pictures Of Blistered Genitalia.

WHORE SPLATTERED WALLS, Lofty Storm (2001).

INTO ETERNITY

REGINA, SK, CANADA — *Tim Roth (vocals / guitar), Daniel Nargang (guitar), Scott Krall (bass), Chris McDougall (keyboards), Jim Austin (drums).*

Regina, Saskatchewan based INTO ETERNITY put a new spin on the Progressive Rock scene with their October 2000 eponymous debut by adventurously introducing Death Metal and Gothic influences into the mix. The band featured in its ranks former PERICARDIUM members vocalist / guitarist Tim Roth and bassist Scott Krall alongside drummer Jim Austin. Dutch label DVS Records picked the band up for the debut. Live work to promote this opus included Canadian gigs supporting NEVERMORE plus a valuable appearance at the 'ProgPower Europe' festival.

Following the issue of the 'Dead Or Dreaming' album guitarist Daniel Nargang left the fold. INTO ETERNITY soon regrouped pulling in vocalist Chris Krall and guitar player Jeff Story. The band would act as support act to the reformed DARK ANGEL for North American dates in December 2002. INTO ETERNAL later united with HATE ETERNAL, KATAKLYSM, and DYING FETUS for North American dates in February and March of 2003. Upon conclusion of these dates PERICARDIUM's Rob Doherty took over guitar duties from Jeff Story.

Signing to the German Century Media label the band recorded ten songs in their hometown based Touchwood Studios for 2004's 'Buried In Oblivion' opus. The band parted ways with longtime bassist Scott Krall in March. Troy of DIRTBREED acted as stand in for scheduled live work in Europe as support to NAGLFAR. The band, seeing Adam Sagan of HALYCON taking over from Jim Austin on the drums, undertook European package tour dates allied with KATAKLYSM, MYSTIC CIRCLE and GRAVEWORM in October. INTO ETERNITY announced the addition of singer Stu Block of Vancouver's OMEGA CROM to the group's ranks in January 2005.

US dates scheduled for March had the band partnered with AMORPHIS, SINGLE BULLET THEORY and BEYOND THE EMBRACE. Unfortunately, the band was forced to cancel several of their late March appearances after guitarist Rob Doherty sought emergency medical treatment in Atlanta, Georgia. The musician was diagnosed with pneumonia and the band immediately returned to Canada where Doherty, vocalist Stu Block and guitarist/vocalist Tim Roth were all treated for pneumonia. The group, fully recovered, launched into Canadian gigs then formed up with a Summer package touring bill comprising HATE ETERNAL, INCANTATION, KRISIUN and ALL SHALL PERISH for US gigs in June. INTO ETERNITY were then added to the full HAMMERFALL and EDGUY North American tour billing in August before renewed touring in September found the band opening for Finnish Metal band STRATOVARIUS. Both Tim Roth and Rob Doherty also scheduled time to add guest spots to the KATAKLYSM album 'Road To Devastation'.

On 31st October INTO ETERNITY joined the OPETH and NEVERMORE US tour in Philadelphia. Drummer Adam Sagan opted out in February 2006, being replaced swiftly by original drummer Jim Austin. The band joined up with the MEGADETH headlined 'Gigantour' North American festivals in early September, sharing billing with OPETH, ARCH ENEMY, OVERKILL, LAMB OF GOD, SANCTITY and THE SMASHUP. By December the band roster had shifted once again as new recruits Justin Bender on guitar and ex-BEYOND THE EMBRACE drummer Steve Bolognese were enrolled.

INTO ETERNITY partnered with DESTRUCTION, MUNICIPAL WASTE and HIRAX for the "Thrash Till Death Over North America" shows in January and February 2007. The group returned for a further round of US campaigning in March and April flanking THE HAUNTED and DARK TRANQUILLITY. INTO ETERNITY partnered with REDEMPTION and headliners DREAM THEATER for US shows in July and August.

INTO ETERNITY, DVS Records DVS002 (2000). Torn / Sorrow / Left Behind / The Modern Day / A Frozen Escape / Behind the Disguise / Holding Onto Emptiness / Into Eternity / Speak of the Dead / Silence Through Virtue.
DEAD OR DREAMING, DVS Records (2002). Absolution Of The Soul / Distant Pale Future / Shallow / Unholy (Fields Of The Dead) / Elysium Dream / Selling God / Imagination Overdose / Dead Or Dreaming / Cyber Messiah / Identify.
BURIED IN OBLIVION, Century Media (2004). Splintered Visions / Embraced By Desolation / Three Dimensional Aperture / Beginning Of The End / Point Of Uncertainty / Spiralling Into Depression / Isolation: Part I: Buried In Oblivion / Isolation: Part II: Black Sea Of Agony / Morose Seclusion.
THE SCATTERING OF ASHES, Century Media (2006). Novus Inceptum (Intro) / Severe Emotional Distress / Nothing / Timeless Winter / Out / A Past Beyond Memory / Surrounded By Night / Eternal / Pain Through Breathing / Suspension Of Disbelief / Paralyzed.

INTO THE MOAT

FORT LAUDERDALE, FL, USA — *Earl Ruwell IV (vocals), Kit Wray (guitar), Rob Shaffer (guitar), Joshua Thiel (bass), Matthew Grossman (drums).*

Fort Lauderdale, Florida act INTO THE MOAT, self described as "a technical Metalcore band with elements of Grind, Death Metal", was initiated by drummer Matthew Gossman in May 2001. Gossman, performing all instrumentation, crafted a first set of demos as a solo effort, using these tapes to pull together a viable band unit. The membership formula was stabilised by a quintet ranging in age from 16 to 19 when bass player Kit Wray shifted over to guitar duties in January 2002. Signing to Lovelost Records INTO THE MOAT debuted with the EP 'Means By Which The End Is Justified', produced by Jeremy Staska at Studio 13 and released in May 2003.

INTO THE MOAT signed a deal with Metal Blade Records during May of 2004. US dates allied with PSYOPUS commenced in July with recording of an album being undertaken in October at Mana Recording Studios in Tampa, Florida. Further North American gigs in July had the group allied with A PERFECT MURDER and SOILENT GREEN. Unfortunately bassist Joshua Thiel withdrew citing "medical reasons" before these shows. Mid-tour guitarist Rob Shaffer pulled out too, forcing the band to cancel six gigs. The band hired guitarist Travis LeVrier and resumed road work.

Going into September, the band formed up package shows backed by BETWEEN THE BURIED AND ME, THE BLACK DAHLIA MURDER, and CEPHALIC CARNAGE. In November it was revealed drummer Matthew Grossman was playing guitar for Sludge project GLACIER.

Means By Which The End Is Justified, Lovelost (2003).
THE DESIGN, Metal Blade (2005). Century II / Empty Shell / Dead Before I Stray / Guardian / The Inexorable / Fortitudine / Beyond Treachery / None Shall Pass / Prologue.

INVERTED

SWEDEN — *Henric Heed (vocals), Mats Blomberg (guitar), Larsken Svensson (guitar), Joel Andersson (bass), Kristian Hasselhuhn (drums).*

Gothenburg Death Metal act founded in 1991, debuting that year with the demo 'Tales Of Estaban'. INVERTED at that time featured singer Joakim Almgren, the guitarist pairing Mats Blomberg and Lars-Hakan Svensson, bass player Dan Bengtsson and drummer Kristian Hasselhuhn. Retaining the same band structure a second demo, 'Heaven Defied', preceded signature to the Wild Rags label for 1994's 'Revocation Of The Beast' EP. Switching labels to the Belgian Shiver imprint INVERTED cut the full length album 'Shadowland'. Line up at this juncture comprised vocalist Henric Heed, guitarists Larsen Svensson and Mats Blomberg, the EXEMPT credited bass player Joel Andersson and drummer Kristian Hasselhuhn. INVERTED underwent a radical line up overhaul upfront of the second album 'There Can Be Only One …'. Now fronted by singer Patrik Svensson, the steadfast rhythm section of Andersson and Hasselhuhn were also joined by guitarist Johan Ohlsson.

A new singer in Stefan Lundberg was then introduced but INVERTED folded during 1998, spawning IMMERSED IN BLOOD during October of that year. Lundberg, Ohlsson and Andersson allied themselves with second guitarist Robert Tyborn Axt and the SUPREME MAJESTY credited drummer Joakim Unger for the opening February 1999 demo 'Eine Kleine Deathmusik'.

INVERTED's Johan Ohlsson is also active with Industrial Death Metal act BLESSED.

Split, Wild Rags (1994) (Split single with RESUCITATOR). Split.
Revocation Of The Beast, Wild Rags WRR046 (1995). Revocation Of The Beast / Beyond The Holy Ground / Lost / Into The Sign Of Chaos.
THE SHADOWLAND, Shiver SHR 016 (1995). Diabolical Ceremonies / Condemned / Circle Of Candles / The Infernal Gate / Journey Into Shadowland / Scripture Of Disgrace / The Dark And Bitter Moon / Serenade Of Grief / Crawling Under Lies.
Empire Of Darkness, Regress BTT004 (1995). Empire Of Darkness / Crawling Underbellies.
Diabolical Ceremonies, Voice Of Death (1996) (Split single with CENTINEX). Diabolical Ceremonies.
THERE CAN BE ONLY ONE …, Shiver (1997). Revenge / Fallen Saints / Longing For Darker Times / As The Last Angel Falls / Inverted / Metal Victory / Forever Death / Wrath Of Sin.

INVOCATOR

DENMARK — *Jacob Hansen (vocals / guitar), Flemming C. Lund (guitar), Carsten N. Mikkelsen (bass), Jakob Grundel (drums).*

A Thrash band dating back to 1986 that went under their original title of BLACK CREED, the group's first demo tape was 'Genetic Confusion' in 1988 followed by 'Alterations' the following year. After gigs with EDGE OF SANITY and ENTOMBED the band signed to Swedish label Black Mark. During 1990 the band toured both Denmark and Finland allied with Speed Metal act PRESTIGE.

The band's debut album, 1992's 'Excursion Demise' featuring former V-AXE, GRAFF SPEE and EXTREME FEEDBACK guitarist Jesper Jensen, sold around 10'000 copies in Europe. That same year the band appeared at the prestigious Roskilde festival, although oddly were lumped in on the non Metal day to share a stage uncomfortably with CROWDED HOUSE, TEXAS, THE POGUES and JAMES. The success of 'Excursion's Demise' prompted INVOCATOR to record a further album 'Weave The Apocalypse' and they opened for PARADISE LOST in Europe during 1994. The 'Early Years' album comprised of the band's original demo tapes plus covers of ARTILLERY and DARK ANGEL tracks. Jacob Schultz was replaced by guitarist Perle Hansen for the 'Dying To Live' album.

INVOCATOR, citing a line-up comprising of Jacob Hansen, AUTUMN LEAVES guitarist Flemming C. Lund, bass player Carsten N. Mikkelsen and erstwhile WITHERING SURFACE drummer Jakob Gundel, would reform in 2002 immediately setting to work on a new studio album. 'Through The Flesh To The Soul', set to appear in mid 2003 on the Italian Scarlet label, included a cover version of ASSASSIN's 'Abstract War'. The regrouped band marked an appearance at the November 'Aalborg Metal' festival in Denmark for their live debut.

Flemming C. Lund would work up a Thrash side project in early 2004. Dubbed SCAVENGER the band comprised SLUGS, ex-AUTUMN LEAVES man Boris Tandrup on bass and Morten Sørensen from AURORA, WUTHERING HEIGHTS and PYRAMAZE on drums. Meantime INVOCATOR drummer Jakob Gundel acted as sessioneer for US act MORPHEUS' debut album and, joining forces with Anders Høeg and Mikkel Sandager of MERCENARY, forged a Thrash Metal side project. Jacob Hansen would be found engaging in guest duties too, appearing on the 'Warhead' track on HATESPHERE's 2004 album 'Ballet Of The Brute'. Gaining kudos as an in demand producer, Hansen racked up impressive credits on albums by the likes of MERCENARY, COMMUNIC, HATESPHERE, ROB ROCK, VOLBEAT and RAUNCHY.

Bassist Carsten Mikkelsen exited in September. According to an official statement this was "due to lack of interest". That same month Jacob Hansen joined the ranks of BEYOND TWILIGHT. January of 2005 found drummer Jakob Gundel in the studio firing up a new band unit with MUGSHOT vocalist Kim Orneborg and the erstwhile WITHERING SURFACE pairing of guitarist Allan Tvedebrink and bassist Kasper Boye-Larsen dubbed THE DOWNWARD CANDIDATE. This new unit committed to demos in January produced by KONKHRA and FURIOUS TRAUMA guitarist Lars Mayland.

Jacob Hansen became the new singer of ANUBIS GATE in January 2006. Breaking a three year hiatus, INVOCATOR, comprising Jacob Hansen, Flemming C. Lund, Carsten Mikkelsen and Joakob Grundel, announced a return to live action in 2007.

EXCURSIONS DEMISE, Black Mark BMCD12 (1992). Excursion Demise (... To A Twisted Recess Of Mind) / Forsaken Ones / The Persistence From Memorial Chasm / Absurd Temptation / Schismatic Injective Therapy / Occurrence Concealed / Beyond Insufferable Dormancy / Inner Contrarieties / Alterations.
EARLY YEARS, Diehard RRS943 (1995). Dismal Serfage / Insurrected Despair / Restraint Life / The Scars Remain / Alterations / Occurrence Concealed / The Persistence From Memorial Chasm / Pursuit Of A Rising Necessity / The Eternal War / The Promise Of Agony.
DYING TO LIVE, Progress PCD20 (1995). Dying To Live / Kristendom / Shattered Self / King In A World Of Fools / Search / South Of No North / Living Is It / Astray / For A While / Hole.
THROUGH THE FLESH TO THE SOUL, Scarlet SC 071-2 (2003). Intro / Through The Flesh To The Soul / Writhe In Spit / On My Knees / Flick It On / Infatuated I Am (Speak To Me) / There Is No Saviour / The Chemistry Of Restlessness / Under The Skin / Fire Cleanses All / Sand Between The Teeth.

IRON LUNG

NJ, USA — *Tom Bush (vocals), Steve Seigerman (guitar), Doug Cerrito (guitar), Frank Maggio (bass), Doug Bohn (drums).*

IRON LUNG is rooted in the antecedent act WELT, issuing the 'Paranoid Delusion' EP on Progress Records in 1994. Featured would be SUFFOCATION and AUTOPSY drummer Doug Bohn, ex-SOCIAL DISEASE guitarist Steve Seigerman, the MYSTEMA, CHRONIC HALITOSIS and SOCIAL DISEASE credited vocalist Tom Bush and SUFFOCATION guitarist Doug Cerrito. The band changed names in 1996 to IRON LUNG releasing the 'Chasing Salvation' album on Diehard Records.

Cerrito joined HATE ETERNAL in 1998. In early 2002 ex-IRON LUNG guitarist Frank Maggio united with the veteran scene figure of former MALEVOLENT CREATION, DISGORGED, R.I.P., INCANTATION, HATEPLOW and SUFFOCATION drummer Dave Culross to announce the formation of PUMMEL, working in league with vocalist Tom Bush, bassist Mark Astrin and second guitarist Steve Seigerman. However, by June 2003 Seigerman and Culross had forged STORM.

CHASING SALVATION, Progress (1997). Far Too Late / Jinx / Chasing Salvation / Heliopath / Tolerance / Dying To Get Laid / Reality Check / Sunblock / Birdman.

IRONY OF CHRIST

BRISTOL, UK — *Sacha Darwin (vocals / guitar), Dave MacLean (guitar), Dan Bartlett (bass), Pete Aplin (drums).*

Bristol based melodic Death Metal combo IRONY OF CHRIST was conceived by KACHANA's vocalist / guitarist Sacha Darwin in mid 2001. A triumvirate of former KACHANA members made up the numbers, with Mark Shield on bass, Tom Huskinson on keyboards and Pete Aplin of MULCH and RELENTLESS on the drums. However, with both MULCH and KACHANA recording throughout 2001 IRONY OF CHRIST was put on hold until 2003. A second guitarist, Jon, was enlisted in 2003 but exited shortly after. Nevertheless, a debut EP entitled 'The Eternal War' was recorded in early 2004.

Line-up changes witnessed the departure of Shield and the introduction of Dan Bartlett from SHATTERED and CRANIOSACRAL on bass guitar. Meantime, Darwin opted out of KACHANA to prioritise IRONY OF CHRIST. The formation was bolstered further with the acquisition of lead guitarist Rob Quick. Following tour work, Quick, joining THE ADVOCATE GENERALS, would be superseded by another CRANIOSACRAL man, Dave MacLean.

The Eternal War, Irony Of Christ (2004). Intro / Revelations / Jester / Demons And Angels / Your Own Death / The Eternal Mourning.

IRREVERENCE

MILAN, ITALY — *Ricky Paioro (vocals / guitar), Luca Colombo (guitar), Mauro Passiatore (bass), Davide Firinu (drums).*

Milan Death Metal combo IRREVERENCE was formulated during 1995 by vocalist / guitarist Ricky Paioro and drummer Davide Firinu. By 1997 the band had been through a few temporary members but stabilised with the addition of lead guitarist Luca Petrazzuolo and bass player Giuliano Strozzi. In this formation the group recorded self titled demos in 1998 and 1999 before signing to Stonehenge Records for the album 'Totally Negative Thoughts', this set featuring a cover version of SODOM's 'Agent Orange'. IRREVERENCE then suffered line up changes, with both Strozzi and Petrazzuolo defecting. Regrouping, the band drew in new recruits Stefano Bertolotti on guitar and bassist Mauro Passiatore.

During 2002 IRREVERENCE entered Harris Johns' Spiderhouse studios In Berlin to lay down four tracks for the EP 'Target: Hate', closing with a rendition of DEATH's 'Pull The Plug', emerging in February 2003. Live work ensued, after which Bertolotti exited. Luca Colombo duly filled the vacancy. Christmas of 2004 saw progress stalled when Paioro suffered a car accident, breaking his arm.

January of 2005 found Davide Firinu temping for Thrashers METHEDRAS. Both Firinu and Passiatore also activated side project L'ORDADUNTO, delivering the album 'Porci'. Another related project would be MURDER 16TH, established in early 2006 by the IRREVERENCE duo vocalist / guitarist Ricky Paioro and drummer Davide Firinu together with NEOPHYTE bassist Saverio Mollica.

In April of 2006 IRREVERENCE toured Italy on a package billing shared with GRIMNESS and NUCLEAR SYMPHONY. The band contributed their cover version of TANKARD's 'Beermuda' to the tribute album 'A Tribute To Tankard' included as a bonus disc on the AFM Records 2007 TANKARD release 'Best Case Scenario: 25 Years In Beers'.

TOTALLY NEGATIVE THOUGHTS, Stonehenge Records (2000). In The Chaos / No Hypocrisy / Needless Mind / Memories Will Never Die / Overcome / Dreams For Reality / Nuclear Years / Irreverence (Beyond Reality) / Agent Orange.
Target: Hate, (2003). Hate Has No Name / Red Zone / 3092 / Darkening Their Light / In Thoughts / Pull The Plug.

IRRITATE

LAPPEENRANTA, FINLAND — *Sami Kettunen (vocals / bass), Janne (guitar), Jukkis (drums).*

Lappeenranta's Groove orientated Death Metal band IRRITATE comprises the CONJURATION trio of Visa Witchcraft, Susej and Harald Mentor (a.k.a. Sami Kettunen). The latter also holds credits with NAILGUNNER, INCRIMINATED, solo Black Metal project RIDE FOR REVENGE and SIVIILKURHA whilst Susej also has ties to INCRIMINATED. For live work the band employed veteran drummer Mikko Aspa of CLANDESTINE BLAZE, DEATHSPELL OMEGA, MORBID SAVOURING, GRUNT, STABAT MATER, NICOLE 12, CLINIC OF TORTURE, CREAMFACE and FLESHPRESS repute.

IRRITATE releases included a split outing 'Need To Destroy' on Riotous Assembly Records with GODSTOMPER, a limited edition 7" split single shared with HATED PRINCIPLES through Hostile Regression and a split album in collaboration with UTTER BASTARD. The group also united with EMULGATOR, MURDER COMPANY and DRUNK JUNKEES for the four way 'Grind War Finland' album. A 2004 co-operative release between Fuckitall Records, Bucho Discos and Underground Punk Support saw IRRITATE combining with OLHO DE GATO and SOCIAL CHAOS for '3 Ways Of Armageddon', this including a cover version of HATED PRINCIPLES 'Armed Leftist'. The 2005 'Driven' EP on Agromosh Records featured renditions of BATHORY's 'Possessed' and LÄRM's 'T.V. Spots'.

3 WAYS OF ARMAGEDDON, Bucho Discos (2004) (Split album with SOCIAL CHAOS and OLHO DE GATO). Revenge Track / For The Maximum Death Toll / Back To The Ground / Armed Leftist / Affection = Addiction / The Warlike Groove.

Driven EP, Agromosh (2005). Driven / Vodka Schizo / T.V. Spots / Rock On / Possessed.

ISACAARUM

ČESKÉ BUDĚJOVICE, CZECH REPUBLIC — *Chymus (vocals), Paul The Whipper (guitar), Blood-spitting M. (guitar), Monthy (drums).*

ISACAARUM is a "Sado Black Grind" endeavour founded during 1993 in the town of České Budějovice. First product would be the 1995 demo 'For Blood Is Life ...' followed by a split 7" single shared with SORATH through Epidemie Records. Singer Chymus, alongside INGROWING vocalist Vlakin and guitarist Pouzar, along with ex-INGROWING drummer Milan would also be operational with Noise act LEWD.

The Leviathan label issued the ISACAARUM 'Die Verwandlung' album in 1997, after which the 'For Blood Is Life ...' material was released on CD format as a split offering shared with ENOCHIAN.

The band engaged with INGROWING for the 'Bondage Enforcers' tour of Europe in April 2006.

CURBED, Obscene Productions OBP 034 (2000). XXX—Rapist & Goregasm / Mentulam Caco! / Hydraulic Kamasutra / Black Dressed Narcissist / Mao-sochism 2000 / Twat Blasting Assassins / Ladies' Pussy Bulldozers / Arts Of Farts / Clyster Squad / Spermacerated / Penis Kamikaze / Coitus Hortator.

CUNT HACKERS, Obscene Productions OBP 041 (2001). Cumshot Combat / Bitchbrigade / Anal Razzia / Integrated Vulva Hacker / Isamahaparinibbanasuttam / T.N.T. Clit Orgasm / Climacterium Pleasures / Teenage Cunt Powerplay / Vagina Panzerfaust / Lost Between Tits / Irrumatrix / Curbed.

MENSES EXORCISM, Obscene Productions (2003). Fellatorium / Cock Control / Piss Fighter / G Spot Seppuka / Dildog Troppers / Cummand & Cuntquer / Menstrua / Orgasmatch Offside / Rhythmic Balls / Mea Verpa! / Stormbuggers Fartillery / The Menses Exorcist / Piss Fighter (Live video) / Stormbuggers Fartillery (Live video) / Teenage Cunt Powerplay (Live video).

ISLAND

BONN, GERMANY — *Christian Kolf (vocals / guitar), Florian Toyka (bass), Rafael Calman (drums).*

ISLAND is a Bonn Progressive Death Metal act. Founded in October 2003, the first product emerged the following year in the form of the self-financed 'Orakel' EP. These sessions were recorded at two locations, Studio 308 and Flammenmeer Studio with co-producer Tim Steffens. At this juncture ISLAND comprised vocalist / guitarist Christian Kolf with Florian Toyka on bass and Patrick Schröder, of KLABAUTAMANN and VALBORG, on drums. Kolf had ties with ORBO and VALBORG whilst Toyka had association with KLABAUTAMANN. Patrick Schröder exited in order to prioritise his other act CENTAURUS-A.

The 'Island' arrived in May 2005. That same year Kolf and Toyka activated the Sludge side act WOBURN HOUSE. For ISLAND commitments, the pair pulled in a session drummer, Martin Below of AARDVARKS, GUERILLA, BLOOD RED ANGEL and WOLFEN repute.

ISLAND inducted new drummer Rafael Calman, from ORBO and VALBORG, in September 2006.

Orakel, Island (2004). Serenity / River Source / Grund / Orakel / Journey Through The Jewel / Über Dem Thal.

Island, Island (2005). The White Ghoul / Veritas / Island.

ISOLATED FIELDS

KS, USA — *D.C. (vocals), Andrew Nagorski (guitar), Tim Dzubay (guitar), Pete Tucker (bass / death vocals), Ben Haggard (drums).*

Kansas Black Metal combo ISOLATED FIELDS was initiated in March of 2002 by the erstwhile DESCENSION pairing of Jon Tucker and vocalist D.C. Initial recruits would include Eric Coleman, Danny a.k.a. 'Beavedge', John Kessler and keyboard player Daniel Breathwaite. The group then re-shaped itself to involve Thai Johnson on guitar, Josh Mundy on keyboards and Jason Hadlock on drums with D.C. and Tucker sharing lead vocals. In this formation ISOLATED FIELDS appeared on the 2003 compilation album 'Treasury Of Souls' issued by Lifeless Records, capitalised on by the demo 'Lost In The Soil'.

Ructions hit the band in March of 2003 when both Hadlock and Johnson exited, soon followed by Mundy. ISOLATED FIELDS was put into stasis whilst D.C. assembled another band that Summer, THE LANTERN HILL NIGHTMARE with drummer Ben Haggard, guitarist Tim Dzubay and Josh Veatch. In June of 2003, after Veatch's defection signalled the collapse of THE LANTERN HILL NIGHTMARE, D.C. and Tucker reconstituted ISOLATED FIELDS, drafting the NOCTOPIA and DARKSIDE credited guitarist Travis Niemeyer and ex-STYGIAN, DESCENSION and VENIFICUS bassist Pete Tucker. Finalising the roster would be formative ISOLATED FIELDS keyboard player Daniel Breathwaite and THE LANTERN HILL NIGHTMARE, OF THE FALLEN and CRAVEN drummer Ben Haggard. The new look ISOLATED FIELDS aimed to blend Black, Death and Thrash Metal and in this guise set out on the live trail scoring opening slots for SIX FEET UNDER, BEHEMOTH, DOG FASHION DISCO and SKINLESS.

Founder Jon Tucker bowed out in late 2003, being replaced by Tim Dzubay of ANGRIUS and THE LANTERN HILL NIGHTMARE. Utilising Greg Ponder as producer, the band cut demo tracks in Springfield during February of 2004. 'The Distant Funeral Bells' EP was then released and once more the group was invited to appear on an updated 'Treasury Of Souls' compilation.

September of 2004 marked the departure of Niemeyer, his place being taken by Andrew Nagorski of SOUNDBLIND, [LID] and VIVISECTION. Daniel Breathwaite bailed out in October.

Lost In The Soil, Isolated Fields (2002). Intro / Consistent Torment / Lost In The Soil / Suffering Soul / Outro.

Nothing Left, Isolated Fields (2003). Threshold Of Embodiment / Consistent Torment / Nothing Left / Infantile Delusion.

The Distant Funeral Bells, Isolated Fields (2004). Threshold Of Embodiment / Nothing Left / Infantile Delusion / Dawn Of Erosion / The Distant Funeral Bells.

ISOLE

GÄVLE, SWEDEN — *Daniel Bryntse (vocals), Christer Olsson (guitar), Henrik Lindenmo (bass), Jonas Lindström (drums).*

Gävle Doom Death act ISOLE's history is entrenched in that of formative outfit FORLORN, forged during 1991 by vocalist / drummer Daniel Bryntse (a.k.a. 'Vortex') and guitarist Crister Olsson. Bryntse has a vast array of credits on the Scandinavian Metal scene including terms of duty with COMPLICITY, AUTUMN LEAVES, DAMNAGE, HELLPIKE, MILKTOAST, MOOD, MORANNON, NIGHCHANT, SAVORY, THEORY IN PRACTICE,

STENCH and WITHERED BEAUTY. Bryntse also deputised as live bassist and drummer for SORCERY and, alongside his FORLORN colleague guitarist Per Sandgren, operates WINDWALKER.

The original line up would also include WITHERED BEAUTY and FEBRUARI 93 credited vocalist / guitarist Magnus Björk, guitarist Magnus Helin, bass player Jan Larsson and drummer Kim Molin. The latter exited before the close of the year with Helin following him in 1992.

FORLORN inducted bass player Henrik Lindenmo (a.k.a. 'Goatlord' of MORANNON and fellow Doomsters OUTREMER) to replace Larsen in 1995. However, with Björk quitting in 1996 and Sandgren relocating to Stockholm the group came to a halt. Members then prioritised their other endeavours, Bryntse and Björk with WITHERED BEAUTY, Bryntse and Sandgren with WINDWALKER, Olsson and Lindenmo with HELLPIKE and Bryntse, Olsson and Björk as part of FEBRUARI 93. FORLORN returned for a 2001 demo 'Autumn Leaves' but then underwent line-up changes as P.O. enrolled replacing Henrik Lindenmo. In a period of confusion a 7" single was projected for issue through I Hate Records but P.O. then exited, Lindenmo returned and Per Sandgren took his leave, these changes culminating in a name change to ISOLE. The album 'Forevermore' was recorded in 2004.

ISOLE worked with session man Jonas Lindström of WITHERED BEAUTY on drums in early 2005, this union being made permanent by April. Gigs in Germany and France allied with WORLD BELOW would be announced for November, but then cancelled.

FOREVERMORE, I Hate IHATE010 (2005). The Watcher / Deceiver / Age Of Darkness / Forevermore / Premonitions / Beyond The Black / Moonstone.

The Beyond, I Hate (2006). The Beyond / Beyond The Black II.

THRONE OF VOID, I Hate (2006). Autumn Leaves / Dreams / Green Demon / Throne Of Void / Insomnia / Bleak / Life?

JACK SLATER

GERMANY — *Stefan Horn (vocals), Sobo (guitar), Nandi (guitar), Christian Neumann (bass), Sepp (drums).*

Cologne's JACK SLATER, founded during 1995 by guitarist Alexander 'Sobo' Sobocinski and drummer Sebastian 'Sepp' Mohneke, deliver "Grind-Breaklastiger Death Metal". Early releases included the 1996 demo 'Abhängig', seeing Sobo and Sepp joined by vocalist Alex, guitarist Berndt and bassist Blondie, and the 1998 EP 'Crescendo'. This latter session found Küpper now installed on second guitar and Björn on bass.

The band introduced singer Stefan Horn, a veteran of such acts as MÄHDRESCHA, ZWEKKFORM and KRUSCHKE, in October of 1998 for the promotion session 'Leichenschmaus' in 1999 leading up to the album 'Playcorpse' emerging in 2001 through Gernhart Records. JACK SLATER pulled in ex-DAKRIA and AARDVARKS guitarist Hernando 'Nandi' Ramirez Giraldo and former JOHNNY WALKER TEXAS BOYS bassist Christian Neumann in May of 2003 and 'Metzgore', recorded at Stonehenge Studios in Bonn for Cudgel Agency Records, arrived in March of 2004. During May JACK SLATER put in a burst of European dates billed as 'Thunderstorm Over Europe' alongside BENEDICTION, DIVINE EMPIRE and MASTER.

Stefan Horn is also active with ANGRY CUNT and EROTIK DER MASCHINE. Bassist Christian Neumann is a member of BLOODSHED.

Crescendo, (1998). Selbstbrand / Doch / Exil / Du Selbst.

PLAYCORPSE, Gernhart (2001). Playcorpse / Kinderfresser (Part I) / Falscher Hase / Leichenschmaus / Hackfleischmann / Brute Mord / Kinderfresser (Part II) / Schlachtplatte / Der schmale Grat ....

METZGORE, Cudgel Agency (2004). Eisenwichser / Lynchmob / Metzgore / Sensou / Timmy / Für Elise / Kinderfresser (Part III) / Jack In The Box / Zerschmetterling.

JIGSORE TERROR

SWEDEN — *Moshbastard (vocals / bass), Tobbe Ander (vocals / guitar), Tobbe Eng (guitar), Adde Mitrouliu (drums).*

JIGSORE TERROR comprises vocalist / bassist 'Moshbastard' of BIRDFLESH and HYPNOSIA, the BIRDFLESH credited guitar team of Tobbe Ander and Tobbe Eng with drummer Adde Mitrouliu (a.k.a. Smattro Ansjovis) of SAYYADINA, BIRDFLESH, DETHRONEMENT and GENERAL SURGERY repute.

JIGSORE TERROR signed to France's Listenable Records in early 2004, entering Soundlab studio in Sweden with engineer Mieszko Talarczyk of NASUM repute for the album 'World End Carnage'. The record, which included a cover version of FURBOWL's 'The Needle', saw Dan Swanö of NIGHTINGALE, UNICORN, EDGE OF SANITY, INFESTDEAD, ODYSSEY and PAN-THY-MONIUM adding backing vocals.

WORLD END CARNAGE, Listenable POSH 062 (2004). Gorging On Exposed Arteries / Skeletal Decomposition / Slaughtered Existence / Death Rattle Cacophony / Senseless Slaughter / Rotten Heads / Reeking Death / Insane Torture / Scattered Cranial Remains / Violent Molestations / Corpses On Fire / Feat Of Dismembered Limbs / Brutally Murdered / Bestial Frenzy / World End Carnage.

JOHNNY TRUANT

BRIGHTON, EAST SUSSEX, UK — *Olly Mitchell (vocals), Stuart Hunter (guitar), Reuben Gotto (guitar), James Hunter (bass), Paul Jackson (drums).*

Brighton based Metal band JOHNNY TRUANT released the October 2005 album 'In The Library Of Horrific Events', produced by KILLSWITCH ENGAGE guitarist Adam Dutkiewicz. JOHNNY TRUANT toured Europe alongside AIDEN and BULLET FOR MY VALENTINE in February 2006 upfront of a headline UK series of dates. Guitarist Al Kilcullen opted out, being replaced by SACK TRICK and TWIN ZERO man Reuben Gotto in time for European shows alongside MONEEN and ALEXISONFIRE.

An adventurous side project for Reuben Gotto came with DREAM OF AN OPIUM EATER, a UK/Norwegian Horror Metal collaboration featuring Benny Calvert from KILLING JOKE, Ivar Bjørnson from ENSLAVED plus Julia Ruzicka from MILLION DEAD. This unit debuted at the 2007 edition of the Danish Roskilde Festival.

IN THE LIBRARY OF HORRIFIC EVENTS, Backs (2005). I Love You Even Though You're A Zombie Now / The Bloodening / Realist Surrealist / Dirty Vampire Feeding Frenzy / Throne Vertigo / Vultures / A Day In The Death / Necropolis Junction / I The Exploder / Footprints In The Thunder.

JOÃO

CURITIBA, PR, BRAZIL — *Clovis (vocals), Júlio (guitar), Emannuel (guitar), Augustus (Bass), André (drums).*

Quite incredibly, Grindcore merchants JOÃO, founded in 2003 as a trio of vocalist Clovis, guitarist Júlio and drummer André, debuted with a 98 track self financed album 'Primeiro João' in June of 2003. Studio guests included Osías and Diogo of SERENADE IN DARKNESS, Toddy from INVASAO, Felipe of MIRACLE and VULGATA's Guilherme Born. 2004's follow up 'As The Shadows Death' once again saw studio contributions from Guilherme Born as well as LONGWINTER guitarist Lin. The album included a cover version of ANTIDEMON's 'Libertação II'. By this stage the band had expanded to a quintet with the introduction of second guitarist Emannuel and bassist Augustus.

PRIMEIRO JOÃO, (2003). Introdução do João / Capítulo 1 Versículo 1 / Capítulo 1 Versículo 2 / Capítulo 1 Versículo 3 / Capítulo 1 Versículo 4 / Capítulo 1 Versículo 5 / Capítulo 1 Versículo 6 / Capítulo 1 Versículo 7 / Capítulo 1 Versículo 8 / Capítulo 1 Versículo 9 / 10 / Capítulo 2 Versículo 1 / Capítulo 2 Versículo 2 / Capítulo 2 Versículo 3 / Capítulo 2 Versículo 4 / Capítulo 2 Versículo 5 / Capítulo 2 Versículo 6 / Capítulo 2 Versículo 7 / Capítulo 2 Versículo 8 / Capítulo 2 Versículo 9 / Capítulo 2 Versículo 10 / Capítulo 2 Versículo 11 /

Capítulo 2 Versículo 12 / Capítulo 2 Versículo 13 / Capítulo 2 Versículo 14 / Capítulo 2 Versículo 15 / Capítulo 2 Versículo 16 / Capítulo 2 Versículo 17 / Capítulo 2 Versículo 18 / Capítulo 2 Versículo 19 / Capítulo 2 Versículo 20 / Capítulo 2 Versículo 21 / Capítulo 2 Versículo 22 / Capítulo 2 Versículo 23 / Capítulo 2 Versículo 24 / Capítulo 2 Versículo 25 / Capítulo 2 Versículo 26 / Capítulo 2 Versículo 27 / Capítulo 2 Versículo 28 / Capítulo 2 Versículo 29 / Capítulo 3 Versículo 1 / Capítulo 3 Versículo 2 / Capítulo 3 Versículo 3 / Capítulo 3 Versículo 4 / Capítulo 3 Versículo 5 / Capítulo 3 Versículo 6 / Capítulo 3 Versículo 7 / Capítulo 3 Versículo 8 / Capítulo 3 Versículo 9 / Capítulo 3 Versículo 10 / Capítulo 3 Versículo 11 / Capítulo 3 Versículo 12 / Capítulo 3 Versículo 13 / Capítulo 3 Versículo 14 / Capítulo 3 Versículo 15 / Capítulo 3 Versículo 16 / Capítulo 3 Versículo 17 / Capítulo 3 Versículo 18 / Capítulo 3 Versículo 19 / Capítulo 3 Versículo 20 / Capítulo 3 Versículo 21 / Capítulo 3 Versículo 22 / Capítulo 3 Versículo 23 / Capítulo 3 Versículo 24 / Capítulo 4 Versículo 1 / Capítulo 4 Versículo 2 / Capítulo 4 Versículo 3 / Capítulo 4 Versículo 4 / Capítulo 4 Versículo 5 / Capítulo 4 Versículo 6 / Capítulo 4 Versículo 7 / Capítulo 4 Versículo 8 / Capítulo 4 Versículo 9 / Capítulo 4 Versículo 10 / Capítulo 4 Versículo 11 / Capítulo 4 Versículo 12 / Capítulo 4 Versículo 13 / Capítulo 4 Versículo 14 / Capítulo 4 Versículo 15 / Capítulo 4 Versículo 16 / Capítulo 4 Versículo 17 / Capítulo 4 Versículo 18 / Capítulo 4 Versículo 19 / Capítulo 4 Versículo 20 / Capítulo 4 Versículo 21 / Capítulo 5 Versículo 1 / Capítulo 5 Versículo 2 / Capítulo 5 Versículo 3 / Capítulo 5 Versículo 4 / Capítulo 5 Versículo 5 / Capítulo 5 Versículo 6 / Capítulo 5 Versículo 7 / Capítulo 5 Versículo 8 / Capítulo 5 Versículo 9 / Capítulo 5 Versículo 10 / 11 / Capítulo 5 Versículo 12 / 13 / 14 / Capítulo 5 Versículo 15 / 16 / 17 / 18 / 19 / 20 / Capítulo 5 Versículo 21 / Violent Termination.

AS THE SHADOWS DEATH, João (2004). Alcool / Capitulo 1 Versiculo 6 / Capitulo 2 Versiculo 20 / Capitulo 2 Versiculo 29 / Capitulo 3 Versiculo 15 / Capitulo 3 Versiculo 18 / Capitulo 5 Versiculo 21 / Capitulo 5 Versiculo 7 / Eu Vou para a Praia (c2v26) / Gremlins (c2v1) / João / Libertação II / No War / Nothing Belongs To You / Capitulo 1 Versiculo 7 / Capitulo 1 Versiculo 8 / Capitulo 1 Versiculos 9 E 10 / Capitulo 2 Versiculo 4 / Capitulo 2 Versiculo 5 / Capitulo 2 Versiculo 9 / Capitulo 2 Versiculo 13 / Capitulo 2 Versiculo 15 / Capitulo 2 Versiculo 17 / Capitulo 2 Versiculo 24 / Capitulo 2 Versiculo 25 / Capitulo 2 Versiculo 28 / Capitulo 3 Versiculo 8 / Capitulo 3 Versiculo 10 / Capitulo 3 Versiculo 13 / Capitulo 4 Versiculo 11 / Capitulo 4 Versiculo 12 / Capitulo 4 Versiculo 16 / Capitulo 4 Versiculo 18 / Capitulo 4 Versiculo 21 / Capitulo 5 Versiculo 12 / Capitulo 5 Versiculo 15 / Capitulo 5 Versiculo 19 / João / Gremlins / Capitulo 1 Versiculo 6 / Eu Vou Pra Praia / Alcool / Apresentação Da Banda / Look Down / Diogo / Total Disaster / M.A.D. / Mr. Melodic / Final.

JUDECCA

CAPE CORAL, FL, USA — *Tim Kimbrough (vocals), Travis Haycock (guitar), Bill Smith (bass), Brent Carmany (drums).*

JUDECCA emerged from the fertile Florida Death Metal swamps of the early 90's. In 1992 the Cape Coral three-piece released the demo 'Eternal Rest', followed up by the 'Scenes Of An Obscure Death' session in February of 1993. The following year the band caught the eye of the underground US label Wild Rags, who licensed the early material and re-issued the 'Scenes' EP with the three track 'Eternal Rest' demo as a bonus.

In 1995 the band issued the charmingly titled, EP/single 'Awakened By The Stench of the Dead' which was a precursor to the bands first full-length album. Now fully signed to the expanding Wild Rags label, the debut album 'Beyond, What The Eyes Can't See' came out in 1996 and saw the addition of Tim Kimbrough on vocals. The vocal chores had previously been handled by founder and lyricist Travis Haycock. Also issued would be a split 7" single shared with HORROR OF HORRORS.

Eternal Rest, (1992). Cannibalistic Urge / Religious Decay / Eternal Rest.
Scenes Of An Obscure Death, Judecca (1993). The Realm / Unspeakable Acts / Bodies Found / Evil Born / Left To Die / Necrosis.
Awakened By The Stench Of Blood, Wild Rags (1995). Forensic Pathology / The Black Blood Of Christ / Evil Born.
BEYOND, WHAT THE EYES CAN'T SEE, Wild Rags WRR 078 (1996). The Undead / The Stench Of An Undouched Cunt / Beyond, What The Eyes Can't See / As We Fuck / May You Find Peace / Trauma Induced Coma / Consume The Soul / Forensic Pathology / The Black Blood Of Christ.

JUDGEMENT DAY

HOLLAND — *Jeroen Dammers (vocals), Simone (vocals), Wim Van Burken (guitar), Theo Van Eickelen (guitar), Bus Van Den Bogaard (bass), Nolo (drums).*

A Dutch Death Metal band, JUDGEMENT DAY have toured with SINISTER, PUNGENT STENCH and KRABATHOR. A demo, 'Pathology Of Crowding', arrived in 1994. In addition to their debut album of 1996 vintage the group have had three songs featured on the 'Effigy Of The Possessed' compilation album.

JUDGEMENT DAY boasts the inclusion of veterans from such acts as CENTURION and PLEUROSY. Bass player Theo Van Eekelen also performs in HOUWITSER and the reformed THANATOS. The 7" single 'To Conjure Conjoint Confusion' released on Damnation Records includes a cover version of Canadian veterans SLAUGHTER's 'F.O.D.'.

A short burst of Benelux dates in December 2004 aligned with DISMEMBER and CALLENISH CIRCLE saw the band joined by new bassist Bas van den Boogaard. Rumours suggested ex-drummer Paul Beltman had joined a reformed SINISTER in March 2005.

CIR—CUM—CIS—ION OF THE MAR -TYR,, Arctic Serenades EFFI 006 (1996). Horror Pain / Daily Rituals / The Old Tree / Sexual Intercourse / Invisible Downfall / Clouds Of Mordor / Pathology Of Crowding.
To Conjure Conjoint Confusion, Damnation (2000). To Conjure Conjoint Confusion.

JUGGERMATH

ADELAIDE, SA, AUSTRALIA — *Ben (vocals), Demir (guitar), Nick Seja (guitar), Ozan (bass), Selen (drums).*

Adelaide Death Metal band JUGGERMATH was conceived during 1999 under a formative billing of SPLAATAGORPHUS as a Grindcore quartet comprising vocalist James, guitarist Demir, bassist Ozan and Selen on drums. A demo was recorded in 2000 but after just one live show, a decision was made not to release the session. With James' departure, SPLAATAGORPHUS folded.

The collective re-assembled in 2002 under the revised brand of JUGGERMATH, now fronted by ex-OBSIDIAN vocalist Ben. In September of 2003 the band cut tracks for a proposed demo in collaboration with DEPHILER. However, DEPHILER folded, putting a halt on the project, but enabling guitarist Nick Seja to join the ranks of JUGGERMATH. This new formation debuted live in January 2004 and issued the demo 'In Onslaught Divina'.

In Onslaught Divina, Juggermath (2003). Intro / Miasma In Pestilence / When Hooks Meet Flesh / Aeons Amok / In Onslaught Divina.

JUNGLE ROT

KENOSHA, WI, USA — *Dave Matrise (vocals / guitar), Kevin Forsythe (guitar), James Genenz (bass), Jim Garcia (drums).*

JUNGLE ROT's own particular brand 'Deathgroove', along with their themed album cover artwork's based on the ubiquitous figure of Sergeant Rot, has set them apart from the pack. The band, based in Kenosha, Wisconsin and named after the Vietnamese war version of trenchfoot, arrived in 1994 with a line-up of vocalist / guitarist Jim Bell, vocalist / guitarist Dave Matrise, bassist Chris Djurcic and ex-PRISONER drummer Jim Harte.

With this membership, JUNGLE ROT cut the opening demo 'Rip Off Your Face' in 1995. A second demo that same year, 'Skin The Living' issued on Felch Bucket Music, witnessed such a volume of sales that the sessions were re-released on CD format in 1998 by Pure Death Records. A latter line-up saw the percussion station taken by erstwhile EVIL INCARNATE man Andy Vehnekamp.

JUNGLE ROT's second album 'Slaughter The Weak' was originally issued by Pulverizer Records in 1998. Label problems saw a swift re-release, with different artwork, the following year by Pavement Records. Meantime, a third round of artwork graced the European version licensed to Germany's Morbid Records with the original depictions of dead bodies removed.

With JUNGLE ROT on a roll a mini-album 'Darkness Foretold' was quickly released. The record included the brand new title track, live material and cover versions of CARNIVORE's 'Jesus Hitler', SLAYER's 'Fight Till Death' and SODOM's 'Agent Orange'. This record has proven to be quite a collectors item as it came with a JUNGLE ROT 'Sergeant Rot' comic the cover of which is covered in the by now expected, entrails, brains and gouged eyes.

JUNGLE ROT underwent a major line up overhaul when founding member Jim Bell departed. Former CYANOSIS man Kevin Forsythe took the role and his CYANOSIS colleague Jim Garcia took the drum position from previous incumbent Shawn Johnson. Keeping up with tradition JUNGLE ROT's 2001 album 'Dead And Buried', released on Olympic Records, saw a European license through Season Of Mist Records but with the artwork (you guessed it- dead bodies!) revised to accommodate the censor. A 2004 album, 'Fueled By Hate', emerged through Olympic in June.

Guitarist Chris Djuricic lent his bass skills to Chicago Thrash combo HURTLOCKER during the recording sessions for their new demo 'Begging for Hatred'. JUNGLE ROT would act as openers to the September / October nationwide tour from the heavyweight package comprising DEICIDE, CATTLE DECAPITATION and GOATWHORE.

The band helped forge a heavyweight road alliance, suitably dubbed 'European Decimation', took in April 2005 gigs throughout Italy, Portugal, the UK, Holland and Germany in partnership with CATASTROPHIC, FUNERUS, HEXENHAMMER and INCANTATION. Canadian gigs in June had the group, now featuring FLESHGRIND bassist James Genenz in the guitar role, sharing stages with a package billing of HATE ETERNAL, KRISIUN INTO ETERNITY and ALL SHALL PERISH. The band, signing a new label deal with Crash Music, parted ways with guitarist Genenz in September, re-enlisting former touring stand in Geoff Bub.

JUNGLE ROT, re-enlisting James Genenz, this time on bass guitar, entered the recording studio in February 2006 to cut new album 'War Zone'. Promoting the record, issued in June, JUNGLE ROT partnered with HURTLOCKER, DESOLATION and DEICIDE for US touring throughout September and October.

SKIN THE LIVING, Pure Death (1998). Demon Souls / Destruction And Misery / Eternal Agony / Killing Spree / Rotten Bodies / Black Candle Mass / Awaiting The End / Tomb Of Armenus / Decapitated / Screaming For Life.
DARKNESS FORETOLD, Sounds Of Death (1998). Agent Orange / Fight Till Death / Jesus Hitler / Darkness Foretold / Tomb Of Armenus (Live) / Eternal Agony (Live) / Consumed In Darkness (Live).
SLAUGHTER THE WEAK, Morbid MR054 (1999). Left For Dead / Gore Bag / Infectious / Demigorgon / Consumed In Darkness / Murder One / Butchering Death / World Of Hate / Deadly Force.
DEAD AND BURIED, Olympic 216 (2001). Intro / Immersed In Pain / Virus / Misplaced Anger / Humans Shall Pay / Strangulation Mutilation / Red Skies / Killing Machine / Dead And Buried / Psychotic Cremation / Afterlife / Circle Of Death- Jungle Rot / Another Fix.
FUELED BY HATE, Olympic OLY 0239-2 (2004). Intro / Face Down / Let Them Die / Fractured / Gain Control / Gasping For Air / Low Life / Scars Of The Suffering / Symbols Of Hate / No Surrender / Habit Fulfilled / More Demon Souls.
WAR ZONE, Crash Music Inc. (2006). Victims Of Violence / Cut In Two / Savage Rite / They Gave Their Lives / Strong Shall Survive / Decapitated / Ready For War / Ambushed / Fight For Life / Territoriality / Killing Spree.

KAAMOS

STOCKHOLM, SWEDEN — *Karl Envall (vocals / bass), Nicklas Eriksson (guitar), Konstantin Papavassiliou (guitar), Chris Piss (drums).*

Stockholm's KAAMOS delivered a purely refined strain of Death Metal. The band came into being in mid 1998, emerging from the aftermath of a prior act A MIND CONFUSED, which included KAAMOS guitarists Konstantin Papavassilou and Nicklas Eriksson, the latter also operational with Thrashers SERPENT OBSCENE.

KAAMOS issued a promotional recording and in parallel a limited edition split 7" single in league with DRAUTHUS in February of the following year. By November Thörngren had relinquished his position to Karl Envall. KAAMOS drummer Thomas Åberg was replaced by Chris Piss (actually Cristofer Barkensjö of REPUGNANT) in September 2000, the second demo session 'Curse Of Aeons' being recorded shortly after.

In late 2001 KAAMOS entered the recording studio once more, laying down their eponymous debut album for the Candlelight label. Barkensjö also bashes the skins for GENERAL SURGERY. Cristofer Barkensjö joined up with veteran Death / Doom outfit GRAVE in February 2003.

The band would be back in the studio during April 2004, cutting a new album entitled 'Lucifer Rising'. May dates in Finland saw KAAMOS on a package billing alongside WATAIN, ANXIOUS DEATH and SLUGATHOR. Drummer Chris Barkensjö joined BLACKSHINE in November 2005. Meantime, Imperium Productions re-issued both 'Kaamos' and 'Lucifer Rising' on limited edition, gatefold vinyl format. The following February Barkensjö enrolled himself into the ranks of FACE DOWN.

KAAMOS announced they were to perform their "last gig ever" at the 'Party.San Open Air' festival in August 2006 in Bad Berka, Germany.

Kaamos EP, Dauthus 1899 D/1 (1999) (Limited edition 397 copies). Desecration / Blood Of Chaos.
Promo 1999, Kaamos (1999). Desecration / Blood Of Chaos / Cries Of The Damned.
Curse Of Aeons, Kaamos (2001) (Demo). Prophesies / Curse Of Aeons / Khem / Mass Of The Dead / Descent.
KAAMOS, Candlelight CANDLE073CD (2002). Corpus Vermis / Circle Of Mania / The Storm Of Coming / Khem / Doom Of Man / Blood Of Chaos / Curse Of Aeons / The Chasm / Cries Of The Damned.
Curse Of Aeons, Nuclear Winter NWR666 (2004) (10" vinyl single). Prophesies / Curse Of Aeons / Khem / Mass Of The Dead / Descent.
LUCIFER RISING, Candlelight CANDLE 154 (2005). Black Revelation / Gnosticon / Inaugurating Evil / Theriomorphic Pandaemonium / Dark Void / Lucifer Rising / Sacrament In Red / Mysterious Reversion / Chthonic / Ascent.

KABAK

SAN SALVADOR, EL SALVADOR — *Rodrigo Fatality (vocals / drums), Jorge Grind (guitar), Ciro Rotten (bass).*

KABAK rank as one of the very first Rock bands to attain a record deal in El Salvador. The band formed in San Salvador during October of 1994 citing a line-up of Jorge 'Grind' López on guitar, Julio 'Corpsegore' Garcia on bass and Rodrigo 'Fatality' Artiga on both drums and lead vocals. In 1995 they KABAK cut their five track opening demo with Mexico's American Line Productions entitled '30 Weeks Of Defecation'. Progress was marred though when Garcia suffered a motorcycle accident injuring his right arm, leaving him unable to play bass. Ciro Rotten took his place.

KABAK issued a mini-album 'Mala Praxis' during 2000. The 'Cronicas Del Quirofano' album, produced by BRONCCO's Vicente Sibrián and sporting a truly horrific cover depicting a discarded abortion, arrived in 2002 included upon which were demo tracks and live CD-ROM material.

Bassist Julio Corpsegore would be killed in a bar fight. KABAK folded and it was announced that Artiga had relocated to Finland, founding HOLY GATES. He subsequently joined Finnish Death Metal bands KATAPLEXIA and DEEPRED.

DESCOMPOSICION CEREBRAL, APL Records (1999). Asauras Purulentas (Intro) / Catastrofe Letrinal / Descomposición Cerebral / Supuración / Execrable Electrolisis / Expectoración Necrotisada (Intro) / Macrovomitorium / Necrocomezón / Parásitos Incontrolables De Putrefacción / Ventosos Lacrimogenos.

CRONICAS DEL QUIROFANO, American Line Productions LA-049 (2002). Several Necrosis / Mala Praxis (Breast Cancer) / Cronica Arteritis Posttraumatica / Cataplexia Ante Mortem / Antiperistaltismo Duodenal / Intro / Several Necrosis / Cronica Arteritis Postraumatico / Supuracion / Reversion Genetica Epifenomena / Mala Praxis.

KACHANA

BRISTOL, UK — *Sacha Darwin (vocals), Alexander Sarantis (guitar), Dan Beaufort (guitar), Mark Shield (bass), Tom Huskinson (drums).*

Although branded with a Zimbabwean name KACHANA are in fact Bristol based Death Thrashers. The group was constructed during 1998 when bassist Sacha Darwin forged a union with fellow Bristol University students guitarist Alex Sarantis and drummer Tom Huskinson. Tom Blackford was introduced as lead vocalist but then switched to the second guitar role but would opt out in 1999. Ed Shackelton, of CONCEPT, substituted as second guitarist for a performance at a 'Battle of the Bands' competition in Bath. However, Shackelton soon decamped in order to join OBSIDIAN. At this juncture Darwin moved over to the role of frontman whilst Mark Shield was incorporated on six string bass. In this incarnation KACHANA won the next Rocksoc 'Battle of the Bands'.

KACHANA released a demo in 2001 entitled 'The Blood Eagle', following this up with an appearance at the 'DungeonFest 2001' in Leeds. That same year KACHANA members Sacha Darwin, Mark Shield and Tom Huskinson were also operational with Thrashers CRANIOSACRAL. Cutting the debut album 'Killing Inside' the group augmented their sound by adding former TORSO guitarist Dan Beaufort. A further demo, 'Bleeding The Darkness', arrived in 2004.

In May of 2004 Sacha Darwin opted out to prioritise his other act IRONY OF CHRIST. The band acquired new singer Tom Morton in July, this event signalling a switch towards a more traditional Heavy Metal stance. KACHANA marked a return in 2006 with the demo 'The Plains Of Illyricum'.

Kachana, (1998). Feed My Pain / Taste The Flesh / Triad.

The Blood Eagle, (2001). Triad / Fornicate For Me / Awakening Of The Dead / Racist Man / Blood Eagle.

KILLING INSIDE, Oran Mor Productions ORAN002CD (2003). Severed Skin / Byzantium / Leper Of This Era / Awakening Of The Dead / Hatred Drowned / Killing Inside / Triad / Taste The Flesh / Beyond Repentance / Blood Eagle / Morbid Atrophy.

Bleeding The Darkness, (2004). Buried / Bleeding The Darkness / Destiny.

The Plains Of Illyricum, (2001). Poseidon / The Plains Of Illyricum / Ride / Twist Of The Knife / Master Of Vice / Vipera Aspis.

KADATH

AACHEN, GERMANY — *Holger Friedenberger (vocals), Markus Mouhlen (guitar), Stefan Wilk (guitar), Marc Leclerc (bass), Erling Agebbo (drums).*

Aachen based Death-Grind Metal band KADATH was formulated during 1992, initially entitled CATALEPSY and comprising singer Holger Friedenberger, guitarists Kai and Robert, bassist Tanya and Robin on drums. However, Robin vacated the drum stool within nine months and the band went into stasis until October 1993 when Rolf was drafted as drummer. Another change saw the bass duties being handed over to Marc. As KADATH, inspired by the German band BLOOD, they debuted on the live front in February 2004 in Aachen sharing the stage with Punk act ZSK-5. On the recording front KADATH bowed in with an April 1994 demo cassette 'Face Your Death', which soon sold out of its 400 copies. Further live work saw supports to ASMODINA, INQUISITOR, GUTWRENCH, DAWN and Argentina's VIBRION.

KADATH's 'Into The Eternal Depths Of Sorrow And Desolation' EP, recorded in April 1995, saw subsequent limited release, just 600 copies, in the USA on the Wild Rags label. The band then ejected Robert, branding him an "incredible liar", and drafted Marcus "Mockel" Mouhlen as substitute. More line-up changes then saw the departure of Rolf, eventually replaced by Belgian Erling Agebbo. Touring saw road work with FLESHLESS, DERANGED and SKULL CRUSHER. Unfortunately a planned tour of Europe packaged with FLESHLESS and DISFIGURED CORPSE was chaotically whittled down to just a solitary gig in Hamburg.

A third demo saw light in 1996 after which Kai opted out. KADATH shared a split 7" EP through Paranoia Syndromes with Nottingham's EVOKE, contributing the track 'Disturbance In My Nocturnal Domain', and another split with IMMURED on Stuhlgang Records. The November 1997 EP 'Twisted Tales Of Gruesome Fates' included a cover version of TERRORIZER's 'Corporation Pull-In'. Live dates intensified with gigs in alliance with IMMURED, AGATHOCLES, MALEDICTIVE PIGS, D.A.B., MASTIC SCUM, SUPPOSITORY, INHUME, PLEURISY, BLOCKHEADS, HARMONY DIES, PURGATORY, DEAD INFECTION, KRISIUN, SUFFICIDE, VADER, LAST DAYS OF HUMANITY and CRYPTIC CARNAGE. The group also appeared on the first 'Fuck The Commerce' festival in May 1997.

Teutonic Existence Records released the full-length 'Cruel' album, produced by ex-HOLY MOSES guitarist Andy Classen, in February 1999. However, KADATH then entered a period of inactivity during which Mouhlen took his leave, being superseded by MENTAL ABERRATION's Stefan "Gesuz" Wilk. Mouhlen returned to record the album 'Chasing The Devil', recorded at Gernhart Records Studio in Siegburg for Cudgel Agency, but the band then, following a September show at the 'Morbide Festspiele' in Bischofswerda, lost the services of Agebbo. Mike Heinemann of Duisberg's INFECDEAD took the drum role. KADATH's membership problems continued to plague them throughout 2003 as Mouhlen then second guitarist Wilk exited. However, toward the close of the year former personnel Markus Mouhlen and drummer Erling Agebbo returned.

Face Your Death, (1994). Intro / Infanticide / Face Your Death / Disgrace / Facial Acromegalical Malformation / Rape Of The Soul / Subconscious Fear Of Death / The Tribulation / Horrible Reality.

Into The Eternal Depths Of Sorrow And Desolation, Wild Rags WRR-KAD (1995). Ascension (Intro) / Thoughts Of A Depressive Origin / An Urgent Intention For Self Destruction (Thoughts Part 2) / Prophecy/World's End / The Unavoidable Process Of Our Nature's Collapse / Descension (Outro).

Into The Eternal Depths Of Sorrow And Desolation, (1995). Ascension (Intro) / Thoughts Of A Depressive Origin / An Urgent Intention For Self Destruction / Prophecy / World's End / The Unavoidable Process Of Our Nature's Collapse / Descension (Outro).

Promo 96, (1996). Abusing The Innocents / Disturbance In My Nocturnal Domain / Traumatic Experiences With Horrifying Consequence.

Twisted Tales Of Gruesome Fates, (1997). Abusing The Innocents / Disturbance In My Nocturnal Domain / Traumatic Experiences With Horrifying Consequence / Corporation Pull-In.

Disturbance In My Nocturnal Domain, Paranoia Syndromes (1997) (Split EP with EVOKE). Disturbance In My Nocturnal Domain.

Kadath, Stuhlgang (1997) (Split EP with IMMURED). Abusing The Innocents / Corporation Pull-In.

CRUEL!, Teutonic Existence (1998). Reign Of Inner Pain / Into The Labyrinths Of Deviance / A Fateful Vision Of Our Ruin / Glorifying Destructive Sexuality / The Seven Spheres Of Dante's Inferno / Burnt Alive In A Barn / Paradise For Perverts / Trench Warfare.

CRUEL!, Teutonic Existence (1999). Reign Of Inner Pain / Into The Labyrinths Of Deviance / A Fateful Vision Of Our Ruin / Glorifying Destructive Sexuality / The Seven Spheres Of Dante's Inferno / Burnt Alive In A Barn / Paradise For Perverts / Trench Warfare.

CHASING THE DEVIL, Cudgel Agency (2002). The Investigation (Chapter III) / Thirst For Revenge (Chapter V) / The Devil Of Rostov (Chapter I) / False Confession (Chapter II) / Stalking The Prey (Chapter IV) / A Monster Revealed (Chapter VI) / Epilogue: Coup De Grace.

CHASING THE DEVIL, (2002). The Investigation / Thirst For Revenge / The Devil Of Rostov / False Confession / Stalking The Prey / A Monster Revealed / Epilogue: Coup De Grace.

KALIBAN

LAMMI, FINLAND — *Henri Peltola (vocals / guitar), Toni Kettunen (guitar), Olli Simola (bass), Mertsi Helppi (drums).*

KALIBAN is a melodic Death Metal band, featuring ex-VANGUARD guitarist Henri Peltola, hailing from Lammi. Created in 1994, at first billed as CALIBAN, the band's opening effort would be the July 1995 demo 'Celestial Sounds', after which bassist Olli Simola enrolled. Further promotion sessions included 'From The Darkest Season' in August 1996 and 'Divine Landscapes' in mid 1997. KALIBAN cut the album 'The Tempest Of Thoughts' at Astia Studios in January 2000, eventually securing a deal with Low Frequency Records for a 2002 issue.

Subsequent line-up changes saw Simola exiting and Henri Gylander being switched bass and dual lead vocals. The band also added ex-VELDER guitarist Mikko.

Celestial Sounds, (1995).
From The Darkest Season, (1996).
Divine Landscapes, (1997).
TEMPEST OF THOUGHT, (2002). Orchard / Carnal Cage / The Angel / Forever in Bloom / The Crimson Ark / Call Of Siren / My Song Silent / Time To Burn.

KALIBAS

NY, USA — *Pat Murphy (vocals), Jody Roberts (guitar), Aaron Nichols (guitar), Paul Pieramico (bass), Erik Burke (drums).*

KALIBAS was created in December of 1999, forged by the trio of guitarist Jody Roberts, bassist Paul Pieramico and drummer Erik Burke, subsequently enrolling vocalist Pat Murphy and second guitarist Greg Herman. Erik Burke is a scene veteran of such acts as NUCLEAR ASSAULT, VALPURGA, LETHARGY, SULACO, MUNGBEANDEMON and BLATANT CRAP TASTE.

In April of 2000 the band cut their first product, a 7" single, for the Howling Bull America label. KALIBAS man Greg Hermann, also active with INERTIA and LOW TON, would switch to drums to found Math Metal band PSYOPUS in 2002. Hermann was duly replaced by Aaron Nichols for recording of a split album shared with RUNE, issued in 2003 through Relapse Records.

PRODUCT OF HARD LIVING, Willowtip (2002). Smells Like Menopause / From The Waste Down / All Of Japa / Floating In Concrete / Last Minute Error / Rundown / Take The Plunge / She Wipes From The Back To The Front / Fishing With Dynamite / Semantic Insanity / Reroute The Foul.

KALISIA

MONTPELLIER, FRANCE — *Brett Caldas-Lima (vocals / guitar), Loïc Tenezas (guitar), Gerard Thibaut (bass), Laurent Pouget (keyboards), Laurent Bendahan (drums).*

Progressive Death Metal act KALISIA made their entrance with the December 1994 demo 'Whisper'. A 1995 follow up, 'Skies', subsequently saw a CD re-release the following year on the Adipocere label. The group was conceived in 1994 as vocalist / guitarist Brett Caldas-Lima, keyboard player Laurent Pouget and guitarist Loïc Tenezas joined forces in August of that year with former RANDOMIZE TIMER drummer Laurent Bendahan and bassist Gerard Thibaut from Toulon Death Metal act BLOODY RITUAL.

Brett found time to participate as an active member of FAIRLIGHT during 2001. Band members Caldas-Lima, Tenezas and Thibaut, also formed up the side project THE K-LIGHT PROJECT 3.3 in alliance with FAIRLIGHT personnel. Other outside activities saw Tenezas appearing on the 2001 CHRYSALIS album 'Between Strength and Frailty'. Both Caldas-Lima and Thibaut had both earlier been involved with CHRYSALIS. Thibaut's energies would also be diverted into his own BLISS Electronic concern, later evolving into the more Metal edged EILERA project.

KALISIA added female singer Corinne to the line up in September of 2001 but she was to leave in July of 2002.

Skies EP, Adipocere (1996). Tower Of Vanities / Chimeria / The Lost Soul / The Mental Frames.

KALOPSIA

NEW BRUNSWICK, NJ, USA — *Matt Medeiros (vocals / guitar), Chris Born (guitar), Mike Hussey (bass).*

New Brunswick's KALOPSIA released the demo 'Source Of My Evil' in 2000 as their opening shot. The group had been formulate during late 1999 by vocalist / bassist Matt Medeiros, a member of ESCHATON and RETROVERSION and rounded out by the MALICIOUS DESECRATION pairing of guitarist Steve Horvath and drummer DJ Jarinywich. This trio crafted the 'Source of My Evil' material in August of 2000. Unfortunately this session suffered from what the band described as "horrendous quality", with the guitars being completely scrapped and re-recorded. Mike Stecz was added on second guitar and, in the wake of ESCHATON's demise in 2001, Medeiros focussed his energies into KALOPSIA.

Horvath was dismissed and drums were delegated to ESCHATON and FUNEBRARUM man Brian Jimenez with Jarinywich shifting over to bass guitar. However, Jarinywich decamped in August of 2002 leaving KALOPSIA as a mere duo. Undaunted, the pair travelled to Victor Studios in Montreal, Quebec to work with KATAKLYSM's Jean-Francois Dagenais as producer. Eight songs were laid down but due to KATAKLYSM's intensive tour schedule would see the 'Exquisite Beauty Of The Defiled' tapes unmastered until the Spring of 2003.

KALIPOS then regrouped, enlisting guitarist Chris Born and bassist Mike Hussey. The latter joined the reformed DEHUMANIZED in 2004.

EXQUISITE BEAUTY OF THE DEFILED, (2003). Pleasure In Torture / Tool Shed Therapy / Source Of My Evil / Orgasmic Mutilation / Driven By Voices / Headless And Raped / Realm Of The Dead / Her Obituary Reads....

KAOTHIC

MADRID, SPAIN — *Ciro E. Sanchéz (vocals), Alberto Marin (guitar), Gustavo Romero (bass), Marcos de la Calle (drums).*

Established during early 2001, Madrid Death Metal band KAOTHIC was originally fronted by GLOOM's David Cuñado. Subsequently David Curtonates, of NOT FOR US and TERRORISTARS, took over the vocal role. The band also comprised guitarist Alberto Marin, of SKUNK D.F., ANKHARA and AVULSED repute, the LACK OF LIFE credited bassist Gustavo Romero and drummer Marcos de la Calle, of TERRORISTARS and MISTRESS.

A self-titled, three track demo arrived in 2003, these sessions produced by Big Simon at Sintona 1 studios in Madrid. The January 2005 album 'Order To Chaos' was recorded at M20 Studios in Madrid, again with Big Simon manning the desk. The group donated their cover version of AVULSED's 'Sweet Lobotomy' to the tribute album 'Reflections'.

Another line-up change saw the incorporation of singer Zyrus (Ciro E. Sanchéz).

Kaothic, Kaothic (2003) (Demo). Hypocritical / Raven In The Dark / Sphere.

ORDER TO CHAOS, Avispa (2005). Sphere / Hypocritical / Strange Confusion / Seven Times Seven / Raven In The Dark / Veil Of Shame / Arrows Of Time.

KARKADAN

DITZINGEN, GERMANY — *Robby Beyer (vocals), Philip Oefner (guitar), Johannes Kircher (guitar), Christian Grunenberg (bass), Martin Daniel (drums).*

Saarland's KARKADAN, titled after a mythological Persian beast, blend traditional Heavy Metal riffs with Black Metal extremism. The group was assembled in September of 1997 with an initial line-up incorporated by vocalist Robby 'Azaroth' Beyer, guitarists Florian Spannagel and Michael Zieschang, keyboard player Dennis Klink and Thomas Reeß on the drums. By December Felix Moosmann had been taken on to fulfill the bass role and Zieschang relinquished his position to Daniel Pütz.

Following the 1999 self financed album 'Eternal Black Reflections' Spannagel was forced out due to health reasons. KARKADAN would also bring in Marcel Frano to supplant Reeß. KARKADAN's 'The Lost Secrets' record would be pressed on 10" picture disc format by Supreme Chaos Productions and restricted to 333 copies. The band would be readying a further release, 'Silent Prayers Of The Forlorn Ones', for late 2002. Subsequently, KARKADAN's line-up comprised mainstays Beyer and Pütz flanked by guitarist Philip Oefner, bass player Gruni and drummer Martin Daniel. The 'Utmost Schizophrenia' album was delivered by Supreme Chaos Records in 2004. That same year ex-KARKADAN drummer Stefan Dittrich joined SAIDIAN.

KARKADAN drummer Martin Daniel exited in January 2005, being replaced by Johannes Gronover in May.

ETERNAL BLACK REFLECTIONS, Supreme Chaos SCR-CD002 (1999). Eternal Black Reflections / Niederknieder Todeskampf / Sleepwalker / Requiem Of Yearning / The Calling / Never Ending Love (Ironic Loyalty) / My Ablaze.

EMPIRE OF IUVENES, No Colours NC044 (2001). The Berserker / Empire Of Winter / Burning Gates Of Temples / Mystic Darkness / Fire Of Tartar / Dethroned Tyrant / Sons Of Mayhem / Desecrated Heavens Virgin / Raise The Dead.

THE LOST SECRETS, Supreme Chaos SCR-VL002 (2002) (Limited edition 333 copies). The Journey / Metalforces / The Ancient Times / Untitled.

UTMOST SCHIZOPHRENIA, Supreme Chaos SCR-CD008 (2004). Passing Away / On Your Knees / The Angel's Death / Faint / Frenetic Visions / The Journey / Sea Of Bitterness / The Ancient Time (Video).

KARMASSACRE

LAMBERSART CEDEX, FRANCE — *DeVermisMysteriis (vocals / guitar / bass / programming).*

Anti-fascist Brutal Death / Grind outfit KARMASSACRE is a concept of Lambersart Cedex based DeVermisMysteriis, a scene veteran of such extreme acts as NECROSIS, KRAAL, DISGUST, DAMN NATION and NECROS. The man also has an extracurricular career as a porn movie actor, operates with Parisian Gothic band NOVA ET VETERA as keyboard player and has a further solo venture billed BLIND LEADING THE BLIND.

Debut KARMAMASSACRE product would be a 2004 demo 'Teaches Bitches To Fulfill Wishes'. The 2005 session 'Arbeit Macht Frei' included a re-work of THE CURE's 'A Forest' re-branded 'A Forest (Of Corpses)'. Additional lead vocals came from Mr. LaMort of NOVA ET VETERA. The May 2005 split demo, in collaboration with KADAVERFICKER, saw the guest inclusion of GRONIBARD's Anal Capone and Albatard on vocals for the track 'Squandered'. An exclusive track, 'nUkrain', would be donated to the Akom Records 'Akompilation 2' compilation album. Also projected would be a split 7" single in collusion with Canadians ELECTROCUTIONERDZ, MIXAMOTOSIS and MEZRINE through Swiss label Tempo Blaster.

Teaches Bitches To Fulfill Wishes, Suffer! Music (2004). To Whip (And Whip Again) / Cum Addicted Teens / Perversed.

Arbeit Macht Frei, AG004CDR (2005). Manufactured Elimination (Video) / A Legacy Of Hate / Kein Kampf / When They've Burned Down The Books / Nazional Fanatizm / Manufactured Elimination / A Forest (Of Corpses) / Arbeit Macht Frei / On The Hunt.

Split Promo CD, Suffer! Music AG005CDRP (2005) (Split demo with KADAVERFICKER). A Legacy Of Hate / Kein Kampf / When They've Burned Down The Books / Nazional Fanatizm / Manufactured Elimination / A Forest (Of Corpses) / Arbeit Macht Frei / On The Hunt / Discipline Thru Pain / Eugenism vs Genocide / Squandered / Squandered (feat. Albatard & Anal Capone) / To Whip (And Whip Again) / Cum Addicted Teens / Perversed.

KARNAK

GORIZIA, ITALY — *Alessandro Seravalle (vocals), Gabriele Pala (guitar), Romolo Del Franco (bass), Marco Colella (keyboards), Stefano Rumich (drums).*

The experimental Death Metal unit KARNAK date back to 1993, conceived in Monfalcone, Gorizia by drummer Stefano Rumich under an inaugural title of SUBTRACTION. Under this guise the band, including guitarists Gabriele Pala and Francesco Ponga plus bassist Mauro Meneguzzi, cut the demo 'Eternal', produced by ELISA guitarist Andrea Rigonat, after which a name switch to OBSCENITY occurred. In 1995 a second session 'Pierced Flesh' was offered, featuring Maurizio Menon now on bass, to a growing local fan base and in 1996 the 'Beyond' demo arrived, this with Emiliano Tortul handling four-string duties. OBSCENITY evolved again in 1996, bringing in Ivan Rassu on bass. A third band title, KARNAK was adopted for a self-financed album entitled 'Perverted' during 1997.

The following year erstwhile CENSURA vocalist Seby Di-Martino was enrolled alongside bassist Roberto Sarcina and keyboard player Marco. Soon losing the latter new inductee KARNAK laid down the album 'Melodies Of Sperm Composed'. Self-funded yet again, the original pressing numbered just 150 copies. Upon release Bilo came onboard to handle keyboards but he too soon departed. Ponga too opted out. The Italian Twelfth Planet label subsequently picked up 'Melodies Of Sperm Composed' for a re-press in mid 2000. For concert work the unit inducted second guitarist Andrea Varnier and keyboard player Diego Biloslavo.

In the Autumn of 2002 KARNAK parted ways with DiMartino, necessitating Pala and Sarcino taking charge of lead vocal duties. The band also brought in keyboard player Marco Colella and singer Matteo Weber was inducted for the EP 'Tutti I Colori Del Buio'. KARNAK morphed yet again, enrolling singer Sandro Farina and bassist Livio Tomasin. Another EP, entitled 'Laboratorium', was issued in 2004. KARNAK at this juncture comprised vocalist Alessandro Seravalle, of GARDEN WALL, guitarist Gabriele Pala, bass player Romolo Del Franco, keyboard player Marco Colella with Stefano Rumich on drums.

In 2005 co-founder Francesco Ponga, of POSTMORTEM, returned to the fold to assume the lead vocal role and Emmanuelle Cucit, from SHENEN and TORKE, took over on bass the following year.

PERVERTED, Karnak (1997). Hatred Within / Wings Of Destiny / The Rapture Of Cremation / Shroud For Jesus / Magnify The Absolute Maledicent / Perverted / In Silence / Estrangement Of Hesitation.

MELODIES OF THE SPERM COMPOSED, Twelfth Planet TWP004 (2002). Spermatozombies / Melodies Of Sperm Conposed / A Face Disfigured By Thorns / Gorham / Eyes Of Larva / My Enchanting Normality / Angel Hooked / Pollen Of My Penis / Other Two Days.

Tutti I Colori Del Buio, Karnak (2002). Tutti I Colori Del Buio / MASS / The Others / Daddy / Synthetic Tears / Phobia / Passion Of The Last Supper.

Laboratorium, Karnak (2004). Do We See Through A Microscope? / Simmetria / Quinta Fuarsa / OTX 2 / Boomerang / Model Hamiltonians (Fitting Highly Fictionalized Objects) / Die Beruhmte Katze Von Schrodinger.

KAT

KATOWICE, POLAND — *Roman Kostrzewski (vocals), Poitr Luczyk (guitar), Wojciech Mrowiec (guitar), Tomasz Jagus (bass), Irseneusz Loth (drums).*

KAT were amongst the first Polish Metal bands to make a breakthrough into Western European Rock circles in the mid 80s. In their homeland the group has sold more than a million albums. Founded in Katowice during 1979, KAT's debut Polish release, 1985s 'Metal And Hell' through Ambush Records, was reissued for the Western market in the form of '666'. KAT at this juncture comprised frontman Roman Kostrzewski, guitarists Piotr Luczyk and Jacek Regulski, bass player Tomasz Jagus with Ireneusz Loth on drums. The Poljazz label released '38 Minutes Of Life' in 1987, KAT now operating as a quartet minus Regulski. Following the 1989 album 'Oddech Wymarlich Swiatów' ("The Breath Of Dead Worlds') KAT underwent line-up changes. Losing guitarist Wojciech Mrowiec and bass player Tomasz Jagus the band would regroup with bassist Krzysztof Oset and guitar player Jacek Regulsji.

The 1991 'Bastard' album, released via Metal Mind Productions, found KAT operating more furiously than ever before, capitalising on this with the 1992 concert album 'Live - Jarocin', but the act calmed down considerably for the 1994 'Ballady' effort. Later work fortunately saw KAT back on track.

The 1997 mini-album 'Badz Wariatem, Zagraj Z Latem' (Get Crazy, Play With Kat') the band reworked earlier material alongside new tracks and Techno remixes. Tragically guitarist Jacek Regulski was killed in a motorbike accident on October 29th 1999 and KAT duly suspended activity.

KAT vocalist Roman Kostrzewski has also issued a double album inspired by Anton La Vey's 'Satanic Bible'. This would be followed up by 'Mark Twain: Listy z Ziemi' ("Letters From Earth"). Kostrzewski would also front up ALKATRAZ.

KAT regrouped during 2002 citing a line-up comprising Roman Kostrzewski, guitarists Piotr Luczyk and ALKATRAZ man Valdi Moder, bassist Krzysztof Oset and drummer Ireneusz Loth. A live album and DVD, 'Somewhere In Poland', arrived in 2004.

KAT adopted a new vocalist, Henry Beck, for the October 2005 album 'Mind Cannibals' issued via Mystic Productions. The band put in an extensive European tour that same month packaged with SIX FEET UNDER, BORN FROM PAIN and DEBAUCHERY across France, Austria, Switzerland, Denmark, Holland, Belgium and Germany before acting as support to HELLOWEEN in November in Slovakia, the Czech Republic and Poland.

Ostatni Tabor, MMPR (1985) (7" single). Ostatni Tabor / Noce Szatana.
666, Silverton (1985). Metal I Pieklo / Diabelsk Dom Cz. I / Morderca / Masz Mnie Wampirze / Czas Zemsty / Nole Szatana / Diabelski Dom Cz. III / Wyrocznia / 666 / Czarne Zasepy.
METAL AND HELL, Ambush (1986). Metal And Hell / Killer / Time To Revenge / Devil's House Part I / (You Got Me) Vampire / Devil's Child / Black Hosts / Oracle / Devil's House Part II / 666.
38 MINUTES OF LIFE, Silverton (1988). Intro / Czarne Zastêpy / Diabelski Dom Cz.II / Mag-sex / Morderca / Wyrocznia / Geos z ciemnoœci / Masz mnie wampirze / Porwany obeêdem.
BASTARD, Metal Mind Productions (1991). W Bezsztalnej Bryle Uwieziony / Zawieszony Sznur / Bastard / Ojcze Samotni / N.D.C. / Piwniczne Widziadia / W Sadzie Smiertelnego Piekna / Odmiency / Lza Dla Cieriow Minionych.
ODDECH WYMARLYCH SWIATÓW, Metal Mind Productions (1994). Porwany Obledem / Spisz Jak Kamien / Dziewczyna W Cierniowej Koronie / Diabelski Dom CZ.II / Mag-Sex / Glos Z Ciemnosci / Bramy Zadz.
BALLADY, Silverton (1994). Legenda Wyshiona / Glos Z Ciemnosci / Talizman / Lza Dla Cienlow Minionych / Delirium Tremens / Czas Zemsty / Robak / Bez Pamieci / Niewinnosc.
RÓZE MILOSCI NAJCHETNIEJ PRZYJMUJA SIE NA GROBACH, Silverton (1995). Odi Profanum Vulgus / Purpurowe Gody / Plaszcz Skrytobojcy / Stworzylem Pieknarzecz / Slodki Krem / Wierze / Strzez Sie Plucia Pod Wiater / Szmaragd Bazyliszka.
BADZ WARIATEM, ZAGRAJ Z KATEM, Silverton (1997). Plaszcz Skrytobojcy (Wersja Skrocona) / Wierze (Wersja Zdigitalizowana) / Plasz Skrytobojcy (Wersja Zdigitalizowana) / Trzeba Zasnac (Wersja Skrocona).
SZYDERCZE ZWIERCIADO, Silverton (1997). Cmok-Cmok, Mlask-Mlask / Tak Mi Chce Samotnosc / Loze Wspolne, Lecz Przytulne / Szydercze Zwierciadlo / Spojrzenie / Czemu Mistrze Krzyz W Tornistrze / Oczy Slonc / Trzeba Zasnac.
MIND CANNIBALS, Mystic Productions (2005). Mind Cannibals / Light Or Hell / Judas Kiss / Uninvited Guest / Religious Clash / Dark Hole - The Habitat Of Gods / Coming Home / Puppets On The Strings / Voodoo Time / Ive Been Waiting.

KATAFALK

GRONINGEN, HOLLAND — *Wokkel (vocals), Chris (guitar), Niels (guitar), Jurjen (bass), Martin (drums).*

Groningen based Death Metal act founded by guitarist Christiaan during 1991. KATAFALK's first product would be the demo tape 'Through The Storm'. Former NETTLERASH and LETHARGY guitarist Pier Abe joined KATAFALK in November of 2000. The band toured Holland alongside GOD DETHRONED in 2001 but shortly after these dates suffered a major loss of band personnel. Three members, singer Wokkel, bassist Jurjen and drummer Martin all decamped en masse in order to create OBTUSE. Wokkel would team up with WINTER OF SIN.

Fresh blood was delivered in the form of singer Peter, guitarist Henk Jan and drummer Michiel van der Plicht, erstwhile members of GRINROTH. The group added Washington, USA native Rodney as lead singer in 2002, a man citing prior experience with Black Metal acts SHADOWVOID and HASTUR. This revised version of the band cut its teeth live at the Heerenveen 'Hydrargyrum' festival in April, although ex-member Jurjen substituted for Henk Jan on bass.

In September of 2002 Rodney bowed out and the group duly re-inducted former singer Wokkel. Signing to the Dutch label Cold Blood Industries KATAFALK readied their inaugural album 'Storm Of The Horde' for January of 2003. However, both guitarist Pier Abe and bassist Henk Jan severed ties with the band due to "serious differences of opinion". In a complete about turn, KATAFALK would be rejoined by their former partners singer Wokkel and bassist Jurjen.

Guitarist Christiaan gained KATAFALK some mainstream exposure in mid 2004 when he starred in a TV commercial for Internet company Chello, broadcasted on Dutch MTV, TMF and children's channel Nickelodeon. The clip featured the musician smashing a guitar into the computer of an unsuspecting computer "nerd" to the sounds of the KATAFALK track 'Cannonfodder'.

Drummer Michiel van der Plicht opted out in July 2005 in order to concentrate on his other acts TRAVELERS IN TIME and PROSTITUTE DISFIGUREMENT. He subsequently joined TOXOCARA. KATAFALK self-financed the EP 'Death's Contradiction' in June 2006.

STORM OF THE HORDE, Cold Blood Industries CBI 0301 (2003). Succubus / Aesthetic Vampires / Birthmark 666 / Cannonfodder / Redeemer / Storm Of The Horde / Hatred / Empty Life / Operation Mindloss / Rise Now / One Last Flight / Blind Envy / Baptized In Fire.
Death's Contradiction, Katafalk KO601 (2006). She's My Darkness / Death's Contradiction / God Pollution / War Chant.

KATAKLYSM

QUÉBEC, QC, CANADA — *Aquarius Sylvain Mars Venus (vocals), Jean-François Dagenais (guitar), Maurizio Lacono (bass), Max Duhamel (drums).*

Québec City Death Black act KATAKLYSM, founded in the Autumn of 1991, opened proceedings with the February 1992 demo tape 'The Death Gate Cycle Of Reincarnation'. This wicked slice of extreme audio more than justified their self-styled preferred tag of Northern hyper-blast metal. KATAKLYSM differentiated themselves by imbuing their predilection for torturously wrought, technical Death Metal with an avant-garde slant. Eschewing tired generic themes, KATAKLYSM's lyrical bent and sonic aesthetic veered towards the abstract exploration of universal chaos.

The line-up initially was quoted as vocalist Aquarius Sylvain Mars Venus (Sylvain Houde), guitarists Jean-François Dagenais and Stéphane Côté, bassist Maurizio Iacono and drummer Ariel Saïed. The band signed to the German label Nuclear Blast for a debut 1993 EP 'The Mystical Gate Of Reincarnation', comprising the original demo tracks with an additional song, 'The Orb Of Uncreation'. A further round of studio pre-production resulted in the demo 'The Vortex Of Resurrection'. By this juncture the band was down to a quartet, having lost the services of Stéphane Côté, who forged OBSCENE CRISIS, and introduced Max Duhamel on drums, as evidenced on the Boundless records 1994 7 single 'Vision The Chaos'.

Promoting the sophomore 'Sorcery' effort KATAKLYSM put in their inaugural European shows, including dates with DEICIDE, and became the first Canadian band to tour Mexico. KATAKLYSM's drummer Max Duhamel was forced to leave the band in late 1995 following cartilage damage to his right knee. His replacement was American Nick Miller. This formation laid down the June 1996 work 'Temple Of Knowledge (Kataklysm Part III)'. Unfortunately their next product, the concert 'Northern Hyperblast Live', a barely treated soundboard recording, damaged their ascent somewhat.

By 1998 Duhamel had made his return as the band welcomed in new bassist Stéphane Barbe. A further significant flux saw the exit of Sylvain Houde, Maurizio Iacono taking over the lead vocal role. This transition marked a change of pace toward a more commercial orientation. The band then switched to the Canadian Hypnotic label for the experimental 'Victims Of The Fallen World' album. However, this record saw limited distribution, not gaining a US release.

Resigning with their former label Nuclear Blast KATAKLYSM cut the April 2000 'The Prophecy (Stigmata Of The Immaculate)' outing at Montreal's Victor Studios. Guests included Rob of NECRONOMICON and Mike DiSalvo of CRYPTOPSY. European touring positioned the group on the label packaged 'Nuclear Blast' festivals sharing stages with HYPOCRISY, RAISE HELL, DESTRUCTION and CREMATORY. Three tracks from these concerts were later used on a DVD release.

Touring to promote the September 2001 album 'Epic (The Poetry Of War)', a conceptual undertaking tackling the Roman Empire, KATAKLYSM put in a run of Canadian dates commencing in Quebec on August 4th. American dates were scheduled in alliance with MARDUK but the band would later retract from these shows.

KATAKLYSM announced the recording of a fresh album 'Shadows And Dust' for September 2002 release. The Roman motif was obviously still at the forefront of the band's mind, as opening track 'In Shadows and Dust' used the 'Gladiator' movie theme as its intro. Jean-Francois Dagenais would also be confirmed as acting as producer for famed American Death Metal act MALEVOLENT CREATION's 'The Will To Kill' album.

The band would be announced as headliners of the fifth annual summer 2002 'Death Across America' dates backed up by BEYOND THE EMBRACE, MISERY INDEX and DIVINE EMPIRE. Canadian gigs saw strong support from Montreal's NECRONOMICON and Toronto's BLOOD OF CHRIST. The band put in a short batch of UK dates packaged with HATE ETERNAL and DERANGED before forming up part of an impressive cast for European 'Xmas Festivals' in December in league with SIX FEET UNDER, IMMOLATION, MARDUK and HATE. Later gigs in Holland added veteran Thrashers EXODUS to the bill. Meantime KATAKLYSM frontman Maurizio Iacono's solo project L.O.S.T., having now switched title to STAMINA, was being courted by various major labels.

The band united with HATE ETERNAL, DYING FETUS, and INTO ETERNITY for North American dates in February and March of 2003. However, drummer Max Duhamel retired from the band in late January and J.F. Richard of ION DISSONANCE filled in on the drum stool at short notice. Martin Maurais was enrolled as a permanent replacement in March.

KATAKLYSM united with THE HAUNTED, SHAI HULUD and SKINLESS for extensive US dates throughout the summer. In August the group was back on the festival circuit in Europe with appearances at the German 'Wacken Open Air' and 'Partysan' events with a headliner at the Czech 'Brutal Assault' meeting. Canadian headline gigs preceded a showing at the Las Vegas 'Metalfest' upfront of re-entering the recording studio for a new record. KATAKLYSM also revealed they had been commissioned to record the them track to the Horror movie 'Female Flesh Eaters'. This renewed and ongoing flush of success for the band saw them securing a further long term album deal with the Nuclear Blast label in July. Another run of US headline dates would be cut short in late September as KATAKLYSM headed into the studio to commence work on the 'Serenity In Fire' album. For this outing HYPOCRISY mentor Peter Tägtgren donated a guest vocal appearance, appearing on the track 'For All Our Sins'. Jean-Francois Dagenais made studio time in early 2004 to donate his services to the DEATH tribute album 'Within The Mind' assembled by JAMES MURPHY.

The band formed up part of the 'No More Serenity' headline tour presented by 'Metal Maniacs' magazine in March of 2004. Alongside KATAKLYSM the line up counted MISERY INDEX, CANNAE and THROUGH THE DISCIPLINE. Further valuable promotion came with a promotional video for the album track 'As I Slither'. Scheduled European dates alongside CROWBAR, and appearance at the 'With Full Force' open air festival in Germany, were cancelled as vocalist Maurizio Iacono's wife had the due date of her pregnancy brought forward.

The band would spend the Summer completely re-recording their debut album 'Victims Of This Fallen World'. Believing that the demise of the Hypnotic label had consigned the record to the vaults, the group decided upon a strategy of re-crafting the entire record from scratch in order to make it available once again. However, they would be less than pleased when, in August, it was learned the original version, alongside 'Northern Hyperblast Live', had been licensed for a re-release through Linus Entertainment. KATAKLYSM asked fans to boycott this release.

After European gigs with MYSTIC CIRCLE, INTO ETERNITY and GRAVEWORM, US touring plans for October saw the band flanking NAPALM DEATH and GOATWHORE with off days from this trek plugged by gigs with MACABRE. Opening up 2005, the band toured the US in February partnered with DANZIG and TRIVIUM. However, the band, working on new album 'In the Arms Of Devastation', had parted ways with drummer Martin Maurais due to "personal and professional reasons", bring back Max Duhamel in his stead. That same month some official recognition came the band's way when KATAKLYSM won the 'Best Metal Group' category at the Canadian Indie Music Awards. European headline gigs in June would see support lent by GRAVEWORM and EMINENCE. The band entered the recording studio on 10th July to record 'In The Arms Of Devastation', this set featuring a guest vocal from KITTIE's Morgan Lander and contributions from Tim Roth and Rob Doherty of INTO ETERNITY.

The band announced a touring partnership as part of the December 2005 'X-Mas' festivals in Europe ranked alongside recently resurrected UK Thrashers ONSLAUGHT, EXODUS, OCCULT, UNLEASHED, BEHEMOTH, and PRIMORDIAL. The group formed up a European 'No Mercy' festival package for dates across Germany, Austria, France, Switzerland, Belgium and Holland in April, ranked alongside CANNIBAL CORPSE, GRIMFIST and LEGION OF THE DAMNED. These shows were

KATAKLYSM (pic: J. Binette)

swiftly followed up dates supporting BOLT THROWER. However, KATAKLYSM pulled out of the dates at the end of the tour due to "reasons beyond the band's control". The band was included the 'Metal Crusaders' North American tour, set to take place in May and June 2006 alongside VADER, GRAVEWORM, SPEED\KILL/HATE and THE ABSENCE.

KATAKLYSM teamed up with NEAERA, FEAR MY THOUGHTS and fellow Canadians QUO VADIS for the 'Road To Devastation' European tour in January 2007. That same month Nuclear Blast issued the CD / DVD package 'Live In Deutschland (The Devastation Begins)'. The group then announced "The Trendkiller" US tour commencing February 1st as an alliance with SWORN ENEMY, ALL SHALL PERISH, TOO PURE TO DIE and BLOOD RUNS BLACK. The band was back out on the European touring circuit in early May 2007, heading up the 'Midvinterblot European Tour Part II' dates backed by UNLEASHED and BELPHEGOR then ARKHON INFAUSTUS.

The Death Gate Cycle Of Reincarnation, Socan (1992) (Demo). Frozen In Time (Chapter I: Will Of Suicide) / Mystical Plane Of Evil (Chapter II: Enigma Of The Unknown) / Shrine Of Life (Chapter III: Reborn Through Death).

The Mystical Gate Of Reincarnation EP, Nuclear Blast NB 0093-2 (1993). Frozen In Time (Chapter One: Will Of Suicide) / Mystical Plane Of Evil (Chapter Two: Enigma Of The Unknown) / Shrine Of Life (Chapter Three: Reborn Through Death) / The Orb Of Uncreation.

Vision The Chaos, Boundless T.G. 002 (1994) (7" vinyl). Vision The Chaos (Kataklysm Part I) / Shrine Of Life (Chapter III: Reborn Through Death).

SORCERY, Nuclear Blast NB 0108-2 (1995). Sorcery / Mould In A Breed (Chapter One: Bestial Propogation) / Whirlwind Of Withered Blossoms (Chapter Two: Forgotten Ancestors) / Feeling The Neverworld (Chapter Three: An Infinite Transmigration) / Eldar God / Garden Of Dreams (Chapter One: Supernatural Appearance) / Once ... Upon Possession (Chapter Two: Legacy Of Both Lores) / Dead Zygote (Chapter Three: Dethroned Son) / World Of Treason (Instrumental Vibrations).

TEMPLE OF KNOWLEDGE (KATAKLYSM PART III), Nuclear Blast NB 0157-1 (1996). The Unholy Signature (Segment One—Utterly Significant) / Beckoning The Xul (Segment II—In The Midst Of The Azonei's Dominion) / Point Of Evanescence (Segment III—Of Sheer Perseverance) / Fathers From The Suns (Act I—The Occurred Barrier) / Enhanced By The Lore (Act II—Scholarship Ordained) / In Parallel Horizons (Act III—Spontaneous Aura Projection) / The Awakener (Epoch I—Summon The Legends) / Maelstrom 2010 (Epoch II—Omens About The Great Infernos) / Exode Of Evils (Epoch III—Ladder Of The Thousand Parsecs).

TEMPLE OF KNOWLEDGE (KATAKLYSM PART III), Nuclear Blast NB 0157-2 (1996) (Digipack). The Unholy Signature (Segment One—Utterly Significant) / Beckoning The Xul (Segment II—In The Midst Of The Azonei's Dominion) / Point Of Evanescence (Segment III—Of Sheer Perseverance) / Fathers From The Suns (Act I—The Occurred Barrier) / Enhanced By The Lore (Act II—Scholarship Ordained) / In Parallel Horizons (Act III—Spontaneous Aura Projection) / The Awakener (Epoch I—Summon The Legends) / Maelstrom 2010 (Epoch II—Omens About The Great Infernos) / Exode Of Evils (Epoch III—Ladder Of The Thousand Parsecs) / L'Odysée.

VICTIM OF THE FALLEN WORLD, Hypnotic HYP 1064 (1998). As My World Burns / Imminent Downfall / Feared Resistance / Caged In / Portraits Of Anger / Extreme To The Core / Courage Through Hope / A View From Inside / (God) Head / Embracing Europa / Remember / World Of Treason II.

NORTHERN HYPERBLAST LIVE, Hypnotic HYP 1069 (1998). Maelstrom 2010 / Exode Of Evils / Enchant By The Lore / Sorcery / Eldar God / Fathers From The Sun / Point Of Evanescence / Beckoning On The Xul / The Awakener / Once ... Upon Possession / The Unholy Signature / The Orb Of Uncreation / In Parallel Horizons / Vision The Chaos / Shrine Of Life.

THE PROPHECY (STIGMATA OF THE IMMACULATE), Nuclear Blast NB 0470-2 (2000). 1999:6661:2000 / Manifestation / Stormland / Breeding The Everlast / Laments Of Fear And Despair / Astral Empire / Gateway To Extinction / Machiavellion / Renaissance.

EPIC—THE POETRY OF WAR, Nuclear Blast NB 0621-2 (2001). Il Diavolo In Me / Shivers Of A New World / Era Of The Mercyless (Roma Part I) / As The Glorious Weep (Roma Part II) / Damnation Is Here / Manipulator Of Souls / Wounds / What We Endure / When Time Stands Still.

SHADOWS AND DUST, Nuclear Blast NB 1032-2 (2002). Where The Enemy Sleeps / Beyond Salvation / Illuminati / Bound In Chains / In Shadows & Dust / Centuries (Beneath The Dark Waters) / Face The Face Of War / Chronicles Of The Damned / Years Of Enlightment-Decades In Darkness / Inside The Material Flesh.

SERENITY IN FIRE, Nuclear Blast NB 1227-2 (2004). The Ambassador Of Pain / The Resurrected / As I Slither / For All Our Sins / The Night They Returned / Serenity In Fire / Blood On The Swans / 10 Seconds From The End / The Tragedy I Preach / Under The Bleeding Sun.

Vision The Chaos, Skyscraper Music SM015 (2005) (CD single). Vision The Chaos (Kataklysm Part I) / Shrine Of Life (Chapter III: Reborn Through Death).

IN THE ARMS OF DEVASTATION, Nuclear Blast NB 1527-2 (2006). Temptation's Nest / Let Them Burn / Crippled & Broken / Open Scars / To Reign Again / In Words Of Desperation / Like Angels Weeping The Dark / It Turns To Rust / The Road To Devastation. Chart position: 76 GERMANY.

LIVE IN GERMANY, Nuclear Blast (2007). Like Angels Weeping (The Dark) / Where The Enemy Sleeps / The Resurrected / Let Them Burn / As The Glorious Weep / As I Slither / Manipulator Of Souls / The Ambassador Of Pain / Crippled And Broken / In Shadows And Dust / Face The Face Of War / The Road To Devastation.

KATAPLEXIA

HELSINKI, FINLAND — *Rodrigo Artiga (vocals / drums), Davi Moreira (guitar), Eero Tertsunen (guitar), Miikka Merikallio (bass).*

Helsinki Death Metal combo KATAPLEXIA, created in 2003 by El Salvador native Rodrigo "Fatality" Artiga of KABAK, DISMAL GALE and DEEPRED repute, released the debut album 'Morgue's Reality' through Severe Music in October that year. This set featured Jani Loikas (a.k.a. JL Nokturnal) of HIN ONDE, AZAGHAL, LET ME DREAM, NOCTURNAL WINDS, MEDIEVAL ART and KATAPLEXIA repute on guest guitar. Original bassist Mikael Da Costa was superseded by Miikka Merikallio of NERLICH whilst guitarist Davi Moreira also operates with TALVELLA. Although based in Finland, all the band members were originally of South American origin.

KATAPLEXIA switched labels to Xtreem Music for January 2005's 'Catastrophic Scenes'. Rainer Düsing of THE VAST and EMBEDDED contributed guest vocals.

MORGUE REALITY, Severe Music (2003). Intro / Morgue's Reality / Inner Skin / Through The Corpses / Several Desencarnation / Deeply Infected By The Pestilence / G.O.R.E. / Putrefied War Remains.

CATASTROPHIC SCENES, Xtreem Music (2005). Infested Wounds / Ashes From Our Incinerated Innards / Morgue's Reality / Brutal Addiction / From The Debris / Devastating War / Scenes Of Tragedies.

KATATONIA

AVESTA, SWEDEN — *Jonas Renkse (vocals / guitar), Anders Nyström (guitar / keyboards), Fred Norrman (guitar), Mattias Norrman (bass), Daniel Liljekvist (drums).*

KATATONIA, named after a schizophrenic condition, are celebrated propagators of ambitious and supremely melodic Doom-Death dubbed "Suicide Rock". Avesta based KATATONIA started life as a duo of guitarist Sombreius Blakkheim (a.k.a. Anders Nyström) and vocalist/drummer Lord Seth (real name Jonas Renkse) in 1987. The group, working with EDGE OF SANITY frontman DAN SWANÖ as producer, utilised Gorysound Studios over three days in July 1992 to record the demo 'JHVA Elohim Meth'. 500 copies of this tape were manufactured, 300 manufactured on blue cassettes, 100 on red and 100 transparent.

The 'JHVA Elohim Meth' material was later released in CD form by Dutch label Vic Records, the only change being a subtle re-naming of the first track from the original 'Prologue: Midwinter Intergates' to 'Midwinter Gates'. This time around, Swanö featured amongst the band credits on keyboards under the pseudonym 'Day Disyhrah'. In rapid fashion KATATONIA, having signed to No Fashion Records, added former TEARS OF LUNA bassist Israphael Wing (real name Guillaume Le Huche). Their opening album, 'Dance Of December Souls', was fashioned at Unisound Studios with DAN SWANÖ reconvening both his production role and alter ego 'Day Disyhrah'. Taking just five days in April 1993, KATATONIA re-recorded their original demo tracks and cut fresh songs to form up the album. As a debut, 'Dance Of December Souls' staggered many with its maturity. Resolutely Doom orientated, the record hung on the bleakest, almost hollow production. From the opening siren laments of 'Seven Dreaming Souls' and into first track 'Gateways Of Bereavement', eschewing a chorus in favour of a mantric "Let me die!", KATATONIA's scorn for convention would be apparent from the outset. Having risen from a Black / Death Metal tradition, KATATONIA's origins would break through on the wholly blasphemous 'Without God' whilst their ability to comfortably tackle the epic was illustrated by the monumental 'Velvet Thorns (Of Drynwhyl)' and 'Tombs Of Insomnia'. Typically oblique, the album rose to a finale with 'Dancing December', a composition whose entire lyric comprised one word repeated in whisper.

In addition to this material, the band also contributed two tracks ('Black Erotica' and 'Love Of The Swan') to the Wrong Again Records compilation album 'W.A.R.' in 1995. That same year witnessed the EP 'For Funerals To Come' released through Italian label Avantgarde Music, these songs having been put down onto tape in a day long session at Unisound Recordings the previous September. Further recordings of interest included a split 10" EP through Hammerheart Records with Irish act PRIMORDIAL the following year. Le Huche opted out in 1994, resurfacing as a member of Progressive Metal band MINDWATCH. Coincidently, another MINDWATCH man, Mikael Oretoft, took over the bass vacancy in 1996. Unbeknown to the outside world, KATATONIA had actually folded during this period, but soon succumbed to a creative drive and duly re-assembled.

Blackheim, having just relinquished a position with IN GREY, also had worked up a side project band titled BEWITCHED releasing the 'Diabolical Desecration' album on Osmose Records in 1996. Seth would also be working on his OCTOBER TIDE project in union with UNCANNY and FULMINATION guitarist Fredrik Norrman. This latter musician was then to be inducted into the KATATONIA sphere of operations.

Avantgarde Music issued the acclaimed and hypnotic 'Brave Murder Day' album in 1996, again recorded at Unisound Studios and produced by the ever industrious Dan Swanö. OPETH's Mikael Åkerfeldt featured as studio guest on "distorted" vocals as a foil to Renske's chaste lamentations. KATATONIA performed a short British tour in late 1996 with support acts IN THE WOODS ... and VOICE OF DESTRUCTION. An EP, 'Sounds Of Decay' once more seeing vocal contributions from Mikael Åkerfeldt, was delivered in December 1997.

1998 was ushered in with an EP in January, limited to 1500 hand numbered copies, entitled 'Saw You Drown'. The 'Discouraged Ones' opus followed in April, this self-produced record being crafted at Sunlight Studios with Fred Estby of DISMEMBER and Tomas Skogsberg gaining engineering credits. Once again Mikael Åkerfeldt was in evidence for backing vocals. 'Discouraged Ones', a brave delineation between the doom death of yore and a courageous leap into the unknown, shocked fans with the complete overhaul of the KATATONIA sound. Forsaking speed and aggression the band discovered that utter despair, maudlin and cold bleakness was just as effective, if not doubly more so. As songs became simpler, stripped down to standard rock formats, the message impacted even harder. Needless to say, the band lost fans directly due to this change of path but began to gather in many more newer admirers.

At this juncture, Blackheim and Seth were also in pursuit of another Death Metal project titled DIABOLICAL MASQUERADE. The pair also forged old-school Death Metal project act BLOODBATH with Dan Swanö and OPETH's Mikael Åkerfeldt, both of these individuals again very much in evidence on KATATONIA's masterly 'Tonight's Decision' album released in August 1999. This collection, the first for the Peaceville label, featured the band's first attempt at a cover version, tackling JEFF BUCKLEY's 'Nightmares By The Sea'. 'Tonight's Decision' strode onward from 'Discouraged Ones' in similar fashion, the audibility of Jonas Renkse's deeply introspective lyrics now beginning to elicit deference from a previously suspicious media.

The 2001 KATATONIA 'Teargas' EP, holding two exclusive tracks, would prove another strong release. It also marked the incorporation of two new band members, ex-DELLAMORTE bassist Mattias Norrman and SUBDIVE and WICKED drummer Daniel Liljekvist. By this stage the band had rid itself totally of its formative Death Metal skin and were plunging headlong into deeply disturbing yet oddly melodic workouts, gaining a wider acceptance and recognition for their efforts.

KATATONIA took on the services of faithful studio mentor Dan Swanö to mix their sixth full-length album for early 2003 through Peaceville Records. The band united with FINNTROLL for European touring throughout April and May.

The emergence of 2003's 'Viva Emptiness', a tapestry of morosely compelling and infectious dirges, put KATATONIA firmly into the major league bracket with praise unanimous and global. German gigs to promote the album in April saw BEFORE THE DAWN and DARK SUNS as support. A 2004 release, entitled 'Brave Yester Days' compiled tracks from EPs alongside rarities and the unreleased 'Untrue'. With KATATONIA's status rising rapidly, Black Lodge Records re-issued their early 'Dance of December Souls' album but sparked some criticism from the band who issued an official statement "We do not support this re-issue and take complete distance from its existence". Apparently the re-issue's new artwork and logo, designed to be in keeping with more recent KATATONIA albums, made the band believe these old recordings were being passed off to look like new material. Meantime, Peaceville Records compiled 'The Black Sessions' compilation, a set of post 1998 recordings comprising all the single's b-sides, cover songs and selective songs off 'Discouraged Ones' through 'Viva Emptiness' plus an unreleased track.

Leading up to the band's appearance the October 'Barlo' festival in Holland KATATONIA united with AMARAN for a run of Scandinavian and European gigs. The group then engaged in songwriting for a new album. In early 2005 the rare 1998 'Saw You Drown' EP would be licensed to Infinite Vinyl for a limited edition vinyl release of 1000 hand-numbered copies.

In June KATATONIA entered Fascination Street Studios located in the outskirts of Örebro to craft a new album entitled 'The Great Cold Distance'. The group's debut Russian performances came in September with gigs in Moscow and St. Petersburg. European road work in April and May 2006 saw NOVEMBRE as support band. The band put in a small run of Turkish concerts in September. KATATONIA, MOONSPELL and DAYLIGHT DIES teamed up for a North American tour commencing in October.

KATATONIA

Northern Silence Productions issued the tribute double album 'December Songs' in December 2006. Artists paying homage to KATATONIA included FOSCOR with 'Midwinter Gates' and 'Gateways Of Bereavement', BEATRIK with 'The Northern Silence', FOREST STREAM 'Without God', AEVERON 'Shades Of Emerald Fields', XASTHUR 'Palace Of Frost', WYRD 'In Silence Enshrined', GEIST 'Love Of The Swan', DARK FORTRESS 'Endtime', LOSS 'Brave', FOREST OF SHADOWS 'Rainroom', HELEVORN '12', FORGOTTEN TOMB 'Nowhere', HEL featuring WINTERHEART 'Cold Ways', FARSOT 'I Break', FRAGILE HOLLOW 'Saw You Drown' and OCTOBER FALLS— For Funerals To Come . . .'

A third single from 'The Great Cold Distance' was released in March 2007. 'July' came backed with an exclusive song entitled 'Unfurl' plus a remix of 'Soil's Song' constructed by Swedish artist Krister Linder and a promotional video shot for 'July' directed by Charlie Granberg. 'The Great Cold Distance' was re-issued as a double CD mixed in 5.1 Surround Sound producer Jens Bogren. This variant added the tracks 'Displaced' and 'Dissolving Bonds'.

KATATONIA announced Portuguese and Spanish headline shows for April 2007. The group's live performance from 2006's Summer Breeze open air festival in Germany was released as a double-disc live album/DVD, entitled 'Live Consternation' in May.

Jhva Elohim Meth, (1992) (Demo. Limited edition 500 copies). Prologue: Midwinter Intergates / Without God / Palace Of Frost / Northern Silence / Epilogue: Crimson Tears.

Jhva Elohim Meth ... The Revival EP, Vic VIC 1 (1994). Midvinter Gates (Prologue) / Without God / Palace Of Frost / The Northern Silence / Crimson Tears (Epilogue).

DANCE OF THE DECEMBER SOULS, No Fashion NFR 005 (1995). Seven Dreaming Souls / Gateways Of Bereavement / In Silence Enshrined / Without God / Elohim Meth / Velvet Thorns (Of Drynwhyl) / Tomb Of Insomnia / Dancing December.

For Funerals To Come EP, Avantgarde AV009 (1995). Funeral Wedding / Shades Of Emerald Fields / For Funerals To Come ... / Epistal.

BRAVE MURDER DAY, Avantgarde AV022 (1996). Brave / Murder / Day / Rainroom / 12 / Endtime.

Scarlet Heavens EP, Misanthropy AMAZON 010 (1996) (Split EP with PRIMORDIAL). Scarlet Heavens.

Sounds Of Decay EP, Avantgarde AV024 (1997). Nowhere / At Last / Inside The Fall.

Saw You Drown, Avantgarde AV028 (1998) (Limited edition 1500 hand numbered copies). Saw You Drown / Nerve / Quiet World / Scarlet Heavens.

DISCOURAGED ONES, Avantgarde AV029 (1998). I Break / Stalemate / Deadhouse / Relention / Cold Ways / Gone / Last Resort / Nerve / Saw You Drown / Instrumental / Distrust.

TONIGHT'S DECISION, Peaceville CDVILE 76 (1999). For My Demons / I Am Nothing / In Death, A Song / Had To (Leave) / This Punishment / Right Into The Bliss / No Good Can Come Of This / Strained / A Darkness Coming / Nightmares By The Sea / Black Session.

Teargas EP, Peaceville CDVILES 98 (2001). Teargas / Sulfur / March.

LAST FAIR DEAL GONE DOWN, Peaceville CDVILED 89 (2001). Dispossession / Chrome / We Will Bury You / Teargas / I Transpire / Tonights Music / Clean Today / The Future Of Speech / Passing Bird / Sweet Nurse / Don't Tell A Soul.

Tonight's Music, Peaceville CDVILES 113 (2001). Tonight's Music / Help Me Disappear / O How I Enjoy The Light.

Ghost Of The Sun, Peaceville CDVILE EP5 (2003). Ghost Of The Sun / Criminals / Evidence.

VIVA EMPTINESS, Peaceville CDVILEF 103 (2003). Ghost Of The Sun / Sleeper / Criminals / A Premonition / Will I Arrive / Burn The Remembrance / Wealth / One Year From Now / Walking By A Wire / Complicity / Evidence / Omerta / Inside The City Of Glass. Chart position: 17 FINLAND.

THE BLACK SESSIONS, Peaceville CDVILEB 129 (2005). Teargas / Right Into The Bliss / Criminal / Help Me Disappear / Nerve / The Future Of Speech / Ghost Of The Sun / I Am Nothing / Deadhouse / Passing Bird / Sleeper / Sulfur / No Devotion / Chrome / A Premonition / Dispossession / Cold Ways / Nightmares By The Sea / O How I Enjoy The Light / Evidence / March 4 / I Break / For My Demons / Omerta / Tonights Music / Stalemate / Wait Outside / Fractured / Sweet Nurse / Black Session / Ghost Of The Sun / Criminals / Teargas / I Break / I Am Nothing / Sweet Nurse / Sleeper / Tonight's Music / For My Demon's / Chrome / Future Speech / Complicity / Burn The Remembrance / Evidence / Deadhouse / Murder.

My Twin EP, Peaceville CDVILES 138 (2006). My Twin (Single Edit) / My Twin (Opium Dub) / Displaced / Dissolving Bonds.

THE GREAT COLD DISTANCE, Peaceville CDVILEF 128 (2006). Leaders / Deliberation / Soil's Song / My Twin / Consternation / Follower / Rusted / Increase / July / In The White / The Itch / Journey Through Pressure. Chart positions: 8 FINLAND, 17 HUNGARY, 42 SWEDEN.

Deliberation, Peaceville CDVILES 140 (2006). Deliberation / In The White (Urban dub) / Code Against The Code / Deliberation (Video).

THE GREAT COLD DISTANCE, Peaceville (2007) (CD + DVD). Leaders / Deliberation / Soil's Song / My Twin / Consternation / Follower / Rusted / Increase / July / In The White / The Itch / Journey Through Pressure / Displaced / Dissolving Bonds / Leaders / Deliberation / Soil's Song / My Twin / Consternation / Follower / Rusted / Increase / July / In The White / The Itch / Journey Through Pressure.

KATATONIA: TRIBUTE

SWEDEN — Black Metal label Northern Silence Productions issued the KATATONIA tribute double album 'December Songs' in December 2006. Artists paying homage included Spain's FOSCOR with 'Midwinter Gates' and 'Gateways Of Bereavement', Italy's BEATRIK with 'The Northern Silence', Russian act FOREST STREAM 'Without God', Germany's AEVERON 'Shades Of Emerald Fields', XASTHUR 'Palace Of Frost', WYRD 'In Silence Enshrined', GEIST 'Love Of The Swan', DARK FORTRESS 'Endtime', LOSS 'Brave', FOREST OF SHADOWS 'Rainroom', HELEVORN '12', FORGOTTEN TOMB 'Nowhere', HEL featuring

WINTERHEART 'Cold Ways', FARSOT 'I Break', FRAGILE HOLLOW 'Saw You Drown' and OCTOBER FALLS—For Funerals To Come…'

DECEMBER SONGS—A TRIBUTE TO KATATONIA, Northern Silence Productions (2006). Midwinter Gates (FOSCOR) / Gateways Of Bereavement (FOSCOR) / The Northern Silence (BEATRIK) / Without God (FOREST STREAM) / Shades Of Emerald Fields (AEVERON) / Palace Of Frost (XASTHUR) / In Silence Enshrined (WYRD) / Love Of The Swan (GEIST) / Endtime (DARK FORTRESS) / Brave (LOSS) / Rainroom (FOREST OF SHADOWS) / 12 (HELEVORN) / Nowhere (FORGOTTEN TOMB) / Cold Ways (HEL featuring WINTERHEART) / I Break (FARSOT) / Saw You Drown (FRAGILE HOLLOW) / For Funerals To Come… (OCTOBER FALLS).

KAZJUROL

SWEDEN — *Kjelle (vocals), Pontus (guitar), T-Ban (guitar), Hakan (bass), Bonden (drums).*

KAZJUROL began as a purely amateur project by members of Hardcore band RESCUES IN FUTURE. The band's first commercial release came with a track on a German compilation single entitled 'Breaking The Silence' in 1986. The interest generated by the single track prompted the recording of a the 1987 'Messengers Of Death' EP for Uproar Records and a demo cassette titled 'A Lesson In Love', which surfaced in 1988.

The band eventually released their debut album, 'Dance Tarantella', in 1990 which saw vocalist Kjelle replaced by Tomas Bengtsson. However, by the next release, the 'Bodyslam' EP KAZJUROL had found another frontman in Henka 'Gator' Ahlberg. The EP featured covers of tracks by BAD BRAINS, VENOM, STORMTROOPERS OF DEATH and CRO-MAGS.

The band further displayed their Hardcore / Punk leanings with a cover of a DISCHARGE track on the Burning Heart Records 1991 compilation 'A Tribute Of Memories'. A four track promotional EP, 'Toothcombing…', also emerged.

However, KAZJUROL eventually split, with both guitarists forming Hardcore act BAD DREAMS ALWAYS. Guitarists Pontus and T-Ban very briefly involved themselves with singer Joakim Öhman and drummer Per Karlsson in the final incarnation of SUFFER.

Messengers Of Death, Uproar UPROAR 004 (1987). Messengers Of Death / Stagedive To Hell / Who Needs You?
DANCE TARANTULA, Active ATV12 (1990). A Clockwork Out Of Order / Moment 22 / Than / Honesty, The Right Excuse / Dance Tarantella / Blind Illusions / Three Minator / Echoes From The Past / Stagedive To Hell / guitar), Milan Siraj (guitar), Fany Veselák (bass), Mira Cizkovsk´y (drums).
Bodyslam EP, Burning Heart Heartcore 001 (1991). We Gotta Know / United Forces / PayTo Cym / Countess Bathory.
Hallucinations, Burning Heart Heartcore 002 (1991). Hallucinations / Dance Tarentella / Blue Eyed Devils.
Toothcombing…, Burning Heart (1991) (Promotion release). Hallucinations / The Unholy War / Deathcon 5 / Dance Tarantella.

KEEN OF THE CROW

CA, USA — *Dan Ochoa (vocals), Seth Arthur (guitar), Ron Slater (guitar), Justin Christian (bass), Rhett Davis (drums).*

Southern California Metal band. Former MORGION members drummer Rhett Davis and bassist Justin Christain, along with NEPENTHEAN founder Ron Slater, issued demos under the KEEN OF THE CROW brand in May 2005. A demo, entitled 'Premonition', was recorded in December. A debut album, entitled 'Hyborea', was contracted to Grau Records in May 2006. Following up, a three song EP, entitled 'Premonition', emerged in December.

The band appeared to collapse on March 23rd 2007 when vocalist Don Ochoa plus guitarists Ron Slater and Seth Arthur all exited. A statement read "The departure was due to a culmination of things including a bad tour last year, a poor recording experience with our debut release 'Hyborea', as well as creative and managerial differences. Several attempts were made to resolve the issues but to no avail… That being said, KEEN OF THE CROW as it was is now effectively over."

However, the following week Dan Ochoa, bassist Justin Christian and drummer Rhett Davis refuted this press release, claiming they "regretfully announce the departure of guitarists Ron Slater and Seth Arthur. Obviously, this is quite a loss to KEEN OF THE CROW, but there is no official change of status of the band." Slater and Arthur retorted ""Regardless of what is touted at the stolen KEEN OF THE CROW MySpace page the band is done."

Keen Of The Crow, Keen Of The Crow (2005). Mercurial / Nightbringer / Stygian Black Lotus / A Twilight Vigil / Speaker Of The Suns / The Ravening.

KEKAL

INDONESIA — *Jeff (vocals / guitar), Leo (guitar), Azhar (vocals / bass).*

KEKAL, dating to August 1995, are an extreme Metal band moulding elements of Death, Black and Progressive styles into one unsavoury whole. Debuted with a 1996 demo entitled 'Contre Spiritualia Nequitiae'. The act originally included vocalist Harry who quit following the debut album leaving KEKAL as a trio with guitarist Jeff taking the lead vocal role. Second album 'Beyond The Dead' would see a release in America on the Fleshwalker label. The album '1000 Thoughts Of Violence' was issued in February of 2003 in cassette format by the Indonesian Undying Music label. It would subsequently be picked up for a European CD release by the Dutch Fear Dark concern. KEKAL also donated their rendition of CRADLE OF FILTH's 'Dance Macabre' to the 2003 Cleopatra tribute album 'Covered In Filth'.

Guitarist Jeff (as 'Jefray') is an ex-INNER WARFARE member and also pursues a one man side project EXCISION releasing the 'Visi' album in 2000. In 2004 Jeff was learned to be active with an all new project dubbed ALTERA ENIGMA, a union with ex-PARAMAECIUM member Jason De Ron.

KEKAL released its sixth album, entitled 'The Habit Of Fire', in March 2007 in Europe on Whirlwind Records and in May in North America via Open Grave Records.

BEYOND THE GLIMPSE OF DREAMS, Candlelight Productions (1998). Rotting Youth / Armageddon / Spirits / Deceived Minds / The Conversion / Behind Those Images / Reality / Escaping Eternal Suffering / A Day The Hatred Dies / My Eternal Lover.
EMBRACE THE DEAD, THT Productions (1999). Longing For Truth / Embrace The Dead / The Fearless And The Dedicated / Healing / The Final Call / From Within / Scripture Before Struggle / Millennium.
THE PAINFUL EXPERIENCE, (2001). The Monsters Within / Crave For Solid Ground / Mean Attraction / Like Theres No Other Way To Go / Behind Closed Doors / After The Storm / Given Words / Militia Christi / The Painful Experience / Via Dolorosa.
INTRODUCE US TO YOUR IMMORTALITY, THT Productions (2003). Source Of Existence (Re-recorded version) / The Only Sound Of Rain / Mean Attraction / Embrace The Dead / Default / A Day The Hatred Dies / Crave For Solid Ground / Healing / Behind Those Images / Millennium / Rotting Youth / The Painful Experience / Introduce Me To Immortality (Remix).
1000 THOUGHTS OF VIOLENCE, Fear Dark (2003). Subsession / Once Again It Failed / Vox Diaboli / In Continuum / Paradigma Baru / Artifacts Of Modern Insanity / Violent Society / Subsession II / Default / Beyond Numerical Reasons I: 404 / Beyond Numerical Reasons II: 911 / Beyond Numerical Reasons III: 70x7.
THE HABIT OF FIRE, Whirlwind (2007). Prelude: Worldhate Chronicle / The Gathering Of Ants / Isolated I / Manipulator Generals (Part I Of Dictatorship): I. Failure Is The System, II. The Precaution Of Aftermath, III. Decadence And Excess / Our Urban Industry Runs Monotonously / To Whom It May Concern / Free Association / Historicity And State Of Mind (Part II Of Dictatorship): I. Repeated Patterns, II. Aftermath / Postlude: Saat Kemarau / A Real Life To Fear About / Escapism / What On Earth Am I Here For? / The Habit Of Fire / Subterranean Passageways / A Road Above, A Road Ahead / Finding A Way to Stand Up Again.

KEYDRAGON

NEVADA CITY, CA, USA — *Tamara Venus Star (vocals), Ron Langford (vocals / bass / keyboards), Dan Marshall (vocals), Bobby Blackmon (guitar), Dave Baxley (keyboards), Jason Weisman (drums).*

Grass Valley, California fantasy fuelled Heavy Metal band established by 9TH WAVE singer / keyboard player Ron Langford during 1984. The 2000 album 'Awaken The Lair' included a cover version of BLACK SABBATH's 'Electric Funeral'. 'Drink From The Waters Of War' followed in 2003. The band's fourth album, 'Uncontrollable Forces', highlighted three "tribal" female lead vocalists in Venus, Starlaiit, and Laughter Medicine. KEYDRAGON subsequently dispensed with band members Mississippi Bud and Lily White.

KEYDRAGON introduced two new members in August 2006, singer Tamara Venus Star and drummer Jason Weisman. Fifth album 'Dragon Prophecy' emerged in October.

AWAKEN THE LAIR, Keydragon (2000). The Show / Games They Play / Tripper / Corrupted / Dragon's Will / A Lesson In Pain / Travesty / The Craziest Ride / Dragon Fear / Electric Funeral / Beneath The Claw.

DRINK FROM THE WATERS OF WAR, Keydragon (2003). Drink From The Waters Of War / Calling The Dragon / Dragon War / Perimeter / The Mystic Comes / It's All This And A Hell Of A Lot More / Draconic Power / You Bring Tears To My Eyes / Dragon Companions / Draconis Pyre / I'm Coming For You.

FIRE RED PERCEPTION, Keydragon (2004). Fire Red Perception / The Darkness / The Dragons Den / I Want To See My Life / The Licking Flame / No Way In / Rammin' Jammin' / Head Rush / Battle The Beast / The Lost Kingdom / Twisted Hearts/Broken Minds / Dragons / Tall Tales.

UNCONTROLLABLE FORCES, Keydragon (2005). Siatica / It's That Great Dragon / Uncontrollable Force Of One / Falls Away / What Happens Inside / You Must Bend / Calling You / The Jaded Dragon / Creeping / The Domino Effect / Rage On / Flying With The Dragon / Dragon Dreaming / Sick Day.

KHAOSPHERE

BARI, ITALY — *Claudio Rodia (vocals), Antonio Mele (guitar), Vito De Michele (bass), Enrico Ronchi (keyboards), Guido Penta (drums).*

KHAOSPHERE is an extreme, experimental Black / Death Metal band hailing from Bari. The group was assembled in September 2005 by drummer Guido Penta, keyboard player Enrico Ronchi and lead singer Claudio Rodia. Subsequent additions included rhythm guitarist Nico Lucarelli and lead guitarist Antonio Mele, the unit finally rounded out with bassist Vito De Michele. KHAOSPHERE then engaged upon recording the demo 'Entering The Khaosphere', recording at Roger Studios with producer Micky Giove. Studio guests included Rocco Capri Chiumarulo delivering poetic narration on the track 'Il Giardino della Disarmonia', this song also featuring lead guitarist Damiano Lomolino and double bassist Davide Penta. The latter also made his presence felt on 'Khaosphere'. Guitarist Nico Lucarelli exited in November 2005.

Entering The Khaosphere, Khaosphere (2005). Khaosphere / Before I Rot / Born In Chains / Businesscross / The Incoming Armagedda / Il Giardino Della Disarmonia.

KHERT-NETER

LAPPEENRANTA, FINLAND — *Lars Holm (vocals), Tommi Havo (guitar), Vesa Kääpä (guitar), Anssi Mäkinen (bass), Enrico Huovinen (drums).*

KHERT-NETER, based in Lappeenranta, is a Egyptian themed Death Metal side project from members of Finnish Black Metal bands HORNA and PEST. Initially, BATTLELORE and DEEPRED guitarist Tommi Havo, bassist Jyri Vahvanen (J. Seneter') and drummer Gorthaur of HORNA and BATTLELORE put together a project during 1999 billed KALMISTO. They would sign to the Iso666 label, switching title to KHERT-NETER, for the 2000 album 'Arrival of the Funeral Dogs'. A demo, entitled 'Images Of Khepri', followed in 2003. Drummer Gorthaur would be replaced by Enrico Huovinen of ELDERTHRONES for recording of an unreleased, six-track demo. Upon completion of these sessions Vahvanen departed and Vesa Kääpä, previously of BLIND, was drafted on guitar. The band evolved further with the addition of Anssi Mäkinen and singer Lars Holm.

KHERT-NETER then cut a second album, 'Images Of Khepri', releasing this opus in October 2005 through custom imprint Khert-Neter Productions.

ARRIVAL OF THE FUNERAL DOGS, Khert-Neter (2000). Bringer Of Storms / Arrival Of The Funeral Dogs / Unen-Nefer / :S: / Undead Warhead / Infected Soil / Forbidden Pain.

Images Of Khephri, Khert-Neter (2003) (Demo). Ma"at-Kheru / An Image Of Khepri / Sutekh-Sa-Gaz.

IMAGES OF KHEPHRI, Khert-Neter Productions (2005). Hiding The Face Of The Sun / An Image Of Khepri / The Crown Of Fathers / Illusion Of Life / Everdreaming God / Ma'at-Kheru / Sutekh-Sa-Gaz / Failed Beliefs / A God in My Own Being / The Monument Of Grief.

KILL FOR SATAN

MAWSON, ACT, AUSTRALIA — *Kellhammer (vocals / drums), Necroslush (guitar), Toaster Doom (guitar).*

Black—Thrash act KILL FOR SATAN feature ex-PSYCHRIST member Kellhammer on vocals and drums along with former EXCEED guitarist Toaster Doom. The band was conceived in 2003 as an old school Thrash covers act, with Kellhammer being joined by guitarists Yurionymous (PSYCHRIST's Yuri Ward) and Necroslush with The Pine Island Sasquatch on bass. This formation lasted just one gig, after which Necroslush was replaced by Hellpitt on vocals and guitar. However, Hellpitt too lasted just one concert, a declared "Lack of beer consumption" being a contributing factor to his downfall. KILL FOR SATAN persevered as a trio, penning original material, until boosted back up to quartet status with the introduction of Toaster Doom.

The 2004 album 'Thy Kingdome Undone ...' included a cover version of ARMOURED ANGEL's 'Madame Guillotine'.

THY KINGDOM UNDONE ..., Kill For Satan (2004). The Fourth Power / Hammers Of Hell / Agents Of The Plague / Spawn Of The Maelstrom / Wolves Among The Flock / Pelagic Spectre / Madame Guillotine.

KILL THE ROMANCE

LAHTI, FINLAND — *Ville Hovi (vocals), Tomi Luoma (guitar), Antti Kokkonen (guitar), Raimo Posti (bass), Mika Tanttu (drums).*

Lahti Death Metal combo. Guitarist Antti Kokkonen, guitarist Tomi Luoma, bass player Raimo Posti and drummer Mika Tanttu also hold ties to DROWNED IN LIFE. Kokkonen and Tanttu also have association with PROFANE OMEN whilst Tanttu is ex-BEFORE THE DAWN. Singer Ville Hovi is involved with DOWNFALL whilst Tomi Luoma has SOLACIDE credentials.

KILL THE ROMANCE first put out an eponymous EP during August 2004. 'Logical Killing Project' followed in June 2005. After issue of a five track promotional session dubbed 'Cyanide' the band signed with Locomotive Music in October 2006. The resulting album, entitled 'Take Another Life', emerged in April 2007.

Kill The Romance, Kill The Romance (2004). Pulse Of Negative / Inner Cell / My Savior / New World Man.

Logical Killing Project, (2005). Dark Filth Water / Countdown To Domination / Killers Of Romance / Demons In Me.

TAKE ANOTHER LIFE, Locomotive Music (2007). I'm Alive / Prey / Ghost White Coma / Inner Cell / Trespasser / Friend / Pulse Of Negative / Breath / Worldwide Destruction / My Sweetest Enemy / Dark With Water.

KILLHARMONIC

INDONESIA — *Wawan (vocals), Innu (guitar), Romi (guitar), Alex (bass), Ongky (drums).*

KILLHARMONIC, dating back to 1997, brand themselves as "Symphonichaos Gorechestra Brutal Death Metal". Initially the band comprised former INNER and NECROPOLIS vocalist / guitarist Innu, ex-WASHBRAIN bassist Yoseph and drummer Sandra, another erstwhile INNER and NECROPOLIS man. With Sandra's departure another WASHBRAIN member Wahyu took command of the drums. Yoseph would then decamp but minus a bassist the band inducted lead singer Wawan, formerly of TENGGOROKAN.

Yet another round of changes was still in store for the band though. KILLHARMONIC's next line up incorporated Wawan, Innu, ex-SOLUTION guitarist Octa on the bass and SLOWLY TERROR and FASTINATION man Ongky on drums. Predictably this line up soon fractured with Andri of REFUSCATION coming in on bass guitar. He too would be forced out of the picture when Alex, ex-SLOWLY TERROR and FASTINATION, became the group's latest recruit on bass. Last in would be second guitarist Romi, previously with NO FRONT.

The group got to grips with a debut demo 'Hatred Diminished In Dismembered Head' during June of 2000. These sessions would subsequently be picked up by Rottrevere Records for CD release as a debut album. A second album, 'Hate That Never Set', surfaced in 2002.

HATRED DIMINISHED IN DISMEMBERING HEAD, Rottrevere (2001). Disgusting Homogenity / Hatred Diminished In Dismembered Head / Soup Of Human Flesh / Never Dread / Abortus Criminalis / Symphony Of Hate / Abusement Torment / Homo Homini Cubus.

KILLING CULTURE

LOS ANGELES, CA, USA — *Marcus Peyton (vocals), Scott Sargeant (guitar), Paul Poljiz (bass), Pat Magrath (drums).*

Los Angeles based Brutal headbangers KILLING CULTURE's debut album was produced by ANTHRAX guitarist Scott Ian. The band, featuring former LÄÄZ ROCKIT and WREKKING MACHINE guitarist Scott Sargeant, toured Germany in April 1997 as part of the 'Full Of Hate' touring festival bill alongside OBITUARY, ENTOMBED, DEATH, SAMAEL, NEUROSIS, CROWBAR, STRAPPING YOUNG LAD and CROWBAR.

Ex KILLING CULTURE singer Marcus Peyton unveiled his new band DOPESICK, a union with erstwhile SKINLAB guitarist Adam Albright, would issue an EP 'Vendetta', produced by Juan Urteaga and Scott Sargeant, in July 2002. By August of that year Sargeant would be revealed as working up a new project billed as MURDER LEAGUE ALL-STARS in league with the M.O.D. pairing of controversial frontman Billy Milano and Tim McMurtrie on bass.

KILLING CULTURE, Concrete Edel 0089532 CTR (1996). Twins In Human / Resurrection 2000 / Live / And Hate / Lockfist / World Attraction / The Line / With Strife / Life By Attrition / Verse 19 / Rhetoric God / Slave Of One / Ironside.

KINETIC

GREECE — *Savvas Betinis (vocals / bass), Manolis Mamas (guitar), Stavros Bonikos (guitar), Costas Alexakis (drums).*

KINETIC, founded in 2002 feature former members of WISDOM and BRAINFADE as well as ACID DEATH man Savvas Betinis on bass. The band debuted with a self-titled September 2003 demo. The group cut a Death Metal version of 'Helpless' by US Hard Rockers FIREHOUSE for a Sleaszy Rider Records tribute album 'Firehouse—All They Wrote'. The same label prepared the band's debut album 'The Chains That Bind Us'. Released in November of 2004 the record was also issued as a limited edition digipack, restricted to 1000 copies and adding a bonus video for the track 'Never Ending Winter'.

KINETIC parted ways with female vocalist Mina Giannopoulou due to "musical differences" in January 2007. She would be replaced swiftly by Margaret Staikou. Recordings for a new album, entitled 'Corrosion'. Then ensued.

Kinetic, (2003). Realms Of Nightmare / Holy Instinct / Never Ending Winter.
THE CHAINS THAT BIND US, Sleazy Rider SR-0027 (2004). Into The Nightmare (Intro) / Realms Of Nightmare / Engaging Web / Never Ending Winter / Hate Master / Holy Instinct / Free And Pure / Heed These Words / Message From Beyond / Life Faded / Last Call For Reaction.

KINGDOM OF THE LIE

KĘTRZYN, POLAND — *Daniel Ejmont (vocals / guitar), Pawel Palmowski (guitar), Dariusz Lotek (bass), David Teodorowicz (drums).*

Kętrzyn, brutal Death Metal act KINGDOM OF THE LIE was formed in 1990. Initially the band, comprising vocalist / guitarist Daniel Ejmont, second guitarist Pawel Palmowski and drummer Marcin Matysiak took on the title NECROSOUL. Adding bass player Dariusz Lotek the band subsequently evolved into BLASPHEREREION, issuing one rehearsal demo, then, minus Matysiak, KINGDOM OF THE LIE.

Both guitarist Daniel Ejmont, as 'Edek', and drummer Marcin Matysiak would join IMPURITY, the latter having been replaced by David Teodorowicz. The 1993 demo, 'About The Rising Star', saw guest guitar solos throughout donated by Peter of VADER. A promotional video for the track 'We Are The K' was filmed at the Olsztyn's Theatre Pantomime. Although drummer David Teodorowicz appeared on the cover of 'About The Rising Star' he did not perform on these tracks, where percussion was in fact delegated to a drum machine. KINGDOM OF THE LIE folded during 1994.

About The Rising Star, Mad Lion 001 (1993). We Are The K. / Life Is Lie / Blaspherereion / Everlasting Love / God Satan Nonsense / Kon Dor.

KISS OF DEATH

LECCE, ITALY — *Max Serafino (vocals / rhythm guitar), Marcello Zappatore (lead guitar), Fernando Conte (bass), Dario Congedo (drums).*

KISS OF DEATH is a Lecce based Thrash / Death Metal outfit, debuting with a 1997 demo 'Lies'. A second session, entitled 'Undisputed Reality', was laid down in June of 1998. The would gain further exposure with a track inclusion of a compilation album 'Mighty Killers' assembled by monthly Metal magazine 'Psycho' in December of 1999. A debut album, March 2000's 'Stronger Than Before', would be promoted by an impressive live campaign tallying over fifty concerts in Italy alone.

KISS OF DEATH cut further demos in early 2002, backed by live work including a swathe of festival performances and supports to such artists as SEPULTURA, SAXON, SHELTER, RAW POWER, EXTREMA, LINEA 77, DEATH SS, NECRODEATH, WHITE SKULL, NODE, OPERA IX, SADIST, UNDERTAKERS and NATRON. The group's second album 'Inferno Inc.' would be recorded at Fear Studios in Alfonsine during February of 2004. The first 100 copies included a DVD-ROM comprising three live videos, five studio clips and photos.

Lies, (1997). In My View / Through The Night / No Way Out / Lies / Buy Or Die / What Did You Say / Around Me.
Undisputed Reality, (1998). Burn The Flag / Undisputed Reality / Between Life And Death / Agony / Screams Of Rage.
STRONGER THAN BEFORE, (2000). Uncontrolled Reaction / Stronger Than Before / Envy / Twisted Personality / Eye For An Eye, Tooth For A Tooth / Mind-Fucker / My Darkest Side / Rising Fear.
Promo 2K2 EP, Kick Promotion Agency (2002). House Of Pain / Uncontrolled Reaction / Stronger Than Before.
INFERNO INC., (2004). Three Times Six / Violent Attitude / My World / House Of Pain / New Blood / Bestower Of Death / Sunk Into Hate Complete / Declaration Of War / Inferno Inc.

KIUAS

ESPOO, FINLAND — *Illja Jalkanen (vocals), Mikko Salovaara (guitar), Teemu Tuominen (bass), Atte Tankskanen (bass), Markku Nareneva (drums)*.

A melodic yet blackened style Death Metal band out of Espoo, KIUAS was created during 2000. Vocalist Ilja Jalkanen, bassist Teemu Tuominen and drummer Markku Näreneva would also be active with ICONOFEAR. Military service would stall progress until recording of an inaugural demo, 'The Discipline Of Steel', issued in 2002. 'Born Under The Northern Lights' followed in February 2003. Signing to British label Rage Of Achilles the EP 'Winter In June' emerged in 2004.

KIUAS, OMNIUM GATHERUM, ELENIUM, MANITOU and AMORAL united for the November 2004 'Dead Achilles' tour of Finland. The band's debut full-length album, 'The Spirit Of Ukko' recorded at Studio Tauko, emerged on Spinefarm Records in May 2005. The album 'Reformation' entered the Finnish charts at number 21 in May 2006. Japanese versions of the record added a cover version of JETHRO TULL's 'Hunting Girl'.

The Discipline Of Steel, Independent (2002). Until We Reach The Shore / Behind The Glass / The Wisdom Of Steel / The Discipline Of Steel.
Born Under The Northern Lights EP, Independent (2003). Warrior Soul / Across The Snows / Song For The Fells.
Winter In June, Rage Of Achilles (2004). Winter In June / Warrior Soul / Song For The Fells / Across The Snows.
THE SPIRIT OF UKKO, Spinefarm SPI226CD (2005). The Spirit Of Ukko / On Winds Of Death We Ride / No More Sleep For Me / Warrior Soul / Until We Reach The Shore / Across The Snows / Thorns Of A Black Rose / And The North Star Cried.
REFORMATION, Spinefarm SPI259CD (2006). Race With The Falcons / Through The Ice Age / The New Chapter / Of Ancient Wounds / Child Of Cimmeria / Black Winged Goddess / Heart Of The Serpent / Bleeding Strings / Call Of The Horns / Reformation (Wrath Of The Gods). Chart position: 21 FINLAND.

KOLDBORN

GLAMSBJERG, DENMARK — *Martin Leth (vocals), Henrik (guitar), Kim (bass), Rasmus Salskov (drums)*.

KOLDBORN is a Glamsbjerg based Death Metal band founded in 1997 by guitarist Henrik and drummer Rasmus Salskov, both previously members of Thrash act ICON OF SIN. Joining this duo would be Martin Leth, erstwhile vocalist and bass player for SOLENS SKYGGE, SATURATION and VINTERMØRKE. Second guitarist Casper, also an ex-SATURATION man, enrolled shortly after. This unit bowed in with the Jan Borsing produced 1999 demo 'Blessed By Beyond'. This session scored a recording deal with Diehard Music but an attempt to record a debut album resulted in failure as the band judged the finished tapes to be unworthy of release. A second go at putting together the album, with Jacob Bredahl of BARCODE and HATESPHERE acting as producer, provided a satisfactory end product 'First Enslavement'.

Guitarist Henrik is also an active participant in HATESPHERE, FURIOUS TRAUMA and HUMAN ERUPT. Rasmus Salskov performs as session drummer with DENIAL OF GOD. Leth is a member of STRYCHNOS whilst bassist Kim can also be found in DEATH MACHINE.

By 2003 Leth had exited and that August KOLDBORN incorporated new singer Thomas Villa. The band, switching line-up once again to incorporate singer Lars Bjørn-Hansen and guitarist Bjørn Bihlet, then cut the EP 'Devil Of All Deals' at Borsing Recordings for Ancient Darkness productions.

KOLDBORN entered Smart 'n' Hard Studios with producer Jacob Bredahl in August 2005 to record a new album 'The Uncanny Valley'. The band replaced guitarist Bjørn Bihlet with Jakob Nyholm from DAWN OF DEMISE in May 2006. In August KOLDBORN signed to French imprint Listenable Records.

KOLDBORN (pic: Peter Svendsen)

October concerts saw Mikael Ehlert from HATESPHERE acting as stand in bassist.

Blessed By Beyond, Koldborn (1999) (Demo). Altar Of Your Fate / Sun Of Souls / Breed Nephilim / Blessed By Beyond / End.
Blessed By Beyond, Koldborn (1999) (Limited edition 50 copies). Altar Of Your Fate / Sun Of Souls / Breed Nephilim / Blessed By Beyond / End / The Embrace Of Thanatos.
FIRST ENSLAVEMENT, Koldborn RRS967 (2002). Of Sins Sublime / Wicked Arise Divine / Blessed By Beyond / In Breathless Sighs / All Bowing Heads Roll / Vague Cries (Of Unborn Lives) / Demonride / Sunbroken / Altar Of Your Fate / The Embrace Of Thanatos.
Checkpoint # 4, Diehard (2003) (Split promotion release with 2 TON PREDATOR, GURD, THORIUM & AURORA BOREALIS). Of Sins Sublime.
The Devil Of All Deals, Ancient Darkness Productions ADP 007 (2005) (10" vinyl single limited to 495 copies). Repression / A Stir Of Unreason / Hand-Held Hate / Behind The World / The Devil Of All Deals / Neural Bound.
The Devil Of All Deals, Ancient Darkness Productions ADP 007 (2005). Repression / A Stir Of Unreason / Hand-Held Hate / Behind The World / The Devil Of All Deals.
THE UNCANNY VALLEY, Listenable POSH089 (2006). 28:06:42:12 / Lords Of Stupidity / The Uncanny Valley / A Destiny Predicted / Below A Crushing Earth / Hope Transformed Horizon / Disconnected / Last Message / Repression / Neural Bound / 2:18 / Relativity.

KONKHRA

COPENHAGEN, DENMARK — *Anders Lundemark (vocals / guitar), Kim Mathieson (guitar), Thomas Christiansen (bass), Johnny Nielsen (drums)*.

KONKHRA, who like to label themselves as "Death n' Roll", were founded in Copenhagen during 1988 and initially featured ex-FURIOUS TRAUMA bassist Lars Schmidt. The band got around to recording their debut demo tape in early 1990 with a second attempt the following year.

KONKHRA signed to local label Progress Records and issued the 'Stranded' EP. This official debut, limited to only 3,000 copies, featured sleeve artwork by noted Chicago tattoo artist Guy Aitchison. The release was capitalised on by support slots to acts such as FEAR FACTORY and BRUTAL TRUTH.

With the release of their first full length album in 1993's 'Sexual Affective Disorder', KONKHRA put in an American tour supported by label mates MEATLOCKER and a January 1994 European trek with SUFFOCATION. The third album, 'Spit Or Swallow', was produced by DISMEMBER drummer Fred Estby and was to push KONKHRA to the status of being Progress Records best selling act.

In support of the record the band toured Europe in 1995 on a bill alongside DEICIDE and SUFFOCATION. However, Scandinavian dates alongside IMMOLATION and CANNIBAL CORPSE had KONKHRA succumbing to internal pressures and splitting in two. Following the tour both Nielsen and Mathiesen quit, forging FACELIFT for the 'State Of The Art' EP with lead vocalist Ivan Grosmeyer. For live work FACELIFT employed Lars Mayland of KONKHRA and FURIOUS TRAUMA repute.

KONKHRA duly regrouped adding American ex-TESTAMENT, MACHINE HEAD and ATTITUDE ADJUSTMENT drummer Chris Kontos.

Lundemark meantime also put his efforts into side project DEAMON liaising with ENTOMBED members guitarist Ulf Cederland and drummer Nicke Andersson.

In 1997 KONKHRA started work on a new album 'Weed Out The Weak' as they were brought up to strength with the addition of ex-CANCER, OBITUARY and DISINCARNATE guitarist JAMES MURPHY. Incidentally, KONKHRA's 'Homegrowth' video featured a cover of TERRORISER's 'The Dead Shall Rise' and guest contributions from members of NAPALM DEATH.

The 'Come Down Cold' album saw Kontos replaced by Per M Jensen. Although Murphy contributes guitar once again for live work, starting out on a European support to NAPALM DEATH, Lars Mayland filled in on guitar.

KONKHRA's progress would be stalled by successive illnesses toward the close of 2001 as drummer Johnny Nielsen suffered a hernia followed by further delays as Lundemark underwent operations to remove kidney stones. Erstwhile drummer Chris Kontos announced a new band formation in 2002, THE SERVANTS, for an album 'Mostly Monsters'.

KONKHRA signed to the Italian Code666 label for a 2003 album 'Reality Check'. A rash of European dates throughout late October and throughout November saw KONKHRA headlining over fellow Danes ILLNATH and CORPUS MORTALE with Greek act HOMO IRATUS also in tow. The band would also put in their debut Israeli gig, appearing at the 'Metalist' festival. Another first for the band came in January of 2004 with three South African gigs in Durban, Johannesburg and Cape Town.

KONKHRA announced they were to "take a break" from activities in January of 2005 due to "personal reasons". That March it would be learned the band had parted ways with guitarist Kim Mathieson. KONKHRA, persevering as a trio, announced Australian dates for November where Ward 69 Records had picked up the 'Reality Check' album. Drummer Johnny Nielsen opted out to prioritise family life in April 2006. Replacement Mads Lauridsen was duly drafted weeks later.

Stranded EP, Progress PRL002 (1992). Time Will Destroy / Day-Break / Stranded / Lustration Of The Need / Spread Around / Deathwish.

SEXUAL AFFECTIVE DISORDER, Progress PRL CD7913009 (1993). Center Of The Flesh / Seasonal Affective Disorder / The Dying Art / Visually Intact / Evilution (Exordium Expired) / Lucid Dreams / Blindfolded / Thoughts Abandoned / Chaos To Climb / Empty Frames.

SPIT OR SWALLOW, Progress PCD19 (1995). Centuries / Spit Or Swallow / Life Eraser / Hail The Body, Burden The Spirit / Hooked / Facelift / Scorn Of The Earth / Subconscience / Necrosphere / Hold Another Level.

Facelift, Progress PCD18 (1995). Facelift / Drowning (Dead Dreaming) / Warzone / Basic Facts Of Life.

LIVE ERASER, Progress PCD31 (1996). Hooked / Warzone / Basic Facts Of Life / S.A.D. / The Dying Art / Centuries / Drowning (Dead Dreaming) / Facelift / Subconscience / Life Eraser / Spit Or Swallow.

WEED OUT THE WEAK, Diehard PCD 44 (1997). Heavensent / Time Will Heal / Crown Of The Empire / Kinshasa Highway / Through My Veins / The Reckoning / Misery / Melting / Inhuman / Pain And Sorrow (Segue) / My Belief.

REALITY CHECK, Code 666 Code017 (2003). Warmonger / The Lions Are Hungry / Reality Check / Eye Of Horus / Hellhound On My Trail / Fear Of God / The Coming Of (R)Age / Grapes Of Wrath / Parasite / Day Of The Dog / Lowlife / The Blackest Of Dawns.

KOROVA

INNSBRUCK, AUSTRIA — *Christof Niederwieser (vocals / guitar / keyboards), Georg Razeburger (guitar), Michael Kröll (bass), Moritz Neuner (drums).*

Death Metal band assembled in Innsbruck by mainman Christof Niederwieser (a.k.a. 'Eviga' of DORNENREICH). Drums would be in the hands of the esteemed veteran Moritz Neuner, a man citing an extended credit list with extreme acts such as SIEGFRIED, DORNENREICH, ANGIZIA, NECROLOGY, ABIGOR, ANGRY ANGELS, DARKWELL and Italy's EVENFALL.

Following the 1998 'Dead Like An Angel' album Niederwieser and Neuner, uniting with ELEND's Renard Tschirner, would take the band into a Gothic-Electro direction rebilling the band as KOROVAKILL. Neuner joined Italian act GRAVEWORM in early 2004 and by the close of that year had enrolled into the ranks of veteran German act ATROCITY. By 2005 Neuner was ensconced in the ranks of LEAVES' EYES.

A KISS IN THE CHANNEL FIELD, Napalm NPR 009 (1995). Intro: Der Weltenbrand / Das Kreuz und der Meltzenapfel / After The Fruits Of Ephemeral Pulchritide / Lachrydeus Mittelgard (Slahan Fontagr Inn Awebi) / Entlebt in tristem Morgenblut / Latin Dreams In Turpentine / Intro: Im Teich erlischt ein Bächlein / Awakening From Perpetual Contemplation (Yellow Mahogony Tomb I) / Nordsciltim In The Filth Where All Cull Perambulates Pain / Salomeh, des Teufels Braut / A Kiss In The Charnel Fields.

DEAD LIKE AN ANGEL, (1998). Europa In Flammen / Strangulation Alpha / Our Reality Dissolves / Trip To The Bleeding Planets / Dead Like An Angel / Echoworld Caravans / Der Schlafmann Kommt / Tantra-Nova-Hyper Cannibalism.

KORRODEAD

PORTSMOUTH, UK — *Lee Langley (vocals), Justin Whittle (guitar), Mike (bass), Alex Koutsoudakis (drums).*

Portsmouth based Death Metal unit dating back to July of 1998, founded by the trio of vocalist Lee Langley, guitarist Justin Whittle and bass player Mike. The embryonic KORRODEAD was then joined by a temporary drummer, Emerson Redsull, although this liaison lasted until April of 2000. During this period KORRODEAD cut a twenty minute demo session, reaction to which earned the band a slot at the April 2000 'Day Of Death' festival in London alongside AKERCOCKE, GOREROTTED and INFESTATION.

Redsull finally bowed out to make way for the Greek born Alex Koutsoudakis. A split CD venture with veteran Greek Metal band OBSECRATION was delivered in May of 2002 through the Sleazy Rider label.

ACTS BEYOND THE PALE, Sleazy Rider SR 0002 (2002) (Split album with OBSECRATION). Divine Hammer Blow / Demonic Disciple / Moon Maniac / 44 Calibre Killer / Coagulate (Demo version).

KORRUPTION

MIERCUREA—CIUC, RUMANIA — *Grama Emanuel Florin (vocals), Kato Lajos (guitar), Buna Attila (guitar), Borbely Andras (bass), Turcza Hunor (drums).*

Miercurea—Ciuc based Death Metal band KORRUPTION dates to 1994. The band involved singer 'Death' (a.k.a. Grama Emanuel Florin) of AGONY, SACRUM and VIOLATOR repute, guitarists Kato Lajos and Buna Attila, ex-SACRUM bass player Borbely Andras and another erstwhile SACRUM veteran, Turcza Hunor, on drums. Formatively, KORRUPTION featured drummer Setnescu Norocel and the SACRUM credited Duduj Levente on guitar. Bestial Records released the album 'Slaves Of Darkness' during 1999.

KORRUPTION went into hiatus but returned in 2004 as Mirgilus Siculorum put out the box set 'Korruption'. This comprised the 'Slaves Of Darkness' album plus an hour of concert DVD footage.

SLAVES OF DARKNESS, Bestial (1999). Bad Step / I Hate Violence / Slaves Of Darkness / Korruption / Separated Mentality / Evil In Chain / Kill Yourself / Rathos.

KRABATHOR

UHERSKE HRADISTE, CZECH REPUBLIC — *Christopher (vocals / guitar), Bruno (bass), Skull (drums).*

KRABATHOR date to 1984. The band, initially known as KRABATOR and based out of Uherske Hradiste, issued a glut of demos in the mid 80's including 1988's 'Breath Of Death', 'Total Destruction' and 'Brutal Death' before the project was put on ice as members served their national service for two years. April of 1991 had KRABATHOR back in action with the demo session 'Pocity Detronizace', capitalised on that same August with 'Feelings Of Dethronisation', the band's first with English lyrics. Signing to Czech label Monitor Records KRABATHOR's debut, March 1992's 'Only Our Death Is Welcome', went on to sell some 16'000 copies backed by a video for the track 'Pacifistic Death'. The band membership at this juncture comprised vocalist / guitarist Christopher, guitarist Hire, bassist Bruno and drummer Kopec. 'Cool Mortification', now seeing Martin on guitar, followed in September 1993. In an effort to break Western markets the group signed to Deathvastation Productions for the limited edition 1995 mini-album 'The Rise Of Brutality'.

Drummer Pegas, a veteran of BRUTALIZER and DEHYDRATED, joined the band and KRABATHOR's third effort, September 1995s 'Lies', recorded and mixed at Exponent Studio in Hlohovec in Slovakia with engineers Tomas Kmet and Ratislav Krcmarik, shifted over 15'000 copies enabling a tour of Europe, which saw the band on the road with IMPALED NAZARENE in October.

The Spring of 1996 had the band gigging with CANNIBAL CORPSE, IMMOLATION, GRAVE and ROTTING CHRIST. The band also broke the ice in America performing at the infamous Milwaukee Metalfest. Returning to Europe KRABATHOR resumed activities with shows backing DEICIDE, ENTOMBED, NIGHTFALL, NAPALM DEATH and SINISTER. Headline dates saw support from South Africans GROINCHURN and Germans SANITY DAWN. That same year Soundless Productions re-issued 'The Rise Of Brutality' tracks as a split cassette outing shared with Russia's PANDEMIA. Morbid Records revisited archive tracks with the EP 'Mortal Memories'.

The KRABATHOR duo of bassist Bruno and drummer Skull founded side project HYPNOS in 2000 releasing an eponymous album. Skull kept himself doubly busy by uniting with frontman Christopher in a project titled MARTYR in union with the notorious American Deathster Paul Speckman of MASTER and ABOMINATION fame for the 'Murder: The End Of The Game' album.

In 2004 KRABATHOR would donate their rendition of 'Evil Warriors' to the 'Seven Gates Of Horror' tribute album assembled by the Dutch Karmaggedon Media label in homage to pioneering Bay Area Thrash act POSSESSED. Skull forged yet another band unit that year, Metalcore band BAD FACE also comprising former DECAY vocalist Pawel, ex-HYPNOS, STAGNANT and the SHAARK guitarist R.A.D., former DEPRESION guitarist Dan.

Feelings Of Dethronisation - Pocity Detronizace, Krabathor (1991). Intro / Psychedelic / Eternal / Nesmyslné Mrtvoly / Odsouzený K Zatracení / Pacifistická Smrt.

Feelings Of Dethronisation, Krabathor (1991). Intro / Psychedelic / Eternal /Pacifistic Death.

ONLY OUR DEATH IS WELCOME..., Monitor-MDD (1992). Royal Crown / Psychedelic / Eternal / Convict To Contempt / Before The Carnage / Pacifistic Death / Preparing Your End / Killing My Wrath / Worried Childhood / Madness Of The Dark Shadow.

COOL MORTIFICATION, Monitor (1993). Faces Under The Ice / In The Blazing River / Evil Coroners Of The Mind / The Loop / Without The Following Dawn / Forget The Gods / Absence Of Life / Temporary Reign Of Insignificancy / Absence Of Life (Absence Of Mind mix).

The Rise Of Brutality EP, Deathvastation Productions (1995). The Rise Of Brutality (intro) / Pain That Doesn't Hurt / The Truth About Lies / Unnecessary.

LIES, Morbid MR019 (1995). The Truth About Lies / Unnecessary / Short Report On The Ritual Carnage / Tears, Hope And Hate / Pain Of Bleeding Hearts / Rebirth Of Blasphemy / Imperator (Strikes Again) / Stonedream / Believe.

Mortal Memories EP, Morbid MR 035 (1997). Breath Of Death / Bestial War / Apocrypha / Orthodox / Slavery.

ORTHODOX, Morbid SPV 084 12852 (1998). Orthodox / Liquid / Shit Comes Brown / To Red Ones / Tales Of Your History / Touch The Sun / Body As A Cover / Parasites / About Death.

The Rise Of Brutality EP, War (1999). The Rise Of Brutality (intro) / Pain That Doesn't Hurt / Unnecessarity / The Truth About Lies / Pacifistic Death / Total Destruction.

UNFORTUNATELY DEAD, System Shock (2000). They Are Unfortunately Dead / The Eagles You Can Have / Mirror Of Your Steps / Different Fate / Surviving On Arrogance / To Be Unknown / Living On The Threat Of One Finger / The Evil Men Can Do / Death Through The Centuries.

DISSUADE TRUTH, System Shock IRC 199 (2003). Intro—Dissuade Truth / Dead Hate Screaming / Smell All The Stench / No One / Silence Will Conquer Hate / Burning Bridges / Face The Intruder / Who Is Guilty / Saving Of Mind.

KRISIUN

IJUÍ, RS, BRAZIL — *Alex Carmago (vocals / bass), Moyses Kolesne (guitar / keyboards), Max Kolesne (drums).*

Ijuí, Rio Grande de Sul Death Metal merchants KRISIUN (Latin for "Seers of abomination") include plentiful old school Thrashing as part of their delivery. The band is a totally family affair, comprising three brothers, vocalist / bassist Alex Carmargo, guitarist Moyses Kolesne and drummer Max Kolesne. (Alex uses his mother's maiden name). The band first offered their 1991 demo 'Evil Age', with 'The Plague' following in September 1992. During this phase KRISIUN operated as a quartet, with Altemir Souza on second guitar. Maurício Nogueira then occupied this post briefly before moving on to TORTURE SQUAD, ZOLTAR and IN HELL. A further session, the Tchelo Martins produced 'Curse Of The Evil One', shared with VIOLENT HATE, backed these up in January the following year. Another release in October, laid down at Anonimato Record Studios in São Paulo, included a shared EP's with Germans HARMONY DIES for Rotthenness Records. This led to the 'Unmerciful Order' album on Dynamo Records in March 1994, on which the trio are all credited with the surname Kolesne.

KRISIUN debuted on the European continent with August 1995's 'Black Force Domain'. These tracks, cut at Army Studios in São Paulo, saw production credits going out to Sergio Sakamoto. Germany's G.U.N. label re-issued 'Black Force Domain' during 1997. German dates in the Winter of 1997 saw KRISIUN opening up a billing comprising RICHTHOFEN, DIMMU BORGIR and headliners KREATOR.

'Apocalyptic Revelation' emerged in August 1998, this being the group's first set of tracks recorded outside of Brazil at Musiclab Studios in Germany with Simon Fuhrmann in control of the desk. The band would make a significant impact upon European shores in 1998 ranked on tour alongside NAPALM DEATH, CRADLE OF FILTH and BORKNAGER before embarking on a series of headline dates with support act SOILWORK. February 1999 had KRISIUN involved in their inaugural North American tour alongside INCANTATION and ANGEL CORPSE.

Switching to Century Media Records, the band re-issued 'Black Force Domain' once again in 1999, adding bonus tracks in the form of cover versions of SODOM's 'Nuclear Winter' and a vastly accelerated take on KREATOR's 'Total Death'. KRISIUN's March 2000 album 'Conquerors Of Armageddon' was produced by MORBID ANGEL's Eric Rutan at Stage One Studio in Büchne, Germany. Limited edition variants added bonus cut 'Seas Of Slime'. Touring to promote the album found the band sharing billing with SATYRICON, IMMORTAL and ANGEL CORPSE in America. As ANGEL CORPSE disintegrated mid-tour with the departure of mainman Pete Helmkamp KRISIUN would obligingly loan out Carmago to fulfill vocal duties in order that

ANGEL CORPSE could complete the run of dates. There would be no let up for the band, soon after engaged in European touring on a package billing in alliance with OLD MAN'S CHILD, GORGOROTH and SOUL REAPER.

The Tchello Martin produced 'Ageless Venomous' arrived in 2001 prompting a full scale global workout which saw KRISIUN performing in Europe, North America, South America, Russia and Japan. The band by now had risen to headliner status for the 'Thrash 'Em All' festivals throughout Poland and Russia topping a bill of VADER, LUX OCCULTA and BEHEMOTH. November of 2001 had the band on the road in the UK and Ireland for seven shows with CANNIBAL CORPSE and KREATOR, this union transferring to Europe before hooking up with MARDUK, DARK FUNERAL, NILE and VOMITORY to participate in the hugely successful sold out 'X-Mass' festivals.

Sadly, news arrived in 2002 that former KRISIUN guitarist Altemir Souza was killed in a motorbike accident. KRISIUN would co-headline a run of dates with VADER across mainland Europe from late August 2002 supported by DECAPITATED and PREJUDICE. 'Works Of Carnage', sporting a rendition of VENOM's 'In League With Satan' and produced by OBLIVEON guitarist Pierre Rémillard, arrived in October 2003 and the band announced touring plans for the US in November, forming up a billing comprising HATE ETERNAL, DEICIDE and CATTLE DECAPITATION. KRISIUN resumed live work in 2004 acting as support to MORBID ANGEL's extensive set of European dates commencing February 20th in Hardenberg, Holland. Further European shows that November dubbed the 'Clash Of Demigods' saw the band forming up a package billing with BEHEMOTH, RAGNAROK and INCANTATION. The 'Bloodshed' album, released by Century Media in October, would comprise eight new recordings alongside tracks from the rare 1993 'Unmerciful Order' EP.

KRISIUN formed up with a Summer 2005 package touring bill comprising HATE ETERNAL, INCANTATION, INTO ETERNITY and ALL SHALL PERISH for US gigs in June, after which the band entered Stage One Studios in Bühne, Germany with producer Andy Classen to craft a new album 'Assassination'. European dates would be announced for August, including Prague's 'Brutal Assault' festival, Germany's 'Party San Open Air' event and the Muotathal, 'Mountains of Death' festival in Switzerland.

'Assassination' arrived in February 2006. KRISIUN scheduled April 2006 US tour dates combined with MORBID ANGEL, Canadians DESPISED ICON and Polish Black Metal band BEHEMOTH. US dates for September and October saw the band hooking up with SIX FEET UNDER, DECAPITATED and ABYSMAL DAWN. Intended live work in December across Europe was to see the band hooking up with SIX FEET UNDER, GOREFEST, BELPHEGOR and DARZAMAT for the 'X-Mass' festivals. However, the group withdrew from these shows.

The Plague, (1992). Sinner's Scorn / Evil Mastermind / Prophecies Of the Plague.
Curse Of The Evil One, (1993) (Split EP with VIOLENT HATRED). Sinner's Scorn / Evil Mastermind / Prophecies Of The Plague / The Dead Are Rising Up.
Krisiun / Harmony Dies, Rotthenness (1993) (Split EP with HARMONY DIES). Rises From Black / Agonize The Ending.
UNMERCIFUL ORDER, Dynamo (1994). They Call Me Death / Unmerciful Order / Crosses Towards Hell / Agonize The Ending / Summons Of Irreligious / Meaning Of Terror / Infected Core / Insurrected Path (Depth Classic) / Rises From The Black.
BLACK FORCE DOMAIN, Great Unlimited Noises GUN147 (1995). Black Force Domain / Messiah Of The Double Cross / Hunter Of Souls / Blind Possession / Evil Mastermind / Infamous Glory / Respected To Perish Below / Meanest Evil / Obsession By Evil Force / Sacrifice Of The Unborn.
APOCALYPTIC REVELATION, Great Unlimited Noises GUN163 (1998). Creations Scourge / Kings Of Killing / Apocalyptic Victory / Aborticide (In The Crypts Of Holiness) / March Of The Black Hordes / Vengeances Revelation / Rites Of Defamation / Meaning Of Terror / Rises From Black.
CONQUERORS OF ARMEGEDDON, Century Media 77259-2 (2000). Intro- Ravager / Abyssal Gates / Soul Devourer / Messiah's Abomination / Cursed Scrolls / Conquerors Of Armageddon / Hatred Inherit / Iron Stakes / Endless Madness Descends.
AGELESS VENOMOUS, Century Media 77367-2 (2001). Perpetuation / Dawn Of Flagellation / Ageless Venomous / Evil Gods Havoc / Eyes Of Eternal Scourge / Saviour´s Blood / Serpents Specters / Ravenous Hordes / Diableros / Sepulchral Oath.
WORKS OF CARNAGE, Century Media 8167-2 (2003). Thorns Of Heaven / Murderer / Ethereal World / Works Of Carnage / Slaughtering Void / Scourged Centuries / War Ritual / Wolfen Tyranny / Sentinel Of The Fallen Earth / Shadows / In League With Satan / Outro.
BLOODSHED, Century Media 77567-2 (2004). Slain Fate / Ominous / Servant Of Emptiness / Eons / Hateful Nature / Visions Beyond / Voodoo / They Call Me Death / Unmerciful Order / Crosses Toward Hell / Infected Core / Outro/MMIV.
ASSASSINATION, Century Media 77667-2 (2006). Bloodcraft / Natural Genocide / Vicious Wrath / Refusal / H.O.G. (House Of God) / Father's Perversion / Suicidal Savagery / Doomed / United In Deception / Decimated / Summon / Sweet Revenge.

KRONOS

THAON LES VOSGES, FRANCE — *Kristof (vocals), Grams (guitar), Tems (guitar), Tom (bass), Michaël Saccoman (drums).*

KRONOS began life as a Thaon Les Vosges teen Thrash Metal band during 1994 comprising vocalist / guitarist Marot, fourteen year old guitarist Grams, vocalist / bassist Jeremy and drummer Michaël Saccoman, the latter being the youngest at just thirteen. During 1996 Kristof was added as lead vocalist and Tems came in as replacement for Marot. This change of membership prompted a shift in style to Death Metal, evident on their 1997 demo tape 'Outrance'. Tom came in on bass during 2000 as KRONOS began to pursue an even less refined and more brutal Death Metal character, sharing a split promotion release with NONE DIVINE.

The 'Titan's Awakening' album would bear witness to two different issues with revised artwork, the latter variant being released through the Warpath label. KRONOS switch to Xtreem Music for 2003's 'Colossal Titan Strife'. In 2005 Kristof guested on Saint Etienne Death Metal band BENIGHTED's 'Identisick' album.

'The Hellenic Terror' surfaced in 2007.

TITAN'S AWAKENING, Warpath (2002). Mashkith / Sysiphe / Enslaved By The Madness / Bloodtower / Eternal Mindtrap / Outrance / Sadistik Retribution / Warmaggedawn / Dismember / Disease Of Good / Demence Of The Gnomish Warriors / Supreme Nordik Reign.
COLOSSAL TITAN STRIFE, Xtreem Music (2003). Mythological Bloodbath / Colossal Titan Strife / Submission / Opplomak / With Eaque Sword / Aeternum Pharaos Curse / Haterealm / Monumental Carnage / Phaeton / Kronos / Infernal Worms Fields.
THE HELLENIC TERROR, (2007). The Road Of Salvation / Bringers Of Disorder / … Until The End Of Time / Suffocate The Ignorant / A Huge Cataclysm / Tricephalic Hellkeeper / Petrifying Beauty—Part 1: Divine Vengeance / Petrifying Beauty—Part 2: The Murderous Reflection / Ouranian Cyclops / Maze Of Oblivion.

KRUEGER

CARACAS, VENEZUELA — *Carlos Sánchez (vocals), Gaetano Iannuzzi (guitar), Daniel Soto (bass), Kristoffer López (drums).*

An infamous Caracas 'Porno-Death' Metal band. KRUEGER, not to be confused with their Brazilian counterparts, trade in the harshest forms of Death Metal laced with equally repugnant lyrical subject matter. The origins of KRUEGER can be traced back to a founding formation in 1990, the band manifesting itself as a unit comprising lead vocalist C.A.S.N. (Carlos Sánchez), lead guitarist Gaetano Iannuzzi, rhythm guitarist Dennys Mattey, bass player Ramfis Tagliafico and Willianhell Salvatierra on the drums. This first variant of the band cut the 1991 single 'Spirit Of The Orgasm'. This self financed effort rapidly sold out of its manufacturing run of 600 copies.

1992 brought about changes with former STRATUZ man Bernardo Borrat supplanting Mattey. KRUEGER's second incarnation issued two singles that year in 'Krueger Live' and 'Lupus'. That year the group made its first live excursions outside of Venezuela, performing in front of 5,000 fans at a Colombian festival. The 1994 album 'Obsecration Of Pain', graced in a photographic sleeve depicting a gaping vagina, would see Daniel Soto installed on bass guitar. Limited to just 500 copies 'Obsecration Of Pain' is now a highly sought after rarity. Touring that year had the band partnered with KREATOR and POST MORTEM. Meantime, Ianuzzi would busy himself as part of Black Metal band LIGNUM CRUCIS.

The 'Granuloma Inguinal' album, once again with sleeve art continuing the female genitalia theme, was delivered in 1998. KRUEGER personnel drummer Willianhell Salvatierra and guitarist Bernardo Borrat split away to found LEAVES just prior to live work to promote the record. KRUEGER pulled in former BAPHOMETH man Javier Vázquez and ex-POST MORTEM member Miguel Ortega as substitutes. Showing comradeship with his former colleagues, initially Carlos Sánchez also acted as stand in vocalist for LEAVES.

The following year Javier Vasquez dropped out and KRUEGER pulled in former GENOCIDIO and TINIEBLAS man José Correa for recording of the album 'Fetid Love'. Ortega was next to exit and live work to promote the album saw former member Gaetano Iannuzzi re-installed. 2000 brought about yet more changes as a cover version of W.A.S.P.'s 'Arena Of Pleasure', donated to a Dwell Records tribute album, found the LANDSCAPES and EIGHTH SIN credited Alejandro Ayala installed on the drum kit.

The band's career was celebrated with the 'Decade Of Perversion' compilation released through Melomaniac. Once again the band shifted shape though with the ASMODEO, TORRE DE MARFIL and TIERRA DEL DRAGON veteran Kristoffer López taking command of the drums. In 2002 the KRUEGER credited José Correa enrolled as drummer with NATASTOR.

In 2006 the band contributed their version of MASACRE's 'Brutales Masacres' to the tribute album 'Bajo El Signo De La Violencia'. KRUEGER recorded a 2006 album 'Psicopathias Sexualis' in 2006 for Melomaniac Metalmedia Records. These sessions were produced by MONSTROSITY drummer Lee Harrison at WPB Studios in Florida.

OBSECRACION AL DOLOR, Melomaniac Metalmedia (1994). Vomito De Frutas / Suffering Conscience / Lupus / Inhuman Sacrifice / Death By Infection / Coito Anal.
GRANULOMA INGUINAL, Melomaniac Metalmedia (1998). Intro / Fetofilia / Granuloma Inguinal / Your Pussy Stinks / Mental Mediocrity / Dark / El Ocaso Del Tiempo / Birongo / MG+ / Outro / El Señor De Las Moscas / Welcome / Eyaculacion Etilica.
FETID LOVE, Independent (2000). Chapter I: Initiating The Anal Experience—Intro / Chapter I: Initiating The Anal Experience—Fetid Love / Chapter I: Initiating The Anal Experience—Shitting With The Devil / Chapter I: Initiating The Anal Experience—Jason / Chapter I: Initiating The Anal Experience—Cuando El Cuerpo Les Pide Pa'dentro / Chapter II: XXX Extasy—Lupus / Chapter II: XXX Extasy—Vómito De Frutas / Chapter II: XXX Extasy—Dark / Chapter II: XXX Extasy—Fetofilia / Chapter III: Inside The Ultra-Perverse Tecno—Sound Mix / Chapter IV: The Imperium Of Anal God—Anal God / Chapter IV: The Imperium Of Anal God—Lesbian Sodomy Society.
DECADE OF PERVERSION, Melomaniac Metalmedia (2003). Decade Of Perversion / Granuloma Inguinal / Lupus / A Morbid Tale Of Children / Dark / Vómitos De Frutas / Shittin' With The Devil / Anal God / Fetid God / El Ocaso Del Tiempo / Coito Anal / Cuando El Cuerpo Te Pide Pa´Dentro / Jason / Your Pussy Stink / Fetofilia / I Don't Know / Arena Of Pleasure.
PSICOPATHIAS SEXUALIS, Melomaniac Metalmedia MMR019 (2006).

KRYZALID

FRANCE — *Nicolas Langlois (vocals / guitar), Micos Orger (vocals / guitar), Laurent Carpentier (bass), Olivier Canton (drums).*

Technical Death-Thrashers KRYZALID, hailing from France, began life billed as SUDDEN DEATH during 1999. In this incarnation their opening gig would be conducted with Franck on vocals, Micos Orger and Nicolas Langlois on guitars, MALEDICTION's Olivier Messaoui standing in on bass and Mathieu on the drums. New bass man Laurent Carpentier enrolled in April of 2000.

The exit of Franck signalled a name switch to KRYZALID as Langlois and Orger took on shared responsibilities for the lead vocals. May of 2003 saw the incorporation of TRIDUS ELASTICUS and BURGUL TORKHAÏN credited Olivier Canton on drums, this unit cutting the EP 'The Beginning . . .'.

The Beginning . . . , Kryzalid (2003). Walk Or Croak / To Remain In Obscurity / Little Savage / Sadness.

KUTABARE

MELBOURNE, VIC, AUSTRALIA — *Damon Bloodstorm (vocals), Sean Sevantez (guitar), Steve Culpitt (bass), Pete Limbspasm (drums).*

Melbourne Death Metal band KUTABARE was formulated in December 2000, manifested by the UNDINISM and ABOMINATOR credited bassist Steve Culpitt (a.k.a. Steve Undinism / Haruko Yamashita) and UNDINISM guitarist Sean Sevantez. Rounding out the band would be drummer Pete Limspasm and vocalist Damon "Bloodstorm", a scene veteran of CORPSE MOLESTATION, BESTIAL WARLUST and ABOMINATOR. First product would be a ten track demo CD-R in March 2001.

KUTABARE's live inauguration came on 26th January 2002 alongside FUCK . . . I'M DEAD and VAGINAL CARNAGE at the Arthouse in Melbourne. In February 2003 Culpitt and Sevantez reformed UNDINISM, operating the two bands in parallel.

The KUTABARE album 'Finger Food Fetish For Morbidly Abnormal' was recorded at St. Andrews Studios in Cheltenham, Victoria, Australia over just three days in May 2003. The sessions were mastered by MORTICIAN's Roger Beaujard through Primitive Recordings in Pennsylvania, USA that September.

FINGER FOOD FETISH FOR THE MORBIDLY ABNORMAL, Razorback (2003). Religiously Frustrated / Moistened Cunt / Frotage The Fromage / Siamese Twins / Rime Of The Ancient Marinated Corpse / Dildo Of Death / Alien Intelligence / Maggot Laced Meal / Assassin / Guinea Worm.

L.O.S.T.

BUCHAREST, RUMANIA — *BB Hanneman (vocals / guitar), Vlad Buşcă (vocals / bass), Bogdan Vişan (guitar), Dragoş Hălmagi (keyboards), Dorin Costea (drums).*

Bucharest melodic Death Metal act L.O.S.T. was forged during March of 2004 by ABIGAIL veterans vocalist / bassist Vlad Buşcă, keyboard player Dragoş Hălmagi and drummer George Angel Tudor. The latter also held DUST credits whilst Buşcă held a tradition with TORNADO and CRONOS. This trio would soon be joined by guitarist BB Hanneman, citing prior affiliations with ADRENALINE, CRONOS, ABIGAIL, ICON OF SIN and MAGMA.

L.O.S.T. soon entered Recreate Studios to cut the two song demo 'Ziua Ce Vine'. The group debuted live in Bucharest on 5th November, their inaugural gig sharing the stage with ENTHRALLMENT and AVATAR.

Ziua Ce Vine, L.O.S.T. (2004). Ziua Ce Vine / Lost Breath.
LAST BREATH, Meta4 Productions META4 001 (2005). Ziua Ce Vine / Clipa / Last Breath / Dreams In Black / No More . . . .

LACRIMA CHRISTI

KASSEL, GERMANY — *Daniel Richter (vocals / bass), Gregor Zelazny (vocals / guitar), Daniel Kuhlmey (keyboards), Marco Gebert (drums).*

Progressive Death Metal act LACRIMA CHRISTI was assembled in Kassel during 1994 by ex-members of IMMORTALIS and ABSZESS. Initially the band boasted two guitars but following completion of the 1995 demo 'Raeder Des Schicksals' Karsten Goebel exited. Two tracks from these sessions would also feature on the compilation albums 'D.E.W.' through Nacht und Nebel Records and 'Only Death Is Real Volume 1'.

LACRIMA CHRISTI added keyboard player Daniel Kuhlmey in 1996 and cut the debut album 'Spiegel' two years later. An alternate mix of a track entitled 'Hypocrite' from this outing also surfaced on the 'Death-O-Phobia 6' compilation released via Earth A.D. Their second effort, 'Maskenball', was delivered in 2000.

SPIEGEL, Lacrima Christi (1999). Tango Of Bitterness / Raeder Des Schicksals / I Hear Black / Hypocrite / Kyrie Eleison / Fear—Spitting In His Face / Ninja—Killermachine? / Pathed Roads Of Deceit.
MASKENBALL, Independent (2000). Final Attack / Angry Grief / Christs For Lions Part II / Maskenball / Midnight / Dance Zombie Dance / Teufelsflöte / Bloodstone / Thrilling Moments.

LAKUPAAVI

HELSINKI, FINLAND — *Luxus Kristus (vocals), Pentti Orvokki (vocals), Vitun Mitu (guitar), The Sieg Heil Man (guitar), Dead Editor (bass), Pave Perestroika (drums).*

Helsinki "audio terrorists" LAKUPAAVI ("The Licorice Pope") actually comprises members of MOONSORROW. The album 'Raah Raah Blääh' came about in strange circumstances. MOONSORROW released a spoof press statement prior to their 'Verisäkeet' claiming they had adopted a new direction and their next release was to be entitled 'Raah Raah Blääh'. Various media outlets reported this as fact and, in honour of this achievement, the MOONSORROW musicians decided to go ahead and record the album anyway, as 23 bursts of brutal Hardcore styled Metal under the title LAKUPAAVI. The album cover depicted Jesus as Adolf Hitler and archbishop Desmond Tutu as Heinrich Himmler.

Drummer Ville Sorvali is also known for his work with AMORAL, AHTI and CRYPT.

RAAH RAAH BLÄÄH, Lakupaavi (2005). Kuolema Taidehomoille ... Ja Muille! / Puutarhurin Painajainen / Myin Lapsesi Jammu- Sedälle / Vitun Runkkarit Ja Muut / Saatanan Lehmä / Homo Jeesus / Saatanan Saksalaiset, Teistä Ei oo Mihinkään / Shitter Limited on Maailman Paras Bändi (feat. Vitummoista Pörinää) / Vapauttakaa Matti Nykänen / Matti Vanhanen on Homo Joka Ei Kestä Viinaa / Juutalaiskysymys? / Morjens!!!! / Anna Pillua Jonne Aaron (Heti) / Vitun Verhoilijavitunmestari / Perspillu ja Hyvät Vitut (Puh Runku) / Se Hyvä Biisi / Kumipaskiainen / Hakaristi on Oikeesti Kaunis / Bjarne Kallis Työnnä Risti Vittu Perseeseen / Ime Meisseliä Silikoni-Janita / Outro: Viikset / Vitun Hevivitunkaraokevitunhomot / Kuolema Taidehomoille (Richard Rape mix).

LAMENT

MEXICO — *Marco Perez (vocals), Iram (bass), Abel Gomez Torres (vocals / drums).*

Christian Mexico City based Death Metal act LAMENT, previously entitled BEHEADED, were founded during 1993. Unfortunately the bands original drummer Arturo Guzman would die before the act landed a deal. Signing to Steve Rowe of MORTIFICATION's label Rowe Productions LAMENT debuted with the Jeff Scheetz produced 'Tears Of A Leper'. Although Scheetz would also contribute with lead guitar LAMENT would stand out from the crowd by employing the bass guitar as a prominent lead instrument.

Following this release vocalist Marco Perez quit the band. Drummer Abel Gomez Torres took over the lead vocal role for the 1998 album 'Through The Reflection' recorded for Finnish Christian Metal label Little Rose Productions.

TEARS OF A LEPER, Rowe Productions (1997). Sacrifice Of Righteousness / From Pain To Hope / The Mystery Of Iniquity / Rivers Of Loneliness / Legal / Terminating Existence / Absolute Predominance / Tears Of A Leper / A Cry Of Anguish / Chaos Of Darkness.
THROUGH THE REFLECTION, Little Rose Productions (1998). Through The Reflection / Come Near / 1250 Dead Without Reason / A Dream At Sunset / The Wind Of My Heart / A Cry Near The Forest / Roars Of Wind / Tears ... Instruments For Reflection.
BREATHLESS, Kingdom (2001). The Sadness Of Your Steps / Breathless / Ocean Of Feelings / As An Eagle Flies / Silent Hero / Confronting The Past / Forgotten Warriors / Mist In My Eyes / Brothers In Battle / Within My Dreams.

LECHEROUS NOCTURNE

GREENVILLE, SC, USA — *Hohenstein (vocals), Chris Lollis (vocals / guitar), Kreishloff (guitar), Joe Payne (bass), Clay Lytle (drums).*

Greenville, South Carolina Death Metal band LECHEROUS NOCTURNE was formulated in 1997 at the hands of guitarist Kreishloff and vocalist Hohenstein, both former members of Thrash act DOMINION. Hohenstein also held down duties as frontman for Atlanta's NARCOLEPSY. Second guitarist Chris Lollis of DESECRATION repute was inducted and Clay Lytle of FATAL AGGRESSION was recruited on drums. Even without a bass player the band unit got to work on the live circuit, acting as openers for a whole host of name acts including ANGELCORPSE, NILE, IMMOLATION and KRISIUN.

In 2000 Lytle bowed out and the group relocated to Colorado to cut a set of demos. Dissatisfied with a stand in drummer these tapes were consigned to the vaults. LECHEROUS NOCTURNE duly made their way back to South Carolina, re-recruited Lytle and pulled in his FATAL AGGRESSION band mate Chad Bradley on bass. The debut album arrived in March of 2003.

Gigs in mid 2004 found the high profile figure of NILE guitarist Dallas Toller-Wade acting as stand in drummer. September of 2004 marked the addition of bassist Joe Payne, ex-LUST OF DECAY. The NILE connection was strengthened in 2005 when guitarist Kreishloff acted as stand in bassist for NILE's April US tour dates.

LECHEROUS NOCTURNE entered SoundLab Studio in Columbia in mid July to commence crafting their full-length debut album, given a provisional title of 'Adoration Of The Blade'. The band severed ties with bassist Joe Payne in October, rather unkindly stating this was due to "lack of experience and enthusiasm". The group announced they had contracted with Deepsend Records in January 2006. Mike Poggione from EXECRATION, SCAB MAGGOT, TRIVIUM, MONSTROSITY and CAPHARNAUM subsequently enrolled as new bassist. In August the following year Poggione joined the reformation line-up of Tampa, Florida's EULOGY.

LECHEROUS NOCTURNE, Independent (2003). Autoerotic Asphyxiation / Consider The Following / Phalluscidal / Horrorgasm / Singe Este Viata / Coitus Per Anum.

LEGACY

VANTAA, FINLAND — *Pekka Koivisto (guitar), Oscar Wollsten (bass), Teemu Hartikka (drums).*

Vantaa Death Metal act. LEGACY debuted with the three song demo 'Legacy Of Pain', followed by 'Bethroned With Death' in 2003 and August 2004's 'Dismal Symphony'. The group had been created as simply LEGACY in 2002 comprising guitarist Pekka Koivisto, bassist Oscar Wollsten and drummer Teemu Hartikka. The Spring 2003 demo set 'Legacy Of Pain' was tracked under the name of LEGACY whilst the December 2003 session 'Betrothed With Death' signalled the switch to THY LEGACY. Although the band had used GORESOAKED and MENSURA man Perttu Saarsalmi as session drummer Jussi Vaalasmaa took control of the drum position in early 2004. Guitar player Pekka Koivisto has an affiliation with GORESOAKED.

The THY LEGACY demo 'Reverse Exorcism' arrived in February 2005 with the 'Blood Work Theories' emerging in April 2006.

Legacy Of Pain, Thy Legacy (2003) (Demo). You Can't Stop The Hate / Legacy Of Pain / Endless Dream.

LEGION

LYSÁ NAD LABEM, CZECH REPUBLIC — *Zdenìk Kuchaø (vocals / guitar), Roman Studený (bass), Daniel Kuèera (drums).*

Lysá nad Labem Death Metal trio LEGION, comprising vocalist / guitarist Zdenìk Kuchaø, bass player Roman Studený with Daniel Kuèera on drums, started life billed as KREMATÖRR. In this guise they released the demo 'Mrtvoly' in 1994. They switch title to GUTTED in 1995 for another demo 'Slepá Debilita' before adopting the LEGION brand for 'Normal Is Not To Believe', recorded at KenahBosm Studio in Èelákovice during July 1997 with engineer Jiøí Zajíèek.

A further demo, 'Christians' in 1998, hosting cover renditions of SIX FEET UNDER's 'Tomorrows Victim', KRABATHOR's 'Imperator' and SEPULTURA's 'Territory', was followed by the album 'Tortured Voices Live', a concert recording taped in Lysá nad Labem on February 28th 1998 also including the KRABATHOR cover version 'Imperator'.

Another promotional session, billed 'Death Is Not Enough', surfaced in May 2002. Produced by Dominik Pecka at OPRO Studios in Kosmonosy. The band cut three originals plus another swathe of covers, including no less than three MORTICIAN tracks 'Bloodcraving', 'Devoured Alive' and 'Incinerated' plus takes on VADER's 'Carnal', BRUJERIA's 'La Ley De Plomo' and HYPOCRISY's 'Roswell 47'.

Normal Is Not To Believe, Legion (1997) (Legion). Carnage Of Christianity / Tortured Voices / Desire / Nìmota / Reincarnate / Normal Is Not To Believe … / Legion Age.

TORTURED VOICES LIVE, (1998). Tortured Voices / Carnage Of Christianity / Desire / Nemota / The Act In The Sign Of The Death / Normal Is Not To Believe / Imperator.

Christians, (1998) (Demo). Clerical Sickness / Christians / The Act Is In The Sign Of Death / Normal Is Not To Believe / Evil Will Be / Tomorrows Victim / Imperator / Territory.

Death Is Not Enough, (2002) (Demo). Without Him We Shall Live On / The Beast Of Vatican / Sin / Roswell 47 / La Ley De Plomo / Bloodcraving / Devoured Alive / Incinerated / Carnal.

LEGION

ITALY — *Gianluca (vocals / bass), Luca (guitar), Andreas (guitar), Steve (drums).*

The initial LEGION line-up, formulated in 1998, comprised a trio of vocalist / bassist Gianluca, guitarist Michele and drummer Steve. A change in tack that October witnessed the departure of Michele, replaced by Luca and Andreas. LEGION's 2000 live opus 'Live Repulsion' hosted a glut of cover versions including renditions of DEATH's 'Leprosy, 'The Philosopher' and 'Spirit Crusher' alongside SEPULTURA's 'Troops Of Doom', DARK TRANQUILLITY's 'Edenspring' and AT THE GATES 'Blinded By Fear'.

The LEGION track 'Obsession' would be featured on the TAO Records compilation 'Together As One' whilst 'Generation's Crime' figured on the 'Guardians Of Darkness' collection put together by Lethe Warden Productions.

Feelings Of Repulsion EP, Independent (2000). Intro / Full Of Hate / Obsession / Generation's Crime / Introspective.

LIVE REPULSION, Independent (2000). Full Of Hate / Suffocation Of Ideals / Blinded By Fear / Dead Inside / Spirit Crusher / Obsession / Edenspring / Instrumental / Troops Of Doom / Leprosy / The Philosopher.

LEGION OF THE DAMNED

LIMBURG, HOLLAND — *Maurice Swinkles (vocals), Richard Ebisch (guitar), Twan Fleuren (bass), Erik Fleuren (drums).*

Announced during early 2006, LEGION OF THE DAMNED was actually a continuation of leading Black-Thrash Metal act OCCULT, founded in 1990 by ex-BESTIAL SUMMONING vocalist Sephiroth. He would later drop the corpsepaint and revert to his real name of Maurice Swinkle. OCCULT vocalist Rachel Heyzer was previously a member of Death Metal band PATHOLOGY. Heyzer would later double up duties by fronting the veteran Death Metal act SINISTER for their 'Creative Killings' record.

UK and European dates projected into October 2003, dubbed the 'Bonded By Metal' trek, found the band forming up a billing comprising EXODUS, AGENT STEEL, NUCLEAR ASSAULT, MORTICIAN, GOD DETHRONED, and CALLENISH CIRCLE. As the year closed OCCULT announced they had signed to the Karmageddon Media label for a new album 'Elegy For The Weak'. This opus would see production credits going to former HOLY MOSES guitarist Andy Classen.

Early 2004 would see the issue of the band's debut DVD through Lowlifemedia Productions. Entitled 'To Be Thrashed–By Occult' it comprised live footage from recent gigs and early club performances, interviews with present and past band members, onstage jams with PENTACLE and DESASTER as well as promotional video clips for 'Killing for Recreation' and 'Doomsday Destroyer'. A short burst of Benelux dates in September 2004 saw the band united with CALLENISH CIRCLE, DISMEMBER and HEARSE. That same month the band entered Stage One studios in Bühne, Germany with producer Andy Classen to craft their sixth album.

The band announced a touring partnership as part of the December 2005 'X-Mas' festivals in Europe ranked alongside recently resurrected UK Thrashers ONSLAUGHT, EXODUS, KATAKLYSM, UNLEASHED, BEHEMOTH, and PRIMORDIAL. Following these gigs OCCULT adopted the new title LEGION OF THE DAMNED. The band formed up a European 'No Mercy' festival package for dates across Germany, Austria, France, Switzerland, Belgium and Holland in April, ranked alongside KATAKLYSM, GRIMFIST and CANNIBAL CORPSE. The band's appearance at the Gelsenkirchen 'Rock Hard' festival in Germany during June was taped and subsequently the track 'Legion Of The Damned' was included on the 'Rock Hard' magazine compilation album 'Rock Hard: Das Festival 2006'.

Second album 'Sons Of The Jackal' arrived in January 2007, impressively entering the national German charts at number 54. LEGION OF THE DAMNED acted as support to CELTIC FROST and KREATOR for European tour dates in March. That April War Anthem Records re-issued 'Sons Of The Jackal' on vinyl as a limited edition run of 500 pieces.

MALEVOLENT RAPTURE, Massacre MAS CD0498 (2006). Legion Of The Damned / Death's Head March / Werewolf Corpse / Into The Eye Of The Storm / Malevolent Rapture / Demonfist / Taste Of The Whip / Bleed For Me / Scourging The Crowned King / Killing For Recreation.

SONS OF THE JACKAL, Massacre (2007). Chart position: 54 GERMANY.

LEHAVOTH

HAIFA, ISRAEL — *Ariel Conan (vocals), Ach Shelo (guitar), Pixel (guitar), Evil Haim (bass), Nir Nakov (drums).*

Death Metal act LEHAVOTH, based in Haifa, comprises vocalist Yuval Talmor (a.k.a. Molech), the guitar duo of Gal Cohen (a.k.a. Pixel) and Nir Gutraiman (a.k.a. Ach Shelo), bassist Haim Benyamini (a.k.a. Evil Haim) and drummer Nir Doliner. An earlier incarnation had featured Evox from Doom band CHRISTINE and Thrashers ENDLESSIGHS as keyboard player. However, this version of the band split in 1999, only to be promptly reformed by Molech and Pixel. Evox subsequently forged solo Black Metal concern BLACK LANDSCAPES.

The new look LEHAVOTH debuted in 1999 with the demo 'Brit Ha'Orvim', followed in 2001 by the 'Iconoclastic' session. LEHAVOTH's rhythm section of bassist Evil Haim and drummer Nir Nakov would also prove active participants of NAIL WITHIN with Nakov also holding down membership of SALEM, Nir Gutraiman subsequently joining him in that band in 2002.

The band participated in a three way split album for the Spew label in 2003, sharing vinyl with SUTURE and LEUKORRHEA. However, singer Moloch parted ways with the band in April of 2004. A rapid replacement was found in Ariel Conan of Grindcore band WHOREXCORE. LEHAVOTH scored a coup by gaining the opening slot to DARK FUNERAL's first ever Israeli show in Tel Aviv during November.

HATRED SHAPED MAN, Fadeless (2003). Catterpiller / Ghost Nation / Non-Civilized / 2nd Practice / Iconoclastic / Reptile / Rodents Among Us / Hatred Shaped Man / Storming Thy Earth / Burning The Seeds.

LENG TCH'E

GHENT, BELGIUM — *Boris (vocals), Jan (guitar), Nicolas (bass), Tony Van den Eynde (drums).*

"Razorgrind" outfit LENG TCH'E, so titled after the renowned Chinese torture of a death by a thousand cuts, formative drummer Sven is in fact ABORTED frontman Gurgloroth 'Svencho' Sven De Caluwé. The band began life in Ghent under the billing of ANAL TORTURE, forged by Sven and DARK AGES guitarist Glen along with vocalist Isaac and bass player Kevin in early 2001. LENG TCH'E signed to the Italian Spew label for the opening 2002 album 'Death By A Thousand Cuts'. Almost immediately the band ran into problems with the track 'Fuck Eddy De Dapper', which due to legal constraints was re-titled 'Fuck Censorship' from the second pressing onwards. A split 7" single shared with BLACK OPS, entitled 'Razorgrind, was next to arrive, this set hosting the HEMDALE cover version 'Overflow'.

The band would employ Israeli guitarist Nir 'The Goat' Doliner of LEHAVOTH, even undertaking gigs in Israel opening for AMON AMARTH. Unable to secure a bassist Nicolas would switch from guitar to cover this role. Eventually the distance factor for Doliner prevented a full time role. In early 2004 therefore the band inducted Geert as second guitarist. Another line-up casualty would be Nicolas, who left the band in order to relocate to New Zealand. The band enrolled former PYAEMIA bassist Frank Rizzo as guitarist in late 2003. Meantime, Isaac fired up a Noise side project billed as PERMANENT DEATH whilst vocalist Sven De Caluwé would front IN-QUEST for an album.

The band's second album, 'Manmadepredator', would be scheduled for May 2004 release. LENG TCH'E proposed split releases in 2004 with FUCK... I'M DEAD for No Escape Recs and a split 7" single with GRONIBARD on Bones Brigade Records. Guitarist Rizzo decamped in August, being replaced in November by Jan of SPLEEN. In early 2005 the band inducted Boris of SUPPOSITORY as new frontman, debuting this revised line-up at the 30th April 'Face Your Underground' festival in Antwerp.

LENG TCH'E contracted to Relapse Records in March, scheduling a Summer release date for new album 'Process Of Elimination'. The band played May US East Coast dates packaged with IMPALED, MALIGNANCY and ABORTED. The band partnered with Quebec natives FUCK THE FACTS plus GORGASM and BENEATH THE MASSACRE for a Canadian tour commencing 1st May 2006 Ottawa, Ontario. In September Bones Brigade paired the band with French Grindcore combo WARSCARS for a split album 'The Musical Propaganda Of Sociologic Warfare'. Amongst the LENG TCH'E tracks would be an unexpected cover version of MÖTLEY CRÜE's 'Looks That Kill'.

The 'Marasmus' opus was recorded between July and September 2006 at CCR Studios, then mixed at Studio Fredman by Fredrik Nordström in September and finally mastered at West West Side Music by Alan Dauches. Guests in the studio would include Avital Tamir of BETZEFER vocalising on 'Confluence of Consumers' whilst Mehdi of DEDICATED added his vocals to both '1-800-Apathy' and 'Trauma & Scourge'.

To coincide with the release of the 'Marasmus album the band announced plans to embark on a European tour commencing March 23rd 2007 playing alongside THE ACACIA STRAIN and Holland's THE ARCHITECHT. In July the band inducted new drummer Tony Van den Eynde, previously of THE SEVENTH.

DEATH BY A THOUSAND CUTS, The Spew Records (2002). Initiate Murder Sequence / Strangled By Underwear / Hypocriscene / I Know Where You've Shit Last Summer / Fuck Eddy De Dapper / Inferior Superiorism / Get Rid Of The Rock In Your Name / Cockporn / The Regular Know It All / Chasms / Schizotrendic / The Scheme / Straight Outta Boerecote II / Mosh Of The Clowns / Human Ignorance / Graveyard Shift / Delusions Of Grandeur / T.P. / (Hidden track).

Razorgrind, The Spew Records (2002). (Split 7 single with BLACK OPS). Delusions Of Grandeur / Overflow / Necro-Dildo 69 / More Evil Than You Can Handle.

MANMADEPREDATOR, The Spew Records (2003). The Meaning Of Life / Public Enema No. 1 / Too Stupid To Live / 5 Minutes Of Fame / You Fat Prick / The Queen Of Egoism / Time Is Against Me / The Happy Retard / Popularity Contest / Sleazebag / God = Mass Hysteria / All Hippies Are Dropouts / I'm Afraid Of People / Life Is An S.T.D. / Still From Da Hood / Nothing To Be Proud Of / Fuck Off Coz I Hate You All / Sick Brutal Gore Bastard (Keep It Fucking Sick) / Crucial 4 Life.

THE PROCESS OF ELIMINATION, Relapse (2006). Fist Of Leng Tch'e / Don't Touch My Spandex / Overkill Bill / Another Hit Single / Bobby-Joe's Slumber Party / Remote Controlled / Glamourgirl Concubine / Ingest/Dissent / Schematic / Man's Inhumanity To Man / Motorgringing / Fat Camp / Icon Resizer / Derisive Conscience / Patriotic Pleasure / Plastic Motive / Testosterone Collar / Scene Scenery / Clarity Denied / Mediocrity Contest / P.I.M.P. / Reality? TV / Alliance Of Blockheads / Terminal Excess Patient.

A MUSICAL PROPAGANDA FOR SOCIOLOGIC WARFARE, Bones Brigade (2006). (Split album with WARSCARS). Confluence Of Consumers / Pattern / Sole Of Mistrust / The Divine Collapse / Self-Pity As A Daily Routine / Convenient Subverting / As Tolerance Subdued / Submissive Manifesto / Looks That Kill.

MARASMUS, Relapse (2007). Lucid Denial / 1-800-APATHY / Tightrope Propaganda / Nonsense Status / Tainted Righteousness / Marasmus / Confluence Of Consumers / The White Noise / Obsession Defined / Abstained / The Sycophant / Social Disgust / The Divine Collapse / Submissive Manifesto / Pattern / Trauma&Scourge.

LET ME DREAM

RIIHIMÄKI, FINLAND — *Tuuka Koskinen (vocals), Jani Koskela (vocals / guitar), Juhana Stolt (guitar), Marko Tuominen (bass), Jari Koskela (keyboards), Marko Jokinen (drums).*

A Riihimäki Doom / Death Metal act that also incorporate elements of Black Metal into their sound. The band date back to 1989 when vocalist / guitarist Jani Koskela and drummer Janne Peltoranta forged CONGESTION. Teemu Peltoranta would join the duo on keyboards in 1991 and guitarist Marko Pitkanen would be installed but quickly departed. Around this timeframe an opening, untitled three song demo was recorded, this session featuring a cover version of CELTIC FROST's 'Dethroned Emperor'. The demo 'Third Dimension' was then laid down after which Marko Tuominen was enrolled for bass duties and a further tape arrived 'Bed Of The Ancient River'. CONGESTION would also tackle their first live gigs during 1993 but Teemu Peltoranta was to depart, replaced by Jari Koskela for a Finnish tour guesting for Argentinean act VIBRION.

The band's demo, 'Bed Of The Ancient River', had by this stage come to the attention of the French Adipocere label and, switching title to LET ME DREAM, the group issued their debut album 'My Dear Succubus' in 1995. Shortly after the album release LET ME DREAM pulled in guitarist Jarno Keskinen but this latest recruit would enjoy only a fleeting tenure.

LET ME DREAM took on a national support tour to TWO WITCHES before going back into the studio for two more demo recordings 'The Maze' and 'Medley Rain'. Their next move was to found their own label imprint, Succubus Records, releasing 'Medley Rain' as a mini album. The vacant guitar spot was filled at this juncture by Juhana Stolt. Another round of Finnish dates found LET ME DREAM as part of a package billing with TWO WITCHES and British band MIDNIGHT CONFIGURATION.

As a deal for a second album was struck with Italian concern Nocturnal Music Jani Koskela relinquished the lead vocal mantle to Tuuka Koskinen. LET ME DREAM would then participate in their first foreign show, an appearance at 'Hells Gate 999' festival in Talinen, Estonia.

The 'Greyscales' album would be promoted by a Finnish support tour to ENSIFERUM and FINNTROLL capitalised on by a further batch of shows with ANCIENT RITES.

In March of 2001 Janne Peltoranta decamped and Marko Jokinen of SINSATIONAL duly stepped into the breech. LET ME DREAM issued a two song promo in 2003 as a foretaste of the 'Soulshine' album.

LET ME DREAM's third album, 'Soulshine', was finally released in May 2006 via Germany's Black Bards Entertainment. The band teamed up with TÝR and DIE APOKALYPTISCHEN REITER for European dates in September.

MY DEAR SUCCUBUS, Adipocere CDAR 027 (1995). Centuries Of Longing / Throne Of Dominating Force / The Sight / Burnt Into My Mind / Once In These Misty Fields / When The Sun Rises In The South / Thousand Decades Ago ... / Ned Of The Ancient River / In Agony Of My Soul / A Clear Line Of Sanity / When I Ride To Beyond / My Dear Succubus / Outro: A Cold Wind Blows.

The Maze, (1996). The Maze / My Doom / The Spear In Your Hand / Wolfborn.

Medley Rain, Succubus (1998). Medley Rain / Windride / Julia / From Passion To Void.

The Maze EP, Succubus (1999). The Maze / Into The Deep Blue Sea / My Dear Succubus (Live) / Wolfborn (Live).

GREYSCALE, Nocturnal Music NM014 (2000). The Maze / City Of Snow / The Spear In Your Hand / Medley Rain / The Crown / Julia / Into The Deep Blue Sea / Love Street 13 / Wolfborn / Outro: Medley Rain (Keyboard version).

Soulshine, Succubus (2003) (Promotion release. 50 copies). Soulshine / Roses On The Silver Plate / The Maze (Video).

LETHAL CURSE

SÃO PAULO, SP, BRAZIL — *Jhair Carvalho (vocals / bass), Alex Rodrigues (guitar), Paulo Moura (guitar / keyboards), Pedro Alzaga (drums).*

São Paulo Death Metal band LETHAL CURSE was assembled during 1992, the opening line up counting lead vocalist and bass player Jhair Carvalho, guitarist Alex Rodrigues with Frederick Stocco on the drums, cutting a 1993 demo 'Return To Obscurity'. LETHAL CURSE also featured on the compilation album 'The Winds Of A New Millennium I' and supported SARCOFAGO in 1993 and ANATHEMA the following year. This trio remained stable until 1997 when Stocco was superseded by new drummer Pedro Alzaga and Paulo Moura drafted on keyboards.

Cogumelo Records took the band on to record their first album, 1998's 'Rape The Innocence', this closing with a cover version of BATHORY's '13 Candles'. Brazilian dates had LETHAL CURSE acting as openers for ROTTING CHRIST. European exposure was afforded by inclusion on the Belgian sampler 'Sometimes Death Is Better'. Jhair Carvalho bowed out in 2001.

RAPE THE INNOCENCE, Cogumelo (1998). Like An Ever Black Skies / Return To Obscurity / Everlasting Alone / Infamous Creation / Tormentfilled / Bloodshed And Dream / Tragic Serenade / Desolation (Of Absolute Emptyness) / 13 Candles.

LETHERIA

VAASA, FINLAND — *Matthias Pellinen (vocals / guitar), H. Häkkinen (guitar), J.Kilpala (bass), J. Vehkaperä (drums).*

Vaasa Death Metal band LETHERIA, founded in late 1998 by guitarists Matthias Pellinen and H. Häkkinen, released a debut demo 'The Profane Oath' in 1999, these sessions including keyboard player and cellist J. Katriina Ranta. Drummer J. Vehkaperä and bassist J. Alakylmänen enrolled later that year. LETHERIA were back in the studio for the demos 2000's 'Lethal', recorded at Tuonela Studio Oy in Tornio, and December's 'Thornweed'. A track from this second set of songs, 'Hymn Of The Fallen', was included on the Low Frequency Records compilation album 'NorthernBreeze 2'.

The 'Doomcrush' set was delivered in 2003. Both J. Ranta and J. Alakylmänen exited in 2005. The demo 'Rancid & Profane', featuring new bass player J. Kilpala, arrived in 2006.

Lethal, Letheria (2000) (Demo). The Guillotine / Lothlorien Burning / Rohirrim / Colour My World.

Thornweed, Letheria (2000) (Demo). Hymn Of The Fallen / Scars / Black Feathers.

Doomcrush, Letheria (2003) (Demo). Suffer / Rabifen 1,5mlx 3i.v. / Epiloque And Exitus / Doomcrush.

Rancid & Profane, Letheria (2006) (Demo). Forced / Under The Boot Of Satan / The Nothing / Godkiller.

LETHIAN DREAMS

PARIS, FRANCE — *Kyrinla (vocals / guitar), Lethe (vocals / guitar), Kweletsy (bass), Darkened (keyboards), Valtyr (drums).*

Paris based LETHIAN DREAMS, founded in 2002 by female vocalist / lead guitarist Kyrinla and male vocalist / rhythm guitarist Lethe in 2002, were first operational as DYING WISH. The demo 'Mournful Whispers' arrived in 2003. Female bassist Kweletsy was added in June and in August of that year the group inducted the FOGZARD and INBORN SUFFERING credited keyboard player Darkened (Seb). Last in would be drummer Valtyr that September. In January of 2004 Kweletsy quit, being replaced by NINGIZZIA and INBORN SUFFERING's Stéphane Peudupin.

Maintaining their positions in LETHIAN DREAMS, both Carline and Matthieu would join Belgian act IN SOMNIS during July 2004. Seb exited in December. A new singer, Sephi, was introduced in January 2005.

Mournful Whispers, Lethian Dreams (2003). Intro / Thy Will Be Done / Last Winter Night / Mournful Whispers.

Lost In Grief, (2004). Sea Of Sadness / Lost In Grief / Toward The Void / Taking Away My Sanity / For A Brighter Death.

LEUKORRHEA

DENNISPORT, MA, USA — *Nate DeMontigny (vocals), Ron Greene (guitar), Rob Brown (guitar), Lucas (bass), Mike McPherson (drums).*

LEUKORRHEA is a Dennisport, Massachusetts Grind-Death Metal act less than subtly named after an abnormal vaginal discharge, were founded in August of 2000 by vocalist Nate DeMontigny, guitar player Adam Ford and erstwhile GODLESS RISING drummer Mike McPherson. Shortly after second guitarist Bob and bassist Nick would augment the line-up. A three track demo, 'Hymns Of The Rotting', surfaced in December 2000.

A membership change saw the introduction of bassist Damian Malgeri. LEUKORRHEA signed to the Forever Underground label in May of 2001, dispensing with Nick and drafting Lucas, previously with BANE OF EXISTENCE, as replacement. In August of 2001 the debut album 'Hatefucked And Tortured' was released. Substituting for Ford, the band pulled in the esteemed figure of erstwhile VITAL REMAINS guitarist Ron Greene during May of 2002. However, Greene left the band the following November in order to concentrate on his priority act CAST OF VENGEANCE. A 2002 split album 'Putrikorrhea' was shared with Texans PUTRILAGE.

The band contributed their rendition of DEATH's 'The Philosopher' to the 'Together As One' 2003 tribute album assembled by the Spanish Mondongo Canibale label. That October a split album via Amputated Vein Records, billed 'Denied Existence', had LEUKORRHEA allied with ETERNAL RUIN. The following month another split outing saw issue, 'The Sick, The Dead, The Rotten' on he Spew Records had the group sharing space with SUTURE and Israel's LEHAVOTH.

Signing to Primitive Recordings the band's second full-length album 'Breeding Salvation', engineered by MORTICIANs Roger Beaujard, was put out in March 2005. These sessions saw guitar duties divided between Ron Greene and Allen Florentine.

Hymns Of The Rotting, (2000). (Demo). Hymns Of The Rotting / Mistaken Identity / Tied Down And Strung Up.
HATEFUCKED AND TORTURED, Forever Underground (2001). Resurrect The Nekromantik / Mistaken Identity / Bloodbath Of Carnage / Dead In The Dark / Hatred Foreseen / Tied Down And Strung Up / Humanity's Victim / Hymns Of The Rotting / Vaginal Hemophilia.
PUTRIKORRHEA, The Spew Records (2002) (Split album with PUTRILAGE). Bodies In The Quagmire / Sodomy (Pedophile In You) / In The Name Of Blasphemy.
DENIED EXISTENCE, Amputated Vein (2003) (Split album with ETERNAL RUIN). Ripped Five Ways From Sunday / Starving For Violent Perversions / RopeBurn Destiny / Ill Conceived Mind / Resurrect The Necromantik (Live).
THE SICK, THE DEAD, THE ROTTEN, The Spew Records (2003) (Split album with LEHAVOTH and SUTURE). Sodomy (Pedophile In You) / In The Name Of Blasphemy / Bodies In The Quagmire.
BREEDING SALVATION , Primitive Recordings(2005). Breeding Salvation / False Oath / Digesting The Dead / Toxic Targets / Flesh Formed To Art / Consumed By Fire / Skinfection / Masks Of Flesh / Sodomy (Pedophile In You) / Starving For Violent Perversions / Bloodbath Of Carnage /Tied Down And Strung Up.

LIERS IN WAIT

GOTHENBURG, SWEDEN — *Christoffer Jonsson (vocals), Kristian Wåhlin (guitar), Matthias Gustafson (bass), Hans Nilsson (drums).*

Gothenburg Death Metal band featuring the talents of ex-GROTESQUE man Kristian Wåhlin. Originally the group was formed up by Kristian Wåhlin on guitar and Hans Nilsson on drums together with second guitarist Jörgen Johansson, previously of AWESOME NOCTURNE and DEMOLITION, along with AWESOME NOCTURNE and BRAINDEAD member Mattias Lindeblad on bass. However, both Johansson and Lindeblad were soon to opt out, with the bass position being filled by Mattias Gustavsson of TURNING CROSSES and CONQUEST repute. In this formation, LIERS IN WAIT utilized the services of THERION vocalist Christoffer Jonsson to record the EP 'Spiritually Uncontrolled Art' during October 1991 at Sunlight Studios with producer Tomas Skogsberg, released the following year by Dolores Records. A fluid guitar roster involved GROTESQUE's Alf Svensson, Jörgen Johansson and INFESTATION's Anders Björler. Tomas Lindberg of GROTESQUE and AT THE GATES also tried out on vocals.

During mid 1992 LIERS IN WAIT inducted new singer Johan and guitarist Moses Jonathon Elfström. That same year, billed as 'Chris Steele', Wåhlin, taking on the role of drummer, issued the side project EP 'Cursed Lands' under the DECOLLATION banner. A promotional video for the LIERS IN WAIT song 'Maleficent Dreamvoid' was filmed in September and in March 1993 LIERS IN WAIT put in live concerts in Poland. However, at this juncture both Nilsson and Elfström decamped to forge CRYSTAL AGE. Johan then switched to guitar whilst Mats took over on drums to track a full-length album for Listenable records 1994 at Montezuma recordings. Unfortunately the group fractured again that September, with both Mats and Gustavsson taking their leave. EUCHARIST's Daniel Erlandsson briefly manned the drums prior to jumping ship to DIABOLIQUE.

LIERS IN WAIT's only other recording came in the form of a 1995 cover version of 'Angel Of Death', again seeing Hans Nilsson returning on drums, donated to the SLAYER tribute album 'Slatanic Slaughter Vol II'.

Nilsson later joined LUCIFERON. Both Wåhlin and Nilsson founded DIABOLIQUE for a 1998 album. Daniel Erlandsson scored credits with ARMAGEDDON, ARCH ENEMY, REVENGIA and THE END.

Black Sun Records re-issued 'Spiritually Uncontrolled Art' in 1996 with new cover art. Kristian Wåhlin became a well known cover artist, executing such memorable sleeve designs as AT THE GATES 'Slaughter Of The Soul', EMPEROR's 'In The Nightside Eclipse', BATHORY's 'Blood On Ice', DARK TRANQUILLITY's 'The Gallery', DISMEMBER's 'Massive Killing Capacity' amongst many others.

Spiritually Uncontrolled Art, Dolores DOL007 (1992). Overlord / Bleeding Shrines Of Stone / Maleficent Dreamvoid / Liers In Wait / Gateways.
Spiritually Uncontrolled Art, Black Sun BS08 (1996). Overlord / Bleeding Shrines Of Stone / Maleficent Dreamvoid / Liers In Wait / Gateways.

LIGATURE

LONDON, UK — *Mark Blennerhassett (vocals), Dan Beaufort (guitar), Alan Temple (guitar), Laurent Lecoq (bass), Steve Temple (drums).*

London Death Metal band LIGATAGE was created under the less than tasteful title of CUNTZ in 1996 by singer Mark Blennerhassett and guitarist Martin Machin. The band would be rounded out the following year by guitarist Alan Temple, bassist Laurent Lecoq and drummer Steve Temple. The demo 'Extinction Agenda' was released in August 1999.

The EP 'The Abolition Of Guilt', produced by Dave Chang and recorded at Philia Studios in Henley-on-Thames, was crafted in January of 2002. Machin exited in April to forge MORATORIUM and the band duly introduced guitarist Andy Galloway, also active with KILLING MODE, BLITZKRIEG, REIGN OF EREBUS and ACOLYTE'S RUIN. The band evolved briefly into ABATTOIR before adopting the LIGATURE brand.

As the band worked on a full lengthy album in mid 2004 Galloway decided to opt out in order to prioritise REIGN OF EREBUS. He would be superseded by Dan Beaufort of KACHANA and 7TH CHILD.

Extinction Agenda, (1999). Persona Non Grata / Law Unto My Own / Deity Of Destruction.
The Abolition Of Guilt, Ligature (2000). Pain Is My Shadow / Empathy For The Devil / Twisted Innocence / Diminished Responsibility.

LIGHT THIS CITY

SAN FRANCISCO, CA, USA — *Laura Nichol (vocals), Brian Forbes (guitar), Nick Koenig (guitar), Mike Dias (bass), Ben Murray (drums).*

The San Francisco trio of vocalist Laura Nichol, bassist Mike Dias and drummer Ben Murray founded LIGHT THIS CITY in 2002, aiming to fuse NWoSDM with the classic Bay Area Thrash sound. After issue of the September 2003 album 'The Hero Cycle', delivered by Reflections of Ruin Records, the group shed the guitar team of Tyler Gamlen and Steven Shirley and duly inducted new guitarists Brian Forbes and Nick Koenig.

LIGHT THIS CITY signed to Prosthetic Records in 2005. Second offering 'Remains Of The Gods' was recorded by producer Zack Ohren at Castle Ultimate Studios in Oakland during March 2006. THE BLACK DAHLIA MURDER vocalist Trevor Strnad guested. Prosthetic issued 'Facing The Thousand' in September 2006. Concerts in December had the band aligned with ION DISSONANCE, NIGHTS LIKE THESE and AS BLOOD RUNS BLACK.

LIGHT THIS CITY filmed their first video, for the song 'The Unwelcome Savior', in Los Angeles during early February 2007 with Director Darren Doane. US touring to coincide witnessed dates alongside ALL THAT REMAINS, after which they confirmed a support slot on a two week tour with fellow California bands THE FACELESS and ANTAGONIST throughout February and March, closing this run with an appearance at the Santa Ana 'California Metalfest'. The band then featured on the April 'School of Rock' nationwide tour flanking HORSE THE BAND, THE NUMBER TWELVE LOOKS LIKE YOU and SO MANY DYNAMOS before acting as support to ALL THAT REMAINS in May.

VITAL REMAINS teamed up with LIGHT THIS CITY and WITH PASSION for summer US shows.

THE HERO CYCLE, Reflections Of Ruin ROR001 (2004).

REMAINS OF THE GODS, Prosthetic (2005). Remains Of The Gods / Obituary / Guardian In A Passerby / Hunt / Letter To My Abuser / Fractured By The Fall / Static Masses / Guiding The North Star / Your Devoted Victim / Last Catastrophe.

FACING THE THOUSAND, Prosthetic (2006). Facing The Thousand / Cradle For A King / The Unwelcome Savior / Exile / Maddening Swarm / City Of The Snares / The Eagle / Fear Of Heights / Tracks Of Decay / Like Every Song's Our Last.

LIMB FROM LIMB

NJ, USA — *Chris Lindemuth (vocals), Rob Boger (guitar), Drew Murphy (bass), Vin Murphy (drums).*

Death Metal act assembled as NO SOUL TO SELL by the Murphy brothers, bassist Drew and drummer Vin—both ex-RELEASE THE HOUNDS, during 1999. The founding line up featured lead vocalist Nick Leonetti and guitarist Rob Boger. However, Nick Shedlock was then added as second vocalist. Leonetti opted out in 2001 and the group duly installed Chris Lindemuth. Confusingly, Leonetti rejoined as the band took on the new title of EVISCERATE. With Leonetti discharging himself once again the band then evolved into LIMB FROM LIMB.

A four song 2002 demo would be followed up by a second session the following year, this featuring material recorded live at The Saint in Asbury Park. Working with engineer Eric Kvortek LIMB FROM LIMB then cut the 'Nothing Will Survive' album.

NOTHING WILL SURVIVE, Independent (2003). Death Perception / Destroyer Of Man / Prototypes / Drowned in Your Own Blood / Origami / In The Name Of God / End Of Time.

LITHURIA

HELSINKI, FINLAND — *Jesse R. (vocals), Kride L. (guitar), Jose V. (guitar), Perttu Kurttila (drums).*

Helsinki brutal Death Metal band LITHURIA is fronted by singer Jesse R. of THORNGOAT and DIARRHEA VOMIT with drummer Perttu Kurttila of NORTHWORLD and Power Metal band TRIONFALE. The group, rounded out by second guitarist Jose V., would employ both Konsta Kaikkonen of EX-ALTE, BLOODSTAINED, GORESOAKED and NORTHWORLD plus Mika Oinonen of SINCLINED and CARNAL CREATION in the session bass role.

Kurttila activated Grindcore side project CLUTCH MENTAL HOSPITAL. Session players naturally included LITHURIA guitarist Kride L. and singer Jesse R. for the improvised, one take demo 'Dentist From Hell', recorded in September 2005. 'Disgorging Your Broken Cogs 05.2' followed in similar fashion that October.

LITHURIA's 'Rehearsalroom Demo 05', recorded in October, included a rendition of GOREROTTED's 'Zombie Graveyard Rape Bonanza'.

Rehearsalroom Demo 05, Lithuria (2005). Gardens Of Decomposion / Cryptic Perversion / Zombie Graveyard Rape Bonanza.

LIVIDITY

CHAMPAIGN, IL, USA — *Von Young (vocals), Dave Kibler (guitar), Chris Campbell (bass), Garrett Scanlan (drums).*

Illinois infamous LIVIDITY started life in Champaign as a solo venture of guitarist Dave Kibler during 1993. A three track demo emerged, three tracks namely 'Mortal Impalement', 'Altar Pieces', and an instrumental named 'Spewing Chunks' all recorded with a Yamaha drum machine, after which vocalist and drummer Tommy Davis was inducted for a further 1995 nine track session 'Ritual Of Mortal Impalement'. Some of these songs would also be featured on a split demo tape in collaboration with MORGUE FETUS distributed by Skin Her Alive Productions.

In mid 1995 LIVIDITY was brought up to full strength with the addition of guitarist Matt Bishop and bassist Aaron Heath. This line-up would issue the 'Rejoice In Morbidity' tape for Polish label Immortal Records. LIVIDITY then switched over to Ohio's Ablated Records. However, shortly before recording new tracks for the 1997 album 'Fetish For The Sick' Heath was supplanted by Mike Smith. Further ructions before the close of the year saw Nick Null taking command of the drum stool as Davis made his exit. A notorious live album 'Show Us Your Tits' crept out in 1999 leading in turn to the millennium released 'The Age Of Clitoral Decay', both on United Guttural Records.

In June 1999 LIVIDITY took their brand of brutal Death Metal onto the European continent, touring alongside the likes of FLESHLESS, SANATORIUM, GODLESS TRUTH, PERVERSIST, AMORPH PNEUMA, 4 SEATS 4 INVALIDES and MONOLITH. The German Death Metal aficionados Cudgel Agency would also pair off LIVIDITY with Teutonic act PROFANITY for a limited edition split 7" single, 'The Urge To Splurge, in 2000. New York's Razorback Records also included the group's cover version of 'Bloody Pit Of Horror' on an IMPETIGO tribute album.

Tragedy would strike LIVIDITY with the premature death of Nick Null, the drummer suffering a heart attack on July 23rd 2000. Aaron Heath rejoined the fold on bass and James Whitehurst took on drum responsibilities before former GORGASM and INCESTUOUS man Derek Hoffman would step into the breach as replacement. In 2002 Germanys Morbid Records issued the album '...'Til Only The Sick Remain'. However, Hoffmann joined FLESHGRIND in August of 2002.

LIVIDITY headed up a package billing of MASTER, Austrias MASTIC SCUM and Polands DAMNABLE for European touring in March of 2003. Bassist Aaron Harper exited later that same year. Chris Campbell was enrolled in December. LIVIDITY enrolled new guitarist Chris Campbell in early 2004. The band parted ways with drummer James Whitehurst for "personal reasons" in August.

Jordan Varela joined on drums and LIVIDITY co-headlined the 'Fuck The Commerce' festival in Germany alongside ENTOMBED in May 2005. In June LIVIDITY inducted Shaun LaCanne of PUTRID PILE on guitar as Matt Bishop had suffered a hand injury. That September, Bishop bowed out, being replaced by Von Young from DEADEN. It transpired that Bishop, together with another ex-LIVIDITY man, guitarist Aaron Harper and drummer Robert Brody, had forged a new act entitled HUMAN ARTIFACTS.

The album 2006 'Used, Abused And Left For Dead' was conceived as a collaboration between Epitomite Productions and Morbid Records. The band also put out a split 7" single in alliance with TERRORISM through Disembowel Records. Garrett Scanlan then enrolled in time for US and Canadian headliners in July 2006. Morbid would also release a DVD featuring footage captured at the 'Fuck The Commerce' festival as a shared product with WACO JESUS. Belgium's Vomi D'Pore Records announced another split 7" single for 2007 in union with NECROCANNIBALISTIC VOMITORIUM.

Lividity, Skin Her Alive Productions (1995). (Split demo with MORGUE FETUS). Graveyard Delicacy / The Urge To Splurge / Food / Process Of Disembowelment / Feasting On Mankind / Immortal Impact / Devour Humanity.
Ritual Of Mortal Impalement , Lividity (1995). (Demo). Graveyard Delicacy / The Urge To Splurge / Food / Process Of Disembowelment / Feasting On Mankind / Immortal Impact / Mortal Impalement / Immortal Impact (Live rehearsal) / Food (Live rehearsal) / Graveyard Delicacy (Live rehearsal) / The Urge To Splurge (Live rehearsal) / Tampered Flesh (Live rehearsal) /Altar Pieces.
Rejoice In Morbidity, Immortal (1995). (Demo). Tampered Flesh / Rectal Wench / Fetal Scabs / Orifice Reconstruction.
FETISH FOR THE SICK, Ablated ABLTD001 (1997). Laceration Of An Unclean Cunt / Feasting On Mankind / Immortal Impact / Randomly Raped Rectum / Graveyard Delicacy / Pussy Lover / Brains For Lubrication / Devour Humanity / My Cock It Bleeds / Process Of Disembowelment / Rectal Wench.
SHOW US YOUR TITS - LIVE, United Guttural (1999). Rectal Wench / Feasting On Mankind / Devour Humanity / Lacerations Of An Unclean Twat / Graveyard Delicacy / Stench Of Virginity / Process Of Disembowelment / Pussy Lover / Orifice Reconstruction / Immortal Impact / Randomly Raped Rectum / My Cock It Bleeds / Brains For Lubrication / Fetal Scabs / Tortured Flesh - Rectal Wench / Fetal Scabs / Orifice Reconstruction.
The Urge To Splurge, Cudgel Agency (2000) (Split single with PROFANITY). Bloody Pit Of Horror / The Urge To Splurge / Stench Of Virginity
AGE OF CLITORAL DECAY, Erebos ERE 021 (2000). Oozing Vaginal Discharge / The Urge To Splurge / Chamber Of Bone / Anal Action Wife / Stench Of Virginity / Food / Dismembering Her Lifeless Corpse / Bloody Pit Of Horror / Sodomy Ritual.
TIL ONLY THE SICK REMAIN , Morbid (2002). T.L.C. (Tight 'Lil Cunt) / Coated With My Semen / Unrelenting Homicidal Obsession / A Woman's Place Is On My Face / Second Cumming (Pussy Lover Part 2) / Snack Size Tits / Anal Autopsy / Fetal Scabs / Conception Through Ingestion.
USED, ABUSED AND LEFT FOR DEAD, Morbid (2006). Raped For Rent / Gore Epitomite / Seven19 / Deviant Pleasures / The Cumming Of The Trilogy (Pussy Lover pt. 3) / Exhibition Of Carnage / Used, Abused And Left For Dead / Hero Of Dementia / No Time For Lube / Stench Of Virginity (Sonic Version) / The Urge To Splurge / Bound In Skin / Phallic Beat Down.

LIVING SACRIFICE

LITTLE ROCK, AR, USA — *Bruce Fitzhugh (vocals / guitar), Rocky Gray (guitar), Arthur Green (bass), Matt Putman (percussion), Lance Garvin (drums).*

Noted Christian Death Metal band, founded in Little Rock, Arkansas during the Autumn of 1989 by vocalist / bassist D.J., guitarist Bruce Fitzhugh and drummer Lance Garvin. This teenage act would be joined by second guitarist Jason Truby during 1990. Their debut demo that year, a four song effort, was deemed "horrible" by the band and not officially released. However, D.J. copied 300 on his mother's stereo to be sold for cost. Although not to the band's liking, the demo did secure a deal with Christian Metal label REX Records. Their debut eponymous album, produced by Doug Mann and BELIEVER's Kurt Bachman, sparked a run of East Coast dates with CRUCIFIED. With this success, the band was soon back in the recording studio to cut follow up 'Nonexistent' before more touring then the 1994 'Inhabit' opus. Stylistically LIVING SACRIFICE opened as a straight down the line Thrash act for their eponymous 1991 debut but would develop into a full flown Death Metal machine complete with guttural vocals by the follow up 'Non Existent'. Tracks from this album would be radically remixed by CIRCLE OF DUST for a compilation 'Metamorphosis'.

D.J. fronted LIVING SACRIFICE for the first trio of albums before leaving. Guitarist Bruce Fitshugh took over the lead vocal position and Chris Truby, Jason's brother, stepped in on bass. Switching labels to Solid State, LIVING SACRIFICE conceived the 'Reborn' album, recorded at Poynter's Palace in Little Rock, by Barry Poynter in January 1997.

LIVING SACRIFICE underwent a further period of flux in 1998 when the Truby brothers guitarist Jason and bassist Chris decamped. The band briefly pulled in bass player Jay Stacy before finding former ESOCHARIS man Arthur Green as permanent replacement. LIVING SACRIFICE also added another ex-ESOCHARIS member Cory Putman on guitar in 1998. In this incarnation the band put in live shows in Sweden and Norway, after which Rocky Gray, a former member of SHREDDED CORPSE, joined on guitar. A subsequent recruit, in 2000, would be Matt Putman from ESOCHARIS on percussion. Guitarist Rocky Gray and drummer Lance Garvin would also be operational with the side project SOUL EMBRACED. The fifth LIVING SACRIFICE record, 'The Hammering Process', emerged in June of 2000 through Solid State Records with 'Conceived In Fire' delivered in 2002.

Clenched Fist Records issued a LIVING SACRIFICE tribute album during 2001 featuring such acts as MORDECAI, DIRGE, CRIMSON THORN, SOUL EMBRACED, KEKAL, NAILED PROMISE, SOTERIOS and MINDRAGE.

With Gray taking time out to act as drummer for the hugely successful EVANESCENCE vocalist / guitarist Bruce Fitzhugh dropped out of the line up in January of 2003. An erstwhile band member, guitarist Jason Truby, joined the high profile P.O.D. in February. LIVING SACRIFICE announced their intention to disband, bowing out with a final appearance at the Illinois 'Cornerstone' Christian Metal festival in July.

In early 2004 Lance Garvin involved himself in a collusion with GODHEAD singer Jason Miller, DROWNING POOL frontman Jason Jones along with PRONG and TOMMY LEE bassist Marty O'Brien on the track 'The End Has Come', slated for the soundtrack to the comic book movie 'The Punisher'. That same year Jason Truby prepared an ambitious solo album entitled 'String Theory'. Employing no less than nineteen different types of guitar, the record apparently claimed to be recorded with a "patent pending recording technique that captured some of the most ground breaking acoustic sounds ever recorded."

LIVING SACRIFICE, Rex (1991). Violence / Internal Unrest / Second Death / Obstruction / Walls Of Separation / Phargx Imas / No Grave Concern / Dealing With Ignorance / Prodigal / Anorexia Spiritual.
NON EXISTANT, Rex (1992). Emerge / Enthroned / Nonexistent / Haven Of Blasphemy / ... To Nothing / Void Expression / Atonement / Distorted / Chemical Straightjacket / Without Distinction.
INHABIT, Rex (1994). In The Shadow / Not Beneath / Sorrow Banished / Unseen / Inhabit / Breathing Murder / Mind Distant / Darkened / Indwelling / Departure.
REBORN, Solid State SS4E (1997). Reborn Empowered / Truth Solution / Threatened / Awakening / 180 / No Longer / Something More / Sellout / Spirit Fall / Presence Of God / Reject / Liar.
THE HAMMERING PROCESS, Solid State SS35 (2000). Flatline / Bloodwork / Not My Own / Local Vengeance Killing / Altered Life / Hand Of The Dead / Burn The End / Hidden / Perfect / Conditional.
CONCEIVED IN FIRE, Solid State TND39688 (2002). Imminent War / Symbiotic / 3x3 We Carried Your Body / Poisoning / Send Your Regrets / Subtle Alliance / Into Again / Separation / Black Seeds / Ignite / Distrust / Martyr / Reach For The Sky.

LOCKUP

SWEDEN / UK / USA — *Tomas Lindberg (vocals), Jesse Pintado (guitar), Shane Embury (bass), Nick Barker (drums).*

LOCKUP

A multi-national collaboration between NAPALM DEATH's Shane Embury and DIMMU BORGIR and ex-CRADLE OF FILTH drummer Nick Barker together with Peter Tägtgren of Sweden's HYPOCRISY and Embury's American NAPALM DEATH band mate guitarist Jesse Pintado.

The resulting debut album, which featured many songs originally destined for Pintado's side outfit TERRORIZER, was highly successful, even breaking the national charts in Germany and receiving many magazine 'Album of the month' awards. The album was produced by ex-SABBAT guitarist Andy Sneap.

LOCKUP undertook a European tour in 2000 with THE CROWN and ex-AT THE GATES singer Tomas Lindberg substituting for Tägtgren. The band were supported by DECAPITATED and CORPORATION 187. Barker also figured anonymously in the notorious 'Mexican' Death Metal project BRUJERIA. Centred upon FEAR FACTORY's Dino Cazares and FAITH NO MORE's Jim Gould Barker aided on the 2000 'Brujerizmo' album.

LOCKUP added erstwhile CANCER guitarist Barry Savage to the line-up in early 2002 for touring purposes. The band then embarked upon Japanese and European dates throughout the summer. Further shows would be slated in Europe, including the 'Wacken Open Air' festival, but then cancelled when NAPALM DEATH went over schedule on recording of their 'Order Of The Leech' album. Fans would be somewhat placated by news that the Japanese LOCKUP dates had been recorded for a live album, recorded at Club Quattro in Nagoya on June 28th 2002, set for release through Toys Factory Records in Japan and Shane Embury's label Feto Records in Europe. In August 2003 Tomas Lindberg and Nick Barker stood in as session members for NIGHTRAGE's debut gig at the 'Göteborgs Kalaset' festival in Sweden. The singer would also guest for veteran Swedish Crustcore outfit DISFEAR, appearing on their 'Powerload' EP.

Sad news emerged on August 27th with the passing of former band member Jesse Pintado. The guitarist had died from liver failure at the Erasmus MC hospital in Holland.

In September Shane Embury, in collaboration with MISTRESS and ANAAL NATHRAKH's Mick Kenney, announced the formation of new label Feto Records. This imprint served as an outlet for Kenney's EXPLODER, MISTRESS and PROFESSOR FATE projects and Embury's 'Live in Japan' opus from LOCKUP. Nick Barker joined Bay Area Thrash veterans TESTAMENT in January 2007.

PLEASURES PAVE SEWERS, Nuclear Blast NB 439-2 (1999). After Life In Purgatory / Submission / Triple Six Sucks Angels / Delirium / Pretenders Of The Throne / Slow Bleed Gorgon—Pleasures Pave Sewers / Ego Pawn / The Dreams Are Sacrificed / Tragic Faith / Darkness Of Ignorance / Salvation Thru Destruction / Leech Eclipse / Fever Landscapes.
HATE BREEDS SUFFERING, Nuclear Blast NB6592 (2002). Feeding The Opiate / Castrate The Wreckage / Violent Reprisal / Detestation / Retrogression / Slaughterous Ways / Dead Sea Scroll Deception / Hate Breeds Suffering / Catharsis / Jesus Virus / Broken World / Horns Of Venus / High Tide In A Sea Of Blood / Cascade Leviathan / Fake Somebody/Real Nobody / Sixth Extinction.
PLAY FAST OR DIE: LIVE IN JAPAN, (2006).

LONG VOYAGE BACK

BRIGHTON, VIC, AUSTRALIA — LONG VOYAGE BACK was founded by the veteran HOBBS' ANGEL OF DEATH and DESTRÖYER 666 bass player Phil Gresik. In his previous act DESTRÖYER 666 the man had gone under the nom de guerre of Bullet Eater.

LONG VOYAGE BACK debuted with an eponymous outing released through the Destruktive Kommandoh label in 1998. The second album, 1999's 'Long Voyage Back II', saw drums courtesy of Sham of DEPRESSION and NOTHING SACRED with female vocals from Mel Watson and Sam Lohs. A split 7" single, 'Poison Blood', arrived in November of 2001 shared with fellow Aussies ANATOMY. LONG VOYAGE BACK's third album, 'Close To Animal', was released by Modern Invasion Music in 2002.

For live appearances Gresik employed guitarist Nick Maurer, backing singers Amber Willems and Ngami with ex-BLOOD DUSTER, ABRAMELIN and FRACTURE man Euan Herriot on the drums.

LONG VOYAGE BACK, Destruktive Kommandoh DSTK7664-2CD (1998). Long Voyage Back / Poison Blood / Towards The Sun / The Search / Reflection / Nomadic Paths.
LONG VOYAGE BACK II, Modern Invasion MIM7328-2CD (1999). Naked And Wounded / Ghosts Of The Past / Pyrrhic Battle / Heavy Stone / Behind The Eyes / The Struggle / The Pitiless Reality.
Poison Blood, Bleed BLEED 005 (2001) (Split single with ANATOMY). Poison Blood.
CLOSE TO ANIMAL, Modern Invasion MIM73352CD (2002). Oceans / The Call / Close To Animal / The Lower Road / Deep And Hallowed / Towards The Sun / Change Your Mind / Naiad.

LORD BLASPHEMER

CHICAGO, IL, USA — *Erik Pertl (vocals / bass), Eric Hersemann (guitar), Narcyz Fortuna (drums).*

Chicago extreme Metal act LORD BLASPHEMER dated back to 1989. The band's second demo, 1991's 'We Love To Kill', provoked interest from a number of labels, including the UK Peaceville concern, but the band folded. At the hand of bass player / vocalist Erik Pertl a revised incarnation of the band rose up once more in 1997, re-debuting with the demos 'Spiral Caverns Of The Occult' in 1998 and 'Visions Of Hatred' in 1999. The album 'Tales Of Misanthropy, Bloodlust And Mass Homicide' was recorded with the aid of session drums from Jim Kerley. In April 2002 Narcyz Fortuna of HURT LOCKER enrolled as drummer.

Guitarist Eric Hersemann decamped in 2002 to join Florida's DIABOLIC. Josh Trevino took his place and former comrade Jim Kerley also resumed his position at the drum kit. Hersemann enrolled into the ranks of HATE ETERNAL in May 2005. Eric Hersemann subsequently forged the GIGAN project in union with HATE ETERNAL vocalist / guitarist Randy Piro and drummer Grover Norton.

TALES OF MISANTHROPY, BLOODLUST AND MASS HOMICIDE, Metal War MWP 002 (2002). Bestial Bacchanal / Bloodbaths Of The Mental Inquisition: Karmageddon / Mutations With Bloodlust In Their Eyes / Cursed By The Spirit Of Thorn / Spiral Caverns Of The Occult / Wading Through A Mulch Of The Dead.

LORD GORE

PORTLAND, OR, USA — *Gurge (vocals), SCSI (guitar), Maniac Killer (guitar), Jesus H Dump (bass), Colon Bowel (drums).*

Portland, Oregon Grind act. LORD GORE's Maniac Killer (a.k.a. Neil Smith) also holds ties to MANIAC KILLER and FRIGHTMARE. Early band members included vocalist Nihilist (a.k.a. Nekro von Gore) of IN MEMORIUM, ABAZAGORATH and THY INFERNAL repute and drummer Surgeon General Redrum. LORD GORE's recorded output commenced with the 2001 demos 'Dark Lords Of The Cyst' and 'Massive Deconstructive Surgery'. Razorback Records issued 'The Autophagus Orgy' album in 2002.

As part of the Death Metal WHORE duo Maniac Killer also published the 'Unfinished Business' album in 2004 through Moribund Records. Meantime, LORD GORE returned with the 'Resickened' opus. Split offerings projected for 2005 included a shared album with Australians BLOOD DUSTER and Belgian act LENG TCH'E on Deepsend Records and an alliance with BIOLOCH on No Escape Records.

LORD GORE announced they were to disband in January 2007.

THE AUTOPHAGUS ORGY, Razorback (2002). Intro / Morgue Whore / Krash Kourse In Psychopathology / Rape Camp / The Forgotten Flesh / The Last Supper (The Autophagus) / Involuntary Vaginal Vermin Slut / Post Coital Eruption / Nekro-Erotic Art / Zombie Molestation (Raped By The Dead) / Lord Gore / Breakfast At The Manchester Morgue.
RESICKENED, Razorback (2004).

LORDS OF DARKNESS

GUADALAJARA, MEXICO — *Lord Dekral (vocals / bass), Lord Goradragh (guitar), Lord Volker (guitar), Lord Raxemmv (drums).*

LORDS OF DARKNESS is a Guadalajara based, Power styled Black Metal band convened in October of 2000. The founding quintet comprised singer Martín Guerrero, guitarists Lord Goradragh Silentium Eternus and Leonel Zapién, bassist Lord Odium Dekral and drummer Lord Fáfner. Guitarist Lord Goradragh Silentium Eternus entered the fold in 2001 with second guitarist Lord Volker enrolling the following year. LORDS OF DARKNESS first committed themselves to the recording studio for the 2002 demo 'Valley Of Tears'. By this stage original drummer Lord Fáfner bowed out in 2003 and the band persevered by utilising the stand in services of Abraham Banda of EK and MELANCHOLY.

A demo, 'The Night Of Raven Comes ...', was delivered in 2004.

Valley Of Tears, Pancho Villa (2002). Sempiternal Torment / Valley Of Tears / Legions Of Hell / L'abbraccio Di Morte.
THE NIGHT OF RAVEN COMES ..., Lords Of Darkness (2003). In The Night Of Raven / Valley Of Tears / Nocturnalis Vento Silente.
INFERNAL MALEVOLENCE, Pancho Villa (2005). Ice Winds / Infernal Malevolence / Anathema / The Wood Of Fallen Angels / Carnal Rites / Rotten Cross / Extermination / Valley Of Tears.

LOS SIN NOMBRE

LINKÖPING, SWEDEN — *Pär Palm (vocals), Saul Camara (guitar), Jimmie Fornell (guitar), Jack Karlsson (bass), Steve Mills (drums).*

Linköping Death Metal band LOS SIN NOMBRE was created during February 2002, initially as an ENTOMBED covers outfit. The founding line-up comprised guitarists Arvid and Saul Camara, of CHAMBER OF TORMENT, SOLE SHAKER and DRAGQUEEN LIPSTICK, bassist Jack Karlsson, of Punk band THE FISTICUFFS, and drummer Steve Mills, a veteran of VICIOUS, CHAMBER OF TORMENT and DRAGQUEEN LIPSTICK. A first demo, 'Tate Murders' featuring narration taken from Charles Manson's parole speech in the title track, was recorded with newly installed singer Pär Palm in September 2002. Arvid exited, being replaced by Jimmie Fornell of THE FISTICUFFS, THE MISUNPASSED and VICIOUS. Second session 'Down With Pressure' was recorded in January 2004. A third demo arrived in May 2005.

Tate Murders, Los Sin Nombres (2002). Hate / Inside My Head / Still Standing / Tate Murders.

LOST SOUL

Down With Pressure, (2004). Down With Pressure / Dust / Empire.
Los Sin Nombre, (2005). Chain Reaction / Internal Bleeding / Leave This Soul / Out Of Hell / War.

LOST SOUL

POLAND — *Jacek Grecki (vocals / guitar), Piotr Ostrowski (guitar), Krzysztof Artur Zagorowicz (bass), Adam Sierzega (drums).*

Extreme Polish Death Metal outfit LOST SOUL, self styled as "Cruel death art", came together during 1991, initially comprising vocalist / guitarist Jacek Grecki, bassist Tomasz Fornalski and drummer Adam Sierzega. First product of this alliance was the 1993 demo session 'Eternal Darkness' with the 'Superior Ignotum' recordings, crafted at Fors Studios in the Czech Republic, following in 1994. The 'Superior Ignotum' tape was picked up for a commercial re-release the following year through Baron Records. Although LOST SOUL engendered a presence on the underground circuit the band was put on hiatus for a number of years. Members would subsequently operate with acts such as SHEMHAMFORASH, HOLLOW and ASKALON.

Returning in 1997, boosted with the addition of guitarist Piotr Ostrowski, LOST SOUL entered Olsztyn's Selani Studios in February 1998 to record the cassette 'Now Is Forever ...'., material from which was donated to the Relapse 'Polish Assault' and Novum Vox Mortis 'Disco's Out, Slaughter's In' compilation albums. A heavy touring schedule witnessed Polish supports to VADER, DYING FETUS, KATAKLYSM and MONSTROSITY amongst others. The domestic Metal Mind label picked the band up for the opening album, 2000's 'Scream Of The Mourning Star', issued in North America via Relapse.

Signing a three album deal with Empire Records LOST SOUL cut the 'Ubermensch (Death Of God)' album, recorded in Wroclaw's Tower Studio with BEHEMOTH's Arek Malczewski . Osmose Productions handled this album for Western Europe. The band embarked upon a ten date tour of Poland during October of 2002 co-headlined by MONSTROSITY and Swedes VOMITORY backed by TRAUMA, SCEPTIC, DISSENTER and CONTEMPT. The band parted ways with bassist Krzysztof Artur Zagórowicz following these dates, replacing him with Pawez Michazowski.

LOST SOUL signed to Earache Records subsidiary Wicked World in October of 2004 for the album 'Chaostream'. The band opened for European gigs with VADER in June 2005, these shows including the band's debut British performances. Throughout September and October of 2005 LOST SOUL partnered with VADER, ROTTING CHRIST and ANOREXIA NERVOSA on the 'Blitzkrieg III' European tour.

SCREAM OF THE MOURNING STAR, Relapse RR 6476 (2001). My Kingdom / Divine Satisfaction / Tabernaculum Miser / Highest Pleasure / Malediction / Entrance To Nothingness / We Want God / Nameless / An Eternal Sleep / Unclean.
UBERMENSCH (DEATH OF GOD), Empire EMP 015 CD (2002). The Dawn / No Salvation / Beast Rising / The Source Of Thee /

LOUDBLAST

LOUDBLAST

LILLE, FRANCE — *Stéphane Buriez (guitar / vocals), Nicolas LeClerc (guitar), Francois Jamin (bass), Thierry Pinck (drums).*

Villeneuve d'Asq, Lille based Death Metal band LOUDBLAST formed in 1985 with vocalist / guitarist Stéphane Buriez, guitarist Nicolas Lecclerq, bassist Francois Jamin and drummer Joris Terrier. Opening recording sessions resulted in demo cassettes 'Behind The Dark Mist' in 1985 and 'Ultimate Violence' the following year. The group debuted commercially with the 1987 split LP, shared with AGRESSOR, 'Licensed To Thrash' on New Wave Records. A further four track demo, simply billed 'Loudblast', followed.

The success of this debut record enabled LOUDBLAST to tour Europe with the likes of HOLY MOSES, TANKARD and SODOM. Having recorded a demo entitled 'Bazooka Rehearsal ' in September 1988, which were sold on a mail order basis, LOUDBLAST signed to Jungle Hop Records and released their first full blown album, 'Sensorial Treatment', at the close of 1989. A further release, 'Total Virulence', followed; after which Terrier quit, his place being taken by ex-AGGRESSOR drummer Thierry Pinck.

1991's 'Disincarnate' was produced by noted Death Metal producer Scott Burns at Tampa's Morrisound studios in Florida and notably featured MASSACRE's Kam Lee on guest vocals for the track 'The Horror Within'. Upon its release the group toured as support to CANNIBAL CORPSE in France during mid 1991 before performing at the 'Monsters Of Death' festival the same year alongside MORGOTH, MASSACRE and IMMOLATION.

Following a tour with DEATH in Europe during 1992 the band parted ways with Pinck and adopted a quick replacement in Herve Coquerel. LOUDBLAST's 1993 album 'Sublime Dementia' was once again produced by Burns in Florida. The 1994 mini album 'Cross The Threshold' includes a cover version of SLAYER's 'Mandatory Suicide'.

LOUDBLAST reformed in 2002, bowing back in with the February 2004 opus 'Planet Pandemonium' released through Boycott Records. That same year Stéphane Buriez took on the role of producer for X-VISION album recordings. Subsequently, Listenable Records re-issued the 'Planet Pandemonium' album with new cover art in 2005.

Behind The Dark Mist, Jungle Hop (1985). Evil's Power / Black Death / The Threat / Time To Die / Visions Of Your Fate / Ultimate Fight.

LICENSED TO THRASH, New Wave R.D.S. 024 (1986). Scared To Death / Let The Blood Run Red / Elm Street / Black Death.
Ultimate Violence, (1986). Scared To Death / Elm Street / Time To Die / Eyes Of Mayhem / Forces Of The Dark Side.
Loudblast, (1987). Scared To Death / Let The Blood Run Red / Elm Street / Black Death.
Bazooka Rehearsal, (1988). Ultimate Fight / Visions Of Your Fate / Agony / From Beyond.
SENSORIAL TREATMENT, Jungle Hop JH 117 (1989). Fatal Attraction / From Beyond / Visions Of Your Fate / Agony / Trepanning / Rebirth / Infinite Pleasure / Malignant Growth / Pouss Mouse.
Promo Tape '89, (1989). Rebirth / The Undercover Trues / Malignant Growth / Mors / Pouss.Mouss!
DISINCARNATE, Major (1991). Steering For Paradise / After Thy Thought / Dusk To Dawn / Outlet For Conscience / Disquieting Beliefs / Horror Within / Arrive Into Death Soon / Wrapped In Roses / Shaped Images Of Discarnate Spirits.
SUBLIME DEMENTIA, Noise NO207 (1993). Presumption / Wisdom ... (Farther On) / Turn The Scales / About Solitude / Subject To Spirit / Fire And Ice / In Perpetual Motion / Fancies / Sublime Dementia / My Last Journey.
CROSS THE THRESHOLD, Noise N0223-3 (1993). Malignant Growth / No Tears To Share / Mandatory Suicide / Cross The Threshold / Subject To Spirit / Sublime Dementia.
THE TIMEKEEPER: LIVE 1995, WMD CD122 126 (1995). Intro / Presumption / Wisdom ... Farther On / Subject To Spirit / Cross The Threshold / Steering For Paradise / Shaped Images Of Discarnate Spirits / Fancies / About Solitude / Outlet For Conscience / Fire And Ice / No Tears To Share / Sublime Dementia / Wrapped In Roses / This Dazzling Abyss / Malignant Growth / My Last Journey.
FRAGMENTS, XIII Bis (1998). Man's Own / Flesh / Frozen Tears / Taste Me / Into The Keep / Labyrinth / Vices / Worthy Of Angels / Pleasure Focus / Ecstatic Trance / I Against I / Carpe Diem.
PLANET PANDEMONIUM, Boycott BYCD 7 (2004). Bow Down / The Serpent's Circle / Pain Brothers / Last Sabbath / The Descent / Mindless Mankind / Words Of Vanity / Scarlet Mist / Roaming In Between Worlds / Days In Black. Chart position: 147 FRANCE.

Incinerate / To The New Light! / Soul Hunger / Lords Of Endeavours / Apeiron / Adoration Of Violet / The One You Seek / The Crown.
CHAOSTREAM, Earache (2005). World Of Sin / Godstate / Death Crowns All / Shameful / The Hidden Law / Mortal Cage / Christian Meat / Angel's Cry / The Birth Of Babylon.

LOUDPIPES

SWEDEN — *Nandor Condor (vocals), Freddy Eugene (guitar), Carl Leen (bass), Peter Starwind (drums).*

UNLEASHED guitarist Fredrik Lindgren ('Freddy Eugene') alongside MERCILESS, UNANIMATED, REGURGITATE and FACE DOWN drummer Peter Stärjvind ("Peter Starwind") are members of Punk / Grindcore combo LOUDPIPES. MERCILESS bassist Fredrik Karlen (Carl Leen) is also involved. Lindgren created Stoner Metal act TERRA FIRMA in 1999.

The vinyl version of the 1997 album 'The Downhill Blues' came with exclusive bonus tracks, a live version of 'Don't You Ever' and a studio cut 'Ingo Vs. Floyd'.

During 2001 Stärjvind and Lindgren founded another side act, BORN OF FIRE, issuing the 7" single 'Chosen By The Gods'. Their collaborators in this venture would be guitarist 'Mr. Dim' and Rickard of DISMEMBER and MURDERSQUAD. Lindgren, together with Mr. Dim, then put his energies into a new project, HARMS WAY being assembled in the winter of 2003

THE DOWNHILL BLUES, Osmose Productions KRON-H 10 CD (1997). You Got That Right Punk! / Clean Your Head / Land Of The Free / Morphine Trip / Downhill Blues / Charged With Murder / Take Me Back / Kill 'Em / Stressed To Death / Stupid Stupid / Don't You Ever / Evil Juice / Keep On Lying / Crime In Progress / You Got That Right Punk! (Part 2).

LOVE FORSAKEN

BELLUNO, ITALY — *Danny De Barba (vocals), Mauro Cavasin (guitar), Stefan (bass), Alessandro Sogne (keyboards), Daniele Da Ponte (programming), Pyt (drums).*

Belluno progressive Death Metal band LOVE FORSAKEN debuted in 1999 with the demo 'Inhumanculture'. The band at this juncture comprised singer Piero, guitarists Lecyo (a.k.a. Alessio Fontanella) and Kaba (Mauro Cavasin), bassist Mrvitz

(Mauro Pison), keyboard player Tacca with Tano on the drums. Session female vocals came from Nadia. The EP 'Dead Sun', recorded at GEM Studios in Vicenza and featuring a cover version of DEPECHE MODE's 'Personal Jesus', arrived in 2000, the membership having changed to incorporate Goj on keyboards and new drummer Lupo. A further demo session, 'Suddenly Loki Faces', was crafted at Majestic Studio in Scorzè and issued in 2001. LOVE FORSAKEN's cast had changed yet again, seeing T-Rex on lead vocals, Pronach (Daniele Da Ponte) on programming, Pyt on drums and Abbott (Alessandro Sogne) on keyboards.

LOVE FORSAKEN self-financed the debut album 'Sex, War And Prayers' released in 2004. Singer Danny De Barba also operates with EGEMONIC.

Inhumanculture, Love Forsaken (1999). Lightfull Experience / Bitter Unreal Diary / Puttane / Kabul's Woman / Oceanica.
Dead Sun EP, (2000). Beyond / Kabul's Woman / Oceanica / Personal Jesus / Bitter Unreal Diary / Lightfull Experience.
Suddenly Loki Faces, (2001). Education / The Human Race / Forsaken Love / Beyond.
The Human Race II, (2003). The Human Race II / The Human Race II (Video).
SEX, WAR & PRAYERS, (2004). Diamonds rain / Lightful Experience / Words To The Wind / The Human Race / Forsaken Love / Beyond / Education / Ominous / Sex, War & Prayers.

LOWBROW

FL, USA — *Rick Hornberger (vocals), Allen West (guitar), Ben Meyer (guitar), Richard Bateman (bass), Curt Beeson (drums).*

Death Metal project led by ex-OBITUARY and SIX FEET UNDER guitarist Allen West. Both guitarist Ben Meyer and drummer Curt Beeson are erstwhile members of NASTY SAVAGE and HAVOC MASS whilst bassist Scott Carino was previously with DEATH and FESTER.

Frontman Rick Hornberger was a one time roadie with OBITUARY. The OBITUARY connection continued with drummer Donald Tardy producing the debut LOWBROW album 'Victims At Play'. Issued by Crook'D Records in North America 'Victims At Play' saw a European release in 2000 courtesy of the Hammerheart label. This variant also coming in vinyl formats and with all new artwork.

For the 2002 sophomore effort 'Sex, Violence, Death' Richard Bateman, another former NASTY SAVAGE man besides citing credits with AGENT STEEL, took over bass duties. In December 2004 Curtis Beeson joined FIERCE ATMOSPHERES.

VICTIMS AT PLAY, Crook'D (2000). Flesh Parade / Victims At Play / Non Descript / Done In / Restoration / Fabrication / Disheveled / Co-Dependent / Cold Scale Sounds / Bloody Meat / Interred In Dirt.
SEX, VIOLENCE, DEATH, Massacre (2002). March / Destroy Yourself / Sex, Violence, Death / Addiction / Trophy / Enforcer / The Hatred You Create / Free Ride / Maniac / Rights.

LUCIFERASE

TURKU, FINLAND — *Hell (vocals), Risto Hämäläinen (guitar), Marko Kaikkonen (guitar), Tuomas Yli-Kovero (bass), Harri Hakala (drums).*

Turku's LUCIFERASE, founded in 2000, undertook their first live performance as support to no less than MAYHEM in the Autumn of 2001. The following year the band, then featuring rhythm guitarist Juuso Hänninen, entered Red House Studios to craft the four song demo 'Misery Ritual'. These same tracks saw a commercial re-issue in the Summer of 2003 by the newly established Onyxia label as a split CD with fellow Finnish Death Metal band EXIT WOUNDS.

Guitarist Risto Hämäläinen holds credits with THERION, bassist Tuomas Yli-Kovero is an ex-member of PRIMITIVE whilst drummer Harri Hakala has prior affiliations with ENERCHY and VORDVEN.

Misery Ritual, Onyxia (2003) (Split EP with EXIT WOUNDS). Intro To Embrace / Of Decay And Immorality / Bitter Hopes / Misery Ritual.

LUCIFERION

SWEDEN — *Wojtek Lisiski (vocals / guitar), Mikael Nicklasson (guitar), Martin Furängen (bass), Peter Wiener (drums).*

LUCIFERION's guitarist Micke Nicklasson and drummer Peter Andersson are both ex-SARCAZM, whilst vocalist Wojtek Lisicki previously sang with HIGHLANDER. Nicklasson also sings lead vocal for LIERS IN WAIT. The band was rounded out by another erstwhile HIGHLANDER man, Martin Furängen on bass guitar. Following the recording of the group's debut 'Demonication (The Manifest)' drummer Peter Wiener quit to be superseded by ex-LIERS IN WAIT drummer Hasse Nilsson. The album featured a version of SODOM's 'Blasphemer'. LUCIFERION also covered METALLICA's 'Fight Fire With Fire' for the Black Sun Records tribute album 'Metal Militia'.

Nilsson would join his erstwhile colleague guitarist Kristian Wahlin founding DIABOLIQUE whilst Nicklasson joined DARK TRANQUILITY. Subsequently Lisicki and Furängen revived HIGHLANDER, this act later taking the title of LOST HORIZON.

Fans dedication over a seen year hiatus was rewarded with an all new LUCIFERION album delivered in September of 2003. 'The Apostate' included a cover version of CELTIC FROST's 'The Circle Of Tyrants'. In April of 2005 it was reported that members of LUCIFERION had united with musicians from LOST HORIZON, North American act FOREST OF IMPALED and Poles DAMNATION in a new extreme Metal project.

DEMONICATION (THE MANIFEST), Listenable POSH007 (1994). Intro / On The Wings Of The Emperor / Graced By Fire / Rebel Souls / Satan's Gift / The Manifest / Risus De Lucifer (Suffering Of Christ) / Tears Of The Damned / Blasphemer / The Voyager.
THE APOSTATE, Listenable POSH049 (2003). Intro / The Apostate: I—Under The Eyes Of The Serpents / The Apostate: II—Transcendental Fusion / The Apostate: III—Gods Bring You Away From Yourself / The Apostate: IV—A Strain From Depths / The Apostate: V—The Force Dwells Within / The Apostate: VI—And All The Waste Will Fade / Become Or Be Gone / Destroying By Will / New World To See / Circle Of The Tyrants / Rebel Souls / The Voyager / Satan's Gift (The Crown Of Thorns) / Graced By Fire / Hymns Of Immortals.

LUNA FIELD

STUTTGART, GERMANY — *Benny Rakidzija (vocals), Heiko Krahl (guitar), Marko Sirac (guitar), Alexander Palma (bass), Tomasz Janiszewski (drums).*

Theatric Death Metal band LUNA FIELD was created in Stuttgart during 1998 by vocalist Benny Rakidzija, guitarists Heiko Krahl and M. Sirac, ex-LANFEAR bassist Alexander Palma and DEBAUCHERY's Daniel Sandvoss on drums. Debut product would be a 2001 Tony Fischer produced album 'Close To Prime', subsequently issued through French imprint Season of Mist. A line-up change in 2003 saw the introduction of the DISINFECT and THE EXORIAL credited drummer Tomasz Janiszewski.

LUNA FIELD's 2005 'Diva' album, released by the Greek label Black Lotus, was produced by ATROCITY's Alex Krull. To open 2006 the band hooked up with RESURRECTURIS, MASTER and GOREFEST for 'The Glorious Dead: European Exorcism' European tour set to commence 16th February in Holland. However, in late January the headline band pulled the entire tour. Alexander Palma joined MY DARKEST HATE in March 2006.

CLOSE TO PRIME, Season Of Mist (2003). The Dead Side / Odial / Animated Anchoret / Thief Of The Adour / Anthem About The Breed / The Black Side / Press The Pressure / I Am Free / Witness Of Delusion / Acrid Insanity.
DIVA, Black Lotus BLRCD095 (2005). Godparade / Kill Bastard Kill / Revolution Restart / Camouflage / Moral Masquerade / Jokers / The Great Monologue / Zenith / Full Vanity Fair / Egoism Divine / Diva Messiah.

LUNATIC GODS

MARTIN, SLOVAKIA — *Horar (vocals), Emil (vocals), Hirax (guitar), Luboslav (guitar), Richard (bass) Psycho (drums).*

LUNATIC GODS was founded in Martin during the summer of 1993 with a line-up of guitarist Pavel 'Hirax' Baricak, vocalist Mortis, keyboard player King (a.k.a. Ivan Kral) and drummer Psycho as BESTIALIT. Under this title the band debuted in 1994 by sharing a split CD 'Fuckland' with DEHYDRATED for the Metal Age Productions label. With the addition of second lead singer Emil and bassist Richard BESTIALIT evolved into LUNATIC GODS and shifted musical direction into the realms of atmospheric, symphonic Death Metal.

The Italian Polyphemus label picked the band up for their April 1996 debut 'Inhuman And Insensible' before a switch back to Metal Age Productions resulted in the 1998 follow up 'Sitting By The Fire'. LUNATIC GODS would contribute a track to a METALLICA tribute assembled by Energie Records, also releasing this separately as part of the 'Cuckoo' EP.

During 2000 both Mortis and King departed, the latter launching his own trad Metal band KING for an album 'Royal Metal'. LUNATIC GODS regrouped by pulling in singer Horar and second guitarist Luboslav for the third album 'The Wilderness'.

A 2004 re-issue of 'Inhuman And Insensible' on Hrom Records added bonus tracks 'Cuckoo' and a cover version of METALLICA's 'Phantom Lord'. The 1998 album 'Sitting By The Fire' would also be re-released with extra tracks. That same year new studio album 'Mythus' also arrived.

INHUMAN AND INSENSIBLE, Polyphemus (1996). Don't Fuck Me / Empire Of The Black Sun / My Dead Friend / Child Of War / Fucking Religions / Son Of Bitch / Eternal Pain / Hate.
SITTING BY THE FIRE, Metal Age Productions (1998). Dead But Free / I'll Never Betray / Smile / Return Of Deads Thoughts / The World Is Full Of Lies / Ocean Of Hatred / Echoes Of Sadness / Sitting By The Fire / At The Threshold Of Life / Irreparable.
Cuckoo EP, Epidemie ER 035 (1999).
THE WILDERNESS, Shindy Productions SHINDY 901D56 (2002). Curse / Tormenting World / Fallen Beauty / Doomsday / Battlefield Of Life / Dance Of Salome / Stone / Mystic Way / Bemidbar I / The Wilderness / Bemidbar II.
MYTHUS, (2004). The Earthfolk / Nation Of The Blind / Under The Veil Of The Night / A Beautiful City / Evil Breeds More Evil Still / Visions Collide / Sacrifice / Falling Into Darkness / Mourning The Blessed One / The History Turns / For More Glory.

LUST OF DECAY

USA — *Jay Barnes (vocals), Steve Green (guitar), Pete Stroupe (guitar), Joe Payne (bass), Jordan Varela (drums).*

Death Metal band formulated during 1996 as Hardcore influenced PURE HATE comprising Steve Green on guitar and vocals, Duane Short on guitar, Flounder on bass with Brent Williams on drums. Line up changes within PURE HATE would see Aaron Brown coming in on bass and Jay Barnes adopted as vocalist. When PURE HATE dissolved Green, Barnes and Williams assembled MINDKILL in alliance with guitar player Pete Stroupe and JUNKIE bassist Robert Mcfarland. A demo as MINDKILL was issued before a name switch to DISSENT occurred. As DISSENT the band released the promotion CDR 'Rest In Hell' although before long the band had changed title yet again to LUST OF DECAY.

Both Williams and Mcfarland exited in 2002, the erstwhile drummer joining PUTRILIGE. Jordan Varela, of EPIC OF EMPYREA, became the band's new drummer. LUST OF DECAY cut their debut album 'Infesting The Exhumed' in March of 2002 for Green's own label Comatose Music.

In October Pete Stroupe decided to part ways with the band. For a brief period James Sain of FAT TORTOISE BUTCHER filled the vacancy. Derek Haymore was subsequently hired on as the new bass player. LUST OF DECAY supported IMMOLATION during this period putting on a show as a trio of Barnes, Green and Varela with Sain and Haymore coming out for the encore song. However, shortly afterward Sain soon departed.

In January of 2004 the band, now a four piece recorded and released their second full-length album, 'Kingdom of Corpses'. Lyrically the band chose to stay with a theme of misogynistic, sexual violence for most of the album. Although the lyrics would be considered vile and depraved by most standards the songs were not without the occasional attempt at humour as evidenced by songs like 'Crustacean Masturbation'. The album also included a cover of DEICIDE's, ' Lunatic of God's Creation'.

Varela also operated with extreme Death Metal act DEBODIFIED. LUST OF DECAY bassist Joe Payne joined LECHEROUS NOCTURNE in September of 2004.

INFESTING THE EXHUMED, Comatose Music COMA 001CD (2002). Festering Anal Vomit / Head In A Crock Pot / Engorging The Vaginal Cavity / Erased From Existence / Draped In White / Bloodart / Absence Of Light / Stricken With Disease / Mutilation Tool / Infesting The Exhumed.
KINGDOM OF CORPSES, Comatose Music COMA 007 (2004). Arachnid Anal Infestation / Cranial Incubation / Septic Tank Abortion / Crustacean Masturbation / Predatory Instincts / Lunatic Of God's Creation / Cognitive Decimation / Kingdom Of Corpses / Twelve Gage Intercourse / Oral Asphixiation.

LYCANTROPHY

KUUSAMO, FINLAND — *Vesa Säkkinen (vocals), Vesa Ruokangas (vocals), Mikko Pesonen (vocals), Jari Aho (guitar / bass), Janne Kela (drums).*

LYCANTROPHY was a Death / Thrash Metal band hailing from Kuusamo. Founded during 1987 the act formatively employed A.R.G. bass player Jari Kelloniemi, the late A.R.G. man Pasi Takkula and MORTAL DECAY's Jykä Karjalainen both on drums. First product would be the three track demo 'No Sorrow, No Pain' in 1988. Follow ups included 'Sickness Revealed' and 'Sleepwalker'.

LYCANTROPHY novelly boasted three vocalists, Vesa Säkkinen of A.R.G., Vesa Ruokangas from NATIONAL NAPALM SYNDICATE and Mikko Pesonen. Latter day drummer Janne Kela held credits with CRIMINAL ASSAULT and SACRED CRUCIFIX. Vesa Säkkinen, re-billed as 'Wesleyer', subsequently founded PAIN CONFESSOR.

No Sorrow, No Pain, Lycantrophy (1988). After My Death / Hiding In The Blood / Kill For Me.
Sickness Revealed, (1989). Dismemberment Of Sanity / Buried In Swamp / Open The Gate / After My Death.
Sleepwalker, (1990). Dismemberment Of Sanity / Sleepwalker / Embryonic Cell.

M-26

PELOTAS, RS, BRAZIL — *Jean (vocals), Carla Domingues (vocals), Vitor Neves (guitar), André Lisboa (bass), Gabriel Porto (drums).*

Pelotas Doom Death act M-26 was assembled in 1996, quoting a line up comprising vocalist Ronaldo, guitarist Alexandre Fernandes, bassist André Lisboa and drummer Gabriel for the first demo tape 'Outubro'. During 2000 the band, drawing in singer Carla Domingues, returned with the 'Sentimentos Sombrios...' session. Changes the following year saw Jean taking Ronaldo's place. 'Sentimentos Sombrios...' would then be re-issued in CD EP format, adding the extra track 'Lágrimas de Desidéria'. Following a 2002 performance at the Santa Catarina 'River Rock' festival Vitor Neves, previously with APHELION, substituted for Fernandes.

M-26 female vocalist Carla Domingues is also a member of VETITUM.

Sentimentos Sombrios..., Independent (2002). Entre As Ruínas Do Caos / Vejo A Dor / Lágrimas De Desidéria.

M-90'S

HOLLAND — *Koen Roneijn (vocals), Michiel Bikker (guitar), Mike Ferguson (guitar), Patrick Velis (bass), Fedor Tieleman (drums).*

M-90's debuted in 1996, the initial line up comprising vocalist / bassist Bas Hensing, guitarist Michiel Bikker and EXIVIOUS and SILENT EDGE drummer Iwan Hendrikx. This trio would cut the opening 1996 demo 'Fear; In Your Mind' and 1998 follow up 'Through The Eyes Of Art'. 1998 also saw the introduction of former GRASMOAIER, KUTSCHURFT and DETONATION guitarist Mike Ferguson but the defection of Hensing.

M-90'S third recording session resulted in the 2000 EP 'Lost In The Corn', by this juncture the band comprising Bikker, Iwan Hendrikx, bassist Patrick Velis and VIRULENT singer Daniel Nak.

In 2002 Hendrikx, joining SAHARA DUST (subsequently evolving into EPICA) was superseded by Fedor Tieleman. Hendrikx would join forces with US project QUIETUS in October 2003. Following recording of the 'Desert Of Pangea' album, witnessing a return for Ferguson, Nak bailed out in December of 2003. M-90's inaugurated their new vocalist Koen Roneijn of ENGORGE and DETONATION repute with an April gig at the De Bastille venue in Schoonhoven.

DESERT OF PANGEA, (2003). Plague Patrol / Unleash The Beast / Desert Of Pangea / C-29R / Last Regrets / Random Aggression / Silent Scream.

M.A.S.A.C.R.E.

PERU — *Omar Pizarro (vocals), Raffo McKee (guitar), Martín Tuesta (guitar), Miguel Tuesta (bass), Willy Hermoza (drums).*

M.A.S.A.C.R.E. ("Metal Avanzando Siempre Ante Cualquier Rechazo Existente") began life as MASACRE, releasing 'Sin Piedad' in 1989 and 'En Vivo ... Hasta El Final' in 1998, but would switch titles in order to avoid confusion with their Colombian namesakes. The band's founding 1987 line up comprised singer Miguel Angel Cervantes, guitarists Coqui de Tramontana and Martín Tuesta, bassist Miguel Tuesta and drummer Pierpa. The name switch came with the 2000 album 'Demoldor', the initials M.A.S.A.C.R.E. quoted as standing for "Metal, Avanzando, Siempre, Ante, Cualquier, Rechazo, Existente". Line-up changes saw the band now fronted by Omar Pizarro, with Raffo McKee on guitar and Willy Hermoza manning the drums.

The album 'En Pie De Guerra' was issued in November of 2004. Recording line up for this outing comprised vocalist Omar Pizarro, guitarists Coqui de Tramontana and ex-RESET man Jaqo Sangalli, bassist Miguel Tuesta and the POR HABLA and NATURA credited drummer Hans Menacho.

DEMOLEDER, Independent (2000). Brutalidad / Demoledor / El Predicador / En El Infierno / Estado Terminal / Huellas De Sangre / Perros De Presa / S.I.N. / Tiempos Oscuros.

EN PIE DE GUERRA, Avenger Productions (2004). Reaccionando / Prevalecer / Conciencia Magra / Hambre X Dios / Bela La Traición / Sentencia / En Pie De Guerra / Despertar / La Marcha / Los Niños Del Futuro / Eternidad / Prevail.

M.A.S.A.C.R.E., (2004). Prevail / Awaken / En Pie De Guerra / Conciencia Magra / Despertar.

M.S.I.

HOBART, TAS, AUSTRALIA — *Rick Ring (vocals), Tim Ikin (guitar), Nick Warren (bass), Matthew Chalk (drums).*

Tasmanian Death-Grind act M.S.I. ("Mindless Self Indulgence"), hailing from the capital Hobart, was formulated by members of AZIMUTH, KUCIFER and BAALPHEGOR and cited a founding roster of frontman Rick Ring, guitarist Tim Ikin, bass player Brady Denehey and drummer Russell Menzies. The band released the 1998 cassette 'Testimony Of The Miserable' followed up by 'The Vault Of Horror' in 1999 but would then split away from their original rhythm section. A debut album, 'Rhythmic Slamish', arrived in May of 2000.

Matthew Chalk, vocalist of PSYCROPTIC as well as citing credits with CHEESEGRATER OF CHASTITY and HEMLOCK, was duly installed on the drums with his fellow CHEESEGRATER OF CHASTITY colleague Nick Warren taking on bass guitar duties.

RHYTHMIC SLAMISH, (2000). Bong Gunge / Agrovated / Seven / Meatpig / Gorge Arse / The Suffering / Chosen Path / Vicious Slaughter / Headshot / Rhythmic Slamish / Requiem / She's So Fine.

MACABRE

CHICAGO, IL, USA — *Corporate Death (vocals / guitar), Nefarious (bass), Dennis The Menace (drums).*

Chicago's MACABRE are noted for their ultra-extreme music, dubbed by the band as 'Murder Metal', based around an almost obsessive theme of serial murderers. Frontman C.D. ('Corporate Death') actually owns several paintings by the renowned serial killer John Wayne Gacy given to him personally by the since executed murderer. C.D. even attended the trial of Jeffrey Dahmer for inspiration. Musically, Corporate Death employs possibly the most remarkable, histrionic vocal style guaranteed to give any listener the chills. MACABRE is rounded out by bassist Nefarious and Dennis The Menace on drums.

MACABRE opened their own perversely primordial little shop of horrors in 1987 with the Decomposed Records EP 'Grim Reality', by which early stage the serial killer fetish was already much in evidence with odes to Ed Gein, Albert Fish and the Son of Sam set to a blizzard of Punk and Grindcore. Ingeniously the track 'Mass Murder' was in fact a triptych of instrumentals, 'Sulphuric Acid' being a guitar solo, 'Morbid Curiosity' a bass solo and naturally 'Lethal Injection' a closing drum solo. 1987 demos dubbed 'Shit List' worked their way to 7" single status in 1988, subsequently re-issued by Gore Records in 1990 as a limited run of 777 copies pressed on white vinyl. Meantime, UK label Vinyl Solutions had issued the full-length 'Gloom' opus. MACABRE's appreciation for the world's most loathsome examples of humanity and now extended to incorporate expressions of admiration for Harvey Glatman, David Brom, Patrick Purdy, Fritz Haarman and the elusive Green River murderer.

MACABRE switched to the then fledgling Nuclear Blast label for the April 1993 'Sinister Slaughter' outing, a veritable bloodbath in homage to twenty of their preferred mass murderers. Sleeve artwork cleverly spoofed THE BEATLES 'Sgt. Pepper' montage, substituting celebrities with individuals of a much more malevolent nature. A July 1994 follow up EP, 'Behind The Wall Of Sleep', included the band's first cover version, a remake of the BLACK SABBATH title track.

MACABRE slunk back into the shadows until 1999, re-emerging touting the 'Unabomber' mini-album. 2000's 'Dahmer' album, produced by Neil Kernon, is a concept based around the twisted life of the cannibalistic necrophile mass murderer Jeffrey Dahmer and probably the first Death Metal album to include a twisted remake of a Willie Wonka 'Charlie & The Chocolate Factory' song. The long out of print but much in demand 1987 release 'Grim Reality' was remixed by Neil Kernon for release in 2002 on Decomposed Records. A further outing, 'Morbid Campfire Songs', provided an unexpected slant on the formula, a clutch of acoustic renditions credited to the "Macabre Minstrels" duo of Corporate Death and Nefarious.

The band would confirm a string of dates in Holland and an appearance at the German 'Wacken Open Air' festival. November 2002 shows found the band on the road in North America on a package billing with CANNIBAL CORPSE, CATTLE DECAPITATION and HATE ETERNAL.

The band released the 'Murder Metal' album in 2003 through French label Season Of Mist. A run of European mainland gigs in January and February 2004 had the group allied with

POLTERCHRIST, CEPHALIC CARNAGE and BRUTUS. These shows would include the band's first UK performance, at the London, Camden Underworld, for more than a decade. US shows into March hooked the group up with PREMONITIONS OF WAR, THE END and RUNE.

MACABRE teamed up with Dutch Deathsters THE MONOLITH DEATHCULT and British act SCREAMIN' DEAMON for UK shows in August / September 2005. Their August 26th show at the Bibelot in Dordrecht, Holland would be filmed for the DVD release 'Live in Holland–True Tales of Slaughter And Slaying', issued in July 2006.

Shit List, Macabre (1987). Disease / Ratman / What The Heck Richard Speck (Eight Nurses You Wrecked) / Natural Disaster / Mass Murder II 1) guitar 2) bass 3) drums / Butcher (Live) / Funeral Home (Live).

Grim Reality, Decomposed M1 (1987). Serial Killer / Mr. Albert Fish (Was Children Your Favourite Dish?) / Disease / Mass Murder / Son Of Sam / Hot Rods To Hell / Ed Gein / Natural Disaster.

Shit List, Gore GORE 001 (1988). Butcher (Live) / Funeral Home (Live) / Disease / Ratman / What The Heck Richard Speck (Eight Nurses You Wrecked).

GLOOM, Vinyl Solution SOL 020 (1989). Embalmer / Trampled To Death / Holidays Of Horror / Fritz Haarmann The Butcher / Evil Ole Soul / Harvey Glatmann / David Brom Took An Axe / Cremator / I Need To Kill / Ultra Violent / Rat Man / Hey Laurie Dann / Patrick Purdy Killed Five And Wounded Thirty / Exhumer / Funeral Home.

SINISTER SLAUGHTER, Nuclear Blast NB 070 (1993). Night Stalker / The Ted Bundy Song / Sniper In The Sky / Montreal Massacre / Zodiac / What The Hell Did You Do? / The Boston Strangler / Mary Bell / Reprise / Killing Spree (Postal Killer) / Is It Soup Yet? / White Hen Decapitator / Howard Unrah (What Have You Done Now?) / Gacy's Lot / There Was A Young Man Who Blew Up A Plane / Vampire Of Dusseldorf / Shotgun Peterson / What's That Smell? / Edward Kemper Had A Terrible Temper / What The Heck Richard Speck (8 Nurses You Wrecked) / Albert Was Worse Than Any Fish In The Sea.

Behind The Walls Of Sleep EP, Nuclear Blast NBA 6891-3 (1994). Fishtales / Behind The Wall Of Sleep / Slaughter Thy Poser / Freeze Dried Man.

Nightstalker, Relapse RR-021 (1997). Nightstalker / Is It Soup Yet? / Zodiac / Sniper In The Sky / What The Hell Did You Do (James E. Pough).

UNABOMBER, Decomposed HHR 030 (1999). The Unabomber / Ambassador Hotel / The Brain / David Brom Took An Axe / Dr. Holmes He Stripped Their Bones / Ed Gein / Serial Killer.

DAHMER, Hammerheart HHR 071 (2000). Dog Guts / Hitchhiker / In The Army Now / Grandmother's House / Blood Bank / Exposure / Ambassador Hotel / Cup Of Coffee / Bath House / Jeffrey Dahmer And The Chocolate Factory / Apartment 213 / Drill Bit Lobotomy / Jeffrey Dahmer Blues / McDahmers / Into The Toilet With You / Coming To Chicago / Scrub A Dub Dub / Konerak / Temple Of Bones / Trial / Do The Dahmer / Baptized / Christopher Scarver / Dahmer's Dead / The Brain.

Macabre / Capitalist Casualties, D.B.D. DBD-001 (2001) (Split single with CAPITALIST CASUALTIES). Embalmer / Trampled To Death.

Morbid Campfire Songs, Decomposed (2002). Tom Dooley / The Geins / In The Mountains / The Cat Came Back / Found A Peanut.

GLOOM, Hammerheart HHR 105 (2002). Embalmer / Trampled To Death / Holidays Of Horror / Evil Old Soul / Fritz Haarmann The Butcher / Harvey Glatman (Your Soul Will Rot Forever) / McMassacre (James Huberty) / David Brom Took An Axe / Cremator / Nostradamus / I Need To Kill / Ultra Violent / Rat Man / Hey Laurie Dann / Patrick Purdy Killed Five And Wounded Thirty / Exhumer / Dr Holmes (He Stripped Their Bones) / The Green River Murder (He's Still Out There) / Funeral Home / Disease / Natural Disaster / Ultra Violent (Live) / Fritz Haarman The Butcher (Live) / What The Heck Richard Speck (Eight Nurses You Wrecked) (Live) / Killing Spree (Live) / Mr. Albert Fish (Were Children Your Favorite Dish) (Live) / Funeral Home (Live).

Drill Bit Lobotomy EP, Hater Of God HOG19EP (2003). Drill Bit Lobotomy (Full version) / Coming To Chicago (Instrumental version) / Grandmother's House (Instrumental version).

MURDER METAL, Season Of Mist SOM 076 (2003). Acid Bath Vampire / You're Dying To Be With ME / Fatal Foot Fetish / The Hillside Stranglers / Dorthea's Dead Folks Home / The Iceman / Poison / Warewolf Of Bedburg / Morbid Minister / The Wustenfeld Man Eater / Diary Of Torture / Jack The Ripper / Fritz Haarman Der Metzger.

MACABRE END

VÅLBERG, SWEDEN — *Per Boder (vocals), Jonas Stålhammer (guitar), Ola Sjöberg (guitar), Thomas Johansson (bass), Niklas Nilsson (drums).*

Vålberg's MACABRE END released the 1991 'Consumed By Darkness' EP. A projected second release, 'Nothing Remains Forever', was announced as forthcoming through Relapse Records, but this never transpired. Subsequently, they changed their name to GOD MACABRE releasing an album in 1994. Guitarist Jonas Stålhammer, holding ABHOTH credits, also doubles as vocalist for UTUMNO. Rhythm guitarist Ola Sjöberg would go on to join his fellow ex-MACABRE END colleague Per Boder in Stoners SNAKE MACHINE as bassist, a band which subsequently evolved into SPACE PROBE TAURUS with Sjöberg taking on lead vocal duties. Jonas Stålhammer would also enjoy a term with SPACE PROBE TAURUS as bassist.

Consumed By Darkness, Corpse Grinder CGR001 (1991). Consumed By Darkness / Ceased To Be / Spawn Of Flies.

MACHETAZO

SPAIN — *Carlos Cadaver (vocals), Dopi Dr. Beltan (guitar), Rober (guitar), Chinin El Mescalinas (bass), Marco (drums).*

Initially a Noisecore unit Spain's MACHETAZO would evolve down a path to Goregrind with lter releases. The band debuted a year after their formation with the 1995 demo '46 Cabezas Aplastados Por Un Yunque Oxidado' which featured renditions of A.C. and GUT songs. The tape provoked such an impact on the underground scene it would be re released by Ironia Productions.

MACHETAZO's sophomore effort, the 1998 'Realmente Distruto Comiendo Cadaveres'- this time paying homage to CARCASS and EXTREME NOISE TERROR with covers, would also see a re-release- this time on 10" vinyl format issued by Fudgeworthy Records.

In 1999 MACHEZATO not only abandoned all pretences of Noisecore but indeed most of its membership. At one stage the band was down to a solo endeavour of drummer / guitarist / bassist Dopi Dr. Beltan. Adopting a Grind direction MACHEZATO cut a shared 7" single in collusion with Japanese band CORRUPTED. MACHEZATO's efforts being an original 'Potro De Tortura' and a cover of ST. VITUS's 'Bitter Truth'.

Eventually former member and bass player Chinin El Mescalinas returned for the debut album 'Carne De Cementerio' recorded for the American Razorback concern. In keeping with tradition further covers were included with S.O.B. and ABCESS tracks. Guest vocals were handled by DEFACE man Carlos Cadaver. Vinyl versions of 'Carne De Cementerio', issued in 2002 by Throne Records, added an exclusive cover version of BLACK SABBATH's 'Children Of The Grave'. This variant would be restricted to 1000 copies only, of which 300 would be pressed in red vinyl.

Until now MACHEZATO had been employing the temporary services of OBSESION COMPULSIVA band members to flesh out their own act. However, a live drummer was found with ICON man Marcos, second guitarist Rober and Carlos Cadaver committed fulltime too.

2001 saw a further split single with BODIES LAY BROKEN for the Discos Al Pacino label. One of MACHEZATO's tracks '(El Increible) Prpucio Septico' translating as 'The Incredible Septic Cock'!

Future split singles were planned with IMPALED and DENAK. The second full length album, 'Trono De Huesos' which included a cover version of MOTÖRHEAD's seminal 'Ace Of Spades', arrived in April of 2002 through the Razorback label.

In September the band donated exclusive material to the first of Relapse Records 7" Slimewave Series, this collaborative effort shared with TOTAL FUCKING DESTRUCTION. MACHETAZO toured Spain and Portugal with Sweden's PAGANIZER in December.

REALMENTE DISTRUTO COMIENDO CADAVERAS, Fudgeworthy (1999) (10" vinyl release). Franco Derdeno. No Seas Descarado / Serrando Codos / Tu And Putrefacto Apesta Mas Que El Disco De High Time / Metadona Infantil / (Como Me Gusta) Beber Pus En Un Craneo I, II, III, IV, V / Tropezones (Restos De Carne Humana En La Sopa Del Mediodia) / Desenterramiento. Incineracion Y Gastronomia / Defecacion Maligna (Cagando Plomo II) / Chupa Tripas I, II, III, IV, V, VI, VII / Realmente Disfruto Comiendo Cadaveres / iii Machetazo !!! / Genitales Rancios Y Criadillas Hominidas Trituradas Pa La Zorza Pa Los Chorizos I, II, III, IV / Recien Nacido Ahorcado Con Su Cordon Umbilical (Traqueotomia Urgente) / iii Hostia Como Escuece.II !!! (Despegando El Parpado Y La Pupilacon Un Cuter Oxidado) / Sueno Humedo De Un Enterrador Subnormal / Infeccion Cutanea De Ernesto Apesto / Tira Al Tetraplegico Por La Ventana / Te Va A Quedar El Culo Como La Bandera De Japon (El Regreso Del Tenebroso Desfigurador Anal) / Obsesion Morbosa (Devoro Tu Costra Asquerosa) / Brazo Amputado En Fase De Descomposicion Metido En Una Lata A Ultrapresion / Carnaval Carnaval, El Cadaver Huele Mal / Beso Negro A Una Anciana Con Diarrea Continua Y Abundante / Otitis Aguda / Tatuaje En El Intestino Grueso / Los Pacientes Del Doctor Beltran / El Ataque De Los Cerdos Asesinos / Hedor De Cripta Humeda / ? Te Aterroriza El Ruido Extremo De Mis Flatulencias En Tu Boca? / El Grito De La Vacaburra (El Mescalinas Vomita) / Los Cuentos Del Munon Gangrenoso: El mino Muerto A Palos.

Potro De Tortura, Frigidity (2000) (Split 7" single with CORRUPTED). Potro De Tortura / Bitter Truth.

CARNE DE CEMENTERIO, Razorback (2000). El Enjambre Asesino / (Todos Somos) Alimento De Los Gusanos / La Cara Mazada A Golpes / Humillado Y Descuartizado Por Mongolicosi / Torso / P.U.S. (Purulento Urologo Sarnoso) / Suicide Fuck / Obecede A Tu Demonio Interior / Pudrete Como Un Cerdo / Masticasesos / Las Ninos No Deberian Jugar Con Cosas Muertos / El Ataque De King Ghidorh / Delusion Of Terror / Maruta / Los Cuertos Del Munon Garjrenso II.

La Mascara Del Demonio, Discos Al Pacino (2001) (Split 7" single with BODIES LAY BROKEN). La Mascara Del Demonio / (El Increible) Prepucio Septico / La Venganza De Los Muertos Sin Ojas.

TRONO DE HUESOS, Razorback (2002). Banquete Funerario / Garrote Dil / Enterradas En El Jardin / Un Vestido De Pellejo Humano / Purificación A través Del Dolor / La Flema / Engendro / Trono De Huesos / Bolsas Con Sangre / Yo Fui Un Caníbal Adolescente / Lepra / Ataque Simio / Ace Of Spades / Los Cuentos Del Muñon Gangrenoso.

MACHINERY

STOCKHOLM, SWEDEN — *Michel Isberg (vocals / guitar), Markus Isberg (guitar), Per Lindström (bass), Fredrik Klingwall (keyboards), Johan Westman (drums).*

Stockholm Death-Thrashers formed in late 2001 by former CORPSEGRINDER and DIMENSION singer Michel Isberg and EXTRICATOR drummer Johan Westman. The band's formative years would see an ebb and flow of members as the line-up remained fluid. Included amongst these candidates would be subsequent HYDROGEN singer Niclas Olsson. Isberg's brother Markus briefly found involvement on guitar. In October 2002 MACHINERY utilised Necromorbus Studios to track the demo 'A Part Of Steel In An Endless Machine'. Recording roster for these sessions involved Michel Isberg on vocals and guitar, Johan Westman on drums with Fredrik Öhlund on bass. Markus Isberg was then re-instated but, following the inaugural MACHINERY gig at the MC-Mjölner motorbike club, Öhlund decamped. Second demo, billed 'A Part Of Steel In An Endless Machine—Part II', was recorded in the autumn of 2003, after which ex-DIMENSION bassist Hans Johansson was enrolled.

Necromorbus was again the venue for a third demo, 'Machinery—The Beginning', cut in October 2004. However, Hans Johansson opted out in November 2005. EXTRICATOR's KG West stood in as a temporary member for live work before Per Lindström, of ETERNAL TORMENT, FLAGELLATION, ANIMA MORTE, IN GREY and GOATSODOMIZER, took on bass duties in January 2006, debuting at the 'Mondo Metal Fest' event that month. In May MACHINERY participated on the 'Thrashing The Masses' compilation album, with the tracks 'Rectifier' and 'Unholy Demon', plus the follow up concert.

MACHINERY's debut album 'Degeneration' was recorded during August 2006 at Necromorbus studio with producer Sverker Widgren for release in October through Last Entertainment Productions. Newly employed keyboard player FREDRIK KLINGWALL is a man holding a tradition with acts such as IN GREY, FLAGELLATION, SHADOW OF THE CONCEALED, GOATSODOMIZER, ANIMA MORTE and RISING SHADOWS.

In January 2007 guitarist Markus Isberg left MACHINERY "due to personal reasons," according to a press release. Replacing him in the group's line-up would be Mano Lewys.

Beginning, Machinery (2004) (Demo). Rectifier / Wheel Of Pain / I Divine / Burned / A Generous Day / Feed Me Hatred / Dismembered / Machinery.

Rising, Machinery (2005) (Demo). Unholy Demon / Degeneration / Blacker Than Pain / Reason Is The Rush.

DEGENERATION, Last Entertainment Productions (2006). Salvation For Sale / Degeneration / River Red / Blacker Than Pain / Unholy Demon / Taste Of God / Rectifer / Falling Through The Grid / Satanic Hippie Cannibal.

MAHAVATAR

NEW YORK, NY, USA — *Lizza Hayson (vocals), Karla Williams (guitar), Shahar Mintz (guitar), Szymon Maria Rapacz (bass), Eran Asias (drums).*

Although a relatively new force New York's MAHAVATAR ('Mind Hypnotic Visions Towards Revolution') have made a sizable impact even before any commercial release. Musically MAHAVATAR employ Psych-Doom overlaid with Eastern tribal rhythms to present a uniquely compelling sound.

Israeli dreadlocked vocalist Lizza Hayson (a.k.a. Lizza Hasan) was previously with FORESIGHT and also holds MASTER-LAST credits. In keeping with their eclecticism guitarist Karla Williams hails from Jamaica whilst drummer Peter Lobodzinski is Polish.

The bands original bassist Benjamin Serf was replaced by Eddie Gasior. Later additions saw Itamar Ben-Zakay taking the drum stool and Evan Glantz contributing flute. MAHAVATAR signed to Cruz Del Sur Music, entering the New York Purple Light Studios to record their debut album 'Go With The No!' in February of 2004. Session musicians for these recordings included bassist Szymon Maria Rapacz, keyboard player Miko and drummer T-Bone Motta.

July 2005 found Szymon Maria Rapacz enrolling on a full-time basis alongside new recruits guitarist Shahar Mintz and drummer Roi Star. However, MAHAVATAR was on the look out for another drummer by February 2006. Eran Asias of THE VINYL STASH took over the drum stool in July as Escapi Music issued the album 'From The Sun, The Rain, The Wind, The Soil'.

GO WITH THE NO!, Cruz Del Sur Music CRUZ8 (2005). Cult / By The Numbers / Raw / Open Your Minds / Psychos / Deep Cobble / Anger / The Time Has Come.

FROM THE SUN, THE RAIN, THE WIND, THE SOIL, Escapi Music (2006).

MALAMOR

NEW YORK, NY, USA — *Jason Kolts (vocals), Ben Kolts (guitar), Sean Kennedy (guitar), Dave Markle (bass), Shawn Mann (drums).*

New York Death Metal band MALAMOR (taken to mean "All love is evil") originated in 1993 with an initial line up roster of guitarists Ben Kolts and Sean Kennedy, bass player Carl Carlew and drummer Kevin Sharp. Vocals were handled by Ben Kolt's sibling Jason. By the following year there was a clean sweep in the rhythm section with new recruits being bass player Dave Markle and drummer Shawn Mann. The band made their presence felt with the 1995 demo tape 'Condemn The Rising'.

SUFFOCATION's Frank Mullen added guest lead vocals to MALAMOR's debut album 'Dead To The World'. Sean Kennedy would also activate the brutal Death Grind project INHERIT DISEASE.

MALAMOR would contribute a version of 'Suicide Machine' to a Dwell Records DEATH tribute compilation and more surprisingly added their take of LED ZEPPELIN's 'Out On The Tiles' to another homage affair. The group opened for DYING FETUS and SUFFOCATION for a run of shows in May of 2004.

DEAD TO THE WORLD, Pulverizer (1999).

MALEDICTION

MIDDLESBOROUGH, UK — *Shaun Stephenson (guitar), Rich Mumford (guitar), Darren O'Hara (guitar), Mark Fox (bass), Alistair Dunn (drums).*

Middlesborough Progressive Death Metal act that excited considerable underground interest with their single released on the French Thrash label. MALEDICTION's early line-up consisted of vocalist Shaun Stephenson, guitarists Rich Mumford and Darren O'Hara, bass player Mark Fox and drummer Alistair Dunn. The band debuted with a March 1990, single track Grindcore demo 'Infestation' before the 'System Fear' 7" release on the Thrash label the following year. MALEDICTION released a demo 'Framework Of Condition' in October 1991 which besides new studio tracks featured a live recording of a gig supporting BOLT-THROWER. These sessions were due to include keyboard contributions from SIGH's Mira Kawashima but apparently the band opted to take their Japanese guest to the pub instead! O'Hara would decamp to found Folk / Death Metal act CERECLOTH and was replaced by Mark McGowan. Also emerging in 1992 would be a split cassette release entitled 'A Pungent And Sexual Miasma' shared with the fledgling CRADLE OF FILTH.

A makeshift live album 'Chronicles Of Dissension' arrived in 1993 on the Gargle With Blood label. Also emerging the same year was the yellow vinyl 'Dark Effluvium' EP on the American Psychoslaughter label, although apparently released without the band's knowledge. Phil Slack would take over the drum stool but would soon relinquish his position to a returning Dunn. During 1994 a proposed split EP with American act INCARNIS was recorded but never released. MALEDICTION signed to the Arctic Serenades label recording their projected debut album 'The Millennium Cotillion'. However, with the label's demise the album was shelved. MALEDICTION duly folded.

The band was resurrected during 2000 by Mumford, McGowan and Fox announcing their return with the demo session 'Shades Of Inequity'. The group, recently joined by drummer Barry of Bradford's THE ENCHANTED, plotted a new album, 'The Return Of The Prodigal', for 2002.

Infestation, (1990). Infestation.
System Fear, Thrash (1991). Infestation / Outro / Moulded From within / Waste.
Mould Of An Industrial Horizon, Mangled Beyond Recognition (1991). System Fear / Insect In The Infrastructure.
Framework Of Contortion, (1991). Intro / System Fear / Waste / Murdered From Within / Longterm Result / Insect In The Infrastructure / Infestation / Framework Of Contortion / System Fear (Live) / Murdered From Within (Live) / Waste (Live) / Longterm Result (Live) / Infestation (Live) / Framework Of Contortion (Live).
Malediction, (1992). Weeping Tears Of Covetousness / Doctrine's Eternal Circles / Framework Of Contortion.
A Pungent And Sexual Miasma, (1992) (split cassette with CRADLE OF FILTH). Mould Of An Industrial Horizon / Infestation / Waste / Longterm Result / System Fear / Sick New Facts / Murdered From Within.
Dark Effluvium, Psychoslaughter (1993) (Yellow vinyl). Dark Effluvium / Weeping Tears Of Covetousness / Framework Of Contortion.
CHRONICLES OF DISSECTION, Gargle With Blood GWBCD 001 (1993). Mould Of An Industrial Horizon / Weeping Tears Of Covetousness / Infestation / Framework Of Contortion / Longterm Result / System Fear / Doctrines Eternal Circles.

MALEFACTOR

SALVADOR, BA, BRAZIL — *Vladimir Mendes Senna (vocals), Danilo Coimbra (guitar), Wallace Guerra (guitar), Roberto Souza (bass), Luciano Gonzag Veiga Dias (keyboards), Alexandre Deminco Lemos (drums).*

Brazilian Death Metal. Based in Salvador the band was conceived in 1991 by a set of young teens, vocalist Lord Vladimir Mendes Senna being just fourteen years old whilst drummer Alexandre was only thirteen. Early demos, 'Sickness' in 1993 and 1995's 'Into The Black Order' saw production credits going to Ephendy Steven. During 1996 the track 'Sacramental Embrace' made its way onto the Demise compilation 'The Winds Of A New Millennium Act 2' and further material was featured on the 'DoisDaBahia' collection issued by Uivo Produções bringing the band valuable exposure. MALEFACTOR signed to the Megahard label for debut album 'Celebrate Thy War' in 1999.

MALEFACTOR guitarist Jafet Amoedo decamped in mid 2000 to be replaced by erstwhile MYSTIFIER and GRIDLOCK man Martin Mendonca. Ex-CARNIFIED guitarist Ricardo Sanct enrolled in 2001, replacing Wallace Guerra.

The band donated their rendition of 'King Of A Stellar War' to a ROTTING CHRIST tribute album, entitled 'An Evil Existence For Rotting Christ', released through Recordshop Productions in June of 2004. That same year MALEFACTOR completed work on the 'Barbarian' album for Maniac Records.

CELEBRATE THY WAR, Megahard (1999). Prelude / The Awakening / Estuans Interius / Amon Rising / Marching To The Unknown / Under The Law Of The Sword / Into The Twilight / Celebrate Thy War / Of Shadow And Light (Malefactor) / Secret Of Amon / Vae Solis / Secret Of Amon (Part II).
THE DARKEST THRONE, Demise DMS CD021 (2001). Necrolust In Thulsa Abbey / Into The Silence / Luciferian Times / Breaking The Castles / Prelude To A Battle / Behind The Mirror / The Darkest Throne / A God That Doesn't Lie.

MALEVOLENCE

NEW ZEALAND — *Daryl (vocals / guitar), Julian Price (bass), Tony Corry (drums).*

Auckland Grindcore unit harking back to April 1992. Lead vocalist and band visionary Daryl Tapsell, who numbers credits with LAGERWERFER, DISWOMBLE and BLACKMASS, held auditions which brought forth guitar Craig Bassett, bassist Dean Stoplmann and drummer Bruce Mutch. With this incarnation MALEVOLENCE would put in an inaugural gig to a respectable 300 people in a local town hall. Before the close of the year the band had cut their opening demo 'Mortum Ad Nausea' on a four track machine garnering international media coverage and an increased range of gigs to a growing fan base. The band would make a striking impression with Tapsell alternating between stage uniforms of corpse paint, basque and suspenders!

1993 saw the exit of Bassett as the guitarist opted out to become a guitar tutor. As a trio MALEVOLENCE donated the track 'Black Sabbat' to the Christchurch based compilation 'Epitaph' issued by Suffocating Tapes. However, soon after Stoplmann decamped to found SEPTIMUS

By mid 1994 MALEVOLENCE was back up to strength with the addition of mohawked bassist Julian Price and guitarist Chris Walter.

This line up, which would win the 'Hard, Fast & Heavy' category of the 1996 'Battle Of The Bands' contest, laid down the less than subtle early 1995 EP 'Fuck The Lord', recorded on an eight track recorder at 'The Chicken Farm'. Released in 1996 and distributed through Rukkus mail order 'F.T.L.' pulled in valuable New Zealand radio play for the band. A tour of the North Island, alongside DISWOMBLE and LAGERWERFER, would coincide.

Gigs the same year opening for international visiting artists included supports to IMPALED NAZARENE, BRUTAL TRUTH, ATOMISER and THE VERUKERS.

MALEVOLENCE would record their debut album 'Almost Like Something Completely Sinister' for September 1998 release putting in shows across the North Island with BRUTAL TRUTH once more. Walter would leave after this set of gigs taking MALEVOLENCE back down to trio status. With the break up of BRUTAL TRUTH in 1998 MALEVOLENCE were asked to contribute a track to the Zero Negative tribute opus 'Choice Of A New Generation. The band duly represented themselves with a take on 'Walking Corpse'.

In March of 1999 MALEVOLENCE, with Christchurch act GRIEF, put in a tour of both islands laying groundwork for another opening run of dates with IMPALED NAZARENE in the August. Further exposure came with a track included on the compilation album 'The Last Friday The 13th Of The Millennium'.

A setback occurred in December 1999 when long standing member Bruce Mutch laid down his sticks. Tony Corry, a veteran of SUBRUPTION, RETICENCE, FATAL ERROR and MALAKRINATE, stepped into the breach for a re-launch Auckland gig in June of 2000 guesting for Americans CODE 13.

The band had the track 'It Is Now Safe' included on 'Axe Attack' DJ Paul Martin's 2004 compilation album 'New Zealand Metal Volume 1'. MALEVOLENCE performed at the Auckland 'Underground Fest' event in October of 2004.

ALMOST LIKE SOMETHING COMPLETELY SINISTER, (1998). Too Slow To Die / Vengeance / I'm The One / Vampire's Kiss / Blut Und Liebe / Suburban Execution / The Cage Of The Insane / Riding On The Bus.
Windows 666: 2002 Tour Edition EP, (2002). It Is Now Safe … / Futilistic / Leukwarmia / Prime Mover.
Fuck The Lord, Bleeding Doll (2003). Fuck The Lord / CCF / Bleed / Fuck The Lord (1995 Version) / Blood Dreams (Remix) / Taste For Cold Flesh (1995 Version).
Windows 666 EP, Lycanthropic (2004). Futilistic / Dreams Of Trevor / It is Now Safe (To Turn Off Your Computer) / I'm The One / I Hate / Suburban Execution / Don't Do Me Like Daddy Does.

MALEVOLENCE

LEIRIA, PORTUGAL — *Carlos Cariano (vocals / guitar), Frederico Saraiva (guitar), Aires Pereira (bass), Paulo Pereira (keyboards), Gustavo Costa (drums).*

A Leiria Black Death Metal band that has supported both SINISTER and CRADLE OF FILTH. MALEVOLENCE debuted with the demo 'Pleasure Of Molestation'. 1999's 'Martyralized' was recorded in Sweden, at Fredman Studios with producer Fredrik Nordström, with an all new line-up centred upon surviving founder member vocalist Carlos Cariano (a.k.a. KK). Both Cariano and bass player Rui Capitão had previous association with VOMITORY. The four-stringer, plus one time guitarist Luis Lacerda, also had prior association with PARANOIA.

The album was issued on CD format by Maquiavel Music Entertainment with Psychic Scream Entertainment handling cassette copies for Malaysia and Singapore. In addition, Norwegian imprint Apocalyptic Empire Records released a limited edition of 500 on vinyl picture disc.

Bassist Aires Pereira stepped up a league in June of 2003 by deputising MOONSPELL. Meantime MALEVOLENCE gathered new material together for a mid 2004 demo 'Celebration Of Dysfunctional Becoming'. MALEVOLENCE added session keyboard player Paulo Pereira in 2005.

DOMINIUM, 199 (0). Desespero / Dominium Of Hate / The Burning Picture / Under Inhuman Torch / Enchanted Mask / Swallowed In Black / My Eyes (Throne Of Tears) / Sweet Bloody Vision / Erotica / Ceremonial Gallery.
MARTYRALIZED, Maquiavel Music Entertainment CD 43195 (1999). The Brotherhood Of Christ / Diabolical Eve (Chronicles Of Master Lusitania) / Hunters Of The Red Moon / Les Salls Obscures De Rode Noire XVIII / Thy Extremist Operetta / Insubordination / A Shining Onslaught Of Tyranny / Oceans Of Fire / Martyralized.
Celebration Of Dysfunctional Becoming, (2004). Slithering Angels / Equilibrium In Extremis / Devoured Unlimited / Mechanisms Of Destructive Behavior.

MALEVOLENT CREATION

BUFFALO, NY, USA — *Brett Hoffmann (vocals), Phil Fasciana (guitar), Jon Rubin (guitar), Jason Blachowicz (bass), Dave Culross (drums).*

Brutal, uncompromising Death Metal act, founded in Buffalo, New York and centred on former RESTHAVEN members guitarist Phil Fasciana and vocalist Brett Hoffmann created in 1987. The initial formation had this pairing allied with second guitarist John Rubin, bass player Mark Van Erp and drummer Mark Simpson. An opening demo session in 1989, involving three tracks 'Injected Sufferage', 'Epileptic Seizure' and 'Violent Offspring', saw a restricted distribution of just 100 cassettes. Another three song set, simply dubbed 'Demo 1990', followed, clinching a contract with Roadracer Records.

Their commercial debut, 'The Ten Commandments', saw delivery in September 1990, although the band had shifted shape, Jeff Juszkiewicz taking Rubin's post and Jason Blachowicz substituting for Van Erp. Roadracer had installed the band in their Florida Death Metal hit factory, Tampa's Morrisound to cut these tracks under the guidance of Scott Burns. General consensus highlighted MALEVOLENT CREATION's obvious affection for Bay Area thrash, the band coming across like an accelerated SLAYER. Setting the group apart, Hoffmann's glass-cutting screeching skills offered an alternative to the by now commonplace growls.

Guitarist Jeff Juszkiewicz parted ways with the band in 1991. Swede Peter Tägtgren had also been a member of MALEVOLENT CREATION and MELTDOWN but would return to Sweden to found HYPOCRISY, initially titled SEDITIOUS. In order to complete a planned American tour with DEVASTATION and DEMOLITION HAMMER the band temporarily pulled in the services of MONSTROSITY guitarist, and former MALEVOLENT CREATION member, John Rubin.

For April 1992's 'Retribution', again hacked out at Morrisound with Scott Burns at the desk, the band utilized the services of the SOLSTICE and ABYSMAL credited guitarist Rob Barrett and drummer Alex Marquez.

'Stillborn', retaining a stable line-up plus the addition of Rubin but now engineered by Mark Pinske, followed suit, in October 1993. However, reviews were unkind for a meandering record that lacked the enthusiastic bite of its forerunners and battled a muddy, reverb drenched production. Naturally MALEVOLENT CREATION still hit the live circuit to promote the record, including a stop at the 'Milwaukee Metalfest', three tracks from which surfaced on a four way split album, 'Live Death', issued via Restless Records in collaboration with CANCER, EXHORDER and SUFFOCATION. In 1994 both Fasciana and Barrett had ensconced themselves in the studio with drummer 'Crazy' Larry Hawke kicking off a side project named HATEPLOW.

By 1995 MALEVOLENT CREATION had parted ways with both their label Roadrunner Records, hooking up with the Pavement label, and vocalist Brett Hoffmann who subsequently busied himself guesting for Swiss act SILENT DEATH. Demos were recorded with bassist Jason Blachowicz handling lead vocals plus ex-DISGORGED, SUFFOCATION and R.I.P. drummer Dave Culross and this formation then put down tracks for the August 1996 offering 'Eternal'. A switch of bases had this album executed at Criteria and Inner Face Studios as a self-produced effort.

The 1997 compilation album 'Joe Black', which comprised rare tracks, demos and a take on SLAYER's 'Raining Blood', was a limited edition release.

MALEVOLENT CREATION's 1997 line-up, which included drummer Derek Roddy (following the tragic death of Crazy Larry in May of that year a fire whilst attempting to save his pet dog), saw the band trimmed down with only Blaschowicz and Fasciana remaining from their origins. Roddy would also session for AURORA BOREALIS and later NILE. Newly installed on guitar would be the CREATURE and PAINGOD credited John Paul Soars for a new MALEVOLENT CREATION studio album, 'In Cold Blood', released in 1997.

Hoffman returned for 1998's 'Fine Art Of Murder'. MALEVOLENT CREATION now comprised of Hoffmann, Fasciana, Barret, bassist Gordon Simms and drummer Dave Culross. Blachowicz, Soars and Roddy would all unite to forge DIVINE EMPIRE releasing the 'Redemption' debut and 'Doomed To Inherit' follow up. Soars would also busy himself further operating with SOLSTICE, BURNER and WYNJARA.

In 2000 MALEVOLENT CREATION drummer Dave Culross aided INCANTATION laying down session drums for their 'Infernal Storm' album. The same year found Culross in collusion with Fasciana and Barrett for their HATEPLOW project album 'The Only Law Is Survival'. MALEVOLENT CREATION released the 'Envenomed' album in 2000.

In a display of brotherhood HATEPLOW would support MALEVOLENT CREATION on their February 2001 headlining shows across Europe. Returning from Europe, Hoffmann was arrested upon entry into the United States and imprisoned for parole violation dating back to 1995. The incarceration of their vocalist forced MALEVOLENT CREATION to withdraw from a projected series of American dates planned with MONSTROSITY. This latest incident involving Hoffmann would eventually trigger his removal from the band for a second time, HATEPLOW's Kyle Symons taking the lead vocal mantle in January 2002.

In late 2001 Blachowicz, newly freed from jail after an assault charge, created the female fronted WYKKED WYTCH.

The band would figure as part of the gargantuan European 'No Mercy' touring festival package in March and April 2002. Also on the billing would be VADER, CATASTROPHIC, DESTROYER 666, HYPOCRISY, DISBELIEF, IMMORTAL and OBSCENITY. Jean-François Dagenais of famed Canadian act KATAKLYSM would also be confirmed as acting as producer for MALEVOLENT CREATION's 2002 'The Will To Kill' album. A scheduled Polish tour in October would see the band heading a billing of with VOMITORY and SEPTIC FLESH.

Former drummer Dave Culross was making news, formulating two extreme Metal ventures. One being an alliance with guitarists Frank Maggio, previously with IRON LUNG, EVIL EYE and SOCIAL DISEASE, and Jason Brennan whilst a separate venture had the sticksman formulating ideas with SLIPKNOT guitarist Mick Thompson.

MALEVOLENT CREATION's new album, 'The Will To Kill', would be unveiled in November. Although Justin DiPinto had handled drums in the studio Ariel Alvarado subsequently assumed the role. Breaking a five year hiatus the band toured the Southern states of the USA as support to CANNIBAL CORPSE in December. MALEVOLENT CREATION continued this run of shows throughout January and February 2003 supported at various stages by BLOODLET, REFLUX, DEAD TO FALL, BETWEEN THE BURIED AND ME and DEEDS OF FLESH.

The band's continuing resurgence would be further progressed as MALEVOLENT CREATION, complete now with NILE drummer Tony Laureano onboard, were confirmed as participants in the April 2003 European 'No Mercy' festivals. The group formed up part of a heavyweight billing comprising TESTAMENT, MARDUK, DIE APOKALYPTISCHEN REITER, DEATH ANGEL, PRO-PAIN, NUCLEAR ASSAULT, DARKANE, and CALLENISH CIRCLE. Meantime, erstwhile members Brett Hoffman and Dave Culross were announced as participating in a DEATH tribute album assembled by erstwhile DEATH guitarist JAMES MURPHY.

MALEVOLENT CREATION embarked on their first Brazilian tour since 1991 during July, recording shows for both future DVD and live album use. Jeff Juszkiewicz made a return with his Atlanta based Sludge trio TUALATIN. As MALEVOLENT CREATION renewed ties with Nuclear Blast for a 2004 studio album it would also be announced that drummer Dave Culross had returned to the fold. Scandinavian shows in June saw the band partnering with DYING FETUS.

A pairing of ex-MALEVOLENT CREATION drummers would also be in the news with Alex Marquez reforged links with his former SOLSTICE band mate and guitarist Dennis Munoz in an eighties styled Power Thrash outfit with a working title APOCALYPSE RISING. The quartet would be completed by second guitarist Willy Medina and bass player Mike Marabell. Meantime, Dave Culross' previously announced band formation PUMMEL, working in league with ex-IRON LUNG and SOCIAL DISEASE guitarist Frank Maggio, saw vocalist Tom Bush, bassist Mark Astrin and second guitarist Steve Seigerman completing the line-up.

MALEVOLENT CREATION's July 2004 'Warkult' opus, recorded at Liquid Ghost Recording Studio in Boca Raton, Florida, included a cover rendition of 'Jack The Ripper' originally by cult Australian band HOBB'S ANGEL OF DEATH. Summer festival appearances across Europe to promote the album included 'Rock Hard', 'With Full Force' and 'Up From The Ground' in Germany, 'Skeleton Bash' in Austria, 'Fury Fest' in France, 'Graspop Metal Meeting' in Belgium and 'Rock the Nations' in Istanbul, Turkey. The band ended up not playing the latter show when the promoter failed to supply enough tickets for the band to get to the venue.

Further misfortune struck the band when a planned London Underworld headlining show was cancelled as violent storms in the English channel prevented ferry crossings from France. Returning to the USA MALEVOLENT CREATION commenced home turf live work with a 'Warkult' record release party on July 24th at Fort Lauderdale's Culture Room. Meantime, a live album 'Conquering South America', recorded during the band's 2001 tour of Brazil and engineered by KATAKLYSM guitarist Jean-François Dagenais, surfaced in September.

In October 2004 the APOCALYPSE RISING pairing of Alex Marquez and Dennis Munoz allied with MALEVOLENT CREATION founder Phil Fasciana and former MALEVOLENT CREATION drummer Gus Rios in an all new band project. Former MALEVOLENT CREATION singer Brett Hoffmann resurfaced in January 2005, touting a demo from his new band DOWN THE DRAIN. Summer 2005 dates, commencing in Florida during early July, had MALEVOLENT CREATION packaged with ORIGIN, DIVINE EMPIRE and ANIMOSITY. In September MALEVOLENT CREATION made a concert return to Puerto Rico at the Mayaguez University Plaza supported by INFLAMATORY and SEPULCHRAL, being the first time in over a decade the band had played on the island. The following month the band once again underwent changes, losing guitarist Rob Barret to CANNIBAL CORPSE and bassist Gordon Simms but swiftly replacing them with returning members John Rubin on guitar and Jason Blachowicz on bass.

European shows in January and February 2006 witnessed strong backing from BOLT THROWER, NIGHTRAGE and NECROPHAGIST. For these gigs the group welcomed back original vocalist Brett Hoffmann. The band joined a heavyweight casting of CARPATHIAN FOREST, ROTTING CHRIST, HARM, INCANTATION and NEURAXIS for the 'Domination' European tour, commencing on February 14th at the Warsaw Progresja venue in Poland before hitting Germany, Austria, the Czech Republic, Italy, Belgium, France and Holland.

MALEVOLENT CREATION, as a unit comprising vocalist Brett Hoffmann, guitarists Jon Rubin and Phil Fasciana, bass player Jason Blachowicz and drummer Dave Culross, set to work on fresh album tracks, dubbed 'Doomsday X', during January 2007. Mick Thomson, guitarist for SLIPKNOT, also contributed a guitar solo for the song 'Deliver My Enemy'.

Malevolent Creation, Malevolent Creation (1989) (Demo cassette. Limited edition 100 copies). Injected Sufferage / Epileptic Seizure / Violent Offspring.

Demo 1990, Malevolent Creation (1990) (Demo). Remnants Of Withered Decay / Decadence Within / Impaled Existence.
THE TEN COMMANDMENTS, Roadrunner RC 93611 (1990). Memorial Arrangements / Premature Burial / Remnants Of Withered Decay / Multiple Stab Wounds / Impaled Existence / Thou Shalt Kill! / Sacrifial Annihilation / Decadence Within / Injected Sufferage / Malevolent Creation.
RETRIBUTION, Roadrunner RC 91811 (1992). Eve Of The Apocalypse / Systematic Execution / Slaughter Of The Innocence / Coronation Of Our Domain / No Flesh Shall Be Spared / The Coldest Survive / Monster / Mindlock / Iced.
STILLBORN, Roadrunner RR 90422 (1993). Dominated Resurgency / The Way Of All Flesh / Dominion Of Terror / Geared For Gain / Stillborn / Ordain The Hierarchy / Carnivorous Misgivings / Genetic Affliction / Ethnic Cleansing / Disciple Of Abhorrence.
LIVE DEATH, Restless (1994) (Split live album with EXHORDER, CANCER and SUFFOCATION). Premature Burial / Slaughter Of Innocence / Decadence Within.
JOE BLACK, Volcano 35013 (1996). Joe Black / Self Important Freak / Sadistic Perversity / No Salvation / To Kill / Tasteful Agony / Genetic Affliction / Raining Blood / Remnants For A Withered Decay / Impaled Existence.
ETERNAL, Pavement ZYX 32220 (1996). No Salvation / Blood Brothers / Infernal Desire / Living In Fear / Unearthly / Enslaved / Alliance For War / They Breed / To Kill / Hideous Reprisal / Eternal / Tasteful Agony.
IN COLD BLOOD, Pavement 32258 (1997). Nocturnal Overlord / Prophecy / Compulsive / Narcotic Genocide / Violated / Leech / In Cold Blood / Visions Of Malice / Seven / Preyed Upon / Millions / Condemned / Seizure.
THE FINE ART OF MURDER, Pavement ZYX 32293 (1998). To Die Is At Hand / Manic Demise / Instinct Evolved / Dissect The Eradicated / Mass Graves / The Fine Art Of Murder / Bone Exposed / Purge / Fracture / Rictus Surreal / Scorn / Day Of Lamentation / Scattered Flesh.
MANIFESTATION, Pavement 32341 (2000). Cold Blood / Condemned / Nocturnal Overlord / Fine Art Of Murder / Scorn / Blood Brothers / Impaled Existence / Living In Fear / Manic Demise / To Die Is At Hand / Infernal Desire / Bone Exposed / Alliance Or War / Mass Graves / Joe Black / Self Important Freak / Multiple Stab Wounds / Eve Of The Apocalypse / Slaughter Of Innocence / Monster.
ENVENOMED, Arctic Music Group 91012 (2000). Homicidal Rant / Night Of The Long Knives / Kill Zone / Halved / Serial Dementia / Bloodline Severed / Pursuit Revised / Conflict / Viral Release / The Deviants March / Envenomed.
THE WILL TO KILL, Nuclear Blast NB 1069 (2002). The Will To Kill / Divide And Conquer / The Cardinals Law / Superior Firepower / Lifeblood / Rebirth Of Terror / With Murderous Precision / All That Remains / Pillage And Burn / Burnt Beyond Recognition / Assassin Squad.
WARKULT, Nuclear Blast NB 1293 (2004). Dead March / Pre-emptive Strike / Supremacy Through Annihilation / Murder Reigns / Captured / Merciless / Section 8 / On Grounds Of Battle / Tyrannic Oppression / Ravaged By Conflict / Shock And Awe / Jack The Ripper.
CONQUERING SOUTH AMERICA, Arctic Music Group ARCT 1013 (2004). Eve Of The Apocalypse / Multiple Stab Wounds / Manic Demise / Blood Brothers / Kill Zone / Rebirth Of Terror / Slaughter Of Innocence / To Die Is At Hand / Coronation Of Our Domain / Monster / All That Remains / Alliance Or War / Infernal Desire / Living In Fear / Malevolent Creation.

MALICE GARDEN

CRICIÚMA, SC, BRAZIL — *Ivan Tyrant (vocals), Destroyer (guitar), Opressor (guitar), Astaroth (bass), Sadus (drums).*

Blasphemous Death Metal act founded as RENEGADES during 1998. The band's formative line-up comprised vocalist Reges, the guitar pairing of Opressor and Angelkill, bassist Kataclismoon and drummer Sadus. Adopting the revised title of MALICE GARDEN released the 'Revenge Against Jesus Christ' session during 1999, these recordings seeing the introduction of the FEAR and HALLUCINATIONS credited Ivan Tyrant on lead vocals and bass. Kataclismoon opted out but the band pulled in guitarist Destroyer, a veteran of SPLENDOUR and HALLUCINATIONS. Yet more changes witnessed the exit of Angelkill and the incorporation of FOREST OF DEMONS and HALLUCINATIONS man Astaroth as substitute.

MALICE GARDEN issued a 2002 demo 'Eternal Evil Victory'.

Revenge Against Jesus Christ, Malice Garden (2001). Rise Above The Things / Angel's Fall / Revenge Against Jesus Christ / Renegade Soul.
Eternal Evil Victory, (2002). The Master / Violation Domain / Black Devastation / Malice Garden.

MALIGNANCY

YONKERS, NY, USA — *Danny Nelson (vocals), Ron Kachnic (guitar), Lance Snyder (bass), Roger Beaujard (drums).*

Although founded in 1992 by vocalist Danny Nelson MALIGNANCY is well known by their MORTICIAN connection afforded through guitarists Roger Beaujard and Desmond Tolhurst. The Yonkers act came together when Nelson united with guitarist Javier Velez and drummer Kevin Chamberlain as CARCINOGEN.

Chamberlain soon made his exit as an all new line-up, now billed MALIGNANCY, saw the recruitment of second guitarist Larry Remlin, bass player Frank Madiao and drummer John Marzan. However Remlin would break ranks swiftly as did his fleeting replacement Tom Dorney. The 'Eaten Out From Within' demo bore a MALIGNANCY line-up of Nelson, Velez, Madiao and Marzan. During 1996 MALIGNANCY operated with Lance Snyder on guitar.

Once again the band fractured with just Nelson remaining. Undaunted he built around himself a fresh cadre of drummer Roger Beaujard, guitarist Ron Kachnic and bassist Desmond Tolhurst for a 1997 demo session 'Ignorance Is Bliss'. This tape secured a deal with United Guttural Records who promptly tested the market with a 1998 promotional CD.

MALIGNANCY toured in Europe during 2000 appearing at the Czech Republic 'Brutal Assault' festival prior to December dates in America with GOATWHORE and MORTICIAN. Tolhurst would depart following these dates necessitating former guitarist Lance Snyder coming back into the fold to take over this role.

The 2001 release 'Ignorance Is Bliss' on Primitive Recordings comprises of early demo tracks. A split album in alliance with Czech band INTERVALLE BIZARRE through Shindy Productions would comprise new tracks 'Fibroid Embolism' and 'Mortality Weakness' alongside re-recorded versions of 'Rotten Seed', 'Profitable Extinction' and 'Post Fetal Depression'.

Desmond Tolhurst joined ENGORGE as their new bass player during March of 2002. The band replaced Beaujard with Mike Heller in March of 2003. MALIGNANCY played May 2005 East Coast dates packaged with LENG TCH'E, IMPALED and ABORTED prior to European gigs allied with WORMED of Spain and German act DESPONDENCY for the 'Killing Spree Over Europe' tour commencing at the 'NRW Deathfest' on 16th September.

In the Autumn of 2005 Tolhurst and Kachnic headed up a new band unit, uniting with LEVIATHAN vocalist Shane Tierney and the former DIRTY BROWN EYE rhythm section of bassist Art Micewicz and drummer Jim Horan to forge PRIMER BLACK. MALIGNANCY signed to Willowtip Records in 2006 to record the album 'Inhuman Grotesqueries' at the Carriage House studios in Connecticut.

MALIGNANCY PROMO, United Guttural (1998). Profitable Extinction / Oral Excrement / Intestinal Sodomy / Cerebral Tissue Extraction / Rotten Seed / Ignorance Is Bliss / Your Life Is Shit / Post Fetal Depression.
INTRAUTERINE CANNIBALISM, United Guttural (1999). Rotten Seed / Intrauterine Cannibalism / Intestinal Sodomy / Internal Corruption / Profitable Extinction / Ignorance Is Blis / Your Life Is Shit / Oral Excrement / Waterlogged Corpse / Cerebral Tissue Extraction / Fried Afterbirth / Post Fetal Depression / Bag.
MOTIVATED BY HUNGER, United Guttural (2000). Motivated By Hunger / Vaginal Incisors / Separated Anxiety / Atmosphere Of Decay / Cystic Fibrosis / Intrauterine Cannibalism (Live).
IGNORANCE IS BLISS, Primitive Recordings (2001). Skinned Alive / Cervical Erosion / Gory Fetish / Rotten Seed / Ignorance Is Bliss / Your Life Is Shit / Post Fetal Depression / Profitable Extinction / Oral Excrement / Intestinal Sodomy / Cerebral Tissue Extraction.

FRAILTY OF THE HUMAN CONDITION, Shindy Productions (2002) (Split with INTERVALLE BIZARRE). Fibroid Embolism / Mortality Weakness / Rotten Seed (Re-recorded) / Profitable Extinction (Re-recorded) / Post Fetal Depression (Re-recorded).
INHUMAN GROTESQUERIES, Willowtip (2007).

MALIGNANT INCEPTION

SALT LAKE CITY, UT, USA — *Zakk Muffett (vocals), Ed Price (vocals / guitar), Jon Creager (guitar), Matt Grassberger (bass), Dave Jelsma (keyboards), Todd Weir (drums).*

Salt Lake City Death Grind outfit dating to 1992. Initially the group went under the title of BLACK DEATH and featured vocalist / guitarist Ed Price, who besides his roll fronting a Death Metal band holds down a day job as a school bus driver, guitarist Chad Kasimatis and drummer Steve Lea. This formative group folded with Kasimatis becoming lead singer for NECROTOMY. Subsequently, Price, Kasimatis and Lea decided to re-forge the band in a self styled "Precision Grind" direction. Dave Jelsma would join on bass guitar for an initial set of aborted demos. With the conclusion of these sessions Lea was superseded by Tim Riley of NECROTOMY and CARNAL DECIMATE repute.

The self financed 1997 album 'Black Death' oddly marked a period of inactivity for the band. A second guitarist, Mike Kimball, was recruited but MALIGNANT INCEPTION then went into stasis, with many of the band members involved in higher education. Kimball would subsequently join DYING FETUS.

A reformed MALIGNANT INCEPTION, adding new faces Mike Ventura on second guitar and keyboard player J.R. Torina, underwent a period of flux during 2003. Line up switches first saw drummer Tim Riley exit in May, duly enrolling the DISORDERED credited Todd Weir as replacement in July but then having both Torina and then Ventura opt out in October. The group pulled in second guitarist Robert Strack of HOOGA in January of 2004. However, by October Strack was out of the picture, being replaced by Jon Creager, with Matt Grassberger on bass and Zakk Muffett fronting the band for recording of a new album entitled 'Restraint'. MALIGNANT INCEPTION would also re-issue the debut album 'Black Death' with new cover art.

Line up changes in January 2005 saw guitarist Jon Creager being replaced by Tyler Harvey of DISTANT VISION repute.

BLACK DEATH, Independent (1997). Surviving Off Humanity / Visions / Necromantic / Black Death Part I—Mark Of Malignance / Black Death Part II—The Inception / Dictator Of Adolescence / Dreams Within Dreams / Stained / The Void / Awakenings / The Calling.

MALIGNANT TUMOUR

CZECH REPUBLIC — *Bilos (vocals / bass), Richard (guitar), Marek (drums).*

The industrious Ostrava based Grindcore merchants MALIGNANT TUMOUR, fronted by Martin 'Bilos' Bílek, date to 1993. A year after formation they would bow in with the rehearsal cassette 'Cadaveric Incubator Of Endoparasites', the studio demo 'Symphonies For Pathologist' and a split tape shared with SOLIDIFICATION. 1995 delivered the tape 'Analyse Of Pathological Conceptions' and a collaborative 7" EP 'Malignus Morbus' in union with DECOMPOSED released via Obscene Productions. The same label put out a follow up split 7", entitled 'Forensic Clinicism', in alliance with IMMURED the following year. The 1996 formation of the band would see a rhythm section installed of NEEDFUL THINGS bassist Otto and CEREBRAL TURBULENCY drummer Michal. MALIGNANT TUMOUR's 1996 shared single with MASTIC SCUM 'Sick Sins Syndrome' on Epidemie Records includes AGATHOCLES and REGURGITATE cover versions. Besides his MALIGNANT TUMOUR priorities guitarist Richard would also be operational as a member of Gothic Doom Metal band LOVE HISTORY.

1997 would prove particularly prolific for the band. Bizarre Leprous Productions released a four way split 7" EP with NEGLIGENT COLLATERAL COLLAPSE, C.U.M. and C.S.S.O. as well as the split live cassette with BLOOD, 'Medical Lecture'. Meantime Quirofano Productions released the vinyl album 'Crush Syndrome' whilst Obscene Productions weighed in with the GRIDE split tape 'Pathology'. The shared album 'Eat The Flesh ... And Vomica', released in union with Polish act SQUASH BOWELS, included two AGATHOCLES cover versions 'No Use ... (Hatred)' and 'Go Fucking Nihilist' along with a rendition of DEAD INFECTION's 'Maggots In Your Flesh'.

The 1998 'Rock Stars- Money Wars' shared EP with Polish act DEAD INFECTION included a further AGATHOCLES cover 'Lay Off Me'. There would be little respite in the work ethic for this year, other releases including a three way split with GRIDE and CEREBRAL TURBULENCY via Shindy Productions, an Epidemie Records split 7" with INGROWING, a Psychotherapy Distribution shared cassette with NEUROPATIA and the tapes 'Killing For Profit' and 'From Grind Gore ... To Mince Core'.

Sick Sins Syndrome EP, Epidemie (1996) (7" split single with MASTIC SCUM). Endocarditis Streptoccia Acuta / Affections Of Outlet Urinary Way / A Start At Least / Lyssa / Grind Gut Wrenching / Desensitized.
Swarms Of Virulency EP, Epidemie (1996) (7" split single with INGROWING). Dysecteria Bacillaris / Acute Haemmorrhagical Necrosis Of Pancreas / Lymphogranuloma Veneres / Chronical Myeloid Leukemia / Herpos Labialis / Climax-Menopause-Polyuria.
EAT THE FLESH ... AND VOMICA, Obscene Productions (1997) (Split album with SQUASH BOWELS). Maggots In Your Flesh / Epiphilitis / Acute Haemorrhagical Necrosis Of Pancreas / Subacute Endocarditis / Decubitis / Mors Praenatalis / Pephigus Vulgaris / Disease Of Oral Cavities / No Use ... (Hatred) / Pertussis / Diptheria / Idiopathic Colitis Ulcerosa / Mucormycosis Of Gastrointestinal Tract / Parasitical Cysts / Dysenteria Bacillaris / Embryopathia / Purulent Attack / Reason To Hate / Necrotic Urocystitis With Ammoniacal Fermentation / Putrefaction Decomposition / Impetigo Contagiosa / Intravascular Disseminated Coagulate / Ingrowing Of The Alien Things In The Body / Pulmonary Collapse / Go Fucking Nihilist / Waterhouse-Fridrichsen Syndrome.
Rock Stars- Money Wars EP, Morbid (1998) (7" split single with DEAD INFECTION). Nature Warning / Human Extinction / This Filth Stinks / Lay Off Me / Government Shitheads / Hope Against A System / Mendacious T-Levision / Violence Against Fascistic Cunts.
DAWN OF A NEW AGE, (2003). Death Is Near—Reign Of Hell / Plastic Existence / Up Your Fucking Arse / Dawn Of A New Age / Peel The Cancer / Nightmare Reality / Wounded / Status Quo / Get To Attack / A Boring Drunken Sod / Nazis Raus / Nature's Warning For Human Extinction / Aalio Ala Lyo Oolio Laikkyy / Destroy / Shit Heil / Behind The Mirror / Paskaa Sistema / Mediareality / Punk To Punx / Everlasting Penetration / Temples Of Consumption / Wat Je Zegt Dat Ben Je Zelf / Stop The Mob / ... And Man Made The End / Mercenaries Of War / Katjusia.
DEMO / SINGLES COLLECTION '94-'98, Extremist EXR 021 (2003).

MANGLED

HOLLAND — *Pepijn Houwen (vocals), Harold Gielen (guitar), Erwin Hemsen (guitar), Loek Peters (bass), Floris de Jonge (drums).*

MANGLED emerged in 1989 led by the trio of vocalist Pepijn Howen, drummer Wilko Reynders and guitarist Erwin Hermsen. By 1991 second guitarist Harald Gielen and bass player Paul Dunn had completed the line up for recording of the inaugural 1992 three track demo tape 'Cadaverous'. A sophomore promotional cassette 'Perish' was issued the following year attracting the attention of the Wild Rags label who promptly re-issued the session on CD format.

However, 1995 would see the departure of Dunn and also later of Reynders. The latter's place was taken by Floris De Jonge for recording of the '... In Emptiness' album. MANGLED would also be brought back up to strength with the addition of INHUMANE man Loek Peeters.

Promoting the 'Ancient Times' album, a concept work based on the depravities of the Roman empire released on former member Wilko Reynders label Fadeless, MANGLED toured Europe in alliance with Italians Natron and Sweden's CENTINEX. November 1999 saw a further burst of live activity sharing billing with VOMITORY, DAWN OF DECAY and DERANGED.

MANGLED would cut their version of 'Visions From The Dark Side' for a 2000 MORBID ANGEL tribute album. The band would later see inclusion on a CANNIBAL CORPSE homage compilation released by Dwell Records with 'A Skull Full Of Maggots'.

Hermsen would act as producer for INHUME's 2000 album 'Decomposing From Inside'. Harold Gielen forged a side act in Mathcore Metal band CHARLIE*ADLER, in 2003, alongside former COLLISION man Wouter Wagemans on lead vocals, guitarist Johan van Gestel of GAAR, KUTABARE and VLEISBOEUM, second guitarist Roel in 't Zandt from GRAMOXONE with Niek van Lin from CONCUBINE, SIN and VLEISBOEUM on the drums. Meantime, MANGLED signed to Fadeless Records for a 2004 album, issuing the limited edition EP 'Carnal Abhorrence' as a foretaste.

In 2005 Floris de Jonge, in alliance with the DISAVOWED pairing of vocalists Joey Sta and Robbet Kok, ex-LENG TCH'E bassist Rizzo plus lead guitarist Pranger, fired up the Death Metal project ARSEBREED, recording the album 'Munching The Rotten'.

Perish, Wild Rags (1995). The Emptiness Of Being / Unbearable / The 7th Key / When Fall Reaches Awareness / Call Of Silence / Perished Innocence.
In Emptiness, Wild Rags (1997). Bathe In Blood / Psychodead / Call Of Silence (Live).
ANCIENT TIMES, Fadeless (1998). Raise My Fist In The Face Of God / Eve Of Mourning / In Ancient Times I: De Christianis / Bathe In Blood / Era: Odium / Goatrider / The Sleeping Paradise / In Ancient Times II: Erotica / In Ancient Times III: Bellum Gallicum / Mangled.
MOST PAINFUL WAYS, Hammerheart (2001). Hate / Blood Fed Orgasm / Evilterrestrial / Mortifying Body Parts / Warfare Embowelment / Revelation Of Soulside Pain / Hellrose Place / Formaldehyde / Scream And Bleed / Spontaneous Human Combustion.
Carnal Abhorrence EP, Fadeless (2004). Carnal Abhorrence / Body Dismorphic Disorder / A Skull Full Of Maggots / Visions From The Darkside.

MANGLED TORSOS

GERMANY — *Olli (vocals / guitar), Frank (bass), Patrick (drums).*

Formed in the summer of 1990, MANGLED TORSOS describe themselves as a very aggressive, fun Grindcore project and explained that the choice of band name highlighted this philosophy to the max.

1992 saw the recording of the group's first demo, 'Incalculate Of Your Subconscious', after which Frank replaced MANGLED TORSOS' original bassist.

In the spring of '93 the 2 track EP 'Anatomia Reformata' appeared as a limited edition of a mere 360 copies. Morbid Records promptly stepped in to sign the group.

In addition to the two albums released since 1994, the band have supported the likes of DEAD, AGATHOCLES, MIASMA, BLOOD and PYOGENESIS.

DRAWINGS OF THE DEAD, Morbid MR 013 CD (1994). Intro / Unsuspecting Sacrifice / Lost Emotions / Drawings Of The Dead / Morphea / Deranged Body Love / Malignant Tumor / Dehuminization / Dissemble.

MANIAS

ALBUQUERQUE, NM, USA — *Drew M. Ruiz (vocals / guitar), Galen Baudhuin (guitar), Robert Montoya (bass), Eric Lucero (drums).*

Founded in 1993 by guitarist/vocalist Drew M. Ruiz and bassist "Bloody" Gary Garcia, MANIAS is a brutal Death / Grind band out of Albuquerque, New Mexico. Originally the band planned on recording in two distinct languages, as SALE SANGRA for the Mexican audience in Spanish, and as MANIAS for the USA. However, this self styled "Brutal Bilingual" idea soon settled simply on the one band title.

The group hit a multitude of problems as Garcia was ejected in 1995 and, according to the band's own accounts, Ruiz was sentenced to 5 years in Federal Prison for transporting a quantity of marijuana. Entrapment Records issued a compilation of archive demos dubbed 'Identity Crisis', featuring a sessioning Matt Loftus on drums, but MANIAS had to wait until March of 2003 when Ruiz, after 40 months in jail, was released on probation. Having added bassist Rob Jaramillo and drummer Eric Lucero MANIAS cut the 2003 'Vivisection' EP.

MANIAS projected a full length album, entitled 'And Blood Soaked The World', for 2004 issue through D.W.S. Records.

Vivisection, Manias (2003). Decimate / Mastubar Mutual / Vivisection / Avarice Gone Mad / (Untitled).

MARAMON

LINDESBERG, SWEDEN — *Peter Ristiharju (vocals), Henrik Tranemyr (guitar), Christer Karlsson (guitar), Denny Axelsson (bass / vocals), Pär Hjulström (drums).*

MARAMON, created as a high school act in Lindesberg, Örebro during November 2001, include erstwhile DALSKOG personnel vocalist Peter Ristiharju and guitarist Christer Karlsson. The band's opening demo, 'Sömn' ('Sleep'), was cut in 2002 without the services of a bassist. Subsequently inducting Tobias Matsson on bass, MARAMON got to grips with a second promotion session 'Dödens Rike'.

MARAMON, dispensing with keyboard player Christian Persson, added a third guitarist in 2004 in Rickard Källqwist whilst Pär Hjulström, previously of AMARAN, took over the drum position from Kalle Jansson. Both Ola Högblom and bassist Tobias Matsson departed, new man on bass being Stefan. MARAMON shifted shape again in 2005, the revised line-up being a trio of vocalist Peter Ristiharju, guitarist Christer Karlsson and bass player Stefan Andersson. The band projected a new album 'Me, Myself, I' through Karmageddon Media in November. However, the band then severed ties with the label. MARAMON's membership roll would flux further, introducing Denny Axelsson on bass of CALM and SWEDISH MASSACRE and vocals with Henrik Tranemyr of THE BEREAVED on guitar.

Sömn, Maramon (2002). Drömmarnas Avgrund / Hednaland / Sömn.
ME, MYSELF, I, Maramon Ind. (2006). Paralysis / Me, Myself, I / Machine Of Eternity / Soul Caged / Thoughts / Why? / Manipulator.

MARE DIBERE

SAO GONCALO, RJ, BRAZIL — *Lord Arkaine (vocals), Rodrigo Ulver (guitar), Valheron (guitar), Marcus Barbatus (bass), Raphael Levithus (keyboards / vocals), M.S. Gomes (drums).*

Rio de Janeiro Death / Doom styled Black Metal band MARE DIBERE (Hebrew for "Lord Of Destruction") was created in late 2002. The band's members, then also including guitarist Marcus Barbatus, previously operated with DESTRUCTION OF THE SKY, LYKANTHROPIA, NECROWAR and RAVISHMENT. During 2005 MARE DIBERE introduced new guitarist Gilliardy 'Valheron' Souza, replacing Thiago, a seasoned campaigner holding credits with acts such as Death Metal act NECROWAR, solo project VALHERON and Doomsters RAVISHMENT.

Line-up changes saw the exit of bassist Lariucci, being replaced by Marcus Barbatus, besides being a former MARE DIBERE man also an ex-member of UNEARTHLY, IMPERADOR BELIAL and VIKING THRONE. The roster now also comprised singer Lord Arkaine, guitarists Rodrigo 'Ulver' Freire and Gilliardy Valheron, keyboard player Raphael Levithus and drummer M.S. Gomes.

SIGNUM TRIUMPHANT, Mare Dibere (2006). The Horseman / Flight Of Tiamat / Abomination / Crowning The Witchcraft Night Princess / Comtesse Burana / Chronicles And Chants Of War / Emperor Vladmir Sword / Voodoo Ritual / Garden Of Darkness.

MARTTYYRIOPERAATIO

JOUTSENO, FINLAND — *Aksu (vocals), Liisa (guitar), Oula Kerkelä (bass), Jori Sara-Aho (drums).*

Joutseno Grindcore merchants MARTTYYRIOPERAATIO ("Martyr operation"), founded by guitarist Liisa and drummer Jori Sara-Aho, of SKULLFUCK, DEADARLINGS and NAILGUNNER, in autumn 2004, include bass player Oula Kerkelä, holding affiliations with CRONUS, GROTESK, LOCADRE, DEATH TOLL 80K and VERENPERINTÖ. The original formation was intended to included Frederic Vanmassenhove of Belgian band ABORTED but distance factors negated this proposal. The first MARTTYYRIOPERAATIO demo, entitled 'Teloittaja Saapuu', saw thirteen tracks being recorded in just six hours on 10th September 2005. Following on from these sessions the group inducted singer Aki.

Teloittaja Saapuu, Marttyyrioperaatio (2005). Ydinsota / Oksennan Suolia / Sisäelinräjähdys / Mahanahan Suikaleita / Köysi On Huono Vaihtoehto / Mätäpaiserepeämä / Happohyökkäys / Helvetinmoinen Teurastus / Oksasilppurionnettomuus / Syön Itseni / Epidemia / Visva / Teloitus: I Teloittaja Saapuu, II Lataus, III Tähtäys, IV Laukaus, V Kuolema.

MARTYR

TROIS-RIVIÈRES, QC, CANADA — *Francois Mongrain (vocals / bass), Daniel Mongrain (guitar), Pier-Luc Lampron (guitar), Patrice Hamelin (drums).*

Technical Trois-Rivières, Québec Death Metal. MARTYR, founded in 1994, opened proceedings with the September 1995 demo session 'Ostrogoth'. Two versions were issued, a three track effort and a secondary tape adding extra track 'Neverending Strife'. A second demo cassette, 'Non Conformis', arrived in 1997. The November 1997 album 'Hopeless Hopes' was a self financed affair. Following recording drummer François Richard made way for Patrice Hamelin. In 1998 MARTYR put in a showing at the infamous Milwaukee Metalfest. Guitarist Daniel Mongrain, whilst retaining his ties to MARTYR, would join GORGUTS in the Autumn of 1999 appearing on their 'From Wisdom To Hate' album. The guitarist also has associations with QUO VADIS and Florida's CAPHARNAUM.

MARTYR's second album 'Warp Zone', featuring GORGUTS vocalist Luc LeMay as guest, arrived in 2000. Co-founder guitarist Pier-Luc Lampron exited in 2001. In October 2004 Dan Mongrain acted as stand in guitarist for CRYPTOPSY.

MARTYR entered Wild Studios in St-Zenon, Quebec in December 2005 with producer Yannick St-Amand to record their third album. As it transpired, 'Feeding The Abscess' released in October 2006, eventually scored a Pierre Rémillard production credit. The album closed with a cover version of VOIVOD's 'Brain Scan', this seeing guest contributions from Blacky (Jean-Yves Theriault) of VOIVOD. To launch the album a show at Montreal's Medley venue on November 11th saw Blacky again guesting on 'Brain Scan'. Mordam Music Group gave 'Feeding The Abscess' a USA release in February 2007.

Non Conformis, Martyr (1997) (Demo). Non Conformis / Prototype / Ostrogoth / Ars Nova.

HOPELESS HOPES, Martyr (1997). Hopeless Hopes / Prototype / Elementals / Non Conformis / Ostrogoth / The Blinds Reflection / Inner Peace / Ars Nova / Nipsky.

WARP ZONE, (2000). Warp Zone / Virtual Emotions / Endless Vortex Towards Erasing Destiny / Deserted Waters / Carpe Diem / The Fortune-Teller / Speechless / Retry? Abort? Ignore? / Realms Of Reverie.

EXTRACTING THE CORE—LIVE 2001, Skyscraper Music (2001). Warp Zone / Speechless / Inner Peace / Virtual Emotions / Endless Vortex Towards Erasing Destiny / Hopeless Hopes / Retry? Abort? Ignore? / Carpe Diem / Prototype.

Ostrogoth, Martyr (2006) (Demo). Prototype / Ostrogoth / Ars Nova.

FEEDING THE ABCESS, Galy 48 (2006). Perpetual Healing (Infinite Pain) / Lost In Sanity / Feast Of Vermin / Interlude—Desolate Ruins / Havoc / Nameless, Faceless, Neverborn / Silent Science / Felony / Part I : Echoes Of The Unseen / Part II : Romancing Ghouls / Part III : Stasis Field / Part IV : Shellshocked / Brain Scan.

MASACRE

MEDELLÍN, COLOMBIA — *Alex Oquendo (vocals), Jorge Londoño (guitar), Rafael Muñoz (guitar), Alvaro Alvarez (bass), Victor Gallego (drums).*

Foremost on the Colombian Death Metal scene. MASACRE, hailing from Medellín, originated during 1988 with an inaugural line-up of vocalist Alex "Trapeator" Oquendo, guitarists Toño and Juancho with drummer Mauricio Montoya. The group hit the scene with an infamous brace of 1989 demos 'Colombia ... Imperio Del Terror' and 'Cancer De Nuestros Dias'. Commercially, MASACRE made their entrance in 1990 with the mini album 'Ola De Violencia'. Self financed, this EP was restricted to just 500 copies and found Qquendo and Montoya joined by guitar players Juan Carlos Gomez and Antonio Guerrero with bass handled by Alejandro Saldarriaga.

The band's notoriety had spread overseas by this time and subsequently MASACRE signed to the French Osmose Productions label for the 1991 album 'Requiem'. By this stage MASACRE was a quartet of Oquendo, guitarist Juan Carlos Gomez, bassist Dilson Díaz and drummer Mauricio Montoya. The 'Ola De Violencia' tapes would also be re-issued as a split album with the notorious North American Black Metal band PROFANATICA.

Extensive touring across South America throughout Colombia, Ecuador, Venezuela and Peru was capitalised on by a further album 'Barbarie Y Sangre En Memoria De Cristo' issued through Mórbida Productions in 1993. The 'Sacro' album came in 1995 with Jorge Londoño being added as second guitarist and Victor Gallego manning the drums. Alvaro Alvarez, previously a member of MURDER and REMEMBRANCE OF PAIN took responsibility for bass on MASACRE's 2001 album 'Muerte Verdadera Muerte', released by Decade Records in Colombia and Hurling Metal in Argentina, included a cover version of the KISS classic 'Strutter' on the domestic version.

The band utilised the services of HATE ETERNAL's Erik Rutan for the 'Total Death' album, recorded at Sirio Studios in Bogota in the Spring of 2003 and noted for being the band's debut English language album. Released the following year, 'Total Death' emerged through the HateWorks imprint in Columbia and Argentine label Hurling Metal. The album saw license to Xtreem Music for Europe the following year.

In 2005 Alex Okendo guested on the DIA DE LOS MUERTOS project album 'Day Of The Dead' assembled by BODY COUNT bassist Vincent Price, and guitarist Andres Jaramillo and drummer Alfonso Pinzon from the Colombian metal act AGONY. Sadly, drummer Victor Gallego died on 3oth October 2005.

Ola De Violencia, Independent (1990) (Limited edition 500 copies). Sangrienta Muerte / Mórbida Implosión / Decadencia.

REQUIEM, Osmose Productions OPCD 002 (1991). Intro—Requiem / Cortejo Fúnebre / Justicia Ramera / Brutales Masacres / Sepulcros En Ruinas / Escoria / Ola De Violencia / Tiempos De Guerra / Conflicto De Paz / Cáncer / Blasfemias.

OLA DE VIOLENCIA, Osmose Productions (1992) (Split album with PROFANATICA). Sangrienta Muerte / Mórbida Implosión / Decadencia / Brutales Masacres / Ola de Violencia.

BARBARIE Y SANGRE EN MEMORIA DE CRISTO, Mórbida Productions (1993). Sarcasmo Divino / Camino Al Calvario / Imperio Del Terror / Una Flor Sobre Mi Tumba.

SACRO, Lorito (1995). Sacro / Orgasmos Oscuros (Paraíso) / Tierra De Lamentos / Confesiones / Dolor Sensato / Mas Allá Del Dolor ... / Funeral Amén / Dios Del Horror / Pecados No Perdonados / Ritos De Muerte / Moral Esclava.

MUERTE VERDADERA MUERTE, Hurling Metal HMR 017 (2001). Espinas / Exodo / Sangre En Mis Manos / Violentada / Símbolos De Héroes / Prepárate A Morir / País En Sangre / Masacrados / Razones De Odio / Strutter.

TOTAL DEATH, Hateworks (2004). Slaves Of Death / Battlefields / Kill Or Get Killed / Soldiers Of The Unknown / Death Metal Forever / Wrath Intense Pain / Oh My God!! / Victims.

MASOCHRIST

HAMILTON, NEW ZEALAND — *Phil (vocals / guitar), Julian (bass), Dane (drums).*

Hamilton's Black / Death Metal band MASOCHRIST was formed in 1998 by drummer Dane and vocalist / guitarist Phil, both erstwhile members of the 1995 act NARKULT, and soon after added Julian on bass guitar to the mix. As the corpse painted MASOCHRIST, the band issued a total of four releases including the 'Nothing Is Forever' album and built up a reputation as one of New Zealand's Death Metal frontrunners. Pre MASOCHRIST, guitarist Julian Baddies had journeyed through such acts as THUNDER MONKEY, SWAMP GOBLIN, DEEP SIX, THE BADDIES and HELL TO PAY. Vocalist / guitarist Phil and drummer Dane had also partnered Baddies in HELL TO PAY, Phil also tracing a band lineage as a guitarist through THE CROWBAR EFFECT and CHURCHBURNER whilst the drummer's musical heritage included DEEP SIX and, as vocalist / bassist a slew of acts including F.I.C., SINFEEDER, ENSHRINE, AZAZEL, ANIMOSITY and GORE STORY.

MASOCHRIST debuted with the two track September 1998 cassette 'Inferno Black'. A self financed CD, 'Nothing Is Forever', surfaced the following year followed by 2000's 'Eternal Antichrist' EP and an eponymous 2001 release, the latter actually recorded back in August 1998.

Following the 2001 MASOCHRIST album 'Last Disaster'- recorded and mixed in a mere four hours, opting for a Doom direction and enlisting Matt Bulldozer on bass, RUIN was founded in late 2001. Both Baddies and frontman Phil operate the 'Lo-Fi' side venture SOUL ECLIPSE in union with Issacha, Dane and Dolf De Borst of THE DATSUNS. Other extracurricular endeavours include Baddies, Phil and Dane in Punk band THE NIGHTMARES, the Grindcore union NAGASAKI MANTRA featuring Baddies, Phil and Dane and the experimental acoustic tones of ANGELS ABLAZE, a project of Baddies and Claire Vincent. Dane also wields the drumsticks in 3 MAN WALL.

Nothing Is Forever EP, (1999). Infinite Folds of Incineration / Return to the Pentagram / The Sign of Satans Return / Inferno Black.

Eternal Antichrist EP, (2000). Flames Of Execution / Unholy Aggressor / White Demons / Infected With The Spirit Of The Deity / Ruin.

Masochrist EP, (2001). Pathways To Misanthropia / Reconciliation Of The Dead / Debris Of Heaven / White Demons / Mark Of Satan / Masochrist.

INFERNO BLACK, (2001) (Cassette release). Pathways to Misanthropia / Debris of Heaven / Reconciliation of the Dead / White Knuckle Hammer / Death's Grinning Angels / Infernal Torment / Mark of Satan / Sealed in Blood.

The Last Disaster EP, (2001). We Come From Hell / Smash The Cross / Crack The Devil Whip / Flames Of Execution / World Full Of Hate.

MASQUE OF INNOCENCE

AMADORA, PORTUGAL — *Marco Nogueira (vocals), Paulo Filipe (guitar), Rui Martins (guitar), Paulo Batista (bass), Hugo Lopes (keyboards), Rui Brito (drums).*

Amadora melodic Death Metal band MASQUE OF INNOCENCE, created in April 1997 by drummer Rui Brito, issued a 1999 demo 'Take O'. Guest female vocals came courtesy of Elisabeth Santos. The band's original line-up featured vocalist Rui Cabral, guitarist Nuno Conceição and bassist Vasco Gonçalves. The group's inaugural live concert took place at the Marquês Rock Club in Lisbon in April of 1998. The vocal reins were taken over during Nuno Damião that same year as MASQUE OF INNOCENCE supported Irish act PRIMORDIAL on their Iberian dates. José Costa took command of bass duties in 1999. More membership shuffles saw the introduction of guitarist João Matos in 2000.

The MASQUE OF INNOCENCE credited João Matos forged the LUNA MARTYR project with vocalist Cris and bassist Vasco from TE DEUM for the 2000 demo 'The Unseen, The Eternal ...'. Matos relinquished his position in MASQUE OF INNOCENCE during 2001. New bass man Carlão was introduced in September 2004.

Take O, Edit Productions (1999). 753 / Emptiness Portrait / Dormant Bliss / Until The End / Wrapped In Tears.

MASSACRE

FL, USA — *Kam Lee (vocals), Rick Rozz (guitar), Terry Butler (bass), Bill Andrews (drums).*

Death Metal act MASSACRE was first noticed internationally as being created by DEATH refugees vocalist Kam Lee (a.k.a. Barney Lee), guitarist Rick Rozz (Frederick DeLillo), bassist Terry Butler and drummer Bill Andrews. As an offshoot of the DEATH family tree, MASSACRE naturally relied on precision riffing and Florida crunch. Kam Lee also figures as a catalyst, cited as the originator of the de-facto death growling style of vocal, which would provide an indelible identity stamp on the genre. Despite their importance, MASSACRE's eminence rests merely on one album and one EP release.

Pre-DEATH Rozz had operated with THATCHER. In actual fact the very first MASSACRE formation was assembled as a covers band, comprising singer Mark Brents, Allen West and the OBITUARY credited JP Chartier on guitar, bassist Scott Blackwood and drummer Bill Andrews. Both Brents and Blackwood would soon be dispensed with as Michael Borders took command of bass. Border's formative acts included CYANIDE, alongside a pre-SIX FEET UNDER pairing of Allen West and Greg Gall.

This formation debuted live with two back to back gigs, the first supported by EXECUTIONER, who later, via XECUTIONER, became known as OBITUARY, and the second as openers to MORBID ANGEL. Following these shows, the Hawaiian native Kam Lee was pulled in as new frontman in early 1985. This version of MASSACRE recorded the inaugural demo, featuring songs 'Aggressive Tyrant', 'Mutilated' and 'Death In Hell'. Chartier exited and Trevor Peres from OBITUARY was auditioned but not chosen.

MASSACRE's second demo, 'Chamber Of Ages' in November, marked the introduction of DEATH and GENITORTURERS guitarist Rick Rozz. In addition, a six song live cassette, the group's first gig with Kam Lee and Rick Rozz recorded at Streets Club in April 1986, was also distributed. MASSACRE's live set at this time notably included the DEATH song 'Corpse Grinder'. Experimenting once again with a twin guitar sound the vacancy was briefly filled for a few shows by Robbie Goodwin. Rumours that the group had signed to Cobra Records for an album given a title of 'From Beyond' proved premature.

More changes saw Borders being superseded by Terry Butler with Goodwin then departing. In 1987, the band was put on hold whilst Rozz, Butler and Andrews sessioned on DEATH's 'Leprosy' album. Lee would forge ABHORRENT EXISTENCE in alliance with Pete Slate of ACHERON and EQUINOX and Mark Lavenia from INCUBUS and EQUINOX.

Within the year MASSACRE got back into gear following completion of DEATH commitments, the new look act seeing

Lee and Rozz flanked by new members Butch Gonzales on bass and former WHIPLASH man Joey Cangelosi on drums. However, both Terry Butler and Bill Andrews soon were back in the fold. MASSACRE got back into the studio on November 9th 1990 to put down six songs for the 'Second Coming' demo. Distributed to a variety of labels, this session met with an offer from UK label Earache Records.

MASSACRE's album inauguration, 'From Beyond', was offered up in July 1991, comprising nine tracks with the first pressing curiously also hosting a single track 7" single of the song 'Provoked Accurser'. Now afforded international exposure, the band's qualities, Kam Lee's commandeering inhuman roar and Rick Rozz's mechanical riffing, set them apart. With the genre still writhing in its birth pangs, 'From Beyond', constructed at Morrissound Studios in Tampa Florida and helmed by British producer Colin Richardson, bridged the gap between Thrash and what was rapidly being recognised as a whole new species—Death Metal.

The band's first European tour, now with second guitarist Steve Swanson, saw Texan's DEVASTATION and German act MORGOTH supporting. The 1992 EP 'Inhuman Condition' featured a version of VENOM's 'Warhead' that include singer Cronos on vocals.

MASSACRE toured Europe in 1993 on a package bill with GRAVE and DEMOLITION HAMMER. Upon their return the band folded with Rozz creating MINDSWEEP.

For July 1996's 'Promise' reformation album, actually recorded at Wolf's Head Studio some two years earlier, MASSACRE drafted in two new members bassist Pete Sison and drummer Syrus Peters. Unfortunately the record, a lethargic sub-Gothic affair complete with a curious rendering of CONCRETE BLONDE's 'Bloodletting' with guest vocals from Christine Whitten, signalled a radical shift away from the band's former glories and would be savaged by fans and media alike. The band struggled on, pulling in vocalist / guitarist Kenny Goodwin, but would soon collapse in contrition.

Lee's industries would be felt across the Florida scene and by 2000 the frontman had created a swathe of acts including KAULDRON, CADAVERIZER, URIZEN and SOUL SKINNER. Announced in April 2006, both vocalist Kam Lee and bassist Terry Butler were revealed to have formed retro Thrash / Death Metal combo DENIAL FIEND, co-assembled by an elite cast comprising guitarist Sam Williams, previously with DOWN BY LAW, and erstwhile NASTY SAVAGE drummer Curt Beeson. In December Kam Lee unveiled plans to release the previously vaulted MASSACRE album 'Second Coming'. Further projects were announced for Lee in early 2007 including working with Matt Olivo of REPULSION on a project called MONSTERSHOCK and adding guest studio vocals to recordings from HATEPLOW.

In April Kam Lee announced a MASSACRE reunion European tour, the band unit comprising Lee, guitarist Steve Swanson, bassist Terry Butler plus DENIAL FIEND members Sam Williams on guitar and Curt Beeson on drums. Only material from 'From Beyond' and 'Inhuman Condition' was aired and Lee was forthright in his objection to any involvement from former colleague Rick Rozz.

Aggressive Tyrant, Massacre (1986) (Demo). Aggressive Tyrant / Death In Hell / Mutilated.

Chambers Of Ages, Massacre (1986) (Demo). Chamber Of Ages / Clangor Of War / From Beyond / Symbolic Immortality.

Provoked, Earache (1989) (Free single with 'From Beyond' LP). Provoked / Accurser.

Second Coming, Massacre (1990) (Demo). Second Coming / Bleed To Death / Devouring Hour / By Reason Of Insanity / Mangled / Psychopain Trip.

FROM BEYOND, Earache MOSH 027 (1991). Dawn Of Eternity / Cryptic Realms / Biohazard / Chamber Of Ages / From Beyond / Defeat Remains / Succubus / Symbolic Immortality / Corpsegrinder.

Inhuman Conditions, Earache MOSH 060T (1992). Inhuman Conditions / Plains Of Insanity / Warhead / Provoked Accurser.

PROMISE, Earache MOSH96 (1996). Nothing / Forever Torn / Black Soil Nest / Promise / Bitter End / Bloodletting / Unnameable / Where Dwells Sadness / Suffering / Inner Demon.

MASTER

CHICAGO, IL, USA — *Paul Speckmann (vocals / bass), Chris Mittelbrun (guitar), Bill Schmidt (drums).*

Chicago's MASTER is but one of the outlets, alongside solo work and DEATHSTRIKE, utilised by Death Metal genius Paul Speckmann. As a vocalist, Speckmann, who had also donated his lungpower to the track 'Forbidden Evil' by Doom combo WAR CRY on the 'Metal Massacre IV' compilation, is able to pour more genuine venomous rage into his vocals than perhaps any other.

As a student, Speckmann's inaugural band at Forest View High School in Arlington Heights was titled WHITE CROSS, this unit featuring a latter day THRUST guitarist Ron Cooke. Speckmann took the lead vocal role in this fledgling act but opted out to pursue bass guitar. In 1982 he joined forces with guitarist Steve Ahlers, second guitarist Marty Fitzgerald, vocalist Rich Rozek plus drummer Joe Iaccino to forge WAR CRY.

Speckmann later formed up the revised WAR CRY rhythm section alongside drummer Bill Schmidt. This pairing, inspired towards a greater degree of aggression apparently due to an airing of VENOM's 'In League With Satan' single, broke away to establish the first proto-organisation of MASTER. This title had been suggested by WITCHSLAYER bassist Rick Manson as a nod of deference to BLACK SABBATH's 'Master Of Reality'.

After failing to secure a suitable guitarist to complete the band, Schmidt drifted off to join the ranks of MAYHEM. Undaunted, Speckmann pulled in TRANSGRESSOR guitarist Chris Mittlebrun to forge DEATH STRIKE, utilising the original MASTER material. This group was rounded out by sixteen year old second guitarist Kirk Miller and drummer John Leprich. DEATH STRIKE cut the 'Fuckin' Death' demo at Open Reel Studios in Lynwood in January 1985, after which Bill Schmidt was re-enrolled on drums. Miller exited too and the MASTER title was adopted once again that July.

The band was embroiled in internal tensions even as it got off the starting blocks. Signing to the Combat label MASTER entered the Seagrapes recording studio to lay down seven tracks for a debut album the following year. Speckmann financed this operation himself, having come into an inheritance from his late father. However, in the midst of these sessions the band broke up and the album was shelved. Conjecture has often pointed the finger of blame towards then manager Kim Fowley's reluctance to accept a five album deal with little advance. This misfortune did not prevent the unmixed tapes leaking onto the underground tape trading market though and before long the name MASTER was being revered across North America and Europe. Another tape circulated would be a rehearsal set recorded by DEVESTATION's Troy Dixler including non album tracks 'Rabid Anger' and 'Live For Free'.

Mittlebrun would join SINDROME and Alex Olvera from ASSAULT was inducted. Combat Records offered a new deal, for an EP release, but once again Fowley re-structured the contract to such a degree the label withdraw the offer. MASTER folded but reformed with the Speckmann/Schmidt/Mittlebrun axis for a one off concert at The Warehouse in Chicago. A tape of this show was widely circulated.

The four song 'Nuke 'Em' demo arrived in 1988. MASTER finally got product into the public domain 1990, the German Nuclear Blast label issuing a split 7" single in collaboration with ABOMINATION. The full-length album of that featured a rendition of BLACK SABBATH's 'Children Of The Grave'. The group was beset by internal problems though. The first draft of 'Master' had featured Jim Martinelli on guitar and Aaron Nickeas on drums but was rejected by the label. Speckmann drew on his erstwhile colleagues Mittelbrun and Schmidt to re-record the entire album.

MASTER's second album, 1991's 'On The Seventh Day God Created... Master', recorded at Morrisound Studios in Tampa by Scott Burns and again put out via Nuclear Blast, features drummer Aaron Nickeas and guest guitar by CYNIC and DEATH man Paul Masvidal, original guitarist Chris Mittelbrun having left for pastures new in SINDROME, a later incarnation of fellow Chicago act DEVESTATION. John Tardy of OBITUARY donated guest vocals to the tracks 'Submerged In Sin' and 'Latitudinarian'. Speckmann released an eponymous solo album almost simultaneously with MASTER's sophomore outing. As it transpired, this set was in fact the original, rejected 'Master' session.

Third effort 'Collection Of Souls' was delivered in 1993. However, MASTER then lost their deal and the next set of tracks was delivered as 'The Final Word' demo in 1995. Moonlight Records put out a split EP, shared with EXCISION, the following year. Fresh label deals were secured for a 1998 album 'Faith Is In Season', SPV Records in Germany issuing the record with a different cover for Europe as opposed to the US edition on Pavement Music.

2000 found Speckmann united with Skull and Christopher from the Czech Republic's KRABATHOR for the MARTYR project and the resulting 'Murder: The End Of The Game' album. MASTER returned in 2001 with the EP 'Follow Your Savior'.

MASTER's long neglected debut record would finally see public airing in 2003, some eighteen years after its initial recording, courtesy of the From Beyond Productions label. In addition to the 1985 tracks this release added three songs from a 1991 demo plus the bonus 'Cut Through The Filth', previously available on the compilation 'Death Is Just The Beginning II'. The reconstituted MASTER formed up a package billing of LIVIDITY, MASTIC SCUM and DAMNABLE for European touring in March of 2003. Bill Schmidt also forged an unlikely alliance with Glam Rock band DIAMOND REXX that same month.

MASTER, OBITUARY and VISCERAL BLEEDING teamed up for the 'The Legends Are Back' dubbed European tour, commencing in early October of 2004. That same year it was learned that former guitarist Chris Mittelbrun has resurfaced as "Mick Mars" in the Chicago based MÖTLEY CRÜE tribute band dubbed THE CRÜE.

In 2004 Californian gore Metal band EXHUMED revealed they had included a rendition of the MASTER song 'Pay To Die' on their covers album entitled 'Regurgitated Requiems: Garbage Daze Re-Regurgitated'. Meantime, MASTER issued 'The Spirit Of The West' album, this session recorded in just four days by Speckmann, guitarist Alex '93' Nejezchleba and drummer Zdenek Pradlovsky.

To open 2006 the band hooked up with RESURRECTURIS, GOREFEST and LUNAFIELD for 'The Glorious Dead: European Exorcism' European tour set to commence 16th February in Holland. However, in late January the headline band pulled the entire tour. The band soon got back in the fray and, alongside ZUUL FX, supported IMPALED NAZARENE's European tour in May 2006. Further European dates set for October were to see TEMPLE OF BRUTALITY and Denmark's SUBMISSION as openers. However, this tour was cancelled shortly before kick off.

In 2007 Displeased Records re-issued MASTER's first two albums, 'Master', adding previously omitted guitar solos and different drums, and 'On the 7th day God Created Master'. A brand new album, 'Slaves To Society', was released on May 11th via Twilight-Vertrieb. The album was recorded at Shaark Studios in Bzenec in the Czech Republic by Paul Speckmann, guitarist Alex Nejezchleba and drummer Zdenek Pradlovsky.

Nuke 'em, Master (1988) (Demo). Nuke 'em / Grim Reality / Most Wanted / Loser.
MASTER, Nuclear Blast NB 040 (1990). Pledge Of Alliance / Unknown Soldier / Mangled Dehumanisation / Pay To Die / Funeral Bitch / Master / Children Of The Grave / Terrorizer / The Truth / Pledge Of Alliance (Original mix) / Re-Entry And Destruction / Terrorizer (Original mix).
AND ON THE 7th DAY GOD CREATED MASTER, Nuclear Blast NB 054CD (1992). What Kind Of God / Latitudinarian / Heathen / Used / Demon / Constant Quarrel / Judgement Of Will / America The Pitiful / Whose Left To Decide / Submerged In Sin.
The Final Word, Master (1995) (Demo). Where Are You Now? / Final word / Prepare For The Fall.
Master / Excision, Moonlight (1996) (Split EP with EXCISION). Cast The First Stone / Fatso / Antidote.
FAITH IS IN SEASON, Pavement (1998). Follow Jesus / Cast The First Stone / Addicted To The Pistol / Imprisoned / Re-Terrorizer / Were About To Fall / Believers Have A Choice / Faith Is Still In Season / Broken Promise / Where Are You Now ? / Butchered By Numbers / Antidote / Spiritual Bankruptcy / Victims Of Jesus / Return To Vietnam / Previously Committed.
LET'S START A WAR, System Shock (2002). Cast One Vote / American Freedom / Miss Misery / Dictators / Lets Start A War / Protégé / Every Dog Has Its Day / Command Your Fate / Purchase A New Handgun / Watch What You Wish For / Disturbed.
UNRELEASED 1985 ALBUM, From Beyond Productions (2003). Master / Unknown Soldier / Mangled Dehumanization / Funeral Bitch / Terrorizer / Pledge Of Allegiance / Re-Entry And Destruction / Constant Quarrel / Judgement Of Will / Submerged In Sin / Cut Through The Filth.
THE SPIRIT OF THE WEST, System Shock (2004). You'll Be Blamed / The Serpent's Tongue / Rites Of Life / Envy / Sign Up / Another Day In Phoenix / Whatever, Wherever, Forever / The Gold Mine / The Perfect Family / Pistols, Whiskey, Coyotes / Long Knives / Ring Of Fire.
FOUR MORE YEARS OF TERROR, Twilight Vertrieb (2005). Race To Extinction / Shoot To Kill / All We've Become / Does One Feel The Pain / Betrayal / Hell Probably Win / Can The Us Be So Great / Lined Up And Punished / Blind Hatred / Line To Kill / Special Skills / To Fight And Die / Everything Is Rotten.
SLAVES TO SOCIETY, Twilight Vertrieb (2007). The Darkest Age / The Final Skull / The Room With Views / Slaves To Society / World Police / In Control / Remnants Of Hate / Anarchy Nearly Lost / Beaten For The Possibility / The Last Chapter / Cheater.

MASTIC SCUM

AUSTRIA — *Will (vocals), Harry (guitar), Steff (bass), Man (drums).*

Grindcore outfit MASTIC SCUM, founded in 1992, debuted the following year with the 'Ephemeral Cerebral Butchery' 12" single. The band has issued split singles with BLOCKHEADS and the 1996 'Riot' EP with Czech's MALIGNANT TUMOUR. Another split outing that year, the 'Fake' album in union with FLESHLESS, saw the band covering the DEAD KENNEDY's 'A Child And His Lawnmower'.

In 1997 drummer Man began doubling up his duties joining BELPHEGOR. A 1997 tape, 'Pure', was shared with MIXOMATOSIS and the following year a further tape 'Hurt', featuring live recordings, was issued in collaboration with SENSELESS. That same year MASTIC SCUM allied themselves with Japan's infamous C.S.S.O. for a split EP for the Ohne Maulkorb Productions label, the Austrians donating a crop of cover versions from the likes of DOCTOR AND THE CRIPPENS, RIGHTEOUS PIGS, UNSEEN TERROR and ELECTRO HIPPIES. A third split cassette, 'Reek' shared with Spain's HAEMORRHAGE, arrived in 2001.

MASTIC SCUM formed up a package billing of LIVIDITY, MASTER and DAMNABLE for European touring in March of 2003. US shows in 2004 to promote the 'Scars' album saw the band putting in a brief burst of August gigs partnered with LIVIDITY followed by an appearance at the 'Central Illinois Metalfest'. The band entered Recordable Studios in December 2004 to cut the album 'Mind'.

Ephemeral Cerebral Butchery EP, Rodel (1993).
Riot EP, Epidemie (1996) (Split single with MALIGNANT TUMOUR). Political Shit / A Load Of Koky / The Human Scum / Rock Out With Your Cock Out.
Fear EP, Stuhlgang (1996) (Split single with BLOCKHEADS).
Riot EP, Stuhlgang (1996) (Split single with MALIGNANT TUMOUR).

Rape EP, Ohne Maulkorb Productions (1998) (Split single with C.S.S.O..

ZERO, Noise Variations (1999). Inhume / Filthkick / I Need A Spliff / Demand The Change / Overdose / L.O.W. / Deaf, Dumb & Blind / Emotive Synergy / Blood Effusion / Arouse Suspicion / Kill The Mute / What In The World? / Lust For Life / Deep Shit / Fuck Authority / Suckass / Exhume.

CRAP, Cudgel Agency CUD 0016 (2002) (Split album with ROTTEN SOUND).

SCAR, Cudgel Agency CUD 021 (2002). Face To Face / Distance To The Truth / Re-progression / The Daily Grind / To Die Is Not Enough / One Track Minded / Turn Inside Out / Liar / The Generation X / Self Respect / Kiss Or Kill / Eyesolation.

MIND, Cudgel Agency (2005).

MAUSOLEUM

PA, USA — *Rick Boast (vocals / drums), Phil Newbaker (guitar), Adam Kegg (guitar), Rob Yench (bass).*

MAUSOLEUM are Pennsylvanian Gore-mongers forged by erstwhile members of NECROTOMIE and INCANTATION. Bassist Rob Yench has prior credits with INCANTATION, EXILE and MORPHEUS DESCENDS with drummer / vocalist Rick Boast having ties to both INCANTATION and NECROTOMIE whilst guitarists Phil Newbaker and Adam Kegg are also NECROTOMIE veterans. Kegg has further affiliation with RENNIS. Signing to Razorback Records the band delivered 'Cadaveric Displays Of Ghoulish Ghastliness' in 2003, this outing including a cover of AUTOPSY's 'Destined To Fester'.

MAUSOLEUM entered the recording studios in June of 2004 to cut their sophomore opus 'Back From The Funeral'. The band would also contribute music to the soundtrack of the Terry King directed Horror flick 'The Brainiac' starring actors Lisa Billhime and Joe Hansard, a remake of the 1961 cult Mexican film 'El Baron del Terror'. Also in the works would be a split offering with MACHETAZO.

CADAVERIC DISPLAYS OF GHOULISH GHASTLINESS, Razorback (2003). Flesh Fiends / Entombed In The Womb / Absolution For The Living Dead / Cadaveric Displays Of Ghoulish Ghastliness / Regurgitated Rebirth / Mortal Extinction / Horrifying World Of Disembodied Souls / Tombs Of The Blind Dead / Destined To Fester.

MAZE OF TORMENT

STRÄNGNÄS, SWEDEN — *Erik Sahlstrom (vocals), Magnus Lindvall (guitar), Rickard Dahlin (guitar), Cloffe Caspersson (bass), Kjell Enblom (drums).*

A Strängnäs Death Metal act named after a MORBID ANGEL song and showing plenty of renaissance Thrash influences. Originally titled TORMENT upon the band's formation in 1994 by former HARMONY members drummer Kjell Enblom and guitarist Peter 'Flesh' Karlsson, the latter also holding EMBRYO and THE MORTICIAN DEAD credentials. The duo was soon joined by VINTERLAND guitarist Pehr Larsson.

The trio, still operating under the name HARMONY, recorded a demo which came to the attention of Deviation Records based in Scotland. Previously, HARMONY debuted with the January 1993 demo tape 'Blood Angels', following this with 'Until I Dream' that October then 'The Radiance From A Star' in 1994. The Arctic Serenades label issued a split album 'The Radiance From A Star', recorded in December 1994 at Studio Skyline, shared with SERENADE during 1995. The band then switched titles to TORMENT for a three track demo. Upon signing to Corrosion Records the band title became MAZE OF TORMENT for the 1996 album 'The Force' produced by EDGE OF SANITY's Dan Swanö. The band line-up at this juncture comprising of vocalist / bassist Pehr Larsson, guitarist Peter Karlsson and drummer Kjell Enblom. Shortly after the release of 'The Force' a deal was struck with Thomas Nyqvist's Iron Fist Productions for the sophomore outing 'Faster Disaster'. Peter Janssen took over bass duties as Larsson concentrated on his lead vocal role.

Larsson would be replaced by Erik Sahlstrom of SERPENT OBSCENE and THE MARBLE ICON. Jansson too lost his place to Kalle Sjodin. MAZE OF TORMENT's 2000 album 'Death Strikes', released by the American Necropolis label, was produced by Jocke Pettersson.

MAZE OF TORMENT would be back for another round in March 2002 with the Necropolis released 'The Unmarked Graves'. Included would be a cover version of MISFITS 'All Hell Breaks Loose'. However, by the close of the year the band severed ties with Necropolis and signed 'The Unmarked Graves', complete with new cover art, over to Hellspawn Records. Singapore based label Konqueror Records would also weigh in with a compilation of archive HARMONY material. During 2002 Karlsson fired up side project THE MORTICIAN DEAD, this unit evolving into DECEIVER.

The group suffered line-up changes in early 2004 as both Peter Karlsson and Kalle Sjödin took their leave, bowing out with a performance at the 'Inferno' festival in Norway. Karlsson duly prioritised DECEIVER. MAZE OF TORMENT signed to Black Lodge Records in June 2004. Cutting a new album, 'Hammers Of Mayhem', the membership was built back up to strength with the acquisition of guitarist Viktor Hemgren, of LUCIEN, MÅNEGARM and SORG, second guitarist Rickard Dahlin, also ex-SORG, and bassist Cloffe Caspersson, a seasoned campaigner of acts such as VEINS OF SUFFERING, QUILMESS and AFTERBURNERZ plus being a familiar voice as DJ on Stockholm's Rockklassiker. The band introduced new guitarist Magnus Lindvall, of SOILS OF FATE, in June 2005.

Billed as FLESH, ex-MAZE OF TORMENT guitarist Peter Karlsson recorded a solo album, 'Dödsångest', that same year on Gothenburg label Iron Fist Productions. In 2006 he allied with DECEIVER bassist Crille Lundin to formulate THROWN for a debut album, entitled 'The Suicidal Kings Occult'.

MAZE OF TORMENT cut the 'Hidden Cruelty' album tracks in September 2006 with producer Berno Paulsson at Berno Studios in Malmö.

THE FORCE, Corrosion CR 6-503-2 (1996). Shapeless In The Dark / Dream Of Blood / Souls Been Left To Die / The Force / Brave The Blizzard / Battle Of The Dead / The Last Candle / Land Unknown.

FASTER DISASTER, Iron Fist Productions (1999). The Reality / Five Inch / Dead Soul / Horror Visions / Ancient Treasure / Faster Disaster / The Devil's Kill / Hide The Light / Bite The Dust.

DEATH STRIKES, Necropolis NR056CD (2000). Death Strikes / Sodomizing Death Spell / Intense Slaughter / This Is Death / Aggressive Bloodhunt / The Infernal Force / The Sadist / Angels From Hell / The Evil Beneath The Flames.

THE UNMARKED GRAVES, Hellspawn (2003). The Evil Remains The Same / Satan Descends / The Unmarked Graves / 13th Disciple / Fortress Of Doom / Demons Rape / Void Of Pain / Enter The Holocaust / Burn Till Death / Blinded By Illusions / Formula XXX / All Hell Breaks Loose.

HAMMERS OF MAYHEM, Black Lodge BLOD 016CD (2005). Beyond The Infernal Gates / F.O.E. (Face Of Evil) / Hammers Of Mayhem / Dead Cold Blood / Servants Of Menace / Into The Bloodswarm / Tyrannizer / The Dead Temple Prayer / Dead Soul / Catharsis / In League With Satan.

HIDDEN CRUELTY, Black Lodge (2007). Breach The Wall / This Vision / Terminate-Obliterate / A Few More Bullets / Hidden Cruelty / The Icons Burden / Death Inhaled / Day Of Passing / Dead Run / he Chasms Flame.

MEATHOLE INFECTION

MONTGOMERY, AL, USA — *Ryan (vocals), Jerm (guitar), Edirol (drums).*

Montgomery, Alabama old school Death Metal band. MEATHOLE INFECTION issued the demo 'Meathole Infection' in June 2006. For 2007 the band announced a whole slew of planned releases, amongst which would be a four way split effort on Triple Penetration Records shared with LINCOLN LOVE LOG, FETUS OMELET and EMBALMED, A split CD-R on Frog Noise allied with BOWEL FETUS, a release via Templar Records as a collaboration with Australia's DEATH IS EVERYTHING, A three way split on Dark Forest Productions with REEKER and RAW SEWAGE, a shared cassette by Bitter About Life with GRIMSBY plus further splits with HORAX, DESICATE, RISING TERROR and DEAD INHUMAN SCUM.

Meathole Infection, Meathole Infection (2006) (Demo). Wretched Rotissarie / Larvicide / Sluts Of The Grave / Pest Infested Rot.

MEGASLAUGHTER

SWEDEN — MEGASLAUGHTER, formed in 1987, was initially known as DINLOYD. Their first demo as MEGASLAUGHTER, 'Death Remains' surfaced in 1989 and garnered the band a deal with French label Thrash Records. After one album MEGASLAUGHTER split in 1992, with vocalist Emil Lilic resurfacing in 1997 fronting MURDER CORPORATION, a project band assembled by members of DERANGED that released the 'Blood Revolution 2050' album. In 1998 both Emil Ilic and Kenneth Arnestedh were to be found in CONCRETE MASS. Former MEGASLAUGHTER bass player Alex Räfling and guitarist Emil Ilic would both be found with the high profile 2003 Metal venture JAGGERNAUT.

Death Remains, (1990) (Demo). Death Remains / False Paradise / Left In Shreds.
Megaslaughter, (1991) (Demo). Intro / Face Of The Deep / Afflicted Flesh / Left In Shreds.
CALLS FROM THE BEYOND, Thrash THR010 (1991). Blood Runs Free / Raise The Dead / False Paradise / Shreds Left Behind / Death Remains / Into The Decay / Calls From The Beyond / Bloodshed.

MELANCHOLIC SEASONS

GERMANY — *Björn Hoppe (vocals), Andi Adler (guitar), Andi Henke (guitar), Alex Haus (bass), Thomas Adler (drums).*

Thrash Metal laced with Scandinavian style Death persuasions. MELANCHOLIC SEASONS came into being during 1995, the first four song demo citing a line up of lead vocalist Holger Jung, guitarists Daniel 'Jesus' Bracevac and Jean-Claude Rettig, bass player Christian 'Hirsel' Sieverding and with Guido Denk on the drums. Shortly after Andi Henke took the place of Rettig. A third demo, released in 1996, found Nico 'Satanas' Seim handling the bass with former BLASPHEMIA man Michael 'Hille' Hillenbrand taking the drum stool thereafter. Seim then decamped, forcing MELANCHOLIC SEASONS to gig minus bass for a period. In the summer of 1999 another BLASPHEMIA member, singer Björn Hoppe, enrolled. With this revised line up MELANCHOLIC SEASONS entered the recording studio to lay down the album 'In My Eyes'. To promote this product the band undertook a spate of club dates utilising Gerd Lücking, guitarist with COURAGOUS and drummer for LIGHTMARE, and former DEADSPAWN musician Dominik Mangelmann as stand in bassists. The band encountered further line up difficulties with the Bracevac usurped by Andi 'der General' Adler.

MELANCHOLIC SEASONS introduced Alex Haus on bass in December of 2002. Ex-bassist Gerd Lücking joined REBELLION as their new drummer in April of 2004. Thomas Adler would be installed as MELANCHOLIC SEASONS drummer that year.

IN MY EYES, (1999). In Your Eyes / This Is Your God / I Am The Evil / Frozen Lyrics / Just A Fuckin' Lullaby / Drowned In Tears.

MENTAL DEMISE

UKRAINE — *Old (vocals), Pinky (guitar), Fester (guitar), Toukan (bass), Tom Grinder (drums).*

Lugansk brutal Death Metal act MENTAL DEMISE forged as a trio comprising vocalist / guitarist Fester, bassist Toukan and drummer Tom Grinder. The band released the 1997 rehearsal recording 'Utopia Of Existence' followed by a February 1998 demo 'Psycho-Penetration', these sessions seeing Old taking lead vocal chores. Second guitarist Pinky was inducted in March of 1998 for gigs in support of this tape.

For the 2000 promotion EP 'Credo Quia Absurdum..?', recorded in the quite unique surroundings of Vaginal Suckers Studios, the group comprised vocalist Old, guitarists Fester and Pinky, bassist S. Vitkovsky and drummer Tom Grinder. The 'Psycho-Penetration' tracks would subsequently be re-issued as a split cassette shared with MENTALITY whilst 'Credo Quia Absurdum..?' saw a re-release on CD shared with ENTRAILS PUTREFACTION in 2001. Live work to push this offering saw MENTAL DEMISE united with Poles HATE for a run of Belarus gigs in November of 2001. Baltus Hash became the group's new bass player shortly after. 'Psycho-Penetration' witnessed a second re-release in 2002 as a cassette shared with DATURA.

Having wrapped up recording for a proposed album 'Disgraceful Sores' MENTAL DEMISE formed up part of an extreme Metal package dubbed 'Grind de Pologne-2' for Polish dates in April of 2003. These shows had the band partnered up with IMPERIAL FOETICIDE, EPITOME, DECAPITATED, DEFORMED, MASTECTOMIA, PATOLOGICUM and ANAL STENCH. The group toured Poland with MINCING FURY AND GUTTURAL CLAMOUR OF QUEER DECAY, PARRICIDE and INCARNATED during November 2005.

Credo Quia Absurdum..?, Moon (2000). Spiritual Atavism—Absurd / Collective Obtrusive Neurosis / Senseless Saint (Prophet-Mattoid).
CREDO QUIA ABSURDUM...?, D.A.C. Productions DAC 017 CD (2001) (Split album with ENTRAILS PUTREFACTION). Spiritual Atavism-Absurd / Collective Obtrusive Neurosis / Senseless Saint (Prophet-Mattoid).

MENTAL HOME

MOSCOW, RUSSIA — *Sergey Dmitriev (vocals / guitar), Denis Samusev (bass), Michael Smirnoff (keyboards), Igor Dmietriev (drums).*

Moscow Death Metal act formed in November 1993. The original MENTAL HOME line-up comprised of the two Dmitriev siblings, vocalist / guitarist Sergey and drummer and keyboard player Igor. Also involved was lead guitarist Roman Povarov and bass player Denis Samusev. Taking an atmospheric Doomladen Death Metal approach the quartet released their inaugural demo session 'Funeral Service' in January of 1994.

Shortly after, the MENTAL HOME returned to the studio and in July of the same year 'Mirrorland' was issued by the domestic Metal Agen concern, soon selling out of its initial 5'000 run.

A setback occurred when Povarov injured his hand in an accident. The guitarist shifted over to keyboards to accommodate his disability and MENTAL HOME drafted Sergey Kalachov for the 'Vale' outing. This album would see a release through Morbid Noizz. Quite spectacularly the album actually sold out after a few months and hit the number one position in the Russian Metal charts.

Despite this upward turn in the bands fortunes Povarov departed. Michael 'Maiden' Smirnoff took not only the vacant keyboard position but also became MENTAL HOME's business manager.

In March of 1997 the band retired to the studio completing the 'Black Art' album by June. With MENTAL HOME's profile riding high the first brace of albums were also reissued.

The bands progress had not gone unnoticed outside of Russia and American based The End Records engineered a deal with the band to release 'Vale' and 'Black Art'.

MIRROR LAND, (1995).
VALE, The End TE001 (1998). Stranger Dove / Southern Calm Waters / Aevin's Cave / The Euphoria / The Vale / My Necklace / Christmas Mercy / Their Finest Voyage.
BLACK ART, The End TE006 (1998). Under The Wing / The Plague Omen / Into The Realms Of Marena / Silent Remembrance / In The Shades Of Inspiration / Pagan Freedom / Winter Art / On A Hand Of The Universe / Tides Of Time.

MENTAL HORROR

UPON THE SHORES OF INNER SEAS, The End (2000). Downstairs / Late To Revise / Eternal Moan / Bliss / Against My Will / Breakdown / Stained / Amidst The Waves '99.

MENTAL HORROR

PORTO ALEGRE, RS, BRAZIL — *Claudio Cardoso (vocals / bass), Adriano Martini (guitar), Robles Dresch (drums).*

MENTAL HORROR formed in 1993 treading the path of a traditional Death Metal band. A demo cassette emerged some two years later after which the band underwent a series of line up changes resulting in only one founder member, vocalist / bassist Claudio Cardoso, remaining by 1997. In September of that year the band was rounded out by the inauguration of guitarist Adriano Martini and drummer Robles Dresch, this new unit bowing in with the February 1998 demo 'Extreme Evolutive Trauma', quickening their pace into a terrifyingly fast speed- Death machine. The sheer extremes MENTAL HORROR achieved with this release generated praise and sizable sales for the tape internationally.

MENTAL HORROR's next move was to cut a split album with QUEIRON for Brazil's Mutilation label. In August of 2001 the full length debut 'Proclaiming Vengeance' was recorded for the Death Vomit label, a subsidiary of Necropolis Records. The album emerged in Europe, complete with bonus tracks, through the Dutch Displeased concern. 'Abyss Of Hypocrisy' followed in September of 2004.

EXTREME EVOLUTIVE TRAUMA, Death Vomit (2000). Intro Of Vengeance / Burning Alive / Genocidal Inquisition / Black Spiritual Void / Rising For Chaos / Screams Of Tiamat / Fragellum Forms / Anguish Seas / Tortured (Bleeding For The Plague) / Profane Spawn / Proclaiming Vengeance.

PROCLAIMING VENGEANCE, Death Vomit D-00103 (2002). Intro Of Vengeance / Burning Alive / Genocidal Inquisition / Black Spiritual Void / Rising From Chaos / Screams Of Tiamat / Flagellum Forms / Anguish Seas / Tortured / Profane Spawn / Proclaiming Vengeance / Burning Alive / Genocidal Inquisition.

ABYSS OF HYPOCRISY, Displeased D-00131 (2004). Purification By Hallowed Flames / Destructor Of Temple / Scourge Of Beast / Angel Of Vengeance / Abyss Of Hypocrisy / Messenger / Vae Solis (Armageddon Song) / Shurpu Baragal / Reborn For Blasphemy / Gigim Xul / Crucify The Liar.

MERCENARY

AALBORG, DENMARK — *Henrik Andersen (vocals / bass), Nikalai Brinkmann (guitar), Rasmus Jacobsen (drums).*

Founded in Aalborg during 1991 as a Thrash act MERCENARY would soon develop distinct Death Metal leanings by the time of their 1993 demo entitled 'Domicile'. Guitarist Nikalau Brinkman is ex-CROSSBONES whilst drummer Rasmus Jacobsen is an erstwhile member of HUMANATICUM. MERCENARY, fronted by Kral (real name Hans Henrik Andersen) would lose his sibling guitarist Jonne along the way but recorded further tracks for a limited demo recording 'Gummizild' produced by Bo Summer of ILLDISPOSED. One of these tracks would also surface on the compilation album 'Fuck You We're From Denmark—Vol. 3'.

MERCENARY's next move was to hook up with INVOCATOR man Jacob Hansen as producer for recording of a June 1996 EP 'Supremacy'. After an eight year term of service drummer Rasmus Jokobsen would lay down his sticks in April 2002. MERCENARY would form part of a package billing with CALLENISH CIRCLE and Ireland's PRIMORDIAL for a short run of gigs in the low countries during September. Meantime, former MERCENARY guitarist Mircea G. Eftemie announced his new band venture MNEMIC in alliance with INVOCATOR session drummer Brian Rasmussen.

MERCENARY parted ways with lead guitarist Signar Petersen in July 2003, the ex-member forging BROADMOOR, drafting the nineteen year old Martin Buus Pedersen as substitute. The departing guitarist duly founded TRANSPARENT, an alliance comprising the LOST, FAILED and LEMURIA credited vocalist Rene Pedersen, guitarist Danny Hove Jensen with Brian 'Brylle' Rasmusen of MNEMIC on drums.

MERCENARY undertook a short burst of Danish dates in March of 2004 allied with Prog Metal band EVERGREY. In the Summer Anders Høeg and Mikkel Sandager announced the formation of a new Thrash project in union with INVOCATOR drummer Jakob Gundel.

MERCENARY signed to the Century Media record label in June for their fourth album, the Jacob Hansen produced '11 Dreams'. It contained a cover of KENT's hit single 'Music Non Stop'. The band would be chosen, alongside fellow Scandinavian acts THE HAUNTED, MNEMIC, HATESPHERE, RAUNCHY, MELTED, BLINDFAULT and STOMPED, to form up the "Nordic Threat" show for the Popkomm 2004 music convention at the Silver Wings in Berlin on 29th September. Subsequent gigs saw further supports to EVERGREY.

During September 2005 MERCENARY partnered with Germany's DEW-SCENTED and US headline act NEVERMORE for European touring. Mikkel Sandager made studio time to guest session on German Hardcore band MAROON's 'When Worlds Collide' album. The group parted ways with Henrik Andersen in March 2006 but by mid the following month still wrapped up recordings for the album 'The Hours That Remain'. Newly introduced to cover bass would be René Pedersen, of LOST, LEMURIA, FAILED and TRANSPARENT.

In June MERCENARY keyboard player Morten Sandager hooked up with PRETTY MAIDS for a brace of shows including the German 'Bang Your Head' festival. Released in August, 'The Hours That Remain' entered the Danish charts at number 67. The record, once again produced by Jacob Hansen, featured studio guests SOILWORK's Björn Strid and HEAVEN SHALL BURN's Marcus Bischoff.

Mikkel Sandager would participate in an "all star" performance at the 'ProgPower' event at Earthlink Live in Atlanta during September, headed up by noted Norwegian vocalist JORN LANDE, involving Zak Stevens of CIRCLE II CIRCLE and ex-SAVATAGE, Lance King of PYRAMAZE, Michele Luppi from VISION DIVINE, Pasi Rantanen of THUNDERSTONE, Michael Eriksen from CIRCUS MAXIMUS and guitarist Mattias "IA" Eklundh of FREAK KITCHEN.

At the Danish Metal Awards 2006, held on November 18th at the Amager Bio venue in Copenhagen, the band landed the honours for 'Album of the Year' with 'The Hours That Remain'. The band had the tracks 'Lost Reality' and 'Eleven Dreams' included on the 'ProgPower USA VIII' DVD compilation in 2007.

... **Domicile**, Mercenary (1993) (Demo). Ignorance / Premature

Burial / Battle Thy Demons / Obscurity / Induration Of Sorrow.

Gummizild, Mercenary (1994) (Demo). One-Eyed Beast / Gateaway / Hour Of Grief (Rehearsal version).

Supremacy, Black Day BDR 001 (1996). Supremacy / Hour Of Grief / One-Eyed Beast / Premature Burial.

FIRST BREATH, Serious Entertainment SE011CD (1998). Symbiotic / World Wide Weep / Horizon / Master Game / Perceptive / Graveart / Next To Nothing / Demon8 / Watching Me / Alternative Ways / Sister Jane / Supremacy.

EVERBLACK, Hammerheart HHR118 (2002). Intro / Everblack / Seize The Night / Screaming From The Heavens / Dead.com / Darkspeed / Bloodrush / A Darker Shade Of Black / Bulletblues / Rescue Me / Alliance—Outro.

11 DREAMS, Century Media 77496-2 (2004). Into The Sea Of Dark Desires / World Hate Center / 11 Dreams / Redestructdead / Firesoul / Sharpen The Edges / Supremacy v2.0 / Music Non Stop / Falling / Times Without Changes / Loneliness.

11 DREAMS, Avalon Marquee MICP-10480 (2004) (Japanese release). Into The Sea Of Dark Desires / World Hate Center / 11 Dreams / Redestructdead / Firesoul / Sharpen The Edges / Supremacy v2.0 / Music Non Stop / Falling / Times Without Changes / Loneliness / 11 Dreams (3-D mix).

11 DREAMS, Century Media 8209-2 (2005) (USA release). Into The Sea Of Dark Desires / World Hate Center / 11 Dreams / Redestructdead / Firesoul / Sharpen The Edges / Supremacy v2.0 / Music Non Stop / Falling / Times Without Changes / 11 Dreams (3-D mix) / 11 Dreams (Radio edit).

THE HOURS THAT REMAIN, Century Media 8296-2 (2006). Redefine Me / Year Of The Plague / My World Is Ending / This Eternal Instant / Lost Reality / Soul Decision / Simplicity Demand / Obscure Indiscretion / My Secret Window / The Hours That Remain. Chart position: 67 DENMARK.

MERLIN

RUSSIA — *Mary Abaza (vocals / bass), Alex Ioffe (guitar), Arteom Nazarov (guitar), Nick Byckoff (drums).*

Female fronted Death Metal formation MERLIN convened in 1992 as a trio of Mary Abaza on bass and lead vocals, guitarist Alex Ioffe and drummer Nick Byckolff. Demos 'Welcome To Hell' and 'Prisoner Of Death' preceded the debut cassette album 'Deathroteque'. MERLIN would sign to the Canadian GWN label for an international release of sophomore outing 'They Must Die' in 1998. Hobgoblin Records would issue the album domestically. Second guitarist Arteom 'Bolt' Nazarov, ex-ANAL PUS, would augment MERLIN the same year.

MERLIN projected an album to be entitled 'Brutal Constructor' for 2003, this release containing a cover version of DEATH's 'Zombie Ritual'. Tragically drummer Nick Byckoff was killed in an auto accident on 13th July.

DEATHROTEQUE, (1996). They Must Die / Holder Of The War / Don't Try / I'm Glad / I Gotta Fall / That's My Time / Black Revenge / Die / Waiting For Death / Leave Me Alone.

THEY MUST DIE, (1998). Unburied / I Want Blood / They'll Never See / They Must Die / Entering The Gates Of Paradise / Don't Waste My Time / Let The Blood Spill / Sixth Victim / R.I.P.

MESS AGE

POLAND — *Rafal Kawalerowski (vocals), Alex Kopczynski (guitar), Sylwester Rybczyk (guitar), Andrzej Osmalek (bass), Dominik Kolodziejczak (drums).*

MESS AGE, formed by an alliance of erstwhile ALIENATOR and AGE CRISIS members, debuted with the October 1998 'Resurrection' tape. The opening line up saw MESS AGE employing both male and female lead vocals in Rafal Kawalerowski and Joanna Paszke backed up by the guitar pairing of Alex Kopczynski on lead and Sylwester Rybczyk on rhythm, bass player Andrzej 'Grooby' Osmalek and drummer Dominik Kolodziejczak.

Further demos, 'Fallen' and 'Reborn' followed in 1999 and 2000. That March the band participated in a package tour of Poland ranked alongside HATE and YATTERING. Subsequently the 'Reborn' tapes were issued as a split CD album through the Demonic label shared with SHADOWS LAND.

Festival appearances saw GHOST's Piotr 'Zvierzak' Kawalerowski standing in temporarily for regular bassist Andrzej Osmalek. However, Paszke quit before the close of the year to forge Thrash act ASBEEL. MESS AGE, opting not to replace her, committed to the November 'Darkzone' tour sharing the stage with YATTERING, SUPREME LORD, DECAPITATED and NYIA to round off 2000.

Conquer Records issued the debut album "Self Convicted' in May of 2002, promotion for which included UK dates. Nergal of BEHEMOTH would add guest vocals to the album track 'Kill The Falsehood'. Andrzej Osmalek joined DEAD BY DAWN in March 2003.

In April of 2003 Artur 'Marysia' Olkowicz, a former member of ADS NOCTEM and OBLIVION, took over the bass position. MESS AGE would be confirmed for an appearance at the UK London Camden Underworld 'London's Death' festival in June. Artur Olkowicz added to his duties by joining up with DEAD BY DAWN. In late 2004 the band united with TRAUMA, WOLFRIDER and TOXIC BONKERS for the Polish 'Divine Perdition' tour. Gigs across Poland in September 2005 saw an alliance with DEMISE.

SELF CONVICTED, Conquer CR004 (2002). Among The Empty Walls / Fulfilled With Nothing / Infected By Deflections / The EXIsTence DOOR / C.O.L.D. / Post Scriptum / Devoured With Famished Eyes / The Scarlet Rings / Kill The Falsehood / Waiting For Miracle.

METALLISK ESEL HIVES

UTSJOKI, FINLAND — *Fleshammer (vocals / rhythm guitar), Vörg (lead guitar), Goretal Carnallity (bass), Vyshüss (keyboards), Eulogy (drums).*

Utsjoki Black Metal band METALLISK ESEL HIVES comprises EXPERI-METAL vocalist / drummer Dàrvik, G-CLAD rhythm guitarist Fleshammer and the SHRAPNEL PILL duo of lead guitar player Vörg and bassist Goretal Carnallity. Formative versions of the band included singer Sven Ortel and drummer Gutburn. The December 2005 demo 'Misanthropic Dillusion In The Galant Chambers' included a cover version of MAYHEM's notorious 'Chainsaw Gutsfuck'. The band followed with the album 'Apni Bahen Day Doo Chudwanay Kay Liya Abb Mujhay'.

The promotional session 'INS[tr00]ME[n]TAL DEMO[n]' saw issue in July 2006.

In August METALLISK ESEL HIVES records the 'NITS' demo, a "mash" of BLACK SABBATH's 'N.I.B.' and NIRVANA's 'Smells Like Teen Spirit'. The album 'Scarred By The Strike From The Scepter Of Light' saw release that same month.

A third album, 'Metallisk Esel Hives III: The Stringore Chronicles' released in September 2006, hosted a cover version of OPETH's 'Demon Of The Fall'. That same month a split album, entitled '3 Floors Down', was issued in collaboration with G-CLAD.

Misanthropic Dillusion In The Galant Chambers, Metallisk Esel Hives (2005). Icycle Formation Of The Frost Bitten Apocalypse / Unholy Freezer Burn Of The Necro-Wolves / Scorn Messiah Draped Over A Seasoned Cross / Warriors Of The Arctic Allegiance / Chainsaw Gutsfuck.

APNI BAHEN DAY DOO CHUDWANAY KAY LIYA ABB MUJHAY, Crimson Finger (2005). Oil Merchants Of The Sandy Crest / Ali Barbarian & The 40 Thieving Arabs / The Turban Enchantment / Sandstorm Of The Entombed Devourment / Rotting Upon Crucifiction / Apni Bahen Day Doo Chudwanay Kay Liya Abb Mujhay / The Pentagonal Scriptures Of Ishtar.

INS[tr00]ME[n]TAL DEMO[n], Crimson Finger (2006) (Demo). 6 / VI / The Square Root Of . . . Four Squared Times Two Plus Eight Minus Two Squared.

N.I.T.S., Crimson Finger (2006) (Demo). N.I.T.S.

SCARRED BY THE STRIKE FROM THE SCEPTER OF LIGHT, Crimson Finger (2006). Impaled On The Spectrum Of Existence / Pulling The Strings That Twitch Immortality / Shattering The Pheared Martyr / Buried Deep Down The Dark Alley / Scarred By The Strike From The Scepter Of Light.

Scarred By The Strike From The Scepter Of Light, Crimson Finger (2006). Scarred By The Strike From The Scepter Of Light / VI / N.I.T.S. / Apni Bahen Day Doo Chudwanay Kay Liya Abb Mujhay / The Pentagonal Scriptures Of Ishtar.

Rehearsal, Crimson Finger (2006) (Rehearsal demo).

3 FLOORS DOWN, Crimson Finger (2006) (Split album with G-CLAD). Sewerpipe Bonger Part 1 (G-CLAD) / Holy Whore (G-CLAD) / G-Clad (G-CLAD) / Iraq, You Break (G-CLAD) / Usawma Beer Garden (G-CLAD) / A Bullet In The Head Is Worth Two In Bush (G-CLAD) / Taliban, Turban, Radioban (G-CLAD) / Terrorism Vs Errorism, The War For Oil (G-CLAD) / Track 9-11 (G-CLAD) / Speak English Or Die (G-CLAD) / Sewerpipe Bonger Pt 2/Bombin' The U.S. Of A. (G-CLAD) / The Pentagonal Scriptures Of Ishtar (METALLISK ESEL HIVES) / Oil Merchants Of The Sandy Crest (METALLISK ESEL HIVES) / Rotting Upon Crucifiction (METALLISK ESEL HIVES).

METALLISK ESEL HIVES III: THE STRINGORE CHRONICLES, Crimson Finger (2006). Intro / Pay For Your Sins / The Dragon's Mane / Avenge The Death / Bringer Of Death / Demon Of The Fall.

METANOIA

TOWNSVILLE, QLD, AUSTRALIA — *Yowie Smith (vocals), Steve Bennett (guitar), Lisa Bennett (bass), Dylan Speerstra (drums).*

Townsville, Queensland based Hardcore Christian, Extreme Death Metal. The band was founded by the Bennett's, guitarist Steve and bass player Lisa (a.k.a. 'Spud'), in the early 90's. In 1994 they recorded a demo called 'Screaming Fetus'. It was a very crude, six-song affair with an explicit cover which left little question as where the band stood on the abortion debate.

Townsville, Queensland based Christian Death Metal band. In 1995 METANOIS put out the 'Akeldema' demo, this established a deal with the Rowe Productions label and contributed four songs to a Rowe compilation release entitled 'Raise The Dead'. Later in the year the band released their debut, 'In Darkness Or In Light', recorded at St. Andrews Studio in Melbourne with MORTIFICATION's Steve Rowe acting as producer. Ian Northey replaced Speerstra on drums shortly after. Further line-up changes followed, Ian Waller from SCREAMS OF CHAOS now manning the drums, and a second album, 'Don't Walk Dead' again on the Rowe label, followed in 1996. For this outing METANOIA allied their Grind influences with choir, violin and even a didgeridoo supplied by Mark Jobst.

In 1998 yet a third album called, 'Time To Die' was released. Simon Pankhurst replaced Yowie Smith as lead vocalist.

Metanoia, (0). Death Of Death / Dead Flesh / Torn By Dogs / Decomposition & Reconstitution (Valley Of Dry Bones) / Ripped In Two / Screaming Fetus.

Akeldama, (1995). Akeldama / Death Of The Innocent / Valley Of Dry Bones / Eternal Destruction.

IN DARKNESS OR IN LIGHT, Rowe Productions ROWE 008 (1995). Acute Obliteration / Enslavement / In Darkness Or In Light / On And On / Dead Flesh / Dimensions Of Life / Son Of Man / Torn By Dogs / Death Of Death / Seventh Seal.

DON'T WALK DEAD, Rowe Productions ROWE 021 (1996). First The Kingdom / Pain / Don't Walk Dead / By His Word / The Blame / Yowie's Hilltop Adventure / Can You Feel It / Reflections / Grave Beyond A Slave / Threshold Of The Annihilation / Kneeling Before Your Throne / Never.

TIME TO DIE, Rowe Productions ROWE 024 (1998). Smashed / Paradise / Now Listen Up / Judge Me Not / Offensive / Time To Die / Corpses / Raped To Reality / Fade / Is To Be Free / Feeling the Fire / Blyth / Lucifer's Seductions.

MICTLAN

LUXEMBOURG — *Mars Dostert (vocals / guitar), Roland Flies (bass), Phil Kessel (drums).*

Melodic Death Metal band MICTLAN was forged in the summer of 1998 by vocalist guitarist Mars Dorstert and bassist Roland Flies, initially joined by guitarist Serge Thinnes and drummer Laurent Hartz. However, this pair lasted a matter of weeks and new drummer Thierry May was duly installed and in this formation MICTLAN debuted live on March 6th 1999. Expanding further, second guitarist Jhemp Even was added to the line-up. Further changes saw Phil Kessel taking over on drums. A demo arrived in early 1999. However, MICTLAN then folded.

Dostert, Flies and Kessel reunited a year later, drawing in Tom Bartholmé on guitar. Jhemp Even rejoined in August 2001, replacing Bartholmé. Both Roland Flies and Jhemp Even operate with Mertzig Power Metal band DREAMS OF NABID.

Mictlan, Mictlan (1999) (Demo). Touch The Sun / Emotions / Mictlan.

MIDIAN

HOLLAND — *Wilmar Taal (vocals), Mike Eijk (guitar), Adrian Rijkeboer (bass), Claudius de Wilde (drums).*

Zaanstad Death Metal act MIDIAN was constructed by erstwhile DELIRIUM, HEXENHAMMER and VLAMMENSEE guitarist Mike Eijk during 1992. Joining him would be singer Wilmar Taal, bass player Erwin Koolen and drummer Claudius de Wilde. However, within a matter of months Koolen was ousted. A 1993 demo, entitled 'War Beyond The Flesh', secured a deal with the Norwegian label Effigy Productions. Being joined at this juncture by bassist Adrian Rijkeboer MIDIAN cut the EP 'Sadistic And Obscene'. MIDIAN folded the following year.

Wilmar Taal has credits with a whole swathe of extreme Metal acts including DELIRIUM, CONSOLATION, ALHAZRED, PANIC, HEXENHAMMER, VLAMMENSEE, TRIPLESIX and THRONE OF DISEASE.

Sadistic And Obscene EP, Effigy Productions (1994).

MIDVINTER

SWEDEN — *Kheeroth (vocals), Damien (guitar / bass), Zathanel (drums).*

The debut album by Death Metallers MIDVINTER, 1997's 'At The Sight Of The Apocalypse Dragon', was produced by KING DIAMOND guitarist Andy La Rocque. The band, founded by a union of erstwhile FOGBOUND and APOLLGON members in 1993, first tested the waters with the 'Midvinternatt' demo. MIDVINTER's initial line-up comprised of vocalist Björn a.k.a. Vlad Morbius, guitarist Damien Midvinter and drummer Krille a.k.a. Kristeian of MELEK TAUS.

MIDVINTER's history now becomes cloudy. A proposed album recording, provisionally entitled 'Norrsken', was apparently curtailed when Damien and Krille came to blows the result of which that the drummer broke three ribs. Damien fled to Greece but was forced to return after suffering a motorbike accident. Supposedly after a short jail term he attempted to resurrect the band. An alliance was struck with BEWITCHED and NAGLFAR personnel Adde and Stolle although this version of MIDVINTER did not gel and the band folded. Unfortunately Björn, according to band sources, was subsequently admitted to a mental hospital.

MIDVINTER was resurrected in 1996 with new members ex-SETHERIAL vocalist Kheeroth (a.k.a. Tobias Fällström) and ex-SETHERIAL and member of SORHIN Zathanel (Anders Löfgren) on drums. Guest musicians on the album included DISSECTION's Jon Nödtveidt and former AT THE GATES and OXIPLEGATZ guitarist Alf Svensson.

Zathanel would later renew his SETHERIAL links founding BLACKWINDS for a 1999 EP in collaboration with his former band colleagues vocalist / guitarist Lord Kraath and drummer Lord Alastor Mysteriis.

Zathanel would also be operational with BLOT MINE alongside erstwhile SETHERIAL colleagues and, in alliance with Kheeroth and BLOT MINE personnel, VÅLNAD UR RYMD. Kheeroth guested in the studio on SORGHEGARD's 2004 'Wardemo' session.

AT THE SIGHT OF THE APOCALYPSE DRAGON, Invasion (1997). Dod Fodd / All Things To End Are Made / Moonbound / Hope Rides On Devils Wings / Dreamslave / Noctiluca In Aeturnum—Of Nights Primeval / Ett Liv Fornekat / De Vises Hymn.

MINAS TIRITH

JESSHEIM, NORWAY — *Frode Forsmo (vocals / bass), Stian Krabol (guitar), Tony Kirkemo (drums).*

Avant-garde black Metal act, titled after J.R.R. Tolkien's 'Lord Of The Rings' trilogy, founded in Jessheim during 1989 with Black persuasions combined with elements of Jazz, Doom and Death Metal. MINAS TIRITH bass guitarist Gottskalk (a.k.a. Frode Forsmo) also has connections with TULUS and OLD MAN'S CHILD.

The band's very first concert was as support to MAYHEM, RED HARVEST and DEATH MISSION. A debut, three song demo entitled 'Tower Of Doom' arrived in 1990. A second session, 'While I Hold The Devil's Hand', was recorded in 1991. Amadeus Records, the band's custom imprint, put out the first commercially available product during October 1992 as the 'Mythology' EP.

MINAS TIRITH signed to the domestic Voices of Wonder label for the 1995 album 'The Art Of Becoming'. A second album, '... Demons Are Forever', arrived in 1996, this time on the FaceFront label.

MINAS TIRITH was re-formulated and, re-signed to Face-Front Records, put out a third album in August 2004 'Dissertation Prophetae'. Promotional live work included a support to VADER at Oslo's Rockefeller and opening for MAYHEM in January 2005 in Hamar and Trondheim.

Singer Frode Forsmo joined resurrected Doom act FUNERAL in 2005. Drummer Tony Kirkemo (as 'Tony White') joined CHROME DIVISION, the Black Rock n' Roll outfit led by DIMMU BORGIR frontman Shagrath.

Tower Of Doom, Minas Tirith (1990) (Demo). Auschwitz / The Curse From God / The Light.
While I Hold The Devil's Hand, Minas Tirith (1991) (Demo). Anti-Eden / Face Of Devine / Longing / Flowers.
Mythology, Amadeus (1992). My Rotting Girl / Heartbeat / Chain Of Grief / Applewine.
THE ART OF BECOMING, Voices Of Wonder 196 (1995). The Living Dead / The Colour Of Nothing / Sympathy From The Devil / The Art Of Becoming / In The Night I Walk / X = 666 / In Union We Die / A Child Is Born In Babylon / Holy Brother.
... DEMONS ARE FOREVER, FaceFront FF003 (1996). Ondtro / Hellfaith / Hellvana (Mother Death) / Mad Alpha (Lunatic-Tac) / In The Purgatory Now / Necromonicon / Brain And The Bee / Satanisms / Beauty And A Beast.
DISSERTATION PROPHETAE, FaceFront (2004). Wisdoms Saberteeht / What Has Eaten Of It All / Enemykind / God Of Gods God / The Day My Life Lost Me / A Lower Heaven / I Am The Night / The Tunnel / Ferry.

MINDFLAIR

KAISERSLAUTERN, GERMANY — *Moshfred (vocals), Boris (guitar), Andreas (guitar), Wuddy (bass), Arthur (drums).*

Kaiserslautern Grindcore-Crust band MINDFLAIR began life in a Death Metal styled incarnation during 1994. A rehearsal demo tape, quaintly entitled "I Fucked Lassie', arrived in 1996. Guitarist Peter would bail out to be replaced by Andreas. Two years later the band cut 'The Multi-Orgasmic Man' demo in a two day recording session. This would be subsequently re-issued as a split cassette shared with UTOPIE. Bassist Wuddy would decamp and MINDFLAIR soldiered on without bass for live work until Wuddy rejoined in 2001.

MINDFLAIR shared further split releases, including a 10" single in collaboration with SUPPOSITORY and a 1999 album with Frenchmen RUNNING GUTS.

MINDFLAIR, (1998) (Split album with BELCHING BEET).
Mindflair EP, Bones Brigade (1999) (Split single with RUNNING GUTS). Miracle Ingredient / Garbage / Mass-Stultification / Purity Of Breeding.
Kruuunk! EP, (2000) (Split single with SUPPOSITORY). Enlarging The Trifle / Puberty Conditioned Murder Career / Political Self Service / Ticket Terror / Power Means Debauch / Minced Meat.
STAGNATION, BB025 (2005).

MINDGRINDER

AKKERHAUGEN, NORWAY — *Cosmocrator (vocals / guitar), Titan (vocals / guitar), Nitrous (guitar), Nex (drums).*

MINDGRINDER, initially billed as MENTAL GARROTER, was established in Akkerhaugen during 1996 as a triumvirate of vocalist / guitarist Cosmocrator, guitarist Nitrous and guitarist / vocalist Titan. Demos included 'Demolition' in 2001 and 'Feeding The Imbeciles' the following year. MINDGRINDER's Cosmocrator established a reputation as member of both SOURCE OF TIDE, as keyboard player, and bass player for ZYKLON, the side venture of EMPEROR members Samoth and Trym. Cosmocrator also sessioned as vocalist for WINDIR's 2002 album '1184'.

During 2003 Cosmocrator aided in forming SCUM, a high profile collaboration of extreme Metal elite players comprising Casey Chaos of US band AMEN and Norwegians Samoth of ZYKLON, and ex-EMPEROR, former EMPEROR and THORNS drummer Bård 'Faust' Eithun and bassist Happy Tom from TURBONEGRO.

Before signing to the Portuguese Sound Riot label for a projected 2003 album release MINDGRINDER issued a brace of demos, 'Demolition' and 'Bless The Imbeciles!', as well as having material featured on the compilation album 'Svartmetal'. Cosmocrator would also act as session drummer for DISIPLIN's 'The DeathRite Sessions' EP.

The band was restructured in January of 2004 as Cosmocrator relinquished his SOURCE OF TIDE ties in order to prioritise MINDGRINDER and the band also bade farewell to the drum computer and welcomed in Dan as drummer. The band also severed their partnership with Sound Riot, signing a new deal with Nocturnal Art Productions, the label owned by Samoth of ZYKLON. A debut album 'MindTech' would be scheduled for April.

In June of 2004 Cosmocrator, working with both Samoth and Trym of ZYKLON and Invictus from DISIPLIN, participated in recordings for a WINDIR tribute album to honour the memory of the late Valfar. In November MINDGRINDER entered Akkerhaugen Lydstudios to craft their second album for Nocturnal Art Productions. Early 2005 saw the introduction of the EVILIZER and DISIPLIN credited Nex on drums.

Demolition 2001, (2001). Sadistic Images / Starspawned Vision / Furious Seas.
Feeding The Imbeciles, (2002). Fire & Equanimity / Regeneration / Feed The Senseless / Sadistic Images / Starspawned Vision / Furious Seas.
MINDTECH, Nocturnal Art Productions (2004). Repulsive Evolution / Regeneration / War Solution / Deception / Starspawned Vision / Human Error / Fire & Equanimity / Sadistic Images / Surviving Gadzooks / Soul Inferno.
RIOT DETONATOR, Nocturnal Art Productions (2005). Warhead / Pathetic Submission / The Rebellion / Transition / Epilogue / Hellfire / Concept Of Honesty / Death's Disciples / Obligation To Prevail.

MINDROT

CA, USA — *Adrian LeRoux (vocals), Dan Kaufman (guitar), Matt Fisher (bass), Evan Killbourne (drums).*

Californian Death Metal unit MINDROT came into being during 1989, instigated by vocalist Adrian LeRoux and former CONFRONTATION singer Matt Fisher, the latter switching to bass guitar. The band was subsequently brought up to full strength with the addition of guitarist Dan Kaufman, drummer

Al Higdon and shortly after erstwhile CANTANKEROUS guitarist Matt Parrillo. This first variant of the band recorded a demo then opted for the band title of MINDROT.

A succession of 7" singles ensued starting with 'Endeavor' in September of 1991 and a split 7" in union with APOCALYPSE the same year. However, Higdon would break ranks and MINDROT pulled in Evan Killbourne for the demo cassette 'Faded Dream'. Parrillo too would then bail out, his position being filled by former RUPTURE guitarist John Flood.

MINDROT began negotiations with several labels but settled on Relapse, issuing the 'Forlorn' EP in July of 1995. The full length 'Dawning' followed in October. After second effort 'Soul', released in March of 1998, both Killbourne and Flood quit and MINDROT subsequently folded.

Latterly Dan Kaufman and Matt Fisher have forged a fresh project entitled SHIVA. Vocalist Adrian LeRoux would join Doomsters MORGION for their 2002 album 'Cloaked By Ages, Crowned In Earth'.

Forlorn EP, Relapse 6914 (1995). Forlorn / Whithersoul / Dreaded Light.

DAWNING, Relapse 6925 (1995). Dawning / Anguish / Burden / Withersoul / Forlorn / Internal Isolation / Across Vast Oceans.

SOUL, Relapse 6967 (1998). Dissipation / Nothing / Suffer Alone / Incandescence / Cold Skin / In Silence / Clemency / Despair.

MINDSNARE

TURIN, ITALY— *Gigi Casini (vocals / bass), Chris Benso (guitar) Marco Boffa (drums).*

Turin's MINDSNARE, originally billed as SATAN'S SLAUGHTER and founded in July of 1989, debuted with a 1990 demo tape 'Satan's Slaughter'. A whole slew of recording sessions then ensued over the years beginning with 1991's 'Chemioterapy'- as CHEMIOTERAPY and featuring Luca Giolo of GREZZO and ARX on drums. Having adopted the band title MINDSNARE, taken from a track on the NAPALM DEATH 'Harmony Corruption' album, the group issued 1992's 'The Dream-Quest Into Unknown'. This session was the first to feature singer Elio Del Grande.

The band was put on hiatus throughout 1993 as guitarist Chris Benso served 12 months national military service in Mozambique. Upon his return MINDSNARE got back to work, releasing the demos 1994's 'Blind' and 1995's 'Icon'. MINDSNARE, ditching their former vocalist and guitarist, pulled in a glut of valuable supports to visiting artists in 1995, opening for MALEVOLENT CREATION, VADER, SACRED SIN and OPPRESSOR.

A live tape arrived in 1996, culled from recordings laid down whilst the band supported KREATOR. The band signed a contract with Cryptic Souls Productions for an album but this deal would go sour. Undaunted MINDSNARE cut the 'Awaiting The Ancients' toward the close of the year and issued it in during 1997. By this juncture MINDSNARE had whittled down its membership to just vocalist / bassist Gigi Casini and guitarist Chris Benso but undertook gigs in France with Max Marzocca of NATRON acting as stand in. Former DEMONRY drummer Marco Boffa enrolled in September.

An EP, 'Hegemony', was delivered in May of 1999. This would be re-issued in album format by the Malaysian Psychic Scream Entertainment label, adding two extra live tracks, that same December. The following year delivered more useful supports to US act DISGORGE and Czechs GODLESS TRUTH.

The group headlined the Vicenza 'Brutal Grind' festival in February of 2002. Following release of 'The Noble Ancestry' album through the US Forever Underground label Marco Boffa departed in February of 2003. Former BASTARD SAINTS man Gianpaolo Ferrotti took the post in March. In 2005 MINDSNARE recorded the album 'From Blood To Dust' on Forever Underground.

Hegemony EP, (1999). Imperial Domain / Stronger Than Any Fate / To Jesus / Monarch Of Prayers / Butchered Human Corpse / Awaiting The Ancients.

HEGEMONY, Psychic Scream (1999). Imperial Domain / Stronger Than Any Fate / To Jesus / Monarch Of Prayers / Butchered Human Corpse / The Ancient's Awakening / Monarch Of Prayers (Live) / The Ancient's Awakening (Live).

HATEFUL ATTITUDE, Psychic Scream (2000). Sothis / Broken Promises / Attitude / Blasted Through Your Head / His Blood In Me / Hatebomb / Obscure Reflections / Monarch Of Prayers / Invocation Of The 4 Gates.

THE NOBLE ANCESTRY, Forever Underground FU 015 (2003). Intro / Blood Of Christ / Reborn From My Death / The Noble Ancestry / Immortal Return / The Waste Land / Ungodly Human / Satan's Breed In Blasphemous Eyes / My War / In The Name Of Kingu.

FROM BLOOD TO DUST, Forever Underground (2005). Along The Shores Of Styx / King Of The Tyrant / Blood And Dust / Beast Among Beasts / Before Human Race / Cassandra's Cry / You Are My Enemy / Mind Snare.

MISCREANT

VÄSTERÅS, SWEDEN — *Johnny Wranning (vocals), Peter Kim (guitar), Peter Johansson (guitar), Magnus Ek (bass), Johan Burman (drums).*

Melodic styled Death Metal from Västerås. MISCREANT's 1993 demo featured contributions from MARDUK's Jocke Göthberg. The group was signed by Wrong Again and released the 'Dreaming Ice' album in 1995. Ex-UTUMNO drummer Pontus Jansson replaced original member Johan Burman. Vocalist Johnny Wranning would later front EBONY TEARS and DOG FACED GODS Following three EBONY TEARS albums, 1998's 'Tortura Insomnia', 1999's 'A Handful Of Nothing' and 'Evil As Hell' in 2001, Wranning exited, forging EYETRAP in November 2000 in collaboration with erstwhile SHATTRD personnel guitarist Fredrik Rhodin, bassist Joakim "Chucken" Rhodin and drummer, Jan Karlsson. In 2004 the singer announced his new band MURGHATROID, a union with ex-THERION drummer Sam Carpenter (a.k.a. Sami Karppinen).

DREAMING ICE, Wrong Again WAR004 (1995). Ashes / Twilight Shadows / Illusions Infinity / Forever Not To Be / The Colonnade In White / Inside The Sadness Part II / Horizon Of Dreams / Naked / Without Grace.

MISERY

BRISBANE, QLD, AUSTRALIA — *Damon Robinson (vocals / bass), L. Kananghis (guitar), Scott Edgar (guitar), Anthony Dwyer (drums).*

A Brisbane, Queensland Death Metal group. Vocalist / bassist Damon Robinson, drummer Anthony Dwyer and guitarist L. Kananghinis are also members of CARDINAL SIN. MISERY date back as far as 1988 issuing two demos 'Sorting Of The Insects' in 1992 and 'Astern Diabolous' in 1993. Their debut album, 'A Necessary Evil', followed the same year. Vocalist Darren Goulding parted ways with the band after support shows to Austrians PUNGENT STENCH and MISERY drafted Moises Contreras. The 1994 'Insidious' EP would feature Contreras but after theses sessions he too left. Bassist Damon Robinson took over the mantle of lead vocalist for the 1995's 'Dark Inspiration' single which led up to the sophomore 1997 album 'Revel In Blasphemy' cut for Warhead Records.

MISERY donated an exclusive cut of 'Holy Devil' to the Australian Metal compilation album 'Legions–Opening Of The Southern Gate' issued by Blacktalon Media in July of 2004.

A NECESSARY EVIL, Velvet Urge (1993). Lifeless / Inverted Prophet / Born Dead / H.I.V. / Septic Octopus / I Endure / Sound Cancer / Body Farm / Sorting Of The Insects / Misery.

Insidious EP, Valve (1994). Seeds Of Doubt / Torn / Venganza Del / Innocent Torture.

Dark Inspiration, Subcide Productions (1995). Dark Inspiration.

REVEL IN BLASPHEMY, Warhead WHCD 18-2 (1997). Godspeak / Act Of War / Plague Of Humanity / Dark Inspirations / Infinite Hate / Morbid Dreams / All That Is Evil / A Song Before Dying / Remembrance / Altered States / Revel In Blasphemy.

CURSES, Venomous (2000). Sweet Oblivion / Intent To Kill / Immortal / Swine / Blood For Blood / There Is No God / Consumate The Virgin / Two Faced / Zealot / Shitmouth / Eyes Wide Shut / The Chosen Fool.

MISERY INDEX

BALTIMORE, MD, USA — *Jason Netherton (vocals / bass), Mike Harrison (guitar), Sparky Voyles (guitar), Kevin Talley (drums).*

MISERY INDEX was created in Baltimore by erstwhile DYING FETUS colleagues drummer Kevin Talley and bass player / vocalist Jason Netherton. Talley also has credits with SUFFOCATION. Also onboard was guitarist Mike Harrison, a veteran citing credits with such extreme Metal acts as MAINFRAME, CADAVER SYMPOSIUM, PESSIMIST, AUTUMN DAWN and SADISTIC TORMENT.

For the 2001 'Overthrow' EP, released on their own Anarcho label, the new band was rounded off with second guitarist Sparky Voyles of M.O.D., DYING FETUS, FEAR OF GOD and SADISTIC TORMENT. Both Voyles and Talley would be involved in a fleeting M.O.D. reunion in the summer of 2001 but would return to action with MISERY INDEX.

During December 2001 it would be learned that Voyles had instigated two side projects namely a Black Metal unit entitled TRUE UNHOLY DEATH in league with PESSIMIST drummer John Gordon and a Grindcore act named CRIMINAL ELEMENT working with DYING FETUS vocalist Vince Matthews.

In early 2002 the band cut two new tracks plus a cover version of DISRUPT's 'Reality Distortion' for a split EP in union with COMMIT SUICIDE. Voyles decamped from the TRUE UNHOLY DEATH project. A further 2002 release would see the re-issue of the 'Overthrow' mini album on a limited-edition 12" vinyl version through Good Life Recordings. The special edition included the full 'Overthrow' roster of tracks on the A side whilst the flip featured recordings from an 88.9 WERS Emerson College Radio live session cut in April.

Kevin Talley would audition for the drummer vacancy in SLAYER during the Spring of 2002, apparently coming close to securing the job. MISERY INDEX would form up part of the fifth annual summer 2002 'Death Across America' dates headlined by KATAKLYSM and backed up by BEYOND THE EMBRACE and DIVINE EMPIRE. In September the band announced they had signed to the German Nuclear Blast label for a new album. 'Retaliate' was recorded at Wild Studios in St. Zenon, Québec with KATAKLYSM's Jean-François Dagenais acting as producer. With the departure of Mike Harrison and Kevin Talley, the latter going on to session for DAATH's 'Futility' album, a new cast was unveiled including new additions second guitarist Bruce Greig, previously with DYING FETUS, TOGETHER WE FALL and NEXT STEP UP, alongside drummer Matt Byers. Talley had exited to pursue a more Rock orientated project billed GRAYSON MANOR. The revamped MISERY INDEX's first move was to plot a split single release in league with Arizona's STRUCTURE OF LIES.

MISERY INDEX would act as co-headliners for a North American package tour in May of 2003, completing a bill of SKINLESS, DIVINE EMPIRE and DYING FETUS. The band would be confirmed as forming up part of the 2003 'X-Mass Festivals' European tour commencing in London on December 7th, making up a strong billing incorporating DESTRUCTION, AMON AMARTH, NILE, DEICIDE, DEW-SCENTED, GRAVEWORM and DISBELIEF.

During November Former MISERY INDEX guitarist/vocalist Mike Harrison made a return, announcing his new outfit KOMMISSAR. Drummer Matt Byers parted ways with MISERY INDEX in March of 2004. Former drummer Kevin Talley filled in whilst a replacement was sought. However, by June Talley was inducted back into the fold as a full time member. The band hit further line-up problems the following month, when guitarist Bruce Greig exited. MISERY INDEX duly re-drafted former member Mike Harrison to fill in for remaining dates, the new look band debuting July 21st date in Buffalo, New York. Unfortunately the band's problems in the drum department would still be ongoing as Talley bailed out to join CHIMAIRA before the close of the month. A swift replacement would be located in Adam Jarvis from St. Louis band ALL WILL FALL.

The band put together a limited 10" vinyl and CD EP entitled 'Dissent', released through the group's own Anarchos Records. Besides an epic, 13 minute title track the EP also comprised Quicktime movies of live and studio footage. Also in the works would be the DVD 'Misery Index DVD Volume 1' featuring a full live set recorded in Athens, Greece during 2003. Back on the road, MISERY INDEX teamed up with NEURAXIS for a short Canadian tour beginning in late October.

2005 gave the band another year of intensive touring, commencing with a round of February concerts allied with SUFFOCATION, BEHEMOTH and CATTLE DECAPITATION then an announced collaboration with IMMOLATION, SKINLESS, WITH PASSION and DEICIDE for US dates in May. To boost their compliment, the band drafted touring guitarist Mark Kloeppel of CAST THE STONE. However, in their own words, MISERY INDEX was "booted" from the DEICIDE tour in early April and duly set about a short burst of headliners with MAGRUDER-GRIND and ROTTEN SOUND.

The former MISERY INDEX duo of Matt Byers and Bruce Greig bounced back onto the scene with COVENANCE, a collaboration with ex-DYING FETUS singer Vince Matthews. Meantime, MISERY INDEX ended their business relationship with Nuclear Blast in September.

Japanese gigs in March 2006 had the band paired with Montreal's NEURAXIS. That same month the band put in its live debut in Puerto Rico with a brace of shows in Quebradillas and Catano whilst ex-drummer Kevin Talley joined the ranks of HATE ETERNAL. In May MISERY INDEX released new album 'Discordia'. Both vinyl versions and the Japanese release added an extra track with a cover version of NASUM's 'Digging In'.

MISERY INDEX lent support to FEAR FACTORY's extensive round of European and UK dates began at the end of March. US road campaigning throughout the summer would be unrelenting. In mid May the band partnered with DISFEAR, PHOBIA and STRONG INTENTION before uniting on June 10th with FROM A SECOND STORY WINDOW, CATTLE DECAPITATION, ANIMOSITY and JOB FOR A COWBOY for a run of gigs into mid July. Concerts in November were backed by INTRONAUT, YAKUZA, BURN IN SILENCE and SWARM OF THE LOTUS. The band then announced they were to team up with NECROPHAGIST, COLDWORKER and BURNING SKIES for a European tour beginning in February 2007. Further dates partnered the group with NECROPHAGIST, ORIGIN and DISKREET.

Overthrow EP, Anarchos 1 (2001). Manufacturing Greed / Your Pain Is Nothing / Blood On Their Hands / Pulling Out The Nails / Dead Shall Rise.

Created To Kill, Bones Brigade 14 (2002) (Split release with DROWNING, BRODEQUIN and ABORTED). Manufacturing Greed / Your Pain Is Nothing.

Misery Index / Commit Suicide, Willowtip WWTP 15-2 (2002) (Split single with COMMIT SUICIDE). My Untold Apocalypse / Alive? / Reality Distortion.

Structure Of Lies / Misery Index, Deep Six DSR 048 (2003) (Split single with STRUCTURE OF LIES). The Living Shall Envy The Dead / Demand The Impossible / Panopticon.

RETALIATE, Nuclear Blast NB 1122-2 (2003). Retaliate / The Lies That Bind / The Great Depression / Angst Ist Die Seele Auf / Demand The Impossible / Order Upheld/Dissent Dissolved / Servants Of Progress / The Unbridgeable Chasm / Bottom Feeders / History Is Rotten.

RETALIATE (LIMITED EDITION), Nuclear Blast NB 1122-1 (2003) (Vinyl edition). Retaliate / The Lies That Bind / The Great Depression / Angst Ist Die Seele Auf / Demand The Impossible / Order Upheld/Dissent Dissolved / Servants Of Progress / The Unbridgeable Chasm / Bottom Feeders / History Is Rotten / Birth Of Ignorance.

Over Throw EP, Anarchos 1.5 (2004). Manufacturing Greed / Your Pain Is Nothing / Blood On Their Hands / Pulling Out The Nails / Dead Shall Rise / Manufactured Goods (Live) / Alive? (Live) / My Untold Apocalypse (Live) / Blood On Their Hands/Pulling Out The Nails (Live) / Spoken Track.

Dissent, Anarchos 3CD (2004). Dissent Part 1 (Sheep And Wolves) / Dissent Part 2 (Exception To The Ruled) / Dissent Part 3 (The Imperial Ambition) / Dissent Part 4 (Multiply By Fire) / Defector (Thinning The Herd).

Dissent, Anarchos 3 (2004) (12" single). Dissent Part 1 (Sheep And Wolves) / Dissent Part 2 (Exception To The Ruled) / Dissent Part 3 (The Imperial Ambition) / Dissent Part 4 (Multiply By Fire) / Defector (Thinning The Herd) / Screaming At A Wall.

Misery Index / Bathtub Shitter, Emetic (2006) (Split single with BATHTUB SHITTER). Conquistadores / Walls Of Confinement.

DISCORDIA, Relapse RR 6675-2 (2006). Unmarked Graves / Conquistadores / Outsourcing Jehovah / Breathing Pestilence / Meet Reality / Sensory Deprivation / The Meduse Stare / Dystopian Nightmares / Discordia / Pandemican.

DISCORDIA (LIMITED EDITION), Relapse RR 6675-1 (2006) (Vinyl). Unmarked Graves / Conquistadores / Outsourcing Jehovah / Breathing Pestilence / Meet Reality / Sensory Deprivation / The Meduse Stare / Dystopian Nightmares / Discordia / Pandemican / Digging In.

MISTRESS

BIRMINGHAM, WEST MIDLANDS, UK — *Dave Cunt (vocals), Misery (guitar), Dirty (bass), Migg (drums).*

"Necro-Doom" out of Birmingham. MISTRESS is not only noted for its individual brand of Doom but for their membership's myriad of other project bands of diverse styles such as SALLY, ANAAL NATHRAKH, FROST, DEADSUNRISING, FROG and FUKPIG. The group was founded in late 1999 as a trio of guitarist Misery, drummer Migg (a.k.a. Mick Kenney) and a singer known in polite company as Dave Cunt. This trio cut the quaintly titled 'Fuck Off' demo, adding bassist Earl from Hardcore merchants AKBAR in April 2000. Drunken from CREEP then took the bass mantle before the four string position for a sophomore demo 'Lord Worm' was handed over to Dirty Von Arse (a.k.a. Darren Donovan), also known as drummer for both KATASTROPHY WIFE and SALLY.

A sizable contingent of MISTRESS perform with 89 style Grindcore act FUKPIG. Migg is drummer for Black Metal bands FROST and ANAAL NATHRAKH and also operates the experimental project PROFESSOR FATE. The drummer also plies his trade with ABOYRM on their 2002 album 'With No Human Intervention' and DISGUST.

MISTRESS signed with Earache Records in mid 2004 for an album billed as 'In Disgust We Trust'. A split 7" with VENOMOUS CONCEPT would also be projected. In July 2005 the band put in an appearance at the 'Dungeonfest 555' festival at The Royal Park Cellars in Leeds. That same month saw the band traversing the UK clubs in alliance with Manchester's BEECHER and Dutch act MALKOVICH.

The Earache Records September 2005 edition of the 'Mistress' re-issue added bonus tracks in covers of METALLICA's 'Whiplash' and TOM WAITS 'Earth Died Screaming'. The 'II: The Chronovisor' re-release added DARKTHRONE's 'In The Shadow Of The Horns' and CROWBAR's 'Like Broken Glass'.

In September 2006 Mick Kenney, in collaboration with NAPALM DEATH's Shane Embury, announced the formation of new label Feto Records. This imprint served as an outlet for Kenney's EXPLODER, featuring MISTRESS bassist Dirty Von Arse as vocalist, and PROFESSOR FATE projects.

MISTRESS toured the UK aligned with NECROSIS in November.

MISTRESS, Rage Of Achilles (2002). Bludgeon / God Of Rock / Goatboy / Necronaut / Stunt Cock / 5th In Line / D.V.D.A. / Rebecca / Lord Worm.

IN DISGUST WE TRUST, Earache (2005).

II: THE CHRONOVISOR, Earache (2005). Ratpiss / Psychic One Inch Punch / Gotaboy / Wanker Colony / The Chronovisor / Hit Bottom / No Memory / Piss For Blood Shit For Brains / 38 / In The Shadow Of The Horns / Like Broken Glass.

MITHRAS

UK — *Rayner Coss (vocals / bass), Leon Macey (guitar), Lee du-Caine (guitar), Ben White (drums).*

Warwickshire Death Metal act founded in 1998 originally billed as IMPERATOR. The band's opening line up comprised of Leon Macey on guitar, Rayner Coss on vocals and bass and drummer Justin Joyce. However, with the reunion of the cult Polish act IMPERATOR the group switched titles to MITHRAS. In this incarnation the band delivered the self financed mini album 'Gods Among Men' in September of 1999, a limited edition of a mere 200 copies. However, Joyce broke the ranks and Macey took over on drums. MITHRAS also enrolled guitarist Steve Crompton.

As MITHRAS the group put in their debut gig at the Birmingham Foundry venue in June of 2000. Further exposure would be garnered from inclusion on the 'No Holy additives Vol. 4' compilation and by October of that year the band welcomed back Joyce into the fold. MITHRAS would follow this with a further EP 'Dreaming In Splendour' in January 2001. Joyce had departed once more in March and Macey was handling both guitar and drums in the studio.

Ben White, also a member of ORBETH, would take Crompton's position as Mithras signed to the Scottish Golden Lake label to record their first full length effort 'Forever Advancing ... Legions'. Macey would deputise for London act THRONE OF NAILS for live work in late 2001. Coss would session on recordings for Scotland's SERENADE. Despite this outside activity MITHRAS cut the 'Bequeath Thy Visions' promotional EP during 2002.

MITHRAS underwent a line up switch in June of 2003, drawing in MOTION SICKNESS guitarist Lee du-Caine and Ben White of ORBETHIUM on the drums. This latter recruitment allowed Leon Macey to concentrate on lead guitar and in this revised formation the band cut a new studio album 'Worlds Beyond The Veil'. Media response would be strong, the record landing the coveted 'Album of the month' accolade at 'Terrorizer' magazine. MITHRAS, acquiring new drummer Sean Broster, signed to the Candlelight label to re-issue the 'Worlds Beyond The Veil' album. A 2006 opus, 'Behind The Shadows Lie Madness', would be constructed during early 2006. SCYTHIAN guitarist Alex de Moller was added to the line-up in June.

GODS AMONG MEN, Mithras (1999).

FOREVER ADVANCING .... LEGIONS, Golden Lake (2001). Forever Advancing ... ... Legions / Trample Their Works / Sloping Altars / Arena Sands / Amidst The Fallen Arches / The Green Wanderer Returns / Wrath Of God / As The Wind Blows / Vae Solis / Dreaming In Splendour / Tomb Of Kings / What Lies Beyond.

Dreaming In Splendour EP, Mithras (2001). Vae Solis / Dreaming In Splendour / Wrath Of God.

WORLDS BEYOND THE VEIL, Golden Lake Productions (2003). Portal To The ... / Worlds Beyond The Veil / Bequeath The Visions / The Caller And The Listener / Break The Worlds Divide / Lords And Masters / Psyrens / Voices In The Void / The Sands Of Time / Search The Endless Planes / They Came And You Were Silent / Transcendence / Beyond The Eyes Of Man.

MOLESTED

BERGEN, NORWAY — *Øystein Garnes Brun (vocals / guitar), Trond Furnes (guitar), Kenneth Lian (bass), Erland Erichsen (drums).*

Bergen based Death Metal band MOLESTED spawned Øystein Garnes Brun to the pioneering Pagan Progressive Metal act BORKNAGAR and drummer Erland "Sersjant" Erichsen to

GORGOROTH. The group had been assembled as PURGATION in May 1991 by Bruun and Erichsen but before long had taken on the revised title of MOLESTED as guitarist Trond Turnes and bass player Kenneth Lian enrolled. Formative demo sessions resulted in the 'Stalk The Dead' promo in 1992. The band would then upgrade to a 24 track studio to cut the second demo 'Unborn Woods In Doom', this securing a record deal with the Effigy label.

Although MOLESTED appeared on track to record a second album, announcing a contract had been signed with the Spanish Repulse label in 1995, the group disbanded sometime in 1997. By this time Brun's new career with BORKNAGAR was already well under way.

Stormvold EP, Effigy EFFIP 004 MCD (1995). The Usurpers Winterblood / Fogflames / Wolves Of Graven Hate / Pyre At The Tarn / Following The Growls.

BLOD-DRAUM, Effigy EFFI 001 (1995). A Strife Won At Wraith / Along The Misty Morass / Unborn Woods In Doom / Following The Growls / Blod-Draum / The Hate From Miasma Storms / Carved By Raven Claws / A Glade Of Ingrown Blood / Forlorn As A Mist Of Grief.

MOMENT MANIACS

NORRKÖPING, SWEDEN — *Jonsson (vocals), Alho (guitar), Jocke (guitar), Roger Svensson (bass), Fredrik Andersson (drums).*

Norrköping Deathcore band MOMENT MANIACS featured an illustrious cast of extreme Punk and Metal elite players on their 1998 album 'Two Fuckin Pieces . . .' issued through Distortion Records. Fronting the band would be the WOLFPACK / WOLFBRIGADE triumvirate of vocalist Jonsson, lead guitarist Alho and guitarist Jocke with a rhythm section comprising Roger 'Bogge' Svensson (a.k.a. B. War) of CHAINED, MARDUK, DEVILS WHOREHOUSE and ALLEGIANCE with the MARDUK, ALLEGIANCE and TRIUMPHATOR credited Fredrik 'Froding' Andersson on drums. Jonsson also has prior credentials with ANTI CIMEX.

In 2005 it was learned that Bogge had initiated the Santa Fe Springs, California based "dark Heavy Rock band" REBELANGELS in union with MARDUK colleague Legion.

TWO FUCKIN' PIECES, Distortion (1999). Forward / Flesh Power Dominion / When I Make You Bleed / No Win Situation / My Loss / Cold Deadly Steel / Haunted / Family Business / Do You Think I Care? / Time For War.

MONASTERY

ZALAEGERSZEG, HUNGARY — *Andres Vincze (vocals), Krisztián Varga (guitar), István Szegi (guitar), Simon Balázs (bass), Róbert Kovács (drums).*

Zalaegerszeg Death Metal crew MONASTERY was forged during 1989. Amongst its ranks featured guitarist Krisztián Varga, from ART OF BUTCHERY, AGE OF AGONY and SEAR BLISS. The band's 1992 cassette album 'Far From Christ', released by Trottel Records, is generally acknowledged as the first domestic Hungarian Death Metal commercial release. Another cassette album, 'Postmortem Aggressive End', arrived in 1994, after which the band folded.

Under drummer Róbert Kovács instigation, MONASTERY resurfaced during 2002, issuing a nine track EP entitled 'Fuck This World' the following year. Misan 666 Records put out the 'Misanthrope' album in 2004. A three song demo was made available for download from the band's website in 2005. In December 2005 singer Krisztian Moricz left the group and Andres Vincze became new frontman.

The 'Play With The Truth' single arrived in 2006. By this juncture the band's style was beginning to lean towards US influenced Metalcore.

FAR FROM CHRIST, Trottel (1992). Prologue (Intro) / Far From Christ / League With Evil / In Witching Of Revenge / Sepsis / There Is No Truth / Darker Side / Devotion / In The Dirt.

POSTMORTEM AGGRESSIVE END, Monastery (1994). Brutal Persecution Of Reason / Terrible Future / Postmortem Aggressive End / Da Pacem Domine / Who Am I / Paralityc Clemency / Self Destruction / Primitive End / Fuckin' Inquisition.

Fuck This World, Monastery (2003). Intro / Dying Earth / Scream / B.L.E.A.D. / Raw / Tuning / Breath / Fuck This World / Outro.

MISANTHROPE, Misan 666 (2004). Psychosis / Died Away World / Save Me / Dope / Misanthrope / Destruction Slave / Coma / Bleed / Clone 6.66 / Noise / Smell Of Blood / Way To Life.

Monastery, Monastery (2005) (Download demo). Shock / Insomnia / Hatefull.

Play With The Truth, Monastery (2006). Play With The Truth / Now / Energy.

MONSTERWORKS

PALMERSTON NORTH, NEW ZEALAND — *Jon (vocals / guitar), Eee (guitar), Hugo (bass), Chris Mills (drums).*

Palmerston North Thrash orientated Metal band founded in 1996. Bassist Ryan, following on from formative four-stringers Chris and Simon, the latter's term lasting just one day, holds BACKYARD BURIAL credentials. MONSTERWORKS debuted in July 1998 with the demo 'Dormant', with 'Delusions Of Grandeur' following in August 1999. The group made their commercial inauguration with the 2001 opus 'Dimensional Urgency', after which Brock relocated to the UK. He would be superseded by Nathan Forbes, having originally made his mark with technical Death Metal act FALCIFORM and holds credits with the experimental Black Metal band ZIRCONIUM as well as DEMIURGE and DRACO AERIUS. MONSTERWORKS followed up with a March 2002 album 'Rogue', issued through Eat Lead And Die Music. The album was recorded in two stages, at The Stomach Studios in Palmerston North during October 2001 and the second at C. Moore Sound in Wellington in February 2002. That March, MONSTERWORKS played their final New Zealand gig.

The band relocated from New Zealand to take up residence in London, England, soon re-enlisting Brock and recording the 'M-Theory' album with the services of a session drummer. Sterghios Moschos took command of the drums in July 2004 but had vacated by the following June. In July the band put in an appearance at the 'Dungeonfest 555' festival at The Royal Park Cellars in Leeds. Casket Records issued the MONSTERWORKS album 'The Precautionary Principle' in 2006.

Mid 2007 saw the release of a new album 'Spacial Operations'.

Dormant, Monsterworks (1998). Macroscope / Cascade / Princess Die / Wasteland / Chopped Into Little Pieces / Simple Ego Shrine / Planet Of The Apes.

Delusions Of Grandeur, (1999). Blokk / Mindstorm / Delusions Of Grandeur / Infernity.

DIMENSIONAL URGENCY, Monsterworks (2001). Primus Exordium / Personal Demons / Redline / Blast Furnace / Dial M For Monster / Dear Abby / In Space (No One Can Hear You Mosh) / Awe Chasm / Chunuk Bair.

ROGUE, Eat Lead And Die Music (2002). Set Up / In The New Age / Tomb Spader / Whoreborn / Nothing / Small Gods / Colossus / Oblique / Blindend / (!?) / No Other Option / Ascension.

M-THEORY, Monsterworks (2003). Latro Praelium / Rogue / Insolence / Supermetal / Redemption / Timebomb / Barricade / Venom Of God / Shatterer Of Worlds / For Glory.

THE PRECAUTIONARY PRINCIPLE, Casket Music CSK074CD (2006). Internal Velocity (Intro) / M-Theory / Screwdriver / It Ends Here Today / Metal Is Everything / Game On / Out Of Control / Hypertrophic Me / Bleed The World / Triumph / The Precautionary Principle / Who Am I / Outro / Charred Vision / Thoroughly Thought Through / Unknown Quantity.

SPACIAL OPERATIONS, Monsterworks (2007). Leaving Home / Firefight / Spacial Forces / November / Stars Malign / Defenders Of The Southern Cross / The Lonely Crown / Hysterical Rapture / Pain And Elation / Parallelysis / Alliance / Exfiltration / Voyage Of Magma Maiden / To Be Continued . . . .

MONSTROSITY

TAMPA, FL, USA — *Brian Werner (vocals), Sam Molina (guitar), Mark English (guitar), Mike Poggione (bass), Lee Harrison (drums).*

Tampa, Florida brutal Death Metal band that, despite an ever fluid line-up, remains centred upon drummer Lee Harrison. Bass player Rob Barrett was a veteran of DARK DECEPTION, SOLSTICE and MALEVOLENT CREATION. Judged in qualitative terms as amongst the very finest practitioners of the genre, MONSTROSITY's efforts have been focussed on high precision rather than a profusion of output.

The group, created during August 1990 in Fort Lauderdale with George "Corpsegrinder" Fisher, nicknamed after one of his early bands, handling lead vocals, debuted in 1991 with the demo 'Horror Infinity', laying down four tracks at Miami's Natural Sound Studios. That same summer the group relocated to Tampa. MONSTROSITY guitarist Jon Rubin stood in for MALEVOLENT CREATION on a temporary basis for their 1991 American tour. Rubin would team up with MALEVOLENT CREATION on a frequent ad hoc basis until finally joining the band full-time.

CYNIC guitarist Jason Gobel guests on MONSTROSITY's 'Imperial Doom' album, their 1991 debut for German label Nuclear Blast Records hewn out at the familiar Morrisound Studios, and would also act as live fill in for a solitary date opening for PESTILENCE and DEATH. Gobel was subsequently replaced by Mark English for their European tour with PESTILENCE in 1992. The undeniable quality of 'Imperial Doom' permeated throughout the metal underground, generating reported sales in excess of 50,000 units.

MONSTROSITY bassist Mark Van Erp was busted on a drugs charge, caught in possession of two ounces of cocaine, and was as such unable to travel outside America. The band swiftly hired CANNIBAL CORPSE guitarist Rob Barret to handle bass, including shows in Lima, Peru and Montreal, Canada in 1995. Touring in Europe saw the band utilizing the services of DEATH's Kelly Conlon as bassist.

For the 1996 'Millennium' album, issued via Conquest Music in the USA and Nuclear Blast in Europe, MONSTROSITY drafted in guitarist Jason Morgan. Lead vocals were recorded by Fisher but after his defection to CANNIBAL CORPSE the band pulled in former EULOGY man Jason Avery for live work. During this time the band hired former NEVERMORE and CHASTAIN guitarist Pat O'Brien to conduct a 1997 tour with allied with VADER and BROKEN HOPE. However. Once these dates were fulfilled O'Brien too decamped to join CANNIBAL CORPSE.

Following recording of 1999's 'In Dark Purity', which closed out with a cover version of SLAYER's 'Angel Of Death', Morgan departed to join MORBID ANGEL and HATE ETERNAL guitarist Erik Rutan's ALAS project. In fact, Morgan had announced his decision to leave prior to recording of 'In Dark Purity' but stayed on to lay down rhythm guitar parts and solos. Initially MONSTROSITY worked with BRUTALITY's Jay Fernandez in the studio but then drafted ex-ETERNAL guitarist Tony Norman. Upon completion of the album sessions the band fired Conlon and substituted him with Mike Poggione of EXECRATION, SCAB MAGGOT and CAPHARNAUM. 'In Dark Purity' closed out with a rendition of SLAYER's 'Angel Of Death'.

The band headed out on a US headline trek throughout September and October 1999 backed by DIMMU BORGIR, SAMAEL and EPOCH OF UNLIGHT. Meantime, Morgan created WYNJARA for a 2000 album whilst Conlon would briefly join VITAL REMAINS in 2001.

MONSTROSITY's December 2000 US tour would see Liverpool Death Metal act DESECRATION as support. After crafting the 2001 live opus 'Enslaving The Masses', this set also hosting archive demo material, Jason Avery quit to concentrate on his career as a tattooist. The band hired Sam Molina, known as

MONSTROSITY

guitarist with Fort Meyers act CALIBOS, to take on lead vocals.

During July and August 2001 MONSTROSITY led the 'Bloodletting North America Pt. 2' tour alongside DEEDS OF FLESH, Dutchmen PYAEMIA, ODIOUS SANCTION and SABBATIC FEAST. The band joined forces with DYING FETUS, VADER and KRISIUN and HOUWITSER for the 'Intervalle Bizarre' European tour during September and October.

October 2002 had the band heading up a ten date tour of Poland backed by a cast of VOMITORY, TRAUMA, SCEPTIC, LOST SOUL, DISSENTER, and CONTEMPT. Kelly Conlon would officially join Boston based Progressive Metal act INFINITY MINUS ONE that same month.

MONSTROSITY guitarist Tony Norman undertook tour work with Gothic Black Metal outfit LOVER OF SIN in Europe during March 2003. Meantime, MONSTROSITY welcomed back original singer Jason Avery to the fold that same month. His replacement, Sam Molina, would stay on as second guitarist. This revised line-up was due to break themselves in with a show in Puerto Rico in May. MONSTROSITY's latest album, 'Rise To Power', arrived in September. Norman once more subbed himself out that year, joining forces with none other than MORBID ANGEL for November US dates.

Still in promotion for 'Rise To Power' the band geared up for a run of 2004 European dates, beginning on 1st May in Zwickau, Germany, partnered with DARK DISCIPLE. Unfortunately the tour was cancelled on 4th May with only a handful of dates being conducted. In a rare admission a statement confirmed "Turnouts have been too bad, losing money day by day is no fun for the bands". Avery quit MONSTROSITY after the tour. He was later replaced by Brian Werner.

Bassist Mike Poggione, retaining his MONSTROSITY links, also teamed up with LECHEROUS NOCTURNE and toured with TRIVIUM as a session bassist in 2004. Tony Norman joined the re-united TERRORIZER in late 2005. MONSTROSITY lined up with DEEDS OF FLESH, VILE and IMPALED for the 'Gutting Europe 4: Triumph In Black' European tour beginning in Poland during late March 2006.

MONSTROSITY set 'Spiritual Apocalypse' as the title of an April 2007 album. Preceding this release the band teamed up with MARDUK, SETHERIAL and CATTLE DECAPITATION for the "Chaos Metal Attack Mexico 2007" tour in February.

IMPERIAL DOOM, Nuclear Blast NB055 (1991). Imperial Doom / Definitive Inquisition / Ceremonial Void / Immense Malignancy / Vicious Mental Thirst / Burden Of Evil / Horror Infinity / Final Cremation / Darkest Dream.

Horror Infinity, Monstrosity (1991) (Demo cassette). Definitive Inquisition / Immense Malignancy / Horror Infinity / The Burden Of Evil.

Darkest Dream, Nuclear Blast NB 055 (1992) (Limited edition 1000 copies. Red vinyl). Darkest Dream / Horror Infinity (Demo version).

The Burden Of Evil, Relapse (1992). The Burden Of Evil / Immense Malignancy.

Monstrosity, Monstrosity (1994) (Demo). Manic / Stormwinds / Slaves And Masters.
MILLENNIUM, Nuclear Blast NB 208-2 (1996). Fatal Millennium / Devious Instinct / Manic / Dream Messiah / Fragments Of Resolution / Manipulation Strain / Slaves And Masters / Mirrors Of Reason / Stormwinds / Seize Of Change.
IN DARK PURITY, Olympic Recordings (1999). The Hunt / Destroying Divinity / Shapeless Domination / The Angels Venom / All Souls Consumed / Dust To Dust / Suffering To The Conquered / The Eye Of Judgement / Perpetual War / Embraced By Apathy / Hymns Of Tragedy / In Dark Purity / The Pillars Of Drear / Angel Of Death.
ENSLAVING THE MASSES, Conquest Music Inc. (2001). Imperial Doom / Ceremonial Void / Darkest Dream / Vicious Metal Thirst / Final Cremation / Definitive Inquisition / Immense Maligamy / Horror Infinity / Burden Of Evil / Manic / Stormwinds / Slaves And Masters / The Eternal Hunt (Live) / Destroying Divinity (Live) / Hymns Of Tragedy (Live) / Fatal Millennium (Live) / Final Cremation (Live) / The Angels Venom (Live) / Perpetual War (Live) / Burden Of Evil (Live) / Deadlock (Live) / Horror Infinity (Live) / Imperial Doom (Live) / Angel Of Death (Live).
LIVE EXTREME BRAZILIAN TOUR 2002, Mutilation 027 (2002). Destroying Divinity—Dust To Dust / Fatal Millennium / The Final Cremation / The Angels Venom / Imperial Doom / Angel Of Death.
RISE TO POWER, Metal Blade 104342 (2003). The Exordium / Awaiting Armageddon / Wave Of Annihilation / The Fall Of Eden / Chemical Reaction / A Casket For The Soul / Rise To Power / Visions Of Violence / From Wrath To Ruin / Abysmal Gods / Shadow Of Obliteration.
SPIRITUAL APOCALYPSE, Metal Blade (2007).

MOONSHINE

SOUTH KOREA — *Amon (vocals / guitar), Vito (guitar), Torr (bass), Giga (drums).*

Claiming to be the first Korean Death Metal band MOONSHINE morphed out of DEATHRASHER, a unit founded in March of 1993. DEATHRASHER would issue a succession of demos beginning with June 1993's 'Malediction And Benediction' and 'Donor With Rotten Guts' in August of the same year. Shortly after founder members vocalist / guitarist Amon and bassist Giga would be joined by Shin and Noh. The latter would decamp within a month but undaunted DEATHRASHER released a third demo tape 'The Torture' in January of 1994. That summer Giga would switch from bass to drums and in 1995 the band was joined by guitarist Yoon in March and bass player Kang in August.

Gigs during this time found the PSYCHOTRON duo of keyboard player Pain and bassist Thorn acting as temporary stand ins. October of 1996 would witness the transition from DEATHRASHER to MOONSHINE. With new man Torr on bass the band would release their debut album 'Shined By Darkness' in December of 1997. Second guitarist Vito augmented the line up in the summer of 1999 as MOONSHINE signed to the Korean arm of Japanese label Pony Canyon resulting in the second opus 'Wake Up The Moon'.

SHINED BY DARKNESS, (1997). Ablaze (Let Me Burn) / Burning Corpse / Here Lies / Domesticated Creatures / Wake Up The Moon / Black Sleeves.
WAKE UP THE MOON, Pony Canyon (2001). Shined By Darkness / Ablaze (Let Me Burn) / Burning Corpse / Ashes Of Thee / Black Sleeves / The Memorable Tide / Wake Up The Moon / The Torture / Les Fleurs Du Mal.

MORBID ANGEL

TAMPA, FL, USA — *David Vincent (vocals / bass), Trey Azagthoth (guitar), Erik Rutan (guitar), Pete Sandoval (drums).*

Blasphemous Death metal act MORBID ANGEL, founded in Tampa, Florida during 1984, broke down the barriers between extreme music and commercial success but seemingly blew their chances of entering the big league with a series of remarks attributed to main man David Vincent being allegedly fascist in nature. The world's Rock media erupted in an outcry against these supposed Nazi leanings. Nevertheless, despite the controversy and the band's denials, MORBID ANGEL had racked up combined sales of over 1'000'000 albums sold by 1998 and, as a new millennium broke, seemed only to solidify their standing. Importantly, the band has built a catalogue of distinction and remained steadfast as genre leaders.

The formative band unit had come together at high school with Trey Azagthoth (real name George Emmanuel III), Dallas Ward and Mike Browning forging ICE. This act subsequently adopted the title HERETIC before discovering another act laying claim to the title. At this juncture Azagthoth suggested MORBID ANGEL. The band's inaugural gigs found the unit honing their skills with cover versions of songs by ANGEL WITCH, SLAYER and MERCYFUL FATE. Having performed initially as a trio the group then brought in singer Kenny Bamber to record a 1985 two song demo of 'Demon Seed' and 'Welcome To Hell'. Bamber exited and MORBID ANGEL persevered as an instrumental act as an interim measure before Dallas Ward took on the lead vocal duties. In August 1985 a demo billed 'The Beginning' comprised a hotch-potch of tracks featuring vocals from both Bamber and Ward.

However, next in line for the frontman role would be vocalist / guitarist Richard Brunelle. Unfortunately Ward was convicted of a drugs offence and incarcerated. This measure forced the band to re-think and, pulling in John Ortega as second guitarist Brunelle was delegated the vocal role. At one stage MORBID ANGEL, albeit fleetingly, rehearsed with a female singer Evilynn. This proposed band structure did not come up to standard though and before long Mike Browning was to try his hand at the vocal role.

With record company interest rising MORBID ANGEL cut a 1986 four song demo, 'Scream Forth Blasphemies', comprising 'Hellspawn', 'Chapel Of Ghouls', 'Angel Of Disease' and 'Abominations'. This tape soon found its way onto the underground trading market spreading the band's reputation globally. What was to be the band's debut album 'Abominations Of Desolation', recorded in North Carolina in May1986, was shelved due to the band disintegrating in an physical argument over Browning's girlfriend. Upon completion of these recordings Browning opted out and John Ortega departed too, later to found MATRICIDE. Georgia native Sterling Von Scarborough, previously fronting his own act INCUBUS, was drafted early that summer to act as vocalist / bassist.

Scarborough, leaving to forge a new INCUBUS with ex-MORBID ANGEL drummer Mike Browning and TERROR guitarist Gino Marino, was supplanted by ex-TERRORIZER man David Vincent. (a.k.a. David Stuppnig) The bassist, previously having led his own act BURIED IN CEMETERY, had been an acquaintance of the band for some time having financed and produced the 'Abominations Of Desolation' sessions. The newly constituted line-up, comprising Vincent, Azagthoth, lead vocalist Michael Manson and drummer Wayne Hartshell, relocated to North Carolina to cut new demos. Manson did not last the pace and dropped out, leaving Vincent to take on the frontman role for MORBID ANGEL's commercial debut the 1988 'Thy Kingdom Come' 7" single released on Switzerland's Splattermaniac label. With this more solid unit MORBID ANGEL's sales began to accelerate as did their worldwide recognition.

Debut album 'Altars Of Madness', cut at Tampa's fabled Morrisound studios, surfaced through leading extreme Metal imprint Earache Records in May 1989. CD versions added an extra track, 'Lord Of All Fevers And Plagues', plus alternate remixes of album tracks with outtake guitar solos. The world's first dose of MORBID ANGEL was positively poisoning and paralysing. Trey Azagthoth and Richard Brunelle had summoned up a snakes nest of riffs that deliberately defied convention, hammering and sliding outside of accepted meters, this near surreal approach providing a platform for even greater experimentation to come. 'Altars Of Madness', undeniably a classic, did have its faults though. A wistful production unfortunately masked much of the bass presence and David Vincent's vocals and lyrics were ineffectual. On the live front, the group participated in the Earache organised "Grindcrusher" tour of Europe that winter shoulder to shoulder with BOLT THROWER, CARCASS and NAPALM DEATH.

'Blessed Are The Sick' was tendered in July 1991. Self-produced at Morrisound, sonically the album corrected many of its predecessors flaws. Adorned in a disturbing J. Delville painting 'Les Tresors De Satan', 'Blessed Are The Sick', despite being a more deliberate and considered body of work, was soon to be held up as one of the most revered albums in extreme metal history. An inceptor to the savagery the band opened a delicate slice of ambience, the first hints of more adventurous adventurism to come in later years. Pointedly, although MORBID ANGEL would be targeted as Satanists for entire decade, their second album dropped the anti-Christian rhetoric in favour of loathing towards humanity in general.

In September 1991, just upfront of a lengthy American tour, MORBID ANGEL's planned debut album 'Abominations Of Desolation' finally saw a release through Earache Records. The album had been bootlegged relentlessly upon the band's ascendancy into the upper echelons of the Thrash ranks.

Guitarist Richard Brunelle drifted away in mid 1992. MORBID ANGEL filled his shoes briefly with former INCUBUS man Gino Marino but before long Brunelle was back. However, Brunelle decamped in the Autumn of 1992 to found EON'S DEAD. A trio of David Vincent, Trey Azagthoth and Pete Sandoval crafted the 'Covenant' album, utilising the familiar Morrisound facilities but enlisting METALLICA producer Flemming Rasmussen to handle desk work. The final tapes were mixed down at Sweet Silence Studios in Copenhagen.

June 1993 saw MORBID ANGEL of such a stature that their 'Covenant' album was signed over to the massive Warner Bros corporation in America, where albums would be released on the label's Giant imprint. Backed by a promotional video clip for 'God Of Emptiness' it would prove the band's biggest commercial success to date, shifting over 130,000 copies in the USA alone. The band closed the membership gap with ex-RIPPING CORPSE and EULOGY guitarist Eric Rutan drafted for European dates. However, for support dates to MOTÖRHEAD and BLACK SABBATH in America during commencing in Connecticut on February 8th 1994 Richard Brunelle made a temporary return. Meantime, an EP of remixes by the cult underground Industrial act LAIBACH surfaced, a groundbreaking move for an extreme Metal act at the time. The 'Laibach remixes' EP came delivered in CD format with black artwork sleeve and a silver clad 12" variant. Meantime, ex-member Sterling Von Scarborough, under the pseudonym 'Nocticula', published a demo, restricted to just 66 copies, under the banner LIBER NOCTICULA.

The May 1995 MORBID ANGEL album 'Domination' witnessed the band's grip on their premier league status strengthening. Their first recorded output to include Erik Rutan, the album also drew considerable criticism from longstanding followers due to its diversion into sludge variations. Vinyl variants came clad in differing artwork to their CD counterparts and the record also saw limited edition releases in a metal tin, restricted to just 1000 copies. A planned 'slime' filled green jewel case sleeve was shelved, with claims of leaking toxic substances being blamed, but nevertheless 'Domination' surpassed the 80,000 sales mark in the USA. MORBID ANGEL undertook an enormous touring schedule throughout 1995 and into 1996. Dates began in their home state of Florida for an American tour before extensively covering Europe until February 1996 saw the band back in America prior top a return trip to Europe. These shows yielded the live album 'Entangled In Chaos'.

The band seemingly suffered a double hammer blow in 1997 not only with the departure of Vincent, so often the band's mouthpiece, but also the collapse of their deal with Warner Bros. Records. However, Azagthoth picked up the pieces and renegotiated a revised deal with their former label, Earache Records, and pulled in ex MERCILESS ONSLAUGHT, CEREMONY and INTERSINE man Steve Tucker to plug the gap left by Vincent.

In 1998 Vincent found himself playing bass in the S&M inspired GENITORTURERS, but then he is the husband of frontwoman Geni after all!

Although Rutan appeared as main songwriter and contributor to the 'Formulas Fatal To The Flesh' album MORBID ANGEL pulled in guitarist Richard Burnelle for live work as Rutan decamped to concentrate on his other two acts ALAS, in union with THERION's Martina Hornbacher-Astner, and HATE ETERNAL. The first 5000 copies of the 'Formulas' opus came with a free bonus CD entitled 'Love Of Lava', comprising of all the guitar solos from the main body of work isolated onto one CD. Sales exceeded 45,000 copies in North America.

However, rehearsals for the tour to promote the record did not go well and with Burnelle being dispensed with Rutan got the call for assistance. Following the 'Formulas Fatal To The Flesh' tour Rutan decamped yet again and produced the 'Conquerors Of Armageddon' album for Brazilian Black Metallers KRISIUN in 2000.

Rutan returned to the fold later in 2000 for the 'Gateways To Annihilation' album, a record that kicks off with an intro of a genuine swamp frog chorus. MORBID ANGEL toured Europe that December headlining an almighty Death Metal package that included ENSLAVED, THE CROWN, BEHEMOTH, HYPNOS and DYING FETUS. US sales of 'Gateways To Annihilation' would fall just short of 40,000 copies.

Upfront of the bands 2001 UK dates it was announced that Tucker would be standing down for personal reasons and to concentrate on his Death Metal 'Super' combo CEREMONY centred upon Tucker, CANNIBAL CORPSE guitarist Pat O'Brien and DISASTRONAUT guitarist Greg Reed. Erstwhile EMPEROR drummer Trym was recruited into CEREMONY during 2002. However, this proposed band unit never materialised.

Drafted in as replacement was HATE ETERNAL's Jared Anderson. American shows had the band supporting PANTERA upfront of their own Winter run of headline dates dubbed the "Extreme Music For Extreme People" tour. Road mates for this burst of live activity would be DEICIDE, SOILENT GREEN, ZYKLON and EXHUMED.

Rutan would busy himself toward the close of 2001 acting as producer for his erstwhile RIPPING CORPSE colleagues for their sophomore DIM MAK release 'Intercepting Fist'. MORBID ANGEL would join MOTÖRHEAD's summer American 2002 'Hammered' tour as guests. Shortly after, Rutan announced his departure from the band in order to concentrate his efforts on HATE ETERNAL. Meantime ex-guitarist Richard Brunelle resurfaced touting his new act PATHS OF POSSESSION.

A MORBID ANGEL tribute album 'Tyrants From The Abyss' was delivered by Necropolis Records in September of 2002 featuring artists such as ZYKLON, VADER, BEHEMOTH, KRISIUN, ANGELCORPSE, IN AETERNUM, INFERNAL and DIABOLIC.

Although various press reports suggested the band was in discussion with former vocalist David Vincent it would be ex-singer Steve Tucker that stepped back up as MORBID ANGEL frontman for a 2003 studio album 'Heretic'. News of another connected project revealed that erstwhile drummer Mike Browning was demoing with the Florida based LISA THE WOLF with Erik Rutan handling production chores.

'Heretic', released in September, saw issue in a virtual slew of variations including a German only box set with complimentary 18 track bonus disc entitled 'Bonus Levels', a double CD version and a picture disc vinyl outing. US dates paired with SUPERJOINT RITUAL saw the band recruiting Tony Norman of MONSTROSITY to handle second guitar duties. A lengthy round of European shows commencing 20th February in Hardenberg, Holland saw Brazilians KRISIUN in support. A promotional video for 'Enshrined By Grace', directed by Pete Bridgewater, depicted the band "performing in an infernal ring of fire whilst the unenlightened masses stare at a mind-numbing screen".

As 'Heretic' exceeded the 20,000 sales figure in the USA, the group continued touring apace across North America into April of 2004 with support coming from SUFFOCATION, SATYRICON and PREMONITIONS OF WAR. Confusingly, MORBID ANGEL's management issued a statement stating the band had severed ties with longterm label Earache Records in July. Within 24 hours Earache fired back with a press release of their own claiming that in fact the band's option still had a further two weeks to run.

Scheduled South America gigs, due to commence in Monterrey, Mexico on 7th August, would be cancelled as reports emerged that Steve Tucker had suffered "massive anxiety attack and had to be hospitalized". The frontman soon responded, stating that he had contracted a lung infection "due to my excessive travel and the variety of weather and environments that I endure in these travels." David Vincent, retaining his role with the GENITORTURERS, duly rejoined MORBID ANGEL for their rescheduled South American dates. MORBID ANGEL announced co-headline US dates in union with SOULFLY for February of 2005, followed by a run of European and Scandinavian shows, supported by Danes HATESPHERE, to take them into April. Meantime, ex-MORBID ANGEL man Steve Tucker was announced as being back on the tour circuit, apparently to act as stand-in bassist for NILE's March European festival dates, but this union never transpired. A scheduled showing at a Portuguese festival in June was put in jeopardy when rhythm guitarist Tony Norman apparently went missing. Although the guitarist eventually turned up alive and well MORBID ANGEL persevered without him, scheduling South American gigs in Brazil, Chile, El Salvador, Guatemala and Mexico for September. The band was announced as engaged in the 'X-Mass Fest Part II' European tour, set to begin in early December and involving ENTHRONED, UNLEASHED, PRIMORDIAL and ENSIFERUM. However, these dates would be pulled after UNLEASHED withdrew.

The erstwhile MORBID ANGEL duo of Jared Anderson and Steve Tucker revealed they were collaborating in February 2006 on a new Death Metal venture. MORBID ANGEL announced April US tour dates combined with Canadians DESPISED ICON, Poles BEHEMOTH and Brazilians KRISIUN. August European festival dates saw a welcome return to the 'Domination' line-up as guitarist Erik Rutan rejoined the fold.

Former MORBID ANGEL vocalist Jared Anderson died in his sleep on Saturday, October 14th 2006 at the age of 30.

The Beginning, (1985). The Gate / Demon Seed / Evil Spells / The Gate / Demon Seed / Evil Spells / Evil Spells / Instrumental / Chaos.

Bleed For The Devil, (1986). Bleed For The Devil / Chapel Of Ghouls / Abominations / Morbid Angel / Hellspawn.

Scream Forth Blasphemies, (1986). Chapel Of Ghouls / Unholy Blasphemies / Abominations / Hellspawn.

Unholy Blasphemies, (1987). Unholy Blasphemies / Chapel Of Ghouls / Evil Spells.

Thy Kingdom Come, Splattermaniac (1988). Thy Kingdom Come / Abominations Of Desolation / Blasphemy Of The Holy Ghost.

ALTARS OF MADNESS, Earache MOSH 11 (1989). Visions From The Darkside / Chapel Of Ghouls / Maze Of Torment / Damnation / Bleed For The Devil.

BLESSED ARE THE SICK, Earache MOSH 31 (1991). Intro / Fall From Grace / Brainstorm / Rebel Lands / Doomsday Celebration / Day Of Suffering / Blessed Are The Sick / Leading The Rats / Thy Kingdom Come / Unholy Blasphemies / Abominations / Desolate Ways / The Ancient Ones / In Remembrance.

ABOMINATIONS OF DESOLATION, Earache MOSH 048 (1991). The Invocation / Chapel Of Ghouls / Unholy Blasphemies / Angel Of Disease / Azagthoth / The Gate / Lord Of Fevers And Plagues / Hell Spawn / Abominations / Demon Seed / Welcome To Hell.

Rapture, (1993) (US promotion release). Rapture / Sworn To The Black / Pain Divine.

MORBID ANGEL

COVENANT, Earache MOSH 081 (1993). Rapture / Pain Divine / World Of Shit / Vengeance Is Mine / Lion's Den / Blood On My Hands / Angel Of Disease / Sworn To Black / Nar Mattaru / God Of Emptiness.

Laibach Remixes EP, Earache MOSH 112T (1994). God Of Emptiness / Sworn To The Black / Sworn To The Black (Laibach remix) / God Of Emptiness (Laibach remix).

DOMINATION, Earache MOSH 134 (1995). Dominate / Where The Slime Live / Eyes To See, Ears To Hear / Melting / Nothing But Fear / Dawn Of The Angry / This Means War / Caesar's Palace / Dreaming / Inquisition (Burn With Me) / Hatework.

ENTANGLED IN CHAOS-LIVE, Earache MOSH 167 (1996). Immortal Rites / Blasphemy Of The Holy Ghost / Sworn To The Black / Lord Of All Fevers And Plagues / Blessed Are The Sick / Day Of Suffering / Chapel Of Ghouls / Maze Of Torment / Rapture / Blood On My Hands / Dominate.

FORMULAS FATAL TO THE FLESH, Earache MOSH 180 (1998). Heaving Earth / Prayer Of Hatred / Bil Ur-Sag / Nothing Is Not / Chambers Of Dis / Disturbance In The Great Slumber / Umulamahri / Hellspawn: The Rebirth / Covenant Of Death / Hymn To A Gas Giant / Invocation Of The Continual One / Ascent Through The Spheres / Hymnos Rituales De Guerra / Trooper.

LOVE OF LAVA, Earache MOSH 180 CDL (1999). Heaving Earth Lava / Heaving Earth Lava 'Alt' / Prayer Of Hatred #1 Lava / Prayer Of Hatred #2 Lava / Prayer Of Hatred #3 Lava / Bil Ur-Sag #1 Lava / Bil Ur-Sag #2 Lava / Bil Ur-Sag #2 Lava 'Alt' / Nothing Is Not Lava / Nothing Is Not Lava 'Alt' / Chambers Of Dis #1 Lava / Chambers Of Dis #1 Lava 'Alt' / Chambers Of Dis #2 Lava / Chambers Of Dis #2 Lava 'Alt' / Umulamahri #1 Lava / Umulamahri #2 Lava / Umulamahri #2 Lava 'Alt' / Umulamahri #3 Lava / Umulamahri #3 Lava 'Alt' / Hellspawn #2 Lava / Hellspawn #3 Lava / Covenant Of Death #1 Lava / Covenant Of Death #2 Lava / Covenant Of Death #3 Lava / Invocation #1 Lava / Invocation #2 Lava / Dominate Lava / Dominate Lava 'Alt' / Dawn Of The Angry #1 Lava / Dawn Of The Angry #1 Lava 'Alt' / Dawn Of The Angry #2 Lava / Burn With Me #1 Lava / Burn With Me #1 Lava 'Alt' / Burn With Me #2 Lava / Burn With Me #2 Lava 'Alt' / Burn With Me #3 Lava / Burn With Me #3 Lava 'Alt' / Eyes To See #1 Lava / Where The Slime Live Lava / Where The Slime Live Lava 'Alt'.

GATEWAYS TO ANNIHILATION, Earache MOSH 235 (2000). Kawazu / Summoning Redemption / Ageless / Still I Am / He Who Sleeps / To The Victor The Spoils / At One With Nothing / Opening Of The Gates / Secured Limitations / Awakening / I / God Of The Forsaken.

HERETIC, Earache MOSH 272 (2003). Cleansed In Pestilence (Blade Of Elohim) / Enshrined By Grace / Beneath The Hollow / Curse The Flesh / Praise The Strength / Stricken Arise / Place Of Many Death / Abyssous / God Of Our Own Divinity / Within Thy Enemy / Memories Of The Past / Victorious March Of Reign The Conqueror / Drum Check / Born Again.

MORBOSIDAD

OAKLAND, CA, USA — *Thomas Stench (vocals), Chip n' Death (guitar), Cuaxo (bass), Raul Varela (drums).*

Underground Black Metal act with IMPALED connections through drummer Raul Varela. Guesting on vocals would be the IMPALED and EXHUMED pairing of Leon del Muerte and Sean McGrath. The band's first offering would be a 1994 demo entitled 'Santisima Muerte', re-issued that same year with additional rehearsal tracks and obscene cover through Iron Fist Domain Productions. MORBOSIDAD's 2000 debut album would be re-issued in 2003 by the Evil Morgue label, this new release adding tracks from the band's 'Santisima Muerte' demo. That same year In Coffin Productions distributed the live cassette album 'Profanando En Vivo (Live Desecration)', limited to 333 hand numbered copies. Another release would be a split offering in alliance with X.E.S. on Nuclear War Now Productions.

French label Bang Or Be Banged Productions released a limited edition EP 'Sexxxual Blasphemous Krucifixxxion' of 300 copies as a split with IRONFIST, comprising of the 1994 rehearsal tapes. This outing also surfaced in Asia through the Singapore based Ravage Records. An album, 'Cojete A Dios Por El Culo' featuring a cover version of BEHERIT's 'Solomon's Gate', saw issue through Evil Morgue in 2004. From Beyond Productions would issue a limited edition split 7" shared with Thailand's SURRENDER OF DIVINITY in early 2005. That same year MORBOSIDAD recorded a NECROVORE track, a Spanish language version, for a projected tribute album planned through From Beyond Productions.

Santisima Muerte, Iron Fist Domain Productions (1994). Tetrico / Castracion Bestial / Matanza / Pacto Satanico / Decompozed Cadaver On The Cross / Castracion Bestial / Putos (Part II) / Tetrico.
Santisima Muerte, (1994). Tetrico / Castracion Bestial / Matanza / Pacto Satanico.
MORBOSIDAD, Quadrivium (2000). Bestial Y Morboso / Esclavos De Hipocrecia / Putos / Pacto Satanico (Parte II) / Putos (Parte II) / Castracion Bestial / Cruxifica Tu Existencia / Tetrico / Cagada De Cristo.
Bajo El Egendro Del Crucificado, Bestial Onslaught (2002). Bajo El Egendro Del Crucificado / In My Blood / War Of Hate / Vomito En La Cruz.
PROFANANDO EN VIVO (LIVE DESECRATION), In Coffin Productions (2003) (Limited edition 333 hand numbered copies). Bestial Y Morboso / Bajo El Egendro Del Crucificado / Cruxifica Tu Existencia / Putos (Part II) / Pacto Satanico / War Of Hate / Castracion Bestial / Tetrico / In My Blood ... / Bastardo Hijo Del Cielo (Bastard Son Of Heaven—New Assault) / Cagada De Christo.
Sexxxual Blasphemous Krucifixxxion, Bang Or Be Banged Productions (2004) (Split EP with IRONFIST). Decomposed Cadaver On The Cross / Castraction Bestial / Putos (Part II) / Tetrico.
COJETE A DIOS POR EL CULO, Evil Morgue (2004). Cadaver Decompuesto En La Cruz / Sangriento Sacrificio Cristiano / Infierno Immortal / Pacto Satanico / Mata En El Nombre De Satanas / Ritual En El Pentagramma / Altar De Sangre Negra / Cojete A Dios Por El Culo / Bestia Del Averno / Muerto En Mi Propia Sangre / Bastardo Hijo Del Cielo / Salomon's Gate / Outro.

MORBUS

GERMANY — *Sascha Wotenick (vocals / guitar), Marius Zöller (guitar), Lars Wieneke (bass), Jörg Heemann (drums).*

MORBUS, manifested during 1994 by vocalist / guitarist Morbus Sascha Wotenick and colleague Marius Zöller on guitar, debuted with an opening demo tape 'Destruction Builds Pain' the following year. In 1997 Lars Wieneke joined the band on bass and Jörg Heemann on the drums for the self-financed album 'Zwinger', recorded at Subsonic Studios with Carlos Silva and released in May 1998. Signing to Godz Greed Records MORBUS, working with former HOLY MOSES guitarist Andy Classen as producer, cut the 'Leibeigen' album in April of 1999 at Stage One Studios.

Heemann opted out but in early 2000 Sven Pollkötter completed the line-up. Lars Wieneke would be next to leave.

Zwinger, (1998). Slanderer Of Addicted Remainz / Beyond / Sardonic / Zwinger / Chaos / Ignorance.
LEIBEIGEN, Godz Greed (1999). Rage Fear Sorrow Shame / Beyond / Leibeigen / Stubborn / Following Man / MDK / Gash / Zwinger / Wizdom Volatile / The Devastating Lightness Of Being.

MORDANT

THESSALONIKI, GREECE — *Maki Manasi (vocals), Kostas Doukopoulos (guitar), Chris Manidaki (guitar / bass), Antoni Vafiadi (drums).*

Thessaloniki's MORDANT is a Death Metal acted created in December of 1997 with an opening line up conceived by guitarist Chris Manidaki and vocalist Angelo Hamilakis, subsequently enrolling second guitarist Tsompanidis Theodore, bassist Kostas Akritidis and drummer Kapetanidis Giannis. In May of the following year this version of the band recorded a two song demo, a song from which was chosen for inclusion on a local CD compilation album. Another demo, 'As Flowers Wither', arrived in April 1999 after which Dimitris Avramidis replaced Akritidis on bass and Makis Manasis took over from Hamilakis as frontman.

MORDANT's band line up proved fluid right up until recording of the debut album 'What Time Can't Touch'. For these sessions Manidaki was responsible for all guitars and bass. Kostas Doukopoulos joined up as second guitarist once the album was complete.

WHAT TIME CAN'T TOUCH, (2002). Primordial Transgression / Human / Malignant Creations / Lost / Enslaved To Destiny / Fear The Time / Outer Heaven / Infernal Anthems / What Time Can't Touch.

MORDICUS

FINLAND — *Robert Aarpo (vocals), Isto Jänönen (guitar), Jani Rytkonen (guitar), Aapi Hämäläinen (bass), Heikki Lappalainen (drums).*

Technical Death Metal outfit MORDICUS bowed in with the 1991 demo cassette 'Abominations Of The Earth', following up on this entrance with a further tape 'Grown Under Shade Of Sorrow' the same year. At this stage MORDICUS was a quartet of vocalist / bassist Robert Arpo, guitarists Jani Rytkonen and Isto Jänönen and drummer Heikki Lappalainen. Before 1991 was out the 'Three Way Dissection' EP had arrived through the American Skindrill Records. MORDICUS would then sign to another American label Wild Rags for 1992's 'Wrathorn' album. The first full-length album, 'Dances From Left' pressed in a limited run of 1500 copies, would be delivered by the French Thrash label in 1993.

The band added bass player Aapi Hämäläinen in 1995 but it would be a full two years before the 'Particular Truths' demo surfaced. MORDICUS recorded the 'Disintegration Groove' album in 2000 for the Yperano label. However, the following year the band learned its planned release through Yperno had been shelved.

Three Way Dissection EP, Skindrill (1991).
DANCES FROM LEFT, Thrash (1993). I Bleed To See / Blood Under Ice / Eternia / Cybernetic Summer / Unholy Wrath / Cosmocrators Of Tartaros / Oceans / Flames Beneath My Sleep / A Thorn In Holy Flesh / Christcide.
WRATHORN, Wild Rags WRR-MUS (1994). Unholy Wrath / Exordium Demorjor / Flames Beneath My Sleep / A Thorn In Holy Flesh / Upon The Throne Of God / Abominations Of The Earth / Eternia / Solar Wind.

DISINTIGRATION GROOVE, Yperano (2000). Rights n' Trials / Equalife / Cloak Of Us All / Lifestyle / Mr. Roots / Atalantas' Race / Border Devil / Saturday Night Crap-o-rama / Search No Integrity / Neo-serious / Babylon Twist / Ritual Despise / Ignore / Black Tide / Re-integration.

MORGOTH

MESCHEDE, GERMANY — *Marc Grewe (vocals), Harry Busse (guitar), Carsten Otterbach (guitar), Sebastian (bass), Rudiger Hennecke (drums).*

Heavily influenced by American Death Metal acts, Meschede's MORGOTH cut their teeth whilst still teenagers with their 1988 six song demo 'Pits of Utumno' followed by a 1989 tape entitled 'Resurrection Absurd'. The latter demo was pressed up for MORGOTH's first EP. Before the release of the 'Cursed' album the group undertook a mammoth tour with OBITUARY and DEMOLITION HAMMER in the autumn of 1990. Earlier in the year the first two EPs were combined as one album. In North America alone this record sold more than 10'000 copies resulting in a 60 date tour with KREATOR.

1991's 'Cursed' album was mixed by Randy Burns and provided MORGOTH with further success, 1994's 'Odium' increasing the group's pulling power and coinciding with a German tour alongside UNLEASHED and TIAMAT.

Amazingly, on the brink of a massive breakthrough, the group split due to personal difficulties between band members. Grewe founded POWER OF EXPRESSION with ex-URGE members releasing an eponymous tribute to B'LAST the same year.

Having been offered the chance to play in Mexico during 1994 MORGOTH reformed and would go on to record a brand new album, 'Feel Sorry For The Fanatic', in 1996. The style was rather different and more modern in its dark, Industrial approach than previous triumphs. A latter day member was former JESTER'S MARCH and HOUSE OF SPIRITS bass player Martin Hirsch.

Post MORGOTH guitarist Carsten Otterbach would enter the realms of artist management handling the affairs of such heavyweights as DIMMU BORGIR, IN FLAMES and ICED EARTH. Former MORGOTH men vocalist Marc Grewe and Sebastian Swart launched their new Thrash Metal band ACTION JACKSON in 2000.

A double CD retrospective launched in January 2005, entitled '1987-1997: The Best of Morgoth', included the 'Pits Of Utumno' demo, the previously unreleased 'Indifferent', an early version of 'TV War' with different lyrics, a demo version of 'Golden Age' plus four promotional videos and two live video cuts recorded in Chemnitz during 1993.

ETERNAL FALL, Century Media 9708-2 (1990). Burnt Identity / Female Infanticide / White Gallery / Pits Of Utumno / Etyernal Sanctity / Dictated Deliverance / Travel / The Afterthoughts / Selected Killing / Lies Of Distrust.
Dictated Deliverance, Century Media 9708-1 (1990) ('Resurrection Absurd' EP). Dictated Deliverance / Travel / The Afterthought / Selected Killings / Lies Of Distrust.
Burnt Identity, Century Media 609711 (1990) ('The Eternal Fall' EP). Burnt Identity / Female Infanticide / White Gallery / Pits Of Utumno / Eternal Sanctity.
CURSED, Century Media 7719-2 (1991). Cursed / Body Count / Exit To Temptation / Unred Imagination / Isolated / Sold Baptism / Suffer Life / Opportunity Is Gone / Darkness.
ODIUM, Century Media CD9749 (1994). Resistance / The Art Of Sinking / Submission / Under The Surface / Drowning Sun / War Inside / Golden Age / Odium.
FEEL SORRY FOR THE FANATIC, Century Media 77119-2 (1996). The Fantastic Decade / Last Laugh / Cash ... / ... And It's Amazing Consequences / Curiosity / Forgotten Days / Souls On A Pleasuretrip / Graceland / Watch The Fortune Wheel / A New Start.

MORGUL

ØSTFOLD, NORWAY — *Jack D. Ripper (vocals / guitar / bass).*

A notoriously disturbing solo act of Jack D. Ripper (a.k.a. Maestro Discordio and Charmock), hailing from Råde, Østfold. MORGUL, named after the J.R.R. Tolkien 'Lord Of The Rings' ;location Minas Morgul in Mirkwood and initially featuring Hex on drums, came together in late 1990, revealing their presence with the demos 'Vargvinter—From The Dark Streams Of Night' and 'In Gowns Flowing Wide', both delivered during 1995. Signing to the Austrian Napalm Records label MORGUL issued their inaugural album, 'Lost In Shadows Grey', in 1997. The 1998 'Parody Of The Mass' album was recorded at Abyss Studio and produced by Mikael Hedlund of HYPOCRISY. For this outing the pair credited themselves as Charmock "Mental disorder & revolting hellharp" and Hex "Severe cranium violation".

Hex decamped in 1999. Switching to Germany's Century Media label, Jack D. Ripper persevered as a solo concern. MORGUL's third effort, January 2000's 'The Horror Grandeur' recorded at Soundsuite Studio in Marseille, Southern France with co-production credits going to Terje Refsnes, was assembled solely by Jack D. Ripper excepting session violin from the SIRENIA, THE SCARR and THE SINS OF THY BELOVED credited Pete Johansen.

MORGUL's March 2001 offering, 'Sketch Of Supposed Murderer', closed out with a cover version of the KISS classic 'She'. April 2002 Jack D. Ripper recorded vocals for Swiss band MERIDIAN's debut album 'The Seventh Sun'.

The band jumped labels again, signing to French concern Season Of Mist for 'All Dead Here ...', released in April 2005. Tom Cuper provided session drums. Jack D. Ripper subsequently relocated to the Detroit, Michigan in the USA.

Vargvinter—From The Dark Streams Of Night, Morgul (1995) (Demo). Blooddebris / Dwelt In The Shadows / Under The Dreary Sky.
In Gowns Flowing Wide, Morgul (1995) (Demo). Riket Som Var / ... And the Wolves Wept / Night's Eternal Majesty / River Of Princess.
LOST IN SHADOWS GREY, Napalm NPR028CD (1997). Enthroned / The Dark Infinity / Hunger Of The Immortals / My Bride ... / River Of Princess.
PARODY OF THE MASS, Napalm (1998). Black Hearts Domain / Healing The Blind / Torn / Ballad Of Revolt / Adoration Of The Profane / Author Of Pain / The End.
THE HORROR GRANDEUR, Century Media 77257-2 (2000). The Horror Grandeur / Ragged Little Dolls / The Murdering Mind / A Third Face / Elegantly Decayed / Cassandra's Nightmare / The Ghost.
SKETCH OF SUPPOSED MURDERER, Century Media 77323-2 (2001). Violent Perfect Illusions / The Dog And The Monster / Dead For A While / Machine / Of Murder And Misfortune / Truth, Liars And Dead Flesh / Stealth / Once Again / She.
ALL DEAD HERE ..., Season Of Mist SOM103 (2005). Intro / The Mask Of Sanity / The Need To Kill / All Dead Here / Sanctus Perversum / Hategrinder / Shackled / Outro / Empty.

MORNALAND

SWEDEN — *Henrik Wenngren (vocals), Tommy Öberg (guitar), Jacob Alm (bass), Joakim Jonsson (drums).*

MORNALAND feature drummer Joakim Jonsson, a man citing affiliations with a multitude of acts such as SKYRUNNER, VORTEX, GANGJÄRN, KOBOLDERS, DREADSTATE, SKINFECTED, DUST and THE MIST OF AVALON. The group was conceived by Jonsson and vocalist Henrik Wenngren during 1995, executing three demo sessions 'Beyond The Dreamers Labyrinth', 'Origin Land' and 'The Journey', of which only the latter would be distributed to the public. It would secure a contract with the German label Path to Enlightenment for inclusion on a 1997 split album shared with ABOMINATOR entitled 'Prelude To World Funeral ...'. Just prior to these sessions MORNALAND enrolled SLUMBER guitarist Tommy Öberg.

Subsequent MORNALAND recordings included various contributions to compilation albums such as the track 'Land Of Dreaming' on 'Voices Of Death' and 'In Dead Skies Looms Tranquility' for the 1999 collection 'From The Underground'. A further release for the band came when Cadla Communications put out the 'In Dead Skies..' EP, compiled from archive demo tracks. That year Jacob Alm of ATHELA and SLUMBER joined as bassist. The demo 'Feathers Of Rapture' emerged in 2000.

Jonsson also operates the solo concern AUTUMN DWELLER, of which 1998 and 2003 recording sessions saw contributions from MORNALAND colleagues Wenngren and lyricist Tommy Öberg. Wenngren also has connections with SKYFIRE, VICIOUS, DUST and ZAVORASH.

In January of 2004 Jonsson teamed up with AXENSTAR to act as touring bassist for European dates. The following month he would record drums for a new SKYFIRE album.

PRELUDE TO WORLD FUNERAL..., Path To Enlightenment (1997) (Split album with ABOMINATOR). Invert / Floating Semblance / Fallen Angels / Mournful Secrets (Part One) / Silent Forest / ... Then Came Dawn ... / Voice In The Wind.

In Dead Skies..., Cadla Communications (1998). Land Of Dreaming / My Last Tear / Labyrinth Of Imagination / Thee Son / In Dead Skies Looms Tranquility.

MORPHEUS

STOCKHOLM, SWEDEN — *David Brink (vocals), Stefan Ekström (guitar), Sebastian Ramstedt (guitar), Johan De Daux (bass), Markus Rüden (drums).*

MORPHEUS was formed in Stockholm by ex-CARBONISED members drummer Markus Rüden and guitarist Stephan Ekström, together with ex-members of EXHUMED. The line-up would be completed by bassist Johan Bergebäck. As MORPHEUS, the group marked their entrance in 1990 with the demo 'Obscurity'. The 1991 single 'In The Arms Of Morpheus' on Opinionate Records features guitarist Janne Rudberg, who left prior to the album to form EXCRUCIATE.

MORPHEUS drafted guitarists Peter Krentzel of CENATARIUM and Henrik Lindgren of THE NEW WIND in 1992 before another CARBONISED man, Stefan Ekström, took the role. However, the band folded following the 1993 'Sons Of Hypnos' release.

Sebastian Ramstedt later made his mark with NECROPHOBIC and NIFELHEIM. Johan Bergebäck also featured in NECROPHOBIC and joined DISMEMBER in September of 2004.

In The Arms Of Morpheus, Opinionate OP003 (1991). In The Arms Of Morpheus.

SON OF HYPNOS, Step One STEP005 (1995). Depths Of Silence / Through The Halls Of Darkness / God Against All / The Third Reich 3797 A.C. / Of Memories Made (The God Of Dreams) / Memento Mori / Among Others / Inflame The Mass / Wonderland / Dreams.

MORPHEUS DESCENDS

NEW YORK, NY, USA — *Tom Stevens (vocals / guitar), Rob Yench (guitar), Andy Newton (bass).*

Esteemed New York Death Metal band created during October of 1990. Both vocalist / guitarist Tom Stevens and guitarist Rob Yench also cite membership of the infamous INCANTATION. MORPHEUS DESCENDS, fronted by Jeff Reimer, made their entrance with a 1990 demo session billed as 'Accelerated Decrepitude'. A 7" double single 'Adipocere' then followed for the underground Seraphic Decay label then a further demo 'Corpse Under Glass'. These sessions would be collected together by the JL America label for the album release 'Ritual Of Infinity'. The band toured heavily across America in 1994 supporting INCANTATION and ANAL CUNT with appearances at the Michigan 'Death Fest 4' and the Milwaukee 'Metal Fest' in both 1994 and 1995, the year of the independently issued 'Chronicles Of The Shadowed Ones'. MORPHEUS DESCENDS would hook up with INCANTATION once again for summer dates alongside ABSU and ENSLAVED. The group restructured, dispensing with Reimer and augmenting their sound with the addition of vocalist / guitarist Tom Stevens, a veteran of NOKTURNEL, SAVAGE DEATH and RIPPING CORPSE. This line-up cut the 1996 mini album 'The Horror Of The Truth'.

In late 1996 Yench and bassist Andy Newton created the side venture BRIMSTONE and in 1997 Yench and Stevens united with INCANTATION. Erstwhile MORPHEUS DESCENDS bassist Andy Newton, under the Pseudonym Lord Typhus Mirinor, would later found Black Metal band FOG.

The 2002 MORPHEUS DESCENDS release, 'Forbidden Path Of Unthinkable Evil' released by former bassist Andy Newton's Dark Horizons label, included a cover version of VENOM's 'Angel Dust' plus material from the 1991 Seraphic Decay 7" single.

Jeff Reimer passed away on 30th August 2005, reportedly as a result of a heroin overdose.

Adipocere, Seraphic Decay (1991).

RITUAL OF INFINITY, JL America (1992). The Way Of All Flesh / Corpse Under Glass / Immortal Coil / Trephanation / Proclaimed Creator / Accelerated Decrepitude / Submerged In Adipocere / Enthralled To Serve / Ritual Of Infinity.

CHRONICLES OF THE SHADOWED ONES, (1995). The Cruciform Hills / Cairn Of Dumitru / Autumn Bleed / Signs Of The Gehenna / Moupho Alde Ferenc Yaborov.

THE HORROR OF THE TRUTH, (1996).

FORBIDDEN PATH OF UNTHINKABLE EVIL, Dark Horizons DHR011 (2002).

MORS PRINCIPIUM EST

PORI, FINLAND — *Ville Viljanen (vocals), Jori Naukio (vocals / guitar), Jarkko Kokko (guitar), Teemu (bass), Toni Nummelin (keyboards), Mikko Sipola (drums).*

MORS PRINCIPUM EST is a Pori, Länsi-Suomen based Death Metal act established during 1999. First product arrived in 2000 with the demo 'Before Birth'. Second session 'Valley Of Sacrifice' followed in 2001 and 'Third Arrival' in 2002. French concern Listenable Records picked the band up for the album 'Inhumanity', produced by Ahti Kortelainen at Tico-Tico Studio and issued in April 2003. Japanese variants added a bonus track 'Hijo De La Luna'. The band roster at this juncture comprised singer Ville Viljanen, guitarists Jarkko Kokko and Jori Haukio, bassist Teemu Heinola, keyboard player Toni Nummelin with Mikko Sipola on drums.

The group added new keyboard player Joonas Kukkola, of CITADEL, in December 2004. The band's second album 'The Unborn' was recorded at Tico Tico Studios in Kemi for an April 2005 release again through Listenable Records. Both digipack and Japanese editions hosted a cover version of MEGADETH's 'Blood Of Heroes'. For their appearance at the 'Rocklinna Metal Fest' on 5th November the band temporarily replaced guitarist Jarkko Kokko with Karri Kuisma.

In January 2006 Listenable Records re-released the first album 'Inhumanity' with all new artwork and with three bonus songs. The band recorded 'Liberation = Termination' at Astia Studio with engineer Anssi Kippo in August for 2007 issue. However, upon completion MORS PRINCIPIUM EST parted ways with guitarist and main songwriter Jori Haukio. The group acquired a session guitarist, Karri Kuisma, to substitute.

Before Birth, Mors Principium Est (2000) (Demo). Forever And A Day / Last Apprentice / Moriere.

Valley Of Sacrifice, Mors Principium Est (2001). Invocation (Intro) / Valley Of Sacrifice Part 1 / Sin Defeats All Hope / Valley Of Sacrifice Part 2.

Third Arrival, Mors Principium Est (2002) (Demo). Another Existence / Eternity's Child / Last Apprentice (2002).

INHUMANITY, Listenable POSH046 (2003). Another Creation / Eternity's Child / In My Words / Inhumanity / D.I.B. / The Lust Called Knowledge / Oblivion / Life In Black / Last Apprentice / Into Illusion.

THE UNBORN, Listenable POSH066 (2005). Pure / The Harmony Remains / Parasites Of Paradise / Two Steps Away / Altered State Consciousness / Spirit Conception / The Unborn / Fragile Flesh / Pressure / The Glass Womb.

INHUMANITY, Listenable (2006). Another Creation / Eternity's Child / In My Words / Inhumanity / D.I.B. / The Lust Called Knowledge / Oblivion / Life In Black / Last Apprentice / Into Illusion / The Lust Called Knowledge (2005 remix) / Inhumanity (Live) / Pure (Live).

THE UNBORN, Listenable (2006) (Digipack). Pure / The Harmony Remains / Parasites Of Paradise / Two Steps Away / Altered State Of Consciousness / Spirit-Conception / The Unborn / Fragile Flesh / Pressure / The Glass Womb / Blood Of Heroes / No More.

LIBERATION=TERMINATION, Listenable POSH092 (2007). Orsus / The Oppressed Will Rise / The Animal Within / Finality / Cleansing Rain / Forgotten / Sinners Defeat / The Distance Between / It Is Done / Terminal Liberation / Lost Beyond Retrieval.

LIBERATION=TERMINATION, Listenable POSH092 (2007). Orsus / The Oppressed Will Rise / The Animal Within / Finality / Cleansing Rain / Forgotten / Sinners Defeat / The Distance Between / It Is Done / Terminal Liberation / Lost Beyond Retrieval.

MORS SUBITA

HAUKIPUDAS, FINLAND — *Antti Haapsamo (vocals), Mika Lammassaari (guitar), Jarkko Kaleva (guitar), Mika Junttila (bass), Juha Haapala (drums).*

MORS SUBITA is a melodic Death Metal band established in Haukipudas during 1999 as ZILSTRONE. The initial formation involved guitarist Mika Lammassaari, his cousin Aki Lammassaari plus drummer Juha Haapala performing covers by the likes of PANTERA, METALLICA, SENTENCED and WHITE ZOMBIE. Deciding to pursue original material the group worked with producer Kari Räty, who also served as session bassist, on a demo. Jarno Rankinen enrolled in mid 2000, quickly followed by guitarist Jukka-Pekka Ellilä, but shortly afterwards Aki Lammassaari exited.

The MORS SUBITA title was adopted during 2002. Further changes then took place as Antti Haapsamo of CATALEPTIC and SEMENTII was drafted as lead singer. However, Jukka-Pekka Ellilä decamped and Jarkko Kaleva took his position. A demo, billed 'Synopsis', arrived in 2003. The band was put into hiatus when Kaleva and Rankinen were obliged to commit to national military service. As it transpired, Rankinen did not return and Mika Junttila, of SANCTIMONIOUS, stepped in as a new bass player for a 2006 self-financed EP 'Epoch'.

Due to a throat injury suffered by CATAMENIA singer Olli-Jukka Mustonen, MORS SUBITA frontman Antti Haapsamo performed much of the vocal work on the fellow Finns 1996 album 'Location: COLD'.

Synopsis, Mors Subita (2003) (Demo). Releaser / Resignation / Sincircus / From Your Side.

Epoch, Mors Subita (2006). Curse Of Nothingness / Greenfield / Spineless / Alone / The Burden.

MORTA SKULD

MILWAUKEE, WI, USA — *Dave Gregor (vocals / guitar), Jason O'Connel (guitar), Jason Hellman (bass), Kent Truckenbrod (drums).*

Deathsters MORTA SKULD were created in 1990 issuing their first demo tape 'Gory Departure' shortly after. MORTA SKULD's sophomore release was a 1991 three track demo tape 'Prolong The Agony' that featured VIOGRESSION drummer Jeff Jaeger. Tracks were 'Through The Eyes Of Death', 'Of Evil' and 'Feast From Within'. The band signed to Deaf Records, a subsidiary of Yorkshire label Peaceville, found a permanent drummer in Kent Truckenbrod after the tape's completion in time for 1993's debut 'Dying Remains'. Touring commenced in promotion of the record with valuable supports to OBITUARY, DEATH, DEICIDE and NAPALM DEATH.

The second album, 1994's 'As Humanity Fades', saw MORTA SKULD out on the road opening for FEAR FACTORY and CANNIBAL CORPSE. The band kept up this work ethic for 1995's 'For All Eternity' guesting for TESTAMENT and MORBID ANGEL. However, the departure of longterm guitarist Jason O'Connell saw MORTA SKULD pull in ex-REALM man Takis Kinis for 1997's 'Surface' album.

MORTA SKULD rounded off the millennium by cutting two tracks for tribute albums—OZZY OSBOURNE's 'Believer' and MERCYFUL FATE's 'Desecration Of Souls', the latter featured on 'The Unholy Sounds Of The Demon Bells—A Tribute To Mercyful Fate' collection issued via Poland's Still Dead Productions.

MORTA SKULD members would re-surface in 2002 brandishing a new act by the name of MS2. This band comprised vocalist Andrew Broas, guitarist Dave Gregor, bass player Jason Hellman and Ed Wallner on drums. This band unit later changed title to 9MM SOLUTION, cutting a Chris Dujuricic produced EP 'The Trial' in 2004.

Takis has scene credentials with a swathe of acts such as K.O.R., WHITE FEAR CHAIN and PROPHIT. During 2004 the six-stringer joined Death Metal outfit DECAPITADO, fronted by DIE KREUZEN's Dan Kubinski.

DYING REMAINS, Peaceville DEAF 11 (1992). Lifeless / Without Sin / Devoured Fears / Dying Remains / Useless To Mankind / Rotting Ways / Withering Seclusion / Hatred Creation / Scarred / Consuming Existence / Presumed Dead.

AS HUMANITY FADES, Peaceville DEAF 64 (1994). Unknown Emotions / A Century Of Ruins / Humanity's Lost / Awakening Destiny / Paradise Of The Masses / No World Escapes / Different Breeds / Sanctuary Denied / Relics / The Sorrow Fields.

FOR ALL ETERNITY, Peaceville CDVILE 57 (1995). Bitter / For All Eternity / Vicious Circle / Justify / Tears / Germ Farm / Second Thought / Crawl Inside / Burning Daylight.

SURFACE, System Shock (1997). The Killing Machine / Save Yourself / The Anger In Disguise / Time Will Never Forget / Surface / Lords Of Discipline / If I Survive / In Nothing We Trust.

MORTAL DECAY

NJ, USA — *Kelly Izquierdo (vocals), John Hartman (guitar), Joe Gordon (guitar), Ron Steinhauer (bass), Anthony Ipri (drums).*

South Jersey Death Metal act formed up in late 1991 as a trio of John Paoline on lead vocals, guitarist John Hartman and drummer Anthony Ipri. MORTAL DECAY, adding guitarist Anthony Divigenze and bassist Brandon Stockl issued the opening demo 'Dawn Of Misery' in February of 1992. After these sessions Divigenzie left to be replaced by Brian Valenti. The band issued a second demo 'Grisly Aftermath' in March of 1993 which further progress and pulled in valuable media exposure. However, both Valenti and Stockl departed at this juncture. Bassist Ron Steinhauer and guitarist Joe Gordon would bring the band back up to strength.

June 1995's demo 'Brutalizing Creations' prompted a bout of nation-wide touring including gigs in Canada. This momentum was stalled though as Paoline exited in early 1996. MORTAL DECAY persevered by inducting Kelly Izquierdo of DEATHRUNE. As such the band signed to the Pulverizer label for their debut July 1997 album 'Sickening Erotic Fanaticism'. Tour promotion with running mates DEADEN saw the band covering the East Coast and the Midwest. MORTAL DECAY's prior demo recordings would be compiled for the 1999 'A Gathering Of Human Artifacts' album.

As 1998 drew to a close Izquierdo was dismissed. MORTAL DECAY continued to gig with erstwhile frontman John Paoline acting as stand in. Izquierdo made a return for the 2000 'Bloodletting' tour billed alongside DISGORGE, DEEDS OF FLESH and CEPHALIC CARNAGE.

Kelly Izquierdo would make his exit once again from the band in March of 2001, during the recording of the 'Forensic' album. John Paoline duly re-took the role of frontman.

The band put in a run of live dates alongside PYREXIA and INTERNAL BLEEDING in July of 2003. European dates throughout September of 2005 had the band hooked up with Malta's BEHEADED and Holland's BRUTUS.

SICKENING EROTIC FANATICISM, Pulveriser (1997). Decomposed With Nitric Acid / Sickening Erotic Fanaticism / Revived Half Dead /

Mediating Through Mayhem / Apparitions / Opening The Graves / Colombian Necktie / Soaking In Entrails / Consume The Rancid Gore / Rejoice In Moribund.

A GATHERING OF HUMAN ARTIFACTS, MDK Entertainment (1999). Ars Moriendi / Dawn Of Misery / Requiem / Postmortem Feast / Mortal Decay / Splendid Decomposition / Bereavement / Rejoice In Moribund / Gruesomely Deceased / Grisly Aftermath / Consume The Rancid Gore / Human Fossils / Apparitions / Revived Half Dead / Opening The Graves / Soaking In Entrails / Delirium.

FORENSIC, Unique Leader Entertainment ULR60007 (2002). My Mind Bleeds Tragedies / Insect To Flesh / Chronicles / Monkey Cage / Beyond Forensic Knowledge / Recollections / Razor Slice Décor / Brutalized And Defiled / Driven Into Hysterics.

MORTAL FORM

HOLLAND — *Edme (vocals), Teun (guitar), Vincent (guitar), Tobias (bass), Bastiaan (drums).*

Formulated in Duiven during 1994 by guitarists Vincent and Teun together with drummer Bastiaan as ODD FUNERAL, a SEPULTURA and BLACK SABBATH covers band. By 1999 the band had adopted a Thrash / Death stance and were pursuing original material. Evolving into MORTAL FORM the group underwent line up changes as vocalist / bassist Tim departed prior to recording of the debut self financed EP 'X-Plore'. The lead vocalist mantle for these sessions was taken by Edme.

In 2000 erstwhile LAB RAT bassist Tobias joined the fold for 'The End Of Times'. The inaugural full length album 'Evil Reborn' arrived in early 2002. Guitarist Teun, retaining his ties with MORTAL FORM, would team up with Gothic Metal band HER ENCHANTMENT during 2001.

EVIL REBORN, (2001). Write My Death / End Of Times / Animal Dynamo / Am I Fooled / Subject Saccharine / Two Bloody Years / Resurrector / Birth In The Cesspool / Shader / P.O.S.

MORTALITY

KINGS LANGLEY, NSW, AUSTRALIA — *Darren Maloney (vocals), Craig Figl (guitar), Luke Ford (bass), Steve Pell (drums).*

Kings Langley, Sydney Death Metal combo MORTALITY, featuring former KILSWITCH drummer Steve Pell, released the demo 'Eternal Life' in February 1993. The EP 'Aggression=Power' followed on Warhead Records, after which the group raised its national profile supporting SEPULTURA. However, both guitarist Darren Jenkins and drummer Rick Fuda opted out, the former joining CRYOGENIC. Staying with Warhead, the full-length 'Structures' album emerged in 1997. Progress was stalled though when frontman Darren Maloney too jumped ship to CRYOGENIC. Remaining band members forged Rap Metal act PORN CADDY. Later associations saw drummer Steve Pell with YOU BLABBED ABOUT MARS, featuring KILSWITCH's guitarist Ruben Sanchez and bassist Rick Sanchez, before rejoining guitarist Craig Figl with THREE POINT TILT. Bassist Luke Ford worked with MANY MACHINES ON NINE.

Aggression=Power, Warhead WH05 (1993). Intro / End Of An Era / Twisted Truth / Underground / Beyond The Call.
Eternal Life, (1993). Substance / Reanimated Corpse / The Living Dead / Violence Beckons Violence.
STRUCTURE, Warhead WHCD16 (1997). D.Form / Slave Drive / What God? / Structure / Inventory / Step / Wonderland Again / Unlearn / Bad Seed / Society In Progress / In Progress.

MORTEM

LIMA, PERU — *Fernan Nebiro (vocals / guitar), Wilber Rosan (guitar), Juan C. Muro (bass), Jaime Garcia (drums).*

The Lima based Death Metal act MORTEM, founded during 1986 by brothers Fernan Nebiro on vocals and guitar and drummer Alvaro Amduscias, first came to attention with the 1989 demo session 'Evil Dead'. The 'Superstition' demo followed in 1989, 'Vomit Of The Earth' in 1992. An earlier credited member, guitarist Janio Cuadros, had been the victim of an ever fluctuating line up which finally settled in 1992 on Nebiro, Amduscias, guitarist Wilber Rosan and bass player Carlos Verastegiu. A further demo ensued titled 'Unearth The Buried Evil' in 1993.

In 1996 MORTEM issued their debut album 'Demon Tales' on the Peruvian Coyote label. MORTEM's 1998 album 'The Devil Speaks In Tongues', their first for German label Merciless Records, includes a cover of the SACRIFICE track 'Turn In Your Grave'. Merciless would also re-issue 'Demons Tales' for the European market. MORTEM's rhythm section was now in the hands of bass player Juan C. Muro and drummer Jaime Garcia.

Sandro Garcia would take the guitar position followed by Christian John in 1999. However, Wilber Rosan would subsequently rejoin for the band's third album 'Decomposed By Possession'. Once again MORTEM produced cover versions, the last two tracks on the album being versions of POSSESSED's 'Satan's Curse' and SLAYER's 'Crypt Of Eternity'.

MORTEM put in a mini tour of Europe in March of 2003 with shows in Gothenburg and Stockholm, Sweden as well as Germany and Holland. The band's debut US show came in June of 2004, performing in Chicago as support to THE CHASM.

DEMON TALES, Merciless MR CD004 (1997). Daemonium Vobiscum / End Of The Christian Era / A Demon's Tale / Satan II / Ungay Man (Mother Of Disease) / Vomit Of The Earth / Unearth The Buried Evil / Demonolatry / Blackened Arts / Tormented By The End.
THE DEVIL SPEAKS IN TONGUES, Merciless (1998). Fiat Obscuritas / Demons Haunt Loudun / Uma, Head Of The Witch / Summoned To Hell / Mutilation Rites / Devil Speaks In Tongues / Posthumous Magic / Turn In Your Grave / Zombie Plague / Sucubus / Lycanthropes (Howling Death) / Moon Of Cannibalism.
DECOMPOSED BY POSSESSION, Merciless MR CD0014 (2000). Death Rules Supreme / Devilled / Blackest Funeral / Morgue Rapist / Hell And Beyond / Curdled Blood / Decomposed By Possession / Noctivagants / Incubus: The Return.

MORTICIAN

NY, USA — *Will Rahmer (vocals / bass), Roger Beaujard (guitar), Desmond Tolhurst (guitar).*

New York Gore Death Metallers founded by ex-INCANTATION frontman, horror movie fan and daytime florist (!) Will Rahmer. (Rahmer's day job has found the man immortalized in the ANAL CUNT song 'Morbid Florist'). The band was named after the character of an undertaker from the movie 'Phantasm'. Early member and guitarist Brian Sekula jumped ship to create BLOODSICK.

MORTICIAN's early drummer Matt Cicero died and since then the band has employed a drum machine in the studio and pulled in session drummers as and when needed for touring. MORTICIAN's 1995 album 'House By The Cemetery' included a version of CELTIC FROST's 'Procreation Of The Wicked'.

The band were unable to tour to promote early releases as both Rahmer and guitarist Roger Beaujard were both on police probation, one for possession of drugs and an unlicensed firearm and one for assault. Road work in 1997 saw FUNERAL PYRE man Vick Novak inducted as drummer. MORTICIAN added guitarist Desmond Tolhurst, from Beaujard's side project MALIGNANCY, for the 'Zombie Apocalypse' album.

The 1999 release 'Chainsaw Dismemberment's cover (depicting a woman with limbs hacked off) was unsurprisingly banned by many record stores. For touring purposes the band pulled in former DEHUMANISE drummer George Torrez.

Beaujard and Tolhurst's project group MALIGNANCY issued the 'Intrauterine Cannibalism' album. For the 2001 MORTICIAN album 'Domain Of Death' the band included two cover versions, namely takes on PUNGENT STENCH's 'Pulsating Protoplasma' and DISASTROUS MURMUR's 'Extra Uterine Pregnancy'. By March of 2002 Tolhurst had teamed up with ENGORGE as their new bass player. MORTICIAN would set September U.S. tour dates with support from SCAR CULTURE, fans being able to purchase advance copies of the new 'Darkest Days Of Horror' CDs at these shows.

UK and European dates projected into October of 2003, dubbed the 'Bonded By Metal' trek, found the band forming up a billing comprising EXODUS, AGENT STEEL, NUCLEAR ASSAULT, GOD DETHRONED, OCCULT and CALLENISH CIRCLE. New man Sam Inzerra, a scene veteran of MORPHEUS DESCENDS and DEADSPEAK, would be installed on drums for this trek. The band got back onto the road in the USA during late September of 2004, with support provided by AKERCOCKE and VEHEMENCE.

To open 2005 MORTICIAN hooked up with INCANTATION, THE CHASM and ARSIS for the 'Winter Migration Broootality' US tour commencing early January. Further gigs were projected with IMPALED and THINE EYES BLEED but the former withdrew, slamming the organisers for "unprofessional booking practices", with the second act also dropping off the bill a few days later.

In the Autumn of 2005 the erstwhile MORTICIAN guitar duo of Desmond Tolhurst and Ron Kachnic headed up a new band unit, uniting with LEVIATHAN vocalist Shane Tierney and the former DIRTY BROWN EYE rhythm section of bassist Art Micewicz and drummer Jim Horan to forge PRIMER BLACK.

MORTICIAN undertook November European shows ranked alongside BLOOD RED THRONE and AKERCOCKE. Unfortunately Will Rahmer found himself arrested by the Polish police following a gig in the Polish city of Zielona Gora on 13th November. The frontman allegedly assaulted a taxi driver with a knife and then stole the taxi cab, driving to the German border where he was detained at Swiecko. Police, arresting him under the charge robbery with a dangerous weapon, found a knife and a set of knuckledusters on his person. Members of AKERCOCKE and BLOOD RED THRONE pooled talents to cover vocals and bass duties in order for MORTICIAN to continue the dates.

Brutally Mutilated, Seraphic Decay (1990). Brutally Mutilated.
HOUSE BY THE CEMETERY, Relapse (1995). Defiler Of The Dead / Barbaric Crueltie / World Domination / Driller Killer / House By The Cemetery / Procreation Of The Wicked / Scum / Gateway To Beyond / Flesheaters / Noturam Demondo.
CHAINSAW DISMEMBERMENT, Relapse (1999). Stab / Fleshripper / Drowned In Your Blood / Mass Mutilation / Mauled Beyond Recognition / Rabid / Bloodshed / Decayed / Final Bloodbath / Island Of The Dead / Brutalized / Slaughtered / The Crazies / Silent Night, Bloody Night / Chainsaw Dismemberment / Psychotic Rage / Funeral Feast / Wolfen / Dark Sanity / Camp Blood / Tormented / Slaughterhouse (Part II) / Barbarian / Rats / Mater Tenebrarum / Splattered / Obliteration / Lords Of The Dead (Mortician Part II).
DOMAIN OF DEATH, Relapse (2001). Brood Of Evil / Maimed And Mutilated / Bonecrusher / The Hatchet Murders / Extinction Of Mankind / Domain Of Death / Cannibalized / Pulsating Protoplasma / Martin (The Vampire) / Telepathic Terror / Mutilation Of The Human Race / Wasteland Of Death / Dr. Gore / Extra Uterine Pregnancy / Tenebrae / Devastation / Necromonicon Exmortis.
THE FINAL BLOODBATH SESSION, Primitive Recordings (2002) Live album. Blown To Pieces / Embalmed Alive / Zombie Apocalypse / Drilling For Brains / Bone Crusher / Domain Of Death / Final Bloodbath / Hacked Up For Barbeque / Chainsaw Dismemberment / Worms / Doctor Gore / Slaughtered / The Crazies / Necrocannibal / Cremated / Redrum / Extinction Of Mankind / Driller Killer / World Damnation / Witches Coven / The Hatchet Murders / Brutally Mutilated / Martin The Vampire / Bloodcraving / Slaughterhouse / Mortician / Lord Of The Dead.
DARKEST DAY OF HORROR, Relapse RR 6562 (2003). Audra / Slowly Eaten / The Bloodseekers / Voodoo Curse / Massacred / Human Puzzle / Chopped To Pieces / Revenge / Mangled / Dead And Buried / Darkest Day Of Horror / Rampage / Cannibalistic Fiends / Carving Flesh / Ghost House / Vaporized / Pledge Night Of Death / Taste For Blood / Disintegrated / The Final Sacrifice.
RE-ANIMATED DEAD FLESH, Crash Music (2005). Werewolves Curse / Burned Alive / Bludgeoned / Marauding Savages / Skinned / Human Beasts / Bloodsoaked Carnage / Unseen Force Of Death / Torn Apart / Axe / Punishment / Re-Animated Dead Flesh / Buzzards / Madman Marz / Return To The Grave / Dismembered / Dead Pit / Crazed For Blood / Slugs / Claws Of Death / Mass Destruction / Be My Victim.

MORTIFER

TUMBA, SWEDEN — *Dementor (vocals / guitar), Heinous (bass / keyboards), Devastator (drums).*

A Tumba based Death Metal act forged by bassist / keyboard player Heinous (a.k.a. Jonas Berndt / 'Goth Gorgon'), prior to his founding of MÖRK GRYNING. Berndt also has association with DIABOLICAL and WYVERN. A two song 1994 demo session featured vocalist Daniel. Far Beyond Human Productions released a second demo, 'Battle Of Titans' featuring guitarist Peter Wendin, in 1996. RAISE HELL and SINS OF OMISSION guitarist Jonas Nilsson also figured in an early line-up. A third MORTIFER set, 1987's 'Running Out Of Time', included a cover version of KREATOR's 'Take Their Lives'. The group then recorded tracks during 1998 for an intended album, given a title 'Masters Of The Universe', but this was never released. MORTIFER's final effort, the single track promotional session 'Harbringer Of Horror', emerged in 1999.

MORTIFER's final roster involved Heinous, Dementor (Danny Eideholm) and drummer Devastator (Dennis Ekdahl) of ATHELA, BLOODSHED, MYSTIC PROPHECY, MOURNFUL, RAISE HELL, RUTTHNA and SINS OF OMISSION.

Running Out Of Time, Far Beyond Human Productions (1987) (Demo). Time For War / Running Out Of Time / Jaws In The Night / Take Their Lives / Real World Dementor / Vlad Dracul Tepes.
Mortifer Promo, Mortifer (1994) (Demo). Infernal Dream / A Touch With Eternity.
Battle Of Titans, Far Beyond Human Productions (1996) (Demo). Darkside / Blade Of The Barbarian / Five Wizards Of The Land Beyond The Forest / Andarnas Land.
Harbringer Of Horror, Mortifer (1999) (Demo). Harbringer Of Horror.

MORTIFICATION

MELBOURNE, VIC, AUSTRALIA — *Steve Rowe (vocals / bass), Michael Carlisle (guitar), Jayson Sherlock (drums).*

MORTIFICATION initially made their mark on the international scene by being, initially, one of a handful of Christian extreme Metal bands. Their evangelistic message was as uncompromising as their music which gave no concessions when pitted against more familiar acts of the genre. Melbourne frontman Steve Rowe cut his teeth with the more mainstream Metal act LIGHTFORCE created in 1987. American label Pure Metal released their debut 1989 album 'Mystical Thieves' as LIGHTFORCE guested for STRYPER on their Australian tour the same year.

1990 Rowe founded MORTIFICATION with guitarist Michael Carlisle and drummer Jayson Sherlock soon signing a deal with American label Intense. MORTIFICATION's sense of industry saw the rapid release of 'Break The Curse', 'Scrolls Of Megilloth' plus the live video 'Grind Planets' and a set up to German label Nuclear Blast for Europe.

MORTIFICATION toured America in 1992 with former VENGEANCE RISING drummer Johnny Vasquez. Rowe had guested as backing vocalist for the fourth VENGEANCE RISING album 'Released Upon The Earth'. Album sales increased with 'Post Momentary Affliction' surpassing the 30'000 sales mark in Europe alone. MORTIFICATION switched drummers once more in 1994 bringing in Phil Gibson for their sixth album 'Blood World'. This feat coincided with Rose's first novel 'Minstrel'.

1995 found MORTIFICATION splintering but with American tour commitments Rose employed Canadian musicians Jason Campbell and Dave Kellogg on guitars and drummer Bill Price for the 'Primitive Rhythm Machine' outing. The band added ex-DELIVERANCE guitarist George Ochoa to record the 'EnVision EvAngelene' record. Rowe was diagnosed with leukemia in 1996 but this has hardly affected the band's work ethic. For 1998's 'Triumph Of Mercy' album on new label Metal Blade Rowe was joined by guitarist Lincoln Bowen and drummer

Keith Bannister. Interestingly MORTIFICATION's first drummer Jayson Sherlock provided the artwork for the album. The band enrolled new guitarist Mick Jelinic on guitar and a new man on the drums in Adam Zaffarese. The latter would be superseded by the RAGEWAR, DIMENTIA, CATWITCH and CYBERGRIND credited Mike Forsberg in 2003. The band's twelfth album, entitled 'Brain Cleaner', was set for a February 2004 release through Rowe Productions. The band confirmed an appearance at the first international 'Revolution Metal Fest' held at the Palacio de los Deportes in Mexico City, Mexico on November 20th alongside fellow Christian artists NARNIA, STRYPER, MORTIFICATION and EXOUSIA. Drummer Mike Forsberg exited in June 2005 as the band were in preparation for an album given an unlikely working title of 'Impaling The Goblin'. This would be changed, apparently so as not to cause offence to "European Orientals", to 'Erasing The Goblin'.

MORTIFICATION announced the addition of drummer Damien Percy to the group's ranks in February 2006. The band teamed up with an all-Christian package comprising NARNIA, ROB ROCK and EXOUSIA for a South and Central American tour in November 2006 hitting Mexico, Guatemala, Honduras, Brazil, Argentina, Colombia and Costa Rica.

MORTIFICATION, Intense FLD 8501 (1991). Until The End / Brutal Warfare / Bathed In Blood / Satan's Doom / Turn / No Return / Break The Curse / New Awakening / Destroyer Beholds / Journey Of Reconciliation / The Majestic Infiltration Of Order.

SCROLLS OF THE MEGILLOTH, Intense FLD 9277 (1992). Nocturnal / Terminate Damnation / Eternal Lamentation / Raise The Chalice / Lymphosarcoma / Scrolls Of The Megilloth / Death Requiem / Necromanicide / Inflamed / Ancient Prophecy.

POST MOMENTARY AFFLICTION, Nuclear Blast NB 0082-2 (1993). Allusions From The Valley Of Darkness / From The Valley Of Shadows / Human Condition / Distarnish Priest / Black Lion Of The Mind / Grind Planetarium / Pride Sanitorium (Reprise) / Overseer / This Momentary Affliction / Flight Of Victory / Impulsation / Liquid Assets / Vital Fluids / The Sea Of Forgetfulness.

LIVE PLANETARIUM, Intense FLD 9468 (1993). Grind Planetarium / Distarnish Priest / Brutal Warfare / Destroyer Beholds / Inflamed / Scrolls Of The Megilloth / Symbiosis / Time Crusaders / Black Snake / From The Valley Of Shadows / Human Condition / Majestic Infiltration Of Order / This Momentary Affliction.

BREAK THE CURSE, Nuclear Blast NB 0101-2 (1994). Blood Sacrifice / Brutal Warfare / Impulsation / Turn / New Beginning / Break The Curse / Illusion Of Life / Your Last Breath / Journey Of Reconciliation / The Majestic Infiltration Of Order / Butchered Mutilation.

BLOOD WORLD, Intense FLD 9488 (1994). Clan Of The Light / Blood World / Starlight / Your Life / Monks Of The High Lord / Symbiosis / Love Song / Live By The Sword / JGSH / Dark Allusion.

Tourniquet / Mortification Collector's Edition CD Single, Intense FLD 9488 (1994) (Split single with TOURNIQUET). Your Life / J.G.S.H. / Love Song / Steve Rowe Talks.

PRIMITIVE RHYTHM MACHINE, Nuclear Blast NB 0134-2 (1995). Primitive Rhythm Machine / Mephibosheth / Seen It All / The True Essence Of Power / Toxic Shock / 40:31 / Gut Wrench / Confused Belief / Providence / Killing Evil.

Noah Sat Down And Listened To The Mortification Live EP While Having A Coffee, Rowe Productions ROWE 015 (1996). Envision A Beginning / Buried Into Obscurity / Steve Talks / Noah Was A Knower / Interview With Steve.

ENVISION EVANGELENE, Nuclear Blast NB 0159-2 (1996). EnVision EvAngelene / Northern Storm / Peace In Our Galaxy / Jehovah Nissi / Buried In Obscurity / Chapel Of Hope / Noah Was A Knower / Crusade For The King.

TRIUMPH OF MERCY, Metal Blade 14192 (1998). At War With War / Triumph Of Mercy / Welcome To The Palodrome / From Your Side / Influence / Drain Dweller / Raw Is The Stonewood Temple / Unified Truth / Visited By An Angel.

HAMMER OF GOD, Metal Blade 14258 (1999). Metal Crusade / Martyrs / Lock Up The Night / In The Woods / Pearl / Hammer Of God / Liberal Mediocrity / Extreme Conditions / Ride The Light / DWAM / Medley / God Rulz / At War With War / Visited By An Angel / Unified Truth / Metal Crusade.

10 YEARS LIVE NOT DEAD, Metal Blade MB 14304 (2000). Dead Man Walking / Buried Into Obscurity / Medley / Martyrs / Peace In The Galaxy / Hammer Of God / Influence / Steve Thanks / Mephibosheth / Chapel Of Hope / Liberal Mediocrity / God Rulz / King Of Kings.

LIVE WITHOUT FEAR, Rowe Productions ROWE 014 (2000). Mephibosheth / Northern Storm / Primitive Rhythm Machine / New Beginnings / Grind Planetarium / Blood World / Steve Talks / The Majestic Infiltration Of Order / Jesus Grind Satan's Head / Killing Evil.

THE SILVER CORD IS SEVERED, Nuclear Blast NB 0583-2 (2001). Metal Blessing / Access Denied / Hardware / Bring The Joy / Standing At The Door Of Death / Whom They Would Kill / I Am A Revolutionary / Forsake The Flesh / Sensitive Nerve Endings / The Silver Cord Is Severed.

RELENTLESS, Rowe Productions ROWE 036 (2002). Intro / Web Of Fire / God Shape Void / Priests Of The Underground / Bring Release / Syncretize / Other Side Of The Coin / Altar Of God / Sorrow / 3 Of A Kind / Arm The Anointed / New York Skies / Apocalyptic Terror.

ERASING THE GOBLIN (LIMITED EDITION), Rowe Productions (2006). Razorback / Erasing The Goblin / The Dead Shall Be Judged / Escape The Blasphemous Tabernacle / Your Time / Forged In Stone / Way Truth Life / Humanitarian / Short Circuit / Dead Man Walking.

MORTIFIED

TALLINN, ESTONIA — *Mart Kalvet (vocals), Kaido Tiits (guitar), Rene Piirkop (guitar), Raimo Jussila (bass), Henry Hinno (drums).*

Tallinn melodic Death Metal band MORTIFIED features singer Mart Kalvet, a scene veteran of NITROUS, DAWN OF GEHENNA, WHISPERING FOREST, TAAK, HERALD and EC-THALION. Guitarist Kaido Tiits holds credits with PREDATORY WAR, TAAK and DAWN OF GEHENNA whilst drummer Henry 'Suss' Hinno has associations with MUST MISSA, MANATARK, SKYDANCER and RATTLER. The demo ' Introitus Mortifer' arrived in 1992 with follow up demo 'Serenity. Tranquillity. Peace.', recorded at Tallinn's Townhall Studios, was issued in December 1993.

Kaido Tiits opted out in 1995, subsequently joining PREDATORY WAR and DAWN OF GEHENNA. He was briefly replaced by Babushkin of RATTLER but the group folded shortly afterward.

Introitus Mortifer, (1992). Intro / Still Proceeding / Eternity In Our Eyes / Twilight Zone.

Serenity. Tranquillity. Peace., Mortified (1993). Intro: Jackhammerrape/ The Manifestation / Oblivion My Brother / The Twilight Zone / Dark Seducing Beauty / Misty Hours / Epitaph For The Mortified / Wilderness / Magic Circle / Solitaire / Outro: Stalk Thy Path / Still Proceeding.

MORTUARY

FRANCE — *Patrick Germonville (vocals), Alexis Baudin (guitar), Christophe De La Fuente (guitar), Jean-Noël Verbecq (bass), Jean-Yves Chateaux (drums).*

Death Metal band, founded initially under the formative title TOTAL DEAD by former SLEUTH EYES singer Patrick Germonville and ex-TRAKTOR bassist Jean-Noël Verbecq, dating to the late 80s. Subsequent recruits included guitarist Gilles Pincet of WOLFEN and in March of 1989, rhythm guitarist Jean Paul Gralak and drummer Guy Pommet. However, by July of that year Gérard Phillipe and Pierre Laurent had also come onboard. A three track demo was cut under the TOTAL DEAD banner before the group relaunched itself as MORTUARY.

MORTUARY's first recording sessions resulted in the 1990 demo 'Below The Marble'. Further tapes, 'In Harmony With Brutality' in 1992 and 'The Mortified Faces' during 1994, followed as the band underwent a succession of line up changes. Pincet departed prior to 'In Harmony With Brutality' to join DEPRAVED and was replaced by Jean Serge Kuhn of DR. MEZCAL. In 1993 Pommet quit, being superseded by Jean-Yves Chateaux. Upon completion of 'The Mortified Faces' Gralak decamped and for a while MORTUARY soldiered on as a quartet until the eventual arrival of Alexis Baudin.

In 1996 the band opted to self finance a debut album 'Hazards Of Creation', that same year enrolling guitarist Christophe De La Fuente. Signing to Thunder Productions MORTUARY followed up with the 1999 Bruce Donini produced 'Eradicate'. Unfortunately both Chateaux and De La Fuente bailed out, leaving the band in an awkward predicament. Christophe Touly became the new man on guitar whilst Dirk Verbeuren, of SCARVE, ABORTED and LYZANXIA repute, took over the drums for a 2001 album 'Agony In Red'.

HAZARDS OF CREATION, Independent (1996). Lands Of Immortality / Dead Heroes For Nothing / Evaporated Landscapes / Prelude To Homicide / Apocalyptic Resurrection / Suffocating Thoughts / Claustrophobia.

ERADICATE, Pavement (1999). A Step Towards Amenta / Killing Waves / Fragments Of Life / Trauma / Ephemeral Funeral / On Silent Paths / Primary Urge / Organ / Misery / Unity Or Extinction / Humanicide / Create—Eradicate.

AGONY IN RED, (2001). Negative / Another Land To Conquer / Elimination / Agony In Red / Carnival Of The Lost Souls / Calvary / Exit / Fifteen Minutes / Televiolence / As I Lay Dying.

MORTUM

KRISTIANSTAD, SWEDEN — *Finna Carlsdoller (vocals), Chrille Anderson (vocals / guitar), Michael Hakansson (vocals / bass), Rille Svensson (guitar), Bartek Nalezinski (drums).*

A Kristianstad Death Metal unit often accused of having Black Metal tendencies, denied by band members. Michael Håkansson is a member of EMBRACED. Chrille Andersson has credits with NON SERVIAM and HELLSPELL. Håkansson also performs with EVERGREY, THE FORSAKEN and was involved with CENOTAPHIA. MORTUM released the 1999 album 'The Druid Ceremony' through Invasion Records.

A large contingent of MORTUM's membership, guitarists Chrille Anderson, Rille Svensson and drummer Bartek Nalezinski, founded melodic Power Metal act SUPREME MAJESTY debuting in June 1999 with the mini-album 'Divine Enigma'. Nalezinski also held associations with INCINERATOR and THE GLADIATOR.

THE DRUID CEREMONY, Invasion (1998). Until Eternity / Punisher / Lady Lost / Night Spawned / The Druid Ceremony / Mother Of Fear / A Cursed Mankind / The Search For You / Outro.

MORTUS POETRY

TORREON COAHUILA, MEXICO — *Morigna (vocals), Abnoba (vocals), Aeon Neox (guitar), Aes Sidhe (guitar), Pit 6a6c6 (bass), Chimaera (drums).*

MORTUS POETRY is a Torreon Coahuila based, female fronted Gothic-Death Metal band. The group was founded in 2003 by former members of PRIEST OF SADNESS and Progressive Death Metal band KLOPFEN KALT, guitarist Poncho Lozano ('Aeon Neox'), vocalist Tony ('Abnoba') and Amaral. They would be joined by ex-SEA OF LIES members drummer Cadena ('Chimaera') and guitarist Jorge ('Aes Sidhe'), and finally, female singer Daniela ('Morigna'). Subsequently Pedro ('Pit 6a6c6') took the bass position.

MORTUS POETRY released the demos 'Enfer Noir' in 2003 and the six song 'Amore Maligna' the following year. The full length 'Deity' album followed in 2005.

Enfer Noir, Mortus Poetry (2003) (Limited edition 200 copies). Enfer Noir / Blasphemy / Euthanasia / Edge Of Sanity.

Amore Maligna, (2004). Intro (Amore Maligna) / In Your Hell / Groue Stabilittat / La Era de La Inocencia / Someday / Endless Suffering / Outro (Exorcism).

DEITY, (2005).

MORTYFEAR

SEINÄJOKI, FINLAND — *Sami Kaste (vocals), Juha Peippola (guitar), Tapio Laitila (guitar), Olli Assola (bass), Henri Yli-Rahko (drums).*

MORTYFEAR is a Seinäjoki based melodic Death Metal act dating to 1999. Upon is formation the band was entitled MORTIFIER and counted a line-up of vocalist Sami Kaste, guitarists Antti Hokkala and Tapio Laitila, bass player Olli Assola and CELESTY and CALDWELL drummer Jere Luokkamäki. Following the release of an opening demo, recorded at AMS Studios by Kimmo Ahola, the band switched title to MORTYFEAR. Following a third demo session Luokkamäki exited. Despite this setback, the band received additional exposure with the inclusion of their track 'Damnation' on the Low Frequency compilation album 'NorthernBreeze 2'.

Anssi Kaunismäki of MISERIA was drafted on the drums in mid 2002, being superseded himself by Henri Yli-Rahko. The guitar position would change too with the introduction of Juha Peippola. A fourth demo was delivered in 2003, followed by the 2004 session 'Let The Fist Do The Talking', recorded at Fantom Studios. A split release shared with ACHREN was planned for December.

Mortyfear, (2001). Ocean That Drowned Itself / Blind Delusion / Brothers Of Birth.

Mortyfear, (2001). Meren Raivo / Damnation.

Mortyfear, (2003). Give Fist Get Respect / Is It Safe To Be Disturbed? / Rotten Corpse.

Let The Fist Do The Talking, Mortyfear (2004). Revelation At The Dawn / I Rather Die And Burn In Hell / Let The Fist Do The Talking / Total Madness / Verestä Syntynyt.

MOURNING

GOUDA, HOLLAND — *Marc van Amelsvort (vocals / bass), René Roza (guitar), Pim (guitar), Andre Van Der Ree (drums).*

Death Metal act MOURNING, from Gouda, date to 1989. The band initially recorded a proposed split album with ETERNAL SOLSTICE in 1990, but this was not released as planned. However, three tracks were culled from these sessions for a demo. With guitarist Pim having quit at the close of 1991, the original split album was finally released in 1992 and original drummer Misha Hak quit just before MOURNING signed a deal with Foundation 2000 Records. Hak later contributed drums to ETERNAL SOLSTICE's debut full length album 'The Wish Is Father To The Thought'.

By coincidence ETERNAL SOLSTICE added Hak's replacement in MOURNING, Andre Van Der Ree, to their line-up in 1994.

Erstwhile MOURNING members vocalist / bassist Marc van Amelsvort, guitarist René Roza and drummer Andre van de Ree forged ROUWEN for a 1997 album 'Rouwkots'.

MOURNING, Midian Creations MID 001 (1992) (Split album with ETERNAL SOLSTICE).

GREETINGS FROM HELL, Foundations 2000 FDN 2006 (1993). Intro—Arma Satani / Sweet Dreams / Demon's Dance / Territorial / Denial Of Your Destiny / Only War And Hell / What? / Deranged Or Dead.

MUCOPUS

ALBANY, NY, USA — *Jason Keyser (vocals), Justin Knipper (guitar), Corey Hall (bass), Kyle Eddy (drums).*

MUCOPUS recorded their debut album at The Slaughterhouse in Rock City Falls, New York in early 2005. Having parted ways with frontman Rich Manzillo in April, MUCOPUS pulled in two SKINLESS veterans to act as stand ins. Singer Jason Keyser handled the vocal duties for MUCOPUS' appearance at the 'Tokyo Deathfest' in Japan, whilst former SKINLESS vocalist Sherwood Webber would join MUCOPUS for an 8th May concert at the Hudson Duster in Troy, New York. Extracurricular activity for MUCOPUS drummer Kyle Eddy saw the sticksman joining INTERNAL BLEEDING for US touring.

MUCOPUS recruited Adam Mason of GORATORY and SEXCREMENT repute as a temporary fill in for vocalist Jason Keyser for their September 2006 European tour dates supported by INFERIA and ROTTENNESS. Having signed to UK based label Grindethic Records the group cut tracks for a split album to be shared with Czech Grind combo MINCING FURY AND GUTTURAL CLAMOUR OF QUEER DECAY.

Mucopus, (2004). Corporation X / Pre-Natal Caesation / Wasted / Superfluous Anomia / Pre-Natal Caesation (Live).

MULCH?!?, Amputated Vein AVR014 (2005). One Is Too Many And A Thousand Is Never Enough / Superfluous Anomia / Pre-Natal Caseation / Language Unheard / Cock Blister / Corporation X / Technology Divine / Borf Snarffle Squirt / Wasted.

MURDER CORPORATION

SWEDEN — *Jens Johansson (vocals), Johan Axelsson (guitar), Dan Bengtsson (bass), Rikard Wermén (drums).*

MURDER CORPORATION is made up from guitarist Johan Axelsson, bassist Dan Bengtsson and drummer Rikard Wermén from DERANGED and fronted by ex-MEGASLAUGHTER vocalist Emil Lilic. Bengtsson also cites INVERTED credits. Hangnail Productions issued a split 7" single, 'Procreate Insanity', shared with VOMITORY in 2001. That same year the album 'Whole Lotta Murder Goin' On' featured a cover of TED NUGENT's 'Cat Scratch Fever'.

The band folded in 2003 with guitarist Johan Axelsson and drummer Rikard Wermén soon firing up a new outfit billed as KILLAMAN in alliance with being frontman Rune Foss of EXEMPT and RECLUSION, second guitarist Roger Johansson of INSISION and bass player Kaspar Larsen of WITHERING SURFACE.

BLOOD REVOLUTION 2050, Qabalah-Repulse QAB 003 (1996). Bulls Eye 8 Straight In The Head / Cyber Genocide / Blood Revolution 2050 / Point Blanc Rage / I'm In Hell.

MURDER CORPORATION, Regain RR 9910-003 (1997). Chaos Killed The World / Out Of Bullets / Point Blank Range / Squeeze The Trigger / Colombian Necktie / Blood Money / Held In Bondage / Self Teached Judges / 9mm Lobotomy / Brand New Scapegoats / Creating Something I Despise / Re-Lease The Prisoners.

Kill!, Planet End PE001 (1998). Violated (Only Rage Remains) / 9mm Lobotomy / Squeeze The Trigger / ... Nameless / Die Laughing / Dog Heaven.

SANTA IS SATAN, Psychic Scream (1998) (Split CD with GRIND BUTO). Fooled By The Fools / Muscle Of Madness / Predator / Children Of The Grave / Out Of Bullets / 12-Gauge Retaliation.

Retract The Hostile, Stormbringer Productions (1998). Retract The Hostile / Forced Into Regression.

Procreate Insanity, Hangnail Productions (2000) (Split 7" with VOMITORY). Procreate Insanity / Hostage Situation.

WHOLE LOTTA MURDER GOIN' ON, Psychic Scream PSDL 9040-2 (2001). Murder In Mind / Forcefed / Procreate Insanity / Violated / Self-Inflicted Virus / Wallow In Greed / Hostage Situation / Highest Power / Self-Teached Judges / Castration Crucifixtion / Retract The Hostile / Forced Into Regression / Buried Alive / Cat Scratch Fever / Chaos Killed The World / Headshot .357 / Held In Bondage / Legalize Murder.

TAGGED AND BAGGED, Displeased D00087 (2001). Kill For Recreation / Bite Your Own Tail / Superior Firepower / Survive / Stashed In The Trunk / Guerilla 2000 / Me Against The World / Worth Shit / Reverse And Despise / Inhuman Endeavor / Interstate Bloodshed.

MURDER IN ART

ÄÄNESKOSKI, FINLAND — *Mikko Nurmi (vocals), Markus Jämsen (guitar), Tomi Kankainen (bass / keyboards), Pasi Pasanen (drums).*

A Death Metal band originally entitled CLAYFORGE, under which title they issued the 1998 demo 'Kult Release'. At this juncture the band cited a line-up roster of vocalist Mikko 'Deepthroat' Nurmi, guitarists Juha 'Speedpick' Raivio and 'Fastfinger' Jämsen, bassist Tomi 'Stormhand' Kankainen and drummer Pasi 'Thunderpedal' Pasanen. The latter had already made his mark with Black Metal veterans MORNINGSTAR. Both guitarist Juha Raivio and bassist Tomi Kankainen had figured in WATERFRONT WEIRDOS.

As MURDER IN ART, and now minus Raivio, the band debuted with the 1999 album 'Scars', featuring re-works of the CLAYFORGE material, for the Mastervox label.

During early 2000 both Juha Raivio and Pasi Pasanen would forge the Stoner band PLUTONIUM ORANGE. The duo also operate a Doom Metal band side venture SWALLOW THE SUN in league with FUNERIS NOCTURNUM personnel. Raivio also features in EMBRAZE. Jämsen has scene affiliations with RAUTAKELLO, MURDER IN ART and SWALLOW THE SUN

SCARS, Mastervox MVXCD8 (1999). Blood Opera / Le Acteur De La Mort / Hell Parade / Demonic Invitation / Nightblade / Haunted Phrases / One Way / Under The Skin / Say No More / Lust Thrill Gain Power / Tired Mind Lost / The City.

MURDER SQUAD

STOCKHOLM, SWEDEN — *Matti Karki (vocals), Uffe Cederland (guitar), Rickard Cabeza (bass), Peter Stjärnvind (drums).*

Stockholm Death Metal band both proudly and blatantly influenced by AUTOPSY. The DISMEMBER duo of vocalist Matti Karkki and guitarist Rickard Cabeza would also collude with ENTOMBED's Uffe Cederlund and Peter Stjärnvind for their MURDER SQUAD project. Both Cabeza and Stjärnvind also operate BORN OF FIRE. Pavement Records issued the 2001 debut 'Unsane, Insane And Mentally Deranged'. Guesting on the 2003 album 'Murderous, Ravenous', would be drummer Chris Reifert of DEATH and AUTOPSY notoriety.

Cabeza added to his long list of extreme Metal citations in the Spring of 2002, acting as tour bassist for premier Black Metal act DARK FUNERAL's North American dates.

RAVENOUS, MURDEROUS, Threeman (2003).

MUTILATED

USA — *Justin Emery (vocals), Russ Crossman (vocals / guitar), Ryan Hall (guitar), Adam Meindel (bass), Tony Cosgrove (drums).*

In February of 2000 guitarists Russ Crossman and Ryan Hall alongside drummer Tony Cosgrove formed DECAPITATOR, this band soon switching title to MUTILATED, cutting an eight song, purely instrumental demo. In January of 2001 singer Justin Emery joined the band and that September the band put in their debut live gig as openers to MORTICIAN and EXHUMED, subsequently appearing at the 'Ohio Death Fest' in April of 2002. Signing to Forever Underground Records the band delivered the first album 'Devirginated Genital Pulp', recorded at Studio One in Racine, Wisconsin during December of 2002.

Tony Cosgrove decamped in August of 2003. He would be replaced by Zach Gibson of CURATE and GUTROT. However, Gibson resigned from his posts in both GUTROT and MUTILATED in June of 2004 in order to join THE BLACK DAHLIA MURDER.

DEVIRGINATED GENITAL PULP, Forever Underground FU018 (2003). Hollowed Out Cunt / Axe Vs. Throat / Female Face Breaker / Lactating Blood / Crush The Skull ... Consume The Contents / Shit Stuffed And Broiled / Her Spaded Anus / Burnt Off Human Face / Impetuous Bloodshed / To Fuck The Rotted.

MUTILATION

MIECHÓW, POLAND — *Slawek (vocals), Pawel (guitar), Tomek (guitar), Piotrek (bass), Marcin (drums).*

Miechów based MUTILATION's 'Possessed By Reality' album included a cover version of BOLT THROWER's 'Cenotaph'. To promote the album MUTILATION formed up part of an extreme Metal tour partnered with fellow Poles ETERNAL TEAR and TROMSNAR with Slovakian Death Metal affiliates CONTEMPT.

Bass player Piotrek (as 'Thyrsus') is also involved with TROMSNAR and GODERAK.

Touring throughout Poland in 2003 the band aligned themselves with the 'Possessed' tour ranked alongside Slovakians CONTEMPT plus domestic artists ETERNAL TEAR and TROMSNAR. The band would form up the 'Days Of Destruction' tour, alongside HATE, ABUSED MAJESTY, ESQUARIAL and PYORRHOEA, throughout Poland in December 2004.

POSSESSED BY REALITY, Empire (2003).

MY DYING BRIDE

HALIFAX, WEST YORKSHIRE, UK — *Aaron Stainthorpe (vocals), Hamish Glencross (guitar), Andrew Craighan (guitar), Ade Jackson (bass), Sarah Stanton (keyboards), Shaun Taylor-Steels (drums).*

MY DYING BRIDE is at the forefront of the British Doom Metal movement that includes such bands as label mates ANATHEMA and PARADISE LOST. MY DYING BRIDE have, bar one infamous aberration, stuck resolutely to their raison d'être. Relentlessly slow, thick, heavy chords allied with remarkably morose lyrics make MY DYING BRIDE a unique proposition and certainly a challenge to the listener. Since its debut, the Halifax based band has remained steadfast in an unwavering pursuit of extreme Metal despite, ironically enjoying the rewards of an international fan base despite the uncommercial nature of its output.

The group is rooted in ABIOSIS, a unit which issued a three track demo 'Noxious Emanation' in 1990. The initial formation numbered vocalist Aaron Stainthorpe, guitarists Andrew Craighan and Calvin Robertshaw plus drummer Rick Miah. Reformed as MY DYING BRIDE in June, the band released the 'Towards The Sinister' demo, noted for its complete absence of bass, recorded over two days in late November at Revolver Studios with Tim Walker manning the production desk. They followed this with the 'God Is Alone' 7" single, restricted to 1000 copies, on the French Listenable label, again utilising both Tim Walker and Revolver Studios in May 1991. The band signed to budding Yorkshire label Peaceville Records to release the 'Symphonaire Infernus Et Spera Empyrum' EP in 1992, debuting new bassist Ade Jackson in the process.

MY DYING BRIDE's first full-length album ,'As The Flower Withers' arriving in May 1992, established the band among press and fans alike. Jointly produced by label mentor Hammy and the band, the record stunned many critics, who struggled to find suitable descriptives to capture the radical nature of this work. In the midst of this confusion, few would disagree that MY DYING BRIDE had, in one fell swoop, turned the Doom genre on its head.

The group had driven deep into the core essence of doom, drastically overhauling every aspect of its composition. The album opened somewhat coyly with an orchestral exercise in deceit before the Latin lyricised 'Sear Me' challenged immediately. Songs were drawn out into near unbearable dirges, capped by the twin violin imbued colossi of 'The Bitterness and the Bereavement' and 'The Return of the Beautiful', Stainthorpe's prose held closer to the great British poets than standard rock n' roll and their deliberately infantile daubed logo also challenged convention. 'As The Flower Withers' was boldly offered up as a cornerstone of a new approach, undoubtedly spawning the successive drone movement.

'As The Flower Withers' provided the opportunity for their first tour of Europe. The progress gained by another EP, 1993's 'The Thrash Of Naked Limbs', was marred by drummer Rick badly damaging his hand, thus cancelling a projected tour with G.G.F.H. Prior to the groundbreaking 1993 'Turn Loose The Swans' album, which came in three different sleeves, the band added violinist / keyboardist Martin to the band and toured Europe once more. 'Turn Loose The Swans', incepting with the piano and violin lament of 'Sear Me MCMXC III' and hinged on the utterly woeful "The Crown Of Sympathy', slowed the pace even further and plunged ever deeper into sluglike doom. Another set of EPs, 'Sexuality Of Bereavement' and 'I Am The Bloody Earth', kept the momentum going during 1994.

'The Angel And The Dark River' was delivered during May 1995 and, in a rare high profile moment of mainstream activity, MY DYING BRIDE gigged as support to IRON MAIDEN across Europe. 'The Angel And The Dark River', six slabs of morose melancholy, marked a shift in the band's strategy, for the first time dropping the Death growl of Stainthorpe in favour of a "clean" vocal delivery. Fans were quick to hail opener 'Cry Of Mankind' as a classic, even though the mind numbing repeat keyboard mantra of the outro dragged on for a full five minutes. Limited editions of this record included a second disc of live material recorded at the Dynamo in Holland.

MY DYING BRIDE's fourth full-length endeavour, 'Like Gods Of The Sun', hit home in October 1996 in similar bleak fashion to its predecessor. Touring in Europe during March 1997 saw the band forming up a package billing alongside THERION, SENTENCED, ORPHANAGE and DARK for the 'Out Of The Dark III' festivals. However, drummer Rick departed and for their 1998 album sessions MY DYING BRIDE pulled in the services of YEAR ZERO and VALLE CRUSIS drummer Mike Unsworth in order to fill the gap. Acquired to handle keyboards would be Yasmine Ahmid of EBONY LAKE.

October 1998 saw MY DYING BRIDE issuing the experimental '34.788%... Complete' album with yet another new drummer ex-DOMINION man Bill Law. The record witnessed a deliberate break from the expected Gothic imagery associated with the band and provided a challenge for their existing fan base. A sharp division of opinion branded the album either as a somnambulistic, self indulgent failure or a richly rewarding diversion. Stainthorpe's vocals on '34.788%... Complete' took on a heavily distorted air, keyboards and samples usurped guitars and song structures ebbed and flowed without formal structure. Undoubtedly the most adventurous assay of the band's entire catalogue came with 'Heroin Chic', a mechanical, expletive infested industrial male / vocal rap duet with a guesting Michelle Richfield of DOMINION.

The band remained strangely inactive on the touring front though as guitarist Calvin Robertshaw departed. He would swiftly be replaced by erstwhile SOLSTICE, SERENITY and KHANG member Lee Baines. The 'Light At The End Of The World' album would be viewed not just as a welcome return to form, including a reprise for Stainthorpe's early growling, after the side step braved by '34.788%... Complete' but even as being one of the finests outings of the genre. For touring commitments in 1999 the band pulled in BAL SAGOTH's Jonny Maudling for live keyboards. The band's more permanent line up was completed with the addition of erstwhile ANATHEMA and SOLSTICE drummer Shaun Taylor-Steels and former SOLSTICE guitarist Hamish Glencross.

An ex-MY DYING BRIDE keyboard player Mark Newby Robson joined CRADLE OF FILTH rebilling himself Mark De Sade.

The 2002 offering 'The Dreadful Hours' included a re-make of 'The Return Of The Beautiful' from the debut record, re-billed as 'Return To The Beautiful'. MY DYING BRIDE themselves witnessed a change of keyboard players in April 2002 when Sarah Stanton took over from Yasmine Ahmed. MY DYING BRIDE also announced the release of their first live album, 'Voice Of The Wretched', the same month. Hamish Glencross and Andrew Craighan launched their BlackDoom Record label in 2003. MY DYING BRIDE put in a short burst of European dates in October of 2003, supported by UK act THE PROPHECY, the first signing to the BlackDoom label.

The band returned in March of 2004 with the album 'Songs Of Darkness, Words Of Light', warning fans in advance that change was in the air and that the track 'My Wine In Silence'

MY DYING BRIDE

was their most commercial effort to date. In late December Shaun Steels injured his ankle in a canoeing accident. The band drafted John Bennett from THE PROPHECY as stand in whilst Steels recovered.

Releases announced in early 2005 included the retrospective box set 'Anti-Diluvian Chronicles', which included new remixes of 'The Wreckage Of My Flesh', 'My Wine In Silence' and 'The Raven And The Rose', plus the live DVD 'Sinamorata', recorded in Antwerp, Belgium during October 2003. This latter release also featured two video shorts made by MY DYING BRIDE fans, 'Hope The Destroyer' and 'My Wine In Silence'.

In September 2005 it was learned that erstwhile keyboard player Martin Powell and his ex-CRADLE OF FILTH colleague guitarist James McIlroy had united with ex-HIMSA guitarist Matt Wicklund in a brand new band project called PREY. Meantime, MY DYING BRIDE returned to live action in the UK during November.

The album 'A Line Of Deathless Kings' was recorded during mid 2006 at Academy Studios in Dewsbury and mixed at Chapel Studios in Lincolnshire. The accompanying single, 'Deeper Down', hitting number 15 on the Finnish charts, was issued as an "Uberdoom" edit with exclusive studio track 'The Child Of Eternity'.

In early 2007 a painting by Aaron Stainthorpe, entitled 'Christs', was utilised as the cover art for Norwegian Doom band SYRACH's album 'Days Of Wrath'. During February the band lost both bassist Adrian Jackson and drummer John Bennet. Taking command of the drums would be the THINE, BAL SAGOTH, BROKEN, THE RAVEN THEORY, THE AXIS OF PERDITION and SERMON OF HYPOCRISY credited Dan Mullins.

Towards The Sinister, (1990). Symphonaire Infernus Et Spera Empyrium / Vast Choirs / The Grief Of Age / Catching Feathers.
God Is Alone, Listenable (1991). God Is Alone / De Sade Soliloquy.
Symphonaire Infernus Et Spera Empyrum, Peaceville VILE 27T (1992). Symphonaire Infernus / God Is Alone / De Sade Soliloquy.
AS THE FLOWER WITHERS, Peaceville VILE 32 (1992). Silent Dance / Sear Me / The Forever People / The Bitterness And The Bereavement / Vast Choirs / The Return Of The Beautiful / Erotic Literature.
TURN LOOSE THE SWANS, Peaceville VILE 39 (1993). Sear Me MCMXC III / Your River / The Songless Bird / The Snow In My Hand / The Crown Of Sympathy / Turn Loose The Swans / Black God.
The Thrash Of Naked Limbs, Peaceville VILE 37T (1993). The Thrash Of Naked Limbs / Le Cerf Malade / Gather Me Up Forever.
Sexuality Of Bereavement, Peaceville Collectors CC5 (1994). Sexuality Of Bereavement / Crown Of Sympathy.
I Am The Bloody Earth, Peaceville VILE 44T (1994). I Am The Bloody Earth / Transcending (Into The Exquisite) / Crown Of Sympathy (Remix).
TRINITY, Peaceville VILE 46 (1995). I Am The Bloody Earth / Transcending / Crown Of Sympathy / The Thrash Of Naked Limbs / Le Cerf Malade / Gather Me Up Forever / Symphonaire Infernus Et Spera Empyrium / God Is Alone / De Sade Soliliquy / Sexuality Of Bereavement.
THE ANGEL AND THE DARK RIVER, Peaceville VILE 50 (1995). The Cry Of Mankind / From Darkest Skies / Black Vote / A Sea To Suffer In / Two Winters Only / Your Shameful Heaven.
LIKE GODS OF THE SUN, Peaceville VILE 65 (1996). Like Gods Of The Sun / Dark Caress / Grace Unhearing / A Kiss To Remember / All Swept Away / For You / It Will Come / Here In The Throat / For My Fallen Angel.
34.788%... COMPLETE, Peaceville VILE 74 (1998). The Whore, The Cook And The Mother / The Stance Of Evander Sinque / Der Uberlebende / Heroin Chic / Apocalypse Woman / Base Level Erotica / Under Your Wings And Into Your Arms.
THE LIGHT AT THE END OF THE WORLD, Peaceville VILE 79 (1999). She Is The Dark / Edenbeast / The Night He Died / The Light At The End Of The World / The Fever Sea / Into The Lake Of Ghosts / The Isis Script / Christliar / Sear Me III.
THE DREADFUL HOURS, Peaceville VILE 90 (2001). The Dreadful Hours / The Raven And The Rose / Le Figlie Della Tempesta / Black Heart Romance / A Cruel Taste Of Winter / My Hope The Destroyer / The Deepest Of All Hearts / The Return To The Beautiful.
THE VOICE OF THE WRETCHED, Peaceville VILE 117 (2002). She Is The Dark / The Snow In My Hand / The Cry Of Mankind / Turn Loose The Swans / A Cruel Taste Of Winter / Under Your Wings And Into Your Arms / A Kiss To Remember / Your River / The Fever Sea / Symphonaire Infernus Et Spera Empyrium.
SONGS OF DARKNESS, WORDS OF LIGHT, Peaceville VILE 110 (2004). The Wreckage Of My Flesh / The Scarlet Garden / Catherine Blake / My Wine In Silence / The Prize Of Beauty / Blue Lotus / And My Fury Stands Ready / A Doomed Lover.
Deeper Down, Peaceville CDVILES158 (2006). Deeper Down (Uberdoom edit) / The Child Of Eternity / A Kiss To Remember (Live). Chart position: 15 FINLAND.
A LINE OF DEATHLESS KINGS, Peaceville VILE 150 (2006). To Remain Tombless / L'Amour Detruit / I Cannot Be Loved / And I Walk With Them / Thy Raven Wings / Love's Intolerable Pain / One Of Beauty's Daughters / Deeper Down / The Blood, The Wine, The Roses.

MY SILENT WAKE

WESTON SUPER MARE, SOMERSET, UK — *Ian Arkley (vocals / lead guitar), Andi Lee (guitar / bass), Alan Southorn (guitar / bass), Jasen Whyte (drums).*

Weston Super Mare, Somerset Metal band MY SILENT WAKE was forged during May 2005 by two former ASHEN MORTALITY members, vocalist . Guitarist Ian Arkley and guitarist / bassist Andi Lee. They would be joined in this new endeavour by guitarist Alan Southorn of THE OTHER WINDOW and BLOODWORK's Jasen Whyte on drums. Arkley holds a strong tradition on the UK Christian Metal scene with SEVENTH ANGEL. He would also guest on Australian Christian Death Metal act PARAMAECIUM's third album 'A Time To Mourn'

MY SILENT WAKE recorded a two track demo, comprising songs originally projected for ASHEN MORTALITY, at Kewsound Studios in Kewstoke during June 2005. Arkey also operates CENTURY SLEEPER. Bombworks Records released the album 'Shadow Of Sorrow' in March 2006.

MY SILENT WAKE completed tracks for a double album set in February 2007.

My Silent Wake, My Silent Wake (2005). Your Cold Embrace / Encircle.
SHADOW OF SORROW, Bombworks (2006). Wake / Shadow Of Sorrow / Burning / Hunting Season / The Mist / In Darkness / Lost / Through Greenest Meadows / Shadow Reprise / Your Cold Embrace / Encircle.

MYGRAIN

HELSINKI, FINLAND — *Tommyboy (vocals), Resistor (guitar), Matthew (guitar), Jonas Kuhlberg (bass), Eve Kojo (keyboards), DJ Locomotive (drums).*

Helsinki's melodic Death Metal band MYGRAIN was established during 2004, comprising singer Tommyboy, previously with WHAT, MOOD and the NEW SCIENCE BAND, guitarist Resistor, ex-GRIND, NEW SCIENCE BAND, SHAOLIN and SNEAKRAID, and Matthew, formerly also with MOOD and NEW SCIENCE RAID, bass player Jonas Kuhlberg, keyboard player Eve Kojo from EMBERS LEFT and ABLAZE IN HATRED with DJ Locomotive on the drums, an erstwhile member of ... AND OCEANS, DECEIVED and TERRORWHEEL. A first set of demos was recorded in November 2004. A second set, dubbed, 'The Red Frame', followed in April 2005 and scored a label deal with Spinefarm Records. Debut album 'Orbit Dance', issued in April 2006, was recorded at Sound Supreme studio with producer Janne Saksa.

Demo 2004, Mygrain (2004) (Demo). Gentle Blistering / Dark Season / Getaway Lane.
The Red Frame, Mygrain (2005) (Demo). Plastic / Downfall / W.I.F.
ORBIT DANCE, Spinefarm (2006). Plastic / Cold Reflection / W.I.F. / Pitch-Black / Darkbound / Humanimal / Misery Assembly Line / Downfall / Orbit Dance / Veil Of Sun / Hollowgram.

MYRKSKOG

DRAMMEN, NORWAY — *Master V (vocals / bass), Savant M (guitar), Destructhor (guitar), Anders Eek (drums).*

A highly individual approach to the genre makes Drammen's MYRSKOG a unique proposition. The band, founded in 1993, include former SUFFERING members and has had a fluid line-up leading to the 1995 demo 'Apocalyptic Psychotasia—The Murder Tape'. MYRKSKOG's Destructhor (real name Thor Anders Myhren) also features on the 2000 ZYKLON album, the side project of EMPEROR's Samoth and Trym. Drummer Anders Eek ('Secthdaemon'), handling drums on the 2000 Thorbjørn Akkerhaugen produced 'Deathmachine' debut album released through Candlelight Records, has credits with ODIUM, FUNERAL and THE FLESH.

Drummer Bjørn Thomas has also featured in the ranks of MYRKSKOG. Session keyboards were handled by Custer (real name Per Arvid). Frontman Master V (Kenneth Lindberg or 'Konstrukt') also operates a live keyboard player for LIMBONIC ART and holds membership of SIRIUS and DIMENSION F3H. Secthdaemon, acting as frontman, would unite with ZYKLON for a bout of late 2001 touring in America. Guitarist 'Savant M' (a.k.a. Haakon Nicolas Forwald or 'General Kshatriya') cites affiliations with SLAVIA, DISIPLIN and KOLDBRANN.

Promotion of the September 2002 album 'Superior Massacre', also on Candlelight, would see the band on a European package tour commencing in Paris on October 8th. Running mates for the extensive series of dates would be NILE, SINISTER, NO RETURN and EKTOMORF. Eek also operates the Funeral Doom project FALLEN along with INZEKT vocalist Kjetil Ottersen. A demo arrived in 2004.

MYRKSKOG's debut appearance on Swedish soil would be as support to GOD AMONG INSECTS at their 4th September record release party gig at Kelly's in Örebro. June of 2005 saw Forwald joining DISSECTION as bassist. Anders Eek joined Torbjørn Sandvik's GLITTERTIND project in February 2006.

Destructhor delivered a guest guitar solo for the 2007 'Eryx' album by GLORIA MORTI, featuring on the track 'Sands Of Hinnom'.

Apocalyptic Psychotasia—The Murder Tape, Myrkskog (1998) (Demo). A Poignant Scenario Of Death / Death Beauty Lust Ecstasy / A Macabre Death Fare To The Devil.
DEATH MACHINE, Candlelight CANDLE037CD (2000). Discipline Misanthropy / The Hate Syndicate / A Poignant Scenario Of Horror / Sinthetic Lifeworm / Syndrome 9 / Morphinemangle Torture / Deathfare To The Devil / Death Machine / Pilar Deconstruction (Syndrome 9 Remix).
SUPERIOR MASSACRE, Candlelight CANDLE071CD (2002). Domain Of The Superior / Detain The Skin / Trapped In Torment / Indisposable Deaths / Over The Gore / Blood Ejaculation / Utter Human Murder / Bleeding Wrists.

MYSTICA

CHARLEROI, BELGIUM — *X-Noise (vocals), Demeter (guitar), Cathy (guitar / keyboards), Gaborin (bass), Kaosnake (drums).*

Wallonian Black / Death act forged in June of 1999. Initially the band included vocalist X-Noise, a guitarist from ENTHRONED, keyboard player Cathy and the drummer from SCATOPHAGUS. Debuting in October of that year MYSTICA issued the demo 'Follow Your God To The Grave' some three months later. Ex-guitarist Xavier journeyed through DEVOURED and CATARRHAL.

Painkiller Records issued the inaugural album 'Blinded By My Blood' in 2001. 'Human Mutants' was set to follow in September of 2003 but Painkiller Records suspended business. Adding Gaborin on bass guitar, drummer Nordic Reaper would be superseded by Kaosnake whilst guitarist Morgan 696's place was taken by Demeter. 'Human Mutants' finally arrived in 2005 on the resurrected Painkiller label.

Follow Your God To The Grave, (2000). Follow Your God To The Grave / The Death Before The Death / My Malediction / White Princess.
BLINDED BY MY BLOOD, Painkiller (2001). My Malediction / Blinded By My Blood / Mystica / Follow Your God To The Grave / Illusion / Betrayal 666 / For The Love Of God / White Princess.
HUMAN MUTANTS, Painkiller (2003). Black Fire In The Sky (Intro) / Two Dead Angels / Human Mutants / Passage X / Leave Your Soil For Me / Final Devastation / Orgasm Before I Pray / Royal Fascination / Outro.

MYTHIC

PITTSBURGH, PA, USA — *Dana Duffey (vocals / guitar), Mary Bielich (bass), Terry Heggen (drums).*

Although MYTHIC's career was fleeting they certainly left their mark on the Metal scene. Far from being a typical girl Rock group MYTHIC employed the trademark guttural growls of Dana Duffey with guitars tuned way down making them probably the most well known of all female Death Metal acts.

In early 1991, guitarist Dana Duffey contacted the all female Death Metal band DERKETA after seeing them in an underground fanzine.

At that time, the Pittsburgh based DERKETA had actually broken up, unbeknownst to Dana who was living in Toledo, OH at the time. Dana decided to visit Pittsburgh, PA to meet with the remaining members of DERKETA, former WORMHOLE and MASTER MECHANIC bassist Mary Bielich and drummer Terri Heggen.

Duffy relocated to Pittsburgh and the trio began writing music. It was decided that Duffy would also be the vocalist and main lyricist for the band. The name MYTHIC was chosen and the band was officially born. In early June 1991 a three song rehearsal tape was recorded on a 4 track recorder to spread the word throughout the underground scene. The tracks on this tape were 'The Destroyer', 'Scarred For Life' and 'Grande Grimoire'. MYTHIC than played several shows on the East coast including in Rhode Island, Cleveland, Detroit, and Pittsburgh.

Later that same year they recorded an official demo entitled 'The Immortal Realm' which was recorded live. Tracks were: 'Thy Future Forecast', 'The Destroyer', 'The Oracle', 'Taste of the Grave', 'Grande Grimoire' and 'Lament Configuration'.

Within a year of forming they were offered a MCD from PA based Relapse Records for the three song release entitled 'Mourning In The Winter Solstice' was released in 1992 on MCD, 7" record (both traditional black and limited blue vinyl) and cassette. Soon after this release, MYTHIC parted ways with Terri Heggen and a session drummer was used for what would be the final performance at the legendary Milwaukee Metalfest VI.

After the festival, MYTHIC strangely disbanded. Dana promptly formed the notorious Black Metal band act DEMONIC CHRIST.

Bielich went on to join the Doom band NOVEMBERS DOOM, Brian Griffin of BROKEN HOPE's side project EM SINFONIA and by 2001 was a member of PENANCE. She would also figure in the scene as part of the political Punk band BEHIND ENEMY LINES.

Rehearsal Tape June '91, (1991). The Destroyer / Scarred For Life / Grande Grimoire.

The Immortal Realm, (1991). Thy Future Forecast / The Destroyer / The Oracle / Taste Of The Grave / Grande Grimoire / Lament Configuration.

Mourning In The Winter Solstice EP, Relapse (1992). Winter Solstice / Lament Configuration / Spawn Of Absu.

MYTHOPOEIA

PLZEN, CZECH REPUBLIC — *Asura Godwar Gorgon's Ray (vocals), Chicco (guitar), Aziz (guitar), Muf (bass), Lucy (vocals / keyboards), Heon Ostamon (keyboards), Vlad (drums).*

MYTHOPOEIA is a "Hermetic Doom Death" act out of Plzen. Upon their formation in 1993 at the hands of keyboard player Heon Ostamon the band went under the original title of MYTHOPOEIA KINGDOM OF FROST. The 1995 band unit comprised singer Asura Godwar Gorgon's Ray, SORATH credited guitarists Admirerforestae and Francis Empty, bassist Martin Tree, keyboard player Heon Ostamon and drummer Ottar Distress. As the band title truncated to simply MYTHOPOEIA in 1996 third guitarist Johannes Rhodostauroticus R.C. was enrolled for recording of the 8 song demo 'Haaramonia In Microcosmos'. A track from this session, 'It is blood of My Veins', also figured on the Metal Breath compilation album 'Breath Of Doom'.

1997 saw Martin Tree opting out, being replaced by SORATH's Mar Markionem. Another demo, 'Scheps Ankh, Aesch Mezareph, Atropopaia, Michani', was delivered in 1998. Rhodostauroticus opted out upon completion of these tapes and Markionem was shifted over to fill this vacancy. 1999 found MYTHOPOEIA uniting with BREAKING BEDS, GRIND 6.4 and PROMISES for the Czech 'Metal Breath' tour.

MYTHOPOEIA underwent a radical membership overhaul in September of 2000 with only Heon Ostamon and Asura Godwar Gorgon's Ray surviving. Following release of the debut album 'The Golden Leaf Of Oak' ex-GOLD OF ATHANOR guitarist Aziz joined in December of 2001.

Haaramonia In Microcosmos, (1996).

Scheps Ankh, Aesch Mezareph, Atropopaia, Michani, (1999). Aphrodisiakum Of Hermaphrodit / Alms / Demons In The Cosmic Low Of The Changes / Soothsayer / Saba R / Flames EO / Laviah / In A River Bed / Dawn Of Sunflower.

THE GOLDEN LEAF OF OAK, Metal Breath Productions (2001). Old Men Of Desert / Templars Bring Art Of Fire From Orient / Inflammation Of Inner Fire / Body Of Forest In The Mirror Of Desert / King's Entering Into A Temple / My Journey To The Stars / The Red Mercurius In The Oaken Wood / The End Of The Way To The Golden Oak / Crossing By Dragon.

NAIL WITHIN

ISRAEL — *Avital Tamir (vocals), Matan Cohen (guitar), Alex Schuster (guitar), Rotem Inbar (bass), Ido Levi (drums).*

NAIL WITHIN was the by product of a defection from the ranks of Black Metal band AZAZEL by the trio of guitarist Alex Schuster, bass player Evil Haim (a.k.a. Haim Benyamini) of LEHAVOTH and drummer Miko. Initially entitled EMBLAZE the band, bringing in Nir Kakov to replace Miko, subsequently adopted the new title NAIL WITHIN. At this juncture the band comprised lead vocalist Yishai Sweartz, ex-BETRAYER. Drummer Nir Nakov was also employed by SALEM, as sessioneer for ARALLU and LEHAVOTH whilst guitarist Matan Cohen is active with Metalcore band BETZEFER and Schuster operates with Black Metal band ARALLU. Sweartz, besides being active with MOONSKIN, would also engage with the US based underground Metal project SUBTERRANEAN MASQUERADE in 2000.

The band's March 2003 eponymous debut, produced by Harris Johns, included guest appearances from KREATOR frontman Mille Petrozza, ex-AT THE GATES and THE CROWN vocalist Tomas Lindberg and ASSASSIN's Robert Gonnela. Vocalist Yishai Sweartz exited from the band that very same month. Morphing once again, NAIL WITHIN introduced the BETZEFER pairing of singer Avital Tamir and bassist Rotem Inbar.

NAIL WITHIN, Listenable POSH041 (2003). Emblazed / Inhuman Conditions / Dirty-Colored Knife / Bleed Forever / Under The Spell / Elastic / Mental Coffin / My Wallow / King Obscenity / Impure / Last Nail.

NAILDOWN

MIKKELI, FINLAND — *Daniel Freyberg (vocals / guitar), Asko Sartanen (guitar), Matti Hämäläinen (bass), Jarmo Puikkonen (keyboards), Harri Heikkinen (drums).*

Mikkeli based Melodic Rock band NAILDOWN started life billed as ACID UNIVERSE, founded in November 2003 and issuing the demo '200 BPM 'Til Dead' in 2004 under this formative brand. The following year the band evolved into NAILDOWN in 2005. Signing to the Spinefarm label the group re-debuted with the EP 'Eyes Wide Open' that March, this set closing with a cover version of the RAMONES 'Pet Sematary'. The album 'World Domination' duly followed.

NAILDOWN frontman Daniel Freyberg has history with SOURCE OF DEMISE. Bassist Matti Hämäläinen is also operational with MATERIAL BLAST, keyboard player Jarmo Puikkonen is ex-CALEDONIAN whilst guitarist Asko Sartanen has association with both CODEON and IMPERANON. Drummer Harri Heikkinen was replaced by Janne Jukarainen, a scene adept citing credentials with BEEZEBUB, GAURITHOTH, GRAYSCALE, HANGING GARDEN, SHAMRAIN and SOURCE OF DEMISE.

NAILDOWN entered Sound Supreme studio to begin recording its second album, 'Dreamcrusher', in September 2006.

Eyes Wide Open, Spinefarm SPI231CD (2005). Eyes Wide Open / Prolong Your Fate / Pet Sematary.

WORLD DOMINATION, Spinefarm SPI247CD (2005). Reflecting My Descent / Prolong Your Fate / Hollow Syndicate / Evil Deeds / Next Infinity / Eyes Wide Open / Broken Down / World Domination / Fragile Side / Shining Throne.

DREAMCRUSHER, Spinefarm SPI275CD (2007). Dreamcrusher / Judgement Ride / Lame / P.I.B. / Silent Fall / Like I Care / Deep Under The Stones / Save Your Breath / The New Wave.

NAPALM DEATH

BIRMINGHAM, WEST MIDLANDS, UK — *Barney Greenway (vocals), Mitch Harris (guitar), Shane Embury (bass), Danny Herrera (drums).*

An Extreme West Midlands Metal band that not only defined the Grindcore genre but often took it to its absolute limits. Although the present day members are now all familiar faces on the Metal scene, such is the convoluted web of early personnel that by the time of their debut 28 track album 'Scum' no original band members had survived the ongoing line-up turmoil. NAPALM DEATH, founded in Meriden, Birmingham under the original title of CIVIL DEFENCE by vocalist Nick 'Nic Scab' Bullen and drummer Miles 'Rats' Ratledge, came together in 1981 as a Punk high school act. These pre-teens, adopting the NAPALM DEATH tag after the 'Apocalypse Now' movie, would be joined by guitarist Daryl 'Sid' Fideski and bassist Graham Robertson. Fideski opted out and Robertson switched instruments to guitar as Finbar Quinn enrolled on bass. First product arrived in 1982 as the demo cassette 'Punk Is A Rotting Corpse'.

Early gigs saw supports to bands such as THE SUBHUMANS, THE APOSTLES and CHAOS UK. This version of NAPALM

DEATH also contributed a track to the third 'Bullshit Detector' album, after submitting a tape to the organisers Anarcho-Punk act CRASS, before going into stasis. Napalm Death would be relatively inactive throughout 1984, only undertaking one concert that year as a benefit for the miners union.

The band duly regrouped in May 1985 with Bullen on vocals, Justin Broadrick of FINAL on guitar, P-Nut on bass and Rats on the drums. Before long NAPALM DEATH became a trio as P-Nut exited and Bullen took command of bass guitar.

Following recording of a demo entitled 'Hatred Surge' Rats was ejected. The erstwhile drummer subsequently forged WITCH HUNT with another ex-NAPALM DEATH man Finbar Quinn. Meantime, NAPALM DEATH started to veer more towards Thrash when drummer Mick Harris joined, putting in his first live showing on January 18th 1986 as support to THE AMEBIX. Not only did this signal a radical shift in musical direction but Harris also lays claim to the invention of the genre term 'Grindcore'. From that point on NAPALM DEATH would lead the field. Digby Pearson, the owner of the Nottingham based Earache Records, signed the group and in 1986 half of the songs which were to become the 'Scum' debut were committed to tape. Upon completion of these sessions Jim Whitely was incorporated on bass to allow Bullen to concentrate on singing. Whitely contributed to DOOM's first recordings for the 'A Vile Peace' compilation album around this period.

When guitarist Justin Broadrick departed following recording of their initial demos to HEAD OF DAVID, later forming GODFLESH, the band asked WARHAMMER and UNSEEN TERROR man Shane Embury to replace him but this invitation was declined. In his stead Frank Healy of SACRILEGE was inducted but his tenure would be brief, being superseded by guitarist Bill Steer of 'Phoenix Militia' fanzine and vocalist Lee Dorrian. The latter had never been involved with a band before, having just lost the offer of a job as bassist with ICONS OF FILTH when they broke up just prior to his enrollment. As frontman for NAPALM DEATH, Dorrian debuted at The Hand & Heart pub in Coventry on a co-billing with ANTI-SECT and HERESY. This gig would actually see Frank Healy standing in as guitarist for a temporarily absent Bill Steer.

It would be this incarnation of the band that laid down the remaining songs at Rich Bitch Studios in Selly Oak during May 1987, which made up the 'Scum' album. This offering rocked the Heavy Metal world to its very core. Easily ranking as the most ferocious album of the genre to be issued to date NAPALM DEATH's caustic delivery, including on the less than a 1.316 seconds stormer which is 'You Suffer', immediately succeeded in dividing critics and polarising opinions. Importantly, 'Scum' also strongly accented blastbeat drumming. Although Mick Harris was not technically the first to employ this technique, that credit goes to D.R.I.'s Eric Brecht, NAPALM DEATH was certainly the band that brought the new percussive style to public attention and utilised it as a cornerstone of their material.

Whitely quit shortly after the album release, having his position filled in August 1987 for a series of dates supporting D.R.I. on a what was to be temporary basis by Shane Embury, who was later to join on a fulltime basis. The band also contributed tracks to two compilation albums at this time; namely 'North Atlantic Noize Attack' and 'Pathological', and cut two John Peel sessions. Peel's mentoring of the band through a nationally broadcast medium resulted in increased demand for 'Scum' and the resulting cash flow gave considerable impetus to the fledgling Earache label. Typically though, just as Peel had proven a staunch supporter, another Radio One DJ, Steve Wright, represented the other end of the spectrum, using NAPALM DEATH songs as a punishment in his afternoon quiz show.

With the exception of Dorrian all members of the band had ongoing side projects at the time of 'Scum'. Steer formed the brutal CARCASS and secured a deal with Earache Records (to later quit to concentrate on his this project full time), bassist Shane was drumming for UNSEEN TERROR whilst Harris plied his non NAPALM DEATH extracurricular activities with DOOM, EXTREME NOIZE TERROR and UNSEEN TERROR.

Still, second album 'From Enslavement To Obliteration' recorded at Birdsong Studios in Worcester, comprised a staggering 54 tracks, many being mere seconds long, was delivered in 1988. Initial copies came delivered with the bonus of a free five track 7" single EP. The BBC 'Arena' documentary also featured the band in its Heavy Metal special, bringing NAPALM DEATH into the nation's living rooms. Such was the band's world-wide reputation even at this early stage that in July 1989, NAPALM DEATH undertook their first successful tour of Japan.

These dates, conducted with S.O.B., marked the advent of Lee Dorrian's custom label Rise Above with the issue of the 'Live' EP, a collection of tracks recorded in Copenhagen, Roskilde and London. Only 2,500 copies of this 7" single were pressed. A further collaboration with S.O.B. would be the rare 7" flexi-disc split single on the Sound Of Burial label. Earache put out a world record breaking 7" single, packaged with the 'Grindcrusher' compilation album, featuring NAPALM DEATH's one second meisterwerk 'You Suffer' pitched against the ELECTRO HIPPIES 'Mega Armageddon Death Pt.3', also clocking in at just over a second.

On the live front, the group participated in the Earache organised "Grindcrusher" tour of Europe that winter shoulder to shoulder with BOLT THROWER, MORBID ANGEL and CARCASS.

Eventually vocalist Lee Dorrian departed to form the successful CATHEDRAL and former BENEDICTION man Mark Greenway stepped into his shoes. Better known as 'Barney', the new Napalm Death frontman, despite an affection for both Aston Villa and AOR, possessed a primal roar perfectly suited to the band's by now supremely focussed ferocity. Steer had also quit to concentrate on CARCASS and had his position filled by ex-TERRORIZER guitarist Jesse Pintado. The band soon added a second guitarist in ex-RIGHTEOUS PIGS man Mitch Harris and the group set to work once more.

Initial copies of the July 1990 album 'Harmony Corruption', cut at Tampa's Morrisound Studios with producer Scott Burns, came with a free live album, recorded at London's ICA, notably including Justin Broadrick guesting on the GODFLESH cover version 'Avalanche Master Song'. DEICIDE's Glen Benton and OBITUARY's John Tardy acted as studio guests on the studio track 'Unfit Earth'. 'Harmony Corruption', probably the band's most traditional Metal styled offering with songs for the first time expanded beyond the one minute range, gave NAPALM DEATH their first intrusion into the national UK charts, entering at number 67. Early 1991 saw the American leg of the 'Grindcrusher tour with NAPALM DEATH, NOCTURNUS and GODFLESH. An interim EP, 'Mass Appeal Madness' recorded at the Violent Noise Experience Club in March, bridged the gap between albums.

As NAPALM DEATH were due to tour America once more in the summer of 1991 drummer Mickey Harris quit to form Industrial project SCORN, re-uniting with Nic Bullen for this venture. This was not before he had scored some unexpected press attention when arrested in a case of mistaken identity for a jewellers robbery in Derby.

Harris' replacement was American Danny Herrera, who joined in time for the dates which saw NAPALM DEATH on a bill with SICK OF IT ALL, SEPULTURA and SACRED REICH as well as the band's first shows in Russia.

1992's 'Utopia Banished' album, laid down in the Welsh retreat of The Windings in Wrexham with producer Colin Richardson, had NAPALM DEATH eschewing the technicality of its predecessor and immersing themselves deep into ugly Grind once again. Band members illustrated this return to brutality by crediting themselves Mark Greenway "Vocular Armageddon", Jesse Pintado "Dissonant Distorted Delirium No. 1", Mitch Harris "Dissonant Distorted Delirium No. 2", Shane Embury "Sub-end Vexation" and Danny Herrera "Hyper Cans". The band undertook extensive roadwork in Europe with OBITUARY and DISMEMBER and in America alongside CARCASS, CATHEDRAL and BRUTAL TRUTH. Further shows followed in Holland, opening for FAITH NO MORE prior to inaugural South African shows.

Returning from the political turmoil of South Africa, NAPALM DEATH released their version of the DEAD KENNEDY's classic 'Nazi Punks Fuck Off' as a single, donating all proceeds to the anti-racism campaign. The single went on to sell over 10'000 copies and the year was rounded off by a headline Canadian tour.

May 1994 saw the release of 'Fear, Emptiness, Despair', self-produced with engineer Pete Coleman, and a British tour with label mates ENTOMBED. Initial reaction to the album was lukewarm, with media attention mainly focused on ENTOMBED rather than NAPALM DEATH. The band fared better in North America, touring alongside OBITUARY and MACHINE HEAD. The band scored a notable success with the inclusion of the track 'Plague Rages' on the soundtrack album to the film 'Mortal Kombat' which broke the American Billboard top five. Further evidence of a return to form came with the well received 'Greed Killing' mini-album. The full-length, Colin Richardson produced 'Diatribes' would be hewn out at Framework Studios, Birmingham then issued in North America during January 1996 with a bonus split CD 'Cursed To Tour' shared with tour partners AT THE GATES.

In 1996 Embury teamed up with Dan Lilker of BRUTAL TRUTH to record the MALFORMED EARTH BORN album 'Defiance Of The Ugly By The Merely Repulsive'. Embury also forged an alliance with SICK OF IT ALL vocalist Lou Koller in BLOOD FROM THE SOUL and the 'To Spite The Gland That Breeds' album. April of that year found NAPALM DEATH conducting UK headline dates with support from CROWBAR and Swedes FACE DOWN.

Controversy surrounded the band in early 1997 as it was announced that Greenway had departed, one of the reasons being the vocalist's well known fear of flying. The band quickly announced their new frontman to be Phil Vane of EXTREME NOISE TERROR and, in a quite surreal turn of events, within days EXTREME NOISE TERROR put out a press statement concerning their new vocalist for their 'Damage 381' album—Barney Greenway. The ex-NAPALM DEATH man would also found a fresh act entitled NOTHING BUT CONTEMPT. This short lived act included Greenway, CANCER and ASSERT drummer Carl Stokes, NAPALM DEATH guitarist Danny Herrera and SACRIFICIAL ALTAR and ASATRU guitarist Rob Engvikson.

Vane made his mark on a split EP with COALESCE, 'In Tongues We Speak', but upon its release it became apparent that Greenway and NAPALM DEATH had patched up their differences and were back together as recording began for the 'Inside The Torn Apart' album.

NAPALM DEATH conducted a lengthy European tour as support to MACHINE HEAD during April and May 1997, delivering 'Inside The Torn Apart', again having revisiting Frameworks and re-employing Colin Richardson, in June. . This album, mixed down at Chapel Studios in Lincoln, benefited from a boisterous mix crafted by former Sabbat guitarist Andy Sneap. In an attempt to keep themselves in the press, the band issued a split EP with German act FATALITY, a band who won a competition to cover a NAPALM DEATH track to win a space on the release.

NAPALM DEATH toured South America to wind up roadwork for the year, but only after Embury had suffered a head injury requiring stitches he suffered whilst in the line of duty—moshing at an ENTOMBED gig in Nottingham.

Whilst on tour, the band's video, shot for the track 'Breed To Breathe' came under such severe criticism from several European TV stations drastic editing was required. The video featured live footage shot at the notorious New York CBGB's club interspersed with documentary footage of various scenes of brutality.

It worth noting that, amongst all their accomplishments, NAPALM DEATH have made the record books for having recorded the shortest single ever (with a running time of a mere one second) on a record given away free with the Earache Records 'Grindcrusher' compilation album.

In addition to his work in NAPALM DEATH Barney Greenaway is known for his alternative career as a journalist. Having contributed to a number of titles, including 'Raw' and Germany's 'Rock Hard', Barney was found to be penning a computer games column in the late 90s version of 'Kerrang!'

'Words From The Exit Wound', once more overseen by Colin Richardson, was ushered out in October 1998, significantly an uncharacteristically lacklustre effort delivered as a parting shot for Earache. The band signed to new label Dreamcatcher during 1999 following a festival appearance at Germany's legendary 'Wacken Open Air' show. First recordings from this new liaison was the Simon Efemy produced 'Leaders Not Followers' EP, put out that October, which comprised of covers by the likes of DEATH, an obscure demo track 'Back from The Dead' that never made it as an official release, RAWPOWER, Chilean Hardcore act PENTAGRAM, EXCEL, Canada's SLAUGHTER and REPULSION as well as a re-recording of their live favourite 'Nazi Punks Fuck Off'.

Both Embury and Pintado also made a mark later the same year with the their LOCKUP project, a new unit created with Peter Tägtgren of Swedes HYPOCRISY along with ex-CRADLE OF FILTH and DIMMU BORGIR drummer Nick Barker. The resulting album 'Pleasures Pave Sewers' proved extremely successful charting in Germany.

Both Embury and Harris also embroiled themselves in a further side project LITTLE GIANT DRUG with vocalist / guitarist Simon Orme and drummer Simon Hornblower to issue the 2000 album 'Prismcast'.

NAPALM DEATH toured Europe in early 2000 with guests KONKHRA. Later European gigs found Harris performing onstage sitting down, the guitarist having broken his foot falling downstairs in a video shoot. A set of UK dates in April 2001 had NAPALM DEATH supported by DEFENESTRATION.

Later that year Embury's LOCKUP cut a second album, 'Hate Breeds Suffering', released in 2002 with Tomas Lindberg taking Tägtgren's position. The bassist also had his past endeavours with the youthful WARHAMMER resurrected when a vintage track appeared on the 'Britannia Infernus' compilation. NAPALM DEATH returned with their first post-Earache full-length 'Enemy Of The Music Business' in September. This effort, helmed again by Simon Efemey, contained some of the band's most biting lyrical matter, for which successive interviews made clear were directed at the band's erstwhile label.

NAPALM DEATH toured Britain in November 2001 with support from Bristol's ONEDICE. European dates into January of 2002 where upset when bassist Shane Embury was hospitalised for a time with influenza. An unphased NAPALM DEATH completed the shows as a four piece.

As the band busied themselves with a live DVD 'Punishment In Capitals' and recording a new studio opus, the Simon Efemey produced 'Order Of The Leech', word arrived in mid 2002 that Embury was recording a Grindcore 'solo' project album in league with erstwhile FEAR FACTORY drummer Raymond Herrera and CATHEDRAL vocalist Lee Dorrian. It would also be revealed that NAPALM DEATH had tracked two SEPTIC DEATH cover versions 'Terror Rain' and 'Thaw' for use as exclusive tracks on the vinyl version of the album.

December UK gigs were supported by THE GREAT DECEIVER. NAPALM DEATH helped forge an impressive extreme Metal cast for North American dates during January and February of 2003 packaged alongside NILE, STRAPPING YOUNG LAD, THE BERZERKER and DARK TRANQUILITY. Shane Embury made time to guest on NASUM's 'Helvete' album early that year. The NASUM connection was strengthened with the announcement of a split EP shared with the Swedish veterans, NASUM covering the NAPALM DEATH track 'Unchallenged Hate' and NAPALM DEATH replying with NASUM's 'The Masked Face'.

Earache Records issued a mammoth two disc retrospective entitled 'Noise For Music's Sake'. The collection hosted a number of rarities and unreleased recordings including 1987 live take of 'Deceiver' with Mitch Dickinson of UNSEEN TERROR on guitar and a 1986 live version of 'Traitor' from The Mermaid in Birmingham, captured on Shane Embury's tape recorder before he joined the band! On top of a myriad of other activities Embury officially joined "Mexican" extreme Metal band BRUJERIA in July 2003.

Following a run of August German dates NAPALM DEATH revisited their successful 'Leaders Not Followers' EP with a full blown album as a follow on companion. 'Leaders Not Followers Part 2', comprised covers of CRYPTIC SLAUGHTER's 'Lowlife', OFFENDERS 'Face Down In The Dirt', DEVASTATION's 'Devastation', ATTITUDE ADJUSTMENT's 'Dope Fiend', AGNOSTIC FRONT's 'Blind Justice', WEHRMACHT,s 'Night Of Pain', ANTI CIMEX's 'Game Of The Assholes—Victims Of A Bomb Raid', SEPULTURA's 'Troops Of Doom', INSANITY's 'Fire Death Fate', HIRAX 's 'Hate Fear + Power', DAYGLO ABORTIONS's 'Bedtime Story', HELLHAMMER's 'Messiah', KREATOR's Riot Of Violence', DISCHARGE's 'War's Not Fairytale', SIEGE's 'Conform', MASSACRE's Clangor Of War' the MASTER theme 'Master' and DIE KREUZEN's 'I'm Tired'. Notably, the album featured an appearance on two songs by Jim Whitely, the band's original bass player from the groundbreaking 'Scum' album.

August brought news of the formation of a Grind 'Supergroup' VENOMOUS CONCEPT comprising Shane Embury, ex-NAPALM DEATH drummer Mick Harris, MELVINS and FANTOMAS guitarist Buzz Osbourne and former BRUTAL TRUTH singer Kevin Sharp. This unit subsequently strengthened the NAPALM DEATH connection when drummer Danny Herrera took over the drum position. Meantime NAPALM DEATH undertook a round of European gigs throughout November, albeit without the services of guitarist Jesse Pintado. The band revealed 2004 was to commence in a suitably heavy fashion, headlining the January 'Extreme The Dojo VII' tour of Japan alongside NASUM, a reformed ANAL CUNT and PIG DESTROYER.

In May 2004 NAPALM DEATH, seeing a return for guitarist Jesse Pintado after several months lay off due to health issues, signed a worldwide deal with Germany's with Century Media Records for issue of the 'Leaders Not Followers Part 2' album. Pintado also made time to guest on the EP 'Welcome to Reality' from Los Angeles based tribal Punk-Grid band RESISTANT CULTURE. In August of the MAYHEM, TORMENTOR and ABORYM scene veteran Attila Csihar revealed plans for an extreme Metal "supergroup" BORN TO MURDER THIS WORLD, this projected union set to comprise Shane Embury, Mick 'Irrumator' Kenney of ANAAL NATHRAKH, Necrobutcher of MAYHEM and former CRADLE OF FILTH and DIMMU BORGIR drummer Nick Barker.

In September the band entered Foel Studios in North Wales to lay down material for a new studio album 'The Code Is Red ... Long Live The Code'. Former CARCASS frontman Jeff Walker would contribute guest vocals to the track 'Pledge Yourself To You', Jello Biafra of the DEAD KENNEDYS made his presence felt on 'The Great And The Good' whilst HATEBREED's Jamey Jasta featured on 'Instruments Of Persuasion'. US touring plans for October saw the band set to flank KATAKLYSM and GOATWHORE. To close out the year, NAPALM DEATH would be announced as one of the main attractions at the annual 'X-Mass Fest' 2004 roving European festival dates in alliance with MARDUK, FINNTROLL, VADER, THE BLACK DAHLIA MURDER and BELPHEGOR.

To aid victims of the December 2004 Indian Ocean tsunamis NAPALM DEATH, in collaboration with THE HAUNTED and HEAVEN SHALL BURN, participated in the issue of a special single release. The band donated the new song 'The Great And The Good', featuring former DEAD KENNEDYS frontman Jello Biafra on guest vocals. These singles, restricted to just 1000 hand numbered copies, would be for sale only at NAPALM DEATH's Bochum and London shows in January 2005. Billed as part of the ANAAL NATHRAKH line-up, Embury cut a BBC Radio session at Maida Vale Studios on 18th March.

On 16th April NAPALM DEATH conducted its first concert in Indonesia, performing at the Ancol Beach, Jakarta with local Grindsters TENGKORAK as support. Oddly, the event, which saw record crowds, would be sponsored by the Gudang Garam tobacco company. Upon their return home the band filmed a promotional video for the track 'Silence Is Deafening' with director Roger Johansson.

European NAPALM DEATH tour dates in the Summer had the band supported by MOST PRECIOUS BLOOD and DIECAST. To celebrate Japanese dates Shane Embury teamed up with Gargamel Toys to produce the Garga-Death toy. These 5" figures, limited to just 150 pieces, being made available only at gigs.

September found Shane Embury involved in a further side project initiated by OLD MAN'S CHILD guitarist Jardar (a.k.a. Jon Øyvind Andersen) in "Dark Death Metal" band INSIDIOUS DISEASE, in collusion with guitarist Silenoz (Sven Atle Kopperud) and drummer Tony Laureano of DIMMU BORGIR, the latter also holding NILE and ANGEL CORPSE credentials.

Brazilian NAPALM DEATH gigs in late October saw support from AÇÃO DIRETA and CLAUSTROFOBIA before engaging with the European 'Persistence' tour in December, ranked alongside AGNOSTIC FRONT, HATEBREED, THE RED CHORD, BORN FROM PAIN, BLEED THE SKY and FULL BLOWN CHAOS. Barney Greenaway made studio time to guest session on German Hardcore band MAROON's 'When Worlds Collide' album.

The band would be back on North American soil in early 2006, packaged with KREATOR, UNDYING and A PERFECT MURDER for gigs in February. In late May NAPALM DEATH entered Foel Studios in Wales to cut a new album. Anneke van Giersbergen from Dutch band THE GATHERING contributed vocal parts. The band's summer schedule was centred on a run of festival appearances including shows at the 'Reborn' festival in Casablanca, Morocco, 'In The Beach' in Spain, 'With Full Force' in Germany, 'Metalparty' and 'Nuvolari Fest' in Italy, the 'Stonehenge' festival in Holland, the 'Brutal Assault' event in the Czech Republic and Poland's 'Hunterfestival'.

Sad news emerged on August 27th with the passing of former band member Jesse Pintado. The guitarist had died from liver failure at the Erasmus MC hospital in Holland.

NAPALM DEATH hit the US touring circuit in September forming up a strong billing alongside HATEBREED, EXODUS, THE BLACK DAHLIA MURDER, DESPISED ICON and FIRST BLOOD. That same month Shane Embury, in collaboration with MISTRESS and ANAAL NATHRAKH's Mick Kenney, announced the formation of new label Feto Records. This imprint served as an outlet for Kenney's EXPLODER, MISTRESS and PROFESSOR FATE projects and Embury's 'Live in Japan' opus from LOCKUP.

NAPALM DEATH hit the road with A LIFE ONCE LOST, DEAD TO FALL, IMPALED, ARSIS and ANIMOSITY throughout November and December as part of the 'Death By Decibels' US tour. The band contributed their version of 'Who Sets The Rules' to the SICK OF IT ALL tribute album 'Our Impact Will Be Felt' assembled by Abacus Recordings for January 2007 release. A European tour was marred when Barney Greenway damaged his tendon onstage on January 24th in Belgrade, Serbia. The singer completed the dates on crutches. Whilst in Bulgaria on the 27th, both Barney Greenway and Mitch Harris laid down

NAPALM DEATH (pic: Linda Aversa)

backing vocals for the song 'Overcome' for album recordings by Hardcore band LAST HOPE at Stain Studio in Sofia

Shows across Europe for March and April 2007 aligned the band with MOONSPELL, ROOT, BEHEMOTH and DEW-SCENTED.

Punk Is A Rotting Corpse, Napalm Death (1982) (Demo). The Crucifixion Of Possessions / Don't Bother / Enough / Dysfunction.

Hatred Surge, Napalm Death (1985) (Demo). What Man Can Do / Instinct Of Survival / Abbatoir / Control / Sacrificed / So Sad / Caught In A Dream / Private Death / Cheswick Green (Live).

Scum, Napalm Death (1986) (Demo). Multinational Corporations / Instinct Of Survival / The Kill / Scum / Caught ... In A Dream / Polluted Minds / Sacrificed / Siege Of Power / Control / Born On Your Knees / Human Garbage / You Suffer.

From Enslavement To Obliteration, Napalm Death (1986) (Demo). Multinational Corporations / Instinct Of Survival / Unclean / Sacrificed / Siege Of Power / Caught ... In A Dream / What Man Can Do / Control / Death By Manipulation / Abattoir / Private Death / The Kill / You Suffer.

SCUM, Earache MOSH 3 (1987). Multinational Corporations / Instinct Of Survival / The Kill / Scum / Caught In A Dream / Polluted Minds / Sacrificed / Stage Of Power / Control / Born On Your Knees / Human Garbage / You Suffer / Life? / Prison Without Walls / Negative Approach / Success? / Deceiver / C.S. / Parasites / Pseudo Youth / Divine Death / As The Machine Rolls On / Common Enemy / Moral Crusade / Stigmatized / M.A.D. / Dragnet.

FROM ENSLAVEMENT TO OBLITERATION, Earache MOSH 8 (1988). Evolved As One / It's A Man's World / Lurid Fairytale / Private Death / Impressions / Unchallenged Hate / Uncertainty Blurs The Vision / Cock Rock Alienation / Retreat To Nowhere / Think For A Minute / Display To Me ... / From Enslavement To Obliteration / Blind To The Truth / Social Sterility / Emotional Suffocation / Practice What You Preach / Inconceivable / Worlds Apart / Obstinate Direction / Mentally Murdered / Sometimes / Make Way.

The Curse, Earache 7 MOSH 8 (1988) (Free single with 'From Enslavement To Obliteration' album). The Curse / Musclehead / Your Achievement? / Dead / Morbid Deceiver.

Repeat At Length, Earache (1988) (flexidisc). Repeat At Length.

You Suffer, Earache (1989) (Split 7" single with ELECTRO HIPPIES. Free with 'Grindcrusher' compilation). You Suffer.

Napalm Death / S.O.B., Sound Of Burial (1989) (7" Flexidisc split with S.O.B.). Multinational Corporations Pt. 2 / Re-address The Problem / Changing Colours / From The Ashes ... / Understanding?!?! / Stalemate.

Mentally Murdered EP, Earache MOSH 14 (1989). Rise Above / Missing Link- Mentally Murdered / Walls Of Confinement / Cause And Effect—No Manual Effort.

Live, Rise Above RISE 001 (1989) (Limited edition 2,500 copies). Multinational Corporations / Unchallenged Hate / The Kill / Lurid Fairytale / Dead / Stigmatized / Deceiver / Make Way! / In Extremis / M.A.D. / Common Enemy / Success? / You Suffer.

Suffer The Children, Earache MOSH 24 (1990). Suffer The Children / Siege Of Power.

Suffer The Children, Earache MOSHT 24 (1990). Suffer The Children / Siege Of Power / Harmony Corruption.

HARMONY CORRUPTION, Earache MOSH 19 (1990). Vision Conquest / If The Truth Be Known / Inner Incineration / Malicious Intent / Unfit Earth / Circle Of Hypocrisy / The Chains That Bind Us / Mind Snare / Extremity Retained / Suffer The Children. Chart position: 67 UK.

Malicious Intent, Earache CAT085 (1990) (Split 7" flexidisc promotion release with JOHN ZORN). Malicious Intent.

Mass Appeal Madness, Earache MOSHT 046 (1991). Mass Appeal Madness / Pride Assassin / Unchallenged Hate / Social Sterility.

Mass Appeal Madness, Earache MOSH 046 (1991) (7" single). Mass Appeal Madness / Pride Assassin.

UTOPIA BANISHED, Earache MOSH 053 (1992). Discordance / I Abstain / Dementia Access / Christening Of The Blind / The World Keeps Turning / Idiosyncratic Araynisms / Cause And Effect / Judicial Slime / Distorting The Medium / Got time To Kill / Upward And Uninterested / Exile / Awake To A Life Of Misery / Contemptuous. Chart position: 58 UK.

World Keeps Turning, Earache MOSH 065T (1992). World Keeps Turning / A Means To An End / Insanity Excursion.

DEATH BY MANIPULATION, Earache MOSH 51CDL (1992). Mass Appeal Madness / Pride Assassin / Unchallenged Hate / Social Sterility / Suffer The Children / Siege Of Power / Harmony Corruption / Rise Above / The Missing Link / Mentally Murdered / Walls Of Confinement / Cause And Effect / No Mental Effort.

One And The Same, Earache MOSH 53L (1992) (Free single with 'Utopia Banished' album). One And The Same / Sick And Tired / Malignant Trait / Killing With Kindness.

THE PEEL SESSIONS, Strange Fruit SFRCD 120 (1993). The Kill / Prison Without Walls / Dead Part One / Deceiver / Lurid Fairytale / In Extremis / Blind To The Trash / Negative Approach / Common Enemy / Obstinate Direction / Life? / You Suffer.

Hung, Columbia (1994) (US promotion release. Brown vinyl). Hung / Truth Drug.

More Than Meets The Eye, Columbia CSK 6046 (1994) (US promotion release). More Than Meets The Eye / Nazi Punks Fuck Off.

Nazi Punks Fuck Off, Earache MOSH 092 (1994). Nazi Punks Fuck Off / Aryanisms / Nazi Punks Fuck Off (Live) / Contemptuous.

FEAR EMPTINESS DESPAIR, Earache MOSH 109 (1994). Twist The Knife (Slowly) / Hung / Remain Nameless / Plague Rages / More Than Meets The Eye / Primed Time / State Of Mind / Armageddon X7 / Retching On The Dirt / Fasting On Deception / Throwaway.

GREED KILLING, Earache MOSH 146 (1995). Greed Killing / My Own Worst Enemy / Self Betrayal / Finer Truths, White Lies / Antibody / All Links Severed / Plague Rages (Live).

DIATRIBES, Earache MOSH 141 (1996). Greed Killing / Glimpse Into Genocide / Ripe For The Breaking / Cursed To Crawl / Cold Forgiveness / My Own Worst Enemy / Just Rewards / Dogma / Take The Strain / Diatribes / Placate, Sedate, Eradicate / Corrosive Elements.

Breed To Breathe, Earache MOSH 185CD (1997) (Includes 'Suffer The Children' by FATALITY). Breed To Breathe / All Intensive Purposes / Stranger Now / Bled Dry / Time Will Come.

In Tongues We Speak EP, Earache MOSH 168CD (1997) (Split EP with COALESCE). Food Chains / Upward And Uninterested.

INSIDE THE TORN APART, Earache MOSH 171 (1997). Breed To Breathe / Birth In Regress / Section / Reflect On Conflict / Down In The Zero / Inside The Torn Apart / If Symptoms Persist / Prelude / Indispose / Purist Realist / Low Point / The Lifeless Alarm.

WORDS FROM THE EXIT WOUND, Earache MOSH 212 (1998). The Infiltrator / Repression Out Of Uniform / Next Of Kin To Chaos / Trio-Degradable- Affixed By Disconcern / Cleanse Impure / Devouring Depraved / Ulterior Exterior / None The Wiser? / Clutching At Barbs / Incendiary Incoming / Thrown Down A Rope / Sceptic In Perspective.

BOOTLEGGED IN JAPAN, Earache MOSH 209 (1999). Antibody / My Own Worst Enemy / More Than Meets The Eye / Hung / Greed Killing / Suffer The Children / Mass Appeal Madness / Cursed To Crawl / Glimpse Into Genocide / I Abstain / Lucid Fairytale / Plague Rages / Cold Forgiveness / Control / Diatribes / Life? / Siege Of Power / If The Truth Be Known / Unchallenged Hate / Nazi Punks Fuck Off / From Enslavement To Obliteration / The Kill / Scum / Ripe For The Breaking.

Leaders Not Followers, Dreamcatcher CRIDE 19M (1999). Politicians / Incinerator / Demonic Possession / Maggots In Your Coffin / Back From The Dead / Nazi Punks Fuck Off / Untitled (Hidden track).

ENEMY OF THE MUSIC BUSINESS, Dreamcatcher CRIDE 33 (2000). Taste The Poison / Next On The List / Constitutional Hell / Vermin / Volume Of Neglect / Thanks For Nothing / Can't Play, Won't Pay / Blunt Against The Cutting Edge / Cure For The Common Complaint / A Necessary Evil / CD (Conservative Shithead Part 2) / Mechanics Of Deceit / (The Public Gets) What The Public Doesn't Want / Fracture In The Equation.

ORDER OF THE LEECH, Spitfire SPT-15172-2 (2002). Continuing War On Stupidity / The Icing On The Hate / Forced To Fear / Narcoleptic / Out Of Sight, Out Of Mind / To Lower Yourself (Blind Servitude) / Lowest Common Denominator / Forewarned Is Disarmed? / Per Capita / Farce And Fiction / Blows To The Body / The Great Capitulator.

LEADERS NOT FOLLOWERS 2, Century Media 77487-2 (2004). Lowlife / Face Down In The Dirt / Devastation / Messiah / Victims Of A Bomb Raid / Fright Night / War's No Fairytale / Conform / Master / Fire Death Fate / Riot Of Violence / Game Of The Arseholes / Clangor Of War / Dope Fiend / I'm Tired / Troops Of Doom / Bedtime Story / Blind Justice / Hate, Fear And Power.

THE CODE IS RED ... LONG LIVE THE CODE, Century Media 77587-2 (2005). Silence Is Deafening / Right You Are / Diplomatic Immunity / Code Is Red ... Long Live The Code / Climate Controllers / Instruments Of Persuasion / The Great And The Good / Sold Short / All Hail The Grey Dawn / Vegetative State / Pay For The Privilege Of Breathing / Pledge Yourself To You / Striding Purposefully Backwards / Morale / Our Pain Is Their Power.

SMEAR CAMPAIGN, Century Media 776872 (2006). Weltschmerz / Sink Fast, Let Go / Fatalist / Puritanical Punishment Beating / Well All Is Said And Done / Freedom Is The Wage Of Sin / In Deference / Short Lived / Identity Crisis / Shattered Existence / Eyes Right Out / Warped Beyond Logic / Rabid Wolves (For Christ) / Deaf And Dumbstruck / Persona Nongrata / Smear Campaign. Chart position: 45 GREECE.

NASUM

ÖREBRO, SWEDEN — *Mieszko Talarczyk (vocals / guitar), Anders Jakobson (guitar / drums), Jesper Liverod (bass).*

Örebro Grindcore. NASUM members Rickard Alriksson and Anders Jakobsson are also members of Gore Metal band NECRONY. The pair got Grindcore side project NASUM into gear during late 1992 shortly after receiving an offer from the notorious German label Poserslaughter to cut a shared 7" split single with Australians BLOODDUSTER. The Swedes contributed their tracks only to find the released single 'Blind World' in union with Belgian veterans AGATHOCLES. NASUM made a dent in musical history with their donation of 9 tracks lasting a mere blistering three and a half minutes for the Swedish compilation album 'Really Fast Volume 9'.

The duo, then joined by guitarist/bassist Mieszko Talarczyk, previously of Örebro Death Metal combo SHAGIDIEL, laid down further songs for a 4 way split album on Talarczyk's own Grindwork Productions label in alliance with fellow Swedes RETALIATION and Japanese bands C.S.S.O. and VIVISECTION. Other songs from these sessions would be included on a split 7" single shared with Americans PSYCHO.

NASUM worked with EDGE OF SANITY's Dan Swanö to record the 'Industrislaven' release, again for Poserslaughter. This record, listed as an album below, features 18 songs but lasts a mere 16 minutes! In order to promote the album NASUM's inaugural gigs were arranged, including a Berlin show with DEAD and MANOS. However, Alriksson bowed out of these shows and NASUM enrolled SUFFER and SERPENT drummer Per Karlsson for the tour. Alriksson would eventually leave the band and after a brief period with FLESHREVELS man Jallo Lehto on the kit NASUM pared down to a duo once more with Jakobsen assuming drum duties. With this line up NASUM recorded tracks for a split release 'Black Illusions' in collaboration with ABSTAIN.

NASUM's reputation had by now attracted international interest and the group signed to American Death Metal specialists Relapse Records for the 1998 album 'Inhale-Exhale'. Initial copies came with a free 7" EP of cover versions comprising of DROPDEAD's 'Bullshit Tradition', S.O.B.'s 'Device', 'REFUSED's 'The Real' and 'Rio De San Atlanta, Manitoba' originally by PROPAGHANDI. The same year saw NASUM paired off with Portland's WARHATE for a further split 7" single.

NASUM boosted the band's strength back up to trio status with the enrollment of BURST's Jesper Liverod on bass in September of 1999. In this incarnation NASUM put in their first American gig at the sprawling Milwaukee Metalfest and managed a slew of further gigs as part of the 'Contamination 99' American tour together with MORGION, EXHUMED, TODAY IS THE DAY and SOILENT GREEN.

In 1999 Jakobsen and Talarczyk created project act KRIGSHOT with guitarist Jallo to release the 'Maktmissbrukare' album. Talarczyk would also act as co-producer for the debut WITHIN REACH album. Anders Jakobson would also form part of the newly reconstituted GENERAL SURGERY line up.

NASUM's 2000 album 'Human 2.0' was once more released by Relapse although a later Japanese release on Ritual Records, re-dubbed 'Human 2.01', saw the addition of extra tracks.

NASUM toured Europe in the autumn of 2000 as support to NAPALM DEATH prior to a string of Scandinavian dates alongside THE HAUNTED. NASUM would be featured on two tribute albums in 2001 with a version of 'Visions Of War' for a DISCHARGE homage and a take of 'Tools Of The Trade' for the Death Vomit Records 'Requiems Of Revulsion' CARCASS tribute.

The May 2003 album 'Helvete' saw Shane Embury of NAPALM DEATH and Jörgen Sandström from ENTOMBED and GRAVE lending support in the studio. The NAPALM DEATH connection was strengthened with the announcement of a split EP shared with the British veterans, NASUM covering the NAPALM DEATH track 'Unchallenged Hate' and NAPALM DEATH replying with NASUM's 'The Masked Face'. Upon completion of recording bassist Jesper Liveröd opted out, prioritising his other act BURST. In his stead came the VICTIMS, ACCURSED, OUTLAST and SAYYADENA credited Jon Lindkvist whilst the band also took the opportunity to upgrade to a quartet, pulling in CREMATORY and REGURGITATE guitarist Urban Skytt. The band revealed 2004 was to commence in a suitably heavy fashion, participating in the January 'Extreme The Dojo VII' tour of Japan alongside ANAL CUNT, NAPALM DEATH and PIG DESTROYER. Open air dates saw the band putting in shows at the French 'Fury Fest' as well as the Finnish 'Tuska' and 'Illosaari' festivals.

In July NASUM switched labels from Relapse to Burning Heart Records, commencing work on the 'Shift' album. That August Jon Lindqvist performed at the 'Pointless Fest' in Philadelphia with DISFEAR, substituting for regular guitarist Uffe Cederlund.

The year ended on a tragic note for NASUM as band leader Mieszko Talarczyk was caught in the tidal waves that engulfed the Indian Ocean just after Christmas. Taking a holiday with his girlfriend on Thailand's Phi Phi Island, Mieszko's girlfriend Emma was injured and hospitalised whilst the singer was reported missing. In February 2005 it was confirmed Mieszko Talarczyk's body had been identified. The musician was buried at the Church of Almby, Örebro on 30th March, his favourite Ibanez guitar being interred with his body.

In May GMR Music Group announced they would be releasing limited edition vinyl picture discs of the three NASUM albums, 'Helvete', 'Human 2.01' and 'Inhale/Exhale' through the Vinyl Maniacs label. A label press statement read "it was the wish of the band to have these done since the remaining band members thought they were something singer Mieszko Talarczyk, who was tragically killed in the tsunami disaster, would have wanted to see."

Anders Jakobson formulated the COLDWORKER project in January 2006, first recruiting RUIN guitar player Anders Bertilsson and RELENTLESS bass player Oskar Pålsson. André Alvinzi of CARNAL GRIEF enrolled as second guitarist in March with ex-PHOBOS man Joel Fornbrant installed as frontman the following month. A debut album, 'The Contaminated Void' followed.

Blind World EP, Poserslaughter (1993) (Split EP with AGATHOCLES).
Grindwork EP, Grindwork Productions (1994) (Split EP with RETALIATION, C.S.S.O and VIVISECTION).
Smile When You're Dead EP, Ax/ction (1995) (Split single with PSYCHO).
INDUSTRISLAVEN, Poserslaughter WIMP014 (1995). Löpande-Bands Principen / Cut To Fit / Fantasibilder / Distortion & Disinformation / Brinn / Krigets Skörd / Mer Rens / Ditt Öde / Ingenting Att Ha! / Revolution / Den Mörka Tiden / Forcefed Opinion / Domehagen / Dolt Under Ytan / I Helvetet / Skithus / Söndermald.
World In Turmoil EP, (1997). World In Turmoil / The Final Confrontation / The Dream / Zombie Society / Sheer Horror / Awake / En Varld Utan Hopp / End / As Time Goes By ... / Our Revolution / Masquerade / Ripped Rage / Law & Order? / Rise / Killed By Your Greed.
Nasum EP, (1998) (Free EP with 'Inhale / Exhale' album). Bullshit Tradition / Device / The Real / Rio de San Atlanta, Manitoba.
INHALE—EXHALE, Relapse (1998). This Is ... / The Masked Face / Digging In / Time To Act! / Disdain And Contempt / I See Lies / Inhale-Exhale / Too Naked To Distort / Theres No Escape / The Rest Is Over / Disappointed / Lagg Om! / You're Obsolete / Tested / Shapeshifter / Feed Them, Kill Them, Skin Them / When Science Fails / Closing In / The World That You Made / The System Has Failed Again / For What Cause? / Fullmatad / Screwed / Shaping The End / The New Firing Squad / No Sign Of Improvement / My Philosophy / I'm Not Silent / The Breathing Furnace / Information Is Free / Burning Inside / A Request For Guidance / Grey / Worldcraft / It's Never Too Late / Du Ar Bevakad / Blinded / Can De Lach.
The Black Illusions, Yellow Dog (1998) (Split single with ABSTAIN).
The Nasum / Warhate Campaign EP, Relapse (1999) (Split EP with WARHATE). ... And You Were Blind To What Lay Beyond The Horizon / Stolen Pride / Silent / Losing Faith.
HUMAN 2.0, Relapse RR 6427 (2000). Mass Hypnosis / A Welcome Breeze Of Stinking Air / Fatal Search / Shadows / Corrosion / Multinational Murderers Network / Parting Is Such Sweet Sorrow / The Black Swarm / Sixteen / Alarm / Detonator / Gargoyles And Grotesques / Nar Dagarna ... / Resistance / The Idiot Parade / Den Svarta Fanan / We're Nothing But Pawns / Defragmentation / Sick System / The Professional League / Old And Tired? / Words To Die For / Riot / The Meaningless Trial / Sometimes Dead Is Better.
HELVETE, Relapse RR 6569 (2003). Violation / Scoop / Living Next Door To Malice / Stormshield / Time To Discharge / Bullshit / Relics / We Curse You All / Doombringer / Just Another Hog / Drop Dead / I Hate People / Go! / The Final Sleep / Slaves To The Grind / Breach Of Integrity / The Everlasting Shame / Your Words Alone / Preview Of Hell / Illogic / Whip / Worst Case Scenario.
SHIFT, Burning Heart (2004). Particles / The Engine Of Death / Twinkle, Twinkle Little Scar / No Paradise For The Damned / Wrath / Fear Is Your Weapon / The Deepest Hole / High On Hate / Pathetic / Circle Of Defeat / Like Cattle / Ros / The Smallest Man / Cornered / Strife / The Clash / Hets / Closer To The End / Fury / Fight Terror With Terror / Ett Inflammerat Sar / Deleted Scenes / Creature / Darkness Falls.
GRIND FINALE, Relapse (2006). Blind World / Think / Scarecrows / No Time To Waste / Total Destruction / Between The Walls / Left In A Dream / Uneventful Occupation / Reasons? / Disforest / Self Vilification / Red Tape Suckers / Re-create The System / Rens / Hurt / Corpse Flesh Genitals / Sawder / A Look At Society / Fucking Murder! / Black Visions (Scarecrows II) / Escape / See The Shit (With Your Own Eyes) / Restrained From The Truth / No Chance / My Fear / Fur / A Game By Society / It's All About The Information / Smile When You're Sad / Blindfolded (By The Media) / Erased / Warfuck / No Chance (Extended noise-remix version) / Cut To Fit / Forcefed Opinion / Domedagen / Left In A Dream / Distortion & Disinformation / Stalemate / Bag / Revolution / What's Life? / Think / Verklighetsflykt / Face Obliteration / Enough! / Dom styr vara lov / Industrielaven / Löpandebandsprincipen / Cut To Fit / Fantasibilder / Distortion & Disinformation / Brinn / Krigets Skörd / Mer Rens / Ditt öde / Ingenting Att Ha! / Revolution / Den Mörka Tiden / Forcefed Opinion / Domedagen / Dolt Under Ytan / I Helvetet / Skithus / Söndermald / Revolution II / World In Turmoil / The Final Confrontation (Scarecrows III) / The Dream / Zombie Society / Sheer Horror / Awake / En Värld Utan Hopp / End / As Time Goes By / Our Revolution / Masquerade / Ripped / Rage / Law & Order? / Rise / Killed By Your Greed / Silent Sanguinary Soil / Evacuate The Earth / The Black Illusions / Disgrace / No Paradise For The Damned / A Change In Your Mind / Dreamland / Last / Dis Sucks / The Leak / Eviscerated (By The Fiend) / Shambler / Lack Of Ammunition / The Machines / Lat inte asen styra ditt liv / Going Nowhere / Generation X / The Soil Bleeds Black.

NATAN

HOUTHALEN, BELGIUM — *JoNatan (vocals / violin), Dries (clean vocals / guitar), Daniel (guitar), Jochen (bass), Claudia (keyboards / female vocals / flute), Ezra (drums / vocals).*

Houthalen's NATAN is rooted in a prior act entitled RELICT, forged in late 1999 and comprising guitarists Dries and Buba with singer Ezra, bass player Ken and drummer Kristof. This band broke up with Ezra going on to front Death Metal act ABJATHAR and Ken joining CULPABLE HOMICIDE. With the eventual collapse of his new band Ezra reunited with Dries and, bringing in violinist Jonatan, created NATAN. Kevin Hensels enrolled on bass guitar but his tenure would be brief, former RELICT bass man Ken taking over his role. Meantime the band was rounded out with the addition of female singer and keyboard player Claudia in December of 2001.

With Ken's priorities laying with CULPABLE HOMICIDE the band drew in Daniel to cover on bass. However, Jonaton decamped in 2002. In a complete overhaul of band members the new look NATAN reformed as Ezra on vocals, Dries on guitar, Daniel switching bass for guitar, new girl Claudia on bass and Steven on the drums. In May of 2003 violinist Sophie entered the ranks but then Stephen exited. Ezra made the move over to the drum stool and Dennie was introduced as NATAN's new frontman. The 'Akeldama' album surfaced in 2003.

NATAN issued the demo 'Nevel' in 2004, released in just 50 copies this including a promotional multi-media section. The audio tracks would be re-issued in remixed and remastered EP format in March of 2005. Line-up changes saw the re-recruitment of JoNatan in July 2005 alongside new singer JonatHan. In August Mexican label Atolinga Records issued the 'Nevel' tracks as a split EP shared with AUGURY, limited to 1000 copies.

AKELDAMA, (2003). Achel Demach Funeral / De Duisternis / Gij Vijand / The Beautiful Darkness / Endless / On Fire / De Klauwaards / Winterforest.
Nevel, Nevel (2004) (limited edition 50 copies). Ochtendmist (Intro) / Abandoned / Evil Silence / Visions Of Fire / My Lost Mind / (Multi-media).
Nevel, (2005). Ochtendmist (Intro) / Abandoned / Evil Silence / Visions Of Fire / My Lost Mind.
Natan/Augury, Atolinga ATO11 CDR (2005) (Split EP with AUGURY. Mexican release. Limited edition 1000 copies). Ochtendmist / Abandoned / Evil Silence / Visions Of Fire / My Lost Mind.

NATASTOR

CARACAS, VENEZUELA — *Paul Quintero (vocals / bass), Ángel Brizuela (guitar), Oswaldo Berroteran (bass), Javier Hernández (drums).*

Caracas based Thrash / Death Metal act NATASTOR started life in 1991 billed as ABADDON. The band's opening formation counted guitarist David 'Ángel' Brizuela and bassist Paul Quintero from the band TINIEBLAS alongside Omar Acosta, actually a roadie for TINIEBLAS, on the drums. During 1994 Oswaldo Berroteran, another TINIEBLAS member, took the place of Quintero. More changes saw the drum position going to ex-BIOPHOBIA man Juan Carlos Figueroa in 1996. The demo 'El Juicio Final' emerged in 1998.

NATASTOR made a return in 2002 with new recruit José Correa of KRUEGER repute on drums. Shortly after Javier Hernández of METAL FUSION replaced him. The '1992 -1996' album, released in 2004, comprised archive tracks remixed by Ing. Nacho Matei at AudioLine Studios in Caracas. NATASTOR's 2005 line-up comprised vocalist / bassist Paul Quintero, guitarists Angel Brizuela and Oswaldo Berroteran with Javier Hernandez on drums.

El Juicio Final, (1998). Jinete Rojo / Descolonización / Jesus / El Juicio Final / Macabre Obsession / Reina De La Noche / Mundo Toxico / Miseria / Dragon Of Metal.

1992 -1996, Natastor (2004). Lección De Muerte / Posesión / Blasfemia / AntiCristo / Inquisición Mental / Poltergeist / Natastor / Contaminacion.

NATASTOR, (2005). Esclavo De La Eternidad / Escape From The Fear's Corner / Prisión De Cristal / Lady Without Face / Dreaming With The Reality / Pensamiento Oscuro / Flying In The Cloudy Sky / Natastor / Blaspheme / Mental Inquisition / Escape From The Fear's Corner (Video).

NATRON

ITALY — *Mike Tarantino (vocals), Domenico Mele (guitar), Fabrizio Cassotta (guitar), Lorenzo Signorile (bass), Max Marzocca (drums).*

Technically mind ultra fast Death Metal band NATRON have been active on the underground scene since 1992, being forged in May of that year initially billed as PIPER OF HAMELIN by drummer Max Marzocca. Becoming NATRON in November 1993 with a line-up comprising Marzocca, vocalist Mike Andriani, guitarists Domenico Mele and Vito Ranieri with Philip Farah on bass. A demo recording heralded their arrival in the shape of 1994's 'Force'. However, in January of the following year both Ranieri and Farah opted out. NATRON opted to pursue a single guitar stance, pulling in Lorenzo Signorile as their new bass player.

Signing to Cryptic Souls Productions an EP entitled 'Unpure' was recorded but would not see a release. Andriani broke away in September and Signorile took over vocal responsibilities. As a trio NATRON released a further demo 'A Taste Of Blood'. Restricted to just 300 copies this tape, combined with intensive live work, garnered a recording contract with Headfucker Records as former PENIS LEACH man Mike Tarantino joined up as new frontman.

In early 1997 Max Marzocca took time out to temp as live drummer for fellow Death Metal act MINDSNARE. NATRON's December 1997 album 'Hung, Drawn & Quartered' was produced by guitarist Tommy Talamanca of SADIST. 1998 would prove industrious for the band, putting in two lengthy tours of Europe and signing to the French Holy Records concern for a four album deal. Both 1999's 'Negative Perils' and 2000's 'Bedtime For Mercy' were recorded at the famous Abyss Studios in Sweden and produced by Tommy Tägtgren. 'Negative Perils' incorporated a spoof of THE POLICE hit 'Message In A Bottle' reworked in a Death Metal style as 'Message In A ... Coffin' whilst 'Bedtime For Mercy' included a cover version of VOIVOD's 'NothingFace' with HYPOCRISY's Peter Tägtgren guesting on vocals.

NATRON combined forces with MISANTHROPE and SEPTIC FLESH for the 1999 'Temple of Humiliations Tour' in 1999. During 2001 the group enrolled Fabrizio "Khol" Cassotta as second guitarist. NATRON drummer Max Marzocca would join THE UNDERTAKERS in early 2002.

In April of 2002 NATRON engaged with Germans NECROPHAGIST and Czechs INTERVALLE BIZARRE for the European 'Spring Of Massacre' shows. In September longstanding bassist Lorenzo Signorile made his exit. PENIS LEACH's Vito Laterza is utilised vas a stand in for recording of the new track 'Red Creeps' for inclusion on a Holy Records 10th anniversary compilation album.

NATRON's November 2004 album 'Livid Corruption' was recorded at Jolly Roger studios in Italy and was mixed at Starstruck studios in Denmark with Anders Lundemark. A promotional video would be filmed for the track 'House Of Festering'. Line-up changes in September of 2005 witnessed the departure of bassist Michael Maggi and re-instatement of former four-stringer Lorenzo Signorile.

The band announced European plans for early 2006 in union with Sweden's DERANGED but subsequently cancelled, apparently due to the Scandinavian act's employment commitments. NATRON re-scheduled shows in union with Dutch act GOD

NATRON

DETHRONED. In mid October both singer Mike Tarantino and bass player Lorenzo Signorile stood down. Replacement vocalist Raffaele Fanelli, of MOTHERLY SIN, was quickly inducted. Ottavio Marzo, guitarist with GOLEM and WARCHILD, took over on bass. The new look NATRON teamed up with DIE APOKALYPTISCHEN REITER and ROTTING FAITH for a European tour commencing November 24th in Milan.

HUNG, DRAWN & QUARTERED, Headfucker HF01 (1997). Elmer The Exhumer / Enthroned In Repulsion / Leechlord / Flesh Of A Sick Virgin / The Stake Crawlers / Undead Awaken / Heretics Consume The Deceased / Morgue Feast.

NEGATIVE PREVAILS, Holy (1999). By the Dawn Of The 13th / Pyheretic / I Bleed Black / Posed To Slaughter / Blood Streams / A Religious Sickopathic / Bewitched By The Engraved / Cozmic Autopsies / Message In A ... Coffin / Negative Prevails.

BEDTIME FOR MERCY, (2000). Overblood / Less Than Human / Bedtime For Mercy / Astroblaster (Dominion Of The Unknown) / A Treacherous Wish / Conspiracy / NothingFace / Crypt Of Sexorcism / SleepDead.

Unpure EP, (2000). Flesh Of A Sick Virgin / Quarantine Of Leprosy / Leechlord / The Unearthed Christ / The Stake Crawlers.

LIVID CORRUPTION, Holy (2004). House Of Festering / Livid / Red Creeps / One Step In Murder / Hatemonger / Flatline / White Worms / Nyctophobic / The Dead Rise Above.

NAUMACHIA

WYSZKÓW, POLAND — *Yarpen (vocals), Andrzej Selwon (guitar), Tomasz Kiliński (guitar), Got (bass), Mariusz Kozon (keyboards), Grzesiek (drums).*

Wyszków based Death Metal act NAUMACHIA was conceived as OVERTURE during 1999 featuring guitarists Tomasz "Soyak" Kilinski, a FAUST and CHAINSAW veteran and also as lead vocalist, and Andrzej "Armand" Selwon with Mariusz "Koshen" Kozon of FAUST handling keyboards. The group's original rhythm section comprised bassist Michal "Kulak" Kulesza and drummer Mariusz "Marianek" Mróz. Replacements would be found in Sebastian "Shock" Adaœ on bass and the FAUST credited Grzegorz "Panzer" Golianek on the drums. Signing to French label Adipocere Records the band cut the 'Wrathorn' album at Hertz Studios in October 2003. NAUMACHIA's membership changed again though with the addition of ex-FAUST man got on bass and ALTER EGO's drummer Grzesiek.

WRATHORN, Adipocere CDAR94 (2005). Intro / Blustud / Vorpal / Diamond / Muertos / Lifeitis / Sickened / Cyberian Dance / Wrathorn.

NECARE

LYNCHBURG, VA, USA — *Amy (vocals), Erin (vocals), Ryan Henry (vocals / guitar / bass / keyboards), Jonathan Greer Cawthon (guitar / keyboards / drums), Andy (guitar), Ben (violin), April (viola), Nick (poetry).*

Virginian "Regal" Doom Metal, taking their title NECARE from the latin "to kill with malice aforethought", originally founded as a duo of versatile multi instrumentalist Ryan Henry and drummer Greer Cawthon. Adding singer Erin Vernon and violinist April Leightty the four track 'Ophelia' EP., following this with the self financed 'Apassionata' outing in 2001. 'Nihilist' Henry operates Black Metal band MALICE in association with guitarist 'Schizo', better known as Chris Molinarco of DIVINE SILENCE.

NECARE's 2001 album includes poems from EVOKEN and FUNEBRARUM man Nick Orlando set to music. NECARE, seemingly down to a duo, signed to Finland's Firebox Records for a 2004 album 'Ruins'.

Ryan Henry contributed vocal parts to 2004 recordings from Swedish Doom-Gothic act DRACONIAN.

Ophelia, (1999). Azrael / Misericordiam / Juliet Consigned To Flames Of Woe / Ophelia.
RITE OF SHROUDS, (2000). The Mourner / Wall Of Voices / My Harrowed Heart Forsaken / Eleanor / Juliet (Reprise) / The Fury / Rite Of Shrouds / Dying Art / Even The Heavens Cried / Appassionata.
APPASSIONATA, (2002). Lux Occulta / Eleanor / Wall Of Voices / The Fury / Juliet (Libera Me) / The Mourner / Even The Heavens Cried / Appassionata.

NECROCIDE

SWEDEN — *Victor Brandt (vocals), Pär Sving (guitar), Roberth Svensson (guitar), Per Söderlund (bass), Tommy Holmer (drums).*

NECROCIDE, including RIMTHURS drummer Tommy Holmer, released a self titled demo in 2000 followed by "The Second Killing" demo in 2002. The band, initially a "vampire" Death Metal duo of Tommy Holmer and Per Söderlund, had started life billed as VAIN. When formative members Erland and Richard decamped the project evolved into SEPULCHRAL, now being fronted by Daniel Westerberg.

In mid 1997 Richard returned to the ranks as bassist for new recordings and the debut SEPULCHRAL gig in January of the following year. That Summer Westerberg exited and Per Söderlund took over as lead vocalist, this move also signalling a switch to Grind orientated Metal and a name change to NECROCIDE. Subsequently, Roberth Svensson of WARGMANE took command of bass, before Svensson and Söderlund changed roles. In 2000 Victor Brandt of TOTALT JÄVLA MÖRKER enrolled as singer for the first official demo.

NECROCIDE released the 'Declaration Of Gore' demo in November of 2003.

Necrocide, Necrocide (2000). Nailed Head / Kill / Bloodstained Corpse / Burning Pain, Freezing Skin / Deformed Face Suicide / Sepulchral / Maimed Bitch.
The Second Killing, (2002). Bloodbath ... And Beyond / Dead, Eaten, Pulverized / Incestuous Necrophilia / Butchery.
Declaration Of Gore, (2003). Intro: The Core Of Savage Hatred / Eat The Foetus / Sodomized By My Axe / Tattered Throat.

NECRODEATH

GENOVA, ITALY — *Flegias (vocals / guitar), Claudio (guitar), Paolo (bass), Peso (drums).*

Genova's NECRODEATH released two late eighties albums, 1987's 'Into The Macabre' and 1989's 'Fragments Of Insanity', before folding, then re-uniting in 2000 for the 'Mater Of All Evil' album. The band had debuted in 1985 with the demo cassette 'The Shining Pentagram' but had in fact been active earlier under the billing GHOSTRIDER, releasing the demo 'Mayhemic Destruction'. NECRODEATH band members vocalist Ingo, guitarist Claudio, bassist Paolo and drummer Peso would also be involved in the 1989 MONDOCANE side project.

The reformed NECRODEATH included vocalist Flegias (a.k.a. Marcelo Santos), also holding down a tradition with CADAVERIA and OPERA IX. Bass player John, a former ZONA and 4WD man, is also active with Industrialists DYNABYTE as well as CADAVERIA.

NECRODEATH bassist John, billed as 'El Sargento', and drummer Peso forged "Flamenco Metal" side project RAZA DE ODIO in 2002, uniting with SADIST singer Zanna, ZØRN guitarist López and flamenco guitarist Paco. Signing to Scarlet Records this outfit issued the 'La Nueva Alarma' debut in October of 2004. The compilation album '20 Years Of Noise' arrived in March 2005.

In December the band revealed that new album recordings, dubbed '100% Hate', featured a guesting Cronos of Black Metal originators VENOM. The group pulled in new rhythm guitarist Pier Gonella, previously a member of LABYRINTH, in early 2006. NECRODEATH toured Europe in May as support to Swedish Black Metal band MARDUK. That same year Gonella and Peso forged side endeavour L.I.V. PROJECT for live work in October and November. Concerts in Italy for NECRODEATH saw METHEDRAS and DELIRIUM X TREMENS as support.

Flegias guested on the SCHIZO album 'Cicatriz Black' in 2007.

The Shining Pentagram, (1985). Necro Thrashing Death / Morbid Mayhem / Iconoclast / Mater Tenebrarum.
INTO THE MACABRE, Nightmare (1988). Agony-The Flag Of The Inverted Cross / At The Mountains Of Madness / Sauthencrom / Mater Tenebraum / Necrosadist / Infernal Decay / Graveyard Of The Innocents / The Undead- Agony (Reprise).
FRAGMENTS OF INSANITY, Metalmaster MET114 (1989). Choose Your Death / Thanatoid / State Of Progressive Annihilation / Metampsychosis / Fragments Of Insanity / Enter My Subconscious / Stillbirth / Eucharistical Sacrifice.
MATER OF ALL EVIL, Scarlet (2000). The Creature / Flame Of Malignance / Black Soul / Hate And Scorn / Iconoclast / Void Of Naxir / Anticipation Of Death / Experiment In Terror / Serpent / At The Roots Of Evil / Fathers.
BLACK AS PITCH, Scarlet (2001). Red As Blood / Riot Of Stars / Burn And Deny / Mortal Consequences / Sacrifice 2K1 / Process Of Violation / Anagaton / Killing Time / Saviours Of Hate / Join The Pain / Church's Black Book.
TON(E)S OF HATE, Scarlet (2003). Mealy-Mouthed Hypocrisy / Perseverance Pays / The Mark Of Dr. Z / The Flag / Queen Of Desire / Petition For Mercy / Last Ton(e)s Of Hate / Evidence From Beyond / Bloodstain Pattern.
100% HELL, Scarlet SC 119-2 (2006). February 5th, 1984 / Forever Slaves / War Paint / Master Of Morphine / The Wave / Theoretical And Artificial / Identity Crisis / Beautiful-Brutal World / Hyperbole / 100% Hell.

NECRODEMON

ELKHART, IN, USA — *Rob Elliott (vocals / guitar), Jeremy Montgomery (bass), Chuck Feldman (drums).*

Elkhart, Indiana's NECRODEMON's first offering was the 1999 demo tape 'Deadly'. As a formative trio the band comprised Rob Elliott on vocals and guitar, Jeremy Montgomery on bass with Aero Charles on the drums. Subsequently Mike Hilton took the bass role and Matt Randall handled guitar and keyboards. Frontman Rob Elliott also has ties to SEPHIROTH and Florida Thrashers LORDES WERRE.

The 2004 NECRODEMON line-up comprised vocalist / guitarist Rob Elliott, guitarist Marty Zeak, bassist Wes Mullvain and Chuck Feldman on the drums. Subsequently both Zeak and Mullvain exited and Jeremy Montgomery was installed on bass. The 'Ice Fields Of Hyperion' album saw release in April 2006.

US shows for the summer of 2007 were announced alongside GODLESS RISING and DOWNLORD.

Deadly Demo 1999, Reaper Records U.S.A. (1999). The Summoning / Rape / The Asp / Journey Through The Continuum ... / ... Mechanical Death / Drop Zone.
HAUNTED EONS, Reaper Records U.S.A. (1999). Journey Through The Continuum ... / ... Mechanical Death / The Summoning / Drop Zone / Necromancer's Lair (Chant Of Making III) / Betraying Christ / Rape / Evil Dead / The Asp.
Non-Divine, Reaper Records U.S.A. (2001). Intro / Non-Divine / Black Magic / The Cthulu Mytho / Prophet Of Doom / Outro.
Incipit Fear, Reaper Records U.S.A. (2003). Intro / Apparition / Prophet Of Doom / Childhood Horror / Mord-Sith / Feed The Worms.

ALLEGIANCE TO THE END, Reaper Records U.S.A. (2003). Non-Divine / Cthulu Mytho / Kingdom Of Shadows / IV / Apparition / Death Of Merlin (Chant Of Making IV) / Feed The Worms / Prophet of Doom / The Meatwagon / Mord-Sith / Galactic Tomb.
ICE FIELDS OF HYPERION, Reaper (2006). The Abominable / Terror In the Arctic / Funeral In The Snow / The Deep Freeze / Avalanche! / Frozen Sorcerer (Chant Of Making V) / Mesopotamia—Warriors Of Ice / Empire Of Winter / Benumbed Suffering / So Cold, So Evil / Hordes of Hyperion.

NECROFOBIA

RIOBAMBA, ECUADOR — *Iván Urquizo (vocals), Santiago Martínez (guitar), Raúl Vaca (bass), Johnny Kalvach (drums).*

Riobamba Death Metal band. NECROFOBIA's opening membership of 1991 comprised Raúl Vaca on vocals and bass, the guitar pairing of Omar Ortíz and Paúl Freire with Johnny Kalvach manning the drums.

The line up for the 'Omnipotente' album incorporated Vaca and Kalvach alongside singer Iván Urquizo, guitarists Germán Fuenmayor and Rafael Veintimilla. In 1998 Danny Guerrero took over from Veintimilla. The group also enrolled ex-PARANOIA drummer Ramiro Vallejo in 1999. That December NECROFOBIA entered Strom Digital Studio in Riobamba to craft the 'Dios Verdugo' album. Further changes saw Byron Cevallos manning the drums in 2001 and the addition of guitarist Santiago Martínez.

Between September of 2003 and June of 2004 the group worked on a new album 'Dark, Deep And Eternal' for Hard Bleeding Records. The band at this juncture counted singer Iván Urquizo, guitarist Santiago Martínez, bassist Raúl Vaca and Johnny Kalvach on the drums.

Necrofobia, Necrofobia (1993). Necrópolis / Fobia / Moco.
Desangrar Dioses, Necrofobia (1994). Bifronte / Desangrar Dioses / Necrópolis / Fobia / Destructor de Almas / Lascivia / Satán Altar / Resurrección.
OMNIPOTENTE, (1998). Satán Altar / De Espaldas A Dios / Necrópolis / Sin Sacramentos / Lascivia / Lázaro / Resurrección.
DIOS VERDUGO, (2001). Acto De Fe / Bestia Carne / Crimen Ritual / Nosferatus / Angel Caido / Dios Verdugo / Estirpe Lacayuna.
DEEP, DARK & ETERNAL, (2004).

NECROMANCER

BURGAS, BULGARIA — *Rossen Grudev (vocals / guitar), Tzvetan Kolev (bass), Irina Boncheva (keyboards), Tihomir Liutzkanov (drums).*

Black Sea based NECROMANCER is recognised as one of the most influential acts on the Bulgarian Death Metal scene. Forged in 1989, they would debut with the cassette album 'Creation Of Darkness' for No Rip Off Productions in 1994. The band's line up at this stage comprised vocalist Svetoslav 'The Rooster' Dimitrov, guitarist Rossen Grudev, bass player Nedelcho Harizanov, keyboard player Lina Petrova and drummer Zdravko Zlatev. The follow up, 1995's 'Memories', released by 0.4.3 Records, would be aptly titled in tribute to Dimitrov who had died in a car accident. Grudev handled lead vocals whilst Tihomir Liutzkanov was installed on drums. This same NECROMANCER line up cut 1998's 'Seven Ways To Die' for the Polish concern Mystic Productions.

Subsequently, Nedelcho Harizanov founded THE REVENGE PROJECT.

CREATION OF DARKNESS, No Rip Off Productions (1994). Under Rule / Forces Of Evil / Are You Ready For? / Eternity / Insanity Is What I Am? / Creation Of Darkness / Immortality / Mortify / Die In Your Dream / Necromancer / Another Life.
MEMORIES, 0.4.3 (1995). Eternal Delay (Intro) / Embrace / The Lowest Heights / From Within / Messenger / Crossroads / Marked For Delete / Confession / Memories.
SEVEN WAYS TO DIE, Mystic Production (1998). Pride / Wrath / Envy / Greed / Lust / Gluttony / Sloth.

NECRONOMICON

CANADA — *Rob (vocals / guitar), Dominik (vocals / bass), Rick (drums).*

Montreal based Death Metal act, mentored by Rob 'The Witch', debuted with the 1991 demo 'Morbid Ritual'. Their next product would not surface until four years later, when the band entered Victor Studios in 1995 to record the Pierre Remillard produced EP 'The Silver Key'. Subsequent live work witnessed showings at both Milwaukee and Montreal Metalfests as well as supports to CRADLE OF FILTH and MERCYFUL FATE. Their full-length debut, 1998's 'Pharaoh Of Gods', would be recorded at Peter Pan Studios and issued by Hypnotic Records. With this label's demise the Unique Leader imprint re-released the record in 2002. An extensive round of Canadian dates in the Autumn of 2002 had NECRONOMICON as part of a strong package billing with KATAKLYSM and BLOOD OF CHRIST. 'The Sacred Medicines' followed in 2003.

NECRONOMICON would be seeking a bass player to replace Dominik for live work in March of 2004 as their regular bass man was forced to withdraw after suffering tendonitis in his right wrist. The group also announced its intent to secure a female lead vocalist. NECRONOMICON announced the addition of bassist Fredrich to the group's ranks in June, the new man first featuring in a promotional video for the track 'Dark Wings Of Deceptions'.

The Silver Key, BC NIC 001 (1996). The Silver Key / Morbid Ritual / The Asylum / Hunting Horror / Cthonians.
PHAROAH OF GODS, Hypnotic (1999). Revelation / The Guardian / The Silver Key / Egypt, The Red Earth / Initiation / Pharaoh Of Gods / The Symbol Of Life / Becoming The Hands That Carry The Spirit / The Daring One (Akhnaton).
THE SACRED MEDICINES, Skyscraper Music SM009 (2003). Through The Door Of Time / Dark Wings Of Deceptions / The Threshold / Behind The Mask / Calling The Spirits / The Sacred Medicines / The Pillar Of Balance / Quetzacoatl / Quest For Vision / Dreaming / Temple Of The Sun.

NECROPHAGIA

WELLSVILLE, OH, USA — *Killjoy (vocals), Frediablo (guitar), Fug (guitar), Iscariah (bass), Mirai Kawashima (keyboards), Wayne Fabra (drums).*

Renowned "Audio Horror" styled proto-Death Metal act, Wellsville, Ohio's NECROPHAGIA bowed in with the November 1984 four song demo cassette 'Rise From The Crypt'. The group, singer Killjoy (a.k.a. Frank Pucci), guitarist Larry Madison, bass player Bill James and drummer Joe Blazer, had been formulated a year earlier, claiming joint rights to birthing the Death Metal formula along with their close allies and enthusiastic tape trading partners, Florida's DEATH. 'Rise From The Crypt' was a crudely hacked out rehearsal recording but perfectly captured the group's ferocity and no holds barred approach to horror worship, a trait that would come to exemplify the band.

Follow ups included 1985's 'Autopsy On The Living Dead' and a brace of 1986 demo 'Death Is Fun' and 'Power Through Darkness'. The 'Nightmare Continues' demo, cut at Peppermint Studios, arrived in 1987. That same year the group signed to Californian label New Renaissance Records, operated by HELLION singer Ann Boleyn, and 'Season Of The Dead' followed swiftly. The record, a truly sinister collection of malevolent curses uttered by Killjoy atop laboured, drudging Metal satiated in reverb, pulled in exemplary reviews. However, NECROPHAGIA split in 1989, torn by directional conflicts of opinion and not fully realising the sizable impact their limited output had made upon the extreme Metal scene. As the years passed, this legacy only grew in weight and importance.

Vocalist KILLJOY formed a new band that bore his name re-signing a deal with New Renaissance for the 'Compelled By Fear' album. Killjoy reformed the band in the late 90's with a fresh line-up of bass player Dustin Havnen, drummer Wayne Fabra and guitarist Anton Crowley. This formation re-debuted with 'Holocausto De La Morte' for Red Stream Records. News rapidly spread throughout the Metal world that 'Anton Crowley' was none other than PANTERA vocalist Phil Anselmo whilst guesting on the track 'The Cross Burns Black' would be the equally notorious Maniac of MAYHEM. Maintaining the momentum, an EP entitled 'Black Blood Vomitorium' surfaced in February 2000. This release proudly sported the proclamation Banned in 31 countries! Other product emerging that year included the unofficial 'Ready For Death' opus and the officially endorsed 'Legacy Of Horror, Gore And Sickness' compilation of 80s era demos.

Killjoy also made time for other endeavours, including his involvement in the 2000 all star Black Metal project EIBON. With a solitary track on the 'Moonfog 2000' compilation album EIBON consisted of Killjoy, MAYHEM's Maniac, SATYRICON's Satyr Wongraven, DARKTHRONE's Fenriz and PANTERA's Phil Anselmo.

The same year found Killjoy fronting VIKING CROWN (with 'Crowley' again) and yet another extreme Metal banding of well known names THE RAVENOUS. Included in the latter project was S.O.D. bassist Dan Lilker and AUTOPSY and ABSCESS guitarist Chris Reifert.

A further Anselmo / Killjoy union would be declared in November 2001, ENOCH boasting the inclusion of Mirai Kawashima from cult Japanese Black Metal band SIGH. As it transpired though, Anselmo never participated.

In mid 2002 NECROPHAGIA announced a complete overhaul of the band line up that saw Phil Anselmo no longer involved. The band now cited a roll call of Killjoy, drummer Wayne Fabra, former IMMORTAL bassist Iscariah, GORELORD and WURDULAK man Frediablo on guitars, Fug of WURDULAK on guitars and Mirai Kawashima of SIGH, CUTTHROAT and ENOCH handling keyboards. The band planned a new album, 'The Divine Art Of Torture', for release through the Season Of Mist label. By August it would be revealed that DAEMONIA's Titta Tani, also lead vocalist for Prog Metal band DGM, had taken the drumming role. NECROPHAGIA at this juncture were crediting themselves as Killjoy "Black blood vomiting and corpse shrieks", Frediablo "Morguefiend masturbator of Hellstrings, Fug "Nekromantic six string suicide", Iscariah "Desecrator of goat's blood and cloven hooves", Mirai "Gran inquisitor of pain, torture and hauntings" and Titta Tani "Tombstones and witchfyre".

Killjoy's stamina for band projects was further tested with the introduction in the summer of 2002 of Black Metal band HELL PIG, a collaboration with SLIPKNOT drummer and MURDERDOLLS guitarist Joey Jordison and WATCHTOWER and DANGEROUS TOYS singer Jason McMaster. Also mooted was a collaboration billed as AMICUSS involving Phil Anselmo, Killjoy, Joey Jordison and AMEN's Casey Chaos.

The 2003 NECROPHAGIA 7" single 'Kindred Of A Dying Kind', limited to 1000 copies, gave fans a worthy collectable item as the A side was an unreleased track dating to 1998 whilst Japanese act SIGH covered NECROPHAGIA's own 'Young Burial'. Iscariah would also be active as bassist for AMOK, the Grind-Thrash venture fronted by AETERNUS and TAAKE vocalist / guitarist Radek (a.k.a. 'Larva') and also working alongside ex-SKYCLAD singer Martin Walkyier in THE CLAN DESTINED.

NECROPHAGIA readied a new studio album 'Harvest Ritual Vol 1: Penance' for 2004 issue. The 'Goblins Be Thine' EP was also released in 2004 through Red Stream. Two DVDs would be in the works too, 'Nightmare Scenarios' and 'NecroTorture/Sickcess', the latter a combination of a live performance filmed in Valencia, Spain with a "gore filled road movie" directed by directed by Fred Vogel and Killjoy.

A further project of guitarist Frediablo also emerged, initially billed as SEVEN GATES OF HELL, but then switched to CHAMBER OF STRENGTH. Recording at Godfed Studios in Norway this solo venture would be self described as "an intense hybrid of Death, Hardcore and modern Metal". In August, Killjoy joined up with the Danish ambient band FORLIS as the group's new vocalist. Meantime, Frediablo's Black Metal project HEMNUR published the 'Ravnsvart' demo in October, also crafting a debut album 'Untamed Norwegian Black Metal' for early 2005 issue through Baphomet Records. The guitarist also readied a third GORELORD album, 'Norwegian Chainsaw Massacre', due in May 2005 via Coffin Records.

As the year closed it was announced NECROPHAGIA had completed the recording of new record 'Harvest Ritual Vol. 1' for the Season of Mist label. The track 'Stitch Her Further' would be co-written by SLIPKNOT's Joey Jordison, who also contributed guest vocals. The summer of 2005 witnessed the first NECROPHAGIA US tour in many years, the band heading up a billing supported by ENGORGE, TYPHUS and SUMERIA. These shows included appearances at the 'Return Of Darkness And Evil' and 'Milwaukee Metal Fest' events. That August, Frediablo relinquished his associations with NECROPHAGIA, GORELORD, WURDULAK and CHAMBER OF STRENGTH to prioritise GRIMFIST. Predictably, NECROPHAGIA returned to the fore once again, issuing a limited edition live album 'Slit Wrists & Casket Rot' before touting the 'Deathtrip 69' album in September. The group further announced an EP release billed 'Satan's Skin'.

NECROPHAGIA announced the addition of DIABOLOS and ex-NOKTURNE guitarist Undead Torment in July 2006.

Rise From The Crypt, Necrophagia (1984) (Demo). Rise From The Crypt / Kill ... / Chainsaw Lust / Demonic Possession.
Autopsy Of The Living Dead, Necrophagia (1985) (Demo). Necrophagia / Vomit.
Death Is Fun, Necrophagia (1985) (Demo). Autopsy Of The Living Dead / Death Is Fun / Communon Of Death / Insane For Blood.
Power Through Darkness, Necrophagia (1986) (Demo). Witchcraft / Power Through Darkness / Young Burial / Chainsaw Lust / Autopsy On The Living Dead.
SEASON OF THE DEAD, New Renaissance NRCD15 (1987). Season Of The Dead / Forbidden Pleasure / Bleeding Torment / Insane For Blood / Reincarnation / Ancient Slumber / Mental Decay / Abomination / Terminal Vision / Painful Discharge / Beyond And Back.
Nightmare Continues, Necrophagia (1987) (Demo cassette). Abomination / Communion Of Death / Young Burial / Black Apparition.
HOLOCAUSTO DE LA MORTE, The Plague PLAGUE 001 (1998). Bloodfreak / Embalmed Yet I Breathe / The Cross Burns Black / Deep Inside, I Plant The Devils Seed / Burning Moon Sickness / Cadaverous Screams Of My Deceased Lover / Children Of The Vortex / Hymns Of Divine Genocide.
DEATH IS FUN, Red Stream (2000). Abomination / Young Burial / Black Apparition / Chainsaw Lust / Intense Mutilation / Autopsy On The Living Dead / Witchcraft / Power Through Darkness / Young Burial (Demo) / Chainsaw Lust (Demo).
Black Blood Vomitorium EP, Red Stream RSR-0131 (2000). And You Will Live In Terror / They Swell Beneath / It Lives In The Woods / Black Blood Vomitorium.
LEGACY OF HORROR, GORE AND SICKNESS, Vinyl Collector's VC 006 (2000). World Funeral / Lust Of The Naked Dead / Hemorage / Ready For Death / Ancient Slumber / Black Apparition / Blood Thirst / Mental Decay / Communion Of Death / Return To Life / Witchcraft / Autopsy Of The Living Dead / Death Is Fun / Communion Of Death / Insane For Blood / Rise From The Crypt / Kill / Chainsaw Lust.
Devil Eyes, Red Stream (2001) (Split single with ANTEAUS). Devil Eyes.
Cannibal Holocaust EP, Season Of Mist SOM 044 (2001). Cannibal Holocaust / Burning Moon Sickness / It Lives In The Woods / Baphomet Rises / Chainsaw Lust / Cannibal Holocaust (Video).
THE DIVINE ART OF TORTURE, Season Of Mist SOM069 (2003). Blaspheme The Body / Upon Frayed Lips Of Silence / Parasite Eve / Maim Attraction / Rue Morgue Disciple / The Sick Room / Conjuring The Unnamable / Flowers Of Flesh And Blood / The Divine Art Of Torture / Ze Do Caixao.
Kindred Of A Dying Kind, Red Stream RSR-0163 (2003) (Split single with SIGH. Limited edition 1000 copies). Kindred Of A Dying Kind.
Goblins Be Thine, Red Stream RSR-0170 (2004). Sadako's Curse / To Sleep With The Dead / Young Burial / The Fog / Goblins Be Thine / Untitled.

HARVEST RITUAL VOL. 1, Red Stream RSR-0181 (2005). The World, The Flesh, The Devil / Dead Skin Slave / Unearthed / Cadavera X / London 13 Demon Street / Return To Texas / Akumu / Stitch Her Further / Excommunicated / Harvest Ritual.

SLIT WRISTS & CASKET ROT, Red Stream RSR-0190 (2006). Requiem For A Black Pope / Upon Frayed Lips Of Silence / Blaspheme The Body / Cannibal Holocaust / Parasite Eve / And You Will Live In Terror / Maim Attraction / Flowers Of Flesh And Blood / Rue Morgue Disciple / Embalmed Yet I Breathe / The Divine Art Of Torture / Ze Do Caixao / Young Burial.

NECROPHAGIST

STUTTGART, GERMANY — *Muhammed Suiçmez (vocals / guitar), Christian Münzner (guitar), Heiko Linzert (bass), Daniel Silva (drums).*

Stuttgart Death Metal band. The album 'Onset Of Putrefaction', besides the exception of one guest guitar solo from FEROCITY's Bjorn Vollmer, was recorded entirely as a solo undertaking by Muhammed Suiçmez. NECROPHAGIST would be brought up to full band strength with the addition of guitarist Christian Münzner, bass guitarist Heiko Linzert and drummer Daniel Silva. In 2003 the band lost their bassist and Silva's place was taken by Hannes Großmann.

NECROPHAGIST was scheduled to support MORBID ANGEL and NILE on European dates in 2005 but would cancel, Muhammed Suiçmez claiming he had "health problems", which prevented him "from performing on stage or leaving Stuttgart". European shows in January and February 2006 witnessed a strong partnership with MALEVOLENT CREATION, NIGHTRAGE and BOLT THROWER. However, NECROPHAGIST then parted ways with guitarist Christian Münzner. Sami Raatikainen, from Finnish band CODEON, substituted.

The group hit North America for an extensive run of US and intended Canadian shows lasting into June. They would be joined on this package tour by ION DISSONANCE from Canada, ARSIS and ALARUM from Australia. However, the Canadian leg was suspended when the band had their passports stolen, making entry across the border impossible.

Christian Münzner teamed up with MAJESTY in May 2006. November saw US dates backing CANNIBAL CORPSE, UNMERCIFUL and DYING FETUS. NECROPHAGIST then announced they were to team up with MISERY INDEX, COLDWORKER and BURNING SKIES for a European tour beginning in February 2007. However, the group was forced to cancel their headlining slot on the first eight scheduled shows due to "unforeseen and out-of-our-control circumstances".

Hannes Grossmann's last stint on drumming duty for NECROPHAGIST came with the band's April 1st 2007 headline show at the California Metalfest in Santa Ana. He would be superseded by the highly travelled Marco Minnemann. The band's next tour outing was to be the 'Summer Slaughter' trek across the USA throughout June and July, headlining with support from DECAPITATED, CEPHALIC CARNAGE, CATTLE DECAPITATION, THE FACELESS, AS BLOOD RUNS BLACK, ARSIS, ION DISSONANCE and BENEATH THE MASSACRE.

ONSET OF PUTREFACTION, Velvet (1999). Foul Body Autopsy / To Breathe In A Casket / Mutilate The Stillborn / Intestinal Incubation / Culinary Hyperversity / Advanced Corpse Tumor / Extreme Unction / Fermented Offal Discharge.

EPITAPH, Relapse (2004). Stabwound / The Stillborn One / Ignominious & Pale / Diminished To Be / Epitaph / Only Ash Remains / Seven / Symbiotic In Theory.

NECROPHILISMA

BOSNIA — *Mirza Selamovic (vocals), Nedzad Bibic (guitar), Vahid Pandur (bass), Mirza Osmanovic (drums).*

Tuzla's Death Metal combo NECROPHILISMA was created during 2001, originally counting a line up of vocalist Mirza Selamovic, guitarist Drazen Mulaosmanovic, bassist Amar Tahirović with Mirza Osmanovic on the drums. This first version of the band crafted the demo 'Hell's Recline' and the live album 'Live Into disgrace', the latter featuring a cover version of KREATOR's 'Lost'. Tahirović then exited, prioritising his other act NO RULES.

NECROPHILISMA commenced recording the studio album 'Unmask death (Servant Of The Damned)' in October of 2002 with new bassist Harsen Kocan onboard. Line up turmoil in early 2003 resulted in the departure of Mulaosmanovic and Harsen. Taking the guitar position would be Nedzad "Nele" Bibic, a veteran of TOXICDEATH, P.B.S., MEPHISTOS and SPORULATE, alongside new bass man Vahid "Vaha" Pandur.

Gigs in July of 2004 saw TOXICDEATH's Sead "Sejo" Hadzic standing in as temporary drummer.

LIVE INTO DISGRACE, Necrophilisma (2002). Disgrace / Seditious End / Lost / Hell's Recline / Down In My Kingdom / Bloody Angel.

UNMASK DEATH (SERVANT OF THE DAMNED), Necrophilisma (2003). Next Obsequies / Natural Ferocity / Evil Breed Evil / In The Name Of The Pure Soul / Wrath / From Death Is Beginning / Blind Hunters / Life Is No Debt / Interior Presage / Killing Brain / Cut The Last Root / Unmask Death.

NECROPHOBIC

STOCKHOLM, SWEDEN — *Anders Strokirk (vocals / bass), Dave Parland (guitar), Tobbe Sidegard (keyboards), Joakim Sterner (drums).*

Stockholm Death Metal act created in 1989. NECROPHOBIC once included ex-DARK FUNERAL guitarist Dave Parland in the ranks. The band's initial demo, 'Slow Asphyxiation', sold a commendable 700 copies, prompting a 1991 three track tape entitled 'Unholy Prophecies', recorded at the ever popular Sunlight studios.

NECROPHOBIC's first commercial release came with an EP titled 'The Call' on U.S. label Wild Rags Records that featured ex-CREMATORY vocalist Stefan Harrvik. A track also followed on a compilation album on Witchhunt Records. The band would then contract to the Black Mark Production label for a run of albums, commencing with 'The Nocturnal Silence' in 1993.

In late 1995 keyboard player Tobbe Sidegard joined fellow Swedes THERION and Parland quit in 1996 to concentrate on his solo outfit BLACKMOON. Undaunted, NECROPHOBIC issued the 'Darkside' album that same year. 1997's 'Darkside' album witnessed a fresh NECROPHOBIC line-up comprised of Tobbe Sidegard on vocals and bass, drummer Joakim Sterner and new guitarist Martin Halfdahn. A third Black Mark Production album, 'The Third Antichrist', arrived in October 1999.

NECROPHOBIC would tour Poland in November of 2002, headlining a package billing also comprising fellow Swedes DIABOLICAL, British band THUS DEFILED along with Polish outfits CORRUPTION, HELL BORN, MESSAGE and UNNAMED. Further shows, allied with SATARIEL and IMPIOUS, took the band into mainland Europe in January of 2003. To coincide with the dates Hammerheart label reissued NECROPHOBIC's first three albums 'The Nocturnal Silence', 'Darkside' and 'The Third Antichrist'.

Johan Bergebäck joined DISMEMBER in September of 2004. Having severed ties with Karmageddon Media during November of 2005, NECROPHOBIC entered Dark Voodoo Studios, working with engineers Anders Bentell and Fredrik Folkare, UNLEASHED guitarist, on a new album, 'Hrimthursum' ("The Frost Giants') for Regain Records.

Slow Asphyxiation, (1990) (Demo). Slow Asphyxiation / Realm Of Terror / Retaliation.

Unholy Prophecies, Wild Rags (1991) (Demo). Sacrificial Rites / Unholy Prophecies / Inborn Evil.

THE NOCTURNAL SILENCE, Black Mark Production BMCD 40 (1993). Awakening / Before The Dawn / Unholy Prophecies / The Nocturnal Silence / Shadows Of The Moon / The Ancients Gate / Sacrificial Rites / Father Of Creation / Where Sinners Burn.

The Call, Wild Rags WRR-NEC (1993). Shadows Of The Moon / The Ancient Gate / Father Of Creation.
Spawned By Evil EP, Black Mark Production BMCD 60 (1996). Spawned By Evil / Die By The Sword / Nightmare / Enter The Eternal Fire.
DARKSIDE, Black Mark Production BMCD 96 (1996). Black Moon Rising / Spawned By Evil / Bloodthirst / Venasectio / Darkside The Call / Descension / Mailing The Holy One / Nifelhel / Christian Slaughter.
THE THIRD ANTICHRIST, Black Mark Production BMCD 146 (1999). Rise Of The Infernal / The Third Of Arrivals / Frozen Empire / Into Armageddon / Eye Of The Storm / The Unhallowed / Isaz / The Throne Of Souls Possessed / He Who Rideth In Rage / Demonic / One Last Step Into The Great Mist.
BLOODHYMNS, Hammerheart HHR098 (2002). Taste Of Black / Dreams Shall Flesh / Act Of Rebellion / Shadowseeds / Mourningsoul / Hellfire / Cult Of Blood / Roots Of Heldrasill / Blood Anthem / Among The Storms.
Tour EP 2003, Hammerheart HHR133 (2003). Before The Dawn / Spawned By Evil / Into Armageddon / Dreams Shall Flesh / Die By The Sword / Nightmare / Enter The Eternal Fire / Ridden With Disease / Moonchild.
HRIMTHURSUM, Regain RR093CD (2006). The Slaughter Of Baby Jesus / Blinded By Light, Enlightened By Darkness / I Strike With Wrath / Age Of Chaos / Bloodshed Eyes / The Crossing / Eternal Winter / Death Immaculate / Sitra Ahra / Serpents (Beneath The Forest Of The Dead) / Black Hate / Hrimthursum.

NECROPOLIS

LONDON, UK— *Sven Olaffsen (vocals), Billy Liesegang (guitar), Trev Thoms (guitar), Keith More (guitar), Algy Ward (bass), Steve Clark (drums).*

The debut album from Black Metallers NECROPOLIS is not all it seems. Drummer Steve Clark, previously with FASTWAY, DESTROYER, ATOMGOD and mentor of Jazz Rock act NETWORK, assembled this band allegedly in an attempt to show the younger genre of Death Metal bands just how this kind of music should be performed. An odd contrast of styles were to make up NECROPOLIS with ex-NINA HAGEN / JOHN WETTON guitarist Billy Liesegang, additional guitars from ASIA and ARENA man KEITH MORE, former TANK, DAMNED and ATOMGOD bassist Algy Ward and erstwhile HAWKWIND guitarist Trev Thoms.

The album, recorded in 1993, includes a guest session from ex-MOTÖRHEAD and FASTWAY guitarist FAST EDDIE CLARKE. Following recording of 'End Of The Line' Clark and Ward resumed activity with NETWORK for the 'Refusal To Comply' album. Ward subsequently resurrected TANK.

END OF THE LINE, Neat Metal NM021 (1997). Victim / Samaritan / A Taste For Killing / Shadowman / 145 Speed Overload / The Bitterness I Taste.

NECROPRIEST

SWEDEN — *Donald Gregory (vocals), Wicked Sylvester (guitar / bass), Napalmor (drums).*

NECROPRIEST began life in the Winter of 2000 as a Death Metal solo project of LITANIA and BEYOND MORTALITY's Napalmor, handling both vocals and drums In the Spring of 2001 Wicked Sylvester was introduced on guitar and bass to record the EP 'The Love We Share'. Two releases emerged in 2002, the album 'Blasphemous Lycantrophy', including a rendition of LED ZEPPELIN's 'Immigrant Song', and EP 'When Theres No More Room In Hell', this second effort seeing Jonne Jumper on guest vocals and a cover version of DANZIG's 'Twist Of Cain'.

Output continued into 2003 with the EP 'Man Made Monsters' and album 'Sell Your Soul'. However, Napalmor quit in January of 2004, being replaced on vocals by Donald Gregory. Napalmor duly returned in March for the demo 'Straight To The Top'.

The Love You Share, Necropriest (2001). I Want To … / Necropriest / Abbra Cadavra / The Love You Share / Night Of The Vampire.
BLASPHEMOUS LYCANTHROPY, Necropriest (2002). Meanest One Alive / A Killer / Immigrant Song / Shadowland / When Good Pets Go Bad / Another Killing Kid / No Redemption For The Damned / Blasphemous Lycanthropy.
SELL YOUR SOUL, Necropriest (2003). Intro / Stop Killing The Dead / Desperation / Evil / Beyond / Sell Your Soul / Human Predator / Outro / Into The Unknown.

NECROSADISTIC GOAT TORTURE

LONDON, UK — *Goatthroat Talkea Schmidt (vocals), GoatCommando Steve Brennan (Guitar), Goatmaster Petr Burov (bass), Goatlord Duncan Jones (drums).*

NECROSADISTIC GOAT TORTURE is a London based Death Metal act manifested during 2003 as a quartet comprising vocalist / guitarist Matt Von Ziegenstein-Pilorz, guitarist Goatess Christine Hell, bass player Goatmaster Petr Alexandrovich Burov and drummer Goatlord Duncan Oliver Jones. The group debuted with the 'Necrosadistic Goat Torture' December 2003 demo. The EP 'One Nation Under Goat' arrived in November 2004.

In December 2006 NECROSADISTIC GOAT TORTURE issued the album 'The Maniac's Banquet'. By early late 2006 the band had re-shaped it's line-up to comprise vocalist Goatthroat Talkea Schmidt, guitarist GoatCommando Steve Brennan, bass player Goatmaster Petr Burov and drummer Goatlord Duncan Jones.

Necrosadistic Goat Torture, Necrosadistic Goat Torture (2003). Morbid Intentions / Primal / Comprehension Day.
One Nation Under Goat, (2004). Morbid Intentions / Anger Overload / Primal / Denial / Godlike.
THE MANIAC'S BANQUET, NGT2 (2006). Nekrolog / Immortals / Deathworm / Faceless / The Maniac's Banquet.

NECROSIS

NORTH HAVEN, CT, USA — *Ryan Early (vocals / guitar), John DeAngelo (guitar), Danielle Gambardella (guitar), Madison Roseberry (bass), Jaime Pompilli (keyboards), Nicole Sestito (drums).*

NECROSIS was formulated under the formative banner of HOLLOW POINT in the Summer of 2002 by vocalist / guitarist Ryan Early and drummer Nicole Sestito. Subsequently, guitarist John DeAngelo was enrolled as initial writing sessions led to a name switch to DRESSED IN BLACK. Early the next year second guitarist Danielle Gambardella was inducted, freeing Ryan Early up to prioritise lead vocals. Further material was penned, prompting another title switch to CORPORAL DOWNFALL, under which brand the demo 'Black Winter' was crafted.

Yet another name change, to NECROSIS, saw the introduction of keyboard player Jaime Pompilli and bassist Madison Roseberry. The band inaugurated itself on the live front on 16th August 2003 performing a rain shortened set alongside ALL UNDONE. The group then went into a lengthy period of stasis, broken with the acquisition of Dave Guckian on bass. The revised formation first performed live on 1st November, at the Polish National Alliance in Wallingford.

NECROSIS then unraveled as both Sestito and Guckian exited. Shortly after this defection Pompilli too opted out. The beginning of 2004 marked a new beginning as the remaining band members took on another title change to become APOSTASY. Bassist Zach Green was adopted in February and APOSTASY's stage debut, complete with drum machine, came on 13th March at a gig dubbed 'Rebfest', held in John DeAngelo's basement. The band put in two more gigs with the drum machine before being offered an album deal through Statue Records of California. Brett Pieper was installed on the drum stool and Rob Spalding for 'Shadows Of The Apocalypse' album recordings commencing in August. However, progress in the studio was minimal and Spalding was let go. The existing tapes would be scrapped and work began afresh, this time billing the album 'Invocation'.

Following a support gig to STRAPPING YOUNG LAD in Hartford in April of 2005 APOSTASY dispensed with Pieper's services.

Black Winter, EarlCore (2003). Pledge Your Allegiance / Sin America / Dressed In Black / Anything To Belong.
MMIII A.D., EarlCore (2003). Anything To Belong / Bloodlust / Dressed In Black / Sin America.
MMIII A.D. SPECIAL EDITION, EarlCore Records (2003). Pledge Your Allegiance (Instrumental) / Dressed In Black / Sin America / Anything To Belong / Bloodlust / Anything To Belong (Black Winter version) / Dressed In Black (Black Winter version) / Pledge Your Allegiance (Black Winter version) / Sin America (Black Winter version).

NECROTIC CHAOS

MALAYSIA — *Adik (vocals / bass), Jadam (guitar), Menthra (guitar), Wira (drums).*

Ipoh based Brutal Death Metal band borne out of the disintegration of GLOTTIS during 1992. Erstwhile members re-united to forge NECROTIC CHAOS, the first incarnation of which consisted of vocalist / bassist Adik, guitarist Is and drummer Jadam. Shortly after second guitarist Dark-E joined the fold. An eponymous 1993 promo tape led to a split demo cassette shared with Singapore Grindsters DEMISOR the following year. Among the five tracks NECROTIC CHAOS contributed would be a BRAIN DEAD cover.

The next step for the band was to include two tracks on the 'Ipoh Metal Militant Supremacist' compilation album released by Ultra Hingax Productions. The band's split album of May 2002 'Splitting The Vulva' would be shared with another Singapore act CARDIAC NECROPSY.

NECROTIC CHAOS during 2002 comprised Adik as frontman, Jadam and Menthra on guitar with Wira on drums. Both Wira and Jadam session for KOFFIN KANSER with Wira also being involved with VOCIFERATION ETERNITY and INFECTIOUS MAGGOTS. Jadam participates in MESMERIZED and GORB. Adik has sessioned for LANGSUYR and BRAIN DEAD.

The 'Regime Grotesque' album, seeing Menthra superseded by Jo-O on guitar, arrived in 2003.

SPLITTING THE VULVA, Dark Artz (2002). Cataclysmical Enlightenment / Forth Abattoir / Infernal Sorcery / The Black Flames Of Hatred.
REGIME GROTESQUE, Ultra Hingax Productions (2003). Fateless Revolution / Perilous Curse Of Supernatural / Regime Grotesque / The Black Flames Of Hatred / Necrochemical Suicide / Cataclysmical Enlightenment / Necrotic Chaos (A Lust Macabre) / Reigns Supreme.

NECROVORE

NEW BRAUNFELS, TX, USA — *Jon DePlachett (vocals / guitar), Bjorn Haga (guitar), Mike Hernandez (bass), Louie Carrizales (drums).*

New Braunfels based NECROVORE is an illustrious name on the American Death-Black Metal scene despite never having officially released product. Frontman Jon DePlachett held scene credits with MATRIX, MESODAEMON and DEATH CORP. The band was founded during the mid 80's's, issuing one raw tape, recorded in the band's practice room on a four track tape machine in March 1987, which ignited their own underground legend. The band's demo 'Divus De Mortuus', recorded by a line-up comprising DePlachett, guitarist Scott Humphrey, former OBSESSED DEATH bassist Ross Stone and drummer Scott Staffney, is undoubtedly one of the founding bedrocks of the Death Metal genre. During 1988 the track 'Slaughtered Remains', a cleaner studio version, was contributed to the New Renaissance compilation album 'Satan's Revenge Part II'.

Line-up changes in the Autumn of 1987 saw Humphrey superseded by ex-OBSESSED DEATH and ANKOU man Bjorn Haga on guitar. With this roster, NECROVORE debuted live in May of 1988 at the San Antonio Cameo Theater. The band commenced work on a second demo session, but this would not be completed. Javier Villegas of HELLPREACHER would man the drums for the latter stages of the band's original career. NECROVORE folded in 1990.

Over the ensuing years there would be persistent rumours of NECROVORE reunions. NECROVORE guitarist Bjorn Haga, as 'Bolder', joined the premier U.S. Black Metal band THORN SPAWN during 1998. Various bootlegs of NECROVORE include a three way split release shared with Florida's INCUBUS and MORBID ANGEL and a split with Brazilians SARCOFAGO.

In 1997 NECROVORE apparently re-united with a new rhythm section of bassist Mike Hernandez and drummer Louie Carrizales, the latter holding a tradition with DEATH, ROTTING CORPSE, DEVASTATION and HELL DOGS. Word arrived in 2002 that new recordings, with the founding members Ross Stone and Scott Staffney back in the fold, were underway.

During 2005 California's MORBOSIDAD recorded a NECROVORE track, a Spanish language version, for a projected tribute album planned through From Beyond Productions.

Divus De Mortuus, Nervure (1987). Mutilated Death / Slaughtered Remains / Divus De Mortuus / Toxic Decay.

NEAPS

ITALY — *Fabio Covelo (vocals / bass), Dario Piggott (guitar), Tom Piggott (drums).*

Death Metal band formed up in 1995 as a trio of frontman Fabio Covelo, guitarist Dario Piggott and drummer Tom Piggott. NEAPS have maintained a stable line up since inception. Fabio Covelo would aid fellow Italian Death Metal band BASTARD SAINTS on their 2000 album. This relationship between the two bands was strengthened with the issue of a shared EP in August of 2001 'Ropes Above An Abyss Of Fury'. NEAPS signed with the German Bones Brigade label for a late 2002 album 'Seven Times Seven'. That same year the band conducted the Polish 'Grind Manifesto 2002' tour packaged with BASTARD SAINTS and Polish outfits PIG NATION, ANTIGUA and TOXIC BONKERS.

He Was Born EP, (1997). Intro / Gate Of Gazer / I'm Born Dead, I'm Born Demon / Cross Every Limit, Cross Every Time (The Pestilence Of The Devil) / Outro.
TRANSFIGURATION TO THE ANCIENT'S FORM, Sothis (2000). Hidden / Immolation For The Abyss / Vision / ... For Our Kingdom / Entwine My Soul.
Ropes Above An Abyss Of Fury EP, (2001) (Split EP with BASTARD SAINTS). Cross Every Limits, Cross Every Time / The Passage.
SEVEN TIMES SEVEN, Broken Bones BB 017 (2002).

NEGLIGENT COLLATERAL COLLAPSE

CZECH REPUBLIC — *Paul (vocals), Brain (guitar), Robocop (guitar / bass), Erich (drums).*

Prague based Grind-Death Metal unit. NEGLIGENT COLLATERAL COLLAPSE released the cassette '28 Minutes Of Silence For All Innocent Victims' in 1996 followed by a split tape with CAT ASEXUAL URGE MOTIVATION entitled 'Spasm Of Extinction' in early 1997 with a four way split 7" EP shared with MALIGNANT TUMOUR, C.U.M. and C.S.S.O. through Bizarre Leprous Productions that same year. In 1998 archive live material dating from 1995 was issued as the 'Massacre Of Nazis In S.P.A.C.E.' tape and in 1999 the 'Homologated Recycled 4D Hippies' demo tape arrived. The 2000 EP 'Feynman' and the full length release in 2002 'Reprocess Segment Database Extender' exhibited the unique influence of quantum physics in the song titles.

The band, in alliance with COCK AND BALL TORTURE, FILTH and DOWNTHROAT partook of a split album in 2001 through Bizarre Leprous Productions.

Feynman, (2000). Intro: Discovery / Superconductivity Research: 'Dry Magnets' / Something Is Shitted With My Analbase / Speaking Wi*th Th*e (Illegal) Devil/ce / Quantum Transport In Optical Lattices / The Principles / Resurrection Of Internal Circulation, Body Application And Human Nervous System / Superstrings: A Theory Of Everything / Unknown Error / The Prayer.

NEGLIGENT COLLATERAL COLLAPSE, Bizarre Leprous Productions (2001) (Split album with COCK AND BALL TORTURE, FILTH & DOWNTHROAT). Feynman's Favourite Quote / Quantum Transport In Optical Lattices / Speaking Wi*th Th*e (Illegal) Devil/ce / Unknown Error / Something Is Shitted With My Analbase / The Principles / Superconductivity Research: 'Dry Magnets' / Runtime Error / Monachus Monachus / Kurt The God / Miss Auschwitz '43 / Máj.

Blue And White, (2001). Blue And White / On The Return Trip Home / Carnal Cacophony.

REPROCESS SEGMENT DATABASE EXTENDER, Obscene Productions OBP 045 (2002). Black Hole Monster In A Spin Releases Energy / Billion Suns / One Thing Is Sure / Buzz / The Paul Dirac Medal And Prize (Gorilla Gorilla Beringei) / A Generalized Lie Derivative And Homothetic Or Killing Vectors In The Geroch-Held-Penrose Formalism / XMM-Newton / Electric Dynamo Effect / Literate Physicist Gets Taste For Fiction / Analysis Of Iron Line / The Hunt / Payload Specialists / Not out / MCG-6-30-15 / New Generation Of Neutrino Experiments Begins—The Ursus Arctos Nelsoni Experiment / Something Is Collapsed In My Analbase / Focuse / On The Return Trip Home / The Brain Is 'Classical' / Two-Dimensional Penrose-Tiled Photonic Quasicrystals: From Diffraction Pattern To Band Structure / Quantum Modelling Of The Mind / Spacetimes Admitting Isolated Horizons / Killing Vector Field / Chain Reaction's Domino Aka Termic Firer / Metamorphosis.

NEMBRIONIC

HOLLAND — *Bor (vocals / guitar), Dennis (guitar), Jamil (bass), Noel Rule (drums).*

Rooted in the Dutch Grindcore act NEMBRIONIC HAMMERDEATH founded in 1988. Following an EP, 'Themes Of An Occult Theory', in 1993 and a split debut album with CONSOLATION entitled 'Tempter' for the Dutch Displeased label the band evolved into simply NEMBRIONIC.

As NEMBRIONIC the band recharged their career with the 1995 opus 'Psycho One Hundred'.

In 1997 a new release 'Bloodcult' was issued, a Mini album version of their previous 'Themes' 7" EP including three brand new numbers and an unreleased track from the archives. A further full album 'Incomplete' arrived in 1998. NEMBRIONIC members united with personnel from CONSOLATION in early 2002 announcing a new, less than subtly titled, act FUCKFACE.

PSYCHO ONE HUNDRED, Displeased D00032 (1995). Kill Them / Coffin On Coffin / Strength Through Hate / Strength Through Pain / Warzone / Modo Grosso / Death To The Harmless / 15 Minutes / In Ebony / Strength Through Power / Psycho 100 / Bulldozer.

BLOODCULT, Displeased D0052 (1997). Warfare Noise / Corroded / Bloodcult / Yog Sotoh / Approach To Coincidence / Against God / Confrontation With Terror.

INCOMPLETE, Displeased (1998). Riotkill / Dawn Of Rage / Hawkeye / Assassinate / Incomplete / Corroded / Warfare / Beastmachine / In Harmony With Blood / Black Heart / Murdered Streaking / Murdered Mooning / Fleshman / Fleshman II / Riotkill-Roadkill.

NEMBRIONIC HAMMERDEATH

HOLLAND — *Bor (vocals / guitar), Dennis (guitar), Jamil (bass), Noel Rule (drums).*

A Dutch Grindcore act founded in 1988. Two years later the band drafted former FRIED FULL RUBBER drummer Noel Rule and CONSOLATION guitarist Dennis. It was to be 1991 before the first NEMBRIONIC HAMMERDEATH demo—'Lyrics Of Your Last Will'—appeared.

The group would then contribute the track 'In Your Own Hell' to the compilation album 'And Justice For None', promoting these releases with support shows to NOCTURNUS, CONFESSOR, CONSOLATION, GRAVE and ALTAR.

An EP, 'Themes On An Occult Theory', in January 1993 pre-empted shows with PESTILENCE before the group shared their debut album with CONSOLATION on the split release 'Tempter'.

TEMPTER,, Displeased (1993). Millionth Beast / Tempter / My Commitment / Yog Sathoth / Approach To Coincidence / In Your Own Hell / Towards The Unholy: I) Thundermarch , II) Waterside, III) Towards, IV) Token, V) Unholy, VI) Endless, VII) Purge.

Themes On An Occult Theory, Displeased D 000021 (1993). Approach To Coincidence / Bow For The Overlord / Yog Sototh / Against God.

PSYCHO 100, Displeased D00032 (1995). Kill Them / Coffin On Coffin / Strength Through Hate / Strength Through Pain / Warzone / Modo Grosso / Death To The Harmless / 15 Minutes / In Ebony / Strength Through Power / Psycho 100 / Bulldozer.

NEMESIS, RTD 397 0021 2 (1997). All About Art / The Godfather / Brothers In Death / Ants That Bleed / Slave To The Land Of The Free / G.H.A.D. / Witness / A Trance Of Masses.

NEMESIS

OSTRAVA, CZECH REPUBLIC — *Radalf (vocals), Martin Dufka (guitar), Lukáš Lednický (guitar), Radim Vaňko (bass), Vladislav Rybka (drums).*

NEMESIS is an Ostrava based Death Metal band. The band incorporated singer Vladimír Tøískala and guitarist Marek Schneider in 1990, debuting in February 1992 with the demo 'Find The Truth' followed by the 'In God We Trust' and 'Final Exit' sessions. Guitarist Lukáš Lednický dropped out in 1992. Founding bassist Tomáš Bláha also bowed out in 1992, being superseded by Petr Danè of DISFIGURED CORPSE and MORSUS and, in turn, by Michal Gašperik. The band donated two tracks, 'Death Is The Only Way' and 'The River', to a Yusic Music compilation cassette 'Creations From A Morbid Society' in 1993.

During 1994 NEMESIS issued the 'Temptation' album through Reflex Records. By 1994 the bass position was in the hands of Radim Vaòko. Dropping out that year would be both Tøískala and Schneider. Monitor Records included the NEMESIS song 'Save The World' on their 1995 compilation album 'Masters Of Czech Metal II' and also contributed to 1997's 'Creations From A Morbid Society II' collection in 1997 with 'Life (Remix)' and 'Save The World (Twisted version)'.

NEMESIS brought back original guitarists Martin Dufka and Lukáš Lednický and introduced Rostislav Kosmák on lead vocals in 2002. The demo 'ProMo deMo destAbility' arrived in 2004. Two NEMESIS tracks, 'Consciousness' and a re-recorded version of 'In God We Trust', saw inclusion on the 2005 Panda Music compilation 'Metal Chaos 7'. The 2006 NEMESIS line-up comprised singer Radalf, guitarists Martin Dufka and Lukáš Lednický, bass player Radim Vaňko with Vladislav Rybka on drums.

In God We Trust, Nemesis (1992) (Demo). In God We Trust / Inhumanity / Failed Exit / Cloud Of Blind.

Final Exit, Nemesis (1992) (Demo). In God We Trust / Inhumanity / Final Exit.

Find The Truth, Nemesis (1992) (Demo). Find The Truth / Sektor 6 / Jezis / No Future.

TEMPTATION, Relflex (1994). Fall To Oblivion / The Blind / Equilibrium / Be One's Own Master / Life / Save The World / The River / A Boy.

ProMo deMo destAbility, Nemesis (2004) (Demo). Inhumanity (Re-recorded) / Fratricidal Fight / Groundless Fear / Find The Truth (Re-recorded).

NEMESIS IRAE

GENLY, BELGIUM — *Anthony (vocals), Richard Tiborcz (guitar), Frederick (guitar), Frank (bass), Kris (drums).*

NEMESIS IRAE purvey Blackened Death Metal. The group had been founded in 1999 by BAALBERITH members guitarist Frederik and drummer Kris, the latter a veteran of SULFURE and VENEFICE. Initially entitled DESPISE the fledgling band acquired singer Patrice, bassist Frank and guitarist Richard

Tiborcz of ASTAROTH and DRAKKAR. Soon afterward the NEMESIS IRAE title was taken on but in August 2001 Patrice left. For their performance at the 'Metal Attack Fest 2' event Frederick covered on vocals. Frank deputized for DECORPORATE briefly in 2002.

A new singer, Anthony of UNNAMED and SACRUM ENDYNIUM, was located in November of 2002. Frank exited in October 2004.

Opening Insane, Nemesis Irae (2003). Nemesis Irae / Crucify / Astaroth / Nosferatu / Malediction / Sentence.

NEOLITH

SANOK, POLAND — *Levi (vocals), Artur Tabisz (guitar), Conrad Bialas (guitar), Pawel Radko (bass), Jerzy Glod (keyboards), Krzysztof Szantula (drums).*

NEOLITH, hailing from Sanok, debuted in 1993 with the nine song cassette 'Death Comes Slow'. A second tape, 'Journeys Inside The Maze Of Time' during 1995 preceded a 1996 promotion recording. Signing to the Ceremony label NEOLITH put out their first commercially available effort in 1997 with the album 'Trips Through Time And Loneliness'. A switch to the Dogma imprint resulted in 1998's 'Igne Natura Renovabitur Integra', this outing seeing vocal contributions from Malwina Zych of MATRAGONA. NEOLITH demoed again in 2002 with the three song 'Thorn In The Side Of My Enemies'.

Drummer Krzysztof Szantula, replacing previous incumbent Yashin in 2002, and keyboard player Jerzy 'U'Reck' Glod both have LUX OCCULTA connections. A new album, 'Broken Immortality', was slated for 2003.

TRIPS THROUGH TIME AND LONELINESS, Ceremony (1997). Time's Trap Prologue / Tempter From A Maze Of Time / My Time Has Come / Lunathiz Danze / The Shining In Her Eyes / Reborn / Forever Alone / Rethona Yerg Yad / This Is My Kingdom / Left Alone / Goil Of Forgotten Souls.
IGNE NATURA RENOVABITUR INTEGRA, Dogma (1998). Uverture / Unbeliever / Awakening (A Prayer For Dying) / In The Garden Of Forgetfulness / Raven Moon / Curse The Lord / Temple Of The Silent Desire / Souls They Love Forever / My Journey To The Stars / Pagan Chant / Igne Natura Renovabitur Integra.

NEOLITHIC

WARSAW, POLAND — *Piotr Wtulich (vocals / guitar), Miroslaw Szymańczak (guitar), Michał Sarnowski (bass), Robert Bielak (keyboard / violin), Janusz Jastrzębowski (drums).*

Atmospheric Death Metal outfit NEOLITHIC were created in Mlawa during November 1991 and debuted with the 'Terpsychora' rehearsal demo, which included a SAMAEL cover version, followed by 'The Personal Fragment Of Life' demo, laid down in June 1993 at Modern Sound Studio in Gdynia with engineer Bogdan Kuźmiński, both distributed by Kassandra Promotion. At this stage NEOLITHIC involved vocalist / guitarist Piotr Wtulich, second guitarist Mirek Szymańczak, bass player Michał Sarnowski, GROAN and CARNAL drummer Janusz Jastrzębowski whilst keyboards and violin were delegated to Robert Bielak of GROAN. This recording was later re-released in by Loud Out in 1994 on cassette and then CD format by Adipocere Records. The first album, 'For Destroy The Lament', arrived in 1995 on Adipocere. Sarnowski lost his position as NEOLITHIC welcomed in replacement Tomek Włodarski. The role of frontman was assigned to Maciek Taff, citing GEISHA GONER, KASHTANY, ROOTWATER and TESTOR credentials. An EP, recorded at Selani Studio and simply titled 'Neolithic', surfaced in 1997 on Mystic Production. This set saw a 2003 re-issue adding an extra track, a cover version of CREAM's 'Sunshine Of Your Love'. NEOLITHIC migrated their home base from Mlawa to Warsaw during 1998.

By February 2003 NEOLITHIC, as featured on third album 'My Beautiful Enemy', cut at Serakos Sudio, would be crediting a line-up of vocalists Nick Wolverine and Kay, guitarist Mrek, VESANIA bassist Orion, keyboard player Zo||k and Pablo on drums. Wolverine also fronted BLINDEAD. Empire Records issued the 'Team 666' EP, recorded at Studio Hendrix in Lublin with engineer Malta Rocco, that December. NEOLITHIC would morph again to feature singer Maciek Taff, guitarists Piotr Wtulich and Art, bassist Orion plus Dary, of PYORRHOEA, SUNWHEEL, VADER and VESANIA, on the drums. For live work Anioł of CORRUPTION took Orion's place, the latter temping for BEHEMOTH.

In December 2006 Daray announced the formation of side project MASACHIST, co-formed by Thrufel, guitarist from AZARATH and YATTERING.

THE PERSONAL FRAGMENT OF LIFE, Adipocere AR 028 (1995). Intro / Wickedness Of The Objects / Nightly Friends / Unupdate Museum (In Memory Of Bruno Schulz) / Undesirable Return / Landscape.
FOR DESTROY THE LAMENT, Adipocere AR 033 (1995). For Destroy / The Lament / Oddity / Gardens Of Phantasms / Szacunek Dla Zmarlego / Last Fix / Chattles / Choreografia / Stainded-Glass Window.
Neolithic, Mystic Productions (1997). 1990 Avenue / Night Insane City / Nowhen, Nowhere / Every Sunday People / Newborn—Reborn / The Short Human Story.
MY BEAUTIFUL ENEMY, Mystic Productions (2003). Pledge / Darkness / My Beautiful Enemy / A Fire Inside / Falling Down / Love? / Love, Sex, Desire / Rebel / Love? (Video).
Team 666 EP, Empire (2003). Intro / Hellboy / Dying / Team 666 / My Beautiful Enemy 2 / Team 666 (Video) / Love? (Video) / The coverage of 'Love?' / Szacunek Dla Zmarlego (Video) / History.

NEOPLASMAH

SEIXAL, PORTUGAL — *Sofia (vocals), Zé Melkor (guitar), Vitor (guitar), Alexandre (bass), Rolando Barros (drums).*

Seixal Death Metal band NEOPLASMAH date to 1997, issuing the demo 'Interstellar Experiences' in 1999. The band features drummer Ronaldo Barros, a man holding credits with SACRED SIN, GROG and NEPHTYS. Dark Music Records issued the album 'Sidereal Passage' during 2004.

Guitarist Zé Melkor (a.k.a. José Marreiros) cites NEPTHYS and THE FIRSTBORN affiliations. Bassist Alexandre operates with GROG and BLEEDING DISPLAY. He would also act as stand in live bassist for HEMATOMA during 2003.

The band also put in an appearance at the 2003 'Steel Warriors Rebellion VI' festival alongside ENTHRONED, INTERNAL SUFFERING, KATATONIA, FINNTROLL, HOLOCAUSTO CANIBAL, ATTICK DEMONS, PITCH BLACK, CORPUS CHRISTII, IN THY FLESH, AXE MURDERERS, AGONIZED, THANATOSCHIZO, FLAGELLUM DEI and ETERNAL MOURNING,

SIDEREAL PASSAGE, Dark Music (2004). Intro / Interplanetary Inner Sanctum / Dome Of Electric Karma / Out Of The Void Into The Storm / Dimensional Threshold / Vortex Voyagers.

NEPAL

ARGENTINA — *Larry Zabala (vocals), Javier Bagala (guitar), Beto Vazquez (bass), Marcelo Ponce (drums).*

Highly regarded Heavy Metal act. NEPAL was initiated during 1984 by lead vocalist Claudio 'Larry' Zavala, guitarist Javier Bagala and bass guitarist Alberto 'Beto' Vazquez. They would first record in July of 1988, laying down tracks for the demo 'Aquellos Bastardos'. Following live work a second tape, 'Nepal II', arrived in 1989. Dario Galvan was enrolled on the drums in February of 1992 for the third demo offering 'Capitulo '92' and, signing to Metal Command Records, NEPAL recorded their opening album 'Raza De Traidores'. Subsequent live shows included a valuable support to KREATOR.

The "Idealogica" album followed in October of 1995, supported by shows as opening act to ANGRA. In 1996 the band also donated their Thrash styled cover rendition of 'Love Gun' to the Sleaze Records KISS tribute 'Gritalo Fuerte'.

The 1997 album 'Manifiesto' included cover versions of BLACK SABBATH's 'Children Of The Grave' and V8's 'Lanzado Al Mundo Hoy'. The line up at this juncture comprised Larry Zavala, Bagalá, Vázquez and drummer Facundo Vega. This album was recorded both in London, England and in Germany and featured a wealth of guest players including Martin Walkyier and Georgina Biddle from SKYCLAD, the ANGRA pairing of Andre Matos and Kiko Loureiro, Hansi Kürsch of BLIND GUARDIAN and keyboard player Carlos Teso Ruggiero. Live promotion witnessed guest slots to both MOONSPELL and BLIND GUARDIAN.

In 2001 Vasquez assembled the highly ambitious BETO VASQUEZ INFINITY concept, his live band comprising former NEPAL colleagues Marcelo Ponce and Javier Bagalá, HUMANIMAL guitarist Pablo Soler, SHANGRI LA singer Max Ditamo, flautist Lilah Bertolini, keyboard player Danilo Moschen and guitarist Gonzalo Iglesias.

RAZA DE TRAIDORES, Metal Command (1993). Falsos Profetas (A Esos) / Raza De Traidores / Devorando Al Tiempo / Justicia Maldita / Represor / La Señal Del Metal / Aquellos Bastardos / Te Destruiré.
IDEALOGIA, NEMS (1995). Escenio / Realidades / Ideología / Guerra Sucia / Paredes De Hierro / Enfriando Las Heridas / Golpea / Katmandu / Herederos Del Miedo / Predicando La Mentira.
MANIFIESTO, NEMS (1997). La Saga / Perfil Siniestro / Besando La Tierra / Más Allá Del Asfalto / Children Of The Grave / Lukumi / Estadio Chico / Lanzado Al Mundo Hoy / Nadaísmo / Ciegos De Poder / Besando La Tierra.
X-Plore EP, Mortal Form (1999). The Midwinter Epos / Silence Of The Masses / Torment Of The Soul / Choose Your Priority.
The End Of Times EP, Mortal Form (2000). The End of Times / Real Life Circle / Subject: Saccharine.

NEPENTHE

PERUGIA, ITALY — *Federico (vocals), Michele (guitar), Giovanni (guitar), Paolo (bass), Ivan (keyboards), Alessio (drums).*

Perugia Death Metal band NEPENTHE was created in 2000 by guitarist Michele and Alex alongside singer Giulio, second guitarist Fabio and bassist Euro. Within a year the formation had changed to incorporate vocalist Cristian and bassist Antonio but before 2001 had closed both Cristian and Fabio had opted out. NEPENTHE was gradually restructured, drawing in guitarist Giovanni in April 2002 and vocalist / bassist Federico in 2003. NEPENTHE issued a 2004 demo, which included a cover version of CHILDREN OF BODOM's 'Bed Of Razors'. Added to the ranks would be singer Sonia and bassist Lestat, although they both departed soon after. Paolo duly assumed the bass position.

2004 Demo, Nepenthe (2004). Winter Of Souls / The Secret Mirror Of Life / Through The Eyes Of Emptiness / Altar / Bed Of Razors.

NEPENTHE

KANSAS CITY, MO, USA — *Joe Gameson (vocals), Patrick Brown (guitar), Alex Blume (bass), Chris Overton (drums).*

Kansas City, Missouri Death Metal act dating to 1992. First product came in the form of a 1993 demo cassette 'The Conqueror Worm'. A 7" single issued in 1995 by Eternal Darkness Creations, 'Ligiea', featured a B side cover version of TIAMAT's 'In The Shrines Of The Kingly Dead'. A concert demo, February 1995's 'Live At Howards', also included this same TIAMAT track plus a rendition of 'Jaws Of Satan', originally by SATHANAS. Following issue of the July 1997 EP 'In Death Overshadow Thee Advance' the band evolved into LIGEIA. Alex Blume would go on to join ARES KINGDOM.

Blume unveiled a heavyweight side project in late 2006, BLASPHEMIC CRUELTY comprising ANGEL CORPSE guitarist Gene Palubicki with Gina Ambrosio, briefly involved with ANGEL CORPSE, on drums. An album, entitled 'The Devil's Mayhem', was prepared for 2007 issue.

The Conqueror Worm, Eternal Darkness Creations (1993) (Demo). The Conqueror Worm / Gleaming Eyes Of Darkness / On The Cheer Of An Eternity.
Ligiea, Eternal Darkness Creations (1995) (7' vinyl single). The Conqueror Worm / In The Shrines Of The Kingly Dead.
Live At Howard's, Eternal Darkness Creations (1995) (Live demo). Cain & Abel / Jaws Of Satan / The Conqueror Worm / Oblivion / The Joyous Dead Man / In The Shrines Of The Kingly Dead.
In Death Overshadow Thee Advance, Eternal Darkness Creations (1997). Oblivion (The Joyous Dead Man) / In Death Overshadow Thee / Be Still Of Ashen Glory.

NEPHASTH

PORTO ALEGRE, RS, BRAZIL — *Fabio Lentino (vocals / bass), Marcos Moura (guitar), Rafael Barros (guitar), Mauricio Weimar (drums).*

NEPHASTH was conceived during 1997 under the original title of INTERIOR SOUL. In this guise the group issued two demos, an opening eponymous effort and follow up 'The Merciless Face Of Evil'. Notable supports were also lent to KRISIUN and REBAELLIUN prior to the name change. Relapse Records then re-issued tracks from the 'The Merciless Face Of Evil' as part of the 'Brazilian Assault' compilation album.

NEPHASTH signed to the Polish Empire Records label for a 2001 debut album 'Immortal Unholy Triumph' before touring Brazil as support to Polish veterans VADER during November 2002. The band then entered the studio to lay down the 'Conceived By Inhuman Blood' album.

IMMORTALITY UNHOLY TRIUMPH, Empire EMP 004 CD (2002). The Wrath Will Be The Fire / Screams For The Supreme Force / Useless Cross / Merciless Controller / Flames Triumph / Gloomy Words / False Pride / Empty Holy Reaching / Visions Of Fury / Inquiring Fear.
CONCEIVED BY INHUMAN BLOOD, Empire (2003). Damned Knowledge / I Reign / Conceived By Inhuman Blood / Hate Earth / Dying End / Ignis Victory / Domination Is My Name / Crucify Again / You Have Lost / Bleeding Mortal Lament / Fear The Truth.

NERLICH

HELSINKI, FINLAND — *Miikka Merikallio (vocals / guitar), Davi Moreira (guitar), Hanna Kauppinen (bass), Teemu Mutka (drums).*

NERLICH is an "old school" Death Metal band created in Helsinki as DEVASTATION MACHINE in 2002. Successive line-up changes, which included the entry and exit of drummers Viktor, Jonttu and Niko as well as guitarist Mikko Agnus, led up to the Autumn of 2003 and the name switch to NERLICH. The group's first demos were cut in February 2004 by Miikka Merikallio on vocals and bass, guitarist Jarno Nurmi and the SARNATH and PHLEGETHON credited drummer Lasse Pyykkö. Subsequently, Pyykkö exited, eventually reforging PHLEGETHON and founding COFFINS OF CYST, and Merikallio switched from bass to guitar as an early member, Pekka Johansson, rejoined on bass. Teemu Mutka, of ACABÓ EL SILENCIO, DEEP RED, AZAGHAL, CARCASE INC. and CADAVERIC INCUBATOR, joined as the band's drummer for a second set of recordings 'Insane Creations—Inorganic Echoes' in October of 2004. SLUGATHOR's Tommi Grönqvist would donate the cover art.

NERLICH's debut live performance came in November, sharing a billing alongside WITHERIA. During 2005 Jarno Nurmi briefly joined the ranks of SLUGATHOR. His replacement would be Otso Kirvelä for a short period. Hanna Kauppinen of GIRL GERMS took over the bass position. In April that same year the Nihilistic Holocaust label put NERLICH tracks alongside DECOHERENCE and GORGASM for a split album billed 'Embalmed Madness'.

NERVECELL (pic: Sami Al-Turki)

In May 2006 Conqueror The Thorns Records compiled archive demo tracks for the exhaustively titled 'Substantial Alteration Of The Cadaver As The

Insects Breed In It's Entrails—The Stench Is Stimulating Senses (Causing Orgasm)'. Recording a new album, 'Defabricated Process', for late 2006 release, NERLICH signed to Old School Metal Records.

Nerlich, Nerlich (2004) (Demo). Flesh Deformation / Dissolve The Bodies / Machine Of Devastation / Altered Form Of Life.

Insane Creations—Inorganic Echoes, Nerlich (2004). Degenerating Process / Dissolve The Bodies / Inorganic Subhuman Echoes / Condemned / Flesh Deformation.

EMBALMED MADNESS, Nihilistic Holocaust (2005) (Split EP with DECOHERENCE and GORGASM). Degenerating Process (NERLICH) / Condemned (NERLICH) / Inorganic Subhuman Echoes (NERLICH) / Dissolve The Bodies (NERLICH) / Flesh Deformation (NERLICH) / The Cabalistic Show (DECOHERENCE) / Ode To Joy (DECOHERENCE) / Synopsis Prosaique (DECOHERENCE) / Pig's Bloated Face (GORGASM) / Hunt To The Weaks (GORGASM) / Rusted Nails Attack (GORGASM) / Beware Of Tramps (GORGASM).

SUBSTANTIAL ALTERATION OF THE CADAVER AS THE INSECTS BREED IN IT'S ENTRAILS—THE STENCH IS STIMULATING SENSES (CAUSING ORGASM), Conqueror The Thorns (2006). Defabricated (Intro) / Substantial Alteration / Condemned / On Sarcastic Impact / Perverted Butcher / Degenerating Process / Dissolve The Bodies / Inorganic Subhuman Echoes / Condemned / Flesh Deformation / Machine Of Devastation / Flesh Deformation / Dissolve The Bodies / Altered Form Of Life / Flesh Deformation (Duck remix).

Promo 2005, Nerlich (2006) (Demo). Defabricated (Intro) / Substantial Alteration / Condemned / On Sarcastic Impact / Perverted Butcher / Degenerating Process / Inorganic Subhuman Echoes.

DEFABRICATED PROCESS, Old School Metal (2006). Defabricated Process / Substantial Alteration / Insane Creations / Inorganic Echoes / Entity Of Sickness / Imminent Reprisal / Mask For The Faceless / Condemned / On Sarcastic Impact.

NERVECELL

DUBAI, UNITED ARAB EMIRATES — *Rajeh Khazaal (vocals / bass), Rami Mustafa (guitar), Barnaby Ribeiro (guitar), Alan (drums).*

Dubai Deathcore combo NERVECELL, comprising vocalist / bassist Rajeh "James" Khazaal and guitarists Barnaby "Barney" Ribeiro and Rami Mustafa, released the 'Human Chaos' demo in late 2004, these sessions recorded by Kiran Sequeira and featuring studio drummer Alan Madhavan.

On 25th March 2005 the band gained the honours of supporting THE DARKNESS, SEPULTURA and MACHINE HEAD, performed in Dubai at the Rugby Country Club, marking the first such occasion for a Western Metal band in the Gulf.

NERVECELL teamed up with Australian acts THE FUROR and AETURNUS DOMINION for the "Metalstock Road Rage" Tour, commencing at Australia's Arthouse in Melbourne on Friday, March 30th 2007, followed by five more shows including Adelaide, Wagga Wagga, Wollongong, Canberra and Sydney.

Human Chaos, Nerve Damage Productions (2004). Signs Of The End / Vastlands Of Abomination / The Darkened / Human Chaos / Demolition.

NERVOCHAOS

SÃO PAULO, SP, BRAZIL — *César (vocals / guitar), Fabio (guitar), Fabiano (bass), Eduardo Lane (drums).*

Death / Grind merchants NERVOCHAOS came into being in September of 1996. The initial group comprised a quartet of erstwhile SIEGRID INGRID personnel vocalist / guitarist Sidney, bassist Thomas, guitarist Goober and drummer Eduardo Lane. Joining them would be former GRUNKS and CHEMICAL DISASTER vocalist Marcelo Miranda. Both Sidney and Goober both had prior experience with SKULLKRUSHER whilst Lane had also operated with REPULSA and Thomas with ACID STORM. This unit issued the October 1996 demo 'Nervochaos'.

NERVOCHAOS signed to the Tumba label for 1998's debut album 'Pay Back Time'. Subsequently the band contributed their rendition of 'Turn Face' to a BRUTAL TRUTH tribute album. Sometime later ex-BRUTAL man Gordo took command of vocals and Thomas lost his position to former BROKEN HEADS and ZERO VISION man Hareton. A demo, 'Disfigured Christ', surfaced in 2000. Meantime, Miranda gained credits with Black Metal band CANIS LUPUS (as 'Lord Vargathron') and OLAM EIN SOF.

Upon completion of the 2001 'Infernal Legion' 34 date tour the group yet again lost personnel when both Sidney and bassist Hareton decamped. in Ex-PUS bassist Walter was enrolled in 2002. NERVOCHAOS were still operational during 2003, releasing the four song demo 'Necro Satanic Cult' and cutting a rendition of MOTÖRHEAD's 'Iron Fist' for a tribute album. However, by this stage Cesar had taken on lead vocal duties and the band was re-established incorporating new members ex-ZOLTAR guitarist Fabio and former TRETA bassist Fabiano.

NervoChaos, (1996). Liar, Loser / Pain Haze / I Hate Your God / Hate Face.

PAY BACK TIME, Tumba (1998). Just The Truth / I Hate Your God / Revolt / No Self Respect / Mighty Justice / Pain Haze / Bastard Fog / Traitor / Rotten Flesh / Hate Face / Liar, Loser / The Way To Pay / Nervochaos.

Disfigured Christ, (2001). Envy / When The Mask Falls Down / Pure Hemp / Speechless.

LEGION OF SPIRITS INFERNAL, Tumba (2002). Cold Feelings / Envy / Conventional Lives / Our Fury / Speechless / Repulsive World / Satanic Domain / Let The Bible Burn / Upside Down Crosses / Mortal Decay / When The Mask Falls Down / Those Behind The Light / Legion Of Spirits Infernal / Pure Hemp.

Necro Satanic Cult, (2003). Cursed Soul / Everlasting Death / Nailed To The Bed Of Worms / Putrid Pleasures.

NETHERBIRD

JÖNKÖPING, SWEDEN — *Nephente (vocals), Grim (guitar), Bizmark (guitar).*

Jönköping Doom edged Death Metal act. NETHERBIRD debuted with the 2005 'Boulevard Black' single, laid down at Studio Underground in Västerås. Augmenting core members guitarists Bizmark and FEAR THE FUTURE's Grim with singer Nephente, of SULPHUR SOULS, BENIGHTED and FEAR THE FUTURE, would be guitarist Alexxx, the NIGHTRAGE and DISSECTION credited bassist Brice LeClercq, pianists Tranquil Chaos and Ivar Edding plus THE CROWN and ANGEL BLAKE drummer Janne Saarenpää.

In early 2007 the band laid down tracks at Studio Fredman in Hyssna for an EP entitled 'Lighthouse Eternal (Laterna Magika)'. The AT THE GATES, CRADLE OF FILTH, NEEDLEYE and NEMHAIN credited drummer Adrian Erlandsson sessioned.

Boulevard Black, Netherbird (2005). Boulevard Black / Boulevard Black (Piano Reprise).

NETTLETHRONE

ANKARA, TURKEY — *Nazmi Can Dogan (vocals), Tankut Aydinliyim (guitar), Burak Tansel (guitar), Mert Tartaç (bass), Kaya Özgen Yalçin (drums).*

Ankara Death Metal act NETTLETHRONE was forged during 2000 by guitarists Tankut Aydinliyim and Burak Tansel, building up to a full unit with the addition of vocalist / drummer Nazmi Can Dogan and bassist Ali. The latter exited during 2002 and the group persevered with a succession of short term bass players until Ali made a return to record the demo 'Ruins Of The Humanity' at Zoosound Studios in 2003.

NETTLETHRONE, drafting SUICIDE, ANOREXIA and LOST INFINITY and FLATGROUND man Çaglar Yürüt as session drummer, then worked with Erkan Tatoglu of SUICIDE and Cüneyt Çaglayan of OMINOUS GRIEF as producers for the April 2004 demo 'Blueprint'. Subsequently, Ender Erisen enrolled as bassist and Kaya Özgen Yalçin of DESPISED and LOST INFINITY was drafted on drums. Following an opening burst of live gigs the bass position switched to incorporate DECIMATION's Mert Tartaç. NETTLETHRONE would spend 2005 crafting a debut album.

Blueprint, Nettlethrone (2004). Ascendancy / The Call From Within / Flamelift Supremacy / Blueprint / Disintegrate.

NEURAXIS

MONTREAL, QC, CANADA — *Ian Campbell (vocals), Steven Henry (guitar), Robin Milley (guitar), Yan Thiel (bass), Alexandre Erian (drums).*

NEURAXIS is a Montreal based brutal Grind-Death unit founded by guitarist Steven Henry, a seasoned campaigner of WINDS OF WAR, HANG OVER and GREEN THE GREY, during 1993. In 1994 the band would be brought up to strength with the addition of vocalist Michel Brisebois, guitarist Felipé Quinzonos and bassist Yan Thiel. Early live shows would be conducted with the aid of a drum machine until Mathies Royal joined the fold in the summer of 1995. However, signaling the start of numerous line-up changes to dog NEURAXIS' career, Brisebois made his exit, joining AGONY.

Maynard Moore would step into the breech as the new NEURAXIS frontman and in November 1996 the band set about recording their debut album, 'Imagery' produced by KATAKLYSM guitarist Jean Francois Dagenais and released by the Neoblast label in February 1997. Indonesian label Extreme Souls Productions would pick up the license for an Asian cassette release. Prior to the release though of 'Imagery' Quinzonos bailed out. His place would be filled by CURSED guitarist Robin Milley. Promoting the album NEURAXIS put in a myriad of guest slots to the likes of international artists such as BORKNAGER, DYING FETUS, WITCHERY and SUFFOCATION.

Moore would be usurped by Chris Alsop but further ructions witnessed the departure of Royal. Temporarily the band maneuvered Thiel over to the drum kit. In January of 1999 erstwhile ELEMENTS drummer Martin Auger would sit in on a session basis for recording of the July 'In Silence' EP. A permanent drummer would be located by the April, with HIDDEN PRIDE man Alexandre Erian being enrolled.

Alsop would be the next casualty, his vacancy being rapidly filled by Ian Campbell, also singer with DARK VOMIT and SPIRITUAL MIGHT. With this line up NEURAXIS cut the 2001 album 'A Passage To Forlorn'.

Henry also pursues other endeavours outside of NEURAXIS including URBAN ALIEN, the IDIOPATHETICS alongside erstwhile WINDS OF WAR colleagues, Black Metal band AXIOMISED and as vocalist for WACKY PACK. Erian also operates a side project in union with ex NECROTIC MUTATION guitarist Eric Jaarn and former VOCIFERATION singer Marie-Helene. Milley and ex-vocalist Chris Alsop would also maintain another group entitled TORN WITHIN.

NEURAXIS united with BIRDFLESH and HELLBLAZER for European shows in September of 2003, sessioning on drums would be Etienne Gallo, a veteran of AUGURY and DISEMBARKATION. Back on the road, the band teamed up with MISERY INDEX for a short Canadian tour beginning in late October 2004.

During early 2005 Rob Milley united with the former QUO VADIS members guitarist/vocalist Arie Itman and bassist Remy Beauchamp alongside drummer Tommy Kinnon in a new band called JESTER. NEURAXIS entered the studio in May to cut a new album 'Trilateral Progression' for a September release via Willowtip Records, working with Yannick St Amand of DESPISED ICON as engineer and Jason Suecof from CAPHARNAUM on the mix. The record was mastered by Scott Hull of PIG DESTROYER. Also in the works for July issue through Willowtip would be a 34 track retrospective compilation billed 'Truth Imagery Passage'.

NEURAXIS surprisingly announced the departure of founding member and guitarist, Steven Henry, a thirteen year veteran, in January 2006. Reduced to a quartet, the band teamed up with STRONG INTENTION for US shows in February 2006. Japanese gigs in March had the band paired with MISERY INDEX. The following month the group pulled in ex-QUO VADIS touring guitarist Will Seghers for a US tour throughout April and May alongside NECROPHAGIST, ARSIS, ALARUM, CATTLE DECAPITATION and THINE EYES BLEED. The band announced the addition of guitarist Will Seghers as a permanent member in October.

The band joined a heavyweight casting of CARPATHIAN FOREST, MALEVOLENT CREATION, HARM, INCANTATION and ROTTING CHRIST for the 'Domination' European tour, commencing on February 14th at the Warsaw Progresja venue in Poland before hitting Germany, Austria, the Czech Republic, Italy, Belgium, France and Holland.

IMAGERY, Neoblast NBR-97-01 (1996). Intro / A Temporal Calamity / Oscilliated To Intelligence / Cyberwar / Inquisition On Mortality / Lid To Your Soul / Reasons Of Being / Atmospheric Holocaust / Psycho-Waves / A Drift ... Driftwood / The Drop.

In Silence EP, Neuraxis (1999). In Silence / Dreamrock / Imagery / Blind The Vision That Shatters.

Virtuosity EP, Neuraxis (1999). Virtuosity (Blind Lead The Blind) / The Art Of Sadness / Link.

A PASSAGE INTO FORLORN, Neoblast NBR-01-03 (2001). Unite / Virtuosity / Art Of Sadness / Link Of Innocence / Blind The Vision That Shatters / To Pacify / The Drop / Forlorn ....

TRUTH BEYOND ..., Morbid (2003). ... Of Divinity / Impulse / Fractionized / Xenobiotic / Reflections / Imagery / Momento / Structures / Mutiny / Essence / Neurasthenic / Truth Beyond Recognition.

TRILATERAL PROGRESSION, Willowtip WT038 (2005). Introspect / Clarity / Thought Adjuster / Shatter The Wisdom / Monitoring The Mind / A Currative Struggle / Chamber Of Guardians / Caricature / Axioms / The Apex.

NEUROSIS

OAKLAND, CA, USA — *Scott Kelly (vocals / guitar), Steve Von Till (vocals / guitar), Dave Edwardson (bass), Jason Roeder (drums).*

Described as groundbreaking Death Metal and avant-garde Hardcore, the ever challenging NEUROSIS have doggedly refused to be compartmentalised. The teenage NEUROSIS started as an Oakland trio in the mid 80's. Guitarist Scott Kelly and bassist Dave Edwardson had formed up the Jason Storey fronted VIOLENT COERCION, splitting this band in December 1985 to found a fresh endeavour. Drummer Jason Roeder enrolled and until January of 1987 NEOROSIS performed as a trio until the acquisition of second guitarist Chad Salter.

NEUROSIS made their first mark with the 1987 album 'Pain Of Mind' on the Alchemy label, the cover artwork notably executed by Kelly and Edwardson's erstwhile band colleague

Jason Storey. Salter exited and the group drafted 'Pete' to record the Lookout! Records 'Aberration' 7 single.

In March 1989 the group added guitarist Steve Von Till for the 'Word As Law' album. With this outing the band made an indelible mark on the Rock scene with eclectic Alt Rock which blends a myriad of styles including even Gothic and Medieval overlaid with spiritually infused lyrical content. As such NEUROSIS are one of the very few bands to truly set themselves apart from the pack. In April 1991 NEUROSIS' ambitions to break out of Hardcore constrictions took a major step forward by introducing Simon McIlroy on keyboards and film projectionist Adam Kendall. The band added ex-CHRIST ON PARADE keyboard Player Noah to their line-up for live work.

NEUROSIS signed to the Alternative Tentacles label for the 'Souls At Zero' album, confounding critics with a record that borrowed from Grunge, Gothic and Metal interspersed with string and woodwind as well as narrative passages from celluloid sources such as 'Triumph Of The Will' and 'Star Wars'.

Their 1996 'Through Silver In Blood' album, complete with an opening twelve minute title track, would land the group deserved accolades and opened up the NEUROSIS catalogue to the mainstream Rock public. April of 1997 found the band back on European soil, forming up the 'Full Of Hate' Easter festivals alongside OBITUARY, DEATH, SAMAEL, ENTOMBED, CROWBAR, KILLING CULTURE and STRAPPING YOUNG LAD. Touring in the UK witnessed support gigs to ENTOMBED during September and October. The 1999 'Times Of Grace' album was produced by the renowned Steve Albini. NEUROSIS toured America with TODAY IS THE DAY and UNSANE. European tour dates in October had the band partnered with Canadian veterans VOIVOD.

Aside from NEUROSIS, the band members would also operational with a conceptual side project titled TRIBES OF NEUROT under which guise they released the split 'Static Migration' CD together with WALKING TIME BOMBS in 1998.

Edwardson sessioned for NOISEGATE on their 1999 album. Vocalist Scott Kelly and keyboard player Noah Landis debuted their new band BLOOD AND TIME in 2003 with the album 'At The Foot Of The Garden'. NEUROSIS worked with Steve Albini once more for the 2004 album 'The Eye Of Every Storm', mixed at Electrical Audio Studios in Chicago. The band put in a special extended live set on 21st July at the Great American Music Hall in San Francisco, California to premier the material.

The band wrapped up sessions for the 'Given To The Rising' album in February 2007.

PAIN OF MIND, Alchemy VM 105 (1987). Pain Of Mind / Self Taught Infection / Reasons To Hide / Black / Training / Progress / Stalemate / Bury What's Dead / Geneticide / Ingrown / United Sheep / Dominoes Fall / Life On Your Knees / Grey.
Aberration, Lookout (1988).
THE WORD AS LAW, Lookout LOOKOUT CD 21 (1989). Double-Edged Sword / The Choice / Obsequious Obsolescence / To What End? / Tomorrow's Reality / Common Inconsistencies / Insensitivity / Blisters / Life On Your Knees / Pain Of Mind / Grey / United Sheep / Pollution / Day Of The Lords.
Empty, Alternative Tentacles (1990).
SOULS AT ZERO, Alternative Tentacles VIRUS 109 (1992). To Crawl Under One's Skin / Souls At Zero / Zero / Flight / The Web / Sterile Vision / A Chronological For Survival / Stripped / Takehnase / Empty.
ENEMY OF THE SUN, Alternative Tentacles VIRUS 134 (1993). Lost / Raze The Stray / Burning Flesh In The Year Of The Pig / Cold Ascending / Lexicon / Enemy Of The Sun / The Time Of The Beasts / Cleanse.
THROUGH SILVER IN BLOOD, Relapse RR 6938 (1996). Through Silver In Blood / Rehumanize / Eye / Purify / Locust Star / Strength Of Fates / Become The Ocean / Aeon / Enclosure In Flame.
TIMES OF GRACE, Relapse RR 6419 (1999). Suspended In Light / Doorway / Under The Surface / Last You'll Know / Belief / Exist / End Of The Harvest / Descent / Away / Times Of Grace / Road To Sovereignty.
SOVEREIGN, Music For Nations CDMFNM258 (2000). Prayer / An Offering / Flood / Sovereign.
A SUN THAT NEVER SETS, Relapse RR64962 (2001). Erode / The Tide / From The Hill / A Sun That Never Sets / Falling Unknown / From Where Its Roots Run / Crawling Back In / Watchfire / Resound / Stones From The Sky.
LIVE IN LYONS, Neurot (2002). Doorway / Lost / Offering / Away / Locust Star / Times Of Grace.
LIVE IN STOCKHOLM, Neurot (2003). Flood / The Doorway / Lost / Belief / An Offering / Locust Star / Under The Surface / Times Of Grace.
THE EYE OF EVERY STORM, Relapse (2004). Burn / No River To Take Me Home / The Eye Of Every Storm / Left To Wander / Shelter / A Season In The Sky / Bridges / I Can See You.

NEUROSIS INC.

COLOMBIA — *Carlos Nuñez (vocals), Jorge Mackenzie (guitar), Luis C. Osorio (guitar), Mauricio Reyes (guitar), Jorge Pinilla (bass),.*

Bogotá's Death Metal act NEUROSIS INC. (Originally entitled simply NEUROSIS) came together in August of 1987, formulated by guitarist Jorge Mackenzie. The group debuted in 1991 with the Spanish language demo 'Mas Alla De La Demencia', soon selling out of its 1000 copies. The inaugural album, 'Verdum 1916' for Talisman Music, followed in 1995 and touring included the band's first trip out of Colombia into Ecuadar alongside Mexican Death Metal band CENOTAPH. A second studio album, entitled 'Karma', saw issue in October of 1996. However, the well known North American NEUROSIS contacted the band at this juncture and so as to avoid confusion the Colombians evolved into NEUROSIS INC.

A live album 'Odas En Concierto', recorded on December 5th, 1998 in Bogotá, saw covers of SLAYER's 'Black Magic' and MOTÖRHEAD's 'Ace Of Spades' alongside four new studio songs. The two month tour that followed, dubbed the 'Disturbing the Continent 1999' dates, saw the group traversing Colombia, Ecuador, Peru, Bolivia, Chile and Argentina. NEUROSIS INC., adding singer Harold Escobar, issued a split CD 'The Trial' shared with RITUAL in 2001. Included would be a cover version of BLACK SABBATH's 'Children Of The Grave'.

The band has subsequently re-titled themselves as WAR MESSIAH and in 2002 counted a line up comprising vocalist Harold Escobar, guitarists Jorge Mackenzie and Camilo Rodríguez, bass player William Suárez and drummer Hamilton Castro.

VERDUN 1916, Talisman Music (1995). The Eyes Of The Soul / Politician / Military Sacrifice / Deprived Of Liberty / Full Of Thorns / Verdun 1916 / Involución / Intro (El Lamento) / El Paso Del Tiempo No Cura / Bautizados En Rencor / Marea Negra / Convención Ancestral.
KARMA, Neuro Music (1996). Karma / Pain (The Sad Fact) / The White Man / Love After Death / Inner Hate / Third Reich / Open Wound / Deprived Of Liberty (Live).
ODAS EN CONCIERTO, Neuro Music (1999). Oda Al Traidor / Verdun 1916 / Convención Ancestral / Involución / Full Of Thorns / Third Reich / La Profecía / The White Man / Military Sacrifice / Open Wound / El Paso Del Tiempo No Cura / Politicians / Black Magic / Ace Of Spades.
THE TRIAL, Neuro Music (2001) (Split album with RITUAL). The Trial / Battle For Fire / As The Bombs Fall / Children Of The Grave.
15 ANOS DE GUERRA, The Box Records (2003). Verdun 1916 / Involución / Bautizados En Rencor / El Paso Del Tiempo No Cura / Open Wound / Third Reich / Oda Al Traidor / Lágrimas / The Trial / Battle For Fire / As The Bombs Fall / Children Of The Grave / La Profecía (demo) / Lejos de La Sanidad Mental (Demo).

NEVOLUTION

REYKJAVÍK, ICELAND — *Heimir Ólafur Hjartarson (vocals / bass), Gunnar Sigurður Valdimarson (guitar), Ágúst Örn Pálsson (guitar), Heiðar Brynjarson (drums).*

NEVOLUTION was forged in December of 2003 by the former ANUBIS triumvirate of vocalist / bassist Heimir Ólafur Hjartarson, guitarist Gunnar Sigurður Valdimarsson and drummer

Ágúst Örn Pálsson. The band would be rounded out by second guitarist Jakob Jónsson, coincidentally another ANUBIS veteran. Within a short time Pálsson was forced out due to a "serious mental condition", being replaced by PROZAC and DELTA 9 man Heiðar Brynjarsson for demo recordings in January of 2004. That May saw Jónsson exiting and the return of Pálsson in the role of guitarist. 'The Jumpstop Theory' demo would be lent promotion by a video clip for 'Nothology' shot by director Baldvin Zophoníasson.

The Jumpstop Theory, Nevolution (2004). Prologue To Nothing / Die For Anything / Nothology / Sea Of Faces / The Left Hand Of God.

NEWBREED

BIELSKO-BIAŁA, POLAND — *Tomasz Wolonciej (vocals / guitar), Piotr Białkowski (guitar), Andrzej Czul (bass), Stanislaw Wolonciej (drums).*

NEWBREED, created in Bielsko-Biała during November 1999 by brothers vocalist / guitarist Thomasz and drummer Stanislaw Wołonciej, debuted with the November 2000 demo 'Solitary'. Apocalypse Productions released the album 'The New Way Of Human Existence' in 2002. In October of 2003, promoting the 'Lost' EP, the band partnered with VILGEFORTZ and VEDONIST for the nationwide 'The Lost Killing Scream' tour. During 2004 NEWBREED musicians fired up a side project billed SPACEBRAIN. Other endeavours found Tomasz contributing vocals to recordings from DIGITAL SUICIDE and Stanislaw supplying drums for SERPENTIA.

March of 2004 found NEWBREED allied with VEDONIST and SERPENTIA for the second installment of 'The Lost Killing Scream' dates. That August guitarist Thomas Czul exited, being swiftly replaced by Piotr "Bjorn" Białkowski of LADY TEMPTRESS.

Solitary, Newbreed (2000). Fantasy / Roam Into The Nowhere / Forgiveness For Myself / Solitary (Between Clouds) / Alert.
THE NEW WAY OF HUMAN EXISTENCE, Apocalypse Productions (2002). Somewhere / Fantasy / No Hope / My Own Nothingness / 1984 / The Sadness & The Silence / Forgiveness For Myself / Inside The Processor.
Lost, (2003). A Leaf / Shelter / If I Were The Rain / Of Our Loneliness / Lost.

NIGHT IN GALES

GERMANY — *Christian Müller (vocals), Frank Basten (guitar), Jens Basten (guitar), Tobias Bruchmann (bass), Christian Bass (drums).*

Delivering modern, Scandinavian style Death Metal this German outfit released an EP 'Sylphlike' in 1995. NIGHT IN GALES was forged the same year staking their claim with a six track demo CD 'Sylphlike' resulting in a deal with Nuclear Blast Records. The band's debut was produced by Wolfgang Stach. Touring during late 1999 would see Uwe Werning of DEW SCENTED temporarily occupying the drum stool.

The 2000 album was produced by Harris Johns and featured a raucous cover of the ALANNAH MYLES hit 'Black Velvet'. Johns would also handle production for 2001's 'Necrodynamic' although the band had switched to pastures new with Massacre Records. For the first time NIGHT IN GALES saw a domestic Russian release with the album being issued there by Art Music.

NIGHT IN GALES toured Japan in March of 2001 alongside DEW SCENTED and DEFLESHED. Drummer Christian Bass bade farewell in September of 2002 in order to concentrate on a fresh band venture called DEADSOIL with in league with ex-members of COPYKILL and DRIFT. His replacement would be announced in February of 2003 as Adriano Ricci of BLOOD RED ANGEL, CORONATION, GRIND INC. and TORTURE CHAMBER. Guitarist Jens Basten joined DEADSOIL in May of 2004.

Sylphlike EP, Night In Gales (1995). Bleed Afresh / Sylplike / Avoid Secret Vanity / Mindspawn / When The Lightning Starts / Flowing Spring.
TOWARDS THE TWILIGHT, Nuclear Blast (1997). A Twilight Kiss / Of Beauty's Embrace / Razor / From Ebony Skies / Autumn Water / Slavesrun / Through Ashen Meadows / Avoid Secret Vanity / Tragedians.
THUNDERBEAST, Nuclear Blast (1998). Intruder / Darkzone Anthem / Perihelion / Crystalthorns Call / Feverfeast / Thunderbeast / I Am The Dungeon God / Blackfleshed / The Distortion / Stormchild / Heroes Of Starfall / From Ebony Skies.
NAILWORK, Nuclear Blast NB 444-2 (2000). Nailwork / Blades In Laughter / Wormsong / All Scissors Smile / How To Eat A Scythe / Black Velvet / Filthfinger / The Tenmiletongue / Hearselights / Down The Throat / Quicksilver Spine.
NECRODYNAMIC, Massacre MAS CD0273 (2001). The Last Livin' Song / Doomdrugged / Blackelectric / Tombtrippin' / Deadmouth Daisies / Song Of Something / Right From The Morgue / Go Get Some Death / The Zeronaut / Counting Flies.

NIGHTRAGE

GREECE / SWEDEN — *Marios Iliopoulos (vocals / guitar), Gus G. (vocals / guitar), Brice Leclercq (bass), Fotis Bernardo (drums).*

Although credited as a Swedish entity NIGHTRAGE was originally formulated in Greece. NIGHTRAGE, featuring Gus G. (a.k.a. Kostas Karamitroudis) of DREAM EVIL and FIREWIND with EXHUMATION guitarist Marios Iliopoulos, have released two self titled demos. The first in 2001 and the second in 2002. During 2003 the band, signing to the German Century Media label for an album entitled 'Sweet Vengeance', welcomed onboard some heavyweight names from the Swedish Metal scene in EVERGREY vocalist Tom S. Englund, THE GREAT DECEIVER and AT THE GATES credited Tomas Lindberg with THE HAUNTED and INVOCATOR drummer Per M. Jensen.

NIGHTRAGE made their live debut at the 11th August 'Göteborgs Kalaset' festival in Sweden, the live line-up comprising Tomas Lindberg on vocals, guitarist Marios Iliopoulos, bassist Brice Leclercq and the DIMMU BORGIR, CRADLE OF FILTH, BRUJERIA and LOCK UP drummer Nick Barker.

The band, having enrolled new Greek drummer Fotis Bernardo of SEPTIC FLESH repute and bassist Henric Karlsson, entered Studio Fredman with producer Fredrik Nordström in August to cut their second album 'Descent Into Chaos'. Korean versions added an extra bonus track in the form of an "extended demo" of 'Gloomy Daydreams'. Brice Leclercq duly joined the notorious DISSECTION in 2004. In extracurricular activity, Gus G. donated guitar parts to Japanese avant-garde Metal act SIGH's controversial 'Gallows Gallery' album.

NIGHTRAGE teamed up with ARCH ENEMY, THE HAUNTED and DARK TRANQUILLITY for a one off, all Swedish Metal bash at London's Forum on 17th December. In early 2005 it would be revealed that Fotis Bernardo had forged THE DEVILWORX project in alliance with the SEPTIC FLESH duo of vocalist / bassist Spiros Antoniou ('Set<'H>') and guitarist Chris Antoniou.

Gus G. joined ARCH ENEMY in mid 2005 as the group's touring guitarist after regular six-stringer Christopher Amott bowed out of that band in order to "fully concentrate on his studies". NIGHTRAGE, switching singer Tomas Lindberg to new man Jimmie Strimell of PAINFIELD, DEAD BY APRIL and DEATHDESTRUCTION repute, announced a September 2005, five week US road partnership dubbed the 'International Extreme Music Festival' in collaboration with GOD DETHRONED, BYZANTINE, EPOCH OF UNLIGHT, HELL WITHIN and LILITU. The group enlisted Pierre Lysell from the Swedish bands THE PROVENANCE and NONE as session guitarist for this trek. However, following the 1st October gig at Chicago's Metro the band withdrew from the tour.

European shows in January and February 2006 witnessed a strong partnership with MALEVOLENT CREATION,

NECROPHAGIST and BOLT THROWER. Guitarist Gus G opted out upon completion of these shows in order to prioritise FIREWIND. The band, severing ties with Century Media Records in May and switching to Germany's Lifeforce Records, was confirmed as partnering with VADER and BLOODTHORN November shows in Denmark, Norway, Sweden and Finland. Pierre Lysell was once again utilised as second guitarist whilst drums were delegated to new recruit Alex Svenningson, previously of MINDFALL.

NIGHTRAGE entered Hansen studios in Ribe, Denmark on December 1st with producer Jacob Hansen to cut fresh album tracks. In January 2007 NIGHTRAGE announced an album title of 'A New Disease Is Born'. Shortly thereafter second guitarist Constantine was installed within the ranks. Meantime, Jimmie Strimmell was revealed to be working with a high profile side act, DEAD BY APRIL, featuring RAPTURE, DRAGONLAND and THE RETURNING guitarist Olof Mörck, guitarist Martin Meyerman of M.A.N, bassist Staffan Persson of WHEN WE FALL plus drummer Richard Evansand, whose scene credentials included SORCEROR, MANIC DEPRESSION, IT'S ALIVE, SOUTHPAW, DOG FACED GODS, DEMONOID, THERION, LIONS SHARE and EBONY TEARS.

SWEET VENGEANCE, Century Media CD 8136-2 (2003). The Tremor / The Glow Of The Setting Sun / Hero / Elusive Emotion / Gloomy Daydreams / Macabre Apparition / In My Heart / Ethereal / Circle Of Pain / At The Ends Of The Earth / The Howls Of The Wolves.
DESCENT INTO CHAOS, Century Media (2005). Being Nothing / Phantasma / Poems / Descent Into Chaos / Frozen / Drug / Silent Solitude / Omen / Release / Solus / Jubilant Cry / Reality Vs. Truth.
A NEW DISEASE IS BORN, Lifeforce (2007). Spiral / Reconcile / Death-Like Silence / A Condemned Club / Scars Of The Past / De-Fame / Scathing / Surge Of Pity / Encircle / Drone / Spiritual Impulse / A New Disease Is Born.

NIHILIST

STOCKHOLM, SWEDEN — *Lars-Göran Petrov (vocals), Alex Hellid (guitar), Uffe Cederland (guitar), Johnny Hedlund (bass), Nicke Andersson (drums).*

Stockholm's NIHILIST mark the genesis of two of Sweden's leading Metal acts, ENTOMBED and UNLEASHED. NIHILIST was forged by teenagers under the BRAINWARP banner during 1987. Initiated by drummer Nicke Andersson the first unit involved school friends singer Daniel "Dudde" Strachal, guitarist Alex Hellid and Leif Cuzner on bass. Strachal soon opted out, later resurfacing behind the LOBOTOMY drum kit, and the band briefly rehearsed with Mattias "Buffla" Boström on the microphone. However, upon entering the Stockholm's Studio Z in March 1988 to cut their first set of demos it would be Lars-Göran Petrov, drummer of MORBID, employed as session singer. Another MORBID man, Ulf Cederlund, handled secondary guitar duties for what would be the Leif Martinsson engineered demo 'Premature Autopsy'.

For subsequent live shows the band was joined by Petrov and new bass guitarist Johnny Hedlund as Cuzner switched to guitar. Over two days in December 1988 this formation utilised Sunlight Studios in Stockholm, and a then unknown producer Tomas Skogsberg, in December to craft a further three song demo, 'Only Shreds Remain'. Once leaked onto the tape trading market the NIHILIST name rapidly garnered enthusiastic support. Until this juncture the only cutting edge Death Metal circulating was emanating from the UK and USA. With 'Only Shreds Remain', NIHILIST had initiated what was to be a tidal flow from Scandinavia.

Leif Cuzner was reluctantly forced out of operations when his family relocated to Canada. In his stead came their former session ally Ulf Cederland, at the time attempting to kick start his own INFURATION project. Another round of Swedish club dates ensued before a return to recording was prompted at the invitation of 'Metalion' (a.k.a. Jon Kristiansen), owner of the fabled 'Slayer' fanzine. The journalist was attempting to assemble a split release set to feature PARADISE LOST, CARCASS and BOLT THROWER to launch his Head Not Found label, requesting NIHILIST also contribute material. although the band laid down the new track 'Morbid Devourment' for this purpose the proposed release never transpired. The song was then mooted for inclusion on a compilation album 'Brutal Jaevla Död', but this too failed to eventuate.

Persevering, NIHILIST set about constructing the 'Drowned' demo in August 1989, including a cover rendition of REPULSION's 'Radiation Sickness'. Just after these sessions, internal disagreements froze out Johnny Hedlund. The bass player soon set up anew with the powerful UNLEASHED, whilst the remainder, adding ex-CARBONISED bassist Lars Rosenberg, forged ENTOMBED. Around this period Nicke Andersson was also dividing his duties singing with TREBLINKA, the pre-TIAMAT extreme Death Metal combo out of Täby.

The debut single, 1989's 'Severe Burns' on Bloody Rude Defect Records, was originally the demo "Drowned", whilst a second single, 'Radiation Sickness' in 1991, turned out to be a semi-official bootleg. Post ENTOMBED drummer Nicke Andersson would become Nicke Royale for his role in THE HELLACOPTERS.

Threeman Recordings issued a collection of NIHILIST recordings in April 2005. Sadly, founding NIHILIST guitarist Leif Cuzner passed away in Montreal, Canada in June 2006.

Only Shreds Remain, (1988) (Demo). Abnormally Deceased / Revel In Flesh / Face Of Evil.
Severe Burns, Bloody Rude Defect BRD001 (1989). Severe Burns / When Life Has Ceased.
Radiation Sickness, Bootleg (1991). Radiation Sickness / Face Of Evil / Morbid Devourment.
Premature Autopsy, (1998) (Demo). Sentenced To Death / Supposed To Rot / Carnal Leftovers.
THE NIHILIST DEMOS, Candlelight (2005). Sentenced To Death / Supposed To Rot / Carnal Leftovers / Abnormally Deceased / Revel In Flesh / Face Of Evil / Severe Burns / When Life Has Ceased / Morbid Devourment / Radiation Sickness / Face Of Evil / But Life Goes On / Shreds Of Flesh / Truth Beyond.

NILE

GREENVILLE, NC, USA — *Karl Sanders (vocals / guitar), Dallas Toller Wade (guitar), Chief Spires (bass), Pete Hammoura (drums).*

NILE is an "Ithyphallic" Greenville, North Carolina Death Metal band that is justifiably being touted as the next major league contender. Nothing if not ambitious, infusing all of their work with exclusively arranged ancient Egyptian themes, NILE have forged a reputation for precise attention to detail spanning the execution of their music, accuracy of translated texts to the expansive explanatory annotations that embellish each CD booklet. The initial quartet of frontman KARL SANDERS, bassist Chief Spires and drummer Pete Hammoura issued two demos on their own Anubis Records label.

In 1995 the five-track demo, 'Festivals Of Atonement' was issued, after which guitarist John Elhers augmented the band roster. In 1996 they followed it up with the three track demo 'Ramses-Bringer Of War', the title cut being directly inspired by Holst's seminal classical work 'Mars–Bringer Of War'. These demos lead them to a very brief business relationship with Visceral Productions who reissued the 'Ramses' demo in 1997. However, this label was to collapse before anything could be arranged and NILE were soon snapped up by Relapse Records, the band augmenting their sound with the addition of second guitarist Dallas Toller Wade after the departure of Elhers.

In April 1998 the band released their debut, 'Amongst The Catacombs of Nephren-Ka' on the Relapse label. Adding an air of mystique to the affair would be credits listing choir chants apparently by the Gyuto Drupka Tibetan Monks led by the Khamtul Incarnation of Lobsang Kampa, Damaru human skull drums attributed to Mahala Kapala and thigh bone flutes and Turkish gongs played by Drilbu Dungkar. This exoticism masked what was, in fact, a supremely brutal and ripping death metal desert sandstorm holding aloft the pulsating 'Die Rache Krieg Lied Der Assyriche', on which Sanders Egyptian obsession manifested itself in an eerie incantation.

Extensive touring followed and eager to capitalize on the success of this innovative and respected band Relapse reissued the first two demos in early 2000, entitled 'In The Beginning', being remastered and came with alternate artwork.

NILE toured North America in 2000 supported by INCANTATION and IMPALED. Unfortunately, Hammoura damaged his arm to such a degree he was unable to perform on the September 2000 'Black Seeds Of Vengeance' album. Derek Roddy of MALEVOLENT CREATION and AURORA BOREALIS stepped in for the studio duties whilst Tony Laureano took over the mantle for live work.

When released, 'Black Seeds Of Vengeance' would break NILE from the cult underground into the Death Metal mainstream putting the focus on the band as long-term contenders. The album, which had taken over a year to compose and arrange, featured a vast array of instrumentation as diverse as tablas, African choirs, Tibetan doom drums, gongs and sitars. The 2000 Hammerheart release 'In The Beginning' combines the two early mini albums 1995's 'Festivals Of Atonement' and 1997's 'Ramses Bringer Of War'.

Following European touring in early 2001 longstanding bassist Chief Spires decamped, being superseded by the DEMONIC CHRIST and DARKMOON credited Jon Vesano. A new studio album, In The Darkened Shrines', would be scheduled for September 2002 release through Relapse. American headline dates would be announced with ARCH ENEMY, HATE ETERNAL and ORIGIN slated to support. NILE would also journey to Japan to appear at the Tokyo 'Beast Fest' extreme music festival in December. The band's status had risen to such a level that US dates were being projected into January 2003 with NILE headlining over a full Metal package of NAPALM DEATH, DARK TRANQUILITY, STRAPPING YOUNG LAD and Australians THE BERSERKER.

Drummer Tony Laureano joined MALEVOLENT CREATION's live roster in March for their April 2003 European 'No Mercy' festivals. NILE's live schedule intensified with September North American dates dubbed 'The Art Of Noise 2'. This run of shows saw the band allied with KREATOR, VADER, AMON AMARTH and GOATWHORE. The band would be confirmed as headliners for the 'X-Mass Festivals' European tour commencing in London on December 7th, heading up a strong billing incorporating DESTRUCTION, AMON AMARTH, DEICIDE, GRAVEWORM, DEW-SCENTED, MISERY INDEX and DISBELIEF.

In September 2003 former NILE members vocalist / bassist Chief Spires and guitarist John Ehlers joined forces in a new band called SHAITAN MAZAR. Mid 2004 found Karl Sanders donating a guest guitar solo to the track 'Xul' included on the 'Demigod' album from Polish Death Metal veterans BEHEMOTH. Drummer Tony Laureano joined Norwegian Black Metal act DIMMU BORGIR on a session basis for the duration of their Summer 'Ozzfest' dates, regular sticksman Reno Kiilerich having been unable to obtain a U.S. work visa.

During downtime for NILE in mid 2004 guitarist Dallas Toller-Wade would be acting as stand in drummer for Greenville, South Carolina band LECHEROUS NOCTURNE. Meantime, KARL SANDERS, working with singer Mike Breazeale, worked up a solo album entitled 'Saurian Meditation' for October issue. NILE drafted Greek drummer George Kollias, a veteran of NIGHTFALL, THE CIRCLE OF ZAPHYAN and SICKENING HORROR to record the 'Annihilation Of The Wicked' album. Limited edition variants of the album came packaged with Serpent-Ankh pendant, colour album poster, vinyl sticker and embroidered patch.

In February 2005 NILE severed ties with bassist Jon Vesano, inducting the MORBID ANGEL credited Steve Tucker as stand in for live work. However, Tucker's union with the band never transpired and nineteen year old Joe Payne took up bass duties in his stead. In addition, Dallas Toller Wade would assume lead vocal duties. The band forged a road alliance with SIX FEET UNDER, DARK FUNERAL, DISBELIEF, DYING FETUS, WYKKED WYTCH and CATARACT for the 'No Mercy Festivals 2005' European tour beginning in early March. The group then scheduled US tour dates for April of 2005 in partnership with headliners KING DIAMOND, Poles BEHEMOTH and THE BLACK DAHLIA MURDER. This latter batch of gigs saw Krieshloff of DOMINION and LECHEROUS NOCTURNE repute occupying the bass role. Impressively, 'Annihilation Of The Wicked' debuted on the national Swedish charts in June at number 27. A promotional video for the track 'Sacrifice Unto Sebek' was shot on location in Atlanta, Georgia with director Chad Rullman.

Further gigs announced for the US with CHIMAIRA, ALL THAT REMAINS, and 3 INCHES OF BLOOD were announced but the band would then withdraw their participation citing "scheduling conflicts". Meantime, ex-NILE drummer Tony Laureano would be performing live on the European festival circuit with DIMMU BORGIR, subsequently joining another Norwegian Black Metal band, 1349.

Live work breaking into 2006 saw the band teaming up with HYPOCRISY, SOILENT GREEN, RAGING SPEEDHORN, DECAPITATED and WITH PASSION for a North American tour commencing in early January. The group then participated in the 'Extreme The Dojo Vol. 15' shows in Japan with THE HAUNTED and EXODUS in late February. NILE signed to the Nuclear Blast label in May.

Karl Sanders guested on Brazilian Doom duo AMARNA SKY's December 2006 album 'Rising Heresy', featuring on the track 'Beyond The Horizon (Legacy Of Light)'. Fresh album recordings were conducted at Sound Lab Studios in Columbia, South Carolina from February 26th 2007 with 'Ithyphallic' being mixed in April.

NILE embarked on a headlining tour of Australia in May 2007 supported by Polish technical Death Metal act DECAPITATED. The group joined the OZZY OSBOURNE headlined 'Ozzfest' extravaganza for arena dates throughout June and July across the USA. 'Off-Fest' headliners were conducted backed by Taiwanese outfit CHTHONIC.

Nile, Nile (1994) (Demo). Le Chant Du Cygre / Worship The Animal / Nepenthe / Surrounded By Fright / Mecca.

Festivals Of Atonement, Anubis (1995) (Demo). Divine Intent / The Black Hand Of Set / Wrought / Immortality Through Art / Godless—Extinct.

Ramses Bringer Of War, Anubis (1996) (Demo). The Howling Of The Jinn / Ramses Bringer Of War / Die Rache Krieg Lied Der Assyriche.

Ramses Bringer Of War, Visceral Productions VP-007-CD-S (1997). The Howling Of The Jinn / Ramses Bringer Of War / Die Rache Krieg Lied Der Assyriche.

AMONGST THE CATACOMBS OF NEPHREN-KA, Relapse RR 6983 (1998). Smashing The Antiu / Barra Edinazzu / Kudurru Maglu / Serpent Headed Mask / Ramses Bringer Of War / Stones Of Sorrow / Die Rache Krieg Lied Der Assyriche / The Howling Of The Jinn / Pestilence And Iniquity / Opening Of The Mouth / Beneath Eternal Oceans Of Sand.

BLACK SEEDS OF VENGEANCE, Relapse RR 6448 (2000). Invocation Of The Gate Of Aat-Ankh-Es-En-Amenti / Black Seeds Of Vengeance / Defiling The Gates Of Ishtar / The Black Flame / Libation Unto The Shades Who Lurk In The Shadows Of The Temple Of Anhur / Masturbating The War God / Multitude Of Foes / Chapter For Transforming Into A Snake / Nas Akhu Khan She En Asbiu / To Dream Of Ur / The Nameless City Of The Accursed / Khetti Satha Shemsu.

IN THE BEGINNING, Relapse RR 6449 (2000). Divine Intent / The Black Hand Of Set / Wrought / Immortality Through Art / Godless—Extinct / The Howling Of The Jinn / Ramses Bringer Of War / Die Rache Krieg Lied Der Assyriche.

AMONGST THE CATACOMBS OF NEPHREN-KA, Toy's Factory TFCK-87239 (2000) (Japanese release). Smashing The Antiu / Barra Edinazzu / Kudurru Maglu / Serpent Headed Mask / Ramses Bringer

Of War / Stones Of Sorrow / Die Rache Krieg Lied Der Assyriche / The Howling Of The Jinn / Pestilence And Iniquity / Opening Of The Mouth / Beneath Eternal Oceans Of Sand / The Black Hand Of Set.

BLACK SEEDS OF VENGEANCE, Toy's Factory TFCK-87238 (2000). Invocation Of The Gate Of Aat-Ankh-Es-En-Amenti / Black Seeds Of Vengeance / Defiling The Gates Of Ishtar / The Black Flame / Libation Unto The Shades Who Lurk In The Shadows Of The Temple Of Anhur / Masturbating The War God / Multitude Of Foes / Chapter For Transforming Into A Snake / Nas Akhu Khan She En Asbiu / To Dream Of Ur / The Nameless City Of The Accursed / Khetti Satha Shemsu / Wrought.

IN THE DARKENED SHRINES, Relapse RR 6542 (2002). The Blessed Dead / Execration Text / Sarcophagus / Kheftiu Asar Butchiu / Unas Slayer Of The Gods / Churning The Maelstrom / I Whisper In The Ear Of The Dead / Wind Of Horus / In Their Darkened Shrines I: Hall Of Saurian Entombment / In Their Darkened Shrines II: Invocation To Seditious Heresy / In Their Darkened Shrines III: Destruction Of The Temple Of The Enemies of Ra / In Their Darkened Shrines IV: Ruins.

ANNIHILATION OF THE WICKED, Relapse RR 6630 (2005). Dusk Falls Upon The Temple Of The Serpent On The Mount Of Sunrise / Cast Down The Heretic / Sacrifice Unto Sebek / User-Maat-Re / Burning Pits Of The Duat / Chapter Of Obeisance Before Giving Breath To The Inert One In The Presence Of The Crescent Shaped Horns / Lashed To The Slave Stick / Spawn Of Uamenti / Annihilation Of The Wicked / Von Unaussprechlichen Kulten. Chart position: 27 SWEDEN.

ANNIHILATION OF THE WICKED, Universal YSCY-1001 (2005) (Japanese release). Dusk Falls Upon The Temple Of The Serpent On The Mount Of Sunrise / Cast Down The Heretic / Sacrifice Unto Sebek / User-Maat-Re / Burning Pits Of The Duat / Chapter Of Obeisance Before Giving Breath To The Inert One In The Presence Of The Crescent Shaped Horns / Lashed To The Slave Stick / Spawn Of Uamenti / Annihilation Of The Wicked / Von Unaussprechlichen Kulten / SSS Haa Set Yoth.

ITHYPHALLIC, Nuclear Blast (2007). What Can Be Safely Written / As He Creates So He Destroys / Ithyphallic / Papyrus Containing The Spell To Preserve Its Possessor / Eat Of The Dead / Laying Fire Upon Apep / The Essential Salts / The Infinity Of Stone / The Language Of The Shadows / Even The Gods Must Die. Chart position: 13 SWEDEN.

NINNGHIZHIDA

GERMANY — *Mephistopholes (vocals / guitar), Baalberith (guitar), Ash Saan (keyboards), Lightning Bolt (drums).*

A blasphemous German Death Metal combo previously signed to the now defunct Invasion label. NINNGHIZHIDDA, who debuted with the demo 'The Horned Serpent', recorded their opening 'Blasphemy' album with a line up of vocalist / guitarist Mephistopholes (Patrick Kalla), guitarist Baalberith (Renè Bogdanski), keyboard player Dr. Faustus and drummer Kerberos.

Later additions to NINNGHIZHIDDA included vocalist / bassist Zagan in the spring of 1998 and also Ventor. With the demise of Invasion Records NINNGHIZHIDDA cut a self financed three track EP 'Mistress Of The Night'. However, Zagan, Ventor and Dr. Faustus would all break away from the band prior to their signature with Dutch label Displeased for a second album.

The bands line-up for the 2002 'Demigod' opus stood at frontman Mephistopholes, guitarist Baalberith, keyboard player Ash Saan (Sascha George) and drummer Lightning Bolt (Markus Aust- also known as Tsatthoggua). Meantime the Dutch Displeased Records label were set to re-issue the band's debut album 'Blasphemy' with bonus tracks later the same year.

Sascha George joined INSIGNIUM in August of 2001. Ex-NINNGHIZIDDA keyboard player Sascha Risseler worked with Recklinghausen Gothic Metal band STORMGARD in 2004.

BLASPHEMY, Invasion (1998). Moonlight Serenade / Of Demons And Witches (Part I) / Baphomet (In The Name Of . . .) / Reach The Jewels Gleam / Of Demons And Witches (Part II) / Dressed In Mourning / The Horned Serpent / Crucify The Lambs Of Christ / Deny Thy Philosophy / Nailed Upon A Cross / Ode To Thy Horned Majesty.

Mistress Of The Night EP, (2000). Mistress Of The Night / Conquering What Once Was / Rape (The Virgin Mary).

DEMIGOD, Displeased (2002). Prowling Sin / Fools Of Christ / Rape (The Virgin Mary) / Mistress Of The Night / The Awakening / March Of The Servants / Conquering What Once Was / Demigod / Siesta In A-Minor / Ode II The Horned Majesty / Finale.

NO DAWN

STEINKJER, NORWAY — *Tor Erik Simensen (vocals), Steinar Forfang (guitar), Tor Egil Solberg (guitar), Ludvik Brandsegg (bass), Kent Skjeflo (drums).*

Steinkjer based Death Metal combo NO DAWN was created in the Summer of 2002 by guitarists Kaki and ex-COMBUSTION men Steinar Forfang with bass player Ludvik Brandsegg, the latter also an active participant of ETERNAL DEMENTIA. In early 2003 drummer Polly was enrolled, he in turn drawing in Cato Skivik of ALLFADER as his own replacement as he took on the lead vocal role. For the groups first gig, held at the Rismelen, Steinkjer on 9th August 2003, NO DAWN performed a set comprising IN FLAMES and AT THE GATES covers.

With the band pursuing original material, Polly vacated the role of frontman in favour of ETERNAL DEMENTIA, SKAMBITT and ex-RAGNAROK's Tor Erik Simensen. That November Kaki was superseded by Tor Egil Solberg. Further changes witnessed the departure of Skivik in February of 2004, being substituted by Kent Skjeflo of DYING BREED, INANE and COMBUSTION repute.

No Dawn, No Dawn (2004).

NO MERCY

PIEDIMONTE MATESE, ITALY — *Marco Stanzione (vocals), Roberto Navarra (guitar), Alfredo Tranchedone (guitar), Emilio Toscano (bass), Marcantonio Rapa (drums).*

Piedimonte Matese Death / Thrash act NO MERCY was founded as a Thrash covers act during 1997 by guitarist Roberto Navarra and drummer Marcantonio Rapa. The formative line-up proved fluid but was stabilised in 2000 with the introduction of singer Marco Stanzione and bassist Vincenzo Di Biase from Gothic Metal act REMEMBRANCE. Live work culminated in the recording of demos in 2002. However, 2003 brought about line-up changes with the induction of second guitarist Alfredo Tranchedone but the exit of Di Biase. The latter would be superseded by Emilio Toscano, a veteran of Prog-Metal act MIND COLOUR.

NO MERCY entered Temple of Noise Studios in Rome in November 2003 to lay down the album 'Thy Will Be Done', these sessions including a cover version of SLAYER's 'Reign In Blood'.

Demo 2002, No Mercy Promo (2002). Unknown Dimension / Cyber Dark Era / Your Sweet Blood Tears / Too Hard.

THY WILL BE DONE, No Mercy Ind. (2005). Intro / Thy Will Be Done You Will Die Alone / Pure Merciless / Where Is Your Jesus Now? / Redemption Through Hate / Thy Will Be Done.

NOBILITAS NIGRA

POLAND — *Vicomte Kveldulv (vocals / guitar / drums), Kniaz Krig (vocals / guitar / bass / drums).*

Extreme Black-Grind act NOBILITAS NIGRA (Latin for "Black Gentry") deal in brutal, hyper-blast bursts of speed mere seconds in duration. Although wishing to remain anonymous it is believed the duo of Vicomte Kveldulv and Kniaz Krig to be Jan Rajkow-Krzywicki and Jerzy Rajkow-Krzywicki of Dark Rock band APRIL ETHEREAL and Funeral Doom outfit OKTOR. The band's thirty three song debut demo 'Celebrating The Northern Altar' was recorded in just three days during early 1999 at Delirium Tremens Studios. Kveldulv and Krig reunited in October 1999 to cut 'Gloria Sathanas'. Third set 'The Only True Armageddon' emerged in May 2000 through Goat Horns Productions.

The track 'Cadaverous Legions' on the August 2003 album 'Coming Straight With Vengeance' featured guest female vocals courtesy of Morbid Queen Of The Night.

Celebrating The Northern Altar, (1999). Intro / Slaughter / Satan/Lucifer / Decapitated Ones / Enter The Palace Of Satan / Armageddon / Beast / Butchered By The Black Priest / Satanas / I Vomit Blood / Skyld / Driven By The Frost / Invocation For Power / Killer / Krig / Thou Shall Rise / Hymn To My Motherland / No One Shall Survive / The Rising Moon Upon The Fiords / The Dungeon Of Power Enthroned / The Northern Path Of Infinite Truth / Infernal Passage / Storming The Paradise / The Wings Of The North / Our Fathers' Crusade Through Medieval Darkness / Diary Of A Hellslaughter / The Beast, The Victim And The Mother / On The Nightside Of The Northern Forest / Triumphant Beast / The Black Wind / Satan Rules / The Ultimate Judgement Of Souls / The Last Massacre.

GLORIA SATHANAS, (1999). Intro / Black Horde (Of Vengeance) / Sabbath / Total War / Get Your Axe / Bellum / The Horned Beast / Belial / Voodoo / Islam / Hare Krishna / The Beginning / The End / Time To Die / Hail Satan / In The Name Of Lucifer / Hell-Born / Malediction / Destiny / Feelings / Lucifer My King / Your Fate / Satanismo Muerte / Oslo / United / Final Step / Norwegian Fog / Facing Satan / The Meeting / Ingenting Att Ha / Thor / Chasing The Victim / No Help, No Future / Death In The Sky / The Last Vision / Solution / Belzebub / Entering Astaroth's Domain / Gift / Blood / In Nomine Sathanas / Ancient / One Last Word.

THE ONLY TRUE ARMAGEDDON, Goat Horns Productions (2000). Intro / Slow Death / Hell Warriors / Your Corpse Is My Life / A Battle To Win / Bloodshed Agony / Calling The Madness / Die Bastard / Electric Escape / Haunted / Decapitation Of The Holy Ones / Calm / Half Human Half Demon / World Sarcofago / He Died In The Skies / Suicidal Incantations.

COMING STRAIGHT WITH A VENGEANCE, (2003). 6:00:01 / Preludium To Annihilation / 7:06:30 / World Of The Dead Arising / 8:00:02 / Prophecy Of The Blind Ones / 9:28:11 / 11:47:58 / Annihilation Begins / 13:09:43 / The Bells Of Doom / 14:32:26 / At The Gates Of Hell / 15:18:03 / Smell Of Terror / 16:51:40 / Cadaverous Legions / 18:02:31 / The First Day Of Battle / 18:40:09 / A Dying Myth / 20:00:03 / A Blood Red Heaven And The Fall Of God / 21:27:46 / Eight Relics / 22:49:13 / Back On The Cross / 23:28:24 / The Birth Of The Time Of The Dead / 23:28:29 / Youre Frozen With Last Scream / 23:41:12 / Heaven Is Crying / 23:59:49 / Pure Hatred (2003 A.B.).

NOCTAMBULANT GRIMNESS

HOLLAND — *Patrick (vocals), Tjaard Walstra (guitar), Corry Kussendrager (bass), Marije Kortstra (keyboards / string instruments), Folkert van der Leest (drums).*

Blackened Death Metal. Starting off life as a part time band in 1998, originally billed as NOCTURNITY, with AUTUMN's Jeroen Bakker on the drums and Horca on keyboards, then NOCTAMBULANT GRIMNESS, the band released demos in 2000, 'After The Slumbering Gloom', and an untitled second session in October of 2002. The band lost singer Berry upon completion of the first demo. A former drummer, Marco de Vos, left the band in 2000 and died in September the following year.

Replacing Bakker would be the NO FUN FOR ME, POLITICAL ABUSE and LEGACY OF HATE credited Folkert van der Leest with former MARTYRS OF MORGOTH's Marije Kortstra superseding Horca. Bassist Corry Kussendrager was a member of QUIDDITY. The band also included singer Patrick Bransma of NECROMONICAL CRUCIFIXION.

With guitarist André quitting, a LEGACY OF HATE guitarist Dicky would be introduced in October of 2001 but left in December, as did van der Leest. The tribulation continued as Kussendrager bowed out in February of 2002, although the group did find a replacement guitarist in Tjaard Walstra of NECROMONICAL CRUCIFIXION. Fortunately Kussendrager returned in May but Patrick would depart in November of 2002. Mark took over but he too exited in 2003. Guitarist Jeroen also bailed out that same year.

The band, adding ex-MON'STRUM singer Dirk-Jan Faber and now describing themselves as "Nethermetal", subsequently evolved into NOCTA in November of 2003. An EP, 'P.E.R.I.O.D.', was projected for Summer 2004 release. Kortstra is also an active member of DARKWOODS, as bass guitarist.

Noctambulant Grimness, Noctambulant Grimness (2002) (Demo). Insane / The Hope That Tears Will Bind / The Slumbering Gloom.

NOCTURNAL BREED

NORWAY — *Destroyer (vocals), A.E. Rattlehead (guitar), Ben Hellion (guitar), Tex Terror (drums).*

Although Scandinavia threw up a confusion of side project acts in the late 90s put together by various Black Metal musicians made good, NOCTURNAL BREED boast more pedigree than most. A distinctly retro old style Death Metal offering performed by members of DIMMU BORGIR, LORD KAOS, SATYRICON, COVENANT and GEHENNA. NOCTURNAL BREED had in fact been operating much earlier with a pre-DIMMU BORGIR founding member Erkjetter Silenoz on guitar going under the stage name of Ed Dominator. NOCTURNAL BREED debuted in 1997 with an EP, 'Raping Europe', for Hammerheart Records, this five track 12" single including a cover rendition of W.A.S.P.'s 'I'm Alive'. The 'Agressor' album followed in October 1997, these sessions sporting a cover of DEATH's 'Evil Dead' and a wry shot at JETHRO TULL's classic 'Locomotive Breath' under the guise 'Locomotive Death'. To coincide with tour work, NOCTURNAL BREED issued a 10" vinyl picture disc entitled 'Raping Europe '97'. That same year Hammerheart put out the 'Triumph Of The Blasphemer' EP and the momentum was maintained by a second full-length offering, 'No Retreat... No Surrender' in November 1998.

NOCTURNAL BREED's third album, 'Tools Of The Trade', surfaced in 1999 on the Holycaust label. The band at this juncture was quoted as vocalist / bassist Destroyer, lead guitarist I. Maztor, rhythm guitarist Ben Hellion and former NUCTEMERON drummer Tex Terror. Frontman 'Tom Bombakill' (a.k.a. Tom Kvålsvoll), also a member of Doom merchants PARADIGMA, would join DHG under the stage name 'Thrawn' during March of 2002, replacing Jens Ryland. Kvålsvoll would also lend vocals to the HAGALAZ'S RUNEDANCE album 'Volven'. Session drums came from Tjodalv (a.k.a. Ian Kenneth Åkesson) of DIMMU BORGIR and SUSPERIA.

Prostata Records put out archive NOCTURNAL BREED album outtakes as the 'Warthog' EP in 2004. Neseblod Records then weighed in with a further three early tracks, dating from 1999, on the 'Motörmouth' 7" EP, a limited edition of 500 copies of which 100 would be manufactured in yellow vinyl. Duplicate Records too released collectable NOCTURNAL BREED product with gatefold split EPs 'Überthrash' and 'Überthrash', both shared with AURA NOIR, AUDIOPAIN and INFERNO.

NOCTURNAL BREED parted ways with guitarist Tom Kvålsvoll in June 2005, citing "internal conflicts". September saw the recruitment of the COCKROACH CLAN, CREST OF DARKNESS and HAMMERHEART credited A.E. Rattlehead as replacement. NOCTURNAL BREED, having wrapped up recording of a new album 'Code Of Conduct', severed ties with Painkiller Records in June 2006.

The group signed with Polish imprint Agonia Records for a 2007 album entitled 'Fields Of Rot'.

Raping The Angels, Nocturnal Breed (1996) (Demo). Bloodsnarl / Nocturnal Breed / Rape The Angels / Dead Dominions.

Black Cult, Nocturnal Breed (1997) (Demo). Intro / Revelation 666 / Alcoholic Rites / In Torture / Locomotive Death.

AGGRESSOR, Hammerheart HHR 011 (1997). Rape The Angels / Frantic Aggressor / Maggot Master / Nocturnal Breed / Evil Dead / Metal Storm Rebels / Dead Dominions / Alcoholic Rites / Revelation 666 / Blaster / Locomotive Death.

Raping Europe '97, Hammerheart HHR 011PD (1997) (10" picture vinyl single limited to 300 copies). Still Alive / Screaming For A Leather Bitch / Rape The Angels / Dead Dominion / I'm Alive.

Triumph Of The Blasphemer, Hammerheart HHR 022 (1998). Triumph Of The Blasphemer / Screaming For A Leather Bitch / I'm Alive / Frantic Aggressor / Evil Dead.

NO RETREAT ... NO SURRENDER, Hammerheart HHR 026 (1998). The Artillery Command / Thrash The Redeemer / Warhorse / Killernecro / No Retreat ... No Surrender / Beyond Control / Sodomite / Fists Of Fury / Under The Blade / Roadkill Maze / Possessed / Armageddon Nights / Outro-Insane Tyrant.

Armageddon Nights, Nocturnal Breed (1999) (Demo). Necro Cruel / Possessed / Armageddon Nights / Return Of The Tyrant.
THE TOOLS OF THE TRADE, Holycaust S810-07 (2000). Give 'em Hell / Slaughter Division / Resistance Is Futile / The Tools Of The Trade / Down By Law / The Sabbath Man / Skeleton Of Sin / Black Tooth Grin / Silvertongue Devil / Ballcrusher / Knuckledust / Scarred.
Überthrash, Duplicate DUPLO 666 (2004) (Split single with AURA NOIR, AUDIOPAIN and INFERNO. Limited edition 500 copies). Code Of Conduct.
Warthog, Prostata (2004). Warthog / Triumph Of The Blasphemer.
Motörmouth, Neseblod (2004) (Limited edition 500 copies). Motörmouth / Judas Breed / Dead And Done.
Überthrash II, Duplicate DUPLO 15 (2005) (Split single with AURA NOIR, AUDIOPAIN and INFERNO. Limited edition 500 copies). Scything Harrow (Mother Whore edit).
FIELDS OF ROT, (2007).

NOCTURNUS

TAMPA, FL, USA — *Mike Browning (vocals / drums), Mike Davis (guitar), Sean McNennerey (guitar), Jeff Estes (bass), Louis Panzer (keyboards).*

Tampa Death Metal act NOCTURNUS are widely credited with being one of the prime instigators of keyboard driven technical styled Death Metal. The group was manifested during June of 1988 by ex-MORBID ANGEL and INCUBUS drummer/ lead vocalist Mike Browning, guitarist Gino Marino, bassist Jeff Estes and eighteen year old guitarist Mike Davis. The addition of keyboard player Louis Panzer in September of that year would undoubtedly succeed in putting the band into the realms of the unique. Their inaugural demo effort, the four song effort 'The Science Of Horror', immediately secured a recording contract with the Nottingham based cutting edge label Earache Records.

For their debut 'The Key' NOCTURNUS, seeing Sean McNenney replacing Gino Marino, plied a unique combination when it came to plying their particular brand of Death Metal unafraid to add the keyboards of Panzer well upfront and with lead vocals being handled by Browning. MASSACRE's Kam Lee adds backing vocals. Meantime bassist Jeff Estes made way for James Sullivan for touring which included dates BOLT-THROWER across the UK capitalised on by the US 'Grindcrusher' tour alongside GODFLESH and NAPALM DEATH. Meantime former member Gino Marino relocated to Atlanta, Georgia to found EUPHORIA.

1992's 'Thresholds' saw the band adopt a more conformist approach by adding former TORTURED SOUL vocalist Dan Izzo to the line up allowing Browning to prioritise the drums. Further changes saw Estes superseded by Chad Anderson. For subsequent touring NOCTURNUS drafted Jim O'Sullivan on bass who was in turn substituted by Emo Mowery for shows in league with CONFESSOR in 1991.

Browning quit to work with ACHERON, appearing on their 1994 albums 'Hail Victory', 'Satanic Victory' and 'Lex Talionis'. In a further change Sullivan lost his place and NOCTURNUS utilised the talents of Chris Anderson in the studio although a more permanent position went to ex FALLEN IDOLS man Emo Mowery. The band toured Europe together with CONFESSOR in 1992. The following year an eponymous two track EP emerged on the Seattle based Moribund label, this seeing new drummer James Marcinek of ASTAROTH installed. Although fans acknowledged this EP as being a return to form the group folded shortly after recording.

Ex-drummer Mike Browning would be found pursuing an eclectic range of products such as DEACON SCREECH, ASH, WOLF AND HAWK and DEVINE ESSENCE. Rising out of the ashes of NOCTURNUS during 1999 the former players vocalist / drummer Mike Browning, guitarist Gino Marino and bassist Richard Bateman forged NOCTURNUS A.D. in union with second guitarist Mike Walkowski. During 2000 this band distanced itself from prior connections, re-billing itself as AFTER DEATH.

NOCTURNUS resurfaced in 2000 with a fresh vocalist Emo Mowery and a new album 'Ethereal Tomb'. Mowery would also form part of ex-CRIMSON GLORY man Wade Black's SECTOR 9 line up as bass player.

Polish Death Metal band SCEPTIC would offer up their rendition of 'Arctic Crypt' on their 2001 album 'Pathetic Being'. In a surprise move NOCTURNUS disbanded during early May of 2002 as both Mowery and Browning announced their departure. The former NOCTURNUS pairing of guitarist Mike Davis and bassist/vocalist Emo Mowery rapidly enlisted the services of SEVEN WITCHES and ex-CRIMSON GLORY singer Wade Black for a fresh band project.

THE KEY, Earache MOSH 23 (1990). Lake Of Fire / Standing In Blood / Visions From Beyond The Grave / Neolithic / BC-AD (Before Christ- After Death) / Andromeda Strain / Droid Sector / Destroying The Manger / Empire Of The Sands.
THRESHOLDS, Earache MOSH55 (1992). Climate Controller / Tribal Vodoun / Nocturne In B.M. / Arctic Crypt / Aquatic / Subterranean Infiltrator / After Reality / Gridzone.
Possess The Priest, Morbid Sounds DEAD 02EP (1994). Possess The Priest / Mummified.
ETHEREAL TOMB, Season Of Mist (2000). Orbital Decay / Apostle Of Evil / Edge Of Darkness / The Killing / Séance For The Trident / Paranormal State / The Science Of Horror / Outland.

NOIZ

GERMANY — *Stefan Schulze (vocals / bass), Elling Golz (guitar), Torben Golz (guitar), Thomas Schulze (drums).*

Christian Death Metal band founded in July 1991 by Thomas Schulze on keyboards, Elling Golz on guitar and Stefan Schulze on bass. The band's initial formation employed a drum machine until Schulze switched to drums in 1992. NOIZ debuted live in November of 1993. However, by December of 1994 the band had folded with Golz joining SEVENTH AVENUE and the Schulze siblings teaming up with CHILDREN OF SILENCE.

NOIZ was reborn during 1997 as the erstwhile members all decamped from their respective bands. A demo arrived in April of 1998 and a full blown album 'Seeds Of The Living' in December of the following year. Torben Golz joined as second guitarist in the summer of 2000.

The official NOIZ website won a gold "Metal for Christ" award. During 2002, after a period of inactivity, NOIZ announced their new music was to lean more toward Grindcore with Black Metal influences.

SEEDS OF THE LIVING, (1999). Abolition Of Idolatry / Baptism And Shelter / Believer's New Life / Bless The Lord / Charity / Crown Of Thorns / Destined To Die / Destruction Of Wisdom / Glory / God's Love / Majestic / My Light / Overpassing / Pain / Pathway / Presence Of Darkness / Radical / Save / Stronger / Tombstones / Waiting For Damnation.

NOMAD

OPOCZNO, POLAND — *Bleyzabel (vocals), Patrick (guitar), Nemeless (guitar), Herman (bass), Rodzyn (drums).*

Opoczno's NOMAD was forged as a quartet in 1994, subsequently adding second vocalist Bleyzabel. 1996 saw the group entering Salman Studios in Bialystok to lay down the 'Disorder' demo. October of 1997 produced a second demo recording, 'The Tail Of Substance'. Dates to promote this release had NOMAD packaged with LUX OCCULTA, CHRIST AGONY, HATE and HERESY for a Polish tour.

NOMAD's 'The Devilish Whirl' album, issued in Poland through Novum Vox Mortis, saw Russian distribution in cassette form through Flame Productions. Renewed live action had NOMAD on the road for a mini-tour with BEHEMOTH and DEVILYN. The 'Demonic Verses (Blessed Are Those Who Kill Jesus)' was to surface in 2003 through Baphomet Records.

Disorder, (1996). The Slanderer / I'm Waiting For Wind / Dies Irae (Day Of Wrath) / To Burn At Dawn.

THE TAIL OF SUBSTANCE, (1997). The Slept Scream / Dirty White Wings / Merciful Agony / Mercy Is Fear / Psychical Degradation / Silent That Picture / The Quartered Dependence / The Blade Of Inquisition / Nameless Throne / Burn Into Your Hell.

THE DEVILISH WHIRL, Novum Vox Mortis (1999). Intro / Confidence / War In The Name Of Impale / Groping The Secret Corpses / A Constructive Image / I—An Alchemist Of My Analysis / The Pile Of Burning Roses / The Black Domination.

DEMONIC VERSES (BLESSED ARE THOSE WHO KILL JESUS), Baphomet (2003). Demonic Verses / The Branch Of Cool Progeny / Raging Arsenals Of Waves / Blazing Mind / Insurrection / My Key / In The King's Hands / The Symphony Of Demonic Sounds.

NOMENMORTIS

SLOVAKIA — *Martin Lukac (vocals), Peter (guitar), Martin (guitar), Erik (bass), Robo (drums).*

A brutal Death Metal combo, NOMENMORTIS originally arrived on the scene in the Spring of 1992 billed as NOMEN MORTIS with a line-up of vocalist Martin, bass guitarist Ivo and drummer Rolo. The band would be finalised with the addition of guitarists Marián and Dano. NOMEN MORTIS got to grips with a six track promotional recording in May of 1993 simply entitled 'Unofficial '93'. By September of the same year the band was active on the live circuit.

In January of 1994 a second tape emerged 'Around The House It Is Good' but Marián later decamped in April. NOMEN MORTIS persevered issuing the 'Twilight Of Humanity' session in August, the band distributing over 1'000 copies to various media sources. More live action followed including festival appearances before Dano opted out in early 1995. His replacement would be Igor but their new recruit's apparent serious health concerns suspended band activity for some considerable time.

By 1996 both Rolo and Mato discharged themselves from duty leaving Martin as the solitary member. Undaunted the singer reconstituted the band under the revised handle of NOMENMORTIS finally pulling together a full membership roster by May of 1997. The new look NOMENMORTIS consisted of Martin, guitarists Mat'o and Šano Suchácek, bass player Tomas and CONTEMPT drummer Robo.

NOMENMORTIS cut their debut album in April of 1999 entitled 'How I Learn to Bleed ... For The Things I Wish To Forget'. As a search for a label to release the product was on Mat'o left in July and was duly replaced by Peter in August. Tracks from the album sessions would appear on various compilations including 'Lacerations Of Brutality Vol. 1' issued by the American Razorback label and a Polish 'Burin' Abyss' fanzine CD.

May 2000 witnessed the induction of Erik on bass and shortly after NOMENMORTIS signed to the Japanese Jackhammer Music label to release the album in August. However, the line-up problems continued unabated, Šano Suchácek drifting off to join DEMENTOR and also pursuing his Progressive Metal project NOSTRUM. His position on guitar was taken by Martin.

HOW I LEARN TO BLEED ... FOR THE THINGS I WISH TO FORGET, Jackhammer Music LRW 018 (2000). Mercy Dies Right Now (Intro) / War Chant Of The Hated Spawn / Maggot Tribe / Tedd Deireadh—Conjunction For Armaggeddon / Left There Something To Live For? / Seen Through The Thorns Of Despair / Empyrium Of Mist / Something Almost Buried / Another Starblaze ... Another Tragedy?—The Swans Are Flying Towards The Flames / Unholy Voices Of Reason—Godexpeller / Outcry Of Senseless Sacrificed—Let Me Die At Last / Eternal Shadow Has Arrived (Outro).

NOMICON

HELSINKI, FINLAND — *Ceasar (vocals / bass), Trooper (guitar), Azhemin (guitar), Agathon (drums).*

Although trading under the pseudonyms Ceasar, Trooper, Azhemin and Agathon, Helsinki's NOMICON in fact comprises a quartet of Finnish Metal elite. Vocalist / bass player Ceasar (a.k.a. Tommi Launonen), having association with COARSE, GANDALF, GLOOMY GRIM, SOULGRIND, TENEBRAE and WALHALLA, is the primary motivator behind the project, which is generally regarded as a solo undertaking.

Launonen would be supported by guitarist Trooper, in fact Roope Latvala, of CHILDREN OF BODOM, DEMENTIA, LATVALA BROS, STONE, SINERGY, WALHALLA, WALTARI and WARMEN, rhythm guitar player Azhemin (Miika Niemelï), from RAVEN, SHAPE OF DESPAIR, SOULGRIND, THY SERPENT, WANDERER and WINTERMOON. Additional female vocals would be supplied by Whisper Lilith (Tanya Kemppainen) of SOULGRIND, LULLACRY and GLOOMY GRIM.

NOMICON's first presence was felt in 1990 with the inclusion of the track 'Contrast' on the Hard Blast Records, four way split 7" EP 'More Than Death vol.1' in alliance with SHUD, RADIATION SICKNESS and Dutch band NOCTURN. A three song demo, entitled 'Tri-Angle', surfaced in February 1991 with another single, 'De Rerum Natura', that same year.

In 1995 Belgian label Shiver Records partnered NOMICON with SARNATH for a split album entitled 'The Me'. Originally these tracks had been recorded for a UK label, Tombstone Records, but then shelved until a new deal had been located. Shiver then issued the full-length 'Yellow' album in 1997. This album, recorded at WALTARI's rehearsal rooms with equipment on loan from STRATOVARIUS, saw Janne Parviainen from WALTARI on session studio drums. Limited live work saw NOMICON taking the stage as a trio comprising Whisper, Ceasar and Trooper plus programmed drums.

A demo the following year, produced by Jussi Heikkinen, preceded the 2001 'Halla' album issued through Sagitarius Productions. By this juncture NOMICON had enlisted drummer Agathon (Ykä) being a veteran of AIRDASH, BARATHRUM, CORPORAL PUNISHMENT, GLOOMY GRIM, SOULGRIND, THY SERPENT and WALHALLA.

More Than Death vol.1, Hard Blast (1990) (Split 7" vinyl EP with SHUD, NOCTURN and RADIATION SICKNESS). Last Breath (SHUD) / Contrast (NOMICON) / Graveyard Without Crosses (NOCTURN) / Disfigured Retard (RADIATION SICKNESS).

Tri-Angle, Nomicon (1991) (Demo). In A Logic / To Material / Development.

De Rerum Natura, Nomicon (1992) (7" vinyl single). Pursuit / ... Of The Tightness.

THE ME / NORTHODOX, Shiver SHR011 (1995) (Split album with SARNATH). Category Mistake (NOMICON) / No Thing (NOMICON) / Occurrence (NOMICON) / Self (NOMICON) / Aged (NOMICON) / To Observe (NOMICON) / Conversion (NOMICON) / Talking About ... (NOMICON) / Arguing (NOMICON) / In The Flames Of Midsummer Pyre (SARNATH) / Silence Of The Lambs (SARNATH) / Covenant (SARNATH) / Walking Through Her Shrine (SARNATH) / The Fantome Reign (Kali Yuga) (SARNATH) / Marian Luostari (SARNATH).

YELLOW, Shiver SHR 022 (1997). Flight / Shade / Claritas / Northsky (Left Behind) / Down Below / Deep Waters / Predestination / Sermon / Fall / Mecca.

Nomicon, Nomicon (1998) (Demo). A Search (Beginning) / Denial / Saint.

HALLA, Sagitarius Productions (2001). Arrival / God Weaker Than Me / Denial / Saint / A Search / Grief / Tribe / Sacrifice / Demolished.

NOMINON

JÖNKÖPING, SWEDEN — *Jonas Mattsson (vocals / guitar), Juha Sulasalmi (guitar), Lenny Blade (bass), Perr Karlsson (drums).*

Jönköping Death Metal act founded during January 1993 by guitarist Juha Sulasalmi and vocalist Peter Nilsson following the demise of their previous band endeavour CHORONZON. As a duo, also performing in parallel as members of DION FORTUNE, they released two demos 'Daemon I' and 'Daemon II', both in 1993. This latter NOMINON session would see credits going out to Fafnir "howlings", Vvhorrkkh on guitar and Iaka on drums. However, in reality the tracks were once again recorded by just Juha Sulasalmi and Peter Nilsson.

NOMINON would put into stasis during 1994 but returned the following with a line-up comprising Sulasalmi on drums, vocalist Nicke Holstensson, guitarist Christian Cederborg, second guitarist Jonas Mattson of Thrash Metal act INCINERATOR and ex-DION FORTUNE bassist Tobbe Hellman. Both Cederborg and Mattson were also veterans of XYMONTHRA.

The unit's inaugural live performance came the following February with a gig supporting VERMIN, DISMEMBER and DISSECTION. Cederborg would be removed upon completion of the 'My Flesh' demo, Sulasalmi taking his place on guitar and TYRANT's Emil Dragutinovic taking over on drums. In this incarnation NOMINON cut a second demo that year, succinctly entitled 'Demo II'. The 'Promo '97' tape followed, after which Hellman was forced out and David Svartz of THE LEGION installed in his stead.

NOMINON gained national exposure in 1998 after they were featured on the Swedish television programme 'Sefyr'. Further line-up changes found Lenny Blade, from APOCALYPTIC VISIONS, BULLET, BEYOND DREAMS and INCINERATOR, taking the bass position. The departing Tobbe Hellman subsequently gained credits with OBSCENE and 9TH PLAGUE. That October NOMINON entered Sunlight Studios to record their debut album 'Diabolical Bloodshed', eventually released by X-Treme Records in November of 1999. Just after recording the band had conducted a lighting tour of Germany. They would return as support to WARHAMMER in April of 1999. In outside activity, Lenny Blade acted as guest vocalist on MAZE OF TORMENT's 2000 album 'Death Strikes'.

Emil Dragutinovic bowed out in September 2001. His profile rose considerably as he landed the coveted spot as drummer with premier league Black Metal veterans MARDUK. Dragutinovic also maintained his position with his longterm act THE LEGION. Meantime, NOMINON persevered with drums being handed over to Perr Karlsson. NOMINON vocalist Nicke Holstensson would join THY PRIMORDIAL during June of 2003. By February of 2004 drummer Per Karlsson was installed in the ranks of IN AETERNUM.

With Jonas Mattson now handling lead vocals NOMINON made a return in 2003 with the demo cassette 'Blaspheming The Dead', this featuring a cover version of REPULSION's 'Decomposed'. In February 2004 the band issued EP 'The True Face Of Death' on Nuclear Winter Records. In May the group lost the services of Lenny Blade, the bassist opting to prioritise his other acts INCINERATOR and BULLET. June 2004 saw the recruitment of IMMERSED IN BLOOD man Joel Andersson taking command of bass duties whilst Juha Sulasalmi was to handle lead vocals whilst the band searched for a new singer. Having signed a new album deal with Singapore's Konqueror Records the band would enter Necromorbus Studios in the Autumn. NOMINON also made time to cut a rendition of VOIVOD's 'Live For Violence' for a tribute album released through France's Nihilistic Holocaust Records, as well as a take on WHIPLASH's 'Spit On Your Grave'.

In September NOMINON, enlisting ABSURDO CULTO singer Daniel Garptoft (a.k.a. 'Sick'), joined the 'Thunderstorm Over Europe' tour allied with BENEDICTION and GODHATE. That year the band donated their cover version of 'Live For Violence' to a Nihilistic Holocaust Records tribute album to early VOIVOD. NOMINON, swelling their ranks further with the addition of second guitarist Kristian Strömblad of AD MORTEM, entered Necromorbus studios in Stockholm with engineer Tore Stjerna in January 2005 to cut a new album 'Recremation', once again for Konqueror Records. The vinyl limited edition version, on Blood Harvest Records, added the WHIPLASH cover 'Spit On Your Grave'. European gigs in October and November, traversing Austria, Italy, Switzerland, France, Spain, Portugal, Luxembourg and Holland, saw NOMINON as support act to VITAL REMAINS.

In 2006 Colombian label Trauma Records issued the rarities album 'Remnants Of A Diabolical History', a limited edition of 1000 copies. Included would be alternate versions, the previously unreleased 'Diabolical Bloodshed', covers of WHIPLASH, VOIVOD and REPULSION plus demos. NOMINON announced the induction of IMMEMOREAL, THE INFESTATION, ABSINTH, TRYMHEIM and PROPHANITY man Anders Malmström as new bassist in October.

NOMINON undertook pre-production throughout December then booked two weeks at Necromorbus Studio with producer Tore Stjerna during February 2007 to cut new album tracks, setting 'Terra Necrosis' as the title.

The band partnered with NUNSLAUGHTER and DEMONICAL for European concerts in July 2007.

Daemon 2, (1993). Whispers In The Polar Winds / Ur Skuggorna / Deep Bogs Of Depression / In This Cold Grave Of Mine / Frozen Mist Over Nordur.
Daemon 1, (1993). Intro: Voice Of The Obscure / My Flesh / Blodsblot / Brinn I Skarsald / Outro: In I Aspen.
My Flesh, (1996). Cemetary Of Life / My Flesh / Genocide / Outro.
Demo II, (1996). Consuming Divineness / Servants Of The Moonlight.
Promo '97, (1997). Night Of Damnation / Sodom's Fall / Consuming Divineness / Son Of The Dragon / Cemetery Of Life.
DIABOLICAL BLOODSHED, X-Treme CXR 11052 (1999). Malicious Torment / Sodom's Fall / Night Of Damnation / Servants Of The Moonlight / Cemetery Of Life / Son Of The Dragon / No Holy Ghost Shall Rise / The Sufferer.
Blaspheming The Dead, Nuclear Winter (2003) (Cassette release). Blaspheming The Dead / Invocations / Blessed By Fire / Decomposed.
DAEMONS OF THE PAST, Northern Silence Productions NSP 006 (2004) (Split album with FAFNER). Intro: Voice Of The Obscure / My Flesh / Blodsblot / Brinn I Skarsald / Outro: In I Aspen / Intro / Whispers In The Polar Winds / Ur Skuggorna / Deep Bogs Of Depression / In This Cold Grave Of Mine / Frozen Mist Over Nordur / Outro: Dress Me In Ice / Cemetery Of Life / My Flesh / Genocide / Outro.
The True Face Of Death, Nuclear Winter TPL 017 (2004). White Death / Amityville / The Lost Ones / Phantoms / Afterlife Desire.
Blaspheming The Dead, Nuclear Winter (2005) (7" single). Blaspheming The Dead / Invocations / Blessed By Fire.
RECREMATION, (2005). Submit To Evil / Hordes Of Flies / Buried By Me / The End Written In Blood / Mirror Of Dead Flesh / Sickening / Under The Five-pointed Star / Into Black / Condemned To Die.
REMNANTS OF A DIABOLICAL HISTORY, Trauma (2006) (Limited edition 1000 copies). Blaspheming The Dead / Invocations / Live For Violence / Cemetery Of Life / Servants Of The Moonlight / Diabolical Bloodshed / Spit On Your Grave / Blessed By Fire / Genocide / Decomposed / Sodom's Fall.
TERRA NECROSIS, Deathgasm (2007). Release In Death / Arcanum / Black Chapel / Ebola / Among The Beasts & Ancient Slumber / Life Extinct / Tabula Rasa / Hell Above / Bane Appetite / The Infernal Voyage.

NORDOR

ATHENS, GREECE — *Lordwinter (vocals), False Prophet (vocals / guitar), L.F.G. (bass).*

Athens Black Metal band NORDOR, first established during September 1989, features the GOATVOMIT credited False Prophet and NAER MATERON drummer Warhead. The first stable line-up would see False Prophet joined by guitarist Mardok, bass player Unblessed with Gore on drums. The demo 'Ceremony Of Demonic Brutality' was recorded on May 20th 1991. However, Mardok decamped that September. The remaining trio recorded tracks intended for a 7" single for the Italian label Obscure Plasma Records. When this product failed to materialise the songs were issued by the band in cassette form dubbed 'His Fictitious Grandeur'.

In August 1993 Unblessed left, necessitating False Prophet taking over four-string duties, and Blind Priest took Gore's place on the drums. In this formation NORDOR crafted the third demo 'The Semen Of Satan' in the winter of 1995. NORDOR folded and drummer Gore would subsequently make his mark as lead vocalist for HORRIFIED. Frontman False Prophet went on to NAISSANT. Sleaszy Rider Records combined material from all three demos to assemble the album 'Nordorian Manifestations' in March 2003.

A reformed NORDOR issued the demo 'Honoris Causa-Timhs Eneken', with producer Kane on drums, on June 6th 2006. Warhead enrolled the previous February. L.F.G. joined as bassist in October.

Ceremony Of Demonic Brutality, Nordor (1991) (Demo). The Apocalypse / Indelible Violations / Your Grave Is A Grand Cross.
His Fictitious Grandeur, Nordor (1993) (Demo). The End Of Necronomicon / Inside The Clouds / Labyrinth / The Entering Into The Psychotic Dimension.
To Sperma Tou Satana, Nordor (1997) (Demo). Nystagmus / God Dog / The Calling Of The Nereid / New Age / Virgin Mary's Holly Fuck With The Lilly.
NORDORIAN MANIFESTATIONS, Sleaszy Rider (2003). The Apocalypse / Indelible Violations / Your Grave Is A Grand Cross / The End Of Necronomicon / Inside The Clouds / Labyrinth / The Entering Into The Psychotic Dimensions / Nystagmus / God Dog / The Calling Of The Nereid / New Age / Mary's Holy Fuck With The Lily.
Honoris Causa-Timhs Eneken, Nordor (2006) (Demo).

NORSETH

RI, USA — *Nick Landmesser (vocals / guitar), Kevin Carr (guitar), Jen Grimes (bass), AJ Grimes (drums).*

NORSETH is rooted in the 2001 formation APOCALYPSE, a band comprising vocalist / guitarist Nick Landmesser, guitarist Kevin Carr and drummer AJ Grimes. Endeavouring to pursue a more professional approach the NORSETH title was taken on in 2002. For the next year the line-up remained fluid, employing a variety of vocalists and bassists. This situation would be stabilised in June of 2003 with the acquirement of Jen Grimes on bass. Ryan Moore of REIGN and APHOTIC RIVER enrolled as frontman in early 2004 but his tenure would be brief and a returning Landmesser duly filled the vacancy. NORSETH recorded the EP 'The Hexed Enigma' in late 2004.

Norseth, Norseth (2004). Relapse / Avert The Hour.

NORTHER

FINLAND — *Petri Lindroos (vocals / guitar), Kristian Ranta (guitar), Jukka Koskinen (bass), Tuomas Planman (keyboards), Toni Hallio (drums).*

NORTHER came together in 1996, first gelling as REQUIEM at the hands of vocalist / guitarist Petri Lindroos and drummer Toni Hallio. Later additions in 2000 would be guitarist Kristian Ranta and the Ekroos siblings Sebastian and Joakim. Having taken onboard the revised moniker of NORTHER this quintet's first set of demos secured a deal with the Spinefarm label. However, shortly after signature the Ekroos bailed out. The remaining trio soon inducted bass player Jukka Koskinen and keyboard player Tuomas Planman to cut the debut record 'Dreams Of Endless War'. The 2002 NORTHER album, the Anssi Kippo produced 'Mirror Of Madness', would see a Japanese release through the Avalon Marquee label which included a bonus track in the form of an unexpected cover of SKID ROW's 'Youth Gone Wild'. US editions released via the Century Media label added a bonus video clip. A 2003 EP, entitled 'Spreading Death', included a cover version of MEGADETH's 'Tornado Of Souls'.

Kristian Ranta forged a project band in 2004 entitled GASHOUSE GARDEN, comprising such scene notables as CRAYDAWN guitarist Jaakko Teittinen, the SINERGY, KOTIPELTO, WARMEN credited Lauri Porra on bass and CHILDREN OF BODOM drummer Jaska Raatikainen. Heading up the band would be female singer Mertsa, located whilst singing AC/DC covers with her band CHINA CAT.

In April of 2004 Petri Lindroos temporarily joined ENSIFERUM for tour work to promote the 'Death Unlimited' album. Swedish 'Spinetour' shows in September saw a package billing, partnering the band with FINNTROLL and THE WAKE. The band entered Astia Studios in Lappeenranta during December to record a new EP.

On 5th January 2005 Toni, Pete, Kride and Jukkis gathered with Finland's Metal community at Helsinki's Rock 'n' Roll Station to pay homage to the recently murdered PANTERA / DAMAGEPLAN guitarist Darrell 'Dimebag' Abbott by forming up a one off PANTERA tribute band DIMEN NIMEEN ("In Dime's Name!"). Musicians featured in this collective included Alexi Laiho and Roope Latvala of CHILDREN OF BODOM, Atte Sarkima from AJATARRA, Tony Jelencovich of TRANSPORT LEAGUE, Petteri Hirvanen and Nicke of MONSTERBALL, Ben, Juffi, Erkki, Niko and Silver of AMORAL, Nico, Euge and OJ from GODSPLAGUE amongst many others.

NORTHER entered Studio Fredman in Gothenburg during July to record a new studio album 'Till Death Unites Us'. However, the band parted ways with drummer Toni Hallio. A replacement would be found in VIRTUOCITY's Heikki Saari during November. The 'Scream' single entered the national Finnish charts at number 3 in January. 'Till Death Unites Us' duly charted in Finland at number 6.

NORTHER made an announcement they were set to unite with CANNIBAL CORPSE, KATAKLYSM and LEGION OF THE DAMNED for the April 2006 'No Mercy' European touring festival. However, the band was then forced off the billing before the trek started.

NORTHER's 'No Way Back' EP of February 2007 landed at the top spot on the Finnish charts upon release.

DREAMS OF ENDLESS WAR, Spinefarm (2002). Darkest Time / Last Breath / Released / Endless War / Dream / Victorious One / Nothing Left / The Last Night / Final Countdown. Chart position: 17 FINLAND.
Spreading Death, Spinefarm SPI191CD (2003). Death Unlimited / Tornado Of Souls.
MIRROR OF MADNESS, Avalon Marquee MICP-10357 (2003). Blackhearted / Betrayed / Of Darkness And Light / Midnight Walker / Cry / Everything Is An End / Unleash Hell / Dead / Mirror Of Madness / Frozen Sky / Smash.
DEATH UNLIMITED, Universal UICO-1059 (2004). Intro / Deep Inside / Death Unlimited / Chasm / Vain / A Fallen Star / The Cure / Day Of Redemption / Instrumental / Hollow / Nothing / Going Nowhere / Tornado Of Souls. Chart position: 18 FINLAND.
TILL DEATH UNITES US, Spinefarm (2005). Scream / Throwing My Life Away / The End Of Our Lives / Evil Ladies / Drowning / Die / Everything / Alone In The End / Norther / Omen / Fuck You / Wasted Years. Chart position: 6 FINLAND.
Solution7 EP, Spinefarm SPI228CD (2005). Day Zero / YDKS / Hellhole / Thorn / Chasm (Remix).
Scream, (2006). Scream. Chart position: 3 FINLAND.
No Way Back, (2007). Chart position: 1 FINLAND.

NOSFERATOS

MOSCOW, RUSSIA — *Lucifer (vocals), Acheron (guitar), Thomas (guitar), Jenya-Vanya (drums).*

Moscow Death Metal act NOSFERATOS are rooted in the 1993 formation GODFATHERS, created by vocalist Alexey Kondrin, bass player Charon (Deniss Kopkov) and drummer Mr. Foont. Both Kondrin and Foont had prior experience with STRONG MEAT and HATEWORK. With the introduction of guitarist Roman Osnovin in 1994 the band adopted the revised title of NOSFERATOS, being rounded out the following year by guitarist Sarkisyan Ashot and drummer Andrey 'Hich' Ahin'ko. The group debuted live that same year with a performance at the Moscow 'Thrash Your Mother' festival, after which the demo session 'Dances Of The Dead' was recorded and a track included on the 1996 compilation album 'Kot Of The Mutilated'.

A first attempt to record a projected debut album was aborted and shortly after Kopkov decamped to forge his own Black Metal project THE GATES OF DARKNESS, this group also including for a time Kondrin and Foont. A replacement for Charon was found in Denis Kravtsov. However, a relocation for Osnovin to Estonia, joining the Tallinn based POSTMORTEM, and then Ashot's move to the USA in December of 1997 put the band into hiatus for a lengthy period. Despite this, an album NOSFERATOS had been attempting to finalise for a number of years was finally completed. The 1998 album 'Ventum Inferum De Tenebrae', first manufactured in a run of 100 CDs and 300 cassettes, included a cover version of UNLEASHED's 'The Immortals'. The Ukrainian Moon Records label later picked the album up to distribute a further 1000 tapes.

NOSFERATOS would be re-constructed with Kondrin and Hich utilising the services of guitarist Sasha and bassist Arkady. Before long Sasha had joined the Russian army and Pasha took his place. Matters got confusing in September of 2000 when Hich was ditched and the EXCELLENCY and ASKAL credited Evgeny Ivanov brought in his stead but in November Hich had re-taken his place behind the drum kit for recording of the 'Pandemonium' album. Yet more changes in December of 2001 witnessed the departure of drummer Hich once again and the re-instatement of former percussionist Evgeny Ivanov.

During March of 2002 guitarist Pasha and bassist Arkady exited the band. NOSFERATOS in 2003 comprised vocalist Lucifer (Alexey Kondrin), the guitar pairing of Thomas (Roman Osnovin) and Acheron (Sarkisyan Ashot) with Jenya-Vanya (Evgeny Ivanov) on the drums.

VENTUM INFERUM DE TENEBRAE, (1998). Wandering In The Darkness / Dead In The Cellar / The Immortals / Souls Of Deceased / Zombie Revenge / The Antichrist Time / Evil Spirits Refuge / Dances Of The Dead / Outcast By Hell / Rebirth (Outro).

PANDEMONIUM, Blacksmith Productions (2001). Pandemonium / War Gods / The Scaffold / Autodafe (1478) / March Of The Scottish Vampires / Bloody Woods / Stench Of Temples / Advent Of Gloom ... The Triumph Of Darkness / Anomalous Abominations / Outro.

NOSTROMO

GENEVA, SWITZERLAND — *Javier (vocals), Jerome Pellegrini (guitar), Lad (bass), Maik (drums)*.

Geneva's NOSTROMO was forged during 1996, aiming to mix Thrash with both Hardcore and Grindcore influences. The debut album 'Argue in Autumn' arrived in 1998 on the local Snuff label but had been preceded by demos and the 1997 7" single 'Selfish Blues'. Promoting the album NOSTROMO toured France allied with label mates KNUT, this trek including an appearance at the Rennes 'Superbowl of Hardcore' in 1999.

NOSTROMO released their sophomore effort 'Eyesore' in July 2000 on Mosh Bart Industries. Touring would be extensive, traversing France partnered with ANANDA as support to BOTCH and THE DILLINGER ESCAPE PLAN before gigs with NASUM and NAPALM DEATH. Successive dates saw NOSTROMO journeying into Spain, Germany and Eastern Europe countries. In June 2001 the group returned to Spain as part of a package billing with HOPEFUL, LIKE PETER AT HOME and INSIDE CONFLICT.

The 'Ecce Lex' album, produced by Miesko Talarczyk of NASUM, was recorded for Overcome Records in early 2002.

Selfish Blues, Snuff (1997). Selfish Blues / Lost Souls.

Eyesore, (2000).

ECCE LEX, Overcome (2002). Rude Awakening / What Is Up In Your Cryotube? / Stillborn Prophet / End's Eve / Lab Of Their Will / Sunset Motel / Pull The Pin / Seeking An Exit / Ecce Lex / Feed The Living / Turned Black / Unwillingly And Slow.

HYSTERON-PROTERON, (2004).

NOUMENA

ÄHTÄRI, FINLAND — *Antti Haapanen (vocals), Tuukka Tuomela (guitar), Ville Lamminaho (guitar), Hannu Savolainen (bass), Ilkka Unnbom (drums)*.

Ähtäri melodic Death Metal band NOUMENA features frontman Antti Haapanen of FALMERS, EMULAATTORI SHEOL and CONSPIRACY WITHIN, guitarist Ville Lamminaho, previously of CADAVERS, EMULAATTORI, CONSPIRACY WITHIN and INFERION, second guitarist Tuukka Tuomela of INFERION and CONSPIRACY WITHIN, bass player Hannu Savolainen from CONSPIRACY WITHIN and ex-FALMERS, EMULAATTORI, CADAVERS and INFERION drummer Ilkka Unnbom.

NOUMENA was assembled in 1998, releasing their first demo 'Aeons', recorded at Studio Etnovox by produce Jruha Remsu, in June that same year. The 'For The Fragile One' follow up arrived in 1999. The group scored a deal with a label from Singapore but, whilst cutting tracks for an intended first album, they learned their record company had gone under. That November the group entered Astia Studios with Anssi Kippo and Jussi Jauhiainen behind the desk to cut more demo tracks. The 'Sala' session followed during April 2001, recorded by Arttu Sarvanne and Pekka Nurmi at Studio Watercastle. Australian label Catharsis Records picked up the archive 1999 tracks for issue as the 'Pride / Fall' album released in August 2002.

NOUMENA demoed again in 2004, crafting 'The Tempter' at Studio Tuononen and Old Man's Inn studios. Spikefarm Records released the 'Absence' album, laid down at Savonlinna's Sundi Coop studios, in 2005. NOUMENA utilised Savonlinna's Sundi Coop once again for recording of their third full-length album, 'Anatomy Of Life', in June 2006 via Spikefarm Records.

Aeons, Noumena (1998) (Demo). Phantasmagoria / Solemn Grace / Semper Fi.

For The Fragile One, Noumena (1999) (Demo). Lucid Dreaming / Silent Words / Bleakest Essence / Sin.

Noumena, Noumena (1999) (Demo). Catharsis / The Heralds Of Fall / Overture To An End.

Sala, Noumena (2001) (Demo). King Twisted / Innate 13 / The Doomwatcher / Igniter.

PRIDE / FALL, Catharsis CRCD 001 (2002). The Heralds Of Fall / Unlit / You Dance / Bleakest Essence / Lucid Dreaming / Overture To An End / King Twisted / Innate 13 / Doomwatcher / Ignifer / The Heralds Of Fall (Video).

The Tempter, Noumena (2004) (Demo). Here We Lie / First Drop / Dreamscape / Prey Of The Tempter.

ABSENCE, Spikefarm NAULA 061 (2005). End Of The Century / Everlasting Ward / First Drop / Slain Memories / Day To Depart / Prey Of The Tempter / Here We Lie / All Veiled / Dream & The Escape / Great Anonymous Doom.

ANATOMY OF LIFE, Spikefarm (2006). Misanthropolis / Burden Of Solacement / Retrospection / The Burning / Monument Of Pain / Triumph And Loss / Marionettes / Through The Element / Fire And Water.

NOVEMBRE

ITALY — *Carmelo Orlando (vocals / guitar), Antonio Poletti (guitar), Fabio Vignati (bass), Thomas Negrini (keyboards), Guiseppe Orlando (drums)*.

The Progressive Death Metal outfit NOVEMBRE started life as CATACOMB in 1990, but it wouldn't be before the Orlando brothers, vocalist / guitarist Carmelo and drummer Giuseppe, came to the fold that the pace picked up and, after a few more line-up changes, CATACOMB offered their first demo 'Unreal' in 1991. In 1993 the band issued their first 7" single 'The Return Of The Ark' on the Sacre Sindore label, selling 2,000 copies and leading to shows with AGATHOCLES and CARCASS. Giuseppe Orlando also saw activity with CARNAL RAPTURE.

In 1994, after Thomas Negrini and Fabio Vignati had joined the band, the NOVEMBRE handle was adopted and the group recorded their debut album, 'Wish I Could Dream Again', in Dan Swanö's Unisound studio.

The 1996 album 'Arte Novecento' would include a cover version of DEPECHE MODE's 'Stripped'. Second guitarist Massimiliano Pagliuso joined the group in Spring of 1997. Another change found Alessandro Niola taking over bass in late 1998.

NOVEMBRE

During 2000 Giuseppe Orlando and his erstwhile CARNAL RAPTURE colleague vocalist / guitarist Emilio Trillò, together with guitarist Antonio Poletti, put out a self titled demo credited to GHOULS.

NOVEMBRE would have a go at another cover version on their 2001 'Novembrine Waltz' opus, this time ambitiously tackling KATE BUSH's 'Cloudbusting'. NOVEMBRE toured Europe to promote the album on a package billing with OPETH and KATATONIA.

The band's European April 2004 'Gothic Easter' gigs found guitarist Massimiliano Pagliuso physically absent from the stage but still making his presence felt. Not being able to participate in the opening three shows due to a "sudden and yet unavoidable obligation," the band decided not to cancel any shows, instead utilizing a pre-recorded audio track of Massimiliano's guitar parts. Pagliuso rejoined the band for their Rome gig on 12th April.

That same year Giuseppe Orlando would act as producer for the DEINONYCHUS 'Insomnia' album, recorded in Rome at The Outer Sound Studio. NOVEMBRE signed a recording contract with Peaceville Records in July 2005 for fifth album 'Materia', recorded at Finnvox Studios in Helsinki, Finland. The group supported celebrated Swedes KATATONIA on their April / May 2006 European tour dates. In September Giuseppe Orlando joined the ranks of DEINONYCHUS.

WISH I COULD DREAM AGAIN, Polyphemous POLYPH001 (1995). The Dream Of The Old Boats / Novembre / Its Blood / Night / At Once / Let Me Hate / Sirens In Filth / Swim Seagull In The Sky / The Music / Nostalgia / Its Gaze / Behind My Window / My Seas Of South / Old Lighthouse Tale / The White Eyed / Neanderthal Sands / Christal.
ARTE NOVECENTO, (1996). Pioggia ... January Tunes / Homecoming / Remorse / Stripped / Worn Carilllon / A Memory / Nursery Rhyme / Photograph / Will / Carnival.
CLASSICA, Century Media (2000). Cold Blue Steel / Tales From A Winter Come / Nostalgiaplatz / My Starving Bambina / Love Story / L'epoque Noire (March The 7th 12973 AD) / Onirica East / Foto Blu Infinito / Winter / Outro—Spirit Of The Forest (Tales From A Winter Come- Reprise).
NOVEMBRINE WALTZ, (2001). Distances / Everasia / Come Pierrot / Child Of The Twilight / Cloudbusting / Flower / Valentine (Almost An Instrumental) / Venezia Dismal / Conservatory Resonance.
DREAMS D'AZOUR, Century Media (2002).
Memoria Stoica, Peaceville (2006) (Download EP). Memoria Stoica / Materia / Nostalgiaplatz (Acoustic) / Flower (Acoustic).
MATERIA, Peaceville CDVILE131 (2006). Verne / Memoria Stoica / Vetro / Reason / Aquamarine / Jules / Geppetto / Comedia / The Promise / Materia / Croma / Nothijngrad.

NOWEN

LAHTI, FINLAND — *Lappis (vocals / guitar), Kusmar Rotten (guitar), Terminator X (bass), Vominator (drums).*

Death Metal unit NOWEN was at first formulated as a side concern of WITHERIA guitarist Mikko "Lappis" Lappalainen during 1999, issuing a demo 'From Birth To Death'. Expanding into a band unit, a second demo, 'Cursed Or Blessed', arrived in 2002. Featuring on these sessions would be guitarist Kimmo Korhonen, bassist Jan Huovinen, both of JUMLHÄMÄRÄ and DIM MOONLIGHT, plus drummer Jarkko Turtiainen. An EP, 'Where Hell Begins', was recorded during September 2005, these songs being laid down by Lappalainen, handling vocals, guitar and bass, along with the WALTARI, ENFORCE and FALCHION credited drummer Ville Vehviläinen.

The 2006 band line-up comprised Lappis, Kusmar Rotten, Terminator X and Vominator, respectively Lappalainen, STARLIT BLACK and WITHERIA guitarist Markus Taipale, ex-SLUGATHOR, NIGHT MUST FALL and NERLICH bassist Jarno Nurmi, and Vehviläinen.

Where Hell Begins, Nowen (2005). Pathetic Existence / Breaking Point / Illusions / Where Hell Begins / With Pain.

NUCLEAR DEATH

AZ, USA — *Lori Bravo (vocals / bass), Phil Hampson (guitar), Joel Whitfield (drums).*

This cult-like Thrash/Death act has a certain reputation in the underground for paradoxically being both brutally bad and good at the same time. Founded in March 1986 in Tempe, Arizona the trio had a seldom seen phenomenon, a female vocalist and bassist. The band worked diligently in the underground and produced four demos 'Wake Me When I'm Dead' in 1986, 'Welcome To The Minds Of The Morbid' in 1987, a live ten track demo called 'A Symphony Of Agony' in November 1987 and finally in 1989 the session 'Caveat'.

By then the band was signed to the fledgling cult underground US Metal label, Wild Rags. The debut, 'Bride Of Insect' appeared in 1990. Staying with Wild Rags the band released 'Carrion For Worm' in 1991 which found Steve Cowan replacing Joel Whitfield on drums. The third release, 'For Our Dead' was delivered in 1992 and a subsequent cassette release 'All Creatures Great And Eaten'.

Bravo and Cowan did later leak a promotion recording dubbed 'The Planet Cachexial' credited to NUCLEAR DEATH but it seems the band have been inactive ever since. Extremist Records reissued the first brace of albums as a double package in 2000.

BRIDE OF INSECT, Wild Rags WRR017 (1990). Necrobestiality / Corpse Of Allegiance / Feral Viscera / Stygian Tranquility / Place Of Skulls / Cremation / The Colour Of Blood / The Beloved Whore Celebration / Fetal Lament: Homesick / Bride Of Insect / The Misshapen Horror / Vultures Feeding.
CARRION FOR WORM, Wild Rags WRR019 (1991). Spawn Song / The Human Seed / Proposing To The Impaled / Moribund / Greenflies / Return Of The Feasting Witch / A Dark Country / Lurker In The Closet: A Fairy Tale / Cathedral Of Sleep / Homage To Morpheus / Carrion For Worm / Vampirism.
FOR OUR DEAD, Wild Rags (1992). The Corpse Tree / Days Of The Weak / The Third Antichrist / The Church Of Evil Minds Of Splatterday Saints.

NUNSLAUGHTER

PITTSBURGH, PA, USA — *Don Of The Dead (vocals), Reaper (guitar / bass), Jim Sadist (drums).*

A notorious name in Death and Black Metal circles. NUNSLAUGHTER, not noted for their subtlety, date back to the late 80's with an initial incarnation of bassist Don Of The Dead, guitarist Jer The Butcher, vocalist Gregoroth and drummer Behemoth Bill. This line-up cut the opening 1987 'Ritual Of Darkness' cassette. Both Butcher and Behemoth would exit signalling a prelude to a turbulent career for the band as membership ebbed and flowed with each successive release. NUNSLAUGHTER's second demo, 1989's 'The Rotting Christ', saw the inclusion of guitarist Rick Rancid (Rick Metz) and drummer John Sicko.

1991 witnessed the departure of both Sicko and Gregoroth and the emergence of new drummer Vlad The Impaler as Don Of The Dead took over lead vocal duties for the provocatively titled demo 'Impale The Soul Of Christ On The Inverted Cross Of Death'. In 1993 the inaugural demo 'Ritual Of Darkness' was bootlegged in Brazil on a 7 single. Meantime, NUNSLAUGHTER laid down a fourth demo 'The Guts Of Christ', issued in April 1993, with predictably another skinsman Mark Perversion. 'The Guts Of Christ' was released twice, the first 300 copies in a full colour cover and a further 100 in a green design.

By 1995 NUNSLAUGHTER reconvened the original founding trio of Don, Gregoroth and Butcher. Along with drummer Jim Sadist (Jim Konya) another session 'Face Of Evil' was issued. The line-up did not stay the course though and soon new faces included bass player Chris 213 (Chris Pello) and guitarist Blood (Todd Thozeski) for a split 7 single with BLOODSTICK in 1997. This would herald a NUNSLAUGHTER tradition as further shared singles quickly surfaced shared with CRUCIFER, DECAPITATOR and female act DERKETA.

Later members include guitarist Megiddo and bassist Insidious. European touring in 2000 witnessed the temporary enlistment of SOULLESS guitarist Wayne Richards. The band signed to the German Barbarian Wrath label for the April 2001 album 'Radio Damnation', a 'live in the studio' offering. Yet another split 7" single saw the band sharing vinyl with arch Black Metal act GRAND BELIAL'S KEY for the 'Satan Is Metal's Master' release through the Danish Horror Records label. This release came in three types of coloured vinyl with 222 in 'Splatter green', 333 in gold and 444 pressings in standard black.

The band was put on hold temporarily in early 2002 as Jim Sadist undertook touring duties for 9 SHOCKS TERROR. Nevertheless, the NUNSLAUGHTER release schedule remained unaffected as the Dutch From Beyond Productions announced the release of the 'Waiting To Kill Christ' demo on CD and limited edition double gatefold vinyl. The 'Hell On Belgium' single comprised six tracks recorded at the Frontline venue in Gent, Belgium September 19th 2000.

NUNSLAUGHTER's Jim Sadist, billed as Jim Satanic, would form up part of THE SPAWN OF SATAN project band also involving SOULLESS guitarist Wayne Richards and INTEGRITY, SOULLESS and DECREPIT man Chris Dora on drums for a shared split album with BLOODSICK, another act to feature Jim. Yet another limited edition split 7" single, this time collaborating with CENTINEX, had the band offering a cover version of RUNNING WILD's 'Preacher' on the 'Hail Germania' EP. A new full-length album, 'Goat', saw issue in 2003, released in Europe by Revenge Productions and Metal War Productions in the USA.

NUNSLAUGHTER would tour Australia during August 2003, supported by Adelaide occult Death Metal band STARGAZER and REVEREND KRISS HADES. The 'Cerebus' single followed on Hells Headbanger Records, a limited pressing of 1000 pieces on clear vinyl. The same imprint entered into agreement to successively re-issue all of NUNSLAUGHTER's demos onto 7" EP format. The band then expanded its roster, inducting guitarist Deserter to record tracks for a split EP shared with NOCTURNAL put out through Polish label Agonia Productions.

That year the Swedish TPL imprint put out the 'Hate Your God' album, a collection of rehearsal tracks recorded on October 11th 2002 at Mother Mary's Vagina Rehearsal Studio. In 2004 Malaysian label Rhapsodeath Productions released a split live album with THE SPAWN OF SATAN, taped on July 19th, 2002 at The Revolution in Parma, Ohio. The 2004 EP 'The Supreme Beast', released by Ordealis Records, included a cover version of BLACK TASK's 'Kill Your Enemies'.

In 2006 the Hell's Headbangers label re-issued all the material from demos 'Ritual Of Darkness', 'The Rotting Christ', 'Impale The Soul ...', 'The Guts Of Christ', 'Face Of Evil' and 'Evil Speaks' on 7" singles all pressed on various coloured vinyls and enclosed in a metal box set dubbed 'Demoslaughter'. Only 100 copies were manufactured. Hells Headbangers maintained a steady pace of collectables throughout 2006 including a series of 7" singles culled from their November 2003 Australian dates—' Metal Assault On Adelaide', ' Metal Assault On Sydney', ' Metal Assault On Melbourne' and 'Metal Assault On Brisbane'. Soundtrack from the DVD ' Damned In Japan' also saw issue as a box set of four 7" singles.

The album ' An Evening At War' was to prove unique, as only 100 copies were pressed, ach with individual artwork hand drawn by Necrodamus. Split releases included an alliance with BRODY'S MILITIA, 'Punk As Fuck' featuring MISFITS cover versions, plus collaborations with MUTILATED MESSIAH and Ohio's DESTRUCTOR. The 'Fuck That Cunt' 7" single put out by Hungary's Terranis Productions comprised 2000 era rehearsal recordings including a version of VENOM's 'Hellchild'.

A burst of July 2007 European 'Nordic Nightmare' tour dates saw the support slot going out to Sweden's DEMONICAL and NOMINON.

Ritual Of Darkness, Nunslaughter (1987) (Demo. Limited edition 100 copies). I Am Death / Hells Unholy Fire / Killed By The Cross / NunSlaughter.
Rotting Christ, Nunslaughter (1989) (Demo. Limited edition 300 copies). Burn In Hell / Hells Unholy Fire / Death By The Dead / Killed By The Cross / Cataclysm / I Am Death.
Killed By The Cross EP, Whisper In Darkness (1990) (7' single. Limited edition, 300 red vinyl, 18 white vinyl copies). Burn In Hell / Hell's Unholy Fire / Death By The Dead / Killed By The Cross / I Am Deaths.
Impale The Soul Of Christ On The Inverted Cross Of Death, Nunslaughter (1991) (Demo. Limited edition 600 copies). Impale The Soul Of Christ On The Inverted Cross Of Death / Blasphemy Of The Flesh / Perversion Of Gore / Seas Of Blood / Altar Of The Dead / Inverted Churches / Alive But Dead / Burn In Hell.
The Guts Of Christ, Nunslaughter (1993) (Demo). Ritual Of Darkness / Guts Of Christ / Sacrificial Zombie / You Bleed / Church Of Disgust.
Face Of Evil, Nunslaughter (1995) (Demo. Limited edition 500 copies). Power Of Darkness / Pyre / Lyre / Lucifer / To Defile / Immortality / Face Of Evil / Slaughter The Heavens.
Nunslaughter / Bloodsick, (1997) (Split single with BLOODSICK). INRI (NUNSLAUGHTER) / Power Of Darkness (NUNSLAUGHTER) / Sacrifice (NUNSLAUGHTER) / Fear No God (BLOODSICK) / Smothered With Blood (BLOODSICK).
Blood Devil EP, Revenge Productions RVP 5 (1998) (White vinyl 7" single. Limited edition 1000 copies). Church Bizarre / Midnight Mass / It Is I / Poisoned Priest.
Trafficking With The Devil, The Crucifier Brotherhood International (1998) (Split 7" single with CRUCIFER). If The Dead Could Speak (NUNSLAUGHTER) / Devil Meat (NUNSLAUGHTER) / Black Beast (NUNSLAUGHTER) / Foul Deeds Will Rise (CRUCIFER).
Emperor In Hell, Midnight (1998) (Split single with DEKAPITATOR). Emperor In Hell (NUNSLAUGHTER) / Demon's Gate (NUNSLAUGHTER) / Bring Me The Head Of God (NUNSLAUGHTER) / Haunted By Evil (DEKAPITATOR) / Make Them Die (DEKAPITATOR) / Outro (DEKAPITATOR).
Evil Speaks, Nunslaughter (1999) (Rehearsal demo). Church Bizarre / Poisoned Priest / Armies Of The Dead.
Evil Dreams EP, Evil Dreams (1999) (Split single with DERKETA). Black Horn Of The Ram (NUNSLAUGHTER) / The Devil (NUNSLAUGHTER) / Murder By The Stake (NUNSLAUGHTER) / Intro / Crypts Of Darkness (DERKETA) / Begotten Son (DERKETA).
Trifurcate EP, Warlord WREP 03 (2000) (Italian release. 7" single. Limited edition 1000 copies). Fire / Obsessed With The Vision Of A Satanic Priest / Atheist Ways / The Fucking Witch.
HELL'S UNHOLY FIRE, Revenge Productions RVP 7 CD (2000) (Limited edition 3000 copies). Burn In Hell / Killed By The Cross / Death By The Dead / Perversion Of Gore / The Dead Plague / Cataclysm / Burning Away / Nun Slaughter / Blasphemy / Seas Of Blood / Altar Of The Dead / Satanic / Blood For Blood / Impale The Soul Of Christ On The Inverted Cross Of Death / I Am Death / Hells Unholy Fire.
Hell On Switzerland, Ordealis (2001) (Limited edition 500 copies). Fire / Power Of Darkness / Blood For Blood / The Fucking Witch / I Am Death.

Face Of Evil, Qabalah Productions (2001) (7" single. Limited edition 400 black vinyl, 100 red vinyl). Power Of Darkness / Pyre / Lucifer / To Defile / Immortalize / Face Of Evil / Slaughter The Heavens.

DEVIL METAL, Hell Attacks Productions HA 001 (2001). Intro / Emperor In Hell / The Dead Plague / It Is I / Blood For Blood / Killed By The Cross / Satanic / The Fucking Witch / Burn In Hell / Altar Of The Dead / Midnight Mass / INRI / Fire / Death By The Dead / Obsessed With Visions Of A Satanic Priest / The Dead Plague / NunSlaughter / In The Graveyard / The Black Horn Of The Ram / Midnight Mass / Devil Metal / Atheist Ways.

Hell On Germany, Bloodbath (2001) (Limited edition 500 copies). Face Of Evil / Emperor In Hell / Dead Plague / Midnight Mass / Killed By The Cross / INRI.

Rehearsal 1987, Nunslaughter (2001) (7" vinyl picture disc. Limited edition 1000 copies). I Am Death / NunSlaughter / Hells Unholy Fire / Killed By The Cross.

Satan Is Metal's Master EP, Horror HOR 006 (2001) (Split single with GRAND BELIAL'S KEY. Limited edition 222 splatter, 444 black, 333 gold vinyl). In The Graveyard / Torment / Hellchild.

RADIO DAMNATION, Barbarian Wrath WRATH666-007 (2001). Fire / Obsessed With The Visions Of A Satanic Priest / Midnight Mass / Killed By The Cross / Emperor In Hell / Power Of Darkness / Devil Metal / Death By The Dead / Atheist Ways / I Am Death / Church Bizarre / The Dead Plague / Altar Of The Dead / Blood For Blood / Black Horn Of The Ram / Satanic / It Is I / The Devil / Burn In Hell / I.N.R.I. / Poisoned Priest / Hellchild.

Nunslaughter / Dr. Shrinker, Revenge Productions RVP 10 (2001) (Split 7" single with DR. SHRINKER. Limited edition 500 copies orange vinyl). Ouija (NUNSLAUGHTER) / I Saw Your God Die (NUNSLAUGHTER) / Our Necropsy (DR. SHRINKER).

Satanic Salvation, Apocalyptor (2002) (Split 7" single with DESTRUKTOR. Limited edition 400 black vinyl, 100 red vinyl copies). Brutal Desecration (DESTRUKTOR) / She Lives By Night (NUNSLAUGHTER).

WAITING TO KILL CHRIST, Displeased (2002). The Dead Plague / Midnight Mass / Death By The Dead / In The Graveyard / Torment / I Saw Your God Die / Power Of Darkness / Obsessed With The Visions Of A Satanic Priest / Altar Of The Dead / The Fucking Witch / Fire / Nunslaughter / Bring Me The Head Of God / If The Dead Could Speak—Devil Metal / It Is I / Black Horn Of The Ram / As The Cacodemons Feast / Your Lord Deformed / Atheist Ways / Killed By The Cross / Church Bizarre / Emperor In Hell / INRI / Burn In Hell.

ONE NIGHT IN HELL, War Hammer WHR 004 (2002) (Limited edition 2000 copies). Fire / Death By The Dead / Obsessed With The Visions Of A Satanic Priest / The Dead Plague / Nunslaughter / Power Of Darkness / I Saw Your God Die / In The Graveyard / Church Bizarre / Midnight Mass / Killed By The Cross / Devil Metal / Your Lord Deformed / Black Horn Of The Ram / Emperor In Hell / Bring Me The Head Of God / Atheist Ways / INRI.

Sickened By The Sight Of Christ, Merciless (2002) (Split picture disc with CIANIDE. Limited edition 500 copies). Sickened By The Sight Of Christ (NUNSLAUGHTER) / Trust No One (CIANIDE) / Choose Your Death (CIANIDE).

Hell On Belgium, Menace To Sobriety (2002) (Limited edition 900 copies). In The Graveyard / Obsessed With The Visions Of A Satanic Priest / Burn In Hell / Burning Away / Nunslaughter / Satanic.

Hell On Spain, Christhunt Productions (2002) (7" single. Limited edition 500 copies, 400 black vinyl, 100 white vinyl). Death By The Dead / It Is I / Altar Of The Dead / Atheist Ways / Reign In Blood.

The Guts Of Christ, Qabalah Productions (2002) (Spanish release. 7" single. Limited edition 500 hand numbered copies). Ritual Of Darkness / Guts Of Christ / Sacrificial Zombie / You Bleed / Church Of Disgust.

HELL ON AUSTRIA, Agonia (2003) (Limited edition 300 hand numbered copies). Fire / Death By The Dead / Face Of Evil / The Fucking Witch / Emperor In Hell / Blood For Blood / Church Bizarre / Killed By The Cross / Midnight Mass / Burn In Hell / Atheist Ways / Obsessed With The Visions / Dead Plague / INRI / Power Of Darkness / Hellchild / Altar Of The Dead / Black Horn Of The Ram / Satanic / I Am Death / Devil Metal.

Hail Germania EP, Hell's Headbangers HELLS EP 001 (2003) (Split single with CENTINEX. Limited edition 1000 copies). Preacher (NUNSLAUGHTER) / Enchanted Land (CENTINEX).

Tasting The Blood of Your Savior ... Before His Soul Was Impaled, TPL (2003) (Swedish release. 7" single. Limited edition 515 copies). Blasphemy Of The Flesh / Burning Away / Seas Of Blood / Perversion Of Gore / Inverted Churches / Alive But Dead.

HATE YOUR GOD, TPL (2003). The Crowned And Conquering Hag / You Bleed / The Dead Plague / Power Of Darkness / The Fucking Witch / Midnight Mass / Emperor In Hell / Sacrificial Zombie / I Saw Your God Die / In The Graveyard / As The Cacodemons Feast / Burning Away / Satanic Slut / Altar Of The Dead / Burn In Hell / I Am Death / Angelhunt / Killed By The Cross / Bring Me The Head Of God / Ritual Of Darkness / Nunslaughter / Atheist Ways.

GOAT, Revenge Productions (2003). The Crowned And Conquering Hag / You Bleed / She Lives By Night / Sacrificial Zombie / Immune To Poison / Raid The Convent / As The Cacodemons Feast / Church Of Disgust / Satanic Slut / Ritual Of Darkness / The Guts Of Christ / Thou Art In The Kingdom Of Hell / Angel Hunt / The Sephiroth / Jesus Is Doomed.

Satanic Sluts, Nunslaughter (2003). Satanic Slut / Satanic Slut (Live 12-20-02) / Satanic Slut (Bitch Mix) / Satanic Slut (Live 10-18-02).

Rotting, (2003) (Limited edition 13 copies). Burn In Hell / I Am Death / Metallic Jam / Death By Dead / Cataclysm.

Cerebus, Hells Headbangers (2003). Mother, Cunt, Whore / Cerebus.

NUNSLAUGHTER / THE SPAWN OF SATAN, Rhapsodeath Productions (2004) (Split live album with THE SPAWN OF SATAN). Satanic Slut (NUNSLAUGHTER) / Immune To Poison (NUNSLAUGHTER) / Altar Of The Dead (NUNSLAUGHTER) / Church Of Disgust (NUNSLAUGHTER) / Midnight Mass (NUNSLAUGHTER) / She Lives By Night (NUNSLAUGHTER) / Killed By The Cross (NUNSLAUGHTER) / Obsessed With The Visions Of A Satanic Priest (NUNSLAUGHTER) / Devil's Ransom (THE SPAWN OF SATAN) / Witchcraft (THE SPAWN OF SATAN) / The Master (THE SPAWN OF SATAN) / The Everlasting Terror (THE SPAWN OF SATAN) / Ritual Murder (THE SPAWN OF SATAN).

On Our Way To Hell, Pentagram Warfare (2004) (Split rehearsal demo with VICTIMIZER). I Am Death / Death By The Dead / It Is I / Killed By The Cross / Power Of Darkness / Altar Of The Dead / Seas Of Blood / Ritual Of Darkness / The Dead Plague / Midnight Mass / Devil Metal / Blood For Blood / Inverted Churches / Emperor In Hell / INRI.

Impale The Soul Of Christ ... On The Inverted Cross Of Death, Hells Headbangers (2004) (Double 7" single pack. Limited edition 500 copies). Impale The Soul Of Christ ... On The Inverted Cross Of Death / Blasphemy Of The Flesh / Perversion Of Gore / Seas Of Blood / Altar Of The Dead / Inverted Churches / Alive But Dead / Burn In Hell / Burning Away.

Blasphemer, Nunslaughter (2004) (7" etched single. Limited edition 1000 copies, 500 black vinyl, 500 dark blue vinyl). Blasphemer.

The Supreme Beast, Ordealis (2004) (limited edition 666 hand numbered copies). The Supreme Beast / Phantom / Driving Out The Demons / Kill Your Enemies.

Metal Assault On Canberra, Lahti Metal Inquisition (2004) (Limited edition 7" single. 274 red vinyl, 274 black vinyl). As The Cacodemons Feast / Raid The Convent / Torment / I Saw Your God Die / Angelhunt / Crebus.

Hell On France, Drakkar Productions (2004) (French release. Limited edition 500 copies). Black Horn Of The Ram / Piranha / Hellchild / Ritual Of Darkness / Devil Metal / Church Bizarre.

Ritual Of Darkness, Hells Headbangers (2004). I Am Death / Hells Unholy Fire / Killed By The Cross / Nunslaughter.

The Bog People, My Mind's Eye (2004) (Limited edition 400 copies). Haunted Places / The Bog People / The Cryptic Aeon / Raid The Convent.

Foreshadow, Bestial Onslaught (2004) (split 7" single with GOATLORD. Yellow vinyl). Healing The Possessed (NUNSLAUGHTER) / The Fog (NUNSLAUGHTER) / Voodoo Mass (GOATLORD) / Sacrifice (GOATLORD).

Burn The Cross, Hells Headbangers (2004) (Limited edition 1000 copies). Burn The Cross / Ride My Nightmare / Burn The Cross / All Of The Dead.

Back To The Crypt, Horror HOR 011 (2004) (Split 7" single with SLAUGHTER. Limited edition 1300 copies). Nocturnal Hell (NUNSLAUGHTER) / Damned Be The Souls (NUNSLAUGHTER) / Children Of The Fire (SLAUGHTER) / Hell Hath Returned (SLAUGHTER).

Satan Shitting On Cunt, Deathstrike DR032 (2004) (Split 7" single with KRIEG. Limited edition 666 copies blue vinyl). Leave The Church Behind (NUNSLAUGHTER) / Titan (NUNSLAUGHTER) / Flesh Descending (KRIEG).

Christmassacre, Hells Headbangers HELLS MLP 001 (2004) (12" vinyl single with "Christ Killer" cut out. Individually hand etched). Deathlehem / Unholy Scriptures / Jewrusalem / Unclaimed Cadaver.

Scorn On The 4th Of July, Hells Headbangers HELLS EP 006 (2004) (Split 7" single with SOULLESS. Red splatter vinyl). As The Cacodemons Feast (NUNSLAUGHTER) / Altar Of The Dead (NUNSLAUGHTER) / Bleeding Darkness (SOULLESS) / Downward (SOULLESS).

Slutty Cryptic Mother, Nunslaughter (2005) (Limited edition 33 copies clear vinyl). Mother Cunt Whore / Cryptic Aeon / Satanic Slut.

OPEN SEPULCRE, Obliteration (2005) (Limited edition 999 hand numbered copies). Angelhunt / Church Of Disgust / The Guts Of Christ / The Sephiroth / Death By The Dead / The Dead Plague / Burning Away / Cataclysm (Alternative take) / Hell Yawns Before You / You Say My Name / Unholy Scriptures / Unclaimed Cadaver / Ride My Nightmare / Burn The Cross / Leave The Church Behind / Haunted Places / The Bog People / Haunted Places / Supreme Beast / Driving Out The Demons / Sick Boy / Midnight Mass / Obsessed With The Visions Of A Satanic Priest / In The Graveyard / Raid The Convent / Satanic Slut / Altar Of The Dead.

Bedeviled, Hells Headbangers HELLS EP 010 (2005) (Split 7" single with THRONEUM). Shadow World (NUNSLAUGHTER) / You Say My Name (NUNSLAUGHTER) / Infernal Waves (THRONEUM) / Waiting For Perdition (THRONEUM).

Cut God Out, Hells Headbangers HELLS EP 011 (2005) (Split 7" single with HAEMORRHAGE).

ON OUR WAY TO HELL, Ancient Darkness Productions (2005) (Limited edition 363 copies). I Am Death / Death By The Dead / It Is I / Killed By The Cross / Power Of Darkness / Altar Of The Dead / Seas Of Blood / Ritual Of Darkness / The Dead Plague / Midnight Mass / Devil Metal / Blood For Blood / Inverted Churches / Emperor In Hell / INRI.

The Guts Of Christ—1993 Demo, Hells Headbangers HELLS EP 013 (2005) (7" single. Limited edition 400 hand numbered copies). Ritual Of Darkness / Guts Of Christ / Sacrificial Zombie / You Bleed / Church Of Disgust.

The Guts Of Christ—1993 Demo, Hells Headbangers HELLS PEP 009 (2005) (7" picture disc. Limited edition 100 hand numbered copies). Ritual Of Darkness / Guts Of Christ / Sacrificial Zombie / You Bleed / Church Of Disgust.

The Rotting Christ, Eccocentric 151 (2006) (3" MCD in metal box). Burn In Hell / Hells Unholy Fire / Death By The Dead / Killed By The Cross / Cataclysm / I Am Death.

Nunslaughter / Nocturnal, Agonia (2006) (Split 7" single with NOCTURNAL).

Fathers Of Fright, Nunslaughter (2006) (Limited edition 33 clear vinyl). Impale The Soul / Perversion Of Gore / Burning Away / Seas Of Blood.

Fuck That Cunt, Terranis Productions (2006). It Is I / Blood For Blood / Altar Of The Dead / Atheist Ways / Hellchild / INRI.

NUNSLAUGHTER, Unisound (2006). Death By The Dead / Dead Plague / Hells Unholy Fire / Ouija / Torment / The Fucking Witch / Atheist Ways / Black Horn Of The Ram / Resurrection / Midnight Mass / Black Beast / Devil Metal / Bring Me The Head Of God / Demons Gate / Power Of Darkness / INRI / Cataclysm / Burn In Hell.

Fuck The God In Heaven, Hells Headbangers HELLS 007 (2006) (Picture disc shaped CD single). Damned To The Souls / From The Sea / Your Lord Deformed / Satans Blood.

Fuck The God In Heaven, Hells Headbangers HELLS PLP 009 (2006) (12" picture disc single. Limited 333 copies). Damned To The Souls / From The Sea / Your Lord Deformed / Satans Blood.

Face Of Evil—1995 Demo, Hells Headbangers HELLS PEP 010 (2006) (7" picture disc single. Limited edition 100 copies).

Face Of Evil—1995 Demo, Hells Headbangers HELLS EP 015 (2006) (Limited edition 400 hand numbered copies). Power Of Darkness / Pyre / Lucifer / To Defile / Immortalize / Face Of Evil / Slaughter The Heavens.

GOAT, Hells Headbangers HELLS 006 (2006). The Crowned And Conquering Hag / You Bleed / She Lives By Night / Sacrificial Zombie / Immune To Poison / Raid The Convent / As The Cacodemons Feast / Church Of Disgust / Satanic Slut / Ritual Of Darkness / The Guts Of Christ / Thou Art In The Kingdom Of Hell / Angel Hunt / The Sephiroth / Jesus Is Doomed / Preacher.

Demoslaughter, Hells Headbangers HELLS BOX 001 (2006) (Metal tin box set. 9 7" coloured vinyl singles. Limited edition 100 copies).

Metal Assault On Sydney, Hells Headbangers (2006).

Metal Assault On Melbourne, Hells Headbangers (2006).

Metal Assault On Brisbane, Hells Headbangers (2006).

Metal Assault On Adelaide, Hells Headbangers (2006) (Limited edition 500 copies).

Punk As Fuck, Hells Headbangers (2006) (Split 7" single with BRODY'S MILITIA. Limited edition 500 copies).

NYCTOPHOBIC

GERMANY — *Christian Zimmermann (vocals), Markus Burgert (guitar), Markus Zoen (bass), Tom Will (drums).*

A very brutal Grindcore act founded in 1992 by drummer Tom Will and bassist Markus Zorn. Other early recruits were guitarist Christopher and vocalist Stephan with second guitarist Martin Hub added in June of 1994. NYCOTOPHOBIC are unfortunately blessed with a vocalist whose style makes it rather difficult to understand a word he's singing! We are assured, however, that the group's lyrics can often be very political in nature! Shortly after NYCTOPHOBIC dispensed with Stephan and drafted singer Alex Schulze for a 1995 demo. Tracks from these sessions formed part of their split single 'Four Ways To Misery' on M.M.I. records. This was quickly followed by a further 7" EP 'Negligenced Respect' prior to a split EP with the undisputed kings of the format Belgian fellow Grindsters AGATHOCLES.

Both Christopher and Schulze decamped in December of 1995 and NYCTOPHOBIC enlisted singer Christian Zimmermann and guitarist Markus Bugert for the full length album 'War Criminal Views'.

In 1997 NYCTOPHOBIC toured Europe with EXHUMED and HEMDALE. A further split 7" venture with ENTRAILS was released the same year. A three way split CD shared with MESRINE and Canadian act TRAUMATISM surfaced in 2000.

Four Ways To Misery EP, M.M.I. (1994). Four Ways To Misery.
Split EP, Lull Rex (1994) (Split EP with AGATHOCLES). Split.
Negligenced Respect, M.M.I. (1994). Negligenced Respect.
WAR CRIMINAL VIEWS, Morbid MR 029 (1996). Earthrise / Horrid Truth / Inner Manipulation / Access Denied / Jehova's Liars / Fundamentals / Rapid Eye Movement / Suffer Life / War Criminal Views / The Pain Of A Conquered Being / Racial Hierarchy / The Remaining Silence / War Seeds / Responsibilities / Denial / Destructive Ignorance / Theatric Symbolization Of Life.
Split EP, T&M (1997) (Split EP with ENTRAILS). Split.
NYCTOPHOBIC, Exacerbate Nasty Deteriorated (2000) (Split album with MESRINE and TRAUMATISM). Denial / Skit / War Criminal Views / Jehova's Liars / Skit / Rapid Eye Movement / Access Denied / Skit / Inner Manipulation / The Remaining Silence / Skit / Horrid Truth.
INSECTS, Morbid (2000). They / Taught To Fear / Haze / Walls Of Seclusion / Unconsciously Dead / Co(g)-existence / Never To Be Led / Ill-justice / World Turns Red / Waste Of Time / Restless / Swallow / Spit It Out / Needless Compromises / X / Pride Breeds Rage / Insects / Co(g)-existence (Caught in the Vortex Remix).

NYIA

OLSZTYN, POLAND — *Michal Pawluc (vocals), Jaroslaw Labieniec (guitar), Szymon Czech (guitar), Maciej Banaszewski (bass), Wojciech Szymanski (drums).*

NYIA is an avant-garde Death Metal combo forged by erstwhile IMPURITY, VADER and DIES IRAE guitarist Jaroslaw 'China' Labieniec. After recording the groundbreaking VADER output of 'The Darkest Age', 'Future Of The Past', the 'Sothis' EP and 'De Profundis' Labieniec broke away to create NYIA. Early singers involved with the project included Bogdan Kondracki and YATTERING's Svierszcz. His co-conspirators for a 2000 EP would be former PROPHECY and ENTER CHAOS guitarist Szymon Czech, ex-LENG bassist Maciej Banaszewski, PROPHECY singer Michal Pawluc and the NEUMA and KOBONG credited drummer Wojciech Szymanski.

Signing to the British Candlelight label NYIA cut the 'Head Held High' album at Selani Studio in Olsztyn for May 2004 release.

Nospromo 2000, (2000). Moloch / Niti / Pulap-ka / Naga.
HEAD HELD HIGH, Candlelight CANDLE098CD (2004). Behind The God / Over The Ceaseless Dying / Pails Of Blood / Everything Is A Dream / Foul Adder / The World's Throat / Heads Of The Insane / Only Whats Mine Is True / Bad Daddy / Wherever Youll Be / Head Held High / Nothing Can Stop Procreation.

OBITUARY

BRANDON, FL, USA — *John Tardy (vocals), Trevor Peres (guitar), Allen West (guitar), Daniel Tucker (bass), Donald Tardy (drums).*

Hailing from the same Florida town as NASTY SAVAGE, Brandon's OBITUARY purvey unadulterated brutal Death-gore Metal. The band, one of the first graduates from the sunshine state's Death Metal alumni, started out in 1985 as a school band originally known as EXECUTIONER before the subtle name change to XECUTIONER. With a line-up of guitarist Trevor Peres, with the Tardy brothers, vocalist John and drummer Donald rounding things out—the band issued a self financed single under the original name, EXECUTIONER, 100 copies on 7" vinyl and 500 copies on cassette, 'Metal Up Your Ass' / 'Syco-Pathic Mind' on their own Xecution Music Productions label. Further recordings came in the form of a two song demo 'Find The Arise' and 'Like The Dead' which eventually surfaced on the 'Raging Death' Godly Records compilation.

Adopting the new title of OBITUARY, so as to avoid confusion with Boston's EXECUTIONER, the band initiated recording of a full-length album for Godly Records, but were to sign the tapes over to Roadrunner prior to completion. The 'Slowly We Rot' sessions had been conducted at Morrisound Recording in Tampa, albeit on a primitive 8 track machine, with Scott Burns acting as producer. Although this combination would soon become synonymous with the entire genre, 'Slowly We Rot' was in fact Scott Burns first ever commercial undertaking.

'Slowly We Rot' crawled out into an unsuspecting world in April 1989. Although acts such as DEATH had pre-empted them, OBITUARY certainly took Death Metal beyond the apex of established acceptability, the ferocity and primal nature of Jon Tardy's vocal delivery in particular easily being the most extreme delivered at that time. Of equal import would be the scything nature of guitarists Allen West and Trevor Peres prosecution of duties, carving out fresh musical terrain that opened the floodgates for a Florida infestation of eager disciples, MALEVOLENT CREATION, DEICIDE, MORBID ANGEL, CANNIBAL CORPSE et al. Shunned by the mainstream, its sub-cartoon artwork not aiding exposure, 'Slowly We Rot' was to find a hallowed throne in metal's gutter regions.

The group suffered a setback when bassist Daniel Tucker was officially listed as a missing person in Florida after disappearing on May 1st. Tucker was later found alive in September having seemingly suffered injury and partial amnesia in a car crash. After recovering he chose not to pursue a "Heavy Metal lifestyle'.

Allen West quit in 1990 just as the group had added Frank Watkins to fill the vacancy left by Tucker's decision not to rejoin. West, who subsequently joined SIX FEET UNDER and LOWBROW, was replaced by ex-AGENT STEEL, HALLOWS EVE and DEATH guitarist JAMES MURPHY in time to record the 'Cause Of Death' album, which included a cover of Swiss avant-garde merchants CELTIC FROST's 'Circle Of The Tyrants'. 'Cause Of Death', a more convoluted, at times close to progressive outing, emerged in September 1990.

The band debuted this revised line-up with February 1991 Mexican gigs supported by CENOTAPH, BLOODSOAKED, BLACK THORN and RIPPING FLESH. UK followed dates in May, supported by CEREBRAL FIX. The following year Murphy departed to join British deathsters CANCER and West was reinstated as the band set out touring America opening for SACRED REICH. Third effort 'The End Complete', again produced by Scott Burns, saw issue in April 1992. The band's standing was now such that the album intruded into both the UK and German national charts.

A fourth opus, the supremely tight 'World Demise' of 1994 found OBITUARY slotting in a short European co-headline tour towards the end of the year sharing the billing with Brazilians SEPULTURA, support coming from ROLLINS BAND and VOODOO CULT. OBITUARY toured Europe in 1995 headlining over EYEHATEGOD and PITCHSHIFTER.

'Back From The Dead' was ushered out during 1997 and that April saw OBITUARY back on European soil, heading up the 'Full Of Hate' Easter festivals alongside ENTOMBED, DEATH, SAMAEL, NEUROSIS, CROWBAR, KILLING CULTURE and STRAPPING YOUNG LAD. The band's run had come to a halt though. Shortly afterward the band splintered. In late 1997 Roadrunner chose to re-issue the first two albums in remastered form with the addition of bonus tracks. Fans were kept guessing into the next year with a live album, suitably titled 'Dead', recorded at the Axis in Boston, Massachusetts on September 10th 1997.

Nearly three years of inactivity ensued before fans learned that the group had ceased operations. Peres created a side project titled CATASTROPHIC in 2000. Roadrunner laid a fitting tombstone on OBITUARY's career with the 2001 Anthology release. This collection not only compiled tracks from the four albums to date but also previously unheard demo cuts, including a cover of VENOM's 'Buried Alive' culled from the 'World Demise' sessions. Noteworthy inclusions came from MASSACRE guitarist J.P. Chartier and bassist Jerome Grable on the demo 'Find The Arise'.

In 2002 it emerged that erstwhile drummer Donald Tardy had joined the backing band for the much vaunted ANDREW W.K. Three-fifths of the classic OBITUARY line up, The Tardy brothers along with bassist Frank Watkins, would reunite on stage at the ANDREW W.K. 'Ozzfest' July 27th gig in West Palm Beach, Florida to perform OBITUARY tracks, fuelling rumours of a reformation. The band members finally revealed plans for a new album, billed as 'Frozen In Time', in January of 2004. The group persuaded producer Scott Burns to come out of retirement and revisited Morrisound studios to capture the authenticity. A concession to the modern world came with the employment of producer Mark Prator, utilising his Tampa ProTools studio, Red Room Recorders. Meantime, Trevor Perez allied himself with an unlikely collaborator, donating his skills as studio guests to Rapper MC NECRO's album 'The Pre-Fix For Death'. OBITUARY, MASTER and VISCERAL BLEEDING teamed up for the 'The Legends Are Back' dubbed European tour, commencing in early October.

'Frozen In Time' emerged in July 2005, charting in Germany but just upfront of touring in union with NAPALM DEATH in the USA during the Autumn of 2005 guitarist Allen West announced his departure. However, within 24 hours of that statement West rejoined the band.

OBITUARY headed up European touring in January and February of 2006 with support from SAMAEL and German Hardcore band MAROON. The band played a gig in Barcelona, Spain on 27th January as a quartet when guitarist Trevor Peres unable to fly out of Italy due to severe weather conditions.

The band hooked up with GOJIRA and GOREROTTED for a run of UK dates in August 2006. OBITUARY's August 24th concert at the Stodola Club in Warsaw, Poland was captured on film for release as a DVD, entitled 'Frozen Alive', through Metal Mind Productions. On November 18th the band appeared at the Monterrey Metal Fest event at the at the Coca Cola Auditorium in Mexico alongside BLIND GUARDIAN, CATHEDRAL, U.D.O., EDGUY, BLUDGEON, DEICIDE, LEAVES' EYES, SADUS, VAINGLORY, HYDROGYN and JOE STUMP'S REIGN OF TERROR.

Mexican shows in May 2007 saw SADUS as support.

SLOWLY WE ROT, Roadracer RO 9489-2 (1989). Internal Bleeding / Godly Beings / Till Death / Slowly We Rot / Immortal Visions / Gates To Hell / Words Of Evil / Suffocation / Intoxicated / Deadly Intentions / Blood Soaked / Stinkpuss.

CAUSE OF DEATH, Roadracer RO 9370-2 (1990). Infected / Body Bag / Chopped In Half / Circle Of The Tyrants / Dying / Find The Arise / Cause Of Death / Memories Remain / Turned Inside Out.

OBITUARY (pic: Linda Aversa)

THE END COMPLETE, Roadrunner RR 9201-2 (1992). I'm In Pain / Back To One / Dead Silence / In The End Of Life / Sickness / Corrosive / Killing Time / The End Complete / Rotting Ways. Chart positions: 43 GERMANY, 52 UK.
WORLD DEMISE, Roadrunner RR 8995-2 (1994). Don't Care / World Demise / Buried In / Redefine / Paralyzing / Lost / Solid State / Splattered / Final Thoughts / Boiling Point / Set In Stone / Kill For Me. Chart position: 59 GERMANY.
CAUSE OF DEATH, Roadrunner RR 8767-2 (1997). Infected / Body Bag / Chopped In Half / Circle Of The Tyrants / Dying / Find The Arise / Cause Of Death / Memories Remain / Turned Inside Out / Infected (Demo Version) / Memories Remain (Demo Version) / Chopped In Half (Demo Version).
BACK FROM THE DEAD, Roadrunner RR 8831-2 (1997). Threatening Skies / By The Light / Inverted / Platonic Disease / Download / Rewind / Feed On The weak / Lockdown / Pressure point / Back From The Dead / Bullituary.
DEAD LIVE, Roadrunner RR 8755-2 (1998). Download / Chopped In Half / Turned Inside Out / Threatening Skies / By The Light / Dying / Cause Of Death / I'm In Pain / Rewind / 'Til Death / Kill For Me / Don't Care / Platonic Disease / Back From The Dead / Final Thoughts / Slowly We Rot.
FROZEN IN TIME, Roadrunner RR 8156-2 (2005). Redneck Stomp / On The Floor / Insane / Blindsided / Back Inside / Mindset / Stand Alone / Slow Death / Denied / Lockjaw. Chart positions: 93 GERMANY, 147 FRANCE.

OBLITERATION

NEW YORK, NY, USA — *Jose Guzman (vocals), Thomas Pioli (guitar), Cesar Vallejo (bass), Alex Glass (drums).*

New York Death Metal combo OBLITERATION feature the PUTRIFACT, HEMLOCK and CEREMONIUM credited guitarist Thomas Pioli. The guitarist had also performed bass duties on INCANTATION's 'Onward to Golgotha' tour of 1992. The group issued the 'Winter' demo in 2003. In November of that same year Pioli stepped back into the ranks of INCANTATION as session player for their South American tour. Frontman Jose Guzman exited in April of 2004 and rhythm guitarist Cesar Vallejo soon followed. However, in June Vallejo returned to the fold. Drafting bass player Mike Greenfield OBLITERATION tried out for the 'Ozzfest' festival 'Unsigned band' competition.

That September OBLITERATION rhythm guitarist Cesar Vallejo announced the formation of a brand new Thrash Metal project entitled CREMAINS, an alliance with OBLITERATION session man Christian Vallejo on guitar, the MYSELF AM HELL and ACTIVATOR credited Gabe Mera on second guitars and

OBLITERATION

Javier Medina of BLOOD OF KINGS and SUN DESCENDS on drums. In December Cesar Vallejo quit once again, although would stay on until the band found a replacement.

In April 2006 Thomas Pioli announced OBLITERATION was no more.

Winter, Obliteration demo (2003) (Demo). In The Fields Of Hallucination / Bestial Tribulations / To Greener Plains.

OBSCENE

JÖNKÖPING, SWEDEN — *Henrik Olin (vocals), Mikael Wedin (guitar), Alex Andersson (bass), Olaf Landen (drums).*

Jönköping brutal Death Metal band OBSCENE debuted with a 2001 rehearsal demo. A self-titled demo emerged in 2002 followed up by 2003's 'Laceration Of The Unborn' session, this set including a cover version of MORTICIAN's 'Bone Crusher'. The band also contributed the track 'Gates To The Dead' to the 2003 compilation album 'El Grinding Mafiozos'. OBSCENE bassist Tobbe Hellman held a prior record with DION FORTUNE and NOMINON. Hellman vacated, subsequently joined Black Metal act 9TH PLAGUE in August 2004 but vacated his position there the following July. New man on bass would be Alex Andersson of SVARTNAR. OBSCENE drummer Olaf Landen also sessioned for SVARTNAR.

2005 saw a split release of 'Laceration Of The Unborn' with BESTIAL DEVASTATION through Redrum Records.

Rehearsal '01, Obscene demo (2001). Addiction / Necrophile / Cannibalistic Vomit / Infernal Wrath.
Demo '02, (2002). Presence Of Evil / Gates Of The Dead / Separation / Infected.
Laceration Of The Unborn, (2003). Intro / Appetite For The Dead / Laceration Of The Unborn / Consuming Through Disembowelment / Abstract Form Of A Woman / Bone Crusher.
LACERATION OF THE UNBORN, Redrum (2005) (Split album with BESTIAL DEVASTATION). Intro / Appetite For The Dead / Consuming Through Disembowelment / Laceration Of The Unborn / Abstract Form Of A Woman / Bonecrusher.

OBSCENE CRISIS

QUÉBEC, QC, CANADA — *Eric Fiset (vocals), Stéphane Côté (guitar), Jean-Pierre Côté (guitar), Yan Chamberland (drums).*

Québec Death / Grind outfit OBSCENE CRISIS, notably including twin guitarists Stéphane Côté and Jean-Pierre Côté, was assembled during 1992. Stéphane Côté was an original founder of KATAKLYSM. A six song demo, 'Modern Hypocrisy', was recorded in 1994. Former bassist Yan Thiel forged NEURAXIS that same year. Thiel also held association with ADENINE and TORN WITHIN. Another formative member, drummer Martin Auger, holding ELEMENTS credentials, also split away to join Thiel in NEURAXIS.

OBSCENE CRISIS followed with a self-funded album 'Silence Of The Mind', produced by OBLIVEON guitarist Pierre Rémillard, recorded by singer Eric Fiset, the Côté siblings, bassist Chrystian Boyer with Stephane Chartrand on drums. The band replaced Boyer with Martin Riendeau but folded in 1997. The band was re-structured during 2003, adding EMPATHY DENIED, DYING DAWN and ENRAGED drummer Yan Chamberland, but collapsed without having issued further product.

During 2004 Eric Fiset and Yan Chamberland, working with NEURAXIS guitarist Steven Henry and DYING DAWN bassist Daniel Daris, forged EMPATHY DENIED.

Modern Hypocrisy, Obscene Crisis (1994) (Demo). Intro—La Porte De Truck / Modern Hypocrisy / Terrorist Airline / Dead World Of Illusion / Hunting Safari / Headrush.

SILENCE OF THE MIND, Obscene Crisis (1995). Off Season / Illogical Responsibilities / Headrush / Human / Ecology / Open Mind / Obscenity / Out Of Cage / Animated Hallucination / Street Of Insecurity / Emotional Abusive Consummation.

OBSCENE EULOGY

CANADA / FINLAND — *Tapio Wilska (vocals), Disease (guitar / bass / keyboards / programming), N. Hate (guitar).*

A joint Finnish / Canadian Black Metal concept based in Saint John, New Brunswick. The project is mentored by Disease (a.k.a. Jamie Vautour) of BOUND IN HUMAN FLESH and BEYOND THE GOAT, handling guitar, bass, keyboards, drum programming, together with guitarist N. Hate. OBSCENE EULOGY released a demo called 'A Portal Into Fire' in March 2002 on the Unexpected Death Music label. This session featured guest lead vocals from Mika Luttinen of IMPALED NAZARENE. Baphomet Records re-released these demos as an EP in January the following year, adding an intro 'Rivers Of Blood In The Mind Of Horror'.

Remaining on the Baphomet imprint, OBSCENE EULOGY's full-length album 'Defining Hate: The Truth Undead' emerged in early 2004. For this outing the group was credited as Disease "Population Control", N "Forever Raping the Continuum of Life" and Mika Vitun Luttinen "Preacher of Doom and Unearthly Voice of Hatred". Guests included keyboard player Graeme McCausland, Tapio Wilska on 'Helvettiin' and Killjoy of NECROPHAGIA, contributing lyrics and vocals to the track 'Mortem Paradise'.

Subsequently, Wilska, a scene veteran of LYIJYKOMPPANIA, FINNTROLL, WIZZARD, SETHIAN, NATTVINDENS GRÅT and TOTAL DEVASTATION.

A Portal Into Fire, Unexpected Death Music (2002). Burn Again / Mark Ov The Beast / Pyövelin Kutsu / Hatred In The Form Of A Serpent / By Any Means Necessary / The Portal.

A Portal Into Fire, Baphomet (2003). Rivers Of Blood In The Mind Of Horror / Burn Again / Mark Ov The Beast / Pyövelin Kutsu / Hatred In The Form Of A Serpent / By Any Means Necessary / The Portal.

DEFINING HATE: THE TRUTH UNDEAD, Baphomet (2004). Defining Hate / Jyrsikää Kyrpää / Lehmänsilmät / Elämälle Kiitos / Kuolleen Vitun Himo / Reflection Of The Dead / Itsemurhana Ratkaisu / Helvettiin / Mortem Paradise.

OBSCENITY

OLDENBURG, GERMANY — *Oli (vocals), Henne (guitar), Jens (guitar), Thimo (bass), Sascha (drums).*

OBSCENITY, founded in Oldenburg during 1989, recorded a demo entitled 'Age Of Brutality' in 1991 before the arrival of the debut album on West Virginia Records in 1993. A further demo, 'Amputated Soul', gained the band a deal with D&S Records. Original guitarist Dirk was to be replaced by Jens, whilst the bass player's position was eventually filled on a permanent basis by Thimo.

OBSCENITY toured in Europe supporting the likes of CANNIBAL CORPSE, BENEDICTION, DEATH and SINISTER. The band parted ways with D&S Records in January of 1996 to sign with the Morbid label. In May 2000 the band enrolled Marc-Andrée "Mücke" Dieken on the drums, also an active member of PAIN FOR PLEASURE and Thrashers BK 49.

OBSCENITY would form part of a gargantuan Death Metal tour of Europe in March 2002 promoting new album 'Cold Blooded Murder'. On the bill alongside OBSCENITY would be IMMORTAL, HYPOCRISY, VADER, DISBELIEF, CATASTROPHIC, MALEVOLENT CREATION and DESTROYER 666.

OBSCENITY bassist Alexander Pahl joined DEW-SCENTED in 2003. Drummer Marc Andree Dieken temporarily joined the ranks of DEW SCENTED for 2004 European touring. The group contracted with Armageddon Music for the release of their seventh album, 'Where Sinners Bleed', recorded at Soundlodge studio in Rhauderfehn, for June 2006 release. OBSCENITY parted ways with bassist Alexander Pahl in November.

The band announced the addition of bassist Gregor to the group's ranks in April, the new recruit making his live debut with the band on April 21st at the 'Metal Inferno' festival in Paderborn.

SUFFOCATED TRUTH, West Virginia WVR 084-57262 (1993). Forgotten Past / Utter Disgust / Depression / Ruthless Greed / Fatal Lorosity / Life Beyond / Age Of Brutality / Corrupted Minds / Infestical Plague.

PERVERSION MANKIND, D&S Records DSRCE 021 (1995). Realm Of The Dead / Lost Identity / Amputated Souls / Perversion Mankind / Removal Of Poverty / Para-Dies / Embryonic Execution / Genutopia / The Revenge / Mental Death / Prophecy II.

THE 3rd CHAPTER, Morbid (1996). Jonathan (Intro) / Disgrace Over You / Nuclear Holocaust / Sensation Mongering / Disengaged / I'm Your God / Abducted And Gutted / Still Alive / Tarot / Schattenspiele.

HUMAN BARBECUE, Morbid MR 039 (1998). Eaten From Inside / Human Barbecue / Eternal Life / Infanticide / Soulripper / Lycanthropy / Utter Disgust / Dress Of Skin / Life Beyond / Obscenity / Raining Blood.

DEMO-NIAC—THE 10th ANNIVERSARY ALBUM, Morbid MR055 (1999). Embryonic Execution / Amputated Souls / Mental Death / Para-Dies / Gene-Utopia / Prophecy / Portal To Obscenity- Fatal Curiosity / Age Of Brutality / Utter Disgust / Corrupted Minds.

INTENSE, Morbid (2000). Bleed For Me / Pride Of Creation / Golden Cage / Suck My Vomit / Ripping Your Torso / Final Breath / Phenomenon Time / Mental Emptiness / Return Of The Crows.

COLD BLOODED MURDER, Morbid MR 093 (2002). Intro / The Arrival / Caught In Life / My Dark One / Alien Hand Syndrome / Sleepwalker / Blessed By Nature / Soulpain / Cold Blooded Murder.

WHERE SINNERS BLEED, Armageddon (2006).

OBSCURANT

JYVÄSKYLÄ, FINLAND — *Luukkainen (vocals / guitar), Mika Kaakkolahti (guitar), M. Honkonen (bass), A. Simonen (keyboards), Järvinen (drums).*

Jyväskylä Death Metal band, manifested initially a solo venture of Luukkainen during 2000. After pulling a full band unit together just two gigs convinced Woodcut Records to sign the band in Spring of 2002, the result being debut album 'Lifeform: Dead'.

Luukkainen (a.k.a. 'L.L. Infection') is active with TROLLHEIM'S GROTT, UNVEILED and Black Metal band ALGHAZANTH. OBSCURANT guitarist Mika Kaakkolahti, as 'Thasmorg', also holds down membership of ALGHAZANTH. Bassist M. Honkonen ('Horgath') is a member of Doom act SWALLOW THE SUN and Black Metal band FUNERIS NOCTURNUM. Both keyboard player A. Simonen and drummer Järvinen (a.k.a. 'Gorath Moonthrone') are also ALGHAZANTH personnel with the latter also maintaining the drum position with UNVEILED.

OBSCURANT returned in 2005 with the album 'First Degree Suicide'.

LIFEFORM: DEAD, Woodcut CUT020 (2002). Ending Life / Face In The Mirror / Symbiosis / Destination Lifeless / Death Declaration / The First Day / Resurrection / Obsessed To Kill / Gallery Of Disgust / Dying Request.

FIRST DEGREE SUICIDE, Woodcut CUT038 (2005). In The End / The Redemption / Guardian Angel / First Degree Suicide / A Wasteland / Light From Above / Blinded By Love / Dead Calm Surface / 170603 (Memoir).

OBSECRATION

GREECE — *Kostas Dead (vocals), Manolis Ps. (guitar), John (guitar), Spiros Ruthven (bass), Alexandros (drums).*

Formed in 1991 rooted in the Death Metal acts PARAKMI, MORBID ILLUSION and CURSE. The duo of vocalist Kostas Dead and drummer Jim first forged an alliance in 1989 with the band PARAKMI. This unit would evolve into MORBID ILLUSION with the inclusion of INSANITY bassist Nectarios and guitarist John from NECROMANCY.

In 1990 another name change occurred this time to CURSE as new faces bassist Billy and guitarist Apostolis were welcomed. In 1991 the final name switch came as CURSE became OBSECRATION with Billy switching instruments to bass as Nectarios returned to take over the guitarist's role for the debut demo 'Petrified Remains'. However, the group lost Nectarios in July as he departed to fulfill his national service obligations. In September OBSECRATION plugged the gap by enlisting ex-AVATAR members guitarist Nick and bassist Sotiris for their first gig. Predictably the line-up fractured once again with Billy joining EPIDEMIC and both Nick and Sotiris leaving.

1992 witnessed further changes with the return of Billy and Sotiris as well as new guitarist John for the second demo session 'The Morning Of The Ghoul'. Further live work ensued utilizing the services of erstwhile BLOOD COVERED drummer Angelos to promote the band's first commercial release the 'Oblivious' EP on Molon Lave Records. By March the bass position was temporarily in the care of Spiros from SEPTIC FLESH prior to Leftiris assuming the role.

OBSECRATION cut their full length debut album 'The Inheritors Of Pain', produced by Magus Wampyr Daoloth of NECROMANTIA, for the Dutch Hammerheart label with unsurprisingly a revised line up comprising of Kostas Dead, guitarists Spiros N. and Billy, bassist Spiros Ruthren and drummer Paul

OBSECRATION's line up ebbed and flowed thereafter with John rejoining replacing Spiros N. before he and brother Paul bailed out. By 2000 former LEPROSY members guitarist Manolis and drummer Alexandros were involved. Kostas would become a founder member of TERRA TENEBRAE but would depart prior to recording of their 'Subconscious' album.

Guitarist John and bassist Ruthven of OBSECRATION would session for WOLFCRY on their demo 'The Ivory Tower'. Ruthven would also feature as session bassist on WOLFCRY's subsequent 'Power Within' debut album.

The band would issue a split album in league with KORRODEAD, 'Last Vision Before Obliteration', through the Sleazy Rider label in May 2002. Lead guitarist Manolis Ps. Decamped and the NIGHTFALL credited guitarist George Bokos duly took on the guitar role for recording of the album 'Sins Of The Flesh'. Bokos also sessioned on 2003 demos from SICKENING HORROR.

Oblivious, Molon Lave (1995). Oblivious.
THE INHERITORS OF PAIN, Hammerheart (1995). The Inheritors Of Pain Part I / Horror In The Gothic Genie's Game / For The King Of This World / ... The Usurper From Darkness / Suffering Under The Unnamable Shade / The Serenity Of The Crystal Sentiments / Offsprings Of The Black Dimensions / The Inheritors Of Pain Part II.
OCEANUM OBLIVIONE, Invasion INV015 (2000).
CLUB WOODSTOCK, (2001). Intro / Closed In The Coffin / The Last Vision Before The Obliteration / From The Depths Of Our Dreams (The Inheritors Of Pain Part IV) / State Of Grace / Obsecration / Shadows Of Damnation / Where The Slime Lives / My Vision And My Dream / I Am An Odious Ghoul / The Inheritors Of Pain / Grotesque / The Intruder / Marble Jaws Of Oblivion.
THE LAST VISION BEFORE OBLITERATION, Sleazy Rider SR 0002 (2002) (Split album with KORRODEAD). Black Dahlia From Astral Ocean (Intro) / Closed In The Coffin / The Last Vision Before The Obliteration / From The Depths Of Our Dreams (The Inheritors Of Pain part IV) / State Of Grace / Obsecration / Shadows Of Damnation / Terra Tenebrae (outro).
SINS OF THE FLESH, Sleazy Rider SR 0006 (2002). Ravenous / An Odour Of Decay / (We Are) The Almighty Contract (The Inheritors Of Pain Part V) / Sins Of The Flesh / Dark Goddess Of The Moon / Hordes Of Disgust / Ex-Oblivione / Subconscious Cruelty.

OBTRUNCATION

HOLLAND — *Anton (vocals), Luc van Ravels (guitar), Tibor Lilkes (guitar), Martin Steigenga (drums).*

OBTRUNCATION, claiming to be the "Fastest Dutch Metal band", is a Dordrecht based Death Metal band dating back to 1989, being founded by vocalist Luc van Ravels, guitarist Frank, bassist Roeland and drummer Martin Steigenga. Demos included 'Sanctum's Disruption' in December 1990 and 'Sphere Of The Rotting' the following year, the latter seeing the incorporation of new singer Lawrence Payne and bass player Arjan Meerkerk as van Ravels shifted to guitar. OBTRUNCATION then signed to a French record label, cutting twelve songs for an intended debut album, which never transpired.

The band folded, but would be resurrected during 1998, now sporting a line up of van Ravels and Steigenga being joined by LAMENTATION and B.S.E. singer Lex van den Heuvel (also operating as drummer for BAILED OUT), guitarist Michel Wijngaard and LAMENTATION bass player Marco Besjis.

Singer Anton joined the fold in 2002 with rhythm guitarist Tibor Lilkes, another LAMENTATION member, enrolling in 2003.

THE CALLOUS CONCEPT, Damnation (1997). Parish Of Perdition / Mutual Hatred / Gruesome Assembly / Sanctum's Disruption / A Bedraggled Scheme / Things That Were And Shall Be Again / Aroused By The Deceased / Sphere Of The Rotting / Repudiated Angel / Church Of Delusion / Pernicious Saviour / Witch From Akyrz.

OCEANS OF SADNESS

DESSEL, BELGIUM — *Tijs Vanneste (vocals), Tom Van Cauwenberghe (guitar), Wim Melis (guitar), Jo Van Heghe (bass), Hans Claes (keyboards), Guy Vernelen (drums).*

OCEANS OF SADNESS, a Dessel based Gothic Doom combo, recorded their 2004 album 'Send In The Clowns' at Midas Studio in Lokeren, Belgium with producer Tony De Block. The record was mastered by Attie Bauw. The arrival of 'Send In The Clowns' would be marked by a special release concert at The Eendracht in Dessel, Belgium on 27th October, where the band performed the album in its entirety. Unfortunately, OCEANS OF SADNESS was forced to cancel all scheduled tour dates after their singer, Tijs Vanneste, became hospitalized with a collapsed lung. The singer underwent surgery and was pronounced fit once more in January 2005.

Vanneste would be found active in two extracurricular endeavours in the Spring, his own "strange electronical" concept THE JEF VAN ECHELPOEL EXPERIENCE and with a project of TRIGGERFINGER's Paul Van Bruystegem.

OCEANS OF SADNESS inked a deal with Italy's Scarlet Records in January 2007. The group's fourth album, entitled 'Mirror Palace', was produced by Jens Bogren at Fascination Street Studio in Örebro, Sweden. It included a cover version of ALICE IN CHAINS' 'Them Bones'.

FOR WE ARE, The LSP Company LSP001 (2001). As The Feast Begins / For When You Sleep, My Love / Re-Erase / A Dying Nightingale / Again The Wolf Wins / The Apocalypse / When We Became One / Oceans Of Sadness / Your Faith / How / Judas.
LAUGHING TEARS, CRYING SMILE, LSP Records LSP010 (2002). Sinner's Dream / So Close / One Entire Shield Of Pain / From The Seed To The Flower / Cold / Accepting Our Weakness / We Are Alone / Schizophrenia / Shadows / Try To See.
SEND IN THE CLOWNS, Apache Productions (2004). Communication. Relation. Illusion. / Who's In Control / Wild Mystery / Two Voices / Conflict. Error. Disillusion. Denial. / Eyes Like Fire /

Where Oceans Begin / Ode To The Past / Precious Gold / Frustration. Anger. Resignation. / See The Angels / You've Slain / Hope Is Gone.
MIRROR PALACE, (2007). Mould / Mirror Palace / Cruel Sacrifice / Sleeping Dogs / Intoxicate Me / The Bones / Sheep And Shepherds / Pride And Shame / Silence Is Gold / I Know You Know.

OCTOBER TIDE

SWEDEN — *Mårten Hansen (vocals), Jonas Renske (vocals / drums), Fredrik Norrman (guitar / bass).*

OCTOBER TIDE are the outfit created by KATATONIA's vocalist Jonas Renske, also known under his stage name of 'Lord Seth'. Guitarist Fredrik Norrman, besides citing KATATONIA credentials himself, is an erstwhile member of FULMINATION and UNCANNY. Frontman Mårten Hansen has affiliations to A CANOUROUS QUINTET, VOTUR and SINS OF OMISSION. A 1995 promotional tape preceded the 1997 album 'Rain Without End'. OCTOBER TIDE's 1999 album 'Grey Dawn' was recorded for Avantgarde Records.

Renske involved himself in the BLOODBATH Black Metal supergroup in 1999 alongside his KATATONIA band mate guitarist Blackheim, OPETH's Mikael Akerfeldt and EDGE OF SANITY's Dan Swanö.

RAIN WITHOUT END, Vic VIC003 (1997). 12 Days Of Rain / Ephemeral / All Painted Cold / Sightless / Losing Tomorrow / Blue Gallery / Infinite Submission.
GREY DAWN, Avantgarde (1999). Grey Dawn / October Insight / Sweetness Dies / Heart Of The Dead / Floating / Lost In The Dark—And Then Gone / Into Deep Sleep / Dear Sun.

OF TREES AND ORCHIDS

GERMANY — *Florian Engelke (vocals / guitar), Karsten Schöning (vocals), Sascha Hermesdorf (bass), Heinz Dirk Janssen (drums).*

A supremely inventive Oldenburg based Death Metal act convened in 1997 at the hands of former GALLERY OF DARKNESS guitarist Florian Engelke, lead vocalist Marcel Schomakers, bass player Felix Engelke and Heinz Kassens on the drums. Atypically the band trod a somewhat oblique Metal path, blending elements of classical German literature such as the works of Wolfgang Borchert with extreme melodies. This avant-garde approach would be amply illustrated by the debut album 'Fragmente aus dem Fliessenden', recorded by Florian Engelke and Heinz Kassens along with new guitarist Karsten Schöning of GALLERY OF DARKNESS and DEFORMED. A later addition was to be bass player Dennis Eickenhorst.

During early 2001 Kassens opted out to prioritise his Stoner band THE MILLSTONE. Heinz Dirk Janssen of DESPONDENCY swiftly enrolled to fill the drum vacancy but then Eickenhorst exited. Nevertheless, OF TREES AND ORCHIDS regrouped in the recording studio to cut the sophomore album 'Thought-Cathedral'. The membership for this occasion comprised Engelke, Schöning, Janssen and bass player Sascha Hermesdorf.

OF TREES AND ORCHIDS evolved into INGURGITATING OBLIVION in the midst of recording the August 2001 album 'Cadence And Perspective'.

FRAGMENTE AUS DEM FLIESSENDEN, Independent (1998). Sublimer Sturm I / I Am swimming In The End / Intermezzo / Of Trees And Orchids / Antiquitäten / In Search Of Infinite Cognition (...) / Meine Doktrine / Sublimer Sturm II.
THOUGHT-CATHEDRAL, Independent (2000). Primordial Dullness / Thought-Cathedral / Solitude Reflection On Linear Despair / Beyond The Thought-Cathedrals Gorge / Nyarlathotep / Cocooned By Crawling Chaos / Of Trees And Orchids.

OFFENSE

VALENCIA, SPAIN — *Mariano (vocals / bass), Javi (guitar), Loren (guitar), Wensho (drums).*

Valencia Death / Doom band OFFENSE were formed in 1990 by the trio of Javi, Loren and Wensho. They were soon joined by bassist Fede and vocalist Murgui and this line-up recorded the demos 'The New Crusade' and 'The Cry'. 'Basic' went on to sell more than 1'200 copies.

Tragically, Fede perished in a cycling accident on the 14th December 1990 and this event not only prevented OFFENSE from rehearsing but led to the departure of Murgui. Another demo, 'Basic', surfaced in 1993.

Once over the grief of losing their band mate OFFENSE recruited vocalist/bassist Mariano and the group later signed to Abstract Emotions and issued the 7" 'Shining Down' EP in 1995. An album was to follow

The Cry, (1991). The Cry / Killing Animals / Payaso! / Ive The Reason (And Also The Gun) / On In 92 / (Falsa) Navidad.
The New Crusade, (1991). Parallel Generation / Colonization / Fucking Doubt! / Killing Animals / The Country Of Liberty? / Heroes Of Shit.
Basic, (1993). Eternal Dream / Visions / Natural Hope / Heroes Of Shit (New version) / Orthopedic Smile / Basic.
Shining Down EP, Abstract Emotions (1995). Shining Down / Seating Distress.
ASIDE, Abstract Emotions AE 003 (1995). Seating On Distress / Why? / The Defect / Law Of Life / Shining Dawn / Aside / Basic.
ABSENCE, Neuron (1999). Elgon Shadow / The Hangman / Doll Of Destiny / The Tree Of Wisdom / Useless Innocence / Difficult / Absence / A Letter To God.

OMINOUS

MALMÖ, SWEDEN — *Anders Sjöholm (vocals), Soren Sandved (guitar), Johan Saxin (guitar), Dan Johansson (bass), Joel Cirera (drums).*

Hailing from Malmö, technical Death Metal band OMINOUS trace their history back to 1991. With the introduction of guitarist Soren Sandved the band set about recording their debut demo recordings. Second guitarist Johan Saxin was inducted upfront of a second demo, 1995's 'Sinister Evocation'. At this juncture Anders Sjöholm of MASSGRAV and THE FORSAKEN took command of the lead vocal responsibilities. During 1998 Thomas Lejon of MISTELTEIN and EMBRACED would be the man behind the drum kit. BLINDED's Joél Cirera took on the job in 2001.

OMINOUS signed to the French Holy Records label for their debut album. Sandved would deputise for THE FORSAKEN for live work.

THE SPECTRAL MANIFEST, Holy HOLY56CD (2000). A Piece Of Humanity / Cry For Dawn / Soon To Be Broken / Forever Remains True / Crossing Boundaries / Drained By A Soul / Keep In Graceful Memory / Center Of Gravity / Object Of Lust / Frequent Redemption.
VOID OF INFINITY, Holy HOLY 77 (2002). Onerous / Immersed By Insanity / Blind Without Sight / Load, Aim, Fire / 13 Days / Breath Of A New Dawn / Omnipresent Ill / Dragons Breathe / Temptation.

OMINOUS

NJ, USA — *Victor Gonzalez (vocals / guitar), Drew Kerwin (bass), Jayson Meerholz (drums).*

OMINOUS is a three piece New Jersey based Death Metal band that was formed in the Winter of 2001 by vocalist / guitarist Victor Gonzalez and drummer Jayson Meerholz. This duo would cut an inaugural, four song demo minus bass guitar but by March of 2003 had drafted bassist Eric Dahlberg, performing their first live show on 16th May. OMINOUS would follow this with an appearance at the 'Milwaukee MetalFest' that same year.

Dahlberg was let go in February of 2004 in favour of Josh Hammond, known as a guitarist with acts such as CASKET, SANGUINARY and solo concern NINE-IRON. That March the Yavcon/Mozer company custom built a Victor Gonzalez signature guitar 'The Desecrator'. The band contracted a deal with Chicago-based label Rotting Corpse Records in early 2005. Their debut album, entitled 'Intercorpse', emerged in early 2006. A promotional video for the track '13 Years Of Pain', was directed by Michael Saladino.

OMINOUS, Ominous (2003). Intro / What Is There For Me / Intercorpse / Lifeless / Emptiness / Tears Of Fear / 13 Years Of Pain / Dead Cunt / Rank / The Sleeper / Heart Of Sorrow.

INTERCORPSE, Rotting Corpse (2006). Intro / What Is There For Me / Intercorpse / Lifeless / Emptiness / Doomed With Innocence / Tears Of Fear / Infected Flesh / 13 Years Of Pain / Behind The Shaded Skies / Dead Cunt / Rank / Battered / The Sleeper.

OMNIUM GATHERUM

ADELAIDE, SA, AUSTRALIA — *Brad (vocals), Rocco (guitar), Dave (guitar), Matthew (bass), Johno (drums).*

A Death / Grind combo forged in 1997 by erstwhile SEXUAL INTERCORPSE duo of guitarist Rocco and drummer Johno, subsequently adding bass player Justin and vocalist Brad. Demo sessions in March of 1998 and 1999 preceded the album 'Rectifying Human Rejection', released through Tasmania's Life Fluid Productions. Indonesian label Extreme Souls Production later took the album on for cassette release. For these sessions Justin was superseded by Paul Stewart, also a member of DEATH'S BOUNDARIES. A new 2002 studio recording, 'Anus Sulfurus Opus Windus', featured on a Necrotardation zine compilation album.

With Stewart making his exit, OMNIUM GATHERUM pulled in David Dinsdale as temporary bass man. In early 2004 new recruits guitarist Dave and bassist Matthew entered the fold. OMNIUM GATHERUM personnel Rocco and Johno are both also active with Adelaide Gothic Metal act ... OF THE HUMAN CONDITION.

RECTIFYING HUMAN REJECTION, Life Fluid Productions (2001). Irate Oration / Irate Oration Too / Deeply Felt Intensity / Conspiracy Theory / A Frown On The Face Of Mars / The Wrath Of Parasites / Pedestrian / Insignificunt / Idiosyncrasies Of Others / A / Imperative Revamp / Rectifying Human Rejection / Omnium Gatherum.

OMNIUM GATHERUM

KYMINLINNA, FINLAND — *Antti Filppu (vocals), Harri Pikka (guitar), Markus Vanhala (guitar), Janne Markkanen (bass), Mikko Pennanen (keyboards), Jarmo Pikka (drums).*

A surrealistic Death Metal band hailing from the town of Kyminlinna. Gearing up for the release of the 2003 debut album 'Spirits And August Light', issued by the British Rage Of Achilles label, OMNIUM GATHERUM filmed a video for the track 'Writhen', directed by Ville Salonen. The clip included new keyboardist Jukka Perälä of MANITOU. That same year the OMNIUM GATHERUM credited Aapo Koivisto joined Kotka Death Metal band BREEDING CHAMBER as lead vocalist.

The band entered Sonic Pump Studios in Helsinki with engineer Nino Laurenne during June of 2004 to record an album initially entitled 'Fall Grave Silence' but subsequently switched to 'Years In Waste'.

In 2004 the Progressive Heavy Metal band MANITOU, featuring both Perälä and guitarist Markus Vanhala alongside frontman Markku Pihlaja of BARABBAS and KAIHORO and the OLOS trio of bassist Ismo Laukkanen, drummer Matti Suhonen and guitarist Antti Laurén cut a debut album 'The Mad Moon Rising'. Valhala also divided his duties further between GORE PENETRATION and MALPRACTICE.

The band signed to Nuclear Blast Records in August 2004 in preparation for the album 'Years In Waste', a promotional video upfront of this release being filmed for the track 'The Fall Went Right Through Here'. The album was recorded at Sonic Pump studios in Helsinki with producer Nino Laurenne and engineer Teemu Aalto then mastered at Finnvox studios in Helsinki.

OMNIUM GATHERUM, AMORAL, ELENIUM, MANITOU and KIUAS united for the November 'Dead Achilles' tour of Finland. To coincide with the 9th November release of 'Years In Waste' Nuclear Blast also re-published the band's 'Spirits And August Light' album and 'Steal The Light' EP on one CD with revised artwork and a new layout. December found the group in Pyhtää's Woodbine Garden Studios recording renditions of MEGADETH's 'Hangar 18' and DEATH's 'Suicide Machine'.

The band opened 2005 with a January package tour of Finland allied with BONEGRINDER and headliners DISMEMBER. Vanhala would also help form a one off band to back ex-IRON MAIDEN singer PAUL DIANNO for his appearance at the 'Sirkkelirock Metal Awards' on 8th January at the Tavastia club in Helsinki.

OMNIUM GATHERUM's 2005 live schedule included festival appearances at Germany's 'Party.San Open Air' in Bad Berka and Finnish events the 'Tuska' festival in Helsinki, the 'Jalometalli' festival in Oulu, the 'Dark River' festival in Karhula and the 'Räntämetalli Icehall' festival in Kouvola. The band recorded a further set of demo tracks at Woodbine Garden Studios in January 2006.

Having severed ties with Nuclear Blast Records, the band parted ways with vocalist Antti Filppu in April. The following month Jukka Pelkonen of Vantaa's ELENIUM was confirmed as new vocalist for OMNIUM GATHERUM. UK dates in September, dubbed the 'Under the Earth' tour, saw BLACK RIVER PROJECT as support upfront of an appearance at the Derby 'Bloodstock' festival.

OMNIUM GATHERUM announced signature to Candlelight Records in October. Working with producer Teemu Aalto, they would utilise Southeast Studios in Karhula during early November to cut an album title with the title 'Stuck Here On Snakes Way'. DIABLO frontman Rainer Nygård aided on guest vocals.

In April 2007 the band united with MOONSORROW, SWALLOW THE SUN and DEBAUCHERY for an extensive round of European shows.

Omnium Gatherum EP, Independent (1998). Valley Of Sinep / Gates / Wasteland Of Mind / Foolish Dream / Crater Lake / Rise Again / Gone By The Wind.

Gardens, Temples ... This Hell EP, Independent (1999). Garden Of The Fallen Jesters / Jesters / Those Black Empty Eyes.

Wastrel EP, Independent (2001). Wastrel / Son's Thoughts / Candles For Giordano Bruno / Ammo / Lost And Found.

Steal The Light EP, Rage Of Achilles (2002). Wastrel / Son's Thoughts / Candles For Giordano Bruno / Ammo / Lost And Found.

SPIRITS AND AUGUST LIGHT, Rage Of Achilles ILIAD033 (2003). Writhen / Deathwhite / The Perfumed Garden / Amor Tonight / Cure A Wound / The Emptiness Of Spirit / Wastrel / Son's Thoughts / It Shines.

Omnium Gatherum, (2006). City Red Light / Remember The Frozen / Neither Dead Nor Alive / My Hands Were Tied / Das Wegrecht.

STUCK HERE ON SNAKE'S WAY, Candlelight (2007). The Snake And The Way / Into Sea / Dysnomia / A-Part Of God / Undertaker / Bastard-O / The Third Flame / Just Signs / Truth / Drudgery / In Sane World / Spiritual.

OPETH

SÖRSKOGEN, SWEDEN — *Mikael Åkerfeldt (vocals / guitar), Peter Lindgren (guitar), Martin Méndez (bass), Martin Axenrot (drums).*

Although initially seen as yet another in the long list of albums produced by EDGE OF SANITY's mentor DAN SWANÖ, Sörskogen's OPETH would struggle out of the Scandinavian scene with their groundbreaking 2001 album 'Blackwater Park' to set themselves as a true force for change in the international arena. The group has propagated an unwavering fan base built on an appreciation for OPETH's ability to artfully sculpt often ponderous neo-progressive wanderings into masterpieces of modern Metal. Starting life influenced by the rawer Black

Thrash acts, OPETH has steadily matured into more melancholic landscapes with each successive release.

Vocalist / guitarist Mikael Åkerfeldt and drummer Anders Nordin are ex-ERUPTION players and had known each other as friends since the age of 5. Established during 1987, ERUPTION comprising Åkerfeldt, Nordin, guitarist Nick Döring and bassist Jocke Horney, had mainly pursued death metal covers by the likes of DEATH, BLACK SABBATH and BATHORY. Horney was swiftly replaced by Stephan Claesberg. The musicians first, faltering steps at composing original material produced tracks such as 'Procreation Of Maledictions', 'Obedient Souls', 'Condemned To Hell' and 'Sarcastic Reign', although ERUPTION never demoed or even performed live.

Singer David Isberg's previous band OPETH, centred in the Täby suburb of Stockholm and taking its title from the Opet moon city described by author Wilbur Smith, had floundered when Isberg had attempted to introduce Åkerfeldt into the ranks during 1990. This strategy did not find favour and the main mass of members split off to create CROWLEY, issuing a 1991 demo 'The Gate'. Meantime, the Åkerfeldt and Isberg subsequently combined to reforge the act subtly retitled OPETH. As a budding, occult influenced duo Åkerfeldt and Isberg's inaugural compositions took on titles 'Requiem Of Lost Souls' and 'Mystique Of The Baphomet', subsequently re-worked into 'Mark Of The Damned' and 'Forest Of October' respectively.

ERUPTION colleagues Nick Döring and Anders Nordin were invited to enroll then second guitarist Andreas Dimeo was recruited for OPETH's debut gig, comprising just two songs, supporting THERION, EXCRUCIATE and AUTHORISE in February 1991. However, shortly after both Dimeo and Döring decamped quickly after. The former CRIMSON CAT duo of Kim Pettersson and Johan DeFarfalla plugged the gap for a second show held in Gothenburg sharing the stage with AT THE GATES, THERION, MEGASLAUGHTER, DESECRATOR and SARCAZM. The new pair would also drift off, although Pettersson stayed loyal for a final 1991 concert with ASPHYX and DESULTORY, and more significantly Isberg left for pastures new in LIERS IN WAIT.

Just 3 gigs into their career, OPETH were now starting to pen much moodier material such as the prototype 'Poise Into Celeano', later to mutate into album track 'Advent'. Åkerfeldt took the lead vocal role as he rebuilt the band with ex-SYLT I KRYSSET ("Jam on the cross") guitarist Peter Lindgren and bassist Stephan Guteklint. OPETH never officially cut any demos, although a two track 1994 cassette was leaked comprising 'Forest Of October' and 'In The Mist She Was Standing'. Securing a deal with the British Candlelight Records label the debut album 'Orchid' was cut at Swanö's Unisound Recordings in March 1994 using previous member De Farfalla on session bass, Guteklint journeying on to join MINDWATCH. A double vinyl edition, pressed by Dutch label Displeased, added an extra track with 'Into The Forest of Winter'.

For an extreme Metal album, 'Orchid's presentation, the album cover simply bearing the flower of the same name, proved deceptive. Once past the packaging, fans revelled in a labyrinth of sound, discordant song structures and apparent chaotic structure. Guitars ranged from crunching Death Metal to lilting acoustics, the bass took on an uncharacteristic prominence, percussion was more in keeping with freeform Jazz whilst vocals took on many tongues, from blackened howls, gut wrenching growls to ethereal pure tones. So confusing was this assembly that in the mastering process tracks were misplaced, with the closing segment of 'Requiem' mistakenly tacked onto the beginning of 'The Apostle In Triumph'.

Gigs followed in the Spring of 1995 including a London Astoria show alongside VED BUENS ENDE, HECATE ENTHRONED and IMPALED NAZARENE. OPETH's second album, 'Morningrise' produced once again by Dan Swanö and released in June 1996, was an exercise in oppressive malaise, a quintet of equally morose, lumbering leviathans imbued with near impenetrable poetic filigree. The album left reviewers either perplexed or in awe whilst existing fans lapped up the twenty minute 'Black Rose Immortal', detractors cruelly labelled the band's Progressive Rock persuasions as "boring". 'Morningrise' promoted with a support slot to MORBID ANGEL in the UK and to CRADLE OF FILTH in Europe. Following these dates both Nordin and De Farfalla made their exit. Persevering, Åkerfelt pulled in a brand new rhythm section of Uruguayans bassist Martin Méndez and ex-AMON AMARTH drummer Martin López, both members of REQUIEM AETERNAM.

This latest incarnation of OPETH cut the 'My Arms, Your Hearse' album, described as a "third observation", during the August and September 1997. The band chose a fresh location to have their art "absorbed by the electronical devices", utilising Fredman studios and employing the production team of Frederik Nordström and Anders Fridén. 'My Arms, Your Hearse' was delivered to the public in August 1998 and further UK live action saw supports to CRADLE OF FILTH in December 1998, shortly after which the band signed to new label Peaceville Records. This union resulted in the self-produced album 'Still Life', hammered out at both Fredman Studios and Maestro Musik during April and May 1999 being ushered out in October. Heavier than previous outings, the album benefited from a brighter sonic value and criticism aimed at their meandering approach to songwriting saw tracks cut down in length.

Meantime, a diversion was afforded by STEEL, an impromptu traditional 80's style Heavy Metal liaison between Åkerfeldt and singer DAN SWANÖ with the OPETH credited Peter Lindgren and Anders Nordin supplied the rhythm section. Never intended to become a serious venture, STEEL nevertheless attracted the attention of Near Dark Productions who issued two tracks on a 1998 7" picture disc single entitled 'Heavy Metal Machine'. Åkerfeldt teamed up with Swanö, KATATONIA's Blakkheim (Andres Nyström) and Jonas Renske to create side project BLOODBATH in 2000.

Returning to Fredman Studios, OPETH hopped labels again, to Music For Nations, to generate 'Blackwater Park' in March 2001, these sessions produced by the band in alliance with PORCUPINE TREE frontman Steven Wilson. A limited double CD package, emerging the following year and restricted to just 1000 copies, hosted two extra songs, 'Still Day Beneath The Sun' and 'Patterns In The Ivy II' plus the promotional video clip for 'Harvest'.

OPETH toured the UK in May 2002 supported by ARCH ENEMY. Later that year the group revealed they were planning not one but two new Fredrik Nordström produced studio albums, a 'heavy' album to be mixed by erstwhile SABBAT guitarist Andy Sneap and a 'mellow' record mixed by Steve Wilson. The original concept was to unveil both works simultaneously but label pressure would result in 'Deliverance' arriving in November 2002 and 'Damnation' the following April, and, as it transpired, Wilson also ended up manning the desk for both collections. The band announced North American tour dates for January 2003, billed as the '4 Absent Friends Tour', allied with PARADISE LOST and TAPPING THE VEIN. Subsequent dates in May had the band packaged with LACUNA COIL and BEYOND THE EMBRACE. Dedicated fans were forced to move fast to pick up a 7" single through the Robotic Empire label. OPETH's first ever single release, 'Still Day Beneath The Sun', was limited to 1092 black vinyl and just 150 grey vinyl copies.

The status of 'Deliverance' was affirmed in February when OPETH received a Swedish Grammy award for the record in the 'Best Hard Rock' category. The band united with PORCUPINE TREE for summer North American co-headlining dates. The band drafted SPIRITUAL BEGGARS Hammond organ player Per Wiberg for these shows. October Scandinavian dates had Norwegians EXTOL acting as support. Further gigs projected in Australia for December were curtailed when air flight costs nixed the proposal.

In November Mikael Åkerfeldt would be confirmed as a session guest on the 2004 AYREON concept album 'The Human Equation'. There would be less fortunate news for OPETH that some month as gigs in Chile and Jordan would be pulled, the latter due to a "stress related breakdown" from drummer Martin Lopez and the withdrawal of crew members because of increased terrorist attacks in the Middle East.

OPETH seemingly got back on schedule with their 'Lamentations Over America Tour 2004' commencing in Edmonton, Canada on 20th January. These shows had the band partnered with DEVILDRIVER and Portugal's MOONSPELL. However, the band pulled out of the Edmonton gig as Martin López was still in Sweden. Further reports suggested the drummer was undergoing treatment for panic attacks. Persevering, OPETH gave an abbreviated five song performance in Calgary with a drum technician acting as stand in. STRAPPING YOUNG LAD and DARK ANGEL drummer Gene Hoglan stepped in as stop gap for the January 23rd Vancouver stop, performing on two tracks 'The Drapery Falls' and 'Demon Of The Fall'. Earlier that evening OPETH had played a truncated acoustic set including a take on DEEP PURPLE's 'Soldier Of Fortune'. López returned for the band's Seattle date.

With their label Music For Nations being acquired by the Zomba Music Group in the Summer of 2004, OPETH would find 'themselves without a label. Announcing in April of 2005 that touring keyboard player Per Wiberg had been enrolled as a permanent member of the band, OPETH entered Fascination Street studios in Örebro during May to craft a new album, 'Ghost Reveries', for Roadrunner Records. Mikael Åkerfeldt would see inclusion on the ROADRUNNER UNITED 25th anniversary album 'The All-Stars Sessions', featuring on the track 'Roads' penned by TYPE O NEGATIVE's Josh Silver.

With Martin Lopez temporarily forced out, the drummer undergoing treatment for a blood disorder, OPETH enlisted STRAPPING YOUNG LAD drummer Gene Hoglan to fill in for live work. The Summer of 2005 found the group participating in the US 'Sounds of the Underground' touring extravaganza, a collaboration between independent labels Ferret Music, Prosthetic Records, Trustkill Records and Metal Blade Records. The mammoth billing for these shows saw the band sharing stages with CLUTCH, POISON THE WELL, UNEARTH, FROM AUTUMN TO ASHES, CHIMAIRA, NORMA JEAN, EVERY TIME I DIE, STRAPPING YOUNG LAD, THROWDOWN, HIGH ON FIRE, DEVILDRIVER, ALL THAT REMAINS, A LIFE ONCE LOST and GWAR. Regional additions included MADBALL and TERROR, splitting the East and West portions of the tour respectively, THE RED CHORD on the East Coast, FEAR BEFORE THE MARCH OF FLAMES in the Midwest and Southeast and HIMSA for Western gigs.

Upon release, 'Ghost Reveries' gave OPETH numerous international chart positions in important territories such as the UK and Australia. In the USA the record sold 15,000 copies in its first week of sale to debut impressively at no. 64 on the Billboard charts. Elsewhere, 'Ghost Reveries' made its presence felt in the national sales rankings across Canada, Finland, Denmark, France, Norway, Holland, Italy and Germany. Most impressive of all was a number 9 score in Sweden.

European touring in September saw support from Christian Metal band EXTOL. For these shows, with Lopez still undergoing treatment, OPETH pulled in the much travelled BLOODBATH, WITCHERY, NIFELHEIM, BLASPHEMOUS, MORGUE, COVEN, TRIUMPHATOR, SATANIC SLAUGHTER and N.C.O. drummer Martin Axenrot. OPETH returned to the USA in October, a first leg of dates supported by PELICAN and FIREBALL MINISTRY with NEVERMORE and INTO ETERNITY taking on support duties for the second leg. Unfortunately the first dates would be cancelled as OPETH band members encountered visa delays.

Entering BBC Studios in Maida Vale, London the band cut

OPETH (pic: Dimitri Borellini)

extra tracks for use on a re-release expanded edition of 'Ghost Reveries'. Included would be a 'When', 'The Grand Conjuration' and cover version of DEEP PURPLE's 'Soldier Of Fortune'. European gigs in November and December would be supported by Sweden's BURST. The band's 2006 season of live campaigning opened up in the USA during February alongside DARK TRANQUILLITY and DEVIN TOWNSEND. During these dates the group engaged in special concerts dubbed 'Chronology MCMXCIV- MMV—A Live Observation By Opeth'. Held in New York, Chicago and Los Angeles, these seated shows encompassed a chronological set of material, some never before performed live, from each of their albums released throughout their career.

In mid May, still apparently beset by illness and anxiety attacks, Martin López officially stood down, allowing Martin Axenrot to take the drummer's role on a permanent basis. The band put in a significant appearance at the METALLICA and KORN headlined 'Download' festival in Castle Donington, UK on June 10th. South and Central American shows, taking in Mexico, Chile, Argentina and Brazil, were announced for September and October. However, these shows were curtailed as the band joined up with the MEGADETH headlined 'Gigantour' North American festivals in early September, sharing billing with LAMB OF GOD, ARCH ENEMY, OVERKILL, INTO ETERNITY, SANCTITY and THE SMASHUP.

Roadrunner issued an expanded edition of 'Ghost Reveries' in October, this double CD set adding the DEEP PURPLE cover version 'Soldier Of Fortune', promotional video for 'The Grand Conjuration', a 40 minute documentary 'Beyond Ghost Reveries' and a 5.1 surround sound mix of the entire album. A run of British dates in November saw strong support from PARADISE LOST.

Mikael Åkerfeldt joined CANDLEMASS onstage for their 20th anniversary concert at Stockholm's Kolingsborg on March 31st, performing the song 'At The Gallows End'. In April 2007 OPETH keyboard player Per Wiberg collaborated on a side project with CLUTCH drummer Jean-Paul Gaster and KAMCHATKA guitarist Thomas "Juneor" Andersson.

Promo 1994, (1994) (Demo). Forest Of October / In The Mist She Was Standing.

ORCHID, Candlelight CANDLE010CD (1995). In Mist She Was Standing / Under The Weeping Moon / Silhouette / Forest Of October / The Twilight Is My Robe / Requiem / The Apostle In Triumph.

MORNING RISE, Candlelight CANDLE015CD (1996). Advert / The Night And The Silent Winter / Nectar / Black Rose Immortal / To Bid You Farewell.

MY ARMS, YOUR HEARSE, Candlelight CANDLE025CD (1998). Prologue / April Ethereal / When / Madrigal / The Amen Corner / Demon Of The Fall / Credence / Karma / Epilogue.

STILL LIFE, Peaceville CDVILE78 (1999). The Moon / Godhands Lament / Benighted / Moonlapse Vertigo / Face Of Melinda / Serenity Painted Death / White Cluster.

The Drapery Falls, Koch International (2001) (European promotion release). The Drapery Falls.

BLACKWATER PARK, Music For Nations MFN 264 (2001). The Leper Affinity / Bleak / Harvest / The Drapery Falls / Dirge For November / Funeral Portrait / Patterns In The Sky / Blackwater Park.

BLACKWATER PARK, Music For Nations MFN 284 (2002) (Limited edition double CD). The Leper Affinity / Bleak / Harvest / The Drapery Falls / Dirge For November / The Funeral Portrait / Patterns In The Ivy / Blackwater Park / Still Day Beneath The Sun / Patterns In The Ivy II / Harvest (Video).

DELIVERANCE, Music For Nations MFN 291 (2002). Wreath / Deliverance / A Fair Judgement / For Absent Friends / Master's Apprentices / By The Pain I See In Others.

Still Day Beneath the Sun, Robotic Empire (2003) (Limited edition 7" single. 1092 black vinyl, 150 grey vinyl). Still Day Beneath the Sun / Patterns In The Ivy II.

DAMNATION, Music For Nations MFN 294 (2003). Windowpane / In My Time Of Need / Death Whispered A Lullaby / Closure / Hope Leaves / To Rid The Disease / Ending Credits / Weakness.

Selections From Ghost Reveries, Roadrunner RR PROMO 863 (2005) (Promotion release). The Grand Conjuration (Edit) / Ghost Of Perdition (Edit) / The Grand Conjuration.

GHOST REVERIES, Roadrunner RR 618123-2 (2005). Ghost Of Perdition / The Baying Of The Hounds / Beneath The Mire / Atonement / Reverie/Harlequin Forest / Hours Of Wealth / The Grand Conjuration / Isolation Years. Chart positions: 9 SWEDEN, 11 FINLAND, 21 NORWAY, 35 AUSTRALIA, 38 HOLLAND, 40 GERMANY, 52 ITALY, 56 CANADA, 62 UK, 64 USA, 72 FRANCE, 84 DENMARK.

GHOST REVERIES: SPECIAL EDITION, Roadrunner (2006) (Double CD). Ghost Of Perdition / The Baying Of The Hounds / Beneath The Mire / Atonement / Reverie/Harlequin Forest / Hours Of Wealth / The Grand Conjuration / Isolation Years / Soldier Of Fortune / Beyond Ghost Reveries Documentary / The Grand Conjuration (Video) / Ghost Of Perdition (5.1 Surround Sound Mix) / The Baying Of The Hounds (5.1 Surround Sound Mix) / Beneath The Mire (5.1 Surround Sound Mix) / Atonement (5.1 Surround Sound Mix) / Reverie/Harlequin Forest (5.1 Surround Sound Mix) / Hours Of Wealth (5.1 Surround Sound Mix) / The Grand Conjuration (5.1 Surround Sound Mix) / Isolation Years (5.1 Surround Sound Mix).

OPPRESSOR

CHICAGO, IL, USA — *Tim King (vocals / bass / keyboards), Adam Zadel (guitar), Jim Stopper (guitar), Tom Schofield (drums).*

A Chicago Death Metal band possessing enough originality to set them apart from the crowd. OPPRESSOR debuted with the workmanlike 'World Abomination' demo tape but really got into their stride with the second effort 'As Blood Flows'. This cassette prompted a deal with the Red Light label for debut album 'Solstice Of Oppression' and subsequent European licensing to Music For Nations offshoot Bulletproof Records. In support of the record OPPRESSOR toured America as guests to MALEVOLENT CREATION and Europe as openers for CRADLE OF FILTH.

However, Red Light went into receivership and OPPRESSOR compiled live material and studio outtakes to comprise the 'European Oppression-Live' disc on Megalithic Records. Olympic Recordings duly picked the band up for the third outing 'Agony'. Touring would find OPPRESSOR billed alongside CANNIBAL CORPSE for American dates.

'Elements Of Corrosion' arrived in 1998. Oddly the trio of frontman Tim King, guitarist Adam Zadel and drummer Tom Schoefield would eschew their Death Metal roots and found Nu-Metal band SOIL in league with former BROKEN HOPE man Shaun Glass.

SOLSTICE OF OPPRESSION, Red Light (1994). Seasons / Eclipse Into Eternity / Devour The Soul / … And The Angels Fell (The Suffering) / Prelude To Death / Genocide / Rotted Paradise / As Blood Flows / Dying Inside.

EUROPEAN OPPRESSION LIVE- AS BLOOD FLOWS, Megalithic (1995). And The Angels Fell (Live) / Seasons (Live) / As Blood Flows (Live) / Eclipse Into Eternity (Live) / I Am Darkness (Live) / Looks That Kill / Human Sacrifice ('95 version) / Intro- Eclipse Into Eternity / Devour The Soul / As Blood Flows / Prelude To Death / Genocide / Dying Inside / Eternal Damnation.

AGONY, Olympic Recordings (1996). Gone / Suffersystem / In Exile / Passage / Valley Of Thorns / Re-Define / Sea Of Tears / I Am Darkness / Carnal Voyage.

ELEMENTS OF CORROSION, Serious Entertainment (1999). Corrosion / Kingdom Of The Dead / Blinded / I Despise / Through Their Eyes / Upon The Uncreation / In Malice I Breathe / Vulgar Illusions / Lost In Sorrow.

OPPROBIUM

METAIRE, LA, USA — *Francis M. Howard (vocals / guitar), Luiz Carlos (guitar), André Luiz (bass), Moyses M. Howard (drums).*

Metaire, Louisiana's Christian Death Metal band OPPROBRIUM started life billed as INCUBUS. Having previously issued two albums under their former title, 'Serpent Temptation' in 1988 with bassist Scot Latour and 'Beyond The Unknown' in 1990 with Mark Levenia of ABHORRENT EXISTENCE and EQUINOX on bass, the Brazilian Howard siblings, vocalist / guitarist Francis and drummer Moyses, opted to record a third album. However, the INCUBUS title legally rested with another act, the successful Rap-Rock act on major label Sony, and so the project, following a brief period billed INCUBUS RAGE, was re-branded OPPROBRIUM.

The album 'Discerning Forces', issued by German label Nuclear Blast in 2000, was recorded in Rio de Janeiro with producer Harris Johns. Newly installed on bass would be André Luiz of DEMONOLATRY and IMMUNO AFFINITY repute.

DISCERNING FORCES, Nuclear Blast NB 462-2 (2000). Digitrap / Unclean / Ancient Rebellion / Dark Entanglement / Drowning / Escapism / Merciless Torture / Moments Of despair / Blood Conflict / Awakening To The Filth.

ORIGIN

KA, USA — *Mark Manning (vocals), Paul Ryan (guitar), Jeremy Turner (guitar), Clint Appelhanz (bass), Jeremy Gregg (drums).*

Founded in the summer of 1997 by guitarists Paul Ryan, of DEMONICIDE, and Jeremy Taylor later adding erstwhile guitarist Clint Appelhanz on bass, Mark Manning on vocals and drummer George Fluke. SKINLESS opened for SUFFOCATION in early 1998 prior to recording the inaugural demo 'A Coming Into Existence'. Reaction to this release led to ORIGIN's inclusion as opening act on the monolithic 'Death Across America' nationwide tour with NILE, GORGUTS, CRYPTOPSY and OPPRESSOR. Line-up ructions led to the inclusion of former ANGEL CORPSE drummer John Longstreth in February of 1999. Appelhanz too would be replaced, this time by CEPHALIC CARNAGE veteran Doug Williams.

Touring to break in the new unit would lead to a deal with Death Metal connoisseurs Relapse Records. However, in early 2001 Manning departed to be replaced by former ILL OMEN man Jim Lee. Guitarist Paul Ryan would unite with ENTER SELF drummer Jeremy Gregg and Leon De La Muerte of IMPALED and EXHUMED infamy to create the MURDER CONSTRUCT project.

ORIGIN's John Longstreth would take command of the SKINLESS drum stool in January of 2003, although the ex-drummer subsequently united with EXHUMED. In May of that year Jim Lee became new frontman for VILE. Meantime, Paul Ryan relinquished his tenure with MURDER CONSTRUCT in order to prioritise ORIGIN. In July 2003 Longstreth's place was replaced by Jeremy Gregg. Meantime, Longstreth, following a stint with Hardcore merchants THE RED CHORD, temporarily joined the ranks of DYING FETUS in October of 2004 for

US touring. Gregg subsequently forged ASERAPHYMN. ORIGIN's third album, 'Echoes Of Decimation' released in March 2005, would be recorded with new members vocalist / guitarist Clinton Appelhanz and drummer James King.

Summer 2005 dates, commencing in Florida during early July, had the band packaged with ANIMOSITY, DIVINE EMPIRE and headliners MALEVOLENT CREATION. John Longstreth was back in the spotlight, joining the reformed DIM MAK. In September, citing "personal and creative differences", ORIGIN severed ties with both Clinton Appelhanz and James King. The two ex-members swiftly announced formation of a new project billed UNMERCIFUL in collaboration with singer Tony Reust and former ORIGIN member/CANNIBAL CORPSE touring guitarist Jeremy Turner.

ORIGIN, being re-joined by John Longstreth on drums, laid out extensive US touring for 2006.

A Coming Into Existence, (1998). Lethal Manipulation (The Bonecrusher Chronicles) / Sociocide / Manimal Instincts / Inner Reflections.
ORIGIN, Relapse (2000). Lethal Manipulation / Sociocide / Vomit You Out / Origin / Mental Torment / Manimal Instincts / Infliction / Disease Called Man / Inner Reflections.
INFORMIS, INFINITAS, INHUMANITAS, Relapse (2002). Larvae Of The Lie / Inhuman / Awaken The Suffering / Perversion Of Hate / Portal / Meat For The Beast / Mental Torment / Insurrection / Implosion Of Eternity.
ECHOES OF DECIMATION, Relapse (2005). Reciprocal / Endless Cure / The Burner / Designed To Expire / Cloning The Stillborn / Staring From The Abyss / Amoeba / Debased Humanity / Echoes Of Decimation.

ORIGIN BLOOD

MALMÖ, SWEDEN — *Rob Ahrling (vocals), Robin Sjöstrand (guitar), Simon Niklasson (bass), Brian Petersen (drums).*

ORIGIN BLOOD, hailing from Malmö, is fronted by Rob Ahrling of THE GLADIATOR and SPAWN OF POSSESSION. Ahrling forged the band during 1997 in league with bass player Simon Niklasson, Christian Kapusta and Björn Baumlisberger. The latter was replaced by Morten in 1998. Robin Sjöstrand, of VANITY DIES HARD, enrolled on guitar for proposed album tracks in 2001 dubbed 'La Muerte Del Arte'.

Drums would then be delegated to ex-OMINOUS man Brian Petersen. The debut album 'Mr. Jakker Daw' was recorded in 2004 at Ahrling's own Flat Pig Studios, issued that October through R.A.H.W. Production. ORIGIN BLOOD teamed up with NECROPHOBIC and RAISE HELL for a European tour beginning late September 2006.

MR. JAKKER DAW, R.A.H.W. Production (2004). Godsize / s.o.r.r.o.w. / Fading / Within / Enlightenment / To Have And To Hold / Mr. Jakker Daw / Still I Turn / Headache / The End / Without.

ORPHANAGE

HOLLAND — *Lex Vogelaar (vocals / guitar), Rosan Van Der Aa (vocals), George Oosthoek (vocals), Eric Hoogendoorn (bass), Guus Eikens (keyboards), Erwin Poldermann (drums).*

Dutch outfit ORPHANAGE's driving force is guitarist/vocalist Lex Vogelaaar, a former member of TARGET, and he initially recorded a trial demo with keyboard player Guus Eikens titled 'Morph', which led to the formation of ORPHANAGE. This initial recording also utilized the services of CELESTIAL SEASON vocalists Jason Kohnen and Stefan Ruiters, together with PARALYSIS drummer Stephan Van Haestregt.

As the project evolved into a permanent band ORPHANAGE added bassist Eric Hoogendoorn and vocalist Martine Van Loon, although at the time she was still fronting THE GATHERING. In 1994 this line-up recorded the demo 'Druid', a tape that also featured the talents of THE GATHERING keyboardist Frank Boeijen.

Enrolling yet another vocalist in George Oosthek, ORPHANAGE contributed two tracks to the DFSA Records compilation album 'Paradise Of The Underground' prior to the departure of Van Haestregt. A temporary replacement was found in GOREFEST's Ed Warby. Drummer Erwin Polderman was recruited in time for the debut album 'Oblivion'. Vocalist Rosan Van Der Aa was eventually replaced by Martine Van Loon.

Following the groundbreaking 1996 album 'By Time Alone' (a heady mix of Metal and Gregorian choirs) ORPHANAGE issued the 'At The Mountains Of Madness' EP co-produced by former VENGEANCE man Oscar Holleman. Touring in Europe during March of 1997 saw the band forming up a package billing alongside THERION, SENTENCED, MY DYING BRIDE and DARK for the 'Out Of The Dark III' festivals. ORPHANAGE also put in a showing at the Dynamo festival in 1997.

In 1996 both Hoogendoorn and Poldermann founded a side project SILICON HEAD together with PLEURISY guitarist Axel Becker. SILICON HEAD's debut album 'Bash' was produced by Vogelaar.

In April 2002 George Oosthoek joined PLEURISY. Following issue of the 'Driven' album, September of 2004 would see ORPHANAGE parting ways with keyboardist Lasse Dellbrügge. Ex-ORPHANAGE members George Oosterhoek and Guus Eikens featured on DELAIN's 2006 debut 'Lucidity' album, the project of ex-WITHIN TEMPTATION keyboard player Martijn Westerholt.

OBLIVION, Displeased DSFA 1001 (1995). Chameleon / Weltschmerz / The Case Of Charles Dexter Ward / In The Garden Of Eden / Journey Into The Unknown / Druid / Veils of Blood / Sea Of Dreams / The Collector / Victim Of Fear.
BY TIME ALONE, Displeased DSFA 1004 P (1996). At The Mountains Of Madness / Five Crystals / The Dark Side / Deceiver / Cliffs Of Moher / By Time Alone / Ancient Rhymes / Odyssey / Requiem / Leafless / Deliverance.
At The Mountains Of Madness (Video mix), Displeased DSFA 1008 (1997). At The Mountains Of Madness (Video mix) / Five Crystals (Oscar mix) / The Crumbling Of My Denial (Live) / Sea Of Dreams (Live).
INSIDE, Nuclear Blast NB 510-2 (2000). Grip / Twisted Games / Inside / The Stain / Pain / Deal With The Real / Behold / Weakness Of Flesh / Kick / Drag You Down / From The Cradle To The Grave.
THE BELOVED'S CRY, Raven Music (2000).
The Sign Tour EP, (2004). The Sign / In Den Bergen Des Irrsinns / Inside.
DRIVEN, Nuclear Blast NB 1050-2 (2004). The Sign / Black Magic Mirror / Cold / Prophecies Of Fame / Dead Ground / My Master's Master / Back Gate / In Slavery / Truth Or Lies / Driven / Infinity / Addiction / Beyond The Fall / Ender's Game.
VOICES AND ORGANS, Western Vinyl (2006). Melodikka (Orphanage Intro) / Any Day Now / Trees Are Bending Shades to Shapes / Staircase, Attic And Out The Window / Reaching For Trees In Dreams / Idle Words On Empty Pages #1 / Ghostwriting / Nestlings / Through The City, Through The Lights / As We Grew Young / Sundays / Boychild / Screamer / Singer / Back And Forth / Polyphony Of Banality / Idle Words On Empty Pages #2 / Orphans.

ORPHANED LAND

ISRAEL — *Kobi Farhi (vocals), Yossi Sassi (guitar), Matti Svatitzki (guitar), Uri Zelcha (bass), Sami Bachar (drums).*

ORPHANED LAND purvey their own brand of what has been dubbed "Oriental Metal". The group was founded in 1991 under the original title of RESURRECTION switching to ORPHANED LAND the following year. The band line-up stood at vocalist Kobi Farhi, guitarists Yossi Sassi and Matti Svatitzki, bassist Uri Zelcha and drummer Sami Bachar.

As such the band guested for visiting international artists such as TIAMAT and CATHEDRAL. In 1993 the debut demo 'The Beloveds Cry' was issued immediately creating a media stir. So much so that Greek label Metal Invader would re-release the tape on CD format shortly after. The demo was re-issued by Holy Records in 1994 and yet again by the MDMA label in

EL NORA ALILA, Holy HOLY18CD (1996). Find Your Self, Discover God / Like Fire To Water / The Truth Within / The Path Ahead, A Never Ending Way: The Path Ahead / The Path Ahead, A Never Ending Way: A Never Ending Way / Takasim / Thee By The Father I Pray / Flawless Belief / Joy / Whisper My Name When You Dream / Shir Hama'A lot / El Meod Na'Ala / Of Temptation Born / The Evil Urge / Shir Hashirim.

THE BELOVED'S CRY, Raven Music (2000). Seasons Unite / Above You All / Pits Of Despair / The Beloved's Cry / My Requiem / Orphaned Land—The Storm Still Rages Inside.

MABOOL: THE STORY OF THE THREE SONS OF SEVEN, Century Media (2004). Birth Of The Three (The Unification) / Ocean Land (The Revelation) / The Kiss Of Babylon (The Sins) / A'salk / Halo Dies (The Wrath Of God) / A Call To Awake (The Quest) / Building The Ark / Norra El Norra (Entering The Ark) / The Calm Before The Flood / Mabool (The Flood) / The Storm Still Rages / Rainbow (The Resurrection).

ORTANK

TARNÓW, POLAND — *Mirosław Kożuchowski (vocals), Tomasz Radke (guitar), Marcin Borowiecki (guitar), Bartosz Sendorek (bass), Lukasz Urbanek (drums).*

Tarnów based Death Metal band ORTANK was created in 1998 by guitarist Tomasz Radke and drummer Seweryn. Drummer Lukasz Urbanek, replacing Seweryn in 1999, would feature in STILLBORN and RAVISHED FLESH. Vocalist Mirosław Kożuchowski also fronts FORSAKEN whilst guitarist Marcin Borowiecki is an ex-member of DEVILYN.

In August of 1999 ORTANK entered Manek Studio in Sanok to cut the demo 'Failures Theory-Defective Members Carnival'. A two track demo followed in 2000, after which Bartosz Sendorek of ECLYPSE was enrolled on bass guitar. The 2002 album 'Mental Diaspora Association' included a SADUS cover version 'Valley Of Dry Bones'.

Promo 2000, Ortank (2000). Not Even A Carcass / I'm The Rapist Of Drowned.

MENTAL DIASPORA ASSOCIATION, (2001). Dislocation / I Artificial Indeed / Embodiment Of Thoughts / Hydro Shit Ecstasy / At The Last Expected Moment / Oderint, Dum Metuant / Relic / An Outlet [99% Loathing Extinguished] / A Tribute To Hot Chicks / Valley Of Dry Bones.

OSSUARY

URUGUAY — *David (vocals), Sebb (guitar), Marcelo (guitar), Lobo (bass), Cristian (drums).*

Uruguayan Death Metal formation OSSUARY formed back in 1992 and after a run of demo cassettes and line up ructions would finally get to release their debut 7" single in 2001 with only guitarist Sebb remaining as a founder member. OSSUARY took only two months from their formation to furnish the Metal scene with the opening demo tape 'Cementry'. At this stage the band members were all in their early teens. A further demo 'Inquisition Dreams' arrived the following year but delivered by a changed line up. The membership roster would fluctuate yet again upfront of the third effort, 1995's 'The Black Wind Whispering From The Coast'. These recordings would subsequently be commercially re-issued by the Bolivian Catapult label to mark South American tour dates. Re-dubbed 'Show No Thirsty- Alcoholic Rites' this revised version saw the addition of one extra new track plus Death style covers of MANOWAR's 'Fighting The World' and even MÖTLEY CRÜE's 'Looks That Kill'!

By the time of the 1998 recordings 'We Await The Secret Conspiracy' guitarist Sebb stood alone from the first line up of OSSUARY. The band now consisted of Sebb, second guitarist Marcelo, erstwhile KARKADAM bass player Portugal and former FATELESS drummer Cristian. Portugal would later decamp and OSSUARY pulled in singer David and bassist Lobo, striking a deal with the American Ire Records label for a 7" single 'Destroying The Weak Opposition', limited to 500 copies.

ORPHANED LAND (pic: Itamar Gero)

1999, giving the band the odd historical quirk of having their demo re-issued three times by three different labels.

ORPHANED LAND struck a deal with the French Holy Records organisation for two albums opening proceedings with 1994's 'Sahara' which included reworks of all four demo tracks. The lyrics of 'Sahara' dealt almost exclusively on religious based themes and/or adaptations of writing from various holy scriptures. The 1996 album 'El Norra Alila' also sold well across Europe prompting a fresh deal with the German Century Media label.

The band would also donate their version of 'Mercy' to the PARADISE LOST tribute 'As We Die For Paradise Lost'. In later years ORPHANED LAND underwent line up fluctuations citing a line up roster of Farhi, Sassi, Zelcha, female vocalist Shlomit Levy and keyboard player Itzik Levy. ORPHANED LAND signed to the German Century Media label for a 2003 album 'Mabool— The Story Of The Three Sons Of Seven', recorded by the band themselves in Zaza and Bardo Studios in Tel Aviv. A limited initial pressing contained a bonus disc of an acoustic live show including a medley of archive tracks and a cover version of PARADISE LOST's.

Profound Lore Records re-issued ORPHANED LAND's early Holy Records albums, 1994's 'Sahara' and 1996's 'El Norra Alila' in a double gatefold vinyl format limited to 500 copies each during 2005. The band lent support to KREATOR and TRISTANIA in Mexico during March prior to landing the special guest spot to PARADISE LOST's European tour in April. ORPHANED LAND announced their first US show that same year, performing at the Atlanta, Georgia 'ProgPower USA VI' festival in September.

ORPHANED LAND engaged in European touring in alliance with KNORKATOR, SPELLBOUND, NOISE FOREST and ENSIFERUM during April and May of 2006.

SAHARA, Holy (1994). Sahara: The Sahara's Storm / Sahara: Blessed Be Thy Hate / Sahara: Ornaments Of Gold / Sahara: Aldiar Al Mukadisa -The Holy Land Of Israel / Seasons Unite / The Beloveds Cry / My Requiem / Orphaned Land—The Storm Still Rages Inside ....

Destroying The Weak Opposition, Ire Records (2001) (Limited edition. 500 copies). Kill Your God / Then World Must Burn.

P.C.P.

VINEBURG, CA, USA — *Nasty Nate Clark (vocals), Jeffro Belly (guitar), Mick Thomas (bass), Brian Durham (drums).*

Southern Bay Area Thrashers P.C.P. comprising of sole surviving founder member 'Nasty' Nate Clark on vocals and bass guitar, Jefro Belly on guitar and Brian 'Bandit' Durham on drums. The group originally came together in 1994 with a line up of Nate Clark, Mike Leahy, Sam Moore and Craig Bingham, a union of erstwhile personnel from acts such as PROPHECY and INIFINITY PERCENT. However, a succession of line ups eventually settled with the present trio. Brian Durham, a veteran of such acts as RINGWORM, EXCELSIOR and PADURHAM, was inducted during 1995. Guitarist Jeffro Belly joined in 1996, citing credits with SOCIETY'S PRODUCT and even THE BEVERLEY BEER BELLYS.

P.C.P. issued their debut album, 'Evilhatemotherfucker', during 2000. Bass player Mick Thomas, a former member of CONFUSED, was added in April of 2002.

Clark also operates with VENGEANCE whilst both Durham and Thomas are involved with THE DJN PROJECT.

EVILHATEMOTHERFUCKER, (2000).

PAGAN

PERTH, WA, AUSTRALIA — *Louis Rando (vocals / drums), Griffyn (guitar), Alan (guitar), Skot (bass).*

Perth Black Metal combo PAGAN was created during 1994 but splintered soon after. The band was re-constructed during 1997 by original members guitarist Griffyn and bassist Battle Sledge, drafting drummer Louis Rando. Lord Astoreth joined briefly as frontman but upon his departure Rando added lead vocals to his duties. This line up cut the 1998 album 'Rule Or Ruin' for Nightshade Records. Further changes saw SACRITUAL guitarist Alan enrolling, then Ludichris of MILITANT MASS replaced Battle Sledge. Ludichris was replaced early in 2001 by Skot.

PAGAN would fold, with Griffin forging THE KABAL. Rando would affiliate himself with FOROR and PATHOGEN.

RULE OR RUIN, Nightshade (1998).

PAGANIZER

SWEDEN — *Rogga Johansson (vocals), Dea (guitar), Oskar Nilsson (bass), Mattias Fiebig (drums).*

Old school Thrash / Death Metal unit PAGANIZER was assembled in Gamleby during late 1988 by DEAD SUN members vocalist Rogga Johansson and TERMINAL GRIP guitarist Dea (a.k.a. Andreas Carlsson) with BLIZZARD personnel drummer Jocke and bassist Diener. Jocke also held credits with GENITAL GRINDER. PAGANIZER's demo 'Stormfire' would later be issued as a 1998 shared album 'In Glorys Arms We Will Fall' in collusion with Singapore act ABATTORY. The band, bringing in bassist Oskar Nilsson, would follow this with a full blown debut 'Deadbanger' pressed up by the Malaysian Psychic Scream Entertainment label.

As one of his many side projects Rogga Johansson would aid Black Metal band BLODSRIT on drums. Jocke would quit PAGANIZER in 2000, being superseded by Mattias Fiebig of PORTAL, DARK RITES and BLODSRIT. The band re-grouped but a second album was held up by Malaysian censorship laws. The band decided to find another label who would consent to release the album, ending up with the Forever Underground concern for the 'Promoting Total Death' outing of June 2001.

Rogga Johansson and Diener, enlisting PORTAL guitarist Emil Koveroth and drummer Mattias Fiebig, would evolve the band into CARVE. Johansson would also operate as vocalist for DERANGED.

The band resurfaced in 2002 with the album 'Dead Unburied', recorded at Sunlight Studios with production credited to Thomas Skogsberg and mixing by DAN SWANÖ. Guesting on backing vocals would be the former GRAVE and ENTOMBED man Jörgen Sandström. PAGANIZER made a return to action in April of 2003 with the Mieszko Talarczyk produced album 'Murder Death Kill'. Founder member Dea opted out in July to prioritise his Gothic Metal band ANOTHER LIFE. He was superseded Halvarsson of BLODSRIT and PRIMITIVE SYMPHONY repute. By 2003 a new side project was on the agenda dubbed RIBSPREADER. This unite comprised Johansson, erstwhile PAGANIZER man Andreas Carlsson on guitar and the much travelled DAN SWANÖ on drums. Johansson reinforced the connection with Swanö by featuring as guest vocalist on the EDGE OF SANITY album 'Crimson II'.

PAGANIZER re-signed with Xtreem Music in 2004, entering Soundlab Studios in March with producer Mieszko Talarczyk to cut a new record. The band also donated their rendition of 'Nausea' to the AT THE GATES tribute album, 'Slaughterous Souls—A Tribute to At The Gates' released in September 2004 through Drowned Scream Records. In January of 2005 PAGANIZER announced that they had no line-up and were being "put on ice". However, in early 2005 RIBSPREADER underwent a drastic line-up overhaul, losing the services of Andreas Carlsson, Dan Swanö and Johan Berglund. The revised trio would comprise Rogga Johansson on vocals and guitar, bassist Patrik Halvarsson and drummer Mattias Fiebig, all ex-PAGANIZER members.

Promoting new album 'Carnage Junkie', mixed by Dan Swanö, PAGANIZER toured Spain and Portugal with MACHETAZO in December 2006.

Stormfire, (1998). Wardog Injection / Deathstar / Sinners Burn / The Final Command / Stormfire.
STORMFIRE, Psychic Scream (1998) (Split album with ABBATORY). Wardog Infection / Sinners Burn / Deathstar / The Final Command.
DEADBANGER, Psychic Scream Entertainment PSDL 9016 (1999). Branded By Evil / The Mask Of Evil / Deadbanger / Heads Of The Hydra / Storms To Come / Time To Burn / Sinners Burn / Into The Catacombs / Phantoms / Metal Crusade.
PROMOTING TOTAL DEATH, Forever Underground FU004 (2001). Promoting Total Death / Brutal Way To Die / Only Ashes Remain / 16 Second Massacre / At War / All Hope Is Dead / Cyclone Of Human Atrocity / Life Slips Away / Pain Has A Face.
DEAD UNBURIED, Forever Underground (2002). Even In Hell / Landscapes Made Of Human Skin / Napalm Burial / Lobotomized / Flesh Supremacy / Beyond Redemption / Procreating Death / At Night They Come / Hateconsumed.
MURDER DEATH KILL, Xtreem Music XM 006 (2003). Meateater / Mourning Life / Bleed Unto Me / Shallow Burial / Dead Souls / Crawl To The Cross / Obsessed By Flesh / Du Vaknar Som Död / Formaldehyde Dreams.

PAINSTRUCK

LISBON, PORTUGAL — *Nuno Loureiro (vocals / guitar), Ivo Martins (guitar), João Madeira (bass), Paulo Lafaia (drums).*

Lisbon Death-Thrashers PAINSTRUCK, assembled in August 1997 as BREED MACHINE, include personnel from MERCILESS DEATH, EXILED, SUBLEVEL, DISAFFECTED, MORTIFY, GROG and SQUAD. The founding members counted vocalist / guitarist Nuno Loureiro, guitarist Ricardo Correia, bass player Alexandre Afonso and Paulo Lafaia on drums.

PAINSTRUCK's first album 'Aggressive Ways To Pacify', produced by Luís Barros of TARANTULA at Rec n' Roll studios, was recorded in 1999. It finally emerged on Paranoid Records in June 2001. In the interim both Correira and Afonso departed, being substituted by GROG guitarist Ivo Martins and the DESIRE, WINTER WHISPERS and ARCANE WISDOM credited Ricardo Veloso on bass. Live work to support the record saw

PAINSTRUCK (pic: Ana Carvalho)

valuable supports to BIOHAZARD and an appearance at the SLIPKNOT and DIMMU BORGIR headlined 'Ermal' festival.

Second effort 'A Whole New Perception', recorded at Floyd Studios, arrived in 2002. João Madeira replaced Veloso in mid 2004.

AGGRESSIVE WAYS TO PACIFY, Paranoid (2001). Intro / Warcry / Easy Shot / Dwelling Demon / Wrath Of God / Acidic Essence / Wolves Pack / Scorching Skin / Spit Of Distrust / Into My Life / Paranoid / Misled Nation / F.O.D.E.S. / Power Of The Written Word.

A WHOLE NEW PERCEPTION, Paranoid (2002). A Whole New Perception / Painstruck / Pain Beyond / In Us You Live / Hate Is The Word... / You Are One Step Ahead / Believe The Word / Pierce The Wing / F.P.R.S. / Send In The Crows / Letting Out Loud / Breath In, Killing Time / Tons Of Chances.

PANDEMIA

CZECH REPUBLIC — *Michal Barta (vocals), Alex Marek (guitar), Jaroslav Friedrich (bass), Pavel Kouba (drums).*

Death Metal act created in 1995 by erstwhile SUFFERING personnel vocalist Matthew, guitarist Alex Marek and bass player Jaroslav Friedrich. The bands original drummer was ejected in favour of incomer Pavel Kouba as the group title evolved into PANDEMIA. The 1995 'Dust On The Eyes' demo gave an indicator of what was to come but Matthew would decamp in favour of new frontman Michal Barta after these recordings. A second cassette 'Dance In Vicious Circle' was issued in January of 1997 leading to a domestic tour alongside KRABATHOR and Polish veterans VADER. With the close of these gigs Kouba decamped in April and new drummer Tom was enrolled as PANDEMIA's second demo, united with Death Metal band EXHUMATE, scored a commercial split release courtesy of Anti Nazi Productions. The year ultimately ended on a high note as PANDEMIA guested for DIMMU BORGIR, KRABATHOR, KRISIUN and KREATOR in Prague.

1998 witnessed a valuable high profile support to DEATH in Prague. The second demo proved its staying power by gaining yet another re-release, this time by Lithuanian label Soundless Records as a split collaboration with South Africans GROINCHURN. As 1998 closed PANDEMIA cut new tracks in the studio for a third demo and also spread the word branching out with live gigs in continental Europe.

The third demo would also find a commercial release as Greek label Adenon Productions put the session out with extra tracks, one of which was a DEATH cover version 'Infernal Death'.

American concern Lost Disciple Records would take the band up for the debut album 'Spreading The Message'. Promoting the album PANDEMIA put in performances in Poland and Belgium. Gigs into 2000 saw a full blown European tour billed in alliance with REBAELLIUN, VADER, FLESHCRAWL and VITAL REMAINS.

The year closed off with a run of dates in Spain and Portugal alongside DEVILYN but as 2001 broke a switch in drummers occurred with Marthus (a.k.a. Martin Škaroupka), previously with ENTRAILS, HAPPY DEATH and MELANCHOLY PESSISM taking the drum stool from Tom who was forced out due to illness.

However, by April Marthus had split away from the band and former incumbent Pavel Kouba re-took the position. PANDEMIA issued the second album 'Personal Demon' in 2002, supporting the release as support act to INCANTATION in Europe throughout August. The band commenced recording of a new album 'Riven' in November.

South American licenses for 'Riven' saw the record distributed throughout Argentina, Uruguay, Paraguay and Bolivia by Hurling Metal whilst Hybrid Music took the album on in Peru, Ecuador, Colombia and Venezuela. A South American tour was scheduled for early 2005 but cancelled due to what was described as "several serious reasons". Dates would duly be re-scheduled for April, seeing PANDEMIA roving across Peru, Ecuador, Colombia, Venezuela, Argentina, Uruguay, Chile and Brazil.

PANDEMIA parted ways with guitarist and founding member Alex Marek in November. In November 2006 Martin Škaroupka stepped up into the international league when he was announced as new drummer for CRADLE OF FILTH.

SPREADING THE MESSAGE, Lost Disciple (1999). Intro / Stiffness / Majestic Suffering / Free Strokes / Intro / The Tones Are Weaker / Slavemind / Leaves In The Storm / Spreading The Message / Presentiment Of The Souls / Created Again / Outro.

PERSONAL DEMON, Lost Disciple LDRF 015 (2002). Shores Of Agony / The Right Path / Devious Omen / Personal Demon / Sins Of My Blood / Demonic Time / In This World / Father Of The Lie / Erased From The Earth.

RIVEN, Metal Age Productions (2005).

PANTOKRATOR

VÄXJÖ, SWEDEN — *Karl Walfridsson (vocals), Mattias Johansson (guitar), Jonathan Jansson (guitar), Jonas Wallinder (bass), Rickard Gustafsson (drums).*

PANTOKRATOR is a Växjö based, Christian Death Metal band, created in the Autumn of 1996, by singer Karl Walfridsson and guitarist Mattias Johansson, and learning their craft by performing covers by MORTIFICATION and TOURNIQUET. Boosted to a quartet by the inclusion of bassist Jonas Wallinder and drummer Rickard Gustafsson, opening demos included 'Unclean Plants / Ancient Path' in 1997, 'Even Unto The Ends Of The Earth' in 1998 and 'Allhärskare' in 2000. They would re-issue their 2001 'Songs Of Solomon' demo as a split CD in alliance with SANCTIFICA.

PANTOKRATOR expanded its line-up in 2003 with the addition of second guitarist Jonathan "Steele" Jansson, a musician holding associations with OBSECRATION, CRIMSON MOONLIGHT, AS A REMINDER and SANCTIFICA. Live work during 2005 saw the inclusion of stand in drummer Gustav Elowsson, a member of CRIMSON MOONLIGHT and Jönköping Grindcore outfit EXHALE, as Gustafsson took paternity leave. Rivel Records released the 2003 album 'Blod'.

In June 2006 PANTOKRATOR contracted with the German label Whirlwind Records. The album 'Aurum' was recorded at Slaughterhouse Studios in Halmstad with producer Rickard Bengtsson.

Unclean Plants / Ancient Path, (1997). Mind / Ancient Path / Punish The Evil / Unclean Plants.

Even Unto The Ends Of The Earth, (1998). Even Unto The Ends Of The Earth / Borderland / Via Dolorosa (Path Of Pain) / Olov Skötkonung.

Allhärskare, (2000). Lamentation / Daughter Of The King / Käpplåten / Blod på dina händer / Vals I Burk Moll.

SONGS OF SOLOMON, Pantokratur (2001) (Split album with SANCTIFICA). Ur Intets Mörker / Divine Light / Under Himmelen / Separated By Night / Come Let Us Free / Behind Thy Veil.
BLOD, Rivel Records (2003). Eden / Förbannad Mark / Blod Ropar Från Jorden / Syndafloden / Bundsförvant / Moria Kallar / Tidevarv / O Guds Lamm / Gudablodets Kraft / Evighetens Gryning.

PANZERCHRIST

ÅRHUS, DENMARK — *Lasse Hoile (vocals), Jes Christiansen (guitar), Finn Henriksen (guitar), Nikolaj Brink (bass), Reno Kiilerich (drums).*

An Århus brutal Death Metal / Grindcore quintet. PANZERCHRIST include ex-ILLDISPOSED drummer Michael Enevoldsen in the line-up. Later memberships had female bassist Karina Bundgaard taking the place of Nikolaj Brink. The band name was inspired by the DARKTHRONE album 'Panzerfaust'.

A six track 1995 demo led to a record deal. Guitarist Jens Christensen was added to the group prior to recording of the '6 Seconds To Kill' album. ILLDISPOSED man Bo Summer joined the band for 2000's 'Soul Collector'. The album, sung in German, comprised entirely of songs devoted to second world war German panzers.

Former PANZERCHRIST guitarist Finn Henriksen was later to be found in Norwegian Black Metal band ALLFADER. For recording of a 2003 album, 'Room Service', PANZERCHRIST's line-up stood at ILLDISPOSED man Bo Summers on vocals, guitarists Rasmus Henriksen and Frederik O'Carroll, bassist Michael Enevoldsen with the EXMORTEM credited Reno Kiillerich on the drums. That same year the PANZERCHRIST duo of guitarist/bassist Michael Kopietz of and drummer Reno Kiilerich founded the brutal Death Metal band KOBEAST in collaboration with Søren 'Azazel' Jensen of GRANHAMMER, IRON FIRE and CORPUS MORTALE repute. Both Kopietz and Kiilerich also have affiliations with FROZEN SUN and 12 GAUGE. In late 2003 Reno Kiilerich joined fabled North American Death Metal band VILE. The drummer stepped up a further league in March of the following year when he was recruited as session man for DIMMU BORGIR's European, South American and US 'Ozzfest' festival dates, and in early 2005 would be laying down studio drums for OLD MAN'S CHILD.

In April 2005 former EXMORTEM man Michael Pedersen took over the drum position from Reno Kiilerich. Further changes in the band roster saw the addition of FAIRYTALE ABUSE keyboard player Dea Lillelund as the group worked on new album recordings for the Neurotic label. In January 2006 Kiilerich joined Anglo-Danish collaboration DOWNLORD. Drafting DIE drummer Bent Nyeng, the band entered Antfarm Studio with producer Tue Madsen that month to record the album 'Batallion Beast'. However, no sooner had the band commenced work it was revealed Reno Kiilerich was once again manning the drums. PANZERCHRIST wrapped up these sessions in mid March. Adding another major act to his scoreboard, Kiilerich temped for HATE ETERNAL's European dates in May.

Mighty Music announced it was to reissue PANZERCHRIST's 2003 'Room Service' and 2000 'Soul Collector' albums for December 2006. The Prutten Records sub-division also put out the group's debut 1995 demo on limited-edition vinyl. Meantime, a brand new studio album 'Bello' was projected for 2007.

SIX SECONDS TO KILL, Voices Of Wonder SE003CD (1996). Perfect Kill / Winterlands / Panzer / Frontlines / Virus / Halls Of Oblivion / Reload / Eviscerated Bitch / Gunhead / Last Supper.
OUTPOST FORT EUROPA, Serious Entertainment (1999). Outpost / Skin / Uranium Angel / Fort Europa / Burning / Killing Of The Weak / Flesh In The Scent / Surrender Is Not An Option.
SOUL COLLECTOR, Mighty Music (2000). Leben Will Gewonnen Sein / P2krieg / Der Panzertoter / Panzergrenadier / Schwars Ist Unser Panzer (Ich Batt'einen Kameraden) / Unsere Hochste Chre / Kalt Wie Der Finsternis / Zum Oegenstoss.
ROOM SERVICE, Mighty Music (2003). Tomorrow / Creature / Lies / Suicide / At The Grave / Death Approaches / Metal Church / Roomservice / The Red Rover / Evil.
BATTALION BEAST, Neurotic NRT060010 (2006). The Lean Black Cruisers / The Gods They Do Not Give Us Long / He Is Dead Who Will Not Fight / Infants' Graves / Weep No More / Flame Of The Panzerchrist / Lumps Of Rotting Clay / War In The North / The Spirit Of Soldiers.

PANZERSCHRECK

SANDVIKEN, SWEDEN — *Fredrik Håf (vocals), Rikard Olsson (guitar), Tommy Kvist (guitar), John Falk (bass), Stefan Englund (drums).*

PANZERSCHRECK, named after the WW II German disposable tank destroyer, is a Sandviken, Gävle based Crustcore band founded during 2005 by the RADIOSKUGGA and MEGATRON credited guitarist Tommy and drummer Stefan Englund. They would be joined by second guitarist Rikard Olsson, of GADGET, DISKONTO, SHITSTORM and NAGANA. Fredrik Håf from VULTURE and GARROTED took up the vocalist role and Emppa of SLAVATOR, KNOCKOUT DROPS and DEDAM became bassist.

The group first performed live at the Sandviken Kungen on July 14th 2006, debuting new DEVOURER, EX INFERIS, EXOSUS, RADIOSKUGGA and IN AETERNUM credited bassist John Falk, having replaced Emppa.

Panzerschreck, Panzerschreck (2006) (Demo). Too Damn Deep / Project: A Neverending Mission / Fucker Of All / You Broke My Heart (So I Break Your Face) / Losing Grip.

PARABELLUM

MEDELLIN, COLOMBIA — *Ramón (vocals), Carlos Mario (guitar), John (guitar), Tomás (drums).*

Medellin Death Metal band PARABELLUM was created in early 1983 by guitarist Carlos Mario and drummer Cipriano. The group debuted in 1987 with the two track EP 'Sacrilegio', this limited to 500 copies. A follow up single, 'Mutacion Por Radacion', was released as a 600 copy run in 1988. A further pressing of 'Sacrilegio' was issued in 1992, once again limited to 500 units, although a bootleg also surfaced, adding a third track 'Guerro, Monopolio, Sexo'.

Blasfemia Records issued the 'Tempus Mortis' compilation album in 2005. Limited to 1000 copies the collection comprised the 1987 'Sacrilegio' EP and 1988 'Mutacion Por Radacion' EP plus six previously unreleased rehearsal tracks dating to 1984-'85 and a live video track from the 1985 'La Batalla De Las Bandas' festival.

Sacrilegio, Independent (1987) (Limited edition 500 copies). Madre Muerte / Engendro 666.
Mutacion Por Radiacion, (1988) (Limited edition 600 copies). Bruja Maldita / Mutacion Por Radiacion.

PARACOCCIDIOIDOMICOSISPROCTITISSARCOMUCOSIS

QUERETARO, MEXICO — *Ginecologic Cryptococcidioidomicosis (vocals / drums), Genital Practical Of Sensation (guitar), Dr.Forense (bass).*

Queretaro based "sick porno goke grind" Metal band PARACOCCIDIOIDOMICOSISPROCTITISSARCOMUCOSIS, no doubt one of the most original names around, released a tape in 2001 entitled 'Lynphatic Descomposition Esquistosomiasis' featuring Infeccion Cutanea on vocals and guitar and Ulcera Genital on bass. The band released a split tape with HORRIFIED entitled 'Cullinigus' in 2001. By this juncture the group was credited as vocalist / guitarist Ginecólogo Necrolamedor Clitoral (a.k.a. Isaac), bassist Obstetra Penetrador Himeneal (Cristoph) with Proctólogo Destructor de Esfínteres on drums.

American Line Productions released the 2002 album 'Satyriasis And Nymphomania'. The cover art for this record, a graphic autopsy photograph, was banned in many countries. In January 2004 a split album was released in collaboration with BUTCHER ABC.

Cunnilingus, Maykos (1999) (Demo). Copulation Zoophiliacal With Genital Siphilitic (Part. 2) / Infection Voluptose For The Aroma Of Vaginal Vomit / Scream Clinically For Genitourinarims Orgasm / Proliferation Of The Lust By Ginecologial Suffering / Under The Exciting Dominion Of The Vaginal Obsession / Uroporfirinogenodescarboxilasandome Y Postulandome Con Tu Orgasmia Hexaclorobencenosisticarial Sexo Traumante.

PARACOCCIDIOIDOMICOSISPROCTITISSARCOMUCOSIS / HORRIFIED, Maykos (2001) (Split album with HORRIFIED). Poison Gas Chamber (HORRIFIED) / Trauma (HORRIFIED) / Inside The Coffin (HORRIFIED) / Severe Catatonia In Pathology (HORRIFIED) / Blown To Pieces (HORRIFIED) / Silent Night, Bloody Night (HORRIFIED) / Copulation Zoophiliacal with Genital Siphilitic (Part 2) / Infection Voluptose For The Aroma Of Vaginal Vomit / Scream Clinically For Genitourinarims Orgasm / Proliferation Of The Lust By Ginecologial Suffering / Under The Exciting Dominion Of The Vaginal Obsession / Uroporfirinogenodescarboxilasandome Y Pustulandome Con Tu Anorgasmia Hexaclorobencenosisticarial Sexo Traumante.

SATYRIASIS AND NYMPHOMANIA, American Line Productions LA055 (2002). Toward The Apocalipsex (Intro) / Uroporfironogenodescarboxilandome Y Pustulandome Con Tu Anorgasmita Exaclorobencenosisticarial Sexo Traumatizante / Grotesque Mucopurulence (Disgorge's Sensation) / Slowly Rot With Esclerosis Under Of Endocrinology / Proliferacion De La Lujuria Por Padecimiento Ginecologianal / Succionando Y Excitando Carcinomas Femeninas (Falta De Higiene Genital) / Necroexpulsion Cangrenosa Por Sindrome De Inmuno Deficiencia Adquirida / Putridexpulsion Diphyllobothrium Of The Vaginal Cavity / Psicoiticoproparasitoscopociabscesoinfangiectasiespasmo Y Hematico / Satyriasis And Nymphomania (Apocalipsex End).

PARACOCCIDIOIDOMICOSISPROCTITISSARCOMUCOSIS / BUTCHER ABC, American Line Productions (2004) (Split album with BUTCHER ABC). Copulation Zoophiliacal With Genital Siphilitic (Part. 2) / Infection Voluptose For The Aroma Of Vaginal Vomit / Scream Clinically For Genitourinarims Orgasm / Proliferation Of The Lust By Ginecologial Suffering / Under The Exciting Dominion Of The Vaginal Obsssesion / Uroporfirinogenodescarboxilasandome Y Postulandome Con Tu Orgasmia Hexaclorobencenosisticarial Sexo Traumante.

PARENTAL ADVISORY

VIENNA, AUSTRIA — *Inhumate (vocals / bass), Otto (guitar), Sic (guitar), Tomas Zonyga (drums).*

PARENTAL ADVISORY, a Vienna Death Metal act, debuted live on February 14th 1998 alongside ENDLESS FALLING at the Andino venue in the Austrian capitol. The group first issued the 'Butcher' demo during 1999. Live dates to promote this outing included supports to IMMOLATION, SANATORIUM, EMINENCE, KRABATHOR, HYPNOS and DARKEST HOUR plus an appearance at the July 2001 Wiener Neustadt 'Hell On Earth' festival.

'Infested With Zombies', produced by Christian Sutter, followed in September 2000, being marketed beforehand with the Austrian 'Foreskin' tour aligned with SEEDS OF SORROW and CRYOSPHERE. Gregor Marboe, of PENDRAGON, JORMUNGARD, ENDKRIEG, PROJECT X, ESCHATA, CRYOSPHERE and DEFENDER KFS, engineered third demo, 2005's 'Zombie Legion'. Initially the band featured DEFENDER KFS's Rene Binder on drums but in September 2003 he opted out and was substituted by DEFENDER KFS and DEVESTATION man Beisser (a.k.a. Niko Scharf). He would be replaced by SEEDS OF SORROW man Tomas Zonyga in September 2004. PARENTAL ADVISORY in 2005 comprised Inhumate, from SEEDS OF SORROW and MISANTHROPIC MIGHT, guitarist Otto, of PUNISHMENT, and second guitarist Sic (a.k.a. Fredl), from PUNISHMENT and MISANTHROPIC MIGHT.

Butcher, Parental Advisory (1999) (Demo). Butcher / Postmortal Cannibals / Armageddon / Nothing But Dead Remains / Holocaust / Suicide Caust The Death / Just Delusion / About Hatred And Sorrow / Alive And Buried.

Infested With Zombies, Parental Advisory (2000) (Demo). Intro / Infested With Zombies / More Dead Than Alive / Headfuck / Waiting To Die / Mortua Terra / Time For A Blowjob / Spit Or Swallow / Hope's End / Outro.

Zombie Legion, Parental Advisory (2005) (Demo). Killed, Fucked, Devoured / Zombie Legion / Takin' Lives / . . . Of Eating Human Beings.

PARRICIDE

CHEŁM, POLAND — *Tadeusz Jankowski (vocals / bass), Piotr Sabaranski (guitar), Albert Kraczkowski (guitar), Tomasz Luc (drums).*

PARRICIDE is a Chełm based brutal Death Metal act dating back to the Spring of 1990. Following a 1992 rehearsal recording PARRICIDE signed to Baron Records for the July 1994 cassette release 'Fascination Of Indifference'. A 1995 demo, entitled 'Unnailed', led to a further tape release 'Accustomed To Illusion', this time through Morbid Noizz Productions. Throughout their formation until 1997 the group line up stood at vocalist / bassist Mariusz Staniuk, guitarists Albert Kraczkowski and Piotr Sabaranski with Artur Raszka on drums. Subsequently Tomasz Łuć of CLIMATE took over on drums and Tadeusz Jankowski became the new frontman. The 1999 'Crude' album, issued via Jackhammer Music, marked PARRICIDE's CD debut.

PARRICIDE's next offering, August 2001's 'Ill Treat', emerged initially on the Surgical Diathesis label but would swiftly be re-released through Empire Records in all new artwork. 'Kingdom Of Downfall' followed in October of 2003. That November PARRICIDE featured on the split album 'Cut Your Head Before They Do' for the Surgical Diathesis label alongside fellow Polish extreme Metal acts DEFORMED and PATOLOGICUM. Included would be their rendition of CANNIBAL CORPSE's 'Hammer Smashed Face'.

Touring across Poland in April of 2004 saw the band, having inducted DEIVOS and ABUSIVENESS drummer Krzysztof Saran as stand in, united with road partners fellow Poles SQUASH BOWELS and Czech Grind crew CEREBRAL TURBULENCY. The group toured Poland with MINCING FURY AND GUTTURAL CLAMOUR OF QUEER DECAY, MENTAL DEMISE and INCARNATED during November 2005.

Rehearsal Tape /92, (1992) (Rehearsal demo). Disturbing Thoughts / Rot In Peace / Perpetual Fate / Outburst Of Fury / The Barboring Image / Hidden Truth / Cult Of Personality.

FASCINATION OF INDIFFERENCE, Baron (1994). Enslavery / Fascination Of Indifference / Swarving To Solitude / Beyond All This / Nothing To Be Said / State Of Mind / Ability Of Comprehension / Play Your Insanity.

Unnailed—Polish Underground Series, Morbid Noizz (1995). Intro / Unexpected Emptiness / Behind The Scenes / Drown In Misery / Mentally Insane / Pushed Aside.

CRUDE, Jackhammer Music (1999). Conditional Infinity / Nothing Twice / Narrow Minded / Mad Arrives / Indignation / Pandemic Destruction / Intoxicating Despair / Deceived / Lofty Rhetoric.

ILL TREAT, EMP 008 CD (2002). I Feel Nothing / Slavers Of Infirmity / Watched (By Shades) / One Step To Deviation / Deranged / Like The God / Liar / Nothing Consider Aeons / Step Of Evolution / Primordial Fear / Coming Dawn / Burnt Offerings / Hammer Smashed Face.

KINGDOM OF DOWNFALL, Mad Lion (2003). Against Doctrines Of Systems / Terror, The Foundation Of Religion / Dethronement / . . . But Sick / Thoughtlessness / Survival Of The Fittest / Sleepwalker / Daddy's Death / Training / Kingdom Of Downfall / He / Masquerade / Resurrection To Come / Behind The Scenes.

CUT YOUR HEAD BEFORE THEY DO, Surgical Diathesis (2003) (Split album with DEFORMED and PATOLOGICUM). Resurrection To Come / Like The God / Hammer Smashed Face / Slaver's Of Infirmity / Step Of Evolution / Daddys Death.

PARRICIDE

WEST GLAMORGAN, UK — *Martyn Cook (vocals), Julian Hay (guitar), Chris Duffell (guitar), Matthew Didcott (bass), Michael Hourihan (drums).*

West Glamorgan Death Metal band PARRICIDE was formulated during 1994. The band employed Tim Hamill of TORTOISE CORPSE to act as producer for their demo 'Infection', recorded at Sonic Studios, Kidwelly in March 1995. The group's original formation comprised singer Martyn Cook, guitarists Julian Hay and Chris Duffell and bassist Mike Hourihan. Unable to locate a drummer, Hourihan switched instruments in time for the band's first concert and Matthew Didcott was installed on bass.

In September 1996 Jeremy Ward replaced Duffell and Chris Thomas enrolled on bass. In this formation PARRICIDE undertook a UK tour and dates in the Czech Republic. The band signed with French label Thunder Records, although no product was forthcoming and PARRICIDE dissolved. Both Julian Hay and Michael Hourihan joined DESECRATION. PARRICIDE briefly reformed for a batch of concerts before faltering again.

In 2004 Michael Hourihan, then a member of NECKBRACE, invited his former PARRICIDE colleagues Chris Duffell and Martyn Cook to join the band. That same year Michael Hourihan joined up with the reformed Glam band TIGERTAILZ. He would also man the drums with EXTREME NOISE TERROR.

Infection, Parricide (1995) (Demo). Infection / Termination / Decades Of Death / Curse The Cross / Mental Incarceration.

PASSENGER

SWEDEN — *Anders Friden (vocals), Niclas Engelin (guitar), Håkan Skoger (bass), Patrik J. Sten (drums).*

PASSENGER is a 2003 project fronted by IN FLAMES vocalist Anders Friden alongside GARDENIAN guitarist Niclas Engelin (formerly of IN FLAMES), HEADPLATE bassist Håkan Skoger and ex-TRANSPORT LEAGUE drummer Patrik J. Sten. The band signed to the Century Media label for an eponymous album release.

European gigs in December saw the band sharing a bill comprising MOONSPELL, LACUNA COIL and POISONBLACK. The band entered the recording studio in March 2004 to cut a new album. With Friden active on the touring front with IN FLAMES Engelin and Sten forged a fresh band venture entitled KEROZENE a collaboration with bassist Robert Hakemo, ex-GARDENIAN and GOOSEFLESH, along with vocalist Mikael Skager. The band cut recordings for their debut album early in the year, mixing it at Studio Fredman in Gothenburg during April. Sten also acted as co-producer for the 2004 album of THE HAUNTED and shortly afterward re-entered the same studios to lay down session drums for Minnesota based melodic Death Metal band THE FIFTH SUN's album 'The Moment Of Truth'.

In March of 2005 a new Metal formation was announced with ENGEL, a Gothenburg based quintet featuring Niclas Engelin in union with guitarist Marcus Sunesson, ex-THE CROWN, drummer Morbid Mojjo (a.k.a. Daniel Moilanen), a veteran of MINDSNARE, SANDALINAS, RUNEMAGICK, DRACENA, RELEVANT FEW and LORD BELIAL, bassist Robert Hakemo, ex-GARDENIAN and GOOSEFLESH together with vocalist Mangan Klavborn.

In November 2006 Niklas Engelin filled in for his old act IN FLAMES, subbing for Jesper Strömblad, who was "sitting out the group's current tour in order to deal with some personal issues'.

PASSENGER, Century Media 8109-2 (2003). In Reverse / In My Head / For You / Just The Same / Carnival Diaries / Circus / Rain / Circles / I Die Slowly / Used / Eyes Of My Mind.

PASSENGER, Toy's Factory TFCK-87319 (2003) (Japanese release). In Reverse / In My Head / For You / Just The Same / Carnival Diaries / Circus / Rain / I Die Slowly / Used / Eyes Of My Mind / Drowning City.

PATHOGEN

PERTH, WA, AUSTRALIA — *Justin Norton (vocals), Aidan Barton (guitar), Adam Ferguson (guitar), Dave Sandstrom (bass), Mark Boeijen (drums).*

Perth Death Metal band PATHOGEN, founded by guitarist Aidan Barton date to 1995. The group's original rhythm section comprised bass player Phil Norman with Gavin Irving on drums. John Cuyperus occupied the second guitar position. Line-up changes the following year saw the introduction of bassist Mark Rodregez then in quick succession Louis Dunstan. PATHOGEN cut the 1996 'Tyranny Of Hatred' demo, recorded by Al Smith at Bergerk Studios. Meantime, Dave Sandstrom took over on guitar. Second demo 'Nightfall' was produced by Al Smith at VHS Studios in 1997.

PATHOGEN went through a further change in 1998, losing both Sandstrom and Dunstan. The bassist created melodic death Metal outfit VESPER'S DESCENT. The following year Gavin Irving was superseded by Mark Boeijen, of VESPER'S DESCENT, as Dave Sandstrom returned on bass. Sandstrom was also performing double duties with ENFORCE between 2000 and 2001. In 2001 ex-CHOKE guitarist Glenn Dyson was incorporated.

An ex-PATHOGEN singer, Cain Cressall, activated MALIGNANT MONSTER in 2003, this unit also involving PATHOGEN mentor guitarist Aidan Barton on the demo 'Welcome To Your Doom', released in 2004, and September 2005 album 'Foul Play'.

Prime Cuts released the debut album 'Bloodline', engineered by Aidan Barton at Sovereign Studios, in April 2005. PATHOGEN opened for THE BLACK DAHLIA MURDER's first Australian tour in August 2006 then for ARCH ENEMY in October. Both drummer Ben Mazzarol and vocalist Michael Lenane exited in February 2007. Former member Mark Boeijen, also operational with VOYAGER, resumed his post on the drums whilst Cain Cressall, of MALIGNANT MONSTER and CENTAUR, took on vocal responsibilities.

Tyranny Of Hatred, Pathogen (1996) (Demo). Eviscerated / Grimoire / Liberty / Denigrate / Blood Of Ancients / Tyranny Of Hatred.

Nightfall, Pathogen (1997) (Demo). Warchild / My Little Cow / Beyond Repent / Nightfall / Bleed My Soul Pt.1 / Bleed My Soul Pt.2.

BLOODLINE, Prime Cuts (2005). ... / Identity Theft / Beyond Repent / Bleeding Eye / Fallen Kind / Shallow / Eviscerated / C.O.W. / Nightfall / Bleed My Soul (Pt. I) / Warchild / Tyranny Of Hatred / ....

PATHOLOGIST

OSTRAVA, CZECH REPUBLIC — *Martin Cvilink (vocals), Daniel Hary (guitar / bass), Stanislav Mazur (drums).*

Ostrava's infamous Gore-Grind outfit PATHOLOGIST were certainly out to push the genre to the extreme with their debut 1990 cassette 'Sexual Cadaveric Mysophilia', this boasting an incredible 385 tracks over 45 minutes. The group, comprising singer Martin 'Cyklo' Cvilink, guitarist Daniel Hary 'Harok' and Stanislav 'Stanley' Mazur on drums, traces its roots to the 1987 formations FUCKING DEATH and SARKOM, adopting the PATHOLOGIST brand in January of 1990.

The band would better their first achievement though with the 'Medical Jurisprudence' tape of 1991, cramming 974 tracks into just 30 minutes of playing time. PATHOLOGIST applied the brakes for the 1992 album 'Putrefactive And Cadaverous Odes About Necroticism', this comprising a sober 12 songs. This album would see release in December 1992, before a re-release in November of 1993 on M.A.B. Records and second, remastered re-issue in December 1994 on Radiation Records, a division of Nuclear Blast Records. Gigs to promote this album witnessed valuable supports to PARADISE LOST, ROOT, TIAMAT, KRABATHOR and CADAVEROUS CONDITION.

'Grinding Opus Of Forensic Medical Problems', put out by Radiation Records in December of 1994, would only host a mere 9 songs. PATHOLOGIST members also operate Noise-Grind band the ONANY BOYS, releasing a split 1996 single in union with GROSSMEMBER.

PUTREFACTIVE AND CADAVEROUS ODES ABOUT NECROTICISM, M.A.B. MAB 002 (1992). Putrefactive And Cadaverous Odes About Necroticism / Malignant Introduction / Open The Dissection Ward / Reck With Suppuration / Cadaveric Metamorphoses / Genital Pathological Perversity / Tumorous Defects And Diseases / Anatomical Necropsy / Progression Of Putrefaction (Part II) / Decomposition Of Corpses / Carcass Dismemberment / Vomitory Corporal Dysfunction / Rotten Outroduction.

GRINDING OPUS OF FORENSIC MEDICAL, M.A.B. MAB 008 (1995). Paroxysmal Prelude / Cannibalistic Disfigurement / Putrescence / Cadavers In Medical Jurisprudence / Uterogestation To Abortion / Exhumed Dead Body / Infectious Agonizing Parasitism / Gynaecological Sickness / Secretion Of Ejaculate.

PATHS OF POSSESSION

FL, USA — *George Fisher (vocals), Jay Fossen (guitar), Richard Burnelle (guitar), Randy Butman (bass), Ridley (drums).*

Florida's PATHS OF POSSESSION is a high profile Death Metal outfit fronted up by erstwhile CANNIBAL CORPSE frontman George "Corpsegrinder" Fisher, MORBID ANGEL guitarist Richard Brunelle and WITHERED EARTH bassist Randy Butman. Initially the band went under the formative handle of SWOLLEN. Following a 2001 demo 'Legacy In Ashes' their commercial debut would come in 2003 as a restricted run of 1000 split albums allied with Fort Pierce, Florida band DARK FAITH issued through Splattergod Records.

PATHS OF POSSESSION contracted with Metal Blade Records in early 2005, entering Mana Recording Studios in Tampa, Florida with the HATE ETERNAL and MORBID ANGEL credited Erik Rutan as producer to record their album 'Promises In Blood'. Ex-PATHS OF POSSESSION drummer Nick Goodyear joined DARK FAITH.

February 2006 saw an announcement detailing PATHS OF POSSESSION singer Nick Goodyear's induction into an all new band billed PROMETHEAN HORDE alongside BLASTMASTERS members guitarist Jeff Parrish and bassist Jesse Jolly. The group utilised Mana Recording Studios once again in January 2007 to record its sophomore album, given a working title 'The End Of The Hour'. PATHS OF POSSESSION lined up a North American tour with DARK FAITH and VIVISECT in July.

LEGACY IN ASHES, SplatterGods (2002). Darklands / Cold Vengeance / Legacy In Ashes / The Second Coming / Bring Me The Head Of Christ / Trial By Torture / The Dawn Brings War / Army Of Death.

PROMISES IN BLOOD, Metal Blade (2005). Darklands / Butcher's Bargain / Bleed The Meek / The Second Coming / Where The Empty Gods Lie / Heart For A Heart / In My Eyes / Erzsebet / Promises In Blood / Bring Me The Head Of Christ / Through The Fiery Halls / The Icy Flow Of Death.

PENTACLE

BLADEL, HOLLAND — *Wannes Gubbels (vocals / bass), Alex Verhoeven (guitar), Mike Verhoeven (guitar), Robert Smissaert (drums).*

Created as a blasphemous Death Metal quartet in 1989, PENTACLE's first product was the 1992 demo tape 'Caressed By Both Sides', which featured four original tracks plus a version of HELLHAMMER's 'The Reaper'. A further demo, 'Winds Of The Fall', was issued in 1993 as the band gained live experience opening for ASPHYX, ANATHEMA, SAMAEL and ANCIENT RITES. The band's growing exposure led to a track, 'A Dance Beyond', on the 1994 DSFA Records compilation album 'Paradise Of The Underground' shortly followed by the debut single 'Exalted Journey'. Originally distributed by Damnation Records, inaugural pressings comprised five tracks including HELLHAMMER's 'The Reaper'. This track would be omitted from subsequent pressings released through Displeased Records.

A 1998 full-length album, '... Rides The Moonstorm' released by Damnation Records, saw the inclusion of a cover version of 'Spell Of The Pentagram' by Chilean band PENTAGRAM. A highly collectable item emerged in 2000 with the Iron Pegasus release '... In League With ...', a split release shared with DESASTER featuring DESASTER's rendition of PENTACLE's own 'A Serpent In Bloodred' whilst PENTACLE covered their allies 'In A Winter Battle'. This opus would be pressed on 500 black vinyl, 333 on "Pussy red" vinyl and 100 picture discs.

The EP 'Ancient Death' emerged in 2001, second pressings via Dark Realm Records in 2002 adding a bonus track in 'Souls Blood'. That year To The Death Records also published a split EP in collaboration with Sweden's REPUGNANT. In 2004 PENTACLE would donate their rendition of 'The Beasts Of The Apocalypse' to the 'Seven Gates Of Horror' tribute album assembled by the Dutch Karmageddon Media label in homage to pioneering Bay Area Thrash act POSSESSED.

A proposed split 10" to be shared BLOOD STORM with entitled 'Archaic Undead Fury', although announced, would not in fact transpire. The band entered Harrow Productions studio in Losser during October to craft a new album entitled 'Under The Black Cross', a conceptual outing based on events in March 1942, for Iron Pegasus Records. A limited edition vinyl variant was pressed with 600 copies on traditional black and 150 in blood red vinyl.

Unfortunately, in mid 2005, guitar player Mike Verhoeven suffered a serious injury to his right arm, putting him out of action for a lengthy period. PENTACLE therefore continued live work as a trio. In November 2005 From Beyond Productions issued the 'Archaic Undead Fury' as a 10" single, limited to 999 copies. PENTACLE lined up March 2006 European dates in alliance with THEE PLAGUE OF GENTLEMEN.

Caressed By Both Sides, (1992) (Demo). A Mind In Flames / Belief From Below / Son Of The Dawn / Denial Of God / The Reaper.

Winds Of The Fall, (1993) (Demo). Buried In Mankind´s Sleep / Descending Of The Soul / My Fall / Deepness Of The Depths / Winds Of The Fall.

Exalted Journey, Midian Creations (1995). Exalted Journey / Son Of The Dawn.

The Fifth Moon EP, Displeased D00047 (1996). Black At Heart / A Serpent In Blood Red / The Flame's Masquerade (Her Sun Is The Moon) / Adoring An Endless Dawn.

... RIDES THE MOONSTORM, Damnation (1998). Rides The Moonstorm / Veil Of Sulphur / Yielding To The Sceptor Of Flesh / For I Am Chaos / Raised By Nights Chaos / Baptism In A Fiery Void / Spell Of The Pentagram / Deepness Of The Depths / Scythes.

... In League With ..., Iron Pegasus (2000) (Split EP with DESASTER). In A Winter Battle / Soul's Blood.

Ancient Death, Damnation (2001). Prophet Of Perdition / Descending Of The Soul / Legion Of Doom / Immolated In Flames / Witch Of Hell / Walking Upon Damnation's Land.

Ancient Death, Dark Realm (2002). Prophet Of Perdition / Descending Of The Soul / Legion Of Doom / Immolated In Flames / Witch Of Hell / Walking Upon Damnation's Land / Soul's Blood.

Dunkel Besatthet, To The Death (2002) (Split EP with REPUGNANT). The Beasts Of The Apocalypse.

UNDER THE BLACK CROSS, Pentacle (2005). Into The Fiery Jaws / Raise The White Ensign! / March Of The Campbletown / A Devil's Shooting Gallery / The Utmost Desolation / (Storming Through) A Hail Of Steel / The Last Fight (ML 306's Stand) / Awaiting The Blast Of Death.

Archaic Undead Fury, From Beyond Productions FBP-056 (2005) (10" vinyl. Limited edition 999 copies). Hellish Descend / Blast Them The Sky.

PERNICIOUS

ALMELO, HOLLAND — *Coen Tabak (vocals), Maikel Ekkerink (guitar), Laurens Bos (guitar), Henri Andres (bass), Mark Knoop (drums).*

PERNICIOUS was established in Almelo during the Spring of 1994 with an introductory roll call comprising lead vocalist Coen Tabak, guitarists Maikel Ekkerink and Laurens Bos, bassist Henri Andres and drummer Mark Knoop. The 'Ancient Stupidity' demo followed in 1996 and a debut album 'Art Of

Aggression' was delivered in 1997. After the release of the 'Bloodlust' album on Teutonic Existence Records Lauens Bos suffered a debilitating accident at work losing half of his middle finger. Undaunted, Bos maintained his position in the band. 2002 proved turbulent for the band, despite recording of a third album with the projected, albeit less than savoury, title of 'Cunteater'. In October Henri Andres stepped down but was swiftly replaced in November by former ULCERATE FESTER man Vincent. However, further bad luck hit home when frontman Coen Tabak opted out. Although the third album, having had the title changed to 'A Carnal Age', was ready for release PERNICIOUS announced they were to fold in January of 2003. Mark Knoop had already joined EXTREEM ECZEEM by October of 2002.

Ancient Stupidity, (1996) (Demo). Intro / Ancient Stupidity / Your Way / Days Of The Underworld / Outro.
ART OF AGGRESSION, Independent (1998). Through The Gleams Of Death / Fake / Ancient Stupidity / Circle Of Lies / Your Way / Meant To Be / And I / Suffer Your God / Eternity Falls / Inner Confessions.
BLOODLUST, Teutonic Existence (2000). Bloodlust / Slowly Been Poisoned / Sever And Spliced / Hypnotized / Mission To Kill / Pernicious / Spellbound / Blood In My Eyes / Child Of Darkness / Illusions.

PERSECUTION

SYDNEY, NSW, AUSTRALIA — *Rod Hunt (vocals), Jody Bartolo (vocals), Dave Neil (guitar / keyboards), Adam Gillis (guitar / bass), Peter Kotevski (drums).*

PERSECUTION is a Sydney Death Metal band that emerged in the early 1990's. In July 1992 they recorded a demo called 'Encapsulated' and, after a few internal changes, the band signed to the relatively new Australian Death Metal specialty record label, Warhead Records. The debut EP, entitled 'Beseiged', came out in 1994. Scott Mullins had appeared on the demo as the drummer but replaced by Nick Hunt in 1995. Hunt himself was replaced by Pete Kotevski for the EP in 1996.

The band, now with a dual vocal attack firmly entrenched, jumped to the Underclass label and released their debut full-length album, 'Thick Face, Black Heart', in 1996. As recently as 2002 members Neil, Bartolo and Gillis played in a hardcore band called UNCLEAN.

Encapsulated, Slightly Persecuted (1992). Wargod / Night Warriors / New 3rd / Encapsulated.
Besieged, (1994). Intro/Indignant / Besieged / Instrumental H.G.C. / Victims / Deadly / Outro.

PERSECUTION

OELSNITZ, GERMANY — *Steffen Thümmel (vocals / bass), Sascha (guitar), Sebastian Schindler (guitar), Volker Schettler (keyboards), Maik Fleckeisen (drums).*

Oelsnitz, Neuwürschnitz based Gothic, melodic Death Metal act founded in 1995. To date PERSECUTION have released three demo sessions, 1996's 'Wozu noch Lieden', recorded with a line-up of vocalist / bassist Steffen Thümmel, guitarist Sascha Ehrlich, keyboard player Aline Langner and drummer Peter Schubert, 1998's 'First Vision' and 'Nightfall In Mind' in October 2000. Drummer Maik ''Flecky'' Fleckeisen also operates with another Gothic Metal outfit BLACK SWAN whilst keyboard player Volker Schettler also shares duties with ESCAPE FROM DIASPAR. PERSECUTION's Steffen Thümmel, also known as 'Ecthelion' of ANDRAS, has a solo Black Metal project ISENBURG, issuing the album 'Erzgebirge' via Black Attakk in 2004.

PERSECUTION's late guitarist Sascha Ehrlich, who died in November 2002, had his position filled by CREDIBLE man Robby.

Wozu Noch Leiden!?, Persecution (1996). Wozu Noch Leiden!? / Diktator / Mach Es War / Dreck.

Nightfall Of Mind, (2000). Freedom / Another Coming Race / Nightfall Of Mind.
MENTAL CHAOS, (2002). Shine / The Sinner Takes It All / Freedom / The Tower Of Barad-Dûr / Sacrosant Nation? / Boiling Blood / Luminous Dark / The Mourning / Trinity In Man.

PESSIMIST

BALTIMORE, MD, USA — *Ralph Runyan (vocals / bass), Kelly McLauchlin (guitar), Bill Hayden (guitar), John Grden (drums).*

Self styled 'Dungeon Metal' act PESSIMIST trace their history as far back as 1989 when guitarist Kelly McLauchlin, a veteran of RESISTANCE, DEATH FORCE (which at one stage included erstwhile DARK ANGEL vocalist Don Diote) and Grindcore act DEMOLITION cut the project 'Tunnel Vision' demo. In 1992 McLauchlin then became involved with the Tampa, Florida act CAULDRON, which featured a pre-ICED EARTH Matt Barlow. As PESSIMIST, McLauchlin laid down a second demo session 'Dark Reality' during 1993, with the 'Dark Reality II' set arriving a year later. For these recordings the band unit comprised Kelly McLauchlin, singer Rob Kline, bassist Tom Kimbler and drummer Rob Westbrook.

Further material, entitled the 'Absence Of Light' EP, arrived in 1995 via Purgatory Productions, by this stage PESSIMIST having an overhaul of the rhythm section, newly incorporating bass player Tony Pernia and drummer Chris Pernia. The promotion release 'Let The Demons Rest' secured a deal with Lost Disciple Records in 1997 for the debut album 'Cult Of The Initiated' and 1999 follow up 'Blood For the Gods'. That same year PESSIMIST donated their rendition of 'The Pestilence' to a Full Moon Productions KREATOR tribute.

During 1999 the band enrolled former DWELLING MADNESS man Gary Daniels as an addition to a line up. Before long Eric Little took over bass and Joe Roffeld, of FORGOTTEN SOULS and DWELLING MADNESS, became the band's new drummer. PESSIMIST would make their mark on the burgeoning tribute scene by donating renditions MEGADETH's 'Killing Is My Business And Business Is Good' to the 1999 Dwell compilation 'Megaded' and a version of DEATH's '1000 Eyes' to the Dwell 'Demonic Plague' collection. The band, promoting the album 'Blood For The Gods', also undertook a brief European tour in August of 1999 before splintering yet again. In the summer of 2000 Daniels, Roffeld and Little resurrected DWELLING MADNESS.

McLauchlin assembled a completely revised line-up of PESSIMIST in 2000, recruits included former FEAR OF GOD men guitarist Bill Hayden and drummer John Grden with frontman Ralph 'Reaper' Runyan, previously a member of New Jersey's CORRUPTURE. Following an appearance at the California 'November To Dismember' event he band re-signed a with Lost Disciple, enlisting the esteemed figure of MORBID ANGEL and HATE ETERNAL guitarist Erik Rutan to produce the 2002 release, 'Slaughtering The Faithful'.

Meantime ex-members Rob Kline, bassist Tony Pirna and drummer Chris Pirna subsequently forged EXCATHEDRA, a band that in turn morphed into PSYCHOTOGEN for the 2001 album 'Perverse And Unnatural Practices'.

Dave Brenzeal of TROKKAR and an ex-colleague of McLauchlin's in CAULDRON, would temporarily take the PESSIMIST drum stool. During December of 2001 Grden would found Black Metal act TRUE UNHOLY DEATH in alliance with MISERY INDEX guitarist Sparky Voyles. As 2002 broke PESSIMIST pulled in yet another member of CORRUPTURE, this time the new recruit being drummer Mick Kimock. Once more though the drum stool would change hands when in September Mike Perigo of CADAVER SYMPOSIUM took on the task for live work. PESSIMIST's October North American headline dates had the support element divided into three portions, REFLUX taking on the first batch of shows followed by MORTALITY then PSYPHERIA.

Kelly McLauchlin was reported to have rejoined DIABOLIC in January of 2003, but in actuality this did not transpire. The guitarist, in union with the former DIABOLIC founding members vocalist / bassist Paul Ouellette, guitarist Jerry Mortellaro and drummer Aantar Lee Coates, also forged UNHOLY GHOST. McLauchlin also found time to guest session on the 2003 BLACK MASS album 'Voices Of Fate'.

By early 2004 Grden was operational with FIRES OF GOMORRAH in league with ex-BLACK MASS guitarist The Blasphemous One (a.k.a. (Russ Strahan). In February, former vocalist Rob Kline, active with HATRED UNLEASHED, was announced as having joined the newly reformed FLESHTIZED. Kelly McLauchlin exited from UNHOLY GHOST in February 2005 in order to prioritise PESSIMIST. The band formation counted Reaper, guitarists Kelly McLauchlin and Bill Hayden with Chris Pernia on drums.

September 2006 saw an announcement from McLauchlin stating "In order to lay the band to rest with some dignity, I must announce that PESSIMIST is on indefinite hiatus."

CULT OF THE INITIATED, Lost Disciple LDRF002 (1997). The Stench Of Decay / Let The Demons Rest / Cult Of The Initiated / Drunk With The Blood Of The Saints / DungeonLorde / Pyrosexual / Innocence Defiled / Unholy Union.

BLOOD FOR THE GODS, Lost Disciple LDRF006 (1999). Century Of Lies / Unspeakable Terror / Psychological Autopsy / Demonic Embrace / Mens Rea / Whore Of The Undead / Unborn (Father) / Tunnel Rats / Wretched Of The Earth.

SLAUGHTERING THE FAITHFUL, Lost Disciple LDRF014 (2002). Requiem / Baptized In Blasphemy / Summoned To Suffer / Embodiment Of Impurity / Slaughtering The Faithful / Infernal Abyss / Metempsychosis / Resurrected Torment / Stripped Of Immortality.

PESTILENCE

ENSCHEDE, HOLLAND — *Patrick Mameli (vocals / guitar), Patrick Uterwyck (guitar), Jeroen Paul Thesseling (bass), Marco Foddis (drums).*

A popular Death Grindcore Metal outfit that has seen considerable album sales in Europe in spite of an ever fluctuating line-up. During the late eighties and early nineties the Enschede based PESTILENCE reigned as the leading Dutch Death Metal band, releasing a string of influential records. PESTILENCE was conceived in Spring 1986 and were originally a trio of guitarist Randy Meinhard, drummer Marco Foddis and vocalist / guitarist Patrick Mameli. As a three piece PESTILENCE released their first 1987 demo 'Dysentry'. The group later added vocalist / bassist Martin Van Drunen, who assumed vocal duties from Mameli, and cut another demo entitled 'The Pennance'. The debut album, 1988's 'Malleus Malificarum', was produced by Kalle Trapp for Roadrunner Records.

PESTILENCE underwent a major line-up reshuffle with Foddis and Meinhard quitting. Meinhard, replaced by former THERIAC man Patrick Uterwijk, joined SACROSANCT and later SUBMISSION. Van Drunen concentrated from this point purely on vocals. The band executed dates in Holland throughout February 1990 with AUTOPSY and BOLT THROWER on the 'Bloodbrothers' tour.

Vocalist Van Drunen quit following 1989 'Consuming Impulse' to join ASPHYX, SUBMISSION and later BOLT THROWER. For 'Testimony Of The Ancients', arriving in September 1991 and recorded at Morrisound Recording in Tampa, Florida by Scott Burns, PESTILENCE employed the services of keyboard player Kent Smith and CYNIC bassist Tony Choy. The band played a brace of concerts in Mexico during November 1991 supported by CANNIBAL CORPSE, BLACK THORN, CENOPTAPH and HARDWARE.

The band's last album, May 1993's 'Spheres', was co-produced by Mameli and Steve Fontano. Dutchman Jeroen Thesseling joined PESTILENCE as a permanent bassist in late 1993 but following European dates with CYNIC the band folded.

Martin Van Drunen resurfaced in mid 2002 debuting his new act DEATH BY DAWN on the European live circuit. Patrick Mameli made studio time in early 2004 to donate his services to the DEATH tribute album 'Within The Mind' assembled by JAMES MURPHY. Meantime, former PESTILENCE bassist Jeroen Paul Thesseling embarked upon an entirely different form of music by forming his own flamenco troupe.

Early 2005 found former PESTILENCE members Martin Van Drunen and Jeroen Paul Thesseling collaborating with KING LOCUST guitarist Niels Drieënhuizen in a new band entitled PROJEKT TABUN. The trio entered Studio Het Lab in Schaarsbergen to put down initial recordings.

In 2006 Jeroen Paul Thesseling announced the formation of ENSEMBLE SALAZHAR. That November Polish label Metal Mind Productions re-issued the compilation 'Mind Reflections' as a limited, hand numbered run of 2000 copies.

In January 2007 it would be learned that Martin Van Drunen had joined forces with THANATOS guitarists Stephan Gebédi and Paul Baayens, GOREFEST drummer Ed Warby and former HOUWITSER bass player Theo van Eekelen in a new band unit dubbed HAIL OF BULLETS. Another PESTILENCE offshoot saw Patrick Mameli forging C-187 in alliance with M.A.N, ex-TRANSPORT LEAGUE and MNEMIC vocalist Tony Jelencovich, ATHEIST and ex-CYNIC bassist Tony Choy plus CYNIC and ex-DEATH drummer Sean Reinert.

Dysentery Demo '87, (1987). Against The Innocent / Delirical Life / Traitor's Gate / Throne Of Death.

The Penance, (1987). Into Hades (Intro) / Before The Penance / Affectation / Fight The Plague.

MALLEUS MALIFICARUM, Roadrunner RR 9159-1 (1988). Malleus Malificarum / Antromorphia / Parricide / Subordinate To The Domination / Extreme Unction / Commandment / Chemotherapy / Bacterial Surgery / Cycle Of Existence / Orculum Infame / Systematic Instruction.

CONSUMING IMPULSE, Roadrunner RR 9421 (1989). Dehydrated / Process Of Suffocation / Suspended Animation / The Trauma / Chronic Infection / Out Of The Body / Echoes Of Death / Deify Thy Master / Proliferous Souls / Reduced To Ashes.

TESTIMONY OF THE ANCIENTS, Roadracer RO 9285 (1991). The Secrecies Of Horror / Bitterness / Twisted Truth / Darkening / Lost Souls / Blood / Land Of Tears / Free Us From Temptation / Prophetic Revelations / Impure / Testimony / Souless / Presence Of The Dead / Mindwarp / Stigmatized / In Sorrow.

SPHERES, Roadrunner RR 9081 (1993). Mind Reflections / Multiple Beings / The Level Of Perception / Aurian Eyes / Soul Search / Personal Energy / Voices From Within / Spheres / Changing Perspective / Phileas / Demise Of Time.

PHANTASM

MILWAUKEE, WI, USA — *Tony Brandt (vocals / drums), Doug Schoeneck (guitar), Scott McKillop (guitar), Lee Groth (bass).*

Milwaukee, Wisconsin's PHANTASM, borne out of the ashes of HUMAN EVIL in 1988 by vocalist / drummer Tony Brandt and guitarist Scott McKillop, issued the demos 'Lycanthropy' in April of 1991 and 'The Abominable' in October of the following year. The former session included erstwhile DR. SHRINKER man Matt Grassberger on bass guitar whilst 'The Abominable' tapes saw Brandt and McKillop joined by second guitarist Doug Schoeneck and THANATOPSIS bass man Steve Somers. In side activity, both Brandt and McKillop sessioned on the DR. SHRINKER demo 'The Eponym'.

'The Abominable', oddly for a Death Metal band featuring a cover version of THE YARDBIRDS sixties hit 'For Your Love', was re-pressed on CD format by the Chicago based Monsterdisc label in 1995. The band subsequently featured Todd Klug and former MORTAL DREAD bassist Lee Groth but dissolved toward the close of 1995. Doug Schoeneck subsequently founded SPIRIT CREEK whilst Brandt and Lee Groth created MAD LAUGHTER.

THE ABOMINABLE, Monsterdisc (1995). A Souls Nightmare / Sewed Back To Life / Heavier Than Hell / Breeders of Hatred / For Your Love / The Abominable / Gut Suckers / Palace Of Blood.

PHANTASMA

KOŠICE, SLOVAKIA — *Andy Duc (vocals / guitar), Rudolf Kurilla (guitar), Richard Dermek (bass), Rastislav Fabian (keyboards), Radovan Timko (drums).*

PHANTASMA, an atmospheric Death Metal act out of Kosice, was founded by vocalist / guitarist Andy Duc and guitarist Roland Kurilla in 1992. Drafting Radoslav Timko the trio cut the demo 'Destroyed 'Cause He Believed" in 1993, after which Timko was forced to exit due to his national military service obligations. PHANTASMA pulled in new guitarist Leviathan and bassist Jesus. Signing to Metal Age Productions they laid down tracks for 'Welcome To Heaven', released in 1994.

Black Labyrinth Productions released the 'Jazz For Jesus' cassette in 1996. Both Kurilla and Jesus decamped that same year. PHANTASMA reformulated, enlisting guitarist Rudrige, keyboard player Rastislav Fabian and Ryhak on drums. In March 1998 the band recorded the 'Jahve' album for Rock Extremum, issued in 1999.

WELCOME TO HEAVEN, Metal Age Productions (1994). The Judgement Day / Back From The Past / Unnamed Grave / Last Homage / Welcome To Heaven (Part I) / Welcome To Heaven (Part II) / The Eternal / A Falling Head / The Wedding Night / Emotional Dullness / Ave Satanas.

JAZZ FOR JESUS, Black Labyrinth Productions (1996). We'll Meet In Hell Again / Their Sword Was Hard Indeed! / A Shore / Get Away! / Jesus Is Just A Stone / A Document About Jesus Death / I Trust In God Only / Sans Commentaire / Jazz For Jesus / Ave Satanas—Songs Of Demons.

JAHVE, Rock Extremum ISP 0018 (1999). Eternal Horizon / Vision / Mission / Depraved / Disease Called Religion / Ave Sathanas III / Oasis Of Loneliness / You Must Kill Him / Noctis / Jahve / Mangy Dogs.

PHAZM

NANCY, FRANCE — *Pierhryck (guitar), Pathryck (guitar), Mahx (bass), Dyrhk (drums).*

Nancy's Deathcore act PHAZM, created during 2003 by erstwhile SCARVE guitarists Pierhryck (a.k.a. Pierrick Valence) and Pathryck (Patrick Martin), debuted with a three track demo. These sessions saw drums handled by Dyrhk, (Dirk Verbeuren), also of SCARVE. Bassist Olivia Scemama, previously a member of NO RETURN, was replaced by Mahx. Scemama also gained credits with Black Metal band BALROG and in December 2005 joined Belgian Death Metal act ABORTED.

PHAZM signed to Osmose Productions for the 2004 album 'Hate At First Seed'. These tracks had been cut in Denmark the previous December with producer Jacob Hansen. Included would be a cover version of MOTÖRHEAD's 'Dogs'. European shows for January 2005 found PHAZM in union with YYRKOON and IMPALED NAZARENE. PHAZM then underwent a membership change as Verbeuren's priorities with SCARVE and SOILWORK forced him out of the picture. Cedric of SOLEKAHN acted as replacement.

In September 2006 PHAZM launched second album 'Antebellum Death 'n' Roll', recorded at Midnight Studios again through Osmose Productions. Initial copies came with an extra DVD disc of live material recorded in Nancy. PHAZM united with Poland's DECAPITATED for extensive European touring throughout February 2007.

HATE AT FIRST SEED, Osmose Productions OPCD 166 (2004). Inchaos / What A Wonderful Death / Resinous Balm / Forest Recipe / Devoured Tenderness / Vicious Seed / Fleshback / Loneliness / Dogs.

ANTEBELLUM DEATH 'N' ROLL, Osmose Productions (2006). How To Become A God / Hunger / Black 'n' Roll / So White, So Blue, So Cold / My Darkest Desire / Damballah / Decay / The Bright Side Of Death / Sabbath / Mr. Toodling / Lorelindorenan / Burarum.

PHLEGETHON

JOENSUU, FINLAND — *Jussi Nyblom (vocals / bass), Teemu Hannonen (guitar), Juha Tykkyläinen (guitar), Lasse Pyykkö (drums).*

A Joensuu Doom / Death Metal band established during 1988, PHLEGETHON is named from Greek mythology, being one of the five principal rivers of fire in the realms of Hades. Initially the band was formed as a trio of guitarists Teemu Hannonen and Juha Tykkyläinen with Lasse Pyykkö on drums. A demo cassette, recorded without bass and entitled 'Visio Dei Beatifica', was issued in October 1989. Having drafted bassist Jussi Nyblom a second session 'Neutral Forest', featuring Jukka Timonen on keyboards, followed in June 1990. In 1991 PHLEGETHON tracks recorded between February, with Hannonen on lead vocals, and re-tracked in May with Jussi Nyblom now as vocalist, at Mix Man Studio were put out by Swiss label Witchhunt Records as the 'Fresco Lungs' EP. This was re-issued on CD format in 1992, adding two newly recorded tracks 'Stone Me' and 'Without Tea Waters'.

PHLEGETHON folded in 1992 but reformed three years later. A three song demo cassette, simply titled 'Promo 1995', resulted that November. However, Saku Hurskainen recorded all lead guitar parts. Drummer Lasse Pyykkö was later to be found as a member of SARNATH. In 2003 Pyykkö forged NERLICH in union with vocalist / bassist Miikka Merikallio and guitarist Jarno Nurmi.

Lasse Pyykkö, Juha Tykkyläinen and Saku Hurskainen refounded PHLEGETHON to record the 2006 demo 'Totem Within'. The first brace of demos saw reissue as the 2006 album 'Visions From The Forestside'. A February 2007 two track demo billed 'Lava Poetry' comprised 'The Unreal Locations Of The Period Of Stones' and 'Petrified Hermits'.

In early 2007 PHLEGETHON members vocalist Jussi Nyblom and drummer Lasse Pyykkö formulated high speed Death / Grindcore Metal band COFFINS OF CYST.

Visio Dei Beatifica, Phlegethon (1989) (Demo). Intro—Endless Horse / The Brethren In Provenance / Sunset Of Golgotha / Those That Are Sent Forth / Encapsulation Of The Ark Of The Covenant / Acrimonious Elysium.

Neutral Forest, Phlegethon (1990) (Demo). Female Sabbath / During My Hollow Trinity / Into The Halls Of Theory / Ornaments.

Fresco Lungs, Witchunt WIHU 9208 (1992). Stone Me / Without Tea Waters / 0-520 / Encapsulation Of The Ark Of The Covenant / Ornaments / The Golden Face.

Promo 1995, Phlegethon (1995) (Demo). Karma Vest / Teaser's Whine / Crystal Limbs.

Totem Within, Phlegethon (2006) (Demo).

VISIONS FROM THE FORESTSIDE, (2006). Intro: Endless Horse / The Brethren In Provenance / Sunset Of Golgotha / Those That Are Sent Forth / Encapsulation Of The Ark Of The Covenant / Acrimonious Elysium / Female Sabbath / During My Hollow Trinity / Into The Halls Of Theory / Ornament / End Of Eternity (1988 rehearsal) / Golden Face (Live 1991).

Lava Poetry, Phlegethon (2007) (Demo). The Unreal Locations Of The Period Of Stones / Petrified Hermits.

PHOBIA

ORANGE COUNTY, CA, USA — *Shane McLachlan (vocals), Steve Burda (guitar), Bruce Reeves (bass), Matt Mills (drums).*

Socio- politically minded Grindcore act with both Punk and Thrash tendencies. Founded in 1990 PHOBIA soon issued the opening 'What Went Wrong?' demo. PHOBIA would bow in commercially with the 'All That Remains' album on Relapse Records and a split live 12" single shared with PLUTOCRACY in 1993.

1994 saw the issue of the 'Return To Desolation' EP, drum sessions for which were laid down by FEAR FACTORY's Raymond Herrera. A West Coast tour ensued alongside Hardcore acts LACK OF INTEREST and CAPITALIST CASUALTIES.

The band's debut album, 'Means Of Existence', would be released by Slap-A-Ham in 1998 followed up by a nationwide American touring schedule. In 1999 PHOBIA would tour Europe and the UK releasing a split 7" with Japanese band CORRUPTED. The same year witnessed a hectic two month, 50 date tour of mainland Europe supporting such acts as IMMOLATION, HARD TO SWALLOW and STATE OF FILTH.

PHOBIA's 2001 album for Necropolis Records subsidiary Death Vomit 'Serenity Through Pain' included a cover of FINAL CONFLICT's 'Private War'.

Drummer Matt Mills parted ways with the band in mid 2002, replaced by Ramond Yuckmouth Herrera once again. PHOBIA also announced plans for a split release in alliance with RESIST and EXIST. In May of 2004 PHOBIA headed up the US 'Grind The East Coast' tour with running mates Finland's ROTTEN SOUND, STRONG INTENTION and for later shows CIRCLE OF DEAD CHILDREN. Gigs on the West Coast in May 2006 saw a union with DISFEAR, STRONG INTENTION and 9 SHOCKS TERROR.

PHOBIA allied themselves with EXTREME NOISE TERROR for US concerts in May 2007.

ALL THAT REMAINS, Relapse (1990).

Live Split EP, Misanthropic (1993) (Split single with PLUTOCRACY).

Return To Desolation EP, Relapse (1994). Degrading Humanity / Sickening Discretion / Depraved / Hitler Killa!

Enslaved, Slap A Ham SLAP029 (1997). Enslaved.

MEANS OF EXISTENCE, Slap A Ham SLAP047 (1998). Rape Theft Murder / Taxes At Work / Stink Head / Morally Content / Blood Sport / Discommunicate / Piece Of Mind / Means Of Existence / Snail / Scars / Another Social Disease / State And Enemy / Systematically Imprisoned / Suffer For Arrogance / Infant Suffering / Cheap Life / Ruined.

Phobia, (1999) (Split single with CORRUPTED).

DESTROYING THE MASSES, Pessimiser (1999).

RETURN TO DESOLATION, Relapse RLP6903 (2001). Degrading Humanity / Sickening Discretion / Depraved / Hitler Killa! / Emptiness / All That Remains / Chemical Fear / Internal Rot / Festering Instinct / Unchained Mind / Degrading Humanity—Dead Nazis / Dead Nazis.

SERENITY THROUGH PAIN, Deathvomit DVR015CD (2001). Death Threat / God Is Grace / Mercy Killing / Mental Incarceration / Hooray For Jesus / Closure / White Devil / D.F.F.D. / Fueled By Pride / Poison My Mind / Pathetic Minds / Sieg Help / Wounds Through Punishment / Slave To Religion / Bush / Ways Of Destruction / Sovereign / You / You Suffer / Social Sheep / Rid Self Condemnation / Private War.

PIG DESTROYER

USA — *J.R. Hayes (vocals), Scott Hull (guitar), Brian Harvey (drums).*

Side outfit of AGORAPHOBIC NOSEBLEED man Jay Randall. PIG DESTROYER's '38 Counts Of Battery' album included CARCASS cover versions 'Exhume To Consume', 'Regurgitation Of Giblets' and 'Genital Grinder' along with a take on THE MELVINS 'Oven'. The CARCASS renditions also appeared on a limited edition split EP release with Boston Doom mongers ISIS. Before the year was out PIG DESTROYER had followed up with the equally brutal 'Prowler In The Yard'.

The band revealed 2004 was to commence in a suitably heavy fashion, participating in the January 'Extreme The Dojo VII' tour of Japan alongside NASUM, NAPALM DEATH and ANAL CUNT. That July the band completed work on the 'Terrifyer' album, this opus coming completing with a bonus, half hour DVD track entitled 'Natasha', mixed in 5.1 surround sound. Joining PIG DESTROYER on a 'Terrorizer' magazine sponsored 'Grind Over UK' tour, commencing 12th November in Nottingham at the Old Angel pub, would be TOTAL FUCKING DESTRUCTION, Doom duo HALO and the UK's NARCOSIS.

The band would contribute their rendition of 'Claude' to a 2005 MELVINS tribute album, 'We Reach: The Music Of The Melvins', through Fractured Transmitter Records.

EXPLOSIONS IN WARD 6, Reservoir RSVR023CD (1998). Deflower / Tentacle / Yellow Line Transfer / Under The Fingernails / Elfin / Unwitting Valentine / Endgame / Oven / Three Second Apocalypse / Treblinka / Fingers In The Throat / My Fellow Vermin / One Funeral Too Many / Higher Forms Of Pornography / Honeymoon / Alcatraz Metaphors / Flesh Upon Gear / Pixie.

PIG DESTROYER, Robotic Empire (1999) (Split album with GNOB). Blond Prostitute / Patterns Of Failure / Rejection Fetish / Dark Satellites / Purity Undone / Forgotten Child / White Sand / Painter Of Dead Girls / Down In The Streets.

Genital Grinder, Relapse (2000) (Split EP with ISIS). Genital Grinder / Regurgitation Of Giblets / Exhumed To Consume.

PROWLER IN THE YARD, Relapse RR6485-2 (2001). Jennifer . Scatology Homework. Trojan Whore. Ghost Of A Bullet. Heart And Crossbones. Strangled With A Halo / Cheerleader Corpses / Scatology Homework / Trojan Whore / Ghost Of A Bullet / Heart And Crossbones / Strangled With A Halo / Intimate Slavery / Mapplethorpe Grey / Evacuating Heaven / Tickets To The Car Crash / Naked Trees / Sheet Metal Girl / Preacher Crawling / Pornographic Memory / Murder Blossom / Body Scout / Snuff Film At Eleven / Hyperviolet / Starbelly / Junkyard God / Piss Angel.

38 COUNTS OF BATTERY, Relapse RR6471-2 (2001). Deflower / Tentacle / Yellow Line Transfer / Under The Fingernails / Elfin / Unwitting Valentine / Oven / Three Second Apocalypse / Treblinka / Fingers In The Throat / My Fellow Vermin / Endgame / One Funeral Too Many / Higher Forms Of Pornography / Honeymoon / Alcatraz Metaphors / Flesh Upon Gear / Pixie / Genital Grinder- Regurgitation Of Giblets / Exhume To Consume / Burning Of Sodom / Delusional Supremacy / Alcatraz Metaphors / Treblinka / Seven And Thirteen / Scouring The Wreckage / Torquemada / Frailty In Numbers / Suicide Through Decay / Dark Satellite / Seven And Thirteen / Flag Burner / Delusional Supremacy / Martyr To The Plague / Ruination / Synthetic Utopia / Monolith / Frailty In Numbers.

PIG DESTROYER, Robotic Empire (2002) (Split album with BENUMB). Hymn / Task Masker / Black Centipede / Immune To Life / Fuck You Up / Contagion / Black Dice.

TERRIFYER, Relapse (2004). Pretty In Casts / Boy Constrictor / Scarlet Hourglass / Thumbsucker / Gravedancer / Lost Cause / Sourheart / Towering Flesh / Song Of Filth / Verminess / Torture Ballad / Restraining Order Blues / Carrion Fairy / Downpour Girl / Soft Assassin / Dead Carnations / Crippled Horses / The Gentleman / Crawl Of Time / Terrifyer / Natasha.

PLEURISY

HOLLAND — *Johan Wesdijk (vocals), Mathieu Van Hamersvelt (vocals), Axel Becker (guitar), Alex Seegers (guitar), Bas Van Den Bogaard (bass), Edwin Nederkoorn (drums).*

Death Metal band PLEURISY employed two lead vocalists, Johan Wesdijk credited with 'screams' and Mathieu Van Hamersvelt for 'grunts'. The group debuted in 1993 with the five track promo tape 'My Favourite Girl'. A further cassette 'Degenerated To A Human Life' followed in 1995, tracks from also surfaced on the EP 'Unholy Spheres'. That same year guitarist Axel Becker, in collusion with ORPHANAGE members bass player Eric Hoogendoorn and Poldermann founded a side project SILICON HEAD.

During 2001 Wesdijk bowed out and was superseded by Roy Vermeulen. However, by early 2002 Vermeulen had parted ways with the band. By April George Oosthoek of ORPHANAGE had assumed the role.

Unholy Spheres EP, (1996). Any Day (Intro) / Living In Oblivion / In Darkness—Mortification Of Flesh / Unholy Spheres / Devastating Authorization.

EXPERIENCE THE SACRILEGE, Power (2000). Mission Transformed / Experience The Sacrilege / Bid Your Pleasures / Gone From The Sun / Ineluki / Divinity In Decay / Witchcraft / Trail Of Destination / In Darkness (Mortification Of Flesh).

DAZED AND DERANGED, (2003).

POLLUTED INHERITANCE

HOLLAND — *Ronald Camonier (vocals / guitar), Erwin Wesdorp (guitar), Menno de Fouw (bass), Friso Van Wijk (drums).*

A Death / Thrash band created during 1989 with the union of erstwhile POLLUTION guitarists Ronald Camonier and Erwin Wesdorp with the former rhythm section of SACRAMENT, bassist Menno de Fouw and drummer Friso Van Wijk. The band would induct lead singer Jean-Paul Hoorman in 1990 and proceeded to cut an inaugural six track demo, 'Afterlife', in August of 1991. However, despite this progress, Hoorman opted out and Camonier took over the lead vocal mantle.

POLLUTED IN HERITANCE, having first donated no less than three of their 'Afterlife' demo tracks to the 'Cries Of The Unborn' compilation album, landed a deal with the West Virginia label. The band's debut album 'Ecocide' was produced by HOLY MOSES man Andy Classen but a severe setback was suffered when West Virginia folded.

POLLUTED INHERITANCE cut a further demo session in April of 1994 which duly scored the 'Demo of the month' rating in Aardschock magazine. A new deal was struck with the DSFA label for second outing 'Betrayed' and the group toured Holland as guests to ORPHANAGE. Splitting with DSFA the band would spend a lengthy period away from the limelight preparing new material, finally signing to the Belgian Rokorola label for the 2001 album 'Into Darkness'. In early 2001 bassist Menno de Fouw announced his departure, the band recruiting bassist Stefan Vrieswijk in his stead.

TAKOJ SE DAVA DOL, 91995) (0).
ECOCIDE, West Virginia WVR SPV 084-57312 (1992). Faces / Dissolved / Eaten / Memories Of Sadness / Substance Of Existence / Fear / Stillborn / After Life / Rottings / Look Inside.
BETRAYED, Displeased DSFA 1002 (1996). Intro / Forgotten Cause / Mental Connection / Elimination / Betrayed / Emptiness / Drowning (In Faith) / Indulge / Never To Be Free / Need Me / My Voice.
INTO DARKNESS, Rokarola (2001).

POSTMORTEM

BERLIN, GERMANY — *Matthias Reutz (vocals), Marcus Marth (guitar), Dirk Olesch (guitar), Tilo Voigtlaender (bass), Marco Thäle (drums).*

A Death Metal band from Berlin, POSTMORTEM released their first demo, 'Secret Lunacy', in 1991. A second tape, 'Last Aid To Die', appeared the following year before the band signed to the Frankfurt based Husky Records in 1993. The group sold more than 4,000 copies of their debut album 'Screams Of Blackness' before Dirk Olesch left the group. POSTMORTEM's follow up album, 'The Age Of Mass Murder', was issued in March 1997.

The group has so far played with acts like MORBID ANGEL, HATE SQUAD, CEMETARY, ATROCITY, IN FLAMES, CREMATORY and PYOGENESIS.

The 'Der Totmacher' EP includes a twisted cover version of 'Anna', the song made famous by German Electronic Pop band TRIO. 1998's 'Repulsion' offering boasts a radical cover workout of AC/DC's 'Sin City'. The 2003 EP 'Join The Figh7 Club' incorporated a rendition of the BEASTIE BOYS 'Fight For Your Right'. Drummer Marko Thäle joined FATAL EMBRACE in mid 2003.

SCREAMS OF BLACKNESS, Husky (1993). God Et Sins / Suicide / Reincarnation / Dreamland / Buried Alive / Lunacy / Bad Times / Shadows Of Memory / Assvibrator / Deathcontrol / Destroy The World / Treibjagd / Gutes Gefuehl.
Der Totmacher EP, Morbid MR031 CD (1996). Pink Giant / Der Totmacher / Autumn Rose / Postmortem / Anna.
THE AGE OF MASS MURDER, Morbid 033 CD (1997). And / Welcome / In / Our / World / Of / Violence / And / Serial / Crime! / Listen To.. / The Baby!!! / Albert 'Cannibal' Fish / To Henry Lee Lucas (From Otis) / Co-Ed Killer / The Manson Cult / Der Totmacher / Green River / Your Innocence / The Age Of Massmurder / Rosa Riese / The Son Of Sam / Are We Not Men? / 25 Cromwell Street.
REPULSION, Morbid MR 046 (1998). Epitomize / Clockwork Black / Gutterballs / Bleeding / Beyond The Bounds / Witches Burn / Over The Line / Heiligenschein / Sin City / Inside The Clockwork / Better Beware / Dreadful Sins / Black Trinity / Sick And Twisted / Follow The Hypocrite / Epitaph.
Join The Figh7 Club EP, Independent (2003). Final Master / Freaky Monster / Fightin' The Club / Blood For Blood / XX_Bastard / Fight For Your Right.

POVERTY

SAN FRANCISCO, CA, USA — *Sean Riggen (vocals), Scott Dodge (guitar), Lou Gilberto (bass), Bud Mills (drums).*

San Francisco Death Metal act POVERTY was formulated in 1989 by guitarist Scott Dodge, bassist Lou Gilberto and two former members of INFERNAL FORCES. Following Bay Area live work and a brace of demo tapes POVERTY changed its line-up in 1991, inaugurating the INSANITY credited Buddy Mills on the drums. In 1998 the eight song demo 'Poverty Sucks' saw publication. However, the band then went into stasis for a number of years as the entire line up enrolled into INSANITY.

With INSANITY, the group released one album before coming to a halt. POVERTY was resurrected once more in 2001. The EP 'Global Destruction' emerged in December 2003.

Global Destruction, Independent (2003). Thou Shalt Kill / Chemical Sweat / Over Before It Begins / Gutter Dead / Toe Tag.

PRECIPICE

GAINESVILLE, FL, USA — *R.J. Hagenow (vocals), Andy Adcock (guitar), Will McClanahan (guitar), Lori Volce (bass), Dave Silverstein (drums).*

Gainesville, Florida Death / Thrash act PRECIPICE includes the erstwhile HELLWITCH pairing of guitarist Andy Adcock and drummer Dave Silverstein. The pair also have ties to GARDY LOO. PRECIPICE aimed to break free from the Death / Thrash genre restrictions, introducing a diverse array of musical persuasions ranging through Jazz, Punk and Fusion. The group's first product would be a 1994 demo 'The Foundation'. These tracks were laid down by Adcock, Silverstein, guest vocalist John "The Klingon" Gauthier, second guitarist Allan Godfrey and bassist John Mortensen. A second session, 'Bloody Kill' recorded at Ibus Recording Studios in Pinellas Park, followed in 1995, now seeing R.J. Hagenow on lead vocals, John Paul and Jimbo on bass. PRECIPICE cut a debut album 'Prophet Of Doom' in 2000 at Morrisound Recording Studios with producer Jim Morris.

The Foundation, Precipice (1994). Degeneration / Dementia / Cycle Of Extinction / Power Of Fear.
Bloody Kill, (1995). Engulfed In Flames / World After War / Black Sun Rising.
PROPHET OF DOOM, Crook' D (2001). Challenges / Lords Of Darkness / Degeneration / Blind Rage / Prophet Of Doom / Bloody Kill / Socio-Violence / Involuntary Skinhead.

PREJUDICE

BELGIUM — *Erik (vocals), Davy Tunicki (guitar), Def (guitar), Sammy (bass), Frank Vangeneugden (drums).*

Death Metal band PREJUDICE was founded in June 1993, debuting live in December that same year. Opening demos included 'Violent New Breed' in 1994 and 'Jaundiced Eye' in 1996. On the album front, PREJUDICE delivered the 'Broken Promises' opus for the Teutonic Existence label during 1998. Switching to Painkiller Records the band followed up with 'Reality' in October 2001.

In 2004 band members involved themselves with Black Metal side act EX INFERIS, guitarist Davy Tunicki and drummer Frank Vangeneugden working alongside singer Stefan C., guitarist Kevin Thoné and bassist Steven Bynens of SOLIPSIST to cut a self-titled demo.

Taking PREJUDICE into 2004, and promoting a new album 'Dominion Of Chaos', would be January European dates, the band packaged alongside American high profile acts HATE ETERNAL, DEEDS OF FLESH and DYING FETUS. The band then were set to form up part of the 2004 European heavyweight 'No Mercy' festivals commencing March 29th, sharing billing with SPAWN OF POSSESSION, HYPOCRISY, KATAKLYSM, CARPATHIAN FOREST, VOMITORY, CANNIBAL CORPSE and EXHUMED. However, the band was forced out of the tour in February, PREJUDICE issuing a strong condemnation of their record company in the process. That November, PREJUDICE hooked up with Maltese band BEHEADED for European dates. More shows in October, dubbed the 'All Over Absorbing' tour, found the band on a package billing with Portuguese act GOLDENPYRE, Ukrainians FLESHGORE and ROTTENNESS from Mexico.

In May of 2005 PREJUDICE entered Excess studios in Rotterdam to cut tracks for a split record to be shared with ROTTENNESS and CARNAL DECAY from Switzerland for release through Spain's Grotesque Productions. As the year closed the group contracted with Greece's Sleaszy Rider Records for a new album. The same label also reissued all of PREJUDICE's previous albums, 1996's 'Broken Promises' adding early demos as bonus tracks, a re-mixed version of 2001's 'Reality' and 2003's 'Dominion Of Chaos' re-mastered. Spring touring across Europe to promote these releases saw tour dates alongside SUHRIM.

Citing "Personal reasons", the band parted ways with drummer Frank Vangeneugden in April 2006. The group installed the SOLIPSIST and MOTHRA credited Cristophe Piette as session drummer for live work. Bassist Greco exited in July.

PREJUDICE returned to Excess studio in Rotterdam in April 2007 to start tracking their fourth album.

Violent New Breed, (1994). A Stranger Within / Abused Minds / Prejudice / Social Dispossal / A Violent New Breed.
Jaundiced Eye, (1996). Two Minded / Second Guess / Social Disposal / Perpetual Pain / Prejudice.
BROKEN PROMISES, Teutonic Existence (1998). Society's Victim / Eyes Only / As Long As It Lasts / Serial Minds / Second Guess / Last Scream / Shadows Of Society / Perpetual Pain / Prejudice / Broken Promises.
REALITY, Painkiller (2001). New Breed / Act Of Despair / Deformity / Dictated Lives / Embrace / Betrayed / In-Vitro / Shadowed Thoughts / Vicious Conduct / Nuclear Malediction / Spheres.
DOMINION OF CHAOS, Painkiller (2004). Suffer / Unobtrusive Hatebreed / Undecided / Obsolete / Destructive Soul / Convicted / Resolved / Remains.

PRIMEVAL

HOUSTON, TX, USA — *John Benavides (vocals), Victor Fernandez (guitar), Juan Fernandez (bass), Welden Roberts (drums).*

PRIMEVAL is a Houston based Death Metal act founded in 1995 by the fusion of two prior acts RELAYER and IMPRECATION, number vocalist Kevin, guitarist John Quiroz and the Fernandez siblings guitarist Victor, bass player Juan and drummer Omar. Shortly after laying down an initial set of demos tragedy struck the band when, on the 11ith of March, Victor, Omar and older brother Mario were involved in an auto accident which claimed the lives of both Omar and Mario. Victor too would be seriously injured but, after eventually recovering from a comatose state, opted to reconstruct the band. Rudy Delgado would be the man chosen to fill the drum position.

PRIMEVAL reconstituted itself further as the DISTORTED RAGE credited John Benavides was brought in to handle lead vocals for the track 'Sub Species' on a new demo 'Condemned', leading up to the 1997 album release 'Temptation'. In 1998 PRIMEVAL were back in the studio cutting a further demo entitled 'Scorn Of Incubus'. Welden Roberts of LEGION repute would then take command of the drums.

TEMPTATION, Visceral Productions (1997). Intro / Origin / Temptation / Stand Your Ground / The Sleeper Has Awaken / Question / L.A.L. / The Replicant / Manipulator.

PROCREATION

BC, CANADA — *Jay Schneider (vocals), Carlos Coraza (guitar), Jim Martin (bass), Johnny Prizmic (drums).*

The pre-BLASPHEMY act PROCREATION, active between 1989 and 1993, delivered a 1990 demo 'Rebirth Into Evil' with a second set, 'Coming Of Hate', arriving in 1991. Both sessions were recorded at the Fiasco Brothers Studio in New Westminister, British Columbia. The band's founding line up comprised singer Jay "Hippieshredder" Schneider, guitarists Mike Death of WITCHES HAMMER and Carlo Coraza, bassist Jim Martin and Tom Komisarski. By the time the group folded they would be down to a quartet, minus Death and seeing WITCHES HAMMER man Johnny Prizmic on the drums.

In 2004 the Californian Nuclear War Now! Label re-issued both demos as the 180 gramm black vinyl album 'Incantations Of Demonic Lust For Corpses Of The Fallen'. 200 copies were issued in the 'Die hard' format, pressed as a picture disc and coming in a gatefold jacket with a booklet, poster, patch and sticker.

INCANTATIONS OF DEMONIC LUST FOR CORPSES OF THE FALLEN, Nuclear War Now! Productions ANTI-GOTH 017 (2004). Intro / Morbid Reality / Caking Blood / After Life / Darkest Force / Tomb Of Assyria / Darkest Force / Rebirth Into Evil / The Coming Of Hate / Tomb Of Assyria.

PROFANE OMEN

LAHTI, FINLAND — *Jules Näveri (vocals), Antti Kokkonen (guitar), Williami Kurki (guitar), Tomppa Saarenketo (bass), Samuli Mikkonen (drums).*

Thrash Metal band PROFANE OMEN, founded in Lahti by guitarist Janne Tolonen and drummer Länä Varjola in 1999, opened proceedings with the demos 'Profane Omen' in 1999 and 'Bittersweet Omen', featuring a cover version of MIDNIGHT OIL's 'Beds Are Burning', in 2000. The inaugural line-up also counted lead vocalist Jules Näveri, second guitarist Bönde Pöllänen and bass player Jukka Keisala. Pöllänen would depart and WRECK OIL's Williami Kurki enrolled as two more sessions arrived the following year in 'Fuck The Beast' and 'Load Of Lead'. Further turmoil ensued in the ranks as both founder members Tolonen and Varjola exited. PROFANE OMEN swiftly regrouped by inducting the DROWNED IN LIFE pairing of guitarist Antti Kokkonen, also of KILL THE ROMANCE, and the BEFORE THE DAWN and KILL THE ROMANCE credited drummer Mika Tanttu. With this line-up PROFANE OMEN cut the August 2002 EP 'Label In Black'.

Bassist Jukka Keisala exited in mid 2003 in order to prioritise MISERY INC. He would be superseded by WRECK OIL's Tomppa Saarenketo. PROFANE OMEN issued the 'Adrenaline' EP in August 2004.

Signing with Dethrone Music in January 2006 the band utilised Hideaway and Villvox studios, working with producer Ville Sorvali, to craft a new album. New man on the drums would be Samuli Mikkonen, scene veteran of ANSUR, ARCADIAN NOCTURNE, END BEGINS and UHRILEHTO. 'Beaten Into Submission' arrived in September.

On February 16th 2007 PROFANE OMEN was honoured with the "Rookie of the Year" award at the Finnish Metal Awards, which were held during the Finnish Metal Expo at the Cable Factory in Helsinki, Finland.

Bittersweet Omen, (2000). Everlasting / Beds Are Burning / Lullaby (To The Other Side) / So Close, Too Far / From Cradle To Grave ....
Fuck The Beast, (2001). Through The Dark / 'til Death Do Us One / Psykho.
Load Of Lead, (2001). Load Of Lead / Painbox / ... Hate ....
Throw Your Stones, Independent (2002). Throw Your Stones / Wildchild.
Label Of Black EP, Independent (2002). Are You A God? / Throw Your Stones / Father / Label Of Black / Burial Hymn.
C2H40, (2003). - / God In A Bottle / Kneel Before My Name / D.H.C.

PROFANE OMEN (pic: Markus Lehto)

Adrenaline, (2004). Adrenaline / Enemies / Adrenaline (Video).
BEATEN INTO SUBMISSION, Dethrone Music (2006). Intro / Adrenaline / Painbox / FMH (Fuck Me Hollow) / Enemies / Gunshot/Mindset / Rew / Pit Of My Thoughts / God In A Bottle / Damaged Justice. Chart position: 28 FINLAND.

PROFANITY

GERMANY — *Thomas Sartor (vocals / guitar), Martl (bass), Armin (drums).*

Bobingen Death Metal act PROFANITY began life with distinct Black overtones but would shed these predilections with successive releases. The opening shot in 1994 came with 'The Transitory' demo followed up by 1995's 'Into The Unforeseen'. Undergoing a line up shift PROFANITY would then induct the rhythm section of bassist Martl and drummer Armin into the ranks. However, Martl would depart and in came four stringer Daniel for recording of the debut album 'Shadows To Fall'.

PROFANITY got out on the road promoting this release putting in gigs with KRABATHOR and CANNIBAL CORPSE as well as having a valuable slot at the 'Fuck The Commerce' festivals.

Signing to the German Death Metal specialists Cudgel Agency PROFANITY cut two tracks, including a cover of POSSESSED's 'The Exorcist', for a split 7" single with Americans LIVIDITY. December of 1998 found Daniel being enticed away to join melodic Rockers REACTOR and the resulting vacancy was once again filled by Martl.

A split 2002 EP 'Humade Me Flesh' with REGURGITATION, would include cover versions of TERRORIZER's 'Fear Of Napalm' and DEATH's 'Zombie Ritual', evolved into a solo release when the American band bowed out due to not having a current drummer. PROFANITY geared up for touring the same April as part of the 'Art Of Sickness' European dates billed alongside CRYPTOPSY, HAEMORRHAGE and SPAWN.

Drowned In Dusk, Cudgel Agency (1997) (Split 7" single with LIVIDITY). Drowned In Dusk / The Exorcist.
SHADOWS TO FALL, (1997). Soulburn ... The Weeping Willow / Shallow Ruins / Fall Of The Shadows / Like A Razorblade / Darkened Watersky / Into The Unforseen / Bloodflow / An Age Of Growing Tragedy.
SLAUGHTERING THOUGHTS, Cudgel Agency CUD005 (2000). Intro / During The Hours Of Darkness / Drowned In Dusk / Soultornado- Hate Burn Inside / The Springs Within / Giants Of Void Vortex / Soulitude / Strangulated With Thoughts / When Colour Becomes Pallor.
Humade Me Flesh EP, (2002). Humade Me Flesh / Zombie Ritual / Fear Of Napalm.

PROJECT: FAILING FLESH

VIENNA, VA, USA — *Eric Forrest (vocals), Tim Gutierrez (guitar), Kevin 131 (guitar).*

PROJECT: FAILING FLESH was the 2002 band assembled in Vienna, Virginia by VOIVID 'Phobos' era frontman Eric Forrest. The singer, prior to having joined the Canadian avant-garde Thrash legends a member of LIQUID INDIAN and THUNDER CIRCUS, had left VOIVOD following severe injuries received on the road in Germany. Kevin '131' has credits with GARDEN OF SHADOWS, TWISTED TOWER DIRE, BRAVE and WHILE HEAVEN WEPT.

The group signed a label deal with the Dutch Karmageddon Media concern for debut album 'A Beautiful Sickness', this opus closing out with a cover of VENOM's 'Warhead'. The band commenced cutting a self-produced second album 'The Conjoined' at Assembly Line Studios in Virginia in early 2004, these sessions lasting well into mid 2005.

PROJECT: FAILING FLESH, having wrapped up recording of 'The Conjoined' album, parted ways with Karmageddon Media in vocally acrimonious circumstances during September 2006. The group signed over to Burning Star Records, based in Greece, the following month. 'The Conjoined' was finally issued in March 2007.

A BEAUTIFUL SICKNESS, Karmageddon Media KARMA 013 (2004) (European release). A Beautiful Sickness / Planet Dead / 9mm Movie / Scene Of The Crime / Entrance Wound / Long Silent Voices / Dementia Pugilistica / Taste Of The Lie / Highwire Act / Warhead.
A BEAUTIFUL SICKNESS, Candlelight CDL0193CD (2004) (North American release). A Beautiful Sickness / Planet Dead / 9mm Movie / Scene Of The Crime / Entrance Wound / Long Silent Voices / Dementia Pugilistica / Taste Of The Lie / Highwire Act / Warhead.
THE CONJOINED, Burning Star BSRCD0018 (2005). Motionless / Through The Broken Lens / Regenerate / The Conjoined / Unsight Unseen / Eve Of Demise / Final Act Of Treachery / Surface Noise / Second Impact Syndrome / Synesthesia / Hand That You've Been Dealt.

PROMETHEAN

FINLAND — *Timo Livari (vocals), Matti Selin (guitar), Jani Yliniva (guitar), Esa Juujärvi (bass), Jaakko Tuomivaara (keyboards), Viljami Jauhiainen (flute), Sami Lehtiniemi (drums).*

PROMETHEAN featured the former BLACK CRUCIFIXION members vocalist / guitarist Timo Iivari (a.k.a. 'Fornicator') and bass guitarist Esa Henrik Juujärvi ('Blacksoul'). PROMETHEAN was found as a trio in 1994 comprising Timo Livari, Esa Juujärvi and guitarist Matti Selin.

The Italian Avantgarde label published the album 'Gazing The Invisible' in January 1997, this record seeing the band as a quintet having acquired Sami Lehtiniemi on drums and Viljami Jauhiainen on the flute. They would then add second guitarist Jani Yliniva and keyboard player Jaakko Tuomivaara, holding prior credits with BLACK SWAN, for the follow up 'Somber Regards' during 1998.

GAZING THE INVISIBLE, Avantgarde AV 019 (1997). Eternal Fall / Polygon / Gazing / The / Invisible / Don't Mind The Dancer / All Blue Is Beautiful / The Kiss Of All That Reminded / Flowing Towards.
SOMBER REGARDS, Avantgarde AV 032 (1998). Rat Dance / It's The Light / Blazah / Self Portraits / Somber Regards / Spiderland / Penny Whistle + Attack Of Überwermi.

PROMISQES

OGDEN, UT, USA — *Lori Medcalfe Hemphill (vocals / guitar), Dena Turk (guitar), Serena (bass), Ben Murphy (drums).*

All female Death Metal outfit dating to August of 1995, forged by vocalist / guitarist Lori Medcalfe Hemphill and drummer Jeanette Smith. Although entitled PROMISQES the band name was often mistakenly billed as 'Promisques'. The initial pairing of Hemphill and Smith cut a demo entitled 'Immortal Thoughts' which never saw commercial release. Dena Turk came onboard as bassist in November of 1996 and trio released the debut album 'Monarchy Of Evil' in September of 1997. Subsequently Serena was drafted on bass and Turk reverted to her familiar role as lead guitarist. Tour work saw supports to DEICIDE and CANNIBAL CORPSE as well as an appearance at the Milwaukee Metalfest XII event. Ben Murphy took over the drum stool in 1998.

MONARCHY OF EVIL, S.I.S. (1997). Monarchy Of Evil / Immortal Thoughts / Anger Within / The Beast / Deathstrumental / Shards Of Glass / Satan Satan Satan / Satan's Friend / Future Prophecy / Satan's Victory.
GEHENNA, (2000).

PROPHECY

TX, USA — *Ryno Isbell (vocals), James Parks II (vocals / guitar), Eric Croson (bass / vocals), Scott Horne (drums).*

PROPHECY was founded in Shreveport, Louisiana by guitarist James Parks II. However, with the addition of guitarist Joe 'Boogie' Dunlap PROPHECY relocated to Fort Worth, Texas in 1995, soon recruiting Phil Holland on lead vocals for the March 1996 demo cassette 'It Shall Come To Pass'. Live work in 1998 witnessed package touring with DYING FETUS and DEEDS OF FLESH followed by a co-headlining run with DIVINE EMPIRE. Festival appearances that year included gigs at 'Grindfest' and 'Michigan International Metalfest'. PROPHECY also made its mark in 1999 at 'Grindfest II', 'Ohio Deathfest' and 'November To Dismember' festival.

Drummer Billy Bonsal, a veteran of SMOKEBOMB, NUX VOMICA and Punk act McBAIN, joined the band in the summer of 2000. Burt Buchanan became the band's latest bassist in September of 2001.

The band enrolled a fresh rhythm section in November of 2003, comprising DEMONSEED bassist Eric Croson and drummer Rick Hawkins. The 2004 PROPHECY line up saw the departure of guitarist Jeff Hernandez and would be fronted by singer Ryan 'Ryno' Isbell. Dates in Europe saw headline action supported by GODLESS TRUTH with the band also topping the bill at the 'Extreme Texas Metalfest II'. The following year found the band working on a new album 'Don't Fuckin' Mess With Texas'.

FORETOLD... FORESEEN, Corpse Gristle CGR 002 (1998). Core Of Depression / Human Atrocity / Feasting On The Flesh / Diggin' A Pit / Inner Reality / Assembled By Death / Ebolic Regurgitation / Prophecy.
Prophecy EP, Pigeon Shit Agency (1999) (Split EP with PERVERSIST). Ebolic Regurgitation / Feasting On The Flesh.
PROPHECY, (2000) (Split album with CRYPTIC). Feasting On The Flesh / Diggin' A Pit / Inner Reality / Driven By Fear.
IT SHALL COME TO PASS, Corpse Gristle CGR 007 (2001). Assembled By Death / Ebolic Regurgitation / Driven By Fear / Inner Reality / Prophecy / Feasting On The Flesh / Diggin' A Pit / Tortured By Deceit.
OUR DOMAIN, Forever Underground (2002). Our Domain / Tortured By Deceit / Destined To Fall / Inevitable Fate / All You Can Fuck And Eat / Gurgling Menstrual Phlegm / Beaten, Broken And Butchered / Keep It Fuckin' Brutal / Questions Never Answered / The Shit.
FORETOLD... FORESEEN, Goregiastic (2005).

PROPHECY OF DEATH

PONTA DELGADA, PORTUGAL — *Nélio Tavares (vocals / guitar), Pablo Sousa (guitar), Miguel Pacheco (bass), Pablo Andrade (drums).*

Ponta Delgada, Azores Death Metal band PROPHECY OF DEATH was initiated during 1993. Originally the group featured singer João Ferreira, guitarists Pablo Sousa and Nélio Tavares with a rhythm section of bassist Marco Cabral and drummer Mario Bulhões. The band opened proceedings in 1994 with the demo cassette 'Beyond Darkness'. The single track 'Immortality' followed that August with a four tracker billed 'Honour' issued in August 1995. A concert recording, 'Live in Ponta Delgada', saw issue in September 1997. The song 'Punished' was included on a 1998 compilation album 'Novas Ondas 98'.

PROPHECY OF DEATH folded during 2001. Between 2004 and mid 2006 Nélio Tavares also fronted SACRED TEARS.

Beyond Darkness, Prophecy of Death (1994) (Demo). Devil / Life After Death / Welcome To The Dark Side / Beyond Darkness.
Immortality, Prophecy of Death (1994) (Demo). Immortality.
Honour, Prophecy of Death (1995) (Demo).
Live In Ponta Delgada, Prophecy of Death (1997) (Demo).
Live At Coliseu, Prophecy of Death (1998) (Demo).

PROSTITUTE DISFIGUREMENT

GRONINGEN, HOLLAND — *Niels (vocals), Roel (guitar), Niels (guitar), Patrick (bass), Michiel van der Plicht (drums).*

Groningen Death Metal / Grind band went by the names ACRID and DISFIGURED before settling on the name PROSTITUTE DISFIGUREMENT. The German Morbid label issued 'Deeds Of Derangement' in 2003. Signing with Neurotic Records the group's third album, 'Left In Grisly Fashion', was recorded at Studio Excess. The record included guest vocal appearances from Robbe K of DISAVOWED and ARSEBREED plus Joey of PYAEMIA and ARSEBREED. Drummer Eric would be superseded by Michiel van der Plicht of KATAFALK and TRAVELERS IN TIME.

European dates scheduled for May 2005 witnessed an alliance with VOMITORY, ROTTEN SOUND and EXHUMED. Promoting the album 'Left In Grisly Fashion', the band allied with DEICIDE, WYKKED WYTCH and VISCERAL BLEEDING for European shows throughout October and November, taking in the UK, Ireland, France, Belgium, Holland, Germany, Switzerland, Austria, Hungary, Croatia, Czech Republic, Spain and Italy.

Live work planned in December across Europe was to see the band hooking up with GOREFEST, MADDER MORTEM, TRAIL OF TEARS, BELPHEGOR and DARZAMAT for the 'X-Mass' festivals set to commence December 8th at the Berlin K17 venue. However, this entire trek was cancelled just days beforehand.

PROSTITUTE DISFIGUREMENT entered Stage One Studios in Germany on April 28th 2007 with producer Andy Classen to record its fourth full-length album 'Descendants Of Depravity'.

EMBALMED MADNESS, Dismemberment (2001). Slaughterhouse Sledgehammer / Feasting On Remains / Choking On Defecation / Bloodless / Rotting Away Is Better Than Being Gay / Chainsaw Abortion / Knifeslasher / Disemboweled / On Her Guts I Cum / Prostitute Disfigurement / Cadaver Blowjob / Dissector.
DEEDS OF DERANGEMENT, Morbid MR 103 (2003). Inside To Expose / Swollen / Deformed Slut / Postal Devirginized / Deeds Of Derangement / She's Not Coming Home Tonight / Repulsive To Kill / G-B Massacre / Cum Covered Stabwounds / Screaming In Agony / Skinned & Sodomized.
LEFT IN GRISLY FASHION, Neurotic NRT050005 (2006). Body To Ravage / Freaking On The Mutilated / Left In Grisly Fashion / The Corpse Garden / Bluedrum Torso / Victims Of The Absurd / Shotgun Horror / Disemboweled / In Death's Decay / Bloodlust Redemption.

PSICORRAGIA

LIMA, PERU — *Mario Romanet Rivas (vocals / bass), Mito Espíritu (guitar), Alick González Mujica (guitar), Antonio Duncan Pérez (keyboards), Daniel Ladrón de Guevara (drums).*

Melancholic and experimental Death Doom outfit established by vocalist / bassist Mario Romanet and dating to 1994. After numerous line up shuffles, which featured guitarist Frame Milón along the way, the introduction of guitarist Alick González Mujica and pianist Antonio Duncan Pérez in 1997 afforded some stability, resulting in the 1998 six track demo session 'Otoño' ('Autumn') to which Víctor Degollar donated his skills on violin.

Degollar would break away from the band and Erick Reynaga took over the role. However, when Reynaga too decamped PSICORRAGIA opted to forgo this instrument indefinably and remain a quintet.

American Line Productions subsequently signed PSICORRAGIA for the 'La Pasión De Lo Mortal' album. Former member Victor Degollar aided on string parts for the recording. Rhythm guitarist Marco Borra Ramírez would be replaced by the KRANIUM and SARCOMA credited Mito Espíritu. Another change saw drummer Manuel Saavedra Chamolí replaced by Daniel Ladrón de Guevara.

Otoño, (1998). Jardin De Las Delicias / Sueño De Muerte / Arida Verdad / Melancolía / Otoño / Descarnado Final / Aspid.

LA PASION DE LO MORTAL, American Line Productions LA-046 (2001). Vagitus / Padecer Solamente / Otono / Nuestro Rio De Recuerdos / Estrofas A La Muerte / Amen / La Misma Historia / Aspid.

PSYCHOFAGIST

ITALY — *Wrath (vocals / bass), Steph (guitar), Simone (drums).*

Death Metal act out of the North Eastern Italian town of Novara and previously operational as BEDEVILED. The group's original 2001 line up comprised vocalist / bassist Wrath, guitarists Steph and Andre with Grom on the drums. However, both Andre and Grom soon exited, the latter hooking up with high profile Norwegian Black Metal band ANCIENT. Bizza was duly installed on the drums for recording of a track 'Deepest Infliction', this song included on the local compilation 'Nubilaria Vol.II' issued by Huginn Productions. As BEDEVILLED morphed into PSYCHOFAGIST a new singer by the name of Conra was inducted for recording of demos. Unfortunately both Conra and Bizza decamped upon completion of these sessions.

PSYCHOFAGIST signed to the Japanese Amputated Vein label to share an April 2003 split album 'Selfless Spite' with Belgian act HYBRID VISCERY. Simon from BASTARD SAINTS enrolled as the new PSYCHOFAGIST drummer that same month.

SELFLESS SPITE, Amputated Vein AVR004 (2003). Fobia D'essere / Asphyxiating Harmony / Icons In Mortal Unconscious / Bygone Genesis / Re-manufacture Of Mental Violence.

PSYCHOTOGEN

BALTIMORE, MD, USA — *Rob Kline (vocals), Jeremy Grande (guitar), Tony Pernia (bass), Chris Pernis (drums).*

Baltimore's PSYCHOTOGEN was borne out of a fresh alliance between erstwhile PESSIMIST members vocalist Rob Kline and the sibling rhythm section of bassist Tony and drummer Chris Pernia. Joining the band in it's original 1999 incarnation as EXCATHEDRA would be guitarists Jeremy Grande and Mike Baron. As EXCATHEDRA the group cut a demo session and put in an appearance at the 2000 Milwaukee Metal Fest.

With the departure of Baron the group switched title to PSYCHOTOGEN. The 2001 'Perverse And Unnatural Practices' album was a self financed affair.

The group parted ways with vocalist and founding member Rob Kline in February of 2003. A Ron Vento produced album planned for that year, 'The Calculus Of Evil', initially saw Greg Puciato of THE DILLINGER ESCAPE PLAN in line to handle vocals. By March it was revealed that erstwhile MISERY INDEX man Mike Harrison was in the frame. The album included an unaccredited cover version of JUDAS PRIEST's 'All Guns Blazing'. PSYCHOTOGEN switched frontmen in February of 2004, vocalist Larry Gamber taking Harrison's place. That same month, former vocalist Rob Kline, active with HATRED UNLEASHED, was announced as having joined the newly reformed FLESHTIZED.

PERVERSE AND UNNATURAL PRACTICES, (2001). Venom In The Voice / Chaingod / Cathexis / In The Dust Of Your Own Nothingness / Tear At The Flesh / Follow Me (Into Hell) / Psycotogen / Death Of The Old Ways.

THE CALCULUS OF EVIL, Crash Music (2003). Might Is Right / Den Of Wolves / Poison Sleep / The Gilded Slave / Descending / Thy Will Be Done / Psychotogen II / Lying In Wait / All Guns Blazing.

PSYCROPTIC

HOBART, TAS, AUSTRALIA — *Jason Peppiatt (vocals), Joe Haley (guitar), Cameron Grant (bass), David Haley (drums).*

Tasmanian Death Metal comprising the Haley brothers, guitarist Joe and drummer David, both veterans of DISSEMINATE. David Haley also cites a prior tradition with JESTER DESTINY and MINDLESS VIOLENCE whilst Joe Haley is also ex-DIONYSIS. Lead vocalist Matthew Chalk is an erstwhile member of HEMLOCK and THE BLEEDING NOSES whilst bassist Cameron Grant was previously with DIONYSIS and MAGORIA.

Hobart based PSYCROPTIC issued the self financed 'The Isle Of Disenchantment' in 2000, recorded at Red Planet Recordings in Hobart. A cassette version of the album was also licensed to Aarack Records for Indonesia. Live work to promote this release across Australia included festival showings at the 'Metal For The Brain' and 'High Voltage' events. The follow up 'Scepter Of The Ancients', again recorded at Red Planet, arrived through the Unique Leader label in 2003. PSYCROPTIC landed a valuable support slot to INCANTATION. This run of dates further enhanced the international focus on the band when David Haley played drums for the headliners at the 'Bloodlust' festival after INCANTATION drummer Kyle Severn was injured in a car accident during the tour.

The band would act as support to US outfit DEEDS OF FLESH on their June and July 2004 Australian dates. Further shows had the band allied with DISMEMBER, ANATA and SANATORIUM for a full European tour commencing 3rd November in Nürnberg, Germany.

David Haley united with multi-instrumentalist Alex Pope on vocals, guitars and bass to forge Black Metal act RUINS. This act contracted to Neurotic Records for release of a 2005 debut album 'Spun Forth As Dark Nets'. However, the band severed ties with vocalist Matthew Chalk in February, the ex-member concentrating on his other acts M.S.I. and GOREVERK. The band, drafting Jason Peppiatt, a veteran of BORN HEADLESS, YORTA and Black Metal band BOLVERK, as new vocalist, announced a road union with VILE and DECREPIT BIRTH for the 'Bloodletting North America' Summer tour. However, this proposition would then be scotched in favour of US gigs in October allied with DEEDS OF FLESH. Meantime, on Australian soil, the group supported HATE ETERNAL's June dates.

PSYCROPTIC signed a recording agreement with Neurotic Records for the group's third full-length album, entitled 'Symbols Of Failure'. In October 2006 the band supported CANNIBAL CORPSE. Later that same month Dave Haley sessioned drums on Belgian act ABORTED's 'Slaughter & Apparatus: A Methodical Overture' album.

The group announced they would be hooking up with VISCERAL BLEEDING and DEICIDE for a European tour in January 2007. However, PSYCROPTIC was forced to drop off the tour four days before the trek's completion when guitarist Joe Haley was hospitalized due to illness following the show in Essen, Germany on January 26th.

THE ISLE OF DISENCHANTMENT, Independent (2001). Carnival Of Vulgarity / The Sword Of Uncreation / Condemned By Discontent / Netherworld Reality / The Isle Of Disenchantment / Of Dull Eyes Borne / Psycroptipath / Beneath The Ground We Dwell / The Labyrinth.

THE SCEPTER OF THE ANCIENTS, Independent PSY 002 (2003). The Color Of Sleep / Battling The Misery Of Organon / Lacertine Forest / Psycrology / Skin Coffin / Cruelty Incarnate / The Valley Of Winds Breath And Dragons Fire / A Planetary Discipline / The Scepter Of Jaar-Gilon.

SYMBOLS OF FAILURE, Neurotic NRT060008 (2006). Alpha Breed / Missionaries Of A Future To Come / Merchants Of Deceit / Minions: The Fallen / Repairing The Dimensional Cluster / Epoch Of The Gods / Our Evolutionary Architecture / An Experiment In Transience / Cleansing A Misguided Path.

PSYOPUS

ROCHESTER, NY, USA — *Adam Frappolli (vocals), Christopher Arp (guitar), Fred DeCoste (bass), Greg Herman (drums).*

Rochester Math-Grind outfit PSYOPUS debuted with an eponymous 2003 demo. The band had been created a year earlier by lead vocalist Adam Frappolli, guitar Christopher Arp, bassist Fred DeCoste from WITHERED EARTH, VALPURGA and HATE MACHINE and drummer Greg Herman of KALIBAS, INERTIA, VALPURGA and LOW TON. Arp had not only made his name by winning a regional 'Guitarmageddon' contest but also came highly placed in LIMP BIZKIT's notorious 2002 talent search. Herman held a repute as a technical yet exceptionally fast Grind drummer, once clocked in the studio at delivering 225 beats per minute.

Black Market Activities issued the album 'Ideas For Reference' in 2004, recorded at Watchmen Studios with engineer Doug White, but by that October PSYOPUS had signed to Metal Blade Records. The band partnered with ION DISSONANCE and SWARM OF THE LOTUS for US touring throughout July and August 2005.

November 2006 US dates had PSYOPUS aligned with HEAVY HEAVY LOW LOW and SEE YOU NEXT TUESDAY. The album 'Our Puzzling Encounters Considered' arrived in February 2007. First signs of live activity for the band in 2007 came with a lengthy run of US shows DYSRHYTHMIA and BEHOLD ... THE ARCTOPUS throughout March and April. Further US concerts in April had the band aligned with JOB FOR A COWBOY and CANNIBAL CORPSE.

IDEAS OF REFERENCE, (2004).
OUR PUZZLING ENCOUNTERS CONSIDERED, Metal Blade 14602 (2007). The Pig Keeper's Daughter / 2 / Scissor Fuck Paper Doll / Whore Meet Liar / Insects / Imogenis Puzzle Pt.2 / Play Some Skynyrd / Kill Us / Siobhan's Song / Happy Valentine's Day / Our Puzzling Encounters Considered.

PSYPHERIA

CA, USA — *Adam Roberts (vocals / bass), John Oster (guitar), Mike Hurley (guitar), Lyle Livingston (keyboards), Cory Valdez (drums).*

Centred on guitarist John Oster, by day a school teacher, and drummer Cory Valdez the beginnings of PSYPHERIA can be tracked back to the 1991 act ENTHRONED. Various demos ensued before Lyle Livingston came onboard as lead vocalist during December of 1993. In this guise ENTHRONED cut the demos 'Gears' and 'Absence Of Life'. However, prior to recording of the next session 'Thy Flesh Consumed' Livingston was discovered to have nodes on his vocal chords and instructed by doctors to cease singing. Not wishing to give up the band the former singer shifted his role to that of keyboard player as ENTHRONED pulled in Rob Martin on vocals and bass, subsequently recording a further demo tape 'Gothic Disturbance'.

April of 1997 brought about the departure of Martin though. Undaunted, PSYPHERIA drafted Tom Persons of PESSIMIST and SADISTIC TORMENT repute on bass. He in turn would manoeuvre to guitar when OSMIUM veteran Rob Lumbre joined as bass player in February of 1998.

Although the 1998 'Gothic Disturbance' album was recorded as a quartet of Tom Persons on lead vocals and bass, guitarist John Oster, Lyle Livingston on keyboards and Cory Valdez on the drums this line up did not remain stable. Both Persons and Lumbre quit to forge their own act MUCUS MEMBRANE in late 2000. Making up the numbers PSYPHERIA's roll call was brought back up to strength with the incorporation of vocalist / bassist Adam Roberts of THE NEW PLAGUE and guitarist Mike Hurley.

Lyle Livingston is also operative as keyboard player for DRAGONLORD.

GOTHIC DISTURBANCE, (1998). Overmodulated / Tocatta In Death Minor / Gothic Disturbance / Lord Of Worms / Liquefied / Injection / Immortal Hate.
Plague's End EP, (2001). Labyrinth Of Suffering / Digital Black / Insensate.
EMBRACE THE MUTATION, Heretic Sound (2002). Flesh Must Burn / Cathartic Degeneration / Shatterer Of Worlds / Taste The Dead / Systemic Confrontation / Insensate / Digital Black / Labyrinth Of Suffering.

PULMONARY ABSCESS

HOLLAND — *Marijn de Zeeuw (vocals / bass), Edwin Kruize (vocals / guitar), Iwan Heskamp (guitar), Bert de Groot (drums).*

PULMONARY ABSCESS was forged as a trio comprising guitarist Edwin Kruize, bass player Jordi Bergboer and drummer Bert de Groot during 1989. PULMONARY ABSCESS, adding second guitarist Jurgen, released the demo 'Branded For Life' in 1992, after which the band trimmed down to just Kruize and de Groot. In February 1993 Bas van de Griek enrolled on guitar and the band entered the studio to cut the 'Definition Of Torture' session. As live work increased, vocalist Paul Wormgoor was added to the fold.

Just upfront of recording the October 1994 'Slave Of Darkness' tape bassist Floor Wolters was incorporated. However, upon completion both Walters and Bas van de Griek exited to join the ranks of GENETIC WISDOM. Opting for a complete re-think, PULMONARY ABSCESS responded by drafting two bassists, re-enrolling Jordi Bergboer and also bringing in Marijn de Zeeuw. A new campaign of live work ensued but in May of 1998 Bergboer bailed out for Hardcore outfit CON-CRETE. Ronald Wensink filled the gap for the EP 'Depths'. In parallel, both Edwin Kruize and Marijn de Zeeuw would be active as members of SOLARISIS.

Wormgoor in 1999 and de Zeeuw duly assumed lead vocal responsibilities. PULMONARY ABSCESS persevered on the live circuit as a trio before introducing the SOLARISIS and DEIFICATION credited Iwan Heskamp on guitar. In December of 2001 this quartet entered the Ground Zero Studios in Zutphen to start recording a full length album 'The Greedy Illness'.

Depths, Independent (1998). Hidden Reality / Cancer / The Everlasting Power / To The Roots Of Life / The Child Inside.
THE GREEDY ILLNESS, Independent (2002). The Presence Of Absence / The Greedy Illness / Mortal Sun / Suffocating Inheritance / This Is The World We Live In / Free Your Mind / Wishmaster / McDriveby / The End.

PUNGENT STENCH

VIENNA, AUSTRIA — *Martin Shirenc (vocals / guitar), Jacek Perkowski (bass), Alex Wank (drums).*

Vienna's PUNGENT STENCH, involving erstwhile CARNAGE personnel vocalist / guitarist Martin Shirenc ('Don Cochino'), bass player Jacek Perkowski ('Pitbull Jack') and drummer Alex Wank ('Rector Stench'), deal in deliberately sick and overgrossed song content and imagery designed to shock. Their controversial and clinically corrupt canon of work fostered feverish appreciation, as each record found fresh ways in which to disgust the mainstream.

PUNGENT STENCH began life as a Death-Grind machine but gradually introduced groove into the proceedings as their profile rose. Having debuted with the 1988 demo 'Mucus Secretion', a split EP with DISHARMONIC ORCHESTRA followed in 1989. The group toured with MASTER and ABOMINATION during 1990 in order to promote their debut album, 'For God Your Soul ... For Me Your Flesh', issued in 'splatter' vinyl and the cover of which was distastefully adorned with severed limbs. That same year Nuclear Blast issued the split 7" single, 'Blood, Pus And Gastric Juice', in collaboration with BENEDICTION.

In October 1991 copies of the 'Been Caught Buttering' album were confiscated by British customs due to concern about the sleeve photograph depicting a sawn in half decapitated head. However, the album was eventually passed as the photograph had been on display in various art galleries previously. To celebrate, the band then manufactured a picture disc version.

Naturally, PUNGENT STENCH lapped up the controversy and toured hard, capitalising on the shock value they created. Dates included gigs in Israel and American shows with BRUTAL TRUTH and INCANTATION. The band would even make it out as far as New Zealand.

The April 1993 'Dirty Rhymes And Psychotronic Beats' EP is worth noting as it features covers of THE MENTORS' legendary 'Four 'F' Club' and WARP SPASMs 'Why Can The Bodies Fly'. European headline dates in April through to June of 1994, promoting the 'Club Mondo Bizarre—For Members Only' album, saw the band supported by MACABRE and BRUTAL TRUTH. In now traditional style, this latest record's original pornographic pastiche cover art was banned in Germany.

A spate of extracurricular activity found drummer Alex Wank forming the Industrial group SPINE whilst Shirenc created HOLLENTHON and then forged KREUZWEG OST with Silenius of SUMMONING.

Following a lengthy absence from the scene the Nuclear Blast label would issue the comeback 'Masters Of Moral- Servants Of Sin' album during November of 2001. Live dates that year saw the incorporation of SCENT OF PARADISE, BELPHEGOR and PATHETIC man Mario Klausner on bass guitar. The band's 'Holy Inquisition 2002' tour would commence in Warsaw, Poland during September and wend its way through the low countries, Russia and the Ukraine before gigs in their native Austria supported by CADAVEROUS CONDITION. As 2003 broke PUNGENT STENCH travelled as far as Australia and New Zealand for gigs in January, these latter shows supported by Kiwis MALEVOLENCE. A short burst of dates in February, dubbed the 'Rotting With Your Christ' tour, found the band on North American soil packaged with INCANTATION, BEYOND THE EMBRACE and RUNE. The year would be rounded out by November European headline gigs with support from London Gore Metal outfit GOREROTTED. In early 2004 Mario Klausner announced his departure in order to fully concentrate on his own band COLLAPSE 7. . Klausner was replaced in February by Fabio Testi.

PUNGENT STENCH's new album, 'Ampeauty', would be set for a September 2004 release through Nuclear Blast Records. Martin Shirenc played bass on the 'Ampeauty album'. Testi was removed from the equation in December 2004 and Klausner briefly returned, before departing again citing family reasons. A new bass payer was then recruited in 'El Gore' (a.k.a. Gregor Marboe). Gore's tradition included credits with bands such as PENDRAGON, DEFENDER KFS, JORMUNGARD, ENDKRIEG, PROJECT X, ESCHATA, CRYOSPHERE and even as drummer for KULDEBLOD.

The band toured New Zealand once more in March 2005 with support from such local acts as BACKYARD BURIAL, MEATYARD, 8 FOOT SATIVA and ULCERATE. British shows then ensued, followed up by festival appearances at events such as the 'Grind Your Mother Fest' in Italy, 'Obscene Extreme' in the Czech Republic and 'Metallic Noise' in Germany. Another round of European gigs took the band through until the end of the year. European shows in January 2006 saw EISREGEN as support. The group launched into a North American tour in May but withdrew mid trek, Alex Wank announcing "under these extreme chaotic and fucked up conditions, we just can't continue this so-called tour". The group did perform prior engagements at New York City's CBGB's on May 26th and the 'Maryland Deathfest' event on May 28th.

Following Greek gigs in February 2007 PUNGENT STENCH toured Europe heading up the "A Splatterday Night Part Two" dates with GOREROTTED and GRIMNESS 69 closing with a run of Spanish shows.

Pungent Stench, Nuclear Blast NB 019 (1989) (Split EP with DISHARMONIC ORCHESTRA). Pulsating Protoplasma / Dead Body Love / Miscarriage / In The Vault / Rip You Without Care / Festered Offals / Pungent Stench.
Extreme Deformity, Nuclear Blast NB 024 (1989). Extreme Deformity / Mucous Secretion / Molecular Disembowlment.
Blood, Pus And Gastric Juice, Nuclear Blast NB 031 (1990) (Split 7" single with BENEDICTION). Blood, Pus And Gastric Juice.
FOR GOD YOUR SOUL . . . FOR ME YOUR FLESH, Nuclear Blast NB 029-2 (1990). Intro / Extreme Deformity / Hypnos / For God Your Soul, For Me Your Flesh / Just Let Me Rot / Pungent Stench / Bonesawer / Embalmed In Sulphuric Acid / Blood, Pus And Gastric Juice / Suspended / Animation / A Small Lunch.
BEEN CAUGHT BUTTERING, Nuclear Blast NB052-2 (1991). Shrunken And Mummified Bitch / Happy Re-Birthday / Games Of Humiliation / S.M.A.S.H. / Brainpan Blues / And Only Hunger Remains / Sputter Supper / Sick Bizarre Defaced Creation / Splatterday Night Fever.
Dirty Rhymes And Psychotronic Beats EP, Nuclear Blast NB 078 (1993). Praise The Names Of The Musical Assassins / Viva La Muerte / Why Can The Bodies Fly / Blood, Pus And Gastric Juice / Horny Little Piggie Bank / Four 'F' Club / Blood, Pus And Gastric Juice (Tekkno-House mix).
CLUB MONDO BIZARRE—FOR MEMBERS ONLY, Nuclear Blast NB 079-2 (1994). True Life / Klyster Boogie / Choked Just For A Joke / Hydrocephalus / I'm A Family Man / Treatments Of Pain / In Search Of The Perfect Torture / Practice Suicide / Fuck Bizarre / Rape-Pagar Con La Misma Moneda.
CLUB MONDO BIZARRE—FOR MEMBERS ONLY, Nuclear Blast NB 079-2 (1994). True Life / Klyster Boogie / Choked Just For A Joke / Hydrocephalus / I'm A Family Man / Treatments Of Pain / In Search Of The Perfect Torture / Practice Suicide / Fuck Bizarre / Rape—Pagar Con La Misma Moneda / Klyster Boogie (Karaoke Version) / Hydrocephalus (Karaoke Version) / Treatments Of Pain (Karaoke Version) / Rape-Pagar Con La Misma Moneda (Karaoke Version).
PRAISE THE NAMES OF THE MUSICAL ASSASSINS, Nuclear Blast (1997). Pulsating Protoplasma / Dead Body Love / Miscarriage / In The Vault / Rip You Without Care / Festered Offals / Pungent Stench / Extreme Deformity / Mucous Secretion / Molecular Disembowlment / The Ballad Of Naked Homeboys / Daddy Cruel / Tony / Madcatmachopsychoromantik / Extreme Deformity / Festered Offals / Pulsating Protoplasm / Pungent Stench / Embalmed In Sulphuric Acid.
MASTERS OF MORAL- SERVANTS OF SIN, Nuclear Blast NB 677-2 (2001). Loot, Shoot, Electrocute / School's Out Forever / Dairy Of A Nurse / The Convent Of Sin / Rex Peadophilus / Suffer The Little Children / To Come Unto Me / Viva Il Vaticano / Mortuary Love Affair / The Testament Of Stench.
AMPEUATY, Nuclear Blast NB 1331-2 (2004). Lynndie (She-Wolf Of Abu Ghraib) / Invisible Empire / The Amp Hymn / The Passion Of Lucifer / Got Mail / Human Garbage / Apotemnophiliac / No Guts, No Glory / Same Shit—Different Asshole / Fear The Grand Inquisitor.

PUNISHED EARTH

BELGIUM — *Fred (vocals), Val (guitar), Ludo (guitar), Patrick (bass), Manni (drums).*

PUNISHED EARTH, assembled in March of 1997, released a brace of demos upfront of their Uxicon Records debut album 'Frankenstein'. The band had been brought together by erstwhile members of RISING NATION as a quartet of vocalist Fred, guitarist Axel, bass player Tanya and Horst on drums. They would perform their first low key gig in November of 1997 at Fred's birthday party.

Initial demos, recorded at their rehearsal studio The Fridge, came in February of 1998, capitalised on by a support to MORTICIAN in Ludwigshafen, Germany and an appearance at the 'Wee Lewaat' festival that August. However, in October Horst quit, being replaced in less than 24 hours by Manni. February of 1999 saw another demo, this leading to the contract with Uxicon. Further line up changes came in June though with the exit of Tanya.

Still as a bass less trio PUNISHED EARTH entered the Underworld Recordings Studios in Lemiers, Holland in January of 2000 to craft 'Frankenstein'. That May they located Patrick to fill the bass vacancy. With 'Frankenstein's release in August the band undertook an exhaustive live schedule opening for acts such as AGATHOCLES, REPUGNANCE, LAST DAYS OF HUMANITY, INTESTINAL DISEASE, SUBLIME CADAVERIC DECOMPOSITION, INGROWING, KADATH, SUHRIM, CARNAL FORGE, MORTICIAN, INHUMATE, MALIGNANT TUMOUR, MUCUPURULENT, CRIPPLE BASTARD, HOUWITSER and PREJUDICE amongst others.

Second album 'Ruined Empire' was recorded at Transpunk Studios in October of 2001. Following two years of live inactivity the band, having replaced Axel with Val on guitar, returned to the live arena at the Frontline venue in Gent supporting NATRON and MASTIC SCUM in May of 2004. PUNISHED EARTH announced a revised line up in November, the band now comprising vocalist Fred, guitarists Ludo and Val, bass player Patrick and drummer Mani.

FRANKENSTEIN, Uxicon UX 014 (2000). Awakening Of The Flesh / Under Authority / Watery Mouth At The First Sight / Run Amok / Decade Of Misanthropy / Final State / Religious Suppression / The Whale / New World Order / Maniac With The Skrewdriver / In The Name Of Democracy / Superficial World / Desperate Wish (Breakdown) / Pedofile In The Neighbourhood / Punished Earth / Weak Is The Flesh (Outro).

PUNISHMENT

VIENNA, AUSTRIA — *Andreas Öcsi (vocals), Fredl (guitar), Otto (guitar), Matthias Arncnik (drums).*

Brutal Death Metal act PUNISHMENT, hailing from Vienna, was created during 1998 by DECEPTION singer Andreas Öcsi. The band line-up fractured, seeing guitarists Peter Spatzierer and Florian Kunz plus drummer Martin Lugmayer opting out to found a new Hardcore styled and called BEAT THE DEVIL. Flo also forged TORTUGA. Ex-bass player Eugen M. Pagany went on to EMPYRE, DISMAL, FESTERING FLESH and VERDAMMNIS.

A revised PUNISHMENT featured DECEPTION drummer Matthias Arncnik, the PARENTAL ADVISORY credited Otto on guitar and Fredl, from PARENTAL ADVISORY and MISANTHROPIC MIGHT, as 'Sic', also on guitar. PUNISHMENT shared their debut 2003 album, 'Chronicles Of Sickness' on Skull Fucked Productions, with French act 7TH NEMESIS. Both acts combined forces for a European and UK tour throughout October.

PUNISHMENT, Skull Fucked Productions SFP002 (2003) (Split album with 7TH NEMESIS). Godsick / Graveyard Earth / The Enemies Behind / Bullet Time / The Die Is Cast / Come With Me.

PURGATORY

SACHSEN, GERMANY — *Sick (vocals), Rene (vocals / guitar), Torsten (bass), Lutz (drums).*

Sachsen Death Metal / Grindcore act, PURGATORY formed in 1989 and released two EPs and three demos before the debut album arrived in 1996. The group have supported NAPALM DEATH, CANNIBAL CORPSE, SAMAEL, ENTOMBED, KRABATHOR and EMINENZ in their short time together. Third album 'Blessed With Flames Of Hate' featured a cover version of ASPHYX's 'The Rack'. PURGATORY supported AMON AMARTH for a tour of Germany in December 2000.

PURGATORY, having incorporated former WARSPITE bassist Andy in December of 2002, shared a split 10" single with POLYMORPH in 2003 on the G.U.C. label, contributing the AUTOPSY cover version 'Fiend For Blood' and a rendition of TERRORIZER's 'Corporation Pull-In'.

The band's January 2006 album, 'Luciferianism', included a cover of LEMMING PROJECT's 'Judasböcke'. Recorded at Soundart Recording studios in Rosslau and produced by Björn Langkopf of VIU DRAKH, the album saw LEMMING PROJECT's Hendrik "Hazy" Vangerow guesting.

Sadistic Spell EP, Perverted Taste MOMO 009 (1995). Frozen Braincells / Paroxysm Of Mortal Lust / Sadistic Spell / Necromanical Necropsy.

PsycopathiaSexualis EP, Perverted Taste MOMO 002 (1995). Masturbation Of Bowels / Childs Of Perversion / Necrocannibalistical Insanity / Psychopathia Sexualis.

DAMAGE DONE BY WORMS, Perverted Taste PT015 (1996). Orgy Of Sickness Dreams / Deep Under The Light / Sodomizing Time / Robes Of Skin / Psychopathia Sexualis Pt II / Necrocannibalistical Insanity / Brought Of Incest / Irresolute Subjection / Final Breath / Frozen Braincells / Paroxysm Of Mortal Lust / Sadistical Spell / Necronomical Necrosy.

Purgatory, Perverted Taste MOMO 009 (1997) (Split single with SEIRIM). Ulcer Of Hate / Tormented Flesh.

BESTIAL, Perverted Taste PT022 (1998). My Blood / Ulcer Of Hate / Immolation Of The Weak / The Bestial / Back From The Shadowlands / Your Soul Will Never Rest / Malignant Spawn / Enslaved By Madness / Tormented Flesh / Burned.

BLESSED WITH FLAMES OF HATE, Perverted Taste PT031 (2000). Damned And Betrayed / Visions Beyond Light / The Daimonion / March Of The Eminent Beast / Pharynx Of Evil / Captured Souls / Blessed With Flames / In Blasphemy / ... And Blood Flows / The Rack.

Purgatory, G.U.C. G.U.C. 009-03 (2003) (Split single with POLYMORPH). Fiend For Blood / Corporation Pull-In / Captured Souls (Live).

LUCIFERIANISM, Animate (2006). Bloodsoil Revelation / Death World Struggle / Seeds Of Annihilation / In Fervent Eyes / The Serpents Creation / The Inexorable Darkness / Judasböcke / None Divine Passion / Luciferic.

PUTREFY

IRELAND — *Jason Bariskill (vocals), Connor Brown (guitar), Alan Gill (guitar), Aaron Irvine (bass), Jason McLaughlin (drums).*

PUTREFY was founded in October of 1992, citing a line up of vocalist Chuck, guitarist Jeff, bassist Mark and Jason McLaughlin on the drums. They would make their first mark with the 1993 'Presumed Dead' demo, recorded at Big River Studios, Londonderry, reaction to which prompted an offer from the Italian Isolated Records for a split CD single shared with ALTERED VISION. Upon completion of these sessions the band acquired second guitarist Mark Loughran from Belfast act HELPLESS. However, following a 1995 support gig to Welsh Death Metal band DESECRATION in Belfast the band broke up.

Jason McLaughlin, together with guitarist Ricky and bass player Aaron Irvine, made an attempt to resurrect the band in 1998 but this was short-lived. Another attempt, in 2000, saw the band briefly fronted by Dave Penny. Original singer Chuck returned and that December the group entered Novatech Studios in Glengormley to record a four song demo, including a cover of DEATH's 'Mutilation'. These tapes were not deemed satisfactory enough for release though. Ricky exited, to be replaced by Connor Brown. More changes witnessed the departure once more of Chuck and, in October 2001, the addition of second ex-ART OF DAMAGE guitarist Nel whilst Jason Bariskill of EPOCH joined on vocals.

In May of 2002 PUTREFY recorded the '4 On 4' demo to coincide with a tour in alliance with ABADDON INCARNATE and DESECRATION. Once these gigs were completed this demo would be enhanced with new intros, a remix and the addition of a live track under a new title 'Lust So Vile'. Nel opted out and PUTREFY continued gigging into 2003 as a quartet. Notable amongst these gigs was an appearance at the MACABRE headlined 'Obscene Extreme' festival in Trutnov in the Czech Republic. In July Grind Ethic Records re-released 'Lust So Vile' in MCD format.

PUTREFY added the SEVERANCE, AGONIST, CORPSECANDLE and VOMITOUS credited Alan Gill on second guitar in December 2003.

Presumed Dead, Putrefy (1993). Splattered / Boiled In A Grave / Putrefied Lust / Presumed Dead.

Putrefy EP, Isolated (1995) (Split EP with ALTERED VISION). Intestinal Vomit / Carved Up Bitch / Cryonic Zombies.
Putrefy Promo 2000, (2000) (Unreleased). 40 Ton Bloodbath / Unearthed / Intestinal Vomit (2000 version) / Mutilation.
4 On 4, (2002). Mutilated Slutfuck / Hung By The Tongue / Pig Fucker / Twelve Gauge Facelift.
Lust So Vile, (2002). Mutilated Slutfuck / Hung By The Tongue / Pig Fucker / Twelve Gauge Facelift / Pleasures (With A Pick-Axe).

PUTRIFACT

PATERSON, NJ, USA — *Omar (vocals / drums), Tom Pioli (guitar), Art (guitar), Victor (bass).*

Paterson, New Jersey Death Metal combo PUTRIFACT published a June 1990 rehearsal recording and a 7" single, 'Visceral Devourment', on the After World label. The group would include guitarist Craig Pillard, a scene veteran of solo project NOCTURNAL CRYPT, AGGRESSIVE INTENT, CARNAGE, DESECRATOR and the high profile INCANTATION, in the ranks until 1991, when he was replaced by Tom Pioli.

PUTRIFACT members Tom Pioli and bassist Victor went on to CEREMONIUM and also performed bass duties on INCANTATION's 'Onward to Golgotha' tour of 1992. Pioli also figured in OBLITERATION and under the pseudonym of 'Azalin' became involved with Dan Lilker's HEMLOCK. Pillard, also briefly associated with CEREMONIUM, would later feature in DISCIPLES OF MOCKERY. Pioli would also reforge his links with INCANTATION, acting as session touring guitarist for their November 2003 South American dates.

Visceral Devourment, After World AWR003 (1991). Visceral Devourment.

PUTRILAGE

TX, USA — *Aaron Mendiola (vocals), Anthony Guerrero (guitar), Llamar Vasquez (guitar), Chris Herrera (bass), Chris Salazar (drums).*

Texan Gore Metal band PUTRILAGE include former MALEFICENT vocalist Aaron Mendiola. Created in January of 1999 by CARRION personnel guitarists Llamar Vasquez and Anthony Guerrero, drummer Chris Salazar in addition to bassist Chris Herrera and Aaron Mendiola. That August PUTRILAGE recorded the debut demo 'Gorenography'. In early 2000 the band signed to Corpse Gristle Records for the album 'Devouring The Gutted'. 2001 would prove turbulent as the band severed ties with Corpse Gristle. Internal ructions in March witnessed Herrera being replaced Dan Briseno. In June Salazar quit, his position being taken by Scott Henneke. Two months later Salazar was welcomed back into the fold. The album was signed over to the Forever Underground label but in November Briseno opted out. PUTRILAGE filled the vacancy on bass with the induction of DISEMBOWEL's Eddie Blanquiz.

'Devouring The Gutted' finally saw a belated release in March of 2002. A short run of dates in North America, which included the New Jersey 'Metalfest', to promote the record found PUTRILAGE packaged with LEUKHORREA and Maltese band BEHEADED. With touring complete Salazar exited once again, creating GORED. Brent Williams, citing credits with South Carolina's LUST OF DECAY, was drafted as new drummer but his tenure was brief.

A 2002 split album 'Putrikorrhea' was shared with LEUKHORREA.

PUTRIKORRHEA, The Spew Records (2002) (Split album with LEUKHORREA). Engorged With Lacerations / Intentions To Mutilate / Voluntary Amputation.
DEVOURING THE GUTTED, Forever Underground (2002). Devouring The Gutted / Defleshed And Decapitated / Until Shes Dead / Facial Bowel Release / Vomit Lubrication / Gourmet Of Vaginal Hemorrhaging / Gorenography / Feasting On Scabs / Hack, Slash, Cut ... You Bleed / Crumbled Genitals / The Art Of Flesh.

PYAEMIA

HOLLAND — *Joel Sta (vocals / guitar), Anton (guitar), Frank Rizzo (bass), Robbert Vrijenhoek (drums).*

Signing to the American Unique Leader label for their 2001 opus 'Cerebral Cereal' would afford PYAEMIA the opportunity of touring the States. Throughout July and August the Dutchmen made up the ranks in the MONSTROSITY led 'Bloodletting North America Pt. 2' tour alongside DEEDS OF FLESH, ODIOUS SANCTION and SABBATIC FEAST. However, upon their return longstanding bassist Frank Rizzo bowed out. For European shows PYAEMIA drafted the services of SEVERE TORTURE man Patrick as stand in.

By late 2003 Frank Rizzo was ensconced with the ranks of Grindcore act LENG TCH'E, having switched roles to that of guitarist. Frontman Joey (a.k.a. Joel Sta), also a member of ARSEBREED, would add guest vocal sessions to PROSTITUTE DISFIGUREMENT's 2005 album 'Left In Grisly Fashion'. After being out of action for most of the year due to a wrist injury suffered by drummer Robbert Vrijenhoek, PYAEMIA announced they were to cease activities in December 2005. Joel Sta and former bass player Frank Stijnen would still be active with ARSEBREED.

CRANIAL BLOWOUT, (1998). Carried In Proboscis / Cranial Blowout / Blood Spewed In My Face / Sugar Spiced Anus / Everlasting Torture.
CEREBRAL CEREAL, Unique Leader Entertainment (2001). Gorging On Mucus And Bile / Cerebral Cereal / Sugar Spiced Anus / Impaled On Stakes / Blood Spewed On My Face / Carried In Proboscis / Malodorous Rancidity / Cranial Blowout / Everlasting Torture.

PYORRHOEA

WARSAW, POLAND — *Chryste (vocals), A.D. Gore (guitar), Lukas (guitar), Cyprian (bass), Desecrate (drums).*

PYORRHOEA (medical terminology for a discharge of pus) is a Warsaw Death Metal band formed up from members of HATE, VESANIA and DEVILYN. The group, established in 2001 by guitarist Andy Blakk and bassist Cyprian then cemented by SPHERE and REVELATION OF DOOM singer Analripper and drummer Daray, debuted in June 2002 with the demo cassette 'Pyorrhoea, Promo 2002'. New guitarist A.D.Gore, of CENTURION and MESMERIZED, joined the band that November.

The band's commercial debut 'Desire For Torment', recorded in November 2003 at Hertz Studios, would be the first in a three album deal for Empire Records. However, upon completion of recording Andy Blakk would subsequently be forced out due to health issues. His place would be taken by Max from EVIL TWIN. Max quit shortly afterwards, leaving PYORRHOEA to persevere on the live circuit as a quartet. 'Desire For Torment' was issued in August 2004. As the year closed the band drafted Lukas on second guitar, a veteran of ABUSED MAJESTY and SPHERE.

With drummer Daray temping for VADER the group drafted the NAAMAH, GORTAL and DESECRATED Krzysztof Szałkowski to man the drums. The band would form up the 'Days Of Destruction' tour, alongside HATE, ABUSED MAJESTY, ESQARIAL and MUTILATION, throughout Poland that December.

Further changes came with the departure of Analripper, his position being taken in early 2005 by GORTAL's Chryste. Empire issued 'The Eleventh: Thou Shalt Be My Slave' in April 2006.

Pyorrhoea, (2002). Consume You / Hung On A Hook / Chainsaw Dance / Crushed / Excited By Stench / Mynameisevaiamsixteenyearsoldiamstillvirginismyfatheragay? / Pigsty End.
DESIRE FOR TORMENT, Empire (2004). Slave / Excrements On Your Face / Masskill Symptom / Bondage Punishment Torture / Suicidal Masturbation / Anal Arousal / Addicted To Killing / S.W.Y.T.E.Y.O.S. / Consume You / Desire For Torment / Chainsaw Dance / 0108 / Hung On A Hook / Dead Orgy Scene.

THE ELEVENTH: THOU SHALT BE MY SLAVE, Empire (2006). Blow / Rules Of Slavery / Stolen Freedom / Miserable Existence / Hidden Under Sanctity / Bad Monk / Natural Born Enemies / Your Master—Your God / Liberation / Nothing He Can Do / Everlusting / Far From Truth / Forbidden Extasy / Rape.

PYPHOMGERTUM

MEXICO — *Alfonso Ruiz (vocals), Pablo Rosales (guitar), Oskar Baltazar (guitar), Angel Flores (bass), Jorge Rubio (drums).*

PYPHOMGERTUM was assembled in March of 1992, debuting with the demos 'Anacreon' and 'To The Mesphil'. The band garnered international attention in 1994 as they shared a split album release 'The Dark Light' on Bellphegot Records with DAWN of Sweden. Following issue of the 1996 album 'Gorific Carnal Confessions' the group underwent a major line up shift with only lead vocalist Alfonso Ruiz and drummer Jorge Rubio surviving. The pair duly inducted erstwhile EXECREATION personnel guitarist Eduardo Guevara and bass player Hector Marquez. Another new recruit would be former ZAMAK man Antonoi Ruiz.

Further ructions resulted in the band losing their singer. New demos entitled 'Inside Tabbing' were laid down with guest vocals from Antimo Buonanno of DISGORGE. Finally Eric Olguin of VISCERAL took on the role of frontman.

THE DARK LIGHT, Bellphegot (1994) (Split album with DAWN). Satan's Sadness (Intro) / The Black Bizarre Flesh / Sodomy Of The Souls / The Dark Light / Fear Of Satan / Mesphil / Odes To An Evil Dead (Outro).

GORIFIC CARNAL CONFESSIONS, Bellphegot (1996). For The Bestiality Of The Dead / Naked Perversions / Guts Over The Obelisk / Zombified / Smashing The Carnal Universe / Death Is Our Only Word / Pyphomgertum (The Firstborn Dimension) / Incisions / Phaidescorm.

PYREXIA

NEW YORK, NY, USA — *Darryl Wagner (vocals), Tony Caravella (guitar), Guy Marchais (guitar), Chris Basile (bass), Mike Andrekio (drums).*

A New York Deathcore unit with blasphemous overtones. The 1993 album 'Sermon Of Mockery' would see PYREXIA counting a band line-up of vocalist Darryl Wagner, guitarists Guy Marchais and Tony Caravella, bass player Chris Basile and drummer Mike Andrekio. A re-issue of the debut during 1999 by Pathos Productions, added 'Liturgy Of Impurity'. Keith DeVito took over the lead vocal mantle for the 1995 EP 'Hated, Anger And Disgust'. PYREXIA's third effort, the 1997 album 'System Of The Animal', witnessed further changes, DeVito and Basile, the latter having switched to guitar, being joined by bass player Ryan Harrison and drummer Rob Maresca. DeVito would be loaned out for European tour dates as stand in frontman for SUFFOCATION. Guitarist Guy Marchais would later join INTERNAL BLEEDING and CATASTROPHIC. There is a further INTERNAL BLEEDING connection with bass player Brian Hobbie.

During 2001 vocalist Keith DeVito, guitarist Guy Marchais, bassist Brian Hobbie and drummer Rob Maresca united with former OBITUARY guitarist Trevor Peres in order to create CATASTROPHIC. PYREXIA reformed in late 2002, putting in a run of live dates alongside MORTAL DECAY in July 2003. For these gigs the MALEVOLENT CREATION credited Justin Dipinto manned the drums. PYREXIA members guitarist Chris Basile and bassist Jay Snell subsequently joined STORM. PYREXIA returned with 'Cruelty Beyond Submission', released in 2004 by Crash Music.

PYREXIA released the album 'Age Of The Wicked", on January 23rd 2007 via Unique Leader Records.

SERMON OF MOCKERY, Drowned Productions (1993). Sermon Of Mockery / Resurrection / Abominat / The Uncreation / God / Demigod / Inhumanity / Lithurgy Of Impurity.

HatredAngerAndDisgust EP, Mockery (1995). Hatred, Anger And Disgust / Bludgeoned By Deformity / The Enshrined.

SYSTEM OF THE ANIMAL, Voices Of Wonder SE007CD (1998). Confrontation / Downsized / System Of The Animal / Closure / Purging The Nemesis / Day One / Unscathed / G.F.Y.S. (Go Fuck Your Self).

CRUELITY BEYOND SUBMISSION, REX REX 001 (2004). Life Long Hate / Ode To Brinn / No Apologies / Confrontation / Closure / System Of The Animal / Hatred Anger And Discust / Bludgeoned By Deformity / Sermon Of Mockery.

PYURIA

FINLAND — *Osku Mäki (vocals / guitar), Tapani Kasurinen (guitar), Valtteri Wilén (bass), Sami Maanpää (drums).*

Uncompromising brutal Death Metal band, founded during 1996 by vocalist / guitarist Oskari Mäki and drummer Sami Siirtola. This duo was soon joined by bass player Jukka-Pekka Suominen and second guitarist Tomi Korkiakangas. This line-up cut a four track, self-titled demo in 1998. Briefly installing singer "Pete", a second demo, the two song 'Suprapubic Pain', emerged the following year. Following sessions for a 1999 EP entitled 'Baroquean Menuets For Oesophagus' PYURIA inducted new member Tapani Kasurinen on guitar. New drummer Sami Maanpää was located in August 2002. Further changes saw Valtteri Wilén taking over bass duties. Signing to Crash Music Inc. the group recorded the album 'Calliphora Vomitoria Introitus' for release in January 2005.

Bassist Valtteri Wilén has association with Norwegian band RILKÁ, fronted by female singer Maya Liittokivi and featuring INTRIGUE and SORG guitarist Knut E. Bakkevold.

Pyuria, Pyuria (1997). Disease / Psycho / Ebony Ice / Permissiveness.

Pyuria, (1997). Disease / Psycho / Ebony Ice / Permissiveness.

Suprapubic Pain, (1998). Abattoir Around / Northern Candlejam.

Baroquean Menuets For Oesophagus EP, (1999). Festered Hate / The Garden Of Pyeden / Syndicate Of Sickness / Porfuria Waltz.

Sublime Metrics Reallocation EP, (2003). To Breathe One's Last / Formaldehyde Bride—Subcutaneous Phagocytosis / Douleur Mortelle / Murder Metaframe / Nemesis Mausoleum / In Rotten Remains Forgotten Names Lie.

CALLIPHORA VOMITORIA INTROITUS, Crash (2004). To Breathe One's Last / In Rotten Remains Forgotten Names Lie / Douleur Mortelle / Murder Metaframe / Nemesis Mausoleum / Formaldehyde Bride-Subcutaneous Phagosytosis / Ghoulish / Field Court-Marshall / Flaunting Moldering Metrics.

QUEST OF AIDANCE

SKÖVDE, SWEDEN — *Christian Älvestam (vocals / guitar), Christian Lundgren (guitar), Anders Johansson (bass), Henrik Schönström (drums).*

QUEST OF AIDANCE, a quite uniquely Arnold Schwarzenneger themed Grind / Death Metal combo, is based in Skövde. Founded in 2004 the band involves vocalist / guitarist Christian Älvestam, of INCAPACITY, SOLAR DAWN, SCAR SYMMETRY, TORCHBEARER, UNMOORED and ZONARIA, guitarist Christian Lundgren of CARNALIZED, bass player Anders Johansson also of CARNALIZED with Henrik Schönström on drums, the latter associated with INCAPACITY, SOLAR DAWN, TORCHBEARER, TRAUMATIZED and UNMOORED.

First QUEST OF AIDANCE product would be a July 2004 demo 'Human Trophy' recorded at Flatpig Studios in Malmö with producer Robert Ahrling. Pulverised Records issued the album 'Fallen Man Collection' the following year.

Human Trophy, Quest Of Aidance (2005) (Demo). Intro / Distant World Arrival / The Hunter And The Prey / Vanishment / Man Is The Harvest / Cranial Works Of Art / 7th Target / Yield.

FALLEN MAN COLLECTION, Pulverised ASH 017 MCD (2006). Imminence / Distant World Arrival / The Hunter And The Prey / Vanishment / Man Is The Harvest / Cranial Works Of Art / 7th Target / Yield.

QUO VADIS

MONTRÉAL, QC, CANADA — *Stephane Paré (vocals), Bart Frydrychowicz (vocals / guitar), William Seghers (guitar), Dominique Lapointe (bass), Roxanne Constantin (keyboards), Yanic Bercier (drums).*

QUO VADIS was forged in Montréal as a 1992 covers act by vocalist / guitarist / violinist Arie Itman, guitarist Bart Frydrychowicz and drummer Yanic Bercier, subsequently drafting bassist Remy Beauchamp in 1995. For live work the band pulled in classically trained soprano guest vocalist Sebrina Lipari. Utilising engineer Pierre Remillard QUO VADIS cut their self financed 'Forever . . .' debut album in 1996. Favourable reviews for the band's technical brand of violin spiced Death Metal generated licensing deals with EarthAD Records in Germany and Immortal Records in Poland.

In 1999 QUO VADIS signed to Hypnotic Records, working with Pierre Remillard on second album 'Day Into Night', capitalised on by 2002's 'Passage In Time', this release a compilation of remixes, live tracks and the group's original 1995 demo tracks.

Both Itman and Beauchamp would both exit, seeing Stephane Paré take over the lead vocal role. CRYPTOPSY's Alex Auburn substituted temporarily for QUO VADIS in March of 2003. To record the band's third album Steve DiGiorgio of TESTAMENT, SADUS, DEATH, CONTROL DENIED and SADUS repute was enrolled as session bassist. QUO VADIS incorporated bassist Dominique 'Forest' Lapointe of ATHERETIC, SATANIZED, B.A.R.F. and AUGURY repute alongside guitarist William Seghers for Summer 2004 shows.

A new album, initially entitled 'To The Bitter End' but then changed to 'Defiant Imagination' and accompanied by a promotional video for the track 'In Contempt', was set for November issue through Fusion3/Skyscraper Records.

During early 2005 former QUO VADIS members guitarist/vocalist Arie Itman and bassist Remy Beauchamp teamed up with NEURAXIS and TORN WITHIN guitarist Rob Milley and drummer Tommy Kinnon in a new band called JESTER. Meantime, Roxanne Constantin recorded keyboards for AVEN AURA's debut 'The Shadow Of Idols' in February. QUO VADIS put in their debut shows in Germany during March, appearing at the 'Darkrise Metal Night' and 'Bowels-Supper Fest III' events. A gig on 7th May at The Medley in Montreal, supported by DESPISED ICON, AUGURY, SOUL OF DARKNESS and ASHES OF EDEN, saw the band performing the 'Defiant Imagination' album in its entirety for future DVD release.

Will Seghers joined NEURAXIS in April 2006. QUO VADIS teamed up with NEAERA, FEAR MY THOUGHTS and fellow Canadian headliners KATAKLYSM for the 'Road To Devastation' European tour in January 2007.

FOREVER . . . , Vomit (1996). Legions Of The Betrayed / As I Feed The Flames Of Hate / Carpae Deum / Mystery / Inner Capsule (Element Of The Ensemble Part II) / Pantheon Of Tears / Zero Hour / The Day The Universe Changed / Nocturnal Reflections / Sans Abris.

DAY INTO NIGHT, Hypnotic (2000). Absolution (Element Of The Ensemble III) / Dysgenics / Hunter/Killer / Hunter/Killer : Endgame / Let It Burn / Dream / On The Shores Of Ithaka / Night Of The Roses / I Believe / Mute Requiem / Cadences Of Absonance.

PASSAGE IN TIME, Skyscraper (2001). Vital Signs 2000 / As One / The Hunted (Hunter-Killer Remix) / Dysgenics (Live) / Point Of No Return—Mute Requiem (Live) / Element Of The Ensemble (Demo 1995) / Sons Of Greed (Demo 1995) / Vital Signs (Demo 1995) / Sadness (Demo 1995).

DEFIANT IMAGINATION, Fusion3/Skyscraper (2003). Silence Calls The Storm / In Contempt / Break The Cycle / Tunnel Effect (Element Of The Ensemble IV) / To The Bitter End / In Articulo Mortis / Fate's Descent / Dead Man's Diary / Ego Intuo Et Servo Te.

R.U. DEAD?

GERMANY — *Chris (vocals), Gero (guitar), Uli H. (guitar), Mad (bass), Rüdiger (drums).*

Guitarist Uli Hildenbrand is an erstwhile member of infamous proto Black Metal band POISON, the guitarist going under the title 'Angel Of Death' in his previous outfit. R.U. DEAD? came together in 1989 releasing the five track 'Simply Dead' demo the following year. Promotion included live dates with NAPALM DEATH, PROTECTOR and ASPHYX. More demos followed in 1991 and 1992. Tracks were lifted from the latter for a 7" EP on Morbid Records titled 'Hypnos'. However, guitarist Gero departed to join FLESHCRAWL and R.U. DEAD? split.

In 1994 Gero quit FLESHCRAWL to reform R.U. DEAD? with previous members in a revised look featuring Gero on vocals and new recruit Almir taking over his guitar duties. The group released a four track CD 'Nothing Will Be Forgiven' in 1995.

Nothing Will Be Forgiven EP, Schädel 001 (1995). When Your Heart Turns Black / And The Moon Whispers / Horrid Tomorrow / Doomworld.

A Thought Before The Kill, Abschadel Produktionen (1996). One Past Zero / A Thought Before The Kill / Profession Of Faith.

COMPLETELY DEAD, Majestic Union (2002). One Past Zero / A Thought Before The Kill / Profession Of Faith / And The Moon Whispers / When Your Heart Turns Black / Horrid Tomorrow / Doomworld / Hypnos / The Tombs Have Not Been Sealed.

RAISE HELL

STOCKHOLM, SWEDEN — *Jonas Nilsson (vocals / guitar), Torstein Wickberg (guitar), Niklas Sjostrom (bass), Dennis Ekdahl (drums).*

Much lauded Stockholm Death Metal combo founded in 1995 as IN COLD BLOOD by vocalist / guitarist Jonas Hilsson, bass player Niklas Sjöström and guitarist Torstein Wickberg. The following year drummer Dennis Ekdahl completed the rankings. The band, very much rooted in the Black Metal scene, were all still in their mid teens by the time the band was finalised leading to jibes about them being "the Death Metal HANSON".

In the summer of 1997 IN COLD BLOOD issued their only demo 'Nailed'. A record company bidding war erupted, which included the Earache label, after which Germany's Nuclear Blast emerged as the victors. However, at this point was an American Hardcore act of same title was discovered hence the name switch to RAISE HELL.

By the time 1998 debut 'Holy Target' arrived RAISE HELL's average band member age was just 18. The record displayed a remarkable maturity for an act so young blending Death and Thrash Metal with unashamed anti-Christian lyrics. The group got straight into gear touring Europe to promote the album alongside DISMEMBER, AGATHODAIMON, NIGHT IN GALES and CHILDREN OF BODOM. During 1999 Niklas Sjöström made time to session bass guitar on DARK EDEN's 'Winterland' demos. The 2000 album 'Not Dead Yet' found RAISE HELL manoeuvring away from their Black Metal roots.

Ekdahl also drums for SINS OF OMISSION and has credits also with MÖRK GRYNING and MYSTIC PROPHECY. The drummer would also feature on Progressive Metal band ATHELA's 'Spectral' demo and take up temporary residency with fellow Swedish Death Metal band BLOODSHED for touring in Finland during December of 2001.

RAISE HELL's October 2002 album 'Wicked Is My Game', released by Nuclear Blast Records, saw production credits going to IN FLAMES vocalist Anders Friden and Frederik Reinedahl.

In February 2003 Jonas Nilsson bowed out, being swiftly replaced by former DRIFTAWAY man Jimmy Fjällendahl. RAISE HELL signed to Black Lodge Records in September of 2004. They entered Sheepvalley Productions in Stockholm during April 2005 to record their fourth album. 'City Of The Damned', was released in May 2006 via Black Lodge Records. RAISE HELL teamed up with NECROPHOBIC and Malmö's ORIGIN BLOOD for a European tour beginning late September.

HOLY TARGET, Nuclear Blast (1998). The March Of Devil's Soldiers / Raise The Dead / Beautiful As Fire / Holy Target / Legions Of Creeps / The Red Ripper / Black Visions / Mattered Out / Superior Powers.

NOT DEAD YET, Nuclear Blast NB 443-2 (2000). Dance With The Devil / Babes / Back Attack / Devilyn / Not Dead Yet / No Puls / User Of Poison / He Is Coming / Soulcollector.

WICKED IS MY GAME, Nuclear Blast NB 1053-2 (2002). Hellborn / Nightwatcher / The Haunted House / Wicked Is My Game / In My Cell / Another Side / Death Race / Devil May Care / Destiny Deceiver.

HOLY TARGET & NOT DEAD YET, Irond CD 02-407 (2003) (Russian release). Dance With The Devil / Babes / Back Attack / Devilyn / Not Dead Yet / No Puls / User Of Poison / He Is Coming / Soulcollector / The March Of Devil's Soldiers / Raise The Devil / Beautiful As Fire / Holy Target / Legions Of Creeps / The Red Ripper / Black Visions / Mattered Out / Superior powers.

To The Gallows, Black Lodge (2006). To The Gallows / Open Your Mind.

CITY OF THE DAMNED, Black Lodge BLOD 031CD (2006). Devil's Station / City Of The Damned / Like Clowns We Crawl / Reaper's Calling / Open Your Mind / Ghost I Carry / My Shadow / To The Gallows / I / Rising.

RAMPAGE

AUGUSTA, GA, USA — *Lord Vic Naughty (vocals / guitar), Earwhig Ringworm (guitar), Tom Coffinsmasher (bass), Paul Bearer (drums).*

Georgia's schizophrenic Death Metal band RAMPAGE have proved an elusive beast to categorize. Many albums are deliberately humourous whilst increasingly latter day albums are deadly serious affairs, in particular the overtly Black Metal 'Bellum Infinitium' concept outing.

The band's first attempt at a formation was as far back as 1989 with Lord Vic Naughty on bass, Paul Bearer on guitar and Sexxxual Rush (real name Ben) on vocals. This unit soon disbanded and it would not be until 1995 when Lord Vic and Bearer, the latter now on drums, reunited. In 1997 the mini album 'Misogyny- Thy Name Is Woman' was issued followed shortly after by the full length 'This End Up'. Although a less tongue in cheek affair 'This End Up' would still obviously mimic POSSESSED's infamous logo and include an irreverent take on 'Jailhouse Rock'.

In 1998 RAMPAGE undertook the 'Gore To Your Door' tour in alliance with GORTICIAN. For these shows Lord Vic pulled in guitarist X Re, bassist Sven Hemlock and drummer Aldo Eniwan. Predictably the band would break up while on the road with roadies taking over musical duties in order to fulfill the dates.

Lord Vic would combine RAMPAGE with FESTERING SORE for a split EP including original 'Doom Metal' along side takes on VENOM's 'Leave Me In Hell' and IMMORTAL's 'Unsilent Storms In The North Abyss'. An admittedly 'fake' live album 'Cummin' Atcha Live, with suitably pornographic cover photograph, followed before recording of the ambitious 'Bellum Infinitium'. Despite being a weighty affair the album would include versions of the KISS classic 'War Machine' and DARKTHRONE's 'In The Shadow Of The Horns'.

Besides RAMPAGE Lord Vic has scored production credits with Toronto Black Metal band MEGIDDO, FESTERING SORE and Doom purveyors EYES OF LIGEIA. The man also operates the spoof Metal Rap band THE GUYS WHO WEAR BLACK TOO MUCH in collaboration with GORTICIAN's High C as well as putting his efforts into a further side venture, DEATH BEAST, in league with Stan Dementor of SONG OF MELKOR, NECROTIC BEHEST and SADOMANIAC.

Further split albums were planned for including unions projected with CHERNOBOG and ENBILULUGUGAL although reportedly RAMPAGE had by this time become purely a Lord Vic solo venture. RAMPAGE did cut a homage to HELLHAMMER by revisiting their renowned 'Apocalyptic Raids' EP. Released by Lord Vic's own Unsung Heroes label the EP, 'Apocalyptic Raids 2001' found RAMPAGE taking on half the tracks whilst MEGIDDO took on the other three. RAMPAGE also shared a further split release, 'New World Blasphemy' with SONG OF MELKOR and CROSS SODOMY.

The 2001 album 'Monolith To An Abandoned Past' sported a rendition of BLACK SABBATH's 'Wheels Of Confusion'. A new lead vocalist, Aerik Von, would first feature on the 2004 EP 'Displeasures Of The Flesh', this featuring two BLACK SABBATH covers in 'N.I.B.' and 'Behind The Wall Of Sleep'.

MISOGYNY- THY NAME IS WOMAN, Unsung Heroes (1998). The Wigglesnake Blues / Kill Ya Tonite / Deadrot / The Round Mound Of Rebound / Cocsucker / Deathcrush / Bloody Leg (The Wifebeatah Mix).

THIS END UP, Unsung Heroes (1998). Bloody Leg / Burn In Hell / Ticket To Hell / Satanic Symphony / Satanic Death / Heavens Gate / The Sceptre / Rampage / The Gates Of The Abyss / Six Bells At Midnight / Eye Of The Hellstorm / Jailhouse Rock '98 (The Emperor Mix) / Witches Sabbath XXX.

Doom Metal EP, Unsung Heroes (1999) (Split EP with FESTERING SORE). Doom Metal / Leave Me In Hell / Unsilent Storms In The North Abyss.

CUMMIN' ATCHA LIVE, Unsung Heroes (1999). Bloody Leg / Born In Hell (On The Bayou) / Deadrot / Satanic Death / The Gates Of The Abyss / Cocksucker / Buried Alive- Money For Nothin' / Six Bells At Midnight / Rampage / Ticket To Hell / The Round Mound Of Rebound / Twisted Minds / Storm Over Avalon / Wanderlust.

BELLUM INFINITIUM, Unsung Heroes (2000). Up From The Depths- Rainbow Skies / Sisters Of Death / Storm Over Avalon / The Wakening- Soulsword / Excalibur / Nemesis / The Vow / The Final Day- Into The Great Beyond- Orbis Tertiius / War Machine / In The Shadow Of The Horns.

APOCALYPTIC RAIDS 2001, Unsung Heroes UHR054 (2001) (Split album with MEGIDDO). Massacra / Whorus/Aggressor / Messiah.

NEW WORLD BLASPHEMY, Unsung Heroes (2001) (Split album with SONG OF MELKOR and CROSS SODOMY). Black Flames Light My Path To Damnation / Ritual Curse.

MONOLITH TO THE ABANDONED PAST, Unsung Heroes UHR049 (2001). Doomsayer / Wanderlust / Doom Metal / Whitechapel / Cursed With Existence / Monolith To An Abandoned Past / Wheels Of Confusion / The Straightener / Neptune's Realm / Rapture Of The Deep / Funeral Fog.

Displeasures Of The Flesh, Unsung Heroes (2004). Doomsayer / Displeasures Of The Flesh / Wasp / Behind The Walls Of Sleep / Bassically / N.I.B. / The Wrath Of Satans Whore.

RAVAGE

DÜSSELDORF, GERMANY — *Jan Michels (vocals), Daniel Pietzsch (guitar), Demian Heuke (guitar), Bernd Steuer (bass), Dennis Thiele (drums).*

Düsseldorf Death Metal combo RAVAGE was created in August 1999 by guitarists Demian Heuke and Daniel Pietzsch, lead vocalist Jan Michels and Stefan Raduschefski on the drums. The latter would soon bow out and in February of 2000 the band welcomed onboard new drummer Dennis Thiele. During early 2001 RAVAGE cut the first demo 'To Kill And Destroy'. The band line up would be brought up to strength in mid 2001 with the introduction of bassist Frank Schneiders. However, after a period of extensive gigging this latest recruit decamped. Bernd Steuer took his place for RAVAGE's 2003 album 'Infernal Devastation', produced by Alex Sokolovski.

The subtly titled 'Get Fucking Slaughtered' arrived in 2005. Guitarist Daniel Pietzsch exited in February.

INFERNAL DEVASTATION, Ravage (2003). Blasphemic War / Disinfestation / Infinite Hate / Execution Call / Drowning In Blood / Day Of Devastation / Totalravage.

GET FUCKING SLAUGHTERED, (2005). Introduction / Get Fucking Slaughtered / Havoc Command / Nuclear Storm / Holycaust / Devilish Strike / Riddled / Vow Of Desecration / Into Your Demise / Blazing Chaos (Death Upon The Nazarene) / Bloody Revenge.

RAVAGER

MEXICO — *Antimo (vocals / bass), Eric (guitar), Samuel (guitar), Oscar Garcia (drums).*

Blasphemic Death Metal act forged in 1997 under the banner of DOMAIN. This title would be switched to RAVAGER upon learning of the already established German melodic Rock act

DOMAIN. RAVAGER include Antimo Buonnano of Grindcore merchants DISGORGE in the ranks.

The February 2002 album 'Storm Of Sin' would be commissioned by the French Osmose Productions label and produced by MORBID ANGEL live sound engineer Juan Gonzales.

RAVAGER folded during December of 2003, Antimo and Oscar Garcia both joining forces with Singapore based veterans IMPIETY. That same year Garcia and Buonnano also allying themselves with DISGORGE, CENOTAPH and BLOODREAPING guitarist Eduardo Guevara, founding Black-Death Metal trio HACAVITZ.

STORM OF SIN, Osmose Productions OPCD 126 (2002). Infernal Redemption / Blasphemic Iniquity / Scorn To The Holy Existence / Ironstorm / Maze Of Extermination / Those Who Lie In Wait / Storming Horror / Chained To Inferno / Initiation Of The Unholy War / Praise The Lord Of Two Faces.

NAZZGUL RISING, Osmose OPCD 153 (2004). Nuclear Vomiting Warcraft / Hades Rises / Of Fire Revealed / Foretold / Crest Fallen Of Divinity / As Shadows Corrupts / In The Depths / Antagonist Grim / Through Honour And Fury / Fourth To Naxzgul.

RE-PULSE

FINLAND — *Katja Pieksämäki (vocals), Mika Niskanen (guitar), Risto Turpeinen (guitar), Harri Paulamäki (bass), Margit Tornio (keyboards), Marko Pieksämäki (drums).*

Melodic Death Metal band RE-PULSE is fronted by Katja Pieksämäki. The group was assembled in the spring of 1991 by guitarist Mika Niskanen and drummer Marko Pieksämäki, the debut line-up also including Jyrki Järvenpää on bass and Christer Åman on second guitar. During 1992 RE-PULSE drafted guitarist Juha Haukipuro, with new bass player Marko Solonen arriving the following year. During 1999 Harri Paulamäki replaced Solonen. The group's first demo, entitled 'Eyes Of Fire', saw issue in 2000. Employed on vocals during 2003, and featuring on the demo session 'Neverforever', would be Alex Felder.

RE-PULSE recorded the demos 'True Emotions' in 2004 and 'Far Away From Here' the following year. Further changes in 2005 found Risto Turpeinen acquired on second guitar.

True Emotions, True Emotions (2004). True Emotions / The Haze Of A Dream / Meant To Be / Nothing Lasts Forever.

Far Away From Here, Re-pulse (2005). Far Away From Here / Somehow Things Got Wrong / The Flames Of Deceit / The Heart Of Darkness / Realms Unseen.

REALITY GREY

ACQUAVIVA, ITALY — *Tommaso Montenegro (vocals), Giuseppe Maselli (guitar), Antonello Addabbo (guitar), Alessandro Giustino (bass), Donato Cosmo (drums).*

Acquaviva's REALITY GREY was conceived during 2000 as a Thrash-Crossover act comprising singer Emanuele Vaira, guitarist Antonello Addabbo, bass player Vito Montenegro and drummer Donato Cosmo. Second guitarist Giuseppe Maselli was added in 2003. The band moved into melodic Death Metal territory with the acquisition of new frontman Tommaso Montenegro and bassist Alessandro Giustino, as evidenced on the 2004 demo 'Reborn In Apathy'.

During 2006 REALITY GREY recorded and its debut album, 'Darkest Days Are Yet to Come', with GOLEM, WARCHILD and NATRON guitarist Ottavio Marzo acting as producer. The track 'Never Again' was on the Razar Ice free compilation album 'Songs From The Crypt'.

Reborn In Apathy, Reality Grey (2004). Reborn In Apathy (Intro) / Screaming Out / My Hell / F.U.

REBAELLIUN

PORTO ALEGRE, RS, BRAZIL — *Marcello Marzari (vocals / bass), Ronaldo Lima (guitar), Fabiano Penna (guitar), Sandro Moreira (drums).*

Death Metal band led by guitarist Fabiano Penna founded in 1996. REBAELLIUN opened proceedings with the 1999 'At War' EP, this outing witnessing a line up of vocalist / bassist Marcello Marzari, guitarists Fabiano Penna and Ronaldo Lima with Sandro Moreira on the drums.

The 2000 'Bringer Of War' EP, recorded as a trio minus Lima, closed out with a cover rendition of MORBID ANGEL's 'Day Of Suffering'. That year REBAELLIUN guested for LIMBONIC ART and ANCIENT in Brazil and later formed part of the 'No Mercy' Festivals across Europe together with VADER, FLESHCRAWL and VITAL REMAINS. For the 'Annihilation' album, produced by ex-HOLY MOSES guitarist Andy Classen, former BLESSED man Lohy Fabiano took over as frontman and bassist and Ronaldo Lima returned on guitar. Fabiano Penna would join Black Metal act HORNED GOD.

At War EP, (1999). At War / Spawning The Rebellion.
Bringer Of War EP, (2000). Agonizing By My Hands / Bringer Of War / Kings Of The Unholy Blood / Day Of Suffering.
ANNIHILATION, (2001). Annihilation / Rebellious Vengeance / Steel Siege / Red Spikes / Unleash The Fire / Unborn Consecration / God Of A Burned Land / Bringer Of War / Defying The Plague.

RECLUSION

GOTHENBURG, SWEDEN — *Rune Foss (vocals / guitar), Mattias Bolander (guitar), Pasi Jaskara (bass), Marek Dobrowolski (drums).*

Based in Gothenburg Death-Thrashers RECLUSION, fronted by Rune Foss of EXEMPT and KILLAMAN, comprise two Swedes, a Finn and a Norwegian. Initially the band went under the title DAWN OF TIME prior to evolving into DROWNED for a debut demo and subsequently RECLUSION. Signing to the French Listenable label, RECLUSION's debut album 'Shell Of Pain' saw production credits going out to KING DIAMOND guitarist Andy La Rocque.

In early 2005 it would be learned drummer Marek Dobrowolski had joined ex-THE CROWN singer Johan Lindstrand's new band project ONE MAN ARMY AND THE UNDEAD QUARTET. RECLUSION parted ways with lead guitarist Toni Korhonen in March. RECLUSION announced the addition of guitarist Mattias Bolander to the group's ranks in June.

SHELL OF PAIN, Listenable POSH 032 (2001). Shelter From Pain / Impulsive / Pressure / Reclusion / The Quest / Sacred Ground / Unspoken Fear / A Force Of One / Speak The Truth.

RED HARVEST

OSLO, NORWAY — *Ofu Kahn (vocals / guitar), TurboNatas (guitar), Thomas Brandt (bass), Lrz (programming), Erik Wroldsen (drums).*

Oslo's RED HARVEST kicked off their career with distinct Thrash Metal leanings but had introduced Industrial elements with each successive release. The band held its roots in the late eighties Heavy Metal band ARCTIC THUNDER, formulated in February 1987 by vocalist / guitarist Jimmy, bassist Thomas Brandt and with drummer Cato Bekkevold, also having credits with DEMONIC. ARCTIC THUNDER persevered until 1989, after which the members formulated RED HARVEST, pulling in second guitarist Jan Nygaard.

The band debuted with the demos 'Occultia' in December 1989 and 'Psychotica' in 1990. The following year RED HARVEST performed its inaugural concert outside of Norway, at Sveadale in Sweden. Recording for the Black Mark label the band had its commercial debut, the album 'Nomindsland', issued in April 1992. Touring to promote this release included

UK support gigs to CADAVER, one or two of these gigs also seeing a fledging CRADLE OF FILTH on the billing.

Contracting to new record label Voices Of Wonder the group, utilising studio keyboards from Lars R. Sorensen, crafted a second album 'There's Beauty In The Purity Of Sadness'. A promotional video was filmed for the track 'Wounds' but promptly banned from Norwegian television due to its explicit content, depicting executions and human suffering. Strangely, MTV in the USA did air the clip. Further product included the donation of three tracks to the 'The Reincarnation Of The Sun' compilation on Dunkel Records. Gigs in Norway were to be capitalised on by a series of German dates but these would be cancelled due to illness on Bekkevold's part.

In 1994 RED HARVEST guitarist Jan F. Nygaard departed and the group had added guitarist Ketil Eggum of DUNKELHEIT and keyboard player Lars R. Sorensen, their former studio colleague. This version of RED HARVEST laid down the 1995 EP 'The Maztür Nation', promoted by a video clip for the track 'Enlighten The Child' and touring across Europe. Third album 'Hybreed' emerged in 1996, once again bolstered by a video, to 'The Burning Wheel', and gigs across Europe.

Drummer Cato Bekkevold would bow out upon completion of support gigs with TYPE O NEGATIVE during 1997, subsequently scoring credits with ENSLAVED and ASHES TO ASHES. Under the pseudonym 'CA-2' Bekkevold had also sessioned on the 2002 SIRIUS album 'Spectral Transition—Dimension Sirius'. New man behind the drum kit would be TRIVIAL ACT's Erik Wroldsen. The band soon engaged themselves in the studio yet again, producing the EP 'New Rage World Music' in 1998. A label switch to the Nocturnal Art imprint the following year would be marked by the delivery of the fourth album opus 'Cold Dark Matter', featuring DARKTHRONE's Fenriz as guest musician, in 1999. RED HARVEST supported MAYHEM on their September 2000 European dates, which saw the band traversing ten countries. 'Cold Dark Matter' found a North American outlet via Relapse Records, this variant adding bonus material culled from 'New Rage World Music'.

RED HARVEST's 1999 album 'New Rage World Music' would be re-issued in 2001 by Nocturnal Art Productions with a bonus live version of 'Absolut Dunkel:Heit' recorded in Vienna and studio tracks which included a guesting Maniac from MAYHEM on vocals. That Summer work on a follow up album commenced and in December producer Neil Kernon travelled to Norway to commit 'Sick Transit Gloria Mundi' (a slight bastardization of Latin for 'Thus Passes The Glory Of The World') to tape. Norwegian and UK gigs ensued and such was the acclaim garnered by the band that RED HARVEST found themselves nominated for Norwegian Grammy awards.

RED HARVEST keyboard player Lrz (Lars R. Sorensen) surfaced as part of the hard hitting Black Metal trio MEZZERSCHMITT for the 'Weltherrschaft' EP. Although anonymous this project saw Lrz working alongside MAYHEM guitarist Blasphemer ('Herr Schmitt') and drummer Hellhammer ('Hauptmann Hammer'). Sorensen also sessioned for SIRIUS. Another side venture found the RED HARVEST pairing of Thomas 'Bølla' Brandt and Bolt Bergsten forging traditionalist Thrash outfit WAKLEVÖREN.

British shows in late 2002 saw a batch of shows in December headlined by THE BERZERKER and including LABRAT and INSISION. A limited edition remix single, shared as a split release with ZYKLON, surfaced in March 2003. The band undertook a November European package tour, allied with AETERNUS and 1349. August saw the band utilising the internet as media with a web only release 'Antipax Mundial Total', comprising remixes and video footage.

The 2004 RED HARVEST opus 'Internal Punishment Programs', promoted with a promotional video for the track 'Anatomy Of The Unknown', was recorded at Subsonic Society Studios and mixed by Fredrik Nordström at Studio Fredman

RED HARVEST

in Gothenburg. Nocturnal Art Productions issued the record in Europe during September whilst Candlelight handled an early October US release.

In March 2005 RED HARVEST amicably parted ways with Nocturnal Art Productions. The band signed to the French concern Season Of Mist in April. September shows in Europe and Scandinavia had the band forming up a package comprising ARCTURUS, NATTEFROST, CONFESSOR and TSJUDER. European and Scandinavian touring commencing late September had the band in alliance with ARCTURUS for the 'Shipwrecked In Europe' dates. The band also made studio time to record a cover version of RAMONES' 'Somebody Put Something In My Drink" for the 'Scandinavian Tribute to The Ramones' tribute album.

RED HARVEST teamed up with SUSPERIA and GRIMFIST for a UK tour in October 2006. A new album, 'A Greater Darkness', was set for February 2007 release. The band performed 'A Greater Darkness' in full at an album release party concert held on February 23rd at Club Maiden in Oslo.

Occultia, Red Harvest (1989) (Demo). Embrace Of Misery / Beneath The Mask / Spirit Of The Serpent.

Psychotica, Red Harvest (1990) (Demo). Face The Fact / Acid / Sane In Solitude / Faithful Unto Deat / D-F Song.

NOMINDSLAND, Black Mark BMCD 19 (1991). The Cure / Righteous Majority / Acid / No Next Generation / Machines Way / (Live And Pay) The Holy Way / Crackman / Face The Fact / Wrong Arm Of The Law.

THE REINCARNATION OF THE SUN, Dunkel Productions DPCD 001 (1994) (Split album with VALHALL, ANSTALT, REMYL, DUNKELHEIT, PILEDRIVER and HUMID). Primal / Receival Of Truth / Resist.

VOICES OF WONDER—A COMPILATION, Voices Of Wonder VOW036 (1994) (Split album with MOTORPSYCHO, HEDGE HOG, OMEN, RUN DOG RUN and WONDERFUL WORLD). Resist / Mindblazt / Wounds.

THERE'S BEAUTY IN THE PURITY OF SADNESS, Voices Of Wonder VOW039 CD (1994). Wounds / Naked / Resist / Mindblazt / Mastodome / Shivers / (?) / Mother Of All / Alpha Beta Gamma L.E.A.K. / Sadness / The Art Of Radiation.

The Maztür Nation EP, Voices Of Wonder VOW046 (1995). The Harder They Fall / Enlighten The Child / Dream Awake / Tears.

HYBREED, Voices Of Wonder VOW052 (1996). Maztür Nation / The Lone Walk / Mutant / After All ... / Ozrham / On Sacred Ground / The Harder They Fall / Underwater / Monumental / In Deep / The Burning Wheel.

NEW RAGE WORLD MUSIC, Voices Of Wonder VOW072 (1999). Ad Noctum / Move Or Be Moved (Preview) / Swallow The Sun / Pity The Bastard / Concrete Steel Vs. The Brain (PTB Remix).

COLD DARK MATTER, Nocturnal Art Productions ECLIPSE 014 (2000). Omnipotent / Last Call / Absolut Dunkelheit / Cold Dark Matter / Junk-O-Rama / Fix Hammer Fix / The Itching Scull / Death In Cyborg Era / Move Or Be Moved.

COLD DARK MATTER, Relapse RLP6479 (2001). Omnipotent / Last Call / Absolut Dunkelheit / Cold Dark Matter / Junk-O-Rama / Fix Hammer Fix / The Itching Scull / Death In Cyborg Era / Move Or Be Moved / Ad Noctum / Move Or Be Moved (Preview) / Swallow The Sun / Pity The Bastard.

NEW WORLD RAGE MUSIC, Red Harvest ECLIPSE 019 (2001). Ad Noctum / Move Or Be Moved (Preview) / Swallow The Sun / Pity The Bastard / Concrete Steel Vs. The Brain (PTB Remix) / Final Scorn / Absolut Dunkel:Heit (Live) / The Supreme Truth / Terrorsonic Zodiac.
SICK TRANSIT GLORIA MUNDI, Nocturnal Art Productions ECLIPSE 20 (2002). U.G.X. / AEP / GodTech / Humanoia / Dead / Cybernaut / Beyond The End / Desolation / Sick Transit Gloria Mundi / Dead Men Don't Rape / WeltSchmertz / [Dead End].
SICK TRANSIT GLORIA MUNDI, Relapse RLP6537 (2002) (USA release). U.G.X. / A.E.P. / GodTech / Humanoia / Dead / Cybernaut / Beyond The End / Desolation / Sick Transit Gloria Mundi / Dead Men Don't Rape / WeltSchmertz / [Dead End] / Re-Hammer-Mix.
Zyklon / Red Harvest, Nocturnal Art Productions ECLIPSE 025 (2003) (Split 7" with ZYKLON). Re-Hammer-Mix.
INTERNAL PUNISHMENT PROGRAMS, Nocturnal Art Productions ECLIPSE 27 (2004). Anatomy Of The Unknown / Fall Of Fate / Abstract Morality Junction / Mekanizm / Symbol Of Decay / Teknocrate / Synthesize My DNA / Wormz / 4-4-1-8 / Internal Punishment Programs.
A GREATER DARKNESS, Season Of Mist SOM 144 (2007). Antidote / Hole In Me / Dead Cities / Mouth Of Madness / Beyond The Limits Of Physical Experience / Icons Of Fear ... The Curse Of The Universe / I Sweat W.O.M.D. / Warthemes / Distorted Eyes / Proprioception.

REDRUM

KIRUNA, SWEDEN — *Phan Cullhaven (vocals / bass), Muerte (guitar), Mr. Rocker (guitar), Deathking (drums).*

Kiruna Death Metal act ANNIHILATION was rooted in the band antecedent REDRUM, an act that had previously issued the December 2000 'Murder Industry' demo. REDRUM had been created by former APOCALYPTIC VISIONS and NAGRIM drummer Deathking alongside guitarist Muerte (a.k.a. Mårten Eliasson), former ELEM and AMSVARTNER vocalist / guitarist Phan 'Phanskap' Cullhaven and bassist Tsenjo. With Tjenso's departure in February 2002 Cullhaven took over the bass role as the band name switched to ANNIHILATION. Following an inaugural live performance the group added guitarist Mr. Rocker. The 'Analsex66' demo arrived in 2003.

Cullhaven is also an active member of VREDE and Thrashers DEADLOCK.

Murder Industry, Redrum (2000) (Demo). When The Nightmares Comes Haunt You / Faith Of Religion / Dead By Faith / World In Chaos And Fire / Experimental Desires By Death.

REGURGITATE

SWEDEN — *Rikard Jansson (vocals), Urban Skytt (guitar), Glenn Sykes (bass), Jocke Pettersson (drums).*

Extreme Grindcore act that relish in the most sickening subject matters. The band was created as a trio of vocalist Rikard Jansson, guitarist Mats Nordrup (also drummer with GENERAL SURGERY and CREMATORY) and drummer Peter Stjarnvind. The latter has an enviable list of credits with acts such as UNANIMATED, FACE DOWN, MERCILESS and LOUD PIPES.

REGURGITATE debuted with the 1994 cassette 'Concrete Human Torture' which found REGURGITATE in a rather more politically inclined mode than the full on Gore that was to come. For recording of the split album with Germany's DEAD for the infamous Poserslaughter label Nordrup took up drum duties as Stjarnvind's other acts became his priority. CREMATORY guitarist Urban Skytt laid down guitars. However, Nordrup would make his exit and the band re-grouped with Stjarnvind back on drums, Skytt joining full time and another former CREMATORY man bassist Joppe Hanson completing the roster. This quartet cut the 'Effortless Regurgitation Of Bright Red Blood' album. Issued in 1999 the album includes an AGATHOCLES cover version. That same year a new drummer was sought as Stjarnvind's commitments to ENTOMBED and LOUDPIPES took priority. Drafted would be Jocke Pettersson, a seasoned campaigner citing a tradition with DAWN, UNMOORED, SOLAR DAWN, RETALIATION, KIDS ARE SICK and THY PRIMORDIAL.

The album covers are not for the faint hearted. The 2000 album 'Carnivorous Erection', recorded at Örebro's Soundlab Studios with NASUMs Mieszko Talarczyk as producer, had its release delayed due to furor caused by the album artwork which featured a rather vicious penis with bared teeth! That August the band cut tracks for a split 7" shared with GORE BEYOND NECROPSY.

2001 saw REGURGITATE tackling live work, undertaking their fifth concert of their career at Stockholm's Kafé 44 with Terje Andersson of ARSEDESTROYER as stand in bassist. Further performances included appearances at the 'Fuck the Commerce IV' festival in Germany, 'Obscene Extreme' festival in the Czech Republic and a brief tour in Europe in union with $KRUPEL and ENTRAILS MASSACRE. Between gigs the group laid down tracks for the 'Hatefilled Vengeance' release, once again with Mieszko Talarczyk behind the desk.

Early 2002 saw the recruitment of a permanent bassist in American Glenn Sykes, having prior duties with VOMIT SPAWN and CARDIOVASCULAR SUB-HYPOTHERMIA. This version of the band first performed in Germany that February. In July REGURGITATE hooked up with SUPPOSITORY and ENTRAILS MASSACRE for a run of eleven shows across Germany, Czech Republic and Slovakia. The 'Deviant' album was recorded that November.

With Jocke Pettersson out of action due to a back injury, NASUM's Anders Jakobson filled in on drums for shows at the 'Just Killers—No Fillers Fest' and 'Morbide Festspiele' events. Guitarist Urban Skytt joined NASUM in September. Bassist Glenn Sykes aided GENERAL SURGERY as stand in musician during January 2004.

REGURGITATE commenced recording of a new album in March 2006. The band announced the addition of bassist Johan Jansson, having association with a swathe of acts such as PYOSISFIED, HATRED, SIDEBURNERS, ASOCIAL, FLESHREVELS, FULMINATION, FROSTHEIM, UNCURBED, INTERMENT, DEMONICAL and DELLAMORTE, to the group's ranks in September. The new man made his live debut at a concert with MASSGRAV on the 30th at Pub Bastun in Marihamn, Åland. In early December the band laid down tracks for use on a split release in collaboration with SKULLHOG.

REGURGITATE teamed up with ROTTEN SOUND for a Finnish mini-tour in February 2007.

REGURGITATE, Poserslaughter (1994) (Split album with DEAD). Cannibalistic Miscarriage / Praedilctio For Mennohagia / Organic Convulsions / Expelling Pyorrhoea / Purulent Vulvectomy / Morbid Reality / Terror Reign / Fear? / Desensitized / Generic Words.
Brainscrambler, Glued Stamp (1995) (7" split single with PSYCHOTIC NOISE). Brainscrambler / Regurgitated Giblets / Internal Bleeding / Methylated Bile / Liquid Excrements / Carnal Cacophony / Vomit Breath / Suicide.
EFFORTLESS REGURGITATION OF BRIGHT RED BLOOD, Relapse (1999). Intro: The Act Of Intestinal Regurgitation / Disgorging Foetus / Confluent Macular Drug Eruption / Bullous Impetigo / Fleshfeast / Anorectal Ulceration / Vulva Fermentation / Multicystic Kidney / Mucupurulent Offal Grinder / Total Dismemberment Of A Female Corpse / Carnal Cacophony / Vomit Breath / Complete Rectal Prolapse / Testicular Trauma / Genital Cancer / Malignant Tumor / Diffuse Systemic Scerosis / Owner Of A Necrotic Intestine / Newborn Regurgitation / Torsion Of The Testicle / Worm Eaten Rectum / Chronic Lymphatic Leukemie / Meatal Ulcer / Purulent Discharge From The Urethra / Vaginal Obstriction / Cloudy, Grayish Vomitus / Fleshmangler / Splattered Brains / Bulging Vaginal Septum / Acute Urinary Infection / Severe Necroses Of The Face / Bleeding Peptic Ulcer / Face Mutilation / Extensive Ulcerate Tumor / Tumescent Foetal Fluids To Expurgate / Carbonized Bowels / Effortless Regurgitation Of Bright Red Blood.
CARNIVOROUS ERECTION, Relapse RLP6465 (2000). You're About To Fuckin' Die / Domination Through Mutilation / Escort Service Of The Dead / Obscene Body Slayings / Fecal Freak / Humiliated In Your Own Blood / Just Another Stillborn / Parade Of The Decapitated Midgets / Ruptured Remains In A Doggybag / Copious Head Carnage / Carnivorous Erection / Relentless Pursuit Of Human Flesh / Dismantle The Afterbirth / Choked In Shit / Funeral Genocide / Rancid Head Of Splatter / Rage Against Humanity / To Boil A Corpse / Bloody Pile Of

Human Waste / Drenched In Cattleblood / Carbonated Death / Skull Of Shit And Sludge / Desperate Need For Violation / 37 Stabwounds / Vomified (Regurgitated To The Core) / Headless She Died / Breath Like Rotten Meat / I Wanna Kill / Claw Hammer Castration / Festering Embryonic Vomit / Smeared With Bloodmixed Semen / The Pulsating Feast / Stinking Genital Warts / Pyronecrobestiality / Self Disembowelment / Savage Gorewhore / The Combustion And Consumption Of Pyorrheic Waste.

DEVIANT, Relapse RR 6565 (2003). Drowning In Filth / Embrace Obscenity And Kiss The Eruption Of Destruction / Seal Your Doom / Grotesque Anoplasty / Blind Fiends Of Chaos / Visions Of Sodomy / Severe Necrotic Manifesto / Aniihilation Meets Depravation / Amphigory / Screams Of Death Your God Won't Hear / Reeking Hellhole / Lethean Sleep / Waging War On Benevolence / Exterminate The Virtuous / Alone In Oblivion / Deviant Malpractice / The Ultimate Enslavement / Systematic Demoralization / Unfed / Manipulation Reigns Supreme / Charred Remains / Crossed Out Existence / Vice And Iniquity / Lobotochrist / Twisted Rhymes Of Perversion / Depopultaion Of The Human Race / Life Falls Before Our Feet.

HATE FILLED VENGEANCE, Relapse RR 6491 (2003). Confluent Macular Drug Eruption / Vulva Fermentation / Complete Rectal Prolapse / Testicular Trauma / Cloudy, Grayish Vomitus / Fleshmangler / Bulging Vaginal Septum / Bleeding Peptic Ulcer / Deranged Menarche Injection / Drastical Decapitation / Dmethic Jizz Treatment / Destined To Burn / Hatefilled Vengeance / 666 Casualties / Deathlike … / Choke That Piggy / Devastation And Nuclear Apocalypse / Disciples Of Obliteration.

SICKENING BLISS, Relapse (2006). Bliss / Abducens Eminence / Euphoric State Of Butchery / Cocoon Of Filth / Putrid Serenity / Tenderizing The Malformed / Violent Necrophilic Climax / Cavernous Sores / Reborn In Latrinic Ecstasy / Bleed On Me / Gutrot Hogfrenzy / Undying Lust For Cadaverous Molestation / Battered With A Brick / Devoured By Ghouls / Addiction (An Unconditional Love For Blasphemous Perversions) / (We Are) Sadistic Hateful Scum / Worm Eater / Perish In Blood / Upheaval Of Human Entrails / Bathed In Feculence / Bestial Sons Of Devastation / Defile / Deterioration Of Grated Genitals / Excremental Investment / Hacksaw Hysterectomy / Catatonic Possession.

REGURGITATION

USA — *Jim Plotkin (vocals / guitar), Henry Veggian (bass), Mike McNeice (drums).*

REGURGITATION published two 1987 demo tapes, 'Bathroom Rules' and 'Organic Backwash'. Two tracks from the latter session, 'Pesticide' and 'Laryngitis' would subsequently be included on the New Renaissance Records compilation album 'Speed Metal Hell Volume Three'. Line-up changes saw drummer Ralph Pimentell being replaced by Mike McNiece. Frontman Jim Plotkin later went on to achieve notoriety with O.L.D.

Plotkin would also act as touring guitarist for fellow Earache act SCORN and pursue leftfield projects such as FLUX, SOLARUS, KRANKY and TRIFFID PROJECT. Plotkin would issue two worthy 1996 releases, the solo album 'The Joy Of Disease' and a collaboration with SCORN's Mick Harris simply billed as PLOTKIN / HARRIS for the 'Collapse' album. He would also rack up credits with ATOMSMASHER, the latter in league with DISCORDANCE AXIS drummer Dave Witte and DJ Speedranch.

Bathroom's Rule, Regurgitation (1987). Laryngitis / Implosion / Aggravated Assault / Pissant / Dead By Dawn / Bathroom's Rule.
Organic Backwash, (1987). Laryngitis / SS / Pesticide.

REGURGITATION

OH, USA — *Ben Deskns (vocals / guitar), Tony Tipton (guitar), Brian Baxter (vocals / bass), Dan Baker (drums).*

REGURGITATION, assembled in 1994 by vocalist / guitarist Ben Deskns and guitarist Tony Tipton, underwent constant line up fluctuations during their early years. Nevertheless, a 1996 demo 'Conceived Through Vomit' emerged before the band was judged stable with the drafting of vocalist / bassist Brian Baxter and drummer Dan Baker.

In October of 2001 guitarist Tony Tipton made a return to the line-up. A planned split EP with German act PROFANITY was shelved due to a lack of drummer. REGURGITATION added new drummer Jason Trecazzi during March of 2002. Former FLESHTIZED and current EPOCH OF UNLIGHT guitarist / vocalist Casey Robertson joined the band in July.

Bassist Brian Baxter joined GORGASM during November of 2002. In late 2003 the REGURGITATION trio of guitarists Ben Deskins and Tony

Tipton with drummer Jason Trecazzi founded NECROTIC DISGORGEMENT. Joining the fold would be DISLIMB and NUNSLAUGHTER bassist Rob Lesniak and the EROTIC INCISIONS and CLEAN FLESH credited frontman Joe Wolffe.

TALES OF NECROPHILIA, Ablated ABLTD002 (1999). Out Of The Womb / Repulsive Genital Disfigurement / Seed Of The Sanguinary / Acid Enema / Fermenting Vaginal Excrements / Menstrual Cykill / Cadaveric Impregnation / Fetal Suffocation.

REIGN OF DECAY

GERMANY — *Helge Stang (vocals), Michael Zech (guitar), Martin Fuchs (guitar), Thomas Kiris (bass), Thomas Taube (drums).*

Munich Death Metal act REIGN OF DECAY was formed in the Summer of 1996 by vocalist Michael Heller, guitarist Martin Fuchs and ODEM ARCARUM drummer Thomas 'C.A.' Taube. A fluid formative line-up would see some settling with the introduction of ATROPIN bassist Thomas Kiris toward the close of the year. This line up cut the inaugural demo 'The Great Fall'.

In 1998 second guitarist Michael Zech, as 'Lord Arioch' founder member of ODEM ARCARUM, entered the line-up for recording of a second demo, 'Obtuse Mankind'. A third session, entitled 'Clockwork', followed in 1999. However, progress was stalled when Heller exited. In 2002 both Taube and Zech joined Black Metal band SAEL. The pair would vacate this position by the following year.

New singer Helge Stang was incorporated into REIGN OF DECAY June of 2003.

Clockwork, Reign Of Decay (1999). Coldplanet / Obtuse Mankind / Clockwork / Pandemonium Of Souls / B.H. 9 / Mindflow (Live).

REIGN OF TERROR

CANBERRA, ACT, AUSTRALIA — *Michael Reggae (vocals / guitar), Glen Luck (bass), Victor (drums).*

Canberra Death Metal act REIGN OF TERROR made their entrance with the 1997 demo session 'Scavenge The Dead'. The band line up comprised of founder member and mainstay vocalist Michael Reggae, guitarist / bassist Nathan and keyboard player / drummer Victor.

REIGN OF TERROR issued the 'Under Blackened Skies' mini album the following year, Nathan having made his departure in favour of new guitarist Jeff.

A 1999 demo, 'Death Shall Be The Season', followed. The year proved to herald a period of debilitating line up changes and in February the band folded. Reggae resurrected the clan in April drafting drummer Ben and in August the band put in useful supports to Finns IMPALED NAZARENE, NEVERMORE and countrymen DESTROYER 666. However, August saw the departure of Ben and his subsequent replacement by Chris of DISRUPTURE.

In February of 2000 guitarist Greg was added to the line up and REIGN OF TERROR donated a track to the 'Down Underground Vol. 3' compilation album. By September, with Jeff, Chris and Greg all bowing out REIGN OF TERROR split yet again. It would be November when Reggae pulled the band back together with a fresh line up comprising of bass player Tom and drummer Adam. The following month Kurt would augment the band on second guitar. In April of 2001 REIGN OF TERROR replaced Tom with erstwhile ARMOURED ANGEL mentor Glen 'Lucy' Luck.

As of October 2001 REIGN OF TERROR's line up stood at Reggae, bass player Lucy and a returning Victor on drums.

UNDER BLACKENED SKIES, (1998). My Undying Love (I Will Always Dismember You) / Under Blackened Skies / Lords Of The Black Earth / Her Funeral Beauty / The Inversion.

RELEVANT FEW

GOTHENBURG, SWEDEN — *Henke Svensson (vocals), Johan Nilsson (guitar), Kristian Lampila (guitar), Robert Hakemo (bass), Morbid Mojjo (drums).*

Gothenburg Grindsters assembled in October of 2000, debuting live as support act to NASUM just two months later. RELEVANT FEW feature GARDENIAN and ex-GOOSEFLESH bass player Robert Hakemo and DRACENA, MINDSNARE, SANDALINAS, RUNEMAGICK and LORD BELIAL credited drummer Morbid Mojjo (a.k.a. Daniel Moilanen). Formatively, the group also included ABANDON guitarist Johan Nilsson.

A February 2001 demo session secured a contract with the Swedish No Tolerance label for the first album 'Who Are Those Of Leadership?'. A tour ranked alongside NAPALM DEATH was secured but the band would be forced to withdraw when singer J.C. quit the band. Henke Svensson was drafted for an appearance at the May 2002 'Fuck The Commerce V' festival in Neiden, Germany. Moilanen bailed out upon completion of the sophomore album 'The Art Of Today', issued in November of 2003, but made a return in December.

The band recorded a cover of NUCLEAR ASSAULT's 'Critical Mass' in December of 2003 for use on a compilation album issued through Evigt Lidande Productions. The same label also readied a live album entitled 'Live: Revolution!', recorded at a June 2002 show in Pianobaren, Trollhättan. The November 2003 album 'The Art Of Today' would witness a swift re-issue through New Hawen Records the following year. Mojjo decamped but made a return in mid 2004. However, Moilanen also performed with Horror Metal act NOTRE DAME for the band's Summer festivals appearances as a stand in for original drummer Mannequin De Sade, who was sidelined due to an apparent "self-inflicted injury."

RELEVANT FEW opened for VADER's Gothenburg gig in August before uniting with GADGET for a run of German "Born to Booze, Live to Grind" dates the following month. In September Moilanen officially joined NOTRE DAME. The band would act as support to DEICIDE on their November Swedish shows.

In March 2005 Morbid Mojjo re-emerged as member of the new band ENGEL, a Gothenburg based quintet also featuring guitarists Marcus Sunesson, ex-THE CROWN, Niclas Engelin, of PASSENGER, GARDENIAN and IN FLAMES repute, bassist Robert Hakemo, ex-GARDENIAN and GOOSEFLESH together with vocalist Mangan Klavborn.

RELEVANT FEW line-up changes saw vocalist Henke Svensson leaving the group due to "a lack of interest and dedication" and being duly replaced by the group's previous frontman, Johan Carlzon. In August 2006 Robert Hakemo joined M.A.N.

WHO ARE THOSE OF LEADERSHIP?, No Tolerance ZERO 004 (2002). Who Are Those of Leadership? / Dress Code Evil / Muddleheads / Scaling The Fortress / The Scars & The Shame / Solution Revolution! / Armed & Scared / Nation Corrupt / Justice According To Pigs / Severed Scars / Eyes Of Liberation / Not Meant To Be/Brown Sound / Ninepin / Hate Towards People's Hate / Interloper / Fake Healer / Sewer Of The System / Exceeding Anxiety.

THE ART OF TODAY, No Tolerance ZERO 007 (2003). Is There No Hope? / No Savior / The White Disease / Pressure's On / Intro / Lustrous Pattern / Extinct Utopia / Dull—Shit! / Choice Of Contempt / Crisis / What Lies Beneath / T.A.O.T. / Doomsday Celebration / Apt For Idiocy / Shiny Miserable People / Crowd Bites Wolves / Piles / Oral Mutual Thieves / 20-11-02 / 110th Floor / Shop-Worn Veracity / Prey Of Progress / Burst Out / Azsir—Ittna / Act Of Ignorance.

RENAISSANCE

BELGIUM — *Santiago Janssens (vocals), Bert Wilmaers (guitar), Peter Vallon (guitar), Chriss Ons (guitar / keyboards), Dirk Vollon (bass).*

RENAISSANCE are a Doom-Death act founded in November 1991. Throughout the course of their career and through successive works the part has steadily drifted into a Gothic tinged Progressive Metal sound. The original formation of the band numbered vocalist Santiago Janssens, guitarist Domingo Smets, ex-CHRONIC DEATH guitarist / keyboard player Chriss Ons, bass player Dirk Vollon, keyboard player Veronique Aerts and drummer Jürgen De Wispelare. This unit recorded an opening demo dubbed 'Archway', released in 1992 but would then be wrought by line-up changes with De Wispelare, Aerts and Smets making their exit. Smets would subsequently feature in AGATHOCLES and ANCIENT RITES.

A split EP for the After Dark label shared with Black Metal band ANCIENT RITES arrived in January of 1993 swiftly followed by single through the Shiver label, splitting the 13 minute epic 'Tired Blood- Vaudeville' over two sides of vinyl..

Despite the departure of Dirk Vollon, RENAISSANCE cut the conceptual first album 'The Death Of Art', utilising the services of session musicians. For a time the band also operated under the revised title of RINASCIMENTO in an effort to avoid confusion with the noted UK Folk act. Under this title a limited edition album, 'Rinascimento Demos 1995-1998', emerged.

The RENAISSANCE triumvirate of Chriss Ons, Santiago Janssens and Dirk Vollon would reunite in 2000 but little progress was made. By 2001 Vollon had broke away to join SHADOWDANCE, subsequently ZERO GRAVITY, and bassist Kris Trappeniers had joined the fold. Latterly the band evolved into RED NUCLEUS. Trappeniers broke away from this band in 2003. Janssens guested on the ZERO GRAVITY April 2003 demo 'Synchronicity'.

Dirk Vollon joined the AHRÁYEPH project of ANCIENT RITES guitarist Raf Jansen during 2006.

Windows, After Dark (1993) (Split single with ANCIENT RITES). Windows.

Tired Blood—Vaudeville, Shiver (1993). Tired Blood / Vaudeville.

THE DEATH OF ART, Shiver SHR 006 (1994). The Death Of Art / Archway.

RENASCENT

HELSINKI, FINLAND — *Barry Halldan (vocals), Eero Tertsunen (guitar), Voitto Rintala (bass), Mikaela Akrenius (keyboards), Jani Stefanovic (drums).*

Helsinki's RENASCENT is a Christian Death Metal act rooted in the 1995 SEPULTURA covers combo CROSSEXAMINATION forged by drummer Jani Stefanovic and guitarist Eero Tertsunen. Gradually pursuing original material the group evolved into SABAOTH but would fold in 1998. Subsequently, Tertsunen founded a fresh act billed KREMATOR whilst Stefanovic teamed up with AM I BLOOD in 2000 for a brief spell. The pair reunited in a new project billed TRAIL OF TEARS, this unit also including keyboard player Mikaela Akrenius, but this act stalled when Stefanovic relocated to Sweden to join SINS OF OMISSION. Meantime, Tertsunen would pursue work with HALLOWED and CANNU GNU.

Quite novelly, Tertsunen and Akrenius, opting to form a new band, performed their inaugural gig at their own wedding in the Spring of 2002. Although the pair aimed to secure Stefanovich for their band they "waited for God's schedule". The drummer did indeed return from Sweden and, with the induction of the CRUCIFERAE and WORSHIP FACTORY credited bassist Voitto Rintala, RENASCENT was borne. First product the 'Demon's Quest' EP saw Tertsunen handling lead vocals. In 2003 Tertsunen and Akrenius united with Puerto Rican singer Miseria to forge Black Metal side project KASTIMONIA.

The band added ex-DARKENED singer Barry Halldan in August 2004 and shortly afterward drafted Pekka Taina from BLOODED and SOTAHUUTO as a session member on rhythm guitar.

During early 2005 the industrious Jani Stefanovic would also be active with both DIVINEFIRE, a project in union with NARNIA and AUDIOVISION vocalist Christian Rivel, and as sessioneer for CRIMSON MOONLIGHT. In March 2005 RENASCENT recorded its first full-length album, entitled 'Through Darkness', in Skara, Sweden. The album was issued in Japan that June through King Records.

Former RENASCENT man Barry Haldan sessioned for MISERATION, another endeavour of Jani Stefanovic, in 2006.

Demons' Quest, Renascent (2004). In The Midst Of Persecution / Circus Of Flesh / Demons' Quest / Son Of God.
THROUGH DARKNESS, King (2005). In Hell / Corrosion Of Emotions / Scenes Of A Tragedy / Through Darkness / Sustain Me / Arise / The Last Journey / Wisdom Calls / Warriors Of The Morning / Exodus / Majestic / Son Of God.

REPUDIATE

FRANCE — *Mitch Hell (vocals), Nico (guitar), David (guitar), Arnaud (bass), P.O. (drums).*

REPUDIATE was forged as a trio of vocalist Mitch Hell in alliance with guitarists Nico and David during 2001. The band brought in drummer P.O., also active as keyboard player in CERBER, in May of that year and filled the vacant bass position with Arnaud of CERBER and SENTENCE repute by August. Newly constituted REPUDIATE laid down an inaugural 9 song session entitled 'Neurasthenia'.

During 2002 the group contributed their track 'Hangman Smile' to the compilation album 'El Grinding Mafiozos' released through Nihilistic Holocaust. In October a split album, shared with fellow Frenchmen GERBE OF LIFE, was delivered through Skullfucked Promotions.

NEURASTHENIA, Independent (2002). Melody For Murderer / Ocean Of Storm / Death By Brutality / Your Fate / Asa Foetida / Repudiated / Hangman Smile / Spiritual Ways / Bloody Thorns.
DEVOTED TO BETRAYAL, (2003). Hangmans' Smile / Spiritual Ways / Bloody Thorns / Sodomination / Glory Of Repent / From The Cowshed To The Cross / Ocean Of Storm (Version II) / Manipulation / Resquiescat In Pace / Devoted To Betrayal.

REPULSION

MI, USA — *Scott Carlson (vocals / bass), Aaron Freeman (guitar), Matt Olivo (guitar), Dave Grave (drums).*

Highly influential Death-Grind Metal band cited by many of todays protagonists of the genre as a direct influence. Previously known as GENOCIDE and issuing the 1985 cassette 'Violent Death', the group's first product under their new title would be the 1986 demo tape 'Stench Of Burning Flesh'. Guitarist Aaron Freeman was previously a member of PAIN. In 1994 ex-REPULSION bassist Scott Carlson joined British Doomsters CATHEDRAL for live work.

NAPALM DEATH paid homage to REPULSION by covering 'Maggots In Your Coffin' on their 2000 'Leaders Not Followers' album. The 2002 album re-release collected together album tracks, the 'Excruciation' 7" single cuts, 'Repulsion' demo songs and a bonus disc replete with rare demo material plus a live radio broadcast from GENOCIDE.

In July of 2003, after a fifteen year absence from the Metal scene, REPULSION reformed. The line up of vocalist / bassist Scott Carlson, guitarists Aaron Freeman and Matt Olivo with Dave "Grave" Holingshead on the drums were announced as headline act the 2003 Milwaukee Metalfest. In 2004 Guitarist Aaron Freeman exited, being superseded by EXHUMED (and briefly EXODUS) man Matt Harvey. October of 2004 witnessed a European live appearance at the French 'Tattoo the Mind' festival and, in January 2005, a showing at the 'Trauma Fest' in Madrid, Spain. However, with regular drummer Dave Hollingshead unable to commit to these shows the band drafted CRETIN and EXHUMED man Col Jones.

In January 2007 it was learned Matt Olivo was working up a fresh project entitled MONSTERSHOCK in union with Kam Lee of MASSACRE, DEATH and DENIAL FIEND repute.

HORRIFIED, Necropolis NECRO 002CD (1989). Stench Of Burning Death / Acid Bath / Radiation Sickness / Splattered Cadavers / Festering Boils / Eaten Alive / Slaughter Of The Innocent / Pestilent Decay / Decomposed.
Excruciation, (1991). Excruciation / Helga (Lost Her Head).
HORRIFIED 2002, Repulse RR 6563 (2002).

REQUIEM

LOURES, PORTUGAL — *Miguel Bastos (vocals / guitar), António Pires (guitar), Leonardo Guerra (bass), Ricardo Simões (keyboards), Robert Kudlek (drums).*

A progressive, Gothic Doom outfit developed in Loures during 1996. REQUIEM underwent a radical line-up overhaul during January of 2003. Founder members vocalist / guitarist Miguel Bastos and bass player Leonardo Guerra would be joined by fresh blood in the form of LEGACY OF DARKNESS and ENATHON guitarist António Pires and the DIVINE LUST, CIBORIUM and OVER credited keyboard player Ricardo Simões. In addition, longstanding drummer Luís Nunes decamped, being superseded by Robert Kudlek, known for his work with German band CHINCHILLA.

Miguel Bastos can also be found as member of Electronica Side project NAAMAH. António Pires also cites membership of SCI-FI PRO-JECT.

Requiem Aeternam Dona Eis EP, Independent (2002). Requiem Aeternam Dona Eis / Tormentor / Path To Perfection / Abandon's Wrath / Die Welt Ist Mein.

REQUIEM

SCHÜBELBACH, SWITZERLAND — *Michi Kuster (vocals / bass), Philipp Klauser (guitar), Ralph Inderbitzin (guitar), Reto Croalo (drums).*

REQUIEM are a US styled Death Metal outfit created in Schübelbach during 1997 by the guitar pairing of Philipp Klauser and Ralph Inderbitzin with Roger Kradolfer on the drums. Klauser's prior experience included Thrash act IMMORTAL VISION, Death Metal band INTESTINES, the Gothic act SCHATTENWELT and Punks OPELGANG. Inderbitzin had been a member of Black Metal band HEXENTANZ.

With the induction of vocalist / bassist Michi Kuster, from Black Metal crew MOONFOG, the band set out on the live trail in 1998, switching drummers to Adi Fuhrer in mid 1999. The addition of Fuhrer signalled a direction change to US Death Metal, evident on the March 2001 EP 'Nameless Grave'.

REQUIEM signed to the German Revenge Productions label in 2002 for a debut album 'Formed At Birth'. However, just prior to recording Fuhrer decamped and Reto Croala, of PUNISH, stepped in as replacement. A bonus track, a remix of 'Fuck-Kill-Die', saw guest session vocals from MUTILATION's Necro-Hase.

REQUIEM signed to the US label Reality Entertainment in 2003. The band was now sporting an all new look line up comprising Kuster, guitarists Klauser and Inderbitzin, the MESSIAH credited bassist Patrick Hersche and a rejoined drummer Adi Fuhrer for recording of a new album 'Government Denies Knowledge'. These sessions included a cover of TERRORIZER's 'Dead Shall Rise'.

REQUIEM signed a five album deal with German label Massacre Records in August 2005. First product of this union would be 'Government Denies Knowledge', recorded by Dede Felix at Dedx Studios in Wil, Switzerland and mixed by Jean-François Dagenais of KATAKLYSM at JFD Studio in Laval,

Québec, Canada. September European gigs saw supports to VITAL REMAINS.

Nameless Grave EP, Fastbeast Entertainment (2001). World Downfall (Intro) / Threads In Hands / Full Of Lies / Murder U.S.A. / Nameless Grave / Ignorant Answer.
FORMED AT BIRTH, Revenge Productions (2003). River Of Blood / Child Of A New Generation / Mind Control / Formed At Birth / Alone / Sentenced To Death / Murder U.S.A. / Kill-Fuck-Die / Living In Misery / Murder U.S.A. (Blackbird remix) / Fuck-Kill-Die (Brutal Death version).
GOVERNMENT DENIES KNOWLEDGE, Massacre MAS-CD 0501 (2006). Government Denies Knowledge / Bloodcult / Nothing Seen, Nothing Heard, Nothing Done / Falling Down / No Answer (Ignorant Answer 2004) / Diary Of A Damaged Brain / Near Dark / Resurrection Of The Gods / The Mutilator / Dead Shall Rise.

REQUIEM

TN, USA — *Jason Smith (vocals), Randy Robertson (guitar), John Henderson (bass), Tino LoSicco (drums).*

Tennessee's REQUIEM, releasing a November 1993 demo 'As The Image Slowly Fades ...', was the forerunner to EPOCH OF UNLIGHT. ENRAPTURED personnel drummer Tino LoSicco and vocalist Jason Smith united with bassist Danny Murphy and guitarist Justin Jones and by 1993 the band, substituting Murphy for John Henderson, had switched titled to REQUIEM. Subsequently the band, now seeing Randy Robertson substituting for Jones, finally became EPOCH OF UNLIGHT during 1994.

Band members credits include vocalist Jason Smith and guitarist Justin Jones with ENRAPTURED, guitarist Randy Robertson with EPOCH OF UNLIGHT and CHAOS SYMPHONY whilst drummer Tino LoSicco has associations with ENRAPTURED, EPOCH OF UNLIGHT and SUBTERRANEAN MASQUERADE.

As The Image Slowly Fades ..., Requiem Ind. (1993). Tetragrammaton / Solitude Reverie / Rapture's Cease / Ascension / Posthumous (An Afterworld) / As The Image Slowly Fades ... / Outro.

RESPONSE NEGATIVE

FL, USA — *Nick Barlow (vocals), Bobby Gustafson (guitar), Mark Dykstra (guitar), Andrew Goodyer (bass), James McCourt (drums).*

RESPONSE NEGATIVE is a Florida based Death / Thrash Metal band, founded in September 2001 by Mark Dykstra, known for the inclusion of former OVERKILL, CYCLE SLUTS FROM HELL, SKREW and GRIP INC. guitarist Bobby Gustafson. Initially Dykstra was joined by singer ex-FISTED and UNIT 17 man Nick Barlow, bassist Tony Viera, Gustafson and drummer James McCourt. Subsequently, Andrew Goodyer of NIHILITY, OSIRIS RISING and IN HUMAN FORM, took command of the bass position. A self-titled, five track EP emerged in 2004.

The RESPONSE NEGATIVE project, according to statements from Bobby Gustafson citing "lack of professionalism and drive from within the band", folded in April 2005. However, within days of this press release drummer Jim McCourt responded, claiming the band was "far from over" and would persevere, minus Gustafson.

In February 2006 RESPONSE NEGATIVE replaced Bobby Gustafson with Claude Fernandez and also added bassist Ruben Trevino to the group's ranks. The new look band debuted on March 4th as support to MONSTROSITY at The Factory in Fort Lauderdale.

Response Negative, Response Negative (2004). All Out War / Silent Son / Etched In Sickness / Carnivorous Lust / Faithless.

RESURRECTED

GERMANY — *Carsten Scholz (vocals), Thomas Granzow (guitar), Stefan Bays (bass), Michael Scholz (drums).*

Black tinged Death Metal act RESURRECTED was formed by the Scholz brothers vocalist Carsten and drummer Michael in 1993 together with guitarist Thomas Mayer. This latter member would be replaced by Thomas Granzow before the close of the year. In 1994 RESURRECTED opened proceedings with the demo 'Darkside Of Reality'. Two further cassettes ensued 'Sinner Of An Unable God' and 1996's 'The Lament Of Configuration'.

A deal was struck with Underground Productions for the release of the 7" single 'Bloodline' in 1997 before Eaststar Records offered RESURRECTED an album deal. However, soon after the release of the 'Raping Whores' opus the two parties severed links as RESURRECTED signed to Death Metal specialists Perverted Taste.

Promotion for the second album Faireless To The Flesh', which included a rendition of DEICIDE's 'Sacrificial Suicide', saw European touring alongside FLESHGRIND and label mates COERCION. The band also put in a showing at the 16th annual Milwaukee Metalfest.

RESURRECTED had their debut album re-issued on the Perverted Taste label and for the American market United Guttural Records released second effort 'Faireless To The Flesh' although the latter version was minus the cover track 'Sacrificial Suicide'.

A third album, 'Butchered In Excrement' produced by Olaf Oebels, emerged in 2001. The band's appearance at the 'Fuck The Commerce III' festival that year would be captured for a live split album shared with FLESHGRIND. RESURRECTED's 2003 studio album 'Blood Spilled' hosted a cover rendition of NAPALM DEATH's 'Mass Appeal Madness'.

RESURRECTED lost the services of drummer Michael Scholz in March 2006. Sessions for a new album, 'Endless Sea Of Loss', were completed at Soundlodge Studio with Adriano Ricci of GRIND INC. and NIGHT IN GALES. In May RESURRECTED announced the addition of SKULLBREAKER drummer Hazim Fouad to the group's ranks.

Bloodline, Underground Productions (1997). Bloodline.
RAPING WHORES, Eaststar (1998). ... As Heaven Declines / Rotten And Worthless / Hook Handed Demon / Damned By Temptation / Suffer My Insanity / Blessed By The Priest / Pray The Lord ... / Impiety Breed / Nailed On Cross (Let Him Fester) / Wide Open Cunt.
FAIRELESS TO THE FLESH, Perverted Taste PT027 (2000). Intro / Two Faces, One More Fist / React With Hate / Premature Ejaculation / Unceremonious Promiscuous / Raping Whores / Christcunt / Denomination / Embellish / Virgin Immaculate / Sacrificial Suicide.
BUTCHERED IN EXCREMENT, Perverted Taste (2001). The Beginning Of Terror (Intro) / Dripping With Blood / Deadly Lessons / Wait To Suffer / Macabre Fuckfest / Infecting The Crypts / Ophidicism / Entangled In Madness / Butchered In Excrement / Conquered Suffering.
LIVE AT THE FUCK THE COMMERCE III, (2002) (Split album with FLESHGRIND). Rotten And Worthless / Wide Open Cunt / Raping Whores / Sacrificial Suicide.
BLOOD SPILLED, Perverted Taste PT 062 (2003). A Sacrificed Murder—Introduction / Prepare For The Siege / Faireless To The Flesh / The Ultimate Damnation (Reprisal) / Rest Before The Bloodstorm / Necronymphomaniac / Mass Appeal Madness / Divine Illumination / The Rapist / Blood Spilled.
ENDLESS SEA OF LOSS, Morbid (2006). Intro / Hidden By Disguise / Seducer Of Mankind / Bloodmarked / Until You Kill Yourself / Smouldering Human Compost / ... And She Loves It Anal / An Obseding End / End Of A Decade / Outro.

RESURRECTION

TAMPA, FL, USA — *Paul Degoyler (vocals), John Astl (guitar), Charlie Haines (guitar), Dave Scott (bass), Alex Marquez (drums).*

The solitary 1993 album 'Embalmed Existence' from Tampa, Florida Death Metal crew RESURRECTION, released through Germany's Nuclear Blast Records, is generally regarded as a lost classic of the genre. The record includes a souped up cover version of KISS' 'War Machine'. Former RESURRECTION drummer Kevin Astl returned to the scene in November 2003 in league with CANNIBAL CORPSE guitarist Jack Owen and female second guitarist Analia Pizzaro in a brand new "Aggro Hard Rock" band project called ADRIFT.

RESURRECTION headed into Red Room Recorders with producer/engineer Mark Prator in December 2006 to cut four new tracks for an intended EP. The band line-up involved vocalist Paul DeGolyer, guitarist John Astl, COUNCIL OF THE FALLEN bassist Scott Patrick and drummer Kevin Astl.

EMBALMED EXISTENCE, Nuclear Blast 6057 (1993). Disembodied / Rage Within / Embalmed Existence / Smell Of Blood / Torture Chamber / Eyes Of Blind / Test Of Fate / Pure Be Damned / War Machine.

RESURRECTURIS

FERMO, ITALY — *Alberto Svampa (vocals), Carlo Strappa (guitar), Janos Muri (guitar), Gianluca Mandolesi (bass), Omar Moretti (drums).*

Fermo based powerful Metal act with Death Metal tendencies RESURRECTURIS, forged in 1990 by guitarist Carlo Strappa, arrived with the 1993 demo 'No Flesh Shall Be Spared'. In 1996 vocalist Jerry di Tullio and second guitarist Janos Muri entered the fold. A further effort 'Evil Confounding Evil', which saw a US pressing as an MCD through Wild Rags Records. The band's third session, the David Lenci produced 'Corpses' led to a record deal with the Dutch Diamond label. Meantime, two demo outtakes were published on a split 7" 'Leichname Fur Immer' shared with Doom Metal band GRIEF OF GOD on the German label Quamby Hill Records label.

RESSURECTURIS utilized the female vocals of guitarist Carlo Strappa's sister Gloria on the 'Nocturnal' album, this limited to a vinyl manufacturing run of just 300 copies. The Hungarian label Backwoods Productions would also aid the cause by releasing a double cassette box entitled 'Nocturnal Corpses (Forever)' comprising the debut album, all antecedent demos, outtakes and cover material.

Drummer Omar Moretti was inducted during 1998 and the following year Ivan di Marco took over the vocal position. The new look RESURRECTURIS undertook an intensive European 'Suicidal Mission' tour commencing March of 2000 taking in Belgium, Portugal and Slovenia. Unfortunately the dates were marred by a car crash, which injured the band members. After nearly ten years, bassist Gianluca Bassi quit the band, his replacement being Gianluca Mandolesi. Further recordings ensued but in 2001 RESURRECTURIS splintered.

2003 witnessed a comeback for the band, complete with new bassist Manuel Coccia, for the album 'The Cuckoo Clocks Of Hell', directly inspired by the Victor Janos directed cult underground movie 'Last House On Dead End Street'. The 'The Cuckoo Clocks Of Hell' record had actually been recorded back in 2001, but shelved after the band broke up. Alberto Svampa became the new RESURRECTURIS singer in 2004. Later that year 'The Cuckoo Clocks Of Hell' was re-issued by the Mondongo Canibale label.

Guitarist Janos Murri joined Austrian Thrashers DEMOLITION for European touring in December 2005. The band hooked up with GOREFEST, MASTER and LUNA FIELD for 'The Glorious Dead: European Exorcism' European tour set to commence 16th February in Holland. However, in late January the headline band pulled the entire tour. The band soon got back into the fray and supported IMPALED NAZARENE's European tour in April 2006.

RESURRECTURIS entered Acme Recording Studio on December 11th to record their third album.

Evil Confronting Evil, Wild Rags WRR-094 (1996). Sui Fuochi Fatui / Mi Guardo Dentro / No Dreams Allowed / Stem The Bloodbath / Il Male Contro Il Male / I Copri Privi Di Vita.

NOCTURNAL, Diamond (1999). Nocturnal / Freeze Frame / Il Male Contro Il Male / Dark Moods / Born Defeated / No Cheating Allowed / Isole / Abisso Notturno / Flashes (Then The End) / Midnight Letter.

THE CUCKOO CLOCKS OF HELL, Independent (2003). The Last Sun / The Hate / Living Reification / In Arts Death / Helmet Logic / I Corpi Privi Di Vita.

RESUSCITATOR

CA, USA — *Summoner (vocals / bass), Sacbe (guitar), Sardonic Wrath (keyboards), Aggressive Beater (drums).*

RESUSCITATOR issued two demos during 1993, an opening eponymous tape followed by the 'Satan Falls To Earth' session. Contracted to Wild Rags Records, the 'Initiation' EP followed, with the line-up consisting of 'Beast' on vocals, Juan on guitar, Fernando Guzman on guitar, J. Luis Aguillera on bass and rounded out by Armando Fernandez on drums, after which the band structure was afflicted by a series of member changes as personnel adopted new stage names. Summoner was installed on vocals and bass guitar during 1994, drummer Fyre enrolled the following year and Sardonic Wrath was added on keyboards in 1996. Aggressive Beater would then take over the drum position as Sacbe was incorporated on guitar. Bassist Soulless decamped in 1998 and Summoner duly took over bass duties once again.

The band signed to From Beyond Productions for a re-issue of their 2003 debut album 'Cursed Visions From His Infernal Realm', this version being completely remixed and re-mastered. A brand new album, 'A Warrior's Death', followed. In early 2004 the band announced that vocalist Summoner would no longer perform live with the band, but was to remain part of the group for songwriting sessions as well as all recordings. All vocal duties in a live situation were delegated to guitarist Sacbe. The band wrapped up recording of a new album, provisionally titled 'A Warrior's Death', in March of 2004. The band line up at this juncture stood at Sacbe on vocals and guitar, second guitarist Obscurer, bassist Altsoba and drummer Zonck. RESUSCITATOR united with THE CHASM and THROCULT for September tour dates.

Initiation EP, Wild Rags WWR 048 (1993). Father Of Obscurity / Inciation / Black Funeral / Servants Of The Darkest Throne / Grant Us The Passage / Legions From The Past.

CURSED VISIONS FROM HIS INFERNAL REALM, (2001). Into The Abyss / Inherit The Wisdom Of Darkness / Battles In Blood / Madicion / Cursed Visions From His Infernal Realm / Hell Storms / End Of My Mortal Life.

A WARRIOR'S DEATH, Displeased FBP033 (2004). My Black Writings (Intro) / In The Night's Silence / Blessings Of Satan / Father Of Obscurity / Messengers Of The Immortal Throne / Legions From The Past / Initiation / Pazzuzu / Blackened Sky.

RETALIATION

SWEDEN — *Henke Forrs (vocals / bass), Andreas Carlsson (vocals / guitar), Jonas Albrektsson (guitar), Jocke Pettersson (drums).*

Stark, uncompromising Death-Grind Metal band RETALIATION came together in 1993. Founded by former NEFARIOUS man Henke Forrs ("Dedicated rape and string terrors") and guitarist Andreas Carlsson ("Sonic Torture and pain") RETALIATION at first employed a drum machine for their opening 1993 demo 'Acrid Genital Spew'. By the following year RETALIATION had pulled in second guitarist Jonas Albrektsson ("666 string holocaust and genocide") and drummer Jocke Pettersson (" Assault and battery discharges") for the sophomore cassette session 'Devestating Doctrine Dismemberment'. Pettersson's credentials included THY PRIMORDIAL, DAWN, NIDEN DIVISION 187 and MAZE OF TORMENT and UNMOORED.

RETALIATION's debut commercial release came courtesy of the German Death Metal aficionados Regurgitated Semen

Records and a split 7" single with GUT entitled 'The Misanthrope'. It was during 1994 that RETALIATION performed their first, and to date only, gig on a billing with THY PRIMORDIAL and DAWN.

RETALIATION then featured on the now renowned 3" 4 way split CD 'Grindwork' ranking alongside fellow Swedes NASUM and Japanese acts VIVISECTION and C.S.S.O. Italian label Headfucker then picked up the band for a split 7" single 'Pray For War' in allegiance with American Deathsters EXHUMED. In keeping with the bands no holds barred style the single sleeve artwork featured a photograph of a firing squad victim. In 1999 Pettersson joined infamous Grind outfit REGURGITATE. The same label would issue RETALIATION's debut album 'The Execution'.

In 2000 RETALIATION shared a further split 7" single, this time with Australian band THE KILL for the American Mortville label. The single included a cover version SKITSYSTEM's 'Jag Värar'.

The Misanthrope, Regurgitated Semen (1994) (Split single with GUT). Intro / Nailgun Rectal Entry / The Undertaker / Lowlife / Disfigured Stillborn Intercourse / The Misanthrope / Dethrone The Dictator / Corrupted / Outro.
Grindwork EP, Grindwork Productions (1995) (4 way single with C.S.S.O., VIVISECTION and NASUM).
Pray For War EP, Headfucker (1996) (Split single with EXHUMED). Retribution / Like Cancer On Society / Strife / Born Of Chaos / Distrust / Pray For War / Fierce / Path Of The Derelict / The Anti-Filanthrope / 9mm / Killing The World.
THE EXECUTION, Headfucker (1999). Genocide Angels / All In Your Head / Suicidal Disease / Anorectic Epileptic / No One Knows My Grave / Sick Of Complacence / Black Malice / Inferior / Given A Reason / Never / Crushing Defeat / War! War! War! / Like Weeds / Another Dead Hero / Ignorance / Last Stop / The Rest Of Me / Return To Zero / The Harsh Bitter Truth / Time To Pray / Unjustifiable Existence / Sans Mercy—Outro.
Suicidal Disease EP, Mortville (2000) (Split single with THE KILL). Blindside / Slaves Of Faith / Jag Värar / Black Malice (Holocaust remix).

RHESTUS

IBIRAMA, SC, BRAZIL — *Alex (vocals / guitar), Charles Da Silva (guitar), Valda (bass), Jailson (drums).*

RHESTUS, hailing from Rio do Sul in Santa Catarina and founded in March of 1993, released the demos 'Had A World' in 1996 and 'Heroes Of Doomsday' during 1999. The band would self finance the November 2003 album 'Embryo Of The Endless Sands'.

The opening RHESTUS formation had comprised erstwhile members of Punk band ANONIMATO and Metal group DELEATOR, singer Avanei, the guitar pairing of Juarez and Rogério, the latter a member of FLESH GRINDER, bass player Cláudio and drummer Jailson. Following the 'Had A World' demo ESCORIA bassist Valda enrolled. Further changes occurred in 1998 as Juarez decamped and Alex 'Fantasma' took over the vocal / guitar role and Emerson became second guitarist for recording of 'Heroes Of The Doomsday'.

Célio Junior replaced Emerson in 2000. The following year saw founder member Jailson exiting. He would be superseded by Marcão of RYTHUAL but Jailson then duly made a return to record the Michael Schindler produced album 'Embryo Of The Endless Sands' in March of 2002. The band added ex-TRANSYLVANIA guitarist Charles Da Silva in June of 2004.

EMBRYO OF THE RESTLESS SANDS, Rhestus (2003). Inside A Torn Apart / Bullet In Point / Insane War / Die Like A Dog / Tsavo: The Place Of Slaughter / Njord Hymn / Big Anesthesia / Cancer / Sacrificed By Mistake / Doomsday / Eternal Sorrow.

RIBSPREADER

SWEDEN — *Rogga Johansson (vocals / guitar), Patrik Halvarsson (bass), Mattias Fiebig (drums).*

RIBSPREADER, assembled during 2004 and debuting with the April 'Bolted To The Cross' album for New Aeon Media, consists of current and former PAGANIZER members, Rogga Johansson and erstwhile PAGANIZER man Andreas Carlsson on guitar, along with the esteemed DAN SWANÖ on drums and lead guitars. Swanö is an influential figure in the extreme Scandinavian Metal scene, citing involvement in acts as diverse as UNICORN, PAN-THY-MONIUM, GODSEND, WOUNDED KNEE and NIGHTINGALE among others. Johansson, also a veteran of DEAD SUN, BLODSRIT, CARVE and DERANGED, reinforced the connection with Swanö by featuring as guest vocalist on the EDGE OF SANITY album 'Crimson II'.

RIBSPREADER cut a 2004 album at Soundlab Studios in Örebro, entitled 'Congregating the Sick' for Holland's Karmageddon Media, in August. The group added THIS HAVEN drummer Johan Berglund for these sessions. In early 2005 RIBSPREADER underwent a drastic line-up overhaul, losing the services of Andreas Carlsson, Dan Swanö and Johan Berglund. The revised trio would comprise Rogga Johansson on vocals and guitar, bassist Patrik Halvarsson and drummer Mattias Fiebig, all ex-PAGANIZER members. Fiebig holds scene credits with PORTAL, DARK RITES and BLODSRIT.

2005 saw Rogga Johansson's involvement in a high profile side-project, the Västervik Progressive Death Metal band DEAD END WORLD. Bowing in with a demo billed 'The Isolation', Johansson would be joined by Jonas Granvik of WITHOUT GRIEF on "Death vocals" and TAD MOROSE veteran Kristian 'Krille' Andrén on "Melodic" vocals, guitarist Simon Johansson of MEMORY GARDEN and FIREGOD and Patrik Johansson, holding YNGWIE MALMSTEEN, STORMWIND and WITHOUT GRIEF credits, on drums.

RIBSPREADER signed to Malaysian label Summers End Records for a 2006 album, 'Church Of The Zombie (Re-Excavated Death)', announcing this outing would be restricted to a limited edition of 600 copies. However, this release was curtailed due to the label fearing confiscation by government authorities. A further new album, billed 'Serenity In Obscenity', would be signed to Dutch label VIC Records and a split single with MACHETAZO would also be projected.

BOLTED TO THE CROSS, New Aeon Media (2004). Dead Forever / Beneath The Cenotaph / Heavenless / The Unblessed / As You Bleed / Hollow Beliefs / Morbidity Awoken / Sole Sufferer.
CONGREGATING THE SICK, Karmageddon Media (2005). Dead To The World / Maggots (Fucking Maggots) / Morbid Reflections / Autopsy Obsessed / Bleeding You Dry / Worms Inside Your Coffin / The Crawling / Breeding Sickness / Not Dead But Buried.

RISE

LOS ANGELES, CA, USA — *Istvan Lendvay (vocals / guitar), Kosuke Hashida (guitar), Johnson Wang (bass / keyboards), Jaime Vivar (drums).*

A Satanically charged Death Metal outfit formed in 1990 by the illustrious EVIL DEAD pairing of guitarist Albert Gonzales and drummer Rob Alaniz. Just prior to forging RISE Gonzalez had stepped off a nationwide tour as live guitarist for DEATH. In August of 1993 RISE added Rik Hansen of INSIDIOUS on second guitar and sometime later Istvan Lendvay, of Hungarian act EQUIMANITHORN, on vocals. Initial 1993 demo recordings, entitled 'Life Into Ever Black', were duly pressed up onto CD EP format by Wild Rags Records during 1995. RISE cut their debut album 'Shadow Of Ruins' in September of 1995 but this did not see release until May of 1996.

NOCTUARY's Joey Van Fossen filled in for live shows after Hansen departed. Alaniz quit to join NOCTUARY. Gonzales too sessioned on NOCTUARY's 2000 album "When Fires Breed Blood'. A latter day RISE guitarist would be the INHUMAN VISIONS and ABYSMAL DAWN credited Charles Elliott.

During 2004 Istvan Lendvay enrolled into the ranks of premier Polish Black Metal band BEHEMOTH. Subsequently, RISE added THE CAUTERIZED guitarist Kosuke Hashida.

Life Into Ever Black EP, Wild Rags WRR064 (1995). Life Into Ever Black / Deathrow / Storm Of Sorrow / Captured In A Dream.

SHADOW OF RUINS, Nigma (1996). Keresztales / Revenge Flowing Through / Sinning (Koszos Krisztus) / Deathrow / Thy Domain / The Vicious Icon / Abandoned / Dismembered Destiny / Sea Of Blood / Captured In A Dream / Shadow Of Ruins.

SLAVES OF ILLUSION, Nephilim (2000). Quest For Freedom / Ruined Soul / Slaves Of Illusion / Scars Remain / Life Into Ever Black / Weakness Spread By Fear / Void Of Despair / Messiah / Awaiting The Holocaust / Bitter End.

DIVINE AETERNUM, Nephilim (2000). Quest For Freedom / Ruined Soul / Slaves Of Illusion / Scars Remain / Life Into Ever Black / Weakness Spread By Fear / Void Of Despair / Messiah / Awaiting The Holocaust / The Bitter End.

RITUAL CARNAGE

JAPAN — *Damian Montgomery (vocals / bass), Masami Yamada (guitar), Wataru Yamada (guitar), Naoya Hamaii (drums).*

Tokyo Speed Death Metal crew RITUAL CARNAGE, founded in 1994 and fronted by Florida native 'Nasty' Damian Montgomery. RITUAL CARNAGE has been wrought by internal dissention with an ever flowing stream of ex-members but has steadfastly managed to retain loyal support. Within the genre RITUAL CARNAGE are recognised as one of the elite of the scene.

Montgomery was previously bass player with PAGAN FAITH in Florida before he was transferred to Tokyo on a tour of duty with the U.S. Air Force. In Japan Montgomery joined Hardcore outfit S.I.C. This tenure lasted until 1988 with Montgomery returning to America.

In 1993 Montgomery, training to be a tattooist, relocated back to Japan and the following year teamed up with the band SCRAP TAMBOURINE. This led in turn to his formation of RITUAL CARNAGE where initially he was joined by SECTION 8 drummer Alex Amedy and bassist Bill Jokela. The line up soon morphed with BLOODSHOWER members guitarist Ken and drummer Shinjiro Sawada complementing Montgomery on a 1996 demo session. These two recruits would decamp soon after in order to concentrate on BLOODSHOWER.

Undeterred Montgomery reassembled RITUAL CARNAGE with Amedy making a return to the drum stool and bassist Hideo Ideno. This version of the band undertook one gig during 1997. Former CRACKED BRAIN guitarist Eddie joined the fold in August for two support gigs to MORTICIAN in Tokyo.

The band recorded their 'The Highest Law' album at Morrisound Studios in Florida. The album sees guest appearances from MORBID ANGEL / RIPPING CORPSE guitarist Erik Rutan and CANNIBAL CORPSE's 'Corpsgrinder' Fisher. These recordings secured a deal for a European release with the French concern Osmose Productions.

RITUAL CARNAGE yet again underwent a transformation with ex CRACKED BRAIN drummer Naoya Hamaii supplanting Amedy and Shige Kamazawa taking over guitar as Montgomery adopted the role of lead vocalist. This would be short-lived though as in June of 1998 Idemo broke ranks and Montgomery added bass guitar to his duties. In this incarnation RITUAL CARNAGE undertook European touring with Osmose label mates IMPALED NAZARENE and DRILLER KILLER. In March of the following year the band would also accompany IMPALED NAZARENE on their Japanese dates. The live activity to promote 'The Highest Law' did not end there though as RITUAL CARNAGE journeyed back to Europe for further gigs with BENEDICTION and IMMORTAL as well as guesting for Swedish Black Metal premier league act MARDUK on their tour of Japan in June.

The solidity displayed by the band came to an end with the close of gigging as Kamazawa departed. In his stead the band enrolled the DISGUST and GRIM FORCE credited guitarist Katsuyuki Nakabayashi for recording of a sophomore album 'Every Nerve Alive'. The album reaped controversy in Malaysia where it's no holds barred lyric sheet was deemed offensive and removed before distribution. Promotion included dates in the Eastern European countries in alliance with Czechs KRABATHOR before Nakabayashi too took leave.

In December of 1999 the TYRANT veteran Hidenori Tanaki filled the six string vacancy. RITUAL CARNAGE would cut tracks for tribute albums on Dwell Records namely VENOM's 'Welcome To Hell' and KREATOR's 'Impossible To Cure'. Predictably RITUAL CARNAGE was assailed once again by line up fluctuations as Tanaki split away on acrimonious terms. The band responded by augmenting the band with two new guitarists, the Yamada brothers Masami and Wataru, both of KING'S EVIL. The renewed band guested for VADER's September Japanese tour and later for DISMEMBER.

The band laid down further songs for tribute albums with two MOTÖRHEAD tracks 'One Track Mind' and 'Mean Machine' for a homage by German label Remedy. Montgomery would also contribute vocal parts to SIGH's 'Scenario IV- Dead Dreams' album.

Eddie Van Koide would then become the occupier of the RITUAL CARNAGE lead guitarist slot. 2001 gigs had the band doing the rounds of Japan with GOD DETHRONED and KRABATHOR. A 2002 album, announced as 'The Birth Of Tragedy', would include a cover version of DEATH's 'Infernal Death'. Digipack and vinyl variants, both issued in restricted numbers, was to have added two exclusive cuts 'Evil Will Avenge' and Dialogue Of Bullets'. However, due to a manufacturing slip up these two songs were excluded, the band having to post the bonus cuts as MP3s on the internet as a consolation. Yet again the band line up had fluxed with Wataru Yamada coming in on second guitar and Naoya Hamaii returning on the drums.

THE HIGHEST LAW, Osmose Productions OPCD 073 (1998). Servant Of The Black / The Unjust (Must Die) / Succumb To The Beast / The Highest Law / Master / Domain Of Death / Chaos And Mayhem / Damnator / Metal Forces / Attack / Onslaught- Death Metal.

EVERY NERVE ALIVE, Osmose Productions OPCD 089 (2000). Awaiting The Kill / 8th Great Hell / Death, Judgement, Fate / Burning Red, Burn 'Til Death / End Of An Ace / World Wide War / Scars Of Battle / Every Nerve Alive / The Wrath / Escape From The Light / Far East Aggressors / Hit The Lights / F.O.A.D. / No Compromise / End's Demise.

THE BIRTH OF TRAGEDY, Osmose Productions OP132CD (2002). The Sixth Sense / The Birth Of Tragedy / Burning Eyes Of Rage / Paradox Of Democracy / Fall Of The Empire / Shroud Of Secrecy / Sanity's Thin Line / Grave New World / Dawn To Decadence / Psycho-Sadistic Psychosis / Infernal Death.

I, INFIDEL, Osmose Productions OPCD 170 (2005). Imprisoned Secret / The Perfect Strain / I, Infidel / Thirst For Blood / These Chains / Do Not Resuscitate / Axiom / Straight To The Nether Regions / Room 101 / Twilight Of The All Too Human / Terror Ends Here / I Am War.

ROOT

BRNO, CZECH REPUBLIC — *Jiri Valter (vocals / bass), Dan Janacek (guitar), Rene Kostelnak (drums).*

Premier blasphemous Death Metal act ROOT, then just a founding duo of vocalist Big Boss (a.k.a. Jiri Valter) and guitarist Blackie, debuted with the 1987 demo cassette 'Reap Of Hell'. The band, hailing from Brno, debuted live in September 1988 and subsequently issued two further demos 'War Of Rats' and 'Messengers From Darkness', all three of these sessions seeing Big Boss manning the drums. Vocalist Dr. Fé (a.k.a. Zelezo) was sacked in 1989, founding Black Metal band AMON. Signing to Zera Records the group's first album, 'Zjeveni', was delivered in 1991. ROOT gained further exposure by including their version of the Czech folk song 'Hrbitov' to the compilation album 'Death Metal Session'.

ROOT's sophomore outing, entitled 'Hell Symphony' and their first English language attempt, spread word into Europe as the British Cacophonous label picked the album up for distribution. Switching to Monitor Records the 'The Temple In The Underworld' album, promoted with a video to the song 'Aposiopesis', arrived in 1993. Internal disputes would put the band on hiatus until a 1996 comeback with the conceptual 'Kargeras'.

Redblack Records released ROOT's fifth album 'The Book' in 1999, also re-releasing the debut 'Zjeveni' with the additional track 'Hrbitov'. Both 'Hell Symphony' and 'Kargeras' were given the re-issue treatment to, adding extra live tracks to each. ROOT showed no signs of slowing down in 2001 in spite of the fact that Big Boss celebrated his 50th birthday. In late 2002 ROOT' Big Black alongside guitarist Ashok, bassist Igor and ONSET keyboard player Tudy formulated the EQUIRHODONT side project for an album release through Shindy Productions. Meantime Blackie busied himself with his other band projects CALES and ENTRAILS.

A collection of ROOT's formative demos surfaced on CD in early 2003 billed as 'Dema'. ROOT, still maintaining an active gig schedule throughout the year with gigs across Germany and Serbia, projected an album for Autumn of 2003 provisionally billed as 'Madness Of The Graves'. The band line up at this juncture comprised vocalist Big Boss, guitarists Blackie and Ashok, bass player Igor and drummer Evil.

Monster Nation issued the 'Capturing Sweden—Live in Falkenberg' concert recordings in November 2005. Captured at the 2001 '2 Heavy 4 You' festival', only 500 copies were manufactured.

In early 2006 Big Boss' services were requested as guest vocalist on the Norwegian Viking Metal band HELHEIM's album 'The Journeys And Experiences Of Death'. A ROOT EP issued in May that year, 'Casilda' on Shindy Productions included cover versions of THE BEATLES 'Strawberry Fields Forever' and JIMI HENDRIX's 'Little Wing'.

The band was added to the 2007 European tour commencing March 31st at Planet Music in Vienna, Austria featuring MOONSPELL, NAPALM DEATH, BEHEMOTH and DEW-SCENTED.

Reap Of Hell, Root (1988) (Demo). Intro: Root / Litanie K Satanovi / 7 Jezdcù / Píseò Pro Rootana / Høbitov / Outro: Zvony.
War Of Rats, Root (1988) (Demo). ... A Zemì Se Otevøela / Král Dogra / Volání O Pomoc / Dogrova øíše.
Messengers From Darkness, Root (1989) (Demo). Pøíchod Poslù / Rootanùv Pøíchod / Poslové Z Temnot / Útìk A Trest / 666 / Stín A Prokletí / Otvírání Hrobù / Prázdný Hrob / Zrození Rootanova Syna.
ZJEVENI, Zetvas (1990). Intro / Zjeveni / Aralyon / Vyslech / Upaleni / Pisen Pro Satana / 666 / 7 Cernych Jezdcu / Demon / Znameni / Cesta Zkazy.
HELL SYMPHONY, Cacophonus NIHIL 11 (1992). Beelzebub / Belial / Lucifer / Abaddon / Asmodeus / Satan / Leviathan / Astaroth / Loki / The Prayers (T. Raudelaire) / The Oath / Satan's March.
THE TEMPLE IN THE UNDERWORLD, Monitor 0100864331 (1994). Intro / Casilda's Song / The Temple In The Underworld / Aposiopesis / The Solitude / Voices From ... / The Wall / The Old Ones / Message / My Name ....
KÄRGERÄS, Black Hole (1996). Lykorian / Kargeras Prologue / Kargeras / Prophet's Song / Rulbrah / Rodaxx / Old Man / Old Woman / Equirhodont—Grandiose Magus / Dygon—Monstrosity / Trygan—Sexton / Dum Vivimus, Vivamus.
THE BOOK, Redblack MRB 004 (1999). The Book / The Mystical Words Of The Wise / The Curse—Durron / Why? / Corabeu—Part I / Corabeu—Part II / The Birth / Lykorian / The Message Of The Time / Remember Me! / Darkoutro—... Toccata—Prestissimo Molto.
BLACK SEAL, Redblack MRB 014 (2002). The Festival Of Destruction / The Incantation Of Thessalonian Women / Nativity / His Eyes Were Dark / Black Seal / The Faith / Salamandra / Necromancy / Theriak / The Mirror Of Soul / Liber Prohibitus / ... Before I Leave!
DEMA, Lava Productions (2003). Intro (Beethoven Allegro) / Litanie K Satanovi / Sedm Jezdcù / Píseò Pro Satana / Høbitov / 7 Synù Satana / ... A Zemì Se Otevøela / Král Dogra / Volání O Pomoc / Dogrova Øíše / Intro (Pøíchod Poslù) / Rootanùv Pochod / Poslové Z Temnot / Útìk A Trest / 666 / Stín Prokletí / Otvírání Hrobu / Prázdný Hrob / Zrození Rootanova Syna / Outro / Procitnutí / Soud / Zjeveni / Aralyon / Výslech / Upalení / Cesta Zkázy / Procitnutí 2 / ... A Zemì Se Otevøela (Live) / Píseò Pro Rootana (Live) / 7 Èerných Jezdcù (Live) / Volání O Pomoc (Live) / Høbitov (Live).
MADNESS OF THE GRAVES, Redblack (2003). Omen / Then (The Tale About Destiny) / Madness Of The Graves (Calling) / Talking Bones (The Story Of Legacy) / Endowment (Refused Message) / Tree (Power Of Calling) / Autumn (Legend About Life) / In the Heart Of Darkness (Ballad Of Ancient Realms) / The Last Gate (The Story Of Demons) / Afterwards (The Tale At The End).
CAPTURING SWEDEN—LIVE IN FALKENBURG, Monster Nation (2005) (double vinyl album. Limited edition 500 copies). The Wall / The Temple In The Underworld / Lucifer / Leviathan / The Old Ones / Message / Casilda's Song / Aposiopesis / Zjeveni / The Curse—Durron / Remember Me / Trygän-Sexton / 666 / Pisen Pro Satana / Hrbitov.
Casilda, Shindy Productions (2006). Little Wing / Strawberry Fields Forever / Casilda's Song (Hyperion version) / Casilda's Song (Illegal Orchestra version) / Human / Casilda's Song (Live video).

ROSE FUNERAL

CINCINNATI, OH, USA — *Destin Armstrong (vocals), Drey Armstrong (guitar), Tony Younce (guitar), Craig Binaut (bass), Ryan Gardner (drums).*

Cincinnati, Ohio Death Metal band ROSE FUNERAL was founded during the autumn of 2005 by vocalist Ray Hughes, bassist Destin Armstrong, guitarists Tony Younce and Drey Armstrong plus drummer Ryan Gardner. ROSE FUNERAL issued the demo 'Buried Beneath The Blood' in March 2006. After these sessions, Hughes quit and Destin Armstrong took over lead vocal duties whilst Craig Binaut was added on bass. That August the EP 'Crucify.Kill.Rot' followed, this outing scoring a deal with UK label Siege of Amida Records.

June 2007 dates had the band packaged with MONSTER OF FLORENCE leading into an extensive run alongside 1931. August shows flanked HORIZONTAL ORANGE and FATAL AFIRE.

CRUCIFY.KILL.ROT, Siege Of Amida (2007).

ROSICRUCIAN

SWEDEN — *Lars Linden (guitar / vocals), Magnus Söderman (Guitar), Johan Wiegal (keyboards), Fredrik Jacobsnon (bass), Patrik Marchente (drums).*

Previously known as ATROCITY with vocalist Glyn Grimwade. Adopted the title ROSICRUCIAN in 1989 when the first demo 'Initiation Into Nothingness' was recorded. The band added second guitarist Lars Linden after the release of their second demo in 1990. Grimwade opted to leave after the 'Silence' album and was duly replaced by ex-MEZZROW frontman Ulf Petersson. Finding themselves without a drummer the drums on the second album 'No Cause For Celebration' were handled by Johnny Bergman of MR. HANGPIKE. ROSICRUCIAN finally located a permanent drummer in Andreas Wallström in late 1994.

Frontman Lars Linden, guitarist Magnus Söderman and bass player Fredrik Jacobsen later formed SLAPDASH releasing the 'Bound' album in 1996. The following year Söderman, also active with LOST SOULS, involved himself in the ZEALION project band and by 1998 was a member of Metal covers band POWERAGE. 2001 found Lars Lindén a member of Death Thrashers CARNAL FORGE. Early 2004 found Magnus Söderman guesting on the VICIOUS album 'Vile, Vicious & Victorious'.

SILENCE, Black Mark BMCD 25 (1993). Column Of Grey / Way Of All Flesh / Within The Silence / Esoteric Traditions / Autocratic Faith / Nothing But Something Remains / Aren't You Bored Enough / Back In The Habit / Defy The Opposition / Do You Know Who You're Crucifying.
NO CAUSE FOR CELEBRATION, Black Mark BMCD 57 (1994). Much About Nothing / Classic Guitar / Parts Of Me / No Cause For Celebration / Stench Of Life / Stagnation Of Emotions / Words Without Meaning / The Opening Of Glory End / Naked Face Down / A Moment Of War / Jazz Blues.

ROTTEN SOUND

FINLAND — *Keijo Bagge (vocals), Mike Aalto (guitar), Juha Ylikoski (guitar), Pekka Ranta (bass), Kai Hahto (drums).*

Grind merchants debuted with a string of 7" singles commencing with 1994's suitably titled 'Sick Bastard' for Genet Records. Both vocalist Keijo Bagge and drummer Kai Hahto are erstwhile VOMITURITION members. The drummer, also known as 'Generis', cites credits with ENOCHIAN CRESCENT, AGRESSOR, WINTERSUN and WINGS. Guitarist 'Gaunt' also operates with Black Metal bands AND OCEANS and BLACK DAWN. The 'Splitted Alive' EP would be shared with fellow Finns CONTROL MECHANISM. Their burgeoning reputation eventually resulted in a deal with the Repulse label for 1998's Ahti Kortelainen produced 'Under Pressure' album. Following the 1999 release 'Drain', which debuted second guitarist Juha Ylikoski, the band signed to the American Necropolis label subsidiary Deathvomit for the mini-album 'Still Psycho', which included a cover version of CARCASS's 'Reek Of Putrefaction'. Touring in Europe to promote 'Still Psycho' found ROTTEN SOUND packaged with label mates IN AETURNUM as well as HATEPLOW and MALEVOLENT CREATION.

The band's 2002 album 'Murderworks' would stir controversy in Europe where the sleeve art was deemed too "offensive" for release although in America the album was released with the original artwork. Commencing with an appearance at the 'Obscene Extreme' festival ROTTEN SOUND embarked upon headline European tour dates, suitably billed as 'Murdering Europe', supported by FLESHLESS and LYKATHEA AFLAME.

The band toured Europe in June of 2003 alongside Florida's HATEPLOW and Germany's DEBAUCHERY. Ex-guitarist Juha Ylikoski meantime teamed up with THROES OF DAWN.

In May of 2004 the band headed up the US 'Grind The East Coast' tour with running mates PHOBIA, STRONG INTENTION and for later shows CIRCLE OF DEAD CHILDREN. The band's next album 'Exit' was recorded at Soundlab studio in Örebro, Sweden with engineer Mieszko Talarczyk. Impressively, 'Exit' landed on the national Finnish album charts at number 22. ROTTEN SOUND teamed up with DISFEAR for Scandinavian dates in March of 2005. European dates scheduled for May witnessed an alliance with VOMITORY, EXHUMED and PROSTITUTE DISFIGUREMENT. The band engaged in an extensive round of Scandinavian and European dates allied with SAYYADINA, CAUSE FOR EFFECT and TOTAL DEVASTATION in early 2006. However, drummer Kai Hahto opted out in order to concentrate more on his family and his other outfit WINTERSUN. He would be replaced by Sami Latva of DEATHBOUND. In June ROTTEN SOUND's 'Consumed To Contaminate' EP, recorded at Sound Supreme Studios by Janne Saksa, hit number 2 on the Finnish charts.

ROTTEN SOUND teamed up with REGURGITATE for a Finnish mini-tour in February 2007.

Sick Bastard EP, Genet GEN 10 (1995). Köyhyys / Koiranyrjö / Verta Ja Suolenpätkiä / Lottovoitto / Painajainen / Splatteria Ja Horroria / E-Pillerin Kevät / Jatkuva Hulluus / Lekalla Päähän / Tautinen Äpärä.
Psychotic Veterinarian, SOA Records 35 (1995). Chainsaw Is God / I Disappear Into Darkness / Nymphomaniac / Police Raped A Pensioner / Anal Sadist / Brains Putrefy / Mom / Fanatic Motherfucker / Cry / Observers / Poverty.
Loosin' Face, Anomie PUT-015 (1996) (Picture disc). Social Rinse / Loosin' Face / Black Rain Of Bureaucrazy / Subordinated / Saviour—Pressurewave / Nerves / I, A Product / The Guard Of The Paradise / Renewer / Corporate Fuck / Your Fault / Acoustics Of The Silence / Behind Our Backs / Veenom / Burtsum / A Religion?
Splitted Alive, I.D.S. IODS-001 (1997) (Split EP with CONTROL MECHANISM). Vicious Circle / Apart.
UNDER PRESSURE, Repulse RPS026CD (1998). Dominion / Controlled Mind / Stages / Under Pressure / I, A Product / Insomnia / Natural / Skinsaw / Corporate Fuck / Vicious Circle / Social Rinse / Debility / Principles Of Abuse / Saviour-Pressurewave / Jesus Christ Fanclub / Loosin' Face / Renewer / Subordinated / Shut Down / Affected / Nerves / Guard Of The Paradise.
DRAIN, Repulse RPS040CD (1999). Calm / Dirty Currency / Bastard Behaviour / Alone At Last / Drain / Braindead / Narrow Mind / Dark Highway / Inversion / Vanity / Super Satan / Cartender / Coldvenience / Abusement Park / Loser.
STILL PSYCHO, Necropolis NR062 MCD (2000). Perfection / Ignorance / StrongMan / DisInterest / Lack Of Awareness / Reek Of Putrefaction.
8 Hours Of Lobotomy, MCR Company MCR-160 (2001) (Split 7" with UNHOLY GRAVE). 8 Hours Of Lobotomy / Dead Shall Rise / Nanking Atrocity.
MURDERWORKS, Deathvomit (2002). Targets / Void / Revenge / Lies / Doom / IQ / Insects / Seeds / Suffer / Obey / Edge / Lobotomy / Insane / Agony.
Seeds Of Hate, Cudgel Agency CUD 016 (2002) (Split MCD with MASTIC SCUM). Seeds / Insine / StrongMan / DisInterest.
EXIT, Spinefarm SPI 214CD (2005). Exit / Burden / Sell Your Soul / V.S.A. / Follow / Maggots / Slave / Mass Suicide / Soil / Fail And Fall / Greed / Slay / Western Cancer / Nation / Havoc / Traitor / XXI / The Weak. Chart position: 22 FINLAND.
Consumed To Contaminate, Spinefarm (2006). Decay / Loss / Crime / GDP / CTC / Flesh / Fear / Time. Chart position: 2 FINLAND.
CONSUME TO CONTAMINATE, Spinefarm (2006).

ROYAL ANGUISH

OCALA, FL, USA — *Mark Knowles (vocals / guitar), Katy Decker (vocals), Marius Kozlowski (guitar), Sean Tibbetts (bass), Kaitee Elliott (keyboards), Anthony Smith (drums).*

ROYAL ANGUISH is an Ocala, Florida based Christian Death Metal act forged by Matt Knowles during 1991. An early line-up saw Knowles ranked alongside guitarist Bryan Murray, bass player Paul Mattox and drummer Damion Smith. In 1993 the band published the EP 'Shocking The Priest', recorded at Impressions Audio in Fort Lauderdale, ROYAL ANGUISH standing at Knowles, Murray, bassist Alex Frasier and drummer Tommy Taylor. An album, 'The Chronicles Of Autumn Sorrow', was crafted during the Winter of 1995 but would remain shelved. Yet again the band line up had altered dramatically with Knowles and Frasier now allied with lead guitarist Dee Mulligan, female singer Terra Cay, keyboard player Drew Damon Grounds and drummer Damion Smith. Former GATE 22 drummer Anthony Smith enrolled in 1999.

In 2002 ROYAL ANGUISH, in a partnership with MISTRAL, contributed the track 'Mary Did You Know' to the seasonal compilation album 'A Brutal Christmas'. Band membership at this juncture found Knowles joined by vocalist / guitarist Henrik Ryosa, bassist Anthony Smith and female vocalist Melody Dove. That same year re-mastered tracks from the 'Shocking The Priest' sessions were included on a three way split album shared with TORTURED CONSCIENCE and SOUL OF THE SAVIOR.

ROYAL ANGUISH published the 'Mysterion' album in 2003, the group now being credited as a duo of Knowles and Smith. Sessioning in the studio would be singers Katy Decker, Melody Dove and Courtney Chadwick, guitarists Henrik Ryosa, Chad Bailey, Howard Card and Corey Steger along with violinist Devon Hawk.

2004 finally saw the issue on album of 'The Chronicles Of Autumn Sorrow' recordings and yet further line-up changes as Don Wisby exited in order to prioritise his other act EVERSINCEVE and bassist Andy Funk was replaced by Greg Andrews. Erik Rutan of HATE ETERNAL and MORBID ANGEL repute would act as producer for a December 2004 EP entitled 'Tales of Sullen Eyes', crafted at Mana Studios in Tampa. Shortly after recording the band added new bassist Sean Tibbetts. ROYAL ANGUISH signed to Dutch label Fear Dark in June 2005.

ROYAL ANGUISH drummer J.R. Daniels joined San Diego's CATTLE DECAPITATION in April 2006. That same year both Katy Decker and Marius Kozlowski exited to prioritise MENA BRINNO.

ROYAL ANGUISH announced the addition of guitarist Asgrim, of YETI, COUNCIL OF THE FALLEN and CHALICE, and drummer Tom Klinesmith, previously with ENIGMATIC PARANOIA, NIGHTSBANE and MORBID SACRIFICE, to the group's ranks in January 2007.

Shocking The Priest, A.R.T. records (1993). Deny / Die Inside / Shocking The Priest / Rest In Pieces.

MYSTERION, (2003). One Last Time / Atmosphere / Come Run With Me / Homeland / My Own Despair / Haunted Whispers / I Close My Eyes / Autumn Sorrow / Green Pastures Await / I Close My Eyes (Moonlight version).

THE CHRONICLES OF AUTUMN SORROW, Bombworks (2004). Commencement / Ceremonial Suicide / Unfulfilled / Celestial Embrace / Land Of The Free / Silence / Feel The Blood / Element Of Fear / The Chronicles Of Autumn Sorrow / Green Pastures Await / Tortured Visions / Consummation / Retrospect.

Tales Of Sullen Eyes, Royal Anguish (2004). Twisted Angel / Until I'm Dead / The Loneliness Of One / The Tale Of Sullen Eyes / Tortured Visions.

RUDRA

SINGAPORE — *Kathi (vocals / bass), Kannan (guitar), Selvam (guitar), Shiva (drums).*

Self styled "Vedic Metal" band named after the Hindu God of destruction and created as RUDHRA in 1992 as a Death Black Metal trio of vocalist / bassist Kathi, guitarist Bala and drummer Shiva. The band would feature on numerous compilation albums including 'Battle Of The Bands', 'Made In Singapore' and 'The Birth Of Death', RUDHRA issued their own demo 'The Past' in 1994.

The band would fold in 1996 but Kathi and Shiva pulled the act back together newly billed as RUDRA by the end of the year with new guitarist Alvin. MANIFEST guitarist Burhan would fill in on a temporary basis until the resumption of duties from Bala.

The band contributed their rendition of DEATH's 'Forgotten Past' to the 'Together As One' 2003 tribute album assembled by the Spanish Mondongo Canibale label. RUDRA would undertake their debut North American shows in July of 2004, touring alongside RAISING KUBRICK. That same year the group signed to Demonzend Records for a new album 'Brahmavidya: Primodial I', this label also re-releasing RUDRA's debut album with all new artwork and bonus tracks taken from the 1995 demo 'The Past'.

RUDRA, having severed ties with Demonzend Records, scheduled US dates for January 2007. Relocating to Australia, guitarist Kannan bowed out in March.

RUDRA, Candlelight (1998). Obeisance / Bliss Divine / Black / Mahamaya / The Ancient One / Atman / War Legion / For The Dying / Sin No War (Demo) / Ananda (Demo).

THE ARYAN CRUSADE, Trishul (2001). Aryaputra / Hymns To Thee / Anantarupa / Malevolent Creed / Burnt At The Stakes / Rudrapatni / Amen / Homage To The Seers / Manifesto Of The Demented / Atmavichara / Sad But True / My Soul Is Marching On / I.

KURUKSHETRA, Trishul TR 004 (2003). Justified Aggression / Apostasy / God Of Delusion / Absolute One / Negate / Mithya / In The Vision Of The Blind / Temple Of Nothingness / Highlands Of Tranquility / Ye Immortal One / Asura Mardhini.

BRAHMAVIDYA: PRIMORDIAL I, DemonZend (2005). Twilight Of Duality / Ananya Chaitanya / The Pathless Path To The Knowable Unknown / There The Sun Never Shines / Veil Of Maya / Ageless Consciousness, I Am / Meditations On The Mahavakya / Aham Brahmasmi / Shivoham / In The Fourth Quarter: Turiya.

RUNIC

SPAIN — *Juan (vocals), Iván (guitar), Jose (guitar), Eneas (keyboards), Rivas (drums).*

RUNIC is a Castellón Viking Metal band employing elements of melodic Death and ancestral Pagan influences. Initiated in mid 2001 RUNIC's first recordings emerged as the six track 'Awaiting The Sound Of The Unavoidable', recorded at Rocketes Studios by TEMPLARIO guitarist Alberto and comprising five originals and a Metal adaptation of the Basil Poledouris 'Conan the Barbarian' soundtrack movie theme. Guests for these sessions include Fran of TEMPLARIO on flute and bagpipes.

Guitarist Vicente Gil exited in October of 2002, a replacement being found in Iván the following April. RUNIC signed to Germany's Massacre Records in October 2005 for an album entitled 'Liar Flags'.

Awaiting The Sound Of The Unavoidable, Independent (2001). The Arrival Of The Troops / Playing With Gods / Showdown / Seed Of Unrest / Prophecy Of A New World / The Search.

LIAR FLAGS, Massacre (2006). When The Demons Ride / Liar Flags / Zasi Days Of Aghrapur / Pt. II Lost Empire / Predecessor / To The Fallen Ones / Vs. Myself / Nau / And A New Journey Begins ....

S.N.I.F.F.

PUERTO RICO — *Chris Godkiller (vocals / guitar), Edwin Torres (guitar), Christian Quintana (bass), Christian Rivera (drums).*

Self-styled "Alcoholic Sexually Perverted Heavy Fucking Metal Metal" band S.N.I.F.F. was formed in 1999 by drummer Christian Rivera and guitarist Edwin Torres, adding second guitar player Annibal Cardona and bassist Jonathan Ruiz. The group was completed with the addition of ex-SEPULCHRAL frontman Christian Mercedes Túa ("Chris Godkiller"). Annibal Cardona departed in 2001.

S.N.I.F.F. recorded a 2001 demo, 'Eyes Of Blood', after which Tito Crowbar of MISERIA took over on bass guitar. The band fractured as Torres quit then, in 2003, Christian Rivera joined ALMA BLANCA. Godkiller persevered with a completely revised band line-up involving guitarist Reynaldo, bassist Cheo and drummer Edil. This version floundered too and Godkiller duly reformed SEPULCHRAL.

S.N.I.F.F. was resurrected in 2006.

Eyes Of Blood, Sniff (2001) (Demo). Odio / Hipocrecia / Human Falling / Love Is Dead.

S.O.B.

JAPAN — *Naoto (vocals), Oseki (guitar), Kawataka (bass), Ito (keyboards), Yasue (drums).*

S.O.B. is recognised as one of the earliest of Japanese Grindcore acts, debuting in 1986 with the nine song 7" single 'Leave Me Alone'. S.O.B. came to international recognition with a shared release in union with NAPALM DEATH in 1990. The 'Thrash Night' EP, a 500 limited gatefold red vinyl 7", was issued through Lee Dorrian of CATHEDRAL's Rise Above label and feature backing vocals by Dorrian and Shane Embury of NAPALM DEATH contributing bass on the song 'Deceiver'.

With original singer Yoshitomo 'Tottsuan' Suzuki committing suicide in June of 1995 the band drafted BRUTAL TRUTH's Kevin Sharp as temporary stand in before Naoto of RISE FROM THE DEAD made the role permanent. At this juncture S.O.B.'s musical emphasis shifted as samplers and keyboards took a keener role.

Leave Me Alone EP, Selfish (1986). Not Me / Give Me Advice / Fat Women / SDI & ABM / Knock Out / Sudden Rise Of Desire / Leave Me Alone / Slap In The Face / Thrash Night (Freak Out).

Don't Be Swindle EP, Selfish (1987). Raging In Hell / Violent Anger / Hear Nothing For You / Influence Of Slime / Hysteric To Temptation / Insane / S.O.B. / I'm A Dreamer / Let's Go Beach / Don't Be Swindle / Look Like Devil / Fuck Or Die / Heads Or Tails? / Don't Your Back / Speed My Way / Speak Mouth Fuck You / Revival / To Be Continued.

S.O.B. EP, Sounds Of Burial (1989) (Split EP with NAPALM DEATH). Repeat At Length / Humanity Of Stupidity / Deceiver Part II / Device.

Thrash Night EP, Rise Above (1989). Raging In Hell / Give Me Advice / Don't Your Back / S.O.B. / Nightmare / No Control / Fuck Or Die / Thrash Night.

Suck Up Brain Or Fuck Ya Brain?, Sounds Of Burial (1990). Suck Up Brain Or Fuck Ya Brain? / Nightmare.

WHAT'S THE TRUTH?, Toy's Factory (1990). Over The Line / Meddlesome Heart / Unseen Terror / Look Like Devil II (Hell) / Obsessed With Wickedness / What's The Truth? / Never / Senseless Fantasy / Repeat At Length / Why?

GATE OF DOOM, Toy's Factory (1993). G.O.D. / Delusion Of Terror / Trapped In Cancer / Human Error?! / Mind Empty Of Happiness / Downfall Of Civilization / Ultimate End Of Earth / Invisible Shadows / Inner Hypocrisy / Death's Inevitable-G.O.D.

VICIOUS WORLD, Toy's Factory (1994). Public Eye / Radiate / Rise Above Yourself / Crisis Prophecy / Killing Field / Vicious World / Morbid Attitude / Collision / Re-evolution / Jacobs.

S.U.P.

FRANCE — *Fabrice Loez (vocals / guitar), Ludovic Loez (guitar), Frédéric Fievez (bass), Thierry Berger (drums).*

A French Death Doom Metal band with Gothic influences. The band started life billed as SUPURATION. In this incarnation the group released the 1991 demo 'Sultry Obsession' and two albums, the second, 'Still In The Spheres', including a cover of TEARS FOR FEARS' 'Shout'. The group toured Europe partnered with SUFFOCATION in 1994 prior to recording the 'Anomoly' album. This recording marked a switch in band title to S.U.P. ('Spherical Unit Provided')

In 1995 a limited edition CD emerged (only 500 copies were pressed) entitled '9092' containing a number of tracks previously only released as singles or on compilation albums between 1990 and 1992. The group would tour with Swiss outfit CORONER in early 1996. S.U.P. signed to Holy Records in 1997, commencing this contract with the album 'Room Seven'. February of 1998 saw a re-issue of 'The Cube', re-credited to S.U.P. and adding tracks from the 'Still In The Spheres' outing. Upfront of the 'Chronophobia' album the band would lose the services of bass guitarist Laurent Bessault. Nevertheless the band toured Europe that Winter in union with ANATHEMA and into the Spring of 2000 acoss France partnered with GLOOMY GRIM and DIVISION ALPHA. The revisionism of their back catalogue continued apace with 'Anomoly', the record re-released in 2000 brandishing an array of remixes, acoustic takes and demos.

Such would be the band's influence that Inner Sides Productions released a double CD tribute set 'A Vision Of S.U.P.' artists paying homage included SKELETON CREW, GRIMORIA, CARNIVAL IN COAL, CATACOMB, BLACKLODGE, HYPNOSIS, INNER SOUL, NOMED, AEONS, DIVISION ALPHA, MISANTHROPE and NOCTURNAL FEARS amongst many others. Ludovic Loez would guest on an irreverent cover of GENESIS's 'Mama' included on the CARNIVAL IN COAL 'French Cancan' album of 1999.

S.U.P. issued the CD / DVD live set 'To Live Alone' in 2001 with a new studio album 'Angelus' arriving in 2002.

TRANSFER, Revelation REV 005 (1996). Ocean Of Faces (D-Än Mix) / Ocean Of Faces (Acoustic Version) / Pain Injection (Limb Mix) / Ocean Of Faces (Cradle Mix) / The Work (Acoustic) / Pain Injection (Demo Version) / In Those Times (Demo Version) / The Work (Demo Version).

ROOM SEVEN, Holy (1997). Deliverance / Bangs In My Head / Real Nature / My Heart On My Tongue / Room Seven / World Of Cushions / A Blue Sweetness / The Calling / Snake-Eyes / The Fall Is Too Long / Fallacy / Imaginary Life.

THE CUBE, Holy (1998). Prelude / Souls Speculum / Elevation / 138.JP.08 / The Cube / Through The Transparent Partitions / Spherical Inner-Sides / The Accomplishment / 4TX.31B / The Dim Light / The Crack / The Cleansing / Variation On Theme 4TX.31B.

CHRONOPHOBIA, Holy (1999). ... But All Has Changed / My Isolation / No Rejuvenation / Chronophobia / Room Eleven / Twins / Like A Wicker Man That Will Never Burn! / Overwhelming Lethargy / Machinations / Strange Impulse.

ANOMOLY 2000, Holy (2000). Anomaly / Pain Injection / In Those Times / The Work / Ocean Of Faces / In The Deepest Silence / Dialogue (D-an And T-on) / D-an' s Last Order / Reset / Ocean Of Faces (D-an mix) / Ocean Of Faces (acoustic version) / Pain Injection (Limb mix) / Ocean Of Faces (Cradles mix) / The Work (Acoustic version) / Pain Injection (1995 demo) / In Those Times (1995 demo) / The Work (1995 demo).

TO LIVE ALONE, Holy (2001). Twins / Bangs In My Head / Pain Injection / Chronophobia / Room Eleven / i308.jp.08 / Room Seven / Like A Wicker Man That Will Never Burn! / Strange Impulse / The Cube / 100 Years / Angel / Fou / Back From The Garden / Shout.

ANGELUS, Holy (2002). Ex Animo / Declivis / Originus / Resurrectio Animalis / Labimente / Umbrifer / Pendere Animi / Valefacio / Liberatio / Jampridem.

SACRAMENTUM

GOTHENBURG, SWEDEN — *Nissé Karlen (vocals), Anders Brolycke (guitar), Johan Norrrman (guitar), Freddy Andersson (bass), Niklas Rudolfsson (drums).*

A Gothenburg Death Metal five-piece, SACRAMENTUM's vocalist Nissé Karlen was previously with RUNEMAGICK. Karlen formed the group as TUMULUS and recorded a demo in 1993 entitled 'Sedes Imporium'. In 1994 the group, comprising Nils 'Nissé' Karlen, guitarist Anders Brolycke, bass player Freddy Andersson with Mikael Rydén on drums, released their self-produced promo EP, 'Finis Maloum', this set produced by EDGE OF SANITY mainman DAN SWANÖ at Unisound Studios and later released commercially by Adipocere Records. However, after the departure of bassist Freddy Andersson, Nissé Karlen doubled up on bass whilst former DECAMORAN and DISSECTION guitarist Johan Norrman also played in the group for a period.

The 1994 SACRAMENTUM album, 'Far Away From The Sun', again produced by DAN SWANÖ. Century Media Records issued 'The Coming Of Chaos' album in September 1997. These sessions were laid down at Los Angered Recordings with KING DIAMOND guitarist Andy LaRocque acting as producer. By this juncture SACRAMENTUM involved a trio of Karlén, Brolycke and drummer Niklas Rudolfsson, the latter a scene veteran holding association with BELLS OF DOOM, DEATHWITCH, DOMEDAG, DRACENA, SWORDMASTER, VARULV, RUNEMAGICK and THE FUNERAL ORCHESTRA.

Second album 'Thy Black Destiny', again with Andy LaRocque operating behind the desk, arrived in January 1999 for Century Media. Nissé Karlen would add guest vocals to the 1999 BENEATH demo 'Everything Ends' and on LORD BELIAL's 'Unholy Crusade'. Zenor Records of Brazil re-issued 'Far Away From The Sun' and 'Finis Malorum' in 2006.

Sedes Imporium, Sacramentum (1992) (Cassette demo). Intro / Sedes Impiorum / Stormbringer / Seasons Of The Dark Souls / Nocturnal Flame / Within Thy Circle / Outro.

Finis Malorum EP, Northern Production EVIL001 (1994). Moonfog / Travel With The Northern Winds / Devide Et Impera / Pagan Fire / Finis Malorum (Outro).

Finis Malorum EP, Adipocere AR023 (1995). Moonfog / Travel With The Northern Winds / Devide Et Impera / Pagan Fire / Finis Malorum (Outro).

FAR WAY FROM THE SUN, Adipocere AR034 (1996). Fog's Kiss / Far Away From The Sun / Blood Shall Be Spilled / When Night Surrounds Me / Cries From A Restless Soul / Obsolete Tears / Beyond All Horizons / The Vision And The Voice / Outro—Darkness Falls For Me / Far Away From The Sun (Part Two).

THE COMING OF CHAOS, Century Media 77178-2 (1997). Dreamdeath / ... As Obsidian / Awaken Chaos / Burning Lust / Abyss Of Time / Portal Of Blood / Black Destiny / To The Sound Of Storms / The Coming Of Chaos.

THY BLACK DESTINY, Century Media 77924-2 (1999). Iron Winds / The Manifestation / Shun The Light / Demoneaeon / Overlord / Death Obsession / Spiritual Winter / Raptures Paradise—Peccata Mortali / Weave Of Illusion / Thy Black Destiny.

SACRAPHYX

CAPE TOWN, SOUTH AFRICA — *Adam van der Riet (vocals / bass), George Schoombee (guitar), Alec Surridge (guitar), John Killin (drums).*

Cape Town Death Metal combo SACRAPHYX issued the 2003 'Shades Of Hate' album through Witchdoctor Records. The band date back to a 1993 formation, instigated by guitarist Alec Surridge and vocalist Tom Stewart, subsequently enrolling drummer Andrew Hodson then second guitarist Chris Maritz. During 1994 the group drafted bassist Craig Og Burns for recording of the demo 'Blinded'. The following year saw Maritz' position handed over to dental student George Schoombee. 1996 saw further changes as bass guitar was delegated to Ryan Johanssen then Johan Piek. 1997 saw the recording and release of the 'Disincarnate' EP.

The SACRAPHYX line up evolved further that April as Francois Knoetze took command of the drums. A 1999 album entitled 'Eighth Day' proved a spectacular success, being promoted by Johannesburg tours with P.I.T.T. and having sold out within 2 months of first pressing. Festival performances saw showings at the 'Metallennium' event and 'Wolseley Open Air'.

Adrian Langeveld became the latest drummer to answer the call in time for 2000 tour partnered with GROINCHURN. Upon completion of these dates Stewart decamped, being superseded by ex-POTHOLE frontman Adam van der Riet. In this formation SACRAPHYX put on their inaugural European gig by featuring on the August 2001 'Wacken Open Air' festival in Germany. Unfortunately the year ended with yet another defection, as Alec Surridge departed.

SACRAPHYX bounced back in January 2003 with the 'Cause & Effect' EP, capitalising on this with an opening slot to THE HAUNTED, seeing new man John Killin on drums. More high profile concerts were witnessed by a support to ENTOMBED in May, after which another POTHOLE veteran, Jacques Hugo, joined the band.

SACRAPHYX acted as support for KONKHRA's January 2004 gigs.

SHADES OF HATE, Witchdoctor (2003). Shades Of Hate / Pulling Teeth / Ungodly / Contempt / Burn / I Feel Nothing / Anti-Crust / Anger Management / Cold Day In Hell / Crackhead.

SACRASPHEMY

WESEL, GERMANY — *Darius Widera (vocals), Marek Widera (guitar), Felix R. (guitar), David R. (bass), Mathias Q. (keyboards), Lukas Raupp (drums).*

Dark Metal outfit SACRASPHEMY was initiated during the Spring of 2002 as a quartet of guitarists Marek Widera and Felix R, bassist David R and keyboard player Mathias Q. They would shortly afterward be joined by dual lead singers Dirk K, of Oberhausen's CHAOS, and Verena M. However, Dirk M vacated his position in January of 2003. Utilising Felix R and drummer Lukas Raupp on vocals, SACRASPHEMY cut the opening demo 'Neidingswerk'. That June Raupp enrolled into the ranks of ABADDON and in August Verena M exited.

SACRASPHEMY persevered by enlisting the ABADDON and NEBULAR MOON credited Darius Widera as new frontman. 2004 line-up changes saw Matthias T. taking command of bass duties and the relinquishing of the drums by Raupp due to "sudden deafness". SACRASPHEMY subsequently utilised a drum computer for live work.

Neidingswerk, Sacrasphemy (2003). I Ravenes Skygge / Flamme Des Hasses / Vikingstorm / Seelenmord / Neidingswerk / Hereditary Disease.

SACRED CRUCIFIX

OULU, FINLAND — *Miku Mertanen (vocals / bass), Tommi Määttä (guitar), Sami Taimela (guitar), Janne Kela (drums).*

Oulu Death Metal band founded in 1987 under an original billing of CRIMINAL ASSAULT. This unit, comprising singer Hannu, Tommi Määttä and Sami Taimela on guitar, Miku Mertanen on bass and Janne Kela of LYCANTROPHY on drums, released a three song demo in 1988. However, dissatisfaction with Hannu's performance led to his dismissal and, newly titled as SACRED CRUCIFIX the band issued a follow up demo 'Realm Of Darkness' in June 1989. This tape secured valuable underground acclaim but progress was stalled when both Määttä and Kela were drafted for their national military service and Mertanen relocated to Sweden.

SACRED CRUCIFIX regrouped in 1993, bringing onboard new faces Tommo on vocals, Jarkko on guitar and bassist Essi. A further demo tape was recorded but did not meet with the band's expectations.

The band resurrected itself during October of 2002, enlisting BURNING POINT's Jukka Kyrö on guitar alongside Tommi Määttä. However, Kyrö's responsibilities with his main act soon forced him out of the picture and Tero Kemppainen took over the position. His stay too would be brief and in November of 2003 original member Sami Taimela was welcomed back into the fold. SACRED CRUCIFIX signed an album deal with Poison Arrow Records in January 2004, recording a new album entitled 'Aeon Of Chaos' at Tonebox Studio in Oulu. The record was mastered at Finnvox in Helsinki.

The group engaged in the 'Creatures from the North' tour of Finland throughout February and March, sharing stages with MAPLE CROSS and NATIONAL NAPALM SYNDICATE. A limited edition, three way split EP, featuring new song 'The Last Path' was distributed during this trek through Verikauha Records.

Demo #1, Sacred Crucifix (1988) (Demo). Brain Death / Beyond The Cross.
Realms Of Darkness, Sacred Crucifix (1989) (Demo). The Fear—Requiem / Braindead / Beyond The Cross / Realms Of Darkness.
Demo 1990, Sacred Crucifix (1990) (Demo). Vlad The Staker / Chosen One / 13 / Deep In Unknown / Wise.
Demo 1994, Sacred Crucifix (1994) (Demo). Inseparable Dream / Caelum Sperare / Vlad The Staker / Unsound World / Under The Sun Below The Sky / Chosen One.
Promo 2003, Sacred Crucifix (2003) (Demo). Aeon Of Chaos / Three Times The 12th Letter / Still Here / The Painhour.
AEON OF CHAOS, Poison Arrow PAR003 (2004). Aeon Of Chaos / Gone / Low Nobility / 3 Times The 12th Letter / To Wallachia (Vlad Dracul) / The Creature From The North / The Painhour / Requiem / 13 / Still Here / Chosen One.
Creatures From The North EP, Verikauha VKR-17034 (2005) (Split EP with MAPLE CROSS and NATIONAL NAPALM SYNDICATE). The Last Path.

SACRED SIN

SINTRA, PORTUGAL — *José Costa (vocals / bass), Nuno Gonçalves (guitar), Pedro Miguel (guitar), Ronaldo Barros (drums).*

Sintra Death Metal act SACRED SIN was created during 1991 by a line-up comprising vocalist / bassist José Costa, guitarists To Pica and Rui Dias, keyboard player Carlos Caseiro and drummer Miguel Maorao, erstwhile members of NECROPHILIAC, MASSACRE and SILENT SCREAM. Maorao would be succeeded by Eduardo Dico in 1993. Another SACRED SIN credited drummer, Jorge Gonçalves, would go on to form Progressive Metal band FALLACY. The band toured Portugal in the Summer of that year promoting their 7" EP 'The Shades Behind' with the full-length album 'Darkside' leading to festival appearances. Other shows would include supports to MANOWAR, TIAMAT, NAPALM DEATH and SENTENCED. Quito Nishal replaced Dias on guitar in 1994. A second pressing of 'Darkside' included a live EP and SACRED SIN's work ethic paid off when they inked a deal with major label BMG.

The 1995 'Eye M God' album was to provide SACRED SIN, now with ex-DISAFFECTED man Quim Aries on drums, with a European tour support to MALEVOLENT CREATION. Joaquim Aires took command of the drums and Arthur Jorge was incorporated on keyboards in 1996, appearing on the following year's 'Anguish . . . Harvest' outing. However, a further switch in drummers found Danilo Warick installed in 1999. Founder member To Pica relinquished his position that year and was replaced by Pedro Miguel, a veteran of UNDERTAKER, PARANORMAL WALTZ and CRYSTAL DRAGON.

SACRED SIN would cut cover tracks for two tribute albums in 2001, namely VENOM and TARANTULA songs. That year Ronaldo Barros of GROG, NEOPLASMAH and NEPTHYS assumed drum duties.

The Shades Behind, Slime (1992). The Shades Behind.
DARKSIDE, Musica Alternavata MA001 (1993). Darkside / In The Veins Of Rotting Flesh / Ode To My Crucifying Lord / Deliverance / The Chapel Of The Lost Souls / Requiem ... For Mankind / Gravestone Without Name / Suffocate In Torment / Life—A Process Revealed / Terminal Collapse / A Monastery In Darkness / The Shades Behind.
EYE M GOD, Dinamite DT 95012 (1995). Intro / Evocation Of The Depraved / Inductive Compulsion / Eye M God / Death-Bearing Machine / The Nighthag (Nocturnal Queen) / One With God / Guilt Has No Past / A Human Jigsaw / Link To Nothingness / Dead Mind Breed / The Endless Path Of Hecate.
ANGUISH ... I HARVEST, (1998). Ghoul Plagued Darkness / Thirteenth Moon / Lead Of Insects / Firethrone / Profane / (Hope) Still Searching / Aghast / Astral / Feathers Black / The Shining Trapezoid.
TRANSLUCID DREAM MIRROR, Demolition DEMCD 111 (2001). Translucid Dream Mirror / La Clef De Grands Miseres / Ravish The Soul / Sukunft Kenntnis / Gift Of Second Sight / Malificai Genii / Extra Natural Mediator / Mel Lacrimae In Tenebrae / Transmutation / By The Wyvern We Flowed / Prelude To Phenomena / Unbridled Hate / The Shadow Gate.
HEKATON, Demolition (2003).

SACRED TEARS

SAN MIGUEL, PORTUGAL — *Susana Oliveira (vocals), Ruben Ferreira (guitar), Fabio Alonso (guitar), Milton Costa (drums).*

San Miguel, Açores Doom-Death outfit dating to 2002. The group was formulated by drummer Rui Dias, guitarists Ruben Ferreira, from STRAPPING LUCY and EON ZERO, and Fabio Alonso and originally featured bassist Rui Cabral. The following year was a point of membership turbulence as many musicians came and went including bassist Ricardo Botelho, keyboard player Bruno Santos, having association with of Ponta Delgada's SLITH, IN PECCATVM and Gothic solo project A DREAM OF POE, singers Bruno Aguiar and Paulo Pacheco who were in turn superseded by Felipe Raposo and Jenny Teixeira. A single song demo, 'A Cradle Song', arrived in 2003.

In 2004 SACRED TEARS witnessed the exit of founders Rua Dias and Rui Cabral plus Felipe Raposo, Jenny Teixeira. Nelio Tavares, from PROPHECY OF DEATH was duly installed on vocals whilst Milton Costa took command of the drums. Tavares, Botelho and Santos bowed out in 2006. Nebur Records distributed second demo 'Whispers Of Loneliness' in June 2006.

A Cradle Song, Sacred Tears (2003) (Demo). A Cradle Song.
Whispers Of Loneliness, Nebur (2006) (Demo). Whispers Of Loneliness / New Blood / The Return Of Winter / Mysterious Light ... (In The Dark).

SACRIFICE

TORONTO, ON, CANADA — *Rob Urbinati (vocals / guitar), Joe Rico (guitar), Scott Watts (bass), Gus Pynn (drums).*

Toronto's SACRIFICE left an indelible legacy on the extreme Metal scene inspiring legions of North American acts. Teenagers vocalist / guitarist Rob Urbinati and guitarist Joe Rico formulated the band in 1983, building up to a full band by hiring vocalist John Baldy, bassist Scott Watts and drummer Andrew Banks. This formation started out by tackling BLACK SABBATH, EXCITER, METALLICA and JUDAS PRIEST covers before elevating to their own brand of Speed Metal. Drummers came and went in quick succession, Banks being succeeded by Craig Boyle who in turn lost his post to Ernst Flach. A series of rehearsal tapes saw local distribution, one three track affair which made it onto the underground tape trading market comprising a METALLICA cover version 'The Four Horsemen' plus 'Turn In Your Grave' and 'Warriors Of Death'. Aiding local Thrash comrades, both Rob Urbinati and Joe Rico guested on the 1984 SLAUGHTER demo 'Bloody Karnage'.

SACRIFICE debuted live opening for local Glam Rock outfit HERRENVOLK, fronted by a pre-SKID ROW Sebastian Bach, on January 12th 1985 at Larry's Hideaway in Toronto. The band's set comprised EXCITER, SLAYER and METALLICA covers and proved to be the last with John Baldy, who was fired shortly afterward. Boyle too decamped, joining LETHAL PRESENCE, Gus Pynn stabilised the percussion department. SACRIFICE recorded the demo, 'The Exorcism' funded by Brian Taylor of local record store The Record Peddler, at Accusonic Studios in June 1985.

Signing to the Diabolic Force imprint of Fringe Records, SACRIFICE delivered their opening Brian Taylor produced album 'Torment In Fire'. Although horrifically under produced the record, delivered in June 1986, did generate a strong response on the burgeoning Thrash scene. Just as 'Torment In Fire' was issued the group was back in the studios preparing more new material, including demoing up a version of DISCHARGE's 'The Possibility Of Life's Destruction'. On the live front, SACRIFICE built up a loyal following in the city by opening for bands such as SLAYER, EXODUS, MEGADETH and KING DIAMOND. In October 1986 the group shared the billing of the Montreal Spectrum 'No Speed Limit' festival alongside POSSESSED, D.R.I., AGGRESSION and AGNOSTIC FRONT amongst others.

In early 1987 SACRIFICE made their first foray into the USA, conducting MidWest shows backing STRAW DOGS and CORROSION OF CONFORMITY, these gigs preceding recording of second album 'Forward To Termination'. Introducing near Progressive elements, SACRIFICE benefited hugely from an improved production and Canadian sales were boosted by regular television airing of the promotional video 'Re-animation'. 'Forward To Termination' gained licenses worldwide with Metal Blade in the United States and Roadrunner in Europe. Performing in the USA again had SACRIFICE alongside KING DIAMOND, TROUBLE, NUCLEAR ASSAULT, DEATH, DEATH ANGEL and HALLOW'S EVE, at the inaugural 'Milwaukee Metal Fest' event. No cohesive live campaign was entered into though as projected tours in alliance with BLOOD FEAST and then with DEATH ANGEL fell through due to lack of finances, although a short run of shows with NUCLEAR ASSAULT took them back into the MidWest. Another scheduled set of gigs, HIRAX and AT WAR, was also pulled. Hooking up with NUCLEAR ASSAULT once more SACRIFICE embarked on Canadian dates in July 1988 then put themselves back into recording mode for a three song demo that December just upfront of East Coast concerts opening for MOTÖRHEAD.

Third offering 'Soldiers Of Misfortune' was to emerge via Diabolic Force during October 1990. Although Metal Blade took the record for the USA no European license was forthcoming. Canadian gigs in September 1990 witnessed a road union with label mates RAZOR.

In early 1991 drummer Gus Pynn made way for former DARK LEGION man Mike Rosenthal, himself quickly superseded by ex-HERRICK pounder Darren Foster. However, Foster's tenure was fleeting and Michael Rosenthal took up the drum position. On July 27th 1991, SACRIFICE played the 'Milwaukee Metal Fest' again, the billing including artists such as CYCLONE TEMPLE, DEICIDE, MASSACRE, NAPALM DEATH and SEPULTURA. US touring then ensued that October together with BELIEVER and BOLT THROWER.

Working with RAZOR guitar player Dave Carlo acting as producer the band recorded a fourth album 'Apocalypse Inside' for Metal Blade Records. However, the line-up then fractured as once the sessions were completed Scott Watts was ousted in favour of INTERZONE's Kevin Wimberley to tour the record in July 1993 across the USA with GOREFEST and DEATH. It wasn't enough to buck the downward trend on Thrash sales though and, dropped by Metal Blade, SACRIFICE folded.

Frontman Rob Urbinati later created INTERZONE for the 1999 'Cydonia' album. By late 2002 Urbinati was touting a fresh act entitled TENET comprising of Death Metal veterans drummer Gene Hoglan of DARK ANGEL and DEATH fame, STRAPPING YOUNG LAD guitarist Jed Simon, erstwhile GRIP INC. bassist Stuart Carruthers plus ex-FORBIDDEN and TESTAMENT guitarist Glen Alvelais.

In late 2004 the Brazilian label Marquee Records announced they were set to re-issue catalogue albums 1986's 'Torment In Fire', 1987's 'Forward To Termination' and 1990's 'Soldiers Of Misfortune'. In addition, there would be a live album culled from 1989 concert recordings. The 'Torment In Fire' release came as a double CD, limited-edition hand-numbered slipcase adding extra tracks culled from 'The Exorcism' demo plus no less than 22 live tracks recorded at Larry's Hideaway, Toronto in 1984 and from 1986 gigs in Toronto and Quebec. The re-issue of 'Forward To Termination' added album demos plus live tracks recorded in Kitchener, Ontario during 1986, Toronto in 1987 and Rochester, New York in 1988.

In early 2005 Urbinati would also fire up side project WAR AMP, a Blues based retro-Doom outfit involving former JAWW and SOULSTORM members. The following year SACRIFICE, comprising vocalist / guitarist Rob Urbinati, guitarist Joe Rico, bassist Scott Watts and drummer Gus Pynn, reunited. The band put in a one off headline appearance at the September 23rd 'Day Of The Equinox II' festival held at the Opera House in Toronto.

TORMENT IN FIRE, Metal Blade 72159 (1986). The Awakening / Sacrifice / Turn In Your Grave / Homicidal Breath / Warrior Of Death / Infernal Visions / Burned At The Stake / Necromonicon / The Exorcism / Possession / Decapitation / Beyond Death.
FORWARD TO TERMINATION, Diabolic Force (1987). Forward To Termination / Terror Strikes / Re-Animation / Afterlife / Flames Of Armageddon / Cyanide / Light Of The End / Pyrokinesis.
SOLDIERS OF MISFORTUNE, Diabolic Force (1991). As The World Burns / Soldiers Of Misfortune / In Defiance / Existence Within Eternity / Pawn Of Prophecy / Lost Through Time / A Storm In The Silence / Truth / After The Rain.
APOCALYPSE INSIDE, Metal Blade 14267 (1993). My Eyes See Red / Apocalypse Inside / Flesh / Salvation / Beneath What You See / Incarcerated / Ruins Of The Old / The Lost / Freedom Slave.

SACRIFICIAL SLAUGHTER

ANAHEIM, CA, USA — *Steve Worley (vocals), Chuck Hill (guitar), Kyle Slominski (bass), Steve Warth (drums).*

Anaheim, California Death Metal band founded in 1999 by singer Steve 'Crusty' Worley. Since formation the band has endured a succession of line-up changes with ex-members including guitarists Bob Babcock, Paul Coultrop and Derek Faulk, bass players Scott Vogt and Adam Kinnick with Kelly Benavidez, Seth Leavitt, Nick Varkatzas, Jon May and Alfonso Paz all having occupied the drum stool.

SACRIFICIAL SLAUGHTER guitarist Kyle Slominski also operates with NECROSIS, DECEPTION and REGURGITATED COW FETUS. The Warth Vader label, drummer Steve Warth's custom imprint, issued a 2002 album 'The Rebirth'. A demo, 'Jackhammer Sodomy', followed in 2003.

THE REBIRTH, Warth Vader (2002). Decapitated Carcass (Intro) / Cannibal Feast With Satan / Evil Servant Of God / Self Sacrifice / Mummified Fetus / Zombie Dead Come Alive To Fuck / Brought By Fire / Apothecary Of Death / Sawed In Half / Sacrificial Slaughter / Apothecary Of Death (Live) / Sawed In Half (Live).

SACRIFICIUM

WEINSTADT, GERMANY — *Claudio Enzler (vocals), Ulrike Uhlmann (guitar), Oliver Tesch (guitar), Samuel Herbrich (bass), Mario Henning (drums).*

SACRIFICIUM is a Christian Death Metal band based out of Weinstadt. The group was founded during 1994 in a Thrash Metal vein but switched to more aggressive Death Metal the following year. A self titled opening demo arrived in 1996 with a second session, entitled 'Mortal Fear' recorded at Tritonus Studios, following in 1999, after which the band lost its singer. Live work was conducted with session players.

The debut album 'Cold Black Piece Of Flesh' was recorded in May 2002, being released that December through Whirlwind Records. Bassist Manuel Kerkow exited in the Spring of 2003, being superseded by Samuel Herbrich. In November of 2004 SACRIFICIUM recorded tracks for the 'Escaping The Stupor' release.

SACRIFICIUM signed to the Greek label Black Lotus Records in September 2005 for the album 'Escaping The Stupor'. Claudio Enzler joined MY DARKEST HATE in March 2006.

Sacrificium, (1996). Death To Death / False Friend / For You / Verify Error.
Mortal Fear, (1999). Pauper's Grave / In Your Eyes / Psalm Of An Unborn.
COLD BLACK PIECE OF FLESH, Whirlwind (2002). Cold Black Piece Of Flesh / Come Closer / Existence / Killing With Style / Zustand Tod / Labyrinth / Kill Me / Psalm Of An Unborn / Pauper's Grave / Vast.
ESCAPING THE STUPOR, Black Lotus (2006). Canvas / Towards The Edge Of Degeneration / I Am The Enemy / Pierced By Death / Extinction Of Mankind / Shivering / Tremendum / As Silence Dies / Revelation Of Justice / Of Traumatic Memories And Tears / Nothing From You.

SACROSANCT

HOLLAND — *Michel Lucarelli (vocals), Randy Meinhard (guitar), Michel Cerrone (guitar), Christian Colli (bass), Marco Foddis (drums).*

Noted Death Metal formation SACROSANCT featured founders guitarist Randy Meinhard and drummer Marco Foddis, both previously with PESTILENCE. The band, featuring Michel Lucarelli on vocals and second guitarist Michel Cerrone, debuted during 1989 with the demo 'The Die is Cast', this scoring a contract with No Remorse Records for a 1990 album 'The Truth—What It Is'. However, both Lucarelli and Remco then exited to forge IMPERIUM. SACROSANCT duly drafted Gerrit Knol on guitar, Christian Colli on bass and PHAROAH's drummer Haico van Atticum.

The album 'Recesses For The Depraved' was recorded at Dust Music Studios in Germany with producer Michael Stotzel. SACROSANCT toured Germany in 1992 as support to DARK ANGEL following which Michael Lucarelli and Gerrit Knol departed, although this didn't prevent the group from contributing the song 'Shining Through' to the 'Stop War' compilation album.

The 1993 'Tragic Intense' album featured ex-PHAROAH musicians vocalist Collin Kock and guitarist Mike Kock and was produced by then TORCHURE vocalist S.L. Coe. In 1994 both Meinhard and Colli joined SUBMISSION, the short lived band assembled by ex-PESTILENCE and ASPHYX vocalist Martin Van Drunen.

During 2006 Gerrit Knol, and another SACROSANCT credited musician—drummer Ronny Scholten, joined WHY SHE KILLS.

TRUTH IS—WHAT IS, No Remorse NRR 1009 (1990). Dimension Of Violence / Execrated (They Will Be) / Skin To Skin / The Sickened Thrill / Terminal Suicide / Disputed Death / Catalepsy / Truth Is- What Is / The Die Is Cast / Injured.
RECESSES FOR THE DEPRAVED, 1MF (1991). Illusive Supremacy / Like Preached Directions / Astrayed Thoughts / Mortal Remains / Hidden Crimes Untold / Enter The Sanctum / With Malice Prepense / The Silence Of Being.
TRAGIC INTENSE, 1MF 377.003-2 (1993). From Deep Below / Godforesaken / Shining Through / Fainted / At Least Pain Lasts / The Gathering Of The Tribes / The Breed Within.

SADIST (pic: Dimitri Borellini)

SADIST

GENOA, ITALY — *Andy (vocals / bass), Tommy Talamanca (guitar), Trevor (bass), Oinos (drums).*

Previously known as NECRODEATH and formed in Genoa during 1991, under the original moniker the Italians released the 'Into The Macabre' record before switching to the SADIST handle and promptly coming up with the 'Black Screams' 7" single for Italian label Obscure Plasma. The single sold around 2'500 copies, but following its release original vocalist Fabio quit and thus bassist Andy took over singing duties.

After touring through Italy, Portugal and France, SADIST signed to Nosferatu Records and recorded the 1993 'Above The Light' debut album before a parting of the ways occurred with Andy and SADIST drafted in vocalist Zanna and bassist Chicco. Both appeared on the 1996 'Tribe' album prior to SADIST reuniting with Andy. 'Tribe' was recorded in England at the Rhythm Studio. Guitarist Tommy Talamanca produced the debut album from extreme Death Metal band NATRON in 1998. SADIST latterly pulled in former THY NATURE and NODE drummer Oinos for session work. The band issued the 'Lego album in 2000, this seeing a drastic diversion towards a more commercial style, but then folded.

Tommy Talamanca would act as producer for INFECTION CODE's 2004 album 'Sterile', this opus also seeing Trevor acting as studio guest. In 2005 the SADIST legacy was given a boost when Czech label Beyond Productions announced they were to issue re-mastered variants of the band's first two albums. 'Above The Light', re-issued in December, added two bonus tracks.

2007 album recordings featured GOBLIN keyboard player Claudio Simonetti as studio guest on a reworking of the 1993 instrumental track 'Sadist'. The eponymous album was issued in Europe in April via Beyond Productions.

Black Screams, Obscure Plasma (1991). Black Screams.
ABOVE THE LIGHT, Nosferatu NOSF001 (1993). Nadir / Breathin' Cancer / Enslaver Of Lies / Sometimes They Come Back / Hell In Myself / Desert Divinities / Sadist / Happiness n' Sorrow.
TRIBE, Rising Sun CD34435 (1996). Escogido / India / From Bellatrix To Betelgeuse / Den Siste Kamp / Tribe / Spiral Of The Winter Ghosts / The Ninth Wave / The Reign Of Asmat.
CRUST, Displeased D00056 (1997). Perversion Lust Orgasm / The Path / Fools And Dolts / Holy … / Ovariotomy / Instinct / Obsession Compulsion / … Crust / I Rape You / Christmas Beat.
LEGO, KMG (2000). * / A Tender Fable / Its Not Good / Meat / Flies On Me / Fog / Plastic Star / Flowing Out Red / I Want It / Welcome To My Zoo / Small Great Child / Dodgy Fuckin Cow / Deline / Dog Sledge Man / Cappuccetto Grosso.
SADIST, Beyond Productions (2007). Jagriti / One Thousand Memories / I Feel You Climb / Embracing The Form Of Life / Tearing Away / Kopto / Excited And Desirous / Different Melodies / Invisible / Hope To Be Deaf / Sadist.

SADISTIC INTENT

LOS ANGELES, CA, USA — *Bay Cortez (vocals / bass), Rick Cortez (guitar), Vincent Cervera (guitar), Emilio Marquez (drums).*

SADISTIC INTENT have a lineage stretching back as far as 1987. The band, originally led by vocalist Enrique Chavez, cut the 1989 demo 'Conflict Within' then signed to the Wild Rags label for the 1990 EP 'Impending Doom'. Following tours of America and Mexico the band would break free from Wild Rags on rather acrimonious terms issuing the limited edition self financed 7" single 'A Calm Before The Storm'.

Line up troubles afflicted the band for the next few years before a newly resettled line up cut the 'Resurrection' mini album in 1994. A further demo session 'Ancient Black Earth' ensued the following year which was pressed up as a limited edition run CD in 1996. The same year SADISTIC INTENT were included on the CELTIC FROST tribute album 'In Memory Of' with their version of 'Return To The Eve'. Live action saw the band undertaking tours of America and Mexico as well as putting in a showing at the legendary Milwaukee Metalfest.

In 1998 SADISTIC INTENT shared space on a shared 7" single with Germany's UNGOD. 1999 found the band on another homage album, this time honouring POSSESSED with the novel addition of erstwhile POSSESSED singer Jeff Becarra on guesting vocals. The POSSESSED track, 'The Exorcist, would later be picked up for release as a 7" picture disc single by the German Iron Pegasus label. As the band set about recording of a new album 'The Second Coming' in October of 2001, with AGENT STEEL guitarist Bernie Versailles handling production duties, a further tribute affair had SADISTIC INTENT donating to a SLAYER collection. However, by September of 2002 'A Second Coming' was still far from completion.

It would be reported that SADISTIC INTENT drummer Emilio Marquez replaced FEAR FACTORY's Raymond Herrera in both ASESSINO and BRUJERIA during September of 2002 although this would be swiftly denied.

Impending Doom EP, Wild Rags (1990). Lurking Terror / Existence / Morbid Faith / Impending Doom.
A Calm Before The Storm, Sadistic Intent (1991). Second Coming / Dark Predictions.
RESURRECTION, Dark Realm (1994). Resurrection / Asphyxiation / Conflict Within / Dark Predictions / Condemned In Misery / A Mass For Tortured Souls.
Ancient Black Earth EP, Dark Realm (1996). Untimely End / Ancient Black Earth / Funerals Obscure.
Eternal Darkness, (1997) (Split single with UNGOD. Limited edition 1000 copies). Eternal Darkness.
THE SECOND COMING OF DARKNESS, Necropolis (2000).
Morbid Faith, Iron Pegasus (2002). Morbid Faith / The Exorcist.

SADUS

ANTIOCH, CA, USA — *Darren Travis (vocals / guitar), Rob Moore (guitar), Steve DiGeorgio (bass), Jon Allen (drums).*

SADUS came together as a quartet in 1984 of vocalist Darren Travis, guitarist Rob Moore, bassist Steve DiGeorgio and drummer Jon Allen, although it was to be two years until the first fruits of this liaison came into being with the 1986 'D.T.P.' ('Death To Posers') demo tape. These sessions led directly to the inclusion of two tracks on the 1987 'Raging Death' compilation album. Quick to capitalise on this achievement SADUS stuck their hands in their pockets to self finance the debut album pulling in METAL CHURCH guitarist John Marshall as producer. The pace of progress was quickened as a deal with label Roadrunner Records was secured resulting in a further album

'Swallowed In Black' and touring with the likes of SEPULTURA and OBITUARY.

SADUS was put on ice for 1991 as DiGeorgio opted to assist DEATH for their 'Human' album. With this added exposure Roadrunner re-released the 'Illusions' debut retitled 'Chemical Exposure' as SADUS regrouped for a summer American tour opening for MORBID ANGEL. Although a further album for Roadrunner, 1992's 'A Vision Of Misery', resulted in a European headline tour, SADUS found itself label less upon their return. Further setbacks occurred when DiGeorgio was enticed back to DEATH for the 'Individual Thought Patterns' album and a subsequent year long bout of touring. DiGeorgio was to return for club shows with SADUS but before any momentum could be gained Moore bailed out.

SADUS continued as a trio crafting the Scott Burns produced 'Elements Of Anger' in 1997. The in demand DiGeorgio, along with drummer Jon Allen, also operated a side project DRAGONHEART (later DRAGONLORD) with ex-VICIOUS RUMOURS and present day TESTAMENT guitarist Steve Smyth and his fellow TESTAMENT six-stringer Eric Peterson. DiGeorgio teamed up with ICED EARTH in late 2000.

News during the summer of 2002 would reveal that frontman Darren Travis and bassist Steve DiGeorgio was embarking on another all star union billed as SUICIDE SHIFT. The project allied the SADUS pairing with TESTAMENT vocalist Chuck Billy as well as drummer Per Moller Jensen of THE HAUNTED and guest guitar from the much travelled TESTAMENT, DEATH and CANCER guitarist JAMES MURPHY.

The Hammerheart label would put the band's original 'Death To Posers' 1986 demo onto CD in 2003, adding a brace of cuts from a 1988 session 'Certain Death' as a bonus.

SADUS announced they were to partner up with fellow Thrash veterans NASTY SAVAGE and high profile Finnish act FINNTROLL for European mainland dates in December. However, just days after the official press release confirming these shows the band withdrew as drummer Jon Allen's commitments to his 11 year old daughter, who had just undergone open heart surgery, took precedence.

Despite Steve DiGeorgio commitments in 2004 to TESTAMENT, the band did increase activity that year. In April the group toured Europe, taking in shows in Greece, Italy, Sweden and appearing at Norway's 'Inferno' festival in Oslo. DiGeorgio then took time out to record with ARTENSION then hit the European festival circuit with TESTAMENT. Gigs in August marked a first for SADUS as they toured Chile alongside TORTURER whilst on South American dates. New SADUS material would be laid down throughout September and October before DiGeorgio joined the ranks of SEBASTIAN BACH's band for further European touring in December. The bassist would also be announced as a contributor to recordings for Norwegian act SCARIOT in early 2005.

SADUS, together with producer Børge Finstad, entered Trident Studios in Pacheco, California to record their fifth album for a late Summer release via Mascot Records. In March 2006 Jon Allen manned the drum kit for live work with TESTAMENT. That same month found DiGeorgio involving himself in a studio collaboration with singer Björn Strid, of SOILWORK, TERROR 2000 and COLDSEED, Glen Alvelais from FORBIDDEN, TESTAMENT and LD/50 and Jeremy Colson of the STEVE VAI band, MARTY FRIEDMAN, MICHAEL SCHENKER, APARTMENT 26, DALI'S DILEMMA and LD/50 repute.

On November 18th the band appeared at the Monterrey Metal Fest event at the at the Coca Cola Auditorium in Mexico alongside BLIND GUARDIAN, CATHEDRAL, U.D.O., EDGUY, OBITUARY, DEICIDE, LEAVES' EYES, BLUDGEON, VAINGLORY, HYDROGYN and JOE STUMP'S REIGN OF TERROR.

SADUS was announced as teaming up with DESTRUCTION, HIRAX and MUNICIPAL WASTE for a North American tour throughout January and February 2007. However, the group

SADUS (pic: Linda Aversa)

dropped off these dates as New Year broke. SADUS lined up the South American 'Fuera Por Sangre' dates hitting Venezuela, Ecuador and Colombia in April prior to supporting OBITUARY in Mexico during May.

ILLUSIONS, Sadus (1988). Certain Death / Undead / Sadus Attack / Torture / And Then You Die / Hands Of Fate / Twisted Face / Fight Or Die / Illusions (Chemical Exposure).

SWALLOWED IN BLACK, Roadracer RO 93682 (1990). Black / Man Infestation / Last Abide / The Wake / In Your Face / Good Ridn'z / False Incarnation / Images / Powers Of Hate / Arise / Oracle Of Omission.

CHEMICAL EXPOSURE, Roadrunner RO 92592 (1991). Certain Death / Undead / Sadus Attack / Torture / And Then You Die / Hands Of Fate / Twisted Face / Fight Or Die / Illusions / Chemical Exposure.

A VISION OF MISERY, Roadrunner (1992). Through The Eyes Of Greed / Valley Of Dry Bones / Machines / Slave To Misery / Throwing Away The Day / Facelift / Deceptive Perceptions / Under The Knife / Echoes Of Forever.

CHRONICLES OF CHAOS, Mascot M 7025-2 (1997). Certain Death / Undead / Sadus Attack / Torture / Hands Of Fate / Illusions / Man Infestation / Good Rid'nz / Powers Of Hate / Arise / Oracle Of Obmission / Through The Eyes Of Greed / Valley Of Dry Bones / Slave To Misery / Facelift / Deceptive Perceptions / Echoes Of Forever.

ELEMENTS OF ANGER, Mascot M 7026-2 (1997). Aggression / Crutch / Words Of War / Safety In Numbers / Mask / Fuel / Power Of One / Stronger Than Life / Unreality / In The End.

OUT FOR BLOOD, Mascot (2006).

SAMAEL

SION, SWITZERLAND — *Vorphalack (Vocals / guitar), Masmiseîm (bass), Xytraguptor (drums).*

Proud to be recognised as one of the gloomiest bands in Europe. Over a series of finely crafted albums Sion's SAMAEL have built up an enviable reputation for quality Metal with a unique touch. 1999's 'Eternal' was widely acknowledged to be a classic of the genre. SAMAEL heralded their arrival with the 1987 demo recording titled 'Into The Infernal Storm Of Evil'. This session, crafted by vocalist / guitarist Vorphalack with Pat Charvet on drums, showed a band bursting with ambition but not yet in possession of the technical ability or experience to get their message across. Nevertheless, the chamber-like echo applied to the vocals hinted at a greater majesty to come. A second demo, 'Macabre Operetta', saw issue the following year, after which Charvet bowed out to join MISERY.

The group's 1989's 'Medieval Prophecy' three track EP, recorded as a duo of Vorphalack, credited with "vociferations" and his drumming brother Xytraguptor, featured a cover of HELLHAMMER's 'The Third Of The Storm' whilst demo track 'Into The Dark' was re-worked, bolting on a further five minutes duration, as 'Into The Pentagram'. Issued through Necrosound Records, two sleeve variations of Medieval Prophecy saw release, adding to collectability. SAMAEL's next release in 1990 was the demo tape 'From Dark To Black'.

Signing to the then newly established French label Osmose Productions SAMAEL published the 'Worship Him' album in June 1990, notably boasting the catalogue number OPCD001. For this creative congress, recorded in Taurus Studios that March, the band unit was enhanced with the addition of Masmiseîm (a.k.a. Christophe Mermod). 'Worship Him' unexpectedly generated substantial sales, eventually surpassing the 100,000 sales mark in Europe alone. Follow up 'Blood Ritual' arrived in December 1992 for German imprint Century Media Records. The record was cut at T & T Studios in Gelsenkirchen, Germany with production credits going to GRIP INC. guitarist Waldemar Sorychta.

A 7" picture disc EP, 'After The Sepulture' comprising a re-recorded variant of the title track and a cover of VENOM's 'Manitou', limited to just 500 copies, emerged in 1993. SAMAEL's next full-length offering, 'Ceremony Of Opposites' with Waldemar Sorychta once again manning the production desk, saw release in February 1994. With SAMAEL's profile rising, Century Media also issued a compilation of the 'Worship Him' and Blood Ritual' material as the November 1994 compilation '1987-1992'. The May 1995 'Rebellion' mini album, laid down at Woodhouse Studio, Hagen in Germany, boasted a cover of ALICE COOPER's 'I Love The Dead'. Also included would be an unlisted, "hidden" track 'Static Journey'.

The group added keyboard player Rudolphe H. for live dates in 1995 with SENTENCED and for the recording of August 1996's 'Passage' all drum parts were programmed and Xytraguptor (later simply 'Xytra' then 'Xy') assumed a new role as keyboard player. 'Passage' marked a new phase in the group's career, introducing heavily industrialised elements. Initial copies of 'Passages' came complete with a bonus disc entitled 'Xytras's Passage', this being a totally instrumental, ambient classical remix variations on the album by Xytra plus re-worked archive material 'Wintersonnenwende' and 'Der Stamm Kains'.

A second guitarist, Khaos from French Death Metallers GORGON, was also brought in for recording and live dates. SAMAEL's relationship to SENTENCED was strengthened as Vorphalack added backing vocals to the Finn's 'Down' outing. Xytra's's skills in the studio would be recognised outside of SAMAEL, gaining production credits on two albums, 'Sleep Of The Angels' and 'A Dead Poem' by Greek Black Metal veterans ROTTING CHRIST. Xy also operated his own label Parallel Union Records in collaboration with War D. of ALASTIS.

April of 1997 found the band back on European soil, heading up the 'Full Of Hate' Easter festivals alongside OBITUARY, DEATH, ENTOMBED, NEUROSIS, CROWBAR, KILLING CULTURE and STRAPPING YOUNG LAD.

The mini-album 'Exodus' was issued in June 1998. Promoting the 'Eternal' full-length, released in July 1999, the band headed out on a US trek throughout September and October that year bolstered by MONSTROSITY, DIMMU BORGIR and EPOCH OF

SAMAEL

UNLIGHT.

Upfront of schedule European summer festival performances guitarist Kaos announced his departure in mid 2002. As 2003 broke the band acted as special guests to UK veteran Doomsters CATHEDRAL and Hungarian newcomers WITHOUT FACE on a lengthy trek throughout Europe throughout January and February. SAMAEL united with STRAPPING YOUNG LAD and CATHEDRAL for September North American dates dubbed the 'Redemption' tour. Product that year came in the form of an elaborate DVD set 'Black Trip' filmed at three concerts, 'Summer Breeze' festival in Germany 2002, Chicago in 1994 and Poland 1996. Century Media also collected together the entire band output for the mammoth box set 'Since The Creation' in December.

In 2004 the band, having fulfilled their contract to Century Media, signed a new label deal with Sweden's Regain Records for Europe and Asia but established their own imprint Galactical Recordings for the rest of the world. A new album, 'Reign Of Light' co-produced by Waldemar Sorychta, was set to arrive in the Summer. A listening session for the media took place on 10th August at the HR Giger museum in Switzerland. 'Reign Of Light' would subsequently be picked up by the Nuclear Blast label for a December US release as that same month the band conducted European dates in union with Electro-Metal merchants OOMPH! and Marseille's DAGOBA.

That same year the band would have their classic cut 'Into The Pentagram' chosen as a pioneering piece of music for a compilation assembled by DARKTHRONE drummer Fenriz, released through Peaceville Records and entitled 'Fenriz Presents The Best Of Old School Black Metal'. An EP, 'One Earth' in June 2005, included a cover version of DEPECHE MODE's 'I Feel You'.

Xy fractured his wrist in a snowboard accident during December, forcing him out of live work for a period. Nevertheless, SAMAEL lined up European touring in January and February of 2006 packaged with OBITUARY and MAROON as the archive collection 'Era One & Lesson In Magic #1' hit the shelves. This double disc involved Electro material originally put down onto tape in 2002 and further ambient styled tracks recorded in 2003.

Vorph guested on TRISTANIA's 2006 album 'Illumination'. SAMAEL set to work on pre-production tracks with producer Waldemar Sorychta in July.

Into The Infernal Storm Of Evil, (1987). Intro / The Messenger Of The Light / The knowledge Of The Ancient Kingdom / Into The Dark.
Macabre Operetta, (1988). Blood Ritual / Crown Of Evil / Macabre Operetta.
Medieval Prophecy, Necrosound (1989). Into The Pentagram / The Dark (Extensive version) / The Third Of The Storms.
From Dark To Black, (1990). Morbid Metal / Knowledge Of The Ancient Kingdom.

WORSHIP HIM, Osmose Productions OPCD001 (1990). Sleep Of Death / Worship Him / Knowledge of the Ancient Kingdom / Morbid Metal / Rite Of Cthulhu / The Black Face / Into The Pentagram / Messengers Of The Light / Last Benediction / The Dark.

BLOOD RITUAL, Century Media CM97372 (1992). Epilogue / Beyond The Nothingness / Poison Infiltration / After The Sepulture / Macabre Operetta / Blood Ritual / Since The Creation / With The Gleam Of Torches / Total Consecration / Bestial Devotion / Until The Chaos.

After The Sepulture, (1993) (Limited edition 500 copies). After The Sepulture (New Version) / Manitou.

CEREMONY OF OPPOSITES, Century Media 77064-2P (1994) (Promotion release). Black Trip / Celebration Of The Fourth / Son Of Earth / 'Til We Meet Again … / Mask Of The Red Death / Baphomet's Throne / Flagellation / Crown / To Our Martyrs / Ceremony Of Opposites.

CEREMONY OF OPPOSITES, Century Media CD 77064-2 (1994). Black Trip / Celebration Of The Fourth / Son Of Earth / 'Til We Meet Again / Mask Of The Red Death / Baphomet's Throne / Flagellation / Crown / To Our Martyrs / Ceremony Of Opposites.

Rebellion EP, Century Media 770992 (1995). Rebellion / After The Sepulture / Into The Pentagram / I Love The Dead / Static Journey.

PASSAGE, Century Media CD 77127-2 (1996). Rain / Shining Kingdom / Angel's Decay / My Saviour / Jupiterian Vibe / The Ones / Liquid Souls / Moonskin / Born Under Saturn / Chosen Race / A Man In Your Head.

EXODUS, Century Media 77210-2 (1998). Exodus / Tribes Of Cain / Son Of Earth / Winter Solstice / Ceremony Of The Opposites / From Malkuth To Kether.

ETERNAL, Century Media 771852 (1999). Year Zero / Ailleurs / Together / Ways / The Cross / Us / Supra Karma / I / Nautilus And Zeppelin / Infra Galaxia / Berg / Radiant Star.

Telepath, Regain RR057CDS (2004). Telepath / Inch'Allah / Telepathic (Remix) / Inch'Allah (Karaoke version) / Telepathic (Instrumental version).

REIGN OF LIGHT, Regain RR055CD (2004). Moongate / Inch Allah / High Above / Reign Of Light / On Earth / Telepath / Oriental Dawn / As The Sun / Further / Heliopolis / Door Of Celestial Peace. Chart positions: 66 SWITZERLAND, 153 FRANCE.

On Earth, Regain RR061CD (2005). On Earth (Album version) / I Feel You / On Earth (Northern Summer mix) / Auf der Erde / Telepath (Video) / On Earth (Live in Paris).

ERA ONE, Century Media 776252 (2006). Era One / Universal Soul / Sound Of Galaxies / Beyond / Night Ride / Diamond's Drops / Home / Voyage / Above As Below / Koh-I-Noor / Connection / Reading Mind / Red Onction / Flying High / Overcome / Inside Stairs / One With Everything / Silent Words / Wealth And Fortune.

SOLAR SOUL, Nuclear Blast NB 1898-2 (2007). Solar Soul / Promised Land / Slavocracy / Western Ground / On The Rise / Alliance / Suspended Time / Valkyries' New Ride / Ave! / Quasar Waves / Olympus.

SAMMATH NAUR

BYDGOSZCZ, POLAND — *Levan (vocals), Sigmar (guitar), Valeo (guitar), Tas (bass), Demetrius (keyboards), Lestath (drums).*

Bydgoszcz Black / Death outfit fronted by Levan of GRAVE OF SHADOWS. Guitarist Sigmar is ex-LEGIONS OF DEATH, second guitarist Valeo is active with MORTIS DEI, bassist Tas is ex-LAND OF ANGER whilst drummer Lestath is another LEGIONS OF DEATH member. The band was founded by the guitar duo of Sigmar and Saturnus during 1999, with Uzurpator of LEGIONS OF DEATH taking on vocals and Lestath the drums. However, this first unit soon fractured with both Saturnus and Uzurpator exiting. New blood would be found by drawing in SECOND TEMPTER and DEMOGORGON guitarist Tempter (a.k.a. Jarek "Ziomal" Ziółkowski), keyboard player Demetrius and bassist Morgoth.

In November of 2001 Saturnus returned in the lead vocal role to record the album 'The Wall Of Sleep'. A projected 2002 follow up, to be entitled 'The Forever War', was delayed by line up problems. First Saturnus left once again, forcing SAMMATH NAUR to undertake gigs as an instrumental act, then Morgoth departed too. Valeo filled the bass vacancy before switching to guitar. Levan would be inducted as new singer to complete 'The Forever War' sessions. In 2003 the SAMMATH NAUR credited Jarek Ziółkowski joined LICH GATE.

SAMMATH NAUR co-headlined the November 2004 'Extreme Blast Attack' tour of Poland alongside DECEPTION, EFFECT MURDER and PENTHAUSE. Valeo joined VESANIA in August 2005.

The band formed up the Polish 'Rebel Angels' tour in April 2007 featuring DARZAMAT, CRIONICS and HATE.

THE FOREVER WAR, Sammath Naur (2004). Enemy Of The Sun / The March Of Liberators / The Forever War (Part I) / The Forever War (Part II) / Rise Of The Five Winds / True Mankind Desire.

SANATORIUM

ZILINA, SLOVAKIA — *Martin Belobrad (vocals / bass), Onecque (guitar), Dzordz (drums).*

Zilina based SANATORIUM are not only the leading Death Metal force in Slovakia but their frontman Martin Belobrad is the prime motivator behind Erebos Productions as well as acting as tour promoter for international Metal acts touring the country. The band originated in Žilina during 1991 as a project of guitarist Onecque and Stasho. By 1994 the band unit, having gone through many changes settled at Martin Belobrad on vocals and bass, guitarists Onecque and Warmo with Alky on the drums and in May of that year SANATORIUM put in their first live concert.

SANATORIUM arrived with a 1995 demo cassette 'Subculture' followed by 'Autumn Shadows'. This second tape would be re-issued by Czech label View Beyond on a 7" single in May of 1997. A third demo 'Necrologue' emerged in 1998. A line up change saw Milan taking over the drum position at this juncture. Their 1999 album 'Arrival Of The Forgotten Ones' was ably promoted by a run of European dates allied with FLESHLESS and American's LIVIDITY. After these dates Warmo exited and SANATORIUM opted to persevere as a trio for a second leg of shows as support to CENTINEX traversing Europe in November. With these gigs at a conclusion Dzordz took over from Milan as 2000 brought yet more live work as guests to SEPSISM in March.

SANATORIUM's 2001 album saw a guest vocal performance from Miroslav of GOREOPSY. Live dates had the band partnered on the road in March with Mexicans DISGORGE and in the Autumn with Sweden's SOILS OF FATE. The band signed to the New York based Sevared imprint for 2003's 'Goresoaked Reincarnation' album, this outing including a cover version of SINISTER's 'Bastard Saints'.

2004 shows had the band allied with DISMEMBER, PSYCROPTIC and ANATA for a full European tour commencing 3rd November in Nürnberg, Germany.

Fetus Rape EP, Forensick (1993) (Limited edition 1500 copies). Oral Fistfuck / Violent Intercourse / Fetus Rape / Goresoaked Reincarnation / In Capture Of Necrophile Visions / Killing.

Autumn Shadows, View Beyond (1997). Tears / In The Dawn Of Time / Autumn Shadows / Strange Primeval Maze Of Souls / Sexual Intercourse Of Demons.

ARRIVAL OF THE FORGOTTEN ONES, Erebos Productions ERE011 (1999). Throne Of The Undead / Necrologue Written In Forest / Race Of The Dimension Unknown / Diseases Awareness Of Reality / Cemetery Of Memories / Guardians Of Deceitful Dawn / Evolution Of Decay / Autumn Shadows / Red Moon / Minulost.

INTERNAL WOMB CANNABALISM, Forensick (2001). Symptoms / Postmortal Gorephobia / Killing / That Cunts Name Is Heather / Intravenous Ejaculation / Penis Epidermis Inflammation / The False Prophet / Bovine Spongiform Encephalopathy / Dunwich Morgue / Dead Virgin Whore / Internal Womb Cannibalism / Final Goremageddon.

GORESOAKED REINCARNATION, Sevared SR005 (2003). Intro / In Capture Of Necrophile Visions / Goresoaked Reincarnation / Consumption Of Remnants Of A Miscarriage / Deeds Of Pedophile / Orgasm Of 7—Year Old Girl Breached By Pneumatic Drill / Purification Of Soul Through Disfiguration Of Body / Outro / Bastard Saints.

SANCTIFICATION

ÖSTERSUND, SWEDEN — *Mathias Mohlin (vocals), Tomas Elofsson (guitar), Marcus Edvardsson (guitar), Nils Fjällström (drums).*

Östersund's SANCTIFICATION, spawned in the Summer of 2001 by members from the late DIVINE DESECRATION and drummer Nils Fjällström from CHASTISEMENT, ODHINN, SOULDRAINER and AEON, deal in brutal, blasphemic Death Metal. The initial formation would also count guitarist Daniel Dlimi of AEON and THE EQUINOX OV THE GODS, PROSERPHINE guitarist Tomas Elofsson and singer Mathias Mohlin. Dlimi would decamp in late 2001 in order to prioritise AEON.

SANCTIFICATION cut their debut demo in November of 2001, after which Peter Jönsson was introduced on bass guitar. The band would debut on the live front during the Spring of 2002 at the Old Courthouse in Östersund. However, with Jönsson unable to commit Jörgen Bylander of DEFACED CREATION and DERANGED took over bass duties for this concert whilst Daniel Dlimi also made a brief return on guitar.

SANCTIFICATION would add CHASTISEMENT and SOULDRAINER guitarist Marcus Edvardsson in 2003. That same year, maintaining his SANCTIFICATION post, Fjällström joined IN BATTLE. Ex-member Daniel Dlimi followed the lead into IN BATTLE in 2004. Tomas Elofsson would also be making a name for himself as a member of GOD AMONG INSECTS, and would also join IN BATTLE during September.

The band issued the debut album 'Misantropic Salvation' for Remission Records. September saw a valuable support date to CANNIBAL CORPSE in Trondheim, Norway.

2006 witnessed the formation of neo-Thrash Metal act ENDLESS TORTURE, a union between Marcus Edvardsson, A*TEEM vocalist Peter Mellgren plus Tom Åsvold, from PAINCRAZE and DIMENSION34, on drums.

Sanctification, Sanctification (2002) (Demo). Misantropic Salvation / Summoning The Ancient One's / Untitled (Instrumental) / Untitled (Instrumental).
Promo '04, Sanctification (2004) (Demo). Thirst For Blood / Untitled / New World Order (Live) / Summoning The Ancient Ones (Live).
MISANTHROPIC SALVATION, Remission RMR 006 (2004). Unleashing The Demons / Haunted / Summoning The Ancient Ones / Slay Christianity / New World Order / Into Our Torment We Dwell / Consumed By Life / Misanthropic Salvation / Feed Upon Christian Souls / Supreme Pain / Necrolord / Disembowelment.

SANCTIMONY

RIGA, LATVIA — *Jânis Bolsaks (vocals), Viesturs Grīnbergs (guitar), Jânis Aizkalns (guitar), Denis Denisenko (bass), Kārlis Jakubonis (drums).*

Riga's Death n' Roll mob SANCTIMONY, established during 1994, released the July 1996 demo 'When The Sun Was God' through Phoenix Studio. Formative band members would include Jānis Levists and the SKYFORGER credited Rihards on guitar, plus bassists Sergey, of HUSKVARN, DISTANT LIGHT and NEGLECTED FIELDS, and Ugis. Father Productions released the Jānis Levits produced album 'Eternal Suffering' in 1999. That same year the group introduced new members former BRUTE CHANT guitarist Jānis Aizkalns and bassist Denis Denisenko, also member of PRETERNATURAL. Demos were cut in 2001, but not released to the public, and a follow up, two track session emerged in 2003.

Drummer Kārlis Jakubonis is also a member of NEGLECTED FIELDS. SANCTIMONY credited vocalist Ruslan would join FLAYING. Although he departed this act in 2004 another SANCTIMONY member, guitarist Viesturs Grīnbergs, subsequently joined the same outfit. SANCTIMONY grabbed the honours of opening for both DISMEMBER and WHITESNAKE on home turf during 2004. The following year further notable supports included shows with ENTOMBED and JUDAS PRIEST.

Platforma Records issued SANCTIMONY's second album, 'Devil And Men' recorded at Sound Division Studio, in June 2005. This set included cover version's of THE POLICE's 'Synchronicity II' and BLACK SABBATH's 'The Void'. The band's third opus, 'Hell In Stereo' sporting a rendition of AC/DC's 'Back In Black' and laid down in May 2006 at Wolk recordings studio in Riga, arrived in February 2007 via Aghast Records.

When The Sun Was God, Phoenix Studio (1996) (Demo). Intro / First Cross / Eternal Suffering / Kas Tie Tädi, Kas Dziedāja / The Castle Mound / March Of The Knight / The Lost.
ETERNAL SUFFERING, Father Productions (1999). Christ Church / The Castle Mound / Autumn / The Lost / Eternal Suffering / The Pray / First Cross / Quark and Sanctimony Orchestra- Satan Fallus.
Sanctimony, Sanctimony (2003) (Demo). Super Hero / Devil And Men.
DEVIL AND MEN, Platforma (2005). Devil And Men / Lover / Living In Hell / Gone / Super Hero / Being Called Disaster / Criminal / Sounds / Back Down / A Dollar Story / Synchronicity II / Into The Void.
HELL IN STEREO, Aghast (2007). Toyman / Heading Mexico / Runaway / Demons Ways / Lord Of Scum / A Call For Rock / Nightmare / Madman's Enemy / Monsters / Final Pain / Thrill / Pleasure Dome / Back In Black.

SANGUINARY

HOLLAND — *Alex Fridricks (vocals), Steven Gerrits (guitar), Bert Dijkhuis (bass), Arie Dijkhuis (drums).*

Groningen Death Metal. Forged during early 1995 SANGUINARY's first line up included vocalist Alex Fridricks, guitarists Bert Dijkhuis and Bas, bass player Roelf with drums from Arie Dijkhuis. Prior to the band's inauguration gig in 1998 Bas departed. A promotion tape was cut in 1999 after which Roelf too left. Herman took on the bass role and Steven Gerrits that of second guitar. This version of the band recorded the 'Bloody Death' demo of 2000.

SANGUINARY's demo 'Promo 2001' included a cover version of DEATH's 'Evil Dead'. In June of 2002 Gerrits decamped in order to found NEONBLACK. His place would be taken by Mark but within a matter of weeks Gerrits made a return, ousting his replacement.

GUTTED- THE FINAL ASSAULT..., (2002). From Hell / Auto-da-fé / Sturmtiger / Bleeding / Division Death / Faceless Death / Aftermath.

SARCASM

SWEDEN — *Heval Bozarslan (vocals), Fredrik Wallenberg (guitar), Dave Janney (bass), Henrik Forslund (drums).*

SARCASM was one of Sweden's more illustrious and elusive of Death Metal names. Founded in October of 1990 by vocalist Heval Bozarslan and guitarist Fredrik Wallenberg. This duo was soon joined by bass player Dave Janney and drummer Henrik Forslund to complete the line up for the 1992 'In Hate' demo.

Within months another tape surfaced suitably entitled 'Dark'. By late 1993 Forslund switched instruments over to guitar and SARCASM drafted Oscar Karlsson on the skins. Now a quintet the group released a third promotional cassette 'A Touch Of The Burning Red Sunset'.

SARCASM would undergo line up turbulence as Wallenberg departed to be supplanted by Anders Erikkson for the recording of the debut album 'Burial Dimensions'. However, the ructions within the band would stall its release and SARCASM duly split. Oskar Karlsson made a significant impact upon the Swedish Metal scene as a member of SCHEITAN, GATES OF ISHTAR, THE DUSKFALL and DEFLESHED.

Despite achieving no commercial release SARCASM's reputation remained and in 1999 the American Breath Of Night label would issue the demos on CD format titled 'A Touch Of The Burning Red Sunset'.

SARCASM would reform with reformed with Bozarslan, Janney and Eriksson joined by Simon Winroth.

Dark, Sarcasm (1993) (Demo). Neverafter / You Bleed (I Enjoy).
Sarcasm, Sarcasm (1993) (Unreleased demo). Through Tears Of Gold / Scattered Ashes / Never For Your God / For Those Who Lied.
A Touch Of The Burning Red Sunset, Sarcasm (1994) (Demo). Dark / Upon The Mountains Of Glorious End / Through Tears Of Gold / A Touch Of The Burning Red Sunset.
A TOUCH OF THE BURNING RED SUNSET, Breath Of Night BON4CD (1998). Dark / Upon The Mountains Of Glory / Through The Tears Of God / Never After / You Bleed (I Enjoy) / Nail Her Up / Pile Of Bodies / In Hate ... / A Touch Of The Burning Red Sunset.
Scattered Ashes, Danza Ipnotica BUIO 004 (2000) (7" vinyl picture disc). Scattered Ashes / Pile Of Bodies.
In Hate ..., Sarcasm (2002) (Demo). Nail Her Up / Pile Of Bodies / In Hate ....

SARCOFAGO

BRAZIL — *Wagner Lamounier (vocals / guitar), Gerald Minelli (bass), M. Joker (drums).*

An esteemed veteran act on the South American Death Metal scene. The Satanically inspired SARCOFAGO employ Death Metal with distinct Punk leanings allied to blasphemous lyrics. Rather alarmingly guests on the 'Rotting' album included Oswaldo Pussy Ripper and Eugenio Dead Zone. Adverts for the album announced "Formed by Wagner Antichrist who left SEPULTURA because they were too commercial!"

SARCOFAGO debuted with the 1986 demo 'Satanic Lust' leaving no pretensions as to which musical direction the band was headed. The equally to the point demos 'The Black Vomit' and 'Christ's Death' ensued upfront of the first full length album 'I.N.R.I.'.

For 1991's 'The Laws Of Scourge' the band comprised of vocalist / guitarist Wagner 'Antichrist' Lamounier, guitarist Fabio Jhosko, bass player Gerald 'Incubus' Minelli and drummer Lucio Olliver. OVERDOSE mainman Claidio David would provide backing vocals. The following year Finnish Black Metal outfit IMPALED NAZARENE cut a cover version of 'The Black Vomit' on their 'Goat Perversion' EP.

SARCOFAGO were still an active concern in 2000 delivering the uncompromising as ever 'Crust' EP. In 2004 the legacy of the 'I.N.R.I.' debut was strengthened as Nuclear War Now Productions issued a limited edition picture disc vinyl album, this issue adding extra tracks taken from the 'Warfare Noise I' compilation. The first 300 of these pressings came packaged as a "die hard" edition in a different sleeve, including poster, booklet, sticker and patch. That same year the band would have their classic cut 'Satanic Lust' chosen as a pioneering piece of music for a compilation assembled by DARKTHRONE drummer Fenriz, released through Peaceville Records and entitled 'Fenriz Presents The Best Of Old School Black Metal'.

I.N.R.I, Cogumelo (1987). Satanic Lust / Desecration Of Virgin / Nightmare / I.N.R.I. / Christ's Death / Satanas / Ready To Fuck / Deathrash / The Last Slaughter / Recrucify / The Black Vomit.
ROTTING, Cogumelo (1989). The Lust / Alcoholic Coma / Tracy / Rotting / Sex, Drinks And Metal / Nightmare.
THE LOST TAPES OF COGUMELO, Cogumelo (1990).
THE LAWS OF SCOURGE, Under One Flag CDFLAG 66 (1990). The Laws Of Scourge / Piercings / Midnight Queen / Screeches From The Silence / Prelude To A Suicide / The Black Vomit / Secrets Of A Window / Little Julie / Crush, Kill, Destroy.
HATE, Cogumelo (1995). Intro / Song For My Death / Pact Of Cum / The God's Faeces / Satanic Terrorism / Orgy Of Flies / Hate / The Phantom / Rhabdovirus (The Pitbull's Curse) / Anal Vomit / The Beggar's Uprising.
DECADE OF DECAY, Cogumelo (1996). The Loss Of Innocence / Orgy Of Flies / Hate / The God's Faeces / Song For My Death / Midnight Queen / Screeches From The Silence / Piercings / Crush, Kill, Destroy / Nightmare / Rotting / I.N.R.I. / Desecration Of Virgin / Recrucify / The Black Vomit / Satanic Lust / Christ's Death / The Anal Rape Of God / Satanas / Third Slaughter.
THE WORST, Cogumelo (1997). The End (Intro) / The Worst / Army Of The Damned / God Bless The Whores / Plunged In Blood / Satanic Lust / The Necrophiliac / Shave Your Head / Purification Process.
Crust EP, (2000). Sonic Images Of The New Millennium Decay / Day Of The Dead / F.O.M.B.M. (Fuck Off The Melodic Black Metal) / Crust.

SARCOPHAGUS

DE KALB, IL, USA — *Andrew Jay Harris (vocals / guitar), Daniel Guenther (guitar), Marcus Matthew Kolar (bass), Duane Timlin (drums).*

Blasphemous Death Metal band SARCOPHAGUS are in fact yet another outlet for the creative forces of Andrew Jay Harris, more commonly known as Akhenaten of JUDAS ISCARIOT and WELTMACHT alongside Lord Imperial of KRIEG. Harris also owns Breath Of Night Records and has issued the one off JESUS FUCKING CHRIST single 'Unalive At Golgotha'.

Debuted with the demo 'Cursed Are The Dead' in 1991. At this point the band comprised of Harris, bassist Marcus Matthew Kolar, vocalist Frank Drago, guitarist Michael Matejka and drummer Paul Bruneau. A stream of demos followed including 'Sarcophagus' in 1993 (bootlegged on a 7" single the following year), 'Der Ubermensch' and 'Apathy' in 1995. By 1994 though SARCOPHAGUS was down to a duo of Harris and Kolar.

A projected album on the Interment label to be titled 'Thirteen Songs' was announced but never released. 1997 saw SARCOPHAGUS up to full band strength with the enlistment of guitarist Daniel Guenther and FOREST OF IMPALED drummer Duane Timlin.

One of Harris' side concerns WELTMACHT also includes Timlin under the pseudonym of Cryptic Winter.

Akhenaten would relocate to Germany for later JUDAS ISCARIOT releases and would also become live bass player for the infamous Czech Black Metal act MANIAC BUTCHER. Bassist Marcus Kolar loaned himself out to NACHTMYSTIUM on a session basis in November of 2001 to participate in that band's debut live performance.

FOR WE ... WHO ARE CONSUMED BY DARKNESS, Pulverizer (1996). Godless / Our Black Autumn / Die Totenmaske / Fuck Pig / Agony's Tale / Wrath / Damned Below Judas / Si Piangiamo Or Dunque Uniti / Breath Of Night.
SARCOPHAGUS- DEADNOISE- UBERMENSCH, Pulverizer (1996). Sarcophagus / Human Machines / Morbid Dreams / Banned From The Altar / From The Cross / Masquerade / Mental Atrocities / Black / The Absence / Die Totenmaske / Fuck Pig / Si Piangiamo Or Dunque Uniti / Ubermensch.
REQUIEM TO THE DEATH OF PASSION, Nightfall (1997). From The Ruin Of Paradise / The Dark Lord Of Impurity / Requiem To The Death Of Passion / In Silent Death / Of Fire Surrounding All The Heavens / Bastard Sons Of Ignorance / Infernal Supremacy / The Pagan Battlefield.

SARGATANAS REIGN

NORRKÖPING, SWEDEN — *Jonas Mattson (vocals), Kristoffer Andersson (guitar), Marcus Lundberg (guitar), Niklas Samuelsson (bass), Stefan Kronqvist (drums).*

Norrköping Black / Death act assembled during 1997 by the trio of guitarist Ushatar (a.k.a. Kristoffer Andersson) and Marcus Lundberg with 'Vrashtar' (a.k.a. Stefan Kronqvist) of DARK REALM and ANGST on the drums. Lundberg had prior involvement with ANTIPATHY, MORTUUM and UNTRINITY. Initially billed simply as SARGATANAS the group added the 'Reign' appellation as the musical style drifted into Death Metal territory. Demos in 1998 included 'Sargatanas', recorded by Ushatar, Vrashtar, Lundberg and bassist Johan 'Jojje' Ericsson, and 'Satanic Hymns'. This second session was laid down by the duo of Ushatar and Vrashtar.

Signing to I Hate Records the band bowed in commercially with a March 2001 EP entitled 'Hellucination'. In 2002 the group enrolled the ALLEGIANCE, CARDINAL SIN, PAIN, GRAVITY, DEAR MUTANT and OVERFLASH and MARDUK veteran Magnus 'Devo' Andersson as lead vocalist and the ANTIPATHY, U-238 and SHADOWS OF GRIEF credited Niklas Samuelsson on bass. The group debuted that year with the 'Euthanasia ... Last Resort' album. Vinyl versions, limited to 525 copies,

SARGATANAS REIGN

added an extra track in a cover version of G.G. ALLIN's "Highest Power'.

The SARGATANAS REIGN duo of guitarist Kristoffer Andersson and bassist Niklas Samuelsson would form up part of the resurrected CARDINAL SIN during 2003. That same year Kristoffer Andersson forged the LAUG TIMOR project in collaboration with former EMPERIOUS guitarist Johan Jönsson.

Magnus Andersson was ousted in April 2004, being swiftly replaced by Jonas Mattsson. Later that year SARGATANAS REIGN signed a deal with Blooddawn Productions/Regain Records, entering Endarker studio in Norrköping with producer Devo Andersson to cut the album 'Bloodwork'.

SARGATANAS REIGN parted ways with bassist Niklas Samuelsson in January 2006. Singer Jonas Mattsson duly took on bass duties. Kristoffer Andersson joined THE LEGION in June. The networking continued in September, with both Jonas Mattson and Marcus Lundberg enrolling into the ranks of ELIZIUM.

The God Below, Sargatanas Reign (1998) (Demo). Intro / The God Below / Sargatanas / I Am / La Voisin.

Satanic Hymns, Sargatanas Reign (1998) (Demo). The Dead Can't Rest / We Have Won The War / Sargatanas / I Speak For Him / I Am / Into Battle.

Sargatanas, Sargatanas Reign (1998) (Demo). Eternal Eclipse / A Carnage In Heaven / Satans Well / Suicide, Art Of Beauty / Outro.

Hellucination, I Hate IHATE 001 (2001) (7" vinyl EP). Hellucination / Amon / Twist The Knife In Christ / Evangelical Clitorial.

EUTHANASIA ... LAST RESORT, I Hate IHATE CD 002 (2002) (CD release). Killing Spree Supreme / In Pain / Drowning / Euthanasia / Last Resort / Hate / Evangelical Clitorial / Epicedium / Modus Operandi / Amon.

EUTHANASIA ... LAST RESORT, IHATE LP 002 (2002) (Vinyl album limited to 525 copies). Killing Spree Supreme / In Pain / Drowning / Euthanasia / Last Resort / Hate / Evangelical Clitorial / Epicedium / Modus Operandi / Amon / Highest Power.

BLOODWORK, Blooddawn BLOOD 021 (2005). Preface / Techniques Of Torture / Chaos Theory / Sliver / Come Greet Me Crawlers / Hellnation / Blood Katharsis / The "Parnassus" Journal / Blindfolded / Kevlar Throat.

SARPANITUM

BIRMINGHAM, UK — *Dan Lowndes (vocals), Andy Techakosit (vocals / bass), Tom Innocente (guitar), Tom Hyde (guitar).*

Birmingham Death Metal band SARPANITUM featured the TENEBROUS AEON trio of vocalist / bassist Andy Techakosit, guitarist Tom Hyde and drummer Barry French. Heavily influenced by ancient Mesopotamian and Sumerian mythological themes the band debuted with the 2003 demo 'The Agushaya Hymn', these sessions recorded by the founding duo of Techakosit and guitarist Jack Galbraith, both formerly of TREPHINED. Techakosit also held affiliations with DARK EARTH and MENSTRUAL GNAW. University studies then intervened and the project was put on hold. However, Techakosit later joined TENEBROUS AEON but with this band folding in July of 2004 he, bringing along Hyde and French, re-founded SARPANITUM, adding Tom Innocente of SERPENS, MORTHVARGR and PHANTOM on guitar.

French decamped in September of 2004. SARPANITUM would enroll new lead singer Dan Knowles, ex-DISEMBOWELLED and STILLBORN DECAY as well as also holding credits with IMINDAIN in October. Techakosit, in the guitar role, also proved active with ENSANGUINED whilst Hyde participates with SPOILT.

The Agushaya Hymn, Sarpanitum (2003). The Agushaya Hymn: Chapter I / The Agushaya Hymn: Chapter II.

SATANIC SLAUGHTER

LINKÖPING, SWEDEN — *Andreas Deblén (vocals), Ztephan Dark (guitar), Stefan Johansson (guitar), Fille Carlsson (bass), Martin Axenrot (drums).*

Linköping's SATANIC SLAUGHTER is one of Scandinavia's older Black Death Metal acts having formed in 1985. Previous to this date the band went under the politically incorrect name of EVIL CUNT. Of the original line-up, only the ORCHRISTE credited guitarist Ztephan "Dark" Karlsson remains. Original bassist Goat became a pyromaniac and now reportedly resides in a mental hospital.

SATANIC SLAUGHTER's name was first felt on the Swedish Metal scene in 1985. Joining Ztephan Dark would be vocalist Moto Jacobsson, bassist Ron B. Goat and TOTAL DEATH drummer Pontus Sjösten. The second guitar position proved fluid, with Mikki Fixx, Jörgen Sjöström and Patrik Strandberg all serving terms in 1985. A second drummer was also installed that year in Peter Svedenhammar. SATANIC SLAUGHTER evolved in 1987 with the recruitment of Toxine (a.k.a. Tony Kampner) on guitar and drummer Mique. Both vocalist Toxine and drummer Mique had also been members of TOTAL DEATH whilst Mique had also been involved in MORGUE. Toxine would cut his teeth on the Rock scene with his debut Punk act PASSIVA MONGOLOIDER as far back as 1979.

The band evolved once again in rapid fashion, Dark drawing in new members Jonas Hagberg on guitar, Patrik Kulman as bassist with Robert Falstedt on the drums. The following year numbers were boosted with the addition of singer Andy Gustavsson and SATANIC SLAUGHTER released their demo 'One Night In Hell' during 1988.

SATANIC SLAUGHTER re-shaped again in 1989, the new cast comprising Dark, guitarist Janne Karlsson and bassist Peter Blomberg. Occupying the drum stool in 1989 would be Gerry Malmström and Evert Karlsson. Unfortunately, in December the band was put on ice as Dark was imprisoned, convicted of assault. The man would later join MORBIDITY, CRUZIFIED ANGEL and MORGUE. The band got back together in 1992 with members of SÉANCE, including vocalist Toxine, drummer Mique and guitarists Patrick Jensen and Richard Corpse were involved. A reunion concert took place at Linköping's Skylten venue, alongside SÉANCE, on 20th November 1994.

The self-titled debut album, recorded at Unisound studios and produced by Patrik Jensen, was issued in 1996 through Necropolis Records. Second effort 'Land Of The Unholy Souls', with production credits going to DAN SWANÖ, emerged in 1997. However, that same year SATANIC SLAUGHTER collapsed yet again, this time due to time honoured musical differences. Dark resolved himself to pick up the pieces with all the other ex-members creating the high profile act WITCHERY. Jensen also became a member of THE HAUNTED.

The band was re-constituted in 1997, introducing Filip Carlsson on guitar, a scene veteran of ANCIENT DIGGER OF GRAVES, DAISY CHAIN, THORNCLAD, HÖST, DEMONS TO PREFER,

SPITEFUL and CORPORATION 187, guitarist Kecke Ljungberg of MORGUE plus Robert Eng on drums, also holding credits with HÖST and CORPORATION 187, for a run of German gigs in April of 1998 alongside LORD BELIAL and HATOR. In 1999 SATANIC SLAUGHTER brought in former BLASPHEMOUS, MORGUE, COVEN and TRIUMPHATOR drummer Martin 'Axenroth' Axenroth (a.k.a. 'Demon Pounding Devestator' in NIFELHEIM) to replace Robert Eng.

The 2000 line-up comprised of Dark, Axenroth, guitarist Christian Ljungberg, vocalist Andreas Deblén and bassist Filip Carlsson. This unit, promoting the album 'Afterlife Kingdom' delivered by Loud n´Proud Records, toured across Europe in alliance with Norwegian act RAGNAROK in December. By the time the band were gearing up for a September 2002 album 'Banished To The Underworld' Stefan Johansson had taken Ljungberg's place on guitar. Further touring saw European gigs in April with road partners LORD BELIAL and CORPORATION 187.

Axenrot would also be found as a member of N.C.O. ('Nephenzy Chaos Order') for their 2003 opus 'Pure Black Disease'. The drummer added to his roster of official projects by joining the Blackheim and DAN SWANÖ mentored BLOODBATH in March of 2004. That November SATANIC SLAUGHTER toured Europe with support from fellow Swedes MISERICORDIA and Czech outfit AVENGER.

In August 2005 Martin Axenrot temporarily joined the ranks of OPETH for European touring, covering for regular drummer Martin López who was forced out due to medical concerns. SATANIC SLAUGHTER announced they were to reform in early 2006, Ztephan Dark, Stefan Johansson and Simon Axenrot being joined by new drummer Fredrik Nilsson of MISERICORDIA.

Ztephan Dark, suffering from a heart condition, died in April 2006.

Satanic Slaughter, Satanic Slaughter (1988) (Demo). Violent Massacre / One Night In Hell / Satanic Queen.
SATANIC SLAUGHTER, Necropolis NR004 (1995). Immortal Death / Forever I Burn / Dark Ritual / Into The Catacombs / Breath Of The Serpent That Rules The Cold World / On Black Wings / Nocturnal Presence / Legion Of Hades / Divine Exorcism / I'll Await My Lord / Embraced By Darkness / Domine Lucipheros.
LAND OF THE UNHOLY SOULS, Necropolis NR014 (1996). Intro / Hatred Of God / Servant Of Satan / Satanic Queen / Demons Feast / Forever I Burn / Legion Of Hades / Breath Of The Serpent That Rules The Cold World / Immortal Death / Land Of The Unholy Souls / One Night In Hell / Dark Ritual / Forever I Burn.
AFTERLIFE KINGDOM, Loud n' Proud LNP012 (2000). The Arrival—Afterlife Kingdom / Nocturnal Crimson Nightmare / When Darkness Prevails / Divine Repulsion / Through The Dark Profound / Autumn / Ad Noctum / Flag Of Hate.
BANISHED FROM THE UNDERWORLD, Black Sun BS 025 (2002). Bringers Of Armageddon / Banished From The Underworld / Dark Temptation / Towards Damnations End / Infernal / Antichrist / Apocalyptic War / One Night In Hell / Season Of Sorrow / Ending In Misery.

SATANIZED

GOTHENBURG, SWEDEN — *Per Alexandersson (vocals), Jon Nödtveidt (guitar), Johan Norman (guitar), Thomas Backelin (bass), Tobias Kellgren (drums).*

SATANIZED was a precursor to the infamous DISSECTION. The band released a single, two song demo in 1991 and performed a solitary gig that November. Guitarists Jon Nödtveidt, an ex-member of OPHTHALAMIA, THE BLACK and SIREN'S YELL, and Johan Norman, together with drummer Tobias Kellgren, then prioritised DISSECTION. Singer Per 'Goat' Alexandersson was to work with NIFELHEIM whilst bassist Thomas Backelin would figure as a member of DECAMERON and LORD BELIAL. Both Kellgren and Norman also featured in DECAMERON and SOULREAPER, the drummer also working with SEVENTH ONE whilst Norman would also donate his services to SACRAMENTUM and RUNEMAGICK.

The two SATANIZED demo tracks, 'Satanized' and 'Born In Fire', would feature on the retrospective DISSECTION release 'The Past Is Alive'. Kellgren joined up as touring member of IN FLAMES during October 2005, as regular drummer Daniel Svensson, awaiting the birth of his second child, sat out these shows.

Jon Nödtveidt closed his career in a manner befitting his philosophies, committing suicide in August. DISSECTION band members released a statement claiming "he was more focussed, happier and stronger than ever" and "he chose to end his life by his own hands. As a true Satanist he led his life in the way he wanted and ended it when he felt that he had fulfilled his self-created destiny".

Nödtveidt, 31 years old, was found dead at his apartment in Hässelby, a suburb of Stockholm, on August 16th. Newspapers reported he had surrounded himself by candles and had a copy of Anton La Vey's 'The Satanic Bible'. Nödtveidt had ended his life with a shot to the head. Shortly beforehand he had told friends he was "going to Transylvania".

Satanized, Satanized (1991) (Demo). Satanized / Born In Fire.

SATARIEL

SWEDEN — *Pär Johansson (vocals), Mikael Grankvist (guitar), Magnus Alakangas (guitar / keyboards), Mikael Degerman (bass), Robert Sundelin (drums).*

SATARIEL was a 1993 union of erstwhile members of defunct outfits BEHEADED and DAWN OF DARKNESS namely vocalist Pär Johansson on vocals, guitarist Magnus Alakangas and bassist Mikael Degerman. A later recruit was guitarist Mikael Grankvist for the debut demo 'This Heavens Fall'. SATARIEL added Mats Ömalm after this recording but his exit followed swiftly after.

1995 also saw the departure of Grankvist. Further changes apparent on the second session 'Hellfuck' included the addition of guitarist Fredrik Andersson and drummer Andreas Nilzon. By 1996 Nilzon was out of the picture and Robert Sundelin of NECROMICON took the drum stool position. However, SATARIEL was put on ice for a lengthy period when both Sundelin and Degerman undertook their military service. When SATARIEL reformed Grankvist too was back in the fold for the debut album 'Lady Lust Lilith' on Pulverized Records. That same year found Sundelin taking on extracurricular drum duties with DEATHBOUND.

SATARIEL guitarist Mikael Grankvist also operates in THE MOANING. Johansson also spent time with SOULASH, a band founded by GATES OF ISHTAR guitarist Mikael Sandorf. However, he would exit this formation before their name switch to THE DUSKFALL.

Between 1993 and 1995 Johansson also put time into his side project BELSEMAR releasing the demos 'De Svarta Gudarnas Sömn' and 'Epistles Of Pain'. Allied with NECROPHOBIC and IMPIOUS, the band toured mainland Europe in January of 2003. Pär Johansson and Mikael Degerman were to be found as a participant in the Death / Thrash formation TORCHBEARER that same year, a collaboration between SOLAR DAWN, UNMOORED and SATARIEL personnel.

SATARIEL entered Dug Out Studios in Uppsala in late March utilising the production team of Daniel Bergstrand and erstwhile MISERY LOVES CO. guitarist Örjan Örnkloo to record their third album 'Hydra' for Greece's Black Lotus Records. However, this alliance did not produce results and a full year later the band switched labels to Cold Records.

Thy Heavens Fall, Satariel (1993) (Demo). Intro—The Winds Of Witchcraft / Dark Are All Paths—The Burden / Drowning In The Stream Of Memories / God Of Eternal Lands—Drowning Part II / Desecration Black—Rape The Holy Heavens / Outro—Thy Heavens Fall.
Desecration Black, Satariel (1994) (Demo). Desecration Black.

SATARIEL (pic: Andreas Wallström)

Hellfuck Demo 95, Satariel (1995) (Demo). Four Moons Till Rising / Hellfuck / Violent Dance / Yet To Be / Into The Void.

Promo 96, Satariel (1996) (Demo). The Great Necropolis—Bahomet Erected / The Well Of The Artist / A Vision Of An Ending.

LADY LUST LILITH, Pulverised ASH 005 CD (1998). Devils Dozen XIII / The Well Of The Artist / Four Moons Till Rising / The Span Of The Shadows / Lady Lust Lilith / The Great Necropolis—Baphomet Erected / Behind What's I / They're Sheep To Be Slain / A Vision Of An Ending / Greeting Immortality.

Promo 2000, Satariel (2000) (Demo). Betrayer Love / Devil At My Shoulder / Doveshooter / Stranger World.

PHOBOS AND DAIMOS, Hammerheart HHR089 (2002). Sodomy Eve / Coffin Gateways / Stranger World / The Claim / Betrayer Love / The Sun Is Grey / Holy Trinity / Death Come Cover Me / Zenithal Man / Doveshooter / Greater Than God.

HYDRA, Regain RR069 (2005). The Freedom Fall / Be You Angel, Be You Beast / Claw The Clouds / Vengeance Is Hers / For Galaxies To Clash / The Springwise / Scattering The Timeweb / 300 Years Old / Nihil Juggernaut / No God Lovers.

Chifra, Pulverised ASH 019 MCD (2006). Hogtied Angel / Slithering / Chifra / Flies Halo / Hogtied Angel (Video).

SATURNUS

COPENHAGEN, DENMARK — *Thomas A.G. Jensen (vocals), Kim Larsen (guitar), Brian Hansen (bass), Anders Ro Nielsen (keyboards), Jesper Saltoft (drums / keyboards).*

A Copenhagen Doom / Death band initially titled ASSESINO. The band can trace its history back to the 1991 union of vocalist Thomas A.G. Jenson, guitarists Kim Sindahl and Christian Brenner, bass player Brian Hansen and drummer Pouli Choir as ASSESINO. The band actually split but reunited with fresh recruit Jesper Saltoft. A period of flux ensued with Sindahl decamping and guitarist Michael Andersen and keyboard player Anders Ro Nielsen being drafted. At this stage the unit opted for the new title of SATURNUS.

1994 saw the inclusion of guitarist Kim Larsen and the following year the exit of Andersen. A support gig to Britain's Doom mongers MY DYING BRIDE made a weighty impression on the band who acknowledge their shift in style to a gloomy, melancholic style from this juncture.

SATURNUS cut their debut album 'Paradise Belongs To You' for the Euphonious label which included new drummer Morten Skrubbeltrang. Promoting the album SATURNUS ambitiously employed an 8 piece choir for live gigs.

After a Flemming Rasmussen produced mini album 'For The Loveless Lonely Nights', which included live material culled from the band's 1997 'Roskilde' festival performance, a switch in drummers had Peter Poulsen joining in time for the Flemming Rasmussen produced 'Martyre' album.

SATURNUS suffered further internal strife in 1999 with new enlistees being PUSH drummer Morten Plenge, former GOTHIC DOMAIN guitarist Tais Pedersen and bassist Peter Heede.

Both Larsen and Nielsen sessioned on BLAZING ETERNITY's debut album of 2000. Nielsen also found time for a further project entitled OUT OF SIGHT. Plenge would join Power Metal band IRON FIRE in November 2000 for their 'On The Edge' album.

In 1999 Larsen decamped. The guitarist debuted his Folk influenced solo project OF THE WAND AND THE MOON with the 'Nighttime Nightryhmes' album which found SATURNUS drummer Jesper Saltoft as session guest. 'Emptiness, Emptiness, Emptiness' followed in 2001. Meantime Larsen, along with SATURNUS colleagues Hansen and Saltoft, also busied themselves with the Gothic Rock band THE LOVELESS. SATURNUS persevered with an ever fluctuating line-up which by September of 2001 stood at Thomas A.G. Jensen on vocals, guitarists Peter Poulsen and Tais Pedersen, bass player Lennart Jacobsen (joining in August 2001), Anders Ro Nielsen on keyboards and drummer Henrik Glass. The new rhythm section saw Glass being an erstwhile member of BEG TO DIFFER whilst Jacobsen held credits with SUSPECT, SYMPOSION and Black Metal unit MIDNATT. Jacobsen also busies himself with his other act ILLUMINOUS.

In early October 2005 SATURNUS recently entered Sweet Silence Studios in Denmark, working again with producer Flemming Rasmussen, to commence recording their third full-length album, 'Veronica Decides To Die', for Finland's Firebox Records. MERCYFUL FATE and FORCE OF EVIL guitarist Michael Denner contributed guest solos.

Saturnus, Saturnus (1994) (Demo). Limbs Of Crystal Clear / Beware Of The Atheist.

Paradise Belongs To You, Saturnus (1996) (Demo). Paradise Belongs To You / Pilgrimage Of Sorrow / Lament For This Treacherous World / The Underworld / Astral Dawn / As We Dance The Paths Of Fire Or Solace.

PARADISE BELONGS TO YOU, Euphonious PHONI005 (1996). Belongs To You / Christ Goodbye / As We Dance The Path Of Fire And Solace / Pilgrimage Of Sorrow / The Fall Of Nakkiel (Nakkiel Has Fallen) / Astral Dawn / I Love Thee / The Underworld / Lament For This Treacherous World.

For The Loveless Lonely Nights, Euphonious PHONI012 (1998). Starres / For Your Demons / Thou Art Free / Christ Goodbye (Live) / Rise of Nakkiel (Live) / Consecreation.

MARTYRE, Euphonious PHONI014 (2000). 7 / Inflame Thy heart / Empty handed / Noir / A Poem (Written In Moonlight) / Softly On The Path You Fade / Thou Art Free / Drown My Sorrow / Lost My Way / Loss (In Memoriam) / Thus My Heart Weepeth For Thee / In You Shinning Eyes.

Rehearsal Studio Tracks, Saturnus (2004) (Demo). All Alone / Embraced By Darkness / I Long / Murky Waters / Raven God / To The Dreams.

VERONICA DECIDES TO DIE, Firebox FIRECD033 (2006). I Long / Pretend / Descending / Rain Wash Me / All Alone / Embraced By Darkness / To The Dreams / Murky Waters.

SAXORIOR

GERMANY — *Matthias Eschrich (vocals / guitar), Kai Uwe Schneider (guitar), Uwe Vogt (bass), Frank Nitzsche (keyboards), Timo Pfeifer (drums).*

Dresden's SAXORIOR ('Saxon Warrior'), offering Pagan Black tinged Death Metal, was created in January of 1994 as a quartet comprising vocalist / guitarist Matthias Eschrich, guitarist Kai-Uwe Schneider, both ex-members of TITAN, bass player Uwe Vogt and drummer Dirk David. The band debuted in June that same year with the demo 'The First Fight'. Upon completion of these sessions Timo Pfeiffer from CORPSESS took over the drum role for the November 1995 self financed album 'Return From The Dark Side'. Having enrolled keyboard player Frank Nitzsche to thicken their live sound, gigging to promote the album witnessed valuable support slots to the likes of EMINENZ, BENEDICTION and ICED EARTH. An EP, 'Beyond Conceptions', followed in the Spring of 1996.

SAXORIOR busied themselves on the live circuit over the next two years, acting as openers to the likes of EISREGEN, DUNKELGRAFEN, RUTHLESS and ENSLAVED. New material then emerged with the inclusion of the track 'Burning Stone' on a G.U.C. compilation album in November of 1998. Impressed enough to sign the band, G.U.C. delivered the band's next album 'Portent Of Eternity' in 1999. However, line up changes marked the introduction of new drummer Michael Mann in May of 2000.

SAXORIOR returned with the 2001 'Saxot' opus', this album, although built up of Wagnerian conceptual pieces based upon ancient Germanic heroes Wittekind and Karl The Great, sporting an ambitious cover version of MIKE OLDFIELD's 'Tubular Bells'. SAXORIOR issued a limited edition, vinyl only album during 2003 entitled 'Von Rache Und Schmerz'. This outing, comprising live and studio tracks, included a cover rendition of AC/DC's 'For Those About To Rock' fronted by a guesting Gorgoroth from Australian act BALTAK. Signing to Battlegod Productions SAXORIOR set about recording a new album 'Never Ending Battles'.

RETURN FROM THE DARK SIDE, Independent (1995). ... From The Dark Side / Recommendation To Die / Compromise For Destruction / In Search Of Life / World Of Emptiness / August The Strong / Marching In Sorrow / Morbid Nightmares / Dropped By Justice / No Comment.
Beyond Conceptions, Independent (1996). In Relation Of Other Dimensions / Eyes Of Death / Hatred For Ignorance.
PORTENT OF ETERNITY, G.U.C. (1999). Arrival/Intro / One Step Into Eternity / Burning Stone / Hagen von Tronje / Einzug in Walhalla / Coma / In Memory / The Might Of Fire / Creatures Of Time / Leaving For Another World.
SAXOT, G.U.C. (2001). Welcome To Another World / Root Of Time / Misguided Promise / Battle Of Wittekind / Vicious Circle / Hic Nulla Pax / Fire Of Retaliation / Overture / Siegfried / Tubular Bells.
VON RACHE UND SCHMERZ, (2003) (Limited edition 500 copies). Schmerz / Rache / August The Strong / Eyes Of Death / For Those About To Rock / Intro (Live) / Siegfried (Live) / Hic Nulla Pax (Live) / Hatred For Ignorance (Live) / Tubular Bells (Live).
NEVER ENDING BATTLES, Battlegod Productions (2004). Disaster Is Coming / Never Ending War / Expiation / Reasons Of War / The Old Spruce In The Wolfsschlucht / Blade Of Revenge / Pain / Father / Dem Meister / For Those About To Rock.

SAYYADINA

SWEDEN — *Ove Wiksten (vocals), Jon Lindqvist (guitar), Andreas Eriksson (bass), Adde (drums).*

SAYYADINA, taking their band name from a character in the 'Dune' Sci-Fi novel, was formed in September of 2000 with a line up of VICTIMS and ACCURSED vocalist / guitarist Jon Lindqvist, BIRDFLESH bass player Andreas Eriksson along with SCAMP and I QUIT drummer Ove Wiksten. Having made their live debut at Kafé 44 in Stockholm during January 2001, cut fourteen studio tracks the following month. Five of these tracks emerged as their share of a split 7" single 'The Inevitable Truth' in union with BRUCE BANNER, Eriksson's other act, on the Sounds Of Betrayal label. Subsequent dates across Germany, Holland, Belgium, France and Switzerland saw the two parties on tour together that July. That same September a further ten songs were recorded at Sunlight Studio in Stockholm. Of these, six were featured on the 'Solace Denied' EP, 200 of which were manufactured in collectable clear vinyl, whilst two more songs were donated to the 'Polar Grinder' compilation album manufactured by Putrid Filth Conspiracy.

A third studio session, taking place in February 2002, generated material for the 'Swedish Assault' compilation through Relapse Records and a split 7" single allied with Japanese Thrash act NO VALUE. This release, pressed on both black and red vinyl, would be restricted to 500 copies. SAYYADINA booked an April 2002 with road partners SECOND THOUGHT but drummer Ove Wiksten suffered a sprained shoulder. To compensate, the band shifted Ove to the lead vocal position and drafted ex-BIRDFLESH, JIGSORE TERROR and DETHRONEMENT man Adde (a.k.a. Smattro Ansjovis Mitroulis) on the drums. Adde, maintaining his ties to SAYYADINA, would also subsequently enroll into the ranks of notorious Death Metal act GENERAL SURGERY.

SAYYADINA, together with CYNESS, toured Europe in January 2004. Quite incredibly the band shared a track on the July 2005 'Unlawful Grindcore Assembly' 7" split single issued by Nuclear Barbecue Party Records as a collaborative effort with EMBALMING THEATRE, PESTILENT DECAY, GATE, WATCH ME BURN, BLOODRED BACTERIA, MIERDA PARA TODOS, CARA DE MIL PUTASOS, FETUS EATERS, DEADFOOD, THE KILL, TU CARNE, WASTEOID, PINATA LAZER, UNHOLY GRAVE, GORED FACE, GODSTOMPER, KERUM, NUKEM, UNHOLY SEMEN, 2 MINUTADREKA and COPROPHAGIGS.

The band engaged in an extensive round of Scandinavian and European dates allied with ROTTEN SOUND, CAUSE FOR EFFECT and TOTAL DEVASTATION in early 2006.

In March 2007 Ove Wiksten laid down a set of retro-Punk tracks under the project title NICE IDIOT at Studio Garget, this union featuring FINGERSPITZENGEFÜHL and GENERAL SURGERY's Mikael Van Tuominen on lead vocals, FACE DOWN and GENERAL SURGERY man Joacim Carlsson on guitar plus MASSGRAV's Johan Norsebäck on bass.

The Inevitable Truth, Sounds Of Betrayal EIGHTH (2001) (Split EP with BRUCE BANNER). Nothing / Prozac Generation / The Revenge / The Awakening / Their Control.
Solace Denied, Sounds Of Betrayal THIRTEENTH (2002). Someday I Will Kill / Line Them Up / From Ashes / När Allting Faller / Black Rose / Med Livet Som Insats.
SWEDISH ASSAULT, Relapse RR 6556-2 (2002) (Split 2 CD with ASSEL, GENOCIDE SUPERSTAR, GADGET, BIRDFLESH and DISFEAR). Retaliation / Civilization / Automation / Compulsion / Stagnation / Confrontation / Outrage.
Sayyadina, Sounds Of Betrayal TWENTYSECOND (2003) (Split EP with NO VALUE. Limited edition 500 copies). Oppression / Future Digits / Razor Discipline / Solitude / Last Days Make The Least.
FEAR GAVE US WINGS, Sound Pollution (CD release) (2004). 18 Hrs / Dear Diary / Holy War / All This Fear / Under Ondskans Pupill / Homegrown Terrorism / Blind Och Döv Eller Bara Dum I Huvet? / Losing Faith / Civilized Control / Neglected / Proffs På Låtsas / Sick Of This World / Turned Inside Out / Three Strikes / Loss / Oppression / Bent Out Of Shape / Enjoy The Silence (While You Can) / Med Livet Som Insats.
Unlawful Grindcore Assembly, Nuclear Barbecue Party NBP010 (2005) (Split 7" single).

SCABBARD

CZECH REPUBLIC — *Alex (vocals / bass), Pavel (guitar), Libor (guitar), Sura (drums).*

Having been a part of the defunct Czech bands BASTARDS and INVAR, assorted members of these bands grouped together under the SCABBARD banner in 1992 and recorded the 'Soudny Den' demo in October of that year. A second tape, 'Nonsense War', surfaced five months later. Two demo tracks, 'Holy Demagogy' and 'Raped', subsequently turned up on a compilation album as the group toured with KRABATHOR and DARKSIDE.

In June 1994 the group added new vocalist Marek, previously with D.M.C. Returning to the studio in order to record a third demo ('Better To Die'), SCABBARD would evolve from a brutal Death Metal package into something a little more melodically inclined. However, Marek was replaced by Petr after a year, the new vocalist previously with BETRAYER. He was to debut on a tour with DESTRUCTION and DEBUSTROL before joining the band in the studio in order to record their first ever album.

BEGINNING OF EXTINCTION, Deathvastation DVT 004 (1996). Last Performance / The Hall Of Souls / Tao / Better To Die / Message Of Truth / Poltergeist / Beginning Of Extinction / Materialized Insanity / The Soul / The Good In Mankind Has Died / Tveret.

SCAFFOLD

SLOVENIA — *Aleš Drolc (vocals), Gorazd Maèek (guitar), Aljoša Orloviè (guitar), Sebastjan Skupek (bass), Robi Kovaèiè (drums).*

SCAFFOLD came into being during 1993 at the hands of guitarist Martin Pecar and drummer Robert Kovacic. The initial band unit was brought up to full compliment with the addition of bassist David Tercek and, in 1994, second guitarist Ivan Kljun. Unfortunately both Kljun and Tercek soon departed but by the summer of 1994 Matjaž Korošec had taken over the bass position. Korošec's cousin Damir Marušic enrolled as the band, then titled OFENZIVA, set about live work. Aleš Drolc came onboard as lead vocalist in 1995 as the group adopted the revised name of SCAFFOLD.

Further line-up changes found INFINITY's Gorazd Macek newly introduced on guitar and Pecar was replaced by Peter Caric. In this incarnation SCAFFOLD supported CANNIBAL CORPSE, KRABATHOR and MORTALITY at a show in Ljubljana during 1998. Yet again the band roster shifted its axis, fresh recruits being found in LEPONEX and BODYMINDSOUL bassist Sebastijan Skupek then guitarist Aljoša Orlovic.

SCAFFOLD released the mini album 'Evil Empire, Morbid World' in 2003.

Drummer Robert Kovacic also holds down drum duties with fellow Death Metal act NECROSED, Industrialists NOXIOUS BEAUTY and DUSK DELIGHT.

EVIL EMPIRE, MORBID WORLD, Independent (2003). Evil Empire, Morbid World / Crush The Rules / Irritably Cutting / Torture Through Thoughts / Wasted Energy.

SCAR SYMMETRY

SWEDEN — *Christian Älvestam (vocals), Jonas Kjellgren (guitar), Per Nilsson (guitar), Kenneth Seil (bass), Henrik Ohlsson (drums).*

SCAR SYMMETRY is an "all star" melodic Death Metal band forged during 2004. The cast comprises veteran figures such as the INCAPACITY, UNMOORED, SOLAR DAWN and TORCHBEARER credited Christian Älvestam on vocals, the guitar pairing of Jonas Kjellgren from CARNAL FORGE, DELLAMORTE and CENTINEX with Per Nilsson of ALTERED AEON, bassist Kenneth Seil and drummer Henrik Ohlsson, the latter able to boast a wealth of associations to acts such as ADVERSARY, LEGIA, ALTERED AEON, MUTANT, DIABOLICAL, THRAWN and THEORY IN PRACTICE. The industrious Älvestam has an extended roll call of band endeavours such as CARNALIZED, ANDUIN '98, EVENDIM, LORD OF THRONES, ORGY OF FLESH, SATTYG, RED SKIES DAWNING, THE STINK BUG COLLECTIVE and DEN TIDLÖSA EVIGHETEN.

A debut album for Metal Blade Records, entitled 'Symmetric In Design' issued in February 2005, was produced by Kjellgren at Black Lounge Studios. Tokuma Records issued the album in Japan in April. Per Nilsson enrolled into the ranks of WORLD BELOW in January 2005, just upfront of the record release. SCAR SYMMETRY switched labels to Nuclear Blast in June. In January 2006 Christian Älvestam enrolled into ANGEL BLAKE, a new band assembled by MNEMIC and ex-TRANSPORT LEAGUE vocalist Tony Jelencovich.

SCAR SYMMETRY joined the 'Metal Hammer' sponsored 'European Neckbreaker's Ball' 2006 tour, also featuring HYPOCRISY, SOILWORK and ONE MAN ARMY AND THE UNDEAD QUARTET, commencing 11th April in Denmark. New album 'Pitch Black Progress' arrived in early May. SCAR SYMMETRY subsequently teaming up with Norway's COMMUNIC for the 'Waves of Pitch Black Decay' European tour in late September. Christian Älvestam donated guest vocals to ZONARIA's 2006 debut album 'Rendered In Vain', featuring on the track 'Attending Annihilation'.

Seeds Of Rebellion, Scar Symmetry (2004) (Demo). Seeds Of Rebellion.
SYMMETRIC IN DESIGN, Nuclear Blast NB 1516-2 (2005). Chaosweaver / 2012—The Demise Of The 5th Sun / Dominion / Underneath The Surface / Reborn / Veil Of Illusions / Obscure Alliance / Hybrid Cult / Orchestrate The Infinite / Detach From The Outcome / Seeds Of Rebellion / The Eleventh Sphere.
PITCH BLACK PROGRESS, Avalon Marquee MICP-10588 (2006) (Japanese release). The Illusionist / Slaves To The Subliminal / Mind Machine / Pitch Black Progress / Calculate The Apocalypse / Dreaming 24/7 / Abstracted / The Kaleidoscopic God / Retaliator / Oscillation Point / The Path Of Least Resistance / Carved In Stone / Deviate From The Form.
PITCH BLACK PROGRESS, Nuclear Blast NB 1482-2 (2006). The Illusionist / Slaves To The Subliminal / Mind Machine / Pitch Black Progress / Calculate The Apocalypse / Dreaming 24/7 / Abstracted / The Kaleidoscopic God / Retaliator / Oscillation Point / The Path Of Least Resistance.
PITCH BLACK PROGRESS, Dream On PARK-9062 (2006) (South Korean release). The Illusionist / Slaves To The Subliminal / Mind Machine / Pitch Black Progress / Calculate The Apocalypse / Dreaming 24/7 / Abstracted / The Kaleidoscopic God / Retaliator / Oscillation Point / The Path Of Least Resistance / Carved In Stone / Deviate From The Form / Dominion / Reborn / Seeds Of Rebellion.

SCARIOT

KRISTIANSAND, NORWAY — *Oddleif Stensland (vocals), Daniel Olaisen (guitar), Frank Orland (guitar), Stefan Schulz (bass), Tor A. Andersen (drums).*

SCARIOT was created in Kristiansand by erstwhile SATYRICON guitarist Daniel Olaison and Anders Kobro of IN THE WOODS and CARPATHIAN FOREST. Also featured was TRAIL OF TEARS "growling" vocalist Ronnie Thorsen and "clean" vocals courtesy of GUARDIANS OF TIME frontman Bernt Fjellstad with session members guitarist Hugo Isaksen and bassist Bonne Thorson. Initially the band was entitled PEGASUS but after discovery of the Australian act of the same name adopted ISCARIOT, this duly evolving into SCARIOT.

After the debut album 'Death Forlorn', issued in September 2000 through British label Demolition Records, SCARIOT trimmed down to a duo of Olaisen and Thorsen. The band by early 2001 had been brought back up to strength with Olaisen joined by ODYSSEY guitarist Frank Orland, vocalist Inge J. Tobiassen, INHERIT bassist Stefan Schulz and drummer Freddy Bolso.

Olaisen also operated, albeit under the guise of 'Død', with the retro Death Metal project BLOOD RED THRONE with former SATYRICON and EMPEROR member Tchort. He was also active with COBALT 60, appearing on the 'Meat Hook Ballet' album. Thorsen would guest on BLOOD RED THRONE's inaugural demo 'Deathmix 2000'.

The band would cut a new album 'Tongueless God' for 2001 release for Demolition Records. Still signed to Demolition the band split with the label before the album was released. Technically 'Tongueless God' was never released, although the band manufactured some copies on their own. SCARIOT, now with APOSTASY and OPUS FORGOTTEN man Tor A. Andersen on the drums, would dispense with the services of Tobiassen in November 2001, announcing the induction of a new singer, Oddleif Stensland of CLAIRVOYA and INGERMANLAND, in the Spring 2002.

Stensland and drummer Tor Atle Andersen, alongside the DIMENSION PSYCHOSPHERE and INGERMANLAND credited Erik Mortensen on bass, founded the Progressive Metal side project COMMUNIC in 2003. The trio debuted with the demo 'Conspiracy In Mind', soon signing to the Nuclear Blast label. Touring in Scandinavia saw the band forming up the billing for the October 2003 'Scream Magazine Metal Tour' comprising headliners EINHERJER alongside LUMSK and GRIFFIN. In November Spiritual Beast issued the album 'Strange To Numbers'.

Reports emerged in early 2005 that SCARIOT, now solely mentored by founder Daniel Olaisen, was employing the TESTAMENT, SADUS, DEATH, DRAGONLORD and SEBASTIAN BACH credited Steve DiGiorgio with Asgeir Mickelson of SPIRAL ARCHITECT and BORKNAGAR on drums for on new recordings.

The band entered Top Room Studios in January 2006, working with producer Børge Finstad.

Bernt Fjellstad fired up another new project in 2006, Thrash Metal band RULES OF ENGAGEMENT. In August SCARIOT, having signed to Facefront Records, scrapped a previously announced album title of 'The Grand Design' in favour of 'Momentum Shift'.

Loosing Faith, Scariot (1998) (Demo).

Demo '99, Scariot (1999) (Demo).

Fear/Addiction, Scariot (1999) (Demo).

DEATHFORLORN, Demolition DEMCD 107 (2000). Crimson Tears / Sister / The Bad Man / Within / False Power / Resurrection / Remains Of Dreams / Cruisin'.

TONGUELESS GOD, Scariot (2001). Clear Mind / The Last Frontier / The Cynic / Death Request / Close To Hell / Tongueless God / Closing The Gates / Misery Fields / Darkenized.

Pinion Dark, Scariot (2002) (Demo).

Pushing For Perfection, Scariot (2002) (Demo). Instrument Of Policy / Inside The Frame / Pushing For Perfection.

STRANGE TO NUMBERS, Spiritual Beast SBCD-1009 (2003) (Japanese release). Monopolize / Strange To Numbers / Prospects Unknown / Broken Circle—Cutting Glass / Lady X / Pushing For Perfection / Clear Mind / E Pollution / Inner Mica / Instrument Of Policy / Inside The Frame.

STRANGE TO NUMBERS, Face Front FF022CD (2004). Monopolize / Strange To Numbers / Prospects Unknown / Broken Circle—Cutting Glass / Lady X / Pushing For Perfection / Clear Mind / E Pollution / Inner Mica.

MONUMENTUM SHIFT, FaceFront (2007).

SCARVE

NANCY, FRANCE — *Pierrick Valence (vocals), Guillaume Bideau (vocals), Patrick Martin (guitar), Sylvain Coudret (guitar), Loïc Colin (bass), Dirk Verbeuren (drums).*

Nancy based Death Metal act created in the opening weeks of 1994. SCARVE's original summer 1994 demo cassette found the band citing a line up of lead vocalist Fred Bartolomucci, ex-METAL DEATH guitarist Patrick Martin, bass player David Fioraso with Dirk Verbeuren on the drums, the latter a veteran of S.P.I.T., MELTDOWN, Black Metal band ANAON and SHRED. The band's second recording arrived in August of 1996 as the six track Bruno Donini produced and self financed EP ' Six Tears Of Sorrow'. By this juncture Sylvain Coudret had been added as second guitarist.

During 1998 SCARVE supplanted Bartolomucci with two lead singers Guillaume Bideau and Alain Germonville. The 'Translucence' album, issued by the Furtive Metal concern in February of 2000 as a limited edition digipack, closed out with a rendition of LED ZEPPELIN's 'Friends'. Previously fan club members had been treated to an exclusive two track demo CD as a taster entitled 'Opacity'. Bassist Julien Thibers had featured on 'Opacity' but for the album recording proper Philippe Elter came onboard. The album would be granted a Europe wide re-release in April courtesy of War Music. Later that year a four track fan club only EP emerged, comprising one studio track and three live tracks. Loïc Colin took the four string role in September of 2001 and Pierrick Valence of BURNING CLOUD entered the fold as second vocalist that October.

SCARVE's March 2002 Daniel Bergstrand produced album 'Luminiferous' contained a cover version of ENTOMBED's 'Serpent Speech'. The record would be subsequently picked up for US license by World War III Records in October. Live promotion in Europe, dubbed the 'Machinery' tour, had SCARVE allied with road mates NO RETURN, DEW SCENTED and RAIN in April. Further European touring in October found SCARVE on a mighty package billing alongside NILE, SINISTER, NO RETURN and MYRKSKOG.

SCARVE's Guillaume Bideau provided both vocals and percussion for his side project THE CUBE's debut 2003 album

SCARVE

'Stand Up Direction Body'. Meantime Dirk Verbeuren maintained a hectic schedule laying down session drums for MORTUARY's 'Agony In Red', LYZANXIA's 'Mindcrimes', ABORTED's 'Goremageddon' as well as for EOSTENEM. In 2003 the man was sessioning for Israeli band ETERNAL GRAY.

SCARVE side projects abounded in 2003 with singer Pierrick Valence, guitarist Sylvain Coudret and drummer Dirk Verbeuren teaming up with their sound engineer Alan Leeroy, guitarist for ANAON, for a Celtic Metal endeavour entitled STENVAL. The same SCARVE trio, alongside NO RETURN and GARWALL bassist Olivia founded PHAZM.

SCARVE's third album 'Irradiant' was recorded at Dug-Out Studio in Uppsala, Sweden with producers Daniel Bergstrand and erstwhile MISERY LOVES CO. guitarist Örjan Örnkloo. Guesting would be DEFLESHED vocalist/bassist Gustaf Jorde whilst MESHUGGAH guitarist FREDRIK THORDENDAL features a guest guitar solo on the track 'Asphyxiate'. The band filmed a live promotional video for the track 'Mirthless Perspectives'.

Now with some international repute behind him Dirk Verbeuren teamed up as stand in for acclaimed Swedish act SOILWORK for their February 2004 European tour dates. Verbeuren then stepped in as substitute drummer for Belgian gore-mongers ABORTED's live dates and then sessioned on INFINITED HATE's 'Heaven Termination' album. The drummer enrolled into the ranks of YYRKOON for dates in January 2005. SCARVE re-grouped to act as support to MESHUGGAH's June European tour. The band featured the exclusive live track 'Fireproven' on the 2005 Listenable Records French Metal compilation 'Revolution Calling'.

Dirk Verbeuren sessioned for Swiss band SYBREED in 2006. That May SCARVE utilised Dug-Out Studios in Uppsala, Sweden to cut a new album with producer Daniel Bergstrand. However, mid session, singer Guillaume Bideau opted out in order to join Danish band MNEMIC. SCARVE persevered, drafting the services of Swedish vocalist Lawrence Mackrory, of DARKANE, THE MIST OF AVALON, ANDROMEDA, SEETHINGS and F.K.Ü. repute, on a session basis for new album 'The Undercurrent'.

Six Tears Of Sorrow EP, Independent SCAR02CD96 (1996) (Limited edition 1000 copies). Liquefied Silhouettes / Shelly's Dead / Blackloader / Torn Underneath / I.M.D.I. / Anchored In Melancholy.

Opacity EP, Independent SCAR04CD99 (1999) (Fan Club release—200 copies). Heaven-Sent (Demo version) / Your Solid Waters (Demo version).

TRANSLUCENCE, Furtive Metal FUR001 (2000). NerveCurrent9 / Your Solid Waters / Heven-Sent / The Seed Unsown / A New Dawn / Freaqualized / Luminiferous / FleshPlunge / Sunken Sin-King / Translucence / Friends.

Fanclub EP, Independent SCAR06CD00 (2000). Friends (Demo) / Heaven-Sent (Live) / Sunken Sin-King (Live) / BlackLoader (Live).

LUMINIFEROUS, Listenable POSH 036 (2002). Emulate The Soul / Alteration / CrustScraper / Capsized / Luminiferous 2.0 / The Resonating Cycle / The Path To Apoptosis / Futile Resilient / Serpent Speech / Infertile Ways / The Day After / Blackloader (2002 Upgrade).

IRRADIANT, Listenable POSH048 (2004). Mirthless Perspectives / An Emptier Void / Irradiant / Asphyxiate / HyperConscience / The Perfect Disaster / Molten Scars / FireProven / Boiling Calm.

SCATTERED REMNANTS

FITCHBURG, MA, USA — *Jason Hendershaw (vocals), Rob Settergren (guitar), Jamie Harman (guitar), Dan Egan (bass), Steve Gonsalves (drums).*

Massachusetts Death Metal band SCATTERED REMNANTS, created in 1992, arrived on the scene with the 1994 promotional tape 'Procreating Mass Carnage'. The following year a CD EP 'Inherent Perversion' followed and shortly after the initial demo would be re-released on CD format.

However, SCATTERED REMNANTS rhythm section of bassist Ron Miles and drummer Eric Roy, a veteran of DESOLATE, had decamped previously and the band were dealt another blow when guitarist Jay Sarate quit too. The latter's position was taken by Jamie Harman.

Signing to the Repulse label the band drafted former EXHUMED bassist Dan Egan and utilised the services of session drummer Steve Gonsalves to record the 1998 'Destined To Fail' album. Egan later joined ALL THAT REMAINS, featuring on the 2002 album 'Behind Silence And Solitude'. The 2002 Deepsend SCATTERED REMNANTS release 'Indulgence In Masochism' is a collection of early demo works.

Inherent Perversion, (1995). Inherent Perversion.
Procreating Mass Carnage, (1997). Procreating Mass Carnage.
DESTINED TO FAIL, Repulse RPS 035CD (1998). Destined To Fail / Lamentation Of Tortured Souls / Draped In Sorrow / At The Right Of Nothingness / As Whores / Angelic Redemption / Virtuous Abandonment / Vaginal Vomit.
INDULGENCE IN MASOCHISM, Deepsend DSR003 (2002). Profanation Of Christ / Ridding Genital Flesh / Anal Birth / Cranial Defilement / Amidst The Afterbirth / As The First Tear Of Blood Falls / Vaginal Vomit / Inherent Perversion / Aborted Salvation / Destined To Fail / Lamentation Of Tortured Souls / Draped In Sorrow / At The Right Hand Of Nothingness / As Whores / Angelic Redemption / Virtuous Abandonment.

SCAVENGER

DENMARK — *Kasper Thomsen (vocals), Flemming C. Lund (vocals / guitar), Boris Tandrup (bass), Morten Gade Sørensen (drums).*

SCAVENGER, assembled in 2001, feature INVOCATOR's Flemming C. Lund on lead vocals and guitar, the SLUGS, INTO DEMENTIA, SUBMISSION and AUTUMN LEAVES bassist Boris Tandrup and drummer Morten Gade Sørensen. The latter has a wealth of credits on the Danish Metal scene including ENDEMECY, ENCRYPTION, DELIQUESCENCE, INTO DEMENTIA, NEPENTHE, SCORNFUL, AURORA, SUBMISSION, WUTHERING HEIGHTS and PYRAMAZE.

SCAVENGER entered Hansen Studios, working with producer Jacob Hansen, to cut demo tracks in 2004. Guesting as lead vocalist for these recordings would be the DARKANE, THE MIST OF AVALON, ANDROMEDA, SEETHINGS and ENEMY IS US credited Lawrence Mackrory. SCAVENGER, now fronted by Kasper Thomsen of RAUNCHY, laid down a further three demo tracks in May 2005 at Hansen studios in Ribe, working with producer Jacob Hansen once again. The group switched title to THE ARCANE ORDER, signing to Metal Blade Records the band engaged with Hansen to record their debut album.

Promo 2005, Scavenger (2005). Servants Of A Darker World / Breathe The Poison / The Sanity Insane.

SCENT OF FLESH

IMATRA, FINLAND — *Niko Ahokas (vocals), Matti Viisainen (guitar), Herkko Miiki (guitar), Sofian Gezuri (bass), Antti Suikkanen (drums).*

SCENT OF FLESH is an Imatra based brutal Death Metal band dating to 2000. The 'Drowned Into The Darkness' demo was recorded in January of 2001. For these recordings the band employed a three guitar line up comprising lead vocalist Niko Ahokas, guitarists Matti Viisainen, Herkko Miiki and Markus Toivonen, bassist Sofian Gezuri with Antti Suikkanen on the drums. Relocating to Tampere, Toivonen left the band in the summer of 2001. SCENT OF FLESH persevered as a quintet, cutting the sophomore demo 'Towards Eternal Lost', which secured a deal with the Greek Black Lotus label.

Switching labels to Firebox Records the band issued the 2004 album 'Valour In Hatred'. SCENT OF FLESH parted ways with guitarist Herkko Miikki in November of 2004. The band, issuing an EP 'Become Malignity', acted as openers for the CHAOSBREED and GRAVE shows in Finland in March 2005. In July 2006 singer Niko Ahokas opted out and guitarist Matti Viisainen took over the vocal role. Firebox Records put out the 'Deform In Torture' album in 2007. That February Samu Viisainen switched over to the guitar role whilst Jari Haapasalo from SOLIUM XI was inducted on bass.

Drowned Into The Darkness, Scent Of Flesh (2001) (Demo). Drowned Into The Darkness / Feed The Greed / Cemetery Fields / Nightly.
Towards Eternal Lost, Scent Of Flesh (2001) (Demo). Dark Years Of Carnage / Rotten, Shattered, Burned And Spoiled / Towards Eternal Lost.
ROARING DEPTHS OF INSANITY, Black Lotus BLRCD 043 (2002). Cursed To Suffer / Eternity In Torment / Dark Years Of Carnage / Witness My Madness / Drowned Into The Darkness / Rotten, Shattered, Burned And Spoiled / Feed The Greed / Beneath The Tombstones / Towards Eternal Lost / Reign In Violent Perfection.
VALOR IN HATRED, Firebox FIRECD 017 (2004). Valor In Hatred / Art Of Beheading / Circle Of Dark Beliefs / Visions Of Death / Descent To Dark Clarity / Unleashed Be The Ungodly / Suicidal Cannibalism / The Last Awakening.
Become Malignity, Firebox FIRECD 031 (2005). Become Malignity / All Flesh To Consume / Our Own Archnemesis / Second Awakening.
DEFORM IN TORTURE, Firebox (2007). Living But Stillborn / At The Stake Of Mercy / Deform In Torture / Last Act Of Power / Relentless Hands / Delusions Of Deity / One Holy Truth / Our Own Archnemesis.

SCEPTIC

CAXIAS DO SUL, RS, BRAZIL — *Lander Artur (vocals / guitar), Maurício Corrêa (guitar / drum programming), Marcelo Nunez (bass).*

SCEPTIC, a technical yet brutal edged Death Metal band, was initiated during June of 2002 by ex-SANGRIA guitarist Lander Artur, former SEDUCED BY SUICIDE six stringer Maurício Corrêa and bassist Marcelo Nunez, previously a member of ARES WRATH, CRUCIFIED BASTARD and MELANCHOLIC ART. Initially Rafael Froner of TERRIFY occupied the drum position but he would be superseded by the PREDATOR credited Roberto Cecatto. A further change in September of 2003 saw João Vieira from MELANCHOLIC ART enrolled as the new SCEPTIC drummer.

The band, switching title to THE SCEPTIC, would work on a five song demo in March of 2004. The 'Psychopathological' EP would be recorded with the aid of programmed drums at Brave Metal Studios, after which THE SCEPTIC drafted new drummer Marcos Conti. The band then trimmed down to a trio.

PSYCHOPATHOLOGICAL, (2005).

SCEPTIC

POLAND — *Michal Skotniczny (vocals), Jack Hiro (guitar), Czesiek Semia (guitar), Pawel Kolasa (bass), Maciek Zieba (drums).*

Death Metal act SCEPTIC was originally entitled TORMENTOR upon its formation during 1994. Initially the band comprised of guitarist Jack Hiro, drummer Maciek Zieba and second guitar player Dariusz Styczen. With the name switch to SCEPTIC Styczen made way for Jacek Mrozek and Arek Strawiarski took command of the lead vocal role as the band weighed in with an opening demo tape in 1996. A further cassette, the eight song 'Beyond Reality' released in 1997, witnessed the induction of bass player Pawel Kolasa from ATHROPIA RED SUN.

SCEPTIC would undergo a radical line up shuffle in 1998 emerging as a new look quartet of Hiro, Kolasa and new faces drummer Kuba Kogut and vocalist Marcin Ubas. This version of SCEPTIC cut a two song demo which secured a deal with the Massive management team.

Adding Czesiek Semia on secondary guitar SCEPTIC recorded their debut album 'Blind Existence'. Post recording live work included appearances at the 'Thrash 'Em All' and 'Mystic' festivals. 'Blind Existence' would be issued in November of 1999 through Mystic Productions.

As 2000 dawned so did yet another round of personnel changes. Urbas bowed out due to time constraints conflicting with his occupation as a professional sprinter and Michal Senajko took his place. Further ructions were resolved when erstwhile drummer Maciek Zieba re-assumed his position. The band put in a second showing at the 'Thrash 'Em All' festival and in September entered the studio to deliver a second album, provisionally titled 'Lost Identity', produced by Szymon Czech. Material included a cover of the NOCTURNUS track 'Arctic Crypt'. Mid way through these sessions Senajko's place was taken by CRIONICS man Michael Skotniczny. The album, adopting a revised title of 'Pathetic Being', saw a release through the Empire label in Poland, Last Episode in Germany and Crash Music in North America.

Jack Hiro also operates as part of the DIE IRAE project band of VADER men Doc and Mauser. The band embarked upon a ten date tour of Poland during October of 2002 co-headlined by MONSTROSITY and Swedes VOMITORY backed by TRAUMA, DISSENTER, LOST SOUL and CONTEMPT. The 2003 album 'Unbeliever's Script' would be licensed to the British based Candlelight label for global distribution. SCEPTIC underwent a major change in 2004 as Weronika Zbieg from TOTEM took over vocal duties, substituting for Marcin Urbas. Her baptism of fire took place in early April at Akwarium Club in Olkusz, the band sharing a billing with ATROPHIA RED SUN, DUST and MIST.

BLIND EXISTENCE, Mystic Productions (1999). Die From Within / Interior Of Life / Blind Existence / Outworld / Sceptic / Senseless / Painful Silence / Sadistic Aggression / Beyond Reality / Imprisoned.
PATHETIC BEING, Empire EMP 002 (2001). Intro / Ancient Portal / Pathetic Being / Only Lies / Ancestor Of All Powers / Incapable Rulers / Lost Identity / Arctic Crypt / Particles Of Time / Children's Eyes.
UNBELIEVER'S SCRIPT, Empire (2003). Unbeliever's Script / Illusion Possessor / Controlled By Mind / Soul Controller / Shapeless Entity / Knowledge Gatherer / Voices From The Past / Spiritually Tormented / Waves Of Destruction.

SCEPTICAL SCHIZO

NOORMARKKU, FINLAND — *Joonas Sukanen (vocals / guitar), Jukka Sillanpää (guitar), Toni Rakkolainen (bass), Mikko Lappalainen (drums).*

SCEPTICAL SCHIZO is a Doom Death act hailing from Noormarkku, Pori. Fronted by Joonas Sukanen, the band included guitarist Jukka Sillanpää, bassist Toni Rakkolainen with Mikko Lappalainen on drums. A demo was delivered in 1989, which closed out with a twisted version of the KISS Disco classic 'I Was Made For Loving You' re-branded 'I Was Made For Killing You'. The 'Dispossessed' and 'Danse Macabre' demos arrived in 1990. A fourth promotion cassette, 'The Four Seasons', surfaced in 1991.

SCEPTICAL SCHIZO put out a self-financed 7" single in 1992 after which the Italian Wounded Love label released a January 1993 single entitled 'The Plight'. The following year the band took on a Gothic Rock stance and, re-branded as LAVRA, published the album 'Bluenothing'. Both Jukka Sillanpää and Mikko Lappalainen also joined AS DIVINE GRACE. Sillanpää also held association with SYNDICATE, THIS EMPTY FLOW, F and FUNCUNT.

Demo #1, Sceptical Schizo (1989) (Demo). Intro / Holy War / Disguised Insanity / Forbidden Games / The Nightmare / I Was Made For Killing You.
Danse Macabre, Sceptical Schizo (1990) (Demo). Comfortable? (Open Your Eyes) / Fruits Of Wrath / Battlefields / Thoughts Of The Dead.
Dispossessed, Sceptical Schizo (1990) (Demo). Intro: The Rocker / Sepulchral Scene / Brainwash / Meaning Of Existence / Victim Of Perversity / Peerless Pastor.
The Four Seasons, Sceptical Schizo (1991) (Demo). (Spring) Illusion Of Sleep / (Summer) I Came To Grief / (Autumn) Falling Leaves (And My Fears Became To Life) / (Winter) Wrapped In Darkness I Grieve.
Sceptical Schizo, Sceptical Schizo (1992) (7" vinyl single). Into The Suction Of Blue / Withdrawn.
The Plight, Wounded Love WLR-93001 (1993) (7" vinyl single). Tightrope Ballet / Sixteen Gardens Of Plight.

SCHEITAN

LULEÅ, SWEDEN — *Lotta Högberg (vocals), Pierre Törnkvist (vocals / guitar / bass), Göran Norman (keyboards), Oskar Karlsson (drums).*

A Black Metal project formed in Luleå by THE EVERDAWN vocalist Pierre Törnkvist and THE EVERDAWN and GATES OF ISHTAR drummer Oskar Karlsson, both had originally recorded only one track to find a suitable label for the project but, in the end, an entire conceptual record was cut for Invasion Records. 'Travelling In Ancient Times' was released in November 1996. 'Bezerk 2000' followed in February 1998. Century Media Records signed the band for the 'Nemesis', issued in September 1999. For SCHEITAN's third effort the group enrolled keyboard player Göran Norman and singer Lotta Högberg.

Törnkvist, a former member of DECORTICATION, also opted to reform side band THE EVERDAWN. Törnkvist also operates in THE MOANING. By 2002 both Törnkvist and Karlsson were to be found in the Death n' Roll act HELLTRAIN.

TRAVELLING IN ANCIENT TIMES, Invasion I.R. 024 (1996). October Journey / Autumn Departure / Riding The Icewinds / December At Fullmoon / In Battle With Angels / Leaving The Mortals / Devastating Heaven / Portals Of Might.
BEZERK 2000, Invasion I.R. 033 (1998). Raincoat / Exitways / Soulside / Sad To Say / V / Terror / Bombraid Over Wastelands / Bezerk 2000 / The Scheitan.
NEMESIS, Century Media 77261-2 (1999). Fury Flow / Psyched / Black Rain / Marionette / Forgive Me / A Silent Hum / Ways / My Isle / Emergency.

SCREAMING AFTERBIRTH

WEST ALLIS, WI, USA — *KP Ripper (vocals), DK Destroyer (guitar), Sticky Privates (guitar), Captain Party (bass), JJ Blaze (drums).*

West Allis, Wisconsin based SCREAMING AFTERBIRTH debuted in 2000 with two demos, a self titled effort and 'Leatherface'. The 'Puke Pile' debut album emerged the following year. The band line-up comprised vocalist KP Ripper, guitarists DK "30 Pack" Destroyer and Sticky Privates, bassist Captain Party with JJ Blaze on drums. In 2003 the band would lay down tracks, including a rendition of TERRORIZER's 'Fear Of Napalm', for a five way split album on United Guttural Records in league with BOUND AND GAGGED, PUTRID PILE, SCREAMING GUTTURAL and DYSCRASIA. European tour dates took the band across Europe in July of 2004 including shows at the Czech 'Extreme Obscene' festival and the Belgian 'DeathMetal.be' festival.

Signing to Bizarre Leprous Records SCREAMING AFTERBIRTH cut the 'Drunk On Feces' album for 2004, this including a cover version of MORTICIAN's 'Cremated' and BLOOD's 'Insomina'. In December SCREAMING AFTERBIRTH drummer Jesse Kehoe joined FLESHGRIND.

PUKE PILE, United Guttural (2002). Entangled In Entrails / Stump Fucked Piss Flaps / Open Pussy Surgery / Anal Volcano / Completely Stuffed Bitch / Writhing And Contorting / Cottage Cheese Between Her Legs / Epidural Emissions / No Orifice Shall Remain / Mongloid Whore / Puke Pile / Stabbing Faces And Kicking Guts.

DRUNK ON FECES, Bizarre Leprous (2004). Drunk On Feces / Stink Of Rapes / Dishevelled Scatter / Truck Stop Raper / Septic / Clit Sized Penis Penis Sized Clit / Drenched In DNA / Anal Volcano / Cremated / Judeop Zoophilism / Fuck Off / Blowtorch Lynchings / Completely Stuffed Bitch / Skunk Butt Gutter Pussy / Alcoholocaust / Insomnia.

SCULPTURED

PORTLAND, OR, USA — *Brian Yager (vocals), Don Anderson (vocals / guitar / keyboards), Jason Walton (bass), Clint Idsinga (trombone), Burke Harris (trumpet), John Schlegel (drums).*

Mentored by AGALLOCH's Don Anderson Portland's SCULPTURED attempt to take Death Metal into uncharted waters. Anderson provides gruff vocals and the bulk of the instrumentation whilst Brian Yager contributes clean vocals. Bass guitar comes courtesy of AGALLOCH and ESPECIALLY LIKELY SLOTH man Jason Walton. The sombreness of SCULPTURED's musical landscape was enhanced by the novel use of a horn section. John Haughm of AGALLOCH took over on drums for the 2000 'Apollo Ends' album.

In April 2006 the band was joined by drummer Dave Murray, known for his work with ESTRADASPHERE, the DESERTS OF TRAUN, DAEDELUS and THOLUS, to record third album 'Embodiment'.

THE SPEAR OF THE LILY IS AUREOLED, The End TE004 (1999). Together With The Seasons / Almond Beauty / Lit By The Light Of Morning / Fashioned By Blood And Tears / Fulfillment In Tragedy For Cello And Flute / Her Silence / Our Illuminated Tomb.

APOLLO ENDS, The End TE010 (2000). Washing My Hands Of It / Above The 60th Parallel / Snow Covers All / Between Goldberg / Apollo Destroys, Apollo Creates / Song To Fall On Deaf Ears / Summary.

SCURVY

VÄSBY, SWEDEN — *Fredrik Andersson (vocals / bass), Johan Wallin (guitar), Martin Person (drums).*

Väsby Metal band. With GALLOW's demise both vocalist / guitarist Niklas Eriksson and guitarist Johan Wallin founded MAGGOTS. Their erstwhile GALLOW drumming compatriot Fredrik Andersson was also drafted into this new band but adopting the new role of bass as this band evolved into SCURVY. Martin Persson of PATHOLOG assumed drum duties. However, Andersson bailed out before recording of a 2000 demo, produced by DISMEMBER's Fred Estby. Perverted Taste issued the 'Tombstone Tales' album in 2002 and in November SCURVY shared the split EP 'Funeral Fist Fucker' on Noise Variations with MORSGATT.

Wallin also operates with Death Metal act REPUGNANT. Person is active with Crustcore outfit SLAGANFALL.

Demo 1, (2000). Forklift Massacre / Grandpa Reaper / (In) Sideburns / Deathwish.

Forklift Massacre, Perverted Taste (2001) (Split EP with DEATH REALITY). Forklift Massacre / Grandpa Reaper.

TOMBSTONE TALES, Perverted Taste PT 085 (2002). Restal Resurrection / Covered In Puke / Obese / Crimes Against Humanity / Tales From The Sewer / Cadaverator / Scurvy / Det Är Nu Det Är Dags Att Kröka / Death By Masturbation / Unchallenged Hate.

Funeral Fist Fucker, Noise Variations (2002) (Split EP with MORSGATT). I Hope You Choke / Deathwish Pt. III / Poppy Seed Cake / Necromaniac.

SEAR

HELSINKI, FINLAND — *Harri Hyytiäinen (vocals), Matias Helle (guitar), J. Hentunen (guitar), Thomas Vee (bass), Lauri Laaksonen (drums).*

Helsinki Black Metal band SEAR, created during 2001 by vocalist Tapsa Kuusela, of HORNA and KORGONTHURUS, and guitarist Matias Helle. The band subsequently pulled in GALLERY OF TRAGEDIES drummer Lauri Laaksonen to supplant Tony Steel. SEAR published the 2004 demo 'Realm Of Lies Falling Down'. SEAR's debut album, 'Begin the Celebrations Of Sin', was released in May 2005 via Dynamic Arts Records. The group parted ways with both original singer Tapsa Kuusela and bassist Mika Nieminen, drafting new personnel vocalist Harri Hyytiäinen and bassist T. Landen in January 2006. Hyytiäinen scene credentials included association with AVATHAR, BARANDUIN, CATALEPTIC, NEKROFUK KVLT and NUCLEAR HAMMER. Guitar player Sami Wass was replaced by J. Hentunen.

SEAR's next opus, 'Lamentations Of Destruction', recorded at studio Ruho and mixed by Santeri Salmi, was wrapped up in December.

Realm Of Lies Falling Down, Sear (2004) (Demo). Vade Retro Deus / Blindfolded Fuck / Monument / Weeping Flesh / Scythe Of Blasphemy.

BEGIN THE CELEBRATIONS OF SIN, Dynamic Arts (2005). Intro / .Lobotomy With A Crucifix / Bless The Child / Scythe Of Blasphemy (Kiss The Goat) / Mankind's Last Breath / Vade Retro Deus / Temptations Of The Flesh / Monument 666 / Blindfolded Fuck / Viimeinen Voitelu.

LAMENTATIONS OF DESTRUCTION, (2007). Introduction / Pedon Käsky / Heaven Ablaze / One Throne / Fire & Death / Purgatory / Destination / Violation Of The Soul / The Burning / Hate & Scorn, Crowned With Horns / Weeping Flesh.

SEARING MEADOW

TURKU, FINLAND — *Mika Ikonen (vocals / guitar), Ville Pekkala (guitar), Sasu Haapanen (guitar), Ville Korhonen (bass), Antti Hakkala (drums).*

Turku Death Metal combo SEARING MEADOW was manifested in the Summer of 2000 by vocalist / guitarist Mika Ikonen and guitarist Ville Pekkala. Shortly after Ville Korhonen was installed on bass guitar. The following year Antti Hakkala joined the band on drums. That October SEARING MEADOW tracked three songs for the 'Slowly Creeping' release. A second session, 'Once Adored' arrived in November of 2001 with third set 'Enduring Enchantment' delivered in November of 2002.

SEARING MEADOW signed to Rising Realm Records in early 2004. The band would cut their debut Kari Nieminen produced album 'Corroding From Inside' at Musamuusa Studios in March. In December the group was joined by Sasu Haapanen as third guitarist. Line-up changes in June of 2005 marked the introduction of FALL OF THE LEAFE bassist Miska Lehtivuori. Crash Music Inc. gave 'Corroding From Inside' a long overdue North American release in July.

In 2005 SEARING MEADOW members frontman Mika Ikonen, Miska Lehtivuori and Antti Hakkala collaborated with guitarist Juhani Sanna from KOLONNA to forge ABLAZE IN HATRED, issuing the September opening demo 'Closure Of Life'. The band scheduled demo recordings for February 2007 at Noisecamp Studios.

Slowly Creeping In, (2000). The Haunted Age / Crying Nightmist / Bleeding Mercy / Drifting In Darkness.

Once Adored, Independent (2001). These Evening Tears / Promises So Deep / Crystalblood.

Enduring Enchantment, Independent (2002). Wasted Heroes / Mirror Of Irony / Three Names For Denial.

SECT OF EXECRATION

AUSTIN, TX, USA — *Steven Watkins (vocals / guitar), Gabriel Ayala (vocals / guitar), Daniel Hearne (bass), Jeremy Peterson (drums).*

Brutal Death Metal from Austin, Texas. Formerly known as MALTHUSIA and successively POGROMY, following a self-titled 2001 demo SECT OF EXECRATION released the 'Baptised Through Blasphemy' album in 2002 on the Texas Death Metal Underground label. SECT OF EXECRATION guitar player Steven Watkins is also active with IMAGES OF VIOLENCE and, alongside IMAGES OF VIOLENCE colleagues singer John Zig and bassist Mark Denton plus DISGORGE and CINERARY drummer Rick Myers, studio project SARCOLYTIC. Drummer Jeremy Peterson is ex-PROPHECY. The group also employed Daniel Hearne, covering both bass and guitar roles.

SECT OF EXECRATION would be whittled down to a duo of Watkins and drummer Dobber Beverly of INGURGITATE and BRACED FOR NAILS repute. Beverly also operated as guitarist for IMAGES OF VIOLENCE.

BAPTISED THROUGH BLASPHEMY, TXDM TXDM 008 (2001). Exanimating The Deity / Scriptural Manipulations / Baptized Through Blasphemy / Hatred Is Bliss / How Feeble The Words Of Christ / Disgusted By The Faith.

Sect Of Execration, Sect Of Execration (2001) (Demo). Deadly Resurrection / Exanimating The Deity / Scriptural Manipulations / Sucking The Putrid Lactation.

SEEDS OF SORROW

VIENNA, AUSTRIA — *Alex Aigner (vocals), David Guger (guitar), Sigurd Krieger (guitar), Markus Marath (bass), Tomas Zonyga (drums).*

Vienna Death Metal band SEEDS OF SORROW debuted in August 1995 with the Dimitri Metzeltin produced EP 'Final Blast'. Live work included a notable support to OBITUARY at the Rockhaus, Vienna in May 1997 and opening for KRABATHOR at Hodonin, Czech Republic in December. Gigs became higher profile in 1998, guesting for VADER at the Shelter, Vienna in February and on October 22nd opening up for CANNIBAL CORPSE, INFERNAL MAJESTY and DARK FUNERAL at the Arena, Vienna. In 1998 former SEEDS OF SORROW guitarist Markus Schlögl forged CRYOSPHERE working with his brother, ex-PENDRAGON guitar player Oliver Schlögl.

Demonware Records put out the 1998 album 'Bleeding Eyes'. These sessions were recorded at Vienna Power Station that July with producer Michael Zastoupil. 'Bleeding Eyes' was presented to the public on December 19th with a release party at Vienna's Shelter venue. In April 1999 SEEDS OF SORROW supported SINISTER in the Czech Republic. The band's biggest concert to date came that June at the 'Rock in Allhau' festival, featuring on a billing alongside W.A.S.P., KREATOR, SODOM, RAGE and MANOWAR. June 2000 witnessed another major event for the band, participating on the 'Monsters of Metal Festival' in Sommerarena backing SLAYER and TESTAMENT. The band also made their presence felt at the 'Donauinsel' festival that same month and the 'Noise Art' event, with CANNIBAL CORPSE, SODOM and VADER, in July.

The Ulrich Guggenberger produced 'Phoenix Rising' single was issued in 2001. SEEDS OF SORROW united with Denmark's EXMORTEM and Dutch act MANGLED for the 'Attack Europe' tour in October. On June 16th SEEDS OF SORROW supported MOTÖRHEAD at the Vienna Arena. In August the group played the Vienna 'Metal Fest', sharing the stage with NIGHTWISH and TIAMAT.

Metal Age Productions signed SEEDS OF SORROW for the 2003 album 'Immortal Junkies'. These tracks, which included a cover version of MEGADETH's 'Symphony Of Destruction', were laid down at Metamorphosis Studios in Vienna with George Sukopp acting as engineer.

Drummer Tomas Zonyga joined PARENTAL ADVISORY in September 2004.

Final Blast EP, Whorehouse (1995). Intro / Bury The Dead / Aggression / Fears Unleashed Upon Me / Open Grave / Crush My Head.

BLEEDING EYES, Demonware (1998). Esod Red Ni Natas / Bleeding Eyes / Angry God / Kinderfucker / Lay Down To Die / Schizophreniac / Under My Skin / Judgement Day / Eternal Silence.

Phoenix Rising, Demonware (2001). Eat Shit / Illuminati / Injaculation / Ejaculation Of An Unknown God.

IMMORTAL JUNKIES, Metal Age Productions (2003).

SEMPER TYRANNIS

RUTHERFORD, NJ, USA — *Greg Bueno (vocals / guitar), Alex Tomaszewski (vocals / guitar), Eric Koppel (bass / keyboards), Alex Zetelski (drums).*

Rutherford, New Jersey melodic Death Metal band SEMPER TYRANNIS was initiated during March of 2002 by guitarists Alex Tomaszewski and Greg Bueno, the latter previously with 16W. Still as yet unnamed, the first band unit was built up with the incorporation of vocalist Rob Van Winkle, bass player Steve Montanez and Andrew Resch on the drums. By June drummer Mike Gardner had been inducted, followed briefly by Roger Smith on bass guitar. In the Autumn another 16W man, Eric Koppel, took over bass as they started to shift emphasis from covers to original material.

Their first, fully instrumental, gig would be conducted in October under the banner of MINDSTORM CONSPIRACY. After this show Kyle Kolich was enrolled as lead vocalist. Gardner was ousted in November, due to a difference of opinion in musical tastes, and Alex Zetelski duly took command of the drums.

SEMPER TYRANNIS, minus Kolich, recorded an eponymous 2004 demo. The 'Casting Dark In Morning Light' session was released in November.

Semper Tyrannis, (2004). Avoiding Sun / The Sky Is Forever Ours / War Procession.

Casting Dark In Morning Light, Semper Tyrannis (2004). Winds In Crimson Twilight / Eternity / The Sky Is Forever Ours / A Prophet Of Man's Fall.

SENTENCED

MUHOS, FINLAND — *Ville Laihiala (vocals), Miika Tenkula (guitar), Sami Lopakka (guitar), Taneli Jarwa (bass), Sami Kukkohovi (bass), Vesa Ranta (drums).*

A Muhos based Death Metal band that leaned more towards the NWoBHM 80s Thrash sound as each album progressed until later works shifted ground to a Doom-Death direction. Indeed, the band's classic British Rock influences were so evident the 1994 EP even went so far as to cover IRON MAIDEN's 'The Trooper'. With a population of less than 10,000, prior to the arrival of SENTENCED, Muhos' only contribution to the international world of entertainment had been the 1975 Miss Universe winner, Armi Kuusela.

SENTENCED was created during 1989 in Muhos, located near the northern city of Oulu, by the trio of guitarists Miika Tenkalu and Sami Lopakka along with drummer Vesa Ranta. These three had actually been performing together under an antecedent brand of DEFORMITY during 1988, Ranta having succeeded Tuure Heikkilä, before switching styles, from Thrash to Death, and titles. In this incarnation the band cut their inaugural demo sessions in November the following year dubbed 'When Death Join Us'. After recording, SENTENCED's numbers were brought up to full strength with the addition of vocalist / bassist Taneli Jarwa. Based on a second promotional recording, June 1991's 'Rotting Ways To Misery', they scored a deal with the French Thrash label for the Ahti Kortelainen produced debut album 'Shadows Of The Past' issued that November. A no frills Death Metal assault, 'Shadows Of The Past' saw guitarist Miika Tenkalu handling lead vocals.

The band also included the track 'Desperationed Future' on a free split EP, the mis-spelt 'Cronology Of Death', collaborating with BLUUURGH..., XENOPHOBIA and Sweden's CARBONIZED, for 'Thrash Your Brain' fanzine as a limited edition of 500 copies. SENTENCED then cut a further demo, 'Journey To Pohjola', in March 1992. These efforts garnered the band praiseworthy media coverage internationally prompting a fresh deal with the domestic Spinefarm label. June 1993's sophomore outing 'North From Here', the first record on which Taneli Jarwa took command of the vocals, would see the band adding a greater degree of melody to their work whilst retaining the technical edge. The group's next move was to a two track demo in 1994, comprising 'Glow Of 1000 Suns' and 'Amok Runs', as a tool to gain a new label deal.

The October 1993 EP 'The Trooper', recorded at Tico-Tico Studios in Kemi for new label Century Media, kept the faithful happy until the arrival of 'Amok' in January 1995. This album succeeding in selling over 35'000 units, with Japanese copies enhanced by two extra songs, 'Dreamlands' and 'Obsession'. SENTENCED toured Europe with TIAMAT and SAMAEL as Century Media re-released the bands first brace of albums to a wider audience. Ever eager to experiment, the September 1995 EP 'Love And Death' included a version of BILLY IDOL's 'White Wedding'.

Jarwa, quaintly billed as 'The fuck you man', often toured and recorded as bassist for IMPALED NAZARENE when the SENTENCED schedule allowed, featuring first on their 1992 'Sadogoat' EP and follow up album 'Tol Cormpt Norz Norz Norz'. However, Jarwa had departed following the 'Love And Death' EP and his place on bass was filled by Niko Karppinen, of LEGENDA and MAPLE CROSS on a session basis, whilst former BREED man Ville Laihiala took over lead vocals for the 1996 Waldemar Sorychta produced 'Down' album. Backing vocals came courtesy of Vorph of SAMAEL with female accompaniment from Birgit Zacher. The bands new lead vocalist brought another new dimension the SENTENCED sound as Laihiala opted for a clean vocal style more suited the more recent, doomier outings. Global touring had SENTENCED hitting their stride with dates in Europe, America and Japan. SENTENCED also formed part of the billing for the December 1996 'Dark Winter Nights' touring festival alongside DEPRESSIVE AGE, LACRIMOSA, THE GATHERING and DREAMS OF SANITY. Touring in Europe during March of 1997 saw the band forming up a package billing alongside THERION, MY DYING BRIDE, ORPHANAGE and DARK for the 'Out Of The Dark III' festivals.

The June 1998 opus 'Frozen', which found bassist Sami Kukkohovi of BREED and MYTHOS added to the roster, would once again be produced by Sorychta. Japanese copies hosted a traditional extra song, 'No Tomorrow'. A "gold" digipack edition increased the song quota by adding no less than four cover versions, namely W.A.S.P.'s ' I Wanna Be Somebody', RADIOHEAD's 'Creep', FAITH NO MORE's 'Digging The Grave' and THE ANIMALS 'House Of The Rising Sun'.

The January 2000 'Crimson' album, crafted at Tico Tico, would lend recognition to SENTENCED's status as it reached the coveted number 1 position in the Finnish album charts. Later in the same year the album would be re-launched on picture disc vinyl format. Meantime, erstwhile frontman Taneli Jarwa resurfaced fronting THE BLACK LEAGUE the same year.

In February of 2001 Century Media repackaged the 'Amok' and 'Love & Death' records on a single CD re-release. Laihiala was also to be revealed as in collaboration with Jesper Strömblad of IN FLAMES on an extracurricular band project.

SENTENCED bounced back in style during May 2002 with the Hiili Hiilesmaa produced album 'The Cold White Light', their 'No One There' single charting at the number 2 position in Finland. Shortly after the album itself hit the top spot in its first week of release, gaining Gold sales certification for 15'000 units sold. The musical transformation was by now complete, the SENTENCED journey having brought them up to an album that was focussed on groove, atmosphere and melancholic balladry.

A month's worth of North American dates commenced in San Francisco on September 16th backing up headliners IN FLAMES with strong support from KILLSWITCH ENGAGE and LACUNA COIL. The band shortly after unveiled an extensive European tour schedule for October, supported by LACUNA COIL. Further North American shows had SENTENCED combining forces with LACUNA COIL, IN FLAMES and DARK TRANQUILITY. Enrolled into the band unit for these gigs would be keyboard player Antti Pikkarainen from the band THE RMS.

SENTENCED bassist Sami Kukkohovi readied his side venture SOLUTION 13 (formerly CONFUSION RED) for their debut album release in November through Low Frequency Records. SENTENCED vocalist Ville Laihiala's own extracurricular endeavour POISONBLACK (formatively SHADOWLANDS), which saw the singer operating as guitarist in league with CHARON's frontman Juha-Pekka Leppäluoto, also announced his debut 'Escapexstacy'.

The band revealed a spirit of local patronage in September, recording their first ever Finnish language song 'Routasydän' for use as a theme song for their hometown of Oulu's ice hockey team Oulun Kärpät. However, this diversion would backfire on the band in spectacular fashion when a local newspaper alleged that the lyric "Sisu, veri ja kunnia" ("courage, blood and honour") displayed Nazi sympathies because it was similar to an oath sworn by the Hitler Jugend organisation from World War II. SENTENCED vehemently denied such assertions but the Oulun Kärpät team pulled the song from their events nonetheless. The band had the last word though, performing the song in front of a crowd of over 30,000 in celebration of the team winning the Finnish championship in April of 2004.

Early 2004 found Ville Laihiala engaged in POISONBLACK activities as well as finding the time to add a guest vocal to the 'Sweet & Deceitful' album from Glam Hard Rock outfit NEGATIVE, this record hitting number 1 on the Finnish charts. SENTENCED's Summer dates included festival performances at the 'Rock The Nations' event in Istanbul, Turkey, 'Athens Open Air' in Greece, 'Gates of Metal' in Sweden and 'Summer Breeze' in Germany. The band then selected Hiili Hiilesmaa as producer to craft a new studio album during November.

As 2005 drew in the band was subject to conjecture that their next album might be their last. In early February guitarist Sami Lopakka announced "The title of the new album is 'The Funeral Album', and with it we, SENTENCED, are coming to the end of our road. This album will be our last one. The decision is mutual, thoroughly thought over and final. Metaphorically speaking, this is a mass suicide of five." A preceding single, 'Ever-Frost' released only in Finland, duly entered the domestic charts at no. 1. SENTENCED performed their swan song live performance at the August 2005 'Wacken Open Air' festival in Germany. 'The Funeral Album' entered the national Finnish album charts at no. 1. Japanese variants added bonus live tracks in 'Brief Is The Light' and 'Nepenthe'.

SENTENCED announced that their final live show, held on 1st October 2005 at Club Teatria in Oulu, would be recorded and filmed for future product. With tickets selling out in less than an hour, the band added a further show for 30th September.

When Death Join Us, (1990). Hallucinations / When Death Join Us / Shadows Of The Past / Obscurity ... / Desperationed Future.
Rotting Ways To Misery, (1991). Rotting Ways To Misery / Disengagement / Suffocated Beginning Of Life / Under The Suffer / Descending Curtain Of Death / The Truth.
SHADOWS OF THE PAST, Thrash THR015-NR340 (1991). When The Moment Of Death Arrives / Rot To Dead / Disengagement / Rotting Ways To Misery / The Truth / Suffocated Beginning Of Life / Beyond The Distant Valleys / Under The Suffer / Descending Curtain Of Death.
Journey To Pohjola, (1992). Wings / In Memoriam / Mythic Silence—As They Wander In The Mist.

NORTH FROM HERE, Spinefarm SPI 13CD (1993). My Sky Is Darker Than Thine / Wings / Fields Of Blood / Harvester Of Hate / Capture Of Fire / Awaiting The Winter Frost / Beyond The Wall Of Sleep / Northern Lights / Epic.

The Trooper EP, Spinefarm SPI 15 (1993). The Trooper / Desert By Night / In Memoriam / Awaiting The Winter Frost.

Demo 1994, (1994) (Demo). Glow Of 1000 Suns / Amok Runs.

AMOK, Century Media 77076-2 (1995). The War Ain't Over! / Phenix / New Age Messiah / Forever Lost / Funeral Spring / Nepenthe / Dance On The Graves (Lil 'Siztah') / Moon Magick / The Golden Stream Of Lapland.

Love And Death EP, Century Media 77101-2 (1995). The Way I Wanna Go / Obsession / Dreamlands / White Wedding / Love And Death.

DOWN, Century Media 77146-2 (1996). Intro—The Gate / Noose / Shadegrown / Bleed / Keep My Grave Open / Crumbling Down (Give Up Hope) / Sun Won't Shine / Ode To The End / 0132 / Warrior Of Life (Reaper Redeemer) / I'll Throw The First Rock.

FROZEN—GOLD EDITION, Century Media 77246G-2 (1998) (Digipack). The Suicider / Dead Leaves / For The Love I Bear / Creep / Digging The Grave / Kaamos / Farewell / One With Misery / Grave Sweet Grave / Burn / Drown Together / Let Go (The Last Chapter) / The Rain Comes Falling Down / Mourn / I Wanna Be Somebody / House Of The Rising Sun.

FROZEN, Century Media 77246-2 (1998). Kaamos / Farewell / Dead Leaves / For The Love I Bear / One With Misery / The Suicider / The Rain Comes Falling Down / Grave Sweet Grave / Burn / Drown Together / Let Go (The Last Chapter) / Mourn. Chart position: 73 GERMANY.

Killing Me, Killing You, Century Media (1999). Killing Me, Killing You / Dead Moon Rising.

CRIMSON, Century Media 77346-2 (2000). Bleed In My Arms / Home In Despair / Fragile / No More Beating As One / Broken / Killing Me, Killing You / Dead Moon Rising / The River / One More Day / With Bitterness And Joy / My Slowing Heart. Chart position: 47 GERMANY.

THE COLD WHITE LIGHT, Century Media 8146-2 (2002) (North American release). Konevitsan Kirkonkellot / Cross My Heart And Hope To Die / Brief Is The Light / Neverlasting / Aika Multaa Muistot (Everything Is Nothing) / Excuse Me While I Kill Myself / Blood & Tears / You Are The One / Guilt And Regret / The Luxury Of A Grave / No One There / Killing Me Killing You (Video).

No One There, Century Media (2002). No One There (desolate single version) / Blood & Tears.

THE COLD WHITE LIGHT, Century Media 77446-2 (2002). Konevitsan Kirkonkellot / Cross My Heart And Hope To Die / Brief Is The Light / Neverlasting / Aika Multaa Muistot (Everything Is Nothing) / Excuse Me While I Kill Myself / Blood & Tears / You Are The One / Guilt And Regret / The Luxury Of A Grave / No One There. Chart positions: 1 FINLAND, 5 SWEDEN, 45 GERMANY.

Routasydän, (2003). Routasydän.

Ever-Frost, Century Media (2005). Ever-Frost / Despair-Ridden Hearts. Chart position: 1 FINLAND.

THE FUNERAL ALBUM, Century Media 8246-2 (2005). May Today Become The Day / Ever-Frost / We Are But Falling Leaves / Her Last 5 Minutes / Where Waters Fall Frozen / Despair-Ridden Hearts / Vengeance Is Mine / A Long Way To Nowhere / Consider Us Dead / Lower The Flags / Drain Me / Karu / End Of The Road. Chart positions: 1 FINLAND, 49 GERMANY, 59 AUSTRIA.

BURIED ALIVE, Century Media 8352-2 (2007). Funeral Intro / Where Winters Fall Frozen / May Today Become The Day / Neverlasting / Bleed / The Rain Comes Falling Down / Ever-Frost / Sun Won't Shine / Dead Moon Rising / Despair-Ridden Hearts / Broken / The Suicider / Excuse Me While I Kill / The War Ain't Over / Nepenthe / Northern Lights / The Way I Wanna Go / Dance On The Graves (Lil' Siztah) / Noose / Aika Multaa Muistot / Farewell / No One There / Drown Together / Cross My Heart And Hope To Die / Brief Is The Light / Vengeance Is Mine / End Of The Road.

FROZEN, NightOfTheVinylDead (2007) (Limited edition 500 copies only on ice clear vinyl). Kaamos / Farewell / Dead Leaves / For The Love I Bear / The Suicider / Rain Comes Falling Down / Grave Sweet Grave / Burn / Drown Together / Let Go (The Last Chapter) / Mourn.

SEPSISM

PACOIMA, CA, USA — *Fernando Avila (vocals), Leon Morrison (guitar), Armando Madrigal (bass), Phillip Hernandez (drums).*

California's SEPSISM, although created in 1990, have taken 9 years to issue their debut album due to a series of ongoing line up fluctuations. The band's only surviving founder members are vocalist Fernando Avila and drummer Phillip Hernandez. Guitarist Leon Morrison joined the ranks in 1993 and SEPSISM was boosted to a twin guitar act with the inclusion of Danny Halstead the following year. Halstead would appear on the 'Severe Carnal Butchery' demo but broke ranks shortly after.

A 1996 demo session 'Necrotic Flesh Rot' led to an album deal with Repulse Records and the enlistment of bassist Armando 'Mondo' Madrigal.

By 2000 Madrigal was out of the picture and in his stead came Danny Bourlier. This latest recruits tenure was predictably brief though.

Guitarist Salvador Altamirano was pulled in for European dates in April / May of 2000. However, with the dates completed Altamirano too would part ways with SEPSISM.

The band added bass player Raffi Roumdikian in the fall of 2001. The Spanish Repulse label would also announce the CD release of the band's much sought after debut demo 'Severe Carnal Butchery'.

PURULENT DECOMPOSITION, Repulse RPS 038 CD (1999). Surgical Atrocity / Pathological Disfigurement / Necrotic Flesh Rot / Shredded In Cannibalistic Violence / Dissection / Internal Fermentation / Uterocasket / Brutally Butchered / Murdering At Random / Veneno En Lasangre / Punctured Internal Organs / Born Into Oblivion.

SEVERE CARNAL BUTCHERY, Repulse (2001). Sadistically Mangled And Devoured / Sodomizing The Exhumed / Vulgar Strangulation / Removal of Putrid Entrails / Blistering Burnt Mutilage / Punctured Internal Organs (Live) / Sadistically Mangled And Devoured (Live) / Uterocasket (Live) / Dissection (Live) / Surgical Atrociy (Live).

TO PREVAIL IN DISGUST, From Beyond Productions FBP-012 (2003).

SEPTIC BREED

MALMÖ, SWEDEN — *Stefan Holm (guitar), Patrick Persson (guitar), Nicke Grabowski (drums).*

A youthful technically minded Death Metal combo, starting out in 1997 titled SEPTIC BREED, hailing from the Malmö-Helsingborg area of Southern Sweden. Drummer Nicke Grabowski, previously with Grindcore act A.I.S., had formulated the band with guitarist Stefan Holm, initially to just jam old Thrash material. With the introduction of second guitarist Patrick Persson the band opted to pursue the craft of penning original material. A debut demo session was delivered as SEPTIC BREED, March 1998's 'Patterns Of Delusive Design', produced by DARKANE's Klas Ideberg and fronted by Grabowski's former A.I.S. singer.

A 2000 Tommy Tägtgren produced demo session 'The Reaper', now with the band labelled as THE FORSAKEN and featuring MASSGRAV and OMINOUS vocalist Anders Sjöholm and Michael Håkansson of EVERGREY, CENOTAPHIA and EMBRACED on bass, soon secured a deal with German label Century Media.

Patterns Of Delusive Design, Skånemangel 001 (1998) (Demo). Patterns Of Delusive Design (Intro) / Psychotic Masterpiece / The Greed Of The Forsaken / Humanity Deformed / Reapers Chamber.

SEPTIC FLESH

GREECE — *Spiros Antoniou (vocals / bass), Chis Antoniou (guitar), Sotiris (guitar), Kostas (drums).*

SEPTIC FLESH describe themselves as "Dreamy Emotional Death" and the band first made their mark with the track 'Melting Brains', which appeared on numerous compilation albums. In early 1991 this was capitalized on by the 5 track demo 'Forgotten Path'. The tape sold well, shifting 800 copies. Their debut vinyl came in the form of the mini album 'Temple Of The Lost Race', which surfaced in early 1992. A further demo, this time highlighting their talents on the solitary track 'Morpheus-The Dream Lord' secured a deal with Holy Records.

Sotiris teamed up with Gunnar Theys of ANCIENT RITES and the industrious Magus Wampyr Daoloth of NECROMANTIA to forge the DANSE MACABRE project but bowed out before completion.

SEPTIC FLESH's 1998 release 'A Fallen Temple' found the band re-recording their debut effort and adding new songs. The band subsequently toured Europe as headliner in the spring of 1999 on the 'Temple Of Humiliations' dates with support from MISANTHROPE and NATRON.

Chris Antoniou, in union with Natalie Rassoulis who had contributed vocals to the last two records, issued a self titled side project album CHAOSTAR in 2000. All the members of SEPTIC FLESH contributed and it would soon be learned that CHAOSTAR had in reportedly completely superseded SEPTIC FLESH. A further 2000 release, 'Forgotten Paths', is a collection of early demos.

However, SEPTIC FLESH would make a return, announcing a 2002 album 'Sumerian Daemons'. Live promotion was to include an October run of Polish gigs in union with VOMITORY and MALEVOLENT CREATION as well as European dates the following month in league with DISMEMBER, SINISTER and THYRFING. Embarking upon a mammoth string of further European shows throughout October and November of 2002 the band created part of a deadly union for the 'Generation Armageddon' festival tour. Joining the band would be Norway's BLOOD RED THRONE, Ireland's PRIMORDIAL, Belgium's ANCIENT RITES, and Swedish heavyweights DISMEMBER and IMPIOUS.

Spiros Antoniou also involves himself in the THOU ART LORD side concern. Manning the drums for these 2002 concerts would be Fotis Bernardo of NIGHTRAGE.

Major line up changes in January of 2003 saw SEPTIC FLESH severing ties with keyboard player George Z and drummer Akis. The erstwhile CASUS BELI members Bob Katsionis and the INNER WISH credited Fotis Giannakopoulos took these respective positions. The band also inducted a new touring guitarist in ENSEMBLE man Alex Haritakis. The 'Generation Armageddon' title would be used once more for a second leg of European shows in May of 2003, the band forming a live alliance with PRIMORDIAL, THYRFING, ANCIENT RITES, BLOOD RED THRONE and SKYFIRE.

The Russian Irond label began a series of SEPTIC FLESH licensed releases throughout 2003. Included would be a unique version of 'The Eldest Cosmonaut' EP with added tracks from the 1991 12" single "Temple Of The Lost Race'.

SEPTIC FLESH manager George Zacharopoulos announced the band had decided to call it quits in November of 2003. SEPTIC FLESH drummer Fotis Bernardo joined the Greek / Swedish act NIGHTRAGE in 2004. Two SEPTIC FLESH members, Bob Katsionis and Fotis Giannakopoulos featured on guitar virtuoso Overlord's 2005 PERPETUAL album. In early 2005 it was revealed that Spiros Antoniou, Chris Antoniou and drummer Fotis Bernardo had forged a new venture billed as THE DEVILWORX.

MYSTIC PLACES OF DAWN, Holy HOLY05 (1994). Mystic Places Of Dawn / Crescent Moon / Return To Carthage / The Underwater Garden / Pale Beauty Of The Past / Chasing The Chimera / Behind The Iron Mask / (Morpheus) The Dream Lord / Mythos- Part One: Elegy, Part Two: Time Unbounded.
ESOPTRON, Holy HOLY13 (1995). Breaking Of The Inner Seal / Esoptron / Burning Phoenix / Astral sea / Rain / Ice Castle / Celebration / Succubus Priestess / So Clean, So Empty / The Eyes Of The Set / Narcissism.
OPHIDIAN WHEEL, Holy (1997). The Future Belongs To The Brave / The Ophidian Wheel / Phallic Litanies / Razor Blades Of Guilt / Tarturus / On The Topmost Step Of The Earth / Microcosmos / Geometry In Static / Sharmanic Kite / Heaven Below / Enchantment.
A FALLEN TEMPLE, Holy (1998). Brotherhood Of The Fallen Knights / The Eldest Cosmonaut / Marble Smiling Face / Underworld Act I / Temple Of The Last Race / The Crypt / Setting Of The Two Suns / Erebus / Underworld Act II / The Eldest Cosmonaut (Dark version).
The Eldest Cosmonaut, Holy (1998). The Eldest Cosmonaut / Underworld Act III / Finale / Woman Of The Rings.
REVOLUTION DNA, Holy (1999). Science / Chaostar / Radioactive / Little Music Box / Revolution / Nephilim Sons / DNA / Telescope / Last Ship To Nowhere / Dictatorship Of The Mediocre / Android / Arctic Circle / Age Of A New Messiah.
FORGOTTEN PATHS (THE EARLY DAYS), Black Lotus BLRCD 017 (2000). Intro / Power Of The Dark / Melting Brains / Unholy Ritual / Curse Of Death / Forgotten Path / Outro / Power Of The Dark (Live) / Forgotten Path (Live) / Melting Brains (Live).
THE ELDEST COSMONAUT, Irond CD 03-611 (2003) (Russian release). The Eldest Cosmonaut (Video remix) / Underworld Act III / Finale / Woman Of The Rings (Remastered) / Erebus / Another Reality / Temple Of The Lost Race / Setting Of The Two Suns.

SERBERUS

DENVER, CO, USA — *Ivan Alcala (vocals / guitar), Dave Otero (vocals / guitar), Patrick Russell (bass), Corey Melanson (drums).*

Accomplished Melodic Death Metal from Denver, Colorado. A self financed mini album 'In Eternity' arrived during 2000 seeing SERBERUS with a line up of vocalist / guitarist Ivan Alcala, vocalist / guitarist Dave Otero, bass player Aaron Meacham and drummer Corey Melanson.

At the close of the year Meacham made way for Patrick Russell as the band set to work on a full length album 'Our Dying Grace', this featuring a cover version of DESTRUCTION's 'Curse The Gods'. Russell subsequently joined EMBER and would act as stand in guitarist for Grind outfit CEPHALIC CARNAGE. Former SERBERUS drummer Jeremy Portz later figured in THROCULT, SYNTHETIC DELUSION and had a brief spell with EMBER.

IN ETERNITY, (2000). Ancinet Throne / Dark Dream / In Eternity / Gates Of Fire / Ancient Throne (Live).
OUR DYING GRACE, (2001). Prologue / Our Dying Grace / Dark Dream / Ancient Throne / Curse Of The Gods (Destruction).
DESCENSION, Crash (2002). Falling Into The Abyss / Our Dying Grace / Dark Dream / Ancient Throne / Creed Of War / Gates Of Fire / In Eternity.

SERENADE

GLASGOW, SCOTLAND, UK — *John Alexander (vocals), Fraser McGartland (guitar), Gerry Magee (guitar), Stephen Mitchell (bass), Graeme McGartland (drums).*

A Glasgow rooted Doom Metal band forged during March 1994. Previous to this the bulk of the band members had operated in IMMORTAL RITES. As SERENADE they heralded their arrival with the demo tape 'Let Loose The Beauty Within'. This release would subsequently be re-issued as an official cassette EP by Deviation Records. Later still these sessions would be allied to material from HARMONY for a split CD release on Arctic Serenades.

SERENADE's first full length opus, 'The 28th Parallel' issued by Deviation, would prove to be a conceptual piece based upon the discoveries of Christopher Columbus. The album generated laudatory reviews but SERENADE's gig schedule was spartan. The sophomore outing, 1998's 'The Chaos They Create' took the concept theme into an obscurer destination, the storyline this time regarding the struggles of a Celtic farming family.

At this juncture SERENADE split away from Deviation Records and also suffered major internal turbulence. Guitarist Gerry Magee broke away and bass player Stephen Mitchell relocated to Aberdeen.

For the 'Plague Of Time' EP release, distributed by the group's own label Golden Lake Productions, SERENADE trimmed down to a trio with guitarist Fraser McGartland taking on bass duties for recording. A latter day band line up saw the induction of new personnel MITHRAS vocalist Rayner Coss and guitarist Adam Chapman.

SERENADE members are also committed to the Stoner side venture MONGOOSE III.

Let Loose The Beauty Within EP, Arctic Serenades SERE 008 (1995) (Split CD with HARMONY). Where The River Flows End / Let Loose The Beauty Within / Born Into Sorrow / Casting The Flash.

THE 28TH PARALLEL, Deviation (1996). Introduction: 1492 / Daring To Dream / The Hearing / Ocean Of Despair / Beyond The Mist / Arrival / San Salvador / The Encounter / Homeward / Eden / To Face The Glory / Eden After The All / This Was Their World / Eternal Dream.

THE CHAOS THEY CREATE, Deviation (1998). The Raptures Of The Moribund / Blue Empyreans / Embracing Weave Of Wheat / Sundown Angels / Flames Dance / Woeful Third Season / Chaos... / The Hermit And The Wolves / Rains Wash Away (Parts 1 To 3).

Plague Of Time EP, Golden Lake Productions (2001). Depth Of The Bleeding Angel / Plague Of Time / Casting The Flesh- Say Hello To Hell.

THE SERPENTS DANCE, Golden Lake Productions GOLD007CD (2002). Into The Serpents Dance / Slaves Of Chaos / Dying Light / March Of Darkness / Betrayal Of Faith / Armageddon Comes / Evenslaughter / Nevermore.

SERMON

MOSCOW, RUSSIA — *Pavel Suslov (vocals / guitar), Serge Smagin (guitar), Vasili Rumjantsev (bass), Dmitri Osipov (drums).*

Moscow Death / Thrash Metal band SERMON was established by guitarist/vocalist Pavel Suslov under the name SS-20 in the Autumn of 1990. Formative demos recorded between 1991 to 1994 included the sessions 'Infernal Life' and 'Preacher Of Death'. During 1994 Suslov assembled an all new membership, also using this opportunity to retitle the band SERMON. In this new guise the band cut the demo 'Through Eternity' in the spring of 1996. The underground US label Wild Rags released the album 'From Death To Death' in 1998, SERMON following this with 'Frustration' in the Spring of 1999. This ten track outing featured three re-recorded demo tracks from 'Through Eternity' plus an unexpected cover version of SMOKIE's Pop hit 'What Can I Do'. In 2003 band signed with Soyuz Music.

FROM DEATH TO DEATH, Wild Rags WRR 112 (1998). I Want To Reach The Dawn / Another's Spring (Kills Me) / Forever Lost / Eternal Progress / Sad Clown / Crying Skies / I'm Terrified / No Place / The Beginning Of The Day / Zatmenie.

HYPERTONIA, (1999). Into Another World (Intro) / Take Me With You / In The Name Of Daughter / Amid Three Coffins / Life Is Hell / Temptation / Pray / Hypertonia / I'm Alone / What Can I Do.

FRUSTRATION, Soyuz SM 738-03 (2003). Frustration / After Me / Scorn / 2 Souls / That Is All / Where The Earth Blooms / Only Winter / Give Me Your Soul / My Cross / Wherever I May Roam.

SERPENS AEON

SEATTLE, WA, USA — *Luis Martinez (vocals / bass), Erick Diaz (guitar), Brian Stephens (guitar), Matt Cason (drums).*

Death Metal band SERPENS AEON was forged in late 1997 by vocalist / guitarist Luis Martinez and guitarist Erick Diaz, both founder members of the esteemed Mexican act THE CHASM. Rounding off the first inductees would be Mike Krutsinger of IN MEMORIUM and DARKENWOOD on Bass. With Krutsinger decamping to concentrate on his priority act IN MEMORIUM second guitarist Chris Rapier joined December of 1998 as Martinez switched instruments to cover bass.

A succession of drummers followed before SERPENS AEON settled on Chris Alexander in late 1999. His place would be taken in June of the following year by Matt Cason of DRAWN AND QUARTERED. After the recording of demo sessions Rapier decamped in February of 2002. Stepping on guitar would be Brian Stephens, frontman for SEMESUS and, under the pseudonym 'Dantven', keyboard player / drummer with Black Metal band INQUINOK.

DAWN OF KOUATL, Moribund DEAD 46 (2003). Forsaken Thy God / Within The Realms Of Serpens / Winds Of Hatred / Nectar Of Godz / Under The Fifth Sun / Cosmic Jaws / Circle Of Serpens.

SERPENT

STOCKHOLM, SWEDEN — *Piotr Wawrzeniuk (vocals), Johan Lundell (guitar), Lars Rosenberg (bass), Per Karlsson (drums).*

Stockholms SERPENT date back to 1993 when the band were formed as a side project by then ENTOMBED bassist Lars Rosenberg and CONCRETE SLEEP / THERION's bassist Andreas Wahl. The band soon enlisted THERION drummer Piotr Wawrzeniuk on vocals and drums before completing the line up with guitarist Johan Lundell.

Wahl departed in 1994 and was replaced by Ulf Samuelsson of SUFFER. Drummer Per Karlsson, another former SUFFER compatriot, joined SERPENT following recording of the debut album.

Unsatisfied with the reception to the debut album, SERPENT split from Radiation Records before undergoing an even more traumatic event when Rosenberg left the fold. Ironically, his swift replacement was none other than Wahl. This line up soon got back into action by donating a fresh recording, a song titled 'The Fog', to a couple of compilation albums prompting a deal with Heathendoom Music.

Karlsson joined T.A.R. in January 1997.

IN THE GARDEN OF SERPENT, Radiation RAD006 (1996). Fly With The Flow / Save From Ourselves / The Order / Stoned The Dawn / Magic / Lost Dreams / Frozen Cosmos / In Memorium / Drown / Corpse City.

AUTUMN RIDE, Heathendoom HDMCD005 (1997). Prologue / Dimension Zero / The Shot / Chasing The Dragon / Autumn Ride / The Fog / Mars's Boogie / Live Through This.

SERPENT OBSCENE

SWEDEN — *Erik Tormentor (vocals), Nicklas Eriksson (guitar), Johan Thorngren (guitar), Jonas Eriksson (drums).*

Thrash edged Death Metal convened during 1997, SERPENT OBSCENE released their inaugural demo 'Behold The Beginning' that same year. Vocalist Erik Tormentor is an ex-MARBLE ICON member. SERPENT OBSCENE guitarists Nicklas Eriksson and Johan Thorngren are former members of A MIND CONFUSED. The pair would create a side act KAAMOS in mid 1998. Although Eriksson still operates with KAAMOS Thorngren left their ranks in 1999.

SERPENT OBSCENE's 1999 'Massacre' demo secured an album deal with the Necropolis label. Following issue of the debut album Jonas Eriksson exited in March of 2001. He would be superseded by KAAMOS man Christofer Barkensjö as the band undertook gigs in Germany.

SERPENT OBSCENE, Necropolis (2000). Devastation / Serpent Prophecy / Sadistic Abuse / Rapid Fire / Pestilent Seed (The Plague) / Evil Rites / Morbid Horror / Violent Torture / Act Of Aggression.

DEVASTATION, Sound Pollution (2003). The Rotten / Chaos Reign Supreme / Beyond Recognition / Torture Slave / Terror From The Sky / Legacy Of The Wicked / Face The Inferno / Under Siege / War Is On / Perversion Prevails.

SERPENTOR

BENSCHOP, HOLLAND — *Jos Manders (vocals), Wico Oostveen (guitar), Leon van Midden (bass), Maarten Kooymans (drums).*

Benschop Death Metal band SERPENTOR, founded in May of 1998 by bassist Leon van Midden of XANTOSSA repute, issued the 2001 EP 'Incarnation Of Evil', recorded at Franky's Recording Kitchen and engineered by Berthus Westerhuis. The band also included erstwhile members of Ijsselstein Thrash act EXPIRE, singer Jos Manders and guitarist Wico Oostveen. With the departure of both Manders and Oostveen, the surviving trio of vocalist / bassist Leon van Midden, guitarist Philip Nugteren and drummer Maarten 'Trigs' Kooymans took on a harder, more brutal direction re-tagged as XERPENTOR. A three track demo, simply entitled 'Promo 2003', would be their first offering.

SEVERE TORTURE

Incarnation Of Evil, Serpentor (2001). Throne Of Death / Evil Incarnate / Forces Of The Dark.

SEVERE TORTURE

HOLLAND — *Dennis (vocals), Thijs (guitar), Patrick (bass), Seth (drums).*

Beginning life in 1997 SEVERE TORTURE comprised CENTURION members drummer Seth and bassist Patrick alongside vocalist Erik and guitarists Thijs and Jelle. This version of the band cut the 1998 'Baptized' demo before Eric quit to team up with SINISTER. Undaunted, SEVERE TORTURE enrolled Dennis as a replacement but following a support gig to IMMOLATION guitarist Jelle departed. The band resolved to persevere as a four piece for an appearance at the Tilburg 'No Mercy' festival and touring into Eastern Europe with Polish act DAMNATION.

A two track vinyl promotional single was issued on Damnation Records upfront of their debut album 'Feasting On Blood'. During 2001 bassist Patrick filled in as temporary stand in for fellow Dutch Death Metal brethren PYAEMIA.

SEVERE TORTURE would tour America in April of 2002 on a package billing with DISGORGE, DEEDS OF FLESH and DISAVOWAL. A further run of European shows would be scheduled commencing September 19th in Eindhoven, Holland, a month's worth of dates supporting DEW SCENTED and CANNIBAL CORPSE. In June of 2003 the band added a second guitarist to the ranks, the DEW SCENTED and BLO.TORCH credited Marvin Vriesde.

SEVERE TORTURE acted as support to DYING FETUS for their Scandinavian shows in June of 2004. A live album, 'Blood Letting' released by Karmageddon Media in February 2005, featured a cover version of the PESTILENCE song 'Lost Souls'. Just previous to this release the band had entered Excess Studios in Rotterdam to lay down new tracks. SEVERE TORTURE signed to Earache Records in June.

UK dates in March 2007 saw a partnership with Huddersfield's EVILE and Welsh gore mongers DESECRATION.

Pray For Nothing, Damnation (2000). Pray For Nothing / Rest In Flames.
FEASTING ON BLOOD, Hammerheart (2000). Feces For Jesus / Blood / Decomposing Bitch / Baptized In Virginal Liquid / Twist The Cross / Butchery Of The Soul / Rest In Flames / Severe Torture / Pray For Nothing / Vomiting Christ.
Lambs Of A God, Hammerheart (2001). Lambs Of A God / Taking Down The Descender.
Butchery Of The Soul EP, Hammerheart (2002). Butchery Of The Soul / Rest In Flames / Pray For Nothing / Lambs Of A god / Taking Down The Descender / Perverse Suffering.
MISANTHROPIC CARNAGE, Hammerheart (2002). Mutilation Of The Flesh / Meant To Suffer / Carnivorous Force / Misanthropic Carnage / Blinded I Slaughter / Impelled To Kill / Castrated / Forever To Burn / Your Blood Is Mine.
BLOOD LETTING, Karmageddon Media (2005). Feces For Jesus / Baptized In Virginal Liquid / Decomposing Bitch / Impelled To Kill / Mutilation Of The Flesh / Butchery Of The Soul / Carnivorous Force / Misanthropic Carnage / Pray For Nothing / Lost Souls / 'Till The End / Severe Torture / Baptized In Virginal Liquid / Lambs Of A God / Taking Down The Descender.
FALL OF THE DESPISED, Earache (2005). Endless Strain Of Cadavers / Sawn Off / Unconditional Annihilation / Consuming The Dying / Impulsive Mutilation / Dead From The Waist Up / Decree Of Darkness / Enshrined In Madness / End Of Christ / Fall Of The Despised.

SEVERED SAVIOR

USA — *Dusty Boisjolie (vocals), Shon Benham (guitar), Murray Fitzpatrick (bass), Troy Fullerton (drums).*

Death Metal act previously known as CHRIST DENIED upon their formation in 1997 by guitarists Murray Fitzpatrick and Tom Stoltz. Joining this duo would be drummer Greg White and bassist Armondo Avalos. During 1998 Stoltz relocated to Hawaii and former WHERE? Guitarist Mike Gilbert took his position. The following year Gilbert's WHERE? Colleague drummer Troy Fullerton was inducted and shortly after vocalist Dusty Boisjolie completed the line up.

Up to full strength CHRIST DENIED recorded a demo session in 1999 billed as 'Puddle Of Gore'. However, the band was then made aware of a European act of the same title and thus switched titles to SEVERED SAVIOR, debuting under their new brand in August of 2000 at a show opening for DISGORGE and DEEDS OF FLESH. Soon after Avalos made his exit and SEVERED SAVIOR opted to continue on the live circuit as a quartet with Fitzpatrick taking on bass duties.

Eventually erstwhile DEEDS OF FLESH man Jared Deaver was inducted. Deaver made his recording mark with the band recording three tracks included on the November 2001 album 'Forced To Bleed'. Just before the album was issued Gilbert took his leave. SEVERED SAVIOR pulled in Rob Lumbre of MUCUS MEMBRANE and PSYPHERIA. The multi talented Lumbre also citing credits as a drummer for PUNISHER and bassist for OSMIUM.

SEVERED SAVIOR were dealt a huge blow when Rob Lumbre was killed in a car accident on the 5th of January 2002. The band inducted Jason Kramer on second guitar in February as they geared up for an album for the Unique Leader label titled 'Brutality Is Law'. Subsequently Shon Benham was pulled in on guitar but in 2003 Jared Deaver exited. Tom Stolz would also found time to deputize on bass for FUNERAL AGE. In July of 2004 SEVERED SAVIOR landed the role as opening act for CANNIBAL CORSE and THE BLACK DAHLIA MURDER.

SEVERED SAVIOR guitarist Shon Benham stood in as temporary bassist for GOATWHORE on their November 2004 US dates.

FORCED TO BLEED, Disfigured (2001). Fuck The Humans / Forced To Bleed / DeadSpeak / Fecalpheliac / Bury The Whore / Puddle Of Gore / Steel Toe Abortion / Molesting The Dead.

SEXTRASH

BELO HORIZONTE, MG, BRAZIL — *Pussy Ripper (vocals), Damned Sentry (guitar), Tomy Simmons (bass), D.D. Crazy (drums).*

SEXTRASH was created in Belo Horisonte during 1987 by former SARCOFAGO drummer D.D. Crazy. The group debuted in 1989 with the three track 'XXX' EP for the French Maggot label. The band's final album output would be 1992's 'Funeral Serenade' as singer Pussy Ripper (a.k.a. Oswald Scheid) was killed in an auto accident in 1997.

SEXTRASH announced a return to action in the Spring of 2005, signing a new album deal with Cogumelo Records. The band at this juncture comprised singer Doom, guitarist Marck, bass player Kruegger and Quake on the drums. One of the re-activated group's first moves was to act as openers for KREATOR in their hometown, Belo Horizonte. SEXTRASH album recordings in late 2005, 'Rape From Hell', would be produced by former SARCOFAGO bassist Gerald Minelli.

XXX EP, Maggot (1989). Jack The Ripper / Sadistic Screams / Extreme Noise Terror.
SEXUAL CARNAGE, Cogumelo (1991). Intro / Psychoneurosis / Delirium Tremens / The Insatiable Pleasure Of Delight / Seduced By Evil / Alcoholic Mosh / Obscene Symphony / Black Church / Night Pigs / Genital Tumor.
FUNERAL SERENADE, Cogumelo (1992).
SEXUAL CARNAGE / XXX, Cogumelo (2000). Intro / Psychoneurosis / Delirium Tremens / The Insatiable Pleasure Of Delight / Seduced By Evil / Alcoholic Mosh / Obscene Symphony / Black Church / Night Pigs / Genital Tumor / Jack The Ripper / Sadistic Screams / Extreme Noise Terror / Intro (Penetration) / Satanás.
RAPE FROM HELL, Cogumelo CG 0079 (2006). Suck Me / Brutal Sex / Chemical Orgy / Fuck In All / Possessed By Cruelty / Maze Of The Damn Madness / Rape From Hell / Lust / Money And Violence / Obscure Doors / Sweet Suffering / Tchambs.

SHADOW'S VEIL

BELGIUM — *Jeroen Jochems (vocals / guitar), Jan Bergmans (guitar), Hans Van Gaeveren (bass), Stefaan De Beckker (drums).*

SHADOW'S VEIL, a melodic Black / Death Metal band with overtones of epic Metal, was forged in the Autumn of 2000 by STIGMATEM vocalist / guitarist Jeroen Jochems and drummer Stefaan De Beckker, soon joined by guitarist Jan Bergmans and ex-STIGMATEM bassist Steven Bergmans. Initially a covers outfit, the band crafted their first original composition 'The Veil' in March of 2001. Liesbet Claeys joined as flute player toward the close of the year. The inaugural recording, entitled 'Cast A Shadow', was laid down at the Trax Studios in Ghent during February of 2002. Liesbet left the band in June 2003.

Upon completion of recording the October 2004 demo 'Shadow Lands' bassist Steven Bergmans exited, being replaced by Hans Van Gaeveren of HORNY MOSES.

Cast A Shadow, (2002). Collapse Of Humanity / At The Gates / The Veil / Break The Chains / Guided By The Northern Wind.
Shadow Lands, Shadows Veil (2004). Break The Chains / Shadow / The Veil / As The Wolves Gather For The Hunt / Collapse Of Humanity / Ruined Heart / Along The Mountainside.

SHADOWBREED

HOLLAND — *Remigius (vocals), Rodj (guitar), Dann (guitar), Rob (bass), Sjoerd Rokx (drums).*

Death Metal with pedigree. SHADOWBREED, hailing from the north of Holland, was forged during 1998 by a quartet of erstwhile MORGANOM members- vocalist Remigius, 7 string guitarist Rodj, 6 string guitarist Dann, bassist Rob and drummer Oll. Rodj and Rob also citing credits with Black Metal act BI FROST.

The band would record tracks for a limited edition 7" single, 'Avatar' / 'Path In The Dark', with Painkiller Records but these sessions would be expanded upon to become a debut mini album 'The Light Of The Shadow' issued by Hammerheart Records subsidiary Unveiling The Wicked in September of 1999. Post recording bassist Rob would make way for another ex BI FROST member Kasper.

Touring in May of 2000 found SHADOWBREED on the road in Europe sharing billing with THYRFING and PRIMORDIAL. The band would also issue the five track promotional CD 'Pure Violations'. However, by December of 2000 longstanding drummer Oll decamped. Sjoerd Rokx, yet another BI FROST refugee, would replace him.

After the issue of their second album 'Only Shadows Remain' for Painkiller Kasper departed and original four stringer Rob rejoined the fold.

THE LIGHT OF THE SHADOW, Unveiling The Wicked (1999). Path In The Dark / Unfinished Business / Wail Of The Banshee / Avatar / Dying Hour.
ONLY SHADOWS REMAIN, Painkiller PKR016LP (2001).

SHADOWS LAND

STARGARD SZCZECIŃSKI, POLAND — *Aro 666 (vocals / guitar), Ra.F. Buzzer (guitar), Paul (bass), T. Borys (samples), J. Nerexo (drums).*

SHADOWS LAND began life in Stargard Szczeciński as an ultra heavy Doom-Death act, proffering the Andrzej Bomba produced 'Epitaph' demo of 1997 as evidence. Upon completion of a second promotion recording in 1999, 'Smell Of Pain', the band introduced two new players, bassist Pith from PERVERSE and the TORQUEMADA and DEATH CERTIFICATE credited drummer J. Nerexo. This version of the band debuted live in 2000 at the Wejherowo 'Devil's Night' festival. Increased live activity in Poland saw SHADOWS LAND supporting visiting international artists such as Mexicans DISGORGE, German bands SUDDEN DEATH and PROFANITY and Swiss act REQUIEM. The April 2002 'Hellish Damned' tour had SHADOWS LAND packaged with SUDDEN DEATH and REQUIEM.

SHADOWS LAND conducted the 'Hellish Damned III' tour of Poland in September 2005 allied with countrymen PERVERSE and Portuguese acts GOLDENPYRE and NECROSE. Empire Records issued the April 2006 album 'Terminus Ante Quem'. Studio guests for the tracks laid down at Hertz Studio included guitarist Br.Martin of PHAETON and CRUENTUS programmer Kruen. This set was licensed to Osmose Productions for European release.

SHADOWS LAND live guitarist Thrufel, of YATTERING and AZARATH, announced the side project MASACHIST, a union with drummer Daray, of VADER, VESANIA and NEOLITHIC, in December 2006.

ANTE CHRISTUM (NATUM), Empire (2003). Hybrid / My Name Are Three Sixes / Z Page Ia-idion Odmicalzo... / Decimel / Last Way / Vortex / You Are God / I'm Dead / Flash / B.O.R.Y.S. Six / Smell Of Pain / Pagan Fears / Instant Kamera (Video).
TERMINUS ANTE QUEM, Osmose Productions OPCD 181 (2006). The Absolute / Narcotic Vision / The Energy Of Masses / Interlude / Hunger Of Infinity / Efface Yourself / And The Master Says... / Lux Nox / Space Of Light.

SHADOWS OF SUNSET

LIETO, FINLAND — *Aki Järvinen (vocals / guitar), Jani Heinonen (guitar), Pasi Uotila (bass), Atte Mäkelä (drums).*

SHADOWS OF SUNSET was conceived in Lieto during the Autumn of 1993 under the moniker IMPOSED SILENCE by vocalist / guitarist Jani Heinonen, bass player Pasi Uotila and former CRIMSON MIDWINTER drummer Atte Mäkelä. This trio recorded the old school Death Metal demo 'Torn Angels Of Divine' in July 1995. Re-branded as SHADOWS OF SUNSET, and installing Aki Järvinen of NIGHTSIDE on second guitar, the band then set out on the live trail. A second demo, 'Fires Of The Soon Dead Moon', arrived the following July.

SHADOWS OF SUNSET signed to Fadeless Records for the four song EP 'Reflection From Afar'. A third demo, 'Mirror Of Bestiality', emerged in 1999, after which the name change to TORN occurred. Järvinen and Mäkelä assembled an all new band including guitarist T. Sinisterror (a.k.a. Tuomas Karppinen) of TORTURE KILLER and FUNERAL FEAST plus bassist Tuomo Latvala, the latter a veteran of TORTURE KILLER, DEEPRED and DEMIGOD.

TORN entered Mika Haapasalo's Pop Studios in Loimaa in July 2001 to record new tracks billed as 'Violent Ecstasy', although these sessions saw only Järvinen handling guitars as Karppinen had damaged his arm in an accident just prior to this date. Severe Music took these recordings on for commercial release. Mäkelä was forced to bow out due to injury and Latvala switched from bass to drums. Kai Huovinen was inducted to cover on bass.

Re-billed as 'Gurglenator', Aki Järvinen founded GORETORTURE for a 2004 album 'Promised To Kill You Last ... I Lied'. The SHADOWS OF SUNSET credited Daimos666 joined BARATHRUM in February 2005.

Fires Of The Soon Dead Sun, (1996). Images Of The Darkest Nature's Wrath / Until The Fires Of Dawn / Beyond Emptiness / Craving Of Pleasure.

Reflection From Afar EP, Fadeless (1997). Reflection From Afar / The Darkred Veil / An Ode For The Blackened Moon / The Beckoning Shadows.

SHEOLGEENNA

CHILE — *Darkon (vocals), Draconis (guitar), Marcelo Contreras (guitar), Anekkiannye (bass), Pablo Clares (drums).*

SHEOLGEENA, a self styled "Primigenian evil Death Metal" act from Valdivia and created in March of 1997, released the 1999 demo 'Emerged From Outside Skies'. These sessions were laid down in 1997 by vocalist Darkon, guitarists Warrior (a.k.a. Marcelo Contreras) and Maximiliano Castro, bass player Mario Quiñileo and drummer Miguel Angel Avendaño. Membership shuffles saw guitarist Draconis and bass player Manuel Martin entering the fold in August of 1998.

Some bad luck befell the band in September of 2000 when Avendaño suffered a fractured leg. For live work SHEOLGEENA took on the services of TEOFOBIA and GNENESHEN drummer Hug-O-Toth. However, Avendaño subsequently opted out of the group and Hug-O-Toth maintained his position. In addition DESTRAL bass player Juan Vitagliano also came onboard. By April of 2001 Hug-O-Toth had stepped down to allow the EXECRATOR and TOTTEN KORPS credited Pablo Clares to assume the drummers mantle.

The debut album 'The Dark Chambers ... (Shukra Kteis, Maher-Salalhas-Baz)' emerged in 2002. After recording yet another new face behind the bass guitar, Anekkiannye, was inducted.

THE DARK CHAMBERS ... (SHUKRA KTEIS, MAHER-SALAHAS-BAZ), Rawforce Productions (2002). Trameron Psykje Domain / Emerged From Outside Skies / Iccha Shukra / Physika, Mystica, Tenibria / Artmagika-Shoget / Shamadi / Cursed Eon Of Eternal Bonfire / Apocrifos / Perpetus Panthey Edenic Na-Fal / Kheprer Kheprou Scaraboeus Sacer.

SHOT INJECTION

GOTHENBURG, SWEDEN — *Kristian Forsell (vocals), Seb Westman (guitar), Patrick Moehlenbrock (guitar), Fredrik Larsson (bass), Niclas Jonsson (drums).*

Gothenburg's SHOT INJECTION features ex-CRYSTAL AGE and HAMMERFALL bassist Fredrik Larsson, also operating in parallel as a member of DEATH DESTRUCTION. SHOT INJECTION was formulated during early 2005 by singer Kristian Forsell and guitar player Seb Westman, subsequently enrolling ex-NONE guitarist Patrick Moehlenbrock and drummer Niclas Jonsson of THAGIRION.

The band cut demos in April 2006, dubbed 'Fear Comes Full Circle', at Division One Studios in Gothenburg with EVERGREY's Tom S Englund acting as producer. Drafting former ROACH bassist Filip Svensson the group then utilised Division One Studios once again in June to cut an album entitled 'Eleven Triple Manifest'. M.A.N and ex-MNEMIC frontman Tony Jelencovich guested on the track 'Follow My Chaos'. Tom S Englund also contributed once again, donating vocals to the song 'Suicide Scenario'. SHOT INJECTION drafted new bass player Erik Samuelsson in July as Larsson jumped over to EVERGREY.

SHOT INJECTION entered Studio Fredman in Gothenburg on September 23rd to cut new tracks for the album 'World Of Coma'. Fredrik Larsson rejoined the HAMMERFALL ranks in April 2007.

Fear Comes Full Circle, Shot Injection (2006) (Demo). Picturing Our Downfall / Fragile White / Bleed The Lies.

Eleven Triple Manifest, Shot Injection (2006) (Demo). Follow My Chaos / Suicide Scenario / Eleven.

SHROUD

MALM, NORWAY — *Psyber-X (vocals), Aztralic (guitar), Sorg (bass), Spectraliz (keyboards), Drake (drums).*

Malm Black Metal band issued the demo 'World Beyond Time' in 1998 as their opening gambit. The group had been formulated by guitarist Aztralic and drummer Drake in 1997. Handling vocals and bass would be Arathorn with Njord on keyboards. Following the 'World Beyond Time' sessions, Psyber-X was introduced as lead singer, followed by further changes with the introduction of Sorg as keyboard player and second guitar player Veles. That winter, after Arathorn's dismissal, the second demo 'Mountainstorms' was recorded. However, SHROUD then went their separate ways.

In 2003 Aztralic, Drake and Psyber-X, inducting Spectraliz on keyboards, reunited. The demo 'Paragons Of Excellence' was crafted, after which Drake opted out. SHROUD issued the demo 'Exploring The Revolutional Aspects' in July 2005. Guest female vocals came courtesy of Wysteria.

World Beyond Time, (1998). World Beyond Time / Ondskapens Ring.
Mountainstorms, (1999). Mountainstorms / The Conquest Of The Mighty Crown Of Darkness / Ondskapens Ring / World Beyond Time.
Rehearsal Demo, (2004). The Art Of Blasphemy / The Malice Of Heaven And Hell / No Longer Of Dust Or Human Blood.
Paragons Of Excellence, (2005). The Art Of Blasphemy / The Malice Of Heaven And Hell / Argent Silver Plata / No Longer Of Dust Or Human Blood.
Exploring The Revolutional Aspects, Shroud (2005). Illusions Meant For Stars And Pure Flesh / Extinction Of The Programmed Mind / Revolution Extreme / The 3rd Eye And The Ghost.

SICKENING HORROR

GREECE — *George Antipatis (vocals / guitar), Ilias Daras (bass), George Kollias (drums).*

Death Metal act founded in January 2002 by vocalist / guitarist George Antipatis, THE CIRCLE OF ZAPHYAN bassist Ilias Daras and George Kollias on drums. SICKENING HORROR's 2003 demo, featuring NIGHTFALL and OBSECRATION guitarist George Bokos, was recorded that November at Zero Gravity Studios. SICKENING HORROR drummer George Kollias gained international recognition with NIGHTFALL, SYSTEM SHOCK, THE CIRCLE OF ZAPHYAN and as member of premier US Death Metal act NILE for their 'Annihilation Of The Wicked' album. Kollias also featured on NOCTA's 'Wicked Woman' album.

In November 2006 SICKENING HORROR contracted with Neurotic Records. The group's next album, entitled 'When Landscapes Bled Backwards', was mixed and mastered by Neil Kernon. Drummer George Kollias quit SICKENING HORROR in February 2006.

Sickening Horror, Sickening Horror (2003). The Most Discursive Expression / Through Blackness It Crawls / Sub Sound Of Decomposing Images.

SIEGE OF HATE

FORTALEZA, CE, BRAZIL — *Bruno Gabai (vocals), Ricarte Neto (vocals / guitar), George Frizzo (bass), Saulo Oliveira (drums).*

Fortaleza Death-Grind Metal band SIEGE OF HATE, created in April of 1997, include the INSANITY and GRIEFGIVER credited Bruno Gabai on lead vocals, vocalist / guitarist Ricarte

Neto, INSANITY bassist George Frizzo and drummer Saulo Oliveira of BRIETAL and SOMBERLAIN repute. The initial formation saw Gabai alongside OBSKURE guitarist Amaudson Ximenes, later inducting Ricarte Neto on bass guitar and OBSKURE drummer Wilker D'Angelo. This band debuted with the demo 'Return To Ashes' during April of 1998. Four tracks from this demo would feature on the 'Atitude Vol.II' compilation album released by Independencia Records with another song being donated to the 'Noise For Deaf' compilation through Rotthenness Records and also the 2000 collection 'Planet Metal n°2'.

SIEGE OF HATE underwent line up changes in April of 1999, losing both D'Angelo and Ximenes but introducing George Frizzo on bass and shifting Neto to guitar.

'Return To Ashes' saw a 2002 CD re-issue adding a slew of bonus tracks including live songs and cover versions of DORSAL ATLANTICA's 'Dor', SARCOFAGO's 'Hate' and MOTÖRHEAD's 'Bomber'.

The 2003 album 'Subversive By Nature', released by Encore Records in Brazil and New Aeon Media in Europe, included a D.R.I. cover 'No Religion'. For these recordings Gabai handled drums, the band incorporating Thiago Feijó of KAPRUK as new sticksman shortly after. Saulo Oliveira took command of the drums in November of 2003.

RETURN TO ASHES, Siege of Hate (2002). Obscene Truth / Self Defense Contradictions / Ridiculous Dignity / Subversive By Nature / Nightmares Of War / Siege Of Hate / Forthcoming Holocaust / Misleaders / Leprous / Nightmares Of War (Live) / Fake (Live) / Dor (Live) / Self Defense Contradictions (Live) / Forthcoming Holocaust (Live) / Hate (Live) / Downfall (Live) / Siege Of Hate (Live) / The Chosen Ones (Live) / Bomber (Live) / Misleaders (Live).

SUBVERSIVE BY NATURE, Encore (2003). Say Your Prayers / Subversive By Nature / From The Top To The Fall / The Walls Built Inside Us / Nightmares Of War / The Chosen Ones / Fake / Obscene Truth / Downfall / Trust / Siege Of Hate / Forthcoming Holocaust / Martyr Of Fools / Fairyland / The Future Is Your Gift / This Is For Real / Self Defense Contradictions / No Religion / Misleaders / U.S.A.

SIKSAKUBUR

INDONESIA — *Japra (vocals), Andre (guitar), Yudi Of Authority (bass), Andyan Gorust (drums).*

SIKSAKUBUR (meaning "Torment in the Grave") had their two opening albums 'Back To Vengeance' and 'The Carnage' packaged as a double offering for Western markets in 2003 through From Beyond Productions. The group, self acknowledged SEPULTURA devotees, was founded as a trio in 1996 comprising vocalist / guitarist Ade Godel, bassist Bembenx and drummer Andyan Gorust. Moving away from their Thrash roots into Grind territory the band line-up evolved to incorporate Ade Godel on lead vocals, guitarists Rosadist and Bembenx, bassist Has and Andyan Gorust on the drums. In mid 1998 Burgenk was inducted on bass. SIKSAKUBUR morphed further in order to record the 2000 debut 'The Carnage', these sessions conducted by vocalist Japra, guitarist Ade Godel, bass player Burgenk and drummer Andyan Gorust.

Gorust joined both VILE and ABSOLUTE DEFIANCE in 2001. SIKSAKUBUR announced an all new line up for mid 2003 comprising vocalist Japra, guitarist Andre, bassist Yudi "Bebek" of Authority and drummer Andyan "Gorust".

THE CARNAGE, Extreme Souls Productions (2000). Into Your Sickening Intestines / Horrifying Demise / Fattened For Killing / Genital Feasting By Ejaculated Carnivore / Disharmonic Revived / Decayed Flesh / To Devour The Carrion / Malicious Diabolism / Uncivilized.

BACK TO VENGEANCE / THE CARNAGE, From Beyond Productions FBP 015 (2003).

SILENT AGONY

ZALAEGERSZEG, HUNGARY — *Kálmán Pápai (vocals), Péter Méhes (guitar), Lajos Nagy (guitar), Krisztián Tóth (bass), Balázs Kovács (drums).*

SILENT AGONY was a precursor to AGE OF AGONY, a blasphemous Zalalövő, Zalaegerszeg based Death Metal act formulated during 2002. Previous to this date the group had operated under the brand SILENT AGONY. Created in 1995, SILENT AGONY comprised Kálmán Pápai on vocals, guitarists Péter Méhes and Lajos Nagy, bass player Krisztián Tóth with Balázs Kovács. In this guise they issued demos 'Agony' in 1999 and 'Poisoned Tears' in 2001.

The group would go through a succession of early guitarists including Krisztián Varga, from ART OF BUTCHERY, MONASTERY and SEAR BLISS, Péter Méhes and Viktor Apagyi before stabilising with Lajos Nagy solely handling six-string duties as they evolved into AGE OF AGONY. A three track, self-titled demo emerged that same year, with a second set billed 'The Dark Conquers All' following in 2003. AGE OF AGONY struck a deal with Kárpátia Productions for the 2005 debut album 'War, Hate, Blasphemy'.

Agony, Silent Agony (1999) (Demo). Nice Day To Die / A Life Left Behind / Like You Were Dead.

Poisoned Tears, Silent Agony (2001) (Demo). The Prophecy / Silent Agony / Clean Blood / Haunting In The Fog.

SILENT SCYTHE

SWEDEN — *Fredrik Eriksson (vocals), Tommi Djukin (vocals / guitar), Peter Henningsson (guitar), Peter Ogestad (bass), Johan Strende (drums).*

SILENT SCYTHE, initiated by former CARNAL LUST and BRIMSTONE vocalist / guitarist Tommi Djukin in October of 1999, put out the 2002 demo 'Death Is Coming' as their opening shot. The band would feature IMPALE, LEGION and PLANET DEEP guitarist Peter Henningsson alongside Djukin's BRIMSTONE colleague, as well as IMPALE and SPINELESS credited, Johan Strende on the drums. Bassist Anders Prykebrant would be superseded by ex-TWILIGHT SYMPHONY man Peter Ogestad. SILENT SCYTHE debuted with a self financed album entitled 'Longing For Sorrow'.

Signing to the Dutch label New Aeon Media the band put out debut as a re-issue, re-titled as the 'Suffer In Silence' album in 2004. Although Tobbe Jansson cut the vocals for this opus, bar Death growls courtesy of Djukin, he would be replaced shortly after completion of the tracks by CRIMSON TIDE's Fredrik Eriksson.

SUFFER IN SILENCE, New Aeon Media (2004). Intro / Longing For Sorrow / Old World Disorder / My Only Family (My Only Enemy) / Backstabber / Suffer In Silence / To Each His Own / Feather.

SILENT SOULS

GERMANY — *Alexander Hartmann (vocals / guitar), John Kleemann (vocals / guitar), Björn Beinborn (bass), Jan Spänhoff (drums).*

SILENT SOULS is a Weifenbach Death Metal formation founded in August of 1992 comprising vocalist / guitarist Alexander Hartmann, vocalist / bassist John Kleemann, guitarist Matthias Hubich and drummer Andreas Henkel. A demo, 'Seal The Fear', was delivered in 1994 but in November of that year the group dissolved.

SILENT SOULS would remanifest in 1996, Hartmann, Kleemann and Henkel recruiting Christian Otto on bass the following year for a debut album 'Behind The Gates Of Passion'. A German mini tour saw SILENT SOULS ranked alongside THORNS, SLEEPING GODS and SCION. Björn Beinborn took over on bass later that year and Jochen Märte became the band's new drummer in 1999. The drum position would then switch to Patrick Nördling in 2000 then in turn to Jan Spänhoff. This latest recruit would exit in April of 2001.

BEHIND THE GATES OF PASSION, Independent (1997). Behind The Gates / Silent Souls / Depths Of Gray / Withered One / Blurred Plains / Ridicule Shape / Rain.

ESCAPE, Independent (2000). Intro / Escape / Channel Life / Conversion Denied / Great Relief / Revive / I Drown / Bodyless Innocence / I Pass Away / Path Of Lies.

SINISTER

SCHIEDAM, HOLLAND — *Aad Kloosterwaard (vocals), Alex Paul (guitar), Bas van den Bogaard (bass), Paul Beltman (drums).*

Premier Schiedam Death Metal act SINISTER has enjoyed two flushes of popularity and respect, first as recognised Euro pioneers of the genre then as a revitalised and female fronted force spearheading the return of Death Metal in mainland Europe. The band formed in April 1988 as a trio of frontman Mike van Mastrigt, guitarist Ron van de Polder and drummer Aad Kloosterwaard adding bassist Corzas in January 1989. This line-up recorded the 'Perpetual Damnation' demo on March 17th 1990, involving four originals and an unlisted cover of SLAYER's 'Praise Of Death'. Sales of the tape were strong, with over 1800 sold in 18 months, and SINISTER toured supporting ENTOMBED and DISHARMONIC ORCHESTRA. Seraphic Decay Records delivered a three track 7" EP in August 1991, Swiss label Witchhunt Records, an imprint noted for picking out influential bands, also weighed in with a 7" single 'Putrefying Remains' in September and the following year Sicktone put together two tracks as a split 7" single shared with Dutch / Swedish alliance MONASTERY. This outfit notably comprised SINISTER members Ron van de Polder and Aad Kloosterwaard in collaboration with ENTOMBED's Lars Rosenberg.

Corzas left in May 1991 and bass duties were handed over to SEMPITERNAL DEATHREIGN's Frank Faase. Another line-up shuffle saw Ron van de Polder moving over to bass as SINISTER added second guitarist André Tolhuis (a.k.a. André Tolhuizen) of VULTURE. Their second demo, 1991's Sacramental Carnage, had secured enough interest to land a deal with Nuclear Blast. That same September SINISTER toured as support to ATROCITY. More touring opened up 1992 as SINISTER gained a valuable support slot to MORGOTH.

Debut album 'Cross The Styx' was produced at Mainstreet Studio Fautspach in Germany by ATROCITY's singer Alexander Krull. 'The Styx' tendered a tirade of mechanically minded, thrash infused death metal far ahead of its time and duly won instant plaudits. The band toured to promote 'Cross The Styx' by opening for DEICIDE, ENTOMBED, CANNIBAL CORPSE and ATROCITY among others.

SINISTER's second album, 'Diabolical Summoning', was recorded at TNT Studios in Gelsenkirchen during March 1993 and produced by Colin Richardson, with a third album appearing in 1995 entitled 'Hate'. By this juncture SINISTER was down to operating as a trio, Mike van Mastrigt, Aad Kloosterwaard with Bart van Wallenberg handling both guitar and bass. Promoting this opus the band put in European headline dates in February 1996 together with CREEPMIME, AVULSED and DARKSEED. A stop gap 1996 EP, 'Bastard Saints', marked the introduction of the SEVERE TORTURE credited bassist Michel Alderliefsten. This outing created consternation as it displayed a seismic shift towards American Nu influences, new songs being arranged in a much simpler fashion and, most controversially, two archive cuts, 'Cross The Styx' and 'Epoch Of Denial', being completely refashioned in similar, stripped down style.

Again SINISTER re-formulated, Aad Kloosterwaard with Bart van Wallenberg bringing in new singer Eric de Windt, from SEVERE TORTURE, and bass player Alex Paul to record the Vincent Dijkers co-produced 1998 'Aggressive Measures' album. In side operations, Mike van Mastrigt and Aad Kloosterwaard founded HOUWITSER in 1997 for the 'Death ... But Not Buried' album, released in 1998. Mike van Mastrigt would also later front DEATHSQUAD.

Vocalist Eric de Windt decamped in August 1999, after which Joost Silvrants of Grindcore outfit INHUME and DROWNING IN TEARS took care of the vocal role until SINISTER surprised many by adopting a female lead singer Rachel Heyzer of OCCULT. Heyzer, a lady in possession of a mighty roar that would shame most male Death Metal vocalists, made her debut with the Hans Pieters produced 'Creative Killings' album. SINISTER switched from Nuclear Blast to the Hammerheart label, licensed in America to the Martyr Music Group, for the November 2001 release of 'Creative Killings'. The album included a cover version of POSSESSED's 'Storm In Your Mind'.

Aad Kloosterwaard would also occupy the drum stool for Death act THANATOS but would vacate this position in August 2001.

By early 2002 the SINISTER ranks saw departure of longstanding guitar player Bart van Wallenberg and subsequent the induction of CANTARA and GOD DETHRONED guitarist Pascal Grevinga for touring purposes. SINISTER would be announced as support to NILE's October European tour. Further European dates for November would be announced with the band forming up a package bill comprising SEPTIC FLESH, DISMEMBER and THYRFING. The band had their efforts rewarded by re-signing to Nuclear Blast label for a new studio album 'Savage Or Grace'.

Former SINISTER singer Mike van Mastrigt resurfaced in late 2002 in a new band union DEATH SQUAD working with ex-RADIATHOR guitarist Walter Tjwa, second guitarist J.G. and drummer Michel.

The band made further upward progress with the album 'Savage Or Grace' but adjusted its line up in August 2003, ousting both guitarist Pascal Grevinga and bassist Alex Paul. Guitarist Ron van de Polder, who had been involved in the song writing process for 1992's 'Cross The Styx' and 'Savage Or Grace', stepped in as replacement as the new look trio immediately set to work on a new album 'Heaven Termination'. This renewed burst of activity also manifested itself in a side project, INFINITED HATE comprising the full SINISTER triumvirate of Heyzer, van de Polder and Kloosterwaard. The first INFINITED HATE album was titled 'Revel In Bloodshed', being released in 2003. Follow up 'Heaven Termination' was released in 2005.

In 2004 SINISTER would donate their rendition of 'Storm In My Mind' to the 'Seven Gates Of Horror' tribute album assembled by the Karmageddon Media label in homage to pioneering Bay Area Thrash act POSSESSED. After 16 years of delivering extreme Metal, SINISTER folded in April 2004.

Word arrived in March 2005 that SINISTER, comprising a revised casting seeing Aad Kloosterwaard handling vocals, Paul Beltman, ex-JUDGEMENT DAY, on drums and Alex Paul on bass and guitar, had reformed yet again. Bas van den Boogard, also ex-JUDGEMENT DAY, was subsequently added on bass. The band entered Stage One studio in Germany to cut new album, 'Afterburner' in December for April 2006 release via Nuclear Blast. That October Aad Kloosterwaard sessioned guest vocals on demos for SUPREME PAIN. Retaining his SINISTER ties, he subsequently joined this old school Death Metal band, which featured Erwin Harreman on bass and guitar and Robert Kovacic of SCAFFOLD on drums. In March 2007 SUPREME PAIN signed a deal with the US based label Comatose Music, owned by Steve Green of LUST OF DECAY, for a debut album 'Cadaver Pleasures'.

The band teamed up with ENTHRONED, VEXED and NECROART for a short Italian tour in May 2007.

Compulsory Resignation, Seraphic Decay 019 (1990). Compulsory Resignation / Spiritual Immolation / Putrefying Remains.

Putrefying Remains, Witchhunt 9103 (1990) (7" single). Putrefying Remains / Spiritual Immolation.

SINISTER

Perpetual Damnation, Sinister (1990) (Demo). Compulsory Resignation / Perpetual Damnation / Putrefying Remains / Spiritual Immolation / Praise Of Death.
Sinister, Sicktone 3 (1991) (Split 7" with MONASTERY). Perpetual Damnation / Putrefying Remains.
CROSS THE STYX, Nuclear Blast NB 061-2 (1992). Carnificinia Scelesta / Perennial Mourning / Sacramental Carnage / Doomed / Spiritual Immolation / Cross The Styx / Compulsory Resignation / Corridors To The Abyss / Putrefying Remains / Epoch Of Denial / Perpetual Damnation / Outro.
DIABOLICAL SUMMONING, Nuclear Blast NB 081-2 (1993). Sadistic Intent / Magnified Wrath / Diabolical Summoning / Sense Of Demise / Leviathan / Desecrated Flesh / Tribes Of The Moon / Mystical Illusions.
HATE, Nuclear Blast NB 131-2 (1995). Awaiting The Absu / Embodiment Of Chaos / Art Of The Damned / Unseen Darkness / 18th Century Hellfire / To Mega Therion / The Cursed Mayhem / The Bloodfeast.
Bastard Saints EP, Nuclear Blast NB183-2 (1996). Bastard Saints / Reborn From Hatred / Rebel's Dome / Cross The Styx / Epoch Of Denial.
AGGRESSIVE MEASURES, Nuclear Blast NB 332-2 (1998). The Upcoming / Aggressive Measures / Beyond The Superstition / Into The Forgotten / Enslave The Weak / Fake Redemption / Chained In Reality / Emerged With Hate / Blood Follows The Blood.
CREATIVE KILLINGS, Hammerheart HHR 075 (2001). Relic Of Possession / Bleeding Towards The Wendigo / Creative Killings / Judicious Murder / Reviving The Dead / Early Gothic Horror / Moralistic Suffering / Altering The Beast / Season Of The Wicked / Storm In My Mind.
SAVAGE OR GRACE, Nuclear Blast NB 1051-2 (2003). Rise Of The Predator / Savage Or Grace / Barbaric Order / The Age Of Murder / Conception Of Sin / Chapel Desecration / Dominion / Collapse Rewind / Apocalypse In Time.
AFTERBURNER, Nuclear Blast NB 1617-2 (2006). The Grey Massacre / Altruistic Suicide / Men Down / Afterburner / Presage Of The Mindless / Into Submission / The Riot Crossfire / Flesh Of The Servant.

SINNERS BLEED

BERLIN, GERMANY — *Jan Geidner (vocals), Sebastian Ankert (guitar), Pele Geltat (guitar), Gunnar Seifert (bass), Eric Krebs (drums).*

Berlin Death Metal act SINNERS BLEED was assembled in 1997, issuing the demo 'The Awakening' two years later. A second tape, 2000's 'Restless', saw promotion by way of support gigs to acts such as HAEMORRHAGE, PROFANITY and CRYPTOPSY. SINNERS BLEED's self-financed album 'From Womb To Tomb', recorded Soundforge Studios in Berlin and produced by Andreas Hilbert, arrived in April of 2003. However, shortly after release guitarist Pele Geltat decamped and for an appearance at that year's 'Fuck The Commerce' festival SINNERS BLEED drafted new man Lille. Response to 'From Womb To Tomb' would get the band selected to be one of the few unsigned acts to perform at Norway's 'Inferno' festival in 2004. an ex-SINNERS BLEED guitarist, Tesk Pörksen, went on to ANENCEPHALUS and DAZED.

The band drafted ex-FATAL EMBRACE guitarist Vincent LaBoor in April 2006. SINNERS BLEED entered Soundforge studio in Berlin with producer Andreas Hilbert again on October 16th to start work on a second album.

FROM WOMB TO TOMB, Independent (2003). Agony Of Self Denial / The Ludo Game / Deathbringer / Sinner's Lust / Daemons / Injected Lies / Invisible Knowledge / From Womb To Tomb / Bound.

SINS OF OMISSION

STOCKHOLM, SWEDEN — *Mårten Hansen (vocals), Martin Persson (guitar), Matthias Eklund (guitar), Thomas Fällgren (bass), Dennis Ekdahl (drums).*

SINS OF OMISSION, founded in Stockholm in 1996 as TO THE GRIND by ex-members of acts such as BESERK, METEPSYCHOSIS and MOURNFUL, initially comprised of MOURNFUL and WYVERN singer Toni Kocmut, guitarists Martin Persson, citing BERSERK, DISMEMBER and MÖRK GRYNING credits, and Johan Paulsson, bass player Thomas Fällgren and drummer Dennis Ekdahl, the latter a veteran of ATHELA, MOURNFUL and MYSTIC PROPHECY. The idea behind the band was to blend the technicalities of modern Swedish Death Metal with the refinement of traditional Heavy Metal. Both Persson and Ekdahl had also performed as live sessioneers for MÖRK GRYNING in 1996 whilst Persson and Kocmut session on albums by THYRFING. Shortly after formation guitarist Jonas Nilsson and bassist Thomas Fällgren enrolled.

Still billed as TO THE GRIND the band debuted live in April 1997, their opening gig being supported by THYRFING, IN COLD BLOOD and THE MARBLE ICON. Invited to appear on a compilation album, the group cut two songs, 'Burn The Night' and 'Reap The Storm'. However, the album did not materialise and TO THE GRIND utilised these tracks as their first promotional effort. However, Nilsson decamped in the Summer of 1997 and with Kocmut switching to guitar the band operated for a while minus a lead vocalist.

Rebilling themselves as SINS OF OMISSION the group's ad hoc demo received favourable responses back from Nuclear Blast, Earache and Wrong Again records. Eventually the band signed to Black Sun Records to craft the opening album 'The Creation', recorded at Studio Fredman in Gothenburg and engineered and supervised by Fredrik Nordström and Anders Fridén. This effort featured Kocmut on lead vocals. This situation was solved as SINS OF OMISSION added former A CANOUROUS QUINTET and OCTOBER TIDE vocalist Mårten Hansen. Following a brief burst of European gigs in Holland and Belgium Kocmut exited and Mattias Eklund stepped in. The new recruit cited a wealth of underground Metal experience with such acts as MÖRK GRYNING (as 'Avatar'), MORTUM, as 'Mephisto', Death Metallers REPUGNANT, MORTIFER, FIST FIRST, VANISHED, REQUIEM and, as 'Necropounder', drummer for "Crack Metal" band CACHTICE. Drummer Dennis Ekdahl also performed with RAISE HELL whilst Mårten Hansen would front VOTUR.

In February 2001 SINS OF OMISSION recorded their second album, the Pelle Säter and Lasse Lindén engineered 'Flesh On Your Bones', at Studio Underground in Västerås. Later that year the group drafted new drummer Jani Stefanovich from Finnish acts SABAOTH and AM I BLOOD. His tenure lasted until 2003 when he relocated to Finland to found Christian Death Metal band RENASCENT. In 2006 Stefanovich drummed on HILASTHERION's debut album.

THE CREATION, Black Sun (1999). Eager For The Fray / Reap The Storm / The Creation / Burn The Night / The Experiment / Let Them March / The Serpentine Route / To The Grind / Exhibition Of Sins.
FLESH ON YOUR BONES, Black Sun (2001). Intro / The Secret Agenda / Pound For Pound / Revolution / Angel Killers / The Rape ... / ... Of Innocence / A Wicked Slaughterhouse Tale / The Grinder / Sinners Redemption / Angel Of Death / The Sentinel.

SIX FEET UNDER

TAMPA, FL, USA — *Chris Barnes (vocals), Allen West (guitar), Terry Butler (bass), Greg Gall (drums).*

Tampa, Florida Death Metal combo SIX FEET UNDER was initially created as a side project by CANNIBAL CORPSE frontman Chris Barnes, OBITUARY guitarist Allen West and erstwhile MASSACRE / DEATH bassist Terry Butler. Greg Gall of LAST RITE assumed command of the drums. Barnes had fronted CANNIBAL CORPSE for their most notorious slash-fests 1990's 'Eaten Back To Life', 1991's 'Butchered At Birth', 1992's 'Tomb Of The Mutilated' and 'The Bleeding' in 1994. SIX FEET UNDER had already been instigated before recording of his swansong CANNIBAL CORPSE opus.

This lineage alone guaranteed an immediate profile and swift acquisition by Metal Blade Records. The debut album, 'Haunted' produced by Brian Slagel and Scott Burns at Morrisound Studios and issued in September 1995, predictably kept up the gore factor of the various band members previous acts and consistent touring pushed the release past the 35'000 sales mark. 'Haunted' took on a rumbling, groove laden path as opposed to the musicians prior endeavours, its catchiness triggering debate as to whether SIX FEET UNDER had strayed too far from Death Metal norms. Regardless, the European audience latched onto the fresh formula from the start, providing the group with a stable platform of operations for the future.

With Barnes obviously placing his priorities SIX FEET UNDER, the unit subsequently evolved into a fully fledged band when the singer was ejected from his previous host. SIX FEET UNDER grasped the opportunity and hit Europe foursquare in the summer of 1996. A live mini-album, October 1996's 'Alive And Dead', comprised of cuts recorded during the previous bout of European touring at Pratteln in Switzerland and Hengelo in Holland, two fresh studio recordings plus a version of JUDAS PRIEST's 'Grinder', these last three tracks laid down at Criteria Studios in Miami. The release plugged a gap between bouts of studio recording whilst West was committed to the latest OBITUARY album.

SIX FEET UNDER's sophomore outing, 'Warpath' sporting a rendition of NWoBHM act HOLOCAUST's 'Death Or Glory' and housed in a striking neon green jewel case, arrived in September 1997. However, the group suffered an unexpected blow when Allen West opted out.

The band uncompromisingly returned to action with 'Maximum Violence' in July 1999, a record that garnered healthy reviews and included a KISS cover 'War Machine' to boot. The group had drawn in the MASSACRE and LAST RITE credited guitarist Steve Swanson to supersede West. Impressively, 'Maximum Violence' surpassed the 100,000 sales mark, a rarity for a Death Metal record in those times. Has momentum gathered, Metal Blade re-issued the album as a two disc set adding a crop of live tracks. Japanese versions naturally cane blessed with extra material, namely takes on IRON MAIDEN's 'Wrathchild' and THIN LIZZY's 'Jailbreak'.

By 2000 West had created his own act LOWBROW with NASTY SAVAGE men Ben Meyer and Curt Beeson and DEATH bassist Scott Carino. Matt Cohen briefly joined the SIX FEET UNDER ranks.

SIX FEET UNDER's 'Graveyard Classics' album, ushered out in October 2000, was a compilation of cover versions of artists such as AC/DC, BLACK SABBATH, SEX PISTOLS, DEAD KENNEDYS, EXODUS, SAVATAGE, VENOM and JIMI HENDRIX. John Bush of ANTHRAX / ARMORED SAINT also guests on vocals for a version of the SCORPIONS 'Blackout'.

The band resumed action in August 2001 with new outing 'True Carnage'. The album included BODY COUNT vocalist and famed Rapper ICE T as guest vocalist on the track 'One Bullet Left' and Karyn Crisis of CRISIS sparring with Chris Barnes on the track 'Sick and Twisted'. This latter track was trumpeted as the first ever Death Metal male / female duet. Japanese editions added a bonus track, a live version of 'Torture Killers'.

'True Carnage' would give SIX FEET UNDER valuable commercial success in Europe charting in both Germany and Austria. However, the promotional video for 'The Day The Dead Walked' was turned down by both MTV and MTV2 due to its supposed extreme nature.

SIX FEET UNDER undertook a lengthy bout of American touring in the summer of 2002, commencing in Houston, Texas on the 31st of May supported by SKINLESS and SWORN ENEMY. The band's June 14th Minnesota gig would be recorded for a DVD and a live album release. September 2002 tour plans for North America had the band paired up with HATEBREED. The band would head up an impressive cast for European 'Xmas Festivals' in December strongly supported by MARDUK, IMMOLATION, KATAKLYSM, DYING FETUS and HATE. Later gigs in Holland added veteran Thrashers EXODUS to the bill.

The group maintained the momentum for September 2003's 'Bringer Of Blood' outing, the album giving SIX FEET UNDER their highest advance sales figures to date landing at no. 36 on the national German charts. SIX FEET UNDER set 'Kings Of The Roadkill' as their January US shows, these gigs seeing support from FULL BLOWN CHAOS and BILE. The group teamed up with label mates CRIMINAL and FLESHCRAWL for a two-week European tour throughout February and March of 2004. Headline shows in the USA throughout April saw a variety of support acts at various stages including THE RED CHORD, THE BLACK DAHLIA MURDER, ON BROKEN WINGS, MISERY SIGNALS, BURY YOUR DEAD and THE HEAVILS.

In readiness for the 'Graveyard Classics II' album, promoted upfront by a promotional video for a cover version of AC/DC's 'Rock n' Roll Ain't Noise Pollution', a further round of North American shows throughout August and September would be bolstered by opening acts MISERY SIGNALS, INTERNAL BLEEDING and PREMONITIONS OF WAR. With teaser press statements being delivered quoting 'Graveyard Classics II' as being a "unique" album it would be learned that the band had indeed stuck to their word—by covering an entire album, namely AC/DC's seminal 'Back In Black'.

Losing no momentum, by 1st October that band was back in Morrisound Studios recording a brand new album billed '13' for 2005 issue. In January the band filmed a promotional video for the track 'Shadow Of The Reaper', directed by Gary Smithson and featuring actors Meagan Crawford and Aaron Kinser. SIX FEET UNDER forged a road alliance with NILE, DARK FUNERAL, DISBELIEF, DYING FETUS, WYKKED WYTCH and CATARACT for the 'No Mercy Festivals 2005' European tour beginning in early March. SIX FEET UNDER teamed up with BYZANTINE, BLOODSIMPLE and GIZMACHI for US "Masters of Brutality" dates announced as commencing in July. However, this trek would be postponed and the band instead hooked up with a package billing comprising CHIMAIRA, ALL THAT REMAINS and 3 INCHES OF BLOOD. European shows to close out the year saw British act MANTAS as openers.

A retrospective four CD box set, entitled 'A Decade In The Grave', saw release in late November. The compilation comprised two discs of archive album tracks, a 21 track live DVD and rare sessions from demos dating back to 1985 plus rehearsal recordings. The band put in an extensive European tour in October 2005 packaged with KAT, BORN FROM PAIN and DEBAUCHERY across France, Austria, Switzerland, Denmark, Holland, Belgium and Germany.

In November Chris Barnes announced that he was to session lead vocals on the 'Swarm!' album from Finnish Death Metal band TORTURE KILLER, released in February 2006 through Metal Blade Records. US dates for September and October 2006 saw the band hooking up with KRISIUN, DECAPITATED and ABYSMAL DAWN. Live work in December across Europe was to see the band joining up with DARZAMAT, GOREFEST,

BELPHEGOR and KRISIUN for the 'X-Mass' festivals. However, the group pulled out of these concerts.

A fresh album, entitled 'Commandment', was slated for April 2007 issue through Metal Blade.

HAUNTED, Metal Blade 14093-2 (1995). The Enemy Inside / Silent Violence / Lycanthropy / Still Alive / Beneath A Black Sky / Human Target / Remains Of You / Suffering In Ecstasy / Tomorrows Victim / Torn To The Bone / Haunted.

ALIVE AND DEAD, Metal Blade 14118-2 (1996). Insect / Drowning / Grinder / Suffering In Ecstasy (Live) / Human Target (Live) / Lycanthropy (Live) / Beneath A Black Sky (Live).

WARPATH, Metal Blade 14128-2 (1997). War Is Coming / Nonexistence / A Journey Into Darkness / Animal Instinct / Death Or Glory / Burning Blood / Manipulation / 4:20 / Revenge Of The Zombie / As I Die / Night Visions / Caged And Disgraced.

MAXIMUM VIOLENCE, Metal Blade 14243-2 (1999). Feasting On The Blood Of The Insane / Bonesaw / Victim Of The Paranoid / Short Cut To Hell / No Warning Shot / War Machine / Mass Murder Rampage / Brainwashed / Torture Killer / This Graveyard Earth / Hacked To Pieces. Chart position: 68 GERMANY.

GRAVEYARD CLASSICS, Metal Blade 14341 (2000). Holocaust / TNT / Piranha / Son Of A Bitch / Stepping Stone / Confused / California Uber Alles / Smoke On The Water / Blackout / Purple Haze / In League With Satan.

TRUE CARNAGE, Metal Blade 14375-2 (2001). Impulse To Disembowel / Day The Dead Walked / It Never Dies / Murderers / Waiting For Decay / One Bullet Left / Knife, Gun, Axe / Snakes / Sick And Twisted / Cadaver Mutilator / Necrosociety. Chart positions: 40 GERMANY, 69 AUSTRIA.

Amerika The Brutal, Metal Blade 3984-14444-2 DJ (2003). Amerika The Brutal / Bringer Of Blood.

BRINGER OF BLOOD, Metal Blade 14444-2 (2003). Sick In The Head / Amerika The Brutal / My Hatred / Murdered In The Basement / When Skin Turns Blue / Bringer Of Blood / Ugly / Braindead / Blind And Gagged / Claustrophobic / Escape From The Grave. Chart position: 36 GERMANY.

GRAVEYARD CLASSICS 2, Metal Blade 14496-2 (2004). Hells Bells / Shoot To Thrill / What Do You Do For Money Honey / Givin' The Dog A Bone / Let Me Put My Love Into You / Back In Black / You Shook Me All Night Long / Have A Drink On Me / Shake A Leg / Rock n' Roll Ain't Noise Pollution.

13, Metal Blade 14527-2 (2005). Decomposition Of The Human Race / Somewhere In The Darkness / Rest In Pieces / Wormfood / 13 / Shadow Of The Reaper / Deathklaat / The Poison Hand / This Suicide / The Art Of Headhunting / Stump. Chart positions: 51 GERMANY, 62 AUSTRIA.

COMMANDMENT, Metal Blade (2007). Doomsday / Thou Shall Kill / Zombie Executioner / The Edge Of The Hatchet / Bled To Death / Resurrection Of The Rotten / As The Blade Turns / The Evil Eye / In A Vacant Grave / Ghosts Of The Undead.

SKELETAL EMBRACE

THETFORD, NORFOLK, UK — *Dean (vocals), Sean (guitar), Chris (guitar), Gavin (bass), Lloyd (drums).*

Norfolk Progressive Death Metal band SKELETAL EMBRACE was manifested during 1998 by erstwhile CARRION bassist Chris. Crafting his new compositions into the self financed 'A Landscape of Whorethorns' release, Chris employed his former CARRION bandmates singer Dean, guitarist Dale and drummer Lloyd. The band was bolstered by the arrival of Sean and Mark, joining the fold as guitarist and bass player respectively. In this guise the band cut a second recording session entitled 'Portrait Of The Thirteenth Requiem'.

SKELETAL EMBRACE's next challenge would be the full length 2004 album 'Seven Cobwebs Breeding'. By this juncture the bass role had been re-assigned to Gavin.

A Landscape Of Whorethorns, (1999). Naked As The Autumn Swans / Romance (The Eternal Bride) / The Carnality Of The Carvidae.

Portrait Of The Thirteenth Requiem, (2001). As Like A Nightingale On Fire / Weaving Horns For A Spine / Into The Shadows Of Spires / Eden Bathed In Hollow Grace.

SEVEN COBWEBS BREEDING, Skeletal Embrace (2003). Talons In Deism / Crown Of Pallid Shadows / Within It's Hooks And Scales / Silhouette Of Her Wings / The Fire Whisperer.

SKINLESS

NEW YORK, NY, USA — *Jayson Keyser (vocals), Noah Carpenter (guitar), Joe Keyser (bass), Bob Beaulac (drums).*

SKINLESS issued the 'Swollen Heaps' promotional tape upfront of their debut album 'Progression Towards Evil'. The band, centred upon guitarist Noah Carpenter, has been wrought by ongoing line up fluctuations since its inception in 1992. Bob Beaulac of SYMPTOM HATE and DISCIPLES OF BERKOWITZ was added on drums in early 1997 and Joe Keyser in November of the same year. SKINLESS would support MORTICIAN on an American tour following release of the 'Progression Towards Evil' debut.

In 2001 SKINLESS issued a split 7" single on the Cudgel label in collusion with MALEDICTIVE PIGS. Bob Beaulac bade his farewell during October 2001. He was swiftly replaced by erstwhile MORTICIAN and DEHUMANISED man George Torres. However, by September of the following year Torres was out of the picture, with Bob Beaulac temping for tour dates as openers to SIX FEET UNDER. ORIGIN's John Longstreth, also known as an erstwhile member of ANGEL CORPSE, was the man taking command of the drum stool in January of 2003.

The band allied themselves with THE CROWN and MONOLITH for the 'Crowning Europe In Terror' tour in March and April of 2003. SKINLESS would act as co-headliners for a North American package tour in May of 2003, completing a bill of MISERY INDEX, DIVINE EMPIRE and DYING FETUS. Giving themselves little respite the band then united with THE HAUNTED and SHAI HULUD for North American touring throughout May and June.

Drummer John Longstreth was to exit in early 2004 to join EXHUMED, being replaced by the man he originally superseded, Bob Beaulac. However, by that May Longstreth was ensconced in Metalcore outfit THE RED CHORD then temporarily joined the ranks of DYING FETUS in October for US touring. The following month vocalist Sherwood Webber left the SKINLESS ranks, replaced in January of 2005 by the DETRIMENT credited Jason Keyser. The band collaborated with IMMOLATION, WITH PASSION, MISERY INDEX and DEICIDE for US dates in May 2005.

Two SKINLESS veterans would act as stand ins for MUCOPUS for live work. Singer Jason Keyser handled the vocal duties for MUCOPUS' appearance at the 'Tokyo Deathfest' in Japan, whilst former SKINLESS vocalist Sherwood Webber would join MUCOPUS for an 8th May concert at the Hudson Duster in Troy, New York. John Longstreth was back in the spotlight in July, joining the reformed DIM MAK.

In early December SKINLESS entered Maxtrax Studio in Albany, New York to start recording new album, 'Trample the Weak, Hurdle the Dead' for June 2006 issue. New Zealand concerts in Auckland and Hamilton in November were supported by DAWN OF AZAZEL.

European concerts, along with DYING FETUS, CATTLE DECAPITATION and WAR FROM A HARLOT'S MOUTH, witnessed shows across Germany, France, Italy, Austria, Belgium, Holland, Norway, Denmark Ireland and the UK in May 2007. SUFFOCATION teamed up with IMMOLATION and SKINLESS for a North American tour beginning late October.

PROGRESSION TOWARDS EVIL, United Guttural (1998). Confines Of Human Flesh / Extermination Of My Filthy Species / Tampon Lollipops / Milk And Innards / Cuntamination / Scum Cookie / Bobbing For Heads / Fetus Goulash / Crispy Kids.

FORESHADOWING OUR DEMISE, Relapse (2001). Foreshadowing Our Demise / Smothered / The Optimist / Salvage What's Left / Tug Of War Intestines / Affirmation Of Hatred / Enslavement / Merrie Melody / Pool Of Stool.

FROM SACRIFICE TO SURVIVAL, Relapse (2003). The Front Line Of Sanity / Escalate Discord / Deathwork / A False Sense Of Security / From Sacrifice To Survival / Battle Perpetual Will / Miscreant / Dead Conscience / Don't Risk Infection.

TRAMPLE THE WEAK, HURDLE THE DEAD, Relapse (2006). Overlord / A Unilateral Disgust / Deviation Will Not Be Tolerated / Trample The Weak, Hurdle The Dead / Spoils Of The Sycophant / Endvisioned / Execution Of Reason / Wicked World.

SKLEROTIKZ

THESSALONIKI, GREECE — *Sotiris Vafiadis (vocals), Marios Giannopoulos (vocals), Makis Lazaridis (lead guitar), Konstantinos Bikos (rhythm guitar), George Sbokos (bass), Sakis Vlahos (drums).*

Thessaloniki Thrashers SKLEROTIKZ was founded under the UNCANNY brand in September 2004 by singers Spyros Emanouilidis and Marios Giannopoulos, lead guitarist Makis Lazaridis, of DIHASMENES ALITHIES and SPLITDAWN, rhythm guitarist Simos Lazaridis plus drummer Sakis Vlahos from DIHASMENES ALITHIES. This formation remained stable until June 2005, when both Emanouilidis and Lazaridis opted out.

That November UNCANNY evolved into SKLEROTIKZ, inducting new personnel Sotiris Vafiadis on vocals, Konstantinos Bikos on rhythm guitar and Nick Ritsis on bass guitar. However, in February 2006 Ritsis departed, due to national military obligations, and George Sbokos took his place. SKLEROTIKZ released the demo 'Equation Of Information Theory', recorded at Rock Sound Studio, Thessaloniki with engineer Giorgos Brigos, in August 2006.

Equation Of Information Theory, Sklerotikz (2006) (Demo). Bloody Resurrection / United / Tormented Soul / The Serpent's Kiss / Our Pictures Are Fading In My Mind (Faded Memories).

SLAUGHTER

SCARBOROUGH, ON, CANADA — *Dave Hewson (vocals / guitar), Terry Sadler (vocals / bass), Ron Sumners (drums).*

SLAUGHTER are a revered name amongst the annals of the Thrash / Death Metal genre. The band, raised in Scarborough, Ontario, was created during August of 1984. Co-founder Terry Sadler, handling vocals and bass guitar, was already a seasoned veteran of the local Toronto scene having served terms with BLIND AMBITION, BLISSMASS, LIZZY BORDEN, MEGOLITH, METAL FATIGUE, NAZZ, and THE HALO OF FLIES. Along with vocalist / guitarist Dave Hewson and drummer Ron Sumners, Sadler forged SLAUGHTERHOUSE, soon truncating the title to SLAUGHTER.

The group made their mark with the opening demo sessions 'Meatcleaver' and 'Bloody Karnage', the latter featuring Joe Rico and Rob Urbinati of SACRIFICE as guest players. Third set 'Surrender Or Die' followed in 1985 and rapidly spread throughout the underground tape trading grapevine, even impacting on the demo top ten charts in leading UK magazine 'Metal Forces'. Their live debut came with the "Live Karnage" event alongside SACRIFICE on March 25th 1985 at Toronto's Larry's Hideaway venue, their set being distributed straight from the soundboard as the 'Live Karnage' demo, brazenly sporting their influences with covers of HELLHAMMER's 'Massacra' and VENOM's 'Witching Hour'. That same May another gig opening for SACRIFICE, at Gilmore's in Toronto, was recorded live for the 'Live Bedlam' demo.

Local radio DJ Brian Taylor secured the rights to the demo 'Surrender Or Die', releasing this commercially as the first release issued by Attic Records subsidiary Diabolic Force. SLAUGHTER capitalised on this with the debut album 'Strappado', recorded again for Diabolic Force at Future Sound in Toronto with Brian Taylor behind the desk in just 24 hours. Although cut in February 1986 'Strappado' remained vaulted for a lengthy period due to financial constraints. Beforehand the promotional three track single 'One Foot In The Grave', limited to 1000 copies, emerged.

Earlier the same year SLAUGHTER had been joined by DEATH frontman Chuck Schuldiner. Having relocated from Florida Schuldiner's tenure lasted a matter of weeks before he journeyed back home to re-activate DEATH. Live work would be restricted to a grand total of just fifteen concerts, the largest of which was held in July 1986 as support to CELTIC FROST and VOIVOD at the Toronto Concert House.

Sumners made his exit during September 1986 and, after fleetingly employing STORM and DEATH ADDER drummer Scott Day, the group re-structured with former LETHAL PRESENCE guitarist Bobby Sadzak and, in May 1987, drummer Brian Lourie. Finally, in mid 1987, the much delayed 'Strappado' was delivered, immediately drawing ecstatic reviews. SLAUGHTER cut a further album 'Paranormal' in July 1988 but these tapes would never see the light of day. Metal Blade Records showed interest, prompted by the band's December 1988 demo 'The Dark', and the track 'The Fourth Dimension' taken from the Paranormal demo was duly included on the 'Metal Massacre Ten' compilation released in 1990.

Further ructions hit the band in 1992 when Sadler bade his farewell, having initially quit in 1988, then returning in 1989, before quitting again in 1990. Hewson would then form an alliance with guitarist Bobby Sadzak, bassist Mike Dalton and drummer Brian Lourie creating STRAPPADO, this move being prompted by the chart success of the Las Vegas hair band of the same name. This new unit only issued the two sessions, 'Fatal Judgement' and 'Not Dead Yet', before splitting. However, the Headache label fanned the flames of the burgeoning SLAUGHTER legend by issuing a bootleg CD 'Strappado'.

SLAUGHTER was resurrected in order to donate a version of 'Dethroned Emperor' to a 1996 CELTIC FROST tribute album. This revised version of the band would collapse once again although Hewson and Sadzak, together with singer Kelly Montico, subsequently created the Industrial outfit INNER THOUGHT releasing 'Worldy Separation' in 1994 and the 1996 follow up 'Perspectives'. In 1999 pioneering UK Grindcore act NAPALM DEATH paid homage by rendering their version of 'Incinerator' on their EP 'Leaders Not Followers' and Utopian Vision Music published the 'Surrender Or Die' demos on CD format, complete with additional tracks recorded at the time but left off the demo.

A slew of SLAUGHTER re-releases arrived during 2000 including the shelved 'Paranormal', live cuts and demos. The German Nuclear Blast label would re-issue 'Strappado' complete with an extra CD compiled of live recordings from SLAUGHTER's inaugural March 1985 gig and rehearsal tapes. The band's legacy was given further prominence during 2004 when Hells Headbangers Records released 'Fuck Of Death', a compilation of the January 23rd 1986 rehearsal recordings conducted with late DEATH frontman Chuck Schuldiner. This vinyl only outing would be restricted to 1000 copies, the first 100 pressed on coloured vinyl with 500 manufactured as picture discs. Further tracks arrived in the form of a split 7" single on Horror Records of Denmark in collusion with NUNSLAUGHTER, the infamous Pittsburgh Death Metal band also paying tribute on their side of vinyl with a cover of SLAUGHTER's 'Nocturnal Hell'.

Meatcleaver, (1984). Age Of Deception / Eve Of Darkness / Surrender Or Die / Children Of The Fire / Hell Hath Returned / Meatcleaver / Slaughter-House / Instro-Metal / Annihilation / Strappado / Total Retribution.
Bloody Karnage, (1984). Disintegrator / Incinerator / One Foot In The Grave / Forged In The Furnace Of Hell / Bloody Karnage.
Surrender Or Die, (1985). Disintegrator / Incinerator / Main To Please / Tyrant Of Hell / Shadow Of Death / Death Dealer / One Foot In The Grave.
Live Karnage, (1985). Disintergrator—Incinerator / One Foot In The Grave / Shadow Of Death / Massacra / Death Dealer / Tales Of The Macabre / Maim To Please / Strappado / Eve Of Darkness / Tyrant Of Hell / Witching Hour / Bloody Karnage.
Nocturnal Hell EP, Fan Club (1986) (Fan Club edition. 1000 copies). Nocturnal Hell / One Foot In The Grave / Tortured Souls.
STRAPPADO, Diabolic Force FPL 3028 (1987). Strappado / The Curse / Disintegrater / Incinerator / Parasites / F.O.D. / Tortured Souls / Nocturnal Hell / Tales Of The Macabre.

NOT DEAD YET, Slaughter (1990). Not Dead Yet / Flake / Threshold Of Pain / Time Warp / Death Comes Ripping Through You / The Dark / Astral Projector / Telepathic Screams.

SURRENDER OR DIE, Utopian Vision Music (1999). Disintegrater / Incinerator / Maim To Please / Tyrant Of Hell / Shadow Of Death / Death Dealer / One Foot In The Grave / Surrender Or Die / Eve Of Darkness / Massacra / Strappado / Tales Of The Macabre / Cult Of The Dead.

NOT DEAD YET / PARANORMAL, Nuclear Blast NB 663 (2001). Not Dead Yet / Flake / Threshold Of Pain / Timewarp / Death Comes Ripping Through You / The Dark / Astral Projector / Telepathic Screams / Schizo / Galactic Dynamics / Coffin Of Ice / The Fourth Dimension / The Curse (Live) / Tortured Souls (Live) / Nocturnal Hell (Live) / Incinerator (Live).

STRAPPADO, Nuclear Blast NB 662 (2001). Disintegrater / Incinerator / Nocturnal Hell / F.O.D. / Tortured Souls / Parasites / The Curse / Strappado / Maim To Please / One Foot In The Grave / Tyrant Of Hell / Death Dealer / Tales Of The Macabre / Disintegrater/Incinerator (Live) / One Foot In The Grave (Live) / Shadow Of Death (Live) / Massacra (Live) / Death Dealer (Live) / Tales Of The Macabre (Live) / Maim To Please (Live) / Strappado (Live) / Eve Of Darkness (Live) / Tyrant Of Hell (Live) / Witching Hour (Live) / Bloody Karnage (Live) / (Hidden rehearsal track).

FUCK OF DEATH, Hells Headbangers HELLS PLP 002 (2004) (Limited edition 1000 copies). Evil Dead / Legion Of Doom / Nocturnal Hell / The Curse / Fuck Of Death / Parasites / One Foot In The Grave / Maim To Please—Strappado / Tortured Souls / Death Dealer / Tyrant Of Hell.

Slaughter / Nunslaughter, Horror HOR 011 (2004) (Split 7" single with NUNSLAUGHTER. Limited edition 1030 copies). Children Of Fire / Hell Hath Returned.

SLOW AGONY

ASUNCIÓN, PARAGUAY — *David Arriola (vocals), Angel Giménez (guitar), Eulogio Garcia (bass), Marcelo Arriola (drums).*

Asunción Death Metal band dating to March 1991. The band's first formation counted vocalist / bassist David Arriola, guitarists Erwin Leguizamón and Daniel Torres with Marcelo Arriola on the drums. In September of 1994 bassist Eulogio García was enrolled. Also credited would be 'Berkhaial' of Black Metal bands DIABOLICAL, TANTRUM, BAALBERITH and WISDOM repute. SLOW AGONY's debut came in 1995 with the demo 'Fall Into The Oblivion', after which Torres decamped to be replaced by Víctor Sarría, with the 'Live' cassette following in 1998 and 'Weakness Cast Aside' in 1999. SLOW AGONY featured on the 2000 four way split demo 'Purgatory Unchained I' shared with NECROPSY, RIPPER and WISDOM. Their first CD format album, 'Crumbling Empires', emerged that same year. Infected Voice Productions released this as a cassette variant for the Peruvian market.

SLOW AGONY featured tracks on a 2002 three way split album 'Sudamerica Brutal 2' published by Argentine label Hurling Metal alongside 1917 and SLOW DEATH. Sarria exited that March, the band soon plugging the vacancy with Ángel Giménez. Kamikaze Records issued the band's second full length album, the Rodolfo Brugada produced 'Spiritual Euphoria', that August. Brothers David and Marcelo Arriola founded a Death Rock outfit called THE PROFANE in July 2003.

Fall Into The Oblivion, (1995). Along The Obscure Land / Dawn Confusion / A Perfect Vision Of Death / Resurrection Of The Real God / Fall Into The Oblivion / Lord Obscurity.

Live, Covenant (1998). Fall Into The Oblivion / Resurrection Of The Real God / A Perfect Vision Of Death / Twisted Reality.

Weakness Cast Aside, Covenant (1999). Ecstasies Pain / Tragedies / Scream Arena / Blackend Arts / Hear The Winds Of The Holocaust / All The Weak Cling To Your Lie.

Purgatory Unchained I, Covenant (2000). A Perfect Vision Of Death / Twisted Reality / Hear The Wings Of Holocaust.

CRUMBLING EMPIRES, Covenant (2001). Sources Of Evil Unleash / Twisted Reality / Falling Crown / Fall Into The Oblivion / Chemicals Dreams / Along The Obscure Land / Starving Eyes / Dawn Confusion / Torment Build Inside / Tragedy / Scream Arena / All The Weak Cling To Your Lie.

CRUMBLING EMPIRES, Infected Voice Productions (2001) (Peruvian release). Sources Of Evil Unleash / Twisted Reality / Falling Down / Fall Into The Oblivion / Chemical Dreams / Along The Obscure Land / Starving Eyes / Dawn Confusion / Torment Build Inside / Tragedy / Scream Arena / All The Weak Cling To Your Lie.

SUDAMERICA BRUTAL 2, Hurling Metal (2002) (split album with SLOW DEATH and 1917). Blessing This Belief / The Rebirth Of Chaos / Crumbling Empires / Fall Into The Oblivion / Dawn Confusion / Chemicals Dreams / All The Weak Cling To Your Lie.

SPIRITUAL EUPHORIA, Kamikaze (2002). The Rebirth Of Chaos / The Kiss Profane / The Age Of Awakening / The Accuser / Slave Of Pain / Humanity Exiled / Hear The Winds Of Holocaust / Dogma-Pervertion / Blessing This Belief / A Circle Of Hunger / Crumbling Empires.

SLUDGE

SWITZERLAND — *Nico (vocals), Marco (guitar), Christophe (bass), Patrick (drums).*

SLUDGE, featuring SAMAEL guitarist Makro, recorded their first EP 'Sweet Daisy' for Godhead Records with producer Tomas Skogsberg at the Sunlight Studios in Sweden during 1996. They returned to Sunlight Studios in the end of 1997 to record their first full length album 'The Well', releasing this through Headstrong Records in 1998. A heavy touring schedule would witness European supports to the likes of MACHINE HEAD, ENTOMBED, CATHEDRAL, SAMAEL, CROWBAR, TESTAMENT, DIE KRUPPS, ANATHEMA, STUCK MOJO and SPIRITUAL BEGGARS.

Working with producer Fredrik Nordström the band soon followed up with second album 'Scarecrow Messiah', partnering with CROWBAR for European gigs in the Summer of 2001. SLUDGE then was put on the back burner as Makro toured with SAMAEL.

The band signed a deal with Denmark's Mighty Music in September of 2004. The resulting album 'Yellow Acid Rain' was recorded in Switzerland and mixed by Fredrik Nordström at Studio Fredman in Gothenburg, Sweden.

SLUDGE returned in 2006, although sporting a completely revised roster of players. Newly installed on vocals would be Odin from UNFOLD and HOUSTON SWING ENGINE, whilst bass guitar was now in the hands of Ukrainian musician Ulik.

SWEET DAISY, Godhead GOD 021 (1996). Sweet Daisy / Long I Thought / Loneliness / Fly Away.

SCARECROW MESSIAH, Headstrong (2000).

YELLOW ACID RAIN, Mighty Music PMZ027-2 (2004).

SLUGATHOR

ESPOO, FINLAND — *Axu Laakso (vocals), Tommi Grönqvist (guitar), Antti Oinonen (guitar), Juuso Heikkilä (bass), Ilmari Jalas (drums).*

Espoo's SLUGATHOR was forged in the Autumn of 1999 by lead vocalist Nebiros, guitarist Tommi Grönqvist, bassist Tatte and drummer Immu (Ilmari Jalas). The quartet debuted with a brace of 2000 demos 'Delicacies Of The Cadaver' in March and 'Fabric Of The Multiverse'. Both of these sessions would be subsequently released by the German based Perverted Taste label as limited edition 7" singles. In early 2001 SLUGATHOR underwent a major line-up overhaul with founders Tommi Grönqvist and Ilmari Jalas being joined by new musicians Axu Laakso on vocals and guitarists Tuoppi (a.k.a. Tuomas Lintulaakso) of DE LIRIUM'S ORDER, and Antti Oinonen, the latter a member of DEEP RED and holding APOPLEXY, EXCREMENT and, as "Necroterror", CADAVERIC INCUBATOR credentials. Laakso's scene associations included DEEP RED, GOATHORDE, NIGHT MUST FALL and THORNGOAT.

SLUGATHOR's 2002 split single for Snuff Records, 'Creation .44', shared with DEEP RED, seeing Tommi on bass guitar, included a cover version of BOLT THROWER's 'Remembrance'. A concert recorded at the Semifinal, Helsinki in December 2002 would be released in Poland by the Time After Time label as a live cassette 'Crush Skulls And Bones'. The band signed to the Polish Agonia label for their inaugural album 'Unleashing The Slugathron' in late 2003. A cassette version was issued in Finland, restricted to 333 copies, by Northern Sound.

May 2004 dates in Finland saw WATAIN on a package billing alongside WATAIN, ANXIOUS DEATH and KAAMOS. That same year the group recorded further demos, from which the song 'Legions Of The Undead' was included on the compilation album 'Metal On Metal—Finnish Undergound Metal Collection'.

Tragedy hit the band on April 15th 2005 when Tuomas Lintulaakso was stabbed to death. In the wake of this event Oinonen briefly switched back to guitar from bass whilst Jarno Nurmi of NERLICH, NOWEN and NIGHT MUST FALL tried out on bass. Oinonen resumed his post on guitar and Juuso Heikkilä from NIGHT MUST FALL, GENERAL WINTER and TYRANNY filled the bass position. In this formation SLUGATHOR appeared at the festivals 'Murder Art' in Moscow, Russia and 'Jalometalli' in Oulu, Finland.

In 2006 drummer Ilmari Jalas, as 'Imperator', forged SATANIC TORMENT involving a quartet of scene veterans from the underground extreme Metal scene with singer H. Necrophiliac Ju Von Nen, of DEVIL LEE ROT, EVOKED CURSE, GOATSODOMY, SACRIFICIAL DAGGER, TRISTITIA, PAGAN RITES and WITCHTIGER, guitarist Kaosbringer, from NEUTRON HAMMER, SACRIFICIAL DAGGER and SYÖPÄ, and bassist Tooloud of EVIL ANGEL, EVOKED CURSE and GOATSODOMY.

In June 2006 Time Before Time Records released the SLUGATHOR album 'Circle Of Death', recorded by a trio of Laakso, Grönqvist and Jalas. REVEREND BIZARRE's Albert Witchfinder guested in the studio. The closing song 'Legions Of The Undead' featured lead guitar work by the late Tuomas Lintulaakso. Terranis Productions released a split 7" single, limited to 300 copies in alliance with AGE OF AGONY. SLUGATHOR donated two tracks including a cover version of TORMENTOR's 'Tormentor'.

Delicacies Of The Cadaver, Perverted Taste (2000) (7' vinyl single). Delicacies Of The Cadaver / Burning Within / Abhorrent Copulation Machine.
Fabric Of The Multiverse, Slugathor (2000) (Demo). Fabric Of The Multiverse / Lord Of all (Unborn) / Slugathor / Reflection Continuum.
Delicacies Of The Cadaver, Slugathor (2000) (Demo). Delicacies Of The Cadaver / Burning Within / Abhorrent Copulation Machine.
Fabric Of The Multiverse, Perverted Taste (2001). Fabric Of The Multiverse / Lord Of All (Unborn) / Slugathor / Reflection Continuum.
Creation .44, Snuff (2002) (Split 7' single with DEEP RED). Seeds Of Torment (SLUGATHOR) / Remembrance (SLUGATHOR) / Creation .44 (DEEP RED) / Trap Them And Kill Them (DEEP RED).
Slugathor, Slugathor (2002) (Demo). Delicacies Of The Cadaver / All Must Die / Lord Of All (Unborn) / Extinction.
Crush Skulls And Bones, Time Before Time (2003) (Live cassette demo. Limited edition 333 copies). Lord Of All (Unborn) / All Must Die / Extinction / Seeds Of Torment / Abhorrent Copulation Machine / Fabric Of The Multiverse / Delicacies Of The Cadaver.
UNLEASHING THE SLUGATHRON, Agonia (2003). Delicacies Of The Cadaver / All Must Die / Bleed For Me / Lord Of All (Unborn) / Suffering Endlessly / Fabric Of The Multiverse / Instinct To Kill / Phenomenon Of Doom / Extinction / Abhorrent Copulation Machine.
Promo 2004, Slugathor (2004) (Demo). Slow And Painful Death / Temple Of Shadows (Apocalyptic Visions) / Legions Of The Undead.
Slugathor / Age Of Agony, Terranis Productions (2006) (Split 7" vinyl single with AGE OF AGONY. Limited edition 300 copies). Reign Of The Supreme (SLUGATHOR) / Tormentor (SLUGATHOR) / Question (AGE OF AGONY) / She Lives By Night (AGE OF AGONY).
CIRCLE OF DEATH, Time Before Time (2006). Cycle Of Destruction / Slow And Painful Death / Bestial Chaos / Crypt Of The Dead / Journey Into Oblivion / Final Ceremony / Temple Of Shadows (Apocalyptic Visions) / Legions Of The Undead.

SOILENT GREEN

NEW ORLEANS, LA, USA — *Ben Falgoust II (vocals), Brian Patton (guitar), Donovan Punch (guitar), Scott Williams(bass), Tommy Buckley (drums).*

New Orleans SOILENT GREEN, somewhat akin to the famous Sci-Fi food substitute the band is named after, blend an unspeakable mix of influences ranging through Grindcore, Sludge and Blues based Southern Rock. The band's discordant style of galloping Grindcore juxtaposed with quagmire like viscosity has both confounded critics and generated admiration from the extreme Metal scene. SOILENT GREEN guitarist Brian Patton is also a member of EYEHATEGOD.

SOILENT GREEN gelled together in 1988 comprising erstwhile NUCLEAR CRUCIFIXION guitar players Donovan Punch and Brian Patton with drummer Tommy Buckley. NUCLEAR CRUCIFIXION operated with Punch and Patton involved with vocalist Glenn Rambo, bassist David Moran and drummer Darren Schallenburg. This unit put out the demo sessions 'Killing Ourselves To Live' and 'Torture Of Humanity' prior to Punch, Patton and Rambo founding SOILENT GREEN. The band's line-up would prove fluid and momentum was slowed when Patton took up position in the more active EYEHATEGOD.

The group stabilised with the introduction of bassist Scott Williams in 1992, lead singer Louis Benjamin Falgoust II of PARALYSIS being inducted the following year. This version of the band cut the opening album, 'Pussysoul', for Dwell Records during 1995. Promotion on the road in North America witnessed gigs with EXTREME NOISE TERROR. It is known that during that year Tommy Buckley also auditioned for MACHINE HEAD.

The group also recorded tracks for what transpired to be a split 10" single with GRIEF, and made an appearance on the 'Cry Now, Cry Later' double 7" single compilation, both of these releases issued by Pessimiser/Theologian Records.

Patton's schedule with EYEHATEGOD resulted in a sallow year for SOILENT GREEN in 1996 but 1997 opened in style, the band acting as guests to PANTERA and CLUTCH on a string of Texan dates. Tracks would be laid down with engineer Keith Falgoust before further road activity in union with CRISIS, ANAL CUNT and CHOKE before hooking up in December with PANTERA, ANTHRAX and COAL CHAMBER in Florida and Mississippi.

SOILENT GREEN switched labels to the Relapse concern for the February 1998 'A String Of Lies' EP swiftly capitalised on by the full length 'Sewn Mouth Secrets'. Between these releases the group put in live dates with BRUTAL TRUTH upfront of a showing at the 'Milwaukee Metalfest'. Another two month round of gigs resumed as part of the 'Nawleans Swamp Tour' in alliance with CROWBAR and EYEHATEGOD.

SOILENT GREEN paid respect to the originators of Doom BLACK SABBATH in unique fashion by donating a track billed as 'Lord Of The Southern Priest', actually a medley of 'Lord Of This World', 'The Sign Of The Southern Cross' and 'Disturbing The Priest', to the Hydrahead tribute compilation 'In These Black Days—Volume 6'.

In downtime Patton resumed activities with EYEHATEGOD whilst Falgoust formed an unholy alliance with CROWBAR guitarist Sammy Duet to found GOATWHORE for 2000's 'The Eclipse Of Ages Into Black' album.

Donovan bowed out in 1999 and Falgoust's colleague in GOATWHORE Ben Stout maneuvered over to fill the SOILENT GREEN guitar vacancy. A third album was recorded, provisionally entitled 'The Devil Wears A Lamb's Skin', eventually emerging as 'A Deleted Symphony For The Beaten Down' in 2001. US dates had SOILENT GREEN navigating the country as part of the 'Extreme Music For Extreme People' tour.

The band announced another bout of North American touring, commencing 16th January 2002, in alliance with headliners GWAR and GOD FORBID. In December of 2001 however, the band would be involved in a road accident while travelling in the Washington area. Their van skidded on black ice, leaving guitarist Brian Patton and bassist Scott Williams with broken bones. As a result SOILENT GREEN cancelled all shows.

Quite bizarrely Scott Williams sustained another injury to his as yet unhealed shoulder in another auto accident. With dates in Japan scheduled in league with EYEHATEGOD the band rapidly drafted fill in bassist Jonny Modell.

After a due period of recuperation the band jumped back onboard the GWAR tour but in a quite surreal turn of events the band was involved in a second van accident on the 11th of April that injured vocalist Ben Falgoust and stand-in tour bassist Jonny Modell. Falgoust had been forced to avoid an out of control car and the band's vehicle smashed into the back of an 18 wheel truck. The singer came off worst breaking two legs but Modell received a broken collar bone. None too surprisingly SOILENT GREEN was forced off the tour yet again.

Amidst all of SOILENT GREEN's trouble one ray of light emerged with the announcement that Ben Falgoust and Jay Branch of SKINCRAWL's new label Incision Records were gearing up for a debut release, a limited edition split 7" affair between SOILENT GREEN and none other than EYEHATEGOD. Restricted to just 2,000 pieces the record was made even more collectable by the fact that 500 of these would be in either clear or coloured swirl vinyl.

In mid 2002 Relapse re-issued 'A Deleted Symphony for the Beaten Down' in a limited run of 1000 gatefold packaged vinyl pressings. 900 of these rarities came in clear green vinyl with an even scarcer 100 copies manufactured in clear vinyl. In August Tommy Buckley would session for JONES LOUNGE, the new band of former EXHORDER vocalist Kyle Thomas.

The group introduced new blood in April of 2003 in the form of second guitarist Tony White and bassist Scott Crochet. SOILENT GREEN, THE BLACK DAHLIA MURDER and LICKGOLDENSKY united for a Summer package tour of the USA commencing 30th July in Fort Lauderdale, Florida. Tragic news came that same month as former SOILENT GREEN bassist Scott Williams was found dead from gunshot wounds on 26th April. Apparently police discovered two bodies in his Gretna, Louisiana apartment, one they were treating as murder and the other suicide. Subsequent reports suggested Williams colleague Tracey Terry, following an argument at a restaurant, shot the musician in the head with a .38 caliber revolver, then killed himself.

Paying tribute to their late colleague SOILENT GREEN united with GOATWHORE, VALUME NOB, ANGEL DUST and RAT IN A BUCKET for a 18th June benefit gig held at The Howlin' Wolf in New Orleans. Dates in January of 2005 saw the band partnering with BEHEMOTH and SUFFOCATION. That same month the band entered Mana Recording Studios in Tampa, Florida with HATE ETERNAL's Erik Rutan acting as producer to cut the album 'Confrontation'. Also projected would be a split 7" single shared with SULACO through Bloated Goat Records. North American gigs in July had the group backed up by A PERFECT MURDER and INTO THE MOAT. A further leg of dates, stretching through until September, saw Oakland's WATCH THEM DIE as support. Tragically, in the wake of Hurricane Katrina's devastation in the New Orleans area, former SOILENT GREEN vocalist Glenn Rambo was found dead in his Violet home.

Live work breaking into 2006 saw the band teaming up with HYPOCRISY, NILE, RAGING SPEEDHORN, DECAPITATED and WITH PASSION for a North American tour commencing in early January. Further US shows throughout June had the band working alongside THE ACACIA STRAIN and DEMIRICOUS.

PUSSYSOUL, Dwell (1995). Thirteen Days A Week / Slapfuck / Falling From A 65 Storey Building / Lips As So Of Blood / The Wrong Of Way / Needlescrape / Zebra Zombies / Keep Crawling / Twitch Of An Eye / Golfers Just Love Punishment / Love None / Branding Of Thieves.

A String Of Lies EP, Relapse RR6985 (1998). Sewn Mouth Secrets / Cat With Nine Claws / Felt Nothing.

SEWN MOUTH SECRETS, Relapse RR 6405 (1998). It Was Just An Accident / So Hatred / Build Fear / Looking Through Nails / Breed In Weakness / Cold Steel Kiss / Openless / Her Unsober Ways / Sewn Mouth Secrets / Walk A Year In My Mind / Gagged Whore / Emptiness Found / Sticks And Stones.

A DELETED SYMPHONY FOR THE BEATEN DOWN, Relapse RLP6481 (2001). Hand Me Downs / A Grown Man / Swallowhole / Afterthought Of A Genius / An Addicts Lover / Later Days / Clockwork Of Innocence / Daydreaming The Color Of Blood / Last One In The Noose / She Cheated On You Twice.

CONFRONTATION, Relapse (2005). Scarlet Sunrise / Leaves Of Three / A Scream Trapped Underwater / Forgive And Regret / 12 Oz. Prophet / Southern Spirit Suite / Pretty Smiles & Shattered Teeth / Liquor & Cigarettes / Theory Of Pride In Tragedy / Fingernails On A Chalkboard / Paper Cut / They Lie To Hide The Truth / Another Cheap Brand Of Luck / This Glass House Of Broken Words / A Permanent Solution To A Temporary Problem.

SOILS OF FATE

SWEDEN — *Henke Krants (vocals / bass), Mange Lindvall (guitar), Trevor Kolbjer (guitar), Jocke (drums).*

Ultraspeed Death Metal act SOILS OF FATE date back to 1995 and the union of vocalist / bassist Henke Crantz and guitarist Mange Lindvall. This duo issued the 1997 demo 'Pain . . . Has A Face' before adding second guitarist Trevor Kolbjer.

This newest recruit lasted a year before bailing out. SOILS OF FATE, finally with a drummer named Jocke, issued a three track promotional CD entitled 'Blood Serology' on their own Empty Veins Music imprint. Upon the release of the debut album 'Sandstorm' Jocke too made his exit. In 1998 an ex-SOILS OF FATE drummer Nicke Karlsson united with the former AD INFINITUM pairing of guitarist Micke Jakobsson and bassist Janne De Sade to found PANDEMONIC.

The 2003 SOILS OF FATE album 'Crime Syndicate', which included a cover version of SUFFOCATION's 'Devoid Of Truth', saw drum duties delegated to Kevin Talley of DYING FETUS, SUFFOCATION and MISERY INDEX repute with DEVOURMENT's Ruben Rosas aiding on backing vocals.

SANDSTORM, Retribute (2001). Life Hijacker / Sandstorm / .44 / Stripped Humanity / Half My Blood / Blunted On Reality / Assassins.

CRIME SYNDICATE, Forensick FM 005 (2003). Killaz Beware / Omertá (Men Of Honor—Codex Of Silence) / Blood Money / VS. / Crack / Murder, Inc. / Flowing Under Skin 2.0 / Insider / Devoid Of Truth.

SOILWORK

HELSINGBORG, SWEDEN — *Björn Strid (vocals), Peter Wichers (guitar), Ludvig Svartz (guitar), Ola Flink (bass), Carlos Del Olmo (keyboards), Jimmy Persson (drums).*

Helsingborg act SOILWORK's initial trademark was to blend a heady mixture of Thrash and Death Metal but latter releases, marked by the turning point 'A Predator's Portrait' album, have seen the band mature apace by injecting huge amounts of melody making them serious contenders for greatness. As such, the band's schedule accelerated markedly to involve lengthy bouts of international touring.

Initially the group, instigated during 1995, operated billed as INFERIOR BREED but as SOILWORK opened proceedings with the 1997 demo 'In Dreams We Fall Into The Eternal Lake'. The band structure at this point involved frontman Björn Strid, going under the name of 'Speed', guitarist Peter Vicious' (a.k.a. Peter Wichers), second guitarist Ludvig Svartz and drummer Jimmy Persson. A former bassist, Carl-Gustav Döös, had decamped beforehand, as had a formative guitarist Mattias Nilsson, the latter resurfacing with KAYSER.

A copy of 'In Dreams We Fall Into The Eternal Lake' was given to ARCH ENEMY guitarist Mike Amott who, obviously impressed, passed it onto various labels spurring a number of offers. The May 1998 album 'Steel Bath Suicide', released through French label Listenable Records, was produced by Fredrik Nordström at Fredman studios. The band that constructed these tracks now incorporated Ola Flink on bass and Carlos Del Olmo Holmberg handling keyboards. Japanese versions were augmented with the traditionally expected extra tracks with 'Disintegrated Skies' and a cover version of DEEP PURPLE's 'Burn'. Road promotion had SOILWORK proffering their wares on European stages backing NAGLFAR, DARKANE and KRISIUN.

Listenable kept the band on for a further round of Death—Thrash in October 1999's 'The Chainheart Machine', again a Fredrik Nordström produced effort witnessing the employment of the 'Jaffa quartet' massed violin section of Ullik Johansson, Julia Petersson, Amanda Ingvaldsson, Fanny Petersson, Alva Ingvaldsson and Katalin Tibell. Newly installed on drums would be Henry Ranta and a new guitarist, Ola Frenning, to replace the departed Svartz. Whilst still locked in stereotypical "Gothenburg Death" territory, SOILWORK adventurously maximised on twin lead guitar harmony playing to good effect. Japanese editions added bonus cut 'Shadowchild'. The European touring circuit was to feel the force of SOILWORK once again when the band supported CANNIBAL CORPSE, DEFLESHED and MARDUK prior to their first live engagement in Japan paired with DARK TRANQUILLITY. Another notable recording executed that same year would be their interpretation of MERCYFUL FATE's 'Egypt', featured on 'The Unholy Sounds Of The Demon Bells—A Tribute To Mercyful Fate' collection issued via Poland's Still Dead Productions.

In outside activity, Peter Wichers would add session guitar to CONSTRUCDEAD's 2000 EP 'Turn'. SOILWORK signed to Germany's Nuclear Blast label for the 'A Predator's Portrait' album, launched in February 2001. This is where SOILWORK hit the crossroads of their career, not fully embracing experimentation but adopting more melody and significantly dropping Björn Strid's previously favoured Death growls for a cleaner approach. Fredrik Nordström maintained his position as producer, Eskil Simonsson provided samples and studio guests included notable figures Mattias IA Eklundh of FREAK KITCHEN, donating a guitar solo to 'Needlefeast' and OPETH's Mikael Åkerfeldt vocalising on the title track. In the Far East, 'A Predator's Portrait' hosted extra cut 'Asylum Dance'.

They would return to the studio in October 2001 with new keyboard man Sven Karlsson, of EVERGREY repute, and producer DEVIN TOWNSEND in tow, this union seeing the Canadian's influence leaving a firm impression on the band. SOILWORK's burgeoning reputation was heightened by the delivery of a March 2002 album 'Natural Born Chaos'. Strid's vocal parts were now almost wholly delivered clean and Karlsson's keyboard atmospherics figured prominently, including the use of Hammond organ on "Black Star Deceiver". Townsend's lush production breathed new life into the band, who adopted his techniques for future outings.

The band toured America during the summer packaged with HYPOCRISY and KILLSWITCH ENGAGE. One notable gig being at the San Jose Cactus Club where Chuck Billy of TESTAMENT lent backing vocals to the track 'Follow The Hollow'. SOILWORK joined IN FLAMES and PAIN for touring in mainland Europe during October.

Members of SOILWORK, in alliance with DARKANE personnel and CONSTRUCDEAD drummer Erik Thyselius also operated the project band TERROR 2000. Bassist Ola Flink would also be active with HATELIGHT, issuing the demos 'Word Ammunition' and 'Ricochet' in 2002 and 2003 respectively.

The band entered Helsingborg's Queenstreet Recording studios with the trusted Fredrik Nordström during mid December to cut their fifth album. Backing vocals for these sessions came courtesy of HATELIGHT's Jens Broman. 'Figure Number Five', issued by Nuclear Blast in April, became the recipient of quite huge acclaim in the Metal world. A novel promotional video for the track 'Rejection Role' saw the band in a turf war with the members of IN FLAMES. Touring in North America saw the band hooking up with headliners IN FLAMES and road partners CHIMAIRA and UNEARTH for a month long trek commencing June 26th in Toronto, Canada. However, the band would lose the services of drummer Henry Ranta beforehand, swiftly replacing him with the EBONY TEARS, DOG FACED GODS, Funksters IT'S ALIVE, MANIC DEPRESSION, SOUTHPAW, EYEBALL and SORCERER credited Richard Evensand. The new recruit debuted with the band at the Gelsenkirchen, Germany 'Rock Hard' festival.

The band put in a showing at the ARCH ENEMY headlined Busan International Rock Festival at Daedepo Beach in Korea on August 8th before uniting with CHILDREN OF BODOM for a Japanese tour in September. A further bout of November US shows saw the band partnered with premier British Black Metal band CRADLE OF FILTH and TYPE O NEGATIVE. Rickard Evansand joined CHIMAIRA during December. SOILWORK, pulling in Dirk Verbeuren from French Thrashers SCARVE as substitute on drums, undertook a headline tour of the UK in February 2004 supported by fellow Swedes THE FORSAKEN. The band then partnered with Thrash veterans ANTHRAX and KILLSWITCH ENGAGE for Australian and Japanese dates in April 2004. Verbeuren then stepped in as substitute drummer for Belgian gore-mongers ABORTED's live dates.

Björn Strid would lend guest vocals to Italian melodic Death Metal band DISARMONIA MUNDI's 2004 album 'Fragments Of D-Generation'. SOILWORK, after festival appearances at 'With Full Force' in Germany, 'Roskilde' in Denmark and the 'Tuska' event in Finland, would enter Studio Kuling in Örebro during September to work with producer Daniel Bergstrand on their sixth album, billed 'Stabbing The Drama', projected for early 2005 issue. European digipacks added extra track 'Wherever Thorns May Grow' whilst Japanese variants were also boosted with an additional song, 'Killed By Ignition'. . US dates for January 2005 had the band packaged with DARK TRANQUILLITY and HYPOCRISY.

SOILWORK's profile rose significantly as 'Stabbing The Drama' entered the national Swedish album charts at an impressive number 14 in late February. Notably, the album also marked first time chart entries for the band in Austria, Finland and France. The band had their track 'Stabbing The Drama' featured on the soundtrack to the 'Rainbow Six Lockdown' game issued by 3volution Productions. The following month Björn Strid revealed he had fired up a new side project dubbed COLDSEED in a collaboration with BLIND GUARDIAN drummer Thomen Stauch, guitarists Thorsten Praest and Gonzalo Alfageme Lopez and the BLIND GUARDIAN and SIEGES EVEN bassist Oli Holzwarth. Strid also put in a guest vocal appearance on German Thrash act DESTRUCTION's 'Inventor Of Evil' album.

Throughout the Summer of 2005 SOILWORK joined the mammoth cast of bands on the US 'Ozzfest' tour alongside such industry giants as BLACK SABBATH, IRON MAIDEN and VELVET REVOLVER. The trek's 13th August Mountain View, California stop proved notable for the band as they were joined onstage by guesting TESTAMENT frontman Chuck Billy for the track 'Follow The Hollow'. Scandinavian, UK and European dates in October saw CONSTRUCDEAD as support. November 8th, at New York's Irving Plaza, marked the start of another US tour, the band forming up a bill comprising FEAR FACTORY, DARKANE and STRAPPING YOUNG LAD.

Guitarist Peter Wichers announced his departure in mid December. Early 2006 found Björn Strid involving himself in a studio collaboration with bassist Steve DiGiorgio, of SADUS, SEBASTIAN BACH, TESTAMENT and DEATH, Glen Alvelais from FORBIDDEN, TESTAMENT and LD/50 and Jeremy Colson of the STEVE VAI band, MARTY FRIEDMAN, MICHAEL SCHENKER, APARTMENT 26, DALI'S DILEMMA and LD/50 repute.

A replacement guitarist would be installed in April 2006, the new man being Daniel Antonsson of DIMENSION ZERO and PATHOS repute. SOILWORK joined the 'Metal Hammer' sponsored 'European Neckbreaker's Ball' 2006 tour, also featuring

SOILWORK (pic: David Falk)

HYPOCRISY, SCAR SYMMETRY and ONE MAN ARMY AND THE UNDEAD QUARTET, commencing 11th April in Denmark.

A whole slew of European open air appearances took the band through the summer. However, unable to secure flights in time for drummer Dirk Verbeuren, residing in Los Angeles, the band pulled in DARKANE's Peter Wildoer for 'Festimad' in Madrid, Spain plus shows in Piteå and Malmö. The band was set to put in a significant appearance at the GUNS N' ROSES headlined 'Download' festival in Castle Donington, UK on June 11th. However, guitarist Ola Frenning suffered a "vascular spasm", forcing a cancellation.

That same month word arrived that Peter Wichers was in collaboration with SANCTUARY and NEVERMORE singer Warrel Dane, working on his debut solo album. The band's appearance at the German 'Rock Hard' festival in June was taped and subsequently the track 'Stabbing The Drama' was included on the 'Rock Hard' magazine compilation album 'Rock Hard: Das Festival 2006'.

September 2006 UK shows were supported by French Thrashers LYZANXIA. The group returned for another North American tour commencing October 5th at the Jaxx venue in West Springfield, Virginia taking along DARKEST HOUR, MNEMIC and THREAT SIGNAL for 'The Last Stab' dates into mid November. On November 7th SOILWORK were announced as replaced a cancelling SIX FEET UNDER as the headliner of the X-mas Festivals tour, scheduled to kick off at the Berlin K17 venue December 8th, alongside GOREFEST, BELPHEGOR, TRAIL OF TEARS and DARZAMAT. However, the following day the band's agency denied this, saying the group was unable to participate.

SOILWORK announced in early March 2007 that Daniel Antonsson, from DIMENSION ZERO and PATHOS, had secured the guitar position.

In Dreams We Fall Into The Eternal Lake, (1997). Bound To Illusions / My Need / In Dreams We Fall Into The Eternal Lake / In A Close Encounter / Skin After Skin.
STEEL BATH SUICIDE, Listenable POSH 012 (1998). Entering The Angel Diabolique / Sadistic Lullaby / My Need / Skin After Skin / Wings Of Domain / Steelbath Suicide / In A Close Encounter / Centro De Predomino / Razorlives / Demon In Veins / The Aardvark Trail / Sadistic Lullabye.
THE CHAINHEART MACHINE, Listenable POSH 017 (1999). The Chainheart Machine / Bulletbeast / Millionflame / Generation Speedkill (Nice Dirty Day For Public Suicide) / Neon Rebels / Possessing The Angels / Spirits Of Future Sun / Machine Gun Majesty / Room No 99.
A PREDATOR'S PORTRAIT, Nuclear Blast NB 582-2 (2001). Bastard Chain / Like An Average Stalker / Needlefeast / Neurotica Rampage / The Analyst / Grand Failure Anthem / Structure Divine / Shadowchild / Final Fatal Force / A Predator's Portrait.
NATURAL BORN CHAOS, Nuclear Blast NB 581-2 (2002). Follow The Hollow / As We Speak / The Flameout / Natural Born Chaos / Mindfields / The Bringer / Black Star Deceiver / Mercury Shadow / No More Angels / Soilworker's Song Of The Damned / Kvicksilver.
FIGURE NUMBER FIVE, Nuclear Blast NB 1108-2 (2003). Rejection Role / Overload / Figure Number Five / Strangler / Light The Torch / Departure Plan / Cranking The Sirens / Brickwalker / The Mindmaker / Distortion Sleep / Downfall 24. Chart position: 59 SWEDEN.
Rejection Role, Nuclear Blast NB 1137-2 (2003). Rejection Role / Departure Plan.
Light The Torch, Nuclear Blast NB 1223-2 (2003). Light The Torch / Figure Number Five / Light The Torch (Video).
The Early Chapters, Listenable POSH 054 (2004). Burn / Disintigrated Skies / Gypsy / Shadow Child / Aardvark Trail (Live).
Stabbing The Drama, Nuclear Blast NB 1417-2 (2005). Stabbing The Drama / Asylum Dance. Chart position: 7 FINLAND.
STABBING THE DRAMA, Nuclear Blast NB 1416-2 (2005) (Limited edition digipack). Stabbing The Drama / One With The Flies / Weapon Of Vanity / The Crestfallen / Nerve / Stalemate / Distance / Observation Slave / Fate In Motion / Blind Eye Halo / If Possible / Wherever Thorns May Grow. Chart positions: 14 SWEDEN, 19 FINLAND, 52 GERMANY, 63 AUSTRIA, 143 FRANCE.
STABBING THE DRAMA, Nuclear Blast NB 1377-2 (2005). Stabbing The Drama / One With The Flies / Weapon Of Vanity / The Crestfallen / Nerve / Stalemate / Distance / Observation Slave / Fate In Motion / Blind Eye Halo / If Possible.

SOLAR DAWN

SKÖVDE, SWEDEN — *Christian Älvestam (vocals / guitar), Anders Edlund (guitar), Robert Karlsson (bass), Henrik Schönström (drums).*

Skövde based Death Metal merchants SOLAR DAWN first saw assembly by the guitar pairing of Andreas Månsson and Anders Edlund of VORHEES as JARAWYNJA during 1997. Utilising Christian Älvestam of UNMOORED as session vocalist and Marcus Engström on the drums the formative band cut the opening Black-Thrash styled demo 'The Festival Of Fools' in 1998. This quartet, albeit now leaning more toward melodic Death Metal territory and enlisting Linus Abrahamsson on bass, remained in force to lay down a further session in 2000 dubbed 'Desideratum'. The Danish Mighty Music label took these recordings for release as an EP in February of 2001, re-titled 'Frost-Work', their first product under the SOLAR DAWN banner.

SOLAR DAWN's next target was a full blown album, which necessitated the recruitment of a drummer. Jocke Pettersson, an established veteran of such artists as DAWN, CRANIUM, THY PRIMORDIAL, UNMOORED, REGURGITATE, NIDEN DIVISION 187 and MAZE OF TORMENT, stepped in to fulfill duties for the Tommy Tägtgren produced album 'Equinoctium'. Upon completion of the record SOLAR DAWN enrolled Henrik Schönström, holding both TRAUMATIZED and UNMOORED credits, as their new drummer.

Månsson made his exit in 2002, the same year SOLAR DAWN inducted Robert Karlsson of FACEBREAKER, EDGE OF SANITY and PAN-THY-MONIUM repute on bass guitar.

Besides his duties with SOLAR DAWN frontman Christian Älvestam has an extended roll call of band endeavours such as CARNALIZED, ANDUIN '98, EVENDIM, LORD OF THRONES, ORGY OF FLESH, SATTYG, RED SKIES DAWNING, THE STINK BUG COLLECTIVE and DEN TIDLÖSA EVIGHETEN. During 2003 Christian Älvestam and Henrik Schönström featured in the Death / Thrash Metal project TORCHBEARER. The following year Christian Älvestam would be found fronting Jonas Kjellgren's SCAR SYMMETRY band for their 'Symmetric In Design' debut.

SOLAR DAWN folded in February 2005 with an announcement stating "Ladies and gentlemen, we have decided to bury SOLAR DAWN once and for all!", adding "without genuine commitment, there's really no point in continuing." Christian Älvestam donated guest vocals to ZONARIA's 2006 debut album 'Rendered In Vain', featuring on the track 'Attending Annihilation'.

Frost-Work EP, Mighty Music PMZ 018 (2001). Artistic Blasphemy / Punished By Silence / Arisen Composure.

EQUINOCTIUM, Mighty Music PMZ 020 (2002). Deicidal Beliefs / Punished By Silence / Spellbinder / Deep In Mourning / Artistic Blasphemy / Vulturous Need / Broken-Winged / Autumns.

SOLARISIS

HOLLAND — *Gijs van Ouwerkerk (vocals / bass), Bart de Zeeuw (guitar), Joop Kartouw (guitar), Frank Klein Douwel (keyboards), Robert Molenaar (drums).*

Enschede's SOLARISIS, delivering a melodically styled band of Death Metal, opened up with the March 1996 demo 'Ecliptica'. The 'Illumination' session followed later that same year. Although SOLARISIS had been formulated in October 1995 for these first two demos, and indeed for the first four years of operation, it was maintained as a solo endeavour of Gijs van Ouwerkerk.

Inducting the PULMONARY ABCESS pairing of Edwin Kruize and Marijn de Zeeuw, the quirkily titled album, 'Holland Is Made Of Tofu', surfaced on the German Morbid label. After this recording the band cut their rendition of the SCORPIONS 'Animal Magnetism' for a Dwell Records tribute collection 'Another Piece Of Metal' and METALLICA's 'Nothing Else Matters' to 'Overload 2'.

SOLARISIS were found in the studio again in 2002, these recordings resulting in the 'Towards Extinction' promo EP. An album provisionally billed as 'Of Plague Proportions' was projected for 2003.

HOLLAND IS MADE OF TOFU, Morbid (1999). Life Is Better Unborn / Alchemy / My Fair Share Of Solitude / Insect Season / Essence Among The Stars / Under The Sun / Bootje Varen / Breed Of Burden / Race Me To Eden / In Your Cradle / Transcendence.

Towards Extinction EP, Independent (2002). Farewell My Serpentine / Why Worship / Towards Extinction / Solar Metal / The Min Min Lights (Outro).

SOLITARY

PRESTON, LANCASHIRE, UK — *Richard Sherrington (vocals / guitar), Andy Mellor (guitar), Michael Parkl (bass), Roy Miller (drums).*

A stoic British Metal band that has endured more than it's fair share of line up ructions over the course of years. SOLITARY came together in Preston, Lancashire during July of 1995 citing a line up of frontman Richard Sherrington on vocals and guitar, guitarist Dave Herbert, bass player Rob Hewitt and drummer Tristan Callaghan. In this incarnation SOLITARY cut an inaugural demo entitled 'Desolate'. Songwriting contributions for this effort, released in March of 1995, were on hand from Chris Astley of XENTRIX.

A second promotional cassette 'Fear' followed in January of 1996. In July Paul Mortimer took the bass position as SOLITARY got to grips with a further demo 'The Human Condition'. Most of these tracks would subsequently emerge as an EP of the same name. Herbert would opt out in the September for a career as a Policeman. The vacant guitar spot was duly filled by Matthew Costello and shortly after Jason Clark was enrolled as SOLITARY's new drummer.

The band signed a record deal with the Holier Than Thou concern the following year as yet more line up fluctuations hit home. Anthony Cox would replace Clark and Julian Heywood was the new man on bass guitar. The turbulence did not end

SOLITARY

there though as in February of the following year Cox departed and Simon Tomlinson came in on drums.

Just as SOLITARY were gearing up for recording of the debut album Heywood decamped and Gareth Harrop became the group's latest four stringer. A UK club tour was undertaken in the summer pre-empting the release of 'Nothing Changes' which arrived in November. Welcome support gigs to the likes of REIGN, KILL II THIS and Swedes DERANGED found Chris Gaughan now occupying the guitarist's role but by the following February erstwhile member Matt Costello rejoined the ranks.

Negotiations were finalised for the Dutch label Roxson to license the album for Europe but predictably SOLITARY hit further membership problems as Tomlinson bade farewell in June. Roy Miller was the next drummer on call. In adverse times SOLITARY learnt that Roxson had gone into receivership as had their UK label's distributor. A UK tour also had more than it's fair share of bad luck with 5 out of 9 dates being cancelled.

During 2000 SOLITARY's line up remained in a state of flux. Costello departed yet again but his substitute, Stuart Armriding, remained with the band only briefly with an acrimonious split resolving itself with the induction of guitarist Paul Morrison. It would be a familiar tale for 2001. Dave Marshall took over on bass whilst Matt Costello rejoined for his third tenure. SOLITARY would soon lose Costello's services yet again though, replacing him with erstwhile VOID and SOMA guitarist Gaz Wilkinson. Fluxing yet again, SOLITARY's 2004 roster included Andy Mellor on lead guitar and Michael Park on bass.

NOTHING CHANGES, Holier Than Thou HTT/TIF002 (1999). Within Temptation / Clutching Straws / The Downward Spiral / No Reason / A Second Chance / Twisted / Bitterness / Fear / Nothing Changes.

SOMBER

STOCKHOLM, SWEDEN — *Christian Fernandes (vocals / guitar), Mattias Bergner (guitar), Mattias Cederstam (bass), Olle Linderdahl (drums).*

Formed in 1993 out of the ashes of two once rival underground bands in the Stockholm suburb of Sollentuna, SOMBER was a young Death Metal unit consisting of vocalist and guitarist Christian Fernandes, guitarist Mattias Bergner, bassist Mattias Cederstam and Olle Linderdahl on drums. Only after these four members assembled did the name SOMBER come into being. In Mattias Cerderstam's previous band, a dispute with the frontman resulted in the creation of a second band. When the two band dissolved Mattias would end up joining members of the later band.

By 1995 the band had gained somewhat of a reputation in the underground by constant gigging and the release of their debut demo 'Dragonfly'. Word of SOMBER reached the label Black Mark Productions which showed interest and considered signing the act. This would fail to transpire as, according to the band, the label backed out in the last moment.

The following year SOMBER released their sophomore and final demo entitled 'Dragonfly / Daybreak' which was a combination of new material along with their previous demo. Instead of increasing their live activity in order to further support their new release, the band only played a minor amount of gigs during 1996. Tension grew within the band after being discouraged by lack of progress and no label deal. By this time the end was looming as drummer Olle Linderdahl quit, being temporarily replaced by SS (whom in the future would play in LUCIEN). Shorty thereafter, Christian Fernandes would also quit and the band would cease to exist.

Olle Linderdahl later went on to join SORG bassist Olle Bodin and guitarist Mikael Ribeiro in forming the Gothic Doom act OUT OF HAND which released the 'A Dream' demo in 1997. Mattias Bergner would then eventually join forces with guitarist Mikael Ribeiro from OUT OF HAND to form the Thrash Metal act CYANIDE in the year 2000.

Dragonfly, Somber (1995) (Demo). Afraid / The Mermaid / A Black Dragonfly / Soulfused / Shadows I / In Sanity / Shadows II.

Dragonfly / Daybreak, Somber (1996) (Demo). Afraid / The Mermaid / A Black Dragonfly / Soulfused / Shadows I / In Sanity / Shadows II / The Black Dome / Daughter Of Pain / Serenade / Caged / Hollow / Daybreak / Azure.

SOMBERLAIN

FORTALEZA, CE, BRAZIL — *Marco Aurélio (vocals), Fabrício Carvalho (guitar), Yuri Leite (guitar), Delano Lima (bass), Romulo Filho (drums).*

Fortaleza blackened Death Metal band SOMBERLAIN was forged during 2002 by the VEKUM, TIGLATH and GRIEFGIVER credited Delano Lima on bass guitar. First product would be the March 2002 EP 'Awakening In The Darkness', Lima drafting studio musicians singer Savage, guitarist Luciano Abreu and drummer Bruno César for these sessions. In August of 2002 ex-TRIARCHY man Marco Aurélio Sales de Freitas assumed the vocal role.

SOMBERLAIN's line up would enter a period of fluidity, with ex-members including ARK OF SIN guitarist Eduardo Melo, guitarist Cassiano Rocha and bassist Rômulo Filho, drummer Saulo Oliveira from SIEGE OF HATE and BRIETAL as well as HUMAN GOD's John Cley.

For recording of June 2004's 'Humanity's Funeral' SOMBERLAIN comprised Marco Aurélio on vocals, the guitar pairing of Fabrício Carvalho and FROZEN FIRE's Hélio Yuri Araújo Leite, bassist Delano Lima and Rômulo Filho on drums. SOMBERLAIN gained a valuable support slot to CANNIBAL CORPSE in June of 2004. In October Rômulo Filho joined FROZEN FIRE.

In early 2005 SOMBERLAIN acquired a new drummer in Bruno Gabai, previously with INSANITY. This formation set about recording a debut album in late January 2006. SOMBERLAIN then announced the addition of ARK OF SIN guitarist Diego Lucena to their ranks in September.

Awakening In The Darkness, Somberlain (2002). Awakening In The Darkness / Morbid War Against Cowardice / My Darkness / The Miserable's Throne.

Humanity's Funeral, Somberlain (2004). Evolvement Martyrdom / Humanity's Funeral / The Mourning / Intentions of The Human Esteem.

SONIC SYNDICATE

FALKENBURG, SWEDEN — *Richard Sjunnesson (vocals), Roger Sjunnesson (guitar), Robin Sjunnesson (guitar), Karin Axlesson (bass), Andreas Mårtensson (keyboards), Kristoffer Bäcklund (drums).*

SONIC SYNDICATE is a Falkenberg melodic Death Metal band, originally founded as FALLEN ANGELS and centred on the Sjunnesson brothers, singer Richard and guitarists Roger and Robin. In the Spring of 2002 the siblings found themselves without a band as their previous act, Power Metal combo TUNES OF SILENCE, had just folded. FALLEN ANGELS was crafted that Autumn, going on to produce the demos 'Fall From Heaven' and 'Black Lotus' in 2003 with 'Extinction' being delivered in 2004. That year bassist Magnus Svensson was replaced by Karin Axlesson.

The band switched title to SONIC SYNDICATE, signing to Florida's Pivotal Rockordings for an August 2005 album 'Eden Fire', recorded at StudioMega in Varberg. SONIC SYNDICATE joined forces with fellow Swedish metal artists AVATAR and INEVITABLE END for the 'Sweden United–Metal' tour commencing in late January 2006. SONIC SYNDICATE parted ways with drummer Kristoffer Bäcklund in early February. John "Runken" Bengtsson of DØDZ stepped in as replacement.

The group made the news in July when SONIC SYNDICATE scored a contract with Nuclear Blast Records, winning a band contest comprising 1,500 entrants judged by a jury consisting of the Nuclear Blast staff and representatives from European magazines. SONIC SYNDICATE entered Black Lounge Studios in Avesta on November 20th 2006 with producer Jonas Kjellgren to cut album tracks. 'Only Inhuman' arrived in May 2007.

EDEN FIRE, Pivotal Rockordings PR001 (2005). Helix Reign—Chronicles Of A Broken Covenant / Jailbreak / Enhance My Nightmare / History Repeats Itself Extinction—A Sinwar Quadrilogy / Zion Must Fall / Misanthropic Coil / Lament Of Innocence / Prelude To Extinction Black Lotus—The Shadow Flora / Soulstone Splinter / Crowned In Despair / Where The Black Lotus Grows.

ONLY INHUMAN, Nuclear Blast (2007). Aftermath / Blue Eyed Fiend / Psychic Suicide / Double Agent / Enclave / Denied / Callous / Only Inhuman / All About Us / Unknown Entity / Flashback.

SORCERY

SWEDEN — *Ola Malmström (vocals), Fredrik Nygren (guitar), Magnus Karlsson (guitar), Mikael Jansson (bass), Paul Johansson (drums).*

Gävle based Death Metal act SORCERY, founded during 1986 by erstwhile members of ACID QUEEN lead vocalist Ola Malmström, guitarist Paul Johansson, bassist Magnus Karlsson-Mård and drummer Patrik L. Johansson. The Johanssons and Karlsson-Mård also held prior credits with CURSE. Second guitarist Peter Sjöberg was inducted in 1987 but left shortly after, subsequently joining MUTANT, RIVENDELL and THEORY IN PRACTICE in later years. As SORCERY, and newly installing Joakim Hansson on the drums, they released the 1988 'Ancient Creations' demo as their opening shot. Another demo, 1989's 'Unholy Crusade' preceded a self titled 1990 mini album. Second guitarist Peter Hedman was enrolled during 1991. The album 'Bloodchilling Tales' was delivered on the Underground label.

In October 1991 singer Ola Malmström and bassist Mikael Jansson forged a fresh outfit FEAR MY SOLITUDE, a productive Doom venture issuing a string of demos including the opening 'When Life Ends' in 1992, 'Morscretia' in 1993, 'Dancing With Solitariness' of 1994 and 1995's 'Melancholicology'. Drummer Paul Johansson, switching roles to guitar, later figured in an early line up of IN AETERNUM. Fredrik Nygren joined ASHRAM. The band fractured and rebuilt itself on numerous occasions in the years to follow. A 1993 line up comprised Ola Malmström, Paul Johansson, bassist Erik Olsson and a returned Patrik L. Johansson on drums. Olsson would then be usurped by former member Magnus Karlsson-Mård. A 1997 variation of the band found SAPFEIRA bassist Linda Adamsson and THEORY IN PRACTICE, FORLORN, AUTUMN LEAVES, WINDWALKER and WITHERED BEAUTY man Daniel 'Vortex' Bryntse on the drums.

The German No Colour label re-released 'Bloodchilling Tales' in 1998 with two extra tracks. Fellow Swedes MARTYRUM paid tribute to SORCERY by covering their track 'Lucifer's Legions' on a 2003 demo, Ola Malmström providing guest vocals for this rendition. Malmström, Paul Johansson and Mikael Jansson subsequently founded Doom outfit OUTREMER in the Summer of 2002.

Rivers Of The Dead, Thrash THR005 (1990). Rivers Of The Dead / The Rite Of Sacrafice.

BLOOD CHILLING TALES, Underground UGR003 (1991). Intro—Bloodchilling Tales / Legacy Of Blood / The Rite Of Sacrifice / Death / Dragons Of The Burning Twilight / Rivers Of The Dead / Immortality Given / Descend To The Ashes / Lucifer's Legions / By These Words.

ETERNITY, Arise ARISE 011 (1998). Penitence / Eternity / Fighting Myself / Before And Now / The Hunt And The Regret / Lost In The Night / No More Wasted Time / Silence Is My Friend / Forever / Son Of The Sky.

SORROW

NEW YORK, NY, USA — *Andy Marchione (vocals / bass), Brett Clarin (guitar), Billy Rogan (guitar), Mike Hymson (drums).*

A Doom fuelled, lethargic Death Metal act with a political edge to their lyrics. The band was previously known as APPARITION, releasing the demo 'Human Fear' in 1989 upfront of their 7" single 'We're Not Sick, And You're Not Evil' for the Relapse label. For a short period Andy Marchione's position as lead singer was temporarily filled by guitarist Billy Rogan. In a tragic accident Marchione had suffered carbon monoxide poisoning in a car. Marchione went into a coma from which he eventually recovered but unfortunately the girl who was with him died.

After two albums Roadrunner dropped the band which promptly folded. Following the collapse of SORROW ex-members founded Ambient Doomsters JOURNEY INTO DARKNESS. Drummer Mike Hymson would go on to DYSTOPIA before founding Nu-edged Metal act WEHATEJULIA in alliance with PSYCHO's Larry Forman.

FORGOTTEN SUNRISE, Roadrunner (1991). Awaiting The Savior / Eternally Forgotten / Curse The Sunrise / A Waste Cry For Hope.

HATRED AND DISGUST, Roadrunner (1992). Insatiable / Forced Repression / Illusion Of Freedom / Human Error / Separative Adjectives / Unjustified Reluctance.

SOTAJUMALA

JYVÄSKYLÄ, FINLAND — *M. Luukkainen (vocals), K. Orbinski (guitar), J. Häkkinen (guitar), T. Otsala (bass), Timo Häkkinen (drums).*

SOTAJUMALA ("Wargod"), despite hailing from Jyväskylä, cite the Florida Death Metal tradition as a direct inspiration. The band, founded in 1998 by bassist T. Otsala and guitarist K. Orbinski, took on a stable form during 2000 with the introduction of guitarists Jyrki Häkkinen and P. Lapio, drummer Arttu Romo, of AGON ORIGIN and IKUINEN KAAMOS, and singer H. Lastu. Häkkinen's credits spanned such outfits as WIZZARD, AGON ORIGIN, GAURITHOTH, NEKROKRIST SS, NJARFRAR and WÅRPATH. This line-up entered the Sundicoop Studios in Savonlinna with producer Tuomo Valtonen to cut their first, eponymous demo in September of 2001. However, upon completion of these sessions Lapio departed.

H. Lastu opted out in the Summer of 2002, paving the way for the strangely monikered '105' to take over for the EP 'Panssarikolonna', recorded at Watercastle Studio, Jyväskylä. Woodcut Records issued the full length 'Death Metal Finland' album in 2004. Live work to promote this opus would see Järvinen of ALGHAZANTH, UNVEILED and OBSCURANT manning the drums. Subsequently M. Luukkainen of UNVEILED, HORNA, EMPYREAN BANE, OBSCURANT, DEATHBOUND and ALGHAZANTH repute took over the lead vocal position whilst drums were delegated to Timo Häkkinen from WHEREVICTIMSLIE, ATAKHAMA and FUNERIS NOCTURNUM.

SOUL DEMISE

The band shared a split release with TORTURE KILLER through Woodcut Records during September 2005, this outing reaching no. 10 in the national Finnish charts.

Sotajumala, (2001). Sotajumala / Pelkuri / 105 Päivää / Verimaa, Isänmaa.

Panssarikolonna, Woodcut CUT023 (2003). Panssarikolonna / Sodan Kauhu / Nimettömäksi Jäänyt / Verimaa, Isänmaa.

DEATH METAL FINLAND, Woodcut CUT030 (2004). Intro / Meidän Maa / Elämän Vihollinen / Syyttömien Veri / Kuolleet / Rakkaudesta Sotaan / Panssarikolonna / Sisu Sinivalkoinen / Sotajumala / Vanki / Pommitus.

Sotajumala, Woodcut (2005) (Split EP with TORTURE KILLER). 8:15 / Blind, Torture, Kill. Chart position: 10 FINLAND.

SOUL DEMISE

GERMANY — *Roman Zimmerhackel (vocals), Andreas Schuhmeier (guitar), Alex Hagenauer (guitar), Andreas Bradl (bass), Roland Jahoda (drums).*

Death Thrashers SOUL DEMISE, founded as INHUMAN during October of 1993, opened proceedings with the November demo 'Incantations'. The band's inaugural line-up incorporated lead vocalist Jürgen "Eumel" Aumann, guitarist Andreas Schuhmeier, bassist Andreas Bradl, second guitarist Martin Werthammer and drummer Andreas Brückelim. Subsequently fresh blood was introduced in the form of former CON-FUSION guitarist Alex Windorfer and ex-IVORY drummer Roland Jahoda. The 'Inners Fears' album of 1996 was supported by a barrage of over 150 live dates that year supporting the likes of MORBID ANGEL, SINISTER, DYING FETUS and VADER amongst others over the next two years. However, a name switch to SOUL DEMISE then occurred and the band re-debuted with the EP 'Farewell To The Flesh' in September of 1998. A further round of touring witnessed opening slots to KRISIUN, DERANGED and SOILWORK.

'Beyond Human Conception' was issued by the Gutter Records label in 2000. A limited edition picture disc vinyl variant was restricted to just 333 copies. Resulting live dates, packaged with DESTROYER 666, DECAPITATED and IMMOLATION, culminated in the departure of long standing lead vocalist Jürgen 'Eumel' Aumann to VIOLATION. The band line up then stood at vocalist Thomas Bachmeier, guitarist Andreas Schuhmeier, bass player Andreas Bradl with Roland Jahoda on drums. Subsequently SOUL DEMISE located a new singer in Roman Zimmerhackel. This new incarnation of the band got straight back onto the live circuit acting as guests to NAPALM DEATH. For the 2003 album 'In Vain' SOUL DEMISE signed to the French Season Of Mist label.

The band donated their rendition of 'Forever Blind' to the AT THE GATES tribute album, 'Slaughterous Souls—A Tribute to At The Gates' released in September 2004 through Drowned Scream Records.

BEYOND HUMAN PERCEPTION, Gutted GUT CD0031 (2000).
IN VAIN, Season Of Mist SOM 057 (2003). In Vain / Naïve / Trapped In A Body / Inside My Emptiness / Amnesia / Cancer / Darkness Within / Eventually We Die / Towards The Gate / Downwards To Deliverance / Passing Away.

SOUL EMBRACED

AR, USA — *Chad Moore (vocals), Rocky Gray (guitar), John Lecompt (guitar), Arthur Green (bass), Lance Garvin (drums).*

SOUL EMBRACED, a grinding Death Metal band forged during 1998, was formulated by guitarist Rocky Gray and drummer David Sroczynski, both erstwhile members of SHREDDED CORPSE, having featured on the 1996 EP 'Exhumed And Molested'. The first incarnation of SOUL EMBRACED cut one track for an inclusion on a compilation album prior to splintering when Gray joined the higher profile Christian Thrash act LIVING SACRIFICE. Sroczynski duly joined THY PAIN.

In 1999 Gray resurrected the name, enrolling vocalist Chad Moore and LIVING SACRIFICE drummer Lance Garvin. A 1999 EP 'Fleshless' preceded the full length 2001 album 'For The Incomplete' on Clenched Fist Records. 'This is My Blood' was delivered by Solid State the same year with a revamped version of 'For The Incomplete', clad in new artwork with extra tracks, being issued by Blood And Ink the following year. For live work SOUL EMBRACED employed MINDRAGE guitarist John Lecompt and ESOCHARIS and LIVING SACRIFICE bassist Arthur Green. SOUL EMBRACED would also feature on a LIVING SACRIFICE tribute album, offering their rendition of 'Truth Solution'.

Gray subsequently found himself thrust into the international spotlight as drummer for multi-platinum act EVANESCENCE. John Lecomt would also join him in the same band. One of SOUL EMBRACED's numbers, 'My Tourniquet', would be reworked by EVANESCENCE for their massively successful 'Fallen' album.

A 2003 SOUL EMBRACED album 'Immune', produced by Barry Pointer and recorded at Pointers Palace in Little Rock, Arkansas, emerged in February through Solid State. Despite the escalating success of EVANESCENCE Rocky Gray resurrected SOUL EMBRACED during late 2006. The reformed band featured two new members, Jack Wiese on guitar and Jeff Bowie on bass.

Fleshless EP, Independent (1999). Sacrificium—Suffer No More / Cleansed / Separation / Fleshless / Without Sight.
FOR THE INCOMPLETE, Clenched Fist (2001). Unborn / Screams Unseen / Ascend Into Thy Embrace / My Tourniquet / Forgiveness In Solitude / Devour Gomorrah / Exhumed / Sacrificium—Suffer No More / Cleansed / Separation / Fleshless.
THIS IS MY BLOOD, Solid State (2002). I Fade Away / The Scorn Of Death's Kiss / Helpless In Wither / Angels In Raven Hearts / Evolver / End What Has Begun / Buried In / The Cold Stare Of Dead Eyes / My Name Is Legion / Scars Remain / Still As You / Kingdom Of Shadows / Leech.
FOR THE INCOMPLETE, Blood And Ink (2002).
IMMUNE, Solid State (2003). Immune To Emotion / The Hero / I Bury You / Abandoned / Someone Just Walked Across My Grave / Someday / Existence In Despair / On Your Own / Seems Like Forever / Shadow World.

SOUL REAPER

SWEDEN — *Christoffer Hjertén (vocals), Johan Norman (guitar), Stefan Karlsson (guitar), Mikael Lang (bass), Tobias Kjellgren (drums).*

Originally titled REAPER and forged by two erstwhile members of DISSECTION drummer Tobias Kjellgren and guitarist Johan Norman. The drummer also boasts an enviable tradition with DECAMERON, SWORDMASTER and SACRAMENTUM. Original second guitarist Mattias Eliasson would relinquish his post to former TEARS OF SAHARA man Christoffer Hermansson for recording of the 'Written In Blood' album. Hermansson in turn exited in order to found Power Metal band SEVENTH ONE opening the way for Stefan Karlsson.

Kellgren would join Hermansson in SEVENTH ONE for the debut 2002 album 'Sacrifice'. SOUL REAPER contracted themselves to the Hammerheart label for a new album 'Life Erazer', produced by KING DIAMOND guitarist Andy LaRocque.

WRITTEN IN BLOOD, Nuclear Blast NB 403-2 (2000). The Sign / Written In Blood / Satanized / Seal Of Degradation / Ungodly / Subterreanean Night / Labyrinth Of The Deathlord.

SOULBURN

HOLLAND — *Wannes Gubbels (vocals / bass), Eric Daniels (guitar), Bob Bagchus (drums).*

SOULBURN was assembled by guitarist Eric Daniels and drummer Bob Bagchus, both previously members of premier Death Metal band ASPHYX. The duo was joined by erstwhile PENTACLE vocalist / bassist Wannes Gubbels. Indeed, for all intents and purposes SOULBURN was a continuation of ASPHYX under another guise. The 'Feeding On Angels' debut arrived in June of 1998 on the Century Media label. SOULBURN invariably included such ASPHYX classics as Abomination Echoes', 'Vermin' and 'The Sickening Dwell' in their live set and once rehearsals got underway for a further album the band members realised the new material was sounding much more in an ASPHYX vein, so duly reverted back to their former title.

A 2000 album, 'On The Wings Of Inferno' recorded at Harrow Production Studios in Losser, found ASPHYX, back to their more familiar band as a mark of respect to late band mate Theo Loomans, as a duo of Wannes Gubbles, Eric Daniel and Bog Bagchus. However, after its release ASPHYX announced their retirement.

FEEDING ON ANGELS, Century Media CD 77217-2 (1998). Enter The Flames Of Soulburn / Hellish Entrapment / Crypts Of The Black / Hymn Of The Forsaken / Feeding On Angels / Storming Hordes / Throne Of Hatred / Behold The Funeral Candle / . . . The Flames Of Soulburn.

SOULDRAINER

ÖSTERSUND, SWEDEN — *Johan Klitkou (vocals), Marcus Edvardsson (guitar), Daniel Dlimi (guitar), Jocke Wassberg (bass), Nils Fjällström (drums).*

SOULDRAINER is an Östersund based Death Metal combo dating to a foundation by the CHASTISEMENT credited guitarist Marcus Edvardsson in 1998. Initially commenced as a solo venture by 1999 CHASTISEMENT singer Johan Klitkou then band colleague and drummer Nils Fjällström had enrolled, Edvardsson handling guitar, bass and programmed keyboards. In this format the trio crafted the August 2000 demo 'Daemon II Daemon'.

In 2001 Fjällström would find time to activate the brutal Death Metal band SANCTIFICATION in league with GOD AMONG INSECTS guitarist Tomas Elofsson. The drummer would also be operational as a member of Black Metal band ODHINN. Meantime, SOULDRAINER was brought up to strength in 2003 with the addition of second guitarist Daniel Dlimi, of SANCTIFICATION, THE EQUINOX OV THE GODS and AEON, plus AND ANGELS WEPT and DEFACED CREATION bass player Jocke Wassberg.

The SOULDRAINER membership became entangled with IN BATTLE during 2003 with Fjällström performing double duty with both bands and Edvardsson acting as session member for IN BATTLE and also joining the ranks of SANCTIFICATION. The following year Dlimi would also join IN BATTLE. 2006 witnessed the formation of neo-Thrash Metal act ENDLESS TORTURE, a union between Marcus Edvardsson, A*TEEM vocalist Peter Mellgren plus Tom Åsvold, from PAINCRAZE and DIMENSION34, on drums.

The band contracted with Holland's Mascot Records in November 2006 for a debut album billed 'Reborn', recorded Marcus Edvardsson at Manic Motion Studio and mixed and mastered by Marcus Edvardsson.

REBORN, Mascot (2007). First Row In Hell / Internal Suicide / The Others / To The Promised Land / Daemon To Daemon / Reborn / Everyday Hero / Black XIII / They All Die / Angel Song.

SOULFALLEN

JYVÄSKYLÄ, FINLAND — *Kai Leikola (vocals / bass), Mikko Luontama (guitar), Tuomas Ekholm (keyboards), Jimmy Salmi (drums).*

Jyväskylä Melodic Death Metal band, founded in 1996 and previously known as BLACKSMITH. Under this former title the group recorded the January 1999 session 'Beneath A Thick Satin Moon' at Watercastle Studio in Jyväskylä with a recording line up comprising vocalist / bassist Kai Leikola, guitarist Christian Jörgensen, keyboard player Turo Marttila and drummer Juha Pesonen. 'Outcast / Forlorn' followed in 2000, this outing seeing the band joined by second guitarist Mikko Luontama. However, obligatory military service put the band on hold for much of the year.

Only Leikola would remain as the transition to SOULFALLEN took place in 2002. New personnel would be Tuomas Ekholm as keyboard player and drummer Jimmy Salmi for a 2004 EP 'Dark Remains'.

A 2006 demo, 'Death Of The Tyrant', emerged in 2006. The following February SOULFALLEN signed to Off Records.

Dark Remains, Soulfallen (2004). Assailed / Where Frozen Dreams Lie / A Silent Farewell.

SOULFORGE

MONTREAL, QC, CANADA — *Michel Bernatchez (vocals / guitar), Yves Bordeleau (guitar), Eric Verrier (bass), Fred Lavallée (keyboards), Pascal Cimone (drums).*

Montreal's SOULFORGE originally went by the title of HAUNTED upon their inception in 1997 at the hands of guitarist Yves Bordeleau and drummer Pascal Cimone. Recording a demo as HAUNTED with vocalist Jean-François Jacques the band set about working the Montreal gig circuit. A switch in singers saw Anne Kudowsky entering the fold but this alliance did not last and during 2000 HAUNTED folded. After a four month hiatus the members regrouped as SOULFORGE, introducing Fred Lavallée on keyboards and having Michel Bernatchez take on the lead vocal role. The album 'Duality' surfaced in 2002 on Great White North Records.

January of 2005 found SOULFORGE in the studio recording a new album with Jean-François Dagenais of KATAKLYSM acting as producer.

DUALITY, Great White North GWN010 (2002). Loophole / Bloodline / Telepathic Bug / Heading Nowhere / Be My Guest / The Dreamstorm / Awakening / Behind The Gates / Vinland / Omniscient / Ethereal.

SOULGRIND

FINLAND — *Ceasar T. Launonen (vocals), Ms. W.Lilith (vocals), Jussi Heikkinen (guitar / bass), Luopio (keyboards), Agathon Frosteus (drums).*

SOULGRIND is the extra curricular project of TENEBRAE's Jussi Heikkinen. The man works constantly in collaboration with other Death Metal musicians on the albums issued under the SOULGRIND banner. For example, 'Ladit AD 1999: Bi-httpotp' was recorded with DEMENTIA's Roope Latvala, Juke Eräkangas, Sauli Kivilahti, Henrick Laine and Kirsi Reunenen on female vocals.

Founded in the early 90's the band/project issued a debut 7" single in 1993 on the obscure M.M.I. label ("Malodorous Mangled Innards"). A full-length, 'La Matanza, El Himmo Pagano', followed in 1994 and soon after the 'Black Orchid' EP in early 1995. Later that same year the band released their sophomore full-length album, 'L.A.T.I.D. A.D.' still at home on the M.M.I. concern. Clocking at over 70 minutes, the band had introduced many Gothic elements to their sound.

The deal with M.M.I. was not to last for long as the band foundered for a year but eventually released the very obscure, 'Whitsongs' in 1997. The band had landed on a tiny label in Argentina called Icarus Records. The line-up however, at this juncture was relatively stable and consisted of Lord J. Heikkinen, Whisper, Luopio, Agathon Frosteus, and Caeser T. MacLaunone.

Drummer Agathon Frosteus (a.k.a. Ykä) also has credits with THY SERPENT, WALHALLA, CORPORAL PUNISHMENT, NOMICON, BARATHRUM and GLOOMY GRIM, keyboard player Luopio is of THY SERPENT whilst vocalist Caesar T. Launonen is a NOMICON member. The 2002 album 'Into The Dark Vales Of Death' released on the French Holy label featured former LULLACRY singer Tanya on backing vocals under the pseudonym of 'Whisper Lilith'. Subsequently Kemppainen would be announced as joining the band on a full time basis.

In May of 2003 SOULGRIND's Lord Heikkinen joined guitarist Toni Näykki's Death metal outfit TWILIGHT OPHERA as the group's bassist. SOULGRIND entered the recording studio in January of 2004 to commence work on the 'Omnino Veritas' album. However, these sessions never surfaced.

That September the group announced they were to employ D Studios in Klaukkala to craft tracks for a release entitled 'The Prophecy Of The Paganblood'. The album featured a guest appearance on lead guitar by CHILDREN OF BODOM's Roope Latvala. A bonus disc with this album comprised video clips for 'Tearflower' and 'Song Of Mantsi' plus demo and rehearsal recordings and unreleased tracks.

SOULGRIND gave 'Pakana' as the projected title for a 2006 album with recording commencing in June. In side activity, Jussi Heikkinen joined a new Speed Metal band called FIERCE as a bass player. SOULGRIND severed ties with bassist JP in August, citing "personal differences".

Santa Sangra EP, MMI (1993). Santa Sangra.
LA MATANZA, EL HIMMO PAGANO, MMI M.M.I. 011 CD (1994). Summoning / Kuoto / Santa Sangre / La Matanza, El Himmo Pagano / Black Abyss, Deep Enterium / Dark Misty Trail / Inner Chain Of Perversions / The Pit / Virginity, A Sanctum Of The Red / Ainomonus (Outro).
LUST AND DEATH IN TUONELA A.D. 1999: BLACK INDUSTRIALHOLOCAUST THROUGH THE PANDEMONIUM OF THE BIZARRE, MMI M.M.I. 020 (1995). Introitus Nostrodamus 1999 / Black Orchid / Darkseed Lust / As Shadows Whisper The Shine / Shamanic Ecstacy / Spin Of Life / The Pandemonium Of The Bizarre / Immortal Desire / Industrial Holocaust (Inferia) / The End Of All.
Black Orchid, MMI MMI 018 (1995). Black Orchid / In My Darkest Sabbath / Anal Christ Pose.
WHITSONGS, Icarus ICARUS1 (1997). Nermi / The Girl And The Boyar's Son / Oterma And Katerma / Tumma / Revenge / Maids Of Hiisi / Blue Cross (Motherland) / The Dark One / Tuoni's Eyes / The Song Of Mantsi / Halempi / The Serf's Son / Tuuri.
KALMA, Holy HOLY48CD (1999). Kalma / Goatride / Secrecy Supreme / Remembrance Through Deep Red Masquerade / Cage / Across The Field Of Thought / Seed (A Sermon In Stone) / Black Lust / Harsh Mother Time / Pagan Pride.
ELIXIR MYSTICA, Holy HOLY64CD (2001). Liekki / Elixir Mystica / Black Stone March / HateLoveChaos / Tearflower / Shadowrain / Evolution / Grey Shades Of Love / Kuun Lapset, Pimeän Voima / Earth Ghost Waltz / Ugri The Key.
INTO THE DARK VALES OF DEATH, Holy HOLY 76 (2002). Into The Dark / Lurid Circle / Rutjas Rapids Through The River Of The Otherworld / Odious Emotions / The Swan And The Fox / Dance Through The Macabre Void / Soulpanders / Beyond Good And Evil / Until Love Kills / Umpijaan Taistelijat.
THE ORIGINS OF THE PAGANBLOOD, Holy HOLY99CD (2005). The Valley / Northlander / When Those Nights Have Circled Over / Red River / The Tree Of Life / Autumn / Flesh Marionette / Paganblood / The Watchful Eye And The Old Way / Circle Of Pain And Glory.

PAKANA, Holy (2007). Through The Gates Of Desperation / The Soul Of The Battle / Pakana / The Second Over Tuoni's Realm / As Bronze May Be Much Beautified / Lost Gardens Beyond The Sunset / Against The Grain / Northbound Reverend / The Path Of Screams / Wheel / Frost Shines Blue.

SOULHAVOC

KOTKA, FINLAND — *Ilkka Lönnqvist (vocals / guitar), Arto Hannula (guitar), Teemu Romppanen (bass), Jaakko Toivonen (drums).*

Kotka melodic Death Metal band SOULHAVOC issued the demo 'While You Thought I Was Dead', recorded at Woodbine Garden Studios with producer Teemu Aalto, in 2005. Extra exposure was garnered by the inclusion of demo track 'Circle Is Closing' on the Risestar Music compilation album 'The Iron Force'. Following these sessions, which saw the band fronted by singer Ville Putkonen, drummer Hessu Mutikainen was replaced by Jaakko Toivonen. A further line-up change saw bassist Janne Boman superseded by Teemu Romppanen.

For the debut concert, held at The Factory in Helsinki, SOULHAVOC employed session guitarist Teemu Karttunen. Yet another change in the membership resulted in Ilkka Lönnqvist taking over from Ville Putkonen.

While You Thought I Was Dead, Soulhavoc (2005). Hollowclones / Convicted To Life / The Halo Of Snake / Circle Is Closing.

SOULLESS

CLEVELAND, OH, USA — *Jim Lippucci (vocals), Wayne Richards (guitar), Jim Corrick (guitar), Tony Daprano (bass), Chris Dorn (drums).*

SOULLESS evolved out of Cleveland Thrashers BLOODSICK during 1997. BLOODSICK was founded upon former DECREPIT drummer Chris Dorn, ex-DECIMATION vocalist Jim Lippucci, guitarists Brian Sekula, formerly with MORTICIAN, and Todd Thozeski and bassist Chris Pello.

Sekula's exit saw the enlistment of erstwhile APT. 213 and BLOODSICK guitarist Jerry Kessler and when both Pello and Thozeski quit the numbers were made up with Kessler's former APT. 213 colleague Tony Daprano on bass and second guitarist Wayne Richards. With such a radical facelift the band opted for the revised title of SOULLESS.

Following recording of the 1999 debut album 'The Darkening Of Days' Kessler bowed out to be supplanted by former HOLY GHOST, DAHMER and ALL THAT IS EVIL man Jim Corrick. Richards meantime would deputize for the notorious NUNSLAUGHTER as live guitarist for their 2000 European shows.

Extracurricular activity would see SOULLESS put in showings on a veritable slew of tribute albums having cut renditions of OZZY OSBOURNE's 'The Ultimate Sin', JUDAS PRIEST's 'Hell Bent For Leather', W.A.S.P.'s 'Tormentor' and METALLICA's 'Motorbreath'.

Dorn and Richards would form up part of THE SPAWN OF SATAN 2002 project band also involving NUNSLAUGHTER's Jim Satanic for a shared split album with BLOODSICK. Crash Music re-issued the 'Agony's Lament' album in 2003.

In October 2006 SOULLESS announced they had signed with Japanese label WorldChaos Productions for an album 'Forever Defiant', recorded at Spider Studios in Strongsville, Ohio with producer Ben Schigel and mastered by Jonas Kjellgren at Black Lounge Studios.

THE DARKENING OF DAYS, ME001CD (1999). Devilish / Abandoned To Bleed / Turn / Blissfully Damned / Crumble Beneath / Down Hell's Path / Emptiness Domain / Hellbent / Lost / The Darkening Of Days.
AGONY'S LAMENT, Worldchaos Productions KDM-010 (2002). Bleeding Darkness / Agonies / Lament / The Soulscythe / Empty Darkness / Terror Of Twilight / Downward / Exile / Suffer The Fallen / The Fleet Of Fury.

SOULLESS HEART

HANNOVER, GERMANY — *Magnus Martin (vocals), Wladimir Bernhardt (guitar), Dmitriy Banchevskiy (guitar), Vlad Rumyantsev (bass), Florian Rienkens (drums).*

Hannover Death Metal act SOULLESS HEART was formulated in February 2003 by guitarist Dmitry Banchevskiy and Drummer Florian Rienkens, subsequently enlisting second guitarist Stefan Strathmeier and bassist Erik Heß. However, Strathmeier was quickly superseded by Wladimir Bernhardt. In April the band recorded the EP 'Prisoner Of The Night'.

In 2004 a three track live demo surfaced. The group also issued a split album with Spanish band SADOK, this set including a cover version of IRON MAIDEN's 'Aces High'. Erik Heß exited towards the close of 2004. SOULLESS HEART regrouped during 2005, adding singer Magnus Martin and bass player Vlad Rumyantsev. A 2006 album, entitled 'Crystal Death', was issued.

Prisoner Of The Night, Soulless Heart (2003). Intro / Death Of The Antichrist / Terror / Prisoner Of The Night / Mights Of Evil / Storms Of Hate.
Live 2004, Soulless Heart (2004) (Demo). Dying Time Is Fun / Lunatic Silence / Mights Of Evil.
SOULLESS HEART / SADOK, (2004) (Split album with SADOK). Death Of The Antichrist (SOULLESS HEART) / Prisoner Of The Night (SOULLESS HEART) / Mights Of Evil (SOULLESS HEART) / Maybe You Die (SOULLESS HEART) / Soulless Heart (SOULLESS HEART) / Aces High (SOULLESS HEART) / Artificial (SADOK) / La Mirada De Lo Incierto (SADOK) / 03 Epitaph (SADOK) / Confusion (SADOK).
Maybe You Die, Soulless Heart (2004). Soulless Heart / Maybe You Die / Aces High / Prisoner Of The Night (Video).
CRYSTAL DEATH, Soulless Heart (2006). Intro / Double-Edged Switchblade / Crystal Death / Axis Of Evil / Death Of The Antichrist / Lost Truth / Prisoner Of The Night / Lunatic Silence / Battle Of The Gods / Mights Of Evil / Soulless Heart.

SOULS ON FIRE

IRAPUATO, MEXICO — *Jesus Bravo (vocals), Nelson St.Marie (lead guitar), Jorge Inukai (lead guitar), Oscar Lopez (bass), Oscar Piñon (drums).*

Irapuato, Guanajuato Heavy Metal band SOULS ON FIRE was forged during 1998 by former TARANTULA and STARFLEET guitarist Nelson St. Marie and ex-AGONY LORDS frontman Jesus Bravo. This founding pair would be joined by another AGONY LORDS veteran, bassist Oscar Lopez, then second guitarist Eduardo Gomez with Luis S. Marie on drums. This formation crafted the opening 'Mythic' demo, following which Tony Martinez of DIES IRAE took over the drum position.

The band set to work recording an album during 2003 but during these sessions both Gomez and Martinez opted out. It would not be until late 2004 that Oscar Piñon of AGONY LORDS was installed on the drum stool and Jorge Inukai joined on lead guitar to complete the 'Fire Demons' album. Mexican label The Art Records issued the record in 2005.

FIREDEMONS, The Art (2005). Firedemon / Archangel / Enemy / Blackened Wings Of The Warrior / Embracing Shadows / Stormbringer / Hellwithin / Army Of Darkness / Until The Glory Fades Away.

SOULSCAR

VANCOUVER, BC, CANADA — *Andrew Staehling (vocals / guitar), Stas Mikheev (guitar), Brent McKenzie (bass), Igor Cheifot (drums).*

Vancouver's SOULSCAR employ Death Metal with a healthy injection of prime era Thrash influences. The band came together in 1997 issuing a stream of demos in 1998's 'Lost In Life', 1999's 'Escaping' and 2000 'Abandoned'. These three sessions were all conducted as solo efforts by Andrew Staehling. The 2000 'Abandoned' album release is a collection of earlier demo tracks produced by Jeff Waters of ANNIHILATOR. Yet another

Waters produced promotion release, 'Python' featuring bassist Brent McKenzie, was recorded in 2001, although never publicly released, upfront of the 'Character Assassination' record. Sessioning on this outing would be drummer Chris Warunki.

Second album 'Victim Impact Statement' was issued in October of 2004 through Galy Records. SOULSCAR's 2004 band line-up comprised Andrew Staehling, Brent Mackenzie, second guitarist Stas Mikheev and drummer Igor Cheifot.

ABANDONED, (2000). S.S.R.I. (Intro) / Cutter / Your Absence, My End / Abandoned / Ever Alone / This Was My Life / Selfmutilation / Bliss Killer / Escaping / Deathbringer-Surrender / Escaping / Lost In Life.

CHARACTER ASSASSINATION, Soulscar SSCAR01 (2002). Fatalist Mantra / Interceptor / Sacrifices / Living Nightmare / Relentless / It Takes A Wolf / The Voyeur / Character Assassination / A Reprieve.

VICTIM IMPACT STATEMENT, Galy GALY 030 (2004). Unmade / Death Anxiety / Cast Aside / Hell Bitch / Without A Shadow / Ultimatum / Regressor / Alive Awake / To The Pain / Victim Impact Statement.

SPAWN OF POSSESSION

SWEDEN — *Dennis Röndum (vocals / drums), Jonas Bryssling (guitar), Jonas Karlsson (guitar), Niklas Dewerud (bass).*

A sick yet technically inclined Death Metal outfit founded in 1997. Formative members bass player Jonas Hagström and guitarist David Lindstrom would soon make their exit leaving SPAWN OF POSSESSION as a trio of guitarists Jonas Bryssling, ex-HEDEON, and Jonas Karlsson, of DESOLATION, alongside vocalist and drummer Dennis Röndum, the latter another HEDEON veteran and also active with VISCERAL BLEEDING as frontman. The group debuted with the August 2000 EP 'The Forbidden'.

A second EP, 'Church Of Deviance' released during 2001 saw the enrollment of VISCERAL BLEEDING bassist Niklas Dewerud. Live gigs in early 2002 found a guesting Emil Dragutinovic of LEGION, NOMINON and MARDUK as guest lead vocalist. The band would be announced as heading up the February 2002 'Gutting Europe III' tour topping a bill comprising DISAVOWED, MANGLED, INHUMANE and VILE.

During 2002 Dennis Röndum united with the BUTCHERY duo of guitarist Juha Helttunen and drummer Tobias Israelsson to found STRANGULATION for the demo 'Carnage In Heaven'. A new album, 'Cabinet', arrived in 2003 through Unique Leader Records, this seeing Dennis Röndum handling all lead vocal duties. Although the band announced Kelly Izquierdo of MORTAL DECAY as being their new singer in fact for ensuing dates across Europe the band drafted DISRUPTION frontman Jonas Renvakter as stand in.

SPAWN OF POSSESSION formed up part of the 2004 European heavyweight 'No Mercy' festivals commencing 29th March, sharing billing with CANNIBAL CORPSE, HYPOCRISY, KATAKLYSM, CARPATHIAN FOREST, VOMITORY, PREJUDICE and EXHUMED. In June the band performed at the Italian 'Grind Your Mother' festival.

The band set 'Noctambulant' as the title of a 2006 album, recorded at Pama Studios in Kristianopel in January with producer Magnus Sedenberg. The group hooked up with HATE ETERNAL, FALL OF SERENITY and SHADOWSLAND for European touring in May covering the UK, Germany, France, Spain, Italy, Holland, Hungary, Czech Republic and Belgium.

Dennis Röndum quit in May 2007, claiming "lack of interest in drumming" as a deciding factor.

The Forbidden EP, (2000). Intro (Sick) / Dead And Grotesque / The Forbidden / Dirty Priest.

Church Of Deviance EP, (2001). Inner Conflict / Spawn Of Possession / Church Of Deviance.

CABINET, Unique Leader (2003). Lamashtu / Swarm Of The Formless / Hidden In Flesh / A Presence Inexplicable / Dirty Priest / Spawn Of Possession / Inner Conflict / Cabinet / The Forbidden / Church Of Deviance / Uncle Damfee.

NOCTAMBULANT, Neurotic NRT060009 (2006). Inception / Lash By Lash / Solemn They Await / Render My Prey / Eve Of Contempt / Sour Flow / By A Thousand Deaths Fulfilled / Dead & Grotesque / In My Own Greed / Scorched.

SPAZZ

REDWOOD CITY, CA, USA — *Chris Dodge (vocals / bass), Dan Lactose (guitar), Max Ward (drums).*

Crusting Grindcore act SPAZZ emerged with an eponymous single on frontman Chris Dodge's own Slap A Ham label. The follow up was a cassette 'Blasted In Bangkok' given away at the sophomore SPAZZ live gig. A whole barrage of split 7" singles would ensue. SPAZZ issued a split single with BRUTAL TRUTH that included the track 'Nuge On A Stick', a track that comprised of a humourous but barbed attack on TED NUGENT's hunting activities. The 'Funky Ass Little Platter' single is in fact a band spoof. The record does exist but only as 1" diameter toy records. Only 14 copies were made.

A further split effort with BLACK ARMY JACKET had SPAZZ covering tracks from such Hardcore veterans as SICK OF IT ALL, STRAIGHT AHEAD and YOUTH OF TODAY.

SPAZZ folded in January of 2001. Dodge would put together an alliance with DISCORDANCE AXIS drummer Dave Witte billed simply as CHRIS DODGE-DAVE WITTE for a 2001 album 'East West Blast Fest"

SWEATIN' TO THE OLDIES, (1997). Gary's Free Time—Intro / Crocket / One Ghetto To The Next / Return To The Wall Of Death / Who Writes Your Rules? / Mighty Morphin Power Violence / Thrice The Heiney / Hot Dog Water Popsicle In The Hand Of Eric Wood / Problems In The Homeland / I Hate The Kids / Spudboy / Smoking Don's Crackhole / Dirt The Purity / Knuckle Scraper / Box II (Yates Goes To Africa) / Spazz vs Mother Nature / Nuge On A Stick / Donger / Gnome Servant / DJ Tinkle Fingers Diplomatic Services / Hard Boiled / 4 Times A Day / All Urban Outfield / Lethal / Hot Dog Water Popsicle In The Hand Of Eric Wood / The Box / Dropping Many Ravers / In The Name Of ... / Might For Right / Loach, Mad At The World / Tripper / Uniform / Bore / Hard Boiled / All Urban Outfield / Weeedeater / Bled Dry / Closet / No Room / Ghost Dance / Hug Yourself / You Gotta Mold It / Lethal / Anemonie / Gas Pump / Enterslavement / Hard Boiled (Live) / Burning Tongue (Live) / Kiss Of The Sasquatsch (Live) / Hot Dog Water Popsicle In The Hand Of Eric Wood (Live) / Danliftingbanner (Live) / Gertie / Enterslavement / Uniform / No Thought / Pressure / Burnt / Our Scene / Biter / Precision Fastening / Lost Cause.

SPHERE

WARSAW, POLAND — *Analripper (vocals), Cthulhu (guitar), Lukas (guitar), Burning (bass), Thorn (drums).*

Warsaw technical Death Metal band SPHERE, founded in 2000, notably features ex-members of HATE and PYORRHOEA. The band's original formation, performing cover versions by DEATH and TIAMAT at first counting singer Jasiek, guitarists Bolek and Val with Thorn on drums, would undergo numerous transformations. Bolek would be the first to leave, being replaced by Lechu whilst Zeras took the bass position. However, this unit proved fragile and by February 2003 only Val and Thorn remained. Regrouping, now fronted by Sapen with Łukasz on guitar and Burning on bass, SPHERE cut their first demo 'Spiritual Dope', recorded at Diamond Studio in Kraków with producer Dominik Burzym, during 2004.

SPHERE signed with Empire Records for a January 2007 debut album, entitled 'Damned Souls Rituals' and recorded at Zed Studios. The band comprised vocalist Andrzej (Analripper) of REVELATION OF DOOM and PYORRHOEA, guitarists Lukas, of PYORRHOEA and ABUSED MAJESTY, and Kuba, bass player Adam (Burning), of MAESTUS, with Michael (Thorn) on drums, of AMOK, UNEVEN TORMENT and ZYWIOLAK.

Spiritual Dope, Sphere (2004) (Demo). Intro / Of The Martyrdom / Spiritual Dope / Cthulhu Rises.

DAMNED SOULS RITUALS, Empire (2007). Vomit The Soul / Saved From Heaven / Greed / Why Don't You Just Kill Yourself? / Next Morning's Mass / Sin Of 17 / Invincible Majority / Ritual Of Rotten Flesh / Hate Legalised Inside / Grandnekromother / Ultimate Saviour / Damned Souls Rituals.

SPINAL CORD

BUSKO ZDRÓJ, POLAND — *Michał Bachrij (vocals), Piotr Smodrzewski (guitar), Krystian Wojdas (guitar), Novy (bass), Sebastian Łuszczek (drums).*

SPINAL CORD is a Busko Zdrój based Death Metal combo starting out in August of 1999. The initial line up comprised lead vocalist Michał 'Barney' Bachrij, guitarist Piotr 'Smoq' Smodrzewski, bassist Michał 'Boba' Dobaj and two musicians from DEVILYN in guitarist Krystian Wojdas and drummer Sebastian Łuszczek. Their first works would come in the form of a three song demo recorded at Lublin's Hendrix Studios in April of 2000. Touring Poland that same year SPINAL CORD formed up part of the 'Millennium' tour sharing stages with BEHEMOTH, DEVILYN and NOMAD. Further recordings followed, being produced by Grzegorz Piwkowski. SPINAL CORD gigged throughout 2001 and into 2002 before recordings began in November at the Screw Factory Studios in Debicy for the debut album 'Remedy'. The record would be picked up by Empire Records for a May 2003 release. Crash Music Inc. licensed the record for North American issue in August of 2004.

The band suffered a line-up change in November of 2003 as bassist Boba exited. He would be replaced by Novy of VADER repute. SPINAL CORD's second album, 'Stigmata Of Life' once again cut at Screw Factory, would be completed in December 2004. Vocalist Barney also enrolled into the ranks of Thrashcore band RISE UP to front their demo 'Unforseeable World'.

REMEDY, Empire (2003). Intro / Breeder Of Corruption / Apocalypse Time / Remedy / Agony / Mtch-Mts (New Life) / Fake / Chosen No More / Blind Ignorant / Art / Tears / There's Nothing.
STIGMATA OF LIFE, Empire (2004). Burn Them All / Body Dismorphy / Retrospection / Mind Killer / Amphitheatre / Storm / Ramirez / Beg For A Fast Death / Stigmatized Possessed / Critical Moment (Dead End) / Epitaph / Exile.

SPIRAL MADNESS

POLAND — *Zephyr (vocals / bass), Twarog (guitar), Seler (guitar), Wielebny (drums).*

Warsaw's SPIRAL MADNESS, dating back to 1996, released the 2000 demo 'Graveland'. The group had been raised from the demise of antecedent act VINEGAR, a band dating back to 1992. Ex-VINEGAR members Zephyr and Lysy (Baldhead) met with guitarist Chmura (Cloud), but this union did not manifest itself proper until 1999, as the short-lived MORGENSTERN project. Shortly afterward though, the first incarnation of SPIRAL MADNESS assembled, counting vocalist / bassist Zephyr, guitarist Chmura and Jack on drums. Upon completion of the June 2000 'Graveland' sessions Jack, apparently unenthusiastic about proposed live work, exited. SPIRAL MADNESS duly regrouped, pulling in ex-drummer of CLAYMORE Deny and second guitarist Viking.

A second session, 'Death n' Roll', arrived in 2002. However, in October of that year Viking departed. As 2003 loomed the band inducted second guitarist Seler (Celery) and drummer Wielebny (Reverend), both holding MARTIAN credentials. With this line up SPIRAL MADNESS crafted the album 'The Berserk Crowning'. Included would be a re-worked VINEGAR track 'world Of Ash' and a Polish language bonus track 'Koszmar'. The group suffered the loss of founder Chmura in 2004 but drafted substitute Twarog (Curds) that April.

THE BERSERK CROWNING, Spiral Madness 03 (2004). Intro / Despair / Final Day / Spiral Madness / My Heart / Becoming Like Steel / One Question / Graveland / Wolfhearts / Helpless / My Reflection / World Is Ash / Faded Night / Misery Of Merciless / Koszmar.

SQUASH BOWELS

BIAŁYSTOK, POLAND — *Mariosch (vocals), Lechu (guitar), Paluch (bass), Rogal (drums).*

Białystok Grindcore band SQUASH BOWELS made their presence felt with the demo tape 'Dead?!' followed up by further recordings 'Fürgott'. A split album with MALIGNANT TUMOUR led in turn to a shared cassette with French spoofsters INFECTED PUSSY. A further split tape was issued in alliance with SM SNIPER as well as another promotional tape 'International Devastation'.

The first pressing of SQUASH BOWELS 'Dreams Come True ... In Death' album featured a photograph of a dead body on the cover. Probably not wishing to be accused of stereotyping the second issue saw a change- to a photo of a woman being attacked by an axe.

The 1996 7" single 'Something Nice' was graced, presumably in a display of Grindcore irony, with a cover photograph of a disembodied woman. Split single releases included collaborations with Japan's CATASEXUAL URGE MOTIVATION, Mexico's DISGORGE and Sweden's BIRDFLESH. During 1999 a split album shared with COCK AND BALL TORTURE included a cover version of NAPALM DEATH's 'Multinational Corporations'. A split tape offering also emerged 'A tribute To serial Killers' shared with INCARNATED, ENFEEBLEMENT and NEUROPATHIA. Hyenzym Records issued a split EP in collaboration with Malmö's SEWN SHUT in 2002.

SQUASH BOWELS 2003 release 'For Dead God— International Devastation' collected together the band's early demos. Obscene Productions put out the 'No Mercy' studio album in 2004, this outing being recorded by the trio of Pierscień on vocals and guitar, Artur on bass and Psychoradek on the drums. Touring across Poland in April of 2004 saw the band united with road partners fellow Poles PARRICIDE and Czech Grind crew CEREBRAL TURBULENCY. The band partnered with NEEDFUL THINGS for a rash of Czech gigs in the Winter.

DREAMS COME TRUE ... IN DEATH, Obscene Productions (1995) (Split album with MALIGNANT TUMOR). Intro / Lustmord / Tested Creatures / Regulation People's Fear / Human Acceleration / Holy Lies / A Suspect / Infanticide / Pseudo—Faces / Victims ... / Right To Live / Live Like A Dream / More Our Colours / Deadly Sick / The Mass Sickening / Old Things / Dash Of Life.
LIVE '95, (1995). Intro / Noise Product / The Grind Core-spondent / Logopedic Formalism / Soundmind / The Mass Sickening / Human Acceleration / Right To Live / Multinational Corporation.
SQUASH BOWELS, Extermination (1996) (Split album with CATASEXUAL URGE MOTIVATION). Intro—Last Warnings / Medical Exhibition / Logopedic Formalism / Stumpers / The Grind Core-spondent / Soundmind.
SOMETHING NICE, Obliteration (1996). Noise Product / Surge Of Assurance / The Grind Core-Spondent / New Standards / A Suspect / More Our Colours.
SQUASH BOWELS, Bizarre Leprous Productions (1998) (Split album with DISGORGE). Fear / Blood Supply / Who Is Gay? / Grind Your Head / Hesta La Vista Baby / Radio Hit / Material Under Test / Murder On Street.
SQUASH BOWELS, Bizarre Leprous Productions (1999) (Split album with COCK AND BALL TORTURE). Intro / Wo-man / Regulation / Human Barbecue / Pseudo Faces / Shit In W.C. / M.I.P. / Right To Live / Multinational Corporations.
TNYRIBAL, Obscene Productions OBP 032 (2000). Stranger Mind / Dark Corridors / Zema Inpa / Zonhori Nteve / Bad Sector / Black Thing.
THE MASS ROTTING- THE MASS SICKENING, Obscene Productions OBP 044 (2002). Screams Saints Pig Dead / Breaking Those Who Suspend To Talk / Strong Will / When Memories Came Back / Dead Nature / Life Business / The Mass Rotting / The Mass Sickening / Behind Pain Hides Hate / Regulations People Fear / Life & Death / Handsome Scum / Triumph Of Act Revenge / Naive Distress / Childhood.

FOR DEAD GOD—INTERNATIONAL DEVESTATION, Obscene Productions OBP 050 (2003). Guzzling Away From Inside / The Sickening Interpersonal Relations / Human Accelerations / Greetings From Poland / Right To Live / Mutilations Corporations / Disharmonized Voices / Noise Product / Surge Of Assurance / A Suspect / New Standards / More Our Colours / Medical Exhibition / Logopedic Formalism / Stumpers / The Grind Core-spondent / Soundmind / Year-Noise-Chaos / Regulations Peoples Fear / Tested Creatures / Lustmord / More Our Colours / Victims ... / Human Accelerations / Old Things / Mad Dentist / Liberate Me / The Rotting / Vulture Ritual / Flesh Grinder.

NO MERCY, Obscene Productions (2004). No Mercy / Garrotte / Vulture Ritual / Guillotine In Lunapark / Squabble / Flesh Grinder / Dead Stumble / Human Extinction / Splinter Off Blood / Saint Father Pedophile / Inclement Instructor / Blood Supply / Face In Cowpox / UFO-Rider.

STABWOUND

GOTHENBURG, SWEDEN — *Uffe Nylin (vocals), Per Ahre (vocals / guitar), Fredrik Linfjard (guitar), Mikka Häkki (bass), Viktor Linder (drums).*

Gothenburg brutal Death Metal act STABWOUND was created in 2000 by vocalist / guitarist Ante and bassist Freddy, subsequently drafting drummer Oskar and guitarist Per Ahre. STABWOUND released the 2002 demo 'Malicious Addiction', after which Viktor Linder assumed the drum position. Another change saw Freddy's exit. 'Bloodsoaked Serenades', with Ahre recording bass parts, arrived in November 2003 via Italian label The Flood Records. These sessions included a cover version of DYING FETUS' 'Kill Your Mother Rape Your Dog'.

'Human Boundaries' saw issue in April 2004 through US imprint Brutal Records. Henke Crant from SOILS OF FATE sessioned vocals on the tracks 'Trans Gender Mutilation' and 'Divine Gluttony'. STABWOUND undertook US touring that same year. The band folded in April 2005 with the main contingent of musicians forming Hardcore outfit NERVE.

Vocalist Uffe Nylin also fronts LAST WORDS WRITTEN, CRANIAL DEVOURMENT, MYSOGYNY, RUINOUS and British Brutal Death Metal act INVOCATE in alliance with vocalist Oliver, of OCULAR FORNICATION and CREPITATION and Dan, of IMINDAIN, CREPITATION and SARPANITUM, handling guitar, bass and programming.

Malicious Addiction, Stabwound (2002) (Demo). Family Remains / Cleansing The World / As I Watch You Bleed / Consume My Flesh.

Bloodsoaked Serenades, The Flood (2003). Intestinal Impalement / Red Worms Erected / Bloated Brain Implow / Ancient Art Of Gutting / As I Watch You Bleed Again / Kill Your Mother Rape Your Dog / Ancient Art Of Gutting (Video).

HUMAN BOUNDARIES, Brutal (2004). Molding Through Sloth / Devouring Deficiency / Red Worms Erected / Facial Skin And Tissue Removal / Trans Gender Mutilation / Disgorging Pieces Of Broken Glass / Divine Gluttony / Morgue Abductions / Unspeakable Perversions / Aqualung.

STARGAZER

ADELAIDE, SA, AUSTRALIA — *The Serpent Inquisitor (vocals / drums), The Great Righteous Destroyer (vocals / bass), Pilgrim (guitar),.*

STARGAZER is an Adelaide occult based Death Metal trio convened during 1995, opening proceedings with the 'Gloat' demo followed by a 7" single 'Borne' for Dream Sovereign Productions in 1997. At this juncture vocalist / drummer Paul Murphy exited, being replaced by Phoenix Chrysalis. With this revised line up the band cut the 'Harbinger' outing for Dies Irae Productions in mid 2000, this release being a split alliance with INVOCATION.

Phoenix Chrysalis then decamped, forcing STARGAZER into a two year hiatus. This was finally broken with the issue of a split single with American Black Metal act ARGHOSOLENT 'Magikkian' via Hellflame Productions.

The band shifted shape in the Summer of 2003 with Pilgrim taking on guitar duties and The Serpent Inquisitor manning the drums. STARGAZER would support INCANTATION in June of 2003 then teamed up with the cult US underground act NUNSLAUGHTER for a batch of Australian shows throughout August.

Borne EP, Dream Sovereign Productions (1997). Darkest Nether From The Solstice Pits / Abstract Flames Burn White / A Mist Falls / Ride The Everglade Of Reogniroro.

HARBINGER, Dies Irae Productions (2000). Conquer / Perennial Fire / Totalitarian Worm Holes / Lust In Pyramis / Interrestrial Black Twilights / Conspirators Wind / Abstract Flames Burn White / Outro.

Magikkian, Hellflame Productions (2002) (Split single with ARGHOSOLENT). Magikkian / Amidst Fireflies And Haunted Trees.

STATE OF INTEGRITY

BRISBANE, QLD, AUSTRALIA — *Aaron Franklin (vocals), Brendan Rhodes (guitar), Ben Clayphan (bass), Nick Rhodes (drums).*

A harsh Metal band out of the Bayside area of Brisbane, STATE OF INTEGRITY was formulated during 2003 featuring vocalist Aaron Franklin, guitarist Brendan Rhodes, bassist Ben Clayphan with Nick Rhodes on drums. A demo, 'State Of Integrity', arrived promoted by the band's live inauguration came in September 2003. The following June STATE OF INTEGRITY supported visiting US act EXHUMED. 2004 also saw the issue of a second promotional outing 'Will It Forever Be'. 2005 album recordings, 'The Fourth Season Of Revelations' being finalised in March and issued in June through MGM Distribution.

New Zealand touring that September witnessed supports to 8 FOOT SATIVA, performing in Auckland, Wellington, Christchurch and Dunedin. Meantime, Sinbad Productions took on 'The Fourth Season Of Revelations' for a USA license in August 2006 whilst Globalroutes Distribution handled the record for New Zealand in September. Returning to New Zealand, STATE OF INTEGRITY partnered with SINATE for a run of shows throughout November.

State Of Integrity, State Of Integrity (2003) (Demo). Bulletproof / Societys Perception / Miss U.

Will It Forever Be, State Of Integrity (2004) (Demo). Will It Forever Be / Protected / Societys Perception.

THE FOURTH SEASON OF REVELATIONS, MGM Distribution (2005). The Fourth Season Of Revelations / Constricted / Forgotten Enemies / Miss U / We Stand Alone / Protected / Society Perception / East vs West / Listen (Self Belief) / Timez Of Reality / (88).

STEEP

TAMPERE, FINLAND — *Samuli Kuusinen (vocals), Teemu Mätäsjärvi (guitar), Jukka Holm (guitar), Tuomas Granlund (bass), Riku Niemelä (drums).*

STEEP is a Tampere based Death Metal act founded in 1997 by guitarist Frank Moberg of HIDDEN, CRYSTALIC and KILL ME GENTLY. Originally the group, involving guitarists Josku Kaarnametsä and Joonas Kaarnametsä with Ossi Toivonen on bass, pursued a Grunge direction but took on a harder edge with Moberg's departure. STEEP was re-assembled after a hiatus during 2002, now comprising singer Samuli "Samurai" Kuusinen, previously with UTTERVOID, guitarist Teemu "Hyeena" Mätäsjärvi of NOCTURN and KIELEKE, second guitarist Jukka "Jäyhä" Holm, bassist Tuomas "Turska" Granlund and drummer Riku "Rambo" Niemelä. Entering Fantom Studios in Tampere during November 2002 the band cut tracks for a demo entitled 'Rearrange', released in January 2003.

The demo 'Undisclosed' emerged in March 2004. Their track 'Silence Is Not Golden' would be included on the 2005 Xtreem Music compilation in Spain 'Xtreemities Vol.5'. Signing to Dies Irae Records STEEP issued their inaugural album 'Silence is Not Golden' in January 2006.

Rearrange, Steep (2003) (Demo). Rearrange / Saints / Head 1st / Truth.

Undisclosed, Lost Mind (2004) (Demo). Complete Lack Of Ideals And Integrity / Redefine / Mouth / Change / Lost Minds / Undisclosed.

SILENCE IS NOT GOLDEN, Dies Irae IRAE 004 (2006). Silence is Not Golden / Rise / Thousand Years / Redefine / Devouring / Fingerthroat / Sweet Leech / Legions Of Hate / Unnatural Disaster / All Dead / The Empire Of Grief / Complete Lack Of Ideals And Integrity / Change / Saints.

STILLBIRTH

ITALY — *Grezzo (vocals), Lorenzo Corti (guitar), Mauro Dell'oro (bass), Edo Sala (drums).*

STILLBIRTH was founded during 1996 as CLONING TECHNOLOGY by ex-PROFANATUM members guitarist Pepe and bass player Mauro Dell'oro together with rhythm guitarist Lorenzo Corti. Demo recordings in 2000 would be cut with Grezzo on vocals and drummer Andrea Rossi. The track 'The Endless Ice Of Soul' featured on the 2002 Dawn Of Sadness compilation album 'Screams From Italy Vol VI.' Live work witnessed supports to ELDRITCH, THE HAUNTED and WITCHERY.

In October of 2003 the band, having trimmed down to a trio, entered Temple of Noise Studios in Rom,e to lay down the EP 'Trauma'. STILLBIRTH, losing drummer Luca Ciambrone in May 2005, added new sticksman Edo Sala in July.

Trauma, Stillbirth (2005).

STILLBORN

MIELEC, POLAND — *Tomasz Ziêba (vocals / guitar), Andrzej Tabor (bass), Lukasz Urbanek (drums).*

STILLBORN, a Mielec based blasphemous Death Metal band dating to 1997, debuted in the Spring of 1999 with the demo 'Mirrormaze'. The group's initial formation counted singer Lukasz Marchewka, guitarist Tomasz Ziêba, former ECLYPSE bass player Andrzej Tabor and drummer Rafal Rzany. The second session 'Die In Torment 666' followed in mid 2001. Early 2004 found the band, having seen Marchewka decamp and Tomasz taking over lead vocals, putting out a further demo, 'Announcement Of Forthcoming Desecration' and sharing a split release with AZARATH billed 'Death Monsters' through Time Before Time Records. STILLBORN signed to Pagan Records for a debut album entitled 'Satanas El Grande'. This set of songs would include a cover version of ROTTING CHRIST's 'The Sign Of Evil Existence'. Rzany would be replaced on drums by Lukasz Urbanek of ORTANK and RAVISHED FLESH.

Mirrormaze, (1999). Crave For Killing / Hefaystos / Die In Torment / Mailed Hessus / Mirrormaze / Morphine Laboratory / Stillborn / Artror City.

Die In Torment 666, (2001). Keep Dying / Blasphemous Perversion / Whore / Millennium Of Hatred / Blood, Chains & Whips / Iconoclast / God Is Good.

SATANAS EL GRANDE, Pagan (2004). Pactum Inferni / Massacre / Satanas El Grande / Anti-God, Anti-Human / Execrable Lord Pretender / Thousand Faced Bitch / March Of Armageddon Warriors / Wrath, Death And Destruction / Holymother Fucker / The Sign Of Evil Existence.

Announcement Of Forthcoming Desecration, (2004). Thousand Faced Bitch / Anti God, Anti Human / Wrath, Death And Destruction.

DEATH MONSTERS, Time Before Time (2004) (Split with AZARATH). Thousand Faced Bitch / Anti-God, Anti-Human / Wrath, Death And Destruction.

STRONG INTENTION

MD, USA — A Maryland Grind based Hardcore outfit formed in 1993, STRONG INTENTION released the 'What's At Stake' demo in 1993 as their opening shot. However, by 1995 line-up fractures had reduced the band down to just founding guitarist Zac. The following year the band re-formed around a new membership with Zac now handling lead vocals, Adam guitar, John on bass and drums delegated to Joey, re-focusing the musical emphasis on speed, evident on the debut 7" EP for Crucial Blast. Pressed up in four batches of 1000 units, the 'Strong Intention' EP would first be manufactured in red vinyl. The ensuing years witnessed yet more line-up shuffles. A 1998 split EP, shared with EVERYBODY GETS HURT, emerged on Fistfight Records in 1998.

In May of 2002 STRONG INTENTION conducted an East Coast tour in alliance with Italians CRIPPLE BASTARDS. Releases included the 2001 inaugural album 'What Else Can We Do But Fight Back', recorded with Zac handling bass, Adam guitar and Andy the drums, the EP 'Each Day Lived An Act Of Defiance' through California's Six Weeks imprint, the 'Extermination Vision' album for Coalition Records and a split EP shared with Germany's Y.

February of 2004 marked another flux in musicians with the integration of Greg and Mough installed on guitar and former PESSIMIST man John on drums. This new roster cut its teeth as part of a package 'Grind The East Coast' US tour united with Los Angeles Grind veterans PHOBIA, Finland's ROTTEN SOUND and CIRCLE OF DEAD CHILDREN. Follow up gigs witnessed a six week Summer haul opening for D.R.I.

STRONG INTENTION lost the services of Greg in early 2005, pulling in Mark MG as temporary substitute. The band introduced permanent second guitarist Chaz in April. Having signed to Goodfellow Records, the band headed out on tour with INTERNAL BLEEDING, BODIES IN THE GEARS OF THE APPARATUS and KILL THE CLIENT in May. The group teamed up with NEURAXIS for US shows in February 2006. Gigs on the West Coast in May saw a union with DISFEAR from Sweden, PHOBIA and 9 SHOCKS TERROR.

What's At Stake, Strong Intention (1993). Innocent Lives / Grim Future / Tomorrows Lost / Self Centred / Measure Of Justice / Where I Stand / What's At Stake.

Strong Intention, Crucial Blast (1996). Make Up Your Mind / Thin Line / Fades Away / No Regard / What's At Stake / Why Be Something That You're Not.

Strong Intention, Fistfight (1998) (Split EP with EVERYBODY GETS HURT). Blinded / Liar / All My Hate / Unjust View.

EACH DAY LIVED ... AN ACT OF DEFIANCE, Six Weeks (2000). Seized / System Failure / It's Not The Time Clock I'm Punching Next / Bullshit Hatred / No Way Out / Pushed To The Back / Nightmares Over / I'm Not Buying It / Curtain Call / Wrench In The Machine.

WHAT ELSE CAN WE DO BUT FIGHT BACK, Six Weeks (2001). Up The Fronts / Model Citizen / Say Anything / Lines In The Sand / Consumer Sucker / A Dry Socket / 1000 Clowns / Code Of The Righteous / Sanitized / Take It Back / Unjust View / Prefabricated / Economic Outpatient / Make Up Your Mind / Artifice Of Faith / Fight Back / All My Hate / Blinded / Liar / Pig Blood Blues / On The Brink Of Help / Tomorrows Lost / It's Only Fear … / Holes In The Wall.

EXTERMINATION VISION, Coalition (2002). Panic In Zero Year / Rat Factory / Beautiful World / Suffocation / Impulse Armageddon / Earthgrave / Slash And Burn / Biased / Betray Humanity / Third Space Gorrilia Generator / Resign Ourselves To Failure / Slaughter Intelligence / Coercion Of The Weak / Next Of Kin.

Strong Intention, Vendetta Mob (2004) (Split with Y). Monuments Of Shit / The Carnivore / A Great Unraveling / Contamination Wolves.

SUBLUSTRIS

HOLLAND — *Arjaan Kampman (vocals), Niels Jansen (guitar), Gert Lozeman (guitar), Jan van den Hoorn (bass), Chiels Lozeman (drums).*

SUBLUSTRIS evolved from CANISTER, a Heavy Metal act originated during 1995 quoting a line-up of guitarists Sebastian den Oudsten, from EMBODIMENT, and Niels Jansen, bassist Martijn Weeda and drummer Ton de Haan. In February of 1996 the band marked a change in pace to a Death Metal style, inducting dual lead vocalists Chiel Lozeman and Arjaan Kampman but losing den Oudsten's services to ART OF PREMONITION. That April Ton de Haan exited. CANISTER would be inactive until August when Lozeman was installed on drums. The group shortly afterward evolved into SUBLUSTRIS.

With this change of title the band enrolled second guitarist Gert-Jan Maichiels. Weeda departed in August 1997, but returned in June 1998 to oust his brief replacement, Marc Brouwer of AMOEBE. Further changes in October 1998 had Gert Lozeman assuming second guitar duties as the band entered QSA Studios in Utrecht with producer Vincent Dijkers for the demo 'This Is Where They Are Stashed'.

Niels Jansen subsequently figured in AMOEBE. Arjaan Kampman would front ART OF PREMONITION. Den Oudsten rejoined THE EMBODIMENT in 2000.

This Is Where They Are Stashed, Sublustris (1999). Following The Stench / Ungracefully Exposed / Carnal Departure.

SUBTENEBRAS

CHILE — *Nicole Auger (vocals), Juan Escobar (vocals / guitar), Mario Maldonado (guitar), Claudio Albornoz (bass), R. Guzmán (keyboards), Alejandro Chacana (drums).*

SUBTENEBRAS, created in 1999 and fronted by Nicole Auger, is a Black edged, Santiago Doom-Death band featuring Juan Escobar of LAPSUS DEI. The group was first assembled as VITA SUBTENEBRAS featuring singer Guillermo, guitarists Juan Escobar and Hugo Bravo, bassist Fredez, keyboard player Moris Elalam with Esteban Zenteno on drums. However, the 2000 'Teufel' demo saw both Escobar and Zenteno sharing lead vocals, with back up from Camila. New recruits by this stage would be guitarist Diego and bass player Pablo. Re-billed as SUBTENEBRAS, the band drafted Nicole Auger for recording of the demo 'Una Vida Bajo Las Tinieblas'.

Line-up changes saw keyboard player Moris Elalam replaced by R. Guzmán and drummer Esteban Zenteno superseded by Alejandro Chacana. Also newly installed would be second guitarist Mario Maldonado and bassist Claudio Albornoz. A self titled demo emerged in 2003.

Subtenebras, Subtenebras (2003). Non Perpetual / Palabras / Darknomatopella / El Parásito / Inmortal VI.

SUFFER

FAGERSTA, SWEDEN — *Joakim Öhman (vocals), Ulf Samuelsson (guitar), Patrik Andersson (bass), Per Karlsson (drums).*

Fagersta / Lindesberg Deathsters SUFFER date to 1988, when the first line-up comprised of vocalist Joakim Öhman, bassist Patrik Andersson and drummer Conny Granqvist. A demo, 'Cemetery Inhabitants', surfaced in December 1989. The group added guitarist Ronny Eide, editor of 'Morbid' fanzine, in 1990, but a line-up shuffle saw Granqvist depart in favour of ex-MAMACLAW, WORTOX and ALTAR drummer Per Karlsson. A second demo, entitled 'Manifestation Of God', was recorded at Sunlight Studio in Stockholm with producer Tomas Skogsberg and released in 1991. Utilising Sunlight Studio once again, SUFFER cut three tracks, two of which emerged on the 'On Sour Ground' EP, issued via French imprint New Wave in 1993, and the third, 'Wrong Side Of Life', remaining unused, originally intended for a proposed compilation album.

In January 1992 guitarist Ronny Eide left the band, being replaced by Uffe Samuelsson. This revised version of SUFFER put out the 'Global Warming' EP in May 1993. Another EP, 'Thrashing The North Away', was recorded live in Lulea. Released in December, only 300 copies were pressed. Following the release of the 1995 'Structures' album, produced by Tomas Skogsberg and DISMEMBER drummer Fred Estby issued through the Austrian Napalm label, SUFFER splintered. Andersson opted out to join IN BETWEEN DAYS. With only and Joakim Öhman and Per Karlsson remaining, a brief attempt to keep the band going by inducting guitarists T-Ban and Pontus from KAZJUROL proved short-lived. Öhman attempted a resurrection of SUFFER, with erstwhile members of ABHOTH guitarist Jörgen Kristensen and drummer Mats Blückert, but this would not come to fruition.

Guitarist Ulf Samuelsson joined the THERION offshoot band SERPENT for their 'In The Garden Of The Serpent' album. He was joined by a further SUFFER member drummer Per Karlsson in 1996. The following year Karlsson joined T.A.R., featuring on the albums 'Fear Of Life' and 'Tar And Feathers For The Millennium'. The sticksman also activated Megagrind Productions, serving the extreme Metal scene with a stream of album releases.

Per Karlsson would join NOMINION during November 2001. Jörgen Kristensen joined DEAD AWAKEN the following year. Mats Blückert enrolled himself into GODHATE in April 2006.

Cemetery Inhabitants, (1989) (Demo). Intro: "The Desolation" / Granulate Sorcery / Intense Brainconvulsions / Cemetery Inhabitants / Reduced From Life.

Manifestion Of God, (1991) (Demo). Sleeping Beauty / Human Flesh / Infectious / Manifestion Of God.

On Sour Ground, New Wave NWR EP039 (1993). On Sour Ground / My Grief.

Global Warning EP, Napalm NPRCD 002 (1993). Impressive Turns / Infectious / Global Warning / Wrong Side Of Life.

Thrashing The North Away EP, Immortal Underground IUPEP001 (1993) (Limited edition 300 copies). Human Flesh (Live) / Wrong Side Of Life (Live).

STRUCTURES, Napalm NPRCD006 (1994). Temporary Sane / Passionate Structures / Lie Within / Selected Genes / A Frenetic Mind / Maginary Homecoming / The Killing Culture / Freedom Of Speech.

SUFFERAGE

HAMBURG, GERMANY — *Jasmin (vocals), Lasse (guitar), Olli (bass), Ole (drums).*

SUFFERAGE is a female fronted Death Metal act out of Hamburg founded in March 2000. Singer Jasmin's formative years were conducted as guitarist with school Punk band A.S.S.T. then as singer for LENINS ERBEN and SÄUREATTACKE. Both guitarist Lasse and drummer Ole, after paying their dues in a METALLICA covers band, are ex-members of Thrash Metal band COMMON CRY. Bassist Olli is also operational with SCYTHE. First product was a 2001 demo billed as 'Birth'. A self-financed album, 'Raw Meat Experience', followed in 2003. SUFFERAGE issued a live DVD, 'Zerhacken Wacken', in 2005. Signing to Remedy Records the 'Bloodspawn' album arrived in November 2006.

Birth, Sufferage (2001) (Demo). Intro / Necormantic / Request Death / Lack Of Intelligence / Pacifistic / Bloodshed / Allen Voran / Outro.

RAW MEAT EXPERIENCE, Sufferage (2003). Dinner For One / Self Hatred Call / At Enmity With This World / Demons / One Behind You / Raw Meat Experience / Buried Alive / Ceremonial War / Civilized / I Hate My Cunt / The Extraordinary Unexciting Adventures Of Mr. Schischinski / Neurotic (Live) / Necromantic (Live).

BLOODSPAWN, Remedy (2006). Trained To Kill / Hate Is Warm And Red / Allday Life / What About / A Shadow Of Your Own (Disfigured Soul) / Grey And Wet And Cold / Not My Place / Prophecies Of A Coming Scenario / Just Another Trend / Stop Corruption / Enticing Lies.

SUFFOCATE BASTARD

HERTEN, GERMANY — *Stefan Brinkmann (vocals), Patrick Czerny (guitar), David Adamietz (guitar), Karsten Boehnke (bass), Thorsten Bertram (drums).*

Herten based, brutal Death Metal band SUFFOCATE BASTARD, created in 2000 by singer Stefan Brinkmann, formatively included musicians such as drummers Mike Brown and Sascha Fichtner. SUFFOCATE BASTARD issued the 2004 demo 'Architects Of Perversity'. These sessions would be recorded by a band line-up comprising vocalist Stefan Brinkmann, guitarist Patrick Czerny, guitarist / bassist David Adamietz and former PARANOIZ drummer Meik Bartnick. The SUFFOCATE BASTARD rhythm section subsequently changed to incorporate bassist Karsten Boehnke, ex-ETERNAL DIRGE and MUSTY

GUTS, and drummer Thorsten Bertram, ex-PROVOCATION and CASTIGATE.

Architects Of Perversity, Suffocate Bastard (2004). Intro / Architects Of Perversity / Cold Eyes Of Murder / In The Whirls Of Spiritual Violence / Winds Of Stench And Poisoned Atmosphere Of Bliss Happiness / Suffocate Bastard.

SUFFOCATION

NEW YORK, NY, USA — *Frank Mullen (vocals), Doug Cerrito (guitar), Terrance Hobbs (guitar), Derek Boyer (bass), Dave Culross (drums).*

Now regarded as one of the most influential original Death Metal combos, New York's SUFFOCATION led the way in deconstructing their art down to the finest, microscopic components, building songs of infinite complexity. Very often their tracks compressed enough riffage to fuel an entire album, this obsessive devotion to their craft taking the methodology soon firing up a new branch of the Death Metal family tree.

SUFFOCATION was initially founded as SOCIAL DISEASE during 1986. The band debuted with a line-up of vocalist Frank Mullen, guitarists Doug Cerrito and Terrance Hobbs, bassist Josh Barohn and drummer Mike Smith. This unit arrived with the 3 track demo tape 'Reincremation' during April 1990.

SUFFOCATION's inaugural EP release 'Human Waste' emerged in May 1991, issued by Nuclear Blast Records in Europe and Relapse Records, as this influential label's first ever release, in America. The title track been lifted straight from the antecedent demo but the newly recorded tracks barely surpassed it in terms of production quality. Where SUFFOCATION did score was in their rampantly excessive use of riffing, managing to congest a bewildering welter of riffs into space normally reserved for a then genre standard of a handful. In this respect, SUFFOCATION immediately set themselves apart.

The band would switch labels to Roadrunner turning round the album 'Effigy Of The Forgotten' in October the same year. This release included re-recorded versions of the 1990 demo tracks 'Involuntary Slaughter' and 'Reincremation', the latter featuring guest vocals from singer George 'Corpsegrinder' Fisher alongside 'Mass Obliteration'. Again SUFFOCATION focussed on their now trademark attention to extreme detail, with massed nano-thrash riffing, Mullen's inhuman bellow and unrelenting blast beats. Soon afterwards, Chris Richards took the four string position.

The May 1993 opus 'Breeding The Spawn' saw Terrance Hobbs and Paul Bagin helming production. In 1994 SUFFOCATION donated the track 'Infecting The Crypts' to the 'Live Death' compilation album, though by this time Doug Bohn filled in behind the drum kit.

Bohn joined gore mongers AUTOPSY prior to founding WELT with his SUFFOCATION colleague Doug Cerrito on guitar for the 1994 'Paranoid Delusion' EP, an act that changed names in 1996 to IRON LUNG releasing the 'Chasing Salvation' album on Diehard Records. Following touring to promote SUFFOCATION's May 1995 Scott Burns produced album 'Pierced From Within' drummer Doug Bohn decamped. His place was taken by DISGORGED and MALEVOLENT CREATION man Dave Culross to record the EP 'Despise The Sun', distributed via the band's management company Vulture Records during 1998. . This outing, witnessing a re-work from the 'Human Waste' EP, 'Catatonia', with minimal promotion, unfortunately languished in obscurity.

The exalted position afforded SUFFOCATION after a decade of output could not sustain the band though and the group ceased activities. During 1998 guitarist Doug Cerrito joined HATE ETERNAL for their 'Conquering The Throne' album, the act founded by RIPPING CORPSE and MORBID ANGEL guitarist Erik Rutan. Culross would rejoin MALEVOLENT CREATION.

Highlighting the undoubted impact SUFFOCATION had upon the scene Greek label Repulsive Echo compiled a 2001 tribute album with an all international cast. SUFFOCATION were duly paid homage by their country mates PROPHECY, DEVOURMENT, PUTRILAGE, SEVERED SAVIOR, INTERNAL BLEEDING and DETRIMENTAL as well as Canadians ROTTING, Australians MISCREANT, Finns DEEP RED, Spains WORMED, Japan's VOMIT REMNANTS, Greeks INVERACITY, Dutch bands PYAEMIA and DISAVOWAL, Germans HARMONY DIES and even BEHEADED from Malta.

Reports surfaced in August 2002 that SUFFOCATION were set to re-unite citing a line up of vocalist Frank Mullens, guitar players Terrance Hobbs and the PYREXIA and INTERNAL BLEEDING credited Guy Marchais, bassist Josh Barohn and drummer Mike Smith. To complement this news, Relapse picked up the neglected 'Despise The Sun' EP for re-release. By late 2003 the band had set 'Souls To Deny', released in April 2004, as a title for a new album. A promotional video clip for the track 'Surgery of Impalement' was filmed at Philadelphia's infamous Eastern State Penitentiary, noted for having held notorious gangster Al Capone.

The group, having switched bassists once again and bringing onboard former DECREPIT BIRTH man Derek Boyer, continued touring apace across North America into April of 2004 as part of MORBID ANGEL's 'American Heretic' dates partnered with SATYRICON and PREMONITIONS OF WAR. Extending live work into May, the band hooked up with DYING FETUS and MALAMOR. Dates in January 2005 saw SUFFOCATION partnering with BEHEMOTH and SOILENT GREEN. As this trek extended into February the band retained BEHEMOTH as road partners but also added CATTLE DECAPITATION and Minneapolis outfit DEVILINSIDE. Road work continued throughout 2005, witnessing October and November shows packaged with CRYPTOPSY, CEPHALIC CARNAGE, ABORTED and WITH PASSION. Mike Smith also made time to see inclusion on the October released ROADRUNNER UNITED 25th anniversary album 'The All-Stars Sessions', helming the drum kit for the Matt Heafy compiled 'Dawn Of A Golden Age'.

SUFFOCATION announced touring plans for the summer of 2006, kicking of the 'Sthress' tour in July alongside POISON THE WELL, IT DIES TODAY, HIMSA, DARKEST HOUR, BURY YOUR DEAD, SHADOWS FALL, THROWDOWN and STILL REMAINS. A new self-titled album was released in September 2006. The band united with headliners FEAR FACTORY, HYPOCRISY and Polish act DECAPITATED for US shows in October 2006. Unfortunately, major transportation problems, described by the band as "fraudulent bus companies", led to the cancellation of the first three shows in Cedar Falls, Iowa, Papillion in Nebraska and Fort Collins in Colorado.

SUFFOCATION teamed up with IMMOLATION and SKINLESS for a North American tour beginning late October 2007.

Reincremation, Suffocation (1990) (Demo). Human Waste / Involuntary Slaughter / Reincremation.

Human Waste EP, Nuclear Blast NB 051 CD (1991). Infecting The Crypts / Synthetically Revived / Mass Obliteration / Catatonia / Jesus Wept / Human Waste.

EFFIGY OF THE FORGOTTEN, Roadrunner RC 9275-2 (1991). Liege Of Inveracity / Effigy Of The Forgotten / Infecting The Crypts / Seeds Of The Suffering / Habitual Infamy / Reincremation / Mass Obliteration / Involuntary Slaughter / Jesus Wept.

BREEDING THE SPAWN, Roadrunner RR 9113-2 (1993). Beginning Of Sorrow / Breeding The Spawn / Epitaph Of The Credulous / Marital Decimation / Prelude To Repulsion / Anomalistic Offerings / Ornaments Of Decrepency / Ignorant Deprivation.

PIERCED FROM WITHIN, Roadrunner (1995). Pierced From Within / Thrones Of Blood / Depths Of Depravity / Suspended In Tribulation / Torn Into Enthrallment / The Invoking / Synthetically Revived / Brood Of Hatred / Breeding The Spawn.

Despise The Sun EP, Vulture Entertainment RR 6527-2 (1998). Funeral Inception / Devoid Of Truth / Despise The Sun / Bloodchurn / Catatonia (Grind mix).

SOULS TO DENY, Relapse RR 6586-2 (2004). Deceit / To Weep Once More / Souls To Deny / Surgery Of Impalement / Demise Of The Clone / Subconsciously Enslaved / Immortally Condemned / Tomes Of Acrimony.

LIVE IN QUEBEC, Relapse (2006) (Only available through online store). Infecting The Crypts / Thrones Of Blood / Surgery Of Impalement / Catatonia / Liege Of Inveracity / Despise The Sun / Subconsciously Enslaved / Immortally Condemned / Effigy Of The Forgotten / Tomes Of Acrimony / Breeding The Spawn / Pierced From Within / Funeral Inception.

SUFFOCATION, Relapse (2006). Oblivion / Abomination Reborn / Redemption / Bind Torture Kill / Inis Conceived / Translucent Patterns Of Delirium / Creed Of The Infidel / Regrets / Entrails Of You / The End Of Ends / Prelude To Repulsion.

SUFFOKATOR

OULU, FINLAND — *Herr Kriegmeister (vocals), Dieqo Death (guitar), Ettra718 (bass), Jonas Lindberg (drums).*

Oulu based Grindcore / Death Metal endeavour. Under various pseudonyms, such as J.S., Caine Infest, J.S. GRVHM and I.C. Cholera, frontman Herr Kriegmeister (real name Joni Soini) also manifested VACUI SEGNO, CHOLERA, TRSX, FROM THE NORTH and ARAS. Hellbourg Records debuted the solo endeavour with a July 2005 EP split with SPLITZEN. Skullyard Records followed swiftly that same month with another split EP, 'Fear The Suffocater', this time in collaboration with NÄKKILEPÄ KANADAAN. Quickfire successive releases included the 'Massacrematory' and 'Chambers' EPs in August. That September the compilation 'Complikation' was issued.

For concerts Herr Kriegmeister was joined by SPLITZEN guitarist Dieqo Death, bass player Ettra718, of TYR and FROM THE NORTH, plus Jonas Lindberg of FORNJOTR on the drums.

The project subsequently took on a revised title of HERR SUFFOKATOR in 2006, issuing the 'Suffocation' EP through Skullyard Records.

Suffokator / Splitzen, Hellbourg (2005) (Split EP with SPLITZEN). Fear The Suffokator / Näkkileipää Kanadaan.

Fear The Suffocater, Skullyard (2005) (Split 7" vinyl EP with NÄKKILEPÄ KANADAAN). Fear The Suffocater.

Massacrematory, Skullyard (2005). Intro / Massacrematory / Verikuorma.

Chambers, Skullyard (2005). Intro / Chambers pt.1 / Chambers pt.2.

COMPLIKATION, Skullyard (2005). Fear The Suffocator / Näkkileipää Kanadaan / Intro / Massacrematory / Verikuorma / Introdukktion / Chambers pt.1 / Chambers pt.2.

Kirva, Skullyard (2005). Maksahuuhtelu / Disagreeable Grind 'n' Roll Disturbance / Kirva / Project Autopsy / Riippa.

SUHRIM

BELGIUM — *Johan Antonissen (vocals / bass), Jeroen Vingerhoed (guitar), Timmy De Beukeleer (guitar), Paul Brunson (drums).*

Noted Death Metal act founded as far back as 1989 by vocalist / bassist Johan 'Jolle' Antonissen. The band made their entrance with the October 1989 Thrash influenced tape 'Return From The Sepulchre', SUHRIM at this juncture comprising of Antonissen on bass, singer Kurt Mampay, guitarist Jurgen Leclerq and drummer Paul Brunson. The group would dispense with Mampay allowing Antonissen to take over lead vocals for a follow up live tape 'Agashura's Deicide'. A third tape, 'Mountain Of Skulls', found SUHRIM as a trio of Antonissen, Brunson and guitarist Jerry Jacobs.

SUHRIM's line-up would flux once more a track 'Lord Of Dreams' included on the Shiver Records 'Sometimes Death Is Better' compilation, bringing in guitarist Luc Niels and vocalist Kenny Verspreet. These two latest recruits would decamp and the band would then induct FATAL OBSESSION guitarist Bart Vergaert for the 'Revenge' demo. SUHRIM would persevere with the demo format with 1998's offering 'Do You Still Have The Guts?'

After yet another demo, 'Life Sucks And Then You Die' which included a cover version ACCEPT's 'Fast As A Shark', SUHRIM operated for many years as a duo of Antonissen and Vergaert although a full band, including another ex FATAL OBSESSION man guitar player Timmy De Beukeleer, would be built up for the 2000 demo 'Gore Is The End'. SUHRIM released a limited edition album 'Unidentified Flying Body Parts' through the Hybreed label in 2002. The first pressing of 500 soon sold out. Later that same year Steven 'Stardust' De Herdt departed, his place swiftly being filled by Paul Brunson- actually the band's original drummer having last been a SUHRIM member some seven years previous. SUHRIM members would also be operational with the MANTIIS project band in union with personnel from Portugues act DECAYED.

In 2004 the band, having added former DISOWN guitarist Jeroen Vingerhoed, marked a return with the less than subtly entitled album 'The Cunt Collector'. October touring in Southern Europe had the group partnering with Portuguese act SACRED SIN. However, the band encountered problems with their new album prior to manufacture as the pressing plant refused to handle the manufacture due to "obscene imagery and language". The album, retitled 'The C*** Collector' would be re-pressed in digipack version with new cover art.

In February 2007 SUHRIM cut their third album, entitled 'Happy Hour', working with producers Wojtek and Slawek Wieslawscy at Hertz Studios in Bialystok, Poland.

UNIDENTIFIED FLYING BODY PARTS, Hybreed (2002). Mutilated Corpse / U.F.B. / Old Bomb Fucked Bitch / As You Bleed / House Of Gore / Headdrilling The Odysee / Joyride / 666 / Hymn Of The Underdog / Shitlover / Shai Hulud / Headdrilling The Sequel.

OLD SCARS FRESH WOUND, Pulsarlight PRSCD010-DVD001 (2004) (CD / DVD release). Intro / Thoughts Without An End / Sudden Death / Mutilated / Scorn / Roasted Cunt With A Slice Of Lemon / Having A Ball / Gore Is The End / 5/6 Billion Death / Necrophile / Bodies Sink Shit Floats / The Hammer / Check The Penis (Millennium Bug) / Unidentified Flying Bodyparts / Old Bomb Fucked Bitch / Thoughts Without An End / Sudden Death / Mutilated / Scorn / Roasted Cunt With A Slice Of Lemon / As You Bleed / Head Drilling-The Odyssey / Head Drilling-The Sequel.

THE CUNT COLLECTOR, Pulsarlight PRSCD012 (2004). Crushed Smashed Mangled / To Eat / The Cunt Collector / Crushed Vagina / Fistfucked In The Throat / Sacrilege Christianity / Your Rotting Lips / Delicious / There Is No God But Man / Wake Up And Smell The Pus / C4 The Nitro Chewing Gum / Bubba.

SUICIDE

TURKEY — *Erkan Tatoglu (vocals), Hakan Kuscu (guitar), Esad Erbil (bass), Çaglar Yürüt (drums).*

Death Metal band SUICIDE was initiated by ex-SCALPRUM guitar player Erkan Tatoglu in 1989, debuting live in front of an audience over a thousand strong at the Talip Cinema venue in Ankara during 1991. The band endured numerous fluctuations in the line-up, at one stage seeing OMINOUS GRIEF's Cüneyt Çaglayan as session guitarist and SAPIK INEK's Baris Efendioglu on bass. The group would switch Tatoglu to the lead vocal role in 1994 as Hakan Kuscu of DEAD MOSH, ROTTEN APPLE, ONE NIGHT STAND and DARKPHASE took command of guitar duties. Esad Erbil, another ONE NIGHT STAND veteran, joined in 1995 on bass. The group debuted commercially with the EP release 'Spiritual Mess' in 2000.

In 2003 Çaglar Yürüt, citing credits with OMINOUS GRIEF, FLATGROUND, ANOREXIA, NETTLETHRONE and LOST INFINITY, took over on drums from longstanding member Cem Devrim Dursun. With this line-up SUICIDE undertook a massive 50 date concert tour of Turkey. The album 'One Of Your Neighbours' emerged in 2004. That same year Erkan Tatoglu and Cüneyt Çaglayan acted as producers for the NETTLETHRONE demo 'Blueprint'.

Spiritual Mess, Zoo Music (2000). Spiritual Mess / Struggle That Never Ends / Mud / Suicide Pact.

ONE OF YOUR NEIGHBOURS, Suicide (2004). Buried Alive / Struggle That Never Ends / One Of Your Neighbours / Hell Star / Spiritual Mess / Crimson River / Gore / Mud / Terror Preached / Sole War / Worms Stuck On A Sphere / Suicide Pact / Virtual Realm / Merchants Of Misery.

SUICIDE

SUICIDE CULTURE

SEATTLE, WA, USA — *Kevin Bedra (vocals / guitar), Greg Hartung (bass), Josh Hannenberger (drums).*

Washington Death Metal band SUICIDE CULTURE issued a self titled 1998 album through Kill To Music Records. Line-up changes would see the departure of vocalist Paul English, guitarist Lucas Jaeger, bassist Terry McCorriston and drummer Mike Sillifrant. A final 2000 line up comprised vocalist / guitarist Kevin Bedra, bass player Greg Hartung and SCORCHED EARTH drummer Josh Hannenberger. 2003 EP sessions 'Fistful of Christ', issued through Thousand Funerals Music, were originally intended to be a SUICIDE CULTURE release but band members felt the switch in musical direction was great enough to warrant a change of name to that of FUNERAL AGE. Guesting as vocalist would be former SUICIDE CULTURE man Paul English, also of VS. THE WORLD and ALCHEMY.

Of the former members Lucas Jaeger would feature in MINCERY, SLEEP TERROR and VILE whilst Terry McCorriston holds SCORCHED EARTH credits.

SUICIDE CULTURE, Kill To Music (1998).

SUICIDE SILENCE

RIVERSIDE, CA, USA — *Mitch Lucker (vocals), Chris Garza (guitar), Mark Heylmun (guitar), Mike Bodkins (bass), Alex Lopez (drums).*

Riverside, California Death-Grindsters SUICIDE SILENCE, created in late 2002, issued the 2004 demos 'Older Demo' and 'Newer Demo' in 2004, following up with the 'Live At The Showcase' session in June 2005. The group underwent a succession of membership changes, with formative members including singer Tanner Womack, guitarist Josh Tufano, bassists Michael Olheiser and Chris Grucelski plus drummers Josh Goddard and Justin Tufano. The band introduced the NOCTURNAL SYMPHONY credited guitarist Mark Heylmun and drummer Alex Lopez, a scene veteran of THE RED DAWN, THE FUNERAL PYRE and BLACKHEART EULOGY repute.

Third Degree Records issued the 'Suicide Silence' EP in September 2005. To coincide with a UK tour, this release, adding videos for both 'Destruction Of A Statue' and "Distorted Thought Of Addiction', was re-issued a year later by UK label In At The Deep End Records. November and December US concerts saw SUICIDE SILENCE backing DIECAST, SWORN ENEMY and SEPULTURA.

Having switched labels to Century Media Records, SUICIDE SILENCE wrapped up album recordings with producer John Travis in mid April 2007. The band hooked up with the BURY YOUR DEAD headlined the 'Don't Call It A Comeback' tour beginning April 20th at the Montage Music Hall in Rochester, New York lasting into mid May flanking fellow openers STICK TO YOUR GUNS and SINCE THE FLOOD.

Demo 2003, Suicide Silence (2003) (Demo). Soak In Tears / Victim Of Tragedy / Stand Strong.

The Older Demo, Suicide Silence (2004) (Demo). To Death / Distorted Thought Of Addiction / Stand Strong / Destruction Of A Statue.

Suicide Silence, Third Degree (2005). Ending Is The Beginning / Swarm / About A Plane Crash / Distorted Thought Of Addiction / Destruction Of A Statue (Live).

Suicide Silence, In At The Deep End (2006) (UK release). Ending Is The Beginning / Swarm / About A Plane Crash / Distorted Thought Of Addiction / Destruction Of A Statue (Live) / Destruction Of A Statue (Video) / Distorted Thought Of Addiction (Video).

SUICIDE SOLUTION

SINGAPORE — *Elsa Faith (vocals), Joe Suicide (guitar), V.Vinz Vinod (guitar), Fadz (drums).*

One of Singapore's most respected names on the underground Metal circuit. SUICIDE SOLUTION, taking their title from the OZZY OSBOURNE classic, date to a 1995 formation. As teenagers they cut their first demo that same year and rapidly became a major draw on the local gig circuit. The band issued the album 'The Dark Adventures' through Spider Records in 1998. The SUICIDE SOLUTION band line-up for these recordings would involve Joe 'Suicide' Ferdinands on vocals and guitar, bass and drums and Sonya Tracey on vocals and guitar. For live work the band employed bassist Alex Tan and drummer Alvin Tan. However, the original line-up then disbanded.

Founding member guitarist Joe Suicide reformed the group with vocalist "Evil" Elsa Faith in November 1999, making a slight amendment to the band name to $UICIDE $OLUTION and switching the musical direction of the band into a heavier and darker "Horror Metal" musical direction, self-described as being "laced with sinful horror imagery, b-movie dialogue and prurient socio-political lyrics, providing a disparaging yet diverse musical platform of pure sonic mayhem". Guitarist V. Vinz had prior credits with CHAOS AFTERMATH, PREDATORY, RASA and NARASIMHA whilst bassist Ash also operates as frontman for V3H3M3NT. On drums would be Fadz of RASPATUL.

$UICIDE $OLUTION would spend 2004 crafting a new album entitled 'Halloween Holocaust'. Both Elsa Faith and Joe Suicide would also session on the KIYAMAT EP 'Prepare For War'. Bassist Ash exited in December. The band included the track 'Shock Hammer Kill Spill' on the Demonzend April 2005 compilation album 'The Arcane Art Of Defiance Vol. 1'.

THE DARK ADVENTURES, Spider SS7981X (1998) (limited edition 1000 copies). Dung & Donuts / Ghoulish Creep / Everybody Wants To Hurt You / Pocketful Of Posies / Taste The Sin / Basement / Vile Sunshine / Suck Station / Lean On Myself / Malice In Wonderland / Fear / Obsessional Neurosis.

SUMMONER

ITALY — *Claudio Passeri (vocals), Dalia Orsi (vocals), Giorgio Belltrami (guitar), Ugo Apicella (guitar), Luca Cinsani (bass), Stefano Magni (keyboards), Massimo Corbani (drums).*

SUMMONER are a Gothic infused Black / Death Metal act convened in January of 2001 by former personnel from the recently dissolved DEATH SEAGULL'S SCREAM, guitarist Giorgio Belltrami, keyboard player Stefano Magni and drummer Massimo Corbani. Initially SUMMONER was fronted by a female vocalist but this idea was abandoned as Paulo Cattaneo took the lead vocal role. The band was completed with the addition of bass player Luca Cinsani.

Valuable support slots to LACUNA COIL followed before SUMMONER issued the four track self financed EP 'Summoner's Sign'. Second guitarist Igor would be added to the ranks shortly after. The band readied a debut full length album 'Winter Solstice' for December 2003, these recordings featuring Dhilorz from ANCIENT and Daniel Botti of NODE appearing as special guest on vocals.

Summoner's Sign EP, (2001). The Maskplague / Tears I've Shed / Summoner Sign / Vicious Fruit.

WINTER SOLSTICE, (2003). Following Your Insight / Winter Solstice / Gaia Flowered Mantle / The Epoch Of Stillness / In Dreamy Lullabies / My Epitaph / Renewed / Forever Fellows.

SUPURATION

FRANCE — *Fabrice Loez (vocals / guitar), Ludovic Loez (guitar), Laurent Bessault (bass), Thierry Berger (drums).*

A French Death Doom Metal band with Gothic influences. The band started life billed as SUPURATION but would later adopt the new title of S.U.P.. In this formative incarnation the group released the 1991 demo 'Sultry Obsession' and two albums, the second, 'Still In The Spheres', including a cover of TEARS FOR FEARS' 'Shout'. The group toured Europe partnered with SUFFOCATION in 1994 prior to recording the 'Anomoly' album. This recording marked a switch in band title to S.U.P. ('Spherical Unit Provided')

In 1995 a limited edition CD emerged (only 500 copies were pressed) entitled '9092' containing a number of tracks previously only released as singles or on compilation albums between 1990 and 1992. The group would tour with Swiss outfit CORONER in early 1996. S.U.P. signed to Holy Records in 1997, commencing this contract with the album 'Room Seven'. February of 1998 saw a re-issue of 'The Cube', re-credited to S.U.P. and adding tracks from the 'Still In The Spheres' outing. Upfront of the 'Chronophobia' album the band would lose the services of bass guitarist Laurent Bessault. Nevertheless the band toured Europe that Winter in union with ANATHEMA and into the Spring of 2000 across France partnered with GLOOMY GRIM and DIVISION ALPHA. The revisionism of their back catalogue continued apace with 'Anomoly', the record re-released in 2000 brandishing an array of remixes, acoustic takes and demos.

Such would be the band's influence that Inner Sides Productions released a double CD tribute set 'A Vision Of S.U.P.' artists paying homage included SKELETON CREW, GRIMORIA, CATACOMB, BLACKLODGE, HYPNOSIS, INNER SOUL, NOMED, AEONS, DIVISION ALPHA, MISANTHROPE and NOCTURNAL FEARS amongst many others. S.U.P. issued the CD / DVD live set 'To Live Alone' in 2001 with a new studio album 'Angelus' arriving in 2002.

SULTRY OBSESSION, (1990). Hypertrophy / Sordid & Outrageous Emanation / Sultry Obsession / Reveries Of A Bloated Cadaver.

9092, PIAS (1992). The Creeping Unknown / Isolated / In Remembrance Of A Coma / Sultry Obsession / 138.JP.08 / Sojourn In The Absurd / Empheral Paradise / Reveries Of A Bloated Cadaver / In Remembrance Of A Coma / 138.JP.38 / Half Dead / Hypertrophy / Sultry Obsession / Reveries Of A Bloated Cadaver.

STILL IN THE SPHERE, Reincarnate SUP 08 CD (1994). The Crack / The Cleansing / Back From The Garden / Variation On The Theme 4TX.31B / Shout.

THE CUBE, Reincarnate SUP 07 CD (1994). Prelude / The Elevation / Soul's Speculum / 1308.jp.08 / The Cube / Through The Transparent Partitions / Spherical Inner-Sides / The Accomplishment / 4tx.31b / The Dim Light.

ANOMALY, Revolution REV 003 (1995). Anomaly / Pain Injection / In Those Times / The Work / Ocean Of Faces / In The Deepest Silence / Dialogue / D-AN's Last Order / Reset / D-AN SUP V1.1.

SURROGOAT

KRUUSAAUK, ESTONIA — *Luix (vocals / guitar), Mihkel Luiga (guitar), Jaanus Ehte (guitar), Enor Niinemägi (bass), Rauno Veeroja (drums).*

Kruusaauk act SURROGOAT created as a raw Black Metal act in 1999 by METSALINE drummer Rauno Veeroja and Kalmistu of BEYOND ACVILON on bass, soon being joined by guitarist Mart Paadik. The group would be rounded out by vocalist / guitarist 'Luix' (a.k.a. Kristjan Luiga). 2000 saw the departure of Paadik as the group switched to a Death Metal stance to record the Urmas Voevodin produced, August 2001 demo 'Excuses For Oppression'. Bringing in 'Imperaator' Alvar Kana from IRDHING on second guitar, SURROGOAT put in their inaugural live performance on 17th November 2001 in Kruusaauk.

Kalmistu exited in 2002, being superseded by Enor Niinemägi. Ghost from TARBATU would briefly figure as a band member at this juncture, being replaced by former ORG man Mihkel Luiga in mid 2003. Following a September support gig to BEHEMOTH, Alvar was replaced by Jaanus Ehte, a veteran of ORG and MORIGAN. SURROGOAT published the 2004 demo 'Landscapes Of Condolence', recorded at Musicworks Studios in Tallinn by Arne Holm.

Excuses For Oppression, Surrogoat (2001). Mentally Handicapped / Ruderoads / Excuses For Oppression / Modern Inspirations / Mentally Handicapped (6LEGZ remix).

Landscapes Of Condolence, (2004). Rottenminded Clerk / World War III / El Niño Satánicos / Rise From Below / Demonic Rain / Into The Misery.

SUTURE

BATON ROUGE, LA, USA — *Jayson Ramsey (vocals), Jason McIntyre (guitar), Lance Strickland (guitar), Bruno Munzler (bass), Brent Smith (drums).*

Baton Rouge extreme Death Metal band. SUTURE debuted in with the 'In Cryptic Bliss' demo followed in 2000 with the forceful 'Deconstructing Anatomy' session. Tracks from both of these recordings would be re-worked for the inaugural album 'Carnivorous Urge To Kill' released by Deepsend Records in October of 2002.

Bassist Bruno Muenzler, an ex-NECROTOMY member, also operates with ENDOMINION and WOLF SYSTEM. A SUTURE credited drummer, Eric Parks, went on to work with Texan outfits SCARLINE and RHOME. By early 2005 Parks had enrolled into the ranks of DEVOURMENT.

In June 2006 SUTURE contracted with Unmatched Brutality for the album 'Skeletal Vortex'.

CARNIVOROUS URGE TO KILL, Deepsend DSR005 (2002). Deconstructing Anatomy / Bonesaw / Bloodsoaked / Hemorrhage Head / Masticated Recrudesce / Torn From Mortal Coil / Still Inside / Carcinoma Contagion / Systematic Removal Of Vitality.

SWALLOW THE SUN

JYVÄSKYLÄ, FINLAND — *Mikko Kotamäki (vocals), Markus Jämsen (guitar), Juha Raivio (guitar), M. Honkonen (bass), Aleksi Munter (keyboards), Pasi Pasanen (drums).*

Jyväskylä based Doomsters SWALLOW THE SUN, created in Spring 2000 by PLUTONIUM ORANGE guitarist Juha Raivio and drummer Pasi Pasanen, also citing credits with PLUTONIUM ORANGE as well as MORNINGSTAR and MURDER IN ART. Subsequent to initial rehearsals the duo was augmented by Mikko Kotamäki of FUNERIS NOCTURNUM, ENTER MY SILENCE and TROLLHEIM's GROTT on vocals and second guitarist Markus Jämsen from RAUTAKELLO, MURDER IN ART and CLAYFORGE. SWALLOW THE SUN would soon after be brought up to full strength with the incorporation of FUNERIS NOCTURNUM players of keyboard player Aleksi Munter ('Ruho') and bassist M. Honkonen ('Horgath'), the latter also having ties to OBSCURANT.

SWALLOW THE SUN issued the 2003 demo 'Out Of The Gloomy Light', this session securing the band a deal with the Firebox label. The resulting album, 'The Morning Never Came' recorded at Sam's Workshop with producer Sami Kokko, emerged in November. Olympic Recordings licensed the album for a US release in early 2005.

During November 2004 Mikko Kotamäki relinquished his position in ENTER MY SILENCE in order to prioritise SWALLOW

THE SUN. The band entered Sam's Workshop studios in Lutakko in January 2005 with producer Sami Kokko to commence recording their second album. A preceding single, 'Forgive Her ...', boasting a cover of the CANDLEMASS classic 'Solitude' featuring guest vocals by REVEREND BIZARRE's Albert Magus, was issued as a limited edition release. The single charted at number 4 on the national charts. A 2005 compilation inclusion of note would be the track 'Silence Of The Womb' featured on the 'Code Red' album, an exclusive collection given to US Marine Corps soldiers active duty in the Middle East.

The August 2005 'Ghosts Of Loss' album entered the Finnish charts at number 8. Aleksi Munter made time to guest on demos from fellow Jyväskylä Metal band GHOST BRIGADE.

SWALLOW THE SUN frontman Mikko Kotamäki, maintaining his links to his priority act, joined Black Metal band ALGHAZANTH as their new vocalist in January 2006. That April the band signed a new label deal with Spinefarm Records, cutting album tracks during October at Seawolf Studios in Helsinki. Jonas Renkse of KATATONIA featured as a guest on the track 'The Justice of Suffering'. A February 2007 release date for 'Hope' was announced, the album entering the Finnish charts at number 3. Upfront of this the lead in single 'Don't Fall Asleep' included a cover version of the TIMO RAUTIAINEN & TRIO NISKALAUKAUS song 'Alavilla Mailla', with AMORPHIS singer Tomi Joutsen on vocals.

MOONSORROW, DEBAUCHERY and OMNIUM GATHERUM teamed up with SWALLOW THE SUN for a European tour throughout March and April 2007.

Out Of This Gloomy Light, Swallow The Sun (2003) (Demo). Through Her Silvery Body / Out Of This Gloomy Light / Swallow / Under The Waves.

THE MORNING NEVER CAME, Firebox FIRECD 012 (2003). Through Her Silvery Body / Deadly Nightshade / Out Of This Gloomy Light / Swallow / Hold This Woe / Silence Of The Womb / Under The Waves / The Morning Never Came.

THE MORNING NEVER CAME, Olympic Recordings 243 (2005) (USA release). Through Her Silvery Body / Deadly Nightshade / Out Of This Gloomy Light / Swallow / Hold This Woe / Silence Of The Womb / Under The Waves / The Morning Never Came / Solitude.

Forgive Her ..., FIRECDS 026 (2005). Forgive Her ... / Solitude. Chart position: 4 FINLAND.

GHOSTS OF LOSS, Firebox FIRECD 027L (2005) (CD + DVD). The Giant / Descending Winters / Psychopath's Lair / Forgive Her ... / Fragile / Ghost Of Laura Palmer / Gloom, Beauty And Despair / The Ship / Descending Winters (Promo video) / Swallow (Horror Pt.1) (Live) / Deadly Nightshade (Live) / Through Her Silvery Body (Live) / Psychopath's Lair (Live).

GHOSTS OF LOSS, Firebox FIRECD 027 (2005). The Giant / Descending Winters / Psychopath's Lair / Forgive Her ... / Fragile / Ghost Of Laura Palmer / Gloom, Beauty And Despair / The Ship. Chart position: 8 FINLAND.

HOPE, Spinefarm SPI 272CD (2006) (Promotion release). Hope / These Hours Of Despair / The Justice Of Suffering / Don't Fall Asleep (Horror Pt. 2) / Too Cold For Tears / The Empty Skies / No Light, No Hope / Doomed To Walk The Earth.

HOPE, Spinefarm SPI 272CD (2007). Hope / These Hours Of Despair / The Justice Of Suffering / Don't Fall Asleep (Horror Pt. 2) / Too Cold For Tears / The Empty Skies / No Light, No Hope / Doomed To Walk The Earth. Chart position: 3 FINLAND.

SWARRRM

JAPAN — *Hatada (vocals), Kapo (guitar), Futoshi (bass), Chowrow (drums).*

Japanese Grindcore act SWARRRM, created in 1996 and fronted by Hatada of Hardcore act GAMY, debuted in 1998 with the 'Chaos & Grind' recordings with TagRag Records reissuing this album in new artwork the following year. The same label also issued a split 7" single shared with FORCE and in 2000 the band collaborated with FUGAKU and Swiss act EDGE OF SPIRIT on another split release. Full length album 'Against Again' was issued in 2000 through God Door Records prior to a further split, this time in union with ATOMIC FIREBALL.

2002 witnessed yet more split outings, with BLOODRED BACTERIA and an EP with NARCOSIS via Crucifidos Pelo Systema. HG Fact published 'Nise Kyuseishu Domo' in 2003.

Swarrm, God Door (2000) (Split with ATOMIC FIREBALL).

AGAINST AGAIN, God Door (2000). Brain / Never Believe / Illitate / Defiant Attitude / Hear My Voice / Despair / Self-Abhorrence / H.T.D. / Pain / Hatred / Intent To Kill / Against Again.

NISE KYUSEISHU DOMO, HG Fact (2003). Scilence / Disturb / Gobbleegegook / Flummux / Don't Mess With Texas / Parasite / Nise Kyuseishu Domo / Vanish / Herzog / Damn / Grasser / Putrecence.

SWEDISH MASSACRE

KUNGSÖR, SWEDEN — *Denny Axelsson (vocals), Jon Peterson (guitar), Anders Lind (guitar), Kristoffer Johansson (drums).*

Kungsör Death / Thrashers established in 2002 by erstwhile members of HARDKAZE and WITHIN REACH, singer Denny Axelsson, guitarist Jon Petersson and drummer Kristoffer Johansson. First product would be the single 'Eyes Of Reflection' recorded at Evelon Studios during February 2004 by with producer Palle Svensson. The title track gained extra exposure with an inclusion on the compilation album 'Metal Ostentation'. Further promotional tracks would be recorded at Evil Bertil Studios in December 2004 with Andreas Öhrn behind the desk. Former SWEDISH MASSACRE man Denny Axelsson, opting out in October 2005, holds ties to both CALM and MARAMON.

Eyes Of Reflection, Swedish Massacre (2004). Eyes Of Reflection / Kids In Satan's Service.

SWEET SORROW

LJUBLJANA, SLOVENIA — *Valentin Bufolin (vocals), Peter Caric (guitar), Jernej Vrecar (guitar), Aljosa Us (bass), Peter Gale (drums).*

Ljubljana Death Metal act SWEET SORROW was founded in 1996 by vocalist Sebastijan Pregelj, guitarist Uros Kejzar and bass player Aljosa Us. The formative band went through a succession of early drummers until this post was stabilised by ex-WEEPING WILLOW man Mitja Radic in time for their first five track demo. Helmut Franges was then hired as second guitarist. However, SWEET SORROW replaced both guitarists with Ziga Hodnik, previously of HELPLESS, and drafted female singer Ursa Kavsek for recording winter 1997 demos at Studio Gong.

An album, 'Breaking The Silence', was prepared for Raspberry Records in November 1998. The group then installed second guitarist Pero Caric, formerly of HELPLESS and SCAFFOLD. In late 1999 Ales Berlot was inducted as new drummer. In July 2000 SWEET SORROW utilised Chinatown Studios to record a second album 'On Life And Death' for Poseidon Records. In mid 2002 SWEET SORROW donated the track 'Do Pekla' to a Slovenian Metal compilation album.

As 2002 closed the group underwent a major transformation, leaving only Us and Garic remaining. Replacements would be found in singer Valentin Bufolin and drummer Peter Gale, after which the band engaged in the "Slovenian Sudden Strike" tour. Second guitarist Sims joined in October 2003. Throughout April 2004 SWEET SORROW cut tracks for their third album. With these tracks completed Sims was superseded by session guitarist Jey from NEGLIGENCE. That November Rok Marolt, ex-CHERNOZYOM and MAGNUS NOCTUM, took the second guitar spot. However, the fluidity in the guitar department continued unabated as a few months later Marolt lost his place to Blaz Kavcic, who left in October 2005. Next in line for the vacancy would be Jernej Vrecar. A demo, entitled 'Northland', followed.

ON LIFE AND DEATH, Poseidon CDM112 (2001).

SWOLLEN

DENMARK — *Mads Haarløv (vocals / guitar), Thomas Fagerlind (bass), Jacob Olsen (drums).*

Death Metal combo SWOLLEN was forged by erstwhile INIQUITY compatriots vocalist / guitarist Mads Haarløv and drummer Jacob Olsen. Following issue of the EP 'The Breathless Waiting' in 1996 and a 1998 demo SWOLLEN folded. Both Haarløv and bassist Thomas Fagerlind subsequently joined INIQUITY. Three tracks from the 1998 SWOLLEN demos emerged on INIQUITY's 'Five Across The Eyes' release. In later years Fagerlind joined THORIUM and DAEMON. Haarløv sessioned for CORPUS MORTALE and aided in the formation of STRANGLER. Late 2004 saw Fagerlind operating with DOWNLORD, the band led by BOLT THROWER and BENEDICTION singer Dave Ingram.

The Breathless Waiting, Swollen (1996) (Demo). Carnal Realm / Subside In Flesh / The Breathless Waiting.

SWORDMASTER

SWEDEN — *Andreas Bergh (vocals), Emil Nödtveidt (guitar), Kenneth Gagfner (bass), Tobias Kjellgren (drums).*

SWORDMASTER date to 1993 and their foundation by guitarist Nightmare (real name Emil Nödtveidt). Nightmare also plays with OPHTHALAMIA and is the brother of the imprisoned DISSECTION mentor Jon. Following the mini album release on Florida's Full Moon Productions, drummer Tobias Kjellgren joined DECAMERON. He would eventually rejoin DISSECTION for their December 1995 European tour. His replacement in SWORDMASTER was another ex-DISSECTION member, Ole Öhman.

The 'Wrath Of Time' mini-album was re-released on vinyl format in 1996, limited to 1000 copies and with two extra tracks; 'Metallic Devastation' and 'Claws Of Death (Conspiracy)'. The band, crediting themselves as vocalist Whiplasher, guitarists Nightmare and Beast Electric, bassist Thunderbolt and drummer Terror, signed to Osmose Productions the same year but would start to draw themselves away from Black Metal and into straightforward Thrash tinged Heavy Metal with each successive release. A further evolution into more modern, Industrial edged sounds prompted a name switch to DEATHSTARS. The band also took on a radical image change for the album 'Synthetic Generation'. The record first surfaced in Sweden during March of 2002 on LED Recordings but would be picked up for European release by the German Nuclear Blast label the following year.

Wraths Of Time EP, Full Moon Productions FMP004v (0) (12" vinyl EP limited to 1000 copies). Wraths Of Time / Upon Blood And Ashes / Metallic Devastation / Conspiracy—Preview / Outro.
MORIBUND TRANSGORIA, SPV 008-08091 (0) (Vinyl release). Deathspawn Of The Eibound / Towards Erotomech Eye / The Angels And The Masters / Metalmorphosis—The Sweat Of Cain / Sulphur Skelethrones / Moribund Transgoria / Doom At Motordome / The Grotesque Xtravaganza.
Swordmaster, Swordmaster (1994) (Cassette rehearsal demo). True Nocturnal Spirit / In Starlit Chambers—Carpathian Woe / Outro—Sic Transit Gloria Mundi.
Wraths Of Time EP, Full Moon Productions FMP004 (1995). Wraths Of Time / Upon Blood And Ashes / Conspiracy—Preview / Outro.
Wraths Of Time, Mystic Productions 012 (1996) (Cassette split release with ZYKLON-B). Wraths Of Time / Upon Blood And Ashes / Conspiracy—Preview.
POSTMORTEM TALES, Osmose Productions OPCD 055 (1997). Intro: Indeathstries—The Masters' Possession / Crust To Dust / Postmortem Tales / Past Redemption / Claws Of Death / Blood Legacy / The Serpent Season / Metallic Devastation / Black Ace.
DEATHRAIDER, SPV 076-20552 (1998). Deathraider 2000 / Firefall Of The Fireball / Necronaut Psychout / Iron Corpse / Stand For The Fire Demon.
DEATHRAIDER, Osmose Productions OPCD 058 (1998) (CD release). Deathraider 2000 / Firefall Of The Fireball / Necronaut Psychout / Iron Corpse / Stand For The Fire Demon.
DEATHRAIDER, Osmose Productions OPPIC 058 (1998) (12" vinyl picture disc limited to 300 copies). Deathraider 2000 / Firefall Of The Fireball / Necronaut Psychout / Iron Corpse / Whisky Driver / The Black Ace / Stand For The Fire Demon.
MORIBUND TRANSGORIA, Osmose Productions VINYL OPLP 084 (1999) (Vinyl release). Deathspawn Of The Eibound / Towards Erotomech Eye / The Angels And The Masters / Metalmorphosis—The Sweat Of Cain / Sulphur Skelethrones / Moribund Transgoria / Doom At Motordome / The Grotesque Xtravaganza.
MORIBUND TRANSGORIA, Osmose Productions OPCD 084 (1999). Deathspawn Of The Eibound / Towards Erotomech Eye / The Angels And The Masters / Metalmorphosis—The Sweat Of Cain / Sulphur Skelethrones / Moribund Transgoria / Doom At Motordome / The Grotesque Xtravaganza.
MORIBUND TRANSGORIA, SPV 084-08092 (1999). Deathspawn Of The Eibound / Towards Erotomech Eye / The Angels And The Masters / Metalmorphosis—The Sweat Of Cain / Sulphur Skelethrones / Moribund Transgoria / Doom At Motordome / The Grotesque Xtravaganza.

SYMPATHY

CARONPORT, SK, CANADA — The Black / Death Metal styled SYMPATHY is a one-man project of the Caronport, Saskatchewan based Dharok (a.k.a. Derek James), active as SYMPATHY since 1990. An initial set of musicians would depart to leave Dharok as a solo artist and in this guise SYMPATHY released the demo sessions 'Arrogance And Ignorance' in 1993, 'Age Of Darkness' in 1995 and 'Realms Of Chaos' in 1996. In 2001 SYMPATHY signed with the Dutch label Fear Dark for the 'Invocation' album, recording at Port Trax Studios.

Tim Roth and Rob Doherty of INTO ETERNITY guested on the February 2004 follow up 'Arcane Path'. SYMPATHY relocated to Toronto, Ontario later that same year. The Monumentum Scandinavia label put out the August 2005 EP, 'Abyssal Throne', limiting this release to 850 copies.

INVOCATION, Fear Dark FD007 (2002). Invocation / Fey Illusion / Occupy / Circle Of Light / Final Ordeal / Cup Of Demons / Arise / Realm Of Disease / Prelude And Toccata In E Minor / Christus Factus Est / Immolation Of The Dragon / Death Of The Immortals.
ARCANE PATH, Fear Dark (2004). Introduction / Adept Arcana / The Shining Ones / Lord Of All Terrors / In Mine Own Image / Bearing The Plague / Adorned In Apostasy / Love Me And Despair / The Red League / Twilight And Rebirth / Surrounded By The Dead.
ABYSSAL THRONE, Monumentum Scandinavia (2005) (Limited edition 850 copies). Depths Of The Earth / Insipid / Immolation Of The Dragon / Ascendency / Occupy / Torn Into Enthrallment.

SYRACH

KALANDSEIDET, NORWAY — *Kenneth Olsen (vocals), Rolv-Erik Berge (guitar), Noralf Venaas (guitar), Ørjan Setvik (bass), Adam Suleiman (drums).*

Initially created as a tribute project to the British Heavy Metal movement SYRACH was forged in Kalandseidet during 1993 by vocalist / drummer Kenneth Olsen and guitarist Torbjørn Hatlestad, subsequently incorporating Rolv-Erik Berge on bass guitar. Frode Rødsjø ('Hrymr') of HELHEIM contributed studio drums to the opening 1993 'Helferd' demo. Rødsjø hung on throughout 1994 as SYRACH performed live but eventually opted out to prioritise HELHEIM.

A second session, '... Nor The Frail Perception', arrived in 1995 with a compilation collection of demos, billed 'Speak Of The Purest Snow ... Sleep In The Sadness' emerged the following year. Upon completion Berge switched to guitar and SYRACH inducted a fresh rhythm section of bassist Nils Inge Bruarøy and Ørjan Olsen on the drums. With this revised line-up the band signed to the German Autonomy Productions label for the album 'Silent Seas'. After UK dates in late 1997 Hatlestad departed and Nils Inge Bruarøy took the guitar position. SYRACH recorded the 'The Twilight Enigma' demo in 1998. 'The Stigma Sessions' followed in 2000.

Herbrand Larsen from ENSLAVED produced album sessions during mid 2006. The group then inducted Noralf Venås on guitar and Suleiman on drums. January 2007 album recordings featured OCTAVIA SPERATI's Silje Wergeland as guest vocalist. The resulting product, entitled 'Days Of Wrath', saw issue via Ripper Management in March. Notably, a painting by MY DYING BRIDE vocalist Aaron Stainthorpe, 'Christs', was utilised as the cover art.

In April 2007 the SYRACH line-up underwent a change, the band subsequently comprising vocalist Kenneth Olsen, guitarist Rolv-Erik Berge, second guitarist Noralf Venaas (a.k.a. "Reichborn"), bassist Ørjan Setvik ("Hjarandr") and drummer Adam Suleiman.

Helferd, Syrach (1994) (Demo). Ante Mortem Nemo Beatus Est / Devil Woman.

... Nor The Frail Perception, Morbid Metal (1995) (Cassette demo). Sadness (Intro) / At Lord's Door / Longing Forcease / Requiscat In Pace / ... Nor The Frail Perception / Outro.

Speak Of The Purest Snow ... Sleep In The Sadness, Syrach (1996) (Demo). Ante Mortem Nemo Beatus Est / Devil Woman / Sadness (Intro) / At Lord's Door / Longing Forcease / Requiscat In Pace / ... Nor The Frail Perception / Outro.

SILENT SEAS, Autonomy Productions APRO 027 (1997). ... Nor The Frail Perception / Jaded Funeral / ... Of Dragons Tears / (As Years Go By In) Silence / A Centenarian Odyssey / Outro: De Doedes Tjern.

The Twilight Enigma, Syrach (1998) (Demo). Semper Ardens / A Death Tear / The Twilight Enigma.

The Stigma Sessions, Syrach (2000) (Demo). Stigma Diabolikum / Come Dæmons.

DAYS OF WRATH, Ripper Management (2007). Are You Able To Breathe Fire? / Semper Ardens / The Firm Grip Of Death / Stigma Diabolikum / Come Daemons / Nine Fallen Men / A Death Tear / The Twilight Enigma.

SYSTEM SHOCK

NORRKÖPING, SWEDEN — *Dimitris Loakimogloul (vocals), Lukas Bergis (guitar), Olle Sundfeldt (bass), Slathis Cassios (keyboards), Markus Engström (drums).*

Norrköping Death Metal act founded during 2003. Initially the band included NIGHTFALL, NILE, NOCTA, SICKENING HORROR and THE CIRCLE OF ZAPHYAN drummer George Kolias. SYSTEM SHOCK's September 2004 debut 'Arctic Inside', released by the Dutch New Aeon Media label, was recorded at Tico-Tico Studios in Finland and produced by MIDNIGHT SCREAM credited guitarist Lukas Bergis. Artwork was conceived by DARK TRANQUILLITY guitarist Niklas Sundin. Following these sessions Olle Sundfeldt was recruited on bass and drummer George Kollias was superseded by Markus Engström, a scene veteran of ... AND SHE DIED, BLOODWRATH, CHAOS LEGION, DEADLY NIGHTSHADE, SOLAR DAWN, THORON and WAR ENSEMBLE.

Belgian label Mausoleum Records issued the 'Escape' album in December 2006. SYSTEM SHOCK drafted new drummer Kim Gustavsson, also drummer for DEVIANT BREED and guitar player in BETWEEN MIND.

ARCTIC INSIDE, Karmageddon Media KARMA050 (2004). Devilwish / Orbital / Fading Star / Moonlight / Cult Of Orion / Safe Inside / Bleed It Off / Arctic Circle.

ESCAPE, Mausoleum (2006). Getting What We Asked For / Escape / Engine Failure / No Life, No Home / Broken In Two / A Note And A Gun / Bleed / Mountains Of Madness / Salvation In Stone.

SYSTEM:OBSCURE

OSLO, NORWAY — *Balfori (vocals), Steinar Gundersen (guitar), Lars Norberg (bass), Bugge Wesseltoft (Hammond organ), Tony Laureano (drums).*

Oslo's SYSTEM:OBSCURE, described as "savagely innovative" Black Metal, was formulated during 2005 and involves a cast of seasoned extreme Metal veterans. Vocals are handled by Balfori (a.k.a. (Lars Larsen) of LUNARIS, ALVHEIM and 1349, guitar from Steinar Gundersen of SPIRAL ARCHITECT and SATYRICON, fretless bass from Lars Norberg of SPIRAL ARCHITECT, ANESTHESIA and SATYRICON, Hammond organ by Bugge Wesseltoft with the NILE, ACHERON, AURORA BOREALIS, GOD DETHRONED, MALEVOLENT CREATION, DIMMU BORGIR and ANGEL CORPSE credited Tony Laureano on drums. A three song demo preceded album recordings in early 2007.

System:Obscure, System:Obscure (2006) (Demo).

SÉANCE

LINKÖPING, SWEDEN — *Johan Larsson (vocals), Patrick Jensen (guitar), Tony Kampner (guitar), Bino (bass), Mique Flesh (drums).*

SÉANCE came into being from an amalgamation of two Linköping acts ORCHRISTE, featuring singer Johan Larsson and guitarist Patrick Jensen having released the 1989 demo 'Necromonicon', and TOTAL DEATH in 1990, the band name SÉANCE coming from an ORCHRISTE song title. December 1990 saw the first SÉANCE gig, with the Swedes playing alongside MERCILESS and TOXAEMIA. A second concert was conducted as support for DISHARMONIC ORCHESTRA.

The group's first demo, 'Levitised Spirit', was released in August 1991and gained the band a deal with Black Mark Records. After the release of the 1992 'Fornever Laid To Rest' album, recorded at Berno Studio in Malmö with producer Berno Paulsson, bassist Bino (Christian Karlsson) lost his place to ex-MORGUE man Rickard Limfeldt. Second album 'Saltrubbed Eyes', again crafted at Berno Studio with Berno Paulsson behind the desk, followed for Black Mark in 1993. In 1996 the band contributed their version of 'Post Mortem' to the SLAYER tribute album 'Slatanic Slaughter I'.

Both Patrick Jensen and Bino relocated to Gothenburg during 1997, intending to form a new act with AT THE GATES man Adrian Erlandsson, leaving Johan Larsson, Tony Kampner and Mique Flesh to continue on as SÉANCE. The band intended on recording a fresh album for Necropolis Records but this never eventuated. When the group dissolved, various members founded trad Metal act WITCHERY. As well as WITCHERY, drummer Mique Flesh, vocalist Toxine (a.k.a. Tony Kampner) and guitarists Patrick Jensen and Richard also performed in SATANIC SLAUGHTER. Jensen subsequently formed THE HAUNTED with former AT THE GATES personnel. Karlsson went on to join DIABOLIQUE. Mique Flesh forged FREEVIL during 2006.

Levitised Spirit, Séance (1991) (Cassette demo). Haunted / Reincarnage / Blood Of The Gates / The Blessing Of Death / Sin.

FORNEVER LAID TO REST, Black Mark Production BMCD 17 (1992). Who Will Not Be Dead / Reincarnage / Blessing Of Death / Sin / Haunted / Forever Laid To Rest / Necromonicon / Wind Of Gehenna / Inferna Cabbala.

SALTRUBBED EYES, Black Mark Production BMCD 44 (1994). Soulerosion / 13th Moon / Saltrubbed Eyes / Controlled Bleeding / Angelmeat (Part II) / Til Death Do Us Join / Sanctum / Skinless / Hidden Under Scars.

TAKETH

SWEDEN — *David Dahl (vocals), Mikael Lindqvist (guitar), Lars Walfridsson (bass), Johan Dahl (drums).*

Originally named PERGANON by founders guitarist Mikael Lindqvist and vocalist David Dahl this Death Metal act from Sweden originally wrote the first few songs on acoustic guitars while the two of them were in the army. Once out of military service bassist Martin and drummer Johan Dahl were added to the ranks. The new band cut a three track demo was recorded with the songs 'Betrayed', 'Game of Nothingness' and 'Edge of Desperation' in November 2000. In 2001 the band went search for a rhythm guitarist to let David, who was playing guitar in conjunction with his vocals, more time to focus on the vocals.

Thus Tobias joined as the second guitarist. Later that spring a new demo was recorded but later that year the band decided to take a break. 2002 saw the band reform under new name TAKETH with Jonas Karlsson replacing Martin on bass and Emil Karlsson replacing Tobias with the guitar duties. In 2003 both Jonas Karlsson and Emil Karlsson joined ADMONISH. Lars Walfridsson took over on bass.

His Majesty, Taketh (2002) (Demo). Thorns / Soothing Prescence / Betrayed / Saved By Grace.

Live Demo, Taketh (2003) (Demo). Can You See Me Now? / Soothing Prescence / Hide / Sic Transit Gloria Mundi / Du Är.

FREAKSHOW, Fear Dark FD 021 (2005). Welcome / Evil / Ignore / Not Quite Right / Consequence (Of Abusing Human Weakness) / Silence / Freakshow / Paths And Crossroads / Högmod / Your Master / Mind Numbing Crap / Past The Horizon / Bring Me Water / A New Day.

TENEBRARUM

COLOMBIA — *Juan Carlo Henao (vocals), David Rivera (guitar / violin), Julián Rivera (bass), David Guerrero (drums).*

Taking their title from a song of the same name from the Italian band NECRODEATH Medellín Death Metal act TENEBRARUM was founded in 1989, assembled initially by guitarist David Rivera alongside Juan Alvear and Esteban Rivera. However, by 1990 both Juan Alvear and Esteban Rivera had decamped, replaced by , Mauricio Montoya and vocalist Mario Aponte. In March of 1992 TENEBRARUM was completely reconstituted as David Rivera recruited a brand new line up comprising vocalist César Restrepo, bass player Walter Tamayo and Daniel Builes on the drums. This unit issued the demo 'Visiones Del Horror' but by November of that year Restrepo had exited and Mario Aponte re-appointed as singer. In addition Dora Vélez was introduced on female vocals.

The album 'El Vuelo De Las Almas' emerged in 1994 after which Juan Carlos Henao was appointed on guitar. The 1996 outing 'Sol Negro' comprises the debut album tracks, archive demo and live material. That year Builes exited and Andres Meza took up the vacancy. Further line up shuffles witnessed the departure of Aponte. TENEBRARUM used this opportunity to manoeuvre away from Aponte's high pitched Black Metal vocal stylings and introduced the baritone voice of Cesar Vasquez for lead vocals with Juan Carlos Henao adding to this with Death growls. In this incarnation the band recorded the 'Divine War' album, issued in August of 1997.

The fluidity in the ranks continued unabated and 1998 signalled the decampment of both Meza and Tamayo. A fresh rhythm section of bassist Julian Rivera and Jorge Mejia was duly installed. However, after a live performance at the 'Rock Al Parque' festival to over 50,000 Rock fans Cesar decided to go, necessitating Henao taking onboard all vocal duties.

TENEBRARUM signed to the Transylvania Music label in 2000, marking their ten year anniversary with an album entitled 'X', this affair incorporating six re-recorded older songs and two new tracks. David Guerrero supplanted Mejia in January of 2001 for the 'Voices' album, this record ambitiously finding the band employing a full chamber orchestra and female backing vocals to good effect.

EL VUELO DE LAS ALMAS, Voodoo VDR002 (1994).

BLOOD AND TEARS, Voodoo VDR002 (1995).

SOL NEGRO, Voodoo VDR003 (1996).

X, Transylvania Music TM003LP (2000).

VOICES, Voodoo VDR005 (2001). Intro / Search / Voices / Rites / Traveller / Battle / Sadness / Visions / Tears / Enlightenment / End.

DIVINE WAR, Voodoo VDR006 (2002).

TERROR

SWEDEN — *Jon Nödtveidt (vocals), Anders Björler (guitar), Jonas Björler (bass), Adrian Erlandsson (drums).*

A short-lived act that manifested itself in 1995. Although boasting an enviable tradition of AT THE GATES and DISSECTION, after a solitary demo, recorded at Studio Fredman in Gothenburg, TERROR folded. Joining the AT THE GATES triumvirate of guitarist Anders Björler, bass player Jonas Björler, both also ex-INFESTATION personnel, and drummer Adrian Erlandsson would be the notorious DISSECTION and THE BLACK frontman Jon Nödtveidt. Both AT THE GATES and DISSECTION shared rehearsal space from 1993 onwards when had Nödtveidt relocated his band to Gothenburg from Strömstad.

Nödtveidt also connections with a myriad of Swedish extreme Metal ventures such as SIREN'S YELL, NECROPHOBIC, DE INFERNALI, NIFELHEIM, SATANIZED and OPHTHALAMIA. In early 1998 Nödtveidt was arrested on suspicion of the murder of an Algerian homosexual. Nödtveit would ultimately be imprisoned for the crime.

Post AT THE GATES, the Björler siblings and Erlandson were to be found with a further high profile act THE HAUNTED. Erlandsson later found prominence with CRADLE OF FILTH.

Jon Nödtveidt closed his career in a manner befitting his philosophies, committing suicide in August. DISSECTION band members released a statement claiming "he was more focussed, happier and stronger than ever" and "he chose to end his life by his own hands. As a true Satanist he led his life in the way he wanted and ended it when he felt that he had fulfilled his self-created destiny".

Nödtveidt, 31 years old, was found dead at his apartment in Hässelby, a suburb of Stockholm, on August 16th. Newspapers reported he had surrounded himself by candles and had a copy of Anton La Vey's 'The Satanic Bible'. Nödtveidt had ended his life with a shot to the head. Shortly beforehand he had told friends he was "going to Transylvania".

Terror, Terror (1995) (Demo). Radiation / Destruction / Terror.

TERRORIZER

LOS ANGELES, CA, USA — *Oscar Garcia (vocals), Jesse Pintado (guitar), David Vincent (drums), Pete Sandoval (drums).*

An illustrious name on the extreme Metal underground circuit, TERRORIZER's original life span would be short, sharp and utterly brutal and, if not for the philanthropic nature of an influential fan, NAPALM DEATH's Shane Embury, nearly lost to obscurity. Los Angeles based TERRORIZER comprised the NAUSEA pairing of singer Oscar Garcia and guitarist Jesse Pintado, subsequently of NAPALM DEATH repute, alongside bassist Alfred 'Garvey' Estrada and MORBID ANGEL drummer Pete Sandoval.

TERRORIZER had reputedly taken their name from the MASTER song of the same title, often performing MASTER's 'Funeral Bitch' at live shows. The band had actually gone its separate ways before Earache Records requested the 'World Downfall' album, released in November 1989 at the insistence of Shane Embury. For these sessions MORBID ANGEL's David Vincent stood in on bass, all cut within a marathon eight hours.

Polish Deathsters VADER covered TERRORIZER's 'Fear Of Napalm' and 'Storm Of Stress' on their 1996 'Future Of The Past' album. New York's EXIT 13 also rendered 'Storm Of Stress' that same year.

Pintado's induction into NAPALM DEATH signalled the end for the band although there would be persistent rumours of a TERRORIZER reformation. By 2003 both Oscar Garcia Alfred Estrada were fronting NAUSEA

TERRORIZER finally relented in late 2005 and succumbed to a reunion and swiftly signing to Century Media Records. Joining guitarist Jesse Pintado and drummer Pete Sandoval in the

TERRORIZER

new roster would be RESISTANT CULTURE vocalist Tony Militia (a.k.a. Anthony Rezhawk) and the ETERNAL, MORBID ANGEL and MONSTROSITY credited guitarist Tony Norman. Comeback album 'Darker Days Ahead', recorded at Juan "Punchy" Gonzalez' Diet of Worms Studios, emerged in August 2006.

Sad news emerged on August 27th with the passing of band member Jesse Pintado. The guitarist had died from liver failure at the Erasmus MC hospital in Holland.

Nightmares, Terrorizer (1987) (Demo). Nightmares / Benedictions / Mayhem / Terror / Crematorium / The Dead Shall Rise.

Terrorizer, Terrorizer (1988) (Demo). Ripped To Shreds / Corporation Pull-In / After World Obliteration / Human Prey / Strategic Warheads / Fallout / Infestation.

WORLD DOWNFALL, Earache MOSH 16 (1989). World Obliteration / Fear Of Napalm / Corporation Pull In / Resurrection / Need To Live / Dead Shall Rise / Injustice / Storm Of Stress / Human Prey / Condemned System / Enslaved By Propaganda / Whirlwind Struggle / World Downfall / Ripped To Shreds.

DARKER DAYS AHEAD, Century Media (2006). Inevitable / Darker Days Ahead / Crematorium / Fallout / Doomed Forever / Mayhem / Blind Army / Nightmare / Legacy Of Brutality / Dead Shall Rise '06 / Victim Of Greed / Ghost Train.

TEXTURES

TILBURG, HOLLAND — *Pieter Verpaalen (vocals), Jochem Jacobs (vocals / guitar), Bart Hennephof (guitar), Dennis Aarts (bass), Richard Rietdijk (keyboards), Stef Broks (drums).*

Tilburg based progressive Death Metal act established in 2001 by members of EMPTY, frontman Rom De Leeuw, bassist Dennis Aarts and drummer Stef Broks. TEXTURES debuted for Listenable Records with the 2003 album 'Polars'. The TEXTURES credited guitarist 'Bastærd' also operates fellow Death Metal act BRUTUS. After signing a recording deal with the French based Listenable Records TEXTURES parted ways with singer Pieter Verpaalen in January 2004, replacing him with ex-BRAINSHAKE man Eric Kalsbeek.

High profile gigs in June included an appearance at the French 'Fury' festival and notable supports to MESHUGGAH, MORBID ANGEL and THE DILLINGER ESCAPE PLAN. Gaining further exposure, the band would win the coveted Essent Award for 'most promising act'. Not only did this benefit the band by way of a major promotional push but also granted them inclusion on the billing at the Netherlands' largest festival, 'Lowlands', in August. However, bassist Dennis Aarts would be diagnosed with pneumothorax that same month and, being hospitalised, would relinquish his position to IN-TENSION's Robin Zielhorst to complete the shows. Further touring across Europe in October had the band allied with Australians ALCHEMIST.

In early 2005 Eric Kalsbeek forged a new Hardcore venture billed SENGAIA in collaboration with 37 STABWOUNDZ member drummer Roy Moonen. In April the band signed to Garden Of Exile Records for the 'Maelstrom' EP. TEXTURES marked a return in 2006 with the full-length album 'Drawing Corcles, delivered through Listenable Records. The band hooked up with TWIN ZERO for UK dates in July. TEXTURES supported ARCH ENEMY in Europe during December.

In January 2007 Jochem Jacobs acted as co-producer on album recordings for Utrecht's DETONATION. European concerts, kicking off on March 29th at the Magnet Club in Berlin, Germany witnessed a package deal with MISERY SIGNALS and ALL THAT REMAINS. For UK dates ETERNAL LORD were added to the billing.

POLARS, Listenable POSH058 (2003). Swandive / Ostensibly Impregnable / Young Man / Transgression / The Barrier / Effluent / Polars / Heave.

DRAWING CIRCLES, Listenable (2006). Drive / Regenesis / Denying Gravity / Illumination / Stream Of Consciousness / Upwards / Circular / Millstone / Touching The Absolute / Surreal State Of Enlightenment.

THALES

HELSINKI, FINLAND — *Karri Suoraniemi (vocals), Lasse Kristiansen (guitar), Jani Mikkonen (guitar), Juha Tretjakov (bass), Juuso Backman (drums).*

Progressive, Melodic Death Metal from Helsinki. THALES came together during 2001 when long term friends Juuso Backman, Jani Mikkonen and Lasse Kristiansen, all guitarists initially, decided upon forming a band. In order to start building this unit Backman switched to the drums and a bassist, Juha Tretjakov, was found by advertising on the web. A purely instrumental demo, '2001's 'A World Beyond', was recorded before Mika Kantola completed the band on vocals. Following rehearsals in Hernesaari this latest candidate drifted away.

THALES pulled in FARMAKON's Marko Eskola for their first recordings but his priorities soon forced him out of the band. A further advert found Karri Suoraniemi. The band put in their inaugural live show on 26th November 2004 at the Factory in Helsinki sharing the stage with CANTATA SANGUI. Bass player Juha Tretjakov also acts as frontman for DEADLIGHT.

A World Beyond, Thales (2001) (Instrumental demo). Solace / Desolation / Pellucid Lake / A World Beyond.

Promo 2003, Thales (2003) (Demo). Eerie Presence / Defective.

Ad Mortis Infinitvm, Thales (2004) (Demo). Ad Mortis Infinitum / Make-Believe Logic.

THANATOS

ROTTERDAM, HOLLAND — *Stephen Gebédí (vocals / guitar), Paul Baayens (guitar), Marco de Bruin (bass), Yuri Rinkel (drums).*

Rotterdam Thrash band THANATOS tend to stand out from the crowd with some inventive songs. THANATOS actually lay claim to being Holland's first Death Metal act having formed in 1984 with a line up of Stephen Gebédí, guitarist Remco De Maaijer and drummer Marcel Van Arnhem. This version of the band released the 'Speed Kills' demo prior to folding in 1985.

Gebédí reformed THANATOS for another demo session entitled 'Rebirth'. Van Arnhem returned along with new bass player André Scherpenberg. Rob De Bruijn would take over the drum stool but departed soon after. Another new recruit in 1987 was former SECOND HELL guitarist Mark Staffhorst.

Scherpenberg quit to join VIGILANT necessitating KILLER FORCE guitarist Erwin De Brouwer to handle bass guitar. However, soon De Brouwer would shift to guitar as Ed Boeser of KILLING ELEVATOR maneuvered into the bassist's job.

The group issued a 1987 demo entitled 'The Day Before Tomorrow', notable for featuring the live track 'Progressive Destructor' and followed this with a 1989 tape 'Omnicoitor'. Following their album for Shark Records, 'Emerging From The Netherworlds' produced by Ulli Pössel, they released another demo in 1991 featuring five tracks before Shark came up with a second record, the Pössel produced 'Realms Of Ecstasy', in 1992. Despite having two albums in the stores THANATOS were far from happy with their label and were vocal in their vehemence. Naturally the two parties went their separate ways.

THANATOS split with Gebédê and De Brouwer created CHURCH OF INDULGENCE in allegiance with bassist Peter Van Wees and drummer Dirk Bruinenberg. This band ground to a halt as De Brouwer united with ex-THANATOS man Ed Boeser in the alternative Rock act SMALLTOWN and Van Wees joined INCOMING. Bruinenberg would ally himself with the high profile act ELEGY.

THANATOS returned in 1999 with ex-CREMATION guitarist Paul Baayens, SINISTER and HOUWITSER drummer Aad Kloosterwaard along with HOUWITSER and JUDGEMENT DAY bassist Theo Van Eekelen in the ranks for the 'Angelic Encounters' album, recorded at Excess Studios, Rotterdam. A limited edition digipack included the bonus track 'Corpse Grinder'. That same year the Hammerheart label re-issued both 'Emerging From The Netherworlds' and 'Realms Of Ecstasy' complete with extra tracks.

A 2002 mini album 'Beyond Terror' included a cover of CELTIC FROST's 'Into The Crypt Of Rays'. For these recordings the rhythm section was now occupied by bassist Marco de Bruin and drummer Yuri Rinkel, the latter also known as 'Y. Xul' of Black Metal outfits FUNERAL WINDS, LIAR OF GOLGOTHA and INFERI. Rinkel also operates ABODE OF THE BLESSED. 'Beyond Terror' comprised two sets of recordings with tracks laid down at Dynamo Studio in Rotterdam during January of 2002 plus a ten hour session at Capture Sound Studios in June.

THANATOS signed to the Greek Black Lotus Records in mid 2003 for recording of the album 'Undead.Unholy.Divine'. This outing, recorded at Excess studios in Rotterdam and co-produced by the band and Hans Pieters, would be mixed by world renowned Metal producer Attie Bauw and featured former GOREFEST man Ed Warby and MELECHESH's Ashmedi on backing vocals.

During May of 2004, Yinkel deputised with Mesopotamian Black Metal band MELECHESH for live dates. THANATOS announced they were to record two new tracks at Excess Studios in Rotterdam in late June 2005, a brand new version of 'And Jesus Wept', from 1992's 'Realm Of Ecstasy' and a cover of DARK ANGEL's 'The Burning Of Sodom'. It would also be reported that frontman Stephan Gebédi was "facing a serious affection of the nerves in his wrist and his neck", delaying album recordings.

THANATOS finally entered Excess Studios in Rotterdam on 23rd February 2006 to begin recording their fifth full-length album, giving a tentative title of 'Justified Genocide'. Unfortunately mid way through these sessions the band's label, Black Lotus Records, ceased operations. In January 2007 it would be learned that THANATOS guitarists Stephan Gebédi and Paul Baayens had joined forces with former PESTILENCE and ASPHYX singer Martin Van Drunen, GOREFEST drummer Ed Warby and former HOUWITSER bass player Theo van Eekelen in a new band unit dubbed HAIL OF BULLETS.

EMERGING FROM THE NETHERWORLDS, Shark 015 (1990). Dawn Of The Dead / Outward Of The Inward / Bodily Dismemberment / Infernal Deceit / The Day Before Tomorrow / War / Rebirth / Progressive Destructor / Imposters Infiltration / Omnicoitor / Dolor Satanae.

THANATOS (pic: Simone Penners)

REALMS OF ECSTASY, Shark 025 (1992). Intro—And Jesus Wept / Tied Up Sliced Up / Realm Of Ecstasy / Mankind's Afterbirth / In Praise Of Lust / Perpetual Misery / Human Combustion / Reincarnation / Terminal Breath.

ANGELIC ENCOUNTERS, Hammerheart 7202000152 (2000). Angelic Encounters / In Utter Darkness / Sincere Chainsaw Salvation / Infuriated / The Howling / Gods Of War / The Devil's Concubine / Speed Kills / Thou Shalt Rot / Corpsegrinder.

BEYOND TERROR, Baphomet BAPH112 (2002). Beyond Terror / Devour The Living / Rites Of Retaliation / Angelic Encounters / Satan's Curse / Into The Crypt Of Rays.

UNDEAD.UNHOLY.DIVINE., Black Lotus BLRCD063 (2004). Lambs To The Slaughter / Undead.Unholy.Divine. / Eraser / Beyond Terror / The Sign Of Sadako / Servants Of Hatred / Devour The Living / Godforsaken / The Suffering / The Sweet Suffering.

The Burning Of Sodom, Konqueror KR 008 EP (2006). The Burning Of Sodom / And Jesus Wept.

THAT OLD BLACK MAGIC

GRENOBLE, FRANCE — *Vader Moloch (vocals / guitar), Zarrach Baal Taag (guitar), S. Crumb (bass), Chris (drums).*

Grenoble Death Metal combo THAT OLD BLACK MAGIC, created in September 1997, started as initially a solo project of the CEREMONIA, DREAMERS, CARBOLIC BLOOD, SPIRITUAL DEATH and VORACIOUS GOD credited Vader Moloch. An opening seven track demo, 'Reborn In Sacrifice', arrived in September 1998. Expanding to a full band unit, guitarist Zarrach Baal Taag, of WHORE HUNT and WHISKEY OF BLOOD, joined the project in November 1999 and S. Crumb, of EMBERS, TYDIRIUM and DARK AGE repute, took on bass duties that December. This trio cut a second demo, billed '... Perverted Mind', in April of 2000. The position of drummer was filled by Hell Bathorr (Thierry Pujos) in October and in January 2001 a third session, 'Tormentor' featuring a live version of BLACK SABBATH's anthem 'Black Sabbath', arrived.

A 2004 EP would include a cover version of DEPECHE MODE's 'Enjoy The Silence'. The album 'Join The Madness', complete with disturbing artwork by famous photographer Gottfried Helnwein, was delivered in 2003. Hell Bathorr departed in April 2005, replaced by ex-STRIKEBACK man Chris.

Reborn In Sacrifice, (1999). Reborn In Sacrifice / Nergal / Sadistic Breath / The Wake Of Hate / The Final Quest / Damnation Gates / Legend Of The Black Sword.

... Perverted Mind, (2000). Sadism Way / Dual Spirit / Kahos / Gates / Cenobite / Staring Through The Eyes Of Blood.

Tormentor, (2001). Sexct / Tormentor / Green Creeping Filth / Tormentor (Live) / Black Sabbath (Live) / Staring Through The Eyes Of Blood (Live).

JOIN THE MADNESS, That Old Black Magic (2003). Warriors Of God / Death Is Not Dead / Last Ones / Forever / Screams In Paradise / Incarnation Divine / Obsession.

THE ABSENCE

TAMPA, FL, USA — *Jamie Stewart (vocals), Patrick Pintavalle (guitar), Peter Joseph (guitar), Nicholas Calaci (bass), Jeramie Kling (drums).*

Tampa, Florida Metal band THE ABSENCE was forged during 2001 by vocalist Jamie Stewart and guitarist Patrick Pintavalle. The opening formation included CUMSHOTTE's Justin Grant on drums, then Christopher Tolan on second guitar. The band's inaugural live performance came in the Autumn of 2002 as opening act for Atlanta's MASTODON. The following Spring Stewart and Pintavalle worked with second guitarist Peter Joseph and drummer Jeramie Kling on an intended side project. However, this unit gelled so well that, following line-up tribulation after a gig with SIX FEET UNDER, the two musicians were inducted into THE ABSENCE. Less than a month later the group was rounding out with bassist Nicholas Calaci.

An intensive local schedule would find the band sharing stages with the likes of CANNIBAL CORPSE, IMMOLATION, GRAVE, SIX FEET UNDER, YNGWIE MALMSTEEN, NAPALM DEATH, SUPERJOINT RITUAL, DARK TRANQUILLITY, GEORGE LYNCH, UNEARTH, NILE and STRAPPING YOUNG LAD. In February of 2004 the band entered the fabled Morrisound Studios to craft a three track EP.

THE ABSENCE recorded their debut album 'From Your Grave' at Manna Studios in April 2005 with HATE ETERNAL's Erik Rutan acting as producer. In October the band formed a touring union dubbed "Metal Blade Records Young Guns Tour" with THE CLASSIC STRUGGLE and LOSA. The band was included the 'Metal Crusaders' North American tour, set to take place in May and June 2006 alongside KATAKLYSM, GRAVEWORM, NUCLEAR ASSAULT, SPEED\KILL/HATE and VADER. The group was then set to unite with Swedish veterans DISMEMBER, GRAVE plus ENTOMBED for a US West Coast tour in December. However, the band withdrew citing "several unresolved problems with our booking agent".

In early 2007 THE ABSENCE set 'Riders Of The Plague' as the title of its sophomore album. The record featured guest appearances by guitarists JAMES MURPHY, of DEATH, CANCER and TESTAMENT, Jonas Kjellgren and Per Nilsson, from SCAR SYMMETRY, Santiago Dobles, of AGHORA, as well as guest vocals by Jonas Granvik, of WITHOUT GRIEF and EDGE OF SANITY.

FROM YOUR GRAVE, Metal Blade (2005). Intro / A Breath Beneath / Necropolis / From Your Grave / Heaven Ablaze / Summoning The Darkness / Shattered / I, Deceiver / My Ruin / Seven Demons.
RIDERS OF THE PLAGUE, (2007).

THE ABYSS

STOCKHOLM, SWEDEN — *Mikael Hedlund (vocals / guitar), Lars Szöke (guitar), Peter Tägtgren (bass / drums).*

THE ABYSS is the Stockholm side project of HYPOCRISY members Peter Tägtgren, Mikael Hedlund and Lars Szöke, the latter also having been a member of EPITAPH and, alongside Tägtgren, CONQUEST. For this band the musicians switched roles from their more familiar responsibilities, Peter Tägtgren moving to drums and drummer Lars Szöke and bassist Mikael Hedlund both playing guitars. The March 1995 album 'The Other Side', released by German label Nuclear Blast, features a version of HELLHAMMER's 'Massacra' track. 'Summon The Beast' followed in November 1996.

Bassist / drummer Tägtgren still fronts the ever more successful HYPOCRISY. In addition he would become a member of ALGAION, LOCK UP and issues highly successful solo projects as PAIN.

THE OTHER SIDE, Nuclear Blast NB 0126-2 (1995). Marutukku / Tjänare Af Besten / Psycomantum / Massacra / Mörkrets Vandring / Sorgens Dal / Slukad / Förintelsens Tid Äro Kommen.

THE ABSENCE (pic: Jesse Angelo)

SUMMON THE BEAST, Nuclear Blast NB 0209-2 (1996). Satan's Majestic Empire / Blessed With The Wrath Of Evil / Damned / Summon The Beast / The Hymn / Cursed / Feasting The Remains Of Heaven / The Arrival.

THE ACCURSED

NEW BEDFORD, MA, USA — *Jonathan Helme (vocals), Loki (guitar), Timothy Giblin (guitar), George Pacheco (bass), Chris Helme (drums).*

New Bedford, Massachusetts based THE ACCURSED credit themselves as vocalist Jonathan Helme "Throat & Arson", guitarists Loki "Six string slaughter" and Timothy Giblin "Axes and razorblades", bassist George Pacheco "Bassassination" and drummer Chris Helme "Battery". The 2002 'Straight From Hell' demo, recorded in The Syrofoam Room by BEYOND THE EMBRACE's Oscar Gouviea and which included a cover of DEATH's 'The Philosopher', featured guitar work from Chris Fitzgerald.

THE ACCURSED signed to Screaming Ferret Records for a full-length album 'Seasons Of The Scythe'. Promotional copies of the album added four cover versions in HELLOWEEN's 'I Want Out', IRON MAIDEN's 'Wasted Years', METALLICA's 'Jump In The Fire' and CARCASS' 'Heartwork'.

Guitarist Chris Ellingsen returned to the fold in April 2006. 'Seasons Of The Scythe' arrived on Halloween 2006.

THE ACCURSED (pic: Bruce Bettis)

Straight To Hell, The Accursed (2002). To Live On Borrowed Time / The Black Thrash / Aftermath Of Sorrow / World's Divide / Autumn's Twilight / The Philosopher / Maniacal Menace (Straight To Hell) / The Final Farewell.

SEASONS OF THE SCYTHE, Screaming Ferret (2006). Deities And Demigods / Sawtoothsmile / Seasons Of The Scythe / Fire Of 1000 Cries / I Am Famine / Aftermath Of Sorrow / The Rider / Land Of The Dead / Slaughter Of The Gods / Cold Is The Grave / Funeral March / The Black Thrash / Armageddon Eulogy.

THE AGONY SCENE

TULSA, OK, USA — *Michael Williams (vocals), Johnny Lloyd (guitar), Chris Emmons (guitar), Matthew Shannon (bass), Brent Masters (drums).*

Tulsa Metalcore outfit THE AGONY SCENE had their 2003 Solid State Records eponymous release produced by KILLSWITCH ENGAGE's Adam Dutkiewicz. Touring saw dates with DEMON HUNTER, AS I LAY DYING and BELOVED, followed by the 'Van's Off The Wall' tour allied with AVENGED SEVENFOLD and the SUICIDE MACHINES. THE AGONY SCENE signed to Roadrunner Records in May of 2004.

The band formed up a package billing comprising IF HOPE DIES, FEAR BEFORE THE MARCH OF FLAMES and ZAO for US tour dates in January 2005. They joined the Roadrunner 'Roadrage' tour with TRIVIUM, 3 INCHES OF BLOOD, STILL REMAINS in March. AGONY SCENE teamed up with the STRAPPING YOUNG LAD headlined US and Canadian dates throughout April and May, partnering with REFLUX and MISERY SIGNALS. Live work extended throughout the mid-year period in an alliance with SCARS OF TOMORROW, HIMSA and THE ESOTERIC on the 'Dirty Black Summer' trek. The band joined forces with the DANZIG headlined 'Blackest of the Black' US dates commencing in September, these shows accompanied by CHIMAIRA, BEHEMOTH, HIMSA and MORTIIS, prior to engaging in a November run alongside NODES OF RANVIER, SCARLET and BECOMING THE ARCHETYPE. Maintaining their road ethic, UK gigs in December saw a strong package billing allied with LAMB OF GOD and DEVILDRIVER.

The band's relentless live campaigning continued unabated into 2006 as they forged a road union in North America throughout March with THROWDOWN, THE BLACK DAHLIA MURDER and THE RED CHORD.

The band parted ways with drummer Brent Masters in June. In March 2007 the group entered the studio with producer Andreas Magnusson to cut their first album for Abacus Recordings,

THE AGONY SCENE, Solid State (2003). We Bury Our Dead At Dawn / Habeas Corpus / Judas / Lines Of Suicide / Eyes Sewn Shut / Nausea / Shotgun Wedding / Vivid / Paint It Black / The Damned.

THE DARKEST RED, Roadrunner (2005). Prelude / Darkest Red / Scars Of Your Disease / Screams Turn Into Silence / Sacrifice / Prey / Procession / Suffer / My Dark Desire / Scapegoat / Forever Abandoned.

THE AGONY SCENE

THE APPARATUS

NORWAY — *Vegard Harkjerr (vocals), Ketil Sæther (guitar), Øystein Iversen (guitar), Sondre Øien (bass), Per Spjøtvold (keyboards).*

Melodic Death Metal band THE APPARATUS was created during 1999, the opening formation, founded by guitarists Øystein Iversen and Ketil Sæther, member of LUMSK and ex-of AD INFEROS, alongside ATROX keyboard player Per Spjøtvold being joined by drummer Kim Sætre then Sondre Øien on of LUMSK, TIMBER FALLS and AD INFEROS bass guitar and lead vocalist Lars Klingenberg. The group would debut with an Autumn 2000 demo entitled 'We Crawl To Nothing'. Subsequently, Vegard Harkjerr of PREDATOR and ANTARES took over the vocal role for the 'Lost: Crossed' session, recorded in early 2002 in three days at Skansen Lydstudio in Trondheim.

During 2002 Ketil Sæther and Per Spjøtvold activated Grind side project GOAT THE HEAD in alliance with LUMSK and TIMBER FALLS man Espen. Meantime, THE APPARATUS had their track 'The Revelation' featured on the compilation album 'The Metal Underground Vol.1'. In September Sæther exited, the band enlisting Rune Holm of THE EMBRACED as substitute. However, Sæther returned in April of 2003.

On 30th January THE APPARATUS, as support to KEEP OF KALESSIN at Blæst in Trondheim, performed their last concert with Kim Sætre, the former drummer opting out to prioritise his Progressive Rock act TIMBER FALLS. THE APPARATUS 2004 debut album 'Heathen Agenda', released by the UK based Dreamcatcher label in early 2005, was recorded at Godt Selskap Studio in Trondheim. An outtake track, 'All Is Nothing', would be utilised for use on a compilation album.

THE APPARATUS parted ways with co-founding member and songwriter Øystein Iversen due to "irreconcilable differences" in September.

We Crawl To Nothing—Demo 2001, The Apparatus (2001) (Demo). New Existence / All Is Nothing / When I Saw The Final Sight / Divine Decay.

Lost : Crossed, The Apparatus (2002) (Demo). Prologue / The Revelation / Worms / Lost : Crossed / Thanatos.

Promo, The Apparatus (2003) (Demo). Otherplace / Revelation / Worms.

HEATHEN AGENDA, Dreamcatcher CRIDE 062 (2004). Other Place / Thanatos / Travesty / Emotional Abduction / Ballistic Bleach / Lost: Crossed / The Revelation / Guidance / Worms.

THE BEAUTY OF DYING

HÄMEENLINNA, FINLAND — *Pasi Lehtinen (vocals), Marko Saarinen (guitar), Teemu Raunio (guitar), Marcus Moberg (bass), Janne Honkanen (drums).*

Hämeenlinna Death / Thrash act, mentored by 20/20 VISION, SHARPEVILLE and AGUSTA BELLS guitarist Marko Saarinen, starting out under a formative title of THE BEAUTY OF DYING. During 2000 the band was built up with the incorporation of singer Pasi Lehtinen, BLASHEMIA, JALOSTAMO and ARCADIAN drummer Janne "Homicide" Honkanen with the SHARPEVILLE credited Marcus Moberg on bass. Some six months later Teemu Raunio, of WITHERED GARDEN, was added on second guitar.

In September of 2001 THE BEAUTY OF DYING cut their debut, three song demo 'First Kill'. Their inaugural concert would be held at the Lahti 'Hellbound 3' event on 8th March 2002 sharing the stage with MUSTAN KUUN LAPSET, BEFORE THE DAWN, GLORIA MORTI, NOWEN and FUNERIS NOCTURNUM. Following this gig the band, drafting Jussi Leppänen to replace Raunio, adopted the DEAD SAMARITAN title. A promotional session entitled 'Dark Matter' was laid down in January of 2003. The demo 'Bone Hill Revelation', limited to 200 copies, was issued in July 2004.

First Kill, The Beauty Of Dying (2001) (Demo). Under Fire / First Kill / Point Blank Range.

THE BEREAVED

ÅSBRO, SWEDEN — *Jonny Westerback (vocals / guitar), Henrik Tranemyr (guitar), Mikael Nilsson (bass), Tony Thorén (keyboards), Tobhias Ljung (drums).*

Åsbro melodic Death Metal band THE BEREAVED started out under the title CLONE, coming together during 1998, the product of bassist Mikael Nilsson and JONNY WONG guitarist Henrik Tranemyr's desire to create a new Metal band. Before long the founding duo was joined by singer Jonny Westerback and second guitarist Tonka. JONNY WONG Tobhias Ljung stood in for the initial sessions. By November of 1999 Jimmy Johansson had assumed the lead vocal mantle. CLONE did not enjoy much luck during 2000, recording a demo, which the band judged unfit to release, and recording a version of 'Welcome To Dying' for a BLIND GUARDIAN tribute album. This latter session was also deemed not up to par and the group unsurprisingly parted ways with Johansson as Westerback and Ljung took over the vocal duties.

The band pulled in singer Mikael Reini and a second stab at cutting a demo gave more favourable results. During June of that year the band learned of the death of their original singer Jimmy Johansson, the former frontman dying peacefully in his sleep in Spain. CLONE, despite dispensing with Reini, issued the November 2002 demo 'Inverted Icons', produced by DIONYSUS drummer Ronny Milianowicz.

The band subsequently switched title to THE BEREAVED, issuing the album 'Darkened Silhouette' in 2004 through Greek label Black Lotus Records.

DARKENED SILHOUETTE, Black Lotus BLRCD070 (2004). Soaked Mud Remain / Silverspoon / The Bereaved / Vital Organ Theft / Hollow Child / My Dying Pride / Pathetic / Devil's Deal / Angels Ablaze / Fatal Human Rapture / Lines In Shape / The Abyss.

THE BERZERKER

MELBOURNE, VIC, AUSTRALIA — *The Berzerker (vocals), Matt Wilcox (guitar), Ed Lacey (guitar), Sam Bean (bass), Dave Gray (drums).*

Caustic industrial edged Death Metal out of Melbourne, Australia fronted by the originally anonymous 'The Berzerker' (a.k.a. Luke Kenny). THE BERZERKER came into being during 1995, issuing an array of EP releases across the globe on labels such as Speedcore in Germany, Widerstand in Austria and Industrial Strength in North America. In 1998 a triptych of MORBID ANGEL remixes, 'Day Of Suffering', 'Abominations' and 'The Ancient Ones', secured a recording contract with the Earache label.

Controversy was on the agenda from the word go as 'The Berzerker' album came under fire from governing television bodies in the UK, banning the promotional short for the track 'Reality' due to "excessive strobe lighting and horrific images". Undaunted THE BERZERKER set of an extensive North American tour throughout early 2001 billed as the 'Crush The Opposition' tour in league with DYING FETUS, SKINLESS and GORGUTS. For these shows the band members, remaining anonymous, wore suitably frightening masks to hide their identities. However, in August THE BERZERKER shed the session guitarist, bass player and drummer previously employed on the U.S. dates and re-built an entirely new band unit, included in which would be ABRAMELIN and STEEL AFFLICTION guitarist Matt Wilcock.

In support of a second album 'Dissimulate' THE BERZERKER would undertake headline shows in Australia in October 2002 supported by ABRAMELIN. Into November the band hooked up with a package billing comprising VADER, IMMOLATION and ORIGIN for gigs across the USA. British shows saw a batch of shows in December supported by LABRAT, RED HARVEST and INSISION. Gigs in North America for January and February of 2003 had the band in alliance with an impressive extreme Metal cast of NILE, NAPALM DEATH, STRAPPING YOUNG LAD and DARK TRANQUILITY.

The group released their debut DVD, 'The Principles And Practices Of The Berzerker' in March 2004. A new album, 'World Of Lies', would be set for 2005. The following year bassist Sam Bean activated solo Death Metal project THE SENSELESS.

THE BERZERKER toured the UK once more in March 2006, supported by HAPPY FACE, MADMAN IS ABSOLUTE and York's RSJ.

THE BERZERKER, Earache MOSH222 (1999). Reality / Forever / Burnt / Pain / Cannibal Rights / Massacre / Chronological Order Of Putrefaction / Deform / Slit Down / February / Mono Grind / Ignorance / Humanity / Ninety Five / Ode To Nash.
DISSIMULATE, Earache MOSH259 (2002). Disregard / No One Wins / Failure / The Principles And Practices Of Embalming / Death Reveals / Compromise / Betrayal / Last Mistake / Painless / Pure Hatred / Paradox / Abandonment / Corporal Jigsaw Quandry.
WORLD OF LIES, Earache (2006). Committed To Nothing / Black Heart / All About You / Burn The Evil / World Of Tomorrow / Follow Me / "Y" / As The World Waits / Afterlife / Never Hated More / Free Yourself / Constant Pain / .... / Farewell.
ANIMOSITY, (2007).

THE BLACK DAHLIA MURDER

DETROIT, MI, USA — *Trevor Strnad (vocals), Brian Eschbach (guitar), John Kempainen (guitar) Bart Williams (bass), Pierre Langois (drums).*

Leading Detroit Metalcore act THE BLACK DAHLIA MURDER take their title after the murder of actress Elizabeth Short, known by many as 'The Black Dahlia'. On January 15th, 1947, her body, severed in two at the waist, was discovered in a vacant lot of the 3800 block of South Norton Avenue in the Leimert Park neighbourhood of Los Angeles. The brutality of the crime, and speculation regarding rumours of henna in her hair, the initials 'BD' carved into her body, grass reportedly forced into her vagina and post-death sodomy served to make the murder one of the most infamous unsolved cases.

The group issued the 2001 demo 'What A Horrible Night To Have A Curse'. An EP, 'A Cold Blooded Epitaph', followed. THE

BLACK DAHLIA MURDER, SOILENT GREEN and LICKGOLDENSKY united for a Summer package tour of the USA commencing 30th July in Fort Lauderdale, Florida. However, the band was forced to pull out of the tour due to "personal reasons", later revealed to be the sudden exit of bassist David Lock. Following these shows the band, with SET ABLAZE's Joe Boccuto installed on bass, allied with HATE ETERNAL, EVERGREY and headliners ARCH ENEMY for a short but intensive run of US 'Anthems Of Rebellion' dates in August. Temporarily filling in as lead vocalist would be Anthony Ezzi of New Jersey's ARSON.

By October both Trevor Strnad and David Lock had rejoined the band. Touring throughout March 2004 was to see the band hooked up with ENTOMBED but the Swedes subsequently cancelled. Nevertheless, they did strike up a touring union with label mates AS I LAY DYING alongside EVERY TIME I DIE and SCARLET for shows commencing later that same month. However, drummer Cory Grady was ousted in June "due to personal and professional conflicts", being succeeded by Zach Gibson of Death metallers GUTROT and MUTILIATED. Grady subsequently joined PREMONITIONS OF WAR.

Renewed touring in mid Summer had the band hooked up with CANNIBAL CORPSE and SEVERED SAVIOR, preceding a run of headliners backed by CATTLE DECAPITATION and GOATWHORE. To close out the year, the band would be announced as one of the main attractions at the annual 'X-Mass Fest' 2004 roving European festival dates in alliance with NAPALM DEATH, MARDUK, VADER, FINNTROLL and BELPHEGOR. The band then scheduled US tour dates for April and May of 2005 in alliance with NILE, Poles BEHEMOTH and headliners KING DIAMOND. Going into September, THE BLACK DAHLIA MURDER headed up shows backed by BETWEEN THE BURIED AND ME, CEPHALIC CARNAGE, and INTO THE MOAT.

Drummer Zach Gibson took his leave in late October in somewhat acrimonious circumstances, departing in order to rejoin his former act GUTROT with a stinging verbal attack on his ex-band mates. As it was revealed that bassist David Lock had also taken his leave the band fired back a retort claiming "Both are gone cause they couldn't actually play our material". A run of November Canadian dates, set to be backed by THE END and A LIFE ONCE LOST, was duly cancelled. Dates in Korea and Japan would see the installation of fresh rhythm section TODAY I WAIT bassist Bart Williams and the internationally renowned figure of Tony Laureano, of DIMMU BORGIR, NILE, INSIDIOUS DISEASE and ANGEL CORPSE repute, on drums.

THE BLACK DAHLIA MURDER teamed up with Belgian Hardcore act LIAR for a European tour during January and February 2006. However, new drummer Pierre Langlois was denied entry to the USA from his native Canada, forcing the band to miss gigs in Minneapolis and Chicago. In the interim, former CHIMAIRA skinsman Kevin Talley stepped in. The band's relentless live campaigning continued unabated into 2006 as they forged a road union in North America throughout March with THROWDOWN, THE AGONY SCENE and THE RED CHORD.

With the installation of a brand new rhythm section, bassist Bart Williams from TODAY I WAIT and drummer Pierre Langois of Canadian bands FROZEN SHADOWS and TENEBRAE, the group subsequently engaged in a gigantic roving festival billing with the 'Sounds Of The Underground' tour throughout the summer, commencing in Cleveland, Ohio on July 8th, partnered with IN FLAMES, TRIVIUM, CANNIBAL CORPSE, GWAR, TERROR, AS I LAY DYING, BEHEMOTH, THE CHARIOT and THROUGH THE EYES OF THE DEAD. The group hit the US touring circuit again in September forming up a strong billing alongside HATEBREED, EXODUS, NAPALM DEATH, DESPISED ICON and FIRST BLOOD.

The group enrolled Shannon Lucas, previously of ALL THAT REMAINS, as new drummer in March 2007.

What A Horrible Night To Have A Curse, The Black Dahlia Murder (2001) (Demo). All My Best Friends Are Bullets / To You, Contortionist / The Middle Goes Down / This Ain't No Fuckin' Love Song / (The Chorus Sang) A Dead Refrain / The Hive.

A Cold Blooded Epitaph, Lovelost 1 (2002). Closed Casket Requiem / The Blackest Incarnation / Burning The Hive / Paint It Black (Hidden track).

The Metal Blade Demo, The Black Dahlia Murder (2002) (Demo). Of Darkness Spawned / Supreme Elder Misanthropy / Thy Horror Cosmic.

UNHALLOWED, Metal Blade 14442-2 (2003). Unhallowed / Funeral Thirst / Elder Misanthropy / Contagion / When The Last Grave Has Emptied / Thy Horror Cosmic / The Blackest Incarnation / Hymn For The Wretched / Closed Casket Requiem / Apex.

3 Song Sampler, Metal Blade (2005) (Promotion release). I'm Charming / A Vulgar Picture / Novelty Crosses.

MIASMA, Metal Blade 14536-2 (2005). Built For Sin / I'm Charming / Flies / Statutory Rape / A Vulgar Picture / Novelty Cross / Vice Campaign / Miscarriage / Spite Suicide / Miasma.

THE CHASM

MEXICO — *Daniel Corchado (vocals), Julio Viterbo (guitar), Alfonso Polo (bass), Antonio Leon (drums).*

Mexican Death Black band THE CHASM, who opened their career with the demo 'Awaiting The Day Of Liberation', relocated to Ohio. Initial recordings in Mexico were issued through the Bellphegot label. The band's mentor and founder is former CENOTAPH man guitarist Daniel Corchada. Vocalist / guitarist Luis Martinez and guitarist Erick Diaz, founder members of the band, would relocate to Seattle, Washington to found a fresh act SERPENS AEON.

Corchada would loan himself out to the infamous INCANTATION in mid 1997. The group has undergone many changes in line-up and by 1999 was down to a duo of Corchado and drummer Antonio Leon. Numbers were boosted with the recruitment of another erstwhile CENOTAPH and SHUB NIGGURATH member Julio Viterbo.

The 2000 album 'Processions To The Infraworld', released by Dwell on CD format and Sempiternal Productions for vinyl variants, saw the enlistment of bassist Roberto Valle of CENOTAPH and THE ONLY FORGOTTEN but he would soon bail out in favour of former ALLUSION four stringer Alfonso Polo.

THE CHASM has cut versions of KREATOR and DESTRUCTION songs for tribute albums. 2000 found the band increasing their tally of covers by donating 'Metalstorm-Face The Slayer' to a Dwell Records SLAYER homage. Bassist Alfonso Polo decamped in June of 2003. For a headline September showing at the 'Aztec Underground Legions' festival in Chicago the band enlisted the temporary services of DARKNESS ETERNAL man George Velaetis on bass.

THE CHASM entered Soto Sound Studios, Palatine, Illinois during April of 2004 to prepare for a new album. Gigs that Summer saw INFINITUM OBSCURE frontman Roberto Lizarraga being utilised as bassist. Recording at Soto Sound Studios in Illinois the band crafted 'The Spell Of Retribution' album for November issue through Wicked World. Vinyl versions, limited to 500 copies, would be clad in exclusive artwork. Winter 2004 gigs allied with MORTICIAN found THE CHASM taking on bassist Ivan Galdamez of Chicago's WHORRID as touring member. To open 2005 the band hooked up with INCANTATION, MORTICIAN and ARSIS for the 'Winter Migration Broootality' US tour commencing early January.

PROCREATION OF THE INNER TEMPLE, Bellphegot BELLCD 95011-2 (1994). Conqueror Of The Mourningstar / A Dream Of An Astral Spectrum (To An Eternal Hate) / Confessions Of Strange Anxiety / Honoris Lux Infinitus (A Whipper To The Moon) / The Day Of Liberation / The Lonely Walker (My Pride And My Wrath) / The Cosmos Within / Stair To Aspirations.

FOR THE LOST YEARS, Reborn CD001 (1995). The Gravefields / Secret Winds Of Temptation / The Pastfinder / Deathcult For Eternity / Ascention Of Majestic Ruins / Our Time will Come ... / Procreation Of The Inner Temple / An Arcanum Faded / Torn (By The Sunrise) / My Tideless Seas / Lost Yesterdays Impossible Tomorrows.

THE CHASM

DEATHCULT FOR ETERNITY: THE TRIUMPH, Oz Productions (1998). Revenge Rises- Drowned In Mournful Blood / No Mercy (Our Time Is Near) / I'm The Hateful Raven / A Portal To Nowhere / Channeling The Bleeding Over The Dream's Remains / Possessed By Past Tragedies (Tragic Shadows) / Apocalypse / In Superior Torment ... / The Triumph (Of My Loss).

PROCESSION TO THE INFRA WORLD, Dwell (2000). Spectral Sons Of Mictlan / The Scars Of My Journey / At The Edge Of Nebulah Mortis / Fading ... / Return Of The Banished / Cosmic Landscapes Of Sorrow / Architects Of Melancholic Apocalypses / Storm Of Revelations.

REACHING THE VEIL OF DEATH, Lux Inframundis (2001). Root Of Damnation / Reaching The Veil Of Death / The Gravefields / This Spiritual Profanity / Embrace My Funeral / Cut-Throat.

CONJURATION OF THE SPECTRAL EMPIRE, Lux Inframundis (2002). Deathcult Arrival / The Conjuration / Dark Cloud / The Ecstasy Of Pain And Destruction / Brand The Mournful Liberation / Master Of The Arcane Torment / Travelling Through Chaos (I, The Pastfinder II) / Reveal The Truth / A Soulstorm Bleeds Over The Horizon / Procession To The Infraworld.

THE SPELL OF RETRIBUTION, Wicked World (2003). From The Curse, A Scourge ... / The Omnipotent Codex / Conqueror & Warlord / Manifest My Intervention / Fortress / Retribution Of The Lost Years (I, The Pastfinder III) / Conjuring The New Apocalypse / The Eclipse: Monument To The Empire: I—Sentence And Burden / The Eclipse: Monument To The Empire: II—The Voyage / The Eclipse: Monument To The Empire: III—The Restitution / Remains Of The Covenant / Eternal Cycle Of Delusion.

THE CIRCLE OF ZAPHYAN

GREECE — *Apollon Zigomalas (vocals), Athanassios Aggelis (guitar / keyboards), Antonis Kollaros (drums).*

Highly experimental Death Metal act THE CIRCLE OF ZAPHYAN debuted in 2002 with the three song demo 'Sublimation', upfront of recordings for an album 'Biochemical Psychosynthesis Eternal'. The group had been formed that same year by guitarist Athanassios Aggelis, ex-NIGHTFALL man Kostas Savvidis subsequently adding singer Apollon Zigomalas. A later addition to the fold would be the NIGHTFALL and SICKENING HORROR credited George Kollias on drums.

THE CIRCLE OF ZAPHYAN, utilising Ilias Daras of SICKENING HORROR on session bass guitar, published the EP 'Flesh Without Soul' in 2004. The group drafted new drummer Antonis Kollaros in late September after Kollias was drafted into the ranks of American act NILE.

Sublimation, The Circle Of Zaphyan (2002). Desolate Inner Dimensions / (Thou Art) The Flesh Of The Universe / Nuclear Paradise.

Flesh Without Soul, (2004). Flesh Without Soul / Your Inner Wasteland To Behold.

THE COUNTY MEDICAL EXAMINERS

USA — *Dr. Morton Fairbanks, MD. (vocals / guitar), Michelle Hayes (vocals / bass), Dr. Jack Putnam, MD. (vocals / drums).*

A quite unique proposition in the annals of extreme Metal, Grindcore combo THE COUNTY MEDICAL EXAMINERS, founded in mid 2001, purport to be real-life pathologists with an "unhealthy adoration of and fixation on CARCASS". Formed under pseudonyms by guitarist Dr. Morton Fairbanks M.D. and drummer Dr. Jack Putnam M.D. the band apparently involves 63 year old Dr. Guy Radcliffe, replacing former bassist Michelle Hayes.

THE COUNTY MEDICAL EXAMINERS album debut was followed up by a split release shared with Sweden's GENERAL SURGERY through Razorback Records. The band signed to Relapse Records in April 2006 for the album 'Olidous Operettas', completing this set, recorded at Tillinghast Workshop, in October.

FORENSIC FUGES AND MEDICOLEGAL MEDLEYS, Razorback (2002). Autopsy Suite / Medicocriminal Entomology / Vitreous Humor / Epicedium For Epidermal Slippage / $NH_2(CH_2)_4NH_2$ & $C_5H_{14}N_2$ (Putrescine & Cadaverine) / Organ Harvest (The Anatomical Gift Act) / Rigor Mortis: Posthumous Muscular Rigidity / Algor Mortis: The Linear Rate Of Cadaveric Cooling / Livor Mortis: Gravitational Blood Pooling / Pugilistic Burn Postures / Y-Shaped Thoracoabdominal Incision / $Y = 1285/X$.

THE CROWN

TROLLHÄTTAN, SWEDEN — *Johan Lindstrand (vocals), Marcus Sunesson (guitar), Marko Trevonen (guitar), Magnus Osfelt (bass), Janne Saarenpää (drums).*

Trollhättan Death Metal combo previously known as CROWN OF THORNS. Although often confused with Jean Beuvoir's American Melodic Rock act, Sweden's CROWN OF THORNS, founded in 1990 by ex-IMPIOUS vocalist Johan Lindstrandt and very much in the Grindcore mould, were a much heavier proposition altogether. Over time THE CROWN rapidly developed into a premier technical Death Metal outfit. CROWN OF THORNS first hit the tape trading scene with an impressive demo, 1993's 'Forever Heaven Gone'. Shortly after its release the band got to play the Swedish Hultsfred festival alongside ENTOMBED and IGGY POP but lost guitarist Robert Österberg to Punk act ÖLHÄVERS. His replacement was Marcus Sunesson who cut his teeth with the 1994 demo 'Forget The Light'. This tape scored them a deal with Black Sun Records for the debut album 'The Burning'. CROWN OF THORNS also made their mark on the SLAYER tribute album 'Slaytanic Slaughter' contributing their take on 'Mandatory Suicide'.

The band's sophomore outing 'Eternal Death' continued the trend and yet again the Swedes were adding to another tribute album, this time nailing a cover of 'Arise' for the SEPULTURA homage 'Sepultural Feast'.

Continued threat of litigation from the American CROWN OF THORNS resulted in the band adopting the title THE CROWN in 1997. Undaunted the band toured Europe in early 1998 on a billing with SACRILEGE resulting directly in a deal with American label Metal Blade for third album 'Hell Is Here'.

To promote the record THE CROWN embarked on further European dates on a Black Metal festival package bill of IMPALED NAZARENE, EMPEROR, MORBID ANGEL and PECCATUM. A further cover version ensued, this time a crack at BATHORY's 'Burnin' Leather' for the 'Power From The North' compilation.

THE CROWN toured Europe in December 2000 as part of an almighty Death Metal package that included ENSLAVED, MORBID ANGEL, BEHEMOTH, HYPNOS and DYING FETUS.

THE CROWN guitarist Marcus Sunesson would join THE HAUNTED for American touring in 2001. Drummer Janne Saarenpää would deputise for GOD DETHRONED for their 'No Mercy' festival appearances. A further round of American dates, commencing in Tampa, Florida on the 24th April 2002, saw support from DARKEST HOUR and ALL THAT REMAINS. The 'Crowned In Terror' album would witness a huge leap in sales and exposure for the band, surpassing sales of all previous albums combined and even entering the national Swedish album charts at no. 8.

Thomas Lindberg would also guest on shared lead vocals in union with KREATOR frontman Mille Petrozza for the track 'Dirty Coloured Knife' on the 2002 album from Israeli metal act EMBLAZE. The singer, along with Marcus Sunneson also sessioned on DARKEST HOUR's 'Hidden Hands Of A Sadist Nation' album.

In a surprise move Lindberg split from THE CROWN in early June rejoining his former act THE GREAT DECEIVER. The band swiftly reinstating original vocalist Johan Lindstrand, albeit with both parties stressing the temporary nature of the union, for their appearance at Finland's 'Tuska Metal' festival and the German Bad Berka 'San Open Air' event. However, in late September Lindstrand confirmed that he had re-joined on a permanent basis.

THE CROWN allied themselves with SKINLESS and MONOLITH for the 'Crowning Europe In Terror' tour in March and April of 2003. The band returned later that year with a new studio album 'Possessed 13'. A limited edition two disc set of the album added both the band's 1993 'Forever Heaven Gone' and 1994 'Forget The Light' demos, a 1992 demo track 'Last Rite', a cover of BATHORY's 'Burnin' Leather' and a 2000 demo version of 'Rebel Angel'. Solidifying their reunion with Lindstrand the band even re-entered the recording studio to manufacture a new version of their 2002 album release 'Crowned In Terror' with Lindstrand replacing Tomas Lindberg's vocals. A further round of November touring on the European mainland saw THE CROWN hooked up with road partners DARKEST HOUR and MONOLITH DEATHCULT.

Although the October 2003 album 'Possessed 13' scored laudatory reviews the band struggled to get onto any decent tour packages. On the 7th of March of 2004 the band called it quits, drummer Janne Saarenpää candidly admitting via an official web posting that the band's inability to match the quality of their music with good business sense had led to their downfall.

The album 'Crowned Unholy', issued in August of 2004, would actually be a remake of the band's fifth album 'Crowned In Terror'. This revised version added re-recorded vocal tracks by Johan Lindstrand, re-recorded bass tracks by Magnus Olsfelt and a brand new intro programmed by drummer Janne Saarenpää. Also included would be a DVD entitled 'The Crown Invades Karlsruhe', documenting a show on THE CROWN's final tour in Karlsruhe, Germany on 24th November 2003.

Johan Lindstrand would front INCAPACITY for a one off gig on 1st October at the Belsepub in Gothenburg supporting IMPIOUS. In December Lindstrand has announced the formation of his brand new project, billed ONE MAN ARMY AND THE UNDEAD QUARTET. Entering Deadline Studios, and working with Valle Adzic of IMPIOUS as engineer, this venture cut the opening demo 'When Hatred Comes To Life'. Meantime, THE CROWN drummer Janne Saarenpää recorded for Canadian act AVEN AURA in mid 2004 on their debut album 'The Shadow Of Idols'.

In March of 2005 Marcus Sunesson re-emerged as member of the new band ENGEL, a Gothenburg based quintet also featuring guitarist Niclas Engelin, of PASSENGER, GARDENIAN and IN FLAMES repute, drummer Morbid Mojjo (a.k.a. Daniel Moilanen), a veteran of MINDSNARE, SANDALINAS, RUNEMAGICK, DRACENA, RELEVANT FEW and LORD BELIAL, bassist Robert Hakemo, ex-GARDENIAN and GOOSEFLESH together with vocalist Mangan Klavborn. Meantime, guitarist Marko Tervonen was in collaboration with TRANSPORT LEAGUE frontman Tony Jelencovich in a new unit billed ANGEL BLAKE. This project soon scored a label deal with Metal Blade Records and also subsequently drafted Janne Saarenpää on drums. Tervonen would also retain ties with his former THE CROWN colleague bassist Magnus Osfelt, acting as producer for the four-stringers STOLEN POLICECAR project. Johan Lindstrand spread his talents by also signing up as new frontman for INCAPACITY in December.

HELL IS HERE, Metal Blade 14193-2 (1998). The Poison / At The End / 1999—Revolution 666 / Dying Of The Heart / Electric Night / Black Lightning / The Devil And The Darkness / Give You Hell / Body And Soul / Mysterion / Death By My Side.

DEATHRACE KING, Metal Blade 14296-2 (2000). Deathexplosion / Executioner (Slayer Of The Light) / Back From The Grave / Devil Gate Ride / Vengeance / Angel Rebel / I Won't Follow / Blitzkrieg Witchcraft / Dead Man's Song / Total Satan / Killing Star (Superbia Luxuria XXX).

CROWNED IN TERROR, Metal Blade 14394-2 (2002). Introduction—House Of Hades / Crowned In Terror / Under The Whip / Drugged Unholy / World Below / The Speed Of Darkness / Out For Blood / (I Am) Hell / Death Is The Hunter / Satanist / Death Metal Holocaust. Chart position: 8 SWEDEN.

POSSESSED 13, Metal Blade 14446-2 (2003). No Tomorrow / Face Of Destruction / Deep Hit Of Death / Deliverance / Cold Is The Grave / Dream Bloody Hell / Morningstar Rising / Are You Morbid? / Bow To None / Kill 'Em All / Natashead Overdrive / Zombiefied / Dawn Of Emptiness / In Memoriam. Chart position: 54 SWEDEN.

CROWNED UNHOLY, Metal Blade 14497 (2004) (CD + DVD). House Of Hades / Crowned In Terror / Under The Whip / Drugged Unholy / World Below / The Speed Of Darkness / Out For Blood / (I Am) Hell / Death Is The Hunter / Satanist / Death Metal Holocaust / No Tomorrow / Face Of Destruction—Deep Hit Of Death / Deathexplosion / World Below / Deliverance / Blitzkrieg Witchcraft / Cold Is The Grave / Zombiefied / Dream Bloody Hell—Kill 'Em All / Under The Whip / Bow To None / Total Satan / House Of Hades—Crowned In Terror / 1999—Revolution 666.

THE DECAY THEORY

SHADYSIDE, OH, USA — *Mike Stead (vocals), Eric Klein (guitar), John Williams (guitar), Jae Littleton (bass), Cole Apser (drums).*

Founded in March of 2002, THE DECAY THEORY's founding line up comprised the erstwhile VLAD duo of singer Mike Stead and guitarist Eric "Lunchbox" Klein in union with former HAVOK man Jae Littleton and Ryan Cook on the drums, the latter relocated from Germany. However, Cook opted out and in July the CRITERIA credited Jeb Millard took command of the drums, although his tenure would last only until that September. Pat Blon of MIDPOINT 77 briefly took on drum duties in December before Mike Markus of 77 IN OCTOBER and HAVOK assumed the role. At this juncture the group also added Christina Martin, another HAVOK member, on second guitar.

In the Autumn of 2003 Markus decamped. Minus a drummer, Stead, Klein and Littleton forged ahead with side project FA-Q. Eventually THE DECAY THEORY regrouped by enlisting Andrew D'Cagna on drums. Further evolvement saw the introduction of second guitarist John 'Corpse' Williams and another drummer, Cole Asper. The demo 'Noise Inventory' was published in March of 2004.

Noise Inventory, Good Enough (2004). Darkness / Infernal Harvest / Suicidal King / Bleeding My Mind.

THE DEVIANT

STAVANGER, NORWAY — *Dolgar (vocals / bass), Violator (lead guitar), E.N. Death (rhythm guitar), Blod (drums).*

Blasphemic Death Metal band THE DEVIANT was formulated in Stavanger during 2003 by erstwhile 122 STAB WOUNDS members vocalist / bassist Sanrabb, drummer Blod and rhythm guitarist E.N. Death (a.k.a. Frode Sivertsen), also connected with ANTAIOS, FORLORN and GEHENNA. Blod (Jan Egil Fosse) has prior involvement with ANTAIOS, FORLORN, GEHENNA whilst Sanrabb has affiliations with GEHENNA, FORLORN, SATYRICON, BLOOD RED THRONE and SHADOW SEASON.

THE DEVIANT

Dolgar took Sanrabb's position following the 'Intimate Skinning' demo. Tabu Recordings issued the album 'Ravenous Deathworship' in November 2005. Lyrics to the tracks 'Intimate Skinnin' and 'Sadosadistic' would be contributed by Dirge Rep (Per Husebø), a well known veteran of 122 STAB WOUNDS, DESSPO HALLELUJAH, AURA NOIR, GEHENNA, ENSLAVED, ORCUSTUS and NEETZACH amongst others.

RAVENOUS DEATHWORSHIP, Tabu Recordings TABU 016CD (2005). Merciless / Genocide / Serpent / Intimate Skinning / Venom Of Mankind / Purity Of Hate / Sadosadistic / Perfect State Of Death / Resurrection Of Hate.

THE DILLINGER ESCAPE PLAN

NJ, USA — *Greg Puciato (vocals), Ben Wienman (guitar), Brian Benoit (guitar), Liam (bass), Chris Pennie (drums).*

THE DILLINGER ESCAPE PLAN are recognised as being frontrunners of the 'Math Metal' genre, purveying a Jazz-Metal hybrid marked by discordant time signatures topped by Greg Puciato's piercing vocal stylings. The New Jersey band is rooted in the Hardcore act ARCANE, this unit comprising Minikakis, guitarists Ben Wienman and Derrick Brantley, bassist Adam Doll and drummer Chris Pennie. Re-billed as THE DILLINGER ESCAPE PLAN, the band performed just two gigs before Brantley exited. A demo prompted Now or Never Records to offer a recording contract and as the band's first tour was organised John Fulton stepped up to fill the guitar vacancy.

The group's completely new approach to Hardcore soon made waves on the live circuit resulting in a swift offer from Relapse Records. Fulton opted out upfront of recording the Relapse debut, 1998's three song 'Under The Running Board' EP, on which Wienman handled all guitar duties. The band also shared a split EP with fellow New Jerseyites NORA through Ferret Records. In 1999 the band hit the Rock world foursquare with the full length opus 'Calculating Infinity'. Unfortunately, Adam Doll lost his position in the band due to a car accident which left him paralyzed. The group duly pulled in Jeff Wood for live work as guitarist Ben Wienman took over bass duties in the studio. Wood would later join FLOOD, the band assembled in 1998 by guitarist Scott Roberts of THE SPUDMONSTERS, vocalist Robb Brock and former AGNOSTIC FRONT and MADBALL drummer Will Sheplar.

THE DILLINGER ESCAPE PLAN toured America in 1998 with BOTCH and JESUIT. Following these dates the band recruited guitarist Brian Benoit from JESUIT in time for a further tour with MR. BUNGLE. Minakakis then announced his departure, bowing out with some farewell gigs including the Japanese 'Beast Feast' festival. During this period the band also undertook a handful of purely instrumental gigs whilst actively searching for a new frontman. Novelly, the group planted a vocal free version of the song '43% Burnt' on their website in order for potential applicants to download and use as an audition piece. In the interim, a performance at the 'Krazy Fest' in Louisville, Kentucky saw COALESCE singer Sean Ingram as guest frontman. Studio work found Mike Patton donating his skills and the band also laid down a brace of tracks for a BLACK FLAG tribute collection.

Greg Puciato was brought on board as new vocalist in October 2001, debuting at the CMJ Music Festival in New York. The band, now signed to Epitaph Records, announced their return in the Spring of 2002 with a mini album, 'Irony Is A Dead Scene', produced by ex-NUMBER FIVE man Chris Badami. The prospect of this record created a buzz when it was learned that former FAITH NO MORE vocalist Mike Patton had contributed guest lead vocals. The band also announced a proposal to record a split album with California's ICARUS LINE.

THE DILLINGER ESCAPE PLAN would be confirmed for a high profile round of European gigs opening for SYSTEM OF A DOWN including the UK's Leeds and Reading festivals. North American dates throughout September and October saw ICARUS LINE as opening act.

Greg Puciato was set to session as guest vocalist on PSYCHOTOGEN's 'The Calculus Of Evil' 2003 album but these plans were later dropped. Former singer Dimitri Minakakis allied himself with ex-members of Philadelphia act KNIVES OUT in a fresh band called TOKYO in early 2003. THE DILLINGER ESCAPE PLAN would form up part of the 'Take Action' festival tour of North America. Commencing in Minneapolis on 11th September and running through until mid October the dates would be designed to raise awareness and funding for the youth suicide prevention body The National Hopeline Network. Sharing the festival billing would be POISON THE WELL, SHADOWS FALL, FURTHER SEEMS FOREVER, AVENGED SEVENFOLD, DEATH BY STEREO, EIGHTEEN VISIONS, SHAI HULUD, THIS DAY FORWARD, BLACK CROSS and SINCE BY MAN. Headline gigs in the UK during December saw support from CULT OF LUNA. A further round of extensive US dates saw the band uniting with THE LOCUST and YOUR ENEMIES FRIENDS for gigs throughout January and February 2004.

In an unexpected move, THE DILLINGER ESCAPE PLAN donated their rendition of 'My Michelle' to the GUNS N' ROSES tribute album 'Bring You To Your Knees' released by Inertia Records in March.

The band entered Mission and Water recording studios with producer Steve Evetts in April to craft a new studio opus 'Miss Machine'. Upfront promotion included a video for the track 'Panasonic Youth' directed by Josh Graham. UK dates in June of 2004 had BURST partnering with BURST, MONO and BLOOD VALLEY. US shows in July, dubbed the 'Fucking With The Lights On' tour, had the band employing a swathe of up and coming acts as support including THE BRONX, PLANES MISTAKEN FOR STARS, DECEHEDRON, READ YELLOW and DAUGHTERS.

'Miss Machine' would hit no. 106 on the Billboard album charts, selling over 11,000 copies in its first week of release, making it the highest charting record in Relapse Records history. US headline dates, billed 'Miss Machine Gets Pregnant', running through September, October and November saw the band heading up a billing of ZAO, MISERY SIGNALS and EVERY TIME I DIE. Various legs also saw the addition of DROWNINGMAN, BAD ACID TRIP and WYOMING. However, in October guitarist Brian Benoit suffered a pinched nerve in his arm and was forced to sit out the set of dates. Despite this, THE DILLINGER ESCAPE PLAN then launched into European dates commencing 8th November in Hamburg, Germany, with BURST and POISON THE WELL providing support.

European gigs for the Spring of 2005 would be jeopardised by a succession of ailments. Brian Benoit's previous injuries became aggravated by non-stop touring and ex-FENIX TX guitarist James Love filled in until Benoit had made a recovery. However, the band was assailed by injury yet again when Ben Weinman was involved in an automobile accident that left him in hospital. Nevertheless, the band still launched into touring but Weinman's injuries would be enough to see him black out

THE DILLINGER ESCAPE PLAN (pic: Kate Thompson)

on stage in Spain. THE DILLINGER ESCAPE PLAN was forced to postpone three weeks worth of dates, returning to action on 18th June at the 'Fields of Rock' festival in Holland.

THE DILLINGER ESCAPE PLAN joined the 'Gigantour' festival trek, headlined by MEGADETH and DREAM THEATER, for US action in late July 2005, cementing a bill also comprising FEAR FACTORY, SYMPHONY X, DRY KILL LOGIC, and West Virginians BOBAFLEX and NEVERMORE. The band was forced to withdraw from the last few shows when guitarist Ben Wienman suffered an arm injury in Atlantic City. In September the band maintained the road ethic, hooking up with ZAO, UNEARTH and A LIFE ONCE LOST.

The band would contribute their rendition of 'Honey Bucket' to a MELVINS tribute album, 'We Reach: The Music Of The Melvins', through Fractured Transmitter Records. Back on the road, November gigs in the USA and Canada would be backed up by BETWEEN THE BURIED AND ME and HELLA.

The group recorded an exclusive cover version of SOUNDGARDEN's 'Jesus Christ Pose' for inclusion on UK magazine 'Kerrang!'s 25th anniversary issue cover mount CD, 'High Voltage', issued in May 2006. Throughout June and July THE DILLINGER ESCAPE PLAN toured the USA backed by AFI then DYSRHYTHMIA. However, guitarist Ben Wienman was forced out in early August in order to "deal with some personal issues".

Working with producer Steve Evetts, THE DILLINGER ESCAPE PLAN cut album tracks in February 2007.

Under The Running Board EP, Relapse RR64102 (1998). Mullet Burden / Sandbox Magician / Abe The Cop.

CALCULATING INFINITY, Relapse RR 6427 (1999). Sugar Coated Sour / 43% Burnt / Jim Fear / *#... / Destro's Secret / Running Board / Clip the Apex ... Accept Instruction / Calculating Infinity / 4th Grade Dropout / Weekend Sex Change / Variations On A Cocktail Dress.

Irony Is A Dead Scene EP, Epitaph 5665806128 (2002). Hollywood Squares / Pig Latin / When Good Dogs Do Bad Things / Come To Daddy.

THE DILLINGER ESCAPE PLAN, Earache MOSH256 (2002). Proceed With Caution / I Love Secret Agents / Monticello / Cleopatra's Sling / Caffeine / Three For Flinching.

MISS MACHINE, Relapse RR65872 (2004). Panasonic Youth / Sunshine The Werewolf / Highway Robbery / Van Damsel / Phone Home / We Are The Storm / Crutch Field Tongs / Setting Fire To Sleeping Giants / Baby's First Coffin / Unretrofied / The Perfect Design. Chart position: 106 USA.

THE DUSKFALL

LULEÅ, SWEDEN — *Kai Jaakola (vocals), Mikael Sandorf (guitar), Kaj Molin (bass), Oskar Karlsson (drums).*

Luleå based, melodically inclined Death Metal act. THE DUSKFALL, created in January of 1999, feature lead guitarist Mikael Sandorf and drummer Oskar Karlsson from GATES OF ISHTAR. Initially the idea was to create just a loose jam band with Glenn Svensson on guitar and Sandorf playing the drums but with the addition of bassist Tommy Konu of DEATHBOUND, Per Johansson of SATARIEL and BELSEMAR on vocals and second guitarist Jonny Ahlgren the project, under the inaugural title of SOULASH, took on the concept of a full band for the demo 'Tears Are Soulash'. Switching title to THE DUSKFALL the band dispensed with both Johansson and Ahlgren but pulled in Urban Carlsson to handle drum duties. Soon incorporated on bass would be Kaj Molin.

Oskar Karlsson, also citing credits with THE EVERDAWN, joined up as new drummer during July 2001. That same September the band enrolled Kai Jaakkola of NECROMICON and DEATHBOUND as well as Andreas Ekberg on bass. The debut album 'Frailty', recorded for the Greek Black Lotus Records, included guest appearances from DARKANE and SEETHINGS guitarist Lawrence Mackrory and HELL's Magnus Olsson.

THE DUSKFALL enrolled guitarist Joachim Lindbäck for recording of the December 2003 album 'Source', recorded at Dug-Out studios in Uppsala. However, by early 2004 Lindbäck was out and the group enrolled Lars Lofven from DEFLESHED as temporary substitute for live shows. The band inducted session guitarist Antti Lindholm, from Finnish act LAMBS, as stand in during May. In October THE DUSKFALL announced they had signed a new label deal with Nuclear Blast Records, projecting a Daniel Bergstrand produced album, 'Lifetime Supply Of Guilt', for 2005. However, that January they would sever ties with bassist Kaj Molin and draft Marco Eronen from Hardcore band RAISED FIST for live work.

THE DUSKFALL parted ways with Marco Eronen in July 2006, the bassist opting out in order to prioritise his other act RAISED FIST. His place would be taken by Matte Järnil, ex-21ST IMPACT.

Scheduled German concerts for January 2007, including the 'Winternoise' festival, were cancelled when Mikael Sandorf was sidelined "due to personal problems".

Deliverance, Duskfall (2001) (Demo). Dawnskies / None / Taking Control / You're The Light / Tune Of Slaughtered Hearts.

FRAILTY, Duskfall BLRCD041 (2002). The Light / Age Of Errors / Agoraphobic / Poison The Waters / None / Farewell Song / Frailty / Tune Of Slaughtered Hearts / Just Follow / Deliverance.

SOURCE, Black Lotus BLRCD060 (2003). Case Closed / Striving To Have Nothing / The Grand Scheme / Source / Not A Good Sign / Guidance / Lead Astray / The Destroyer.

LIFETIME SUPPLY OF GUILT, Nuclear Blast NB 1491-2 (2005). Trust Is Overrated / The Shallow End / Break The Pact / A Stubborn Soul / Shoot It In / Going Down Screaming / Hours Are Wasted / Sympathy Has Decreased / Downright Dreadful / Relive Your Fall.

THE ELYSIAN FIELDS

GREECE — *Bill A., Mikhalis Katsikas, Marinos A..*

THE ELYSIAN FIELDS is essentially a duo of guitarist / bassist / pianist Mikhalis Katsikas and the mysterious 'Bill'.

The group actually made its entrance in 1994 billed as DESULPHARISE and touting a Death Metal charged demo 'Nihilistic Era'. With the name switch to ELYSIAN FIELDS the following year the subsequent demo session found the pair shifting into Doom territory.

The debut album 'Adelain', issued by Greek label Unisound during 1995, garnered healthy praise in the Rock media. The group, subtly altering the band title to THE ELYSIAN FIELDS, would later sign to the British Wicked World concern for the sophomore 'We ... The Enlightened'.

The band switched to the Greek label Black Lotus and recorded a third CD '12Ablaze' in early 1999. It finally saw the light of day in 2001

Katsikas also operates side venture HAVORUM.

ADELAIN, Unisound (1995). I Of Forever / As One / Un Sentiment / I Was Dying Once Again / Of Purity And Black / Foredoomed Elegy / Father Forgive Them (For They Don't Know) / Elysian Fields / Deicide / The Auspice.
WE ... THE ENLIGHTENED, Wicked World WICK02CD (1998). Their Blood Be On Us / I Am The Unknown Sky / Until The Night Cries Rise In The Heart / ... And The Everdawn Faded Away / Shall They Come Forth Unto Us / Arcana Caelestia / The End Shall Be Tragically Fulfilled / The Last Star Of Heaven Falls / Wither, Oh Divine, Wither.
12 ABLAZE, Black Lotus BLR CD 029 (2001). Ensheild My Hate Eternal / Of Dawns, Perished Tranquility / Rapture And The Mourning Virtue / Weak We Stand Before Them / Ablazing 12 / A Serenade Like Blood Caress / Even If I Could Forgive / The Entreaty Unsung / As The Light Disappears.
SUFFERING G.O.D. ALMIGHTY, Black Lotus (2005). Aeons' Unlight / I Am Your Willing Darkness / Suffering G.O.D. Almighty / Ravished With Thee Light / Unleashing The Propaganda / I See The Lie Behind All Truths / An Overture Of Sorrows Unfolding / All Those Tristful Winters / Anathema Unveiled.

THE EMBODIMENT

HARDERWIJK, HOLLAND — *Peter Hagen (vocals / guitar), Erik-Jan Brinker (guitar), Danny van Helden (bass), Martijn van Gene (drums).*

Harderwijk Death-Thrashers. THE EMBODIMENT was originally gathered as EMBODIMENT in 1994 by vocalist / guitarists Peter Hagen and Erik-Jan Brinker along with drummer Martijn van Gene and bassist Sebastiaan den Oudsten. Den Oudsten exited in 1996 to join up with CANISTER, subsequently going on to ART OF PREMONITION. The band put in its first concert on 13th December 1996, after which den Oudsten returned to the ranks as EMBODIMENT entered QSA Studios in Utrecht with producer Vincent Dijkers to craft the demo 'All Because Of Lust' in January 1998.

Bassist Danny van Helden was inducted during 2000 and shortly afterward the group subtly revised its title to THE EMBODIMENT. An EP, 'Razor Cut Reality', emerged in 2002. Peter Hagen went on to join Groningen's ENRAGED in 2004. THE EMBODIMENT released the 'Legion' album in October 2006. The band donated the track 'Y2K' to the 2006 compilation album 'Blown To Pieces 4' issued by FearSomeRecords.

Razor Cut Reality, Independent (2002). Careless / Victims Of Retaliation / I'm Despair / 45 Years.
LEGION, (2006).

THE EMBRACED

TRONDHEIM, NORWAY — *Frank Bøkseth (vocals), Rune Holm (guitar), Rocco (guitar), Tom Wahl (bass), Vargon (drums).*

Trondheim melodic Death Metal band, founded in 1997 and then featuring ex-SEPTIC GRAVE drummer Jørgen Bjørnstrøm. Following issue of the debut album, 'In My Dreams ... I Am Armageddon' for Aftermath Music in August of 1998, Bjørnstrøm relocated back to his native Sweden and Vargon of HELLSTORM assumed control of the drums. In the interim a limited edition 7" single 'Songs Of Death' emerged.

Vocalist Frank Bøkseth then exited as the band prepared for a second album 'The Birth'. As such, session vocals to record the album at Skansen Lydstudios in Trondheim. were handled by Mads Eriksen. Bøkseth made a return in the Summer of 2000. This album would be licensed to Soundholic Records for Japanese release. However, further defections witnessed the departure of both guitarist Geir Frode Stavsøien and bass player Daniel Set. The group duly went into a lengthy hiatus.

During 2002 guitarist Rune Holm would act as stand in guitarist for THE APPARATUS. On 22nd November 2003 THE EMBRACED, with Tom Wahl of ANTI DEPRESSIVE DELIVERY, MAELSTRÖM, KILLING FOR COMPANY, BETHZAIDA, MIST ENTICER, ATROX, MINSTREL, GODSEND, STONES OF OCTOBER and EVIL PENIS on bass and Rocco on second guitar, returned to the live stage.

IN MY DREAMS ... I AM ARMAGEDDON, Aftermath Music CHAPTER I (1998). In My Dreams (I Am Armageddon) / Dreamspawn / Remnants Of A Scorched World / Remains Of Life / Split / The Last Embrace / The Demon Storm / As Darkness Falls / Autumn Leaves.
Songs Of Death, Aftermath Music CHAPTER VI (2000). Song Of Death / Dark Embracement.
THE BIRTH, Soundholic TKCS-85007 (2000) (Japanese release). The Birth (Intro) / A Path That Never Ends / The Beautiful Angels / The Plague Divine / Apart / Daughter Of The Lupus Moon / Thymus / Last Departure / Song Of Death.
THE BIRTH, Aftermath Music CHAPTER VIII (2001). The Birth (Intro) / A Path That Never Ends / The Beautiful Angels / The Plague Divine / Apart / Daughter Of The Lupus Moon / Thymus / Last Departure.

THE ENCHANTED

UK — *Tony Wildwood (vocals / guitar), Robb Philpotts (guitar), Adam Thomas (bass), Jamie Sykes (drums).*

Bradford Metal band whose self financed album 'Trust In Death And Rebirth' features erstwhile BURNING WITCH and THORR'S HAMMER drummer Jamie Sykes. The band evolved during 1997, founded by the former DARK EMBRACE musicians guitarist Tony Wildwood and bassist Daryl Parson, vocalist Kate, drummer Barry and PARONIRA guitarist Robb Philpotts. Tony also cited prior credits with NECROMANCER. This line-up undertook just two gigs and cut the debut demo tape 'Freedom To Perceive'.

Kate would depart, to concentrate on studies but also to sing for local act MAYA, and THE ENCHANTED pulled in vocalist Natalie from IN DYING GRACE. A second tape, 'Pagan Metal', arrive with this version of the band before Natalie was ousted. In May of 2000 Barry left to team up with the reformed MALEDICTION and THE ENCHANTED duly enrolled Jamie Sykes, recently returned from band activity in North America. In 2002 the track 'Forever In Your Dream' would be included on the Arcane Productions sampler 'Deathfest—The Art Of Extremity'. Following the release of the debut 'Trust In Death And Rebirth' album Sykes would leave the band in November of 2002. However, within a matter of weeks he would be back in the fold.

Bass player Daryl Parson dropped out in March of 2003, being superseded by Adam Thomas of EPITAPH, BORN INTO SODOM and RUINS OF AMBER repute. THE ENCHANTED acted as support to Norwegian Viking Metal veterans ENSLAVED for their one off January 2004 performance at London's Camden Underground. Sykes left yet again in June, being briefly replaced by Robb Philpotts brother Vinnie, of TORTOISE WALTZ and actually an early BLOODSTREAM singer, on a temporary basis. At this same juncture, Robb Philpotts, retaining his ties to THE ENCHANTED, would join BLOODSTREAM as their new frontman.

Tony Wildwood would be announced as guitarist for Nottingham based Pagan collective THE CLAN DESTINED, a Heathen Metal band spearheaded by ex-SABBAT and SKYCLAD singer

Martin Walkyier alongside bassist Iscariah of IMMORTAL repute. In February of 2005 Jamie Sykes re-assumed THE ENCHANTED drum stool. Sykes would also be found working with Doomsters ATAVIST.

TRUST IN DEATH AND REBIRTH, Sinister Realm SINR001 (2002). The Portal / The Eternal Hourglass / Waiting In The Shadow World / Disposable Planet / Facing The Beast / As Silence Deepens / Soulburn / Forever In Your Dream / Celtica / Devastation.

THE EVERSCATHED

CHICAGO, IL, USA — *Bill Frickenstein (vocals / bass), Brice Dalzell (guitar / vocals), Tim Frickenstein (drums).*

Chicago Death Metal trio THE EVERSCATHED is rooted in the antecedent ENMORTEM, established during 1996, comprised brothers vocalist / bassist Bill Frickenstein and drummer Tim Frickenstein alongside guitar player Brian Laurence. ENMORTEM issued the 1997 demo 'Bleeding The Sorrow', after which Laurence bowed out. Tom Flanagan was drafted on guitar for a second demo session, 1999's tuned down, doomier 'Their Blood I Offer The King'. Later that same year the trio utilised Sheffield Studio to record 'Manifestations Of Infernal Disgust'.

At this juncture the Frickenstein siblings forged side project WARSHIP in collaboration with guitarist Brice Dalzell of CORPSE VOMIT repute. Dalzell then quit CORPSE VOMIT, joining up with ENMORTEM. The quartet version of the band did not last long and Flanagan soon exited. A June 2000 demo cassette 'Barbaric Displeasure' was cut at RK Studios. The group subsequently evolved into THE EVERSCATHED as tracks were laid down for a debut album entitled 'Razors Of Unrest' in 2002. The band also issued the January 2003 demo 'Halted Glory'.

However, a major setback hit the band as Dalzell was severely injured at work, severing a nerve in his fretting arm. Just as Dalzell had fully recovered, a further accident ensued. In early 2005, Bill Frickenstein was to undergo surgery as he was injured too, tearing the bicep on his fretting arm.

A further demo, '... Again The Chains', arrived in June 2005. THE EVERSCATHED signed to Open Grave Records in May 2006 for the album 'Razors Of Unrest'.

Halted Glory, The Everscathed (2003). Halted Glory / Wounds Of Confusion.

... Again The Chains, (2005). Shackled By Failure / The Everscathed.

RAZORS OF UNREST, Open Grave (2006). Overthrow The Sphere Of Existence / Raging In Unrest / Halted Glory / Wounds Of Confusion / Surgical Theater / The Everscathed / Evil Bleeds On / Shackled By Failure / Cries Of Damnation's Rebirth / ... To The Place Of Death Begotten.

THE EXORIAL

STUTTGART, GERMANY — *Tobias Mohl (vocals), Markus Sailer (guitar), Jochen Scholtysik (guitar), Martin Nagel (bass), Tomasz Janiszewski (drums).*

Stuttgart Death Metal band THE EXORIAL features ex-DISINFECT members guitarist Markus Sailer and drummer Tomasz Janiszewski. Founded in 1998 by Sailer, Janiszewski, guitarist Jochen Scholtysik and bassist Martin Nagel THE EXORIAL was at first fronted by Jazek Janiszewski. The group debuted with a self-titled demo in 2000, leading to supports with PROFANITY, IMMURED and AGATHODAIMON, after which Tobias "Donnergurgler" Mohl assumed the role of lead vocalist. THE EXORIAL's second promotional session, 'Neither Dream Nor Reality' recorded at Exponent Studios in Slovakia, followed in 2002. The latter joined theatric Death Metal combo LUNAFIELD in 2003.

The Exorial, The Exorial (2000). Bullet Proof / D.L.I. / Infame Deadline / Release / Suffer To Exhale.

Neither Dream Nor Reality, (2002). Intro / Sexorial / Infame Deadline / D.L.I. / Release / Bullet Proof / Neither Dream Nor Reality / Nothing To Loose / Suffer To Exhale / Nocturnal Born Killer.

THE FALLEN

ORANGE COUNTY, CA, USA — *Mike Granat (vocals / guitar), Mark Venier (guitar), Bryan Klinger (bass), Henry Higgs (drums).*

Stoic Metal campaigners THE FALLEN, founded as THE CRESTFALLEN during 1992, endured nearly a decade of struggle and successive demo releases before finally landing a record deal in 2001. The group was convened as a trio of vocalist / guitarist Mike Granat, guitarist Mark Venier and drummer Max Wolff mixing traditional Metal with newer Death and retro Thrash influences. With the addition of bass player Bryan Klinger the band became known as THE FALLEN.

A demo cassette, 'The Perfect Darkness Of Death', arrived in 1993 which found the group fronted by lead vocalist Wagner Pierera. However, THE FALLEN was back to a quartet for 1994's 'Eventually Nothing Remained' session with Granet taking the lead vocal mantle. Wolff would be out of the picture by the band's third and fourth attempts, 1995's 'Turning Hollow' and the following year's 'Bloodletting: Victims Of The Order', drums being simply credited to 'Greg'. Keith Gordon took the drum stool for the 1997 session 'Bloodrush'.

THE FALLEN, now with Henry Higgs placed on drums, committed to CD for the first time with their 1999 three track EP 'Sector - 7G'. A self-financed full-length album 'The Tones In Which We Speak' emerged in 2000 leading to a deal with the Metal Blade label and the subsequent Bill Metoyer produced 'Front Toward Enemy'. By March of 2003 THE FALLEN had severed ties with drummer Max Wolff, replacing him with John Skaare. Another casualty would be singer Mike Granat, who opted out in July. However, despite announcing this officially, THE FALLEN then refuted this statement within days.

Sector- 7G EP, (1999). To Dust / Descend From Heaven / Bound In Thorns.

THE TONES IN WHICH WE SPEAK, (2000). Suffer With It / The Tones In Which We Speak / All For None / Harbinger / Turning Hollow / Sunken Ploy / To Dust / Descend From Heaven / Bound In Thorns / Bloodwash.

FRONT TOWARDS ENEMY, Metal Blade 3984-14398-2 (2002). Short Fuse / Blessings / What I Have Become / Keep Suffering / The Hopeless & The Frail / Front Toward Enemy / Shifting Our Vision / Killswitch / In Loathing / From Fragile To Strength / Eleven Years.

THE FLESH

DRAMMEN, NORWAY — *Einar Fredriksen (vocals / bass), Espen Simonsen (guitar), Morten Vaeng (guitar), Anders Eek (drums).*

THE FLESH was an exceptionally brutal Death Metal band formed in 1993 in Drammen, near Oslo. The quartet features two ex-members of FUNERAL, bassist Einar Fredriksen and drummer Anders Eek, and was originally conceived as a side project from the duo's mothership. Prior to debuting with the 'Storming The Heaven's Gate' EP for the Arctic Serenades label THE FLESH had received some rave reviews for their 1994 'Ice Cold Macabre Lust' demo.

THE FLESH guitarist Espen Simonsen would work with Sunndalsøra Black Metal act ENTHRAL. Frontman Einar Fredriksen, also holding an earlier association with MYSTICUM, would join PARADIGMA in 1997. Fredriksen committed suicide on 10th January 2003.

Anders Eek joined Torbjørn Sandvik's GLITTERTIND project in February 2006.

Icecold Macabre Lust, The Flesh (1994) (Demo). Graveyard Bound / Black Book's Tool / Icecold Macabre Lust / Winter People.

Storming The Heaven's Gate, Arctic Serenades SERE 004 (1995). The Weeping Of Wrists / Inadvertent Battery / Last Day Of Your Life / Inhuman Misbehaviour.

THE FORSAKEN

MALMÖ, SWEDEN — Anders Sjöholm (vocals), Stefan Holm (guitar), Patrick Persson (guitar), Michael Håkansson (bass), Nicke Grabowski (drums).

A youthful technically minded Death Metal combo, starting out in 1997 titled SEPTIC BREED, hailing from the Malmö-Helsingborg area of Southern Sweden. THE FORSAKEN cannily combine melody with blast beats and an obvious musical prowess. Drummer Nicke Grabowski, previously with Grindcore act A.I.S., had formulated the band with guitarist Stefan Holm, initially to just jam old Thrash material. With the introduction of second guitarist Patrick Persson the band opted to pursue the craft of penning original material. A debut demo session was delivered as SEPTIC BREED, March 1998's 'Patterns Of Delusive Design', produced by DARKANE's Klas Ideberg and fronted by Grabowski's former A.I.S. singer.

A 2000 Tommy Tägtgren produced demo session 'The Reaper', now with the band labelled as THE FORSAKEN and featuring MASSGRAV and OMINOUS vocalist Anders Sjöholm and Michael Håkansson of EVERGREY, CENOTAPHIA and EMBRACED on bass, soon secured a deal with German label Century Media.

Tommy Tägtgren would once again work with the band on their debut 2001 record 'Manifest Of Hate'. THE FORSAKEN would land a valuable European tour supporting NILE, THE HAUNTED and CARNAL FORGE. However, Håkansson's conflicting duties with EVERGREY would necessitate the temporary enlistment of OMINOUS guitarist Soren Sandved to fulfill the bass role for these dates. Hakansson made his exit in October 2001 in order to focus on his priority act EVERGREY. Guitarist Patrick Persson would take command of bass duties for recording of the follow up album 'Arts Of Desolation'.

THE FORSAKEN's third outing, November 2003's 'Traces Of The Past' produced by Tommy Tägtgren and marking the arrival of bass player Stefan Berg, closed out with a cover rendition of METALLICA's 'Blackened'. The group acted as support to SOILWORK's February 2004 UK tour. US versions, issued in June, added a glut of bonus tracks in covers of METALLICA's 'Creeping Death', SLAYER's 'Spirit In Black' and GRAVE's 'You'll Never See' alongside a previously unreleased original 'Project: The New Breed 666'.

Reaper-99, The Forsaken (1999) (Demo). Truth Of God / Daemon Breed / Project: The New Breed 666.
MANIFEST OF HATE, Century Media 77318-2 (2001). Manifest Of Hate / Incinerate / Truth Of God / Collector Of Thoughts / Soulshade / Seers Hatred / Betrayal Within Individuals / Dehumanized / Daemon Breed / Inseminated By The Beast.
MANIFEST OF HATE, The Forsaken KICP-822 (2001) (Japanese release). Manifest Of Hate / Incinerate / Truth Of God / Collector Of Thoughts / Soulshade / Seers Hatred / Betrayal Within Individuals / Dehumanized / Daemon Breed / Inseminated By The Beast / Project: The New Breed 666.
ARTS OF DESOLATION, Century Media 77418-2 (2002) (European release). Incubator / The Hatebreed / Cold Flesh Colony / Dethroned / Embedded Insanity / The Second Manifest / Injected Terror / Human Chapter X / Scars / Mental Degeneration.
ARTS OF DESOLATION, Century Media 81182-2 (2002) (USA release). Incubator / The Hatebreed / Cold Flesh Colony / Dethroned / Embedded Insanity / The Second Manifest / Injected Terror / Human Chapter X / Scars / Mental Degeneration / Human Prey.
ARTS OF DESOLATION, King KICP-886 (2002) (Japanese release). Incubator / The Hatebreed / Cold Flesh Colony / Dethroned / Embedded Insanity / The Second Manifest / Injected Terror / Human Chapter X / Scars / Mental Degeneration / Human Prey / Creeping Death.
TRACES OF THE PAST, Century Media 77518-2 (2003). A Time To Die / One More Kill / Acid With Acid–Piece By Piece / Glitches Will Tell / Traces Of The Past / Serpent's Tongue / God Of Demise / Massive Machinery / The Empire / First Weapon Of Choice / Blackened.
TRACES OF THE PAST, King KICP-984 (2004). A Time To Die / One More Kill / Acid With Acid–Piece By Piece / Glitches Will Tell / Traces Of The Past / Serpent's Tongue / God Of Demise / Massive Machinery / The Empire / First Weapon Of Choice / Blackened / Shredding My Skin / Counteract The Dead.

THE FUNERAL PYRE (pic: Karen Jerzyk)

THE FUNERAL PYRE

LA HABRA, CA, USA — John Strachan (vocals), Jimmy (guitar), Adam Campbell (bass), Daniella (keyboards), Alex (drums).

THE FUNERAL PYRE is a La Habra, California based melodic Death Metal band founded during 2003 having morphed from an antecedent act billed ENVILENT. Formatively the band included SUICIDE SILENCE, BLACKHEART EULOGY and THE RED DAWN man Alex Lopez. The three song demo 'October' emerged that same year. A self-financed full-length album, 'Immersed By The Flames Of Mankind', arrived in 2004.

THE FUNERAL PYRE shared a 2006 split 7" vinyl single with LEECH entitled 'The First Book Of The Kings' on Forest Moon Records. A limited edition of 342 copies, half were pressed in clear vinyl, the remainder on red and grey swirl. Signing to Creator-Destructor Records second album 'The Nature Of Betrayal' saw release in August. US concerts throughout November were conducted with APIARY.

Prosthetic Records gave 'The Nature Of Betrayal' a re-release in March 2007.

October, The Funeral Pyre (2003) (Demo). A Gradual Awakening / World Of Vengeance / Isengard Unleashed.
IMMERSED BY THE FLAMES OF MANKIND, The Funeral Pyre (2004). The Wrath / World Of Vengeance / Sight Through Bleeding Eyes / Lies Of Eternity / A Fallacy Carved In Stone / A Gradual Awakening / Immersed By The Flames Of Mankind / Isengard Unleashed.
The First Book Of The Kings, Forest Moon (2006) (Split 7" vinyl single with LEECH. Limited edition 342 copies). The Last Breath Of Man (THE FUNERAL PYRE) / On The Eve Of Battle (LEECH) / The Greatest Burden (LEECH).
THE NATURE OF BETRAYAL, Creator-Destructor (2006). 200 Years / In The Wake / Here The Sun Never Shines / The Nature Of Betrayal / Plague That Leads To Extinction / Victims / Stealing The Air Of Life / Ending The Eternal Reign.

THE LOCUST

SAN DIEGO, CA, USA — Justin Pearson (vocals / bass), Bobby Bray (guitar), Joey Karam (keyboards), Gabe Serbian (drums).

Formed during the mid nineties THE LOCUST, a heady brew of Hardcore, Punk and Grind, was founded by frontman and bassist Justin Pearson, a veteran of acts such as STRUGGLE, BRAIN TOURNIQUET, SWING KIDS and CRIMSON CURSE. Formative members included BRAIN TOURNIQUET guitarist Dylan Scharf, second guitarist Bobby Bray, TARANTULA HAWK keyboard player Dave Warshaw and drummer Dave Astor.

Getting into their stride the band issued split product with JENNY PICCOLO, ARAB ON RADAR and MAN IS THE BASTARD. The band unit endured a succession of line-up changes but maintained their presence on the live circuit both in the USA and Europe. THE LOCUST's debut eponymous album, all 13 minutes of it, arrived in vinyl format the Autumn of 1998 on the GSL label. The entire pressing of 2000 copies swiftly sold out and a CD re-issue in May of 1999 followed suit as touring extended its reach into Japan. The following year a drum n' bass double 12" set of the track 'Well I'll Be a Monkey's Uncle' was released as part of GSL's LAB Remix Series. 2000 also witnessed the departure of original drummer David Astor, being superseded by Gabe Serbian from vegetarian Grind act CATTLE DECAPITATION.

THE LOCUST gigged in Japan for the second time during 2001, headlining five shows and supporting AT THE DRIVE IN at four more. A notable release would be the 2001 'Flight Of The Wounded Locust' EP, which comprised four 7" singles that locked together in a jigsaw. Five new tracks also saw release as a split EP shared with Tokyo's MELT BANANA. US headline gigs spanned the country for a six week stint prior to THE LOCUST acting as guests for ROCKET FROM THE CRYPT. With a third round of European dates fulfilled Gabe Serbian then united with ALEC EMPIRE and MERZBOW for a one-off performance at Japan's 'Fuji Rock' festival that July.

THE LOCUST members are naturally employed in a myriad of side ventures. The triumvirate of guitarist Bobby Bray, bassist Justin Pearson and drummer Gabe Serbian also operate with HOLY MOLAR working with former CHARLES BRONSON vocalist Mark McCoy. Pearson is also active with SOME GIRLS. Keyboard player Joey Karam is to be found on the live circuit as drummer for DEATH DRUG and LE SHOK.

THE LOCUST's 2003 offering 'Plague Landscapes' was produced by FUDGE TUNNEL's Alex Newport. THE LOCUST would open dates for ANDREW W.K. and FIREBALL MINISTRY's May 2004 US dates.

The band undertook a short run of West Coast dates in February 2005 alongside EX MODELS, THE PLOT TO BLOW UP THE EIFFEL TOWER and UPSILON ACRUX. An EP, 'Safety Second, Body Last', would be issued in March. THE LOCUST, FANTOMAS and TRIO CONVULSANT formed up the 2005 US 'Geek' tour in April.

PLAGUE LANDSCAPES, Epitaph (2003). Recyclable Body Fluids In Human Form / Identity Exchange Program Rectum Return Policy / Solar Panel Asses / Live From The Russian Compound / Earwax Halo Manufactured For The Champion In All Of Us / Wet Dream War Machine / Listen, The Mighty Ear Is Here / Who Wants A Dose Of The Clap? / Teenage Mustache / How To Become A Virgin / Anything Jesus Does I Can Do Better / Late For A Double Date With A Pile Of Atoms In The Water Closet / File Under 'Soft Core Seizures' / Practiced Hatred / Psst! Is That A Halfie In Your Pants? / The Half-Eaten Sausage Would You Like To See You In His Office / Pulling The Christmas Pig By The Wrong Pair Of Ears / Can We Get Another Nail In The Coffin Of Culture Theft? / Your Mantel Disguised As A Psychic Sasquatch / Twenty-Three Lubed Up Schizophrenics With Delusions Of Grandeur / Captain Gaydar It's Time To Wind Your Clock Again / Priest With The Sexually Transmitted Diseases, Get Out Of My Bed / Pickup Truck Full Of Forty Minutes.

THE LUST I SEEK

ALAVUS, FINLAND — *Juha Wuorinen (vocals), Kalle Suhonen (guitar), Jussi Pekkala (guitar), Antti Ojala (bass), Tomi Valkealahti (drums).*

Alavus based Doom Death outfit THE LUST I SEEK, founded during 2001, released the demo 'Where Shadows Grow Silent'. The group had been created by the DEMONITAR pairing of vocalist Juha Wuorinen and guitarist Jussi Pekkala, subsequently incorporating Tomi Valkealahti, another DEMONITAR man, on the drums. Formative members also included Sissala and Lehtonen, but this pair would soon depart being replaced by bassist Antti Ojala, of METATRIEL and DEMONITAR, and second guitarist Kalle Suhonen.

Progress with THE LUST I SEEK was slowed after the demo release as both Wuorinen and Valkealahti had to undertake

THE LOCUST

their national military service duties. Upon their return the group put in gigs, including support to SPIRITUS MORTIS, and set about recording the 2004 follow up 'Serpent Scripts'. In 2005 the band recorded tracks for a split release with FUNERAL PLANET. The 'Ancient' single saw release in March 2006.

Where Shadows Grow Silent, The Lust I Seek (2003) (Demo). Frozen Roses (For Thy Grave) / For My Sins / Where Shadows Grow Silent / The Silent Light.

Serpent Scripts, The Lust I Seek (2004) (Demo). Beyond The Grace Divine / Crowned In Damnation / Anno Pandemonia.

Ancient, The Lust I Seek (2006). Carpathian Desire / Faces In The Mist.

THE MEADS OF ASPHODEL

HODDESDON, HERTFORDSHIRE, UK — *Metatron (vocals), Azrael (guitar), Deorth (keyboards), Urakbaramel (drums).*

THE MEADS OF ASPHODEL, based out of Hoddesdon, Hertfordshire, is a left field Black Metal act that infuse their material with strong Arabian and avant-garde influences. The band make no bones about their religious beliefs, their website hosting a game entitled 'Shoot Jesus' penis off'! THE MEADS OF ASPHODEL was convened in 1998 by vocalist Metatron and Jaldaboath (a.k.a. James Fogarty or 'Mr. Fog') of EWIGKEIT, soon adding Zephon and Urakbaramel on drums. A succession of demos ensued starting with 'Bemoaning Of Metatron' in 1998, 'Metatron And The Red Gleaming Serpent' in 1999 and finally 2000's 'The Watchers Of Catal Huyuk'. The demo track 'Angelwhore' would be donated to Godreah compilation 'No Holy Additives Volume 2' whilst another demo cut 'The Watchers Of Catal Huyuk' made it onto Moongleam's 'The Silent Shining' collection'.

THE MEADS OF ASPHODEL 2001 debut 'The Excommunication Of Christ' would make a great impression upon the scene. Notable guest appearances included Space Rock veteran Huw Lloyd Langton of HAWKWIND appearing on a version HAWKWIND's 'Assault And Battery', Kobold of OLD FOREST and A.C. Wild (Alberto Contini) of cult Italian act BULLDOZER. The band also pay homage to the Punk / Metal inspiration of G.B.H. by including a cover version.

The band would contribute a version of BULLDOZER's 'Neurodelini' to a tribute EP compiled by Warlord Records. Metatron would also pay back a favour to OLD FOREST, adding guest vocals to a track 'Necrophiliac' on their 2002 album. Plans were also projected for a split 10" release shared with Norwegian Black Metal veterans MAYHEM, this resulting in the May 2002 release 'Jihad'. Limited to 666 copies 'Jihad' came as a picture disc featuring two, rare archive MAYHEM tracks.

Reports emerged during mid October that the band had been wrought by an acrimonious split, forcing both Jaldaboath and The Mad Mulla out of the picture and leaving Metatron in sole charge of the project. Fogarty duly prioritised solo concern EWIGKEIT. By December the group had announced the addition of bassist Deorth and guitarist/keyboardist Azrael.

A new studio album 'Exhuming The Grave Of Yeshua' was unveiled for 2003. Studio guests included former HAWKWIND members HUW LLOYD LANGTON and ALAN DAVEY, Mirai of SIGH, Vincent Crowley of ACHERON and Paul Carter from THUS DEFILED. Metatron and J.D Tait would also work up a Punk covers album under the banner THE THIEVES OF FATE. This collaboration included Evo of WARFARE and Paul Fox of THE RUTS.

THE MEADS OF ASPHODEL issued 'The Mill Hill Sessions' album in October of 2004 through Godreah Records, once again featuring guest appearances by HAWKWIND's ALAN DAVEY and HUW LLOYD LANGTON on bass and lead guitar. The album incorporated a cover of SEPULTURA's 'Refuse/Resist'. The band's industry continued apace with an early 2005 release 'The Damascus Steel', seeing Mirai of SIGH as guest and a cover version of HAWKWIND's 'Sword Of The East'. Yet more endeavours found the band working with Italian label Warlord Records for a split 7" single of BULLDOZER covers shared with FROSTMOON ECLIPSE. Meantime, J.D Jait, Urakbarammel and L. Cornel fired up side project WORMS OF SABNOCK for an album release via Mordgrimm Records.

The band would also be projecting a working title of 'The Passion And Death Of Iesous' as a third full length album. THE MEADS OF ASPHODEL issued an EP, 'In The Name Of God, Welcome To Planet Genocide', in July 2006 through Firestorm Records. A 2007 split album collaboration shared with THUS DEFILED featured cover versions of ANGELIC UPSTARTS 'Liddle Towers', CONFLICT's 'From Protest to Resistance', STIFF LITTLE FINGERS 'Straw Dogs', UK SUBS 'C.I.D.' and COCKNEY REJECTS 'Bad Man'.

THE EXCOMMUNICATION OF CHRIST, Supernal FERLY005CD (2001). The Excommunication Of Christ / Angelwhore / The Watchers Of Catal Huyuk / Agrat Bat Malab / Weeping Tears Of Angel Light / Bene Ha Elohim / Assault And Battery / Jezebel And The Philistines / Pale Bread Hunger / Rise In Godless Hell / Disembodied Voices Of Melchizedek / Falling With Lightning Rays Beamed Through The Blazing Firmament Towards The Untended Burial Ground Of Bharsag / Calling All Monsters.

Jihad EP, Supernal FERLY007PD (2002) (Split picture disc single with MAYHEM. Limited edition of 666 copies). Intro / Jihad: The Grisly Din Of Killing Steel / Paradise / Another God In Another Place.

EXHUMING THE GRAVE OF YESHUAH, Supernal FERLY 010 (2003). Intro—Exhuming The Grave Of Yeshua / God Is Rome / Blood Blasted Holy War / 80 Grains Of Sand / Guts For Sale / Utopia / Sons Of Anak Rise / A Healer Made God / Sluts Of The Netherworld / On Graven Images I Glide Beyond The Monstrous Gates Of Pandemonium To Face The Baptized Warriors Of Yahweh In The Skull Littered Plain Of Esdraelon / Book Of Dreams.

THE MEATSHITS

USA — *Robert Deathrage (vocals), Leyla Shelton, Doug Carranza, Aaron Copelan, Vince Castillo, Andy Garcia.*

An infamous name on the American underground circuit. The band, founded in 1987 previously known as CHEMICAL DEPENDENCY and led by Robert Deathrage a.k.a. M.C. Cuntkiller, are renowned for their sickening mixture of hardcore pornography and brutal Death soaked Grindcore. THE MEATSHITS issued a barrage of offensive demo cassettes and were one of the very first bands to utilize sampling. The group's trademark unsavoury titles included 'Frectate Fumes', 'Meet The Shits', 'Menstrual Samples', 'Bowel Rot', Regurgitated Semen', 'Let There Be Shit', 'Fuck Frenzy' and 'Genital Infection'.

A slew of split singles followed over the years as THE MEATSHITS struck up vinyl alliances with ANAL MASSAKER, DEAD, ANAL CUNT, BUTT AUGER CRAP, CATATONIC EXISTENCE, PSYCHO, Japan's C.S.S.O. and NECROPHILIACS.

ECSTACY OF DEATH, (0). Depravity / There Is No God / Children Of Rape / Menstrual Bloodlust / First Blow Job / Perverted Vengeance / Shit On Your Grave / The Devil Made Me Do It / Bulimic Excretion / Orgasmic Euphoria / Finger Fuck Surprise / Poor Feminine Hygiene / Bow To The Penis God / In You I Cum / Act Of Love / Anal Quickie-Act Of Hate / Cock Rock Faggots / Septic Jesus / Orgasm Of Cardiac Arrest / Bloodbath Cleansing / Forced Into Submission / Meat Rabbit / Revenge On A World Full Of Cunts / Eat My Fuck / Hairless But Hard / Isolated And Gang Raped / Sex Life / Cocaine Cunt Numb / Violent Outburst Of Sodomy / Elvis Is Still Dead / Manipulation Of Mankind / Fag Killer / Three Way Fuck / Would You Please Die / Surgically Removed Vagina / Runaway Sex Slave / Hermaphrodite Horror / Forbidden Fruit / Fornication / Mental Midget / Ignorance Is Bliss / She Never Says No / Ejaculation Evacuation / Don't Have A Nice Day / Disposal Of Human Garbage / Cum On Your Fucking Face / Excrement Infection Of The Male Urethra / A.C. (Anal Cunt) / Intelligence Refused / She Likes It Hard / Strenuous Fuck / F.B.M. / Bathe In Holy Excrement.

Crack Slave, Wicked Sick 4 (1991) (7" split single with ANAL CUNT). Crack Slave / Eternal Misery / Time For Sex / Test Tube Butt Baby / Lust For Death / Nose Candy / Bible Belt / Porno Palace / Rotting Fuckhole / Bullshit Lottery / Feverish Fucking / Oriental Orgasms / No Holes Barred / Body Heat / Drunk And Horny / The Golden Shower Girls / Censor Shit / Gallons Of Cum / Let There Be Shit / Acid Rain Meltdown.

Proud To Be An Asshole, Ax/ction ACT 15 (1992) (7 split single with PSYCHO). Proud To Be An Asshole / Greek Sex / Drive It Home / Tongue Probe / Harmony Excretion / Ice Slut / Orgasm Plasma / Face Hole / Fuck Fart / Meat Sauce / Dildo Girls / Wall To Wall Fucking / Negative Feedback / Fuck-Suck Action / Semen Sealed Asshole / Fuck Rush / No Solution / Maggot Puke / French Fuck / Sex Smells.

Final Exit, Regurgitated Semen RSR003 (1992). Final Exit / Fuck Attack / Fuck The Wet Spot / Vaginal Fallout / Get Naked Cunt / Pussy Fart / Love Song / Butt Pus / Lip Service / Pulsating Vaginal Infection / Bobbing For Stools / Brown Sugar / Anal Majesty / Vulgar Display / Church Approval / Sex For Profit (Not For Fun) / Ninety Proof Holy Water / Masterpiece Of Defecation / Legacy Of Shit / Cancerous Foreskin / A.I.D.S. Victim / Fuck Frenzy (Thrash version) / Regurgitated Semen / Regurgitated Semen (Part II) / The Meat Shits.

Live Split EP, Regurgitated Semen RSR002 (1992) (Double 7" split single with W.B.I.).

Make Me Cum, Psycho Mania PMR005 (1993). Moan Of Orgasm / Make Me Cum / Hugs And Drugs / Midnight Snack / Bizarre Fetish / Fingered / Working Girl / Mutated Testicle / Fear Of Sex / Torn Hymen / Cold Cunt / Anal Worship / Half Eaten Pussy / Bought The Farm / Skid Row Graduate / Stagnant Pussy Fumes / Blood In Your Stools / Slap Happy Pappy / Human Extinction / Am I Shit? / Alcoholic Aphrodisiac / Hypersexual Nymphomaniac / Stinking In The Earth / Sexual Death Sentence / Latex Euphoria / Dis-Pleasure / Spray Of Secretion / Vaginal Hell / Sexual Wasteland / Erotic Oblivion / Talk Dirty To Me / Introduction To Anal Sex.

Sexual Abuse EP, Gutted GR008 (1993). Sexual Abuse / Psychotic Interlude / Public Execution / The Meat Shits Part VI / In Pain / Incubator Of Death / You Wish You Were Me / Going Mental / This Is The End.

Rape Bait EP, Morbid Granny M666001MC (1994) (7" split single with CATATONIC EXISTENCE). Mind Control / Lucky Stuff / Waterworks / Sushi Girls / Potty Pals / Hypocrite Shit / Another Orgasm / Fighting Words / Fucked From Behind / Concentration Of Hate / Back To The Seventies / Backfired / Eve Of Your Death / Hate Dance.

Another Day Of Death EP, Regurgitated Semen RSR007 (1994) (7" split single with NECROPHILIACS). Get Ready To Deep Throat / Leaving In Pieces / Dripping In Sweat / Cum Spurting / Vaginal Leprosy / Slippery When Erect / Genital Hospital / Sex Novelty / Another Day Of Death.

Punishment (Tomb Of The Guardian Angel), Morbid (1995) (7" split single with C.S.S.O.). Punishment (Tomb Of The Guardian Angel) / Seven Year Jock Itch / Semen Splurge / Lick Up The Blood / ... Of Hate / Back To The Seventies / Backfire / Eye Of Your Death / G.G. Is Now Death / Burn In Her Lies / Mistake Fuck.

Take This And Eat It EP, Hellion (1995). Intro / Sexual Abuse / Hatred Speaks / Fucked Up Part II / Mental Skip / Incubator Of Death / I Spy (Masturbation) / You Should Have Thanked Me / Pink In Your Face / Stay Hard And Fuck / Dirty Old Farts / Mr. Stinky / Go Fuck Yourself / Anal Rampage / Vacuum Cunt / Piece Of Fuck / Barbaric Bitch Beater / Emotion Sickness / Death On All Fours / Fucked Up Part III / Outro.

Sewer In My Mind EP, Gulli GR007 (1995) (7" split single with DEAD). Homosexual Slaughter (Demon Wind Re-mix) / Barbaric Bitch Beater (Scissors Re-mix) / Homosexist (M.R.R.) / Another Brutal Fucked Up Song / Floats On The Water (Shit) / Perversion Spree / San Francisco Gay Massacre / Bursting Fluids (On Her Face) / Faggot (Freak) / Outro (I Hate Their Kind).

THE MONOLITH DEATHCULT

HOLLAND — *Robin Kok (vocals / bass), Michiel Dekker (vocals / guitar), Martijn Moes (guitar), Sjoerd Visch (drums).*

THE MONOLITH DEATHCULT's debut album, 'The Apotheosis', was released in 2002 through Cold Blood Industries. The band comprises vocalist / bassist Robin Kok of EXPOSING INNARDS, SLAYNE and LEGION repute, vocalist / guitarist Michiel Dekker of DEAD HEAD, BEYOND BELIEF and ETERNAL CONSPIRACY, guitarist Martijn Moes from LEGION, TOXOCARA and ETERNAL CONSPIRACY and drummer Sjoerd Visch, the latter of ALTAR, BEYOND BELIEF and TO ELYSIUM. Touring to promote the first release included European dates with THE CROWN and SKINLESS. Live work saw the inclusion of guitarist Jos van den Brand, a scene veteran of ACROSTICHON, MASTER, OUTBURST and CRUSTACEAN.

THE MONOLITH DEATHCULT signed to Karmageddon Media in July of 2004 for their second album 'The White Crematorium'. In September the band expanded their line up by drafting keyboard player Carsten Altena. Having already contributed synthesizers, samples and orchestras on both 'The Apotheosis' and the 'The White Crematorium', Altena is also known for his role as guitarist for Thrash act IZEGRIM and choirmaster of the ROYAL MAKHACHKALA STRING ORCHESTRA.

THE MONOLITH DEATHCULT teamed up with US Deathsters MACABRE and British act SCREAMIN' DEAMON for UK shows in August / September 2005.

During November 2006 THE MONOLITH DEATHCULT contracted a new deal with Mascot Records, entering Ground Zero studio with producer Pascal Altena for fresh album recordings the following month.

THE APOTHEOSIS, Cold Blood Industries CBI 0303 (2003). Doomed To Slaughter / Forest Of Flesh / Cathedral Of Corpses (Slayer Of Jihad Part I) / The Malleus Malificarum Manuscript / The Apotheosis / The Deserved Reputation Of Cruelty / The Desecration Of The Black Stone (Slayer Of Jihad Part II) / Der Kriegmeister / Colosseum Carnage.

THE WHITE CREMATORIUM, Karmageddon Media (2005).

THE NUMBER TWELVE LOOKS LIKE YOU

BERGEN COUNTY, NJ, USA — *Jase (vocals), Justin (vocals), Alex (guitar), Jamie (guitar), Smoogs (bass), Chree (drums).*

Bergen County, New Jersey's THE NUMBER TWELVE LOOKS LIKE YOU successfully blend Hardcore attitude with Grind Metal riffing, Jazz leanings and Screamo stylings. The group signed to Brutal Records for an EP, 'Put On Your Red Glasses', in March 2003. The band toured the East and Midwest in July 2004 sharing stages with END OF ALL and ION DISSONANCE. New York's Eyeball Records picked the band up in October,

THE MONOLITH DEATHCULT (pic: Cindy van Stralendorf)

issuing the EP 'An Inch Of Gold For An Inch Of Time' recorded at Stained Glass Studios, Paramus, featuring an inspired cover of THE KNACK's 'My Sharona', in January 2005. The full-length 'Nuclear. Sad. Nuclear' saw release in June.

2006 opened with a rash of US dates across January and February in collusion with ED GEIN and THROUGH THE EYES OF THE DEAD. The band partnered with YAKUZA, THE JONBENET and HEAVY HEAVY LOW LOW into July.

THE NUMBER TWELVE LOOKS LIKE YOU partnered up with CANCER BATS, FROM A SECOND STORY WINDOW and SPEAKERFIRE for January and February 2007 US dates. The band then featured on the April 'School of Rock' nationwide tour flanking HORSE THE BAND, LIGHT THIS CITY and SO MANY DYNAMOS. Summer dates throughout July and August had the band involved in the gargantuan 'Sounds Of The Underground' touring festival accompanied by JOB FOR A COWBOY, NECRO, GWAR, CHIMAIRA, AMON AMARTH, THE ACACIA STRAIN, HEAVY HEAVY LOW LOW, GOATWHORE, THIS IS HELL, THE DEVIL WEARS PRADA, DARKEST HOUR and EVERY TIME I DIE amongst others.

Put On Your Red Glasses, Brutal (2003). Civeta Dei / Blue Dress / Bambi The Hooker And A Case Of Beer / Jesus And Tori / Don't Get Blood On My Prada Shoes.

An Inch Of Gold For An Inch Of Time, Eyeball (2005).

NUCLEAR.SAD.NUCLEAR, Eyeball (2005). The Devil's Dick Disaster / Texas Dolly / Clarissa Explains Cuntainment / Track Four / The Proud Parents Convention Held At The ER / An Aptly Fictional Description / Like A Cat / Remembrance Dialogue / An Exercise In Self Portraiture: Go Shoot Yourself / Operating On A Re-Run Episode / Track Eleven / Category.

THE PLAGUE

STOCKHOLM, SWEDEN — *Mårten Hansen (vocals), Leo Pignon (guitar), Linus Nirbrant (guitar), Jesper Löfgren (bass), Fredrik Andersson (drums).*

Formed in early 2005, the Kungsängen / Stockholm based THE PLAGUE involved former members of esteemed Black / Death Metal band A CANOROUS QUINTET. This antecedent act had issued an October 1994 EP, 'As Tears' released through Chaos Productions, two albums for No Fashion Records, 1996's 'Silence Of The World Beyond', recorded at Abyss Studios with HYPOCRISY's Peter Tägtgren acting as producer, and 'The Only Pure Hate' in 1998 crafted at Sunlight Studios with Tomas Skogsberg behind the desk, but would fold that same year.

Guitarist Leo Pignon later forged a similar Black Metal outfit NIDEN DIV. 187 with members of DAWN and THY PRIMORDIAL releasing two albums 'Towards Judgement' and 'Impergium' on Necropolis Records. Drummer Fredrik Andersson is better known for his role in premier Swedish Black Metal band MARDUK. Andersson also boasts credits with AMON AMARTH, TRIUMPHATOR and ALLEGIANCE.

Vocalist Mårten Hansen guested on OCTOBER TIDE's 1999 album 'Grey Dawn'. By 2000 both guitarist Linus Nirbrant and Andersson were involved with GUIDANCE OF SIN. The following year Andersson's services were requested by AMON AMARTH. The drummer also found space, alongside Pignon, to launch side venture CURRICULUM MORTIS in union with Mattias Leinikka from GUIDANCE OF SIN as lead vocalist. The debut demo 'Into Death' surfaced in 2003.

Andersson started up a fresh project band in 2003, LAID TO REST being a Death / Thrash Metal project featuring KAPUT! and ORCHARDS OF ODENWRATH guitarist Zack Z. Former members of A CANOROUS QUINTET, Mårten Hansen, Leo Pignon, Linus Nirbrant, Jesper Löfgren and Fredrik Andersson embarked upon a new band project, THE PLAGUE, in early 2005. In February 2006 the group, working with producer Linus Nirbrant, cut the demo 'Let The World Burn' at Offbeat studio in Stockholm. However, during these sessions the group switched title to THIS ENDING.

Let The World Burn, The Plague Demo (2006). Seed Of Destruction / Plague Angel / Let The World Burn.

THE PROJECT HATE

ÖREBRO, SWEDEN — *Jonna Enckell (vocals), Jörgen Sandström (vocals), Lord Kenth Philipson (guitar), Petter Freed (guitar).*

THE PROJECT HATE is a Swedish Electro-Gothic Death Metal unit founded in 1998 by erstwhile GRAVE and ENTOMBED vocalist Jörgen Sandström in league with former LEUKEMIA, ROSICRUCIAN, ODYSSEY, LAME and HOUSE OF USHER guitarist Kenth Philipson (a.k.a. 'Lord K'). Lord K had initially assembled a project entitled DEADMARCH upon his relocation to Örebro, this venture upon the incorporation of Sandström, subsequently evolving into THE PROJECT HATE. The duo demoed up material the following year with Dan Swanö of EDGE OF SANITY acting as producer and ENTOMBED's L-G Petrov contributing backing vocals.

These sessions secured a deal with the German Massacre label and, adding singer Mia Ståhl, culminated in the release of 'Cybersonic Superchrist' in February of 2000. The August 2001 sophomore release 'When We Are Done ... Your Flesh Will Be Ours' was produced by Mieszko Talarczyk of NASUM. The group bolstered their sound with the addition of 2 TON PREDATOR guitarist Petter Freed and PAIN OF SALVATION bass player and FROZEN EYES guitarist Magnus Johansson in 2000. A live album, 'Killing Hellsinki', arrived later that same year, this release incorporating the 1999 demos.

THE PROJECT HATE parted ways with singer Mia Ståhl during October. Signing to the Dutch Mascot label the band entered the studio to record a new album billed as 'The Project Hate—Deadmarch, The Initiation of Blasphemy'. Female singer Jo Enckell, previously with BOUND, was incorporated into the band during January of 2003. By April the album title had been changed to 'Hate, Dominate, Congregate, Eliminate' with its release now given over to Threeman Recordings, the label owned by ENTOMBED. DARK FUNERAL's Emperor Magus Caligula contributed backing vocals.

In October of 2003 it would be learned that THE PROJECT HATE duo of Lord K and Jörgen Sandström had united with SANCTIFICATION bassist Tomas Elofsson and VOMITORY drummer Tobias Gustafsson to found an "old school" Death Metal band entitled GOD AMONG INSECTS. In early 2004 Sandström also enrolled himself into VICIOUS ART, a Death / Thrash act forged by former DARK FUNERAL and DOMINION CALIGULA members Mattias 'Dominion' Mäkelä and Robert 'Gaahnfaust' Lundin. Another record he featured on would be a 2004 album from THE MIGHTY NIMBUS, featuring on a cover of the SAINT VITUS track 'Born Too Late'.

THE PROJECT HATE

THE PROJECT HATE scheduled to record once again at Soundlab Studios in February 2005 with Mieszko Talarczyk of NASUM and GENOCIDE SUPERSTARS acting as producer. Due to Talarczyk's tragic loss in the Indian Ocean tsunami disaster the band switched to utilising DAN SWANÖ, recording at his studio in Örebro. Session bass work on the album, dubbed 'Armageddon March Eternal (Symphonies Of Slit Wrists)', came supplied by Michael Håkansson of EVERGREY. The track 'At The Entrance to Hell's Unholy Fire' featured backing vocals by "The Troops of Devastation", an assemblage of scene notables comprising Gustaf Jorde of DEFLESHED, Jonas Granvik of WITHOUT GRIEF and DEAD END WORLD, Morten Hansen of ACQ, Linus Ekström of INTO DESOLATION and PANDEMONIC, Anders Eriksson of HYDRA, Tobbe Sillman of GUIDANCE OF SIN, Jocke Widfeldt and Matti Mäkelä of VICIOUS ART, Insulter of Jesus Christ! From DAMNATION, Jonas Torndal of GRAVE, Anders Schultz from UNLEASHED and Björn Åkesson of CELTIC FROSTFLAKES.

In November Kenth Philipson joined the touring ranks of VOMITORY as fill-in guitarist for the recently departed Ulf Dalegren for gigs UK, Ireland, The Netherlands and Sweden.

Jörgen Sandström announced the formation of a deliberately retro-Death Metal band project entitled DEATH BREATH in collaboration with his erstwhile ENTOMBED colleague and THE HELLACOPTERS frontman Nicke Andersson with THUNDER EXPRESS man Robert Persson on guitar.

THE PROJECT HATE commenced work on fresh album recordings in October 2006. Michael Håkansson joined ALL ENDS in April 2007.

The Project Hate, The Project Hate (1998) (Demo). With Desperate Hands So Numb / Selfconstructive Once Again / Oceans Of Endless Tears.

CYBERSONIC SUPERCHRIST, Massacre MASCD 239 (2000). The Divine Burning Of Angels / The Swarming Of Whores / Self-Constructive Once Again / Shape, Memory, Murder / Nine Spectrums Of Impurity / Soul Infliction / Oceans Of Seemingly Endless Bleeding / Christianity Delete / With Desperate Hands So Numb.

WHEN WE ARE DONE ... YOUR FLESH WILL BE OURS, Massacre MASCD 284 (2001). I Smell Like Jesus ... Dead / Can't Wait / Hallucination / Believing Is Bleeding / Hate Incarnate / Forsaken By The Naked Light Of Day / Blessed Are We To Be Lied Upon / Disciples Of The Apocalypse / In Sickness And In Hell / Dividead.

KILLING HELLSINKI, Threeman TRECD008 (2002). I Smell Like Jesus ... Dead / Forsaken By The Naked Light Of Day / Can't Wait / The Divine Burning Of Angels / Christianity Delete / With Desperate Hands So Numb / With Desperate Hands So Numb (Demo) / Selfconstructive Once Again (Demo) / Oceans Of Seemingly Endless Bleeding (Demo).

HATE, DOMINATE, CONGREGATE, ELIMINATE, Threeman TRECD010 (2003). Hate / Nailed / Dominate / Deviate / Congregate / Burn / Eliminate / Weep.

DEADMARCH: INITIATION OF BLASPHEMY, www.theprojecthate.net (2005). Angels Misled / Bloodstained / The Crucified Starts To Reek / Divinity Erased / Everloving / So I Mourn / Soulrain / Sear The Son.

MCMXICX: ARMAGEDDON MARCH ETERNAL—SYMPHONIES OF SLIT WRISTS, Threeman TRECD019 (2005). At The Entrance To Hell's Unholy Fire / The Bleeding Eyes Of A Breeding Whore / I See

Nothing But Flesh / Resurrected For Massive Torture / We Couldn't Be Further From The Truce / Godslaughtering Murder Machine / Symphony Of The Deceived / Loveless, Godless, Flawless.

THE RED CHORD

REVERE, MA, USA — *Guy Kozowyk (vocals), Kevin Rampelberg (guitar), Gunface (guitar), Gregory Weeks (bass), John Dow (drums).*

Northern Massachusetts Grind-edged Hardcore outfit THE RED CHORD, including erstwhile ICTUS personnel vocalist Guy Kozowyk and guitarist Kevin Rampelberg, took their name from a line signifying a slit throat in Alan Berg's stage play 'Wozzeck'. The band debuted live in August of 2000 at the Cafe Mio in Taunton, Massachusetts sharing the stage with UNDYING and BLOOD HAS BEEN SHED. Line-up changes then saw the introduction of second guitarist Mike 'Gunface' and Adam Wentworth of BEYOND THE SIXTH SEAL. The inaugural album, 'Fused Together In Revolving Doors' released on the Robotic Empire imprint, was recorded with producer Andrew Schneider over just four days in December of 2001.

THE RED CHORD adopted a new rhythm section as 2004 dawned, losing the services of bass player Adam Wentworth, going on to join PREMONITIONS OF WAR, and drummer Mike Justain, maintaining his involvement in UNEARTH. As replacements the band drafted Gregory Weeks of BEYOND THE SIXTH SEAL and DEAD WATER DROWNING's Jon Dow on drums. Touring throughout April had THE RED CHORD partnered with SIX FEET UNDER, BURY YOUR DEAD, THE HEAVILS and ON BROKEN WINGS.

The debut 'Fused Together In Revolving Doors' would be the subject of a lavish re-issue in 2004, adding demo tracks, a full concert performance and the video clip for 'Dreaming In Dog Years'. The band signed to Black Market Activities Records, a subsidiary of Metal Blade, in March. New man behind the drum kit in May would be John Longstreth of ORIGIN, ANGEL CORPSE, SKINLESS and EXHUMED. However, by September Longstreth was out, temporarily joining DYING FETUS in October (and subsequently the reunited DIM MAK), and former drummer Mike Justain was acting as stand in. The band entered Planet Z Studios in Hadley, Massachusetts on 1st November with producer Zeuss to craft their sophomore full-length album 'Clients'. They would spend much of that month auditioning potential drummers, finally selecting EVISCERATE's Brad Fickeisen.

US touring in March of 2005 had THE RED CHORD announcing a touring partnership with DROWNINGMAN then embarking on April dates BURY YOUR DEAD, A LIFE ONCE LOST and IF HOPE DIES. To coincide the band filmed a promotional video for the track 'Antman' with director Dave Brodsky. The band put in Autumn US dates in partnership with BETWEEN THE BURIED AND ME, THE ACACIA STRAIN and FROM A SECOND STORY WINDOW. Maintaining the road ethic, the band allied with HIGH ON FIRE, THE CHARIOT and EVERY TIME I DIE for a month long, 27 city trek launching on 7th September in Poughkeepsie, New York. Crossing the Atlantic, THE RED CHORD engaged with the European 'Persistence' tour in December, ranked alongside AGNOSTIC FRONT, HATEBREED, NAPALM DEATH, BORN FROM PAIN, BLEED THE SKY and FULL BLOWN CHAOS.

The band's relentless live campaigning continued unabated into 2006 as they forged a road union in North America throughout February with THROWDOWN, STILL REMAINS and A DOZEN FURIES, then in March alongside THE BLACK DAHLIA MURDER, THROWDOWN and THE AGONY SCENE.

'Ozzfest' loomed for the 2006 summer touring season, the group hitting Canada as a warm up in June, flanking ALL THAT REMAINS, UNEARTH, A LIFE ONCE LOST, WALLS OF JERICHO and IF HOPE DIES, before sharing the festival stages with OZZY OSBOURNE, SYSTEM OF A DOWN, HATEBREED, LACUNA COIL, DISTURBED, BLACK LABEL SOCIETY, UNEARTH, BLEEDING THROUGH, NORMA JEAN, A LIFE ONCE LOST, STRAPPING YOUNG LAD, ATREYU, FULL BLOWN CHAOS, WALLS OF JERICHO, ALL THAT REMAINS and BETWEEN THE BURIED AND ME. May 2007 UK and European shows had the band partnered up with FROM A SECOND STORY WINDOW.

FUSED TOGETHER IN REVOLVING DOORS, Robotic Empire (2002). Nihilist / That Certain Special Ugly / Catalepsy / Like A Train Through A Pigeon / He Was Stretching, And Then He Climbed Up There / Breed The Cancer / L Formation / Dreaming In Dog Years / Sixteen Bit Fingerprint.

CLIENTS, Metal Blade (2005). Fixation On Plastics / Lay The Tarp / Black Santa / Clients / Upper Decker / Hospice Residence / Dragon Wagon / Love On The Concrete / Blue Line Cretin / He Was Dead When I Got There.

THE REVENGE PROJECT

BURGAS, BULGARIA — *MaxPain (vocals), Staffa (vocals / guitar), (vocals / guitar), Sevar (bass), Kalhas (drums).*

THE REVENGE PROJECT is a collective of musicians from prominent Bulgarian extreme Metal bands. The original formation included singer G.McManus, guitarists Deimos (a.k.a. "Lord Deimos Infernal Frost" or Zlatin Atanasov) of DIABOLISM and Staffa (Stanislav Vassilev) of KARTZER, NECROMANCER bassist Nedelcho Harizanov and drummer Kalhas of KOROZY and BIOPHOBIA, performing a debut gig at the 'Metal Sound' festival in Shoumen during 2001. Subsequently MaxPain of EXHUMATION took over vocals and KOROZY's Astaroth enrolled as bassist.

THE REVENGE PROJECT released a 2002 demo entitled 'No Chance To See The Sun Again'. Staffa, Deimoz and Astaroth would also be operational with Industrial project HIERONYMUS BOSCH. THE REVENGE PROJECT returned in 2004 with a demo 'The End Is Coming'. This would be promoted by supports in Bulgaria to both VADER and SODOM. The band signed with the Stain Studio label for a full-length album in 2005.

No Chance To See The Sun Again, The Revenge Project (2002). No Chance To See The Sun Again / Anger To Dwell / The Deadly Dance / The Heart.

The End Is Coming, (2004).

THE SCOURGER

HELSINKI, FINLAND — *Jari Hurskainen (vocals), Timo Nyberg (guitar), Jani Luttinen (guitar), Kimmo Kammonen (bass), Seppo Tarvainen (drums).*

Helsinki melodic Death Metal combo THE SCOURGER dates to 2003, quoting an opening formation as former GANDALF singer Jari Hurskainen, guitarists Pekka Hämäläinen with Seppo Tarvainen on the drums. A demo that year, hosting a cover version of 'Cold' originally by AT THE GATES, was recorded as a trio. Expanding, the group then introduced the GANDALF and DIVINE DECAY credited Timo Nyberg on second guitar. However, Hämäläinen opted out to be superseded by Harri Hytönen, another GANDALF adept also having CUBEHEAD ties. Alec Hirst-Gee from DIVINE DECAY and SURBURBAN TRIBE aided as session bassist for songwriting sessions.

Next product would be an EP, 'To The Slayground', released in February 2005. These tracks had been recorded at Moonman Studios in Karjaa with BLAKE's Aaro Seppovaara acting as producer. For these recordings the group enlisted AIRDASH and GANDALF bassist Kirka Sainio.

Making the bass position permanent would be ONE ORPHAN MORE's Kimmo Kammonen. Quite incredibly, the band's next single, 'Hatehead' in July, went straight into the national Finnish charts at number 1.

Jani Luttinen of THE WAKE took the second guitar post from Hytonen, this new line-up debuting with a hometown support to TRIVIUM in October 2005. THE SCOURGER issued a full-length album, 'Blind Date With Violence' again produced by Aaro Seppovaara, in January 2006. That May Jani Luttinen injured his hand, necessitating WARMEN's Antti Wirman stepping in as substitute.

In June German label Cyclone Empire took the album on for European license. This version added cover versions of SLAYER, 'Ghosts Of War', and TESTAMENT's 'Over The Wall'. The EP 'Maximum Intensity' entered the Finnish charts at no. 3, rising to number 2 the following week. THE SCOURGER commenced fresh album recordings in early January 2007 at Seawolf Studios in Helsinki.

The Scourger, The Scourger (2003) (Demo). The Fool Circle / Pain Zone / Maximum Intensity / Cold.
To The Slayground, Stay Heavy SHR 001-2 (2005). Slayground / Soul Seducer / The Greediness / Crossfire Of Lies / Malediction Of Heredity / Black Worms.
Hatehead, Stay Heavy SHR 002-2 (2005). Hatehead / Vicious Circle. Chart position: 1 FINLAND.
BLIND DATE WITH VIOLENCE, Stay Heavy SHR 003-2 (2006). Decline Of Conformity—Grading:Deranged / Hatehead / Maximum Intensity / Enslaved To Faith / The Oath & The Lie / Chapter Thirteen / Pain Zone / Exodus Day / Feast Of The Carnivore.
Maximum Intensity, Stay Heavy SHR 004-2 (2006). Maximum Intensity / Ghosts Of War / Over The Wall. Chart position: 2 FINLAND.

THE SEVENTH DELIRIUM

BARCELONA, SPAIN — *Jonathan Barrena (vocals), Elena Uría (vocals), Patxi Valdés (guitar), Jonathan Aparicio (guitar), Juanjo Ruíz (bass), Mireia Muset (keyboards), Luis Uría (drums).*

THE SEVENTH DELIRIUM is a seven piece, Barcelona, Catalonia based melodic Death Metal operation featuring dual lead vocalists Jonathan Barrena and Elena Uría. The group was forged during 1998 by guitarist Jonathon Aparicio and bassist Jonathon Barrena, later drawing in second guitar player Luis Uría and drummer Raúl Lari, then singer Mireia Muset. The latter would be replaced by Elena Urìa to record a three track demo at Estudios Jorbasa.

Lari was to withdraw, due to national military obligations, and the group evolved to see Juanjo Ruìz handling bass and Barrena switching to the guitar role. This version of the band cut further demos at Maratón Records studios. THE SEVENTH DELIRIUM evolved once again as Barrena concentrated on lead vocals whilst Patxi Valdés came into the fold as second guitarist. A third round of demos was then laid down in Barcelona's Control Room studios. A self-financed album, 'The Book Of Sorrows', emerged during December 2002.

THE BOOK OF SORROWS, 7th Delirium (2002). House Of Thousand Eyes / Rotten Flower / About The Damned / Last Dance Of Berseker / Eve Of Destruccion / The Saddest Room / Shall We Die? / Bones Of Woe.

THE TOMBERS

ITALY — *Il Colonnello (vocals), The Redeemer (guitar), Leo Glass (bass), Fabio (drums).*

Novara Black-Death Metal combo THE TOMBERS was created in 1997 by Leo Glass, former bassist with Punk outfit THE BASTARDS. Both singer Il Colonnello, joining in 2001 and noted for wielding a chainsaw onstage, and guitarist The Redeemer also operate Black Metal acts FRANGAR and HIEMS. Il Colonnello is also a member of Grindcore unit RECTO RECTORS. THE TOMBERS cut a 2003 album 'Until You Are Dead', this opus recorded at One Voice Studios in Chivasso and including a cover of VENOM's 'Countess Bathory'.

Supporting ENTHRONED in June an over eager fan threw a real cow's head into the audience, hospitalizing an unfortunate crowd member. THE TOMBERS offered a free demo as compensation! The band toured Italy as support to BLOOD RED THRONE and GORGOROTH that September.

UNTIL YOU ARE DEAD, The Tombers (2003). World's End / Insect Invasion / Necromantic / Dark Crusade / Funeral For You / Killer Madness / White Death / Countess Bathory / Intermezzo / Maybe I'm Mad / Liquid Flesh / Vomito Etilico / The Bastards.

THEORY IN PRACTICE

SANDVIKEN, SWEDEN — *Henrik Ohlsson (vocals / drums), Peter Lake (guitar), Mattias Engstrand (bass).*

A precision Death Metal act with Euro-Thrash overtones. THEORY IN PRACTICE was formed up in Sandviken during mid 1995 by former INCARNATION vocalist / guitarist Johan Ekman along with RIVENDELL personnel bassist / keyboard player Mattias Engstrand and guitarist Peter Lake (a.k.a. Peter Sjöberg), the latter also citing previous membership of SORCERY. Drummer Henrik Ohlsson had prior credits with LEGIA and ADVERSARY. The group debuted with the demo session 'Submissive'.

A Tomas Skogsberg produced debut, 'Third Eye Function', arrived on the Singapore based Pulverized imprint after which Ekman departed. Initially reports suggested that Daniel Bryntse of WITHERED BEAUTY, FORLORN and WINDWALKER was set to act as replacement but this proposed union failed to materialise. THEORY IN PRACTICE's sophomore album 'Armageddon Theories', produced by Tommy Tägtgren at the world renowned Abyss Studios and seeing drummer Henrik Ohlsson taking charge of lead vocals, was originally released on Pulverized label in 1999. However, it would see a subsequent re-release with all new artwork some two years later courtesy of the French Listenable concern. The band mooted a band name switch to MONUMENT and later RAPTURE but these plans were then curtailed. Between these releases band members drummer Henrik Ohlsson and guitarist Peter Lake fired up another more Black Metal inclined band unit entitled MUTANT, resulting in 'The Aeonic Majesty' album.

Drummer Henrik Ohlsson would co-found the Occult based Thrash Metal side endeavour THRAWN in union with Kjell Andersson of AZOTIC REIGN in 2001, resulting in a demo 'Light Creates Shadows'. This band would evolve into ALTERED AEON. The drummer also held ties to DIABOLICAL.

Quite bizarrely THEORY IN PRACTICE's third album, 'Colonizing The Sun' issued in 2002, contained a cover rendition of SPARKS' 'This Town Ain't Big Enough for Both of Us'.

Submissive, Theory In Practice (1996) (Demo).
THIRD EYE FUNCTION, Pulverised ASH003CD (1997). Submissive / The Third Eye Function / Astral Eyes / Self Alternative / Worlds Within Worlds (The Ethereal Withdrawal) / The Expiring Utopia / Theoretical Conviction / Void Of Origin / Inexplicable Nature.
THE ARMAGEDDON THEORIES, Pulverized ASH009CD (1999). Dehumanized / The Visionaire / Departure / Prophecies / Carnage Earth / Embryo / Posthuman Era / Embodied For War.
COLONIZING THE SUN, Listenable POSH-035 (2002). Colonizing The Sun / Conspiracy In Cloning / The Psychomantum Litany (Chronicle Excerpt) / Shapeshifter / Ashen Apocrypha / That Clockwork That Counts Aeons / Illuminati / Replica Dawn / This Town Ain't Big Enough For Both Of Us.

THIS ENDING

STOCKHOLM, SWEDEN — *Mårten Hansen (vocals), Leo Pignon (guitar), Linus Nirbrant (guitar), Jesper Löfgren (bass), Fredrik Andersson (drums).*

Formed in early 2005, the Kungsängen / Stockholm based THIS ENDING, created as THE PLAGUE, involved former members of esteemed Black / Death Metal band A CANOROUS QUINTET. This antecedent act had issued an October 1994 EP, 'As Tears' released through Chaos Productions, two albums for No Fashion Records, 1996's 'Silence Of The World Beyond', recorded at Abyss Studios with HYPOCRISY's Peter Tägtgren acting as producer, and 'The Only Pure Hate' in 1998 crafted at

Sunlight Studios with Tomas Skogsberg behind the desk, but would fold that same year.

Guitarist Leo Pignon later forged a similar Black Metal outfit NIDEN DIV. 187 with members of DAWN and THY PRIMORDIAL releasing two albums 'Towards Judgement' and 'Impergium' on Necropolis Records. Drummer Fredrik Andersson is better known for his role in premier Swedish Black Metal band MARDUK. Andersson also boasts credits with AMON AMARTH, TRIUMPHATOR and ALLEGIANCE.

Vocalist Mårten Hansen guested on OCTOBER TIDE's 1999 album 'Grey Dawn'. By 2000 both guitarist Linus Nirbrant and Andersson were involved with GUIDANCE OF SIN. The following year Andersson's services were requested by AMON AMARTH. The drummer also found space, alongside Pignon, to launch side venture CURRICULUM MORTIS in union with Mattias Leinikka from GUIDANCE OF SIN as lead vocalist. The debut demo 'Into Death' surfaced in 2003.

Andersson started up a fresh project band in 2003, LAID TO REST being a Death / Thrash Metal project featuring KAPUT! and ORCHARDS OF ODENWRATH guitarist Zack Z. Former members of A CANOROUS QUINTET, Mårten Hansen, Leo Pignon, Linus Nirbrant, Jesper Löfgren and Fredrik Andersson embarked upon a new band project, THE PLAGUE, in early 2005. In February 2006 the group, working with producer Linus Nirbrant, cut the demo 'Let The World Burn' at Offbeat studio in Stockholm. However, during these sessions the group switched title to THIS ENDING. The album 'Inside The Machine', released on December 1st, was again crafted utilising the Nirbrant / Offbeat Studios formula.

Let The World Burn, This Ending (2006) (Reissue of 'The Plague' demo). Seed Of Destruction / Plague Angel / Let The World Burn.

INSIDE THE MACHINE, Metal Blade MB 14603-2 (2006). Seed Of Destruction / Inside The Machine / Pitch Black / Plague Angel / Lidless Eyes / Armageddon / Nailed Down / Let The World Burn / Into Pain / This Ending.

THORAZINE

CALGARY, AB, CANADA — *Pete Redecopp (vocals), Joe Sikorski (guitar), Matt McDonald (guitar), Lance Davis (bass), Ryan O'Neill (drums).*

Calgary's THORAZINE is often quoted as Alberta's leading Death Metal outfit debuting with a demo in 1997. Injected Productions issued the album 'Seed The Black Sky' during 1999. Founding bassist Don Stenhouse exited to join PERICARDIUM. Switching to Deathgasm Records THORAZINE's second album 'Geneticide' emerged in 2002. At this juncture THORAZINE would be credited with a roster of vocalist Shane Hawco "Crepitis Asphyxiations", guitarists Joe Sikorski "Corrosive Benevolent Distortions" and Jeff Taylor-Beitz "Razorwire Priesthood", bassist Dave "Ultimo" Rooks "Undertone Pain Injector" and drummer Scott Tanner "Malicious Death Pulse".

Subsequently the band included the CHUPACABRA, K.F.H., SNOWAXE and D.F.A. credited drummer Ryan O'Neill. Shortly after THORAZINE recorded their third and final album, 'The Day The Ash Blacked Out The Sun', vocalist Shane Hawco stepped down, relocating to Edmonton to join Wes Sontag's SECTION VIII, being replaced by Pete Redecopp of M.S.C. and D.F.A. However, upon release of the record in January 2004 the band dissolved.

Post THORAZINE, bassist Lance Davis co-founded BLACKSKY. Guitarist Joe Sikorski joined BLACKSKY and CAVEAT. Redecopp and O'Neill stayed together in a new Grind orientated formation dubbed EVERYTHING IS DEAD. This act would be short-lived though and, together with Cory Hutchison the duo founded NOISE CONVULSION. Bassist Dave Rooks joined OCCAMS RAZOR whilst Jeff Taylor-Beitz, as "Sannhet Nebelwerfer", figured in TWO RAVENS and OPERATION WINTER MIST.

The THORAZINE credited Scott Tanner, also holding EON credits, joined up with Black Metal act OPERATION WINTER MIST in May 2005.

Thorazine, Thorazine (1997). Intro / Demise / Diabolic Illusions / Corporate Messiah / Tortured Existence / Thorazine / Blind Lead The Blind / 187 / Rite To Die / Cross Of Emptiness / Children Of Redemption / Silent As They Dream / Solitude / Buried Alive / Epitaph.

SEED THE BLACK SKY, Injected Productions (1999). C.L.A.B.T. (Cunt Like Bear Trap) / The Pride / Rapid Desecration / Wall Of Corpses / Fuck Sanity / Flatline / Into The Light.

GENETICIDE, Deathgasm DG-08 (2002). Into The Chaos / Aborted / Blind Eat The Blind / Geneticide / Fifth Victim / Here I Lay Rotten / Malpractice Makes Perfect / Curbstomp Execution / Injecting Utopia / Baptized In Excrement / Infanticide / Iron Hook Purification / Tortured Existence.

THE DAY THE ASH BLACKED OUT THE SUN, Deathgasm DG-016 (2004). Compromise / Beastial Insemination / The Day The Ash Blacked Out The Sun / The Zone / Behind Cold Eyes / My Brothers Keeper / Raping Under God / U.N. Holy War / Sewn By Numbers.

THORIUM

SWEDEN / DENMARK — *Michael H. Anderson (vocals), Morten Ryberg (guitar), Allan Tvelebakk (guitar), Jonas Lindblood (guitar), Jesper Frost (drums).*

The Danish / Swedish collaboration THORIUM boasts no less than three guitarists with bass duties reportedly delegated out to whichever one is the most drunk at the time. Jonas Lindblood (Linblad) has credits with TAETRE whilst drummer Jesper Frost is known from INIQUITY. The band produced an outstanding Black Death Metal record but fell foul of their record company Diehard who relinquished the band's contract due to apparent Nazi lyrics. The situation was a huge misunderstanding and Diehard resigned the group.

Vocalist Michael H. Anderson, guitarists Morten Ryberg and Allan Tvelebakk are all erstwhile members of WITHERING SURFACE. Ryberg, a veteran of cult act ARISE, also plays with INFERNAL TORMENT.

The 2002 album 'Unleashing The Demons' closed out with a cover version of CANCER's 'Cancer Fucking Cancer'. Jesper Frost joined melodic Death Metal act ECITON in early 2005. That August THORIUM cut a three track demo at Berno Studios in Malmö. 2005 saw Frost operating with DOWNLORD, the band led by BOLT THROWER and BENEDICTION singer Dave Ingram.

OCEAN OF BLASPHEMY, Diehard RRS948 (2000). Crest For War / Abomination Of God / Crypts Of Chaos / Impaled / Betrayed By God / Countless Ways To Die / Ocean Of Blasphemy / Desecrating The Graves / Dawn Of Flames / Lunatic Of God's Creation.

UNLEASHING THE DEMONS, Progress PCD59 (2002). Unleashing The Demons / Nocturnal Prophet Of Destruction / Mark Of Wrath / Hateful Vengeance / Infestation Of Salvation / Throne Of Infernal Fire / Warlust / Altars Of Blood / Construction Of Chaos / Mangled Screams / Cancer Fucking Cancer.

Checkpoint # 4, Diehard (2003) (Split promotion release with KOLDBORN, GURD, 2 TON PREDATOR and AURORA BOREALIS). Infestation Of Salvation.

Thorium, www.thorium666.com (2005) (Internet download demo). Cast from Hell / Sinful Death / Malignant Darkness.

THORNAFIRE

CHILE — *Antonio Acuña (vocals), Víctor MacNamara (guitar), Alejandro Lizana (guitar), Alexis Muñoz (bass), Andrés González (drums).*

THORNAFIRE feature former SILENTIUM and DOMINUS XUL drummer Andrés González and his ex-DOMINUS XUL colleague Alejandro Lizana on guitar. The band was founded during November of 1998 and originally included singer Antonio Acuña on vocals, Victor Mac-Namara on guitars, MELEK TAUS guitarist David Liempi and drummer Victor Vegara. This version of THORNAFIRE cut the 1999 demo 'Granted For All Sombreness'.

Both Liempi and Vegara exited in 2001. Enrolling drummer Eduardo Diaz THORNAFIRE recorded the EP 'Mortus Tenebrae Surrectus', this outing including a cover version of ATOMIC AGRESSOR's 'The Hallucination'. Subsequently Lizana and González took their positions. A 2004 demo entitled 'Sin And Flesh Devotion' secured a label deal with Ibex Moon Records, the imprint owned by INCANTATION's John McEntee. THORNAFIRE duly commenced work on the album 'Exacerbated Gnostic Manifestation'.

Mortus Tenebrae Surrectus EP, Skull (2001). The Arrival (Of Ablazed Hordes) / Avernal Empire / Scorching Iron Thorns / From Grand And Darkest Conversion / Risen From Somberness / The Hallucination / Those Funeral And Sorcering Voices.

THOU SHALT SUFFER

NOTODDEN, NORWAY — *Ihsahn.*

Avant-garde styled, obscure Death Metal from Notodden created during 1991 featuring EMPEROR personnel Samoth (a.k.a. Tomas Thormodsæter Haugen), Ihsahn (Vegard Sverre Tveitan) and Ildjarn (Vidar Vaaer). The band went through a slew of formative titles before settling on THOU SHALT SUFFER. Initially founded in Akkerhaugen as DARK DEVICE then XERASIA, the formative trio comprised vocalist / bassist Finn Arne Nielsen, guitarist Tomas Thormodsæther Haugen with Ronny Johnson on drums. A 1990 live rehearsal demo was issued under the XERASIA banner prior to a name change EMBRYONIC, having replaced Nielsen with Vegard Sverre Tveitan and releasing the demo 'The Land Of Lost Souls', recorded in November 1990 at Notodden Lydstudio. Subsequently the act morphed again into THOU SHALT SUFFER.

THOU SHALT SUFFER was created by Ihsahn and Samoth in parallel to EMPEROR's formation. Session drums would be supplied by Thorbjørn Akkerhaugen, proprietor of Akkerhaugen Lydstudios. First product was a 1991 7" single released through Distorted Harmony entitled 'Open Mysteries Of Your Creations', limited to 1100 copies. Also emerging that year would be a rehearsal demo and the 'Into The Woods Of Belial' set.

Subsequently, Ihsahn continued the venture as a solo undertaking, delving into more ambient landscapes. Although THOU SHALT SUFFER remained a background force to his main activities, with the archive demo sessions 'Into The Woods Of Belial' surfacing in 1997 on Samoth's own Nocturnal Art Productions, the Candlelight label collected together archive demos for a 2001 release 'Somnium'.

Ihsahn has a wealth of extreme Metal affiliations besides THOU SHALT SUFFER and EMPEROR including ARCTURUS, ILDJARN, PECCATUM, ULVER, STAR OF ASH and WONGRAVEN. An IHSAHN solo album, ' 'The Adversary', saw release in April 2006.

Open Mysteries Of Your Creations EP, Distorted Harmony DH05 (1991) (7" vinyl single. Limited edition 1100 copies). Painful Void Of Time / Spectral Prophecy.
Into The Woods Of Belial, Thou Shalt Suffer (1991) (Cassette demo). Into The Woods Of Belial / I Seek The Path Of Obscurity / Chimera Dimension / The Goat Of A Thousand Young / Succumb To Vestigia Terrent.
Thou Shalt Suffer, Thou Shalt Suffer (1994) (Rehearsal demo). Into The Woods Of Belial / The Goat Of A Thousand Young / Chimera Dimension / I Seek The Path Of Obscurity (Burb mix) / . . . Obscurity Supreme.
INTO THE WOODS OF BELIAL, Nocturnal Art Productions ECLIPSE 007 (1997). Into The Woods Of Belial / I Seek The Path Of Obscurity / Chimera Dimension / The Goat Of A Thousand Young / Succumb To Vestigia Terrent / Painful Void Of Time / Spectral Prophecy / Into The Woods Of Belial / The Goat Of A Thousand Young / Chimera Dimension / I Seek The Path Of Obscurity (Burp mix) / . . . Obscurity Supreme.
SOMNIUM, Candlelight CANDLE 049CD (2000). Solum Visio Perfecta Est / Solum Somnium Completum Est / Solum Haec Visio Potest Mihi Dare / Absolutam Commoventem Suavitatem / Solum Hoc Somnium Est Verum Mihi / Non Possum Vivere Ante / Meum Sommium Esse Veritatem / Solum Tunc Possum Vivere / Vivam In Meo Somnio / Numquam Peribo.

THRALLDOM

NEW YORK, NY, USA — New York blackened Death Metal band THRALLDOM is fronted by vocalist / guitarist Killusion of VILLAINS and Doom outfit UNEARTHLY TRANCE. Only 15 copies of the opening 1997 demo 'Impious Survival Séance' were released. A second session, the 'Phoenix', was only slightly more generously distributed to the tune of 20 copies. THRALLDOM released the 2003 demo 'Beast Eye Opened To The Sky'.

Deathstrike Records released a yellow vinyl EP, 'The Seven Heads Of The Lion Serpent', restricted to 777 copies in 2005. The album 'A Shaman Steering The Vessel Of Vastness' emerged through Profound Lore in March 2006. Later that same year Killusion announced the demise of THRALLDOM and fired up a fresh project billed DRIFTING COLLISION, weighing in with the EP 'External Paranormal System'.

Impious Survival Séance, Thralldom (1997) (Demo. Limited edition 15 copies). Hung From Eye-Lids / Amidst The Fog / Crown Of The Unearthly Trance / Immersed As The Sun Sets.
Phoenix EP, Thralldom (1999) (Limited edition 20 copies). Telepathic Currents / 4th Dimensional Warpath / Immersed / The Darkest Green / Phoenix.
Veins/Crown, Thralldom (1999) (Demo). Veins Sewn Together / Crown Of The Unearthly Trance.
Warsteiner Sessions, Thralldom (2001) (Demo). Warsteiner / Nuclear Hate / Decrepit Foul Laughter / Reign Of The Magus / When Winter Arrives.
Promo 2002, Regimental (2002) (Demo. Limited edition 55 hand numbered copies). Nuclear Hate / Warsteiner.
A Murderous Magus Of The Morphogenetic Grid EP, Regimental REG002EP (2002) (Blue vinyl. Limited edition 555 copies). Ritual Plateau / Stimulus Corrosion / Nuclear Hate / Heathen From The Aether.
Distress And The Inversionist, Humanless Recordings (2003) (Limited edition 555 copies). Distress And The Inversionist.
The Seven Heads Of The Lion Serpent, Deathstrike DR036 (2005) (Limited edition 777 copies. Yellow vinyl). The Expiration Is Sweeter Than Death / Holy Mother Of Abominations / Waratah.
BLACK SUN RESISTANCE, Total Holocaust (2005) (Limited edition 1000 copies). No Return / Diminishing Daylight / Do Not Speak Of It Until The Gun Is Fired / Stealing Gold Out Of A Pocket Of A Corpse / Soothsayer Of The Red Moon / Sin Is Necessary (As Is Air) / A Gathering To Invoke The Gnostic Bomb.
A SHAMAN STEERING THE VESSEL OF VASTNESS, Profound Lore (2006). Anticipation Of An Obituary / Quantum Frost / Only The Dead Speak The Truth / The Wolf Will Never Die / Ultra-Extinction / Narrow Road / The Mentu Dynasty.

THROCULT

DENVER, CO, USA — *Inferno (vocals / guitar), Gremor Azazel (guitar), Forneus Amon (bass), Lord Naberius (drums).*

Denver, Colorado based, electronically charged blasphemous Death Metal act. THROCULT, previously entitled THROAT CULTURE, debuted in 2001 with the 'De-Facto' album. During July of 2002 the band would appoint Ivan Alcala, a former SERBERUS member, as second guitarist. Bassist Cassie Belday would also deputise for live work with DEADSPEAK.

In September, after laying down a pre-production promotion EP 'Hunted' as a taster for a forthcoming album 'The Flower Of Flesh And Blood', THROCULT parted ways with drummer Dustin Parsons. The band were quick in replacing him with erstwhile SERBERUS and SYNTHETIC DELUSION skinsman Jeremy Portz. This new recruit would also enjoy a very brief association with EMBER as stand in drummer.

Keyboard player Jeremy Fisher (a.k.a. 'Scab') also operates side endeavour NICARAGUAN DEATH SQUAD. Vocalist

Chris Vigil is also employed with REV23. Fisher is no longer a THROCULT member.

In August of 2003 Chris Vigil parted ways with the band. The following month bassist Cassandra "Cassie" Begay was ousted, THROCULT duly replaced her and united with Rudy Hernandez of the SLAYER tribute band DIVINE INTERVENTION. Further changes saw drummer Jeremy Portz opting out in December to concentrate on his studies leaving the official line up standing as vocalist / guitarist Inferno (a.k.a. Ivan Alcala), guitarist Gremor Azazel (Nick Jackson), bass player Forneus Amon (Dave Borusch) and Lord Naberius (David Csicsely) on the drums. The band entered Flatline Audio Studios in June of 2004 with producer Dave Otero to commence recording a new album, originally entitled 'Order Of The Lunar Temple' but then switched to 'Stormbringer—Conjuration Of The Nighthorde', for Crash Music.

With guitarist Nick Jackson exiting in January 2005 THROCULT pulled in SILENCER's Dan Lynn as substitute for live work.

DE-FACTO, (2001). Japanese School Girl / Abused / Follow Me / Missing / La Fin De Monde / Soul Keeper / Green River / De-Facto.

Hunted EP, (2002) (USA promotion release). Kill Or Be Killed / Hunted / Eclipse Of The Blood Moon.

Soldiers Of A Blackened War EP, Crash Music Inc. (2003). The Uprising / Dark Cloud Holocaust / Hunted / Salem / Eclipse Of The Blood Moon / Kill Or Be Killed / Elipsis.

SOLDIERS OF A BLACKENED WAR, (2003). The Uprising / Dark Cloud Holocaust / Hunted / Salem / Eclipse Of The Blood Moon / Kill Or Be Killed / Ellipsis.

THROMDARR

FINLAND — A revered name of the Finnish extreme Metal scene, nevertheless, THROMDARR have issued only one album in over a decade of existence with 1998's 'Northstorm Arrives'. The group had previously been operational as NECROBIOSIS, releasing a 1991 demo "Consume The Lifeless Cadaver' under this title, but switched to THROMDARR the following year in order to quell confusion with another NECROBIOSIS hailing from Uusikaupunki. THROMDARR debuted with a 1992 cassette 'As A Wind Cries' and would issue a further 1997 demo 'Winds Of The Fall' upfront of the album. The band did re-surface in 2001 touting a three track demo CDR comprising of the tracks 'Hornblower', 'Burn For The Eternity' and 'An Old Oak Tree'.

Little is known publicly of THROMDARR's membership although Tobias Kellgren also operates with the equally esteemed and mysterious Doom band SKEPTICISM. An ex-THROMDARR bassist, Marko Tuominen, also a member of PARALYSIS and BLIND REALITY, would join Gothic Rock act LET ME DREAM in 1993.

As A Wind Cries, Thromdarr (1992) (Demo). Dawn Of The Samhain (Intro) / Dragonmyrmidon / Nocturnal Inner Torment / Prologue Of Satan (Outro).

Winter Of Flames, Thromdarr (1993) (Demo).

Silverthrone, Thromdarr (1995) (Demo).

Winds Of The Fall, Thromdarr (1998) (Demo).

NORTHSTORM ARRIVES, Solistitium SOL029 (1998). NorthStorm Arrives / An Eclipse Over The Mountains / Eyes Of Crystal / Path Leads Over The Stone Bridge / Ravens At The Lake / A Crown Of Black Thorns / Silver Throne / The Embrace Of Cold / By Thy Arrows.

Demo '03, Thromdarr (2003) (Demo).

THRONE OF CHAOS

ESPOO, FINLAND — *Tuomas Nieminen (vocals), Joiku Harmaja (guitar), Taneli Kiljunen (guitar), Rasmus Nora (bass), Carl Sjöblom (keyboards), Teemu Laitenen (drums).*

A classy Espoo based Death Metal act, imbued with melody and a sense of adventurism. Following demos 'Equilibrium' in 1996 and the 1997 EP 'Fata Morgana' THRONE OF CHAOS, featuring THY SERPENT drummer Teemu 'Snake' Laitinen, weighed in with the 2000 'Menace And Prayer' album for the Spinefarm subsidiary Spikefarm label. Alongside Laitenen the album saw a recording line-up of guitarists Joiku Harmaja and Taneli Kiljunen—the latter handling lead vocals, bassist Rasmus Nora and keyboard player Carl Sjöblom. Although impressive the album did not exactly stand out from the standard Scandinavian fare, something which the broader musical span of follow up 'Pervertigo', recorded at Studio Fredman in Gothenburg, certainly did. Niklas Isfeldt of DREAM EVIL aided on guest vocals alongside second vocalist Pasi Nykänen, crafting an album whose aggression was tempered by bursts of psychedelia.

THRONE OF CHAOS evolved into TOC for the October 2003 album 'Loss Angeles'. Issued by Spinefarm Records the album included a cover version of DEEP PURPLE's seminal 'Smoke On The Water'. Limited edition variants also hosted a rendition of JUDAS PRIEST's 'Night Crawler'.

The change in band title also marked a clear switch in style. Early works had been firmly placed in the Death Metal arena but a gradual leaning towards more adventurous realms led to TOC's Progressive Rock output. At this same juncture frontman Taneli Kiljunen backed away from the microphone, having damaged his throat. New lead singer Tuomas Nieminen held credits with BRIDE ADORNED and ADAMANTRA. 'Loss Angeles' saw release across Europe through Universal Music, in Japan via Avalon Marquee and was issued in North America by the Inside Out Music imprint.

Drummer Teemu Laitinen joined DIVERCIA for their 2004 album 'Cycle Of Zero'. Nieminen contributed as guest vocalist on CROWPATH's 'Red On Chrome' album. TOC folded in August 2005.

Equilibrium, Throne Of Chaos (1996) (Demo). Equilibrium / Pagan Tears / Soul Journey / Withering / ... And My Silence Is Eternal.

Fata Morgana, Throne Of Chaos (1997) (Demo). Valkyrie Reborn / Everlasting / Never In A Dream / Towards Glory.

MENACE AND PRAYER, Spikefarm NAULA 007 (2000). From Clarity To Insanity / The Scaffold Scenario / Cold Bits Of Fire / Bloodstained Prophecy / Menace And Prayer / Synthetia / Opus Void / Divanity.

MENACE AND PRAYER, Avalon Marquee MICP-10198 (2000) (Japanese release). From Clarity To Insanity / The Scaffold Scenario / Cold Bits Of Fire / Bloodstained Prophecy / Menace And Prayer / Synthetia / Opus Void / Divanity / Never In A Dream / Towards Glory.

Truth And Tragedy, Spinefarm SPI 154CD (2002). Truth And Tragedy / Night Crawler.

PERVERTIGO, Spinefarm SPI 156CD (2002). Johnny B. Dead / Pervertigo / The System / No Nothing / Fistfucking And Alienseed / Truth And Tragedy / Sleep / Reason To Be / Game.

PERVERTIGO, Avalon Marquee MICP-10316 (2002) (Japanese release). Johnny B. Dead / Pervertigo / The System / No Nothing / Fistfucking And Alienseed / Truth And Tragedy / Sleep / Reason To Be / Game / Nightcrawler.

LOSS ANGELES, Spinefarm SPI 190CD (2003). The Window / Mary Lou Is Dead / Acid Highway / Gothamburg / Blue Lady / Wait / The Blue Lady Suite / Break-a-neck / Bite The Bullet / Smoke On The Water.

LOSS ANGELES, Avalon Marquee MICP-10427 (2004) (Japanese release). The Window / Mary Lou Is Dead / Acid Highway / Gothamburg / Blue Lady / Wait / The Blue Lady Suite / Break-a-neck / Bite The Bullet / Smoke On The Water / Los Angeles, Los Angeles.

THRONEAEON

VÄSTERÅS, SWEDEN — *Tony Freed (vocals / guitar), Jens Klovengård (guitar), Andreas Dahlström (bass), Roger Sundquist (drums).*

Västerås based THRONEAEON date back to a 1991 formation convened by drummer Roger Sundquist. In their formative stages the group was entitled SHADOWS AT DAWN and subsequently AUTUMNAL. This early act drew in vocalist / guitarist Tony Freed the following year and by 1994 Andreas Dahlström had assumed the bass position and Göran Eriksson second guitar. During 1995 the new title of THRONEAEON was adopted, a demo being delivered in December of that year. Based upon this tape Swedish label Voices Of Death offered a split album deal which the band declined and instead put their efforts into the 'Carnage' demo.

In April of 1999 the Danish label Helgrind Productions issued 'The Sardonic Wrath' four track EP. In October 1999 Göran Eriksson made his exit, THRONEAEON plugging the vacancy with Jenz Klovegård of ABHOTH repute. A year later Hammerheart Records in Holland signed the band, re-releasing 'The Sardonic Wrath' as a precursor for a full length studio album. Promoting 'Neither Of Gods' THRONEAEON toured Europe in September of 2001 alongside BENEDICTION.

Founder member Roger Sundquist would leave in July of 2002. However, as Sundquist rejoined, Andreas Dahlström broke ranks in October being superseded by another ABHOTH member Magnus Wall. Shortly after releasing the 2003 album 'Godhate' the band switched title to GODHATE. Wall would vacate his post toward the close of 2003, replaced by Claes 'Clabbe' Ramberg, ironically the same man who had replaced Wall in ABHOTH. Wall joined MAUSOLEUM to record their demo 'Fluctuating Senses' as well as Power Metal band HATERUSH, featuring on the 2004 album 'Mark Of The Warrior'.

Claes Ramberg joined the ranks of IN AETERNUM in February 2006.

Throneaeon, Throneaeon (1995) (Demo). Before The Throne Of Stone / Liers-In-Wait / Upon The Sinners Cross / Ancestral Belief / North Winds Of Hate.
Carnage, Throneaeon (1997) (Demo). Carnage Of The Children / Ancestral Belief / Upon The Sinners Cross / Sacrilegious Feast.
With Sardonic Wrath EP, Helgrind Productions HEL001 (1999). Despise For God / Sardonic Wrath / Blasphemous Prediction / Entwined To The Lies Of The Light.
With Sardonic Wrath EP, The Plague 003 (2001). Despise For God / Sardonic Wrath / Blasphemous Prediction / Entwined To The Lies Of The Light.
NEITHER OF GODS, Hammerheart HHR102 (2001). Neither Of Gods / Thru Sinfulness / Above The Aware / In All And Nothing / Seven In Heaven Seven On Earth / Blackened To Be / The Serpent Unfolds / Strength On The Flesh / From On High / Enemys Of Thy God / 5211131103 / As It Has Come To End . . . .
GODHATE, Forensick FM 007 (2003). Oblivion / Heading Inwards / In Loathing (For Your God) / To Forever Be / Laid To Waste / Genocide In Grace / Divine Soul / Blackwinged / On The Highest Throne.

THRONEUM

POLAND — *Tomasz (vocals / guitar / bass), Marek (vocals / bass), Aleksander (drums).*

A Polish extreme Death Metal trio convened originally as THRONE during 1996. THRONEUM credit themselves as Tomasz with "Volkanics & orgasmic deathscythe", Marek on "Strangulation bulldozer & vomitations" and Aleksander as "Nekroblasts & nailthrower". The founding duo of Tomasz Hanuszkiewicz and Karol both handled lead vocals, guitar and bass, with drummer Aleksander augmenting the band in August of 1997. The THRONE triumvirate cut a debut demo session 'Beyond The Numbers And Creatures' in the summer of 1998 but in November Aleksander quit.

The erstwhile drummer made a return to the fold in March 2000 as the band, aware of another act holding the same title, evolved into THRONEUM. A second promotional demo 'The Underground Storms Eternally' arrived but then the band hit a further setback when founder member Karol quit. THRONEUM soon engaged Marek as replacement and set about recording tracks for a split CD with Mexican act THE LIGHT OF THE DARK entitled 'Brotherhood In Darkness' for Toaj Records. THRONEUM then cut a full length album 'Old Death's Lair' for the Japanese label Weird Truth Productions. For 2002 THRONEUM projected a further split release, with Poland's ANIMA DAMNATA, entitled 'Gods Of Abhorrence' and two shared 7" singles in league with Dutchmen THE REBELLION for the Macabre Operetta label and with HANGOVER for Alefcium Records. The Brazilian Vampira label would also announce a scheme to re-issue the original THRONEUM demos in CD format.

2003 found the German label Sombre Records re-issuing 'Old Death's Lair' in a limited run of just 350 vinyl albums, adding an extra track in a cover of SAMAEL's 'Rite Of Cthulhu'. The 'Mutiny Of Death' album included covers of both CIANIDE and ASPHYX. A new studio album entitled 'Pestilent Death' would be cut for Apocalyptor Records in late 2004.

In mid 2005 From Beyond Productions issued a split EP, naturally limited to 666 copies, shared with Finnish band INCRIMINATED. In January 2007 the group announced they were to participate on a four-way split CD in collaboration with Sweden's BESTIAL MOCKERY, Virginia's CRUCIFER, and US outfit SATHANAS through Time Before Time Records. The band also cut tracks for a collaborative outing with REVELATION OF DOOM for Pagan Records entitled 'Total Regression!'.

OLD DEATH'S LAIR, Weird Truth Productions WT 010 (2001). The Key / Rites Of Forefathers / Reign Of War / Immolation's Fear / Tortures' Mask / Creeping And Trustful / Domination To Fall / Ancient Mother Whore / Black Thrash Till Death / Future Is Like A Funeral / Serpentine Transformation / Doomsday / Last Revelation.
Bestial Antihuman Evil EP, Weird Truth Productions WT 011 (2002). Godless Antihuman Evil / Death From Beyond Hell / Fuck Me Dead / In The Depth Of Sulphur Sea / Madness Destroys.
BROTHERHOOD IN DARKNESS, Toaj (2002) (Split album with THE LIGHT OF THE DARK). Hail Old Spirits / Mutiny Of Death / Ancient Mother Whore / Light And Cause / Closed Circle.
GODS OF ABHORRENCE, Pagan MOONCD 033 (2002) (Split album with ANIMA DAMNATA. Limited edition 666 copies). Morbid Death Terror / Black Leather Whore Fucks / Tombs Call / Ritual Asphyxia / War & Sodomy / Infernal Tanks Attack / Lunatic Of God's Creation / Reborn In Gehenna (Outro).
MUTINY OF DEATH, Pagan MOON 038 (2003). The Great Executor / Freedom With Fires Of Hell / Pure Total Death / Goat Archangels Of Lust / From Belial / Worship From Chaos / Hell-Leprous-Slaughter-Reign / New Nightmare Plague Has Born / Gravedancer / Black Souls' Crucifixion / Streams Of Ancient Wisdom / Funeral.
Throneum/Incriminated, From Beyond Productions FBP-039 (2005) (Split single with INCRIMINATED. Limited edition 666 copies). Orders Of Doom / Bloody Parchment Persist.

THROUGH THE EYES OF THE DEAD

FLORENCE, SC, USA — *Anthony Gunnels (vocals), Justin Longshore (guitar), Chris Anderson (guitar), Jake Ososkie (bass), Josh Kulick (drums).*

Florence, South Carolina Metalcore band THROUGH THE EYES OF THE DEAD initially featured former TELL HER I SAID GOODBYE members guitarist Justin Longshare, bass player Jeff Springs, second guitarist Richard Turbeville and drummer Dayton Cantley. The band, joined by vocalist Anthony Gunnels, debuted with a 5 track EP, 'The Scars Of Ages', for Lovelost Records in January 2003.

THROUGH THE EYES OF THE DEAD underwent major lineup changes, drafting new faces Chris Anderson on guitar, Jake Ososkie on bass and Josh Kulick on the drums. Promoting the album 'Bloodlust' through Prosthetic Records, THROUGH THE EYES OF THE DEAD hooked up with ION DISSONANCE, SUMMER'S END and THE RED DEATH for September 2005 US touring. Upon completion of these dates the band jumped onto further gigs with THE RED DEATH and EMBRACE THE END, which segued into November gigs bolstered by THE KNIFE TRADE and THE CLASSIC STRUGGLE. Meantime, ex-members Jeff Springs, Richard Turbeville and Dayton Cantley, in alliance with singer vocalist Damon Welch and bassist David Hasselbring, set to work on a fresh band project dubbed FROM GRAVES OF VALOR.

2006 opened with a rash of US dates across January and February in collusion with ED GEIN and THE NUMBER TWELVE

THROUGH THE EYES OF THE DEAD (pic: Karen Jerzyk)

LOOKS LIKE YOU. The group announced they were to team up with the reformed WILL HAVEN and CROWBAR for a UK tour in March. In April the group hit the US campaign trail once again, this time with CEPHALIC CARNAGE, SCARLET and A LIFE ONCE LOST in tow. June concerts would be undertaken sharing stages with TERROR and DEATH BEFORE DISHONOR.

The band subsequently engaged in a gigantic roving festival billing with the 'Sounds Of The Underground' tour throughout the summer, commencing in Cleveland, Ohio on July 8th, partnered with IN FLAMES, TRIVIUM, CANNIBAL CORPSE, GWAR, TERROR, THE BLACK DAHLIA MURDER, BEHEMOTH, THE CHARIOT and AS I LAY DYING. The group formed up another package tour, the 'Sanctity Of Brothers' expedition ranking them alongside TERROR, ANIMOSITY, UNEARTH and BLEEDING THROUGH in September.

THROUGH THE EYES OF THE DEAD toured the United States from Virginia to the West Coast returning to South Carolina throughout November, headlining over Prosthetic label mates THE ACACIA STRAIN plus FROM A SECOND STORY WINDOW and IF HOPE DIES.

A second album, entitled 'Malice' was recorded commencing February 16th 2007 at Mana Studios in St. Petersburg, Florida with HATE ETERNAL's Erik Rutan at the production helm. In March the band revealed that Nate Johnson, of DEADWATER DROWNING, BURNT LIKE THE SUN and PREMONITIONS OF WAR, had enrolled as new vocalist.

THROUGH THE EYES OF THE DEAD were rapidly back into touring mode, forming up a set of European shows throughout May alongside DEAD TO FALL, ION DISSONANCE and DYING FETUS hitting Germany, the UK, Poland, Denmark, Croatia and Belgium. THROUGH THE EYES OF THE DEAD embarked on a month long North American tour in June sharing stages with THE RED CHORD, DESPISED ICON, ALL SHALL PERISH, SEE YOU NEXT TUESDAY and GENGHIS TRON.

The Scars Of Ages, Lovelost (2003). Beneath Dying Skies / Autumn Tint Of Gold / Forever Ends Today / Between The Gardens That Bathe In Blood / To Take Comfort (In Yesterday's Scars).

BLOODLUST, Razor & Tie (2005). Intro / Two Inches From A Main Artery / When Everything Becomes Nothing / Bringer Of Truth / Beneath Dying Skies / The Black Death And It's Aftermath / Truest Shade Of Crimson / With Eyes Ever Turned Inward / Force Fed Trauma / The Decaying Process / Outro.

THURISAZ

BELGIUM — *Peter Theuwen (vocals / guitar), Mattias Theuwen (guitar), Lars Vereecke (bass), Kobe Cannière (keyboards), Pepijn De Raeymaecker (drums).*

THURISAZ is a melodic Black / Death Metal act from Wervik, founded under the banner of MODILIUM during 1997. The 'Never To Return' debut demo was followed by 'The Last Embrace', this second set marking the introduction of keyboard player Kobe Cannière. A third promotional recording, 'Anno Viroviacum', was cut in 2003. The group debuted in March of 2004 with the EP 'Scent Of A Dream', recorded at CCR Studios. Live work in early 2004 witnessed supports to MANIC MOVEMENT and SIX FEET UNDER. TwoFatMen Productions put out 'Scent Of A Dream' as a full length album in September.

The group scheduled dates for a European tour in November 2006, sharing stages with by NOVEMBERS DOOM, AGALLOCH and Denmark's SATURNUS.

Scent Of A Dream, Independent (2004). A Timeless Flame / Scent Of A Dream / Years Of Silence / When Images Are Fading / Anno Viroviacum / Endless ....

THY DISEASE

KRAKÓW, POLAND — *Psycho (vocals), Dario (guitar), Pepo (guitar), Marco (bass), Qba (keyboards), Pinocchio (drums).*

Kraków Death Metal act THY DISEASE, who boast the unlikely inclusion of Pinocchio on drums, features the former SCEPTIC pairing of vocalist Psycho and guitarist Dario. The band was formulated in 1999 and issued the four track 'Art Of Decadence' offering before the year was out.

THY DISEASE would ambitiously offer a rendition of MADONNA's 'Frozen' featuring Anna Wojtkowiak of CENTURIA on guest lead vocals for their 2001 record 'Devilish Act Of Creation'. The group also cut a rendition of VADER's 'Sothis' although this did not make the final running order.

The 2002 album 'Cold Skin Obsession' closed with a cover version of DEATH's 'Without Judgement'. In May of that year Pinocchio was replaced on the drum stool by Alizee666 (a.k.a. Maciek Kowalski) of CRIONICS and TROMSNAR repute.

Together with personnel from SCEPTIC, DECAPITATED, SERPENTIA and CRIONICS band members operate the brutal Death Metal act ANAL STENCH.

DEVILISH ACT OF CREATION, Metal Mind Productions (2001). Condemnation Of Whores / Angel Ashamed / Impure Lust / Crashing The Soul / Finding God / The Wish / New Slaughter / Art Of Decadence / Cursed / My Serpent / Frozen / Act Of Creation.

COLD SKIN OBSESSION, Metal Mind Productions (2002). Perfect Form / Blade Intimacy / War Is Mine / Ultimate Reign / The Last Of The Mohicans / Cold / Redemption in ... Pain / Nihilistic Tranquillity / Qualbuhu La Jadruqqu / Without Judgement.

THY FLESH CONSUMED

HALIFAX, NS, CANADA — *Peter Mestre (vocals), Dave Burns (guitar), Dan Jamieson (guitar), Randy Jeddry (bass), Gerald Smith (drums).*

Halifax, Nova Scotia Metal Black—Grind band founded in November of 2001 by the SLOTH pairing of guitarist Dan Jamieson and drummer Gerald Smith, the latter also citing credits with GORBAGE, THE WANKLIN FAMILY and SYSTEM SHIT. Previously this pair had been building a project by the title of EXISTENCH but this fell by the wayside as THY FLESH CONSUMED gathered momentum. Following second guitarist John Haight's departure after just one gig, the band would be rounded out by lead vocalist Peter "Pneumatic" Mestre and bassist Randy "Crust" Jeddry for the 2002 album 'Dawn Of The Impurity Design', this release restricted to just 100 copies.

Boosting their numbers once again THY FLESH CONSUMED inducted former BURNING MOON and READY FOR EDDIE guitarist Dave Burns for a second album, 2003's 'End Of Blind Obedience'. This record closed out with a rendition of BLASPHEMY's 'Atomic Nuclear Desolation'.

DAWN OF THE IMPURITY DESIGN, Independent (2002) (Limited edition 100 copies). From The Hand Of Man / Cessation And Purulence / Apathy Level Increase / Beneath The Poison Sky / Mind Collapse / Regression Into ... Nightmare / Suffocating In The Synthetic / Dawn Of The Impurity Design / A Creation Through Psychosis / Burial For Your God.

END OF BLIND OBEDIENCE, CDN (2003). Divided And Conquered / Depreciated Life Worth / Fist Of The Iconaclast / Let Mankind Bleed / Bound To Malevolence / Prelude To Desolation / Torture Overture / Of All Abomination / Homocide Pact / End Of Blind Obedience / Atomic Nuclear Desolation.

THY LEGACY

VANTAA, FINLAND — *Oscar Wollsten (vocals / bass), Pekka Koivisto (guitar / keyboards), Veikko Ringvall (drums).*

Vantaa Death Metal act. THY LEGACY debuted with the three song demo 'Legacy Of Pain', followed by 'Bethroned With Death' in 2003 and August 2004's 'Dismal Symphony'. The group had been created as simply LEGACY in 2002 comprising guitarist Pekka Koivisto, bassist Oscar Wollsten and drummer Teemu Hartikka. The Spring 2003 demo set 'Legacy Of Pain' was tracked under the former name of LEGACY whilst the December 2003 session 'Betrothed With Death' signalled the switch to THY LEGACY. Although the band had used GORESOAKED and MENSURA man Perttu Saarsalmi as session drummer Jussi Vaalasmaa took control of the drum position in early 2004. Guitar player Pekka Koivisto has an affiliation with GORESOAKED.

Guitarist Joonas Vepsä enrolled briefly before Sampo Riikonen of MENSURA joined the band in November 2004 as a second guitarist, but soon opted out. The THY LEGACY demo 'Reverse Exorcism' arrived in February 2005. Jussi Vaalasmaa withdrew in December, being replaced by Veikko Ringvall. The 'Blood Work Theories' emerged in April 2006.

Bethroned With Death, Thy Legacy (2003) (Demo). Nekropolis / Metal Till' The End / Bethroned With Death / Legacy Of Pain / Deathwish / Outro.
Dismal Symphony, Thy Legacy (2004) (Demo). Salt On Rotten Flesh / Bury Me / Mortally Shredded.
Reverse Exorcism, Thy Legacy (2005) (Demo). Reverse Exorcism / Vile Crematory / Relapse Of Remains.
Blood Work Theories, Thy Legacy (2006) (Demo). Embryonic Display Of Life / Blood Work Theory / Distant Suffocation.

THY SERPENT

FINLAND — *Luopio (vocals / bass / keyboards), Azhemin (vocals / keyboards), Sami Tenetz (guitar), Agathon (drums).*

Doom Death Metal band THY SERPENT formed in 1992 as guitarist Sami Tenetz began recording rehearsal tapes followed by more professional sounding demos, including January 1994's 'Frozen Memory'. With interest from Spinefarm Records Tenetz opted to recruit band members to a project he had worked on single handedly up to that point. After a number of changes, a stable group of musicians were found that enabled recording of September 1996's 'Forest Of Witchery' meisterwerk to be commenced. However, Spinefarm went on record to state that THY SERPENT would never play live. Drummer Agathon Frosteus (a.k.a. Ykä) held affiliations with AIRDASH, GLOOMY GRIM, WALHALLA, NOMICON, BARATHRUM and CORPORAL PUNISHMENT. Second opus 'Lord Of Twilight' arrived in February 1997. That same year the group shared a collaborative three way split single, 'Only Dust Moves . . .' with CHILDREN OF BODOM and NIGHTWISH.

The May 1998 album, 'Christcrusher', saw the notable inclusion of CHILDREN OF BODOM guitarist Alexi Laiho into the ranks. Members of the band involved themselves with BARATHRUM for the 2000 side project act SHAPE OF DESPAIR issuing the 'Shades of . . .' album.

THY SERPENT man Tomi Ullgren also performs as guitarist with RAPTURE. THY SERPENT credited drummer Teemu Laitinen, also a member of THRONE OF CHAOS, joined DIVERCIA for their 2004 album 'Cycle Of Zero'.

Frozen Memory, Thy Serpent (1994) (Demo). Intro / Unknown / Frozen Memory / The Sky Is Falling / Just A Shadow In The Darkness.
Into Everlasting Fire, Thy Serpent (1995). The Forest Of Blåkulla / In Blackened Dreams / Ode To The Witches (Part I) / 24th Of August 1628 / Hear My Darkest Calls / Ode To The Witches (Part II).
FOREST OF WITCHERY, Thy Serpent SPI 36CD (1996). Flowers Of Witchery Abloom / Of Darkness And Light / Traveller Of Unknown Plains / Only Dust Moves . . . / Like A Funeral Veil Of Melancholy / Wine From Tears.
LORDS OF TWILIGHT, Spinefarm SPI 42CD (1997). Prometheus Unbound / The Forest Of Blåkulla / Ode To The Witches—Part IV / In Blackened Dreams / As Mist Descends From the Hills / Unknown / Epic Torment / In Blackened Dreams / Ode To The Witches—Part III.
Nightwish The Carpenter, Spinefarm SPI 46CD (1997) (Split single with CHILDREN OF BODOM and NIGHTWISH). Only Dust Moves . . . .
CHRISTCRUSHER, Spinefarm SPI 56CD (1998). Chambers Of The Starwatchers / Curtain Of Treachery / Thou Bade Nothingness / Go Free The Wolves / Circles Of Pain / Christcrusher / Crystalmoors / Calm Blinking.
Death EP, Spinefarm SPI 102CD (2000). Deathbearer / Wounds Of Death / Sleep In Oblivion / Parasites.

THYABHORRENT

SARPSBORG, NORWAY — *Occultus (vocals), Knegg (guitar), Biffen (guitar), Sleepy (bass), Persen (drums).*

Sarpsborg's THYABHORRENT, founded as ABHORRENT in 1989, released the demo 'Occultus Brujeria' in May 1990. In December that same year the group evolved into THYABHORRENT for the 7" single 'Death Rides At Dawn' for the Seraphic Decay label. Stian Johansen, a.k.a. 'Occultus' or 'Cultoculous' and editor of the underground fanzine Sepulchral Noise, would briefly perform with MAYHEM during 1991 following the death of singer Dead. Demos 'Incopnitus From Arcustus' and rehearsal set 'The Conclusion Phase' followed the same year.

Occultus subsequently forged PERDITION HEARSE for a 1993 demo 'Mala Fide', then Gothic outfit SHADOW DANCERS.

Death Rides At Dawn, Seraphic Decay SCAM-012 (1990). Death Rides At Dawn / Condemnation / Occultus Brujeria.
The Conclusion Phase, Thyabhorrent (1991) (Rehearsal demo). Death Rides At Dawn / Condemnation / Occultus Brujeria / Wails Of Passion / Decayed Deserver.
Incognitus From Orcustus, Thyabhorrent (1991) (Demo). Incognitus From Orcustus / Death Rides At Dawn / Wails Of Passion / Occultus Brujeria / Decayed Preserver.

TIAMAT

TÄBY, SWEDEN — *Johan Edlund (vocals / guitar), Magnus Sahlgrem (guitar), Johnny Hagel (bass), Lars Sköld (drums).*

A Gothic Death Metal combo out of Täby, masterminded by Johan Edlund, that has evolved chameleon like with each successive release. Less tastefully known in their formative years as TREBLINKA, during which time vocalist Johan Edlund also pursued his gruesome side project GENERAL SURGERY, the Swedish quartet adopted the title of the Sumerian goddess of chaos and mythical planet TIAMAT. The band has evolved from a derivative Speed Metal / Death act to a more substantial stance in offering aggression with adventurous Progressive variances. This makeover gave TIAMAT access to the underground, yet considerable European Dark Wave club scene.

As TREBLINKA the band consisted of vocalist/guitarist Johan Edlund ("Lucifer Hellslaughter"), bassist Klas Wistedt, guitarist Stefan Lagergren ("Emetic") and drummer Andreas Holmberg ("Najse Auschwitzer"). This unit released the 1988 demo 'Crawling In Vomits' and follow up tape 'The Sign Of The Pentagram' in 1989. Also emerging that year would be the 'Severe Abomination' EP on Mould In Hell Records. A later incarnation of TREBLINKA also included Nicke Andersson of ENTOMBED repute.

The group issued the September 1990 debut album 'Sumerian Cry', laid down at Sunlight Studios, through C.M.F.T. Productions. The band that recorded this work was firmly entrenched in Black Metal, evidenced by an album cover brandishing pentagrams and inverted crosses, harsh riffing driven by blast beats and musicians caked in corpsepaint and studded with nails. Once the tracks were completed a decision was made to switch from the controversial TREBLINKA to a more palatable TIAMAT, debuting live under their new banner on April 6th 1990 in Stockholm. 'Sumerian Cry' was, in truth, a fairly basic affair, marred by some amateurish drumming and some ill conceived attempts at experimentation, such as a clumsy 'Evilized'. Nonetheless, 'Sumerian Cry' succeeded in getting the TIAMAT brand onto the European Metal scene. However, from this point onwards the band would be rocked with constant re-shuffling of personnel. For the Thomas Skogsberg engineered 'A Winter Shadow' single, released in December 1990 by CBR Records, the band personnel would be credited as Hellslaughter, guitarist A.D. Lord (a.k.a. Thomas Petersson), bass player Jorgen Thullberg ("Juck the Ripper") and drummer Oakbeach (Niklas Ekstrand).

Locating a stable base of operations with German imprint Century Media, TIAMAT toured Europe in 1991 with label mates UNLEASHED. Staying out in the live environment, TIAMAT allied with DEATH for German concerts in February. September 1991's 'The Astral Sleep' album saw both Lagergren and Holmberg depart for EXPULSION and the record was recorded by vocalist/guitarist Johan Edlund, guitarist Thomas Petersson, bassist Jörgen Thullberg and drummer Lars Sköld with Jonas Malmsten aiding on keyboards. 'The Astral Sleep' was conceived at Woodhouse Studios in Dortmund, with production being delegated to GRIP INC. guitarist Waldemar Sorychta, who also added a guitar solo to the track 'Ancient Entity'. Europe again felt the force of the TIAMAT onstage experience in October as the group, together with PARADISE LOST, hit Belgium, Holland, Denmark, Sweden, Germany, Poland, Slovakia, Slovenia, Hungary and Italy. The campaigning carried on into the New Year, another circuit of the continent being conducted alongside SAMAEL and UNLEASHED. In April Tiamat hopped onboard a further brutal package, comprising CANNIBAL CORPSE, DEATH and CARCASS.

The band's 1992 line-up for the atmospheric third effort 'Clouds', issued that September, comprised Edlund, Petersson, ex-SORCEROR bassist Johnny Hagel, keyboard player Kenneth Roos and drummer Niklas Ekstrand. 'The Sleeping Beauty- Live In Israel' record was recorded in Tel Aviv on June 3rd 1993 prior to dealing Germany another blow backed by MORGOTH and TANKARD. Later shows found the band touring alongside MORGOTH, UNLEASHED and, into 1994, VOODOO CULT and CREMATORY. Petersson and Roos took their leave, requiring Johan Edlund to carry on with an all new formation that included bassist Johnny Hagel.

September 1994's Space Rock charged 'Wildhoney' album found the band expanding into fresh vistas of sound. In the studio, Birgit Zacher lent female vocal colour, keyboards contributed were by Waldemar Sorychta and the group's confidence resulted in no less than four instrumentals, 'Wildhoney', '25th Floor', 'Kaleidoscope' and 'Planets'. The single choice, 'Gaia', a six-track EP released in 1995, included a cover version of PINK FLOYD's 'When You're In' as one of the additional tracks. Predictably the line-up fluxed yet again with Ekstrand and Petersson discharging themselves and drummer Lars Sköld welcomed back into the fold. Former CELEBORN guitarist Magnus Sahlgren sessioned on 'Wildhoney' and was kept on for tour work. Sahlgren subsequently joined DISMEMBER and LAKE OF TEARS.

The band toured as support to TYPE O NEGATIVE in Europe during 1994 and attacked 1995 with an exhaustive round of dates flanking SENTENCED. TIAMAT also successfully headlined the 1995 Dynamo Festival in Holland. A sizable coup was then to be had with a tour of the USA, Europe and Britain as support to BLACK SABBATH. The same year a limited edition album, 'A Musical History Of Tiamat', would give fans further live material in the form of an extra CD.

April 1997's Dirk Draeger produced 'A Deeper Kind Of Slumber' heralded another shift in TIAMAT's musical landscape as Edlund, now employing a near Gregorian vocal timbre, ventured into unashamed and uncompromising Progressive Rock territory. Members of German band THE INCHTABOKATABLES enhanced proceedings with string arrangements. Collectors would be appeased when Century Media issued 'A Deeper Kind Of Slumber' in two sets of cover art, one for Europe and another for the USA. Naturally the ebb and flow of band members continued unabated too with CEMETARY's Anders Iwers enrolling on guitar as in a straight swap Johnny Hagel joined CEMETARY. The ex-TIAMAT man would later be found ensconced in SUNDOWN before pursuing his own CINNAMON SPIRAL and LITHIUM projects. Meanwhile further internal manouevres in TIAMAT saw Iwers shifting to bass when Petersson rejoined later. Once dates with THE GATHERING had been fulfilled in September, Iwers would also find extracurricular activities deputising for Italian act LACUNA COIL after both their guitarists pulled out of an October 1997 tour at short notice.

TIAMAT returned with the August 1999 Gothic infused, grittier guitar heavy 'Skeleton Skeletron' outing. A preceding EP, 'Brighter Than The Sun', had included a rendition of the ROLLING STONES staple 'Sympathy For The Devil'. European dates in November saw the band supported by ANATHEMA but Petersson bailed out yet again. The band, complete once more with a yoyo-ing Petersson bouncing back, got to grips with a November European package tour alongside running mates ANATHEMA and TRISTANIA.

Johan Edlund struck out on a no frills Gothic Rock n' Roll direction with the 2001 solo side project LUCYFIRE. Scoring a deal with SPV Records LUCYFIRE issued 'This Dollar Saved My Life at Whitehorse'. Edlund, billing himself as "Notorious PIG" for the LUCYFIRE endeavour also assembled a live band for an appearance at the 'Mera Luna' festival in Hildesheim, Germany. The same year leading German Gothic Rock act LOVE LIKE BLOOD would cover 'Whatever That Hurts' for their covers album 'Chronology Of A Love Affair'.

A February 2002 TIAMAT album, the Lars H. Nissen produced 'Judas Christ', which once again garnered the band chart success in Sweden, would see American variants adding the bonus cut 'Cold Last Supper' plus a video clip of 'Vote For Love'. Peter Tägtgren of HYPOCRISY and PAIN guested on the track 'Spine'. 'Judas Christ' triggered European gigs opened up by MOONSPELL and FLOWING TEARS in March.

European summer festival appearances throughout July and August for the band included showings at the German 'Zillo' and 'Summer Breeze' events as well as Spain's 'Rock Machina' festival, the Czech 'Brutal Assault' open air gig and the Viennese 'Metalfest'. TIAMAT would embark upon touring in mainland Europe as part of a co-billing with PAIN. Regular guitarist Thomas Petersson would be unable to participate, being replaced temporarily by SOUTHFORK's Henrik Bergqvist as DARK TRANQUILLITY's Martin Brändström handled keyboard duties.

A brand new Johan Edlund produced TIAMAT album, 'Prey' delivered in October of 2003, would be preceded by the single 'Cain', this release including a cover version of W.A.S.P.'s 'Sleeping (In The Fire)'. Former TIAMAT touring keyboard player P.A. Danielsson was killed in a car accident in Italy on 26th November 2004. He was 35 years old.

The band reported a European road alliance with SIRENIA, THEATRE OF TRAGEDY and PAIN to take them through late 2004 and into 2005. For these concerts the band would be joined by TALISMAN guitarist Fredrik "Kulle" Åkesson, replacing regular guitarist Thomas Petersson detained by "parental duties", and DARK TRANQUILLITY keyboard player Martin

Brändström. TIAMAT live concerts took place in Greece in February 2005. The band made festival appearances in 2006 and released a DVD, entitled 'The Church Of Tiamat', in May 2006.

With TIAMAT drummer Lars Sköld delegated production duties, Johan Edlund's LUCYFIRE side project undertook work on album recordings in November 2006.

SUMERIAN CRY, C.M.F.T. Productions CMFT 6 (1990). Intro: Sumerian Cry Part I / In The Shrines Of The Kingly Dead / The Malicious Paradise / Necrophagous Shadows / Apotheosis Of Morbidity / Nocturnal Funeral / Altar Flame / Evilized / Where The Serpents Ever Dwell / Outro / Sumerian Cry Part II / The Sign Of The Pentagram.

A Winter Shadow, CBR CBR-S-125 (1990). A Winter Shadow / Ancient Entity.

THE ASTRAL SLEEP, Century Media 9722-2 (1991). Neo Aeon / Lady Temptress / Mountain Of Doom / Dead Boys Quire / Sumerian Cry (Part III) / On Golden Wings / Ancient Entity / The Southernmost Voyage / Angels Far Beyond / I Am The King (Of Dreams) / A Winter Shadow / The Seal.

CLOUDS, Century Media 84 9736-2 (1992). In A Dream / Clouds / Smell Of Incense / A Caress Of Stars / The Sleeping Beauty / Forever Burning Flames / The Scapegoat / Undressed.

THE SLEEPING BEAUTY—LIVE IN ISRAEL, Century Media 77065 (1994). In A Dream / Ancient Entity / The Sleeping Beauty / Mountains Of Doom / Angels Far Beyond.

WILDHONEY, Century Media 77080-2 (1994). Wildhoney / Whatever That Hurts / The Ar / 25th Floor / Gaia / Visionaire / Kaleidoscope / Do You Dream Of Me? / Planets / A Pocket Size Sun. Chart position: 29 GERMANY.

Gaia EP, Century Media 77089-2 (1994). Gaia (Video edit) / The Ar (Radio edit) / When You're In / Whatever That Hurts (Video edit) / The Ar (Industrial mix) / Visionaire (Remix Longform version).

THE MUSICAL HISTORY OF TIAMAT, Century Media LC6975 (1995). Where The Serpents Ever Dwell / The Sign Of The Pentagram / Ancient Entity / Dead Boys Choir / The Southernmost Voyage / A Winter Shadow / Smell Of Insence / A Caress Of Stars / The Sleeping Beauty / When You're In / Visionaire / Do You Dream Of Me? / A Pocket Sized Sun / Whatever That Hurts (Live) / The Ar (Live) / In A Dream (Live) / 25th Floor (Live) / Gaia (Live) / Visionaire (Live) / Kaleidoscope (Live) / Do You Dream Of Me? (Live) / The Sleeping Beauty (Live) / A Pocket Sized Sun (Live).

A DEEPER KIND OF SLUMBER, Century Media 77180-2 (1997). Seed / Teonanacatl / Trillion Zillion Centipedes / The Desolate One / Atlantis As A Lover / Alteration X / Four Leary Biscuits / Only In My Tears It Lasts / The Whores Of Babylon / Kite / Phantasma / Mount Marilyn / A Deeper Kind Of Slumber. Chart positions: 29 GERMANY, 39 SWEDEN.

A DEEPER KIND OF SLUMBER, JVC Victor VICP-60034 (1997) (Japanese release). Seed / Teonanacatl / Trillion Zillion Centipedes / The Desolate One / Atlantis As A Lover / Alteration X / Four Leary Biscuits / Only In My Tears It Lasts / The Whores Of Babylon / Kite / Phantasma / Mount Marilyn / A Deeper Kind Of Slumber / Only In My Tears It Lasts (The Cat mix) / Three Leary Biscuits.

Cold Seed, Century Media 77167-2 (1997). Cold Seed / Only In My Tears It Lasts (The Cat mix) / Three Leary Biscuits.

Brighter Than The Sun, Century Media 77279-3 (1999). Brighter Than The Sun (Radio edit) / Sympathy For The Devil / Children Of The Underworld / Brighter Than The Sun.

SKELETON SKELETRON, Century Media 77280-2 (1999). Church Of Tiamat / Brighter Than The Sun / Dust Is Our Fare / To Have And Have Not / For Her Pleasure / Diyala / Sympathy For The Devil / Best Friend Money Can Buy / As Long As You're Mine / Lucy. Chart positions: 19 GERMANY, 56 SWEDEN.

SKELETON SKELETRON, JVC Victor VICP-60886 (1999) (Japanese release). Church Of Tiamat / Brighter Than The Sun / Dust Is Our Fare / To Have And Have Not / For Her Pleasure / Diyala / Sympathy For The Devil / Best Friend Money Can Buy / As Long As You're Mine / Lucy / Children Of The Underworld.

For Her Pleasure, Century Media 77281-3 (1999). For Her Pleasure (edit) / Lucy (Demon mix—remixed by Element & The Short Romans) / Brighter Than The Sun (Bullsrun mix—remixed by Tarsia) / As Long As You Are Mine (Lodmalm's Cocktail Club A Go-Go mix).

JUDAS CHRIST, JVC Victor VICP-61717 (2002) (Japanese release). The Return Of The Son Of Nothing / So Much For Suicide / Vote For Love / The Truth's For Sale / Fireflower / Sumer By Night / Love Is As Good As Soma / Angel Holograms / Spine / I Am In Love With Myself / Heaven Of High / Too Far Gone / Vote For Love (Video).

JUDAS CHRIST (LIMITED EDITION), Century Media 77380-0 (2002). The Return Of The Son Of Nothing / So Much For Suicide / Vote For Love / The Truth's For Sale / Fireflower / Sumer By Night / Love Is As Good As Soma / Angel Holograms / Spine / I Am In Love With Myself / Heaven Of High / Too Far Gone / Sixshooter / However You Look At It You Loose / Vote For Love (Video).

JUDAS CHRIST, Century Media 77380-2 (2002). The Return Of The Son Of Nothing / So Much For Suicide / Vote For Love / The Truth's For Sale / Fireflower / Sumer By Night / Love Is As Good As Soma / Angel Holograms / Spine / I Am In Love With Myself / Heaven Of High / Too Far Gone. Chart positions: 28 GERMANY, 52 SWEDEN.

Cain, Century Media 77479-3 (2003). Cain (Radio edit) / Love In Chains / Sleeping (In The Fire).

PREY, Century Media 77480-2 (2003). Cain / Ten Thousand Tentacles / Wings Of Heaven / Love In Chains / Divided / Carry Your Cross And I'll Carry Mine / Triple Cross / Light In Extension / Prey / The Garden Of Heathen / Clovenhoof / Nihil / The Pentagram. Chart position: 83 GERMANY.

TIBURON

SWITZERLAND — *Manuel Alberati (vocals), Monika Bolliger (vocals), Emilio Barrantes (guitar), Peter Erni (guitar), Patrick Smonig (bass).*

October of 1992 witnessed the launch of the Swiss Death Metal act TIBURÓN. The group was assembled by lead vocalist Manuel Alberati with guitarist Emilio Barrantes. During March of 1993 this duo was supplemented by a drummer simply known as M.S. and in September of that same year Pipo Muntwyler took on bass guitar to complete the line up. Ludi DeTotaro subsequently took command of the drums for recording of the December 1994 mini album 'The Underdark'. However, Di Totaro departed soon after and TIBURON soldiered on utilising a drum machine.

The 'Join Us' full length album followed and was capitalised on with a picture disc release, 'Tales Of Malice', in November of 1997. This issue being limited to just 100 copies. Peter Erni augmented the band on second guitar that December. Once again TIBURON released another limited edition picture disc EP, 'Sphereshifting' arriving in May of 1998. With the band's music evolving rapidly the decision to take onboard female vocals signalled the incorporation of Monika Bolliger in August. Patrick Smonig supplanted Muntwyler toward the close of 1999.

The 'Tiburon Ataca' album is a collection of tracks from the picture disc rarities. TIBURON's next move was the late 2000 demo 'Death Rate Sequencer'. May of 2002 found TIBURON sharing space with ANIMAL CANNIBAL PROCESS on a split 7" single "Total Fucking Chaos'.

THE UNDER DARK, Opus Dei SPV 65-96782 (1994). Drifting Into Blackness / Extinction / In Morte Liberatio / Zak / Between Death & Life.

JOIN US, (1996). Drop By Drop / Beyond / Join Us / Sysruction / The Higher Grounds / Onslaught / The Nihilist / Feuerwalze / Eternity / Nazca / When I'm Dead / Outro.

Tales Of Malice EP, (1997) (Picture disc. Limited edition 100 copies). Malice / Lord Darkness / Beyond / Join Us.

TIBURON ATACA, Opus Dei (1998). Terror / Necropolis / Sphereshifting / Deathcall / Malice / Lord Darkness / Drop By Drop / Eternity / The Higher Grounds.

Sphereshifting EP, (1998) (Picture disc. Limited edition 100 copies). Terror / Necropolis / Sphereshifting / Deathcall / Final Voyage.

Total Fucking Chaos EP, (2002) (Split single with ANIMAL CANNIBAL PROCESS). Angel Of Revenge / Total Fucking Chaos.

TO SEPARATE THE FLESH FROM THE BONES

FINLAND — *Herr Archstein (vocals / guitar), Rot Weiler (bass), Pus Sypope (drums).*

TO SEPARATE THE FLESH FROM THE BONES is a 2003 Grindcore project assembled anonymously by members of AMORPHIS and H.I.M.. Retaining their secrecy the band projected an album 'For Those About To Rot' for Autumn 2004 issue.

TO SEPARATE THE FLESH FROM THE BONES

The band comprised ex-AMORPHIS man Pasi Koskinen ('Herr Archstein') on vocals and guitar, AMORPHIS bassist Niclas Etelävuori ('Rot Weiler') and H.I.M. drummer Mika "Kaasu" ("Gas Lipstick") Karppinen ('Pus Sypope'). The debut 'Utopia Sadistica' album emerged in November of 2004 through Spikefarm Records, this outing featuring a guesting Jeff Walker (a.k.a. J. Offalmangler') of CARCASS.

TO SEPARATE THE FLESH FROM THE BONES, along with Jeff Walker as guest and sharing the stage with DIABLO, OMNIUM GATHERUM and SARA, appeared at 'The Fragile Art of Existence—Tribute to Chuck Schuldiner' benefit concert at Klubi in Tampere held on 18th December.

For Those About To Rot, Spikefarm NAULA051 (2004). Infected Rectum / Breast-Fed By Blood / Rotten Vagina / Filthy Cunt / Genital Massacre / Chainsaw Fuck / Die Like A Wimp / Flesh That Lies Beneath / Fistfucked 'til Death / Spermjerker.
UTOPIA SADISTICA, Spikefarm NAULA058 (2004). Meatbash / Cold Cuts / Rotten Siege / The Final Extinction / Preternatural Pervert / Meretricious Murderess / Disconsolated Suffer / Pussyfer / Amputated Whore / Conflagration / Absolute Holocaust / Mass Of Vipers / Brain Drain Faucet / The Rot / Art Of Aggression / The Spoon / Bare Your Wounds For Me / Reek Of Excrete / The Revolt / Mutilated Virgin Slut / Profanity / Drowned In Semen / The Manticore / Drunk & Nauseous / Condition Dead.

TOMBTHROAT

LUDWIGSHAFEN, GERMANY — *Evil Ass (vocals), Björn Köppler (guitar), Peter Hildenbrand (guitar), Alexander Wenz (drums).*

Death-Grind combo TOMBTHROAT developed in 1996 from a Black Metal band featuring guitarist Björn Köppler and drummer Alexander Wenz. This duo's prior track record included Grindcore bands NECROPHALLUS and BANAL plus Black Metal acts ANGMAR and BAAL. Both musicians are also operational with "Surf n' Proll" band BIERVERNICHTER and RIOT PIGS whilst Köppler also holds an affiliation to DISCOURAGED.

Installed on bass guitar would be Stefan Analmastersadofuck. An early frontman, Dirk, vacated and 'Evil Ass' of Hardcore band KICK UP enrolled for demo recordings, dubbed 'Demo 9999', in 1999. Stefan then exited, due to "female oppression", and Evil Arn of COMING DOWN substituted temporarily. Ewool (a.k.a. Wolfram Schellenberg) of DISEMBOWELED and FRAGMENTS OF UNBECOMING then assumed the bass role for recording of the EP 'Evil Fuckin' Zombie Riot' in January 2000.

TOMBTHROAT once more lost their bassist and utilised the temporary services of Evil Knut from Mannheim's MUNDO MUERTO until they acquired Peter Hildenbrand of DEI TENEBRARUM and DISCOURAGED repute. However, with Hildebrand's switch to guitar the band was once again on the lookout for another bassist. Another promotional session, 'The Revenge Of Evil', surfaced in June 2002. 'Slaughtered, Cutted And Pissed On' followed a year later. TOMBTHROAT signed to Twilight Records for release of the album 'Out Of The Tomb', issued in February 2005. The band allied with VITAL REMAINS and LIFTHRASIL for European touring in October.

Demo 9999, (1999). Crying Corpse / Power & Glory / Rocken, Saufen, Ficken / Feuertod / Bloody Pain / Björn / Prophecy Of Rage.
Evil Fucking Zombie Riot, (2000). My Sweet Hatchet / Blood, Sweat 'n' Beers / Crying Corpse / Vier / Selfinflicted Slavery / Dance On The Graves / Blown Fuse / Power & Glory / Fleshlust / Björn / Rocken, Saufen, Ficken / Mosh Until Death / Bloodsuckers / Metal Bitch / Evil Fucking Zombie Riot.
The Revenge Of Evil, (2002). The Revenge Of Evil / Burnt Beyond Recognition / Zombie Crushing Cunts / Underground Bastards / Chainsaw Riot.
Slaughtered, Cutted And Pissed On, (2003). Introduction / Slaughtered, Cutted And Pissed On / Death Fucking Metal / Dark Force Rising / Forever War / Death From Above.
OUT OF THE TOMB, Twilight (2005). Arise To Victory / The Revenge Of Evil / Slaughtered, Cutted & Pissed On / Malignant Blessings / Zombie Crushing Cunts / Forever War / Phobia / Underground Bastards / Death Fucking Metal / Bad Blood / Burnt Beyond Recognition / Bloodday Sunny Bloodday / Out Of The Tomb / Death From Above / Darkforce Rising / Chainsaw Riot.

TORCHBEARER

SWEDEN — *Pär Johansson (vocals), Christian Älvestam (guitar), Göran Johansson (guitar), Mikael Degerman (bass), Henrik Schönström (drums).*

TORCHBEARER, a Black tinged Thrash / Death Metal outfit assembled in 2003 comprises SATARIEL vocalist Pär Johansson, also a campaigner of THE DUSKFALL, DAWN OF DARKNESS and solo concern BELSEMAR. Joining the singer would be the UNMOORED, SOLAR DAWN and INCAPACITY pairing of guitarist Christian Älvestam and drummer Henrik Schönström, alongside the SETHERIAL, IMPIOUS, RINGHORNE and CHAOSDAEMON credited guitarist Göran Johansson. Bassist Mikael Degerman is active with SATARIEL and has held membership of STRIKEFORCE 666 and DAWN OF DARKNESS. Schönström also drums for TRAUMATIZED. The industrious Älvestam has an extended roll call of band endeavours such as CARNALIZED, ANDUIN '98, EVENDIM, LORD OF THRONES, ORGY OF FLESH, SATTYG, RED SKIES DAWNING, THE STINK BUG COLLECTIVE and DEN TIDLÖSA EVIGHETEN.

A debut album 'Yersinia Pestis', recorded at Black Lounge Studios in Sweden with CARNAL FORGE and CENTINEX guitarist Jonas Kjellgren acting as producer, was delivered in March of 2004. That same year Christian Älvestam would be found fronting Jonas Kjellgren's SCAR SYMMETRY band for their 'Symmetric In Design' debut.

TORCHBEARER's second album, 'Warnaments', recorded at Panic Room studios with producer Thomas Johansson, saw release in April 2006 through Regain Records. Christian Älvestam donated guest vocals to ZONARIA's 2006 debut album 'Rendered In Vain', featuring on the track 'Attending Annihilation'. TORCHBEARER members re-assembled in March 2007 to commence work on a fresh album.

YERSINIA PESTIS, Cold 14489-2 (2004). Assail The Creation / Sown Are The Seeds Of Death / Dead Children, Black Rats / Faith Bled Dry / Bearer Of The Torch / Pest Cometh / Fad Advanced Closure / Thus Came Dying Unto Kaffa / Shorespread God / Failure's Dawn.
WARNAMENTS, Regain RR106CD (2006). Dark Clouds Gathering / Last Line Of Defence / Burial Waters, Deepsome Graves / Swift Turns Of War / The Stale Drownings / Battlespawn / Where Night Is Total / Sealer Of Fates / The Blunt Weapon.

TORN

TURKU, FINLAND — *Aki Järvinen (vocals / guitar), T. Sinisterror (guitar), Kai Huovinen (bass), Tuomo Latvala (drums).*

TORN was conceived in Turku during the Autumn of 1993 under the moniker IMPOSED SILENCE by vocalist / guitarist Jani Heinonen, bass player Pasi Uotila and drummer Atte Mäkelä. This trio recorded the old school Death Metal demo 'Torn Angels Of Divine' in July of 1995. Re-branded as SHADOWS OF SUNSET, and installing Aki Järvinen on second guitar, the band then set out on the live trail. A second demo, 'Fires Of The Soon Dead Moon', arrived the following July.

SHADOWS OF SUNSET signed to Fadeless Records for the four song EP 'Reflection From Afar'. A third demo, 'Mirror Of Bestiality', emerged in 1999, after which the name change to TORN occurred. Järvinen and Mäkelä assembled an all new band including guitarist T. Sinisterror (a.k.a. Tuomas Karppinen) of TORTURE KILLER and FUNERAL FEAST and bassist Tuomo Latvala, the latter a veteran of TORTURE KILLER, DEEPRED and DEMIGOD.

TORN entered Mika Haapasalo's Pop Studios in Loimaa in July 2001 to record new tracks billed as 'Violent Ecstasy', although these sessions saw only Järvinen handling guitars as Karppinen had damaged his arm in an accident just prior to this date. Severe Music took these recordings on for commercial release in February 2002. Mäkelä was forced to bow out due to injury and Latvala switched from bass to drums. Kai Huovinen was inducted to cover on bass.

TORN folded in November 2004, announcing "Thanks & farewell to all supporters, stay brutal". Re-billed as 'Gurglenator', Aki Järvinen founded GORETORTURE for a 2004 album 'Promised To Kill You Last ... I Lied'.

Live At Old School, Torn (2002) (CD-R and internet download demo). Fatal Release / Inhuman Fantasies / Insane Paradox / Devoured Existence / Martyr / Cenotaph / Hypochrist / Opponent Of Humanity / Flag Of Hate.
VIOLENT EXCSTASY, Severe Music SVR 003 (2002). Inhuman Fantasies / Fatal Release / Hypochrist / Spawn Of Hatred / Devoured Existence / Martyr / Infinite Dead Mass / Opponent Of Humanity.
Wrapped In A Mantle Of Anger, Torn (2004) (Demo). Insane Paradox / Beyond Mortal Scopes / Wrapped In A Mantle Of Anger.

TORTHARRY

CZECH REPUBLIC — *Martin Vacek (vocals / bass), Jarda Rubeš (guitar), Dan Pavlík (guitar), Miloslav Jirman (drums).*

TORTHARRY was created in August 1991 by the rhythm section of bassist Martin Vacek and drummer Miloslav "Juan" Jirman, the pair having first encountered each other as 13 year olds in the band IMAGO. This band evolved into EXECUTOR during 1988 with the addition of guitarist Jarda Rubeš. Taking on a Death Metal stance the band re-billed itself as TORTHARRY and debuted with a demo titled 'Mezi Nebem A Peklem' in September of 1991, after which 17 year old guitarist Daniel Pavlík enrolled. This session was then followed by another demo, entitled 'Flames Of Eternity', in 1992 and, utilising lyric writer Štefan Ležoviè, 'Incriminated' in 1993. The band donated two tracks, 'Nightmare' and 'Incriminated, to a Yusic Music compilation cassette 'Creations From A Morbid Society' in 1993.

In early 1994 TORTHARRY crafted the album 'When The Memories Are Free', with Vacek and Pavlík sharing lead vocals. The band submitted a track to a Czech METALLICA tribute album '10 Years After ... A Tribute To Cliff Burton' in 1996, recorded at the Hacienda Studios owned by Miloš "Dodo" Doležal. This would also serve as the venue for their next album 'Book Of Dreams'. Live promotion saw the band extending their reach by taking to stages in Germany, Austria, Poland, Slovakia, Switzerland and Portugal.

A third album, 'Unseen' produced by Doležal, was laid down in February of 1999. TORTHARRY also donated their rendition of 'Pull The Plug' to the Dwell Records DEATH tribute album 'Demonic Plague'. The 'White' album was released by CBR Records in 2003.

Incriminated, Independent (1993). Nightmare / To The Death / Eternal Insanity / Incriminated / Time Of Decay.
WHEN THE MEMORIES ARE FREE, Independent (1994). If I Was / I'm Afraid / Day Has Died / The Noble / Inner Frost / Clouds / Sunshine / Thirtees / Moonlight / The Lost One / When The Memories Are Free / To The Death.
BOOK OF DREAMS, Independent (1997). Arrival / Late / Tell Me / All Of That ... / Stain / Just A Feeling / I'm Not Sure / Dumb / Don't Ask / Strach.
UNSEEN, CBR (1999). Dusktale / The Chosen / Unseen / The Eternal / Out Of Today / In The Desert / Hymn Of Twilight / Acceptance / Ending Of Slavery / Stain / Nightmare / Outro.
WHITE, CBR (2003). Intro / The Defilement / Of Soul And Flesh / A Foe Inside / Forest Meditation / Revelation / Illuminations / The Abandoned / Prayer / Remembrance / Path To Silence / Eternal Journey / Acts And Thoughts.

TORTURE ETERNAL

UPPLANDS VÄSBY, SWEDEN — *Ari (vocals), Rikard Bjernegård (guitar), Tobbe (guitar), Linus Nylén (drums).*

TORTURE ETERNAL is an Upplands Väsby Death Metal group established during 2003 under the title NECROPHILIUM. A first demo was released that same year titled 'Sickness And Dismembered Gutsorgasmus' through Sorrow Embraced Records. The band underwent many line-up changes, being fronted at one stage by HERETIQUE and VITUPERATION's Sebastian Zingerman. Jonas Mähl, of VITUPERATION, has also featured in the ranks. Guitarist Rikard Bjernegård, as 'Nattram', also operated with Black Metal band FROSTRIKE.

The TORTURE ETERNAL album 'Mentally Killed Before The Birth' followed in 2005.

With TORTURE ETERNAL's demise guitarist Tobbe and drummer 'Soilslasher' (a.k.a. Linus Nylén) founded GODPHOBIA. Shugatraa (Jonas Mähl) also mentored solo project ÅNGEST and operated Black Metal project ANNIHILATE in alliance with Sinneskog, of INTERRED, issuing the January 2007 demo 'My Path'.

Sickness And Dismembered Gutsorgasmus, Sorrow Embraced (2003) (Demo). Devoured By Demons / Necrofuck Insania / Destroy The Human Race / Torture Eternal / A Butchers Thoughts / The Final Cut / Wormeaten / I Hate You.
MENTALLY KILLED BEFORE THE BIRTH, Sorrow Embraced (2005). Intro (Dark Industrial Waves) / Totally Aggressive And Cold / Mentally Killed Before the Birth / Alone In Hell Cold / End Of All And Nothing In Particular / Necrophilian Psychotic Autopsy / Fuck You / Christianity Denied / Darklife In Stoneversion / Grey Distorted Playgrounds / The Last Gate Of Despair / Outro (In Empty Darkness).

TORTURE KILLER

PORI, FINLAND — *Matti Liuke (vocals), Taneli Hatakka (guitar), Tuomas Karppinen (guitar), Jari Laine (guitar), Tuomo Latvala (drums).*

Pori's TORTURE KILLER, fronted by Matti Liuke, a.k.a. 'Centurion' of ANNIHILATUS and featuring guitarist Tuomas 'T. Sinisterror' Karppinen of TORN and FUNERAL FEAST, signed to the Hammerheart label for a 2003 album 'For Maggots To Devour'. On drums would be Tuomo Latvala from DEMIGOD, TORN and DEEPRED. Latvala, together with guitarist Taneli 'Korpse' Hatakka, previously drummer for ANNIHILATUS, would forge side project AN, issuing a 2003 7" single 'Pure Northern Hell' with Centurion aiding on session vocals.

Bassist Torniainen was added to the TORTURE KILLER ranks in March 2004. In September, just three days before scheduled touring, singer Matti Like was ejected, being swiftly replaced by Sallinen of FUNERAL FEAST for a split 7" single shared with SOTAJUMALA on the Woodcut label.

Finding themselves without a frontman once again during 2005 the band solved the problem in spectacular fashion by announcing in November that SIX FEET UNDER and ex-CANNIBAL CORPSE vocalist Chris Barnes had agreed to join to lay down vocals on second album 'Swarm!'

FOR MAGGOTS TO DEVOUR, Karmageddon Media KARMA001 (2003). Flesh Breaks To Open Wounds / Sadistic Violation / Motivated To Kill / Necrophag / Fuck Them When They Bleed / No Time To Bleed / Torture To Death / Gore Terror / Strangulation.

Sotajumala / Torture Killer, Woodcut CUT040 (2005) (Split single with SOTAJUMALA). Day Of Cadavers / Defiled And Dead.

SWARM!, Metal Blade 14558-2 (2006). Swarm! / Forever Dead / A Funeral For The Masses / Multiple Counts Of Murder / Obsessed With Homicide / Sadistic / Cannibal Gluttony / I Killed You / Heading Towards The Butchery / A Violent Scene Of Death.

TORTURE SQUAD

SÃO PAULO, SP, BRAZIL — *Vítor Rodrigues (vocals), Maurício Nogueira (guitar), Castor (bass), Amílcar Christófaro (drums).*

São Paulo Death Metal crew TORTURE SQUAD was formed in 1989 as a Thrash / Crossover power trio of vocalist / bassist Marcelo Dirceu, guitarist Cristiano Fusco and drummer Marcelo Fusco. However, by the following year Cristiano Fusco was left to build up an entirely new band unit, pulling in singer Vitor Rodrigues, guitarist Fúlvio Pelli and drummer Amilcar Chistófaro, all previously with Thrash band REASONS TO HEAVEN, and bassist Castor. This version of TORTURE SQUAD first demoed that year with the 'A Soul In Hell' session.

Their first album, 'Shivering' limited to 1000 copies, emerged in 1995 through Destroyer Records. 'Asylum Of Shadows' followed in December of 1999. In early 2001 the band donated the track 'Mandate For Freedom' to Die Hard Records conceptual 'William Shakespeare's Hamlet' opus, after which 'The Unholy Spell' album was released. Promotion for this record included an appearance at the São Paulo Extreme Metal Fest and MTV play for a promotional video for the track 'Abduction Was The Case'.

A ten year tenure would be broken as founder Cristiano Fusco exited. TORTURE SQUAD drafted Maurício Nogueira as replacement. The 'Pandemonium' album arrived in 2003 with a live CD / DVD outing 'Death, Chaos And Torture Alive' delivered in 2004.

TORTURE SQUAD, working with producers Marcello Pompeu and KORZUS guitarist Heroes Trench, entered the recording studio in June 2006 to craft a new album.

SHIVERING, (1995). Torture Till Die / Criminal Brutality / Shivering / Suffocation / A Soul In Hell / Dreadful Lies / Darkness Hides The Light.

ASYLUM OF SHADOWS, Destroyer (1999). Convulsion / Shades Of The Evil / Asylum Of Shadows / Murder Of a God / Agonies In Your Brain / Mad Illusion / The Hangman's Call / Come To Torture / Finally The Disgrace Reigns.

THE UNHOLY SPELL, (2001). The Unholy Spell / War Monger / Spiritual Cancer / Abduction Was The Case / The Host / Area 51 / Welcome Home (The House Of Eternal Night) / Under The Wings Of Empire / A Soul In Hell.

PANDEMONIUM, (2003). Intro / Horror And Torture / Towers On Fire / World Of Misery / Leather Apron / Out Of Control / Pandemonium / Requiem For The Headless Rider / The Curse Of Sleep Hollow.

DEATH, CHAOS AND TORTURE ALIVE, (2004). Intro/Horror And Torture / Towers On Fire / Convulsion / The Unholy Spell / A Soul In Hell / Pandemonium / Murder Of A God / Abduction Was The Case / World Of Misery / Area 51 / Out Of Control / The Host.

TOTAL DEVASTATION

KARHULA, FINLAND — *Jaakko Heinonen (vocals), Saku Hakuli (guitar), Harri Pikka (guitar), Pasi Hakuli (bass), Lauri Pikka (keyboards), Jarmo Pikka (drums).*

TOTAL DEVASTATION, hailing from Karhula, debuted commercially in 2003 with the 'Roadmap Of Pain' album issued through Firebox Records. Previously the group had published a string of demos such as 'Blood Culture' and 'Roadmap Of Pain' during 1998, 'Divine—Ecstasy' in 2001 and ' The band's second album, 'Reclusion' recorded at Sound Supreme Studios with producer Janne Saksa and issued by Firebox Records in February 2005, featured a guest appearance by ROTTEN SOUND singer Keijo "G" Niinimaa on the track 'Divine'. A limited edition version of the album contained a cover of AUTOPSY's 'In The Grip Of Winter'.

The group engaged in an extensive round of Scandinavian and European dates allied with ROTTEN SOUND, SAYYADINA and CAUSE FOR EFFECT in early 2006. The group then entered Sound Supreme studios on April 22nd to commence recording of their third album, entitled 'Wreck'.

Blood Culture, Polttouhri Productions PU#07 (1998) (Demo). Voices In My Head / Blood Culture / Point Black / The End.

Roadmap Of Pain, Polttouhri Productions PU#02 (1998) (Demo). No Future / Maniac / Total Devastation / Machine Vs. Man / Gestapo (Kuolema) / Blood Culture / Roadmap Of Pain / Scolesiasis / Dawn Of Terror.

Fallen Mankind, Polttouhri Productions PU#26 (2000) (Demo). Mind Crusher / Chemical Visions / Fallen Mankind.

Divine—Ecstasy, Polttouhri Productions PU#46 (2001) (Demo). I Am God / Burn Yourself / Let It Bleed / Prepare To Die.

Left Hand Of The Devil, Total Devastation (2002) (Demo). Left Hand Of The Devil / Fleshing / Disguise / Production Peak / Mayhem Machine.

ROADMAP OF PAIN, Firebox FIRECD006 (2003). I Am God / Struggling From Chokehold / Disguise / Fragments / Production Peak / Left Hand Of The Devil / Fleshing / Let It Bleed / Prepare To Die / Ignoring Pain.

RECLUSION, Firebox FIRECD018 (2005). Murderous / Divine / They Stand On 3 / Reclusion / Full Circle / Converted Illusion / Ground Zero / Repentance / Well Of The Dead / No Surrender / Bleeding Time.

RECLUSION (LIMITED EDITION), Firebox FIRECD018 (2005). Murderous / Divine / They Stand On 3 / Reclusion / Full Circle / Converted Illusion / Ground Zero / Repentance / Well Of The Dead / No Surrender / Bleeding Time / In The Grip Of Winter / Reclusion (Video).

TOTAL FUCKING DESTRUCTION

PA, USA — *Pngdum (vocals / guitar), Herzog (vocals / guitar), Joe (bass), Hoak (drums).*

Pennsylvania Grind act TOTAL FUCKING DESTRUCTION feature former BRUTAL TRUTH drummer/vocalist Richard Hoak. Joining TOTAL FUCKING DESTRUCTION on a 'Terrorizer' magazine sponsored 'Grind Over UK' tour in November of 2004 would be PIG DESTROYER, Doom duo HALO and the UK's NARCOSIS.

In 2006 the band donated their rendition 'Kill Your Boss' of to raise funds for the EYEHATEGOD musicians on the Emetic Records assembled benefit CD 'For The Sick—A Tribute To Eyehategod'. In September TOTAL FUCKING DESTRUCTION donated exclusive material to the first of Relapse Records 7" Slimewave Series, this collaborative effort shared with MACHETAZO.

In January 2007 TOTAL FUCKING DESTRUCTION announced signature to Translation Loss Records for a debut album entitled "Zen And The Art Of Total Fucking Destruction', a mix of studio, acoustic and live tracks. The group partnered with BRUTAL TRUTH for UK dates in February.

3 WAY OF ARMAGEDDON, Obliteration (2001) (3 way split with NUCLEAR DEVASTATION and C.S.S.O.). Boxcutter / Fear Of A Black Metal Planet / Supervirus One / Supervirus Two / Supervirus Three / Metal Emergency / Jesus (Entering From The Rear) / Grim Corpses / Pig's Head / Intense Negative Vibration / Chromatic Blackness / Supervirus Four / Supervirus Five / Boxcutter / Boxcutter / Four Songs Live at the CBGB's mad grinderz ball,4/8/2000.

TOTTEN KORPS

CHILE — *Ricardo Reyes (vocals), Fernando Toro (guitar), Francisco Torres (guitar), Victor Trujillo (bass), Sergio Aravena (drums).*

TOTTEN KORPS is a Santiago based Death Metal band created during 1989 with the inaugural demo session 'The King Of Hell Reclaims His Throne' arriving a year later. A second 5 track demo, 'Our Almighty Lords', was subsequently issued as a mini album by Hellion Records in 1993. However, due to line up fluctuations the band folded.

In 1998 founder members singer Gerardo Valenzuela and guitarist Fernando Toro resurrected the band, fresh blood being brought in with second guitarist Francisco Torres, bassist Cristian Ort'z and Sergio Aravena on drums. TOTTEN KORPS in this renewed form would be signed by the Spanish Repulse label but the recordings intended for a debut album were deemed by both parties to be unfit to release. TOTTEN KORPS and Repulse parted ways as the band suffered a further fracture with both Torres and Valenzuela bailing out. Ortz took over the lead vocal mantle and Cristian Soto came in on guitar to bring the band back up to strength.

The group's second attempt at a debut 'Tharnheim: Ati-Lan-Nhi, Cyclopean Crypts Of Citadels' arrived in October 2001 on the American World War III label. TOTTEN KORPS would be in for another major overhaul of their line up though with Ort'z and Soto departing. Ricardo Reyes took over on vocals, Francisco Torres resumed his former position on guitar and Victor Trujillo took the bass position.

OUR ALMIGHTY LORDS, Hellion (1993). The King Of Hell Reclaims His Throne / From The Crypts, Putrid Cadavers Rise / The Buried Wizard, In The Millennium Of Obscurity / Totten Korps / Our Almighty Lords.
THARNHEIM: ATI-LAN-NHI, CYCLOPEAN CRYPTS OF CITADELS, World War III (2001). Intro / The Ancient Demoniac Celebration / Slaughter Nocturnal Butcher / Tharnheim; Athi-Land-Nhi, Ciclopean Crypts Of Citadels / The Black Horde Of The Surdic Gods / Our Almighty Lords / Imperator Of The Black Abyss / Das Schwarze Korps / Totten Korps / Avohej; The God-Dog Of Nazareth / The 7th Blasphemies Of Sacred Sacrament.

TOXICDEATH

TUZLA, BOSNIA — *Edin Begovic (vocals), Nedzad Bibic (guitar), Asmir Osmanovic (bass), Sead Hadzic (drums).*

Brutal, technical Death Metal outfit out of Tuzla. TOXICDEATH debuted with the demos 'Daemo Of Madness' in 2000 and 'Pathfinder' during 2001. TOXICDEATH's 2002 promotional album featured cover versions of SLAYER's 'Black Magic' and KREATOR's 'Coma Of Souls'. During early 2003 guitarist Nedzad "Nele" Bibic, retaining his commitments to TOXICDEATH, also joined NECROPHILISMA. Bibic also held credits with P.B.S., MEPHISTO and SPORULATE.

Drummer Sead Hadzic acted as stand in live member for NECROPHILISMA in mid 2004. TOXICDEATH's October 2004 album 'Contamination closed out with a bonus cover of KREATOR's 'Under The Guillotine'.

TOXICDEATH's second album 'Techniques Of Darkness' was recorded in February 2007 for Walk Records.

Pathfinder, (2001). Ancient's Law / When The Day Became Night / Demons Of Madness / Pathfinder / Land Of Primitives / Against The Reality.
LIVE TILL DEATH, Independent (2002). Darkness Of Infinity (Intro) / Death Metal Infection / Demons Of Madness / Coma Of Souls / Pathfinder / Raining Blood / Black Magic / Black Metal.
CONTAMINATION, WalkRecords (2004). Opening A Window To The Past / Darkness Of Infinity / Death Metal Infection / Law Of The Ancients / Pathfinder / Temporal Vortex / Dark Depth / Contaminated Hate / Ludilo / Demons Of Madness / Molecular Collapse / When The Day Became Night / Sins Of Mankind / Under The Guillotine.

TOXOCARA

GRONINGEN, HOLLAND — *Kevin Quilligan (vocals), Martijn Moes (guitar), Vince Zwarts (guitar), Anne van Doorn (bass), Michiel van der Plicht (drums).*

Groningen Death Metal band TOXOCARA was founded in 2003. Formative line-up changes, which saw the exit of the KATAFALK and PROSTITUTE DISFIGUREMENT associated guitarist Niels van Wijk, eventually settled to see a stable unit comprising EREBUS singer Kevin Quilligan, guitarists Vince Zwarts, ex-SEIZURE, and Martijn Moes, of LEGION, THE MONOLITH DEATHCULT, ex-ETERNAL CONSPIRACY and ex-BEYOND BELIEF, erstwhile SANGUINARY bassist Anne van Doorn with the TRAVELERS IN TIME, KATAFALK and PROSTITUTE DISFIGUREMENT credited Michiel van der Plicht on drums.

In September 2004 TOXOCARA entered the studio for the 'Visceral Larval Migrans' demo sessions. In August 2005 the debut album 'Imminent Repulsion (Suffice To Prevent)' was laid down for issue through Sevared Records. A second album, 'Cold Stone Chaos', was projected for 2007.

Visceral Larval Migrans, Toxocara (2004) (Demo). The Blood Road / Visceral Larval Migrans / Mortal Intrepid Frigate / Insomnia.
IMMINENT REPULSION (SUFFICE TO PREVENT), Sevared SR-024 (2005). T34 (Silhouette Of Death) / Blast Wave Diffraction / Suffice To Prevent / The Blood Road (Ho Chi Minh Trail) / Egoist Existence / Visceral Larvel Migrans / Imminent Repulsion / Insomnia / Der Rattenkrieg (Fortress Stalingrad) / Mortal Intrepid Frigate (The Battle Of The Nile).

TRASOS

PADOVA, ITALY — *Fabio (vocals / bass), Alex (guitar), Federico (guitar), Raffaele (keyboards), Fudo (drums).*

Scandinavian styled Death Metal from Italy, founded in Padova during January 2003. TRASOS comprises ex-INSANIA and DELIRIUM vocalist / bassist Fabio, SOULPIT guitarist Federico, also ex-SILENT RITES and CLAYMORE, former METNAL guitarist Alex, TANIST keyboard player Raffaele and drummer Fudo, also active with ALGOL and TRIFIXION and holding prior credits with MAELSTROM, INSANIA, DELIRIUM and FUNEREAL DUSK.

TRASOS was initially created by Fudo in alliance with guitarist Giulio of DELIRIUM, PROCLIVITY GLOOM and CHRONIC HATE, singer Davide, second guitarist French and bassist Alberto. Next to enroll, in March of 2003, would be Raffaele. Changes then saw the departure of both Alberto and Raffaele but the recruitment of bassist Fabio. Next to go would be Davide and Giulio, the role of guitarist being filled by Federico with Raffaele returning in July 2003 but French opted out in September.

In mid 2004 ex-AUTUMN LEAVES man Marco joined as the new TRASOS singer. However, before the close of the year this newest member had vacated and Fabio picked up lead vocal duties.

Frozen Souls, Trasos (2005). Alone / Undead / Nightmares / The Train Of The Damned / Illusion.

TRAUMA

POLAND — *Artur Chudewniak (vocals), Jarosław Misterkiewicz (guitar), Patryk Krajnik (guitar), Paweł Krajnik (bass), Arkadiusz Sinica (drums).*

One of Poland's earliest Death Metal bands, TRAUMA debuted in 1992 with the 'Invisible Reality' album for Morbbid

Noizz Productions. A cassette release, 'Comedy Is Over', followed in 1995 before TRAUMA signed to the Pagan label for the 1997 'Daimonion' record. Staying with Pagan, TRAUMA released 'Suffocated In Slumber' and 'Crash Test- Live', both during 2001.

TRAUMA embarked upon a ten date tour of Poland during October of 2002 co-headlined by MONSTROSITY and Swedes VOMITORY backed by SCEPTIC, LOST SOUL, DISSENTER, and CONTEMPT. The 'Unperfect Like A God' album arrived through Empire Records the following year. In late 2004 the band united with MESS AGE, WOLFRIDER and TOXIC BONKERS for the Polish 'Divine Perdition' tour.

COMEDY IS OVER, Pagan MOON002 (1995). Intro / Incertitude / Relief / This Cant Be True / Perfection / Comedy Is Over / Naked Truth / Outro.
DAIMONIAN, Pagan MOON014 (1998). Intro / Suicide / Dust (Kill Me) / Contradictions / Possessed / Name / Outro / The Dawn- No Way Out / Hidden Instincts / Human Race / No Hope / Escape Into The Shadow.
CRASH TEST—LIVE, Pagan MOON 033 (2001).
SUFFOCATED IN SLUMBER, System Shock (2001). A Gruesome Display / Unable To React / Suffocated In Slumber / A Deep Scar / Swallow The Murder / Words Of Hate / Tools Of Mutual Harm / Dust (Kill Me) / ... Bloodshot Eyes.
UNPERFECT LIKE A GOD, Empire CDAR88 (2003). Blade Under Your Throat / The Hidden Seed / The Madness Here / Beyond The Perception / Imperfect Like A God / Make Me Blind / Spiritual Disorder / Perplexity Of Truths / Outrage To Fools.

TREBLINKA

TÄBY, SWEDEN — *Johan Edlund (vocals / guitar), Stefan Lagergren (guitar), Klas Wistedt (bass), Calle Fransson (drums).*

A Death Metal combo out of Täby, masterminded by Johan Edlund. TREBLINKA was the forerunner of leading Alt-Gothic Metal band TIAMAT, a band that has evolved chameleon like with each successive release. Less tastefully known in their formative years as TREBLINKA (during which time vocalist Johan Edlund also pursued his side project GENERAL SURGERY), the Swedish quartet adopted the title of the Sumerian goddess of chaos and mythical planet TIAMAT. The band has evolved from a derivative Speed Metal / Death act to a more substantial stance in offering aggression with adventurous Progressive variances.

As TREBLINKA the band consisted of vocalist/guitarist Johan Hedlund ("Lucifer Hellslaughter"), bassist Klas Wistedt, guitarist Stefan Lagergren ("Emetic") and drummer Andreas Holmberg ("Najse Auschwitzer"). This unit released the 1988 demo 'Crawling In Vomits' and follow up tape 'The Sign Of The Pentagram' in 1989. Also emerging that year would be the ' Severe Abomination' EP.

Upon taking the TIAMAT moniker the group issued debut album 'Sumerian Cry' through CMFT Productions in 1990.

Crawling In Vomits, Treblinka (1988). Crawling In Vomits / Earwigs In Your Veins / Hail To Cruelty / Cadaverous Odour.
Severe Abomination, Mould in Hell MHR-S 001 (1989) (7" single, first release on black vinyl, second release on red vinyl). Severe Abomination / Earwigs In Your Veins.
The Sign Of The Pentagram, Treblinka (1989). Nocturnal Funeral / Evilized / Necrophagious Shadows / Mould In Hell.

TRIBULATION

ARVIKA, SWEDEN — *Johannes Andersson (vocals / bass), Jonathan Hultén (guitar), Adam Zaars (guitar), Jakob Johansson (drums).*

Thrash / Death combo TRIBULATION came together during 2001 under the original branding of HAZARD. The group, hailing from Arvika in the southwest of Sweden, first featured guitarists Jonathan Hultén, of TRAKTOR, and Adam Zaars, TERROR, CORRUPTED and MASS HYPNOSIS bassist Joseph Tholl with Jonas Wikstrand of LEPROSY on drums. This unit cut the demo 'Aggression Within'. The CORRUPTED and LEPROSY credited Olof Wikstrand took over on bass during 2002. Singer Johannes Andersson came on board the following year.

Switching title to TRIBULATION, the band underwent a radical line-up shift in 2004, as both Olaf and Jonas Wikstrand exited. FERAL's Jimmie Frödin briefly occupied the drum stool, for the demo 'Agony Awaits', before Jakob Johansson enrolled. Re-billed as TRIBULATION, they recorded a further demo, 'The Ascending Dead', in June 2005. That same year Jonatan Hultén forged a new outfit billed GUERILLA.

The Ascending Dead, Tribulation (2005) (Demo). Island Of The Flesh Eaters / Cannibal Feast / C.H.V: The Gore Attack / Soul Tribulation.
Putrid Rebirth, Blood Harvest (2006). Dread City Of Death / Zombie Holocaust / Imprisoned In Abhorrence / Churning Sea Of Absu.

TRIVIUM

ALTAMONTE SPRINGS, FL, USA — *Matt Heafy (vocals / guitar), Corey Beaulieu (guitar), Brent Young (bass), Travis Smith (drums).*

An Altamonte Springs, Florida Death / Thrash styled Metal act originally created in 2000 when the group's original singer viewed guitarist Matt Heafy conducting a rendition of THE OFFSPRING's 'Self Esteem' with drummer Travis Smith in order to enter a high school 'Battle of the bands' contest. The name TRIVIUM was chosen, a Latin word meaning the intersection between three schools of learning, namely grammar, rhetoric and logic, as it implied an open mindedness towards varying musical styles. Line-up changes then saw the addition of Brent Young on rhythm guitar and Heafy took over the lead vocal role, following several party gigs. The following year Richie Brown of Black Metal outfit MINDSCAR filled in as bassist for live work but subsequently Young switched instruments to cover this position.

2002 would prove a pivotal year for the group as TRIVIUM claimed top honours at the school 'Battle of the bands' contest, supported national acts PESSIMIST and PISSING RAZORS and Heafy won the local 'Orlando Metal Awards' as best guitarist. A self-financed album would see Jason Suecof of CAPHARNAUM acting as producer as the band found itself being hailed as frontrunners in the New Wave of American Heavy Metal stakes. TRIVIUM, signing to the Lifeforce label for the 'Ember To Inferno' follow up, cut at Audiohammer Studios, added Corey Beaulieu as second guitarist in September 2003.

The group re-entered Audiohammer Studios in mid May 2004 to commence pre-production for their Roadrunner Records debut album, subsequently re-selecting producer Jason Suecof for the final recordings. TRIVIUM acted as support to ICED EARTH and BEYOND THE EMBRACE for Summer shows in the US. The group forged an alliance with MACHINE HEAD and CHIMAIRA for the August 'RoadRage 2004' dates in North America.

TRIVIUM entered Tampa's Morrisound studios on September 13th with Jason Suecof once again for recording of their sophomore album entitled 'Ascendancy'. Mastering would be conducted by ex-SABBAT guitarist Andy Sneap in the UK. In November the group added former METAL MILITIA bassist Paolo Gregoletto to the ranks. The album sold 6,976 copies in its first week of release to debut at number 151 on the US Billboard charts. The band had their track 'Like Light To The Flies' featured on the soundtrack to the 'Rainbow Six Lockdown' game issued by 3volution Productions.

The band opened 2005 with a set of US headlining dates in January, heading up a touring package with ALL THAT REMAINS, IT DIES TODAY and THE ACACIA STRAIN. Gigs into February found the group partnering with DANZIG and KATAKLYSM. They joined the Roadrunner 'Roadrage' tour with 3 INCHES OF BLOOD, THE AGONY SCENE, STILL REMAINS in March prior to April gigs alongside CHIMAIRA. This tour extended into UK dates during May. Initially announced as an opening act on the SLIPKNOT / SHADOWS FALL US arena tour of Spring 2005 the band was forced to drop off the billing due to "Union enforced time constraints".

Matthew Heafy would act as one of five high profile writers contributing to the ROADRUNNER UNITED 25th anniversary album 'The All-Stars Sessions', his songwriting credits featuring amongst four compositions. 'The Dawn Of A Golden Age' utilized lead vocals from Dani Filth of CRADLE OF FILTH, Heafy laying down lead and rhythm guitar parts, while 'I Don't Wanna Be (A Superhero)' boasted vocals by Michale Graves of the MISFITS with lead and rhythm guitar cuts recorded by Heafy. 'Blood And Flames' was sung by ex-KILLSWITCH ENGAGE man Jesse Leach, the ever versatile TRIVIUM frontman donating lead, rhythm and acoustic guitar, not to mention backing vocals—lead, rhythm and acoustic guitar also came courtesy of Heafy on the KING DIAMOND sung 'In The Fire', bandmate Cory Beaulieu supplying lead and rhythm guitars too on this number. Heafy himself vocalised and lent lead guitar services on 'The End' penned by ex-FEAR FACTORY guitarist Dino Cazares.

The TRIVIUM track 'Pull Harder On The Strings Of Your Martyr' gave the band a good degree of extra exposure when it was included on the soundtrack to the Bruce Hunt directed movie 'The Cave', released in August. The band's September and October European dates, taking in the UK, with ALL THAT REMAINS and IT DIES TODAY, then France, Belgium, Holland, Germany, Norway, Sweden and Denmark, saw strong support from ARCH ENEMY. The two bands stuck together for Japanese gigs in October. To coincide with these dates a special tour edition of 'Ascendancy' was issued, adding a bonus disc featuring two previously unreleased tracks and three videos. On 15th December Matt Heafy, Travis Smith and Corey Beaulieu notably joined the ROADRUNNER UNITED conglomerate at the New York Nokia Theater for an all star Metal evening. TRIVIUM included a track 'Washing Me Away In The Tides' on the 'Underworld: Evolution' movie soundtrack.

IN FLAMES, TRIVIUM and DEVILDRIVER pooled their talents for a January 2006 US tour. March had the band scheduled for 'The Crusade III: Ascend Above The Ashes' concerts in the UK and Ireland alongside GOD FORBID and BLOODSIMPLE. The band played their part in honouring METALLICA, contributing their rendition of 'Master Of Puppets' to the album 'Remastered', this set being a complete remake of 'Master Of Puppets' in joint celebration of the twentieth anniversary of the classic album's release and the 25th anniversary of UK Rock magazine Kerrang! In April. Yet another re-issue of the 'Ascendancy' opus would collect this interpretation as an additional bonus track in May.

The band put in a significant appearance at the METALLICA and KORN headlined 'Download' festival in Castle Donington, UK on June 10th. The group subsequently engaged in a gigantic roving festival billing with the US 'Sounds Of The Underground' tour throughout the summer, commencing in Cleveland, Ohio on July 8th, partnered with IN FLAMES, AS I LAY DYING, CANNIBAL CORPSE, GWAR, TERROR, THE BLACK DAHLIA MURDER, BEHEMOTH, THE CHARIOT and THROUGH THE EYES OF THE DEAD.

TRIVIUM's first headline US trek saw them through late September into mid November, supported by THE SWORD, PROTEST THE HERO, SEEMLESS, SANCTITY and CELLADOR. On October 9th 'The Crusade' was officially certified silver status in the UK for sales in excess of 60,000 copies, hitting number 7 on the charts.

The band scored a notable coup, supporting IRON MAIDEN for their massive series of arena dates throughout Europe, UK and Scandinavia for November. Unfortunately the band came in for some unwelcome press when British fans of the headline act turned on the band. At the December 22nd Earl's Court, London show audience members bombarded both frontman

TRIVIUM (pic: Josh Rothstein)

Matt Heafy and bassist Paolo Gregoletto during the song 'Like Light To The Flies' with bottles and water balloons filled with urine.

In January and February 2007 the group put in Japanese headliners followed up a slot on the New Zealand and Australia 'Big Day Out' festivals, on a bill comprising TOOL, THE KILLERS, MUSE, MY CHEMICAL ROMANCE and JET, interspersed with headline shows. The band packaged up with LAMB OF GOD, MACHINE HEAD and GOJIRA for a lengthy run of North American dates commencing on February 16th 2007 at the Palladium Ballroom in Dallas, Texas. During this period Corey Beaulieu managed to find time to guest on the comeback album for cult Heavy Metal band LIZZY BORDEN.

A mammoth European tour kicked off with a two night stand at the Ambassador in Dublin, Ireland on April 8th. Canadian Thrash veterans acted as support for the entire trek, which covered the UK, France, Belgium, Holland, Germany, Poland, Denmark, Sweden, Finland, Norway, Austria, Italy, Spain and Switzerland.

Trivium, Trivium (2003) (Demo). To Burn The Eye / Requiem / Fugue / My Hatred / The Storm / Sworn / Demon.
EMBER TO INFERNO, Lifeforce LFR 040-2 (2003). Inception, The Bleeding Skies / Pillars Of Serpents / If I Could Collapse The Masses / Fugue (A Revelation) / Requiem / Ember To Inferno / Ashes / To Burn The Eye / Falling To Grey / My Hatred / When All Light Dies / A View Of Burning Empires.
EMBER TO INFERNO, Tokuma TKCS-85083 (2003) (Japanese release). Inception, The Bleeding Skies / Pillars Of Serpents / If I Could Collapse The Masses / Fugue (A Revelation) / Requiem / Ember To Inferno / Ashes / To Burn The Eye / Falling To Grey / My Hatred / When All Light Dies / A View Of Burning Empires / The Storm / Sworn.
ASCENDANCY, Roadrunner RRCY-21238 (2005) (Japanese release). The End Of Everything / Rain / Pull Harder On The Strings Of Your Martyr / Drowned And Torn Asunder / Ascendancy / A Gunshot To The Head Of Trepidation / Like Light To The Flies / Dying In Your Arms / The Deceived / Suffocating Sight / Departure / Declaration / Blinding Tears Will Break The Skies / Washing Away Me In The Tides.
ASCENDANCY, Roadrunner 6182512 (2005). The End Of Everything / Rain / Pull Harder On The Strings Of Your Martyr / Drowned And Torn Asunder / Ascendancy / A Gunshot To The Head Of Trepidation / Like Light To The Flies / Dying In Your Arms / The Deceived / Suffocating Sight / Departure / Declaration. Chart position: 151 USA.
Anthem (We Are The Fire), Roadrunner RR PROMO 951 (2006) (Promotion release). Anthem (We Are The Fire) (Clean edit) / Anthem (We Are The Fire) (Edit) / Anthem (We Are The Fire) (album version).
ASCENDANCY (SPECIAL EDITION), Roadrunner 6182518 (2006) (CD + DVD). The End Of Everything / Rain / Pull Harder On The Strings Of Your Martyr / Drowned And Torn Asunder / Ascendancy / A

Gunshot To The Head Of Trepidation / Like Light To The Flies / Dying In Your Arms / The Deceived / Suffocating Sight / Departure / Declaration / Washing Away Me In The Tides / Like Light To The Flies (Video) / Pull Harder On The Strings Of Your Martyr (Video) / Gunshot To The Head Of Trepidation (Video) / Rain (Video) / Rain (Live) / Dying In Your Arms (Live) / Like Light To The Flies (Live) / Gunshot To The Head Of Trepidation (Live) / Pull Harder On The Strings Of Your Martyr (Live).

THE CRUSADE, Roadrunner (2006). Ignition / Detonation / Anthem (We Are The Fire) / This World Can't Tear Us Apart / In Sadness We'll See Her / Entrance Of The Conflagration / The Crusade / Synthetic / Becoming The Dragon. Chart positions: 7 UK, 12 IRELAND, 14 AUSTRALIA, 23 GERMANY, 23 CANADA, 25 USA, 41 SWEDEN, 44 AUSTRIA, 46 JAPAN, 61 NORWAY, 64 HOLLAND, 86 ITALY, 92 SWITZERLAND, 115 FRANCE.

TROLLHEIM'S GROTT

KUOPIO, FINLAND — *Spellgoth (vocals / guitar), Trist (guitar), Korpse (bass), Ruho (keyboards), Troll N. (drums).*

The corpse paint bedecked TROLLHEIM'S GROTT deliver raging speed Metal but are reluctant to apply the term Black Metal to their brand of music. Although bearing a Swedish title, TROLLHEIM'S GROTT emanate from the Finnish town of Kuopio. The band was conceived by vocalist Spellgoth, along with his drumming brother T. Nattefrost (later titled Troll N.), during 1997. The band became a trio with the addition of A. Hellwitch in time for an eponymous 1998 demo. Goreblast would take on bass duties for a self-financed live album simply billed as 'Live 1999'.

TROLLHEIM'S GROTT would subsequently draft Trist of MINOAN in on bass and maneuvered Goreblast over to second guitar. Hellwitch bailed out in 2000 and was replaced by H.G.G. Void for the summer 2000 demo 'Kalt, Trist, Sorg Och Dod'. Further shuffles found Goreblast back to his original four-string ranking and Trist elevated to guitarist. Shortly after this shuffle, Goreblast too decamped. With the band scoring a deal with the Woodcut label Trolldom was inducted as temporary session guitarist. Yet more ructions witnessed the departure of Void as TROLLHEIM'S GROTT brought in Ruho from FUNERIS NOCTURNUM to act as keyboard player. Thereafter, Korpse of DEATHCHAIN, DE LIRIUM'S ORDER and WINTERWOLF assumed the bass mantle. Drummer Troll N. would also be operational alongside Korpse as a member of Thrash Metal band DEATHCHAIN. Korpse also sessioned lead vocals on TWISTED SILENCE's 2002 demos and joined DEMILICH in 2005.

Mikko Kotamäki of TROLLHEIM'S GOTT also cites credits with FUNERIS NOCTURNUM, EMPYREAN BANE, ENTER MY SILENCE and SWALLOW THE SUN. The band also has ties to BLACK DEATH RITUAL. Spellgoth also fronts Industrial Metal act TURMION KÄTILÖT.

Trollheim's Grott, Trollheim's Grott (1998) (Demo limited to 200 copies). Trollheims Grott (Intro) / Polar Werewolf / Grå Varg Och Svart Korp / Christian Fuckers / Jag Drömde Om Fimbulvetr I Natt.
Promo-99, Trollheim's Grott (1999) (Promotion release limited to 25 promo slipcases and 50 jewelcases). Pimeä Metsä, Vaalea Varjo / Scar In My Soul / A Step Towards Divinity.
Chapter I: Silent Is The Dead, Trollheim's Grott (1999) (Demo limited to 25 copies). Dark Glowing / Long Waited Moment / Usva / Cuningas Talwi (Rehearsal) / Yksin Tähtitaivaan Alla (Rehearsal).
LIVE 1999, Trollheim's Grott (1999). Into The Cave Of Trolls / The Curse / Snow Cover My Heart / Into The Pond Of Deadsouls / Beyond The Stargate.
Kalt, Trist, Sorg Och Död, Trollheim's Grott (2000) (Demo limited to 50 copies). Nattvandrare / Parabellum—Prepare For War / Melancholic Thunderstorm / Before The Day Of The Flames / Kalt, Trist, Sorg Och Död.
BIZARRE TROLL TECHNOLOGY, Woodcut CUT016 (2001). Trollgeddon / Trollsyndicate / Conquering With Blasphemy / Bizarre Troll Technology / Amanita Virosa / Mushroomcloud Science / Electronic Genocide / Chased By Trolls.
BLOODSOAKED & ILL-FATED, Woodcut CUT 025 (2003). Dehumanize / Exact Answers And Syndicate Solutions / Syndicate Wormcampaign / Operation: Lick The Fungus / Little Shot Of Scalpels / Syndicate Haunts You Down / Experimentation / Addicted To Lethal Injections.

TUBE

OSLO, NORWAY — *Jonny Painful, Sturt.*

An Industrial edged Oslo Grindcore Black Metal band. The TUBE duo of Sturt and Jonny Painful began life as BLODSHUNGER ("Bloodlust") in 1995, releasing the demo 'Nightside Kingdom'. Oddly the project then took on the demo name as their own title, becoming NIGHTSIDE KINGDOM. In this incarnation the group issued a further demo 'A Storm To Bring The Dark Age' in 1997. Further recordings committed to tape at this time were given the handle of WHIP. Sturt also published the 1998 demo 'Crossing The Crystal Desert' as ALRUNE MADRAGORA.

As TUBE the endeavour first surfaced with the '99/98' recordings. For the second session 'Co-operation With The Devil' TUBE brought in RED HARVEST and DUNKELHEIT man Turbonatas on guitar.

Live work was contemplated but abandoned. Despite this the esteemed Skoll of VED BUENS ENDE, ARCTURUS and ULVER repute joined the formation on bass.

99/98, Tube (1999) (Demo). Doomsday F.War / Satanified / Total Genocide / Cuntwar / Hammering Damnation / The Slithering Demon / Unholly Deathfist / Blessing The Shit.
CO-OPERATION WITH THE DEVIL, Tube (1999). Unholified Through Cunt / SS-Slut / The Final Perversion / Soul Perversion / The Satanic Take Over / Cybersatan Chaoslaw / The Final Countdown / Goat Machine.

TUSKA

KARJAA, FINLAND — *Greger Grönholm (vocals), Urho Tuska (guitar), Tarmo Tuska (bass), Yrjö Tuska (drums).*

Self-styled "Blackcore" band TUSKA ("Agony"), established in Karjaa during 1999, issued the 'Saasta' in April 2001, September's 'Raato' EP, October's 'Orjuus' and June 2002 EP 'Käärmeys', on the Loud'n'Wrong label. A series of line-up changes would witness the shedding of guitarists Juho Tuska and Lalli Tuska plus drummers Igor Kreschnek and Jukka Tuska.

A split album for Bestial Burst, limited to 666 copies and shared with INCRIMINATED entitled 'Ten Hail Marys', arrived in 2003. TUSKA's Greger Grönholm (a.k.a. Matti Tuska) fronts Sludge outfit LOINEN billed as 'Primus'. As 'G.G.' he also heads up Grind outfit VALD and has affiliations to VERESSLIHA, MASOKISMI, DISTRAHERA and SVEN TUBA OCH FISKMASARNA. Bass player Tarmo Tuska (Tuomo Tolonen) has ties to VERESSLIHA, WASARA and VÅLD.

Saasta, Loud'n'Wrong (2001). Tuska / Peto / Kaiva Poika / Veren Jumala / Äijäkristus.
Raato, Loud'n'Wrong (2001). Verta Ja Spermaa / Anaalimessias / Hornaaja / Leprapillu.
Orjuus, Loud'n'Wrong (2001). Ristiinnaulittu Äpärä / Kärsimys / Teurasjäte / Ruumiinhäpäisy / Rektaalirangaistus.
Käärmeys, Loud'n'Wrong (2002). Perseenhornaus / Veresliha / Sielunsurma / Uskonto Orjuuttaa / Suolijeesus.
TEN HAIL MARYS, Bestial Burst BEBU 03 (2003) (Split album with INCRIMINATED. Limited edition 666 copies). Tuska Raatelee / Kyrpääjä / Pahan Hengen Nimeen / Sadonisti / Manala.

TWILIGHT

VAASA, FINLAND — *Kai Jaakkola (vocals), Petri Seikkula (guitar), Tommi Konu (bass), Toni Erkkilä (drums).*

TWILIGHT was a precursor to Vaasa Death Metal band DEATHBOUND. The 2002 DEATHBOUND membership roster boasts a worthy Death Metal pedigree with frontman Kai Jaakkola holding down a reputation with DUSKFALL, NECROMICON and MONSTER SPANK, guitarist Petri Seikkula citing credits with BLACK DAWN as well as AND OCEANS, bassist Tommi Kontz activity with HELLMASKER and drummer Mika Q claiming AND OCEANS, BLACK DAWN and ROTTEN SOUND credentials.

The group has its roots in the early 90's act UNBOUND. By 1995 the title of TWILIGHT had been put into effect, this band starting life with a roster of vocalist Kai Jaakkola, guitarist Petri Seikkula, bassist Tommi Konu and Toni Erkkilä on the drums. In this incarnation TWILIGHT issued a brace of demos 'Twilight', in December 1995, and 'The Melancholy Of The Northern Landscapes' before the band was put on hold due to the intrusion of Finland's national service policy. Activity was sporadic until 1998 when the band regrouped with the addition of BEYOND DREAMS guitarist Fred Andersson and drummer Robert Sundelin of SATARIEL and an ex-member of NECROMICON. Konu, as 'Hellkuntz', participated in recording of the Swedish band HELLMASKER's 'Probably The Best Band In The World' demo. The band recorded the 'Flames Of Madness' demo in September 1999 upon completion of which Andersson's place was taken by NECROMICON's Nick Sundqvist.

During 2000 the decision was taken to revert back to the formative title of UNBOUND due to the increasing media presence of the Italian Power Metal band TWILIGHT. Bringing in Mikael Sandorf on the drums the band laid down a fresh demo 'Elaborate The Torture' in November 2000 before switching the group name again—this time to DEATHBOUND as Blastmor of THYRANE became next in line to occupy the drum stool but by 2002 Mika Q had taken the role.

Melancholy Of Northern Landscapes, Twilight (1995) (Demo). The Spirit / Wings Turn To Ashes / My Final Rest / A Dream Of Winter ... Dying / The Dragon Legions.

Flames Of Madness, Twilight (1999) (Demo). Feel The Repulsion / Phantomside / Drown In The Waves / Flames Of Madness.

TYPHOID

SLOVAKIA — *Roman Regina (vocals / guitar), Rado Godal (guitar), Jozef Flimel (bass), Ďuso Mokry (drums).*

American styled Death / Grind act out of Prievidza. Forged in 1994 as a trio of Roman Regina on guitar, Jozef Flimel on bass guitar and drummer Ďuso Mokry, the band debuted with the 1997 tape 'Intestines Of Immortality'. Upon completion of Mokry's military service TYPHOID followed up with 'Ruptured Self Control' in 1999, released by Immortal Souls Productions. Touring to promote this release saw the introduction of additional vocalist Peter Karaba. Subsequently the archive demo 'Intestines Of Immortality' was re-issued, adding a live rendition of POSSESSED's 'The Exorcist'.

TYPHOID released a further release in 2001 entitled 'Deoxyribonucleaic Acid', this featuring three new songs plus covers of 'Nocturnal Crucifixion' by DYING FETUS and 'Service For A Vacant Coffin' from AUTOPSY. The band added second guitarist Rado Godal of SYNTHETICALLY REVIVED during 2003. TYPHOID cut further demos at Moonset Studios in May of 2004.

INTESTINES OF IMMORTALITY, (1999). Typhoid Fever / Involuntary Suicide / Silence Into Conscience / Way Back / ... Only Naïve Game Of Immortality / Devoid Of Blood / The Exorcist (Live).

RUPTURED SELF CONTROL, Immortal Souls Productions (2000). Ruptured Self Control / Mortal Pregnancy / Painless Treatment / Sudden Death / Killed For Killing / Beyond My Possibilities / Decay And Cleavage Of Typhoid Bacteria.

Deoxyribonucleic Accident, Immortal Souls Productions (2002). Closing Eyes / Deoxyribonucleic Accident / Transcendental Dream / Nocturnal Crucifixion / Service For A Vacant Coffin.

ULCERATE

NEW ZEALAND — *James Wallace (vocals), Michael Hoggard (guitar), Jared Commerer (guitar), Jamie Saint Merat (drums).*

Hamilton Death Metal act previously known as BLOODWREATH. The band was forged during 2000 comprising HATE THEORUM's Michael Hoggard and Jamie Saint Merat on guitars and drums respectively and Bart Fine on bass. Saint Merat also cites credits with MISLED BY LIES. Hoggard and Saint Merat are both also active in MISADVENTURES IN SELF SURGERY. The drummer also operates with ROCK.PAPER.MEATCLEAVER. Subsequently Mark 'Worzel' Seeney took on the role of frontman and Fine was usurped by Phil Smathers, also known as vocalist for MISLED BY LIES.

BLOODWREATH was embroiled in some major line up shifts during mid 2002 triggered by the departure of vocalist Mark Seeney, who left to concentrate on his role as a drummer in RED SHIFT, and dismissal of bass player Phil Smathers. BLOODWREATH duly inducted James Wallace of AS HEAVEN BLEEDS repute into the vocal role as well as pulling in Jared Commerer, a veteran of EYESORE, BLUT and ALTECH, on second guitar. Demos were recorded in September that year.

During 2003 BLOODWREATH evolved into ULCERATE, their first task under their new title acting as support to DAWN OF AZAZEL's January 2003 'Law Of The Strong' tour. An eponymous 2003 demo would be followed by a 2004 session 'The Coming Of Genocide'.

ULCERATE guitarist Michael Hoggard found himself reaping national exposure in 2005 in a most unexpected, and very un-Metal, fashion. He would be featured on the New Zealand television ballroom dancing game show 'Dancing With The Stars' partnering famous sex-change government minister and erstwhile sex industry worker Georgina Beyer.

ULCERATE signed with Neurotic Records in April 2006. That October, promoting the album 'Of Fracture And Failure', the band supported CANNIBAL CORPSE in Auckland and Wellington.

Ulcerate Promo, Independent (2003). Subversive Supremacy / Burnt Offering / Ulceration / Smash The Deceitful.

OF FRACTURE AND FAILURE, (2006). Praise And Negation / Ad Nauseam / The Mask Of The Satyr / Becoming The Lycanthrope / To Fell Goliath / Martyr Of The Soil / Failure / The Coming Of Genocide / Defaeco.

OF FRACTURE AND FAILURE, Neurotic NRT060011 (2006). Praise And Negation / Ad Nauseam / The Mask Of The Satyr / Becoming The Lycanthrope / To Fell Goliath / Martyr Of The Soil / Failure / The Coming Of Genocide / Defaeco.

ULTIMATUM

ALBUQUERQUE, NM, USA — *Scott Waters (vocals), Robert Gutierrez (guitar), Steve Trujillo (guitar), Tom Michaels (bass), Sean Griego (drums).*

One of the leading Christian Death Metal acts. ULTIMATUM was forged in 1992 with lead guitarist Robert Gutierrez also handling lead vocals. Both Gutierrez and initial drummer John Carroll were both erstwhile members of HOLY SACRIFICE whilst guitarist Steve Trujillo was a veteran of both HOLY SACRIFICE and ANGELIC FORCE.

ULTIMATUM first issued the 1993 demo 'Fatal Delay'. Drummer Mike Lynch joined up in 1994 but EXTRACTION's Rick Campbell would deputize for ULTIMATUM's inaugural gig supporting GODFEAR. For recording of a second demo session 'Symphonic Extremies' ULTIMATUM enlisted bassist Tom Michaels.

Lynch would be supplanted in 1996 by Sean Griego for recording of the 'Puppet Of Destruction' album released by Rowe Productions, the label headed by MORTIFICATION main man Steve Rowe. The band signed to German label Gutter Records, a subsidiary of Massacre, for the 2000 album 'The Mechanics Of Perilous Times'. This record included a cover version of VENGEANCE RISING's 'Burn'.

ULTIMATUM would contribute their version of 'Sins Of Omission' to the Dwell Records TESTAMENT tribute 'Jump In The Pit'. In 2001 the band put in an appearance at the annual STRYPER Expo in California. Rob Whitlock superseded Michaels during

2002, the band debuting with this revised line up 'Metal Marti Gras' festival in California that August.

In 2004 Scott Waters formed up with the re-branded VENGEANCE RISING, now billed as ONCE DEAD. ULTIMATUM appeared at the 'Beyond The Mountain' festival in August 2005. During 2006 Roxx Productions issued a limited edition EP entitled 'Til The End', restricted to just 300 copies. ULTIMATUM contracted with Retroactive Records in September for a fourth album 'Into The Pit', recorded at Site 16 Studios in Albuquerque with producer Ysidro Garcia.

Fatal Delay, (1993). Wickedness & Perdition / Fatal Delay / All I Need / Plea For Holiness.
Symphonic Extremities, (1995). Symphonic Extremities / Killing Fields / Black Light / The Grip / Megaton.
SYMPHONIC EXTREMITIES, Juke Box Media (1995). Symphonic Extremities / The Killing Fields / E.N.D. (Erroneous Notion Of Death) / Black Light / Darkest Void / Ode To Noise / The Frip / Fatal Delay / Megaton / Blink / World Of Sin.
PUPPET OF DESTRUCTION, Rowe Productions (1998). Never / Mortal Stomp / Scorn / Puppet Of Destruction / Gutterbox / Repentance / World Of Sin / Crosshope / Conform To Reality / Charged / Power.

UMBRAE

MEXICO — *Macklén Mingura (vocals / guitar), Víctor Hernandez (guitar), Julio Cesar Rodríguez (bass), Mónica San Martín (keyboards), Iván Perales (drums).*

The formative version of melodic Death Metal band UMBRAE was fronted by Victor Hernandez and had keyboards supplied by Galia Mireles, both formerly of MORTIGENA. Mireles had also featured on the 1998 demo 'Luna Muerta' from ZAGROS ATICA. This incarnation of the band self financed the 'Infamous Revelations' release. Initially restricted to a manufacturing run of just 150 copies it would be subsequently re-issued by Concreto Records. After an EP release, the five track 'Beaten', the band enrolled a new keyboard player Monica San Martin, previously of EDAHI.

UMBRAE drummer Iván Perales can also be found on the live circuit with Punk band SEIS PISTOS.

INFAMOUS REVELATIONS, (2000). Beloved Darkness / Final Chapter / Angel Del Abismo / Empty / The Storm's About To Break (Or It Already Has) / La Ultima Brisa Del Verano / Born To Darkness II / Un Lugar Solitario Para Morir / Dead Heaven's Lord / The River Of Melancholy / The Kiss Of Fire / An Infamous Revelation In Two Parts / Beloved Darkness (Reprise).
Beaten EP, (2002). Beaten / White Path To Damnation / Chaos AM / La Barranca / The Edge (Live) / The Sanctity Of Sin (Live).

UNANIMATED

STOCKHOLM, SWEDEN — *Micke Jansson (vocals), Jonas Melberg (guitar), Jonas Bohlin (guitar), Richard Cabeza (bass), Jocke Westman (keyboards), Peter Stjärnvind (drums).*

Death Metal band UNANIMATED was created in Stockholm during 1989. The inaugural line-up of the group found guitarists Chris Alverez and Jonas Melklberg teamed with Richard Cabeza on lead vocals and bass and ex-MERCILESS drummer Peter Stjärnvind. By the time of their first studio demo tape, June 1991's 'Fire Storm', UNANIMATED had replaced Alverez with Jonas Bohlin, whilst Cabeza left for a time to join DISMEMBER. The band drafted in Micke Jansson on lead vocals and MASTICATION's Daniel Lofthagen on bass. In parallel to their tenure with UNANIMATED, Stjärnvind and Cabeza would be actively pursuing Death Metal combo MURDER SQUAD as an alliance with DISMEMBER's Matti Kärki and ENTOMBED's Ulf Cederlund.

Some versions of the first UNANIMATED album, 1994's 'In The Forest Of The Dreaming Dead' released on the No Fashion label, possess a cover of VENOM's 'Buried Alive'. That same year both Stjärnvind and Cabeza, in collaboration with CHARRED REMAINS bassist Björn Gramell activated side venture DAMNATION resulting in the demo 'Divine Darkness'.

For UNANIMATED's second album, 1995's 'Ancient God Of Evil', a record hyped at the time by No Fashion as one that took Death Metal into a new dimension, bass parts were once more handled by Cabeza, although he was still a full time member of DISMEMBER. Subsequently UNANIMATED contributed rendition's of BATHORY's 'Raise The Dead' to the No Fashion 'In Conspiracy With Satan' tribute album and SLAYER's 'Dead Skin Mask' to the 'Slatanic Slaughter' collection.

UNANIMATED split, with Stjärvind joining FACE DOWN and, in 1997, ENTOMBED. Jonas Mellborg enrolled into the ranks of THERION during 1996. Stjärnvind and Cabeza forged BORN OF FIRE in 2001. Cabeza later added to his long list of extreme Metal citations in the Spring of 2002, acting as tour bassist for premier Black Metal act DARK FUNERAL's North American dates whilst the equally industrious Peter Stjärnvind set up yet another new outfit, KRUX.

Rehearsal Demo 1 '90, Unanimated (1990) (Demo). Unholy Funeral / Ancient God Of Evil.
Fire Storm, Unanimated (1991) (Demo). The Call / Through The Gates / The Blackness Of The Fallen Star / Storms From The Skies Of Grief / In The Forest Of The Dreaming Dead.
IN THE FOREST OF THE DREAMING DEAD, No Fashion NFR004 (1994). At Dawn / Whispering Shadows / Blackness Of The Fallen Stars / Fire Storm / Storms From The Skies Of Grief / Through The Gates / Wind Of A Dismal Past / Silence Ends / Moonlight Twilight / In The Forest Of The Dreaming Dead / Cold Northern Breeze.
ANCIENT GOD OF EVIL, No Fashion NFR009 (1995). Life Demise / Eye Of The Greyhound / Oceans Of Time / Dead Calm / Mirielle / The Depths Of A Black Sea / Ruins / Dying Emotions Domain / Die Alone.

UNBOUND

VAASA, FINLAND — *Kai Jaakkola (vocals), Petri Seikkula (guitar), Fred Andersson (guitar), Tommi Konu (bass), Robert Sundelin (drums).*

Vaasa Death Metal band. The group has its roots in the early 90's act UNBOUND but by 1995 the title of TWILIGHT had been put into effect, this band starting life with a roster of vocalist Kai Jaakkola, guitarist Petri Seikkula, bassist Tommi Konu and Toni Erkkilä on the drums. In this incarnation TWILIGHT issued a brace of demos 'Twilight' and 'The Melancholy Of The Northern Landscapes' before the band was put on hold due to the intrusion of Finland's national service policy. Activity was sporadic until 1998 when the band regrouped with the addition of BEYOND DREAMS guitarist Fred Andersson and drummer Robert Sundelin of SATARIEL and an ex-member of NECROMICON. Konu, as 'Hellkuntz', participated in recording of the Swedish band HELLMASKER's 'Probably The Best Band In The World' demo. The band recorded the 'Flames Of Madness' demo in 1999 upon completion of which Andersson's place was taken by NECROMICON's Nick Sundqvist, after a decision was taken to revert back to the formative title of UNBOUND due to the increasing media presence of the Italian Power Metal band TWILIGHT. Bringing in Mikael Sandorf on the drums the band laid down a fresh demo 'Elaborate The Torture' in November 2000 before switching the group name again—this time to DEATHBOUND as Blastmor of THYRANE became next in line to occupy the drum stool but by 2002 Mika Q had taken the role.

DEATHBOUND signed to the Woodcut label for a debut May 2003 album release 'To Cure The Insane—With Insanity'.

Flames Of Madness, Unbound (2000) (Reissue of TWILIGHT demo). Feel The Repulsion / Phantomside / Drown In The Waves / Flames Of Madness.

UNCANNY

AVESTA, SWEDEN — *Jens Törnroos (vocals), Mats Forsell (guitar), Fredrik Norrman (guitar), Christoffer Harborg (bass),*

Kenneth Englund (drums).

Avesta based Death Metal band, founded in 1990. UNCANNY guitarists Mats Forsell and Fredrik Norrman were both former members of FULMINATION. Norrman subsequently joined KATATONIA and OCTOBER TIDE. Drummer Kenneth Englund cites credits with a profusion of acts such as MOONDARK, INTERMENT, PYOSISFIED, DELLAMORTE and CENTINEX.

UNCANNY bowed in with the demo 'Transportation To The Uncanny' in 1991. That June the band shared a split demo with ASOCIAL, ENTRAILS and UNCURBED entitled 'Avesta Mangel'. They followed up with the 'Nyktalgia' session of 1992. The Colombian based Warmaster Records then issued a split album shared with Belgian act ANCIENT RITES. Signing to the Greek Unisound label the band cut the 1994 album 'Splenium For Nyktophobia', this outing being engineered by DAN SWANÖ.

Transportation To The Uncanny, Uncanny (1991) (Demo). Intro / Creeping Persecution Behind The Gates / Transportation To The Uncanny / The Porno Flute / Why My Intestines? / Outro.

Avesta Mangel, Uncanny (1991) (Split demo with ASOCIAL, ENTRAILS and UNCURBED).

Nyktalgia, Uncanny (1992) (Demo). Profligacy Of Power / The Cryptic Trail / Tales From The Tomb / Ceased From Reality / Nyktalgia.

UNCANNY / ANCIENT RITES, Warmaster WAR001 (1993) (Split album with ANCIENT RITES). Ceased From Reality / Determination To Win / Profligacy Of Power / Soul Incest / Why My Intestines? / Brain Access.

SPLENIUM FOR NYKTOPHOBIA, Unisound USR 008 (1994). Elohim / Faces From The Tomb / Brain Access / Timeless / Screaming In Phobia / Enkelbiljetten / Indication Vitalis / Soul Incest / Strangskitten / Towards The Endless Throne / Lepra / The Final Conflict (The Pornoflute Part Two) / Splenium For Nyktophobia.

UNCURBED

SWEDEN — Punk infused Grindcore outfit UNCURBED was established during 1990 by guitarist Conny Enström, bassist Micke Gunnarsson and Johan Jansson. Local gigs that year led to the inclusion of four tracks, including a NAPALM DEATH cover version, recorded at Studio Fragg in June 1991, for inclusion on the split album 'Avesta Mangel' shared with ASOCIAL, ENTRAILS and UNCANNY. Expansion of the ranks in 1992 introduced two dual lead vocalists, Henrik Lindberg and Jens Törnroos, plus second guitarist Nico Knudsen, and this formation cut an eleven track demo at Unisound Studios, working with EDGE OF SANITY's DAN SWANÖ as producer.

Lost & Found Records in Germany took the band on in 1993 and, after recording a further five tracks, the demos were issued as the 'The Strike Of Mankind' album. Touring in Europe witnessed collaborative dates with DISFEAR, also generating a split 7" single between the two acts. Maintaining the Unisound / Swanö formula, UNCURBED delivered a second album, 'Mental Disorder' in 1994. However, Swanö opted out in October, being substituted by TB from ASOCIAL. The group switched labels to the Finn imprint for third album, 1995's 'A Nightmare In Daylight', again crafted at Unisound. Notable Swedish gigs that year saw supports to CHAOS UK and ENGLISH DOGS.

UNCURBED was back in the studio, this time utilising HYPOCRISY's Peter Tägtgren and his Abyss Studios, to deliver the 'Punk & Anger' album, this sixteen song set featuring a rendition of ASOCIAL's 'Frige Alla Fångar'. German concern Yellow Dog Records also issued four tracks as a split EP in union with S.G.R., limited to 1000 copies. Next record 'Peace. Love. Punk. Life... And Other Stories' was laid down at Abyss Studios in April 1997 and intended for issue through Finn Records. Unfortunately the label was experiencing financial difficulties and so US label Sound Pollution picked the album up instead.

The work ethic was maintained as UNCURBED ensconced themselves into Soundlab Studios during January 1999 to produce the 'Keeps The Banner High' album. Founder Micke Gunnarsson exited, being replaced by Kenneth Wiklund of ASOCIAL and HATRED. This version of the band put down eight tracks for a 10" EP, 'Ackord För Frihet', for Retribute Records. Swedish concerts saw Jimmy Lind from CROSSING CHAOS deputising for an unavailable TB. Once the German 'Punx On Parole 2000' tour had been completed, Lind stepped into the band on a full-time basis, as bass player taking Wiklund's position. Four new songs were contributed to compilation albums, 'Against Your System' on Versus Records and 'Really Fast Vol. 11', promoted by live work sharing stages with DRILLER KILLER, DISKONTO, F.D.M., DELLAMORTE and CROSSING CHAOS.

Tommy Tägtgren took on the production mantle for 'Punks On Parole' in February 2001. Tribulation then ensued as the group nearly collapsed due to internal friction. Both singers would decamp, but TB eventually returned to the fold and Steffe of DISKONTO made up the numbers in time for a valuable hometown support to the DEAD KENNEDYS. More new material was then hammered out for inclusion on the 'Rise And Shine' EP, through German label Devil's Shitburner, and a split EP with AUTORITÄR via US label Rescued From Life. UNCURBED then once again pulled in Kenneth Wiklund to handle bass duties.

A significant loss came in 2003 when founder Conny Enström bowed out. However, another original member, Micke Gunnarson, duly took his place.

2004 ushered in another UNCURBED album, 'Welcome To Anarcho City' produced by Tommy Tägtgren at Abyss Studios in May. Three further songs were donated to a split EP with RAJOITUS. In a first for the band, North American dates were undertaken throughout October and November. Power It Up Records released a split 7" single with MY COLD EMBRACE in 2005.

UNCURBED's Johan Jansson also has a wealth of associations across the Metal scene with PYOSISFIED, HATRED, SIDEBURNERS, ASOCIAL, FLESHREVELS, INTERMENT, DELLAMORTE, FROSTHEIM, FULMINATION and CENTINEX. With the collapse of CENTINEX in March 2006 Johan Jansson founded DEMONICAL in union with former CENTINEX colleagues bass player Martin Schulman and drummer Ronnie Bergerståhl, also known for his work with AMARAN and JULIE LAUGHS NO MORE. Johan Jansson joined REGURGITATE in September.

Avesta Mangel, Uncurbed (1991) (Split demo with ASOCIAL, ENTRAILS and UNCANNY).

The Strike Of Mankind, Uncurbed (1992) (Demo).

THE STRIKE OF MANKIND, Lost And Found LF061CD (1993). Death, Violence And Pain / No Life Without Money / They Lie About Your Rights / Hate Your System / Failure Of God / Dictature-Murders / Meanless Preach / Innocent Child / Slave System / Missiles / The End / The Strike Of Mankind / Acting Like Fools / Face The Fact / All This Sickness / Sex Therapy.

Uncurbed / Disfear, Lost And Found LF065 (1993) (Split 7" vinyl single with DISFEAR). The Strike Of Mankind.

Mental Disorder, Lost And Found LF094CD (1994). Riots In Blood / Mental Disorder / No Respect / Victims / Build Up A Front / No More To Say / Warhead / Discrimination Of Humanity.

A NIGHTMARE IN DAYLIGHT, Finn Records 010 (1995). Set It Off / Blochhead / War Incident / Mercanaries Of War / Raise Hate / I Don't Belong / Sick Pleasure / Free Yourself / Dishing Out / Death By A Lie / Society Downfall / World In Chaos / Lost In Sorrow / We Will Never Be.

PUNK AND ANGER, Finn 015 (1996). Punk And Anger / Born Against Your Will / Mind Terror / Eat Shit / Anguish... Life / Reject Yourself / Let The Bastards Pay / A Nightmare In Daylight / Wounded And No Escape / Wasted / Drink It Up / Frige Alla Fangar / Watch Your Back / Nothing To Declare / Strike Of Mankind / Go To Hell—I Hate You.

Uncurbed / Society Gang Rape, Yellow Dog YD 005 (1996) (Split EP with SOCIETY GANG RAPE). My War / Abused And Raped / The Rope Song / Pissaa Ja Paskaa.

PEACELOVEPUNKLIFE... ANDOTHERSTORIES, Sound Pollution POLLUTE 045 (1998). Tomorrow Rebels / System Stinx / Welfare Or Hellfare? / Anarchy And Peace (Brothers And Sisters) / If I Need... I Make!! / Taste Of Tomorrow / Passed Away / Breakout / Realise / Living In A Squat (So What!!?) / Forget The Future—Live In The Past / Never Change / Celebration To The Losers / Liberation Hippies / Government Education / Party Punx.

UNCURBED KEEPS THE BANNER HIGH, Sound Pollution POLLUTE 053 (2000). Why Am I To Be? / Ge Igen Med Dubbel Ranta / Bar-Star / Horrified Future / Freedom Road / Ockupera Mera / Utsliten Och Slangd / Violent Criminal / Luffarens Klagan / Uproar / Riding On The Highlife / Valium Holiday / High Of Hope … / … But High In The Gutter / Skot Du Ditt … Sa Skoter Jag Mitt / Liberation Day / Utsugarnas Afton / Rebell Punx / Samhallets Avskum / Moonshine Harmony.

PUNKS ON PAROLE, Sound Pollution POLLUTE 065 (2002). Punks On Parole / Blow The System / Freedom Party / Kill The Government / Reality Escape / Man Overboard / Choked In Shit / Buy Me Out / Underground Heroes / Share My Stones / Lawless And Poor / Kick 'Em Down / Human Rebel / A Psychedelic Party / Moments Of Anarchy / Punk Never Dies.

Ackord För Frihet / Chords For Freedom, Sound Pollution POLLUTE 072 (2003). Riv Demokratin / The Uncurbed Family / Framtids Visioner / Ingren Forandring / Det Sista Jag Gor / Led Mig Hem / Bryt Mot Alla Lagar / Container Punk.

Uncurbed / Autoritär, Rescued From Life #09 (2004) (Split EP with AUTORITÄR). Obsolete Country Of Sweden / Rebels Of Hate.

Uncurbed / My Cold Embrace, Power It Up P.I.U.# 27 (2005) (Split 7" vinyl single with MY COLD EMBRACE). A Psychedelic Party / Moments Of Anarchy.

WELCOME TO ANARCHO CITY, Sound Pollution POLLUTE 093 (2006). Welcome To Anarcho City / Divorced From Life / The Whore Needs More / Dead Roses / A Gift To Life / Stories From An Outlaw / Capitalist Sucker / Time To Resign / Gutter Romance / Ten Points Road / Dead Without You / Trousers And Junk / Suburban Heroes / Just Another Day / Don't Push Me To Far / Drink My Pain / Nervous Breakdown / The Criminal Race.

UNDER MOONLIGHT SADNESS

MEXICO — *Iván G. Velazquez (vocals), Carlos Bastida (guitar), Jesús Morales (guitar), Marcos Barba (keyboards), Iván Vilchis (drums).*

Mexican Doom embroiled Death Metal band led by former CENOTAPH and PROHIBITORY singer Iván G. 'The Bloodhunter' Velazquez. UNDER MOONLIGHT SADNESS was the product of a 1995 union of former ASGARD and BELLPHEGOR personnel. The opening demo tape 'Echoes Of Ancient Music' proved a success with the band managing to sell over 2000 copies. During 1996 the band reaped the honours of opening act to MERCYFUL FATE's Mexico City gig.

In 1998 the band cut their debut record 'After The Cosmic Gate' for the Oz Records label. The album proved to be an eclectic mix of styles and influences, seeing former SHAMASH bassist Pablo Tames performing cello and even the inclusion of an ancient Aztec instrument the teponaztli. Carlos Bastida was added as second guitarist after the album sessions. Promoting 'After The Cosmic Gate' UNDER MOONLIGHT SADNESS toured Mexico in 1999 heading up the 'Tourmemtor' billing featuring SHAMASH, DISGORGE, BURIED DREAMS and THE ZEPHYR.

Velazquez also fronts two Death Metal acts FOETICIDE and DEW OF NOTHING.

The 2000 album 'Geneticsis' saw guest vocals contributed by CALVARIA's Mario A. Montaño. The band switched title to MOONLORD shortly after.

AFTER THE COSMIC GATE, Oz (1998). In The Gloomy Hemisphere / Arrival Over Crystal Ground / Dying Moon / Behind This Tears / Ancient Rhymes / Reflections In A Dark Mirror / Millenium Of Red Light / Minds Beyond Fear / … / Lost In Silence / Die andere Welt / Slavery Parameters / From Nadir To Zenith / Eclipse Sons / Cosmos Concept Farther Intellect / Meztli / Anthems Of Misanthropy.

GENETICSIS, X Rated (2001). Architects Of Quanta / Unnatural / One With The Infinite / Bloodhunter / Infinite … / Echoes (Intro) / Ethereal Pains / Lord Of Exile Lands / Winter Mourning / Agony Remembrances / A Dream, A Tear ….

UNDER THREAT

BOGOTÁ, COLOMBIA — *John Perez (vocals), Nick Bermudez (guitar), David Bermudez (bass), Alejandro Rojas (drums).*

Death-Thrashers UNDER THREAT were created in Bogotá during 1997 by vocalist John Perez, guitar player Nicolas Bermudez and bassist David Bermudez under a formative title of SKULPTOR. Several membership changes later, and with the inauguration of drummer Alejandro Rojas, SKULPTOR became UNDER THREAT in 1999. Toward the close of that year Transilvania Music issued the album 'Hipostasis'. These sessions, which featured a cover version of SARCOFAGO's 'Piercings', marked a switch from Spanish lyrics to English. In December 2001 the band entered Studio One in Racine, Wisconsin to record 'Behind Mankind's Disguise'. A bout of US summer touring saw the band partnering up with MONSTROSITY, DARK FAITH and BLOOD STAINED DUSK. UNDER THREAT also scored an appearance at the Milwaukee Metalfest. The 'Behind Mankind's Disguise' album was picked up by Conquest Music, the custom imprint of MONSTROSITY's Lee Harrison, for issue in March 2003. Once again the band played at the Milwaukee Metalfest that year.

During summer 2004 the band, having lost the services of second guitarist Eric Leider, entered Studio One again to lay down tracks for next outing 'Deathmosphere'. That October UNDER THREAT performed at their hometown's annual festival 'Rock Al Parque' in Simon Bolivar Park. Barbarian Records from Madison picked up the record for the USA whilst Hateworks Records from Manizales, Colombia distributed across South America and Europe. Jake Sommer was added as second guitarist.

UNDER THREAT musicians guitarist Nick Bermudez and bass player David Bermudez made news in March 2007 when they joined BLAZE, the band of former IRON MAIDEN singer Blaze Bayley.

HIPOSTASIS, Transilvania Music (1999). Poisoned Soul / Learned Helplessness / The Lower Man / Lymbic Zone / Consummatum Est / Unchainment / Syndrome Of Alienation / Hipostasis / Tormenta Interna / Piercings.

BEHIND MANKIND'S DISGUISE, Conquest Music (2003). Blame Game Trap / Face Of Emptiness / Under Threat / Serpent's Lick / Ghost And The Machine / Desperate Human's Path / Behind Mankind's Disguise / The End Of Grace / Infestation / Gates Of Deception / The Warning / Mirrors Of Dejection.

Under Threat, Under Threat (2004) (Demo). Prisoners Of Their Own Betrayal / Read The Codes / Black Innertia Disintegration / Parallel Hells.

DEATHMOSPHERE, Barbarian (2006). Deathmosphere / Kingdom Of Eternal Crisis / Parallel Hells / Echo Shaped Life / Black Inertia Disintegration / Embraced By Disaster / Prisoners Of Their Own Betrayal / Read The Codes / Restrained Hate Coexistance / Third World Blood.

UNDERCROFT

CHILE — *Alvaro Lillo (vocals / bass), Claudio Illanes (guitar), Pablo Cortez (drums).*

UNDERCROFT, created in 1991, debuted with a May 1993 demo 'To The Final Battle'. A second session, 'Demons Awake, Revenge Is Near', followed in November of that year and the debut album 'Twisted Souls' in 1995. Released on the Toxic label 'Twisted Souls' featured an UNDERCROFT line up of Tito Melin on vocals, guitarists Claudio Illanes and Alejandro Landeros, bassist Diego Marin and drummer Pablo Cortez.

The band's 'Re-Demolition' album of 1998 collected together prior demo recordings and added a cover version of NAPALM DEATH's 'Unfit Earth'. UNDERCROFT added guitarist Andre Arancibia but his tenure was short. The band became a quartet comprising vocalist Tito Melín, guitarist Claudio Illanes, bass player Marco Medina with Pablo Cortez on drums. However, former RADICAL man Rodrigo Onetto subsequently took on the bass role.

For August 2000's 'Danza Macabra' album UNDERCROFT sported a line up roster of former EXECRATOR vocalist / bassist Alvaro Lillo, guitarist Claudio Illanes and drummer Pablo Cortez. The band travelled to Sweden in 2001 to work with producer Daniel Bergstrand and signed to the Pavement label for the album 'Evilution'. Meantime, Onetto was enlisted into the ranks of NECROSIS to record the December 2001 album 'Enslaved To The Machine'.

Fully relocated in Hamburg, Germany UNDERCROFT issued the live album 'BastardLiveHamburg' through the Chilean label Negative Entertainment. This record comprised the band's Hamburg December 2003 'Fuck Christmas' show along with three new studio tracks and a video clip for the song 'Evilution'.

TWISTED SOULS, Toxic (1995). I Demand Revenge / Wake Up From Your Dreams / Rumanian Impaler / Open Your Eyes To The Pain / Empire Of Orgies / They Kill For Me / Lords Of Terror / Demons Awake / Beheading False Prophets / Sodom And Gomorrah.
BONEBREAKER, (1997). To The Final Battle / Bone Breaker / Evil Being / I Condemn / Espectral Town / Insane Outcry / Mercy / Road To Desolatation / Sabatical Potion / Law Of Sacrifice / Evotic Song.
RE-DEMOLITION, (1998).
DANZA MACABRE, (2000). Perverse Praise / Dark Water's Captive / Through The Night's Veil / Lapidation / Under The Broken Sign / Blackening The Sun / I'm Prepared To Die / Danza Macabra / Dementia / Maniakiller / Oppressor / Behind The Cassock / In Join With The Devil.
EVILUSION, Pavement (2002). Evilusion / Fake Messiah / Carros De Fuego / Celebration Of Sin / The Cartomancer / The Psychopath / Whispers From Other Sky / Sub Race / Bleed To Death / Bridges To Melissa / Temples Of Carrion.

UNGODLY

SALVADOR, BA, BRAZIL — *Serafin Vila (vocals), Luciano Campos (guitar), Daniel Oliveira (guitar), Fernando Cliff (bass), Alex Rocha (drums).*

Salvador, Bahia Death Metal act UNGODLY date back to 2001, at first being fronted by singer Hiram Fernades. The first stable line-up would settle on CARNIFIELD singer Serafin Vila, guitarist Daniel Oliveira, INSAINTIFICATION bassist Fernando 'Cliff' Costa and drummer Alex. Earlier, INOCULATION guitarist Marcos had figured in the roll call but left for ETERNAL SACRIFICE.

The band added second guitarist Luciano Campos, another INSAINTIFICATION man, in February of 2004. UNGODLY released the 'Hate Celebration' EP in April, working in the studio with producer Thiago Nogueira, ex-drummer of HEADHUNTER D.C. Gigs that Spring saw supports to KRISIUN, HEADHUNTER D.C. and German Thrash veterans DESTRUCTION. In August drummer Alex Rocha exited and Thiago Nogueira took over on a temporary basis.

UNGODLY's self-titled debut album was released in 2006 via Dynamo Records. UNGODLY supported SLAYER in São Paulo and Rio de Janeiro in September.

Hate Celebration EP, Independent (2004). Layed In Ashes / Pestilence Of The Limbo / Hate Celebration.

UNHOLY GHOST

FL, USA — *Paul Ouellette (vocals / bass), Jerry Mortellaro (guitar), Kelly McLauchlin (guitar), David Breazeal (drums).*

UNHOLY GHOST, founded by PESSIMIST mentor and guitarist Kelly McLauchlin during 2003, features the former DIABOLIC founding members vocalist / bassist Paul Ouellette, guitarist Jerry Mortellaro and drummer Aantar Lee Coates. The latter also cites credits with EXMORTIS, NECROSIS and HORROR OF HORRORS. The group signed to the Olympic label for a Juan Gonzalez produced debut album 'Torrential Reign', recorded at the Diet Of Worms studios in Seffner, Florida.

UNHOLY GHOST got out onto the live circuit with an appearance at the 'Sun n' Steel' festival in early March of 2004 at the Pinellas Expo Center in Tampa, Florida. Aantar Lee Coates lost his position following the band's appearance at the July 'Gathering of the Bestial Legion' festival in California. The ex-member duly forged BLASTMASTERS, cutting a Juan Gonzalez produced demo in August.

UNHOLY GHOST became the subject on news in July when Jerry Mortellaro reported his prized Jackson Warrior guitar as being stolen. Within a few days the instrument had been tracked down and Mortellaro's former EULOGY band mate Mike Bearden, branded a "scumbag", had been jailed for the theft.

In October of 2004 UNHOLY GHOST inducted David Breazeal onto the drums, a man citing prior credits with CAULDRON, PESSIMIST and TROKAR. The band partnered with COUNCIL OF THE FALLEN and THE CLASSIC STRUGGLE for the 'Reigning Florida' tour commencing 31st December at New Smyrna Beach. Kelly McLauchlin exited in February 2005 in order to prioritise PESSIMIST. Within days, UNHOLY GHOST announced the addition of former DEICIDE guitarist Eric Hoffman. However, Hoffman himself refuted these claims some weeks later. Drummer David Breazeal announced in April that he had parted ways with UNHOLY GHOST due to "musical differences." Shortly afterward, UNHOLY GHOST drafted the DIABOLIC, BRUTALITY and CRADLE OF FILTH credited Brian Hipp on guitar and scene veteran Gabriel Lewandowski, of NAPHOBIA, HELLWITCH, ACHERON and EQUINOX, on drums.

Aantar Lee Coates joined the resurrected EXMORTIS in mid 2005.

TORRENTIAL REIGN, Olympic (2004). The Calling Of Sin / Soul Disment / Eyes Of Lost / Decimated / Cross Contamination / Denouncication / Entrenched In Warfare / Torn Apart / Under Existence / Torrential Reign / The Apparition.

UNHOLY GRAVE

JAPAN — *Takaho (vocals), Kajisa (guitar), Tadashi (guitar), Ume (bass), Debuzo (drums).*

Renowned Japanese Grindcore act UNHOLY GRAVE have issued a string of shared 7" singles over the years in collusion with such artists as WARSORE, ARSEDESTROYER, CHICKENSHIT, MAD THRASHER, REFORM CONTROL, VIOLENT HEADACHE and ENTRAILS MASSACRE.

In 2001 UNHOLY GRAVE shared a limited edition split 7" single with the industrious Black Thrashers SABBAT, included would be cover versions of TERRORIZER's 'Strategic Warhead' and NAPALM DEATH's 'Cause & Effect'.

Quite incredibly the band shared a track on the July 2005 'Unlawful Grindcore Assembly' 7" split single issued by Nuclear Barbecue Party Records as a collaborative effort with EMBALMING THEATRE, PESTILENT DECAY, GATE, WATCH ME BURN, BLOODRED BACTERIA, MIERDA PARA TODOS, CARA DE MIL PUTASOS, FETUS EATERS, DEADFOOD, THE KILL, TU CARNE, WASTEOID, PINATA LAZER, SAYYADINA, GORED FACE, GODSTOMPER, KERUM, NUKEM, UNHOLY SEMEN, 2 MINUTADREKA and COPROPHAGIGS.

The band engaged in the 'International Grind Assault' East Coast US tour alongside MAGRUDERGRIND, YACOPSAE, and Germany's SANITY'S DAWN in May 2006.

Split, Riotous Assembly RIOT 017 (0) (7" split single with DEPRESSOR).
Split, MCR Company MCR094 (0) (7" split single with CHICKENSHIT).
CRUCIFIED, Eclipse (1995). Maniacal Damage / Human Mummification / Mental Disease / Atrocity- War Of Aggression / Worthless Prize / Korean Residents In Japan / Be Born Poor / Forced Unfair Future / Blind- Death From Overwork / Euthanasia / The Unknown Ghost- Fugitives / Discrimination / Protestant? Catholic? / Shameless Bighead / Mass Imbeciles- Racism / Greedy Pig.
Agonies EP, MCR Company MCR099 (1996) (7" split single with AGATHOCLES). Slaughtered Civilians / My Nightmare / Japan's Warcrime / Confession / Ei Skit Sota / Kim After Kim.
Xeroxed Person, Headfucker HF 04 (1998) (7" split single with CAPTAIN 3 LEG). Xeroxed Person / Zillion Of Bodies / Life After Death / Land For Sacrifice / Mutilated Souls.
Racism, Def American (2000) (7" split single with CAPITALIST CASUALTIES).

Split, The Sky Is Red 001 (2001) (Split single with SABBAT. Limited edition 1000 copies). Nobody Perfect / I Hope It'll Work / Strategic Warhead / Power Hungry / Cause & Effect.

UNHOLY TRINITY

STATEN ISLAND, NY, USA — *Vic Casciotta (vocals / guitar), Mike Koltosky (bass), Alex Farag (drums).*

UNHOLY TRINITY was created by erstwhile THALLIUM members Alex Farag and Vic Casciotta. Initially the duo forged Death Metal band SOLDIERS OF ELIMINATION, alongside Anthony Garbarino and Jack Ferranti, but then left this project. Farag would switch from guitar to drums as they founded UNHOLY TRINITY in February 2004. Andrew Mahler was installed on bass but swiftly vacated his post. The next set of recruits would be lead guitarist Rob Schneck and bassist Andrew Schlissel, these two also only briefly maintaining their positions. UNHOLY TRINITY finally solidified with a line up comprising Vic "Gomorrah" Casciotta on vocals and guitar, Alex "Sodom" Farag on drums and Mike "Hezekiah" Koltosky on bass. UNHOLY TRINITY debuted with the demo 'Pseudomonas Orifice'.

Pseudomonas Orifice, Unholy Trinity (2005). Pseudomonas Orifice / Fall Of Thor / It Came From Sodomy / Incarnating The Beast / Ode To The Northern Winds / Fetal Devourment / Var Reiser Til Valhalla.

UNKNOWN

AREQUIPA, PERU — *Jorge Esteban LLosa (vocals), Miguel Ballón M. (vocals / guitar), Diego Del Carpio C. (guitar), Juan Arce M. (bass), Diego Zimermann (drums).*

UNKNOWN would originally be fronted by singer Rafael Fernandez. His departure saw guitarist Miguel Ballon taking over the lead vocal role. Signing to Prescott Records the band projected the album 'Identity Unknown' for September 2005. Guitarist Diego Del Carpio would be replaced by Clever. Further changes saw the addition of second singer Ronny and bassist Jose Luis Mercado replaced by Jesus Aleman. UNKNOWN subsequently re-enlisted Rafael Fernandez and drafted Santiago Mazeira on bass. Shortly afterward, Gabriel Alvarez R. was to take the bass role. The group format changed yet again when Jorge Esteban Llosa was enrolled as new singer, Diego Del Carpio C. on guitar, Juan Arce M. on bass and Diego Zimermann on the drums.

My Fallen Angel, Unknown (2004). Scream / My Fallen Angel / Tormento / Flechas / Eternal Flames.

IDENTITY UNKNOWN, Prescott (2005). My Fallen Angel / Fire Release / Tormentor / One Smile Is Enough / Twister Mind / Identity Unknown / Under Pressure / Fist Of Fate / Vampire Summoning / You Give Me The Strength / Giving Up, Not For Sire.

UNLEASHED

KUNGSANGEN, SWEDEN — *Johnny Hedlund (vocals / bass), Fredrik Folkare (guitar), Thomas Olsson (guitar), Anders Schultz (drums).*

A stoic Kungsangen based Death Metal band that not only has defied genre stereotypes by maintaining a relatively solid line-up but stuck true to their convictions with each successive album release. UNLEASHED, "Lords of the E chords", enhance their material with ancestral themes and Viking mythology. Featuring ex-NIHILIST guitarist Johnny Hedlund, UNLEASHED recorded demos in 1990 titled 'The Utter Dark' in March and September's '... Revenge' that soon sold out, prompting a deal with Germany's Century Media Records. The group roster saw Hedlund ranked alongside erstwhile DISMEMBER frontman Robert Sennebäck, guitarist Fredrik Lindgren with Anders Schultz on drums. However, Sennebäck rejoined DISMEMBER shortly afterward, leaving Hedlund to take over microphone duties.

Two now rare 7" singles, October 1990's '... Revenge' through CBR Records plus the 'And The Laughter Has Died' EP of 1991, were issued before the group debuted proper with the 'Where No Life Dwells' album in May 1991. Produced by DESPAIR and GRIP INC. guitarist Waldemar Sorychta, the album had been recorded at the Woodhouse Studios in Dortmund, Germany that April. UNLEASHED toured Europe and America during the year as support to MORBID ANGEL.

Returning in May 1992 with 'Shadows In The Deep', again using Waldemar Sorychta as producer and featuring a cover of VENOM's 'Countess Bathory', UNLEASHED toured hard once more to promote the album, including a European headline tour with support acts TIAMAT and SAMAEL before American shows with CANNIBAL CORPSE. Unbeknownst to the band, the group's music, and in particular the album track 'Onward Into Countless Battles', had an influence on the most unexpected of major acts—NIRVANA. Many years later drummer Dave Grohl admitted NIRVANA had re-worked the song to their own ends but felt it too close to the UNLEASHED original to pass off.

The group's third album, October 1993's 'Across The Open Sea', found the band lyrically delving deep into Scandinavian history although oddly it is also notable for including a cover of JUDAS PRIEST's 'Breaking The Law'. UNLEASHED cut a live album during 1993, although the recordings were initially released as a bootleg prior to the band responding by issuing the 'Live in Vienna' album the following year. In addition to his work in UNLEASHED guitarist Fredrik Lindgren was also an member of Punk outfit LOUD PIPES billing himself 'Freddy Eugene'. Lindgren, his last work with UNLEASHED being the February 1995 'Victory' album, created Stoner Metal act TERRA FIRMA in 1999 with COUNT RAVEN vocalist Christian Linderson for an eponymous album. A double live collection, 'Eastern Blood–Hail To Poland', was delivered in November 1996. Lindgren's place had been taken by Fredrik Folkare for June 1997's 'Warrior' opus.

In October of 2002 UNLEASHED, and in particular Johnny Hedlund, had to contend with rumours that the band pursued extreme right wing 'Nazi' politics. Apparently Dave Grohl of FOO FIGHTERS fame had considered Hedlund for inclusion on his extreme Metal PROBOT project until he was advised of the singer's supposed fascist leanings. Hedlund was quick to deny the claims branding them as false and stating "UNLEASHED praises nature, beast and man. Man . . . . regardless of background, place of birth or color of the skin".

UNLEASHED marked a return in August 2002 with the 'Hell's Unleashed' album. They would follow up in July of 2004 with 'Sworn Allegiance', recorded and mixed by Fredrik Folkare at Chrome Studios and mastered by Peter In de Betou of Tailor Maid Productions. The band promoted this release by teaming up with IN BATTLE and YATTERING for a European tour commencing in late November. Anders Schultz featured as backing vocalist on THE PROJECT HATE's 2005 album "Armageddon March Eternal (Symphonies Of Slit Wrists)'. UNLEASHED filmed their 1st July performances at the 'With Full Force' festival in Leipzig and August 'Up From The Ground' festival in Gemünden, Germany for DVD release. During November Fredrik Folkare took time out to engineer album sessions for NECROPHOBIC.

The band announced a touring partnership as part of the December 2005 'X-Mass' festivals in Europe ranked alongside recently resurrected UK Thrashers ONSLAUGHT, EXODUS, KATAKLYSM, OCCULT, BEHEMOTH, and PRIMORDIAL.

To perform at the 'Metalmania' festival in Katowice, Poland in March 2006 the group drafted INCARDINE drummer Jonas Tyskhagen as a temporary replacement for Anders Schultz, who had suffered a lung-collapse. UNLEASHED announced in July they has signed with the German SPV Steamhammer label for new studio album 'Midvinterblot'.

Tyskhagen again sessioned for an appearance at the

'Hellflame' festival on September 2nd in Osnabrück, Germany. European show announced for November, dubbed the "Masters Of Death", had the band lined up with a supremely heavyweight Scandinavian cast of DISMEMBER, ENTOMBED and GRAVE.

UNLEASHED was back out on the European touring circuit in early May 2007, heading up the 'Midvinterblot European Tour Part II' dates backed by KATAKLYSM and BELPHEGOR then ARKHON INFAUSTUS.

The Utter Dark, Unleashed (1990) (Demo). The Dark One / Ancient Dead / Violent Ecstacy.
Revenge, Unleashed (1990) (Demo). The Utter Dark Revenge / Unleashed / Where No Life Dwells.
Revenge EP, CBR CBR-S 124 (1990). The Utterdark Revenge / Unleashed / Where No Life Dwells.
Century Media Promo Tape, Century Media (1990) (Promotional cassette). The Dark One / If They Had Eyes / Dead Forever / Unleashed / Where Life Ends.
And The Laughter Has Died . . . EP, Century Media CM7 020 (1991) (Limited edition. 2000 copies). The Dark One / Where Life Ends.
WHERE NO LIFE DWELLS, Century Media 84 9718 (1991). Where No Life Dwells / Dead Forever / Before The Creation Of Time / For They Shall Be Slain / If They Had Eyes / The Dark One / Into Glory Ride / . . . And The Laughter Has Died / Unleashed / Violent Ecstacy / Where Life Ends.
SHADOWS IN THE DEEP, Century Media 84-9732-2 (1992). The Final Silence / The Immortals / A Life Beyond / Shadows In The Deep / Countess Bathory / Never Ending Hate / Onward Into Countless Battles / Crush The Skull / Bloodbath / Land Of Ice.
LIVE IN VIENNA '93, Century Media 77056-2 (1993). The Final Silence / Bloodbath / Before The Creation Of Time / Shadows In The Deep / Never Ending Hate / If They Had Eyes / Open Wide / Onward Into Countless Battles / Where No Life Dwells / Dead Forever / Countess Bathory / The Immortals / Into Glory Ride / Breaking The Law.
ACROSS THE OPEN SEA, Century Media 77055-2 (1993). To Asgaard We Fly / Open Wide / I Am God / The One Insane / Across The Open Sea / In The Northern Lands / Forever Goodbye (2045) / Execute Them All / Captured / Breaking The Law / The General.
VICTORY, Century Media 77090-2 (1995). Victims Of War / Legal Rapes / Hail The New Age / Defender / In The Name Of God / Precious Land / Berserk / Scream Forth Aggression / Against The Wind / Revenge.
EASTERN BLOOD—HAIL TO POLAND, Unleashed 77118-2 (1996). Execute Them All / The Immortals / Revenge / The Defender / In The Name Of God / Against The World / Victims Of War / Shadows In The Deep / Before The Creation Of Time / Berserk / Into Glory Ride / Dead Forever / If They Had Eyes / For They Shall Be Slain / Unleashed / The Immortals / The Dark One / Into Glory Ride / Shadows In The Deep / Violent Exstasy / Before The Creation Of Time.
WARRIOR, Century Media 77124-2 (1997). Warmachine / In Hellfire / Mediawhore / Down Under Ground / My Life For You / Death Metal Victory / Hero Of The Land / Löngt Nid / Born Deranged / I Have Returned / Ragnarök / Your Pain My Gain / The End.
HELL'S UNLEASHED, Century Media 77424-2 (2002). Don't Want To Be Born / Hell's Unleashed / Demoneater / Fly Raven Fly / Mrs. Minister / Joy In The Sun / Demons Rejoice / We'll Come For You / Triggerman / Dissection Leftovers / Peace, Piece By Piece / Burnt Alive / Your Head Is Mine / Made In Hell.
SWORN ALLEGIANCE, Century Media 77524-2 (2004). Winterland / Destruction (Of The Race Of Men) / Only The Dead / The Longships Are Coming / Helljoy / Insane For Blood / I Bring You Death / Attack! / CEO / One Night In Nazareth / Praised Be The Lord / Metalheads / To Miklagård / Long Live The Beast.
MIDVINTERBLOT, Steamhammer SPV 97952 (2006). Blood Of Lies / This Is Our World Now / We Must Join With Him / Midvinterblot / In Victory Or Defeat / Triumph Of Genocide / The Avenger / Salvation For Mankind / Psycho Killer / The Witch / I Have Sworn Allegiance / Age Of The Warrior / New Dawn Rising / Loyalty And Price / Valhalla Awaits.

UNREAL OVERFLOWS

SPAIN — *Zoilo Santiago (vocals / bass), Francisco J. Pérez (guitar), Pedro Cochón (guitar), Jorge Rosales (drums).*

Death Metal band UNREAL OVERFLOWS was founded by former ABSORBED guitarist Francisco J. Pérez during 2002, being joined by lead vocalist Victor, second guitarist Pedro Cochón, bassist Zoilo Santiago and drummer Jorge Rosales. A demo, 'Point Of A New Departure', was recorded during 2003. Victor then exited and Santiago assumed lead vocal responsibilities. In this revised formation UNREAL OVERFLOWS was offered a recording contract by Xtreem Music in January 2004. The 'Architecture Of Incomprehension' album sessions finally took place at SpaceLab Studio in Trier, Germany during October 2005 with producers Christian Moos and Oliver Philipps.

Points Of A New Departure, Unreal Overflow (2004). A Real Overflow / Godforsaken / The Unavoidable Passage Of Time / In Darkness I Dwell.

UNSANCTUM

LIVERPOOL, UK — *Tom (vocals), Paul (guitar), David (bass), Sean (drums).*

UNSANCTUM was conceived during 2001 by vocalist Tom and guitarist Paul. The debut UNSANCTUM demo would be produced by Micke Kenney (a.k.a. 'Battlesticks' of ANAAL NAKRAATH, MISTRESS and FROST repute), scoring a label deal with Cacophonous Records. Kenney would once again man the desks for the laying down of the inaugural album 'Ignite The Skies'. However, this process, commencing in December of 2002, did not run smoothly and the record finally emerged in 2003. UNSANCTUM toured the UK in August of that year on a package billing with SACCULUS and BURNING SKIES. Further gigs in November saw the band as support to WALLS OF JERICHO.

IGNITE THE SKIES, Cacophonous NIHIL37CD (2003). The Chaosborn / Forests Of The Burning Darkness / As The Ruin Falls / The Laceration / Dawn The Black Winds / Ignite The Skies / Shadows Of Dilligence / New Maps Of Hell / Serpent / Every Waking Moment Dies / Beneath The Fire.

UNSEEN TERROR

BIRMINGHAM, UK — *Mitch Dickinson (vocals / bass), Peter Giles (guitar), Shane Embury (drums).*

UNSEEN TERROR featured a pre-NAPALM DEATH bassist Shane Embury. Vocalist / bassist Mitch Dickinson was also in parallel a member of both HERESY and ANTICHRIST. Both Embury and Dickinson are also erstwhile members of pioneering early eighties Shropshire death Metal act WARHAMMER. In 1987 UNSEEN TERROR had two songs included on the Bailey Brothers compilation album 'Diminished Responsibility' and subsequently scored a label deal with the fledgling Earache label. The album, 'Human Error', was recorded at Rich Bitch Studios in Birmingham during September of 1987. By this stage Embury was already gigging as a member of NAPALM DEATH and, as a further side concern alongside guitarist Pete Giles and former WARHAMMER man Wayne Ashton had founded Death Metal act AZAGTHOTH, putting in one gig in London in December of that year. The band altered its formation upon completion of the record, switching Giles to bass and Dickinson to guitar. Subsequently, DOOM, EXTREME NOIZE TERROR and NAPALM DEATH drummer Mick Harris was announced as the band's new singer. In March of 1988 UNSEEN TERROR cut tracks for airing on John Peel's Radio One show and performed a solitary show in Nottingham that same month with Wayne Aston temping on bass. This line up, and the band, soon collapsed.

The 2001 CD re-issue of 'Human Error' added six extra demo tracks. Pete Giles subsequently re-surfaced in HARMONY AS ONE and SCALPLOCK. In 2004 Californian gore Metal band EXHUMED revealed they had included a rendition of the UNSEEN TERROR song 'Uninformed' on their covers album entitled 'Regurgitated Requiems: Garbage Daze Re-Regurgitated'. Japanese Grind outfit WORLD DOWNFALL paid homage that same year with a take on 'Death Sentence Of The Innocent' included on their EP 'Show Your Colors Vol. 3'.

URKRAFT

HUMAN ERROR, Earache MOSH 4 (1987). Unseen Terror / Oblivion Descends / Divisions / Death Sentence (Of The Innocent) / Normal / Ignorant Scene / Uninformed / Expulsion Of Wrath / Garfield For President / Burned Beyond Recognition / Winds Of Pestilence / Hysteria / In A Shallow Grave / Odie's Revenge / Deliverance / The End Product / To Live And Learn / Charred Remains / Beyond Eternity / Garfield Strikes Again.
THE PEEL SESSIONS, (1988). Incompatible / Burned Beyond Recognition / Oblivion Descends / Divisions / Voice Your Opinion / Strong Enough To Change / Odies Revenge / It's My Life.

URKRAFT

SVENDBORG, DENMARK — *Thomas Strømvig Pedersen (vocals / guitar), Thomas Birk (guitar), Jeppe Tander (bass), Jeppe Eg (keyboards), Mikael Skou Jørgensen (drums).*

Svendborg melodic Death Metal act URKRAFT (a Danish expression for "primitive force") was founded during 1995 by vocalist / guitarist Thomas Strømvig Pedersen, guitarist R. Mørk, bass player Jeppe Tander and Mikael Skou Jørgensen, also a member of Power Metal band UREAS, on the drums. In 2000 the group inducted a new recruit in the CACOPHONY credited Thomas Birk on guitar and, in 2001 keyboard player Tommy Neperus for live work. During 2002 the keyboard position was secured with the enrollment of Jeppe Eg, the man holding credentials with CACOPHONY, BLAZING ETERNITY and MANTICORA.

URKRAFT issued the 'Primordial' demo in 2003. The band, signing to the German Cartel Media, entered the Antfarm recording studio with producer Tue Madsen in January of 2004 to commence work on debut album 'Eternal Cosmic Slaughter'. URKRAFT signed a multi-album deal with Earache Records in the Spring of 2005. URKRAFT duly utilised both Antfarm Studios and producer Tue Madsen once again in mid July to cut a second album 'The Inhuman Aberration'.

URKRAFT joined forces with CANNIBAL CORPSE and DISAVOWED for extensive European dates in February and March 2007.

Verden Vil Bedrages, Urkraft (1996) (Demo). Urkraft (Intro) / Håbets Tyranni / Under Nul—6652 / Sindssyge Eksistens / En Døende Jord / Hvad Blev Der Af Mit Liv? / Vilde Blomster Visner.
Urkraft, Gritt (2000) (Danish promotional release). Af Hele Mit Hjerte / Ukristelig Længsel / Krigsdans / Det Blodbestænkte Fængsel.
2001, Gritt (2001) (Danish promotional release). Knoglerne Skriger / Her Var Aldrig Smukt.
2002 Version 2, Gritt (2002) (Danish promotional release). Nord (Den Förste Krig) / Solen Braender Ihjel / Intet Ansigt / Kloglerne Skriger.
2002 Version 1, Gritt (2002) (Danish promotional release). Nord (Den Første Krig) / Solen Brænder Ihjel / Aldrig Smukt / Kødet Triumferer.
Primordial Promo 2003, Gritt (2003) (Danish promotional release). Cannibal Melancholy / Eternal Cosmic Slaughter / Soulless / The Scarlet Burning.
ETERNAL COSMIC SLAUGHTER, Cartel CM 232-5 (2004). Blessed Be The Human Beast / Paint The City Black / Soulless / Unleash The Will / Eternal Cosmic Slaughter / At The Border Of The Known World / Cannibal Melancholy / Through Your Senses / The Scarlet Burning.

THE INHUMAN ABERRATION, Earache MOSH328 (2006). Too Strong For The Strongest Lord / This Great Summer / Only The Gods / The Inhuman Aberration / Open The Gate / Come No Tomorrow / Watch Your Own Eyes / Liberation / Forsaken / The Pressure Of Our Jaws.

V:28

ARENDAL, NORWAY — *Eddie Risdal (vocals / guitar), Kristoffer Oustad (guitar / programming), Atle Johansen (bass).*

Arendal based "half-human half-machine" Industrial Death Metal act V:28 started life billed as V:O:I:D during 1996. The band comprises ANCESTRAL LEGACY vocalist / guitarist Eddie Risdal "Mindexpander", guitarist / programmer Kristoffer Oustad "Deconstructing engineer" and bassist Atle 'Anton Dead' Johansen "Virtual annihilator". V:O:I:D issued the demos 'Cosmos' in 1998 and 'Galaxy B-28.unreal' during 2001. Risdal also operated parallel outfit SYKDOM in alliance with Arataus Fachthal (a.k.a. Christian Mehus), previously of MISVITA, to issue the 'Hat' demo in 2000.

2002 V:28 demos included 'A Journey Through A World Of Madness', as V:O:I:D, and 'Time Is Empty' in April under the V:28 banner. V:28 performed their debut concert as support act to ENSLAVED in May 2002. Later the same year, drummer Børre Iversen enrolled a support to RED HARVEST and CADAVER INC. in October. However, the group then reverted back to programmed drums.

The album 'NonAnthropogenic', produced by LRZ of RED HARVEST, was recorded at Subsonic Society Studios in June 2003. Grutle Kjellson of ENSLAVED added guest vocals. North American label Vendlus Records issued 'NonAnthropogenic' in November. During late 2004 V:28 started to record the follow up album entitled 'SoulSaviour' at Forbidden Frequencies studios, once utilising LRZ's services as producer. Vendlus issued the album, featuring guest vocals from Kim W. Isaksen of TRIVIAL ACT, in May 2005.

'SoulSaviour' was also released as a limited version in just 28 copies housed in a handmade slipcase, enclosing a CDR with a cover version of the track 'One Last Beath' originally recorded by BLEAK. This version was only sold at the album release party held at Arendal Kulturhus May 20th 2005.

Time Is Empty, V:28 (2002). Execute Schizophrenia / Dead Shing Star / The Human Element / Perspective / The Fall Of Science.
Promotion CD 2003, V:28 (2003). Dead Shining Star / DeConstructor / Cosmic Infinity.
NONANTHROPOGENIC, Vendlus VEND002 (2003). Consumed By Schizophrenia / Dead Shining Star / The Human Element / To Be Tuned / Perspective / Everything But Life / Soldier Of The Neverending War / Purity / The Fall Of Science / Zero Nothing.
SOULSAVIOR, Vendlus VEND008 (2005). The Brightest Light / Unleash The Energy / A Prophecy Written In Uranium / Infected By Life / The Purifying Flames / Solid Structure Unknown / As The Sky Opens / DeConstructor / Dead Men's Choir.

VADER

OLSZTYN, POLAND — *Piotr Wiwczarek (vocals / guitar), Mauser (guitar), Novy (bass), Daray (drums).*

Death-Thrash band hailing from Olsztyn, VADER blitzed the globe with intense drumming and unashamed reliance on esoterica as a staple of their subject matter. VADER's unrelenting and brutal album schedule and seemingly inexhaustible appetite for global touring has elevated the band to the very top of the Polish Metal league. VADER came together in 1986, initially operating very much in the traditional Thrash Metal mould. That same year, VADER's first taste of the studio generated the demo 'Tyrani Piekieł', actually a circulated tape of a live radio broadcast, and December's 'Live In Decay', the band at this juncture comprising lead vocalist Czarny (a.k.a. Robert Czarneta), guitarists Peter (Piotr Wiwczarek) and Vika (Zbigniew Wróblewski), bassist Astaroth (Robert Struczewski) with Belial (Grzegorz Jackowski) on drums. Both Czarneta and Wróblewski decamped to found RAXAS.

The band released a further demo tape, 'Necrolust', working with engineer Władysław Iljaszewicz at Studio PR in Olsztyn in March 1989. Vader was now down to a trio, Peter being joined by bassist Jackie (Jacek Kalisz) and the SLASHING DEATH-credited drummer Krzysztof 'Docent' / 'Doc' Raczkowski. This tape gained VADER a deal with Carnage Records. A deal was struck to subsequently distribute the July 1990 demo 'Morbid Reich', these sessions co-produced by Mariusz Kmiolek at Pro-Studios in Olsztyn. This tape was to go down in Metal history, spectacularly selling in excess of over 10,000 copies.

The band, having inducted ex-IMPURITY and DIES IRAE guitarist Jaroslaw 'China' Labieniec and bassist Shambo (Leszek Rakowski), travelled to the UK to cut their debut record, 'The Ultimate Incantation' laid down at Rhythm Studios with Paul Johnson manning the desk. Upon the release of 'The Ultimate Incantion' in November 1992, VADER toured Europe with BOLT THROWER and GRAVE. Further dates in North America followed with DEICIDE, SUFFOCATION and DISMEMBER.

'The Darkest Age—Live '93', which included a cover of SLAYER's 'Hell Awaits', was recorded in front of a home crowd in Krakow. The 1994 'Sothis' EP witnessed another cover, BLACK SABBATH's anthem 'Black Sabbath', as well as a complete rework of VADER's 1989 track 'The Wrath'.

June 1995 found VADER out on the road in Europe once more touring alongside CRADLE OF FILTH, MALEVOLENT CREATION, OPPRESSOR, DISSECTION and SOLSTICE promoting the Adam Toczko produced 'De Profundis' album. Originally this album had been released domestically via Croon Records, subsequently seeing rapid fire reissues through Conquest Music and Impact Records.

VADER undertook a full European tour in the spring of 1996 as guests to CANNIBAL CORPSE. In 1996 Docent would unite with Cezar of CHRIST AGONY to found a Black Metal side venture MOON. Docent would appear on the first MOON album, 'Daemon's Heart', released in 1997, before relinquishing the role to concentrate on VADER. Keen to display their influences, VADER closed out 1996 with an album comprising entirely of cover versions. 'Future Of The Past' collected renditions of SODOM's 'Outbreak Of Evil', KREATOR's 'Flag Of Hate', TERRORIZER's 'Storm Of Stress' and 'Fear Of Napalm', POSSESSED's 'Death Metal', DARK ANGEL's 'Merciless Death', CELTIC FROST's 'Dethroned Emperor', SLAYER's 'Silent Scream', ANTI-NOWHERE LEAGUE's 'We Are The League', DEPECHE MODE's 'I Feel You' and BLACK SABBATH's 'Black Sabbath'.

The band would be joined by another DIES IRAE man, guitarist Mauser (Maurycy Stefanowicz), during 1997 as Labieniec opted out to found NYIA. That October Impact Records put out the next VADER installment, 'Black To The Blind'. Diligent fans soon noticed that the lyric sheet included an absent track, 'Anamnesis'. This song apparently excised from the final running order by mistake. In August the act hit Japan, a concert at the Tokyo Club Quattro held on the 31st being captured on tape for a live album. 'Anamnesis' finally received a public airing included on the November 1998 mini-album 'Kingdom'.

Wiwczarek produced the debut album by fellow Poles DECAPITATED during 2000 as Vader themselves worked up the 'Litany' opus, released via Metal Blade Records that May. Japanese editions boasted a brace of extra songs, 'Red Dunes' and 'Lord of Desert'. VADER themselves headlined the European 'No Mercy' festivals alongside American' VITAL REMAINS, Brazilians REBAELLIUN and Germany's FLESHCRAWL.

Mauser would find the opportunity to re-activate the DIES IRAE name in 2000 drafting his VADER colleague Docent on drums, SCEPTIC guitarist Hiro and frontman Novy of DEVILYN. This new version of DIES IRAE entered the recording studio in June 2000 with producer Szymon Czech for the debut 'Immolated' album. VADER attacked a further batch of covers with the April 2001 offering 'Reign Forever World', paying homage to DESTRUCTION's 'Total Desaster', JUDAS PRIEST's 'Rapid Fire' and MAYHEM's 'Freezing Moon'.

September 2001 found VADER on the look out for a new bassist as previous occupant of the position Shambo had departed. They found their man with Simon (Konrad Karchut), an ex-member of HUNTER. The band would figure as part of the gargantuan European 'No Mercy' touring festival package in March and April 2002. Also on the billing would be IMMORTAL, CATASTROPHIC, DESTROYER 666, HYPOCRISY, DISBELIEF, MALEVOLENT CREATION and OBSCENITY. That June the 'Revelations' album, recorded at Red Studio, Gdańsk with Wiwczarek acting as producer, arrived via Metal Blade. Studio guests included Nergal of BEHEMOTH vocalising on 'Whispers' and Ureck of LUX OCCULTA featured as session keyboard performer on 'Torch Of War' and 'Revelation Of Black Moses'. Loosely conceptual, 'Revelations' artwork tied together lyrical observations on the 9/11 twin towers disaster. Digipacks hosted an additional track, 'Sons Of Fire'.

VADER toured Japan as headliners in October. The band would headline a run of dates across mainland Europe from late August supported by KRISIUN, DECAPITATED and PREJUDICE. North American shows, commencing 6th of November had the Poles topping a strong Death Metal package of IMMOLATION, CEPHALIC CARNAGE, ORIGIN and DECEMBER. VADER issued a CD single version of THIN LIZZY's 'Angel Of Death' in 2002, restricted to the obligatory 666 copies.

Wiwczarek aided Prog-Metal act CETI on their 2003 album 'Shadow Of The Angel', adding guest vocals to the track 'Falcon's Flight'. The band would part ways with bassist Simon, replacing him in June with the BEHEMOTH and DEVILYN credited Novy (Marcin Norwak). The band would put in an appearance at the gargantuan 'Woodstock 2003' festival in Poland, playing in front of not only national TV cameras but a huge crowd of 400,000 Rock fans. VADER's live schedule intensified with September 2003 Polish gigs marked out with running mates DECAPITATED, FRONTSIDE and VESANIA prior to North American dates dubbed 'The Art Of Noise 2'. This run of shows saw the band allied with KREATOR, NILE, AMON AMARTH and GOATWHORE taking them through October.

An October EP entitled 'Blood' featured two new studio songs 'We Wait' and 'Shape-shifting' alongside cuts from the 'Revelations' sessions that previously had only surfaced as part of foreign license versions of the album, digi-packs and on EPs. Frontman Piotr Wiwczarek readied a solo project PANZER X for the studio in September, cutting the EP 'Steel First'. Novy would join SPINAL CORD as bassist in November 2003.

VADER, working once more with producer Piotr Lukaszewski, set February of 2004 for recording of a new studio album 'The Beast'. However, Doc met with an accident in the studio, seriously injuring his hand and leg. Cancelling the sessions, VADER re-booked studio time at the PR Studios in Gdańsk for a later date, pulling in Daray (Darek Brzozowski) from Polish black metal band VESANIA as a session musician

Upon finalization of these sessions after which the band projected road work in Slovakia and Czech Republic, sharing the stage with HYPNOS. A European tour with MALEVOLENT CREATION, NAGLFAR and BLOOD RED THRONE was to follow in June. The band projected a massive 160 date plus world tour to keep them active throughout the year, including a prestigious opening slot to SLIPKNOT and METALLICA on 31st May to over 50,000 fans at the Silesian Stadium in Chorzów.

Also in 2004 VADER would donate their rendition of 'Death Metal' to the 'Seven Gates Of Horror' tribute album assembled by the Dutch Karmageddon Media label in homage to pioneering Bay Area Thrash act POSSESSED.

A run of European gigs would be interrupted in late August when, en route to Falkenstein, near Leipzig VADER's tour bus was involved in an accident. Although the bus was seriously damaged, fortunately its occupants managed to escape unharmed. US touring plans for October saw the band set to flank NAPALM DEATH, KATAKLYSM and GOATWHORE. However, the band pulled out of these shows due to Piotr Wiwczarek requiring an operation to treat "a minor spinal injury" sustained whilst on tour in Scandinavia.

To close out the year, the band would be announced as one of the main attractions at the annual 'X-Mass Fest' 2004 roving European festival dates in alliance with NAPALM DEATH, MARDUK, FINNTROLL, THE BLACK DAHLIA MURDER and BELPHEGOR. In March of 2005 VADER parted ways with longtime drummer Doc, drafting Daray as substitute. Explaining the exit of Doc, frontman Piotr Wiwczarek explained "Doc pretty hard tried to 'fight' against his weaknesses, which were troubles for all of us."

US shows in April of 2005 had the band packaged with KREATOR, PRO-PAIN and THE AUTUMN OFFERING. The band broke this exhaustive touring schedule by entering Hertz Studios in Bialystok in early July to record an EP with a working title of 'The Art Of War', their first product for new label Sweden's Regain Records. Intros for these sessions would be conducted by Siegmar from VESANIA.

European gigs in June saw LOST SOUL as support act. A Polish tour of September, dubbed 'Blitzkrieg III', saw support from Greek veterans ROTTING CHRIST, fellow Poles LOST SOUL once again and French extreme Metal band ANOREXIA NERVOSA. Tragedy hit the VADER family in August with the announcement that former drummer Krzysztof "Docent" Raczkowski had died. The musician was just 35 years old and had a history of alcohol related problems.

Renewed road work in the USA for VADER continued in late 2005, witnessing November shows packaged with SUFFOCATION, CEPHALIC CARNAGE and ABORTED. The group headlined a memorial show for late drummer Doc at the Proxima Club in Warsaw on 11th December, supported by a local cast comprising CETI, HATE, DEAD INFECTION, LOST SOUL, CORRUPTION, AZARATH, CHAINSAW and VIRGIN SNATCH.

The band was included the 'Metal Crusaders' North American tour, taking place in May and June 2006 alongside KATAKLYSM, GRAVEWORM, DESTRUCTION, SPEED\KILL/HATE and THE ABSENCE. NIGHTRAGE and BLOODTHORN were confirmed as the support acts for the Scandinavian leg of the world tour, taking in Denmark, Norway, Sweden and Finland, in November. The 'Impressions In Blood' album, recorded at Hertz Studio in Bialystok, entered the national Polish charts at number 8 in September. An accompanying promotional video for the song 'Helleluyah (God Is Dead)' was directed by Andrzej Wyrozebski. Regain Records handled the album's European release Candlelight took on US licensing.

Shows during December 2006 in Bosnia, Turkey, Bulgaria, Rumania, Hungary and Serbia saw support from AMON DIN. That same month drummer Daray announced the formation of side project MASACHIST, co-formed by Thrufel, guitarist from AZARATH and YATTERING.

To commemorate VADER's 25th anniversary the band utilised Hertz Studio during March 2007 in order to completely re-record 25 of their best catalogue tracks.

VADER announced headline Australian dates in April 2007, supported by Sydney acts KILLRAZOR and INFERNAL METHOD.

Necrolust, (1989). Decapitated Saints / Reborn In Flames / The Final Massacre / The Wrath.

Morbid Reich, Carnage (1990). From Beyond (Intro) / Chaos / Vicious Circle / Breath Of Centuries / The Final Massacre / Reign-Carrion.

THE ULTIMATE INCANTATION, Earache MOSH 59 (1992). Creation / Dark Age / Vicious Circle / The Crucified Ones / Final Massacre / Testimony / Reign Carrion / Chaos / One Step To Salvation / Demon's Wind / Decapitated Saints / Breath Of Centuries.

VADER (pic: Vlad Nowajczyk)

THE DARKEST AGE—LIVE' 93, Arctic Serenades SERE 007 (1994). Macbeth (intro) / Dark Age / Vicious Circle / Crucified Ones / Demon's Wind / Decapitated Saints / From Beyond (Intro) / Chaos / Reign-Carrion / Testimony / Breath Of Centuries / Omen (Outro) / Hell Awaits.

Sothis EP, Massive MASS 001 MCD (1994). Hymn To The Ancient Ones / Sothis / De Profundis / Vision And The Voice / The Wrath / R'Lyeh / Black Sabbath.

DE PROFUNDIS, System Shock IR-C-067 (1995). Silent Empire / An Act Of Darkness / Blood Of Kingu / Incarnation / Sothis / Revolt / Of Moon, Blood, Dream And Me / Vision And The Voice / Reborn In Flames.

FUTURE OF THE PAST, Impact IR-C-092 (1996). Outbreak Of Evil / Flag Of Hate / Storm Of Stress / Death Metal / Fear Of Napalm / Merciless Death / Dethroned Emperor / Silent Scream / We Are The League / IFY / Black Sabbath.

BLACK TO THE BLIND, Impact IR-C-104 (1997). Heading For Internal Darkness / The Innermost Ambience / Carnal / Fractal Light / True Names / Beast raping / Foetus God / The Red Passage / Distant dream / Black To The Blind.

REBORN IN CHAOS, Hammerheart (1997). Decapitated Saints / Reborn In Flames / The Final Massacre / The Wrath / From Beyond / Chaos / Vicious Circle / Breath Of Centuries / The Final Massacre / Reign-Carrion.

Kingdom EP, Metal Mind Productions MMP CD 0057 (1998). Creatures Of Light And Darkness / Breath Of Centuries / Kingdom / Anamnesis / Inhuman (Disaster mix) / Quicksilver (Blood mix).

LIVE IN JAPAN, Impact IR-C-132-2 (1998). Damien / Sothis / Distant Dream / Black To The Blind / Silent Empire / Blood Of Kings / Carnal / Red Passage / Panzerstoss / Reborn In Flames / Fractal Light / From Beyond / Crucified Ones / Foetus God / Black Sabbath / Reign In Blood / Omen / Dark Age.

Xeper / North, Empire (2000). Xeper / North.

LITANY, Metal Blade 14297-2 (2000). Wings / The One Made Of Dreams / Xefer / Litany / Cold Demons / The Calling / North / Forward To Die!! / A World Of Hurt / The World Made Flesh / The Final Massacre.

REIGN FOREVER WORLD, Metal Blade 076-103182 (2001). Reign Forever World / Frozen Paths / Privilege Of The Gods / Total Disaster / Rapid Fire / Freezing Moon / North (Live) / Forwards To Die!! (Live) / Creatures Of Light And Darkness (Live) / Carnal (Live).

Angel Of Death, Empire EMP 012 CDS-E (2002) (Limited edition 666 copies). Angel Of Death / When Darkness Calls.

REVELATIONS, Metal Blade 3984-14411-2 (2002). Epitaph / The Nomad / Wolftribe / Whisper / As The Fallen Rise / When Darkness Calls / Torch Of War / The Code / Lukewarm Race / Angel Of Death / Revelation Of Black Moses.

Blood EP, Metal Blade 3984-14461-2 (2003). Shape-Shifting / We Wait / Son Of Fire / As The Fallen Rise / Traveller / When Darkness Calls / Angel Of Death.

BLOOD—REIGN FOREVER WORLD, Metal Blade 14461-2 (2003) (USA release). Shape Shifting / We wait / As The Fallen Rise / Son Of Fire / Traveler / When Darkness Calls / Reign Forever World / Frozen Paths / Privilege Of The Gods / Total Desaster / Rapid Fire / Freezing Moon / Creatures Of Light And Darkness (Live) / Carnal (Live) / Red Dunes / Lord Of Desert.

Beware The Beast, Empire (2004). Dark Transmission (333.version) / Stranger In The Mirror / Report from studio (Video) / Dark Transmission (Video).

THE BEAST, Metal Blade 14485-2 (2004). Intro / Out Of The Deep / Dark Transmission / Firebringer / The Sea Came In At Last / Stranger In The Mirror / I Shall Prevail / The Zone / Insomnia / Apopheniac / Choices.

The Art Of War, Regain RR 074 (2005). Para Bellum / This Is The War / Lead Us!!! / Banners On The Wind / What Colour Is Your Blood? / Death In Silence / This Is The War (video).

IMPRESSIONS IN BLOOD, Regain (2006). Between Day And Night / ShadowsFear / As Heavens Collide ... / Helleluyah!!! (God Is Dead) / Field Of Heads / Predator / Warlords / Red Code / Amongst The Ruins / They Live!!! / The Book. Chart position: 8 POLAND.

VAKARM

AMIENS, FRANCE — *Alex (vocals), Benoît Moritz (guitar), Olivier Delplace (guitar), Xavier (bass), Nicklaus Bergen (drums).*

VAKARM is a Death-Grind unit operating out of Northern France created by guitarist Benoît Moritz of UNTOLD, CAAR-CRINOLAS DESCAMISADOS and DSK repute. The project debuted with the 2000 recording 'Brutal Zone'. Recruiting guitarist Olivier Delplace, also citing credits with both DESCAMISADOS and DSK as well as BLINDING FEAR and SEPTICAL MIND, the follow up 'The Sum' was laid down in 2001. Dividing his duties, Benoît Moritz joined BURGUL TORKHÄIN between 2002 and 2004.

Subsequent VAKARM recruits would comprise NO MAMS and FRIZZING BALL singer Alex, INYTIUM bassist Xavier and drummer Nicklaus from DECLINE OF HUMANITY and LIVING DEAD. A live demo, 'Killerfest 2004', then surfaced. Drummer Nicklaus Bergen would also be operational with SHADOW OF THE BEAST.

Brutal Zone, Vakarm (2000). Return To Hatred / Forbidden Gate / Bruised Flesh.

THE SUM, Vakarm (2001). Intro / The Sum / Ritual Mutilation / Forbidden Gate / Rise At The Curtains / Bruised Flesh / Return To Hatred.

VAULTAGE

HOLLAND — *Dennis Droomers (vocals), Rob (guitar), Tom (guitar), Jeroen (bass), Clemens Wijers (keyboards), Ivo Wijers (drums).*

VAULTAGE was created during 2002 by former INGER INDOLIA guitarist Rob in a union with erstwhile ICON OF SIN personnel guitarist Tom and bassist Jeroen. Tom would also cite a tradition with both AMNESIA and DISOLUTION. Keyboard player Clemens Wijers was drawn in from the band DARK MUTATION with the band being completed by drummer Roy and another ex-INGER INDOLIA and CARACH ANGREN man Dennis Droomers handling lead vocals. VAULTAGE debuted with the EP 'Hallucinate Beyond'. Released in September of 2003 this offering saw Bas Maas of AFTER FOREVER guesting on the title track. In March of 2004 Ivo Wijers of CARACH ANGREN took over on drums.

Clemens Wijers is also involved with NVU and CARACH ANGREN. Droomers operates a solo concern LAMMENDAM. VAULTAGE also featured female bassist Anouk ("Countess Sjnoek"), later of Thrash Folk Metal act CHAIN OF DOGS.

Hallucinate Beyond, Independent (2003). Dim Messenger / Infecting Common Self Deceival / Icon Of Sin / Hallucinations Beyond.

VEHEMENCE

AZ, USA — *Nathan Gearhart (vocals), Bjorn Dannov (guitar), John Chavez (guitar), Mark Kozuback (bass), Andrew Schroeder (drums).*

Arizona Melodic Death Metal combo forged in 1995 by former BLUDGEON (the Phoenix version) vocalist Nathan Gearhart and guitarists Bjorn Dannov and Scott Wiegand. The bands rhythm section was completed by drafting in bassist Mark Kozuback and drummer Andrew Schroeder, both of REVOLUTION and Punk band MISTAKEN IDENTITY. A demo emerged in 1998 but on conclusion of recording for the debut album 'The Thoughts From Which I Hide', recorded in November, Wiegand made his exit. VEHEMENCE drafted BRIDES OF CHRIST and DEPRECATED man John Chavez as replacement. The album emerged in August 2000.

VEHEMENCE were set to form part of the 'North American Extermination' tour in 2001 along with BRODEQUIN and Japanese act VOMIT REMNANTS. However, this union fell through and VEHEMENCE successfully took on the dates themselves. The band signed to the Metal Blade label for a 2002 debut 'God Was Created'. Road work included a string of August North American gigs packaged with INCANTATION, DECAPITATED and DEAD TO FALL. The band would also support the reformed NUCLEAR ASSAULT for West Coast dates in January of 2003. The band would be scheduled to be out on the road again in March as part of a mighty package tour aligned with DEICIDE, BEHEMOTH, AMON AMARTH and REVENGE. However, the band was forced to pull out due to illness, vocalist Nathan Gearhart suffering from a sinus infection. Nevertheless, the band set to work on a new studio album billed as 'Helping The World To See', this opus produced by Will Solares and the band at Open Primary Productions/DBD Studios in Maricopa, Arizona. Keyboard player Jason Keesecker bowed out in early November and guitarist Bjorn Dannov handled piano parts during the recordings.

VEHEMENCE put in dates allied with PRONG, DOG FASHION DISCO and ALL THAT REMAINS in late May and early June of 2004. Their live schedule intensified as they hooked up with VITAL REMAINS for one week at the end of August before uniting with CREMATORIUM, ALL SHALL PERISH and ANIMOSITY in September, then with MORTICIAN and AKERCOCKE through until October. This trek would be backed by a promotional video for the track 'We Are All Dying', directed by Elliot Phear. 2005 got off to a difficult start for the band as Nathan Gearhart exited in early January, apparently due to "family obligations". He would rapidly be replaced by ex-FROM A SECOND STORY WINDOW man Sean Vandegrift. However, preliminary West Coast dates saw Bryan Edwards of CLIFTON temping as frontman.

VEHEMENCE forged a touring alliance with CREMATORIUM, THE RED DEATH and ALL SHALL PERISH for US dates in May. By September the group revealed they had installed yet another new singer, Adam Cody of GLASS CASKET. However, in mid October the group disbanded, a statement quoting "Eight years after it all started, we decided that now is the time to throw in the towel". Band members would be quick off the mark with new projects, Gearhart having forged HE WHO BINDS HIMSELF whilst Mark Kozuback, Andy Schroeder and Bjorn Dannov founded ABIGAIL WILLIAMS. Chavez subsequently unveiled his new concept CURSED IN BLACK.

Although VEHEMENCE reunited for a one off gig in February 2006, musicians would still be active with other projects. Mark Kozuback, Andy Schroeder and Bjorn Dannov, together with ABIGAIL WILLIAMS singer Connor Woods and ex-BRIDES OF CHRIST guitarist KC Bradham forged THE SYMMETRY IN CHAOS. In March 2007 it was learned that Mark Kozuback had united with singer Marshall Beck, from REBIRTH, DESCEND and VEXATION and drummer Ken "Sorceron", of ABIGAIL WILLIAMS, in a new conceptual Death Metal project called REIGN OF VENGEANCE.

THE THOUGHTS FROM WHICH I HIDE, Independent (2000). I Take Your Life / Saying Goodbye / Whore Cunt Die / What You've Become / No One Wins / Nameless Faces, Scattered Remnants / Devour The Rotten Flesh / Reconditioning The Flock.

GOD WAS CREATED, Metal Blade (2002). Made For Her Jesus / She Never Noticed Me / Fantasy From Pain / Christ, I Fucking Hate You! / Lusting For Affection / The Last Fantasy Of Christ / I Didn't Kill Her / God Was Created / I Must Not Live / The Lord's Work.

HELPING THE WORLD TO SEE, Metal Blade (2004). By Your Bedside / Kill For God / Trinity Broadcasting (Know Your Enemy) / To The Taste / You Don't Have To Be Afraid Anymore / Alone In Your Presence / Spirit Of The Soldier / Darkness Is Comfort / What Could Go Wrong? / We Are All Dying / Her Beautiful Eyes.

VENGEANCE RISING

LOS ANGELES, CA, USA — *Roger Martinez (vocals / guitar), Larry Farkas (guitar), Doug Thieme (guitar), Roger Dale Martin (bass), Glenn Mancarusco (drums).*

Although one of the leading lights of the Christian Death Metal scene for a lengthy period, the Los Angeles based VENGEANCE RISING would become embroiled in bitter recriminations as vocalist Roger Martinez, now solo, has reportedly disowned his previous beliefs. Martinez, who plotted another anti- Christian VENGEANCE RISING album to be titled 'Realms Of Blasphemy' as well as an expose treatise 'The Lixivium Letters', claims to have been duped into believing in and promoting God.

The band was created in 1985 by former SACRIFICE members along with guitarists Larry Farkas and Doug Thieme along with drummer Glenn Mancaruso. Martinez, previously with PROPHET, was enrolled as singer the following year. The band was initially billed as VENGEANCE but another act of the same name was discovered. The album sleeve, which featured a close up of a nailed crucified hand, actually that of Pastor Bob Beeman, for the Caesar Kalinowski produced debut 'Human Sacrifice' had to be reprinted with the new logo. Tracks on this album were co-written by guitarist Glenn Rogers, subsequently to join DELIVERANCE then HIRAX.

Following the 1990 Ron Goudie produced 'Once Dead' album promotional tour the band splintered. Only Martinez remained to carry on with the name as Farkas, Mancaruso and bassist Roger Dale Martin all quit. Martin founded Biker Blues band TRIPLE ACE whilst the others created DIE HAPPY. Farkas would also figure in SIRCLE OF SILENCE, the band assembled by erstwhile ACCEPT and BANGALORE CHOIR vocalist David Reece.

Meantime, Martinez enrolled guitarist Derek Sean and drummer Chris Hyde of DELIVERANCE for the 'Destruction Comes' opus.

For the 1992 'Released From The Earth' album Martinez employed guitarist Jamie Mitchell, bass player Joe Monsrb'nik and drummer Jonny Vasquez. Backing vocals came courtesy of MORTIFICATION's Steve Rowe, TOURNIQUET men Victor Marcios and David Vasquez and Jimmy Brown of DELIVERANCE. Jonny Vasquez would then join MORTIFICATION for touring.

Touring upon the album release saw DELIVERANCE guitarist George Ochoa as live guitarist. Apparently upon completion of these dates, sometime between 1995 and 1997, Martinez became an atheist. His personal website claimed fresh VENGEANCE RISING recordings were on the way but they did not materialise.

Undeterred by the scandal, Christian Deathsters ULTIMATUM would cover 'Burn' for their third album 'The Mechanics Of Perilous Times'.

Needless to say VENGEANCE RISING remains a hot topic of debate on the Christian music scene. Re-billed as VENGEANCE the group made a surprise return in 2004. With Martinez conspicuous by his absence the band—guitarists Larry Farkas and Doug Thieme, bass player Roger Dale Martin and drummer Glen Mancaruso announced an appearance at the 'Summer Madness' event on 29th August at Chain Reaction in Anaheim, California. A surprise guest vocalist would fill in for Martinez, Scott Waters of ULTIMATUM, was to rise to the challenge. This grouping of musicians, under threat of legal action from Roger Martinez, subsequently unveiled a new band title of ONCE DEAD. In January 2006 guitarist Glenn Rogers, another ex-VENGEANCE RISING member, joined the fold.

Martinez returned to the fore in 2006, announcing an appearance at the August 19th 'Sex, Drugs & Death Metal' festival in Overland, Missouri.

HUMAN SACRIFICE, Intense (1989). Human Sacrifice / Burn / Mulligan Stew / Receive Him / I Love Hating Evil / Fatal Delay / White Throne / Salvation / From The Dead / Ascension / He Is God / Fill This Place With Blood / Beheaded.

ONCE DEAD, Intense (1990). Warfare / Can't Get Out / Cut Into Pieces / Frontal Lobotomy / Herod's Violent Death / The Whipping Post / Arise / Space Truck'in / Out Of The Will / The Wrath To Come / Into The Abyss / Among The Dead / Interruption.

DESTRUCTION COMES, Intense (1991). You Can't Stop It / The Rising / Before The Time / The Sword / He Don't Own Nothing / Countless Corpses / Thanatos / You Will Bow / Hyde Under Pressure / Raeqoul.

RELEASED UPON THE EARTH, Intense (1992). Help Me / The Damnation Of Judas And The Salvation Of The Thief / Released Upon The Earth / Human Dark Potential / Instruments Of Death / Lest You Be Judged / Out Of Bounds / Bishop Of Souls / Tion / You Will Be Hated.

VERMIN

NÄSSJÖ, SWEDEN — *Jimmy Sjøoqvist (vocals / guitar), Moses Shitch (guitar), Johan Svensson (bass), Mathias Adamsson (drums).*

VERMIN, a Swedish Death Metal troupe out of Nässjö, were founded in 1991 issuing a seven track eponymous demo the following year. Further promotional cassettes included 'Life Is Pain' and 'Scum Of The Earth'. The band debuted commercially with the inclusion of one of their tracks on the compilation album 'Requiem Morbid Symphonies Of Death' before Chaos records issued all the VERMIN demos to date collected onto one CD 'Obedience To Insanity' during October 1994.

The second album, 'Plunge Into Oblivion', which saw bassist Johan Svensson replaced by David Melin, included Fred Estby of DISMEMBER.

In early 1997 founder member and guitarist Moses Shtieh decamped. VERMIN underwent a necessary reshuffle shifting Melin to guitar and bringing in bassist Timmy Persson.

The 1998 album 'Millennium Ride' would be issued by No Fashion Records and picked up for an American license by Metal Blade Records in March of 2000. 'Filthy F***king Vermin' emerged in January 2001.

Not to be confused with the Australian Nu-Metal VERMIN.

OBEDIENCE TO INSANITY, Chaos CHAOSCD 01 (1994). In Darkness Dwells (Intro) / Enjoy ? / Cremation Sustained / Into Nothingness / Trapped / Psychic Tomb / Obedience To Insanity (Outro) / Life Is Pain / Corroded Conscience / Internal Emptiness / Lunatic Fanatics / Human Extermination / Among The Tombstones (Intro) / Pile Of Pus / Namtab / Rotting Mass Of Human Flesh / Insain Pain (Intro) / Autopsy For Pleasure / Fated (To Die).

PLUNGE INTO OBLIVION, Chaos CHAOSCD 03 (1995). When Hell Becomes Reality / Slave / Screw / The Silence / Life-See My Sorrow / Enemy / Eternal Love / Denials / Hypochrist / Plunge Into Oblivion / How Many Million / Bitter Hate / San Quentin.

MILLENNIUM RIDE, No Fashion NFR030 (1998). Hungerface / Circle Of Time / Upright Infinity / Demon Soul / Bloodlust / Everlasting / Black / Deviltrip / Broken / Species.

FILTHY F*ING VERMIN**, No Fashion NFR046 (2001). Into—Already Dead / King For A Day / Laughing Face Of Madness / Random Pain / God's Eye / See Ya In Hell / Hate Crimes / Feed The Fire / Monster / Self-Inflicted Fiction Hell / Filthy (Disgusting Vermin) / Shoot.

VERMINOUS

AHUS, SWEDEN — *Germaniac (vocals / guitar), Pelle Melander (guitar), Simon Frödeberg (bass), Agge Johansson (drums).*

Ahus Blasphemous Death Metal outfit VERMINOUS was assembled in August 2002 by vocalist / guitarist Linus 'Germaniac' Björklund, guitarist Pelle Melander and drummer Andreas Johansson. Under a former title of DELVE the group released a 2002 demo and the EP 'The Dead Amongst'. Bass player Simon Frödeberg enrolled in May 2003. Debut product would be the 7" vinyl EP 'Smell The Birth Of Death' released by Nuclear Winter. The Xtreem Music label released the album 'Impious Sacrilege' in July 2003.

VERMINOUS plotted a new album, entitled 'Keepers Of Chaos', for late 2004 release. That same year found VERMINOUS members bassist Simon Frödeberg and drummer Agge Johansson active with EVILDOER, a Death / Thrash combo fronted by WITHIN Y frontman Andreas Solvestrom. The bassist would also be operational with SGT. CARNAGE and INFERNAL HELLFIRE plus solo concern URUZ.

Nuclear Winter re-issued 'Smell The Birth Of Death' set in 2006 as an MCD.

Smell The Birth Of Death EP, Nuclear Winter NWR006 (2003). Intro / Verminous Fluids / Salvation By Extermination / Resuscitation Of The Dead / Chaos In The Flesh.
IMPIOUS SACRILEGE, Xtreem Music XM 008 CD (2003). Intro / Spawn Of Satans Curse / Impious Genocide / Malevolent Effacement / Chanting Of Ghouls / Salvation By Extermination / Of Evil Blood / Grotesque Visions / Rapt In Malignity / Verminous Fluids.
IMPIOUS SACRILEGE, Blood Harvest (2005) (Vinyl release). Intro / Spawn Of Satans Curse / Impious Genocide / Malevolent Effacement / Chanting Of Ghouls / Salvation By Extermination / Of Evil Blood / Grotesque Visions / Rapt In Malignity / Verminous Fluids / Charred Remains.

VEULIAH

SALVADOR, BA, BRAZIL — *Fábio Gouvêa (vocals), Ricardo Sanct (guitar), Júlio Gouvêa (guitar), Márcio Medeiros (bass), Luciano Veiga (keyboards), Léo Rivas (drums).*

VEULIAH guitarist Ricardo Sanct also has ties to MALEFACTOR. The group, offering melodic styled Death Metal, first delivered the 1996 demo tape 'Temple Of Fears'. The group line up at this juncture comprised singer Eduardo Santos, guitarists Alexandre Veiga and Leonardo, bassist Marcio Medeiros, keyboard man Luciano Veiga with Alberto Alpire on the drums.

Further sessions included 'Last Breath' in 1997 with Wallace Guerra installed on guitar, that same year also gaining exposure on the 'DoisdaBahia' compilation, but then suffered with serious line up problems in 1999, stalling progress. The band returned for 2003's 'Black Spirit' demo. The new look line up saw Medeiros and Veiga being joined by vocalist Fabio Gouvêa, guitarists Julio Gouvêa and Ricardo Sanct with Léo Rivas on the drums.

VEULIAH prepared an album entitled 'Deep Visions Of Unreality' in 2004.

DEEP VISIONS OF UNREALITY, Veuliah (2005). Ego Et Alli / The Dead Poet / Immortal Thoughts / The Oldest One / Black Spirit / Helm Beyond / Route Of Mysteries / Virtual Salvation.

VIBRION

ARGENTINA — *Luis Cederborg (vocals / guitar), Guillermo Giusti (guitar), Fabian Fernandez (bass), Gus Cederborg (drums).*

VIBRION, blending Harcore, Grind and Death elements, came together in 1989, recording the demo 'Eradicated Life' in 1991. VIBRION's line up at this juncture comprised the EXISTENCIA DE ODIO credited vocalist / guitarist Luis Cederborg, second guitarist Guillermo Giusti, bass player Fabián Fernandez and drummer Gustavo Cederborg. The Swiss Witchunt label subsequently pressed the demo tracks up as a 7" single and the domestic Advance Records issued sessions, plus live tracks, as a CD album in March of 1994. A 1995 line up shuffle saw Alejandro Mangiacavalli taking Giusti's guitar position.

VIBRION's 1997 album 'Closed Frontiers' included a cover version of AGNOSTIC FRONT's 'Toxic Shock'. By 2002 the band line-up had completely transformed with only Luis 'Guardamagna' Cederborg surviving. New personnel would include guitarist Eric Renwart, bassist Roland Wislet and drummer Charles de Croix.

Eradicated Life EP, Witchunt (1992). Massive Frustration / Immoral Class / Schizoids Obsession / Legal Fights / Erradicated Life.
ERADICATED LIFE, Advance (1994). Massive Frustration / Immoral Class / Schizoids Obsession / Legal Fights / Erradicated Life / Legal Fights (Live) / Schizoids Obsession (Live) / Massive Frustration (Live) / Erradicated Life (Live).
DISEASED, Frost Bite (1995). Incoming Aggression / Metamorphosis / Partner Of The Crimes / Polluted Areas / Erradicated Life / Legal Fights / Full Of Sickness / Massive Frustration / Strange Slow Invasion.
CLOSED FRONTIERS, Frost Bite (1997). Closed Frontiers / Hinterland / Imprisoned / Insufficient System / Message Of Disaster / Defences Fall / Reprisal / Toxic Shock.

VICIOUS

VÄSTERÅS, SWEDEN — *Henke Wenngren (vocals), Pontus Pettersson (guitar), Simon Jarrolf (bass), Fredrik Eriksson (drums).*

Västerås based Death Thrashers. The band began life as a school act of guitarists Pontus Pettersson and Fredde, soon uniting with drummer Adam Hobér of Black Metal act ENTHRALLED. This trio picked the title RAGE ANTHEM initially for the opening demo 'Fire Desires' but would then adopt WARGASM as their banner. Later recruits included bassist Simon Jarrolf and new drummer Erik Wallin.

Although the band issued the mini album 'Pure Evil (Straight From Hell)' during 2001 they would, bringing in another drummer Fredrik Eriksson, subsequently switch band title to VICIOUS. Under their new title the band re-debuted in 2002 with the EP 'Chains Won't Hold It Back'. VICIOUS frontman Henke Wenngren also holds down membership in MORNALAND and SKYFIRE. He would also gain production credits on DEAD AWAKEN's demo "Death Before Dishonour'.

Signing to the Portuguese Sound Riot label VICIOUS cut their debut album 'Vile, Vicious & Victorious' at Studio Underground in Västerås for release in March of 2004. Guesting in the studio would be bass player Petri Kuusisto of CARNAL FORGE and the ROSICRUCIAN, SLAPDASH, ZEALION, POWERAGE and LOST SOULS credited guitarist Magnus Söderman.

Chains Won't Hold It Back, Vicious (2002) (Demo). High On Fire / Deathrash / Feeder Of Evil.
VILE, VICIOUS AND VICTORIOUS, Sound Riot SRP.027 (2004). Beast / Trigger Needs Some Action / High On Fire / Deadicate / Life Corrupted / Deathrash / Boots Of Led / A Vicious Mind / The Feeder Of Evil.

VICIOUS ART

STOCKHOLM, SWEDEN — *Jocke Widfeldt (vocals), Matti Mäkelä (guitar), Tobbe Sillman (guitar), Jörgen Sandström (bass), Robert Lundin (drums).*

VICIOUS ART is a 2004 founded Death / Thrash act forged by former DARK FUNERAL and DOMINION CALIGULA members Mattias 'Dominion' Mäkelä and Robert 'Gaahnfaust' Lundin, also both holding OBSCURITY credentials. The duo subsequently enrolled Jörgen Sandström of GOD AMONG INSECTS, THE PROJECT HATE, KRUX, NASUM and a veteran of ENTOMBED and GRAVE on bass. Secondary guitars would be delegated to Tobbe Sillman of GUIDANCE OF SIN and THE DEAD.

The band would soon sign an album deal with ENTOMBED's Threeman Recordings, 'Fire Falls And The Waiting Waters' being set for a November release. To coincide, VICIOUS ART made their concert debut at the Tantogården venue in Stockholm in 12th November alongside MÖRK GRYNING and NINNUAM.

The VICIOUS ART triumvirate of Tobbe Sillman, Jocke Widfeldt and Matti Mäkelä featured as backing vocalists on THE PROJECT HATE's 2005 album "Armageddon March Eternal (Symphonies Of Slit Wrists)'. Jörgen Sandström also announced the formation of a deliberately retro-Death Metal band project entitled DEATH BREATH in collaboration with his erstwhile ENTOMBED colleague and THE HELLACOPTERS frontman Nicke Andersson with THUNDER EXPRESS man Robert Persson on guitar.

VICIOUS ART issued the 'Weed The Wild' EP in February 2006.

Vicious Art, Vicious Art (2003) (Demo). A Whistler And His Son / The Poet Must Die / Crash Landing / Why Would The Captured Set Free The Flies?

FIRE FALLS AND THE WAITING WATERS, Threeman Recordings TRECD017 (2004). Debria Seems To Be Bleeding / Komodo Lights / Fire Falls / A Whistler And His Gun / Ceremony (The Waiting Waters) / Mother Dying / The Poet Must Die / Cut This Heathen Free / War / Why Would The Captured Set Free The Flies?

Weed The Wild, Vicious Art (2006). Weed The Wild / Tanja Joins The Beating / Exit Wounds.

VICTIM

GERMANY — *Benjamin Jahn (vocals), Konstantin Alogas (guitar), Andreas Böhner (guitar), Andrea Tontsch (bass), Thorsten Fröhlich (drums).*

VICTIM was founded during 1993 at the hands of guitarist Andreas Böhner and drummer Thorsten Fröhlich. Singer Benjamin Jahn was enrolled just prior to recording the debut, self financed 'Faces Of Death' album in 1997. Second guitarist Marc Wolfshöfer was taken onboard upfront of a second outing 'Cocktail Of Brutality'. VICTIM underwent further changes with the exit of Wolfshöfer. Andrea Tontsch was pulled in as bassist in September of 2000 and the second guitar vacancy was finally filled by Konstantin Alogas in mid 2001.

The Japanese Eclipse label combined the two albums for a re-release in May of 2002, limiting this offering to just 1000 copies.

FACES OF DEATH, Independent (1998). Massmurder Puzzle / In War With Belief / Faces Of Death / Such A Religion Can't Survive / Smashed To Pieces / Redemption / A Tribute To Macabre.

COCKTAIL OF BRUTALITY, Independent (2000). Serial License / Bloodshed / Lust Love & Morgue / Dead Man Walking / Differences / Jesus Died Under My Wheels / The Other Way Of Defloration / Life Is Cold Like The Winter / Homicide.

COCKTAIL OF BRUTALITY—FACES OF DEATH, Eclipse (2002) (Japanese release. Limited edition 1000 copies). Intro / Serial License / Bloodshed / Lust Love & Morgue / Dead Man Walking / Differences / Jesus Died Under My Wheels / The Other Way Of Defloration / Life Is Cold Like The Winter / Homicide / Massmurder Puzzle / In War With Belief / Faces Of Death / Such A Religion Can't Survive / Smashed To Pieces / Redemption / A Tribute To Macabre.

VICTIMIZER

SKJERN, DENMARK — *Killhailer (vocals), Henrik Engkjær (guitar), Azter (bass), Atziluth (drums).*

The 2004 band line-up of Skjern based blasphemic Death-Thrashers VICTIMIZER comprised KILL, UNDERGANG and CHURCH BIZARRE man Killhailer on vocals, the EXEKRATOR and FULL MOON LYCANTHROPY credited Henrik Engkjær on guitar, DENIAL OF GOD bassist Azter and drummer Atziluth (a.k.a. Michael Huhle), a scene veteran of RAVISHING, BLACKHORNED, RENEGADETH and GRIMNISMAL. Atziluth would work with DENIAL OF GOD in October 2004.

Erstwhile VICTIMIZER personnel included drummer, later guitarist, C(unt). Molestor, drummer Snuff and guitarist / bassist Dr. Rape. Credited session musicians numbered the DEMON REALM credited Lars Groth on drums and guitarist Suicide Machine. The project had debuted in October 2000 with the three song demo tape 'Skullfucked By Victimizer' complete with cover of MOTÖRHEAD's 'Ace Of Spades'. This would soon sell out and be re-issued in May 2001 then followed by 'Unholy Banners Of War'. Horror Records issued the 'Communist Crusher' EP, featuring a cover version of ALICE COOPER's 'Prince Of Darkness', in December 2003, these sessions including Lars Groth on drums.

The band shared a split cassette release 'Revenge Of The Hellhorde' with NUNSLAUGHTER on the Pentagram Warfare label in September of 2004. Amongst these tracks would be VICTIMIZER's interpretations of NUNSLAUGHTER's 'In The Graveyard' and D.A.D.'s 'True Believer. VICTIMIZER signed to the Australian label Apocalyptor Records in October to re-issue the 'Unholy Banners Of War' demo tracks with additional material in the form of new track 'Reap the nuclear whirlwind', a re-recording of 'Battle Weapons' plus NUNSLAUGHTER and MOTÖRHEAD cover versions. The band also announced a split 7" single shared with TOXIC HOLOCAUST for Hells Headbangers.

The band donated their rendition of 'Tormentor' to the W.A.S.P. tribute album 'Shock Rock Hellions–A Tribute to W.A.S.P.', released by Denmark's Codiac Records in May 2006.

Skullfucked By Victimizer, Victimizer (2000) (Demo, limited to 243 handnumbered copies). Skullfucked By Victimizer / Hell Revealed / Battle Weapons.

Unholy Banners Of War, Victimizer (2001). Devoured By Satan's Flames / Pentagram Warfare / Hell Revealed / Skullfucked By Victimizer / Communist Crusher.

Communist Crusher, Horror HOR 010 (2003) (Limited edition of 666 numbered copies). Bonebreaking Armageddon Metal / Prince Of Darkness / Speed Metal Nightmare / Communist Crusher.

REVENGE OF THE HELLHORDE, Pentagram Warfare (2004) (Split cassette release with NUNSLAUGHTER). Pride Of The Zombie Squad / Hellrevealed! / In The Graveyard / Bonebreaking Armageddon Metal / True Believer / Speed Metal Nightmare / Reap The Nuclear Whirlwind.

Communist Crusher, Horror HOR 010 PD (2005) (Limited edition of 525 numbered 7" picture disc). Bonebreaking Armageddon Metal / Prince Of Darkness / Speed Metal Nightmare / Communist Crusher.

REVENGE OF THE HELLHORDE, Ancient Darkness Productions ADP 008 (2005) (Split vinyl release with NUNSLAUGHTER). Pride Of The Zombie Squad / Hellrevealed! / In The Graveyard / Bonebreaking Armageddon Metal / True Believer / Speed Metal Nightmare / Reap The Nuclear Whirlwind.

VICTIMIZER / ETERNAL PAIN / BETRAYED / FARSCAPE, Deathstrike DR042 (2005) (Split release with ETERNAL PAIN, BETRAYED and FARSCAPE limited to 500 copies). Pride Of The Zombie Squad / Flamethrower Madness.

UNHOLY BANNERS OF WAR, Warfuck WAR666-003 (2006). Devoured By Satan's Flames / Pentagram Warfare / Hell Revealed / Skullfucked By Victimizer / Communist Crusher / Behold The Coming (Intro) / Battleweapons / Ace Of Spades / In The Graveyard / Reap The Nuclear Whirlwind.

VICTIMS OF INTERNAL DECAY

ALBANY, OR, USA — *Lance Thrill (vocals), Terry Geil (guitar), Nick Wusz (guitar), Ron Farris (bass), Pat Wombacher (drums).*

Although an unashamed Death Metal band Oregon's VICTIMS OF INTERNAL DECAY (V.O.I.D.- "Born and raised on beef and trees") are unique in not only pursuing a path of Grunge flavoured extreme Metal but in reputedly having a lead guitarist with one leg! The band heralded their arrival with the 1989 demo session 'Democrazy' with a line up of vocalist Lance Thrill, guitarists Jason Moser and Dave Bruce, bassist Aaron Baird and drummer Pat Wombacher. A second tape followed in 1990 entitled 'Terminal Happenings' which saw Hans Jochimsen on guitar. V.O.I.D.'s third demo, 1991's 'Dead Fish White', had John Eddleman on bass.

The 1993 album witnessed the inclusion of Ron Farris on bass with the aforementioned monoped Terry Geil on guitar. The eponymous album included a version of GREEN RIVER's 'One More Stitch'. The band's line-up would shift again for a

1996 promotional recording 'Resin 67 Session' with Jochimsen replaced by Nick Wusz.

Due to Geil's alleged lack of limb the band are known as "Death on nine legs"!

VICTIMS OF INTERNAL DECAY, Grindcore 89817-4 (1993). Absolute Worship / Bathed In Sickness / Bleed / One More Stitch / Jim's Lament / Consummation / Under The Sun / In Extremis / False Hate / Sterile Nature.

VIGILIA MORTUM

KOHTLA-JARVE, ESTONIA — *Radislav Kaverin (vocals), Denis Savitskiy (guitar), Igor Klyuchnik (guitar), Artur Rozenbush (bass), Sergey Kozakov (drums).*

VIGILIA MORTUM, a Kohtla-Jarve based brutal Death Metal band, began life in 1994 billed as MANUSCRIPT and debuted the following year with the three track 'Inquisition' demo. The opening band formation counted vocalist Radik Kaverin, guitarists Denis Savitski and Sergei Bashilov and bassist Denis Zdanovich. Subsequently, drummer Victor Petrov completed the roster. Line-up changes in the Summer of 1996 saw the exit of Bashilov and the induction of Alex Kobzar on guitar and drummer Sass Kuzmin as the evolution to VIGILIA MORTUM took place. This would be capitalised on with a 1997 cassette 'Transformation To The Dust'. VIGILIA MORTUM's membership would prove constantly fluid, drummer Konstantin Erly saw action between 1996 and 1997 before Sass Kuzmin took over and Roman Denisenko of ARMAGGEDON was installed on guitar as Kobzar decamped to join POSTMORTEM. In 1998 the bass position went to Dmitry Savin as the demo 'Shadows Of The Dead City' emerged. An album, 'Invoking', saw release in 1999. Drummer Alex Safronov bowed out in 2000 and the following year the group lost the services of bass player Denis Zdanovich and guitarist Roma Denisenko.

In 2002 the group was overhauled completely with the introduction of four MEATOPATHY members, guitarists Aleksandr and Dmitriy Samorukov, bassist Pavel and drummer Boris Hreptukov. This entire quartet opted out in 2003.

VIGILIA MORTUM's new album 'Bloody Remorse' would be scheduled for a December 2005 release through Blacksmith Productions.

Transformation To The Dust, Vigilia Mortum (1997). Intro / The Order Of Plague / Dr. Polm / Slave Of Dampground / Fear / Intro 2 / Transformation To The Dust / Creature At The Threshold / Bloody Contract / Outly.
Shadows Of The Dead City, (1998). Shadows Of The Dead City / Vigilia Mortum / A Man.
INVOKING, Vigilia Mortum (1999). Christianity's Ways Of Blood / Either A Killer Or Poet / Vigilia Mortum / Shadows Of The Dead City / The Invoking / A Man / The Happy Dead / Pretty Girl.

VIHALIHA

LOHJA, FINLAND — *Korpse-Eater (high vocals), Fukkhead (low vocals), Gordon (clean vocals / guitar / drums), Frank (bass).*

Lohja based Grindcore / Industrial act VIHALIHA was founded during the Spring of 2003 by vocalists Korpse-Eater and Fukkhead. Adding guitarist Gordon the trio, with the aid of a computer to generate bass and drum parts, cut a four song demo at their home studios in early 2004. After these sessions bassist Frank was enrolled and the band's subsequent April 2004 demo 'Viha' would be limited to 33 hand numbered copies of CD-R and the same quantity of cassette. The 21 song collection 'Liha' followed, being released that August. 6 tracks would also be recorded for a split EP in collaboration with FRENESIS, put out through Korpse-Eater's own Virkkala Rekords in November. Another proposed split release would be projected for a tie-in with British outfit HOMOEROTIC BOB, but this project fell through and the tracks duly surfaced on the 'Rotten Flesh' EP in May 2005. A Christmas only single, 'Grindmass', was issued for the December 2005 festive season.

Viha, Virkkala Independent (2004) (Limited edition 66 hand numbered copies, 33 CD-Rs, 33 cassettes). The Worst Of All / Exit Wounds / Disproportionate Bloodshed / I Kill, You Die / Dead But Screaming / Vesuri, Kirves Ja Veitsi / A Hole In Your Head / No Exit / Saw You Through / Noidankehä / Walking Disease / G.G.F.H. / Grave New World / Cut To Kill / I Severed The Genitals Of Seven People, Dumped The Corpses In The Sewer And Covered Them In Semen / Seal Your Lips / For Maggots To Devour / Bodies Lie Broken / When Insanity Takes Control / Viha.
Liha, Virkkala VIR002 (2004) (CD-R. Limited edition 51 hand numbered copies). The Fucking Insane / I Love / Porn To Die / Night Of The Killing Dead / Anusthesia / (Mas)sacred / Nekrofukk / Mortuary Rape / Decapitated / Deranged / Hiljaisten Ja Ystävällisten Koti / Kingdom Cum / Erectum / Rotten To The Gore / Leikkimaa / Swallow The Cum / Nekromance / Scenery Of Life Bashed Down / Smile When You're Dead / Liha / Lihaa Piiloon.
Vihaliha / Frenesis, Virkkala VIR003 (2004) (Split EP with FRENESIS. Paper slipcase). Unfinished Business / Too Much / Rape At Any Rate / Thrashed, Slashed, Bashed And Trashed / Nightwank / Pull The Trigger / Outro.
Rotten Flesh, Virkkala VIR004 (2005). Tight Chokehold / World Today / Perfectly Perverted / I Wanna Kill / Instrumenstrual / The Bleeding / Painkiller / Behind Your Window / Rotten Flesh.
Grindwank, Virkkala VIR006 (2005) (Split demo with HOLOGEENI). Move I / Move II / Move III / Move IV.
Grindmass, (2005) (split CD-R Christmas single with VÄLILIHA, available only during December 2005).

VII ARCANO

ITALY — *Mirko Scarpa (vocals), Marco Montagna (guitar), Mauro Diciocia (bass), Gilles Schembri (drums).*

Rome's Doom style Deathsters VII ARCANO came into being with the formulation of SEPOLCRUM during 1989 at the hand of guitarist / keyboard player Roberto Cufaro. A band line-up was forged, including guitarist / bassist Marco Montagna, for release of demo sessions 'Anteroom Of The Hell' in 1991 and 'Flowers Upon The Grave' in 1993.

A name switch to VII ARCANO would be marked by a 7" single, 'Gather My Blood Forever', in 1994. At this juncture the band comprised of vocalist Nunziati, Cufaro on guitar, Montagna on bass and De Stefano on keyboards. The band morphed again with the introduction of erstwhile OMICRON vocalist Mirko Scarpa. A former member Lord Vampyr (Alexander) famously created the notorious vampire Black Metal band THEATRE DES VAMPIRES.

However, the band line up fluxed once more upfront of a further promotion tape 'MCMXCIX' as Montagna took over guitar responsibilities, Bomboi came in on bass and Paul Soellner on drums. In 1998 VII ARCANO, undergoing yet further line up changes, Soellner founding KLIMT 1918, which bore witness to the induction of PILGRIM drummer Gilles Schembri and bass player Francesco Frasso, was signed up by the Warlord label.

The resulting 'Inner Deathscapes', produced by NOVEMBRE drummer Giuseppe Orlando, would be revealed as a fine slice of Thrash infused Death Metal. With Frasso departing just prior to recording Marco Montagna took on bass duties in the studio. Vinyl versions of the August 2001 album 'Inner Deathscapes' would include an exclusive bonus track, namely a cover of the KISS classic 'Love Gun'.

Following completion of the 2003 album 'Nothingod', which sported a cover of TESTAMENT's 'Burnt Offerings', VII ARCANO were in rehearsals with a fresh rhythm section of bassist Carlo Paolucci and drummer Francesco Struglia.

Gather My Blood Forever EP, (1994). Walpurgis Fullmoon / Dance With A Dark Dress.
INNER DEATHSCAPES, Warlord WR04CD-5490182 (2001). Intruding / Anticlockwise Cycle Of Dying / Of Suicidal Age / The Inner Deathscape / Echo Calling / Fog Path / Release Into Anguish / Necrotica Art- The Performance / Streams Of Paranoia / Descending.
NOTHINGOD, (2003). Millennium Plague / Furybound / Deathlike Blues / Final Dream / Down The Afterworld / An Assassin Charisma / Burnt Offerings / Murder Parade / Nothingod Manifest (The Crawling Race).

VILE

CONCORD, CA, USA — *Juan Urteaga (vocals), Colin Davis (guitar), Aaron Strong (guitar), Jeff Hughell (bass), Mike Hamilton (drums).*

A renowned name in extreme Death Metal circles. VILE was assembled by guitarist Colin Davis and bassist Matt "Favor" Faivre during 1996, pooling the talents of disbanded groups such as LORDS OF CHAOS, ENTROPY, SPORADIC PSYCHOSIS and THANATOPSIS. With the induction of second guitarist Jim Tkacz the band published a brace of demos, 'Unearthed' and 'Vile-ation', touring in November of 1997 in alliance with DEEDS OF FLESH. Guitarist Aaron Strong of ENTROPY and LORDS OF CHAOS was acquired in 1998.

Shortly after recording VILE's debut 'Stench Of The Deceased' album drummer Mike Hamilton made his exit to join DEEDS OF FLESH. Jim Tkacz jumped ship to DEEDS OF FLESH too. In 2002 the 'Depopulate', featuring MUDSLINGER bassist Lars Von Lowen as session man, was released on Listenable Records for Europe and Unique Leader Records in the USA.

VILE would re-issue 'Stench Of The Deceased' in 2003 to coincide with a European February / March package tour alongside MANGLED, INHUME, DISAVOWED, and SPAWN OF POSSESSION. The new version added three extra live tracks plus an unreleased studio track.

The group severed ties with singer Juan Urteaga in May of 2003, drafting a swift replacement in ILL OMEN, DAEMONICIDE and ORIGIN's James Lee. By August long standing guitarist Aaron Strong was also to depart. VILE put in a run of gigs commencing 12th February 2004 in Houston, Texas that had the band traversing North America in league with EXHUMED, HYPOCRISY and CANNIBAL CORPSE. The band's roll call for these gigs put original members Colin Davis and Matt Faivre alongside ORIGIN vocalist James Lee, lead guitarist Lucas Jaeger, a scene veteran of SUICIDE CULTURE, MINCERY and SLEEP TERROR, and Danish drummer Reno Kiilerich, a veteran of such acts as FROZEN SUN, PANZERCHRIST, 12 GAUGE, EXMORTEM and KOBEAST. The drummer stepped up a further league in March of the following year when he was recruited as session man for DIMMU BORGIR's European, South American and US 'Ozzfest' festival dates.

VILE donated their rendition of 'Cold' to the AT THE GATES tribute album, 'Slaughterous Souls—A Tribute to At The Gates' released in September 2004 through Drowned Scream Records. VILE drafted EXODUS bassist Jack Gibson in January 2005 to record a new album 'The New Age Of Chaos'. The band announced a road union with PSYCROPTIC and DECREPIT BIRTH for the 'Bloodletting North America' Summer tour.

VILE lined up with DEEDS OF FLESH, MONSTROSITY and IMPALED for the 'Gutting Europe 4' European tour beginning in Poland during late March 2006. VILE's line-up for these shows saw Colin Davis joined by an all new cast comprising the DIVINE RAPTURE, AZURE EMOTE and I.C.E. credited Mike Hrubovcak on vocals, J.J. Hrubovcak of DIVINE RAPTURE and MOURNING on second guitar, BLOOD RED THRONE, APOSTASY, UNSPOKEN NAMES, MR. CUCUMBER, DISMAL EUPHONY and THE ALL SEEING I bassist Erlend Caspersen and ex-VITAL REMAINS drummer Marco Pitruzella.

The band partnered with DEEDS OF FLESH, DECREPIT BIRTH and ODIOUS MORTEM on the 'bloodletting North America V' tour of the USA in July 2006.

STENCH OF THE DECEASED, Vile (1999). Abort (The Fetus) / Cradle Of Deceit / Surgery / Alive To Suffer / Stench ... / Terminal Existence / Severed / Persecution.

DEPOPULATE, Listenable (2002). Depopulate / Butchered / Path To Incineration / Retaliation / Engulfing Horde / Eat The Rude / Unit 731 / Interrogation Rites / Bitterness.

THE NEW AGE OF CHAOS, Listenable POSH072 (2005). Devour / Deafening Silence / The New Age Of Chaos / Suicide Warfare / Sentenced To Live / The Burning Shrines / Ritual Decapitation / Worldhunt / Forlorn.

VIOLATION

GERMANY — *Wolfgang Dreiseital (vocals), Alex Schödel (guitar), Larsen Beattie (guitar), Martin Saalfrank (bass), Claudia Reich (keyboards), Andreas Schmidt (drums).*

Melodic Death Metal band VIOLATION was convened by guitarist Alexander Schödel and singer Wolfgang Dreiseitel during 1993. By 1995 the line up had stabilised and counted Schödel, Dreiseitel, Larsen Beattie on second guitar, bassist Martin Saalfrank, keyboard player Claudia Reich and Andreas Schmidt on the drums. As such, VIOLATION recorded the inaugural demo 'Carbonized' in February 1996. Having sold some 600 copies of the tape and reaped favourable media appraisal VIOLATION took the adventurous step of booking Sweden's famous Abyss Studios to record their debut album. This move, coming in October of 1997, despite not being signed to a record company. The gamble paid off and Last Episode Records took the album 'Beyond The Graves'.

Bassist Martin Saalfrank had already signalled his intention to break away from the band prior to these sessions but maintained his duties throughout recording. VIOLATION suffered a further series of blows subsequent to the album release with Dreiseital and Beattie both opting out, the latter to concentrate on his other act CRYPTIC WINTERMOON.

The group enlisted EXTINCTION vocalist Marcus Fiessmann, guitarist Olli Riedel and Jens Löhner of CRYPTIC WINTERMOON on bass and signed to Invasion Records in 1999 for a proposed second album. However, Invasion hit financial troubles and VIOLATION signed their second record 'Moonlight's Child' over to the North American Red Stream Records. Early 2001 witnessed further changes. Jürgen Aumann became the band's new singer and Timo Grefenberg took up bass.

BEYOND THE GRAVES, Last Episode 0073542 LEP (1998). Dark Embrace / Genocide / Thuatra Dé Danann / Carbonized / Bleeding Souls / Invocation / Through The Gates Of Infinity / Bitterness / Fading Flames Of Life.

MOONLIGHT'S CHILD, Red Stream (2000). A Shattered Blind / Downfall / Trapped In Chaos / Path Of Sorrow / Nightshades / Blood Flows Through The Haze Of Time / Mortal Divinity / The Angelmaker / New God Evolution.

VIOLENT ASYLUM

ROMFORD, ESSEX, UK — *Jamie Dodd (vocals), Spencer Carter (guitar), Mark Cole (guitar), Alan Knight (bass), Wes Keenen (drums).*

Although based in Romford, Essex, Death-Thrashers VIOLENT ASYLUM have based their sound entirely on the NWoSDM. The group formed up in October of 2001, the idea actually gelling between guitarists Spencer Carter, previously with KERATOSE, and Mark Cole at a PANTERA gig, and issued the demo 'Decay' the following year. At this juncture the band was entitled DECAY. Initially Ben Prigmore handled both lead vocals and bass but he would be shifted to occupy just the bass role. Gavin from FAULTLINE took the frontman position but shortly after Prigmore exited. He would be superseded by Alan Knight but then Gavin too left. Jamie Dodd came onboard as new singer in time for the 'Decay' sessions.

A second stab at recording a demo, entitled 'Catharsis', signalled the name switch to VIOLENT ASYLUM.

Decay, Violent Asylum (2002). Vile Glory / Scars / Lie To Me / Ashes & Dreams.

Catharsis, (2003). Born From Chaos / Scars / Diabolus / Demise / Relentless.

VIOLENT HEADACHE

SPAIN — *Capo (vocals), Jordi (guitar), Chico (bass), Tonyo (drums).*

Extreme Barcelona act that blend both male and female lead vocals into a genre defying mix of Death Metal, Thrash and Grindcore. The band would issue the demo 'Attack Of The Antijetcore Argaraboys' prior to embarking on a stream of shared single releases with international acts. A 1991 shared release found the band in alliance with Italy's CRIPPLE BASTARDS and the following year VIOLENT HEADACHE united with undisputed kings of the 7" split single genre Belgium' AGATHOCLES. Other combined efforts include releases with CARCASS GRINDER, EXCRETED ALIVE, UNHOLY GRAVE and INTESTINAL DISEASE.

VIOLENT HEADACHE's 2000 album 'Bombs Of Crust' features over 50 tracks originally recorded in 1995.

Split, Psychomania (1991) (7" split single with CRIPPLE BASTARDS).
Starbation, Anaconda (1992) (7" split single with AGATHOCLES).
Condemned Childhood, Blurred 11 (1997) (7" split single with EXCRETED ALIVE). Condemned Childhood.
Trituradora De Cadaveres, Nat (1997) (7" split single with CARCASS GRINDER). Trituradora De Cadaveres.
BOMBS OF CRUST, Six Weeks (2000).

VIRULENCE

BOSTON, MA, USA — *Chris Danecek (vocals), Nick Peyer (guitar), Dave Sheaffer (bass), Darren Cesca (drums).*

VIRULENCE is a Boston, Massachusetts based, brutal styled Death Metal band initiated during 1998. The VIRULENCE pairing of Chris Danecek and drummer Darren Cesca also hold credits with GORATORY and PILLORY. Cesca also has ties to DESSICATE and ENCRIMSON'D. VIRULENCE began life as a trio with Chris Danecek handling lead vocals and bass, Nick Peyer of INCARRION on guitar and Dan Meath, of INCARRION and FACERAKE, on the drums. First product would be the EP 'The Dormant Strains', released in 2000. Following these sessions Dave Sheaffer was introduced on bass.

VIRULENCE released the full length album 'A Conflict Scenario' through Morbid Records in 2001, after which drummer Darren Cesca was drafted for "strategic bombardment and homefront security missions". Danecek and Cesca founded PILLORY in 2003. Darren Cesca joined the ranks of ARSIS in January 2007.

The Dormant Strains, JRB V006 (2000). Meme Epidemics / Evolutionary Masquerade / Cortical Reproductive Abstractions / Branne Cvicene: Defensive Drilling.
A CONFLICT SCENARIO, Morbid MR 091 (2001). Entrance / Reptilian Triangle / Painting / Texture Shock / Evolutionary Masquerade / Cementing With Introspection / Pipeline Dialogue / Your Own Palestine.

VIRULENT BLESSING

TURKU, FINLAND — *Heikki Raisio (vocals), Kalle Salminen (guitar), Tapani Nurminen (guitar), Markus Vainio (bass), Sami Rantanen (drums).*

Turku's Death Metal act VIRULENT BLESSING, established in 2004, comprised former members of TUMULT in guitarist Petri Salmio, also of MAGGOTTHOLAMIA, singer Heikki Raisio, also of RELICS OF DISORDER, and guitarist Kalle Salminen. The band's rhythm section involved bassist Markus Vainio, from MAHAPRALAYA, and the CUMBEAST and MAGGOTTHOLAMIA credited Sami Rantanen on drums.

A self titled demo emerged in 2004. Initially Vesa Suhonen, of CUMBEAST and MAGGOTTHOLAMIA fronted the band, but he would be superseded by Heikki Raisio. MAGGOTTHOLAMIA replaced Salmio.

TUMULT issued the three track promo 'Essence Of Extinction' in 2005. In July the following year Magik Art Entertainment partnered TUMULT with FUNERAL SPEECH, FULLY CONSUMED and VOMINATION on the split album '4 Ways Of Brutality'.

Virulent Blessing, Virulent Blessing (2004). Divine Overdose / I Skin You / Circularsaw Dismemberment.
Essence Of Extinction, Virulent Blessing (2005) (Demo). Celebration Of Human Decay / Ravishing Deceit / Effigy Of The Parasite.
4 WAYS OF BRUTALITY, Magik Art Entertainment (2006) (Split album with VOMINATION, FULLY CONSUMED and FUNERAL SPEECH). A Cold Wind Of Sorrow (VOMINATION) / Yog-Sothoth (VOMINATION) / Vomination (VOMINATION) / Divine Overdose (VIRULENT BLESSING) / Revulsion (VIRULENT BLESSING) / Hate Aspect (VIRULENT BLESSING) / I Skin You (VIRULENT BLESSING) / Flagellation Of The Dead (FUNERAL SPEECH) / Bloody Deeds (FUNERAL SPEECH) / Man Of Peace (FULLY CONSUMED) / Doldrums (FULLY CONSUMED) / Circle Of Hate (FULLY CONSUMED).

VISCERAL BLEEDING

KALMAR, SWEDEN — *Dennis Röndum (vocals), Peter Persson (guitar), Marcus Nilsson (guitar), Calle Löfgren (bass), Tobias Persson (drums).*

Kalmar based extreme Death Metal act forged by guitarist Peter Persson and Niklas Dewerud. Frontman Dennis Röndum would also be active as drummer for SPAWN OF POSSESSION. In their formative stages the band members went under the title of SECRETION. Demos included the 'Internal Decomposition' set in September 2000. Following recording of the April 2002 'Remnants Of Deprivation' album Dewerud become bass player for SPAWN OF POSSESSION. Dewerud would be replaced by Tobias 'Rotten Boy' Persson, former frontman of Hässleholm Death Metal combo LUNGSPIT.

In side activity during 2002, Dennis Röndum united with the BUTCHERY duo of guitarist Juha Helttunen and drummer Tobias Israelsson to aid STRANGULATION on session vocals for the demo 'Carnage In Heaven'.

VISCERAL BLEEDING entered Flatpig Studios in Malmö with producer Robert Ahrling to cut a second album 'As Fury Unfolds' in December 2003. This album title would be subsequently switched to 'Transcend Into Ferocity' as the band signed to Neurotic Records for its release. Vocalist Dennis Röndum decamped in June 2004 in order to prioritise SPAWN OF POSSESSION. The band united with OBITUARY and MASTER for the 'The Legends Are Back' dubbed European tour, commencing in early October 2004.

VISCERAL BLEEDING had their debut album, 'Remnants Of Deprivation', reissued under the revised title of 'Remnants Revived' in April of 2005 by Neurotic Records. This expanded version, having been re-mastered by Scott Hull, added bonus material in the form of cover versions of CANNIBAL CORPSE's 'Stripped, Raped & Strangled' and DISMEMBER's 'Dreaming In Red' plus an alternate version of VISCERAL BLEEDING's own 'Carved Down To The Bone'. The video extras comprised a studio clip and three live songs filmed on the October 2004 tour. VISCERAL BLEEDING partnered with NAILED and CONDEMNED for UK dates in May 2005. The band, drafting new singer Martin Pedersen, allied with DEICIDE, WYKKED WYTCH and PROSTITUTE DISFIGUREMENT for European shows throughout October and November, taking in the UK, Ireland, France, Belgium, Holland, Germany, Switzerland, Austria, Hungary, Croatia, Czech Republic, Spain and Italy. VISCERAL BLEEDING parted ways with guitarist Marcus Nilsson in May 2006. The group announced they would be hooking up with DEICIDE and PSYCROPTIC for a European tour in January 2007.

Internal Decomposition, Visceral Bleeding (2000) (Demo). State Of Putrefaction / Gasping For Air / Explosive Surgery / Time To Retaliate.
REMNANTS OF DEPRIVATION, Retribute RET 008 (2002). Spreader Of Disease (Burn The Bitch) / Carved Down To The Bone / Gasping ... / Remnants Of Deprivation / State Of Putrefaction / To Disgrace Condemned / Time To Retaliate / Butcher Knife Impalement / Explosive Surgery.
TRANSCEND INTO FEROCITY, Neurotic NRT040002 (2004). Merely Parts Remain / Fed To The Dogs / Indulged In Self Mutilation / Fury Unleashed / Trephine The Malformed / All Flesh ... / Clenched Fist

Obedience / Fire Took His Face / When Pain Came To Town / Fury Unleashed (Video).

ABSORBING THE DISARRAY, Neurotic NRT060012 (2006). Bi-polar / Disgust The Vile / Despise Defined / Perpetual Torment Commence / Emulated Sense: Failure / Rip The Flesh / Absorbing The Disarray / Awakened By Blood / Beyond The Realms Of Reason / Bring Forth The Bedlam / Demise Of The One That Conquered / Rip The Flesh (Video) / Disgust The Vile (Video).

VITAL REMAINS

RI, USA — *Jeff Gruslin (vocals), Paul Flynn (guitar), Tony Lazaro (guitar), Joe Lewis (bass), A. Alonzo (drums).*

An illustrious name in Death Metal circles. Although firmly in the Death Metal camp, Rhode Island's VITAL REMAINS infuse their whole being with blasphemous content. The band's first line-up for recording of the demo 'Reduced To Ashes' in 1989 comprised vocalist Jeff Gruslin, guitarists Paul Flynn and Tony Lazaro, bass player Tom Supkow and drummer Chris Dupont. A further tape 'Excruciating Pain', with new drummer 'Ace' Alonzo, and a 7" single for French label Thrash 'The Black Mass'. Recorded in November 1990, 'The Black Mass' shifted over 1500 copies in two weeks. This first commercial outing bolstered the band's reputation and signaled a deal with Deaf Records, a subsidiary of British label Peaceville Records. VITAL REMAINS released the 'Let Us Pray' album in August 1992, issued through Grind Core International in the USA. Peaceville had also issued a 1993 split clear vinyl 7" single, 'Amulet Of The Conquering', on clear vinyl, in collaboration with MORTA SKULD, as part of their exclusive and now exceptionally sought after Collectors Club series. A three month US road alliance across the USA with AUTOPSY, kicking off in May 1993, led into sessions for a second album, 'Into Cold Darkness', released in March 1995. The latter closed out with a cover version of CELTIC FROST's 'Dethroned Emperor'. The band also cut a rendition of VENOM's 'Countess Bathory', this song only included on Peaceville's 1996 compilation 'Under The Sign Of The Sacred Star'.

By the recording of March 1997's 'Forever Underground', the group's first offering for French label Osmose Productions, VITAL REMAINS had trimmed down to a trio of Lazaro, bassist Joseph Lewis and drummer David Suzuki.

VITAL REMAINS were included on the 1999 tribute to JUDAS PRIEST album 'Hell Bent For Metal' covering 'You've Got Another Thing Comin'. Another cover executed that same year would be their interpretation of MERCYFUL FATE's 'To One Far Away / Come To The Sabbath', featured on 'The Unholy Sounds Of The Demon Bells—A Tribute To Mercyful Fate' collection issued via Poland's Still Dead Productions.

Vocalist Jeff Gruslin was replaced by Thorn. VITAL REMAINS released the 'Dawn Of The Apocalypse' album in November 1999. However, in 2000 VITAL REMAINS sacked vocalist Thorns as the remaining band members cited alleged drug abuse. VITAL REMAINS re-hired Gruslin in time for European dates as part of the 'No Mercy' festival package alongside Poland's VADER, Brazil's REBAELLIUN and Germany's FLESHCRAWL.

Late 2000 found Gruslin back on the scene as part of the prominent WOLFEN SOCIETY project, which included erstwhile ACHERON man Vincent Crowley, INCANTATION's Kyle Severn and Lord Ahriman of DARK FUNERAL. The Dutch label Cryonics would re-issue the debut demo 'Reduced To Ashes' in CD format.

The band would enlist ex-MONSTROSITY and DEATH bassist Kelly Conlon but following a brief run with the band he would bail out necessitating lead guitarist Ron Greene taking on bass for the interim. However, in April 2002 vocalist Jake Raymond and lead guitarist Ron Greene parted ways with the band, founding a fresh project entitled CAST OF VENGEANCE in league with former VITAL REMAINS bassist and frontman, Joe Lewis. Greene would also unite with LEUKORRHEA.

In a major coup, the band pulled none other than Glen Benton of DEICIDE infamy in to record lead vocals for the 'Dechristianize' album. Recorded at Morrisound Recordings the recording line-up consisted of Tony Lazaro on guitars and David Suzuki on guitars, leads, bass and drums. VITAL REMAINS debut gig with Benton would be the 2003 Milwaukee Metalfest.

The band hooked up with VEHEMENCE for one week at the end of August 2004. Suzuki would enroll into the ranks of DEICIDE for their October European tour dates. VITAL REMAINS European headline gigs in October and November, traversing Austria, Italy, Switzerland, France, Spain, Portugal, Luxembourg and Holland, saw NOMINON and Germany's HIDDEN IN THE FOG as support act.

In early 2006 ex-VITAL REMAINS drummer Marco Pitruzella joined the ranks of US Death Metal band VILE to conduct their 'Gutting Europe' tour during March and April. The band conducted West Coast "God Killers" shows alongside DEICIDE, seeing Glen Benton doing double frontman duty each night, CREMATORIUM and Oregon's DESOLATION. Shows commencing in late May had VITAL REMAINS hooked up with INCANTATION, SIN OF ANGELS and New Zealanders DAWN OF AZAZEL. VITAL REMAINS teamed up with DISMEMBER, GRAVE, DEMIRICOUS and WITHERED for a North American tour commencing September 29th.

The band line-up at this juncture comprised a core trio of Glen Benton, Dave Suzuki and Tony Lazaro plus live session members bassist Brian Hobbie, from CATASTROPHIC, 420 and INTERNAL BLEEDING, with Antonio Donadeo, from STILLNESS BLADE, UNDERTAKERS, TRAITOR, NECROTORTURE, VIRULENT RE-SHAPES and EXHUMER on drums.

The group, having utilised Mana Recording Studio in Florida, wrapped up new album recordings in mid January 2007. When advance copies of 'Icons Of Evil', set for April issue, were distributed feedback from retailers caused such concern in regard to the cover art, depicting Jesus Christ's hands being pinned to the crucifixion cross, a decision was made to put the album out in a discreet slip case. Tony Lazaro stated "The record's scheduled to come out around Easter, and apparently the subject of Christ being nailed to his cross is a bit extra-sensitive around that time."

VITAL REMAINS teamed up with LIGHT THIS CITY and WITH PASSION for summer US shows.

Reduced To Ashes, Vital Remains (1989) (Demo). Vital Remains / Smoldering Burial / Morbid Death / Reduced To Ashes / More Brains / Slaughter Shack.

Excruciating Pain, (1990) (Demo). Intro / Human Sacrifice / Resurrected / Fallen Angels / Excruciating Pain / Nocturnal Blasphemy / Outro.

The Black Mass, Thrash (1991) (7" single). Of Pure Unholyness / Frozen Terror.

The Black Mass, Thrash THR008 (1991). Of Pure Unholyness / Frozen Terror.

LET US PRAY, Peaceville CDVILE 58 (1992). War In Paradise / Of Pure Unholiness / Ceremony Of The Seventh Circle / Uncultivated Grave / Malevolent Invocation / Isolated Magick / Cult Of The Dead / Frozen Terror / Amulet Of The Conquering.

LET US PRAY, Deaf 009 (1992) (Vinyl). War In Paradise / Of Pure Unholiness / Ceremony Of The Seventh Circle / Uncultivated Grave / Malevolent Invocation / Isolated Magick / Cult Of The Dead / Frozen Terror.

Amulet Of The Conquering, Peaceville Collectors CC 4 (1993) (Limited edition 7" clear vinyl. Split single with MORTA SKULD). Sacrificial Rite (MORTA SKULD) / Amulet Of The Conquering (VITAL REMAINS).

Excruciating Pain, Wild Rags WRR-045 (1995). Intro / Human Sacrifice / Resurrected / Fallen Angels / Excruciating Pain / Nocturnal Blasphemy / Outro.

INTO COLD DARKNESS, Peaceville CDVILE 48 (1995). Immortal Crusade / Under The Moons Fog / Crown Of The Black Hearts / Scrolls

Of A Millenium Past / Into Cold Darkness / Descent Into Hell / Angels Of Blasphemy / Dethroned Emperor.

FOREVER UNDERGROUND, Osmose Productions OPCD 050 (1997). Forever Underground / Battle Ground / I Am God / Farewell To The Messiah / Eastern Journey / Divine In Fire.

REDUCED TO ASHES, Cryronics CRY02 (1999). Vital Remains / Smoldering Ritual / Morbid Death / Reduced To Ashes / More Brains / Slaughter Shack.

DAWN OF THE APOCALYPSE, Osmose Productions OPCD 077 (1999). Intro / Black Magick Curse / Dawn Of The Apocalypse / Sanctity In Blasphemous Ruin / Came No Ray Of Light / Flag Of Victory / Behold The Throne Of Chaos / The Night Has A Thousand Eyes / Societe Des Luciferiens.

DECHRISTIANIZE, Olympic OLY 0229-2 (2003). Let The Killing Begins / Dechristianize / Infidel / Devoured Elysium / Saviour To None… / Failure For All / Unleash Hell / Rush Of Deliverance / At War With God / Entwined By Vengeance.

HORRORS OF HELL, Century Media CMR 8254-2 (2006) (Limited edition 5000 copies). Of Pure Unholyness / Frozen Terror / Human Sacrifice / Resurrected / Fallen Angels / Excruciating Pain / Nocturnal Blasphemy / Vital Remains / Smoldering Burial / Morbid Death / Reduced To Ashes / More Brains / Slaughter Shack.

ICONS OF EVIL, Century Media (2007).

VITALITY

NORWAY — *Sven-Erik Lind (vocals), Bengt Olsson (guitar), Karl Fredrik Lind (guitar), Håvar Wormdahl (bass), Glenn-David Lind (drums).*

VITALITY was a precursor to DROTTNAR, one of a growing number of 'unblack' Christian Black Metal styled acts. The group was formulated during 1996 as VITALITY, boasting an initial roster comprising four family members, brothers and cousins, vocalist Sven-Erik Lind, guitarist Karl Fredrik Lind, bassist Bjarne Peder Lind and drummer Glenn-David Lind. As VITALITY the group issued an opening five song demo in May of 1997. A second tape, 'A White Realm', started to incorporate ancestral and Viking themes and this musical persuasion prompted the adoption of a new title DROTTNAR.

The British based Plankton Records label released the debut album 'Spiritual Battle', assembled from VITALITY and DROTTNAR demo sessions.

Vitality, Vitality (1997) (Demo). Away From The Destruction / Doom Of Antichrist / Missing Souls / Dead And Rotten / Frykt Ikke.

VITUPERATION

STOCKHOLM, SWEDEN — *Jonas Mähl (vocals), Sebastian Zingerman (vocals / guitar), Tor Steinholtz (guitar), Simon Zingerman (bass), Rodrigo Valenzuela (drums).*

Stockholm based Death Metal band fronted by PSYKOTISK, KALL DÖD and TORTURE ETERNAL singer Jonas Mähl. Guitarist Sebbe Zingerman is also a TORTURE ETERNAL member. The group was created in mid 2004 by guitarists Sebastian Zingerman, then of HERETIQUE and also handling lead vocals, and Tor Steinholtz, from DIAMOND. They were joined by Zingerman sibling, Simon, on bass and in early 2005 Joakim Wallgren, of VALKRJA repute, took command of the drums for the band's first concert at Stenhamra Gård. Following this show Jonas Mähl took over as lead vocalist.

VITUPERATION first live demo, 'Live At Bro', was recorded at the Bro Fri Scen on 28th May 2005. 'Nothing Is Sacred', laid down at Offbeat Studio in Järfälla, followed in April 2006. Original drummer Joakim Wallgren, quitting to join DISDAINED, was replaced by Bolivian Rodrigo Valenzuela.

Shugatraa (Jonas Mähl) of VITUPERATION also mentors solo project ÅNGEST and operated Black Metal project ANNIHILATE in alliance with Sinneskog, of INTERRED, issuing the January 2007 demo 'My Path'.

Live At Bro, Vituperation (2005) (Live demo. Limited edition 20 copies). World Of Hate / Nekrofilens Fantasi / She, Myself And I.

Nothing Is Sacred, Vituperation (2006) (Demo). Urge And Need (For The Passion To Bleed) / Nekrofilens Fantasi / She, Myself And I / Humanity Of Life / World Of Hate / Nothing Is Sacred.

VOLATILE

SYDNEY, NSW, AUSTRALIA — *Kane (vocals), Shane (guitar), Demon Frog (bass), Nigel Nofriends (drums).*

Sydney's VOLATILE, renowned for gore soaked live shows involving exploding mannequins. The band first made their presence felt with the track 'Scientific Experiment' on the 'Warhead vol. 1' compilation album. A full length record for Warhead, 'Quarantine', emerged the following year. None too surprisingly had trouble pressing their album 'Get Off The Road Ya Farkin' poofta Bastard!'. Eventually VOLATILE manufactured the album themselves in 1999, following up with the cassette 'Barbecues And Gore'. They called it a day in February of 2003. Guitarist Shane teamed up with BLUDGEONER whilst bassist Demon Frog persevered with his Grindcore outfit EXHIBIT A.

QUARANTINE, Warhead WH17 (1996). Escape Reality / Quarantine / Bleed For Me / Horror Hospital / Scientific Experiment / Dust / Scarred / Friction Rash.

GET OFF THE ROAD YA FARKIN' POOFTA BASTARD!, (1999). Eating Dead Sheilas Cunt / Driller Killer / Lying In Wait / Annoying Shit / Blood Seeps / Gay Mardi Gras Massacre / Pooey Pants / Constable Kick Ass / Bitch Slapping / Flemo Markets / Gook Off / Grease Lightning / Sod Off / Pissed Cunt / Dimension / Monga / 666 / Monga's Revenge.

VOMIT

OSLO, NORWAY — *Kittel Kittilsen (vocals / bass), Lars (guitar), Tommy (guitar), Torben Grue (drums).*

The charmingly named VOMIT were certainly among one the very first of countless bands to use the term 'vomit' (or some variation thereof) as their band name. Oslo's VOMIT were one of the earliest examples of a style that was the predecessor to Black Metal. This is not surprising as vocalist Kittel Kittilsen and drummer Torben Grue eventually joined Norway's Black Metal pioneers MAYHEM in 1988. Prior to the exodus that ultimately resulted in the dissolution of the band, VOMIT recorded a demo on 31st January 1987 entitled 'Rot In Hell'. They remain an interesting footnote in the lineage of extreme Metal.

Kittel Kittelsen would also work with BØRRE OG BlØDERNE and KVIKKSØLVGUTTENE.

Rot In Hell, Vomit demo (1987). Armies Of Hell / Damnation Of Sin / Dark Abyss / Rotting Flesh / Demencid / Telemarksvingen.

VOMIT REMNANTS

JAPAN — *Toshiyasu Kusayanagi (vocals), Takahiro Kuwabara (guitar), Atsoyuki Katou (guitar), Ryo Nagamazu (bass), Keisuke Tsuboi (drums).*

Uncompromising Death Metal from Tokyo in a deliberately mimicked American old school style. VOMIT REMNANTS made their mark with the demos 'In The Name Of Vomit' in 1997 and 'Brutally Violated' a year later. Both of these sessions would feature FLESHMANGLER vocalist Shinjiro who would leave the fold in 1999. For the 'Supreme Entity' album, which included a cover of SOIL OF FATE's 'Faces Of The Deceased', guitarist Toshiyasu Kusayanagi switched to lead vocals.

Touring saw an appearance at the 1999 Ohio 'Deathfest' and European shows in alliance with FLESHLESS and GODLESS TRUTH as the band drafted second guitarist Atsuyuki Katou.

VOMIT REMNANTS toured America in April 2001 on their 'Extermination' dates billed alongside VEHEMENCE, BRODEQUIN and MORGUE. The band would also cut a version of 'Mass Obliteration' for a SUFFOCATION tribute album released by Repulsive Echo Records. Singer Toshiyasu Kusayanagi would subsequently found a new act entitled WOUNDEEP.

The band would feature on the first Tokyo 'Deathfest' in April 2005 at the Shibuya Cyclone, joining a billing comprising ETERNAL RUIN, DISGORGE, GODLESS TRUTH and fellow Japanese bands DISCONFORMITY and WOUNDEEP. VOMIT REMNANTS signed to Unique Leader Records for a debut full-length album.

SUPREME ENTITY, Macabre Mementos (1999). Putrifying Dead Flesh / My Blessed Sickness / Decomposed Of Structure / Rotted Human Waste / Macabre Memories / Engorgement / Faces Of The Deceased / Murderous Thoughts Determined.

INDEFENSIBLE VEHEMENCE, Supreme Musick (2001).

VOMITORY

FORSHAGA, SWEDEN — *Ronnie Olsson (vocals), Ulf Dalgren (guitar), Urban Gustafsson (guitar), Bengt Sund (bass), Tobias Gustafsson (drums).*

Swedish Death Metal originally fronted by Ronnie Olsson, also known as Ronnie Ripper—bassist for GEHENNAH. Olsson had also issued a 1993 demo, 'Grim Clouds', from his solo Black Metal project GRINNING MOON. VOMITORY was first assembled in Forshaga during 1989, the original formation including NEZGAROTH guitarist Ulf Dalegren. Debut product would be the 1992 'Vomitory' demo cassette. Between the June 1993 'Moribund' single, issued via Swiss imprint Witchhunt, and 1997 album 'Raped In Their Own Blood' released on Fadeless Records, VOMITORY released a 1994 demo tape 'Through Sepulcharal Shadows'. Supporting the 'Blood Rapture' album VOMITORY embarked upon a ten date tour of Poland during October of 2002 co-headlining with MONSTROSITY and backed by TRAUMA, SCEPTIC, LOST SOUL, DISSENTER, and CONTEMPT.

In October of 2003 it would be learned that drummer Tobias Gustafsson had united with THE PROJECT HATE duo of guitarist Lord K and vocalist Jörgen Sandström alongside SANCTIFICATION bassist Tomas Elofsson to found an "old school" Death Metal band. Gustafsson would also lend his skills as a producer for the DISOWNED demo 'Progressive Death'.

VOMITORY's fifth album, 'Primal Massacre' recorded at Studio Kuling in Örebro with producer Henrik Larsson, was set for April 2004 release. To promote the record VOMITORY formed up part of the European heavyweight 'No Mercy' festivals commencing 29th March, sharing billing with SPAWN OF POSSESSION, HYPOCRISY, KATAKLYSM, CARPATHIAN FOREST, CANNIBAL CORPSE, PREJUDICE and EXHUMED. VOMITORY lost the services of their frontman, but by September had announced they were to persevere as a quartet. European dates scheduled for May of 2005 witnessed an alliance with EXHUMED, ROTTEN SOUND and PROSTITUTE DISFIGUREMENT. In October VOMITORY, closing a fifteen year tenure, parted ways with guitarist Ulf Dalegren. Scheduled gigs across the UK, Ireland, The Netherlands and Sweden, supported by Welsh act DESECRATION, in November took place as planned with Lord Kenth Philipsson of THE PROJECT HATE and GOD AMONG INSECTS acting as fill-in guitarist. The following month it was announced that VOMITORY had found their new permanent guitarist in DESPIRITED and THE LAW man Peter Östlund.

In September 2006 Animate Records announced it was to re-issue both 1996's 'Raped In Their Own Blood' and 1999's 'Redemption' on limited vinyl versions of 666 copies each. That same year Olsson was fronting a fresh side project, the groove orientated Hard Rock band TURBOCHARGED.

VOMITORY, working with producer Rikard Löfgren, entered Leon Music Studios outside Karlstad on December 3rd to begin recording their sixth album 'Terrorize Brutalize Sodomize'.

Vomitory, Vomitory (1992) (Cassette demo). Moribund / Untouchable Challenge / Undivulged.

Moribund, Witchhunt 9309 (1993). Moribund / Dark Grey Epoch.

Vomitory, Vomitory (1993). On Black Winds Gone / Into A Passage / Silvery Moonlight / Into Winter Through Sorrow / Under Empty Skies.

Through Sepulchral Shadows, Vomitory (1994) (Demo). Through Sepulchral Shadows / Thorns / Sad Fog Over Sinister Runes.

RAPED IN THEIR OWN BLOOD, Fadeless FAD 002 (1996). Nerve Gas Clouds / Raped In Their Own Blood / Dark Grey Epoch / Pure Death / Through Sepulchural Shadows / Inferno / Sad Forgotten Sinister Runes / Into Winter Through Sorrow / Perdition / Thorns.

Vomitory/Murder Corporation, Hangnail Productions (1999) (Split EP with MURDER CORPORATION). The Voyage / Dinga Linga Lena.

1989—1999, Vomitory (1999) (10 year anniversary picture disc. Limited to 667 copies). The Art Of War / Dead Cold / Undivulged / Extremity Retained / Christ Passion.

REDEMPTION, Fadeless FAD 005 (1999). The Voyage / Forty Seconds Bloodbath / Forever In Gloom / Heaps Of Blood / Embraced By Pain / Redemption / Ashes Of Mourning Life / Partly Dead.

REVELATION NAUSEA, Metal Blade MB14350 (2000). Revelation Nausea / The Corpsegrinder Experience / Beneath The Soil / Under Clouds Of Blood / The Art Of War / When Silence Conquers / Chapter Of Pain / The Holocaust / Exhaling Life / 9mm Salvation.

BLOOD RAPTURE, Metal Blade MB14391 (2002). Chaos Fury / Hollow Retribution / Blessed And Forsaken / Madness Prevails / Redeemed In Flames / Nailed, Quartered, Consumed / Eternity Appears / Rotting Hill / Blood Rapture.

PRIMAL MASSACRE, Metal Blade MB14486 (2004). Primal Massacre / Gore Apocalypse / Stray Bullet Kill / Epidemic (Created To Kill) / Demons Divine / Autopsy Extravaganza / Retaliation / Condemned By Pride / Cursed Revelations / Chainsaw Surgery.

TERRORIZE BRUTALIZE SODOMIZE, Metal Blade (2007). Eternal Trail Of Corpses / Scavenging The Slaughtered / Terrorize Brutalize Sodomize / The Burning Black / Defiled And Inferior / March Into Oblivion / Whispers From The Dead / Heresy / Flesh Passion / Cremation Ceremony.

VOMITURITION

VAASA, FINLAND — *Keijo Bagge (vocals), Mika Aalto (guitar), Mikko Hannuksela (guitar), Harri Huhtalla (bass), Kai Hahto (drums).*

VOMITURITION started life in Vaasa as a quartet, founded by the erstwhile CARTILAGE collective of guitarist Mikko Hannuksela, bassist Harri Huhtalla and drummer Kai Hahto. The group's first recordings surfaced a 1992 demo 'Expecto Ressurectionem Mortuorum'. The debut 1992 7" EP, 'Flesheater Musicians On Their Last Supper' on the Laktoosi label, had Matti Kovero on bass and Keijo Bagge, of BURLESQUE and UTTERVOID, on second guitar. VOMITURITION signed to Germany's Invasion Records for a 1994 album entitled 'Head Tales'. The July 1995 album effort 'A Left Over' found Bagge concentrating on lead vocals and Harri Huhtalla on bass.

Post VOMITURITION vocalist Keijo Bagge and guitarist Mika Aalto went on to ROTTEN SOUND. Hahto would also gain credits with ENOCHIAN CRESCENT, WINTERSUN, AGRESSOR, ARTHEMESIA and ROTTEN SOUND. Huhtalla meantime went on to join THROES OF DAWN.

Flesheater Musicians On Their Last Supper, Laktoosi (1992). Flesheater Musicians On Their Last Supper / Entitled Murder / Horrors Of The Mansion / A Journey Through Life.

Expecto Ressurectionem Mortuorum, Vomiturition (1992) (Demo). Absurd Manslaughter / Desecration / Deathlike Silence.

HEAD TALES, Vomiturition I.R. 004CD (1994). Inside The Depths Of Mind / Malignancy / Falling / Close Down Time / One's Belief / Ancient Psychotherapy / Olet Vitun Tyhmä (You're Fucking Stupid).

Promo 95, Vomiturition (1995) (Demo). Debility / Principles Of Abuse / Dominion.

A LEFTOVER, Invasion I.R. 014CD (1995). Sacred Tree The Pain / A Beast Revived / Depression / A Leftover / Head Tales / Insucceded / Expectations / Trifle / Improvement—Unimprovement / Extinction / Abandonment / Malleus Maleficarum.

VORE

VORE

FAYETTEVILLE, AR, USA — *John Voelker (vocals / guitar), Page Townsley (vocals / guitar), Glen Wheeler (bass), Brian Marcinkiewicz (drums).*

Northwestern Arkansas Death Metal act brought into life during 1994 by vocalist / guitarists John Voelker and Page Townsley, both former members of MAUSOLEUM. Inducting drummer Brian Marcinkiewicz, and shortly after bassist Glen Wheeler, VORE was duly assembled. 400 copies of the 1995 'To Devour' demo were manufactured. The response to this session smoothed the way to the EP 'Dead Kings Eyes' delivered in 1997. Further exposure internationally with the band's rendition of 'Inner Self' to the 1999 Dwell Records SEPULTURA tribute 'World Of Pain'. That year the band would also perform at the Milwaukee Metalfest.

Remy Cameron joined VORE as their new drummer in early December 2002. A 2006 opus, entitled 'Maleficus', was recorded by Aaron Allen at Buzzwo studios in Tulsa, Oklahoma and mixed and mastered by Colin Davis at Imperial Mastering in Pecheco, California.

Dead Kings Eyes EP, Frozen Solid (1997). Suffer The Slave / Dead Kings Eyes / Summon The Nameless / Right Cross / Albion / Bring Me Back.
LORD OF STORMS, Frozen Solid (2001). Veils Of Oblivion / Godslayer / Host Of Abominations / To Be God / Lurker Above / Lost Nation / Agony / Opaque / Primordial Conquest / Forging A New Vision.

VULGAR PIGEONS

SAN FRANCISCO, CA, USA — *Paul Ponitkoff (vocals / bass), Mike Gilbert (guitar), Jeff Lenormand (guitar), John Gotelli (drums).*

Despite the quirky band name San Francisco's VULGAR PIGEONS, forged by the former BENUMB rhythm section of bassist Paul Ponitkoff and John Gotelli in September of 1998, deliver starkly uncompromising yet experimental Grindcore style brutal Death Metal. Both Ponitkoff and Gotelli would also be operational with Christian Death Metal band TORTURED CONSCIENCE.

The VULGAR PIGEONS line-up would be rounded off with the addition of guitarists Mike Gilbert and Jeff Lenormand. A debut six track 7" single, 'Citric Snot', released through Nonsense Records, surfaced in the Autumn of 1999 which triggered a hectic schedule of gigging. A second 7", 'Genetic Predisposition', was cut for the Howling Bull label. CD formats added bonus tracks and live material from a KZSU radio session. The band also donated a track 'Skullcap' to the 625 Records compilation 'Barbaric Thrash Detonation'. Live work around this period included a tour of the Pacific North Coast billed with YELLOW MACHINEGUN and a showing at the annual San Bernadino 'November To Dismember' festival.

VULGAR PIGEONS would pique the interest of Necropolis Records offshoot Deathvomit, donating their version of 'Corporeal Jigsore Quandary' to the CARCASS tribute album 'Requiems Of Revulsion'. A full length debut 'Summary Execution', produced by Larry Santiago, would follow.

VULGAR PIGEONS added vocalist Dave Levya, who also operates SHRINE OF SCARS, during March of 2002.

Citric Snot EP, Nonsense (1998). Citric Snot / E.T. In The Gutter / Nothing Left / Silence / Vodka & Salsa / Carney Lansford.
Genetic Predisposition EP, Howling Bull (1999). Pukeweed / Taken From / Quiet / U.T.I. (Urinary Tract Infection) / Adv. Of Doom Rogers.
GENETIC PREDISPOSITION, Howling Bull (2000). Pukeweed / Taken From / Quiet / U.T.I. (Urinary Tract Infection) / Adv. Of Doom Rogers / Citric Snot / E.T. In The Gutter / Nothing Left / Silence / Vodka & Salsa / Carney Lansford / De Atras Para A Delante / Citric Snot (Live) / SkullCap (Live) / SeaSick (Live) / T.F.S. (Time For Sleep) (Live) / Nothing Left (Live).
SUMMARY EXECUTION, Deathvomit (2001). Hymnal Of The Misanthrope / Empty The Streets / Skullcap / Swelling / Carve / Stumbling Into The Crossfire / MSG / Lampshade Desire / Follow The Hum / Flip Off Your Boss / Process Of Elimination / Sunderland Sickness / Police = Shit / Intermission / Pharmaceutical Knockout / River Rat / Aggro-Culture / Colonizing The Nearest Habitual Planet / Corporate Morgue / 100 Feet Off The Roadway / Fuck The Police (Bump) / In The Hands Of A Benevolent Chimpanzee Scientist / Permanent Speechlessness / (T.F.S.) Time For Sleep / Measure Of Loss / Foreshadowing Of Ignorance.

VULTURE

ITAPETININGA, SP, BRAZIL — *Adauto Medeiros Xavier (vocals / guitar), Yuri Schumamn (guitar), Max Schumann (bass), André M. Xavier (drums).*

VULTURE, an Itapetininga based Death Metal outfit dating to 1996, issued the demo tape 'Dreams Of Despair' in 1998 as their opening shot. The group had been founded by guitarist Adauto Medeiros Xavier and vocalist / drummer Marcelo Machado Brizzotti. Subsequently Lucas Guidi was added on bass guitar and Leandro Rodrigues took over on drums.

In 1999 more changes saw the recruitment of second guitarist Yuri Schumamn and new drummer André Barros. The cassette 'Death Metal Live' followed in 1999 upfront of a self-financed 2000 album 'A Call For The Ancients'. VULTURE evolved yet again in 2001, André M. Xavier manning the drums and Felipe Camargo Munhoz enlisted on bass.

VULTURE spent 2004 working on a new album 'Test Of Fire'. This opus saw release in December 2005 through Die Hard Records. Max Schumann would be the new man on bass guitar.

Demo Ensaio 96, (1996) (Demo). Sword Of Thunder / The Death / Deads In Dawn / Torments Of War / Brutal Wrath / Through The Eyes Of Vulture.
Dreams Of Despair, (1998) (Demo). Vampire Empire / Fast To Your End / Confessions Of A Hangman / Dreams Of Despair.
Death Metal Live, (1999) (Demo). Death Metal Ways / Confessions Of A Hangman / Abstract / Vampire Empire / Countess Bathory.
A CALL FOR THE ANCIENTS, Vulture (2000). Prelude To Evil Incarnation / Even Death May Die / Kill Or Not To Kill / Vlad Tepes (The Impaler) / Revenge / Sail Of Charon / The Beast Within / In Darkness / Certificate Of Death.
HELLRAISED ABOMINATIONS, Vulture (2002). Son Of Darkness / Bad Omen / Carpe Necrum / The Vulture's Path / Unholy Inquisition / Dead God.
TEST OF FIRE, Die Hard DHR017 (2005). Lobotomy / Evil War Domination / Dead Man Walking / Silence Of The Lambs / Walls Of Flesh / Vicious Void / Empalação Brutal / Reanimator / World Of The Fallen.

WACO JESUS

IL, USA — *Kevin Menssen (guitar), Dave Kibler (guitar), Nick Null (drums).*

Illinois extreme Grindcore. Founded during 1994 by guitarist Kevin Menssen WACO JESUS cut an opening demo in 1995. Originally Brad of MALEDICTION was responsible for secondary guitar with Jamie on vocals and Takashi on the drums. Line up changes saw the enrollment of LIVIDITY guitarist Dave Kibler and drummer Nick Null in 1997. The scatological collage art for the band's debut 'The Destruction Of Commercial Scum' for United Guttural Records proved the band held no qualms when it came to delivering controversial content. Null died in 2002 but WACO JESUS persevered by enlisting Johnny Baker as replacement.

The photographic sleeve of 2003's 'Filth' record, released by the German Morbid concern, went beyond all that had gone before.

DESTRUCTION OF COMMERCIAL SCUM, United Guttural (1999). Mass Pussy Obliteration / Bleeding To Death / Orally Tortured / A Butt Plug In Your Pussy / Strangled Then Revived / Fist Fucked / Cadaveric Mutilation / Mutilation / Cunt Killer / Virgin Assassin.

FILTH, Morbid MR 101 (2003). Filth / Blast You In The Face With My Semen, Blast You In The Face With My Fist / Punch You In The Cunt / Blinded / The Consequence Of Your Ignorance / Sexual Assault / Orgasm Is The Enemy / Animosity / I Hope He Beats You / Fag Basher.

WARGASM

SWEDEN — *Henke Wenngren (vocals), Pontus Pettersson (guitar), Simon Jarrolf (bass), Fredrik Eriksson (drums).*

Västerås based Death Thrashers. The band began life as a school act of guitarists Pontus Pettersson and Fredde, soon uniting with drummer Adam Hobér of Black Metal act ENTHRALLED. This trio picked the title RAGE ANTHEM initially for the opening demo 'Fire Desires' but would then adopt WARGASM as their banner. Later recruits included bassist Simon Jarrolf and new drummer Erik Wallin.

Although the band issued the mini album 'Pure Evil (Straight From Hell)' during 2001 they would, bringing in another drummer Fredrik Eriksson and MORNALAND and SKYFIRE frontman Henke Wenngren, subsequently switch band title to VICIOUS. Under their new title the band re-debuted in 2002 with the EP 'Chains Won't Hold It Back'.

Pure Evil (Straight From Hell), Wargasm (2001) (Demo). Like A Beast / Thrasher / Spread / Boots Of Led / Death Recrution.

WARHAMMER

UK — *Mike Craddock (vocals / bass), Wayne Ashton (guitar), Mitch Dickinson (guitar), Shane Embury (drums).*

Shropshire's WARHAMMER was a pioneering, if not the first, British Death Metal act. Founded in 1984 the group issued the six song demo tape 'Abattoir Of Death', recorded in one day for the princely sum of fifty pounds, the following year. WARHAMMER, performing covers by SLAYER and HIRAX, only managed two live gigs on the 19th December 1985 in Oswestry and the 27th of the same month in Telford.

Guitarist Mitch Dickinson went on to Birmingham Thrashers SACRILEGE, proto-Metalcore outfit HERESY, ANTICHRIST and UNSEEN TERROR. Drummer Shane Embury subsequently came to notoriety as a bass guitarist with AZAGTOTH—alongside Wayne Ashton, UNSEEN TERROR, LOCK UP, BRUJERIA and most notably as a core member of NAPALM DEATH. For a brief period in 1986 Dickinson and Embury also activated the less than serious LOBSTER CLUB. Aston subsequently figured as a member of MORBID JUDGEMENT.

Word arrived in 2005 that Purist Records was set to make an official release of the WARHAMMER demos.

Abattoir Of Death, Warhammer promo (1985). Halloween / Blood On Satan's Claw / Satan's Angel / Malevolent Sinner / Prophecy / Abattoir Of Death.

Rehearsal, (1985). Halloween / Satan's Angel / Bombs Of Death.

WARHEAD

PERM, RUSSIA — *Eugene Makeev (vocals / bass), Michael Toburdanovskiy (guitar), Dmitry Bersenev (drums).*

Perm based Death Metal band WARHEAD released the 1996 demo 'The Realms Of Fancy' following it up with 'The Various Views Of The Present-Day Reality' session in 1998. WARHEAD at this juncture quoted a roster of erstwhile ESTEBUN members vocalist / bassist Mike (a.k.a. Eugene Makeev), guitarists Dick (Edward Yuzhakov), Ben (Dmitri Bersenev) on drums plus second guitarist Michael Toburdanovsky. Guitarist Edward Yuzhakov exited and a third recording, 'Hate', arrived in 1999 for which the band was credited with a line-up of guitarist Michael Toburdanovsky, vocalist / bassist Eugene Makeev and drummer Dmitri Bersenev. However, Yuzhakov returned in early 2000 as WARHEAD also added female vocals. The album 'Strange Age' followed in 2002.

THE REALMS OF FANCY, Warhead demo (1996). Saint Hate / The Prayer Of The Vampire / Disease / The Place / Son Of The Nature / Difference / Warhead / Energy.

VARIOUS VIEWS OF THE PRESENT DAY REALITY, Drive Sound Production (1998). Fighter / Difference / Drug Addict / My Love / Pain / Warhead / Winter Of The Soul / Strangers In Me / Freedom / Loser / Soul For Sale / She.

HATE, Drive Sound Production (1999). Last Hope / Customs / Break / Bogota Marazmus / The Gale / Empty Eye Sockets / War / Spite.

STRANGE AGE, (2002). Emptiness / Question / Terrorism / Strange Age / Grave Worms / Power / Unity / Lost Soul.

WATCH ME FALL

TURKU, FINLAND — *Niilo Sevänen (vocals), Ville Vänni (guitar), Olli Pekka Suhonen (guitar), Ilari Ojala (bass), Varpu Vahtera (keyboards), Ville Kaisla (drums).*

Gothic inspired melodic Death Metal from Turku. WATCH ME FALL originated in 1996, reportedly operating as a PARADISE LOST covers band. With the recording of a demo based upon original material, and the introduction of keyboard player Varpu Vahtera during 1997, the band took on the title of WATCH ME FALL. Live gigs would be few and far between as the band struggled to remain stable, rocked by numerous line-up changes. One permanent member that did enroll during this period would be bassist Ilari Ojala. By 1998 a second demo session, entitled 'Blood Red Colours', had been issued.

Signing to the independent KTOK Records label WATCH ME FALL added drummer Ville Kaisla and lead singer Niilo Sevänen just upfront of recording their debut album 'Worn'. A second guitar player, Olli-Pekka Suhonen, would augment the group for live work.

During 2004 WATCH ME FALL members guitarist Ville Vänni and bassist Joni Jontte Suodenjärvi forged Death-Thrashers HATEFORM in union with singer Petri Njysvär" Nyström and the ex-MORBID DREAM pairing of guitarist Tomy Speedy Laisto and drummer Tuomas Reisari Vähämaa. Vänni, Vahtera and Sevänen also hold INSOMNIUM credits.

Watch Me Fall, Watch Me Fall (1997) (Demo). I Understand / Curtain Canopy / Deserted To Live / Embittered.

Blood Red Colours, Watch Me Fall (1999) (Demo). Blood Red Colours / Life Left Behind / Waves / For Outcasts / Prison Of Darkness.

WORN, KTOK Records KTOK 0003 (2001). Silent Aeons / Worn Out / More Than Gods Could Dream / Waves / Incoldblood / On Borrowed Time / Dirge For The Final Journey / Winter Within / Discord Symphony.

WATCH MY DYING

BUDAPEST, HUNGARY — *Gábor Veres (vocals), Sándor Bori (guitar), Attila Kovács (guitar), Imre Eszenyi (bass), Zoltán Bordás (drums).*

WATCH MY DYING, a modern Thrash / Death Metal band, was manifested in Esztergom, Hungary during 1999. An opening demo, 'System Error (Rendszerhiba)', was recorded at Pont-Mi Studio in Székesfehérvár in March the following year. Further progress was made when, in May 2000, the group scored a fourth placing in the Pepsi sponsored 'Generation Nexxt' talent competition, broadcast on national television. Live work saw the band increasing its profile with shows at major festivals such as the Slovakian 'Klikk' event and 'Pepsi Sziget' festival.

In September 2002 the band convened at Acoustair Studio, Budapest to record the 'Húsmágnes' EP. Live work across Hungary to promote the outing was extensive but by mid 2004 WATCH MY DYING was ready to lay down a full length album, 'Klausztrofónia', utilising the Bakery and the Grape Studio between July to October for this purpose. Once again the group set out on the road, landing supports to the likes of OPETH, STAMPIN GROUND and DEW-SCENTED. The band also shared the stage at the 'Metal Mania' festival alongside CRADLE OF FILTH, APOCALYPTICA, KATATONIA, MOONSPELL and THE HAUNTED.

WATCH MY DYING released the 'Fényérzékeny' album in November 2006.

Rendszerhiba, Watch My Dying WMD-001 (2000). Systole / Képfakasztó / Digitális Antikrisztus / Túl Jón És Rosszon / Extrasystole.

Húsmágnes EP, Watch My Dying WMD-042 (2002). Terápiarezisztens / Szájzár / Eredeti Testforma / Jelennemlét / Yang / Húsmágnes—Megjön / Húsmágnes—Elmegy.

KLAUSZTTROFONIA, Watch My Dying WMD-666 (2004). Idomtalan / Carbon / Klausztrofónia / Nullpont / Horizont 16:9 / Technika Angyala I. / Technika Angyala II. / Nicht Vor Dem Kind / Gyúlékony Csíra / B-terv / Nyers Hát / Kék Ég, Zöld Fű.

CLAUSTROPHONY, Watch My Dying (2005) (Split album with SZEG). Hope For The Best / I Show You The Way / Leave Me Alone / Bring Me / Carbon / Time Overdose / Plan B / Blues Sky, Green Grass (remix).

FÉNYÉRZÉKENY, Watch My Dying WMD-99 (2006). Elsőbbségi / Fényérzékeny / A Tegező / Sztereotip (Állami Sláger) / Metrikus / OHM / 50 Hz / Háttal Álmodó / Hínár / Om / 9 Kapu.

WEB

RUMANIA — *Dennis Mustafa (vocals), Corneliu Belu (guitar), Costin Beizadea (guitar), Sorin Vlad (bass), Florian Laghia (drums).*

Constanta based WEB, formed in October of 1998, was assembled by guitarist Costin Beizadea and former NECROPOLA and CELESTIAL SANCTUARY bassist Vali 'IngerAlb' Zechiu. In December former ANGELS & TEARS man Nicu Galie joins as vocalist and this trio entered ID Stage Studios to craft the 'Spirits' demo in February of the following year. Narcis Chiamil of INSTINCT would act as sessioneer for these recordings but subsequently joined on a full time basis. WEB expanded further in March with the incorporation of ex-IN CREPUSCULUM guitarist Corneliu Belu. However, the band lost the services of Zechiu, the ex-bassist enrolling successively into MAGICA, Industrial Metal band INGER DE FIER before forging his own solo Dark Ambient concern TELURICA.

WEB performed their first live concert at the Green Hours club in Bucharest in January of 2000, after which MAGICA's Cristi Barla took over on drums. That August Sorin Vlad stepped in as new bassist for recording of a second demo entitled 'First Moods Of Anger'. Fractures among the ranks in May of 2001 saw Barla exiting to join INTERITUS DEI. The group went into hiatus for several months until they located ARON drummer Florian Laghia for a return gig in November at the 'Metalheart' festival. However, Narcis Chiamil re-took his former position on drums in 2003. That July Dennis Mustafa, a seasoned veteran of MYSTIC SIGHT, WATCHTOWER, TEARS BLAME, INTERITUS, ULTRA and FLATLINERS, became WEB's new vocalist as Nicu Galie joined Death Metal band AVSKILD.

SEVERAL MOODS OF ANGER, Web (2004). The Web (Intro) / I Met Myself Again / Pass Away / Fate / Shock System / So I Died / Unexpurgated Reality / Aflicao E Felicidade / Deadly Web / Endless Manipulation.

WEHRWOLFE

CHARLOTTE, NC, USA — *Nathan Ellis (vocals), Chuck Brummond (guitar), Devon (bass), Scott Pletcher (drums).*

Charlotte Death Metal band WEHRWOLFE came into being during 2002 with the split of DARKMOON. This previous act had folded when vocalist Jon Vesano teamed up with NILE, the remaining three musicians, including the DEMONIC CHRIST associated rhythm section of bassist Devon Penrod and drummer Scott Pletcher, forging ahead as WEHRWOLFE by enlisting singer Nathan Ellis. The inaugural version of the band comprised Ellis, guitarists Chuck Brummond, bassist Devon and drummer Scott Pletcher. They would first make their presence known by distributing a two song promo tape at the 2002 'Milwaukee Metalfest'. Signing to Magick Records WEHRWOLFE issued the 2003 album 'Godless We Stand'. WEHRWOLFE also donated their rendition of CRADLE OF FILTH's 'The Principle Of Evil Made Flesh' to the 2003 Cleopatra tribute album 'Covered In Filth'.

In January of 2004 Ellis exited in order to join DAYLIGHT DIES and Devon duly added lead vocals in order to cover. Drummer Scott Pletcher left the ranks in November 2005. The band drafted the REQUIEM, COTHURNUS and THE TORTURE CELL Chris Hathcock as their new sticksman in March 2006.

GODLESS WE STAND, Independent (2002). Intro / Godless We Stand / M1A2 Batallion Of Hate / Stainless Steel Lycanthropy / Bloodstained Honour / Forged Sufferance / The Trinity Undone / Masked Jackal.

WELKIN

BELGIUM — *Demis (vocals), Pepjin (guitar), Davy (guitar), Steven (bass), Frank (drums).*

Death Metal act WELKIN was formulated by bassist Demis and guitarist Pepjin from the Hardcore act PILGRIM, ex-URN personnel guitarist Steven, former URN and LOCUSTA man Jacob on drums and lead vocalist Maarten Verbeke. As WELKIN the band first performed live in April of 1998 but by the December both Jacob and Steven opted out. Building WELKIN back up to full strength Davy was incorporated on guitar and Frank took over the drums although Verbeke too would leave, becoming frontman for Thrash act MANIC MOVEMENT.

In January of 2000 Demis relinquished the bass to concentrate on lead vocals and former member Steven was delegated the four string role. In this incarnation WELKIN cut the demo 'The Untold' in that August. The October 2002 album 'Angel Inside' would see guest vocals delivered by their erstwhile comrade Maarten as well as Svencho from ABORTED.

WELKIN, introducing the FAMILY OF DOG credited Peter Staelens on guitar, made a return during 2003. Whilst Staelens learned the material live work was conducted with stand in guitarist Jacob Illlyrian.

ANGEL INSIDE, Independent (2002). Angel Inside / Sonic Death Monkey / Embraced Reality / La Masquerada / Stages Of Awareness / Black Feathered Wings / Eternal Tides / Wonderland.

WINDHAM HELL

WA, USA — *Leland T. Windham (vocals / guitar / bass), Eric Friesen (guitar).*

One of the few Death Metal acts to stylistically stand head and shoulders above the pack. WINDHAM HELL, originally conceived as WYMONDHAM in 1986, fuse Death Metal with Baroque and neoclassical guitar work as well as infusing their work with a rich ambience.

As a one man project of guitarist Leland T. Windham WINDHAM HELL's first product emerged as the demo session 'Do Not Fear ... Hell Is Here'. A second cassette 'Complete Awareness' surfaced in 1992 landing WINDHAM HELL a deal with Moribund Records.

Windham would be joined by another multi-instrumentalist Eric Friesen for later works.

WINDHAM HELL have, besides their CD output, released a shared tape in 1997 in collaboration with NOTHING.

SOUTH FACING EPITAPH, Moribund (1994). God Swallow / Paste Human / Garmonbozia / Faces Of Carnage / Terror Soak / Human Foot / Tomorrow You're Going To Die / I Remember Drooling / Exsiccation / Wrapped In Plastique / Post.

WINDOW OF SOULS, Moribund (1996). Laceration Of The Soul / Inversion Soil / Clear Blue Plastique / Ionic Abyss / Excarnation / Crepusculum / Corporal Compendia / Ashes In The Green Chair / Sacremonte (Popocatepeti) / Spiritual Bleeding (Faces II) / The Rain / Darkness Deluge / The Last Of Summer.

Windham Hell EP, Order Of The Deaths Head ODH 002 (1998).

REFLECTIVE DEPTHS IMBIBE, Moribund (1999). Postphoria / Nomis Syas Eid / Gathered Suicide / Aeolachrymation (Faces III) / Cold Granitic Bliss / Alpinia / Nocturnally Consumed / Deceased Eternity / Faded Epitaph Crescendo / Lower Levels Of The Skin / Sodflesh / Glacier Walk In Me / Wailing Souls: The Completion Of Awareness / Features Of Euphoria / Safterello Presto.

WINGS

VAASA, FINLAND — *Mikki Salo (vocals), Karri Suoraniemi (guitar), Anssi Hyvärinen (guitar), Harri Kessunmaa (bass), Kai Hahto (drums).*

Certainly not to be confused with Sir Paul McCartneys outfit of the same title. A Vaasa based Death Metal act convened during 1992 by guitarist Karri Suoraniemi of CARTILAGE repute. He would be joined by his CARTILAGE colleague Mikki Salo as vocalist for the 'Thorns On Thy Oaken Throne' EP issued that opening year for French label Adipocere. A full length album, 'Diatribe' released in 1995, surfaced on Salo's own Woodcut label. Also involved in the WINGS venture would be ENOCHIAN CRESCENT's guitarist Anssi Hyvärinen ('Anshelm') and bassist Harri Kessunmaa.

With WINGS demise Suoraniemi, re-billed as 'W.G. Victor', founded ENOCHIAN CRESCENT. Drummer Kai Hahto (a.k.a. Generis), also of CARTILEGE, scored scene credits with ROTTEN SOUND, AGRESSOR, VOMITURITION, WINTERSUN and ENOCHIAN CRESCENT.

Bitterness, Wings (1992) (Demo). Under Autumn Trees / Unfettered Aspiration.

Thorns On Thy Oaken Throne, Adipocere AR 012 (1993) (7" vinyl single). Under Autumn Trees / A Canticle To Forlorn.

The Sun, Wings (1994) (Promotional cassette release). Equidistant / Austere.

DIATRIBE, Woodcut CUT001 (1996). Sunburnt / Eden / Cast Asunder / Thus Far / Unwind / Equidistant / Austere / Deus Ex Machina / Passion Et Resurrection.

WINTER

NEW YORK, NY, USA — *John Alman (vocals / bass), Stephen Flam (guitar), Joe Goncalves (drums).*

New York's WINTER is a hallowed name in Doom Circles. Unfortunately the band garnered this reputation only after its demise. The trio debuted with an eponymous 1989 cassette. The band's solitary album would be recorded by Greg Marchak between April and May of 1990 at S.O.S. Studios in Hempstead. Released by Future Shock Records in 1992, and licensed to Nuclear Blast Records for European issue, these sessions saw Tony Pinnisi handling keyboard duties. A 12" clear vinyl edition was also pressed in Europe. The 1989 demos were given a commercial release in 1994 by Nuclear Blast billed as the 'Eternal Frost' EP. For this issue the track 'Hour Of Doom' would be rebranded as 'Blackwhole' and an instrumental track 'Manifestations I' was added.

Guitarist Stephen Flam subsequently formed THORN, featuring Roy Mayorga of SOULFLY and MEDICATION repute on drums. Nuclear Blast re-issued the 'Winter' album in 1999, adding the 'Eternal Frost' material.

Winter, (1989). Servants Of The Warsmen / Eternal Frost / Winter / Hour Of Doom.

INTO DARKNESS—ETERNAL FROST, NBR (1990). Oppression Freedom / Reprise / Servants Of The Warsmen I / Goden / Power And Might / Destiny / Eternal Frost I / Into Darkness / Servants Of The Warsmen II / Eternal Frost II / Winter / Blackwhole / (Untitled).

Eternal Frost EP, Nuclear Blast (1994). Servants Of The Warsman / Eternal Frost / Winter / Blackwhole / Manifestations I.

WITCHERY

LINKÖPING, SWEDEN — *Toxine (vocals), Patrick Jensen (guitar), Ricard Corpse (guitar), Sharlee D'Angelo (bass), Martin Axenroth (drums).*

Linköping trad Metal act WITCHERY was created in its familiar format during 1997 from the ashes of SÉANCE and SATANIC SLAUGHTER. The band has set itself apart from the crowd by blending elements of Black, Death and retro 'Thrashback' styled Metal, this amalgamation seeing WITCHERY rapidly attaining solid international sales. Musically WITCHERY are unafraid to show their influences as made evident by the frequent 80s Metal cover versions that litter their catalogue. Both vocalist Toxine (a.k.a. Tony Kampner) and drummer Mique (Micke Pettersson) had also been members of TOTAL DEATH whilst Mique had also been involved in MORGUE alongside guitarist Richard Corpse (Rille Rimfält). Toxine would cut his teeth on the Rock scene with his debut Punk act PASSIVA MONGOLOIDER as far back as 1979.

The revised WITCHERY came together when SATANIC SLAUGHTER vocalist Ztephan Dark fired his entire band just days before a scheduled album recording. Undaunted the quartet, Toxine, Corpse, Mique and second guitarist Patrik Jensen, stuck together to found WITCHERY enlisting MERCYFUL FATE and ILLWILL bassist Sharlee D'Angelo (Charles Petter Andreason). The latter's priority commitments to MERCYFUL FATE meant that recording of the debut WITCHERY album, 'Restless And Dead', was delayed until January 1998, sessions being conducted at Blue Hill Studios in Linköping. Necropolis Records in the USA took the band on to issue 'Restless And Dead' in 1998. The band put in their debut show in April 1998 in Copenhagen although minus Richard Corpse who was too ill to perform.

The March 1999 mini-album 'Witchburner', assembled at Los Angered Studio in Gothenburg, with KING DIAMOND guitarist Andy LaRocque taking the production reins, comprises originals plus various covers including ACCEPT's 'Restless And Wild', BLACK SABBATH's 'Neon Knights', W.A.S.P.'s 'I Wanna Be Somebody' and JUDAS PRIEST's 'Riding On The Wind'. WITCHERY put in a showing at the renowned German Wacken Metal festival in 1999. WITCHERY returned in September with the unsavoury 'Dead, Hot And Ready', recorded at Blue Hill Studios. Engaging in their first real bout of touring, the band took to the European stages in January 2000 alongside MOONSPELL and KREATOR following up with a one off US appearance at the New Jersey 'March Metal Meltdown' festival in March. The remainder of the year found band members prioritising ARCH ENEMY, THE HAUNTED and the SÉANCE reunion.

For the 2001 album 'Symphony For The Devil', cut in February at Berno Studios in Malmö, WITCHERY employed scene veteran drummer Martin 'Axe' Axenroth, a man having seen service as 'Demon Pounding Devastator' in NIFELHEIM and with SATANIC SLAUGHTER, BLASPHEMOUS, MORGUE, COVEN and TRIUMPHATOR. MERCYFUL FATE's Hank Shermann added guest guitar to the track 'Hearse Of The Pharaohs', prompting reviewers to remark upon the phonetic similarities with MERCYFUL FATE's own 'Curse Of The Pharaohs'.

Guitarist Patric Jensen, was also operational with THE HAUNTED. Toxine and Corpse also busied themselves with INFERNAL. Mique had a side project entitled RHOCA GIL.

WITCHERY would cut versions of KING DIAMOND's 'The Shrine' and the SCORPIONS 'China White' for tribute albums. Once the band members other commitments had been fulfilled WITCHERY entered Berno Studios in Malmö during August of 2004 to craft a new album. Included would be tracks 'The Wait Of Pyramids', featuring MERCYFUL FATE guitarist Hank Shermann and 'Crossfixation' with a guest appearance by ex-THE CROWN member Marcus Sunesson. The record also saw a remake of SATANIC SLAUGHTER's 'Immortal Death'.

In August 2005 Martin Axenrot temporarily joined the ranks of OPETH for European touring, covering for regular drummer Martin López who was forced out due to medical concerns. The album 'Don't Fear The Reaper' finally emerged in March 2006. That same year Mique Flesh forged FREEVIL alongside ex-DENATA members guitarist Tomas Andersson and bass player Roger Blomberg.

RESTLESS & DEAD, Necropolis NR029 (1998). The Reaper / Witchery / Midnight At The Graveyard / The Hangman / Awaiting The Exorcist / All Evil / House Of Raining Blood / Into Purgatory / Born In The Night / Restless And Dead.

RESTLESS & DEAD, Toy's Factory TFCK-87167 (1998) (Japanese release). The Reaper / Witchery / Midnight At The Graveyard / The Hangman / Awaiting The Exorcist / All Evil / House Of Raining Blood / Into Purgatory / Born In The Night / Restless And Dead / The Howling / Into The Catacombs / Breath Of Serpent That Rules The Cold World.

Witchburner EP, Necropolis NR034 (1999). Fast As A Shark / I Wanna Be Somebody / Riding On The Wind / Neon Knights / The Howling / The Executioner / Witchburner.

DEAD, HOT AND READY, Necropolis NR041 (1999). Demonication / A Paler Shade Of Death / The Guillotine / Resurrection / Full Moon / The Dead And The Dance Done / Dead, Hot And Ready / The Devil's Triangle / Call Of The Coven / On A Black Horse Thru Hell . . . .

DEAD, HOT AND READY, Toy's Factory TFCK-87202 (1999) (Japanese release). Demonication / A Paler Shade Of Death / The Guillotine / Resurrection / Full Moon / The Dead And The Dance Done / Dead, Hot And Ready / The Devil's Triangle / Call Of The Coven / On A Black Horse Thru Hell . . . / Fast As A Shark / I Wanna Be Somebody / Riding On The Wind / Neon Knights / The Howling / The Executioner / Witchburner.

SYMPHONY FOR THE DEVIL, Necropolis NR066 (2001). The Storm / Unholy Wars / Inquisition / Omens / Bone Mill / None Buried Deeper . . . / Wicked / Called For By Death / Hearse Of The Pharaohs / Shallow Grave / Enshrined / The One Within.

SYMPHONY FOR THE DEVIL, Toy's Factory TFCK-87249 (2001) (Japanese release). The Storm / Unholy Wars / Inquisition / Omens / Bone Mill / Enshrined / None Buried Deeper / Wicked / Called For By Death / The One Within / Hearse Of The Pharaohs / Shallow Grave.

DON'T FEAR THE REAPER, Toy's Factory TFCK-87401 (2006) (Japanese release). Disturbing The Beast / Stigmatized / Draw Blood / The Ritual / Ashes / Plague Rider / Damned In Hell / Crossfixation / The Wait Of The Pyramids / Immortal Death / Styx / War Piece / Cannonfodder / Into The Catacombs.

DON'T FEAR THE REAPER, Century Media 77505-2 (2006) (European release). Disturbing The Beast / Stigmatized / Draw Blood / The Ritual / Ashes / Plague Rider / Damned In Hell / Crossfixation / The Wait Of The Pyramids / Immortal Death / Styx / War Piece / Cannonfodder.

DON'T FEAR THE REAPER, Century Media 8205-2 (2006) (USA release). Disturbing The Beast / Stigmatized / Draw Blood / The Ritual / Ashes / Plague Rider / Damned In Hell / Crossfixation / The Wait Of The Pyramids / Immortal Death / Styx / War Piece / Cannonfodder / Legion Of Hades.

WITCHES SABBATH

LAS PALMAS, SPAIN — *Eduardo Rodriguez (vocals / samples / programming), Eduardo Salazar (guitar), Luis Henriquez (bass).*

Las Palmas, Gran Canaria Blackened Death Metal. WITCHES SABBATH was convened during 1997 with an inaugural line-up comprising Eduardo Salazar on vocals and lead guitar, Luis Henriquez on rhythm guitar, Eduardo Rodriguez on bass and Jesus Ojeda on the drums. After just one live performance the band cut the opening demo, 'The Beginning Of A New Age', in 1998. More gigs ensued and a follow up demo entitled 'Darkness Kingdom Coming' was issued in 2000. However, changes saw Henriquez leaving the fold with Ignacio González stepping in as substitute as WITCHES SABBATH were signed to the French Oaken Shield label for a professional CD pressing of 'Darkness Kingdom Coming'.

The band then entered a period of instability as Ojeda exited, replaced by Culi. Luis Henriquez then returned on bass and shortly after Ojeda too re-entered the ranks. However, Ojeda left again in February 2003 and Gonzalez followed that August. Persevering, the band opted not to find a substitute drummer and relied on sequencers. As diversions to their WITCHES SABBATH priorities the band members also engaged in side pursuits with Salazar active with Stoner band CRIMSON STONE, the Electro act DECADENCE, Black Metal combo HELLISH STORM and Doom outfit SOULITUDE, the latter act also featuring Henriquez. The bassist also operated another Doom venture SHADOWMYST. Rodriguez too held a myriad of other ventures including Gothic act AEON, Crossover Thrash band HO3, being singer for ANIMA and live bassist for both WHISPER and THE LAST SIGH.

WITCHES SABBATH cut a 2004 album 'New World Plague' at Ayers Rock studios by Juanjo Sepúlveda for release through Necromance Records.

DARKNESS KINGDOM COMING, (2001).
NEW WORLD PLAGUE, Necromance (2004). False Truth Falls / Bloodshed / The Call Of My Black Spirit / Legions Of Death / Stormwrath / Silent Path To Die / Deep In The Flesh / Her Eternal Realm I—Empress / Her Eternal Realm II—Tribute.

WITHERED

ATLANTA, GA, USA — *Chris Freeman (vocals / guitar), Mike Thompson (guitar), Greg Hess (bass), Wes Kever (drums).*

Atlanta, Georgia's Death Metal combo WITHERED, created in the early Summer of 2003, features the SOCIAL INFESTATION pairing of vocalist / guitarist Chris Freeman and guitarist Mike Thompson. Drummer Wes Kever is ex-PUAKA BALAVA whilst bassist Greg Hess was previously with LEECHMILK. A three song demo emerged in 2004 as a precursor to the Mike Green produced EP 'Order Born From Chaos'. WITHERED issued the 'Memento Mori' album through Lifeforce in September 2005. The band toured the UK as support to MASTODON and HIGH ON FIRE during December.

WITHERED teamed up with VITAL REMAINS, GRAVE, DEMIRICOUS and DISMEMBER for a North American tour beginning in early October. However, drummer Wes Kever exited the following month. The group installed a fresh rhythm section of bassist Mike Longoria and drummer Beau Brandon in February 2007, both members of WAITED. WITHERED's new line-up made its debut on March 1st at The Masquerade in Atlanta sharing the stage with UNLEASHED, KRISIUN, and BELPHEGOR.

Withered, Withered (2004). The Fear And Pain That Cripples Me / Within Your Grief / Like Locusts.
MEMENTO MORI, Lifeforce LFR 056-2 (2005). It's All Said / Within Your Grief / Like Locusts / Silent Grave / Beyond Wrath / Fear And Pain That Cripples Me / Among Sorrow.

WITHERED BEAUTY

SWEDEN — *Daniel Bryntse (vocals / guitar), William Blackmon (guitar), Tobias Björklund (bass), Jonas Lindström (drums).*

A Swedish, melodic Death Black Metal band rooted in the Death Metal act CONSPIRACY of which founder members frontman Daniel Bryntse and guitarist Magnus Björk paid their dues. Bryntse was also earlier a member of STENCH. A brace of mid 90's demos 'Screaming From The Forest' issued in June 1994 and 'Through Silent Skies' led to a deal with the German Nuclear Blast concern. The eponymous April 1998 album was produced by HYPOCRISY's Peter Tägtgren. Following the album Björk departed and guitarist William Blackmon filled the gap. Drummer Jonas Lindström was also employed to take over percussion, previously handled by Bryntse.

Bryntse spreads his talents far and wide appearing as bassist in SORCERY and as a member of WINDWALKER and Doom act

FORLORN. As if all this activity was not enough he operates in Black Metal act MORRAMON under the pseudonym of 'Vortex' and plays live with Punk band KALLT STAÅL besides activity with AUTUMN LEAVES, DAMNAGE, HELLPIKE, MILKTOAST, MOOD, MORANNON, NIGHCHANT and SAVORY.

Screams From The Forest, Withered Beauty (1994) (Demo). In The Dark Of The Night / The Dusk Arrives (The Plague) / Destiny / Screams From The Forest ... / ... Forest Of The Doomed / A Divorce From Death / Land Of The Undead / Paralysed.
Through Silent Skies, Withered Beauty (1995) (Demo). Immortality Is Mine / The Only Adventure / Failure / Broken / Through Silent Skies / As I Fly.
WITHERED BEAUTY, Nuclear Blast NB 0316-2 (1998). Lies / Broken / Veil Of Nothing / The Worm / Through Silent Skies / Twilight Dreaming / Dying Alone / Failure / Joust / He Who Comes With The Dawn.

WITHERED EARTH

ROCHESTER, NY, USA — *Adam Bonacci (vocals), Chris Burgio (guitar), Ron Cortese (guitar), Fred Decoste (bass), John Paradiso (drums).*

Rochester's WITHERED EARTH came into being in 1995 from a union of former DISGORGED members along with drummer John Paradiso of WITHIN. The demo 'Abolish In Thorns' arrived in March of 1995 followed by the 'Icaronycteris' session the following year. Severed Records would issue 'Abolish In Thorns' as a split album shared with archive DISGORGED tracks in November of 2002. Bassist Fred DeCoste, also of HATE MACHINE, would found Math Metal band PSYOPUS that same year.

Adam Bonacci would front up OVERLORD EXTERMINATOR in early 2004, a Black Metal combo assembled by Danny Lilker of NUCLEAR ASSAULT, THE RAVENOUS, S.O.D., HEMLOCK, BRUTAL TRUTH and ANTHRAX reputation and also featuring Lee from COMMIT SUICIDE on bass guitar. This band's presence would be first marked by internet demos posted in February.

FORGOTTEN SUNRISE, (1999). Forgotten Sunrise / The Nocturnium / Heaven Abandon / Dominion Under Angels Graves- The Astral Dread / Eternity Bleeds The Silence / There After The Fallen Praise / Growning / A Violent September Moon / Heaven's Abandon (Live) / Supernatural Terror Unearthed By Two Storms (Live).
ABOLISH IN THORNS, Severed (2002) (Split album with DISGORGED). A Cold Labyrinth Beyond The Dark Towers / Iconoclasm Disintegrates The Flower Of Mortality / Supernatural Terror Unearthed By Storms / Gazing Into A Placid Stream / As Chaos Spreads Like The Plague.
OF WHICH THEY BLEED, Olympic OLY 0231-2 (2003). The Imperial Tribulation / Calculated To Create Terror / Under The Merciless / Ruins / Only Weakness Is Inhuman / Suicide Of Arrangement / BDT / Lifeless, Soulless, Hated And Feared / From Ripe To Spoil / Worlds Without End / Caverns Of The Mind / Of Which They Bleed.

WITHERED GARDEN

TAMPERE, FINLAND — *Ipe (vocals), Teemu Raunio (guitar / bass), Juha (drums).*

Tampere Death Metal act WITHERED GARDEN was formulated during 1995 by vocalist Ipe and guitarist Teemu Raunio. The band underwent formative line-up changes but did issue a rehearsal demo in 1996, followed up by a studio session, 'Watcher In The Nightsky' in 1997. Signing to Dark Moon Records WITHERED GARDEN's commercial inauguration came in 1998 with an EP release 'Exhausted Eden' recorded at Rantajatkat Studios. The band cut tracks for an intended 2001 album, to be called 'Heaven Raped', but this was shelved as the band went into hiatus. Ipe, Raunio and drummer Ruha resurfaced under the revised billing of SIGHTLESS. Teemu Raunio joined THE BEAUTY OF DYING in 2001. WITHERED GARDEN folded in spring 2004.

Withered Garden, Withered Garden (1996) (Demo).
Watcher In The Nightsky, Withered Garden (1997) (Demo). Flame / Call Of Stormcrow / Praise Of Evil Rising High / Watcher In The Nightsky.
Exhausted Eden, Dark Moon (1998). Flame In Your Soul (My Goddess) / Exhausted / Master Melancholia / Redeemer.
Promo '99, Withered Garden (1999) (Demo). Shadowheart / Dance, Dismembered Souls / Another Narcotic Nylon Angel.
HEAVEN RAPED, www.sightless.fi (2001) (Only available as internet download). Death Awaits / Hunger / Wipe Them Out / Sons Of Hellfire / Shadowheart / Dance, Dismembered Souls / Another Narcotic Nylon Angel.

WITHIN Y

GOTHENBURG, SWEDEN — *Andreas Solveström (vocals), Mikael Nordin (guitar), Niknam Moslehi (guitar), Matte Wänerstam (bass), Thim Blom (drums).*

WITHIN Y feature former GARDENIAN and SUNCASE drummer Thim Blom. The Gothenburg based band debuted during 2002 with the demo 'Feeble And Weak', being founded in March of that year by NEMESIS and EVILDOER singer Andreas Solveström along with the MNEMONIC guitar duo of Nikke Almen and Mikael Nordin. Adding Thim Blom to the line up this unit entered Musikbörsen Studios to craft the 'Feeble And Weak' sessions. Matte Wänerstam took on bass for these tracks and would subsequently join WITHIN Y on a full time basis. Off to a flying start, Sweden's largest Rock magazine 'Close Up' awarded the demo a full 10 out of 10.

The band, recording during September of 2003 at Meta4Music Studios in Gothenburg, debuted in March of 2004 with the album 'Extended Mental Dimensions', issued through Holland's Karmageddon Media label. A promotional video for the track 'Face Down' was directed by David Andersson, drummer for Thrash metal band KALIBER. The band parted ways with guitarist Niklas Almen in December. A replacement would be found in Niknam Moslehi during early 2005.

WITHIN Y entered GBG Sound Studios in September to cut a second album 'Portraying Dead Dreams' for release through Gain Records in May 2006. The album charted in Sweden at number 46.

In November it was revealed WITHIN Y members Andreas Solveström and Jonas Larsson had teamed up with KALIBER drummer David Andersson to launch a new side project called ORO. WITHIN Y parted ways with drummer Thim Blom in December. The group pulled in new sticksman Erik Hagström in April 2007.

Feeble And Weak, Within Y (2002) (Demo). Lost In Solitude / Face Down / Feeble And Weak / Things.
EXTENDED MENTAL DIMENSIONS, Karmageddon Media KARMA 020 (2004). Lost In Solitude / God In Silence / Remains Of A Shattered Illusion / Things / Injection / Face Down / Behold / Silently Leaving / Feeble And Weak / Sacred Lies.
New Life, Within Y (2005) (Demo). New Life / Unjust Being / Sensless Murder.
PORTRAYING DEAD DREAMS, Gain GPCD30 (2006). Portraying Dead Dreams / Breeding Murder / Never Forgotten / Beautiful Violence / Unjust / Reckoning Day / As The Dust / Fade Away / Remembered / New Life / Feeding The Disease. Chart position: 46 SWEDEN.

WITHOUT GRIEF

FALUN, SWEDEN — *Jonas Granvik (vocals), Tobias Ols (guitar), Daniel Thide (guitar), Björn Tauman (bass), Patrik Johannsson (drums).*

Falun based melodic Death Metal debuted with an April 1996 demo entitled 'Forever Closed'. WITHOUT GRIEF's September 1997 debut album 'Deflower', issued via Danish label Serious Entertainment, featured guitarist Nicklas Lindh and bassist Ola Berg. November 1999's 'Absorbing The Grief', released by Serious Entertainment once again, saw Björn Tauman of CUDFISH and CHAINWRECK taking over on bass and Daniel

Thide installed on second guitar. Japanese editions of the album, on the Soundholic label, added an exclusive bonus track in the form of a cover of MOTÖRHEAD's 'Iron Fist'.

Post WITHOUT GRIEF guitarist Tobias Ols and Nicklas Lindh together with Ola Berg forged Death / Thrashers 21 LUCIFERS. Drummer Patrik Johannsson would enroll into STORMWIND and YNGWIE MALMSTEEN's band.

WITHOUT GRIEF singer Jonas Granvik resurfaced in 2003, vocalising on EDGE OF SANITY's 'Crimson II' opus. Granvik featured as backing vocalist on THE PROJECT HATE's 2005 album "Armageddon March Eternal (Symphonies Of Slit Wrists)'. That same year two WITHOUT GRIEF personnel, Jonas Granvik and Patrik Johannsson resurfaced as part of Västervik Progressive Death Metal band DEAD END WORLD. Bowing in with a demo billed 'The Isolation' this act saw the pair ranked alongside TAD MOROSE veteran Kristian Andrén on "Melodic" vocals, guitarist Simon Johansson of MEMORY GARDEN and FIREGOD and bassist Roger Johansson of RIBSPREADER and PAGANIZER.

Forever Closed, Without Grief (1996) (Demo). The Fear Of Silence / Betrayer Of Compassion / Suicidal Stroke / Forever Closed.

DEFLOWER, Serious Entertainment SE008CD (1997). Suicidal Stone / The Last Days / Deflower / Shallow Grave / The Failures Crown / Your Empty Eyes / Betrayer Of Compulsion / Vocalise.

ABSORBING THE ASHES, Soundholic SHCD 1-0027 (1999) (Japanese release). Kingdom Of Hatred / Lifeless / Ungodly / Instrumental / To The Evil / Blackborn Soul / Heaven Torn Apart / Only Darkness Lies Ahead / Iron Fist.

ABSORBING THE ASHES, Serious Entertainment SE018CD (1999). Kingdom Of Hatred / Lifeless / Ungodly / Instrumental / To The Evil / Blackborn Soul / Heaven Torn Apart / Only Darkness Lies Ahead.

WOMB

SOUTH PLAINFIELD, NJ, USA — *Craig Pillard (vocals), Ronny Deo (bass), Jim Roe (drums).*

South Plainfield, New Jersey Doom Death outfit WOMB comprised the former INCANTATION and DISCIPLES OF MOCKERY triumvirate vocalist Craig Pillard, bassist Ronny Deo and drummer Jim Roe. Pillard, upon his exit from DISCIPLES OF MOCKERY during 1994, relocated to New York. In the midst of a well documented heroin addiction, Pillard teamed up with both CATTLE PRESS and Doom act CEREMONIUM. Freeing himself from his drug habit the man journeyed back home where he reunited with Deo and Roe in WOMB. The band cut just one, five-track demo, recorded without guitar, prior to re-forming DISCIPLES OF MOCKERY. Necroharmonic Productions published the WOMB demo in 2001 as a split outing shared with 1998 DISCIPLES OF MOCKERY tracks.

Pillard's tradition on the extreme Metal scene extends to tenures with NOCTURNAL CRYPT, AGGRESSIVE INTENT, CARNAGE, METHADRONE, PUTRIFACT and DESECRATOR. During 1999 Pillard activated STÜRMFÜHRER. The WOMB project was re-activated during 2002. Craig Pillard joined Black Metal band EVOKEN in April 2006.

WOMB, Necroharmonic Productions (2000) (Split album with DISCIPLES OF MOCKERY). Bound, Fucked, Humiliated / Thong / Secrete / Borne / Outro.

WOMB OF MAGGOTS

GREECE — *John Minardos (vocals), Jim Koutsoukis (guitar), Lefteris Christou (bass), Chris Benetsanopoulos (keyboards), Katerina Stavropoulou (drums).*

WOMB OF MAGGOTS initiated as a trio comprising bass player Lefteris Christou, keyboard player Chris Benetsanopoulos and drummer Katerina Stavropoulou in April of 2001. Following an eponymous demo cut with the aid of session players Jim Koutsoukis enrolled on guitar. Singer John 'Mineiros' Minardos came in just prior to recording the debut album for Sleaszy Rider Records. 'Life Odium' included a cover version of KREATOR's 'Phobia'. Makis of NEGATIVE CREEPS aided in a guest role and former EN-GARDE vocalist Elisabeth Kotronia makes her presence felt on the title track 'Life Odium'.

Live shows throughout 2002 saw supports to SEPTIC FLESH and ROTTING CHRIST in Greece and also the undertaking of gigs in Bulgaria and Rumania. In 2004 the group switched title to INACTIVE MESSIAH, duly signing to Black Lotus Records.

LIFE ODIUM, Sleaszy Rider SR 0004 (2002). Intro / Chatroom Killer / The Bullet / Animus (Judge) / My Pleasure / Disembowelment / 6De6uS6 / Phobia / Life Odium / Trickery / Nostalgia / Outro.

WORLD OF LIES

USA — *Tony Avila (vocals / guitar), Kevin Ryan (vocals / bass), Paul Suchoski (guitar), Daniel Van Kuren (drums).*

WORLD OF LIES initial line up incorporated former THE HOODS, ASSYRIAN DEEDS and EULOGY vocalist / guitarist Tony Avila, BLED and SHRINE OF SCARS guitarist Chris Dann, SONS OF CHAOS bassist Paul Suchoski and ex-EULOGY man Dave Phillips on drums. The band became a trio comprising Avila, vocalist / bassist Kevin Ryan, also active with KNIFETHRUHEAD, and COWBOY KILLER drummer Daniel Hynes prior to re-inducting Paul Suchoski as a guitarist and bringing in Daniel Van Kuren of KURU (And ex-EULOGY) on drums.

The WORLD OF LIES line up morphed once more in October of 2004, adding guitarist Matt Sutphin and drummer Wayne Scott.

MATERIAL GOD, Independent (2001). Intro / Material God / Lost Faith / Consumed By Hate / Parasitic Humanity / Death Before The Flesh / Disguised / Dismemberment.

WORMFOOD

ROUEN, FRANCE — *E Worm (vocals / guitar), Fred Patte-Brasseur (guitar), Romain Yacono (bass), Timmy Zecevic (piano), Alexis Damien (drums).*

Rouen Gothic Metal formation WORMFOOD was assembled in January of 2001 by vocalist / guitarist Emmanuel ('E Worm') and bassist Romain, previously members of Black Metal bands ALIEN CHRIST and OUTWARD CEREMONY. Their debut five song demo, recorded in May of 2001, saw Youri Gralak and ex-LIVEVIL man Guillaume Pille. The band completed a line-up with the addition of drummer Alexis Damien, previously a member of ONE, BADJADA, DUNE and the FOLSCHWEILER TRIO, for 2003 album sessions. Pianist Timmy Zecevic would be the latest addition.

In 2004 the band entered Walnut Groove Studios in Amiens with Axel Wursthorn of CARNIVAL IN COAL acting as producer for the promotional session 'Jeux d'Enfants'. WORMFOOD added the FUNERALIUM and ATARAXIE credited guitarist Frédéric Patte-Brasseur in December 2004. The band signed to Italian label Code666 for remixed release of 'Jeux d'Enfants', this new variant also adding extra tracks.

WORMFOOD released the 'France' album in November 2005. Limited edition variants added additional material in 'Veni Sancte Spiritus', the TYPE O NEGATIVE cover version 'Femme Chrétienne' ('Christian Woman') plus a rendition of SERGE GAINSBOURG's 'La Décadanse'.

WORMFOOD, Independent (2002). Carpathian Carousel / Human Circus / Abortion Exit / Grandpa's Remission / The Night Of The Elderly / Hunger Anger / Schlachthaus / Licking The Bones / The Dead Bury The Dead / Acouphene.

Jeux d'Enfants, (2004).

FRANCE, Code666 CODE031 (2005). Leçon de Français / Bum Fight / Ecce Homo / TEGBM / Daguerréotype / Miroir de Chair / François Corbier chante la Comptine / Vieux Pédophile / Dark Mummy Cat / = Ø / Love At Last.

WORSHIP FACTORY

OULU, FINLAND — *Lasse Läntelä (vocals), Iikka Hintsa (guitar), Voitto Rintala (bass), Aleksi M. (keyboards), Markus Laakso (violin), Jari Ketola (drums).*

Hailing from Oulu, WORSHIP FACTORY was a Christian themed Gothic Metal band, incorporating violin, that issued a 2000 EP, 'Colours' recorded at Watercastle Studios, through the Little Rose Productions label. The record was famously recorded on CALLISTO guitarist Marcos Molinostelos Guitar Amplification Tower comprising Marshall JCM-800 with 4x12" 1960A. Both violinist Markus Laakso and bassist Voitto Rintala have ties to CRUCIFERAE. The latter also has an association with RENASCENT. Keyboard player Aleksi M. holds RANDOM, SWALLOW THE SUN and TROLLHEIM'S GROTT credits whilst A.Tolonen appears in Finnish Folk-Ambient group NEST.

COLOURS, Little Rose Productions (2000). Intro—Flows Of Eden / Colours / Echoes Of Mourning / Colours Of Creation / Outro—Rising Of Realms.

WOUNDS

HARJAVALTA, FINLAND — *Joakim Soldehed (vocals / bass), Jouni Hertell (guitar), Arto Ovaskainen (drums).*

Harjavalta Black Thrashers founded during 1997 by Joakim Soldehed. Initially WOUNDS, influenced by 80s Thrash, included guitarist P.P. Walkama and drummer Arto Ovaskainen. With the addition of Jouni Hertell on guitar Walkama shifted over to bass duties. In this incarnation the band cut a 1999 rehearsal demo 'Brown In Sight'.

Walkams decamped and the remaining trio duly enlisted Sakari Lajunen as new bassist. However, this latest recruit's tenure lasted a matter of weeks. Out of necessity Hertell performed bass on the subsequent November 1999 WOUNDS demo session 'Brutal Mutations'. Extensive gigging across Finland then ensued upfront of a further promotion recording entitled 'Barbarizing The Death'. Another demo, 'Nuclear Devastation' in June of 2001, secured a contract with the Bestial Burst label. The debut 'Chaos Theory' album was delivered in January of 2002. A demo entitled 'Holocaust Reich' arrived in December 2003. Bestial Burst issued a split album with NAILGUNNER in June 2005 billed 'Thermokuklear Thrash Metal Warfare'. A demo, 'Morbid Holocaust', was delivered in September 2005 being followed up by an album of the same title.

'Stormheit' of WOUNDS also operates with ANIMAL FORESKIN, alongside Arto Ovaskainen, UNCREATION'S DAWN and solo project STORMHEIT. In 2006 WOUNDS personnel "Chico Santiago" (a.k.a. Jouni Hertell), handling vocals, guitar and bass, alongside drummer Däni Manninen (Arto Ovaskainen) issued tracks billed as INFILTRATOR on a split EP with ANIMAL FORESKIN in March 2006. During 2006 The Warlock (a.k.a. Joakim Soldehed), and The Snake (Arto Ovaskainen), issued the January 2007 demo 'The Night Of Sorcery' under the EVIL WITCH banner. The pair also prepared a full-length album, billed 'Temple Of The Iron Witch', for 2007 release.

Rehearsal Tape 1999, Wounds (1999) (Rehearsal cassette demo). Brown Inside / Cold Steel Tonight / Rainbow Fighter.

Brown In Sight, Wounds (1999) (Unreleased demo). Brown In Sight / The Newman Prisma / Rautakirves.

Brutal Mutations, Wounds (1999). Brown Inside / Crematory / Rot Until Reborn.

Barbarizing The Death, Wounds (2000). Barbarizing The Death / Gas Mutations / Crush The Bones / Alien Abduction / Insane / Crematory / Rot Until Reborn.

Nuclear Devastation, Wounds (2001). Nuclear Devastation / Wounded / Mansion Of Mutilations / Butchered For Denial / Chaos Theory (Live).

CHAOS THEORY, Wounds BBRF002CD (2002). Bestial Burst / Death 3 / Extended Death / Alien Abduction / Day Of Doom / Compulsed To Terror / Chaos Theory / Mentally Disposable / Wounded / Nuclear Devastation / Butchered For Denial / Mansion Of Mutilations.

Holocaust Reich, Wounds (2003). Holocaust Reich / Barbarized And Brutalized / Violent Warfare / Ritual Afterlife.

THE DEMO-NIC DESECRATIONS '99-'03, Northern Warrior Productions (2005) (Malaysian release. Limited edition CD-R 100 copies). Holocaust Reich / Barbarized And Brutalized / Violent Warfare / Ritual Afterlife / Nuclear Devastation / Wounded / Mansion Of Mutilations / Butchered For Denial / Barbarizing The Death / Gas Mutations / Crush The Bones / Alien Abduction / Insane / Brown Inside / Crematory / Rot Until Reborn / Brown Inside (Original version) / The Newman Prisma / Rautakirves.

THERMONUKLEAR TRASH METAL WARFARE, Bestial Burst (2005). Holocaust Reich / Barbarized And Brutalized / Violent Warfare / Ritual Afterlife / Brown Inside / Crematory / Rot Until Reborn.

Morbid Holocaust, Wounds (2005) (Demo). Urge To Slaughter / Panzer Attack / Random Kill / Superior Human Race / Holocaust Reich.

MORBID HOLOCAUST, (2006). Crushing Enemy Line / Urge To Slaughter / Random Kill / The Sign Of Persecution / Enforcing With Blast / Kill The World / Holocaust Reich / Storming Death / Retreat Or Die! / Mayhem From Failure / Panzer Attack / Violent Warfare / Destroy The Sun / Superior Human Waste.

Storming Death, Final Punishment (2006). Storming Death / Gas Mutations / Enforcing With Blast / Murdering Reception / Rot Until Reborn.

WRATHAGE

OULU, FINLAND — *Scythe (vocals / bass), D.V. Grim (vocals / guitar), H.Beast (guitar), Janne Kusmin (drums).*

High velocity Black Metal act WRATHAGE was founded in Oulu during 1997. The band's original line up revolved around lead vocalist Olli-Jukka Mustonen, guitarists Joonas Juntunen ('Scythe') and Juuso Juntunen ('Von Grim'), bassist Jani Hurme, keyboard player Tero Nevala and drummer Mika Pakonen. During 1999 Scythe embarked on another venture as vocalist for Thrash act UNBLESSED where he met ex-THYRANE guitarist Joni Kylätie (Hornanvasara) and persuaded him to join WRATHAGE as their new drummer. During 2000 D.V Grim and Scythe cut tracks for an intended EP, to be titled 'As Night Falls', but this was never released.

Marko Heikkinen would also have a spell as a guitarist. The band line-up ebbed and flowed until it settled down with Scythe assuming lead vocal duties, Von Grim and Chaos on guitar and Janne Kusmin on drums. The latter is also a member of KALMAH, SOULHAMMER and the high profile CATAMENIA. Both Scythe and Von Grim also operate Death Metal band GUT FEAST.

WRATHAGE published the 'anNihil[N]ation' demo during the Autumn of 2004. A live DVD recording entitled 'Annihilating', featuring a cover version of DØDHEIMSGARD's 'Ion Storm', captured the band's support slot to DISMEMBER at the Oulu Hevimesta on 22nd January 2005. WRATHAGE entered the studio in February to lay down more demo tracks, resulting in the August release 'Black Light Zodiac'. Line-up changes then saw H.Beast replacing Chaos as the band set about recording the album 'Crawlspace Antipathy' during November.

anNihil[N]ation, Wrathage CD001 (2004). Entering / Before The Monumental Beast / Hellworlds / Terra Limbo / Death.

Black Light Zodiac, Wrathage CD002 (2005). Sadicum / Glory Black / Freezing Fire / The Nation's Demons.

XANTOSSA

UTRECHT, HOLLAND — *Johnny Diepeveen (vocals), Jan-Willen Ligtelijn (guitar), Harry Van Breda (guitar), Jeff McBacon (bass), Edward Vereijken (drums).*

Utrecht Death Metal band XANTOSSA, founded in 1991, issued the demo 'Upcoming Death', cut at Tape Productions in Raamsdonksveer with producer Ton Bouwens as a quartet of vocalist Andre Gielen, guitarist Rob Mans, bassist Theo van Alphen and AITTALA drummer Edward Vereijken. The band recorded the 1995 demo tape 'Drowned In The Black Lakes Of

Sadness' at Beaufort Studios, Bovenkarspel with producer Han Swagerman. Second session 'Godforsaken' was cut a year later at Recorded at Franky's Recording Kitchen with Berthus Westerhuis manning the desk. At this juncture XANTOSSA comprised vocalist Leon van Midden, guitarists Jan-Willen Ligtelijn and Olivier Keun, bass player Rob Mans and drummer Edward Vereijken. However, Leon van Midden exited to create SERPENTOR (evolving into XERPENTOR) in 1998.

XANTOSSA's next offering, simply entitled 'Xantossa', saw vocal duties going out to Kees Ligtelijn and Kevin Verpaalen. This unit remained stable for the 1998 album 'Central Program For Swallowing', produced by Erik de Boer at Harrow Studios in Losser, but disbanded in 1999. Kees Ligtelijn joined BACKWATER whilst Kevin Verpaalen teamed up with SCROTUM.

XANTOSSA duly reformed in 2001, issuing the EP 'Cosmic Cemetery', recorded that November at Sunday Luxuries Studios in Lunteren with producer Menno Fink. 2003 witnessed changes, marking the introduction of second guitarist ex-IN DARKNESS man Harry Van Breda but the exit of Rob Mans. A 2003 compilation of demos, entitled 'A Brutal Reunion', included a cover of MORBID ANGEL's 'God Of Emptiness', recorded by singer Johnny Diepeveen, guitarists Jan-Willen Ligtelijn and Harry Van Breda, former MALICIOUS OBSCURITY, WASTED and THE PROJECT bassist Jeff McBacon and Edward Vereijken on drums. However, in April 2003 reports emerged that XANTOSSA had folded once again, with ex-members forming ADORN.

XANTOSSA was to resurrect itself again though, but vocalist Johnny Diepeveen and co-founding guitar player Jan-Willem Ligtelijn opted out in 2004. New vocalist Sander Boere, previously of ANTIDOLS, was inducted in November 2004. A new demo, "Negative Influence', surfaced in 2005.

Upcoming Death, (1991). Intro: The XantossA / Nonsense Of War / N.A.N. / Nailed Into My Casket / Mortis / Doomed Demolition / False Control.
Drowned In The Black Lakes Of Sadness, Xantossa (1995). Blind Me / Final Deathrow / Upcoming Death / Deny / Drowned In The Black Lakes Of Sadness.
Godforsaken, (1995). Intro / Godforsaken / Imbedded Mind / Genetic Manipulation / Welter In Gore / Redemption (The Downfall).
Xantossa, (1997). Masses To Ashes / Trampoline / Angels Hands / Two For One / Outro.
CENTRAL PROGRAM FOR SWALLOWING, (1998). Please Me / Five Minute Drives / Angels Hands / Me Versus / Two For One / Lemon Tea / Serenity / Prayer For The Common Man / Tramp-O-Line / Masses To Ashes.
Cosmic Cemetery, (2002). The Hunters Trophy / Gutted With Bare Teeth / Cosmic Cemetery.
Negative Influence, (2005). Negative Influence / The End Of Faith / Schizofrenic / Gore Massacre / Your God / Army From Hell.

XENOFANES

STRÄNGNÄS, SWEDEN — *Klabbe Alaphia (vocals), Danne Sporrenstrand (guitar), Jocke Hasth (guitar), Crille Lundin (bass), Mogge Wiklund (drums).*

XENOFANES is a Strängnäs Black / Death act dating to 1993. The group debuted in April 1995 with the three song demo 'In The Shadow Of Naked Trees' recorded at Studio Underground in Västerås. A 1996 promotional session was cut at Rago Studios with Jonas Granvik of WITHOUT GRIEF acting as producer and the following year Cadla Communications issued a split cassette shared with CRANIAL DUST.

Guitarist Daniel Sporrenstrand joined HYPNOSIA during 1999. XENOFANES members resurfaced in trad Metal band DECEIVER. Bassist Crille Lundin, in alliance with Pete Flesh Karlsson of FLESH, DECEIVER and MAZE OF TORMENT, formulated THROWN during 2006 for the album 'The Suicidal Kings Occult'.

In The Shadow Of Naked Trees, Xenofanes (1995) (Demo). In The Shadow Of Naked Trees / Sworn Oath / The Last Sunset.
Promo 96, Xenofanes (1996) (Demo). Operation Suicide / Sence Of Carence / The Journey / Deep Black Cold.
XENOFANES / CRANIAL DUST, Cadla Communications CP003 (1997) (Split album with CRANIAL DUST). Operation Suicide / Sence Of Carence / The Journey / Deep Black Cold.

XENOMORPH

LEIDEN, HOLLAND — *Peter (vocals), Kreft (guitar), Crutch (guitar), Yasper (bass), Marc V (drums).*

Leiden Death Metal combo created during 1994 by ex-COMPOS MENTIS guitarist Coert Zwart, bassist Dennis van Driel and drummer Ciro Palma. The band added former EJACULATE man Kreft as second guitarist the following year but then lost the services of their rhythm section, Palma subsequently finding national recognition as a member of WITHIN TEMPTATION. New members would be bassist Yasper and drummer Marc 'Bomber' V.

XENOMORPH debuted commercially with the album 'Baneful Stealth Desire', released in April 2001 by System Shock Records. However, earlier demo sessions 'Carnificated Dreams' and 'Passion Dance' had been compiled for a CD release entitled 'Acardiacus' by Teutonic Existence Records in 1997.

European dates in 2002, dubbed the 'Death Comes To Your House' tour, saw XENOMORPH traversing the continent in the company of US Death metal veterans MASTER, Czech act KRABATHOR and Poles TRAUMA. The band added former DISSECT guitarist Vincent Scheerman to the ranks the following year as they began to craft tracks for an album 'Necrophilia Mon Amour' scheduled to be released early 2004.

Carnificated Dreams, Xenomorph (1994). Intro / Irrelevent Life / Abandoned (Body) / Carnificated Dreams / Moodswings.
Passion Dance, Xenomorph (1995). Wolf / A Trip To Catatonia / Collector Of Pain / The Frost Is All Over / Passion Dance.
ARCADIACUS, Teutonic Existence (1997). Acardiacus / Irrelevent Life / Abandoned (Body) / Carnificated Dreams / Moodswings / Wolf / A Trip To Catatonia / Collector Of Pain / The Frost Is All Over / Passion Dance.
BANEFUL STEALTH DESIRE, System Shock IR-C-159 (2001). Dragon's Breath / Post-Human (The X-Morph Deathcult) / Blood Of The Stars / Storm Innocent Eve / On The Most Blackened Wings / Bestia Infernali / Last Contribution To Art / Once Upon Armageddon.

XERPENTOR

BENSCHOP, HOLLAND — *Leon van Midden (vocals / bass), Philip Nugteren (guitar), Jolanda Koning (drums).*

Benschop Death Metal band previously entitled SERPENTOR, founded in May of 1998 by bassist Leon van Midden of XANTOSSA repute, issued the 2001 EP 'Incarnation Of Evil', recorded at Franky's Recording Kitchen and engineered by Berthus Westerhuis. The band also included erstwhile members of Ijsselstein Thrash act EXPIRE, singer Jos Manders and guitarist Wico Oostveen. With the departure of both Manders and Oostveen, the surviving trio of vocalist / bassist Leon van Midden, guitarist Philip Nugteren, a scene veteran of ETERNAL SOLSTICE, ROUWEN and DISSECT, and drummer Maarten 'Trigs' Kooymans took on a harder, more brutal direction re-tagged as XERPENTOR. A three track demo, simply entitled 'Promo 2003', would be their first offering.

XERPENTOR donated the track 'Compulsion To Kill' to the 2006 compilation album 'Blown To Pieces 4' issued by FearSomeRecords.

Promo 2003, Xerpentor (2003). Descent Into Hell / Anathemize The Gods / Salvation Through Bleeding.

XYSMA

FINLAND — *Joanitor Mustaco (vocals), Thee Stranius (guitar), Mr Lawny (guitar), Heavenly (bass), Marvellous S. Safe (drums).*

XYSMA developed from a brutal Grind-Death Metal band to see incorporation of classic Doom elements as their career progressed. The band, starting life as REPULSE, comprised vocalist Janitor Muurinen (a.k.a. 'Janitor Mustasch'), guitarists Olli Nurminen ('Olivier Lawny') and DISGRACE's Toni Stranius ('Thee Stranius'), bassist Vesa Litti and drummer Teppo Pulli ('Marvellous Sidney Safe'). Commencing activity in 1988 XYSMA issued the 'Swarming Of The Maggots' session in 1989, this including a NAPALM DEATH cover version 'Deceiver'. Comeback Records released the EP 'Above The Mind Of Morbidity' whilst French label Seraphic Decay Records issued the 'Fata Morgana' 7" single both in 1990. XYSMA's debut album, 'Yeah' recorded at Sunlight Studios, emerged via Comeback in 1991.

In 1992 Kalle Taivainen ('Dr. Heavenly') took over the bass position for the second album 'First & Magical', this set laid down at Music Box

Studio in Pargas, Finland. The group switched to Spinefarm Records for 1994's 'De Luxe'. The following year XYSMA tackled ELVIS PRESLEY's 'The Witch' for a 7" single on the Oskun Divari label. The successive album for Spinefarm, 1996's 'Lotto', saw XYSMA now crediting themselves as 'Joanitor Lottoner', 'Minister Stranius', 'Foreigner Lawny', 'Gablo Heavenly' and 'Orvis Goodnight'. This album closed with the twenty minute plus track 'Bravado', of which eight minutes was pure silence. 1998's 'Girl On The Beach' followed.

Swarming Of The Maggots, (1989). Pulsating Cerebral Slime / Pulverized Necrobrains / Gripping Slaughter / Festering Sore / Procreated From Blood / Sudden Impulse / Unanaesthetic Genitoplasty / Fetid Gurgitation / Fleshsaw / Pathologist Perversities / Priests Fermented In Excrements / Charred Limbs / Drown Oneself / Burbed Rectum / Phrenetic Chainsaw Suicide / Evisceration / Vacant Mind / Deceiver.

Above The Mind Of Morbidity EP, Comeback TC-001 (1990). Foetal Mush / Paradise Of Steaming Cadavers / Entangled In Shreds / Mild Stench Of Rot / Dismemberment In Trance / Cranial Cradle.

Fata Morgana, Seraphic Decay SCAM 009 (1990). On The Hill Of Desecration / Entangled In Shreds (Live) / Embodiment Of Morbidity / Fata Morgana.

YEAH!, Comeback TC-3 (1991). Why Am I? / On The Hill Of Desecration / Uranus Falls / Aspirations / Reflections Of Eternity / First Sunbeams Of The New Beginning / Above The Horizon / Importance Of The Dimensionless Mirage / Until I Reach The Unattainable / There's Only One Sun / Written Into The Sky / Into The Blue Of The Sky.

YEAH/ ABOVE THE MIND OF MORBIDITY, Comeback TCD-3 (1992). Why Am I? / On The Hill Of Desecration / Uranus Falls / Aspirations / Reflections Of Eternity / First Sunbeams Of The New Beginning / Above The Horizon / Importance Of The Dimensionless Mirage / Until I Reach The Unattainable / There's Only One Sun / Written Into The Sky / Into The Blue Of The Sky / Foetal Mush / Paradise Of Steaming Cadavers / Entangled In Shreds / Mild Stench Of Rot / Dismemberment In Trance / Cranial Cradle.

FIRST & MAGICAL, Comeback TCD-5 (1993). One More Time / Souls Are Stolen / Uranus Falls Again / Turning / You Can Call Everything In A Question / My Mind Like A Heron / Clouds Give Me Consolation / Can't Imagine Your Death (Face) / Symbol / It's My Sound.

DELUXE, Spinefarm SPI 020 CD (1994). I Feel Like Lou Reed / Hard Without Tenderness / Nice Pale / Need / Green Gas Station Jacket / Le Mans 66 / So Divine / Getting Emotional / Head Off / So Divine (Reprise) / Viewmaster.

The Witch, Oskun Divari OSKU-003 (1995). The Witch / Love Vein.

LOTTO, Spinefarm SPI 029 CD (1996). Shortest Route / We Just Came Inside / Do'n'Do / New Gel In Town / Aquanaut / Shoes / One Hell Of A Man / The Tram / Millionaire / Bravado.

GIRL ON THE BEACH, Spikefarm SPI 54CD (1998). Fit / I Saw Them Kissing / Lamborghini / Star / Penniless / Girl On The Beach / Three Basic Things / Dennis & Charlie / Life In The Sea / It's About Time / I'm Not Ready To Dance.

YATTERING

POLAND — *Mrcin Swierczynski (vocals/ bass), Marek Chudzikiewivcz (guitar), Mariusz Domaradski (guitar), Marcin Golebiewski (drums).*

Technical Death Metal hailing from Gdansk. YATTERING added guitarist Mariusz Domaradski following 1998's debut 'Human's Pain' album. YATTERING drummer Marcin Golebiewski deputized for VADER in 2000 when their longstanding skinsman Doc had to bow out with an illness. The French Season Of Mist label would re-issue the debut 'Human's Pain' album for European release, adding bonus cuts in the form of cover versions of BRUTAL TRUTH's I'll Neglect' and SLAYER's ' Dittohead'. YATTERING signed to the Candlelight label in late 2002, projecting a March 2003 studio album provisionally billed as 'Genocide'.

The band teamed up with UNLEASHED and IN BATTLE for a European tour commencing in late November of 2004.

HUMAN'S PAIN, Moonlight (1998). Intro / The Feeling / Unnormally Zone / Annihilation Of Fellow Creatures / Demon's Inoculate (Fourfold Change) / Chase Of Thoughts / Sexual Trauma / Lost Within / Escape from The Scheme / Eyes Can See / Taken Due / I'll Neglect / Dittohead / Exterminate.

GENOCIDE, Candlelight CANDLE 087 (2003). Genocide / Schism / Message To M.A.R.I.O. / Non Adapted Socially / Panic In A Sea Of Blood / Inflow (Thought From Outside) / Non Typical Homo / Rapist's Victim / Sentence (To Die) / Temptation Of A Crime / Murderer (You Are) / Living Bomb.

YOUR SHAPELESS BEAUTY

FRANCE — *Nicolas Blachier (vocals), Michel Canavaggia (guitar), Jean-Marc Abate (guitar / keyboards), Révérend Michel (bass), Jérôme Lavail (drums).*

A classically inspired Gothic Doom / Death outfit, YOUR SHAPELESS BEAUTY took shape in October of 1994. The founding line up would comprise lead vocalist Nicolas Blachier, guitarist David Cammal, bass player Cédric N., keyboard player Jean-Marc Abate and drummer Lionel R. The following year witnessed some experimentation within the line up, the group adding female vocals courtesy of Sandrine B., additional guitar by Sylvain O. and subsequently by Sébastien R. A major difference of opinion that July found Blachier and Cammal opting to pursue a Doom stance opposed to the other members who all defected.

This revised version of YOUR SHAPELESS BEAUTY saw Blachier and Cammal joined by Abate making a return on keyboards, the recruitment of Révérend Michel for bass guitar and the temporary employment of a drum machine. Following a set of rehearsal recordings the group introduced second guitarist Michel Canavaggia. As the year closed more demos would be cut but a blow came early in 1996 with the departure of Cammel. Undaunted, YOUR SHAPELESS BEAUTY engaged in live work, culminating with the CD format re-issue of their debut demo by Adipocére Records, this release being restricted to 1500 copies. The band would also bolster its sound with the incorporation of drummer Jean-Marc N.

During January of 1997 the band cut two tracks for issue as a limited edition single 'Songe En Dehors...' through Edge Circle Productions. Their debut album, 'Sycamore Grove', would be recorded in just 11 days in 1998, seeing release in March of 1999, after which Jérôme Lavail assumed the drum position. A second effort, 'Terrorisme Spirituel', arrived in 2001.

YOUR SHAPELESS BEAUTY, Independent (1996). Au Delà Du Voile / Darkness My Bride / Your Shapeless Beauty / Rotten Love / Gothic Visions / Dark Retalations / Those Winds I Shall Ride.

Songe En Dehors... EP, Edge Circle Production (1997) (Limited edition of 500 copies). Le Chant Des Bannis / The Forthcoming Answer.

SYCAMORE GROVE, Adipocere AR047 (1999). Prélude n°3 / Le Berceau De L'ange (Nocturnal Call part III) / The Awakening / On The Wings Of The Black Rain / Equinoctial Desires / An Orchid In My Belfry (Nocturnal Call part II) / Last Ember From The Past / Goddess Of Lust / Récital Pour Une Agonie Céleste / Deities In The Dew / Empyreal Dispair.

TERRORISME SPIRITUEL / INSOUMISSION COMPLETE, Adipocere AR049 (2001). Indulgence Aveugle / Le Chant Des Bannis (Version

2000) (Nocturnal Call part I) / The Forthcoming Answer (Version 2000) / An Orchid In My Belfry (Nocturnal Call part II, Live) / Le Chant Des Bannis (Nocturnal Call part I, Live) / Rotten Love (Live) / On The Wings Of The Black Rain (Live) / Dark Retaliations (Live).

MY SWAN SONG, Adipocere (2002). Wolves Are Not Yours / Mourning Of A New Day / Song For A Ghost / Sine Sole Nihil / Contempt / Of Roaches And Shades … / I'll Be Your Shadow God / The Heretic Side Of Wisdom.

ZARATHUSTRA

GERMANY — *Alastor (vocals), Disruptor (guitar), Kerberos (guitar), F.T. (bass), Mersus (drums).*

A Black Thrash act, ZARATHUSTRA was founded in 1996 citing a line up of vocalist Alastor, guitarists Disruptor and Manox, bassist F.T. and drummer Mersus. The group debuted with the 1997 demo 'Black Perverted Aggression', following up on this with a second tape 'Heroic Zarathustrian Heresy' in 1998. Shortly after this recording Manox made his exit.

For a period ZARATHUSTRA employed the services of Mentor from HOMICIDE on session guitar until June of 1999 when a permanent replacement, Kerberos, was inducted. The second demo would see a re-issue on CD format limited to 1000 copies, upfront of a full length album 'Dogma Antichrist' on the Undercover label. A single 'Nihilistic Terror' and album 'Perpetual Black Force' followed in 2003.

The band entered Necromorbus Studios in Sweden during February 2005 to record an EP entitled 'Contempt'. Vinyl variants of this release, limited to 500 copies, included a cover of 'Sphinx' originally featured on the 1994 album 'Into The Abyss' by pioneering German Black Thrash act POISON.

Heroic Zarathustrian Heresy EP, Undercover UCR-04 (1999). Screams From The Past / 1999 / Oppose What Is False / Of Splendour, Honour, And Bitterness.
DOGMA ANTICHRIST, Undercover UCR06 (2000). Sadistic Spell / Dissenters Blood / Evoken Damnation / Yearning For Deliverance / Bleeding Saint / Torment Written In Flesh / Beyond Infinity / Screams From The Past / Proclaiming The Spirit / Seek The Truth.
Nihilistic Terror, Satan's Hammer (2003) (Limited edition 500 copies). Intro—Existence Of Evil / Lucifer's Domain.
PERPETUAL BLACK FORCE, (2003). Echoes In Eternity / Reverence To Myself / Vulgus Necare / Cosmic Black / Mass Execution / My Pandaemonium / Way Of The Creator / Dynasty Of The Eternal Ones / Of Destroyers And Despisers.
Contempt, Undercover (2005) (Limited edition 1000 copies). Slave Morality / Become Eternal / Master Morality / … Of Serpents And Swords.
Contempt, Undercover (2005) (Limited edition 500 copies). Slave Morality / Become Eternal / Master Morality / … Of Serpents And Swords / Sphinx.

ZEENON

OSLO, NORWAY — *Linn Pedersen (vocals), Linda Aurland (guitar), Elin Henden (bass), Mads Guldbekkhei (drums).*

Oslo's ZEENON, founded in 1995 as SPOOKY BALLOONS by bass player Nina Engen Hansen and Linn Pedersen, operated initially in Industrial tinged Thrash Metal territory. The band, rounded out by guitarist Linda Aurland, paid their dues on the live circuit as a covers act but within their first year built up a solid enough repertoire of original tracks to fuel a crop of self-financed EPs 'Zeenon' and 1996's 'Dhuma'.

Enlisting Tom V. Nilsen on the drums in 2000 ZEENON recorded the 'Against The World' EP. However, Hansen was to be diagnosed with leukemia. Despite this setback the bassist staunchly committed herself to the band's progress. ZEENON donated tracks to compilation albums assembled by Vampiria magazine and Dead Puppy Records 'Sick Music For Sick Children' (a Metallized version of the children's song 'Im A Little Teapot'!) as well as putting in an appearance at the 2001 'Inferno' festival. By the Spring of 2002 Elin Henden of DESIDERIUM was drafted to cover for Hansen, by this stage too weak to perform live. Sadly, on 30th July 2002 Nina Hansen passed away.

That November, with Henden installed as a permanent member, ZEENON laid down the 'Inject The Truth' EP. After Tom V. Nilsen exited in March of 2003, prioritising his other act KOLDBRANN, the band enlisted the services of THE ALLSEEING I and PULVERHUND drummer Mads Guldbekkhei, also announcing their intention to boost their sound by recruiting a second guitarist.

By early 2004 ZEENON had shed their Thrash mantle with the 'Arbor Vitae' EP to become a full on Death Metal act. Following a brief burst of dates as support to VADER the band signed with the UK based Retribute Records. The album 'Blood Vessel Criteria' would be recorded at Strand Studios

Zeenon EP, Zeenon (1995). Z / Even / Versus Black.
Dhuma EP, Zeenon (1996). Die 5 / Propagare / Border Line / Mars Attack.
We Want Your Mind EP, Zeenon (1999). Alienated / InkJet.
Against The World EP, Zeenon (2000). Between 2 Worlds / Absurd / Better If / Utopia / Secret (Of Secrets).
Inject The Truth EP, Zeenon (2002). Food / Alienated / Code Of Life.
Arbor Vitae EP, Zeenon (2004). Superior Control System / Arbor Vitae / Immunization / Post Absurd.
BLOOD VESSEL CRITERIA, Retribute RET 024 (2006). Welcome To The Conic Section / Sense Of Coherence / Immunization / 1 Sag / Cascade Of Blood / Arbor Vitae / Half A Pound Of Dead Meat / Superior Control System.

ZENITE

BELÉM, PA, BRAZIL — *Marcelo Histeria (vocals), Joe Ferry (guitar), Luiz Lobato (bass), Sandro Maués (drums).*

Belém based Death Metal combo ZENITE date back to 1987, debuting with the 1989 demo 'Mistic'. Further sessions included 'The Last Seconds' in 1990 and 1995's 'The End'. ZENITE contributed the track 'Nightmare War' to the 1998 compilation album 'Açaí Pirão'.

By 1999 the band, relocating to São Paulo, had settled on a roster of singer Marcelo Histeria, ex-BLACK MASS guitarist Joe Ferry, bassist Rogério Byron and former MANTRA drummer Sandro Maués. This line up cut the 2000 'Brutal Enigmatics Prophecies' album, after which Luiz Lobato, another BLACK MASS veteran, took the bass position.

ZENITE issued the album 'Tales Of Death' through Ná Figueiredo Records in 2002.

BRUTAL ENIGMATIC PROPHECIES, Ná Figueiredo (2000). 98 mm / Betrayers / Santurine's Widow / Psycho / Blue Sky / Warriors / Nightmare War / Goodbye / N.S.C.F. / Depression / Rainbow In Hell / The End.
TALES OF DEATH, Ná Figueiredo (2002). Torture Voices / Reign Of The Pain / Religious Corporation / Rotten / Black Angel / Invitation To Die / Cursed Bird / Crionics / Satan's Empire.

ZIRCONIUM

WELLINGTON, NEW ZEALAND — *Jolene Tempest (vocals), Maelstrom (guitar), Astrophus (bass), Rosemary (violin), Blizzard (drums).*

Wellington extreme Metal band, featuring FALCIFORM's Nathan Forbes and Jason Hislop, with female vocals from Jolene Tempest and violinist Rosemary. The band credited itself as Jolene Tempest ("Demonic Oration"), guitarist Maelstrom ("Scythe"), bassist Astrophus ("Seismic Pulsation"), violinist Rosemary ("Earthen Ambience") and drummer Blizzard ("Battery"). A self titled demo was recorded in October of 2001 at The House of DuanDemonus and The Castle. Maelstrom would also hold credits with DEMIURGE and MONSTERWORKS.

In 2004 ZIRCONIUM, despite having folded a year earlier, contributed the track 'The Veil Of Negative Existence' to the 'Morbid Music Vol. 1' compilation album. Both Maelstrom and Astrophys joined DRACO AERIUS.

Zirconium, Zirconium (2002). Intro / Tranquil Sky / Fake Embrace / Embedded Within / The Veil of Negative Existence.

ZOLTAR

VOTORANTIM, SP, BRAZIL — *Rodolfo Nekathor (vocals / guitar), Fabrício Exumer (guitar), Mário Deathvastation (bass), Oscar Vision (drums).*

Votorantim based, blasphemous Death Metal band. ZOLTAR started life billed as AGRESSOR in 1994, early members including lead vocalist Heltom and Arnaldo Damiani. Both Damiani and ex-singer Nuno Hellknight journeyed on to THRASHATTACK COMMANDER. Another ex-member, Fabio 'Fubá' Altafim, joined HIPPIE HUNTER. Early drummer Sergio Andrei was superseded by Oscar Vision. The KRISIUN, IN HELL and TORTURE SQUAD credited guitarist Mauricio Nogueira has also served a term of duty with ZOLTAR.

Opening demo sessions would be 1995's 'Masters Of Brutality', 'The Lord' in 1996 and 'Pleasure Of Possession' during 1997. In 2000 the group featured on the Demise compilation 'The Winds Of A New Millenium vol. 3'. Signing to Tumba Records ZOLTAR released the 2002 debut album 'Into The Depths Of Burn'. A demo, 'Indestructible Ancient Armies', followed in 2004.

The Lord, (1996) (Demo). Branded To Pain / Impaler / Spit in The Cross.
Pleasure Of Possession, (1997) (Demo). Innocence Of Death (Intro) / Malicious Malevolence / The Temple Of Evil / Pleasure Of Possession.
INTO THE DEPTHS TO BURN, Tumba (2002). Ancestral Vengeance/Kill Me Angel / The Night Unholy Archangel / Evil Chrucher / Lord Zoltar / War, Fire & Domination / Innocence Of Death / Pleasure Of Possession / Malicious Malevolence / The Temple Of Evil / Decade Of Evil / Braded To Pain / Impaler / Spit In The Cross.
Indestructible Ancient Armies, (2004) (Demo). Into The Chaos / Revenge Over The Enemy / Deciphering Testaments / Slander Cause Suffering / Drastic Unconscious War.

ZOMBIE VOMIT

KANNUS, FINLAND — *Markus Tavasti (vocals), Juha Kellokoski (guitar), Lasse Löytynoja (guitar / bass / drums).*

Kannus Goregrind duo ZOMBIE VOMIT released the demos 'Necro Goat Oath' in 2001 and 'Brutal Approach To Dentism' in 2002. The January 2003 'Certain Death', including a cover version of DEATH's 'Infernal Death', and 'Terror By Haunted' sessions followed in June with 'Unholy Vomit Cült' delivered in 2004. Drummer Lasse Löytynoja has ties to INCARNATE, YDIN, ARSKA and GESCHÜSZTURM. Billed as 'Vomitormentor', he co-founded SINVISION in 2002. Singer Markus Tavasti would also be active with INCARNATE. The singer also held membership of GOATDOMAIN and KURALUTKU. ZOMBIE VOMIT guitarist Juha Kellokoski is another INCARNATE man.

Necrogoatoath, Zombie Vomit (2001). Corpsefukker / Zombie Attack / Lobotomy / Goatcunt / Corpsefukker (Finnish language version).
Brutal Approach To Dentism, Zombie Vomit (2002). Aren't You Hungry? / Open The Anus / Dentist.
Terror By Haunted, Zombie Vomit (2003). Zombie Crucifixion / Terror By Haunted / Masochist / Festering Limbs.
Certain Death, Zombie Vomit (2003). Planet Crusher / 666 Wounds / Infernal Death.
Unholy Vomit Cült, Zombie Vomit (2004). Vomitormentor / Paineenlaukaisu / Torture Engineering Inc. / Unholy Vomit Cült / Exhumed First Love.

ZONARIA

UMEÅ, SWEDEN — *Simon Berglund (vocals / guitar), Emil Nyström (guitar), Jerry Ekman (bass), Emanuel Isaksson (drums).*

Melodic Death Metal combo ZONARIA, established in Umeå, Northern Sweden during 2001 under the title SEAL PRECIOUS and fronted by a fourteen year old singer Simon Berglund, previously of ORUKU SAKI. Guitarist Emil Nyström has association with NUQUERNA. The early formation underwent a series of membership shuffles, at various stages including vocalist Mikael Hammarberg, bassists Christoffer Wikström and Karl Flodin, drummers Simon Carlén, Niklas Lindroth and Claes-Göran Nydahl plus keyboard players Johan Aronsson and INVADER's Gustav Svensson. Stabilising, ZONARIA pulled in ex-ACRIDIAN drummer Emanuel 'Cebbe' Isaksson.

ZONARIA issued a May 2005 demo 'Evolution Overdose'. Bassist Karl Flodin would be replaced by Jerry Ekman. ZONARIA acted as support to IMPALED NAZARENE's April 2006 European tour. ZONARIA signed to Swedmetal Records in October for an album billed 'Rendered In Vain'. The album was recorded at Black Lounge Studios and featured Christian Älvestam, of UNMOORED, SCAR SYMMETRY, TORCHBEARER, SOLAR DAWN, INCAPACITY and ANGEL BLAKE, donating guest vocals to the track 'Attending Annihilation'.

In mid November 2006 ZONARIA contracted a new deal with Pivotal Rockordings before entering Black Lodge Studios on November 20th with producer Per Nilsson. The album sessions were completed mid December.

Evolution Overdose, Zonaria (2005). The Way Back To Before / Evolution Overdose / The Pyromaniac / Imaginary Enemy / A Fool's Mind / Image Of Myself.
Rendered In Vain, Zonaria (2006). Rendered In Vain / Attendin Annihilation / Ravage The Breed.

ZUBROWSKA

TOULOUSE, FRANCE — *Clod (vocals), Ben (vocals), Nutz (guitar), Flo (bass), Ben (drums).*

Toulouse act ZUBROWSKA offer a volatile mix of brutal Death Metal and Hardcore. The group's origins date to November of 2001 and an unnamed combo assembled by guitarists Nutz and Jon with Sam on the drums. By March of the following year the trio had half a dozen original songs readied. Entering a live music contest, Jeunesse Musicale de France, two friends bassist Balt of UNEVEN and vocalist Matt from KAVERN stepped on a temporary basis. Having made the competition finals the group decided upon the name ZUBROWSKA. By April Ben had assumed vocal duties with Flo taking command of drums. They would close the month off with a debut live performance as openers to CEREBRAL TURBULENCY and ALIENATION MENTAL.

ZUBROWSKA's next move would be the recording of a full length album, the band bringing in secondary singer Clod just two weeks prior to the studio date. Signing to the Spanish Xtreem Music label the album 'One On Six', recorded in just six days, emerged in September of 2003. The band featured the track 'Pay To Play' on the 2005 Listenable Records French Metal compilation 'Revolution Calling'.

ONE ON SIX, Xtreem Music (2003). Intro / Forkebabh / Sex, Drugs & Basketball / Do I Look Well? / Happy Pink Town / Smells Like Suicide / I Hate Teen Visions / One On Six / I Talk To The Wind / This Rose For You / Sad Sick World / When Satan Plays Disco People Die.

ZYKLON

NOTODDEN, NORWAY — *Daemon (vocals), Zamoth (guitar), Destructhor (bass), Trym Torson (drums).*

Notodden Death / Black Metal project ZYKLON is a revamping of EMPEROR guitarist Samoth's (a.k.a. Tomas Thormodsæter Haugen or 'Zamoth' as he is known with this project) ZYKLON-B project. The second album, February 2001's 'World Ov Worms' for Candlelight Records, was simply credited now to ZYKLON, thereby losing the direct reference to the holocaust gas at a time when Norwegian Black Metal was being put under the political microscope. Major participants included EMPEROR drummer Trym Torson (a.k.a. Kai Johnny Mosaker) colluding with Destructor of MYRKSKOG. The Dutch label Displeased Records also issued a limited edition vinyl variant of 'World Ov Worms'.

Guesting on the 2000 'World Ov Worms' album is the INFINITE DECAY and LIMBONIC ART credited Daemon (Vidar Jensen), ULVER's 'Trickster G' (actually frontman Garm) and the American fetish star Persephone. Bass guitar for ZYKLON is sessioned by Cosmocrator of SOURCE OF TIDE and MINDGRINDER.

Following their 2001 'Milwaukee Metalfest' appearance vocalist Daemon parted ways with the group. A bout of touring in North America would see Secthdaemon (a.k.a. Anders Eek) of ODIUM, FUNERAL, FALLEN and MYRKSKOG holding down vocal and bass duties.

Zamoth and Lars-Stian of SOURCE OF TIDE would be reported as uniting with former EMPEROR drummer Bård 'Faust' Eithun in an unspecified project. However, this proposition never materialised. Eithun would also be announced as scoring the lyrics for a new ZYKLON release. Trym hooked up with MYRKSKOG man Kshatriya's new DISIPLIN act in 2002.

A limited edition remix single, shared as a split release with RED HARVEST, surfaced in March of 2003. ZYKLON worked towards a sophomore album with producer Fredrik Nordström, 'Aeon', for September issue, these recordings marking the studio inauguration of Secthdaemon. Guest contributions for this opus were delivered by VOID's Ocd and RED HARVEST's Ofu Kahn with lyrical contributions from ex-EMPEROR man Faust. ZYKLON partnered with DARK FUNERAL and GOATWHORE for the 'Extreme The Dojo Volume 9' Japanese gigs in January of 2004. The band then lent support to ARCH ENEMY's February and March European dates. There would be little respite for Trym as the drummer stepped in as stand in member for SATYRICON's April US tour.

In June of 2004 both Zamoth and Trym, working with Cosmocrator of MINDGRINDER and Invictus from DISIPLIN, participated in recordings for a WINDIR tribute album to honour the memory of the late Valfar. ZYKLON set 'Disintegrate' as the working title for a 2005 album. Later that same year Zamoth and Trym re-activated EMPEROR but still forged ahead with plans for the next ZYKLON opus, recording at Akkerhaugen Lydstudios in November.

The group teamed up with ENSLAVED, 1349 and KEEP OF KALESSIN for a UK tour in September 2006. In January 2007 ZYKLON vocalist Secthdamon recorded a guest appearance on the 'Urge To Annihilation' demo from the Norwegian thrash band KILL ALL. Meantime, Destruchtor delivered a guest guitar solo for the 'Eryx' album by GLORIA MORTI, featuring on the track 'Sands Of Hinnom'.

BLOOD TSUNAMI partnered with ZYKLON for UK dates in May.

WORLD OV WORMS, Candlelight CANDLE061CD (2001). Hammer Revelation / Deduced To Overkill / Chaos Deathcult / Storm Detonation / Zycloned / Terrordrome / Worm World / Transcendental War—Battle Between Gods.

Storm Detonation, Nocturnal Art ECLIPSE025 (2003) (Split 7" with RED HARVEST). Storm Detonation.

AEON, Candlelight CANDLE074CD (2004). Psyklon Aeon / Core Solution / Subtle Manipulation / Two Thousand Years / No Name Above The Names / The Prophetic Method / Speciment Eruption / Electric Current / An Eclectic Manner.

DISINTIGRATE, Candlelight CANDLE111CD (2006). In Hindsight / Disintegrate / Ways Of The World / Subversive Faith / A Cold Grave / Vile Ritual / Underdog / Wretched / Vulture / Skinned And Endangered.

Also available from Zonda Books & Garry Sharpe-Young

New Wave of American Heavy Metal
By Garry Sharpe-Young
ISBN 0-9582684-0-1

Heavy Metal is the ultimate survivalist, weathering every trend, every fad. In the mid 90s, in the wake of Grunge, the Metal movement underwent its most radical evolution to date, ushered in by a leaner, meaner crop of purist, aggressive acts in PANTERA, MACHINE HEAD, BIOHAZARD, LIFE OF AGONY, PRONG and SLIPKNOT as Thrash fused with Hardcore and Death Metal.

As the millennium dawned this new found power exploded not only onto the US touring circuit, but also the national album charts giving rise to a new generation of offshoots as Screamo, Emocore and Metalcore.

In the traditional Rockdetector style executive editor Garry Sharpe-Young, exhaustively documents over 600 U.S. and Canadian Alternative Metal, Emocore, Hardcore, Math Metal, Metal, Metalcore, Neo-Thrash and Screamo bands in painstaking detail with extensive historical biographies, line-ups and full discographies including track lists, labels, catalogue numbers and chart positions.

Sabbath Bloody Sabbath: The Battle for Black Sabbath
By Garry Sharpe-Young
ISBN 0-9582684-2-8

Between 1980 and 1997 Tony Iommi and Ozzy Osbourne were involved in a titanic struggle unprecedented in Rock n' Roll history. Both stars would employ the very finest players of the genre in the conflict and produce some of the finest Heavy Metal of the generation in the process. Tony Iommi, the man who without question invented Heavy Metal, pitched vocal legends such as Ronnie James Dio, Ian Gillan, Glenn Hughes and Tony Martin against Ozzy Osbourne's awesome arsenal of guitar innovators Randy Rhoads, Jake E. Lee and Zakk Wylde.

Now the author's two landmark tomes 'Story of the Ozzy Osbourne band' & 'Black Sabbath: Never Say Die' along with new material are combined into one definitive Metal milestone. This meticulously detailed history employs exclusive interviews from the musicians that were sucked into this maelstrom: Tony Iommi, Geezer Butler, Cozy Powell, Ronnie James Dio, Ian Gillan, Glenn Hughes, Ray Gillen, Tony Martin, Geoff Nicholls, Rob Halford, Bob Daisley, Lee Kerslake, Carmine Appice, Tommy Aldridge, Neil Murray, Dave Spitz, Eric Singer, David Donato, Jeff Fenholt, Bobby Rondinelli, Rudy Sarzo, Phil Soussan, Randy Castillo, Bernie Torme, Brad Gillis, Jo Burt, Pete Way, Dana Strum, Terry Chimes, Lita Ford, Steve Vai, Don Airey, Lindsey Bridgewater, Terry Nails, plus many more.

FOR INFORMATION ABOUT NEWER TITLES VISIT

www.zondabooks.com

Also Available from Zonda Books & Garry Sharpe-Young

Thrash Metal
By Garry Sharpe-Young
ISBN 978-0-9582684-3-1

Thrash Metal. At first mocked by the Rock traditionalists Thrash would swamp the hard n' heavy world propelling one of it's own—Metallica, to the very pinnacle of Rock's elite.

In the early 80s Thrash breathed new life into the Rock scene providing older acts with a much needed kick. This new force opened the floodgates to armies of teens armed with flying Vs, bullet belts and a sense of purpose that would fuel genres such as Thrashcore, Crossover and technical Speed Metal. Without Thrash there would be no Death Metal, no Black Metal. That explosion of aggression has seen subsequent afterblasts, most recently Europe and South America has seen a genuine renaissance of Thrash Metal.

Without doubt, Thrash Metal still continues to make its mark in the biggest possible way. The 'big four'—Metallica, Megadeth, Anthrax and Slayer are all documented here in the greatest possible detail with full, up to the minute histories, exclusive photographs and global discographies, which include demos, albums, singles, chart positions, track listings and catalogue numbers. Over 400,000 words leave no stone left unturned in pursuit of knowledge of ex-members, rare recordings and career milestones. The author has interviewed all these major acts. Indeed, he interviewed Metallica's late Cliff Burton just days before his passing. The early days of Megadeth are straight from the mouth of Dave Mustaine.

Also covered are the legion of groundbreaking Bay Area acts such as Metal Church, Testament, Exodus, Death Angel and Hirax. The European Thrash explosion of Kreator, Rage, Destruction, Sodom, Grave Digger and Helloween is also covered in frightening detail. The Pagan Thrash of Sabbat, the avant garde eccentricity of Celtic Frost and the Funk Thrash of Morded—it's all here. The second wave of Thrash with major artists such as Sepultura, Pantera and Machine Head takes the genre right up to the new breed of Thrashers, now a truly world-wide phenomomen. All examined in depth.

Having achieved its quarter of a century, Thrash Metal is not only alive, it is thriving. If you thought this rawest form of Heavy Metal was consigned to the past this book will deliver a rude awakening! Read the book, buy the records and bang that head!!

FOR INFORMATION ABOUT NEWER TITLES VISIT

www.zondabooks.com